REGNUM STUDIES IN GLOBAL CHRISTIANITY

Orthodox Handbook on Ecumenism

REGNUM STUDIES IN GLOBAL CHRISTIANITY
(Previously GLOBAL THEOLOGICAL VOICES series)

Series Preface

The latter part of the twentieth century witnessed a global level of change in Christian dynamics. One significant development was the rise of the churches in the global south, not only in their number but also in their engagement with their socio-cultural contexts. *Regnum Studies in Global Christianity* explores the issues that the global church struggles with, focusing particularly on churches in Africa, Asia, Latin America and Eastern Europe.

The series publishes studies that will help the global church learn not only from past and present, but also from provocative and prophetic voices for the future. The editors and the publisher particularly pray that the series as a public space will encourage the southern churches to make an important contribution to the shaping of a healthy future for global Christianity. The editors invite theological seminaries and universities from around the world to submit relevant scholarly dissertations for possible publication in the series. It is hoped that the series will provide a forum for South-to-South as well as South-to-North dialogues.

Series Editors

Ruth Padilla DeBorst	President, Latin American Theological Fraternity, Santiago, Chile
Hwa Yung	Bishop, The Methodist Church in Malaysia, Petaling Jaya, Malaysia
Wonsuk Ma	Executive Director, Oxford Centre for Mission Studies, Oxford, UK
Damon So	Research Tutor, Oxford Centre for Mission Studies, Oxford, UK
Miroslav Volf	Director, Yale Center for Faith and Culture, New Haven, MA, USA

REGNUM STUDIES IN GLOBAL CHRISTIANITY

ORTHODOX HANDBOOK ON ECUMENISM

Resources for Theological Education

"That they all may be one" (John 17:21)

Editors

Pantelis Kalaitzidis
Thomas FitzGerald
Cyril Hovorun
Aikaterini Pekridou
Nikolaos Asproulis
Guy Liagre
Dietrich Werner

REGNUM BOOKS INTERNATIONAL, OXFORD
(in cooperation with WCC Publications),
Oxford, 2014

First Edition 2014 by Regnum Books International
Regnum is an imprint of the Oxford Centre for Mission Studies
St. Philip and St. James Church
Woodstock Road
Oxford OX2 6HR, UK
www.ocms.ac.uk/regnum

09 08 07 06 05 04 03 8 7 6 5 4 3 2 1

British Library Cataloguing in Publication Data
A catalogue record for this book is available from the British Library

ISBN 978-1-908355-44-7

Typeset by Dr. Nicolae Turcan, Romania – www.nicolaeturcan.ro
(Visiting Associate Professor, Faculty for Orthodox Theology, Babes-Bolyai University, Cluj-Napoca, Romania)

Cover design by Words by Design
www.wordsbydesign.co.uk

Printed and bound in Oxford
for Regnum Books International
by TJ International

Explanation for cover picture:

Christ the Vineyard, 15th century Byzantine icon, Parish Church of Malles, Ierapetra, Crete.

This Byzantine icon depicts Christ as the true vine from the Gospel of John (15:1-7), and symbolically points to the unity of the Church. Jesus Christ is represented here as the founder of the Church (vineyard), while the Apostles, who with their preaching spread the Church's message in the whole of the *oikoumene*, are represented as the branches of the vineyard. On the left and on the right of Christ, St. Peter and St. Paul are seen as the representatives of the West and the East respectively. The whole icon symbolizes the mystery and reality of the unity of the body of Christ in the whole of the inhabited earth.

CONTENTS

Prelims

Prelims

FOREWORD

In recent Church history, the first two decades of the twentieth century are surely considered to be the dawn of a fresh and promising period in Church relations. The pioneering initiatives of the Ecumenical Patriarchate for reconciliation and cooperation – with crucial encyclicals published in 1902, 1904, and 1920 – together with the call of the World Missionary Conference of Edinburgh for a common Christian witness in the world (1910), the formation of the World Alliance for Promoting International Friendship through the Churches (1914), as well as the Preparatory Conferences of the "Faith and Order" and "Life and Work" movements (1920) marked praiseworthy attempts to abandon past practices and lay the foundations of the ecumenical movement. This movement was perceived as an effort of the Christian Churches and many committed Christians to overcome past quarrels and to discern significant denominators for the Churches' common witness and service to the world, thereby preparing the conditions that would facilitate the restoration of their unity.

It should be stressed, however, that although the term "Ecumenical Movement" was used for the first time in the 1920's in order to define this positive development in inter-church relations, the idea of ecumenism is not a recent development in the life of the Church. On the contrary, it could be stated that ecumenism has been at the center of the Church's pastoral ministry since the earliest apostolic times. The Church never considered itself to be a sect or a denomination. It always saw itself as the true Church of God, the Body of Christ, the divine presence and witness in the world. It is this reality that defines both the necessity and the limits of our involvement in the ecumenical movement.

On the one hand, of course, it is true that modern ecumenism emerged from within the Protestant world, as the outcome of its endeavor to present a more coherent image of Protestantism by attempting to reunite the multitude of Protestant denominations on the basis of a common ecclesiological understanding. On the other hand, however, it would be incorrect to attribute the paternity of ecumenism to the Protestant and Anglican world alone. It is a fact that the history of the ecumenical movement, and more particularly of the World Council of Churches, is very closely linked with the Orthodox Church in general and the Ecumenical Patriarchate in particular.

Moreover, it should be remembered that the first concrete proposal to establish a "*Koinonia* of Churches" came from the Church of Constantinople, which, with its well known 1920 Encyclical advocated that the fellowship and cooperation of the Christian Churches were not excluded by the doctrinal differences that otherwise divided them. As W.A. Visser't Hooft once pointed out: "The Church of Constantinople rung the bell of our assembling, for she was among the first in modern history to remind us with its 1920 Encyclical that world Christendom would be disobedient to the will of its Lord and Savior if it did not seek to manifest in the world the unity of the people of God and of the Body of Christ." As was noted in that encyclical addressed "Unto the Churches of Christ Everywhere": Love should be rekindled and strengthened among the churches, so that they should no longer consider one another as strangers or foreigners, but as relatives and part of the household of Christ, and as "fellow heirs, members of the same body and partakers of the promise of God in Christ."

The Ecumenical Patriarchate has always been convinced of its broader ecumenical responsibility in the world. This keen sense of obligation and leadership before other people and before God has inspired manifold initiatives, such as the Patriarchate's tireless efforts to consolidate the unity of the Orthodox Church worldwide, an effort which has often been fraught with national tensions and political divisions. Indeed, the involvement of the Ecumenical Patriarchate in ecumenical encounter and exchange dates back at least to the 16th century with the "Ausgburg-Constantinople" correspondence, which consisted of a series of communications between Lutheran theologians from Tübingen and Ecumenical Patriarch Jeremiah II from 1572 to 1595. Although not dialogues in the formal sense, these exchanges were nonetheless indicative of the general philosophy of the Ecumenical Patriarchate with regard to other churches and other faiths.

The same philosophy has also inspired our encouragement in principle of ecumenical discussions from the early 20th century, while providing the impetus and foundation for several bilateral discussions with other Christian Churches. Beyond the diverse discussions and agreed statements between the Eastern and the Oriental Churches, the most effective and to date fruitful of these theological dialogues have been engaged with the Roman Catholic Church, the Anglican Communion and the Lutheran World Federation. Indeed, even at the cost of much defamation for "betraying" the Gospel truth, we have never restricted these engagements merely to the various Christian confessions. After all, standing as it does on the crossroads of continents, civilizations and faith communities, the vision of the Ecumenical Patriarchate has always embraced the idea and responsibility of serving as a bridge between Christians, Moslems, and Jews.

Why do we participate in the ecumenical movement? The answer is simple: because the mission and vision of the Church require it. The Church cannot escape its responsibility and opportunity to "give an answer to everyone, who asks us to give the reason for the hope that we have – and to do this with gentleness and respect." (1 Peter 3:15) As Orthodox Christians, we have no right to ignore the world around us; this world requires our presence and voice wherever it can be heard, precisely because the Church is the guardian of a universal truth, which we have no right to restrict or confine within our zones of comfort. In fact, we are called to proclaim the fullness of this truth precisely where we feel uncomfortable.

To this end, then, Orthodoxy must be in constant dialogue with the world. The Orthodox Church does not fear dialogue, because truth is not afraid of dialogue. On the contrary, if Orthodoxy is enclosed within itself and not in dialogue with those outside, it will fail in its mission and cease to be the "catholic" and "ecumenical" Church. Instead, it will become introverted and self-contained, a "ghetto" on the margins of history. This is why the great Fathers of the Church never feared dialogue with the spiritual culture of their age, instead even welcoming dialogue with pagan idolaters and philosophers. It is in this spirit that they influenced and transformed the civilization of their time and offered us a truly ecumenical Church. Orthodoxy always remains contemporary and ecumenical, so long as we promote it with humility and interpret it in light of the existential quests and needs of humanity in each given historical period and cultural circumstance.

Today, Orthodoxy is called to continue this dialogue with the outside world in order to provide witness and the life-giving breath of its faith. However, this dialogue cannot reach the outside world unless it first passes through all those who bear the Christian name. And so first we must converse as Christians among ourselves, to resolve our differences, so that our witness to the outside world may be credible. Our endeavor in the cause that all Christians be united is the command of our Lord, who before His passion prayed to His Father "that all [namely, His disciples] may be one, so that the world may believe that you sent me." (John 17:21) It is not possible for the Lord to agonize over the unity of His disciples and for us to remain indifferent about the unity of all Christians. That would constitute betrayal of fidelity and transgression of His will.

For this reason, we wholeheartedly welcome the publication of this Pan-Orthodox Handbook for teaching ecumenism, which is being produced in preparation for the 10th General Assembly of the World Council of Churches in Busan, South Korea, this year. It is our fervent prayer that this volume will restore and revive the ecumenical vision among our Churches and especially among the younger generation, who are called to sustain and expand it in the years to come.

At the Ecumenical Patriarchate, the 3rd of September, 2013

Prayerfully yours,

† BARTHOLOMEW
Archbishop of Constantinople-New Rome
and Ecumenical Patriarch

Orthodox Handbook on Ecumenism

Olav Fykse Tveit

It is my great pleasure to acknowledge the publication of the *Orthodox Handbook on Ecumenism* edited by a group of Orthodox theologians in collaboration with the WCC/ETE Program, the Conference of European Churches, Volos Academy for Theological Studies in Greece, and Holy Cross Greek Orthodox School of Theology in Brookline, Massachusetts. This *Handbook* which is part of a broader ETE project of publishing resource books for theological education and teaching ecumenism in different settings[1] is in many ways a *historic publication*.

The engagement of the Orthodox Churches in the modern efforts for Church unity are broadly known and appreciated. The history of the foundation and development of WCC was profoundly marked by the Orthodox Churches, both Eastern and Oriental. In 1920, the Ecumenical Patriarchate "took an initiative which was without precedent in church history,"[2] namely to extend an invitation to all Christian churches to form a "league of Churches." This initiative was well-received and further developed by representatives of other Christian traditions, and in 1948 the World Council of Churches was founded. From the 147 founding member churches of WCC[3], 5 were Orthodox (3 Eastern Orthodox: the Ecumenical Patriarchate, the Church of Cyprus, and the Church of Greece, and 2 Oriental Orthodox: the Ethiopian Orthodox Tewahedo Church and the Malankara Orthodox Syrian Church), while several other Orthodox churches were present with representatives (the Greek Orthodox Patriarchate of Alexandria and All Africa, the Greek Orthodox Patriarchate of Antioch, the Greek Orthodox Patriarchate of Jerusalem, the Romanian Orthodox Diocese in the USA, the Archdiocese of Russian Orthodox Churches in Western Europe (as it was called at that time), and the Coptic Orthodox Church). A simple enumeration of the Orthodox founding members of WCC clearly shows that almost all those who remained outside the WCC fellowship were based behind the iron curtain that divided the world after the Second World War. During the third WCC Assembly that took place in New Delhi in 1961 and in the years after, Eastern and Oriental Orthodox Churches from the former communist bloc joined WCC. The last Eastern Orthodox Church which became a WCC member was the Orthodox Autocephalous Church of Albania (1994), a church which suffered the most under the communist regime and whose recent history of revival and rebuilding is strongly linked with its deep ecumenical involvement. After the political changes that occurred in the world since 1989, two Orthodox member churches, the Georgian Orthodox Church and the oldest Slavonic Orthodox Church (the Bulgarian Orthodox Church) chose to suspend their membership in WCC and CEC, due to several reasons related with the complex realities existing in Eastern Europe in the post-communist period (although several working relationships remained also to theologians within these churches).

The presence of Orthodox Churches in the membership of WCC decisively influenced its agenda. Orthodox emphasis on seeking unity between member churches, the contribution of Orthodox representatives especially in the commissions of Faith and Order and Mission and Evangelism, the permanent insistence on an osmotic relationship between *martyria*, *diakonia* and *leitourgia* are just a few examples of areas in which the Orthodox brought their values to the ecumenical fellowship.

---

[1] So far three Handbooks of Theological Education have been published: (1) Dietrich Werner, David Esterline, Namsoon Kang, Joshva Rajha, *Handbook of Theological Education in World Christianity*, (Oxford: Regnum, 2010) which is a general introduction in theological education and teaching ecumenism; (2) Isabel Phiri and Dietrich Werner (eds.), *Handbook of Theological Education in Africa*, (Oxford: Regnum, 2013) focused on the African context; (3) Hope Antone, Huang Po Ho, WatiLongchar, BaeHyunju, Dietrich Werner (eds.), *Asian Handbook on Theological Education and Ecumenism*, (Oxford: Regnum, 2013), focused on the Asian context.

[2] W. A. Visser' t Hooft, *The Genesis and Formation of the World Council of Churches*, (WCC Publication, 1982), 1.

[3] Ibid., 63.

In terms of ecumenical theological education, along with the role of the Orthodox Churches and their representatives in developing the Ecumenical Institute in Bossey in Switzerland, representatives of Orthodox Churches in collaboration with Orthodox staff members of WCC and with WCC leadership and the ETE program were permanently preoccupied with developing an ecumenical formation within Orthodox Churches. In this sense, several conferences and consultations were organized by WCC in collaboration with different Orthodox Churches. The last International Inter-Orthodox Consultation of this kind, entitled "The Ecumenical Movement in Theological Education and in the Life of Orthodox Churches", took place from 9-12 November 2012 in Sibiu, Romania, and was organized in collaboration with the Romanian Orthodox Church. It brought together 25 key Orthodox theologians involved in ecumenical education and academic formation and formulated a few key recommendations which took up the earlier "Volos Initiative for Ecumenical Theological Education in Central and Eastern Europe" from 2007 and thus led to the production of this Handbook.

The content of this Handbook was developed by the editorial team in such a way that it can provide both a better understanding of Orthodox approaches on ecumenism as well as an introduction into several aspects of the broader theme of "Orthodox involvement in the ecumenical movement." It supplies propaedeutic articles on the role of Orthodoxy in the world today, on the Orthodox understanding of ecumenism or ecumenical terminology, and presents the ecumenical profiles of several Orthodox hierarchs and theologians involved in ecumenical work. It presents studies about the Orthodox understanding of the main foundations of ecumenism (in biblical, patristic, historical, liturgical, ecclesiological perspectives, etc.), about ecumenical dialogue in various Orthodox Churches and about the history and current level of bilateral dialogues between Orthodox Churches and other Christian traditions. Last, but not least, the present Handbook approaches issues like Orthodox identity today, migration, interreligious dialogue, etc. It is admirable that some chapters courageously treat delicate issues like anti-ecumenism and its causes in Orthodox contexts and the controversial issue of common prayer.

While this Handbook is written by Orthodox authors and is addressed primarily to the Eastern Orthodox, I am sure that it will be useful also for a broader constituency, especially for those who are interested in an Orthodox understanding of Church unity and want to learn more about how the Orthodox perceive and relate to the modern ecumenical movement and other Christian traditions.

Congratulating the editorial team, the ETE program and Volos Academy as well as the authors and all those who contributed to this Handbook, I express my confidence that it will be well received among Orthodox Churches and theological schools, that it will contribute significantly to deepen the dialogue within and between the Orthodox churches and that it will serve properly the purposes for which it was published.

Rev. Dr Olav Fykse Tveit
General Secretary
World Council of Churches (WCC)

Guy Liagre

It is an honour for the Conference of European Churches (CEC) to be a part of the broader project for the preparation of the Orthodox Handbook for Teaching Ecumenism suggested by ETE/WCC in collaboration with CEC, Volos Academy and the Holy Cross Greek Orthodox School of Theology.

The *Conference of European Churches* is an ecumenical fellowship of 114 Churches (Old Catholic, Anglican, Orthodox and Protestant), and in earlier years had produced a directory of European institutions of theological education. It thus facilitated an initial process of networking and exchange, and later acknowledged the importance of theological education again by emphasizing efforts for strengthening the spirit of ecumenical cooperation among the European churches. For this purpose, CEC has organized different consultations of Theological Faculties in Europe in cooperation with the Roman Catholic Theological Faculty of the University of Graz, Austria. This process is still going on. At the Lyon Assembly in 2009, His All Holiness the Ecumenical Patriarch Bartholomew stressed the importance of these efforts as follows: "We duly appreciate the CEC's theological contribution as well as its involvement in promoting programmes designed to improve cooperation between our theological faculties."[1]

In this spirit and continuing a history of good cooperation between ETE and CEC in the area of theological education,[2] the Volos Academy and WCC planned a project together to work on a major resource book for teaching about ecumenism in Orthodox contexts, a project which could facilitate theological education on the ecumenical movement in the family of Orthodox theological faculties, schools, and beyond.

This *Orthodox Handbook on Ecumenism* is the result of this process and intense collaboration. It uncovers the unique vision of history and actual perception of the ecumenical idea in the Orthodox tradition. It underscores that there are many and varied reasons for Orthodoxy's involvement – or the lack of it – in the ecumenical movement. The basic question of this publication is: what have been the long-term effects of the Orthodox Church's involvement in the ecumenical movement over the years? How have the Orthodox benefitted from their collaboration in the ecumenical movement?

Reviewing the titles of the different articles, this publication proves that true ecumenical unity is not the same as imposed uniformity. As one ponders history, reading the articles in this book by Orthodox theologians on ecumenism, one feels awe at the courage and decisiveness of these great figures who were able to overcome stereotypes and long established perceptions. With God's blessing they were able not only to lay foundational stones in the history of Orthodoxy, but also in the history of Ecumenism, contributing to theological progress and a better mutual understanding between Churches both inside and outside the Orthodox tradition. As a result of their labours, Orthodox theology has become a historic factor and transforming element in the ecumenical movement.

In this book, the editors share their conviction that informed discussion and deliberation on these contributions and knowledge of worldwide Orthodox ecumenical achievements are essential if the Orthodox position and witness are to be deemed credible and its participation in the ecumenical movement to remain a manifestation of a common pastoral responsibility. It is also an answer to those outside the Orthodox tradition who are

---

[1] 'The rich future of hope for the Conference of European Churches'. Address by His Holiness the Ecumenical Patriarch Bartholomew I for the 50th anniversary of the Conference of European Churches. http://assembly.ceceurope.org/fileadmin/filer/asse/Assembly/Documents/Official_documents/Bartholomew_EN.pdf (last accessed, September 2013).

[2] See for instance: The future of Ecumenical Theological Education in Eastern and Central Europe. Report of the International Seminar in Sambata de Sus, Rumania, 24-28 September 2008, ed. By Viorel Ionita and Dietrich Werner, CEC/WCC/ETE, Geneva 2009.

interested in understanding and articulating the role and involvement of Orthodox Churches in Ecumenism. Too often the pioneering role played by Orthodoxy in the genesis of the Ecumenical movement and in the foundation of WCC and in the history of CEC is set under a bushel.

As underlined by the former director of the Churches in Dialogue Commission of CEC Father Viorel Ionita, "The faith confessed by the Church is for the Orthodox not a theoretical exposition of the faith with no relation to the moral and liturgical life of the Church. In other words the faith is confessed in this Church not simply mentally or theoretically but also liturgically, spiritually and practically. In this respect the Orthodox expects that what the churches confess doctrinally should also be reflected in their practical life."[3] Many dilemmas tormenting human existence today demand a common Christian awareness of social and ethical issues as well of ecology in the light of Christian Spirituality, as expressed by the WCC inter-Orthodox consultation in 1995.[4] I hope that this publication will support the ecumenical involvement of Orthodox students, scholars and theologians worldwide, but particularly in the Conference of European Churches, in order to sustain the continuation of ecumenical collaboration in the work of Christian Advocacy in the European Institutions and beyond.

These words of greeting would be incomplete without mentioning that the project would not have been possible without the cooperation of a great number of people. It has been an exciting experience, but also time consuming and difficult, especially for those from the Volos Academy and from WCC-ETE who worked hard to receive all the articles, to read them and to manage this common publication. I express my sincere gratitude to them all, together with my predecessor who was director of the CEC Dialogue Commission and former interim general secretary and one of the initiators of the whole project, Father Viorel Ionita from the Romanian Orthodox Church.

May this publication strengthen the ecumenical fellowship and may the *lex credendi* govern the lives of all who march together in their common goal to Christian unity.

Guy Liagre
General Secretary
Conference of European Churches (CEC)

---

[3] V. Ionita, 'The Vision of Unity from an Orthodox perspective', Consultation on "Visions of Unity in our Churches – Points of Convergence", Conference of European Churches, Churches in Dialogue Commission, Budapest, 22-23 June 2011. http://cid.ceceurope.org/fileadmin/filer/cec/CEC_Documents/Press_Release_Attachments/Report_Consultation_Budapest. pdf (last accessed, September 2013).
[4] *The Ecumenical Review*, 48.2 (1996): 185-192. http://onlinelibrary.wiley.com/doi/10.1111/j.1758-6623.1996.tb03465.x/ pdf (last accessed, September 2013).

Metropolitan Ignatius of Demetrias

It is with great joy that I, in my capacity as the Chairman of the Board of Directors of the Volos Academy for Theological Studies, acknowledge the publication of the *Orthodox Handbook on Ecumenism — Resources for Theological Education*, a joint initiative of the World Council of Churches (WCC), the Council of European Churches (CEC), and the Volos Academy.

The Volos Academy for Theological Studies — a Church-related institution, which for more than a decade has productively and creatively ministered the word of God — acts as an open forum of thought and dialogue between the Orthodox Church and the broader scholarly community of intellectuals worldwide. Our city, Volos, the see of our local diocese, and the people who live here have been known throughout history for their tolerance, friendliness and solidarity with all different cultures and religious traditions. It is within this climate that the Volos Academy for Theological Studies was born and has matured, seeking to highlight the inherently ecumenical character of the Christian faith. Being itself a place for critical dialogue with the various contemporary theological, social, intellectual and wider cultural currents and movements, it is struggling with all its might to bring the Orthodox tradition into dialogue not only with other Christian traditions and movements in the West and in the East, but also, due to the particular geographic position of our country, with the broader religious environment and especially the Jewish and Islamic world. Inspired by this vision, the Academy has very successfully organized major international conferences and meetings related not only to the search for the Orthodox self-consciousness, but also to the fostering of a spirit of trust, mutual understanding and reconciliation between sister Churches, faithful Christians and people of different religious and cultural backgrounds. Moreover, for the same reasons, the Volos Academy participates actively in the programs and actions of the ecumenical movement as implemented through the long-standing, vital contribution of the WCC and the CEC.

For the Volos Academy, as an Orthodox Institution faithful to the eucharistic and eschatological understanding of the Christian Tradition and of the church-world relationship, ecumenical theological education is undoubtedly of primordial importance. We believe that the Orthodox Church has to constantly witness to its ecumenical ethos, and all-embracing catholic truth which is embodied in its very historical existence and its mission in the world. By participating in the ecumenical movement, we are convinced that we remain faithful to the deepest consciousness of Orthodoxy, as expressed par excellence in the Divine Liturgy, the very heart of Orthodox life and theology. In this liturgical and principally eucharistic context, the Church experiences the eschatological mystery of unity and prays ceaselessly for its proleptical manifestation or rather realization in history. It prays continually *"for the unity of all"* and asks for *"the unity of the faith and the communion of the Holy Spirit"*, a necessary presupposition that we may *"love one another, that with one mind we may confess: Father, Son, and Holy Spirit, the Trinity, one in Essence and inseparable"* (Liturgy of Saint John Chrysostom). By praying for unity in the Divine Liturgy, the Orthodox Church appeals to the realization of the ancient biblical faith and tradition in every aspect of the ecclesial life. Jesus' high priestly prayer serves as a compass: *"That they may all be one. As You, Father, are in me and I in you, may they also be in us, so that the world may believe that you have sent me. The glory that you have given me I have given them, so that they may be one, as we are one, I in them, and you in me, that they may become completely one, so that the world may know that you have sent me and have loved them even as you have loved me"* (John, 17:21-23). This biblical perspective demonstrates the Trinitarian foundation of ecclesial unity and fraternal love, and the indissoluble bond which links Trinitarian theology, ecclesiology, and anthropology.

Thus the theological curricula have to be ecumenically-oriented and expanded in this direction. Furthermore, when we include ecumenical education in our missionary and pastoral work and agenda, we bear witness to the Gospel's message of the Church's catholicity. Since the apostolic period, the teaching of the word of God, which embraces the *other* despite differences of culture, religion, origin, gender, political and social background, has been a priority in the life of the Church. The opening of our educational institutions, schools and faith communities to the Ecumenical Movement is an act of incarnating the word of God in history and witnessing that the Church exists for all people and the whole creation, for the benefit of the *ecumene* and the world. At the same time, teaching about the "other," learning from the "other" and about the "other" and, moreover, the awareness of the long and rich history of encounter and dialogue with other Christian traditions, provides the necessary means by which the Church will be able to overcome ignorance and stereotypical prejudices, introversion and fundamentalism, theological self-sufficiency and confessional entrenchment.

Inspired and motivated by this biblical and patristic understanding of the ecumenical ethos of Orthodoxy, the "Volos Initiative for Ecumenical Theological Education in Central and Eastern Europe" was inaugurated in February 2007 as a joint initiative between the Ecumenical Theological Education Program of the World Council of Churches (ETE/WCC) and the Volos Academy, highlighted by an important meeting, the final communiqué of which insisted on "increased efforts and proper resources to strengthen ecumenical theological education in Central and Eastern Europe." I am particularly pleased because the "Volos Initiative for Ecumenical Theological Education in Eastern and Central Europe" has now reached a fruitful conclusion with the publication of this *Orthodox Handbook on Ecumenism*. Even though ecumenicity and catholicity are not ancillary properties, but rather constitute integral elements of the Gospel message and the Orthodox tradition, nevertheless today Eastern Orthodoxy seems often hesitant to engage in an open and honest meeting and dialogue with other Christian traditions, due to fear of losing its identity. I hope, therefore, that this Handbook will represent an opportunity for the catholicity and the ecumenical ethos of the Orthodox tradition to emerge, so that whatever reservations there may be can be overcome.

The productive cooperation between the ETE/WCC, the CEC and the Volos Academy has resulted in this unique publication, this *Resource book*, which aims to facilitate theological education about the ecumenical movement within Orthodox theological faculties, schools, seminaries and beyond, and which is envisioned as a significant Orthodox contribution to the 2013 10th General Assembly of WCC in Busan, Korea. We are, indeed, honored by the coming together of all these eminent Orthodox theologians from all over the world, and from various local Orthodox Churches, who, despite the fact that they are not officially representing their respective Churches, nevertheless make valuable contributions to this prestigious volume, and in fact illustrate the strong commitment of these Churches to the Ecumenical dialogue and our common concern for the unity of all Christians.

Before concluding these words of greeting, I would like to express my deep appreciation and sincere gratitude to the editorial team, the contributors, the second readers, the translators and copy editors, the graphic designers, the printing companies, and the publishers for this unique achievement, for all the efforts expended toward the publication of this volume, and the high quality they have reached, but especially to the persons in charge of the three supporting and collaborating institutions (WCC, CEC, Volos Academy).

I hope that this Handbook will render service to the catholicity and ecumenicity of the Church, and will help toward a better awareness and understanding of the tradition of the undivided Church, to which we consider the Orthodox Church a humble servant and faithful witness. With these thoughts I greet the publication of the *Orthodox Handbook on Ecumenism — Resources for Theological Education*, praying for its publishing success and spiritual fruition.

Metropolitan Ignatius of Demetrias
Chairman, Board of Directors of the Volos Academy

PREFACE OF THE EDITORS

From the beginning of her historical involvement with the Ecumenical Movement, in the first decades of the 20th century, the Orthodox Church sought to highlight and build upon the biblical and apostolic roots of Christian unity, a unity which, according to Orthodox theology, is anticipated and experienced in the eucharistic gathering. The highest sacramental experience of the Church is a foretaste of the universal unity which we will fully experience in the Kingdom of God. As Fr. Georges Florovsky put it once, "The Church is *one*. Unity is her very being and nature. It was for the sake of unity that she was established by the Lord. The Church is 'one Body' ... Yet – Christians are divided ... The Christian world is in schism..." and Florovsky would conclude with asking the core question: "*Divisus est Christus*?" giving at the same time the proper answer "No. Emphatically not."[1] In this respect the Orthodox consider their participation in the Ecumenical Movement as a living and consistent witness and service to the unity and the catholicity of the Church, while at the same time they attempt to unveil the tragedy of the current divisions, to overcome the schisms of the Christian churches, and to heal the traumatic memories of the past. As Metropolitan John D. Zizioulas of Pergamon points out:

> The Orthodox participate in the ecumenical movement out of their conviction that the unity of the Church is an inescapable imperative for all Christians. This unity cannot be restored or fulfilled except through the coming together of those who share the same faith in the Triune God and are baptized in His name. [...] The Orthodox, in my understanding at least, participate in the ecumenical movement as a movement of baptized Christians, who are in a state of division because they cannot express the same faith together. In the past this has happened because of a lack of love which is now, thank God, disappearing. In the history of Christianity there has been a great deal of polemic between Christians, and without overcoming this history and the memories of it, it is not possible to move toward eucharistic communion. So the ecumenical movement is the place where all these divided Christians meet in order to examine whether they can love one another and confess the same faith with a view to eucharistic communion.[2]

This "coming together" of people sharing the Christian faith, despite the existent doctrinal (as well as historical, political, social and cultural) differences, towards the honest and true rapprochement and establishment of cordial relations, derives from the heart of the Orthodox ethos and understanding of ecumenism, insofar as this ethos is inspired, among others, by the epoch making Patriarchal Encyclicals of 1902 and 1920.[3] Through her involvement in the ecumenical movement, as well as through its teaching and life in general, the Orthodox Church seeks to respond adequately to the demand of her Lord "that they may all be one...so that the world may believe" (John 17:21), firmly believing that the continuation of confessional divisions constitutes a scandal for the whole of Christianity and a direct opposition to God's will.

Nevertheless, ecumenical commitment for the Orthodox has never been without difficulties, and even frustrations, particularly as the Orthodox came to realize that discussion on crucial theological matters and restoration of Christian unity was not always a priority for their ecumenical partners. On the other hand, the genuine ecumenical spirit of Orthodoxy was frequently overshadowed by historical traumas, or concerns of

---

[1] Georges Florovsky, "The Doctrine of the Church and the Ecumenical Problem," *The Ecumenical Review*, 2 (1950): 152-153.

[2] John D. Zizioulas (Metropolitan of Pergamon), *The One and the Many: Studies on God, Man, the Church, and the World Today*, ed. Fr. Gregory Edwards, (Alhambra: CA, Sebastian Press, 2010), 316-317, 331-332.

[3] See the English version of the two Encyclicals of the Ecumenical Patriarchate of Constantinople in: *The Orthodox Church and the Ecumenical Movement: Documents and Statements 1902-1975*, ed. Constantin G. Patelos, (Geneva: World Council of Churches, 1978), 27-33, 40-43; *Orthodox Visions of Ecumenism: Statements, Messages and Reports on the Ecumenical Movement, 1902-1992*, ed. Gennadios Limouris, (Geneva: WCC Publications, 1994), 1-5, 9-11; Thomas FitzGerald, *The Ecumenical Patriarchate and Christian Unity*, (Brookline, MA: Holy Cross Orthodox Press, 2009), 62-65 (for the Encyclical of 1920).

cultural order, and the ignorance of the "heterodox Other". The lack of an appropriate and coherent ecumenical theological education in Orthodox contexts and an awareness of the various important movements and figures of Western Christian theology and spirituality during the 20th century hinders graduates from Orthodox Schools of Theology from entering into genuine ecumenical conversation and exchange. It is worth noticing that, up to this day, classic works of Western theologians are still untranslated in many of the languages of the traditionally Orthodox countries. Given this situation, ecumenical theological education is of crucial importance for the promotion of a well-articulated ecumenical spirit among Orthodox clerics, theologians, and educated laity, as well as for the sake of mutual understanding and the overcoming of stereotypical images and constructions. As it is pointed out in a recent Inter-Orthodox document:

1. There is a clear need to develop appropriate, fair-minded, non-polemical Orthodox resources and methodologies for teaching about other Christian churches, other religions and the ecumenical movement.
2. It is necessary to prepare an essay book about the history of the ecumenical movement from the Orthodox point of view to be introduced as a part of the teaching curriculum in our theological schools and seminaries.

These were two key recommendations from the International Inter-Orthodox Consultation on "The Ecumenical Movement in Theological Education and in the Life of Orthodox Churches," which took place from 9-12 November 2010 in Sibiu, Romania, which brought together 25 prominent Orthodox theologians and representatives in the ecumenical movement.[4]

The initial impetus for creating a Handbook on teaching ecumenism in Orthodox contexts had already begun in February 2010 as a follow-up of earlier initiatives between the Volos Academy and the Programme on Ecumenical Theological Education of the World Council of Churches (ETE/WCC). During the Sibiu conference of November 2010 and on several other occasions, different voices indicated the need to have a proper reference book for teaching ecumenism in Orthodox theological faculties, seminaries, and academies, as there is still a serious lack of resources for proper and sound teaching of the history and life of the ecumenical movement. Among the several contributors who were involved and brought their own background and historical involvement into this project we should mention the following:

a) The **Volos Academy for Theological Studies in Greece**, which has played a major role in highlighting ecumenical studies and bringing into the debate major issues in contemporary international theological dialogue as well as intra-Orthodox dialogue. In February 2007, the "Volos Initiative for Ecumenical Theological Education in Central and Eastern Europe" was inaugurated as a joint initiative between ETE/WCC and the Volos Academy which urged increased efforts and proper resources to strengthen ecumenical theological education in Central and Eastern Europe.

b) The **Programme on Ecumenical Theological Education** of the World Council of Churches, which follows the constitutional mandate of WCC to increase "ecumenical consciousness of its member churches" and to facilitate the development of proper resources for ecumenical formation in all its member churches. Since its early beginnings, ETE/WCC and its predecessor programme have been interested already in accompanying and strengthening Orthodox theological education. The first major consultation of the newly formed Programme on Theological Education (PTE) which followed the London based Theological Education Fund (TEF) of the International Missionary Council in 1976/1977 was an *International Consultation on Orthodox Theological Education* which was held in Basel from 4-7 July 1978.[5] ETE/WCC also had been involved in various initiatives to cooperate with regard to theological education and ecumenical formation in Orthodox contexts and therefore employed a consultant with

---

[4] See: Final Communiqué from the International Inter-Orthodox Consultation on "The Ecumenical Movement in Theological Education and in the Life of Orthodox Churches," Sibiu, Romania, 9-12 November 2010. Documented also in: http://www.globethics.net/web/ecumenical-theological-education?layoutPlid=13227594 (last accessed, September 2013).

[5] The papers and reports of this consultation (well documented in Ministerial Formation 2, 1978, pp. 16ff) already at that time included two key recommendations which are still of relevance today: The Basel consultation referred to the task of "Orthodox theological schools... to deal seriously with the need to be open to ecumenical demands both inherent in Orthodox tradition and as they are present in contemporary situations". Further, it highlighted the challenges for "setting

an Orthodox background for theological education in Eastern and Central Europe.[6] The ETE/WCC had also published similar major Handbooks on Theological Education for different regions, in which there were always several contributions included from Orthodox theologians.[7] Some of these served as an example for this Handbook.

c) **The Conference of European Churches (CEC)**, which for several years has provided a platform for meetings between theological faculties of Eastern and Western Europe (the so-called Graz process)[8], and which also encouraged the reflection on mission and theological education in Europe. In addition, CEC in cooperation with ETE/WCC held the international seminar on "The Future of Ecumenical Theological Education in Eastern and Central Europe" (24-28 September 2008, Sambata de Sus Monastery, Romania) which also provided a major recommendation to increase the literature and resource books for solid teaching on ecumenism in Eastern European contexts.[9]

d) **Holy Cross Greek Orthodox School of Theology** in Brookline, Massachusetts, has a long history of involvement into ecumenical dialogue both for the Orthodox churches in the North American context and beyond. Its teaching staff has developed a significant ecumenical activity, often taking part as resource persons or as members in various WCC commissions. Holy Cross organized some of the major ecumenical events and conferences, while its publishing house (Holy Cross Orthodox Press) has published a remarkable set of works of ecumenical interest.

e) **SS Cyril and Methodius Theological Institute of Post-Graduate Studies in Moscow**, a leading theological institution of the Russian Orthodox Church. In its curricula and research, it is focused on ecumenical studies and inter-Orthodox relations. It is affiliated with the Department for External Church Relations of the Moscow Patriarchate.

All the institutions mentioned above share the following core convictions: a) that there is a serious need for a common resource book for teaching ecumenism in Orthodox theological faculties and academies; b) that there still is a considerable lack of resources for proper and sound teaching of the history and life of the ecumenical movement; c) that the Orthodox Churches had inspired, contributed to, and profoundly benefited from the ecumenical movement — and this allowed them to meet other Christians and to overcome temptations of isolationism; d) that there is still some need to improve the level of inter-Christian studies and dialogue in Orthodox theological schools in order to promote mutual understanding and to eradicate prejudices; e) that the study of other Christian churches and ecumenism needs to move beyond the framework of comparative or even polemical apologetics.

Inspired by this common view, a group of committed Orthodox theologians and ecumenical partners formed an editorial group to conceptualize a Pan-Orthodox Handbook for Teaching Ecumenism. This publication was planned as a constructive Orthodox contribution to the 10th General Assembly of WCC in Busan, Korea (2013), where a major forum for ecumenical theological education took place as well as other significant ecumenical

---

up an Orthodox Theological Commission to promote permanent relationships among Orthodox theological schools", a demand which partly was realized by bringing into existence the Conference of Orthodox Theological Schools (COTS).

[6] See the final report of Rev. Prof. Dr. Vladimir Fedorov, St. Petersburg, on his work with ETE/WCC, 2009. See: http://www.globethics.net/web/ecumenical-theological-education (documents on Europe) (last accessed at September 2013).

[7] Dietrich Werner, David Esterline, Namsoon Kang, Joshva Rajha, *Handbook of Theological Education in World Christianity*, (Oxford: Regnum, 2010); *Handbook of Theological Education in Africa*, eds. Isabel Phiri and Dietrich Werner, (Oxford: Regnum, 2013); and *Asian Handbook on Theological Education and Ecumenism*, eds. Hope Antone, Huang Po Ho, Wati Lonchar, Bae Hyunju, Dietrich Werner, (Oxford: Regnum, 2013).

[8] See the 3rd Graz Consultation of Theological Faculties in Europe in July 2010, Austria: http://cid.ceceurope.org/fileadmin/filer/cid/Education_and_Formation/Final_statement_Graz_Process.pdf (last accessed at September 2013).

[9] *The Future of Ecumenical Theological Education in Eastern and Central Europe: Full Report of the International Seminar for Young Lecturers and Professors of Theology*, Sambata de Sus, Romania, 24-28 September 2008, (Geneva: Conference of European Churches/Churches in Dialogue Commission-World Council of Churches/Ecumenical Theological Education Programme, 2009), 111ff.

events. An initial process started in the period between December 2010 and March 2011 to develop a draft concept to be shared with a wider group of Orthodox theologians interested in this project. People involved in this first core group stage were Dr. Pantelis Kalaitzidis (Volos Academy), Rev. Prof. Dr. Viorel Ionita (CEC), and Rev. Dr. Dietrich Werner (ETE/WCC).

The first core project outline was presented to a wider group of some 30 Orthodox theologians who were called together for a planning workshop at the Volos Academy, 16-18 October 2011; during this meeting key parameters of the project were affirmed.

Six major goals were decided to guide the beginning editorial work.

The goals of the envisaged publication were defined as follows:

a) To underline the decisive role of the Orthodox Church in the development of the ecumenical movement from its early beginnings, as well as to highlight both how Orthodox churches have contributed to ecumenical theology in general for many decades, and how they have benefitted from the ecumenical movement;

b) To provide access to essential and authentic Orthodox texts relating to the search for Christian unity as well as the understanding of ecumenism and the involvement of Orthodox churches in the ecumenical movement, including providing access to official decisions and statements of Orthodox churches with regard to theological education and ecumenism. Towards this end, a broader selection of the important historical Orthodox texts is available in a digital form in the Digital Reader of Official Texts - CD ROM, that is attached to the back cover of the present Handbook;

c) To address practical aspects of ecumenical dialogue and common Christian witness in diakonia, education, joint witness, pastoral counseling and Christian life which demand for pastoral theological reflection on contemporary areas of church life and action and therefore would combine theological articles with those that were more practical and pastoral;

d) To present materials from Orthodox theologians involved in theological education on ecumenism from different Orthodox churches and to highlight some of the pioneers of Orthodox involvement in ecumenical dialogue;

e) To communicate a proper and theologically sound understanding of ecumenism from an Orthodox perspective, with a dialogical approach reflecting and relating to some prejudices and misperceptions of ecumenism which are still circulating in some Orthodox churches. That is to offer an apologetic Orthodox theology of ecumenism in the most positive sense of the word;

f) To identify proper additional resources which facilitate theological education on ecumenism by providing and pointing to course outlines and curriculum plans (bibliographies, curriculum outlines, lists of websites with additional resources), while at the same time avoiding restricting its audience to academic theologians, and instead reaching out to the interested general public in Orthodox contexts and beyond.

It was also agreed in further deliberations that the Handbook should have nine major sections or chapters:

1) **Introduction**.
2) **Foundations:** Orthodoxy and ecumenism – introduction, historical outline and key historical texts.
3) **Theological Positions:** Selected texts from Orthodox Synods and Bishops Conferences,
4) **Representative Ecumenical Thinkers and their key texts**.
5) **Local Surveys:** Articles on ecumenical dialogue in various Orthodox churches and settings.
6) **Bilateral Dialogues Between Eastern Orthodox and Other Churches:** Selected texts from bilateral dialogues of Orthodox churches on theological and ecclesial issues.
7) **Ecumenical Perspectives of Oriental Orthodox Churches:** A general introduction on the dialogues between Oriental Orthodox churches and other churches and Christian traditions, and articles on ecumenism in various Oriental Orthodox contexts.
8) **Key Themes**: Core themes in Orthodox ecumenism.

9) **Ecumenical Theological Education in Orthodox Schools** – examples for teaching ecumenism in Orthodox contexts.

The editorial team from 2011 onwards consisted of Dr. Pantelis Kalaitzidis, Fr. Dr. Thomas FitzGerald, Fr. Dr. Cyril Hovorun, Aikaterini Pekridou (MTh) and Nikolaos Asproulis (MTh). Rev. Dr. Dietrich Werner from ETE/WCC, Rev. Dr. Kaisamari Hintikka (until 2012) and Rev. Dr. Guy Liagre (after 2012) from CEC, who represented the supporting institutions and also served as advisors to the project and the present publication, while Nikolaos Asproulis from the Volos Academy was mandated to serve also as secretary of the editorial board, taking a large part of the coordinating work and the demanding correspondance with the different authors. Five meetings of the core editorial group and the representatives of the supporting institutions took place in Geneva and Volos between November 2011 and September 2013, for coordinating and managing the editorial process.

The editors of this volume are aware that they build on the previous work of other Orthodox scholars who have produced substantial publications and on Orthodox involvement in the ecumenical movement[10] and that further work by Orthodox in the area of ecumenism is needed. They believe that this Handbook promotes solid biblical teaching on ecumenism that is in line with the principles of the Orthodox tradition. While each article presented here stands for itself and does not necessarily and in every detail represent the common opinion of all editors, the editors are convinced that a solid and sound introduction and survey on essential aspects of Orthodox understanding of Ecumenism can be found within this volume. It is the hope that this volume will contribute to a spiritual ecumenism, which according the late Ecumenical Patriarch Athenagoras I, is at the beginning and heart of true Orthodox ecumenical commitment. When opening the Fourth Pan-Orthodox Conference (Orthodox Center of Chambésy, Switzerland, 1968), the legendary Patriarch of Constantinople stated the following remarkable principle of Orthodox ecumenism:

I do not deny that there are differences between the Churches, but I say that we must change our way of approaching them. And the question of method is in the first place a psychological, or rather a spiritual problem. For centuries there have been conversations between theologians, and they have done nothing except to harden their positions. I have a whole library about it. And why? Because they spoke in fear and distrust of one another, with the desire to defend themselves and to defeat the others. Theology was no longer a pure celebration of the mystery of God. It became a weapon. God himself became a weapon!

I repeat: I do not ignore these difficulties. But I am trying to change the spiritual atmosphere. The restoration of mutual love will enable us to see the questions in a totally different light. We must express the truth which is dear to us – because it protects and celebrates the immensity of the life which is in Christ – we must express it, not so as to repulse the other, so as to force him to admit that he is beaten, but so as to share it with him; and also for its own sake, for its beauty, as a celebration of truth to which we invite our brothers. At the same time we must be ready to listen. For Christians, truth is not opposed to life or love; it expresses their fullness. First of all, we must free these words, these words which tend to collide, from the evil past, from all political, national and cultural hatreds which have nothing to do with Christ. Then we must root them in the deep life of the Church, in the experience of the

---

[10] Among others we mention the following: *Theological Studies and Ecumene. With Reference to the Participation of the Orthodox Church to Inter-Christian Dialogues and their Future*, ed. Stathokosta Vas. (University of Athens-Pedio: Athens, 2013); Thomas FitzGerald, *The Ecumenical Patriarchate and Christian Unity*, (Brookline, Mass: Holy Cross Orthodox Press, 1997, revised edition, 2009); Aram I Catholicos of Syria, *In Search of Ecumenical Vision* (Antelias, Lebanon: Armenian Catholicosate of Cilicia, 2001); Todor Sabev, *The Orthodox Churches in the WCC. Towards the Future*. (Geneva: WCC Publications - Bialystock: Syndesmos, 1996); George Lemopoulos, *The Ecumenical Movement, the Churches of the World Council of Churches : An Orthodox Contribution to the Reflection Process on the "Common Understanding and Vision of the WCC"* (Geneva: WCC, 1996); *Orthodox Vision on Ecumenism: Statements, Messages and Reports on the Ecumenical Movement, 1902-1992*, ed. Gennadios Limouris, (Geneva: WCC Publications, 1994); Ion Bria, *Orthodoxy And Ecumenism: A New Theological Discourse*, (Geneva: WCC, 1994); Ion Bria, *The Sense Of Ecumenical Tradition: The Ecumenical Witness And Vision Of The Orthodox*, (Geneva: WCC Publications, 1991); *Go Forth In Peace: Orthodox Perspectives On Mission*. WCC mission series no 7, ed. Ion Bria (Geneva: WCC, 1986); *The Orthodox Church in the Ecumenical Movement: Documents and Statements, 1902-1975*, ed. Constantin George Patelos, (Geneva: WCC, 1978).

Resurrection which it is their mission to serve. We must always weigh our words in the balance of life and death and the Resurrection.

Those who accuse me of sacrificing Orthodoxy to a blind obsession with love, have a very poor conception of the truth. They make it into a system which they possess, which reassures them, when what it really is, is the living glorification of the living God, with all the risks involved in creative life. And we don't possess God; it is He who holds us and fills us with His presence in proportion to our humility and love. Only by love can we glorify the God of love, only by giving and sharing and sacrificing oneself can one glorify the God who, to save us, sacrificed himself and went to death, the death of the cross.[11]

We the editors are grateful to the wide spectrum of contributors from different Orthodox churches who have offered time and expertise for this volume, often in circumstances which were neither easy nor favourable, considering the situation and context in which some Orthodox churches find themselves at present. It should be noted at this point that each contributor express his or her own position without in any case representing officially his or her respected Church. We also express thanks to all who gave advice concerning the structure and content of the Handbook, particularly to Mr. Yorgo Lemopoulos, Deputy General Secretary of WCC and to V. Rev. Lecturer Dr. Daniel Buda, WCC's programme executive for church and ecumenical relations. We need also to express our deep gratitude to V. Rev. Prof. Dr. Viorel Ionita, Former General Secretary par Interim of CEC, for his valuable contribution to the early stage of the project and the development of the draft concept and outline of the Handbook. Our sincere thanks go also to people that helped with the communication or correspondence with various authors as well as to people who graciously accepted to serve as second readers, content and language editors, copy editors or translators like Dr. Paul Ladouceur (Trinity College, University of Toronto and Université de Sherbrooke), Prof. Dr. Petros Vassiliadis (Aristotle University of Thessaloniki), Dr. Rutham Gill (CEC), Rev. Dr. Gregory Edwards (Volos Academy), Rev. George Anagnostoulis (Volos Academy), George Vlantis, MTh (University of Munich and Volos Academy), Filoktimon Stamatopoulos - Samaras (Volos Academy), Sofia Kounavi (Volos Academy), Vallila Giannoutaki (Volos Academy), Dr. Michael Hjälm (Orthodox Church of Finland), Matthew Baker MTh (Fordham University, NA, USA) and Dr. Jeremy Wallace (King College, New York City) who had the responsibility of the general linguistic editing of the Handbook.[12] We also express gratitude for the cordial encouragement and support from which this project has benefitted through ETE/WCC, CEC, and the EKD churches in Hannover. Finally we give thanks to our colleagues of the Romanian Institute for Inter-Orthodox, Inter-Confessional, and Inter-Religious Studies (INTER, Cluj-Napoca), particularly to Nicolae Turcan, who have done the typesetting for this opus magnum, as well as to Maria Nanou, MA (Volos), for the proposal of the cover picture.

We hope and pray that this Handbook will inspire and deepen the passion of Orthodox theologians to search and to contribute to the unity of Christians unity in the mission of Christ which is at the heart of the ecumenical vocation.

The Editors
Pantelis Kalaitzidis
Thomas FitzGerald
Cyril Hovorun
Aikaterini Pekridou
Nikolaos Asproulis
Guy Liagre
Dietrich Werner

---

[11] For Ecumenical Patriarch Athenagoras' Address, see Olivier Clément, *Dialogues avec le Patriarche Athénagoras,* (Paris: Fayard, 1976), 310-311, 313-314.. Source for the English translation of this excerpt: http://www.stpaulsirvine.org/html/athenagoras.htm (last accessed, September 2013).

[12] We also explicitly mention the names of the following second readers and translators: Paraskevi Arapoglou, Stephanos Salzman, James Lillie, Chris Henson, Elaine Griffiths and Nikolaos Petropoulos.

LIST OF CONTRIBUTORS

Emmanuel Adamakis: Ecumenical Patriarchate; Metropolitan of France; President of KEK/CEC (Conference of European Churches); President of the Assembly of the Orthodox Bishops in France; Co-president of the Council of Christian Churches of France; Co-president of the World Conference of Religions for Peace (WCRP). E-mail: metropolite.emmanuel@gmail.com

Nareg Alemezian: Armenian Apostolic Orthodox Church – Holy See Catholicos of Cilicia (Antelias-Lebanon); Ecumenical Officer and Dean of the Theological Seminary, World Council of Churches Central Committee member; Chair of the Conference of Secretaries of the Christian World Communions.

Nikolaos Asproulis: Orthodox Church of Greece; MTh; PhD student; Academic member of Volos Academy for Theological Studies, member of the editorial department of the official theological Journal of the Church of Greece *Theologia*; Coordinator of NELCEE (Network for Ecumenical Learning in Central and Eastern Europe (2013-); Co-Editor of "Orthodox Handbook on Ecumenism. Resources for Theological Education". E-mail: asprou@acadimia.gr

Pavel Aurel: Romanian Orthodox Church, Professor and Dean at the Andrei Şaguna Faculty of Orthodox Theology, Lucian Blaga University of Sibiu, Romania. E-mail: aurelpavel@yahoo.com

Daniel Ayuch: Greek Orthodox Patriarchate of Antioch; Professor of New Testament, St. John of Damascus Institute of Theology at the University of Balamand in Lebanon, Assistant to the Dean for Academic Affairs. E-mail: dayuch@balamand.edu.lb

Augoustinos Bairactaris: Ecumenical Patriarchate; Assistant Professor at the University Ecclesiastical Academy of Heraklion – Crete; Priest; Academic member of Volos Academy for Theological Studies. E-mail: augustinos_bairactaris@yahoo.gr

Matthew Baker: Greek Orthodox Archdiocese of America; MTh; Priest. E-mail: matthew.j.baker77@gmail.com

Ştefăniţă Barbu: Romanian Orthodox Church; Mth; Rector of the "Descent of The Holy Spirit" Church – Liège (Belgium). E-mail: pr.stefan.barbu@gmail.com

Athanasios Basdekis: Ecumenical Patriarchate; Orthodox theologian; Employed in the National Council of Churches in Germany as orthodox Secretary. E-mail: basdekis@t-online.de

Marios Begzos: Orthodox Church of Greece; Faculty Member of the University of Athens/Greece; Dean and Professor in the Faculty of Theology; Member of the Societas Oecumenica - European Society for Ecumenical Research. E-mail: mbegzos@theol.uoa.gr

Tesfaye Ayalkibet Berhanu: Ethiopian Orthodox Tewahedo Church (Ethiopia, South Africa), PhD student, School of Religion, Philosophy and Classics at the University of KwaZulu-Natal in South Africa. E-mail:ayalkibet@gmail.com

Metropolitan Bishoy: Coptic Orthodox Church; Metropolitan of Damietta, Kafr El-Sheikh and the Monastery of Saint Demiana, Barrari, Belkas, Egypt; Former secretary of the Coptic Orthodox Holy Synod since 1985. E-mail: demiana@demiana.org

Radu Bordeianu: Romanian Orthodox Archdiocese in the Americas; Associate Professor, Duquesne University, United States of America; President of the Orthodox Theological Society in America; Priest. E-mail: bordeianur@duq.edu

Iosif Bosch: Ecumenical Patriarchate; Bishop of Patara; Chancellor of the Archdiocese of Buenos Aires and South America; Member of WCC ECHOS Commission on Youth; Member of WCC JWG with the Roman Catholic Church. E-mail: iosifbosch@hotmail.com

Peter Bouteneff: Orthodox Church in America; Professor at St. Vladimir's Orthodox Theological Seminary in New York, USA; Executive Secretary of Faith and Order at the World Council of Churches (1995-2000); Member of the Faith and Order Commission of the NCCCUSA (2003-2012); Consultant to the Orthodox Church of America's Commission for External Affairs and Inter-Church Relations (2001-today). E-mail:petercb123@verizon.net

Daniel Buda: Archpriest of the Romanian Orthodox Church; Program Executive for Church and Ecumenical Relations in the World Council of Churches, Geneva, Switzerland; Lecturer for Church History in the Orthodox Theological Faculty "Saint Andrei Şaguna" of University "Lucian Blaga", Sibiu, Romania. E-mail: Daniel.Buda@wcc-coe.org

Alkiviadis Calivas: Ecumenical Patriarchate; Priest; Emeritus Professor of Liturgics, Holy Cross Greek Orthodox School of Theology, Brookline, MA USA; former President and Dean of Holy Cross; former member of the North American Orthodox-Catholic Bilateral Consultation. E-mail: acalivas@msn.com

Christine Chaillot: Ecumenical Patriarchate; author and editor of several books on the Eastern Orthodox and Oriental Orthodox Churches and also on the Dialogue between them. E-mail: acchaillot@hotmail.com

Demetrios Charbak: Greek Orthodox Patriarchate of Antioch and all the East; Bishop; Syria Professor of Ecumenical Movement at the university of Balamand in Lebanon; Member of the International Committee for dialogue between the Orthodox and Roman Catholic Churches. E-mail: demetrios.charbak@yahoo.com

Emmanuel Clapsis: Ecumenical Patriarchate; Archbishop Iakovos Professor, Holy Cross Greek Orthodox Theological School; Priest; Vice Moderator of the Faith and Order Commission of the World Council of Churches (1991-1998) and commissioner of Faith and Order Commission of the U.S. National Council of Churches (1985-1991); member of the formal delegation to the Seventh, Eighth and Ninth Assemblies of WCC in Canberra, Australia (1991), in Harare Zimbabwe (1998) and Porto Alegre, Brazil (2005); Former member of the Reference Group that informs and accompanies the work of the World Council of Churches During the Decade to Overcome Violence (2001-2010). E-mail: eclapsis@hchc.edu

Geevarghese Mor Coorilos: Metropolitan of Niranam diocese of the Jacobite Syrian Orthodox Church; Moderator of the Commission on World Mission and Evangelism (CWME); Chairperson of the Student Christian Movement of India (SCMI). E-mail: gcoorilos@gmail.com

Seraphim Danchaert: Greek Orthodox Archdiocese of America; Director of Strategy, Princeton Theological Seminary. E-mail: seraphim.danckaert@ptsem.edu_

Konstantinos Delikonstantis: Ecumenical Patriarchate; Professor of Philosophy and Systematic Theology, Faculty of Theology, University of Athens and Institute of Postgraduate Studies in Orthodox Theology, Chambésy/Genève; Theological Consultant to the Ecumenical Patriarchate. E-mail: kdelikos@theol.uoa.gr

Amal Dibo: Orthodox Church of Antioch; Instructor in the Civilization Sequence Program at the American University of Beirut; lecturer and advisor at the WSCF and the Middle East Council of Churches. E-mail: amaldibo@gmail.com

Alexei Dikarev: Russian Orthodox Church; Staff-member of the Department for External Church Relations of the Moscow Patriarchate; Faculty Member of SS. Cyril and Methodius Theological Institute of Post-Graduate and Doctoral Studies. E-mail: alexdikarev@mail.ru

Ivan Dimitrov: Orthodox Church of Bulgaria; Professor Emeritus of New Testament at Faculty of Theology of St. Kliment Ohridski Sofia University; Former Director of the Department for Religious Affairs with the Council of Ministers of Bulgaria; Initiator for the creation of the Interreligious Council in Bulgaria; Former member of different commissions of WCC. E-mail: ivand@theo.uni-sofia.bg

Irinej Dobrijevic: Serbian Orthodox Church; M.Div. Bishop of the Metropolis of Australia and New Zealand; Chairman, National Heads of Churches of Australia; Member, World Council of Churches Central Committee, Permanent Committee on Consensus an Collaboration, Moderator, 10th Assembly Public Issues Committee, Busan (2013); Co-Moderator, Conference of European Churches 50th Anniversary Assembly, Lyon (2009); Member of the Jasenovac Committee and the Permanent Missions Board of the Holy Synod of Bishops of the Serbian Orthodox Church; Advisory Council of the Njegos Endowment for Serbian Studies at Columbia University, New York; Communications Committee of the Board of Directors of St Vladimir's Seminary, Crestwood; Senior Lecturer, Loyola University, Chicago (1992-1996) and Guest Lecturer, Theological Faculty of the Serbian Orthodox Church, Belgrade (1996-1997). E-mail: irinej@earthlink.net

Christoph D'Aloisio: Exarchate of the Ecumenical Patriarchate for the Russian Orthodox Churches in Western Europe; Priest; Professor of Dogmatic Theology at the Orthodox Institute Saint-John-the-Theologian in Brussels, Belgium; President of Syndesmos, the World Fellowship of Orthodox Youth; Member of the Continuation Committee on Ecumenism in the 21st century. E-mail: christophe.daloisio@orthodoxie.be

Bishara Ebeid: Greek Orthodox Church; Mth in patristic theology and Arab Christian litterateur (Pontifical Oriental Institute, Rome). E-mail: bisharaebeid@gmail.com

Vladimir Fedorov: Archpriest of the Russian Orthodox Church; Director of the Orthodox Research Institute of Missiology, Ecumenism and New Religious Movements; President of Interchurch Partnership, St Petersburg, Russia. Assistant Professor of the Psychological Department, St Petersburg State University; Former Consultant of the ETE Program WCC for Eastern and Central Europe. E-mail: vffedorov@yahoo.com

Thomas FitzGerald: Ecumenical Patriarchate; Protopresbyter; Professor of Church History and Historical Theology at Holy Cross Greek Orthodox School of Theology, Brookline, MA, USA; Dean of the faculty (2006-2013); Orthodox Executive Secretary and Member of the Orthodox–Roman Catholic Bilateral Theological Consultation in North America; Consultant, Committee for Ecumenical Relations and Committee on Theological Education, Assembly of Canonical Orthodox Bishops; Editor, The Greek Orthodox Theological Review Executive Director, WCC, Programme Unit I on Unity and Renewal 1994-2000. E-mail: tfitzgerald@hchc.edu

Brandon Gallaher: Orthodox theologian; British Academy Postdoctoral Fellow (Oct. 2011-Jan. 2015); Faculty of Theology and Religion, Regent's Park College, University of Oxford; member of the Parish of St Nicholas the Wonderworker in Oxford, UK (Moscow Patriarchate); He specializes in and has published widely on modern Orthodox theology. He has been involved with Hindu-Christian dialogue and Islamic-Christian dialogue (through the Building Bridges Seminar, Georgetown University) and is participating in a consultation with the World Council of Churches (WCC) on ecclesiology in the context of religious plurality. E-mail: brandon.gallaher@theology.ox.ac.uk

Paul Gavrilyuk: Aquinas Chair in Theology and Philosophy, Theology Department, University of St Thomas, Saint Paul, Minnesota, USA; Deacon in the Orthodox Church in America, Holy Trinity Church, Saint Paul, Minnesota, USA. E-mail: PLGAVRILYUK@stthomas.edu

Vladimir Gerka: Orthodox Church in Slovakia; Orthodox Theological Faculty of University of Presov; Board member of Fellowship of Orthodox Youth in Slovakia; SYNDESMOS Local correspondent for Slovakia. E-mail: vladimirg@orthodox.sk

Tamara Grdzelidze: Orthodox Church of Georgia; Programme Executive within the Faith and Order Secretariat of the World Council of Churches in Geneva, Switzerland; PhD Oxford University, Doctorate in Medieval Georgian Literature, Tbilisi State University. E-mail: tgrdzelidze@gmail.com

Perry Theodore Hamalis: Greek Orthodox Archdiocese of America; Cecelia Schneller Mueller Professor of Religion, North Central College (Illinois, U.S.A.); Trustee, Hellenic College and Holy Cross Greek Orthodox School of Theology; Outside Consultant for Faith and Order Commission, WCC. E-mail: pthamalis@noctrl.edu

Oliver Herbel: Orthodox Church in America; Rector, Holy Resurrection Orthodox Mission, Fargo, North Dakota; Chaplain, North Dakota Air National Guard. E-mail: froliverherbel@cableone.net

Bishop Hovakim: Armenian Apostolic Orthodox Church; Former Director of the Inter - Church Office of the Mother See of Holy Etchmiadzin; Lecturer at the Gevorkian Seminary and the Vaskenian Academy on the History of the Universal and Armenian Churches; Former member of the Central Committee of the CEC since 2009 and as the Ecumenical Officer of the Armenian Church to the World Council of Churches since 2004; Member of the Trustee Committee of the Armenian Round Table Charitable Foundation.

Cyril Hovorun: Russian Orthodox Church; Research fellow at Yale University; Priest. E-mail: hovorun@gmail.com

Heiki (Theodoros) Huttunen: Orthodox Church of Finland; Priest of the Holy Metropolis of Helsinki; General secretary of the Finnish Ecumenical Council; Member of the WCC central committee (Porto Alegre to

Busan); WCC Youth Director 1985-98; President of Syndesmos 1992-1995; Mth; Lecturer in the St. Platon Orthodox Theological Seminary in Tallinn. E-mail: heikki.huttunen@ekumenia.fi

Benedict Ioannou: Orthodox Church of Cyprus; Priest in charge of the Church of Panagia Phaneromeni in Nicosia; Permanent Representative of the Ecumenical Patriarchate to the World Council of Churches (1999-2008). E-mail: benedict.2008@yahoo.com

Viorel Ionita: Romanian Orthodox Church; Priest; Professor Emeritus of the Orthodox Theological Faculty of the University Bucharest; Former Director of the Conference of European Churches. E-mail: pr.vionita@yahoo.com

Vaclav Jezek: Orthodox Church of the Czech lands and Slovakia; Lecturer at Orthodox theological faculty of the Prešov University, Slovakia; Orthodox Priest; Currently involved in issues relating to inter Orthodox relations in the context of Ethiopia. E-mail: vaclavjezek111@gmail.com

Rastko Jovic: Serbian Orthodox Church; PhD; Associate at the Educational Institute at the Theological Faculty in Belgrade; Teacher of Religious Education; Member of the WCC group "Movers for Gender Justice". E-mail: rastko.jovic@hotmail.com

Pantelis Kalaitzidis: Orthodox Church of Greece; Director of Volos Academy for Theological Studies; Editor of the series "Doxa & Praxis: Exploring Orthodox Theology, A joint project of Volos Academy and WCC; Lecturer of Systematic Theology in Hellenic Open University. E-mail: pkalaitz@acadimia.gr

Kyriaki Karidoyanes-FitzGerard: Ecumenical Patriarchate; PhD, Adjunct Professor of Theology at Holy Cross Greek Orthodox School of Theology in Brookline, Massachusetts; Founder of St. Catherine's Vision, an association of theologians and lay leaders; Representative of the Ecumenical Patriarchate of the WCC Faith and Order Commission from 1985 to 1999. E-mail: drkfitzgerald@gmail.com

Eleni Kasselouri-Hatzivassiliadi: Orthodox Church of Greece; Orthodox Biblical Scholar; Academic Staff of the Hellenic Open University; Member of the Steering Group of Women's Voices and Visions Program of WCC ; Co-opted staff and Bible Facilitator at the 9th General Assembly of WCC, Porto Allegre, Brazil. E-mail: ekasselouri@gmail.com

Ioustinos-Ioannis Kefalouros: Orthodox Church of Greece; Priest in Thessaloniki (Greece); MTh. E-mail: father.ioustinos@gmail.com

Leonid Kirshkovsky: Archpriest. Director of External Affairs and Interchurch Relations, Orthodox Church in America. Has served as President of the National Council of the Churches of Christ in the the USA, Moderator of Christian Churches Together in the USA, Moderator of Religions for Peace. Member of the World Council of Churches from 1983 to 2013. E-mail: leonid@oca.org

George K. M. Kondothra: Professor of Systematic and Patristic Theology; Priest of Malankara Orthodox Syrian Church, India; Special Advisor on Ecumenism and External Church Affairs to HH the Catholicos, Member, Central Committee of the WCC. E-mail: frkmgeorge@hotmail.com

Miltiadis Konstantinou: Orthodox Church of Greece; Faculty Member of Aristotle University of Thessaloniki/Greece; Professor in the Faculty of Theology; Member of the United Bible Societies Global Board and its Church Relations Committee; Chairman of the UBS Committee on Translation Policy and of the Board of the "Hellenic Society of Biblical Studies"; Delegate of the Church of Greece to the International Commission of the Anglican-Orthodox Theological Dialogue (ICAOTD). E-mail: mkon@theo.auth.gr

Anna Koulouris: Greek Orthodox Church, Archdiocese of America; Reporter and media representative of the Greek Orthodox Patriarchate of Jerusalem. E-mail: anna@annakoulouris.com

Valentin Kozhuharov: Bulgarian Orthodox Church; Freelance Researcher and Lecturer in Christian education and in Missiology at theological schools in Bulgaria, Hungary and UK; Formerly (2002-2009) missionary at the Department for religious education and catechization of the Moscow Patriarchate of the Russian Orthodox Church. E-mail: valentin_kozhuharov@yahoo.co.uk

Koshy Vaidyan Kumpalathu: Malankara (Indian) Orthodox Syrian Church; Faculty Member of Sruthi School of Liturgical Music, Orthodox Theological Seminary, Kottayam, India; Faculty Member of St.

Basil Bible School, Kerala, India; Director of The Ministry of Human Empowerment of the Diocese of Kollam of the Orthodox Church of India. E-mail: frvaidyan@yahoo.com

Paul Ladouceur: Orthodox Church in America (OCA), Archdiocese of Canada; Orthodox theologian and writer; Lecturer in the Orthodox theology programmes of the Université de Sherbrooke and Trinity College, University of Toronto; Responsible for the French-language web site Pages Orthodoxes La Transfiguration, the electronic newsletter Lumière du Thabor; Member of the Governing Board and the Commission on Faith and Witness of the Canadian Council of Churches. E-mail: thabor@megaweb.ca

Ioan Vasile Leb: Romanian Orthodox Church; Professor Doctor of General Church History University "Babes-Bolyai" Cluj-Napoca, Faculty of Orthodox Theology. E-mail: lebioan@yahoo.com

Nicolae Adrian Lemeni: Lecturer at the Faculty of the Orthodox Theology, Bucharest University; Director of the Centre of the Dialogue and Research in Theology, Science and Philosophy, Bucharest University; He has a large activity in the ecumenical and inter-religious dialogue (Ecumenical Institute from Bossey, Catholic Institute from Paris) and much participation to the meetings regarding the ecumenical and inter-religious dialogue to the national and international level (especially as State Secretary for Religious Affairs in 2005-2012). E-mail: adrian.lemeni@gmail.com

Georges (Yorgo) Lemopoulos: Ecumenical Patriarchate; Deputy General Secretary of the WCC; Church interim Representative to the WCC; Mth. E-mail: Yorgo.Lemopoulos@wcc-coe.org

Guy Liagre: General Secretary Conference of European Churches (CEC); Former president United Protestant Church in Belgium; Former Lecturer Modern Church History Protestant Theological Faculty Brussels. E-mail: Guy.Liagre@cec-kek.org

Grigorios Liantas: Orthodox Church of Greece; Assistant Professor of Inter-Orthodox and Inter-Christian Relations and Ecclesiastical Politics, University Ecclesiastical Academy of Thessaloniki; Committee Member of the Patriarchate of Alexandria, and its Representative in Inter-Orthodox Committee of Bioethics. E-mail: grliantas@yahoo.com

Gennadios Limouris: Ecumenical Patriarchate of Constantinople; Metropolitan of Sassima; Professor of Orthodox theology and canon law; Member of the WCC executive and central committees since 2002; Leader in various dialogues between Orthodox Christians and Baptists, Lutherans, Methodists and Roman Catholics.

Bogdan Lubardic: Serbian Orthodox Church; Assistant Professor at the Faculty of Orthodox Theology of Belgrade University; Regular and official member of the International Commission for Anglican-Orthodox Theological Dialogue (ICAOTD). E-mail: blubardic@pbf.rs

George Martzelos: Orthodox Church of Greece; Professor of Dogmatics in the Theological Faculty of Thessaloniki/Greece; Member of the Central Committee of WCC; Member of the special Committee of the Theological Dialogue between the Eastern Orthodox and Oriental Orthodox Churches, E-mail: martzelo@theo.auth.gr

John McGuckin: Archpriest; Romanian Orthodox Church; Nielsen Professor of Church History, Union Theological Seminar; Professor of Byzantine Christian Studies, Columbia University, New York; President of the Sophia Institute (for the advanced study of Eastern Christian Culture); Fellow of the British Royal Historical Society. E-mail: Jam401@columbia.edu

Pekka Metso: Finnish Orthodox Church; Acting Professor of Practical Theology (Orthodox Theology) in the University of Eastern Finland. E-mail: pekka.metso@uef.fi

Nicolae Moşoiu: Romanian Orthodox Church; Priest; Associate Professor at the Orthodox Faculty "Saint Andrei Şaguna", Sibiu, Romania; formerly member of the Central Committee and of the Commission on World Mission and Evangelism of the World Council of Churches. E-mail: nicolaemosoiu@yahoo.com

Bassam Antoine Nassif: Greek Orthodox Church of Antioch; General Secretary of the St. John of Damascus Institute of Theology, University of Balamand; Assistant Professor of Pastoral Theology and Marriage Counseling in Balamand; Priest in Mount Lebanon. E-mail: bassam.nassif@balamand.edu.lb

Bradley Nassif: Antiochian Orthodox Church of North America; Professor of Biblical and Theological Studies, North Park University, Chicago; Visiting Professor, Holy Cross Greek Orthodox School of Theology, Brookline, MA. E-mail: blnassif@yahoo.com

Philoxenos Mattias Nayis: Syrian Oriental Orthodox Church; Archbishop of the Diocese of the Syrian-Orthodox Church in Germany; Second Patriarchal assistant and administrator of the St. Ephraim Theological College in Ma'arrat Saidnaya.

Legesse Nigussu: World Council of Churches, Programme Executive for Africa. E-mail: nle@wcc-coe.org

Nikos Nissiotis (+1924-1986): Orthodox Church of Greece; Professor of Philosophy of Religion in Athens University, Greece (1965-1986); Associate General Secretary of WCC (1968-72); Moderator of the WCC Commission on Faith and Order (1977-82).

John Njoroge: Greek Orthodox Patriarchate of Alexandria; Priest; Lecturer in Mission, Biblical and Ecumenical Studies Department of Theology and Religious Studies Kenya Methodist; Priest University. E-mail: ngigenjoroge@yahoo.com

Godfrey Hugh O' Donell: Priest; Romanian Orthodox Church in Ireland; President of the Irish Council of Churches and Co-Chair of the Inter-Church Meeting with the Roman Catholic Church in Ireland; Mth. E-mail: godfreyhugh@gmail.com

Dorin Oancea: Romanian Orthodox Church; Metropolitanate of Transylvania, Orhtodox Theological Faculty "Andrei Şaguna" in Sibiu. E-mail: oancead@yahoo.com.

Ioan Ovidiu: Romanian Orthodox Church; Faculty Member of Philipps-Universität Marburg (Germany); formerly Academic Researcher at the Institute for Ecumenical Research Sibiu (Romania); formerly Coordinator of NELCEE (Network for Ecumenical Learning in Central and Eastern Europe); E-mail: ovidiu_ioan@hotmail.com

Athanasios N. Papathanasiou: Orthodox Church of Greece; Lay Theologian; Tutor, Hellenic Open University; Editor-in-chief of the quarterly Synaxi (Athens); Member of The European Society for Intercultural Theology and Interreligious Studies (ESITIS). E-mail: paptam@windowslive.com

Grigorios Papathomas: Orthodox Church of Greece; Professor of Canon Law at the Faculty of Theology of the State University of Athens and at the "Saint Sergius" Orthodox Institute of Theology in Paris; President of EFOST (Brussels). E-mail: grigorios.papathomas@wanadoo.fr

Henryk Paprocki: Orthodox Church in Poland; Theologian.

Alina Patru: Romanian Orthodox Church; Lecturer at the Orthodox Theological Faculty "Andrei Şagna", University of Sibiu, Romania; Lecturer at the Humboldt Postdoctoral Research Fellow, Department for Religious Studies of The University of Bonn, Germany. E-mail: patru_alina_ro@yahoo.com

Stanislau Paulau: Belarusian Orthodox Church (Moscow Patriarchate); M.Th, M.A. (Intercultural Theology); PhD candidate and research assistant in the Institute of Ecumenical Theology and Oriental Church and Mission History at the University of Göttingen (Germany). E-mail: stanislau.paulau@theologie.uni-goettingen.de

Aikaterini Pekridou: Orthodox Church of Greece; Doctoral Candidate at the Irish School of Ecumenics, Trinity College Dublin; Former member of the Churches in Dialogue Commission of the Conference of European Churches; Member of the Dublin City Interfaith Forum; Academic member of Volos Academy for Theological Studies. E-mail: pekridoa@tcd.ie.

Vlassios Pheidas: Orthodox Church of Greece; Emeritus Professor of Theological Faculty, Athens University; Former Dean and Professor of the Orthodox Theological Center of the Ecumenical Patriarchate in Chambésy, Switzerland; Member of various Committees in Bilateral inter-Christian dialogues.

Rauno Pietarinen: Orthodox Church in Finland; Former Rector of the Orthodox Seminary, Joensuu, Finland; Coordinator of the International Working Group on Orthodox Theological Education; Priest in Ivalo, Lapland. E-mail: rauno.pietarinen@ort.fi

Michael Plekon: Orthodox Church in America (OCA); Faculty Member of Baruch College of the City University of New York; Professor in the department of Sociology/Anthropology and in the program in

Religion and Culture; Archpriest attached to St. Gregory the Theologian Church, Wappingers Falls NY. E-mail: michael.plekon@baruch.cuny.edu

Radu Preda: Orthodox Church of Romania; Associate Professor of Social Theology, Babes-Bolyai, Cluj-Napoca, Romania; Director of the Romanian Insitute for Inter-Christian, Inter-Confessional, Inter-Religious Studies (INTER). E-mail: teologiasociala@gmail.com

Dhimiter Qosja: Orthodox Church in Albania ; Mth. E-mail: qosjadim@yahoo.com

Teva Regule: Orthodox Church in America, MDiv. Holy Cross Greek Orthodox School of Theology, Brookline, Mass. USA; Orthodox consultant to a variety of ecumenical gatherings sponsored by the World Council of Churches, including the assemblies in Harare and Porto Allegre, and consultations in Stoney Pt. (NY), Geneva, Volos (Greece), and Durres (Albania). E-mail: TEVA@MIT.EDU

Elena Sadovnikova: PhD in Haematology, During 1990s worked as a research scientist for ICRF and Imperial College, London, UK, specialising in cancer immunology. Took an active part in the life of metropolitan Anthony's London parish. Member of the Council of Metropolitan Anthony's of Sourozh Spiritual Legacy Foundation, Moscow, Russia.

Hieromonk Christopher Savage: Orthodox Church in America; Monk of New Skete Monastery, Cambridge, NY, USA. E-mail: brchristopher@newskete.org

Chrysostomos-Georges Savvatos: Orthodox Church of Greece; Metropolitan of Messinia; Professor of University in Athens; Member of Dialogue International between Orthodox and Roman-Catholic Churches. E-mail: mitropolis_messinias@yahoo.gr

Marian Simion: Lecturer in Government at Harvard University, Extension School; Postdoctoral Research Fellow at Harvard Divinity School; Sub-deacon in the Romanian Orthodox Archdiocese of the Americas; Assistant Director of the Boston Theological Institute. E-mail: marian.simion@bc.edu

Augustin Sokolovsky: Deacon, Russian Orthodox Church, Moscow Patriarchate; Co-Director of Doctoral Program "De Civitate Hominis. Theology in the Age of Post-Ecumenism", University of Fribourg, Switzerland; Member of the International Coordination of the Week of Prayer for Christian Unity, WCC – Faith & Order. E-mail: rev.dr.sokolovski@gmail.com

Vassiliki Stathokosta: Orthodox Church of Greece; Faculty Member of National and Kapodistrian University of Athens/Greece; Assistant Professor in the Faculty of Theology for "Orthodox Theology and the Ecumenical Movement". E-mail: vstathokosta@theol.uoa.gr

Dragica Tadic-Papanikolaou: Serbian Orthodox Church; MTh; Formerly Project Manager at Christian Cultural Center, Belgrade. E-mail: drtadic@yahoo.com

Wedad Abbas Tawfik: Coptic Orthodox Church of Egypt; Professor of Theology at the Post Graduate Institute of Coptic Studies in Cairo, Egypt, and at the Coptic Seminary in Germany; Member of Faith and Order Plenary Commission; Executive Member of the Circle of African Women Theologians. E-mail: wedadt@yahoo.com

Elizabeth Theokritoff: Orthodox Church in America; Independent scholar and theological translator; occasional lecturer at Institute for Orthodox Christian Studies, Cambridge; Former Secretary of the Fellowship of St Alban and St Sergius (London). E-mail: e.theokritoff@some.oxon.org

Sister Theoktisti (Emsley): Nun of the Holy Monastery of St. John the Forerunner, Anatoli - Agia, Greece; PhD. E-mail: imtp.anatoli@gmail.com

Vasileios Thermos: Orthodox Church of Greece; Doctorate of Theology (Athens University); Child and Adolescent Psychiatrist; Priest. E-mail: thermosv@otenet.gr

Ciprian Toroczkai: Romanian Orthodox Church; Assistant Professor at the Andrei Şaguna Faculty of Orthodox Theology, Lucian Blaga University of Sibiu, Romania. E-mail: torocipri@gmail.com

Georges Tsetsis: Grand Protopresbyter of the Ecumenical Patriarchate; Former Deputy Director of the Commission on Inter-Church Aid, Refugee and World Service of the World Council of Churches (1965-1985) and Permanent Representative of the Ecumenical Patriarchate to the WCC (1985-2000); Member of the Central and Executive Committees of the WCC. E-mail: gtsetsis@bluewin.ch

Stylianos Tsompanidis: Orthodox Church of Greece; Associate Professor of ecumenical theology and ecumenical social ethics in the School of Theology of the Aristotle University of Thessaloniki. E-mail: stsompa@theo.auth.gr

Petros Vassiliadis: Orthodox Church of Greece; Professor Emeritus of the University of Thessaloniki; Former Orthodox commissioner of CWME of the WCC. E-mail: pv@theo.auth.gr

Natallia Vasilevich: Orthodox Church of Belarus; Director of Centre Ecumena. E-mail: ecumena@ecumena.by

Juljia Vidovic: Serbian Orthodox Church, PhD candidate at the Catholic Institute of Paris and Orthodox Institute "Saint-Serge"; Member of the Governing Board of CEC. E-mail: julijavidovic@yahoo.fr

Georgios Vlantis: Theologian; M.Th. (Philosophy of Religion); Assistant of the Chair of Orthodox Systematic Theology, Faculty of Orthodox Theology, Ludwig-Maximilians-Universität, Munich; Member of the Academic team of the Volos Academy for Theological Studies. E-mail: drosiotis@yahoo.gr

Athanasios Vletsis: Ecumenical Patriarchate; Professor of Orthodox Systematic Theology (Dogmatics, Ethics, Ecumenical Theology), Faculty of Orthodox Theology, Ludwig–Maximilians–Universität, Munich, Germany. E-mail: Athanasios.Vletsis@gmx.de

Antony C. Vrame: Greek Orthodox Archdiocese of America (Ecumenical Patriarchate); Director of Department of Religious Education, Greek Orthodox Archdiocese of America; Chair, Faith and Order, National Council of Churches USA; Associate Professor, Holy Cross Greek Orthodox School of Theology, Brookline, Mass., USA. E-mail: tvrame@goarch.org

Ramy Wannous: Greek Orthodox Patriarchate of Antioch; Assistant Professor of Church History; Priest; E-mail: ramy.wannous@balamand.edu.lb

Dietrich Werner: Pastor of the Northelbian Lutheran Church in North Germany; Director of the Programme on Ecumenical Theological Education (ETE) in the World Council of Churches in Geneva; Co-founder of the Global Digital Library for Theology and Ecumenism (GlobeTheoLib) and key editor of "Handbook on Theological Education in World Christianity" (2010),"African Handbook of Theological Education"(2012), "Asian Handbook on Theological Education for Christian unity and common witness."(2013). E-mail: dietrich.werner@brot-fuer-die-welt.de

Stavros Yangazoglou: Orthodox Church of Greece; Consultant at the Greek Ministry of Education and Religious Affairs/Institute of Educational Policy; Lecturer at the Hellenic Open University/Postgraduate Studies in Orthodox Theology; Director of the quarterly journal *Theologia*/Church of Greece. E-mail: stavrosyang@gmail.com

Anastasios Yannoulatos: Archbishop of Tirana, Durrës and All Albania; Primate and Head of the Holy Synod of the Autocephalous Orthodox Church of Albania; Professor Emeritus of the National University of Athens; Honorary Member of the Academy of Athens; Co-president of the Central Committee of the World Council of Churches; Honorary President of the World Conference of Religions for Peace.

Angeliki Ziaka: Orthodox Church of Greece; Assistant Professor on the Study of Religion and Interreligious Dialogue and Visiting Professor at the Department of Political Sciences, Aristotle University of Thessaloniki; Member of Board of Directors of the Volos Academy for Theological Studies. E-mail: ziaka@theo.auth.gr

Metropolitan John Zizioulas: Ecumenical Patriarchate; Metropolitan of Pergamon; Co-President of the Joint International Commission for theological dialogue between the Catholic Church and the Orthodox Church; Professor of Universities of Edinburg, Glasgow, King's College London, Thessaloniki.

Stavros Zoumboulakis: Orthodox Church of Greece; Writer, President of the Biblical Foundation "Artos Zoes", Athens, Greece; President of the Board of Trustees of the National Library of Greece.

PART I

ORTHODOX CHURCHES
IN THE ECUMENICAL MOVEMENT – AN INTRODUCTION

(1) THE ROLE OF ORTHODOXY IN WORLD CHRISTIANITY TODAY – HISTORICAL, DEMOGRAPHIC AND THEOLOGICAL PERSPECTIVES – AN INTRODUCTION

Fr. John McGuckin

A Setting of the Scene

If the world's media turns its attention to the Church today it begins by habitually imagining the Christian world in one of only two vestures: the Roman Catholic or the Protestant. This has almost become the default way of thinking about Christianity. To point out that such a categorization only gives half the picture, since it leaves out of consideration Eastern Christianity, would be genuinely puzzling to most contemporary journalists and indeed to ordinary people. Is it not true that Roman Catholicism and Protestantism have spread across the globe – from the Amazon to Alaska, and from Texas to China? Anyone speaking today about Eastern Christianity needs, of necessity, to explain themselves: such is the almost complete exclusion of the multi-cultural ethos of the early churches in modern consciousness, and the wholesale suppression (in so many iterations of European history and theology books) of the record of the Byzantine Empire, that vastly extended form of Christian civilisation which nurtured, shaped, and dominated Christian consciousness for more than a millennium in its formative youth, and which continues to inform so many aspects of the culture and life of the most ancient Orthodox families of churches.

But a moment of thought will make anyone with even a cursory knowledge of Christianity take pause and realize the folly of elevating Roman Catholic and Protestant versions of Christianity as axiomatic, for were they not both deeply shaped by their own Renaissance oppositional clashes? And is not this early modern perspective a very late vantage point to comprehend so antique and apocalyptic a religious system as inspires Christian core values? Simply put, the religion of Jesus was from the Orient. It was passed on to European civilisation (both in its Protestant and Catholic forms) predominantly in Greek. Its earliest Gospels, liturgies, creeds, hymns, and apostolic letters all came in Greek. Its first great theologians and poets all composed in Greek; even when they lived in Rome the name of the Saviour, *Yeshu*, would have been comprehensible to the majority only when passed on in Greek, as *Jesus*. It is this ancient Greco-Roman Christian matrix of thought that runs in an unbroken line from the age of the Apostles, through New Testament times, on into the formative age of the great theologians and creed-makers of Christendom, embracing and sponsoring the ascent of Christian imperial civilization through its war-torn Middle Ages, and even down into the modern era as the shared culture and ethos of the Orthodox churches. The Orthodox world is heir to a vastly ancient and profound tradition. Its garments are dyed purple in the blood of martyrs; and still redolent of the perfume of innumerable saints and mystics who, in an unbroken lineage, illuminate its distinctive Christian ethos. Yet, for the most part, its history and spiritual writings are generally unknown in European and American Church life; its ritual practices (if ever witnessed) seem obscure and unapproachable, and its record of achievement remains a closed book. This is not merely a calamity for the Orthodox world itself, which is undoubtedly marginalized by it; but a factor that tragically limits and distorts western Christianity's own understanding of itself, its origins, and its potential future.

Things are certainly changing in respect to this marginalization of the Orthodox world, and have been since the latter part of the 20th century. It is relatively common now (unheard of a generation ago) to see Orthodox Icons play a large part in the devotional life of both Catholics and Protestants; and numerous series of translations have been made of the great writers of the Orthodox Christian East, bringing old masterpieces back to new life in European versions. The works of great luminaries (such as Ephrem of Edessa, Isaac of Niniveh, Symeon the New Theologian, and Gregory Palamas, to name only a few) are being taken up widely by the western Christian world as acknowledged masters of the spiritual life. Indeed the whole systemic structure of theology that lies behind such fascinating writers is being looked at again with new eyes, and Neo-Kantian forms of dogmatization (which had been so prevalent in western theological circles) are being rightly taken down from their pedestals. The Orthodox Church's approach to major dogmatic structures, accordingly, is being newly appreciated by theologians habituated to different modalities of discourse. Deification theory (*theiopoiesis kata charin*), so fundamental to Orthodox soteriology, is now seen to complement Latin Atonement theology, not to contradict it; and the customary Orthodox affirmations of the unity of all modes of Christian discourse (that is, how spirituality can never be separated from dogmatics, or ecclesiology and sacramentality) is once more reaching appreciative ears.

At the end of the 20th century, world Orthodoxy finally came back into the light of political freedoms that had been denied it for more than five centuries. At the dawn of the 21st century, for the first time in many generations, it slowly began to rebuild its university schools, its libraries and institutions that had been so extensively suppressed, often violently so, under the oppressive conditions of political and religious overlords. Today world Orthodoxy is poised as a major force to return to the table of international Christian discourse: both addressing the Church internally (offering to Christian brothers and sisters of different traditions the benefit of its own wisdoms, and being ready to learn from their experiences) and 'externally' as the Church of Christ, charismatically and kerygmatically addressing a wider world which in many cases has either never been Christian, or has largely drifted away from its ancestral Christian heritage. World Orthodoxy in this present era is readying itself to make its sonorous voice heard once more. It has passed from being an 'eastern' minority faction of the Christian world, to being embedded, after three generations of extensive emigrations, all over the Americas, Australasia, and Western Europe. In comparison to world figures for Roman Catholicism or global Protestantism, Orthodoxy may still be seen sociologically as a third force; even so its numbers are very large and its internal coherence immensely (and unusually) strong across the Christian world, making it in its newly liberated condition, a voice that will resonate loudly and with exceptional confidence and energy in the 21st century.

A Very Brief Introduction to Orthodox Church Culture

The Orthodox Christian world is a family of churches in complete communion with one another. Orthodox understand the Church to be essentially a communion of grace and love. They approach the definition of what church is (New Testament: *ekklesia,* or the elect assembly) by reference to the foundational terms of charismatic union and universal fidelity to foundational tradition. This is given expression in the four cardinal terms the Nicene Creed uses to describe the Church as: 'One, holy, catholic, and apostolic.' In the course of history the communion of the Orthodox has sometimes been disrupted. Today the Eastern Orthodox recognize that an Orthodox communion existed on almost all levels between themselves and their western Catholic counterparts (despite differences in language and ritual) throughout most of the first millennium; but that increasing alienations of ritual practice and doctrinal positions led to a growing separation between the eastern and western Catholic churches after the 13th century until by the 14th most recognized that a long term 'separation' (ecclesiastically known as a schism) was in effect. The so-called 'Great Schism' of 1054 was one of a series of minor, temporary separations between the Byzantine and Latin churches: and was not the great divide later text books have often made of it. The real alienation of the churches came a few centuries later, and it has not been healed to this day although ecumenical relations from the early 20th century onward between Orthodox and Roman Catholics have been greatly improved.

Orthodoxy took several generations before it collectively recognized what had happened in the western church at the time of the Reformation; and generally took much longer to place the Protestant churches in its theological 'world-map' of ecclesial belonging. It concurred with the Protestant movements in their almost unanimous attempts to curb the ecclesial scope of the authority of the papacy; and it agreed with the biblical tenor of the reformed theologians. On the other hand it found Protestantism's curtailed ecclesiology, rejection of sacramental forms and traditional practices, and numerous other doctrinal stances, to be profoundly at variance with what it took to be core elements of the Catholic Christian tradition.

In the Eastern Christian world proper, in ancient Byzantine times, there were many other instances of local Orthodox churches falling in and out of communion with one another, for a variety of reasons: some doctrinal and some political. One very large set of fall-outs, that have never been resolved, concerned the question of the reception of the authority of 'Ecumenical Councils.' While all the Orthodox were agreed that an ecumenical council (having 'world-wide' authoritative status for Christendom) laid down international law and protocol for all the churches; there was disagreement over which of the great councils actually counted as ecumenical. Subtle and confused Christological arguments, between the fifth and sixth centuries, in the Greek, Coptic, Ethiopic and Armenian churches, led to large-scale conflicts and divisions that were exacerbated and, to an extent, massively extended by Islamic invasion of traditional Christian territories in Asia Minor and Africa. These Christological disruptions and issues remaining over the classification of the great councils, led to a division between the Eastern Orthodox and the so-called Oriental Orthodox. The latter are now commonly referred to as the 'Non-Chalcedonian Orthodox.' The various families of Orthodox churches have immense amounts in common with each other and recognize the commonality of spirit; yet are still divided from full communion over the question of adhering to seven great councils or simply the first three. Many great strides took place in the 20th century towards renewed dialogue between the families of the Byzantine Orthodox (Greek, Antiochene, Romanian, Russian and other Slavic churches) and the Oriental Orthodox (Armenian, Coptic, Ethiopic, Syrian, Malabar). These two ancient ecclesial divisions (between the Byzantine and Latin traditions, of 800 years' standing; and between Byzantine and Oriental Christian churches, of 1400 years' standing) are what the Orthodox generally hope for as the 'first to be healed' in any significant ecumenical advancement of our time. All three traditions, Latin, Byzantine, and Oriental, concur on the fundamentals of the authoritative 'markers' of Christian tradition: namely, the vivifying presence in the Church of the Risen Lord and his energizing Spirit; the ongoing charismatic inspiration of the Church collectively as gathering of saints; the centrality of inspired scripture as a guide to the 'Mind of the Lord'; the continuing guidance of the Church and the energization of its spiritual life in the sacraments and life of holiness of its members (regarded collectively as the holy tradition); and the manner in which its ordained ministers (especially the bishops) authoritatively guide it along the road of the conciliar canons (church law) which also have a revered status. Obviously world Protestantism would itself concur with many of the elements itemized above; but not with all of them. The agreement with that collective, however, (despite many significant internal differences in details of application of the principles) is something that still characterizes the three ancient families of churches; orientating them differently from the newer families of western churches that devolved from an (often violent) separation from late medieval Latin Catholicism.

Orthodox Church Organization Today

The Eastern Orthodox world today is comprised of various families of national churches in full communion and theological agreement with one another, who hold that their collective solidarity on all critical matters of faith and ritual practice stands as a key witness to enduring Orthodox Christian authenticity. Their common corporate organisation flows out of the New Testament and early Christian principles of local churches gathered under bishops, arranged in larger Metropolitan provincial synods, and this eventually culminating in the expression of the ancient Pentarchy of Patriarchates (the practical role of governance the five greatest Christian sees expressed internationally in ancient times) which was felt to express a global sense of different Christian cultures in harmony with the whole. The ancient Pentarchy afforded the five greatest Christian churches of the old world a special status as international supervisors of Christian communion, and was comprised of the cities (mainly the episcopal courts) of Rome, Constantinople, Alexandria, Antioch, and Jerusalem. After the Orthodox-Latin separation only four patriarchates remained in Orthodox communion, Rome having fallen away in the understanding of the East. To this four, other patriarchal sees were added in later times, as 'newer' nation-churches gained status. In addition status was also afforded to other significant (generally smaller) 'Autocephalous' Orthodox churches (a term which means: in charge of their own affairs), and other Autonomous Orthodox churches (a term designating those churches which have large degrees of independence but which are still attached to their original 'founder churches' by remaining organisational ties). These Autonomous churches are an extension of the 'International character' of world Orthodoxy that prevailed in antiquity within the Pentarchy of patriarchates that constituted the Christian Roman Empire. The exact organizational pattern of the Orthodox churches now as follows:

A. Four Ancient Patriarchates: Constantinople (Istanbul), Alexandria, Antioch, and Jerusalem.

B. Eleven Autocephalous Churches (with the dates of their recognition as such): Cyprus (431); Sinai (1575); Russia (1589); Greece (1850); Bulgaria (1945); Serbia (1879); Romania (1885); Georgia (1917); Poland (1924); Albania (1937); The Czech Lands and Slovakia (1998).

C. Four Autonomous Churches: Finland (1923. From the Patriarchate of Constantinople); Estonia (1923. From the Patriarchate of Constantinople); Japan (1970. From the Patriarchate of Moscow); China (1957. From the Patriarchate of Moscow). No one of these Autonomous Churches is unanimously recognised as such by the Orthodox Churches' consensus. The Orthodox Church in America is currently 'in controversial process' of belonging to this group (in the sense that it is still in the position of gaining world-wide Orthodox recognition). Originally a daughter-church of Russia, it assumed Autocephalous status in 1970 with the blessing of the Patriarchate of Moscow. The Autocephaly has not been acknowledged by the Patriarchate of Constantinople or the majority of other Orthodox churches, though its Autonomous status would be apparently now *de facto*. To these three major groupings of Orthodox churches we ought also to add a fourth dimension namely:

D. Various 'Diaspora' Churches. The so-called Diaspora churches are the Orthodox of different ethnic groupings who for historical reasons, such as immigration or trade over past generations, have been removed from their original homelands and now reside in what were formerly seen as 'western' countries. Orthodoxy is now deeply rooted in most parts of Western Europe and America, as the old geographical simplicities have increasingly been blurred by global mobility. There are, for example, incomparably more Orthodox belonging to the Patriarchate of Constantinople living in North America, than there are in the old heartlands of Thrace, Asia Minor, or Greece. There are also more Orthodox living in Britain today than there are Baptists. The Diaspora Orthodox are organized in the form of missionary extensions of the synods of the 'Home churches.' For example, the Romanian Archdiocese of the Two Americas is led by a Romanian Archbishop based in North America, who is a reporting member of the Home Synod of the Church of Romania. The Greek Orthodox Archdiocese in Great Britain is equally named for an otherwise defunct see in Asia Minor called Thyateira, to show symbolically that its Archbishop is really a member of the Synod of the Church of Constantinople, but at the same time, and in a spirit of ecumenical sensitivity, to avoid giving the name of the city or of the local church (London) to the Orthodox Archbishop. These historical subterfuges continue in the present moment marking the no-man's-land between how long a local Orthodox church can be a missionary extension from another homeland, and how long it has to be rooted in a new territory before being eligible for consideration as 'indigenous'. Fundamental to Orthodox understandings of Church is that the Local Church is the Church in its totality. Many western territories (and America is a prime example) have, however, been occupied by Greek, Russian, Romanian, Syrian and many other Orthodox 'missions' for many hundreds of years now, and have not yet been able to decide on how many generations it takes for them to become indigenous Orthodox, rather than members of a historical immigrant mission. Discussions of this modern problem of 'jurisdictional coherence' occupy many of the bishops of such diaspora territories today.

The Orthodox and the Concept of Ecumenicity

The Patriarch of Constantinople, Germanos, at the dawn of the 20ᵗʰ century, was one of the leading church figures of the time who called and worked for a greater sense of unity and cooperation in world Christian affairs. As such, he is rightly seen as a founder of the modern ecumenical movement, and he was a pioneer who brought the Orthodox churches into what is now a long-standing ecumenical dialogue. Ecumenics in ancient Orthodox thought meant the issue of maintaining a 'world-wide' solidarity in communion on basics of faith and practice in the churches. It has tended, in the 20ᵗʰ century, to assume a new meaning of dialogue between divided churches over issues of faith and practice, in the cause of re-establishing understanding, and possible eventual reunion of divided believers. At the logical heart of the latter concept of ecumenical rapprochement lies the notion of ecclesiology: or what one understands to be the nature of the Church. Orthodoxy has precise ideas on what the Church is, which determine many of its attitudes. In the first place it is heavily influenced by its history in dealing with Church divisions in antiquity. In many of the ancient Orthodox canons of the Eastern Church (laws accumulated over centuries of episcopal synods) there are instructions dealing with how to manage church division. Following the lead of the new Testament *Letters of John*, which was a position developed by many of the early Fathers (theologians) of the Church, Orthodox teachers have generally accepted the position that a separation from the Church cannot happen when both parties continue to belong fully to the Church: in other words unity is quintessentially important to Church belonging, and a rupture of unity means that one party has 'departed from' the Church. From the 3ʳᵈ century theologians went on to refine this insight by adding degrees of differentiation to it, by means of two distinct terms: heresy and schism. The first Greek words means 'division' while the second connotes 'ripping'. In ecclesiastical usage the first signifies a severe disjunction caused by disagreements involving fundamental matters of faith or morals; while the second means a lesser form of disunity caused by organizational, or less central ideational differences. These two terms became the primary ways that Orthodoxy navigated the idea of Christian ecumenical union for most of its past. Its canons laid down that no Orthodox must continue to relate to heresy in any of its forms or manifestations after it had been recognized, on the grounds that it was a particular form of apostasy. This complete rejection of heresy (and the organizational contexts in which it existed) was seen to be a necessary apocalyptic response to a great eschatological sin against Church unity. Today this attitude is often difficult to understand by many non-Orthodox thinkers, who do not have such a rooting in the ancient contexts of thought, especially the manner in which the mystery of the existence of the Church was seen to be 'eschatological'. Those who approach ecumenical and ecclesiastical matters primarily from historical and sociological perspectives (such as from contemporary theories of group interaction and reconciliation negotiation) often find the Orthodox approaches to the Ecumenical movement to be rigid and hard to understand. The deeply eschatological context of Orthodox ecclesiology needs to be more carefully explained by the Orthodox. Without this background, the regularly heard claims from Orthodox commentators on the ecumenical movement that Orthodoxy 'simply is' the Church; not part of it, but the totality of it; can often be read as chauvinism that refuses to take cognizance of the real nature of global Christianity; or at least as a sign of bad faith, in the sense that those appearing to take part in ecumenical discussions are really only intending to speak, not to hear; to proselytize, not to appreciate the legitimate variety of Christian identities. The best of Orthodox ecumenists do not imply these ends when they insist, in eschatological theological terms, on refusing to allow the notion of Church to be partitioned, and on claiming to possess, purely and uncorruptibly, the authentic tradition of the Christian Church. Some Orthodox, however, make a wooden linear logic out of this eschatological insight, and go on to claim that since the Orthodox are the Church, all other forms of Christian denominations are 'not-Church', and some even go on to designate them as heretical and consequently claim Orthodoxy is prohibited from being involved in anything to do with them. Such thinkers equate their peculiar muddling of the past with the defence of ancient tradition, and blithely cling to the narrowest and most uncharitable of formulations that completely neglect the more fundamental fact that 'Church' means, above all else, God's unstoppable energy of salvation in the world. This kind of closing out brother and sister Christians in an excessively rigid understanding of God's large Ark of

Salvation has, nevertheless, not commanded the allegiance of the majority of the Orthodox world, which sees in the attempt to brand Ecumenism as a modern Pan-heresy a rather myopic refusal to recognize the working of the Holy Spirit in the life of the non-Orthodox churches. For this reason most Orthodox theologians and the more cultured of the Orthodox hierarchs have encouraged greater efforts in world ecumenical *fora* so that these difficult and complex matters of theology, and practical life, can be further developed.

Many great strides have been taken in the 20th century and the modern ecumenical movement has undoubtedly led to a much deeper appreciation of the 'real' positions of the different churches, as distinct from the often wooden world of apologetic that previously stood in for genuine learning and accurate mutual understanding. Orthodoxy's unique witness to what being Church is has never been more important in the counsels of the world ecumenical movement than today: both for its own ongoing understanding of the realities of Christianity in its third millennium, as well as for the benefit of the churches with whom it can dialogue.

All Orthodox who love and value their church are evangelically compelled to be enthusiastically joined with Christ's Arch-priestly prayer: 'That they all may be one.'

Bibliography

1) Benz, E., *The Eastern Orthodox Church: Its Thought and Life*, (Chicago: Aldine, 1963).
2) Casiday, A. (ed.), *The Orthodox Christian World*, (London: Routledge, 2012).
3) Clément, O., *L'Église orthodoxe*, (Paris: Presses Universitaires de France, 1985).
4) Constantelos, D. J., *The Greek Orthodox Church: Faith, History, Practice*, (New York: Seabury Press, 1967).
5) McGuckin, J.-A., *The Orthodox Church. An Introduction to its History, Theology & Spiritual Culture*, (Oxford & New York: Blackwell-Wiley, 2008).
6) Idem, 'The Orthodox Church and the Ecumenical Imperative.' *International Journal of Orthodox Theology*, Bamberg University, 2.2 (2011): 44-59.
7) Pelikan, J., *The Christian Tradition, vol. 1: The Emergence of the Catholic Traditio*, (Chicago: The University of Chicago Press, 1971).
8) Idem, *The Christian Tradition, vol. 2: The Spirit of Eastern Christendom*, (Chicago: The University of Chicago Press, 1974).
9) Soumakis, F. (ed), *Power & Authority in Eastern Christian Experience,* Sophia Studies in Orthodox Theology, vol. 3, (New York: Theotokos Press, 2011).

(2) How to Understand Christian Unity (Ecumenism) in Relation to Orthodox Identity? – A First Theological Approach

Fr. Thomas FitzGerald

The Orthodox Church honors Jesus Christ as her Lord and proclaims His Gospel of salvation to the world. As St. John says: "God so loved the world that he sent his only son…" (John 3:16). The Person, who was known, loved, and followed by the first disciples in Palestine nearly two thousand years ago, is the same Risen Lord and Savior who is known, loved, and followed today through the life of the Orthodox Church. This community of faith was established by Christ with the call of the first apostles and disciples (Matt. 4:19). It was enlivened by the Holy Spirit on the day of Pentecost (Acts 2:1). The Church is an essential part of God's plan of salvation. Through the life of the Church, persons have the opportunity to know God and to experience His love, mercy and goodness. The Living God "wishes that all be saved and come to the knowledge of truth" (1 Tim. 2:4).

Christ and His Church

Fundamental to the Orthodox understanding of Church is the salutary knowledge of God and His self-disclosure. The content of this divine revelation is centered upon the coming of Christ who is the fulfillment of the Law and the prophets of Ancient Israel. Through the divine revelation in Christ, the believers have come to know the One God as Father, Son and Holy Spirit. As St. Paul boldly says: "All this is from God who through Christ reconciled us to himself and gave us the ministry of reconciliation" (1 Cor. 2:5).

As Christ revealed the mystery of the one God, Father, Son and Holy Spirit, the Church continues to make Him known and to praise Him in her worship. As Christ revealed the love of the Father for His sons and daughters, the Church continues to proclaim the dignity of the human person created in His image and likeness. As Christ reconciled humanity to the Father, His Church continues to be the sign of reconciliation throughout the world. As Christ revealed the value of the physical world created by God, the Church affirms that we grow closer to God in the midst of the physical creation.

The Orthodox Church affirms her direct continuity with the community of believers which Christ established, and with the faith of the Apostles. The distinctive identity of the Orthodox Church is rooted in her relationship to Christ and His Gospel. The very images of the Church which are found in the New Testament, and which were also used by the Fathers, relate the community of believers to Christ and his saving activity. The Church, for example, is described as the "Body of Christ" (1 Cor. 12:27), as the "household of God in the Spirit" (Eph. 2:22), and as "a royal priesthood, a holy nation, God's own people" (1 Pet. 2:9). In using these and other images, the deepest identity of the Church is affirmed. This identity reflects the distinctive relationship between the persons of the Holy Trinity and the members of the Church. This community of believers is not simply another association of persons which has its genesis in human inspiration. Rather, persons of faith who are members of the Church have been incorporated into Christ and have become participants in the mighty acts of God.

The Eucharistic Community

The reality of the Church is manifested in a specific and concrete way in the celebration of the Eucharist. It is the most important act of communal worship for Orthodox Christians and the center of the Church's liturgical life. In obedience to the command of the Lord given at the Last Supper (Luke 22:19), the community of believers gathers at the Eucharist. The believers hear the Word of God, offer prayers, present the gifts of bread and wine, profess the faith, recall the mighty acts of God, seek the blessing of the Spirit, and receive Holy Communion as an expression of union with Christ and with one another. Through the reception of Holy Communion, the believers share in the new life in Christ. With the conclusion of the Eucharist, the believers depart to live faithfully as Christ's disciples in the world.

There is an intimate relationship between the worship of the Church and the faith of the Church. The Orthodox affirm the ancient Christian dictum: the rule of prayer is the rule of faith: *lex orandi est lex credendi*. This means that the faith of the Church is expressed through her worship. It is expressed in her Scriptures. It is also expressed in the prayers, creed, hymns, icons and rituals of worship. The Eucharist and all other acts of worship express the Apostolic faith. It is through acts of worship the Triune God is honored, and it is through worship that our personal faith in the Living God is nurtured and strengthened.

The centrality of the Eucharist does not diminish the other expressions of Church life. Indeed, the rich expressions of the Church's faith are nurtured and guided by the Eucharist. Because she professes the Apostolic faith, the Church is a missionary community. She seeks to spread the Gospel to all nations and peoples. Because of her faith, the Church is a philanthropic community. She cares especially for those who are physically or spiritually ill, those who are poor and those who are marginalized. Because of her faith, the Church is a reconciling community. She seeks to be an instrument of God's reconciling love in the world.

Apostolic Faith and Unity

There is an intimate relationship between the Apostolic faith and the unity of the church. Already in the New Testament period, there was a clear recognition of the need both to maintain the Apostolic Faith with accuracy and to maintain the unity of the church. St. Paul was especially mindful of this relationship. On the one hand, he criticized the divisions among Christians and on the other he admonished them to be faithful to the authentic teaching. Writing to the Corinthians, for example, Paul declared that there should be "no divisions in the body" (1 Cor. 12:25). And, in his letter to the Ephesians, Paul called upon them to "maintain the unity of the spirit in the bond of peace. There is one body and one Spirit, just as you were called to the one hope of your calling, one Lord, one Faith, one baptism, one God and father of all, who is above all and through all and in all" (Eph. 4:3-6).

Throughout the early centuries of the Church, the great Fathers and Mothers also recognized the need both to maintain the Apostolic Faith free from distortion and to maintain the unity of the church. As teachers of the Gospel, they recognized that the Apostolic Faith bore witness to the truth of God and was a necessary guide to salvation. Distortions of the Faith of the Church meant that persons could be misguided in their relationship with God, one another and the creation. Their salvation was in jeopardy.

Likewise, the early Fathers and Mothers recognized that the disunity of the churches was not to be easily tolerated. They expressed a firm desire not only to uphold the Apostolic Faith but also to struggle to overcome divisions among regional church communities. The disunity of those who professed faith in Christ inhibited the Gospel message and weakened the witness of Christians in the world.

So, the Church was ready to enter into dialogue with those divided Christians who truly sought reconciliation and unity. In so doing, the Church sought to distinguish between legitimate diversity of expression related to culture, language and theological emphasis, and truly doctrinal differences which were divisive and harmful to salvation.

While forcefully affirming the Apostolic Faith, St. Athanasius, St. Basil and St. John Chrysostom sought to reconcile the various Arian groups and others in the fourth century. St. Cyril of Alexandria acted to heal the division with the Church of Antioch in 433. St. Maximos the Confessor refused to accept false accusations made against the Western Christians in the seventh century. Despite being criticized by extremists, St. Methodios of Constantinople sought to reconcile the Iconoclasts after the Council of 843. St. Photios of Constantinople restored communion with the Church of Rome at the Council of 879 and also sought to reconcile the Church of Armenia. And, St. Mark of Ephesus participated in theological dialogue with Western Christians in the fifteenth century. These Fathers recognized an obligation to be seekers of reconciliation in the name of Christ. They knew that Christian divisions, in the words of St. Basil, were "nothing less than a disaster."[1]

Indeed, the history of the great Ecumenical Councils demonstrates similar concerns. The Councils were called to examine and address distorted teachings and the tragic divisions they caused. In their decisions, the Councils opposed heresies and bore witness to the Apostolic Faith using terminology of their day. At the same time, the Councils were devoted to reconciling where possible separated churches and Christians through the common profession of the Apostolic Faith expressed especially through the celebration of the Eucharist.

The Contemporary Witness

The Orthodox Church has taught that her involvement in the contemporary quest for the reconciliation and unity of divided churches is in keeping with the spirit found in the concerns and actions of these fathers and the great Councils. Today, the participation of the Orthodox Church in various aspects of the ecumenical movement expresses the firm desire to teach the Apostolic faith free from distortion and the desire to heal divisions among Christians where there is good intention.

The Encyclical of the Ecumenical Patriarchate in 1920 is a profoundly significant text which marks the beginning of the contemporary ecumenical movement in the wake of the tragedy of World War I.[2] In this document, addressed to all the churches, the Patriarchate calls upon the churches to come out of their isolation and to look for opportunities for dialogue, cooperation, and common witness. It proposed the establishment of a League of churches where representatives would meet together. This proposal eventually contributed to the establishment of the World Council of Churches in 1948. The document provided a basis for early Orthodox involvement in the "Faith and Order" and "Life and Work" movements in the 1920s and 1930s.

While the encyclical of the Ecumenical Patriarchate encouraged dialogue, it did not address a number of serious issues, chief of which is the question of the ecclesiological status of Western churches and confessions. As the involvement of the Orthodox Church in ecumenical dialogues increased in subsequent decades, this has remained a question which has received different responses from Orthodox theologians.

In her encounters with others, the Orthodox Church has affirmed her identity of preserving the Apostolic Faith and of being in continuity with the Church established by Christ and enlivened by the Spirit at Pentecost. At the same time, the Orthodox Church has acknowledged its obligation to contribute to the unity of the separated churches.

The Third Pre-Conciliar Pan-Orthodox Conference (1986) expressed this conviction when it declared.

> The Orthodox Church has always sought to draw the different Christian churches and Confessions into a joint pilgrimage aiming at searching (for) the lost unity of Christians so that all might reach the unity of faith. .. The Orthodox Church, which unceasingly prays "for the union of all," has taken part in the ecumenical movement since its inception and has contributed to its formation and further development. In fact the Orthodox Church, due to the ecumenical spirit by which she is distinguished has, through the history, fought for the restoration of Christian unity Therefore the Orthodox participation in the ecumenical movement does not run counter to the nature and history of the Orthodox Church. It constitutes the consistent expression of the apostolic faith within new historical conditions, in order to respond to new existential demands.[3]

---

[1] St. Basil the Great, *Epistle* 203.
[2] "The Encyclical of the Ecumenical Patriarchate," in Thomas FitzGerald, *The Ecumenical Patriarchate and Christian Unity* (Brookline, MA: Holy Cross Orthodox Press, 2009), 62-65.
[3] "Statement from the Third Pan-Orthodox Pre-Conciliar Conference," in FitzGerald, *The Ecumenical Patriarchate and Christian Unity*, 74-75.

Part I: Orthodox Churches in the Ecumenical Movement – an Introduction

With the leadership of the Ecumenical Patriarchate, all the Autocephalous Orthodox churches have formally committed themselves to ecumenical dialogue with other churches and Christian traditions. Rooted in the church's identity, this dialogue ultimately aims at reconciliation and unity in obedience to the prayer of the Lord for his disciples "that they all may be one" (John 17:6). This healing process is not an easy one. Many of the divisions date back centuries. Most have been compounded by linguistic, cultural and political factors. Yet, the old reasons for divisions must be seriously examined free from polemics and misunderstandings. And, more recent teachings and practices of other churches can not be ignored.

The reconciliation of Christians and the restoration of the visible unity of the divided churches cannot come about through a disregard for the truth of the Apostolic Faith in all its richness and fullness. True Christian unity cannot be founded upon falsehood on a cosmetic agreement, which pretends that there is agreement on essential issues. In the various dialogues, the Orthodox have consistently taught that true reconciliation and genuine unity must be found in the common understanding and acceptance of the Apostolic faith, the "faith which was once for all delivered to the saints" (Jude 3).

Bibliography

1. Aghiorgoussis, Maximos (Metropolitan), *Together in Christ: Studies in Ecclesiology and Ecumenism*, (Brookline, MA: Holy Cross Orthodox Press, 2012).
2. FitzGerald, Thomas, *The Ecumenical Patriarchate and Christian Unity*, (Brookline, MA: Holy Cross Orthodox Press, 2009).
3. Limouris, Gennadios (ed.), *Orthodox Visions of Ecumenism*, (Geneva: WCC Publications, 1994).
4. Patelos, Constantin G. (ed.), *The Orthodox Church and the Ecumenical Movement*, (Geneva: WCC Publications, 1978).
5. Zizioulas, John D. (Metropolitan of Pergamon), *Being as Communion*, (Crestwood, NY: St. Vladimir's Seminary Press, 1985), 67-122.

(3) OFFICIAL TEXTS ON ECUMENISM - A SYSTEMATIC INTRODUCTION

Fr. Cyril Hovorun

A theological perspective, which later on would be embodied in the texts produced by the *Faith and Order* and WCC, was articulated at the conclusion of the World missionary conference in Edinburgh in 1910 by the Nobel Peace Prize winner John Mott: 'We go out <…> with a larger acquaintanceship, with deeper realization of this fellowship <…> Our best days are ahead of us because we have a larger Christ.'[1] This vision soon went beyond the Protestant churches and became shared by other traditions, including the Orthodox. Remarkable in this regard is an encyclical letter of the Ecumenical Patriarchate promulgated in 1920. Referring to the newly established League of Nations, the encyclical suggested a concrete program of the Christian ecumenism according to the pattern of the League. At that time, this program was remarkably progressive. It urged the ecumenically-minded churches to approach each other

'a) By the acceptance of a uniform calendar for the celebration of the great Christian feasts at the same time by all the churches.

b) By the exchange of brotherly letters on the occasion of the great feasts of the churches' year as is customary, and on other exceptional occasions.

c) By close relationships between the representatives of all churches wherever they may be.

d) By relationships between the theological schools and the professors of theology; by the exchange of theological and ecclesiastical reviews, and of other works published in each church.

e) By exchanging students for further training among the seminaries of the different churches.

f) By convoking pan-Christian conferences in order to examine questions of common interest to all the churches.

g) By impartial and deeper historical study of doctrinal differences both by the seminaries and in books.

h) By mutual respect for the customs and practices in different churches.

i) By allowing each other the use of chapels and cemeteries for the funerals and burials of believers of other confessions dying in foreign lands.

j) By the settlement of the question of mixed marriages among the confessions.

k) Lastly, by wholehearted mutual assistance for the churches in their endeavours for religious advancement, charity and so on.'[2]

Since then, the ecumenical theology has developed dramatically. The task of constructing ecumenical theology was commissioned into the *Faith and Order*, which initially was an independent movement and later on became incorporated to the World Council of Churches as its commission.[3] The task of this commission was defined as to work out theological documents for further consideration by the WCC, particularly at its general

---

[1] *The International Missionary Council: Addresses and Papers of John JR. Mott*, vol. 5, (New York: Association Press, 1947), 19-20.

[2] Available online on the website of the Permanent Delegation of the Ecumenical Patriarchate to the World Council of Churches: http://www.ecupatria.org/encyclical1920.htm [last accessed November 10, 2012].

[3] See information on the website of the WCC: http://www.oikoumene.org/en/who-are-we/organization-structure/con-sultative-bodies/faith-and-order.html [last accessed November 10, 2012]. Also Günther Gassmann, What is Faith and Order?: http://www.oikoumene.org/en/resources/documents/wcc-commissions/faith-and-order-commission/xii-essays/what-is-faith-and-order-ga14nther-gassmann.html [last accessed November 10, 2012]; Mary Tanner, What is Faith and Order?: http://www.oikoumene.org/en/resources/documents/wcc-commissions/faith-and-order-commission/xii-essays/what-is-faith-and-order-mary-tanner.html [last accessed November 10, 2012].

assemblies. Theological insights of the *Faith and Order* / WCC evolved from a mere comparativistics to the well-elaborated concepts of unity.[4]

As early as in 1937, the *Faith and Order* adopted a concept of an *organic union*, which is

'the unity of a living organism, with the diversity characteristic of the members of a healthy body <...>

In a Church so united the ultimate loyalty of every member would be given to the whole body and not to any part of it. Its members would move freely from one part to another and find every privilege of membership open to them. The sacraments would be the sacraments of the whole body. The ministry would be accepted by all as a ministry of the whole body.'[5]

The General assembly of the WCC in New Delhi (1961) brought the idea of the organic union of Christians further, by identifying its dynamic manifestations. This

'organic and transcendent unity of faith, life and love[6] <...> is being made visible as all in each place who are baptized into Jesus Christ and confess him as Lord and Saviour are brought by the Holy Spirit into one fully committed fellowship, holding the one apostolic faith preaching the one Gospel, breaking the one bread, joining in common prayer, and having a corporate life reaching out in witness and service to all and who at the same time are united with the whole Christian fellowship in all places and all ages in such wise that ministry and members are accepted by all, and that all can act and speak together as occasion requires for the tasks to which God calls his people.'[7]

New Delhi suggested that churches follow the way of self-denial and deconstruction of own identities:

'We all confess that sinful self-will operates to keep us separated and that in our human ignorance we cannot discern clearly the lines of God's design for the future. But it is our firm hope that through the Holy Spirit God's will as it is witnessed to in Holy Scripture will be more and more disclosed to us and in us. The achievement of unity will involve nothing less than a death and rebirth of many forms of church life as we have known them. We believe that nothing less costly can finally suffice...'[8]

This approach can be characterised as 'kenotic'. It is essential for achieving organic union of the churches, but indicates a painful way to this goal. This way did not find real support from the churches. As a result, the idea of organic union was transformed into a concept of *conciliar fellowship*. The *Faith and Order*, having discussed the latter at its consultations in Louvain (1971) and Salamanca (1973), recommended it for acceptance by the WCC in the following terms:

---

[4] In exploration of this development, I follow Thomas Best in his chapter on 'Ecclesiology and ecumenism' in Gerard Mannion and Lewis Seymour Mudge, *The Routledge Companion to the Christian Church*, (London; New York: Routledge, 2008), 410-413.
[5] Leonard Hodgson, *The Second World Conference on Faith and Order, Held at Edinburgh, August 3-18, 1937*, (New York: The Macmillan company, 1938), 252.
[6] New Delhi Statement on Unity, §26 in 3rd assembly of the WCC, (New Delhi, 1961). Available online on the website of the WCC: http://www.oikoumene.org/en/resources/documents/assembly/new-delhi-1961/new-delhi-statement-on-unity. html [last accessed November 10, 2012].
[7] New Delhi Statement on Unity, §2 in 3rd assembly of the WCC, (New Delhi, 1961). Available online on the website of the WCC: http://www.oikoumene.org/en/resources/documents/assembly/new-delhi-1961/new-delhi-statement-on-unity. html [last accessed November 10, 2012].
[8] New Delhi Statement on Unity, on the website of the WCC: http://www.oikoumene.org/en/resources/documents/assembly/ new-delhi-1961/new-delhi-statement-on-unity.html [last accessed on November 10, 2012].

'The one Church is to be envisioned as a conciliar fellowship of local churches which are themselves truly united. In this conciliar fellowship, each local church possesses, in communion with the others, the fullness of catholicity, witnesses to the same apostolic faith, and therefore recognizes the others as belonging to the same Church of Christ and guided by the same Spirit.'[9]

This concept was accepted by the general assembly of the WCC in Nairobi (1975), which made some clarifications about it:

'The term (conciliar fellowship - *CH*) is intended to describe an aspect of the life of the one undivided Church *at all levels* (italics - *WCC*). In the first place, it expresses the unity of church separated by distance, culture and time, a unity which is publicly manifested when the representatives of these local churches gather together for a common meeting. It also refers to a quality of life within each local church; it underlines the fact that true unity is not monolithic, does not override the special gifts given to each member and to each local church, but rather cherishes and protects them.'[10]

The General assembly of the WCC in Vancouver (1983) identified three marks of the desired unity:

'A common understanding of the apostolic faith; a common confession of the apostolic faith including full mutual recognition of baptism, the eucharist and ministry; and common ways of decision-making and teaching authoritatively.'[11]

In these evaluations, Vancouver relied on the outcome of the *Faith and Order* plenary commission in Bangalore (1978). So far, the theological work of the *Faith and Order* and WCC was concentrated on identifying features of a unity, which would be acceptable by the churches. Both *organic union* and *conciliar fellowship* were ideal models of unity. Realising that this is not enough, the WCC started to elaborate models, which would combine the ideal models of unity with the harsh ecumenical realities of the divided churches. As a result, two theological models were brought to table: *communion of communions*, and *reconciled diversity*. The former one considered major ecclesial traditions as *typoi*, which are, in the words of Thomas Best,

'to be preserved for the enrichment of the church as a whole, but to be set within a larger ecclesial framework. In its original formulation this included common sacraments and dogma, as well as a basic structure for ministry in which the bishop of Rome would exercise a unique ministry on behalf of unity.'[12]

The model of reconciled diversity sees confessions as 'legitimate expressions of diversity within the one body of Christ, each preserving certain aspects of Christian faith and life for the benefit of the church as a whole.'[13] This model contains a rather unrealistic proposal that the diversities, which are to be reconciled, should not include dividing features, and the churches have to get rid of them. Another weak point of this model was lack of framework, within which the diversities could be reconciled.

This deficiency was addressed by a theological matrix of *koinonia*. It has became a main matrix of the ecumenical theology and serves the ecumenical movement in this capacity even now. *Koinonia* was referred

[9] Report of Section II: What unity requires, sect. II, §3 in Fifth Assembly of the WCC, (Nairobi, 1975), in Michael Kinnamon and Brian Cope, *The Ecumenical Movement: an Anthology of KeyTexts and Voices*, (WCC Publications, 1997), 110.

[10] Report of Section II: What unity requires, sect. II, §4. Fifth Assembly of the WCC, (Nairobi, 1975), in ibid. 110-111.

[11] Mannion and Mudge, *The Routledge Companion to the Christian Church*, 411.

[12] Mannion and Mudge, *The Routledge Companion to the Christian Church*, 411.

[13] Mannion and Mudge, *The Routledge Companion to the Christian Church*, 412.

to as early as in New Delhi (1961)[14] and found its full expression at the General assembly of the WCC in Canberra (1991):

'The unity of the Church to which we are called is a koinonia given and expressed in the common confession of the apostolic faith; a common sacramental life entered by the one baptism and celebrated together in one eucharistic fellowship; a common life in which members and ministries are mutually recognized and reconciled; and a common mission witnessing to all people to the gospel of God's grace and serving the whole of creation. The goal of the search for full communion is realized when all the churches are able to recognize in one another the one, holy, catholic and apostolic church in its fullness. This full communion will be expressed on the local and the universal levels through conciliar forms of life and action. In such communion churches are bound in all aspects of their life together at all levels in confessing the one faith and engaging in worship and witness, deliberation and action.'[15]

A next important step in framing ecumenical theology was a convergence text *Nature and mission of the Church*[16] published in 2005. The purpose of this study conducted by the *Faith and Order* was declared

'to give expression to what the churches can now say together about the nature and mission of the Church and, within that agreement, to explore the extent to which the remaining church-dividing issues may be overcome' (§5).

The method of convergence implemented in this study, in the words of Thomas Best,

'focuses on points at which the churches are approaching another in their understanding and practise. Those involved are expected to remain true to their ecclesial identities and convictions, even as they seek understandings and formulations to express ecclesial truths which are yet deeper than the issues which divide us.'[17]

Common ecclesiological formulas, however, do not exclude disagreements on the Church-related theological matters. In the *Nature and Mission of the Church*, disagreements were placed in 'grey boxes' and treated with more care than earlier. This change of attitude to the differences in understanding of the

---

[14] 'The word "fellowship" (*koinonia*) has been chosen because it describes what the Church truly is. "Fellowship" clearly implies that the Church is not merely an institution or organization. It is a fellowship of those who are called together by the Holy Spirit and in baptism confess Christ as Lord and Saviour. They are thus "fully committed" to him and to one another. Such a fellowship means for those who participate in it nothing less than a renewed mind and spirit, a full participation in common praise and prayer, the shared realities of penitence and forgiveness, mutuality in suffering and joy, listening together to the same Gospel, responding in faith, obedience and service, joining in the one mission of Christ in the world, a self-forgetting love for all for whom Christ died, and the reconciling grace which breaks down every wall of race, colour, caste, tribe, sex, class and nation. Neither does this "fellowship" imply a rigid uniformity of structure, organization or government. A lively variety marks corporate life in the one Body of one Spirit.'
   New Delhi Statement on Unity, §10, in 3rd assembly of the WCC, (New Delhi, 1961). Available online on the website of the WCC: http://www.oikoumene.org/en/resources/documents/assembly/new-delhi-1961/new-delhi-statement-on-unity. html [last accessed November 11, 2012].
[15] The Unity of the Church: Gift and Calling - The Canberra Statement, §2.1. This unity statement was produced by the *Faith and Order* commission and adopted by the seventh Assembly of the World Council of Churches held in Canberra (1991). The document is available online on the website of the WCC: http://www.oikoumene.org/gr/resources/documents/wcc-commissions/faith-and-order-commission/i-unity-the-church-and-its-mission/the-unity-of-the-church-gift-and-calling-the-canberra-statement.html [last accessed November 11, 2012].
[16] Faith and Order Paper 198, available on the website of the WCC: http://www.oikoumene.org/fileadmin/files/wcc-main/documents/p2/FO2005_198_en.pdf [last accessed November 10, 2012].
[17] Mannion and Mudge, *The Routledge Companion to the Christian Church*, 403-405.

Church signified a shift in the ecumenical theology. This became more comprehensive to the divergences of different theological traditions. An important contribution to this shift was made by the *Special Commission on Orthodox participation in the WCC* established in 1998 at the 8th General Assembly of the Council in Harare. In exploring the nature of the Church, the *Nature and Mission of the Church* summarised it in the following statement:

'The Church exists for the glory and praise of God, to serve the reconciliation of humankind, in obedience to the command of Christ. It is the will of God that the communion in Christ, which is realised in the Church, should embrace the whole creation (cf. Eph 1:10). The Church, as communion, is instrumental to God's ultimate purpose (cf. Rom 8:19-21; Col 1:18-20)' (§33).

The mission of the Church is defined as follows:

'It is God's design to gather all creation under the Lordship of Christ (cf. Eph 1:10), and to bring humanity and all creation into communion. As a reflection of the communion in the Triune God, the Church is God's instrument in fulfilling this goal. The Church is called to manifest God's mercy to humanity, and to bring humanity to its purpose – to praise and glorify God together with all the heavenly hosts. The mission of the Church is to serve the purpose of God as a gift given to the world in order that all may believe (cf. John 17:21)' (§34).

In 2006, at its General assembly in Porto Allegre, the WCC adopted a document *Called to be the One Church*[18], subtitled as 'An invitation to the churches to renew their commitment to the search for unity and to deepen their dialogue.' This document summarised achievements of the ecumenical theology in the previous studies under the auspice of the WCC and invited the churches to answer the following questions, which need to be addressed for further advances towards unity:

'a. To what extent can each discern the faithful expression of the apostolic faith in their own life, prayer, and witness and in that of other churches?
b. Where does each perceive fidelity to Christ in the faith and life of the others?
c. Does each recognize a common pattern of Christian initiation, grounded in baptism, in the life of the others?
d. Why do some believe that it is necessary, others permissible, others not possible to share the Lord's Supper with those of other churches?
e. In what ways is each able to recognize the ordered ministries of the others?
f. To what extent can each share the spirituality of the others?
g. How will each stand with the others to contend with problems such as social and political hegemonies, persecution, oppression, poverty, and violence?
h. To what extent will each participate in the apostolic mission of the others?
i. To what extent can each share with the others in faith formation and theological education?
j. How fully can each participate in common prayer and in the worship of others?' (§14)

Apart from setting the theological framework for the ecumenical movement, the *Faith and Order* commission continued its work on particular aspects of the Church unity. At its plenary session in Lima (1982), the commission adopted a convergence text called *Baptism, Eucharist and Ministry* (BEM).[19] This text became a

[18] Published on the website of the WCC: http://www.oikoumene.org/en/resources/documents/assembly/porto-alegre-2006/1-statements-documents-adopted/christian-unity-and-message-to-the-churches/called-to-be-the-iyne-church-revised-draft.html [last accessed November 10, 2012].
[19] Baptism, Eucharist and Ministry - Faith and Order Paper No. 111 ('Lima text'). Available online on the website of the WCC http://www.oikoumene.org/en/resources/documents/wcc-commissions/faith-and-order-commission/i-unity-the-church-and-its-mission/baptism-eucharist-and-ministry-faith-and-order-paper-no-111-the-lima-text/baptism-eucharist-and-ministry.html#c10470 [last accessed November 11, 2012].

milestone of the ecumenical movement. A long series of consultations preceded it[20] and after its adoption, it was widely received and discussed in the churches.[21]

The document addresses three constituting aspects of the Church, which are also its sacraments: baptism, Eucharist and ministry. They are considered, on the one hand, from the perspective of their ecumenical contribution: namely how they serve as points of convergence between the churches. On the other hand, they are interpreted to fit major theological traditions. Thus, baptism, according to the BEM,

> 'is a sign and seal of our common discipleship. Through baptism, Christians are brought into union with Christ, with each other and with the Church of every time and place. Our common baptism, which unites us to Christ in faith, is thus a basic bond of unity. We are one people and are called to confess and serve one Lord in each place and in all the world. The union with Christ which we share through baptism has important implications for Christian unity. "There is <…> one baptism, one God and Father of us all" (Eph. 4:4—6). When baptismal unity is realized in one holy, catholic, apostolic Church, a genuine Christian witness can be made to the healing and reconciling love of God. Therefore, our one baptism into Christ constitutes a call to the churches to overcome their divisions and visibly manifest their fellowship' (Baptism, §6).

The ecumenical meaning of Eucharist the BEM expresses in the following words:

---

[20] This story is described in the preface to the document: 'The three statements are the fruit of a 50-year process of study stretching back to the first Faith and Order Conference at Lausanne in 1927. The material has been discussed and revised by the Faith and Order Commission at Accra (1974), Bangalore (1978) and Lima (1982). Between the Plenary Commission meetings, a steering group on Baptism, Eucharist and Ministry has worked further on the drafting, especially after September 1979 under the presidency of Frère Max Thurian of the Taizé Community.

The ecumenical documents also reflect ongoing consultation and collaboration between the Commission members (approved by the churches) and with the local churches themselves. The World Council's Fifth Assembly (Nairobi 1975) authorized the distribution for the churches' study of an earlier draft text (Faith and Order Paper No. 73). Most significantly, over a hundred churches from virtually every geographical area and ecclesiastical tradition returned detailed comments. These were carefully analysed at a 1977 consultation in Cret-Berard (Faith and Order Paper No. 84).

Meanwhile particularly difficult problems were also analysed at special ecumenical consultations held on the themes of infant and believers' baptism in Louisville, 1978 (Faith and Order Paper No. 97), on episkopé (oversight) and the episcopate in Geneva, 1979 (Faith and Order Paper No. 102). The draft text was also reviewed by representatives of Orthodox Churches in Chambésy, 1979. In conclusion, the Faith and Order Commission was again authorized by the World Council's Central Committee (Dresden, 1981) to transmit its finally revised document (the "Lima text" of 1982) to the churches, along with the request for their official response as a vital step in the ecumenical process of reception.

This work has not been achieved by the Faith and Order Commission alone. Baptism, eucharist and ministry have been investigated in many ecumenical dialogues. The two main types of interchurch conversations, the bilateral and the multilateral, have proved to be complementary and mutually beneficial. This is clearly demonstrated in the three reports of the Forum on Bilateral Conversations: "Concepts of Unity" (1978), "Consensus on Agreed Statements" (1979), and "Authority and Reception" (1980), subsequently published in Faith and Order Paper No. 107. Consequently, the Faith and Order Commission in its own multilateral consideration of the three themes has tried to build as much as possible on the specific findings of the bilateral conversations. Indeed, one of the tasks of the Commission is to evaluate the net result of all these particular efforts for the ecumenical movement as a whole.' Website of the WCC: http://www.oikoumene.org/en/resources/documents/wcc-commissions/faith-and-order-commission/i-unity-the-church-and-its-mission/baptism-eucharist-and-ministry-faith-and-order-paper-no-111-the-lima-text/baptism-eucharist-and-ministry.html#c10470 [last accessed November 11, 2012].

[21] According to Thomas Best, 'By the year 2000 BEM, translated into almost 40 languages, had become the most widely studied of all ecumenical texts. It had received official responses from about 190 churches (and many more from other sources) and had been studied in faculties, lay academies and church education classes around the world. It continues to inspire formal agreements among churches, and to inform theological work done ecumenically and within individual churches. These are signs that BEM has been "received" in a substantial way by the churches and within the ecumenical movement.' Mannion and Mudge, *The Routledge Companion to the Christian Church*, 408-409.

'The eucharistic communion with Christ who nourishes the life of the Church is at the same time communion within the body of Christ which is the Church. The sharing in one bread and the common cup in a given place demonstrates and effects the oneness of the sharers with Christ and with their fellow sharers in all times and places. It is in the eucharist that the community of God's people is fully manifested. Eucharistic celebrations always have to do with the whole Church, and the whole Church is involved in each local eucharistic celebration. In so far as a church claims to be a manifestation of the whole Church, it will take care to order its own life in ways which take seriously the interests and concerns of other churches' (Eucharist, §19).

Ministry is treated in the BEM with care, as there are many forms, practices and interpretations of ministry in different traditions. However, all the churches would agree, according to the document, that

'[i]n order to fulfil its mission, the Church needs persons who are publicly and continually responsible for pointing to its fundamental dependence on Jesus Christ, and thereby provide, within a multiplicity of gifts, a focus of its unity. The ministry of such persons, who since very early times have been ordained, is constitutive for the life and witness of the Church' (Ministry, §8).

Faith and Order continued its work on the issues raised in the BEM. A recent study text, *One Baptism: Towards Mutual Recognition*[22] developed further the insights of the BEM regarding baptism. It comes out of the belief that

'[t]he mutual recognition of baptism is fundamental to the churches' search for visible unity. Insofar as it has been achieved, it has become a basis for the churches' increasing common witness, worship and service' (§79).

The study thus addresses difficulties on the way to the mutual recognition of baptism. Theological work of the *Faith and Order* and WCC in general continues. It remains focused on the theological meaning of Church unity. It also assists other theological traditions to comprehend this meaning and adopt it in their own texts. In the framework of the WCC, theological traditions exchange and converge. They enrich each other and learn more about themselves.

Bibliography:

Basdekis, Athanasios, *Orthodoxe Kirche und ökumenische Bewegung. Dokumente - Erklärungen - Berichte 1900-2006*, (Frankfurt am Main: Verlag Otto Lembeck, 2006).

Best, Thomas, "Ecclesiology and ecumenism," in Gerard Mannion and Lewis Seymour Mudge, *The Routledge Companion to the Christian Church*, (London; New York: Routledge, 2008), 410-413.

Kinnamon, Michael, and Brian E. Cope, *The Ecumenical Movement: An Anthology of Key Texts and Voices*. (Geneva: WCC Publications, 1997).

---

[22] One Baptism: towards mutual recognition. A study text. Faith and Order Paper No. 210. Available online on the website of the WCC: http://www.oikoumene.org/fileadmin/files/wcc-main/documents/p2/2011/One_Baptism_Corrected_for_reprint. pdf [last accessed November 11]

Part I: Orthodox Churches in the Ecumenical Movement – an Introduction

(4) Ecumenism of Faith and Ecumenism of History: Distorted Images of Ecumenism in the Today's Orthodox Perspective

Dn. Augustin Sokolovski

Who does believe, is free.
Huldrych Zwingli[1]

Credere di credere - or to the origins of the ecumenical movement

Dogma and history will meet; righteousness and peace will kiss each other (cf. Ps. 85:10). When one takes a close look at what is called the "ecumenical movement", it seems that we are dealing with a real success story, which does not happen often in history. An awareness of the historicity of dogmatic divisions has led Christians to an awareness of the need for reconciliation, prompting the search for unity and longing for it. Unity in this sense means a reconciliation of dogma and history. From this perspective, an ecumenical history becomes a chronology of successes. An outside observer begins to be haunted by an obsessive sense of idyll. In 1948, the Orthodox Church (or the Orthodox Churches) joined the ecumenical movement, or, what is however equivalent to it, joined the World Council of Churches. It should be noted immediately, that for a sensitive Slavic, ear an overlap of notion "council" in the English version of the name of the organization in Geneva with the notion of Ecumenical Council of the ancient Church sounds quite numinous. Starting from the very establishment (of the Council in Geneva), a convincingly long track record of joint activities and meetings, mutual visits, trips and acquaintanceships have grown. Our well-documented century has preserved sufficient evidence of theological works and interviews.[2]

Contradictions have been overcome by joint declarations; not: misunderstandings, by explanations; thus charting the way forward for work on dogmatic and canonical agreement. In the words of veterans of the ecumenical movement one can hear an amazing taste of nostalgia - nostalgic enthusiasm for what the ecumenical movement is and what it was. A beginner in this issue would think that we talk about something else, not about the Oikoumene the way it was and *is*.

Simultaneously it could be noted that the Orthodox members of the ecumenical movement, are usually perceived by others with mindful courtesy. They are acknowledged to have an unwritten right to perceive things with skepticism, since they joined the achievements of the ecumenical civilization somewhat late, and, for some objective political reasons of the recent history, not to the full degree. Nevertheless, their skepticism towards ecumenism cannot be explained only by this. The desire to understand the reasons is often the cause of impatience. This reflection is intended to explain this impatience at least partly.

Seeing is believing ... In autumn of 1997, a very representative ecumenical delegation, led by the General Secretary of the World Council of Churches at that time, had been visiting principal theological schools of the Moscow Patriarchate in the Holy Trinity-Sergius Lavra.[3] There is no need to describe what had happened then. It is only necessary to note that ecumenism, as such, was pointedly rejected by the students and monks present in the hall and was filibustered in a very, very open form. Of course, on the next day many of the students had admitted that the response of the audience to the words of the participants of the delegation had been too harsh

---

[1] *Wer glaubt ist frei. Aus den Schriften des Reformators Ulrich Zwingli*, (Vienne, 1984), 134.

[2] An interesting overview is presented in the collection of articles: *Православие Экуменизм. Документы и материалы 1902-1998*, (Moscow, 1999).

[3] At the very beginning of his seminary years, the author of this contribution attended this incredibly important event, which went surprisingly unnoticed.

and unconstructive. But their collective student *sensus fidelium* had convinced them that they were right. The main argument of the students, regardless of their exposure to theological knowledge, was based upon their ignorance about what was said, done and signed at the ecumenical level on behalf of their Church. They did not know why it was done. However, being young Orthodox Christians, newly arrived in the church, behind their shoulders they recognized an experience of struggle for the survival of the Russian Church in the era of communism. It is in this struggle for survival, that the Church had joined the ecumenical movement. Yet, this argument was no longer seen as relevant to them. They belonged to another generation. They also knew that participation in ecumenical programs had been encouraged by the communist government for propaganda purposes. Thus, it was unexpected for those observing the process from the West, but rather expected and logical for the "people of the East" that the Oikoumene has become a symbol of persecutions.

They also knew the way that their "Fathers in faith", that is theologians, bishops and the Church Fathers of the glorious past of the Orthodox tradition[4] - were taught, and how every Orthodox believer used to know this - perceived "ecumenism" in a negative way.[5] The fact that the Church Fathers had lived and worked in a completely different context remains unaddressed in the Orthodox theological hermeneutics. Around the same time (I do not mean the time of the Fathers, but the time of the visit of the WCC delegation to the Academy) some Orthodox Churches had left the ecumenical movement represented by the Council of Churches: Serbian, Bulgarian, and Georgian. A revolution took place in this autumn of ecumenism. After all, when all at once begin to think differently, what is it, if not a revolution?[6] And, as often happens to revolutions, a preceding success story pure and simple gives rise to them.[7]

"The ecumenical fusion of horizons"[8], or How do we believe in what others believe?

The Orthodox Church is the true Church of Christ established by our Lord and Saviour Himself, the Church confirmed and sustained by the Holy Spirit, the Church about which the Saviour Himself has said: "I will build my Church; and the gates of hell shall not prevail against it" (Mt. 16:18). She is the One, Holy, Catholic (Conciliar) and Apostolic Church, the keeper and provider of the Holy Sacraments throughout the world, "the pillar and ground of the truth" (1 Tim. 3:15). She bears full responsibility for the proclamation of the truth of Christ's Gospel, as well as full power to witness to "the faith which was once delivered unto the saints" (Jude 3)[9]. These words of a recent document on Basic principles on the attitude of the Russian Orthodox Church to the non-Orthodox[10] allow us to make a kind of a methodological leap to another topic. Let's try to disengage

---

[4] A hermeneutic principle that "the Father of the Church" is any theologian and writer canonized in the Church, regardless of his affiliation to the era of "Ancient Undivided Church" is a very important fact for understanding the perception of ecumenism in the Orthodox Church. An axiom of the Orthodox identity claims that each generation is called and is capable of producing "the Fathers of the Church."

[5] An issue of necessary, but missing contextualization of this concept, that is the one on the degree to which our perception of the ecumenical movement and a negative perception by the Fathers of schisms and doctrinal divisions in the Church of their time are identical, is not usually considered and is perceived as positively solved.

[6] Cf. Paul Hazard, *La crise de la conscience européenne* (I), (Paris 1994), 4.

[7] This "revolutionary" aspect of the events taken place, a radical change in paradigms of perception of the recent past of their Church, in my opinion, is absolutely not taken into account. And it is exactly a revolutionary character of the events happened that explains much. It involves a certain amount of surprise, irrationality and unexplainability of events. This neglect leads to a focus of attention on minor things. See in more detail on this subject: Johannes Oeldemann, *Orthodoxe Kirche im ökumenischen Dialog. Positionen, Probleme, Perspektiven*, (Paderborn 2004).

[8] Germ.: Horizontverschmelzung.

[9] Official text of the document: http://www.mospat.ru/en/documents/attitude-to-the-non-orthodox/i/ (last accessed 15 September 2013).

[10] It is interesting, that the term "инославие" (in the text: "non-Orthodox"), as used in the original Russian text of the document, is neutral in itself and differs quite radically from the term "heterodoxy" given in the French version – "hétéro-

ourselves from what was said in the previous sections, since it is too pessimistic. Let's try to build the argument in such a way, as if the ecumenical movement, with all its ups and downs, had never existed and ask ourselves: what do Christians of different traditions know of each other? Speaking of "Tradition", I deliberately avoid using the word "confession." In other words, what is the perception of the Traditions of each other, what doctrinal themes draw their attention if they wish to distance themselves from others, or, conversely, to come to a common denominator?

To begin with, let us take Orthodoxy and Catholicism as an example. In order not to search for a long time, let us open any standard Orthodox textbook on "Comparative theology", which is used in Orthodox theological schools up until now. Let us carefully examine which topics divide the Orthodox and Catholic Christianity. Like centuries ago, it is the question of the Filioque in the doctrine of the Trinity, purgatory in eschatology, infallibility and jurisdictional primacy of the bishop of Rome in the doctrine of the Church. Added to this are numerous issues in Mariology – the Orthodox dogmatics do not use that term, preferring to consider Marian mystery in the framework of general Christological and soteriological section - as well as in the doctrine on sacraments and in the field of spirituality. We can talk about it for a long time in detail; however, the whole spectrum of the themes indicated hardly reflects the agenda of modern Western theology. Political correctness, required from theology these days, would formulate a possible replica of a competent Western theologian concerning the just described.[11] "Fusion of horizons" of Western European Christianity with the ever-growing body of African, Latin American and Asian Catholicism - that is the Church of the future Ecclesia Catholica - irrevocably this leads to a "shift of horizons" of the theological Oikoumene. In other words, what motivates us in faith and what we "believe" about the faith of others is quite different in modern Orthodox and Catholic theology. Let us note: we speak of "comparative" theology rather than of "ecumenical." If we take as an example not the Orthodox-Catholic, but the Orthodox-Evangelical "axis of good" of world Christianity, then the discrepancy between current theological interest and goal-setting will be even more striking. In the Orthodox theological mind there is still a belief that, when starting the Reformation, Martin Luther would have certainly become Orthodox, if he had known the Orthodox tradition. For all the pathos of his protest had been directed against the papacy and its abuses. Orthodoxy has always opposed the Roman primacy. Being loyal to the tradition of the Ancient Undivided Church, it has saved itself from all the abuses, which Luther opposed. This is the Orthodox belief, in such a way the future clergy members are taught in the seminary.

The choice of words is seldom random. As we have just mentioned, the study of other Christian traditions has long been called an "ecumenical theology" in the Catholic and Protestant theology, whereas in the Orthodox - only partly. In the Russian theological school only a comparative theology is taught. *Nomen est omen?*

The Fröhlicher Wechsel or the prospects of ecumenism

What has just been said makes a simple statement, that the word "ecumenism" is not perceived positively in the Orthodox world. This can only be acknowledged and it makes no sense to deny it. However, it is the unwillingness to acknowledge this simple fact of the rejection of the notion "ecumenism" in the collective perception of Orthodoxy that makes it impossible to understand what had happened. *To live is to die ...*

---

doxie". The latter is originally pejorative and implies an explicit non-orthodoxiness of the interlocutor in the perception of Orthodoxy. The German term "Andersglaubende" is more neutral, however, in the reverse translation, it literally means, rather, "the one of the different faith", or "the one of the other faith" rather than the non-Orthodox.

[11] Of course, an interest in traditional themes has been and will always remain at the center of attention of theologians-experts on these topics, as well as those professional ecumenists who have been traditionally engaged in classic dogmatic confrontations of traditions. As an example, compare with an article of M.-A. Vannier on the need for a new formulation of the issue of the Filioque and its articulation by the doctrinal authority of the Catholic Church: "L' rapport de la Clarification sur le Filioque", *Revue des Sciences Religieuses* 75:1 (2001): 97-112.

Paradoxically, it is exactly in recognition of this bankruptcy of "ecumenism" on a conceptual level that progress on the way for a search for Christian unity, otherwise known as Oikoumene, is made possible. As an introduction to the argument, I want to cite the words of the Patriarch of Moscow and All Russia Cyril[12]: "On the day of his enthronement, Pope Benedict XVI has honored me with a personal audience. [...] The Catholic and the Orthodox Church in the world today are the sole natural allies in the hard opposition, separating today supporters of secular liberalism and carriers of Christian tradition. We can defend Christian values together with the Catholics. And we already have an experience of such collaboration. For example, during the preparation of the draft of the European Constitution we had conducted active dialogue with the Catholic Church, and by doing so, we had come to a mutual understanding."[13] "In considering such words, one needs to understand what it speaks about and what it does not. The words "the sole natural allies" can be interpreted in two ways. This dual interpretation finds its match in the understanding of what ecumenism is and what it is not.

A kind of an axiom of the ecumenical movement is to divide the participants into three groups: the Orthodox, Catholic and Protestant. This classification is self-evident, self-sufficient and does not imply additional divisions. However, the history of the ecumenical movement always gives us examples of relationships and alliances within the Oikoumene, which result in, and often set as a goal a transformation of the "triad of traditions" of the Christian world into the binomial. Thus, it was characteristic of Orthodoxy to see in Protestantism a "natural ally" in the ideological opposition to Catholicism,[14] bilateral theological dialogues of the Catholic Church with traditions of Protestantism have virtually ignored the third observer, this time an outsider, represented by the Eastern Churches. In turn, the latest attempt to negotiate a "strategic alliance" to combat secularism and liberalism between the Orthodox and the Catholic side had given and will always give an impression of the union aimed at elimination of the "odd man out"; a friendship against someone. This instrumentalisation of ecumenism remains unnoticed by an absolute majority of not only outside observers, but of the direct participants. However, it is one of the key engines, a sort of an original sin of the ecumenical movement.

The opposite vector for the interpretation of the words about the "strategic alliance" of the Traditions lies within the understanding that every Christian tradition carries its unique hermeneutics, irreversible history, exclusive vocation. In fact, we are talking about the inadmissibility of the instrumentalisation of ecumenism, the need for its proper definition, which would make it identical to the Christian vocation, the existence of a Christian in the world.

Another problematic factor in the perception of ecumenical processes is a somewhat lacking historical consciousness. It manifests itself primarily in the frequent lack of awareness that the world has changed a lot since the beginning of the ecumenical movement. The world of the early and the mid 20th century - the "golden age of the Christian Oikoumene" - is not the world of the 21st century. A century ago, say, in 1910, the Christian world first became aware of its non-unity. A century later, say, in 2010, Christians live in a world that is increasingly no longer calling itself a Christian one. "For everything there is a season, and a time for every matter under heaven" (Eccl. 3:1).

It has already been said that in modern Orthodox discourse, the term "ecumenism" has passed into the category of "negative" concepts. This can be particularly and obviously traced in Russian-speaking Orthodoxy, where the bloom of the ecumenical movement coincided with the domination of the communist ideology. By coincidence, in Russian, the terms "communism" and "ecumenism" rhyme perfectly. This could have negative connotations in the theologically and philosophically unprepared minds of simple believers. Nature abhors a vacuum, and therefore any displaced notion is replaced by a certain counterpart when necessary. Sometimes such counterparts become a viable alternative, which will eventually efface not only the forgotten notion but its

---

[12] Then Metropolitan of Smolensk and Kaliningrad.

[13] Kyrill, Patriarch von Moskau und der ganzen Rus', *Freiheit und Verantwortung im Einklang. Zeugnisse für den Aufbruch zu einer neuen Weltgemeinschaft Freiheit und Verantwortung im Einklang*, (Fribourg, 2009), 87.

[14] Compare the remark above about Martin Luther and the Orthodoxy.

negative content as well. The search for such an alternative begins spontaneously, *nolens volens.* In the context of the notion "ecumenism", this solution is intellectually more cost effective than trying to give this notion a new, positive and non-defamatory meaning. It is noteworthy that the first trend, that is, the replacement of the notion, is ongoing in modern Russian-speaking Orthodoxy, the latter one - in other Orthodox traditions.[15] Thus, in Russian theological language, the notion of "ecumenism" in its positive value is virtually displaced by the syntagma "Inter-Christian dialogue." Here are several aspects of this usage: 1). If the word "ecumenism" spontaneously recalls the times of persecution and lack of freedom suffered by the Russian Church during the Soviet rule, the notion of "Inter-Christian dialogue" is perceived as a new one, and therefore associated with the times of the newfound freedom of the Church in the state and the society, 2). "Ecumenism" is perceived as a kind of displacement of the horizons of the Tradition, in which the Christian unity becomes an imperative of the aspiration to lose the own identity, and 3). The use of the word "dialogue" opens new perspectives, which the "Oikoumene of the past" failed to implement. What is especially meant here are the common testimony and the common mission.

In many respects, the now-unpopular word "mission" is used here to emphasize that the described reformatting of the discourse does not mean at all that we are going from the doctrinal genre of the Oikoumene of theological discussions to an a-dogmatic practical ecumenism. A little more than a century ago, in 1910, the World Missionary Conference was held in Edinburgh. For the Christian world, this event was marked by the realization that division makes the Christian testimony unconvincing in the world. The momentum imparted by the Conference - in spite of the upheavals of the two World Wars - led to the creation of the World Council of Churches in 1948. The ecumenical movement has received the status of a public institution committed by its very existence to testify to the unity of the Christendom. The light of faith had to shine brighter. "That all of them may be one, Father, just as you are in me and I am in you. May they also be in us so that the world may believe that you have sent me." (John 17:21). Due to the institutionalization of the Oikoumene, the call that "all of them may be one" has become the bedrock of the ecumenical movement. But the call itself was suddenly reformatted. Having become an end in itself, it moved the center of gravity of the processes to the consideration and the accentuation of the differences. Therefore, in today's perspective, the return of the Oikoumene to life means the revival of the initial momentum of Edinburgh, suggesting that the mission is not "practice rather than doctrine," but "practice of doctrine experienced by faith." This "happy replacement" of notions (German: der fröhliche Wechsel) means, above all, the question of what it means to be a Christian in the world and to belong to a particular Christian tradition at the same time. This opens the possibility of a new apprehension of the so-called confessional differences in Christianity.

Every Christian denomination is aware of its authenticity in the face of the apostolic tradition. This awareness should not become a legitimization of the division, but be transformed into a true confession, which would give to the common Christian testimony the credibility of a mission. This makes possible the return to the original understanding of the term "catholic", containing the wealth of completeness, *kat'holon* (in Greek). The catholicity of the Church would in this case mean not the membership in the Roman tradition or jurisdiction, but the ability to integrate the different and the whole, the real presence and the possibility of the existence of the Church overcoming the boundaries of the perceived non-unity, an *ecclesia extra ecclesiam*. In this context, Orthodoxy would mean not the limitation of the doctrinal space in relation to any non-Orthodoxy, but the ability and the chance to carry and to declare to the others the glory of God, His genuine praise in the world and for the world [Doxa].The inter-Christian dialogue becomes a topos of the common testimony, the mission of the

---

[15] Speaking of the change in the conceptual series, I do not mean a kind of a postmodern reformatting of ecumenism, in which no real future is presumed. Cf. Wolfgang Thönissen, *Dogma und Symbol. Eine ökumenische Hermeneutik,* (Freiburg i.Br. 2008), 10: "Begriffe, vielmehr ihre Anwendung auf die ökumenische Situation, leisten keine Orientierung mehr, sondern führen in die Irre.Statt ständig an Einheitsbegriffen herumzudoktern, sollte ein zureichender Begriff der Different ausgearbeitet werden, der das Problem der Einheit und Vielfalt erklären könne. Dahinter verbirgt sich freilich, schaut man näher hin, die von vielen vorgetragene Überzeugung von der Unaufhebbarkeit der Differenz; diese wird als das ökumenische Problem schlechthin identifiziert".

Church, an Engagement, a consciousness that our belief is leading now here and now. Formulated in such a way, the way of Oikoumene will be freely acceptable for all Orthodox Christians.

In conclusion, we present the words of one of those who are now referred to as "veterans of ecumenism" - a phrase which, in our opinion, sufficiently expresses the ambivalence of the historical path of the movement for the Christian unity. In one interview on the difficulties of the Catholic-Protestant Ecumenism, the director of the Institute of Oriental Churches in Regensburg, prelate Klaus Wyrwoll speaks of ecumenism not in terms of the past, as perhaps all have become accustomed to, but in terms of the future: "Everywhere where Christians meet each other precisely as Christians, where they pray, celebrate, live and bear testimony to their faith, they become each other's authentic tests of faith, can learn from each other, and together cognize the signs of time. The Christian truth is inexhaustible, and in each new moment in the history it gives birth to a new world. [...] The time (Ger. der Kairos) of the acts of God, comes suddenly, getting past the guard of the chronology of our pre-planned time." And here I can only repeat what was said once by Dietrich Bonhoeffer: "Our commitment is in the prayer and in the deeds of righteousness; it is in the hope for His time."[16]

Bibliography

Huntington, Samuel P. *Kampf der Kulturen. Die Neugestaltung der Weltpolitik im 21. Jahrhundert*, (München-Wien 1998).

Morerod, Charles, *Oecuménisme et philosophie. Questions philosophiques pour renouveler le dialogue*, (Paris 2004).

Oeldeman, Johannes, *Einheit der Christen – Wunsch oder Wirklichkeit?*, (Regensburg 2009).

Patriarch Kyrill, *Freiheit und Verantwortung im Einklang*, (Fribourg 2009).

Špidlík, Tomáš, *Die russische Idee. Eine andere Sicht des Menschen*, (Würzburg 2002).

Suttner, Ernst Christoph, *Staaten und Kirchen in der Völkerwelt des östlichen Europa. Entwicklungen der Neuzeit* (= Studia Oecumenica Friburgensia 49), (Fribourg Schweiz 2007).

Thesing Josef, Uertz Rudolf (Hg.), *Die Grundlagen der Sozialdoktrin der Russisch-Orthodoxen Kirche*, (Sankt-Augustin 2001).

Thönissen, Wolfgang, *Dogma und Symbol. Eine ökumenische Hermeneutik*, (Freiburg i.Br. 2008).

---

[16] "Die 'Ökumene der Profile lenkt' vom entscheidenden Schritt ab - Prälat Wyrwoll zum Stand der katholisch-evangelischen Beziehungen». Von Ralf Magagnoli, *KNA Ökumenische Informationen* 4.26 (2010): 12ff.

Part I: Orthodox Churches in the Ecumenical Movement – an Introduction

(5) Ecumenical Challenges in the Practical Life and Pastoral Praxis of Orthodox Churches

Fr. Alkiviadis Calivas

Introduction: Overcoming the tragedy and scandal of disunity

Today, when the world has become a global village, we must recognize that the division of Christians is both a tragedy and a scandal; it is the vexing problem of Christian history that is in need of healing. In today's world, which is filled with all manner of strife and division, Christians have the sacred duty to advance the cause of unity for the sake of their common ancestry; for the sake of the saving truths of the Gospel; and for the sake of their common witness in response to the Lord's command to "make disciples of all nations" (Matt. 28:19). Above all, the pursuit of unity, as a duty and an obligation, rests in the fact that unity is not simply a characteristic or attribute of the Church but is constituent of her very life. Ecumenical engagements endure not for the purpose of creating unity — it already exists — but that divided Christians may search for their origins in the one undivided Church.[1]

In the effort to make Christ's prayer for unity a reality, "that they may all be one…so that the world may believe" (Jn. 17:21), the Orthodox Church has a special obligation and responsibility. This obligation, as Father Georges Florovsky reminds us, comes from the fact that the Orthodox Church represents the voice of Christian antiquity and embodies not a particular tradition but the uninterrupted Tradition of the undivided Church.[2]

In the paragraphs that follow, I will endeavor to set forth several foundational principles, which have guided the participation of the Orthodox Church in the ecumenical movement.

Unity of the faith is both a gift and a vocation

The first of these principles is that the concern for unity in the faith is embedded in the conscience and the prayer of the Church and in the conscience of every attentive worshipper. For example, at every corporate worship service Orthodox Christians pray "For peace in the whole world, for the stability of the holy churches of God, and for the union of all."[3] At several intervals during the day, as part of the Daily Office,[4] we recite the prayer, "Ο εν παντι καιρω και παση ωρα — Christ our God, who at all times and in all places," which includes the entreaty, "Encompass us with Your holy angels, so that guided and guarded by their Host, we may attain the unity of the faith and the comprehension of Your ineffable glory." The intercessions of the Anaphora of the Divine Liturgy of St. Basil includes the request, "reunite the separated, lead back those who are in error and unite them to Your holy, catholic, and apostolic Church."

The Anaphora of St. Basil also stresses that unity in its vertical and horizontal dimension is a fruit or benefit of Holy Communion: "…so that all of us who partake of the one Bread and Cup may be united with

---

[1] See Nikos Nissiotis, "The Witness and the Service of Eastern Orthodoxy to the One Undivided Church," in Constantin G. Patelos (ed.), *The Orthodox Church in the Ecumenical Movement* (Geneva, 1978), 241.

[2] Georges Florovsky, "The Eastern Orthodox Church and the Ecumenical Movement," in *Theology Today*, 7.1 (1950): 68-79.

[3] One in a series of petitions that constitute the Great Synapte or Litany, which is said at every Vesper service, Orthros, Divine Liturgy, and other sacred services.

[4] The prayer is common to the office of the four Hours, the Apodeipnon, and the Midnight service, all of which, together with the Vespers and Orthros, comprise the Daily Office of the Church.

one another in the communion of the one Holy Spirit."[5] The communion of the Holy Spirit (vertical) makes possible the communion of the faithful with one another (horizontal).

The theme of unity is repeated again in the litany of the Pre-Communion rites of the three Divine Liturgies of the Byzantine or Constantinopolitan Rite (St. Basil, St. John Chrysostom, and the Pre-Sanctified): "Having prayed for the unity of the faith and for the communion of the Holy Spirit, let us commit ourselves, and one another, and our whole life to Christ our God." The Church, echoing the Scriptures in its message of openness and tolerance (Luke 9:50), is continually pointing us through her rule of prayer towards unity, reconciliation, and forgiveness, the foundational elements of which are truth and love (John 17:15-23).

By praying for the unity of the faith we acknowledge and confess that unity is not simply a human feat but a precious gift that comes from God. Simultaneously, we acknowledge that this gift is also a vocation and a duty: the ministry of reconciliation (2 Cor. 5: 18-21), through which God's saving love touches, heals, and illumines human lives and relationships. The love shown by Christ is the model of an authentic Christian life. We are called to imitate His humility and selflessness. Love calls for love. Therefore, as agents and ambassadors of Christ, our vocation is to mediate His grace and love and thereby create the possibilities by which the condition of enmity is changed into friendship. This constitutes another foundational principle, which the legendary Ecumenical Patriarch Athenagoras underscored in the 1952 Encyclical of the Ecumenical Patriarchate regarding the Church's role in the ecumenical movement:

> The task of rapprochement and cooperation between all Christian confessions and organizations is a sacred obligation and a holy duty, derived from their own function and mission...The Orthodox Church in her participation in the pan-Christian movement has sought to make known and to impart to the heterodox the riches of her faith, worship, and order and her spiritual and ascetic experience, as well as to inform herself about their new methods and their conceptions of church life and activity, things of great value that the Orthodox Church could not possess and foster, on account of the particular conditions in which she lived.[6]

The role of the Orthodox Church in the ecumenical movement has been considerable and at times even decisive,[7] as evidenced by the important initiatives of the Ecumenical Patriarchate from the dawn of the 20th century to the present time in cooperation with the other autocephalous Orthodox Churches.[8] Of particular importance are two ground-breaking Encyclicals of the Ecumenical Patriarchate issued in 1902 and in 1920. Also of great value are the Statements that Orthodox delegations have issued at various ecumenical forums to express the fundamental agreements but also the significant differences which exist between the churches.[9]

---

[5] Fr. Robert F. Taft, the distinguished liturgical scholar, notes that the theme of unity, implicit in the Anaphora of St. John Chrysostom and explicit in the Anaphora of St. Basil, is the oldest and most basic fruit of Holy Communion. See his *A History of the Liturgy of St. John Chrysostom: The PreCommunion Rites*, volume V (Rome 2000), 123.

[6] "Encyclical of Ecumenical Patriarchate," issued on January 31, 1952 in C. Patelos (ed.), *The Orthodox Church in the Ecumenical Movement*, 44-45.

[7] See, for example, the essays and the documentary anthology complied by Gennadios Limouris, *Orthodox Visions of Ecumenism: Statements and Reports on the Ecumenical Movement* (Geneva 1994). See also three collections of Orthodox Responses to the consensus document of the WCC *Baptism, Eucharist and Ministry,* Faith and Order paper 111: George Tsetsis, *A Synthesis of the Responses of the Orthodox Churches to the Lima Document* (Geneva 1987), Gennadios Limouris, *Orthodox Perspectives on 'Baptism, Eucharist and Ministry'* (Geneva 1985) and *St. Vladimir's Theological Quarterly*, 27:45 (1983).

[8] See Thomas FitzGerald, *The Ecumenical Patriarchate and Christian Unity* (Brookline, MA 2009).

[9] By way of example see the collections of statements in Thomas FitzGerald and Emmanuel Gratsias (eds), *Restoring the Unity in Faith: The Orthodox-Oriental Orthodox Theological Dialogue* (Brookline, MA 2007), and John Borelli and John H. Erickson (eds), *The Quest for Unity: Orthodox and Catholics in Dialogue* (Crestwood, NY 1996).

The Patriarchal Encyclicals of 1902 and 1920

In 1902 the Ecumenical Patriarchate of Constantinople issued a Patriarchal and Synodical Encyclical setting forth a bold agenda by calling the Orthodox Churches to consider several issues. Of these, some pertained to internal matters of the Orthodox Churches, while others to the establishment of meaningful relations with the Roman Catholics and Protestants. While some of the issues regarding the inner life of the Church have yet to be resolved,[10] the proposal for ecumenical engagements was eventually accepted and acted upon with varying degrees of participation and success. However, to be productive, ecumenical engagements require the unwavering commitment of the Orthodox Churches to the ecumenical movement – the third foundational principle.[11]

Each generation is charged with the responsibility to respond enthusiastically to the call for unity, and to do it in the spirit put forth by Patriarch Joachim III and the Holy Synod of Constantinople in the Encyclical of 1902, which, in part, reads as follows:

> If, as in every matter which is impossible with men but possible with God, we cannot yet hope for the union of all as ever being possible, yet because divine grace is constantly active and men are being guided in paths of evangelical love and peace, one must consider very carefully whether it might be possible to prepare the (at present) anomalous way which leads to such a goal and to find points of encounter and contact, or even to turn a blind eye to certain irregularities until the completion in due course of the whole task, whereby might be fulfilled to our joint satisfaction and benefit our Lord and God and Savior Jesus Christ's saying about one flock and one shepherd.[12]

In the aftermath of the devastations of the First World War, the Ecumenical Patriarchate of Constantinople once again took the initiative. In 1920 it issued an Encyclical calling on all Christian Churches to overcome the spirit of mistrust, to heal ancient enmities, and to manifest to the world the power of Christian love through the establishment of a *koinonia* (a fellowship or league) of churches to promote Christian fellowship and cooperation in the struggle for justice and charity against the evils that cause divisions and undermine the dignity of people. The Patriarchal Encyclical was addressed, "*Unto the Churches of Christ Everywhere,*" and began with the exhortation of the Apostle Peter, "Love one another earnestly from the heart" (1 Peter 1: 22).[13]

The Encyclicals of 1902 and 1920 harbor no illusions. They both recognize that the chief obstacle to full unity are the doctrinal differences between the churches. Yet, both Encyclicals dare to conclude that this most serious of concerns should not preclude the rapprochement between the Churches, thereby giving expression to the fourth foundational principle for ecumenical engagements, stated thusly in the Encyclical of 1920: "Our own Church holds that rapprochement between the various Christian Churches and fellowship between them is not excluded by the doctrinal differences which exist between them. In our opinion such a rapprochement is highly desirable and necessary."[14] In fact, the establishment of cordial relations serve "the preparation and

---

[10] Among other things, the Encyclical touched upon the question of a common calendar and date of Pascha, issues, for example, that remain unresolved.

[11] See Todor Sabev, *The Orthodox Churches in the World Council of Churches: Towards the Future* (Geneva 1996). The author, a former Deputy General Secretary of the WCC and Church Historian, offers the reader "some basic information and reflection with a view to enhance inter-Orthodox discussion, encounter with ecumenical partners, and common input towards a renewed vision of the WCC."

[12] "Patriarchal and Synodical Encyclical of 1902," in C. Patelos (ed.), *The Orthodox Church in the Ecumenical Movement*, 30. The Encyclical was issued on 12 June 1902. This and other Encyclicals of the Ecumenical Patriarchate related to Christian unity have been also published by Thomas FitzGerald, *The Ecumenical Patriarchate and Christian Unity* (Brookline, MA 2009).

[13] "Encyclical of the Ecumenical Patriarchate, 1920," in C. Patelos (ed.), *The Orthodox Church in the Ecumenical Movement*, 40-43, T. FitzGerald, *The Ecumenical Patriarchate and Christian Unity*, 62-65, and G. Limouris, *Orthodox Visions of Ecumenism*, 9-11.

[14] Ibid. 40, 62, and 9 respectively.

advancement of that blessed union which will be completed in the future in accordance with the will of God."[15] The churches are urged to move beyond old enmities and controversies, which "have so often jeopardized attempts at reunion," by rekindling bonds of "friendship and kindly disposition" towards one another.

Several years ago, Ecumenical Patriarch Bartholomew echoed similar sentiments when he said, "While it is true that the Orthodox Church invites everyone to the unity of the one faith, she does not make brotherliness and love dependent upon this, nor does she manifest her concern only for those who adhere to her. Rather she loves all people."[16]

The conciliatory language and tone of the 1902 and 1920 Encyclicals should not escape our attention. The 1920 Encyclical is addressed to "the Churches of Christ everywhere," thereby according ecclesial status and character to the heterodox, recognizing them not as strangers but as estranged relatives who share a common heritage and promise. "We consider that above all, love should be rekindled and strengthened among the churches, so that they should no more consider one another as strangers and foreigners, but as relatives, and as being a part of the household of Christ and "fellow heirs, members of the same body and partakers of the promise of God in Christ" (Ephes. 3:6).

The Encyclical of 1920 made two proposals, which were deemed essential for the establishment of cordial relations between the churches. It also offered eleven suggestions for the building up of trust and cooperation among the churches. In addition, it listed several dangers that "attack the very foundations of the Christian faith and the essence of Christian life and society." The first of the two proposals addressed the issue of proselytism, i.e., the concerted effort to entice adherents of other confessions. The Encyclical called for the elimination of proselytism,[17] because it breeds mistrust and bitterness and disturbs the inner peace of the churches.

The second proposal of the Encyclical was an invitation to the churches to exert sincere efforts to rekindle and strengthen bonds of love and mutual respect. Towards this end, the Encyclical put forward eleven concrete suggestions — practical and pastoral in nature — which many would say were visionary and ground-breaking. It called for the study and acceptance of a uniform calendar for the celebration of the great Christian feasts. It also called for the pursuit of a deeper historical study of the doctrinal differences by seminaries and theologians. To aid this process, the Encyclical asked for the cultivation of close relationships between local churches, theological schools, and professors of theology and the exchange of students for further training between the seminaries of different churches. The Encyclical also sought to address several pastoral concerns calling for the fostering of mutual respect for the customs and practices of the different churches; the convocation of pan-Christian conferences to examine questions of common interest; the facilitation of funerals and burials of believers dying in foreign lands; and the settlement of questions pertaining to mixed marriages. This list of proposals sets forth another foundational principle. Ecumenical engagements can become the forums where pastoral issues are discussed and, when possible, resolved through sound theological reflection.[18]

The Encyclical of 1920 also listed several dangers threatening the Churches in the aftermath of World War I; dangers which "attack the very foundation of the Christian faith and the essence of Christian life and society." Among the "unhealthy symptoms," which "worsen already existing wounds and open other new ones," the En-

---

[15] Ibid.

[16] Patriarch Bartholomew, "Ithika Dilimmata tis Pagkosmiopoiiseos" ("Moral Dilemmas of Globalization"), *Peiraïki Ekklesia* (March 1999), 8, 9.

[17] Proselytism was (and continues to be) a matter of deep concern for all the Orthodox Churches. The matter was raised by the Churches in reaction to the Encyclical of 1902 and addressed by the Ecumenical Patriarchate in the "Response to the Reactions of the Local Orthodox Churches," which was issued in 1904. The Patriarchate noted the following. "The difficulties are increased by the manifold attempts of the Roman Church and of many Protestants to poach and proselytize in the domestic folds of our Orthodox Church. It is indeed very dangerous, and quite contrary to the Christian calling, for Christians to attack Christians or to suborn and foment trouble among the faithful: as Scripture has it, 'traversing land and sea to make one proselyte' (Matt.23:15). We all feel pain and are deeply wounded when we see souls…seduced and led astray…" in C. Patelos (ed.), *The Orthodox Church in the Ecumenical Movement*, 36.

[18] Theological dialogues do not lead, as some believe, to doctrinal relativism, to the dilution of the Church's faith.

Part I: Orthodox Churches in the Ecumenical Movement – an Introduction

cyclical listed the following: the great lack of respect even for the elementary principles of justice and charity; the unchecked licentiousness and indecency being perpetrated under the cloak of freedom, emancipation, and the cultivation of fine art; and the deification of wealth and the contempt for the higher ideals. The list of dangers sounds familiar — a portrayal, many would say, of our own times. Despite the wondrous and unprecedented achievements of modern science that have greatly improved human lives since the time the Encyclical was first promulgated, respect for the higher ideals appears to be in short supply now as it was then. The state of irreligion continues to spread, as more and more people are being drawn into its web. The times, now as then, call for greater efforts by the Church to enrapture people with the transforming power of the Gospel and the truths of the Faith.

Unity: its theological foundations

Dogmas are not just a set of obscure propositions and concepts about God but vital and authoritative truths that bring salvation and have practical significance for the everyday life of the Church and the world.[19] The concept of unity as a theological principle is derived chiefly from the two foundational dogmas of the Church: the Holy Trinity and the Incarnation. The concept of unity originates in the doctrine of the Holy Trinity — the inseparable union between the three Hypostases of the Godhead. The one true God is personal and transcendent and has revealed Himself as Trinity in the work of salvation in historical events.[20] He is one being or one essence (ουσία) in three hypostases or three distinct and particular persons. God's unity and His trinity are full realities. "In God, essence and person are co-fundamental, neither is prior to the other."[21] "The Holy Trinity," as Bishop Kallistos Ware notes, "is a mystery of unity in diversity, and of diversity in unity."[22] Citing St. Gregory the Theologian and St. John of Damascus, he adds: "The divine is indivisible in its divisions," for the persons are "united yet not confused, distinct yet not divided."[23]

The concept of unity also originates in the mystery of the Incarnation. The Son and Word of God, the second Person of the Holy Trinity "became flesh and dwelt among us, full of grace and truth" (John 1:14). In the one undivided Person of Jesus Christ, the incarnate Son of God, we contemplate the union of two natures, the divine and the human, which, according to the dogmatic definition of the Fourth Ecumenical Synod of Chalcedon, are united without confusion, without change, without division, and without separation.

The Church's search for unity is inspired also by the desire and intention of the Savior and Founder of the Church that all who believe in Him 'may be one' (John 17:11). It is also founded upon the conviction that Orthodoxy, by the grace of God, has maintained an unbroken continuity with the Church of Pentecost by preserving the Apostolic faith and polity unadulterated. Furthermore, it is based on the Orthodox approach to salvation, which is essentially therapeutic in nature and on the Orthodox understanding of the holy sacraments as manifestations of the age to come, by which we share in the life-giving acts of Christ and engage the salvific, transforming, and empowering love of the Triune God, which heals and reconciles.

Orthodoxy and the search for Christian unity

The Orthodox believe that the unity of the Church is an existential fact. There is no room in Orthodox ecclesiology for the branch theory or any other kind of theory that seeks not only to rationalize and justify division, separation, or fragmentation but to normalize it. The Church can only be one — μια — because she is the Body

---

[19] John D. Zizioulas, *Lectures in Christian Dogmatics*, edited by Douglas H. Knight (London and New York 2008), 6, 40
[20] Dumitru Staniloae, *Theology and the Church* (Crestwood, NY 1980), 74 and J. D. Zizioulas, *Lectures in Christian Dogmatics*, 42-43 See also John Meyendorff, *Byzantine Theology* (New York 1979), 180-186 and Jaroslav Pelikan, *The Christian Tradition: A History of the Development of Doctrine*, vol. 1 (Chicago and London 1971), 211-225.
[21] J. D. Zizioulas, *Lectures in Christian Dogmatics*, 54.
[22] Timothy Ware (Bishop Kallistos), *The Orthodox Church* (New Edition, London 1997), 211.
[23] Ibid. (St. Gregory the Theologian, *Orations,* 31:14 and St. John of Damascus, *On the Orthodox Faith.* 1:8).

of Christ and the Temple of the Holy Spirit. Hence, the center of operation of the Holy Spirit can only be the historical and visible one, holy, catholic, and apostolic Church and this Church is the Orthodox Church. This truth — another foundational principle which guides the Church's involvement in ecumenical affairs — was set forth clearly and succinctly by the representatives of the Greek Orthodox Church at the North American Faith and Order Study Conference, held in Oberlin, Ohio in 1957.

> The Unity we seek, is for us a given unity which has never been lost, and, as a divine gift and an essential mark of Christian existence, could not have been lost. This unity in the Church of Christ is for us a unity in the historical Church, in the fullness of faith, in the fullness of continuous sacramental life. For us, this unity is embodied in the Orthodox Church, which has kept, *catholikos* and *anelleipos,* both the integrity of the Apostolic Faith and the integrity of the Apostolic Order.[24]

When affirming this truth, however, we must be careful not to conclude or argue that outside the canonical limits of the Orthodox Church there is only darkness and impoverishment and thereby deny completely and fully the presence of grace in other Christian bodies. Metropolitan John of Pergamon reminds us that "It is certainly not easy to exclude from the realm and the operation of the Holy Spirit so many Christians who do not belong to the Orthodox Church. There are saints outside the Orthodox Church."[25]

Leontios of Jerusalem, a theologian of the sixth century, had already enunciated this principle:

> It is often possible to observe gifts of miracles among orthodox and heterodox persons alike, not on account of ortho-doxy alone...but on account of the particular individual's natural simplicity and humility and even more, innocence of soul, or on account of his gentle and sympathetic disposition and, to put it simply, his greater personal fitness for so great a gift over the others who share his faith. If the capacity for miracle-working really is present in anyone on account of his opinion alone, then everyone who took the same doctrinal stance must always have miracles in the same way. To tell the truth, though, teachers of the faith often aren't miracle-workers; it is those they have taught who perform signs.[26]

In the spirit of the Fathers and echoing the canonical and liturgical tradition of the Church, Bishop Kallistos Ware provides us with a concise but insightful principle or rule by which to understand our role in the ecumenical movement and our relationship with other Christian communities.

> We know where the Church is but we cannot be sure where the Church is not. There is only one Church, but there are many different ways of being related to this one Church, and many different ways of being separated from it.

---

[24] "Statement by the Representatives of the Greek Orthodox Church at the North American Faith and Order Study Conference." The Conference was held in Oberlin, Ohio (3-10 September 1957). The statement is available on *http://www.orthodoxresearchinstitute.org/* A similar statement was issued by the Third Pan-Orthodox Pre-Conciliar Conference of 1986: "The Orthodox Church, faithful to her ecclesiology, to the identity of her inner structure and to the teaching of the undivided Church, in participating in the fellowship of the WCC, does not accept the idea of parity of denominations and cannot accept Church unity as an interdenominational adjustment." In *Episkepsis* 369 (1986): 14.

[25] John Zizioulas, "Orthodox Ecclesiology and the Ecumenical Movement," in *Sourozh*, vol. 21 (1985): 22, cited in E. Clapsis, *Orthodoxy in Conversation – Orthodox Ecumenical Engagements* (Geneva and Brookline, MA, 2000), p. 118.

[26] Leontius of Jerusalem, *Against the Monophysites: Testimonies of the saints and Aporiae,* edited and translated by Patrick T. R. Gray (Oxford 2006), 157. Also, Leontius of Jerusalem, *Quaestiones*, in *PG* 86, part 2, 1896-1897. I am grateful to Prof. Christos Arabatzis of the Theological School of the Aristotle University of Thessaloniki for bringing this text to my attention.

Some non-Orthodox are very close indeed to Orthodoxy, others less so; some are friendly to the Orthodox Church, others indifferent or hostile.[27]

The canonical boundaries of the Church are real and essential, but they are not absolute.[28] St. Basil, for example, taught that certain schismatic groups should be treated as having vestiges of the Church and are, therefore, "*still of the Church — ως ετι εκ της εκκλησίας οντων.*"[29] In fact, the canonical and liturgical tradition relating to the reception of converts clearly accords ecclesial significance to some heterodox churches and communities.[30] What is valid in a heterodox community is that which remains with them as their portion of the inner core of the Church. Having kept the core of the catholic faith, these ecclesial communities are held together in a certain unity with the one true Church. The Church not only knows, transmits, and preserves the truth, she also recognizes it and rejoices when she finds it in other places.[31]

Nikos Nissiotis made the point that "if Orthodoxy silently accepts that there is salvation in other churches outside its limits [then] the presence and witness of the Eastern Orthodox Churches and their witness to the unbroken Orthodox tradition can help all the historical Churches to recover their own true life."[32] And he adds, "This means in practice that Orthodoxy must give up its defensive, confessional-apologetic-polemic attitude, and in the glory of the Holy Spirit, become a mighty river of life, filling the gaps, complementing opposites, overcoming enmities, and driving forward towards reunion.[33]

Throughout her history, but more vigorously in our own times, despite the hesitation within some circles and the strong opposition within others, the Orthodox Churches have engaged the ecumenical dialogues responsibly and prayerfully in the belief that the pursuit of the unity of faith is an inescapable imperative for all Christians. This unity, as Metropolitan John of Pergamon notes, "cannot be restored or fulfilled except through the coming together of those who share the same faith in the Triune God and are baptized in His name. The fellowship that results from this coming together on such a basis and for such a purpose cannot but bear an ecclesiological significance, the precise nature of which will have to be defined."[34]

---

[27] Timothy Ware, *The Orthodox Church* (second edition), 308.

[28] See Emmanuel Clapsis, *Orthodoxy in Conversation*. In this volume of essays, Father Clapsis provides the reader with insightful reflections on issues that pertain to Christian unity and other relevant matters. In the essay, "The Boundaries of the Church: An Orthodox Debate," p. 120, he states that contemporary Orthodox theologians "seem to agree that, while the one, holy, catholic, and apostolic Church is the Orthodox Church, this does not mean that other Christian churches and communions are void of ecclesiological significance to the extent that in their lives church structures and aspects of the catholic faith have been preserved."

[29] St. Basil, *Letter 188 – To Amphilochios*. St Basil identified three kinds of groups that are outside the canonical boundaries of the Church, heretics, schismatics, and dissenters (illicit communities, παρασυναγωγαι). His description of these groups is especially important (*Letter 188:1*). The heretics are groups that understand the Triune God in radically different and highly deficient, unrecognizable, and irreconcilable ways. Hence, their baptism is considered null and void. Schismatics, on the other hand, are groups of Christians who are separated from the Church for holding opinions that, while dissimilar, are reparable and resolvable. Dissenters or Dissidents are groups that form rival and illicit communities in opposition to legitimate ecclesial authority.

[30] See A. Calivas, "Receiving Converts into the Orthodox Church: Lessons from the Canonical and Liturgical Tradition," in *The Greek Orthodox Theological Review (GOTR*, hereinafter*)*, 54 (2009): 1-4.

[31] See Thomas Hopko, "Tasks Facing the Orthodox in the 'Reception' Process of BEM," in *GOTR*, 30.2 (1985): 236.

[32] Nikos Nissiotis, "The Witness and the Service of Eastern Orthodoxy to the One Undivided Church," 237, 238. Of special interest is Nissiotis' definition of the term *historic Churches*. He writes, "By 'historic churches' we mean churches which confess in terms of the Nicene Creed the whole of the Divine Economy of the Revelation in the Church of God the Holy Trinity, and which believe in the continuation of this event by the Holy Spirit in and through the Church by acts culminating in the Sacraments and the Word, administered by those set apart to do so." 233.

[33] Ibid. 238.

[34] Metropolitan John Zizioulas, "The Self-Understanding of the Orthodox and their Participation in the Ecumenical Movement," in George Lemopoulos (ed.), *The Ecumenical Movement of the Churches and the World Council of Churches*

The 'coming together' of which we speak, however, does not mean or require the absorption of other churches and communities — another of the foundational principles. Archbishop Germanos of Thyateira, representing the Ecumenical Patriarchate at the first "Faith and Order" Conference in 1927, enunciated this thusly:

> Although the Orthodox Church considers unity in faith a primary condition of reunion of the Churches, yet it rejects that exclusive theory according to which one Church, regarding itself as the one true church, insists that those who seek reunion with it shall enter its own realm. Such a conception of reunion, amounting to the absorption of the other Churches, is in every way opposed to the spirit existing in the Orthodox Church, which has always distinguished between unity on the one hand and uniformity on the other...As a consequence, only those things which have a direct reference to the Faith and which are by general consent accepted should be considered obligatory and as making for unity.[35]

The involvement of the Orthodox Churches in various local, national, and international councils and consultations has, for the most part, proven to be beneficial both to us and to our partners and interlocutors in the ecumenical movement. We have all been enriched by these encounters[36] and "have derived much comfort from the experience that, although divided by dogmatic differences, we are one with our brethren in the faith in our Lord and Savior Jesus Christ."[37] Through these encounters centuries of estrangement and suspicion have been overcome.[38] For this, we express gratitude to the many inspired church leaders and theologians for their valiant efforts and decisive actions in seizing the historical moments and opportunities to serve the cause of Christian unity.

Moved by a spirit of humility, love, and openness — and aware of St. Paul's words that we are "earthen vessels, that the excellence of the power may be of God" (2 Cor. 4:7) — these visionaries of the Faith chose

---

(Geneva 1996), 46.

[35] Archbishop Germanos of Thyateira, "The Call to Unity." The text was first published in *Faith and Order-Proceedings of the World Conference* (Lausanne, 1927), and more recently by C. Patelos (ed.), *The Orthodox Church in the Ecumenical Movement*, 132-136. The cited text is on p. 134. The rule expressed by Archbishop Germanos, as he notes, is based on the Encyclical Letter of Patriarch Photios the Great to Pope Nicholas I, in which we read: "In cases where the thing disregarded is not a matter of faith and does not involve disobedience to any general or catholic decree, a man capable of judging would be right in deciding that neither those who observe them nor those who have not received them act wrongly." A statement, similar to that of Archbishop Germanos, was made by the Orthodox Consultation on "The Church's Struggle for Justice and Unity," held on the island of Crete, March 1975: "The Orthodox Church does not expect that other Christians be converted to Orthodoxy in its historical and cultural reality of the past and the present and to become members of the Orthodox Church. Its desire is that all should strive in their own churches and traditions to deepen the fullness of the Apostolic faith embodied in a fully ecclesial life. No church is therefore required to uproot itself, to cut itself off from its cultural heritage or to lose its distinctive character. Each would contribute to the enrichment of all." In C. Patelos (ed.), *The Orthodox Church in the Ecumenical Movement*, 123. In sharp contrast to this ecclesiological and missiological principle is the claim of universal jurisdiction by the bishop of Rome, which essentially means that ecclesial fullness is possible only through communion with the bishop of Rome. The Unia (or the Eastern Catholic Churches) is an example of this kind of ecclesiology. On the issue of Uniatism see the documents of the Joint International Commission and Official Dialogues in the United States in John Borelli and John H. Erickson (eds), *The Quest for Unity: Orthodox and Catholics in Dialogue* (Crestwood, NY 1996), 159-190; and Kondothra M. George, "Local and Universal: Uniatism as an Ecclesiological Issue," in *One World*, 180 (November 1992) and in G. Limouris, *Orthodox Visions of Ecumenism*, 228-232.

[36] See, for example, Metropolitan Emilianos Timiadis, *What the Orthodox Church Owes to the West* (Brookline 1991), and Donald Fairbairn, *Eastern Orthodoxy Through Western Eyes* (Louisville-London 2002).

[37] From the Statement read by Archbishop Germanos of Thyateira at the First World Conference on "Faith and Order," in C. Patelos (ed.), *The Orthodox Church in the Ecumenical Movement*, 82.

[38] Troublesome historical circumstances, such as the Unia and other attempts at dominance and proselytism by Western Christians, gave rise to deep-seated antipathies among the Orthodox populace. See, for example, the description on the state of church affairs in the 18th century by the learned theologian Eustratios Argenti, in Timothy Ware, *Eustratios Argenti: A Study of the Greek Church Under Turkish Rule* (Oxford 1964), 78-79.

Part I: Orthodox Churches in the Ecumenical Movement – an Introduction

good will and patience over hostility and bigotry that are born of ignorance, intolerance, and hubris. Mindful of the apostolic saying, "God desires all men to be saved and to come to the knowledge of the truth" (1 Tim. 2:4), men and women of faith who have engaged the ecumenical dialogue, in the past and in the present, speak the truth in love in the knowledge that love casts out fear (1 John 4:19) and that the truth has the power to free, heal, reconcile, and sanctify.

Grass-roots ecumenism

The same spirit of love and sincerity has produced forms of grass-roots ecumenism, which are especially evident in the multi-cultural and multi-religious societies in which many Orthodox Christians live today. In such societies ecumenical engagements are not a theory or a luxury but a way of life, a practical need. They are conducted not as officially sanctioned consultations but as part of daily life in various public contexts and forums, which include consortia of theological schools, local ministerial associations, community councils, civic institutions, schools, hospitals, neighborhoods, and especially families in which the spouses are of different faiths. Every day, in contexts such as these Orthodox clerics and laypeople encounter other Christians, people of other faiths, and people of no faith. The circumstances require them to engage the other "ecumenically," that is, with a spirit of respect, humility, and openness, but also with faithfulness to the Church's faith and discipline. Grass-roots ecumenism softens prejudices and enmities but it also places the wounds of division in full view; divisions that beg for resolution and healing.

The tragedy of Christian disunity is especially evident and painful in mixed marriages. The inability of the non-Orthodox spouse to share fully in the sacramental life of the Church is a painful reality. While full integration in the life of the Church is limited by this sad fact, the Church nonetheless has a special responsibility to honor, welcome, and embrace the non-Orthodox spouse and to encourage and nurture to the highest possible degree his or her ties to the Church, as the spouse and parent of those who are full members of the community.

A roadmap for ecumenical relations

We have learned by experience that the search for Christian unity is an arduous, complex, and delicate task. Its ultimate goal is the unity of faith and the sharing of the same Bread and Cup at the same Holy Table, because the Eucharist is the mystery of Christ and the realization of the Church as the unbroken unity of His one body. Hence, as Fr. Georges Florovsky noted, the Eucharist is a doctrinal witness and not simply an expression of human brotherhood.[39] The Church's unity is constituted by the unity of the Holy Spirit, who is the Spirit of Truth. The Divine Liturgy — the sacred rite by which the Orthodox Church celebrates the sacrament of the holy Eucharist — inspires us to action in favor of unity. The order (τάξη) and structure (δομή) of the Divine Liturgy provides us with a roadmap which delineates the way to unity, defines its meaning, and gives expression to the several basic principles of the endeavor.

Four acts of the Divine Liturgy are especially significant in this regard. The first act is the proclamation of the Word of God at the beginning of the Divine Liturgy. It is a public act, open to all, so that the world may hear the message of the Gospel and believe. The Scriptures constitute a sign of the common heritage of all Christians who share the belief in the Holy Trinity and in the divinity of Jesus Christ, the Son and Word of God made flesh.

The second act is the Kiss of Peace that follows later in the Divine Liturgy. It can be interpreted as an invitation for rapprochement, as an act of mutual forgiveness and acceptance, and as a call to all who claim Jesus

[39] Fr. Georges Florovsky, "The Elements of Liturgy," in G. Patelos (ed.), *The Orthodox Church in the Ecumenical Movement*, 177-179.

Christ as Lord to set aside old prejudices and enmities. The Kiss of Peace, an essential element of Christian worship from the beginning, is an invitation extended to all Christians to manifest Christ's love in the world by working jointly in the struggle for justice, peace, freedom, equality, and every other godly work.

The recitation of the Creed, which comes after the Kiss of Peace is the third act. It stands as a reminder to everyone that the desired blessed union of the Churches can be restored and fulfilled only through substantive theological work, so that "the faith which was once delivered to the saints" (Jude 3) may be properly understood, formulated, affirmed, and embraced by all. Only then can Christians gather at one Table — the fourth act — to share together the Bread and Cup of Life — the Eucharist — as the expression and fulfillment of their unity in love and in faith.

True unity begins with the acknowledgment by Christians of their common spiritual ancestry. It is advanced through a spirit of cooperation between the Churches and their engagement in common godly endeavors, all of which must lead to an earnest desire and a real effort to resolve their confessional and doctrinal differences which are the root cause of their disunity.

Every work of fellowship and concord should be a path to the realization of the fullness of truth in conformity with the mind of the undivided Church. True unity is that which manifests and discloses the perennial identity of the Church's faith. For this reason, the Eucharist is not an instrument of reunion, a means for achieving Christian unity. It is, rather, the very sign of that union based on doctrinal truths and canonical harmony already held and possessed in common. Hence, it is not possible to approach Holy Communion by way of hospitality.[40] St. Justin the Martyr tells us that this was the Church's practice from the earliest days: "This food we call Eucharist and no one may share it unless he believes our teaching is true…and lives as Christ taught."[41]

The Church: keeper and witness of the message of Revelation

The Church is not only the vigilant keeper and interpreter of the message of revelation but also its passionate, heroic, and humble witness. The Church is the evangelical community of love and peace, infinitely compassionate and tolerant, even when she is scorned and wronged. She is the Body of Christ, the extension and fullness of the incarnation, which draws the brokenness of the world within her communion of unity, love, and truth. Thus regardless of differences in conceptual language, theological presuppositions, or spiritual traditions the Orthodox Church is obliged to engage other Christians and even people of other religions for the sake of the truth, to which she bears witness.

As the authentic depository of the apostolic kerygma and tradition, the Orthodox Church is able to discern what is authentically of the undivided Church wherever it is found. As the bearer of the Light, the Church has the capacity to discern the existence of light — however bright or dim — beyond her borders.

However, in contemplating and enacting her lofty calling and mission to the world the Church must never lose sight of the world's brokenness and tragic unfulfillment — the stark historical reality of sin which subverts the truth, betrays love, and destabilizes human relationships. Nikos Nissiotis reminds us that an authentic ecclesiology has to be mindful of the "curious and unique dialectic between unshaken communion in *essence* and brokenness in *existence* in the whole creation. This is because the *ecclesia* as sacramental communion is absolutely holy… but all men yet remain sinful and in broken relationship both in the ecclesial communion and in the world."[42]

---

[40] Metropolitan Paulos Mar Gregorios of the Malankara Orthodox Syrian Church notes that the term *intercommunion* and the expression *eucharistic hospitality* make no theological sense and adds, how can one "offer communion to those who are not in communion." See his brief comment, "Eucharistic Hospitality: Not a Question of Hospitality. A Comment," in G. Limouris, *Orthodox Visions of Ecumenism*, 233.

[41] St. Justin the Martyr, *Apologia* 1: 65, 66.

[42] Nikos A. Nissiotis, "The Church as a Sacramental Vision and the Challenge of Christian Witness," in G. Limouris (ed.), *Church, Kingdom, World: the Church as Mystery and Prophetic Sign*, (Geneva 1986), 109.

Every undertaking, even the most noble, requires that we take into account the human condition in its fallen state which places limits on all our efforts and claims. At the same time, however, we know by faith that the primal wound of the original sin — estrangement from God, the world, the neighbor, and the self — has been healed by Christ. What man failed to do, God accomplished through the incarnation of His only-begotten Son, our Lord and Savior Jesus Christ. God Himself bridged the essential gulf between created and uncreated nature. "A closer union than this between God and His creation there could not be. God Himself became one of His creatures."[43] The union of two perfect natures, the divine and the human, in the one Person of God the Word illumines all human relationships and gives them meaning and purpose. If God in His goodness bent the heavens to heal our infirmities (Phil. 2:5-8; Heb. 2:9, 14-15), could we, who are called to manifest His love and make known His truth, do less? *"In the Holy Spirit, divine inspiration, good will, understanding, peace, and blessing are imparted to all..."*[44]

Bibliography

Borelli, John and Erickson, John H. (eds), *The Quest for Unity: Orthodox and Catholics in Dialogue*, (Crestwood, NY 1996).

Calivas, A., "Receiving Converts into the Orthodox Church: Lessons from the Canonical and Liturgical Tradition," in *The Greek Orthodox Theological Review (GOTR)*, (2009).

Clapsis, E., *Orthodoxy in Conversation – Orthodox Ecumenical Engagements*, (Geneva and Brookline, MA 2000).

FitzGerald, Thomas and Gratsias, Emmanuel (eds.), *Restoring the Unity in Faith: The Orthodox-Oriental Orthodox Theological Dialogue*, (Brookline, MA 2007).

FitzGerald, Thomas, *The Ecumenical Patriarchate and Christian Unity*, (Brookline, MA 2009).

Florovsky, Georges, "The Eastern Orthodox Church in the Ecumenical Movement," in *Theology Today* 7.1 (1950).

Hopko, Thomas, "Tasks Facing the Orthodox in the 'Reception' Process of BEM," in *GOTR* 30.2 (1985).

Limouris, Gennadios, *Orthodox Visions of Ecumenism: Statements and Reports on the Ecumenical Movement* (Geneva, 1994).

Limouris, Gennadios, *Orthodox Perspectives on 'Baptism, Eucharist and Ministry'*, WCC Faith and Order, (Geneva, 1985).

Nissiotis, Nikos A., "The Witness and the Service of Eastern Orthodoxy to the One Undivided Church," in Constantin G. Patelos (ed.), *The Orthodox Church in the Ecumenical Movement*, (Geneva, 1978), 231-241.

Sabev, Todor, *The Orthodox Churches in the World Council of Churches: Towards the Future*, (Geneva, 1996).

Tsetsis, George, "A Synthesis of the Responses of the Orthodox Churches to the Lima Document", *Baptism, Eucharist and Ministry*, WCC Faith and Order paper 111 (Geneva, 1987).

Zizioulas, John D., *Lectures in Christian Dogmatics*, edited by Douglas H. Knight (London and New York 2008).

Zizioulas, John "Orthodox Ecclesiology and the Ecumenical Movement," in *Sourozh* 21 (1985).

Zizioulas, John, "The Self-Understanding of the Orthodox and their Participation in the Ecumenical Movement," in George Lemopoulos (ed.), *The Ecumenical Movement of the Churches and the World Council of Churches*, (Geneva, 1996).

---

[43] T. Ware, *The Orthodox Church*, 210.

[44] Hymn of the Second Antiphon of the Anavathmoi of the Sixth Tone of the Sunday Orthros.

Fr. Rauno Pietarinen

One of the first things that I learned at seminary, many years ago, was that Christians have never been the majority in any country, at any time. I had mistakenly thought that this had been the case in both the Byzantine and Russian Empires. But the late, great Professor John Meyendorff pointed out that even in both these instances, the majority of the population only formally belonging to the Church. Those in living communion with the Church have always been a minority in their own countries — and even within their own Churches.

In the current situation, therefore, we do well to refer to a 'majority Church' as simply the largest Church in any given country or region.

According to the Gospels, the path of a Christian is difficult, but at the same time wonderful. The difficulty means that only a few choose to follow Christ in such a way that they remain in Christ, and Christ in them. Although the line between the committed and the indifferent Christian is thin, there is in the tradition of the Orthodox Church, however, criteria for true communion with the Church.

The most important criterion is eucharistic communion. Without it, man is but an "associate" member of the Body of Christ. Eucharistic communion in turn, requires awareness of the continuing correction in one's life through repentance. That consciousness is maintained by personal prayer, reading of the Scripture and participation in liturgical life. Awareness of one's own development, in turn, leads people to the healing sacraments of the Church. Here the Sacrament of Repentance (Healing) plays an important role as one tries to explore specifically whether there is in one's soul a real awareness of the need for healing — and how this awareness is put into action. An experienced confessor acts like a good doctor. He not only seeks quick relief of symptoms, but seeks "wellness" in guiding the repentant's whole life into change according to the Gospel's teaching.

In her early history the Church had to decide whether to keep weaker brothers and sisters within the Church. At the end of the fourth century, as persecution of Christians was waning, the question was raised concerning those who had fallen during the persecutions (Lapsi). The Confessors, who had suffered a great deal, resolved this problem by suggesting that the lapsed be taken back to the Church - but only through repentance. Thus the Church avoided becoming nothing more than a small elite community of ascetics — and at the same time obligated to at least try to do better.

We have a similar situation today. The Church does not abandon its weaker members, but She expects them to try to do better. Thus even within the Church there is always a minority/majority division. For just as in Confessors' era, those today who have made great spiritual progress, and have become partakers of the Glory of God already in this world, are the most loving and forgiving. Their love for us, who are inferior to them, gently guides us towards the right path.

The Church as an Oppressed Minority in Society

There have been times, however, such as during the Ottoman and Communist eras that oppression shook away the merely formal members of the Church. Church activities were largely reduced to liturgical services — and even that could cause great inconvenience to believers. Christians, of any kind, became not only a minority, but an ill-treated minority. While personal, private connections within the Church were often strengthened, missionary and diaconal activity necessarily declined.

Modern organizational theory teaches that in a network there should not only be sufficient flexibility, but at the same time, a necessary flow of information between different cells and the center. Flexibility means, for example, sufficient autonomy to act at the local level without constant contact to the center. Steep subordination to a central administration guarantees the flow of information, but it may also shatter the entire network if the network is attacked from the outside. At the same time, fully self-governing groups rarely survive as organizations, because they lack connection to leadership and other branches.

The survival of the Church under Ottoman rule or communist totalitarian states is based on God's Providence, which revealed the Church's optimal model of governance. While each local eucharistic community manifests the fullness of the Church, none of these communities can legitimately function without its connection to the bishop, and to other Churches. Moreover, each parish, however small or oppressed, always affects its surrounding community. As long as the local members of the Church rise up to Mount Tabor and are united to Transfigured Christ in the Eucharist, on a regular basis, the Church will always remain a shining light on the mountain that no-one can miss.

Too tight of a connection between the Church and the State has caused persecution of minority religions. In general, the background was the State's concern about political unity, which sometimes led the Church to persecute minorities. Religious intolerance could also be spread by the very same people who had themselves suffered from persecution. The harassed become a harasser — unless the love of Christ could work in people's hearts. Overall, the earthly power of the Church has been generally proved detrimental. As fire is a good servant but a bad master, so too a powerful Church is tempted to give fire and the sword, not love, the upper hand.

The 20th century Brings Orthodoxy to the West

The 20th century brought much confusion to local Orthodox Churches all over the world. The emergence of the Soviet Union and its aggressive political expansion into many Eastern European countries led to a massive emigration of these peoples into all of Western Europe and the Americas. Orthodox believers found themselves in situations where their environment had little sympathy or understanding to their faith. They faced both prejudice and even social pressure to conform to local religious norms. However, Orthodox parishes were established. And, the Church became for many the only place with a living connection to the old country's (former) culture and life.

On the positive side, the Orthodox Church gradually became familiar to many Western nations. Ecclesiologically problematic was the strong commitment of these emigrant Churches to the old country's language and customs. National epithets began to commonly appear in front of the words 'Orthodox Christian': hence, Greek-, Russian-, Romanian-, Serbian-, Carpatho–Russian Orthodox. The Church lost an opportunity to be seen as truly universal, as was required by her own vocation. Links with the old country, when possible, were maintained, but they were hampered by political polarization.

The last century was also notable for Orthodox Christians for the emergence of ecumenism within Orthodoxy. Now to be found among other churches and even other religions, the Orthodox were forced to articulate the very substance of their own faith in new languages and new ways. The dialogue began, and it benefited both the local majority churches and the Orthodox Christian minority. In many cases, other Churches were of great help to Orthodox when they looked for buildings in which to worship and also in other practical matters.

In this regard, the World Council of Churches and the Conference of European Churches were invaluable links between the Churches. They also provided a forum in which the Orthodox themselves had the opportunity and possibility of meeting each other. As a result the first Pan-Orthodox Conference, to begin planning the long-proposed Great and Holy Synod, was held in Rhodes in 1961 at the invitation of the Patriarch of Constantinople, Athenagoras. Based on their ecumenical experiences in the WCC, Orthodox youth established SYNDESMOS, the World's Fellowship of Orthodox Youth in 1953. For decades SYNDESMOS played a pivotal and important role in bringing together Orthodox youth living in both minority and majority situations. After all, it was the only pan-Orthodox organization for decades. SYNDESMOS also invited all Orthodox theological schools to join in 1968, thus enabling the formal involvement of Eastern European Orthodox youth. For it was particularly the youth who felt the urgency of international contacts when living in minority situations — whether in small Orthodox communities in Western Europe, or under oppression in Eastern Europe or the Middle East.

Orthodox Minorities in the West

Living in the minority usually meant economic difficulties as well as religious and social ones. Priests often had to support themselves through another occupation as well. And even when they did not have to take a second job, an Orthodox priest wages were very low. Emigrant communities were often terribly divided by a variety of disputes - political, social and ecclesiological. Ecclesiastical items were difficult to obtain. Even more problematic for Orthodox Christians was the fact that the surrounding society lived in a different rhythm - both in terms of time and culture - than what believers were used to.

And there were other problems: Worship in the language of the old country did not attract crowds except a few linguistic enthusiasts. Social activities were exclusive to "our people", whichever "people" that may have been. Resources were scarce and potential financial assistance was directed to one's "own". Diaconal and missionary work were neglected. On the other hand, the ethos of Diaconia had already been lost in the old country: Communists did not allow diaconal service to society by Churches with the exception of financial support for "peace work".

The situation became radically different after the collapse of the Soviet Union and the Eastern Bloc. Since the 1990s, with freedom to move abroad restored, a new wave of emigration occurred. Many new emigrants left because of financial rather than political reasons. And once again the ecclesiological principle, that a given area can have only one bishop, was forgotten. Dioceses and parishes were once again established on an ethnic basis. When co-operation could have meant strength and a more visible presence for Orthodoxy, our Churches chose division — and thus, ultimately, a minority role once again. Common sense would suggest both North America and Western Europe should have their own autocephalous Orthodox Churches, each of which would have multi-cultural parishes, able to serve their first generation members in their own languages, and later generations in the local language. In this regard, we have departed far from the surrounding reality, and our own ecclesiology.

The Baltic Sea is surrounded by nine states, of which, in religious terms, Lutherans, Catholics and Orthodox predominate. The area is interesting because all these confessions are in the majority at least in one coastal State, and in the minority in more than one. In Poland, the Catholics are in majority whereas in the Nordic countries, Russia and the Baltic states they are a minority. Lutherans are the majority in the Nordic countries, but in Russia, the Baltic states and Poland they are minority. Orthodox believers are in majority in Russia, but in the minority in the Nordic countries, the Baltic states and Poland.

The region's network of Churches (Theobalt) brought up some years ago the majority/minority issue on its agenda. Measures to promote co-operation among the Churches in helping migrant workers and in stopping trafficking in human beings were widely discussed. At the same time, though, it became possible to compare the attitudes of each Church concerning its majority and the minority position. The question was: When in majority position, do we deal with minorities in the same way as we expect others to deal with us when we ourselves are in the minority? This question remains. If we insist on minority rights for our people, but refuse to give those rights to other Christian minorities when we are in the majority, how is this possible, or just?

The Experience of the Orthodox Church in Finland

The Finnish Orthodox Church is a spiritual daughter of the Russian Church. After the Russian Revolution the Finnish Orthodox Church sought recognition, and was received as an autonomous Church under the jurisdiction of the Patriarchate of Constantinople, in 1923. However, The State of Finland, which had become independent in 1917, legally confirmed this position of the Orthodox Church at that same time. An ecclesiastical Seminary was founded in 1918, also with state support. When the Orthodox Church of Finland lost approximately 90% of its property in World War II, the Finnish Parliament enacted a law granting large financial support to the Orthodox Church. As a result, numerous Churches, Parish Halls and cemeteries were built around the country.

Orthodox Christians have always been a small minority in Finland. At present, Finland has a population of almost 5.5 million, of which approximately 60,000 are Orthodox Christians. The constitution grants both the Orthodox and Lutheran (majority) churches full freedom to decide their own affairs. The government supports the Orthodox Church on certain salaries and buildings, as well as to provide necessary support in restoring historical Church buildings. Both the Lutheran and the Orthodox Churches have a right to tax. This Church tax is collected only from members of their respective Churches and the state (as the tax collector) charges the Churches a fair compensation for collecting it. The tax is about 1% of income.

Churches insist that this tax does not constitute state aid to Churches, rather, it is the Churches, levy upon their own members. If a person leaves the Church, he does not pay Church tax any more. Thus the State cannot count on this money as a source of income. Church taxes are paid to the local parishes, which then cover their employees' salaries, building maintenance etc. The Church tax covers in many Parishes as much as 90% of their expenses.

When the Finnish Orthodox Church adopted the Gregorian (or "new") Calendar in the 1920s, there were rumors abroad that this was done under pressure from the State. It was, however, the Church's own decision. And, it was blessed by the Ecumenical Patriarch. And whereas the Lutheran Church agreed in 1973, at the State's request, to move certain ecclesiastical holidays to Saturday, the Orthodox Church never moved those feasts, nor was it required to do so. These feasts were returned to their rightful dates by the Lutheran Church in 1992.

The only case when the State put pressure to the Orthodox Church in Finland was after the Second World War, when the Russian Orthodox Church, at the initiative of the Soviet Government, called on the Orthodox Church in Finland to return to the jurisdiction of the Moscow Patriarchate. Finnish State representatives recommended the transition to appease the Soviets, but Archbishop Herman (Aav) postponed the meeting of the clergy-laity council year after year. As only the clergy-laity council could decide the matter, the situation remained open from 1947 to 1957. The Russian Church finally gave up.

During the 20th century the Finnish Lutheran Church could have made life for the Orthodox really difficult. Immediately after independence, the Lutheran Church did not oppose the state giving the Orthodox Church a specific position as a religious minority. Then again, after World War II, the Lutheran Church did not oppose the Law on reconstruction of the Orthodox property. Lutherans did not act against their Christian sisters and brothers, and thus contributed to the future of the Orthodoxy in Finland. In more recent years, they have shown great sympathy and support for the Orthodox Church, both at the national and local level.

Civilized countries like Finland have well understood the principle that minorities always need a bigger share of attention and support than their size would indicate. If the Finnish Orthodox had received only one per cent of the attention of Finnish society, the situation of my Church today would be quite different. In part the state's attitude reflects the historical fact that Orthodox Christians have been present in Finland for over 1,000 years. This historical memory applies to other cultural minorities in Finland as well, including the Swedish-speaking population (Swedish is the second official language in Finland), the Sami people and the Roma. Swedish speakers have their own TV channel in the state broadcast network; the Sami have their own radio channel (which broadcasts in three different Sami languages) and the Roma have radio programs in their own language as well.

The school system is a major supporter of minorities. Orthodox pupils have their own religious instruction, which the schools themselves pay for, if there are a minimum of three Orthodox pupils in the municipality. Orthodox textbooks are published by the state. State radio and TV both broadcast Orthodox liturgies on a regular basis. Orthodox military conscripts are given pastoral care and education by their own clergy. The

University of Eastern Finland in Joensuu has a theological department with Orthodox and Western sections. Orthodox theology students do their own liturgical, homiletic and practical exercises at the Joensuu Orthodox Seminary, which the Orthodox Church owns and the state funds. The Seminary has also a dormitory for students and its own chapel.

Orthodox bishops in Finland are in regular contact with Lutheran bishops, leaders of other faiths and civil authorities. Our bishops can thus convey our Church's position on matters concerning not only the Church, but also on wider societal issues.

For the small Orthodox Church in Finland the situation is good. Relations with the Lutheran Church and the state are both excellent. In many cases the Lutheran Church apparently feels that cooperation with the Orthodox is of importance to them as well. When they invite this small Orthodox Church to the table, they hear not only the Orthodox position, but another Finnish view. In important theological and moral issues the Orthodox Church in Finland does not, of course, have its own policy, but we reflect universal and traditional Orthodox thinking.

Bibliography

Ambrosius (Father), "The Finnish Orthodox Church," in Ion Bria (ed.), *Martyria-Mission: The Witness of the Orthodox Churches Today*, (Geneva: WCC, 1980).

Arvola, Pekka and Kallonen Tuomas (eds), *12 Windows on Orthodoxy in Finland*, (Helsinki: Publications Committee for Orthodox Literature, 2010).

Huttunen, Heikki, "Wittnessing in a secular situation: Reflections on the Orthodox Church of Finland," in: *Ortodoksia* 49, 2002: 194 - 207.

Report of CEC consultation on "Religious Freedom: Majority and Minority Churches in Europe in their Relations to the State", December 2012; see: http://www.leuenberg.net/node/1514; see also: http://www.leuenberg.net/node/1513 (last accessed September, 2013).

CEC Document on Minimal Standards for Churches and Communities of Faith and Conviction, 21 November 2009. German and English Flyer: Hearing on Minimal Rights for Churches and Communities of Faith and Convictions, 13th Lyon Assembly July 2009: http://csc.ceceurope.org/index.php?id=1659; see also: http://csc.ceceurope.org/index.php?id=1659 (last accessed September, 2013).

http://en.wikipedia.org/wiki/Finnish_Orthodox_Church (last accessed September, 2013).

http://orthodoxwiki.org/Church_of_Finland (last accessed September, 2013).

http://en.wikipedia.org/wiki/Evangelical_Lutheran_Church_of_Finland (last accessed September, 2013).

http://en.wikipedia.org/wiki/Roman_Catholicism_in_Finland (last accessed September, 2013).

(7) INTRODUCTION TO MAJOR ECUMENICAL ORGANIZATIONS WITH RELEVANCE FOR ORTHODOX CHURCHES[1]

Athanasios Basdekis

In this article an attempt is made to introduce briefly the Orthodox to the history, activities and general relevance of three major ecumenical organizations, in which the Orthodox Church participates actively since their beginning.

a. World Council of Churches (WCC)

The World Council of Churches was founded in Amsterdam, the Netherlands in 1948. From the 147 founding member churches of WCC, 5 were Orthodox (3 Eastern Orthodox: Ecumenical Patriarchate, Church of Cyprus, Church of Greece, and 2 Oriental Orthodox: Ethiopian Orthodox Tewahedo Church, and Malankara Orthodox Syrian Church), while several other Orthodox churches were present with representatives (Greek Orthodox Patriarchate of Alexandria and All Africa, Greek Orthodox Patriarchate of Antioch, Greek Orthodox Patriarchate of Jerusalem, the Romanian Orthodox Diocese in the USA, the Archdiocese of Russian Orthodox Churches in Western Europe (as it was called at that time), and the Coptic Orthodox Church). Many other Orthodox Churches became members of WCC over time, while others (such as the Orthodox Church of Georgia and the Church of Bulgaria) left the Council during the 1990s due to the fact that they were did not agree with some of the Council's decisions.

The World Council of Churches emerged out of the merger of two other Inter-Christian Movements of the 20th century. The first one was the Faith and Order Movement and the other was the Life and Work Movement. The World Council of Churches merged with the International Missionary Council in 1960-1961 and with the World Council of Christian Education in 1971.

Today in the World Council of Churches 349 member churches from over 120 countries work together representing about 560 million faithful people. Several other church, inter-Christian organizations and assemblies, such as National Council of Churches, participate in the Council's works having the right to express themselves in the Central Committee Meetings and Assemblies.

The fact that the Roman Catholic Church, so far, has not become a member of the WCC, purely due to ecclesiological reasons, is noteworthy. Still, it fully and on equal terms collaborates with the Faith and Order Commission which deals with clearly theological issues, as well as with the Commission on World Mission and Evangelism. At the same time, the Roman Catholic Church collaborates with the WCC on the preparation, issuing and celebration of the so-called Week of Prayer for Christian Unity. Among the existing groups of the WCC there is the significant Joint Working Group which for many years has been dealing with theological issues and has issued really interesting theological texts on various matters.

WCC is based in Geneva, Switzerland. The Ecumenical Institute at Bossey pertains to WCC. The Ecumenical Institute at Bossey, which is located some 17 km outside Geneva serves as a major place for ecumenical formation and learning for young scholars and theologians from a wider spectrum of Christian churches all around the world.

According to the WCC it is stated: "The World Council of Churches is a fellowship of churches which confess the Lord Jesus Christ as God and Savior according to the scriptures, and therefore seek to fulfill together their common calling to the glory of the one God, Father, Son and Holy Spirit."

---

[1] The present article has been initially published as part of a wider section dealing with the Ecumenical Movement in general in Ath. Basdekis *We and the Others, The Orthodox Church and the other Churches and denominations*, (Athens, 2012), 260-277 (in Greek).

In the historical Toronto Statement (1950) of the Central Committee, which until now is considered as the ecclesiastical charter of the Council, it is clarified that "*The World Council of Churches is not and must never become a super-church*".

The organizational structure of the WCC consists of: a) the Assembly which meets every eight years, b) a presidential body of eight elected members, c) the Central Committee, consisting of 150 members, and d) the Executive Committee, consisting of 25 members. These bodies are overseen by the eight-member presidential body and the Moderator along with two Vice Moderators coming from the Central and the Executive Committees, who are aided in their work by the Council's General Secretary who is elected by the Central Committee every seven years. In the eight-member Presidential body, an Oriental Orthodox as well as an Eastern Orthodox delegate has always been elected. So, today members of the presidential body are Archbishop Dr Anastasios (Yannoulatos) of Tirana and all Albania and the late Patriarch Abune Paulos of the Ethiopian Orthodox Tewahedo Church. It is also worth noting that the Armenian Patriarch Catholicos Aram Kesischian, from 1991 to 2006 was Moderator of the Central and Executive Committee of the WCC.

The General Secretaries of WCC from its founding in 1948 until today are: W.A. Visser´t Hooft (1948-1966, Netherlands), Eugen Carson Blake (1966-1972, U.S.A.), Philip Potter (1972-1985, Caribbean- Dominican Republic), Emilio Castro (1985-1992, Uruguay), Konrad Raiser (1993-2003, Germany), Samuel Kobia (2004-2010, Kenya) and Olav Fykse Tveit, 2001- present, Norway).

WCC's General Assemblies (1948-2006) took place in the following countries, each each with their own focus:
- 1st Amsterdam, Netherlands in 1948, "Man's Disorder and God's Design",
- 2nd Evanston, U.S.A. in 1954, "Christ- the Hope of the World",
- 3rd New Delhi, India in 1961, "Jesus Christ, the Light of the World",
- 4th Uppsala, Sweden in 1968, "Behold, I make all things new",
- 5th Nairobi, Kenya in 1975, "Jesus Christ Frees and Unites",
- 6th Vancouver, Canada in 1983, "Jesus Christ – The Life of the World",
- 7th Canberra, Australia in 1991, "Come Holy Spirit – Renew the Whole Creation",
- 8th Harare, Zimbabwe in 1998, "Turn to God – Rejoice in Hope",
- 9th Porto Alegre, Brazil in 2006, "God in your Grace, Transform the World".
- 10th Busan, Republic of Korea in 2013, "God of Life, lead us to Justice and Peace."

The work of the WCC until the Busan assembly was focused around the following six Commissions:
- The WCC and the Ecumenical Movement in the 20th century,
- Church Unity, World Mission and Spirituality,
- Public Witness, Justice and Peace,
- Justice, Peace and Integrity of Creation,
- Education and Ecumenical Formation, and
- Inter-religious Dialogue and Collaboration.

The main issues the WCC has dealt with over the last decades, according to my point of view, are the following:
- Unity schemes and models: How must we understand and pursue the Unification of the Churches?
- Nicene Creed and Filioque,
- Baptism, Eucharist and Ministry,
- Church, Synodality and Apostolicity of the Church,
- Prayer for Church Unity ("Week of Prayer for Christian Unity" and "Prayer Cycle").
- Racial Discrimination and Human Rights,
- Justice, Peace, and Creation Integrity,
- Ministry and inter-church assistance.

There are many significant Orthodox personalities that have served and still serve not only the Church but also Orthodoxy during the almost one hundred year course of the Ecumenical Movement and the WCC. I will only mention here some particularly significant personalities: The Metropolitans of Thyatira Germanos,

Chalcedon Melitonas, Myron and later Ephesus Chrysostom, Cartagena Parthenios who later became Patriarch of Alexandria, Laodicea Ignatius who later became Patriarch of Antioch, Leningrad Nicodemus, Pergamon Ioannis, Smolensk Cyril who is today Patriarch of Moscow, Bishop of Androusa Anastasios who today is Archbishop of Tirana, along with many professors such as Halmikar Alivizatos, Stephan Chankov, Nikolaos Nissiotis, Fr. Georges Florovsky, Fr. Vitalius Borovoy, Fr. Ioan Bria, Vasileios Ioannidis, Ioannis Karmiris, Gerasimos Konidaris and Vasilieios Stavridis.[2]

There is also a Permanent Delegation of the Ecumenical Patriarchate at the main building site of the Ecumenical Organizations in Geneva. Some of the permanent delegates of the Ecumenical Patriarchate have been the Bishop of Melita Iakovos and later Archbishop of North and South America, the Metropolitan of Silivria Emilianos, the Great Archpriest of the Ecumenical Patriarchate Fr. Georges Tsetsis, and the dean Benediktos Ioannou. Deputy General Secretary of the Council today is another Orthodox theologian of the Ecumenical Patriarchate Georgios Lemopoulos, who ministers his Church by being the permanent representative of the Ecumenical Patriarchate at the WCC. It is of great importance here to highlight the fact that the mere existence of the WCC and the Ecumenical Movement itself would be inconceivable without the participation and the collaboration of the Orthodox Church. Without the participation of Orthodox Churches, and taking into consideration the fact that the Roman Catholic Church is not a participating member, the WCC would otherwise be a clearly Protestant organization.

Apart from the renowned Encyclicals by the Ecumenical Patriarchate in 1902, 1904 and 1920, we also have many significant Orthodox and inter-Orthodox texts[3] regarding the contribution the Ecumenical Patriarchate and other Autocephalus Churches had in the Ecumenical Movement in the 20th century and especially in the course of the WCC. Some of these texts I will briefly mention:

- Patriarchal Encyclical of 1952,
- Speech of the Ecumenical Patriarch Athenagoras during his visit at the WCC in November 1967,
- Proclamation of the Ecumenical Patriarchate for the twenty-five years of the WCC in 1973,
- Proclamation of the Patriarchate of Moscow for the twenty-five years of the WCC in 1973,
- Decision of the Third Pre-Synodal Pan-Orthodox Conference in 1986,
- Speech of the Ecumenical Patriarch Dimitrios during his visit at the WCC in December 1987,
- Announcement of the Ecumenical Patriarchate on the forty years of the WCC in 1988,
- Speech of the Ecumenical Patriarch Bartholomew during his visit at the WCC in December 1995, and
- Speech of the Ecumenical Patriarch Bartholomew on the celebration of the sixty years of the WCC in February 2008 at St. Peter's Cathedral in Geneva.[4] Besides the above mentioned Orthodox texts, all the texts that the Primates and delegates of Orthodox Churches have issued and continue to issue on the events of the many Conferences and issues dealt with by the WCC are of great importance for the contribution of the Orthodox Churches in the matter of the Churches Unification through the efforts of the WCC. I have included about one hundred of these works in a publication in German under the title "Orthodox Church and Ecumenical Movement. Documents and Declarations 1900-2006".[5] In this book are published in German with citations in Greek publications all of the above mentioned Orthodox texts regarding the WCC.

---

[2] Georgios Tsetsis, *Ecumenical Annals. A contribution to the history of WCC* (Katerini, 1987), 77 (in Greek).

[3] For the contribution of the Ecumenical Patriarchate and the Orthodox Church in the WCC and the Ecumenical Movement in general, three books of George Tsetsis are of great significance: a) *Ecumenical Annals. A contribution to the history of WCC* (Katerini 1987) (in Greek), b) *The contribution of Ecumenical Patriarchate to the foundation of WCC* (Katerini 1988) (in Greek), and c) *Ecumenical Throne and Oikoumene. Official Patriarchal Documents* (Katerini 1989). See also *Basdekis Athanasios,* Orthodoxe Kirche und Ökumenische Bewegung. Dokumente-Erklärungen-Berichte 1900-2006, (Frankfurt am Main 2006).

[4] *Episkepsis* 685 (2008): 22-29.

[5] Basdekis Athanasios, *Orthodoxe Kirche und Ökumenische Bewegung. Dokumente-Erklärungen-Berichte 1900-2006,* (Frankfurt am Main 2006), 896.

In the second text on the Third Pan-Orthodox Conference under the title "Orthodox Church and Ecumenical Movement" the Orthodox Churches express their unanimous and solid belief that "…the Orthodox Church constitutes an entity giving true witness of faith and tradition of the One, Holy, Catholic and Apostolic Church…it believes that it holds a central place in the matter of the promotion of Christian unity within the contemporary world" (§ IV. 1). In other words, according to the Orthodox Church the issue of Church unification is not just a simple matter but also a sacred duty, therefore it is impermissible for Orthodoxy not to get involved in the Ecumenical Movement and not to participate in the efforts for the unification of the Churches.

This realization along with the document-decision on the forthcoming Pan-Orthodox Conference constitutes a logical result of both the stance and the actions of the Orthodox Churches since the beginning of the 20th century. These actions were aiming at the Churches' collaboration and unity promotion, the way it is described and pursued through the WCC.

Within the frame of such an a priori positive stance towards the Ecumenical Movement and the World Council of Churches, the Orthodox Churches did not leave out any complaints or problems. These problems arose over time out of some of the programs as well as priorities the WCC had set, when i.e. it digressed from its original aim, the unification of the Churches. Let us not forget that one of the most important ecclesiological principles the WCC has set is that the World Council of Churches is not and must never become a super-church, as many people coming from the Protestant environment would wish, but instead a Council of Churches in the service and ministry of its member Churches.

Such "Orthodox protests" have been a frequent phenomenon during the course of the WCC. The most renowned as well as significant among them, according to my opinion are the following two: a) Sofia's Desiderata, which was a series of issues raised and clarified by the Orthodox delegates in an inter Orthodox Conference held in Sofia in 1981, and b) the findings of an Inter-Orthodox Conference in Thessaloniki in 1998. We could even consider the establishment of the Special Commission for the Collaboration of the Orthodox Churches in the WCC with its accompanying declaration document *(Special commission Final paper)* of 2002,[6] as a part of the general Orthodox protest stance within the WCC. I wish to conclude this chapter with an excerpt from the Ecumenical Patriarch Bartholomew on the event of the sixty year anniversary of the WCC at St. Peter's Cathedral in Geneva in 2008:

"We should recognize that during these sixty years, and especially during its last two decades the course of the World Council of Churches, has been quite turbulent. This is due to the fact that there have been many variations of theological, ecclesiological, cultural and ethical nature. These variations have been affecting the brotherly relations among the members and have gradually been leading to the crisis we had to face twenty years ago, on the eve of the fifty year anniversary of the WCC and just a few months prior to the 8th General Assembly in Harare, Zimbabwe. That crisis was instantly attributed to the differences between the Orthodox and the Protestant members of the Council. However, it constituted a crisis among people belonging to different theological and church traditions, among Churches applying a different reading on the text of the Holy Scriptures, even different perceptions of ethical and socio-political issues. Still, we can say that this specific crisis had a positive outcome, allowing in the end, under a spirit of sincerity, humility and without any feelings created by ulterior motives, the development of a dialogue which led to the overcoming of long standing difficulties that had been poisoning our brotherly relations. At the same time a new thrust was given to the continuance of our common course towards unity…I am deeply happy because the visions the member Churches have towards the fulfillment of unity under the same faith and around the same Eucharistic Meal, in God's grace, remains at the center of the Council's activities. Hence, the cardinal significance and the primary role of the WCC, especially of the Faith and Order Commission, in its involvement in the very essence of the Council regarding the ecclesiological issue along with the pursuit for the Christian Unity. We, yet, have before us a long standing and difficult mission, a common course in love, responsibility and mutual respect towards the Tradition and Teaching of our Savior Christ's Church"[7].

---

[6] All these documents have been published in my abovementioned work "*Orthodoxe Kirche und Ökumenische Bewegung*". See also Dagmar Heller/Barbara Rudolph, *Die Orthodoxen im Ökumenischen Rat der Kirche. Dokumente, Hintergründe, Kommentare und Visionen*, Beiheft zur Ökumenischen Rundschau 74, (Frankfurt am Main 2004).
[7] *Episkepsis* 685 (2008): 26.

Part I: Orthodox Churches in the Ecumenical Movement – an Introduction

b. Conference of European Churches (CEC)

The second important ecumenical organization after the WCC is the Conference of European Churches (CEC). In contrast to the World Council of Churches in which Churches from all over the world collaborate, the members of the CEC are churches from Europe.

The CEC was founded in Nyberg, Denmark in 1959, during the "Cold War Era" after World War II. Significant church personalities from various Churches of both the western and the eastern European territory decided to collaborate in order to assist their Churches, which existed back then under different political, financial and social competing systems, to overcome the traumas caused by the war, and also to contribute in mutual understanding, reconciliation of the peoples and the prevalence of peace.

The CEC has the same theological founding principle as the WCC: "The Conference of European Churches is an ecumenical fellowship of Churches in Europe which confess the Lord Jesus Christ as God and Savior according to the Scriptures and therefore seek to fulfill their common calling to the glory of the one God, Father, Son and Holy Spirit." (CEC Constitution).

After preliminary, exploratory discussions in 1953 and 1957, the first Assembly took place in Nyberg, Denmark in 1959. In this founding assembly delegates from 40 European countries took part, with many Orthodox Churches among them. Today 114 Churches collaborate in CEC (Orthodox, Lutheran-Protestant, Anglican, Old Catholic and Pentecostal Churches) from 37 countries. More than 40 other ecumenical organizations, National Councils of Churches and Organizations in partnership collaborate with CEC. The Roman Catholic Church is not a member of the CEC, as it is not a member of the WCC. However they have a close collaboration mainly through Concilium Conferendarium Episcopalium Europae (Council of European Roman Catholic Bishops' Conferences (CCEE) and the Commission of the Bishops' Conferences of the European Community (COMECE)).

The highest authority of CEC is the General Assembly, which is assisted by a twenty-member Governing Board. Today the President of the Conference is the former Anglican Bishop of Guildford, the Rt Rev. Christopher Hill.

Many significant Orthodox personalities have served as Presidents of the Conference, such as the Blessed Patriarch of Moscow, Alexios II, the Metropolitan of Switzerland Ieremias and up until recently the Metropolitan of France Emmanuel. Members of the former Presidium have also been the Archbishop of Tirana and all Albania, Anastasios and the Patriarch of Romania Daniel from Moldova, as well as the Metropolitan of Sasima Gennadios. Among the members of the general assembly we can also find names such as, Dr. Alexandros Papaderos, ex-director of the Orthodox Academy of Crete, the Great Archpriest Georges Tsetsis, Professor Grigorios Larentzakis as delegates of the Ecumenical Patriarchate, and Mrs. Katerina Karkala-Zorba (The Church of Greece). The most reverent professor Dr. Viorel Ionitsa of the Patriarchate of Romania has been working for many years as an Orthodox Theologian at the main offices of the Conference in Geneva in the function of director for the former Churches in Dialogue Commission and has been serving from 2010 till 2012 as its acting Secretary General.

The General Assembly is called every five years. Since the founding of the Conference in 1959 until today, fourteen General Assemblies of the CEC have taken place. The first one was called in Nyberg, Denmark in 1959, the eighth at the Orthodox Academy of Crete in 1979, and the last one in Budapest, Hungary in 2013. The Conference has offices and delegations in many international organizations in Geneva, Brussels and Strasbourg.

In 1999 the CEC merged with the European Ecumenical Commission for Church and Society (EECCS) working in the field of church and society in European matters.

The CEC today is active in different domains, i.e. European Affairs; Human rights; Migrants in Europe; Ecclesiology and theology; ecumenical and interreligious dialogue; *Unity and Mission; Human enhancement; Globalization; Sunday protection.*

The CEC issues an electronic news bulletin as well as the proceedings of the General Assemblies. At times it publishes issues on important matters such as globalization, poverty, human rights, etc.

Charta Oecumenica

The CEC has always worked with the WCC, and is in close collaboration with the Council of European Roman Catholic Bishops' Conferences. The most significant fruit of this collaboration is the publication of the Charta Oecumenica, signed in 2001.[8] The *Charta* was signed on behalf of the CEC by the Metropolitan of Switzerland Ieremias and includes many interesting fundamental principles and expressions, such as the One, Holy, Catholic and Apostolic Church. It is based on the Nicene Creed (381) and does not include the Filioque, it is also very specific about the importance of collaboration regarding the visible unity of the European Churches, the shared responsibility and co-operation for the unity of European countries, the reconciliation of European peoples, the protection of Creation and the dialogue with other religions, especially Judaism and Islam.

Charta Oecumenica constitutes the fruit of two very important European Ecumenical Assemblies of the CEC and the Council of European Roman Catholic Bishops' Conferences: the first one took place in Basel Switzerland in 1989 and the second in Graz, Austria in 1997. A third European Ecumenical Assembly took place in Sibiu, Romania in 2007.

The Ecumenical Patriarch Bartholomew, during his speech in the opening ceremony of the 13th European Ecumenical Assembly on 5 September 2007 in Sibiu, Romania, praised the importance of Charta Oecumenica and the significance of ecumenical dialogue in the following words:

> "Of course we are aware that *Charta Oecumenica* does not constitute a Charter of a super-Church, nor do we consider it to be an infallible document. However, besides the omissions that it may have, it still remains the result of an intensive as well as responsible inter-church collaboration as well as a really profound depiction of the powerful will the European Churches display towards the continuation and enrichment of their collaboration for the new European mutual understanding...
>
> We implicitly support and promote every ecumenical, equal theological dialogue, which we regard as absolutely necessary...for without any dialogue it is impossible to succeed what we pursue, which is the Christian reconciliation, communion and unity...we therefore, repeat and highlight that each and every Orthodox, and we personally, remain stable in our belief that we are obliged to do whatever it takes in order to promote the sacred pursuit of the restoration of complete church and sacramental communion among the Churches on the basis of mutual love and respect for the individual experience expressions of the Apostolic faith."[9]

In Germany, the Churches that collaborate within the Ecumenical Assembly of German Churches, among them some Orthodox too, co-signed in Berlin in 2003, within the procedures of Ökumenischer Kirchentag the aforementioned Charta Oecumenica, highlighting the importance of this Declaration for the German Churches in general.

Problems and Perspectives of the CEC

As it was made clear during the 13th General Assembly of the CEC in Lyon, France in 2009, the Conference faces today the need for a reconsideration of its programs, strategy and work mode. This need is clearly highlighted in the Message of the Assembly: "The Assembly, in looking at the future, has established a working group to carry out a revision of the CEC as a whole, including a common purpose, vision and a setting of strategic goals, and which structures serve this goal in an optimal way."[10]

---

[8] *Charta Oecumenica* has been published by the CEC in 2001 and has been translated in many languages, Greek being one of them.
[9] The speech oft he Ecumenical Patriarch Bartholomew, is available, among other documents on the website oft he Ecumenical Patriarchate (2011).
[10] The message of the 13th Assembly of the CEC (15-21.07.2009) is available on the website of the Ecumenical Patriarchate (2011).

Part I: Orthodox Churches in the Ecumenical Movement – an Introduction

Prior to this Assembly the members of the Inter-Orthodox Preliminary Commission during their meeting in Ierapetra, Crete in April 2009, called the Orthodox Churches of Bulgaria and Georgia to reconsider their participation as full members of the CEC and the WCC, which they had decided to terminate during the 90s. The delegates in this meeting also expressed their regret for the decision of the Russian Orthodox Church to suspend its participation in the CEC. Next, they highlighted the need for a revision of the goals and mode of work of the Conference and pointed out in the common announcement that:

"We are deeply worried for the present situation regarding the many ongoing, albeit not complete programs of the CEC, as well as for the degree of transparency and accounting obligation during each decision making process. This is why we suggest the radical revision of the standing criteria regarding the approval as well as the execution of any program or action… Being fully aware of our commitment, as Orthodox Churches, to promote the goals of the CEC, but taking into account at the same time the difficulty we are having into making our voices heard, we ask that the 13th General Assembly should adopt a more consensual method of decision making processes, following the positive experience of the WCC."[11]

The 14th General Assembly, when the revision of the Conference was fulfilled, took place in Budapest, Hungary in July 2013.

c. Middle East Council of Churches (MECC)[12]

The Middle East Council of Churches is a fellowship of churches relating itself to the main stream of the modern ecumenical movement, the same which gave birth to the World Council and other regional ecumenical councils throughout the world.

The first and most remarkable feature of the Middle East Council of Churches (MECC) is its setting. It was through the Middle East that Abraham, his children and grandchildren migrated. Here the ancient Hebrew tribes wandered; the judges, prophets, priests, kings, singers and sages who gave voice to scripture were nurtured here. And it was here that the Incarnation took place, and the redeeming ministry of Christ fulfilled. The Church was born in the Middle East, and here the early controversies played themselves out and the first divisions in the Church occurred. The people and churches which form the council are the direct heirs of all of that. And the vibrant ecumenical movement to which the council gives expression in this region is a profound healing process. A glimpse of the Tree of Life whose leaves are "for the healing of the nations" (Rev. 22:2) is somehow not so distant here.

The second feature is geo-political. Powerful forces swirl and eddy in this region. They break out from time to time in violence. Death, misery and exploitation are no strangers. Economic forces, ethnic movements, big power pressures, religious passions … they make for a heady mix of variables drawing in influences and interests from around the world, and predators abound. In the midst of this, for the past quarter century there has been the MECC, committed to witness and serve in Christ's name. The circumstances of human dysfunction place upon it an overwhelming burden. People in the Middle East have reason to be suspicious of those who say they want to do them good. Wolves in sheep's clothing have been plentiful. In a region overwhelmingly Muslim in complexion, it is remarkable that the council, an indigenous Christian agency, should retain the credibility rating it does. It has worked quietly and effectively as an agent of mercy and reconciliation in war-torn Lebanon; it has interceded in the delicate dialogue between the Palestinians and the world, preparing some of the more important pathways that led to the peace process; it was early on the

---

[11] *The Common Announcement of the Inter Orthodox Preliminary Meeting, among other documents is available on the Ecumenical Patriarchate website* (2011).

[12] This last section on MECC was complemented by the editor of this chapter, based on the official website of the Council: http://www.mec-churches.org/about_mecc.htm (last accessed, October 2013).

scene in post-war Iraq; it initiated discussions within Arab society to engage both Muslims and Christians in the examination of what should go into building a just and peaceful civil society; and it has participated in some momentous initiatives of Christian reconciliation. There is a pivotal quality to the MECC, and that pivot has integrity. Having a legacy directly tied into the early days of the ecumenical movement, the Council has served in another remarkable way. Because of its long-standing partnerships with churches and Christian agencies both in the West and in the East, it depicts as no other body in this region that the love of Christ transcends barriers and makes of humanity one people. By the sheer fact of its existence it is a testimony to the fact that healing can happen.

Finally, there is the intimacy of the Council. The twelve to fourteen million souls who claim Christ's name in the Middle East are few in number when compared to the constituents of similar ecumenical associations elsewhere. But being small means that people know each other, and there is a bond of kinship that is rather special. It is no accident, therefore, that the Council chose to organize itself as a family of families—the Eastern Orthodox, the Oriental Orthodox, the Catholic and Protestant families. Each makes its contribution to the witness of all. This, then, is the Middle East Council of Churches. We invite you to become better acquainted with it.

(translated by Paraskevi Arapoglou)

Part I: Orthodox Churches in the Ecumenical Movement – an Introduction

(8) TERMINOLOGICAL ORIENTATIONS
- A SHORT INTRODUCTION INTO AN ECUMENICAL GLOSSARY

Marian Gh. Simion/Fr. Daniel Buda

During the past century, the ecumenical discourse has been recognized both as a choice and as a necessity. As a choice, it was primarily spawned by an intellectual effort to eliminate theological disparity and confusion, to improve relationships, and maybe to comprehend and eventually reconcile cross-cultural differences. As a necessity, however, the ecumenical discourse was urged by the need to heal traumatic memories of unfortunate events that haunted churches at various points in history, as well as by the need of the Christian minorities to build coalitions with the wider Christian family, whenever these were subjects of discrimination, and human rights violations.

It is also a matter of reality that today, the Orthodox Christians use several languages in their daily life, in liturgical services, as well as in writing theology. While some of the Orthodox Churches still maintain their classical liturgical languages (i.e. Church Slavonic, Liturgical Greek, and Classical Georgian), Orthodox theology is written and expressed exclusively in vernacular languages (e.g. Albanian, Arabic, Bulgarian, Czech, Finish, Georgian, Greek, Polish, Romanian, Russian, Serbian, Slovakian, and so on), and one cannot speak of an Orthodox lingua franca. Just for the sake of illustration, an episode that took place at WCC Assembly in Nairobi, Kenya (1975) had made a clear display of the linguistic diversity of Orthodox Christianity. When the Orthodox participants in Nairobi were invited by the Assembly moderator to sing "Christ is Risen," each national group sang the Easter troparion in its own language.[1]

The ongoing process of globalization combined with a growing Orthodox Diaspora, beyond the geographic boundaries of historic Orthodox Christianity; seem to have triggered the production of a growing body of theological literature in languages such as English, German and French. Furthermore, with the growing Orthodox presence in Africa (as a result of various mission projects conducted by the Patriarchate of Alexandria and All Africa), a similar phenomenon seems to develop, with Orthodox theology being written in several African (especially Sub-Saharian) languages.

With this dynamic in mind, the future of the pan-Orthodox and ecumenical discourses can only be enhanced within the comfort of a reliable terminology; a terminology which has yet to be adopted by the lingua franca of our contemporary world. Not to be exclusively prescriptive, this requisite terminology ought to be imbued with cohesiveness and semantic elegance not only in the interest of linguistic parity, but also in the interest of building more reliable venues of communication. It will be on these shared venues that the new minds will be comforted by the resonance of a theological expression that would educe the underexplored mysteries of faith.

The engagement of the Orthodox Churches in the ecumenical movement triggered additional challenges to the Orthodox theology. First of all, it encouraged the use of English as a communication language among the Orthodox as well. For example, English was the language used in the Pre-Assembly meeting for the Orthodox delegates (which took place in the island of Kos, Greece, from 11-17 October 2012), even though from 35 delegates representing the Orthodox Churches, only one was a native English speaker. Within the ecumenical movement, in order to be understood by their ecumenical partners of dialogue, the Orthodox representatives are asked to articulate their theology in languages that are, in most cases, foreign to them. Conversely, in order to make the results of the ecumenical work available to their own Churches, the Orthodox representatives need to translate ecumenical documents in their national languages. This reality triggers serious challenges, with regard to specific terminology that becomes subject to dogmatic nuances and theological accuracy. It

---

[1] This episode is described by Thomas Hopko, "Constance Tarasar, Orthodox at Nairobi" in *St. Vladimir's Theological Quarterly* 20.1-2 (1976): 40.

often becomes a difficult dynamic to determine how various theological expressions are used, understood and translated in different confessional, cultural and linguistic contexts.

In general, terminological parity had often been the subject of various conversations and controversies. Controversies were usually in line with political attitudes that emerged between subcultures engaged in espousing the message of the Gospel in an ad locum fashion. Fortunately, the contemporary theological discourse has prevailed in making the question of terminology responsible (if not the scapegoat), for various unfortunate events, such as the Chalcedonian split, a case in which it was generally recognized that it was terminological disparity that generated the tragic partition between Eastern and Oriental churches. Therefore, given the contemporary political will to clarify old confusions, to correct mistakes of history and to make the language an improved venue for communication, the creation of a comprehensive glossary in the contemporary lingua franca, represents a real chance to recreate the oikoumene, at least in the way we communicate.

In a way, the authors of this paper have the audacity to launch a call for the creation of an English lexicon where key terminology would be specifically and comprehensively introduced and explained. This lexicon should serve as a heuristic device for the forthcoming generation of theologians; to enable them to communicate across the theological persuasions and cultural traditions. The goal of such work is to adopt a meaningful and focused terminology that each Orthodox language and subculture can fully subscribe to; as well as a terminology that would go beyond Orthodoxy and serve as a heuristic device in ecumenical and interfaith conversations. Yet, terminological parity represents a devious task faced by those theologians daring to bridge the historical gap of semantics. It is a devious task because it requires theological knowledge, spiritual depth, linguistic expertise and sensibility to historical events that influenced the development of the theological nuances of contemporary vocabulary.

Therefore, the aim of this paper is to serve as a call for the development of a future pan-Orthodox and ecumenical English glossary, and to begin by offering some prolegomena toward a future agenda and structure of such a reference work. Additional rationales that make such a project imperative are geopolitical and statistic in nature, so as to improve political, trans-cultural and interfaith communication. For instance, Orthodox Christianity is located at the cross-road of history and civilizations proving its vital importance in communication between cultures and civilizations. Furthermore, Orthodox Christianity represents a large segment of Christianity and of the religious world in general, as current data on global Christianity indicates that from the total of the global Christian population 50% are Catholic, 37% Protestant, and 12% Orthodox Christians.[2]

Just to generate some appetite for this theological undertaking, in this article the authors will tap into several cases of terms simply to exemplify how such terms, when translated into English, not only project conflicting hermeneutics, but also easily trigger miscommunications.

(1) Oikoumene/Ecumenical/Ecumenical Movement

"Oikoumene"[3] derives from "oikein", "to inhabit", and it is used in reference to the idea of "inhabited earth" or "the whole world." Since the Hellenistic period, "oikoumene" was primarily used in a geo-cultural sense and in reference to the Greco-Roman empire; to mark the distinction between the civilized world and the territories inhabited by the uncivilized barbarians. In the biblical writings, "oikoumene" is used as synonym for "earth" (Ps. 24:1), with political (Luke 4:5-7; 2:1; Acts 17:6; Revelation 16:14), and even eschatological (Hebrews 2:5) connotations, as "coming oikoumene."[4] In the 19th century, the term "ecumenical" was used in the context of Evangelical Alliance and YMCA as a notion expressing the overcoming of national, confessional and social

[2] Global Christianity: *A Report on the Size and Distribution of the World's Christian Population* (Washington, D.C.: Pew Research Center's Forum on Religion & Public Life, 2011), 21.

[3] Konrad Raiser, art. *Oikoumene in Dictionary of the Ecumenical Movement*, 2nd Edition, Nicholas Lossky etc. (eds.), (Geneva: WCC Publications, 2002), 840-841 with indicated bibliography.

[4] George Johnston, "Oikoumenē and Kosmos in the New Testament" in *New Testament Studies* 10.3 (1964): 352-360.

Part I: Orthodox Churches in the Ecumenical Movement – an Introduction

---

borders. At the beginning of 20th Century, due to impulses given by Nathan Söderblom, the expression "ecumenical" as a movement (a.k.a. "ecumenical movement") became a classical definition incorporating various efforts for Christian unity.[5] The term "ecumenism" was used for the first time by Yves Congar in 1937 in his book *Chrétiens Désunis. Principes d'un oecuménisme catolique.*

At the end of 1990s, a report of WCC Orthodox Task Force stated that the word "ecumenical" and the expression "ecumenical movement" have different understandings in different Christian traditions. For the Orthodox "'ecumenical movement' refers specifically to the quest for Christian reconciliation and unity." In the Protestant context sometimes "ecumenical movement" is used to describe "inter-Protestant activities" or "to refer to a wide range of associations devoted to particular causes and often involving non-Christians. It can also be taken to refer to a vague post-denominational reality."[6]

The Common Understanding and Vision (CUV)[7] document attempted to bring some clarification regarding the understanding of the word "ecumenical." In chapter 2, there are six paragraphs on "The meaning of 'ecumenical': There is agreement that the term 'ecumenical' embraces the quest for Christian unity, common witness in the worldwide task of mission and evangelism, and commitment to diakonia and to the promotion of justice and peace. But there is no authoritative definition of the term, and it is in fact used to characterize a wide range of activities, ideas and organizational arrangements."[8] It is strongly recommended to use the expression "ecumenical movement" only in singular, expressing in this way "the vitality and coherence of the one ecumenical movement."[9]

(2) Liturgy/worship/prayer/devotion

Another expression that not only goes beyond the linguistic confines, but can also create an organic tension in ecumenical conversations is the use of the word "liturgy". In a Protestant setting "liturgy" represents both a standardized form of worship (e.g., Lutheran, Reformed, Anglican, Methodist, Pentecostal, Free Church, etc.,),[10] as well as a general and occasional act of worship open to spontaneous spiritual creativity, artistic expressions, and poetry.[11] In the Orthodox setting however, "liturgy" is exclusively linked to the Eucharistic experience, and, as such, it is regarded as "the Locus of Truth," and the privilege of the Orthodox only, through apostolic succession.[12] Considering that worship is one of the most intimate components of religion in general, an "inappropriate" use of a "commonly" shared terminology can often be perceived as an intrusion into one's religious intimacy. Consequently, an expression such as "ecumenical liturgy" can easily be perceived as a deliberate attempt to trivialize the central and most intimate component of the Orthodox worship.

[5] Reinhard Frieling, *Der Weg des ökumenischen Gedankes. Eine Ökumenekunde*, (Göttingen, 1912), 5-6.
[6] Orthodox-WCC Relations. A Contribution from the Orthodox Task force 28 January 1998, chapter 3 Fundamental Orthodox questions – ambiguity of terminology, in Thomas FitzGerald and Peter Bouteneff (eds.), *Turn to god Rejoice in Peace. Orthodox Reflections on the Way to Harare*, (Geneva: WCC Publications, 1998), 175.
[7] "The Common Understanding and Vision Document" in *Ecumenical Review* 51.1 (1999): 96-113.
[8] CUV, 101-102.
[9] CUV, 97.
[10] J.F. White "Liturgies in America" in Daniel G. Reid (Coordinating Editor). *Dictionary of Christianity in America*, (Downers Grove, IL: Intervarsity Press, 1990), 662-664.
[11] In 2010 the schools of the Boston Theological Institute served as the fourth and final of the major conferences commemorating the 1910 World Missionary Conference in Edinburgh. As described by the main organizers of this conference, Todd M. Johnson & Rodney L. Petersen "[a] special conference program of worship songs and prayers was compiled and led by Harvard Divinity School Student Tracey Wispelwey of the Restoration Project. [...] Wispelwey, being attentive to the global nature of the conference purview and constituency, employed variosu musical styles and liturgies [emphasis added] focused on mission and world Christianity." Todd M. Johnson & Rodney L. Petersen. 2012 Boston: *The Changing Contours of World Mission and Christianity*. (Eugene OR: Pickwick Publications, 2012), xxii.
[12] John D. Zizioulas *Being as Communion*, (Crestwood, NY: SVS Press, 1993), 114-122.

(3) Catholicity/Sobornicity/universality

Another case of linguistic disparity and confusion is the way in which the Creed–and liturgical texts in general–have been translated into English. Members of the Orthodox Diaspora who settled into the English-speaking world have usually translated their own liturgical texts from the languages they inherited as an immigrant community (e.g. Slavonic, Greek, Romanian, etc.), thus giving birth to English versions that are often theologically inaccurate, and structurally defective and confusing to the Orthodox congregation. Over a decade ago, the Greek Orthodox Metropolitan Isaiah of Denver, while President of Holy Cross Greek Orthodox School of Theology, was decrying the widespread use of the mistranslations of liturgical literature. As he put it, "[t]he more one compares the English translations with the original Greek regarding the Divine Liturgy, as well as the other services and prayers of the Church, the more frightened one becomes with the gross errors, some of which render heretical meanings to particular words and phrases."[13] One obvious case is the English version of the Creed, particularly the semantics used in defining the Church. It is well known that while the original Greek defines the Church as one universal phenomenon of faith in Christ, rooted into the faith of the apostles,[14] the Russian[15] and the Romanian[16] translations have adopted the Slavonic term "sobornaya", perhaps as to redefine the Orthodox Church more in a structural-administrative fashion, and emphasize its synodal configuration.[17] Considering the choices faced by Prince Vladimir, when picking out Orthodoxy over Roman-Catholicism as the official faith of the Russians–as detailed by the Russian Chronicle–it is to be presumed that the word katholikin was to be avoided, and replaced by a term situated at a safe distance from inferring any affiliation with the Catholic Church. This linguistic twist is also present in contemporary reference works, such as the official Catechism of the Romanian Orthodox Church which insists to define the term "sobornicească" exclusively as an universal phenomenon of faith, that is "the union of everyone with everything,"[18] in a decentralized fashion,[19] and less around the idea of a centralized structure of power. Nevertheless, the English translations of the Creed have generally insisted in maintaining the original Greek term of "katholikin," translated as "Catholic". Needless to say, for an Orthodox Diaspora that settled in a religious culture that is predominantly Protestant (with a strong Roman Catholic presence), this situation often triggered confusion of identity, when questions such as "are we Catholic?," were being asked.

***

In light of the three examples given above, it is clear that the ecumenical conversation has reached a point in which English language needs to be more specific, while the meaning of Orthodox terminology be properly

---

[13] Bishop Isaiah of Denver, *Liturgical Mistranslations*, (Denver: Greek Orthodox Diocese of Denver, 1997), 1.

[14] The original Greek version reads as: Εἰς μίαν, ἁγίαν, <u>καθολικὴν</u> καὶ ἀποστολικὴν ἐκκλησίαν.

[15] The Original Russian version reads as: Единой Святой <u>Соборной</u> и Апостольской Церкви.

[16] The Romanian version reads as: Una Sfântă <u>Soborniceasc</u>ă şi Apostolească Biserică.

[17] Lucian Turcescu "Stăniloae's Sacramental Theology in Dialogue with Afanasiev's Eucharistic Ecclesiology" (Presentation at the 4th Symposium of Romanian Spirituality, St. Paul University, Ottawa, March 5, 2011) http://www.romarch.org/ro/pags.php?id=3262 (Last accessed: September 27, 2013)

[18] Învăţătura de credinţă creştină ortodoxă: tipărită cu aprobarea Sfântului Sinod al Bisericii Ortodoxe Române şi cu binecuvântarea şi purtarea de grijă a Preafericitului Părinte Teoctis, Patriarhul Bisericii Ortodoxe Române. Editura Institutului Biblic şi de Misiune al Bisericii Ortodoxe Române: Bucureşti, 2000, p.139

[19] Petru Movilă's Confession of Orthodox Faith, which was adopted by all Eastern Orthodox Patriarchates following the Synod of Iaşi of 1640, states about this article from the creed that "the Universal Church did not receive its name and title from a special place because these are local churches, such as the one from Ephesus, Philadelphia, Laudicea, Antioch, Jerusalem, Rome, Alexandria, etc." (Ecclesiam Catholicam a nullo loco etiam principaliori nomen et titulum accipere, quandoquidem hae Ecclesiae sunt particulares, nempe Ephesiensis, Philadelphiensis, Laodicensis, Antiochena, Hierosolymitana, Romana Alexandrina etc.,) cf. Petru Movilă Mărturisirea Ortodoxă a credinţei universale şi apostolice a Bisericii Orientale, trans. Traian Diaconescu (Iaşi: Institutul European, 2001), 101.

explained; thus calling for the creation of an ecumenical glossary. Yet, in accomplishing such a task, one must be aware of several aspects that need to be taken into consideration. In general, the structure of such a project needs to be built around the idea of creating a comprehensive glossary which will also include general terms that would reflect the conceptual parity between Orthodox and Catholic and Protestant theological traditions. In order to be created and then adopted as such, this project should be perceived as a neutral reference work that would enable each Orthodox Christian to feel ownership into it. Therefore it is mandatory to be inclusive of each tradition, ethnicity and subculture in the selection process, while maintaining high standards of academic and ecclesiastic integrity.

Here are a few principles that shall stay at the basis of such a glossary:

a. One must start from the presumption that each religious tradition is representative of dominant cultural orientations that alter (if not redefine) the presumably shared terminology.

b. Some religious traditions view themselves strictly in a structural sense, while others tend to gravitate toward a religious consciousness, where institutional bureaucracy is highly volatile. For example, in numerous instances local spirituality can often be regarded as a system of meaning and as a basis for religious identity, thus lacking a contractual status of institutional affiliation and membership.

c. By associating ecumenical experience exclusively with elite communication, ecumenical leaders lack the necessary tools in identifying the strengths and weaknesses of a desired reconciliation.

d. An editorial team of linguists and theologians with strong philological and cultural expertise shall be formed in order to identify a list of terms and expressions that should be included in the glossary;

e. The editorial team shall identify potential authors who are able to write comprehensive articles on the identified terms and expressions. Preferably two or more authors shall be invited to jointly define a term/expression;

f. Each article shall focus on the etymology; contextual understandings in major Christian confessions (and in key ecumenical documents), as well as by prominent theologians. Some proposals of how the respective term/expression shall or shall not be translated into major languages used by the Orthodox, ought to be given;

g. In case a term expression is biblical or patristic, or it appears in liturgical texts, special emphasis shall be given to the respective meaning;

h. Authors could propose a clear definition of a meaning of a term/expression, especially to those that create serious misunderstanding;

i. The editorial team who oversees of the project shall ensure the coherence of the glossary by suggesting which terms/expressions are in immediate connection.

j. Last but not least, the proposed epigrammatic lexicon should also include key terms and expressions that separate the Christian family from the perspective of each branch, which will be correlated based on conceptual parity. The concepts will be correlated based on situations involving the individual (e.g., leadership, spiritual authority, gender, etc); the institution (e.g., administrative structure, protocol, titles, canonical authority, etc.), and spiritualities (e.g., cultural expressions that have meaning and offer parity with theological concepts.)

***

It is our hope that, in light of the above examples, one can recognize the need for an English ecumenical glossary, aimed to explain the fundamental terminology used in ecumenical texts. Undoubtedly, the adoption of a new terminology into the English vocabulary ought to express the nuances of the Orthodox faith as expressed by every culture and subculture touched or encountered by the Orthodox faith.

Bibliography

"The Common Understanding and Vision Document" in *Ecumenical Review* 51.1 (1999), 96-113.

"Orthodox-WCC Relations. A Contribution from the Orthodox Task force 28 January 1998", chapter 3 Fundamental Orthodox questions – ambiguity of terminology, in Thomas FitzGerald and Peter Bouteneff (eds.), *Turn to god Rejoice in Peace. Orthodox Reflections on the Way to Harare*, (Geneva: WCC Publications, 1998), 171-178.

Reinhard Frieling, *Der Weg des ökumenischen Gedankes. Eine Ökumenekunde*, (Göttingen, 1912).

Bishop Isaiah of Denver, *Liturgical Mistranslations*, (Denver: Greek Orthodox Diocese of Denver, 1997).

George Johnston, "Oikoumenē and Kosmos in the New Testament" in *New Testament Studies* 10.3 (1964): 352-360.

Gennadios Limouris, *Orthodox Visions of Ecumenism. Statements, Messages and Reposts on the Ecumenical Movement 1902-1992*, (Geneva: WCC Publications, 1994).

Konrad Raiser, art. *Oikoumene in Dictionary of the Ecumenical Movement*, 2nd Edition, Nicholas Lossky etc. (eds.), (Geneva: WCC Publications, 2002), 840-84.

Lucian Turcescu, "Stăniloae's Sacramental Theology in Dialogue with Afanasiev's Eucharistic Ecclesiology" (Presentation at the 4th Symposium of Romanian Spirituality, St. Paul University, Ottawa, March 5, 2011) http://www.romarch.org/pags.php?id=3262 (Last accessed: September 27, 2013).

J.F. White "Liturgies in America" in Daniel G. Reid (Coordinating Editor), *Dictionary of Christianity in America*, (Downers Grove, IL: Intervarsity Press, 1990), 662-664.

John D. Zizioulas, *Being as Communion*, (Crestwood, NY: SVS Press, 1993).

http://ecumenism.net/glossary

Ecumenical glossary: Glossaire oecumenique. Ökumenische Terminologie. Terms in current use. (World Council of Churches, 1967) (in English, German, French)

Part II

Orthodoxy and Ecumenism - Foundations

Ivan Dimitrov

The Orthodox Churches were involved in the ecumenical movement from its very beginnings. Two important documents of the Patriarchate of Constantinople, the circular Synodical and Patriarchal letters of 1902 and 1920, essentially marked the beginning of the Orthodox involvement in this modern initiative of world Christianity, which later resulted in the participation of the Orthodox Church in WCC. The involvement of the Orthodox Church as a family of local Orthodox autocephalous Churches in the Ecumenical movement enjoys the agreement and support of all Orthodox Patriarchates and Autocephalous Churches.[1] Nevertheless, for some Orthodox Christians, especially the traditionalist, it remains a challenge. Particularly in the Internet age, where news, documents and images are transferred swiftly from one end of the earth to the other, ecumenical activities create challenges for people who live in a spiritual environment, which makes it difficult for them to understand the actions of their brothers living in a completely different environment, in another country, in another society.

There is also another point of view which needs to be underlined. If ecumenical relations are a challenge for some or many Christians, we cannot ignore the simple fact that this challenge does not come from men and women or from human institutions, but from the Lord Himself. He is always present in the history of humanity and directs his people, the new Israel, on roads which are sometimes new and unexpected. More specifically, it is my conviction that the very development of history encouraged the Orthodox Churches to enter the ecumenical movement. And because every major development in history cannot be seen except as an opportunity for new ways to testify to and witness to, the Gospel, i.e. the divine truth in it, we should interpret positively the challenges that arose as a result of migration and mixture of peoples and beliefs, which gradually became more and more widespread during the 20th century.[2]

The last century was really the epoch of conscious and sincere concern about the unity of the Church of Jesus Christ. Church leaders and theologians from different denominations were discussing the lack of Christian unity, as well as possible ways to recover it. The most secure way of approaching the issue of Christian unity, i.e. Church unity, was to re-read the Bible, the only indisputable authority among Christians, without of course neglecting the Apostolic Tradition.

For all those who believe in Jesus Christ as their Lord and Savior, unity is a clear command given by Jesus Christ to his followers. This will of Jesus is clearly attested in the Gospels and highlighted in the apostolic writings. Therefore, Orthodox Christians (and not only Orthodox) are motivated by the Bible itself to participate in efforts for the unity of the Church. This conscious and active participation of the Orthodox Church in the ecumenical movement is not based on situational considerations or any other interest, but is in line with Christ's prayer to God the Father for his followers: "that they may all be one" (John 17:21).

Jesus prayed to his Father for his disciples to preserve the unity of faith in him, and on the basis of the unity of the faith to be a community in him, to be a Church "in Christ". But he did not speak specifically to his disciples, that they should be united, to be one, because their unity was self-evident as a result of their loyalty to the words and deeds of their divine teacher. At the same time, Jesus clearly showed them the danger of divisions when instructing them to have love for one another (John 13:34-35), to love to the point of sacrificing

---

[1] Especially after a decision of the 3rd Pan-Orthodox Preconciliar Conference (Chambésy, 1986). As a part of the process of preparation for a Pan-Orthodox council, delegates from the Eastern Orthodox churches met in Chambésy in 1986 to discuss, among other issues, ecumenism and participation in WCC and CEC.

[2] Rev. Georgios Basioudis, "Biblical Challenges and Ecumenical Movement," in I. Petrou-St. Tsompanidis-M. Goutzioudis (eds.), *The Ecumenical Dialogue in the 21st Century: Realities-Problems-Prospects*, (Thessaloniki, 2013) (in Greek).

for one another (John 15:13), to be humble, avoiding even the thought of superiority over one another (Matt. 20:26-28). The danger of division and domination has always existed, so the apostles in their speeches and letters pay close attention to this issue. St. Paul the Apostle wrote to the Corinthian Christians: "Now I exhort you, brethren, by the name of our Lord Jesus Christ, that you all agree and that there be no divisions among you, but that you be made complete in the same mind and in the same judgment" (1 Cor. 1:10 ff.).

Considering the issue of unity theologically, we can say that, inspired and repulsed by their faith, led by the Spirit of God (Rom. 8:14), and in every way encouraged and supported by the grace of God, Christians are entirely dedicated to serve the good of human society, creatively defining and implementing the concrete forms and specific manifestations of this service with their "renewed mind" by which they know "from experience what is good and acceptable and perfect will of God" (Rom. 12:2). They form the behavior and activities in the service of human society as found in the Gospel's life-giving values and guiding principles, without being to formal and schematic, but always with the understanding of their God-given talent and commissioned ministry (1 Cor. 12:4-5), while also recognizing the signs of the times (Mat. 16:3, Luke 12:56) and testing the spirits (1 John 4:1).

Here I want to draw our attention to the following. It is important not to consider one of the most powerful words of the Lord to the Church as an appeal to the masses in general: "May they all be one: as thou, Father, art in me, and I in thee, that they also may be in Us one, that the world may believe that thou hast sent me" (John 17:21). For in these divine words, we see that Christ differentiates between these "all" to be one, and the "world" that should "believe." Christ is not saying: "May they all be one with the world," because then neither will "they" be one, nor will the world believe. "They" are the disciples of the Lord, completely faithful to the truth of Christ. This faithfulness namely makes them one in the unity of the Holy Trinity. Everyone who fell from this divine truth, also fell from the Church and spiritually switches to the "world," which still needs to believe. The overwhelming majority of humanity from the Fall until the time of Christ was in sin and separated from God, and any apparent unity they achieve is not accepted by God. We can see clearly how some disciples of Christ have become part of this unbelieving world. The Church has always offered its assistance to them as neighbors, but the prayer "to be one" can no longer refer to them as the truth of God cannot comply with human variability, the fruit of sin. We must earnestly pray for them: "To return to the unity which they alone have left."

Christ's plea "that they may all be one" (John 17:21) does not concern human organizational or institutional unity; it is something beyond that! Critical voices say, "Ecumenism is the desire of some within a number of Christian denominations to achieve a sort of institutional 'oneness'." A few see an ideal of just one Christian organization wholly united in purpose and doctrine. But in John 17, Jesus did not pray for something like that. His words in verse 21 clearly show that Jesus wanted the Church to be one in the very sense that there is oneness between Jesus and the Father, and that, through this very "oneness", the world may believe that God had sent Jesus. Quite obviously the oneness between Jesus and the Father is a oneness of complete unity of purpose and love. Through this unity of purpose, the world was to recognize who Jesus Christ was. And one more point: this "oneness" or unity of Jesus' disciples was already accomplished when he uttered his prayer. Because Jesus had revealed himself to his own and his own had accepted him! Therefore Jesus prayed that the Church should be "perfect in one" (John 17:23).

Christ prayed for a certain category of people — those whom God the Father had given to Him. There is no trace of universalism. Moreover, Jesus did not ask His Father to unite them, but to keep them in a unity that already exists, already functions, as evidenced by the verb forms in use. This is not an external unity inherent in normal human association; it is neither a unity of belief, not one of love and peace in God. According to the context it is a unity of life, granted by the common coexistence in the name of God (better: granted by the unity that exists among the persons of the Holy Trinity).

Of course, this does not mean that disciples must remain a small closed community or that unity is a static value. On the contrary, as the Savior said, "the kingdom of heaven is like leaven" (Mat. 13:33). Therefore, unity is perceived as a dynamic value. Believers constantly joined the Apostles "through their word" (John 17:20), but it will still be the same unity, building on the unity of the Holy Trinity.[3]

Researching different theological writings on the subject of ecumenism and unity of the Church one can easily see that the main problem around whith disunity is not in a diverse understanding of the commandments of Christ about the unity of his disciples and followers, but rather the different understanding of what the Church is.[4]

In the New Testament, there are only few passages speaking about unity of the followers of Christ or refer to problems of divisions and how to avoid them.

In this regard, one Orthodox theologian has stated, "The ecumenical attitude of Orthodoxy does not derive only from the firm and inviolable will of the Lord 'May they all be one' (John 17:21), but also from the firm belief that the goal of God's providence is the unity of all things (see 'that God may be all in all,' 1 Cor. 15:28) and 'the summing up in Christ' of all things, of the whole creation (Eph. 1:10, cf. Col. 3:11 etc.)."[5]

The problem of strife in the church at Corinth, which caused certain divisions in the middle of the first century, was not caused by different opinions with regard to doctrinal views. Rather it was caused by conflicts about personalities. St. Paul the Apostle is critical of all parties, which were formed by the followers of Paul, Apollos, Peter and even Christ. Everyone could explain the cause (or the causes) of the different parties, but nobody can excuse their existence, especially in the Church of Christ. There are also certain indications as to the cause of divisions in Corinth. E.g., the "Christ party" may have consisted of those commending themselves (2 Cor. 10:12), called "super-apostles" by Paul (*2 Cor.* 11:5). The whole idea of a disunited assembly is unthinkable. Therefore we always should remember Paul's rhetorical question: "Is Christ divided? Was Paul (or someone else) crucified for you, other than Christ himself?" (1 Cor. 1:13)[6]

If we study the question of Christian unity using the Bible, we should basically research the texts of the New Testament, although a theological study might profitably begin with the Old Testament, which presents such a wide variety of literary forms and thereby prepares a more sophisticated approach to the word of God.

The epistle to the Ephesians offers very interesting and important thoughts on the unity of Christ's Church: "There is one body and one Spirit, just as also you were called in one hope of your calling; one Lord, one faith, one baptism, one God and Father of all who is over all and through all and in all" (Eph. 4:4-6). With this imposing summation, Ephesians sets forth the unity of Christian faith and community, grounding it ultimately in the one

---

[3] Dimitrov, Ivan, *High-priestly prayer of our Lord Jesus Christ (Exegetical analyse of John 17)*, (Sofia, 1995) [in Bulgarian].

[4] Nevertheless the famous Sweden theologian David Hedegard wrote in this regard: "In spite of different interpretations the New Testament church was not split into different church groups, so as to experience one leadership taking charge and, at times, condemning another. A controlling denominational leadership is not the solution to keep the assembly from threats to the unity, whether they would come from the outside or the inside. The key is the individual's commitment to the Christ of the Bible and a life which would bear testimony to such a confession." (Frandell, Bruno W, *Contending for the Faith – The Apologetic Theology of David Hedegard*, (Newburgh, Indiana, 2011), 363. Cf. Hedegård, David, *Församling, Dop, Samfund*, (Stockholm, 1932), 56. Idem, *Ecumenism and the Bible*, (Amsterdam: International Council of Christian Churches, 1954.)

[5] P. Vassiliadis, "The Orthodox Church and the Quest for the Visible Unity," in: *Orthodoxy and the Unity of All*, edited by the Holy Monastery of Koutloumousion, (Mt. Athos 1996), 140 [in Greek].

[6] There is a certain opposition to the ecumenical movement from the side of so called charismatic evangelical groups, who accuse the churches participating in the WCC, saying that the "ecumenical types mostly just represent the two or three largest denominations and seek greater influence, power and control for their own group by negotiation"; according to them the ecumenical movement seeks "to achieve a 'oneness' which would be purely cosmetic, that is, a oneness which would be 'for appearances only'." Contrary to this opinion the Orthodox churches, members of Conference of European Churches, stated: "We, Orthodox, treat our non-Orthodox brothers with love, 'for by one Spirit we were all baptized… and all were made to drink of one Spirit' (1 Cor. 12:12). 'There are varieties of gifts, but the same Spirit; and there are varieties of service, but the same Lord' (1 Cor. 12:4-5). Our common service to Christian unity in the world, in the power of the Holy Spirit, secures our ecumenical fellowship even more firmly within the framework of the Conference of European Churches" ("Unity in the Spirit – Diversity in the Churches", 205).

Part II: Orthodoxy and Ecumenism - Foundations

God. The logic is entirely straightforward: the oneness of God, Jesus Christ, Christian confession, liturgy, and eschatology plainly imply the oneness of the body, the Church. In an apparent allusion to 1 Cor. 12, Ephesians refers to the Church as one body (see also Eph. 1:22-23, where body and Church are explicitly equated).

"Church" (or 'ecclesia' from ἐκκλησία = gathering, assembly) quickly became the generic term for the individual Christian congregations, as well as for the congregation as a whole, and so it has remained. Nevertheless, the New Testament has different ways of referring to the Christian community. It is not only the Body of Christ but the people of God (1 Petr. 2:9-10), God's building (1 Cor. 3:9), the family of faith (Gal. 6:10; cf. Eph. 2:19), God's temple (1 Cor. 3:16-17), the elect lady (2 John 1), etc., so that some theologians may legitimately speak of images of the Church in the New Testament. Although these images reflect a healthy variety in the ways the Church is conceived in the New Testament, most of them also convey a sense of its unity. The emphasis of Ephesians on Church unity accurately represents the bearing of the New Testament as a whole, even if comparable statements are seldom found elsewhere. This emphasis on unity did not, however, exclude diversity, as the wealth of images already suggests. In fact St. Paul defends the legitimacy of diverse gifts and functions within the Church as the work of the one Spirit (1 Cor. 12); they are necessary, moreover, for the Church's well-being.

The apostle regards his own ministry as being "in the priestly service of the gospel of God" (Rom. 15:16), which he relates on the one hand to his collection among the gentile churches of an offering for the Jerusalem church (vv. 22-29) and on the other to the praise of God by both Jews and gentiles (vv. 9-13). In either case, St. Paul has in view the unity of the Church as God's people; in both doxology and in a quite concrete act of generosity and helpfulness which had engaged him for some time (see Gal. 2:10; 1 Cor. 16:1-3; 2 Cor. 8:9). In its own way, Ephesians reflects the successful culmination of St. Paul's ministry in its emphasis upon the accomplishment of union between Jews and gentiles as the very essence of the work of Christ and consequently of the gospel St. Paul preached (Eph. 2:11-3:6).

The Apostle Paul's earlier controversy with the so-called Judaizers was a concrete expression of his own sense that the unity of the Church is essential to the appropriation of the gospel. Thus the approval of the pillar apostles was of crucial importance to him (Gal. 2:6-10). Paul found the behavior of the apostle Peter at Antioch (Gal 2:11,16) to be intolerable not only because it implied a defective soteriology (vv. 17-21), but because it involved a concession to the circumcision party (v. 12) that threatened the unity of the Church and therefore the gospel. While St. Paul did not in principle object to circumcision and observance of food laws among Jewish believers, he insisted upon the unity of the Church in its table fellowship and Eucharist, and thus he ran afoul of those who gave such practices priority. The apostolic decree of Acts (15:19-21, 23-29) looks like an effort to resolve such problems by laying down minimal food restrictions which all Christians should observe in order to keep the unity also in this regard. In any case both the controversy of St. Paul and the apostolic decree were efforts to protect the unity of Christians, not only in theory but in practice and particularly in worship.

It is necessary to indicate also the view expressed by some Orthodox Christians that the institutionalization of the ecumenical movement brings negativity to it: "If ecumenism was not organized in the way it is, if it was not one of the world's phenomena ending in -ism, but simply the embodiment of pure human desire to communicate with the neighbor (in the Christian sense), it would be much more acceptable to all, because it would really be cultivated by the quiet everyday acts of Christian love and stay consistent with it and only with it. Because in its natural form it is nothing else but Christ's answer to the question 'Who is my neighbor' (Luke 10:29)."

The simple answer to this opinion could be that the ecumenical movement was organized not in order to be a mere organization, closed and tending to exclusivity, but rather because of the need of more easy and regular contacts among the Christians from different churches in the struggle for the quest for unity in front of the unbelieving world. It does mean therefore that every organization, ecclesial character and orientation like WCC, instead of aiming at a kind of successful debate, should seek through mutual recommendations to investigate and "understand what the will of the Lord is" (Eph. 5:17).

From the Christian point of view, our neighbor is every human being and for that reason we are forbidden to condemn, to counsel proudly on the differences with him. The neighbor, the human being next to us, for us is not good or bad, orthodox or heretic, but a human being like us, fellow in the flesh, God's creation, the image of God. If Jesus Christ Himself was "eating and drinking" with the sinners, how can we also being sinners abhor our neighbor?[7]

In our times, we live next door, sometimes are part of the same family, or work in the same place with Catholics, Protestants, with people from other religions and with atheists, of course. We do not repel them for religious reasons, but we accept them as our equals. Many everyday examples are in support of this quiet, natural and constructive "practical ecumenism" which is based on Christ's answer to the big question: "Who is my neighbor?" And every Christian owes a sincere answer to this question.

Bibliography

1. Basioudis, Rev. Georgios, "Biblical Challenges and Ecumenical Movement," in I. Petrou-St. Tsompan-idis-M. Goutzioudis (eds.), *The Ecumenical Dialogue in the 21st Century: Realities-Problems-Prospects*, (Thessaloniki, 2013).
2. Clapsis, Emmanuel, *Orthodoxy in Conversation. Orthodox Ecumenical Engagements*, (Geneva and Brookline, MA 2000).
3. Dimitrov, Ivan, *High-priestly prayer of our Lord Jesus Christ (Exegetical analysis of John 17)*, (Sofia, 1995) [in Bulgarian].
4. FitzGerald T. - P. Bouteneff (eds.), *Turn to God – Rejoice in Hope: Orthodox Reflections on the Way to Harare*, (Geneva, 1998).
5. Hedegård, David, *Ecumenism and the Bible*, (Amsterdam, 1954).
6. Smith, D. Moody, "New Testament and Christian Unity," *Dictionary of the Ecumenical Movement*, (Geneva, 2002), 819-821.
7. Sabev, Todor, *The Orthodox Churches in the World Council of Churches: Towards the Future*, (WCC Publications, Geneva/Bialystok, 1996).
8. Vassiliadis, Petros, "The Orthodox Church and the Quest for Visible Unity," in: *Orthodoxy and the Union of All*, edited by the Holy Monastery of Koutloumousion, (Mt. Athos, 1996), 139-151 [in Greek].
9. Vassiliadou, Anastasia, *The Orthodox Participation in the WCC in the Light of the Decisions of the Special Committee* (a Master's degree dissertation), Aristotle University of Thessaloniki 2005 [in Greek]: http://www.academia.edu/1913273/H (last accessed, September 2013).
10. Weber, Hans-Ruedi, "The Bible in Today's Ecumenical Movement," *The Ecumenical Review*, 23.4, (1971), 335-346.
11. "Unity in the Spirit – Diversity in the Churches," Report of the Conference of European Churches' Assembly VIII, Crete, 18-25 October 1979.

---

[7] This exact Gospel rule was always the inspiration for the Bulgarian society and the Bulgarian Orthodox Church in the rescue of Bulgarian Jews. And this act always remained in the memory of our generations so pure and natural that nobody has described this as a reprehensible "attempt at rapprochement between religions."

(10) THE ECUMENICAL CHARACTER OF THE BIBLE AS A CHALLENGE FOR THE BIBLICAL STUDIES IN ORTHODOX TEACHING TODAY[1]

Miltiadis Konstantinou

A few decades ago it was widely recognized that the European civilization was mainly based on, and inspired by, the Bible; today it seems that the Bible no longer has this indisputable force, at least in terms of the civilization of contemporary Europe. Europe can no longer be characterized as a Christian continent, since the Christians constitute a minority of its population and the term "post-Christian era" is almost established as a new field of the human sciences.

When we turn to biblical studies, it is widely accepted that the 20th century was the century of triumph of the critical method. The famous historical-critical method, the foundations of which were traced back in the 19th century, was fully predominant in the academic interpretation of the Bible, at least until the mid-1970s.

However, before the end of that century, the historical-critical method of interpretation did not seem to be capable of preserving its sovereignty. It appeared to be on the verge of collapsing under "attacks" by a whole series of new interpretative methods that developed over the past years and claimed to replace it. For example, if von Rad and Noth could discuss a few decades ago about whether a text belongs to the period of Israel before or after the amphictyony period, today the theory of amphictyony is not only out of discussion, but even the question is unthinkable, since the largest part of the Old Testament texts dates back in the Postexilic Period. There is also the well known dispute in the 50s between the W.F. Albright and A. Alt Institutes about the settlement of the tribes of Israel in Canaan. Today no one discusses about how and when the Israelites reached Canaan, but the question of whether they ever settled there once is put forward instead. In addition to this, there is an intense conflict among scholars about whether one who writes the history of Israel is even obliged to take the Bible into consideration; a question that would be unthinkable back in the 60s. Finally, one should refer, indicatively, to the aforementioned new interpretative approaches to the Bible. Their common feature is that they no longer start by analyzing the text through a classical approach according to its various levels, sources or its peers, but rather they try to interpret it as a whole in the form it has received today.

The common denominator of all these new interpretative approaches to the Bible is that they are based on methods developed outside the framework of theology. This change is so radical, so that the names of these new methods, indicative of their "secular" origin, are used in English by the scholars around the world, even by the Germans, who were regarded to be pioneers in the field of the biblical study: post-structuralism, semiotics, feminism, liberation hermeneutics, reader-oriented criticism, psychological and ecological readings, new historism, newer literary criticism, etc. The use of English terms indicates another important change noted mainly in the field of biblical studies. In Germany and in countries that follow the German model in University education (such as Greece), biblical studies develop exclusively in the framework of Theological Schools, as a branch of Theology. On the contrary, in America, (the source of almost any new interpretative method), and in the wider Anglo-Saxon world and numerous European countries (French, Italy), biblical studies are usually independent from theological studies, thus allowing closer communication and collaboration between the biblical scholars and their colleagues from other branches of the Humanities.

Undoubtedly, the aforementioned advances are not irrelevant to what is usually vaguely called the "globalization" of research. The term "globalization or "internationalization" is a neologism, introduced over the last years in theological language as well, causing various debates. The term originates from the field of Economy

[1] The present paper was presented by the author at the International Scientific Conference "Theological Studies and Ecumene - With reference to the participation of the Orthodox Church to the Inter-Christian Dialogues and their future", Inter-Orthodox Center of Penteli/Athens, 12-13 March 2012. It is published here for the first time with the necessary adjustments (Ed.).

and indicates, among others, the creation and development of a capital market over the last thirty years, based on monetary fluctuations. Any transaction in this market can be made instantaneously, 24 hours a day, via a keyboard from any part of the world. This market is not monitored by a national or even international political center, yet it holds entire nations hostage, by controlling the value of their currency. Control of the currency simply means control of the value of goods. In that way, it accentuates the differences between the rich and the poor countries, multiplying respectively the exchange rate surplus and deficit. Even in the developed countries, it intensifies conflicts between groups with different economic interests, making it impossible to resolve them in the standard political procedure. Globalization works against social cohesion, as businesses move all around the world on the sole criterion of achieving competitiveness.[2] From this point of view, globalization acquires not only an economic but also an immense moral interest.

Nevertheless, apart from the potential importance of the term "globalization" for the economy and its impact on the society, the changes it has caused extend over every aspect of life. Maybe one could say that the most important change takes place in the field of the exchange of ideas. As in the case of speculation, one can exchange ideas all over the world through the Internet or other electronic means. This is the case for instance with the exchange of ideas between the First and the Third World. In the past, the programmes of theological studies in the Third World would copy the European-American models; today the situation has been reversed. In this direction the debate that emerged around the famous "Contextual Theology" or the effort of developing an "Asian Theology"[3] are quite indicative. This reality could be regarded as reversing the classical saying of Karl Marx according to which "the ideas of the ruling class are the prevailing ideas at any time". A closer look at this shows that globalization also includes the idea of the ruling class serving the class privileges of those propagandizing it.

This is obvious in the case of the exchanges between students and professors. In the past, scholars from the First World used to go and teach in the Third World. Then, the situation changed and the students from the Third World studied at the First World universities, in order to get their PhDs and return to their countries to convey what they had learned. Over the last years, the situation has changed once again. Various well-known universities, adopting the principles of competitiveness, try to procure and include among their teaching staff, distinguished scholars from the Third World. The consequence is the following paradox: Third World students go to prominent, First World universities to study Third World-related issues, close to professors coming from the Third World as well. So the whole discussion about ideas emanating from or concerning the non-privileged ones is conducted once more in the institutions of the privileged ones. These institutions on the other hand, although they keep creating new problematics, inspired by the ideas of the Third World scholars, respond usually to their appeal for help, by sending obsolete ideas in the form of books that they no longer use.

One of the consequences of globalization in the field of biblical studies is the turn over the last years of research interest towards the study of the Bible from the point of view of the disadvantaged groups. Despite the positive results of such a turn (and undoubtedly there are many), the truth is that "the privileged" theologians, tired from the use of the historical-critical method, which they have pushed to its limits, are now looking for new sources of inspiration in the Third World interpretations. In that way, the poor countries pay out their debts to the rich countries in the form of a spiritual capital, ending up even poorer. Consequently, it is not the human being and its needs at the heart of the biblical hermeneutics, but the service of interests of specific persons or groups.

---

[2] David Jobling, "Globalization in Biblical Studies/Biblical Studies" *Globalization, Biblical Interpretation, A Journal of Contemporary Approaches* 1.1 (1993): 97.

[3] The international journal Biblical Interpretation, specialized in new hermeneutical methods, apart from various relevant articles published from time to time, has dedicated a certain issue on the Asian Hermeneutics: R.S. Sugirtharajah (guest ed.), "Commitment, Context and Text: Examples of Asian Hermeneutics", *Biblical Interpretation, A Journal of Contemporary Approaches* 2.3 (1994). The same journal had devoted its previous issue on the popular, cultural traditions: Alice Bach (guest ed.), "The Bible and Popular Culture", *Biblical Interpretation, A Journal of Contemporary Approaches*, 2.1 (1994).

Part II: Orthodoxy and Ecumenism - Foundations

In addition, the globalization of biblical studies, despite the impression this term might create, did not lead to research homogenization, union of all scholars of the world to a common research goal, but it led instead to legitimization and accentuation of the peculiarities and unique interpretation approaches. Contemporary hermeneutics not only questioned the hopes of modernism for objectivity but also declared that objectivity cannot and actually should not be achieved, since every apparently objective analysis is now understood as an effort of supporting the established centers of political, economic, academic or religious power, from the oppression of which the researcher has to free himself.[4]

What is certain is that here in particular as with the globalization of research in general, two basic principles – or "myths" according the modern view- that legitimized the scholarly research in the past were shaken: the mainly theoretical, German, Hegelian principle of "spirit dialectic" and the mainly active, French (cf. Enlightenment, French Revolution) principle of the "man's emancipation". The consequence of the collapse of these two old principles is their replacement by a new one: that of "functionality" which helps the system work better. Since then, this new principle legitimates any research[5].

Under these conditions, the question of legitimization of biblical studies is put forward. When this question is asked at a personal, ecclesiastical or even academic level, the answer seems quite profound. At the personal level, anyone can study the Bible, because it is regarded as the word of God and therefore important for Christian piety. At the ecclesiastical level, one can study the Bible considering that new interpretive approaches can enrich the spiritual life of the faithful. Respectively, one can study the Bible at the academic level in order to place the biblical texts in the framework of the history of their religions or as a literary genre belonging to the past etc. However when the question is asked at the level of society, the answer is much more complicated. In this regard one could easily ask: why should a secular state, (i.e. in Greek or elsewhere), should fund biblical studies in the university? How does criticism of the Bible improve the function of the social system in virtue of the principle described above?

In our modern era, all the "myths" that used to legitimize science or knowledge, or operate as a foundation for the development of societies (such as the nation-state, etc.) now seem useless and irrelevant. The present devaluation of these myths, even without a total collapse of the fabric of society, undoubtedly led to the formation of closed and self-referent groups, where each group was dedicated to its own concerns. This sort of closed groups had already been formed in the field of theological studies due to the fragmentation of the cognitive object of Theology into branches (Hermeneutics, Systematic, Historical, and Practical) and the scientific specialization as well. Hence one could also find closed groups even within these various branches. These groups develop their own problematic and terminology and they are totally indifferent about the respective concerns of other groups. The users of the historical-critical method for example, cannot follow the problematic and terminology of those who work with new hermeneutic methods and viceversa.[6] In this case it is impossible to talk about wider programmes or common goals, but only about individual programmes. If the above assertion about the devaluation or even collapse of the various myths has a grain of truth, then the spread of the New Era/Age ideology, which nourishes radical individualism, according to which everyone creates their own myth, can be explained: the basic motto of this movement seems to be: "create your own myth".

---

[4] Terence J. Keegan, "Biblical Criticism and the Challenge of Postmodernism", *Biblical Interpretation, A Journal of Contemporary Approaches* 3.1 (1995): 1.

[5] Mark Coleridge, "Life in the Crypt or Why Bother with Biblical Studies?", *Biblical Interpretation, A Journal of Contemporary Approaches* 2.2 (1994): 141-142.

[6] The statement of the British Old Testament specialist in the University of Sheffield, David J.A. Clines: "When I was a beginner in research, I used to think it my duty to read everything anyone had written on my text; but now I will not even send on inter-library loan for an article if I suspect that the author is not interested in my questions or if I have reason to believe that the national conditions under which that author operates will make it likely that he or she will be dancing to a form-critical tune, for example, when I am setting about a feminist Interpretation or experimenting with a deconstruction". D.J.A. Clines, "Possibilities and Priorities of Biblical Interpretation in an International Perspective", *Biblical Interpretation, A Journal of Contemporary Approaches* 1.1 (1993): 71.

Against this situation and given that the Bible, outside the Christian community in modern Europe, has lost its previous authority while the religion is continuously marginalized in the public sphere, two possibilities are still available for biblical hermeneutics. The first one is to continue following an anachronistic, out-dated hermeneutical way as if nothing has changed, and the Bible still plays an important role in European society. The second possibility consists in an attempt to recapture the lost territory, by changing its paradigm and opening itself to a wider cultural dialogue with other branches such as philological criticism, psychoanalysis, philosophy, literature, linguistics, semiotics, feminist studies, sociology etc.

It is obvious that in the first case, the interpretation is understood as a completely self-referent reality of a closed group that addresses only itself. The development of social media over the last years has largely facilitated this isolation. It is not a random fact that new blogs continuously appear for various fundamentalist groups, which address a very specific and limited audience, without the possibility of being in a constructive dialogue with other groups which are always denounced as being heretic. Nevertheless, even the second possibility, referring to wider cultural dialogue, seems to be rather difficult. However biblical hermeneutics is obliged today to enter into fields beyond the boundaries of religious groups and open a constant discussion with them. In this context one should not look for a monophonic paradigm. In contrast, the discovery of biblical hermeneutics' polyphony seems to be the new paradigm or rather challenge, as a result of the very polyphony of the Bible. Hence, the profit from this adoption of new hermeneutical approaches would be the acknowledgment that the Bible, while it is the word of God, speaks with many voices and they all speak at once· God speaks polyphonically. In the framework of the World Council of Churches, this acknowledgment has led to the transformation of the original project "Gospel and Culture" to "Gospel and Cultures". There is only one and the same Gospel, but it is now acknowledged that this same Gospel can be expressed, preached and interpreted through various cultural systems.

In a constantly changing and globalized world, where cultures strive to keep their particular dignity, the only way to make the Bible's message relevant for humanity today is to make use of the various available voices in order to properly express it. There is no right and wrong reading of the biblical text according to a post-modern approach. Both reader and the text are part of a broader cultural system. An endless variety of meanings can be given from the encounter between reader and text. The aim of the interpreter today is not to answer the question "what does the text mean?", but to help the reader reach new meanings.[7]

It is true that the aforementioned method is not something entirely new. The Apostle Paul himself, when he declared that Christians of other nations should not be circumcised, actually provided a new reading of the already existent Christian tradition, a reading quite different from that of other Christian communities. It should be noted that when Paul addressed the early leaders of Christianity, who held a different understanding of the tradition, they finally approved his reading. This example of the Apostle Paul proves once again how fruitful the dialogue between different cultural traditions can be. According to Acts, Paul discontinued his missionary trips for two years and stayed in Ephesus, where, apart from the synagogue, he visited daily for 5 hours (from 11 a.m. to 4 p.m.) the school of Tyrannus (Acts 19:8-10) listening and teaching. It is not accidental that in his Epistles related to Ephesus (i.e. 1st to the Corinthians, to the Colossians and to the Ephesians) there is an adjustment of the Jewish term "Hohma" (=wisdom) to the Hellenistic perception of word and wisdom that prepared the ground for the prologue to the fourth Gospel. One could find the same reality regarding the terms "deliberate" or "discuss" in the New Testament, where three of the occurrences are related to the stay of Paul at Ephesus. Over the following centuries, when Marcion sought a canon that would speak in one voice, Orthodoxy preferred the polyphony of the Gospels. The entire history of the Christian Church is a procedure of advances, including disputes and conflicts and continuous new readings of the biblical text.

Therefore, any attempt to reflect on a question such as *"what is the main idea of Paul's thought?"*, would possibly lead to various legitimate answers, even if some of them may be more functional than others. The ac-

---

[7] Terence J. Keegan, "Biblical Criticism and the Challenge of Postmodernism", *Biblical Interpretation, A journal of Contemporary Approaches* 3.1 (1995), 7-8.

Part II: Orthodoxy and Ecumenism - Foundations

knowledgment of this polyphony of the Bible itself and its interpretation could be beneficial at multiple levels. At an academic level, it means a resistance to exclusive interpretative methods, which leads to a radical specialization and excludes any polyphony. At the same time it means readiness for a possible collaboration with other branches and eagerness for dialogue with those branches which wish to abandon any dispute or division of the past, like that between the Bible and the Natural Sciences. At the social level now the acknowledgment of the Bible's polyphony provides biblical scholars with a vision about the possibility and necessity of the dialogue between the various cultural groups. The Bible's polyphony could be considered as the proper model and foundation for the development of a society of dialogue. At the same time this polyphony would be able to inspire the hope that there is an alternative way between the totalitarianism and individualism which jointly constitute the most important consequences of the globalization of economy. Yet the great progress that is expected by the acceptance of post-modern hermeneutics is related to the inter-ecclesiastical and inter-religious dialogue. The positivist interpretations of the Bible offer of course the possibility of dialogue or even consensus on some issues, yet they do not overcome the differences that separate the various communities of faithful people. By realizing that every reading of the biblical text is a reading coming from the reader's context, we reach the conclusion that the differences of the interpretation are the result of the different context of the readers. The dialogue in this case, instead of dealing with the endless effort of compromising on the various interpretations, should deal with the various connections that emerge from these interpretations. This sort of dialogue would be more productive than the limited consensus on the results of the positivist methods. Finally, another parameter related to the acknowledgment of the Bible's polyphony and ecumenicity, has to do with the very future of the Orthodox Church. Orthodoxy today is obliged to deal with an almost tragic dilemma, as the one faced by Judaism during the 1st century AD: either she will be engaged to an honest and open dialogue with the modern world based on the various possibilities offered by her faith, tradition and certainly the Holy Scriptures or she will be closed on and refolded to herself. The decisive choice of Judaism towards the second option led it to decay, leaving the way open for Christianity to conquer the world. Therefore, it is of great importance for Orthodoxy nowadays to take the right decision in order to overcome the profound historical impasses of Judaism.

Bibliography

Alice Bach (guest ed.), "The Bible and Popular Culture", *Biblical Interpretation, A Journal of Contemporary Approaches* 2.1 (1994).

David Jobling, "Globalization in Biblical Studies/Biblical Studies in Globalization", in *Biblical Interpretation, A Journal of Contemporary Approaches* 1.1 (1993): 96-110.

Miltiadis Konstantinou, "Old Testament Canon and Text in the Greek-speaking Orthodox Church", in S. Crisp & M. Jinbachian (ed.), *Text Theology & Translation, Essays in Honor of Jan de Waard*, (UBS, 2004), 89-107

Miltiadis Konstantinou, "Bible Translation and National Identity: the Greek Case", *International Journal for the Study of the Christian Church* 12.2 (2012): 176-186.

N. Matsoukas, "Holy Scripture and Tradition According to the Hermeneutical Principles of the Ancient Church", *Bulletin of Biblical Studies* 4 (1985): 41-50 (in Greek).

R.S. Sugirtharajah (guest ed.), "Commitment, Context and Text: Examples of Asian Hermeneutics", *Biblical Interpretation, A Journal of Contemporary Approaches* 2.3 (1994).

Ton Veerkamp, *Autonomie und Egalität, Politik und Ideologie in der Schrift*, (Alektor-Verlag / Berlin 1992).

(11) Foundations for Ecumenism in Patristic Theology and Church History

Fr. Daniel Buda

Introduction

This article will try to highlight the most important contribution that the study and research of Patristic Theology and Church History could bring to ecumenical theology and understanding. It was written from an Orthodox perspective and primarily used sources produced by Orthodox authors; however the intention was to bring a contribution for the benefit of the whole *oikoumene*. The first part, dedicated to the foundations for ecumenism in Patristic theology begins with a few notional definitions which are absolutely necessary for an appropriate understanding of the role of patristic studies in ecumenical theology today. The role of patristic theology for Orthodox ecumenical theology emerges from the authority of the Church Fathers in Orthodox theology. Different understandings of their authority also determine their role in ecumenical theology today. While Orthodox and Roman-Catholics appeal with a certain preference to Patristic authority, in the Protestant tradition this type of authority plays a rather marginal role. The most important contributions of Patristic theology to ecumenical theology are presented in a systematic way and are based on concrete examples. The "neo-patristic synthesis" initiated in Orthodox theology as well as the role of modern patristic editions for promoting ecumenism are briefly presented. The first part of this article ends with a brief presentation of the challenges presented by the wrong understanding and implementation of patristic theology today.

The second part deals with the foundations for ecumenism in Church history. It contains two parts: the first one is a short analysis of how history is perceived in Orthodox theology and the second part presents the role of the study of church history for ecumenical theology from an Orthodox perspective.

I. Patristic Theology

Terminological definitions. Under "*Patristics*" or "*Patrology*" (also *"Patristic theology"*) one finds "the academic discipline dedicated to the study of the fathers … i. e. the life and writings of 'fathers'."[1] *Stricto sensus* patrology deals with Church Fathers who lived in the age from after the apostolic period (beginning of the second century) to the 8th and 9th centuries (St. John of Damascus and St. Photios the Great). For Latin patristics, the period is extended up to the medieval theologian Bernard of Clairvaux.[2] A more inclusive approach to patrology would include also those authors who do not enjoy the status and authority of a Church Father whether because of moral or doctrinal condemnations (like Origen, Diodore of Tarsus, Theodore of Mopsuestia, Theodoret of Cyrus, etc.) but the study of their life and works presents a certain interest for understanding the patristic period with all its implications.

Patrology is strongly connected "with the idea of Tradition which implied continuity and consistency in the teaching of the church at all times." Therefore "in the Orthodox church the patristic legacy provides the main authoritative direction for understanding and interpreting the content of Scripture."[3] The *Church Fathers* who enjoy a high "patristic status" in contemporary Orthodoxy include "those definitive and highly authoritative theologians of the church in its classical ages who represent purity of doctrine allied with great

---

[1] John Meyendorff, art. "Patristics," in *Dictionary of the Ecumenical Movement,* 2nd Edition, Nicholas Lossky etc. (eds.), (Geneva: WCC Publications, 2002), 887-889.

[2] John A. McGuckin, art. "Patristics" in *The Encyclopaedia of Eastern Orthodox Christianity,* John Anthony McGuckin (ed.), (Wiley-Blackwell, 2011), 440-441.

[3] J. Meyendorff, "Patristics", 887.

holiness of life; a life that manifests the indwelling of the Holy Spirit in their acts and their consciousness, such that they are not merely good speculative thinkers, or interesting religious writers as such, but rather substantial guides to the will of God, and Spirit-bearers (*pneumatophoroi*) whose doctrine and advice can be trusted as conveying the authentic Orthodox tradition of faith and piety."[4]

The status and authority of a Church Father is strongly connected with the notion of *patristic consensus* (*consensus patrum*): no single individual can be seen as an exclusive interpreter of Tradition or enjoy "canonical" status. However, "collectively, and by the consensus of the fathers among themselves, and by the manner in which they stand in a stream of defence of the ecumenical faith of the church, they together comprise a library of immense prestige and authority. They are thus collectively strong and concrete evidence for the central tradition of the Orthodox Church. That is why the church affords them a very high theological authority, not as great as the Scriptures or the ecumenical councils, but certainly alongside the latter; for it was from their writings that the doctrine of the great councils generally emerged."[5] As J. Meyendorff observed, "there are contradictions on individual issues between otherwise very authoritative fathers. The real content of transmitted truth should be sought where there is unquestionable consensus. Sometimes the consensus is easier to be defined in terms of theological methodology or a general approach to issues, rather than in actual theological formulations. One speaks then of the *sense of the fathers*."[6] The "sense of the Fathers" means to interpret Scripture in their spirit and to theologize in the manner they theologized. For a modern Orthodox theologian, abundant quotations of proof texts from patristic authors are not the guarantee of a genuine "sense of the fathers". Rather, this requires a "true consistency" and "a unity of method and congeniality of approach"[7] in dealing with patristic theology today.

The concept of "*patristic witnesses*" which is strongly linked with the notion of patristic authority can be found in the earliest patristic writings. Prominent figures of the early Church like Ignatius of Antioch, Polycarp of Smyrna or Clement of Rome enjoyed a special status and therefore a special authority in their own period of time. The idea of authority of the fathers had grown especially in the period of the "collective defence against heterodoxy." In particular, the anti-Arian front formed in the 4th century offered the opportunity for such a growth. St. Athanasius the Great in his *Life of Antony* addressed to Christians from the West[8] presented St. Antony as "one of the great fathers who personally represents a standard of truth, holiness and Orthodoxy." Sts. Gregory the Great and Basil the Great presented Athanasius as "pillar of Orthodoxy for his defence of Nicaea." By the 5th century, the concept of "authoritative fathers" was well developed. *Florilegia* i. e. collections of patristic texts on certain, especially doctrinal subjects were published in order to defend the true faith. Canon 7 of the Council of Ephesus (431) presents the attenders in the council as defenders and propagators of the "theology of the fathers." The definition of Faith of the Council of Chalcedon (451) understand itself as "following … the holy fathers."[9] At the end of the so-called "patristic period," St. John of Damascus defined the Tradition of the church as the "boundaries put up by our Fathers,"[10] and the proclamation that was made in 842 in Constantinople on the Sunday of Orthodoxy stated solemnly: "this faith is apostolic, this faith is patristic, this faith is Orthodox."[11]

---

[4] J. A. McGuckin, "Patristics," 441.

[5] J. A. McGuckin, "Patristics," 441.

[6] John Meyendorff, "Patristics," 888.

[7] John Meyendorff, *Byzantine Theology. Historical Trends and Doctrinal Themes*, (New York: Fordham University Press, 1979), 128.

[8] Adolf Martin Ritter, *Alte Kirche*, 9th edition, (Neukirchener Verlag, 2007), 249.

[9] J. A. McGuckin, "Patristics," 441-442.

[10] *Third Apology Against Those Who Decry Holy Images*, PG 94, 1356C.

[11] Hilarion Alfeyev, "The Faith of the Fathers. The Patristic Background of the Orthodox Faith and the Study of the Fathers on the Threshold of the 21st Century," *St. Vladimir's Theological Quarterly* 51.4 (2007): 371.

Foundations for ecumenism in Patristic theology

The starting point of the role of patristic theology for ecumenical theology today is the authority of the Church Fathers and its different understandings in the main Christian traditions involved in ecumenical dialogue. While in the Orthodox Church the Church Fathers enjoy a special authority which is also widely recognized in the Roman-Catholic Church in the same manner, their authority has a different understanding in the Protestant tradition. In spite of the fact that the basic Protestant principal *sola Scriptura* makes them understand only the Bible as being the "unique – or at least a very privileged – sources of divine revelation", Calvin, Luther and Melanchthon "looked at the fathers with great respect as authoritative commenters on scriptural texts."[12] The fathers of the Reformations studied the writings of the Church Fathers being convinced that they objectively reflect the realities of the early church to which they wanted to return.[13] J. Meyendorff observed that the appeal to the Church Fathers rather enhances the importance of the Scripture than diminish it: "one cannot discover the mind of Christianity without referring to the fathers, recognizing that the specific authority of scripture is enhanced rather than diminished when one studies the ways in which it was read and understood throughout the centuries."[14]

For ecumenical theology, the most important foundations provided by the Church Fathers emerge from their role as *exempla* for posterity. These foundations could be summarized as following:

1. The Church Fathers struggled for church unity. Unity of the Church is one of the fundamental preoccupations of the Church Father's writings. It is enough to mention Clement of Alexandria (especially with his *Paedagogos – The Tutor* and *The Stromata*), Cyprian of Carthage with his *The Unity of the Church,* Serapion of Thmuis with his *Euchologion* or Basil the Great with his correspondence to understand that the Church Fathers struggled for church unity. They could not accept any division within the Church, whether it was created by a schism or by a heresy. In their entire life and work the Church Fathers stood for the unity of the Church of Jesus Christ. Regarding the model of unity proposed by the Church Fathers, there is only one possibility: the return of those who left the Church into communion.

2. The Church Fathers were involved in theological dialogue. It is obvious that the Fathers of the Church very often theologized for the refutation of the heretics and schismatics, but this attitude did not hold them from initiating dialogue with those who left the community of the church. There are many examples which emphasize the desire of the Church Fathers for dialogue. The entire neo-Arian controversy which dominated the life of the Church between 325-381 is a good example of a very polemical, tense but coherent dialogue between the Nicene party led until his death (373) by Athanasius of Alexandria and several forms of neo-Arianism. Saint Basil the Great was part of a careful dialogue with those who could not accept without any reservations the divinity of the Holy Spirit. A classic example of theological dialogue in which the Church Fathers were the main actors is the so called "Union of 433" between the Antiochian party led by John of Antioch and the Alexandrian party led by Cyril of Alexandria. The council of Ephesus (431) could not reach any consensus. In fact in 431 in Ephesus there were two separate synods of the two doctrinal parties which anathematized each other. The separation between the two big theological and ecclesial centres of Christianity, Antioch and Alexandria was unacceptable in the eyes of their leaders, John of Antioch and Cyril of Alexandria. After a long and difficult dialogue, they agreed on a dogmatic formula which re-established full communion.[15] Another good example

---

[12] John Meyendorff, art. "Patristics," 888.

[13] See for example the recent study of Adolf Martin Ritter, "Das Chrysostomosbild in der Tradition des deutschen Luthertums bis Johann Albrecht Bengel (gest. 1752)," in *Studia Chrysostomica. Aufsätze zu Weg, Werk and Wirkung des Johannes Chrysostomus (ca. 349-407)*, Studien und Texte zu Antike und Christentum 71, (Tübingen, 2012), 155-182 speaks about the role that the writing of St. John Chrysostom plays in German Lutheranism up to Johann Albrecht Bengel. It is amazing how extensive the Church Fathers were used in the Lutheran theology of that time.

[14] John Meyendorff, art. "Patristics," 889.

[15] John A. McGuckin, *St. Cyril of Alexandria. The Christological Controversy, its History, Theology, and Texts*, (New York: Leiden, 1994), 107-125.

of permanent dialogue with schismatic groups in order to bring them in the communion of the Church is Saint Augustine who managed to bring into Church communion the group of tertullianists (a separate group founded by Tertullian at the end of his life) and who maintained dialogue with the Donatists.

3. The Church Fathers were against isolation of any kind. The Church Fathers entered into dialogue with other religions, with the society they were living in, with the challenges of their times. The Church Fathers initiated dialogues, many of them polemical, with Judaism, Paganism and philosophy. The purpose of such dialogues was mainly apologetic, but some of the Church Fathers, like Justin Martyr or Clement of Alexandria also looked for finding common points between Christianity and pagan philosophy and religions. The Church Fathers also criticized sharply the immorality of Greco-Roman society, proposing a Christian alternative to it. After the "Constantinian shift" (konstantinische Wende) when the Greco-Roman society became more or less "Christian" the Church Fathers stopped criticizing the society in its entirety but continued to reject certain practices that were not in line with the teaching of the Gospel. The dialogue with philosophy continued. It is important to underline that the most important Church Fathers of the golden age of patrology like John Chrysostom, Basil the Great or Gregory of Nazianzus were educated at the best profane schools of their times. All these examples are evidence that isolation of any kind cannot be sustained with the example of Church Fathers.

There are two other aspects related to the role of patrology in ecumenical theology today that have to be mentioned here separately, as being part of the modern history of patristic studies and research.

1. *"Neo-patristic synthesis" in Orthodox theology.* Georges Florovsky[16] (1893-1979) is the main initiator of the "neo-patristic synthesis" which became "the dominant paradigm for Orthodox theology and ecumenical activity."[17] Florovsky was the one who at the 1936 (29 November – 6 December). First Pan-Orthodox Congress of Theologians in Athens, Greece, in two papers[18] presented a call to return to the Fathers. The first paper, presented in German, entitled "Western Influences in Russian Theology" argued that Russian theology had been "entirely disfigured by Western influence." In the last centuries a "forcible *pseudomorphosis* of Orthodox thought, first under Latin, later under German and English influence took place." The Orthodox were forced "to think in essentially alien categories to express themselves in foreign concepts." Afterwards Florovsky suggested a "redirection" of Orthodox theology and a "radical return to the ignored and forgotten sources of Patristic Orthodoxy."[19] The second paper entitled "Patristics and Modern Theology" was presented in English and contains a call addressed to Orthodox theologians to return to the "creative fire of the Fathers, to restore … the patristic spirit." This call to "return to the Fathers" was followed by many Orthodox theologians and formed the dominant approach in Orthodox theology of the 20th and 21st centuries, with immediate implications for Orthodox involvement in ecumenical dialogue.

2. *Last but not least*, it should be mentioned that modern Patristic editions and Patristic studies are in many ways a product of ecumenical collaboration. Publication in printed form of the writing of the Church Fathers began in the 16th century in Western Europe. Some publications involved "interesting ecumenical concerns."[20]

---

[16] For Georges Florovky's biography see Ans J. van der Bent, art. "Florovsky, Georges Vasilievich," in *Dictionary of the Ecumenical Movement* ... 477; Andrew Blane (ed.), *Georges Florovsky – Russian Intellectual and Orthodox Churchman*, (Crestwood, N.Y.: St. Vladimir Theological Seminary Press, 1993).

[17] Brandon Gallaher, "'Waiting for the Barbarians': Identity and Polemicism in the Neo-Patristic Synthesis of Georges Florovsky," *Modern Theology* 27.4 (2011): 659. This study contains details about Florovsky's neo-patristic synthesis and the way it was presented and argues that key ideas of this synthesis are taken not from Eastern patristic sources, but from some Western sources. For an analysis of a possible influence of Jesuit scholars over the Orthodox patristic revival movement using as starting point a note written in pencil by Florovsky on an offprint of his speech presented in Athens in 1936 see Ivana Noble and Tim Noble, "A Latin Appropriation of Christian Hellenism: Florovsky's Marginal Note to 'Patristics and Modern Theology' and its Possible Addressee," in *St. Vladimir's Theological Quarterly* 56.3 (2012): 269-288.

[18] See *Procès-Verbaux du premier congrès de théologie orthodoxe à Athènes. 29 Novembre – 6 Décembre 1936,* Hamilcar S. Alivisatos (ed.), (Athens, 1939).

[19] Brandon Gallaher, "Waiting for the Barbarians …," 664.

[20] J. Meyendorff, art. "Patristics," 888.

For example, the "Maurist" edition was published by the French Benedictines of St. Maur with the generous support of the French King Louis XIV who was interested in finding in early Christian literature "some support for gallicanism". The publication by Nikodemos of the Hagiorite of *Philokalia* in 1782 was possible only with the support of Western contracts. The collections of Jean-Paul Migne's *Patrologia Graeca* (162 vols.) and *Patrologia Latina* (221 vols.) "are also in their own way an ecumenical witness." In 1882 Adolf von Harnack launched the Patristic series *Texte und Untersuchungen zur Geschichte der altchristlichen Literatur* which was meant to serve as a basis for studying early Christianity in a Protestant context. The so-called Oxford movement within Anglicanism used the writing of early Christian fathers as a tool for Anglo-Catholic revival" Eduard Pusey, John Keble and Cardinal Neumann edited the series *Library of the Fathers* (45 vols Oxford 1838-1888).[21] The revival of patristic studies in France and Germany after the Second World War created a new approach to theology, and "on the patristic basis, dialogue with other Christians, particularly the Orthodox, was becoming easier."[22] The French series *Sources Chrétiennes* which was started in Paris 1941 by Henri de Lubac and Jean Daniélou attempted consciously "to restore the tradition of the early church within Catholicism, thus making ecumenical dialogue easier." What is the "obvious importance" of these "great enterprises", i.e. publication of Patristic collections? An authoritative response was formulated by J. Meyendorff: "to grasp the mind of the Christian community before the occurrence of historical schisms, splits and other crises. The result, more often than not, was a better understanding of what is absolute and permanent in the Christian faith and what is of relative importance, determined by passing historical factors." [23]

All these collections of patristic writings were extensively used by Orthodox theologians involved in the patristic renaissance and stimulated the publication of similar collections by Orthodox editors. It is obvious that the Orthodox neo-patristic movement profited extensively from the Patristic editions and research initiated both by Roman-Catholics and Protestants. Nowadays it is impossible to initiate Patristic research from an Orthodox perspective without using the results of research initiated by Roman-Catholic and Protestant colleagues.

The "neo-patristic synthesis" which was launched by G. Florovsky and became so influential in the Orthodox theology of 20th and 21st centuries needs to be protected against several threats that became very visible in certain Orthodox settings. J. Meyendorff warned already that there are temptations to transform the notion "Return to the Fathers" into a "slogan or a conservative panacea." Sergei Bulgakov warned that Orthodox theology of patristic origin is perceived by some as having a kind of "Talmudic authority" which is incontestable and could be quoted as a definitive sentence whenever necessary: "Orthodox theology is not the Talmud, and a real veneration of the Fathers must reverence not the letter but the spirit. The writings of the Holy Fathers must have a guiding authority, yet be applied with discernment."[24] Metropolitan Hilarion Alfeyev also drew attention to those groups within the Orthodox Church who pretend to "vigilantly guard Orthodoxy against the infectious trends of modern times" by "fearfully rejecting the challenges of modernity, they dedicate all their time to preserving what they perceive as the traditional teaching of the Orthodox Church, explaining that in the present time of 'universal apostasy' there is no place for any creative understanding of Tradition, since everything had been clarified by the Fathers centuries earlier."[25]

Instead of such anachronisms which kill the vivacity of the tradition, Metropolitan Kallistos Ware proposes an inspiring connection of Orthodox theology of the 21st century with the Church Fathers in such a way that "... tradition lives on. The age of the fathers didn't stop in the fifth century or the seventh century. We could have holy fathers now in the 21st century equal to the ancient fathers."[26] In one of his programmatic works recently published, Metropolitan Kallistos pledged a renewal of Orthodox Christianity in the spirit of the Church Fathers

[21] J. Meyendorff, art. "Patristics", 888.
[22] J. Meyendorff, art. "Patristics," 889.
[23] John Meyendorff, art. "Patristics," 888.
[24] S. Bulgakov, "Dogma and Dogmatic Theology," in *Tradition Alive*, Michael Plekon (ed.), (Lanham, 2003), 70-71.
[25] Hilarion Alfeyev, "The Faith of the Fathers ...," 372.
[26] "The Fullness and the Centre," interview by David Neff, *Christianity Today*, (July 2011): 39.

Part II: Orthodoxy and Ecumenism - Foundations

"for the benefit of the whole oikoumene."[27] It is obvious that the neo-patristic movement which dominates Orthodox theology today has a dominant ecumenical dimension.

The most appropriate way to overcome the recent situation in the ecumenical movement which was characterized in the statement of the participants in the Pre-Assembly for the preparation for the 10th WCC Assembly as being dominated by a lack of interest in unity and lack of a clear vision about the nature of this unity would be "to go back to the theological and moral teachings and practices of the early Church by moving to a patristic understanding of the Holy Scriptures and ethical values: A re-reading together of the patristic heritage would enable us all to find common ground, and this will give the churches in the WCC the ability to move forward and to revitalize the whole ecumenical movement."[28]

II. Church history

History of the Church in Orthodox understanding. G. Florovsky stated that "Christianity is history by its very essence." This means that there is no abstract Christian message that can be detached from any historical context. There is no eternal truth "which could be formulated in some supra-historical propositions."[29] These affirmations summarize the importance of history for Orthodox Christianity. History is the medium where this world was prepared to receive its Redeemer, the Son of God incarnated in history at a time that can be determined quite precisely and his spiritual body, which is his Church, grows throughout history. History of humanity and history of salvation are intimately inter-related.

Another important aspect of the perception of history in Orthodox understanding is the conviction that "the God-given, ontological and invisible unity of the Body of Christ" was "realized and preserved in history." The Orthodox "believe that this unity (i. e. of the Body of Christ) has existed continuously and without interruption in the Orthodox Church, its doctrine, its sacraments and its essential order – even if its members, either as individuals or as a historic fellowship, fail to realize and manifest the implications of this divine gift." The Orthodox are convinced that "the undivided Church has existed in the past and still does today" and is to be identified with the Orthodox Church.[30]

Foundations for ecumenism in Church History

It was affirmed that it is typical for the Orthodox to call "to return to the bosom of the mother church of the first centuries" or, with other words, "to rediscover the common roots of Christianity."[31] This preference to appeal to the past emphasizes the role of Church History studies for the Orthodox tradition, including its importance for ecumenical theology and understanding. An intensive study of ancient church history emphasized the reality that the primitive church was not so ideal and homogenous as it appeared. It emphasized also that the struggle for the unity of the Church is not a new dimension of the Church, but it existed always. For the Orthodox it is very important to highlight the reality that the efforts for church unity are not a tendency that appeared recently. Unfortunately the most prominent monograph on the history of the ecumenical movement[32] begins with 1517 giving the impression that efforts for church unity started with the Reformation. This monograph contains a short chapter (24 pages) which presents the struggle for unity before 1517, however the brief approach strongly contradicts the detailed research on the period after the beginning of the Reformation.

[27] Metropolitan Kallistos Ware, *Orthodox Theology in the Twenty-First Century,* (Geneva: WCC Publications, 2012), 7.
[28] The Pre-Assembly took place in the island of Kos, Greece, from 11-17 October 2012. Here was quoted the paragraph 23 of the "Inter-Orthodox Pre-Assembly Consultation Statement."
[29] G. Florovsky, "The Eastern Orthodox and the Ecumenical Movement," *Theology Today* 7.1 (1950): 75.
[30] Ion Bria, "Living in the one Tradition," *The Ecumenical Review* 26.2 (1974): 225.
[31] Tamara Grdzelidze, "Ecumenism, Orthodoxy", in John Anthony McGuckin (ed.), *The Encyclopedia of Eastern Orthodox Christianity* vol. I, (Wiley-Blackwell, 2011), 212.
[32] *A History of the Ecumenical Movement,* Ruth Rouse, Stephen Charles Neill (eds.), (Geneva: WCC Publicaions, 2004).

An objective study of Church history should highlight that any time the Church was confronted with a separation caused either by heresy or by a schism, efforts for re-establishing church unity were initiated. The entire neo-Arian controversy (325-381) was an effort to find a solution for unifying the different Arian groups with the Church which confessed the Nicene Christology. After 451, when major groups of believers, especially from Egypt, Syria and Palestine left the communion of the Church, major efforts were initiated for re-establishing Church unity. Immediately after the Great Schism (1054), a dialogue between Eastern and Western Churches was established. Some of these efforts for church unity are linked with negative and painful experiences like the involvement of political and non-ecclesial aspects, forced unions that were unpopular and therefore impossible to be implemented, but history in general offers negative examples in order that they might be avoided by the next generations.

Georges Florovsky spoke about the "Western captivity" of the Orthodox mind, referring to the textbooks of Orthodox dogmatics which appeared in the Orthodox East after the eighteenth century. In terms of Church History studies in the Orthodox context, this "Western captivity" could be translated in the following terms: for a long period, starting even earlier than the textbooks of Orthodox dogmatics to which G. Florovsky is referring to, Orthodox theologians used to take information about the Roman Catholic Church from Protestant sources and information about the Protestant Churches from Catholic sources, both published in the time of confessionalism or following the principles of it. That is why church history textbooks written by Orthodox authors sometimes contain both anti-Catholic and anti-Protestant affirmations that have nothing to do with the historical reality. Very often such church history textbooks contain wrong information, tendentious affir-mations and spread prejudices about other mainline Christian confessions. In order to avoid this in the future, *de-confessionalization of church history as a science* and the support of the ecumenical Church history in Orthodox context is urgently necessary.[33] Such a de-confessionalization is a process that needs to take place in all Christian traditions and cannot be unilateral process taking place for instance only in the Orthodox tradition. De-confesionalization of Church History as a science does not mean having the same opinion on all matters related to the past or avoiding delicate aspects of the past, but presenting an objective study of Church history based primarily on sources and using the newest authentic research as secondary bibliography.

"Ecumenical Church History" is a concept that is in vogue among historians today. A definition of this concept has been formulated in an early"ecumenical Church History"[34] book: "an attempt of historians and theologians belonging to the mainline Christian confessions to achieve a common presentation of Church History." This approach represents a clear break with the past, since the authors acknowledge that "the study of Church History was ... one of the main means of fighting in the inter-Christian polemics."[35] The method used by this project was the following: each chapter had been distributed to two authors, one Protestant and one Roman-Catholic who decided among themselves which chapter to write. They wrote the distributed chapters separately. Afterwards each author read the work of the other author. In the case that one of the authors could not agree "from his confessional point of view" with an affirmation of his colleague, and after discussions it was not possible to find a common solution, he was allowed to insert notes in italic type. However, there are two exceptions from this method. Part IV of this project dedicated to the History of Orthodox Churches was written by an Orthodox author and was "viewed" ("durchgesehen") by a Protestant and a Roman-Catholic Church historian. The last chapter was written by three authors belonging to the mainline Christian confessions.

We can conclude with Paul Schrodt that "an ecumenical history of the church is a step in the right direction. What had been practiced in biblical studies for a generation ... is still only in a developing stage in general

---

[33] Daniel Buda,"Kirchengeschichte als Wissenschaft. Versuch einer orthodoxen Perspektive," in *Kirchengeschichte als Wissenschaft,* Bernd Jaspert (ed.), (Aschendorff Verlag, 2013), 48.

[34] Raymund Kottje and Bernd Moeller, *Ökumenische Kirchengeschichte,* vol. I (Mainz/München, 1970).

[35] Ebd. P. V. German original: "Versuch, Historiker und Theologen der grossen christlichen Konfessionen zu einer gemein-schaftlichen Darstellung der Kirchengeschichte ... die kirchenhistorische Wissenschaft ist... eines der Hauptkampfmittel in der innerchristlichen Auseinandersetzungen gewesen" (my own translation from German to English).

Part II: Orthodoxy and Ecumenism - Foundations

church histories. Yet inasmuch as responsible ecumenism is characterized by the unprejudiced pursuit of the truth, each confession must begin to see itself and its place in history as others see it."[36]

As G. Florovsky noted, Orthodoxy stands for the "common heritage of the universal church" as "Patristic tradition."[37] This common heritage includes, of course, also the post-patristic Church history. It is our duty as Orthodox involved in the ecumenical efforts for unity to remind our dialogue partners that a permanent appeal to history (patrology is included!) can bring inspiring ideas for ecumenical theology.

Bibliography

Hilarion Alfeyev, "The Faith of the Fathers. The Patristic Background of the Orthodox Faith and the Study of the Fathers on the Threshold of the 21st Century," *St. Vladimir's Theological Quarterly* 51.4 (2007): 371-393.

Ion Bria, "Living in the one Tradition," *The Ecumenical Review* 26.2 (1974): 224-233.

Daniel Buda, "Kirchengeschichte als Wissenschaft. Versuch einer orthodoxen Perspektive," in *Kirchengeschichte als Wissenschaft*, Bernd Jaspert (ed.), (Aschendorff Verlag, 2013), 42-52.

Sergei Bulgakov, "Dogma and Dogmatic Theology," in *Tradition Alive*, Michael Plekon (ed.), (Lanham, 2003), 67-80.

Georges Florovsky, "The Eastern Orthodox and the Ecumenical Movement," *Theology Today* 7.1 (1950): 68-79.

Brandon Gallaher, "'Waiting for the Barbarians': Identity and Polemicism in the Neo-Patristic Synthesis of Georges Florovsky," *Modern Theology* 27.4 (2011): 659-691.

John A. McGuckin, art. "Patristics," in *The Encyclopedia of Eastern Orthodox Christianity,* John Anthony McGuckin (ed.), (Wiley-Blackwell, 2011), 440-442.

John Meyendorff, "Patristics," in *Dictionary of the Ecumenical Movement,* Nicholas Lossky etc. (eds), (Geneva: WCC Publications, 2002), 887-889.

Johannes Quasten, *Patrology,* 4 vols, (Notre Dame, IN, 1986).

Metropolitan Kallistos Ware, *Orthodox Theology in the Twenty-First Century*, (Geneva: WCC Publications, 2012).

---

[36] Paul Schrodt, Ökumenische Kirchengeschichte, vol. 3: Neuzeit *Journal of Ecclesiastical History* 14.2 (1977): 340.
[37] G. Florovsky, "The Eastern Orthodox and the Ecumenical Movement … ," 72.

(12) Ecclesiological Foundations for Ecumenism

Fr. Cyril Hovorun

Unity as nature of the Church

The idea of the Church and the idea of unity of Christ's disciples were born together, as twins. Both are rooted in the New Testament. Approximately in the same time when Christ said to Peter "You are Peter, and on this rock I will build my Church,"[1] he prayed to the Father that his disciples "will all be one."[2] Unity is not simply the bene esse of the Church, but its esse.[3] Unity and Church are synonyms, as John Chrysostom testified: "The name of the Church is not one of separation but of unity and harmony."[4]

The Fathers of Church referenced the Church mostly from the perspective of its unity. Ecclesiological passages are sparse in the patristic literature. When they occur, in most cases they stress the idea of the Church unity. The Fathers insisted that in order to be faithful to its nature and its call, the Church has to take care of its unity. When the unity was disturbed and divisions occurred, they received them as a painful tragedy.

Since the earliest centuries of Christianity, unity of the Church had two meanings. The one implied preservation of integrity of the existent community, unity of faith, and communion between the members. From this perspective, the Church took care to overcome internal divisions and sectarian tendencies. The other meaning of unity provisioned a missionary outreach of the Church to all people who were not yet in communion with it, as well as overcoming the existent divisions.

These two meanings of unity stem from the developments in the first Christian community, which from its foundation by the incarnate Word and the Spirit experienced two dynamics of development, one introverted and the other extroverted. The one kept the community together and the other urged its members to step out and go preaching. The former one was initially embodied in the community of Jerusalem, while the other, in Antioch. A harmonious combination of the two dynamics was not something given. The first disciples of Christ had to make effort to balance them. They did not always succeed, as the conflict of Paul with some "old" disciples from Jerusalem shows.[5] Communities often became either excessively introverted or too extroverted. In the first case they were in danger of turning into isolated sects. In the second case, they became exposed to the threats of internal divisions and disintegration. Only by balancing the two dynamics could the communities keep together and preserve the Church's unity.

Symbols of unity

We cannot find any comprehensive definition of Church unity in Christian literature until only recently, as there were also no definitions of the Church proper. It is arguable whether the Church and its unity can be defined at all. In the words of Georges Florovsky,

> "It is impossible to start with a formal definition of the Church. For, strictly speaking, there is none which could claim any doctrinal authority. None can be found in the Fathers. No definition has been given by the Ecumenical Councils. In the doctrinal summaries, drafted on various occasions in the Eastern Orthodox Church in the seventeenth

---

[1] Matt 16:18.
[2] John 17:21.
[3] Eric W Gritsch, *The Church as Institution: From Doctrinal Pluriformity to Magisterial Mutuality*, (1979), 453.
[4] In 1 Cor 1.1 as quoted in Thomas P Halton, *The Church*, (Wilmington, Del.: M. Glazier, 1985), 56
[5] Gal 2:11-14.

century and taken often (but wrongly for the 'symbolic books'), again no definition of the Church was given, except a reference to the relevant clause of the Creed, followed by some comments."[6]

Instead of trying to define the Church, early Christian authors, including New Testament writers, made use of images. The imagery that they developed is rich and diverse. Paul Minear identified 96 images of the Church in the New Testament alone.[7] Both scriptural and patristic images present the Church not as a flat intellectual construct, but as a multidimensional and spherical living reality, which cannot be captured by definitions. In the words of John Chrysostom,

"The Church is many things: at one time a bride, at another a daughter, now a virgin, now a handmaid, now a queen; at one time barren, at another a garden; at one time fertile, at another a lily, at another a fountain. Therefore, when you hear these names beware of regarding them as physical <...> A mountain is not a virgin, a virgin is not a bride, a queen is not a servant; yet the Church is all these things. Why? Because these are spiritual, not physical, realities, and the spiritual is a vast ocean."[8]

All images that have been applied to the Church speak about its unity. They envisage the unity in both senses mentioned earlier, as integrity of a local community and as an all-embracing outreach of the universal Church to the world.

Ekklesia

The very word "Church", (ekklesia, in Greek) should not be considered as a term, but rather as a symbol of the new reality that emerged out of the group of followers of Jesus Christ, through the outpouring of the Holy Spirit. As a term, this word can be misleading. Historically, it denoted a gathering of citizens who convened for various issues related to their *polis*.

As a symbol of the Church, the word *ekklesia* means, on the one hand, call and election. On the other, it implies universality of the Church, as far as the Greek *ekklesia* spoke on behalf of and decided for the entire *polis*. Essential in the symbolism of *ekklesia* is coming together "in one place".[9] This implied holding everything in common[10], sharing charismatic gifts[11] and participation in the Eucharist.[12] These factors were regarded by the early Church as important for sustaining the integrity of any Christian community.

People of God

From the ancient Greek world, the newly born Christian community borrowed for its self-identification the image of *ekklesia*. From the Jewish world, it borrowed the symbol of "people of God" (*qahal Yahweh*).[13] This image should not be applied to the Church without reservations, in a non-metaphorical sense.[14] From the perspective of Christian ecclesiology, people of God should be perceived differently than from the Jewish perspective, as has been stressed by Clement of Alexandria:

---

[6] Georges Florovsky, "The Church: Her Nature and Task," in *Collected Works of Georges Florovsky*, vol. 1, (Bücherver-triebsanstalt, Vaduz, Europa, 1987), 57.

[7] Paul S Minear, *Images of the Church in the New Testament*, (Philadelphia: Westminster Press, 1960).

[8] *On the fall of Eutropius* in Halton, *The Church*, 14.

[9] Act 2:1; 1 Cor 7:5.

[10] Act 2:44.

[11] 1 Cor 14:23.

[12] 1 Cor 11:20.

[13] Ex 19:5; Isa 43:20-21; Hos 2:23. See Michael Baily, "The People of God in the Old Testament," *The Furrow* 9.1 (1958): 3-13; Minear, *Images of the Church in the New Testament*, 67-71.

[14] Avery Dulles, *Models of the Church, A Doubleday Image Book*, (Doubleday Religious Publishing Group, 1991), 58.

"The New People, in contrast to the Old, are young, because they have heard the new good tidings. The fertile time of life is this unageing youth of ours during which we are always at our intellectual prime, ever young, ever childlike, ever new. For those who have partaken of the New Word must themselves be new. Whatever partakes of eternity ipso facto assumes the qualities of the incorruptible. Therefore the name 'childhood' is for us a life-long season of spring, because the truth abiding in us is ageless and our being, made to overflow with that truth, is ageless too. For wisdom is ever fruitful, ever fixed unchangeably on the same truths, ever constant."[15]

A principle difference between the concept of people of God in the Old and New Testaments is that the former confines this notion to only one chosen people, Israel, while the latter includes many, virtually all people on earth. This difference probably became a reason why the Church adopted for its self-identification the word "ekklesia" and not *qahal*. The image of people of God is still a powerful representation of the universality of the Church, on the one hand, and of the Church's unity, on the other. All humanity now belongs to God. As Church, it constitutes one entity, which remains undivided by national, cultural or any other background.

There are a number of New Testament images of the Church connected with the people of God: Israel[16], chosen race[17], holy nation[18], Abraham's sons[19] and others.

Kingdom of God

Far more frequently than the images of *ekklesia* and *qahal*, the New Testament evokes the image of the "kingdom of God." Jesus Christ himself used it many times in direct speech.[20] Posterior patristic hermeneutics identified the "kingdom of God" with the Church and simultaneously placed the kingdom ahead of the Church. The early text of *Didache*, for instance, describes the kingdom, on the one hand, as a Eucharistic event that happens here and now:

"As this broken bread was scattered upon the mountains, but was brought together and became one, so let thy Church be gathered together from the ends of the earth into thy Kingdom, for thine is the glory and the power through Jesus Christ forever."[21]

On the other hand, the kingdom for the author of *Didache* is something which is prepared for the Church, where it should enter after having been delivered from evil and made perfect: "Remember, Lord, thy Church, to deliver it from all evil and to make it perfect in thy love, and gather it together in its holiness from the four winds to thy kingdom which thou hast prepared for it."[22]

Modern hermeneutics agrees with such double interpretation of the kingdom as simultaneously coinciding and exceeding the Church.[23] Although the kingdom of God proclaimed by Christ is an eschatological category, it is simultaneously present here and now. It is based on the communion of the members of the Church with God and with each other. Hans Küng remarks in this regard:

---

[15] *Paidagogos* 1.5.20 as quoted in Halton, *The Church*, 64-65.

[16] Gal 6:16; see Minear, *Images of the Church in the New Testament*, 71-72.

[17] 1 Pet 2:9; see ibid. 72-73.

[18] 1 Pet 2:9; see ibid. 73.

[19] Gal 3:29; Rom 4:16; see ibid. 76-78.

[20] Matt 12:28; 19:24; 21:31; 21:43; Mark 1:15; 4:11; 4:26; 4:30; 9:1; 9:47; 10:14; 10:15; 10:23-25; 12:34; 14:25; Luke 4:43; 6:20; 7:28; 8:10; 9:27; 9:60; 9:62; 10:9; 10:11; 11:20; 13:18; 13:20; 13:28-29; 16:16; 17:20-21; 18:16; 18:17; 18:24-25; 21:31; 22:16; 22:18; John 3:3; 3:5.

[21] *Didache* 9.4; transl. by Kirsopp Lake available online in the Library of early Christian writings http://www.earlychristianwritings.com/text/didache-lake.html (last accessed March 20, 2013).

[22] *Didache* 10.5; transl. by Kirsopp Lake available online in the Library of early Christian writings http://www.earlychristianwritings.com/text/didache-lake.html (last accessed March 20, 2013).

[23] See Hans Küng, *The Church* (New York: Sheed & Ward, 1967), 88-96.

"In general Jesus' picture of the kingdom, if we exclude passages of editorial framework and decoration borrowed from apocalyptic material, is remarkably restrained in comparison with apocalyptic literature. Apocalyptic calcula- tions as to when the end will come are rejected, for "the kingdom of God is not coming with signs to be observed" (Luke 17:20), only the Father knows the day and the hour (Mark 13:32). Judgment, resurrection of the dead and future glory are not painted in detail. Images like that of the feast are not literal descriptions of the kingdom of God, but are intended to emphasize its reality: they point not to pleasures of the table but to communion with God and with one's fellow men."[24]

The image of the kingdom of God is a powerful witness about the universal and all-embracing character of the ecclesial unity. As the above passage from *Didache* makes clear, the Church-kingdom reaches the ends of the earth. It puts different elements together and makes them one. The Church cannot be confined to one place or time. It reaches everywhere, because God is omnipresent. It is as universal as God. Küng rightly remarks in this regard: "the term *basileia* should not be taken to mean a kingdom, an area of dominion situated in place and time, but simply God's rule: the reign of the king."[25]

New creation

The kingdom of God comes as God's new creation.[26] They both manifest the Church. Paul particularly pre- sented the Church as a new creation[27]: "If anyone is in Christ, he is a new creation; what is old has passed away - look, what is new has come!"[28] This radical language echoes Paul's universalist vision of the Church. The Church, for him, constitutes a new reality in comparison with anything that existed before, including old Israel. Paul's allusion to the creation of the world can be interpreted as interchangeability of the novelty of the Church and the universal character of the Christian community. Paul stressed connection between novelty and universality in another passage:

"You have put off the old man with its practices and have been clothed with the new man that is being renewed in knowledge according to the image of the one who created it. Here there is neither Greek nor Jew, circumcised or uncircumcised, barbarian, Scythian, slave or free, but Christ is all and in all."[29]

"New man" is an image that correlates with the image of the "new creation." Like the latter, it underlines the universal character of the Church. Its universality is not only quantitative, but also qualitative. It bridges divisions that were considered the profoundest in the ancient world: religious, national, and social.

The New Testament has a number of other images that concur with the imagery of the new creation. Thus, James used a more moderate and traditional language of "first fruits", which expresses the same idea: "By his sovereign plan he gave us birth through the message of truth, that we would be a kind of firstfruits of all he created."[30]

Body of Christ

The imagery of the Church as the body of Christ has been confined to the Pauline corpus only.[31] Paul developed the language of body in continuation with the language of people of God. He stressed that the Church as body

[24] ibid. 49-50.
[25] ibid. 50.
[26] Minear, *Images of the Church in the New Testament*, 119.
[27] See ibid. 111-116.
[28] 2 Cor 5:17.
[29] Col 3:9-11.
[30] James 1:18.
[31] Eph 1:22; 1:23; 3:10; 3:21; 5:23; 5:24; 5:25; 5:27; 5:29; 5:32; Col 1:18; 1:24.

is not self-sufficient and needs Christ as its head. At the same time, this image helped Paul to illustrate how diversity of gifts and calls can coexist in one Church without tearing it into pieces.[32]

Although the Scripture referred to the image of the Church as the body of Christ less frequently than, for instance, to the image of kingdom of God, it became the most popular in the later theological literature. In the patristic era, this happened because of the Arian and Christological controversies that gave impulse to the incarnational ecclesiology. Basil of Caesarea, for instance, referred to the image of body when he tried to heal the divisions, which were caused to the Church by the Arian controversy:

> "For the same Lord who divided the islands from the mainland by sea, bound island Christians to mainland Christians by love. Nothing, brethren, separates us from one another but deliberate estrangement. We have one Lord, one faith, one hope <...> The hands need each other. The feet steady each other. The eyes possess their clear apprehension from joint agreement."[33]

In terms of symbolism of the ecclesial unity, the image of body emphasises the integrity of the entire Church. At the same time, it makes the borders of the Church much sharper than other images. This image encourages thinking that the space of the Church at some point suddenly ends and then the space without grace and salvation begins. One should not, however, forget that the body is not a definition of the Church; it is an image alongside other images of the Church.

Temple of the Holy Spirit

A more inclusive image of the Church was that of the temple. The image of temple is connected with the image of body. Paul said that believers are God's temple.[34] He drew this analogy because both the Temple in Jerusalem and the bodies of Christians host the Holy Spirit. Paul implied that a local congregation[35] and the universal Christian community[36] also constitute a temple. The image of the Temple in Jerusalem was employed in the New Testament primarily because of its association with the Spirit[37], to stress the pneumatological aspect of the Church. When Paul referred to the imagery of temple he always spoke of the Spirit. Church thus is a temple as far as it hosts the Holy Spirit. Irenaeus of Lyons developed further the New Testament imagery of temple. The Church, for him, is a vessel of the Spirit,

> "We receive our faith from the Church and keep it safe; and it is a precious deposit stored in a fine vessel, ever renewing its vitality through the Spirit of God, and causing the renewal of the vessel in which it is stored. For the gift of God has been entrusted to the Church, as the breath of life to created man, that all members by receiving it should be made alive. And herein has been bestowed on us our means of communion with Christ, namely the Holy Spirit, the pledge of immortality, the strengthening of our faith, the ladder by which we ascend to God. For the Apostle says, "God has set up in the Church apostles, prophets, teachers" (1 Cor 12:28) and all the other means of the Spirit's workings. But they have no share in this Spirit who do not join in the activity of the Church <...> For where the Church is, there is the Spirit of God, and where the Spirit of God is, there is the Church and every kind of grace. The Spirit is truth. Therefore those who have no share in the Spirit are not nourished and given life at their mother's breast; nor do they enjoy the sparkling fountain that issues from the body of Christ."[38]

---

[32] Rom 12:4-8; 1 Cor 12:4-7.

[33] *Ep.* 203 in Halton, *The Church*, 53-54.

[34] 1 Cor 6:19; see Nijay K Gupta, *Worship That Makes Sense to Paul a New Approach to the Theology and Ethics of Paul's Cultic Metaphors*, (Berlin; New York: De Gruyter, 2010).

[35] 1 Cor 3:16-17.

[36] Eph 2:21.

[37] Minear, *Images of the Church in the New Testament*, 97.

[38] *Adv. haer.* III.24 [TLG 1447.002] as quoted in Halton, *The Church*, 38-39.

It is noteworthy that although Irenaeus closely linked the Church and the Spirit, he did not confine the Spirit to the Church. This was also the idea behind the Scriptural image of the Church as the Temple. The divine *Shekhinah* (הניכש) that marked the particular presence of God in the Temple was nevertheless not locked within its limits. This makes the image of the Temple more open than the image of the body. The Church presented as the Temple is more inclusive and reaches beyond its visible borders.

Irenaeus in the above passage equated the Spirit with truth. In drawing the equilateral triangle Church-Spirit-truth, he could have relied on 1 Tim 3:15, which pictured a similar triangle: the household of God - the Church of the living God - the support and bulwark of the truth. The latter image that identifies the Church with truth is important for the later developments in ecclesiology, when acceptance of the same Orthodoxy of doctrine became an important criterion of belonging to the Church. Those who dissented from the Orthodoxy were regarded as stepping out of the Church.

Bride and mother

The New Testament and the early Christian literature developed a rich feminine imagery of the Church. Female figures from the Old and New Testaments became some of the most popular kinds of images employed to represent the Church. In the Old Testament, the symbolism of the Church was recognised in the figures of Eve[39], Susanna[40], and others.

In the New Testament, John the Baptist in the narrative of the Gospel according to John first witnessed the Messiah as a bridegroom.[41] Under the bride, John apparently implied the Messianic community.[42] More explicit in this regard was Paul, who presented the local community in Corinth as a bride of Christ: "I am jealous for you with godly jealousy, because I promised you in marriage to one husband, to present you as a pure virgin to Christ."[43] The Revelation of John applied the image of bride to the Church in its fullness: "And I saw the holy city - the new Jerusalem - descending out of heaven from God, made ready like a bride adorned for her husband."[44] This picture made some interpreters speak of the Church as a reality that existed from the beginning of the world, almost in a Platonic way. Origen, for instance, commented:

> "Do not believe that the Bride, that is, the Church, has existed only since the Savior's Incarnation. She exists since the beginning of the human race and even since the creation of the world."[45]

The book of the Revelation supplied another female image for the Church, the "Messiah's Mother"[46]:

> "Then a great sign appeared in heaven: a woman clothed with the sun, and with the moon under her feet, and on her head was a crown of twelve stars. She was pregnant and was screaming in labor pains, struggling to give birth."[47]

---

[39] See, for instance, Augustine: "Adam, the figure of Christ, Eve, the figure of the Church, whence she was called the mother of the living. When was Eve fashioned? While Adam slept. When did the sacraments of the Church flow from the side of Christ? When He slept on the cross" (*Enarr. in ps.* 40.10 as quoted in ibid. 25).

[40] Hippolytus in his commentary on Daniel interpreted the episode of Susanna walking in the garden under the surveillance of the two lusty elders (Dan 13:1-64) as speaking about the Church. Both Susanna and the garden become figures of the Church. Babylon is the world and the two elders are persecutors of the Church. The hot day on which Susanna wanted to bathe in the garden (Dan 13:15) is the day of the Pascha. The Church bathed like Susanna stands as a pure bride before God. See ibid. 22.

[41] John 3:29.

[42] Minear, *Images of the Church in the New Testament*, 55.

[43] 2 Cor 11:2.

[44] Rev 21:2.

[45] *In Cant* 11.8 as quoted in Halton, *The Church*, 35.

[46] Minear, *Images of the Church in the New Testament*, 53-54.

[47] Rev 12:1-2.

The later hermeneutical literature translated this apocalyptic language to a "non-apocalyptic"[48] image of Mary. Hippolytus was among the first who established this connection in his work *Against Antichrist*:

> "The Church never ceases to give birth to the Logos. 'And she brought forth a man-child to rule all nations' says the text: the perfect man that is Christ, the child of God, both God and man. And the Church brings forth this Christ when she teaches all nations. Admittedly, he is thinking about the Church, but his words can also apply to Mary."[49]

Mary, thus, became considered in early patristic hermeneutics as the mother of all Christians. Her motherhood was transferred to the Church. The image of the Church as mother spread widely throughout the Christian *oecumene*, particularly in North Africa.[50] In Alexandria, for instance, Clement hailed the Church as mother with reference to Isaiah:

> "'Their children', Scripture says, 'shall be put upon the shoulders, and they shall be comforted held on the knees, is a mother comforts, so will I comfort you' (Isa 66:12-13). A mother draws her children close to her. We seek our mother, the Church."[51]

The female imagery of the Church and particularly the image of mother became popular in the Christian world as a reaction to the divisions. It was promoted to demonstrate that the Church is a value in itself. This value, on the one hand, is attractive, as a bride can be. On the other hand, those who reject it in effect threaten their salvation, as Cyprian of Carthage put it in his famous saying: "He can no longer have God for his Father, who has not the Church for his mother."[52] This imagery, thus, became a powerful tool in protecting the Church's unity. Simultaneously, it ascribed to the Church more subjectivity and even more independence vis-à-vis Christ.

"Marks" of the Church

The Council of Nicaea (325) included among other articles of the Orthodox doctrine four "marks" of the Church: one, holy, catholic, and apostolic. The difference of the marks from the images is that they are more sophisticated and conceptualised. Marks are summaries of images. They also reflect the history of the discovery by the Church of its own identity. For this reason, it is also possible to consider marks as identities of the Church. In some sense, they are self-identities, because in identifying its marks, the Church was not only an object, but also a subject of the inquiry.

It is commonly accepted that the Nicene creed contains the most comprehensive list of the marks of the Church. Although these marks/identities have the authority of an Ecumenical Council and enjoy a complete reception by all Christians through all centuries of the Church's history, they are not unhistorical. They reflected concerns of the Church in a given period of time as a result of particular problems. Not only in its Trinitarian or Christological formulas, but also in its ecclesiological part, the creed reflected the situation of the first quarter of the 4th century. It actually summarised the ecclesiological self-consciousness of the Christian communities of the pre-Constantine era.

What makes the marks of the Church relevant for all times is that they address the issues of the unity of the Church. In this sense, they are not different from the images of the Church. Each of the four marks approaches the unity differently.

---

[48] ibid. 54.
[49] *De antichr.* 6 as quoted in Halton, *The Church*, 17.
[50] See Bradley M Peper, *The Development of Mater Ecclesia in North African Ecclesiology*, (Vanderbilt University, 2011) (unpublished dissertation).
[51] *Paidagogos* 1.5,21 as quoted in Halton, *The Church*, 46.
[52] *De unitate* 6 [CPL 0041].

Two of them, "one" and "catholic," correspond to the dynamic of expansion of the Church and best express its universal character. "One" means not just numerical oneness and uniqueness of the Church, but also and primarily its unity and all-embracing character. This character is stressed even more in the predicative "catholic." As Cyril of Jerusalem explained in his Catechism:

> "This Church is called catholic because it is spread throughout the world from end to end of the earth; also because it teaches universally and completely all the doctrines which men should know concerning things visible and invisible, heavenly and earthly; and because it subjects to right worship all mankind, rulers and ruled, lettered and unlettered; further because it treats and heals universally all sorts of sin committed by soul and body; and it possesses in itself every conceivable virtue, whether in deeds, words, or in spiritual gifts of every kind."[53]

"Catholic" in the context of the beginning of the 4th century also meant "non-sectarian." Catholic communities considered it important to stay together, regardless of their disagreements and diversities. They shared the mentality of belonging to one universal community. This mentality was open enough to accept diversities of other communities. It opposed to the mentality of closedness and particularism, which believed that only what I hold is true. Optatus of Milevis eloquently expounded the difference between the two mentalities, with reference to the Donatist schism:

> "You my brother Parmenian, have said that (the Church) is with you alone. This, I presume, is because, in your pride, you are eager to claim some special holiness for yourselves, so that the Church may be where you please, and not where you do not want it. And so, in order that she may be with you in a small corner of Africa, one corner in one small region, is she not to be with us in another part of Africa? Is she not to be in Spain, in Gaul, in Italy, where you are not? If you insist that she is with you only, is she not to be in Pannonia, in Dacia, Moesia, Thrace, Achaia, Macedonia and all of Greece, where you are not? To enable you to argue that she is with you, she is banished from Pontus, Galatia, Cappadocia, Pamphylia, Phrygia, Cilicia, the three Syrias, the two Armenias, all of Egypt and Mesopotamia where you are not. And is she not to be in countless islands and innumerable provinces where you are not? Where in that case shall be the application of the Catholic name, since the Church is called Catholic precisely because she is in accordance with reason and is scattered all over the world? For if you limit the Church just as you please into a narrow corner, if you withdraw whole peoples from her communion, where will that be which the Son of God has merited, where will that be which the Father has freely granted to Him, saying: 'I will give to thee the nations for thine inheritance, and the ends of the earth for Thy possession' (Ps 2:8)."[54]

The other two marks of the Church, "holy" and "apostolic," describe the quality of the ecclesial unity and universality. They counter-balance the dynamic of the Church's growth *ad extra* by focusing on the integrity of the Christian community, sharing of one faith, participating in one Spirit. The quality of holiness means that the Church is far more than just an organisation. It struggles to imitate God in his holiness, as Gregory of Nyssa put it:

> "It is not possible for Christ not to be justice, purity, truth, and estrangement from all evil, nor is it possible to be a Christian, that is, truly a Christian, without displaying in oneself a participation in these virtues. If one might give a definition of Christianity we shall define it as follows: Christianity is an imitation of the divine nature."[55]

By participation in God's holiness, the Church also takes part in his oneness. Holiness makes the Church one and catholic, safeguards it from splits and accommodates in unity all diversities, which are compatible with the holy.

---

[53] *Catechesis* 18.23 as quoted in ibid. 84.
[54] *Contra Parmenianum* 2.1 [CPL 244] as quoted in ibid. 86.
[55] *What it means to call oneself a Christian* in ibid. 152.

The creed refers to apostolicity as a factor that preserves the integrity of the ecclesial community. In the early Christian centuries, it served as a main criterion of unity. The reasons were obvious: various Christian communities were in communion with each other through the apostles who either directly or indirectly through their disciples had established them. It was not only apostolicity of faith and doctrinal traditions that mattered, but primarily apostolicity of the origins. During the time, however, apostolicity of origins gradually turned to the apostolicity of faith and of episcopal succession. Although this change was a reduction of the original notion of apostolicity, it turned into an important practical instrument of securing unity of the Church: those bishops who did not have proper apostolic succession in their ordinations, were excluded from the ecclesial communion, together with their communities. This secured healthy relations between the communities and preserved the unity of the Church at the large scales.

Bibliography

Afanasiev, Nicholas. "Una Sancta." *Irenikon* 36 (1963): 436–475.

Baktis, Peter Anthony. "Ministry and Ecclesiology in the Orthodox Responses to BEM." *Journal of Ecumenical Studies* 33.2 (1996): 173–186.

Best, Thomas F, and Martin Robra. *Ecclesiology and Ethics: Ecumenical Ethical Engagement, Moral Formation and the Nature of the Church*, (Geneva: WCC Publications, 1997).

Bobrinskoy, Boris. *The Mystery of the Church: a Course in Orthodox Dogmatic Theology*, (Crestwood, N.Y.: St. Vladimir's Seminary Press, 2012).

Bordeianu, Radu. *Dumitru Staniloae: an Ecumenical Ecclesiology. Ecclesiological Investigations*, (London; New York: T&T Clark, 2011).

Bouyer, Louis. *L'incarnation et l'Église-Corps du Christ dans la théologie de Saint Athanase*, (Paris: Éditions du Cerf, 1943).

Braaten, Carl E. *Mother Church: Ecclesiology and Ecumenism*, (Minneapolis, Minn.: Fortress Press, 1998).

Burkhard, John J. *Apostolicity Then and Now: an Ecumenical Church in a Postmodern World. A Michael Glazier Boo*, (Collegeville, Minn.: Liturgical Press, 2004).

Carter, David. "Ecumenical Ecclesiology: Unity, Diversity and Otherness in a Fragmented World." *Ecclesiology* 7.3 (September 1, 2011): 403–406.

Clark, Francis. "Trends in Ecumenical Ecclesiology." *Heythrop Journal* 4.3 (July 1963): 264–272.

Di Berardino, Angelo. *We Believe in One Holy Catholic and Apostolic Church. Ancient Christian Doctrine*, (InterVarsity Press, 2010).

Evans, G R. *The Church and the Churches: Toward an Ecumenical Ecclesiology*, (Cambridge; New York: Cambridge University Press, 1994).

Fuchs, Lorelei F. *Koinonia and the Quest for an Ecumenical Ecclesiology: From Foundations Through Dialogue to Symbolic Competence for Communionality*, (Grand Rapids, Mich.: William B. Eerdmans Pub. Co., 2008).

Kärkkäinen, Veli-Matti. *An Introduction to Ecclesiology: Ecumenical, Historical & Global Perspectives* (InterVarsity Press, 2002).

Kinnamon, Michael. Ecumenical Ecclesiology: One Church of Christ for the Sake of the World, *Journal of Ecumenical Studies*, 44.3 (Summer, 2009): 341-351.

Küng, Hans. *Theology for the Third Millennium: an Ecumenical View*, (New York: Doubleday, 1988).

Tavard, George Henry. *The Church, Community of Salvation: an Ecumenical Ecclesiology. New Theology Studies*, (Liturgical Press, 1992).

Tjørhom, Ola, and Geoffrey Wainwright. *Visible Church, Visible Unity: Ecumenical Ecclesiology and "the Great Tradition of the Church."* (Unitas Books, Liturgical Press, 2004).

(13) A Theological Affirmation of God's Action outside the Canonical Boundaries of the Church[1]

Athanasios N. Papathanasiou

Introduction

The question as to whether God acts salvifically outside the Church, and what happens to those unreached by the Church's proclamation, is a question as old as the Church herself. In the case that one acknowledges the primacy of God's love and mercy, the answer seems clear: in several ways, obvious or unseen, God is always and everywhere at work, inviting all to the Kingdom. This is, in broad outline, the answer many theologians of the ancient Church, such as Justin, Irenaeus and Clement of Alexandria gave—reflected also in the tradition on Christ's descent into Hell.[2] Over the course of history, however, this answer, instead of being developed, was rather bypassed. An institutionalistic theology prevailed, which on the one hand understands the Church as the organization or structure that "contains" Christ, and on the other hand sees the Holy Spirit as Christ's "byproduct", in the sense that it is merely what he grants to the members of the Church only. This is, in short, the notorious "Christomonism", much discussed in recent decades as a grave impasse of western theology.

The narrowness of Christomonism, together with the reinforcement of the question about God's salvific activity *extra muros* in modern times (due to the awareness that the bounds of history have gone beyond whatever the first Christians could imagine, and millions of people are to remain non-evangelized), has resulted in fervent dialogue in recent years, particularly in the field of Missiology. By way of an example one could mention Paul Tillich's and Karl Rahner's contributions, as well as the ongoing debate over exclusivism, inclusivism, and pluralism that has been going on since the 1970s. The shaping of theologies that affirm God's universal action without relativizing Christian uniqueness remains a major task.

The dispute

In this perspective it has been acknowledged that Orthodox theology has made a significant contribution through its participation in the ecumenical movement, especially since the 1960s. Contrary to the Spirit's "subordination" to the Son within the framework of the *Filioque*, the insistence by some Orthodox theologians that there are two distinctive economies, that of the Son and that of the Spirit, opened up the horizons of the discussion. Calling upon Trinitarian theology, these thinkers brought to the fore the role of the Holy Spirit, not only as the Person who is being sent by Christ, but also as the Person who has been creatively present throughout the world from the very first moment of the creation (not just after the Incarnation) and who even made the Son's incarnation possible. It was this awareness of the universal action of the Spirit that, ever since, triggered the recognition of God's presence in all good deeds and in the life of all people, regardless of their religious identity.

As early as 1944, the Orthodox theologian Vladimir Lossky claimed that

> Intimately linked as they are in the common work upon earth, the Son and the Spirit remain nevertheless in the same work two persons independent the one from the other as to their hypostatic being. It is for this reason that

---

[1] This text in its full version was originally published in *Communio Viatorum* 53.3 (2011): 40-55. Here it is published slightly abridged, and with the addition of the subtitle.

[2] Justin, *First Apology* 46, Patrologia Graeca (hereinafter, PG) 6, 397C; Irenaeus, *Against Heresies* 3, 6, 1, PG 7, 724B-C; Clement of Alexandria, *Miscellanies* 5, PG 9, 9-206; 1 Peter 3:18-19.

the personal advent of the Holy Spirit does not have the character of a work which is subordinate, and in some sort functional in relation to that of the Son.[3]

As a matter of fact, what Lossky intended to examine was the ecclesiastical experience; not the question of where the boundaries of the Church lie or God's presence beyond them. However, the dynamics of his position facilitated the thoughts of the next generation. In 1971 the Orthodox bishop Georges Khodr spoke at the WCC Central Committee Meeting, Addis Ababa, Ethiopia.[4] He referred his audience to Lossky and stressed the hypostatic independence of the Persons. Nonetheless, at the same time he underlined that "between the two economies [that of the Son and that of the Spirit] there is reciprocity and a mutual service", and insisted that Christ himself is mystically present in every good-intended human deed, even in the realm of other religions.

> At the present moment the Church is the sacrament of this future unity, the unity of both "those whom the Church will have baptized and those whom the church's bridegroom will have baptized", to use Nicholas Cabazilas's wonderful expression.[5]

I will focus on this "wonderful expression" in the second part of this paper. But first let us take a glimpse at the itinerary of the "hypostatic independence" idea. Almost ten years later, in January 1990, Khodr participated in a WCC consultation in Baar, Switzerland on the issues posed by pluralistic theology. He repeated the tenet of the Son's "eternal reciprocity with the Spirit",[6] however he decisively emphasized the need to discern the distinct economy of the Spirit. He mentioned the Spirit's work with the prophets of the Old Testament and concluded:

> The Spirit here preceded, in his salvific action, the historical Jesus. That was the economy of the prophets according to Irenaeus's affirmation: "There is but one the same God who, from beginning to end, through various economies, came in assistance to mankind" [...] [The Church's] function is to read through the mystery of which it is the sign, all other signs sent by God through all times and in various religions in view of the full revelation at the end of history.[7]

Though Lossky had initiated the whole speculation, and other important Orthodox theologians worked on it more or less critically, it was Khodr who made a considerable impact on ecumenical mission discussions. Several theologians of various denominational origins were inspired by his view, so that in the following decades ecumenical theology has experienced an explosion of interest in Pneumatology. Paul Knitter, a participant in the Baar consultation, declared characteristically that in Khodr's lecture "the Holy Spirit was descending upon us and was leading us out of the Christological impasse by leading us more deeply into the Christological mystery."[8] The fact is, however, that many pushed hypostatic independence to its extremes, developing Pneumatologies almost in antagonism to Christology—something that I am not sure at all was part of Khodr's intention. Kirsteen Kim aptly notes:

---

[3] Vladimir Lossky, *The Mystical Theology of the Eastern Church,* (New York: St Vladimir's Seminary Press, 1976), 159.
[4] Georges Khodr, "Christianity in a Pluralistic World. The Economy of the Holy Spirit", *The Ecumenical Review* 23.2 (1971), 118-128.
[5] Georges Khodr, "Christianity", op.cit., 127.
[6] Georges Khodr, "An Orthodox Perspective of Inter-Religious Dialogue", *Current Dialogue* 19 (1991): 25 and 27.
[7] Georges Khodr, "An Orthodox Perspective", op.cit., 26 (Irenaeus's quotation is *Contra Haereses* 3, 12, 13, PG 7, 907A).
[8] Paul F. Knitter, "A new Pentecost? A Pneumatological Theology of Religions", *Current Dialogue* 19 (1991): 35.

Part II: Orthodoxy and Ecumenism - Foundations

The suggestion by Lossky and others of a certain "hypostatic independence" implied to some Protestant and Catholic theologians a way of using pneumatology to distinguish the universal work of God in the world from its particularly Christian aspects, thus marginalizing the institutional church or explicit Christian confession in theology, if these proved awkward. Such a distinction was certainly not the intention of Lossky, who called the church "the centre of the universe", and it could certainly be contrary to Orthodox tradition to suggest that the Spirit's mission is in any way subversive of the church or the Christian community.[9]

What, eventually, proved to be at the stake with this pneumatocentric shift, was Christology! For some of the said theologians Christology has to do with the Church only (consequently it can hardly be related to the universal activity of God), while Pneumatology comprises the process of opening up to the world.

In my thinking the "hypostatic independence" needs to be interpreted in ways that neither fragment the Trinity nor negate Christ's finality. First of all, we must take into serious consideration the fact that in Old Testament times it was not only the Spirit that acted world-wide, as Khodr stresses. It was also the Logos, the yet pre-incarnate Son. It is important to keep this in mind, because it affirms the Trinitarian base of revelation. Second, now we would go even beyond this and speak about the universal presence of the *incarnate* Son. No one-sidedness is implied here. The incarnate Son that is, the Christ event, has been Spirit conditioned; he has been a historical reality and, at the same time, an eschatological intervention in history, but free from the bondage of it. The recognition that not only the Spirit but also Christ himself has cosmic dimensions is of immense importance, since it takes into account the biblical assurance that the entire creation—not only the members of the Church—are going to encounter Christ at the eschaton (1 Cor.15: 28). So, as I said on another occasion,[10] "we should not talk about 'hypostatic independence' of the Spirit, but about the seeming-paradox of 'relational independence'. I mean that the Spirit is free to act wherever it pleases, but it always leads mystically to the Trinity and its Kingdom. The conclusion of the book of Revelation is especially characteristic: Not only the Church, but also the Spirit anticipates the eschatological Christ. 'The Spirit and the Bride say, Come! [...] Amen. Come, Lord Jesus!' (Rev. 22:17, 20)."

In this direction the scrutiny of Cabasilas's "wonderful expression", mentioned laconically by Khodr, may be of some help.

Nicholas Cabasilas was a fourteenth-century Orthodox theologian (d. 1371), renowned for his liturgical theology in East and West and recently (1983) canonized by the Orthodox Church. He is very often referred to in relation to Eucharistic theology and the mystical union between Christ and the faithful. Yet, apart from this "centripetal" theology (I mean the theology that focuses on the Church within), his "centrifugal" views (that is, those having to do with the opening up of the Trinity and the Church to the world outside the Church) are mostly ignored. As we will see, he voices a view which would be enumerated together with the inclusivism of Justin, Irenaeus and Clement. Apparently Cabasilas's theological agenda was not that of modern discussion. So on the one hand we have to approach his view without succumbing to anachronism and, on the other hand, we have to discern the dynamics of his agenda and the perspectives it can open.

An "inside" - "outside" osmosis

Cabasilas's "wonderful expression" is found in his work *The Life in Christ*.[11] The entire work is dedicated to the three sacraments which, according to the author, incorporate the faithful in Christ: Baptism, Chrismation and the Eucharist.

[9] Kirsteen Kim, *The Holy Spirit in the World. A Global Conversation*, (London: SPCK - Orbis Books, 2008), 54.
[10] See my "Journey to the Center of Gravity: Christian Mission One Century after Edinbourgh 1910", *2010 Boston. The Changing Contours of World Mission and Christianity*, eds. Todd M. Johnson, Rodney L. Petersen, Gina A. Bellofato, Travis L. Myers, (Oregon: Pickwick Publications, 2012), 67-83.
[11] Nicholas Cabasilas, *The Life in Christ* (tr. Carmino J. De Catanzaro), *The Life in Christ*, (Crestwood, NY: St. Vladimir's Seminary Press,1974).

For Cabasilas "to be baptized [...] is [...] to receive our very being and nature, having previously being nothing".[12] It initiates a procedure that finds its completion at the holy Eucharist.[13] So it seems clear that for Cabasilas no one can be saved without finding his way into full membership in the established Church. However a careful examination may show that his horizon was broader, precisely because he acknowledged God's surprisingly unpredictable manner of acting. In a valuable chapter, where he mentions the numerous martyrs (the "choir of the martyrs") as the example of the utmost love for Christ,[14] he points out that

> It happened that many ended up in this choir even though they had not been washed, i.e., had not been baptized with water by the Church, yet the Church's Bridegroom Himself baptized them. To many He gave a cloud from heaven, or water sprang from the earth of its own accord, and so He baptized them. Most of them, however, He invisibly re-created. Just as the members of the Church, such as Paul and others like him, should complete what is lacking in Christ, so it is not incongruous if the Head of the Church supplies what is lacking in the Church. If there are some members who appear to be helping the Head, how much more fitting if it is that the Head Himself should add that which is lacking for the members.[15]

What we should single out in the first place in this chapter is a strange understanding of church membership. Cabasilas speaks about people who have encountered Christ and have been incorporated into his Church, but without having been canonically baptized and without having any actual relationship with the established Church; they have not been baptized in a community, they have not been baptized by an ordained minister, they have not been baptized by water, and, besides, they have never partaken in the Eucharist, which is supposed to comprise the very essence of the Church! It seems that Cabasilas is willing to expand the Christological and Pneumatological boundaries of the Church so that they embrace the canonically unchurched! Apparently he reclaims an ancient conviction of the Church, which recognized several types of non-canonical baptism, such as baptism by blood (the martyrdom of those who confessed Christian faith without having been baptized), and the baptism of desire (the disposition of those who yearn to be baptized, but reasons unconnected to their will—e.g. sudden death—stopped them from proceeding). But Cabasilas develops this tradition in a rather unusual direction and deepens the theological insights, as we shall now explore.

As is well known, St Paul has emphasized that the faithful and the Church are the complement of Christ, "the fullness of Him who fills everything in any way" (Col. 1:24; also Eph. 1:23). This view has been well-attested in traditional theology. One could look at John Chrysostom[16] and the Russian bishop Theophan the Recluse (1815-1894), cited by Georges Florovsky:

> He Himself is complete and all-perfect, but not yet has he drawn mankind to Himself in final completeness. It is only gradually that mankind enters into communion with Him and so gives a new fullness to His work, which thereby attains its full accomplishment.[17]

Cabasilas, then, reverses and completes this view, stressing the fact that Christ has being working where the Church is not. In this manner Cabasilas is speaking about the exciting idea of *Missio Dei*, which has fervently been discussed by ecumenical Christians since 1952 in several tones. God is the missionary par excellence, who ceaselessly works for the salvation of his creation, and the church is a deacon of his mission, a witness of his

---

[12] Cabasilas, op.cit., 66.

[13] Cabasilas, op.cit., 67.

[14] Myrrha Lot-Borodine, "Le martyre comme témoignage de l' amour de Dieu d' aprés Nicolas Cabasilas", *Irénikon* 27 (1954): 157-166.

[15] Cabasilas, op.cit., 88-89, 92-93.

[16] John Chrysostom, *On the epistle to the Ephesians*, I, 3, PG 62, 26.

[17] Georges Florovsky, "The catholicity of the Church", idem, *Bible, Church, Tradition*, (Belmond: Büchervertriebsanstalt, 1987), 39.

love for the entire world and a foretaste of the Kingdom to where he is calling the universe. So the Cabasilean *Missio Dei* bears two specific characteristics:

1. The agent is the *incarnate* Christ. Cabasilas points out that what has radically changed human fate has been the divine incarnation and death. After these deeds it is God himself who encounters human persons; not only words and laws—even if these are words and laws of divine origin, as happened in the Old Testament era.[18]

2. Cabasilas explicitly states that there are saints (not just "people", in general) who accepted truth neither by means of listening to the Church's preaching nor by observing miracles, but through a mystical baptism that Christ himself had the initiative to perform for them.[19] "The word of teaching seems to have had no effect. The power of Baptism brought it all about."[20] Cabasilas brings to the fore the example of three certain martyrs in the early centuries: Porphyrius, Gelasius and Ardalion, all mime actors who used to mock Christians.

Cabasilas narrates that Porphyrius had the chance to hear many things about Christ and see miracles, but remained adamant in his denial. One day he was mimicking Christian baptism and pretending to baptize himself. Yet the Grace of God touched him in reality and when he came out of the water he confessed Christ and finally was martyred for him. The same happened with Gelasius. The case of Ardalion differs. He played the role of a Christian martyr in torture. His fellow-actors hanged him naked upon a cross. Then, all of a sudden he accepted Christ, declared his faith and was driven to martyrdom.[21]

With all three Cabasilas is speaking about *eros*, the fiery love that Christ himself generated "invading" the actors' hearts. Especially for Adralion he enthusiastically notes: As soon as the actor uttered his lines, that he loved Christ, "he at once began to love Christ [...]. For other men the good proceeds to the mouth 'from the good treasure of the heart' (Mt. 12:35), but for Adralion the treasure of foods above flowed from his heart to his mouth".[22] At this point one could object. Doesn't the uttering of the name of Christ seem like a magic spell here, since it appears to operate regardless of the man's disposition? Cabasilas would definitely answer "no". What he tries to describe is a mystical and wholehearted act of consent. Christ "laid hold on him [Ardalion] and attached him, so that He *persuaded* him of the things which he formerly could not bear even to hear".[23] Besides, a Christian "believes without compulsion and governs his conduct by the power of God, and not by laws".[24]

What might be the sources of Cabasilas? First of all, tradition itself, for the veneration of these martyrs became established very quickly. In the 5th century, for example, Theodoret of Cyrus praises the sainthood of mimics who had experienced sudden conversion and were finally martyred.[25] But as far as literary sources are concerned, we may suppose that Cabasilas was a reader of the *Synaxarium Ecclesiae Constantinopolitanae* (composed in the 10th century)[26] and the *Menologium* of the emperor Basil II (composed a little later than 979, utilizing the *Synaxarium*).[27] A glimpse at these hagiographical texts may help us understand Cabasilas better.

Porphyrius's memory is celebrated on 15 September. He was beheaded in 361, having acted in a play ordered by the emperor Julian the so-called the Apostate for the celebration of his birthday. The *Synaxarium* provides the detail that Porphyrius evoked the Trinity when pretending to baptize himself.[28]

---

[18] Cabasilas, op.cit., 91-92.
[19] Cabasilas, op.cit., 92.
[20] Cabasilas, op.cit., 94.
[21] Cabasilas, op.cit., 92 (Porphyrius), 92-93 (Gelasius), 93 (Ardalion).
[22] Cabasilas, op.cit., 93.
[23] Cabasilas, op.cit., 93.
[24] Cabasilas, op.cit., 94.
[25] Theodoret of Cyrus, *Sermon 8, On the martyrs*, PG 83, 1032D-1033A.
[26] Hippolytus Delehaye (ed.), *Synaxarium Ecclesiae Constantinopolitanae*, Bollandists, Brussels 1902, col. 801.
[27] *Menologium*, PG 117, 19A-614C.
[28] *Synaxarium*, op. cit, col. 47. See also *Acta Sanctorum*, Septembris, v. 5, (Brussels, 1755), 37. Yet the *Synaxarium* does not mention the baptism at all. Porphyrius appears to be executed for publicly criticizing Julian for his apostasy

There is also another martyr Porphyrius, also an actor, who was put to death in 270 (his feast-day is on 4 November),[29] but Cabasilas does not refer to him. He was baptized on the stage by another mimic, who played the bishop. After that Porphyrius was catechized by angels, while many among the audience accepted the Christian faith and were miraculously baptized by a sudden rainshower.[30] In several versions of the martyrdom the action of the Holy Spirit has been underlined.[31] I suspect that Cabasilas preferred to mention the other Porphyrius because his story contains an immediate action of Christ himself; neither a third person performed the sacrament nor did angels teach. Exactly the opposite happens with the canonist Balsamon (12th c.), which is, I think, characteristic of what I said earlier about Cabasilas's openness. Balsamon comments on the 4 November martyrdom when discussing the validity of a sacrament performed by someone who is not an ordained minister.[32] He neither mentions the 15 September martyrdom nor deals with the issues raised by the mystical action of Christ.

Regarding Gelasius, the texts give only the information that he is commemorated on 26 or 27 February[33] and was beheaded or stoned in 297.[34]

Ardalion (whose feast-day is on 18 or 17, or 14 April[35]) was burnt alive during the reign of Maximian Galerius (305-311). Of all three, his story is the most extreme example of a mystical encounter with Christ, since it contains no hint of conventional baptism, not even in the sense of a mockery. So a comparison between the hagiographical account and Cabasilas's comments can show how freely and almost passionately he theologizes on this martyrdom. He inserts or rather invents a baptism, in the sense that he calls this personal and unconventional activity of Christ a "baptism", apparently trying to stress that there is no affinity with God without a relationship to Christ and the Spirit, without a relationship to one's fellow human beings, and without a real transformation of human life; in few words, without what baptism stands for. Furthermore, in Adralion's case Cabasilas accentuates a very special encounter with Christ: the encounter through the experience of suffering. What may be implied here is an important theological trend which concedes that Christ is on the side and in the position of all who suffer pain and injustice.

In Cabasilas's baptismal theology overall one has to take into account its strong Trinitarian presuppositions, which astonishingly remind one of modern quests mentioned at the beginning of this paper.

> When those who perform baptism invoke God over the act of washing it is not by the common name 'God' that they call the Trinity [...]. But rather they proclaim the proper nature of each of the Persons with more precision and exactitude [...]. Even though it is by one single act that the Trinity has saved our race, yet each of the blessed Persons is said to have contributed something of His own [...]. The Father has re-shaped us, by means of the Son we were re-shaped, but "it is the Spirit who gives life" (John 6:63). The Trinity was foreshadowed even at the first creation. Then the Father created, and the Son was the hand for Him who created, but the Paraclete was the breath for him who inbreathed the life.[36]

Cabasilas's Christocentrism is never divorced from the Spirit's blow. "The new law", he says, "is spiritual because the Spirit works everything",[37] shaping —I would add— the new creation, the Church which surprisingly extends wherever God wills.

---

[29] The *Menologium*, op. cit. 144A, names Emperor Aurelian, while V.D.V., "Une Passion inédite de S. Porphyre le Mime", *Analecta Bollandiana* 29 (1910): 264, Emperor Diocletian.

[30] *Synaxarium*, col. 193-194. *Acta Sanctorum*, Novembris IIa, Brussels 1894, 230B.

[31] V.D.V., op. cit., 271, *Acta Sanctorum*, op. cit., 231 A.

[32] G.A. Rallis - M. Potlis, *Syntagma ton theion kai ieron kanonon.* [Collection of the divine and holy Canons], III, (Athens: 1853), 277, 279-280.

[33] *Synaxarium*, op. cit., col. 492-494. See also *Acta Sanctorum*, Februarii, v. 3. 675.

[34] V.D.V., op. cit, 263-264.

[35] *Synaxarium*, op. cit., col. 612; *Menologium*, op. cit., 408C-D; *Acta Sanctorum*, Aprilis, II, (Brussels, 1675), 213, 521 respectively.

[36] Cabasilas, op.cit., 73-74.

[37] Cabasilas, op.cit., 95.

Part II: Orthodoxy and Ecumenism - Foundations

Conclusion

The three martyrdoms share a common characteristic of great importance. The mimics had neither interest nor desire prior to Christ's initiative, and this differentiates their case from the baptism by blood of those who had been intending to enter the Church but who had not yet been able to do so (for example the *Apostolic Tradition*, 3rd c., as well as the *Apostolic Constitutions*, late 4th c., speak about a catechumen "who has been baptized in his own blood"[38]). They do not even appear as infidels of good disposition and intentions, but, quite the opposite, as the worst type of person, hostile to Christianity and morally degenerate, the opposite of a virtuous martyr. "Nothing could be meaner than a mime or more philosophical than a martyr."[39] So, when Cabasilas draws his theological inspiration from these martyrdoms, he strives to show that Christ acts in unseen and unforeseen ways at the darkest ends of human reality, and that everyone is the subject of God's care. Whenever Cabasilas refers to people who have denied their salvation, he always means those who have intentionally declined the doctor (Christ) and remained blind.[40] He does not deal with adjacent issues which have been posed by modern discourse, such as Christ's presence in the good intentions of people of other religious persuasions or anonymous Christians. Yet, the dynamics of his view and his assurance that Christ acts mystically everywhere, are sound criteria for any further discussion. In any event the biblical tenet that in the life of many people Christ will remain present yet unknown until the end of history (Mt. 25:37-45) encompasses an insuperable challenge to all our theological schemes.

Bibliography

D' Costa Gavin (ed.), *Christian Uniqueness Reconsidered: the Myth of a Pluralist Theology of Religions*, (Maryknoll , NY: Orbis Books, 1990).

Florovsky Georges, "The Limits of the Church", *The Church Quarterly Review*, 117.233 (October 1933): 117-131.

Florovsky Georges, "The Church: Her Nature and Task", idem, *Bible, Church, Tradition: An Eastern Orthodox View*, (Vaduz: Büchervertriebanstalt, 1987), 57-72.

Khodr Georges, "Christianity in a Pluralistic World. The Economy of the Holy Spirit", *The Ecumenical Review*, 23.2 (1971): 118-128; reprinted in: Constantin G. Patelos (ed.), *The Orthodox Church and the Ecumenical Movement: Documents and Statements 1902-1975*, (Geneva: World Council of Churches, 1978), 297-307.

Khodr George, "An Orthodox Perspective of Inter-Religious Dialogue", *Current Dialogue* 19 (1991), 25-27.

Kim Kirsteen, *The Holy Spirit in the World: A Global Conversation*, (New York: Orbis Books, London, 2008).

Papathanasiou Athanasios N., "Journey to the Center of Gravity: Christian Mission One Century after Edinburgh 1910", *2010 Boston. The Changing Contours of World Mission and Christianity*, eds. Todd M. Johnson, Rodney L. Petersen, Gina A. Bellofato, Travis L. Myers, (Oregon: Pickwick Publications, 2012), 67-83.

Papathanasiou Athanasios N., "The Church as Mission: Fr. Alexander Schmemann's Liturgical Theology Revisited", *Proche-Orient Chrétien* 60 (2010): 6-41.

---

[38] *The Apostolic Tradition of Hippolytus* 2, 19, trans. Burton Scott Easton, (Ann Arbor: Cambridge University Press, 1962), 44.
[39] Cabasilas, op. cit., 93.
[40] Cabasilas, op. cit., 81- 83.

(14) Toward an Ecumenical Ethos in Orthodox Theology and Education

Antony C. Vrame

The ecumenical ethos of Orthodox thought manifests itself in theological education in two general, albeit not mutually exclusive, contexts. First, there is the Orthodox Christian setting: a seminary or graduate school of theology, or a university where we see Orthodox Christian instructors teaching almost exclusively Orthodox Christian students about Orthodox Christianity. In this setting, even after honoring the academic values of freedom of thought and critical inquiry, an instructor probably expects but cannot require the topic studied to have an impact on the personal and professional lives of students, ranging from making a deeper commitment to their faith tradition to shaping the skills of a minister for an Orthodox community. Second, we find non-Orthodox Christian settings, of which there can be many. These environments are ecumenical (inter-Christian), interreligious, secular, state-sponsored, religious but not Orthodox (e.g. a Roman Catholic university), or without any religious affiliation at all. In these settings, we usually find an Orthodox Christian instructor teaching mostly non-Orthodox students (perhaps with some or no Orthodox Christian students) about Orthodox Christianity. In this setting, most likely an instructor cannot expect the exposure to Orthodoxy to have a personal, transformational, experience on the student, as seen in the first setting.

In both settings, Orthodox Christianity is being taught, as His Eminence Metropolitan John D. Zizioulas argues, in a confessional manner and not as ecumenically as one might hope. As he writes, "They (Orthodox theological schools – and by extension their faculties) do not take into account, either in their curriculum or in their teaching staff, the needs of the Church as a whole but of a particular confessional Church."[1] It should be immediately noted that this is not only an Orthodox issue. The second context does add the diverse perspectives of the students as well as the culture of the educational setting, where critique and dialogue may be more appreciated or expected than in the Orthodox context that is struggling to shape the identity and agency of the student, especially for ministry in the Orthodox Church. In both settings though, Zizioulas properly points out that Orthodox Christianity is treated as a specialized subject or specialized branch of Christian thought or religious studies, without much connection to the other areas of thought or across the curriculum. For example, Church History is still taught in most places with a focus on East *or* West, not East *and* West (even as this dichotomy should have been overcome after a century of ecumenical life).

In the two contexts we see the challenge facing theology and theological education, that of fostering a mature Orthodox Christian identity and agency in students and one that engages them with the *oikoumene*. The Jewish educator Michael Rosenak asks the question quite effectively: "How *does* one really educate a young person, really *help* a young person to become loyal, disciplined by the regimen of revealed norms and, at the same time, curious, open and endowed with an expansive spirituality? What is the 'recipe' for blending piety and humility with a more-than-scholastic intelligence and faculty of criticism?"[2] The dichotomy he presents is one of education for loyalty to one's faith tradition, acceptance of its basic tenets, and observant of its practices and yet doing so in a manner that leaves the believer able to think critically about one's faith tradition, open minded to learning from one's encounter with the world, and contribute to that world. In addition, how can one "harvest" the fruits of ecumenical and inter-religious dialogues?

---

[1] John D. Zizioulas, "The Ecumenical Dimensions of Orthodox Theological Education," *The One and the Many: Studies on God, Man, the Church, and the World Today*, ed. Fr. Gregory Edwards, (Alhambra, California: Sebastian Press, 2010), 355.

[2] Michael Rosenak, *Commandments and concerns: Jewish religious education in secular society*, (Philadelphia, Pennsylvania: The Jewish Publication Society, 1987), 257.

The ecumenical ethos in Orthodox theology does offer the potential for bridging these dichotomies by transcending confessionalism and addressing the concerns of the *oikoumene*, by engaging theology dialogically, and by engaging theology critically.

The Concerns of the *Oikoumene* Transcend Confessionalism

When theology becomes self-referential and does not address the concerns of the world, the *oikoumene*, it becomes irrelevant and stagnant. The words of Christ, "I came that they may have life, and have it abundantly" (John 10:10) are strengthened when theology is life-giving and speaks to the deep issues of the contemporary person in a manner that is accessible and comprehensible.

Orthodox education is still content with demonstrating religious difference, antiquity, and peculiarity as a community. By focusing almost to an absurd extreme on confessional concerns, we leave little time for the deep concerns of the world today. This makes us appear increasingly irrelevant to the important conversations of the world and thus ill-prepared for dialogue with the other.

Theology and theological education cannot afford to neglect "the weightier matters of the law: justice and mercy and faith" (Matt. 23:23), even as the Church still must educate for the particularity of the community. Thankfully, the environmental concern of the Ecumenical Patriarchate has moved us beyond this, but there are many more concerns in our world today than even the environment. These tend to be the deep issues of faith – prayer, ascetic disciplines, justice, security and hope in a time of uncertainty and fear, peace and violence, etc. – not the "religious trivia"[3] of confessional particularity, even as colorful and interesting as it might be.

A dialogical approach

Metropolitan John D. Zizioulas writes, "Dialogue is a step further than tolerance. It involves the recognition that the other, the different, exists not simply in order to exist–that is what tolerance means–but exists as someone who has something to say to me, which I have to listen to seriously, relate to my own convictions, and judge under and in light of those convictions."[4]

One task of theological education is to present both one's own faith tradition and also the faith tradition of another accurately, in as non-judgmental attitude as one can, because no matter what our position is towards the religious other, our appropriate stance is to respect the faith commitments of the religious other. The ability to compare and contrast is central to dialogue, but dialogue and comparative religion is not the same thing.

A dialogical approach to theological education requires an openness and willingness to engage the "religious other" whether in face-to-face dialogue or in dialogue with the sources of the other's faith tradition. There are plenty of examples where meaningful dialogue has occurred for theological students: the Seminarians Interacting program of the National Council of Christians and Jews; the New Fire Movement of the National Council of Churches in Christ, USA; ecumenical consortia such as the Boston Theological Institute or the Graduate Theological Union in Berkeley, California. In Berkeley, they say "we live ecumenically," by which they mean dialogue across religious lines is a daily occurrence, from the classroom, to the library (there is just one for the entire consortium), to the faculty meeting (in addition to meetings of a particular school, faculty meet according to areas or disciplines to plan academic life).

---

[3] The sentiments of John Boojamra about Orthodox Christian education might also be applied to our theological education, "Because we have focused our attention on children, we have distorted the Church by simplifying it so it can be understood; Christian education has reduced it to facts, dates, numbers and doctrines that can be presented in a classroom in a forty-five minute period." John Boojamra, *Foundations for Orthodox Christian Education*, (Crestwood, NY: St. Vladimir's Seminary Press, 1989), 9.

[4] John D. Zizioulas, "The Orthodox Church and the Third Millennium," *The One and the Many: Studies on God, Man, the Church, and the World Today*, ed. Fr. Gregory Edwards, (Alhambra, California: Sebastian Press, 2010), 398.

A critical approach

Our educational practice cannot be content with mere repetition and transmission of religious facts and information. Information abounds. The church lives in an open environment, an open system, due to the forces of globalization and communication technology; many have called it a "flattening" effect. We can "google" the answer to just about any religious question. Because we recognize that the Church cannot control where people receive their information, the educational task must be more mindful of critical thought about that information. Learners can be taught to challenge the information they encounter and think critically about it, if for no other reason than that some information they receive is reliable and some far less so.

Critical thought has served the Church by clarifying its teachings leading to the development of the life of the Church. As Fr. Alkiviadis Calivas writes, "Critical theological reflection is essential to the church because, on the one hand, it helps preserve the identity of her message, while on the other hand it prompts the continuous progress into the inexhaustible meaning of the mystery of salvation."[5] The great thinkers of the church have always been rigorous and disciplined in their approach to matters of Faith, asking and wrestling with difficult questions, seeking accuracy and clarity, fearlessly pursuing an argument to articulate the apostolic faith. In today's information abundant era, this level of critical engagement serves to enhance theology and theological education.

Bibliography

Bouboutsis, Elias, *Singing in a Strange Land: The Ancient Future of Orthodox Pluralism,* (Brookline, Massachusetts: Holy Cross Orthodox Press, 2010).

Calivas, Alkiviadis, "Theology and Theologians: An Orthodox Perspective," in R. Peterson with N. Rourke (eds), *Theological Literacy for the Twenty-first century*, (Grand Rapids, Michigan: Eerdmans, 2002), 23-38.

Clapsis, Emmanuel (ed.), *The Orthodox Churches in a Pluralistic World: An Ecumenical Conversation,* (Geneva/Brookline, Massachusetts: WCC Publications/Holy Cross Orthodox Press, 2004).

Ford, John, "Theological Language and Ecumenical Methdology," in T. Campbell, A. Riggs, G. Stafford (eds), *Ancient Faith and American-born Churches*, (New York: Paulist Press, 2006), 15-23.

Yannoulatos, Abp. Anastasios, *Mission in Christ's Way: An Orthodox Understanding of Mission*, (Holy Cross Orthodox Press, Brookline, Massachusetts, 2010).

Zizioulas, John D. (Metropolitan of Pergamon), *The One and the Many: Studies on God, Man, the Church, and the World Today*, edited by Fr. Gregory Edwards, (Alhambra, California: Sebastian Press, 2010).

---

[5] Alkiviadis Calivas, "Theology and Theologians: An Orthodox Perspective," in R. Peterson with N. Rourke (eds), *Theological Literacy for the Twenty-first century*, (Grand Rapids, Michigan: Eerdmans, 2002), 27.

(15) HISTORICAL ROAD MAP OF ORTHODOX INVOLVEMENT IN THE ECUMENICAL MOVEMENT[1]

Georges Lemopoulos

1. 1902-1904: "Inter-Orthodox relations" and "Ecumenical Movement" belong together

In the very beginning of the 20th century, the Ecumenical Patriarch wrote letters to all heads of the (Eastern) Orthodox Churches inviting them to:

- revitalize the inter-Orthodox relations through the preparation of a Great and Holy Council of the Orthodox church;
- consider the possibility of inaugurating bi-lateral theological dialogues with Christian Churches (particularly those who had respected Orthodoxy and had not developed systematic proselytistic campaigns in predominately Orthodox lands).

These letters were written after long period of tribulations for many Orthodox Churches (most of them living in countries recently liberated from the Ottoman yoke) and after the first positive experiences of having bi-lateral theological dialogues with the Anglican and Old Catholic Churches (mid-19th century).

Orthodox Churches, in their majority, responded positively to this double invitation which marked the beginning of the Orthodox participation in the contemporary ecumenical movement.

2. A "Church-centered" proposal suggesting the formation of a "koinonia of Churches", precursor of the World Council of Churches

In 1920, the Ecumenical Patriarchate issued an Encyclical Letter "Unto the Churches of Christ Everywhere" inviting them to consider the formation of a "League (koinonia/fellowship) of Churches", just as the governments had done a few years before with the formation of the "League of Nations".

The "Missionary Movement", as well as the "Faith and Order" and "Life and Work" movements had already started, led by outstanding Church leaders and theologians. However, according to Dr. Visser't Hooft, the Encyclical of the Ecumenical Patriarchate was one of the two "Church-centered" and "Church-oriented" documents (together with an article by Archbishop Söderblom) laying the foundations for the nature and structure of the World Council of Churches. Later, the first General Secretary of the WCC wrote:

> "The Ecumenical Patriarchate (…) took an initiative which was without precedent in church history (....) The Church of Constantinople became the first church to plan for a permanent organ of fellowship and cooperation between the churches".

The Encyclical suggested two measures for the rapprochement of the Churches:

- to remove the mutual mistrust and bitterness between Churches (arising particularly from proselytism), and
- to rekindle and strengthen love among the churches, so that they do not consider one another as strangers and foreigners, but as relatives, as "fellow heirs" (*Eph.* 3:6).

---

[1] The reader of this contribution to a volume with purely academic educational purposes may be surprised that the presentation does not follow strict academic rules, but rather privileges the educational dimension. Indeed, what follows is only an introduction, an unpretentious guide, a plain list of important dates and events, a compilation of information available in many sources and many forms, offered here with the hope of facilitating the understanding of the origins, the importance, the challenges, and the prospects of Orthodox participation in the WCC. For example, there are no references in the body of the text, most of which are drawn from the rich bibliography included at the end of the presentation.

Two fundamental observations may be formulated at this point:
- in a very early stage, the Encyclical marked the determination of the Ecumenical Patriarchate (and of many other Orthodox theologians and Churches) to actively participate in the ecumenical movement;
- the Encyclical is one of the many official Orthodox documents that would accompany the WCC encouraging and/or critically assessing its activities, according to the circumstances. This spirit of the Encyclical was reflected in other documents issued by the Ecumenical Patriarchate, such as the Encyclical marking the 25th anniversary of the Council and Ecumenical Patriarch Bartholomew's speech on the occasion of the 60th anniversary of the WCC.

3. 1948: Orthodox Churches are among the founding members of the WCC

Contrary to what is normally believed, Orthodox Churches (both Eastern and Oriental) were among the founding members of the WCC and thus present in the Amsterdam Assembly. These Churches were the Ecumenical Patriarchate, the Archdiocese of the Greek Orthodox Patriarchate of Antioch in the USA, the Church of Cyprus, the Church of Greece, and the Ethiopian Orthodox Church.

It is true, however, that in 1948 an Orthodox gathering in Moscow severely criticized the new instrument of the ecumenical movement and urged those Orthodox Churches present not to participate in its membership. This meeting obviously reflected the dynamics of the political context of that time. However, it has created serious difficulties more recently, particularly when the question about the "political" or "ecclesial" reasons for Orthodox participation in the WCC was raised after the fall of the iron curtain.

4. 1950: The "ecclesiological debate" is central to the WCC- The "Toronto Statement"

Immediately after the formation of the World Council of Churches, Orthodox theologians started asking the sharpest ecclesiological questions about the new "fellowship of Churches".

Though they would constitute a tiny minority at that time, Orthodox theologians have contributed substantially to the Toronto Statement on "The Church, the Churches and the World Council of Churches: The ecclesiological significance of the World Council of Churches". To a very large extent, this document remains the foundation that allows many Orthodox to participate in the World Council of Churches, particularly because the document states and clarifies what the WCC "is" and what the WCC "is not".

The most essential points here are the fact that Orthodox theologians:
- considered very seriously the new phenomenon of divided churches committed to coming together and forming a "fellowship", and
- have deliberately decided to be part of this new "fellowship" of divided Churches, despite all their ecclesiological hesitations and obstacles.

5. 1961: Most of the Orthodox Churches join the membership of the WCC

The 3rd Assembly of the WCC marked a new beginning for Orthodox participation in the Council. After a long and careful process of building relationships in the midst of the Cold War, most of the Churches living in the then "Second World" (under the Eastern European communist regimes) joined the WCC membership.

Much later, this fact was severely criticized. Churches in the West accused the Council of compromising with the totalitarian regimes and for not speaking out loudly against violations of fundamental rights. Conservative Orthodox in these countries argued that their Church hierarchies followed the "political logic" and served the interests of their governments.

Heads of the Orthodox Churches, however, openly and on several occasions, recognized that their Churches received unique ecclesial, moral and financial support during difficult years and circumstances. Membership in the wider ecumenical family allowed their Churches to continue offering their witness and their service within their respective societies.

6. 1967: An informal theological dialogue between Eastern and Oriental Orthodox begins

For the first time after many centuries of separation, Eastern and Oriental Orthodox Churches were encouraged by the WCC to enter into a theological dialogue with the aim of clarifying their Christological teaching. Several meetings organized by "Faith and Order" paved the way for the official bi-lateral theological dialogue between the two families.

7. 1975-1981: Official bi-lateral theological dialogues are prepared and conducted

The 1st Pre-conciliar Pan-Orthodox Conference (Geneva, 1975) encouraged the (Eastern) Orthodox Churches to conduct bi-lateral theological dialogues. Soon after this decision, such dialogues with the Oriental Orthodox Churches, the Anglican Communion, the Old Catholic Church; the Lutheran World Federation, the World Alliance of Reformed Churches were inaugurated. The dialogue with the Roman Catholic Church needed more time for careful preparation and began only in 1981.

Christology was at the center of discussions between the Eastern and Oriental Orthodox; Trinitarian theology and the foundation of ecclesiology ("koinonia") was the starting point for the dialogue with the Roman Catholic Church; a full theological and ecclesiological agenda was dealt with in the dialogue with both the Anglicans and Old Catholics.

On the positive side, these theological dialogues brought ecclesial traditions closer to each other (for example, Orthodox and Lutherans and Orthodox and Reformed, as they did not have common historical roots) and allowed them to discover and affirm their common theological convictions.

From the perspective of the unfinished agendas, it was really unfortunate that the two dialogues that were successfully completed from a theological point of view (with the Old Catholics and the Oriental Orthodox) did not have any concrete ecclesial implications. Their reception posed serious problems which were not solved until today.

8. 1981: Orthodox difficulties within the WCC surface: The Sofia Consultation

As the Council began growing rapidly (in the 60s and 70s) and its worldwide ecumenical authority and influence became more and more visible, there have been some temptations to re-interpret its nature. This was coupled with an institutional/structural uneasiness of the Orthodox who gradually became aware of their "minority" situation within the Council.

The Orthodox consultation in Sofia expressed unanimity among the Orthodox in considering the WCC as a platform for theological dialogue and a tool for inter-Church cooperation. It has expressed however serious reservations about any claim for doctrinal authority or "ecclesiological" significance.

The Consultation listed a series of fundamental Orthodox concerns: ecclesiological, theological, institutional, procedural, etc.

As a result of the consultation, important corrections were made in the relationship between the WCC and the Orthodox member Churches (e.g. an article in the WCC Rules allowing member Churches to oppose whenever a voting procedure was proposed on fundamental matters of faith; participation of all Orthodox Churches in all the governing and consultative bodies of the WCC at a minimum rate of 25% etc.).

This was an early signal of what followed much later and lead to the Special Commission.

9. 1986: The WCC on the agenda of the 3rd Pre-conciliar Pan-Orthodox Conference

The implementation of the recommendations formulated in Sofia and the success of the Assembly in Vancouver (1983) offered a positive framework to the 3rd Pre-Conciliar Pan-Orthodox Conference (Geneva, 1986), which strongly reaffirmed Orthodox participation in the ecumenical movement in general and in the WCC in particular, stating that:

"Orthodox participation in the ecumenical movement does not run counter to the nature and history of the Orthodox Church. It constitutes the consistent expression of the apostolic faith within new historical conditions, in order to respond to new historical demands".

Moreover, the Conference recognized the multi-faceted ecumenical contribution of the World Council of Churches:

"The WCC, as an instrument of its member churches, does not confine itself to maintaining a multilateral dialogue within the framework of the Faith and Order Commission. Its manifold activities in the fields of evangelism, diakonia, health, theological education, interfaith dialogue, combating racism and promoting peace and justice, respond to particular needs of the churches and of the world today and provide an opportunity for common witness and action. The Orthodox Church appreciates this multidimensional activity of the WCC and fully cooperates in the above-mentioned fields, within the limits of her possibilities".

This positive assessment did not last for a long time. As radical socio-political changes occurred in Eastern Europe, affecting Church and ecumenical relations, the potential impact of this Conference was somehow lost. Instead, pertinent questions came from the Orthodox side criticizing (sometimes quite severely) the WCC.

10. 1994: "All Orthodox Churches" are now members of the WCC

In 1994, the Autocephalous Orthodox Church of Albania, a Church raised from its ashes after decades of state atheism, joined the WCC membership making it possible to state – with some sense of pride – that "now, all canonical Eastern and Oriental Orthodox Churches were members of the WCC". Indeed, the Eastern and Oriental Orthodox Churches were now the only ecclesial tradition (probably followed to some extent by the Anglican Communion) to be fully present in the WCC despite internal tensions, a variety of schools of thoughts and, even, conservative (sometimes fundamentalist) positions and streams.

11. 1998: New difficulties with Orthodox participation in the WCC

During the years that followed the fall of the Berlin Wall (1989), major changes occurred in Orthodox attitudes vis-à-vis the WCC.

Harsh questions of a broader ecumenical character emerged. The Orthodox Church of Georgia and the Orthodox Church of Bulgaria suddenly and unexpectedly withdrew from membership in the WCC, mainly in order to preserve unity and peace in the Church, very seriously threatened by pressures from fundamentalist circles. The Council of Bishops of the Russian Orthodox Church and the Holy Synod of Bishops of the Serbian Orthodox Church requested a new pan-Orthodox discussion on Orthodox participation in the WCC.

Consequently, in May 1998, representatives of Eastern Orthodox Churches gathered in Thessaloniki, Greece, to state that their churches were "no longer satisfied with the present forms of Orthodox membership in the WCC", and to ask that the structures of the WCC be "radically changed". Once again the issues raised were ecclesiological (nature of the fellowship; understanding of membership), theological (ordination of women; inclusive language; ethical issues), institutional (the predominant Protestant "ethos" of the WCC and the permanent minority situation of the Orthodox).

Recognizing the importance of this situation, the WCC Assembly in Harare (meeting a few months after Thessaloniki) responded by appointing a Special Commission on Orthodox Participation in the WCC, mandated "to make proposals concerning the necessary changes in structure, style and ethos of the Council". The nature and scope of this response prompted Dr Konrad Raiser, General Secretary of the WCC, to affirm that "never before in its fifty years of history has the WCC taken its Orthodox member churches as seriously as with this decision of the Harare assembly".

12. 2003: The Central Committee adopts the report of the Special Commission

As the Special Commission started its work, it became clear that it would be insufficient to address solely structural adjustments. The Commission saw that deeper changes in the style and ethos of the Council's work and life would require attention. Therefore the Commission addressed several issues ranging from membership and decision-making to ethical issues and common prayer.

The most important finding and affirmation of the Commission would be the following statement:

"Ecclesiological issues embrace all of the matters under the consideration of the Special Commission: response to social and ethical issues, common prayer at WCC gatherings, matters of membership and representation, as well as how decisions are made together."

And the most important challenge the Special Commission addressed to the members of the fellowship in the WCC is encapsulated in the following two questions:

"To the Orthodox: "Is there space for other churches in Orthodox ecclesiology? How would this space and its limits be described?" To the churches within the tradition of the Reformation: "How does your church understand, maintain and express your belonging to the one, holy, catholic and apostolic church?" Exploring these questions would lead to a greater clarity of how churches belonging to the fellowship of the WCC relate to each other and to the World Council. It would also invite them to reflect on the implications of including baptism in the name of the Father, Son and Holy Spirit, as a criterion for membership in the Council."

13. 2006: The 9th Assembly in Porto Allegro: A new beginning?

The 9th Assembly adopted a number of radical constitutional changes resulting from the final report of the Special Commission:
- new criteria for membership (introducing a series of theological considerations); new rules for conducting meetings (consensus method).
- the "ecclesiological challenge" will be at the very centre of all the life and work of member Churches (what is the nature of the fellowship? what is the specific character of the Council as a fellowship of Churches? etc.)

Orthodox Handbook on Ecumenism

- the "ethos of fellowship" (as embodied in the possibility for spiritual discernment offered by the consensus method) should prevail to an "institutional logic";
- consensus is a means leading to the building of a "common mind"; therefore, it is based on listening and discernment, avoiding confrontation or polarization;
- a common spiritual journey (including common prayer) is not only desirable, but constitutes the heart of our commitment to Christian unity.

14. An attempt to describe the "harvest"-a tentative assessment of Orthodox participation

Was it really important for the Orthodox to participate in the ecumenical movement and the WCC? If so, what would be the results? Here is an attempt to provide a very tentative exploratory list:
- the WCC has been both a forum for theological dialogue on Christian unity and a platform for encounter between the Orthodox Churches;
- participation in the ecumenical movement allowed Orthodox Churches to transcend all forms of isolation imposed on them by political developments;
- participation in the ecumenical movement and the WCC allowed Orthodox Churches to experience a series of renewal movements: biblical, missiological, diaconal, academic;
- encouraged by the vision of the WCC, Orthodox youth took certain initiatives and have actively participated in the above-mentioned renewal;
- the WCC very often spoke and acted on matters of peace, justice and human rights related to particular conditions in which the local Orthodox Churches involved were not free to articulate their position or to affect the situation;
- through its resource sharing mechanisms, the Council provided human and material resources for the development of educational and diaconal services of the Orthodox Churches.

The contributions of the Orthodox could also be, tentatively, listed as follows:
- Orthodox theologians reminded with persistence the centrality and importance of "ecclesiology" and participated in all efforts to find new ways and new formulations allowing Churches to articulate their unity/communion;
- Orthodox theologians offered new perspectives grounded on Trinitarian theology (the Basis of the WCC; theology of "koinonia"; theology of the Holy Spirit);
- Orthodox Churches challenged the classical western missiology of Church expansion, underlining the importance of *Missio Dei* (the aim of our mission is the glorification of God's name), of liturgical life (incorporation to a worshipping community), of culture (that has the possibility to "incarnate" the gospel);
- Orthodox theological and pastoral experience suggested very strongly the ecclesial, sacramental and spiritual dimensions of diakonia ("sacrament of the brother and sister");

There is a rich bibliography on the above mentioned points. A brief and comprehensive assessment is offered by Dr. Konrad Rasier, General Secretary of the WCC (1993-2004). According to Dr. Konrad Raiser, the most important Orthodox contribution to the WCC was the "consistent expression of the Orthodox commitment to the ecumenical fellowship of churches, which has been re-affirmed in response to questions and sometimes harsh criticism from within". And the "second major Orthodox contribution to unfolding the self-understanding of the WCC" was to establish the christocentric affirmation of its Basis (the confession of "the Lord Jesus Christ as God and Savior") in a Trinitarian setting ("to the glory of the one God, Father, Son and Holy Spirit").

Dr. Konrad Raiser also referred to other Orthodox contributions, such as the awareness of conciliarity – i.e. "the fact that the church in all times needs assemblies to represent it and has in fact felt this need" as "a fundamental dimension in the understanding of the church" –, the decisive influence of Orthodox thinking in the convergence documents on Baptism, Eucharist and Ministry – "particularly in terms of emphasis on the role of the Holy Spirit"– and the "understanding of the missionary vocation of the church as well as of its diaconal service".

Part II: Orthodoxy and Ecumenism - Foundations

15. Some questions for today and tomorrow

Looking at Orthodox participation from the perspective of the ongoing programmatic activities of the Council, it becomes obvious that any assessment of such participation in the Council's life should not be limited to program plans and activities. It should go deeper (i.e. to institutional, strategic and broader ecumenical layers). In this sense, some of the fundamental questions for today and tomorrow could be formulated as follows:

- Where are we after a few years of implementation of the main findings of the Special Commission? Is an evaluation needed?
- How do we make sure that Orthodox Churches and their theologians actively participate in key debates/ processes (e.g. on ecclesiology; mission; ecumenism in the 21st century; spirituality and common prayer, etc.) and that their voice is heard and seriously taken into consideration?
- How could Orthodox theologians contribute to a motivating and assembling discourse (in French, "un discours mobilisateur") for the ecumenical movement in general and the WCC in particular?
- What would be the specific Orthodox contribution to the dialogue of religions (particularly today, as a natural continuation of the ground-breaking reflections by Orthodox Church leaders and theologians in the past decades)?
- How do we convince, encourage and assist some Orthodox Churches who seem to gradually lose their interest in the activities of the Council? The phenomenon of decreasing interest in the ecumenical movement is not limited to the Orthodox Churches. Yet, it is important to look at it from an Orthodox perspective by taking into consideration the precious legacy of Orthodox initiatives and leadership within the movement.
- How do we assist Orthodox Churches in their efforts to face internal pressures from conservative/ fundamentalist circles? Rising fundamentalism, as a consequence of both ecclesial and socio-political developments, is a fact. Orthodox Churches are facing this challenge to a very large extent. It is important though to re-articulate the fundamental principles of Orthodox commitment to the ecumenical movement and pay particular attention to the proper education and preparation of, particularly, the younger generations.
- How do Orthodox Churches assess new ecumenical initiatives (e.g. the Global Christian Forum)?
- What is the attitude/assessment of Orthodox Churches with regard to new ecumenical instruments (ENI, EAA, ACT, etc.)?

These questions are important for the future of the ecumenical movement and the WCC. They are closely related to an ongoing reflection process, more specifically to *ecumenism in the 21st century*. All the questions could be turned around and addressed to other church and confessional families participating in the ecumenical movement and in the WCC. Therefore, an intense dialogue on some of them could be beneficial.

Bibliography

Amba Bishoy, Metropolitan of Damiette, "Common prayer in WCC meetings", *The Ecumenical Review* 54.1-2 (2002): 38ff.

Bartholomew, His All Holiness Ecumenical Patriarch, *Homily at the 60th anniversary of the World Council of Churches*, Geneva: St Peter's Cathedral, 2008. In: http://www.oikoumene.org/en/resources/documents/central-committee/geneva-2008/reports-and-documents/homily-by-the-ecumenical-patriarch-hah-bartholomew.html (last accessed September 2013)

Basdekis Athanasios (Hrsg.), *Orthodox Kirche und Oekumenische Bewegung. Dokumente – Erklärungen – Berichte 1900-2006*, (Frankfurt: Lembeck/Bonifatius, 2006).

Fitzgerald Thomas & Bouteneff Peter, *Turn to God, Rejoice in Hope -- Orthodox Reflections on the Way to Harare*, (WCC-Orthodox Task Force, 1988).

Florovsky G., "The Orthodox Church and the World Council of Churches" *St Vladimir's Seminary Quarterly* 2 (1954): 111-118.

Lemopoulos George (editor), *The Ecumenical Movement, the Churches and the World Council of Churches: an Orthodox contribution to the reflection process on "The common understanding and vision of the WCC"*, (Geneva: Orthodox Centre of the Ecumenical Patriarchate, 1995).

Limouris Gennadios (editor), *Orthodox vision of ecumenism: statements, messages and reports on the Ecumenical Movement, 1902-1992*, (Geneva: WCC, 1994).

Nikodim of Leningrad, "The Russian Orthodox and the Ecumenical Movement", *The Ecumenical Review* 21(1969): 116-119.

Nissiotis N. A., "The ecclesiological significance of inter-church diakonia", *The Ecumenical Review* 13.2 (1961): 191-202.

Raiser Konrad, *The importance of the Orthodox contribution to the WCC*, http://www.oikoumene.org/en/resources/documents/wcc-programmes/ecumenical-movement-in-the-21st-century/member-churches/special-commission-on-participation-of-orthodox-churches/03-06-03-orthodox-contribution-to-the-wcc.html (last accessed September 2013)

Sabev Todor, *The Sofia Consultation – Orthodox Involvement in the World Council of Churches*, (Geneva: WCC,1982).

Tsetsis Georges, "Amsterdam 1948: the Meaning of the Orthodox presence", *The Ecumenical Review* 40.3-4 (1988): 440-445.

W.A. Visser't Hooft, *The Genesis and Formation of the WCC*, (Geneva: WCC,1972).

Zernov N., "The Eastern Churches and the Ecumenical Movement in the 20th Century", Rouse-Neill (ed.), *A History of the Ecumenical Movement*, (London, 1967), 645-674.

(16) ORTHODOX PARTICIPATION IN THE ECUMENICAL MOVEMENT – A DETAILED HISTORICAL SURVEY

Stylianos C. Tsompanidis

1) The Orthodox participation and contribution to the ecumenical movement - a first approach for the understanding of the reason and extent of involvement

The main event and a characteristic mark of the history of the Church in the 20th century is the genesis and the evolution of the ecumenical movement. Although the second millennium of Christianity was colored by division, it ends with an optimistic and hopeful perspective related to ecumenical efforts for its overcoming. The modern ecumenical movement is the practical desire for finding opportunities to know each other better, for mutual cooperation despite theological differences, and for strengthening the common faith and mutual witness of the Christian truth in the modern world.

The history of the modern Ecumenical Movement and specifically the history and the background of its worldwide and regional institutions, the World Council of Churches (WCC) and the Conference of European Churches (CEC), are deeply connected to Orthodox Churches. The Orthodox Churches felt right from the start, in the midst of rapid sociopolitical changes and crisis, the necessity for the unity of the churches and their mutual testimony in a world that looked in a new direction. The Orthodox Churches contributed decisively to the creation of the ecumenical movement, firstly with the formation of the movements of "Life and Work" and "Faith and Order" which led to the formation of the WCC.[1]

In the beginning of the 20th century, Orthodoxy enters the scene of the ecumenical movement with a direct and effective action: in 1902 and in 1904 the Ecumenical Patriarch of Constantinople Joachim III sent Encyclicals[2] to the heads of the autocephalous Orthodox Churches. His specific emphasis is on the need of promoting the unity of the Orthodox Churches and dialogue with the Roman Catholic Church, the Oriental Orthodox Churches and Protestantism. The importance of those letters is significant. From the Orthodox point of view these are the first official documents which talk about the importance of strengthening the connection between the Orthodox Churches and their relations, and to enlarge them into a wider ecumenical perspective related to the rest of the Christian churches. They express with intensity the Orthodox concern for the unity of the world and its progress in the Christian life.

The decision of the Russian Church Synod in 1918 to create a "section for the unification of churches" with the following foundation was critical: "The Council of the Orthodox Church of Russia, which shall meet under those difficult circumstances for all the Christian church, would be responsible before history, if it didn't put forth the issue of the unification of Christian churches and if it didn't direct this matter according to the circumstances."[3] The Russian Church also supported ecumenism according to its experience from dialogues with Anglicans and Old Catholics since the 19th century and its involvement in the movement "Faith and Order",

---

[1] The most specific and original study on this issue is the doctoral thesis of G. Tsetsis, *The Contribution of the Ecumenical Patriarchate in the formation of the World Council of Churches* (Katerini: Tertios, 1988) (in Greek). See also N. Zernov, "The Eastern Churches and the Ecumenical Movement in the Twentieth Century", in: *A History of the Ecumenical Movement 1517-1948*, R. Rouse – St. C. Neil (eds.), vol. 1, (Geneva: WCC, 1986), 645-674.

[2] See "Patriarchal and Synodical Encyclical of 1902" and "Response to the reactions of the Local Orthodox Churches", in: G. Limouris (ed.), *Orthodox Visions of Ecumenism: Statements, Messages and Reports on the Ecumenical Movement, 1902-1992*, (Geneva: WCC, 1994), 1-5 and 5-8.

[3] It is referred according to V. Borovoj, "Die Russische Orthodoxe Kirche und der Ökumenische Rat der Kirchen", H. Vorster (Hgr.), *Ökumene lohnt sich*, (Beiheft zur Ökumenischen Rundschau 68), (Frankfurt: Lembeck, 1998), 286.

when it made its first steps. Because of the circumstances which were created after the Russian Revolution, the initiatives of the Russian Church were drowned in the making.

A "milestone" of the history of the Ecumenical movement and a "limited expression of Orthodox ecumenism" is the initiative which the Ecumenical Patriarchate took in 1920 which came as a consequence of the last two letters from Joachim III. Even before the complete formation of the two Worldwide Movements of the Ecumenical Movement, the Patriarchate of Constantinople addressed a Synodical Encyclical called "Unto the Churches of Christ everywhere."[4] It asked all of them to overcome the spirit of disbelief and to show the power of love by creating a "League of Churches" similar to the "League of Nations" which has just been formed.[5] The Encyclical points out that, despite existing doctrinal differences, it is possible to have a rapprochement between the churches and society, specifically in social and moral matters "for the preparation and advancement of that blessed Union."[6]

The importance of the Letter of the Ecumenical Patriarchate in 1920 in boosting Orthodox Churches was so great that it was compared to the importance of the World Missionary Conference for the Protestants in Edinburgh in 1910.[7] Therefore it was known as "the constituting treaty of the participation of Orthodoxy in the ecumenical movement". It is also important for the ecumenical movement as a whole. It gave all churches a plan, perfect in theory and applicable in practice, for the course of the relations and the cooperation between churches. Many of the articles of this plan were implemented only later. The first General Secretary and historian of the WCC, Visser't Hooft, complimenting the initiative of the Ecumenical Patriarchate, mentioned that the Church of Constantinople formed a great principle when he said that the cooperation of the churches in practical matters must not be postponed until the complete dogmatic agreement, but also that this cooperation would prepare the road to such a reunification. This principle was one of the basic prerequisites of the ecumenical movement, Visser't Hooft said.[8]

This statement did not mean that the Orthodox Church refused to discuss dogmatic matters. Since the World Conference of the Movement "Faith and Order" in Lausanne (1927) special emphasis was given to theological discussions which took place. However, agreement on dogmatic matters was not yet possible at this early stage of the ecumenical movement. Therefore it was a realistic position and strategy to focus on cooperation in practical matters, so that the churches would not stay in conflict caused by endless discussions about the matter of unification, while pressing matters of people in real life situations and ethical challenges required direct, coordinated inter-Christian intervention and cooperation at this point in time.

In the next two decades, the Orthodox Church was successfully able to monitor developments, to participate actively in the formation of the precursor movements of WCC, to participate efficiently in them and, finally, to contribute to the creation of the WCC itself. Orthodox hierarchs, priests and university professors such as Metropolitan of Thyateira Germanos (Strenopoulos), Archbishop of Sofia Stefan, Bishop Novi Sad Irenei, Chrysostomos Papadopoulos (later Archbishop of Athens), Leo Zander, Georges Florovsky, Stefan Zankov, Hamilkar Alivisatos, Constantinos Dyovouniotis, Dimitrios Balanos, and Sergei Boulgakov played major roles and are considered founders of the Ecumenical Movement.

The Orthodox participation during the first years, when the ecumenical movement was in its first steps, was taking place under a unique set of historical circumstances (destruction of Asia Minor, migration of huge pop-

---

[4] See "Encyclical of the Ecumenical Patriarchate, 1920", in: G. Limouris (ed.), *Orthodox Visions of Ecumenism*, 9-11. For the ecclesiastical , political and social frame of the circular see. G. Tsetsis, *The Contribution of the Ecumenical Patriarchate*, 73f.

[5] "Encyclical of the Ecumenical Patriarchate, 1920", 11.

[6] Ibid., 9.

[7] See, J. Oeldemann, *Orthodoxe Kirchen im Ökumenischen Dialog. Positionen, Probleme, Perspektiven*, (Paderborn: Bonifatius, 2004), 19.

[8] See V. Stavridis – Ev. Varella, *History of the Ecumenical Movement*, (Analecta Vlatadon 47), (Thessaloniki: Patriarchal Institute of Patristic Studies, 1996) (in Greek). Cf. WCC, *Minutes and reports of the Twelfth Meeting of the Central Committee, Rhodes, Ceece, August 19-27, 1959*, (Geneva, 1959), 95-97.

Part II: Orthodoxy and Ecumenism - Foundations

ulations after the Lausanne Treaty 1923, Russian Revolution). Despite all the difficulties the positive presence of the Orthodox Churches in the ecumenical movement was not incidental nor was it driven by any "church politic". It was the natural result of the ecumenical spirit which describes itself and stems from the saying and unbreakable rule of Christ "that all may be one", as well as its unshakeable belief that the supreme goal of the divine Economy is the unification of all by Christ, the consummation of the whole creation. It is the vision "for the union of all" for which the Orthodox Church prays incessantly for centuries now.

The achievements of the first decades of the formation and development of the ecumenical movement, which were deeply influenced by Orthodox contributions, still form the character and the profile of the ecumenical movement. Maybe the greatest of all these is the formation of an appropriate ecumenical climate and a related state of mind which is interested in mutual understanding and cooperation.

The history of the ecumenical effort as it unfolded within the series of General Assemblies of the WCC is a common history. The Orthodox participation in the common course of Christians was declared right and appropriate from the very start. The spirit of freedom and genuine universality of the Orthodox Church helped it to "overlook" what existed outside of Orthodoxy in terms of strength and life of Christianity and allowed it not to follow the initial negative stance and politics of "non possumus" of the Roman Catholic Church. Therefore, Orthodox Churches followed a course of humility and acquiescence and showed a willingness for cooperation and dialogue. En route the Orthodox opinions and positions were expressed *from within* and they can easily be tracked in the reports of the General Assemblies. Based on the spirit of catholicity and opposed to the "long addiction of division", Orthodoxy desired to be inside the Ecumenical Movement and the WCC, but maintained a continuous reminder that every common act and witness within the ecumenical fellowship should remain to be inspired by the basic goal of the churches in the ecumenical fellowship, to rediscover the apostolic tradition and to return to the simplicity and completeness of Christian faith, in order to conform in harmony with all which was believed everywhere, always and by everyone ("id tenemus quod ubique, quod semper, quod ab omnibus creditum est").[9]

The Orthodox representatives at the 3rd General Assembly of WCC in New Delhi 1961 declared, in a critical tone, that they understood the ecumenical movement as *"ecumenism in time"* (a fundamental thesis of G. Florovsky), in contrast to the perception of Protestant partners which emphasized ecumenism as *"ecumenism in space"*, in other words the effort which intends an agreement between the Christian confessions as they exist now. In the text they have tabled as a "Contribution" the dialogue concerning the unification of Church in underlining: "The immediate objective of the ecumenical search is, according to the Orthodox understanding, a reintegration of the Christian mind, a recovery of apostolic tradition, a fullness of Christian vision and belief, in agreement with all ages".[10]

This was the perception of the Orthodox since the first time at the 1st World Conference of the Movement "Faith and Order" in Lausanne 1927, stating that "reunion can take place only on the basis of the common faith and confession of the ancient, undivided Church…"[11]

The "Contribution" of the Orthodox ended with the confirmation that the Orthodox Church was willing to participate in this common ecumenical effort, as authority and witness preserving the treasure of apostolic faith and church tradition unchanged.[12] The willingness for cooperation was expressed by the Orthodox in their important Statements during the 2nd General Assembly as well as in the 3rd worldwide Conference of "Faith and Order" at Lund 1952. In the latter they urge: "Let us all be brothers in Christ and work and pray together for unity and show to unbelievers everywhere that Christianity is the religion of love…"[13]

---

[9] See for instance what Ham. Alivisatos writes in: "On the nature of the Church from an orthodox view", *Theologia* 21 (1950): 34, 35 (in Greek) · Cf. G. Tsetsis, "The Meaning of the Orthodox Presence", *Ecumenical Review* 40 (1988): 440-445.

[10] "Third Assembly of the World Council of Churches", in G. Limouris (ed.), *Orthodox Visions of Ecumenism*, 31.

[11] "First World Conference on Faith and Order, Lausanne, Switzerland, 1927", in G. Limouris (ed.), *Orthodox Visions of Ecumenism*, 13.

[12] "Third Assembly of the World Council of Churches", in G. Limouris (ed.), *Orthodox Visions of Ecumenism*, 31.

[13] "Third World Conference on Faith and Order, Lund, Sweden, 1952", in G. Limouris (ed.), *Orthodox Visions of Ecumenism*, 25.

At this point a clarification is necessary. When the Orthodox talk about returning to a common tradition of the undivided Church, they do not mean this from a denominational point of view. They don't support an "ecumenical theology of return". Orthodox theologians had underlined this during the WCC Assembly in New Delhi where in their text "Contribution" it reads: "No static restoration of old forms is anticipated, but rather a dynamic recovery of the perennial ethos, which alone can secure the true agreement 'of all ages'."[14]

However, what should always come first for the Orthodox is the creation of an "atmosphere of patience" - the greatest and most promising "ecumenical virtue" according to Alivisatos and Florovsky. First of all, the development of friendship and the removal of ignorance, misunderstanding, and acrimony was of great importance along with the cooperation of Christian churches in moral, educational, social and political matters and issues related to the impact of the Gospel on people. "When this would take place" – Hamilkar Alivisatos one of the initiators of ecumenical movement, said – "two thirds of the word for the unification, which depends on human thoughts has already been made. The rest is in the hands of God, and He will look ahead for it."[15] This proved to be a very realistic statement and method, which has been fruitful after all those years of dialogue and the creation of an atmosphere of trust and patience.[16]

Progressively, the Orthodox participation in the ecumenical movement and in the life of the WCC increased. The influence of the Orthodox Churches became more powerful, valuable and creative with the highlight of the 6th General Assembly in Vancouver in 1983. Many times, it forced the Council to change its course.[17]

After the "crisis" of the relationship of the Orthodox Church towards the WCC in the 90's, the overall work of the General Assemblies in Harare (1998) and in Porto Alegre (2006) was related to the renewal of the institutional operations of the Council and the adjustment of its future activities, which were connected with the search for the meaning of the nature and the purpose of Church confronting the challenges of globalization. Specifically, modifications made during the 9th General Assembly at Porto Alegre relating to the process of decision making in the Council and the definition of criteria during the process of adding new members to the WCC, has created a new base not just for the unconditional participation of the Orthodox Churches in the ecumenical movement, but also for a substantial upgrade of their role in the WCC.[18]

Through the different phases of the history of the Council, Orthodox Churches have developed a comprehensive perception of the effort for Christian unity as well as of common witness for justice, peace, human rights and the integrity of creation.[19] According to this understanding, unity and witness, church and people, spiritual and missionary social dimension, history and eschatology, liturgy and diakonia are closely connected.

Besides some prejudices which have come up from time to time, Orthodox Churches have contributed to a deepened perception of Christian universalism, contributing to a wider perspective of the ecumenical mission and the presence and witness of churches of the world. Orthodox contributions have led to the substantial

[14] "Third Assembly of the World Council of Churches", in G. Limouris (ed.), *Orthodox Visions of Ecumenism*, 31.

[15] Ham. Alivizatos "The Greek Orthodox Church's unbroken continuation with the undivided Church" *Ekklesiastikos Pharos* 33 (1934), 425 (in Greek).

[16] Cf. my *"For the union of all"* - *The Contribution of the Orthodox Church and Theology to the World Council of Churches* (in Greek) with foreword by Alexandros K. Papaderos, (Thessaloniki: Pournaras, 2008), ch. C.

[17] See G. Lemopoulos, *Structure and Function of WCC. Descriptive exposition of its legislative, administrative, consultative and executive bodies with reference to the role of the Orthodox Churches,* (Thessaloniki: Pournaras, 2012) esp. 165ff (in Greek).

[18] See Metropolitan Ignatios of Dimitrias, "Report on the 9th General Assembly of the World Council of Churches (WCC)" (in Greek) and Vl. Pheidas, "The Orthodox Church and the 9th General Assembly of WCC", *Ekklesia* 83 (2006): 361-364 and 457-461(in Greek).

[19] More on this in S. Tsompanidis, *Orthodoxie und Ökumene: Gemeinsam auf dem Weg zu Gerechtigkeit, Frieden und Bewahrung der Schöpfung.* Mit einem Vorwort von Ulrich Duchrow, (Ökumenische Studie 10), (Münster/Hamburg/London, Lit, 1999).

Part II: Orthodoxy and Ecumenism - Foundations

renewal of a trinitarian theology, to the perception that the unity of the church is founded in the koinonia of a triune God, and to a new discovery of conciliarity and conciliar forms of life in the understanding of the ecumenical fellowship of churches. Orthodox contributions have also emphasized the central place that the Eucharistic communion has for dialogue, a Eucharistic cosmic perception of life and the consequent formation of an ecologically sensitive theology of creation, as well as an understanding of diakonia and social engagement as "liturgy after the Liturgy."[20]

Crucial insights based on a holistic approach for a common ecumenical vocation and on the Eucharist, have informed and inspired two inter-Orthodox meetings: The Inter-Orthodox Consultation on "The Ecumenical nature of the Orthodox witness"[21] at the New Valamo Monastery in Finland 1977 and the Inter-Orthodox Consultation on "An Orthodox Approach to Diakonia"[22] in the Orthodox Academy of Crete 1978. These Consultations realize and formulate the completeness, consistency and integrity of the ecumenical calling and vocation, which goes beyond all the divisions and polarizations between vertical and horizontal dimensions, Divine Liturgy and social responsibility or other polarities. It is necessary to mention the conclusion of the Crete Consultation: "Christian diakonia is not an optional action, duty or moral stance in relation to the needy, additional to our community in Christ, but an indispensable expression of that community, which has its source in the Eucharistic and liturgical life of the church. It is a 'liturgy after the liturgy', and it is in this sense that diakonia is described as a judgement upon our history (Mt 25:31-46)."[23]

The recognition of the meaning of the liturgical experience, of sacraments and Eucharist for the identity, the unity, the witness and the social involvement of the Church, led the WCC during the General Assembly in Vancouver (1983) to express a "Eucharistic Vision"[24] for the unity of the Church and humanity. The "Eucharistic approach" is the most visible and the most valuable contribution of the Orthodox Church to the Ecumenical Movement. Many, such as Konrad Raiser, Margot Käßmann, Martin Robra, Ulrich Duchrow, have recognized that the "Eucharistic vision" in which unity and social and moral responsibility of the Church are connected, is a "gift" of the Orthodox Church to the ecumenical movement.[25] Henceforth, the motivations from the Orthodox Churches will remain an unbreakable part of theological thinking of the WCC. Reminding everybody of the relevance of the tradition of the first church is and remains a crucial contribution and correcting element for the ecumenical movement. This contribution of the Orthodox Church is due to the theological work of people like Nikos Nissiotis, Vitaly Borovoy, Metropolitan John (Zizioulas) of Pergamon, Archbishop of Albania Anastasios, Ion Bria, Georges Tsetsis, Alexandros Papaderos, Georges Lemopoulos.

[20] For the origin of the term and the contribution of Anastasios Yannoulatos (now Archbishop of Albania), Fr. Ion Bria and Al. Papaderos see by Tsompanidis, *Orthodoxie und Ökumene*, 169-183.
[21] The report and the contributions of this important Consultation at the New Valamo Monastery see in: *The New Valamo Consultation. The Ecumenical nature of the Orthodox witness*, (ed.) (Geneva: WCC/Orthodox Task Force, 1977). See also "Report of an Inter-Orthodox Consultation 'The Ecumenical Nature of the Orthodox Witness', New Valamo, Finland, 24-30 September 1977", in G. Limouris (ed.), *Orthodox Visions of Ecumenism*, 66-69.
[22] See "Report from the Work Groups of an Inter-orthodox Consultation 'An Orthodox Approach to Diakonia', Chania, Crete, 20-25 November 1978", in G. Limouris (ed.), *Orthodox Visions of Ecumenism*, op. cit, 70.
[23] See David Gill (ed.), *Gathered for Life. Official Report of the Sixth Assembly of the World Council of Churches*, (Geneva, WCC, 1983), 44f. More on the Orthodox contribution to this issue and its ecumenical significance see S. Tsompanidis, *Orthodoxie und Ökumene and Margot Käßmann, Die Eucharistische Vision. Armut und Reichtum als Anfrage an die Einheit der Kirche in der Diskussion des Ökumenischen Rates* (München / Mainz, 1992).
[24] See for instance: WCC, CUV document 2.4.: http://www.oikoumene.org/en/resources/documents/assembly/2006-porto-alegre/3-preparatory-and-background-documents/common-understanding-and-vision-of-the-wcc-cuv
[25] See for instance the lecture by Rev. Dr Konrad Raiser at an international symposium in Thessaloniki, Greece, 1-3 June 2003, idem, "The importance of the Orthodox contribution to the WCC" (in Greek), in: P. Vassiliadis (ed.), *Orthodox Theology and Ecumenical Dialogue*, (Athens: Apostoliki Diakonia, 2005), 32-54, 44ff. In English http://orthodoxeurope.org/page/7/4/1.aspx [last accessed on 04-06-12] and in site of the WCC.

Orthodox Handbook on Ecumenism

2) The ecclesiastical and theological basis of the participation of the Orthodox Church in the ecumenical movement - deepening the reason for and the extent of ecumenical participation

Until now we referred to the presence and the participation of the Orthodox Movement in the World Council of Churches, their contributions to the foundation and then to the formation of the WCC. The reasons to what extent and for what purpose Orthodox churches participate in the ecumenical movement and efforts for the rehabilitation of the unity of Christians were reasonably clear according to has been mentioned before. Nevertheless, some crucial questions need further explanation, particularly those related to the self-understanding of the Orthodox Church and its relationship to other Christian or non-Christian communities which defined themselves as churches. The perception of other Christian churches within Orthodox ecclesial self-understanding is one of the most sensitive and difficult matters. It affects also the way in which Orthodox Churches are actually related to other Christian churches, the understanding of the goal of the ecumenical movement, and Orthodox participation in it.

Even today there is not a single and unanimous answer from Orthodox Churches concerning the question of the ecclesiastical heterodox communities, and no clear answer is given whether they are recognized as churches or not. Here the answer is really difficult, as there is a wide range of different answers from the Orthodox point of view.[26] Although almost all of the Orthodox agree on the basic points of ecclesiology, they do not completely agree on everything which has to do with the practical consequences of Orthodox teachings.[27] In this sense, the Special Commission of the WCC concerning the Orthodox participation at the WCC touches the ecclesiological nerve when it addresses the question: *"Is there space for other churches in the Orthodox ecclesiology? How can this space and its limits be described?"*[28] The answer to this question is of decisive importance for the progress of ecumenical dialogue in the future. Already the history of the ecumenical movement has shown that the participation of the Orthodox Church in the ecumenical dialogue has contributed to the refinement of the Orthodox position and has led to a certain Pan-Orthodox agreement.

The following attitude prevailed in the Orthodox Church concerning their attitude to other Christian communities. We first mention the general characteristics of this attitude and then analyze more specifically some of the crucial texts.[29]

The Orthodox Church, according to its self-consciousness, is the bearer of the faith and tradition of the one, holy, catholic and apostolic church of Christ. On the other hand it also admits the reality of the existence of other churches and confessions in the life of Christianity. This double acceptance and recognition helps to define what Orthodoxy is for others and what other Christian communities are for Orthodoxy; it allows Orthodoxy to define its position and stance towards the other churches. The recognition of the ontological and historical existence of other churches does not mean either acceptance of the dogmatic teachings of the churches or a way to confirm their teaching. This particular point has been clearly mentioned in the statement of Toronto (1950). Recognition of each other means and presupposes that there is not a hostile tension between different ecclesial speakers and at the same time that the speakers are equals. This equality is not considered as being in possession of the same truth, but in the same position of receptivity which all the speakers share in terms of being open to the same life and the possession of truth.[30]

---

[26] Overview of the debate among Orthodox theologians about the position of the other churches in the Orthodox self-consciousness see in Emm. Clapsis, *Orthodoxy in Conversation – Orthodox Ecumenical Engagements,* (Geneva / Brookline: WCC, 2000), 1-10 and 114-126.

[27] Kallistos Ware, *The Orthodox Church,* (Athens: Akritas, 1996) (in Greek), 485.

[28] Section B, para. 16 (author's emphasis).

[29] For the following paragraphs see my studies *"For the union of all" - The Contribution*, 213-234. S. Tsompanidis, "The Church and the churches in the ecumenical movement", *International journal for the Study of the Christian Church* 12 (2012): 148-163.

[30] See the very important remarks of N. Matsoukas, *Ecumenical Movement: History – Theology,* (Thessaloniki: Pournaras, 2003), 13f (in Greek).

The main feature of the definition of the stance of the Orthodox Church is its willingness to sustain its openness for cooperation, understanding and continuous dialogue. That is why it participated from the start in the ecumenical movement and contributed in its formation and evolution. The Orthodox Church never abandoned dialogue or suggested a way of mere disinterested coexistence, of conflict or of assimilation or merger and absorption of other churches.

The double admission, that the Orthodox Church is both the one, holy, catholic and apostolic Church of Christ and that it recognizes the ontological existence of other churches, moves in the dialectic of the austerity of *akribeia* and the sensitivity of *oikonomia*, a distinction of Church boundaries according to canonical and charismatic understandings which do not always coincide.[31] Even when - according to the Statement of Toronto - it does not recognize some churches or acknowledge them as churches in the complete meaning of the word, it does not remove them from dialogue. On the other hand, Orthodoxy insists on conversation with the objective of following and shaping the course towards unity. Therefore Orthodoxy continues to emphasize the understanding of the ecumenical movement as a movement in search of the "other".[32]

The Orthodox believe that they represent the one and only church, but they do not raise the Orthodox Church as a judge on the ecclesial identity or on of the rest of Christian communities. This is expressed with the following famous statement of the Orthodox Church: "We know where the church is, but we don't have the power to judge and to nominate where church isn't".

All the above are responsible positions of the Orthodox Church concerning the nature of the Orthodox participation in the ecumenical movement and its primary instrument, the WCC, which are formulated in formal ecclesiastical documents, encyclicals, proclamations, messages, statements, These and Pan-Orthodox texts provide a clear testimony and clarification of faith, self-consciousness and its relation with other Christian churches and communities.

Even in the beginning, from the World Conference of "Faith and Order" (1927) to the General Assembly in New Delhi, the Orthodox articulated separate statements expressing, from time to time, their reservations for the decisions and theological statements of the ecumenical meetings especially in the World Conference of "Faith and Order" in Lund 1952 and in the 2nd General Assembly in Evanston 1954: "*We would not pass judgment upon those of the separated communions*"[33] and "*We do not come to criticize other Churches* but to help them, to illumine their mind in a brotherly manner by informing them about the teaching of the One, Holy, Catholic, and Apostolic Church which is the Greek Orthodox Church, unchanged since the apostolic era."[34]

In this era, the influence and impact of G. Florovsky is obvious, who once said: "In no way am I willing to set someone 'outside of the church'. The 'judgment' was given to the Son. No one was appointed to forestall His judgment."[35] It still is one issue to reflect about a Christian community in terms of whether it has the proper features of the church in its full meaning, and quite another issue to remove this Christian community from the very meaning of being "church".

The recognition of the existential reality and identity of other Christian churches is the basis for the participation of the Orthodox Church in the ecumenical movement.

That is the spirit which was expressed in a unanimous statement the Third Pre-conciliar Pan-Orthodox Conference in Chambésy /Geneva in 1986 examining the subject "Relations of the Orthodox Church towards

---

[31] On this crucial issue see the important article of G. Florovsky, "The Boundaries of the Church", in: G. Florovsky, *Ecumenism I: A Doctrinal Approach*, (Collected Works, Volume XIII), (Vaduz/Belmond Mass: Buchervertriebsanstalt, 1989), 36-45.

[32] Cf. Al. Papaderos, *Ecumenism: Call and Challenge* (in Greek), (Chania, 1984), 45 and N. Matsoukas, "Ecumenicity of Orthodoxy", *Scholarly Annual of the Theological School of Thessaloniki* 8 (1998): 286 (in Greek).

[33] "Second Assembly of the World Council of churches, Evanston, USA, 1954", in G. Limouris (ed.), *Orthodox Visions of Ecumenism, 29*, b) 3 (author's emphasis).

[34] "Third World Conference on Faith and Order, Lund, Sweden, 1952", in G. Limouris (ed.), *Orthodox Visions of Ecumenism*, 25 (author's emphasis).

[35] G. Florovsky, "'Inter-Communio': Confessional Loyalty in the Ecumenical Movement", G. Florovsky, *Issues of Orthodox Theology*, (Athens: Artos Zoes, 1989), 211-220, 220 (in Greek).

the rest of Christianity". This document is, until today, the most official and important position articulated on a Pan-Orthodox level considering the matter of the relations between Orthodox and other Christian churches. The Third Pre-conciliar Pan-Orthodox Conference said: "The Orthodox Church, which is the one, holy, catholic and apostolic Church, *is fully aware of its responsibility for the unity of the Christian world, recognizes the real existence of all Christian churches and confessions*, but also believes that all the relationships which it maintains with them must be founded on the quickest and most objective clarification possible of the whole ecclesiological question."[36]

From the very beginning of the ecumenical movement the Orthodox have defined their position starting from the basis that the undeniable reality of the existence of the other churches cannot be ignored. This is what the Letters of the Ecumenical Patriarchate witnessed to in the early 20th century which were mentioned above.

In the same sense, it was Metropolitan of Leningrad Nikodim, who during the decade of the 60s explained the reasons which forced the Church of Russia to be a member of WCC: He said that this was the result of brotherly love, which does not tolerate divisions between Christians, and also the need to coordinate the efforts of all the Christian churches in the common work of the diakonia of humanity.[37]

One of the most clear theological and ecclesiastical foundations of the Orthodox participation in the ecumenical movement is the report of the Inter-Orthodox Consultation in New Valamo of Finland in 1977, which dealt with the subject "The ecumenical nature of the Orthodox witness". The report underlines: "… the participation of the Orthodox in the ecumenical movement of today is not, in principle, a revolution in the history of Orthodoxy, but it is a natural consequence of the constant prayer of the church 'for the union of all'. It constitutes another attempt, like those made in the Patristic period, to apply the apostolic faith to new historical situations and existential demands. What is in a sense new today, is the fact that this attempt is being made together with other Christian bodies with whom there is no full unity. It is here that the difficulties arise, but it is precisely here that there also are many signs of real hope for growing fellowship, understanding and cooperation."[38]

This documentation of the ecumenical character of the Orthodox gained value and weight with the decisions of the Third Pre-Conciliar Pan-Orthodox Conference in Chambésy 1986, which not only ratified the above, but also moved to further clarifications concerning the motives and the nature of the participation of the Orthodox Churches in the ecumenical movement and its institution. The text on "The Orthodox Church and the Ecumenical Movement" says in an official and clear way:

> "The Orthodox Church, in her profound conviction and ecclesiastical consciousness of being the bearer of and witness to the faith and tradition of the One, Holy, Catholic and Apostolic Church, firmly believes that she occupies a central place in matters relating to the promotion of Christian unity within the contemporary world…The Orthodox Church has always sought to draw the different Christian Churches and Confessions into a joint pilgrimage aiming at searching the lost unity of Christians, so that all might reach the unity of faith. The Orthodox Church, which unceasingly prays 'for the union of all', has taken part in the ecumenical movement since its inception and has contributed to its formation and further development. In fact, the Orthodox Church, due to the ecumenical spirit by which she is distinguished, has, through history, fought for the restoration of Christian unity. Therefore, the Orthodox participation in the ecumenical movement does not run counter to the nature and history of the Orthodox Church. It constitutes the consistent expression of the apostolic faith within new historical conditions, in order to respond to new existential demands…This many-faceted ecumenical activity derives from the sense of responsibility and from

---

[36] See "Relations of the Orthodox Church with the Whole Christian World" *Episkepsis* 17.369 (1986): 9 (in Greek), (author's emphasis).

[37] See. Metropolitan Nikodim, "The Russian Orthodox Church and the Ecumenical Movement", *ER* 21 (1969): 116-129 and G. Limouris (ed.), *Orthodox Visions of Ecumenism*, 40-49.

[38] "Report of an Inter-Orthodox Consultation 'The Ecumenical Nature…'", in G. Limouris (ed.), *Orthodox Visions of Ecumenism,* esp. 68.

the conviction that coexistence, mutual understanding, cooperation and common efforts towards Christian unity are essential, so as 'not to hinder the Gospel of Christ' (I Cor. 9,12)."[39]

Along with the ecclesiological foundations of the participation of the Orthodox Church in the ecumenical movement, the Third Pre-Conciliar Pan-Orthodox Conference reaffirmed the urgent need for a common Christian witness so that the efforts of all Christian churches and denominations could gain more weight and strength. It stressed that a comprehensive approach and a common commitment of the Church is needed more than ever before because of the disruptive and destructive forces that threaten all life. The unanimous statements from all Orthodox Churches in the Third Pre-Conciliar Pan-Orthodox Conference (1986) under the subject "The Contribution of the Orthodox Church to the Realization of Peace, Justice, Freedom, Fraternity and Love among People and to the Elimination of Racial and other Discriminations"[40] clarified that this concern does not have an exclusive character. It concerns not only all Christians, but all religions and is consistent with the interests of all humanity.[41] Referring to the contribution of Orthodoxy in the modern world, which should mainly be a witness of love and diakonia, the text states:

"We, Orthodox Christians, have – by reason of the fact that we have had access to the meaning of salvation – a duty to fight against disease, misfortune, fear; because we have had access to the experience of peace, we cannot remain indifferent to its absence from society today; because we have benefited from God's justice, we are fighting for further justice in the world and for the elimination of all oppression; because we daily experience God's mercy, we are fighting all fanaticism and intolerance between persons and nations; because we continually proclaim the incarnation of God and the divinization of man, we defend human rights for all individuals and all peoples... because, we are nourished by the body and blood of our Lord in the holy Eucharist, we experience the need to share God's gifts with our brothers and sisters, we have a better understanding of hunger and privation and fight for their abolition; because we expect a new earth and a new heaven where an absolute justice will reign, we fight here and now for the rebirth and renewal of the human being and society."[42]

This text has an impressive relevance for Christian presence in the world and is a solid basis for the development of Orthodox witness in the modern world.

3) Problems and perspectives of the ecumenical "koinonia" through encounter and dialogue

The Orthodox presence in the ecumenical koinonia has the form of giving and taking. It is a mutual enrichment and mutual challenge. However, the procedures for dialogue and the growth in koinonia were neither easy nor smooth. Although there is a positive side, it had and still has many problematic sides and has encountered many difficulties, contrasts, controversies, disappointments and tensions. These were pointed out from time to time by the Declaration of the Ecumenical Patriarchate on the occasion of the 25th Anniversary of the WCC (1973), the Inter-Orthodox Conference in Sofia (1981), the Third Pre-Conciliar Pan-Orthodox Conference (1986), with a separate statement in Canberra Assembly (1991), the Inter-Orthodox Consultations in Chambésy (1991, 1995), the Inter-Orthodox meeting in Thessaloniki (1998), by the Orthodox Churches of Russia and Romania and the Ecumenical Patriarchate in the frame of the studies during the 90s, which aimed at the reconfiguration the nature and purpose of the WCC.

---

[39] See "Decisions of the Third Pre-Conciliar Pan-Orthodox Conference on 'The Orthodox Church and the Ecumenical Movement', (Chambésy, Switzerland, 1986)", in G. Limouris (ed.), *Orthodox Visions of Ecumenism,* 112-115, 112f.
[40] See the original text-decision in Greek, in *Episkepsis* 17.369 (1986): 18-26.
[41] Ibid., 18.
[42] Ibid, 25f. (para. H, 2). Here quoted from Vl. Pheidas, "Peace and Justice: Theological Foundations", in G. Limouris (ed.), *Justice, Peace and Integrity of Creation. Insights from Orthodoxy*, (Geneva: WCC, 1990), 115.

Through these meetings an extensive catalogue of points is raised which explain why there are still reasons for the distance of the Orthodox from the WCC and incidents which have blocked or still block a fruitful participation in the Council (e.g. the insistence on implementing intercommunio, the use of so-called "inclusive language" in the translation of the Bible, in the Liturgy and in Theology, the adoption of very liberal approaches in pastoral and ethical issues, the institutional profile of the Council, particularly the manner of representation and decision making).[43]

These critical points were turned into resentment when, during the celebration of the 50th Jubilee since the establishment of the WCC, signs of uncertainty in the Council began to appear in relation to the understanding of the koinonia of the churches and doubts related to the future of the ecumenical movement as a whole. There was such disappointment after so many years of intensive search for the unity of the Church, that the way to full communion still has not been opened yet. The idea of Christian mission in a world of religious and cultural pluralism was bringing up new questions. The tradition of ecumenical social ethics was loaded with intolerable burdens in the effort to respond to the impacts of globalization in the life of human societies. Eventually, criticism of the Orthodox took alarming proportions, when rapid socio-political changes came into the social and political contexts of Eastern Europe and altered the situation of Orthodox Churches which had been repressed for decades. As a result, morbid aspects of fundamentalist and nationalist exacerbations and some strong anti-Western and anti-ecumenical spirits began to prevail in some contexts. While criticism from Orthodox Churches and from those who know and interpret their positions, had as background its concern for the universal dimension and tasks of the ecumenical movement, there also came different criticism from a group of extremist tendencies driven by a fanatical spirit of intolerance and often marked by ignorance or even deliberate disinformation which argued that any contact with the heterodox is a deviation from the strict and canonical ecclesiological principles of orthodoxy and should be characterized as traitorous and heretical.[44]

Within this climate, it was suggested by the Orthodox Churches[45] and approved by the Council at the 8th Assembly at Harare (1998), that a Special Commission on Orthodox Participation in the WCC would be held in order "to study and analyze the whole spectrum of issues related to orthodox participation in the WCC" and "to make proposals concerning the changes in structure, style and ethos of the Council". The changes were substantial and radical and provide Orthodox Churches more opportunities to act fairly towards other members of the WCC based on their own ecclesiological identity.[46]

It was impressive that the effort to avoid a crisis that could have led to the collapse of the WCC instead highlighted the fellowship of WCC member-Churches as a community which has a tremendous ability to avoid unnecessary friction and to process and settle conflicts and to apply wisdom in order to move ahead jointly.

During the process of the Special Commission, a heated debate took place which also led to the realization that unilateralism would be shifting the responsibility to only one side and therefore would not be appropriate for the Orthodox criticism. It also became more clear that if the integration of Orthodox Churches

---

[43] The Consultation in Chambésy (1995) summarizes the complains (desiderata) and the difficulties of the Orthodox participation in WCC (see G. Lemopoulos (ed.), *The Ecumenical Movement, the Churches and the World Council of Churches: an Orthodox contribution to the reflection process on "The Common Understanding and Vision of the WCC"*, (Geneva: WCC/Syndesmos, 1996), 13ff, para. 22-34) and the Pan-Orthodox Meeting in Thessaloniki (1998) (see "Evaluation of new facts in the relations of Orthodoxy and the ecumenical movement" (in Greek), *Enimerosis* 14 (1998): 3-6. In English see in the site of WCC. In German : "Bewertung neuer Fakten in den Beziehungen zwischen der Orthodoxie und der ökumenischen Bewegung, Thessaloniki", in Ath. Basdekis (ed.), *Orthodoxe Kirche und Ökumenische Bewegung. Dokumente – Erklärungen – Berichte 1900-2006*, (Frankfurt a.M.: Lembeck/Bonifatius, 2006), 723-727.

[44] For the anti-ecumenical climate that was emerged after the serious and rapid socio-political changes in Eastern Europe with characteristic examples, the fundamentalist mentality and the intolerance see e.g. G. Tsetsis in *Enimerosis* 13 (1997): 10; 14 (1998): 5-6 (in Greek).

[45] See "Evaluation of new facts in the relations of Orthodoxy and the ecumenical movement", para. 16.

[46] See Vl. Pheidas, "The Orthodox Church and the 9th General Assembly of WCC", 457-461.

Part II: Orthodoxy and Ecumenism - Foundations

in the WCC is seen as unnatural and their presence ineffective or their "voices are not heard" and the multilateral dialogue is seen as being in a credibility crisis, this is not only due to the unsatisfactory structure
and internal problems of the Council, but also to a large extent due to disagreements and internal problems
of Orthodox Churches (like excessive trends to nationalism and the autocephalous factor, lack of internal
discipline in implementing decisions taken at a Pan-Orthodox level, schisms within the local Orthodox
Churches, Orthodox indifferences to the sensitivity of the WCC related to great historic challenges of our
times, ignorance with regard to the pleroma of the Church and the lack of awareness and participation in
ecumenical events and endeavors).

However, these weak points of Orthodoxy were not seen as insurmountable difficulties that would
cause irreparable damage to its unity and seriously impair its ecumenical conscience. All organized events,
initiatives, and activities during the 20th century, such as the Encyclicals of the Ecumenical Patriarchate (1902, 1904, 1920), the conferences of Orthodox theology (e.g. in 1936 and 1976 in Athens and the
Inter-orthodox theological Symposium in Thessaloniki 1972), the Pan-Orthodox Conferences and the
Pan-Orthodox process to the Holy and Great Synod of the Orthodox Church are efforts to witness and
promote the unity of the Orthodox Churches and to seek opportunities to mitigate some differences and
misunderstandings. This course has renewed the self-understanding of the Orthodox Church and helped to
rediscover its catholic consciousness and to keep its ecumenicity alive. Without institutions that express
the unity and the catholicity of the Orthodox Church and its self-examination, it would be impossible to
attempt a coherent representation and commitment to the ecumenical movement.[47] Any initiative of the
Orthodox Church to co-operate in the ecumenical movement was accompanied and is still accompanied
by an automatic movement for closer relations between the Orthodox Churches themselves and the renewal of their life.

In this way, Orthodoxy gradually but steadily came out from behind the walls of introspection which also
had made Orthodoxy closed to other Christians who until recently knew Orthodoxy only from Handbooks of
Apologetics. Orthodoxy moved from monologue to dialogue, from reaction to action, from the position of an
observer to real participation and from simple contribution to full cooperation.

Despite some trends in the ecumenical movement that hinder dialogue and despite the recognition that the
road that leads to unity is still long and dangerous, the Orthodox Church did not give up. Orthodox Churches
reaffirmed that they will remain loyal to the ecumenical task, since it arises from the explicit command of
Christ "that all may be one". This is why Orthodox Churches will continue to pray "for the oikoumene" and
"for the union for all" and to transform into action this long theological and liturgical tradition. Orthodox
Churches considered the WCC as a "common home"[48] and "blessed organ"[49] of the Churches, which allows
cooperation for the promotion of Christian unity and the common treatment of various problems of humankind and the world. Eventually, it is this history of ecumenical involvement which cultivated a catholic and
ecumenical attitude of Orthodoxy in the modern world, which really leaves space for the existence of others
and is sensitive towards people and life.

It is true that the ecumenical movement, particularly the WCC, has been for churches, as was characteristically
said at some time, an intrusive "gadfly" that embroiders the lazy horse and sometimes disturbs and awakens.
The very encounter which happens in the oikoumene in the meeting between one church with another church,
is really an encounter with the "irritating you", and as such always brings an enriching as well as sometimes
irritating effect.[50]

---

[47] See N. Matsoukas, *Ecumenical Movement*, 235.

[48] Ibid., 239.

[49] "Official Welcome speech to the WCC by Ecumenical Patriarch Bartholomew, 11 December 1995", *Enimerosis* 11 (1995): 17 (in Greek).

[50] See Al. Papaderos, "The 'gadfly' on trial: the 'political' commitment of the WCC", in Al. Papaderos, *Ecumenism: Call and Challenge*, 16-43, 29 (in Greek). English in: *Voices of Unity*, (Geneva: WCC, 1983), 78-91.

Bibliography

Alivizatos, Hamilkar, "The Greek Orthodox Church's unbroken continuation with the undivided Church", *Ekklesiastikos Pharos* 33 (1934): 421-442.

Basdekis, Athanassios, (ed.), *Orthodoxe Kirche und Ökumenische Bewegung. Dokumente – Erklärungen – Berichte 1900-2006*, (Frankfurt a.M.: Lembeck/Bonifatius, 2006).

Clapsis, Emmanuel, *Orthodoxy in Conversation – Orthodox Ecumenical Engagements,* (Geneva / Brookline: WCC, 2000).

Florovsky, Georges, "The Boundaries of the Church", in G. Florovsky, *Ecumenism I: A Doctrinal Approach,* (Collected Works, Volume XIII), (Vaduz/Belmond Mass: Buchervertriebsanstalt, 1989), 36-45.

Limouris, Gannadios (ed.), *Orthodox Visions of Ecumenism: Statements, Messages and Reports on the Ecumenical Movement, 1902-1992*, (Geneva: WCC, 1994).

Lemopoulos, Georges, (ed.), *The Ecumenical Movement, the Churches and the World Council of Churches: an Orthodox contribution to the reflection process on "The Common Understanding and Vision of the WCC"*, (Geneva/Bialystok: WCC/Syndesmos, 1996).

Lemopoulos Georges, *Structure and Function of WCC. Descriptive exposition of its legislative, administrative, consultative and executive bodies with reference to the role of the Orthodox Churches* (in Greek), (Thessaloniki: Pournaras, 2012) (in Greek).

Matsoukas, Nikos, *Ecumenical Movement: History – Theology*, (Thessaloniki: Pournaras, 2003) (in Greek).

Papaderos, Alexandros, *Ecumenism: Call and Challenge*, (Chania, 1984) (in Greek).

Raiser, Konrad, "The importance of the Orthodox contribution to the WCC" (in Greek), in Petros Vassiliadis (ed.), *Orthodox Theology and Ecumenical Dialogue*, (Athens: Apostoliki Diakonia, 2005), 32-54."Relations of the Orthodox Church with the Whole Christian World", *Episkepsis* 17.369 (1986): 9-13 (in Greek).

"Relations of the Orthodox Church with the Whole Christian World", *Episkepsis*, 17, No. 369 (1986): 9-13(in Greek).

Stavridis, Vassilios –Varella, Evangelia, *History of the Ecumenical Movement* (Analecta Vlatadon 47), (Thessaloniki: Patriarchal Institute of Patristic Studies, 1996) (in Greek).

Tsetsis, Georges, *The Contribution of the Ecumenical Patriarchate in the formation of the World Council of Churches*, (Katerini: Tertios, 1988) (in Greek).

Tsompanidis, Stylianos, *Orthodoxie und Ökumene: Gemeinsam auf dem Weg zu Gerechtigkeit, Frieden und Bewahrung der Schöpfung*. Mit einem Vorwort von Ulrich Duchrow, (Ökumenische Studie 10), (Münster/Hamburg/London: Lit, 1999).

Tsompanidis, Stylianos, *"For the union of all' - The Contribution of the Orthodox Church and Theology to the World Council of Churches* with Foreword of Alexandros K. Papaderos, (Thessaloniki: Pournaras, 2008) (in Greek).

(17) Pan-orthodox Decisions on the Ecumenical Relations of Orthodox Churches – A Survey and Historical Account

Fr. Viorel Ionita

On the 12 June 1902, the Ecumenical Patriarch Joachim III (1878-1884 and 1901-1912) published a Patriarchal and Synodal Encyclical, considered as "the first ecumenical act of the ecumenical Patriarchate in the history of the ecumenical movement."[1] In his letter the Ecumenical Patriarch proposed a more intensive cooperation between all local Orthodox Churches in order "to seek the mind of the most holy autocephalous Churches on the subject of our present and future relations with the two great growths of Christianity, viz. the Western Church and the Church of the Protestants".[2] Along this concern of the Ecumenical throne, in January 1920 the Ecumenical Patriarchate published the Encyclical Letter addressed "*Unto the Churches of Christ everywhere*", which stated that "the rapprochement between the various Christian Churches and fellowship is highly desirable and necessary"[3] This Encyclical Latter rightly considered as the *Magna Charta* for the Orthodox involvement in the Ecumenical Movement recommended a series of actions which are still to be fulfilled.

The first Inter-Orthodox gathering which made some decisions with direct implications for the relationship between the Orthodox Church and other Christian Churches was the Pan-Orthodox Congress convened by the Ecumenical Patriarch Meletios the 4th (1921-1923) from 10 May to 8 June 1923.[4] One of the recommendations made at this congress was the correction of the Julian calendar in all Orthodox Churches. Following this recommendation several local Orthodox Churches corrected their calendar while others did not. This situation still existing today is one of the obstacles towards a common date for Easter. In connection with this Inter-Orthodox Congress a debate started within the Orthodox Churches about the possibility of organising an Ecumenical Council. In this respect an Inter-Orthodox Commission met from 8-13 June 1930 at the Vatopedi Monastery on the Mount Athos in order to establish a list of topics to be discussed at the Pre-Synod, which was considered at that time as a preparatory step for the Ecumenical Council. At this meeting a first list of 17 large themes was elaborated mainly with reference to the renewal of the life and the mission of the Orthodox Church in the 20th century. The seventh theme in this list recommended the "definition of the relations between the Orthodox Church and the heterodox Churches both in the East as well as in the West, namely: a) relations in the spirit of love with the Oriental Orthodox Churches as well as with the Old-Catholic and the Anglican Churches, which do not proselytise among the Orthodox and b) careful and defensive relations with the Churches which are proselytising among the Orthodox Churches, namely the Catholic, Protestant, Baptist and Adventist Churches.[5]

The way in which the relationship between the Orthodox Church and the other Churches was expressed in 1930 was first of all determined by the fact that the Orthodox suffered from the proselytism of some Western churches and secondly from the perspective of a possible rapprochement with some of these Churches, first of all with the Oriental Orthodox and secondly with two Western Churches, namely the Old-Catholics as well

---

[1] Athanasios Basdekis, *Orthodoxe Kirche und Ŝkumenische Bewegung. Dukumente – Erklärungen – Berichte,* 1900-2006, (Lembrck/Bonifatius, 2006), 1.

[2] *The Orthodox Church in the Ecumenical Movement. Documents and Statements 1902-1975*, Constantin G. Patelos (ed.), (Geneva: WCC Publications, 1978), 30.

[3] Ibid., 40.

[4] Patrick Viscuso, *A Quest for reform of the Orthodox Church. The 1923 Pan-Orthodox Congress. An Analysis and Translation of its Acts and Decisions,* (Berkeley, CA: Inter-Orthodox Press, 2006), xviii.

[5] See Anne Jensen, *Die Zukunft der Orthodoxie. Konzilspläne und Kirchenstrukturen,* (Benzinger Verlag, 1986), 28.

as the Anglicans, which showed interest in a communion with the Orthodox already during the second half of the 19th century.

Another important Orthodox gathering for the Ecumenical involvement of the Orthodox Church before the Second World War was the first Congress of the Orthodox Theological Faculties, held in Athens from 29 November – 6 December 1936. The statement published at the end of this congress stated in point number seven, that "as we see in the ecumenical activity for the unity of the Church as well as in the activity for the Practical Christendom an expression of the new awareness for Church and Theology, the congress appreciated this movement and ensured that it is ready to contribute to this activity in an Orthodox spirit."[6]

The first Inter-Orthodox gathering after the Second World War with implications for the Orthodox involvement in the Ecumenical Movement was the Church Conference of Heads and Representatives of Orthodox Autocephalous Churches organised from 8-17 July 1948 in Moscow by the Russian Orthodox Church on the 500th celebration of its autocephaly. At this conference the following four topics were discussed and separate statements were adopted an each of them:

1. the Vatican and the Orthodox Church;
2. the validity of the Anglican ordinations;
3. the Orthodox calendar and
4. the Orthodox Church and the Ecumenical Movement.

In relation to the Roman Catholic Church, the Moscow Conference adopted a very strong statement condemning the proselytising actions of this Church among Orthodox believers. The validity of the Anglican Ordinations was discussed in Moscow, because this issue was very much debated during the years before the Second World War. In its statement, the Moscow Conference decided that the recognition of the Anglican Ordinations could be taken into consideration only if the head of this Church would express clearly and officially the wish of this Church to be united with the Orthodox Church. A decision in relation to the Orthodox calendar was necessary because the Orthodox Churches were following different calendars after the Pan-Orthodox Congress from 1923. In this respect the Moscow Conference recommended that as long as there is no a more precise calendar to be adopted by all local Orthodox Churches, in order to celebrate together at least the Resurrection of the Lord, the most important Christian feast, all the local Orthodox Churches were obliged to celebrate Easter according to the Julian calendar. This decision is still valid in the Eastern Orthodox Churches. In relation to the Ecumenical Movement, the Moscow Conference reacted to the invitation addressed to each local Orthodox Church to attend the first Assembly of the World Council of Churches (WCC), planned to take place 22 August – 4 September 1948 in Amsterdam. This Assembly constituted at the same time the foundation of the world wide ecumenical organisation based in Geneva. Among the difficulties the Moscow Conference had in relation to the formation of the WCC was first of all in relation to the danger that this organisation would become an "Ecumenical Church" and second to the fact that the "reduction of the requirements and conditions for unity" were reduced "to the simple recognition of Christ as our Lord", which "lowers the Christian faith to such a degree as to be accessible even to the devils (James 2:19, Matt 8:29, Mk 5:7)."[7] The Moscow decisions were actually very useful for the development of the WCC, as this organisation improved its self understanding by adopting in 1950 a decision, taken by its Central Committee, in which this organisation was defined as a tool for the rapprochement of the Churches rather than as a Super-church or an Ecumenical Church. Also in relation to the Orthodox criticism that the basis for the Church unity cannot be reduced only to the faith in Jesus Christ was rightly taken into consideration by the WCC, which at its 3rd Assembly (New Delhi, 1961) enlarged its basis to a Trinitarian formula.

The Ecumenical Patriarch Athenagoras (1948-1972) soon after his enthronement started preparations for a Synod of the Orthodox Church by organising the series of Pan-Orthodox Conferences. After intensive prepa-

---

[6] *Proces-Vebaux du Premier Congres de Theologie Orthodoxe a Athenes*, 29 Novembre – 6 Decembre 1936, Hamilcar S. Alivisatos (ed.), (Athenes: 1939), 467.

[7] *Orthodox Visions of Ecumenism. Statements, Messages and Reports on the Ecumenical Movement, 1902-1992*, Gennadios Limouris (ed.), (Geneva: WCC Publications, 1994), 19.

Part II: Orthodoxy and Ecumenism - Foundations

rations the first Pan-Orthodox Conference took place from 24 September to 1 November 1961 on the island of Rhodes. At this conference the list of themes established at the Vatopedi Monastery was further elaborated into eight large chapters. The 5th chapter, entitled "The relationship of the Orthodox Church with the rest of the Christian World," proposed a study of bringing closer and uniting the Churches according to the following scheme:[8]

1. Orthodoxy and the Lesser Ancient Oriental Churches, for "cultivation of friendly relations with a view to establishing a union with them";
2. Orthodoxy and the Roman Catholic Church, in order to undertake a) a "study of the positive and negative points between the two Churches: 1. in faith; 2. in administration; and 3. in church activities (especially propaganda, proselytising, the Uniates) and b) cultivation of relations in the spirit of Christian love, with particular reference to the points anticipated in the Patriarchal Encyclical of 1920";
3. Orthodoxy and the Churches and Confessions emanating from the Reformation: a) Confessions lying further from Orthodoxy (1.Lutheranism; 2. Calvinism, 3. Methodism; 4. Other Protestant Confessions); b) Confessions lying nearer to Orthodoxy: (1. Anglican Church and 2. Episcopalians in general).
4. Orthodoxy and Old Catholicism: advancement of relations with them in the spirit of former theological discussions and their intention and inclination to unite with the Orthodox Church.
5. Orthodoxy and the Ecumenical Movement: a) the presence and participation of the Orthodox Church in the ecumenical movement in the spirit of the Patriarchal Encyclical of 1920; b) study of theology and other subjects related to the assumptions of the Orthodox Church's participation in the ecumenical movement; c) the importance and the contributions of the Orthodox participation as a whole in the direction of ecumenical thinking and action.[9]

The first Pan-Orthodox Conference was very successful and it had a large echo not only among the local Orthodox Churches but also among the other Christian Churches[10] also because the Roman Catholic Church was preparing the Second Vatican Council and many theologians hoped for some common actions between these two churches. It was also the wish of the Ecumenical Patriarch Athenagoras to improve the relationship between the Orthodox Church and the Roman Catholic Church. Therefore the second Pan-Orthodox Conference, held once again on the island of Rhodes from 26-29 September 1963 discussed the issue of sending Orthodox representatives to the Second Vatican Council as well as the question of an official dialogue between these two churches. On the first point it was decided that each Autocephalous Orthodox Church should decide on its own whether or not to send delegates to the Vatican Council and on the second point it was decided that an official theological dialogue with the Roman Catholic Church cannot be initiated before the end of the Vatican Council.[11] The question of clarification about the official theological dialogue between the Orthodox Church and the Roman Catholic Church was precisely the task of the 3rd Pan-Orthodox Conference, held again on the island of Rhodes from 1-15 November 1964. This conference recommended that a future official theological dialogue between the Orthodox and the Roman Catholic churches should be done only on an equal basis[12] as well as on the prerequisite that the Roman Catholic church will renounce its proselytising actions among Orthodox Christians.

Finally the third Pan-Orthodox Conference recommended that the Ecumenical Patriarchate undertake the preparations for dialogue on one side with the Anglican Church and on the other side with the Old Catholic Church. In this respect an Inter-Orthodox Conference was organised from 1-15 September 1966 in Belgrade, Serbia (former Yugoslavia), which established the criteria as well as the guidelines for the

---

[8] Ibid., 32.
[9] Ibid., 33.
[10] N.A. Nissiotis "La Conference Pan-Orthodoxe de Rhodes" *Contacts- Revue francaise de l'Orthodoxie* 37.1 (1962), 54.
[11] O. Rousseau, "La trisieme conference panorthodoxe de Rhodes" *Irénikon* 4 (1964): 488.
[12] Olivier Clement, "La trisieme conference de Rhodes", *Contacts- Revue francaise de l'Orthodoxie* 49 (1965): 56.

dialogue of the Orthodox Church with these two western Churches.[13] Through the first three Pan-Orthodox Conferences, which were considered as a relevant progress of the relations and cooperation between the local Orthodox Churches,[14] all these Churches were invited to study the themes as an act of preparation for the Orthodox Synod. On this basis the fourth Pan-Orthodox Conference, held from 8-16 June 1968 at the new established Centre of the Ecumenical Patriarchate in Chambésy, near Geneva, Switzerland, recommended to the Ecumenical Patriarchate to establish a working plan for the preparation of a great Inter- or Pan-Orthodox Synod, which should take decisions on the themes established at the first Pan-or-thodox Conference, from Rhodes 1961.[15] In this respect a Secretariat for the preparation of the Synod was established at Chambésy, as well as an Inter-Orthodox Preparatory Commission with the task to prepare the agenda of the first Pre-Conciliar Pan-Orthodox Conference as soon as possible. As for the involvement of the Orthodox Church in the ecumenical movement, this conference took a resolution in 9 points with some clear guidelines for a more constructive cooperation of all local Orthodox Churches within the WCC, by underlining that the Orthodox Church "is an organic member" of the WCC, and "her firm resolve, with all the means at her disposal, theological and other, to contribute to the advancement and the success of all the WCC's work."[16]

Along the recommendations of the fourth Pan-Orthodox Conference, the first meeting of the Inter-Orthodox Preparatory Commission for the Orthodox Synod, at its first meeting, held from 16-28 July 1971 at Chambésy, recommended that new, much shorter list of themes should be adopted by the first Pre-Conciliar Pan-Orthodox Conference, which took place from 21-28 November 1976, at Chambésy. At this conference it was definitively decided that the Synod to be prepared by the Orthodox Churches in a Pan-Orthodox process should be called "The Great and Holy Synod of the Orthodox Church". Another important decision taken at this conference was to adopt a new list of 10 themes on which the Great and Holy Synod of the Orthodox Church shall take concrete decisions. These themes are:

1. Orthodox Diaspora;
2. Autocephaly and how it is to be proclaimed;
3. Autonomy and how it is to be proclaimed;
4. Orthodox Diptychs;
5. the question of the common calendar;
6. the impediments for marriage;
7. fasting ordinances;
8. the relations of the Orthodox Church with the other Christian churches;
9. The Orthodox Church and the Ecumenical Movement and
10. the contribution of the local Orthodox Churches to the accomplishment of the Christians ideals for peace, freedom, fraternity, and of love between people as well as for the elimination of the racial discrimination.[17]

From these themes on which the future Great and Holy Synod of the Orthodox Church should take decisions, two of them refer to the ecumenical relations of the Orthodox Church. The third Pre-Conciliar Pan-Orthodox Conference, which took place again at Chambésy, from 28 October to 6 November 1986, also elaborated among other things the texts on the two ecumenical themes, which are sent directly to the Great and Holy Synod of the Orthodox Church.[18] The texts on the relations between the Orthodox Church and the other Christian Church-

---

[13] Irinäus Trotzke OSB, "Die panorthodoxe Konferenz von Belgrad", in *UNA SANCTA. Zeitschrift für ökumenische Begegnung* 21 (1966): 278.

[14] Erich Bryner, *Die Ostkirchen vom 18. bis zum 20. Jahrhundert,* (Evangelische Verlagsanstalt: 1996), 27.

[15] Idem, op. cit.

[16] *Orthodox Visions of Ecumenism...*, op. cit. 38.

[17] Vlassios I. Pheidas, *Droit Canon. Une perspective orthodoxe.* Analacta Chambesiana 1, (Chambésy, Genève: 1998), 161.

[18] Secrétariat pour la préparation du saint et grand Concile de l'Église orthodoxe, *IIIe Conférence Panorthodoxe Préconciliaire, Chambésy, 28 octobre – 6 novembre 1986,* (Geneva: Centre orthodoxe du Patriarcat oecuménique, 2000).

es is related to the bilateral official theological dialogues between the Orthodox Church and the following churches: Anglican, Old Catholic, Oriental Orthodox, Roman-Catholic, Lutheran and Reformed. The text on the Orthodox Church and the ecumenical movement underlined that the "Orthodox Church, in her profound conviction and ecclesiastical consciousness of being the bearer of and the witness to the faith and tradition of the One, Holy Catholic and Apostolic Church, firmly believes that she occupies a central place in matters relating to the promotion of Christian unity within the contemporary world."[19]

After some consideration of the identity and self-understanding of the Orthodox Church the text from 1986 indicates also that the "Orthodox Church, however, faithful to her ecclesiology, to the identity of her internal structure and to the teaching of the undivided Church, while participating in the WCC, does not accept the idea of the "equality of confessions" and cannot consider Church unity as an inter-confessional adjustment. In this spirit, the unity which is sought within the WCC cannot simply be the product of theological agreements alone. God calls every Christian to the unity of faith which is lived in the sacraments and the tradition, as experienced in the Orthodox Church."[20]

At the end of the text elaborated by the third Pre-Conciliar Pan-Orthodox Conference proposed the following points for immediate action:

"1. It is essential to create within the World Council of Churches, the Conference of European Churches and other inter-Christian organisations, the necessary conditions which will enable the Orthodox Churches to act on an equal footing with the other members of the above-mentioned organisations. It is therefore necessary to work out new regulations in the WCC and the other ecumenical organisations, in order to enable the Orthodox Church to bear her witness and give her theological contribution, as expected by her partners in the Ecumenical Movement. More particularly, concerning the relations of the Orthodox Church with the WCC, it is necessary to deal with those of the "Sofia desiderata", on which so far there has not been any decision.

2. The Orthodox Church, while participating in multilateral theological dialogue within the framework of the Faith and Order Commission, should find ways of coordinating her efforts, especially with respect to the ecclesiological criteria of her participation in this dialogue."[21]

The third Pre-Conciliar Pan-Orthodox Conference decided that although these texts are to be presented as they are to the Great and Holy Synod of the Orthodox Church for deliberation, nevertheless they could be put into practice by the local Orthodox Churches. In other words, these decisions constitute the most official guidelines for the Ecumenical Involvement of the Orthodox as they are taken in common by all the local Orthodox Churches.

Bibliograpy

1. Athanasios Basdekis, *Orthodoxe Kirche und okumenische Bewegung. Dukumente – Erklarungen – Berichte, 1900-2006*, (Lembrck/Bonifatius: 2006).
2. Constantin G. Patelos (ed.), *The Orthodox Church in the Ecumenical Movement. Documents and Statements 1902-1975*, (Geneva: World Council of Churches, 1978).
3. Anne Jensen, *Die Zukunft der Orthodoxie. Konzilspläne und Kirchenstrukturen*, (Benzinger Verlag, 1986)
4. Gennadios Limouris (ed.), *Orthodox Visions of Ecumenism. Statements, Messages and Reports on the Ecumenical Movement, 1902-1992*, (Geneva: WCC Publications, 1994).
5. Hamilcar Alivisatos (ed.), *Procès-Veraux du Premier Congrès de Théologie Orthodoxe à Athènes*, (Athènes, 1939).
6. Olivier Clément, *Dialogues avec le patriarche Athénagoras*, (Paris, 1969).

---

[19] *Orthodox Visions of Ecumenism...*, op. cit., 112.
[20] Ibid., 113.
[21] Ibid., 115.

7. Metropolite Damaskinos Papandreou, *On the Way to the Great and Holy Synode, Problems and Perspectives*, (Athens, 1990) (in Greek).
8. George E. Matsoukas, *Orthodox Christianity at the Crossroads. A Great Council of the Church – When and Why*, (Bloomington, USA, 2009).
9. "Orthodoxie et dialogues oecumèniques", *Revue Contacts* 240 (2012).

Fr. Daniel Buda

Introduction

It must be specified from the very beginning that this article will refer only to well-articulated and constructive criticism formulated by Orthodox Churches through their official representatives or by some prominent orthodox theologians or church leaders vis-à-vis the ecumenical movement and especially about the World Council of Churches (WCC). Any form of criticism formulated by fundamentalist Orthodox groups or individuals, without a real basis in reality and making use of conspiracy theories, will be totally ignored here. It is obvious that this study cannot contain all the criticism formulated by every document issued by Orthodox meetings or formulated by Orthodox theologians and church leaders. It concentrates on criticism formulated by the most important documents produced by significant Orthodox gatherings, and it gives voice to some prominent individual voices.

On the critical role of Orthodox Churches in the Ecumenical Movement

A. Before the foundation of WCC

Already the Patriarchal and Synodical Encyclical of 1902 of the Ecumenical Patriarch Joachim III, speaking about the desire for unity with all those who believe in Christ, sets out frankly the fact that the different doctrinal positions create obstacles on the journey to unity.[1] The Encyclical of the Ecumenical Patriarchate, 1920,[2] issued on behalf of the Ecumenical Patriarchate by Metropolitan Doroteos of Brussa, in that time *locum tenens* of the Patriarchal See of Constantinople, which is considered "foundational to the ecumenical movement in general"[3] especially because of the proposal to create "a permanent organ of fellowship and cooperation between the churches"[4] warns about "prejudices, practices or pretensions, the difficulties which have so often jeopardized attempts at reunion in the past may arise or be brought up" again. However it expressed the hope that "they cannot and should not create an invincible and insuperable obstacle."[5]

At the First World Conference of Faith and Order, Lausanne, Switzerland, 1927, the Orthodox participants issued a statement[6] in which they expressed their regret that, with the exception of the first Report, they cannot agree with the other Reports produced by that World Conference. The reasons mentioned were that "the bases assumed for the foundation of the Reports … are inconsistent with the principles of the Orthodox Church" and that these documents "set off from the consideration that the Scriptures were the only source of revelation, and did not recognize the Nicene-Constantinopolitan Creed as the common symbol of Christian faith; nor did they refer to the threefold priestly ministry instituted by Christ."[7] However, the Orthodox mentioned that already in

---

[1] Athanasios Basdekis (ed.), *Orthodoxe Kirche und ökumenische Bewegung. Dokumente – Erklärungen –Berichte*, (Frankfurt: Verlag, 2006), 1-8 (hereinafter quoted as "Ath. Basdekis"); Gennadios Limouris (ed.), *Orthodox Visions of Ecumenism. Statements, Messages and Reports on the Ecumenical Movement 1902-1992*, (Geneva: WCC Publications, 1994), 1-5 (hereinafter quoted as "G. Limouris").

[2] See Ath. Basdekis, document 3, 16-20; G. Limouris, 9-11.

[3] Tamara Grdzelidze, *Ecumenism, Orthodoxy and* in *The Encyclopedia of Eastern Orthodox Christianity*, John Anthony McGuckin (ed.), vol. I, (Wiley-Blackwell, 2001), 209.

[4] W. A. Visser`t Hooft, *The Genesis and Formation of the World Council of Churches*, (Geneva: WCC Publications, 1982), 1.

[5] G. Limouris, 9.

[6] See Ath. Basdekis, document 4, 21-26; G. Limouris, 12-14.

[7] Grdzelidze, *Ecumenism, Orthodoxy and* in *The Encyclopedia…*, 210.

the preliminary Faith and Order conference in Geneva 1920, their representatives "recommended that before any discussion of the reunion of the Church in faith and order, a League of Churches should be established for their mutual co-operation in regard to the social and moral principles of Christendom."[8] A similar statement[9] was issued after the Second Conference on Faith and Order, Edinburgh, Scotland, 1937 which analysed the Reports of the conference and concluded that "they (i. e. the reports") express many fundamental agreements which exist between us and our Christian brethren on many points." However, the statement continues, "they contain a long series of statements in regard to which significant differences exist of such weight that we found it necessary to formulate the Orthodox standpoint upon them in a series of short footnotes."[10] This decision to formulate a separate "Orthodox standpoint" was repeated many times by Orthodox delegates participating in major ecumenical events of the next decades of the common ecumenical journey.

In August 1948 in Amsterdam, 147 churches from 44 countries formed the foundation of the World Council of Churches.[11] Eleven Orthodox Churches (eight Eastern and three Oriental Orthodox Churches) were founding members. In spite of the fact that some Orthodox saw the foundation of the WCC as a realization of their demand expressed in the previously quoted documents, Orthodox contribution to the idea and foundation of WCC was overshadowed by the decision of an Assembly of some Orthodox church leaders[12] which took place in Moscow in July 1948 under the presidency of Patriarch Alexei of Moscow, not to attend the Assembly in Amsterdam and eventually to stay away from WCC. This decision had been taken with 14 votes out of 17,[13] obviously under the pressure of the Soviet communist regime. The meeting in Moscow issued a resolution[14] which was very critical to the ecumenical movement and WCC: "We have come to a complete and joint understanding that at the present time influence is being exerted on the Orthodox Church by other confessions from at least two directions. On the one hand, the Papacy … On the other, Protestantism in all its vast diversity … here (i. e. with Protestantism) Orthodoxy faces a still greater temptation – to turn aside from its seeking the Kingdom of God and enter a political arena which is foreign to its purpose. This is the practical aim of the ecumenical movement today." What follows are five reasons why the Orthodox Churches shall stay away from WCC and the ecumenical movement which could be summarized as following: (a) the purpose of the ecumenical movement as expressed in the formation of WCC is not in accord with the ideals of Christianity and the aim of the Church as understood in the Orthodox tradition; (b) the use of social and political activities for the creation of "an Ecumenical Church as an international influence" is comparable with the temptation faced by Jesus Christ in the desert; (c) the ecumenical movement "in its present scheme" lost faith in the possibility of union in the Holy, Catholic and Apostolic Church and created WCC which is overwhelming Protestant and is aimed at a "self-protection of Protestantism"; (d) because of the inconsistency of the previous discussion around the ecumenical idea, the ecumenical movement offers "no assurance for the work of uniting the Churches by the ways and means of grace"; (e) the reduction of the requirements for unity only to the simple recognition of Christ as Lord is sharply criticized. Therefore "our conference of heads and representatives of Autocephalic Orthodox Churches, having prayerfully invoked the presence

---

[8] G. Limouris, 12.

[9] See Ath. Basdekis, document 5, 27-32; G. Limouris, 15-17.

[10] G. Limouris, 15.

[11] W. A. Visser`t Hooft, *The Genesis and Formation…*, 63-64.

[12] The following Orthodox Churches were represented at the meeting in Moscow: Patriarchate of Alexandria, Patriarchate of Antioch, Moscow Patriarchate, Patriarchate of Georgia, Patriarchate of Serbia, Patriarchate of Romania, Patriarchate of Bulgaria, Autocephalous Orthodox Church in Poland, Albanian Orthodox Church and the Orthodox Church in Czech Lands and Slovakia. (Ath. Basdekis, 33). It is important to underline that the decision to stay away from WCC was followed only by those Orthodox Churches which were under the communist regimes. The old patriarchates of Alexandria and Antioch decided to be founding members of WCC.

[13] For other details related with the Moscow gathering of some Orthodox leaders see Alexander de Weymarn, The official Report of the Moscow Conference in 1948 in *Ecumenical Review*, 2.4 (1950): 406.

[14] See Ath. Basdekis, document 6, 33-39; G. Limouris, 18-19.

of the Holy Spirit has decided: to inform the World Council of Churches, in reply to the invitation we have all received to participate in the Amsterdam Assembly as members, that all the national Orthodox Churches taking part in the present Conference are obliged to decline participation in the ecumenical movement in its present form."[15] Fortunately expressions like "at the present time", "today" or "in its present form" referring to the ecumenical movement and WCC left open the possibility of joining later for the Orthodox Churches living under communist regimes. This happened in 1961 during the Third WCC Assembly in New Delhi and in the years following it.

W. A. Visser`t Hooft considered, for good reasons, that the period of WCC "formation" lasted until 1950 when the WCC Central Committee gathered at Toronto in 1950 adopted a statement entitled "The Church, the Churches and the World Council of Churches. Ecclesiological significance of the World Council of Churches", better known simply as "Toronto Statement,"[16] which defined the identity of WCC (what WCC is and what WCC is not). The critical position of the Orthodox in Toronto could be summarized as follows: "the Orthodox concern was to avoid identifying the WCC as a church in itself, a super-church, membership of which implied any specific doctrine concerning the nature of global church unity."[17] This judgement is confirmed years later by another Orthodox theologian, who, speaking about how the Toronto Statement was received in the different traditions involved in WCC, wrote that "for the Orthodox this (i.e. "Toronto Statement") is the great charter of the WCC, and the main guarantee of the immunity and integrity of their ecclesiology within the membership of the WCC."[18]

B. After the foundation of WCC

In many ways, the participation of the Orthodox Churches in WCC and other ecumenical organizations was determined by the following dilemma: should the Orthodox Churches participate as full members in an ecumenical organization together with the large variety of churches that resulted mainly from the Reformation or should they instead stay away and eventually give priority to a dialogue with the Roman Catholic Church with whom the Orthodox Church is doctrinally and ethically nearer, in spite of difficult and painful experiences of the past? From the perspective of "non-Orthodox" membership of WCC, it is crucial to have Orthodox Churches as full member in WCC; otherwise WCC is, more or less, just an "inter-Protestant federation." These two dilemmas fundamentally influenced WCC life since its creation and determined the critical voice of the Orthodox regarding WCC. Here are two examples provided by well-known Orthodox theologians who were deeply involved in the ecumenical work, especially within WCC. Speaking in an ecclesiological context (i.e. about the possibility for the Orthodox to recognize other groups of Christians as Churches), the Romanian Orthodox theologian Ion Bria, who for many years worked in the WCC, expressed the following dilemma: "We (i.e. the Orthodox) are well aware that Orthodox participation in the fellowship of the World Council of Churches comes far from naturally or easily to us. It is a standing challenge, which implies a good deal of tension, of internal struggle, of critical decisions."[19] Speaking about the structures and procedures of WCC, the American-Orthodox theologian and Church historian John Meyendorff considers that these are a source of permanent tensions. Therefore he wrote at a certain moment of difficulties: "Quite clearly, the Orthodox

---

[15] G. Limouris, 19.

[16] For the text of "Toronto Statement" see W. A. Visser` Hooft, *The Genesis and Formation ...*, 112-120. For general information see Morris West, art. "Toronto Statement" in *Dictionary of the Ecumenical Movement*, Nicholas Lossky et al (eds.), 2nd edition, (Geneva: WCC Publications, 2002), 1137-1139.

[17] Tamara Grdzelidze, *Ecumenism, Orthodoxy and ...*, 212.

[18] Vitaly Borovoy, "The ecclesial significance of the WCC: the legacy and promise of Toronto", in *Ecumenical Review* 24.2 (1985): 506. See about the contribution of G. Florovsky in the discussions in Toronto, as acknowledged by W. A. Visser`t Hooft, *The Genesis and Formation ...*, 78.

[19] Ion Bria, "Living in the one Tradition: an Orthodox contribution to the question of unity", in *The Ecumenical Review* 26.2 (1974): 231.

Churches cannot fully identify themselves with the Council (i.e. WCC). This creates a permanent tension, which is painful both to the Orthodox and to the Protestants."[20]

The statement of the Orthodox delegates at the second Assembly of WCC, Evanston, USA, 1954[21] expressed "general agreement" with the report of the Advisory Commission of the Assembly and made some remarks on aspects that were "not fully acceptable" to them. The most important are the remarks on the Unity statement presented at Evanston. It was reaffirmed that "from the Orthodox viewpoint, re-union of Christendom with which the WCC is concerned can be achieved solely on the basis of the total, dogmatic Faith of the early, undivided Church without either subtraction or alteration."[22] Another critical remark is also of ecclesiological nature. The report of the Advisory committee suggested that "the road which the Church must take in restoring unity is that of repentance." The Orthodox comment to this was: "We must recognize that there have been and there are imperfections and failures within the life and witness of Christian believers, but we reject the notion that the Church herself, being the Body of Christ and the repository of revealed Truth and the 'whole operation of the holy spirit could be affected by human sin. Therefore, we cannot speak of the repentance of the Church which is intrinsically holy and unerring."[23]

The Third Assembly of the WCC, New Delhi, India, 1961 is a milestone in the Orthodox involvement in the ecumenical movement, especially in WCC, due to the fact that several Orthodox Churches from, in that time, communist countries agreed to join WCC in the New Delhi Assembly or in the years after. However, the statement presented by the Orthodox delegates is more critical than expected.[24] It states, surprisingly, that "the ecumenical movement as it is embodied in the WCC, had begun by Protestant initiative." It is added that this aspect "must be especially emphasized now, when almost all churches of the Orthodox Communion have entered the membership of the World Council." Afterwards, the statement speaks about different understanding of the ecumenical problems: while "denominationalism" is the primary problem of the Protestant world being "quite natural" to it and "uncongenial" for the Orthodox, "schism" is the basic Orthodox ecumenical problem. "Denominationalism" is problematic for the Orthodox because "they cannot accept the idea of a 'parity of denomination' and cannot visualize Christian Reunion just as an interdenominational adjustment ... The Orthodox Church is not a confession, one of many, one among the many. For the Orthodox, the Orthodox Church is just the Church". Instead of an "ecumenism in space" understood as "agreement between various denominations" which is "quite inadequate and incomplete", the Orthodox proposed an "ecumenism in time" understood as finding the common ground from which all denominations derive their existence."[25] After such a clear presentation of different understanding of unity, it is not a surprise that the first Pan-Orthodox Conference gathered also in 1961 in Rhodes, Greece, in a "Study of ways of bringing closer and uniting the Churches in a Pan-Orthodox perspective" does not even mention WCC, but only the ecumenical movement in general and "the presence and participation of the Orthodox Church ... in the spirit of the Patriarchal Encyclical of 1920.[26] Totally different is the situation of the Resolution[27] of the Fourth Pan-Orthodox Conference, Chambésy, Switzerland, 1968 which expressed "the common mind of the Orthodox Church, that she is an organic member of the WCC, and her form resolve, with all the means at her disposal, theological and other, to contribute to the advancement and the success of all the WCC`s work."[28]

---

[20] John Meyendorff, *Orthodoxy and the Ecumenical challenge* in *Witness to the World*, (Crestwood, NY: St. Vladimir's Seminary Press, 1987), 23.

[21] See Ath. Basdekis, document 11, 59-62; G. Limouris, 26-29.

[22] G. Limouris, 28.

[23] G. Limouris, 29.

[24] See Ath. Basdekis, document 19, 92-94; G. Limouris, 30-31.

[25] G. Lemouris, 31.

[26] G. Lemouris, 32-33.

[27] G. Limouris, 38-30

[28] G. Limouris, 38.

The 4th WCC Assembly in Uppsala, Sweden, 1968 was in many ways a difficult Assembly. It was dominated by the spirit and decisions of a conference on church and society organized in Geneva in 1966 which spoke about the so-called "theology of revolution" meaning the revolutionary character of the message of Jesus Christ. The Geneva conference issued an "appeal to the churches" reflecting on the future role of churches in society. The Uppsala Assembly spoke more about renewal of churches than about "theology of revolution", having as its starting point the Assembly theme "Behold, I make all things new"[29], however "renewal" appeared suspicious to the Orthodox. For many Orthodox, the Uppsala Assembly gave a different direction to the ecumenical work. John Meyendorff wrote in 1983, after the Vancouver Assembly, looking back at the Uppsala Assembly, that: "It is clear ... that the Fourth Assembly reflected a radical turn 'to the left' away from the traditional ecumenical search for Church unity and towards solidarity with radical movements seeking to change society and the world."[30] This change in direction was sharply criticized by other Orthodox.[31] The tensions continued also after the Assembly. In 1969, Dr. Eugene Blake, the General Secretary of WCC of that time, recognized in a speech delivered to the Central Committee in the summer of 1969 that "our Orthodox constituency is deeply troubled by any trend which can be interpreted as a shallow western activism." John Meyendorff commented on Blake's words, as following: "This is a recognition that the Orthodox witness in the World Council is not carried on in vain."[32]

The East-West polarization from the late 1960s and the different priorities of WCC membership made John Meyendorff warn, in the early 1970s, when he was President of Faith and Order, against the danger of the ecumenical movement losing the momentum and coherence and its determination for the quest of visible unity, if contextuality one-sidely were to be adopted as the main principle in ecumenical discussions and put to the extreme at the expense of "catholicity" of the church. Around 30 years later, Petros Vassiliadis observes that Meyendorff's reservations "were proved right."[33] In 1973, John Meyendorff observed self-critically, that "There is in the Orthodox Church a growing reaction against 'ecumenism'. Ecumenism is viewed mainly as clerical pageantry, empty speech-making, futile conference-going and inter-ecclesial redtape. A vocal and frightened minority invokes the canons forbidding prayer with heretics and proclaims that the Orthodox faith goes down the drain at every ecumenical event."[34]

The Orthodox preparatory meeting for the 5th WCC Assembly (Nairobi, 1975), which took place at the monastery of Cernica, Romania, reviewed WCC work in the last years. A report on the meeting published by John Meyendorff stated that "it is well known that recent trends in the World Council, which were described as 'secularism' and defined as an exaggerated 'horizontalism' ... were sharply criticized by the Orthodox in the recent years. In different forms, the patriarchs of Constantinople and Moscow have made their criticisms at the meeting of the Central Committee in Geneva (1973). The Holy Synod of the Orthodox Church in America had published a lengthy Encyclical 'On Christian Unity and Ecumenism', where this issue was taken up with

---

[29] Reinhard Frieling, *Der Weg des ökumenischen Gedankes. Eine Ökumenekunde*, (Göttingen: 1992), 84-86.

[30] The Vancouver Assembly: A Preliminary Evaluation, Witness to the World, 35.

[31] For a good review of Orthodox criticism on new ecumenical directions taken by WCC after Uppsala, see Robert G. Stephanopoulos, *Reflections on Orthodox Ecumenical Directions after Uppsala* in *Journal of Ecumenical Studies* 9.2 (1972): 301-317, esp. 312-313.

[32] John Meyendorff, *On <Secular> Christianity*, in *Witness to the World ...*, 41.

[33] Petros Vasilliadis, Eleni Kasselouri, Pantelis Kalaizidis, *Theological Education in the Orthodox World* in *Handbook of Theological Education in World Christianity. Theological Perspectives – Regional Surveys – Ecumenical Trends*, Dietrich Werner, David Esterline, Namsoon Kang, Joshva Raja (eds.), (Oxford: 2010), 605. Petros Vasilliadis rightly had observed that, while ,contextuality', i.e. the recognition of the contextual character of theology, is a legitimate hermeneutical concern in the ecumenical debate on theological education, it should be kept in balance with the principle of the 'catholicity of theology': "The future of ecumenical theological education lies in reconciling these two currents of modern ecumenism. Orthodox theological institutions must immediately start a process in order to soften the existing antithesis between contextuality and catholicity." (ibid., 606).

[34] John Meyendorff, *True and False Ecumenism*, in *Witness to the World ...*, 45.

force."[35] A detailed report of the Nairobi Assembly from an Orthodox perspective was published by Thomas Hopko and Constance Tarasar, delegates of the Orthodox Church in America.[36] Their report contains some critical remarks on the WCC Assembly in Nairobi, as well as some self-criticism on the way Orthodox delegates acted in that Assembly. A source of frustration for the Orthodox in Nairobi was the nature of worship: they were almost totally Protestant. The issue of women ordination appeared, very likely for the first time in a WCC Assembly and "the Orthodox opinions were not heard." Also "the Orthodox delegates were often directly and openly attacked as provincial or obstinate for not participating in the general Eucharists or for not allowing others to participate in the Orthodox Liturgy."[37] They self-criticized the "national parochialism" of a great number of Orthodox delegates involved too much in politics at the costs of the common Orthodox witness within the Assembly, a "super-Orthodox" tendency to drown the documents in heavy theological terminology, and the lack of effort among the Orthodox to speak with one voice. In conclusion "the Orthodox cannot really rejoice too much over Nairobi". Some spoke of the "agony of the Orthodox" in WCC activities.[38]

A more official and critical evaluation of the Nairobi Assembly has been done by the Russian Orthodox Church in a 17 page typed letter, signed by Patriarch Pimen and the members of the Holy Synod of the Russian Orthodox church and addressed to the WCC Central Committee moderator of that time, Archbishop Scott and WCC General Secretary, Philip Potter. The letter was circulated with all the heads of the Orthodox Autocephalous Churches, and shared with all members of the WCC Central Committee.[39] The letter welcomes the missionary concern as expressed in the Assembly, but it warns that "missionary activity and 'common witness' without unity in faith and in basic canonical structure does not contribute to true unity, and even can be an obstacle if the confessional differences are artificially silenced." It mentions that some participants at the Assembly affirmed that one day WCC could become a "Church Council" and rejects any idea that WCC is, in any sense, a "super-church" or has any independent "ecclesial significance." The letter complains of the criticism formulated about the Orthodox in Nairobi because of their refusal to practice "intercommunion" and urges further studies of Baptism and the meaning of the Eucharist and sacerdotal ministry. The letter welcomes in principal inter-religious dialogue and dialogue with "secular ideologies", but "exclude *a priori* any possible 'convergence' of Christianity with those ideologies and any form of religious syncretism." Critical remarks are made on the Assembly's recommendation that those churches which admit female ordination should not abstain from it "out of ecumenical considerations." While mentioning that "we do not see reasons to object to any solution of this problem (i.e. female ordination) in confessions which do not recognize the priesthood as a sacrament" the letter rejects "secular categories" as being able to define a solution for the church and defines female ordination as "unknown" in the New Testament and Holy Tradition. Relevant also are complaints regarding worship and the fact that the Orthodox are isolated in the midst of a Protestant majority.

After such a heavy critique formulated by the largest WCC member church, several efforts have been done both by Orthodox Churches and by WCC to identify the difficulties faced by the Orthodox in WCC and to improve WCC's agenda in those points that were criticized by the Orthodox. A consultation of Orthodox theologians on "The Ecumenical Nature of Orthodox Witness" was organized by the Orthodox Task Force of WCC in New Valamo, Finland from 24-30 September 1977 which tried to formulate the principles of Orthodox

---

[35] John Meyendorff, "Confessing Christ today: Orthodox consultation prepares for fourth assembly of the World Council of Churches" in *St. Vladimir's Theological Quarterly,* 18.4 (1974): 193-194 (N. B.: the title is wrong: it presents the consultation preparing the Orthodox delegates for the fifth WCC Assembly). The reports of the Cernica consultation were published also by Nikos Nissiotis, "Confessing Christ Today: reports of groups at a consultation of Orthodox theologians" in *International Review of Mission* 64.1 (1975): 79-94.

[36] Thomas Hopko, Constance Tarasar, "Orthodox at Nairobi" in *St. Vladimir's Theological Quarterly* 20.1-2 (1976): 37-42.

[37] Ibid., 40.

[38] Ibid., 40.

[39] Ath. Basdekis, document 33, 191-209. See also John Meyendorff, "An Evaluation of Nairobi by the Church of Russia" in *St. Vladimir's Theological Quarterly* 1 (1976): 42-45 who presents a summary of the letter. In my presentation, I followed Meyendorff's review.

Part II: Orthodoxy and Ecumenism - Foundations

engagement in modern ecumenical movement.[40] More important for the Orthodox participation in WCC was the consultation organized by Eastern Orthodox Churches and WCC in Sofia, Bulgaria, 23-31 May 1981 on "Orthodox Involvement in the WCC."[41] The report contains four parts, an introduction and a conclusion. After talking about "the Orthodox understanding of ecumenism and participation in the WCC" (part 1), the document turns to "Orthodox experiences and problems in the WCC" (part 2). First are mentioned the positive aspects of Orthodox participation in the WCC: WCC was instrumental in promoting ecumenical consciousness in countries of many Orthodox Churches; it encouraged dialogue between Eastern and Oriental Orthodox Churches; WCC "rendered great service to the cause of Christian unity and unity of human kind" through its various activities. The "problems emerging from the Orthodox participation in the WCC" fall under three points: (1) "Because of the working style of the Council, from time to time the Orthodox feel uneasy in it. They have not always had the opportunity to promote their priorities in the programmatic undertaking of the Council. On the contrary, issues alien to the Orthodox tradition and ethos are adopted on the Council's agenda as priority issues, such as the question of the ordination of women to priesthood;" (2) "The language used and the methodology of elaborating theological statements have not always been sufficiently transparent to allow Orthodox positions to emerge and become an integral part of documents from the WCC bodies;" (3) "The Council, being primarily a Council of Churches, member churches should have the right of appointing their representatives to the various bodies of WCC."[42] The third part of the document entitled "Perspectives of Orthodox contributions to the activities of the WCC" contains concrete proposals on how Orthodox participation and visibility in WCC should be improved. The Sofia consultation was also the first one which proposed a "family model" with reference to decision-making procedures in WCC.

Orthodox theologians who constantly observed the life of WCC continued to formulate critiques on its agenda. In 1982, John Meyendorff observed that "the ecumenical movement, as represented by the WCC ... apparently forgot its original goal. Since theological differences between various Christian churches or groups seemed insurmountable, impatient activists within Protestantism, obsessed with a vision of the world full of poverty and obvious injustice, began to identify Christianity with a dream of social revolution which in fact served as a substitute for the Christian faith in the Resurrection. Very few had enough historical experience and human wisdom to realize that the same despair and the same dreams had led earlier generations to revolutions which eventually enslaved humanity and killed the human spirit."[43]

The Orthodox delegates for the 6th WCC Assembly, Vancouver, 1983, met in a preparatory meeting in Damascus from 5-10 February 1982. In the communiqué[44] issued after the meeting, the Orthodox warned "not to be pressured into any minimalist conceptions of Christian unity and therefore of 'intercommunion'" which is defined as being foreign to the Orthodox tradition. "We should not be asked or pressured to be unfaithful to that tradition (i.e. authentic tradition) on the basis of some argument which appears rational and Scripture-based. Our memories are long, and we have the experience of being led astray by arguments which looked rational and were based on Scripture"[45] – added a participant in the pre-assembly meeting in Damascus. Orthodox participation in the Vancouver Assembly, both in theological discussions as well as in worship improved significantly, as Professor Aurel Jivi, Romanian Orthodox Church delegate stated in a report on the Assembly. He concluded by saying that "the Orthodox participation in this Assembly (i. e. in Vancouver) has again proved their deep commitment to the cause of church unity as well as their conviction that the WCC constitutes the best framework within which Christian churches can advance the road leading to unity."[46]

[40] See "Report of an Inter-Orthodox Consultation 'The Ecumenical Nature of Orthodox Witness'", New Valamo, Finland, 20-24 September 1977 in G. Limouris, 66-69.
[41] For the text of the report, see Ath. Basdekis, Document 44, 300-314 and G. Limouris, 87-94.
[42] G. Limouris, 90-91.
[43] John Meyendorff, "An Ecumenical Advance?" in *Witness to the World* ..., 38.
[44] See Ath. Basdekis, document 45, 315-333; G. Limouris, 95-104.
[45] G. Limouris, 104.
[46] Aurel Jivi, "Orthodox Participation at Vancouver" in *Ecumenical Review* 36.2 (1984), 177.

The Third Pre-Conciliar Pan-Orthodox Conference gathered in Chambésy, Switzerland from 28 October – 6 November 1986 formulated a decision on "The Orthodox Church and the Ecumenical Movement"[47] in the spirit of the previous Orthodox consultations in New Valamo and Sofia. It reaffirms the ecumenical commitment of the Orthodox Churches and their involvement in WCC as "one of the principal bodies of the contemporary ecumenical movement" and underlines that "the Orthodox Church ... does not accept the idea of the 'equality of confessions' and cannot consider Church unity as an interconfessional adjustment." It expresses also "concern ... about the ongoing enlargement of the WCC, resulting from the admission of different Christian communities as new members. Such a development will reduce in the long term the Orthodox participation in the various governing and consultative bodies of the WCC and will be detrimental to a healthy ecumenical dialogue within the Council."[48] The document contains also a few "points requiring immediate action" which are meant to improve Orthodox participation in WCC life and activities.

In the 7th WCC Assembly, in Canberra 1991, Eastern and Oriental Orthodox delegates presented a document called "Reflections of Orthodox Participants addressed to the Seventh Assembly of the WCC,"[49] expressing "some concerns ... that have been developing among the Orthodox since the last Assembly." These concerns were: restoration of the unity of the Church seems not to be anymore the main priority of the ecumenical movement; an increasing departure from the Basis of WCC; inter-religious dialogue should be developed on the basis of theological criteria "which will define the limits of diversity"; changing process of decision-making in the WCC (critic on the system of quotes). All these concerns "and other tendencies and developments question – in Orthodox opinion – the very nature and identity of the Council." The document harshly criticizes critic on the speech delivered by the Korean female theologian Mrs. Chung Hyun Kyung (without mentioning her name): "it is with alarm that the Orthodox have heard some presentations on the theme of this Assembly. ... some people tend to affirm with very great ease the presence of the Holy Spirit in many movements and developments without discernment."[50]

Shortly after the Canberra Assembly, the Orthodox Churches (both Eastern and Oriental) organized a consultation in Chambésy, Switzerland, 12-16 September 1991 to reflect on their experience in the last WCC Assembly. The report[51] contains three parts: (I) Presuppositions of Involvement for the Orthodox in ecumenical movement and the WCC; (II) Some Problems for the Orthodox in the WCC; (III) Towards an Improved Orthodox participation in the ecumenical movement. The main presuppositions formulated were: primary purpose of WCC is "to work for the restoration of unity among Christians" which means "full ecclesial unity, that is, unity in doctrinal teaching, sacramental life and polity"; re-commitment to the constitutional Basis of WCC; WCC is a council of churches, not a council of individuals, groups, movements etc.; within WCC, the Orthodox Churches should be the only ones responsible for their representation; doctrinal issues in the WCC structures should be considered as an essential element of each church's membership. The main problems mentioned were: the feeling shared by many Orthodox that WCC is drifting away from the Toronto Statement; "syncretistic accommodation in WCC activities especially in relationship with inter-religious dialogue; "tendencies within the WCC towards a one-sided 'horizontalism' which tends to disconnect social, political, environmental problems from our commitment to the Gospel of Jesus Christ"; "Inter-communion" and "Eucharistic hospitality" are criticized: "to share in the common cup while maintaining fundamental differences in faith, order and ministry does not make sense to the Orthodox, because it violates a major element of the meaning and significance of the Eucharist." In order to improve Orthodox participation in the ecumenical movement, the report proposed: to involve all levels of Orthodox Churches in ecumenical work; to improve Orthodox witness within ecumenical circles as a response

---

[47] Ath. Basdekis, document 51, 379-405; G. Limouris, 112-115.
[48] G. Limouris, 113.
[49] Ath. Basdekis, document 63, 545-549; G. Limouris, 177-179.
[50] Tony Kireopoulos, "A Cronicle of SVS Response to the WCC Assemblies", in *St. Vladimir's Theological Quarterly* 36.1-2 (1992): 159-175 describes this episode as a "sensation" created by the media and defined it as "only a minor incident within a serious aspect of the ecumenical crisis we are in today." (173)
[51] See Ath. Basdekis, document 65, 561-571; G. Limouris, 189-194.

to an express need for knowing Orthodoxy better; to take initiatives in responding to main areas of modern life instead of simply reacting to similar initiatives coming from other churches.

It is important also to mention here the consultative process on the theme "Towards a Common Understanding and Vision on the WCC" (CUV) and the Orthodox contribution and critical approach to it. The CUV process of consultations emerged after the WCC Central Committee meetings in Moscow (1989) and Geneva (1990). In Moscow, the General Secretary of WCC, Emilio Castro, was asked by the Central Committee to initiate a process of consultation on: (1) the common understanding and vision of WCC; (2) the relationship of WCC to its member churches; (3) the relationship of the WCC to its member churches and other Christian groups.[52] A small task force, under the leadership of WCC general secretary was hired to draft the CUV document. An advanced form of the CUV document was shared with delegates of Eastern and Oriental Orthodox Churches gathered at Chambésy in June 1995. They produced a document called "Common Understanding and Vision of the WCC: Preliminary Observations on the Reflection Process."[53] An entire chapter of the document deals with the difficulties or "dilemmas" faced by the Orthodox in WCC and in the ecumenical movement. They are classified under three different categories:

- *theological* (results of the theological dialogue are not satisfactory; tendencies to address topics without sufficient attention being given to theological perspectives; tendency to accept a certain relativity of Christian faith which seems to minimalize the concept of heresy; concern about the limits of acceptable diversity; different ecclesiological understanding and proselytism; "new radical theologies" emerging in many WCC member churches which promote inclusive language, women`s ordination, new sexual morals, abortion; refusal to accept any tampering with the language of the Scripture, any attempt to re-write the Scriptures or to confront them with the beliefs or ideology of any culture, denominations or movement; religious syncretism;)
- *cultural* (tendencies within WCC to consider the Orthodox as being "of the East" and their theology as being without relevance for the West; WCC is succumbing to the pressure of secular values, considering them universal and acceptable for all churches and cultures) and
- *procedural* (feeling of the Orthodox members in WCC governing bodies that they are a numerical minority; WCC is taking political position and actions without sufficient consultation with the local churches concerned; WCC should review its resource-sharing policy and methodology in order to respect the priorities established by local churches themselves; number of Orthodox staff members should be increased).

Separately under the interrogative category "New possibilities or new sources of tensions?", the following two issues are mentioned: concern is expressed that growing non-Orthodox membership in WCC will have "a deleterious effect on Orthodox involvement with regard to the issue of balanced participation"[54]; youth and female participation in WCC life should be proposed, not imposed.

The CUV process could not solve the big challenges faced by the Orthodox churches in their relationships with WCC. Deeply challenged by the profound political, social and economic changes which occurred in Eastern Europe after the fall of the communist regimes, Orthodox Churches reconsidered their place in WCC and in the ecumenical movement. The Georgian Orthodox Church has withdrawn from membership in the WCC and the conference of European Churches in May 1997. On 9 April 1998, the Holy Synod of the Bulgarian Orthodox Church decided to suspend its membership in WCC. The Council of Bishops of the Russian Orthodox Church and the Holy Synod of bishops of the Serbian Orthodox Church have requested a Pan-Orthodox discussion of Orthodox participation in the WCC.

---

[52] For a presentation of the genesis and development of the CUV process see Marlin Van Eldener, "Towards a Common Understanding and Vision" in *Ecumenical Review* 43.1 (1991), 138-145.

[53] See the final document in *Turn to God Rejoice in Hope. Orthodox Reflections On the Way to Harare,* Thomas FitzGerald, Peter Bouteneff (eds.), (Geneva: WCC Publications, 1998), 53-61.

[54] Ibid., 60.

In such a situation, two Orthodox meetings tried to manage this crisis. The first meeting took place in Thessaloniki, Greece, from 29 April – 2 May 1998 after an invitation of His All Holiness Ecumenical Patriarch Bartolomew and as a response to the request of the Russian and Serbian Churches. It issued an *Evaluation of New Facts in the Relations of Orthodoxy and the Ecumenical Movement*[55] which firstly underlined "the necessity for continuing Orthodox participation in various forms of Inter-Christian activity." The term "ecumenical" is avoided, probably because a previous paragraph explains that the "theme of ecumenism" is used by "extremist groups" to criticize the Church leadership. The document mentions along with positive aspects of Orthodox participation in WCC, "certain developments within some Protestant members of the Council that are reflected in the debates of the WCC and are regarded as unacceptable by the Orthodox." These are: intercommunion with non-Orthodox, inclusive language, ordination of women, the rights of sexual minorities and certain tendencies relating to religious minorities. The increasing estrangement between Orthodox and non-Orthodox constituency of WCC is clearly described: "After a century of Orthodox participation in the ecumenical movement and fifty years in the WCC in particular, we do not perceive sufficient progress in the multilateral theological discussion between Christians. On the contrary, the gap between the Orthodox and the Protestants is becoming wider as the aforementioned tendencies within certain Protestant denominations are becoming stronger (paragraph 10)." Finally, the Thessaloniki Statement recommends unanimous but sharply limited Orthodox participation at the Harare Assembly and proposes that a "Mixed Theological Commission" should be created after Harare to discuss "acceptable forms for Orthodox participation in the ecumenical movement and the radical restructuring of the WCC.[56] The second meeting, which took place immediately afterwards was the Orthodox Pre-Assembly meeting for the preparation of Orthodox delegates to participate in the 8th WCC Assembly, Harare, Zimbabwe, held at St. Ephraim Theological Seminary, near Damascus Syria, 7-13 May 1998. The statement of the Pre-Assembly meeting in St. Ephraim Theological Seminary acknowledged that "the relationships of the Orthodox to the WCC have become a matter of serious study." Reasons for this are: the Orthodox have become victims of proselytism, some ecumenical actors no longer have as their goal the restoration of Christian unity, values crisis, the moral stances taken by certain Christian groups. The statement also affirms that "there is a perception that the fellowship between Orthodox and Protestants in the Council is weakening, and that the Orthodox find it more difficult to make a contribution to the Council's agenda. These two inter-related problems need to be taken into account in the consideration of all areas of the Council's life, from the staff to the governing bodies and their commitments."[57]

Under these circumstances, the WCC 8th Assembly, Harare, 1998 took place in a time when "the local Orthodox churches have been debating their involvement in the ecumenical movement perhaps more hotly than ever before and a time when relations between the Orthodox churches and the WCC … were particularly strained" as Peter Bouteneff, American Orthodox theologian and participant in the Assembly stated.[58] The Orthodox participation and behaviour in the Harare Assembly was dominated by the Thessaloniki Statement.

Following the request formulated in Thessaloniki, a Special Commission on Orthodox participation in the WCC was created. The Commission was composed of an equal number of representatives appointed by Eastern and Oriental Orthodox Churches and representatives of other WCC member churches. After four meetings which took place between December 1999 and May 2002, the commission issued its final report which was accepted by the Central Committee meeting in September 2002. Even if the process of the Special Commission was sharply criticized by some Orthodox theologians like Ion Bria,[59] the final report[60] deals in an acceptable way

---

[55] Thomas FitzGerald and Peter Bouteneff, *Turn to God …*, 136-138.
[56] Ibid., 137-138.
[57] "Final Statement of the Orthodox Pre-Assembly Meeting" (before Harare) in *Turn to God Rejoice in Hope …*, 9-10.
[58] Peter Bouteneff, "The Orthodox at the Harare Assembly" in *St. Vladimir's Theological Quarterly* 43.1 (1999): 79.
[59] Ion Bria, "Widening the Ecclesiological Basis of the Ecumenical Fellowship" in *Ecumenical Review* 56.2 (2004): 199-210.
[60] See http://www.oikoumene.org/en/resources/documents/assembly/2006-porto-alegre/3-preparatory-and-background-documents/final-report-of-the-special-commission-on-orthodox-participation-in-the-wcc (last accessed September 2013). For a printed form see "Final Report of the Special Commission on Orthodox Participation in the WCC" in *Greek Orthodox Theological Review* (Spring/Summer 2004): 155-178.

Part II: Orthodoxy and Ecumenism - Foundations

with issues raised by the Orthodox, like ecclesiology, approach of social and ethical issues in WCC, common prayer, consensus decision-making, membership and representation in WCC.[61]

The Pre-Assembly Orthodox preparatory meeting for the 9th WCC Assembly, Porto Alegre, 2006 which took place on the island of Rhodes was a good opportunity to make the first considerations on the work and recommendations of the Special Commission on Orthodox participation in the WCC. The 3rd chapter of the final communiqué is a first evaluation of the experience of the spirit and ethos of the Special Commission. Two aspects are analysed in details: ecclesiology and consensus. Especially the implementation of consensus instead of making decisions from a parliamentary voting system is greeted as "the most visible result of the Special Commission."[62] The WCC Assembly in Porto Alegre went quite well for the Orthodox.[63] The major achievement of the Porto Alegre Assembly was the confirmation of a previous decision of WCC Central Committee to establish a Permanent Committee on Consensus and Collaboration to be formed by 50% Orthodox members and 50% members representing other WCC member churches, whose mandate would be to watch over the implementation of the spirit and ethos of the Special Commission.

The recent Pre-Assembly for the preparation for the delegates of the Orthodox Churches for the 10th WCC Assembly, Busan, Korea, which took place on the island of Kos, Greece, from 11-17 October 2012, formulated the following critical remarks on the current state of the ecumenical movement: "Orthodox churches – both Eastern and Oriental – call for a stronger focus in the WCC on the search for Christian Unity. We often hear comments about the crisis in the ecumenical movement and about the lack of interest in unity or the lack of a clear vision about the nature of this unity. To a greater extend, this is a consequence of the fact that the idea of visible unity is seen as unrealistic by many ecumenical partners, the Orthodox among them. We see this as a consequence of the developments taking place in some member churches over the last forty years (e.g., the ordination of women, different approaches to moral and ethical issues, etc.). The gap between member churches is thus growing wider. On the other hand, the growing participation in the ecumenical movement of Churches which are not members of the WCC and which bring to the dialogue new ecclesiological considerations and new understandings of unity as mission, add new challenges to the search for unity, particularly when such churches apply for WCC membership."[64] This statement proposes also that "the most appropriate way to solve this solution" is "to go back to the theological and moral teaching and practices of the early Church."

Concluding remarks

This short overview of Orthodox criticism on the ecumenical movement and WCC should be concluded by emphasizing the following summary remarks:

- The Orthodox were quite critical with the ecumenical movement and with WCC. They criticized the unity models proposed by the Protestant partners, the still existing prejudices, practices and difficulties emerging from the past, the WCC agenda and structures, proselytism, the "Protestant dominance" in WCC, inclusive language, newly developed approaches of moral values etc.;
- The fact that the same criticism is repeated by several Orthodox meetings could be interpreted as a sign that the issues raised by the Orthodox were not really heard by their partners in WCC;

[61] For an Orthodox interpretation of the final report of the Special Commission see Peter Bouteneff, "The Report of the Special Commission on Orthodox Participation in the world Council of Churches: an introduction" in *Ecumenical Review* 55.1 (2003): 49-55;

[62] Metropolitan Gennadios of Sassima (ed.), *Grace in Abundance. Orthodox Reflections on the Way to Porto Alegre*, (Geneva: WCC Publications, 2005), 8.

[63] See Antoine Arjakovsky, "Porto Alegre's redefinition of ecumenism and the transformation of Orthodoxy" in *Ecumenical Review* 58.3 (2006): 265-279.

[64] See http://www.oikoumene.org/en/resources/documents/executive-committee/2013-03/orthodox-pre-assembly-report (last accessed September 2013).

- Orthodox criticism, even if sometimes formulated in quite hard terms, tried to be constructive and to propose alternative solutions;
- While criticising the ecumenical movement, the WCC or their partners within the Council, the Orthodox did not forget to be self-critical;
- In order to ensure a genuine contribution to the modern ecumenical movement and, when necessary, a constructive critical approach, more coherent training and theological formation on Orthodox participation in the ecumenical movement is needed;
- Challenged on the one hand by their brothers and sisters within the ecumenical movement and on the other by their own Orthodox fellows, sometimes Orthodox ecumenists put more emphasis on what has not been the reason for the Orthodox participation in the modern ecumenical movement, i. e. not "to water down Orthodox witness, (or) to accept a Protestant view of Christianity and to drop the claim of Orthodoxy to be true Church of Christ"[65], rather than to highlight the main reasons for Orthodox involvement in the ecumenical movement, i.e. its genuine and permanent concern for the unity of the Church of Christ.

Bibliography

Athanasios Basdekis (ed.), *Orthodoxe Kirche und ökumenische Bewegung. Dokumente – Erklärungen – Berichte,* (Frankfurt am Main: Lembeck, 2006) provides easy access in German to significant documents for the engagement of Orthodox Churches in the ecumenical movement. A footnote attached to each document indicates other sources where the respective document was published in different languages;

Peter Bouteneff, "The Orthodox at the Harare Assembly" in *St. Vladimir's Theological Quarterly* 43.1 (1999): 79-84;

Peter Bouteneff, "The Report of the Special Commission on Orthodox Participation in the world Council of Churches: an introduction" in *Ecumenical Review* 55.1 (2003): 49-55;

Thomas FitzGerard and Peter Bouteneff (eds.), *Turn to God Rejoice in Peace. Orthodox Reflections on the Way to Harare,* (Geneva: WCC Publications, 1998); it contents important Orthodox documents issued between 1995-1998;

Tamara Grdzelidze, *Ecumenism, Orthodoxy and* in *The Encyclopedia of Eastern Orthodox Christianity,* John Anthony McGuckin (ed.), vol. I, (Wiley-Blackwell, 2001), 208-215;

Aurel Jivi, "Orthodox participation at Vancouver" in *Ecumenical Review* 36 :2 (1984), p. 174-177;

Tony Kireopoulos, "A Cronicle of SVS Response to the WCC Assemblies", in *St. Vladimir's Theological Quarterly* 36.1-2 (1992): 159-175;

Gennadios Limouris, *Orthodox Visions of Ecumenism. Statements, Messages and Reports on the Ecumenical Movement 1902-1992,* (Geneva: WCC Publications, 1994) useful as resource book in English;

John Meyendorff, *Witness to the World,* (Crestwood, NY: St. Vladimir's Seminary Press, 1987);

Robert G. Stephanopoulos, "Reflections on Orthodox Ecumenical Directions after Uppsala" in *Journal of Ecumenical Studies* 9.2 (1972): 301-317.

---

[65] John Meyendorff, *The Ecumenical Dilemma* in *Witness to the World* ..., 25.

(19) Theological, Historical, and Cultural Reasons for Anti-ecumenical Movements in Eastern Orthodoxy

Pantelis Kalaitzidis

The emergence of the ecumenical movement, in which Eastern Orthodoxy played a decisive role, has been recorded as a major development in the Christian history of the 20th century. In fact, some examples which signify the importance of Eastern Orthodoxy in the emergence of Ecumenism are the two famous encyclicals (1902 and 1920) issued by the Ecumenical Patriarchate of Constantinople appealing for Christian unity and inter-church cooperation, but also for the creation of a "league" of churches; the decision of the Great Council of Moscow of the Russian Orthodox Church to establish a Department for Christian unity (1918). Finally, the active participation of many distinguished Orthodox ecclesiastical and theological figures (such as the Archbishop of Athens Chrysostomos Papadopoulos, the bishops Germanos of Thyatira and Irinej of Novi Sad, the fathers Sergius Bulgakov, Georges Florovsky, and Lev Gilet, and the lay theologians Leon Zander, Nicholas Glubokovsky, Hamilcar Alivizatos, Stefan Zankof, etc.) in the first ecumenical meetings of "Faith and Order" and "Life and Work", and their constructive as well as enriching contributions in the beginnings of the ecumenical theological reflection worldwide were admittedly of significant importance for the emergence of Ecumenism and the consolidation of the ecumenical idea among Christians and churches.

However, despite this positive role, it is also a fact that negative reactions to Ecumenism and distorted images of it appeared very early in Eastern Orthodoxy. The Patriarchal Encyclical of 1902 was not positively received by all Orthodox churches. Besides the violent anti-ecumenical reactions of the Greek Old Calendarists, which had already begun in the interwar period, it is also noteworthy that in the 1948 Founding Assembly of the World Council of Churches in Amsterdam, in spite of the presence of numerous official representatives of Eastern Orthodox churches, only three of them (the Ecumenical Patriarchate, the Church of Cyprus, the Church of Greece) were eventually listed among the founding members of the major forum for the ecumenical dialogue and inter-Christian cooperation. The rest of the Orthodox churches, either remained sceptical or "neutral" towards this major ecclesial ecumenical development, or even openly disagreed (mainly because of the political situation of that time, shaped in most cases by the communist regimes) with the founding and the ecumenical vision of the World Council of Churches. This meant that they signed or endorsed the Moscow Document issued at the end of the Moscow Consultation of the Orthodox Churches held at the initiative of the Russian Orthodox Church (1948). Some Eastern Orthodox churches began joining the WCC from 1952 onwards (such as the Greek-Orthodox Patriarchate of Antioch), but the majority of the Orthodox churches finally became WCC members only in 1961 at the third General Assembly in New Delhi (and some of them even later, up to 1973), while two Eastern Orthodox churches, i.e. the Georgian Orthodox Church and the Bulgarian Orthodox Church suspended their membership to the WCC (the first one in 1997 and the second only one year later).

Many significant events in the second half of the 20th century undoubtedly marked the ecumenical commitment of Eastern Orthodoxy. The majority of the Orthodox Churches became members not only of the WCC, but also of the Council of European Churches (CEC) after 1959. By meeting with Pope Paul VI in Jerusalem (1964), the Ecumenical Patriarch Athenagoras I, sent to the Christians worldwide a bold and meaningful message of reconciliation, forgiveness, and overcoming the painful rivalries of the past and its traumatic memories, inaugurating thus the "dialogue of charity." Following the initiative of the Ecumenical Patriarchate of Constantinople, all Orthodox churches entered into a longstanding theological dialogue with the Roman Catholic Church, the so-called dialogue of truth (from 1980 until today). Parallel to this official theological dialogue, the Orthodox churches, under the leadership of the Ecumenical Patriarchate, engaged in many other official theological dialogues, as for example with the Oriental Orthodox (non-Chalcedonian) churches, the Anglican Church, the Old Catholic Church, the Lutheran churches, the Reformed churches, etc. An initial theological agreement was reached with the Old Catholic Church (1987) without, however, achieving full sacramental communion because of some disagreement in issues such as intercommunion and women's ordination; the final doctrinal agreement of crucial importance on the Christological issue was signed jointly by the Eastern Orthodox churches and the Oriental Orthodox (non-Chalcedonian) churches (1990), which clearly stated that the two church-families explicitly acknowledged sharing the same and identical Christological faith. However, this was not followed by any impact in the life of the respective churches, and did not lead to the next step, i.e. the restoration of the full ecclesial and Eucharistic communion, despite the agreement reached on a series of Proposals for the lifting of the Anathemas and towards the restoration of ecclesial communion at the 1993 Chambésy meeting (mainly because of pending issues regarding the recognition on behalf of the Orientals of the 4th, 5th, 6th, and 7th Ecumenical Councils, and of the mutual lifting of the anathemas, but also because of the hesitations expressed on the part of the Russian Orthodox Church, and the strong reactions of some monasteries in Mount-Athos).

In spite of this pan-Orthodox agreement regarding the Orthodox membership to WCC and more broadly to the participation in the ecumenical movement (confirmed once again, and in a very solemn way at the 3rd Pre-Conciliar Pan-Orthodox Conference in Chambésy, 1986), and despite the unequivocal ecumenical engagement and orientation of contemporary leading Orthodox theologians like Archbishop Anastasios of Albania, Metropolitans Anthony Bloom of Sourozh, John Zizioulas of Pergamon, Georges Khodr of Mount-Lebanon, and Kallistos Ware of Diokleia, Frs Georges Florovksy, Dumitru Stăniloae, John Meyendorff, Ion Bria, Cyril Argenti, Professors Nikos Nissiotis, Olivier Clément, Todor Sabev, Gerassimos Konidaris, Savas Agourides, and others, a powerful anti-ecumenical trend was from the very beginning persistently present in Eastern Orthodoxy, having a great impact on many domains of the ecclesial life and theological education. If for many decades this trend was mostly active and aggressive in the context of the Orthodox Church of Greece (for the reasons I will try to explain later in my text), after the fall of communism and the consequent political and socio-cultural turbulences, it also became visible, and even influential, in the Orthodox countries of Central and Eastern Europe.

How could anyone then explain this "Orthodox" reluctance or, even, animosity, towards the ecumenical idea? Why is a church tradition with a rich universalistic past and a diachronic ecumenical ethos, facing today a strong and tenacious fundamentalist anti-ecumenical polemics? Which are the historical, social and theological reasons for the strengthening of anti-ecumenical movements and feelings in the context of Eastern Orthodoxy? In this article I will attempt to provide some insights and give some answers to this complex and multifaceted issue.

I. Persistent Ambiguity of the Orthodox Participation in the Ecumenical Movement

Despite the institutional participation of all canonical autocephalous Orthodox churches in the ecumenical movement and their fruitful and constructive contribution in many crucial issues; despite the leading role of distinguished Eastern Orthodox theologians as the ones cited in the previous section of this article, in promoting ecumenical understanding and theological reflection towards Christian unity, it seems that from the Orthodox side, especially in the monastic milieus, the low clergy and the grassroots, there has always been a standing suspicion to, if not an open rejection of, the ecumenical movement.

As the leading Greek biblical scholar, Professor Savas Agourides (very active ecumenist during the 60s and 70s) reminds us:

> There were strong reactions against the participation of the Orthodox Church in the ecumenical movement. The argument that was put forward in order to override these reactions was that Orthodox participation will be a witness to the undivided Church of the first millennium and an invitation of return to its tradition and roots. [...] We

entered the ecumenical movement with unrealistic visionary perceptions of the first millennium, which was neither undivided, nor perfect and without need of reformation. We entered it because of the other's salvation; but, so did the others towards us. [...] It is for the above-mentioned reasons that the Orthodox attitude towards the ecumenical movement from its beginning until today has been defensive. As it happens with other partners within the World Council of Churches, Orthodoxy expresses claims of supremacy which have been proved ineffectual. It would be essential for the participation of our church in the ecumenical movement if it is firstly going to experience a spiritual and theological renewal with the dynamic recovery of the Holy Spirit and the historico-critical approach of pending issues. Then the spirit of sincerity, modesty and love can break the ice of centuries. Something must be done within the churches. Only then something new could rise in their relations.

This defensive attitude was aggravated for different reasons and by unfortunate events, as for example by the Old Calendarist schism in the Orthodox Church of Greece (1924) or the establishment of the Synod of Bishops of the Russian Church Abroad in the Sremski Karlovci, Serbia (1922, 1927), later named the "Russian Orthodox Church Outside Russia" (ROCOR), as a reaction to the compromise of the Russian Orthodox Church in Bolshevik Russia with the communist atheist regime. The extreme reactions of a rather small, but extremely conservative part of the Orthodox faithful (with an anti-modern, anti-ecumenical, anti-Western agenda), against any reformation or change in the church life, led many local Orthodox Churches, hierarchs and lay theologians to the adoption of an ambiguous stance towards the ecumenical movement: with some rare exceptions, the general rule was that, while they were fully participating in the ecumenical meetings and discussions, the official ecumenical representatives of the Orthodox Churches systematically avoided speaking during these meetings to a wider audience within their churches, as they never openly addressed their flock or their theological students' issues and concerns commonly raised with other Christians during the ecumenical gatherings. The official Orthodox representatives used to use for decades a dual language: one ecumenical *ad extra*, and one conservative and defensive (but not principally anti-ecumenical) *ad intra*. As a result of this ambiguity, despite the initial positive attitude of Eastern Orthodoxy towards ecumenical movement, the Orthodox faithful remained alienated from, and finally became suspicious of, the search for Christian unity and the efforts towards ecumenical understanding. To this overall "Orthodox" ambiguity we must mention two notable exceptions: a) the Ecumenical Patriarchate of Constantinople, whose Patriarchs and hierarchs in general showed even at the dawn of the 20th century a rare ecumenical awareness, being from the beginning warmly committed to the ecumenical idea, whereas its professors of theology at the Theological School of Chalki used to share with their students their own ecumenical experience and participation in inter-Christian theological meetings; and b) the Greek-Orthodox Patriarchate of Antioch (Syria and Lebanon); especially after the renewal brought about by the creation of the "Mouvement de Jeunesse Orthodoxe" (Youth Orthodox Movement, 1942), this Church engaged in a sincere and fervent ecumenical spirit, and worked, through biblical, patristic and liturgical renewal, towards deeper faith, repentance, and reconciliation among Christians.

In order for us to understand this "Orthodox" reluctance towards the ecumenical movement, it seems that we have to go deeper into the question, as very often for many Orthodox churches, monastics, or lay theologians, this ambiguity, and this dual language, and even anti-ecumenical stance imply: the understanding of ecumenical movement mainly or exclusively as a return to Orthodoxy; the successive losses of Orthodox universalism; the exclusivist ecclesiological models and the non-recognition of the "ecclesiological status" of the other Christian churches and Confessions; historical reasons as the Westrern aggressiveness and the traumatic historical experience of Orthodox peoples, which decisively contributed to the formation of Orthodox fundamentalism, anti-Westernism, and anti-ecumenism; the way in which the famous "Return to Fathers" was understood and applied to the East-West relationship; and last, but not least, the unresolved relationship of Orthodoxy and Modernity.

II. The Understanding of Ecumenical Movement as a Return to Orthodoxy
and the Exclusivist Orthodox Ecclesiological Models

According to the recent analysis by Professor Athanasios Vletsis of Munich University, the fundamental thesis of Orthodox ecclesiology regarding the issue under discussion, at least as it is recorded and witnessed in the official texts and statements issued at the occasions of the Orthodox or the ecumenical meetings, does not seem to leave room for any dualism between an idealized image of the catholicity of the church and its concrete, visible, and institutional expression within the Orthodox Church, since "the Orthodox Church is the One, Holy, Catholic, and Apostolic Church which we confess in the Creed" (3rd Pre-Conciliar Pan-Orthodox Conference, Chambésy, Geneva, 1986); or to put it in a more drastic way, according to the wording of the Orthodox representatives in the 3rd General Assembly of the WCC, in New Delhi, in 1961: "For the Orthodox, the Orthodox Church *is* precisely the Church;" and, finally, according to the *Toronto Declaration* of 1950 (adopted by the Central Committee of WCC): "Membership in the WCC does not imply the acceptance of a specific doctrine concerning the nature of Church unity [...] Membership does not imply that each Church must regard the other member Churches as Churches in the true and full sense of the word."

Orthodox then, according to Timothy (Kallistos) Ware in his classic work *The Orthodox Church*, "by participating [sc. in WCC], do not thereby imply that they regard all Christian confessions as equal, nor do they compromise the Orthodox claim to be the true Church. [...] In view of this explicit statement [...], Orthodox can take part in the Ecumenical Movement without endangering their Orthodoxy. And if Orthodox *can* take part, then they *must* do so: for since they believe the Orthodox faith to be true, it is their duty to bear witness to that faith as widely as possible." The Orthodox participation in the ecumenical movement is then not only understood as a witness to the undivided church, and as an invitation to the other Christians to return to the common tradition of the first millennium (as another wording of the final document of the 3rd Pre-Conciliar Pan-Orthodox Conference of Chambésy maintains), but very often it is related to the expectation that this search for the common biblical and patristic sources and the return to the roots would eventually lead to the conversion of the Western Christians to Orthodoxy. In this more or less exclusivist ecclesiological perspective, ecumenical dialogue was justified by the very fact that it should one day lead to the acknowledgment by all Christians of the truth and authentic faith preserved in the Orthodox Church. But to the extent that such a return did not take place, and Western Christians continued to follow their respective church tradition, and even introduce reformations and canonical changes in many church life domains, frustration and disappointment were considerably increased among the Orthodox, along with suspicion and rejection towards ecumenical dialogue.

Of course the Orthodox constantly appealed to the need for all Christians (the Orthodox included) to return to the tradition of the undivided Church, but by identifying this tradition exclusively with the Eastern Church, and by assigning to the other Christian churches and Confessions a status of deficient or partial ecclesiality, they finally come to imply that they should all return to Orthodoxy.

The same ambiguity can be observed in the issue of the recognition of the Baptism of the other Christians: Despite the general rule prevailing until the 18th century of receiving Western Christians who wish to convert to the Orthodox Church only through Chrismation, and without re-baptizing them (which implies the recognition of their Baptism); despite a fundamental theological agreement reached between the Eastern Orthodox and the Roman Catholic churches in the Trinitarian, Christological, ecclesiological and sacramental domains—including a common vision of baptismal initiation—as it is recorded in the Munich (1982), Bari (1987), and Valamo (1988) documents, there is not any explicit recognition on behalf of the majority of the Orthodox churches of the baptism of the Western Christians, not even of that celebrated in the Roman Catholic Church. A hopeful exception to this general negative rule is the fact that almost all the Orthodox churches in Germany signed the Magdeburg Declaration (2007) mutually recognizing the Baptism of the other Christian churches.

If the ecumenical movement is "a great move of conversion and repentance" (Jürgen Moltmann), then it may be time for the Orthodox to recognize their own mistakes and failures for which they need to ask forgiveness, clarify the topics and issues they should reconsider in the light of the common tradition of the undivided Church.

In any case, according to the prevailing idea among many clerics, monastics, and lay Orthodox (which is not the one maintained in the institutional level), this return should not only include the acceptance by Westerners of the Orthodox position in key dogmatic issues such as, for example, the *filioque* or papal primacy and infallibility, the distinction in essence and uncreated energies in God, purgatory, and the theory on the satisfaction of divine justice by the Cross of Jesus Christ, etc., but should also move to the liturgical rite, to canonical matters or even to local customs and practices. There has not been any serious discussion among the Orthodox regarding the nature and the origins of the differences separating us from Christians of other traditions, i.e. the effort to distinguish and discern which of the differences we have with the Westerns (Catholics, Anglicans, Protestants) and the Oriental Orthodox, those which touch the very core of the ecclesial faith and those which are just a reflection or an expression of the cultural, social or political context of each place and time.

The example of the recent canonical practice of women's ordination adopted by the mainstream Protestant churches, as well as by the Anglican Church, and the Old Catholic Church, but strongly rejected by the Orthodox Church, is an indicative one, and high revelatory of the prevailing mentality. In recent times, the Orthodox have tried to respond to the challenges posed by the feminist movement and feminist theologies on many occasions, particularly at the Rhodes Consultation in 1988, which mainly focused on the elaboration of arguments against women's ordination. Despite the overall negative Orthodox attitude, in more recent years the opinion has gained ground (even among distinguished Orthodox hierarchs and theologians) that, apart from the argument of "tradition," there seems to be no other serious theological reason hindering the ordination of women. As early as 1968, John D. Zizioulas (now Metropolitan of Pergamon in the Ecumenical Patriarchate), maintained that "on the question of the ordination of women, Orthodox theologians could find no theological reasons against such an ordination. Yet the entire matter is so deeply tied up with their tradition that they would find it difficult in their majority to endorse without reservations the rather enthusiastic statements of the paper." For his part, Metropolitan of Diokleia Kallistos Ware, in a book written in collaboration with the late French Orthodox theologian Elisabeth Behr-Sigel, had to recognize that in the light of patristic anthropology and of Orthodox theology, there are no serious theological arguments against women's ordination, except the argument of "tradition." Despite the fact that canonical matters in Orthodoxy have always been subject to revisions and reformations, insofar as they do not affect the fundamental doctrines of our faith, i.e. Trinitarian or/and Christological doctrines, and the growing consensus among distinguished Orthodox theologians regarding the non-theological character of "Orthodox" arguments against women's ordination, it is clear that the Orthodox Church is constantly refusing to seriously consider and discuss this issue, appealing to the criterion of "tradition" which is in fact identified with the structures and perceptions of the traditional patriarchal societies of the Middle East in which Orthodoxy is mainly shaped, and to which it owes its historical and cultural physiognomy. In addition, as it is well-known, the adoption of women's ordination by the Old Catholic, Anglican, and mainstream Protestant churches, and its rejection by the Orthodox Church, constitutes a source of serious discordance and friction in their ecumenical relations. With regard to the relationship of the Orthodox Church with the Old Catholic Church, it was even one of the reasons of failing to achieve full sacramental communion, despite the initial theological agreement which was reached between the two churches in 1987. If the Orthodox Church could be criticized for its rejection of a "new" canonical practice on the basis of its fixation on non-theological/cultural factors, the Western churches on the other hand, which adopted the ordination of women, could in their turn be criticized for their lack of ecumenical sensitivity, since they had not tried to raise this issue in their dialogue with the Orthodox Church prior to the final adoption of this practice. In addition, by adopting

Orthodox Handbook on Ecumenism

women's ordination without taking into account Orthodoxy's difficulties in this matter (even of cultural order), Western mainstream churches demonstrated once again their eurocentric spirit and their feeling of cultural superiority and sense of progress, insofar as they expect that the Eastern Christians can walk within a few decades a journey for which Western Christians needed many centuries and the landmarks of Enlightenment, modernity, and post-modern pluralistic societies.

As a result of the above lack on behalf of the Orthodox of a clear distinction between theological and non-theological factors, every different practice or belief in the life of the non-Orthodox churches, every diverging formula or wording in the latter's dogmatic tradition immediately acquires for many of the Orthodox faithful the status of doctrinal distortion, which must be abandoned and overcome if we aspire to union and communion in the same Eucharistic chalice. For many Orthodox it is still difficult to see unity in diversity or to reach church unity through the legitimate church's diversities, while, despite a positive approach to otherness articulated nowadays by leading Orthodox theologians, it seems that on behalf of the Eastern Orthodox it is painful to accept theological pluralism as well as to reconcile the uniqueness of the true faith with the acceptance of otherness, the particularity of Orthodoxy with the ecumenicity and the catholicity of the church. In a bold statement Fr. Georges Florovsky went so far as to maintain that the catholicity of Christendom requires inseparably both the Christian West and the Christian East. He is not speaking yet of the catholicity of the church, but merely of the Christian civilization:

> In any case, both societies, Western and Eastern Orthodox, have the same ancestry and the same historical roots, and have succeeded the same parental society, Hellenic and Roman. It would be inexact to consider them simply as parallel developments, for parallel lines have no common points, and our two societies have obviously at least one point in common, namely their starting point: They are obviously off-springs of the same root. [...] One may call them sister-civilizations. And I venture to suggest, these sisters were Siamese twins. One knows but too well, that even with a skillful surgeon the separation of the Siamese twins is a risky and dubious operation. I am afraid this is precisely what has happened. The main feature, or rather the major tragedy of European history, or actually of the history of Christendom, was that these two Christian Societies broke away from each other, and a historian runs a heavy risk of misconceiving and misconstruing the history of either Society, if he dares to ignore this basic fact. The point is that neither is self-explanatory, neither is intelligible, when taken separately. Both Societies are but fragments of a disrupted world, and they belong together despite the Schism. Only in the perspective of this Christian disruption is the history both of the East and the West truly intelligible. A self-explanatory character of Western Society is but a deceiving fiction, and a very dangerous and misleading fiction it is indeed. Western Christendom is not, and never was, an independent world, but a part or just a fragment of the wider whole. So is Eastern Christendom too. The only intelligible field of study would be Christendom as a whole.

Today, there is an increasing tendency within Eastern Orthodoxy of ignoring the other parts of Christianity, a tendency towards uniformity and homogeneity. Legitimate theological pluralism and unity in diversity are not only treated with suspicion when it comes to Christians of other traditions, but even within the Orthodox Christians themselves. An example would be that of the predominance in all Orthodox places, faculties or seminaries of the "neo-patristic synthesis" over the Russian School theology, and the henceforth mandatory character for all Orthodox theologians of the famous "return to the Fathers"; or, to use another example, the insertion of models and practices of spirituality, or of elements of the liturgical rite (architecture, iconography, music), originated in the Greek or Russian "mother churches" in the Orthodox missions in Africa and Asia without any serious concern for enculturation. These could all be considered as indicative signs of this ecclesial and theological uniformity affecting today's Orthodoxy and preventing a genuine ecumenical spirit among the Orthodox faithful. However, in order to understand and explain the above defensive attitude chiefly characterized by ecclesiological exclusivism and theological uniformity, we have to be aware of the successive losses of Orthodox universalism which determined, to a great extent, the theological background of the Orthodox anti-ecumenical movements and shaped their physiognomy and agenda.

Part II: Orthodoxy and Ecumenism - Foundations

III. The Successive Losses of Orthodox Universalism

Eastern Orthodoxy, as it is maintained in the Final Document of the 3rd Pre-Conciliar Pan-Orthodox Conference of Chambésy, Geneva (1986), kept alive the consciousness that it is the catholic Church. According to the same pan-Orthodox document, the Orthodox Church, in its profound conviction and ecclesiastical consciousness of being the bearer of and the witness to the faith and tradition of the One, Holy, Catholic, and Apostolic Church, firmly believes that it occupies a central place in matters relating to the promotion of Christian unity within the contemporary world. This understanding of the catholicity of the church, chiefly and primarily experienced in the Eucharist, and formulated within the theology of the local church and through Eucharistic ecclesiology, was not without consequences for the historical course of the church, since it was, later and in a second stage, linked, in many regards, to the universalistic vision of a Christian empire, i.e. the Roman/Byzantine empire (which was claiming to incarnate and to realize the Kingdom of God on earth), in which the Emperor was supposed to be "in place of Christ."

However, to the extent that this catholic and universalistic vision was related to the Byzantine theocracy, to the Roman/Byzantine *oikoumene* and the imperial power, it was (and still is) suffering by a series of multiple—mainly historical and political—losses related, in their turn, to the retreat, diminution, and finally demise of the Roman/Byzantine empire, losses which seriously affected the sense of the catholic and universalistic consciousness of Orthodoxy. We Orthodox identify this consciousness greatly with Byzantium and its vision, that the Empire's demise in 1453 appears to have opened an incurable wound in our ecclesiological constitution and the way in which we materialize the relationship between local and universal church, between the particular and the catholic. In fact it is difficult to decide if our vision of catholicity arises from the Eucharistic experience and its ensuing ecclesiological principles or from the imperial unity and the reality of the Roman/Byzantine *oikoumene*. In other words, whether it could be considered as Eucharistic and ecclesial or political and cultural. Even worse, for many Orthodox these two visions of catholicity and universality are just nothing else but identical!

If the catholicity and universality of the church was really linked with the Empire, then we can easily understand why the first serious loss happened during the 5th century, the period of the Christological debates, a loss which was related to the schism between the Eastern Orthodox and the Oriental Orthodox (non-Chalcedonian) churches. But, as it is commonly admitted today, behind their distinct dogmatic definitions one can henceforth find the same Christological faith in these two church families. However this was not admitted at that time, and caused the first great schism in Christendom, when after the Fourth Ecumenical Council of Chalcedon (451), the Oriental Christians separated themselves from the Imperial Byzantine church (not only for theological, but also for political, cultural and ethnic reasons, i.e. as a reaction to the oppression of their ethnic particularity by the imperial power, and to the further Hellenization which was somehow an unavoidable effect of the Byzantine dominion). Along with their loss came that of the Oriental regions of Byzantium (mainly Syria, Palestine, Egypt), but also the Semitic and Syrian tradition, and the non-ontological/non-philosophical, and mere narrative, understanding of Christian faith and theology. Eastern Orthodoxy gradually became mainly Greek in its cultural expression and liturgical experience. That was especially brought about through the homogenization of the liturgical rites, and the gradual disappearance from the Eastern Orthodox landscape of the existing multiplicity of liturgical traditions of the ancient church and that of Egypt, Syria, Armenia (like the liturgy of St. James, Brother of the Lord, the Eucharistic Anaphoras of "Didachè" and the *Sacramentary of Sarapion of Thmuis*, the liturgy of St. Marcus, the liturgy of the so-called "Apostolic Constitutions," etc.). In addition to that, the *"lex orandi"* so important for the Orthodox ecclesiological and theological self-consciousness came to be identified exclusively with the Byzantine liturgical tradition, and therefore to the belief that only within the frame of this tradition could the authentic experience of holiness and divine-human communion (θέωσις) be acquired. It is noteworthy, in regard to what has been said here, that for centuries now (and especially after the great schism between the West and the East), the Orthodox have not known or experienced other liturgical rites than the Byzantine one. Furthermore they have not

Orthodox Handbook on Ecumenism

known, studied, or accepted other patristic tradition than that of the Greek Fathers, almost totally ignoring the Syrian and the Latin church Fathers.

The same applies, mutatis mutandis, in the case of the 1054 great schism between the Eastern and the Western churches, a schism for which today we are aware that despite the existing theological and ecclesiological disputes, a major role should also be attributed to cultural and political reasons. It is of great importance that the separation of the Christian East and Christian West, affected terribly Christian universalism, and helped to increase tendencies towards particularism. If, after this significant politico-religious split, the West became more aggressive, seeking after its dominion, expansion, and supremacy to the detriment of Christian East, the latter became more defensive and suspicious, and at the same time less universalistic, seeking how to be protected from both Latin and Muslim (Arab first, and later Turkish) conquest.

The fall of Constantinople to the Ottoman Turks (1453), and the ensuing Turkish rule imposed on all Orthodox countries and regions (except Russia), as well as the posterior, in the period of Enlightenment, adoption of the principle of nationalities from all the Orthodox peoples, and the concomitant nationalization and Statism of Orthodox churches during the 19th century, along with the quite new reality of these peoples to live in homogenous "Orthodox" and ethnically "pure" states or societies, contributed to a great extend in the eclipse of Orthodox universalism, and the adoption of a defensive anti-ecumenical stance.

IV. The Ethno-religious Narrative of Orthodox Fundamentalism and Anti-ecumenism, and the Historical Roots of Orthodox Anti-Westernism

All the above mentioned elements, which have decisively contributed to the shaping of the Orthodox anti-ecumenical spirit, are also to be related to a defensive perception of the Orthodox identity, common to all traditional Orthodox peoples. According to this identity understanding, ecumenism is perceived as a threat to the authentic Orthodox consciousness and tradition, as a betrayal of the genuine Orthodox identity, along with religious syncretism, globalization, and multicultural societies. However, this defensive perception of Orthodox identity, particularly stressed during the globalization era, is not only connected to a certain loss of the universalistic vision in Eastern Orthodoxy, but also to an ethno-religious narrative (which is a key element of the Orthodox fundamentalism) and to the historical roots of Orthodox anti-Westernism.

Our reference to anti-Westernism should by no means be taken as a rejection of the legitimate Orthodox critiques of the West for its deviations from the tradition of the undivided church; nor does it signify a disagreement with moderate assessments of the fundamental differences between the two branches of Christianity and/ or the intrinsic problems and impasses plaguing the West. Instead, what we are referring to is the simplistic ideological construction, the one-sided, inaccurate, and condemnatory critique which sees in the West nothing but errors and heresies (while praising the Eastern Church for its doctrinal purity and uprightness). Such an ideological construction continues to see East-West relations in terms of unabated confrontation and division, often in flagrant disregard for historical accuracy, thus discounting ten centuries of common Christian life and ecclesial communion. It also disregards the second Christian millennium whose historical picture seems to be quite more complex and rich than the customary one constituted only by the separation, and the permanent hostility, animosity, and confrontation between Eastern and Western Christians. In the words of Timothy (Kallistos) Ware, who in his PhD thesis (1964) offered us a fine description of the Greek Church under Turkish rule,

Yet if an underlying hostility towards Rome is never entirely absent, it is surprising how little it is in evidence in the Greek world of the seventeenth century. Despite occasional outbreaks of hostility, particularly at Constantinople and Jerusalem, encounters between Orthodox and Roman Catholics were often extraordinarily cordial. Mixed marriages were frequent; the two sides took active part in one another's services; Western missionaries, with full permission from the Orthodox authorities, preached in Orthodox churches and heard the confessions of the Orthodox faithful; Orthodox received communion from Roman Catholic priests, while Greek converts to Rome were often told by the Western missionaries to receive communion as before at Orthodox altars; a Roman Catholic was accepted as godparent at an Orthodox baptism, and vice versa. Both sides frequently acted as if the schism between east and west did not exist. The Latin missionaries, in the absence of any bishop of their own, behaved towards the local Orthodox bishop as though they recognized him as their ordinary; the Orthodox authorities for their part, so far from repudiating the missionaries as intruders, welcomed them as friends and allies, and encouraged them to undertake pastoral work among the Greek population. Instances of common worship and *communicatio in sacris* during the seventeenth century are so frequent that only a few examples can be mentioned here.

Of course the above description is taking into account only one side of the problem, since no one could undervalue the disastrous effects and the tragic consequences of the events which followed the great schism between the East and the West, and the latter's attempt towards both spiritual and religious colonization, and politico-economic submission of the East. The remainder of this attempt is still perceptible in our days, and it is made evident by a strong suspicion, and even rejection of everything that comes from the Westerners, the ones who were taken to be the responsible for the fall of Byzantium, and the destruction of the Eastern Christendom. Following again the pertinent analysis contained in the same work by Timothy (Kallistos) Ware,

> Long before the end of the Byzantine Empire, Orthodox had come to regard the Roman Catholic Church with misgiving and suspicion. Quite apart from doctrinal questions, the sack of Constantinople by the Crusaders in 1204 was something (so it has rightly been observed) which "Christians of the east could neither forgive nor forget." The reunion Council of Ferrara-Florence in 1438-39 had in the end done more to widen than to bridge the gulf. Looking back on the Council, Greeks in later generations felt that they had somehow been tricked and deceived when they went to the west: they felt that the Latins had taken advantage of their political weakness in order to extract religious concessions from them; they felt that they had been forced against their better judgement into signing an act of submission in which they did not really believe. Historically this is certainly an over-simplification of what actually happened at the Council; but such was the "legend" which later grew up among the Greeks. For them Florence was not an encouraging precedent for the future but an awful warning.

These anti-Western feelings and suspicions were much more aggravated after aggressive Roman Catholic proselytism deployed in Orthodox settings, and particularly as a reaction to Uniatism (the establishment of Greek-Catholic churches, but also Syrian-Catholic, Coptic-Catholic, Armenian-Catholic churches, etc.) which gained some success in Eastern Europe and the Middle-East, and which led in 1755 to the decision of the Ecumenical Patriarchate and the other Orthodox Patriarchs of the East to re-baptize all Roman Catholics wishing to enter into the communion of the Orthodox Church (this decision was in force until the end of 19th century). The Protestant and Anglican proselytism practiced during the 19th and the first half of 20th century at the expense of the local Orthodox communities in Asia Minor (Anatolia) and the Middle East has only increased suspicion, rejection and hostility against any initiative coming from Christians of the West. It is sad to remember that until very recently (and in some cases, in Eastern Europe and Russia, even today), all proselytizing activities by Western Christians, both Roman Catholics and Protestants in traditionally Orthodox settings, were directed almost exclusively at Orthodox Christians, and never at Muslims or faithful of other religions. Despite the formal condemnation of these kinds of proselytizing activities in official documents (as in the 1990 Freising Roman Catholic-Orthodox Document, the 1993 Balamand Roman Catholic-Orthodox Agreement, or relevant official Documents of the mainstream Protestant churches), there has not been to my knowledge a process of the "healing of memories" on this issue, nor a clear request for forgiveness on behalf of Western churches for their disastrous policy in the Christian East.

The relationship between Greek theology (which serves here as a paradigm for the Orthodox world) and the West has nearly always been one of ambivalence: on the one hand, the Greek (and the wider Orthodox) side has shown a pronounced rejection and a radical critique of its Western counterpart, which has recently been justified in the name of authenticity and faithfulness to Orthodoxy, and is usually accompanied by an attitude of triumphalism against Western digressions and heresies. On the other hand, Greek theology is fairly replete with observable and tangible influences and loans from the West, which sometimes border on scholarly heteronomy or even a secret admiration for the accomplishments, dynamism, and high scholarly and academic standards of Western theology. The diachronic, thus, views of Orthodox theologians on this matter run across a wide spectrum, ranging as they do from the near absence of an East-West polarity and the critical or even friendly dialogue with the West (usually accompanied by the adoption of its theological agenda and its academic/critical methods), down to the radical denunciation and demonization of the entire Western tradition, an identity-centered entrenchment, and the promotion of an anti-Western and anti-ecumenical spirit.

The fact remains, however, that during the 20th century, both the Russian theology of the diaspora, and contemporary Greek theology bloomed and further grew in a dialogical context with the West, as opposed to one given to fanaticism and Orthodox introversion. At any rate, Western theology itself in all its diversity, has already gone a long way towards self-criticism, just as it has fought hard to liberate itself from the fetters of neo-Scholasticism and dry rationalism, while in search of the tradition of the undivided church, as it was rediscovered by pioneering Western theologians, and in dialogue with the contemporary world. The rediscovery of the eschatological identity of the church (particularly in German Protestantism), the renewal movements in Roman Catholic theology, such as the "Ressourcement" and the Patristic movement best portrayed by the Fourvière School in Lyon and its reputable publication series, the "Sources Chrétiennes," or the demand for liturgical renewal, the reconnection between Bible and worship, and even the social commitment of both church and theology, are only some instances of self-criticism and rehabilitation shown by Western theology, all related to the movement known as "nouvelle théologie."

It will certainly strike some as paradoxical, or even scandalous, that it was in fact the dialogical intersection with Western developments which paved the way for the renaissance of Orthodox theology in the 20th century and its liberation from the "Babylonian captivity" in Western scholastic or pietistic theology. Indeed, there is no denying that Orthodox theology (in its Greek and Russian diaspora versions alike) was led out of its provincial introversion and defensive self-sufficiency largely thanks to the opportunities and challenges which it was afforded by participation in the ecumenical dialogue. The latter has played a key role in the intellectual maturation of 20th century Orthodoxy, both in terms of the more well-known Orthodox theologians of the Russian diaspora, and in terms of the authentic theological synthesis in Greek-speaking thought, such as the theology of personhood.

Soon, however, the Orthodox vision shrunk hopelessly, and dialogue gave way to aphorisms, polemics and shadowboxing with the West, or better yet, a caricature of the contemporary West, which came to be identified with absolute evil or even with the Antichrist. Besides the growing influence of the monastic, and more precisely Athonite milieus, this unfortunate lapse was also due to a progressive drift from a purely theological to a cultural and, eventually, Greek-centered, or even nationalistic, discourse (featuring an emphasis on the search for the Greek Orthodox identity and uniqueness), as a result of the near-total predominance of theologians like Christos Yannaras or Fr. John Romanides. Orthodox theologians became then increasingly receptive to the polarizing hermeneutic of "Orthodox East versus heterodox or heretical West" (initiated by the Russian diaspora theologian Vladimir Lossky, and the radical apophaticism, the over-emphasis on the *filioque* issue, and the simplistic scheme of Eastern personalism versus Western essentialism that he proposed), which in turn contributed to the popularization of the tendency to juxtapose the "noblest" version of Orthodoxy against the most problem-ridden and outdated version of Western Christendom. The contemporary West is still seen in Greece, as well as in the wider Orthodox world, through this selfsame deforming prism, as well as despite the substantial Western progress in such areas as patristic studies, the theology of the local church, and Eucharistic ecclesiology. As a result, Orthodoxy can be observed to be retreating from its ecumenical and inter-denominational contacts, a move which is not unrelated to the aforementioned demand for the "return to tradition" and the rediscovery of an authentic, untainted Orthodoxy, rid of Western influences, as it was systematically promoted by the famous "return to the Fathers" movement.

Part II: Orthodoxy and Ecumenism - Foundations

The reaction, however, of the above leading Orthodox theological figures and of Orthodox monastic milieus against academic scholasticism and the Western mindset in general is inconceivable without the agonizing search for the authentic Orthodox identity (rid of the Western fetters imposed upon it during the course of its "Babylonian captivity"), and the demand for the rediscovery of the genuine Hellenic spirit as it was exemplified in the Roman/Byzantine empire, a political formation which collapsed under the repeated attacks of Western Christians and Muslims, but whose spirit continues radiating among the Orthodox peoples. This is the reason we cannot understand Orthodox anti-ecumenism without taking into account the powerful ethno-religious narrative which is directly connected to the historical roots of Orthodox anti-Westernism. Yet, Orthodox anti-Westernism has not only theological/ecclesiastic, but also historic/political, origins and is deeply rooted and lived within a collective social conscience.

A unique moment of this historic and political anti-Westernism, with particular importance on our subject, is the Byzantine anti-Westernism, and even more, the phenomenon that, according to Greek biblical professor Savas Agourides, goes by the name of "Byzantine Political Orthodoxy." This phenomenon involves a peculiar perception of "realized eschatology" and of voluntary instrumentalization of Orthodoxy, animated by the strong conviction that the Byzantine empire was identified with God's right hand that governs the world using the Patriarch as His left hand. This conception led to the identification of divine and human affairs, divine providence and worldly (Byzantine) history, Christian eschatological expectation within the world/historic perspective, transforming automatically in this way the Empire's enemies into enemies of the Orthodox faith (prior declaration of Orthodoxy as state religion, the *de facto* conversion of Orthodoxy's enemies into enemies of the empire, etc.). The Greek biblical scholar, based on Hélène Ahrweiler's work entitled "The Political Ideology of the Byzantine Empire" and rendering the novel political tendencies that the well-known Byzantinist scholar describes as "Greek-Orthodox patriotism," will remind us that in Byzantium, after Constantinople's recovery from the Franks in 1261, a deep passion is expressed about Orthodoxy and Constantinople, a kind of holy war not against the Turks but this time against Westerners. "The Byzantines' deposit of inconceivable humiliation and the resentment about their historic fate has sadly been expressed through "utopian ideological constructions unable to fortify the country from the adventures that would surely await it in the future. The Christian notion of repentance is often completely absent in these cases. Our adversaries, in other words some other people, should bear the guilt on their arms."

Since the 1204 signpost and up until today, the motives and reasons for the emergence, cultivation and tension of anti-Western feelings throughout the Greek and the Orthodox East have been multiplied. They are constantly constituted and present as repeated themes within numerous books, journal papers, and newspapers articles of Orthodox theologians and intellectuals, which hold the West as responsible for all the sufferings and historical adventures of Orthodox peoples. The Greek case is again very characteristic in this regard.

In fact, for centuries, Hellenism—and, with it, Greek-speaking Orthodoxy, and to a wider extent Eastern Orthodoxy—has been experiencing radical and painful changes throughout its history. The most important of these involve the fact that while for centuries it was at the epicenter of history, political and economic power, literature, arts, and culture; with the conquest of Constantinople by the Franks in 1204, the Frankish rule that followed, the fall of Byzantium to the Ottoman Turks in 1453, and finally with the Asia Minor Catastrophe and the population exchange with Turkey in 1922-23, Hellenism has now been consigned to the margins of history and simply become a provincial power. Hellenism (which serves again here as a paradigm for the whole of Orthodoxy) has ceased to be the center of the world, and Greece, since its liberation from the Turks (1830, 1832) is a small, unstable Balkan country on the edge of Europe, which exists and survives only with the help and assistance of the Great Powers of each era. This picture changed only recently with Greece's accession to the institutions of the European Union and the Euro zone, but the mistakes made by successive Greek governments have plunged the country into an unprecedented financial crisis and have made the Greeks, once again, feel humiliated. The Greeks' usual response to this humiliation is to tout the accomplishments and virtues of their glorious ancestors—primarily the ancient Greeks, but also the Byzantines for those closest to the Church. This last point, however, is an attitude which has been characterizing Hellenism for decades now, if not centuries: Greeks live and operate in the world more on the basis of the accomplishments of the past than on something they can display as an achievement or reality in the present. The invocation of the past makes up for the lack of a constructive present. And this attitude is directly connected with the founding myth of modern Hellenism, which pervades their collective imagination, foreign policy, education, and their understanding of history. Of course, this also applies to the dominant ecclesiastical rationale, as well as theology and its orientation, which most of the time do not seem able to abandon the church's celebrated "national" role and their lament for the loss of universal Hellenism, nor can they seem willing to recover from the historical wound inflicted by their nostalgia for, and sanctification of, the lost empire, their myth of a "Christian" society, and their dream of a holistic unity. Similar ethno-religious trajectories and attendant mythologies can easily be found, *mutatis mutandis*, in the other Orthodox peoples of Balkan and Eastern Europe, too, regardless whether it is about "Holy Russia", the "Third Rome," the Slavophil movement, the medieval Christian kingdom of Serbia, the "Serbian people as the servant of God," the Latin character and uniqueness of Romanian Orthodoxy, etc.

The Greeks, and the Orthodox in general, were so closely identified with Byzantium that the fall of the Empire in 1453 appears to have inflicted an incurable wound. From that date onward, the Greeks have felt orphaned and handicapped, with the sense that history stole something from them which it ought to give back; they are thus waiting for this restoration and their vindication within history. The greatest challenge for Hellenism around the world, but also for all Orthodoxy in general, is to overcome this historical trauma, to right itself and discern its mission in today's world, without reference to ancient Greece or Byzantium. However, Orthodoxy, both Greek-speaking and non-Greek-speaking (although to different extents), draws its legitimacy from Byzantium, and all its points of references—i.e., the source of its liturgical tradition, the rhetorical forms of its *kerygma*, and the theology of the Fathers and the Councils—trace back to Byzantium.

Quite the opposite happens in today's context, marked by the economic crisis and the faltering of Europe. As the Greek Orthodox theologian Stavros Yangazoglou, editor of the official academic journal of the Church of Greece *Theologia*, points out in a recent article,

> Today, forty years after the overthrow of the Greek military regime, the paradoxical intertwining of ultra-religious groups within the rightwing returns to the spotlight, reminding us of other times and situations. In some religious circles they systematically have been cultivating the imaginary making of enemies who are constantly threatening Orthodoxy and the nation. Those enemies are not only external but also internal. This confessional entrenchment of contemporary Orthodoxy often leads to the refusal of ecumenical and interreligious dialogue, since the conception of possessing the absolute truth is *de facto* engrained in the Orthodox people for ancestral or local reasons, physical or ethnic nationality. Within the ecclesiastical domain, Orthodoxy's enemies and traitors are those in favor of the ecumenical movement, those who are chosen as institutional representatives of local Orthodox Churches to discuss with the heterodox West. Even those who care about inter-Orthodox unity and ecumenical expression of local Orthodox Churches and work for the future Pan-Orthodox Council fall under the same category. If in the past these trends used to be confined to the Old Calendarist circles, nowadays they are to be found within the institutional church and have created a lobby which puts pressure on the Orthodox Church of Greece. On the pretext of saving Orthodoxy from heresy, the heterodox West and ecumenism, several conservative lay, monastic, and—only recently—clerical milieus assumed the role of police and prosecutor of the church. They often claim infallible authority and place themselves above the canonical ecclesiastical structure of the church. This trend understands the church as an ideological and denominational array rather than as an expression of communion, catholicity and universality. [...] Today we witness a strange osmosis between fundamentalists and nationalists. It is not by chance that even Archbishop Anastasios of Albania, the man who devoted his life to and ministered in theology and the church, is accused by these groups of being "internationalist" and "ecumenical." In some theological and ecclesiastical circles, mostly bottomless aphasia, endless conspiracy theorists and internet bloggers reveal a peculiar kind of religious nationalism. "Without national

Part II: Orthodoxy and Ecumenism - Foundations

identity the church cannot function" or "good and supreme [is] the Orthodox support to immigrants, but we leave the Greeks aside ... bishops who provide assistance to immigrants often belong to similar parties of atheism." Often in fundamentalist circles, faith proves to be a sanctimonious ideology and cultivates a deep conservatism, it does not want and does not seek any kind of dialogue, it only wants its absolute predominance.

The fact is even more serious if we move from the Greek context to another Orthodox place like Russia. We are still facing the same extreme phenomena as those described this time by Russian Orthodox intellectual Alexei Bodrov, the Rector of St. Andrews Biblical Theological Institute,

An additional problem is that an authoritative state needs an authoritative church. So given the problems of our society and the state there is no surprise with the recent campaign against human rights as a foreign (Western) concept launched by the Russian Orthodox Church leadership. There is a profound anti-Western attitude. East-East dialogue (e.g. Orthodox-Muslim) is much easier than East-West (e.g. Orthodox-Catholic or Protestant). Theology is not an issue here. Religion is widely used in politics at all levels in Russia (even though Russia is a profoundly secular county with a very low level of active church goers). It should be clear that the Orthodox truth cannot be used as an ideology or a political instrument, and yet Orthodoxy has become a new state ideology. It is perceived more that the national tradition, culture and the Orthodox Church is *de facto* the state church. *Political Orthodoxy* is strong and influential (in its very conservative form) and has nothing to do with theology or spirituality. It is not a religion, it is an ideology. Recent sociological polls tell us that about 20% of Orthodox do not believe in God and thus 13-15% of people are 'Orthodox non-believers' and they certainly can influence politics. Political Orthodox groups and movements are numerous and different, but all of them are nationalistic, anti-Western and antidemocratic.

Especially for Russia and Eastern Europe it should be noted that after the fall of the Berlin wall, and the collapse of the communist system in this predominantly Orthodox part of Europe, anti-ecumenical movements were considerably reinforced. As professor Stelios Tsompanidis from Aristotle University of Thessaloniki points out, "The downfall of the 'socialist system' marked the revival of fundamentalism and nationalism, mainly featured as anti-ecumenism and anti-Westernism. The ecumenical movement was considered to be the incarnation of devastating powers of internationalism and cosmopolitanism as well as the contemporary form of heresy." In this context, according to the pertinent analysis of Fr. Georges Tsetsis, in order for the various Orthodox fundamentalist groups in Eastern Europe to convert people to their ideas and establish their own conventicle, they fought against the primates of churches with canonical jurisdiction, criticizing bishops and theological scholars for being sympathetic to and in collusion with ecumenism, and theological minimalism, demanding the immediate termination of any kind of contact with Western Christianity. We should also take into account the fact that, after the painful experience of many decades under a totalitarian system, with strict control not only of political, philosophical or religious beliefs but also of everyday life, in which even the right of traveling and the freedom of having contacts with the West was limited to an élite of privileged people, ecumenical figures of Eastern European churches were seriously suspected, and consequently scorned and discredited, because they were seen as traitors and collaborators of the Communist Party, since they were among the very few people who were permitted to travel abroad and have any contacts with the Westerners.

V. Anti-ecumenism as a Specific Form
of Orthodox Fundamentalism and Anti-modernism

The search for Christian unity and the overcoming of schisms and church divisions has always been at the center of church life and liturgical prayer ever since the first Christian centuries. Yet, the ecumenical movement is a phenomenon of modern times, since it implies a "paradigm shift" affecting wide domains of intellectual and spiritual life, including issues of dialogue and human rights, religious freedom and tolerance, otherness and acceptance of diversity. Although ancient and contemporary theological dialogues aim at the same goal, i.e.

Christian unity, doctrinal agreement, and full Eucharistic communion, the way these dialogues are performed is very different, and this difference is due to the radical changes that were brought about by modernity. To the extent that the ecumenical movement is related to modern times, the tentative or even problematic relationship of Orthodoxy to modernity (explaining the serious difficulty the former has in communicating its message to the latter) could also be considered as one more reason for fundamentalist Orthodox animosity towards the ecumenical movement.

As it is well known from the current sociological discussion, fundamentalist movements are usually, through their discourses and actions, responding to the challenges of modernity. The cause of the birth of fundamentalism itself is modernity and, by extension, the revolution that modernity brought into all fields (the relationship between religion and politics as well as between the sacred and the secular, the disengagement of societies and the individual from religious influence, new hermeneutical approaches to the Bible and sacred texts, the re-examination of the relationship between faith and science, the re-evaluation of nature and the natural world, etc.). This is why fundamentalism is incomprehensible outside the context of modernity and can only be understood as a reaction to it.

For mainly historical reasons, the Orthodox world did not inherently participate in the phenomenon of modernity and did not experience the Renaissance, the Reformation and Counter-Reformation, the religious wars and the Enlightenment, the French and Industrial Revolutions, the rise of the individual and individuality, human rights, and the secular nation-state. For this reason, everything that has been characterized as an achievement of modernity seems to be alien to Orthodoxy, which still has not really engaged modernity. This is why, according to many, Orthodox Christianity has a difficulty in communicating with the modern and contemporary world; and this could explain, I would add, the ambiguity and the dual language of many Orthodox representatives in the ecumenical movement mentioned in previous section (ecumenical language *ad extra*, conservative and defensive, but not principally anti-ecumenical, *ad intra*), since it seems that only at the high ecclesiastical and theological level, although only to some point, the Orthodox are aware of the radical changes brought about by modernity, while the Orthodox faithful remained alienated from, and finally became suspicious of, the efforts towards ecumenical understanding.

From an Orthodox Christian perspective, the crucial question that arises from this state of affairs—especially in our contemporary situation, which is characterized by the re-appearance of national and religious conflicts, the temptation towards fundamentalism, and the rise of traditionalism, along with globalization, universalism, and the transition from modernity to post-modernity—can be summarized as: *Did Orthodoxy come to a halt before modernity?* Or, to put it in a different way: Does Orthodox Christian theology only operate within traditional environments? Do its theological and liturgical symbolisms, as well as its way of preaching, the structure of church administration, and the established conceptions about the relationship between the sacred and the secular, religion and politics, and the church and state, only borrow models and imagery from agrarian societies? Has Orthodox Christianity accepted the achievements of modernity and its consequences for religious, social, and cultural fields, or do we Orthodox long for the organizational schemes and structures of our glorious past (the Byzantine/imperial in particular)? Perhaps we still dream—in accordance with the imported logic of fundamentalism—of a return to pre-modernity, turning away from the gains of modernity and even interpreting post-modernity as the church's *revenge* against modernity? On this point, could we be mimicking the anti-modernist reaction of the Roman Catholic Church before it came to terms (mostly after the Second Vatican Council) with the new reality and decided to deal with modernity through dialogue and dialectic?

It is time for Orthodoxy to stop being afraid of modernity and to try to get into a serious dialogue with it. It has to be admitted that, from the Orthodox point of view, with some rare exceptions, a dialogue between modernity and Orthodoxy has never seriously taken place. A fruitful meeting and even a synthesis (why not?) between Orthodoxy and modernity are still needed. Orthodoxy seems to be systematically avoiding such a meeting, while modernity seems to ignore Orthodox Christianity and its deeper spiritual truth. The Orthodox Church and its theology can no longer ignore modernity and act as if they are living in traditional or pre-modern

Part II: Orthodoxy and Ecumenism - Foundations

societies. To persist along this line would mean denying the very essence of incarnational theology, for it is in this historical, social and cultural context of modernity and post-modernity that the church is called to fulfill its mission, and that it is once again called to embody the truth of Christianity about God, the world and humankind.

VI. The "Return to the Fathers": ## Its Interpretations and Implications for the Issue of Ecumenism

Some of the Orthodox theologians of the new generation (very few, to be honest) have begun over the last several years to criticize the uncritical way in which many Orthodox theologians all subscribed to the famous "return to the Fathers." In fact, the way this famous "return to the Fathers" was understood and practiced, led, in some cases, to a "fundamentalism of tradition" or to a "fundamentalism of the Fathers," which prevented Orthodoxy from remaining an integrated part of the modern world, and getting into critical dialogue with Christian West. As it is well known, in the First Orthodox Theological Congress, which was held in Athens in 1936, Fr. Georges Florovsky, perhaps the greatest Eastern Orthodox theologian of the 20th century and modern Orthodoxy's most important ecumenical figure, proclaimed Orthodox theology's need to "return to the Fathers" and to be released from its "Babylonian captivity" to Western theology in terms of its language, its presuppositions, and its thinking. His call was quickly adopted and shared by many theologians of the Russian diaspora, while he also gathered fervent supporters in traditionally Orthodox countries, such as Serbia, Romania, and Greece. Thus, the theological movement of the "return to the Fathers" became the hallmark of, and the dominant "paradigm" for, Orthodox theology for the better part of the 20th century. For many this was considered its primary task, to such a degree that this celebrated "return to the Fathers" and the effort to "de-Westernize" Orthodox theology overshadowed all other theological questions and other Orthodox theological trends, as well as all the challenges the modern world had posed—and continues to pose—to Orthodox theology.

The 20th century was, therefore, a time of renewal for Orthodox theology. However, at the same time it was also—precisely because of the way in which this "return to the Fathers" was perceived (especially by some of the so-called "heirs" of Florovsky's legacy) and of the corresponding program to "de-Westernize" Orthodox theology—a time of introversion, conservatism, and of a static or fundamentalist understanding of the concept of Tradition, which very often came to be equated with traditionalism.

A critical reappraisal of the consequences of this "return to the Fathers" and the subsequent over-emphasis on patristic studies would bring into light, among other things: 1) the neglect and devaluation of biblical studies; 2) an ahistorical approach to patristic theology leading to a subsequent exaltation of traditionalism; 3) a tendency towards introversion and Orthodox theology's near total absence from the major theological developments and trends of the 20th century; 4) the polarization of East and West, and the cultivation and consolidation of an anti-Western and anti-ecumenical spirit; and 5) a weak theological response to the challenges posed by the modern world and, more generally, the unresolved theological issues still remaining in the relationship between Orthodoxy and modernity.

More specifically, regarding consequence number 4): Judging from the results, it can hardly be denied that the "return to the Fathers" (as was the case with Vladimir Lossky, Fr. Justin Popovic, Christos Yannaras, Fr. John Romanides, etc.) has contributed decisively—although negatively—to the polarization between East and West, to Orthodoxy's uncritical rejection of the West, and to the cultivation and consolidation of an anti-Western and anti-ecumenical spirit, which moves beyond the historical facts, and re-stages reality by continuing to read the relationship between the East and the West as a relationship of constant confrontation, conflict, and division, thus erasing ten centuries of common Christian life and ecclesial communion.

Here we run into a major paradox, which is worth attempting to analyze. Fr. Georges Florovsky, who was the main proponent of the "return to the Fathers," and the most important theologian both within this movement and within Orthodoxy as a whole during the 20th century, was reared not only on patristic literature, hymnology, and even the Bible, but also by the great works of contemporary Western theology, which he took into consideration or with which he was in constant dialogue (A. von Harnack, K. Barth, E. Brunner, Yv. Congar, H. de Lubac, L. Bouyer, E. L. Mascal, R. Bultmann, A. Nygren, J. A. Moehler, E. Mersch, P. Batiffol, G. L. Prestige, G. Kittel, Et. Gilson, J. Lebreton, P. Tillich, and R. Collinwood, H. Marrou et al.). Moreover, Florovsky never adopted the idea of a polarization between the East and the West as a methodological tool; he utilized the Latin Fathers, such as Augustine, in his ecclesiological works; he wrote many of his classic studies for an ecumenical audience or as an Orthodox contribution to ecumenical meetings; and, above all, he was always quick to maintain that the catholicity of Christian civilization could not exist only with the West, just as it could not exist only with the East, and that catholicity requires both lungs of the Christendom, Western and Eastern, like Siamese twins. However, the movement for a "return to the Fathers" was significantly influenced by the participation and the work of other theologians (Vladimir Lossky, Justin Popovic, et al.), while the positions and the general theological line of thought which ultimately prevailed was, in many fields, at odds with Florovsky's positions, such as, most notably, an intense anti-Westernism and anti-ecumenism. The Fathers and their theology were often seen as the unique characteristic and exclusive property of the East—thus blatantly ignoring the Christian West's important contributions in rediscovering the Fathers—, while more than a few times patristic theology was used to wage an outdated and illogical invective against the West. Thus Orthodoxy was seen as having the wealth and authenticity of the Fathers' thought, a rich liturgical experience, and mystical theology, while the spiritually emaciated West lacked all these things and instead was content with scholasticism and pietism, theological rationalism, and legalism. As a result, younger Orthodox theologians, particularly in traditionally Orthodox countries, assimilated not only the interpretive schema of an Orthodox East versus a heretical West, but it also became commonplace for them to contrast, in a self-satisfied way, the better version which is Orthodoxy (expressed by the Cappadocian Fathers, Maximus the Confessor, so-called "mystical" theology, St. Gregory Palamas, the Russian theology of the Diaspora, etc.) with the inferior version represented by the West (with its scholastic theology, the problematic parts of Thomas Aquinas, the Holy Inquisition, a theology of legalism and pietism, etc.). This is how the modern West today remains understood in many Orthodox countries. Despite the significant progress that has taken place in the fields of patristic studies, the theology of the local church, and Eucharistic ecclesiology, the West is still seen through this distorted lens for reasons of convenience and simplicity or, more simply, because of ignorance. This climate has abetted in depriving the newer Orthodox theological generation of the right, as well as the possibility, of becoming familiar and interacting with the fundamental works of Western theology, which remain, for the most part, untranslated or unknown in the Orthodox world. We have thus forgotten how much Russian diaspora theology, as well as the "return to the Fathers" movement itself, owes to the West; the Orthodox theology of the second half of the 20th century has lost, in other words, its sense of history and interaction.

VII. The Growing Influence of the Monastic Milieu

We cannot understand the Orthodox reactions to the ecumenical movement without taking into account the decisive role, and growing influence of, the monastic milieu on the Orthodox faithful and their idea of Ecumenism. Over the past few decades, Orthodox monasticism has undergone a remarkable spiritual renewal and significant economic, and in some cases even political, empowerment, which first took place at the end of the 60s on Mount Athos, Greece. Later, this renewal spread to the whole Orthodox world, both in traditional Orthodox countries (such as those in Eastern Europe) and in diaspora, North America and the Church of Antioch (Syria and Lebanon) being the last places where the Athonite model was exported.

Monasticism has always represented the most conservative understanding of the Orthodox tradition, and it used to be the most militant anti-Western, anti-modern, and anti-ecumenical element within the Orthodox Church. Despite this fact and the risks this overemphasis on monasticism implies, pre-eminent Eastern Orthodox theologians from different local Orthodox churches praised monasticism and placed their hopes for the renewal of the church in the monastic renewal, hailing the Athonite renaissance of the 70s and the 80s as the most significant ecclesial event of modern times! Monastic renewal nowadays is taking place all over the Orthodox world, displaying as an obvious result, among other things, the strengthening of fundamentalism and anti-ecumenism, while the exaggerated role of the charismatic elders who place themselves above the ecclesial community and its conciliar expressions practically annuls the centrality of the Eucharist and the traditional hierarchical constitution of the church, its unity, and its Eucharistic ecclesiology. In addition, Orthodox monasticism is becoming more and more visible by its tendency to patronize the ecclesial body and to engage in a worldly fundamentalist activism, which aims at defending the values of "country, religion, and family." Furthermore, there is a growing tendency among monastic milieus of frequent and open accusations aimed at Orthodox patriarchs, bishops and lay theologians, especially those involved in the ecumenical movement, charging them with theological minimalism and the betrayal of Orthodoxy.

One gets the impression that nowadays many of the monks, especially on Mount Athos, seek to be considered as the ultimate authority and the genuine voice of Orthodoxy, believing that many local Orthodox Churches have been diverted from the proper and authentic Orthodox path. In the present circumstances, it is clear, in our view, that even decisions taken at a Pan-Orthodox level (like that of the 3rd Pre-Conciliar Pan-Orthodox Consultation of Chambésy, 1986, concerning the participation of the Orthodox Church in the Ecumenical Movement), cannot be accepted in practice, if they do not get the prior approval of the ultra-Orthodox movements, as these movements continue to exert a kind of spiritual and ecclesial supervision over the Orthodox throughout the world, a sort of universal jurisdiction over local churches. It is time, *kairos*, for our church leaders and for all of us to end this caricature of fidelity to the tradition, these Orthodox ayatollahs who believe themselves to be responsible for Orthodoxy all around the world, while denouncing the Pope of Rome for its claims to primacy and universal jurisdiction. They are doing exactly what they accuse of others, although not as individuals but as a college of elders, as the magisterium of the most enlightened spiritual fathers!

VIII. In Place of Conclusion

The Orthodox Church cannot deny its dialogic and charitable ethos, its long tradition of catholicity and ecumenicity. It has always been in favor of dialogue, both for theological and for pastoral reasons, as it is stated at the very beginning of the official document issued at the end of the 3rd Pre-Conciliar Pan-Orthodox Conference, in Chambésy, Geneva, in 1986. A church which refuses to dialogue with the world and its problems, which is not willing to converse with the "other" and which does not acknowledge what this "other" has to offer in such a dialogue, in reality ceases to function as a church, ekklesia, in the sense that it refutes the most important *consequence* of Incarnation: "the gathering together of one in all things in Christ", in the sense of recapitulation (Eph 1:10, cf Eph 3:2, Gal 3:28, 4:4, Col 1:16, 3:11). This means the reception, as well as the transfiguration, of the created from the uncreated, the assumption in the face of the Incarnate Son and Word of the whole human nature and history of the tragedy and the pursuit of the fallen man. However, this need for, as well as the intensifying duty to, dialogue (in other words, the Orthodox ethos) derives from the theological self-consciousness and nature of the Trinitarian God, constituting nothing else but a community of divine people in dialogue under love. This exact divine Being is the Trinitarian mode of existence which is understood by Patristic theology, as well as by contemporary Orthodox theology, especially Greek-speaking, as "Being as Communion" and "Being as Dialogue."

In the midst of current challenges, and in our rapidly changing world, the Orthodox, strengthened by the spiritual richness of our abundant tradition and the genuine and remarkable theological syntheses we have achieved on behalf of the tradition of the undivided church, should give a new sense to and a renewed impetus in our participation to the ecumenical movement. The genuine Orthodox spirit has to reject not only any fundamentalist temptation and the anti-ecumenist, anti-Western, ethno-religious narrative, but also what lies behind this defensive attitude, mainly an introversionist spirit and exclusivist claims.

Orthodox Handbook on Ecumenism

A contemporary Orthodox spiritual father, elder Porphyrios, spoke out, commenting on the authentic Orthodox ethos, "Fundamentalism has nothing to do with Christ. You should be a true Christian. Then nobody will be misunderstood by you, on the contrary your love 'will always stand firm.' Even when addressing a man of another religion you should behave like a Christian. In other words, you should be kind and show him respect regardless of his religion." If this is pretty much the case concerning other religions' believers, then we can imagine what should be applied to believers of other Christian traditions, and how those who oppose the ecumenical movement and try to defend ideological Orthodoxy are exposed by the intimate tradition of Orthodoxy! Orthodoxy should not be a historical outcast. Its place is at the center of progress, of vanguard, of development, of transition and finally of man's and the entire world's transfiguration so that they can be an image of God's Kingdom. This crucial task has to be continued within the hands of those who truly care about Orthodoxy's ecumenical witness and mission. They cannot lose their nerve in the face of inquisitive attacks and defamations or against fearful reactions and conservative reservations which clearly indicate smattering and insecurity. If we allow these harmful reactions to dominate the public sphere of our church, they will lead Orthodoxy to a historic marginalization in the 21st century.

Bibliography

Agourides, Savas, "Critical Evaluation of the Current Theological Issues," in: idem, *Visions and Acts*, (Athens: "Artos Zoes," 1991), 186-199 [in Greek].

Agourides, Savvas, "Western Europe, Byzantium, and Modern Greece: The Importance of Theological and Non-Theological Factors in the Relations East-West," *Koinonia Politon* [Civil Society] 7 (2001): 36-49 [in Greek].

Ahrweiler, Hélène, *L'idéologie politique de l'empire byzantin*, (Paris: PUF, 1975).

Behr-Sigel, Elisabeth and Ware, Kallistos, *The Ordination of Women in the Orthodox Church,* (Geneva: WCC Publications, 2000).

Bodrov, Alexei, "Relations Between the Russian Orthodox Church and the Military," in: Semegnish Asfaw-Alexios Chehadeh-Marian Gh. Simion (eds), *Just Peace: Orthodox Perspectives*, (Geneva: WCC Publications, 2012), 42-48.

Clapsis, Emmanuel, *Orthodoxy in Conversation: Orthodox Ecumenical Engagements,* (Geneva/Brookline: WCC Publications/Holy Cross Orthodox Press, 2000).

Clark, Elmer T., "Non-Theological Factors in Religious Diversity," *The Ecumenical Review* 3 (1951): 347-356.

Comité mixte Catholique-Orthodoxe en France, *Catholiques et Orthodoxes: Les enjeux de l'Uniatisme, dans le sillage de Balamand*, (Paris: Bayard Editions/Fleurus/Mame/Les Editions du Cerf, 2004).

Congar, Yves, *After Nine Hundred Years: The Background of the Schism Between the Eastern and Western Churches*, (New York: Fordham University Press, 1959).

Demacopoulos, George, and Papanikolaou, Aristotle (eds), *Orthodox Constructions of he West*, (New York: Fordham University Press, 2013).

Florovsky, Georges, "The Legacy and The Task of Orthodox Theology," *Anglican Theological Review* 31 (1949): 65-66.

Florovsky, Georges, "The Boundaries of the Church", in: *Ecumenism I: A Doctrinal Approach,* Volume Thirteen in the Collected Works of Georges Florovsky, (Vaduz, Europa: Buchervertriebsanstalt, 1989), 36-45.

Jenkins, Daniel, "The Ecumenical Movement and its 'Non-Theological Factors'," *The Ecumenical Review* 3 (1951): 339-346.

Kalaitzidis, Pantelis, *Orthodoxy and Modernity: An Introduction*, (Athens: Indiktos, 2007 [in Greek], under publication in English by St Vladimir's Seminary Press: New York).

Kalaitzidis, Pantelis, "From the 'Return to the Fathers' to the Need for a Modern Orthodox Theology," *St Vladimir's Theological Quarterly* 54 (2010): 5-36.

Part II: Orthodoxy and Ecumenism - Foundations

Kalaitzidis, Pantelis, "Orthodox Theological Education in the Postmodernity Era: Challenges, Questions and Ambivalences," in: D. Werner-D. Esterline-N. Kang-J. Raja (eds), *Handbook of Theological Education in World Christianity: Theological Perspectives, Regional Surveys, Ecumenical Trends*, (Oxford: Regnum Books International, 2010), 614-622.

Kalaitzidis, Pantelis, "Orthodoxy and Hellenism in Contemporary Greece", *St Vladimir's Theological Quarterly* 54 (2010): 365-420.

Käßmann, Margot, *Die Eucharistische Vision. Armut und Reichtum als Anfrage an die Einheit der Kirche in der Diskussion des Ökumenischen Rates,* (München/Mainz, 1992), especially chapter 2: Ausgangspunkt in der Eiheitsdebatte, paragraph 2.1: "Nicht-Theologische" Faktoren, 38-51.

Küng, Hans-Moltmann, Jürgen (eds), *Fundamentalism as an Ecumenical Challenge*, Concilium journal Special issue, (London: SCM Press, 1992).

Meyendorff, John, *Imperial Unity and Christian Divisions: The Church 450-680 AD*, (Crestwood, NY: St. Vladimir's Seminary Press, 1989).

Nichols, Aidan, *Rome and the Eastern Churches: A Study in Schism*, Revised edition, (San Francisco: Ignatius Press, 2010).

Oeldemann, Johannes, *Orthodoxe Kirchen im ökumenischen Dialog. Positionen, Probleme, Perspektiven*, (Paderborn: Bonifatius, 2004), especially chapter 5: Historische Erblasten und kulturelle Eigenarten–Probleme im Dialog mit der Orthodoxie, 117-146.

Stavrou, Michel, "Relations œcuméniques et reconnaissance du baptême des autres Eglises," *Contacts* 243 (2013): 519-533.

Tsetsis, Georges, *The Contribution of the Ecumenical Patriarchate in the Formation of the World Council of Churches*, (Katerini: Tertios, 1988) [in Greek].

Tsompanidis, Stelios, *"For the Unity of All": The Contribution of Orthodox Church and Theology to the World Council of Churches*, (Thessaloniki: Pournaras, 2008) [in Greek].

Vletsis, Athanasios, "Return to Orthodoxy: What is the Model of Church's Unity for the Orthodox Church?", in: Ioannis Petrou, Stylianos Tsompanidis, Moschos Gkoutsioudis (eds), *The Ecumenical Dialogue in the 21st Century*, (Thessaloniki: Vanias Publications, 2013) [in Greek].

Ware, Timothy (Kallistos), *The Orthodox Church*, (Penguin Books, 1963).

Ware, Timothy (Kallistos), *Eustratios Argenti: A Study of the Greek Church under Turkish Rule*, (Oxford: Clarendon Press, 1964).

Yannaras, Christos, *Orthodoxy and the West: Hellenic Self-identity in the Modern Age*, translated by Peter Chamberas and Norman Russell, (Brookline, MA: Holy Cross Orthodox Press, 2006).

Zizioulas, John D., "Comments on the Study paper of the Faith and Order Commission on 'The Meaning of Ordination'," *Study Encounter* 4 (1968): 192-194.

Zizioulas, John D. (Metropolitan of Pergamon), *The One and the Many: Studies on God, Man, the Church, and the World Today*, edited by Fr. Gregory Edwards, (Alhambra: CA, Sebastian Press, 2010).

Church and the World: The Unity of the Church and the Renewal of Human Community, A Faith and Order Study Document, Faith and Order Paper No. 151, Geneva: WCC Publications, 1990.

World Conference on Faith and Order, *The Non-Theological Factors in the Making and Un-making of Church Union*, Report No. 3, Prepared by the Commission on the Church's Unity in Life and Worship, Edinburgh, 1937.

"That they all may be one," *Synaxi* 11 (1984).

(20) Distorted Images of Ecumenism – Historical and Theological Reasons for the Difficulties in developing a proper Understanding of Ecumenism in the Russian Context

Vladimir Fedorov

The contemplations on the subject of this chapter are limited by the context of the confessional, political and linguistic culture the author has lived in and in which he was educated. To cover all the contexts in a brief paper does not seem possible. Yet there are many countries where Orthodoxy prevails or is present that have many characteristics in common. Furthermore, the Union of Soviet Socialist Republics (USSR) and post-communist Russia are also a special contexts which needs the mentioning of some additional determinants.

A thorough analysis of this issue has been put forth in Fr. Tom Stransky's article "Criticism of the Ecumenical Movement and of the WCC."[1] Fr. Stransky identified four general categories of criticisms of the ecumenical movement: theological, ecclesiological, political and institutional. He wrote: "Some of these criticisms are based on deliberate or unintended caricatures and judgments shaped from a distance."[2] Such exaggerated images are still prevailing in the minds of Christians (not only Orthodox) in Russia and other East European countries.

As far back as sixty years ago the first General Secretary of the World Council of Churches Willem Adolf Visser't Hooft wrote in his famous essay on the meaning of the word 'ecumenical':

> "For although 'ecumenical', in the sense of 'that which concerns the unity and the world-wide mission of the Church of Jesus Christ', is widely used and now generally understood, that is not the meaning traditionally assigned to the word. Yet this new usage seems to have established itself, with a good prospect of permanence, in at least ten European languages, and even in ecclesiastical Latin".[3]

Visser't Hooft commented on seven meanings of the word. Since then, the word "ecumenical" has come to widen its usage (e.g. "related to interfaith dialoguing"), some of the occurrences being questionable. Interestingly, it can be observed that misunderstandings of and negative connotations to the word 'ecumenism' were partly developed due to the very fact of this word becoming "substantivized" (i.e. transformed into a subject: ecumenism) from what originally was solely understood as an adjective ('ecumenical'). This is now one of the most frequently occurring causes for the rejection of the concept of 'ecumenism' by the Russian speaking milieu. The meaning of the word remains unclear and vague for people for whom Church related terms are alien and not familiar. Therefore the term 'ecumenism' in Russian popular consciousness often is associated with some theory or teaching that has come to the East from the West and therefore is suspicious. The original Greek root of the word is left unrecognized, while the suffix "ism", leads to connotations with 'communism' or similar words which are only received and viewed negatively. Few would at the same time be aware of the fact that for instance the positive notions of 'Romanticism' or "Idealism" which refer to periods in intellectual history have the same "technical" suffix. As far as Christian believers and church-attendants are concerned, there are good chances that those who have not graduated from a theological school are familiar with the word 'ecumenism' only in the context of the slogan "Ecumenism is the worst of *all heresies* of the 20th centuries"

---

[1] Tom Stransky, "Criticism of the Ecumenical Movement and of the WCC," in *Dictionary of the Ecumenical Movement*, (Geneva: WCC Publications, 2002), 278-282.

[2] Ibid., 278.

[3] Willem Adolf Visser't Hooft, The word 'ecumenical' - its history and use, in: "Appendix 1," in Ruth Rouse and Stephen Neill (ed.), *A History of the Ecumenical Movement* 1517-1948, v. I, (Geneva: WCC, 1993), 739.

("modern heresy of heresies" or *"pan-heresy")* coined by its opponents. The danger of distortion of the concept of 'ecumenism' already starts therefore when ecumenism is presented and treated as a doctrine imported from the West and as a closed ideology.

If however we understand ecumenism as a movement of the faithful, a quest and striving for Christian missionary unity, we need to realize that "the unity which 'Ecumenism' is concerned about is a concept which makes it impossible to be labeled as the key term of a 'heresy'. There is a distinction between good 'ecumenism' and bad 'ecumenism'." That is what a prominent Orthodox theologian of the past century, Fr. Alexander Schmemann reminds us all of.

> "And as long as the Orthodox are permitted to fight for the 'good' one against the 'bad' one, as long as their voice is heard, as long as their consensus (with a few possible exceptions) remains obvious and in fact increases, the question of the usefulness of Orthodox participation in ecumenical events may be debated as well as that of our tactics, greater unity, better preparation, etc., but there should be no room for accusations of betrayal and innuendos of all kinds."[4]

Strictly speaking, it is by no accident that there is no article on "ecumenism" as such in the Dictionary of the Ecumenical Movement. But instead there are many articles which combine the attribute "ecumenical" with different expressions of the life and sharing of churches together (like: associations, conferences, councils, decade, directories, learning, prayer, sharing of resources). The subject-term 'ecumenism' however, although it is a secondary term, is circulating in the conversations and essays of modern Western culture. The Decree of the Vatican II "Unitatis Redintegratio" was also called a "decree on ecumenism". Later on, the Pontifical Council for Promoting Christian Unity published directories for application of "principles and norms on ecumenism."[5]

One can find definitions of "ecumenism" in popular or encyclopedic editions, for example, in the Encyclopedia Britannica: "Ecumenism - the movement or tendency toward worldwide Christian unity or cooperation. The term, of recent origin, emphasizes what is viewed as the universality of the Christian churches." But there are still too many Orthodox countries, first of all, in post-communist Europe, where the lack of information on the history of the concept of 'ecumenism' and the misusage of this word is dramatic.

Both Visser't Hooft's essay on the understanding of 'ecumenical' and the definition of the Encyclopedia Britannica emphasize the missionary dimension of the concept of being 'ecumenical', as this word is related to the striving to attain unity. This rootedness of the concept of 'ecumenical' in a missionary understanding of the church is very important indeed. It is because of the missionary vision and obligation of the participants of the 1910 Edinburgh World Missions Conference and their subsequent followers that the term "ecumenical" was chosen to signify a commitment to unity and world-wide missionary outreach of the Church.

It should also be realized that the concept of being 'ecumenical' did not so much present a clearcut strategy, pre-conceived plan or policy, as a longing and tendency towards worldwide Christian unity, which included an attitude of openness to contacts with other churches and inter-confessional collaboration. At the same time, ecumenism remained related to a missionary vision of the church involved in global communication of the Gospel to the whole of the inhabited earth..

For the context of post-soviet Russia, the absence of religious education and seventy years of atheism as the prevailing ideology resulted in almost total religious ignorance. However, within the walls of the three centers of theological education that survived in the USSR through the waves of persecution, the topic of ecumenism emerged with new vitality when the Russian Orthodox Church (ROC), i. e. the Moscow Patriarchate, joined the Conference of European Churches (CEC) in 1959 and the World Council of Churches (WCC) in 1961. The Moscow Council of Heads and Representatives of Orthodox Churches responded to

---

[4] Fr. Alexander Schmemann, "On The 'Sorrowful Epistle' of Metropolitan Philaret," The Orthodox Church, November 1969, 5, 8. See http://shmeman.ru/modules/myarticles/article_storyid_162.html (last accessed, September 2013)

[5] In particular on March 25th, 1993. http://www.vatican.va/roman_curia/pontifical_councils/chrstuni/general-docs/rc_pc_chrstuni_doc_19930325_directory_en.html (last accessed, September 2013).

the invitation addressed to the ROC in 1948 to participate in the First Assembly of the WCC which was to be held in Amsterdam quite coldly: "We inform the World Council of Churches, in reply to the invitations received by all of us to take part in the Amsterdam Assembly in the capacity of members of it, that all Local Orthodox Churches participating in the present Meeting are compelled to refuse to participate in the Ecumenical Movement in its present form." The resolution was signed by the heads of the Russian, Georgian, Serbian, Rumanian, Bulgarian, Polish, Albanian and Czechoslovakian Churches and by representatives of the Churches of Antioch and Alexandria.

After 1961, the climate and connotations of ecumenism changed again as neither professors of theology nor students could now say anything against the word "ecumenical" because it was taken to bear a special reference to inter-confessional Christian contacts. One could still shed some doubt on the appropriateness or meaning of such contacts with other Christian bodies, but the term 'ecumenical' as such could not be put into question anymore. There were already criticisms of ecumenism who argued that the participation of the ROC in the New Delhi Assembly was solely an expression of servile obedience to the Communist Party. Strangely however, in 1948, in the time of the Cold War, the position of the ROC was not associated with the communist ideology. It was during the tense atmosphere of the early 1960s, that leading Soviet ideologists felt forced to make the West take the USSR as a socialist state with a human face, i.e. with a faith sanctioned by the state authorities. In reality, these were the years of most severe ideological persecution of religion and ill-treatment of believers and also the years of the mass closings of churches and monasteries. But ecumenical contacts in this period for the Russian Orthodox Church also were a unique chance to gain international religious and political support. Until now, many critics of ecumenical activities underestimated the strategy of the Moscow Patriarchy in the 60s through the 80s. Its strategy also was an expression of some elements of opposition over against the atheist regime. But even today, when we must oppose not only atheism, but also the ever growing danger of global secularization, ecumenical strategies are also on the agenda.

In Russia, the trend of accusing 'ecumenism' of heresy began to appear during late 80s and early 90s. It was caused by the increasing contacts of the Russians with Western European and American believers from the Russian Orthodox Church Outside of Russia (ROCOR), who in their turn tended to stick to the anti-ecumenical argumentation of the members of the Old Calendar Greek Schism. Typical is the speech of the Archbishop Vitaly (Ustinov)[6] from the ROCOR, after the 1968 WCC General Assembly:

> Ecumenism is the heresy of heresies, because until now every separate heresy in the history of the Church has striven itself to stand in the place of the true Church, while the ecumenical movement, having united all heresies, invites them all together to honor themselves as the one true Church. Here ancient Arianism, Monophysitism, Monothelitism, Iconoclasm, Pelagianism, and simply every possible superstition of the contemporary sects under completely different names, have united and charged to assault the Church. This phenomenon is undoubtedly of an apocalyptic character. The devil has fought in turn, almost in sequence, with Christ's Truth set forth in the Nicene Symbol of Faith, and has come now to the final and most vitally important paragraph of the Creed: "I believe in One, Holy, Catholic and Apostolic Church."[7]

In his criticism, Archbishop Vitaly emphasized that the ecumenical movement was prepared and inspired by a special world-view of pseudo-Christianity – while neglecting and ignoring totally the fact that the ecumenical movement is rooted in the bosom of the YMCA, YWCA, SCM, and other similar Christian organizations. In Archbishop Vitaly's view, which is shared by many Orthodox believers, the most obvious reason and rationale for ecumenism is to be found in the world and strategies of *Freemasonry* which strives to establish a secret world government and which – according to his view - in every manner inspires, aids and finances all that is going on in ecumenism. There is no real sense in going into the details of this conspiracy theory. To see how

---

[6] Metropolitan, primate of the Orthodox Church Outside of Russia (1985 – 2001).

[7] Archbishop Vitaly of Montreal and Canada, "A Report to the Sobor of Bishops of the Russian Orthodox Church Outside of Russia," see http://orthodoxinfo.com/ecumenism/vitaly.aspx (last accessed, September 2013).

Part II: Orthodoxy and Ecumenism - Foundations

false documents were manufactured for accusations of every thinkable trouble, may these be now Masons, or Jews or Jesuits, it is sufficient to read Umberto Eco's *Prague Cemetery*.

It is noteworthy that Archbishop Vitaly widens the notion of ecumenism which initially referred to nothing more than the Christian phenomenon of inter-confessional collaboration, to include also the issue of attitude towards non-Christian faiths and to put them in parallel to other Christian confessions which are as unacceptable for him as non-Christian faiths.

"All other religions, so-called Christian, monotheistic or pagan, all without the slightest exception, whether it be Catholicism, Protestantism, Islam or Buddhism—all are obstacles placed by the devil as his traps between the Church of Christ and the whole human race. Only in personal relationships with those of different faiths, for the sake of church economy, for the sake simply of knowledge and criticism, we can view certain of them as more capable of becoming Orthodox and others as farther away, but in principle they all without exception belong to falsehood, having nothing in common with truth… Thus all these religions are they that have accepted food from the devil: here is the subtle seductiveness of Francis of Assisi in one vessel, and beside it nirvana in another, and there Mohammed, Luther, Calvin, Henry VIII, with food corresponding to their tastes."

Cardinal Walter Kasper in his presentation at the event marking the 40th anniversary of the Joint Working Group between the Roman Catholic Church and the WCC remarked:

"We cannot overlook the theological, political and institutional critique of the ecumenical movement, which comes not only from so-called fundamentalist groups but from some venerable old churches and serious theologians as well. For some of them ecumenism has become a negative term, equivalent to syncretism, doctrinal relativism and indifferentism."[8]

Identification of ecumenism with syncretism ranks among the most absurd, however still recent common judgments. To give an example, a professor at the Moscow Orthodox Theological Academy issued a book titled *Challenge of Ecumenism* which according to its annotation "focused on an intent to unite different religions. This intent has been articulated by a quantity of sects."[9] In his foreword, Prof. Kuraev observed that "the newspaper-minded masses take the word ecumenism as a substitute for the disreputable word 'syncretism,' the former approximating in its connotation to theosophical slogans of the 'Religious brotherhood' or 'Unity of religions' type. So I, too, will not differentiate between ecumenism and syncretism in this book and will use the word ecumenism in the meaning people most often ascribe to it nowadays."[10] Instead of demonstrating the incompatibility of the two notions by saying that syncretism is unacceptable the author makes the reader think that ecumenism is unacceptable as syncretism is anyhow.

Many opponents treat ecumenism as the most noticeable manifestation of Protestant, Catholic and Orthodox modernism.[11] However, the notion of modernism deserves special attention. In obscurant and fundamentalist circles, it serves to be another abusive label. Ideologists of the struggle against modernism explain the word as "…introducing into the Church theology of a wide set of heresies, philosophical views, scientific ideas, cultural mages, ideological and social clichés and above all, superstitions – for the sake of renewal and modification of the Church to be in keeping with progress. …modernism is gradually conforming to disorderly revolutionary shifts of life of the human society with the ideal ultimate aim of complete reconciliation with course of events

---

[8] "The ecumenical movement in the 21st century - A contribution from the PCPCU," see http://www.oikoumene.org/en/resources/documents/wcc-commissions/joint-working-group-between-the-roman-catholic-church-and-the-wcc/the-ecumenical-movement-in-the-21st-century.html (last accessed, September 2013).
[9] Deacon Andrey Kuraev, Vyizov *Challenge of Ecumenism*, (Moscow: Publishing Department of the Russian Orthodox Church, 2007), 2.
[10] Ibid., 4.
[11] http://www.antimodern.ru/ecumenism.html

which is taken as establishment of Kingdom of God on Earth."[12] Such a picture is usually based on false prem-ises and on the conviction that theology should not evolve by definition. Often this is accompanied by a whole strand of theological thinking, which is denying creativity in exegetics and hermeneutics.

The concept of Orthodoxy as being mainly traditional, conservative and resistant to any contemporary influences which is implanted in the minds of the Orthodox believers makes our situation often confused. It is frequently said that renewal, aggiornamento, is contradictory to Orthodoxy. Orthodoxy certainly is about the tradition of fiat and in that sense traditional, but Orthodoxy always is about a living tradition. Yes, it is conservative, but in the sense that it serves the preaching and the conservation of the eternal values of the Gospel. The Church as a Theandric organism cannot but interact with the social milieu and cannot but look for a language to communicate to those who are to listen to the Gospel today. Missiological reasoning for such a position can start from the notion of "inculturation" introduced into missiology in the last quarter of the 20th century. Since horizontal, geographical inculturation is readily apparent, it seems natural to admit chronological inculturation as well.

Another blame put on ecumenism is related to the so-called "branch theory" which is reputedly adhered to by ecumenists. The branch theory is the theory that, though the Church may have fallen into schism within itself and its several provinces or groups of provinces be out of communion with each other, but each may still be a branch of the one Church of Christ, provided that it continues to hold the faith of the original undi-vided Church and to maintain the Apostolic Succession of its bishops. The branch theory, as it is contended by many Anglican theologians, describes the condition of the Church at the present time, which consists now of three main branches Roman-Catholic, Orthodox and Anglican.[13] William Palmer (1803–1885), an Oxford theologian, was the principle originator of this Branch Theory. The theory was then popularized during the Oxford Movement, particularly through the work of the Tractarians. However, some leaders of the movement became dissatisfied and later became Roman Catholics. A majority of participants in the ecumenical movement are Protestants. But as the branch theory excludes Protestant ecclesial bodies from the one true church as they are judged to lack Apostolic Succession, it is obvious that not much support for the theory could emerge from the Protestant Churches. It is also a statement of fact that Orthodoxy rejects the "branch theory."

For anti-ecumenical polemics there are always some new faults to be found in those who stand for ecu-menism. "Ecumenists have in general developed the following newfangled theologies: 'Baptismal theology', the theology of 'Sister Churches', the theology of the 'Wider Church', the theology of 'Cultural Pluralism', the theology of 'Common Service', 'Interfaith theology'."[14] Each of these swift accusations deserves some unhurried and detailed response and polemics.

But today there is also something more solid that can serve as a common basis for arguing for ecumenism: these are Orthodox ecclesiology and missiology. The Orthodox teaching on the Church was deepened through the 20th century and is still developing further. And Orthodox missiology has contributed to analyzing the current situation and creating awareness of the role of the Church in society and in the world and thus will also help to evaluate the natural and pragmatic need of searching for various forms of inter-confessional Christian collaboration in today's social contexts.

His Holiness, Patriarch of Moscow and all Russia Kirill, is of the opinion that one of the reasons of enmity towards ecumenism typical of the Russian popular consciousness lies in the fact that for many years, due to political motives it was only the theological elite who where involved in ecumenical activities when the ROC was taking part in the work of the WCC. It was only the new (post-communist) situation which made allowances for the Church to look both at the ecumenical movement and the WCC from the standpoint of

---

[12] http://antimodern.wordpress.com/2009/02/09/%D0%BC%D0%BE%D0%B4%D0%B5%D1%80%D0%B-D%D0%B8%D0%B7%D0%BC/ (last accessed, September 2013).
[13] *The Oxford Dictionary of the Christian Church*, Edited by F. I. Cross, (Oxford University Press, 1997), 232.
[14] http://www.synodinresistance.org/Theology_en/TheologyofAntiEcumenism.html (last accessed, September 2013).

common believers for the first time, not of its theological elite."[15] Patriarch Kirill reminds us that participation of the Orthodox believers in the ecumenical movement is prompted by a missionary imperative. "Saving and defending purity of the Orthodox faith, we must share our Orthodox faith with every inquirer, leaving that which follows for God's will."[16]

A survey of negative attitudes towards ecumenism in communities of different Christian confessions leaves an impression that sometimes antagonistic attitudes do not only correlate with confessional worldviews, but rather also with a certain psychological type of personality. Characteristic of this type are rigorism which sometimes turns into fanaticism, authoritarianism, disposition to pharisaism, a tendency to literal interpretation of the sacral texts and canons, lack of exegetic and hermeneutic taste, a complex of enemy hunting and relying on conspiracy theories. With regard to social and political preferences, people of this personality type tend to reject democracy, underestimate the principle of liberty of conscience, have an antipathy towards religious tolerance and a readiness to rely upon external forces in struggling against heterodoxy. Usually such a personality type is often found behind the religious fundamentalist type, but this topic would require a more detailed and special investigation.

---

[15] Cited after Hilarion (Alfeev) Metropolitan of Volokolamsk. *Patriarch Kirill: life and worldview*, (Moscow, 2010), 434.
[16] Ibid., 435.

Sister Theoktisti Emsley

Introduction

It is important to make clear at the beginning that being an Orthodox nun in the Greek tradition, I am not a specialist but someone who experiences the ecumenical Orthodox monastic tradition. Thus I will talk about my reflections on this subject, pointing out some of the difficulties involved. To begin with there is a difficulty in using the term *ecumenism - οἰκουμενισμός*. This refers to something other than the adjective *ecumenical - οἰκουμενικός,* or universal, which we should use in order not to be misunderstood:

The adjective *οἰκουμενικός* is used in a different way as the nouns *οἰκουμενιστής* or *οἰκουμενισμός:*
ecumenical ecumenist ecumenism.

The understanding of *οἰκουμενική* is not the same as *οἰκουμενιστική;* there is a great difference between an "Ecumenical Church" and an "Ecumenist Church". An ecumenist church understands itself to be a gathering of all the churches and religions together, choosing which elements they want to keep and which they want to discard. So for example they might say let us have the liturgy from the Orthodox, the organization from the Roman Catholics and the emphasis on the Bible from the Protestants, thus we have in today's terms a "copy and paste church".

Ecumenism makes comparisons between traditions, but not for conclusions about the truth of any one tradition, only for some middle ground between the churches. The ecumenical dialogue on the other hand is a necessary precondition of mutual understanding, and that mutual understanding is a precondition of mutual trust as well as providing the condition for all people to cooperate and to coexist. Dialogue is the only path pleasing to God.

The Orthodox Church, in all humility, believes itself to be the 'One, Holy, Catholic and Apostolic Church'. It is called ecumenical because it unfolds itself in the entire world and contains all of the universal truth, thus the understanding of "ecumenical" is linked to the understanding of "catholic" confessed in the Creed: "One, Holy, Catholic and Apostolic Church".

The ecumenical Tradition

In the New Testament we find the word *οἰκουμένη,* having the sense of a noun, denoting the "inhabited land". In Matthew for example, the gospel is for all nations (Matt 24:14), in Luke it is for "the world" (Luke 21:26), and in the Acts of the Apostles, for "the Roman Empire" (Acts 19:27). We know that we are all made in the image of God whether we are Orthodox, Roman Catholics or Protestants. Revelation tells us that God held out hope and the promise that we should all walk in the light of the city of God and that all the beings of the earth shall bring the glory and honour of the nations into it (cf. Rev. 21:24-26). This is the scriptural basis for engaging in the ecumenical dialogue.

The Fathers of the Church use *οἰκουμενικός* to denote the whole world. An ecumenical attitude can be found in St. John Climacus in his discourse "To the Shepherd" when he is talking about how those pastors who are strong in faith should respond positively when they are invited by heretics in a spirit of trust and goodwill.

The first seven Councils of the undivided Church, which determined and defined Orthodox doctrine, are the Ecumenical Councils, for the then Christian world. These are accepted by both Eastern and Western churches.

The Patriarch of Constantinople is known as the Ecumenical Patriarch; he furthers the collaboration between the local autocephalous and autonomous churches of the Orthodox world and offers unfailing ecumenical charity and courtesy to all, whether they are Orthodox or not.

There are those who see "ecumenism as the greatest heresy of the 20th century, preaching about a dogmatic and religious syncretism, leading to a kind of pan-religiousness, making equal all Christian denominations and other religions". Greek theologian Athanasios Frangopoulos for example believes that: "Ecumenism is a new heresy that has appeared in our days ... we Orthodox must stand far apart. Indeed, we ought to fight against it by enlightening those Orthodox who are ignorant of ecumenism and what it entails".

Bishop Kallistos Ware, on the other hand, cites the opinions of theologians who see ecumenism not just as a positive action of the Orthodox Church, but as a necessary response to other Christian groups that do not share the same environment, the same attitude, the same spiritual identity and intention as Orthodoxy. This "ecumenical" attitude does not abandon Orthodoxy. "Orthodoxy has no need of fanaticism or bigotry to protect itself." Orthodoxy is greater than that.

Bishop Anthony Bloom reminds us that: "At the beginning, the Ecumenical Movement was the only place where Christians separated from long ago could meet each other in good will, come to know each other and share in the experiences of hundreds of years. What would be the outcome of such meetings was not discussed in advance: there was a belief that Christ would unite us. But the theological commissions began to lose their way in complicated theological 'labyrinths', and then got out of them by being satisfied with insubstantial agreements. But such 'agreements' devalue the task itself: the search for Truth has already been forgotten". He continues "the Christian world is like a tree: through their roots all Christian communities are in the past, in the Undivided Church (although there were divisions even at the very beginning, but they were regarded with wise toleration by Apostle Paul), but to return to those days is impossible. From the depths of the earth in which we are all rooted, tree trunks have grown, stretching up parallel to each other. The way to unity is to grow straight upwards until all tops fuse into one. Christians must realize the Gospel in their lives and only then will the tops fuse into unity." "But for this to happen," according to Bishop Anthony Bloom, "it is necessary to take a firm decision; so long as there is no such decision we cannot, as in the past, 'collaborate' in theological quests, although the Orthodox Church has made a considerable contribution in the area of Trinitarian theology. We must continue our collaboration, but only after seeking new ways."

The ecumenical discussions today aim at establishing a theological dialogue and an understanding of the great problem of ecclesiology. Any rapprochement can only come about through prayer, humility, repentance and forgiveness. Dialogue does not mean arriving at a "common acceptance of a minimum standard of common faith, through a decision to ignore differences and difficulties or to embrace all differences as a kind of acceptable variety. ... (It) must be pursued within the framework of the undivided Church – that is, the Church before the Schism".

The annulment of the anathemas of 1054 signed by Patriarch Athenagoras and Pope Paul VI in 1965 meant that the "symbol of division" was replaced by a "symbol of love" and can be seen as the point of departure for the ecumenical dialogue. The issue is not who erred first, or who erred more or less. That is an unworthy approach; it is a question of the salvation of the world. The participation of the Orthodox Church in the ecumenical dialogue is based on the conviction that the Orthodox must contribute to the restoration of unity, bearing witness to the one undivided Church of the Apostles, the Fathers and the ecumenical councils.

The problem of syncretism however is very real: a mixing of faiths and religions by which elements of different world views are assimilated into each other, resulting in a change in the nature of them, and the emergence of a new and revised set of beliefs. It removes absolutes and works on the assumption that any belief can be adopted, re-shaped, discarded or denied depending on whether it suits the new environment. It involves adding other beliefs to Christian doctrine, with the intention of supplementing the salvation provided by Jesus and springs from lack of faith in Christ's saving power. Syncretism is not compatible with true Christianity. In fact, any modification to Biblical law and principle for the sake of a "better" religion is heresy (Cf. Rev 22:18-19).

It is here that Orthodox monasticism can show a way forward. Monasticism was and is *ecumenical*, it is not limited to one nation or race or place; it is not limited in any way. It spread where the spirit called the early monks and nuns. The historical roots of monasticism lie in Scripture. In the Old Testament Elijah serves as the monastic prototype. In the New Testament, John the Baptist is the model of ascetic life. St. Paul stands as one of its first theological exponents of celibacy. Orthodox monastics could be found anywhere in the οἰκουμένη, that is all over the then known world.

The essential and definitive traits which constitute monasticism are the indelible impressions and characteristics of the undivided Church; these are theological - patristic, liturgical, and ecclesiological.

The *ecumenical* Orthodox Monastic Tradition

As in the parable of the publican who finds favour with God through his prayer for mercy (Luke 18:9-14), the monk or nun who in prayer has a humble remembrance of sin and repentance, finds the spiritual fruitfulness of repentant sorrow and so finds favour with God. What characterizes the monk or nun is humble prayer, repentance, patience, love of neighbor and forgiveness.

This attitude is necessary for our Orthodox Church. Only when we have the courage to recognize our wounds can we begin the path of healing. At least the term "ecumenical dialogue" is not unknown, this is one step on the way, but self-knowledge and self-criticism are a *sine qua non* for continuation of an ecumenical dialogue.

We would do well to keep in mind the advice given by St. Basil to a young man who sought a greater knowledge of God: "If you wish to learn, you must first unlearn". This coupled with the saying from the Book of Ecclesiastes: "For in much wisdom is much vexation, and those who increase in knowledge increase in sorrow" (Eccles. 1:18), provide a sound basis for moving forward. The real work of healing in dialogue takes place when the issues that divide us are acknowledged and honestly examined with genuine love, patience and pain.

Divisions between churches or in monasteries are a scandal as they imply a division of the body of Christ. The gospel of John gives us the example of remaining whole and undivided, when the Roman soldiers cast lots for the tunic of Jesus (John 19: 23b-24) a symbol of the unity of the Church as the undivided body of Christ. We are all created for fellowship and communion with God. The image of God within us signifies not only relationship with God but also relationship with one another.

Orthodox monasticism provides us with a different set of values, an alternative way of living without compromise. It seeks to change the world with prayer, silence and humility rather than through power and imposition, in the fear of God, with sincerity and prudence. Monastics play a great role in deepening the understanding of Orthodoxy and in extending the study and knowledge of Orthodoxy, thus awakening and contributing to the need of ecumenical dialogue, to share and not to divide. The path of monasticism, that of perfect charity has not always been obvious when we think of the ecumenical dialogue; it has even been at times a contradiction on the part of some of its members of hindering any possible reconciliation between Christians and between churches. The idea of communication and reconciliation was bitterly rejected at various times in our history, even in some quarters to the present day. Today there is awareness that the ecumenical dialogue needs the contribution of the monastics.

The monastics renounce themselves for the sake of God and for other people. This is a love which implies a sacrifice: the greater the sacrifice, the greater the love. If monasticism is the acceptance of Christ who comes: "I was a stranger and you welcomed me" (Matt. 25:35), this means the acceptance and love of whoever arrives, even the unexpected and the unannounced. This love is lived in obedience to a freely chosen way of life that is centered on the worship of God and a gradual transformation of the passions into spiritual energy under the guidance of a spiritual father or mother.

The importance of obedience to a spiritual father or mother is underlined from the first emergence of monasticism. This is a theme constantly emphasized in the Apophthegmata or Sayings of the Desert Fathers: "The old Men used to say: 'if you see a young monk climbing up to heaven by his own will, grasp him by the feet and throw him down, for this is to his profit ... if a man has faith in another and renders himself up to him in full submission, he has no need to attend to the commandment of God, but he needs only to entrust his entire will into the hands of his father. Then he will be blameless before God, for God requires nothing from beginners so much as self-stripping through obedience'."

The Desert Fathers speak about the relationship between the spiritual child and the spiritual guide. Abba Poemen tells his brother that he should not be the legislator for others but rather lead them by example. He suggests that the brother will teach and guide his disciples through his own actions and how he leads his own life. This is a model that spiritual guides in society, outside of a monastic setting, could also employ to direct and teach the faithful, their spiritual children. The spiritual guide should provide discernment and guidance, not to be a force but to serve as a guide along the Christian journey.

When Christ said to deny oneself, take up one's cross, and follow Him, He meant that one must put aside one's own will and follow the example of Christ's love for others and obedience to the will of His Father in heaven (Matthew 16:24). Christ emphasizes this even more in Mark (12:30-31), when He reminds us of the two greatest commandments: to love God and to love one's neighbor (Cf. 1 Cor. 1:17-25). True unity should be pursued above all in the spiritual life as a path which accepts the weakness of the cross, in which the power of God can triumph.

Spiritual fathers and mothers are characterized by their wisdom which is manifested through their humility, generosity, compassion and willingness to accept the imperfections and shortcomings of life. We find ourselves attracted by their open-heartedness in giving and receiving love. Their attitude towards others is marked by compassion, and they are sensitive to those who are in different places on life's journey. Because our Scriptures and tradition hold spiritual guides in great respect the Orthodox Church, which has kept alive the tradition of the spiritual father and mother, is uniquely positioned to reclaim their value. While authentic spiritual guidance is ultimately achieved through years of discernment, prayer and deep thought about one's faith, time spent in a monastery can serve a guide on the spiritual journey, particularly important for those involved in the ecumenical dialogue.

Ecumenical Orthodox Monasticism Today

When we speak about the ecumenical dimension of the monastic tradition and practice we are talking about a canonical practice in the Orthodox Church everywhere in the *οἰκουμένη*. Monks and nuns come from different cultures and countries, the only real meeting they can have, however, is through prayer. We can fantasize about a unity as monks and nuns, we can fantasize about a unity of the churches and denominations in that we all go back to the first centuries and begin again as one Church. But without prayer and humility this does not lead us anywhere. We are dreaming of something unrealistic.

Orthodox monasticism is a way to live a real ecumenical life, but truth and freedom have to be the basis of monastic life. This means that we cannot opt for an artificial unity of monks and nuns but that we have to live out the pain of our division. Monasticism is founded in our churches and has to live out the truth and canonical practice of our churches; this entails living the continual pain of division and thus making present the need for humble prayer. Here we all must base our lives on some of the virtues that are particularly cultivated in monastic life: we need prayer, we need humility, we need patience, and we need to "reset" ourselves to the teaching of Jesus Christ. Only something like this will unite us.

The monastic virtue of humility is the key; it teaches us the way forward – to find our mistakes and not to repeat them again. In order to become "one" we need repentance (*metanoia*). What divided us? Egoism, church politics, historical events and stubbornness divided us. How can we now correct this mess we have made? We need to change ourselves in order to see our mistakes, not just political and historical but also our personal mistakes and misunderstandings, which we do not easily get over; and we need to ask for forgiveness, not from the media or from the balcony, but deep down and in our everyday life. It is here that the monastic tradition, which carries along with it the same spirit of the first Church through the centuries, can give an example and can teach us how to do this with humility and a clean heart.

We live, however, in the tradition of the Church, we live with our sacraments and all that we have come to know and love in the Church. How can we approach another when we see for example that the liturgy and the sacraments look different, that they have developed differently? We need to go back and see how this happened in order to move forward. Unity does not mean to be under one head and to be all exactly the same, but to accept each other and be reconciled. This is what the monastics try and do every day.

We need to find dogmatic reconciliation. This is very specific and we need the specialists and theologians to discuss and find a common expression of these dogmatic issues. There has to be some result, something final, saying "this and this we have in common dogmatically". There will still be differences because of the varying development of symbolism in the churches, the liturgical, the "para-liturgical", the rituals, etc. Here we find the role of the spiritual father or mother in the monastery. They are, so to speak, the theologian and specialists who pray and guide and unite their community in love, compassion and patience despite it being made up of very varying individuals. With wisdom and discernment they hold fast onto the essentials, but know when and how to adapt and include different developments.

There must be a space in the Church for each nation and their culture. In the wider ecumenical perspective, it cannot be right making Africans ignore their own great musical tradition and making them sing Byzantine music in their church or to celebrate Greek and Russian feasts (at times political ones) rather than their own. This is a nationalistic rather than an ecumenical approach to the Church. A further "mistake" is the insistence on keeping Byzantium alive at all costs. In Greece, Byzantium has its place, through the language, geography and culture, but this is clearly not the case for the whole *ecumenical* world. The discernment of the spiritual father or mother of the monastery gives the right place due to each member of the community. All belong to the same community all need the love and acceptance of all the community, but this can be expressed in ways that are specific to the different individuals.

Thirst for Unity

A first step towards unity is to see if Christians today have a "thirst" for unity? We need to see if there is a "thirst for ecumenism". If the churches do not rouse Christians for Christian life in general they will have no understanding for the need for unity. If you have real "thirst" you are prepared to do anything to quench this thirst. If you have no thirst, then you probably have no interest. If this is the case then the whole ecumenical dialogue is just a theoretical discussion, abstract and far removed from the reality of the members of the Church today – a waste of time!

The role of the monastic is to pray intensively for this "thirst" for all Christians and pray for a deeper interest in Orthodoxy, first and foremost from our own Orthodox faithful. We must not close our doors to those Christians who do not know us and to those who show the first steps of interest, we have to be open and welcoming. We need a "pure ecumenism", which is not heretical. This can show to the world the truth and beauty of Orthodoxy and then show the path to unity. This path can only be found through intensive prayer. Our Church prays every day in the liturgy for unity of the whole world; this does not mean to lose our richness or something, but to open our heart to the whole world the οἰκουμένη.

We are made in the image and likeness of God, we are all icons of God; not only does it not help to insult all other Christian confessions but it is going against the specific teaching of Jesus Christ to love one another. Unfortunately some of our monasteries are selling books which just do that. There are books which pretend to explain the Orthodox Church but give misinformation and insult other Christian confessions without saying anything really constructive, or teaching about Orthodoxy, its beauty and richness. Orthodoxy does not need to explain itself in term of others and their "mistakes", it is more than that, and it is a pity when books stoop down to that level. Another terrible thing that happens is that people reading these books throw them away with remarks such as: "if this is all the Orthodox Church is, then I am not interested", or: "you would think they could get their facts right before writing such nonsense", or even worse: "I thought of becoming Orthodox before reading this, but not now". These are remarks we have heard in our monasteries. Instead of showing the way to Orthodoxy, we are pushing people off the path to God!!!

Other religions and confessions were a "taboo" for the Orthodox people for a long time based on fear, wars, and the crusades etc., inherited from past experiences. The world where Orthodoxy flourished was historically closed, these countries were not free and had little or no good contact with other Christians, for them it was "Orthodoxy or hell", and they did not know that there were Christians other than themselves. This is now no longer the case and the fear needs to be overcome in order to move on and heal the past wounds. We need good information available for our own Orthodox faithful (and priests) to deepen our understanding of our faith and equip us to share this faith with others.

It is here that Orthodox monasticism can help very much with the maxim "do not criticize". In humble recognition of oneself the absurdity of criticism of others becomes apparent. Only those who are closed to the working of God in their hearts can judge others without compassion. In our monasteries we see the development of the new-comer, who perhaps at the beginning "doesn't suffer fools gladly", who moves then to the ever deeper insight of their own sinfulness and gradually awakens to a completely new attitude to those who think and act differently. This is a necessary path for everyone who seriously engages in any kind of ecumenical dialogue.

The Orthodox Church has always accepted, in theory and applied in practice, the principle of tolerance towards other religious faiths as a corollary of absolute respect towards human freedom which constitutes a basic element of its faith.

It is clear that every religion asserts that it holds within its belief system the absolute truth concerning God and the world, the latter of which also incorporates humanity. For the coexistence of all peoples and religions the realization that we all are God's creation is essential. Dialogue brings people closer through understanding of the other. This is because God always, and in many ways, is in dialogue with us. God is seeking the free offering of our heart.

The conciliatory role of Christianity can only be initiated and sustained by, and through, the voice and ear of genuine tolerance. The virtue of tolerance, together with the virtue of diversity, reflect the divine attributes of love maintained in the essence of God, perfectly and infinitely.

The human person is the main concern of God, and through the dialogue between God and man one arrives at perfect goodness and love. The human person seeks communion with himself and God but unless one has communion with "others," he will not be able to come to God.

Pentecost: an Ecumenical Message

The message of the Resurrection was: "Go therefore and make disciples of all nations" (Matt 28:19). The message of Pentecost was to go to preach to all nations, that is why "All of them were filled with the Holy Spirit and began to speak in other languages, as the Spirit gave them ability" (Acts 2:4). There were to give light, to give Christianity, to give the gospel to the whole world, to those who did not speak their language. This is the ecumenical message.

Orthodox monasticism has a similar ecumenical message; it is possible to live canonically in all the οἰκουμέ-νη. This can unite everyone. Monastic life is "epiclesis" in action, invocation of the descent of the Holy Spirit which at Pentecost was the power of the plural unity, communion in the distinction of gifts (Acts 2: 1-3). A monastic can be anyone who tries to live according to the same traditional pattern or model, living in chastity, poverty and obedience. This monastic basis is lived out through experience and not through theory; it is made real and can thus serve as an example for the ecumenical dialogue.

Orthodox monastic life in every age requires a life of conversion, or a return to the sources, to the Gospel. If the end of the ecumenical dialogue, the "pure" ecumenical dialogue, is unity then this will have to be preceded by an interest in, and a concern for, unity. The virtues cultivated in monasticism can be the basis for this movement towards unity, especially prayer, humility, reconciliation, forgiveness and respect of the other. The recognition of one's own mistakes and the forgiveness of the other is the last thing a monastic does every evening after the last community prayer. The monastic asks for forgiveness from the Geronda /Gerondissa (Abbott/Abbess), who is in the place of Christ for the community. This act has a great symbolic value and plays a great role in the cohesion of a community. This asking for forgiveness can be the mode for beginning the path towards understanding, forgiveness and unity.

Orthodox involvement in ecumenism is a missionary responsibility. As in any missionary situation, a person's actual conversion to Orthodoxy is left up to God, but the responsibility lies with the Orthodox to be present and witness to their apostolic faith, to teach, and also to learn from the encounter. This will only succeed if the missionaries know how to deal sensitively with the experience those interested in Orthodoxy bring with them. Even many Orthodox Christians are ignorant of the real basis of their own faith and are very confused, knowing only a few bits about other religions and confessions. This is true everywhere: Asia, Africa, Americas, and Europe. It is not just a question of education but of spiritual guidance. Our monasteries are doing much in this area, but much more still needs to be done, especially among our own faithful.

Conclusion

The Patristic revival has been an essential factor in Orthodox involvement in the ecumenical dialogue. If monastics understand and truly respond to this Patristic revival they can respond to the call of interior unification, of lived communion, of ever-renewed reconciliation, of continual mercy, then they will be servants of unity of the ecumenical dialogue. By this we do not mean, or want, or agree with, the idea to create a church by taking bits from here and there to create a church that has everything. We mean the capacity to go two miles with those who ask us to go one (Cf. Matt. 5:41). It needs a passion for the body of Christ.

The Ecumenical Patriarch in "Speaking the Truth in Love" tells us: "The bonds of friendship among divided churches and the bridges by which we can overcome our divisions are indispensable, now more than ever. Love is essential, so that dialogue between our churches can occur in all freedom and trust".

This is the challenge we all need to face, particularly monastics who can show others the way through their example of prayer, humility and forgiveness.

A great monastic spiritual guide of our times, Fr. Porphyrios of Kafsokayvia tells us: "…if we live in unity we will be happy and we will live in Paradise. Our every neighbor is 'flesh of our flesh'. … This is the great mystery of our Church: that we all become one in God. … There is nothing better than this unity. This is the Church. This is the Orthodox faith."

Bibliography

Bloom, Anthony, *Ecumenism: Orthodox-Roman Catholic Encounters, and the Ecumenical Patriarchate*, (London 1997).
Bartholomew, Ecumenical Patriarch, *Speaking the Truth in Love*, (New York 2011).
Frangopoulos, Athanasios, *Our Orthodox Christian Faith*, (Athens 2000) [in Greek].
Ware, Timothy (Kallistos), *The Orthodox Church*, (London 1963).
Wounded by Love: The life and wisdom of Elder Porphyrios, (Evia, Greece 2005) [in Greek].

PART III

REPRESENTATIVE ORTHODOX THEOLOGIANS REFLECTING ON ECUMENISM

(22) Ecumenical Theologians and Important Leaders from Orthodox Tradition – General Introduction

Nikolaos Asproulis

Anti-ecumenical voices and dangerous attitudes of fundamentalism and religious nationalism feature in many parts of the Orthodox world in the early twenty-first century. It is in this context that a comprehensive introduction to major representative Orthodox ecumenical figures and great thinkers, presenting especially their contributions to the ecumenical movement, is both challenging and an urgent necessity. The Orthodox Church must be seen not only as an institution or an organization (at the local level), or a communion of organizations (at the ecumenical level) but more importantly also as a "way of being,"[1] or "a combination of personalities,"[2] into which the faithful are grafted through Baptism, Chrismation and the Eucharist, thus providing the means for the gradual fulfillment of *theosis* or deification in the Orthodox ascetic and spiritual vocabulary. To consider Orthodox contributions to ecumenism, it is necessary to take into account not only the official statements of the Churches but especially the personal, individual efforts of eminent theologians and figures who contributed both formally and informally to the origins and development of the ecumenical movement itself. These distinguished thinkers and ecumenical figures, with their deep ecumenical commitment to the *catholic* nature of the *apostolic* faith despite the different obstacles they encountered, contributed to the inspiration of the ecumenical movement in the early the 20th century, bringing a traditional Orthodox *ethos* of openness, sincere dialogue and reconciliation with all Christian Churches and Traditions and a wide range of intellectual, religious, cultural, social, political trends and ideas. This chapter thus highlights the contributions of the major Orthodox figures toward the fulfillment of the *inherent* ecumenical premise of the Eastern and Oriental Orthodox Churches.

The individual chapters concerning the major ecumenical thinkers and figures emphasize in particular these basic aspects of their lives and writings:

1. *Theological contribution*: The majority of the ecumenical thinkers and figures covered in this chapter articulated and promoted a creative theological vision with respect to an Orthodox understanding of ecumenism. In this perspective, by the use of relevant *conceptual* tools such as the *biblical*, *patristic* or *modern* theological terminology of "communion" and "personhood" (for example, John Zizioulas), "sobornost" or "sobornicity" (Nicholas Afanasiev and Dumitru Staniloae), they sought to present in convergence with other the Christian Traditions, the dialogical, perichoretic and inclusive nature of the *catholicity* of the Church as it has been traditionally understood by Orthodoxy. At the same time they provided an overview and also the fundamental features of the *ecclesiality* of major Christian Traditions such as the Anglican Church and the Roman Catholic Church, with a view towards a possible rapprochement in the future (such as Sergius Bulgakov, Nikos Nissiotis and Ioan Bria).

2. *Canonical and Charismatic borders:* One basic argument of this dynamic and positive attitude of Eastern and Oriental Orthodoxy toward the embracement in the first place of the Christian "other" and also of all humanity, is the bold and to some provocative distinction between the *canonical* and *charismatic* borders of the Church. This distinction is rooted in the thought of Augustine, a Father of the undivided Church too often neglected in the East. This perspective, while generally considered a *theologoumenon* – a theological opinion not binding on the Church as a whole -, could provide the necessary import and foundation for Orthodox to acknowledge the real presence of the Trinitarian God in the current state of *schism* and *division* between the Christian Churches and Communities. This theological argument, grounded in Scripture and the Fathers of the

---

[1] John Zizioulas, *Being as Communion*, (Crestwood NY: St Vladimir's Press: 1985), 15.
[2] Georges Florovsky "The Church: Her Nature and Task," in Georges Florovsky, *Bible, Church, Tradition*, (Collected Works vol. 1) (Belmont MA: 1975), 67.

Church, should not be seen as a form of *relativism*, an accusation which is often brought against the ecumenical commitment of the Orthodox Churches. It is rather a proper and helpful concept towards the sincere and genuine encounter of the Orthodox Christian with other Christians and with the followers of other religions. In this perspective it is inappropriate and indeed unacceptable to claim that God the Trinity continuously reveals itself and acts in history only within the Orthodox Church. As Christ said, the Spirit "blows everywhere he wills" (cf. Jn 3:8). The important distinction between the canonical and the charismatic limits of the Church is advanced by many modern Orthodox theologians, such as Sergius Bulgakov, Georges Florovsky and Georges Khodr. This approach permits the affirmation of the truth of the Orthodox Church among other Churches, as the *One, Holy, Catholic* and *Apostolic* Church on the one hand and on the other hand acquires an inherent *soteriological* perspective, since it allows God the Father to work by his "two hands", the Son and the Holy Spirit (St Irenaeus), toward "divine – human communion", in other words the *theosis* of the whole creation.

3. *Critical approach to the ecumenical movement:* Despite this positive, even challenging Orthodox attitude toward the *re-uniting* of all Christians, many Orthodox thinkers and figures have been critical of a certain "secular" tendency, which occurred in the general perspective and vision of the World Council of Churches and the Conference of European Churches CEC, the main ecumenical organizations. In this perspective, a strong focus of *institutional* ecumenism toward a predominantly political, social, cultural agenda, with an accompanying reduction in attention devoted to the theological and doctrinal issues that constitute the central core of Christian *dis*-unity, appears to be a major departure of the very original vision of the ecumenical movement. While this critique has some merit, at the same time it is widely recognized that the current global context of serious social, financial and environmental problems obliges the Christian Churches to increase their *ethical* and humanitarian concerns, in the light of a *vital* and *contextual* re-*interpretation* of the Gospel and the apostolic and patristic Tradition, to provide modern society with answers to its existential needs. However this "ethical" *unity* and co-operation between the Christian Churches should not in any case be regarded as a substitute to the "doctrinal" *union*, since there can be no love (or ethics) without truth (or dogma).

This chapter does not pretend to present an exhaustive overview of the contribution of all the eminent thinkers or figures of Eastern Orthodox and Oriental Churches in the 20th century. Its purpose is rather to provide an introduction to the contributions of major and representative Orthodox figures to the rapprochement of all Christian Traditions, inspired by the biblical message "that they all may be one" (Jn 17:21). This chapter hopes to provide an important *reference* for the continuous and creative involvement of Orthodoxy in the ecumenical movement.[3]

---

[3] The reader will find recommended bibliography for further reading at the end of the presentation of every individual ecumenical thinker or figure.

Orthodox Handbook on Ecumenism

Fr. Michael Plekon

Introduction

When asked about the ecumenical and theological contributions of the Orthodox Church, some would name Metropolitan Anthony of Sourozh, George Florovsky and Vladimir Lossky; others, Alexander Schmemann and John Meyendorff. Many of these were émigrés connected with St. Sergius Theological Institute in Paris. In their assessments of the important contributions of the last century, such theologians as Hilarion Alfeyev, Kallistos Ware and Boris Bobrinskoy all name Father Nicholas Afanasiev as the one who rediscovered the "eucharistic ecclesiology" of the Church's first centuries and who highlighted the significance of this in the Church of our time.

Biographical note

Afanasiev was born in Odessa in 1893. His interests ran from mathematics to natural science and medicine but the Russian civil war interrupted his studies. He served in the White Army and saw the horrors of warfare first hand before emigrating. He first lived and worked in Belgrade after studying there under the great historian Dobroklonsky. He married, and then taught in FYRO Macedonia at a secondary school.

Both at Belgrade and in Paris where he finally came to study and teach, Afanasiev received scholarships from western Christian institutions. In Paris he began teaching in 1930 at St. Sergius, funded by the American YMCA as well as by the Anglican Church both from England and America. Afanasiev was ordained priest in 1940 and during World War II he served a parish in Tunisia. Returning to St. Sergius in 1947, he taught and served as an administrator and episcopal consultant. He was a participant in numerous important groups with ecumenical connections, including the Russian Student Christian Movement, the Fellowship of St. Alban and St. Sergius and the Holy Trinity Fraternity in Paris. As a faculty member at St. Sergius along with colleague Cyprian Kern, established the liturgical week of study, fellowship and prayer in 1953, an annual conference that continues to this day. In the early photos of conference participants, the ecumenical vision and thrust is remarkable – we see Max Thurian, Joachim Jeremias, Irenée Dalmais, Lambert Beaudoin, Charles Dumont, Bernard Botte, among many other Catholic and Protestant scholars. Later in his life, Afanasiev was invited as Orthodox observer to the last sessions of Vatican II and was present in Rome for the lifting of the anathemas of the schism by Pope Paul VI and Patriarch Athenagoras I.

Afanasiev's work on eucharistic ecclesiology is reflected in Vatican II's dogmatic constitution on the Church, *Lumen gentium*. His writings were cited in the council's working sessions and drafts. Even after his death, in 1966, Afanasiev's eucharistic ecclesiology featured prominently in the "Lima Document" of the World Council of Churches *Baptism, Eucharist, Ministry* (1982), as well as in the *Catechism of the Roman Catholic Church*. Afanasiev is cited and discussed by subsequent scholars such as John Zizioulas, J.-M.R. Tillard, Paul McPartlan, Kallistos Ware, Aidan Nichols, Alexander Schmemann, John Meyendorff. And a new generation of scholars continues to be committed to his legacy, including myself, Stefan Barbu, Victor Alexandrov, Radu Bordeianu and Anastasia Wooden.

Afanasiev's Theological and ecumenical vision

Afanasiev's writings are marked by great erudition in fields as diverse as church history, liturgical theology, the councils and canon law. His prose is careful, deliberate, yet he himself said that his own blood and his tears were the source for his research and writing and his colleague Alexander Schmemann said that he had one vision—a truly consuming love for the Church, and this was the "hidden fire" behind his technical, meticulous writing. From the start of his career, there was, as noted, a constant ecumenical involvement and appeal. In his later work Afanasiev explicitly focused on what it would take to heal the schism between the Catholic and Orthodox churches in writings such as "Una sancta" and "The Eucharist, the principal link between the Catholics and the Orthodox." Equally as profound is his exploration of the early Church in *The Church of the Holy Spirit* (1975) and the essays that were to have comprised his unfinished work *The Limits of the Church.* Afanasiev's vision of the Church:

> The People of God, whom God formed for Himself in the New Covenant, are gathered by God in Christ's body. The baptized come into being as one body at the Eucharist. Thus the Eucharist, in the words of pseudo-Areopagite, is the sacrament of the assembly, but the assembly of the People of God "in Christ" is the Church... The Eucharist is the center towards which everything aspires and in which everything is gathered. "This is my body", but the body is realized in the Eucharist. Where the body is, there is Christ. And the opposite: where Christ is there is his body...There is no assembly in the Church without con-celebration nor is there con-celebration without the assembly. There is no supper without participants nor are there participants in the supper without the one who heads it.[1]

For Afanasiev, the Church comes before and is the necessary condition of the sacraments, the scriptures, the preaching of the Gospel and works of loving kindness to the neighbour. The Church is also the source and location of the hierarchy, all of the clergy and people. Only those washed, sealed and ordained to be God's priests, kings and prophets in baptism can later be called by the ecclesial community to receive the laying on of hands to serve them, to preside, preach and lead them in the work of service to the world. Ordination is for service of the community, without separating those so ordained into a different, higher caste, as Afanasiev makes clear from the oldest ordination prayers. This eucharistic and conciliar ecclesiology was the understanding as well as the shape and practice of ecclesial life in the first five centuries. Afanasiev also insists that to be theologians we must also be diligent historians, not shying away from the realities of human life but rather honestly studying and portraying them, since they are the means by which the Spirit works in the world.

"The Church makes the Eucharist, the Eucharist makes the Church"

> "The Church of God is in Christ" since the people of God are gathered by God "in Christ" and thus it belongs to God as Christ belongs to him. From this follows the identity of the Church with the Eucharist and the identity of the local Church with the Church of God, which is actualized each time during her Eucharistic assembly...Members of the local church become members of the body of Christ and all that are gathered together for the Eucharistic assembly are "The Church of God in Christ"... The Church is where the Eucharist is celebrated, and where the Eucharist is celebrated, there is the Church. This is the fundamental principle of the Eucharistic ecclesiology revealed by Paul.[2]

Afanasiev's careful historical analysis of the early Church is quite unlike what we experience today. This eucharistic Church was intensely communal, ruled by love, not law. There is no clerical caste in it, separated from the non-consecrated, "worldly" laity.

---

[1] *The Lord's Supper*, trans. Alvian Smirensky, forthcoming.
[2] Ibid., chapter 1.

The Church is God's people, and every faithful in the Church belongs to this people. He is *laikos,* a laic. "The gifts and the call of God are irrevocable" (Rom 11:29), therefore one cannot be in the Church and not be a laic, *laikos* -- a member of God's people. Every one in the Church is a laic and all together are God's people and each one is called, as a priest of God, to offer spiritual sacrifices to Him through Jesus Christ. [3]

The presiders of eucharistic assemblies, as Cyprian of Carthage says, "do nothing without their presbyters, deacons and people." Those who lead do so because they serve the community as Christ does. The presiders come from the rank and file membership, are elected by the community and then ordained to serve in, for and with that community. The idea of the *proestos/hegumen* or bishop-presbyter being *above* or *other* than the community, of such a one celebrating the liturgy or making any decisions *without* the community would have been unimaginable.

> Authority is part of the life of the Church which has this ministry of administration. But the ecclesial authority ought to conform to the nature of the Church and not be in conflict with her. If such authority claims to be superior to the Church then it must also be superior to Christ. This is why the Church can never be founded, nor her authority based upon a juridical principle, for the law is external to, outside of Love. Such authority cannot belong to the vicars of Christ on earth, since God has not delegated his power to anyone, but has put all people in submission to Christ, "put all things under his feet." In the Church, which is Love, there is only the power of love. God gives the pastors not the charism of power but that of love and, by his mediation, the power of love. The bishops who exercise the ministry of administration are the representatives of the power of love. ... There can be no other foundation of power in the Church, for Christ is the only foundation of power in her...The power of Christ in the Church is the power of Love, acquired by the love which he has for us. [4]

Afanasiev taught many different courses at the St Sergius Institute – about "initiation" or entry into the Church through baptism/chrismation, the reception of those from other Churches, the ordination of the clergy, as well as courses on marriage, monasticism, the councils of the Church, canon law, the history of the early Church and of the Russian Church. He wrote on the priesthood of all the baptized, the laity, as well as on the development and decadence of the liturgy.

Afanasiev's view of ecclesiology integrates the sacraments into the life of the Christian community as well as the individual Christian. Afanasiev does not value the Eucharist to the detriment of baptism as the centre of the Church's life. Neither does he restrict the actions of the ecclesial community, both the leaders and the membership, to liturgical worship alone. Preaching, teaching and administration of the community's affairs as well as ministry to the society – all are pivotal to his vision.

Baptism is fundamental for him, since this is the consecration/ordination of each and every Christian to the priesthood of all believers, and also to the status of prophet and king in the Kingdom. (1 Peter 2: 4-10):

> The apostolic church did not know the separation of clerics from laics in our meaning of the words and it did not have the terms themselves in its usage. This is a basic fact of the ecclesial life in the primitive era but it would be wrong to infer from this fact that ministry in the Church was exhausted by the notion of the priestly ministry, common for all. It was a ministry of the Church. Another fact of the life of the primitive Church was the diversity of ministries. The same Spirit by whom all were baptized into one body and of whom all were made to drink distributes particular gifts to each one "for the common good," (*sympheron*) (1 Cor 12:7) for action and service within the Church.
>
> And the gifts were that some should be apostles, some prophets, some evangelists, some pastors and teachers, to equip the saints for the work of ministry, for building up the body of Christ. (Eph 4:11-12)

---

[3] *The Church of the Holy Spirit*, trans. Vitaly Permiakov, ed. Michael Plekon, (University of Notre Dame Press, 2007), 10.
[4] Ibid., 273.

Part III: Representative Orthodox Theologians reflecting on Ecumenism

The diversity of ministries stems from the "organic" nature of the Church. Each of her members occupies in it his own position and place, proper to him alone. "God arranged the organs in the body, each one of them, as he chose." (1 Cor 12:18) In a living organism, place and position of its members depends on the functions executed by them. So in Christ's body diverse ministries are associated with the place and position of the members. The gifts of the Spirit are not given for their own sake, as a reward of some sort but for ministry in the Church and they are given to those who already have drunk of the Spirit.[5]

Conclusions

These are the most important ways in which Afanasiev, and indeed others with him, expressed the relationships, the connections among all the sacraments and the Christian life:

- All Christian life begins with the new life in Christ given in the washing of baptism and in the seal of the Holy Spirit, the chrismation or "Christification" (Mother Maria Skobtsova) of the sacrament of initiation.[6]

- The Church is the community of Love, where Love, not status, law or power rules.

- Every sacramental action refers us back to Baptism and the Eucharist, for as Afanasiev intuited and Schmemann made explicit, these are first and foremost *Paschal* sacraments, sacraments in which we die and are raised with Christ.

- Every vocation and sacramental event is rooted in Baptism and the Eucharist, for example, ordination is the setting apart of Christians for the service of presiding and preaching and counseling and administration in the ecclesial community. As Afanasiev's friend, the lay theologian Paul Evdokimov described it, (borrowing from John Chrysostom) the "sacrament of love," marriage, joins together men and women into a relationship that is an image of Christ and the Church.[7] Their homes become as Chrysostom called them, "miniature churches". There is no vocation that cannot be a life of praise and thanksgiving and love that is essentially eucharistic.

- The Church gathers all together into one, one with Christ. Afanasiev puts forward the somewhat striking ecclesiological mathematics of the fullness of each local church, over against a universalistic ecclesiology which sees each church as only a part of the great Church. The formula is 1+1+1=1. While each local church is complete, the local church in all its fullness also needs to be in communion, in fact *must* be in communion with all the rest of the churches.

Bibliography

Nicholas Afanasiev, *The Church of the Holy Spirit*, Vitaly Permiakov, trans., Michael Plekon, ed., (University of Notre Dame Press, 2007).

Nicholas Afanasiev, "'Una sancta," "The Church's Canons: Changeable or Unchangeable," "The Eucharist: The Principal Link Between the Catholics and the Orthodox," in *Tradition Alive: On the Church and the Christian Life in Our Time, Readings from the Eastern Church*, Michael Plekon, ed., (Lanham MD: Rowman & Littlefield, Sheed & Ward, 2003).

Aidan Nichols, *Theology in the Russian Diaspora: Church, Fathers, Eucharist in Nikolai Afanas'ev, 1893-1966*, (Cambridge: Cambridge University Press, 1989).

---

[5] *The Church of the Holy Spirit*, 14-15.

[6] *Mother Maria Skobtsova: Essential Writings*, trans. Richard Pevear and Larissa Volokhonsky, (Maryknoll NY: Orbis, 2003), 174.

[7] *The Sacrament of Love*, trans. Anthony P. Gythiel and Victoria Steadman, (Crestwood NY: St. Vladimir's Seminary Press, 1995).

Michael Plekon, *Living Icons: Persons of Faith in the Eastern Church*, (University of Notre Dame Press, 2002).

Paul Valliere, *Modern Russian Theology*, (Grand Rapids MI: Eerdmans, 2000).

Antoine Arjakovsky, *The Way: Religious Thinkers of the Russian Emigration in Paris and their Journal,* Jerry Ryan, trans., John A. Jillions and Michael Plekon, eds., (University of Notre Dame Press, 2013).

Part III: Representative Orthodox Theologians reflecting on Ecumenism

(24) Hamilkar S. Alivizatos

Vassiliki El. Stathokosta

Hamilkar Alivizatos is a major figure in Greek theology and in the ecumenical movement of the twentieth century. He received international recognition; in May 1945 he was honoured by the Church of England with the Lambeth Cross for his services to the Anglican-Orthodox dialogue[1] and in Greece elected a member of the Academy of Athens (1962)[2].

Born in May 1887 in Cephalonia, a distant island of the Ionian Sea, he studied theology in Athens from 1904 to 1908, then in Leipzig and in Berlin, from 1908 to 1912, under the guidance of great specialists in Church history and canon law.[3] During his studies he was actively engaged in the theological discourse of his time that helped him on his return to Greece.[4] In 1919, he became a professor in the School of Theology at the University of Athens.[5] Unlike most professors of his time, he was also engaged in social activity that sprung from his Christian faith, as a manifestation of witness of Orthodox faith and *diakonia* to the people of God. He served the Church of Greece as a theologian, specialized in canon law, and was noted for his ability to deal with crucial administrative Church matters as well as the Church-State relationship.[6]

Hamilkar Alivizatos contributed to the development of theology and ecumenism not only at a local but also at an international level[7] that affected Christianity worldwide. He is recognized as one of the pioneers of Orthodox participation in the ecumenical movement together with Metropolitan Germanos Strenopoulos of Thyateira, Father Georges Florovsky and Stephan Zankov of Bulgaria[8] (although in Greece his many contributions are not well known).[9]

Hamilkar Alivizatos devoted himself to efforts to promote Christian unity between West and East. He was a friend and a close associate of leading figures of the ecumenical movement, such as Visser't Hooft. Their persistent and methodical joint efforts to clarify the aims of this movement led to a positive response of the Greek-speaking Orthodox Churches and to their participation in the ecumenical movement. Alivizatos contrib-

---

[1] V. Stathokosta, "Relations between the Orthodox and the Anglicans in the Twentieth Century: A Reason to Consider the Present and the Future of the Theological Dialogue", in *Ecclesiology* 8.3 (2012): 350-374.

[2] See http://www.academyofathens.gr.

[3] Ger. Konidaris, *Ο Αμίλκας Σ. Αλιβιζάτος (1887-1969) εν τη Εκκλησιαστική Ιστορία της Ελλάδος (O Amilkas S. Alivizatos en ti Ekklesiastiki Istoria tis Ellados* - Hamilkar S. Alivizatos in the Church History of Greece), 8-10.

[4] V. Stathokosta, *Η Θεολογική και Οικουμενική Σκέψη στην Ελλάδα κατά τον 20ο αιώνα - Η συμβολή του Αμίλκα Σ. Αλιβιζάτου* (H Theologiki kai Oikoumeniki Skepsi stin Ellada kata ton 20o aiona – H symvoli toy Amilka S. Alivizatou - The Theological and Ecumenical Thought in Greece during the 20th century – The Contribution of Hamilkar Alivizatos) in V. Stathokosta, Ορθόδοξη Θεολογία και Οικουμένη: Μελέτες - Άρθρα (Orthodoxi Theologia kai Oikoumeni: Meletes – Arthra -Orthodox Theology and Ecumene: Studies - Articles), (Athens: Parresia, 2011), 107-112 (in Greek).

[5] Ger. Konidaris, *Ο Αμίλκας Σ. Αλιβιζάτος* (Hamilkar S. Alivizatos), op. cit., 8-10 (in Greek).

[6] V. Stathokosta, *The Theological and Ecumenical Thought in Greece during the 20th century*, op.cit., 113-126.

[7] Cf. Visser 'T Hooft, *The Genesis and Formation of the World Council of Churches*, (Geneva: WCC, 1982), 6, 64, 83; Rouse & Neill, *A history of the ecumenical movement 1517-1948*, (Geneva, 1953), 658.

[8] See indicatively G. Tsetsis, *Οικουμενικά Ανάλεκτα, Συμβολή στην ιστορία του Παγκοσμίου Συμβουλίου Εκκλησιών (Oikumenica Analekta, Symboli stin istoria toy Pagkosmiou Symbouliou Ekklision* - Ecumenica Analekta, Contribution in the History of the World Council of Churches), (Tertios, Katerini, 1987), 134 (in Greek). V. Stathokosta, *Σχέσεις της Εκκλησίας της Ελλάδος με το Παγκόσμιο Συμβούλιο Εκκλησιών, 1948-1961. Με βάση το αρχειακό υλικό του ΠΣΕ (Sxeseis tis Ekklesias tis Ellados me to Pagkosmio Symvoulio Ekklesion, 1948-1961. Me basi to arxeiako yliko tou PSE* - 'The relationship between the Church of Greece and the World Council of Churches 1948-1961, based on the Archives of the WCC' (PhD diss. in Greek, University of Thessaloniki, 1999), 314 (in Greek).

[9] For further information and evaluation of his activity and work see V. Stathokosta, *The Theological and Ecumenical Thought in Greece during the 20th century*, op.cit., 103-156.

uted directly to the organisation of the official visit of leaders of the Faith and Order Movement to the Orthodox Churches in the Balkans in 1919,[10] as well as that of the delegation of the World Council of Churches in early 1947. It was during this visit that the Orthodox Churches confirmed their willingness to participate in the First Assembly of the WCC as founding members.[11]

Alivizatos was commissioned by the Ecumenical Patriarchate to introduce the proposal of the Ecumenical Patriarchate to "all Churches of Christ" according the example of the "Koinonia of Nations", at the preliminary congress of Faith and Order in Geneva in 1920. He inspired and organised the First Congress of Orthodox Theology in 1936 in Athens (although this meeting is remembered largely for the contributions of Father Georges Florovsky, who also put forward publically the call for a renewal of Orthodox theology based on patristic thought).[12] Alivizatos was also instrumental in promoting the celebrations commemorating the 1900 years since the arrival of St Paul in Greece (1951). Both were to pioneer efforts for the development of inter-Orthodox cooperation and openness of the Orthodox Church to the world.[13] Alivizatos was the official delegate of the Church of Greece in both the Faith and Order and the Life and Work Movements, as well as in the General Assemblies, the Central Committee and in other WCC bodies. In Greece he served as the director of the Committee of the Holy Synod of the Church of Greece on Inter-Church Aid and Relations with the Foreign Churches, as the permanent representative of Church World Service[14] and as director of Inter-Church Aid and Service to Refugees of the WCC, which collaborated with the United Nations High Commissioner for Refugees.[15] He also had an active role in the Committee of the Churches on International Affairs of the WCC.[16] In all these positions Alivizatos enjoyed the confidence of the Holy Synod of the Church of Greece.[17]

Hamilkar Alivizatos, Meletios Metaxakis (who served as Archbishop of Athens and later as Ecumenical Patriarchate), Chrysostomos Papadopoulos (Archbishop of Athens) and Germanos of Thyateira (Strenopoulos) were the visionaries and the leaders of the Greek-speaking Orthodox for the development of inter-Christian and inter-Church relations in the twentieth century. They were the pioneers and leaders who promoted the renaissance of the Church and theology and for the advancement of the Church and theology in Greek society and abroad. Their work prepared the way for their successors, such as Nikos Nissiotis and Savvas Agourides, who can be considered Alivizatos' followers, as well as many others who developed modern Greek theological thought.

The Theological Work and Contribution of Prof. Hamilkar Alivizatos

Hamilkar Alivizatos had a solid Orthodox theological formation and ecclesiastical experience and his approach to theology and ecumenism was open-minded. These characterised his ecumenical orientation and led him to undertake numerous initiatives. In addition to those mentioned above, he was editor of the periodical *Orthodoxos Skepsis* (Orthodox Thought), published in 1957.[18] *Orthodoxos Skepsis* recorded the concern of the 1950s for the present and the future of the Orthodox Church and theology, for its opening to the world and to the ecumenical movement. Certain thoughts and concerns expressed in this pioneering periodical at that time are still timely.

Church revival, the training of clergy and Church involvement in social work were three crucial areas that attracted Alivizatos' interest and served as a springboard for his active participation in the ecumenical movement. In this context he supported the work of the *Apostoliki Diakonia* of the Greek Orthodox Church.

---

[10] See V. Stathokosta, '*The relationship between the Church of Greece and the WCC'*, op.cit., 41-43.

[11] V. Stathokosta, op.cit., 314-315.

[12] V. Stathokosta, *The Theological and Ecumenical Thought in Greece during the 20th century*, op.cit, 145-148.

[13] V. Stathokosta, op.cit., 148-150.

[14] See Ger. Konidaris, op.cit, 32.

[15] V. Stathokosta, '*The relationship between the Church of Greece and the WCC'*, op.cit., 373, 380-382.

[16] See V. Stathokosta, op.cit., 361-417.

[17] See V. Stathokosta, *The Theological and Ecumenical Thought in Greece during the 20th century*, op.cit., 103-14.

[18] See V. Stathokosta, op.cit., 122-124.

Part III: Representative Orthodox Theologians reflecting on Ecumenism

Among its activities was a project for the establishment of the School for Social Welfare for the formation of "Diaconesses", post-graduate social workers level (1957). This project was supported by the WCC. Thus Alivizatos contributed to the development of social activity of the Church of Greece, which took a leading role in Greek society[19]. The results of these endeavours were innovative at that time. For Alivizatos, social diakonia was the fruit of Christianity, and thus he believed that the Church should pioneer in social work.[20]

Hamilkar Alivizatos' Priority: The Return to Genuine Patristic Thought

Inter-Orthodox and inter-Church relations were priorities for Alivizatos. By his writings and other activities he expressed the theological arguments in favour of the ecumenical movement and the promotion of Church efforts for dialogue and cooperation, according the wish and prayer of Christ "that may all be one" (John 17: 21)[21].

An important characteristic of his theology, as well as that of many who supported Orthodox participation in the ecumenical movement, was a return to the genuine patristic thought.[22] His conviction was that this was the only way to assure the fruitful growth of theology. He underlined the need for the development of theological thought and discipline without barriers, in a spirit of freedom and critical analysis, taking into consideration new theological achievements, regardless of their confessional origin. Moreover, he posed as an essential condition for the achievement of these goals the systematic detection and removal of foreign elements, which had unwittingly ("ασυναισθήτως") entered Orthodox theology in the past. This outlook marked the First Conference of Orthodox Theology in 1936, that Orthodox theology "bears many subsequent alien influences".[23] He attributed these influences to contacts the Orthodox had with non-Orthodox theology in the past, where there was "ignorance of things", "a low-level of theological education" and "emancipation reluctance" (e.g. fear that they might be manipulated) on the part of the Orthodox. The results of these foreign influences were mostly harmful to the ecumenical movement.[24] However, there is no doubt that the twentieth century offered a different framework for cooperation among Churches. Alivizatos made significant contributions to the understanding of the new reality of inter-Church relationships, to the genesis and development of the modern ecumenical movement, to the openness of Orthodoxy to the world, to the growth of Orthodox theology with fidelity to the spirit of patristic teaching of the Orthodox Church.

From the time of his involvement in the work of the World Alliance for International Friendship through the Churches in 1914[25] (he served as president), until the Fourth WCC General Assembly in Uppsala in 1968, (as a representative of the Patriarchate of Jerusalem), Alivizatos left his mark in many ecumenical congresses

---

[19] See V. Stathokosta, op.cit., 118-120.

[20] It is worth mention Alivizatos' commitment for the relief of the immediate needs of the earthquake victims during the earthquakes his birthplace, the Ionian Islands, suffered in August 1953, by ensuring essential humanitarian aid from foreign Churches and the WCC. Furthermore, aid was given by the WCC for the future development of the island of Cephalonia. See relative archive material in V. Stathokosta, 'The relationship between the Church of Greece and the WCC', op.cit., 402-405.

[21] See Alivizatos' theological argumentation in V. Stathokosta, *The Theological and Ecumenical Thought in Greece during the 20th century*, op.cit., 127-145

[22] H.S. Alivizatos, *Αι σύγχροναι θεολογικαί τάσεις εν τη Ελληνική Ορθοδοξία*, Ανάτυπον εκ της «Θεολογίας», τόμ. Κ΄ (1949), Αθήνα 1949, (*Ai sygxronai theologikai taseis en ti Elliniki Orthodoxia* - Modern Theological Trends in Greek Theology, Reprint from "Theology", vol. II, Athens 1949), 17 (in Greek). Cf. H.S. Alivizatos, *Ανασκόπησις και Προοπτική*, *Orthodoxos Skepsis* 15.1 (1958): 1-5 (in Greek).

[23] See H.S. Alivisatos three works: 1) *La position actuelle de la Theologie Orthodoxe*, 1939, 24 ff; 2); *Αι σύγχροναι θεολογικαί τάσεις*, (Modern Theological Trends in Greek Theology), op.cit.; 3) *Ανασκόπησις και Προοπτική* (Review and Prospect) op.cit., 1-5 (4-5).

[24] H.S. Alivisatos, *Modern Theological Trends in Greek Theology*, op.cit., 18-19.

[25] See V. Stathokosta, 'The relationship between the Church of Greece and the WCC', op.cit., 34-37.

and studies. He contributed to the formation of ecumenical theology, to the development of Orthodox theology and to the theological maturing of the WCC. His activities for the rapprochement between East and West and his leading role in the ecumenical movement from its early days were recognized by the General Secretary of the WCC, Visser' t Hooft, and by others, such as Edmund Schlink, distinguished theologian and pioneer of the ecumenical movement.[26]

Bibliography

Alivisatos H.S., Αι σύγχροναι θεολογικαί τάσεις εν τη Ελληνική Ορθοδοξία, Ανάτυπον εκ της «Θεολογίας», τόμ. Κ΄ (1949), Αθήνα 1949, [(*Ai sygxronai theologikai taseis en ti Elliniki Orthodoxia* - Modern Theological Trends in Greek Theology, offprint from *Theologia* 20 (1949), Athens 1949)].

Alivisatos H.S., Ανασκόπησις και προοπτική, in *Orthodoxos Skepsis* 15.1 (1958): 1-5.

Alivisatos H.S., Η Ελληνική Ορθόδοξος Εκκλησία, Σειρά μαθημάτων περί της Ελληνικής Ορθοδόξου Εκκλησίας δοθέντων εις το Πανεπιστήμιον και το Οικουμενικόν Ινστιτούτον του Σικάγου κατ'Απρίλιον 1953 και Ιούλιον 1954, Ανάτυπον εκ της ΕΕΘΣΠΑ, Αθήνα 1955, (*H Elliniki Orthodoxos Ekklisia, Seira mathomaton peri tis Ellinikis Orthodoxou Ekklisias dothenton eis to Panepistimion kai to Oikoumenikon Institouton toy Sikagou kat'Aprilion 1953 kai Ioulion 1954* - Greek Orthodox Church, Courses on Greek Orthodox Church given at the University and the Ecumenical Institute of Chicago in April 1953 and July 1954, Reprint from ΕΕΘΣΠΑ, Athens 1955) (in Greek).

Alivisatos H.S., *La position actuelle de la Theologie Orthodoxe*, 1939.

Konidaris Ger., Ο Αμίλκας Σ. Αλιβιζάτος (1887-1969) εν τη Εκκλησιαστική Ιστορία της Ελλάδος [*O Amilkas S. Alivizatos en ti Ekklisiastiki Istoria tis Ellados* - Hamilkar S. Alivizatos (1887-1969) in the Church History of Greece] (in Greek).

Stathokosta V., Σχέσεις της Ε.τ.Ε. με το Παγκόσμιο Συμβούλιο των Εκκλησιών, 1948-1961, με βάση το αρχειακό υλικό του Π.Σ.Ε., διδ. διατριβή, Θεσσαλονίκη 1999 (*Sxeseis tis Ekklesias tis Ellados me to Pagkosmio Symvoulio Ekklesion, 1948-1961. Me basi to arxeiako yliko tou PSE* - V. Stathokosta, 'The relationship between the Church of Greece and the World Council of Churches 1948-1961, based on the Archives of the WCC'(PhD diss. in Greek, University of Thessaloniki, 1999) (in Greek).

Stathokosta V., Η Θεολογική και Οικουμενική Σκέψη στην Ελλάδα κατά τον 20ο αιώνα - Η συμβολή του Αμίλκα Σ. Αλιβιζάτου (*H Theologiki kai Oikoumeniki Skepsi stin Ellada kata ton 20o aiona – H symvoli toy Amilka S. Alivizatou* - The Theological and Ecumenical Thought in Greece during the 20th century – The Contribution of Hamilkar Alivizatos) in V. Stathokosta, Ορθόδοξη Θεολογία και Οικουμένη: Μελέτες - Άρθρα (*Orhtodoxi Theologia kai Oikoumeni: Meletes – Arthra* -Orthodox Theology and Ecumene: Studies - Articles - Orthodox Theology and Ecumene: Studies - Articles), (Athens, Parresia, 2011) (in Greek).

Tsetsis George (Great Protopresbyter), Οικουμενικά Ανάλεκτα. Συμβολή στην ιστορία του Παγκοσμίου Συμβουλίου Εκκλησιών, «Τέρτιος», Κατερίνη 1987 (*Oikumenica Analekta, Symboli stin istoria toy Pagkosmiou Symbouliou Ekklision* - Ecumenica Analekta, Contribution in the History of the World Council of Churches), Tertios: Katerini, 1987) (in Greek).

Yannaras Chr., Ορθοδοξία και Δύση στη νεώτερη Ελλάδα, εκδ. Δόμος, Αθήνα 1992 (Athens, 1992) (in Greek).

---

[26] E. Schlink, "The nature of Christian Hope", in *The Ecumenical Review* 4.3 (1952): 284-290.

Part III: Representative Orthodox Theologians reflecting on Ecumenism

(25) ECUMENICAL PATRIARCH ATHENAGORAS

Fr. Augoustinos Bairactaris

The Ecumenical Patriarch of Constantinople Athenagoras is undoubtedly the ecclesiastical personality who contributed the most to the rapprochement between the Christian East and West during the 20th century. He embodied in himself the desire of the Ecumenical Throne, as expressed in the Synodical Encyclical letters of 1902, 1904 and 1920, that the Orthodox Church would lead in the establishment of an ecumenical forum, the so-called "League of Churches", which would be able to bring the Christian Churches closer together. In this context, he laid the foundation of the collaborative and diaconal contact of the whole of Orthodoxy with the World Council of Churches, which was founded in August 1948, i.e. just before his election as Patriarch of Constantinople.[1] He believed that the Orthodox East and the Protestant West could jointly formulate the appropriate conditions which would favor Christian unity and the common testimony of the Gospel to the world.[2] At the same time, he was absolutely convinced that, in this ecumenical and inter-Christian venture, the participation of the Roman Catholic Church was more than necessary.

Patriarch Athenagoras considered the Ecumenical Movement as a unique opportunity and an inter-church tool, which on the one hand would make every effort to overcome points of conflict which were formed in the evolution of the historical progress of the Churches, and on the other hand would help those traumatized by war and poverty by offering them charity and solidarity.[3] Through cooperation, every spiritual force would emerge which would create a unified Christian front against the moral evil threatening to destroy the religiousness of society.[4] It could therefore be argued that through his action and historical initiatives, he created a new path in the theological affairs of the Orthodox Church through its participation in the ecumenical movement in general,[5] leading Orthodoxy away from provincialism, introversion, nationalism and isolation.[6]

Faithful to the vision of the universal unity sought by Christians, inter-Church relations between Orthodoxy and Roman Catholicism, which were previously characterized by mutual suspicion and lack of trust, were transformed positively through formal meetings with Pope Paul VI, the mutual lifting of anathemas at the end of the Second Vatican Synod, and the writing of the *Volume of Love*.[7] Patriarch Athenagoras preached that the unity of all people is the duty of all Christians, since Christians are brothers and members of Christ. He regarded the 20th century as the given opportunity in time to establish ecumenical love and brotherhood. The embrace of love and peace between Pope Paul VI and Patriarch Athenagoras during their meeting in Jerusalem

---

[1] George Tsetsis, *The Contribution of the Ecumenical Patriarchate in establishing the World Council of Churches* (Tertios: Katerini 1988), 166 (in Greek).

[2] George Tsetsis, *Ecumenical Annals - Contribution to the History of the World Council of Churches* (Tertios: Katerini, 1987), 127 (in Greek).

[3] George Tsetsis, «La dimension sociale de l'engagement Orthodoxe dans le Movement Oecuménique,» in *Études Théologiques*, vol.6 (Orthodoxie et Mouvement Oecuménique, ed.Centre Orthodoxe du Patriarcat Oecuménique: Chambésy -Genève, 1986), 219: "*Ainsi, Athénagoras Ier encourageait les Églises à coordonner leurs efforts afin d'affronter en commun les grandes problèmes de l'humanité et de coopérer au sein du COE dont le but principal est la collaboration des Églises dans le domaine social et pratique.*"

[4] Stylianos Tsompanidis, *The Contribution of the Orthodox Church and Theology in the World Council of Churches,* (Pournaras: Thessaloniki, 2008), 43 (in Greek).

[5] John Kalogirou, *Athenagoras, the Ecumenical Patriarch, the man from Epirus* (Company of Epirus Studies: Ioannina 1975), 278 (in Greek).

[6] Hamilkar Alivisatos, *Procès - Verbaux du Premier Congrés de Théologie Orthodoxe à Athènes 29 Nov. - 6 Dec. 1936* (Athènes, 1939), 45.

[7] Nikos Matsoukas, *Ecumenical movement - History Theology* (Pournaras: Thessaloniki, 1996), 226 (in Greek).

in January 1964 was not a move to impress public opinion, but the real expression of their deep faith that all this is done for the glory of the name of Christ and for the good of humanity.

Thus, within such a context a "dialogue of love" was established between the Old and New Rome, which lasted for ten whole years, leading eventually to the inauguration of official theological dialogue, which was described as a "dialogue of truth"[8]; a dialogue of cooperation and preparation between two Churches, which now considered one another as "Sister Church". The immediate aim of dialogue is the clarification and thorough theological study of both the *unifying* and the *dividing* points between the two ecclesiastical traditions and theologies, while the ultimate aim is the union of the two Churches on the basis of the common faith as was realized in the first ten centuries.[9]

At the same time, the Primate of Orthodoxy never failed to mention at every opportunity that the motive of the Orthodox participation in the WCC was to bear witness to the modern world of the treasure of faith, of worship and of the richness of tradition, as had been experienced and preserved by the Orthodox Church. Patriarch Athenagoras always desired that Orthodoxy, portrayed with dynamism and prestige in the international forum, would fit in its particular place and its historical mission in the inter-Christian world.[10] Indeed to serve this need he went on to establish the Permanent Delegation of the Ecumenical Patriarchate at the headquarters of the WCC in Geneva, placing as its head the Metropolitan of Melitis Iakovos (later Archbishop of America).

He considered ecclesiastical narcissism and stagnation, which are born out of the feelings of complacency and self-satisfaction for past achievements, to be significant obstacles for the development of ecumenical dialogue between the Churches. According to Athenagoras, the Churches' innovation and spirituality is the fundamental prerequisite for the achievement of ecclesial unity between members of the WCC. This innovation of the Churches and the Christian people is closely related to Christian unity.[11] The Church must constantly move forward in the Holy Spirit without being bound by a rigid, conservative tradition which is identified with the sterile repetition of the past, customs and habits.[12]

The vision of Athenagoras as the Primate of the Church of Constantinople was a Church characterized by the common Gospel, the common Eucharistic practice and the diocesan system as a way of administration.[13] In that ecclesiastical framework, the various Confessions of Faith would be defined among each other as "Sister Churches" on the basis of their Apostolic faith, their Patristic tradition and the grace of the Holy Spirit. In this context, he even recognized the existence of the Roman primacy, albeit not in its current form, as a canonical authoritarian center of the universal Church, but considered it as a *primacy of love*, which is not placed *over* the Church, but in the center and on the basis of Christian brotherhood. In other words, he approached and understood *primacy* through the perspective of functional ministry for the benefit of the wider ecclesial reality.[14]

His main concern was the restoration of Eucharistic communion, which he perceived not only as restoration of the unity of faith, but also as an anticipation of this unity through the power of love in Christ.[15] East and

---

[8] Aidan Nichols OP, *Rome and the Eastern Churches - A Study in Schism* (Ignatius Press: San Francisco, 2010), 356.

[9] Jeffrey Gros, Eamon McManus, and Ann Riggs, *Introduction to Ecumenism* (Paulist Pres: New York 1998), 164.

[10] George Tsetsis (ed.), "Patriarchal Encyclical of 1952," in the *Ecumenical Throne and Oikoumene - Official Patriarchical Texts*, (Tertios: Katerini, 1989), 73 (in Greek).

[11] George Tsetsis, ed., "The speech of the Ecumenical Patriarch Athenagoras the 1st during his visit to the WCC (6 November 1967), in *Ecumenical Throne and Oikoumene, ibid*, 85.

[12] Georges Florovsky, "The Ethos of the Orthodox Church," in *Orthodoxy - A Faith and Order Dialogue*, Faith and Order Paper No. 30 (WCC, 1960), 40.

[13] Basileios Stavridis and Evangelia Varella, *History of the Ecumenical Movement* in the series *Analects of Vlatades* vol. 47 (Patriarchal Institute of Patristic Studies: Thessaloniki, 1996), 363: *"The immediate object of universal inquiry, according to the Orthodox conception, is the revival of Christian cognition, the restoration of the apostolic tradition, the completeness of the Christian intuition and faith according to all the centuries"* (originally in Greek).

[14] Olivier Clément, "Athenagoras (Aristokles Pyrou)," in *Dictionary of the Ecumenical Movement* (WCC: Geneva, 2002), 76.

[15] W. A. Visser't Hooft, *Memoirs* (WCC: Geneva, 1973), 274-275: *"When does a man express his deepest desire?, asked the Patriarch. And he answered himself: When he formulates his last will. And where do we find the last will of our Lord?*

Part III: Representative Orthodox Theologians reflecting on Ecumenism

West, according to Patriarch Athenagoras, are characterized both by their differences and their similarities. For that reason, he considered as an imperative need the purification of the memory of the Church from sins and from the historical burdens of the past. As a result of this position, he was not a champion of *apologetic* theology, which until then was used routinely by the theologians of the two Churches, but rather a conveyor of the *loving*, one could say, Johannine theology. He used to assert that theology is a celebration of the mystery of God and not a weapon which is used against the other. Without downplaying the existent differences, he was convinced that mutual love among Christians and common faith in Christ have the power to illuminate differences in such a way that each Church can approach the other without be alienated from it.[16] In addition to the seventeenth chapter of the Gospel of John, Paul's Epistle to the Philippians also inspired his views: "And look out for one another's interests, not just for your own."[17] In other words, only through sacrificial love for each other which leads to the resurrection can we feel the true fullness in God. "It is the sharing, the humility and the reconciliation which makes us fully and truly Orthodox, not in order to keep the truth for ourselves, but to use it for the unity of all as a form of testimony of the undivided Church," as stated by the late Ecumenical Patriarch.[18]

Meanwhile, Patriarch Athenagoras, in his 1952 Encyclical (which indirectly addressed the Orthodox Churches and directly, the World Council of Churches), clearly defined the limits of the participation of Orthodox representatives in the diversified commissions of WCC—preconditions which corresponded to the climate of inter-Church relations of that time. The document specifically highlighted that cooperation between the Churches should be related to social and practical issues, but not doctrinal issues, as long as the Churches are deeply divided doctrinally.[19] In addition, it clearly states that Orthodox clerical representatives should be as reserved as possible "in worship congregations with the heterodox, [since they are] contrary to the sacred canons and blunt the confessional sensitivity in faith of the Orthodox."[20] That is why he encourages them to celebrate Orthodox services so as to emphasize the "glory and grandeur of the Orthodox Worship before the eyes of the heterodox."[21]

Moreover, Patriarch Athenagoras also gave special attention to inter-Orthodox relations. Repeatedly, he sought through meetings and encyclicals letters to achieve rapprochement and cooperation between the Orthodox Churches in all areas, as he looked for a wider common stance and a *consensus* on the way decisions were taken on issues relating to the Orthodox Churches. Specifically, in the Patriarchal Encyclicals, he announced to the individual Orthodox Autocephalous Churches and to the Patriarchates, the decision of the Holy Synod to convene a Pan-Orthodox Conference on the island of Rhodes in September 1961. Thus, the First Pan-Orthodox Conference was held between 24 September and 1 October 1961 and compiled a list of issues for the forthcoming Pre-Synod which suggested fostering friendly relations with the Non-Chalcedonian or Oriental Orthodox Churches towards the restoration of the unity and the study of history, faith and worship of these Churches, and cooperation with them in ecumenical Conferences on pastoral issues.

The Second and Third Pan-Orthodox Conferences were also held in Rhodes. The Second (from 26 September until 1 October 1963) decided to start a dialogue with the Roman Catholics "on an equal footing." The Third

---

In the high-priestly prayer in the seventeenth chapter of St. John. Now, that prayer is all about unity and love. That is what we have so often forgotten in our theological quarrels. That is what the Ecumenical Movement must bring back ... We should now really look forward to the time when all Christians would break the bread together."

[16] Castanos de Medicis, *Athénagoras I, l'apport de l'Orthodoxie à l'Oecuménisme* (Age d'Homme: Lausanne, 1968), 37.
[17] Phil. 2:4.
[18] Olivier Clément, *Dialogues avec le Patriarche Athénagoras* (Fayard : Paris, 1969), 391.
[19] Alexandros Papaderos, *Ecumenism: Call and Challenge* (Orthodox Academy of Crete: Chania, 1984) 38 (in Greek).
[20] Compare, George Tsetsis, "Patriarchal Encyclical of 1952," op. cit. 74. See, Metropolitan of Sassima Gennadios (Limouris), *Orthodox Visions of Ecumenism: Statements, Messages and Reports on the Ecumenical Movement 1902-1992* (WCC: Geneva, 1994), 34-37.
[21] Compare to George Tsetsis, "Patriarchal Encyclical of 1952," 74.

(convened between 1 and 15 November 1964) decided, in relation to the dialogue with the Roman Catholics, that it was also necessary to prepare and create appropriate conditions for dialogue with the Anglicans and the Old Catholics. For this purpose, the Third Conference immediately formed two special Inter-Orthodox Theological Commissions for the continuation of theological cooperation.

The Fourth Pan-Orthodox Conference took place from 8 to 15 June 1968 in Chambésy, Switzerland. During that consultation, participants first decided to pursue immediately the convening of a Holy and Great Synod of the Orthodox Church, and, instead of convening a Pre-Synod, to convene gradually successive Pre-Synod Pan-Orthodox Conferences as well as an Inter-Orthodox Preparatory Commission. Second, it was decided to continue the systematic preparation of theological dialogue with heterodox Christians, mainly through the participation of Orthodoxy in the various working Committees of the WCC. Moreover, a decision was taken to begin theological dialogue between the Orthodox Church and the Non-Chalcedonian Churches. Finally, during Patriarch Athenagoras's leadership, the First Inter-Orthodox Preparatory Commission of the Holy and Great Synod was also convened in Chambésy, from 16 to 28 July 1971, where proposals were presented on six issues of the agenda of the First Pan-Orthodox Conference.[22]

The ultimate and decisive criterion in every thought and action of the Patriarch Athenagoras, whether referring to the Orthodox, or to other Christians, was his love for the other, a way of life that resulted from the absolute faith and trust in the person of Christ. At the crucial and important question, "How are we to move?", he replied saying that no Christian Church has the right to remain in isolation, nor to proclaim that there is no need of the fellow Christians brothers. Furthermore, no one has the right to say that, Christians outside of its own *yard* lack ties with Christ. The more a Church is possessed by the self-consciousness that it lives in the truth of the Lord, the more owes and has the responsibility to cooperate and converse with everyone in order to build the Body of Christ.[23]

Bibliography

1. Aidan Nichols O.P., *Rome and the Eastern Churches – A Study in Schism* (Ignatius Press: San Francisco, 2010).
2. Olivier Clément, "Athenagoras (Aristokles Pyrou)," in *Dictionary of the Ecumenical Movement* (WCC: Geneva, 2002).
3. Olivier Clément, *Dialogues avec le Patriarche Athénagoras* (Fayard: Paris, 1969).
4. Jeffrey Gros, Eamon Mc Manus, and Ann Riggs, *Introduction to Ecumenism* (Paulist Press: New York, 1998).
5. Georges Florovsky, "The Ethos of the Orthodox Church," in *Orthodoxy – A Faith and Order Dialogue*, Faith and Order Paper No. 30 (WCC, 1960).
6. Metropolitan of Sassima Gennadios (Limouris), *Orthodox Visions of Ecumenism. Statements, Messages and Reports on the Ecumenical Movement 1902-1992* (WCC: Geneva, 1994).
7. Constantin Patelos, *The Orthodox Church in the Ecumenical Movement* (Geneva, 1978).
8. W. A. Visser 't Hooft, *Memoirs* (WCC: Geneva, 1973).
9. Ioannis Kalogirou, *Athenagoras, the Ecumenical Patriarch from Epirus* (Epirus Company Studies: Ioannina, 1975) (in Greek).
10. Basilios Stavridis and Evangelia Varella, *The History of Ecumenical Movement* (Patriarchal Foundation for Patristic Studies: Thessaloniki, 1996) (in Greek).
11. *Tomos Agapis (Volume of Love) Vatican – Phanar (1958 – 1970)* (Rome – Istanbul, 1971).

---

[22] Metropolitan of Switzerland Damaskinos, *Orthodoxy and World* (Tertios: Katerini, 1993), 365-366 (in Greek).

[23] As above, George Tsetsis (ed.), "The speech of the Ecumenical Patriarch Athenagoras the 1st during his visit to the WCC (6 November 1967)" 83.

Part III: Representative Orthodox Theologians reflecting on Ecumenism

12. George Tsetsis, *The Contribution of the Ecumenical Patriarchate to the foundation of WCC* (Tertios: Katerini, 1988) (in Greek).
13. Stylianos Tsompanidis, *The Contribution of the Orthodox Church and Theology to the WCC* (Pournaras: Thessaloniki, 2008) (in Greek).

(translated by Fr. Georges Anagnostoulis)

(26) Ecumenical Patriarch Bartholomew

Fr. Augoustinos Bairactaris

Ecumenical Patriarch Bartholomew is one of the most important religious figures of our epoch. After his election as the 270th Archbishop of Constantinople and Ecumenical Patriarch of New Rome, Patriarch Bartholomew, with a spirit of reconciliation that springs from love of neighbor and with a disposition for true dialogue, held a series of official visits to the headquarters of various Christian Churches, confessions and religions around the world, initiating a practice of living contact and an exchange of opinions on issues concerning the relationship between religion, society and the environment. The vision of Patriarch Bartholomew, which he faithfully follows from the beginning, is a belief in the dynamic and intellectual virtues which humanity can bring forth through universal tolerance, which is founded on dialogue, solidarity, humility, brotherhood and the belief in one God.[1] Only in this way— that is, through the inspired role and word of religious leaders in spite of the differences they may have in culture, economy, religion and language—can the peaceful coexistence and cooperation between peoples be achieved.

As a consequence, Patriarch Bartholmew's tenure is characterized by his emphasis on, and initiative in, inter-Christian and inter-religious dialogue, as well as by the Inter-Orthodox cooperation he pursues at all levels. Indeed, he himself has led five Congregations of the Primates of the Orthodox Churches with the goal of achieving a united testimony of Orthodoxy "in one mouth and one heart" within the world. Moreover, the Ecumenical Patriarch's activity, during his more than twenty years at the patriarchal throne of Constantinople, is related to and embodied in his struggles and agony for Orthodox people worldwide, his treatment of the negative effects of the divisions still plaguing Christianity, and his belief that the Church is called to give a constant witness to modern people.

The relationship between the Ecumenical Patriarch Bartholomew and the World Council of Churches began very early in 1968 when he was a member of the delegation of the Patriarchate to the General Assembly of the Council in Uppsala. For fifteen consecutive years he was a member of the "Faith and Order" committee. Afterward, he served as its Vice President for eight years. He actively took part in the preparation and publication of the famous *B.E.M.* text *(Baptism, Eucharist, and Ministry)* which is probably the most representative ecclesiological text of WCC.[2] He participated in most delegations of the Ecumenical Patriarchate in bilateral inter-Orthodox, and multi-lateral ecumenical, inter-Christian dialogues. In particular, he took part in the General Assembly of the WCC in Uppsala in 1968, Vancouver in 1983 and in Canberra in 1991, where he was elected member to the Central Committee of the Council. In addition, in 1990 at the Orthodox center of Chambésy in Geneva, he chaired the Inter-Orthodox Preparatory Committee of the Holy and Great Synod on the issue of the Orthodox Diaspora.[3]

Ecumenical Patriarch Bartholomew not only continued the work of his predecessors Athenagoras and Demetrios regarding inter-Christian theological dialogues (especially with the Roman Catholics, Lutherans,

---

[1] Ecumenical Patriarch Bartholomew, "The Interfaith Meeting of Brussels," *Episkepsis* 603 (2001): 7: "The famous tragic events of September 11th of the expiring year require us to reveal to all peoples the peaceful and peace-loving face of God and to dispel the impression that God blesses human sacrifice ... Wherefore we warmly request ourselves and each other to abandon any political approach to the issue of peace outside this hall and to give to our faithful and to the whole world undistorted the peace-making message one and only true God."

[2] *Baptism, Eucharist and Ministry*, Faith and Order Paper No.111 (WCC: Geneva, 1982). Cf. Augoustinos Bairaktaris, *Baptism and Ecumenical Dialogue - An Orthodox approach* (Pournaras: Thessaloniki, 2010), 269-291 (in Greek).

[3] Yorgo Lemopoulos, "Bartholomew (Dimitrios Arhondonis)," in the *Dictionary of the Ecumenical Movement,* (WCC: Geneva, 2002), 102.

Anglicans, Old Catholics, Reformed and Oriental Orthodox), in a spirit of love and truth and always in accordance with the received resolutions at a pan-Orthodox level,[4] but it could be said that he gave a broader sense and a new impetus and dynamism towards the dynamic witness of the Orthodox Church in the modern world.[5] Moreover, he promoted the unbroken relationship between the Ecumenical Patriarchate and the Ecumenical Movement, a relationship inaugurated by the famous Encyclical Letters of the Ecumenical Throne (1902, 1904, 1920).[6]

Particularly, the theological dialogue with the Roman Catholic Church continued despite the difficulties encountered in the early 90s because of the emergent situation in Eastern Europe, mainly related to the Unia, as a consequence of the collapse of the Communism in the USSR.[7] Both sides attempted to give a definitive solution to the thorny issue of the Unia through the Balamand text (17-24 June 1993) entitled "Uniatism, method of union of the past and the present search for full communion."[8] Contrary to the initial ambitions, the formal theological dialogue seemed to be driven to an impasse, portraying to the world a state of stagnation and a lack of any substantive result. However, the theological dialogue between Phanar and Vatican found the necessary space and time to re-establish and overcome their theological obstacles which were raised after the failure of the meeting in Baltimore (2000). Especially, the 9th General Assembly of the Joint Theological Commission held in Belgrade (2006) served as the impetus for renewed dialogue, culminating in the publication of a very important Ravenna document (13 October 2007) entitled "Ecclesiological and canonical consequences of the sacramental nature of the Church Ecclesial Communion, Conciliarity and Authority." The position of Patriarch Bartholomew on the relationship between Orthodoxy and Roman Catholicism is defined by his belief that the common admission that "we have found the Messiah", of the two brothers-in-the-flesh Peter (founder of the Church of Rome) and Andrew (founder of the Church of Constantinople) is something that makes them brothers spiritually, beyond the flesh. As Patriarch Bartholomew specifically mentions at the throne Feast of St. Andrew: "*The Churches of Rome and Constantinople are obliged to rediscover the common voice of the two Apostles, their common confession of faith and the body and blood of Christ their 'full brother', so that the world is able to believe in the Messiah, whom 'they found', the two founders of these two Churches.*"[9] Christ being in our midst joins what had been in opposition.[10] That is why the two Churches should behave and live with each other as *sister Churches*.[11]

In contrast to the globalized economy, which tends to dominate in all sectors of society by imposing a dangerous uniformity in the way of life and thinking of the people, the inspired Patriarch counter-proposes the establishment of a globalized inter-Christian and inter-faith dialogue, which ought to be based on honesty and equality, starting from the exercise of self-criticism and humility. The common goal of these dialogues is the peaceful coexistence and cooperation between religions and the people. It should be taken for granted that the participation of religions in dialogue does not mean the confusion or mixing of religious teachings, nor does it mean the ignorance of the existent differences. Nevertheless, as Patriarch Bartholomew asserts, one should

---

[4] Metropolitan of Switzerland Damaskinos, *Orthodoxy and World* (Tertios: Katerini, 1993), 365-377 (in Greek).

[5] Olivier Clément, "Witnessing in a Secularized Society," in *Your will be done - Orthodoxy in Mission*, (WCC & Tertios: Geneva, 1989), 117-135.

[6] Emmanuel Clapsis, *Orthodoxy in Conversation - Orthodox Ecumenical Engagements* (WCC & Holy Cross Orthodox Press: Brookline Massachusetts, 2000), 1-10.

[7] George Martzelos, *Orthodoxy and Contemporary Dialogues* (Pournaras: Thessaloniki, 2008), 239ff (in Greek).

[8] George Martzelos & Peter Hofrichter, eds., *The Official Theological Dialogue between Orthodox and Roman Catholic Churches* in the series *Ecumeni - Dialogue and concerns*, vol. 3 (Paratiritis: Thessaloniki, 1998), 86-93 (in Greek).

[9] *Address by his Holiness the Ecumenical Patriarch Bartholomew to the Delegation of the Church of Rome at the Throne feast of the Ecumenical Patriarchate* (30 November 2011), 2.

[10] Cyril of Alexandria, *Memorial to Ioannis* 1, 14, PG 73, 161C: "Because all of us and the common person of humanity in Christ revives."

[11] Augustinos Bairactaris, "Une interprétation ecclésiologique et théologique de l 'expression' églises soeurs' vis-à-vis le contenu de terme 'églises locales'," in *Inheritance* 36 (2004): 119-140.

take into account the necessity of fostering solidarity and brotherhood so as to eliminate the forces of fear, racism and intolerance.[12] Through dialogue, isolation and narcissism, which characterize "the original sin" of modern humanity, is abandoned, since any notion of limit and self-sufficiency have been lost.[13]

Moreover, nobody can ignore that one of the main initiatives of the aforementioned Patriarch was and is the defense of the religious rights of minorities and the protection of freedom, speech and worship.[14] The sacredness of the human person and the protection of human life constitute eternal evangelical virtues which should characterize every age and society. As the Primate of Orthodoxy used to repeat emphatically: "*every crime committed supposedly in the name of religion is a crime against the religion itself and an insult to God.*"[15] The freedom of human consciousness and the unrestricted exercise of the religious beliefs of all the people, without distinction, are fundamental Orthodox principles which Patriarch Bartholomew presents in every possible occasion. In opposition to the absoluteness which religious dogmatism and fanaticism generates, Patriarch Bartholomew participates in various social, economic and political forums,[16] because the ecclesiastical word must be heard so that it can act effectively to reshape European and global reality.[17]

Moreover, Patriarch Bartholomew is an example and model for those who seek and believe that Christians can achieve the transformation and conversion of people's hearts by the grace of God. In other words, the Ecumenical Patriarch professes the biblical vision of a harmonious and peaceful coexistence of people despite their cultural, linguistic, religious, social and political diversity. Diversity and cultural multiformity no longer constitute a threat of social or religious unrest and instability, but they are approached as evidence of human richness and religious pluralism.[18] Those who contribute to the religious diversity in our society are also our neighbors, and we are called to live with them in harmony.[19]

---

[12] Ecumenical Patriarch Bartholomew, *In the World, Yet not of the World - Social and Global Initiatives of Ecumenical Patriarch Bartholomew*, ed. by John Chryssavgis (Fordham University Press: New York, 2010), 75.

[13] The Ecumenical Patriarch Bartholomew notes accordingly, in his speech at his award of an honorary Ph.D. in the Faculty of Biological and Conservatory Farming and Floriculture in Kalamata in February 2010: *"The common root of all forms of human destructiveness is indeed the self-glorification of the man, the 'complex of God', as it has been named. In the place of the deposed God did not seat the 'enlightened man', but the arrogant 'human-god'."* See related "Theological Annals" in *Theology* 1 (2010): 340-344 (in Greek).

[14] Ecumenical Patriarch Bartholomew, "Globalization: Ethical Dilemmas," in Greek Daily Newspaper *Eleftherotypia* (03-02-1999), 9: "But we wish that it is ensured to members of the Orthodox minority in the world, but also of every other cultural minority, the possibility to retain its particular characteristics and its culture ... already many times as Ecumenical Patriarchate and personally, we have invited the followers of dissenting religions and ideologies and interests to the cessation of conflicts, conciliation and cooperation on the practical field."

[15] Ecumenical Patriarch Bartholomew, *Encountering the Mystery - Understanding Orthodox Christianity Today*, ed. John Chryssavgis (The Doubleday Broadway Publishing Group: New York, 2008), 136.

[16] The Ecumenical Patriarch Bartholomew has sent messages and given general talks to both the European Parliament and the U.S. Congress. Also, he has given talks at Unesco and the World Economic Forum and has been awarded several honorary doctorate degrees from universities of Greece, as well as of other countries (USA, England, Belgium, Australia, Russia, Romania).

[17] Message by His All Holiness Ecumenical Patriarch Bartholomew at the 11th "Euroasian Economic Summit," Istanbul, 3 May 2008: "*In this way it becomes evident that not only does religion play a pivotal role in people's personal lives throughout the world, but religion also plays a critical role as a force of social and institutional mobilization on a variety of levels ... And it is involvement that highlights the supreme purpose and calling of humanity to transcend political or religious differences in order to transform the entire world for the glory of God. Modern society requires increasing efforts from the Christian faith to fulfill itself and to help this society to go deeper in its humaneness.*"

[18] Metropolitan of Constantia and Famagusta Basil, *The Religious and Ethnic Pluralism of the New Society of the World* (Armos: Athens, 2002), 46-47 (in Greek). Cf. George Tsetsis, "We and others. Orthodoxy in dialogue," in *Roadside* 1 (1992): 25: "By meeting the other we should perhaps henceforth cease treating him, as it often happens, as a potential enemy of Orthodoxy, but regard him as a fellow man, being also molded in the image and likeness of God."

[19] Metropolitan of Ephesus Chrysostomos, "Orthodoxy and Religious diversity" in P. Kalaitzidis and N. Ntontos eds., *Orthodoxy and Modernity* (Indiktos: Athens, 2007), 168 (in Greek).

Part III: Representative Orthodox Theologians reflecting on Ecumenism

Religious, cultural, and even inter-Christian dialogues present a counterbalance to the ideology of *fundamentalism* which has grown to a dangerous degree.[20] For these reasons, the Ecumenical Patriarchate (by its honorary Primacy and through specific theological committees) participates in and also organizes international and interfaith meetings and symposia with the aim to foster a culture of peace, tolerance and reconciliation among people[21] for their *goodwill*, contrary to the phenomena of violence and terrorism.[22] So the Ecumenical Patriarch Bartholomew has widely become known for his willingness to build *bridges of dialogue and peace* between Christianity, Judaism and Islam.[23]

Finally, thanks to the activities of the Ecumenical Patriarch Bartholomew, the close connection between the ecological problem and the ecclesiological dimension of the relationships of man to Creation, man to neighbor, and by extension Creator and the created being has been highlighted.[24] His basic conviction is that our attitude towards creation reflects the way we behave to our neighbor, because the goal of humanity is closely connected to the preservation of the Trinitarian God's created world.[25] Therefore, through conferences, seminars and academic meetings, focusing on the sustainability and integrity of the environment, Patriarch Bartholomew has contributed to the emergence of an environmental conscience, having also put forward from time to time the necessity of taking concrete measures towards the protection of the ecological heritage for the future generations.[26]

---

[20] Metropolitan of Dimitrias Ignatius, "The Dialogue of Religions and Civilizations, and the promotion of mutual respect, peaceful coexistence and tolerance of the different" (2011-04-14) in http://www.amen.gr/index.php?mod = news & op = article & aid = 5355 (last accessed 03/09/2013): "... mission of the religion is the welcoming and hospitality of the other, the different, which portrays the par excellence Other, the God; that mission of the Christians and those who believe in God is to be on the side of the victims of History, the 'least brothers' of Christ, that the task of the religion is, finally, the healing of the wounds of historical violence, the replacement the violence by forgiveness and conciliation."

[21] Archbishop of Tirana Anastasios, *Facing the World, Orthodox Christian Essays on Global Concerns* (WCC: Geneva, 2003), 193.

[22] Metropolitan of Constantia and Famagusta Basil, "Ecumenical Patriarch Bartholomew - Twenty years of Glorious Patriarchy (1991-2011)," in *Spiritual Service* 12 (2011): 3.

[23] Ecumenical Patriarch Bartholomew, *Encountering the Mystery - A contemporary reading of Orthodoxy* (Akritas: Athens, 2008), 328 (in Greek).

[24] Ecumenical Patriarch Bartholomew, *On Earth As In Heaven: Ecological Vision and Initiatives of Ecumenical Patriarch Bartholomew*, ed. John Chryssavgis (Fordham University Press: New York, 2011), 38.

[25] Ecumenical Patriarch Bartholomew, *Cosmic Grace, Humble Prayer: The Ecological Vision of the Green Patriarch Bartholomew I*, ed. John Chryssavgis (William Eerdmans Publishing Company & Grand Rapids: Michigan/ Cambridge UK, 2003), 47ff.

[26] At this point it is necessary to mention the most well-known and internationally recognized activity of Ecumenical Patriarch Bartholomew regarding the responsible stance which the religions, the peoples and the cultures must take in relation to the environment. Thanks to a series of specific actions, conferences and events, with the environment as the central theme, the Ecumenical Patriarch of Constantinople Bartholomew proves in practice his anxiety and interest in environmental sustainability. At the same time, inter alia, he organized from 1994 to 1998 a series of Ecological Conferences at the Theological School of Halki (Turkey) with a variety of topics directly related to the environmental issue. He also sanctioned the realization of the floating Symposia on seas and rivers in different geographical areas of the planet. The so-called "Patmos Circle" so far includes the organizing of the following eight waterborne symposia: 1. "Revelation and Environment" – Patmos-Greece (1995), 2. "Religion - Science - Environment: The Black Sea in distress" - Black Sea (1997), 3. "Danube: River of Life" - The Danube (1999), 4. "Adriatic: A Sea Endangered, a common goal" - Adriatic (2002), 5. "The Baltic Sea: Common Heritage and Responsibility" - Baltic (2003), 6. "Amazon: Source of Life" - Amazon (2006), 7. "Arctic: Mirror of Life" - Arctic (2007), 8. "Mississippi: Restoring the Balance" - Mississippi (2009). Finally, he has established a special Inter-Orthodox Commission to study and address the ecological problem. Therefore, it could be said that rightly has been given the title of the "Green Patriarch". See in connection, Ecumenical Patriarch Bartholomew, *Messages and Homilies on the Environment* (Fanarion: Athens, 2002).

Bibliography

1. Ecumenical Patriarch Bartholomew, *Cosmic Grace, Humble Prayer: The Ecological Vision of the Green Patriarch Bartholomew I*, ed. John Chryssavgis (William Eerdmans Publishing Company & Grand Rapids: Michigan/Cambridge U.K., 2003).
2. Ecumenical Patriarch Bartholomew, *Encountering the Mystery – Understanding Orthodox Christianity Today,* ed. John Chryssavgis (The Doubleday Broadway Publishing Group: New York, 2008).
3. Ecumenical Patriarch Bartholomew, *In the World, Yet not of the World – Social and Global Initiatives of Ecumenical Patriarch Bartholomew*, ed. John Chryssavgis (Fordham University Press: New York, 2010).
4. Ecumenical Patriarch Bartholomew, *On Earth As In Heaven: Ecological Vision and Initiatives of Ecumenical Patriarch Bartholomew*, ed. John Chryssavgis (Fordham University Press: New York, 2011).
5. Message by His All Holiness Ecumenical Patriarch Bartholomew at the 11th "Euro-Asian Economic Summit," Istanbul, 3 May 2008.
6. Ecumenical Patriarch Bartholomew, *Messages and Homilies on the Environment* (Fanarion: Athens, 2002) (in Greek).
7. Ecumenical Patriarch Bartholomew, *Encountering the Mystery. Understanding Orthodox Christianity Today* (Doubleday: 2008).
8. Archbishop of Tirana Anastasios, *Facing the World, Orthodox Christian Essays on Global Concerns*, (WCC: Geneva, 2003).
9. Metropolitan of Switzerland Damaskinos (Papandreou), *Orthodoxy and the world* (Tertios: Katerini,1993) (in Greek).
10. Metropolitan of Constantia and Famagusta Basil, *The religious and ethnic pluralism of the new society of the world* (Armos: Athens, 2002) (in Greek).
11. Olivier Clément, "Witnessing in a Secularized Society," in *Your will be done – Orthodoxy in Mission*, (WCC & Tertios: Geneva, 1989), 117-135.
12. Yorgo Lemopoulos, "Bartholomew (Dimitrios Arhondonis)," in *Dictionary of the Ecumenical Movement*, (WCC: Geneva, 2002),102-103.
13. Emmanuel Clapsis, *Orthodoxy in Conversation – Orthodox Ecumenical Engagements* (WCC & Holy Cross Orthodox Press: Brookline Massachusetts, 2000).
14. George Martzelos, *Orthodoxy and Contemporary Dialogues* (Pournaras: Thessaloniki, 2008) (in Greek).
15. Augoustinos Bairactaris, *Baptism and Ecumenical Dialogue - An Orthodox approach* (Pournaras: Thessaloniki, 2010), 269-291 (in Greek).

(translated by Fr. George Anagnostoulis)

Part III: Representative Orthodox Theologians reflecting on Ecumenism

(27) Elisabeth Behr-Sigel

Paul Ladouceur

Elisabeth Behr-Sigel was one of the leading Orthodox theologians of the twentieth century, a luminous presence whose long and varied life reflected a constant commitment to truth, human dignity and the Church as the Kingdom of God, as much here and now as in the eschaton.[1] Born in 1907 of a French Lutheran father and a Jewish mother, she initially studied philosophy and in 1927 she was one of the first women to be admitted to the Faculty of Protestant Theology at the University of Strasbourg. As an adolescent she was active in a Protestant student organisation, the Fédération universelle des associations chrétiennes d'étudiants (FUACE). Through this association and her theological studies, she met many of the French Protestant leaders of the inter-war period. She also met Russian students at the university and through them she had her first contacts with the Orthodox Church. She spent a year at the Protestant Faculty in Paris and became acquainted with Father Lev Gillet, who remained a life-long friend and who received her into the Orthodox Church in December 1929. She also met many of the leading younger Orthodox theologians in Paris, such as Paul Evdokimov, Vladimir Lossky and Evgraph Kovalevsky, as well as the older generation, represented by Sergius Bulgakov, Nicholas Berdiaev and Saint Maria of Paris (Mother Maria Skobtsova).

After completing her studies at Strasbourg, she did a master's degree in Germany with a thesis on sainthood in the Russian Orthodox Church.[2] In 1931-32 she served as an unordained lay minister in the Evangelical Lutheran Church of France in a rural community in Alsace. This truly ecumenical service – as a young Orthodox woman ministering to a Protestant community – represented a unique pastoral experience which would prove valuable much later in life, when she became deeply involved in ecumenical dialogues on the role of women in the Church.[3]

She resigned this ministry to marry André Behr, an Orthodox Russian, in February 1931. The Behrs lived in Nancy, in the east of France, and it was there that the couple's three children were born. Beginning in 1939, Elisabeth pursued a career in education. During the German occupation of France in World War II, the Behrs frequently hosted a clandestine ecumenical group including Orthodox, Catholics and Protestants, united in Christian opposition to Nazi ideology, for mutual support, theological discussions and resistance activities.

After the war, Father Lev Gillet, who took up residence in England in 1938, invited her to participate in a meeting of the Fellowship of Saint Alban and Saint Sergius, an association founded to promote understanding between Orthodox and Anglicans. Subsequently, Elisabeth Behr-Sigel became one the leading Orthodox participants in the Fellowship's activities, together with Fr. Lev, and Vladimir Lossky. In 1951 she began research on the nineteenth-century Russian theologian Alexander Bukharev, under the well-known Slavic scholar Pierre Pascal, and completed a doctorate in 1976.[4]

---

[1] For the life of Elisabeth Behr-Sigel, see her biography by Olga Lossky, *Toward the Endless Day: The Life of Elisabeth Behr-Sigel* (Notre Dame IN: University of Notre Dame Press, 2010); Elisabeth Behr-Sigel's short autobiographical essay "My Journey to the Orthodox Church" and Lyn Breck "Nearly a Century of Life" in Elisabeth Behr-Sigel, *Discerning the Signs of the Times. The Vision of Elisabeth Behr-Sigel* (Yonkers NY: St Vladimir's Seminary Press, 2001). For an overview of her theology and writings see Paul Ladouceur, "Pensée et œuvre littéraire d'Élisabeth Behr-Sigel", *Contacts, Revue française d'orthodoxie* 59 (2007): 220.

[2] A revised and expanded version was published as *Prière et sainteté dans l'Église russe* (Paris: Le Cerf, 1950 ; Abbaye de Bellefontaine (SO 39), 1982).

[3] See her reflections on this experience in the Introduction to *The Ministry of Women in the Church* (Torrance CA: Oakwood Publications, 1987), and in "My Itinerary to the Orthodox Church".

[4] Her doctoral thesis was published as *Alexandre Boukarev – Un théologien de l'Église orthodoxe russe en dialogue avec le monde moderne* (Paris: Beauchesne, 1977).

Although she lived in the east of France, Elisabeth Behr-Sigel remained in close contact with the French Orthodox community in Paris, travelling frequently to participate in meetings organised by her friends, such as Paul Evdokimov. Evdokimov worked for many years for the Protestant social assistance organisation CIMADE (Comité inter-mouvements pour l'accueil des évacués) and regularly organised ecumenical gatherings at which Elisabeth participated, together with Father Lev Gillet and other Orthodox figures. In 1959 Elisabeth joined the editorial committee of the major French Orthodox theological periodical *Contacts*, which published many of her articles on Orthodox theology and spirituality and on ecumenism. In addition, she became involved in correspondence courses on Orthodox theology and spirituality, which were soon incorporated into the Saint Sergius Institute of Orthodox Theology in Paris. Her course on Orthodox spirituality was published under the title *The Place of the Heart*.[5]

After the death of her husband in 1968, she moved to Paris and became deeply involved in the advancement of the French Orthodox community, in collaboration with Olivier Clément, Father Lev Gillet and others, and in international ecumenical activities.

Other ecumenical involvement over the years included participation in ecumenical publications and organisations. In the late 1940s, she collaborated with other leading Orthodox theologians, such as Vladimir Lossky, Paul Evdokimov and Myrra Lot-Borodin, in the ecumenical theological periodical launched by Catholic intellectuals, *Dieu Vivant*. Her principal contribution was an important article on the Jesus Prayer.[6] For many years she was active, with other Orthodox such as Fr. Cyrille Argenti and Fr. Michel Evdokimov (son of Paul Evdokimov), in an ecumenical anti-torture organization, Action des chrétiens pour l'abolition de la torture (ACAT), serving as its vice-president from 1981 to 1993. She regularly taught at the Ecumenical Centre in Bossey, Switzerland, an educational institute of the WCC, at the Catholic Faculty of Lyons, and at the Institut supérieur d'études œcuméniques (established by the Catholic, Protestant and Orthodox schools of theology in Paris). Until the late 1990s she also continued to participate in symposia organised under the auspices of the WCC.

Women in Society and in the Church.

Until the end of World War II Elisabeth Behr-Sigel's main ecumenical activities were largely of a personal nature, arising from her Protestant background and theological studies, her service as lay minister to a Protestant community and her involvement in the ecumenical group during the War. From the late 1940s until the mid-1970s, her ecumenical involvement revolved around her participation in the Fellowship of St. Alban and St. Sergius, her ecumenical teaching activities and her contributions to the periodical *Dieu Vivant* and to the ecumenical activities organised by Paul Evdokimov.

In the mid-1970s, already in her late 60s, Elisabeth Behr-Sigel became deeply involved in the social and theological issue of the role of women in the Church and it was in this context that she made her most well-known ecumenical contributions. She was introduced into global ecumenical circles, especially the World Council of Churches (WCC), by leading Orthodox ecumenical figures such as Metropolitan Emilianos Timiadis, representative of the Ecumenical Patriarch at the WCC headquarters in Geneva, and her friend Paul Evdokimov. Encouraged by Metropolitan Émilianos, Metropolitan Anthony Bloom, Father Lev Gillet and later Bishop Kallistos Ware, she became the leading Orthodox representative in Orthodox and ecumenical discussions on the role of women in society and the Church. Her initial public involvement in this area was in 1976, when she was invited to give the opening talk at a meeting of Orthodox women, the first of its kind, organised by the WCC at the women's monastery in Agapia, Romania.[7] It was here that she raised for the

---

[5] *The Place of the Heart: An Introduction to Orthodox Spirituality* (Torrance CA: Oakwood Publications, 1992).

[6] "Le Mystère de la spiritualité orthodoxe", *Dieu Vivant*, 8 (Seuil, 1947). Reprinted in *La douloureuse joie, Aperçus sur la prière personnelle de l'Orient chrétien* (Abbaye de Bellefontaine (SO 14), 1974).

[7] For her opening talk at Agapia see "The meaning of the participation of women in the life of the Church," C. Tarasar and I. Kirillova, eds., *Orthodox Women, Their Role and Participation in the Orthodox Church* (Geneva: WCC, 1977); reprinted in Elisabeth Behr-Sigel, *The Ministry of Women in the Church* (Torrance CA: Oakwood Publications, 1987).

Part III: Representative Orthodox Theologians reflecting on Ecumenism

first time in an Orthodox context the delicate question of the ordination of women to the priesthood. Prior to this meeting, Orthodox declarations on the role of women in the Church, especially on the sensitive issue of the ordination of women, were elaborated almost entirely in the absence of participation of women. With the rise of the "women's liberation" movement in the 1960s, the question of women in the Church had become a major issue in many Churches and in the ecumenical movement, with a number of Protestant Churches and the Anglican Church debating and eventually approving the ordination of women. Orthodox representatives in ecumenical fora were asked to explain the thinking of the Orthodox Church on this issue, especially the question of ordination. It was largely due to WCC initiatives that the Orthodox Churches were encouraged to listen to the voices of Orthodox women on these issues.

For the two decades following the Agapia meeting, Elisabeth Behr-Sigel was the principal Orthodox voice on questions of women in society and the Church. In 1974 the Faith and Order Commission of the WCC proposed a major project on "The Community of Women and Men in the Church," a project approved by the WCC Assembly in Nairobi in 1975. The Agapia meeting took place in the context of this project and after the meeting Behr-Sigel took the lead Orthodox role in the development of the project, participating in subsequent meetings in Strasbourg-Klingenthal (1978), Niederaltaich (1979) and the final conference in Sheffield (1981). By then the question of the ordination of women dominated all other aspects of the role of women in the Church, but the final report of the Sheffield meeting was ill-received by representatives of Orthodox Churches on the Central Committee of the WCC, since it appeared to open the door to the ordination of women.[8] A related issue for the Orthodox Churches concerned the maintenance of ecumenical dialogues with those Churches which eventually decided to ordain women. For Elisabeth Behr-Sigel, it was clear that this step does not entail an essential aspect of the Apostolic faith, but rather is compatible with ecclesial communion in keeping with the maxim *In necessariis unitas, in dubiis libertas, in omnibus caritas* ("unity in necessary things; liberty in doubtful things; charity in all things"). In this light there is no reason for Orthodox Churches to break relationships with those Churches which ordain women.[9]

Mindful of questions relating to the role of women in other Christian denominations, Behr-Sigel nonetheless addressed herself primarily to the Orthodox Church. Her well-researched reflections on women in the Church were based especially on an attentive reading of Scripture, the experience of the early Church and patristic anthropology. Many of her talks at WCC meetings and in other contexts were published by the WCC and in the French periodical *Contacts*, and form a lasting reference of her thinking on women in society and the Church, which is likely her most important and enduring theological contribution.[10]

Although Elisabeth Behr-Sigel favoured the ordination of women to the priesthood in the Orthodox Church, she concentrated her energies more on the boarder question of the role of women in the Orthodox Church. She was well aware of Orthodox sensitivities on this issue and was inclined to urge reflection and reform of thinking and practices grounded on Biblical and patristic teaching of the ontological equality of men and women, rather than shrill denunciations of male domination. Nonetheless her calm, well-founded theological reflections were influential in expanding Orthodox thinking on women in general and specifically on the ordination of women. For example, she had a fruitful dialogue with Bishop Kallistos Ware on this issue, including the joint authorship of a book containing the views of each (*The Ordination of Women in the Orthodox Church*, 2000). Whereas initially Bp Kallistos opposed the ordination of women, by 1999 he accepted that neither the arguments against the ordination of women, nor those in favour are decisive, that there are "no easy answers", but the question of woman's ministry in the Church must be approached "with

---

[8] Constance Parvey, ed., *The Community of Women and Men in the Church: A Report of the WCC Conference, Sheffield, England, 1981* (Geneva: WCC, 1983). See Elisabeth Behr-Sigel's assessment of Sheffield and its aftermath in her Introduction to *The Ministry of Women in the Church*, 11-13.

[9] Introduction to *The Ministry of Women in the Church*, 17.

[10] Many of Elisabeth Behr-Sigel's most important writings on women are collected in three volumes: *The Ministry of Women in the Church*; *Discerning the Signs of the Times*; and *The Ordination of Women*. See the Bibliography for full references.

an open mind and an open heart".[11] It is likely that other Orthodox theologians have also been influenced by Elisabeth Behr-Sigel's thinking on this issue. Unquestionably her thinking on women in Church remains a landmark and reference in Orthodox theological reflection on this complex issue. Her involvement in the issue of women and the Church illustrates, possibly more than any other single issue, the complex interplay between Orthodox participation in the ecumenical movement and the development of Orthodox thinking on a theological and ecclesial issue.

Active to the very end of her life, Elisabeth Behr-Sigel died on 5 November 2005 at the venerable age of 98.

Bibliography

This Bibliography contains principal references to Elisabeth Behr-Sigel's ecumenical thought and activities, especially relating to women in the Church, available in English. Many of her important articles and conference interventions are contained in *The Ministry of Women in the Church* and in *Discerning the Signs of the Times*. For additional articles and other writings in French, see the Bibliography in Olga Lossky,

The Ministry of Women in the Church (Torrance CA: Oakwood Publications, 1987).

"The Orthodox Women in a United Europe", *Mary Martha*, 4, 1, 1995.

"The community of women and men: What does this mean for a prophetic and sacramental Church", *Mary Martha*, 4, 2, 1996.

The Ordination of Women in the Orthodox Church (with Kallistos Ware) (Geneva: WCC Publications, 2000).

Discerning the Signs of the Times. The Vision of Elisabeth Behr-Sigel (Yonkers NY: St Vladimir's Seminary Press, 2001).

"The ordination of women: a point of contention in ecumenical dialogue", *St Vladimir's Theological Quarterly* 48.1 (2004): 49-66.

---

[11] Compare the very different essays by Bp Kallistos Ware, both under the title "Man, Woman and the Priesthood of Christ", in the two editions of the book edited by Thomas Hopko, *Women and the Priesthood* (Yonkers NY: St Vladimir's Seminary Press, 1983 and 1999). Quotations are from the 1999 edition, p. 52.

Part III: Representative Orthodox Theologians reflecting on Ecumenism

Fr. Nicolae Moşoiu

"I consider you are the only one capable of doing a highly appropriate interpretation of my writing, because you are the only one who thinks personally, creatively, the only Romanian theologian from the generations after me, troubled about problems and with resources for a new, subtle, poetic expression. Perhaps, if you would undertake to do such a work, more elaborate, which would mean to take further the Romanian theological thought - you would do a great service to the endeavours of making the creative spirit of the Romanian Orthodoxy, known."

"I remain firmly convinced that you're after me, the only theologian who thinks lively, originally, capable of other and other personal insights and broad personal syntheses. Each of the others has one attribute: diligence, logical thinking and sentiment. You have them all. You've got the whole complexity of a theologian."

(Excerpts from two letters addressed by Father Professor Dumitru Stăniloae to Father Professor Ion Bria, dated: 30.12.1978, respectively 02.06.1979)

Fr. Ioan Bria and his involvement into the Ecumenical Movement

Orthodox priest, professor and director in the World Council of Churches in Geneva, Father Ion Bria (1929-2002) contributed decisively to the development of Orthodox theology and ecumenism in the twentieth century, opening the road for the third millennium. He served altar and academy with great dedication, charming many students and countless people of different confessions who heard him or read his writings. He made the profession of priest and teacher of theology a true *profession of faith*. Saint Gregory the Theologian stated that familiarity with God - *pros Theon oikeioteta* - make others become familiar - *allous oikeioun* with God too, through word and example. Father Bria was endowed with such familiarity with God, which he made transparent in a humble and therefore engaging manner. The same familiarity conferred him the full dignity, fairness, optimism and permanent commitment in *missio Dei Triunius*.

Professor at the Theological Seminary in Buzau, then at the Theological Institute in Bucharest, Father Bria was involved in the ecumenical movement beginning in 1973, leading several departments of the Council of Churches, the only "umbrella" for Orthodox Churches in countries with totalitarian regimes. In 1995 he accepted an invitation from Father Dean Mircea Păcurariu, despite the effort and implicit shortcomings, to become associate professor at the Faculty of Theology Andrei Saguna at the University of Sibiu, occupying the Chair of Dogmatic and Ecumenical Theology from 1995 to 1999.

Father Professor Bria was the author or co-author of 32 books, 18 collections of courses and academic lectures and more than 280 studies and articles. He published in the areas of dogmatic theology, missiology, ecumenism and theological hermeneutics. The originality of his work, his theological thought and his method is undeniable.

During his doctoral studies, Father Ion Bria benefited from the guidance of Father Professor Dumitru Stăniloae and Professor Nicholae Chiţescu, and it was for this reason that he so easily touched, in his early writings, the core teaching of Saints Maximus the Confessor, Symeon the New Theologian and Gregory Palamas, understanding, that they are defining thinkers for Orthodox identity. Subsequently positioning his work in the most important international ecumenical organization, he was able to make Orthodoxy and "the Romanian soul" better known in the world. He is the Romanian theologian who published the most books and studies abroad, who delivered the most conferences outside the country, and who attended the most international ecumenical meetings, including the General Assemblies of the WCC: Nairobi (1975), Vancouver (1983), Canberra (1991) and Harare (1998).

Father Bria campaigned against the tendency to define Orthodoxy by comparison (more often the Orthodox can tell you what they are not than what they are), always stressing that Orthodoxy has its own identity. At the same time he emphasized the specificity of Romanian Orthodoxy and insisted on its distinctiveness from the *pan-Hellenic* and *pan-Slavic* trends, which consciously or unconsciously acquired importance in Romania. For Father Bria, Orthodoxy is for everyone, but its genius lies in how it grafts onto the stem of various peoples, becoming a constituent part of their being and history; it is therefore unacceptable that Orthodoxy should be exclusively circumscribed to a certain people.

Before Father Ion Bria came in Sibiu[1] in 1995 as associate professor, he had written a very valuable handbook entitled: *Tratat de Teologie Dogmatică şi Ecumenică*[2] (*Treatise of Dogmatic and Ecumenical Theology*). Since this book has not yet been translated into English, we will make some references to the second part which deals with the ecumenical themes.

Father Ion Bria emphasizes that Ecumenical Theology was termed *Symbolic Theology* in the past, a term officially derived from the *symbols of faith* confessed by different Christian denominations. But this comparative representation was far from being free from digressions and ambiguities. For example, denominations were sometimes presented and analyzed rather by way of contrast, one opposing another or to others, with considerable emphasis on highlighting differences, Orthodoxy being placed between Catholicism and Protestantism as an intermediary dogmatic entity. For this reason, ecumenical conversations brought up a "reciprocal ecclesiological ignorance," not only as a mutual incomplete representation, but also as a lack of moral reciprocal commitment.

What is the status and meaning of Ecumenical Theology today when an increasing number of schools of theology have introduced *Ecumenism* as a theological subject? How can its function (as orientation, programme and reforms) be determined within the internal relationship between dogmatic theology, missiology and ecclesiology? What critical role has Ecumenical Theology in relation to the outcomes of theological, bilateral and ecumenical dialogues in which the Orthodox Churches are involved?

The scope and the principles of ecumenical theology according to Fr. Ioan Bria's ecumenical vision

Ecumenical Theology does not have clearly defined borders as a theological field of study; its field of study is still provisional. Here are some principles of ecumenical theology:

1) The point of reference for ecumenical theology is dogmatic theology as taught at the Faculty of Theology. Christian dogmatic theology has been preserved by the Orthodox Tradition but it is not therefore a denominational or confessional theology reduced to the simple expression of a "Confession of Faith". Dogmatic theology studies Christian theology *per se*, for all. Faculties of Theology in public universities are not institutions of Orthodox higher education and for this reason its graduates are theologians in a general sense, not only specialists in Orthodox theology.

2) Ecumenical theology presents other denominations, Churches or particular theological traditions in an integral manner, so that their "confessionalism" should be understood not simplistically, but in its entire complexity (using various expressions, including symbols of faith, catechisms, worship, specialised literature and confessional texts). The aim is to penetrate deeply into the specific tradition of that denomination in order to reveal the so-called *vesitigia Ecclesiae*, that is, its specific doctrine and mission within the universal Church and to seize its *ethos*, its way of relating to a historical identity, particular and universal at the same time.

3) The current view of other Churches and Christian denominations is nowadays influenced by the outcomes of ecumenical dialogues, which are either bilateral or multilateral. For this reason considerable importance

---

[1] In 2009 at the Faculty of Theology in Sibiu was organized an international conference dedicated to the late Father Ion Bria (1929-2002) with the theme: *The Relevance of Reverend Professor Ion Bria's work for contemporary society and for the life of the Church. New Directions in the Research of Church Doctrine, Mission, and Unity*; see the volume of the conference on www.ecum.ro/infoecum/file/doc_ecum/lucrari_simpozion_Ion_Bria.pdf (Last accessed May, 2013)

[2] Published in Sibiu, 1996, in Bucharest, 1999 and in Sibiu, 2009

Part III: Representative Orthodox Theologians reflecting on Ecumenism

should be given to the documents and convergences achieved through such dialogues, for example the document *Baptism, Eucharist, Ministry* of the World Council of the Churches (1982).

4) Ecumenical Theology closely examines what is being done within the global ecumenical movement as well as within local ecumenism, aiming to motivate theologically the common Christian witness and above all the mutual recognition of baptism and the practice of Eucharistic communion.

5) Theological education and the ecumenical formation of students and future priests are inextricable. This double expertise, theological and ecumenical, is absolutely necessary today when priests are confronted with all types of movements, groups and missions which, instead of uniting Christians, divides them.

Basic ecumenical premises of Bria's *Treatise of Ecumenical Theology*

Consequently, Father Bria advances additional objectives in his *Treatise of Ecumenical Theology*:

Descriptively: to present briefly the characteristics of the Church *Una Sancta* as ecclesial reality (doctrinal, sacramental, institutional) tangible in the Orthodox Church. The Orthodox Church is not monolithic, but it avoided, in its historical evolution and organization, internal ruptures and incoherencies: heresies, schisms, sects, thereby preserving the universal insight of the community from Pentecost in Jerusalem, even though it spread through the *oecumenia*.

Methodologically: to make structural comparisons among Christian denominations, having as a unifying point of reference the theological and practical convergences (also called agreements or declarations of faith), arising from bilateral or multilateral ecumenical dialogues. In this view, traditions may appear united and separate, dispersed and convergent at the same time. Some tensions can be reconverted and integrated into a reliable and coherent communion.

Hermeneutically: to discern, in the layout of denominations what represents legitimate confessional identity and what is inflexible confessionalism, the extent to which the principles and theological doctrines displayed in confessional texts form "common rationales" which foster mutual recognition, reconciliation and visible unity. What are the ecumenical drawbacks in the confessional approach which must be retrieved or questioned?

Ecumenical: to observe how the ecumenical movement evolves in relation to the contemporary history of the Churches, religions, and human society in general. What is the *metanoia* (conversion) of the Churches at the end of the millennium? Spiritual reconciliation? Structural change? Or the apology of the truth of Christianity? What are the qualities of today's Christianity and its place in the struggle for global reconciliation, solving ethnical conflicts which arose after the end of the Cold War in Europe? The history of the Churches, united or separate, is not simply a confessional phenomenon but a social, cultural and political phenomenon.

Regarding the *"comparative display"* of confessions, which is the object of Ecumenical Theology, two series of questions can be tackled:

1) *On the one hand*: how are the history and doctrine of Christian denominations in today's ecumenical theology presented, either in the specialized fields of study at the faculties and theological institutes, or in the textbooks and published studies? What are the criteria used to classify them and what type of vocabulary is used to describe their doctrine and spirituality, either in relation to Orthodoxy or in today's ecumenical context? Where do the Protestant Reform of the 16th century and the modern ecumenical movement fall within the universal history of the Church?

2) *On the other hand:* what new theological elements for the assessment of Christian denominations have been outlined by the bilateral and ecumenical dialogues, by the attempts and negotiations for unity, by the reality of local and regional structures? Where do agreement texts or ecumenical convergences fall in the studies of Symbolic Theology, in catechesis and in religious publications? What image does Catholicism demonstrate after the lifting of the *anathema* between Rome and Constantinople, after Vatican II? What profile does Protestantism have in the light of the ecumenical movement and bilateral dialogues with Orthodoxy? What new

ecclesiological significance has this *"fellowship of churches"*, the World Council of Churches, where Orthodoxy is not only represented but also participates? To what extent does the fact that the Roman-Catholic Church is not part of this *fellowship* limit the possibilities of the Orthodox people to understand Catholicism from a wider perspective? What chances are there for a history of confessions to be written from an ecumenical perspective?

Some Churches, including the Orthodox Churches, have published "Ecumenical Guidelines", guidelines concerning Christians' ecumenical behaviour, mainly in the field of hospitality and Eucharist communion. These guidelines, though representing theological convictions, are not formally addressed to schools of theology and to those who teach Symbolic Theology and ecumenism under various forms.

On the Pan-Orthodox level, official documents orientating systematic and ecumenical theology have not been issued thus far. The theme "Orthodoxy's Interrelationship with other Christian Churches and with the Ecumenical Movement" is on the agenda of the long-awaited Pan-Orthodox Council. Intending to facilitate the Council's study of this theme, the Orthodox Centre in Chambesy organized a seminar on theological matters between 27 April and 20 May 1985. The documents from this seminar were sent for reflection to the Third Preparatory Pan-Orthodox Conference, which also dealt with the topic of "Orthodoxy and the Ecumenical Movement".

The Roman Catholic "Decree on Ecumenism" is of dogmatic relevance. Following Vatican II, Catholicism uses a series of concentric circles to place the non-Roman Catholic denominations in relation to the centre, which is the Roman Church. There are sister Churches, Churches and ecclesiastic communities which are situated around this centre, some close, some farther away. For this reason the Council developed a theological concept of high ecumenical value, namely the hierarchy of truths, stating that not all the doctrines of the Roman Catholic Church have the same compulsory dogmatic authority, without any order, to rebuild Christian visible unity.

After this important introduction, Father Ion Bria gives a useful survey of the confessional configuration of today's Christianity, followed by "The place of Orthodoxy in the ecumenical community". When we refer to the Orthodox Church or to Orthodoxy, we refer to the local Orthodox Churches which confess the same apostolic teaching, use the Byzantine rite, are autonomous and autocephalous, having their own synods, without canonical dependence on another local Church.

Orthodoxy does not consider itself as one among many Christian denominations and does not identify its doctrine with a historical confessional text. From Saint Ignatius of Antioch, it preserved the idea that the *catholicity* of the Church is offered by the Orthodox character of the norm of faith. The Church is "catholic" if she confesses the true Orthodox doctrine, in conformity with the apostolic rule; Orthodoxy implies the theological sense of *catholicity*.

The next chapter is dedicated to the history of the ecumenical movement, but it also contains important statements such as: "The ecumenical movement is comprehensive and indivisible". There is only "one" ecumenical movement open to all the Churches, and no Church can claim to be the centre of this movement, which is larger than any particular Church and which includes all the Churches. It is not a federation of non-Roman Churches, but an inclusive communion; that is why the Roman Catholic Church is not excluded. The World Council of Churches must not be identified with the ecumenical movement. Even if the World Council should include all the Churches, the ecumenical movement would always be something inclusive. The World Council of Churches is a fruit, a tool of the ecumenical movement, an attempt to express more visibly and more structurally the fellowship discovered by the Churches in the ecumenical movement. But the ecumenical movement extends beyond the World Council of Churches. Of course, this does not mean that belonging to the World Council of Churches is of no importance. On the contrary, being admitted to the Council is a decisive step for every Church as it means entering into a "conciliar community" or a "conciliar process".

Concerning the Orthodox Church and the ecumenical movement, Father Bria underlines that in the period 1948 to 1980, the Orthodox elaborated ecclesiological criteria and principles of positive collaboration with the World Council of Churches. The main point is that the ecumenical issue is not the unity of the Church *per se*, which is God's gift and is preserved in a historic and visible way in the Orthodox Church – *Una Sancta*

Part III: Representative Orthodox Theologians reflecting on Ecumenism

- but the historical divisions between the Christians. The schism does not lie within the Church, but in the separation of the Christian confessions from the undivided Church, which directly continues the apostolic and patristic Tradition.

The restoration of the visible unity of the Church is not a question of ecclesial centralism, nor of uniformity or confessional plurality, but of integration and synthesis of common faith, of unity in diversity and in communion. There is an organic relationship between the unity of faith and the Eucharistic communion and the task of ecumenism is to rediscover the "Eucharistic basis" of the visible unity.

Unfortunately, after the Canberra General Assembly in 1991, the relationship between the Orthodox Churches and the WCC saw a critical phase. However, some of the main problems were resolved after the Harare General Assembly as a result of the work of the Special Commission established to deal with WCC-Orthodox relations.

In the message of the Primates of the Orthodox Churches (1992) we can read:

"Moved by the spirit of reconciliation, the Orthodox Church has participated actively for many decades in the effort towards the restoration of *Christian unity*, which constitutes the express and inviolable command of the Lord (John 17:21). The participation of the Orthodox Church as a whole in the *World Council of Churches* aims precisely at this. It is for this reason that she does not approve of any tendency to undermine this initial aim for the sake of other interests and expediencies. For the same reason the Orthodox strongly disapprove of certain recent developments within the ecumenical context, such as the ordination of women to the priesthood and the use of inclusive language in reference to God, which creates serious obstacles to the restoration of unity."[3]

The Primates of the Orthodox Churches refer to the same problematic issue in their Patmos message (1995), noting that the recent crisis and deviations in the ecumenical movement force the Orthodox Churches to oppose these deviations and promote the authentic tradition of the Church. Some of these deviations are identified as the ordination of women, inclusive language with reference to God, the acceptance of homosexuality and lesbianism as moral sexual orientations.[4]

In that context, two Orthodox Churches withdrew from the WCC: the Church of Georgia in 1997 and the Church of Bulgaria in 1998. Because of these tensions, it was decided at Harare to establish a special commission to deal with the issues raised by the Orthodox. The final report of the Special Commission on Orthodox Participation in the WCC was published [5] and it seems that some of the problems have been solved.

Father Bria identifies also seven ecclesiological theses with ecumenical implications: the concept of visible, historical unity; *vestigia ecclesiae* (tangible signs of apostolicity and catholicity preserved in a variety of forms and structures); the "boundaries" of the Church (some Orthodox theologians refer to the "charismatic boundaries" of the Church); *oikonomia* as an ecumenical typology; the reception of theological convergences which arise from ecumenical dialogues; uniatism; and the use of the Byzantine rite.

According to Father Bria, the principles[6] of the Orthodox ecclesiology are that:

The Church is one and only one; she is a historical entity (see the Nairobi Assembly);

The Church is an eschatological entity and the Orthodox must always remind others about the eschatological perspective of the Church;

The Church is a relational entity; the Church is where the Holy Spirit is and where the Spirit binds together the past and present, a present open to the future. Orthodox are also involved in the ecumenical movement to remind all about the importance of Tradition and its creative reception at the same time. The ecumenical movement must perceive the mystery of the Church from the point of view of a permanent reception.

---

[3] "Message of the Primates of the Most Holy Orthodox Churches", in Gennadios Limouris ed., *Orthodox Visions of Ecumenism. Statements, Messages and Reports on the Ecumenical Movement*: 1902-1992, (Geneva: WCC Publications, 1992), 197.
[4] See the developments in the Episcopalian Church (USA) of recent times.
[5] *The Ecumenical Review*, 55.1 (January 2003): 4-38.
[6] They are presented concisely here.

The Church is a sacramental entity. This is another question on which the Orthodox contribution to the ecumenical movement should concentrate. It could be the most difficult aspect, because it must have as a prerequisite Eucharistic communion, which Orthodox Churches refuse to non-Orthodox. Engaging this issue involves broad range of issues, but what is crucial is that Eucharistic communion must not cease to be the goal (the Orthodox will say "the ultimate goal") of the ecumenical movement. The importance of keeping this issue central lies in the fact that by it, the WCC preserves its non-secular nature, which otherwise would be lost. The document on *Baptism, Eucharist, Ministry* (BEM) is a good start and it reveals a great potential for future progress. With this document, the Protestant Churches truly moved on to sacramental theology, specifically Eucharistic theology and this is a significant step. The question that the Orthodox will have to answer soon, if this sacramental concept continues to influence the problematic of the ecumenical movement, is this: to what extent does the recognition of Baptism require the recognition of ecclesiology?

Conclusion

As Father Ion Bria always emphasized, it is very important to be aware of all the changes and challenges present in our world, the new global village; to be aware of the need to renew the understandings of education theories; to reach an authentic culture of dialogue in teaching - as expressed in the New Testament, where Christ engaged in dialogue with different persons and the salvation started from their own great problems; to be aware that it is wrong to separate theology from spirituality, the witness in the world from *martyria*, from martyrdom; to be aware of the holistic[7] character of theological education and ministerial formation "which is grounded in worship, and combines and inter-relates spirituality, academic excellence, mission and evangelism, justice and peace, pastoral sensitivity and competence and the formation of character. For it brings together education of:

> the ear to hear God's word and cry of God's people;
> the heart to heed and respond to the suffering;
> the tongue to speak to both the weary and the arrogant;
> the hands to work with the lowly;
> the mind to reflect on the good news of the Gospel;
> the will to respond to God's call;
> the spirit to wait on God in prayer, to struggle and wrestle with God, to be
> silent in penitence and humility and to intercede for the Church and the world;
> the body to be the temple of the Holy Spirit".[8]

Bibliography

Gennadios Limouris ed., *Orthodox Visions of Ecumenism. Statements, Messages and Reports on the Ecumenical Movement*:1902-1992 , (Geneva: WCC Publications, 1992).

Ioan Bria *Romania. Orthodox Identity at a Crossroads of Europe*, (Geneva: WCC Publications, 1995).

---

[7] The term "mission" also carries a "holistic understanding: the proclamation and sharing of the good news of the gospel by word (*kerygma*), deed (*diakonia*), prayer and worship (*leiturgia*) and the everyday witness of the Christian life (*martyria*); teaching as building up and strengthening people in their relationship with God and each other; and healing as wholeness and reconciliation into *koinonia* - communion with God, communion with people, and communion with creation as a whole" - fragment from the document "Mission and Evangelism in Unity Today," in *"You are the Light of the World" Statements on Mission by the World Council of Churches 1980-2005*, (Geneva: WCC Publications, 2005), 63.

[8] John S. Pobee (ed.), *Towards Viable Theological Education: Ecumenical Imperative,Catalyst of Renewal*, (Geneva: WCC Publications, 1997), 1.

The Liturgy after the Liturgy. Mission and witness from an Orthodox Perspective, (Geneva: WCC Publications, 1996).

"La Théologie Orthodoxie aujourd'hui en Roumanie. La Theologie dans l'Église et dans le Monde", in *Les Études Theologiques de Chambesy* 4 (1984): 167-175.

"Reflections on Mission Theology and Methodology", in *International Review of Mission*, 73.289 (1984): 66-72.

"L'Orthodoxie et le Mouvement Oecumenique. Contribution orthodoxe au domaine de la mission", in *Études Theologiques*, no. 6, Éditions du Centre Orthodoxe de Chambesy, 1986, 201-215.

(29) Fr. Sergius Bulgakov

Brandon Gallaher

Sergius Nicolaevich Bulgakov (1871-1944), one of the leading Orthodox theologians of the twentieth century, was actively involved in the ecumenical movement from shortly after his coming to the West in 1923 until ill health caused his premature retirement from this work in 1939. His ecumenical theology reflects a rich and challenging vision of engagement with other Christians. While Bulgakov grounds his ecumenism on Orthodoxy's claim to be the Church of Christ on earth, he forswears all triumphalism. Many of his ideas on Church unity were formative in the modern Orthodox vision of ecumenism. Other Orthodox theologians both formulated their theologies in reaction to his thought and tacitly borrowed his ideas.[1]

Sergius Bulgakov was born in Livny (Orel province) in Russia on 16 June 1871 to a family from the Russian clerical caste.[2] Like many intellectuals of his generation, Bulgakov left the Church after a religious crisis forced him to leave junior seminary abruptly. In the late 1880s and the 1890s, he studied law, economics, philology, philosophy and literature in Moscow and then pursued graduate work in political economy in Moscow and in Germany, while teaching part-time at the Moscow Technical School. In these years he was a convinced Marxist and atheist. However, after a series of religious experiences that he later saw as visions of 'Sophia' or 'Holy Wisdom', he became more and more disenchanted with Marxism as a system and as a quasi-religion. He subsequently taught political economy in Kiev (1901-6), immersed himself in philosophical idealism and was particularly influenced by Feodor Dostoyevsky and the sophiology of Vladimir Solov'ev (1853-1900). In this period, he was gradually moving closer to Orthodoxy. This took the form, for example, of his involvement in Christian socialist politics - he served as a deputy in the Second Duma (1907). By 1906, now professor of economy at Moscow's Commercial Institute and lecturer at the University of Moscow (eventually becoming professor there), Bulgakov completely rejected Marxism, which he saw as a twisted pseudo-religion. His return home to Orthodoxy and the Church was consummated in the autumn of 1908 at a remote northern skete. There, after having met the starets of the community, who received him back into the Church like the prodigal son, he sealed his conversion with participation in the Eucharist.

In the years to come his involvement with the Church became more intense. His writings from about 1917 onwards were almost entirely theological. He served as a lay delegate to the All-Russian Church Council of 1917-1918 and in June 1918, by the blessing of Patriarch Tikhon (Bellavin) of Moscow (1865-1925), Bulgakov was ordained to the priesthood. The combination of this ordination and his well-known opposition to Bolshevism eventually led Bulgakov into exile in December 1922 along with many other intellectuals whom the Bolsheviks expelled from the new U.S.S.R. He spent three years in Prague lecturing on canon law at the Russian law institute at Charles University. In 1925, Metropolitan Evlogii (Georgievskii) (1868-1946), the Russian bishop responsible for the Russian Orthodox Church in Western Europe, invited Bulgakov to become the professor of dogmatic theology at the new Saint Sergius Orthodox Theological Institute in Paris.

Bulgakov's literary output was huge. He wrote on everything from systematic theology (several dogmatic treatises, often grouped under two 'trilogies'), iconography and Biblical commentary to political philosophy, history, sociology and law, critiques of German Idealism (which he saw as a series of forms of Trinitarian heresy) and philosophy of language. Many of these works, especially his second systematic trilogy, are centred on the

---

[1] See Paul Gavrilyuk, *Georges Florovsky and the Russian Religious Renaissance* (Oxford: Oxford University Press, forthcoming 2014) and Brandon Gallaher, 'The 'Sophiological' Origins of Vladimir Lossky's Apophaticism', *Scottish Journal of Theology*, 66.3 (July 2013): 278-298.

[2] See Gallaher, 'Bulgakov's Ecumenical Thought', *Sobornost* 24.1 (2002): 24-55 and 'Bulgakov and intercommunion', *Sobornost* 24.2 (2002): 9-28.

highly controversial notion of 'sophiology' or theology of Holy Wisdom (actively opposed by both Georges Florovsky and Vladimir Lossky). Bulgakov continued to teach at the Saint Sergius Institute, serving both as professor of dogmatic theology and as dean, until his death from cancer on 12 July 1944.

Bulgakov's ecumenical involvement was deep and wide. It was motivated by his apocalyptic belief that, following the rise of 'Satanic' Bolshevism, humanity was in the last times and that the Anti-Christ could only be defeated by the sacramental reunion of the Churches led by the Russian Orthodox Church - he echoes here the finale of Solove'v's 'Tale of the Anti-Christ.' His initial introduction to ecumenism was through has participation in the first congress of the Russian Christian Student Movement (RCSM), held in Pšerov, Czechoslovakia from 1-7 October 1923. The RCSM was established to bring together Russian Christian youth, initially in Russia then in the emigration, both Orthodox and also Protestants, in order to encourage them in community, a wholistic Christian vision and to counter Bolshevism. Each day of the conference was opened with a liturgy served by Bulgakov. There was also a strong eschatological sense in the participants who saw themselves as members of a post-Constantinian Church dedicated to the 'churching' of all of life and (for the Orthodox) the mission of witnessing to Orthodoxy in the West. Both the Eucharist and a strong sense of an eschatological call for reunion of the Churches became the hallmarks of Bulgakov's ecumenism. This conference was financed by the Young Men's Christian Association (YMCA) and the World Student Christian Federation (WSCF) and it lead Bulgakov to subsequent fruitful collaboration with John Mott (1865-1955), the Secretary General of the YMCA, and Paul B. Anderson (1894-1985), a secretary of the YMCA assigned to work with Russian refugees in Europe.

Bulgakov subsequently attended the early conferences of Faith and Order (Lausanne, 1927, and Edinburgh, 1937) and Life and Work (Oxford, 1937), movements that paved the way for the foundation of the World Council of Churches (WCC). He was one of the most important Orthodox representatives at these meetings and other ecumenical gatherings until he was obliged to cease his ecumenical involvement for health reasons in the spring of 1939. At the Lausanne and Edinburgh conferences, Bulgakov challenged the Protestant majority by advocating the veneration of the Virgin Mary as the Mother of God, Theotokos. He held that Mary was the mystical head of humanity in the Church, the Bride of the Lamb. He encouraged the conference delegates to name Mary in prayer because her veneration was crucial for the reunion of the Churches since she is at the heart of the very unity of the Church as the Body of Christ.

Bulgakov's contacts with Anglicanism were particularly important for his developing ecumenical theology. He participated in the First Anglo-Russian Congress at St Albans from 11 to 15 January, 1927, where he presented an important paper, 'The Church and Non-Orthodoxy'.[3] The ideas contained in this paper underlay Georges Florovsky's now classic essay, 'The Limits of the Church.'[4] Through an analysis of the Patristic canonical literature, Bulgakov contends that the sacraments of the non-Orthodox can be understood as 'of the Church', so that one cannot argue that the spiritual and canonical limits of the Orthodox Church coincide and that there is only darkness outside of Orthodoxy.[5] The following year, at the Second Anglo-Russian Congress (28 December 1927 to 2 January 1928), Bulgakov was one of the founders of Fellowship of St. Alban and St. Sergius, a key ecumenical organization initially dedicated to Orthodox-Anglican (and now Eastern-Western Christian) relations and one of the most important international forums for Orthodox ecumenical involvement. Bulgakov was elected vice-president of the Fellowship and attended all of its meetings until 1939.

---

[3] See 'Fr. Sergius Bulgakov's *Outlines of the Teaching About the Church: Address given at the Orthodox & Anglo-Catholic Conference', found at* <http://www.sobornost.org/Archives_Bulgakov-Outlines-of-the-Teaching-about-the-Church_Dec1926-Jan1927.pdf> (Last accessed: 20 July 2013).

[4] Georges Florovsky, 'The Limits of the Church', *Church Quarterly Review* 117.233 (1933): 117-131. Recollected in *The Patristic Witness of Georges Florovsky: Essential Theological Writings*, eds. Brandon Gallaher and Paul Ladouceur (forthcoming T & T Clark-Bloomsbury, 2014).

[5] Published here: 'Ocherki ucheniia o tserkvi. (III) Tserkov' i "Inoslavie', *Put'* 4 (1926): 3-26 ('Outlines of the Teaching about the Church—The Church and Non-Orthodoxy', *American Church Monthly* 30.6 (1931): 411-423 and 31.1 (1932): 13-26 (abridged).

From the beginning the celebration on alternate mornings of the Eucharist according to the Anglican or the Orthodox rites and alternate evenings of Orthodox Vespers or Anglican Evensong structured the conference itself. In was in the context of the participation of Orthodox and Anglicans in each other's liturgy (without sacramental communion) that Bulgakov advanced a proposal for partial intercommunion between the Anglicans and the Orthodox. He first proposed partial intercommunion between the Anglican and Orthodox members of the Fellowship in June 1933. The Anglican and Orthodox members had already, he claimed, achieved 'a substantial dogmatic agreement with one another [...] more complete than that which exists within the Anglican Church itself'[6] and therefore 'spiritual intercommunion' already existed in shared worship (the 'sacrament of prayer')[7] and similar liturgical forms in the service developed for the Fellowship and the Molèben. In light of these commonalities, the Fellowship, Bulgakov argued, needed to move from the realm of ideas to concrete realization through creative catholic action. Here he was trying to formalize in sacramental terms the then widespread opinion that the Orthodox and Anglican Churches were one in doctrine, worship and polity (many Orthodox Churches then acknowledging the validity of Anglican orders) and should therefore formally re-establish communion. Moreover, at that time there existed an extensive 'economic' intercommunion between the two Churches: in cases of extremity, Orthodox and Anglican laity were often blessed by their bishops to partake of one another's sacraments.

In the Fellowship conferences of 1934 and 1935, Bulgakov refined what was an initially vague intuition. He situated his proposals within a sacramental and canonical nexus. His basic idea was for a mutual episcopal 'sacramental blessing' of Orthodox and Anglican Fellowship members, both ordained and lay, to partake of communion at one another's altars at Fellowship conferences; this would serve as a sort of seed leading to the eventual complete unity of the two Churches.[8] In the case of the Orthodox, the blessing or sacramental sanction would come from Met. Evlogii of the Russian exarchate under Constantinople and Evlogii would ask for a corresponding blessing from the Patriarch of Constantinople. In the case of the Anglicans, the appropriate blessing would come from the diocesan bishop or from the Archbishop of Canterbury. Anglican and Orthodox bishops alike would confer the blessing on the Fellowship priest of the other Church so that the blessing would be fully mutual. Orthodox bishops would bless Anglican priests to communicate at the Orthodox liturgy, to concelebrate with Russian priests if they so desired and to communicate Orthodox and Anglican laity in the Fellowship who wish to participate in these celebrations. Likewise, in an analogous fashion, which Bulgakov left to the Anglicans to determine, the Anglican bishop would bless the Orthodox priest to participate in intercommunion with Anglican clergy and laity. The particular sacramental blessing of Anglican laity to participate in intercommunion at Orthodox altars could take either the form of a blessing by a bishop but, more preferably, the form of Chrismation with the invocation of the Trinity by a priest. This latter rite is of course the standard Russian way of receiving converts to Orthodoxy, though Bulgakov was using it to acknowledge the tacit Orthodox ecclesial status of these Christians. The final version of Bulgakov's proposals was ultimately rejected in June 1935 by the Fellowship council (with particularly strong opposition by Florovsky)[9] before, however, it could be discussed in open session at the conference.

---

[6] 'General Report of the Fellowship Conference, June 1933', *Journal of the Fellowship of St Alban and St Sergius* [=*JFAS*], 20 (1933): 12-16 at 12.

[7] Nicholas Zernov and Evgeny Lampert, 'The Fellowship and the Anglican-Orthodox Intercommunion', *Sobornost* 21 (May 1940): 9-15 at 11.

[8] See 'Partial Intercommunion'. ('Notes and Comments by Fr. S. Bulgakov for Advisory Committee and Fellowship Exec.).' Dated '3.V.1935', *FASOxon* in white envelope with writing 'to Deacon Stephen Platt', Summarized at A. F. Dobbie-Bateman, 'Footnotes (IX)--*In quos fines saeculorum*', *Sobornost'*, 30 (December 1944): pp.6-8 at 7-8 (To be published as an appendix to my article, 'Great and full of Grace': Partial Intercommunion and Sophiology in Sergii Bulgakov' in *Festschrift for Michael Plekon* (Rollinsford, NH: Orthodox Research Institute. 2013), 69-121.

[9] See Brandon Gallaher, '"Waiting for the Barbarians": Identity and Polemicism in the Neo-Patristic Synthesis of Georges Florovsky', *Modern Theology* 27.4 (October 2011): 659-691 and Paul Ladouceur, '"Aimons-nous les uns les autres': Serge Bulgakov et Georges Florovsky', *Contacts* 237 (Janvier-Mars 2012): 56-87.

Part III: Representative Orthodox Theologians reflecting on Ecumenism

The theology that lay behind Bulgakov's proposals was focused on the Eucharist and on presenting an 'icon' of Orthodoxy to the West. Indeed, the Orthodox were called, Bulgakov argued, in the ecumenical movement to witness perpetually to non-Orthodox concerning the uniqueness of the Orthodox Church as the One, Holy, Catholic and Apostolic Church, which bears within herself the fullness of the faith. The Orthodox Church *is* the Church itself and Bulgakov rejected the so-called 'branch theory' of the Church (according to which each distinct Church is a 'branch' of the Church of Christ).[10] The Church, for Bulgakov, is a divine-human organism which is a spiritual reality incarnated in the world: visible and invisible, institutional and historical as well as spiritual and eternal. The invisible universal Church, *Una Sancta,* Orthodoxy as such, is, Bulgakov argued, like the ancient Jewish temple composed of two circles and all baptized Christians belong to her and are in a sense Orthodox insofar as they are Christian. In the inner circle, the holy of holies, is the visible empirical Church which coincides with the canonical family of Churches known as Eastern Orthodoxy, but in the larger circle, the court of the temple, are the other Christian confessions. These groups have to a lesser or greater degree 'a grain of Orthodoxy' insofar as they are related to the 'Orthodox' centre of the temple with its fullness of divine-human life but all Churches are alike ecclesial, tacitly Orthodox.[11]

Bulgakov's emphasis on ecumenism as a form of witness to the truth of Orthodoxy became (ironically under the influence of his sometime opponent Florovsky who was influenced by him) the fundamental theology for Orthodox involvement in the ecumenical movement. However, Bulgakov's version of this now standard position is not triumphalistic. He argues that the Orthodox need to learn from their non-Orthodox Christian brothers and sisters and become convicted and changed by these encounters. He sees Christian reunion in Orthodoxy not as a "Byzantinisation" of the non-Orthodox but the entry of the non-Orthodox more deeply into their specific identity as Anglican, Lutheran, Roman Catholic etc. in entering into communion with the Church. Furthermore, in arguing against the majority of Orthodox in favour of intercommunion as a means to unity of the Churches, Bulgakov suggested that the means of reunion or reintegration of non-Orthodox into the Orthodox Church is not through complete theological agreement as worked out in detail by appointed committees of theologians from two Churches and approved by their respective hierarchs in a reunion council (e.g. Ferrara-Florence (1438-1445)). Rather, reunion, if it comes, will emerge through a gradual 'molecular' process that begins in common worship that presupposed a basic or essential union in faith. The example of St. Basil with the semi-Arians was often utilized in this context.[12] Thus sacramental reunion with the Anglicans was based on a "living minimum" of dogma (i.e. the central dogmas of the faith including Christology and Trinitarian theology) grounded in the Eucharist.[13] This position was in contrast to an abstract maximalism[14] that simply asserted the particular Eastern Orthodox teaching of the moment without attention to its age or context, and an abstract minimalism that appealed to the lowest common theological denominator.[15] Thus the 'living minimum' of dogma on which the entry into communion would be based was simply Orthodoxy.[16] Bulgakov's proposed episcopal 'sacramental blessing' for Intercommunion was therefore in the service of a gradual reuniting or reintegration of non-Orthodox Churches with Orthodoxy through acknowledging that the non-Orthodox were already in some sense Orthodox and tacit members of the Orthodox Church.

[10] See Bulgakov, *The Bride of the Lamb* (Edinburgh/Grand Rapids, Mich.: T & T Clark/Eerdmans, 2002), 310 [*Nevesta Agntsa* (Paris: YMCA Press, 1945), 337] and 'The Church and Non-Orthodoxy' (1931), 419 ['Tserkov' i "Inoslavie"', 10].

[11] Bulgakov, *The Orthodox Church* (Crestwood, NY: St. Vladimir's Seminary Press, [1932] 1988), 188 [*Pravoslavie: Ocherki ucheniia Pravoslavnoi Tserkvi* (Kiev: Lybid, 1991), 228].

[12] See Anton Kartashev, 'The Paths Towards the Reunion of the Churches', *JFAS* 26 (1934): 7-13 at 11 (This and other related articles are recollected in Michael Plekon, ed., *Tradition Alive: On the Church and the Christian Life in Our Time- -Readings from the Eastern Church* (Lanham, MD: Rowman and Littlefield Pub. Inc., 2003)).

[13] Bulgakov, 'Ways to Church Reunion', *Sobornost* 2 (1935): 7-15 at 8.

[14] Ibid., 7-9, 12-13.

[15] *The Orthodox Church*, 188 [ibid., 228].

[16] Ibid., 188-189 [ibid., 228-229] and see Kartashev 'Intercommunion and Dogmatic Agreement', *Sobornost* 4 (1935): 41-48 at 43 and 46.

Christian sacraments, even if defective as in the case of the non-Orthodox, are 'a call to universality'[17] being *of* the empirical Church, insofar as they are celebrated in it, but are *from* the invisible Church above. Echoing Augustine, Bulgakov contends that non-Orthodox sacraments from baptism to ordination are, to a greater or lesser degree, depending on the nature of the schism, merely ineffective in schism although most certainly not non-existent. In short, the Church exists outside of its own walls: *ecclesia extra muros*.[18] What Bulgakov was doing in proposing limited intercommunion between Anglican and Orthodox was acknowledging that the baptism, orders *and* the Eucharist of the Anglicans, while sacramentally defective, were basically Orthodox realities which regained their true force in communion with the Orthodox Church. Communion was both thus the means *and* the end or crown of reunion.

Bulgakov's ecumenical theology has not lost its power to inspire as well as to challenge. In its day, it mostly challenged, both Orthodox and non-Orthodox, and therefore the essential Orthodoxy of his basic ecumenical position was lost to his contemporaries. He held that in Orthodoxy's engagement with other Christians it must with all humility and love both witness to itself as the true Church, insofar as it embodies the fullness of the Catholic faith, and call those Christians to return to sacramental union with her.

Bibliography

Sergius Bulgakov was an extremely prolific author over a long career, writing on theology, philosophy, economics, law, history and the social sciences. Many of his later theological writings are now available in translations in English, French, German and Italian. For a detailed bibliography of his work see Kliment Naumov, *Bibliographie Des Œuvres de Serge Boulgakov* (Paris: Institut D'Études Slaves, 1984). The Bibliography below lists only his most relevant writings relevant to ecumenism available in English.

Collections:

Father Sergius Bulgakov 1871-1944. A Collection of articles by Fr. Bulgakov for the Fellowship of St. Alban and St. Sergius (London: Fellowship of St. Alban and St. Sergius, 1969).

Tradition Alive: On the Church and the Christian Life in Our Time--Readings from the Eastern Church, Michael Plekon, ed. (Lanham, MD: Rowman and Littlefield Pub. Inc., 2003), 51-80.

Individual works:

'By Jacob's Well—John iv. 23 (On the Actual Unity of the Divided Church in Faith, Prayer and Sacraments)', *Journal of the Fellowship of St Alban and St Sergius* [=*JFAS*], 22 (December 1933): 7-17 recollected in *Father Sergius Bulgakov 1871-1944*, 1-11 and *Tradition Alive*, 55-66.

'The Church's Ministry' [1927] in *Faith and Order: Proceedings of the World Conference—Lausanne, August 3-21, 1927,* ed. H. N. Bate (Garden City, NY: Doubleday, Doran & Co., Inc., 1928), 258-263.

Churchly Joy: Orthodox Devotions for the Church Year, trans. Boris Jakim (Grand Rapids, Mich./Cambridge: Eerdmans, 2008 [1938]).

'The Church Universal', *Journal of the Fellowship of St Alban and St Sergius*, 25 (September 1934), 10-15 recollected in *Father Sergius Bulgakov 1871-1944*, 16-21.

'Does Orthodoxy Possess An Outward Authority of Dogmatic Infallibility?', *The Christian East*, 7.1 (April 1926), 12-24.

'The Hierarchy and the Sacraments' in *The Ministry and the Sacraments: Report of the Theological Commission Appointed by the Continuation Committee of the Faith and Order Movement* (London: Student Christian Movement Press, 1937), 95-123.

'"One Holy, Catholic And Apostolic Church"', *JFAS* 12 (1931): 17-31.

The Orthodox Church [1932] (Crestwood, NY: St. Vladimir's Seminary Press, 1988).

---

[17] Bulgakov, 'The Church Universal', *JFAS* 25 (1934): 10-15 at 11.

[18] 'The Church and Non-Orthodoxy' (1931), 310-314 ['Tserkov' i "Inoslavie"', 337-341].

Part III: Representative Orthodox Theologians reflecting on Ecumenism

'Outlines of the Teaching about the Church--The Church and Non-Orthodoxy', *American Church Monthly,* 30.6 (1931): 411-423 and 31.1 (1932): 13-26.

'The Papal Encyclical and the Lausanne Conference', *The Christian East*, 9.3 (1928): 116-127.

'The Question of the Veneration of the Virgin Mary at the Edinburgh Conference', *Sobornost'*, 12 (1937): 28-31.

'Spiritual Intercommunion', *Sobornost'* 4 (1935): 3-7; recollected in *Father Sergius Bulgakov 1871-1944*, 29-32.

The Vatican Dogma (South Canaan, PA.: St Tikhon's Press, 1959).

'Ways to Church Reunion', *Sobornost,* 2 (June 1935): 7-15; recollected in *Father Sergius Bulgakov 1871-1944*, 22-28.

Fr. Ioustinos-Ioannis Kefalouros

Since the division of the One Church of Christ, the ecumenical dialogue has been a key concern of various Christian denominations. Through bilateral dialogues and organizations such as the World Council of Churches and the Council of European Churches, Christians have used ecumenical discussion and debate to find ways of concurrence and cooperation in topics relating to common concerns. Starting with the common faith in Jesus Christ and the Bible, the ecumenical movement is an attempt to mitigate theological differences, ultimately aiming at Christian unity.

Ever since mid-19th century, the first Christian moves to the dialogue between the Christian Churches started making their appearance. It is obvious that communication was not easy after so many centuries of silence. The contribution of individuals played an important role, as it always happens at moments in history. At this critical historic juncture, it would be a delinquency not to mention the names of two great religious personalities : the Ecumenical Patriarch Athenagoras A from the East and Pope Paul VI from the West, who were rightfully called "Peacemakers". Additionally, there were all those around them, lay theologians and clergy, who contributed to the ecumenical dialogue in order to become a reality today and not just a keen desire.

1. Olivier Clément and Orthodox Christian Thought

Olivier Clément was one of those who lived near the golden era of the Ecumenical Movement, and he succeeded through his writings to highlight aspects of Orthodox theology, embracing modern humanity who seeks answers to key existential issues, whether belonging to the West or the East. His book *Dialogues Avec Le Patriarche Athenagoras* was a benchmark in the ecumenical movement, as it managed to convey – both in Europe and the Western world - the vision and the agony of Patriarch Athenagoras for the unity of Christian Churches and the requirement of the times for a common course.

Olivier Clément was born on 17 November 1921 at Aniane (Languedoc), France, a region with a tragic religious history. Surrounded by anti-Christian peasants and teachers, Olivier Clément was not driven to baptism, nor did he receive any religious education. "I had never entered a Church, nor had it ever crossed my mind", he confesses.[1]

After a long quest in various forms of atheism and Asian spirituality, he discovers Christ, largely thanks to the study of Fyodor Dostoyevski, Nikolas Berdiaev and Vladimir Lossky. At the age of thirty he was baptized Christian and embraced Orthodoxy in the Orthodox francophone parish of the Patriarch of Moscow in Paris, but later moved to Constantinople's Russian Exarchate at St. Sergius Orthodox Theological Institute.

He conducted studies in History and postgraduate studies on the subject: "Pierre le Vénérable, abbé de Cluny". He was a student of Alphonse Dupront, one of the founders of Christian anthropology, who worked during the Resistance over the last war years. He taught in Paris for some time, at Lycée Louis-le-Grand.

After his conversion to Orthodoxy, he attended theology courses organized by the Patriarchate of Moscow, under Professors Vladimir Lossky, Leonid Ouspensky and Fr. Sofronios, spiritual disciple of St. Silouan. After the untimely death of Lossky, he published several of his hand-written works. He taught Christian ethics and church history at the Institute of St. Sergius in Paris, as well as the Catholic Institute of the same city, as part of the Higher Institute of Ecumenical Studies.

---

[1] Olivier Clément : *Ce temps qui appele l'Église* (Maistros Publications : Athens 2004), 8 (in Greek).

He was director to the Descleé de Brouwer publishing house of the Orthodox series "Théopanie" and editor of the Orthodox journal *Contacts* and also a doctor of Theology of St. Sergius Institute in Paris, as well as professor emeritus at the Theological Institute in Bucharest and the Catholic University of Louvain (Belgium).

During the Soviet regime, he fought with the poet Pierre-Emmanuel for the Christians of Russia. He was president of the faithful writers, Christians, Jews and Muslims (1976-1994). He collaborated in the Galimard, Universalis and l'Histoire de la sainteté encyclopedia series. Olivier Clément died in Paris on 15 January 2009 at the age of 87.

2. Olivier Clément's contribution to the Ecumenical Movement

There is no doubt that Olivier Clément was one of the greatest Orthodox theologians and thinkers of the 20th century. Raised in the West he was knowledgeable of Western culture and able through his personal contact with the Orthodox Tradition and Theology, to channel unknown aspects of Orthodox spirituality into Western environments. His writings, in terms of the Ecumenical Movement, provide a broader approach for the perspective of Orthodox Theology, which is now perceived as the common ground on which the East and the West can commune. For Clément, the encounter between Orthodoxy and the Western world, the spirit of novelty and non-Christian religions was a point of reference. Man, freedom, rebellion of the spirit, outrivaling nihilism, the relationship between Islam and Christianity, the cosmic universe, are just some of the topics addressed to in his texts.

Clément stands in a formidable line of Orthodox theologians whose ministries in the West developed through writing, teaching and pastoral care. Their return to patristic sources and Eucharistic renewal opened them to the work of the Spirit in the church and in the world, a work they embraced with passion and courage. Clément inherited their dynamic and creative intellectual achievements and became a witness to the openness and hope of the Christian message for all men and women. He became part of the re-articulation of the patristic renewal and ressourcement, which enriched Christian Churches during the twentieth century and fostered a real and new ecumenism between Christians. The theologian émigrés to the West had a renewed sense of confidence and joy in their Orthodox faith, which humanly speaking could have been crushed by contemporary nihilism, ignorance, and Western suspicion of the Eastern Church; the sense of liberty and mysticism characteristic of Orthodoxy enabled Clément to break free from a culture of death.[2]

Clément shared their vision that theology necessarily is linked to spirituality; he worked to make Orthodox theology more widely known and to establish unity between West and East at the highest ecclesial levels, a unity that must come from within and not be imposed by ecclesial authority or power. Deeply moved by John Paul II's invitation to write *Via Crusis*, he responded positively and saw it as an opening between the churches. Neither did he neglect to listen to and serve the needs of ordinary men and women, young and old, in their quest for truth. He offered an ecclesial vision, firmly rooted in the tradition of the Churches, yet open and full of hope for humanity. His *corpus* of writings was wide-ranging; even after his retirement he continued to exert a great deal of influence on Orthodox thinkers in the West and to engage with students.

It is true that we will not find Clément in leadership positions of the several Ecumenical Movement Commissions. This was not because he was incapable. Rather, he has his own aversion to this kind of conformism. Therefore, if we would like to trace out Olivier Clément's Ecumenical profile, we should mostly focus on his writing and essays, which are imbued by the belief that the alternative suggestion of Orthodoxy towards any kind of materialism is the transcendence of death through the mystery of Resurrection. He is so focused on the mystery of the Cross and the Resurrection that one feels nothing can actually exist and live within the Church without this dipole of the course from Crucifixion to Resurrection. "The Resurrection, the miracle of

---

[2] Stefanie Hugh-Donovan, "Olivier Clément on Orthodox theological thought and ecclesiology in the West", *International Journal for the Study of the Christian Church* 10.2-3, (2010): 125.

miracles, gives meaning to history just like it does to global attraction", as he writes shortly after the passing of Patriarch Athenagoras.[3]

For Olivier Clément it is indispensable that modern man experiences Resurrection through the mystery of Holy Eucharist, not in an idealistic or verbal manner but fully in the Church where the Body of Christ is the fundamental place, where the truth, which is life, reveals itself, offers itself and becomes our own flesh and blood.[4] Olivier Clément becomes ecumenical just because he manages, in his own unique way, by talking and writing about an Orthodox Christianity to go beyond the surface of an Orthodoxy which is trapped in external shapes of a static Tradition, and enters the sheer entity, the heart of this Faith that renounces death, because the whole of the Church must endlessly attest: Christ is risen and there is no such thing as nil[5].

Orthodoxy affirmed for Clément that Christianity opens men and women in the Holy Spirit, to an infinite experience, that the true masters of history are men and women of prayer, the Church is a mystery of the Transfiguration: only the light and the life that radiates from the Resurrected One can give sense to the modern exploration of the cosmos and of man himself.

Writing in 2002, Clément confirms his assessment of the situation of the Church in the world: there is no longer a place today for a church that dominates. Christians can no longer impose, only propose humbly and with generosity. In a world that is saturated with media, words and consumerism, the person of prayer offers something which cannot be bought and sold: a joy and compassion that radiates out to others. The Christian presence must essentially be a witness to the life that is lived in Christ; it is the face of the person that radiates this truth and light.[6] Clément has devoted his Christian life and corpus of work to a 'renewed understanding of the human person in the light of our relationship to God' and a life-long quest not only to encourage further unity between Eastern and Western Christians but with all cultures and peoples.

Why did Clément's encounter with Christ lead to Orthodoxy and not Catholicism, the national ecclesial denomination of France? He found the neo-Scholasticism of contemporary Catholic theology 'dry', the Catholic exclusiveness of the 'perfect society' prior to Vatican II, too closed. Clément's choice of the Orthodox Church points us to the origins, ecclesiology and fruitful creativity of the theologians of the Russian diaspora, to which he was introduced as a young teacher in Paris. A characteristic of émigré theology was the notion of *sobornost*, defined as freedom, unity and conciliarity. It carries the meaning that church life is 'collaborative and yet hierarchical', building up the Body of Christ. Clément notes that, for Christians of the first centuries, there was no ecclesiology *per se* but affirms that the Church was above all the Body of Christ. 'It is the Eucharist that makes the Church the Body of Christ. The Eucharist is the "mystery of mysteries."[7]

3. Epilogue

Clément grew up in a predominantly non-ecclesial, 'de-Christianized' area of France in which he received no parental education. This left a significant gap in his familiarity and understanding of Catholicism. This seemed to influence some of his reflection and understanding of the Catholic Church before and after the Second Vatican Council. Clément found the Orthodox tradition of Christianity in adulthood. The religious history of the Laguedoc area of his birth continued to exert a strong influence on the twentieth-century culture in the area of Clément' s upbringing, and therefore influenced his subsequent choices. He highlights this fact in his writing. His life was already marked by the earlier world and context, but he emerged as a person in communion, a

---

[3] Olivier Clément, "Athenagoras A", *Episkepsis* 58 (1972): 25-28.

[4] Olivier Clément, *Ce temps qui appele l'Église*, (Athens: Maistros Publications, 2004), 20 (in Greek).

[5] Olivier Clément , *Ce temps qui appele l'Église*, (Athens: Maistros Publications, 2004), 32 (in Greek).

[6] Clément, Petite boussole spirituele, 122.

[7] Stefanie Hugh-Donovan, "Olivier Clément on Orthodox theological thought and ecclesiology in the West", *International Journal for the Study of the Christian Church* 10.2-3 (2010): 119-120.

Part III: Representative Orthodox Theologians reflecting on Ecumenism

Christian beacon of ecumenical desire. As his theological vision he distanced himself from Vladimir Lossky's critiques of the Catholic tradition and the West, which he considered over time as partial.

He responded to John Paul II's request in 1995 for ecumenical discussion with his book *Rome Autrement*, an Orthodox theological reflection on papal primacy. Clément favored the conciliar structure of Orthodoxy but criticized Orthodox nationalist models. He spoke out against intolerance and his views were not always well received by some parts of the Russian Orthodox Church, although his theological writings are read by significant sections of a Russian Orthodox intelligentsia, particularly that which emerged in the Russian post-Soviet era.

From his European upbringing and atheist family background he developed distinctive insights and intuitions into the identity crisis experienced by those who lived in the culture of Western nihilism that pervaded intellectual and political life. Atheism, which Clément judged to be crafted by a Christian theological atomism, became a major preoccupation in his analysis of contemporary life; religion must not become a collection of abstract concepts. His profound and sympathetic understanding of Western society and politics formed an important aspect of his identity, significant in his emergence as an Eastern Orthodox thinker; his original theological contribution to modern Orthodox thought and dialogue between Eastern and Western Christians was made from within and as part of Western Tradition.

Bibliography

Olivier Clément, *Roots of Christian Mysticism: Texts from Patristic Era with Commentary Jean-Claude Barreau*, (London: New City Press, 1995).

-, *You Are Peter: An Orthodox Reflection on the Exercise of Papal Primacy*, (New City Press: London 2003)

-, *Taize: A Meaning to Life*, (Chicago: GIA , 1997).

-, *Three Prayers: The Lord's Prayer, O Heavenly King, the Prayer of Saint*, (Crestwood, NY: St. Vladimir's Seminary Press, 2000).

-, *On Human Being: A spiritual anthropology (Theology and Faith)*, (London: New City Press, 2000).

-, *Dialogues Avec Le Patriarche Athenagoras*, (Paris, Fayard, 1969).

-, *Le Chemin de Croix à Rome, Desclée de Brouwer*, (Paris: 1998).

-, *The Church of Orthodoxy (Religions of Humanity)*, (New York: Chelsea House Publications, 2002).

-, *Conversations With Ecumenical Patriarch Bartholomew I*, (New York: St. Vladimir's Seminary Press, 1997).

-, *Berdiaev, un philosophe russe en France*, (Paris: Desclee de Brouwer, 1991).

-, *The Spirit of Solzhenitsyn*, (Barnes & Noble Books , New York 1976).

-, *Ce temps qui appele l'Église*, (Athens: Maistros Publishers, 2004) (in Greek).

Matthew Baker/Seraphim Danckaert

Father Georges Florovsky (1893-1979) was the leading architect of Orthodox ecumenism in the twentieth century. He combined magnanimity towards non-Orthodox with faithful adherence to patristic Orthodoxy, exhibiting the courage to present his views without reserve in all forums, both Orthodox and non-Orthodox. Florovsky maintained lasting ecumenical commitments, but warned against any ecumenical endeavour that would settle for doctrinal minimalism or privilege common action over theological engagement.

Ecumenical Career

Florovsky's ecumenical involvement began in 1926 in the discussion group founded by Nicholas Berdyaev in Paris. This gathering brought together leading Orthodox, Roman Catholic and Protestant thinkers. Soon after, Florovsky joined the Fellowship of St. Alban and St. Sergius, founded to promote unity among Orthodox and Anglicans. His first public theological reflections were offered in these contexts. Ordained in 1932, Florovsky frequently lectured in Great Britain, where he was enthusiastically received.

These activities expanded with the 1937 Edinburgh Conference on Faith and Order, where Florovsky was elected as Orthodox representative to the "Committee of Fourteen" charged with drafting the constitution of the future World Council of Churches (WCC). At the founding Assembly of the WCC in Amsterdam (1948), he played a critical role, leading to his appointment to the Central Committee and election to the Executive Committee of the WCC, on which he served until 1961. He remained a principled and fearless Orthodox voice in ecumenical meetings into his final decade, his last major event being the meeting of the Faith and Order Commission in Louvain in 1971.

Philosophy

Florovsky's ecumenism has deep roots in his historical philosophy. Eschewing both raw empiricism and the direct intuitionism of idealists, Florovsky stresses not only the interpreted character of facts, but also the contingent, synthetic character of the categories by which experience is interpreted: what appears retrospectively as "fact" or a closed, necessary determination of thought was once prospectively open—the action of a free subject. Following the economic "singularism" of Peter Struve, Florovsky considers the acting person to be the subject of history, refusing to grant any fixed hypostatic character to race, nation, or civilization. The historical "whole" is an ever-shifting nexus of interacting persons-in-relation. True solidarity exists in Christ, in whom alone freedom coincides with "organic" oneness—an eschatological unity, transcending natural realities, and built up historically through faith and sacrament. Already by the mid-1920s, while insisting on the seriousness of schism and conflicting doctrines of salvation, Florovsky emphasized that faith in Christ still binds together Christian East and West.

This early anti-determinist philosophy informs Florovsky's later strenuous resistance to all attempts to explain Christian divisions by reference to psychological-cultural "types"—whether to magnify or to relativise divisions (as distinct from Lev Karsavin, Leon Zander, Vladimir Lossky and John Romanides). Any suggestion of historical inevitability of schisms, following the retrospective tendency to posit necessary causal links between events, is to be rejected. Christian communities are composed of free persons; the history of doctrine must not be thought to follow patterns of logical deduction or organic evolution. Precisely in this light, however, we cannot act as if events had never happened: though they might have been avoided or overcome, historic conflicts gave birth to doctrines subsequently determinative for particular traditions. Yet a changed historical perspective, Florovsky held, might also reveal a wider acceptable consensus.

Ecumenical Theology

In Florovsky's account, the main ecumenical problem is the "paradox" of schism. The Church is one—the Christian world lies in division. Faith in Jesus as God and Saviour creates a real *ontological* bond. Yet the divisions are no less ontological—marking separations, not only in love and creed, but the very experience of faith. In the phrase "separated brethren," the adjective weighs as heavily as the noun. True ecumenism demands a "theology of the abnormal."

This "paradox" is expressed acutely in the distinction between the Church's canonical and charismatic borders. Contrary to what some have claimed, Florovsky reiterated the views expressed in his 1933 article, "The Limits of the Church,"[1] many times throughout his multi-decade career, with no sign of changes in his position. Florovsky rejects the over-rigorist tendency amongst some Orthodox to deny categorically the existence of sacraments beyond canonical boundaries. He regards the "economic" interpretation concerning reception of heterodox as a doubtful theological opinion, not the teaching of the Church. Where Eastern Christians often appeal simply to canons, Florovsky credits Western theologians for raising the question in a properly theological light, and calls on Orthodox theologians to appropriate Augustine's theology of sacraments in schism. While the simplicity and clarity of Saint Cyprian's theory ("There is no salvation outside the Church") have a certain intellectual appeal, Augustine's more nuanced *theologoumenon* makes the most theological sense of the Church's historic practice. This does not mean, however, that canonical boundaries can be ignored. Intercommunion without full unity in faith is impossible. We are thus left with a sharp "antimony"—a scandal whose bitterness should inspire Christians to undertake the search for full doctrinal agreement.

Concretely, the greatest ecumenical problem in Florovsky's view concerns Rome. In contrast with the views of Vladimir Lossky, Florovsky views the *filioque* largely as a canonical matter and rejects as unhistorical the attempt to deduce "papism" by some necessary logic from the *filioque*; theologically, a synthesis of Cappadocian and Augustinian triadology is not, in his view, impossible. The primary divider is the papal claims, reflecting a false doctrine of Church unity. Yet Florovsky is clear: the Spirit of God still breathes in the Roman Church; the holy sacrifice is still offered. In contrast, he discerns in the communities issued from the Reformation, a departure from priesthood and historic Church order.

While Florovsky constantly strove to direct the ecumenical conversation towards ecclesiology, he underscores nonetheless that existing divisions concern the whole of faith, involving doctrines of God, Christ, Mary, man and—not least—the understanding of history implied in these doctrines. Florovsky observes a certain "hyper-historicism" in Roman Christological consciousness—as if the Ascension marked Christ's exit from history, leaving his "deputy" behind to govern. In Protestantism, conversely, Florovsky detects a "hyper-eschatological" reduction of history: human striving is undervalued; sacraments become nearly Old Testament signs; the Church's historic visibility is not fully recognized. The Reformation divorce of "Jerusalem" from "Athens" marks yet another departure. It was in defending Christian metaphysics against the perceived fideism of early dialectical theologians that Florovsky introduced his call for return to the "Christianized Hellenism" of the Fathers of both East and West.[2]

---

[1] *Church Quarterly Review* 117.233 (1933): 117–131.
[2] See for example his call at the 1936 meeting of Orthodox theologians in Athens in Hamilcar S. Alivisatos: *Procès–verbaux du premier Congrès de théologie orthodoxe à Athènes, 29 novembre – 6 décembre 1936* (Athens: Pyrsos, 1939), 238–242, and reprinted in *Diaconia* 4.3 (1969): 227–232.

Florovsky regarded the recovery of patristic theology as ecumenically crucial. It is in this light that his 1937 masterwork, *Puti Russkogo Bogoslovija* [The Ways of Russian Theology]—a book meant for Russian readers, which Florovsky intended to revise for translation—must be understood. His sharp critique of Westernizing "pseudomorphosis" was aimed, not at the West *per se*, but at a Russian theology alienated from its own liturgical sources and unmoored from its roots in patristic theology, as well as a spirit of "servile imitation" that made real ecumenical confrontation impossible. Florovsky's alternative is *not* isolation, but "free encounter with the West", conducted on the common recovered ground of patristic and classical conciliar theology, which Orthodoxy claims as her own. It was this vision that accompanied his concepts of "neo-patristic synthesis" and "ecumenism in time" which, he stressed, were closely correlated.

"Ecumenism in time" searches the shared past of apostolic tradition, seeking recovery of a "common mind." Florovsky celebrated the decision of the Third World Conference of Faith and Order in Lund, Sweden, in 1952 to retire the confessional method of "comparative theology" in favour of a more historical approach. Florovsky's goal, however, is "ecumenical synthesis," rooted in the Fathers but responsive to questions surrounding present divisions. Such a synthesis presumes discrimination: not every belief can be reconciled. Agreement in truth requires conversion, response to a divine gift. The Orthodox uniquely remind all Christians of the faith of the "undivided Church." Culturally speaking, however, the East too is a "fragment" and must also enlarge its theological vision, avoiding exaggerating local particularities. Christian unity understood as "universal conversion to Orthodoxy" entails neither submission to the East nor rigid uniformity, but rather "agreement with all the ages" and "mutual acknowledgement in the truth."

The 1954 Evanston Assembly of the World Council of Churches marked the zenith of Florovsky's ecumenical activities. There, together with his friend Archbishop Michael Constantinides, primate of the Greek Orthodox Archdiocese of America, Florovsky led the Orthodox delegation in a serious challenge to the Protestant presuppositions of the Assembly, in the form of two separate Orthodox statements: on the main Assembly theme of Christian hope, and on the Faith and Order document regarding Christian disunity. While the first response was critical, the second repudiated outright the approach of the Faith and Order report towards Christian reunion as entirely unacceptable to the Orthodox Church. Only a complete return to the total faith and episcopal order of the Catholic and Apostolic Church of the Seven Ecumenical Councils can produce the desired unity. Nor should this unity be understood only eschatologically, for it exists as a continuous historical reality. Orthodox is bound to confess their conviction that the Church has preserved fully the apostolic faith. These points were further elaborated in the Orthodox statement at the 1957 Conference on Faith and Order (Oberlin, Ohio), which Florovsky also authored, and which is still considered one of the best statements of Orthodox ecclesiological self-understanding in the ecumenical movement.

Criticism and Conflict

In Florovsky's view, the Amsterdam and Evanston Assemblies of the WCC were "high level," as serious theologians kept the focus on substantive issues. However, the WCC began going "downhill" afterwards due to proliferation of staff in the Life and Work Commission and a reduction in the Faith and Order Commission; the influence of authoritative theologians weakened. In 1971 Florovsky stated: "The result was decisions made by men who are ignorant of dogma and ignorant of Church history, tradition, Christian culture. Hence they feel that what we need to do is find what we have in common, then forget the rest, not realizing that "the rest" is what makes up the individuality of the traditions and denominations, and one does not simply forget them for the sake of unity, since it is a superficial, unreal, and certainly not a lasting unity. When there is ignorance of this sort it means that in dialogue, which I am entirely in favour of, these individuals do not represent Protestantism, or Orthodoxy, or Rome at all, but rather their own stupidities."[3]

---

[3] Verbal comment recorded by Florovsky's secretary, Masha Vorobiova, August 8, 1971, Andrew Blane archive.

Part III: Representative Orthodox Theologians reflecting on Ecumenism

Such changes dovetailed with shifts in Orthodox leadership. The 1958 death of Archbishop Michael was, in Florovsky's words, "a great blow."[4] There were strong disagreements between Florovsky and Michael's successor, Archbishop Iakovos Koukouzis (1911-2005), who served as WCC co-president from 1959 to 1968. From the start, Iakovos insisted there be no separate Orthodox statements as there had been at Evanston. Representing the Ecumenical Patriarchate at the Third WCC Assembly in Delhi in 1961, Florovsky flouted this directive, leading forty Orthodox representatives together with Bishop Athenagoras Kokkinakis in a statement reiterating the Orthodox ecclesiological terms of involvement. Absent from the delegation, Iakovos issued his own communiqué that there was no Orthodox statement; the "Florovsky statement," however, had already been published. A similar, but less publicized conflict occurred at the Fourth World Conference on Faith and Order in Montreal in 1963, occasioned by Iakovos' support of a referendum ascribing ecclesial status to the WCC—in contradiction to the 1950 "Toronto Statement" of the WCC Central Committee, which Florovsky had been instrumental in getting passed.

Tensions between Florovsky and WCC secretary Willem Visser't Hooft also came to a head in a conflict at the 1959 Pan-Orthodox Conference in Rhodes, the details of which were never made public. Florovsky strongly supported official dialogue with the Roman Catholic Church, but objected to the insistence of Visser't Hooft and Iakovos that Protestants be included: he felt that the WCC, threatened by an Orthodox-Rome alliance, was attempting to control the dialogue. Florovsky followed Vatican II with positive interest, noting a return to ancient tradition and more conciliar structures. The Jerusalem meeting of Patriarch Athenagoras and Pope Paul VI in 1964 was a hopeful sign, but required more careful "molecular" theological work: the "dialogue of love" must be joined with the dialogue of truth. Without sound doctrinal foundations, outward signs of reconciliation, such as the lifting of the 1054 anathemas, would prove illusory and only alienate the faithful.

In Florovsky's view, problems were caused in the WCC by inattention to doctrine, as well as by the increasing influence of political agendas. The secularizing trend in theology also signalled a crisis of faith. The Fourth WCC Assembly in Uppsala in 1968 was hardly an ecumenical event: there was little interest in the Church, no Christian note; the event resembled a UN meeting, the focus turned to race and war. This political turn, Florovsky held, was driven not only by pragmatism but also impatience with theological dialogue, making the problems of the ecumenical movement "perhaps insoluble."

Conclusion

For all his strictures, Florovsky remained committed to ecumenism to the end of his life. In interviews of his last decade, he defended continued Orthodox participation in the WCC, noting the influence of Orthodox participants in turning the conversation to ecclesiology and introducing patristic studies into the Faith and Order Commission. Orthodox responsibility to the Christian world makes ecumenical witness imperative. And Orthodox have also learned from other Christians. Ecumenical encounter reawakened Orthodox theologians to neglected elements of their own tradition, challenging them to renew or clarify Orthodox teaching, especially on the Church. In this regard, ecumenism had encouraged greater seriousness about theology in general. Looking forward, Florovsky held out hope for serious theological work, particularly in light of the increased ecumenical involvement of Roman Catholics.

All the same, Florovsky remarked repeatedly that he expected no spectacular new developments in the near future. Just as he had done since the 1930s, he stressed that the chief ecumenical virtue is patience. One must carry "the Cross of patience," avoiding over-hastiness. The work is urgent; the victory rests with the Lord.

Archbishop Basil Krivocheine once remarked that Florovsky showed the Orthodox that they could be ecumenical without betraying Orthodoxy. While he left much undone, and the situation has changed since his day,

---

[4] Maria Psareva, ed., "Переписка Протопресвитера Георгия Граббе с Протоиереями Георгием Флоровским и Александром Шмеманом", *Вестник Р.Х.Д.* № 189 (2005), 210-218, at 213.

Florovsky laid perennial foundations, which will guide generations to come. His example was marked by bold candour in speaking the truth, sympathetic willingness to learn from other Christians, absolute confidence in the universal vocation of Orthodoxy, and an ability to hold together polarities that many lesser spirits would pry apart. In his own words: "I am neither Eastern nor Western, but just abide by the perennial truth of the Christian message."[5]

Bibliography

The Collected Works of Georges Florovsky are not comprehensive or reliable; the volumes on ecumenism are especially poor. Recourse to the original articles is advised.

Primary
"The Limits of the Church," *Church Quarterly Review* 117:233 (1933), 117-31.
"Проблематика христианского воссоединения," *Путь* (Feb 1933), 1-15.
"Determinations and Distinctions: Ecumenical Aims and Doubts," *Sobornost* 4:3 (1948), 126-132.
"The Legacy and the Task of Orthodox Theology," *Anglican Theological Review* 31:2 (1949), 65-71.
"Une vue sur l'Assemblée d'Amsterdam," *Irénikon* 22:1 (1949), 4-25.
"Confessional Loyalty in the Ecumenical Movement," *Student World* 53:1 (1950), 59–70.
"The Eastern Orthodox Church and the Ecumenical Movement," *Theology Today* 7:1 (1950), 68-79.
"The Ethos of the Orthodox Church," *Ecumenical Review* 12:2 (1960), 183-198.
"The Problem of Ecumenical Encounter," in E. J. B. Fry and A. H. Armstrong, eds., *Re-Discovering Eastern Christendom* (London: Darton, Longman & Todd, 1963), 63-76.
"Знамение Пререкаемо," *Вестник Русского Студенческого Христианского Движения*, 72-73:1-2 (1964): 1-7.
"Interview with Georges Florovsky," *Concern* 3:4 (Fall 1968): 9-12, 27.

Secondary
Matthew Baker, "Neopatristic Synthesis and Ecumenism: Towards the 'Reintegration' of Christian Tradition," in Andrii Krawchuk and Thomas Bremer, eds., *Eastern Orthodox Encounters of Identity and Otherness* (Palgrave-MacMillan, 2013, forthcoming).
Andrew Blane, ed., *Georges Florovsky: Russian Intellectual – Orthodox Churchman* (Yonkers NY: St Vladimir's Seminary Press.,1993).

---

[5] Unpublished talk, "The Vision of Unity," in Georges Florovsky Papers, Carton 3, Folder 1955; Department of Rare Books and Special Collections, Princeton University Library.

Part III: Representative Orthodox Theologians reflecting on Ecumenism

(32) METROPOLITAN GERMANOS OF THYATIRA

Grigorios Liantas

A) Biographical note

The Metropolitan of Thyateira Germanos Strinopoulos[1] was born in 1872 in the village of Delliones in Eastern Thrace (Greece). He studied philosophy and theology at the Theological School of Halki and the Universities of Leipzig, Strasbourg and Lausanne. In 1903 he received a doctorate from the University of Leipzig. He was professor and School Principal of the Theological School of Halki until 1922. In 1912 he was elected Metropolitan of Seleucia, and in 1922, during the tenure of Patriarch Meletius the IV, (Metaxakis), he was elected Metropolitan of Thyateira, based in London.

In 1939 he was one of three fellow candidates at the election of the Patriarch of Alexandria. Metropolitan Thyateira Germanos, apart from teaching in Halki and his tenure at the Metropolis of Thyateira, worked intensively in the field of inter-Orthodox and inter-Christian relations and also as a prolific writer.[2]

B) Contribution to the promotion of ecumenical and inter-Christian relations

The contribution of Metropolitan Germanos in the inter-Christian relations has been of great importance. He effectively promoted relationship between Orthodox and Anglicans and Orthodox and Old Catholics in the decade 1920-1930.[3]

He motivated and embodied the path toward the right direction of the relationship with other Christian Churches and the ecumenical movement, which the Ecumenical Patriarchate followed at the time.

The name of the Germanos Strinopoulos is closely related to the history of the ecumenical movement, at least on the part of the Orthodox participation and cooperation. Indeed, he is placed among the pioneers of this movement and among the most senior of the Ecumenist figures.[4] He joined the ecumenical movement in 1920, through the faculty club of Halki, acquiring an active role and participation in the drafting of the "Synodical Encyclical Letter of the Church of Constantinople to the Worldwide Churches of Christ (1920)," and he participated in all the global inter-Christian conferences which contributed to the founding of the World Council of Churches (WCC). He has been a member of the Committee of Fourteen, which paved the way for the merging of the movements "Faith and Order" and "Life and Work" into the World Council of Churches.[5]

During the same period, Germanos actively participated in the Movement as a representative of the Ecumenical Patriarchate and President of the Orthodox delegations.

What is striking, however, is that the Church of Constantinople, which, at the beginning of the century, especially with 1920 Encyclical Letter, played the leading part in the whole affair of Christian Unity, in the World Conferences "Faith and Order" and "Life and Work", which took place between 1925 and 1937, did not send any official representative, coming directly from the Phanar. In all these conferences, the Ecumenical Patriarchate was represented by officials who ministered in the diaspora, led by the Metropolitan of Thyateira Germanos.[6]

---

[1] George Tsetsis, *The contribution of Ecumenical Patriarchate in the foundation of WCC* (Katerini: Tertios, 1988), 277-278 (in Greek).

[2] Vasilios Stavridis, *The Holy Theological School of Halki* (Kyriakidis: Thessaloniki, 1988), 130 (in Greek).

[3] Ibid., 131-132.

[4] Ibid.

[5] George Tsetsis, *The contribution*, op. cit. 277-278.

[6] Ibid, 122.

C) Participation in ecumenical meetings and consultations

Metropolitan Germanos attended the Faith and Order conferences in Geneva (1920), Lausanne (1927) and Edinburgh (1937); the Life and Work conferences in Geneva (1920), Stockholm (1925) and Oxford (1937); the conferences of the World Federation of International Friendship through the Churches in the beginning of the WCC from 1938 onwards and the First General Assembly of the WCC in Amsterdam (1948), where he was elected as one of the six presidents of the Council[7].

D) Theological contribution

In Metropolitan of Thyateira Germanos, the Patriarchate had an excellent spokesman of the ecclesiastical tradition of Phanar, but also the most appropriate interlocutor on ecumenical issues, as he himself was the one who had a leading role in drafting the 1920 Encyclical Letter and was a preeminent expert on the issue of the union of Churches.

Metropolitan of Thyateira Germanos, because of his many pursuits, never issued independent major writings. He left, nevertheless, many valuable treatises, over 100, in journals and collected volumes referring to Anglican society, the ecumenical movement and inter-Christian relations.[8]

For his contribution and his work he was honored with the title of Doctor of Theology from the universities of Oxford, New York and Athens. The WCC dedicated a private hall in his honor at the ecumenical center of Geneva.[9]

E) Conclusions

Metropolitan of Thyateira Germanos,[10] a representative of the Ecumenical Patriarchate at the ecumenical meetings and consultations which convened between 1920 and 1938 and resulted in the foundation of the WCC, played a leading role in the Ecumenical Movement. Therefore he is rightly regarded as one of its eminent pioneers. His constant concern was to provide the Orthodox witness to the various phases of the ecumenical developments, as well as to be vigilant that the WCC will be shaped on the spirit and principles expressed by the 1920 Encyclical Letter.

Bibliography

1. John Karmiris, *The Dogmatic and Symbolic Monuments of the Orthodox Catholic Church*, volumes I-II, (Graz, 1968)
2. Basilios Stavridis, *The Holy Theological School of Halki*, (Thessaloniki: Kyriakidis, 1988) (in Greek)
3. Basilios Stavridis, *Bibliography of the Ecumenical Movement 1960 - 1970* (Athens: 1972) (in Greek)
4. Basilios Stavridis – Evagelia Varella *History of the Ecumenical Movement*, (Patriarchal Foundation for Patristic Studies: Thessaloniki, 1996) (in Greek)
5. George Tsetsis, *Ecumenical Annals*, (Tertios: Katerini, 1987) (in Greek)
6. George Tsetsis, *The contribution of the Ecumenical Patriarchate in the foundation of the WCC*, (Tertios: Katerini, 1988) (in Greek)

---

[7] Vasilios Stavridis, *The Holy Theological School*... op. cit., 132.

[8] Ibid.

[9] Ibid.

[10] George Tsetsis, *The contribution*, op. cit., 195.

Part III: Representative Orthodox Theologians reflecting on Ecumenism

7. George Tsetsis, "Ecumenical Patriarchate and the World Council of Churches", in *400 years Phanar*, (Ecumenical Patriarchate: Istanbul 2001), 543-574

8. Metropolitan of Thyateira Germanos, "Unitarian Movement, General Conference of Churches" *Ecclesiastical Truth* 41 (1921): 235-236

9. Ad. Keller, "Germanos Strenopoulos", *Welt Kirchen Lexicon*, 477-478

10. *Anglican Commemoration of the Twentieth Anniversary of Archbishop Germanos Arrival in London* (London, 1943)

11. Metropolitan Germanos of Thyateira, "Methods of Cooperation and Federative Efforts Among the Churches (1925)", *The Orthodox Church in the Ecumenical Movement*, (Patelos, ed.), (Geneva: WCC, 1978), 127-131

12. Metropolitan Germanos of Thyateira, "The Call to Unity (1927)", *The Orthodox Church in the Ecumenical Movement*, (Patelos, ed.), (Geneva: WCC, 1978), 132-136.

(translated by Fr. George Anagnostoulis)

(33) Archbishop Iakovos of North and South America

Grigorios Liantas

Biographical note

Archbishop Iakovos[1] was born as Dimitrios Koukouzis in 1911 at Saint Theodore (on Imvros island, Turkey). He graduated from the Holy Theological School of Halki in July 1934 and in November of the same year he was ordained deacon, taking the name Iakovos. He continued his studies at Harvard University.

He served the "Great Church of Christ" of Constantinople in various positions and on 17 December 1954, upon the recommendation of the Ecumenical Patriarch Athenagoras to the Holy and Sacred Synod of the Ecumenical Patriarchate, he was elected Metropolitan of Melitis and was appointed as the first permanent representative of the Ecumenical Patriarchate to the World Council of Churches (WCC).[2]

According to the pioneer of the Ecumenical Movement and the first General Secretary of the WCC (1948-1966) W. Visser 't Hooft, "the Patriarch's decision in 1955 to appoint a permanent representative of the Ecumenical Patriarchate at the headquarters of the WCC and the placement of Iakovos, a warm friend of the Ecumenical Movement, as first representative, had a profound effect on relations of the WCC with Orthodoxy".[3]

Indeed, Iakovos of Melitis soon imposed himself in Geneva as a first-class ecclesiastical figure. Visser't Hooft,[4] after a few months' acquaintance and cooperation with him, felt the need to write to the Patriarch Athenagoras, expressing his deep gratitude for his presence in Geneva as Representative of the Ecumenical Patriarchate. He claimed that Iakovos' close contacts with the members of staff led them to become better acquainted with the Orthodox Church.

B) Theological contribution

Iakovos of Melitis, consistent with the line of the Ecumenical Patriarchate and the Patriarch Athenagoras, has always presented a genuine Orthodox witness to the WCC, firmly believing that Orthodoxy, having a deep sense of its history and tradition, was called to play a central role in the effort to reconstruct the divided Christianity.[5]

Since he first took up his duties, he engaged in contacts and actions, which very soon made his presence in the Council dynamic, so as to seriously influence the General Secretariat and its executives commissions on their decisions. In addition he played an important role on issues that concerned the relations between the Orthodox and WCC, particularly the issue of the participation of all local Orthodox Churches as member-Churches therein.

His four-year presence at the WCC as Permanent Representative of the Ecumenical Patriarchate has been particularly important for the history of the Council during the first decade of its activities in the inter-Christian world, as a center of the Ecumenical Movement, as well as for the history of the Patriarchic Office in WCC.

It should be noted[6] that at the WCC, Metropolitan Iakovos soon managed to foster and develop himself into a valuable adviser thanks to his experience, his sound theological training and knowledge of the current eccle-

---

[1] George Bebis "Iakovos" *Religious and Ethical Encyclopedia* vol. 6 (Athens, 1965), 655 (in Greek).

[2] Ibid.

[3] Georges Tsetsis, *Ecumenical Annals* (Katerini: Tertios 1987), 134 (in Greek).

[4] Ibid, 139-140.

[5] Ibid, 140-141.

[6] George Tsetsis "Iakovos, Archbishop of America", *Enimerosis* 19.2 (2005): 11-12.

siastical and theological issues, his consistent treatment of sensitive situations and his administrative abilities. His close contacts with the members of the staff of WCC led to their familiarizing with the orthodox faith.

Being fully conscious of the Ecumenical Throne's peaceful stance and desire for cooperation, he struggled so that the witness of Orthodoxy and its tradition might be heard and received with respect.[7]

Archbishop Iakovos realized in time the responsibility of cooperating with the WCC in order to promote the ideal of Christian unity and was the forerunner in marking the difficult path of ecumenical contacts.

C) Participation in committees

Iakovos was a member of WCC delegations and was elected as one of the Presidents of the Council at the 1959 General Committee meeting.

It is worth noting that Iakovos in 1959 was received by Pope John XXIII at the Vatican.[8] He was the first Greek Orthodox bishop who visited the Primate of the Roman Catholic Church. For a long time, until 1959 there had been no official communication between the two Churches, neither correspondence and exchange of delegates, nor personal meetings between the Patriarchs and Popes of Rome. For this reason, 1959 should be considered as the year of the beginning of the new climate between the two Churches.[9]

Iakovos' mission to the Vatican was secret, but official. During his discussion with Pope John XXIII Archbishop Iakovos presented Patriarch Athenagoras' intention, his audacity, and the courage of his conviction to correct the Pope's view of restoring the Christian unity by the return of all to the Roman Catholic Church and the subjugation of all under the Pope's authority and primacy. Undoubtedly, Archbishop Iakovos had been cordially received by Pope John XXIII and the discussion between them took place in an honest and objective spirit.[10]

D) Conclusions

Iakovos' tenure at the WCC was not only regarded as the link between Phanar and Geneva, but also as the source that supplied the WCC with the richness of Orthodox theology and tradition during that time. During his ministry, he has been very active regarding the promotion of the Ecumenical Patriarchate and of the true ecumenical spirit of the Orthodox Church, thus becoming a worldwide recognized ecclesiastical figure. He represented the Ecumenical Patriarchate, as well as other Orthodox Patriarchates, at the WCC conferences and committees and successfully accomplished all the missions assigned to him. Rightly then, he is still considered as a leading authority on pan-Christian and ecumenical issues.[11]

Bibliography

1. Gregorios Larentzakis, "The right path towards the Christian cooperation and unity», http://www.amen.gr (last accessed 12/08/2012) (in Greek).
2. Grigorios Liantas, *Inter-Orthodox ministry of the Ecumenical Patriarchate and the Church of Greece and the contribution of the two Churches in the bilateral theological dialogues with the Roman Catholic Church and the Church of the Old Catholics*, (Thessaloniki: K. Sphakianakis, 2005) (in Greek)

---

[7] Ibid, 12

[8] Grigorios Larentzakis "The right path towards the Christian cooperation and unity" available at the website www.amen.gr (in Greek, last accessed 12-8-2012).

[9] Ibid.

[10] Ibid.

[11] George Bebis, op. cit. 656.

3. George Malouchos, *I, Iakovos*, (Athens: Livanis, 2002) (in Greek)

4. George Bebis, "Iakovos" , *Religious and Ethical Encyclopedia*, (Athens, 1965), v. 6, 655-657 (in Greek)

5. Basilios Stavridis – Evagelia Varella, *History of the Ecumenical Movement*, (Thessaloniki, 1996) (in Greek)

6. George Tsetsis, *Ecumenical Annals,* (Katerini: Tertios, 1987)

7. George Tsetsis, *The contribution of the Ecumenical Patriarchate in establishing the World Council of Churches*, (Katerini: Tertios, 1988) (in Greek)

8. George Tsetsis, "Archbishop of America Iakovos" *Enimerosis* 19.2 (2005): 10-15.

9. Iakovos of America "Towards New Delhi (The true nature of the WCC)" *Apostolos Andreas* 11 (1961): 523-525 (in Greek)

10. Vasilios Koukousas, *History of the Orthodox Church of America, based on the sources*, (Thessaloniki: Pournaras, 2010) (in Greek)

11. Visser't Hooft, WA, *The Genesis and Formation of the WCC*, (Geneva: WCC, 1982)

12. Iakovos of America, "Der beitrag der ostlichen Orthodoxie zur oekumenischen Bewegung", Lutherische Rundschau 2 (1959/1969): 166-177

13. Archbishop Iakovos Koukoujis, "The Contribution of Eastern Orthodoxy to the Ecumenical Movement (1959)", *The Orthodox Church in the Ecumenical Movement*, (Patelos, C., ed.), (Geneva: WCC, 1978), 209-219

14. T. Gazouleas, *And running across ... A pilgrimage of Iakovos of America to Greece*, (New York: Pilgrimage Publishing Incorporated, 1991).

(translated by Fr. George Anagnostoulis)

(34) METROPOLITAN GEORGES KHODR OF MOUNT LEBANON

Amal Dibo

Biographical note

Georges (Khodr) is the Metropolitan of the Archdiocese of Byblos and Botrys and Mount Lebanon in the Church of Antioch. He was born in Tripoli, Lebanon on 6 July 1923 and studied law at Saint Joseph University in Beirut where he graduated in 1944.

On 16 March 1942, he co-founded the Orthodox Youth Movement (known as MJO - Mouvement de la Jeunesse Orthodoxe) that invigorated spiritual life in Antioch and enhanced its contribution to the life of the Orthodox Church.

In 1952 Father Georges graduated from St. Sergius Orthodox Theological Institute in Paris with a diploma in theology, and, on 19 December 1954, he was ordained a priest and was assigned to the parish of Mina (the Port) of Tripoli in 1955. During these years, Father Georges was very active as a theologian, pastor, and spiritual father. He received three doctorates *Honoris Causa* in 1968 from St. Vladimir's Orthodox Seminary in New York, in 1988 from the Faculty of Protestant Theology in Paris, and in 2007 from St. Sergius Orthodox Theological Institute in Paris.

Metropolitan Georges taught Arab Civilization at the Lebanese University and pastoral theology at St. John of Damascus Institute of Theology at Balamand University in Lebanon. He has been active in ecumenical conferences and in dialogue with scholars of Islam, representing the Church of Antioch in pan-Orthodox and ecumenical meetings and inter-religious conferences.

He is a prolific writer of many articles, sermons and academic papers, several of them collected and published in some 30 books. Most of his writings are in Arabic along with a number of papers and lectures in French. Few translations are available in English. His book "Laou hakaytou masra at-toufoula" (Eng. trans. "If I were to reflect on childhood's journey") is translated into French, English, and Russian, along with other lectures and articles.

The ecumenical and theological contribution of Metropolitan Georges Khodr

In addition to his gifted personality, two major aspects of Metropolitan Georges Khodr have predisposed him to be a man of multi-cultural, multi-religious and multi-confessional dialogue, namely being an Antiochian Bishop and a Lebanese born citizen.

Indeed, both the Antiochian Church and Lebanon, by their very nature and composition, represent such a variation of Christian communities that it is impossible for any of their representatives to practice ministry in isolation. Imperatively, this wide variety fosters a type of existential ecumenical communication that covers a wide range of axis and praxis amidst a majority Muslim population.

Antioch, where "the disciples were called Christians for the first time," today hosts a number of Christian traditions that developed through time into distinctive Churches, all part of the Eastern Christian world. The head of all these sister Churches carries the title of Patriarch of Antioch: the Orthodox, the Maronites, the Syriacs, the Melkites, the Jacobites. They live and witness in an alien surrounding, namely the land of Islam which had extended its rule across the Near East over the centuries. The rule of Islam, more tolerant in its first centuries, became increasingly invasive and imposing, resulting in the capture and subjugation of formerly Christian cities: Constantinople in 1453 under the Ottomans and the cities of Antioch, and Iskenderun in 1939.

The wars in the Middle East, increasing at the beginning of the 21st century, have swept across major countries and cities where Eastern Christians have continued to live and witness. Though massacres and destructions have caused an intense movement of emigration such as in Iraq, Lebanon and most recently and dramatically in Syria, facing this tragic destiny, most Christians and more particularly their religious leaders have, by virtue of their faith, no other means of resistance than to cling to their homeland and witness their presence through dialogue and peaceful means.

At a smaller, yet more complex, scale, Lebanon (which counts eighteen religious denominations grouped in two large religions, Christianity and Islam, along with a minority Jewish community in the last century) has to meet additional challenges that demand concerted efforts to protect life and keep a peaceful existence. Though Lebanon remains to date the sole country in the Arab East headed by a Christian president, the Christian population -which presented until recent past a majority of Maronites, Melkites, Greek Orthodox, Armenian Orthodox, Catholics and Protestants, Syriac Orthodox and Catholics and Protestants of smaller denominations- is significantly diminishing over the years.

Since 1970, Metropolitan Georges Khodr has led the Episcopate of Byblos (3rd millennium BC) and Botrys (14th century BC)- two major cities of ancient civilization to which was added the large area of Mount Lebanon under the Mutassarrifiyah in the administration of the Levant after the World Wars. This area is geographically at the heart of the troubled area of the East which carries a historical legacy of threats and faces a number of challenges in order to protect the bare existence of its members and their witness.

This brief but quite necessary overview of the mosaic ground on which Metropolitan Georges stands along with a closer look at his life is indispensable for allowing us to perceive and understand his ecumenical contribution and ministry.

a. The dialogue of religions

Bishop Georges was born under the French Mandate in the Muslim city of Tripoli north of Lebanon and was raised there until the age of eighteen. As most of the high quality schools at that time were run by French Catholic missionaries, he was sent to the Catholic École des Frères Chrétiens. The school was located in the center of the city, amidst the Greek Orthodox Cathedral and its bishopric, neighboring a Syriac Catholic Church, a Melkite Greek bishopric and its church and two Maronites Churches, all clustered in the small area of the Souks, shouldering four major mosques. Since his childhood, he was accustomed to the Muezzin call for prayer at different hours of the day, and more so to hear this call mixed with the bells of his Church and chants of the Resurrection at dawn on Easter morning. The small boy did not seem to be annoyed by the Muezzin proclaiming that "there is no God but God" and that "God was the greatest." While attending the Liturgy that was celebrated in Arabic and in Greek, he must have developed an affinity with the text of the Koran which he recognized later in his life to be a miracle of the Arabic language. Endowed with a real talent for Arabic and sensible to its richness, he soon discerned the newness which the Christian message expressed in Arabic and had ascribed to the Arabic language itself and to the thinking of Muslims in the Orient. Indeed a breadth of biblical texts had infiltrated the Arabic classical texts. The Arabic Literary Renaissance was made by Christian writers who added a dimension of freedom, new imagery and symbolism to modern Arabic writing. Later on in his life, Georges Khodr, who was then a priest, became, for seven years, a professor of Arabic Civilization at the Lebanese University. As such, he elucidated the objective historical reality of a tolerant Islam and highlighted the contributions of Christians in the early periods of its reign, bearing in his mind the great figure of Saint John of Damascus (675-753), a man who participated in Muslim-Christian dialogue (who, like his father and grandfather, was minister of finance under the Omayyad Caliphs). Trained with an objective Cartesian mind, Georges Khodr was convincing and attractive to the intellectual Muslims who looked up to him at every opportunity for a sound and positive dialogue between Christianity and Islam so vital for Lebanon. He soon became the natural point of reference. He is known to have created within the

Part III: Representative Orthodox Theologians reflecting on Ecumenism

Arabic language a specific vocabulary and a divinely inspired message. His witnessing to Christianity coupled with his deep and sound knowledge of Islam and the Koran was not witnessing exclusively to Orthodoxy. All other Christian denominations recognized him as their spokesman and a solid and mutual respect linked him with open-minded scholars from the other Christian Churches, to name but one, the late Father Youakim Moubarak (1924-1995) from the Maronite Church.

Through his dialogue with Islam, Georges Khodr witnessed to an ecumenical understanding and relationship with the other Christian communities in Lebanon and worldwide. At the Lahore International Islamic Conference in 1974 he was mandated by the late Patriarch Elias Muawed IV to prepare the speech which carried the voice of Christians of the Middle East to the world of Islam. His weekly editorials appeared uninterruptedly over 70 years in the widely-read daily newspaper "An-Nahar", spread Christian values and a new approach to current issues in socio-political life and revealed to Muslim and Christian readers an ecumenical message.

b. Sister Churches

His acquaintance with the other Christian families started early in his life. As mentioned earlier, he studied at l'École des Frères, where he acquired proficiency in the French language and a sound Cartesian training along with the "catéchism catholique" that the brothers offered to all the pupils. He recalls that, for no reason he could know, the brother in charge of the class of Christian education summoned him once to answer this question: "Georges Khodr, stand up and tell me why the Orthodox Church is neither Holy, nor One, nor Apostolic, nor Catholic"! The young Georges carried this exhortation as positively as can be. In the course of his studies at the Jésuites, Saint-Joseph University in Beirut, when he was pursuing his Law degree, Georges Khodr investigated in-depth the history of the Church, probably in search for the right answer to that old question. Thus, the richness of the Orthodox Tradition, not well-known to traditional believers in the 30s of last century, was revealed to him. He was going to invest his whole life in revealing the treasures of Orthodoxy to all Arabic speaking Christians of various Churches. Initiating a deep and responsible dialogue with leaders of sister Churches, Khodr referred to the common heritage of the Church, pointing out with an acute sense of discernment and precision the essential common faith of early Christianity while acknowledging the cultural and spiritual input of the various Churches along the centuries.

In Paris, where he was pursuing his theological studies at Saint Sergius, he began his pan-Orthodox and ecumenical journey. His close contacts with the Russian Orthodox Émigrés, Father Nikita Struve, Father Paul Evdokimov and others, the French Orthodox intellectual (former Catholic) Olivier Clement, the first Orthodox female theologian in Europe Elisabeth Behr-Sigel, the Maronite Lebanese priest Youakim Moubarak, consolidated his conviction in the Universal Church and deepened his responsibility to reveal the input of the Antiochian legacy. In Lebanon, he developed close contacts and mutual appreciation with the Melkite Catholic priest Father Jean Corbon, author of l'Eglise des Arabes (1977) and the Romanian Orthodox theologian André Scrima, in his search for a common and ecumenical witness.

His first contacts with Protestants took place during his stay in Paris, when he was made a member of the youth commission at the World Council of Churches in 1948.[1] His respect for the faithful, loyal and good-willing Protestants and their organized efforts to offer Christians a serious platform for encountering each other away from the Catholic proselytism he had suffered from back at home, invited him into the world of Ecumenism. He served the Middle East Council of Churches in its various commissions and responded positively to a number of Ecumenical Conferences at the WACC.[2]

[1] George Khodr, attended as an Arab youth delegate of the Orthodox Church of Antioch the First Assembly of the World Council of Churches, Amsterdam, Netherlands, in 1948.

[2] The WCC and Dialogue with men of other faiths. Debats 1/11/1971 Document WCC Central Committee, Addis Ababa, 1971. The Fifth World Conference on Faith and Order met in Santiago de Compostela, Spain 3-14, August 1993, around the theme "Towards Koinonia in Faith, Life and Witness".8/1993 Document Metropolitan Georges KHODR (Lebanon),

In 1964, he was invited to Bossey the Ecumenical Institute at Chambesy in Switzerland to give a six-month course. In all his ecumenical, encounters Georges Khodr was known to be intransigent with regards to articles of dogmatic faith; his mastery in theological knowledge, his thoughtful argumentation, and his thorough loyalty to the legacy of the Church Fathers protected him from any syncretism or compromise. This strong advocate of Orthodoxy was however wounded by the obstacles that were standing in the way of a Pan-Orthodox Council.

In 1989, he participated in the Joint Committee meeting that brought together the Chalcedonians and non-Chalcedonians in Egypt and resulted in the "Corinthian Declaration" in relation to the person of Jesus Christ.

In 1993, he joined the Meeting of the International Committee for the theological dialogue between Catholics and Orthodox that took place in Balamand. The meeting investigated the issue of "uniatism" that was considered as an obsolete formula for Church "unity". However this document was followed up with less seriousness than it deserved, both by the Orthodox and the Catholics.

c. The unity in love and mutual recognition

Metropolitan Georges' concern for the distance between the Orthodox and Catholic Church was no longer focused on theological views afterward. He had experienced great encounters and knew better that the unity of the Churches is a gift of God for men of good will. Confident in the great love and deep understanding of Pope Jean Paul II, he answered his Holiness' swift friendly question: "What is the last obstacle between you and us?" Metropolitan Georges answered, "It is You, your Holiness!" He founded his saying on the declaration of the Melkite Church who signed in 1995 a declaration written by Mgr Elias Zoghbi in 1975, known under the name "the double communion", pointing at the communion of faith with the Orthodox Church and the communion with Rome recognizing the Pope as Primus inter-pares as it was the case in the first century of Christianity.

He could acknowledge and cherish with gratitude every step that the other Churches would make towards Orthodoxy. He visited their monasteries with awe and admiration. At the Roman Catholic Benedictine Monastery of Chevetogne where he met his friend and ecumenical partner in the Commission on Faith and Order of the WCC, late Father Emmanuel Lanne and Monsignor Michel Van Parys. He was full of praise to witness the living Ecumenism as they celebrated the divine Byzantine and Slavonic liturgy and their commitment to the early Fathers of the Church.

It is at the ecumenical monastic community of Bose during the Orthodox theological Conferences, where he was invited as key-note speaker, that he was won over by the true spirit of ecumenism. One might think that what reconciled him with the ecumenical endeavor at these conferences, where Orthodox theologians and scholars from the various Orthodox Churches met with scholars from other denominations, was the seriousness, the mastery and depth of the papers and discussions. These were certainly valuable and made him encounter men of God who praised Him and revealed His truth and beauty in all Churches of the East and the West. But what was more convincing for Metropolitan Georges was the collegiality, the fraternal community, and the "agape" that brought the members of the many Orthodox Churches together in the evangelical hospitality of Bose.

At the end the desired answer to the brother of the Écoles Chrétiennes was found: it is in the hospitality, the respect, the deep knowledge and love of the Catholic Brother Enzo Bianci and each member of his Community for Orthodoxy, that the seventy year old question was made trivial. In his late eighties, Metropolitan Georges had found the answer that challenged him in his youth.

Bibliography

Al Mawarina wal Orthoox fi Hadrati ar-Rabb, "The Maronites and the Orthodox in the Presence of the Lord," in *An–Nahar*, 19 January 2013.

Greek Orthodox. Ecumenical Center, Geneva: Official celebration of the World Council of Churches' 50th anniversary, September 22, 1998.

Part III: Representative Orthodox Theologians reflecting on Ecumenism

Metropolitan Georges Khodr, "Le Combat Spirituel pour l'Unité de l'Église", *Irénikon* 82.2-3 (2009).

_____, «Dialogue des Religions et des Cultures,» paper presented at the Colloquium: "Cultures, Religions et Conflicts", Unesco & the International Center for Human Sciences at Byblos, Lebanon, 19-21 September 2002.

_____, "Le Liban Religieux", *Proche Orient* 5-6 (September, 1994).

_____, "Christian Mission and Witness in the Middle East", Washington D.C., 7 February 1994.

_____, *L'Appel de l'Esprit Église et société*, (Paris: Editions de Cerf, 2001).

_____, *Et si je disais les Chemins de l'Enfance* (Paris: Editions de Cerf, 2001).

Fr. Oliver Herbel

Introduction

Fr. John Meyendorff (1926-1992) (like Alexander Schmemann as well)[1] is noted for many things by many people. His impact upon American Orthodox Christianity has been significant, shaping both St. Vladimir's Orthodox Theological Seminary and *St. Vladimir's Orthodox Theological Quarterly* (originally named *St. Vladimir's Orthodox Seminary Quarterly*). It should be noted that his work was neither independent of, nor separate from, the work of others, such as Fr. Georges Florovsky (1893-1979). Nonetheless, his work is important with respect to engaging the West and Ecumenical concerns. This becomes noticeable when one takes a historical perspective, for his ecumenical work directly addressed the tension that Orthodox in America, indeed, Orthodox worldwide, exhibit: that between reacting against the ecumenical other and embracing what is good and true within the ecumenical other. For both Meyendorff (and Schmemann), healthy ecumenism was an Orthodox responsibility and required a balance between discerning what could be claimed as true within others and sharing the Orthodox conviction that true unity could only be found in the fullness of the Orthodox faith.

Earlier in American Russian Orthodox history, Orthodoxy exhibited this very tension, responding at times in a reactionary manner and at other times with openness. Orthodox Christians reacted against Protestant missionaries who had begun to target Orthodox Native Alaskans, following the 1867 sale of Alaska to the United States of America.[2] On the other hand, in 1870, the rector of the Russian Orthodox chapel in New York City, Nicholas Bjerring, promoted ecumenical engagement.[3] Additionally, Archbishop Tikhon (who served the Russian Mission in America from 1898 to 1907) and Archimandrite Theoklitos Triantafilides (who served the Russian Mission from 1895 until his death in 1916) responded by building relationships with non-Orthodox Christians in other parts of America.[4] This tension between reacting to and embracing the ecumenical other remained in place even right up to the arrival of John Meyendorff (and Alexander Schmemann) in the United States, as evidenced by Fr. Georges Florovsky (1893-1979). According to Florovsky, in order to engage the West anew, one first had to address the *pseudomorphosis* that had occurred to Eastern Orthodoxy due to

---

[1] The present paper should be read in parallel to that on Fr. A. Schmemann (ed.).

[2] The literature concerning Protestant missionary schools and Americanization attempts is extensive. For this feature in Alaska, one may consult Ted G. Hinckley, *The Americanization of Alaska, 1867-1897* (Palo Alto: Pacific Books, 1972) and *Alaskan John G. Brady, Missionary, Businessman, Judge, and Governor, 1878-1918* (Columbus, OH: Ohio State University Press, 1982) as well as Clifton Bates and Michael Oleksa, *Conflicting Landscapes: American Schooling/Alaskan Natives* (Fairbanks: University of Alaska Press, 2011). Orthodox defense of the Natives (in part) led to the conversions of the Tlingits. See Sergei Kan, *Memory Eternal: Tlingit Culture and Russian Orthodox Christianity Through Two Centuries* (Seattle: University of Washington Press, 1999), 245-77 and Michael Oleksa, *Orthodox Alaska: A Theology of Mission* (Crestwood, NY: St. Vladimir's Seminary Press, 1992), 171.

[3] For an in-depth look at Bjerring's career, see my article "A Catholic, Presbyterian, and Orthodox Journey: The Changing Church Affiliation and Enduring Social Vision of Nicholas Bjerring," *Zeitschrift fur Neuere Theologiegeschichte/Journal for the History of Modern Theology* 14.1 (2007): 49-80. Bjerring was a Danish immigrant who had converted from Lutheranism to Roman Catholicism in Europe, prior to his immigration and subsequent conversion to Orthodox Christianity. He became a Presbyterian pastor in 1883 and Roman Catholic again, shortly before his death in 1900.

[4] See Peter Carl Haskell, "Archbishop Tikhon and Bishop Grafton: An Early Chapter in Anglo-Orthodox Relations in the New World, Part One" *St. Vladimir's Orthodox Theological Quarterly* 11.4 (1967): 193, 198-9. It should be noted that Tikhon went on to become the Patriarch of the Russian Orthodox Church and due to his ministerial career, especially the latter portion during and following October, 1917, he was canonized as an Orthodox saint. On Triantafilides' ecumenical work see "Associated Charities Committees at Work," *Galveston Daily News* February 11, 1910.

negative Western influences.[5] Because of it, Orthodox theology had become a Western, scholastic caricature, making it a "pseudomorph" (a false form).

The concern with this tension would likewise characterize the ecumenical work of Meyendorff (and Schmemann). Their visions, however, sought to balance out this tension. Achieving the proper balance was to enable Orthodoxy to engage the West in a healthier manner and toward this end, their extensive engagement with ecumenism aided them.

A Biographical Introduction to Fr. John Meyendorff[6]

John Meyendorff was born in Paris in 1926 to a Baltic-German-Russian family. He studied at the St. Sergius Institute and at the Sorbonne, the arts, languages, and humanities faculties of the University of Paris. Meyendorff received a *Licence-ès-lettres* from the Sorbonne as well as a *Diplôme d'études supérieures* (equivalent of an M.A.) in 1949. He completed his theological training in 1949 at St. Sergius as well and continued on to earn the prestigious *Doctorat-ès-Lettres* from the Sorbonne in 1958. In 1959, after having taught church history at St. Sergius Orthodox Theological Institute, he moved to New York, where he accepted the position of professor of church history and patristics at St. Vladimir's Seminary. Meyendorff later served as the dean of St. Vladimir's Seminary from 1984 until shortly before his death in 1992. Meyendorff's engagement with the American academy extended beyond St. Vladimir's Seminary and included significant work with Harvard University's Dumbarton Oaks Research Library and Collection as well as teaching at Fordham University.

The importance of the American scene, combined with his French émigré background, inspired him to dedicate a lot of his writing to the issue of "diaspora." He believed such a notion, with its requisite requirement that such "diaspora" communities must be under the guidance of a foreign "mother church" was incorrect. Indeed, this is no small point when assessing Meyendorff's importance to ecumenism, for he believed that an emphasis on "diaspora" was contradictory to a catholic and apostolic Christianity. In keeping with this, on a practical level, he was a founding member of Syndesmos, an international Orthodox Christian youth movement, which began in 1953. Earlier in his life he had been a member of the Russian Student Christian Movement, which was dedicated to a holistic eucharistic vision and the presentation of Orthodoxy to the West.

He also involved himself in institutional ecumenism. Meyendorff served as a representative of the Orthodox Church to the World Council of Churches (WCC). In that capacity, he participated in several WCC Assemblies, chaired the Commission on Faith and Order from 1967 to 1976, and served on the WCC Central Committee. For Meyendorff, a proper ecumenical vision was a matter of great importance.

Meyendorff's Ecumenical Engagement with Western Christianity

Meyendorff directly discussed this Orthodox tension between reacting polemically to the West and engaging in healthy ecumenical dialogue. Like Florovsky before him, Meyendorff relied on an earlier patristic period and believed the Orthodox understanding of the "Catholic Church" required "new theologies, new

---

[5] On this point and Florovsky's anti-Westernism in general, see Paul Gavrilyuk, "Florovsky's Christian Hellenism: A Critical Evaluation," (paper presented at the conference "'Neopatristic Synthesis or Post-Patristic Theology: Can Orthodox Theology Be Contextual?," Volos Academy of Theological Studies, Volos, Greece, June 2010). This paper has since been edited and will be forthcoming as "Orthodox Constructions of the West," in *The Constructions of the 'West' in Eastern Orthodox Theology*, ed. George Demacopoulos and Aristotle Papanikolaou (New York: Fordham University Press, forthcoming). See also, Brandon Gallaher, "'Waiting for the Barbarians': Identity and Polemicism in the Neo-Patristic Synthesis of Georges Florovsky," *Modern Theology* 27.4 (2011): 659-691.

[6] For lengthier biographies, see Michael Plekon, *Living Icons: Persons of Faith in the Eastern Church* (Notre Dame, IN: Notre Dame University Press, 2002), 178-233.

formulations of doctrine," rather than mere repetition of past statements.[7] Also, like Florovsky, he saw Orthodoxy's (especially Russian Orthodoxy's) problems as stemming from the West. According to Meyendorff, the real challenge for the Church came not from internal events such the liturgical reforms of the 16th century Russian Patriarch Nikon, but from the West: Latin-oriented scholarship introduced through the mediations of the Kiev Academy, Enlightenment principles imposed upon society by Peter I and Catherine II, the nineteenth century influence of European literature and culture upon Russia, and the Marxist revolution of the twentieth century.[8]

The concern for how to relate to the West was important to him and he saw Orthodoxy's mission as one of engaged evangelism, wherein one ought to distinguish between "good" and "wrong" ecumenism.[9] Meyendorff made the distinction between good and wrong ecumenism in the context of responding to the claim made by some Orthodox that ecumenism was a heresy. Ecumenism, so the charge went, was heretical because it muted, if not contradicted, Orthodoxy's claim to be the Church founded by Christ through the Apostles. He agreed that there was a "danger in accepting relativism, superficiality, and secularism (conservative or radical) as a valid principle of our ecumenical movement" but he also believed that Orthodoxy must avoid the danger of becoming nothing more than an "introverted sect."[10] Good ecumenism struck a balance between these two poles. To strike that balance, Meyendorff argued that what the Orthodox needed to do was to define ecumenism as "an authentic search for truth in love."[11] Ecumenism included listening and learning, but doing so while also acknowledging that Orthodoxy is "the Church of God" and being prepared to share that conviction with other Christians.[12] He believed this sharing was necessary because ecumenism too often became relativistic in Protestant circles or subject to an outside fallible authority (the papacy) in Roman Catholic circles.[13] According to Meyendorff's engaged evangelism approach, therefore, there is something misguided and lacking within Western Christianity and Orthodoxy must remain true to what she is, lovingly being open to discerning truth in non-Orthodox Christians but also sharing with them the central conviction of unity within Orthodoxy. Incidentally, it should be noted that Meyendorff's position is not very far removed from that of one of his theological mentors, Fr. Georges Florovsky.[14]

He articulated this approach to ecumenism as the second part of a three point platform for authentic witness, broadly conceived. In this tripartite approach to engaging the world, Meyendorff noted the need for emulating the Fathers of the Church in order to be traditional (but not merely conservative), ecumenical (in a "good" way), and the Church (rather than a denomination or a sect).[15] Meyendorff saw these as key components to the acculturation of Orthodoxy, or the Christianization of a culture, which he believed "remains our task as teachers, as preachers, as scholars, as theologians."[16] Evidence of this commitment may also be found in his long-standing tenure as editor of the *St. Vladimir's Theological Quarterly* (initially named the *St. Vladimir's Seminary Quarterly*). Admittedly, Meyendorff was primarily involved at St. Vladimir's Seminary but he did not see the Seminary as a sectarian enterprise, as shown by the various symposia and events held at the seminary and his own work at Harvard, Dumbarton Oaks, and Fordham. For Meyendorff, good ecumenism was part and parcel of the Christian witness to world at large.

---

[7] John Meyendorff, *Witness to the World* (Crestwood, NY: St. Vladimir's Seminary Press, 1987), 55, 80.

[8] John Meyendorff, "Introduction," *The Legacy of St. Vladimir* (Crestwood, NY: St. Vladimir's Seminary Press, 1990), 13.

[9] Meyendorff, *Witness to the World*, 42-4.

[10] Ibid., 43-44.

[11] Ibid., 46.

[12] Ibid., 14-15.

[13] Ibid., 17.

[14] Florovsky argued polemically against the West and believed ecumenism was, essentially, evangelism, but yet retained an ecumenical compassion and historical pragmatism that enabled him to see the good in non-Orthodox. For more on this, see Brandon Gallaher, "'Waiting for the Barbarians'," especially 663-8.

[15] Meyendorff, "Introduction," 15-17.

[16] Ibid., 20.

Conclusion

Meyendorff's ecumenical thinking was characterized by a tension between reacting against Western Christian errors affecting Orthodoxy on the one hand, and embracing what was good and true within non-Orthodox Christians on the other hand. A balance between the two may be seen in Meyendorff's "good ecumenism". This "good" ecumenism required a balance between listening and learning on the one hand and proclaiming the Orthodox conviction that unity could be found in Orthodox Christianity on the other.

Bibliography

Meyendorff, John. *Byzantine Theology: Historical Trends and Doctrinal Themes*, (New York: Fordham University Press, 1979).

____. *Catholicity and the Church*, (Crestwood, New York: St. Vladimir's Seminary Press, 1983).

____. "Introduction." In *The Legacy of St. Vladimir*, (Crestwood, New York: St. Vladimir's Seminary Press. 1990).

____. *Living Tradition: Orthodox Witness in the Contemporary World*, (Crestwood, New York: St. Vladimir's Seminary Press, 1998).

____. *Rome, Constantinople, Moscow: Historical and Theological Studies*, (Crestwood, New York: St. Vladimir's Seminary Press, 1996).

____. *Witness to the World*, (Crestwood, New York: St. Vladimir's Seminary Press. 1987).

(36) Nikos Nissiotis

Grigorios Liantas

A) Biographical note

Nikos Nissiotis, Professor of Philosophy of Religion at the Theological School of Athens (1965-1986), was born in Athens in 1924. He studied at the Theological School of Athens with postgraduate studies in Switzerland and Belgium. He received his doctorate in theology in 1956.

He worked at the World Council of Churches (WCC) and the Ecumenical Institute of Bossey for approximately twenty years (1956-1974). Since the very first years of his tenure Nissiotis insisted on the importance of the ecumenical movement, on the priority of the liturgical, mystical and sacramental element of the Orthodox witness.[1] He established the annual liturgy of the Seminar of Orthodox theology during the Holy Week, at the Ecumenical Institute, where sixty heterodox persons, every year, were initiated into the liturgical life of Orthodoxy and were taught the theology of the Church. During its 25 years of operation, over a thousand western Christians have experienced Orthodox spirituality there and lived the Eastern tradition in its worshiping practice. He served as Professor of Theology at the University of Geneva (1962-1974) and Dean of the Graduate School of Ecumenical Studies (1966-1974). He is considered as an original pioneer of the ecumenical theology.

B) Participation in executive positions of the WCC and in various ecumenical meetings and consultations

He offered his services to the WCC, apart from the Ecumenical Institute and the Geneva headquarters, reaching up to the position of Deputy General Secretary of the WCC (1968-1972). As an Orthodox observer he represented the WCC at the Second Vatican Council (1963), and he participated also in the works of the Pan-Orthodox Conferences of the island of Rhodes – Greece (1961 and 1964).

It has very rightly been argued that, "at all and almost certainly at the most fundamental conventions of the ecumenical movement during the last forty years since the foundation of WCC, Nissiotis was the undisputed champion and keynote speaker. Therefore it is not accidental that is also considered as the most famous Greek Orthodox theologian in the Christian world of the postwar era."[2]

He was also chairman of the Department "Faith and Order" of the WCC for five years (1977-1982). The importance of this position becomes obvious if one takes into consideration that the Department "Faith and Order" constitutes the most theological of the fields of activity of the ecumenical movement.[3] After the end of his term, he was unanimously elected president of the "International Academy of Religious Sciences" in Brussels (1984-1986).

As a visiting professor he was invited to and taught at Universities abroad. His academic activity and research work were rewarded with the title of honorary doctorate from the Orthodox Theological Institute of St. Sergius in Paris (1965) and the Universities of Aberdeen in Scotland (1967), Bucharest (1977) and Geneva (1984).

He was honored by the Greek State, the Ecumenical Patriarchate, the International Olympic Committee and other international authorities with decorations, medals and honorary distinctions.

---

[1] Marios Begzos, *The Word as dialogue. A portrait of Nikos Nissiotis* (Thessaloniki: Pournaras, 1991) (in Greek).

[2] Nikos Nissiotis, *From existence to co-existence* (Athens: Maistros, 2004), 246-247 (in Greek).

[3] Ibid.

C) Writings

His writings include about two hundred publications in four languages (Greek, English, French and German), with many translations in other languages. In particular, that which refers to the orthodox theology of ecumenism is expansive and includes over one hundred articles of ecumenical content. Nissiotis did not give a systematic treatise in ecumenical theology, probably due to his sudden death.

D) Theological contribution

A spokesman of peace, reconciliation and understanding, Nissiotis participated in the Ecumenical Movement, aiming to regain the conditions for unity of the Church according to the Orthodox theological tradition, rather than just in the superficial "union of Churches" in the western Christian perception of modern ecumenism. Through inter-Christian dialogues, where he participated for almost forty years as one of the most basic contributors, he promoted the importance of Pneumatology and Trinitarian theology, as the eminently Orthodox contribution to modern ecumenical theology.[4]

Nissiotis regarded Pneumatology as the most fundamental theological contribution of Orthodoxy to the ecumenical Movement. Starting from Trinitarian theology, which he considered as underdeveloped in western Christianity, he attempted to open new ways in ecclesiology based on the Orthodox pneumatology.[5]

In Roman Catholicism, he ascertained the weakness of "patromonism" which consisted in the overstressing of God the Father over the two other persons of the Holy Trinity (Son and Spirit). In the antipode, in Protestantism, he located another kind of overemphasis, that of "Christomonism", namely the overstressing of the person of Son-Christ over the Father and the Spirit. The only proper solution could be found in the Orthodox tradition, which ascribed an eminent theological function to the Holy Spirit and hence excluded every theological monism, preserving the right balance in Trinitarian theology. Nikos Nissiotis called this original theological proposal as "pneumatological Christology" which seems to condition Orthodox ecclesiology.

Therefore, the most important Orthodox contribution to the development of both the self-consciousness of the WCC, and the general theological discussions of the Council, was the introduction of Trinitarian theology. An extended report of this Trinitarian understanding was contained in Nissiotis's speech to the plenary session of the General Assembly in New Delhi in 1961, for the "witness and ministry of the Eastern Orthodox Church in one undivided Church." Nissiotis started from a basic tenet of Orthodox ecclesiology: unity is realized by the energies of the Trinitarian God, as this was precisely experienced by the early Christians in the event of Pentecost. The whole world belongs potentially to this unity. There are no schismatic Churches, but only Churches in a schismatic condition within the one undivided Church. In this perspective the unity is the very life of Pentecost and not anything abstract. Therefore, the unity of the Orthodox Church, as witness and diakonia, is this vibrant reality of Pentecost. Such a unity could gather the Churches, which are in schismatic condition, so that with the blooming of life itself to join the one undivided Church. The conditions of such a unity and witness have direct application in the manner the ecumenical dialogue is conducted. That is why the Orthodox Church cannot invite the others to return to the ancient tradition and the first eight centuries, but only to lead them based on the witness and the ministry to the blooming of the mystery of Pentecost. A call for a return to the ancient tradition renders Orthodoxy (which is the fullness of catholicity and apostolicity) a confessional group which preserves the truth for her. The Orthodox Church does not define in abstract the truth in certain types and bonds. The Church dogmas are the expression of the life of a mystery and not a definite and restrictive description of truth.

---

[4] N. Nissiotis, ibid., 9.
[5] M. Begzos, ibid., 62.

Nissiotis' theological contribution is very important, because without ignoring the uniqueness and exclusivity of the Orthodox Church in history, he gives eminent priority to the divine energies which through the mystery of Pentecost, gather the scattered members to the one undivided Church.

As indeed, Professor Stylianos Tsompanidis very aptly argues, "very early, Nissiotis served a dynamic ecclesiology which has a universal and ecumenical dimension. He did not place all the Churches at the same level, and exceeding the old heresiology, was far from the old confessional entanglements taking into account the new reality of the 'community churches', which are en route to its perfect realization. Moreover, Nissiotis proceeding on the effects on the ecclesiology of invocational pneumatology combined with the ontological, dynamic approach of unity as integration process, he recognizes that beyond the canonical boundaries of the Orthodox Church is an ecclesial reality which he calls 'ecclesiality', elements of which are the mysteries, the doctrines - especially the Creed of Nicaea - Constantinople, as an expression of the common apostolic faith - the missionary and evangelical - diaconal activity, along with the participation in the eschatological hope."[6]

Moreover, for Nissiotis, ecumenism intended the unity of the Church and not the union of the Churches.[7] The ecumenical movement served to rediscover the experience of the truth of faith in Orthodoxy. This restoration of the unity of the Church requires few theological conditions. In this perspective the honest Christian self-criticism in East and West was one of the first conditions of ecumenical dialogue.

Nissiotis, finally, believed that by serving Orthodox theology in the ecumenical movement one could contemplate the ecclesiastical unity.[8] It is also worth noting that Nissiotis significantly contributed, as president of the theological department of the WCC "Faith and Order" (1977-1982), to the implementation of a research program on the three fundamental mysteries of the Church, that is *Baptism, Eucharist and Ministry*, which led to the famous Text from Lima (BEM - 1982). It is even asserted that "with this program, representatives of Protestant confessions were encouraged to carefully look into the sacramental structure of the Church and to realize the ecclesiological nature of Christianity. This disregarded aspect of faith was recalled by the Orthodox theological presence in the ecumenical movement. And exactly on this, Nissiotis decisively contributed with his personal intervention."[9]

E) Conclusions

For Nissiotis the word was dialogue, never monologue. His criticism always started with self-criticism, as he believed that existence means coexistence and survival is linked to living together. Moreover, speaking of dialogue he did not mean "negotiations" or "bargaining", but a meeting of traditions. Lastly, contrary to the various misunderstandings arising from the participation of Orthodoxy in the Ecumenical Movement, he responded that the Ecumenical Movement and primarily, the World Council of Churches, do not intend to lead to "the union of churches", but to the cultivation of the conditions which could contribute to the restoration of the unity of the Church in the future.

Bibliography

1. Marios Begzos, *The Word as dialogue. A portrait of Nikos Nissiotis* (Thessaloniki: Pournaras, 1991) (in Greek)
2. Nikos Nissiotis, *From existence to coexistence* (Athens: Maistros, 2004) (in Greek)

---

[6] Cf. Stylianos Tsompanidis , *The contribution of the Orthodox Church and theology to the WCC*, (Thessaloniki: Pournaras, 2008).

[7] Marios Begzos, ibid,.63.

[8] Ibid.,64.

[9] Ibid.,58.

Part III: Representative Orthodox Theologians reflecting on Ecumenism

3. Basilios Stavridis, - Evaggelia Varella, *History of the Ecumenical Movement* (Thessaloniki: Patriarchal Foundation for Patristic Studies, 1996) (in Greek)

4. George Tsetsis, *Universal Annals* (Katerini: Tertios, 1987) (in Greek)

5. Nikos Nissiotis, "The Witness and the Service of Eastern Orthodoxy to the One Undivided Church (1961)", *The Orthodox Church in the Ecumenical Movement.* (C. Patelos, ed.), (Geneva: WCC, 1978), 231-241

6. Nikos Nissiotis, "Spirit, Church and Ministry", *Theology Today*, 19 (1963): 484-499

7. Nikos Nissiotis, "Pneumatologie orthodoxe", *Le Saint Esprit,* (1963): 85-106

8. Nikos Nissiotis, "Die Bedeutung der Trinitaetslehre fuer Leben und Theologie der Kirche", *Die Theologie der Ostkirche*, (1964): 19-63

9. Nikos Nissiotis, "The Third Panorthodox Conference" *Orthodox Presence* 1 (1964): 189-195

10. Nikos Nissiotis, "Types and Problems of Ecumenical Dialogue", *Ecumenical Rewiew* 18 (1966): 39-57

11. Nikos Nissiotis, "The Degree on Ecumenism: Ten Years After", *Studia Anselmiana* 71 (1974): 158-167

12. Nikos Nissiotis, "A credible reception of BEM in the churches", *Mid-Stream* 26 (1987): 1-21

13. Nikos Nissiotis, "Ecumenical implications of Second Vatican Synod" *Modern Steps* 61 (1987): 4-15

14. J.Kallarangatt, "The Ecumenical Theology of Nikos Nissiotis", *Christian Orient* 11 (1990): 173-186

15. Apostolos Nicolaidis, *The ecumenical adventures of Christianity* (Athens: Grigoris Publ., 2008) (in Greek)

16. Stylianos Tsompanidis, *The contribution of the Orthodox Church and theology to the WCC* (Thessaloniki: Pournaras, 2008) (in Greek).

(translated by Fr. George Anagnostoulis)

Fr. Augoustinos Bairactaris

Biographical note

The Metropolitan of Andrianoupolis, former [Metropolitan] of Switzerland, Damaskinos Papandreou was born in Kato Hrysovitsa of Aetolia (Greece) in 1936, coming from a family of clergy. He was one of the most important pioneers and founders of the spirit of the Ecumenical movement within the Orthodox Church in the 20th century. Having received his early theological formation in the Halki Theological Seminary (an island near to Instabul-Turkey,1955-1959), he then moved to Germany for postgraduate studies at the Universities of Bonn and Marburg (1959-1965) in the fields of Philosophy of Religion and Comparative Religion Studies. After completing his studies and following a decision of the Holy and Sacred Synod of the Ecumenical Patriarchate in 1965 he became abbot - director of the newly established Orthodox monastic center of Taizé in France. In 1970 he was elected once again by the Holy and Sacred Synod of the Ecumenical Patriarchate as Metropolitan of Tranoupolis, while a year earlier he was appointed Head of the Orthodox Center of the Ecumenical Patriarchate in Chambésy, Geneva (1969) with the future prospect to assist in upgrading and reorganizing the inter-Orthodox and inter-Church initiatives of the Ecumenical Patriarchate. At the same time and in this context, as the capabilities and qualities of the charismatic Damaskinos were firstly evaluated, he was appointed Head of the Secretariat by the late Ecumenical Patriarch Athenagoras for the preparation of the Holy and Great Synod of the Orthodox Church. Thus, he undertook the arduous and difficult task of coordinating the preparatory work of the Pre-Synodic Inter-Orthodox Committees and of the Pan-Orthodox Conferences. The year 1982 is an important date for Damaskinos, as he was elected by the Holy and Sacred Synod of the Ecumenical Patriarchate, first Metropolitan of Switzerland and Hexarch of Central Europe, expanding this way his duties with the pastoral care of the Orthodox of Central Europe, acquiring temples, establishing parishes, founding the youth office and creating a charitable foundation.

The theological contribution of Metropolitan of Switzerland Damaskinos

Damaskinos as Metropolitan of Switzerland (1982-2003), nurtured in the spirit and the ecclesiastical practice of the Ecumenical Patriarchate, had a vision based on three pillars: firstly, the strengthening of the relations among the Orthodox through the synodic process and the living communication, secondly, the establishing and intensifying of the inter-Christian dialogues with the Christians of the West, and thirdly, the founding of the academic dialogue among the monotheistic religions with ultimate aim the peaceful coexistence of the peoples. Therefore, it is on that triple purpose that he devoted his life, his ministry and his theological studies.

Enthusiastic, visionary and a hopeful man by nature, he did not hesitate to innovate. One of the guiding principles of his life was that *"we would never sacrifice the truth, but on the contrary will sacrifice everything for the truth."* For this reason, both his words and writings are characterized by the distinction between the essential and the non-essential element, emphasizing the former.[1] All of his moves evidence his interest in the current situation of the world in the fields of religion, politics, economy and culture.

His open mind towards the Ecumenical movement and Ecumenism in general, his theological competence which he drew from the study of Patristic texts, and his scientific-critical position to the other religions, have

---

[1] Costas Mygdalis, "Damaskinos Papandreou: the Prelate, the Leader" in *Church - Oikoumene - Politics, Tribute to the Metropolitan of Andrianoupolis Damaskinos* (Athens: Interparliamentary Assembly on Orthodoxy, 2007), 455 ff (in Greek).

provided him all the necessary elements, so that based on the Church Tradition to overcome the fear of the openness and relationship with the other Christian Churches, the other religions and with contemporary society. His faith in God and love to man encouraged him and gave him an invincible hope, something which prompted him to find the possibilities that lie within difficulties.[2] For Damaskinos the dilemma of fidelity to tradition or renewal did not exist. He detested the "idolization" of Tradition, or its endorsement as a museum exhibit, as he was looking for a dynamic Tradition, which would be incarnated in the *now*, in the current historical condition, and will be in direct contact with the contemporary man.[3]

Damaskinos being indeed himself a man of tolerance and communication, believed and worked towards a united and peaceful Europe, where respect for one another will prevail and fanaticism and intolerance will be absent, so that society would be led from a formal to a substantial tolerance and acceptance of the other.[4] And all that does not simply portray an idealist, but a man of deeds. Realizing the signs of the times he constantly emphasized the necessity for interfaith dialogue.[5] A key point for Damaskinos was the education of youth, which would be the guarantor and the bearer of the spiritual weight for the achievement of peace and harmony among the peoples. He despised religious introversion and religious intolerance, while on the contrary he encouraged the truth as practice and witness, which can only be achieved through dialogue.

He realized, as early as the 70s, that the threat to the peace among the peoples of Europe would not come from the side of religion, but from the idolization of matter and the glorification of power. For this reason he called on the religious leaders and institutions to cooperate peacefully and together to go against the intellectual obsolescence of man. In other words, the theologian Damaskinos had managed to think and act without denominational or religious labels. He had therefore deeply understood that inter-religious dialogue could heal the wounds of the historical past and minister to the contemporary confused man.[6] To achieve this, it is necessary to defend peace, social justice and human rights regardless of religion. Thus he emphasized on every occasion that the inter-Christian and inter-religious dialogues tie in with the substance and nature of the Orthodox Church, as in the first case the dialogues attempt to restore ecclesiastical unity, while in the second they seek the peaceful coexistence and the nurturing of mutual respect.

This perspective resulted in his direct involvement in the meetings of the World Council of Churches as a representative of the Ecumenical Patriarchate. In particular, in 1968 he took part in the Fourth General Assembly of the WCC in Uppsala, where he was appointed member of the Faith and Order committee. Therefore, during his ecumenical involvement he served since 1980 as co-chairman of the Theological Committee on the dialogue between the Orthodox Church and Old Catholic and as co-chairman of the Theological Commission on the dialogue between the Eastern Orthodox and the Oriental Orthodox. Moreover, it is noteworthy that we was invited by the Pope John Paul II in 1981 to deliver a speech to the Hierarchy of the Roman Catholic Church in St. Peter's Basilica on the occasion of the celebration of the 1600th anniversary of the Second Ecumenical Council. Also, due to the universal magnitude of his personality and his international contribution he served as a member of the International Academy of Religious Sciences, the Foundation *Pro Oriente*, the Conference of European Churches (CEC), the European Society of Culture and finally as Corresponding member of the Athens Academy. He has been honored as few contemporary academic theologians, receiving the title of Honorary Doctor from 14 different University theological faculties.

[2] Damaskinos Papandreou, *Orthodox and United Europe* (Katerini: Tertios, 1989), 19-21 (in Greek).
[3] Maria Brun, *Damaskinos Papandreou First Metropolitan of Switzerland 1969 - 2003*, (Athens: 2011), 665.
[4] Metropolitan of Switzerland Damaskinos, "Religion and Society in Modern European reality" in *Église et État en Europe*, in the series Études Théologiques, vol.11, (Geneva: Centre Orthodoxe de Chambésy, 1996), 63.
[5] Metropolitan Damaskinos Papandreou, "Le Dialogue de l 'Eglise Orthodoxe avec le Judaisme et l' Islam. Experiences de conflict, de reconciliation et de coexistence", in Maria Brun - Wilhelm Schneemelcher, *Thanksgiving, Festschrift für Damaskinos Papandreou, Metropolit der Schweiz* (Athens: 1996), 343-355.
[6] Metropolitan of Switzerland Damaskinos, "Religion and Society in contemporary European reality," in *Religion et Société*, in the series Études Théologiques, vol.12, (Geneva: Centre Orthodoxe de Chambésy, 1996), 89.

As the Director of the Orthodox Centre in Chambesy, Geneva he worked towards the academic collaboration with theological faculties and with other intellectual institutions of Switzerland, but also of the wider European area. At the same time the central aim of the Ecumenical Orthodox center was defined and clarified as follows:

- Informing the Christian West about Orthodox worship, tradition and theology. The Theological Seminars held regularly in the Center with scholarly proposals, recommendations and discussions on various topics contributed to this end.
- Promoting the unity and the resolution of various issues between the Orthodox Churches and serving as the center of the pan-Orthodox meetings.
- Cultivating the ecumenical spirit and inter-Christian relations with other Churches and Faiths with the ultimate aim of promoting the wider unity.
- Convening of the Joint Working Committees of bilateral or multilateral theological dialogues of the Orthodox Church with the other Christian Churches.[7]

Finally, it is worth noting that Metropolitan Damaskinos sought to connect between theology and pastoral care, so as to ensure the necessary organic reciprocal inclusion between theory and practice. In this perspective he stressed that the role of Orthodoxy, especially in the 20th century, must be contemporary, universal and without polarizations. He advocated the principle that Orthodoxy is responsible answer urgent issues of humanity, such as the human rights, the dignity of the person, the prevalence of the ideals of peace, justice and love and the respect for creation.[8]

In this effort he did not stop proposing solutions and dealing with difficult theological questions, mainly related to ecclesiology. *What does it mean for the Orthodox Church to have unity with the rest of the Churches? On the basis of which ecclesiological criterion is the distinction made between the notions of "Church" and "Confession"? How is it possible to speak of one Church, i.e. the Orthodox, and of many Churches outside of Orthodoxy, without contradicting ourselves? Is it possible for a Church to equate the limits of the One, Holy, Catholic and Apostolic Church with its own and yet to accept the same ecclesiological elements in other Churches without creating an internal problem in its self-consciousness?[9]* In these difficult ecclesiastical questions, he sought through his studies and action to give essential answers. So when he spoke on theological issues he approached it from the perspective that what we will experience in the eschaton, is the consistency of the whole and the harmony of all regardless of gender, race, age, social status, moral or political affiliation. In the Spirit of adoption of the Father all people, according to Damaskinos, become children of God and through baptism they participate in the celebration of the Holy Eucharist, which renews our communion with God Himself.[10]

Bibliography

1. Damaskinos Papandreou - Metropolitan of Switzerland, *Orthodoxy and United Europe*, (Katerini: Tertios, 1989) (in Greek).
2. Damaskinos Papandreou - Metropolitan of Switzerland, *Orthodoxy and World*, (Katerini: Tertios, 1993) (in Greek).
3. Damaskinos Papandreou - Metropolitan of Switzerland, *Theological Dialogues. An Orthodox Perspective,*(Thessaloniki: 1986) (in Greek).
4. Metropolitan of Switzerland Damaskinos, "Religion and Society in Modern European reality" in *Église et État en Europe*, in the series Études Théologiques, vol.11, (Geneva: Centre Orthodoxe de Chambésy, 1996), 53-70.

---

[7] *Damaskinos Papandreou – Metropolitan of Switzerland* (Athens: 1990), 21-22.
[8] Damaskinos Papandreou - Metropolitan of Switzerland, *Orthodoxy and World* (Katerini: Tertios, 1993), 71 (in Greek).
[9] "Proceedings of the Inter-Orthodox Preparatory Commission, Chambesy 16-28/07/1971" in *Episkepsis* 41 (1971): 15.
[10] Maria Brun, *Damaskinos Papandreou first Metropolitan of Switzerland 1969 - 2003*, op. cit. 693-695.

Part III: Representative Orthodox Theologians reflecting on Ecumenism

5. Metropolitan Damaskinos Papandreou, "Le Dialogue de l 'Eglise Orthodoxe avec le Judaisme et l' Islam. Experiences de conflict, de reconciliation et de coexistence", in Maria Brun - Wilhelm Schneemelcher, *Thanksgiving, Festschrift für Damaskinos Papandreou, Metropolit der Schweiz*, (Athens: 1996), 343-355.

6. Metropolitan of Switzerland Damaskinos, "Religion and Society in Modern European reality", in *Religion et Société*, in the series Études Théologiques, vol.12, (Geneva: Centre Orthodoxe de Chambésy, 1996), 75-92.

7. *Damaskinos Papandreou - Metropolitan of Switzerland*, (Athens: 1990).

8. Maria Brun, *Damaskinos Papandreou – first Metropolitan of Switzerland 1969 - 2003*, (Athens: 2011) (bilingual edition, Greek-English).

9. Vasilios Karagiannis, Bishop of Trimithunta, "The Metropolitan of Andrianoupolis Damaskinos and my spiritual roots" in *Church - Oikoumene - Politics, Tribute to the Metropolitan of Andrianoupolis Damaskinos*, (Ahtens: Interparliamentary Assembly on Orthodoxy, 2007), 325-336 (in Greek).

10. Costas Mygdales, "Damaskinos A. Papandreou: the Prelate, the Leader", in *Church - Oikoumene - Politics, Tribute to the Metropolitan of Andrianoupolis Damaskinos*, (Athens: Inter-parliamentary Assembly on Orthodoxy, 2007), 455-466 (in Greek).

(translated by Fr. George Anagnostoulis)

Fr. Oliver Herbel

A Biographical Introduction to Fr. Alexander Schmemann[1]

Schmemann was born in 1921 in Tallinn, Estonia, to a Russian family of German origin. He studied at St. Sergius Orthodox Theological Institute in Paris from 1940 to 1945, was ordained a priest in 1946, and lectured there from 1946 to 1951. During this time, Schmemann studied under Sergius Bulgakov, a renowned theologian, though Kyprian Kern (1899-1960) had the most theological influence upon Schmemann. During his time in Paris, Schmemann was exposed to an ecumenical liturgical movement that was part of the *ressourcement* movement, a movement committed to a return to earlier patristic and liturgical sources. Kyprian Kern and Nicholas Afanasiev (1893-1966) helped organize ecumenical liturgical gatherings. Through these week-long gatherings, Schmemann became familiar with the liturgical and historical work of important Roman Catholic theologians such as Dom Botte, Louis Bouyer, Jean Daniélou, Yves Congar, Dom Gregory Dix, and Henri de Lubac. This meant Schmemann's theological vision itself was an ecumenical enterprise, even while he retained his strong commitment to the Orthodox Church. This vision concentrated upon the Church living out her baptism by being gathered around the Eucharist, the sacrament that overcomes the divisions of the world and offers all to God, infusing all of creation with the gift of redemption. In this way, humanity serves as the priest of creation, not because certain men are "separated" from the rest as "ordained priests," but because the Orthodox Church as a whole exists to serve in this priestly life.

In 1951, Schmemann accepted a teaching position at St. Vladimir's Orthodox Theological Seminary in New York, primarily for financial reasons. It was while teaching there that he would later complete his doctorate in 1959 from St. Sergius Institute. He served as Professor of Liturgical Theology from 1951 to 1983 and concurrently as dean of the seminary from 1962 until his death in 1983. During his time at St. Vladimir's Seminary, Schmemann also served as an adjunct instructor at Union Theological Seminary, General Theological Seminary, New York University, and Columbia University, bringing his theology to a complete ecumenical circle—ecumenical in development and ecumenical in dissemination.[2]

Schmemann was more concerned with secularism and engaging Western culture than with institutional ecumenism per se, though he did participate in such ecumenism, as evidenced by his presence at the 1954 Assembly of the World Council of Churches in Evanston, Illinois, his participation in the Fellowship of St. Alban and St. Sergius and his role as an Orthodox observer at Rome's Second Vatican Council.[3] Because Schmemann's theological vision was broader than institutional ecumenism, it affected not only theologians, but also clergy and laity. He gave thousands of "Sunday Talks" for Radio Liberty. These talks addressed the basics of the faith for those living inside the USSR. He also served as an advisor to the Holy Synod of Bishops of the Metropolia, later the Orthodox Church in America. The Metropolia was known as such due to its history. Following the Russian Revolution in 1917-1918, Metropolitan Platon found himself exiled in North America and took the helm of the North American archdiocese. In 1924, the diocese declared itself self-governing in response to the concern of collusion between the Soviet government and the Russian Orthodox Church. For this reason, it became known as the "Metropolia." While advising the bishops,

---

[1] The present paper should be read in parallel to that on Fr. John Meyendorff (ed.)

[2] A helpful summary may be found within Schmemann's obituary in the *New York Times*, December 14, 1983. Schmemann's work at Columbia proved influential on Paul Valliere. See his *Modern Russian Theology: Bukharev, Soloviev, Bulgakov* (Grand Rapids: Eerdmans, 2000), 373.

[3] See David Rodney Fox, "Beyond Secularism: The Theological Vision of Alexander Schmemann," Ph.D. diss. (Drew University, 2006).

Schmemann helped engineer a rapprochement with the Russian Orthodox Church. In 1970, the Metropolia was granted completely independent governing prerogatives ("autocephaly") and full communion with the Russian Orthodox Church.

Schmemann's Ecumenical Engagement with Western Christianity

In one of Schmemann's key texts, *For the Life of the World*, one encounters an extended argument against the dichotomy between the "sacred" and the "profane," a theme that characterizes his overall thought.[4] The book itself was written for an ecumenical body of college-age Christians and was intended as a study guide for primarily non-Orthodox students attending the 1963 Conference of the National Student Christian Federation in Athens, Ohio. The purpose of these conferences was to provide students with full resources while simultaneously encouraging the students to become their own leaders.[5] Schmemann's *For the Life of the World* was one such resource guide, which subsequently became much more widely popular. It was a work that resonated with a perspective on the university that he continued to hold, believing an institution existed "to bring new generations into a live inheritance of culture, and also, of course, into real freedom, into a critical search for truth."[6]

Schmemann's ecumenical endeavor for Christian youth parallels his liturgical scholarship, which began in Paris, when he studied and taught at the St. Sergius Orthodox Theological Institute. Many of the liturgical questions explored by Roman Catholic theologians had come to interest Schmemann's teachers and colleagues and so influenced him.[7] One issue of special note was the exploration of ecclesiology and how lay people are not merely consenting observers in the Church. Nicholas Afanasiev was especially important in this way, emphasizing the local Eucharistic gathering as the Body of Christ, which influenced Roman Catholic discussions as well as Schmemann.[8] For Schmemann, then, ecumenism was often grounded in theological exchange, from Roman Catholic theologians to an ecumenical youth gathering in America.

It should not be thought, however, that Schmemann engaged non-Orthodox Christian thought uncritically. On the contrary, Schmemann often expressed a strong reaction against Western theology, which he labeled "scientific theology." For Schmemann, this was an errant entity that had even affected seminary life, including St. Vladimir's Seminary itself. "The very idea and principle of a seminary (*as inherited from the West*), is ambiguous. It is precisely in seminaries that developed, on the one hand, the clericalization of theology, and, on the other, the religious fixation of Christianity."[9] In fact, Schmemann could be quite dismissive of Western theology, reducing it to "false dilemmas and dichotomies."[10] The very notion of a false dilemma, however, is a standard category of Western philosophy itself and one that is not restricted only to Western Christians, as Schmemann himself unfortunately demonstrated when he dichotomized and created a false dilemma between "scientific theology" and the "experience" of the Church.[11] There is, in other words, within Schmemann's thought, that same tension between reaction and embrace found in earlier Orthodox thinkers. Schmemann nuanced this somewhat. The West should not be simplistically rejected but must be actively engaged since it is the source

---

[4] Alexander Schmemann, *For the Life of the World* (Crestwood, NY: St. Vladimir's Seminary Press, 1973).

[5] Douglas Sloan, *Faith and Knowledge: Mainline Protestantism and American Higher Education* (Louisville, KY: Westminster John Knox Press, 1994), 79.

[6] Julianna Schmemann, trans., *The Journals of Father Alexander Schmemann, 1973-1983* (Crestwood, NY: St. Vladimir's Seminary Press, 2000), 194.

[7] William C. Mills, *Church, World, Kingdom: The Eucharistic Foundation of Alexander Schmemann's Pastoral Theology.* (Chicago: Liturgy Training Publications, 2012), 37-9.

[8] Ibid., 41.

[9] Julianna Schmemann, 174-5, emphasis in the original.

[10] Ibid., 150.

[11] Ibid., 209.

of Orthodox theological problems. It is his response to this very tension that enabled Schmemann to write *For the Life of the World* for, as he noted near the beginning of that work, "nowhere in the Bible do we find the dichotomies which for us are the self-evident framework of all approaches to religion."[12] This beginning point became his concluding point, when he turned to discuss the Orthodox approach, which was "either obscured or simply ignored during the long dependence of Orthodox theology on Western, mainly Latin, systems and thought forms."[13] The West was to be engaged, but Orthodoxy had also been corrupted by Western theology. The solution to the tension was the liturgical life of the Orthodox Church.[14]

For Schmemann, the high point of the liturgical answer could be found in the Eucharist, for it is through eucharistically centered worship that the whole (of those gathered) becomes greater than the sum of its parts (the individuals).[15] This greater sum included the act of bearing witness to Christ as well as the lifting up of the world into the Kingdom of Heaven, for "the Eucharist is the entrance of the Church into the joy of its Lord."[16] It is while being in a state of true thanksgiving that the Orthodox Christian is able to balance the tension between witnessing to and lifting up.

The tension itself is probably best seen in Schmemann's participation in the Hartford "Appeal for Theological Affirmation," a 1975 ecumenical statement written at Hartford Seminary Foundation in Connecticut, to address theological errors that the signers saw as rampant within Christianity at the time.[17] In an essay concerning the statement, Schmemann interpreted Orthodox silence in response to the appeal as demonstrating that Orthodoxy has always viewed Christianity in a way fundamentally different from Western Christians.[18] In light of this, Schmemann placed himself in the position of an interpreter and sought to explain the importance of the Hartford Appeal to the Orthodox and the silence of the Orthodox to Western Christians. Schmemann believed his work as ambassador between the two worlds could help further the ecumenical movement in that the Hartford Appeal could create the kind of real, profound encounter that needed to happen between Western Christians and the Orthodox. For Schmemann, this would only be possible if the Orthodox themselves took the appeal as a challenge—as an opportunity—to show how "the total, absolute, and truly apophatic transcendence of God and his real and wonderful presence in this created, fallen, and redeemed world" worked in a real way in the here and now.

Conclusion

Schmemann's ecumenical thinking was characterized by a tension between reacting against Western Christian errors affecting Orthodoxy on the one hand, and embracing what was good and true within non-Orthodox Christians on the other hand. A balance between the two may be seen in Schmemann's Eucharistic-centered response to the sacred/profane dichotomy. Schmemann (as Meyendorff) could be critical of the West and Western Christianity, but did not place the blame for all of Orthodoxy's problems upon the West. This healthy ecumenism required a balance between listening and learning on the one hand and proclaiming the Orthodox conviction that unity could be found in Orthodox Christianity on the other.

---

[12] Schmemann, *For the Life of the World*, 14.

[13] Ibid., 145.

[14] Ibid., 150.

[15] Ibid., 25.

[16] Ibid., 26.

[17] "The Hartford "Appeal for Theological Affirmation," *Mid-Stream* 14:3 (1975): 439-444.

[18] Schmemann, "The Ecumenical Agony," in *Church, World Mission* (Crestwood, NY: St. Vladimir's Seminary Press, 1979), 198. The essay was initially published as an essay in a volume of essays dedicated to the Hartford Appeal: Peter L. Berger and John Neuhaus, eds., *Against the World For the Word: The Hartford Appeal and the Future of American Religion* (NY: Seabury Press, 1976).

Bibliography

Schmemann, Alexander. *Church, World Mission: Reflections on Orthodoxy and the West.* (Crestwood, New York: St. Vladimir's Seminary Press, 1979).

-. *The Eucharist.* Crestwood, (New York: St. Vladimir's Seminary Press, 2000).

-. *For the Life of the World.* (Crestwood, New York: St. Vladimir's Seminary Press, 1973).

-. *Great Lent: Journey to Pascha.* (Crestwood, New York: St. Vladimir's Seminary Press, 1974).

-. *The Journals of Father Alexander Schmemann, 1973-1983,* translated by Julianna Schmemann. (Crestwood, New York: St. Vladimir's Seminary Press, 2000).

-. *Liturgy and Tradition: Theological Reflections of Alexander Schmemann,* Edited by Thomas Fisch. (Crestwood, New York: St. Vladimir's Seminary Press, 1990).

-. *Of Water and the Spirit: A Liturgical Study of Baptism.* (Crestwood, New York: St. Vladimir's Seminary Press, 2000).

Fr. Michael Plekon

Introduction

In the Eastern Church, usually several times during the services, the deacon or priest makes a circuit of the church building, censing all the icons on the walls, those on the icon screen before the altar as well as the altar area itself. At the conclusion of this rite, he turns and faces the congregation and then censes them. Visitors often can grasp the reverence that the censing makes to the images of Christ, the Virgin Mary and numerous angels and saints that cover the inside of the church. God and the friends of God are due reverence. But what about the women and men gathered? Are they not ordinary, imperfect, even sinful souls? One writer, whose small church was routinely filled not only with neighbourhood members but also with many impoverished, homeless, distraught individuals, had a different take on this ritual. She said that in censing those gathered for the service, no matter their failures or successes in life, the celebrant was indeed giving reverence to "living icons," God incarnate in his children, no matter who they are.

Biographical note

That writer was Elizaveta Pilenko, known later on as a nun, Mother Maria. She was born 1891 in Riga into an upper class family with an estate close to the Black Sea and, after the death of her father, she moved to winter quarters in a stylish part of St. Petersburg. Her talents were diverse—poetry, drawing, painting, later politics and philosophy, eventually even theology. Her memoirs of growing up reveal a rich cultural experience, and her life, even as a young woman, was amazingly cosmopolitan. As a child she was a favourite of the Ober-Procurator Constantine Pobedonostsev, a high official in the Imperial adminstration. Her literary talents drew her into the circles of the poets Alexander Blok and Vyacheslav Ivanov. Her relationship with Blok is startling, in her own description of it. She was not just an admirer, student or protégé, but a confidant and counsellor, and this as a teenager! She was among the first women allowed to study theology at the St. Petersburg Academy and was the first woman mayor of her family's country home, Anapa. In adolescence and young adulthood she was not only swept up in Silver Age literary circles but also the turbulent political scene in Russia. Politically engaged, she came close to execution by the Bolsheviks as a counterrevolutionary and later, as mayor of Anapa she would be put on trial by the retreating White Army.

If her cultural and political existence was complex, even more so was her personal life. An early marriage to a fellow intellectual was quickly terminated. There was another relationship and a child, Gaiana. A second marriage also ended in separation but an amicable one. Anastasia and Yuri (George), another daughter and a son, were born but they would lose Nastia as a small child to meningitis. Gaiana died of mysterious causes as a young adult after she returned to the Soviet Union. Yuri grew up at Mother Maria's hostel in Paris.

Such a complex and rich personality Liza was—a Bohemian, artistic, nonconformist political activist, later passionate servant of the poor, the homeless and those hunted by the Nazis. Those who wrote remembrances of her—Constantin Mochulsky, Sophie Pilenko, her mother, Jacqueline Perry d'Alincourt, Genevieve de Gaulle, Dominique Desanti, Metropolitan Anthony Bloom, Sophie Koloumzine and Elisabeth Behr-Sigel among others, did so with mixed feelings of admiration, affection and sadness. The death of her second daughter Nastia plunged Liza into a personal crisis on many levels. Already deeply committed to assisting suffering émigrés, Liza's spiritual transformation pushed her further and further into religious life. Her religious divorce finalized, she received monastic tonsure and the habit from Metropolitan Evlogy, head of the Russian Orthodox Church in Western Europe. Though several friends were dubious about a monastic vocation—Nicholas Berdyaev, Frs. Sergius Bulgakov and Lev Gillet—they recognized her commitment to caring for those in need and supported her work as Mother Maria. A true visionary, Met. Evlogy told her that the world and its suffering people would now become her monastery.

Theological-ecumenical vision

She would put into practice this vision of a life of Christian service, later to be called "Orthodox Action," the name of the group of which she was a co-founder. From the very beginning her vision and her work were ecumenical. She was funded in part by the American YMCA as were other Orthodox educational and intellectual projects in Paris. She was close to the Fellowship of St. Alban and St. Sergius, the first ecumenical Orthodox-Anglican organization, through Bulgakov. First on Villa de Saxe, then on Rue de Lourmel in Paris and further out in Noisy-le-Grand, Mother Maria somehow found the financial resources to open houses of hospitality, where meals, shelter, fellowship and medical and other services were available to any in need. The chapel became the heart of the hostels, and just as in her writings for various journals, the love of God was linked inextricably to the love and service of the neighbour in need. Criticized by companion nuns and another chaplain for not attending all the services in the chapel, Mother Maria needed to do much more. She scoured Les Halles markets for surplus or day old produce, meat and other food the merchants would give her. She had organized the cooking of meals as well as the providing of other services. The service of the sister or brother was the continuation of the liturgy, "outside the church."[1] She could see no opposition or distinction between the love of God and of the neighbour. The two great gospel commandments were for her in reality just one invitation to love.

> Christ gave us two commandments: to love God and to love our fellow man. Everything else, even the commandments contained in the Beatitudes, is merely an elaboration of these two commandments, which contain within themselves the totality of Christ's "Good News." Furthermore, Christ's earthly life is nothing other than the revelation of the mystery of love of God and love of the neighbour. These are, in sum, not only the true but the only measure of all things. And it is remarkable that their truth is found only in the way they are linked together. Love for man alone leads us into the blind alley of an anti-Christian humanism, out of which the only exit is, at times, the rejection of the individual human being and love toward him in the name of all mankind. Love for God without love for man, however, is condemned: "You hypocrite, how can you love God whom you have not seen, if you hate your brother whom you have seen" (1 Jn 4:20). Their linkage is not simply a combination of two great truths taken from two spiritual worlds. Their linkage is the union of two parts of a single whole.[2]

As cosmopolitan as her life had been in Russia, it remained so in Paris and it was also intensely ecclesial. Alongside her work directing the hostels, Mother Maria sustained a lively intellectual life, participating in study groups and periodicals led by major Russian intellectual figures such as Nicholas Berdyaev, Sergius Bulgakov, Ilya Fundaminsky and George Fedotov. These groups were ecumenical at the root, often comprised of Catholic as well as Protestant and Orthodox intellectuals, many of who attended the gatherings of the various circles and contributed to the important periodical Berdyaev edited, *The Way*. Mother Maria was a frequent contributor as well. Many of her essays were contributions to debate about what shape the Christian life should take, as well as on the rise of Fascism and impending war. While respecting the tradition of prayer, church services, the feasts and fasts, Mother Maria would not accept all of Christian faith being reduced to these activities and certainly not a legalistic observance of them. In the many essays in which she engaged in this debate, Mother

---

[1] Mother Maria, *Essential Writings*, 82, 183-186.
[2] *Essential Writings*, 173-174.

Maria's rebuttal is radical, fearless, confident. In rediscovering the "liturgy after the liturgy," the service of the neighbour rooted in worship, she was faithful to the early church and far ahead of her time, much like Dorothy Day and Catherine deHueck, her contemporaries.

In "A Justification of Pharisaism," she rejected the subservience of the Church to any authority, political, economic, social or ethnic.[3] Mother Maria, clearly under the influence of historian George Fedotov, demythologizes "Holy Russia." Like Fedotov, she looked with discernment at the actual historical figures of the Russian tradition, while at the same time revering their legacy as still living and relevant. In her arguments for outreach to those in need, she cites in the first place, the Gospels but then the example of Nilus of Sora, Sergius of Radonezh, Seraphim of Sarov, on the evangelical poverty of Joseph of Volokholamsk. She examines various forms of Christian faith and engagement at length in "Types of religious Lives."[4]

Mother Maria's theological vision resembles that of the "Paris School" of which she is a member. Paul Valliere has insightfully profiled their outlook and legacy, one of ecumenical openness to other churches and progressive, open to the modern world.[5] Bulgakov and Berdyaev were mentors, but Mother Maria retained her own distinctive style and view, as Natalia Ermolaev argues.[6] Yet she shared many perspectives with them, on the Russian tradition, on ecumenical work with other Christians, on the need for political and social engagement.[7] These are rooted in the vision of "the humanity of God." (*Bogochelovechestvo*)—the Incarnation as God embracing humanity, with the invitation to us to do the same. One can find this affirmation in essays such as "The Second Gospel Commandment, "Love without Limits," and in a distinctive way in "On the Imitation of the Mother of God."[8] The Incarnation, God's becoming human through the Virgin Mary, was her dogmatic foundation. The Incarnation must then be lived out, put into practice by those who bear the name of Christ. In so doing they continue Christ's work "Christifying," bringing all creation into Christ.[9]

> In several essays in 1939, Mother Maria reflected on the growing power of Fascism in Europe. In one essay written in late 1939, she writes about the "Guardians of Freedom"–those who stood up against the threats to the human person, to freedom and to Christianity in those apocalyptic times. The "guardians of freedom" which Mother Maria explicitly praises are the Roman Catholic, Anglican and Protestant Churches, which voiced their opposition to threats to freedom.[10]

The work in Mother Maria's hostels became more intense with the invasion of France and the occupation of Paris in 1940. Feeding and housing those in need had been difficult enough in the years preceding but with the occupation, the task became almost impossible. Yet Mother Maria found ways in which to utilize the increasingly scarce resources. She applied for and received recognition as a public canteen from the municipal government, and thus was able to get supplies and subsidies. As her biographers and those remembering her witness, with the cooperation of her chaplain, Fr. Dmitri Klepinin, she began to protect and hide those hunted by the Gestapo—Jews but also members of the Resistance, those with opposition political views. Some were dispersed to secure houses and hiding in the country. Others were supplied baptismal certificates and membership in the hostel's parish community. The Gospel mandate to love the neighbour took on its most radical challenge in those days.

---

[3] *Essential Writings*, 114-120.

[4] Ibid., 88-101.

[5] *Modern Russian Theology: Bukharev, Soloviev, Bulgakov*, Grand Rapids MI: Eerdmans, 2000, 347-403.

[6] "The Motherhood of God: Mother Maria Skobtsova's Poetry and Theology," PhD. dissertation, Columbia University, 2010.

[7] See my anthology of texts in translation from these thinkers of the Paris School, including almost 2/3 of those from their 1937 manifesto collection, *Zhivoe predanie* ("Living Tradition")—*Tradition Alive: An Anthology on the Church and the Christian Life in Our Time*, Sheed & Ward/Rowan & Littlefield, 2003.

[8] *Essential Writings*, 43-58, 94-101, 59-72.

[9] Ibid. 181-184.

[10] "The Guardians of Freedom" (1939), French translation in Sainte Marie de Paris, *Le Jour du Saint-Esprit*, ed. Paul Ladouceur, Paris: Le Cerf, 2011, 525-538.

In July, 1942, almost 7,000 Jewish citizens, over 4,000 of these children, were rounded up by the Vichy government as part of the Reich's "solution" of the "Jewish problem." They were held in summer heat at the Velodrome d'Hiver, a cycling stadium in Paris, without food and limited water and facilities. Mother Maria was there day and night, bringing food, consoling, and according to reports, smuggling out some young children in trash cans.[11] How she was reported to the Gestapo remains unclear—it may have been an insider, it may have been one of her enemies in the larger Russian community. She had many then, and still has critics and detractors today who question her faith as well as her monastic life. And when the Gestapo came to arrest her for hiding Jews in her hostels, they took Fr. Dmitri as well, for he had completed baptismal certificates to protect them and defied the interrogating officer by pointing out Jesus' Jewishness.[12] Both Mother Maria and Fr. Dmitri, as well as Yuri, her son and the hostel's treasurer, Ilya Fundaminsky, died in Nazi camps, the men from dysentery and pneumonia and slave labour. According to one account Mother Maria volunteered to take the place of another woman being sent to the gas chambers on 31 March 1945, Western Holy Saturday, just weeks before Ravensbrück's liberation by the Allies. In 2004 the four were canonised by Orthodox Church.[13]

Conclusion

We cannot see the Church as a sort of aesthetic perfection and limit ourselves to aesthetic swooning. Our God-given freedom calls us to activity and struggle. And it would be a great lie to tell searching souls: "Go to church, because there you will find peace." The opposite is true. She tells those who are at peace and asleep: "Go to church, because there you will feel real anguish for your sins, for your perdition, for the world's sins and perdition. There you will feel an unappeasable hunger for Christ's truth. There, instead of becoming lukewarm, you will be set on fire; instead of pacified, you will become alarmed; instead of learning the wisdom of this world you will become fools for Christ."[14]

Mother Maria's urgent sense of the Gospel command to love God and to love and serve the neighbour dominated her activity. She was canonised, as some of the liturgical texts for her and her companions say, as "witnesses to the truth and preachers of holiness" in their effort to save those marked for destruction. Her rambunctious personality, nonconformist life and radical dedication to serving the poor seem to be the stuff of which heroes are made. It was not necessarily viewed as such in her own time and milieu. Several of her colleagues who were quite sympathetic and supportive of her efforts at best had mixed feelings about her and her work. To still others she was a scandal, with her explosive demeanour and ragamuffin crew. The nuns who joined her eventually left for a more traditional monastic setting. Few came to her defence when arrested by the Gestapo. Today her writings still evoke criticism. Metropolitan Anthony (Bloom) of Sourozh has written that in his youth and pride, he was embarrassed by her life and work. Yet, he had the courage to recognize both her idiosyncrasies and her witness, calling her a "saint of our day and for our day." Jean-Marie Cardinal Lustiger of Paris was at the canonization services for Mother Maria and her companions on 1-2 May 2004, at the Russian Orthodox cathedral. He called her a universal saint and urged all to celebrate the new saints on 20 July, their common feast day.

---

[11] See the account of this in Jim Forest, *Silent as a Stone*, Crestwood NY: St. Vladimir's Seminary Press, 2007.

[12] Hélène Arjakovsky-Klèpinine, daughter of Fr. Dimitri, has published his biography. The English version is *Dimitri's Cross: The Life and Letters of St. Dimitri Klepinin,* Conciliar Press, 2008.

[13] . Much information on the canonization as well as photos of icons of the new saints can be viewed at: http://www.in-communion.org/st-maria-skobtsova-resources/

[14] *Essential Writings*, 113.

Bibliography

Sainte Marie de Paris (Mère Marie Skobtsov, 1891-1945), *Le Jour du Saint-Esprit*, ed. Paul Ladouceur, trans. Hélène Arjakovsky-Klépinine, Françoise Lhoest, Bertrand Jeuffrain, Alexandre Nicolsky, Nikita Struve, Jérôme Lefert, (Paris: Cerf, 2011).

Sergei Hackel, *Pearl of Great Price: The Life of Mother Maria Skobtsova 1891-1945*, (Crestwood NY: St. Vladimir's Seminary Press, 1981).

Michael Plekon, *Living Icons: Persons of Faith in the Eastern Church*, (University of Notre Dame Press, 2002).

Dominique Desanti, *La sainte et la incroyante*, (Paris: Bayard, 2007).

Mother Maria Skobtsova: Essential Writings, trans. Richard Pevear and Larissa Volokhonsky, (Maryknoll NY: Orbis, 2002).

Antoine Arjakovsky, *The Way: Religious Thinkers of the Russian Emigration in Paris and their Journal*, Michael Plekon and John A. Jillions, eds., Jerry Ryan, trans., (University of Notre Dame Press, 2013).

Part III: Representative Orthodox Theologians reflecting on Ecumenism

Fr. Ştefăniţă Barbu

Fr. Dumitru Stăniloae's (1903-1993) theological personality has been rightfully compared with that of Georges Florovsky, Eduard Schillebeeckx,[1] Karl Barth, Karl Rahner and Hans Urs von Balthasar.[2] Although Stăniloae did not intend to write an ecumenical theology, his work is nonetheless deeply ecumenical, as Ioan Săuca[3] and others remark.[4] We will offer here a brief account of Stăniloae's contribution to ecumenism by focusing on his participation in the ecumenical movement as well as on his understanding of unity and "open sobornicity".

Stăniloae is known for being one of the first modern Orthodox theologians to bring to light Gregory Palamas and the theology of the uncreated energies (1938), for his enriched translation into Romanian of the *Philokalia* (12 vols.) (1946-1948; 1976-1992), and for his *Orthodox Dogmatic Theology* (3 vols.) (1978). His entire *corpus* is very substantial over 1,149 titles, including 20 original books, 33 translations of which 24 are from the Greek Fathers, 210 studies of theology, ethics and history published in various theological journals and several hundred newspaper articles.[5] Among his publications are 65 articles, notes and comments dedicated to ecumenical issues.[6]

Beside his academic work, Stăniloae was also an active participant in the ecumenical movement, taking part in the following ecumenical gatherings: Addis Ababa (1971) – the first Orthodox-Non-Chalcedonian meeting; Goslar (1979), Iasi (1980), and Hüllhorst (1982) – meetings between the Romanian Orthodox Church and the Evangelischen Kirche in Deutschland (EKD); München (1982)[7] - the second plenary meeting of the Orthodox-Roman Catholic International Commission of Dialogue, which seems to have produced a positive change in his attitudes towards Roman Catholic theology.[8]

In many of his studies and interviews concerning ecumenical issues, Stăniloae is critical[9] towards the teachings of other Christian Churches.[10] Bordeianu contends that several factors determined some of Stăniloae's sharp

[1] Ion Bria, 'The Creative Vision of D. Stăniloae: An Introduction to His Theological Thought', in *The Ecumenical Review* 33.1 (1981): 53-59, 53.

[2] Lucian Turcescu, 'Introduction', in Lucian Turcescu (ed.), *Dumitru Stăniloae: Tradition and Modernity in Theology*, (Iaşi-Oxford-Palm Beach-Portland: The Center for Romanian Studies, 2002), 7-14, 8.

[3] Ioan Săuca, 'The Church Beyond Our Boundaries/ The Ecumenical Vocation of Orthodoxy', in *The Ecumenical Review* 56.2 (2004): 211-225, 223. Cf. Roberson, 'Dumitru Stăniloae on Christian Unity', 105; †Daniel Ciobotea, 'Părintele Dumitru Stăniloae – teolog al ortodoxiei ecumenice', in *Anuarul Facultaţii de Teologie,* (Bucuresti: Universitatea Bucureşti, 2004): 65-67.

[4] However, as some theologians have recently observed, Stăniloae's work seems to be used in more recent times for supporting an Orthodox anti-ecumenical movement. Cf. Radu Bordeianu, *Dumitru Stăniloae: An Ecumenical Ecclesiology,* (London: T&T Clark, 2011), 5.

[5] Bordeianu, *Dumitru Stăniloae,* 2.

[6] Gheorghe Anghelescu – Ioan Ică Jr., 'Opera păr. prof. Stăniloae. Bibliografie sistematică', în Ioan I. Ică jr. (ed.), *Persoană şi Comuniune: Prinos de cinstire Părintelui Profesor Academician Dumitru Stăniloae,* (Sibiu: Editura Arhiepiscopiei Ortodoxe Sibiu, 1993): 20-67;

[7] Aurel Pavel - Ciprian Iulian Toroczkai, *Adevărul şi falsul ecumenism: Perspective ortodoxe asupra dialogului dintre creştini,* (Sibiu: Editura Universitaţii Lucian Blaga, 2010), 136.

[8] Ronald G. Roberson, 'Dumitru Stăniloae on Christian Unity', in Turcescu (ed.), *Dumitru Stăniloae,* 104-125, 113.

[9] Bordeianu, *Dumitru Stăniloae,* 20-21.

[10] See for example his studies: 'Învăţătura despre Maica Domnului la ortodocşi şi catolici', în *Ortodoxia* 2 (1950): 559-609; 'Dumnezeiasca Euharistie în cele trei confesiuni', în *Ortodoxia* 5 (1953): 46-115; 'Starea sufletelor după judecata particulară în învăţătura ortodoxă si catolică', în *Ortodoxia* 5 (1953): 546-614; 'Fiinţa Tainelor în cele trei confesiuni', în *Ortodoxia* 8 (1956): 3-28; 'Starea primordială a omului despre păcatul ereditar judecată din punct de vedere ortodox', în *Ortodoxia* 9

positions, such as the fact that "he was not current with the developments in the theologies that he criticized because of his isolation behind the Iron Curtain," or because of his "personal experience with the Byzantine Catholic proselytism in his native region of Transylvania." Furthermore, Bordeianu contends that at times Stăniloae uses inappropriate generalizations, some of his sources being hard to trace.

Stăniloae rejected any form of inter-communion as a partial unity among Christian denominations as long as outstanding doctrinal issues were not resolved, or in other words as long as the same doctrines are not shared by all those involved in the dialogue, avoiding thus, in his opinion, the danger of relativism.[11] When having to choose between unity in truth and unity in love, a proposal forwarded by Brother Roger Schultz of Taizé, Stăniloae argues for a unity in truth and in love, the two being in fact two faces of the same coin.[12]

Unquestionably, for Stăniloae, "Church unity is a doctrinal unity."[13] In close dependence on this doctrinal unity he places the sacramental unity and the hierarchical unity.[14] However, Stăniloae's reflection on "unity" as one of the four marks of the Church begins by acknowledging that in fact there is one single Church because, quoting St. Ignatius of Antioch, "One is the Body of the Lord Jesus and one is His blood shed for us; one is the bread given to all and one is the cup shared to all."[15] Furthermore, drawing on Gregory of Nyssa, Stăniloae concedes that the unity of the Church has been realized in Christ through His Incarnation.[16] Therefore, "Wherever Christ is, there is unity."[17] "Division is the fight of all against all for temporary and singular things, or each one's fight against many in order to take hold of as many things as possible."[18] Therefore it is the sign of an egoistic existence. In this sense, the ecumenical movement, as an attempt to re-establish unity, appears to be a divinely inspired event.[19]

Stăniloae introduces a gradation in the "ecclesiality" of non-Orthodox communities, which he calls "not fully churches", although some of them are closer than others to this fullness.[20] Yet although only the Orthodox Church can be fully called "the Church", Stăniloae contends that "In some sense, the Church comprises all the confessions separated from her, due to the fact that they could not separate themselves completely from her."[21] Through the fact that the other Churches know Christ only partially, they have still received the quality of being church, and by this they have been called to become fully churches.[22] Thus Stăniloae, in spite of his many criticisms of non-Orthodox Churches, as well as the fact that he considers the Orthodox Church as the only true Church, still acknowledges the ecclesiality, although incomplete, of other communities. His thinking

(1957): 195-215; 'Doctrina ortodoxă si catolică despre păcatul strămoşesc', în *Ortodoxia* 9 (1957): 3-40; 'Doctrina luterană despre justificare si cuvânt si câteva reflecţii ortodoxe', în *Ortodoxia* 35 (1983): 495-509. Some of the critiques addressed in these studies, as well as a somehow pessimistic attitude towards the ecumenical movement are re-encountered in the last part of Stăniloae's life (late 1980s-1993). See for example three interviews: Ioanichie Bălan, *Convorbiri duhovniceşti*, vol. II, (Editura Episcopiei Romanului şi Huşilor, 1988); Sorin Dumitrescu, *7 Dimineţi cu Părintele Stăniloae*, (Bucureşti: Anastasia, s.a.), (interview realized in 1992); Costion Nicolescu, *Teologul în cetate. Părintele Stăniloae şi aria politicii*, (Bucureşti: Christiana, 2003), 110.

[11] Dumitru Stăniloae, 'În problema intercomuniunii', în *Ortodoxia* 4 (1971): 561-584; Dumitru Stăniloae, 'Biserica universală şi sobornicească', în *Ortodoxia* 18.2 (1966): 167-198.

[12] Dumitru Stăniloae, 'Iubire şi adevăr: Pentru o depăşire a dilemei ecumenismului contemporan', în *Ortodoxia* 19 (1967): 283-292.

[13] Dumitru Stăniloae, *Teologia Dogmatică Ortodoxă*, vol. II, (2nd ed., Bucuresti: EIBMBOR, 1997), 173. (Henceforth *TDO*. All the translations from Romanian are mine, unless otherwise indicated.)

[14] *TDO*, II, 175.

[15] *TDO*, II, 171.

[16] *TDO*, II, 170.

[17] *TDO*, II, 169.

[18] *TDO*, II, 169.

[19] Dumitru Stăniloae, 'Mişcarea ecumenică şi unitatea creştină în stadiul actual', în *Ortodoxia* 15 (1963): 544-589.

[20] *TDO*, II, 176.

[21] *TDO*, II, 176.

[22] *TDO*, II, 176.

Part III: Representative Orthodox Theologians reflecting on Ecumenism

is thus similar to that of Fr. Georges Florovsky, for example, who advanced the idea that the juridical and the mystical or charismatic borders of the Church do not coincide.[23]

For Stăniloae, the answer to the question "How can Orthodoxy contribute to the ecumenical dialogue?" is found in Orthodoxy's "symphonic character,"[24] which is the manifestation of its sobornicity/catholicity. Thus, Stăniloae contends that "Orthodox sobornicity, as a true organic unity in plurality, can serve as model – even as final goal – for the different Churches in the progress of their ecumenical relations."[25]

Stăniloae dwells more on the idea of sobornicity and its significance for the ecumenical dialogue in his well-known 1971 study "Sobornicitate deschisa" (Open Sobornicity).[26] Stăniloae uses the word "sobornicity" (similar to the Russian word *sobornost*) to translate the Greek *catholikos* of the Nicene-Constantinopolitan Creed. In Stăniloae's writings, sobornicity has a broad range of meanings: "universality", "communion" and "conciliarity".[27] "Sobornicity is Christian universality in the form of communion. (…) It is also all-encompassing unity of the Christian teaching lived by the universal and free Christian community."[28]

Stăniloae's discussion on "open sobornicity" comes in the wake of the document of the Faith and Order Commission on *Scripture and Tradition* (Aarhus, 1964), which emphasized unity in diversity testified in Scripture, reflecting God's various actions and the many ways in which human beings respond to Him. Stăniloae values the document especially for its recommendation that one should not retain exclusively one single aspect or interpretation of the Bible, thereby running the risk of misunderstanding the richness of God's revelation.[29] Stăniloae wishes to apply the same recommendation not only to interpreting the Bible but also to any theological affirmation. Thus he argues that:

God makes himself known and works through acts, words and images, always different, for He does not exhaust his being in any of them, but through all of them He reveals Himself. One should not disregard any of them since God has found them worthy to be used, yet one must not regard any of those belonging to the revelation and to the history of piety until now as fully expressing God, thereby excluding for the future other possible modes of expressing God… One must not attach oneself to any or to all of these modes as to the final reality, as Bonhoefer and Congar say, because all are penultimate. All have to be transparences of God, because each one of them indicates something from His being. Furthermore, one has to admit as well new modes of expressing God, or rather, our relationship with Him. This means that one has to recognize that all Christian modes of expressing God have a certain value, and at the same time a certain lack of fullness, a degree of relativity. Both these attitudes of Christian conscience can help us progress on the road of Christian unity. To cling only to some modes of expressing God as to the ultimate and exclusive reality means to experience His presence in a very limited way, or not at all, and to absolutise our diversity, not seeing through this diversity the Same One God… And this holds us in division, since each one considers that through one's way of living and expressing God one lives and expresses Him completely, and that one's way is the only way to live and express God.[30]

---

[23] Cf. Georges Florovsky, 'The Doctrine of the Church and the Ecumenical Problem', in *The Ecumenical Review* 2.2 (1950): 152-161; Georges Florovsky, 'The Limits of the Church', in *The Church Quarterly Review* 233 (1933): 117-131. See also our study 'Ecclesiality, Sacraments of Initiation, and the Orthodox-Roman Catholic Dialogue: New Prespectives', in P. De Mey (ed.), *The Arduous Journey from Consensus to Communio: Ecclesiology in the Bilaterals*, (Leuven: Peeters Publishers, 2012).
[24] Dumitru Stăniloae, *Theology and the Church*, Trans. by Robert Barringer, (New York: St. Vladimir's Seminary Press, 1980), 221.
[25] Stăniloae, *Theology and the Church*, 221.
[26] Dumitru Stăniloae, 'Sobornicitate deschisă', în *Ortodoxia* (1971): 165-180. This study received lately increased attention from the part of ecclesiologists and ecumenists. See for example: Lucian Turcescu, 'Eucharistic Ecclesiology of Open Sobornicity?', în Turcescu (ed.), *Dumitru Stăniloae*, 83-103; or Roberson's already mentioned study on 'Dumitru Stăniloae on Christian Unity', as well as the first chapter of Bordeianu's *Dumitru Stăniloae: An Ecumenical Ecclesiology* which bares the title 'Open Sobornicity: Stăniloae's Interaction with the West', 13-40.
[27] Cf. *TDO*, II, 186.
[28] Stăniloae, 'Sobornicitate deschisă', 172.
[29] Stăniloae, 'Sobornicitate deschisă', 172.
[30] Stăniloae, 'Sobornicitate deschisă', 173.

This perspective mirrors Orthodoxy's understanding of deification as a continuing process of growth in holiness, of which Stăniloae has been a great promoter.[31] At the same time Stăniloae assimilates all forms through which God is revealed with icons, which only point towards transcendence and do not exhaust the mystery of God, but only mediate it.[32]

Stăniloae considers that not only the non-Orthodox Churches but also the Orthodox Church could benefit greatly from practicing an open sobornicity by considering, for example, those elements that have been to a large extent over-stressed by the other Christian traditions.[33]

By this concept of open sobornicity Stăniloae offers Orthodoxy and the ecumenical movement a rich instrument and working method, which calls for transcending all the concepts and images used by various traditions to express and reveal God. It is at the same time an incentive for the Orthodox to deepen the mystery of God and to go beyond the centuries-old formulations that have become to a great extent ossified.

Bibliography

Works by Dumitru Stăniloae (in translation)

Théologie ascétique et mystique de l'Église orthodoxe. (Paris: Cerf, 2011).

Eternity and Time. (Oxford: SLG Press, 2001).

Die Eucharistie als Quelle des geistlichen Lebens. (Köln : Koinonia-Oriens, 2004).

Orthodox Spirituality: A Practical Guide For the Faithful and A Definitive Manual For the Scholar. (South Canaan (PA): St. Tikhon's Religious Center, 2003).

Dieu est amour. (Genève : Labor et Fides, 1980).

Le génie de l'Orthodoxie : introduction. (Paris : Desclée de Brouwer, 1985).

Theology and the Church. (Crestwood (NY): St Vladimir's Seminary Press, 1980).

Orthodox Dogmatic Theology, Vol. 1: Revelation and Knowledge of the Triune God (Continuum, 2000); *Vol. 2: The World: Creation and Deification* (T&T Clark, 2002); *Vol. 3 The Person of Jesus Christ as God and Savior* (Holy Cross Orthodox Press, 2011).

Cogoni, Daniele, Cristian Crisan and Andrei Ştefan Mărcuş. *Il genio teologico di padre Dumitru Stăniloae : prospettive antropologiche, teologiche e sacramentali.* (Assisi: Cittadella, 2010).

Miller, Charles. *The Gift of the World: An Introduction to the Theology of Dumitru Stăniloae.* (Edinburgh: T&T Clark, 2000).

Robertson, Ronald G. *Contemporary Orthodox Ecclesiology: The Contribution of Dumitru Stăniloae and Younger Colleagues.* (Romae: Typis Pontificiae Universitatis Gregorianae, 1988).

---

[31] Cf. Emil Bartoş, *Deification in Eastern Orthodox Theology: An Evaluation and Critique of the Theology of Dumitru Stăniloae,* (Carlisle, UK: Pater Noster Press, 1999).

[32] Stăniloae, 'Sobornicitate deschisă', 178.

[33] Stăniloae, 'Sobornicitate deschisă', 175.

Part III: Representative Orthodox Theologians reflecting on Ecumenism

(41) Metropolitan Kallistos Ware of Diokleia

Tamara Grdzelidze

Biographical Note

Metropolitan Kallistos (born Timothy Ware in 1934) is one of the most widely known Orthodox theologians of the late twentieth century and the beginning of the twenty-first century. His books *The Orthodox Church* (1963) and *The Orthodox Way* (1979) are widely read both among Orthodox and non-Orthodox and are standard and easily accessible references to Orthodoxy. His translations of the Orthodox liturgical books and participation in the translation of *The Philokalia*,[1] a collection of major ascetic and spiritual texts from the fourth to the fourteenth centuries, are valuable contributions to Orthodox liturgy and spirituality.

Timothy Ware was born in an Anglican family in England and became Orthodox after a long process of contact with Orthodoxy and personal reflection, described in a short autobiographical text.[2] He was educated at Westminster School, London, and continued studying Classics and subsequently Theology at the University of Oxford (Magdalene College). He was received in the Orthodox Church (Ecumenical Patriarchate) in 1958, and was ordained deacon in 1965 and priest in 1966. He took monastic vows at the monastery of St. John the Theologian on the island of Patmos, Greece.

Ecumenical Involvement

Metropolitan Kallistos has played an important role in ecumenical relations of the Orthodox Church. With a good understanding of the Anglican tradition, he helped especially with rapprochement of the Anglican Communion and the Orthodox Church. He took an active role in the Fellowship of St. Alban and St. Sergius, founded in 1928 to promote understanding and unity between the Anglican and the Orthodox Churches, and he was a co-editor of *Sobornost*, the journal of the Fellowship. From 1973 until 1984 Bp. Kallistos was a delegate to the Anglican-Orthodox Joint Discussions and since 2007, he has co-chaired the International Commission of Anglican-Orthodox Theological Dialogue. He has been a leader of the Orthodox-Anglican pilgrimages.

Among his other ecumenical activities, in the 1990s he was a co-chairman of the committee for the proposed Orthodox- Methodist international dialogue. He was a patron of the Society of the Blessed Virgin Mary and has been a member of the Joint Coordinating Committee for the Theological Dialogue between the Roman Catholic Church and the Orthodox Church. He is the chairman of the group Friends of Orthodoxy on Iona and has been a leading figure and president of the Society of Friends of Mount Athos.

For many decades Metropolitan Kallistos has preached and taught about Orthodoxy and the Orthodox Church to a wide range of both Orthodox and non-Orthodox audiences and he is widely read in many non-Orthodox circles. A 1969 article on Orthodox-Catholic theological issues reflects on the theology of Vatican II (1962-5), highlighting the importance of discussion between Orthodox and Catholics on the role of the papacy. The article is hopeful regarding the future Orthodox-Catholic discussions around this issue, because Vatican II supplemented the teaching on *Pastor Aeternus* with statements on the episcopate and the People of God.[3]

---

[1] The *Philokalia*, The Complete Text compiled by St Nikodimos of the Holy Mountain and St Makarios of Corinth, Translated edited by G.E.H. Palmer, Philip Sherrard and Kallistos Ware, volumes 1-4 (Faber and Faber: London, 1979-1995).

[2] See "Strange yet Familiar: My Journey to the Orthodox Church," in Kallistos Ware, *The Inner Kingdom*, The Collected Works, Vol.1 (Crestwood NY: St Vladimir's Seminary Press, 2000).

[3] Kallistos Ware , "Primacy, Collegiality, and the People of God" (first delivered as the Headly lecture given at Belmont Abbey, Hereford, on 27 November 1969), *Eastern Churches Review* 3.1 (1970): 18-29.

Papal primacy became the most significant topic at the Orthodox-Catholic dialogue in Ravenna in 2007. According to Metropolitan Kallistos, 'the Ravenna statement constitutes merely an initial prelude or overture, doing no more than opening up the whole question of papal primacy.'[4] But at the same time it gave signs of hope for the understanding of the ministry of the Bishop of Rome in terms of Apostolic Canon 34: "The bishops of each province (ethnos) must recognise the one who is first (*protos*) amongst them, and consider him to be their head (*kephale*), and not do anything important without his consent (*gnome*); each bishop may only do what concerns his own diocese (*paroikia*) and its dependent territories. But the first (*protos*) cannot do anything without the consent of all. For in this way concord (*homonoia*) will prevail, and God will be praised through the Lord in the Holy Spirit."[5]

Theological Vision

Even when Metropolitan Kallistos' theology does not deliberately refer to intra-Christian issues, it contributes to the ecumenical formation of the Orthodox themselves. At the heart of his theological focus lies the search for salvation, reflected in the manifold aspects of Orthodox spirituality: the liturgical tradition, the Jesus prayer, ascetic practices, the balance between contemplation and praxis, with the Fathers of the Church as living examples of deep meditation on the truths of Christianity and purity of heart in their own lives. Another important theme for Bp. Kallistos is God's creation, which is to be protected by those created in God's image and likeness. His wide-ranging knowledge of Christianity together with his breadth of culture allows him to situate aspects of the Orthodox tradition in the context of Christian and world history and spirituality. His writings and sermons welcome all those who seek God, providing an open, welcoming and nourishing atmosphere for Christians of various traditions as well as non-Christians. The "theology of transfiguration", as Metropolitan Kallistos calls it, implies neither pietism nor abdication to secularism. Bishop Kallistos' theological vision, drawing on philosophical principles and modern psychology, permit a dialogue with modernity.

Metropolitan Kallistos combines a profound awareness of both the patristic heritage, including apophatic theology, and the Orthodox theological flowering of the twentieth century, many of whose most prominent figures he knew personally.

Bibliography

Eustratios Argenti: A Study of the Greek Church under Turkish Rule, (Clarendon, 1964).

The Orthodox Church, (Penguin, 1963; revised edition, 1993).

The Festal Menaion, (Tr. Mother Mary and Archimandrite Kallistos Ware) (Faber & Faber, 1977).

The Lenten Triodion, (Tr. Mother Mary and Archimandrite Kallistos Ware) (Faber and Faber, 1978; St. Tikhon's Seminary Press, 2002).

The Orthodox Way, (Mowbray, 1979; St Vladimir's Seminary Press, 1995).

Communion and Intercommunion, (Light & Life, 1980).

The Power of the Name - The Jesus Prayer in Orthodox Spirituality, (SLG Press, 1982).

Praying with Orthodox Tradition, (Abingdon, 1990).

How Are We Saved? The Understanding of Salvation in the Orthodox Tradition, (Light & Life, 1996).

The Inner Kingdom: Collected Works, Vol. 1, (St Vladimir's Seminary Press, 2000).

In the Image of the Trinity: Collected Works, Vol. 2, (St Vladimir's Seminary Press, 2006).

---

[4] Kallistos Ware, "The Orthodox Church and the Primacy of the Pope: Are We Any Closer to a Solution?" Album Accademico 2008-2009 (Pontificio Istituto Orientale, 44-59), 56.

[5] P.-P. Joannou, Discipline générale antique (IVᵉ – IXᵉ s.), vol. 1, no. 2, Les canons des Synodes Particuliers (Grottaferrata (Rome): Tipografia Italo-Orientale S. Nilo, 1962), 24.

Part III: Representative Orthodox Theologians reflecting on Ecumenism

Nikolaos Asproulis

Metropolitan John Zizioulas (1931-) is widely recognized as the most profound ecumenical thinker of the Orthodox Church today. He was a lay theologian before becoming titular Metropolitan of Pergamon, teaching for many years at Glasgow, London and Thessalonica universities. Inspired mainly by the Greek Fathers (in particular Ignatius, the Cappadocians, Maximus the Confessor), but also by modern existentialist trends, his thought, often described as personalist ontology and Eucharistic theology, has sparked animated debate in ecumenical theology and has had enormous influence in inter-Christian dialogue.

In seeking Zizioulas' contribution to the inter-Christian theological and ecumenical scene, we will briefly present both the phases of his involvement in the official ecumenical institutions and inter-church dialogue and primarily his basic theological insights in order to provide a robust assessment of his significant ecumenical contribution.

1. John Zizioulas' involvement in the Faith and Order Commission and the Bilateral Dialogue with the Roman Catholic Church.

a. After his doctoral studies in Athens, Metropolitan John was appointed by the WCC General Committee as Secretary of the Faith and Order Commission in 1967, where he remained until 1970. This event was of great importance for him because he gained precious ecumenical and theological experience, being at the center of the ecumenical inter-Christian movement. He organized many major events, conferences, and meetings, focusing on issues such as the Christological debate between the Oriental and Eastern Orthodox Churches, the importance of Eucharist for the Church life, the meaning of apostolic succession etc. In this context Zizioulas had the opportunity to enrich his general theological vision with the variety and the richness of Christian traditions and to broaden his ecumenical perspective and sensitivity toward the Christian other. Hence, it is not surprising that for him "the Orthodox Church cannot drop out of the ecumenical movement without betraying its own fundamental ecclesiological principles," a perspective not easily accepted by many conservative believers.

According to Zizioulas himself[1] during his work in the secretariat of Faith and Order, two major challenges were raised. On the one hand the restructuring of WCC and the need for the Faith and Order to be incorporated to the central organization with the risk of its absorption, and on the other hand the difficult combination of the Commission's strictly theological agenda (issues related to the dogmatic and doctrinal foundation of the Churches) with horizontalism, the orientation to social issues of the central organization. Zizioulas did not hesitate to address a sharp criticism of the alleged "ecclesial" character of WCC, since he has the opinion that the WCC "cannot be turned into a Church, but it must acquire an ecclesial vision shared by all its member churches,"[2] while in the meantime it could serve as the locus of a creative and healthy encounter between Orthodox and Western Christian Churches and traditions.

In his occasional paper under the title "Faith and Order, Today and Tomorrow", Zizioulas provides a general appreciation of the Commission's heritage, new challenges and future tasks. He considers the decisive advances of the Commission since its foundation (for instance, the focus on the local Church, *Nairobi* document, *Lima*

---

[1] John Zizioulas, *The One and the Many: Studies on God, Man, the Church, and the World Today* (Alhambra CA: Sebastian Press, 2010), 380.
[2] Ibid, 327.

document, the concept of *communion* etc.), "as it were, the *heritage* bequeathed"[3] to the subsequent theological generations. At the same time Zizioulas emphasizes the future task of Faith and Order to respond to the new scientific and technological challenges, in virtue of a culturally relevant hermeneutic of the common tradition. However in order for this purpose to be accomplished, Faith and Order, in Zizioulas' conception should remain, among other things, a "theological enterprise", emphasizing Church's unity in the direction of a common interpretation of the apostolic faith and "hermeneutical re-reception of the Tradition.[4]

b. The bilateral dialogue between the Roman Catholic and Orthodox Churches constitutes the place where Zizioulas' contributions have been of marked influence. Metropolitan John was from the beginning, in early 1980s, an Orthodox member of the Joint International Commission for Theological Dialogue Between the Catholic Church and the Orthodox Church, while in recent years (the second phase of the dialogue, from 2006 onwards), he is co-president of the Commission with Cardinal Kurt Koch of the Roman Catholic Church. The first phase of this dialogue (1980-2000) was extremely important and creative and produced several key-documents (Munich 1982, Bari 1987, New Valaamo 1988, followed by Ravenna 2007 in the second phase) that rendered possible the profound mutual understanding and close rapprochement of the "Sister Churches", by virtue of a common interpretation and understanding of the ecclesiological tradition.

The contribution of Zizioulas' ecclesiological thought was of great influence as is clear from the study of the basic arguments and theological rationale of these documents. For instance, beginning with the Munich document, and through the others, especially the Ravenna document, the central place that the Eucharist occupies as the heart of the Church in relation to its very being and unity, the importance of the bishop and of the synodical institution for the constitution of the Church in various levels (local, regional, universal), the decisive value of the local church as the principle by which the Universal Church manifests itself in the world, a severe and careful theological interpretation of the issue of primacy, are reflections of Zizioulas' well known and widely received Eucharistic ecclesiology, which since 1989 has attracted the interest of international theological scholarship. Even the burning issue between the two Churches, the *filioque*, has been interpreted by Zizioulas with an appeal to the common patristic (for example, Maximus the Confessor) and conciliar (Second Ecumenical Council) tradition, praising an official document of the Pontifical Council for the Promotion of Christian Unity that goes in this direction.[5]

2. The Theological Principles of Zizioulas' Ecumenical Vision.

Metropolitan John Zizioulas is a fertile ecumenical thinker whose ecclesiological thought is of decisive importance for the vital witness of the Orthodox Church within the ecumenical environment. Following both of his teachers at Harvard University, Father Georges Florovsky and Paul Tillich, he sought to articulate an ecumenical vision which was intended to offer a "neo-patristic synthesis" and existential "correlation", "capable of leading the West and the East nearer to their common roots, in the context of the existential quest of the modern man."[6] Consequently his very theological project is an inherently ecumenical programme seeking the visible unity of the *Una Sancta*. In this perspective, what are the fundamental theological principles and parameter of his ecumenical vision?

a. The issue of *methodology*: Zizioulas' *existential* dimension is most relevant to his methodology. The task of the Christian theologian is not just to quote or repeat the sayings and the writings of the Holy Fathers of

---

[3] Ibid, 381.

[4] Ibid, 385-386.

[5] See John Zizioulas, "One single source: An Orthodox response to the clarification on the *filioque*",in *The One and the Many*, 41-45. The document of the Pontifical Council is entitled "The Greek and the Latin Traditions Regarding the Procession of the Holy Spirit (Vatican City: Tipografia Vaticana, 1996).

[6] John Zizioulas, *Being as Communion: Studies in Personhood and the Church* (Crestwood NY: St Vladimir's Seminary Press, 1985), 26.

the Church, but most importantly to find the existential relevance of the common Christian Tradition, seeking to address the existential needs of humanity in our days. On one occasion Zizioulas expressed a reservation regarding his difficulty to address the issue of ecclesiology from a specific "Orthodox point of view". The point here was that there is no single "Orthodox point of view", but rather different theological interpretations of the common sources (Scripture, the Fathers, and the Councils). What is important in the ecumenical debate is always the theological presuppositions and not the concrete theses.[7] For this purpose Zizioulas has usually employed ecclesiology (especially with respect to the Eucharist) as the starting point and framework of dealing with Christian dogmatics. Since *Ecclesia* is not only an institution but more importantly "a way of being", that is, a way of relating to God, other people and creation as a whole, dogmatic theology, in the sense of dogmatic hermeneutics, should certainly be at the centre of ecumenical discussions. Drawing on this deep interpretation of the doctrine he attempts to "correlate" the Gospel and the Church to the modern human quest. According to Zizioulas himself, "after a rather long experience in ecumenical discussions, I have come to the conclusion that instead of trying to agree on concrete theological theses we should try to agree on theological principles"[8] as the urgent task of Christian theology towards its engagement into a creative and fruitful dialogue with humanistic and natural sciences.

b. *Trinitarian theology* constitutes one of the fundamental concerns of his theology. Zizioulas distances himself from the Western tendency to combine closely the Economy (God *ad extra*) and Theology (God *ad intra*). Based on the centrality of Eucharistic experience and outlook in the ancient Church, he articulates an image of the Church not only as community but mainly as an icon, reflecting the communion of the Trinitarian persons. The strictly Trinitarian roots of his ecclesiology provide the proper way for overcoming the ever-present problems of *christomonism* and *pneumatomonism*. As in the Trinity, the Father (the One) is the cause of the personal otherness of the other two persons within the context of mutual love and communion (the Many), similarly in the Church the bishop (the one) is the center of the unity and divergence of all the charismata (the many), while at the same time is conditioned by them. The Trinitarian *taxis* (order) of personal relationship and otherness is transferred through the Eucharistic channel into the structure of the Church. Interpreting the important Apostolic Canon 34 in the light of this Trinitarian ecclesiology, Zizioulas highlights the decisive importance of primacy, not only in a local but also in a universal sense, within the context of conciliarity, as a way to overcome successfully the impasse regarding the understanding of the papal primacy, which is still a burning issue between the Roman Catholic and the Orthodox Church.

c. Zizioulas' emphasis on the *eschatological* identity of the Church is certainly of decisive ecumenical importance. Following the overall retrieval of the eschatological vision in Western theology during the early 1920s, he considers eschatology not as one chapter among others in the dogmatic discourse but an outlook, a method of the entire theological enterprise. According to this eschatological perspective, the Church is considered not only as an icon of the Trinity but also or primarily as an icon of the Kingdom of God. This eschatological vision should be reflected in the entire structure and life of the Church which is centered on the Eucharistic *synaxis*. Appropriating this eschatological perspective, Zizioulas challenges the ecumenical movement with the necessity to overcome the constant temptation of deterioration into "ephemeral secular affairs", reminding other Christian Churches and traditions that the Church is "a prophetic sign of the Kingdom".

d. As we have seen, Zizioulas is credited with bringing to the ecumenical agenda of Faith and Order the idea of *communion*, a profoundly Biblical and patristic idea, as a key notion in its theological vision. Based on his interpretation of the Trinitarian being of God and his eschatological ontology, Zizioulas highlights the relational character of the Church, developing a communion ecclesiology. He aspires to render this ecclesiology as the common ground of inter-Christian understanding of the identity, structure, and mission of the Church. In this perspective, according to Metropolitan John, the constant re-reception of the common Tradition of the Church would provide the ecumenical movement with the proper tools in its struggle with many challenges of modernity.

---

[7] J. Zizioulas, "The Mystery of the Church in the Orthodox Tradition", in *The One and The Many*, 136.
[8] Ibid. 137.

e. Because of his emphasis on the Eucharistic identity of the Church, it is noteworthy that Zizioulas praises the Baptism, Eucharist and Ministry Document (BEM, Lima, 1982) as "a good beginning" in keeping the theological and non-secular character of WCC. Hence, for him the *sacramental* moment of the Church is not something secondary in its definition; otherwise the Church would become only an authoritative institution (a Roman Catholic tendency) and activist community (a Protestant tendency) or an archaeological monument (an Orthodox tendency) - in all these cases the Church is seen merely as a *historical* entity. In contrast, the Church as *sacramental* entity, constantly reconstituted by the Holy Spirit, "asks to receive from God what she has already received historically in Christ as if she had not received it all."[9] This epicletic dimension of the Church's life is the pneumatological input of the Orthodox tradition, where the ecclesiology always is determined by the liturgical context. Zizioulas is adamant to bring to the fore this perspective, presenting a more or less balanced interpretation of the relation between Christology and Pneumatology, in the direction of overcoming earlier tensions. Furthermore the sacramental character of the Church preserves the necessary dialectic relationship between history and *eschata*, between Church and the world. Zizioulas frequently reminds us that the Church is "in the world but not of this world", wishing to avoid any kind of conflation or identification of the Church with authoritative and compressive earthly institutions. The absolute priority of the theological criterion in Zizioulas' engagement with the ecumenical discourse should be conceived as a very decisive aspect of his thought, because it helps us to realize that the final word for all things belongs to God.

3. Conclusion

Although Zizioulas can sometimes be a very sharp critic of various forms of Western theology (for instance, his downgrading of Augustine and Aquinas, or his sharp distinction between Eastern personalism and Western essentialism), his overall theological enterprise is a constant attempt to recover the common tradition and patristic roots of Church unity. Following his mentor Georges Florovsky, he recognizes that "ecumenism in time" should precede and be conceived as the very ground of any kind of "ecumenism in space". Considering individualism, that is, ecclesiastical *provincialism,* as the basic problem and a real tragedy for the Orthodox Church, he argues for the necessity for the Churches to rediscover the Eucharistic and conciliar self-understanding of the early Church as the proper way of overcoming the obstacles in the direction of the Christian unity.

Bibliography

McPartlan, Paul, *The Eucharist Makes the Church: Henri de Lubac and John Zizioulas in Dialogue,* (Edinburgh: T & T Clark, 1993).

Papanikolaou, Aristotle, *Being with God: Trinity, Apophaticism, and Divine-Human Communion,* (Notre Dame: University of Notre Dame Press, 2006).

Zizioulas, John, *Being as Communion,* (Crestwood: St Vladimir's Seminary Press, 1985).

- "Preserving God's Creation: Three Lectures on Theology and Ecology", *King's Theological Review* 12 (1989): 1-5, 41-45; 13 (1990): 1-5.
- *Ellinismos kai Christianismos: I synantisi dyo kosmon,* (Athens: Apostoliki Diakonia, 2003) (in Greek).
- *Communion and Otherness,* (Edinburgh: T & T Clark, 2006).
- *Lectures in Christian Dogmatics,* (Edinburgh: T & T Clark, 2008).
- *The One and the Many: Studies on God, Man, the Church, and the World Today,* (Alhambra CA: Sebastian Press, 2010).

---

[9] *Being as Communion,* 185.

(43) Vladimir Lossky

Paul Ladouceur

Biographical introduction

Vladimir Lossky (1903-58) was one of the leading Orthodox theologians of the twentieth century. He is a major figure in the neo-patristic movement in modern Orthodox theology and indeed his book *The Mystical Theology of the Eastern Church* (1944; English translation 1957) is possibly the most significant and influential Orthodox writing of modern times.[1] Lossky's theology focuses strongly on themes such as the importance of apophatism in theology, personalism (the person as distinct from nature, both with respect to God and to humans), the essence-energies distinction in God (Palamism) and the inseparable links among theology, mysticism and spirituality.

Vladimir Lossky was born in Göttingen (Germany) in 1903, where his father, the well-known Russian philosopher Nicolas Lossky, lived temporarily for academic reasons. Vladimir spent his childhood in Saint Petersburg, where he studied history under the religious philosopher and medieval historian Lev Karsavin from 1919 to 1922. The Lossky family was expelled from the Soviet Union in late 1922, and after two years in Prague, Vladimir Lossky received a scholarship to study in Paris. He studied medieval history at the Sorbonne, specialising in medieval Western thought. Lossky followed closely the teaching of the great Catholic medievalist Étienne Gilson and in the late 1920s, developed a strong interest in Western mysticism. This interest eventually focussed on the mysticism of Meister Eckhart, and resulted in a profound study on apophatic theology and knowledge of God in Eckhart, for which he was awarded a doctorate posthumously.[2] It was Eckhart's constant insistence on the incomprehensibility of God that led Lossky to explore apophatism and Palamism in the Orthodox tradition.[3]

Together with other young Russian immigrants in France, especially the Kovalevsky brothers (Eugraph, Maxime and Serge), Lossky played a leading role in the Fraternity of St Photius, established in 1928 to advocate the universality of Orthodoxy and to promote a local expression of universal Orthodoxy in the countries of exile of those fleeing the Russian revolution. For Lossky and other members of the Fraternity, this meant an "enculturation" of Orthodoxy to Western Europe, involving for example rediscovering the ancient roots of the universal Church from the period before the separation between East and West (for example local saints and the ancient Gallic Liturgy) and the use of the local language for liturgy, while maintaining essential Orthodox doctrines. The Fraternity's activities were intended to provide an Orthodox witness in the West, a bridge between the separated parts of Christendom. It is in this context that Lossky became a member of the first French-language parish, the parish of the Transfiguration-Saint Genevieve, established in 1928 with Father Lev Gillet ("A Monk of the Eastern Church") as priest, under Metropolitan Evlogi (Georgievsky). In 1936 Lossky joined the newly-established French-language parish under the Moscow Patriarchate, Notre-Dame-Joie-des-Affligés.

In the mid-1930s, Vladimir Lossky became deeply involved in the painful conflict over the doctrine of the divine Sophia, advanced by the leading Orthodox theologian of the time, Father Sergius Bulgakov. Lossky wrote several texts criticising sophiology, which he regarded as a dangerous doctrine, as well as other aspects of Bulgakov's theology.

---

[1] *Essai sur la théologie mystique de l'Église d'Orient* (Aubier-Montaigne, 1944; Le Cerf, 1990). *The Mystical Theology of the Eastern Church* (James Clarke: London, 1957; Crestwood, NY: St Vladimir's Seminary Press, 1976).

[2] Published as *Théologie négative et connaissance de Dieu chez Maître Eckhart* (J. Vrin, 1960). Forward by Maurice de Gandillac, Preface by Étienne Gilson.

[3] Cf. Rowan Douglas Williams, "The Theology of Vladimir Nikolaievich Lossky: An Exposition and Critique" (unpublished thesis, Oxford University, 1975), 8.

In 1945 the "French Orthodox Mission" under the leadership of the brilliant if erratic Father Eugraph Kovalevsky established the Institut Saint-Denys as a theological school devoted to furthering the development of French-language Orthodoxy. Lossky was the principal theologian connected with the French Orthodox Mission and he became dean of the Institute and professor of dogmatics and Church history. He remained with the Institute until Kovalevsky broke with the Moscow Patriarchate in early 1953; Lossky resigned from the Institute, preferring to remain with Moscow than seeking canonical affiliation elsewhere. He subsequently taught in the context of pastoral courses organised by the Moscow Patriarchate in France and died suddenly in February 1958.

Ecumenical engagement

Vladimir Lossky was engaged in ecumenical dialogues primarily in two contexts, within the institutional framework of the Fellowship of Saint Alban and Saint Sergius, and, on a less structured basis, with French theologians, philosophers and other intellectuals, including non-believers.

The Fellowship was founded in 1928 to promote ties between Orthodox and Anglicans and was very active in the 1930s. Fathers Sergius Bulgakov, Georges Florovsky, Lev Gillet and Sergius Chervernikov were the principal Orthodox participants in the Fellowship in the pre-war period. In August 1947, Vladimir Lossky was invited to participate for the first time in the Fellowship's summer session. In subsequent years, he became one of the leading Orthodox participants in the Fellowship, together with other Orthodox theologians such as Lev Gillet and Elisabeth Behr-Sigel. Lossky enjoyed considerable prestige among the Anglican members of the Fellowship because of his patristic orientation and his approach to "mystical theology" – it was through his involvement with the Fellowship that his *Mystical Theology* was first translated into English and published in 1957. For Rowan Williams, Lossky's stature in many English ecumenical circles grew to the point that "Lossky came to hold the position, occupied by Bulgakov before the war, of chief spokesman for the Orthodox viewpoint."[4]

Beginning in the 1930s, Lossky had frequent contacts with Catholic theologians and philosophers in Paris who turned to the study of the early Fathers of the Church, the *ressourcement* movement which was at the source of the *nouvelle théologie* within the Catholic Church. Lossky participated in the Resistance during World War II, all the while maintaining his intellectual interests, including participation in colloquia organised by the well-known philosopher Marcel Moré. These meetings brought together a wide range of theologians and philosophers and it was here that Lossky delivered a series of conferences in 1944 on Orthodox mystical theology, published in 1944 under the title *Essai sur la théologie mystique de l'Église d'Orient*.

From these colloquia developed a new periodical, *Dieu vivant: Perspectives religieuses et philosophiques*, founded in 1945 by Louis Massignon, Marcel Moré and the future Cardinal Jean Daniélou. The Catholic intellectuals and theologians behind *Dieu vivant* represented a new voice in Catholic theology, long dominated by increasingly arid scholasticism. *Dieu vivant* was a public expression of the "patristic turn" in Catholic theology, begun in the 1930s and its orientation was decidedly "eschatological", often on the fringes of, or even opposed to official Catholic theology. From the start *Dieu vivant* was ecumenically oriented. The editorial committee, which reviewed manuscripts, consisted of a Catholic (Gabriel Marcel), a Protestant (Pierre Burgelin), an Orthodox (Lossky) and a non-believer (the philosopher Jean Hyppolite). Lossky contributed an article on St Gregory Palamas to the first issue of *Dieu vivant* and published another major article in the journal in 1948.[5] During its short existence (1945-55), *Dieu vivant* was an influential if controversial periodical on the French intellectual scene. Other major Orthodox figures who published articles in the journal were Elisabeth Behr-Sigel, Paul Evdokimov and Myrra Lot-Borodin.

---

[4] Rowan Williams, "The Theology of Vladimir Nikolaievich Lossky," 27-8.

[5] Lossky's articles in *Dieu vivant* were "La théologie de la lumière chez saint Grégoire Palamas", *Dieu vivant* 1, 1945; and "Du troisième attribut de l'Église," *Dieu vivant* 10, 1948 (translations in *In the Image and Likeness of God* (Crestwood, NY: St. Vladimir's Seminary Press, 1974).

Part III: Representative Orthodox Theologians reflecting on Ecumenism

Lossky also participated in the *Centre catholique des intellectuels français* (CCIF), founded clandestinely in 1941 by Catholic philosophers and historians as a meeting-place for French Catholic intellectuals to reflect on the place of Catholic Christianity in modern society and to take part in the great intellectual debates of the time. This group was especially active after the war and played an important role in the preparation of the Second Vatican Council. Open to the active participation of non-Catholics and non-believers, several Orthodox thinkers (Lossky, Paul Evdokimov and the iconographer Gregory Krug) were invited to take part in the discussions.[6] Lossky's participation sought in the CCIF "to identify in Western mystical movements those which are related to Eastern spirituality" and "to witness to the universality of Orthodoxy."[7]

In 1939, Vladimir Lossky met Jean Wahl, a renowned French philosopher, forced into exile during World War II. After the war, Lossky participated in the *Collège philosophique*, which Wahl founded in 1946 as a centre for non-conformist intellectuals, an alternative forum to the more conservative Sorbonne. Lossky was a regular participant in the *Collège philosophique*, contributing five major papers to its discussions.[8] In a similar vein, in 1945-46 Lossky gave a series of lectures on the vision of God in patristic and Byzantine theology at the *École pratique des hautes études*, a leading French secular institution for research and higher education affiliated with the Sorbonne.[9]

For the last 15 years of his life, Vladimir Lossky saw his role primarily as witnessing to Orthodoxy in the West; he represented "the creative presence of a theologian at the heart of the flow of ideas", an Orthodox witness "at the heart of Western science and thought" (Olivier Clément).[10] This included not only involvement in confessional institutions such as Catholic and Anglican groups, but also in secular bodies which included non-believers. Lossky was unflinching in his adherence to Orthodox doctrine, yet at the same time fully prepared to enter into fraternal dialogue with Western Christians. Rowan Williams writes that Lossky "clearly regarded it as a part of his theological vocation to identify not only the points of serious divergence between Eastern and Western Christendom, but also points of convergences, the hidden Orthodoxy of the West."[11]

The ecclesiological principles of Lossky's ecumenical outlook

Vladimir Lossky's ecumenical outlook rested on two fundamental principles of his ecclesiology: first, in the "catholicity" of the Church, which, as he emphasizes, is not a geographic notion but rather a recognition of the presence of the whole Truth of the Church in each of its discrete parts, in the image of Christ as the Head of the Church, in the smallest component "where two or three are gathered in my Name" (Mt 18:20), as in the entire Communion of Saints:

Catholicity is not a spatial term indicating the extension of the Church over the entire face of the Earth. It is rather an intrinsic quality present from the beginning and forever proper to the Church, independent of the historical conditions in which her space and numbers can be more or less limited. For the Fathers of the first centuries, the *Katholiké* or *Catholica*, used as a noun, often becomes a synonym for *Ecclesia*, designating a new reality which is not a part of the cosmos, but a totality of a more absolute order. The Church exists in the world, but the world cannot contain her...

---

[6] Lossky participated in discussions of "Transcendence and Negative Theology," "Dogma and Mystery" and "The Myth."

[7] Claire Toupin-Guyot, "Modernité et Christianisme. Le Centre Catholique des intellectuels français (1941-1976). Itinéraire collectif d'un engagement" (Unpublished thesis, Université Lumière Lyon II, 2000).

[8] Lossky's papers at the Collège philosophique were "Ténèbres et lumière dans la connaissance de Dieu," "L'apophase et la théologie trinitaire," "La notion théologique de la personne," "La théologie de l'image" and "La rose et l'abîme (la notion de l'être créé chez Maître Eckhart." All except the last are contained in *In the Image and Likeness of God*.

[9] These lectures were published in French in 1962 and in English as *The Vision of God* (Crestwood, NY: St. Vladimir's Seminary Press, 1983).

[10] Olivier Clément, *Orient-Occident, Deux passeurs, Vladimir Lossky et Paul Evdokimov* (Geneva: Labor et Fides, 1985), 98.

[11] Rowan Williams, "The Theology of Vladimir Nikolaievich Lossky," 8.

The Truth which we confess presents itself in all its objectivity, not as a private opinion, as "my personal theology", but as the teaching of the Church, the *kath' olon*, as the catholic Truth. The mystery of the catholicity of the Church is realised in the plurality of personal consciousnesses as a harmony of unity and multiplicity, in the image of the Holy Trinity which the Church accomplishes in her life: three Consciousnesses, a single Subject; a single "Divine Council" or "Council of Saints" which is the divine catholicity, if we dare to apply this ecclesiological expression to the Holy Trinity. In the ecclesiastic realm, in the becoming of the new creation, a number of personal consciousnesses are the consciousness of the Church only to the extent that they cease being self-awareness and substitute for their own "me" the single subject of the multiple consciousnesses of the Church.[12]

And secondly, Lossky recognises the presence of divine grace in non-Orthodox Christian communities:

Faithful to its vocation to assist the salvation of all, the Church of Christ values every "spark of life," however small, in the dissident communities. In this way it bears witness to the fact that, despite the separation, they still retain a certain link with the unique and life-giving centre, a link that is, so far as we are concerned, "invisible and beyond our understanding." There is only one true Church, the sole bestower of sacramental grace; but there are several ways of being separated from that one true Church, and varying degrees of diminishing ecclesial reality outside its visible limits.[13]

Lossky's ecumenical outlook is also tempered by a vivid awareness of the scandal of Christian disunity: "The absence of unity in the Christian world is a cruel reality, constantly present in the conscience of every Christian concerned with the common destiny of humanity… The wound caused by these separations remains virulent and bleeding…"[14] Yet for Lossky ecumenical involvement, the search for Christian unity, must be based on faithfulness to one's own ecclesial Tradition: "We discover this union of the Churches on condition that we go to the very end in the clear and sincere confession of the faith of our specific and historical Churches or communities, to which alone we are committed."[15]

Lossky rarely presented his views on ecumenism in a systematic fashion, but his personal involvement in a variety of institutions bears witness to his commitment to ecumenical dialogue. In his ecumenical activities he remained faithful to his firm convictions that the Orthodox Church possesses the plenitude of the truth of Christianity and that it is the responsibility of Orthodox to bear witness to this truth in the societies in which they live. In practice this meant both presenting the scriptural and patristic foundations of Orthodox theology and pointing out where Western theologies depart from this tradition to engage in perilous doctrines.

It is in this ecumenical context of contacts with Catholics, Anglicans, Protestants and non-believers that Lossky prepared many of his writings. Indeed, many of his publications consist of written versions of lectures delivered in French in the various religious and secular bodies mentioned above. Lossky's engagement in inter-confessional dialogue is unmistakable. At the same time he is fully committed to the Orthodox tradition and accepts no compromise in the expression of essential Orthodox theological doctrines, which have an inevitable impact on Christian spiritual life. For Lossky, the conflict of ideas and doctrines among modern Christian Churches and communities is real, but the exposition of divergent theologies takes place in a context of openness and respect, a search for truth wherever truth is to be found.

[12] Vladimir Lossky, "La Conscience catholique: Implications anthropologiques du dogme de l'Église," in *À l'Image et à la Ressemblance de Dieu* (Paris: Aubier-Montaigne, 1968), 190-1.
[13] Vladimir Lossky, introductory note to Patriarch Sergius (Stragorodsky), "L'Église du Christ et les communautés dissidentes," in *Messager de l'Exarchat du Patriarche russe en Europe occidentale* 21 (1955): 9-10. Cited by Kallistos Ware, "Strange Yet Familiar: My Journey to the Orthodox Church," *The Inner Kingdom* (Crestwood, NY: St. Vladimir's Seminary Press, 2001), 9.
[14] Vladimir Lossky, "The Doctrine of Grace in the Orthodox Church" [c. 1952], published in *Présence orthodoxe* (Paris), 42 (1979). Introduction and English translation by Paul Ladouceur, forthcoming in *St Vladimir's Theological Quarterly* (2014). See Lossky's introduction to this article below.
[15] Vladimir Lossky, "The Doctrine of Grace in the Orthodox Church."

Part III: Representative Orthodox Theologians reflecting on Ecumenism

Bibliography

Vladimir Lossky wrote mostly in French. Several of his books are transcriptions of lectures or courses taught in Paris or posthumous collections of articles. This bibliography includes the original publication and translations in English where applicable.

I. Works by Vladimir Lossky.

Spor o Sofii [The Controversy over Sophia], (Paris: Confrérie Saint-Photius, 1936).

Essai sur la théologie mystique de l'Église d'Orient, (Paris: Éditions Montaigne, 1944; Le Cerf, 1990; 2004). *The Mystical Theology of the Eastern Church Church*, (James Clarke: London, 1957; Crestwood, NY: St Vladimir's Seminary Press, 1976).

Der Sinn des Ikonen (with Leonid Ouspensky), (Bern and Olten, 1952). *The Meaning of Icons*, (Boston, 1952; Crestwood NY: St Vladimir's Seminary Press, 1989).

Théologie négative et connaissance de Dieu chez Maître Eckhart, (J. Vrin, 1960; 1973; 1998).

Vision de Dieu (Lausanne: Delachaux & Niestlé, 1962). *Vision of God*, (Crestwood NY: St Vladimir's Seminary Press, 1983).

À l'image et à la ressemblance de Dieu, (Paris: Aubier-Montaigne, 1967; Le Cerf, 2006). *In the Image and Likeness of God*, (Crestwood NY: St Vladimir's Seminary Press, 1974).

Théologie dogmatique in: *Messager de l'Exarcat du Patriarche russe en Europe occidentale*, (Paris, 1964-1965); *La Vie spirituelle* 677 (Paris, 1987); (Paris: Le Cerf, 2011). *Orthodox Theology: An Introduction* (Crestwood NY: St Vladimir's Seminary Press, 1978).

La Paternité spirituelle en Russie aux XVIIIième et XIXième siècles (with Nicolas Arseniev), (Bellefontaine [SO 21], 1977).

Sept jours sur les routes de France (Le Cerf, 2001). *Seven Days on the Roads of France*, (Crestwood NY: St Vladimir's Seminary Press, 2012).

Histoire du dogme. Course given by Vladimir Lossky between 1955 and 1958. Unpublished manuscript, recorded and transcribed by Olivier Clément (numerous quotations from this work are contained in Olivier Clément *Orient-Occident, Deux passeurs: Vladimir Lossky et Paul Evdokimov*, (Geneva: Labor et Fides, 1985).

II. Major Works on Vladimir Lossky.

The most important study of Lossky's theology is Rowan Williams' unpublished doctoral thesis:

Rowan Douglas Williams, *The Theology of Vladimir Nikolaievich Lossky: An Exposition and Critique*. Thesis, Oxford University, 1975. Available online at the Oxford University Research Archive (http://ora.ouls. ox.ac.uk). See also his article "The *Via Negativa* and the Foundations of Theology: An Introduction to the Thought of V. N. Lossky," *New Studies in Theology* 1 (1980).

Olivier Clément, *Orient-Occident, Deux passeurs: Vladimir Lossky et Paul Evdokimov*, (Geneva: Labor et Fides, 1985).

Special issue devoted to Vladimir Lossky of the journal *Contacts* (Paris, 31, 106, 1979), 111-238. Articles by Donald A. Alichin, J.R. Bouchet, Olivier Clément, Étienne Gilson, Basil Krivochein, John Meyendorff, and Christos Yannaras.

Juljia Vidovic

St. Justin Popovic shares the position of the entire Orthodox Church on ecumenism. Our dialogue with non-Orthodox is the evangelical responsibility that is specific to the very nature, to the very essence of the Orthodox Church, which is the same Church that the Lord founded on Himself as eternal stone (1 Corinthians 3:11). It is our duty to bear witness to the Risen Lord to the end of the world. This mission was entrusted to the Apostles, and the Orthodox Christians do not have the right today, after two thousand years, to withdraw from it.

However, a profound interest and involvement in the ecumenical movement implies questioning and criticism of it. We should not stand silently by without pointing out the problems that arise within the ecumenical movement when, represented by certain organizations, it begins to meddle in political and national issues while the essential question – the unity of the Christian world – remains in the shadows. How can the Orthodox Church (and indeed other churches) participate in a movement which could ultimately destroy the very foundations of the Christian faith and morals?

As we have concluded that on the one hand, we do not have the right to withdraw from efforts toward ecumenical dialogue, and that on the other, we have ever rising discontent with the development of the broader ecumenical movement, the question is whether it is time to design a new model, a new formula of ecumenism which would allow us to interact with each other and collaborate in a more positive way? This does not mean that we need to, or should, abandon and forget all the important work that has already been done: convergence, better knowledge and understanding of each other impregnated with love, but having the mind and heart to make a step forward. For this new model of dialogue and collaboration we have an inexhaustible source in the works of Justin Popovic, and especially by using his severe criticism of the consideration of ecumenism as an ideology.

Fr. Justin represent what Bishop Athanasius (Yevtic) calls "the Orthodox ecumenism."[1] This means that the whole truth of our Christian faith is the revelation of the Holy Trinity in Christ, in His Incarnation. The body of this truth, as the Fathers of the Church often stated, is the Church as the Body of Christ. Therefore, for us Orthodox, the very real Ecclesiology in our times is derived from, based on and inseparable from Christology. "The union of God and man in Christ, our own union with God, with His creation (= the whole world) and other people, is in the cosmic and, at the same time, in the concrete historical, ecclesiastical body of the Church of Christ. For this reason bridging of all chasm, abyss, and 'dualism' – that cannot exist alongside the Person of Jesus Christ, God-man – is an essential feature of the Orthodox vision of the world and of man, and therefore of the Orthodox 'ecumenism'."[2]

From this movement, which is certainly not a new one, all "Orthodox ecumenists" proceed, i.e. ecumenical people, people not of exclusiveness, but of inclusiveness, comprehensiveness, like Fr. Justin Popovic.[3]

Saint Justin Popovic's (1894-1979) criticism of ecumenism was deeper and more theologically founded than that of Bishop Nikolai.[4] He, as Bishop Athanasius notes, never actively participated in meetings and ecumenical dialogues. However, during his studies in England (1916-1919) inquired after of Bishop Nikolai, who was active, as we have seen.

---

[1] Bishop Athanasius (Yevtic), "Православни икуменизам", in Radovan Bigovic, *Православље и екуменизам*, Хришћански културни центар (Belgrade, 2005), 181.

[2] *Ibid.*

[3] Bishop Athanasius (Yevtic), "О екуменизму", in Radovan Bigovic, *Православље и екуменизам*, Хришћански културни центар (Belgrade, 2005), 201.

[4] Cf. the related article on Bishop Nikolai by the same author (ed.).

When addressing his critique of ecumenical dialogue we must bear in mind the historical context. Justin Popovic spoke during the time of the Ecumenical Patriarch Athenagoras. The latter made several audacious statements, saying that there were no real obstacles to the establishment of the unity of the Church and that the difficulties came only from theologians and theology. Patriarch Athenagoras made statements full of emotion and daring, and gave the impression that a new category of ecumenists had appeared in the Orthodox world. In a testimony on Saint Justin, Irenaeus (Bulovic), one of his faithful disciples and one of the most active representatives of the Serbian Orthodox Church in the ecumenical dialogue of our times, noted: "I feel that voices like that of Father Justin, often harsh and critical, have ensured that the course of events should not take a different direction. Father Justin, this is how I understand it now, after raising this issue with him often, never criticized the idea of dialogue, witness and love. He was himself an extremely open person. But he criticized the ideology of ecumenism, considered as a variant of the 'new Christianity', as an ecclesiological heresy. He felt it as a dangerous heresy and he even forged a new term, now widely used, that of the 'pan-heresy'."[5] But unfortunately in our times, those who most often refer to this term are well below the theological and spiritual level of Justin Popovic.

Those who hold the position that Justin Popovic was an anti-ecumenist most often refer to his study *Orthodox Church and Ecumenism.*[6] However, as noted by his disciple and collaborator, Bishop Athanasius (Yevtic), who perhaps best understood his thought, "this book was not written specifically on that subject, but quickly redacted from the unfinished manuscript of Father Justin, who was then working on the third and final book of Dogmatic Theology, which gives a fuller and richer picture of Justin's ecclesiology."[7]

According to Bishop Athanasius, Justin Popovic does not reject the term "ecumenism", which in his writings is usually identified with the Roman Catholic and Protestant humanistic tendencies toward Christian unity, but following the methodology of the Church Fathers who transformed the terminology of pagan philosophy, he fills this term with a new meaning and content.[8] On this specific point Vladimir Cvetkovic notes that: "as he (Fr. Justin) finds the substitute for humanism in the God-humanism, he also replaces the idea of western ecumenism as a humanistic project with the evangelical and Orthodox ecumenism as the God-human endeavor. In other words, for Saint Justin, as a result of the dwarfing of the God-man Christ by man, first by the infallible man in Rome, and later by infallible human beings all over Europe, Christianity in the West has been reduced to humanism."[9] Here we find clearly recognizable and elaborated Bishop Nikolai's aforementioned critique of a European civilization separated from Christ on the one hand, and of the presence of the secularist tendencies inside the Church on the other. According to St. Justin, in both Roman Catholicism and Protestantism, man as the supreme value replaces the God-man Christ.

But his criticism is also addressed to the Orthodox whose humanistic theorems regarding the plans for a next 'ecumenical' Council of the Orthodox Church have almost nothing in common with the "essential relation to the spiritual life and experience of apostolic Orthodoxy down the ages."[10] We can only wonder if such a spirit

[5] Bishop Irenaeus (Bulovic), "Сербская Церковь и экуменизм", *Церковь и время* 4.7 (1998): 61-62 (in Russian).

[6] St. Justin Popovic, *Православна Црква и Екуменизам,* published in both Serbian and Greek in 1974 by the Serbian Monastery of Chilandar on the Mont Athos Greece. Available online on: http://www.svetosavlje.org/biblioteka/izazovi/justin.htm (last accessed on the 6th of December 2012).

[7] Bishop Athanasius (Yevtic), "Introduction", in St. Justin Popovic, *Записи о екуменизму,* (Манастир Твдош, 2010) 2.
[8] *Ibid.*

[9] Vladimir Cvetkovic, "St. Justin the New (Popovic) on the Church of Christ" in Danckaert, Baker et al. (eds.), *The Body of the Living Church: the Patristic Doctrine of the Church,* St. Vladimir's Seminary Press, Crestwood, New York, forthcoming. (Paper ceded by the author for consultation). (I would like to express my sincere gratitude to the author allowing me to consult and use his unpublished paper for the present article).

[10] St. Justin Popovic, "On a Summoning of the Great Council of the Orthodox Church", letter addressed to Bishop Jovan of Sabac and the Serbian hierarchy on May 7, 1977, with the request to transmit this letter to the Holy Synod and the Council of Bishops of the Serbian Orthodox Church. Available online on: http://www.svetosavlje.org/biblioteka/izazovi/justin.htm (last accessed on the 6th of December 2012).

was present in the preparation of such an important event for the Orthodox Church. In one of his early works *The Inward Mission of Our Church: Bringing About Orthodoxy*, he underlines that:

"The mission of the Church, given by Christ and put into practice by the Holy Fathers, is this: that in the soul of our people be planted and cultivated a sense and awareness that every member of the Orthodox Church is a Catholic Person, a person who is for ever and ever; that each person is Christ's, and is therefore a brother to every human being, a ministering servant to all men and all created things. This is the Christ-given objective of the Church. (…) For our local Church to be the Church of Christ, the Church Catholic, this objective must be brought about continuously among our people. And yet what are the means of accomplishing this God-man objective? Once again, the means are themselves God-man because a God-man objective can only be brought about exclusively by God-man means, never by human ones or by any others. It is on this point that the Church differs radically from anything that is human or of this earth."[11]

Yet at the beginning of the above-mentioned book on ecumenism Fr. Justin wrote:

"Ecumenism is a movement that swarms with numerous questions. And all of these questions, in fact, spring from a desire and emerge into a desire. And that desire wants one thing: the True Church of Christ. And the True Church of Christ holds, and must hold, answers for all questions and sub-questions that ecumenism raises. Because, if the Church of Christ cannot resolve eternal questions of the human spirit, then she is not necessary… Among the creatures man is the most complex and most mysterious one. That is why God came down to earth and became a man… For this reason he remained on earth in His Church, of which He is the head, and she – His Body. She – the True Church of Christ, the Orthodox Church: and in it all the God-man with all his benedictions, with all its perfections."[12]

By this Fr. Justin shows the uniqueness of the God-man event and the reality that is the Church = Christ is the salvation for all modern ecumenical enquiry and wandering and is, at the same time, the only hope of fallen humanity and the world.

This vision of ecumenism is especially developed in his *Notes on ecumenism*, dating from 1972 but only published in 2010. Bishop Athanasius (Yevtic), thanks to whose efforts the *Notes* were published, explains how they were formed at a time when Justin Popovic was working on his book *The Orthodox Church and Ecumenism*.[13] He observes that *Notes on ecumenism* shows all the breadth and depth of Justin Popovic's theology and ecclesiology founded on the very sources of Orthodoxy. "In these *Notes* the real Justin is present: by his language, by his style, literature, polemics, philosophy, theology, and above all, by his confession of the God-man Christ and His Church."[14]

For developing his understanding of "Orthodox ecumenism", as we can read in these *Notes*, Justin Popovic does not refers to any secondary literature of his time but invokes the help of the testified experience of the Scripture and the living Tradition preserved in the Church of Christ. However, methodologically speaking it may represent a kind of lack in Justin's approach of Western Christianity, as Bishop Maxim (Vasiljevic) noted.[15] Justin's methodology was based on the communion with the incarnated historical God-man as he

---

[11] St. Justin Popovic, *The Inward Mission of Our Church: Bringing About Orthodoxy*, Available online on: http://orthodox-info.com/general/inwardmission.aspx (last accessed on the 6th of December 2012).

[12] St. Justin Popovic, *Православна Црква и Екуменизам*, 7.

[13] Bishop Athanasius (Yevtic), "Introduction", in St. Justin Popovic, *Записи о екуменизму*, (Манастир Твдош, 2010) 2.

[14] *Ibid.*

[15] "On observe d'un côté chez nos trois auteurs (including Bishop Athanasius) l'absence d'une lecture approfondie et documentée de la théologie occidentale ; mais d'un autre côté, prévaut l'impression qu'une telle lecture ne servait qu'à confirmer une opinion déjà formée chez ces auteurs orthodoxes. Or, cette opinion avait été formée sous l'influence de la critique russe de la culture occidentale, ainsi que la théologie occidentale. Une telle conclusion nous oblige à définir ce moment comme une imperfection, puis comme la source d'une certaine « vulnérabilité » de leur synthèse, paradigme et proposition. En effet, si leur critique de la théologie occidentale a été établie avec l'aide de l'attitude « préexistante » des

noted: "'Gospel *not according to man*' (Galatians 1:11). There is nothing '*according to man*': neither content, nor method; since nothing can be measured by man nor 'according to man'. Everything (should be) in accordance with the God-man: therefore – (it is) irreducible to humanism or its methods, but everything (should be measured) according to the God-man and man through the God-man."[16]

This does not mean that Fr. Justin was against a thorough work on contemporary theological or any other scholarship, on the contrary, for this it was essential first to be formed at the school of the Church of Christ in order to obtain the mind of Christ (1 Corinthians 2:16).[17] But to "obtain the mind of Christ" and to come to the Truth the first thing that has to be done is repentance, "Repentance leading to knowledge of the truth" (2 Timothy 2:25).[18] Only then will the Truth, which is Christ the God-man Himself, be given for the faith, as Saint Paul stated: first faith, then truth, and at the end love, which is the bond of perfection (Colossians 3:14). From this it becomes apparent that ecumenical dialogue cannot be only a dialogue of love[19]. "Faith is the bearer of truth and Love loves because of the Truth; what was delivered from a lie – deception, love? 'Love speaking the truth' (Ephesians 6:15) 'new' love: Christ – the God-man: delivers from sins, death, from every evil, from every devil: And it is capable of being eternal because it loves what is eternal in man, above all: The Eternal Truth."[20]

After this first important remark, we may proceed by saying that Justin Popovic in his *Notes* elaborates his concept of ecumenism on a central difference between any humanistic ecumenism on the one side, and the "Orthodox ecumenism" on the other.

1) The main problem of the modern European man, according to Justin Popovic, is that he fights against the God-man, and in that fight he degenerates himself into a pseudo-man.[21] What is the cause of this fight? Long patristic tradition gave a comprehensive answer to this important anthropological question, which was summarized by Fr. Justin in his *Notes* by these words: "For only by solving the problem of the God-man, would the problem of man be solved, and also the problem of everything eternal in all human worlds. Therefore: God always has to be in the first place and a criterion for everything, and man should always be in the second place. From God to man: from the God-man to man. The first commandment, and always the first: love of God (*theofilia*), and from it and after it, the second commandment, always the second (Matthew 22:37-39). And all

---

théologiens orthodoxes russes et non à la suite d'une approche personnelle et directe des théologiens occidentaux eux-mêmes, alors une telle critique doit être considérée avec une certaine réserve. En termes simples, si l'approche avait été différente du point de vue méthodologique, alors l'aspect *polémique* de leur théologie aurait été encore plus approfondi et plus solidement fondé. Et peut-être les résultats auraient-ils été en partie différents ?" ("Trois théologiens serbes entre l'Orient et l'Occident. Nicolas Velimirovic, Justin Popovic et Athanase Jevtic", in *Istina* 56 (2011): 72. This confirms also an other important thing that the book *The Orthodox Church and Ecumenism* was not for the western reader.

[16] *Notes on Ecumenism*, 18. "Nothing human, moreover sinful, cannot represent the principal criterion in all spheres of human life and knowledge. Only a pure, passionless and divinized mind can be the criterion but solely by the God-man. This is a divine-mind, divine-will and divine-life: 'We have the mind of Christ' (1 Corinthians 2:16). (…) Without it and beyond it – the entire man lies in eternal darkness and shadow, especially his parts, fragments. All this is a pseudo-gnosis, a pseudo-gnoseology. Thus comes a pseudo-culture, a pseudo-Christianity; everything that doesn't have an organic relation to the God-man is pseudo" (*Notes on Ecumenism*, 16-17).

[17] "Ecumenism. All this is a gnoseological problem. It can only be solved by the Holy Trinity; from the Father through the Son with the Holy Spirit. The Holy Spirit mightily performs, acts, creates and churchifies only in the frame theanthropic and the God-man category" (*Notes on Ecumenism*, 7).

[18] *Notes on Ecumenism*, 7. This is particularly underlined in his letter from 1964 addressed to a future monk and partly published in Fr. Justin Popovic, *На богочовечанском путу*, (Belgrade: 1980), 205-207.

[19] "Ecumenism. 'Dialogue of love': The entire history of the Orthodox Church and Holy Fathers 'speaking the truth in love' (Ephesians 4:15) have constantly be oriented towards you/us/ for centuries; each Father – the dialogue of truth and love in the truth and leading towards the truth. St. Marc of Ephesus – calls to the following: the dialogue of Truth and Love: for Truth and Love are of one essence (homoousios) in the Church, in the Gospel" (*Notes on Ecumenism*, 19).

[20] *Notes on Ecumenism*, 20. (Cf. *Notes on Ecumenism*, 19).

[21] *Notes on Ecumenism*, 24.

Orthodox Handbook on Ecumenism

the humanism headed by popes, goes the other way round."[22] This leads him to conclude that in comparison to all other heresies, humanistic ecumenism is a "pan-heresy."[23]

The reason for this, according to Fr. Justin, is that humanistic ecumenism falls into the trap of scholasticism and rationalism, which want to measure explain everything by man and only "according to man". And the main problem is that they are guided only by the unquenchable desire to "'conquer' this visible, material world", so as Fr. Justin noticed: "They live by it and they live for the sake of it: every culture is in this and for this, and so is civilization. And what would be the content of man even if he 'gained' the whole world, all the worlds (Matthew 16:26) (...) What is the use of it if by it and because of it, man forfeits his soul which possesses his entire and eternal value, joy and the meaning of his being?"[24] That is why every human work and all human achievements should be viewed from this principal theanthropic criterion, which is the God-man. The very reason for this is that "He alone heals and saves man from humanistic selfishness, narrowness, goal and closing in oneself."[25] In other words, He only can satisfy the unquenchable human desire for life without end. This is also the reason why the Church is principally the Divine Liturgy, and not a worldly or social organization.[26]

2) Now it becomes clear that, as Saint Justin said, the problem of ecumenism presupposes the genuine Church. So, by answering the question of the genuine Church we should be able, at the same time, to give a proper answer to ecumenism.[27] Then what is the Church? According to Fr. Justin, "the Church is the most complex organism in all the world; it comprises everything from all the world: that is why it is impossible to give an integral definition of the Church. Thus her most perfect definition is the God-man and He is her ineffable essence. The God-man embraces everything: from God to atoms. Everything is in God although everything is not God: it is precisely by Him and in Him that everything stays personal, original, on its own: in being and in essence and above all, in personality. For personality is the most mysterious mystery after God himself."[28]

From this very important passage we can draw several conclusions about Saint Justin's understanding of Orthodox ecumenism:

a) the perfect definition of the Church is the God-man Himself, as "her ineffable essence". This is also the reason why he so often insists on the fact that for a proper understanding of ecumenism, and consequently of the Church, the key is to properly comprehend and perceive the God-man Christ and His work.[29]

b) In "the very personhood of the God-man, our Lord Christ, in the Second Hypostasis of the Triune Godhead, is the whole divine and whole human nature. *Perichoresis* = interpenetration - through faith, the holy sacraments and virtues."[30] Ecumenism founded on the God-man becomes "ontologically integral, temporally integral, eternally integral, integral by the Truth. And it is only the God-man who unites everything and everyone in the Church."[31] By the fact that He is a Man, He united to Himself the whole creation, and by the fact that He is at the same time God, He united to Himself everything and all except the sin, death and the devil. And so "the God-man by the Holy Spirit through the Holy Sacraments and holy virtues performs human salvation."[32] Thanks to the theanthropic

---

[22] *Notes on Ecumenism*, 7.

[23] *Notes on Ecumenism*, 7.

[24] *Notes on Ecumenism*, 15.

[25] *Notes on Ecumenism*, 14. Elsewhere he will write: "Until man becomes consubstantial with the Church – the God-man, he remains humanistically alone; always pupating in the narrow pupa of human, in an earthly way" (*Notes on Ecumenism*, 10). But when he is with the God-man, man becomes a "heavenearth, theanthropic being and by God he entirely becomes theanthropic, he divinizes himself" (*Notes on Ecumenism*, 11).

[26] *Notes on Ecumenism*, 11.

[27] *Notes on Ecumenism*, 10.

[28] *Notes on Ecumenism*, 6.

[29] *Notes on Ecumenism*, 4.

[30] *Notes on Ecumenism*, 17.

[31] *Notes on Ecumenism*, 9.

[32] *Notes on Ecumenism*, 27.

humanism, the "man spreads out through all theanthropic dimensions. And all his capacities and components do so. Everything acquires its theanthropic eternity through (the) victory over death, sin and the devil."[33]

c) And finally, according to Fr. Justin, and with this we will finish with this brief presentation of his understanding of ecumenism; though much remains to be said, that goes far beyond the limits of this presentation.[34] "God-manhood is the fundamental catholicity of the Church (=ecumenicity, the same as the relation between the atom and the planet[35]): to the Trinity: but by the God-man who introduces and unites with the Holy Trinity who is the ideal and the reality of the perfect catholicity (=ecumenism): the ideal society and the ideal person: everything is *perichoresis*: everything perfectly united and preserved in that perfect catholicity. Every man is a living image – an icon of the Holy Trinity = therefore the Church as the 'body of the Holy Trinity' is everything and all for him and his trinitarization (being filled with the Holy Trinity)' represents 'human perfection' – in the God-man. That is why the Church is the most perfect workshop for making a perfect man. Everything else apart from the God-man: pseudo-society and pseudo-personalities are an illusory humanistic mixture of everything. Only Christ is everything and everyone."[36]

In conclusion we can say that such an "ecumenism" (from the Greek word *oecumène*, universe) would reflect conciliar and soteriological responsibility of the Church for the salvation of the entire world. We hope that in accordance with Saint Justin Popovic to be representatives of and witnesses to an ecumenism that is not against dialogue, testimony or collaboration, but against all kinds of falsifications and errors. Thus discernment of spirits is a principle that applies perfectly to the ecumenical movement.

Bibliography

"The Philosophy and Religion of Dostoyevski", in *Christian Life (Hriscanski Zivot),* N°1, year I (1922), N° 2-4, year (1923); separate book, (Sremski Karlovci, 1924) (in Serbian)

"The Inward Mission of Our Church", in *Christian Life* 9.2 (1923) (Latter republished more than once in Serbian and Greek)

"The Crisis of Humanism", in *Raskrsnica (Crossroad)* 13-14, (1924) (in Serbian)

The Orthodox Philosophy of Truth: The Dogma of the Orthodox Church. Book. I, (Belgrade, 1932); Book II, (Belgrade, 1935); Book III, (Belgrade 1978) (in Serbian)

About the Progress in the Mill of Death, (Monastir, 1933) (in Serbian)

Dostoyevsky on Europe and the Slavs, (Belgrade, 1940) (in Serbian)

The Philosophy of Life According to St. Sava, (Munich, 1953) (in Serbian)

Philosophical Abyss, (Munich, 1957) (in Serbian)

The Theory of Knowledge of St. Isaac the Syrian, (Athens, vol. 38, 1967, and 2nd. ed., Thessaloniki, 1980) (in Greek)

Man and the God-man: Studies in Orthodox Theology, (Sebastian Press, Western American Diocese, 2009) (in English)

The Orthodox Church and Ecumenism, (Thessaloniki, 1974) (in Serbian and in Greek)

On the Planned Great Council of the Orthodox Church, (Athens, 1977) (in Greek); (Geneva, 1977) (in French); *Orthodox Life,* (Jordanville, New York, N° 1) (1978) (in English)

Orthodox Faith and Life in Christ, (Institute for Byzantine & Modern Greek, 1994) (in English)

Commentary on the Epistles of St. John the Theologian, (Sebastian Press, Western American Diocese, 2009) (in English)

---

[33] *Notes on Ecumenism,* 9.

[34] Cf. Vladimir Cvetkovic, "St. Justin the New (Popovic) on the Church of Christ" in Danckaert, Baker et al. (eds.), *The Body of the Living Church: the Patristic Doctrine of the Church,* (Crestwood, NY: St. Vladimir's Seminary Press), forthcoming.

[35] "In experiencing the Church in all her dimensions, even by atom. Because an atom also contains the entire God-man; just as the entire sun reflects itself in one drop of water" (*Notes on Ecumenism,* 14).

[36] *Notes on Ecumenism,* 6.

(45) Bishop Nikolai Velimirovic

Juljia Vidovic

Saint Nikolai Velimirovic (1880-1956) was bishop of Ohrid and of Zhicha in the Serbian Orthodox Church. As an influential theological writer and a highly gifted orator, he became known as 'the New Chrysostom.'[1] Bishop Nikolai strongly supported the unity of all Orthodox Churches and established particularly good relationships with the Anglican, the Old Catholic and the American Episcopalian Church. His presence in England during the years of the Great War did much to strengthen the friendship between the Church of England and the Eastern Orthodox Churches in general, and the Serbian Church in particular. His original Christian eloquence made a deep impression and his warm personality won him many friends. As the Bishop of London wrote at the time: "Father Nikolai Velimirovic by his simplicity of character and devotion has won all our hearts."[2] In his lifetime, Bishop Nikolai visited the United States of America several times, and perhaps of all Eastern Orthodox churchmen was the best known to America. After his speech at the Institute of Politics in Williamstown, Massachusetts, in 1927, a reporter covering the event wrote,

"His black monk's robe, his long black beard, and his dark, living eyes, set in an oval Slavic face, gave him an appearance which contrasted as strongly with that of conventionally dressed professors and diplomats as did his views of the common problems of world peace contrast with theirs. His charm and urbanity of manner, the completeness of his grasp upon international problems only emphasized the difference in his thought … Bishop Nikolai, speaking from the point of view of a civilization in which men still are more important than institutions, points out that peace or war is a matter of the way men think and feel toward each other, and that all other things are only outgrowths of this. The greatest force for affecting men's attitudes toward each other he believes would be a reunited Christian Church."[3]

Nikolai's attitude toward ecumenism is shown by his participation, as an Orthodox bishop and theologian, in the ecumenical meetings and dialogues between the two World Wars, and later he was present, as the accredited visitor, at the meeting of the World Council of Churches in Evanston, Illinois, in 1954.

In his approach to ecumenism we can distinguish two different phases. In his early works, Bishop Nikolai considered the prerequisite for the achievement of union among the Churches to be not so much agreement in doctrine as mutual love. He wrote in *The Agony of the Church*,

"The Church of England cannot be saved without the Church of the East, nor the Church of Rome without Protestantism; nor can England be saved without Serbia, nor Europe without China, nor America without Africa, nor this generation without the generations past and those to come. We are all one life, one organism. If one part of this organism is sick, all other parts should be suffering. Therefore let the healthy parts of the Church take care of the sick ones. Self-sufficiency means the postponement of the end of the world and the prolongation of human sufferings. It is of no use to change Churches and go from one Church to another seeking salvation: salvation is in every Church as long as a Church thinks and cares in sisterly love for all other Churches, looking upon them as parts of the same body, or there is salvation in no Church so long as a Church thinks and cares only for herself, contemptuously denying the rights, beauty, truth and merits of all other Churches. It is a great thing to love one's Church, as it is a great thing to love one's country, but it is much better to love other Churches and other countries too. Now, in this time, when the whole Christian world is in a convulsive struggle one part against the other, now or never the consciousness of

[1] Cf. Bishop Artemije (Radosavljevic), "The New Chrysostom. Bishop Nicolai 1880-1956", in Bishop Maxim (Vasiljevic), *Treasures New and Old. Writings by and about St. Nicolai Velimirovic*, (California-Vrnjacka Banja: Sebastian Press), 15-59.
[2] Cf. Bishop Maxim (Vasiljevic), *Treasures New and Old. Writings by and about St. Nicolai Velimirovic*, (California-Vrnjacka Banja, Sebastian Press, 2010).
[3] "Living Age", 335-6 (1928-1929).

the desire for one Church of Christ on earth should dawn in our souls, and now or never should the appreciation, right understanding and love for each part of this one Church of Christ on earth dawn in our souls, and now or never should the appreciation, right understanding and love for each part of this one Church begin in our hearts."[4]

It seems that at first he emphasizes only love and has little to say regarding the theology of the Orthodox Church. However, as bishop Athanasius pointed out, this does not mean that he denies the authenticity and uniqueness of the Eastern Orthodox Church, nor does he consider her lacking or defective in any way[5]; rather, in the context of the wartime drama encompassing his and other European nations, he sincerely wishes for the unification of all European Christian communities for their benefit and for the benefit of other Christians in the world.[6] He clearly expresses the Orthodox stance with regard to the ideal of Church unification: "We must return to the only source of Christian strength and majesty – to the spirit of Christ. This rebirth and the revival of Christianity are possible only in a united Church of Christ. This unity is possible only if built on the foundations of the original Church."[7] The above quotation confirms that in Saint Nikolai's opinion, there is continuity in two things: 1) only the Orthodox Church has the plenitude of Christ, but this is not her own treasure but the treasure of Christ accessible to everyone; 2) the relationship of the Orthodox Church with other Churches must be a relationship of love, so that they can recognize the treasure that the Orthodox Church carries.

However this explains also his harsh criticism of two things:

1) The poverty of European civilization. He observes that the spirit of any civilization is inspired by its religion, and whenever we divide a civilization from her religion, she is condemned to die. He states that "the Christian religion, which inspired the greatest things that Europe ever possessed in every point of human activity, was degraded by means of new watchwords: individualism, liberalism, conservatism, nationalism, imperialism, secularism, which in essence meant nothing but the de-christianization of European society, or, in other words, emptiness of European civilization."[8] That leads him to conclude that Europe, in abandoning Christ, abandoned all the greatest things she possessed and clung to the lower, and indeed the lowest, ones.

2) The secularization of the Church. According to Bishop Nikolai, "Liberalism, conservatism, ceremonialism, right, nationalism, imperialism, law, democracy, autocracy, republicanism, socialism, scientific criticism, and similar things have filled Christian theology, Christian service, Christian pulpits as the Christian Gospel. In reality the Christian Gospel is as different from all these worldly ideas and temporal forms as heaven is different from earth. For all these worldly ideas and temporal forms were earthly, bodily – a convulsive attempt to change unhappiness for happiness through the changing of institutions. The Church ought to have been indifferent towards them, pointing always to her principal idea, embodied in Christ. This principal idea never meant a change of external things, of institutions, but rather a change of spirit. All the ideas named above are secular precepts to cure the world's evil, the very poor drugs to heal a sick Europe, outside of the Church and without the Church."[9]

---

[4] Saint Nicolai Velimirovic, *Agony of the Church*, at the online version of the book: http://www.gutenberg.org/cache/epub/20206/pg20206.html (last accessed on the 6 December 2012).

[5] Nikolai's devotion to the Eastern Orthodox Church is clearly expressed in his speech at the meeting of the Anglican-Orthodox Society on 16th of December 1919, convened in the Cathedral of St. Paul in London (in English, with three additional texts: *The Spiritual Rebirth of Europe*, London, 1920), when he talked about the "principles of the Eastern Orthodox Church," which are: 1) the "principle of infallibility" of the Ecumenical Council that represents all local Christian Churches guided by the Holy Spirit and 2) the "principle of inclusiveness," which has been "in the prayers of the Christian East for the unification of all Christians."

[6] Bishop Athanasius (Yevtic), *"The Christology of St. Nikolai, Bishop of Ohrid and Zhicha"*, in Bishop Maxim (Vasiljevic), *Treasures New and Old. Writings by and about St. Nicolai Velimirovic*, (Sebastian Press, California-Vrnjacka Banja, 2010) 146.

[7] Saint Nicolai Velimirovic, *Agony of the Church*, at the online version of the book: http://www.gutenberg.org/cache/epub/20206/pg20206.html (last accessed on the 6 December 2012).

[8] Ibid.

[9] Ibid.

He concludes that the Church ought to give an example to secular Europe: an example of humility, goodness, sacrifice – saintliness. And he asks: "Which of the Churches ought to give this example for the salvation of Europe and of the world?" and answers, "Whichever undertakes to lead the way will be the most glorious Church. For she will lead the whole Church, and through the Church, Europe, and through Europe, the whole world, to holiness and victory, to God and His Kingdom."[10]

As we can see from the passages quoted above, the first period of Nikolai's maturation and thoughtful presentation of his understanding of man, the Church, the world, the global society, and God, is full of quests and questioning, sometimes even rebellion and revolutionary zeal, seeking for something deeper and more holistic. In this period he will write, entirely in the movement of the spirit of his time that "Christianity is not a museum where everything is set from the start, but a workshop in which the roar of labor never stops."[11] All his questing for the grasp of dead ideas and petrified structures of thought and life are in fact the pursuit of and the struggle for a living faith in the living God, the deep inner meaning and structuring of the whole being.

Metropolitan Amphilocus notes, "While being in constant dialogue with Europe and America, in his first period of life, we can say that Bishop Nikolai considered himself, especially toward Europe, as a student."[12] He was tied to the reality of the societal currents and messianic enthusiasms of his time, distinctive to Europe and to European intellectual and ecclesiastical circles in the first half of the twentieth century. But in his mature period, in the wartime and postwar time – sobered by Nazism and Bolshevism, and after experiencing Dachau – he no longer behaved toward Europe as a student but rather as a *prophet* who, in the spirit of the Old Testament prophets, felt responsible for not only for his people but for all the people of Europe and the world without exception.[13]

Nikolai begins in his youth with a kind of ecumenical humanistic vision of the Church, but in deepening his experience of the Church (which was the result of his encounter with Orthodox Russia, the Ohrid of Ss. Clement and Naum, and the Holy Mountain of St. Sava and other Athonite Fathers), he develops a clear distinction between "heterodox churches" and the Orthodox Church. He goes even further in *The Century from Ljubostinja*,[14] writing that in the Christian world only the Orthodox Church holds the Gospel as the only absolute truth and is not governed in the spirit of this century."[15] In many aspects he came close to the ways of the early Christians, the Apostles and Church Fathers, who introduced theology into everyday life, who not only lived by it but also with it.[16] This is the reason why he reproaches most sternly Western Christianity for its easy adaptation to worldly circumstances. Thus the main difference between East and West, according to him, is in "a different understanding of the Gospel of Christ – the West understands it as a theory, one of the theories, and the East as an ascetical struggle (*podvig*), and practice."[17]

However, this does not mean that Bishop Nikolai was no longer open to ecumenical dialogue. That would be in complete opposition to his inner being; that of a truly godly man who realized and achieved a balance

---

[10] Ibid.

[11] Metropolitan Amphilocius (Radovic), "Предговор" in Св. Николај Велимировић, *Изабрана дела Св. Николаја Велимировића*, at the online version of the book: http://www.svetosavlje.org/biblioteka/vlNikolaj/Uvod/Nikolaj000002.htm (last accessed on the 6 December 2012). Metropolitan Amphilocus also notes that "Encouraged and inspired by the great ideas of Western Christian nations, (Nicolai) remained to the end of his life loyal to his perception, which was expressed in sermon, *"Biti ili Delati"* ("To Be or To Do"), where the East is "to be" and the West is "to do." God's is to be *and* to do. That is why only through the unification of being and doing is it possible to find a balance between the human being and human history" (*The Theanthropic Ethos of Bishop Nikolai Velimirovich*", in Bishop Maxim (Vasiljevic), *Treasures New and Old. Writings by and about St. Nicolai Velimirovic*, (Sebastian Press, California-Vrnjacka Banja, 2010, 129-130).

[12] Metropolitan Amphilocius (Radovic), *"The Theanthropic Ethos of Bishop Nikolai Velimirovich"*, 129.

[13] Ibid., 130.

[14] Bishop Nikolai Velimirovic, *Љубостињски стослов*, at the online version of the book: http://www.svetosavlje.org/biblioteka/vlNikolaj/LjubostinjskiStoslov/Nikolaj0605.htm (last accessed on the 6 December 2012).

[15] Ibid.

[16] Cf. Djordje Janic, *Hadji into Eternity*, (Belgrade, 1994).

[17] Ibid.

Part III: Representative Orthodox Theologians reflecting on Ecumenism

between the individual and the general, the material and spiritual, God and man, national and pan-human. He was able to succeed in doing this through the mystery of Christ, the Only Lover of man, as he called Him in one of his final works, in the mystery of Christ's Orthodox Church. Thus we can read in his inspired report from the Second Meeting of the World Council of Churches held in Evanston, Illinois, 15 - 31 August 1954:

"In Evanston, one name brought all together and closer – Jesus Christ"; he continues: "As mentioned later (in the statement of Florovsky)[18] the fact that if each denomination contains only a part of the Christian faith, only the Orthodox Church contains the totality and plenitude of the true faith, 'which was transmitted to the saints once and for all' (Jude 3). Hope in Christ [an allusion to the theme of the meeting] is based on the true and whole faith, for it is written: first faith, then hope and then love, otherwise it is a house without foundation. The same applies to eschatology which was contained in that faith from the beginning. Without such faith, it is difficult to approach with truth the Christ who is considered as the complete Hope, as well as the eschatological Christ who is destined to accomplish human history and to be the eternal Judge. The union of all the churches cannot be achieved through mutual concessions but only by adherence by all to the one true faith in its entirety, as it was bequeathed by the Apostles and formulated at the Ecumenical Councils; in other words, by the return of all Christians in the one and indivisible Church to which belonged the ancestors of all Christians in the entire world during the first ten centuries after Christ. It is the Holy Orthodox Church."[19]

Bibliography

Faith in the Resurrection of Christ as the Fundamental Dogma of the Apostolic Churchi, Doctoral thesis, Bern, 1910 (translated in Serbian, *Collected Works*, vol. 2, Himmelstür, 1986).

Serbia in Light and Darkness, with a Preface by the Archbishop of Canterbury, Green and Co., (London: Longmans, 1916; repr., New York: Cosimo. Classics, 2007)

Beyond Sin and Death, "Collected Works", vol. 6, (Bigz, Valjevo:Beograd, 1996) (in Serbian)

The Religion of Njegosh, "Collected Works", vol. 1, (Bigz, Valjevo:Beograd, 1996) (in Serbian)

Orations on the Universal Man, "Collected Works", vol. 2, (Bigz, Valjevo:Beograd, 1996) (in Serbian)

Prayers by the lake, "Collected Works", vol. 10, (Bigz, Valjevo:Beograd, 1996) (in Serbian)

New Sermons at the Foot of the Mount, "Collected Works", vol. 1, (Bigz, Valjevo:Beograd, 1996) (in Serbian)

Thoughts on Good and Evil, (Serbian Orthodox Parish, Linz, 2001) (in Serbian)

The Prologue from Ohrid, vol.1 and 2, (Sebastian Press, Western American Diocese, 2012) (in English)

Letters from India, "Collected Works", vol. 2, (Bigz, Valjevo:Beograd, 1996) (in Serbian)

The Spiritual Lyrics, (Glas Crkve, Valjevo, 2003) (in Serbian)

The Only Lover of Mankind, "Collected Works", vol. 10, (Bigz, Valjevo:Beograd, 1996) (in Serbian)

The Faith of Educated People, "Collected Works", vol. 17, (Bigz, Valjevo:Beograd, 1997), 41-113 (in Serbian)

The Symbols and Signs, "Collected Works", vol. 3, (Bigz, Valjevo:Beograd, 1996) (in Serbian)

Emmanuel, "Collected Works", vol. 9, (Bigz, Valjevo:Beograd, 1996) (in Serbian)

Cassiana - the Science on Love, "Collected Works", vol. 9, (Bigz, Valjevo:Beograd, 1996) (in Serbian)

The Land of No Return, "Collected Works", vol. 9, (Bigz, Valjevo:Beograd, 1996) (in Serbian)

---

[18] Bishop Maxim (Vasiljevic) pointed out that Nikolai reported accurately the positions taken personally by Father Georges Florovsky and that he adhered completely (cf. "Trois théologiens serbes entre l'Orient et l'Occident. Nicolas Velimirovic, Justin Popovic et Athanase Jevtic", in *Istina* 56 (2011): 63-78 (in French)).

[19] St. Nicolai Velimirovic, "Догађај у Еванстону" first published in review "Слобода" from 20 October 1954 and reprinted in *Collected Works*. Vol. 13, Himmelsthür, 1986, 42-46 (in Serbian).

(46) Metropolitan Mar Gregorios

Fr. Koshy Valdyan

Biographical note

Metropolitan Paulos Gregorios was born Paul Varghese on 9 August 1922 at Tripunithura, Kerala, India in a traditional Christian family. The multi-linguist, Paul Varghese started his career as a freelance journalist. Later after working with the Cochin Transport Company in Kerala, India, he joined the Post & Telegraphs Department in 1942. He took up a job as a teacher in Ethiopia. There he served as the Emperor Haile Selassie's personal aide and advisor. He received his education from Goshen College, Oklahoma University, Princeton and Yale Universities. In 1954, he returned to India with a Masters Degree in Theology. He worked as a Director of the Fellowship house in Alwaye (Kerala) and as a visiting Professor of Union Christian College, Alwaye, Kerala, India. In 1955, he joined the faculty of The Orthodox Theological Seminary, Kottayam, Kerala. He also served as the General Secretary of Orthodox Students Christian Movement.

In 1961 he was ordained as Fr. Paul Varghese by the Catholicos, the supreme head of his Church. Fr. Paul Varghese continued to pursue theological studies. He did his Doctoral studies in Oxford and Germany and received his Doctorate in Theology from Serampore University in Calcutta.

His dissertation submitted to Serampore University was published under the title *Cosmic Man*.[1] It dealt with the relation between God, Humanity and World in the 4th century Eastern Christian Father St. Gregory of Nyssa. It deals with one of the fundamental problems of Christian Theism. As a consequence of St. Augustine's teachings, Christian theology hyperbolized the sinfulness of man. By the influence of the vision of St. Gregory who was a contemporary of Augustine in fourth century, he articulated the basic goodness of human beings who were created in God's image. He renounced the original sin concept which proclaims the transmission of sin as such from generation to generation. His venture was to draw the attention of the church and society to the tremendous human potentiality to be good like God. The *Cosmic Man*, his dissertation depicts this vision of human goodness.

His theological perspective was based upon some fundamental axes: on the one hand the vision of the Kingdom of God, and on the other hand the Christian affirmation of the union of God and humanity in Christ, a perfect union of divinity and humanity without confusion and separation.[2] This cosmic vision enabled him to head numerous important positions in the WCC and other international Committees and institutions. In 1967, he was appointed as the Principal of Orthodox Theological Seminary, Kottayam. In 1975, Fr. Paul Varghese was ordained as a bishop under the name Paulos Gregorios. He later became Metropolitan of the newly formed Diocese of Delhi, a position he held until his death. He established the Delhi Orthodox Centre, where he began such ambitious projects as the *Neeti Shanti Kendra* for promoting peace and justice, and *Sarva Dharma Nilaya* for inter-religious dialogue and cooperation. Mar Gregorios has authored a number of books, apart from numerous periodicals, articles, contributions to symposia and encyclopedias in India and abroad. He died on 24 November 1996.

---

[1] Paulose Mar Gregorios. *Cosmic Man : The Divine Presence : An Analysis of the Place and Role of the Human Race in the Cosmos, in relation to God and the Historical World, in the thought of St. Gregory of Nyssa (ca 330 to ca 395 A. D.)* (New Delhi: Sophia Publications, 1982).

[2] Paulose Mar Gregorios, *A Human God* (Kottayam: Mar Gregorios Foundation, 1992), 69.

Ecumenical Involvement of Mar Gregorios

Mar Gregorios was a theologian who has tried to understand Ecumenism in a holistic way. He came to the ecumenical movement through the ecumenical student activities. His actual involvement in the movement was as a Bible Study leader at the New Delhi Assembly of the World Council of Churches in 1961. From 1962 to 1976, he served the WCC as Associate Secretary and Director of the Division of the Ecumenical Action. In these capacities he visited most of the Protestant and Orthodox Churches of the world. As a staff-member from Asia and especially from the Orthodox tradition, he surprised many of his Western co-workers with an unusual efficiency in planning and performing. He was also an observer at the second Vatican Council of the Roman Catholic Church.

From 1968 to 1961, he was on the Central Committee of the WCC, and, between 1975 and 1983, he was a member of its executive committee. He served also a member of the Faith and Order Commission of the WCC from 1968 to 1975. During 1963 to 1975, he participated in the Joint Working Group between the Roman Catholic Church and the World Council of Churches almost assuming the role of a 'founding member.' Gregorios' sincerity in the ecumenism of Churches is also commendable. His strenuous efforts to reconcile the divided Orthodox families of Eastern Orthodox Churches and Oriental Orthodox Churches are an inspiring model for those who dream of healing the wounds of Church divisions and politics.[3] He along with the representative of the Greek Orthodox Church, Nikos Nissiotis, jointly convened the unofficial conversations (Aarhus-1964, Bristisol-1967, Geneva-1970, Addis Ababa-1971) between theologians of the Oriental Orthodox and Eastern Orthodox Churches. Gregorios writes on their joint efforts as follows:

"We began our joint efforts in 1962 to the Aarhus consultation. There was much skepticism in the beginning about the possible benefits of taking up an issue which had frustrated greater persons in previous centuries. But ours is an age of frequent ecumenical contacts, and our informal gatherings at various meetings of the World Council of Churches gave us new hope. We are both in Geneva at that time. We, Metropolitan Gregorios in the General Secretariat of the World Council of Churches, and professor Nikos Nissiotis at the Ecumenical Institute in Bossey, are very much indebted to the Faith and Order Commission which consistently supported our efforts, Viewed our meetings as a primary concern towards re-establishing Church unity and financed them. We are especially grateful to Lukas Vischer, former Director of the Secretariat to the Faith and Order Commission, who gave us encouragement and support and also took an active part in all four meetings."[4]

He led WCC delegations to major conferences including the UN General Assembly Special Sessions on Disarmament (1983, 1988). In WCC forums and beyond, he persistently opposed apartheid and the old and new colonialism. He chaired the World Conference on Faith, Science and the Future in Cambridge, USA (1979). He was the vice-president of the Christian Peace Conference (1970-90). In 1983 at the Vancouver Assembly of the World Council of Churches, he was elected as the President of the World Council of Churches, a position he held till 1991.

Gregorian Vision of Ecumenism

Mar Gregorios worked hard to promote communal harmony, nuclear disarmament, the end of western imperialism, holistic healing, use of science and technology for a just society, just participation of women in church, etc. He was able to recognize goodness in all human creative expressions of science and technology. He affirmed the goodness of the world which is basically God's Being (Essence) and His Energy converted into matter. While appreciating the contributions of the secular world, he denied the negativities of modernism which is based on reason. Books like *A Light Too Bright, Enlightenment East and West, Worship in a Secular*

---

[3] Joice Thottackkadu, *Prakasathilekku Oru Theertha Yathra* (Biography of Mar Gregorios in Malayalam) (Kottayam: Sophia Publications, 1997), 266.

[4] Paulose Mar Gregorios, William H. Lazareth, Nikos. A. Nissiotis (Eds). *Does Chalcedon Divide or Unite?* (Geneva: WCC, 1981), XI.

Age etc demonstrate his vision on secularism. He paid attention to faith and worship which are essential for the humanization of the world. He insisted that science and technology should be used to address the issues of poverty, ecological issues, war and violence. He was involved in a lot of dialogues at national, international and ecumenical levels. On the word 'dialogue' Gregorios opines that it does not mean simply a conversation between two people. According to him it is, speaking, discoursing, and reasoning through all aspects of a problem thereby correcting each other and moving forward.[5] Gregorios wants to use dialogue as a way to find a common path through reality and through the problems that confront us. Gregorios strongly uphold dialogue of religions: "This is my dream, which religions are constantly in touch with each other, not only to dialogue, but also to see how the unity and the peace of humanity could be maintained and how the religions could provide a different basis for transcending national loyalties than the transnational corporation."[6] Mar Gregorios articulates his Christological conviction on dialogue as follows:

"Love and compassion for the whole creation is the characteristic of Christ. The Church as His body shares in this love and compassion. I as a member of that body have to express that love and compassion in faithfulness, integrity and openness with sympathetic understanding. This is a sufficient and compelling reason for me to engage in dialogue with people of other faiths. It is love in Christ that sends me to dialogue."[7]

According to him orthodoxy and orthopraxy to build up a peaceful society is also an important role of the church in his thought. He calls for a dialogue among religions for peace and welfare of the society while keeping devotion to a particular faith. Ecclesiology and wider Ecumenism seem to be inseparable in his thought. These basic ideas were reflected in his vision on ecumenism.

Mar Gregorios fought for a new world order of freedom and justice, He was in the forefront of international debates on such issues as nuclear disarmament, justice for the poor and the marginalized, concerns of indigenous people across the world, apartheid and racial discrimination, interfaith dialogue, ecumenical vision of one humanity and so on. His critical vision of a new world order was rooted in his spiritual and theological understanding of the Kingdom of God as portrayed by Christ in the Gospels.

He worked towards the reconciliation among Muslim, Hindu, Buddhist, Catholic, Protestant and Orthodox communities. His ecumenical vision was related not merely to inter-Church relationships but also to interreligious relationships. He was one among the few ecumenical leaders who played a very active role in the dialogue with religions, ideologies and international affairs towards the wider unity of humanity and the integrity of creation. Mar Gregorios' involvement in inter-Church and interfaith dialogue developed a theology of dialogue from his thought and experience. His Christo-centric vision on wider ecumenism expressed in his Last Will and Testament:

"Christ is my all. Without him I am nothing all. I share that life with all those in Christ's body....And Christ's love is for all humankind, not just for Christians. It is for the whole humanity that he has died...."[8]

K. M. George observes Mar Gregorios' cosmic ecumenical consciousness:

For him, Christian unity was a part, albeit integral, of the overarching unity of humankind and of all God's creation. So he spent a major chunk of his time, talents and energy for a deeper understanding between religions and for the dialogue with the secular world.[9]

---

[5] Paulose Mar Gregorios *Religion and Dialogue* (New Delhi: MGF and ISPCK, 2000), 219.
[6] Ibid, 224.
[7] Gregorios, *Religion and Dialogue,*157.
[8] K. M. George, Guru Gregorios (1922-1966) in A. Smaranjali (ed.) *Deepthi Annual 1997* (1997), 9.
[9] K. M. George, *Foreword* in Jacob Kurian (ed.) *Paulose Mar Gregorios*: *On Ecumenism* (New Delhi: ISPCK and MGF, 2006), Kottayam, vii, Paulose Mar Gregorios, *Religion and Dialogue* (New Delhi: MGF and ISPCK, 2000), 219.

Part III: Representative Orthodox Theologians reflecting on Ecumenism

Unity of the churches and unity of humanity are interconnected in his thought. For him the Church which is deep-rooted in the mystery of the Trinity `has been called to serve the world by manifesting the love of God towards all humanity of which harmony making mission is integral part. Mar Gregorios articulates his vision on unity based on the Trinitarian unity. As he puts it:

"It is the mystery of all being, because it is the mystery of God's own being as Three in One. And Christ's great high priestly prayer (John 17) prays that all may be one on the pattern of the Father's unity with the Son."[10]

In Gregorian vision, inter-religious dialogue and evangelization are the two important tasks of the Church. Through his life and teaching he proved that one can be a Christian Ecumenical leader without compromising one's faith and also without being fundamentalist. His vision of the Church is closely associated with his global ecumenical consciousness and deep commitment to a just world.

Bibliography

Mar Paulose Gregorios *A Human God*, (Kottayam: Mar Gregorios Foundation, 1992).

Mar Paulose Gregorios, *Cosmic Man : The Divine Presence : An Analysis of the Place and Role of the Human Race in the Cosmos, in relation to God and the Historical World, in the thought of St. Gregory of Nyssa (ca 330 to ca 395 A. D.).* (New Delhi/Kottayam: Sophia Publications, 1982).

Mar Paulose Gregorios, *Enlightenment, East & West: Pointers in the Quest for India's Secular Identity*, (New Delhi: Indian Institute of Advance Study in association with B.R. Publishing Corporation, 1989).

Mar Paulose Gregorios, *Love's Freedom, the Grand Mystery: A Spiritual Autobiography*, K. M. George (ed.) (Kottayam: MGF, 1997).

Mar Paulose Gregorios, *On Ecumenism*, Jacob Kurian (ed.) (Kottayam: ISPCK and MGF, 2006).

Mar Paulose Gregorios, *Religion and Dialogue* (New Delhi: MGF and ISPCK, 2000).

Mar Paulose Gregorios, *Science for Sane Societies*, (New York: Paragon House, 1987).

Paulose Mar Gregorios *Science Technology and the Future of Humanity*, (Kottayam: ISPCK and MGF, 2007).

Mar Paulose Gregorios, *The Freedom of Man: An Inquiry In to Some Roots of the Tension Between Freedom and Authority in Our Society*, (Philadelphia: Westminster, 1972).

Mar Paulose Gregorios, *The Human Presence: An Orthodox View of Nature*, (Geneva: WCC Publications, 1978).

Mar Palose Gregorios, *The Joy of Freedom: Eastern Worship and Modern Man*, (London: Lutterworth, 1967).

Mar Paulose Gregorios, *The Meaning and Nature of Diakonia*, (Geneva, WCC Publications, 1982).

Mar Paulose Gregorios, William H. Lazareth, Nikos. A. Nissiotis (Eds.). *Does Chalcedon Divide or Unite?* (Geneva: WCC Publications, 1981).

---

[10] Paulose Mar Gregorios, *On Ecumenism*, Jacob Kurian (ed) (Kottayam: ISPCK and MGF, 2006), 3.

(47) Pope Shenouda III

Metropolitan Bishoy

His Holiness Pope Shenouda III was the 117th Pope of Alexandria and Patriarch of the Apostolic See of Saint Mark. He believed that Christian unity must be founded upon a unity of faith rather than on a unity of jurisdiction. Guided by this principle, he initiated and monitored theological dialogues with the Eastern Orthodox, Roman Catholic, Anglican and Presbyterian Churches, and with the World Alliance of Reformed Churches.

As the Bishop for Education of the Coptic Orthodox Church between September 1962 and October 1971, Bishop Shenouda's desire for Christian unity became apparent in his participation at several ecumenical meetings. Since the Council of Chalcedon in 451, the Christological question of the nature of Christ had been the main source of division between the Oriental Orthodox Churches and both the Eastern Orthodox Church and the Western Churches. At the Pro Oriente Conference between the Oriental Orthodox Churches and the Roman Catholic Church in Vienna in 1971, Bishop Shenouda espoused a Christological formula which was unanimously agreed upon by the participants and immediately became the basis of subsequent theological agreements between all Churches. Bishop Shenouda's formula was:

> We all believe that our Lord, God and Saviour Jesus Christ the Incarnate Logos is perfect in His Divinity and perfect in His Humanity. He made His Humanity one with His Divinity without mixture, nor mingling, nor confusion nor change. His Divinity was not separated from His Humanity even for a moment or the twinkling of an eye. At the same time we anathematize the doctrines of both Nestorius and Eutyches.

In 1990, Pope Shenouda was granted an honorary doctorate from the University of Bonn in recognition of his role in formulating this agreement and his quest for Church unity.

Bishop Shenouda's sermon during the holy liturgy on 12 September 1971, highlighted his ecumenical vision. He said, "May our Lord and God Jesus Christ who gathered us together in His name from far and different countries, gather us also in His Kingdom, in the Heavenly Jerusalem, singing a new song for the Lord."[1] For Pope Shenouda, ecumenism meant that Christian unity on earth was a bond which would extend into eternity.

During Pope Shenouda's first ecumenical trip, from 3 to 30 October 1972, he visited the Church leaders who attended his enthronement ceremony. His Holiness was the first Pope of Alexandria to make such an ecumenical trip, visiting Russia, Romania, Armenia, Constantinople (modern Turkey), Syria, and Lebanon, where he met with many Patriarchs and heads of Churches.

In May 1973, Pope Shenouda III visited Pope Paul VI in Rome, the first meeting between an Alexandrian and Roman Pontiff since 451. Both Popes signed a Declaration which included a confession of common faith in Christology. At this historic encounter, Pope Shenouda addressed Pope Paul VI saying,

> We feel happy to meet today with Your Holiness as the Supreme Head of the Roman Catholic Church in Christendom and to exchange with your Holiness the holy kiss of peace. We pray humbly that this meeting will have its far reaching results in supporting and strengthening the friendly relations between our two Apostolic Churches. Your Holiness, the friendly relations between our churches have become stronger. Coptic delegations attended sessions of the Vatican Council in 1962. Catholic representatives attended the celebration of (the consecration of St. Mark's Cathedral in Cairo in June 1968). The friendly gift of Your Holiness at the time of the relics of St. Mark has been met with feelings of deep regard and gratitude on behalf of all Copts.

---

[1] Pro Oriente, *Five Vienna Consultation between Theologians of the Oriental Orthodox Churches and the Roman Catholic Church: 1971, 1973, 1976, 1978 and 1988* (Vienna, 1993).

He concluded by saying:

> We are all more ready and more intense in our desire to reach solutions for differences and attain simpler expressions
> of our common faith. Through this present personal meeting we are driving on to a more effective promotion of
> this mutual commitment.

Following this important meeting, a joint commission was established to facilitate inter-communication
between the two Churches. The commission produced an agreed statement on Christology which was signed
by Pope Shenouda III and Pope John Paul II in February 1988.

Pope Shenouda sought ecclesiastical unity on all levels and across all Christian denominations, and he devoted
considerable energy to constructing bridges of love and participation in ecumenical bodies and conferences. In
an address which he gave at an ecumenical forum during the International Week of Prayer for Christian Unity
at St Mark's Cathedral in Cairo in 1974, he again expressed his personal thoughts on ecumenism stating that:

> The whole Christian world is anxious to see the Church unite. Christian people – being fed up with divisions and
> dispersion – are pushing their Church leaders to do something about Church Unity and I am sure that the Holy Spirit
> is inspiring us. Christian Unity will be a magnificent universal achievement for generations to come. Christian Unity
> is God's will, so there shall be one flock and one Shepherd (John 10:16). Christian Unity is essential for faith and
> evangelism. The mere existence of so many Christian divisions and fractions is the greatest stumbling block to the
> world. How can they believe while truth appears to be lost amidst controversy and contradiction? In our ecumenical
> meetings, we should talk about actual beliefs regardless of what happened in the past. We must avoid complex and
> vague expressions. In spite of all the problems that might arise about history, rites, ecumenical councils, and so on,
> we shall achieve good results with love, good spirit and determination. We shall achieve this together. Let us pray
> that we unite in the faith delivered to us by our great fathers who kept it, defended it, and sacrificed their lives for
> it. Let us pray that God works in our hearts and thoughts so that we fulfil His will.

One of Pope Shenouda's ecumenical priorities was the restoration of full communion between the Oriental
(non-Chalcedonian) and Eastern (Chalcedonian) Orthodox Churches. With the support of Pope Shenouda,
official dialogues between the two families of Orthodox Churches took place in 1985 in Chambesy, Switzerland (1987), in Corinth (1989), in Egypt, and in Chambesy (1990). The Christological formula was ratified
by the Chambesy meeting and agreement was reached to begin the process of the mutual lifting of anathemas
on Church Fathers and Councils. To provide an impetus to these dialogues, a pastoral agreement specific to
matrimony for couples within the Orthodox Church of Alexandria (Chalcedonian) and the Coptic Orthodox
Church was signed by Pope Shenouda III and Patriarch Petros VI in April 2001.

In October 1987, the former Archbishop of Canterbury, Dr Robert Runcie, signed the first Declaration
between the leaders of the Coptic Orthodox and Anglican Churches, expressing mutual commitment towards
full unity. In March 1990, Pope Shenouda chaired the meeting of the Oriental Orthodox-Anglican Forum, and
stated that all dialogue should be based on Biblical teachings, particularly when discussing issues such as the
ordination of women, polygamous marriages, and homosexuality. His Holiness stated that:

> The unity of the Church should be unity of faith. The Bible is to be the basis of our dialogue and we must place it in
> front of us and not lean on our understanding (Proverbs 3:5). Through the Holy Bible we become one Church, we
> can have one teaching. Sometimes the word 'variety' is used but there is a great difference between variety and con-
> tradiction. We may rejoice in variety if this variety is not contradicting any commandment of God, if it is according
> to the will of God. We are disappointed in what is called 'new Theology'. People may not believe in many chapters
> of the Holy Bible claiming this is a kind of mythology.

In November 1988, His Holiness initiated the first Coptic-Presbyterian theological dialogue. The joint
committee convened twice in 1989 and once in 1990, addressing the theological dimensions of salvation and

baptism. Although this dialogue was confined to the Presbyterian Church in Egypt, it paved the way for potential reconciliation between the Orthodox and Protestant Churches in the Middle East.

Dialogue commenced between the Coptic Church and the World Alliance of Reformed Churches in Egypt in May 1993. Pope Shenouda chaired the first and second meetings of the forum. In the former, he delivered a lecture on tradition in the Church, and in the latter a talk on Christology. In September 1994, he visited Drie-bergen in Holland, where one of the official dialogue sessions was held between the two Churches.

Pope Shenouda facilitated its close relationship with the Church of Antioch (Syrian Orthodox), the Armenian Church, and the Ethiopian Orthodox Church. In June 1996, in order to deepen the historical, theological, and ecclesiastical bonds between the Coptic, Syrian and Armenian Churches, Pope Shenouda III, Patriarch Mar Ignatius Zakka I, and Patriarch Aram I (the heads of the Churches), agreed to hold an annual meeting to discuss issues of ecumenical importance and develop ways to enrich their joint efforts in ecumenical fields. The first official meeting took place in Egypt in March 1998, in which a joint statement was issued. It was agreed that:

> In our joint testimony of our faith in the Only-begotten Son, the Incarnate Word, our Savior Jesus Christ, we hold fast our Apostolic faith which we received from our fathers the Apostles in the Holy Scriptures, in the Old and New Testaments, in the three Ecumenical Councils: Nicaea (325 AD), Constantinople (381 AD), and Ephesus (431 AD), and the teachings of the holy Fathers who are honored in our three churches...We firmly reject all heretical teachings taught by Arius, Sabillius, Apollinarius, Macedonius, Paul of Samosata, Diodore of Tarsus, Theodore of Mopsuestia, Nestorius, Eutyches, and all who follow their heresies or teach their erroneous heretical principles, and the rest of the heresies...We agreed on the need to maintain a unified position of faith in all theological dialogues. For this reason, henceforth, any theological dialogue with other churches and world Christian communities will be held at the level of the Oriental Orthodox Church Family of the Middle East, hoping to expand this principle to include the church families at large, as is currently, in many dialogues.

Between 25–30 September 1973, Pope Shenouda visited Ethiopia and was received by the late Emperor Haile Selassie. He visited Ethiopia a second time in 2008, when he met the late Abune Paulos, Patriarch of Ethiopia, and other official leaders of Ethiopia. Pope Shenouda also received Abune Paulos in Egypt several times.

Pope Shenouda's ecumenical work also included meeting other patriarchs. The Ecumenical Patriarch of Constantinople visited Pope Shenouda in 1987, and His Holiness visited the Ecumenical Patriarch Bartholomew I on 13-16 September, 2001. The late Patriarch Alexis II, Patriarch of Russia, visited His Holiness; and, in April 2010, Patriarch Cyril, the new Patriarch of Russia, visited Alexandria. In 1988, Pope Shenouda partic-ipated in Russia's global celebration marking the millennium of the introduction of Christianity to Russia. Pope Shenouda was also visited by the Catholic Patriarchs of the Middle East, with its seven patriarchates: the Maronites, Coptic Catholics, Byzantine Catholic Melkites, Latins in Jerusalem, Armenian Catholics, and Syrian Catholics. At the Council of Churches, Pope Shenouda met with the Chaldean Patriarch.

Other ecumenical initiatives of Pope Shenouda include the establishment in 1967 of the Association of Theology in the Near East (ATINA; after 1980, the Association of Theological Institutions in the Middle East (ATIME)). Pope Shenouda was its first president, since he was Bishop for Education at the time.

In Australia in 1991, Pope Shenouda became the first Coptic pope to attend a World Council of Churches assembly. At the conclusion of the assembly, His Holiness was elected as one of eight presidents of the WCC, representing the Oriental Orthodox Churches and the Middle East.

In November 1994, Pope Shenouda headed a delegation of seven members to the Middle East Council of Churches assembly in Cyprus. At the conclusion of this assembly, he was elected one of the four presidents of the Middle East Council of Churches, and at the Jubilee Assembly of the MECC in Lebanon in May 1999, Pope Shenouda was re-elected for another four-year term.

During Pope Shenouda's rule the Coptic Orthodox Church became a member of the All-Africa Council of Churches (AACC) and the National Council of Churches of the United States of America (NCCUSA), and of many regional and national ecumenical councils,

Part III: Representative Orthodox Theologians reflecting on Ecumenism

In all of his ecumenical endeavours Pope Shenouda emphasised fostering amicable relations with other Churches and he often referred to "constructing bridges of love". Indeed, Pope Shenouda's ecumenical vision centred on enhancing the spirit of love amongst all Christian Churches. In his vision, Christian unity is the will of God for His Church and this unity should be a unity of faith and love, to fulfil the words of the Lord Jesus Christ: "That they all may be one" (Jn. 17: 22).

Bibliography

A Collection of Writings By His Holiness Pope Shenouda III, Coptic Orthodox Electronic Publishing (COEP) Australia, 1998 - disc.
The Christian Orthodox e-Reference Library, COEPA -disc.

Books
H.H. Pope Shenouda III, *Comparative Theology*, (London: Coptic Orthodox Publishers Association, 1988).
H.H. Pope Shenouda III, *The Oridnation of Women and Homosexuality*, (London: Coptic Orthodox Publishers Association, 1993).
H.H. Pope Shenouda III, *The Nature of Christ*, (Cairo: Dar El Tebaa El Kwmia, 1997).
H.H. Pope Shenouda III, *The Heresy of Jehovan's Wittnesses*, (Cairo: Baramous Monastery Press, 1993).
H.H. Pope Shenouda III, *Contemplations of the Life of St. Antony the Great*, (San Antonio: St. Antony the Great Coptic Orthodox Church, 1993).
H.H. Pope Shenouda III, *Salvation in the Orthodox Understanding*, (Chicago: St. Mark and St. Bishoy Coptic Orthodox Church).
H.H. Pope Shenouda III, *The Divinity of Christ*, (London: Coptic Orthodox Publishers Association, 1989).
H.H. Pope Shenouda III, *Three Purposeful Stories*, (Maryut, Egypt: St. Mena Monastery Press, 2007).
H.H. Pope Shenouda III, *Quizzes on the Holy Bible*, (Cairo: Dar El Tebaa El Kwmia, 1995).

(Note: The writings of H.H. Pope Shenouda III were in Arabic the abovementioned are translations of few books)

(48) Catholicos Abune Paulos I

Nigussu Legesse

Biographical note

His Holiness Abune Paulos I was born within the territory of the Monastery of Abba Gerima, Medera-Adewa, Central Tigray Region in Ethiopia, on 3 November 1933. He was given the name Gebremedihin at birth. His father, *Afe Memhir* Gebreyohannes Woldeselassie was a priest himself serving as the *Afe Memhir* (literally meaning: the mouth of the head) of the Monastery of Abba Gerima. This means that he functioned as Ambassador of the Monastery of Medera. His mother, Woizero Aradech Tedla was also one of the pious members of the surrounding Abba Gerima Community.

Because of their devotion to the Monastery, his parents offered their son, *Gebremedihin,* to the Monastery of Abba Gerima at the age of five. Then, the young Gebremedihin grew up in the monastery as a member of the monastic community, studying the faith and order of the Church, the service he should carry out, especially, the monastic order and life of the Ethiopian Orthodox Tewahedo Church (EOTC). Then he was allowed to travel to the nearby monasteries (as the old tradition of the Church), to Cheh and Abba Hadera monasteries where he studied the Ethiopian Orthodox Church tradition, namely Zema (hymnology of St. Yared which is peculiar to the Ethiopian Orthodox Church), Mezgebe Kidase (Liturgy and Anaphora), grammar of Geez language under the famous master scholars of the time: Memhirs (i.e. teachers) Wold Hawariat, Gebre Egziabiher, Kidane Mariam, Paulos and Gebre Mariam.

At the completion of his church education, he was ordained a Deacon by His Grace Abune Marcos, and was later ordained a priest by His Grace Abune Yishac. He was then made a monk in Abba Gerima monastery as in the regular service of the monastery. After some years of consecutive services in the monastery, he asked the senior leaders of the monastic community for further modern theological studies. In 1957, His Holiness continued his studies at the Holy Trinity Theological College in Addis Ababa as a boarding student when he was granted permission by the late Patriarch of the Ethiopian Orthodox Tewahedo Church and the then president of the College, His Holiness Abune Theophilos. Here, he studied religious education and completed his elementary and secondary schools. Under the tutorship of the Scholars of the EOTC, His Holiness followed the ancient teachings of the Church: Commentaries of the Old and New Testaments, Tsewatwe Zema (Hymnology and Chants), Geez and Amharic Grammar and Church History both national and international.

The college records indicate that His Holiness was one of the prime high ranking and promising students with outstanding achievements and visionary future leader. As one of the outstanding students of his time, Abune Paulos received prizes at three different occasions from the late Emperor, His Imperial Majesty Haile Selassie I, for standing first among his course mates. During His visits to the college, the Emperor always talked to him and encouraged him in his studies.

On completion of his Church and modern education in the Holy Trinity Theological College, His Holiness was allowed to go for higher studies to the United States of America by the permission of His Holiness Abune Basilios (the first Ethiopian Patriarch) and by the farsightedness of the late Abune Theophilos, where he studied in different prestigious Universities for 16 years. He subsequently secured the following academic awards. In May 1962 he was awarded a Diploma in Theology, from St. Vladimir Russian Orthodox Seminary (New York) with an emphasis on the Theology of the Oriental and Eastern Orthodox Churches. In May 1966 he received Bachelor of Divinity from Berkeley Divinity School at Yale (New Haven), specializing in the theological views and differences in Divinity, between the Oriental, Eastern and Western Churches. In May 1972 his holiness advanced to Master of Theology in Divinity at Princeton Theological Seminary, and finally in May 1988 Abune Paulos received his Doctor of Philosophy in Divinity, at the Princeton University, School of Divinity submitting his ever outstanding theses entitled *"Filisata: the feast of the Assumption of Mary and the Mariologial tradition of the Ethiopian Orthodox Tewahedo Church"*.

Abune Paulos has contributed to Christian Vocation and Pastoral Services in the church for 15 years, as a Deacon, monk and priest- at the monastery of Abba Gerima, 8 years Standing member in the liturgical services of Menbere Tsebaot Holy Trinity Cathedral, Dean of St. Paul's Higher Theological Seminary, Administrator of History, Literary, Evangelical, Newspaper Publication and Radio Department of the EOTC. His Holiness was also the Founding Father of the newly organized Sunday Schools Central Office, Secretary General of the Development and Inter Church AID Commission (DICAC) of the Church including Refugee Services of the EOTC/program and head of the Tensae Zegubae Printing Press.

After completing his Masters Degree in divinity at the Princeton Theological Seminary and enrolling for his PhD Degree, His Holiness was called back to Ethiopia by the Patriarch, Abune Theophilos and was consecrated as a Bishop in September 1975 assuming the name Abune Paulos and was given responsibility for ecumenical affairs of the Church. His consecration, however, angered the Marxist regime of the time who ordered his arrest along with his colleague and the Patriarch Abune Theophilos who consecrated them both.

He was imprisoned for more than 7 years (without charges) for upholding his Christian faith, no crime was committed and no charges were made. In spite of the hardships and restrictions in the prison, he demonstrated his commitment and calling by arranging Bible studies among the prisoners in his daily programmes, risking his own life in a strictly forbidden high security prison environment where any reading materials were not allowed, let alone the Bible. Eventually, he was released from prison and joined the Church to live another difficult life under strict follow up by security forces. The Patriarch, Abune Theophilos, who was arrested with him for consecrating Abune Paulos, never had the opportunity to be released from prison and serve the church again. He was executed while still in prison.

After his release from prison in 1983, the follow up on his movement by the security forces could not allow him to discharge his duties as a bishop and life became difficult for him. He finally decided to live in exile in the United States. Once he arrived in the US to begin a new life in exile, and went back to Princeton University in 1984 to complete his doctoral degree studies. While still in exile, His Holiness was promoted to the rank of Archbishop by the third Patriarch, Abune Tekle Haymanot in 1986.

Life in exile never deterred His Holiness from his commitment to the Church service. He continued his service to Ethiopian Christian exiles who fled the country to escape persecution and settled in the United States of America. He established new frontiers of Church Services in the following states since 1984.

- Holy Saviour's Church in New York City, New York
- Debre Mehiret St. Michael's Church in Dallas, Texas
- Debre Tsion St. Mary's Church in Los Angeles, California
- Debre Selam St. Gabriel's Church in San Diego, California
- More churches in Tampa, Florida; Phoenix, Arizona; and in Las Vegas, Nevada
- He also established six Spiritual Associations in the above Holy Saviour, St. Mary, Kidane Miheret, Abune Gebre Menfes Kidus, St. Michael, and St. Gabriel etc churches for teaching Biblical Education and Faith and Order of the Church for Ethiopians in the Diaspora.

In order to serve the newly organised churches and associations in the USA, His Holiness recruited clergymen from Ethiopian communities in exile including from Greece, Egypt, Sudan, and Kenya and also from mainland Ethiopia.

The end of the Marxist regime in 1991 paved the way for the return of Abune Paulos back to Ethiopia in 1992, after 8 years of life in exile. The year of his return to his country coincided with the election of the fifth Patriarch of the Ethiopian Orthodox Church for which he was one of the candidates.

He was elected by the highest vote in June 1992 by members of the Holy Synod, Church Scholars, administrators of the main monasteries and Cathedrals of EOTC; Heads of departments of the Patriarchate, and representatives of the entire Church community drawn from the clergy, laity and the youth and enthroned as the fifth Patriarch of the Ethiopian Orthodox Church on 12 July 1992.

After taking office as the 5th Patriarch of the church, His Holiness made every effort to disseminate the Gospel, strengthen the administration and broaden the scope of international relations of the Church with a far reaching vision. With the will of God, he succeeded in re-opening the Holy Trinity Theological College in Addis Ababa which was banned and closed by the Godless Marxist regime for nearly 20 years.

He also established the new theological colleges, St. Frumentius Kesate Birhan in Mekele and St. Paul Theological Seminary in Addis Ababa, expanded the number of clergy training centres all over the country and reinstated the Church land and Property of the Sebetta Nunnery and the buildings and property of the Church which were confiscated by the former Marxist Regime. He also inaugurated many new Church buildings both at home and abroad.

His Holiness initiated the construction of church buildings and began many Churches in various parts of country. With the intention of modernising the office set up at the patriarchate, he initiated the construction of the new Patriarchate office complex, the renovation and reconstruction of the old patriarchate and its conversion into a modern Library Museum. These were accomplished by the Leadership and guidance of His Holiness.

The Library Museum is the first of its kind to be constructed in modern style in the Ethiopian Orthodox Church with the objective of making the Library a research and information centre while the Museum is used to keep the belongings and treasures of the church.

In recognition of his outstanding contribution for peace and the welfare of refugees, he was awarded the Nansen Medal for Africa by the United Nations High Commissioner for Refugees (UNHCR) on 28 November 2000.

Ecumenical contribution

In line with the Church's policy of expanding its International relations, he made pastoral and friendly visits to the Holy Land, headquarters of the WCC in Geneva, Constantinople (Turkey), Vienna (Austria), Athens (Greece), the Vatican, EOTC dioceses in Europe, the Caribbean and North America, the Middle East, South Africa, Spain and France.

During his visit to the Holy Land, His Holiness emphasized that our Church is the sole, historical and rightful owner of the Deir Sultan Monastery in Jerusalem and as the only monastery of the black people in the Holy Land constituting the spiritual treasure of the entire black race of the world. In September, 1994 His Holiness attended the International meeting on Peace convened in Assisi, Italy by the Community of Saint Egidio and presented a proposal which could strengthen the quest for Peace.

In October 1997, His Holiness hosted the 7th Assembly of the All Africa Conference of Churches (AACC) that convened in the United Nations Economic Commission for Africa (UNECA) in Addis Ababa, Ethiopia from 1 to 10 October 1997, which was successfully organized and accomplished its tasks.

In September 1998, His Holiness attended an International meeting on Peace held in Bucharest–Rumania and also visited the Rumanian Orthodox Church. In December 1998, His Holiness Participated the 8th Assembly of WCC held in Harare, Zimbabwe.

He has strived to strengthen of the relations of the EOTC with Oriental and Eastern Orthodox Churches and other western churches. On 17 June 1998, he invited and coordinated the national symposium of all religious leaders and prominent public figures to seek a lasting peaceful solution to the problem that has arisen between Ethiopia and Eritrea.

He led the meeting of the Ethiopian religious leaders to the peace talks held with the Eritrean religious leaders repeatedly in Oslo, Norway; Frankfurt, Germany and in New York, U.S.A from 2000 -2001 in order to bring about a peaceful solution to the conflict between the two countries. On 12 November 1999, he took part in the international meeting on peace held in Genoa, Italy by the St. Egidio Community. In September 2001 he took part in the world Summit of Religious and Spiritual leaders held at the United Nation in New York. On 1 October 2001, he attended the World AIDS Day meeting convened in Washington, U.S.A. at the White House.

His Holiness also encouraged and reactivated a number of ecumenical relations including dialogue with the Eastern Churches and theological dialogue with the Roman Catholic Church. To this end, His Holiness organised and hosted the Ninth Joint International Commission for the theological dialogue between the Oriental Orthodox Churches and the Roman Catholic Church in January 2012. He also initiated interfaith dialogue both locally and internationally with the formation of different interfaith forums of religious leaders in the country.

His Holiness also participated in the World Economic Forum, where he delivered historical messages on globalization, analyzing the negative and positive aspects of it warning world leaders against to be prepared and combat it.

In February 2006, His Holiness was elected as one of the eight presidents of the WCC at the 9th Assembly in Porto Alegre, Brazil, a global ecumenical position he assumed for six years till his death in August 2012.

After his election, he continued to strengthen the ecumenical movement by delivering messages of peace and reconciliation to all conflicting parties in Africa and elsewhere in the world:

- 1-5 July 2006, he attended the World Summit of Religious Leaders in Moscow which was inaugurated by President Putin of Russia. His Holiness represented WCC and EOTC and delivered a far reaching message of Peace and reconciliation.
- 17-21 July 2006, he attended another world Religious summit in Washington DC, representing WCC, the All Africa Conference of Churches (AACC) and Africa where he delivered important messages concerning, world peace and overcoming problems of Africa.

After becoming the fifth Patriarch, His Holiness demonstrated an extraordinary level of commitment and dedication to introduce systematic and innovative approaches to advance and enhance the teachings of the church through:

a. Modernizing the church administration
b. Supporting youth and women
c. Designing leadership teaching for the clergy
d. Responding to social, health and educational issues such as HIV/ AIDS Program
e. Encouraging and guiding the church community to participate more actively in development
f. Promoting the teachings of the Bible by making different literature available including the translation of the Holy Bible
g. Promoting communication through interfaith dialogue and advocating for peace and peaceful coexistence with other faiths and denominations
h. Advancing international cooperation through active participation in regional and international Christian Councils such as WCC and AACC

His Holiness expanded the outreach of the church and established parishes and dioceses in the USA, Europe, Middle East, Asia and Africa.

Although he had mapped out a long term strategy for the progress of the Ethiopian Orthodox Church and the improvement of the living conditions of the Ethiopian people, his time span has been untimely curtailed by God who has given him wisdom and providence. God wanted him to cut his journey short and His Holiness passed away suddenly on 15 August 2012. He was accorded a State Funeral and the Service was solemnly performed by Bishops, Heads of Churches from Egypt, Syria, India, the Vatican, the World Council of Churches and the All Africa Conference of Churches in the presence of Government officials, the Diplomatic community, official delegates from all Christian Churches, representatives of various religious groups, civic and interfaith organizations as well as peace loving people of all nations and nationalities.

Orthodox Handbook on Ecumenism

Conclusions

His Holiness shall be remembered forever in view of the following specific characteristics he manifested and the contributions he has so wonderfully made.

1. His devotion and commitment to the service of the Church
2. His response to the call of our Lord Jesus Christ
3. His dedication to help the poor and improve their material and spiritual needs
4. His tireless efforts to envision the needs and development requirements of the Church and the means to equip it with modern management and thoughts
5. His capacity to build institutions for theological education, social services and management infrastructure
6. His commitment to advance knowledge and scientific Christian teaching through research, publication and discussion
7. His personal motivation and commitment to bring about different organizations, religious groups with differing opinions together in a forum for mutual understanding for the betterment of mankind
8. His focus on international cooperation and understanding and maintaining dialogue with other faiths

Part III: Representative Orthodox Theologians reflecting on Ecumenism

Paul Ladouceur

In her biography of Fr. Lev Gillet, Elisabeth Behr-Sigel refers to him as a "universalist, evangelical and mystical free believer."[1] These four adjectives well characterise Lev Gillet's at times perplexing personality and his extremely varied and enigmatic ministry spanning over half a century. His commitment to Orthodoxy, to ecumenism and indeed to interreligious dialogue was deep and unmistakable, yet it was a commitment that expressed itself more in personal encounter and engagement than in formal institutional involvement.

Biographical introduction

Fr. Lev Gillet's life can be considered in three phases: from his birth in 1893 into a pious French Roman Catholic family in central France until joining the Orthodox Church in 1928; the ten years of his ministry in Paris, from 1928 to 1938; and his ministry after he moved to London in 1938 until his death in 1980.

Louis Gillet, Fr. Lev's civil name, had just completed an undergraduate degree in philosophy when he was mobilised at the beginning of World War I. Wounded in the early days of the war, he was captured and spent most of the war as a prisoner in Germany. There he came to know many Russian prisoners and learned Russian. In 1920 he became a novice in the Benedictine Order and the following year he met Metropolitan Andreas Sheptytsky, head of the Galician Church, a Byzantine rite Church united with Rome after the Union of Brest of 1595. Together with his previous contacts with young Russian soldiers, friendship in Rome with other young Benedictines interested in improving relations between the Catholic Church and the Orthodox Churches of Slavic countries, his acquaintance with Sheptytsky was decisive in determining his future orientation. In 1924, Louis Gillet joined Sheptytsky in Lvov, at that time in Poland, now in western Ukraine. He became a monk and was ordained to the priesthood with the intention to work towards the reunion of the Eastern and Western Churches, mainly by example and collaboration in common undertakings. But he soon became dismayed with the intentions of the Catholic Church with respect to Orthodox Russians and in 1926 he obtained a temporary ministry to work with poor Russian immigrants in Nice, France. Following the publication of the anti-ecumenical encyclical *Mortalium animos* by Pope Pius XI in January 1928, Fr. Lev developed contacts with the Russian Church in France and in May 1928 he met Metropolitan Evlogi (Georgievski), head of the Russian Orthodox communities in Western Europe. Metropolitan Evlogi, concerned with the development of a local Orthodox Church in France, invited Fr. Lev to concelebrate the Divine Liturgy with him on 25 May 1928, thereby accepting Fr. Lev into communion with the Orthodox Church.

For the next ten years, Fr. Lev served in a number of pastoral ministries in the Russian community in Paris: as pastor among the younger generation of Russians active in the Russian Student Christian Movement (ACER), including such future prominent figures as Evgraph Kovalevsky, Vladimir Lossky and Paul Evdokimov, all of whom remained life-long friends; as prison chaplain for Russian convicts, including the murderer of the French President Paul Doumer; as friend, confident and collaborator of Mother Maria Skobtsova (Saint Maria of Paris) in her social service activities, and as chaplain of Mother Maria's chapel from 1935 to 1938.

Significantly, in late 1928 Metropolitan Evlogi asked Fr. Lev to head up the first French-language Orthodox parish, thereby laying the groundwork for the "inculturation" of Orthodoxy in France. Many young Russian Orthodox intellectuals, such as Vladimir Lossky, frequented this French-language parish, motivated by a de-

---

[1] Élisabeth Behr-Sigel, *Lev Gille « Un Moine de l'Église d'Orient » : Un libre croyant universaliste, évangélique et mystique* (Paris : Le Cerf, 1993). English version: *Lev Gillet: A Monk of the Eastern Church* (Oxford: Fellowship of St Alban and St Sergius, 1999). The English translation is somewhat unreliable.

sire to promote a local Orthodoxy rather than a perpetuation of an "exile Church". The parish also attracted French converts, notably Elisabeth Behr-Sigel, who became a life-long friend of Fr. Lev and eventually his biographer. In addition to pastoral work in these years, Fr. Lev was also an active writer on theological and spiritual subjects, and he translated, anonymously, Fr. Sergius Bulgakov's book *The Orthodox Church*, first published in French in 1932, then in English in 1935.

Throughout the 1930s, Fr. Lev was one of the main Orthodox participants in the Fellowship of St. Alban and St Sergius, founded to further relations between the Anglican and Orthodox Churches, hopefully leading to the establishment of communion. Fr. Lev participated in many Fellowship meetings, preaching and leading retreats, and he was a frequent contributor to the Fellowship's publication *Sobornost*. Towards the end of the 1930s, Fr. Lev, deeply affected by the persecution of Jews in Nazi Germany and elsewhere, developed close relationships with Jewish communities in France and England and with Jews from Central Europe fleeing persecution. This opening to Christian-Jewish contact and dialogue led into the final phase of his life, his long and varied ministries in England.

In February 1938 Fr. Lev took up residence in London, where he became warden at a hostel set up to receive young Jewish and Jewish-Christian (Christians of Jewish origin) refugees from Germany and Austria. The outbreak of World War II led to complications, since the British authorities considered most of the hostel residents to be "enemy aliens" and finally the hostel was bombed during the Battle of Britain, putting an end to this experiment. Fr. Lev had developed extensive contacts among many Christian communities in Great Britain and his Quaker friends arranged for him to receive a fellowship to write a book on Christian-Jewish relations. For about ten years he was actively involved in the Christian Institute of Jewish Studies in London. Several books emerged from this involvement in Christian–Jewish relations, the most important of which was *Communion in the Messiah, Studies in the Relationship between Judaism and Christianity*, a ground-breaking study first published in 1942.[2]

Throughout his London years, Fr. Lev continued to be active in the Fellowship of St. Alban and St. Sergius, primarily as spiritual "animator" of the Fellowship and as the chaplain of St. Basil's House, the Fellowship's headquarters in London, where he lived from 1948 until his death. During this period, Fr. Lev directed many retreats, mainly for Anglicans, and he wrote a number of books on Orthodox spirituality, several of which became classics, such as *Orthodox Spirituality*, originally written for the Fellowship in 1946, and *The Jesus Prayer*, published in 1950.

Beginning in 1946, Fr. Lev was deeply involved with the spiritual renewal in the Orthodox Church of Antioch initiated by the *Mouvement de jeunesse orthodoxe* (Orthodox Youth Movement). He visited Lebanon almost every year from 1948 to 1978, preaching and writing on spiritual subjects. Many of his finest liturgical writings were first published in Beirut, including his commentary on the Byzantine liturgical year, *The Year of Grace of the Lord*. His writings in the 1960s and 1970s were mostly commentaries on Biblical passages, not learned treatises, but rather meditations on the personal significance of key texts, often in the daring form of a dialogue between the disciple and Jesus.

Ecumenical engagement

In many writings throughout his life, Fr. Lev sought to build bridges between Eastern and Western Christianity, emphasising continuities in spirituality, liturgy and devotions, rather than focussing on differences. This can be seen, for example, in essays on the veneration of the Mother of God in England (Our Lady of Walsingham), the veneration of Saint Joseph in Eastern Christianity, Saint Alban as a model disciple, the "gift of tears" in both East and West and the invocation of the Name of Jesus in the West.[3] In a similar vein, in an essay on papal infallibility and *sobornost* ("conciliarity"), Fr. Lev presents an interpretation of the Roman Catholic doctrine

---

[2] See the Bibliography for full references to Lev Gillet's books.
[3] Articles on these subjects appeared mostly in *Sobornost*, the publication of the Fellowship of St Alban and St Sergius. The essay on the invocation of the Name of Jesus in the West is an appendix to Lev Gillet's book *The Jesus Prayer*.

Part III: Representative Orthodox Theologians reflecting on Ecumenism

of papal infallibility, based on Catholic sources, which seeks to reconcile this doctrine with the Orthodox notion of (*sobornost*).[4] Fr. Lev did not write about his ecumenical perspective or actions, nor about current ecumenical developments.[5]

Although Fr. Lev's ecumenical work was primarily among Anglicans through the Fellowship, he also had contacts with other Christian communities in Britain; he particularly liked the "charismatic" communities, such as the Quakers and the Pentecostalists, often preaching at their services. His "universalist" outlook reached well beyond Christianity, to encompass believers of non-Christian religions, agnostics and even atheists. Although based in London, Fr. Lev was truly an itinerant minister, a pilgrim without borders, responding to calls for his pastoral care wherever they might originate. He continued to support the budding French Orthodox community, preaching, animating retreats, working with young people and writing and acting as spiritual counsellor. He also frequently visited Geneva, where he preached annual retreats for about 15 years, and spoke at meetings of Syndesmos, the international Orthodox youth organisation.

Refusing to "live from the altar", Fr. Lev always sought a source of modest income for his simple needs. After the destruction of the London hostel in 1941 and his scholarship from the Quakers, for a quarter century he worked as researcher for the Spalding Trust and the Union for the Study of Great Religions, organisations founded by the wealthy philanthropist H.N. Spalding to advance world peace by better understanding and respect among religious traditions. Fr. Lev's work consisted mainly in the preparation of bibliographic material – "booklists" – on world religions for publication in the Union's quarterly bulletin – his "monastery" was the reading room of the British Library. This involvement led to his appointment from 1961 to 1965 as Secretary of the World Congress of Faiths, dedicated to furthering dialogue between Christians and other world religions. Among his responsibilities was the organisation of interreligious meetings, including inter-faith services in England several times a month, a formidable challenge. We can see traces of these inter-faith services in his 1971 book *Amour sans limites* (Limitless Love),[6] a series of meditations on divine love which could find echoes among believers of all great world religions. In 1961 Fr. Lev wrote to Elisabeth Behr-Sigel that he had "many moving contacts with Buddhists, Moslems, Baha'is – in my thoughts, meeting and adoring Christ hidden and implicit... In each, I see the Logos... It is Christ – I dare to say – who unifies my life and its manifold ways."[7] Behr-Sigel wrote of his book *Amour sans limites* that "this slender volume is simultaneously the most mystical, the most poetic and also the most theological of the writings of the Monk of the Eastern Church."[8]

Even though Fr. Lev left the Roman Catholic Church because of a disagreement with Rome's policy towards the Orthodox Churches in Slavic countries, he maintained good relations with a number of his former Benedictine brothers who founded the Monastery of Amay in Belgium, which became the Monastery of Chevetogne, dedicated to improving relations with the Eastern Churches through prayer, study and publications. After World War II, Fr. Lev renewed his personal relations with the monks of Chevetogne, who published a number of his writings in their periodical *Irénikon* or as books. Chevetogne itself was not well regarded in many Catholic circles because of its openness to Orthodoxy and in order not to draw attention to the fact that the monastery was publishing writings of a priest who broke with Rome, Fr. Lev's writings appeared under the pseudonym "Un Moine de l'Église d'Orient" (and in English "A Monk of the Eastern Church").

Other ecumenical involvement of Fr. Lev included conferences and preaching at the Ecumenical Institute of Bossey, an educational centre established by the World Council of Churches in the outskirts of Geneva. He also taught at the St Sergius Orthodox Theological Institute in Paris.

---

[4] Lev Gillet, "Papal Infallibility and Sobornost", *Sobornost*, June 1944, 15-17.
[5] Elisabeth Behr-Sigel, followed by several others, attributes to Lev *Gillet* an article on the intercommunion controversy in the Fellowship of St Alban and St Sergius in the mid-1930s. The article in question, which states that sacramental intercommunion is premature, is written from an Anglican perspective and is signed by Rev. C. [Charles] S. *Gillett*, an Anglican divine. Cf. Élisabeth Behr-Sigel, *Un Moine de l'Église d'Orient*, 363 ; *Sobornost* 2.3 (1935).
[6] English translation published as *In Thy Presence* (London: Mowbrays, 1977; SVS Press, 1997).
[7] Cited by Élisabeth Behr-Sigel in *Un Moine de l'Église d'Orient*, 519.
[8] *Un Moine de l'Église d'Orient*, 557.

Theological contribution

Fr. Lev Gillet's approach to ecumenism was above all personal and pastoral. His approach to ecumenism was bringing the Good News of salvation in Christ to all those in need of hearing it, both Orthodox and non-Orthodox, even non-Christians and atheists. Although active in the Fellowship of St. Alban and St. Sergius, he preferred to remain in the background with respect to theological questions and formal ecumenical dialogues, seeking instead personal relationships with those who believe in Christ – and, as we have seen, in a broader ministry with all seekers after the Truth. He was primarily a spiritual counsellor and guide; his charism was the spoken word, which his books reflected. By nature an intellectual, Fr. Lev gradually moved away from a "learned" approach to spirituality, evident in the 1920s and 1930s, to conveying the personal significance of the divine word of God in Scripture. His mastery of the Orthodox tradition is shown for example in his writings on Orthodox spirituality and the Jesus Prayer, while his deceptively simple yet profound meditations on Biblical themes illustrate his pastoral concern to make the word of God relevant to Christians living in a secular society. It is this combination of learning, pastoral focus and sensitivity to the needs of each person who came to him for counsel and guidance that characterised his ecumenical vision and commitment.

Bibliography – Books by Lev Gillet

Most of Fr. Lev Gillet's books were published under the pseudonym "A Monk of trhe Eastern Church". He wrote in both French and English.

Communion in the Messiah, Studies in the Relationship between Judaism and Christianity, (London, Lutterworth Press, 1942 ; 1999; Lutterworth Press, 2003), 260 pp.

Judaism and Christianity: essays presented to the Rev. Paul P. Levertoff, edited by Lev Gillet, (J. B. Shears & Sons: London, [1939]).

An Outline of the History of Modern Jewish Thought, Christian Institute of Jewish Studies, Series A, No. 1, (London, n.d. [c.1940]).

Orthodox Spirituality, (SPCK, London, 1946; Saint Vladimir's Seminary Press, 1978).

Love of Christ : A little anthology from writings and inscriptions of the first three centuries, (Mowbray, London, 1961), 25p.

The Shepherd, (Fellowship of Saint Alban and Saint Sergius, London, 1968).

The Burning Bush, (Fellowship of St Alban and St Sergius, London, 1971. Templegate, Springfield IL, c. 1976; Saint Vladimir's Seminary Press).

Encounter at the Well, (Mowbray, London and Oxford, 1988), 139p. (Contains : "Encounter at the Well", "The Burning Bush" et "The Sheppard").

On the Invocation of the Name of Jesus, (Fellowship of St Alban and St Sergius, London, 1950), 32p. *The Prayer of Jesus*, (Desclee NY/Tournai BE, 1967), 125p. (Borgo Press : San Bernardino CA, reprint 1986). *The Jesus Prayer*, (Templegate, Springfield IL, 1985); (Saint Vladimir's Seminary Press, 1987). Also contained in: *Praying the name of Jesus: The ancient wisdom of the Jesus Prayer*. (Wilfrid Stinissen and Lev Gillet, Ligouri, n.d.), 132p.

Jesus: A Dialogue with the Saviour, (Desclee, NY, 1963). 185p. (Educational Services; Reprint edition, 1990), 184 pp.

A Day with the Lord, (Mowbray, London, 1958). *A Day with Jesus*, (Desclee, NY [1964]). [Same book]

In Thy Presence, (Mowbray, 1977). (Saint Vladimir's Seminary Press, 1977; 1997). 144p.

Serve the Lord with Gladness (Contains "Our Life in the Liturgy" & "Be My Priest"), (Saint Vladimir's Seminary Press).

The Year of Grace of the Lord: A Scriptural and Liturgical Commentary on the Calendar of the Orthodox Church, (Saint Vladimir's Seminary Press, 1980).

Part III: Representative Orthodox Theologians reflecting on Ecumenism

Books in French only:

Notre Père. Introduction à la foi et à la vie chrétienne, Éd. An-Nour, Beyrouth, n.d. ; (Cerf, 1988). 80p

Le Visage de lumière, (Chevetogne, 1966), 229p.

Au Cœur de la fournaise, (Le Cerf/Le sel de la terre, 1998), 160p.

Le Pasteur de nos âmes, Directeur de publication Paul Ladouceur, (YMCA-Press-F.X. de Guibert, 2008).

Kyriaki Karidoyanes-FitzGerard

Biographical Note

Maximos Aghiorgoussis (1935-) is the retired Metropolitan of Pittsburgh (Ecumenical Patriarchate) and the Distinguished Emeritus Professor of Dogmatic Theology at Holy Cross Greek Orthodox School of Theology in Brookline, Massachusetts (USA).

Through his lectures, writings and personal witness, Metropolitan Maximos has been the preeminent dogmatic theologian and exponent of Orthodox ecumenical dialogue in North America. Born on the island of Chios (Greece) on 5 March 1935 to Fr. Evangelos and Pres. Lemonia, he graduated from the Patriarchal Theological School of Halki in 1957. Ordained a deacon in 1957 and a priest in 1959, Maximos completed his graduate studies at the University of Louvain, (Belgium), where he received the Baccalaureate in Philosophy and the Doctorate in Theology in 1964. This led to a period of pastoral service and study in Rome.

Upon the recommendation of Ecumenical Patriarch Athenagoras, Maximos was appointed Professor of Systematic Theology at the Holy Cross School of Theology in 1966 where he remained until 1978 when he was elected Bishop of Diocleia and subsequently bishop for the diocese of Pittsburgh in 1979. He later received the title of Metropolitan of Ainou in 1997. Upon the recommendation of Ecumenical Patriarch Bartholomew, the Holy Synod elevated the diocese to a Metropolis in 2002 and Maximos became the first Metropolitan of Pittsburgh. He remained in this position until his retirement in 2011.

Theological and Ecumenical Perspectives

The experience of studies at the theological School of Halki exposed Maximos to the rich theological perspectives of the Constantinopolitan theological tradition. It provided him with an understanding of theology which was rooted in the Scriptures and Tradition of the Church, nurtured by prayer, expressed in the Eucharist and oriented to the needs of God's people. As he would later say, "authentic theology always has a pastoral spirit because it is concerned with salvation in Christ. This is a process of healing and reconciliation that restores the human person and glorifies the living God." [1]

This period at Halki also provided Maximos with an appreciation of the ecumenical orientation of the Ecumenical Patriarchate. Since the early decades of the twentieth century, the Patriarchate had urged the other Orthodox Churches to emerge from isolation in order to cooperate with each other and to enter into dialogue with the Christian West.[2] As he puts it: "My studies at the Patriarchal School of Halki provided me with valuable perspectives on the causes of Christian divisions and the need to address them." [3] Maximos was deeply influenced by the Patriarchate's perspectives and by the personal commitment to reconciliation of the late Ecumenical Patriarch Athenagoras.

While at Louvain, Maximos studied extensively the writings of St. Basil the Great which led to his doctoral dissertation.[4] At the same time, his personal contacts with Catholic professors led him to recognize two important facts. First, he experienced the desire of many Catholic theologians to become reacquainted with

---

[1] Maximos Aghiorgoussis, *Together in Christ: Studies in Ecclesiology and Ecumenism* (Brookline: Holy Cross Orthodox Press, 2012) vii.

[2] See Thomas FitzGerald, *The Ecumenical Patriarchate and Christian Unity* (Brookline: Holy Cross Orthodox Press, 2009).

[3] Ibid., viii.

[4] Maximos Aghiorgoussis, *La Dialectique de l'Image de Dieu d'Apres Saint Basile le Grand* (Louvain, 1964).

the theological perspectives of the Orthodox Church. It should be remembered that this was a time when there was no formal theological dialogue between the Catholic Church and the Orthodox Church. Second, these and other informal encounters led Maximos to deepen his own commitment to dialogue.[5]

During his period of pastoral service in Rome between 1964 and 1966, Maximos again had the opportunity to meet informally with Catholic theologians at a time of great theological and ecumenical ferment. Upon the recommendation of the late Ecumenical Patriarch Athenagoras, Maximos had the distinctive opportunity to serve as an observer for the Ecumenical Patriarchate at the Second Vatican Council at its third and fourth sessions in 1964 and 1965.

In his writings on ecclesiology and ecumenism, Maximos is a theological companion of Georges Florovsky, John Meyendorff and Metropolitan John Zizioulas whom he greatly admires. Following them, Maximos affirms the importance of the 'return' to the Fathers in contemporary Orthodox theology. Yet, he does not interpret this narrowly. Rather, he sees the "return" also as a recovery of the Scriptures and a deepened appreciation of the Eucharist and liturgical life of the Church. It is through the life of the Church that one gains insight into the reality of the Trinitarian God as revealed by Christ, acquires a vision of His plan for all creation and celebrates His divine victory. Regarding Christian reconciliation, Maximos recognizes that the Christian East and Christian West share in the task of "returning to the Fathers," and renewing their commitment to patristic thought and teaching.[6]

Maximos is a fervent exponent of 'Eucharistic ecclesiology' as thoughtfully developed in recent times by John Zizioulas.[7] He affirms that the writings of Zizioulas "are of paramount importance regarding the patristic and Orthodox teaching that the Church is united around the bishop and the Eucharist." [8] At the same time, Maximos also recognizes that Eucharistic ecclesiology can be enriched by a fuller appreciation of the significance of Baptism. He notes that it "is imperative for our theology and church life to rediscover the baptismal piety of the Church, namely, the paschal experience of Baptism and the Pentecostal experience of Chrismation."[9]

Much of Maximos' writings are devoted to ecumenical topics and reflect his extensive involvement in dialogues. He recognizes that the "tragedy of divisions between the Christian churches continues to be one of the greatest challenges facing us today…The gradual process of reconciling the churches is not merely a matter of good will. It requires a solid and consistent theological reflection that aims at agreement in the historic Apostolic Faith."[10]

Of particular concern to Maximos is the dialogue between the Orthodox and the Catholic Church. He believes that the major historic issues in this division must be recognized, addressed and resolved. Chief among these are the significance of the primacy of the bishop of Rome and developments related to it. These are major themes in his extensive study devoted to the interrelationship of primacy and conciliarity.[11]

At the same time, Maximos also recognizes that the deep relationship between the two churches is distinctive in spite of formal separation. With this in mind, he affirms that the two are truly "sister churches." He holds that a deep and mysterious communion still exists. He states: "There is no doubt that the two churches are not yet in full communion. But to say that there is no communion at all is also inaccurate."[12] His extensive

[5] See Maximos Aghiorgoussis, "East Meets West: Gifts of the Eastern Tradition to the Whole Church", *St Vladimir's Theological Quarterly* 37.1 (1993): 3-22.
[6] *Together in Christ*, 29.
[7] Maximos Aghiorgoussis, "The Holy Eucharist in Ecumenical Dialogue," *Journal of Ecumenical Studies* 13.2 (1976): 204-212.
[8] Ibid., 239.
[9] Maximos Aghiorgoussis, *In the Image of God* (Brookline: Holy Cross Orthodox Press, 1999), 109.
[10] Ibid., viii.
[11] Ibid., 187-200. The chapter is titled "Primacies of Honor: The Development of Primacies in the Life of the Church."
[12] *In the Image of God*, 139.

essay "Sister Churches: Ecclesiological Implications" expresses this conviction. He affirms that the churches "are still 'sisters' with the responsibility to rediscover one another as such and strive for the restoration of full communion with one another."[13]

Maximos has always been sensitive to other critical issues facing the Church today. He has recognized the need of theologians to address these contemporary issues with clarity and conviction. It is important to note that Maximos also served as a pastor throughout the period of his teaching. This provided him with a valuable context to relate theology to the real concerns and needs of the faithful. For example, he has forcefully defended the need for a Great and Holy Council of the Orthodox Church.[14] He has strongly supported efforts to unify the Orthodox in America.[15] And, he has advocated for the restoration of the order of the ordained Diaconate for qualified women.[16] In addressing issues such as these, he has said that "theology must be sensitive towards the needs and concerns of God's people today." [17] He also believes that each of these topics has significant ecumenical consequences.

Participation in Bilateral Dialogues and Other Ecumenical Meetings

Maximos has been especially active in two major bilateral dialogues in North America. First, he served as a member and later the Orthodox chairman of the Lutheran-Orthodox Bilateral Dialogue from 1989 to its suspension in 2005. Maximos' influence can be seen in the three significant statements "Christ in Us and Christ for Us in Lutheran and Orthodox Theology" (1992),[18] "A Common Statement on Faith in the Holy Trinity" (1998)[19] and "Common Response to the Aleppo Statement o the date of Easter/Pascha" (1999).[20]

Likewise, Maximos was appointed a member of the official Orthodox-Catholic Bilateral Consultation in 1968 which was sponsored by the Standing Conference of Canonical Orthodox Bishops, (later the Assembly of Canonical Orthodox Bishops), and the United States Conference of Catholic Bishops. [21] In 1987, he became the Orthodox co-chairman of the Dialogue serving until his retirement in 2011. In this very fruitful dialogue, Maximos was a major contributor of formal papers and informal interventions. He had a significant involvement in the preparation of twenty-five significant Joint Statements from the Dialogue between the years 1969 and 2011.[22]

Of particular importance are two statements which reflect Maximos' deep and creative involvement. First, with his leadership, the Dialogue produced in 2003 the statement entitled "The Filioque: A Church-Dividing Issue?". This extensive statement addresses the major historical and theological issues related to the *Filioque*

[13.] Ibid., xii. His chapter on this topic is entitled: "Sister Churches: Ecclesiological Implications," 153-195.

[14] See, Maximos Aghiorgoussis, "A Theological Apologia for the Forthcoming Great and Holy Council," *The Greek Orthodox Theological Review* 24.2-3 (1979): 117-122.

[15] See Maximos Aghiorgoussis, "Unity in the Orthodox 'Diaspora," in *A New Era Begins: Proceedings of the 1994 Conference of Orthodox Bishops in Ligonier, Pennsylvania,* ed. George Bedrin and Philip Famous (Torrance, CA: OPT Publications, 1996).

[16] Interviews with Metropolitan Maximos, Pittsburgh, 12-13 December 2006 and 24 October 2009.

[17] *Together in Christ*, vii.

[18] "Christ in Us and Christ for Us in Lutheran and Orthodox Theology," in *Salvation in Christ*, ed. John Meyendorff and Robert Tobias (Minneapolis: Augsburg Fortress, 1992), 17-33.

[19] "Lutheran-Orthodox Common Statement on Faith in the Holy Trinity," in *Growing in Consensus II*, ed. Lydia Veliko and Jeffrey Gros, (Washington: Bishops Committee for Ecumenical and Interreligious Affairs Catholic Conference of Catholic Bishops, 2005), 409-413.

[20] "Common Response to the Aleppo Statement on the Date of Easter/Pascha," Ibid., 407-408.

[21] The Canadian Conference of Catholic Bishops became a co-sponsor of the Consultation in 1997.

[22] All of the early documents can be found in *The Quest for Unity: Orthodox and Catholics in Dialogue*, (Crestwood: St. Vladimir's Seminary Press, 1996). Most later statements can be found at http://www.scoba.us/resources/orthodox-catholic.html.

and offers recommendations to the Churches. Second, the Dialogue produced in 2010 a statement entitled "Steps Towards a Reunited Church: A Sketch of an Orthodox-Catholic Vision for the Future." Reflecting previous Dialogue statements, this text is an unprecedented effort to visualize the shape of a reunited Catholic and Orthodox Church, that addresses historic divisive issues and that results in the re-establishment of full communion.

As a professor at Holy Cross Greek Orthodox School of Theology, Maximos generously shared his ecclesiological and ecumenical insights with his students. He frequently discussed the dialogues with his students. In so doing, he recognized the importance of nurturing new generations of clergy and theologians who had a deep appreciation of the Orthodox faith and the desire to share these insights in ecumenical encounters.

After becoming a diocesan bishop in 1979, the ecumenical concerns of Maximos were not diminished. Although he served a vast diocese comprised of 64 large parishes in three states, Maximos found new opportunities to speak of his concern for Christian reconciliation and unity. This is evident in his sermons and in his essays in the *Illuminator*, the newspaper of the Metropolis. There, one can find numerous essays devoted to ecumenical themes and written for a broad audience. [23]

Maximos is deeply respected and honored for his devoted episcopal service in the Metropolis of Pittsburgh, his contribution to the Eparchial Synod of the Greek Orthodox Archdiocese, and his teaching at Christ the Saviour Theological Seminary in Johnstown, Pennsylvania.

As a bishop, Maximos also participated in numerous missions of the National Council of Churches of Christ (NCCUSA), including the Middle-East (1980), the People's Republic of China (1981), and the former USSR (1984). During this period he served as a Vice-President of the National Council of Churches. He participated in World Council of Churches mission to Lebanon (1982) and former Czechoslovakia (1984). He was part of the Patriarchal Delegation to the Sixth General Assembly of the WCC in Vancouver, Canada (1983). He also participated in WCC missions to the former USSR and Czechoslovakia in 1998, to Byelorussia and Ukraine (1992). He represented the Ecumenical Patriarchate at the Fourth Conference of the Roman Catholic Latin American Bishops (CELAM) in Santo Domingo, the Dominican Republic (1992).

Maximos has recognized the importance of Orthodox involvement in local ecumenical and interfaith meetings. He was an active participant of the Christian Associates of Southwest Pennsylvania and in Councils of Churches Pennsylvania, Ohio and West Virginia. He participated in the 12th National Conference of Christians and Jews in Chicago (1990), and served as a member of the organizing committee of the 13th National Conference of Christians and Jews, which was held in Pittsburgh, Pennsylvania (1992).

Through his teaching, theological acumen, sermons and personal witness, Metropolitan Maximos continues to influence generations of clergy, theologians and lay leaders. He is a wise spiritual father and mentor to countless believers.

Bibliography

Maximos Aghiorgoussis, *Together in Christ: Studies in Ecclesiology and Ecumenism,* (Brookline: Holy Cross Press, 2013).

Idem, *In the Image of God* (Brookline: Holy Cross Orthodox Press, 1999).

Idem, *La Dialectique de l'Image de Dieu d'Apres Saint Basile le Grand,* (Louvain, 1964).

Idem, "Orthodox-Catholic Consultation issues Common Statement on the Value of Ecumenical Witness," *The Illuminator* 21.122 (2000): 7-8.

Idem, "East Meets West: Gifts of the Eastern Tradition to the Whole Church," *St Vladimir's Theological Quarterly* 37.1 (1993): 3-22.

---

[23] I am collecting many of these essays for future publication.

Idem, The Ecumenical Patriarchate and the Unity of Orthodoxy," *The Illuminator* 11.81-83 (1990).

Idem, "The Church as a Presupposition for the Proclamation of the Gospel," *The Greek Orthodox Theological Review* 25 (1980): 371-376.

Idem, "Theological and Historical Aspects of Conciliarity: Some Propositions for Discussion," *The Greek Orthodox Theological Review* 24.1 (1979): 5-19.

Idem, "Catholicity of the Church and Nationalism," Savvas Agourides (ed.) *Procès-Verbaux du deuxième Congrès de Théologie Orthodoxe*, (Athens, 1978), 482-485.

Idem, "The Holy Eucharist in Ecumenical Dialogue," *Journal of Ecumenical Studies* 13.2 (1976): 204-212.

Part III: Representative Orthodox Theologians reflecting on Ecumenism

(51) ARCHBISHOP ANASTASIOS YANNOULATOS OF TIRANA AND ALL-ALBANIA[1]

Marios Begzos

Archbishop of Tirana and all-Albania Anastasios (Yiannoulatos) has left such a large impact on global ecclesiastical affairs for well over a century that it is excusably easy to lose sight of a crucial aspect of his public life, meaning his contribution to religious studies and the theology of missions. It is precisely this gap that we are undertaking to cover modestly in this paper, chiefly by means of a brief and concise overview of His Beatitude's pioneering work in Modern Greek theology.

As already mentioned, Archbishop Anastasios' scholarly contribution is twofold, pertaining to world religions and mission. His literary output comprises 15 lengthy scholarly works, written originally in two languages (Greek and English) and translated into 5 more (English, Serbian, Romanian, Bulgarian, and Albanian). This work is further complemented by well over 140 essays published in numerous Festschrifts, scholarly volumes and journals of international repute, in all amounting to an output which has been translated into 10 languages.

A fluent speaker of three European languages (English, French and German), and competent in five more tongues (Spanish, Italian, Russian, Albanian, and Swahili), Anastasios has taught modern Greek language and literature at the prestigious Marburg University in Germany, which has rightly been dubbed the "Mecca of world religious studies," in light of its two outstanding institutes for the study of Comparative Religion, one in the University's Evangelical School of Theology and the other in the Philosophy Department, as well as thanks to the famous "World Religions Collection" housed in it, a legacy bequeathed to the University by Rudolph Otto, the premier expert in the field of Comparative Religion during the first half of the 20th century.

Archbishop Anastasios taught the history of world religions at the Faculty of Theology of the University of Athens for 25 years. In addition to his teaching load, His Beatitude has been the founder and first director (1971-1976) of the Inter-Orthodox Institute of the Church of Greece, located at Penteli Monastery; furthermore, he has served as an External Member of the Academy of Athens (1993), and has been the recipient of honorary doctorates from numerous world class universities, including non- theological faculties such as the School of History and Archaeology of the University of Ioannina (1996), the Department of Political Science of the University of Athens (1998), the Department of International and European Studies of Piraeus University (2001), the Department of Philology of the University of Crete (2002), and the Departments of Physical Medicine, Elementary Education, and Civil Engineering of the University of Patras (2004).

In recognition of his inter-disciplinary scholarship, Archbishop Anastasios has been awarded several covetous prizes, such as the European Pro Humanitate Prix of the Pro Europa Foundation (2001). His Beatitude was moreover invited to lecture on the International Monetary Forum in Davos, Switzerland, in 2003, and was awarded an honorary doctorate from the Boston University School of Theology, in 2004.

Lastly, the Archbishop has been justly praised for his overall contribution by such personages as His All-Holiness, Ecumenical Patriarch Bartholomew, who commend Anastasios as an "exceptional miracle;" Patriarch of Alexandria Theodore B, who described Anastasios as his own example and statue in missionary work; His Eminence, President of the Hellenic Republic Mr. Carolos Papoulias (2005-2015), who said that "should there exist someone who benefited Albania, it is Anastasios."[2]

---

[1] The present article was initially published in Greek in Theologia 84.2 (2013): 237-242.
[2] Athanasios Delikostopoulos *Anastasios, Archbishop of Tirana and All-Albania: The Minister of Reflection, creativeness, and Peace* (Athens: Eptalofos Publications, 2005), 15 (in Greek).

Religious Studies, particularly the history of religions, has been Anastasios Yiannoulatos' chief field of scientific inquiry and endeavor for over 50 years in Greece and abroad, as well as the subject he has skillfully and elegantly taught at the Faculty of Theology of the University of Athens for 25 years (1972-1997). More precisely, his research interests have focused on three particular areas: African Studies, Islamic Studies, and Comparative Religion.

Anastasios pioneered African Studies, i.e. the systematic research into the history of African religions. This was the first time that a Greek expert on world religions embarked on a thorough, on-location study of the religious faiths and experiences of the African Continent, as early as the 60s. The fruit of this long, personal research was his doctoral dissertation, entitled *The M'Ban'Dua Spirits and their Worship Context – An Inquiry into Aspects of African Religiosity in Western Uganda*,[3] which he submitted to the Faculty of Theology of the University of Athens.

This work was followed by a post-doctoral dissertation, entitled *The Lord of Glory: The God of the Kenya Mount Tribes*.[4] Further research papers were subsequently published in his book *Figures of African Ritual: Initiation and Spirit-Possession Eastern of 'Rouenzori.' A Comparative Religion Approach*[5] as well as in his study *Rouhan'ga, the Creator: A Contribution to the Inquiry into the African Beliefs on God and Man*.[6]

The study of Islam was another field championed by the Archbishop of Albania, given the fact that he was the conceiver and author of the first systematic and documented work on Islam written in Modern Greek. His monograph, entitled *Islam: A Comparative Religious Overview*[7] came on quite early for Greece's academic theology, and even long before the West was awakened to the magnitude of the rising force of Islam. Within a span of thirty years, this book has become immensely popular and won wide acclaim, to the point of numbering 15 consequent editions, nowadays being available in the modern Greek idiom, as well as enriched with additional material and an enhanced, updated bibliography.[8]

Another field pioneered by Archbishop Anastasios was Comparative Religion, the systematic and impartial study of the world's great religions. Earlier, he had published in English, then in Greek, his work *The Theses of Christians versus Other Faiths*.[9] Concurrently, he also focused on Japanese religion in his study *The Dawn of Orthodoxy in Japan*[10] which was complemented by his instructive manual *Aspects of Hinduism-Buddhism*.[11]

Among his most thoroughly researched and documented works, however, is *Globalism and Orthodoxy: Studies of Orthodox Reflection*,[12] the fruit of scholarly and intellectual maturity. Lastly, His Beatitude has edited, reviewed, and authored numerous articles and essays in encyclopedias, collective volumes, and in his own, important work, *Traces from the Quest of the Transcendent: A Collection of Papers on World Religions; Religion, Buddhism, Islam, and African Faiths*.[13]

If the Study of Comparative Religion was the "grand love" of Anastasios Yiannoulatos, his "first love" was doubtlessly mission, both as regards Church ministry in five continents, and as it pertains to theological scholarship. Here, it is worth quoting the Archbishop himself: "My African trajectory entailed several phases and experiences. I would dare say that over the long years, I developed a loving relation to that continent."[14]

---

[3] Athens, 1970, 294 pp.
[4] Athens, 1971, 246 pp.
[5] Athens, 1972, 176 pp.
[6] Athens, 1975, 138 pp.
[7] Athens, 1975, 340 pp.
[8] Athens: Akritas Publications, 2004, 506 pp.
[9] Athens, 1975, 144 pp
[10] Athens, 1971, 70 pp.
[11] Athens, 1985, 176 pp.
[12] Athens: Akritas Publications, 2000, 285 pp.
[13] Athens: Akritas Publications, 2004, 493 pp.
[14] In Africa, 2010, 19.

Here, we would do well to flip through the 15 autonomous theological essays on Orthodox missionary theology since 1961, written originally in four different languages (Greek, English, French, and German) and published in world class theological journals, here and abroad, so as to focus more prominently on the Archbishop's major writings from his maturity.

The first major work, among these, is entitled *Mission in the Wake of Christ: Theological Essays and Homilies*[15]. It was followed, one year later, by the historical study *Monks and Mission During the 4th and 9th Centuries.*[16] His overall literary output on missionary activity culminates with the anthology titled *In Africa: Papers, Studies, Assessments, Trajectories.*[17]

In addition to the aforementioned works, Archbishop Anastasios published two more books comprised of essays relating his personal pastoral and ministerial experiences in the Church of Albania. The first of these is titled *God Manifested Himself in the Flesh,*[18] and was translated in Albanian that same year. The other one, is titled *Now All Is Filled with Light,*[19] and is concurrently published in Albanian as well.

An almost unknown, but still very crucial, theological initiative credited to Anastasios, then Bishop of Androussa, was his idea to found a conference center that would also serve as an educational agency sponsored by the Church of Greece. The ensuing foundation that materialized from Anastasios' inception, named the "Inter-Orthodox Center of the Church of Greece," was built in the eastern side of Penteli Holy Monastery. It was founded in 1969 and officially inaugurated in 1971, with Anastasios Yiannoulatos as its first director. Henceforth, for over 40 years, the Center functions continuously along the lines first established in the course of six years (1971-76) by its visionary founder and director, Anastasios Yiannoulatos.

Thankfully, Anastasios' vision for the Inter-Orthodox Center has been consistently supported by the Archbishops of Athens, beginning with Hieronymus the First in the 70s and continuing with his successors, Seraphim (1980-1990), and especially Christodoulos, who renovated the Center's entire building from scratch and added more rooms to it, as well as the current Archbishop of Athens, Hieronymus, who has been instrumental in the revitalization of the Center in terms of mission and function, as a vital theological forum addressing contemporary spiritual, religious and social challenges and witnessing the Gospel to the (post) modern world.

Here, we would be remiss in failing to mention the eloquent theological justification of the Inter-Orthodox Center of the Church of Greece by Archbishop Anastasios, as it is relayed in his booklet "Perspectives and Theological Presuppositions of the Athens Inter-Orthodox Center."[20]

In concluding our brief reference to the scholarly accomplishments of Archbishop Anastasios, we ought to say forthrightly that the quality of his critical reflection is inversely proportional to the small quantity of his published work. If Cyril and Methodius were pronounced the "enlighteners of the Slavs," we would be fully justified, I believe, to grant His Beatitude the title of "enlightener of the peoples," on the basis of his overall missionary and scholarly output. From the remotest reaches of the African continent to Albania, the restless and indefatigable Archbishop of Albania has been complemented, in his institutional and pastoral capacity, by the scholar of Comparative Religion Anastasios Yiannoulatos.

Bibliography

Yannoulatos Anastasios, *Islam: A Comparative Religious Overview* (Athens: Akritas Publications, 2004) (in Greek)

- *Globalism and Orthodoxy: Studies of Orthodox Reflection* (Athens: Akritas Publications, 2000) (in Greek)

---

[15] Athens: Apostoliki Diakonia, 2007, 376 pp.
[16] Athens: Akritas Publications, 2008, 388 pp.
[17] Athens: Apostoliki Diakonia, 2010, 478 pp.
[18] Athens: Maistros Publications, 2006, 166 pp.
[19] Athens: Maistros Publications, 2007, 160 pp.
[20] An offprint of *Ecclesia* journal, vol. 48 (1971), 16 pp.

- *Traces from the Quest of the Transcendent: A Collection of Papers on World Religions; Religion, Buddhism, Islam, and African Faiths* (Athens: Akritas Publications, 2004) (in Greek)
- *Mission in the Wake of Christ: Theological Essays and Homilies* (Athens: Apostoliki Diakonia, 2007) (in Greek)
- *In Africa: Papers, Studies, Assessments, Trajectories* (Athens: Apostoliki Diakonia, 2010) (in Greek)
- *God Manifested Himself in the Flesh* (Athens: Maistros Publications, 2006) (in Greek)

Part III: Representative Orthodox Theologians reflecting on Ecumenism

Bishop Demetrios Charbak

Introduction

The ecumenical movement had acquired great importance since the beginning of the twentieth century, and the relations among the Churches had become one of the top interests for those in charge of them.

The Chair of Antioch had an important role in this movement, and in developing and encouraging the good relations among the Churches in general and in the Middle East in particular, namely in Syria and Lebanon where there are several Christian denominations living together and sharing joy and sorrow.

If we want to talk about the Thrice-Blessed Patriarch Ignatius IV Hazim (1920-2012) and about his thought and his ecumenical role, it will take too long. But maybe the whole thing can be summarized by the Title given to him "Father of Dialogue."[1] This title encompasses a number of His Beatitude's qualities was characterized by, because the one who leads dialogue should be patient, calm, honest, good listener, respectful of one's dialogue partner and uncompromising. Everyone who had met personally His Beatitude knows that he enjoyed all these properties distinctively.

The theological contribution of Patriarch Ignace IV of Antioch

Dialogue has bases, principles and constituents, but all of them are futile if there has been no fertile ground within man's spirit. The spirit of His Beatitude was very fertile. It gave the ecumenical movement multiples of eighty, ninety and hundred. His Thrice-Blessed was very popular in the ecumenical domain for his courage and frankness. Everyone knows that he used to say only what he believes in without partiality or favoritism. He was always motivated by his love for the Church and his sorrow for the splits within it.

He was not ashamed of his Church; on the contrary he was very proud of it and of its weaknesses. He was completely aware of its history and of the events it passed through that negatively affected it. But he had also faith in its future and in its leading role in the formulation of the events of the region as a whole and its essential contribution in building up man and society, producing ecumenical work among the Churches in collaboration in all fields by all the Christians, clergy and laity.

Based on this experience, he used to encourage dialogue which cannot be done without meeting and without knowing each other and loving each other. "The ecumenical work is a collective work based on meeting and on love."[2] He always sought to consolidate this thing in Antioch. "We, in the Chair of Antioch, encourage dialogue among people, especially among the Churches. By dialogue, man would feel that the other is present in front of him and not away from him and from his care and thought. Absence is a sort of death, but dialogue indicates presence, and presence characterizes the living being."[3] As he again put it "We should express the deepest essence of Christianity which is to love each other."[4] and "If you have love within you, then dialogue with you is possible, and without love there would be no dialogue."[5]

---

[1] Hazim, Patriarch Ignatius IV, "Antiochian Ideas", h.
[2] Hazim, Patriarch Ignatius IV, "Antiochian Ideas", 73.
[3] Idem, "Antiochian Ideas", h.
[4] Idem, "Sermons", part two, 73.
[5] Idem, "Antiochian Ideas", 355.

His understanding of unity is quite relevant. It is far from cancellation or exclusion. "Unity does not intend to cancel either or us. The Christian unity in the world is not a cancellation for anyone, but it is love for all."[6] Seeking to achieve unity of Churches was an obsession for him, and he considered it as one of his most important responsibilities. He knew that this was the wish of the Lord who asked in his Farewell Prayer "that they may be one,"[7] and this is also the wish of the faithful Christian who loves God. Therefore, he was one of the first supporters and participants in the Middle East Council of Churches, and he was the Chairman of the Council for many years for the sake of achieving this noble goal. "The Middle East Council of Churches deliberates all the matters that constitute a stumbling block in the face of any rapprochement among the Churches … in an attempt to facilitate the unity of the Christians which is the dream of the whole Christian People."[8] Therefore, he constantly called for the overcoming of difficulties and the removal of obstacles, providing the necessary space for the Spirit to work in the Church. "You know the obstacles in front of the unity, and each one of our Churches should contribute in overcoming them, each according to the historical responsibility incurred on it. The important thing is not to shut down the doors in the face of the Spirit's breezes."[9] He especially deemed that most of the splits in the Church did not take place due to doctrinal reasons, but due to human whims. "The doctrinal differences should not be considered as the main reason behind the divides, where a "multiple" approach to the truth will hold all these differences. The rupture itself, in terms of failure in love, would find at a later phase a 'doctrinal' justification for it, until the separation is confirmed in a legal structure."[10]

Understanding this matter would make the Christians again one Church and one family, and it would eliminate the dispersion experienced by the Christians. "Our conscience would not be in peace except when we know that we are responsible for the condition we are thinking of, and that originally we are not dispersed groups of Christians, but we are one family in origin."[11]

His Thrice-Blessed used to emphasize that the splits that happened in the Church were not because of Jesus Christ. "If you have found a slip, then search for a reason behind it other than Christ."[12] The splits did not take place in the Head of the Church, but they fell on us. "Christ will not split. The holy sacraments will not split. Those who are practicing the holy sacraments are the ones who split."[13] "All of us are requested to walk in one way, so that it would be truly said that the Church of Christ is one. Christ is not split. We are the split, not Him."[14] For this reason, we are responsible for it. "We are not the only ones on Earth, and we will not be the only ones in Heaven. We all believe that Christ is one person, and we have faith that He is a whole God. So, where is the problem? Split does not result from the doctrine, and all the conflicts are ecclesiastical matters caused by man."[15]

The ecumenical contribution of Patriarch Ignace IV of Antioch

His Thrice-Blessed deems that ecumenical work needs courage. The skilled surgeon cannot operate the surgery and complete the treatment if he has not looked at the place of the injury even though the sight is hard and painful. At the same time what is important is not to enjoy looking at the wound and be afraid of commencing the treatment on the pretext that it would be safer not to do so. "I imagine that we are afraid of seeing each

---

[6] Idem, "Antiochian Ideas", 229.

[7] John 17:11

[8] Hazim, Patriarch Ignatius IV, "Antiochian Ideas", 74.

[9] Idem, "Antiochian Ideas", 274.

[10] Idem, "The Church Is You", 125.

[11] Hazim, Patriarch Ignatius IV, "Antiochian Ideas", 97.

[12] Idem, "Antiochian Ideas", 93.

[13] Idem, "Antiochian Ideas", 232.

[14] Idem, "Dialogues", part one, 212.

[15] Idem, "Antiochian Ideas", 211.

other, and I think that we are afraid of confronting intelligently, deeply and seriously those who have beliefs different from our own beliefs. I even think that we like the splits because they are very safe." By healing the wounds Christian witness is made stronger. "Only the Eastern Denominations knew the cohabitation in the East. Thus, we should cure this big wound in order to put the Christian groups on the way of healing, so when the Church retrieves its unity it will be able to hold, in the core of the contemporary nihilism, the testimony of resurrection, and primarily its own resurrection."[16]

The ecumenical work for Patriarch Ignace activated the Orthodox Christian presence in an environment of Islamic majority. "What is important for us is the real Christian collaboration because the Muslim cannot understand the existence of many Christian denominations that talk about Christ, but are not consistent with each other"[17].

He was aware that seeking unity is a decision that should be adopted by all, since the truth does not belong to anyone in particular, but we are all trustees on it. Proceeding in this direction means that unity is "the consensus to live together and the conviction that the differences are a source of richness, without falling in the trap of fabrication. We have to believe that the truth can never be an exclusive property to us, though we are trustees that we do not deserve it."[18]

Our involvement in the ecumenical work in a proper and effective way is initiated, according to his perception, by the understanding of our identity as openness in love towards the other Christian Churches and Traditions, due to a regenerated and permanent expectation that we always work as servants for reconciliation. The ecumenical work of the Church is about the rapprochement and dialogue between the Christians, and not challenge and competition. This attitude is supposed to facilitate the life of the faithful without leading them to dangerous paths. "I think that the Churches through the variety of its references contribute in complicating the life of the Church and its members. I do not understand a reason for the existing differences among them."[19]

The relationship with the other Christian Traditions

Patriarch Ignace had never bargained for half solutions, especially in matters related to faith practices, even if they have been practiced wrongly among some people, as for instance the promoted attitude of having communion with all the Christian Churches and Traditions. "We ourselves are annoyed from the rough practice for serving the Eucharist, which we feel is no more than a disguised preaching."[20]

The danger of Proselytism

Patriarch Ignace was courageous and frank in handling the subject of proselytism which the Churches in the East have suffered from, an issue that caused a lot of wounds, and contributed in enlarging the distance among the Churches. As Patriarch Ignace put it "The thing that the Church suffered from mostly is that one Church hunts the members of another church. This might be the biggest tragedy experienced by the Church"[21]. Hence Patriarch Ignace called for Churches to abandon this sort of strategy which destroys instead of building up the Christian relationship and unity, by adopting a theology of reconciliation. "We are convinced that we cannot give up this strategy of hunting, unless we adopt a real theology in the reconciliation, in which the brother is considered living in the heart of Christ himself."[22]

---

[16] Idem, "The Church Is You", 112.
[17] Hazim, Patriarch Ignatius IV, "Dialogues", Part Two, 93.
[18] Hazim, Patriarch Ignatius IV, "Sermons", Part One, 86.
[19] Idem, "Antiochian Ideas", 211.
[20] Idem, "Antiochian Ideas", 271.
[21] Idem, "The Church Is You", 105.
[22] Idem, "Antiochian Ideas", 271.

The relationship with the Oriental Orthodox Churches

Patriarch Ignace used to concentrate on the relations with the Oriental Orthodox Churches (for instance the Syrian, Copts and Armenian), and particularly the Syrian Church due to its important presence in Syria and Lebanon, and also because of the presence of their Patriarch in Damascus. This situation had allowed continuous meeting and permanent coordination between the two Churches. Patriarch Ignace described those churches as Sister Churches with the full sense of this word. "The Oriental Orthodox Church is a sister Church, the sister with the deep sense of this word."[23]

More than once, he strongly asserted that the Christians, especially in the Oriental Church, are one family and have the same belief that was partitioned by the expressions, terms and political purposes. "Let's not set further difficulties with the other Churches. Instead, let's at least talk about the truthfulness of faith. This is associated with the Holy Trinity and associated with the character of our Lord, Jesus Christ, and whatever is said in this respect is no more than an expression."[24]

His Beatitude also expressed in several speeches the distinctive relationship with the Patriarch of the Syrian Church, both at the personal and the confessional level. "I mention as an example that I have with the Syrian Orthodox Patriarch some kind of unity in belief. This had been written down by our theologians since 1972. But this did not lead actually and directly to the restoration of the partnership."

Conclusion

Patriarch Ignace used to pray fervently for the unity of Churches and for the ecumenical dialogue among the Churches to be fruitful. As he amply put it, "We pray to be able to start anew, all of us together, the Ancient Oriental Churches, the Catholic Churches and the Orthodox Church, an honest, deep and loving dialogue."[25] After his assumption (2012) the ecumenical movement particularly in the Middle East has lost a distinguished figure and a key supporter to this direction.

Bibliography

Hazim, Patriarch Ignatius IV, "The Church Is You", (Damascus: Greek Orthodox Patriarchate, 2005).
-, "Antiochian Ideas", (Damascus: Greek Orthodox Patriarchate, 2004).
-, "Sermons", Two Parts, (Damascus: Greek Orthodox Patriarchate, 2003).
-, "Dialogues", Two Parts, (Damascus: Greek Orthodox Patriarchate, 2001).

---

[23] Hazim, Patriarch Ignatius IV, "Antiochian Ideas", 95.
[24] Idem, "Dialogues", part one, 93.
[25] Idem, "Antiochian Ideas", 272.

Part III: Representative Orthodox Theologians reflecting on Ecumenism

(53) Father Matta el-Maskeen

Christine Chaillot

In 1966, Pastor Otto Meinardu wrote that, in February 1963, Father Matta el-Maskeen and his disciples exerted significant pressure upon the Coptic Orthodox Patriarchate to cancel the proposed meeting of the Executive Committee of the World Council of Churches (WCC) in Cairo. The place of the meeting was subsequently changed to Geneva. Opposed then to the Coptic Church's participation in the WCC, this group of conservative hermits had published altogether three pamphlets (1962, 1963). Later on, Matta evolved a lot in his understanding of ecumenism, in ecumenical spirit and contacts.

Father Matta el-Maskeen (1919 – 2006), Matthew the Poor, is a well-known spiritual personality of the Coptic Orthodox Church of the 20th century. In 1969, he was asked by Pope Kyrillos VI to go and reorganise the historic and famous monastery of Saint Macarius in the Wadi Natroun, in the desert between Cairo and Alexandria. Before that, he had spent about nine years (1960-1969) in the Desert of Wadi Rayan in the Fayum region with a dozen of hermits. There they led a life very similar to the Desert Fathers of the first centuries, staying in caves with minimal resources. Thus, Father Matta acquired a deep ascetic and spiritual experience.

Nowadays many people of all Churches are deeply moved by his writings considered as mystical. One may say that Father Matta el-Maskeen had a spiritual impact in ecumenism through some of his texts, first written in Arabic and then translated. But he had no direct involvement in official theological dialogue. For him this was the concern of the Church authorities.

His involvement was mostly through his prayer together with the prayers of the monks of his monastery. A 1974 letter the monks of Chevetogne in Belgium says the following:

> "Our monastery fully lives the unity of the Church in Spirit and in truth, while waiting for that unity to be realized also at the level of the letter and of the hierarchy. Because of our sincere openness of heart and spirit towards all people, independently of their religious confession, it becomes possible for us to recognise ourselves in the other, or rather to recognise Christ in every human being. For us, Christian unity is living together in Christ through love. The barriers fall by themselves, and the differences disappear. Then remains only the Unique Christ who gathers us all in his holy person.
>
> Theological dialogue must take place, but we leave this to competent people in charge. As for us, we feel that the Unity of Church exists in Christ and that it is, consequently, by the measure in which we unite ourselves to Christ that we discover in Him the fullness of unity. 'If anyone is in Christ, he is a new creature (2 Cor 5:17).' And in this new creature, there are not several but 'one new human being (Eph. 2:15).' We fully live our Orthodox faith, being aware of the truth and spiritual richness which are there. At the same time we know that in Christ, 'there is no longer Greek or Jew, circumcised or uncircumcised, Barbarian, Scythian, slave or free; there is only Christ who is all and in all (Col 3:11).' In this inner rift?, we would like to die every day in sacrifice for the reconciliation of the Churches.
>
> In the monastic life, we have found the best way of union to Christ and thus the best realisation of this new creation which gathers men 'of every nation, race, people and language (Rev 7:9)' in the unity of the Spirit and heart."

Unity is a gift. The grace of the Holy Spirit is the principle of unity and also the principle of unity of the Church. Through the Holy Spirit, people also enter into communion with the Father and the Son.

Christians of all Churches (Orthodox, Catholic, Protestant), as well as many Muslims and even Jews, visit the Monastery of Saint Macarius. Some visitors can attend the monastic prayers or stay for a time of retreat. All are impressed by the peaceful place. Everyone is welcomed as if being Christ.

The Monastery of Saint Macarius is in contact with several monasteries outside Egypt, especially in Europe, for example with Chevetogne (Belgium) and Bellelfontaine (France).

Usually the ecumenical movement is seen as the place where all the divided Christians meet in order to examine whether they can confess the same faith with a view towards eucharistic communion. In his writings, Father Matta looks at ecumenism far beyond simple encounters between people during conferences. He looks at the biblical, theological, ecclesiological and spiritual levels and at the level of mutual love which enable Christians to see the questions in a totally different light.

Like many bishops and priests of the Coptic Orthodox Church, he knows the Gospel very well and quotes it frequently, as the Church Fathers did in the past. Thus his writings can be accepted by all Christians, whether Catholic, Protestant or Orthodox. In his comment on the Epistle to the Ephesians, he speaks of the Unification of humanity in Christ. He has also written on the theology of *theosis*, that is, in Orthodox theology, the process of coming into union with God.

He has written about the Unity of the Church in three main articles.

In "One Christ and One Catholic Church," Father Matta first defines the "catholic" or universal Church, meaning "wholeness", that which transcends the totality of finite existence. The Church, with regard to its universal nature is greater than man, his concepts, his structures and his dogmas.

What is lost is the reality of the infinite nature of the Church which transcends the physical earth as well as thought. The Church has the divine capacity attained through Christ to make every single person one with God.

Through the sacraments all the faithful are brought together into union with the mystical body of Christ, thus becoming one body and one spirit. Therefore, they have access to the nature of the one universal Church. In the eucharistic communion, Christ is thus made one with every man, a new man, newly and purely created in a manner analogous to the image of Christ, a son of God within the unique filiation of Christ. The mystical body of Christ in the Church is that source of power which makes it capable of gathering all within its own unique universal nature.

The Church is Christ's mystical body, with its baptism and its eucharist, the meeting point of all humankind and the only meeting point for all peoples, nations, races, tongues, and colors which dissolves all barriers and disagreements, void of any division, dispute, or discrimination—which is exactly what is meant by the "catholicity" of the Church.

The universal nature of Christ has the power of total reconciliation and the unification of sundry dispositions in such a manner that surpasses the capability of any nature in itself, not only ideas, principles, and dogmas.

In ecumenism, the defects have occurred in the interpretation and in the comprehension of theological terms. The fault in the Church's schism lies not in the nature of the Church, but in the nature of man's inability to conceive and grasp the nature of Christ and the Church. Therefore, we can see that any schism in the concept of the nature of Christ and the Church signals that we have mundanely approached the divine through a fallen mind, that is to say, through an un-divine approach. Every schism that has taken place within the Church implies that man has started to deal with ecclesiastical matters through an ethnocentric and prejudiced mind (which disperses), not in an ecclesiastical or catholic way (which unites).

It is only for the new man that Christ will remain unbreakable, indisputable, and without variation; only for the man who possesses the mind of Christ will the Church remain one, unique, and universal to all people, with the work of the Holy Spirit. The new man must be whole and one, for it is out of one universal nature and one Father that he emerges. And love imposes its divine and universal authority.

When people earnestly renounce their own will and surrender their lives to Christ, through fervent repentance, only then will the life of Christ be manifested in the Church, and then will His Spirit be poured out over it. Then will the Church be one through the grace of God. The catholicity of the Church and its oneness are but the totality of theology.

Father Matta concludes, "We now look forward most eagerly with tears and supplication, with the new man's consciousness, to the Church's catholicity and to its unity all over the world."

In another article, "Christian Unity", Father Matta continues to give spiritual advice towards Christian unity.

The principle of theological unity springs initially from a maturity of faith and from an overflowing spirituality which bursts through the barriers of hate, the variance of thought, the discords of the soul, the inventions

Part III: Representative Orthodox Theologians reflecting on Ecumenism

of the intellect, and the cares of the flesh. If there were indeed a spiritual renaissance, a deep fervor for the faith, unity would have taken the form of a collective and individual return to God, a sweeping movement for conversion, repentance, and begging God for forgiveness.

Our quest for Christian unity must be sought through the Spirit without any interference from the flesh or emotion. I ought, in the first place, to have made a complete renunciation of the "me" and all my emotions in the presence of God, before trying to unite myself with others, in order "That they may be [one] in us (Jn. 17:21)." I should have to love God "with all my heart, and with all my soul, and with all my mind" so as to be able to love others with a unifying love that cannot bring harm to me or to them. The intellect, or intellectual illusion, is a force which emotion exploits—until we reach the state of total abandonment to God. He who unites himself to God undertakes to consider how he should unite himself to all and takes no rest until that union has been accomplished. If, therefore, Christian unity is not realized at the present time, it is because we are seeking it before we have surrendered our whole heart and our whole soul and our whole mind to God; and because we are seeking it outside ourselves, that is to say, we are trying to realize it as a matter for discussion and not within ourselves. Unity is one of the desires of God that Christ revealed to us: "That they may be [one] in us (Jn. 17:21)." It is, therefore, within ourselves that it is to be sought and studied —if, of course, Christ is in fact within our heart ("that Christ may dwell in your hearts through faith [Eph. 3:17]"). To seek unity outside oneself is to deviate into matters of interest and speculation.

Unity is not a subject that can ever be examined theoretically; unity is initially a divine essence and consequently a truth. Unity will become a living fact when all are in God. Unity is an edification of the soul, the gathering together of its powers. This is the concern of the Spirit: the Spirit forgives and pardons, loves and unites.

If we desire a true unity, we must seek it and study it in God, in His presence, not as some theoretical subject separated from God, whatever theological guise it may adopt. Any question concerning unity on the theological plane which cannot find a solution is indeed sufficient proof that the Lord is not present in the midst of the assembly. The Lord's absence necessarily causes one to think again about the aim of the union, the method of seeking it, and the intention of its united members.

Unity without the divine presence is nothing more than an idea, a matter for discussion, or a vain longing. But in the presence of God unity becomes real and visible, overflowing and life-giving, and many live it.

The question in the matter of unity is in a penetrating and decisive manner the question of the presence of the Lord; it is by this presence that unity will be accomplished on the divine plane, and that divisions will be brought to an end. Unity is based on the willingness of each one to receive the divine presence and is not simply a gathering together of the community.

Human logic would like us first to remove the differences so unity could be accomplished, whereas the logic of God, as it is expressed in the inspiration of the second chapter of the Epistle to the Ephesians, requires that unity should be accomplished first, so that the middle partition may be broken down. This is the mutual opposition that exists at the present time in meetings on Christian unity. The necessity forces itself upon us of once more paying attention to the problem of unity, so it can exist according to the way of God. In outward appearance unity is weakness, but in essence it is an immense force, as indivisible as God. The strength of Christian life comes neither from the many nor from "union," but from union with God: "for [it] is God at work in you, both to will and to work for His good pleasure (Ph. 2:13)."

There is a danger that Christian unity could be made to exist out of the instinct for natural union, whether it stems from the weak in order to gain strength or from the powerful in order to increase power. In either case it would be to pursue the temporal life, and that would be incompatible with the practice of Christian life. We should understand that Christian unity is a state of divine weakness over against the world—like that of their Master, who surrendered His infinite power to be crucified by anyone who wished and in whatever way they wished.

Father Matta ends his article with these words: "We wish and we pray that the Churches may have a unity, divine both in appearance and in essence, a unity above the realm of time."

Orthodox Handbook on Ecumenism

In a third article, Father Matta speaks of "True Unity: an Inspiration for the World" where he continues to give his deep vision for the search of Christian unity.

First he shows a very Orthodox stance when he says that doctrine still exists unchanged and that it is a precious living heritage handed down from generation to generation, through living tradition. Then he adds that Christian unity is the greatest demand of faith.

Christ is not asking for unity to the letter or unity of thought and opinion, but unity of the Spirit and of love, with the deep longing for unity of all believers in Him. As for the Spirit, it is the one who establishes one mind, one voice, and one word without any Church being deprived of its special characteristics or the distinctive features of its theology. It is necessary to begin doctrinal dialogue with the Spirit and not with the letter, by receiving the one Christ first. Christ requires a mystical unity for all of us, at the highest level.

The Church unity we seek is not a unity based on temporal or geographical dimensions, nor can it be built on any human or intellectual basis whatever they may be, for Jesus asked that it be first a unity in the Father through Christ himself. Unity will be fulfilled and will take place through the death of the ego of each Church, in order that Christ's self may live in them all. The state of our behavior with regards to Christ is at odds with the true Christ. This is the poisonous root of division which will continue to nourish separation and schism.

The most dangerous of all the things lacking in the divided Churches of today is Christ himself, and him crucified. In the language of dialogue, one may say that what is lacking among the divided churches is a Church that is able to bear responsibility for errors of the past in order to free itself and others from the sin of the present—that is to say schism and disintegration. If such a Church could be found, then unity and reconciliation could take place and love would be victorious. The unity that is granted by the Holy Spirit is still absent. While the Church herself remains divided, she will never be able to pray for the world which is also divided.

The Church cannot offer these powers, potentialities and immortal values to the world through outstanding theologians only, but she must also offer them through the saintly among them, as well as through simple, saintly individuals, the exemplaries of the churches. Hence, regardless of how much we may try to lay the responsibility of unity and change upon the shoulders of the church, in the long run the burden will fall upon the saints of the church. If truly we demand that the process of unity begin immediately, then we must fix our eyes on the elect and the gifted who exist in every church, despite their efforts to escape being seen by men. When our confidence is placed with the poor, the meek, the humble, the pure in heart, and the lovers of the peace that only Christ can give, then and only then will we ever have hope of achieving the true Christian unity that will inspire the world.

Bibliography

Father Matta el Maskeen (Matthew the Poor), *Orthodox Prayer Life*: *The Interior Way*, (Crestwood, NY: St Vladimir's Seminary Press, 2003).

_____, "One Christ and One Catholic Church" in *The Communion of Love* (Crestwood, NY: St Vladimir's Seminary Press, 1984), 215-222. (Also in French: « Un seul Christ et une seule Eglise universelle », in *La Communion d'amour,* Spiritualité Orientale 55, (Bellefontaine 1992), 259-267.

_____, "Christian Unity" in *The Communion of Love*, 223-234. (Also in French: *Prière, Esprit Saint et Unité chrétienne*, Spiritualité Orientale 48, (Bellefontaine 1990), 191-205; and «L'unité chrétienne» in *Irénikon* 58 (1985): 338-350.)

_____, "True Unity: an Inspiration for the World," in *One in Christ,* (Bedfordshire, England: Turvey Abbey, 1993), no 3, 187-198. (Also in French: « L'unité véritable, source d'inspiration pour le monde » in *La Communion d'amour*, 269-299 ; and in *Irénikon* 3 (1991): 365-380.

_____, « Notre vie monastique et l'unité de l'Eglise » in *Prière, Esprit Saint et Unité chrétienne*, 27-29.

Part III: Representative Orthodox Theologians reflecting on Ecumenism

_____, « L'Esprit Saint et le mystère de l'unité dans la diversité » in *Prière, Esprit Saint et Unité chrétienne*, 182-187.

_____, « La Pentecôte » in *Irénikon* 50 (1977): 5-45.

_____, « Le monastère de Saint-Macaire au Désert de Scété (Wadi el Natroun) » in *Irénikon* 51 (1978): 203-215.

_____, « L'Unification de l'humanité dans le Christ : thème théologique fondamental de l'Epître aux Ephésiens » in *Irénikon* 66.3 (1993): 335-346.

_____, « Les faux pas de l'Eglise et la venue du Seigneur » in *Irénikon* 75.2-3 (2002): 230-239.

The French translations of the articles of Father Matta are closer to the original Arabic texts than the translations into English.

Meinardus, O., "The Hermits of Wadi Rayan" in *Studia Orientalia Christiana Collectanea* 11 (1966): 293-317.

Chaillot, C. (ed.), *Towards Unity : The Theological Dialogue Between the Orthodox Church and the Oriental Orthodox Churches,* (Geneva: Inter-Orthodox Dialogue, 1998).

Chaillot, C., *Vie et spiritualité des Églises orthodoxes orientales des traditions syriaque, arménienne, copte et éthiopienne,* (Paris: Le Cerf, 2011).

Fr. Cyril Hovorun

Metropolitan of Leningrad and Novgorod Nikodim (Rotov) (1929-1978) was likely the most important figure in the ecumenical movement on behalf of the Russian Orthodox Church. During his tenure as a chairman of the Department of External Church Relations (DECR) of the Moscow Patriarchate, he was regarded as the most influential official of the Church after the Patriarch. His vision of ecumenism, Church-state relations, and the position of the Church in the society, shaped the relevant policies of the Russian Orthodox Church regarding these issues for decades. Even now the Church greatly embodies Metropolitan Nikodim's ideas and ideals. He expressed these ideas not so much in his writings, which are mostly official statements and speeches, but in his activities and policies. His attitude towards the ecumenical movement was both sincere and instrumental. He believed in the ideal of Christian unity and at the same time used the ecumenical fora to serve the interests of the Russian Church or the Soviet state.

Boris Rotov (his lay name) was born on 15 October 1929 in the village Frolovo in the region of Ryazan in Russia. After having graduated middle school, he enrolled in the faculty of natural sciences at the Ryazan Pedagogical Institute. Soon, however, he decided to dedicate his life to the Church. On 19 August 1947, Archbishop of Yaroslavl' and Rostov Dimitriy (Gradusov) tonsured him a monk with the name Nikodim and ordained him a deacon. On 20 November 1949, the same hierarch ordained him a priest and appointed him to serve in the parishes of the region of Yaroslavl'. In 1950, Nikodim began his theological studies at the Seminary and Academy of Leningrad from which he graduated in 1955 with the degree 'candidate of theology.'

The following year, his remarkable career as a Church diplomat began with his appointment as a member of the Russian Ecclesiastical Mission in Jerusalem. In 1957, he became the head of the Mission. In 1959, he returned to Moscow, where he served for several months as the director of the Chancellery of the Moscow Patriarchate. Then he was promoted to the deputy chairman of the DECR. The following year, on 10 July 1960, he was consecrated a Bishop of Podolsk, as a vicar of the Patriarch of Moscow. He was simultaneously appointed a chairman of the DECR. In this position, Bishop Nikodim dramatically upgraded the profile of this institution and made it the second most influential in the Russian Church after the office of Patriarch.

In 1960, the Holy Synod of the Russian Orthodox Church elected him as a Bishop of Yaroslavl' and Rostov. In 1961, he was chosen as one of the permanent members of the Synod, a group of the most influential hierarchs of the Moscow Patriarchate. The same year, he was elevated to the rank of Archbishop. In 1963, he became a president of the Commission of the Holy Synod on the Christian unity. On 3 August 1963, he was elected Metropolitan of Minsk and Belorussia, and on 9 October of the same year, Metropolitan of Leningrad and Ladoga. In 1967, in addition to his diocese of Leningrad, he became a ruling bishop of the diocese of Novgorod. His title then became Metropolitan of Leningrad and Novgorod. In 1970, in addition to his responsibilities over the parishes of the Russian Orthodox Church in Hungary, Finland, and Japan, of which he was in charge as a chairman of the DECR, Metropolitan Nikodim received under his hierarchical care the parishes in North and South America.

After the death of Patriarch Alexiy I (1970), Metropolitan Nikodim was one of the most eligible candidates to succeed him. However, the local council of the Russian Orthodox Church (1971) chose Metropolitan of Krutitsy and Kolomna Pimen as the next Patriarch of Moscow instead.

In the meantime, the health of Metropolitan Nikodim deteriorated. After a heart attack he asked in 1972 for the Holy Synod to relieve him of the position of the DECR chairman. He remained however a president of the Commission of the Holy Synod on the Christian unity. He was also appointed a Patriarchal exarch to the Western Europe.

Metropolitan Nikodim died on 5 September 1978 after a sixth heart attack during an audience with the Pope John Paul I. He is buried at the St Alexander Nevsky Lavra in St Petersburg.

The overall attitude of Metropolitan Nikodim to the non-Orthodox churches and to the ecumenical movement was open. This attitude was consistent with the policies of the Soviet Union under Khruschev towards peaceful coexistence and détente in the international relations. Metropolitan Nikodim, on the one hand, supported this policy of the Soviet state in his ecumenical activities. On the other hand, he used them to make the Russian Church more open and free from the state control. One of his main concerns was to ease the grip of the Soviet state over the Church and to lead the Church from the ghetto, where it had been encaged by the atheistic regime. Ecumenism was one of the instruments that Metropolitan Nikodim used to achieve these goals.

This does not mean that Metropolitan Nikodim did not believe in the ecumenical ideals. He shared the vision of the Church unity but was also realistic about it. From this realistic perspective, he particularly favoured the relations of the Russian Orthodox Church with the Oriental Churches and the Roman Catholic Church. He believed that unity with these Churches was achievable in the foreseeable future. He made practical steps to a rapprochement with the Oriental Churches particularly in the countries friendly to the Soviet Union. He also managed to send observers of the Russian Orthodox Church to the Second Vatican Council. His personal relations with the hierarchs of both Church families were extremely friendly.

With the support of Metropolitan Nikodim, the Russian Orthodox Church joined the World Council of Churches during the General Assembly of the WCC in New Delhi (1961). He led the Russian delegation at the General Assemblies in Uppsala (1968) and Nairobi (1975). In Uppsala, he was elected a member of the Central Committee of the WCC, and at Nairobi, one of the Council's Presidents.

Metropolitan Nikodim also initiated a number of bilateral dialogues, including those with the Evangelical Church of the Federal Republic of Germany, The Union of the Evangelical Churches in the Democratic Republic of Germany, the Evangelical Lutheran Church of Finland, and the Anglican Churches, *etc*. Even now the Russian Orthodox Church builds its inter-Christian relationships on the ecumenical legacy of Metropolitan Nikodim.

Bibliography

Августин (Никитин), архимандрит. Церковь плененная. Митрополит Никодим (1929-1978) и его эпоха (в воспоминаниях современников). (Tserkov' plenennaja. Mitropolit Nikodim (1929-1978) i jego epokha (v vospominanijah sovremennikov) СПб. : Издательство Санкт-Петербургского университета, 2008.

Александрова Т.Л., Суздальцева Т.В. Русь уходящая. Рассказы митрополита Питирима. (Rus' uhodiaschaja. Rasskazy mitropolita Pitirima), СПб., 2007.

Василий (Кривошеин), архиепископ. Воспоминания. Митрополит Никодим (Ротов). (Vospominanija. Mitropolit Nikodim (Rotov)): www.ubrus.org/data/library/pages/260/Main.htm (18.06.2012)

Васильева О.Ю. Русская Православная Церковь и II Ватиканский Собор. Доклад на международной богословской конференции «Личность в Церкви и обществе». (Russkaja Pravoslavnaja Tserkov' i II Vatikanskiy Sobor. Doklad na mezhdunarodnoj bogoslovskoj konferentsii "Lichnost' v Tserkvi i obschestve"): www.sfi.ru/lib.asp (21.06.2012)

Лилиенфельд, фон, Фэри. Жизнь. Церковь. Наука и вера: Профессор Фэри фон Лилиенфельд рассказывает о себе и своем видении православия и лютеранства. Беседы с проф. Е.М. Верещагиным, состоявшиеся в Германии в 1996-2002 гг. (Zhizn'. Tserkov'. Nauka i vera: Professor Fairy von Lilienfeld rasskazyvaet o sebe i svoem videnii pravoslavia i luteranstva. Besedy s prof. M. Vereschaginym, sostojavshyjesa v Germanii v 1996-2002 g.) М. : Индрик, 2004.

Поспеловский Д.В. Русская Православная Церковь в XX веке. (Russkaja Pravoslavnaja Tserkov' v XX veke) М. : Республика, 1995.

Стойков Василий, прот. Служение церкви и миру. (Sluzhenije tserkvi i miru): www.orthlib.ru/JMP/79_04/17. html (21.06.2012)

Шкаровский М.В. Русская Православная церковь в XX веке. (Russkaja Pravoslavnaja tserkov' v XX veke) М. : Вече, Лепта, 2010.

Шкаровский М.В. Санкт-Петербургские (Ленинградские) Духовные школы во 2-й половине XX — начале XXI века. (Sankt-Peterburgskije (Leningradskije) Dukhovnyje shkolyvo vtoroj polovine XX - nachale XXI veka): religare.ru/2_57537.html (17.06.2012)

Ювеналий, митрополит Крутицкий и Коломенский. Человек Церкви (Chelovek Tserkvi). М. : Издание Московской епархии, 1998

Part III: Representative Orthodox Theologians reflecting on Ecumenism

Elena Sadovnikova/Amal Dibo

Biography

Metropolitan Anthony of Sourozh was born in Lausanne in 1914. He spent his early childhood in Russia and Persia, his father being a member of the Russian Imperial Diplomatic Corps. His mother was the sister of Alexander Scriabin, the composer. During the Russian Revolution the family had to leave Persia, and in 1923 settled in Paris where the future Metropolitan was educated, graduating in physics, chemistry and biology, and taking his doctorate in medicine, at the University of Paris.

In 1939, before leaving for the front as a surgeon in the French army, he secretly professed monastic vows. He was tonsured and received the name Anthony in 1943. During the German occupation of France, he worked as a doctor and took part in the Anti-Fascist movement of the Resistance. After the war he continued practicing as a physician until 1948, when he was ordained to the priesthood and sent to England to serve as Orthodox Chaplain of the Fellowship of St. Alban and St. Sergius. He was appointed vicar of the Russian patriarchal parish in London in 1950, consecrated as Bishop in 1957 and as Archbishop in 1962, in charge of the Russian Orthodox Church in Great Britain and Ireland. In 1963, he was appointed Exarch of the Moscow Patriarchate in Western Europe, and in 1966 was raised to the rank of Metropolitan. At his own request he was released in 1974 from the function of Exarch, in order to devote himself more fully to the pastoral needs of the growing flock of his Diocese and all who come to him seeking advice and help.

Metropolitan Anthony is Honoris Causa Divinity Doctor: of Aberdeen University "for preaching the Word of God and renewing the spiritual life of this country"; of the Moscow Theological Academy for his theological, pastoral and preaching work; of Cambridge University; and of the Kiev Theological Academy, St Petersburg and Minsk Theological Academies. His first books on prayer and the spiritual life (*Living Prayer*, *Meditations on a Theme* and *God and Man*) were published in England, and his texts are now widely published in Russia, both as books and in periodicals and in many languages throughout the world.

His Eminence, Metropolitan Anthony of Sourozh, died peacefully on 4 August 2003 at the age of 89.

Preamble

To understand Metropolitan Anthony's views and ministry, it is imperative to review briefly the formation of the diocese of Sourozh which he served practically all his life, responding in his inspirational unique way to the demanding challenges that addressed the church today.

In 1948, Hieromonk Anthony (Bloom) was appointed Chaplain of the Anglican-Orthodox Fellowship of Saint Alban and Saint Sergius. On 1 September 1950, Hieromonk Anthony became the Rector of the Russian Parish of the Dormition in London. The Parish of the Dormition was not the only Russian Orthodox parish in Great Britain, and by 1957 a number of other parishes appeared, set up by Russian Orthodox communities. This prompted, in 1957, the formation in Great Britain of the Vicariate of Sergievo of the Exarchate of Western Europe (Moscow Patriarchate), with Hieromonk Anthony now becoming Bishop of Sergievo.

Following this, on 10 October 1962, the Diocese of Sourozh was formed, led by Bishop Anthony of Sergievo, who now became Archbishop Anthony of Sourozh. The Russian Church did not name the diocese after a British territory so as not to upset good relations with the Church of England.

For many years the political situation between Great Britain and the Soviet Union meant that the Diocese of Sourozh was able to function in virtual independence of the Moscow Patriarchate. In those years, the culture of the diocese reflected both the Franco-Russian émigré Orthodoxy in which Metropolitan Anthony had spent many of his formative years, as well as the middle-to-high Anglicanism which formed the ecclesial background of many of the English converts to the diocese. Many in the diocese had a long-term vision of the establishment of an autocephalous (self-governed) Orthodox Church in Great Britain.

Metropolitan Anthony himself maintained links with the Moscow Patriarchate to the end of his life. And whilst the Diocese of Sourozh was numerically far smaller than the Greek Orthodox Archdiocese of Thyateira and Great Britain (the local British Diocese of the Ecumenical Patriarchate), Metropolitan Anthony considered the Diocese of Sourozh to be "the Orthodox Church in Britain" *simpliciter*, on the grounds that it was open to all and not only to those of a particular ethnic background (as he took the Diocese of Thyateira to be).

However, some traditionalist ROCOR (Russian Orthodox Outside Russia) criticized the Sourozh diocese for endorsing "an Anglican form of Orthodoxy," led by "a small and ageing clique of intellectuals, very much part of one particular, upper middle-class, Western cultural elitist group, one elderly generation."

With the fall of communism in Russia, a new wave of Russian Orthodox parishioners entered the diocese. Many among this group, attending the diocesan cathedral in London, were unhappy at the (for a Russian Church) non-standard practices which prevailed in the diocese, and sought to bring its liturgical practices and ethos into line with the standard practice as it is understood in the Russian Orthodox Church of the post-Soviet period. For the supporters of such change, this amounted to "normalization"; for its opponents, it constituted Russification. Tension developed within the Cathedral over these issues. Until recently, however, there has been no evidence of such problems elsewhere in the diocese, not even in parishes with significant "new" Russian and British elements.

It has been alleged by British ROCOR clergy that the diocese of Sourozh failed to expand to meet the spiritual needs of newly arrived Orthodox Christians from Russia who lived in areas of the United Kingdom in which the diocese did not have parishes or communities. Such allegations have been confirmed by the commission of the Holy Synod, which has concluded that in recent years "there were not enough Russian-speaking priests in the parish to celebrate services and, in particular, to confess, that English was gradually used more and more as a liturgical language, and that this was disproportionate to the actual number of English people at the Cathedral."

Since May 2006, when the Ennismore Gardens Cathedral had been controversially taken over by the pro-Russian traditionalist faction, and a number of priests and members of the congregation were forced to leave, various new parishes and communities have been opened.

In years prior to the death of Metropolitan Anthony, several problems were noted amongst the clergy of the Diocese, tensions divided the flock between Russians and non-Russians and indeed between the faithful to Metropolitan's Vision and those who followed the practices of the Russian Church of the post-Soviet period. Perhaps the following words of the Moscow appointed Bishop Hilarion illustrate best this dichotomy, as he declared his inability to understand "how the 'style' of Sourozh diocese could be incompatible with his own Russian Orthodox liturgical tradition, and noted that liturgical celebration in the London Cathedral has a style of its own peculiar only to Vladyka Anthony."

Indeed, Metropolitan Anthony left a deep and solid imprint in the life of the Church not only in the Diocese of Sourozh, but also in Great Britain, in Russia, in Europe , in the United States, and among committed Orthodox in various parts of the world. From this brief biographical review we encounter a person endowed with special gifts of the Spirit, who was exposed to rich and varied experiences of life. His multilingual, multicultural, multidisciplinary upbringing and training paved his way to a deep understanding of the universality of Orthodoxy. Heralding the orthodoxy of faith, he never lost sight of the Incarnate Truth which he was keen on experiencing it in the life of the local church, both divine and human.

Part III: Representative Orthodox Theologians reflecting on Ecumenism

The truth in the Living Body of Christ

Metropolitan Anthony's vision of Ecumenism focuses on his concern for the unity in Truth, and starts essentially from the local church, and the experience of the living Body of Christ in his multinational parish in Ennismore Gardens, London.

At the meeting of the Sourozh Diocesan Assembly held at the Russian Cathedral in London on 9 June 2001 Metropolitan Anthony introduced the "major topic of discussion" by reviewing the purpose of the Assembly in the life of the diocese and then going on to consider the nature of ecumenism as it has developed in the past and as it now exists. He challenged the Assembly to "bring to the West Orthodoxy with a capital '0', not a denomination, but a new presence of Christ" and reminded Assembly members that ecumenism is not "a way of compromise" that makes it "easier to be together," but "an attitude of mind that recognizes that Christ is Lord and King."

"Because we are no longer in a Christian world, the Church is becoming more and more as it was in the early centuries. There may still be remnants in tradition, in Christian culture, but the world as such is no longer a Christian world. It has broken down morally, philosophically, theologically, and in so many other ways. But we must proclaim the one thing that we can give, and make people into one body — the Body of Christ, not a body of people who simply agree among themselves what is best for them, but a Body which is Christ's incarnate Presence. Father Sergei Bulgakov said that each of us is an incarnation, an incarnate presence of the Lord Jesus Christ, and together we are the Body of Christ, a body of people who are Christ's own presence, because we are all baptized into Christ, we have all become the limbs of his body, and people should be able to recognize that when they meet us.

Today we live in a world in which ecumenical work, ecumenical relationships have become very different from what they were when I first came here. Then there were clearly defined denominations. There was an attempt at meeting and trying to understand one another. This is now no longer so and much confusion has resulted. Unless we are deeply rooted in a life of prayer, in the life of the Church not as an administration and not as a denomination, but as the Body of Christ, a sense of alienation will follow. We have to realize a different vision and search for a new approach.

First of all Christians are no longer one. They are divided into denominations. For a long time now we have been trying to meet and find a common language. Unfortunately we seem to have found a common language that makes it possible for us to remain separate, and yet to become friends and brothers and sisters. This is not enough. To overcome separation by compromise is not a solution. And to remain separate while pretending to be one is not a solution either; it is a betrayal of Christ and his Gospel. What we must do is to bring to the West Orthodoxy with a capital 'O,' not a denomination, but a new presence of Christ.

When the Russian Orthodox Church became a member of the World Council of Churches we were represented by Bishop Ioann Wendland. I have never forgotten what he said. He addressed the World Council of Churches thus: 'We want to thank you for having accepted us Orthodox into your midst. You may ask yourselves what we bring to you. We do not bring a new denomination; we bring the faith of the Early Church. We have not been capable of living up to it. We hand it over to you and we hope that you will be able to bring forth the fruits that we have proved incapable of bringing forth'. That was the introduction of the Russian Orthodox Church to the World Council of Churches.

There is a supreme truth here: we are not bringing a new denomination, and if we do consider ourselves as a new denomination we are betraying Orthodoxy, and are alien to our vocation. What we must bring is Christ, and the spirit of the Church as it was in the early centuries, before it became recognized by the state and constrained in so many ways. If you look at the history of the Church you will discover all too easily that the Ecumenical Councils were summoned at moments of crisis by order of the state, because the state, the emperors of Byzantium, wanted the Church to be a center of unity for the empire and not an experience in itself. Father Georges Florovsky once said that yes, the Ecumenical Councils were legitimately called, they legitimately proclaimed the truth of Orthodoxy, but they never gave an answer to the heretics and those who had seceded from Orthodoxy. We condemn them, we see them as alien, but we have found no language, no argument to engage them except intellectual, philosophical arguments; and not ones concerned with the essential Christian life. We have fallen into this same state.

Orthodox Handbook on Ecumenism

We argue with denominations, though we argue very little now, as we do not any longer feel the difference between denominations as we felt them fifty, sixty, seventy years ago — but we still do not answer these questions, which should relate to the transfiguration of the world.

A man who played a great role in my discovery of faith, a man who had been a sub-deacon of Patriarch Tikhon and who, with the Patriarch's blessing, became a Protestant and an Evangelical preacher. He wrote that if you argue with someone, he will resist and refuse your arguments. You must always speak above his arguments, so that your interlocutor looks at what you say and says, 'How great it is!' — and thus opens to what you have to convey to him. This is what we must learn to do in the world in which we now live. Ecumenism is no longer a way of compromise, a way of joining together different Churches, and bringing people who believe nearer to each other because the greater the compromise, the easier it is to be together. Ecumenism as we must understand it is an attitude of mind that recognizes that Christ is the Lord and the King of the *ecumene,* the total world, and that our role is to bring to this universal situation a truth which embraces it, engulfs it, and brings it to a greatness, to a flowering, to a beauty which it has not known.

And so, when we think of our Assembly and of our Diocese, our Assembly is a place where we must think out these things and think of them not only with our minds but with our whole being, with all the passion we have, even if we are unworthy of them. I am totally unworthy of what I preach: that is not the point, I will answer for it, for my words I will be judged, and condemned, probably. But the words remain true. And we must be prepared to proclaim the truth, not as an intellectual truth, not as philosophy, but as life. Use words, use all your life — including the Liturgy, not as acts of worship for a closed community but as a way of bringing into the knowledge of Christ and into the knowledge of eternal life the people who are outside.

This is a new ecumenism which must be ours: not an ecumenism of theological discussion and argument, of compromise, and finding ways together, but an ecumenism of people who, however unworthy of what they preach, can nonetheless with wonder say: 'This is what Christ has revealed to me. I want to share it with you. I have never been able to live according to it, you can. Take it and become truly the Body of Christ.'"[1]

Living the Truth in Christ

In the end of 2001 to the beginning of 2002 metropolitan Anthony of Sourozh gave the last series of talks for his English speaking congregation in which he presents in an exceptionally condensed manner his views and understanding of things earthly and divine which he developed in the course of his long eventful life of prayer and pastoral ministry.

The scope of subjects touched upon in this relatively small collection of texts, gathered under the title *On the Light That Shineth in the Darkness*, edited by Avril Payman, is extraordinary wide comprising anthropology, ecclesiology, theology of matter, soteriology, asceticism and mysticism, worship, and prayer, etc. One of the talks presents metropolitan Anthony's views on ecumenism summarising his wide ecumenical experience reflected in other articles and talks, which appeared in the Bulletin of the diocese or in other orthodox or ecumenical publications. This is his last address on the subject and is of particular interest as an expression of his position acquired through whole life experience.

From the first sentences of the talk, metropolitan Anthony places the situation of Christian unity – and disunity – in the context of his general perception of human history as the situation of twilight thus taking as a starting point the fact that it belongs to human history and that Christian disunity is a matter of human dimension rather than of the divine institution.

"We live in a world of twilight where the light shines and at the same time where we are not always able in this light to discern the absolute. The light shines in the darkness and the darkness has not been able to quench it and that is the world in which we live."[2]

---

[1] *Sourozh* 86 (2001): 1-5.

[2] Here and further quotations are from: Metropolitan Anthony of Sourozh, *On the Light That Shineth in Darkness*, ed. Avril Payman, (Moscow: Metropolitan Anthony of Sourozh Foundation, 2010).

Part III: Representative Orthodox Theologians reflecting on Ecumenism

There is strong affirmation in his words that the light of God is there. The separation which exists among Christians originates from their inability to discern the absolute in this light – or the Absolute with the capital "A", Christ Himself, who is the beginning, Alpha "the first member of the Church – the community both human and divine" as metropolitan Anthony puts it, and the end, the Omega, in personal relation and communion with Whom the only possible unity can be reached.

This idea of the inability to discern eternal dimension in the light creating Christian unity is echoed in the quotation often used by metropolitan Anthony. He attributes it to St Philaret of Moscow: the walls that separate the Churches do not reach Heaven. The darkness still exists but it has not been able to quench the light and "this is the world in which we live."

The notion of the twilight of history is one of the major themes of metropolitan Anthony's last series of talks. He points out that with the Fall the world has entered the period of twilight defining twilight as a period of imperfect light between two moments of brilliant light, of a light without a shadow, the light that shone when the world came out of the hand of God and the light at the end of times when *God will be All in all*. On the other hand, twilight means the lack of light, the presence of darkness, and one must not forget it, but the accent should be put on the idea of light. The division among Christians exists and this cannot be overlooked or looked at lightly. In his early paper on Intercommunion, metropolitan Anthony firmly states that it is unacceptable to treat the Communion Table as a crossroads. It is impossible to commune to one Cup and then part, continue on the same mode of disunity, conflict or disagreement.

Darkness has entered history with the Fall and this is something that must be lived through. But at the same time there is another side to it - the perception of light has been affected - we see things *as though through the glass darkly*. In the situation of Christian disunity this inability to see things clearly is manifest in the difficulty of discerning the Absolute in what unites us.

In the image that metropolitan Anthony borrows from Prof. Leo Zander, people united by the "experience rooted God Himself" live in communion as long as they are "linked with mutual love, mutual respect and mutual interest in the way in which the other thinks and expressed himself." The separation comes when the major stress is laid upon the way of expressing the experience, which can be so different that people fail to recognise the same experience in different formulations about faith.

Neither the way of expression nor intellectual considerations in themselves but the lack of "mutual love, mutual respect and mutual interest" is the reason that causes separation. As soon as the focus of interest is transferred from the experience of the other onto own considerations and intellectual statements, relations are shattered. And friends, in a vivid image of Zander, turn their backs on one another and, still feeling the shoulder blades of each other, become infinitely far from each other because they look into opposite directions (into the "vile eternity" of Berdyaev) away from a person and the image of God imprinted in a person which is the only meeting point. Instead of relating to a person - or to the Person, One of the Holy Trinity - the way of expressing things, formulations and creeds are being put forward and become "faith complete", the philosophy of the time or cultural differences take over and the Churches – or two friends in Prof. Zander's image – part.

And as long as the dialogue between them is led on the level of statements about God, however refined, there is little hope of reunion because the language, the ways of expression are different and rooted in different cultures but more importantly because these statements are no more than human attempts of "expressing the inexpressible."

Metropolitan Anthony develops this theme by recalling the notion of metahistory introduced by Fr Sergius Bulgakov for the period described in the first chapters of Genesis, experience of "the world that preceded the Fall" and which "disappeared from the experience and, to a great extent, from the awareness and understanding of man."

"Adam and Eve when they found themselves on an Earth that was no longer paradise, how often did they try to remember what it was to be in a world that knew no sin, that was totally in communion with God in which God Himself was life and reality? They tried to remember, to describe it to themselves, not to forget, to hand it over to their children, and from generation to generation, but the memories faded. What was a hesitant memory for Adam and Eve became the recollection of what Adam and Eve had said to others, and gradually the clarity, the absoluteness of vision that had disappeared even in them became more and more darkened. But there is an old saying: Nature does not put up with emptiness. Whenever there was no way of remembering, when there was a gap that needed to be made sense of, people began to fill the gap not with invention but with an attempt at imagining what had happened."

Hardly any more progress in coming to agreement in ecumenical dialogue is possible after centuries of comparing one blurred obscure image of the vision of God, of man and of the world against the other. The vision is distorted by the dark glass of sin.

But the friends (the Churches in the context of ecumenical dialogue) set upon a long road of searching, a road of inspiration and despair, achievements and failings. They are in search and (putting it into metropolitan Anthony's words), they are searching for truth and there is no other truth then God.

If they turn back towards their friend, transfer their interest from formulations and philosophies to a person, there is hope of finding each other.

"The logic which we used in the past may be replaced by another logic — God's own logic, God's own vision of things, the way He presents things, He conveys them to us: mutual love, mutual respect, at times mutual admiration."

"Then they [the friends] come and face one another and if they ask the right question there is a possibility of coming together. And the question is: What have you learnt about God, about yourself, about life, about the Church since we have parted? Not what you have invented, not what formulations have you coined but what have you learnt at the very depth of your being about the things that are absolutely essential: God himself, you in connection with Him, your own depth and life and the created world and its tragic destinies in which separated-ness, enmity coincide, live together with sacrificial love, with the sacrificial love of the Son of God and of those who were the saints of these separated groups."

Metropolitan Anthony points out that while ecumenical efforts were largely fruitless, the saints of the Churches have in fact found unity – unity in life and faith.

"And when we look at the different saints of the East and West how often we find that they have so much in common, not necessarily in their theology if they express themselves in theological forms, but in their knowledge of God, in their faith in God, in their faithfulness to God."

Together with their Churches the saints have travelled the same road of separated-ness, but along the way they achieved unity because they realize that there is something beyond human attempts at understanding - "God's Revelation and life in God."

Ways to God are one of the main subjects on which metropolitan Anthony meditates in his last series of talks. Ways can be different as long as they are towards God. As he points out speaking about the first chapters of St John's Gospel, the Word was Godwards – towards God, - and this Godward-ness is the only value of the chosen way.

Metropolitan Anthony's view on inter-Church relationships as a road is part of his general vision of the history of mankind as a way to God where twilight of the fallen world coexists with light of the Absolute. The absolute which is present in the relationship of the Churches is their "vocation to live according to the Gospel, to be worthy of God, to be at one with Him in everything He has told us."

In his search for unity in God, metropolitan Anthony goes beyond the relationships within Christian world. If unity is sought in the Absolute, through being God's own, which means "to be with God at one, to live in God, to live for God," kinship with people who proclaim their intrinsic knowledge of Christ by their lives and deeds becomes obvious no matter what Creed they have been taught by the incidents of their culture, time in

Part III: Representative Orthodox Theologians reflecting on Ecumenism

history and surrounding. And he gives an example of an officer "during the war who came six times out of a protected corner to bring back soldiers who had been wounded. He was brought to us, I was then a military surgeon, he was brought to us pierced through by bullets. He was not an Orthodox but could I look at him and say: 'Ha, a heretic.' No, he was a man who had learnt from Christ what Christ stands for, what Christ is: to love to the point of giving one's life and one's death for another to be saved." Metropolitan Anthony also speaks about an unbeliever whose belief in men to the point of giving one's life makes him partaker of the mystery of faith, of ancient and non-Christian religions in which one can find glimpses of true experience and knowledge.

> "We live in the world of twilight but despite our separated-ness, despite differences and conflicts, the light is still there. And here comes not the problem but the reality, the importance of being true to what is in the Gospel or, if you prefer, of living in such a way that God may believe that we are faithful to Him. And on that we can grow more and more one with Him and then the twilight matters less and less because what matters is the light. The surrounding darkness becomes like a mist through which one can walk because one knows that beyond the mist there is the perfect light of the sun."

Bibliography

Metropolitan Anthony of Sourozh, "What can you say about the ecumenical movement, about its positive and negative characteristics and also of your attitude to it?" in *Encounter* (London: Darton, Longman & Todd, 2005). Translated from the Russian by Tatiana Wolff.

_____, "Orthodoxy and various Christian bodies (13 June 2002)" in *On the Light that Shineth in the Darkness*, ed. Avril Payman, (Moscow: Metropolitan Anthony of Sourozh Foundation, 2010), 134-145.

_____, «Nouveaux Besoins et Nouvelles Perspectives Ecuméniques pour les Paroisses en Occident» in *SOP* 265 (2002).

_____, "A Letter to Patriarch Alexis of Moscow and all Russia, 5 February 1997" in *Sourozh* 69 (1997): 17-22. Translated by Elisabeth Obolensky

_____, "Reflexions on 'Some of the Faithful are perplexed'" in *Sourozh* 45 (1991): 7-16. Translated by Benedict Roffey.

_____, "Primacy and Primacies in the Church" in Sourozh 25 (1986), 6-15.

_____, "Reflexions on the Expression, 'The Undivided Church'" in *Messager de l'Exarchat du Patriarche russe en Europe occidentale* 105-108 (1980-81) 69-77.

_____, "Is Fellowship Possible?," extracts from discussions in the Central Committee in *The Ecumenical Review* 24.4 (1972) 465-470.

_____, "Sermon at Vespers for the Week of Prayer for Christian Unity, 23 January 2002" in *Newsletter* 361 (February 2002).

_____, "Vatican II and the Eastern Churches: Two Short Comments (first made at the Hammersmith Christian Unity Conference, May 1965)" in *Eastern Churches Review* 1.1 (1996): 19-21.

Unpublished presentations, Metropolitan Anthony of Sourozh Foundation.

_____, "One in Christ," 22 April 1986.

_____, "Talk to Ecumenical Commission of the Portsmouth Roman Catholic Diocese, on 9 March 1984."

_____, "The Prayer and Sacraments of the Orthodox Church," a talk at an ecumenical gathering organized by Catholics at Grail Center, London, 28 September 1966.

_____, A talk on Ecumenism at St. Basil's House, 25 October 1973.

PART IV

ECUMENICAL DIALOGUE
IN VARIOUS ORTHODOX CHURCHES AND SETTINGS

(56) ECUMENICAL DIALOGUE IN THE PERSPECTIVE OF THE ECUMENICAL PATRIARCHATE

Fr. Georges Tsetsis

Founded by Saint Andrew the Apostle in 38 AD in the strategic triangle where the Golden Horn meets the Bosporus and the Sea of Marmara, the Church of a rather small site, colonized by Byzas the Megarian in 667 BC and called Byzantium, at the beginning was a modest diocese under the jurisdiction of the Metropolitan See of Herakleia, on the shores of the Black Sea. When, however, in 330 by decision of Constantine the Great this city became the capital of the Eastern Roman Empire and was renamed Constantinople/New Rome, the Church of the new Capital acquired consequently a particular significance.

Just fifty years following the inauguration of the new Capital, the Second Ecumenical Council, convoked in 381 in Constantinople, promulgated that *"the Bishop of Constantinople shall have the prerogative of honour after the Bishop of Rome, because Constantinople is New Rome."*[1] Seventy years later, the Fourth Ecumenical Council, convened in 451 in Chalcedon, granted to the bishop of this Church the honour of seniority next to the Bishop of Rome, *"since Constantinople was from now on the See of the Emperor and of the Senate."*[2] At the same time the Council expanded his jurisdiction to territories outside the boundaries of the then known Local Orthodox Churches, and conferred to him pastoral responsibilities throughout the world. Since the 6th century, the Bishop of the new Roman capital was bestowed with the title of Archbishop of Constantinople, New Rome and Ecumenical Patriarch. A postulate that he continues to hold today, together with the prerogative of being the *Primus inter pares* among the Orthodox Hierarchy, and consequently the visible sign of Orthodox unity and coordinator of any Pan-Orthodox activity.

In this leadership position, the Ecumenical Patriarchate played a decisive role in the life and growth of Eastern Christianity. It was from the city of Constantinople that the Slavic nations, (such as the Kievan Russians, the Bulgarians, the Serbs, the Moravians), received in the ninth century the Orthodox faith and together with it they also obtained all those religious, spiritual and artistic elements that deeply influenced their cultural development.

A new chapter in the life and history of the Ecumenical Patriarchate began after the conquest of Constantinople in 1453. One of the first endeavours of the Conqueror Fatih Sultan Mehmet II was to bestow to George Scholarios, an outstanding scholar and theologian of that time, known as Gennadios II, the office of Patriarch, designating him as "Millet başı", namely as the "Head of the Roman Nation". Thus, in addition to his religious rights, the Patriarch was granted prerogatives pertaining to the social and family life of all Orthodox Christians under Ottoman rule, regardless of their ethnic background.

The Ecumenical Patriarchate survived two vast and powerful Empires. Namely, the Eastern Roman (or Byzantine) Empire and the Ottoman Empire. And nowadays, in spite of the alteration of the status and function of the Patriarch as "Millet Başı" in the Republic of Turkey, in the aftermath of the 1923 Lausanne Treaty, the Church of Constantinople continues to fulfil its God-given mission to deliver the "Good news" of the Gospel, to work for the spiritual growth of its flock around the world, to enhance Pan-Orthodox and Pan-Christian unity, to encourage interfaith dialogue, and to call for reconciliation of humankind and for peace in the world.

In accordance with the centuries-old praxis and the ethos of the Orthodox Church, that consisted of taking steps to establish peace and restore fraternal relations when disputes emerged between Christian communities, and firmly believing that the termination of schisms, the repression of heresies, the restoration of peace in the Church and the unity of the entire humankind in Jesus Christ, was an essential part of the mission of the Church,[3] the Ecumenical Patriarchate, considered Church Unity as a major theological and ecclesiological challenge.

---

[1] Canon 3 (Second Ecumenical Council).

[2] Canon 28 (Fourth Ecumenical Council).

[3] Divine Liturgies of *St. Basil the Great* and of *St. John Chrysostom.*

Indeed, both the liturgical praxis and the conciliar history of the Church demonstrate that "ecumenism" in the sense of a mobilization for eliminating the scandal of division, has always been at the very centre of the pastoral ministry of the One, Holy, Catholic and Apostolic Church. And, in spite of severe criticisms articulated by several fundamentalist quarters who qualify ecumenism as the worse heresy of any time, it should be affirmed that there is no substantial difference between the praxis of the early Church and the policy followed today by the Orthodox Church, as far as the issue of Christian unity is concerned. Today, as in the past, while praying *"for the Oikoumene"*, as well as *"for the stability of the Holy Churches of God and for the union of all,"*[4] the Orthodox Church seeks rapprochement and cooperation with the non-Orthodox Churches, be it in the context of bilateral dialogues or in the framework of different ecumenical organizations, because nowadays and as never before, Church unity and interaction are dictated by the world's agenda.

It should be remembered that "Ecumenism", both as a theological challenge and as an effort to restore Christian unity, has already been experienced in the Orthodox Church during the 5th, the 11th and the 16th centuries, when different schisms and separations occurred. And it re-emerged at the beginning of the 20th century, when the Ecumenical Patriarchate took its pioneering initiative in 1920, inviting all the Churches around the world to form a *League of Churches* (Κοινωνία τῶν Ἐκκλησιῶν), in order to foster cooperation and promote unity. An initiative *"without precedent in Church history"*, as Visser't Hooft once stated,[5] that was favourably welcomed by many Protestant Churches and denominations, which, confronted with their own separations, were also trying to unite and thus give a common Christian witness to the world.

The 1920 Encyclical was the obvious follow up of the Encyclicals of Patriarch Joachim III, promulgated in 1902 and 1904. In these two Encyclicals, Joachim III, while pleading for the restoration of Orthodox unity, -severely hit at that time by schisms and territorial disputes-, was also raising the question of establishing fraternal contacts with Western Christians *"remembering that they too believe in the All-Holy Trinity, they glorify the name of our Lord Jesus Christ and hope to be saved by the grace of God."*[6]

The Ecumenical Patriarchate in the early 1920s, (these critical years for its life and witness in the Republic of Turkey), undertook several initiatives to foster Orthodox unity (in 1923, 1930, 1946, 1961), but at the same time it played a pioneering role in the genesis and formation of the World Council of Churches (in 1925, 1938, 1948) and later on of the Conference of European Churches (1959).

Meticulously planned by the Holy Synod of the Ecumenical Patriarchate and convoked by Patriarch Athenagoras in 1961, the First Pan-Orthodox Conference of Rhodes constituted undoubtedly a turning point, not only with regard to inter-Orthodox relations, but also as far as the relations of the Orthodox with Western and Oriental Christendom are concerned This Conference not only paved the way towards convoking the Great Council of the Orthodox Church, but it also proceeded with the evaluation of the Ecumenical Movement and its institutional instruments, and made preliminary plans to inaugurate bilateral theological dialogues with non-Orthodox Churches and Denominations.[7]

The reasons that prompted the Orthodox Church to embark in theological discussions were articulated in the clearest possible way by the Third Pan-Orthodox Pre-conciliar Conference (Chambésy 1986). *"The Orthodox Church"*, this Conference said, *"believes that through dialogue gives witness to its rich spiritual heritage, in view of preparing the path towards unity... (Our Church) recognizes the real existence of all Christian Churches and Confessions. At the same time, she believes that her relations with these Churches and Confessions must be based upon the clarification, as quickly and objectively possible, of the ecclesiological question and particularly of issues concerning their teaching about sacraments, grace, priesthood and apostolic succession"*[8].

---

[4] Idem.
[5] W.A. Visser't Hooft, *The Genesis and Formation of the World Council of Churches*, (Geneva: WCC Publications, 1982) 1.
[6] See the text of the Encyclical in Constantin Patelos (ed.), *The Orthodox Church in the Ecumenical Movement*, (Geneva: WCC Publications, 1978), 34-39. See also in Georges Tsetsis, *The Contribution of the Ecumenical Patriarchate in the Foundation of the World Council of Churches*, (Tertios, 1988), 49 (in Greek).
[7] Minutes of the 1st Pan-orthodox Conference of Rhodes (1961) *Orthodoxia* 37 (1962): 51-83.
[8] Minutes of the 3rd Pan-orthodox Pre-conciliar Conference of Chambésy (1986), *Episkepsis* 369 (1986): 9.

It is precisely in this spirit that the Orthodox Church inaugurated in the last quarter of the past century theological dialogues with the Oriental Pre-Chalcedonian Churches, the Roman Catholic Church, the Anglican Communion, the Old Catholic Church, the Lutheran World Federation, and the World Alliance of Reformed Churches, while she started a few years ago some preliminary conversations with the World Methodist Council, and is now exploring possibilities of conversing with the Baptist World Alliance and the Pentecostals.

Presided and coordinated by the Ecumenical Patriarchate, these dialogues are conducted with a varying degree of success, according to the circumstances and their historical context. Some of them aim at the mutual acquaintance and better understanding of the theology, life and witness of Churches having no particular historical link between them. Others, especially those conducted at the local level, seek cooperation and common action in the resolution of pastoral problems as they arise in the day-to-day life and witness of the Churches in a given local context. While others, in spite of serious theological or ecclesiological problems arising in the course of deliberations, point to the restoration of the full union of Churches, that once upon a time constituted the *One undivided Church*, but in the course of history have found themselves alienated and separated. In this last category belong, undoubtedly, the dialogue of the Orthodox with the Oriental and the Roman Catholic Churches. And it can be added that the bilateral theological dialogues the Orthodox Church undertook with the above Churches, aim precisely at the creation, through a *"dialogue of communication"*, of a better understanding between them, in order to achieve through a *"dialogue of communion"* their visible unity in one faith and in one Eucharistic communion.

The fundamental question regarding both the multilateral dialogues conducted within the wider Ecumenical Movement (World Council of Churches, Conference European of Churches), or in the framework of the bilateral Theological conversations, is whether their "agreed statements" can be accepted or "received" by the believers.

The term *"reception"* denotes a process by which the people of God, guided by the Holy Spirit, accept new answers to emerging issues in the life of the Church, provided that they do not contradict the Apostolic Faith and that are in continuity and harmony with the teachings of the universal Church. This process was applied in the early Church when doctrinal teachings, canons and resolutions of Ecumenical or local Councils were shared with the entire Church around the oikoumene, not simply for information, but primarily for their implementation in the daily life of the faithful. In this process, Christians were able to recognise in these new answers a continuity with the faith and tradition of the One, Holy, Catholic and Apostolic Church. The question at stake is whether this can be achieved today with the bilateral theological conversations that take place in the wider framework of the Ecumenical Movement. The answer could be affirmative, with the proviso however, that the conversing partners, while recognizing the objective difficulties in the path leading to unity, would adopt a methodology which will enable them to articulate anew the common Christian faith affirmed by the Ecumenical Councils of the One undivided Church.

Several years ago an ad hoc Symposium called to evaluate the Lima document on "Baptism, Eucharist and Ministry", pointed out that in the framework of the Ecumenical Movement the notion of *reception* is quite different from the classical Orthodox understanding of the reception of decrees and decisions of Holy Councils. Today, the Symposium said, by the term "reception" we mean *"a step forward in the process of our growing together in mutual trust, towards doctrinal convergence and ultimately towards communion with one another, in continuity with the apostles and the teaching of the Universal Church."* [9]

By focussing on different theological and ecclesiological issues that divided Christendom for many centuries, these dialogues try to reach convergences in order to pave the way leading to Christian unity. The question, however, is whether theological agreements or convergence documents can be meaningful for the people of God or be relevant in the context of the day-to-day life and witness of a local community. The question is pertinent, because, academic dialogues that are based on positions, texts and arguments, but overlook, or even ignore, the pastoral problems of the Churches in a given context, are condemned to remain simply theoretical

---

[9] G. Limouris-N. Vaporis (eds.) *Orthodox Perspectives on Baptism, Eucharist and Ministry* (Brookline, MA: Holy Cross Orthodox Press, 1985), 161.

Part IV: Ecumenical Dialogue in various Orthodox Churches and Settings

exercises, with little impact in the endeavour to restore Christian unity and with no influence in the life of the faithful. This is why, pastoral, social and ethical problems can no longer be excluded both from the bilateral and multilateral dialogues, because analogous to the connection between doctrine and worship is the inseparable connection between *orthodoxia* and *orhtopraxia,* an *orthopraxia,* that makes ethics an indispensable element of any inter-Church dialogue. Church doctrine, spirituality and diaconal action are so intimately related, that they should be all integral part of today's ecumenical dialogue.

As His All Holiness, the Ecumenical Patriarch Bartholomew recently underlined, the *"true dialogue is a gift from God..., (it) is the most fundamental experience of life..., (it) promotes knowledge and science, reveals truths and emotions, abolishes fear and prejudice, cultivates bonds and broadens horizons. Finally, dialogue seeks persuasion, not coercion"*[10].

May these thoughtful Patriarchal words be our motto as we continue struggling in different ways to seek our unity and to give a credible Christian witness in today's secularized society.

Now, what is today our perception with regard to the "reception" of agreed statements elaborated in the bilateral conversations between the Orthodox and the Oriental and the Roman Catholic Churches?

It goes without saying that the same could be affirmed with regard to the outcome of the bilateral dialogues, particularly those we conduct with the Oriental and the Roman Catholic Churches. The unity we seek in their framework cannot be simply the result of an agreed statement. Their aim should be directed towards the understanding of the significance of the Church, particularly her visible structure that gives to human beings the possibility of entering into a new and saving relationship with God and the world.

Without minimizing the value of our dialogues with the Churches and Denominations that emerged as a result of the Reformation, one could affirm that the bilateral conversations of the Orthodox with the Oriental and the Roman Catholic Churches have a particular significance. Not only because of the common heritage of these Churches, but also because at a certain moment of history they were protagonists of the painful schisms of the fifth and eleven centuries, and therefore they have today a debt towards the Lord, namely to restore His broken Body.

The agreement reached between the Orthodox and the Oriental Orthodox Churches on the Christological doctrine, undoubtedly eliminated the most important obstacle in the way towards full union of these two sister traditions of the Christian East. Presently the convergence documents are under study by competent theological commissions in our Churches, particularly so far as the lifting of the anathemas is concerned. Needless to say however that the final authority to receive the agreed statements and apply their contents is of course a Pan-Orthodox Council.

Several Autocephalous Orthodox Churches have welcomed with satisfaction this historical breakthrough, while recognizing that there are some quite important ecclesiological and canonical questions to be resolved before the full union between the Eastern and Oriental Orthodox Churches is proclaimed. Yet, there are clear indications that at least some local Orthodox Churches, having experienced in the past schisms in their own body, (Russia, Georgia, Greece), will be reluctant to "receive" the agreed statements of this dialogue, with the understandable argument that a Church cannot afford an eventual split in her own body, for the sake of union with another Church, considered so far as *heterodox*!

The same could be affirmed with regard to our dialogue with the Roman Catholic Church, particularly after the deadlock that followed the Balamand plenary of the Joint Theological Commission. There is a clear reluctance not only to receive the agreed document of Balamand, (which after all opened new possibilities for fresh examination of those issues that divided the two Churches in the course of history), but even to continue the dialogue, if the issue of Uniatism is not resolved beforehand. The Baltimore plenary gave evidence to this fact. It is interesting to note parenthetically that immediately after the publication of the Balamand agreed statement there were sharp criticisms and reactions, coming not only from some influential Orthodox quarters, (Jerusalem, Athens, Mount Athos), accusing the Orthodox members of the Joint Commission as betrayers of

---

[10] Bartholomew, Ecumenical Patriarch, *Encountering the Mystery* (Doubleday, 2008), 220.

their faith, after having recognized the historical reality of the Uniates today, but also from Uniate circles in Ukraine and Transylvania, who blamed the Roman Catholic members of the Commission for having "sold" them to the Orthodox!!

As Cardinal Edward Cassidy, Roman Catholic co-chairman of the Joint Commission, pointed out immediately after the Baltimore meeting, Uniatism had become the "real core" of Orthodox-Catholic dialogue. He admitted that the issue is too complicated to allow an "easy solution". From his perspective Archbishop Stylianos of Australia, Orthodox co-chairman of this body, also admitted the difficulty, adding however that the whole issue was connected with the primacy and infallibility of the Pope. And certainly he was right.

Concluding remarks

Some thirty five years ago, W.A.Visser't Hooft, in a conference he delivered at the Theological Faculty of Athens, extensively spoke about the spirit that should prevail in any ecumenical encounter and dialogue. And he pertinently remarked that the ecumenical dialogue, which for reasons of politeness or opportunism conceals the real issues, does far more harm than good. *"We need maximum ecumenism,* he said, *in which each Church brings the fullness of its conviction, not minimum ecumenism in which we are left with a meagre common denominator".* I fully agree with this affirmation and I do believe that our bilateral theological dialogues with the Orientals, the Roman Catholics, and indeed with any other Church or Denomination will progress, only if they are conducted in a spirit of frankness and sincerity, even if the issues at stake are painful. After all, the healing of one thousand or six hundred years old wounds is not an easy task.

It is difficult to predict when these two important dialogues of our Church will resume again, because presently, our local Orthodox Churches seem more inclined to cope first with their own internal existential problems, rather than to give priority to relations with the rest of Christendom. When some time in the future however, the Joint Theological Commission, after having resolved satisfactorily the thorny Uniate question, will start again its normal work, it is expected to deal with a very crucial and challenging topic of its original agenda. It reads as follows: *"Ecclesiastical and Canonical Consequences of the Sacramental Structure of the Church: Conciliarity and Authority in the Church".* Quite a programme in perspective! But, it will not be an exaggeration to say that the real dialogue between the Orthodox and the Roman Catholics will start only then!

Before concluding this presentation, I wish to make a general remark that is relevant to all bilateral dialogues in which the Churches are engaged today.

Metropolitan John (Zizioulas) of Pergamon pertinently remarks that *"the catholicity of the Church is not simply a matter of bringing together existing cultures and nations in their present state of concerns,"* but a matter of uniting *"historical identities and traditions, so that they may be transcended in the unity of the body of Christ."* Seen from this perspective therefore, the problem of receiving the outcome of a bilateral dialogue appears to be linked with the problem of ecclesiology. This is why in debating the issue of the reception or acceptance of agreed statements, one has to have in mind the concept of the Church.

Bibliography

1. G. Tsetsis, *Ecumenical Analects-Contribution to the History of the Ecumenical Movement,* (Tertios, 1987) (in Greek)
2. - *The Contribution of the Ecumenical Patriarchate in the Formation of the World Council of Churches,* (Tertios, 1988) (in Greek)
3. - *A Synthesis of Orthodox Responses to BEM,* (Athens, 1988) (in Greek)
4. - "The meaning of the Orthodox Presence in the Ecumenical Movement", *The Ecumenical Review* 40 (1988): 440-445

5. - *Ecumenical Throne and Oikoumene- Official Patriarchal Texts*, (Tertios, 1989) (in Greek)
6. - "An Orthodox Assessment of Ecumenism", *Epistimoniki Parousia Estias Theologon Halkis*, II (1991), 385-408
7. - "What is the World Council's Oikoumene?" *The Ecumenical Review* 43 (1991): 86-89
8. - "Nathan Söderblom and the Orthodox Church" *Tro & Tanke* 7 (1993): 89-102
9. - "The Orthodox Presence in the World Council of Churches" *Analogion* 1 (2001): 80-94 (in Greek)

(57) Ecumenical Dialogue in the Perspective of the Patriarchate of Alexandria

Fr. John Njoroge

A historical Introduction

This article will focus on a brief history and ecumenical journey of the Greek Patriarchate of Alexandria and All Africa.

The Greek Orthodox Patriarchate of Alexandria and All Africa has its headquarters in Alexandria, Egypt and extend its ecclesiastical jurisdiction into the entire Africa. It serves the Eastern Orthodox churches which comprise Greek speaking and Russian speaking Orthodox faithful mainly living and working in major African cities as well as the native African Orthodox communities. The Greek Orthodox Patriarchate of Alexandria and All Africa is ecclesiastically in communion with all Eastern Orthodox patriarchates, autocephalous and autonomous churches in the world. It is a member of the World Council of Churches, All Africa Conference of Churches and Middle East Council of Churches.

According to Eusebius' "Church history" (320 AD) and keeping with the tradition of both the Greek Orthodox Patriarchate of Alexandria and the Coptic Orthodox Church, St. Mark the evangelist, evangelized Alexandria between 43-63AD and eventually, was ordained its first Bishop Annianus in the year 62 AD.[1] The authenticity of Eusebius' records that John Mark established churches in the city of Alexandria[2], can only be supported by the fact that St. Mark was a missionary companion of St. Peter, the apostle to the Jew (Gal 2:8). Therefore, since Alexandria was a home of the largest Jewish community in diaspora, it was very possible for Peter to have sent Mark his spiritual son (1 Peter 5:13) to visit Alexandria. It could be true that Alexandria had been evangelized by 53 AD because of a story of a Christian Jew from Alexandria by the name Apollos, who was evangelising in enthusiastically in Ephesus (Acts 18:24; 1 Cor. 3:4-7) at the time of St. Paul. As noted above the Alexandrian Church has continuously confessed St. Mark the Evangelist as its founder and from the 4th century AD, the see of Alexandria has been called Cathedra Marci ("the throne of Mark"). His symbol is a lion, an emblem that marks the flag of the Greek Orthodox Patriarchate of Alexandria and All Africa. His feast day is September 23rd when a liturgical rite attributed to him is celebrated in Alexandria.[3]

Throughout history, the Alexandrian church has been known for its involvement in the ecumenical arena. First and foremost, the Alexandrian church did not only participate in the ecumenical councils but greatly contributed to the formation of the Christian doctrines through its bishops like Athanasius the Great (298-373 AD). The formation of the Nicene-Constantinople creed and Christian doctrines like that of incarnation has offered to the ecumenical church solutions to the heresies of the time.[4] Secondly the Alexandrian church has given to the ecumenical church the profound allegorical method of interpreting of the Holy Scriptures through its famous catechetical school. One can argue that the Alexandrian catechetical school produced the first Christian thinkers like Clement of Alexandria and Origen who successfully explained the biblical faith philosophically and systematically. Third, the Alexandrian church is known for its monasticism. Ordinary

[1] John Baur, *2000 Years of Christianity in Africa: An African Church History*, (Nairobi: Paulines Publications), 21. Also see Greek Orthodox Patriarchate of Alexandria and All Africa office website "Previous Patriarchs" available at: http://www.patriarchateofalexandria.com.(last accessed on 13/05/2013).

[2] Groves C.P., *The Planting of Christianity in Africa*, Vol. 1 (London: Lutterworth Press, 1964), 35.

[3] Due to the Arab conquest, the Alexandrian liturgical tradition was slowly displaced. It is only in 1585 Patriarch Meletios Pegas of Alexandria copied St. Mark's liturgical manuscript. The same was copied by St. Nectarios of Pentapolis in 1890 but only to be published in Greece in 1955 and in Alexandria in 1960.

[4] Heresies such as Arianism that was introduced by Arius; a Christian priest of Alexandria, Egypt, whose teachings affirmed the created, finite nature of Christ.

Christians like Antony the Great (251-356) the father of monasticism took a total commitment to the following of Christ (Mk 19:17-21) and made it to the desert to live a life of asceticism and contemplation. Monasticism inspired many people like St. Pachomius (292-346) who developed the cenobitical or communal monastic way of life. The flourishing of monasticism in the Egyptian desert brought pilgrims from all over the world and at the same time the desert become the place of encounter between the Christian monks and the Nubian traders along the river Nile. Apparently, through this encounter the historical kingdom of Nubia to become Christian.

Although right from the beginning the Alexandrian church witnessed the Gospel of Christ as one united church, the Fourth Ecumenical Council (451AD) and Arabic conquest (640AD) have affected the unity and prosperity of this church. During that Council, the Alexandrian Church encountered a division namely the "non-Chalcedonian" churches or the "Oriental Orthodox Churches."[5] It is at this juncture that the Coptic Orthodox Church and the Ethiopian Orthodox Church belonging to the Alexandrian church did not agree with the resolutions of the Chalcedonian council on the two natures of Christ, thus on how the Divine and the human natures are united in the person of Jesus Christ.[6] On the other hand, the Greek Orthodox Patriarchate of Alexandria remained faithful to the Chalcedonian family (Patriarchates of Constantinople, Jerusalem, Antioch and Rome) and fully participated in the next three ecumenical councils. For centuries these two Orthodox families remained in separation. Only recently during WCC meetings have they entered into informal and formal theological dialogues.[7]

The Arabic conquest in 640 AD marked a turning point in the history of the church in Egypt.[8] For many Egyptians the coming of the Arabs was a liberation from the Roman yoke. However, the implementation of Islamic policy was discriminative to the minority who opted to remain Christians. These kinds of legislative policies affected also the Greek Orthodox Patriarchate of Alexandria, and because of persecutions the Patriarch and a large number of members fled Egypt. However, after the Turks took Egypt in 1517, a new era dawned for the Egyptian Christians.[9] Persecutions were over and the patriarchate re-opened with few Greek speaking followers.

The Greek Orthodox Patriarchate of Alexandria and the Ecumenical Dialogue

In the present day no church, denomination or religious body can stay in isolation without collaboration and solidarity with other churches, faiths and religious bodies. Ecumenical dialogue is one of the best avenues through which churches are coming to a common understanding, mutual respect and tolerance. Ecumenical dialogue is a necessity for the Greek Patriarchate of Alexandria and All Africa because of its regional witness, its mission activities in south Saharan Africa and its co-existence with Coptic Orthodox Church in a dominate Muslim Egypt. In this aspect, the Alexandrian Patriarchate is active in inter-religious, bilateral and multilateral dialogues both regionally and internationally.

Regionally, meaning in Egypt and in the Middle East, the patriarchate has continually participated in dialogues. Being a member of the Middle East Council of Churches, the Alexandrian Patriarchate has been involved in official and unofficial consultations with the Oriental Orthodox churches. As a result of these consultations,

[5] The use of term 'non-Chalcedonian' is basically to emphasis their disagreeing on the doctrine of Christology that stresses on the two natures of Christ. This doctrine as it has been viewed and practiced by the Eastern Orthodox and the Roman Catholic churches, the so-called chalcedonian churches teaches that Christ has two natures namely, the divine nature and the human nature.
[6] *Dictionary of the Ecumenical Movement* (Geneva: WCC Publications, 2002), 859.
[7] Michael Kinnamon & Brian E. Cope, *The Ecumenical Movement: An Anthology of Key Texts and Voices* (Geneva: WCC Publications, 1997), 484.
[8] Baur, *2000 Years of Christianity in Africa*, 25.
[9] See Member churches of the World Council of Churches, available at http://www.oikoumene.org/en/member-churches/greek-orthodox-patriarchate-of-alexandria-and-all-africa. (last accessed on 10 of May 2013).

a solid Christological agreement has been reached. For example, in a meeting at AnbaBishoy monastery in Egypt in 1989, the two Orthodox families signed a historical agreement stating:

"We have inherited from our fathers in Christ the one apostolic faith and tradition, though as churches we have been in separation from each other for centuries. As two families of Orthodox churches long out of communion with each other, we now pray and trust in God to restore that communion on the basis of the apostolic faith of the undivided church of the first centuries, which we confess in our common creed."[10]

Throughout these unofficial and official meetings, these churches had an ample opportunity through dialogue to come to a common understanding and to issue important signed statements regarding their common faith and Tradition. For example in Geneva 1970 was affirmed:

"The common Tradition of one church in all the important matters- liturgy and spirituality, doctrine and canonical practice, in our understanding of the Holy Trinity, of the incarnation, of the person and work of the Holy Spirit, on the nature of the church as the communion of the saint with its ministry and sacraments, and on the life of the world to come when our lord and saviour shall come in all his glory."[11]

Moreover, in 1993 in Chambesy, a lifting of the anathemas was proposed through the signing of an appropriated ecclesiastical act that would also lift the synodical and personal condemnations. Apparently, with major theological and historical obstacles being removed, there are fresh hopes of a full reconciliation between these two Orthodox Christian families.[12] The reconciliation of these families is ideal in witnessing the mission of the Orthodox Church in the world today. Such reconciliation is a key tool in affirming the oneness of the Orthodox voice bearing public witness on matters of spiritual, pastoral and moral concerns. This can be achieved through constructive dialogue on strong political, cultural and social factors that have played part in breaching communion between the Oriental and Eastern Orthodox churches for 1500 years.[13] Dialogue, used as a mission tool would help these churches to address together the challenging needs in the Middle East. With one united voice they will offer a spiritual guidance and the truth of the Gospel not only to the Orthodox faithful, but also to their Muslim neighbours and beyond.

The Greek Orthodox Patriarchate of Alexandria and All Africa, through ecumenical dialogue, has reached a consensus with the Coptic Church on pastoral issues. One example is the issue of marriages that occur between a Coptic and an Orthodox faithful. This had been signed by the late Patriarch Petros VII of the Greek Orthodox Patriarchate of Alexandria and All Africa and Pope Shenouda III of the Coptic Church. This agreement was officially accepted by the members of Middle East Council of Churches in their general assembly on 4-9 May 2000 in Lebanon. Partially, the report reads:

They also welcomed the pastoral agreement reached between the Coptic Orthodox Church of Alexandria and the Greek Orthodox Patriarchate of Alexandria and All Africa regarding the mutual recognition of the sacraments of holy matrimony blessed in their respective churches in the cases of mix marriages.[14]

The Patriarchate of Alexandria has not limited its ecumenical dialogues and participation regionally, but also participates in international ecumenical organizations like the World Council of Churches (WCC). This

---

[10] *Dictionary of the Ecumenical Movement*, 861.

[11] *Dictionary of the Ecumenical Movement*, 861.

[12] Kallistos Timothy Ware (Metropolitan of Diokleia), *The Orthodox Church* (London: Penguin Books, 1997), 4.

[13] See an article by Rev. John H Erickson, "Beyond Dialogue: The Quest for Eastern and Oriental Orthodox Unity Today that was presented in a Symposium on 1700th Anniversary of Christian Armenia October 27-28, 2000". Available at: http://www.svots.edu/content/beyond-dialogue-quest-eastern-and-oriental-orthodox-unity-today. (Last accessed on 10 May 2013).

[14] See the report of the Third Meeting of the Heads of the Oriental Orthodox Churches in the Middle East that was held on 4-9 May 2000 at Antelias, Lebanon. Available at: http://www.suryoyo.uni-goettingen.de/library/3meeting-orientalchurchs.htm. (Last accessed on 10 May 2013).

Part IV: Ecumenical Dialogue in various Orthodox Churches and Settings

affirms that the Greek Orthodox Patriarchate of Alexandria and All Africa considers ecumenism as part of its very life. This is because as mentioned above, this church actively participated in the seven ecumenical councils and has continued to do so till today. The "unity of all churches of God" is a constant prayer, a petition in the divine services of the Orthodox Church.[15] Therefore, participation of this church and all other Orthodox churches in the ecumenical movement is a reward or an answer from God to this petition. This is well put by Metropolitan Gennadios Limouris who stresses that the participation of the Orthodox Church in the ecumenical movement of today is not, in principle, a revolution in the history of Orthodoxy, but it is a natural consequence of the constant prayer of the church "for the union of all."[16] Jesus Christ prayed to the Father that "all be one just as He is one with the Father" (John 17:21), it is therefore, a divine calling for the entire church to continue praying for the unity of all. As an "ecclesia" that prays for the unity of all, action must be taken so that our practice aligns with our prayers. This is why the Greek Orthodox Patriarchate of Alexandria and All Africa through its leaders like the late Patriarch Parthenios III involves itself in this God given work for unity of all.

The late Patriarch Parthenios III who continued the missionary and ecumenical efforts of his predecessor, His Beatitude Nicolaos VI, would be best described as an "icon of ecumenism" in the Alexandrian church. Patriarch Parthenios has been described by the former WCC general secretary, Konrad Raiser as "one of the outstanding Orthodox leaders of the ecumenical movement."[17] This is because of his charisma in theological knowledge, spiritual wisdom and ecumenical commitment. From 1968 when he was elected to be a member of the Central Committee of the World Council of Churches, to becoming one of its presidents in 1991, Patriarch Parthenios became a trusted Orthodox ecumenical voice. This was through his profound ecumenical speeches, theological and inter-religious dialogues, as well as leadership and open-mindedness to reaching others. In most of his ecumenical speeches, he emphasized a more mission-oriented unity that leads to a dialogue of the whole people of God.[18] He meant that the dialogue of the whole people of God is a dialogue for the churches of God. He interestingly affirms that WCC offers a platform where churches encounter dialogue which is a gift of God. Such deep theological and ecumenical spirited speeches caused him to be invited to address the main theme of the World Council of Churches' Assembly in Canberra in 1991.[19] On theological and inter-religious dialogues, Patriarch Parthenios III represented the Patriarchate of Alexandria in almost all WCC meetings as well as Pan-Orthodox and Inter-Orthodox consultations since 1968. On reaching out to others, he consolidated the Orthodox Mission particularly in Uganda, where he established the Metropolis of Kampala, and Kenya.

The acceptance of the native African Orthodox communities into the Greek Patriarchate of Alexandria is a sign of how the patriarchate was ready to rekindle, seemingly, the forgotten active mission aspect of the One, Holy, Catholic and Apostolic church.[20] Receiving these native African communities led by Fr. Reuben Mukasa of Uganda and Fr. George A. Gathuna of Kenya had a tremendous impact to the entire Orthodox world. As a result, the churches of Greece, Cyprus, America and Finland have been engaged in missionary work in Africa. Through the blessings of the primates of the Alexandrian Church, these churches send missionary personnel into Africa. Likewise, mission organizations have been created in these countries to enhance mission awareness

---

[15] See great litanies in the divine services of the Orthodox Church.
[16] Gennadios Limouris, *The Ecumenical Nature of the Orthodox Witness in Orthodox Visions of Ecumenism*, (Geneva: WCC Publications, 1994), 68.
[17] See former WCC secretary Konrad Raiser, tribute to the Greek Orthodox Patriarchate of Alexandria and All Africa, following the passing on of the late Patriarch Parthenios III dated 26 July 1996.
[18] See a sermon Patriarch Parthenios III preached at an ecumenical service during a WCC Central Committee meeting in Geneva in 1966.
[19] The WCC 7th General Assembly was held on 7-20 February 1991 in Canberra Australia with the Theme: Come, Holy Spirit – Renew the Whole Creation.
[20] John Ngige Njoroge, *The Christian Witness and Orthodox Spirituality in Africa: The dynamism of Orthodox Spirituality as a missionary "case" of the Orthodox witness in Kenya* (unpublished PhD Diss; Thessaloniki, 2011) (in Greek).

among the faithful and offer their prayers and financial support.[21] Apparently, this has made the Alexandrian church to be the most active missionary patriarchate among the Orthodox churches of our times. The reception of the native Orthodox communities by the Alexandrian church has opened a very crucial and constructive missiological dialogue between Orthodoxy and African cultures. This means, Patriarch Parthenios III in his charisma and open-mindedness was ready to offer theological foundations for such a dialogue. A dialogue of such a nature would mean that the Alexandrian church was ready to guide these native Orthodox communities to become authentic African Orthodox local churches. This is through apostolic succession and at the same time going through the process of enculturation. Enculturation would mean the church becoming "local". The church becomes "local" when it takes roots in a given place with all its cultural, natural, social, and any other characteristic that constitutes the life, values and thoughts of the people involved.[22] This is well illustrated in the Divine Liturgy of St. John Chrysostom, where a worshiping community offers to God the "Holy Gifts" as "His Own", i.e. Your own of your own we offer to you.[23]

Conclusion

The Greek Orthodox Patriarchate of Alexandria and All Africa, through its present leader His Beatitude Patriarch Theodoros II, continues with the ecumenical spirited efforts of the late Patriarch Parthenios III. In the present time, the Alexandrian church continues to participate in all international and regional ecumenical gatherings. In most cases, the patriarchate is represented by His Eminence, Metropolitan Seraphim Kykkotis of Zimbabwe and Angola, who heads the office of international church relations of the Patriarchate of Alexandria. The efforts being made by the patriarchate to remain active in the ecumenical movement and inter-religious dialogues is of paramount importance for its mission today. As already mentioned, no church, faith or religion, in today's globalized world can manage to stay in isolation and without solidarity with the other. Therefore, the Greek Orthodox Patriarchate of Alexandria must continue to witness the message of the Gospel, through its active role in bilateral and multilateral dialogues, because of its difficult situation in Egypt and its profound missionary activities in Africa. Its involvements in these dialogues is not a fight for survival, but it is the very calling for the church to engage through prayers, love and sacrifice to achieve visible unity so that the world can believe (John 17: 21). On the other hand, and especially at the present time of human conflicts, injustices and ecological crisis, the Alexandrian church cannot hold back its prophetic voice. It must tell the world the will of God the creator and giver of everything.

Despite the achievements made by the Patriarchate of Alexandria so far, there is much more to be done especially in the mission field. In this, it would be right to suggest new theological and missiological approaches that would dialogue with African cultures. The reason for such dialogue is to offer an appropriate atmosphere for the Orthodox churches in Africa. Africa is a religious continent and 23.6 % of the world Christian population is living in Africa. This suggests that the future of Christianity is in the so-called global south. Therefore, it is time for the Greek Orthodox Patriarchate of Alexandria and All Africa to strength its presence in Africa and let its rich liturgical tradition, theology and spirituality give answers to social, economic and even political problems that are affecting Africa peoples. This can be possible if major Orthodox theological seminaries like Makarios III Seminary in Nairobi deepen their theological training and seek new theological hermeneutical

---

[21] Apostolic Diakonia of the Church of Greece, formally "Porephthentes", Orthodox Missionary Fraternity of Thessaloniki (formerly known as: "Friends of Uganda Northern Greece"), Orthodox Christian Mission Center (OCMC) of the Greek Orthodox Archdiocese of American and Mission Aid from the Church of Finland.

[22] Zizioulas John D., *Being As Communion; Studies in Personhood and the Church* (Crestwood, New York: St. Vladimir's Seminary Press, 2002), 254

[23] See the prayer before the consecration of the Holy Gifts (bread and wine) in the liturgy of St. John Chrysostom. Also, John N. Njoroge "The Orthodox Church in Africa and the Quest for Enculturation: A Challenging Mission paradigm in Today's Orthodoxy", *St. Vladimir's Theological Quarterly* 55.4 (2011): 405-438.

approaches especially in the field of Mission and Evangelism. In addition, Africa is a home of many religions and different Christian denominations. It is therefore important for the Orthodox seminary schools to introduce ecumenical studies in their curriculum. Such initiatives would help the students to be well equipped on how to relate to others and engage constructively in interfaith dialogue when they become leaders in their respective communities.

Bibliography

Constantin G. Patelos (ed.), The Orthodox Church in the Ecumenical Movement: Documents and Statements 1902-1975, (Geneva: WCC Publications, 1978).

Gennadios Limouris, Orthodox Visions of Ecumenism: Statements, Messages and Reports on the Ecumenical Movement 1902-1992, (Geneva: WCC Publications, 1994).

Groves C.P., The Planting of Christianity in Africa, Vol. 1, (London: Lutterworth Press, 1964).

John Baur, 2000 Years of Christianity in Africa: An African Church History, (Nairobi: Paulines Publications, 1994).

Kallistos (Timothy) Ware (Metropolitan of Diokleia), The Orthodox Church, (London: Penguin Books, 1997).

Michael Kinnamon & Brian E. Cope, The Ecumenical Movement: An Anthology of Key Texts and Voices, (Geneva: WCC Publications, 1997).

Zizioulas John D, Being As Communion: Studies in Personhood and the Church, (New York: St. Vladimir's Seminary Press, 2002).

Dictionary of the Ecumenical Movement, (Geneva: WCC Publications, 2002).

John N. Njoroge, "The Orthodox Church in Africa and the Quest for Enculturation: A Challenging Mission paradigm in Today's Orthodoxy", St. Vladimir's Theological Quarterly 55.4, (2011).

-, The Christian Witness and Orthodox Spirituality in Africa: The dynamism of Orthodox Spirituality as a missionary "case" of the orthodox witness in Kenya (unpublished PhD Diss; Thessaloniki, 2011) (in Greek).

John H Erickson, "Beyond Dialogue: The Quest for Eastern and Oriental Orthodox Unity Today". Available at: http://www.svots.edu/content/beyond-dialogue-quest-eastern-and-oriental-orthodox-unity-today (last accessed September 2013).

Greek Orthodox Patriarchate of Alexandria and All Africa official website: http://www.patriarchateofalexandria. com (last accessed September 2013).

Fr. Ramy Wannous

The division among the churches is not a theological reality; it is the reality of sin in the history of the churches, and that cannot be relied on. What is trustworthy is the unity which Christ builds. Division is a fruit of sin and it has no place with the Saviour except in the tears that flow from His eyes. And from those tears we all come and not from the division, until the Lord removes all traces of the separation.[1]

The history of Christianity shows straightforwardly that most of the schisms which took place in the early Christian period were mainly in the East and affected particularly the Antiochian Church. At first glance, these few words might give the impression that in Antioch there is a so-called "schismatic spirit" among believers, or, in other words, one could say that the spirit of ecumenism is lacking between the Christians. In fact, one might say that Antioch lost its utmost call as a Greek city on Semitic territories which sought to bring together different cultures. What Antioch mastered in the early Christian period by being the major area and city to spread the Gospel to the gentiles, faded away in later centuries. As a result, it is not accidental that in this Apostolic See, five patriarchates carry the name of this Church: the Rum-Orthodox Patriarchate,[2] the Syriac Orthodox Patriarchate,[3] the Apostolic Church of the East[4], the Maronite Church[5] and the Melkite Greek Catholic Patriarchate[6] (though the rise of later patriarchate took place later in 1724). It is not my intention here to reflect on this complex situation. In contrast I would like to focus on the current "ecumenical" situation in Antioch. As it will be made clear, Antioch is still more ecumenical than any other place in the world.

According to Georges Khodr, the (Rum-)Orthodox Metropolitan of Mount Lebanon:

> "Nowadays, the Christians of this country (Lebanon) live together with a consciousness of unity which exists though it does not have a legal systematic expression. You accept deep inside you – with an understanding be it deep or shallow – that the other Christian is your brother and that you will not wound him. And that is due to the fact that you have started to love him since thirty or forty years and have become conscious that God is blessed with that attitude of yours. That could be due to the fact that one party among the people no more wants dispute and discord. The reason behind that could be that the difficulties that rise due to the division have become harmful to each other and we find that harm needless. In this overall ambiance of rapprochement among the people, the consciousness of unity among them has increased."[7]

Therefore in this brief paper I will try to explore the reasons behind this ecumenical reality and then raise the question whether this particularly, Antiochian, reality can be used as the proper model for the way that other Orthodox and non-Orthodox Churches conceive their ecumenical involvement.

---

[1] Metr. Khodr. G. "The Maronites and the Orthodox in the Presence of the Lord", in: *Annahar* (19/01/2013) Article reference #: 1848.

[2] I prefer to use the self designation of this church and not the Western term Greek Orthodox.

[3] See Chaillot, Christine. *The Syriac Orthodox Church of Antioch and All the East.* (Geneva: Inter-Orthodox Dialogue, 1988).

[4] See Baumer, Christoph, *The Church of the East, an Illustrated History of Assyrian Christianity* (London and New York: I. B. Tauris, 2006). Also: Baum, Wilhem, & Dietmar Winkler, *The Church of the East: A Concise History* (London and New York: Routledge Curzon, 2003).

[5] See Suermann, Harald, *Histoire des origines de l'Eglise Maronite*, (PUSEK, Kaslik, 2010).

[6] See Tawil, Joseph. *The Patriarchate of Antioch Throughout History: An Introduction* (Boston: Sophia Press 2001).

[7] Metr. Khodr. G. "The Maronites and the Orthodox in the Presence of the Lord", in: *Annahar* (19/01/2013) Article reference #: 1848.

Reasons behind ecumenism in Antioch

Discovering the "Christian neighbour" in the 20th century

The assumption that the peculiar situation in Antioch (i.e. that Christians were forced to come together due to living within a Muslim context)[8] is not plausible and lacks a historical proof. One can easily argue against this theory by saying that Christians of different denominations in Antioch have been living together for over 14 centuries under Islamic or non-Christian rule; so why didn't they seek for unity or at least rapprochement in that period?[9] Apart from the ecumenical spirit which arose in the 20th century and was spread away all over the churches in several continents, there are in my assumption two reasons behind this new tendency: 1. the quest of identity; 2. the presence of charismatic leaders in the above mentioned Churches in Antioch.

The quest of identity

Patriarch Ignatius IV points out to this issue by saying:

> "after the 1960s, it has become clear that the Syrian Orthodox and the Greek Orthodox are moving on the same line, with different verbal formulas on the nature concealing the same doctrine. It has also become clear that some of our non-Orthodox brothers, affected by a crisis of identity, are moving towards recovering their Antiochene identity..."[10]

After the rise of nationalism, first in Europe and then in the Middle East, Christians in Antioch belonging to various confessions and living alongside with each other, started raising questions regarding their own identity, not as Orthodox or Catholics or Syriacs, but rather as Christians, especially after they noticed that the boundaries between them started to fade more or more. By this, I solely mean that these Christians started perceiving that being a good Christian does not imply exclusively being Orthodox or Catholic or Protestant in the strict confessional sense. This abolishment of the confessional exclusivity but not at the same time of the peculiarity seems to be the starting point for every honest dialogue. In this perspective an Orthodox Christian started to recognize that Christians belonging to other confessions love also their neighbour, read the Bible and fast maybe more than he does and vice versa. To be more flagrant, a Protestant Christian started realizing that what divides him from other Christians does not exist anymore. For example, he began to understand that the icons in the Orthodox Church are only venerated and not worshiped and that Orthodox priests know the Bible and make use of modern exegetical methods in many cases in their sermons. So this Protestant was forced indirectly to question his peculiarity as Protestant. In this respect one should avoid simplifying everything and should always bear in mind that this happened only on the daily life level not on the theological one. However, it is this sort of communication with Christians of other confessions which brought the Christians closer in Antioch. This peculiar multi-confessional situation, which, as far as I am aware does not exist in any other Orthodox context, constituted the *Dialog des Alltags,* the very daily dialogue, which

---

[8] *Orthodoxie im Dialog: Bilaterale Dialoge der orthodoxen und der orientalisch-orthodoxen Kirchen 1945-1997. Eine Dokumentensammlung.* (Hrg.) von Thomas Bremer, Johannes Oeldemann und Dagmar Stoltmann von Paulinus, (1999), 21. In fact, one of the main reasons for this rapprochement is the mixed-marriages. Every single Christian family in Lebanon and Syria has such marriage among at least one of its members. Thus, the Christian-Christian context and not the Muslim-Christian context pushed the coming together of the Christians in the East.

[9] There is however one aspect related to Islam which is pushing the different Christian denominations to achieve unity mainly the feast of Easter. Christians in Lebanon and Syria feel truly embarresed in front of Muslims, when the laters ask them about crucifing Christ and letting him rise twice. On this level lay people want their churches to find a solution to this scandaleous situation, thinking that when Christians in these countries start celebrating Easter together then they will be the cornerstone in uniting the church again.

[10] See Hazim, Patr. Ignatius IV, *Orthodoxy & the Issues of our Time.* Translated from Arabic by Shaun O'Sullivan, (Balamand 2008), 30.

served as the necessary foundation for the later theological dialogue and bilateral meetings and agreements among Christians in the East.

Georges Khodr argues that Eastern Christianity represents a reality of theological rather than geographical significance.[11] He then clarifies that this expression

"sets the distinction between the theology that developed in the West during the thirteenth century from the Eastern theology that remained faithful to the Patristic thought. But in this article we refer to all the Christians who live in the Arab East; those Easterners that have adopted Roman Catholic thought and systems and those who have not. This is so because there are common components in all the Churches of the East namely the system of the Patriarchate or that of the Synod, or the predominance of an ancient language like the Syriac, the Coptic, the Armenian, and Ethiopian, in the worship services; also, even though these Churches have an ethnic character, yet the use of Arabic is common in the service of worship and prayer. And, except for Ethiopia, we find these people living in the Arab East. Then the Evangelical Protestant movement appeared in this land during the first three decades of the nineteenth century; this movement played an important role in the Arab renaissance and in spreading the principles of the Protestant Reformation and in establishing university education. The above mentioned churches have branched from the ancient root but have some differences and disagreements; yet what brings all these Christians of this region together is their faith in Christ and their following of one Gospel and one Creed. This provides a legitimate foundation for their unity. Needless to say, they experience unity in their love for one another, and in their experience of God and in mutual cooperation in what concerns them. So if one group among them becomes lame for one reason or another, they all limp with them. And a weakness that befalls one group is felt by all…The Christians in general have been in Syria, Lebanon, Palestine and Asia Minor and Egypt before the Gospels were written."[12]

According to Khodr's understanding there are common points among the Christians in the East, mainly in spirituality and asceticism. In this respect faith seems to be the adequate starting point for the Christian unity. Additionally, their common spirituality should be considered as the proper opportunity for the necessary dialogue between them. This would explain the pastoral agreement between the (Rum-)Orthodox Patriarchate and the Syriac-Orthodox Patriarchate in 1991[13]. Indeed, one could find several similarities in the spirituality of both churches. Therefore, it is reasonable that spiritual life could become the solid foundation for this rapprochement. In this case I would assume that this common understanding of spirituality was the basic reason of the agreement of the Rum-Orthodox with only the Syriac Patriarchate. In this regard one can easily realize the Latin influence on the Maronite monasticism, which led to its estrangement from its Eastern Orthodox roots, especially after the 16th century. Thus, as a result, a different sort of spirituality arose among the believers of this church. In addition, neither the Rum-Orthodox Church nor the Syriac Church practiced proselytism (contrary to the Uniates) against each other especially in the modern era. Consequently, mutual respect reigns among both Churches. (We must also keep in mind that the Syriac Church is autocephalous and does not need to ask Rome for permission as is the case by the Uniates[14]).

It is true that one can find flexibility in dialogue on the side of the Rum-Orthodox, which is rarely found among other Orthodox churches. This flexibility is rooted in the fact that in Antioch there is not any church, which is bound to a particular language or nation, in strong contradistinction to the sister churches. In other

---

[11] Khodr, Metr. Georges "Eastern Christians", in: *Annahar* (15/01/2011) Article reference #: 1349. Similar ideas can be found in Khodr's article "Antioch: The Great City of God", in: *Annahar* (16/02/2013) Article reference #: 1860.

[12] Ibid.

[13] *Proche-Orient Chrétien* 41 (1991): 424-426.

[14] A good example regarding the difficulty to reach tangible agreements with and the Uniates is the unsuccessful dialogue between the Melkite Greek Catholic Church and the Rum-Orthodox Patriarchate which took place between the last decades. The dialogue was simply aborted because no further actions could have been done from the Melkite side without the approval of the Roman See. More in Hachem, G. "Un projet de communion ecclésiale dans le patriarcat d'Antioche entre les Eglises grec-orthodoxe et melkite-catholique". *Irenikon* 72.3-4 (1999): 453-478.

words, the Church of Antioch should not be considered as a "national" church. As Metropolitan Georges Khodr put it in his article "The Rum-Orthodox":

> "The Orthodox believers do not mix their religious affiliation and their national loyalty. During the events of 1958, as fragmentation dominated the country, the Orthodox community was one with the Lebanese government against what it considered as regional intervention. During the last civil war, the Orthodox community did not have a militia and the Orthodox Church neither blessed nor condemned its members whenever they had joined a political party or another. It is possible to say, even today, that the entire Orthodox community in Lebanon is Lebanese and there is no calamity in this. One should add further that since 1975, the Orthodox Church has taken explicit positions against Israel, which appeared in the statements of the local Synod headed by the Patriarch, and this was done in total freedom. This position had nothing to do with our love of the holy places; rather it was to vindicate the rights of the Palestinians. We have never talked about the Christians of Palestine, but rather about all the Palestinians."[15]

This non-nationalistic attitude among the Rum-Orthodox is an important aspect in dialogues.

Charismatic church leaders in Antioch

No progress could have been achieved on the level of ecumenism without the ceaseless efforts of some char-ismatic Christian leaders of these churches in the East. In this respect two of the most eminent figures of the Rum-Orthodox Church are undoubtedly the late Patriarch Ignatius IV (Hazim) and Metropolitan Georges Khodr of Mount-Lebanon. These two personalities have determined due to their personal commitment the ecumenical movement and spirit in Antioch.[16]

We have already referred to the way that Metropolitan Georges Khodr understands the Church unity. I will now proceed to the second eminent figure, the Patriarch Ignatius Hazim. The late Antiochian Patriarch has argued that the various divisions which occurred in the East throughout history did not however eliminate the deep feeling of unity between the Christians. According to the same Patriarch, the so-called "Antiochene identity", could be considered as the starting point towards the Church unity.[17] After the discovering of this "identity", Patriarch Ignatius raised the following crucial question "whether the Antiochene unity can move from the level of sentiments to the level of an effective organization. The first level should be the re-ordering of parochial affairs within all our Churches, so that weddings, funerals, other rites, and the basic Christian education follow a similar procedure. However, from a theological standpoint, the new challenge is to render, not the universal but the local or regional Church, the real foundation of the ecclesial life."[18]

---

[15] "The Rum-Orthodox", in *Annahar* (13/03/2010) Article reference #: 557.

[16] Also worth noting the position of the new patriarch John X regarding the unity of the Church, which he briefly tackles in his enthronement homily. Though it is still too early to talk about his thought concerning the ecumenical movement, however, the fact that he mentioned this issue in his speech, shows that the ecumenical work with other churches will be one of the priorities during his era. He says: "Jesus cries when He sees the Christian world divided and when He realizes the distance separating its members, as well as the regression of the ecumenical work in the last years. We have to pray, with Jesus and all brothers belonging to Him, that we 'become one' (John 17: 1). We must understand that this unity is a necessary condition 'that the world may believe' (John 17: 21). Some people's drifting away from faith, their disinterest in God's love, the putting of their hope in humanity apart from the God who created them in His own image, calling them to His likeness, and offering them a way toward deification, all this is a sign, among others, urging us to try and instill har-mony between the oriental and occidental churches, to launch a practical cooperation in the fields of ministry and pastoral care. We also need to encourage dialogue, to get to know each other better and to take brave prophetic initiatives so that we may reach, when God allows, the communion in the one chalice. Only then, can we tell those who ask us about our faith: 'come and see' (John 1: 46), come and witness how our love for each other stems from our love for the One who loved us first and gave His life for us." See http://john-x-enthronement.com/uploads/speech/Enthronement_dicours_Ar.pdf (last accessed, September 2013).

[17] Hazim, Patr. Ignatius IV, *Orthodoxy & the Issues of our Time*. Translated from Arabic by Shaun O'Sullivan, (Balamand 2008), 30.

[18] Ibid.

Patriarch Hazim considered the peculiar religious situation in Antioch as an almost unique phenomenon. Religious plurality and multi-confessional Christian co-existence provide Antioch a good ground and opportunity towards unity. Additionally he highlighted the relevance of the synodical approach as the proper starting point in striving for this unity.[19] By this he did not mean a juridical procedure, but rather "a matter of transcending the shells into which decant ecclesiologies have enclosed us. It is about re-situating ourselves in the living sense of the Holy Tradition of the Councils and Fathers, which offers us the proper way to the mystery of the One Church: first; communion in charity, with all its demands; then, the search for communion in faith; finally, as its fruit, the full communion in Liturgy, which includes the canonical communion of pastors."[20]

Conclusion

In this article an attempt was made to show the particularity of the Antiochian Orthodox Church and its Christian context, which compels the various Christian denominations to strive for unity on the basis of a common understanding. This common basis is what Patriarch Hazim calls the "Antiochian identity". Undoubtedly this situation constitutes a unique feature of the East. Therefore, the power of change and the flexibility in tackling the issue of the Church unity, or rather the Christian unity, could be considered as a proper model for the other Christian churches. At the same time, however, the present challenge in Antioch is this: In which way will the Rum-Orthodox Church be able to spread its faith to the new ecumenical brotherly context? If Antioch succeeds in this task, then this model could inspire other sister Churches.

Bibliography

Baum, Wilhem, & Dietmar Winkler. *The Church of the East: A Concise History*. (London and New York: Routledge Curzon, 2003).

Baumer, Christoph. *The Church of the East, an Illustrated History of Assyrian Christianity*. (London and New York: I. B. Tauris, 2006).

Hachem, G. "Un projet de communion ecclésiale dans le patriarcat d'Antioche entre les Eglises grec-orthodoxe et melkite-catholique" *Irenikon* 72.3-4 (1999): 453-478.

Patr. Hazim, Ignatius IV, *Orthodoxy & the Issues of our Time*. Translated from Arabic by Shaun O'Sullivan, (Balamand: 2008).

Metr. Khodr, Georges. "The Maronites and the Orthodox in the Presence of the Lord." *Annahar*. (19 Jan 2013). Article reference #: 1848.

-"Antioch: The Great City of God." *Annahar* (16 Feb 2013). Article reference #: 1860.

-"Eastern Christians." *Annahar* (15 Jan 2011). Article reference #: 1349.

-"The Rum-Orthodox." *Annahar* (13 Mar 2010). Article reference #: 557.

-"The Maronites and the Orthodox in the Presence of the Lord." *Annahar* (19 jan 2013) Article reference #: 1848.

Tawil, Joseph. *The Patriarchate of Antioch Throughout History: An Introduction*. (Boston: Sophia Press 2001).

---

[19] Ibid. p. 47.
[20] Ibid.

Part IV: Ecumenical Dialogue in various Orthodox Churches and Settings

(59) Ecumenical Dialogue in the Perspective of the Patriarchate of Jerusalem[1]

Anna Koulouris

The epicenter of Christianity has been Jerusalem since the time of Christ, with a legacy that stretches back thousands of years into the Old Testament. The ancient Church of Jerusalem, from which the Greek (Rum) Orthodox Patriarchate of Jerusalem can trace its lineage, was instituted on the day of Pentecost. It was on this day that Christians believe the Holy Spirit descended upon the disciples of Jesus Christ (Acts 2:1-41) and the Gospel spread throughout the world from Jerusalem. By default, this puts the ancient Orthodox Church of Jerusalem, validated by its apostolic succession and marking the exact location of the resurrection, in the perpetual position of facilitating inter-religious dialogue and taking a clear stance on ecumenism between the Christian faiths. It is first necessary to understand the unique role of the Jerusalem Patriarchate on a local level in order to understand comprehensively its relevance to Eastern Orthodoxy and ecumenism in the broadest sense.

The Church of Jerusalem, widely acknowledged as the "Mother of all Christian churches," was elevated to the rank of patriarchate in the year 451 at the Fourth Ecumenical Council held in Chalcedon. As the only local and autocephalous Christian institution in Israel, the patriarchate heads the various Christian communities throughout the Holy Land. Its jurisdiction falls under the political domain of the Hashemite Kingdom of Jordan, Palestinian Authority and Israel and includes almost 200,000 people. Due to its special status that is connected to Jerusalem, the patriarchate enjoys certain rights and privileges but also faces heavy pressures. Some of these pressures include being pulled into conflicting political interests as a result of this jurisdiction that spans three national territories. By definition, the mission of the patriarchate is not a political one, however, a layered history and geographical disposition that places it amid conflict has invited the patriarchate to participate in the region's politics, especially since its esteemed role is to protect the holy shrines, which are often threatened by political circumstances. The Brotherhood of the Holy Sepulcher, the monastic order of the patriarchate, which holds the special responsibility of physically protecting the holy shrines, has succeeded in keeping the holy places accessible to all pilgrims without differentiation. It is locally and internationally understood that without the presence of the patriarchate, most of the holy places would have been destroyed or converted into museums, archeological sites or tourist attractions.[2] Another factor that contributes to the patriarchate's political importance and pivotal role in the current and future status of Jerusalem is its inheritance of property, in addition to tradition and leadership.

The year 637 AD was decisive in many ways for the church. Caliph Omar ibn al Khattab, known to be a stricter enforcer of Islam than the prophet himself,[3] seized Jerusalem from Patriarch Sophronios. The invaders were more fanatically motivated than technically advanced. Byzantine inhabitants handed over their properties to the patriarchate for guardianship and divine services. To this day, the Patriarchate of Jerusalem owns a large percentage of property in the Old City, and numerous churches, monasteries and other properties throughout the Holy Land, including the Israeli Knesset building and residence of Israel's prime minister. In addition, it is the custodian of the Holy Sepulcher Church (Church of the Anastasis), where Jesus Christ was crucified and resurrected. A covenant was made between al Khattab and Patriarch Sophronios, known as "the Covenant of Omar," which is a fundamental agreement that has been the basis of all legal agreements and many business

[1] The first following article on this subject is from Anna Koulouris, while the second one from Bishara Ebeid.
[2] Koulouris, Anna, "The Greek Orthodox Church and the Future of Jerusalem" *Palestine-Israel Journal of Politics, Economics and Culture* 17.12 (2011).
[3] Montefiore, Simon Sebag, *Jerusalem* (New York: Vintage Books, 2011), 182.

arrangements that have taken place from that time until the present between the patriarchate and its respective authorities.[4]

"Unlike the other Christian churches here – and they do have a lot of properties as well – the Greek Orthodox Patriarchate is the only church institution that is independent, autonomous and autocephalous. This means that the properties of the patriarchate are the properties of the country here; the land here. They belong here," says Patriarch Theophilos III.

But property ownership is only one indication of the patriarchate's historical role in the city as an inheritor of spiritual and natural heritage. The patriarchate as an institution also gives legitimacy to historical claims that the Hashemite Kingdom of Jordan and the Palestinian Authority have over the holy places, by upholding the "Covenant of Omar," since both governing bodies have claims to the places when the Muslims took Jerusalem. Today, the relationship between the Patriarchate of Jerusalem and the states within its jurisdiction is a good one. When political tensions arise, the patriarchate does not interfere, holding to its exclusively spiritual mission. However, when the people of the region are negatively affected by the policies of Israel's occupation, the church steps in on a humanitarian level. "We try not to turn ourselves into politicians, but at the same time this does not mean that we do not have compassion for the suffering and the affliction through which people are passing here,"[5] says Patriarch Theophilos III. Since it is a local institution whose attention is focused on the holy places but also on the flock, the patriarchate offers financial assistance to people in need, scholarships to students of any ethnicity and religion, and sends representatives – often the patriarch himself – to visit refugee camps to give aid and spiritual support. When the political issue at the forefront of international discussion is the status of Jerusalem, the patriarch continues to uphold one view:

> "Our purpose is to try, from our position, to contribute to mutual respect and understanding and to peaceful coexistence and symbiosis. This is the duty of the Church. This is why we as churches have officially and repeatedly made statements and expressed our position over the status of Jerusalem. Our position on Jerusalem is that we want it to be an open city, to be accessible to everybody, and that Jerusalem has enough space to accommodate all religious communities. Politically speaking, everybody has claims over Jerusalem and everybody wants Jerusalem to be his or her own capital. But from the religious point of view, Jerusalem is the capital of God."[6]

As custodians of the shrines of the Holy Land, the Patriarchate of Jerusalem is indispensable to both the ancient land and to a large portion of the more than one million people who visit Israel each year as tourists.[7] Its very functions require understanding and mutual respect. Visitors and guests from around the world, from every sect of Christianity, are hosted by the patriarchate on behalf of the original, true Church of the Apostles. "Jerusalem has the privilege and advantage to have been sanctified by the sacrificial blood of our Lord Jesus Christ. The redeeming blood of Jesus Christ has allowed Jerusalem to be a city for believers of all faiths," says Patriarch Theophilos III. Naturally, the essence of Jerusalem is ecumenical.

As it pertains to ecumenical dialogue, the Patriarchate of Jerusalem fully supports the end goal of what these dialogues aim to produce; understanding amongst the faiths in order to achieve unity. However, unity that requires compromising Orthodox doctrine in order to achieve Eucharistic unity is unacceptable. "We have achieved relative – not absolute – ecumenism," says His Eminence Archbishop Aristarchos of Constantina, chief secretary of the Patriarchate of Jerusalem. Absolute ecumenism would entail Eucharistic union and con-celebration, which calls for an Orthodox confession of faith. "The ultimate goal of dialogue is theological unity, but it doesn't depend on us; it's not our decision," says Archbishop Aristarchos.

---

[4] Koulouris, Anna, "The Greek Orthodox Church and the Future of Jerusalem", 232.

[5] Ibid., 233.

[6] Ibid., 234.

[7] Potter, George, Record number of tourists visit the Holy Land in early 2012. *The Times of Israel*. (2012).

Part IV: Ecumenical Dialogue in various Orthodox Churches and Settings

Patriarch Theophilos III says the Patriarchate of Jerusalem seeks "to work and pray all the time, whole-heartedly, for the restoration of the unity between churches." However, he stresses that unity should not be in terms of administration, but rather, of faith. This is a key distinction, which he says is not mutually understood amongst denominations, especially between the Latin (Roman Catholic) and Eastern Orthodox churches, which share catholic and apostolic tradition and are therefore qualified for unity. In the meantime, debate occasionally arises regarding ecclesiastical positions on socially prevalent topics. This year, the Vatican surveyed various churches on their positions of female ordination to the deaconate. There was a firm response from Patriarch Theophilos III, which stated that Churches of apostolic succession do not deviate on issues regarding sacraments, since the Orthodox Church is founded upon Holy Scripture and holy tradition.

During the visit of His Holiness Benedict XVI, Pope of Rome, to Jerusalem in May 2009, Patriarch Theophilos III expressed that the Greek (Rum) Orthodox Church, and more specifically, the Patriarchate of Jerusalem, supports the unity of the faith but not a unity of administration. "They recognize us as a point of reference only; symbolically," he says. At the same time, the Patriarchate of Jerusalem willingly reaches out to the Latin Church on matters that require unity in other ways, such as issues of humanitarian concern and social justice. In his address to the pope, Patriarch Theophilos called upon Christians from every confession to "join forces" and live by the words of the psalm that says, "Steadfast love and faithfulness will meet; righteousness and peace will kiss each other (Ps. 85:10)." He called upon church leaders to attend to the moral task of reconciliation and mutual respect, especially in the Holy Land. Welcoming the pope as not just a pilgrim but as a "messenger of peace," he said that unity of faith is not an end in itself, but a means by which to unite humanity.[8]

The fundamental task of ecumenism for the Patriarchate of Jerusalem is currently to initiate and participate in dialogue that creates presuppositions for peace. This ambition is vital in lands where being Christian, especially Orthodox, is increasingly difficult and dangerous. Interestingly, as a result of ecumenical dialogue, political advancements have been achieved, which in turn have actually helped the Church. For example, in a 2005 message of solidarity with the patriarchate during a time of leadership change, General Secretary of the World Council of Churches at the time, Rev. Dr. Samuel Kobia, wrote, "Please be assured that the World Council of Churches stands firmly with the patriarchate in rejecting this unwarranted interference with the freedom of the Church to choose her own leadership. We will raise this matter directly with representatives of the State of Israel and all the governments concerned in keeping with the principles we expressed previously." The Church of Jerusalem, the first church and uninterrupted continuation of the first Christian community, validates the other Christian Churches by its existence. In return it seeks and may powerfully benefit from the support of these other Churches in order to maintain its very existence.

Not many people worldwide realize there are churches in the Islamic State of Qatar, let alone a Greek Orthodox church, St. Isaac and St. George, under the jurisdiction of the Patriarchate of Jerusalem. The first time an Orthodox priest celebrated Divine Liturgy there was in 1997, by the invitation of the former United States Ambassador to Qatar, Patrick Theros. The priest who celebrated that Divine Liturgy was Archimandrite Theophilos at the time, the current Patriarch of Jerusalem. As a result of their negotiations with the Emir of Qatar Sheikh Hamad bin Khalifa al-Thani, who has recently abdicated power to his son, and the help of the assigned priest Archimandrite Makarios, who was elected an archbishop in March, an agreement was made in 2005 for a plot of land with a symbolic lease to be used for the building of churches in order to accommodate the growing number of expatriates in the country. Six denominations of Christians are approved to build churches and freely worship within the designated area. The Greek Orthodox Church, still under construction, welcomes Christians from all over the Arab world, Greece, Russia, Serbia and the United States. For nearly a decade, Archbishop Makarios, under Patriarch Theophilos III, has fulfilled the needs of the parish and worked to raise the funds for construction. The needs of the flock are wide-ranging in terms of languages, house visits, youth activities, infrastructure challenges, enforcement of Islamic law, growing population, and fast turnover

---

[8] Jerusalem Patriarchate. "Visit of the Pope of Rome Benedict XVI to the Holy Land", *Jerusalem Patriarchate Official News Gate* www.jp-newsgate.net. (2009)

of Doha residents. However, there is a high satisfaction with the spiritual leader. "This church is an example of how to be united as Christians, and also have symbiosis between Muslims in this part of the world," says Archbishop Makarios.

There has been ongoing controversy since the election of Archbishop Makarios of Qatar. The Patriarchate of Antioch, in an official statement of rejection of the election, citing the Geneva agreements, said the pastoral arrangement with Archbishop Makarios should have been temporary. They threatened to cut ties with the Patriarchate of Jerusalem.[9] In response, the Patriarchate of Jerusalem says that as early as 1996, the late Patriarch Diodoros had appointed his representative (Theophilos), which has until this time never elicited a response from Antioch. Patriarch Theophilos III also made a pastoral visit to Doha in 2010, where he served the Divine Liturgy, bolstering the progress of the church there. If relations between the Jerusalem and Antioch Patriarchates are damaged or broken, there will be implications for the flock. Compounded with external political tensions, the fracturing of the two sides will be harmful to the unity that both patriarchates have separately encouraged for future security.

Tensions in the Middle East have steadily risen since the Arab Spring began in Tunisia and Egypt two years ago. The massacre in Syria continues, and Egypt is still struggling to steady itself after its regime change upheaval. The Christian population of the Middle East, already a staggering minority, is further diminishing and losing rights within its respective governments. As far as Jerusalem is concerned, there is a lot to worry about for the Christians. The Jerusalem Municipality master plan for 2020 seeks to manually alter the demographic of East Jerusalem, in which the Patriarchate of Jerusalem and the Christian Quarter are located.[10] Education is an extremely high priority of Patriarch Theophilos III as it relates to surviving and even surmounting the challenges facing the region. "Schools are helping to bring about reconciliation and mutual respect between Islam, Christianity and even Judaism. Our pastoral center is focusing on education, building schools all over the ecclesiastical jurisdiction of the patriarchate. Schools are the only way to educate and provide our young generation with the knowledge of their identity," says Patriarch Theophilos III.

The Patriarchate of Jerusalem owns 18 schools throughout its jurisdiction, has enrolled more than 8,500 students, and employs more than 800 people comprised of both Christians and Muslims. They are located in Amman, Acaba, Remla, Beit Sahour, Ramallah, Taybeh, Fhes, Madaba, Gaza, Jaffa and Jerusalem.[11] "Our schools have existed here since the time of the Ottomans. They are the oldest schools in the Holy Land, because the Greek Orthodox had the only schools in the empire," says the Very Reverend Archimandrite Innokentios of Madaba, Jordan. The patriarchate's schools, which were time capsules in a sense, directly contributed to the preservation of the Arabic language. During 400 years of Ottoman rule, the Greeks, Armenians and Jews continued to operate much of the empire. The two important ministries run by non-Muslims at the time were the Ministry of Foreign Affairs and the Ministry of Finance. The Christians have been part and parcel to the legacy of the Holy Land and its passing empires, as well as co-sufferers with the Jews and Muslims at the hands of the Crusaders who left indelible marks on the land and on history. For this reason, the Christians have maintained a deep-rooted respect for the cultures with which they co-existed. "Orthodox Christians are an indigenous element in this land. We are not newcomers or intruders, and especially educated people know this fact. It all comes down to education," says Archimandrite Innokentios.

The majority of the patriarchal schools are in Madaba. More than half of the students are Muslim and the rest are Christian. The curriculum is dictated by the British Council of Amman, which is important because English is a critical component in the desired skill set of the patriarchal schools so that students have a better

---

[9] Holy Synod of Antioch. The Patriarchate of Antioch's Official Decision on the Patriarchate of Jerusalem's Intrusion in Qatar. *Notes on Arab Orthodoxy.* (2013).

[10] Meir, Margalit. "Jerusalem Municipality's 2020 Master Plan" *The Palestine-Israel Journal of Politics, Economics and Culture* 17.1-2 (2011): 141.

[11] Jerusalem Patriarchate. "Other Schools in the Holy Land" (2012). www.jerusalem-patriarchate.info (last accessed, September 2013).

Part IV: Ecumenical Dialogue in various Orthodox Churches and Settings

chance to be employed. Religion is taught according to the respective religion of the student, taught by the teacher who practices that respective religion.

"Ours are the only schools to have never carried out missionary activity. Others who came tried to proselytize to the local population. The Latins (Romans) and Protestants took advantage of the local congregation here, as they were faced with war and hunger. They were offered free schooling and refuge in return for joining their Churches. For this reason, any non-Orthodox Christian Arabs had converted at some point throughout the years," says Archimandrite Innokentios.

In the year 1917, during the Russian Revolution, the Patriarchate of Jerusalem had fallen into debt following the British Mandate period, which lasted until 1947. During this time, the patriarchate lost numerous properties. But within the past 30 years, substantial change has occurred. There has been about 30,000 square meters of construction added to the patriarchal school properties this past decade. About 200 high school students graduate each year from the schools in Jordan alone. Since the repair of the patriarchate's financial status, much more focus has been reverted to the educational initiatives. Ranking second and third place among all private schools in the Hashemite Kingdom of Jordan, the patriarchal schools are in high demand.

One problem of the past that has been solved with the growth of the schools and influx of highly qualified teachers is that many young people are being offered employment, especially women. "The societies we live in are theocratic, and therefore women can't just take any job, especially in Arab society. For women within an Arab society, to be a teacher is a dignified position; it's not just any job. It commands respect," says Patriarch Theophilos III.

It is an aspiration of Patriarch Theophilos III to re-open the Theological School of the Holy Cross, which closed in 1912 due to financial adversities. He says the facilities are ready for use, and the patriarchate is prepared to host a theological faculty. However, financial resources in order to pay student tuitions and faculty salaries are the main reason for the delay of the school's re-opening.

The Greek (Rum) Orthodox Patriarchate of Jerusalem is a supporter of ecumenism in the capacity that theology, sacraments, and tradition do not deviate from their apostolic succession. The patriarchate has assigned representatives to the central committees of the World Council of Churches as well as the Middle East Council of Churches. It does make a distinction, however, between being ecumenist, which it rejects, versus being ecumenical. The patriarchate's main objective is to participate and benefit from dialogue, disregarding the notion of becoming one in the Eucharist. Clergy consider their responsibilities to be multi-faceted. They are obligated to their duties imparted to them at ordination, while also serving as protectors of the most precious shrines in Christendom. A man's willingness to devote his life to such a cause is usually not discernable by his desire to go to the Holy Land, but rather, to stay. Nevertheless, Jerusalem and the Holy Land will be visited by pilgrims from all faiths undoubtedly for all time. The Patriarchate of Jerusalem continues to uphold its belief that all are welcome to venerate that, which for them, makes Jerusalem the capital of the world, while protecting the holy places for what they once were, and what they will become again.

Bibliography

Montefiore, Simon Sebag, *Jerusalem: The Biography*, (New York: Vintage Books, 2011).
Wagner, Donald E., *Dying in the Land of Promise: Palestine and Palestinian Christianity from Pentecost to 2000*, (London: Melisende, 2001).
Runciman, Steven, *A History of the Crusades* (Cambridge University Press: Cambridge, 1987).
Woods, David, "The 60 Martyrs of Gaza and the Martyrdom of Bishop Sophronius of Jerusalem" *ARAM Periodical* 15 (2003): 129-150.

Betts, Robert Brenton, *The Southern Portals of Byzantium*, (London: The Musical Times Publications Limited, 2009).

Papadopoulos Chrysostomos, *History of the Church of Jerusalem*, (1910) (in Greek).

Al-Sakakini, Khalil, *The Diaries of Khalil Sakakini Volume Two: Orthodox Renaissance, World War I, Exile to Damascus*. (Ramallah: The Institute of Jerusalem Studies, 2004).

Montefiore, Simon Sebag *Jerusalem: The Biography* (New York: Vintage Books, 2011).

Dowling, Theodore Edward, *The Patriarchate of Jerusalem* (London: Society for Promoting Christian Knowledge, 1909).

Gaganiaras Damaskinos *The administrative structure of the Patriarchate of Jerusalem*, (Thessaloniki: Aristotle University of Thessaloniki, 2008) (in Greek).

Katz, Itmar and Kark, Ruth *The Greek Orthodox Patriarchate of Jerusalem and its Congregation: Dissent Over Real Estate*. International Journal Middle East Studies, vol. 37, (New York: Cambridge University Press, 2005).

Bishara Ebeid

The Holy Land where God decided to incarnate and to conclude the economy of salvation, and Jerusalem, the center of the world where God was crucified in the flesh and resurrected, is the place where the Patriarchate of the Greek (Rum) Orthodox Church is settled. Through this paper we would like to point out the role of the Patriarchate in the ecumenical movement and its statement on this movement. We will begin by arguing the historical role of the Patriarchate in the dialogue among Christians, then we will focus on the current situation of the Patriarchate and the ecumenical movement, and end with some critical remarks.

Introduction

When someone talks about the Patriarchate of Jerusalem, one cannot forget the particular situation of the area and how the political and economic conditions reflect the view that the people and the ecclesiastical hierarchy can have on the ongoing situation of the Christian world. One can describe the particularity of this land in one phrase: where the Love was incarnate, where the Prince of the Peace has established his kingdom of Peace, there is no love, there is no peace, it is a zone under conflict.

Talking about the ecumenical movement brings to mind one word "dialogue", meaning discussion in a synodical way. The fact is that ecclesiastical life started in Jerusalem with the apostolic synod in 49 AD[12] The lesson that this synod gives is how to live in unity in diversity, unity in plurality, and demonstrate the message of love that goes to embrace the "other", the "different". And today in the area of Jerusalem, the Holy City, we live with the others, with the different, and one can ask, do we embrace them? Do we try to live in unity in plurality and diversity? To respond to this question, we need to take a historical view of the Patriarchate and the zone.

A Historical view[13]

Egeria during her pilgrimage in the holy land (4th-5th cen.) mentions that when the Bishop of Jerusalem was speaking in Greek, one deacon was translating his speech into Syriac-Aramaic, to make his speech comprehendible

---

[12] Acts 15.

[13] It is not easy to make a historical view with all the details, the nature of our article limit as to point the most important events that could help us to understand better the historic background of the Patriarchate of Jerusalem.

to those who did not understand Greek.[14] This testimony can demonstrate the coexistence of cultures, and respect for diversity in one period of divisions and schisms (Council of Ephesus and Council of Chalcedon). That means that even if Greek was considered the language of the orthodoxy of Chalcedon, the people of Palestine and the Patriarchate had no problem using other languages[15] to serve as one bridge of dialogue with the non- Chalcedonians.

The monasteries of Palestine had special missionary campaigns in Arabia, which means they were in rapport with different cultures.[16] In these monasteries, and because of the particularity of being in the Holy Land, one can notice the plurality in the liturgical life[17] and the liberty in expressing theological views. It is clear that Palestine was the hostile land of a dialogue between Chalcedonians and the non-Chalcedonians.[18] The Origenist monks received hospitality in the monasteries of Jerusalem,[19] and we cannot forget to mention that Caesarea of Palestine was the second home of Origen himself where he found a refuge. All these facts show the openness of the people of Palestine and the Patriarchate of Jerusalem. We absolutely need to see these events of the history of the church of Jerusalem by reading it in their context. This means that having a dialogue in that time is not the same thing when we talk about ecumenism and the ecumenical movement today. But it surely demonstrates the plurality and the acceptance of others in some conditions.

This situation continued under the Arabic conquest of the Holy Land (638 AD). But, we must notice that now we have a new element. The center of control is not Constantinople but the capital of the Arabic empire, al-Medina, Damascus or Baghdad etc., and the language now is a frank language for the Christians of the zone: the Arabic language. The Patriarchate of Jerusalem had begun a new period now. We can say that when Sophronius, the patriarch of the Holy City, gave the keys of Jerusalem to the Caliph 'Umar bin al-Ḥaṭṭab, a new chapter of the history of the Patriarchate began.

In this period we have a lot of works written, especially by the Melkite monks (Chalcedonians) of the monasteries of Jerusalem and the Holy Land, in Arabic, which demonstrate the ecumenical dialogue that led the Patriarchate. It was a challenge that the first Christians who used the Arabic language were Melkites of Palestine and belonged to the Patriarchate of Jerusalem. The oldest, in fact, Christian work written in Arabic, *On the Triune Nature of God* (Sinai Arabic MS 154)[20] comes from this zone and shows how the Christians in this land knew Islam and the Qur'an, and they could write apologetic works to defend their faith and their identity.[21]

Another work that can show us this open minded atmosphere are the letters that were written by Theodore Abū Qurrah, the theologian of the patriarch of Jerusalem Thomas (811-820): one letter was sent to his friend who had been Jacobite and became Melkite, and the another one was sent to the Armenian to ask them to return to the Melkite

---

[14] Egeria, *Itinerarium*, PLS 1, 1091, 47, 4.

[15] S. Griffith, "From Aramaic to Arabic: The Languages of the Monasteries of Palestine in the Byzantine and Early Islamic Periods" in *The Beginnings of Christian Theology in Arabic. Muslim-Christian Encounter in the Early Islamic Period* (Variorum collected studies series 746), (Padstow 2002), X 16 - X 24.

[16] S. Griffith, "The Arabic account of 'Abd al-Masīḥ an-Naǧrānī al-Ġassānī" in *Arabic Christianity in the Monasteries of Ninth Century Palestine* (Variorum collected studies series 380), (Padstow 1992), X 331- X 332. See more in, Derwas J. Chitty, *The Desert a City. An Introduction to the Study of Egyptian and Palestinian Monasticism under the Christian Empire*, (Basil Blackwell and Mott Ltd: Oxford 1966).

[17] S, Griffith, "From Aramaic to Arabic", X 16- X 24.

[18] Cfr, L. Perrone, *La chiesa di Palestina e le controversie cristologiche. Dal concilio di Efeso (431) al secondo concilio di Costantinopoli (553)* (TRSR 18), (Brescia 1980).

[19] Cfr., Elizabeth A. Clark, *The Origenist Controversy. The Cultural Construction of an Early Christian Debate,* (Princeton: Princeton University Press, 1992); eespecially read the first chapter; Derwas J. Chitty, *The Desert a City,* 123-142 (chapter VII).

[20] *Fī Taṭlīṭ al-Lāh al-Wāḥid,* in: *An Arabic version of the Acts of the Apostles and the seven Catholic Epistles from an eighth or ninth century ms. In the Convent of St Katherine on Mount Sinai, with a treatise On the Triune nature of God with translation, from the same codex,* ed. Margaret Gibson, (London, 1899), (English translation) 2-36, (Arabic text) 74-107.

[21] Cf., S. Griffith, *The Church in the Shadow of the Mosque. Christians and Muslims in the World of Islam,* (Princeton-Oxford, 2008), 53ss.

confession. Because of this letter, Abū Qurra went to Armenia to have a dialogue with the theologians there. The same theologian had a dialogue with Muslims mutakallimūn (theologians) in the court of the Caliph al-Ma'mūn.[22]

This view can help us to understand the exact spirit of the Patriarchate in that time, a spirit of dialogue of faith and truth. Having a dialogue means having a longing to the unity of Christians. Again we must read these theological politics in the context of their period.

With the Ottoman Empire we have a new character in the situation of the Holy Land, and especially of the Patriarchate of Jerusalem. Having the knowledge that the Greek patriarch of Jerusalem, Theophanes (1608-1644), went to Istanbul (Constantinople) and submitted documents to the Sultan Murād IV to prove that the privileged position claimed by the Greek Orthodox church with respect to the holy sites had been acknowledged and reaffirmed by the greatest leaders of Islam,[23] we can understand that the division of the Christians divided also the pilgrimages of the Holy Land. And from that time, meaning from the time that the Sultan gave rights to some groups of Christians to have control in some pilgrimages and another time to others, the problems between Christians started to become more complicated. The rights which became a *Status quo* for the Christians are still in practice today, even if there is no more Sultan.[24]

For the Greek patriarchates in the Ottoman Empire we have a new phenomenon: the Hellenization and re-Byzantinization of these patriarchates. Especially in Jerusalem we have the foundation of *The Brotherhood of the Holy Sepulcher*.[25] This fact can demonstrate the new politics of these churches; unfortunately, it was the beginning of a period of enmity between the different groups of Christians, between hierarchy, monks and laity.

Another element of this period that helped to force this division between Christians were the movements of missionaries in the whole Ottoman empire from Europe and Western Christianity (and the Russian Orthodox Church).[26] With these movements we have the start of the phenomenon of proselytism, which left a negative imprint in the memories of the Eastern churches, among them the Patriarchate of Jerusalem.[27] A very logical reaction was the closed politics, and the writings about the falsity of the other Christians. There is no longer an atmosphere of dialogue, but an atmosphere of protection, which had its origins in the time of the Crusades. One glimpse of the works of this period can tell us about the negative atmosphere. Most of these works are polemical works,[28] without a place for a dialogue or discussion, and are absolutely related to the following conditions: historical, political, economical and theological.

Ecumenical Movement and the Patriarchate of Jerusalem

With the start of the Ecumenical Movement in the beginning of the 19th century, we have the start of a new chapter of the life of the devised churches. The patriarchate of Jerusalem was involved in this movement too, because

---

[22] Cf., Samir K. Samir, *Abū Qurrah. Al-sīrah wa-l-marāǧi'*, (Beirut: Dar al-Mashriq, 2000), 33-46.

[23] Cf., Oded Peri, *Christianity under Islam in Jerusalem. The Question of the Holy Sites in Early Ottoman Times*, (Leiden-Boston-Köln: Brill, 2001), 105.

[24] The book of Oded Peri is so important to understand the question of this period, see, *idem*. The last paragraph of the 4th chapter is so illustrative: " Ottoman policy in the Question of the Holy Sites seems to have been a working combination between a religious world view, political sagacity and practical considerations of economic profitability", *idem*, 200.

[25] *Idem*, 98ss.

[26] For more information about this period you can see the 3rd chapter of, Bruce Masters, *Christians and Jews in the Ottoman Arab World. The Roots of Sectarianism*, (Cambridge: Cambridge University Press, 2001).

[27] For the relation between the Papacy in Rome and the Sultan in Istanbul you can see the work, Charles A. Frazee, *Catholics and Sultans. The Church and the Ottoman Empire 1453-1923*, (Cambridge: Cambridge University Press, 1983); its so important to understand the foundation of the oriental catholic churches and their rule in proselytism and the negative relation with the eastern orthodox churches.

[28] You can see the 3rd vol. of the work of G. Graf in which we have the name of works and the authors and a description of each one, Georg Graf, *Geschichte der christlichen arabischen Literatur. Dritter Band: Die Schriftsteller von der Mitte des 15. Bis zum Ende des 19. Jahrhunderts Melchiten und Maroniten*, (Città del Vaticano: Biblioteca Apostolica Vaticana, 1949).

of some reasons and conditions which will talk about in the next paragraphs. After the Ottoman Empire, in the Holy Land after the First World War, we had the English conquest. Then after the Second World War we have in 1948 the foundation of the new state of Israel, which made a very big change to the zone. We can notice that the real necessity of a dialogue within the churches started after the First World War; the churches started to argue their role in the world and how they could help in the establishment of peace.[29] In fact, from the Orthodox perspective we can see this beginning with the encyclical letter of the ecumenical patriarchate Joachim III in 1920.

The Patriarchate of Jerusalem and the Anglicans

The Patriarchate of Jerusalem, due in part to its own diverse population of different Christian confessions and groups and also to other political and economic reasons, started very important and serious ecumenical dialogues, first of all with the Anglican Church. During the Ottoman period, the Russian Orthodox Church helped the Orthodox Church in the Middle East. Such help for the Patriarchate of Jerusalem was so important, because the Russians were a precious economical source. The Hellenization of the patriarchate and the help for the Patriarchate were two reasons that influenced Damianos, the Patriarch of Jerusalem, in that time to approach England for help. We think that the description by Bryn Geffert makes it evident:

> The patriarchate of Jerusalem was every bit as troubled as the patriarchate of Constantinople. Deep divisions separated its laity and parish priests (most of whom were indigenous Arabs) from the Greek monks who governed the Jerusalem synod from their headquarters at the convent of the Brotherhood of the Holy Sepulcher. The Brotherhood elected the patriarch and all members of the Synod, excluding the Arab laity from administrative matters. Russia had long provided economic assistance to the Jerusalem patriarchate, due both to her political interests in the region and her wish to aid the thousand of Russian pilgrims to the Holy Land. But the Great War bankrupted Russia, Russia lost its Orthodox tsar, and Jerusalem lost its main source of income...[30]

The Brotherhood got help from Greece, precisely from Venizelos. Into this situation entered England, which had soon occupied Jerusalem. In this situation the Church of England had its word. Damianos accepted the Anglican's orders, even if the synod did not agree with this decision, showing how the political and economical conditions were behind this approach. And like Bryn Geffert mentioned in his conclusions that "*Greeks and Arabs in Jerusalem each sought to convince their British overseers to support their respective, feuding camps*",[31] England decided to help the Greek side due to a political interest in the area.[32]

This atmosphere between the Patriarchate and the Anglican Church is demonstrated by the Remarks of the Patriarch Theophilos III[33] at the installation of Hosam Naoum as Dean of Saint George's Cathedral in Jerusalem. On 17 May 2012, he said,

> The Anglican Communion has a long and important relationship of particular significance. We remember with warmth the recent pilgrimage to the Holy Land of His Grace the Archbishop of Canterbury, whose commitment to closer relations with the Orthodox Church is well known, and whose support of the Christian communities of the Holy Land has been especially encouraging to us all.

---

[29] Bryn Geffert, *Eastern Orthodox and Anglicans. Diplomacy, Theology, and Politics of Interwar Ecumenism*, (Notre Dame: University of Notre Dame Press, 2010), 32.

[30] Ibid., 94.

[31] Ibid., 448-449.

[32] Ibid., 95s.

[33] We must notice that Theophilos III studied in England (Durham University) and there he received his post-graduate education which means a lot to the rapport between the Church of England and the patriarchate of Jerusalem. See, http://www.jerusalem-patriarchate.info/en/diathrwsh.htm (last accessed, 7.6.2012).

As Orthodox and Anglicans in the Holy Land, we share many of the same challenges as well as many commitments. Most of all we share the commitment of ensuring the well-being and the security of the Christian presence in
the Holy Land. Christianity is native to this region, and we regard the Holy Land as our home. And we understand
that a vital, vibrant Christian presence is essential to the true nature of the Holy Land as a place of genuine religious,
cultural and ethnic diversity and co-existence.[34]

The words of the Patriarch have a big significance to the situation in the Holy Land, and show the reality
of this area, which we will discuss at another point. We wanted by this citation to demonstrate that the rapport
between the Orthodox Patriarchate of Jerusalem and the Anglican Church which started after the First World
War, still exists and behind this rapport there is always an interest. Today we are talking about the support of
the Christians communities of the Holy Land that comes from the Anglican Church and the need for co-existence. This means that the reasons are political and social, at the beginning, and that behind such rapport was
a political and economical motivation.

The Patriarchate of Jerusalem and the WCC

The rapport with the Anglican Church was a first step of the Patriarchate to the ecumenical movement. In 1948
in Amsterdam we have the first assembly of the WCC, the Assembly of the Foundation. In this assembly, the
Patriarchate of Jerusalem was a member of the WCC. But from the eighth assembly held in Harare 1998, the
Patriarchate stopped sending representatives to the assemblies and delegates to the WCC's events, but did not
cancel his participation as a member. With the patriarch Theophilos III, after the Patriarchate being absent in
the 9th assembly too in Porto Alegre 2006, returned to being present in the events of the WCC, meaning a new
start to a new ecumenical period. The symbolic meeting between the Patriarch Theophilos III and the General
Secretary of the WCC Reverend Dr. Olav Tveit can demonstrate this new period, and to make it more clear
we will cite how the patriarchate had expressed this meeting:

His Beatitude pronounced the blessings of Jerusalem to the recently elected General Secretary of the WCC. This
election was made by the Central Committee of the WCC convened during the months of August and September
2009, with duties being assumed from the beginning of the year 2010. Reverend Dr. Olav Tveit, in order for Reverend Dr. Olav Tveit to be able to continue his mission on behalf of the Christian rapprochement for the protection of
human rights and for the peaceful coexistence between nations and religions, as an ecclesiastic and not as a secular
organization, as a place of prayer and of theological dialogue and not as a place of political activities.
    The General Secretary explained to His Beatitude that he strongly wishes to renew communication with the Land
where the Crucifixion and the Resurrection of Christ took place.
    His Beatitude emphasized how important it is for the Patriarchate to contribute to the preservation of the Christian
character of the city of Jerusalem and of its status as an open city to the adherents and believers of all religions.[35]

The interest of the patriarch is so clear: "to contribute to the preservation of the Christian character of the
city of Jerusalem and of its status as an open city to the adherents and believers of all religions." In reality of
the everyday life of the Patriarchate, there is a necessity to say such words. The patriarch spoke also of a unity
among Christians without confusion, which explains his theological view of the ecumenical dialogue, he said,

As you know, the Patriarchate of Jerusalem has long supported and continues to support and encourage, the mission
of the World Council of Churches, a mission that is based firmly in the common witness that we bear to the Triune
God and to the Gospel of our Incarnate Lord Jesus Christ.

---

[34] Cf. http://www.jp-newsgate.net/en/2012/05/17/2035/#more-2035 (last accessed, 7.6.2012).
[35] Cf. http://www.jp-newsgate.net/en/2010/08/29/943/ (Last accessed 7.6.2012).

Part IV: Ecumenical Dialogue in various Orthodox Churches and Settings

The Orthodox Church participates in the life of the World Council of Churches not in order to create some sort of "super Church", but to work together for the unity of all Christians in faith, in the creation of, to use a Chalcedonian phrase, "unity without confusion". In our ecumenical journey we are all obliged to maintain a spirit of Christian love one for the other as well as a spirit of integrity.[36]

The words of the Patriarch are so positive and demonstrate a desire for dialogue to promote the unity of all Christians, the unity of faith, as he said.

The Patriarchate of Jerusalem and the dialogue with the Roman Catholic Church

After the decision of the Pan-Orthodox Synod of Rhodes, which had proclaimed the orthodoxy of the dialogue with the non-Orthodox churches, the Patriarchate of Jerusalem, with respect to this decision took place in the dialogue officially with the Roman Catholic Church. The presence of the Catholics in the Holy Land had a long history; the Patriarchate could help a lot in the dialogue with the Roman Catholic Church if he used representatives from her flock. The representatives of the Patriarchate were Germanos, Metropolitan of Petra, and Prof. Georgios Galitis from the University of Athens. These two have participated in the meeting of Patmos-Rhodes (1980), Munich (1982), Crete (1984), the second part of Bari (1987), Valamo (1988)[37]. After the meeting of Valamo the patriarchate did not send representatives to the meeting in Freezing (1990) and Balamand (1993). According to Frans Bouwen, the Patriarchate of Jerusalem stopped participating in the dialogue in 1989.[38] It is known that the dialogue between the Catholic and Orthodox churches was stopped after the meeting of Balamand for a period, and with the meeting of Emmetsburg-Baltimore (2000) it began again.[39] The Patriarchate of Jerusalem started to send representatives again to the dialogue after the enthroning of the Patriarch Theophilos III. But the road was beginning to be ready during the visit of Pope John Paul II in the Holy Land (Marc 2000).[40] So we see that Theophanis, the Archbishop of Jerash, and Prof. Georgios Galitis are present in the meeting of Belgrade (2006),[41] Ravenna (2007),[42] Paphos (2009)[43] and Vienna (2010).[44]

The decision to return to participate in the dialogue can be clarified by the speech given by the Patriarch Theophilos III during the visit of Pope Benedict XVI in the Holy Land:

Our task is to extend and deepen the moral task of mutual respect, reconciliation, and lasting peace in the Holy Land. In this great work, Christians from every confession are called to join forces. Let our life together model the words of the psalmist, who said "steadfast love and faithfulness will meet; righteousness and peace will kiss each other." (Ps. 84 (85): 10).

---

[36] http://www.jp-newsgate.net/en/2010/09/02/930/ (Last accessed, 7.6.2012).

[37] Cf. Dimitri Salachas, *Il dialogueo teologico ufficiale tra la chiesa cattolico-romana e la chiesa ortodossa.iter e documentazione,* (Bari: Quadernio di o Odigos,1994), 223-243.

[38] Frans Bouwen, "Emmitsburg-Baltimore 2000. VIIIᵉ session plénière de la Commission mixte international pour le dialogueue théologique entre l'Èglise catholique et l' Èglise orthodoxe" *Proche-Orient Chrétien* 50 (2000): 317.

[39] Ibid., 309-314.

[40] We can notice that reading the discource made by the Patriarch Diodoros, see, Frans Bouwen, "Dimensions Ecuménique du pèlerinage du Pape Jean-Paul II en Terre Sainte" *Proche-Orient Chrétien* 50 (2000): 143-149.

[41] Frans Bouwen, "Belgrade 2006. IXᵉ session plénière de la Commission mixte international pour le dialogueue théologique entre l'Èglise catholique et l' Èglise orthodoxe" *Proche-Orient Chrétien* 56 (2006): 280-281 (see note 2 p. 281).

[42] Frans Bouwen, "Ravenne 2007. Xᵉ session plénière de la Commission mixte international pour le dialogueue théologique entre l'Èglise catholique et l' Èglise orthodoxe" *Proche-Orient Chrétien* 58 (2008): 62-63 (see note 2 p. 63).

[43] Frans Bouwen, "Paphos 2009. XIᵉ session plénière de la Commission mixte international pour le dialogueue théologique entre l'Èglise catholique et l' Èglise orthodoxe" *Proche-Orient Chrétien* 60 (2010): 91-92 (see note 13 p. 92).

[44] Frans Bouwen, "Vienne 2010. XIIᵉ session plénière de la Commission mixte international pour le dialogueue théologique entre l'Èglise catholique et l' Èglise orthodoxe" *Proche-Orient Chrétien* 60 (2010): 345-346 (see note 13 p. 345).

In this great task, we are all summoned to move dynamic dialogue- a dialogue between our Churches, as well dialogue between Christians and the believer of our faiths. Let us never forget that the unity of faith to which we Christians are summoned is not an end in itself, but a means by which we witness to the unity of humankind.

Your Holiness, we know that you have come to the Holy Land as a pilgrim, but you are welcome also by the people here as a messenger of peace and reconciliation. At the same time, as Patriarch of Jerusalem, we greet you with the words of the Liturgy of St. John Chrysostom, who exhorts us at every Divine Liturgy to "love one another, that with one mind we may confess Father, Son and Holy Spirit, the consubstantial and undivided trinity."[45]

Theophilos III's message is clear. Christians are called to collaborate and to dialogue to give a witness of Love and Peace, because "Let us never forget that the unity of faith to which we Christians are summoned is not an end in itself, but a means by which we witness to the unity of humankind." This expresses the need for unity, at least in the collaboration and the witnessing, especially in such a land as Palestine, Israel and Jordan where Christians live among Muslims and Jews. These lands need to give a model to live the diversity within the unity.

The Patriarchate of Jerusalem and the dialogue with the Lutheran Church

It is important for us to focus on this dialogue because the last meeting of the joint commission of the dialogue between the Orthodox and the Lutheran churches took place in Bethlehem, and the Patriarch of Jerusalem, Theophilos III, gave a welcoming speech in which he said,

We welcome you to the holy city of Jerusalem with great joy, and we are pleased that you have accepted our invitation to hold your meeting in Bethlehem. In this city, in the place where the eternal Logos became incarnate in Jesus Christ, we celebrate together our common origin in the faith of the Gospel.[46]

For the Patriarch the base of the inter-Christian dialogue is the common origin in the faith of the Gospel. He continued and presented the history of the dialogue between the Orthodox and the Lutheran churches. After that he mentioned:

As the oldest continuous religious Institution in the Holy Land, the Patriarchate of Jerusalem takes seriously our vocation of *diakonia* both to all those, regardless of religious, ethnic or cultural origin, who make this region their home, as well as to all those, of whatever religious affiliation, who come here throughout the year as pilgrims. In this ministry of *diakonia* to humankind and for the sake of the unity of all Christians, we extend to you our appreciation and encouragement.

We look forward to the 15th Plenary Meeting of the Lutheran- Orthodox Joint Commission next year, and to the results of your dialogue in deepening our understanding of the Nature and Attributes of the Church. It is our fervent prayer that, as we can say together the common words of the Nicene-Constantinopolitan Creed, we may also one day be able to share a common understanding of the mystery of the Church, and one day also be able to share the common Chalice. We are fully aware that the road to the fullness of the unity of faith and the communion of the Holy Spirit is difficult and painful. Nevertheless, we have to continue in our efforts in doing our part and the rest we leave in faith to the Lord.[47]

It is clear also that for the Patriarch, the dialogue is a type of diakonia to humankind, and within it the Christians can achieve the unity of faith, which is difficult and painful.

---

[45] Cf. http://www.jp-newsgate.net/en/2009/05/15/670/ (last accessed 18.6.2012).
[46] Cf. http://www.jp-newsgate.net/en/2010/05/26/824/ (last accessed 18.6.2012).
[47] Cf., ibid.

The Patriarchate of Jerusalem and the Middle East Council of Churches (MECC)

With its foundation (May 1974), the Patriarchate of Jerusalem was a member of the MECC. Theophilos III was elected one of the presidents of the MECC for four years, during the 10th assembly in Paphos, Cyprus (November 2011)48. He addressed a speech in this assembly. By this speech we can understand the importance of the Participation of the Patriarchate in the WECC:

As we move forward, we must also re-commit ourselves to the principle that the Council is not a vehicle for the agendas of individual member Churches of their leaders. As a Council, we respect the right of individual Churches and their leaders to speak and act as their circumstances dictate and we all have our own means for the discussion and publication of those matters that affect our own Churches and communities. Yet, at all times, with regard to the ongoing work of this Council, we are to keep our collective mission at the forefront of our work.

With respect to this mission, let us outline the way ahead as we see it ...

My dear sisters and brothers in Christ, the challenges before us are clear; the mission of this Council is paramount. It is our fervent prayer that this Assembly will propose and carry out to a successful completion a specific plan to accomplish all these goals. As we have emphasized, our work together and the strength of the Middle East Council of Churches are of life-saving significance, especially at a time of inevitable change and serious threat to the Christian presence here.[49]

Epilogue

The Middle East is described as a mosaic of religions and confessions, and the Holy Land gives the same image.[50] The Ecumenical Movement, as Florovsky once said, is a road, but to continue to walk in this road, we need to make an effort in practical life; without effort, seriousness and responsibility, we cannot arrive at the end of this road. So in one area like the Holy Land, Christians must give a real image of dialogue, collaboration, unity and love. Taking in consideration what we had presented above, we can understand the importance of the Ecumenical Movement for the Christians of the Holy Land, and how important could be the role of the Greek Orthodox Patriarchate of Jerusalem in the whole issue.

Bibliography

The discourses of Patriarch Theophilos III are quoted from :
1. http://www.jerusalem-patriarchate.info/en/
2. Bouwen Frans, "Belgrade 2006. IXe session plénière de la Commission mixte international pour le dialogue théologique entre l'Église catholique et l'Église orthodoxe" *Proche-Orient Chrétien* 56 (2006): 280-281
3. -, "Dimensions Ecuménique du pèlerinage du Pape Jean-Paul II en Terre Sainte" *Proche-Orient Chrétien* 50 (2000): 143-149.
4. -, "Emmitsburg-Baltimore 2000. VIIIe session plénière de la Commission mixte international pour le dialogueue théologique entre l'Église catholique et l' Église orthodoxe" *Proche-Orient Chrétien* 50 (2000).
5. -, "Paphos 2009. XIe session plénière de la Commission mixte international pour le dialogueue théologique entre l'Église catholique et l' Église orthodoxe" *Proche-Orient Chrétien* 60 (2010): 91-92 .

---

[48] Cf. http://www.jp-newsgate.net/en/2011/11/30/1780/ (last accessed 18.6.2012).
[49] Cf. http://www.jp-newsgate.net/en/2011/11/29/1752/ (last accessed 18.6.2012).
[50] You can see the study of Anthony O'Mahony, *The Christian Communities of Jerusalem and the Holy Land. Studies in History, Religion and Politics*, (Cardiff: University of Wales Press, 2003).

6. -, "Ravenne 2007. X^e session plénière de la Commission mixte international pour le dialogueue théologique entre l'Èglise catholique et l' Èglise orthodoxe" *Proche-Orient Chrétien* 58 (2008): 62-63.

7. -, "Vienne 2010. XIIe session plénière de la Commission mixte international pour le dialogueue théologique entre l'Èglise catholique et l' Èglise orthodoxe" *Proche-Orient Chrétien* 60 (2010): 345-346.

8. Clark Elizabeth A., *The Origenist Controversy. The Cultural Construction of an Early Christian Debate,* (Princeton: Princeton University Press, 1992).

9. Chitty Derwas J., *The Desert a City. An Introduction to the Study of Egyptian and Palestinian Monasticism under the Christian Empire,* (Oxford: Basil Blackwell and Mott Ltd, 1966).

10. Egeria, *Itinerarium,* PLS 1, 1045-1092.

11. *Fī Tatlīt al-Lāh al-Wāḥid,* in: *An Arabic version of the Acts of the Apostles and the seven Catholic Epistles from an eighth or ninth century ms. In the Convent of St Katherine on Mount Sinai, with a treatise On the Triune nature of God with translation, from the same codex,* ed. Margaret Gibson, (London, 1899).

12. Frazee Charles A., *Catholics and Sultans. The Church and the Ottoman Empire 1453-1923,* (Cambridge: Cambridge University Press, 1983).

13. Galitis Georgios, "An inner voice" *Anaplasis* 450 (2011).

14. Geffert Bryn, *Eastern Orthodox and Anglicans. Diplomacy, Theology, and Politics of Interwar Ecumenism,* (Notre Dame: University of Notre Dame Press, 2010).

15. Griffith Sidney, "From Aramaic to Arabic: The Languages of the Monasteries of Palestine in the Byzantine and Early Islamic Periods" in *The Beginnings of Christian Theology in Arabic. Muslim-Christian Encounter in the Early Islamic Period* (Variorum collected studies series 746), (Padstow 2002), X 16- X 24.

16. -, "The Arabic account of 'Abd al-Masīḥ an-Naǧrānī al-Ġassānī" in *Arabic Christianity in the Monasteries of Ninth Century Palestine* (Variorum collected studies series 380), (Padstow 1992), X 331- X 332.

17. -, *The Church in the Shadow of the Mosque. Christians and Muslims in the World of Islam,* (Princeton-Oxford, 2008).

18. Masters Bruce, *Christians and Jews in the Ottoman Arab World. The Roots of Sectarianism,* (Cambridge: Cambridge University Press, 2001).

19. O'Mahony Anthony, *The Christian Communities of Jerusalem and the Holy Land. Studies in History, Religion and Politics,* (Cardiff: University of Wales Press, 2003).

20. Peri Oded, *Christianity under Islam in Jerusalem. The Question of the Holy Sites in Early Ottoman Times,* (Leiden-Boston-Köln: Brill, 2001).

21. Perrone L., *La chiesa di Palestina e le controversie cristologiche. Dal concilio di Efeso (431) al secondo concilio di Costantinopoli (553)* (TRSR 18), (Brescia 1980).

22. Salachas Dimitri, *Il dialogueo teologico ufficiale tra la chiesa cattolico-romana e la chiesa ortodossa.iter e documentazione,* (Bari: Quadernio di o Odigos, 1994).

23. Samir Samir K., *Abū Qurrah. Al-sīrah wa-l-marāǧi',* (Beirut: Dar al-Mashriq, 2000).

Part IV: Ecumenical Dialogue in various Orthodox Churches and Settings

(60) Ecumenical Dialogue in the Perspective of the Russian Orthodox Church

Fr. Cyril Hovorun

In the 19th century

In the times when confessional borders were extremely strong and denominations treated each other as enemies, the Russian Church often demonstrated unusual openness. For instance, as early as in the mid-nineteenth century, metropolitan of Moscow St Filaret (1782-1867) claimed: 'I will dare not to call as false any Church, which believes that Jesus is Christ <...> My justified respect to the teaching of the eastern Church, he continued, does not mean that I judge or accuse western Christians and the western Church.'[1] St Filaret acknowledged that he was unable to affirm that there is no salvific grace outside the Orthodox Church. In the end of his life he wrote: 'An Orthodox Christian is supposed, in the spirit of love, to joyfully find outside of the Orthodox Church a preserved grace.'[2] Another prominent hierarch of that time metropolitan Platon Gorodetsky of Kiev (1803-1891) in the same vein uttered his famous sentence: 'Our earthly walls do not reach the sky.' He said this when he visited a catholic congregation in the town of Korostyshev in Ukraine in 1884. He also called the Orthodox and the Catholic Churches 'cousins'.

The Russian Church embodied this spirit of openness in a number of bilateral dialogues: with the Anglicans, Old Catholics, and non-Chalcedonian Orientals. These dialogues had a full support of the Church authorities and were built on a solid theological ground. The Holy Synod of the Russian Church established a permanent commission for these dialogues. This commission was chaired by the archbishop of Finland and Vyborg, later metropolitan of Saint Petersburg and Ladoga Anthony Vadkovsky (1846-1912). Among leading theologians of that time who participated in the earliest ecumenical dialogues on behalf of the Russian Church was Professor of Church History at the Theological Academy of St Petersburg Vasily Bolotov (1853-1900). He developed first theological principles of ecumenical dialogue in his famous 'Theses on Filioque.'[3] The Church significantly advanced in its dialogue with the three above-mentioned Christian groups, when the World War I began and hindered any further progress towards unity.

Beginning of institutionalised ecumenism

In parallel to the dialogues with the Anglican, Old Catholic, and Oriental Churches, the Russian Church supported the Faith and Order movement that started in the beginning of the 20th century. Among the Russian hierarchs who particularly contributed to this movement were Patriarch of Moscow St Tikhon (1865-1925) and archbishop Platon Rozhdenstvensky (1866-1934). When protopresbyter neomartyr Alexander Khotovitsky (1872-1937) took part in one of the meetings of the movement (in May 1913 in New York), in his address he praised the movement's initiatives and signed a resolution on establishing an executive and conciliatory commissions for the international conference 'Faith and Order.' The preparatory commissions for this conference decided to get approval for their work from the Holy Synod of the Russian Church. Unfortunately, these plans were impeded by the war that started in Europe in 1914. In the meantime, activists of the movement exchanged correspondence with such prominent Russian theologians as Sergey Troitsky (1878-1972), Nikolay Glubokovsky (1863-1937), Vasily Ekzemplyarsky (1875-1933), and others. A number

---

[1] Митр. Филарет Дроздов, *Собрание мнений и отзывов Филарета ... по делам Православной Церкви на Востоке*, Синодальная типография, 1886, 29, 35.

[2] Ibid., 29, 35.

[3] In the periodical Христианское Чтение, 1913.

of publications in the official periodical of the Russian Church 'Tserkovny Vestnik' positively evaluated the intentions of the movement.

The All-Russian local council 1917-1918, which became a crucial point in the history of the Russian Church, regarded highly the issues related to the Christian unity. To discuss these issues, the Council established a special 'Department for the unity of the Churches'. At its last session on 7-20 September 1918, the Council confirmed a resolution, which was elaborated by this Department. In the resolution, the Council blessed all those who work for making closer the Christian unity.

Along with such positive evaluations of the nascent ecumenical movement, there emerged reservations against it. Protagonists of a conservative attitude to the ecumenical movement were metropolitan Anthony Khrapovitsky (1863-1936) and archbishop St Hilarion Troitsky (1886-1929). They rejected ecumenical contacts of the Russian Church and developed a specific understanding of the non-Orthodox Christianity, which was radically exclusive. This understanding had a practical implication in the theory of *oikonomia* regarding acceptance of converts to the Orthodox Church. This theory goes back to the Greek theologians St Nicodeme the Hagiorite (1749-1809) and St Athanasios of Paros (c. 1721-1813), who in the late eighteenth century dealt with the problem of receiving converts from the Roman Catholic Church. They insisted that the normative practise of the Church is to receive everyone through re-baptism. They called this normative practice *akribeia* (ἀκρίβεια). It reflects what the Church truly believes about itself, the mystery, and the salvation. The Church nevertheless allows some concession to those who want to join it. The concession is called *oikonomia* (οἰκονομία). As Nicodeme put it, 'it is not possible to consider *oikonomia*, which sometimes was used by some of the Fathers, either as a law or as a pattern to follow.'[4]

Metropolitan Anthony subscribed to this concept of *oikonomia* and explained it as a means to remove psychological obstacles on the way of the heterodox and schismatics to the true Church, so that they do not feel embarrassed to be treated like pagans or Jews. When they join the Church, the forms of mysteries, which they had received outside it immediately 'get filled' with grace.[5] Archbishop Hilarion made this idea clear:

'The truth of unity of the Church excludes possibility of grace for the sacramental practices in the societies outside the Church[6] <...> The Church is one, and only it can possess all fullness of gracious gifts of the Holy Spirit. Whoever and in whatever way stepped out of the Church, either to heresy, or to schism, or to self-ordered gathering, loses communion with the grace of God. That is why the mysteries, which are accomplished outside the Church cannot act graciously. Only for the benefit of the Church, to facilitate joining it, the rite of baptism is allowed to be not repeated, if it is performed in a correct way outside the Church. This is not because this rite already had been a gracious mystery, but in hope that the gift of grace will be received through the reconciliation with the body of the Church.'[7]

The line of metropolitan Anthony became fully incarnated in the ecclesiology of the 'Russian Orthodox Church Outside Russia' (ROCOR), which he co-founded after the Bolshevik revolution. This Church gradually came to reject all sorts of ecumenism. It went as far as to accuse other Orthodox Churches of being not Orthodox because of their participation in the ecumenical movement and broke relations with them for this reason. For some time, this Church practiced re-baptism of those who joined it from other local Orthodox Churches, particularly from the Moscow patriarchate. The ROCOR believed at that time that salvation is impossible outside its own boundaries. Even those Orthodox who are members of the Churches, which participate in the ecumenical movement, have no chance for salvation.

The *oikonomia* theory was substantially criticised by Fr. Georges Florovsky (1893-1979). He addressed his critique mostly to metropolitan Anthony Khrapovitsky. He argued that it is highly hypocritical to accept

---

[4] Νικόδημος. *Πηδάλιον*, Ἀθῆναι, 1976, 371 (in Greek).
[5] Митр. Антоний Храповицкий, 'Письма к Р.Гардинеру', in: *Вера и Разум* 8 (1916): 887-888.
[6] Архиеп. Иларион Троицкий, *Очерки из истории догмата о Церкви*, Сергиев Посад, 1912, 70.
[7] Ibid., 83.

those who come from the graceless space outside the Church, as the followers of the theory believed, by letting them to understand that there is grace outside. Those who support the idea that the space around the Church is graceless, should not apply *oikonomia*, but must strongly warn that grace can be received only in the Church.[8]

Instead of the *oikonomia* theory, Florovsky started the following line of reasoning concerning the issue of the borders of the Church. On the one hand, he firmly held the idea of one Church as identical with the Orthodox Church. He rejected the theories of branches and invisible Church. On the other hand, he was reasonably ecumenical and allowed some undefined ecclesiality and possibility of salvation outside the Orthodox Church. This theory comprises two elements, one exclusive and the other inclusive. Florovsky tried to reconcile them, without, however, success. He recognised that he could not solve the problem. He eventually had to identify his approach as a question, not as a solution to the problem.[9] The ecclesiology of balances in fact contains more questions than solutions. In this form, it became a theological mainstream in the Orthodox milieu.

Interwar period

After the Bolshevik Revolution of 1917, the Russian Church in the Soviet Union became completely isolated from the international Christian community. However, those parts of the Russian Church that emigrated to the West, continued ecumenical activities, in accordance with the resolution of the Local council 1917-1918. Thus, the first conference on 'Faith and Order' in Geneva (12-20 August 1920) was attended by archbishop Eulogy Georgievsky (1868-1946), who in March 1921 was appointed by the Patriarch Tikhon to manage Russian parishes in Western Europe. Metropolitan Eulogy also participated in the meetings of the World Conference on 'Faith and Order' in 1927 in Lausanne. Together with him, Fr. Sergey Bulgakov (1871-1944), Prof Nikolay Glubokovsky (1863-1937), and Prof Nikolay Arsenyev (1888-1977) took part in the Lausanne conference. Glubokovsky and Arsenyev also participated in preparation of the Stockholm Conference on 'Life and Work' in 1925.

In 1937, two world conferences of the ecumenical movement were convened: on 'Life and Work' in Oxford and on 'Faith and Order' in Edinburgh. Many representatives of the Russian theological tradition took place in both conferences: metropolitan Eulogy Georgievsky, who now was an exarch of the Ecumenical Patriarchate, Fr. Sergiy Bulgakov, Nikolay Berdyaev (1874-1948), Prof Nikolay Glubokovsky, Fr. Vasily Zenkovsky (1881-1962), Prof Nikolay Arsenyev, Prof Anton Kartashov (1875-1960), Prof Boris Vysheslavtsev (1877-1954), Nikolay Zernov (1898-1980), Lev Zander (1893-1964), and others. Fr. Georges Florovky, who also took part in the conferences in Britain, was particularly active in the ecumenical movement. More than fifty years of his life he dedicated to serve the Christian unity. He was a participant of numerous ecumenical conferences, a member of the Commission on 'Faith and Order', and a member of the Central Committee of the World Council of Churches.

After the World War II

After the World War II, the Soviet regime allowed some limited freedom for the Russian Orthodox Church, including international contacts. In February 1946, the Synod of the Russian Church established a Department for External Church Relations. Metropolitan Nikolay Yarushevich of Krutitsy (1892-1961) was appointed its first president. The Russian Church, however, did not engage immediately to the process of establishing the World Council of Churches (1948). It initially opposed this new ecumenical organisation.

---

[8] Прот. Георгий Флоровский, 'О границах Церкви', in *Путь* 44 (1934): 18-19.
[9] Ibid., 26.

The main reason was that the world became politically polarised, and the Russian Church affiliated with one of the two poles. In the late 1940s, the USSR regarded the ecumenical movement as western and anti-Soviet. Because of this, the Russian Church officially expressed a negative attitude to it, as it happened, for instance, at the meeting of Orthodox Primates and representatives in Moscow dedicated to 500 years of the Russian autocephaly.

When the Soviet government in late 1950s - early 1960s decided that participation of the Moscow Patriarchate in the ecumenical movement would facilitate the international tasks of the USSR, the Russian Church joined ecumenical organisations. The Russian Church had to demonstrate to the world 'freedom' of the Soviet society, and to participate in the Soviet campaigns for peace. Thus, in 1958 the Russian Church took an active part in establishing the Christian Peace Conference. In 1959, the Russian Church co-founded the Conference of European Churches (CEC). Soon it joined the World Council of Churches. This decision was taken by the Holy Synod of the Church and approved by the Council of Bishops in 1961. In the same year, the Russian delegation for the first time participated in the General Assembly of WCC, which took place in New Delhi. Since then, the Russian Church has actively participated in the WCC, including its General Assemblies and Commissions, as well as other ecumenical activities. A key figure who shaped the ecumenical policies of the Church at that time was metropolitan of Leningrad and Novgorod Nikodim Rotov (1929-1978).

Although the ecumenical agenda of the Russian Church was strictly controlled by the Soviet state, the Moscow Patriarchate used ecumenical meetings as an opportunity to weaken Soviet pressure on the Church. Owing to ecumenical contacts, many churches and monasteries in the Soviet Union were saved from closure or destruction, as, for instance, the famous Pyukhtitsy monastery.

After collapse of the communist regime

After the collapse of the Soviet Union, the grip of the state on the Russian Church was loosened. At the same time, within the Church, ultra-conservative and anti-ecumenical voices became louder. These two factors changed the stand of the Russian Church against the ecumenical movement. On the one hand, the Church did not have to promote anymore the agenda dictated by the state. On the other hand, it had to take seriously into consideration anti-ecumenical moods among its believers, in order to avoid splits.

A key figure, who rearranged and defined the policies of the Russian Church concerning ecumenism in this period of time, was metropolitan of Smolensk and Kaliningrad Cyril, now Patriarch of Moscow (born 1946). From 1989 to 2009 he chaired the Department for External Church Relations of the Moscow Patriarchate. Metropolitan Cyril was one of those who initiated a Special Commission on Orthodox Participation in the WCC set up at the VIII General Assembly of the WCC in Harare (1998). He was also a person behind the constitutional document of the Russian Church on ecumenism: 'Basic principles of the attitude of the Russian Orthodox Church to heterodoxy.'[10] This document was received by the council of bishops of the Russian Church in 2000.

The document states that the Orthodox Church and the one Church of Christ are fully identical (1.1). Other Christian communities should be considered as fallen apart (1.4). At the same time, as the document continues, 'communities, which have fallen apart, were never considered as completely deprived of the grace of God. Break in Church communion inevitably leads to damages in the life of grace, but not to its complete disappearance' (1.15). The most important objective in relations between the Orthodox Church and other Christian confessions is to restore the God-commanded Christian unity (John 17: 21); it is part of God's providence and belongs to the very essence of Christianity (2.1). Indifference to or rejection of this task is a sin against God's commandment of unity (2.2).

---

[10] Available on the official website of the Moscow Patriarchate: http://www.patriarchia.ru/db/text/418840.html [accessed 25 Sept 2012].

Part IV: Ecumenical Dialogue in various Orthodox Churches and Settings

Ecumenism in the Russian theological institutions

Institutions of theological education in the Russian Orthodox Church always kept in their focus teaching non-Orthodox traditions.[11] The latter were seen from different angles. In this regard, it is interesting how how the relevant subject changed in the seminaries' curricula. In the 19th century, for instance, it was called 'Accusative theology'. In the 20th century, it lost a good deal of accusativity and was branded 'Comparative theology'. Nowadays, Comparative theology is read during 2-4 terms on the undergraduate level.

A discipline called 'History of the western confessions' is traditionally taught in the Theological Academies, on the postgraduate level. It can also be accompanied by special courses on the history and present situation in different Christian denominations. For example, Saint-Petersburg Theological Academy offers the following special courses: Roman Catholic theology, Protestant theology, Western theology in the 20th century, History of Reformation, Comparative liturgics, Protestantism and State system in the USA.

The current situation in the global Christianity, as well as in the ecumenical movement, is the special focus of the Doctoral School of the Russian Orthodox Church. This is a new educational institution established in 2009. It is closely affiliated with the Department of External Church Relations of the Moscow Patriarchate. Both institutions are presided by metropolitan of Volokolamsk Hilarion Alfeyev. A leading unit in the Doctoral School is the chair of External Church Relations, which is responsible for a number of relevant courses, including problems of the Church unity and inter-Christian relations, taught on the master level. A significant number of students of the school write their theses, including doctoral ones, on the subjects of ecumenism and non-Orthodox Churches.

Bibliography

1. Alberigo, Giuseppe, Beozzo José Oscar, Zyablitsev Georgy. *The Holy Russian Church and Western Christianity*, London; Maryknoll, NY: SCM Press; Orbis Books, 1996.
2. Metr. Anthony (Bloom). "Ecumenism: a Russian Statement." *Diakonia: a Quarterly Devoted to Advancing the Orthodox-Catholic Dialogue [Then] to Promoting a Knowledge and Understanding of Eastern Christianity* (1967).
3. Philip, H. "The Russian Orthodox Church and Ecumenism." *Journal of Ecumenical Studies* 46.3 (2011): 353–358.
4. Roberson, Ronald G. "Russian Steps to Unity - the Late Patriarch Alexei II May Have Been Suspicious of the Vatican, but His Legacy of Ecumenism Will Be a Firm Foundation to Build on." *The Tablet.* 262.8772 (2008): 14.
5. Walters, Philip. "Turning Outwards or Turning Inwards? the Russian Orthodox Church Challenged by Fundamentalism." *Nationalities Papers* 35.5 (2007): 853–879.
6. Metr. Kallistos (Ware). "Sobornost and Eucharistic Ecclesiology: Aleksei Khomiakov and His Successors." *International Journal for the Study of the Christian Church* 11.2 (2011): 216–235.
7. Zander, Leon, Duddington Natalie. *Vision and Action : [the Problems of Ecumenism]*, London: Gollancz, 1952.

---

[11] See on this: Vladimir Fedorov, 'Theological Education in the Russian Orthodox Church (in Russia, Ukraine, Belarus)', in *Handbook of Theological Education in World Christianity*, Regnum publishers, 2010 (eds Dietrich Werner and others), 514-524.

(61) Ecumenical Dialogue in the Perspective of the Serbian Orthodox Church

Rastko Jovic

Introduction

With so many ideas concerning WCC in the Serbian Orthodox Church (SOC) we should start our essay with the Constitution of the SOC. In the document which represents the corner stone of understanding the role of the SOC, it is stated under the article 70 that the Holy Synod[1] of the Serbian Orthodox Church is supposed to foster "closeness and unity of the Christian Churches."[2] Taking into account this important document we can clarify the historical, theological and modern situation of the Serbian Orthodox Church towards Ecumenical dialogue.[3]

Historical beginnings

The 1848 Encyclical of the Eastern Patriarchs called for unity of all Christians. This encyclical has been greeted and accepted by all Orthodox churches of the time.[4] Official participation of the SOC in the ecumenical dialogue began early as in 1903. After the invitation of the Ecumenical patriarch from Constantinople Joachim III to all Christian churches to foster unity, the Serbian Church in the Kingdom of Serbia held assembly with all the bishops issuing an important document. In that document the SOC greeted ecumenical efforts and the dialogue. According to that document the SOC recognized that unity was going to be achieved through diversity of local customs of the each Christian church respecting dogmas of the first millennium.[5]

From that period on, the SOC regularly participated in ecumenical dialogues, according to the political situation of the time. After the Second World War the SOC was under the communist yoke.[6] During that period, we can recognize political tensions that directly influenced the ecumenical situation. After the Second World War until 1948, Yugoslavia (where Serbia presented an integral part) had a strong relationship with the Soviet Union. The beginning of the Cold War shaped the position of the USSR in which all projects from the West should be rejected. In order to accomplish this policy of enmity with the West, the Soviet dictator Stalin used all possible means. During the meeting of the Orthodox hierarchs in Moscow 1948, under pressure of the Soviet government, the SOC rejected WCC which has been founded that same year.[7] At the same time the SOC received much of its economic support from the same Protestant Churches in 1949-1952.[8] After the process of de-stalinization in the USSR during the late fifties, Orthodox Churches

---

[1] Holy Synod represents government of the Serbian Orthodox Church which issues decisions and statements on everyday basis.

[2] *Constitution of the Serbian Orthodox Church*, chapter 70.

[3] Ecumenical dialogue is a matter of the Church's mission and soteriological question; Радован Биговић, *Црква и друштво*, (2000), Београд: Хиландарски фонд при Богословском факултету СПЦ, 163.

[4] Свети Ава Јустин, *Записи о екуменизму*, (Требиње: Манастир Тврдош, 2010), 32.

[5] Cf. Дејан Мачковић, „Свете тајне и еклисиологија у савременом екуменском дијалогу", *Српска теологија данас 2009*, (Београд: ПБФ-ИТИ, 2010), 45-59.

[6] During 1945-1960 atheism in Yugoslavia tried to destroy the Serbian Orthodox Church minimizing her function and life. In this period, number of bishops has been reduced for 33%, priests for 50%, theological seminaries for 60%, students for 75%, and Church property for 88%: Љубодраг Димић, *Срби и Југославија*, (Београд: 1998), 87.

[7] Радмила Радић, *Држава и верске заједнице 1945-1970, Књига II*, (Београд: 2002), 180.

[8] Ibid, 190.

held several assemblies in Rhodes, where the third in 1964 accepted participation of the Orthodox in the WCC.[9] The Serbian Orthodox Church became a member in 1965,[10] but even before that a delegation was sent in 1961 to the WCC assembly in New Delhi.[11] In 1968 the Serbian patriarch German was elected as one of the six presidents of the WCC, at the fourth Assembly of the World Council of Churches in Uppsala. During that period he stated, "We, as Orthodox do not have to give up on anything, but we are bound to witness Orthodoxy to other Christians, whichever denomination they are, if we believe that the truth will liberate us."[12] From that period on the SOC has regularly been involved in the work of the WCC depending on political-historical circumstances. We should be aware that communist involvement in the policy of the SOC lasted until 1991. During that period every move of the hierarchs has been carefully watched by the government.[13]

Difficulties in participation in WCC

From 1991-1995, when the civil war broke out in Yugoslavia, political circumstances shaped the policy of the SOC towards WCC.[14] The international community held Serbia responsible for all atrocities in the Yugoslav civil war, which developed anti-Western reactions throughout the country, further complicating the relationship with the WCC.[15] Also, some members of the WCC insisted that the SOC should be expelled from the WCC because of the situation in Yugoslavia.[16] In that period, the Roman Catholic Church acted politically against the unity of Yugoslavia, which only fired up the war.[17] During poverty, war and economic destruction of Serbia during 1991-1999, some Protestant communities took advantage of this terrible situation in Serbia to proselytize directly, weakening the influence of the SOC.[18] Other statements and attacks on the SOC complicated an already difficult position towards Ecumenical dialogue in general. Again, the political situation dictated ecumenical dialogue whether in WCC or in the SOC. The situation became even more complicated after the decisions in 1997 of the Georgian and Bulgarian Orthodox Church to withdraw from WCC. Strong pressure has been brought upon the SOC to follow the decisions of those who withdrew, especially taking into account the difficult relationship between the Western powers and Serbia. In 1997 the

---

[9] Артемије Радосављевић, "Српска црква против екуменизма", *Православље и екуменизам*, (Београд: Хришћански културни центар, 2005), 328.

[10] In 1966 Orthodox churches held *Belgrade Consultations* meeting concerning further dialogue with Anglican and Old Catholic Church : Марко Николић, *Екуменски односи: Српске православне и Римокатоличке 1962-2000. године,* (Београд: Службени гласник, 2011), 75.

[11] Артемије Радосављевић, "Српска црква против екуменизма", *Православље и екуменизам*, (2005), Београд: Хришћански културни центар, 329.

[12] Калезић Д., "Однос СПЦ према екуменизму", *Vrhbosnensia* 4.2, (2000), Сарајево, 228.

[13] Саво Б. Јовић, *Утамничена Црква,* (Београд: Православна реч, 2012); Ivan Bešlić, *Čuvari Jugoslavije: Suradnici UDBE u Bosni i Hercegovini,* (Posušje: Samizdat, 2003)

[14] Before war broke out SOC and Roman Catholic Church in Yugoslavia held several meetings in order to stop the war during 1991, Смиља Аврамов, *Опус Деи: Нови крсташки поход Ватикана,* (Ветерник: Лдиј, 2000), 198.; In Canbera assembly (1991), metropolitan Jovan has been chosen to the Central Committee of the WCC. It was shown that SOC has been well integrated into WCC, Марко Николић, *Екуменски односи: Српске православне и Римокатоличке 1962-2000. године,* (Београд: Службени гласник, 2011), 163.

[15] Владимир Вукашиновић, "Ка новом екуменизму", *Православље и екуменизам,* (Београд: 2005): Хришћански културни центар, 369-379; Different look on Yugoslav crisis: David N. Gibbs, *First Do No Harm: Humanitarian Intervention and the Destruction of Yugoslavia,* (Nashville: Vanderbilt University Press, 2009).

[16] Смиља Аврамов, *Опус Деи: Нови крсташки поход Ватикана* (Ветерник: Лдиј, 2000), 199.

[17] Смиља Аврамов, *Опус Деи: Нови крсташки поход Ватикана* (Ветерник: Лдиј, 2000), 199.

[18] Владимир Вукашиновић, "Ка новом екуменизму", *Православље и екуменизам* (Београд: Хришћански културни центар, 2005), 369-379.

Serbian Orthodox church decided to continue its work in WCC waiting for final decision which should issue Pan-Orthodox forum.[19]

When we discuss nowadays the involvement of the SOC in the work of WCC, we should bear in mind that the SOC is just one of 15 Orthodox autocephalous and autonomous Churches. It needs to accommodate its decisions with Constantinople and, even more, with other Orthodox churches.[20] Also, we should never forget that the difficult political situation between Serbia and most of the Western powers has strong implications on the ecumenical dialogue within the WCC. Some members of the WCC adopted the same campaign against Serbian people in general, imitating the Western mass media.[21] This culminated even more after bombardment of Serbia in 1999, by some of the most developed countries of the West. In 2004 Albanian extremists destroyed more than 50 churches and monasteries, some even more than 600 years old,[22] in the Serbian province Kosovo, in just a few days. Western powers that have been responsible to secure the situation in that area did not do a thing to stop this spiritual genocide over the SOC. A final decision in 2008, when the province Kosovo declared independence from Serbia, made the relationship between Serbia and the majority of Western Powers (which immediately recognized a new state) even more complicated. Taking into account all these political circumstances between Serbia and the West, we can better understand the relationship and problems between the SOC and WCC which many groups equate with the West. This is especially important to bear in mind because the SOC is based in Serbia and the political situation in Serbia affects directly the situation in the SOC.

For these reasons, the SOC has been involved in the work of the WCC, passively sending delegations from time to time to some ecumenical bodies. Disintegration of both countries, Yugoslavia and Serbia, contributed to disappointment in the process of unity on any level. Disintegration of these countries proved the weakness of theology in front of strong political interests. This could be the main reason for the passivism of the SOC in today's dialogue within the WCC. If one country could not remain a unity, how could so many different churches remain a unity? The paradigm of war and disintegration shaped the mentality in the SOC and it will continue to do so in the times to come. To testify to this disinterest and passive protest towards the WCC, we can observe the decisions of the SOC to send a different delegation every year, which does not allow continuity towards the Ecumenical dialogue in the WCC. This can be explained only because of the difficult situation within Serbia, economic and political, but also because of the strong anti-Western sentiments after two decades of conflicts and wars. Because of all the above mentioned problems, ecumenical dialogue led by the SOC in Serbia is much more promising than the one led in the WCC.

New Ecumenical Policy of the SOC

In Serbia, the SOC tries to develop better understanding and communication with other Christian confessions and other religions. In 2006 a theological dialogue between the Roman-Catholic and Orthodox Church was held in Belgrade (Serbia). Patriarch Pavle of the Serbian Orthodox Church accentuated our necessity for unity in his speech.[23] This was one of the many meetings that confirmed the capability of the SOC to work on a dialogue and understanding after many years of political conflicts and wars in Serbia and around it.

---

[19] Decisions of the Holy Synod of the SOC in 1997 and 1999: АСброj 89/зап. 151 (1997); АСброj 12/зап. 56 – (1999). Pan-Orthodox forum has been held 1998 in Thessaloniki, Greece, Марко Николић, Екуменски односи: Српске православне и Римокатоличке 1962-2000. године, (Београд: Службени гласник, 2011), 85-88

[20] Дејан Мачковић, "Свете тајне и еклисиологија у савременом екуменском дијалогу", *Српска теологија данас 2009,* (Београд: ПБФ-ИТИ, 2010), 48.

[21] Смиља Аврамов, *Опус Деи: Нови крсташки поход Ватикана* (Ветерник: Лдиj, 2000), 198.

[22] Savo B. Jovic, *Ethnic Cleansing and Cultural Genocide on Kosovo and Metohija : testimony to the suffering of the Serbian Orthodox Church and Serbian people from 1945 to 2005,* (Belgrade: Informative-publishing house of the Serbian Orthodox Church, 2007).

[23] Радован Биговић, *Православна теологија екуменизма* (Београд: Хришћански културни центар, 2010), 181-183

Part IV: Ecumenical Dialogue in various Orthodox Churches and Settings

The best example of good cooperation between different confessions in Serbia, with positive outcome, has been the initiative of traditional religious groups in Serbia to introduce Religious Education (RE) into Serbian schools in 2001.[24] Fifty years after being canceled, Religious Education has been reestablished in Serbian public schools, allowing traditional communities to have their own confessional teaching. The Serbian Orthodox Church, even though it is the major religious denomination, insisted during the dialogue with the government that all other denominations should have their own RE, respecting diversity and multiculturalism in Serbia.[25] During 2001 traditional religious groups acted together in order to get approval from the government for Religious Education in the schools. The ecumenical atmosphere of the dialogue and cooperation between different churches had a victorious ending for all confessions. The Serbian government decided to reintroduce Religious Education at schools in 2001. That has been a major step towards better understanding the many different religious groups in Serbia. In that sense, Religious Education, even though it is confessional, discovers and examines Christian heritage that is common to Roman Catholics and many protestants that live in Serbia.[26] Also, in its holistic and more comprehensive attitude towards world and life, Religious Education of the Orthodox Church in Serbia is not only compatible to other Christian confessions but also to other religions, providing a solid meeting ground for these differences in a search for a common goal.[27] After more than 10 years of RE in Serbian schools, the SOC is preparing some changes in its curriculum during 2013. The change should achieve two goals: to express and explain ecumenical dimensions of Orthodoxy and, at the same time, to raise tolerant citizens.

After a successful cooperation with other religions to reintroduce RE in Serbia, the SOC initiated a religious body consisting of traditional religious communities in Serbia to have regular meetings in order to foster cooperation and solidarity between themselves. In 2010 an Interreligious council has been constituted, including the SOC, the Roman-Catholics, the Muslims and the Jewish community.[28] All these steps seem to reflect much better policy of the SOC. Instead of understanding Ecumenism as something that comes from the outside (like the WCC) – the Serbian Orthodox Church tries to develop ecumenical dialogue in Serbia. This can provide hope for the future involvement in the WCC, when people in Serbia realize that ecumenical dialogue close to their home gives results from which we all profit – more trust and tolerance between different religious groups.

All these steps have been supported by the Theological Faculty in Belgrade which provided several courses on other confessions and religions: History of Religions, Protestant Theology, Introducing Theology, Roman-Catholic Theology and Ecumenical Theology.[29] Offering these courses at the faculty, the SOC offered a tool to model young generations of the students to cherish different understandings of the world in which they live.

In 2004 Theological Faculty in Belgrade became a part of the University which integrated theological knowledge to other disciplines more effectively and to the society at large. Conferences at the faculty nowadays have more influence than before, radiating throughout the University. The Theological faculty in Belgrade has fruitful cooperation with many different schools and institutions, developing understanding and better knowledge

---

[24] Растко Јовић, "Историјат верске наставе у Србији", *Верска настава у београдским школама* (Београд: ПБФ-ПКИ, 2011), 78-89

[25] In Serbia we have members of SOC 84,5%, Muslims 3,1%, Protestants 0,99%, Roman Catholics 4,97%, Jews 0,008%: Official statistics in Serbia in 2011, www.popis2011.stat.rs

[26] Игнатије Мидић, *Православни катихизис: Приручник за наставнике основних и средњих школа*, , (Београд: Завод за уџбенике и наставна средства, 2003), 20-36

[27] Игнатије Мидић, *Православни катихизис: Приручник за наставнике основних и средњих школа*, , (Београд: Завод за уџбенике и наставна средства, 2003), 6.

[28] Official statement of SOC on the official website of the Serbian Church, http://www.spc.rs/sr/osnovan_medjureligijski_savet_ministarstva_vera_republike_srbije

[29] For these courses (except *History of Religions)* we should be thankful to the late Professor Radovan Bigovic (1956-2012) who introduced them in order to develop ecumenical thinking in young generations of students of theology.

about others.[30] The one that is especially important is the cooperation with the Theological faculty in Zagreb, Croatia. After many years of war and conflict, these two schools overcame a negative political climate in order to develop a better theological and, moreover, Christian witness of cooperation and understanding, being a good example for society at large. What needs to be done in the future is to implement Ecumenical classes in Theological high schools. Many students of the Theological faculty have been educated at Theological high schools. A reform of education at theological high schools is necessary, in order to provide the students with a better understanding of Ecumenism. In the future these students could be more prepared to produce better policy and methods in a dialogue.

Controversy concerning Ecumenism

We should also mention the ones who opposed to the Ecumenical dialogue. The greatest authority that has always been used as an argument against ecumenism in the SOC is Justin Popovic (+1979). A new book with authentic writings of Justin Popovic concerning ecumenism has been published in 2010: *Inscriptions on Ecumenism*.[31] Before that, another one of his books had been published in 1974, regarding the same subject: *Orthodox Church and Ecumenism*.[32] What is obvious in both books is that Justin Popovic is not opposed to ecumenism in general, but against some negative aspects of it.[33] His arguments have been accepted by the Orthodox Church and used in the further dialogue with the WCC in later years.[34] That became more evident after the Canberra Assembly (1991) where the Orthodox churches insisted on theological and not political dialogue.[35] The other Serbian theologian that has been extensively used as an argument against ecumenism within the SOC was Bishop Nikolai Velimirovic[36]. Being an extraordinary person like he was, Velimirovic was much more open-minded than those who misuse and misinterpret him for their own, simple-minded goals. During his life, he studied and lived abroad. Personally, he has been involved in many ecumenical dialogues. In 1954 he was present at the Ecumenical assembly in Evanston.[37] He stated once boldly, "I prayed to God in a Catholic church, in a mosque, in a synagogue and God didn't punish me."[38] These words were obviously pointed to the ones who use Orthodox canons literally in order to avoid dialogue with others. Taking in account both of these theologians of the SOC we can see that they did not criticize Ecumenical dialogue in general. What they essentially criticized is the Orthodox lack of understanding and the aims of Ecumenical meetings, which threaten to become nothing more than "sentimental dialogue of love and pharisaic kindness."[39]

For the last twenty years, the bishop of the SOC in the Serbian province of Kosovo Artemios has been the major representative of anti-Ecumenism. His main idea was to use extensively works of Justin Popovic in his

---

[30] Lateran University from Rome, Theological schools from Germany, Switzerland, France, USA, Russia, Greece and the region.

[31] Свети Ава Јустин, *Записи о екуменизму* (Требиње: Манастир Тврдош, 2010).

[32] Архимандрит Јустин Поповић, *Православна Црква и екуменизам* (Света Гора: Манастир Хиландар, 1974)

[33] Свети Ава Јустин, *Записи о екуменизму* (Требиње: Манастир Тврдош, 2010), 33.

[34] Justin Popovic advised Orthodox Churches in their dialogue in 1976 with very sharp critique of all negative aspects within Orthodox itself. It is obvious that Justin Popovic has been much more open and ecumenical than all of those who used him to justify their lack of understanding, love and energy to have a dialogue with different denominations, cf. Марко Николић, *Екуменски односи: Српске православне и Римокатоличке 1962-2000. године* (Београд: Службени гласник, 2011), 155-158.

[35] Марко Николић, *Екуменски односи: Српске православне и Римокатоличке 1962-2000. године* (Београд: Службени гласник, 2011), 164.

[36] On his idea of ecumenism: Владимир Цветковић, "Перспективе српске теологије у екуменском дијалогу" *Српска теологија данас 2009* (Београд: ПБФ-ИТИ, 2010) 60-61.

[37] Епископ Николај (Велимировић), *Сабрана дела, књига XIII* (Химелстир, 1986), 42-46.

[38] Милан Д. Јанковић, *Епископ Николај – Живот, мисао и дело, Књига II* (Београд, 2002), 843.

[39] Радован Биговић, *Црква и друштво*, (Београд: Хиландарски фонд при Богословском факултету СПЦ, 2000), 165.

own interpretation. Even if Justin was critical to Ecumenism it was in order to make the Church representatives more cautious in the dialogue. On the other hand, bishop Artemios used Justin's works in order to stop the dialogue.[40] In 2010 he was degraded from a bishop to a regular monk and his diocese has been taken away from him. Today he is just one in the midst of those groups that actively advocate against ecumenism and their field of work is mainly on the internet where they collect and consolidate their followers.[41] This is one great paradox of modern times. Traditional believers who want the Church to be more conservative and closed for the outer world, use, at the same time, mainly modern means of communication to gain new supporters.

Future promises

Today we have very different opinions on Ecumenism from bishops, monks and lay persons. And these opinions go from acceptance to complete rejection of any kind of dialogue. [42] The new Patriarch Irineos after his election in 2010 started his efforts to revive ecumenical dialogue. The same year when he was elected, the new Patriarch has been awarded with Pro Oriente award in Vienna, because of his devoted ecumenism. [43] Patriarch Irineos should be praised for changes in the language of the SOC in recent years concerning ecumenism. Even though the political situation is still difficult because of many disintegrative processes in Serbia, the Patriarch is giving new energy and optimism to the dialogue with other confessions. Moreover, in his interview in 2012 he accentuated necessity for deeper ecumenical dialogue giving a new initiative to this process.[44] In his interview to another Serbian magazine he said: "Ecumenism is the desire of all of us to be united by Church and Christianity. Christianity is a religion of Ecumene, with the idea to embrace the whole world. Those who advocate the idea of ecumenism wish from Christianity to be common to all and to be a religion of all Christian Ecumene. We believe in One, Holy, Catholic and Apostolic Church. The idea is that we all belong to one Church, one Christianity and unity in teaching and dogmas. If we accomplish this unity in teaching and dogmas, we'll be united in the everyday life too."[45] In the same interview the Patriarch answered that Ecumenism is an "absolutely real idea, but it is a completely different question whether today's world, in this stage, is capable of accepting this idea. We need to work on it."[46] We should not forget that the SOC is working actively in the Conference of European Churches (CEC). From 2009 the SOC has been represented by two members in the Central Committee of CEC.[47] All these developments represent a good ground for future work.

In 2011, the Ministry of Faith supported interreligious dialogue between Serbia and Indonesia with participation of the SOC.[48] This dialogue incorporated meetings between Christians, Muslims, Hindus and Jews. Again, Serbia and the SOC proved to be good hosts in this type of active Ecumenism. It is planned to continue with this dialogue in the future.

---

[40] Артемије Радосављевић, "Српска црква против екуменизма", *Православље и екуменизам*, (Београд: Хришћански културни центар, 2005) 321-339.

[41] http://www.eparhija-prizren.org/ ; http://www.novinar.de/ ; http://borbazaveru.info/

[42] Cf. Марко Николић, *Екуменски односи: Српске православне и Римокатоличке 1962-2000. године*, (Београд: Службени гласник, 2011), 165-174.

[43] *Православље 1044*, (2010), 2-4; 6-8.

[44] *НИН 3223* (Београд, 2012), 17-22.

[45] DANAS magazine, (2012). http://www.danas.rs/danasrs/drustvo/ekumenizam_je_realna_ideja.55.html?news_id=214173 (last accessed, September 2013).

[46] http://www.danas.rs/danasrs/drustvo/ekumenizam_je_realna_ideja.55.html?news_id=214173 (last accessed, April, 2011)

[47] http://www.ceceurope.org/how-we-work/cec-central-committee-members/ (last accessed September 2013)

[48] Богољуб Шијаковић, "О миру, правди и љубави: Србија и Индонезија у међувјерском дијалогу" : *Огледање у контексту: О знању и вјери, предању и идентитету, цркви и држави*, друго издање, (Београд: Службени гласник, 2011), 104-108

Conclusion

The ambivalent relationship of the SOC towards the WCC and other ecumenical organizations helped pacify those within the SOC who supported radical views against ecumenical movement in general. The moderate and cautious policy of the Holy Synod of the SOC silenced fundamentalist elements within hierarchs and ordinary people. Regular meetings between hierarchs of different confessions do not have the same provocative dimension today like they had before. Visitations of professors from other confessions do not provoke an atmosphere of fear and protest. The Orthodox Church in general and the SOC in particular are still in the process of defining theologically what the WCC is and what the role of the SOC is supposed to be.[49]

The main problem for the SOC and other Orthodox churches in ecumenical dialogue today is lack of some generally acceptable principles, criteria, and methodology in this dialogue. Dialogue has its difficulties but lack of dialogue could be much worse, transforming the SOC into a sect. What we need today is an inter-Orthodox dialogue on ecumenism. Otherwise, if we Orthodox continue the dialogue through diversity and pluralism of opinions on ecumenism itself, we will be more confusing to ourselves and others in the Ecumenical process. The history of the Serbian Orthodox Church gives us hope for a better future. Today's activities of the SOC represent a great pledge for tomorrow, hope for a development of serious theology of ecumenism within WCC and other organizations.

Bibliography

Avramov, Smilja, *Opus Dei: The New Crusade of Vatican* (*Opus Dei Novi krstaški pohod Vatikana),* (Veternik 2000).

Bešlić, Ivan, *Safeguards of Yugoslavia; Associates of the Yugoslav Secret Service in Bosnia and Herzegovina* (*Čuvari Jugoslavije: Suradnici UDBE u Bosni i Hercegovini),* (Posušje, 2003).

Bigović, Radovan, *Church and Society* (*Crkva i društvo),* (Beograd 2000).

Bigović, Radovan, *Church in the Modern Society* (*Crkva u savremenom svetu),* (Beograd 2010).

Bigović, Radovan, (ed.), *Orthodoxy and Ecumenism (Pravoslavlje i ekumenizam)* (Beograd 2005).

Bigović, Radovan, (ed.), *The Orthodox Theology of Ecumenism (Pravoslavna teologija ekumenizma),* (Beograd 2010).

Dimić, Ljubodrag, *Serbs and Yugoslavia (Srbi i Jugoslavija),* (Beograd 1998).

Gibbs, David N., *First Do No Harm: Humanitarian Intervention and the Destruction of Yugoslavia,* (Nashville 2009).

Janković, Milan D., *Bishop Nikolai – Life, Thought and the Work (Episkop Nikolaj – Život, misao i delo, Knjiga II),* (Beograd 2002).

Jović, Rastko, "History of Religious Education in Serbia" ("Istorijat verske nastave u Srbiji", *Verska nastava u beogradskim školama),* (ed.) by Slobodanka Gašić-Pavišić & Ševkušić Slavica, (Beograd 2011), 78-89.

Jovic, Savo B., *Ethnic Cleansing and Cultural Genocide on Kosovo and Metohija : testimony to the suffering of the Serbian orthodox church and Serbian people from 1945 to 2005,* (Belgrade 2007).

Jović, Savo B., *Imprisoned Church (Utamničena Crkva),* (Beograd, 2012).

Kalezić, Dimitrije, "Relationship of the Serbian Orthodox Church towards Ecumenism" ("Odnos SPC prema ekumenizmu"), *Vrhbosnensia* IV/2, (Sarajevo 2000).

Mačković, Dejan, "The Holy Sacraments and Ecclesiology in Current Ecumenical Dialogue" ("Svete tajne i eklisiologija u savremenom ekumenskom dijalogu"), *Srpska teologija danas 2009,* (ed.) by Bogoljub Šijaković, (Beograd 2010), 45-59.

Midić, Ignatije, *The Orthodox Cathecism: Manual for the Teachers in Elementary and High Schools (Pravoslavni katihizis: Priručnik za nastavnike osnovnih i srednjih škola),* (Beograd 2003).

[49] Радован Биговић, *Црква у савременом свету,* (Београд: Службени гласник, 2010) 111-123.

Part IV: Ecumenical Dialogue in various Orthodox Churches and Settings

Nikolić, Marko, *Ecumenical Relations: Serbian Orthodox Church and Roman Catholic Church 1962-2000* (*Ekumenski odnosi: Srpske pravoslavne i Rimokatoličke 1962-2000. Godine),* (Beograd, 2011).

Popović, Justin, *Notes on Ecumenism/ (Zapisi o ekumenizmu),* (Trebinje, 2010).

Popović, Justin, *The Orthodox Church and Ecumenism* (*Pravoslavna Crkva i ekumenizam),* (Sveta Gora, 1974).

Radić, Radmila, *State and Religious Communities 1945-1970* (*Država i verske zajednice 1945-1970, Knjiga II,*) (Beograd, 2002).

Šijaković, Bogoljub, "Concerning Peace, Justice and Love: Serbia and Indonesia in interreligious dialogue" ("O miru, pravdi i ljubavi: Srbija i Indonezija u međuvjerskom dijalogu": *Ogledanje u kontekstu: O znanju i vjeri, predanju i identitetu, crkvi i državi,* drugo izdanje), (Beograd 2011), 104-108.

Velimirović, Nikolaj, *Collected Works XIII* (*Sabrana dela, knjiga XIII),* (Himelstir 1986).

Vladimir Cvetković, "Perspectives of the Serbian Theology in the Ecumenical Dialogue" ("Perspektive srpske teologije u ekumenskom dijalogu", *Srpska teologija danas 2009),* (ed.) by Bogoljub Šijaković, (Beograd, 2010), 60-61.

Vukašinović, Vladimir, "Towards the New Ecumenism" ("Ka novom ekumenizmu", *Pravoslavlje i ekumenizam),* (ed.) by Radovan Bigović, (Beograd 2005), 369-379.

(62) ECUMENICAL DIALOGUE IN THE PERSPECTIVE OF THE ROMANIAN ORTHODOX CHURCH[1]

Fr. Aurel Pavel

Introduction

Teaching Ecumenism within the Faculties of Orthodox Theology in Romania is closely related to the Romanian Orthodox Church's involvement in the ecumenical movement. We can identify three distinct situations: 1) 1920-1948 period, including the years of "stagnation" or "non-involvement", 1948-1961, 2) 1961-1989 Period and 3) From 1990 until today.

1920-1961 Period

The creation of Great Romania in 1918 would be followed by the reorganization of the Romanian Orthodox Church through a new statute written in 1925 (when it was raised to the rank of Patriarchate). Even though the Romanian Orthodox Church did not take part in the Assembly of Edinburgh (1910) it would be involved in the ecumenical movement. Thus, it sent a delegation to the preparatory meeting for the formation of the World Council of Churches, held in Geneva during 9-20 August 1920.[2] It is worth mentioning Romanian participation within the Commission "Faith and Order": a Romanian delegation took part in the first general meeting (3-31 August 1927, in Lausanne).[3]

Reorganization of the Romanian Orthodox Church was accompanied also by the theological education reform. Between 1918-1948 in Romania have functioned three Faculties of Theology (Bucharest, Cernăuți and Chișinău), five Academies in Transylvania and Banat (Sibiu, Cluj, Oradea, Arad and Caransebeș) and more than ten seminars,[4] all in the "old Romania".

The ecumenical relevance of teaching the theological subjects in these Romanian educational institutions was null. On the contrary, the Orthodox theology that was taught in them was a strictly confessional one. In the field of missionary Theology, Vasile Ispir[5] and Petru Deheleanu[6] have imposed themselves. Their work

---

[1] The present paper explores the ecumenical involvement of the Romanian Orthodox Church according to its relevance in the Faculties of Orthodox Theology in Romania. As a case study the author has chosen "Andrei Saguna" Faculty of Theology in Sibiu (ed.).

[2] To this delegation took part Prof. Ph.D Dragomir Demetrescu and Fr. Ph.D Gheorghe Rădulescu from Constanța. See P.I. David, *Ecumenismul, factor de stabilitate în lumea de astăzi (Ecumenical Movement, Stabilizing Factor in Today's World)*, (Bucharest: Gnosis Publishing, 1998), 57-58; Niculae I. Șerbănescu, *Biserica Ortodoxă Română și mișcarea ecumenică (Romanian Orthodox Church and the Ecumenical Movement)*, Ortodoxia (Orthodoxy), 1-2 (1962): 122.

[3] Consisting of Fr. Prof. Ph.D Grigorie Cristescu and Prof. Ph.D Nicolae Colan, both from the Theological Academy in Sibiu, and Fr. Trandafir Scorobeț, counselor at the Metropolitan of Transylvania. On the fifth day of the conference Nectarie Cotlarciuc, Metropolitan of Bucovina, also arrived. See Iuliu Scriban, "Românii, la Congresul creștinesc de la Lausanne (The Romanians at the Christian Congress in Lausanne)", in *Biserica Ortodoxă Română (Romanian Orthodox Church)*, 8 (1927): 497.

[4] Mircea Păcurariu, *Biserica Ortodoxă Română în secolul XX (Romanian Orthodox Church in the Twentieth Century)*, in Christine Chaillot (coord.), *Biserica Ortodoxă din Europa de Est în secolul XX (Orthodox Church in Eastern Europe in the Twentieth Century)*, translation into Romanian by Liliana Donose Samuelsson, (Bucharest: Humanitas Publishing, 2011), 183.

[5] Vasile Ispir, *Sectele religioase din România (Religious Cults in Romania)*, (Arad, 1928); *Idem, Curs de îndrumări misionare (Missionary Guidance Course)*, (Bucharest, 1929).

[6] Petre Deheleanu, *Sectologie (Sectology)*, (Arad, 1948).

mainly focused on the "internal" mission of the Orthodox Church. The main purpose of their writings was to fight against the sects that began to penetrate into and consolidate all over Romania. We should mention that, in combating these new sects, the call was made not only on biblical and theological arguments, but also on arguments of national order, the new religious movements being seen not only as a threat to the true Church of Christ, the Orthodox one, but also as a threat to the preservation of the Romanian national unity (the motivation being their allogeneic origin as well as the external support enjoyed by the representatives of these sects).[7]

The Communist regime in Romania has produced profound changes at a socio-economic and theological level. In August 1948 the new Law on Religions came into force. According to it, in Romania were recognized 14 religious denominations. The Law also stipulated the right of the State to supervise and control all these religious denominations. The State had some "special delegates" to mediate between the religious denominations and the State. In fact, their role was to achieve permanent control over all religious life in Romania. Also, in August 1948 a new Law on Education came into force. This provided for an education exclusively secular and public. The study of religion was forbidden in the schools of all grades and the high schools of some religious groups passed under the Ministry of Education. At the same time were closed the Faculty of Theology of Cernăuți (transferred meantime to Suceava), four theological academies in Transylvania and all the theological seminaries in "Old Romania".

Restriction of activity of Romanian Orthodox Church by the new atheist communist state authorities was made on several fronts, and followed the line imposed by the Soviet State on the Russian Orthodox Church. At the ecumenical level, it should be noted that the Romanian Orthodox Church, like all the other Orthodox Churches of so-called "socialist countries" could not be present at the general assembly in Amsterdam (1948) due to directives from Moscow. Under the sphere of influence of the Soviet Union, the Romanian Orthodox Church has not taken part for more than a decade in any ecumenical assembly. Despite these restrictive measures the ecumenical efforts did not miss. At a strictly theoretical level they have resulted in "The Handbook of Dogmatic and Symbolic Theology", in which were critically discussed the major Christian denominational families. On this basis the ecumenical theology could be later built, and through it the Romanian theology was singled out positively between other Orthodox Churches.

In practice, especially in Transylvania, the so-called "local practical ecumenism" continued to progress, being the living source of the ecumenical theology about which we talked.

1961-1989 Period

A change could occur only after 1958, when the Romanian Communist authorities have adopted a line of national autonomy (un-Sovietisation). Thus, at the third general assembly of the World Council of Churches in New Delhi (19 November to 5 December 1961), were received as members also the Orthodox churches from the "socialist camp" that had not joined in 1948; among them the Romanian Orthodox Church. Starting this year the ecumenical contacts locally and internationally are intensified. Locally, under the watchful eye of the communist authorities, Romania has developed an "ecumenism under the cross"

---

[7] Another name worth to be mentioned here is that of Bishop Grigorie Comșa (1889-1935). In the interwar period he carried out an intense publishing activity antisectarian, regarded mainly against the Baptists and Adventists. He also tried to revive the "apostolate of the laity", as the main defensive measure against these sects' offensive. Among his works we mention: *Pentru neam și lege. Patruzeci de cuvântări împotriva baptiștilor și adventiștilor (For the Nation and Law. Forty Speeches against the Baptists and Adventists)*, (Caransebeș, 1923); *Combaterea catehismului baptiștilor (Combating the Baptist Catechism)*, (Arad, 1926); *Lucrarea diavolească a adventiștilor (The Devilish Work of Adventists)*, (Arad, 1929), *Zece ani de luptă împotriva baptiștilor (Ten Years of Fighting against the Baptist)*, (Arad, 1930); *Apostolatul laic (The Apostolate of the Laity)*, (Arad, 1933); *Biserica misionară (The Missionary Church)*, (Arad, 1928).

the successor of the local practical ecumenism remembered above, through meetings between the heads of the religious denominations and interdenominational theological conferences between the Orthodox, Roman Catholic and Protestant institutes, with the participation of bishops and teachers of the religious denominations. Externally, it must be said that the Romanian Orthodox Church sent representatives to the various ecumenical organizations of the time, such as the Christian Peace Conference, WCC and CEC. Some representatives of the two Theological Institutes from Bucharest and Sibiu played a significant role in the activity of these organisms (Milan Pavel Şesan in the CPC, Ion Bria in the WCC, and Dumitru Popescu in the CEC). In addition it should be noted that most teachers, especially those in the Bible, historical and systematic sections have been engaged in various bilateral and multilateral ecumenical dialogues in which the Romanian Orthodox Church took part. For example, we can mention in this sense Fr. Prof. Ioan Ică senior, Fr. Prof. Ilie Moldovan and lecturer Dorin Oancea, members of the ROC Commission of dialogue with the Evangelical Churches in Germany who took part in its committees – *Faith and Order*, *Life and Work* and *Mission and Evangelism*. Also, the Romanian Orthodox Church attended, through its representatives, all the general meetings of the Conference of European Churches. In this context it should be noted that the outstanding graduates of the Theological Institute from Bucharest and Sibiu were sent to study trainings abroad, which contributed decisively to their ecumenical profiling. We may mention in this context Dumitru Popescu, Dumitru Radu, Ion Bria, Remus Rus, Dumitru Abrudan, Constantin Voicu, Daniel Ciobotea, the current Patriarch of Romania, Nifon Mihăiţă, Casian Crăciun, Viorel Ioniţă, and Aurel Jivi, to mention only those who have left their mark on the ecumenical profile of the theological education of ROC. During this period in particular, the theological substantiation of the new ecumenical orientation provided by the professors from the two Theological Institutes was important. It has also resulted in new approaches of the entire problem within each discipline separately, allowing the assimilation of the ecumenical idea by the graduates that represent today the vast majority of priests in Romania. Significant in this regard were the efforts of the professors from Bucharest Liviu Stan, Emilian Vasilescu, Dumitru Stăniloae and those of their disciples.

Unfortunately, this intensification of the ecumenical contacts and of the theological grounding of ecumenism did not have a corresponding curriculum and did not reflect enough within the two Theological Institutes from Bucharest and Sibiu to have functioned. Here prevails, along with the sectology – a method that continues the style of the communist era – the method of doctrinal-confessional teaching. References on the ecumenical activity of the Orthodox churches, in general, and of the Romanian Orthodox Church, particularly, were made in the Department of Missionary guidance. In Bucharest should be mentioned, particularly, the name of Arch. Prof. Ph.D Peter David (1938-2003).[8]

The major difficulty that has been a problem for the world ecumenical efforts, including our country, is the actual reception of the ecumenical dialogue results at the level of hierarchy and of the believers. In our case, even if in the magazines – the ones that had not been destroyed by the communists – were presented the results of the Orthodox participation to the international ecumenical meetings, they were not received at the level of the hierarchy and of the believers, and mostly, not even at the level of the theologians who used to teach in Bucharest and Sibiu. In this respect should be mentioned here the manual of "Missionary Guidelines" conducted by a group of professors from the University Theological Institute in Bucharest, coordinated by Fr. Prof. Ph.D Dumitru Radu. This manual is written as though the Romanian Orthodox Church would have been totally cut off from the other churches and Christian denominations.

---

[8] Bio-bibliography for Mircea Păcurariu, *Dicţionarul teologilor români (Dictionary of the Romanian Theologians)*, 2nd Edition, (Bucharest, 2002), 151-152. P.I. David followed in the period before 1989 the sectarian line. See the work *Călăuză creştină pentru cunoaşterea şi apărarea dreptei credinţe în faţa prozelitismului sectar (Guide for Understanding and Defending the Christian Orthodox Faith against Sectarian Proselytism)*, Arad, 1987. Over the time he was even more opened to other Christian denominations. We mention in this regard the work: *Ecumenismul, factor de stabilitate în lumea de astăzi (Ecumenical Movement, Stabilizing Factor in Today's World)*, (Bucharest, 1998).

Part IV: Ecumenical Dialogue in various Orthodox Churches and Settings

The Years after 1989

The fall of communism led by Nicolae Ceauşescu in December 1989 brought significant changes to the life of the Romanian Orthodox Church. These changes had repercussions in the ecumenical relations both internally and externally. Thus, after 1990, our country's ecumenical relations have been driven through the creation of the *Ecumenical Association of Churches in Romania* (AIDRom), which includes the Romanian Orthodox Church, the Evangelical Church – Sibiu, the Lutheran Church CA, the Reformed Church, and the Armenian Apostolic Church. Another manifestation of the local ecumenism in Romania is the Interdenominational Bible Society. It was established in May 1992 and it consists of twelve church-confessions. The main activity of this society is spreading the word of God in schools, prisons, homes for the elderly or orphans, and implementation of a translation of the Bible accepted by all members.

Externally this local ecumenism was complemented by the further participation in the existing ecumenical dialogues and meetings organized by the World Council of Churches and the Conference of European Churches. Thus, at pan-Orthodox level, Prof. Ph.D Viorel Ioniţă became a permanent member of the Commission for dialogue with the Lutheran Churches, Arch. Prof. Ph.D Ioan Ică jr. with the Catholic Church and Arch. Prof. Ph.D Dorin Oancea with the World Reformed Alliance, including as Orthodox secretary of the Joint Commission. We mention here a simple example: the important contribution of Romanian Orthodoxy to the document Charta Oecumenica. A particularly significant expression, of the share that the ecumenical concerns of the Romanian theological education have, represents the organizing of the Third General Assembly of European Churches in 2007 in Sibiu, with the active support of the Theological Faculty from this town, known internationally for its ecumenical commitment.

After 1990 the number of Orthodox Theology Faculties increased and the discipline *Misiology and Ecumenism* is being taught also. Here are the professors that are currently teching at the most important Orthodox theological faculties in Romania and their main works, with ecumenical character: Faculty of Orthodox Theology "Patriarch Justinian", from the University of Bucharest: Fr. Lect. Ph.D David Pestroiu[9] and Fr. Lect. Radu Petre Mureşan[10]; Faculty of Orthodox Theology "Dumitru Stăniloae", from the "Al. I. Cuza" University of Iaşi: Fr. Prof. Ph.D Petraru Gheorghe[11]; Faculty of Orthodox Theology from "Babeş Bolyai" University of Cluj-Napoca: Fr. Prof. Ph.D Valer Bel[12] and Fr. Asist. Ph.D Cristian Sonea[13]; Faculty of Orthodox Theology

---

[9] *Martorii lui Iehova – sunt ei creştini? (Jehovah's Witnesses – Are They Christians?)*, in the collection *Călăuză ortodoxă (Orthodox Guide)*, România creştină Publishing, Bucharest, 1999.; *Ortodoxia în faţa prozelitismului Martorilor lui Iehova (Orthodoxy against Proselytism of Jehovah's Witnesses)*, (Bucharest: Insei Print Publishing, 2005).

[10] *Alternative spirituale în România (Spiritual Alternatives in Romania)*, (Sibiu: Agnos Publishing, 2011); *Stilismul în România (Old Style Church in Romania)*, (Sibiu: Agnos Publishing, 2012); *Atitudinea Bisericilor Tradiţionale Europene faţă de prozelitismul advent (The Attitude of the Traditional European Churches towards the Advent Proselytism)*, (Alexandria: Cartea Ortodoxă Publishing, 2012).

[11] *Ortodoxie şi prozelitism (Orthodoxy and Proselytism)*, (Iaşi: Trinitas Publishing, 2000); *Lumea, creaţia lui Dumnezeu. Perspective biblice, teologico-patristice şi ştiinţifice (World, God's Creation. Biblical, Theological-Patristic and Scientific Perspectives)*, (Iaşi: Trinitas Publishing, 2002); *Misiologie ortodoxă. I. Revelaţia lui Dumnezeu şi misiunea Bisericii (Orthodox Missiology. I. Revelation of God and the Church's Mission)*, (Iaşi: Panfilius Publishing, 2002); *Teologie Fundamentală şi Misionară. Ecumenism (Fundamental and Missionary Theology. Ecumenism)*, (Iaşi: Performantica Publishing, 2006); *Secte neoprotestante şi noi mişcări religioase în România (Evangelical Sects and New Religious Movements in Romania)*, (Iaşi: Vasiliana Publishing, 2006); *"Mergând, învăţaţi toate naţiile..." Aspecte din istoria misiunii creştine ("Going, teach all nations..." Aspects of the History of the Christian Mission)*, (Iaşi: St. Mina Publishing, 2012).

[12] *Misiune, parohie, pastoraţie (Mission, Parish, Ministry)*, Bartolomeu Anania (ed.) (Cluj-Napoca, Renaşterea Publishing, 2006); *Iisus Hristos, Fiul lui Dumnezeu şi Mântuitorul lumii (Jesus Christ, Son of God and Savior of the World)*, (Cluj-Napoca: Renaşterea Publishing, 2007); *Teologie şi biserică (Theology and Church)*, Andrei Marga (ed.) (Cluj-Napoca: Cluj Universitarian Press Publishing, 2008).

[13] Sonea Cristian-Sebastian (in collaboration with Chirilă Ioan and Iloaie Ştefan), *Omul în perspectiva întâlnirii cruciforme dintre verticala transcendentului şi orizontala imanentului. Repere de antropologie creştin-ortodoxă (Man in the Perspec-*

from "Aurel Vlaicu" University of Arad: Fr. Prof. Ph.D Tulcan Ioan[14] and Conf. Ph.D Cristinel Ioja[15]; Faculty of Orthodox Theology "Bishop Ph.D Vasile Coman" from the University of Oradea: Fr. Prof. Ph.D Nicu Dumitraşcu[16]; Faculty of Orthodox Theology from the University of Craiova: Lect. Ph.D Gelu Călin[17]; Faculty of Orthodox Theology from the "Ovidius" University of Constanța: Fr. Prof. Ph.D Gheorghe Istodor[18] and Fr. Asist. Ph.D Cosmin Ciocan; Faculty of Orthodox Theology from "1 decembrie 1918" Universității of Alba Iulia: Fr. Prof. Ph.D Mihai Himcinschi[19]; Faculty of Orthodox Theology from the "Valahia" University of Târgoviște: H.E. Nifon Mihăiță.[20]

tive of the Cruciform Meeting between the Vertical of the Transcendence and Horizontal of the Immanence. Highlights of Orthodox Christian Anthropology), in *Repere patristice în raportul dintre ştiinţă şi teologie (Patristic Highlights in the Relationship between Science and Theology)*, (Bucharest: Basilica Publishing, 2009) (chapter pp. 331-391).

[14] *Teologia. Ştiinţa mărturisitoare despre Dumnezeu (Theology. The Science Confessing About God)*, (Sibiu: Oastea Domnului Publishing, 2009).

[15] *Elemente de istorie, doctrină şi practică misionară: o perspectivă ecumenică (Elements of Missionary History, Doctrine and Practice: an Ecumenical Perspective)* (co-author), "Lucian Blaga" (Sibiu: University Publishing, 2006); *Raţiune şi mistică în Teologia Ortodoxă (Rationality and Mystical Orthodox Theology)* (doctoral thesis), (Arad: "Aurel Vlaicu" University Publishing, 2008); *Homo adorans. Între Iisus Hristos şi politeismul lumii contemporane (Homo adorans. Between Jesus Christ and the Polytheism of the Contemporary World)*, (Arad: "Aurel Vlaicu" University Publishing, 2008); *Cosmologie şi soteriologie în gândirea Părinţilor Răsăriteni (Cosmology and Soteriology in the Thought of the Eastern Fathers)*, (Arad: "Aurel Vlaicu" University Publishing, 2008); *Dogmatică şi dogmatişti. Prolegomena privind aprofundarea Teologiei Dogmatice Ortodoxe Române în a doua jumătate a secolului al XX-lea şi începutul secolului al XXI-lea (Dogmatics and Dogmatists. Prolegomena on the the Deepening Romanian Orthodox Dogmatic Theology in the Second half of the Twentieth Century and Early Twenty-First Century)*, (Timişoara: Marineasa Publishing).

[16] *The Mission of the Romanian Orthodox Church and its Challenges*, (Cluj-Napoca: Napoca-Star Publishing, 2002); *Cele Şapte Personalităţi de la Niceea (325), rolul lor în cadrul primelor frământări ecumenice majore ale lumii creştine (The Seven Celebrities of Nicaea (325), Their Role in the First Major Ecumenical Unrests of the Christian World)*, (Cluj-Napoca: Napoca Star Publishing, 2001), 239 pages, reprinted in 2004; *Hristologia Sfântului Atanasie cel Mare, în contextul controverselor ariene şi post-ariene (Christology of Saint Athanasius the Great, in the Context of Arian and Post-Arian Controversies)*, (Cluj-Napoca: Napoca Star Publishing, 1999).

[17] *Teologie şi ştiinţe naturale (Theology and Natural Sciences)*, (co-author), (Craiova: Metropolitan of Oltenia Publishing, 2002); *Science and Theology in dialogue*, (co-author), (Craiova: Universitaria Publishing, 2006) *Relaţia dintre Biserică şi stat privită interconfesional (The Relationship between Church and State from an Interreligious Point of View)*, (Craiova: Universitaria Publishing, 2008) (doctoral thesis).

[18] *M.I.S.A. si Yoga în lumina Ortodoxiei (M.I.S.A. and Yoga in the Light of Orthodoxy)*, 1st Edition, (Constanţa: Archdiocese of Tomis Publishing, 2005); *M.I.S.A. si Yoga în lumina Ortodoxiei (M.I.S.A. and Yoga in the Light of Orthodoxy)*, 2nd Edition, (Bucureşti: Sigma Publishing, 2006); *Iubirea creştină şi provocările contemporane – perspective misionare (Christian Love and Contemporary Challenges - Missionary Perspectives)*, 1st Edition, (Bucureşti: Sigma Publishing, 2006); *Iubirea creştină şi provocările contemporane (Christian Love and Contemporary Challenges – Missionary Perspectives)*, 2nd Edition, (Bucureşti: Sigma Publishing, 2006); *Misiunea creştină ca activitate permanentă şi practică a Bisericii (Christian Mission as Permanent and Practical Activity of the Church)*, (Bucureşti: Sigma Publishing, 2006).

[19] *Misiune şi dialog. Ontologia misionară a Bisericii din perspectiva dialogului interreligios (Mission and Dialogue. The Missionary Ontology of the Church from the Perspective of Interreligious Dialogue)*, (Alba Iulia: Reîntregirea Publishing, 2003); *Doctrina trinitară ca fundament misionar. Relaţia Duhului Sfânt cu Tatăl şi cu Fiul în teologia răsăriteană şi apuseană. Implicaţiile doctrinare şi spirituale ale acesteia (Trinitarian Doctrine as missionary basis. The Relationship of the Holy Spirit with the Father and the Son in the Eastern and Western Theology. Its Doctrinal and Spiritual Implications)*, (Alba Iulia: Reîntregirea Publishing, 2004); *Biserica în societate. Aspecte misionare ale Bisericii în societatea contemporană (Church in Society. Missionary Aspects of the Church in the Contemporary Society)*, (Alba Iulia: Reîntregirea Publishing, 2006); *Misionarismul vieţii ecleziale (The Missionarism of Ecclesial Life)*, (Alba Iulia: Reîntregirea, 2008); *Testimony and Dialogue. Missionary Aspects in Today's Society*, (Alba Iulia: Reîntregirea Publishing, 2008); *Violenţa – o analiză misionară şi teologică (Violence – A Missionary and Theological Analysis)*, (Alba Iulia: Reîntregirea Publishing, 2010).

[20] *Ortodoxie şi Ecumenism (Orthodoxy and Ecumenism)*, (Bucharest: Agora Publishing, 2000); *Misiune şi Viaţă (Mission and Life)*, (Bucharest: ASA Publishing, 2001); *Misiologie Creştină (Christian Misiology)*, (Bucharest: ASA Publishing,

Part IV: Ecumenical Dialogue in various Orthodox Churches and Settings

Information with ecumenical character is transmitted to students are not only in the Department of *Misiology and Ecumenism*. As in the previous period, professors from other academic disciplines (Universal Church History, Dogmatics etc.), especially those involved in the bilateral dialogues or in the World Council of Churches' committees write ecumenical books and studies. Sometimes there may be a discrepancy between how professors of Misiology that keep the "traditional" line of presentation and control of certain sects, even if some of them are members of the Council, and the more tolerant position adopted by the professors of other theological disciplines. We cannot reproduce here an exhaustive list of works and studies with ecumenical character published by the professors working at the Faculties of Orthodox Theology in Romania. Therefore, in the last part of our study we will use as a case study the "Andrei Saguna" Faculty of Theology from Sibiu. We mention that the above statements are illustrated by the specificity of this Romanian superior traditional theological institution.

Case Study: "Andrei Şaguna" Faculty of Orthodox Theology from Sibiu

Established as a "clerical school" in 1786, "Andrei Saguna" Faculty of Theology from Sibiu has functioned ever since then under different names and with different degrees of academic success (Institute, Academy or Faculty). It has a long ecumenical tradition, situated in a Transylvanian town in which have coexisted always a wide variety of ethnic and religious groups. This has left its mark also on the training of teachers and students in the Faculty of Orthodox Theology. The rapprochement between the Christian denominations was also possible due to the ecumenical partnerships which the Faculty has had. An eloquent example is the close cooperation with the Faculty of Lutheran Theology from Sibiu (now a Department of the "Lucian Blaga" University from Sibiu). In this context it should be noted the important organizational role played during the Third General Assembly of Christians in Europe, action that took place with the hierarchical blessing of H.E. Laurenţiu Streza,[21] both as Metropolitan of Transylvania and as Professor of Theology. Here should be also mentioned the 2004 General Assembly of *Societas Oecumenica* organization, an ecumenical reflection organization of theologians from all around the world. With regard to the ecumenical work of the teaching staff, one can say that it continued the previous ecumenical orientation, given a new freedom of expression and exercise. We highlight first of all that one of the professors of the faculty, Aurel Jivi, was elected in the Central Committee of WCC, where he served precisely while defining a new profile of Orthodox participation in the ecumenical movement. He was, until his premature death, the representative of ROC in the pan-Orthodox commission with the Reformed World Alliance, including as Orthodox secretary of the commission, the two functions were taken over later by Arch. Prof. Dorin Oancea. Also, other faculty members are involved in the work of international ecumenical organizations. Thus Fr. Ass. Prof. Ph.D Nicolae Moşoiu is a member of the commission for mission of WCC and lecturer Alina Pătru is part of the the Central Committee of CEC.

Regarding ecumenical dialogues, we mention especially fathers/professors Dorin Oancea and Ioan Ică jr. The first has worked for a long time as a member of the dialogue commission of ROC with the Evangelical Churches in Germany, and continues to be the Orthodox secretary of the commission of dialogue between the Orthodox Churches and the Reformed World Alliance (now World Communion of Reformed Churches).

2005); *Profetul Miheia: Introducere, traducere şi comentariu (Prophet Micah: Introduction, Translation and Commentary)*, (Bucharest: ASA Publishing, 2000); *The Orthodox Church and Ecumenical Movement"*, (in English), (Bucharest: ASA Publishing, 2002) (includes studies, conferences and theological meditations).

[21] Thus continues a tradition of active involvement of the Transylvanian hierarchs from Sibiu in the interchristian dialogue. We mention here especially the Metropolitan Nicolae Bălan, whose ecumenical considerations – see the works Regarding the Unification of the Churches (1909) or Regarding the Reunification of the Churches (1912) – remain valid to this day. See Dorin Oancea, *Ecumenismul în gândirea teologică transilvăneană (The Ecumenical Movement in the Theological Transylvanian Thinking)*, in *Contribuţii transilvănene la teologia ortodoxă (Transylvanian Contributions to the Orthodox Theology)*, (Sibiu, 1988), 344. Also Metropolitan Antonie Plămădeală was a prominent member of the World Council of Churches.

After 1990, a milestone in strengthening the ecumenical dimension of theological study from Sibiu was the appointment of Fr. Professor Ion Bria on the position of associate professor of the Faculty. He had benefited from a large experience in the ecumenical movement (remember that in July 1968 he was elected member in The Board of the Bossey Ecumenical Institute, and from 7 April 1973 he was appointed executive secretary of the committee "Mission and Evangelism"). To the numerous papers and studies with ecumenical character published that far,[22] Fr. Bria has added a special course of Dogmatics with declared ecumenical valences.[23] For the first time the students of a Faculty of Orthodox Theology in Romania had the opportunity to study not only the main dogmas of the Orthodox Church, but also to make an overview of the history and place of Orthodoxy in the ecumenical movement. In the last part of the Treaty was a presentation of the religious configuration of Christianity: Roman Catholicism, Old Catholic, Anglican, Protestant, evangelical movement, Pentecostalism, Unitarianism and sectarian organizations. Then it was shown the place of Orthodoxy in the ecumenical community: una sancta Catolica, then it was gave a history of the ecumenical movement and the Orthodox participation within it. Perhaps the most interesting aspects aimed at the seven ecclesiological thesis with ecumenical implications,[24] that need to be taken into account in order to achieve full unity (Eucharistic) from an Orthodox point of view. Finally, the last part of the ecumenical Section of the Treaty presents ecumenism in the Romanian Theology, focusing on the ecumenical relevance of the most important Romanian theologian of the twentieth century, Father Dumitru Stăniloae (1903-1993).

In our opinion, we can talk about a Stăniloae-Bria "legacy" at the Faculty of Orthodox Theology from Sibiu. This was taken over and assumed by the current teaching staff of this Faculty. I became Head of the Department of Misiology and ecumenism in 2001. I set out in the curriculum for students from the fourth year, last semester, certain topics pertaining to ecumenism. The course structure is as follows:

- Ecumenical Theology. Introduction;
- Origin and Development of the Ecumenical Movement;
- World Council of Churches: Structure and Organization;
- The General Assemblies of the World Council;
- Conference of European Churches: Structure and Organization;
- Nowadays Religious Configuration of Christianity;
- The Place of Orthodoxy in the Ecumenical Community;
- Dogmatic Aspects of the Union of the Churches;
- Coordinates of Ecumenism from an Orthodox Point of View;
- The Romanian Orthodox Church and Nowadays Ecumenism;
- Coordinates of Ecumenical Theology in the Context of Postmodernity;
- Theological and Ecumenical Interfaith Dialogue;
- The Ecumenical Movement in the Twenty-first Century: Disappointments and New Opportunities;
- Anti-Ecumenical Positions;
- Interfaith Dialogue.

---

[22] Among his works we mention the volume *Martyria Mission. The withness of the orthodox churches today*, (Geneve: 1980), *Destinul ortodoxiei (The Destiny of Orthodoxy)*, (Bucharest: 1989), *Ortodoxia în Europa. Locul spiritualității române (Orthodoxy in Europe. The Place of Romanian Spirituality)*, (Iași: 1995) or *Liturghia după Liturghie (The Liturgy after Liturgy)*, (Bucharest: 1996). For bio-bibliographical data see Nicolae Moșoiu (coord.), *Relevanța operei părintelui profesor Ion Bria pentru viața bisericească și socială actuală (The Relevance of the Work of Fr. Prof. Ion Bria for the Today's Religious and Social Life)*, (Sibiu: "Lucian Blaga" University Publishing, 2010), 9-30.

[23] We are talking about a *Curs de Teologie Dogmatică și Ecumenică (Dogmatic and Ecumenical Theology Course)*, (Sibiu, 1996), reprinted as *Tratat de Teologie Dogmatică și Ecumenică (Treaty of Dogmatic and Ecumenical Theology)*, (Bucharest, 1999), respectively (Sibiu, 2009), in two volumes.

[24] These are: the vision of visible, historical unity; vestigia ecclesiae; "the limits" of the Church; the economy as ecumenical typology; reception of the theological convergences resulting from the ecumenical dialogue; the Uniatism; use of "Byzantine Rite".

Part IV: Ecumenical Dialogue in various Orthodox Churches and Settings

Also for the students to form their critical opinion on the pro- and anti-ecumenical Orthodox perspective I wrote together with the assistant at the Systematic section, Cyprian Julian Toroczkai, a book[25] in which we illustrate the two positions: on the one hand, the involvement in the ecumenical dialogue and supporting this involvement on a theological basis, in the works of two of the most important theologians of the twentieth century, Georges Florovsky and Dumitru Stăniloae and, on the other hand, the critical voices who have declared ecumenism as the "pan-heresy of the twentieth century" and repeatedly called out for the Orthodox churches from the World Council of Churches: Justin Popovich and Mount Athos.

The traditional collaboration of the Faculty of Orthodox Theology with the Institute (now Department) of Protestant Theology was strengthened by establishing within the "Lucian Blaga" University of an *Ecumenical Research Center* (in 2005). Also, within the Ecumenical Research Center there is a series of works of the same nature[26].

The teaching staff from the Faculty of Orthodox Theology of Sibiu, as well as those from other Orthodox Faculties of Theology in Romania, together with the students get the chance to study and deepen the main ecumenical documents as well as the possibilities of developing an ecumenical ethos in educational institutions through meetings organized in Sibiu.[27] Finally, the same collaboration is evident in printing of some papers presenting elements of missionary history, doctrine and practice.[28] Finally, it should be noted that the most deserving students of the Faculty benefit each year from study scholarships abroad: Germany, Switzerland, France etc.

---

[25] Aurel Pavel, Ciprian Iulian Toroczkai, *Adevăratul şi falsul ecumenism. Perspective ortodoxe privind dialogul dintre creştini (True and False Ecumenism. Orthodox Perspectives on the Dialogue Between Christians)*, (Sibiu: "Lucian Blaga" University Publishing, 2010).

[26] Under the name of *Documenta Oecumenica*, ERC began publishing a collection of translations. The first volume of this collection opens the series of documents of theological dialogue between the Romanian Orthodox Church and the Evangelical Church in Germany; *Sfânta Scriptură şi Tradiţia Apostolică în mărturisirea Bisericii (Holy Scripture and the Apostolic Tradition in the Confession of the Church)*, (Sibiu: "Lucian Blaga" University Publishing, 2007) and *Sfintele Taine ale Bisericii în Confessio Augustana si Mărturisirile de credinţă ortodoxe din secolele XVI-XVII (Holy Sacraments of the Church in Confessio Augustana and the Orthodox Confessions of the Sixteenth and Seventeenth Centuries)*, (Sibiu: "Lucian Blaga" University Publishing, 2009).

The series *Studia Oecumenica* contains studies on different ecumenical themes. So far six volumes have appeared in this series. These are: Ciprian Burlăcioiu, *Consens şi disensiune în teologia protestantă contemporană. Concordia de la Leuenberg şi Acordul bisericesc Meissen (Consensus and Dissent in the Contemporary Protestant Theology. Concordia from Leuenberg and the Meissen Ecclesiastical Agreement)*, (Sibiu: "Lucian Blaga" University Publishing, 2008); Ion Bria, *Sensul tradiţiei ecumenice. Mărturia si viziunea ecumenică a Bisericii Ortodoxe (The Meaning of the Ecumenical Tradition. The Ecumenical Testimony and Vision of the Orthodox Church)*, (Sibiu: "Lucian Blaga" University Publishing, 2008); Daniel Benga, *Identităţi creştine europene în dialog. De la mişcarea husită la ecumenismul contemporan (European Christian Identities in Dialogue. From the Hussite Movement to the Contemporary Ecumenism)*, (Hermannstadt: "Lucian Blaga" University Publishing); Christoph Klein, *Spovedania in Biserica Evanghelica Saseasca din Transilvania (Confession in the Saxon Evangelical Church from Transylvania)*, (Sibiu: "Lucian Blaga" University Publishing); Cosmin D. Pricop, *Dialogul Bisericilor Ortodoxe cu Federatia Luterana Mondiala, vol. I (The Dialogue of the Orthodox Churches with the Lutheran World Federation, I^st Volume)*, (Sibiu: "Lucian Blaga" University Publishing); Cosmin D. Pricop, *Dialogul Bisericilor Ortodoxe cu Federatia Luterana Mondiala, vol. II (The Dialogue of the Orthodox Churches with the Lutheran World Federation, IInd Volume)*, (Sibiu: "Lucian Blaga" University Publishing); I. A. Tudorie, *De la Reformă la unitatea vizibilă deplină: dialogul teologic dintre anglicani şi luterani (From the Reform to the Full Visible Unity: Theological Dialogue between Anglicans and Lutherans)*, (Sibiu: "Lucian Blaga" University Publishing).

[27] "Ethosul ecumenic în învăţământul teologic din România, Sibiu, 19-20 septembrie 2011" *(The Ecumenical Ethos in the Theological Educational System from Romania, Sibiu, September 19 to 20, 2011)*, in *Revista Ecumenică (The Ecumenical Review)*, Sibiu, 1 (2012): 105-108.

[28] Nicolae Moşoiu (coord.), *Elemente de istorie, doctrină şi practică misionară: o perspectivă ecumenică (Elements of History, Doctrine and Missionary Practice: An Ecumenical Perspective)*, (Sibiu: "Lucian Blaga" University Publishing, 2006).

Final Considerations

The Romanian Orthodox Church, in general, and the Faculty of Orthodox Theology from Sibiu, in particular, are heavily involved in the ecumenical movement. The Transylvanian Theological Educational system through the very historical, social, cultural and religious context had, since its beginnings, a strong ecumenical character. We can thus speak of a genuine "Ecumenical tradition" of the Faculty, which not only the undersigned – responsible for teaching the discipline Misiology and Ecumenism – but its entire teaching staff want to continue to inspire the students being aware of the words spoken by Jesus Christ "that all may be one".[29]

---

[29] For the related rich bibliography one could take into consideration the footnotes of the present article.

Ivan Dimitrov

Ecumenism is a difficult challenge at present in Bulgaria.The Orthodox Church, which went through harsh and painful conditions after the fall of Communism, is very closed on itself and dislikes dialogue with other Christian confessions. One could say that it is rather against this. In fact, several members of the synod of the Bulgarian Orthodox Church readily stress that the only true Christian Church is the Orthodox Church with its Eastern Tradition.

Each case of the local Orthodox Churches as carriers and promoters of the ecumenical idea is characterized by its peculiarities. This is the case also with the Bulgarian Orthodox Church. One of the main qualities of the Orthodox Christian is to be opened to the outside world, the people outside his church and outside his nation or tribe (cf. Mt 28:18). This principle led to the bishops, the clergy and people of the Bulgarian Orthodox Church (BOC) for decades in the 20th century. It was a staple component of the Church politics especially during the imposed schism (1872-1945), when BOC was functionally separated from the other churches in the family of the local Orthodox Churches. In those times BOC was looking for opportunities to be recognized at another level - the level of inter-Christian contacts and in the newly started ecumenical movement. As in 1945 BOC received the recognition of autocephalous church with over-thousand-years history, BOC immediately got involved in the life of the local Orthodox Churches. It actively participated in the meeting of the Orthodox Churches in Moscow in 1948, where ecumenism was actually condemned as heresy, after the report by the Russian Archbishop Seraphim Sobolev, head of the Russian immigrant parishes in Bulgaria. But a little later, in 1961, under political influence, BOC joined the WCC together with other Orthodox churches from the Warsaw bloc countries.[1] Probable reasons for this change are the impressions from the activities of the WCC (established in 1948) and the opportunities that the communist parties in Eastern Europe have seen to spread their influence through active participation in the WCC of the Orthodox and Protestant churches in their countries. Even only the possibility of 'cleaning the image' of the communist countries was sufficient reason to support such participation. Many metropolitans (diocesan bishops) and bishops, other clergy and laity of BOC for nearly four decades, participated actively and successfully in the work of the WCC, were members of different committees and prof. Todor Sabev for 14 years was Deputy Secretary General of the Council. Many ecumenical events were held in Bulgaria. BOC as an institution was consciously involved in the ecumenical movement.

The personal motivation of the majority of participants in various events was indeed purely ideal. They contributed to the extent possible in developing the ecumenical idea and the ecumenical movement, drawing on the experience of other churches, sharing difficulties, seeking support. The Christian brotherhood, existing in WCC, created an atmosphere of friendship and readiness for mutual aid. Recognition of sister churches abroad was important to the position of the Orthodox Church in the country itself. I am sure this was true for the representatives of the other Churches from communist countries. Not least, it should be noted that

---

[1] Dimitrov, Ivan, "Bulgarian Christianity" In: *The Blackwell Companion to Eastern Christianity*, Edited by Ken Parry. (Malden MA, USA 2007), 47-72. Idem, "Die erste Nach-Wende-Generation – Fragen an die bulgarisch-orthodoxe Kirche", In: Verkündigung und Forschung, 56.1 (2011), 83-89. Idem, "Christian Mission Today in a Socialist Country of Yesterday. Impressions from Bulgaria", *International Review of Mission*, 317 (1991): 421-425. Idem, "Oases of Spiritual Life and Witness. The Missionary Work of the Monasteries" in *Bulgaria. You Shall Be My Witnesses. Mission Stories from the Eastern and Oriental Orthodox Churches* (Katerini 1993), 61-65. *Idem*, "The Orthodox Church in Bulgaria Today", *Greek Orthodox Theological Review*, 45.1-4 (2000): 491-511, Idem, "Die Bulgarische Orthodoxe Kirche im europaeischen Kontext" In: *Philia. Eine Zeitschrift fuer Europa. I-II. Frankfurt am Main* (2003), 162-168.

the participation of the Orthodox churches in the WCC has provided the opportunity during the event to meet each other, share and address issues that are of a purely inter-Orthodox or bilateral interest. I can name many such confessional business meetings of Orthodox representatives at General assemblies and other large ecumenical events.

Of course, it should not be excluded that some of the representatives of BOC have participated just for the chance to travel abroad during the known limitations of the communist regime to receive any benefits.[2]

The situation with the ecumenical engagement of BOC changed radically in 1989, when the communist parties lost power, and churches in the former communist countries felt free to determine the line of their conduct. This freedom naturally became a major challenge for the churches. BOC particularly faced many new problems and was unprepared to respond to them. One of these problems was the issue of participation in the ecumenical movement. Under the influence of a number of allegations of non-canonical actions of the BOC in its ecumenical activities, Orthodox believers began to urge the church to leave the WCC. Wide popularity enjoyed the work of two clerics "Orthodoxy and Ecumenism,"[3] where the authors claim, ecumenism is a heresy and the Orthodox Christians ought to abstain from practicing it. The main arguments to reject ecumenism are:

1. The Orthodox Church is the undivided Catholic Church of Christ. All others have dropped out of it and the union can only happen if they return to us.

2. All non-Orthodox are heretics and Orthodox canons prohibit praying with heretics.

3. As we talk to heretics, we legitimize them.

4. When communicating with heretics, we make concessions and fall under their influence.

5. Inter-confessional communion leads to syncretism.

6. World Council of Churches is trying to become a "super-church".

Some of these arguments are right. During previous assemblies, inter-confessional worship really was practiced. This has given rise to protests from Orthodox delegations, resulting separate worship in subsequent assemblies. Not accidentally Albanian Archbishop Anastasios (Yannoulatos), elected by the last General assembly of the WCC as one of the seven presidents of the WCC, in an interview after his election, said, "This is a matter only about assembly. This is not a communion (in sacris). WCC is not a super-church. We should explain that the tradition, which we wear, is not an illusion, but a reality, which goes back to the first millennium. We ought to bear witness to this fact. And often, the most important is not only what we say, but what we are. This is a big challenge: to be an Orthodox Christian in all aspects of life."

In Bulgaria was established real psychosis, albeit in a limited number of Orthodox Christians, but the trouble is that these are the most active believers. Therefore, the editor of a private Orthodox website[4] wrote: "Today, anyone is blamed as an Ecumenist who is not convinced that all Christians outside the Slavic and Greek universe are primarily a dangerous source of spiritual contagion, and then everything else; an Ecumenist in this extended version is anyone who is able to sit quietly in a room with a Protestant, let alone one that comes into any business or personal relationship with 'them'; Ecumenist in a sense is a person who reads theological texts in the English language; Ecumenist is just somebody who I do not know enough. The Ecumenist may be conscious, but may not know that he is of this kind..."

---

[2] See the article of Metodiev, Momchil, "The Ecumenical Activities of the Bulgarian Orthodox Church: Reasons, Motivations, Consequences" In: *Religion in Eastern Europe* 32.3 (2012): 3-12.

[3] These are *Archimandrite Seraphim Alexiev and Archimandrite Sergiy Yazadzhiev*, former associate professors at the Theological Academy. In the meantime as "defenders of the pure Orthodoxy" and fighters against ecumenism as "destructive to the pure faith" they created the Old Calendar Church of Bulgaria. The title of their book, published in Bulgarian language, but soon translated into other languages of traditionally Orthodox nations is "Orthodoxy and ecumenism" (Sofia, 1992).

[4] That is the internet site www.pravoslavie.bg

Under such public pressure, the BOC leadership has decided to leave the WCC and CEC. This decision was not sufficiently grounded; on the other hand the provided argumentation does not necessarily justify such action by the Synod of the Bulgarian Orthodox Church. In May 1998, the Holy Synod of the BOC issued the following statement:

> "Statement of the Holy Synod of the Bulgarian Orthodox Church (BOC) in connection with the participation of the BOC in the ecumenical movement.
>
> After a century of Orthodox participation in the ecumenical movement and half a century of presence in the World Council of Churches (WCC), there was no satisfactory progress in multilateral theological dialogue between Christians. Rather the gap between Orthodox and Protestants became more and more large because of the growth of dozens of new sects in the bosom of certain Protestant churches that disturb consciousness of Orthodox Christians, not only in our country, but also in all Orthodox countries, and stand out many variations from the original intent of the WCC.
>
> In connection with the foregoing, the Holy Synod of the Bulgarian Orthodox Church at its meeting on 9 April 1998 decided to terminate its participation in the WCC, taking into account the deviations of the WCC, and that the BOC in recent years has not done consciously contributions to WCC and hasn't participated in conferences convened by it and froze its membership in the WCC.
>
> On this occasion, from April 29 to May 3, 1998 in Thessaloniki, Cultural Capital of Europe for 1997, a meeting was convened with representatives of all Orthodox churches at the invitation of the Ecumenical Patriarch Bartholomew following the request of the Russian and Serbian Orthodox Church after the withdrawal of the Georgian Orthodox Church from the WCC. At this meeting were discussed the issues about the participation of the Orthodox churches in the Ecumenical movement, the dissatisfaction in the Orthodox countries with their treatment and their disregard in decision-making processes by the WCC.
>
> The Holy Synod of the Bulgarian Orthodox Church declares, that will decide whether to send a representative in Harare, Zimbabwe, to the 8th Assembly of the WCC in December 1998, or will notify in writing the WCC, that we have already ceased our participation in it.
>
> From the office of the Holy Synod of BOC,
> 27th May 1998".

Reactions among the clergy and the faithful in the BOC are mixed. The majority did not approve this decision, thinking that the bishops of the Orthodox Church, which formed its synod, in their helplessness to answer appropriately the attacks from conservative religious circles for "betrayal of the Orthodoxy" have chosen the easiest kind of reaction: "no membership, no problem". There were interesting publications in the media. Highlighting the fact that the Georgian Church has left the WCC, rumors that other Orthodox Churches might leave. It was now time to take stock, but it should always be done very carefully, "sine ira et studio".

The editor of the "Tzarkoven vestnik" ("Church Herald"), the official newspaper of the Holy Synod of the Bulgarian Orthodox Church, responded with sensitivity to the attacks of "treason" against Orthodoxy through participation in the Ecumenical movement:

> "Here we should clarify that between the concepts of communion and communication exists a clear difference. It concludes that the communion includes joint prayers and 'communio in sacris', in the sacraments of Christ. As to the communication through dialogue, theological discussions, explanations and other events outside of the worshiping community - it is something different, something on the order of "earth" relationship. And exactly in it lies the positive side of the Orthodox participation in the WCC till now. However, a large number of distortions occurring in the ideology and practice of the ecumenical movement in the most official appearances cannot go unnoticed.
>
> Ecumenism today has become a symbol of religious relativism and religious 'free-thinking', reaching to the absurd. There are offered teachings profoundly alien to Christianity. On behalf of faith is promoted moral laxity. A form of militant feminism is incited. Proselytism is practiced. In the theological discussions there is no sign of concern for the truth. It is only aimed at overlooking the differences at the expense of external similarities in the name of some

far-fetched and reckless unity, nothing to do with church. The seeking of rapprochement with other religions leads to the apparent retreat from Christianity and Christ."[5]

Other observers of the processes in the BOC on the occasion of its withdrawal from the WCC asked themselves the question: "What does it mean in terms of the doctrine of the Church, the fact that only part of the local churches participate in the WCC as a member? The issue here is not who is "right or wrong" or why some participate and others – not. The question is how this difference relates to the idea of church unity, how it fits into the perspective of a church founded on the one belief, the same principles, the unity of thinking and acting. If we use a simplistic legal analogy, the local churches are "common parts" of the One Holy Catholic and Apostolic Church. This means that everything that happens to some ideal part, take effect for all... So the presence of even just one local church in WCC already means that the Orthodox Church participates there. How we answer this question when we took our "local" decision?"[6]

In the Orthodox context are widely discussed also the reasons for the participation of the Orthodox churches in the WCC. The main defense argument is that the Orthodox Churches participate in the WCC in order to testify about Orthodoxy. Of course, this thesis is formulated precisely and reasoned on theological and historical levels, differently in the local Orthodox Churches. The success of this mission of the Orthodox Church among other Christian communities is difficult to assess. But the Orthodox clergy and theologians believe that, although variable, these successes are available.

There is also another dimension of the problem. Unfortunately today the Orthodox representatives are united not only in their attitude towards other Christian communities in the WCC: even their relationships to one another are contradictory! In recent years, there were cases of broken communion among several other prominent Orthodox churches (Russian and Romanian, Romanian and Jerusalem, etc.). Is it not more appropriate to focus our prayers and thoughts on this concern and the issue of deepening contradictions among the Orthodox Churches, united in one faith and one worship, but now broken, rather than the dubious threat of "ecumenical pan-heresy"?

"The question of the witness of the Orthodox Christians to the rest of the world, or the question of our own Orthodox identity should concern us much more seriously than an artificially created danger of ecumenical indoctrination and the fear to not be publicly known that you run a social project developed with funds from the Protestant social organizations – fear that keeps trembling perhaps hundreds of otherwise decent and loving church people in Bulgaria. We want it or not, in the Christian world occur processes, changes, challenges. We are part of this world. And will understand that more clearly and personally with the development of the processes of globalization, with our new international integrations, with the development of our own Orthodox identity."[7]

It is unworthy to "hide from your shadow", to talk with ourselves only, to wage wars, to be afraid of the questions of the society. Orthodoxy is neither a doctrine which has to be in competition with other doctrines, nor a privilege which puts us beyond any competition. We witness the truth when we are part of it, not only when talking about it. And only the truth will make us free (cf. John 8:32). And we will be free also for this – to love the different and to fight for him, not against him. Only from this starting point can the temptations around the issue of ecumenism be beaten "inside."

The church is invincible because it has the power to love everyone without limits, to know through that love everything and everyone in the way of love of the coming kingdom where "Christ will be all in all". In this love the Church sees the human in his real image and seeks a way to the image of God in him. Another

---

[5] Velichkov, Angel, "Obshtenie, obshtuvane, icumenisam (Communication, Communion, Ecumenism)," in Tsarkoven vestnik (Church Herald) 11 (1998).
[6] *Iliana Alexandrova* as above.
[7] Ibidem.

way we have already seen: we have an enemy, we organize a fight, we have someone to hate. At another time we will look for someone to love.[8]

What is the role of the theological faculties and of the theological education in the formation of ecumenical thinking among future workers of the Orthodox Church - clergy and laity? Unfortunately, they have no role. Due to the misrepresentation of the ecumenical commitment of the BOC in the second half of the 20th century as activities related primarily to the communist regime, today the ecumenical experience and contribution of the Bulgarian church is denied. This happens primarily in the Theological Faculty of Sofia University - the oldest and most reputable faculty in Bulgaria. There is no teaching of ecumenism at any theological school, even in the form of history of the Ecumenical movement. The "fashionable" ultra-conservative notions of the "preservation of Orthodoxy" lead consequently to a total rejection of contacts with non-Orthodox Christians. In this sense, the main line of modern Bulgarian theology is anti-ecumenical, having been expressed opinions such as "a dialogue should not be" (a young lector from the Faculty of Theology of Sofia University) or "students should not be present at activities of other denominations in order not to convert to other faiths" (the dean of the same faculty). It is evident that these positions are in line with the extreme positions of some bishops of the BOC. Whether coordinated or simply influenced, the facts are there. Under such circumstances it is impossible to think about teaching ecumenism at the faculties of theology in Bulgaria. Any ecumenical contact on the local level of some of the Orthodox theologians is a private matter and such contact is seen as "not popular," if not discrediting, for the person practicing it.

What is the future of the BOC in the ecumenical movement? This is an issue of increasing difficulty. Hitherto were often expressed the hope that with the election of a new patriarch in place of the century-old Patriarch Maxim (+6.11.2012) the BOC would change to become more open to the non-Orthodox world. But people who have such hopes, just forget that the policy of the Orthodox Church in Bulgaria is made by the bishops - the members of the Holy Synod, not only by the Patriarch. And still the bishops remain the same, with the same lack of capacity to meet the challenges not only of tomorrow, but even of the present day. This is not a good conclusion for such a survey. But at least it is honest.[9]

Nevertheless in concluding I would like to add that there is still a hope which will never die – this hope does not disappoint (Rom. 5:5). Our hope lies firstly in Christ and secondly in the young generation. The problem with the young generation in BOC, however, that they almost do not have any positive examples to follow. Because the old is gone and a new should be created, we ought to help creating new examples.

Bibliography

Alexandrova, Iliana. Ikumenisym (Ecumenism). – In: http://www.pravoslavie.bg

Dimitrov, Ivan, "Christian Mission Today in a Socialist Country of Yesterday. Impressions from Bulgaria", *International Review of Mission*, 317 (1991): 421-425.

-, "The Orthodox Church in Bulgaria Today" *Greek Orthodox Theological Review*, 45:1-4 (2000): 491-511.

-, "Bulgarian Christianity", in *The Blackwell Companion to Eastern Christianity* Edited by Ken Parry. (Malden MA, USA 2007), 47-72.

Metodiev, Momchil "The Ecumenical Activities of the Bulgarian Orthodox Church: Reasons, Motivations, Consequences" *Religion in Eastern Europe* 32.3 (2012): 3-12.

Sabev, Todor (ed.). *The Sofia Consultation. Orthodox Involvement in the World Council of Churches* (Geneva 1982).

-, *The Orthodox Churches on the World Council of Churches, Towards the Future*, (Geneva/Bialystok: WCC Publications, 1996).

---

[8] Ibidem.

[9] A rather optimistic picture of the situation see in: Sabev, Todor, *Church and Culture in Service to Society and Unity* (V. Tarnovo 2003), p. 364.

-, *Church and Culture in Service to Society and Unity* (V. Tarnovo, 2003).

Seraphim, Archimandrite and Sergey, *Archimandrite,* (Sofia: Orthodoxy and Ecumenism, 1992).

Velichkov, Angel "Obshtenie, obshtuvane, icumenisam" (Communication, Communion, Ecumenism). – Tsar-koven vestnik (Church Herald) 11 (1998).

Tamara Grdzelidze

The population of Kartli/Iberia (East Georgia) was made aware of Christianity from the first century. Christianity was proclaimed in Georgia by the Apostles Andrew, the 'First-called', and Simon the Canaanite.[1] Church tradition also attests to the preaching of the Apostles Bartholomew and Matthias. Mtskheta claims to have preserved the most sacred of all relics for Christians – the robe of Jesus Christ, which had been retrieved from Calvary after the Crucifixion and brought from Jerusalem to the capital by a local Jew named Elioz. Archaeological data and written evidence, such as the Manichaean 'Book of Magic' and the inscription of Kartir the Magus Master, attest to the presence of Christians in East Georgia (Iberia) in the second and third centuries.[2] The first disseminators of the Christian message were Judaeo-Christians in Mtskheta and elsewhere in Kartli.[3] The Church historians Gelasius of Caesarea, Rufinus, Gelasius of Cyzicus, Sozomen, Socrates and Theodoret mention in their works that Armenians and Iberians adopted Christianity during the reign of Constantine, that is, before 337 (the year of the emperor's death).[4] From the very beginning, the Patriarchate of Antioch was regarded as the Mother Church by the Church of Kartli.

Christianity was adopted by the west Georgian state of Egrisi – called 'Lazica' by the Byzantines – at the same time as or earlier than in Kartli. The acts of the Council of Nicaea (325) identify Stratophiles as bishop of Pityos (modern-day Pitsunda, Abkhazia).[5] A Christian cathedral in Pityos, dating from the first half of the fourth century, testifies to the presence of Christianity during the same time. This would indicate that the conversion at least of parts of the population of Lazica took place earlier than the conversion of Kartli.

In the first part of the fourth century, a young woman from Cappadocia named Nino was sent to evangelize the godless people of Kartli (Iberia). Nino arrived at Mtskheta, the capital of Kartli, carrying a simple cross made of vine branches bound by her own hair. Nino started teaching, first converting Queen Nana. For King Mirian, it was not easy to give up his idols. One day, while he was hunting, an eclipse of the sun occurred and King Mirian called on the idols for help. When the idols left his plea unanswered, he remembered the god of Nino, called on him for help and was relieved of his distress. Then the whole royal family of Kartli was converted, and Christianity became the official religion of the state. King Mirian sent ambassadors to the Roman Emperor Constantine the Great requesting clergy. The first bishop in Kartli was consecrated by Eustathios, bishop of Antioch between 325 and 330.

The full separation from the Church of Antioch took place in the eleventh century. The catholicos of Kartli, Melkisedek I (1010-1033), extended his jurisdiction to western Georgia and was given the title of patriarch. Since then the primate of the OCG has been known as the 'Catholicos-Patriarch of All Georgia' and the Church became completely independent in its domestic and foreign affairs. In 1811, however, autocephaly was abolished as a result of the annexation of Georgia by Russia. In March 1917, after over a hundred years' subordination to the Russian Synod, the Georgian hierarchs convoked an assembly of ecclesiastical and secular figures and

---

[1] V. Licheli, 'St Andrew in Samtskhe - Archaeological Proof?', in T. Mgaloblishvili (ed.), *Ancient Christianity in the Caucasus, Iberica Caucasica*, vol.1 (Richmond 1998), 25-37.

[2] T. Mgaloblishvili, 'Introduction', ibid., 4.

[3] T. Mgaloblishvili, I. Gagoshidze, 'The Jewish Diaspora and Early Christianity in Georgia', ibid., 39 ff.

[4] According to Socrates, the adoption of Christianity in Georgia took place around 330, namely, in the year when the philosopher Metrodoros made his journey to India *(Ecclesiastical History* 1.20; 1.19). Historians today agree on a date around the 320's. See for the above mentioned sources: *Georgica, Scriptorum Byzantinorum Excerpta Ad Georgiam Pertinentia*, vol. 1, ed. by A. Gamkrelidze et S. Kaukhchishvili (Tbilisi, 1961).

[5] See H. Gelzer et al. (eds.), *Patrum Nicaenorum Nomina* (Stuttgart and Leipzig, 1995), II.110, p. 65

restored the autocephaly of the OCG. Full recognition came gradually: the Russian Patriarchate only recognized this restored autocephaly in 1943 and the Ecumenical Patriarchate in 1990. On 23 January 1990, the Synod of the Church of Constantinople made a decision to recognize the ancient autocephaly of the Georgian Church and to rank its head as Catholicos-Patriarch of the Church of Georgia. Since the enthronement of Ilias II as Catholicos-Patriarch of All Georgia, the church has revived immensely; this is especially true about its physical constitution: re-opening old churches and building new ones, founding monasteries, ordaining priests, consecrating bishops, establishing theological schools, journals, newspapers, media channels, university. Only the fact that the COG rejects the Ecumenical Movement raises many question concerning the quality of its education and teaching in general.

A short discourse in a rather recent past: After having sent representatives as observers to the Third Assembly in New Delhi in November-December 1961, the Orthodox Church of Georgia requested a full membership in the World Council of Churches.[6] In his reply Visser't Hooft assures that the Central Committee, the highest governing body of the WCC, will consider the application at their meeting in Paris in August 1962 and invited one observer from the Church to attend the Paris meeting. On 19 March 1963, Ephrem II, the Catholicos-Patriarch of All Georgia, in his reply to Visser't Hooft, who congratulated the Patriarch with the membership of his church (written on 19 February 1963), expressed his joy and deep gratitude regarding the membership of the Orthodox Church of Georgia in the WCC. Taking into account the means of communication at that time, also the fact that all foreign correspondence was purposefully checked, the timeline is quite impressive.

In the WCC archives, one can find just enough material to analyze WCC- the Orthodox Church of Georgia relations in 1960 -1997. In a letter to the newly enthroned patriarch of Georgia Ephrem II (1960-1972) the General Secretary of the WCC W.A. Visser't Hooft sent congratulations and expressed regret that "circumstances prevented the delegation of the World Council of Churches to the Patriarchate of Moscow last December from visiting your church, but we would like you to know that we would warmly welcome any possibilities for direct contact with you and other leaders of your church." From the letter it becomes evident that there were some direct contacts between the OCG and the WCC prior to 1960, that the WCC delegation while visiting Moscow was not permitted to visit the OCG. There is an exchange of letters between the two parties in the period of the leadership of Ephrem II, but an official WCC delegation could not reach the OCG. During the short period of leadership by Patriarch David V (1972-1977), the WCC Archives do not have any information whatsoever; only his death was announced, followed by the enthronement of Catholicos-Patriarch Ilias II. Even from this superficial glance, one understands that the Ecumenical Movement and membership in the WCC was seen as beneficial for the autocephalous OCG under the circumstances at that time. Soviet ideology played unpredictable games with the Church, Moscow was preventing OCG from making a direct link with the oecumene and the Ecumenical Patriarchate did not recognise its autocephaly. It must be added to the merits of the two shrewd Patriarchs – Ephrem II and Ilias II – that they found ways for the OCG to connect with the outside world. Unfortunately, with the fall of communism – a great historical event in the life of the peoples and churches of the former Soviet Union – the unqualified interpretation of these links became prevalent in Georgia. The primate of the OCG was accused of collaboration with Soviet government, since control over

[6] "On behalf of the Holy Synod of the oldest Orthodox Church of Georgia and myself, as its head, I address you hereby regarding the membership of the Church of Georgia in the World Council of Churches. We agree to the bases expressed in the first Article of the Constitution of the WCC. We declare that the Orthodox Church of Georgia, existing from the fourth century, is autocephalous, which is a requirement according to the statutes of WCC. The Orthodox Church of Georgia has always attributed first-rate importance to the issue of *rapprochement* between the churches for the sake of consolidation of brotherhood, love and peace among the peoples. The Orthodox Church of Georgia confesses One, Holy Catholic and Apostolic Church, being a member and a part of its catholicity, praying for "the stability of the holy churches of God and for the unity of all" (from The Great Litany of the Liturgy by St. John Chrysostom's, TG.), it is ready to contribute to a great affair of the Christian unity. We hope that the WCC will assign to the Orthodox Church of Georgia a proper place of real membership, among the other real members." (Author's translation from Georgian).

Part IV: Ecumenical Dialogue in various Orthodox Churches and Settings

borders under the totalitarian regime was very tight and only few could pass the iron curtain. On top of that, the Orthodox zealots transmitted to Georgia a myth about the 'ecumenical heresy' which, in combination with the 'collaboration theory', dominated the local Orthodox milieu. As a result of these circumstances the synod of the OCG decided to withdraw its membership from the ecumenical organisations (May1997). It must be noted that the 1990s, especially its second half, was a critical period for the local Orthodox Churches regarding their participation and role in the WCC. However, only two local Orthodox Churches withdrew their membership, Georgia and Bulgaria, in November 1997. In light of the Orthodox ecclesiological principle – one church, one Eucharistic fellowship - the withdrawal from the Ecumenical Movement was not well received by the fellow Orthodox. Neither has it been beneficial for the OCG to stay in isolation and reduce the knowledge and spirit of the ecumenical engagement. Staying in isolation brings short-term fruits and popularity to the church: at present the church has been immensely influential over the majority of population in the country, most of whom are unemployed and marginalised; the church has been used as one of the focal points during the election periods: used, or rather misused, by the governing party as well as by the opposition. Under the current circumstances of isolation and self-sufficiency, the OCG has been trying to assume a diplomatic/political role in difficult relations with Russia. Although there are no visible results from those attempts, for the devoted part of the Georgian population, and they seem to make a large group, such patriotic gestures are taken for granted.

The OCG since recently has been involved in two official dialogues: with the Roman Catholics and with the Anglicans. How many in the Church know about this?

For the COG it is crucial to introduce the ETE at least at a level of the Spiritual Academy, if not seminaries. Hostility towards Ecumenism that prevails in the COG must be first replaced by tolerance. ETE has to manifest also the difficulties for the Christians in today's secularised and pluralistic world. Although Georgia is not as homogenous as it was twenty years ago, the OCG is still the spiritual leader; this leadership somehow, maybe not by its own initiative, minimizes the value of the other spiritualities. The leadership of the OCG largely is due to the policy of preservation of the national identity. The latter, in the view of the majority of believers, has been threatened under the ongoing processes of globalisation and attempted democracy.

Bibliography

1. *Witness through Troubled Times: A History of the Georgian Orthodox Church, 1811 to the Present*, with contributions by N. Abashidze, Z. Abashidze, E. Bubulashvili, G. Saitidze & S. Vardosanidze, eds. Tamara Grdzelidze, Martin George & Lukas Vischer (London: Bennet&Bloom, 2006).
2. "The Georgian Tradition", in *The Orthodox Christian World*, edited by Augustine Casiday (London and New York: Routledge, 2012).
3. T. Mgaloblishvili (ed.) *Ancient Christianity in the Caucasus, Iberica Caucasica*, vol.1 (Richmond:1998).
4. *The Wellspring of Georgian Historiography, The Early Medieval Historical Chronicle, The Conversion of Kartli and the Life of St Nino*, Translated with Introduction, Commentary and Indices by Constantine B. Lerner (Bennet&Bloom, 2004).

(65) Ecumenical Dialogue in the Perspective of the Church of Cyprus

Fr. Benedict Ioannou

The Church of Cyprus, a member of the family of the Eastern Orthodox Churches, is an autocephalous and an apostolic Church founded by the Apostles Paul and Barnabas (see *Acts*). Two Ecumenical Councils confirmed her autocephaly: the 3rd Ecumenical Council in Ephesos (A.D. 431) and the Quinisext Council in Constantinople (A.D. 691). Despite its small size and far from being isolated, the Church of Cyprus has been always participating in ecumenical councils and inter-Orthodox and inter-Christian dialogues.

Following the initiative and leadership of the Ecumenical Patriarchate of Constantinople and responding to the patriarchal encyclical letter of 1920, the Church of Cyprus took part in the conversations[1] and procedures resulting in the foundation of the Commission "Faith and Order" (Lausanne 1927), the World Council of Churches (Amsterdam, 1948) and the Conference of European Churches (Nyborg Strand, Denmark 1959), fully supportive of these organizations and commissions by all means. We should also mention the active participation of the Church of Cyprus in the Middle East Council of Churches (MECC).

In particular, concerning the creation of "Faith and Order", the Church of Cyprus was represented in the Preliminary Meeting at Geneva, 1920, the Lausanne Conference of 1927 and the Edinburgh Conference of 1937.

Regarding the movement "Life and Work", the Church of Cyprus participated in the Universal Christian Conference on Life and Work (Stockholm, 1925), the Universal Christian Council for Life and Work (1930-1938) and the Oxford Conference on Church, Community and State (1937).

Moreover, the Church of Cyprus was constantly being informed about the important meetings, which convened on 9 May 1938 in Utrecht and in Clarens (August 1938). Both meetings were the last stages before the establishment of the World Council of Churches, delayed for ten years because of the second World War.

During all these years, between 1919 and 1948 —the foundation day of the WCC—, there was a continuous exchange of letters and visits between the Church of Cyprus and other ecumenical partners in the framework of inter-Christian relation and cooperation.[2]

The Church of Cyprus participates in the international theological dialogues with the Roman Catholic, the Anglican, the Lutheran and the Oriental Orthodox (pre-Chalcedonian) Churches. She has hosted many of these meetings as well as meetings of the WCC, the CEC and the MECC.

Although there is not official "National Council of Churches" in Cyprus, the main and old Christian Churches on the island (Orthodox Eastern and Oriental, Roman Catholic, Maronite, Anglican and Protestant) have good relations with one another and their leaders meet often.

The Cypriots are quite open to dialogue with other Christian Churches but few of them are actually involved in ecumenical dialogues, meetings or other common Christian activities. As in other parts of the world, especially in the so-called Orthodox countries, the ecumenical movement has not reached the grass roots of the Churches.

---

[1] See for example the letter of Archbishop Kyrillos of Cyprus to Robert H. Gardiner in 1921, where the Archbishop expresses the desire of himself and his Church for the union of the Churches: "*Truly, the soul of every Christian rejoices in seeing how steadily the blessed work for the promotion and realization of the so longed for union of the churches goes on*".
[2] According to the Orthodox Research Institute, in February 1947, a delegation was sent to the WCC to visit the ecclesiastical heads of the Orthodox Churches of Constantinople, Alexandria, Antioch, Cyprus and Athens with the purpose of Orthodox participation within the ecumenical movement and in order to personally invite them to the first General Assembly of the WCC in Amsterdam in 1948. The delegated returned to Geneva with the results of its mission. However, at the Conference of Heads of the Orthodox Churches in Moscow in July 1948, it was decided, "to refuse the invitation to participate in the Ecumenical Movement in its present form". This decision was not signed by the representatives of Constantinople, Jerusalem, Cyprus, Greece and Finland.

In Cyprus, this is not due to any hostility towards the ecumenical movement, but rather to indifference. In other words, the ecumenical movement is not part of their Christian life.

The Orthodox Church is the main religion in Cyprus. Although the Republic of Cyprus does not have an "official" or "state religion", the Constitution gives some special privileges to the Orthodox Church of Cyprus but not to the expenses of the other Churches on the island. Religious freedom is totally guaranteed in Cyprus (but not in the Turkish occupied area of the island). During medieval times the Church of Cyprus was very much oppressed by the Roman-Catholics (Franks and Venetians) and later by the Ottomans. This is perhaps one of the reasons why the Church of Cyprus does not use its "privileged" position against other small Churches on the island.

Churches acting together

As we know, during the war years and especially after World War II, the European Churches and the WCC undertook to assist the prisoners of war and the refugees, plus many other charitable projects.

Cyprus itself was recipient of a significant humanitarian aid by the World Council of Churches after the Turkish invasion of 1974. Moreover the WCC supported the right demand of the people of Cyprus for the liberation of the island from the Turkish army and the reunification of the island through many statements and other initiatives.

The Church of Cyprus has been active in diaconal work and has demonstrated its solidarity to migrants and poor people. In the last twenty to thirty years the Cypriot Church has welcomed thousands of migrants coming especially from the ex- Soviet Union area and the Middle East. Together with the WCC and other ecumenical organizations the Church of Cyprus has fruitfully worked in the area of migration, racism and interfaith relations.

Religious Education

Religious Education is a part of the syllabus of all public schools in Cyprus (primary and secondary). Although it is Christian education and mainly Orthodox Christian faith that is taught, all pupils learn not only about the Orthodox Church but also about other Christian denominations and other religions. A specific chapter is dedicated in the creation and role of the World Council of Churches and the various initiatives for the rapprochement of the Churches and reunification processes from the Medieval to the contemporary times. The non-Orthodox pupils may request to be excluded from the teaching of the Orthodox Christian faith, but they rarely use this right (except perhaps for some Muslims but not all of them). Cypriot pupils learn how to live with people of other faith (even Muslims) and to live in an inclusive society in general. After all, in Cyprus today, it is hard to find a school with Orthodox pupils exclusively.

Perspective

The World Council of Churches, according to its Constitution, "*is a fellowship of churches which confess the Lord Jesus Christ as God and Savior according to the scriptures, and therefore seek to fulfill together their common calling to the glory of the one God, Father, Son and Holy Spirit... It seeks to advance towards this unity, as Jesus prayed for his followers, "so that the world may believe." (John 17:21)*"

The primary purpose of the fellowship of churches in the World Council of Churches is "*to call one another to visible unity in one faith and in one Eucharistic fellowship, expressed in worship and common life in Christ, through witness and service to the world, and to advance towards that unity in order that the world may believe. In seeking koinonia in faith and life, witness and service, the churches through the Council will...*"

Today, the Church of Cyprus continues sharing the same vision and goals of the World Council of Churches and works for the fulfillment of these goals. It is truly committed to the ecumenical movement and collaborates constructively *"in common life in Christ"*. It is represented in the Central and Executive Committee of the WCC by H.E. Metropolitan Vasileios of Constantia-Ammochostos, who serves also as the Moderator of "Faith and Order" Commission. Other bishops represent the Church of Cyprus in the official international theological bilateral dialogues and other ecumenical organizations.

Bibliography

John E. Skoglund and J. Robert Nelson, *Fifty Years of Faith and Order: An Interpretation of the Faith and Order Movement* (New York: Committee for the interseminary Movement of the National Student Christian Federation, 1963).

Histories of the Ecumenical Movement, ed. by Ruth Rouse and Stephen Charles Neill, vol. 1, 1517-1948, and ed. by Harold E. Fey, vol. 2, (1948-1968).

Lukas Vischer, ed., *A Documentary History of the Faith and Order Movement 1927-1963*, (St Louis: Bethany Press, 1963).

Gunther Gassmann, ed., *Documentary History of Faith and Order 1963-1993*, (Geneva: WCC Publications, 1993).

Lausanne 1927 to Santiago de Compostela 1993, Faith and Order Paper No. 160, (Geneva, WCC Publications, 1993).

G. Limouris (ed.), *Orthodox visions of Ecumenism* (Statements, messages and reports on the Ecumenical Movement, 1902-1992), (Geneva, WCC Publications, 1994).

V. Stavridis, Ποία η συμβολή της Ορθοδοξίας εν τη Οικομενική Κινήσει, Αθήνα, 1958 (in Greek).

—, Ιστορία της Οικουμενικής Κινήσεως, εκδ. β΄, Θεσσαλονίκη, 1984 (in Greek).

G. Tsetsis, Η συμβολή της Εκκλησίας Κύπρου εις την ίδρυσιν του Παγκοσμίου Συμβουλίου των Εκκλησιών, *Απόστολος Βαρνάβας*, τεύχ. 1-3, 1976, σελ. 3-10 (in Greek).

—, Αλληλογραφία του Αρχιεπισκόπου Κύπρου Κυρίλλου Γ΄ μετά των Charles Anderson και Robert Gardiner του παγκοσμίου συνεδρίου περί Πίστεως και Τάξεως, *Απόστολος Βαρνάβας*, τεύχ. 4-6, 1976, σελ. 50-54 (in Greek).

Ch. Chrystoforou, *Οι σχέσεις της Εκκλησίας Κύπρου με την Οικουμενική Κίνηση (1919 - 1948)*, Master thesis, Λευκωσία 2005 (in Greek).

(66) ECUMENICAL DIALOGUE IN THE PERSPECTIVE OF THE CHURCH OF GREECE

Vassiliki Stathokosta

Introduction

The study of the relationship between the Church of Greece and the Ecumenical Movement goes back to the very beginning of this Movement. The time we refer to is the late nineteenth and the beginning of the twentieth century, when efforts for dialogue among Christians began and seemed to progress in a very promising way. The Church of Greece alongside the Ecumenical Patriarchate contributed a great deal for the development of inter-Christian relations that gradually led to the formation of the WCC and its first Assembly in 1948. Our research process, based on bibliography and mainly on the WCC's archive material, shows clearly the eagerness and vivid activity of brilliant Greek hierarchs and lay theologians to work for the restoration of Christian unity. They served the ecumenical purpose either as representatives of the Church of Greece or the Ecumenical Patriarchate. Furthermore, Greek theologians participated in delegations of other Patriarchates (Alexandria and Jerusalem) or autocephalous Churches (Church of Cyprus), in ecumenical assemblies and conferences. This participation of the Church of Greece in the Ecumenical Movement is an undeniable fact that counts one century of life and it consistently continues until today.

Brief note on the theological and historical background

The process of the ecumenical involvement of the Orthodox and the Church of Greece in particular, is closely related to the general endeavour for the unity of Christendom as a continuous concern of the Church since the apostolic era and the patristic period of time. Unity is after all the very essence of Christian faith and life, according the Gospel's teaching and the liturgical demand. The Orthodox pray for peace of all the world, stability of the holy churches of God and the unity of all.[1] Orthodoxy as the One, Holy, Catholic and Apostolic Church has a special task to give an Orthodox witness to the world, even to Christians who are separated from the Orthodox; to introduce them to the faith and tradition of the undivided Church of the first eight centuries and the seven Ecumenical Councils, which is common to all. We should always remind others that the great family of Christianity had been united before the separation of the fifteenth (Fourth Ecumenical Synod of Chalcedon, 451), eleventh (the Great Schism, 1054) and sixteenth centuries (the Reformation, 1517).

All these divisions were never accepted as a normal status either in the West or in the East. On the contrary, they were faced as a great failure, a wound inside the body of Church, which ought to be healed. That is why, since the eleventh century, after the Great Schism (1054), efforts for dialogue began but eventually failed as their motives were not purely of a theological origin. Those were rushed efforts sprung mostly from political causes as was the case for Western Church, or from necessity as was the case for Eastern Church. The desire of the West to expand its imperium in the East and the need of the East to find allies for its protection against enemies in its eastern boarders was not a solid basis for dialogue. That is why these efforts for Christian unity ended up with failure, in meetings such as the second synod of Lyon and the Ferrara-Florence synod, leaving behind disappointment and fear for the Orthodox and deteriorating relations between East and West.

---

[1] The Divine Liturgy of Saint John of Damascus: "Ὑπὲρ τῆς εἰρήνης τοῦ σύμπαντος κόσμου, εὐσταθείας τῶν ἁγίων τοῦ Θεοῦ Ἐκκλησιῶν καὶ τῆς τῶν πάντων ἑνώσεως, τοῦ Κυρίου δεηθῶμεν".

A further division in the body of the Western Church, the Reformation, occurred in the sixteenth century. Efforts for inter-Christian relations had been made mainly on the initiative of the Reformation since its early steps when its representatives turned to the Ecumenical Patriarchate. Dialogue between Luther, Melanchthon and theologians from Tubingen Theological School with the Ecumenical Patriarchate was a great step for the Reformation and Orthodoxy to meet each other. At the same time, the Orthodox expressed their interest to find out the principles of Reformation as well as what their expectations should be concerning this new ecclesiastical reality.[2] However, the status of Orthodoxy at that time as subjected to the Ottoman Empire did not allow any further developments.[3] As the late Greek Orthodox theologian Nikos Matsoukas noticed:

> "That position of the Ecumenical Patriarchate meant that it was still open to dialogue and mainly to any possible progress in Ecumenism ... so that later on and in better circumstances a new approach on this matter would be easier."

Actually, a positive evolution occurred when the Anglicans turned to the Orthodox East (seventeenth century onwards) seeking dialogue and agreement in several church matters. As the British Empire expanded all over the world, many Anglicans found themselves living in the East among Orthodox. They approached Orthodox seeking cooperation mainly in pastoral matters (e.g. funerals etc). In this frame the issue of validity of the Anglican orders was raised and Greek theologians alongside Russians and others started to study it in the early twentieth century. Orthodox officially recognized in their meeting at the Holy Mountain, Athos, in 1930, that Anglicans paid respect to Orthodoxy and they did not conduct any proselytism against the Orthodox flock.[4] This observation made dialogue with the Orthodox much easier. These Anglican – Orthodox contacts cultivated a set of good presuppositions for the rapprochement between East and West and the development of the Ecumenical Movement of the twentieth century.[5]

Church of Greece and the Formation of the Ecumenical Movement

Finally, in the early twentieth century different political and social changes shaped a new landscape, enabling church relations. The suffering of humanity due to the two world wars led to an urgent demand for reconciliation and unity; Churches were called to contribute for this purpose giving witness of their faith that peace is Christ according Saint Paul's saying "for he himself is our peace, who has made us both one and has broken down in his flesh the dividing wall of hostility" (Eph. 2:14). Soon they realized they had to put aside their dogmatic differences in order to work together for the preservation of human life and dignity.

That means that in the twentieth century the issue of Christian unity was not only a theological matter but an urgent demand of humanity as well. The issue of giving witness of the Christian faith was a common task for Churches and it was at stake. That is why the twentieth has been characterized as the century of the ecumenical movement. That was the very moment the ecumenical movement was shaped and flourished as efforts for Christian unity were engaged in the West and the East either by Churches or individuals, in a very careful and methodical way. They tried to achieve their aim through two different ways. The first one was going through church cooperation on practical matters and it gradually led to the

---

[2] Dimitrios Mysos had traveled (1559) in West as a representative of the Ecumenical Patriarch Ioasaph II (+1565) trying to find out what the Reformation was about. The contact moved further more when the theologians of Tubingen addressed several times to the Ecumenical Patriarchate.

[3] This is the reason that later on the Ecumenical Patriarch Ieremias II asked the Reformers not to insist on dogmatic discussions anymore but only to keep a friendly relation.

[4] *Minutes of the Preliminary Committee of the Holy, Orthodox Churches convened in the Holy and Great Monastery of Vatopedi at the Holy Mountain, 8-23 June 1930,* (Constantinople 1930) 144.

[5] See V. Stathokosta, "Relations between the Orthodox and the Anglicans in the Twentieth Century: A Reason to Consider the Present and the Future of the Theological Dialogue", *Ecclesiology* 8 (2012): 350–374.

Part IV: Ecumenical Dialogue in various Orthodox Churches and Settings

formation of "Life and Work" (LW) Movement. The second one was through studies and discussions on dogmatic issues and it led to "Faith and Order" Movement (FO). In those efforts of the twentieth century, the first step for inter-Christian dialogue was made mostly by individuals, prominent theologians as well as clergymen from Europe and USA. Greek theologians were present since the beginning and they had been the pioneers on behalf of Orthodoxy for a long time, following the dialogical tradition of the One, Holy, Catholic and Apostolic Church in general and the practice the Ecumenical Patriarchate had inaugurated since the sixteenth century in particular. Because of the political situation in Europe, Greeks were mostly the ones who contacted relations with Western Christians, as other Orthodox living in communist countries did not have such a possibility, especially after 1945.[6] Officially it was the Congress of Moscow in 1948 that condemned the Ecumenical Movement.[7] However, the Russian Diaspora in Paris and elsewhere contributed a great deal with its prominent theologians like Fr. G. Florovsky and others, as members of the delegations of the Ecumenical Patriarchate.[8]

Members of the Church of Greece participated in most of the pioneering ecumenical bodies developed at the first half of the twentieth century, as it was the "World Alliance for International Friendship through the Churches" (1914).[9] Many professors of the Theological Faculty of Athens, such as Am. Alivizatos, Chrysostomos Papadopoulos (Archimandrite and later on Archbishop of Athens and All Greece), K. Dyovouniotis, Gr. Papamichael and D. Balanos were present in this endeavor.[10] Similarly, the Church of Greece supported with eagerness LW and FO from the very beggining. She sent representatives to the ecumenical congresses of LW in Geneva (1920), Stockholm (1925) and Oxford (1937).[11] We should underline that the Orthodox participation in the first congress of LW was a strong motive and an encouragement for the participation of the Anglican and the Old Catholic Church in this movement.[12]

The Church of Greece was supportive to FO and its task to study dogmatic issues and find solutions to problems that dogmatic differences created for Churches. It is worth mentioning that the Church of Greece was informed about this initiative from its very beginning, she expressed her sincere interest and she kept a positive attitude.[13] She considered that the purpose of FO, as the late Prof. Alivizatos wrote:

"was identical to the very desire of Jesus 'that may all be one' (John 17:21)."[14]

---

[6] G. Tsetsis states that their refusal to attend the Assembly was "on grounds that were more political than theological or ecclesiological". See G. Tsetsis, "Introduction to the 'Special Commission': The origin and the work of the 'Special Commission' for the Orthodox participation in the WCC', (Paper presented to the International Conference "Orthodox Theology and Ecumene", Penteli/Athens 12-13 March 2012).

[7] V. Istavridis and Ev. Varella (eds.), Ιστορία της Οικουμενικής Κινήσεως (History of the Ecumenical Movement), (Patriarchal Institute of Patristic Studies, Thessaloniki, 1996), 111 (in Greek).

[8] Ibid, 113.

[9] That was the first time in the history of Christianity that special personalities of Churches from different countries had a close cooperation in order to resolve problems and restore peace among nations, having as a common basis "Christian ideology", according a characteristic expression used at that time. See V. Stathokosta, Ορθόδοξη Θεολογία και Οικουμένη: Μελέτες - Άρθρα (Orthodox Theology and Ecumene: Studies - Articles), (Parrisia, Athens ²2011) (in Greek).

[10] See V. Stathokosta, The relationship between the Church of Greece and the World Council of Churches 1948-1961, based on the Archives of the WCC, (unpublished PhD dissertation, University of Thessaloniki, 1999), 33-37 (in Greek).

[11] Ibid, 63-75.

[12] See R. Rouse and S. C. Neill (eds.), A History of the Ecumenical Movement 1517-1948, (Geneva, 1953), 548-549. Also, Ham. Alivizatos, Η Οικουμενική Κίνησις και η προσπάθεια του Amsterdam (The Ecumenical Movement and the endeavor of Amsterdam), offprint from journal Pimen, (Mitilini, 1950), 31 (in Greek).

[13] In March 1919 a delegation of the preparatory committee of the congress of FO visited under the leadership of R. Gardiner the Church of Greece and had discussions with the Holy Synod. See V. Stathokosta, The relationship between the Church of Greece and the WCC, (1999), 41-43 (in Greek).

[14] H. Alivizatos, Η προσπάθεια του Amsterdam (The Amsterdam Assembly), 20 (in Greek).

Consequently, the Church of Greece took part in the FO congresses in Geneva (1920), Lausanne (1927) and Edinburgh (1937) and contributed a great deal to its work and its theological development.[15]

Her participation in LW and FO, although numerically small, either positive or critical, formed with other participants the decisions of these congresses. At this period of time, starting from 1920 until 1937, the participation of the Orthodox Church was based on the participation of each Autocephalous Church separately. There was not any Pan-Orthodox meeting prior to decide their common attitude, so often there had been different approaches. Briefly, at that time there were two ways of perception and attitude the Orthodox expressed: the first one was expressed by the Greek-speaking delegates who emphasized discussions on practical matters; the other one was expressed by the Slavophones who showed their preference to dogmatic discussion. Greek representatives in those congresses tried to communicate all their work to the Holy Synod as well as to the flock.[16]

However the most important effort for church unity came from Orthodoxy herself and the Mother Church of Constantinople, the Ecumenical Patriarchate. The Orthodox Church not only did not rely on the status of separation of all those centuries but she took a radical initiative for the restoration of unity. The Patriarchic Letters of 1902-1904 and especially the one in 1920 addressed to "all Churches of Christ" showed the way to begin and commit in a serious effort for achieving church unity. In these letters there is a significant contribution of members of the Church of Greece yet not widely known. The contribution of Archbishop of Syros, Tinos and Milos, Alexandros Lykourgos in the formulation of the Patriarchic letters of 1902-1904 and 1920 is one of them.[17] Furthermore, it was Professor Alivizatos from Athens University who presented this Encyclical letter (1920) at the FO congress in Geneva (1920).

Also, not known well enough is the preparatory work that was achieved in 1918 by the Greek delegation to USA and England, where they had discussions with Episcopalians and Anglicans respectively. The Professors of the Theological School of Athens, Archimandrite Chrysostomos Papadopoulos and Hamilkar Alivizatos, authors of the Report to the Holy Synod, concluded:

> "the Anglican Church, 'rejecting the character of Protestantism on one hand and avoiding the extremes of Papacy on the other, is similar to our Church through its teaching and its worship and its religious life. … Our personal observations convinced us that the Anglican Church worships God properly."[18]

We should notice that those contacts had been a decisive step towards the formation of the Ecumenical Movement in general[19].

All these initiatives for church unity went on despite serious obstacles caused by the Second World War and led to the formation of the WCC.

---

[15] See V. Stathokosta, *The relationship between the Church of Greece and the WCC*, 41-63.

[16] Ibid, 75-78

[17] Chrysostomos Savvatos (Metropolitan of Messinia), *Ο Αλέξανδρος Λυκούργος, αρχιεπίσκοπος Σύρου, Τήνου και Μήλου (1866-1875) και η συμβολή του στην ανάπτυξη της οικουμενικής κινήσεως (Alexandros Lykourgos, Archbishop of Syros, Tinos and Milos, 1866-1875, and his contribution in the development of the ecumenical movement)*, Offprint from the honorary volume of the Holy Synod of the Church of Greece in the memory of the Blessed Archbishop of Athens and All Greece Christodoulos, (Athens, 2010) (in Greek).

[18] See the report of professors Archimandrite Chrysostomos Papadopoulos and Hamilcar Alivizatos to the Holy Synod of the Church of Greece: *Ορθοδόξων και Αγγλικανών Θεολογικαί συζητήσεις* (Theological discussions of Orthodox and Anglicans: Brief Report of the unofficial discussion of the Ecclesiastical mission under the Metropolitan of Athens and the delegates of the Anglican Episcopalian Church in America and England, in Athens, 4 February 1919), *Εκκλησιαστικός Κήρυξ* (1919), 518-522 (in Greek).

[19] V. Stathokosta, "Relations between the Orthodox and the Anglicans", *Ecclesiology* 8 (2012), 350–374.

Part IV: Ecumenical Dialogue in various Orthodox Churches and Settings

Church Of Greece And The World Council Of Churches

The work of all these endeavours of the pioneers, churchmen and theologians, as Visser't Hooft, Am. Alivizatos[20] and many others, resulted in the formation of the WCC. In its frame the participation of the Church of Greece took an official, namely an ecclesiastical, character, as it was the case with all member Churches as well. At Amsterdam Greek theologians participated not as individuals but as official church representatives. That was the case in all following general assemblies as the members of the delegations in official conferences of the WCC were and still are, nominated by the Holy Synod of the Church of Greece.

Landmarks in the participation of the Church of Greece in the WCC

1. Amsterdam to New Delhi

Soon after the Second World War, WCC was a very significant event and a certain reality in the Churches' life. The WCC embraced not only a great number of "Churches" and their broad field of activities, but also the variety and intensity of discussions concerning its nature, its aims and the way of its work and function. In these discussions the representatives of the Church of Greece were extremely active, and they contributed a great deal for the clarification of its nature and task. Especially after the Amsterdam Assembly questions of a) the Constitution of the WCC and the presuppositions required by a Christian community to be accepted in the WCC as a church member, b) the relation of the WCC to its member Churches, and c) the ecclesiastical or ecclesiological character of the WCC was elaborated in a more fruitful way that led to further developments in the WCC. It was two years later that the Central Committee in Toronto (1950) gave answers to these burning questions with the text on the Nature of the WCC. Although there was not any Greek participation in Toronto, the work the Orthodox had offered is shown clearly in this very document.[21] These separate Statements they submitted in previous years urged the WCC to formulate and clarify its identity, method of work and theological orientation.

Another landmark in the Ecumenical Movement was the assembly in New Delhi when, following the hard theological work of the Greeks alongside other church representatives, there had been a new formula for the basis of the WCC's Constitution, stating clearly faith in the triune God: "The World Council of Churches is a fellowship of churches which confess the Lord Jesus Christ as God and Saviour according to the Scriptures, and therefore seek to fulfill together their common calling to the glory of the One God, Father, Son and Holy Spirit."

It was important that just prior to New Delhi a Pan-Orthodox meeting took place in Rhodes (24 Sept. - 10 Oct. 1961). Representatives of fourteen Orthodox Autocephalous Churches, (Greeks, Slavs, Romanians and Arabs), positively decided to participate in the ecumenical movement, stressing that the Patriarchal Encyclical of 1920 must remain the basis of all efforts of Orthodox Christianity towards Christian unity.[22] In New Delhi (1961), when the Russians joined the WCC, the Orthodox participation was reinforced and no more Statements were needed as there was enough Orthodox participation that their voice was heard enough.[23]

During these first twelve years of the WCC, the participation of the Greeks was very active indeed. In 1958 - 1974, N. Nissiotis was appointed as a director of the Ecumenical Institute of Bossey. He also served

---

[20] Prof. Alivizatos is recognized as one of the pioneers of the ecumenical movement. Βλ. Visser 't Hooft, *The Genesis and Formation of the World Council of Churches*, (Geneva: WCC, 1982) 6, 64, 83. Also ROUSE & NEILL, *History*, σ. 658 και J. Fr. Woolverton, *Robert H. Gardiner and the reunification of worldwide Christianity in the progressive era*, (Missuri 2005), see indicatively 227 (footnote 57).

[21] See V. Stathokosta, *The relationship between the Church of Greece and the WCC*, 182-185.

[22] Ibid, 278.

[23] V. Istavridis, and Ev. Varella (eds.), *Ιστορία της Οικουμενικής Κινήσεως* (History of the Ecumenical Movement), 160 (in Greek).

as a Deputy General Secretary of the WCC (1967-1972).[24] At the General Assembly in Nairobi (1975) he was elected moderator of the Commission on Faith and Order. Under his leadership the elaboration of the three convergence documents concerning Baptism, Eucharist and Ministry was accomplished.[25] As the late Archbishop of Athens and All Greece, Christodoulos put it:

"Nissiotis was an ambassador of the idea of the participation of all Orthodox Churches in WCC, but mostly he supported something beyond the ordinary, the awareness of all Churches in the whole course of ecumenical movement."[26]

During that period, the Church of Greece contributed to the development and further maturation of the WCC. Prof. Alivizatos was a pioneer of the ecumenical movement; he was the coordinator of the efforts for church unity in West and East. His cooperation and intense efforts with Visser't Hooft resulted in the acceptance of WCC by the Orthodox Churches in the East. The contribution of many Greek hierarchs and professors was also important.[27]

The issues Orthodox representatives introduced to the WCC contributed a great deal to its theological growth as they managed to turn the interest of the WCC to matters of theology and ecclesiology. Due to the persistence of the Orthodox and the theological argumentation they developed, issues of the place of the eucharist in the Church, the sacraments, the place of saints and Holy Mary, church tradition and its continuality, proselytism and religious liberty, were included on the agenda of the WCC.[28] Thus a serious ecumenical dialogue was developed. Their insistence to project the Orthodox teaching concerning the One, Holy, Catholic and Apostolic Church led to the Toronto statement. We will mention no more here since the issue of the Orthodox contribution to the WCC will be studied further in another section of this handbook.[29]

2. The post - New Delhi era

After the New Delhi assembly, a new era started for the Church of Greece and her participation in the WCC. Radical political changes took place in Greece that ended in the abolishment of democracy by a military dictatorship. WCC's efforts to correspond to appeals against tortures that political prisoners suffered and for respect of human rights caused disturbance to its totalitarian Government as well as to church leadership, which abstained from the Uppsala assembly (1968). The attitude of the late Hieronymus Kotsonis, Archbishop of that period (1967-1973) and a prominent professor of University is still a matter of question. Although he was supportive of the participation of the Orthodox and served in the Ecumenical Movement, he suddenly turned to

[24] Ibid, 151

[25] These texts were submitted to the Faith and Order Commission at its meeting in Lima (1982) and they were sent to the Churches with the request for an official response. Konrad Raiser, *The importance of the Orthodox contribution to the WCC, Public lecture by Rev. Dr Konrad Raiser at an international symposium on "Orthodox theology and the future of ecumenical dialogue: perspectives and problems"*, Thessaloniki, Greece, 1-3 June 2003 in http://www.oikoumene.org/en/resources/documents/wcc-programmes/ecumenical-movement-in-the-21st-century/member-churches/special-commission-on-participation-of-orthodox-churches/orthodox-contribution-to-the-wcc.html?print=1_print%20A (last accessed at September 2013).

[26] Archbishop Christodoulos at Ecumenical Institute, Bossey, http://www.oikoumene.org/fileadmin/images/wcc-main/news/spring2006/christodoulos-bossey.pdf (last accessed at September, 2013).

[27] Just to mention some of them: the Metropolitans of Phiotida Amvrosios, of Edessa and Pella and later on of Thessaloniki Panteleimon Papageorgiou, of Korinthos M. Konstantinidis, and bishop of Achaia Panteleimon Karanikolas, archimandrite later on archbishop of Athens and All Greece) Hier. Kotsonis and of the Professors J. Karmiris, G. Konidaris, V. Ioannidis, Balanos, P. Bratsiotis, V. Vellas, K. Bonis, D. Moraitis, N. Nissiotis, S. Agouridis, Ev. Theodorou. See V. Stathokosta, *The relationship between the Church of Greece and the WCC*, 315.

[28] Prior to Toronto statement the General Secretary of WCC visited Greece and he was informed about the theological argumentation developed in Greece. See op.cit., 325-326.

[29] Further information can be found in V. Stathokosta, *The relationship between the Church of Greece and the WCC*, 323-337.

support the dictatorship's decisions, accused the WCC, and even objected to the participation of the Church of Greece.[30] However, there had been Greek theologians that took part in Uppsala as members of other Orthodox delegations.[31] Soon after, that crisis was over when Hieronymus officially confirmed that the Church of Greece should participate in the ecumenical movement.

Definitely, the participation of the Church of Greece in the ecumenical movement is based on the decisions of her Holy Synod, according to the synodical system. However, for the economy of this study we refer to certain periods of time according to the service of different Archbishops, also serving as Presidents of the Holy Synod.

So, especially after 1973 when Seraphim was elected to the Archbishopric (1973-1998), the Greek Church as well as the majority of Orthodox in general developed some reservations towards WCC as its agenda turned to be overfilled with social issues. Greeks protested that this emphasis was harmful for its very essence and definitely for the Orthodox participation.[32] There is no doubt that Seraphim favored the ecumenical orientation of the Church of Greece as he said the following:

"The initiative as well the responsibility belongs to our Ecumenical Patriarchate, the respectful head of Orthodoxy that Church of Greece follows in great respect."[33]

However the abovementioned reservation was kept in 80s as well, as Seraphim did not encourage the participation of the Church of Greece in the WCC although he was not against it. On the contrary, he considered that the Church of Greece has the possibility and the obligation to keep a leading role in dialogue worldwide due to historical and national reasons. He considered that Greek Theological Faculties have theologians of high level for this task which should always be fulfilled in cooperation with the Ecumenical Patriarchate that anyhow has the leading role in this special matter.[34]

The fact that Seraphim was rather indifferent to the WCC was the result of three main factors. First, he became Archbishop at a crucial historical moment when the most urgent need was reconciliation inside the Greek Church,[35] plus reconciliation of Greek society with the institutional church as she was blamed for cooperation with the dictatorship. So, he chose to keep a low profile for the Church. Second, he simultaneously blamed the WCC for its agenda, being of mostly social and not theological character. Third, Seraphim was a genius -but a very practical- man and he could not perceive any particular utility in participation of the Church of Greece in WCC. Besides, he relied on his belief that this was mainly a task for the Ecumenical Patriarchate. However, the participation of the Church of Greece continues but in a rather distant way; WCC was seen mostly as a bureaucratic affair and the participation of the Church of Greece in it as a matter of external church affairs.

[30] N. Zacharopoulos, *Πτυχή των Σχέσεων Εκκλησίας της Ελλάδος – ΠΣΕ στην περίοδο της Δικτατορίας των Συνταγματαρχών*, (An aspect of the Church of Greece –WCC relation during the time of the military dictatorship) offprint from the *Festschrift to Prof. Ioannis Papazachariou*, vol. I (Athens, 1994), 173-190 (in Greek).

[31] E.g. Alivizatos as member of the delegation of the Patriarchate of Jerusalem or as consultants (archimandrite Anastasios Giannoulatos) or secretaries (N. Nissiotis, J. Zizioulas and Dora Gontica). See V. Istavridis, and Ev. Varella (eds.), *Ιστορία της Οικουμενικής Κινήσεως* (History of the Ecumenical Movement), 181-182.

[32] Ibid., 203-204.

[33] Σεραφείμ Α´ Τίκας, *Ενθρονιστήριος λόγος*, 1974 (Archbishop Seraphim I (Tikas), "Enthronement speech", in G. Valssamis (ed.), «Οι προκαθήμενοι Αθηνών και πάσης Ελλάδος», «Εκκλησιαστική Βιβλιοθήκη I. Μητροπόλεως Δημητριάδος» 3, Βόλος 1997. See also, Seraphim (Archbishop of Athens), "Message of his Beatitude to the doxology held in the church of St. Dionysius, protector saint of Athens, 25 May 1990" *Ecclesia* 12 (1-16 Αυγ. 1990): 404.

[34] Archbishop Seraphim I (Tikas), *Enthronement speech*, 226-234 (232).

[35] It was about the intervention of religious organizations etc that acted independently from the Institutional Church of Greece, caused serious problems and disruption of church peace. Seraphim called them for Christian obedience and modesty to their Mother Church and they asked them to contribute for the peace inside her. See Archbishop Seraphim I (Tikas), "Enthronement speech" 226-234 (232).

That attitude went on until the death of Seraphim in 1996. However, the theological contribution of Greek representatives in the ecumenical endeavour kept on.

Despite the above mentioned situation, in the 90s, a revival of the ecumenical interest is noticed in Greece in the field of theological studies, mainly in the Faculty of Theology in Thessaloniki. This interest is manifested in studies, publications, conferences, as well as in theological education at all levels. Theology is characterized by its opening up and its desire to communicate and collaborate with the West. This desire seemed to be favoured by the entrance of Greece in the European Union (1992) as well as by the development of European exchange programmes for studies and teaching in European Universities. So, an opening up of Theology to society and the world and many ecumenical initiatives are noticed, aiming to emphasize the original characteristic of the Church of Christ, e.g. openness and dialogue with the world and its needs in order to witness the Orthodox faith and address to all people the redeeming word of the Gospel. It is worth mentioning the cooperation of the Faculty of Theology in Thessaloniki with the WCC and the Ecumenical Institute of Bossey that gave the fruits of a conference on "Classical Theology and Contectual Theology" (Thessaloniki 1992) and the seminary on "Orthodox Theology and Spirituality" (Thessaloniki 1994). At the same time the "Society for Ecumenical Studies and Inter-Orthodox Relations" (Thessaloniki 1993) was founded under the presidency of Prof. Dr. N. Zacharopoulos and Metropolitan of Ephesos Prof. Chrysostomos Konstantinidis, in order to cultivate inter-Orthodox communication, study of inter-Christian dialogue and promotion of Orthodox theological thought in the modern ecumenical debate.[36]

Later on, archbishop Christodoulos (1996-2008) who was very extroverted highly educated and a brilliant personality had an ecumenical vision himself. He worked for the cultivation of inter-Orthodox and inter-Christian relations.[37] He even paid a visit to WCC in Geneva and he restored the reputation and honored the work of Nikos Nissiotis by establishing a special scholarship in memory of him for ecumenical studies in Bossey.[38]

3. Canberra to Thessaloniki and the Special Commission: Reservations towards the participation in WCC

Meanwhile the Orthodox noticed serious problems in the WCC. Alongside the ecumenical orientation of the Church of Greece in the 90s, the revival of proselytism, an extremely sensitive issue for the Orthodox, came up. WCC was very helpful to the Orthodox by paying attention to their theological argumentation and condemning proselytism as a non Christian, hostile act.[39] Still, there were many unresolved problems related to the theological and ecclesiological dimension of the Orthodox participation in the WCC. As the Great Protopresbyter Georges Tsetsis concludes:

"These problems were at times demonstrated by the Churches of Constantinople, Russia, Romania and Greece, on the occasion of various commemorations or on the eve of General Assemblies of the WCC and other official or unofficial inter-Orthodox entities like the New Valamo Consultation (1977), the Symposium of Sofia (1982) and mostly the Third Preconciliar Pan-Orthodox Conference (1986).

Serious problems occurred especially during the 7th General Assembly in Canberra (1991) caused by the way its main theme on pneumatology was approached by certain speakers.[40] In 1998, just before the 8th Assembly

---

[36] "Foundation of the Society of Ecumenical Studies and Inter-Orthodox Information", in *Enimerosis* 9.3, 1

[37] He met with Pope John-Paul II (Athens, May 2001) and Pope Benedict (Rome, December 2006).

[38] Archbishop Christodoulos at Ecumenical Institute, Bossey, http://www.oikoumene.org/fileadmin/images/wcc-main/news/spring2006/christodoulos-bossey.pdf (last accessed at September 2013).

[39] V. Stathokosta, *Proselytism as an ecumenical problem and the Orthodox contribution to its understanding*, in V. Stathokosta, *"Ορθόδοξη Θεολογία και Οικουμένη: Μελέτες – Άρθρα" (Orthodox Theology and Ecumene: Studies - Articles)*, op. cit. (in Greek).

[40] V. Stathokosta, *Ορθόδοξη θεώρηση της Πνευματολογίας στο πλαίσιο του Π.Σ.Ε. Το παράδειγμα της Ζ´ Γενικής Συνέλευσης του Π.Σ.Ε. Καμπέρρα, 7 – 20 Φεβρουαρίου 1991 Με αναφορές στη Θεολογία της Συνάφειας* (Orthodox approach of

Part IV: Ecumenical Dialogue in various Orthodox Churches and Settings

in Harrare, a joint Orthodox-WCC meeting was held in Thessaloniki to study all these issues. Definitely, both sides wished to strive for the amelioration of their relation. This meeting gave a clear message to WCC about the problems Orthodox face and their pursuits. As the Great Protopresbyter G. Tsetsis underlines:

"This message was that the Orthodox Church can no longer give *"the green light"* to any theological, ethical or social innovation that the various Protestant denominations or lobbies try to impose to the rest of the Christian world through the WCC."[41]

Soon after, at the General Assembly in Harrare, WCC responded to the Orthodox challenge by establishing a "Special Commission for the Orthodox participation in the WCC."[42] The new frame shaped by the Special Commission is the one in which Church of Greece carries on her participation and work in the WCC. The core of the debate developed in this Commission is ecclesiology. Briefly, it addresses the following question to the member Churches:

"To the Orthodox: 'Is there space for other churches in Orthodox ecclesiology? How would this space and its limits be described?' And to the churches of the Reformed: 'How does your church understand, maintain and express your belonging to the One, Holy, Catholic and Apostolic church?'" (para. 16) .[43]

Actually, the Special Commission has tried to examine once more the "ecclesiologic challenge" that Orthodox participation implies to the WCC. A first reaction is already reflected in the Toronto Statement but it does not seem that we have moved any further since then.[44] Rather it is commonly accepted that the whole matter is still an open issue. As his Holiness the Ecumenical Patriarch expresses it:

"Are we today prepared, as member churches, to reaffirm the role of the Council as a privileged ecumenical space, where... the churches will continue to break down the barriers that prevent them from recognizing one another as churches confessing a common faith, administering the same baptism, and celebrating the Eucharist together, so that the community, which is what they now are, can become a communion in the faith, in sacramental life and in witness?".[45]

We should not refer further to the issue of the work and contribution of Special Commission as there is another special study in this handbook.

Pneumatology in the frame of WCC. The example of the 7th General Assembly of WCC. With reference to Contextual Theology) in V. Stathokosta, *Ορθόδοξη Θεολογία και Οικουμένη: Μελέτες - Άρθρα (Orthodox Theology and Ecumene: Studies - Articles)*, op. cit.

[41] See G. Tsetsis, *Introduction to the "Special Commission": The origin and the work of the "Special Commission" for the Orthodox participation in the WCC*, (Paper presented to the International Conference "Orthodox Theology and Ecumene", Penteli/Athens 12-13 March 2012).

[42] Πρβλ K. Raiser, *The importance of the Orthodox contribution to the WCC. Public lecture by Rev. Dr Konrad Raiser at an international symposium on "Orthodox theology and the future of ecumenical dialogue: perspectives and problems"*, Thessaloniki, Greece, 1-3 June 2003 in http://www.oikoumene.org/en/resources/documents/wcc-programmes/ecumenical-movement-in-the-21st-century/member-churches/special-commission-on-participation-of-orthodox-churches/orthodox-contribution-to-the-wcc.html?print=1_print%20A (last accessed at September 2013).

[43] Final report of the Special Commission on Orthodox Participation in the WCC in http://www.oikoumene.org/en/resources/documents/assembly/porto-alegre-2006/3-preparatory-and-background-documents/final-report-of-the-special-commission-on-orthodox-participation-in-the-wcc.html (last accessed at September 2013).

[44] K. Raiser, *The importance of the Orthodox contribution to the WCC.* op. cit.

[45] Speech on the occasion of the 60th anniversary of the World Council of Churches, Saint Pierre Cathedral, Geneva, 17 February 2008 at http://www.ec-patr.org/docdisplay.php?lang=gr&id=876&tla=gr (last accessed at September 2013).

Several Greeks are engaged in studying the issue of ecclesiology and participation in the ongoing discussion. Their work is reflected in the publication of two very important documents: "The nature and mission of the Church: A Stage on the Way to a Common Statement" (Faith and Order Paper 198), published by the WCC, and "The Church of Triune God: The Church of the Triune God: The Cyprus Agreed Statement", which is the last text of that kind the International Commission for the Anglican - Orthodox Theological Dialogue has issued.[46]

The Development of Ecumenical Theological Education in Theological Schools

Theological Faculties in Athens and Thessaloniki Universities are really active in the Ecumenical Movement. There are specialized professors who teach Ecumenical Movement and inter-Christian dialogues. In Athens University there is in the curricula a main course on "Symbolic Theology and Ecumenical Movement". Ecumenical Theological Education is a significant matter for both Faculties.

Recently, one can notice a trend for studying the income of the theological dialogue and its fruits until today, with a certain aim, namely to move further on. That means, in other words, that the ecumenical income should be the springboard for future developments soon. Two meetings held in Athens recently mark this trend. Their agenda and studies referred to the evaluation of this participation all these years. The first one was about "Dialogues of Orthodoxy – The Orthodox Witness" (Faculty of Theology, May 2010) and dealt with the income of the bilateral dialogue between church traditions closer to Orthodoxy (Roman Catholics, Anglicans, and Old Catholis) by the representatives of the Church of Greece (Metropolitan of Messinia - Prof. Dr. Chrysostomos Savvatos and Prof. Dr. M. Konstantinou) and of the Ecumenical Patriarchate (Prof. Dr. K. Delikonstantis) in these dialogues. The speakers focused mostly on the perspectives of these dialogues. The second one was a conference in Penteli Monastery on "Theological Studies and Ecumene: With reference to the participation of the Orthodox Church in the Inter-Christian Dialogues and its future" (March 2011). An evaluation of the work and perspectives of the Special Commission had been achieved in this second meeting by two pioneers of this endeavor, the Great Protopresbyter Fr. Georges Tsetsis and the Deputy Secretary General of the WCC Yorgo Lemopoulos. The meeting engaged in the discussion of the evaluation of the Orthodox – FO relation in which contrbuted the Metropolitan of Konstantia and Ammohostos Vassileios and the well known Mary Tunner, moderator of FO in the past and president of WCC for Europe at this time.

Both meetings were initiatives of the Metropolitan of Messinia Prof. Dr. Chrysostomos Savvatos and they show the desire of the Theological Schools to reclaim the progress of the ecumenical dialogue achieved until now and to contribute themselves, to bring new ideas and claims from and in the ecumenical movement.

Conclusion

The Church of Greece contributed a great deal for the formation and development of the Ecumenical Movement. This contribution started in the late nineteenth – early twentieth century and it is going on until today. Nowadays, Church of Greece counts one hundred years in the ecumenical movement, not as a simple member but as a foundational factor for its genesis and formation and she has a decisive role in the development of the ongoing discussion. She conducts a good fight for achieving dialogue and giving the Orthodox witness ("be ready always to give an answer to every man that asketh you". 1 Pet. 3:15). Orthodox cooperation under the spiritual guidance of the Ecumenical Patriarchate is a guarantee of good results. Also, the existing cooperation

---

[46] A reaction on this text from an Orthodox point of view see V. Stathokosta, "Relations between the Orthodox and the Anglicans in the Twentieth Century: A Reason to Consider the Present and the Future of the Theological Dialogue," *Ecclesiology* 8.3 (2012): 350-374.

Part IV: Ecumenical Dialogue in various Orthodox Churches and Settings

between the institutional church and the Theological Faculties plays a crucial role for achiving a significant contribution in this task. As the deceased Archbishop Seraphim stated:

> "we have at our disposal a theological human resource of the highest quality in our Theological Faculties and we can and we are obliged, due to historical and national reasons as well, to claim a leading position in the world dialogues…."[47]

However, as much as is certain about the participation of the Church of Greece in the WCC since its very beginning, it is also certain that often there are voices claiming to abstain from the ecumenical movement in general. These voices are expressed mostly in the internet in several blogs of traditionalist individuals. However, they have some influence on people as they exercise their anti-ecumenical propaganda in terms of a polemic attack against enemies that intend to destroy the Greek nation and its Orthodox identity. In a time of crisis as it is now in Greece, such a simplistic, "xenophobic" argumentation is easy to be spread. Still, the Church of Greece and the Archbishop Hieronymus II with the Holy Synod keep a serious and responsible attitude towards the WCC approving the participation in it and preserving a good relation as it is the case all these years. Of course, there is more to be done. There is no doubt that the economic crisis in Greece and Europe in general will cause problems to our societies, even the rise of fundamentalism, racism etc. That is why it is an urgent need for Churches to keep on working together.

Bibliography

Ham. Alivisatos, *Η Οικουμενική Κίνησις και η προσπάθεια του Amsterdam* (The Ecumenical Movement and the endeavour of Amsterdam), Offprint from journal «Ποιμήν», (1950) (in Greek).

Βιογραφικόν – εργογραφικόν σημείωμα του μακαριστού Αρχιεπισκόπου Αθηνών και πάσης Ελλάδος κυρού Χριστοδούλου (Biographical and Bibliographical note of the late Archbishop of Athens and All Greece Christodoulos), *Ecclesia* τόμ., 65.2 (2008): 92, http://www.ecclesia.gr/greek/press/ekklisia/2008_februarios. pdf (last accessed at September, 2013) (in Greek).

V. Istavridis and EV. Varrela (eds.), *Ιστορία της Οικουμενικής Κινήσεως* (History of the Ecumenical Movement), (Thessaloniki: Patriarchal Institute of Patristic Studies, 1996) (in Greek).

K. Raiser, *The importance of the Orthodox contribution to the WCC. Public lecture by Rev. Dr Konrad Raiser at an international symposium on "Orthodox theology and the future of ecumenical dialogue: perspectives and problems"*, Thessaloniki, Greece, 1-3 June 2003 in http://www.oikoumene.org/en/resources/documents/ wcc-programmes/ecumenical-movement-in-the-21st-century/member-churches/special-commission-on-par- ticipation-of-orthodox-churches/orthodox-contribution-to-the-wcc.html?print=1_print%20A (last accessed at September 2013).

R. Rouse and S. C. Neill (eds.), *A History of the Ecumenical Movement 1517-1948*, (Geneva, 1953).

Chrysostomos Savvatos (Metropolitan of Messinia), *Ο Αλέξανδρος Λυκούργος, αρχιεπίσκοπος Σύρου, Τήνου και Μήλου (1866-1875) και η συμβολή του στην ανάπτυξη της οικουμενικής κινήσεως (Alexandros Lykourgos, Archbishop of Syros, Tinos and Milos, 1866-1875, and his contribution in the development of the ecumenical movement)*, Offprint from the honorary volume of the Holy Synod of the Church of Greece in the memory of the Blessed Archbishop of Athens and All Greece Christodoulos, (Athens, 2010) (in Greek).

V. Stathokosta, *The relationship between the Church of Greece and the World Council of Churches 1948-1961, based on the Archives of the WCC*, (University of Thessaloniki: PhD diss., 1999) (in Greek).

-, *Ορθόδοξη Θεολογία και Οικουμένη: Μελέτες - Άρθρα (Orthodox Theology and Ecumene: Studies - Articles)*, (Ahtens: Parresia, 2011) (in Greek).

---

[47] Seraphim (Archbishop of Athens), "Enthronement Speech", 230-231.

V. Stathokosta, "Relations between the Orthodox and the Anglicans in the Twentieth Century: A Reason to Consider the Present and the Future of the Theological Dialogue", *Ecclesiology* 8 (2012): 350-374.

G. Tsetsis, *Introduction to the "Special Commission": The origin and the work of the "Special Commission" for the Orthodox participation in the WCC*, Paper presented to the International Conference "Orthodox Theology and Ecumene", (Penteli/Athens, 12-13 March 2012)

Σεραφείμ Α΄ Τίκας, *Ενθρονιστήριος λόγος*, 1974 (Seraphim I Tikas, "Enthronement speech"), in G. Valsamis. (επιμ.), «Οι προκαθήμενοι Αθηνών και πάσης Ελλάδος», «Εκκλησιαστική Βιβλιοθήκη Ι. Μητροπόλεως Δημητριάδος» 3, (Βόλος 1997) (in Greek)

N. Zacharopoulos *Πτυχή των Σχέσεων Εκκλησίας της Ελλάδος – Παγκοσμίου Συμβουλίου των Εκκλησιών στην περίοδο της Δικτατορίας των Συνταγματαρχών, (An aspect of the Church of Greece – WCC relation during the time of the military dictatorship*) in «Festschrift for Prof. Ioannis Zacharopoulos vol. I, (Athens 1994), 173-190 (offprint-in Greek)

Part IV: Ecumenical Dialogue in various Orthodox Churches and Settings

(67) Ecumenical Dialogue in the Perspective of the Orthodox Church in Czech Lands and Slovakia

Ecumenical Dialogue in the Perspective of the Orthodox Church in Czech Lands

Fr. Václav Ježek

The Czech Orthodox tradition draws on the apostolic work of the Byzantine Saints Cyril and Methodius carried on in the ninth century. Ironically, while in this regard the Orthodox Church can claim ancient provenance, the fruits of this mission of saints Cyril and Methodius appeared in other neighbouring Slavic and non –Slavic countries, while in the region of the Czech lands and Moravia, the Eastern tradition practically disappeared for various reasons in the later centuries. Although the work of saints Cyril and Methodius formed the basis of later Czech culture, the ecclesial fruits appeared in other countries.

The Slavic Czech and Moravian environments found themselves at the crossroads of central Europe, heavily influenced by Roman-Catholic culture and the German culture, but also by the nascent Reformation movement, to which the Czech side contributed some notable contributions. All this contributed to a religious and cultural fluidity, which perhaps explains the current situation in this region, which is defined by strong atheism, and to a degree religious pluralism.

In the Czech and Moravian environment the Eastern Christian tradition virtually disappeared after saints Cyril and Methodius and appeared only sporadically through migration or other sporadic endeavours. The great stimulus to the development of Orthodoxy came after the First World War when a group of clergy and laity broke away from the Roman Catholic Church and formed a reformed "Czecho-slovakian church" in 1920. This church was formed by around a hundred former Roman Catholic priests.[1] These former Roman Catholics called for a democratisation of the church, for greater conciliarity and especially for a national church. These ideas found grounding especially due to the historical event of the creation of the Czechoslovak state after the First World War, when the strongly Roman Catholic Austrian-Hungarian Empire fell apart. Roman Catholicism was viewed by many as the oppressor religion, denying the Czechs their national identity. The toleration edict of 1781 viewed the Orthodox Church as a necessary evil in Austria-Hungary, while in 1874 the state gave greater rights to the Orthodox.

This new Czechoslovak church which claimed around half a million faithful struggled from the outset to define its religious theological identity. Very soon two basic trends developed one more or less inclined to Orthodoxy whereas the other to a more Reformed -Protestant basis. The Orthodox movement was more or less exemplified by Bishop Gorazd (Matej Pavlik, 1879-1942) and archbishop Savattiy (Antonin Jindrich Vrabec 1880-1959). Gorazd was later killed by the Nazis for harbouring those who killed the Nazi leader R. Heydrich, and Savattiy ended up in a concentration camp for allegedly baptising Jews. Later this Czechoslovak church was divided and the Orthodox fraction formed their own Orthodox church in 1924, under the care of the Serbian Orthodox church.

Perhaps to the credit of the movement and to Orthodoxy itself all these Orthodox converts and figures were not naive and realised many negative traits that should be avoided in Orthodoxy. In fact, all the protagonists of Orthodoxy were characterised by the fact that they themselves had to undergo an often painful, but spiritually fruitful search for what it means to be Orthodox. This search for identity and definition itself was very fruitful from the ecumenical point of view, since it formed the basis of a positive self-critical approach, which had to define Orthodoxy consciously or unconsciously within an environment where Orthodoxy had little grounding and was virtually nonexistent. Further the nascent Orthodox movement had to struggle in the context of

---

[1] Marek, P., *Pravoslavní v Československu v letech 1918-1942*, (L. Marek, Brno, 2004), 13.

jurisdictional issues. For example, the Patriarch of Constantinople Meletios IV consecrated Savatiy as the archibishop of Czechoslovakia (4 March 1923), while for various reasons the Serbian Orthodox church also played a strong role in the formation of the church.

Bishop Gorazd is of paramount importance as an example of the Czech religious and spiritual environment. He was the embodiment of everyday and grassroots ecumenism. We can state that he was one of the key founders of the modern Orthodox tradition in the Czech area. He began his career as a Roman-Catholic priest, who later on became part of a group of Roman Catholic clergy and laity who wanted to reform the church. He said,

> "In the past, it was politics and the sword, which helped to spread religion....but we have to adopt a different way.... Theologians have to explain the causes of division, and to destroy that which is only a lie and illusion, and to show both sides the real causes of division and that these do not have substance. On both sides there is prejudice...The so-called unhealthy conservatism of the East is not such a mistake as is often portrayed. It is the character of the East that it draws on the great people of earlier ages. All changes appear as a sin against authority of this or that saint. But this surely has its positive sides. If the Eastern churches were not defined by this excessive conservatism, who knows where they would have ended up and who knows what new differences would have emerged between them and us....we then have to study and compare the origin of the differences and to seek a way how to harmonise them...Any central exclamations of unity have to be proceeded by many years of work and development....And if the work of unity should bear results, it cannot be carried on in the spirit of war, polemics, it cannot be irritable, but it has to be carried on peacefully, in a spirit of calm, and commitment. Unity does not lie in words, but in the spirit.... if any unity will emerge, it will emerge thanks to people like saints Cyril and Methodius."[2]

In 1922 Bishop Gorazd embarked on a journey to the United States of America in order to gather information and possible insights into the religious experience there. He made contacts with the Episcopilian church there. This church offered assistance to the nascent ecclesial movement in many ways forming a basis for substantial co-operation. Gorazd's ideas resonated even in the Anglican Church when the then archbishop of Canterbury mentioned the work of Gorazd and drew on resolution 62 of the Lambeth conference from 1908, where the Anglican Church permitted the distribution of baptism and the Eucharist to members of the Orthodox church.[3]

In America, Gorazd formed and organised a number of religious communities which would belong to the Czecho-Slovak ecclesial organisation. Later however, these did not bear fruits for many reasons, especially since they did not receive support both morally and otherwise from Czechoslovakia itself.

The Orthodox Church in the Czech lands and Moravia, from its outset at least in the modern period had to co-operate with all the churches, especially with the Roman Catholic Church and the Protestant churches. In the Czech lands and Moravia the overwhelming majority of the Orthodox were converts, who grew up in other non-Orthodox traditions. This stimulated an important intellectual, theological and spiritual self-reflection in the Orthodox Church. Further, it provided a basis for a self-critical approach, which also was capable of identifying possible negative traits in the life of the Orthodox and was not offered a possibility to dwell in a safe-haven of ideological triumphalism as can be the temptation in "traditional" Orthodox churches.

Orthodox believers in most cases were able to incorporate the positive experiences and traits of other Christian traditions and were able to utilise these in a positive way in their own new experience as Orthodox Christians. By its nature the Orthodox Church in the Czech lands and Moravia could not define itself in opposition to other Christian traditions, but defined itself by being an inclusive organisation.

It seems that the period before the Second World War was a period where the Orthodox church offered alternatives to an existing religious milieu. It was not built by some external mission or pressure, but was rather developed as a consequence of seeking alternatives to an existing religious order and within this order.

---

[2] Lecture given by Gorazd at the slavonic club of the Literary organization at the theological faculty in Olomouc, Šuvarský, J. Biskup Gorazd, *Orthodox Church in Czechoslovakia*, (Prague, 1979), 231.
[3] Šuvarský, J. Biskup Gorazd, *Orthodox Church in Czechoslovakia*, (Prague, 1979), 142.

During the communist period, the Czech and Slovak Orthodox Church participated in many ecumenical activities both abroad and at home, which however were tainted by the communist period and ideology. Participation in the ecumenical movement was further limited by financial resources, political will and the control of the communist government. All ecumenical efforts were understood and portrayed by the government as efforts "towards world peace". Interestingly, there were some figures from Czechoslovakia from all Christian denominations who even sincerely argued for communism as a compatible movement with Christianity.

Currently, the ecumenical movement in the Czech Republic is dictated by a number of presuppositions. First of all, atheism and a historically conditioned aversion to the Church exasperated by the communists provide for a framework were no church can claim some ideological dominant position in the society. Any church working for Christianity has to "apologise" for some negative events in other churches, regardless if these are different churches, since the ordinary theologically or religiously uneducated person attributes blame to the "Church" without discerning between the various churches. This in a way sponsors ecumenical interaction between the churches, since they fight a common enemy that is ignorance, prejudiced hatred or simply atheism. Any mission has to start from the Gospel, and only after a significant catechetical preparation, can there be any talk of denominational difference.

Secondly the Orthodox Church is still a church of converts, even though significant numbers of migrants are beginning to form a significant proportion of believers. Some of these converts, who become priests, bring with them a closed, overtly "romantic" idea of the Orthodox Church, which precludes them from ecumenical work. They are not interested in ecumenism, since the Orthodox Church is seen as self-sufficient. This view is of course unsustainable, since any person coming to the church realises that the Orthodox church is incapable of forming in many areas or situations a self-sustaining community and therefore one has to "co-operate" with his or her environment in order not to be totally isolated, which itself would be ecclesiologically unsustainable, since the "community" is at the heart of the Orthodox mindset. However, others are open to co-operation realising that this will not destroy Orthodoxy and that being inclusive is a fundamental Orthodox trait.

Thirdly, the Orthodox Church in the Czech Republic does not seek to convert others to Orthodoxy. While there is some form of mission, this is subtle. The greatest challenge which the Orthodox Church faces is how to incorporate positive developments into its own framework. It has to draw on the positive experiences and culture of other churches and utilise these within its own tradition in the area of the Czech Republic. Otherwise, it will be limited to the culture of other traditional Orthodox churches and would not offer any viable and salvific possibilities within the national context. In fact, there is great help and support from people who do not join the church, but are sympathetic to Orthodoxy.

Fourthly, it is becoming increasingly obvious in the Czech republic that the success of any given Christian church is dictated by the concrete fruits that it offers or rather produces. Claiming to have and possess the truth, the correct tradition or other intellectual arguments are nothing compared to the concrete expressions of love and sympathy on the parish and individual level. Thus all the churches are on the "market" and are tested according to what they offer and exemplify regardless of what they believe is true. The success of the Orthodox Church hinges on the ability of its priests and faithful to offer the substance of empathy and love. This in a way is positive, since all the churches have to "prove their worth" not merely by defining themselves against the other.

Partly because the churches are finding themselves isolated, and do not have the financial or other capacity to offer a complex service on many fronts, the churches co-operate on a number of levels.[4] This itself contributes to the effective witness of the Christians churches as a whole. It is increasingly becoming obvious that the local parish carries the challenge of implementing good and Christian relationships with other churches.

---

[4] See Ambros, P., *Fórum Pastorálních teologů VI, Pastorační situace jako výzva k ekumenismu, Centrum Aletti Velehrad-Roma*, (Refugium Velehrad, Roma, Olomouc, 2007) .

This micro-ecumenism is dictated not only for a desire for co-operation but in fact it is the only way forward for churches who are in such a difficult Christianity environment as the Czech setting.

The Orthodox Church participates on various ecumenical projects, which accent the overall potential Christian contribution to society at large. For example, the Orthodox Church participates in common ecological projects. Common projects for renewable energy such as windmills draw the various Christian traditions together including the Orthodox Church. In this context the Orthodox Academy in Vilemov organises meetings, ecological projects and theological meetings, which are ecumenically minded. In practically all cases there is mutual co-operation in sharing church buildings between the Orthodox Church and the Protestant churches. There is a common inter-faith radio broadcast.

The Orthodox community in the Czech Republic is small and has some historically conditioned advantages and disadvantages in its life, which have a bearing on ecumenical thought. It does not form a state religion and is formed mainly by members who came from other traditions after self-reflection and intellectual and spiritual journeys. All this is an advantage, since this often presents stimulus to an inclusive interaction with other Christians without feeling threatened. However, the communities are small and cannot suffice as integral spiritually and materially self-sufficient communities. This again stimulates the believer to a more inclusive community minded approach, without of course necessarily denying the salvific value of the Orthodox tradition.

The staunchly antagonistic environment towards the "Church" and the fact that no Church is favoured by the state coupled with a strong critical intellectual tradition display the necessity of co-operation between the Christian churches in the Czech Republic. Further, it also shows the necessity of individual efforts by the Christians to embody the spirit of love and co-operation in their respective contexts.

Recently co-operation between the Czecho-slovak Orthodox church and the ecumenical movements was subjected to a test, since a debate emerged in the Ecumenical Council of Churches on consensual voting, which is supported by the Czech side. It was stated that any movement away from this form of voting would trigger a exodus of the Czech church from this organisation. Another issue relates to the term "ecumenical liturgy" which is rejected, since the liturgical tradition in the Orthodox Church has a specific meaning.

In conclusion we can again draw on Gorazd who in 1940 observed:

"There is an ecumenical movement, but we cannot expect that there will be an ecumenical council soon, which can only take place on a unity of faith. Before we reach this unity of faith, taking into account the difference of opinions, the only way forward is love. Unity will not come from above, it cannot be dictated. The ecumenical movement strives forward mostly to identify that which unites the churches and not which causes division. The worst obstacle to unity is mutual ignorance and repetition of the many but unchecked incriminations. The movement attempts to identify that which is substantial and that which is not substantial, and then on the basis of the discovered substance to reach a common formulation, and by this a unity in faith. Before we reach this stage ecumenism proclaims co-operation in various fields on the basis of love, love which is exemplified by the parable of the good Samaritan, love formulated by expressions from the first centuries of Christianity- 'I refuse the error, but I love the erring human being.'"[5]

Bibliography

Ambros, P., *Fórum Pastorálních teologů VI, Pastorační situace jako výzva k ekumenismu, Centrum Aletti Velehrad-Roma*, Refugium Velehrad, (Roma, Olomouc, 2007)

Marek, P., *Pravoslavní v Československu v letech 1918-1942*, L. (Marek, Brno, 2004)

Šuvarský, J *Biskup Gorazd , Orthodox Church in Czechoslovakia*, (Prague, 1979)

---

[5] Šuvarský, J, *Biskup Gorazd , Orthodox Church in Czechoslovakia*, (Prague, 1979), 233.

Part IV: Ecumenical Dialogue in various Orthodox Churches and Settings

Ecumenical Dialogue in the Perspective of the Orthodox Church in Slovakia

Vladimir Gerka

The Orthodox Church in Slovakia is a part of the autocephalous Orthodox Church in the Czech Lands and Slovakia.

The ecumenical situation and dialogue in Slovakia (the Ecumenical Context)

The current ecumenical relations of the Christian churches in Slovakia are determined by many factors affecting them to a large extent, directly or indirectly:
  a. the dogmatic teaching, canons and traditions of the churches;
  b. the historical development of the churches, as well as the historical relations between them;
  c. the political and societal changes in history of Central Europe, including the territory of Slovakia;
  d. the geographical location of Slovakia, laying on the borders between Eastern and Western Christian traditions, directly reflected in the ecumenical relations;
  e. the gradual formation of ecumenical relations;
  f. the number of the faithful of individual churches;[6]
  g. the geographic distribution of believers according to their membership in individual churches;[7]
  h. the contemporary tendencies.

The ecumenical situation on the territory of today's Slovakia has always been based on the actual possibilities of churches in a given period.

The Slovak territory is not large and the Orthodox Church is not represented by large numbers of believers, although the Orthodox in this area have always played a role in the formation of ecumenical relations and in the historical events which have also had an impact on other surrounding regions.

The statuses of churches, as well as their relationships, have changed significantly in time. Every historical period had its specific characteristics and influenced the formation of the following relations. The background for the understanding of the current ecumenical context in Slovakia is to be found in the following historical milestones.

---

[6] According to the 2011 Population Census, the Slovak Republic had nearly 5.4 million inhabitants, out of which 75 % declared their affiliation to Christian churches. The Roman Catholic Church registers 62.0 % of the population, the Greek Catholic Church 3.8 %, the Evangelical Church of the Augsburg Confession 5.9 %, the Reformed Church 1.8 %, the Orthodox Church 0.9 % of the population. The other registered churches and religious societies such as the Religious Society of Jehovah's Witnesses, Methodist Church, Christian Churches, Apostolic Church, Baptist, Seventh-Day Adventists Church, Brethren Church, Central Union of Jewish Religious Communities, Old Catholic Church, Czechoslovak Hussite Church, New Apostolic Church, the Baha'i community, the Church of Jesus Christ of Latter-Days Saints, count together 1.6 % of the population. 13.4 % of the population considered themselves as religionless and 10.6 % of the population did not revealed their religious affiliation. In the last ten years, a decrease in the number of persons declaring their affiliation to any of the registered churches counting most of the believers was registered, while the population without religion increased. Up to ten percents of the population was not reported as belonging to any religion, yet this fact does not change the overview of the religious structure of the population in Slovakia.
  Source: Základné údaje zo sčítania obyvateľov, domov a bytov 2011. Obyvateľstvo podľa náboženského vyznania. [Basic data from the 2011 Population Census. Population by religion.] (Bratislava: The Statistical Office of the Slovak Republic, 2012), 7–11.
[7] Most numerously represented are the Roman Catholic Church in Western Slovakia, the Evangelical Church of A.C. in Central Slovakia, the Greek-Catholic Church and the Orthodox Church in North-Eastern Slovakia, and the Reformed Church is in the South-Eastern Slovakia. The highest percentage of people without any religion is found in the capital city of Bratislava.

1. Spreading of Christianity and the first struggles between Western and Eastern traditions

Various missionaries came on the territory of today's Slovakia from the East and West. These missions had little success because the Slavs, who took over the territory from 4th to 6th century, did not understand Greek or Latin.

In the 9th century the territories of today's Czech Republic and Slovakia were part of Great Moravian Empire. Great Moravian Prince Rastislav during his reign (846 – 870) tried to free his people so they would not be subjected to foreign nations and could live full lives in Christ. He searched for spiritually and culturally advanced missionaries who would love their faithful. In 862 he asked the Byzantine Emperor Michael III to send such missionaries.[8] Rastislav did not want just any teacher, just any faith, as he already experienced the Frankish mission and saw that faith is a subject of different interpretations among the Christians. He longed for a true and reliable faith. In 863 at his request holy brothers Cyril and Methodius from Byzantium came to Great Moravia. They brought scripture to the Slavs, spread the Christ's Gospel and served the divine services in the understandable living Slavic language.

Prince Rastislav fought with the Franks over the sovereignty of his territory. In doing so, he got into a dispute with his nephew Prince Svätopluk, who at that time collaborated with the Franks. Svätopluk betrayed Rastislav and assisted the Franks in seizing him around the year 870. Prince Rastislav was blinded and died a martyr's death in Regensburg. The Orthodox Church in the Czech Lands and Slovakia canonized Prince Rastislav as saint and equal-to-the-Apostles in 1994.

Svätopluk, after Rastislav, took over Great Moravia. After the death of St. Methodius in 885 Svätopluk together with the Frankish bishop Wiching drove Cyril and Methodius mission from Great Moravia and subsequently raised a Frankish – Latin orientation in the territory. Most of the Slavs who through the mission of Cyril and Methodius accepted Christianity and Eastern rite were forced to accept Latin rite.

2. Gradual Latinisation in 10 – 16 centuries

After the invasion of the Hungarians to the territory of Great Moravia in 906 the Kingdom of Hungary gradually arose. In the years 1000 – 1918 present territory of Slovakia belonged to the Kingdom of Hungary and was exposed to the Hungarian ruling.

The newly established Kingdom of Hungary began to focus more on the West due to the political reasons and so was the Latin rite implemented. Everything that reminded the Orthodox heritage of the mission of Sts Cyril and Methodius was closed; however, it remained in many monasteries for a long period in the Kingdom of Hungary, although they were gradually latinised too.

After the Tatar invasion in 1241 the country was devastated. In an effort to uplift the economy of the Kingdom of Hungary the territory was inhabited by German colonization. This strengthened the Latin rite and western influence on the life of Slavs.

The position of the Orthodox Church on the territory of today's Slovakia was strengthened by Wallachian colonization in the first half of the 14th century that came to this territory from Ukraine-Romanian borderline.

From the 15th century the Orthodox Serbs lived in the southwest of present Slovakia. They had a special status in the Kingdom of Hungary and strengthened Orthodoxy there.

Orthodoxy survived mainly in the northeast of the Kingdom of Hungary where Ruthenians lived (present north-eastern Hungary, eastern Slovakia, south-eastern Poland – Galicia, Carpathian Ukraine), which was significantly affected by good relations with Kievan Rus, where Kievan metropolitans had a significant impact on the spiritual orientation of the Orthodox believers.

---

[8] Rastislav's message to Michael III: „Since our people have cast paganism and hold Christian law and we do not have such a teacher who would in our language explain to us the true Christian faith, so the other regions, when they see us, did the same. Send us then bishop and a teacher of such. Because from you the good law spreads to all sides."
Source: *Život Konštantína-Cyrila.* [The Life of Constantine the Philosopher.] in RATKOŠ, Peter: *Veľkomoravské legendy a povesti.* [The legends and stories of the Great Moravia.] (Bratislava: Tatran, 1994), 36.

Part IV: Ecumenical Dialogue in various Orthodox Churches and Settings

The Orthodox believers in the Kingdom of Hungary belonged to the jurisdiction of Constantinople. After the fall of Constantinople guidance for the Orthodox could only come from the Patriarchal Exarch Metropolitan of Kiev. After the immigration of Serbs to the Kingdom of Hungary this territory officially came under the jurisdiction of the Serbian Orthodox Church.

The Hungarian ruling class despised and humiliated Slavic Ruthenian population if they did not accept the Latin rite. Later Latin hierarchy deemed schismatic everything that was not Latin.

The Reformation and Counter-Reformation had a negative impact on the life of the Orthodox Church in the territory of the Kingdom of Hungary too, particularly due to the power interests of the feudal lords who spiritually and politically subordinated the Orthodox believers.

In the process of the recatolization of the Kingdom of Hungary, starting in the first half of the 17th century, many Protestant families went back to the Catholic Church and influenced the Orthodox believers to go into union with Rome.

3. Union of Uzhhorod 1646

The Catholic feudal lords due to their power interests enacted the Union of Uzhhorod in 1646, which sought to bring Orthodox believers living in the north-eastern part of the Kingdom of Hungary under the power of the Roman Pontiff. Orthodoxy was, against the wishes of the faithful, gradually and forcibly liquidated. Thus, the entire property of the Orthodox Church became the property of the Union, which was constituted as the Greek Catholic Church. The Orthodox believers in the fight with the Union while under the influence of the Reformation and Counter-Reformation adopted the Reformation in some parishes.

4. National and spiritual revival in the 19th century

In the mid-19th century in the Kingdom of Hungary, a large national and spiritual revival of the Slavs occurs as the effect of the national and social oppression by the state power and denationalization. At the same time interest in Orthodoxy appears among some Greek Catholics, Catholics and Protestants. A movement for a return to Orthodoxy emerges in the northeast of the Kingdom of Hungary mainly among Ruthenians. The believers that used the Eastern rite visited places in Tsarist Russia such as Pochajev, Kiev, where they accepted the Orthodoxy. The strongest revival of Orthodoxy came from America, where the local people immigrated for work opportunities. In the United States and Canada they united with the Russian Orthodox Church and returned back home as Orthodox. Austro-Hungarian state power saw this movement as pan-Slavic and hostile to the state. Orthodox faithful living in northeast of the Kingdom of Hungary were not allowed to establish Orthodox parishes and to serve Orthodox services freely. Orthodox clergy was prosecuted as the enemies of Austria-Hungary, Tsarist Russia agents and violators of peace.

5. Beginning of the building of the ecumenical relationships

The Catholic Church in ambition to solve interconfessional problems and rapprochement of churches started to organize Velehrad conferences in years 1907, 1909, 1911, 1924, 1927, 1932, 1936, 1946, etc., which aimed at the questions of the particular periods. This movement was provoked by the conclusions of the 1st Vatican Council, where the Catholic Church in 1870 declared the dogma of papal infallibility.

6. Return to the Orthodoxy

After World War I a large movement for a return to Orthodoxy arises in the newly formed Czechoslovak Republic. In the Czech Republic it was a movement away from Rome. There were 121,000 Orthodox believers in the territory of Mukachevo-Prešov Eparchy in 1930.[9] Almost all of them were under the jurisdiction of the Serbian Orthodox Church and some parishes were under the jurisdiction of the Church of Constantinople.

After World War II there was a great euphoria towards Russia in Czechoslovakia and the movement for a return to the Orthodoxy intensified.

The position of the Orthodox Church in Czechoslovakia was strengthened by the government, because the Czech Orthodox Church was declared illegal for its patriotism and support of some clergy who sheltered the assassins of the German Reich Protector R. Heidrich. Czech Orthodox bishop Gorazd and his colleagues were sentenced to death. Church property was confiscated in favour of the German Empire.

7. Atheistic regime in the years 1948 – 1989 and the period of 1948 – 1968

After the election and change of the democratic system in 1948 churches experienced a difficult reality. Communist government by adopted law[10] took control upon all churches in 1949. Any church activity needed the state permission. Church property was nationalized or controlled by the state. By this rule the state started to pay salaries for priests and the costs of churches' administration offices.

The Communists perceived the Greek Catholic Church in a hostile way, as it did not stand up for the Communist Party but for the Democratic Party during the elections. At the same time they suspected it of assisting the Organization of Ukrainian Nationalists – Bandera faction in rebellion against the Soviet Union.

Communist leaders sought various ways to weaken the position of the Catholic Church, because it, through the Vatican headquarters, had prepared the most effective strategy against the communist pressure, compared to the other confessions. Greek Catholic historians write about this fact: "Dissolution of the Greek Catholic Church in 1950 must be seen in a wider context. It was a part of general hysteria of a new atheistic regime, which ultimately tried to dispose any manifestation of a religion." [11]

In 1950 the political leadership of Czechoslovakia manipulated by Soviet ideology in an effort to weaken Vatican influence organized an official movement in the Greek Catholic Church, which in cooperation with the State declared the Greek Catholic Church in Czechoslovakia illegal. On 28 April 1950 the Great Council of the Greek Catholic clergy and faithful was held in Prešov, which proclaimed the cancellation of the Greek Catholic Church. Consequently all the church buildings, parish houses and the offices of the Church were, by the State regulation, transferred to the Orthodox Church. That property was considered as a heritage of the members of the parish. Other property of the Greek Catholic Church was nationalized. 105 priests converted from the Greek Catholic Church to the Orthodox Church. Majority of the members of the Greek Catholic Church accepted Orthodoxy. Many of them were preparing themselves to conversion to the Orthodox Church. After the dissolution of the Greek Catholic Church, Orthodox priests served only where believers wished that.

Because the event of 1950 was a matter of politics and power, liquidation of the Union was regarded as a cancellation of the remains that affected people by the Catholic feudal lords, when they forced them to leave Orthodoxy for the Union; although, the communist dictatorship brought up the reaction of many people.

---

[9] "Православная церковь на Пряшевщине" [Orthodox Church in Prešov territory.] in *Православный церковный календарь на 1950 год.* [Orthodox Church calendar 1950.] (Praha: Prešov, 1949), 72.

[10] See the Law No. 218/1949 Coll. on economic provision for the churches and religious organizations by the state.

[11] ČITBAJ, František, "Unionizmus a ekumenizmus na území tzv. Prešovska v 20. Storočí" [Unionism and ecumenism in territory of so-called Presovsko in 20th century.] in CORANIČ, Jaroslav – ŠTURÁK, Peter (eds.): *Gréckokatolícka cirkev na Slovensku vo svetle výročí* [Greek Catholic Church in Slovakia in the light of anniversaries.] (Prešov: Gréckokatolícka teologická fakulta Prešovskej univerzity, 2009),161.

Part IV: Ecumenical Dialogue in various Orthodox Churches and Settings

8. The establishment of the Ecumenical Council of Churches in Czechoslovakia

An attempt to create the council of various churches in the interwar period was stopped by World War II. The pressure of atheistic regime on Christian churches was an impulse for them to seek for mutual support, common opinion and ecumenical cooperation.

In 1955 the Ecumenical Council of Churches in Czechoslovakia was founded. Its role was, first of all, to promote the Christian ideas of reciprocity and solidarity in the practice.[12]

9. Period of the years 1968 – 1989

In 1968, due to the democratization process in society and the socio-political situation (Prague Spring) the Greek Catholic Church was re-opened.[13] Many believers returned back to the Greek Catholic Church, because of the strong pressure from the public and state offices that decided where, in which parishes, the Orthodox services could be held. The State government did not allow the Orthodox believers to acquire new worship space, because it did not want further sacred objects. The Greek Catholic Church was allowed but the churches and the church buildings remained property of the Orthodox Church even though they had to be already settled in 1968. However, after the invasion of the armies of Warsaw Pact into Czechoslovakia, political turnover in the society changed the direction of the societal development. Among the believers of both churches strong emotional charge occurred. While the Greek Catholic Church was supported by the Roman Catholic Church and emigration, the Orthodox Church did not have anyone to rely on.[14]

The Orthodox Church found itself in a very difficult situation. It was violently denied entry to the 285 churches[15] and many parish houses. Some priests with their believers converted to the Greek Catholic Church either under strong political and social pressure or for material benefits and social position.

Some people who worked in state government assumed in 1968 that the Orthodox parishes would disappear and the problem would be solved. In many cases, this actually happened. That is why many times the requirements of the Orthodox believers were not heard. Many Orthodox believers perceived ecumenism, as such, as a cover-shield, in particular of the Catholic Church, for the total absorption of the Orthodox Church by all possible means.[16] The Orthodox clergy and believers were disappointed that the rapprochement of both churches is not maintained in a way of professional theological dialogue but by the restoration of the Union. And this created an enormous tension and hostility between the believers of both churches. The Orthodox believers then considered ecumenism as a big delusion. On the other hand, some Lutheran, Reformed and Catholic believers sympathized with the Orthodox.

Ecumenical meetings of the churches in the years 1980 – 1989 were not an open solicitation for a greater religious freedom. The Christians felt the need of being together in the face of an atheistic pressure. The socialist institution tried to use this Christian motive in its favour as a voice of the people – believers in their effort to preserve the peace in the world. On the agenda was the so-called peace theology, which beside other things in the state interest also sought to witness to the religious freedom in the socialist institution.

Ecumenical and peaceful meetings also partially served for mutual exchange of information and building the trust between the government and the churches, where it was also shown that activities of the churches and worship meetings do not endanger the state institution.

---

[12] DRÁB, Pavol *Ekumenizmus na Slovensku* [Ecumenism in Slovakia.] (Prešov: Vydavateľstvo Michala Vaška, 1998), 84.
[13] Government Decree No. 70/1968 Coll. on the Economical Assistance to the Greek Catholic Church by the State.
[14] PEŠEK, Ján – BARNOVSKÝ, Michal: Pod kuratelou moci. Cirkvi na Slovensku v rokoch 1953 – 1970. [Under curate of the power. Churches in Slovakia in years 1953 – 1970.] (Bratislava: Veda, 1999), 205.
[15] GERKA, Milan "Pravoslávna cirkev na Slovensku" [Orthodox Church in Slovakia.] in *Odkaz sv. Cyrila a Metoda.* [The Legacy of the Saints Cyril and Methodius.] 1998) 21, n. 6.
[16] PRUŽINSKÝ, Štefan *Aby všetci jedno boli. Pravoslávie a ekumenizmus.* [That all may be one. Orthodoxy and ecumenism.] (Prešov: Metropolitná rada Pravoslávnej cirkvi na Slovensku, 1997), 37.

10. Velvet Revolution in 1989

After November 1989 and the fall of the socialist atheist establishment, the Christian churches focused more on their own needs.[17] There were efforts of returning church property, teaching of religion, freedom of the press, setting up religious schools, charities and diaconal institutions. At the same time there was also a spiritual awakening and finding the new spiritual horizons of many formal Christians while they were proselytized.

The Orthodox Church in Slovakia at that time was exposed to the great struggle for its survival. Based on the adopted law[18] all churches and buildings, which in 1990 were used by the Orthodox Church, but in 28 April 1950 were the property of the Greek Catholic Church, had to be handed over by the Orthodox Church to the Greek Catholic Church, without any regards to the fact that the believers in 1990 were Orthodox and wanted to remain so.

The problems between Greek Catholic and Orthodox believers were often dealt with emotionally. The State government has sought to help both churches and provided financial assistance, so the both churches were the damaged least. The Orthodox Church has built or acquired a new property – churches, parish and administrative buildings. In the years 1990 – 2000, the Orthodox believers built 120 churches and built or bought 30 parish houses, 2 buildings for a seat of the Bishops, 1 building as a seat for the Metropolitan Council and 2 buildings for the Faculty of Theology.

The Orthodox Church and the faithful are grateful for moral and social help offered by Ecumenical bodies – the World Council of Churches, the Conference of European Churches, the Ecumenical Council of Churches in Czechoslovakia and since 1993 Ecumenical Council of Churches in Slovakia. Thus the loss of ecumenical confidence of the Orthodox believers in Slovakia slowly began to recover.

Later, the two churches began to look for a way to fulfill the obligation to bear witness of the peace. Finally, in 2002 the Framework Agreement on Property Settlement between the Greek Catholic and the Orthodox Churches was signed. After this point the new challenge arises. In the Orthodox Church it is a struggle to retain the faithful, who are often exposed to the temptations of modern liberalism and consumer lifestyle.

11. The formation of the independent states in 1993

Political concerns prompted the division of the Czech and Slovak Federal Republic into two independent states. On 1 January 1993 the Czech Republic and the Slovak Republic were established. This event affected the entire organization of a church life. A new relationship between churches and state started to be built. The Ecumenical Council of Churches in the Czech Republic and the Ecumenical Council of Churches in the Slovak Republic were established. The Orthodox Church in Czechoslovakia did not split and remained united. There were only necessary organizational adjustments and change of the name for the Orthodox Church in the Czech Lands and Slovakia.

Contemporary mutual relations among churches in Slovakia

Understanding the contemporary ecumenical situation in Slovakia from the point of view of the Orthodox Church comes directly from these historical milestones. These milestones also represented measures for possible development of the ecumenical effort. All mentioned historical events express themselves now and form also contemporary tendencies for ecumenical development.

The answer to the question why in this territory in the times of Great Moravia people accepted the faith and Eastern rite from Sts. Cyril and Methodius and their work had spread also to other countries and why today Orthodoxy lives only in one part of this territory and mainly in the territory of Eastern Slovakia and among only a considerably small group of inhabitants, is important not only for the Orthodox Church, but it is also important challenge for the future of the ecumenical discussion in Slovakia.

---

[17] See the Law No. 308/1991 Coll. on The Freedom of Religious Belief and The Status of Churches and Religious Societies.
[18] Legislative Disposal of the Presidium of the Slovak National Council No. 211/1990 Coll. on the Resolution of the property relations between the Greek Catholic Church and the Orthodox Church.

Part IV: Ecumenical Dialogue in various Orthodox Churches and Settings

At the same time it is interesting that the other churches in Slovakia themselves profess the legacy of St. Cyril and St. Methodius and confess it, too. And not only churches, but the Slovak society as a whole. The Constitution of the Slovak Republic as the highest law of the state in its preamble states:

"We, the Slovak nation, bearing in mind the political and cultural heritage of our ancestors and the centuries of experience from the struggles for national existence and our own statehood, mindful of the spiritual heritage of Cyril and Methodius and the historical legacy of Great Moravia, ..., adopt through our representatives this Constitution." [19]

According to previous statement, it is possible to understand the status of the Orthodox Church in Slovakia using two questions, how are the relations of the Orthodox Church in Slovakia with the other churches determined and why are ecumenical contacts so important for the Orthodox Church in Slovakia.

Mutual relations among respective confessions in Slovakia today depend on the number of their believers and on big differences among them in their membership. This decisively determines their status and ecumenical efforts. The majority Roman Catholic Church does not consider ecumenical cooperation as necessary for fulfilling its mission in the conditions of the Slovak society. For such territories this is characteristic also for the presence of the Greek Catholic Church. Relations of the Orthodox Church to the Greek Catholic Church are complicated everywhere and Slovakia is not an exception. Another ecumenical task for the territory of Slovakia is the formation of the Old Catholic Church and its relationship towards the Roman Catholic Church. Churches which developed from the Reformation still consider the history of the Counter-reformation as a barrier for their relationships with the Roman Catholic Church. However, these relationships between the Roman Catholic Church and the Evangelical Church have improved after the visit of the Pope John Paul II in Slovakia in the year 1995.[20]

In general it is possible to say that the contemporary relations among churches in Slovakia are on a relatively good level. Representatives of respective churches visit each other on various occasions related to their lives and they solve together issues of church and State relations. The main goal of the ecumenical movement in Slovakia is seeking a common celebration of visible signs of unity of Christian churches and their cooperation on issues of the life of the churches and their status in the society.[15]

The development of the ecumenical dialogue in Slovakia takes place on three platforms. The first platform is given by the framework of the Roman Catholic Church, which develops certain activities throughout its Board for Ecumenism under the Slovak Bishop's Conference.

The second platform is given by the framework of the Ecumenical Council of Churches in the Slovak Republic. It is a communion of churches which confess Lord Jesus Christ as Saviour and the Head of the Church. They see a common basis for their religious teaching in the Holy Scripture and in the ecumenical confessions of faith (Apostolic, Nicene and of St. Athanasios). By their activity together and by their respective activity they celebrate God the Father, the Son and the Holy Spirit in the Word.[21] It creates an atmosphere of understanding, tolerance, the building of good mutual relations among churches and mutual collaboration. It consists of 8 full member churches and of 4 churches as observers.[22]

Ecumenical Council of Churches in Slovakia works also on issues and activities dealing with relations between the churches and the state by strengthening the legal and societal status of churches in Slovak Re-

---

[19] The Constitution of the Slovak Republic, the Constitutional Law No. 460/ (1992) Coll.

[20] The website of the Ecumenical Council of Churches in Slovakia. http://www.ekumena.sk/Hlavna_stranka/historia.htm (last accessed at September 2013).

[21] Constitution of the Ecumenical Council of Churches in Slovakia. http://ekumena.sk/Hlavna_stranka/statut.htm (last accessed at September 2013).

[22] Full member churches: 1. Evangelical Church of the Augsburg Confession in Slovakia; 2. Reformed Christian Church in Slovakia; 3. Orthodox Church in Slovakia; 4. Brethren Church in Slovak Republic; 5. Evangelical Methodist Church, Slovak area; 6. Czechoslovak Hussite Church in Slovakia; 7. Baptist union in Slovak Republic; 8. Old Catholic Church in Slovakia. Observers: 1. Roman Catholic Church in Slovak Republic and 2. Greek Catholic Church in Slovak Republic represented by Slovak Bishop's Conference; 3. Seventh-Day Adventists Church, Slovakian conference; 4. Apostolic Church in Slovakia.

public.[23] It is dedicated to the issue of the protection of believers before the harmful spiritual movements in the established Centre for the Study of Sects, which publishes the professional magazine *Rozmer*. Every year in January it organises *The Week of Prayers for Christian Unity* and a common ecumenical service which is transmitted television. Also there is a periodic ecumenical radio broadcast. It deals with social issues such as service to people in material need and humanitarian aid at home and abroad. The grant programme *Round Table* played an important role which helped churches in their service in the social sphere after the change of the political system, and at the same time it contributed to building of ecumenical relations. The function of the advocacy which is used among the churches also belongs to the area of strengthening relationships. Orthodox Church participates in Ecumenical pastoral care in armed forces and armed corps. Ecumenical council of Churches in Slovakia cooperates with WCC and CEC.[15]

Among important ecumenical tasks belongs also the building of relations between traditional churches and the so-called free churches. Originally member churches of the Ecumenical Council of Churches were the traditional churches. The so-called free churches such as Baptists, Methodists, Adventists, Brethren Church, and Apostolic Church based themselves in Slovakia in the interwar period or after the World War II and were considered sects by the traditional churches. In the last period on both sides has grown a new generation and proselytization is not the only way to get new members. The contemporary situation offers new possibilities.

The charismatic movement is a phenomena of the ecumenical scene. It spreads in all churches. The smaller a particular Protestant confession in Slovakia, the more difficult it is for it to come to terms with the Charismatic movement. So-called free churches have to face splits quite often.

The third platform for the development of the ecumenical dialogue takes place on a local level. An example is the Ekumena Košice – Ecumenical community of churches in the territory of the town of Košice, which from 1994 helps Christians to get closer to one another and supports tolerance, common recognition and brotherly cooperation by a wide spectrum of activities.[24]

An important expression of the ecumenical cooperation was a 17 year long common effort, a spiritual and theological struggle which was crowned by the publication of the first Slovak ecumenical translation of the Bible in 2007.[25]

The presence and development of ecumenical theological education in schools

Education of the Christians and view on Ecumenism in religious studies at the Orthodox Theological Faculty of the University of Prešov

The Orthodox teachers speak for tolerance to members of the other denominations in religious and theological education but also for the consistency of Holy Orthodoxy on the level appropriate to the age and education of those who are educated.

Although a fair view of the audience on the members of the other denominations is determined by the canons and traditions of the Church, the study of the cause includes the background of the issue of the canons, political and social time, the impact of the philosophical streams of the period and the social status of the society. There are differences in the causes of that doctrine between Orthodox and other denomination member in the 4th – 6th centuries and Orthodox and a denomination member in the 21st century. It is not only the essence of truth itself, but also the reason why the person has taken it and follows it. This is one of the starting points in addressing doctrinal issues among Christians today. In secular society the faithful remain in their faith not only because

---

[23] For example preparation of the Agreement between the Slovak Republic and the Registered Churches and Religious Societies in the Slovak Republic as Law No. 250/2002 Coll. and others important laws and agreements.

[24] Constitution of the Ecumenical community of churches on the territory of the town of Košice. in (Ekumena Košice. Košice: Karnat, 2001) 104, See more <http://ekumena-ke.sk>

[25] Biblia – slovenský ekumenický preklad. [Bible – Slovak Ecumenical Translation.] (Banská Bystrica: Slovenská biblická spoločnosť, 2007).

Part IV: Ecumenical Dialogue in various Orthodox Churches and Settings

of the deep spiritual convictions of the teachings, but also under the influence of traditions and standards of practice of the family community in which they live.

The issue of other confessions has been taught at the Orthodox Theological Faculty of the University of Prešov using the different methods. At the beginning it was *Comparative theology*, which acquainted the listeners with the teaching of the other confessions and with Orthodox criticism of it. Later it further explored of the teaching of the other confessions through the ecumenical movement in the subject *Orthodoxy and Ecumenism*.

Later, in the subject *Ecumenical movement and the Orthodoxy* is given an overview of the history of the ecumenical movement, focusing on the current initiative of the Orthodox Church in the ecumenical movement containing the origin and development of Christian ecumenism, development and complexity of the concept of Ecumenism, the history of the ecumenical movement, predecessors of the ecumenical movement in the 19th century, Orthodoxy and efforts to unify Christianity, the World Council of Churches – its principles, mission and structure, theological content of the General Assemblies of the World Council of Churches, importance of the participation of the Orthodox Church in the ecumenical movement.

Subject *Sectology* deals with the origin, development and belief of the religious communities and sects focusing on their harmfulness and destruction of society. It also deals with the basic concepts and definitions (sect, heresy, and religious community), the cause of the origins of the religious groups and sects, sects division, psychological contexts of the sects, the sects and their destruction of a society, leaders of sects, chiliasmus and charismatic movement.

The subject of *Orthodox and non-Orthodox Christology* surveys transcendental Christology in the works of Karl Rahner, study of the works of Wolfgang Pannenberg and current neopatristic Orthodox Christology in the works of Mantzaridis, Nellas, Yannaras, a survey of Anglo-American efforts to discover the historic Jesus, works of B. Mack, N. T. Wright, C. Testament and a survey of the Christological assumptions of current Christian authors.

Presently, there is a deeper learning and exploration of teaching and certain mind streams in the confessions, as well as efforts to understand the causes of such views and create the most objective and constructive opinions on the non-Orthodox believers. Everything is confronted from the patristic point of view at the issue.

The ecumenical movement in the current world is facing a crisis. Previous ecumenical efforts have not brought the expected unity. In post-socialist countries in the freedom of religion, many believers do not see the need for unity, because they are closed in themselves. We believe that the pressure of consumerism and liberalism will call the theologians to pause and show to the world the true value of Christ's Gospel. Only in this view can Christians find unity in Christ's love, which will help them to depersonalize, to get rid of worldly wisdom, and to understand Christ's truth, which is the only one, and one without which the true Christian unity is unthinkable.

This is an answer to the question of shallow ecumenism, which is explained as the form of unity in diversity. Unity cannot be in diversity, it only can be a diversity of the manifestations of one and the same truth. However, Christians can gain such attitudes if they want to be led by the Spirit of God manifested in the tradition of the Church.

The Orthodox Church proclaims this truth at every liturgy, before the symbol of the faith the believers are called by the words: "Let us love one another, so we unanimously confess." This is a real Ecumenism, and every ecumenical movement, if it aims jointly to love and unanimously to profess, is on the right way to the destination. When it comes to something else it becomes formalism and in its essence remains still a labyrinth, in which believers will remain disappointed.

Finally it is necessary to add that on the occasion of ecumenical contacts it is possible to find inspirations for pastoral care in contemporary society. From this point of view Christian confessions should together recognise reasons for the development of new sects and movements which usually have their origin in the hidden spiritual illnesses of certain Christians and in an inappropriate pastoral care in a respective church community.

The Orthodox Church after the year 1990 not only in Slovakia but also in many other countries had to face proselytizing from various Christian confessions. For this reason the ecumenical movement today in the eyes of many Orthodox believers lost its credibility and authority. It is necessary to evaluate and to change the direction of Ecumenism so that it would be understood as an instrument of knowing better and of getting closer to one another and as an instrument of common resolution of problems in the life of the church. We deal here with the area of belief, ethos, spiritual and social service for an individual and for a given society and with seeking an optimal and common approach of Christians towards themselves and towards the World to which we have to give witness to the Truth of Christ.

Bibliography

Biblia – slovenský ekumenický preklad. [Bible – Slovak Ecumenical Translation.] (Banská Bystrica: Slovenská biblická spoločnosť, 2007).

Čitbaj, František, Unionizmus a ekumenizmus na území tzv. Prešovska v 20. storočí. [Unionism and ecumenism in territory of so-called Presovsko in 20th century.] in CORANIČ, Jaroslav – ŠTURÁK, Peter (eds.) Gréckokatolícka cirkev na Slovensku vo svetle výročí. [Greek Catholic Church in Slovakia in the light of anniversaries.] (Prešov: Gréckokatolícka teologická fakulta Prešovskej univerzity, 2009).

Ekumena Košice. (Košice: Karnat, 2001).

Constitution of the Slovak Republic, the Constitutional Law No. 460/1992 Coll.

Dráb, Pavol, Ekumenizmus na Slovensku. [Ecumenism in Slovakia.] (Prešov: Vydavateľstvo Michala Vaška, 1998).

Ecumenical Council of Churches in Slovakia. <http://www.ekumena.sk>

Gerka, Milan, "Pravoslávna cirkev na Slovensku" [Orthodox Church in Slovakia.] in Odkaz sv. Cyrila a Metoda, n. 6 [The Legacy of the Saints Cyril and Methodius.] 1998) p. 19 – 28.

Ondica, Slavomír et al., Duchovné Slovensko[Spiritual Slovakia.] (Sabinov: Dino et Trnava: Spolok svätého Vojtecha, 2010).

Pešek, Ján – Barnovský, Michal, Pod kuratelou moci. Cirkvi na Slovensku v rokoch 1953 – 1970. [Under curate of the power. Churches in Slovakia in years 1953 – 1970.] (Bratislava: Veda, 1999).

"Православная церковь на Пряшевщине" [Orthodox Church in Prešov territory.] Православный церковный календарь на 1950 год. [Orthodox Church calendar 1950.] (Prešov – Praha, 1949).

Pružinský, Štefan, Aby všetci jedno boli. Pravoslávie a ekumenizmus. [That all may be one. Orthodoxy and ecumenism.] (Prešov: Metropolitná rada Pravoslávnej cirkvi na Slovensku, 1997).

Základné údaje zo sčítania obyvateľov, domov a bytov 2011. Obyvateľstvo podľa náboženského vyznania. [Basic data from the 2011 Population Census. Population by religion.] (Bratislava: The Statistical Office of the Slovak Republic, 2012).

Život Konštantína-Cyrila. [The Life of Constantine the Philosopher.] in RATKOŠ, Peter, Veľkomoravské legendy a povesti. [The legends and stories of the Great Moravia.] (Bratislava: Tatran, 1994).

Dhimiter Qiosia

Albania is a country of the SE Balkan Peninsula without a dominant religion, in which live four traditional religious communities: the Orthodox, the Roman Catholic, the Muslim and the Bektashi. Lately the community of Protestants was recognized. Religious freedom is guaranteed by the constitution since 1998. The state has a separate agreement with every religious community, which was approved and ratified by the parliament.[1] The religious communities in Albania began the process of reconstructing their spiritual and social mission, after a period of hard testing and dramatic developments for decades. The Orthodox Church of Albania, as an integral part of Orthodoxy in the world, but also of Albanian society in a country of various religious communities, without constituting the overwhelming majority, commenced its arduous work. Apart from the work which defines its nature, in order to develop, i.e. a missionary action, a catechetical and a charitable, so as to overpower the great void which was created by the regime, it needed to develop that work in an ecumenical spirit, building ecumenical relationships and experiencing the ecumenical mission, the ecumenical ministry and the ecumenical witness. Therefore this has been a goal from the beginning and remains constantly a challenge for the Orthodox Church in Albania.

Archbishop Anastasios since the first moment of his arrival in Albania on 16 July 1991,[2] taking into account the mentality of the people and respecting them, used to say that, "a forest is no more beautiful when it has only a tree, but another tree grows to support and to help the other." He immediately gave great importance to the communication and cooperation between the Christian communities in Albania, so that there would be a strong voice of Christianity in the diverse religious society of the country. He gave Orthodoxy very quickly the honorary position at home and abroad, in the international inter-Christian activity. He succeeded in receiving its cordial hospitality and covering the needs for the ecumenical activities in Albania. He describes Orthodoxy as "a diamond that has nothing to fear, if it stands next to the others, indeed it will shine even more."[3] On these guidelines the Church of Albania with its initiatives, its participation, or its presence in several meetings, with its deep tradition and its ethos, and especially with the experience and the deep spirit of Anastasios, has contributed to the strengthening of relations and dialogue.

Thus with the Roman Catholic community of Albania, apart from the mutual visits of the heads of the two Christian communities in major festivals of each community, and the joint statements in difficult situations or festival celebrations,[4] meetings have taken place in the context of a mutual acquaintance, cooperation and dialogue. Indeed, between the two theological Schools, the Theological Academy *"Resurrection"* in Saint-Blaise - Durres and the Theological Seminary of the Roman Catholic Church in Shkoder, since 2000 onwards, various topics have developed, aiming at the common acquaintance of worship and spirituality, emphasizing more the common axes of our united tradition. Apart from the Roman Catholic community in Albania, after 1990 there is a strong presence and activity of the various Protestant groups, which number over 100. During the course of their activities in our country, the Orthodox Church came to contact with

---

[1] See "The agreement with the community of the Orthodox Church" no.10057, 22.01.2009, *Government Bulletin*, art.7, 4 (February 2009): 138-147.

[2] See Papazachou, "The first visit to Albania, of the Patriarchal Exarch Mr. Anastasios, *"Gone"*, 549-579.

[3] Anastasios, *In Albania*, 334.

[4] At Easter of 2001 they made a joint statement on: "Vdekjen e ktheu në jetë - Urrejtjen në dashuri" - Deklaratë e përbashkët me rastin e Pashkëve, e Kishave Orthodhokse e Katolike të Shqipërisë" ("Death he turned into life - hate in love" - Joint statement on the occasion of the feast of Easter of the Orthodox and the Roman Catholic Church in Albania") See *"Ngjallja"* No. 5:104, (May 2001) 12.

some groups, of which many appeared with extreme tendencies. Most groups decided to organize together in one body and were recognized by the state as a Christian community under the name Brotherly Evangelical community of Albania (VUSH[5]). Immediately after the official recognition, with the initiative and invitation of the Orthodox Church, there was a meeting of the two communities at the Holy Archdiocese of Tirana. Archbishop Anastasios, head of the delegation, eager and pioneer of inter-Christian and inter-faith meetings, expressed his goodwill towards the guests, highlighting the need for dialogue, mutual acquaintance, cooperation and exchange of views with the prospect of spreading the Gospel to the contemporary society of Albania.[6] In the ambit of cooperation the Christian communities in Albania decided to jointly create the Albanian Bible Society, which is recognized as Inter-Christian SA, and the heads of the Christian churches run that organization in turns. By working together, the translation of the New Testament from the original was made, and it continues with the Old Testament in the modern Albanian language.[7] Taking account of the above, regarding the issue of inter-Christian relations between the Christian communities in Albania during the period 1991-2012, relations have improved significantly, fostering relations of trust, cooperation and love. These ecumenical relations were put into a new perspective, where there is no doubt that the work of the Orthodox Church and Anastasios, remains steadfast. Moreover, Anastasios as a person who contributed to the WCC[8] and with an ecumenical magnitude attached great importance to the full membership of the Church of Albania in the major Christian organizations, without reservations and fears. Thus, the Church of Albania was accepted to CEC in 1992 and to the WCC in 1994, the only institution of the Ecumenical Movement in Albania, contributing to the ecumenical work at local and international level, realizing a task of reconciliation at various levels.

The contribution of the Orthodox Church in the relations between religious communities in Albania

The religious communities in Albania are characterized by a historical tradition between their relations. The presence of all the believers in the festive events of others irrespective of the community they belong to is a testimony, which confirms the practice that developed mainly in the 20th century.[9] Many argue that the religious coexistence in Albania constitutes a positive element in the contemporary Albanian society and consider it a valuable treasure of the country. In many villages and towns, in a condominium, everyone next to each other, regardless of religious faith. The tradition of religious tolerance that exists was further encouraged in the communist era, with the mixed marriages, intensifying until today the phenomenon of different faiths in the members of one family. But today also there are cases where the newlyweds are baptized and come to the Church to get married, regardless of their religious origins. The Primate of the Church of Albania with his great experience as a member of several theological committees in the Department "Dialogue with Men of Other Faiths and Ideologies" of the WCC and the "World Conference on Religion and Peace" and as an expert on the

---

[5] VUSH - Vëllazëria Ungjillore e Shqipërisë (Evangelical Brotherhood of Albania).

[6] See "Takimi përfaqësuesve të Vëllazërisë Ungjillore të Shqipërisë në Kryepiskopatën e Shenjtë" (Meeting of the representatives of the Evangelical Brotherhood of Albania at the Holy Archdiocese), "*Ngjallja*" no.11 (226), November 2011, p.3.

[7] See "Së bashku', në një përkthim të ri të Fjalës së Perëndisë" ("Together" in a new translation of the Word of God), "*Ngjallja*" no.11 (178), (November, 2007), 5.

[8] See Tsobanidou S.: "The Orthodox Church", *History of Orthodoxy*, 292. The 9th General Assembly in Porto Alegre, Brazil in 2006 unanimously elected Anastasios as one of the eight presidents. (In December 2003, the Archbishop was elected one of the two deputies of the CEC).

[9] On 16 November 1990 as the day of the reopening of the first mosque after 23 years in Shkodre, there were present Christians of the two Churches, as it happened with the reopening of the Churches, in which the traditional religious communities in Albania took part together, see http://www.kmsh.al / historiku-i-kmsh-se.html (last accessed at 30.08.2012). At the reception of Anastasios on 16th July at the airport there were present the representatives of the religious communities, see Dhima, Dëshmitë, 112.

issues of Islam has offered an invaluable contribution to interfaith relations. He himself pledged to continue the old tradition of religious tolerance in Albania with sincere support of the peaceful coexistence and mutual respect between the religious communities.[10]

The Church continues to foster relations of trust with the Muslim community. Many argue that Islam in the Balkans, and especially in Albania, should be regarded as a "*European Islam*" in the sense that it is tolerant, open and secular.[11] This community historically belongs to the "*hanefi*" school[12] and is generally characterized by gentleness, maintaining a peaceful form, a religious practice impossible so far.[13]

Considering the old tradition and new reality in the ambit of teaching the lesson of Religious Studies at the Theological Academy "*Resurrection*", there have meetings with teachers of the Muslim community. After 1990, there were individual radical groups, which did not found fertile ground. In any case, the Orthodox Church in Albania is struggling to maintain traditional relations between communities, as they constitute a factor of peaceful coexistence in Albania.

Moreover, in Albania there is the community of Bektashi.[14] Between the two communities there are very good relations, perhaps the best relations between religious communities in Albania.[15] It is obvious because the Bektashi in their overwhelming majority are located in southern Albania, where the Orthodox also live. In the past twenty years, there have been several meetings, visits, seminars and symposiums between religious communities as well as various interfaith conferences by various agencies, to foster the spirit of tolerance and cooperation and to promote it inside and outside Albania.[16] Almost every year an interfaith meeting takes place in the country, which aims to strengthen cooperation and coexistence and the promotion of interfaith harmony in Albania.[17] Taking into account the above, the four traditional religious communities moved jointly to an organized institution. Thus was founded the Interfaith Council of Albania in February 2007, the formation of which was supported by the World Conference of Religions for Peace - WCRP - (Archbishop Anastasios is Honorary President) and was officially recorded as an organization, "expressing what existed actually" according to Archbishop Anastasios.[18]

---

[10] "The enthronement speech of His Beatitude the Archbishop of Tirana and All Albania", *Church* 69 (1992) 517-519, 548-551.

[11] Clayer Nathalie in an interview: "Rrënjët e Islamit në Ballkan" (The roots of Islam in the Balkans) newspaper "*Shqip*", 18 May 2006, 18-19.

[12] This school was founded in the eighth century in Iraq by Ebu Hanife and is generally followed by the Muslims in Turkey, the Balkans and in other countries of the West, such as the UK and Germany. It is considered to be liberal and progressive compared to the other schools of Islam.

[13] See Ziaka A., *Interfaith*, 287 and on.

[14] The Bektashya, which doctrinally belongs to Shiite family, but in Albania, had received a strong influence from Christianity, from which one observes today many elements in the local community. In Albania it was spread through people who were members of the Ottoman administration and spread mainly in southern Albania. After the establishment of the Turkish state in 1925, the Bektashi were expelled from Turkey. The then leader of the community, Salih Niyazi, who was of Albanian origin, moved its headquarters in Albania.

[15] In the Condolences by the Church of Albania to the Bektashi community on the death of their leader, in April 2011, Archbishop Anastasios expressed particular honor to his personality, the love and the efforts for the closest cooperation in the recovery of faith and of the religious harmony in the two decades, see "*Ngjallja*" 219.4 (2011): 1.

[16] See "Konferencë me komunitetet fetare nën kujdesin e Presidentit R. Meidani", (Conference with the religious communities under President R. Meidani), "*Ngjallja*" 75.12 (1998): 1, 2.8. Archbishop Anastasios in his speech stressed: "I believe that in Albania a model of religious coexistence can be build, valuable for application in the wider region of the Balkans," 8.

[17] We can mention the interfaith conference (South East Europe Interfaith Conference) entitled: "Advancing Peace and Stability through Regional Cooperation", 16-19 November 2005, where the Archbishop was one of the main contributors with the theme: "For a peaceful coexistence in the Balkans", see "*Ngjallja*" 155.12 (2005): 1,3. Also the meeting of the NATO, "Science for Peace Project", from 19 September to 1 October 2006, with the participation of the religious communities in Albania. The meeting was attended by various celebrities from the Balkans. See "Ngjallja" 165.10 (2006): 12.

[18] See "Të ofrojmë një model për bashkekzistencën fetare dhe bashkëpunimin harmonic në mbarë Ballkanin", "*Ngjallja*" 170.3 (2007): 4.

In the development of progress of such a reality, the Orthodox Church of Albania instrumentally contributed, as in many other meetings. As a small church among the other Orthodox Churches in the world, it has contributed to the ecumenical activity and the ecumenical forefront of the ecumenical witness, with its Herculean work (taking into account the short period of 20 years and various adverse conditions), thanks to the Enlightened Ecumenical Master and Missionary of our time, Archbishop Anastasios, who in Orthodox teaching with a continuous ecumenical Orthodox vision, raised the level and strengthened the voice of Orthodoxy in the world, revealing its ecumenical content and its eschatological ecumenical certainty. Apart from the various meetings, the Church of Albania with the many educational institutions, kindergartens (17 in total), in which many children from non-Orthodox families attend and then with the other schools (technical schools), primary schools, Tirana (2002) in Durres (2004) and Gjirokastra (2008) and lastly the recent establishment of the University "*Word*" in Tirana, institutions that offer education in the spirit of social solidarity and unconditional love. All of this, with the purpose of assisting in "raising the standard of living, thinking, education, health and culture", in the service of the infrastructure of coexistence among people.[19] Through its work in the field of education and health it has embraced man regardless what believes in and where he belongs. Also, the youth centers offer the timeless values of Christianity and the spiritual feeding the young, especially with the summer camps from which they go through every summer over 1,000 children, involving children from across the country. The youth camps have become spiritual and educational centers, teaching respect of individuality and diversity, friendship and love—all of these serve everyone and are open to Christians and Muslims. We believe that this reality constitutes the essential basis of the "*dialogue of life*" which society experiences. Therefore, what is being done is a form of dialogue "*in the context of life and deeds*",[20] an inter-faith-dialogue at a very good degree.

Also, the Church of Albania has given a major contribution in the efforts for peace in our region. Particularly at the critical moments of the dramatic events, in the former Yugoslavia, in 1993.[21] It has also contributed to the dialogue between religious communities of Skopje in the meeting of Morges, Switzerland from 11-13 June 2001. In the spirit of peace in our region, the Church of Albania was the first to react constructively to the events of Kosovo in 2004.[22] The statement: "No one has the right to use the holy oil of religion to strengthen the fire of armed conflicts. Religion is a holy gift to soften hearts, to heal the wounds and bring peacefully people and the peoples closer"[23] has become a slogan. At the same time he acted practically offering the amount of $ 600,000 to build symbolically on site, a church and a mosque.[24] But previously, the Church of Albania in October 1998, had offered housing in camps, minimum conditions of hygiene, food, clothing and subsiding of the fear and indignation of 33,000 non-Orthodox refugees of Kosovo. Since then, a friendly acquaintance was initiated between ethnic Albanians of Kosovo and the Albanian Church, which continues until today. Indeed since 2001, relations entered a new phase with the summer camps being organized for the children of Kosovo by the Orthodox Church of Albania. Every year during summer many children in the city Malisevo are accommodated, coming from various schools of the city, with a participation of over 600 children, (in 2008 and 2009, the number reached 1800 children). The teachers in charge together with students are active in the schools of the city (the writer has an experience because many times he participated in this project),

---

[19] Anastasiou, *In Albania*, 251.

[20] See Matsoukas, Universal, 245.

[21] From 12 to 16 September 2001 its Conference was held in Sarajevo: "Christians and Muslims in Europe, responsibility and religious commitment in the plural society". In this conference, the Archbishop was awarded by the Foundation "Pro Europa" the prize "Pro Humanitate" for the year 2001 for his contribution to the efforts for peace in the region and beyond.

[22] The statement of the Holy Synod on 24.06.1999 "the various religious communities ... we are called to become inspired workers of reconciliation and peace. To take the lead in building a free and just society, which will respect religious freedom and the individuality of others, who, regardless of what believes in, is still a creation of God and our brother".

[23] See Anastasiou, *Traces,* 404.

[24] See "Një kontribut me një kuptim të veçantë - 600,000 $ USD - për një kishë dhe xhami në Kosovë" (A contribution of particular symbolism - $ 600,000 - for a church and a mosque in Kosovo), "*Ngjallja*" 4 .135 (2004): 1.

Part IV: Ecumenical Dialogue in various Orthodox Churches and Settings

fostering a spirit of solidarity, peace and love, etc..[25] For our activity in Kosovo have expressed their gratitude the community of Malisevo and its schools, rewarding our team and the Archbishop. Our activity has not gone unnoticed by the media in Kosovo.[26]

For his contribution to the Church and to the Albanian society Archbishop Anastasios was honored by the President of the Republic of Albania with the medal "George Kastriotis Skanderbeg" with the following written praise: "*... for the significant contribution and action in the resurrection of spiritual faith and hope for a better future, for the re-establishment worship institutions, as well as for the support and increasing of religious tolerance and harmonious interfaith coexistence of the Albanian people.*"[27] This contribution and appreciation of him, and of the Church of Albania, inside and outside the country, "constitutes a live voice of existence between Christians and Muslims", in our time.[28] In the commemoration of 20 years of Anastasios's election as Archbishop of Albania, the state leadership attended, as well as religious leaders and many other personalities from Albania and abroad, who by their presence honored his ecumenical deed and his ecumenical contribution and that of the Orthodox Church of Albania to the Orthodox faithful, all Christians and Muslims of the country. The anniversary was celebrated in the new magnificent cathedral of the "Resurrection of Christ" in the center of Tirana, which symbolizes what has been achieved in twenty years, "*as a sign of eternal witness of Christ's victory over death .... and will symbolize the resurrection of the Albanian people.*"[29] A resurrection that describes the whole work of the Church[30] through inspiration from the personal experience of the Resurrection, from the whole Church, because it is strength in the execution of its ecumenical work. The Archbishop often reminds us of the passage of Paul: "to know him and the power of the Resurrection of his ..." (Phil. 3:10). That is precisely the secret of his wonderful deed, because it is a deed of miracle. The speech of the Ecumenical Patriarch Bartholomew in completion of the ten years since the enthronement of our Archbishop in his salutation says that: "... the achievements by the Archbishop and Primate of the Most Holy Orthodox Autocephalous Church of Albania during the elapsed decade, we confess that this is an exquisite miracle similar to which in no other Orthodox Church of those that recently left the suffocating pressure of atheistic regimes has been performed."

Bibliography

"The enthronement speech of His Beatitude. Archbishop of Tirana and All Albania", *Church* 69 (1992).

Archbishop Anastasios of Albania, *Traces of searching the transcendental*, (Akritas: Athens, 2006) (in Greek).

Archbishop Anastasios of Albania, *In Albania Cross and Resurrection*, (Livanis: Athens, 2011). (in Greek).

Clayer, Nathalie, interview "Rrënjët e Islamit në Ballkan" (The roots of Islam in the Balkans), "*Shqip*", (18 May 2006).

Delikostopoulos, Athanasios I., Anastasios, Archbishop of Tirana and All Albania - *The pastor of contemplation, creation and peace, publishing house* (Eptalofos: Athens, 2005).

---

[25] We want to remind you that initially the war erupted in the city Malisevo. We started with topics showing that we want to continue the friendship that begun in 1999 and bringing hope to the children after the many traumas of war. Then the issues have to do with the fruits of the Holy Spirit (Gal. 5.22), see "Ngjallja" October 2002, September 2008, August 2009.

[26] We mention the newspaper "Koha Ditore" entitled: "Kampet model shkollash verore - vullnetarë të Kishës Ortodokse Autoqefale të Shqipërisë organizojnë kampe për fëmijë të Malishevës" (The camps - an example of summer schools - volunteers of the Orthodox Autocephalous Church of Albania organize camps for the children of Malisevo), (9 July 2007).

[27] http://www.orthodoxalbania.org/new/index.php?option=com_content&view=article&id=847%3Apresidenti-topi-de-koron-kater-udheheqesit-me-te-larte-komuniteteve (last accessed at 17.09.2012).

[28] Ziaka, "Interfaith Dialogue ...," 532-567, 554.

[29] Delikostopoulos Anastasios, 196.

[30] See, Forest J., *The Resurrection*, 127.

Dhima, Aleko, *Dëshmi të një besimtari të përunjur - Kujtime nga jeta ime në shërbim të Kishës* (Testimonies of a humble believer-remembrances of my life in the service of the Church), (Orthodox Research Institute, Boston 2010).

Ziaka, Angeliki, *Interreligious Dialogues, vol.2, The encounter of Christianity with Islam,* (P. Pournara: Thessaloniki, 2010).

Ziaka, Angeliki, "Interfaith Dialogue" History of Orthodoxy - Orthodoxy in Dialogue (224-369), v.8, Road.

Fletorja, Zyrtare (Bulletin of Government) Art.7, (February 4, 2009) 138-147.

Forest, J., "The Resurrection" in Jim Forest, *The Resurrection of the Church in Albania - Voices of Orthodox Christians,* (WCC publication: Geneva 2002).

Matsoukas, Nikos, *Ecumenical Movement, History - Theology*, (Pournaras: Thessaloniki, 1996) (in Greek).

Papazachos, George, "The first visit to Albania of the Patriarchal Exarch of Mr. Anastasios", in *Gone - Charistirios Volume in honor of Archbishop of Albania Anastasios (Yannoulatos)*, (Armos: Athens 1997).

Tsompanidis, Stylianos, "The Orthodox Church and the World Council of Churches. A "society" of mutual enrichment in the way of pursuit", *History of Orthodoxy - Orthodoxy in Dialogue,* v.8, Road.

"*Ngjallja*" (Resurrection), Monthly Journal of Orthodox Autocephalous Church of Albania, 104.5 (May 2001), 226.11 (November 2011), 178.11 (November 2007), 219.4 (April 2011), 75.12 (December 1998), 155.12 (December 2005), 165.12 (October 2006), 170.3 (March 2007), 237.10, 106.7 (July 2001), 135.4 (April 2004), and 212.9 (September 2010).

"Koha Ditore", Kosovo Albanian newspaper, July 9, 2007.

Electronic Resources

- Official website of the Muslim Community of Albania http://www.kmsh.al (last accessed at 30.08.2012).
- Official website of the Orthodox Autocephalous Church of Albania http://www.orthodoxalbania.org/new (last accessed at 17.09.2012).

(translated by Fr. George Anagnostoulis)

(69) ECUMENICAL DIALOGUE IN THE PERSPECTIVE OF THE ORTHODOX CHURCH IN POLAND

Henryk Paprocki

1. Historical Background

The beginnings of the tradition of Eastern Christianity on Polish lands go back to the times of the mission of the Brother Saints Cyril and Methodius. It is difficult to establish with certainty which Liturgy the brother saints celebrated; nevertheless, the most probable one is considered to be the so-called Liturgy of Saint Peter, which, in accordance with the Byzantine liturgical pattern of the 8th century, comprised the canon of the Roman Mass. Saints Cyril and Methodius brought about a change in the mind-set of the faithful by introducing the language of the people into the Liturgy. The Cyrillic-Methodian mission had a minor impact on what is today Polish territory and did not play any considerable part in the final process of Christianisation.

The political expansion of Poland to the East left much longer-lasting traces. Nonetheless, even until the middle of the 11th century, there existed a Slav hierarchy next to the Latin one and in Krakow a Western Rite was still celebrated in a Slavic language. This practice disappeared definitively only as late as the 15th century. The Orthodox Church found itself within the sphere of influence of Polish politics following the annexation of the principality of Galicia (Halizia) by Casimir the Great. That king went to Constantinople to request that a distinct Orthodox Metropolitanate be established and the Patriarch appointed Anthony, who was the choice of the king, as Metropolitan of Galicia. On the one hand, the Metropolitanate in question included the dioceses of Chelm, Turow, Przemysl and Vladimir in Volhynia. On the other hand, as regards the Polish-Lithuanian union, the lands of the Grand Duchy of Lithuania were now within the sphere of influence of Polish politics.

In the 16th century, because of the pressure exerted by the authorities of the state and of the Roman Catholic Church, a union with Rome was established (at the Council of Brest-Litovsk of 1596). That union did not bring the expected results either for the state or for the Church and, instead of helping consolidate the state, led to long religious wars and to the persecution of the Orthodox who had not accepted the union. This was also one of the causes of the wars between Poland and Muscovy, as a result of which one part of the Lithuanian lands joined the Muscovite state. It was not until the reign of Stanislaw August Poniatowski, at the time of the Great Sejm, that the Pinsk Congregation raised the issue of the freedom of Orthodoxy and of its hierarchical organisation in Poland.

The partitions of Poland shed a new light upon the problem of Orthodoxy and the Union. The latter remained only in the part of Poland which was under Austrian rule. In the Russian part, a large majority of parishes spontaneously returned to Orthodoxy. Nonetheless, because of the disastrous policy of the Russian government, the Uniates of Podlesia[1] were brought back together by force. The period of partitions clearly complicated national and religious relations on the lands of the old Polish Rzeczpospolita [Polish calque of the expression "Res publica"].

The history of Orthodoxy changed radically in 1915, when the authorities of the Russian state gave up the Polish lands. The largest part of the Orthodox population and the clergy were equally evacuated. On Polish lands there were hardly ten priests and two bishops left. The life of the Orthodox Church was almost entirely shattered because of all that. However, active Orthodox Christians remained in some urban centres. In 1918 a mass evacuation started in the opposite direction, and the Patriarchate of Moscow entrusted Bishop Dionizy [Dennis] Waledynski with the organisation of a new diocese, that of Polesia. In 1919 the situation became clearer, but on the part of the Roman Catholic Church massive claims started being laid to the assets of the Orthodox.

---

[1] Podlesia: region of Bialystok. Polesia is located to the south of Podlesia (still called Podlachia).

In 1921 Archbishop Jerzy [George] Jaroszewski arrived in Poland and the state authorities entrusted him with the organisation of the Church; this was confirmed by a decision of Patriarch Tikhon, who raised the Archbishop to the rank of Exarch. However, certain bishops had a negative attitude to the project of organising the Orthodox Church in Poland in accordance with the principle of autocephaly or ecclesial autonomy. Despite the growing difficulties, Archbishop Jerzy, raised in 1922 to the rank of Metropolitan of the province, set up a printing press, a chaplaincy for the Armed Forces, and church fraternities, all of which enabled the Church to return to normal functioning. On 14 June 1922, the Synod of Bishops, relying upon the decision of the Patriarch of Moscow, which stipulated that in case of difficulty in the communication with the Church authorities, the Bishops shall have the right to organise their own dioceses and Metropolitanates without the agreement of the Patriarchate, ruled that it would thenceforth be itself that would make all decisions regarding the affairs of the Church in Poland. After the tragic death of Metropolitan Jerzy in 1923, the Synod elected the aforementioned Bishop Dionizy Waledyński as his successor and addressed itself to the Patriarch of Constantinople with the request that he ratify the choice and grant him the same rights and prerogatives as those of Metropolitan George.

In November 1923, Metropolitan Dionizy addressed a letter to Patriarch Tikhon, requesting that he grant autocephaly to the Church in Poland. The situation of the Russian Church at that time was complicated and there was practically no Synod of Bishops, something which made the observance of the canonical procedure impossible. In that state of affairs the Polish government and the Orthodox Church engaged in talks with the Patriarchate of Constantinople so that the latter may grant autocephaly. In effect, by its *tomos* of 13 November 1924, the Patriarchate granted autocephaly to the Church of Poland, making reference to the situation in which the Metropolitanate of Kiev depended on Constantinople but passing over in silence the period during which it belonged to the Russian Church. This being so, the Church of Russia did not recognise the autocephaly solemnly proclaimed on 17 September 1925.

The internal situation of the Orthodox Church was still complicated at that time because of the neo-Uniate activity of the Catholic Church and the local movements of the Ukrainian and Belarusian populations. On the contrary, the authorities of the state strove hard for the polonization the Church. The most threatening action against Orthodoxy was taken by state authorities in 1938. In that year, 108 Orthodox churches were blown up by those in power.

During the interwar period there were five Orthodox dioceses on the territory of Poland: those of Warsaw, Wilno, Polesia, Volhynia and Grodno (Hrodna); two seminaries (Wilno and Krzemieniec), a theological sixth-form college (in Warsaw), a school of theology (in Dermań, Volhynia), a school for the training of Readers (in Jabłeczna) and the Department of Orthodox Theology at the University of Warsaw, opened on 8 February 1925. The Church also included 9 monasteries, 125 deaneries and 1457 parishes (without counting their subsidiaries). It had around 4.5 million faithful.

The most tragic time in the history of Orthodoxy in Poland began on 1 September 1939. Metropolitan Dionizy was forced to withdraw from the leadership of the Church and all decision-making power passed into the hands of national groups. The occupation authorities established peace in a certain number of Orthodox villages; several people active in the Church died in concentration camps or were shot. The war disrupted the life of the Church, and the Department of Orthodox Theology ceased to exist, just like the seminaries, the printing press and several parishes. During World War II, an important part of the Polish army who emigrated consisted of Orthodox soldiers. There was a chaplaincy for the Armed Forces, headed by Bishop Sawa Sowietow, who had the rank of brigadier.

At the time of the liberation, the Orthodox Church was in a state of serious disorganisation, because of the losses suffered during the war, the lack of a high-ranking clergy and the great reduction of the number of the faithful, mainly as a result of the change of the borders of Poland, the displacement of populations to the Soviet Union, and in the context of the operation "Vistula".[2] On 17 April 1948, the President of the State annulled the recognition previously granted to Metropolitan Dionizy Waledyński of the Orthodox Church. Consequently, the

---

[2] 140,000 Ukrainians were displaced from the southeast of Poland and sent to the North and the West. [Translator's note.]

Minister of Public Administration convoked a "Provisional Governing College of the Orthodox Church", the task of which was to normalise the affairs of autocephaly as well as domestic relations. In 1948, the Russian Church granted autocephaly to the Church of Poland. Shortly after that decision, the Synod of the Church of Poland invited Archbishop Tymoteusz [Timothy] Szretter to the post of *locum tenens* of the Metropolitan and effected a change in the borders of the dioceses. The last regulation of the canonical situation was brought about in 1951, when Archbishop Makary Oksijuk was invited to come from USSR. In 1950, the theological sixth-form college of Warsaw was returned to the Church and subsequently transformed into a seminary, and a Department of Orthodox Theology at the Academy of Christian Theology of Warsaw was founded in 1957. The Church had to draft a new organic statute, because the one of 1938 no longer corresponded to the existing state of affairs. The new statute was approved in 1970. The issue of the publications of the Church was also settled: in 1982 the Church set up its own publishing house. In 1981 the circle of Orthodox Theologians was founded, rallying the youth and publishing its own newsletter, the "Biuletyn Informacyjny K.T.P.". In addition, the Church published a monthly review, "Wiadomości Polskiego Autokefalicznego Kościoła Prawosławnego" [News of the Orthodox Autocephalous Church of Poland], the "Cerkiewny Wiestnik" quarterly [The Church Herald] and calendars in Polish-Russian and Ukrainian versions. After the war, 26 new churches were built, while construction work began on another 28 such as in Hajnówka, Białystok, Zyndranowa, Krynica, and the restoration of the Church of the Supraśl Monastery was undertaken. Because of the change of the political situation, in 1990 a revision of the rules concerning the legal status of the Orthodox Church in Poland began. This status was ratified by the Sejm and signed by the President in 1991. Within that new reality, a Chair of Orthodox Theology was established at the University of Białystok, as well as a school of icon-painting in Bielsk Podlaski for students having completed their secondary education, and a school for the training of Readers in Hajnówka.

Currently, the Orthodox Church in Poland is administratively divided into 6 dioceses:
1. The Archdiocese of Warsaw and Bielsk (6 deaneries, 68 parishes). It comprises the Convent of Saints Martha and Maria in Grabarka, the Monastery of Saka, the Convent of Zaleszany, the 'desert' in the natural reserve of Kudak, the higher seminary of Warsaw, the Department of Orthodox Theology of the Academy of Christian Theology and the publishing house of the Metropolitanate;
2. The diocese of Bialystok and Gdańsk (5 deaneries and 575 parishes). It is in this diocese that the Supraśl Monastery is found, as well as the Convents of Zwierki and Wojnowo;
3. The diocese of Lodz and Poznań (3 deaneries, 12 parishes and 3 subsidiaries);
4. The diocese of Wrocław and Szczeciń (5 deaneries and 41 parishes);
5. The diocese of Przemysl and Nowy Sącz (3 deaneries, 19 parishes and 26 subsidiaries). This diocese was re-established in 1981 and comprises the lands inhabited by the Orthodox Lemkos, the Monastery of Ujkowicy near Przemyśl and a house of religious Sisters in Wysowa.
6. The diocese of Lublin and Chełm (5 deaneries, 28 parishes and 17 subsidiaries). The Stavropegiac Monastery [*i.e. under the direct control of the Metropolitan of Poland — Translator's note*] of Jabłeczna, the house of religious Sisters of Kostomłoty and the Convent of Turkowice are found in this diocese, re-established in 1989 (with Chelm being the oldest Orthodox Episcopal See in Poland, founded in 1205).

In 1994 a diocese for the Armed Forces was created and is currently divided into 6 deaneries and 7 parishes, as well as a Deanery for the Border Guard.

Since 1990 the Orthodox parishes of Brazil are also under the jurisdiction of the Polish Church.

The supreme power within the Church lies with the local council and the Synod of Bishops. There are around 600,000 faithful. The Orthodox Autocephalous Church of Poland is canonically connected with all (fifteen) local Orthodox Churches.

Orthodoxy perceives its participation in the ecumenical movement as part of the witness it offers of the Christianity of the first millennium, of the undivided Church. Almost all Orthodox Churches (apart from those of Georgia, Bulgaria and Jerusalem) are members of the World Council of Churches (Orthodoxy being one of the founding members thereof) and take part in the various debates. The most advanced of these is the dialogue with the pre-Chalcedonian Churches (the Coptic, Ethiopian, Armenian and Syriac ones). A dialogue is also conducted with the Old Catholic Church, the Protestant Churches and the Roman Catholic Church. Generally, the Orthodox Churches are members of the ecumenical organizations found in each country. Thus in Poland, the Orthodox Church is a member of the Polish Ecumenical Council, as well as of the World Council of Churches, the Christian Peace Conference, the Conference of European Churches, and participates in various inter-ecclesial dialogues.

The Church carries out charitable action thanks to various structures, such as the Metropolitan Social Fund, the "Eleos" Charity Centre, different foundations, six retirement homes, canteens for the poor, socio-therapeutic centres and special forms of pastoral care. The Church also deploys cultural activity, thanks to the Orthodox culture centres, publishing and icon-painting actions (there are icon-painting schools); there is also an Orthodox sports organization. One of the staple forms of the activity of Orthodoxy is the existence of Church fraternities at the parish and diocesan levels and throughout Poland. The Brotherhood of Orthodox Youth, founded in 1981, also carries out fruitful work.

There are chaplaincies for students, as well as in hospital, holding cell or prison environments, a police chaplaincy, a fire brigade chaplaincy and others.

Orthodoxy considers that the common witness of all Christians has a great importance in the modern world. This is why it takes part in Services for the Unity of Christians, collaborates with the humanitarian aid or organises it in case of natural disasters both in Poland and abroad.

Since 1998 His Eminence Metropolitan Sawa Hrycuniak is at the head of the Orthodox Church of Poland.

Bibliography

Chodynicki, K., *Kościół prawosławny a Rzeczypospolita Polska*, (Warsaw, 1934).

Łapiński, A., *Zygmunt Stary a Kościół prawosławny*, (Warsaw, 1937).

Mironowicz, A. and L. Adamczuk (eds.), *Kościół prawosławny w Polsce dawniej i dziś*, (Warsaw, 1993).

Mironowicz, A., "Organizacja Kościoła prawosławnego w Rzeczypospolitej do końca XVIII wieku", in *Europa Orientalis*, (Toruń, 1996), 211-218.

Mironowicz, A., *Kościół prawosławny w Polsce*, I-III (Białystok 2001-2005).

(translated by Nikolaos Petropoulos)

Part IV: Ecumenical Dialogue in various Orthodox Churches and Settings

(70) ECUMENICAL DIALOGUE IN THE PERSPECTIVE OF ORTHODOX CHURCHES IN WESTERN EUROPE

Metropolitan Emmanuel

Introduction

Europe is, by its vocation, a promise that was built on the still smoking ashes of the horrors of World War II. It is a promise that such atrocities will never again be witnessed in the history of humanity. Europe is a promise sustained, above all, by dialogue and reconciliation. Dialogue occurs when we note a relational reality in an exchange of words; it signifies a reciprocal gift freely given, and interdependence in our lives. Reconciliation, in turn, is a profound transformation, a metamorphosis. It is the passing from one state to another, from conflict to pacification or at least a more normal situation. But I cannot see any better definition of what reconciliation might be than the expression used in the document cancelling the anathemas of 1054 between the Catholic Church and the Orthodox Church; this document, dating from 1965, speaks of the "purification of memory". Being reconciled means, above all, purifying memory. Unlike relativism, this recognizes a catharsis of history, and rethinks this historical phase in terms of a process of relationship, not of separation. The events remain, but their meaning may evolve.

The construction of Europe is full of metamorphoses in this regard. One of the most evocative reconciliations is doubtless the result of Franco-German rapprochement. Thanks to this reconciliation, enemies became brothers and sisters. The history of these two countries has since been written together, despite the clashes of the past, without wanting here to trace them right back to the wars of religion. Moreover, the history of Orthodoxy in Western Europe and in France has been written within this dialectic.

Is there a French Orthodoxy? With this question I would like to embark on a reflection aiming to inquire into the place, the role, even the special features of the Orthodox Church in France. This question seems to me legitimate, as it opens the doors to other inquiries, notably on the meaning of the very term "Orthodoxy", which today is used in many and varied contexts. These contexts were well identified by Antoine Arjakovsky in a most stimulating intellectual exercise. He started from the ambivalence of the term 'Orthodoxy' such as implied in the expression *lex credendi, lex orandi*, where the definitions of 'belief' cannot be dissociated from worship.[1]

So let me begin by examining the historical process of Orthodoxy in France. I will then analyse the way in which inter-Orthodox relations are organized there. Finally, I will inquire into the concepts of dialogue and of reconciliation in ecumenism and interreligious dialogue as expressions of the openness and mission of French Orthodoxy.

1. From immigration to integration. Some historical markers

The Orthodox Church in France is a 'pluralist' church in origin and language, and also in terms of the sociological and cultural reality of the faithful. It is the result of successive waves of immigration by believers from different countries considered to be traditionally Orthodox. They have lived and worked in France for decades, the oldest families even for a century. France is thus regarded as a hospitable country. Orthodox Christians are diverse in view of their origins, their time of arrival in France and their socio-professional level. Orthodoxy in France reflects Orthodoxy in the world. It is diversified but united by a common bond with the experience of European pluralism and is firmly rooted in the openness of French society.

---

[1] Antoine Arjakovsky, *Qu'est-ce que l'Orthodoxie*, (Paris, 2013).

It goes without saying that the growth of migration by Orthodox population groups towards Western Europe, and France in particular, redrew the map of world Orthodoxy. This started at the end of the 19ᵗʰ century and continued all through the 20ᵗʰ century, for reasons of geopolitical reconfiguration or economic crises. In parallel, these flows of immigrants helped to develop the French religious scene in which Orthodoxy is represented as an entity, despite its small numbers, which probably do not exceed 400,000. Let me list some highlights in the formation of Orthodox communities in France.

Even though you can find traces of an Orthodox colony in Corsica in the 17ᵗʰ century, the first testimonies of an Orthodox presence in France are linked to diplomatic representation. Indeed, the first mention of an Orthodox priest in Paris dates from 1727, after his secondment to the Russian embassy. Less than a century later, a chapel was organised for pastoral ministry to the Orthodox of the capital. The first Greek parish was created in Marseilles in 1820, even before the inauguration of its church building, which was the first one to be erected in France and dedicated to the Dormition of the Mother of God. The Romanian community acquired its first chapel in 1853. The latter disappeared when a new location was chosen a few years later. But the most important event at the end of the 19ᵗʰ century was undoubtedly the inauguration in Paris of the Russian Orthodox cathedral dedicated to St Alexandre Nevsky in 1861. It was built to meet the growing pastoral needs of the Russian Orthodox community of the capital. Other spiritual and church centres were then established in Paris: a new Romanian church in 1892, the Greek cathedral of St Steven in 1895, etc. At the beginning of the 20ᵗʰ century, new churches were constructed in the South of France, e.g. the Cathedral of Saint Nicholas (1912) in Nice, or again on the Atlantic coast.

The 20ᵗʰ century, as already mentioned, was marked by war, conflicts and revolutions. These events generated waves of migration of people seeking refuge in the West. Thus after the occupation of the Dodecanese by Italy, then in 1923 the disaster of Asia Minor, two waves of Greek immigration reached France. The massive arrival of Russian immigrants from 1920 was a consequence of the Bolshevik Revolution. The ecclesiastical dioceses organized themselves in parallel with these new immigrant communities, who were able to establish themselves permanently on the French religious scene.

The political break-up of Europe was to a lesser degree responsible for structuring intra-Orthodox relations in France. In opposition to the Communist government in Russia, an Archbishopric was organised, inspired by the great theological and ecclesiological renewal brought by the Council of Moscow in 1917-1918. To describe the complexity of such a period I will quote the great theologian Olivier Clément:

> "The consolidation and hardening of the Soviet régime produced varying degrees of schism. 1926 saw the constitution of the *Église russe hors frontière* or *Église synodale*, which was a minority group in France and very conservative. In 1931, the new leader of the Russian Patriarchal Church, Metropolitan Sergius, desirous of showing that the Church, while safeguarding its message, was going to integrate loyally into Soviet society, denied the existence of persecutions in Russia to western journalists. This caused a great scandal in Western Europe where a broad movement of prayer for the countless new martyrs arose. The head of the Church of the Russian diaspora, Metropolitan Eulogius, noting that the Patriarchate had lost its freedom, requested protection from Constantinople, the centre of the primacy responsible for the unity and universality of the Orthodox Church. The ecumenical patriarchate then organised an exarchate that embraced more than two thirds of Russian immigrants, while keeping the cathedral of rue Daru [St Alexandre Nevsky], the St Sergius Orthodox Theological Institute and the youth movement called Christian Action of Russian Students."[2]

Orthodoxy in France is pluralist, I repeat, but it has been able to prove sustainable over time. Starting merely as communities of migrants, they were able to crystallise into a diaspora community. That is, they foresaw a future in exile while maintaining their worship and cultural traditions, and opening up to a society that they now had to espouse. The organization and mission of these communities took place in several stages. The creation of the St Sergius Institute of Orthodox Theology played a key role here, as it met a dual need: first,

[2] Olivier Clément, "L'Orthodoxie en France", first Day of Orthodoxy in France, 2001.

Part IV: Ecumenical Dialogue in various Orthodox Churches and Settings

that of training pastors for pastoral needs not only of the churches and communities in the Russian tradition but of all the Orthodox communities on the Continent of Europe. Secondly, the properly pastoral training was added to theological research and intellectual reflections. Father Alexis Kniazeff, the former principal, speaks of the St Sergius Institute as follows:

"One of the non-negligible factors in its development was the climate of freedom it found in the French capital. There it was able to translate into life the liberal principles that dominated his work. It also had the great privilege to fully enjoy academic freedom. Thanks to this freedom, it was able to verify by its own experience that theological reflection is an integral part of religious life."[3]

After the end of World War II, the Orthodox scene continued to evolve: Greeks, Serbs, Romanians, Lebanese, Syrians came to the country. In parallel, a second, even third-generation Orthodoxy formed. The latter was completely integrated into French society, participating even in its *intelligentsia*. Orthodoxy was attractive to the native French as a sign that it was possible for the western and eastern worlds to meet. But the organisation of a French Orthodoxy also posed problems. The old demon of ethnophyletism [division of the church along ethnic lines] had never ceased to tempt Orthodoxy from the end of the 19th century, whether it be by traditional reflexes regarding countries of origin or in the constitution of a militant French Orthodoxy. The destiny of the Orthodox Catholic Church of France is thus significant.[4] Neglected by the Orthodox hierarchy in the 1990s, it did not represent the path chosen by the Orthodox Church in France. For all that, French-speaking communities got underway. Liturgical celebrations in French even became one of the keys to handling Orthodox pluralism at the parish level.

As I tried to show before, the different flows of Orthodox migrants to France led to a greater complexity of the church fabric through the multiplication of jurisdictions. For example, the Greek Church became a Metropolis in 1963, while the exarchate of parishes in the Russian tradition remained under the wing of the Ecumenical Patriarchate. Between 1969 and 1974 a diocese of the Patriarchate of Serbia was founded; in 1980 a Metropolis of the Patriarchate of Romania, at the same time as the Patriarchate of Antioch. It goes without saying that such a mosaic needed to find internal coherence from both the institutional and spiritual point of view. At the spiritual level, it was necessary to bring together the heritages and practices proper to the different local Churches. To this end, an Orthodox fellowship (Fraternité orthodoxe) was founded by young people of different jurisdictions in the 1970s. Father Jean Roberti commented that the creation of this association, with branches at the regional level, is made up of many networks that "have manifested the existence of lively communities in the provinces".[5]

According to the *l'Annuaire de l'Église orthodoxe en France* (directory of the Orthodox Church in France) published in 2010 by the Cantauque monastery, the figures are: 220 parishes grouped in dioceses depending on the Patriarchates of Constantinople, Moscow, Antioch, Serbia, Romania, etc. In France there are currently about 20 monastic communities, two theological colleges and an Orthodox centre for study and research (Patriarchate of Romania), organisations such as the Orthodox Fellowship, youth movements and associations of iconographers. To manage these communities we have nine bishops, of which two are vicar bishops and no less than 300 priests and deacons.

2. The challenges of pan-Orthodox coordination – the Assembly of French Orthodox bishops

In the 20th and 21st century, the Orthodox Church emerged from its traditional, oriental realm. It is quite clear that the Orthodox communities in France participate actively in the intellectual ferment and critical spirit so typical of this country. They contribute constructively to the exchange of ideas, the dialogue of

[3] Alexis Kniazeff, « L'Institut Saint-Serge, de l'Académie d'Autrefois au Rayonnement d'Aujourd'hui », *Point Théologique* 14 (1974): 145.
[4] Cf. Maxime Kovalevsky, *Orthodoxie et Occident. Renaissance d'une Eglise locale*, (Paris, 1990).
[5] Jean Roberti, *Etre orthodoxe en France, Aurjourd'hui*, (Paris 1998), 63.

cultures and they are intermediaries between one society and another, actively promoting the integration of its communities in the social fabric of France. The enthusiastic participation in this secular intellectual adventure, which is always beneficial for the Orthodox peoples, fully demonstrates the spiritual unity and social cohesion of the heritage of the peoples of Europe. The canonical division of the Orthodox Church into local autocephalous churches has followed the logic of dispersion, also extending pastoral activities into the diaspora territories. Nevertheless, this jurisdictional fragmentation of the Orthodox diaspora is by no means in conformity with Orthodox ecclesiology. This fact has been widely commented on. Metropolitan Kallistos Ware sums up the issue very well: "The second obvious problem with which the diaspora is confronted is its division into jurisdictions. However comprehensible this might be from a historical point of view, it is detrimental to the pastoral work of the Orthodox Church among its own members in the West, and to the witness of western Orthodoxy to the outside world."[6] Therefore it is necessary to articulate the canonical tradition of the Orthodox Church founded on both the principle of territoriality and the principle of reality. The members of the Orthodox congregations now live permanently outside national borders, outside the limits of all church jurisdictions, except that recognized by canon law as effectively belonging to the Ecumenical Patriarchate.[7]

Faced with this difficulty, the representatives of the Orthodox diasporas in certain countries took the initiative, for the first time, to create a joint assembly of all Orthodox bishops in order to confront together the new pastoral problems of the Orthodox communities. The Orthodox bishops of France and the United States of America did pioneer work by launching this initiative in the 1960s and set the example of favouring an overall approach to treating the relevant problems. However, it is very important to note that the situation in America is different from that of France. Therefore the Ecumenical Patriarchate, taking the initiative to convene the Holy and Grand Council of the Orthodox Church thanks to the enormous energy and inspiration of Ecumenical Patriarch Athenagoras, attached importance to finding a collegiate response to the question of how to deal with the diaspora. After all, only harmony and agreement around the question of diaspora will permit us to justify a situation of compromise with canonical tradition

In France, the Inter-Episcopal Committee was created in Paris in 1967, before being turned into the Assembly of Orthodox Bishops of France (AEOF) in 1997. Indeed, the canonical organisation of the Orthodox diaspora was studied by the inter-Orthodox preparatory commission bringing together the representatives of all the autocephalous and autonomous Orthodox Churches during the 2009 session decided to convene Orthodox Episcopal assemblies in precise regions in order to coordinate pastoral activity and, more generally, spiritual initiatives. The task of each assembly is defined by its bye-laws. Those of AEOF state:

> "The responsibilities of the Assembly of Orthodox Bishops of France are:
> 1. seeing and contributing to the maintenance of the unity of the Orthodox Church in its theological, ecclesiological, canonical, spiritual and charitable commitments;
> 2. coordinating and promoting activities of common interest in the fields of pastoral work, catechism, liturgical life, religious publishing, mass media and church education;
> 3. relations with other Christian churches and other religions;
> 4. all matters that commit the Orthodox Church in France in its relations with civil society (political, juridical, administrative, media …authorities) (Art. 4)."

Consequently, each diaspora or church community dependent on a particular church jurisdiction will be served by its own clergy at the parish and episcopal level, on the basis of principles defined by the Assembly of the said region. Thus the bishops of the diaspora will face their pastoral problem in collaboration with their local Church (clergy, liturgical books, teaching manuals). Certainly, these arrangements do not resolve the jurisdictional question of the Orthodox diaspora, but – through the conciliar experience - they open up new

---

[6] Kallistos Ware, *L'Orthodoxie*, (Paris, 2002), 239.
[7] 28th canon of the 4th Ecumenical Council of Chalcedon (451).

Part IV: Ecumenical Dialogue in various Orthodox Churches and Settings

prospects for coping with the canonical pitfalls in each region. Hence these Assemblies now have the principal responsibility of seeking solutions to common problems.

It is quite clear that, with this pioneering initiative, the Orthodox Church in France has the theological framework needed to reinforce its internal unity, collaborate constructively on pastoral matters in the interests of the Orthodox population, and bear credible witness to Orthodoxy from near and far. Everyone shares in this responsibility and there is a lot of potential inherent in it. Finally, it bypasses an inward-looking focus on the national identity of each diaspora in order to build one church body in keeping with the unanimous request of the local Orthodox churches. If we remain indifferent today, we will have no grounds for opposition in future: we will be the ones to bear the principal responsibility for all that we judge and criticise.

3. The Orthodox Church in France, dialogue and reconciliation

In Orthodox theology, all dialogue originates in God himself, who makes himself known through the Word. For St John Chrysostomos, this characteristic of divine dialogue must above all be received as a gift given us by God himself. After all, God gives himself, above all, through words: God speaks through the prophets, the apostles, the saints, prayer and nature. God speaks. From the first hours of God's revelation, he has been in relationship, awaiting the consecration of his elected people. If we hold to a broad definition of the term dialogue, as an exchange of words, these words addressed by God to his people are diverse in nature. While some are real conversations, others are vocations, calls, elections – a special field of prophetic action is to bring about a change of heart within the people of God. Indeed, with their proclamation of misfortune and God's judgement, the core of the prophetic message is thus an appeal to conversion. From Amos to Hosea, from Isaiah to Micah, the curse and the imminence of divine judgement must appeal to a change in the life of humankind. The most radical example is still that of the Book of Jonah, in which the prophetic work is followed by an immediate effect. [6]

When the news reached the king of Nineveh, he rose from his throne, removed his robe, covered himself with sackcloth, and sat in ashes. [7] Then he had a proclamation made in Nineveh: "By the decree of the king and his nobles: No human being or animal, no herd or flock, shall taste anything. They shall not feed, nor shall they drink water. [8] Human beings and animals shall be covered with sackcloth, and they shall cry mightily to God. All shall turn from their evil ways and from the violence that is in their hands. [9] Who knows? God may relent and change his mind; he may turn from his fierce anger, so that we do not perish." [10] When God saw what they did, how they turned from their evil ways, God changed his mind about the calamity that he said he would bring upon them; and he did not do it.

Conversion is then assimilated to repentance as the only way to accede to the promise, not just of lifting the divine curse, but of entering into a period of joy and richness. Conversion is reconciliation, a turnaround also called *metanoia*.

From the hypostatic union in the Logos, of humanity and divinity, there follow conditions of a radical change in soteriological perspectives. In a preliminary statement, quoting St Iraneus of Lyon, St Athanasius the Great declared in the 4th century: "God was made man so that man might become God." Exchanging words thus remains a union with the word, and the possibility was granted by the very incarnation of the Logos. The Christian vocation thus becomes acquisition of the Logos, union with Christ and salvation in becoming divine, *theosis*.

Dialogue is a theological paradigm by which conversion becomes not only the point of departure for repentance but that of salvation as union between God and humankind, in a process of reconciliation between the Creator and his creation. We must affirm here that Orthodox theology, on the basis of the mystery of incarnation, affirms the possibility of participating in the divine nature by grace. This deification constitutes our real participation in approaching the divine as far as God can really allow. For the Cappadocian Fathers, as for St

Gregory Palamas in the 14ᵗʰ century, we can participate in uncreated energies, i.e. to quote Olivier Clément, in "the mystery of God himself, of unity in otherness and otherness in unity".

Considering that the unique treasure of every person is being made in the image of God, any racist act constitutes a negation of human dignity and a crime against the Holy Spirit. In the face of a revival of such acts, the social exclusion of national minorities in Europe has grown and their need for protection is increasingly urgent. Entering into dialogue and being reconciled with one another thus means recognising the dignity and freedom of our neighbours. In my view, the commitment of religious people means turning the indeterminate other into a person close to us, making her or him into our neighbour, and respecting his or her individual differences.

The French philosopher Régis Debray, legitimately asked: "When we say *dialogue* what do we mean?" The response is mainly in this affirmation: "Something that has neither meaning nor interest unless it brings into relationship people who think and feel differently from one another." In other words, it is about turning each encounter into a celebration of alterity, to the extent that it generates its own conditions for the possibility of living peacefully together in an attitude of openness and respect. Alexandros Papaderos means the same when he writes:

> "The Church cannot turn in on itself and cut itself off from others: it must always be open to dialogue. Today the Orthodox Church in particular must offer the public some of the elements of its conciliar character able to contribute to accelerating and deepening the process of democratisation within the state and society."[8]

Hence the question of ecumenism is eminently theological and fits into the French context in a special way. Indeed, the experience of diaspora has brought about profound change in perceptions of confessional difference. Geographical relocation has been accompanied by a relocation of attitudes in face of dialogue with other components of Christianity. Beyond the question of otherness, the experience of division among Christians has become acute through their cohabiting in the same space, and this obliges the Orthodox Churches to take a position on ecumenism as a quest for unity. It is not easy to sum up in a few sentences the rich history of ecumenism and of Orthodoxy's link with it. However, we must understand that it is a deep-seated movement promoted by the Ecumenical Patriarchate which has not ceased to grow since the early 20ᵗʰ century. The French context is exemplary here, as it brings together all the conditions favouring a common approach. This fact has been all the more true since the tremendous rapprochement initiated between the Catholic Church and the Orthodox Church on the eve of the Second Vatican Council (1962-1965).

Today the ecumenical dimension is a reality that cannot be ignored in Orthodoxy. It is not just seen in the institutional context, be it in the framework of the Council of Christian Churches of France or in the different bilateral dialogues that we hold. Ecumenism in daily life is powerfully nurtured by the fabric of interpersonal relations, in other words, by the friendship that we are seeing grow between people of different denominations. I dare to believe that the encounter of winding ecumenical paths will permit the realisation of our common desire for unity. I will give one example among many others. Every year, the Catholic Church invites us to celebrate Orthodox vespers in the magnificent cathedral of Notre Dame. This gesture of brotherhood is a strong ecumenical gesture, of common prayer before we are permitted to communicate together from the same chalice. Ecumenism is both dialogue and reconciliation. Or, to put it differently, I will repeat what His Holiness the Ecumenical Patriarch Bartholomew stated in 2008, marking the 60ᵗʰ anniversary of the World Council of Churches: "The bonds of fellowship between divided churches and the bridges to overcome our divisions are indispensable, more now than ever."

Moreover, the modern dialogue between Islam and Christianity in its most varied forms, and primarily in the framework of this meeting, constitutes an essential element in the reconciliation between peoples and interaction between cultures. For almost four decades, consistent efforts have been made to achieve the conditions of fruitful mutual listening. However, a number of tensions between our two religions have surfaced

---

[8] Ingeborg Gabriel, Ulrich Körtner, Alexandros Papaderos, *Trilogy of Social Ethics*, (Philadelphia, 2012), 115.

Part IV: Ecumenical Dialogue in various Orthodox Churches and Settings

following the changes in geopolitical situations, e.g. after the Fall of the Berlin Wall in 1989, and the attacks of 11 September 2001. This last event, as tragic as it was, has informed our representations and thus our ability to dialogue to this day. So it is necessary for us to develop new foundations for our relations, through greater contacts – not just interpersonal, but also institutional – freeing ourselves from the patterns of war which, too often, prevent us from fulfilling our mission. Indeed, both at the multilateral and bilateral level, interreligious dialogue and notably the dialogue between Christianity and Islam could positively influence the spiritual health, even the ethical health of the modern world in crisis. Likewise, our initiative for dialogue today is also part of the process of constituting a set of values able to strengthen the exercise of religious freedom and human rights. In this spirit, the Assembly of Orthodox Bishops of France is engaged, with other religious leaders (in the conference of religions for peace), in promoting constructive dialogue for peace.

Conclusion

The Orthodox Church in France today manifests a unity that faithfully reflects the communion at the heart of its spiritual experience. We can affirm that it is generally integrated into the religious scene of the country, alongside other Christian denominations and also other religions. As we have seen, the situation of Orthodoxy in France is complex, difficult and yet full of promise both in terms of its origins and the emergence of an organisation faithful to its canonical tradition.

Today, the common progress of the peoples of Europe towards accomplishing the great dream of European unity represents for us all a challenge and an appeal to take up the mission of the church, which proclaims, in the name of Christ, the transcending of all the distances and discrimination in the world. This is a challenge and an appeal to harmonise the message of the "hope that is in us" with the spiritual needs of humankind in the multicultural society of our time. The choices of the European peoples have now been demonstrated; they are inspired by Orthodox tradition, and we are called to serve them here and now, to teach by the luminous example of a faith incarnate in time, in the image of our God incarnate in history.

Bibliography

Clément Olivier *Qu'est-ce que l'Église orthodoxe : L'Église orthodoxe en France, juridictions, instituts, églises et chapelles. Bibliographie sommaire orthodoxe*, (Périgueux, Centre œcuménique Enotikon, 1961).

-*L'Église orthodoxe*, (Paris, Presses universitaires de France, coll. "Que sais-je ? n° 949", 1961) (réimpr. 1965, 1985, 1991, 1995, 1988, 2002)

Chaillot Christine, Short History of the Orthodox Church in Western Europe in the 20th century (Paris, 2006)

Roberti Jean, *Etre orthodoxe en France, Aurjourd'hui*, (Paris 1998)

(translated by Elaine Griffiths)

Fr. Thomas FitzGerald

The Orthodox Church in the United States has contributed in a very meaningful manner to the ecumenical movement and dialogues with other Christian churches and communities especially in the past fifty years. This is particularly significant, because the Orthodox Church in the United States, with about 3 million active members, represents a very small minority of Christians in the United States which now has a population of about 313 million. Moreover, members of the Catholic Church and a wide variety of Protestant denomination far outnumber the Orthodox in this vast country. The United States contains 3.79 million square miles (9.83 million km)

The initial immigration of Orthodox believers of various ecclesial and ethnic backgrounds to the great cities of the eastern United States dates from the late 19th and early 20th century. This was complemented by the sale of Alaska by Imperial Russia to the United States in 1867. At the time, there were communities of Orthodox believers there whose presence was traced back to Russian Missions in Russian Alaska beginning in 1794.

Throughout the late 19th and the first half of the 20th century, the relationship of Orthodox believers to other Christian groups varied greatly. Protestant missionaries in Alaska in the late 19th and early 20th centuries had little appreciation of Orthodox Christianity. They frequently sought to convert the Orthodox to Protestantism. In other parts of the United States, however, the Orthodox immigrants frequently received assistance from the Episcopal Church and some other local Protestant congregations. Some of the earliest Orthodox Church buildings were purchased from other Christians and converted into places appropriate for Orthodox worship.

The early history also indicates some significant relationships of Orthodox leaders and Western Christians. While in California, Father John Veniaminov (+1879) (later recognized as Saint Innocent) visited Roman Catholic missions in 1836. He sought opportunities to speak within Jesuit missionaries and learn about their liturgical practices. In the early decades of the twentieth century, both Metropolitan Meletios (Metaxakis) (+1935), later Patriarch of Constantinople, who sought to organize the Greek Orthodox parishes, cultivated cordial relationships with the leaders of the Episcopal Church. Similar relations were established by Archbishop Tikhon (Bellavin) (+1925), later Patriarch of Moscow and eventually honored as a saint, of the Russian Orthodox Archdiocese. During the 1920s, an Anglican and Eastern Orthodox Church Union association was established. Bishop Raphael (Hawaweeny) of Brooklyn, (+1915), later recognized as a saint, served as one of its Orthodox co-president. This group led to the establishment an Anglican-Orthodox Fellowship in the United States in 1934. This served as the American counterpart to the Anglican and Eastern Churches Association founded in England in 1864 and the more famous Fellowship of Sts. Sergius and Alban, begun in England in 1928. These organizations reflected the conviction, held by many at the time, that Anglicanism and Orthodoxy had much in common and that these points of agreement deserved greater study.

The early attempts at building positive relationships and establishing opportunities for prayer and dialogue were frequently damaged, however, by covert and overt attempts by some Protestants to bring Orthodox Christians into their fold. It was also affected by the harsh reaction of some Roman Catholics to the entrance of Eastern Catholics (Uniates) into the Orthodox Church. Throughout the late 19th century and early 20th centuries, many hundreds of Carpatho-Russian immigrants who came to America as Eastern Catholics subsequently joined the Orthodox Church. This frequently created disputes over property rights. The mutual respect and understanding that would later become part of the ecumenical movement were not always central to the relationship among Christian groups in America in the early decades of the 20th century.

The participation of American Orthodox theologians in ecumenical organizations and conferences became more pronounced and more formal especially from the 1950s. The entrance of some American Orthodox clergy and laity into the activities of the National Council of Churches and the World Council of Churches provided them with an opportunity both to bear witness to their faith and to cooperate with Western Christians in activities directed towards the well being of the society.

The National Council of Churches of Christ in the U.S.A. (NCCUSA) was founded in 1950. As a cooperative ecumenical association, it initially reflected a merger of the earlier Evangelical Alliance, founded in 1867, and the Federal Council of Churches of Christ, founded in 1908. Although the new council was dominated by Protestant denominations and Protestant perspectives from the beginning, it was viewed as an American counterpart to the World Council of Churches (WCC), which was established in 1948.

Within the first few years of the establishment of the National Council of Churches, a number of Orthodox jurisdictions formally became members. These included the Syrian (Antiochian) Orthodox Archdiocese, the Russian Orthodox Greek Catholic Church (the Metropolia), the Romanian Orthodox Episcopate, the Ukrainian Orthodox Diocese, and the Greek Orthodox Archdiocese.

At the Second Assembly of the World Council of Churches held in Evanston Illinois in 1954, a number of Orthodox theologians from both Europe and the United States were active participants. Archbishop Michael (Constantinidis) (+1958) the primate of the Greek Orthodox Archdiocese was a representative of the Ecumenical Patriarchate. In addition to delivering one of the keynote addresses, he was also elected as one of the six presidents of the WCC.

The participation of Orthodox in the early work of the WCC and NCCUSA brought to them the rich theological perspectives of the Christian East. Yet, the Orthodox frequently found themselves in meetings with Western Christians who had little or no appreciation of the history and teachings of the Christian East. The Orthodox often engaged in difficult theological deliberations that were dominated by Protestant theological perspectives.

Closely related to the ecumenical concerns was a drive to have the Orthodox Christianity better recognized as a major faith in the United States. This movement began with the desire to have Orthodox military personnel during World War II receive their appropriate religious designation. During the period after the war, committees of Orthodox clergy and laypersons organized to have state governments and federal agencies grant the same recognition to the Orthodox faith that had been given to others. There is no government sponsored church or religion in the United States. Throughout the 1950s and into the early 1960s a number of states and governmental agencies passed resolutions that recognized Orthodox Christianity as a major faith insofar as this could be done legally.

The concern expressed by so many Orthodox over this issue was an important sign that they were looking for greater recognition from the wider society. In earlier decades of the 20th century, the Orthodox were concerned primarily with survival in an environment that was seen as hostile. Bolstered by movements toward greater Pan-Orthodox cooperation and unity as well as the presence of Orthodox theologians in high-level ecumenical forums, many Orthodox now came to believe that the Orthodox faith deserved to be recognized properly as one of the major religious traditions in American society.

The movement towards greater cooperation, witness and unity among the various Orthodox jurisdictions found renewed expression in the establishment of the Standing Conference of Canonical Orthodox Bishops in America (SCOBA) in 1960. Under the leadership of Archbishop Iakovos (Koukouzis) (+2005) the primate of the Greek Orthodox Archdiocese (Ecumenical Patriarchate), SCOBA initially brought together the representatives of eleven jurisdictions of very different ecclesial backgrounds. SCOBA built on earlier pan-Orthodox activities and the longing of many for greater signs of Orthodox unity. With committees comprised of clergy and laity, it immediately sought to coordinate the various national Pan-Orthodox activities which began in the pervious decades. This included programs related to religious education and campus ministry. SCOBA supported the establishment of the Orthodox Theological Society in 1965, an important body bringing together theologians from most jurisdictions.

Ecumenical dialogue was given very high priority by Archbishop Iakovos. He had served at the WCC in Geneva between 1954-1959 as the representative of the Ecumenical Patriarchate. Under his leadership, SCO-BA established formal bilateral theological dialogues with the Episcopal Church (1962), the Roman Catholic Church (1965), the Lutheran Church (1968), and the Reformed Churches (1968). SCOBA established a unique, formal dialogue with Roman Catholic bishops in 1981. SCOBA began a dialogue with Oriental Orthodox Churches in 2000. It also published in 2007 a book containing all the joint statements of the Orthodox and Oriental Orthodox. In order to coordinate these dialogues, SCOBA maintained an Ecumenical Commission.

The North American Orthodox-Catholic Bilateral Consultation has been especially fruitful. This dialogue preceded the international dialogue by about twenty years. The Dialogue is formally sponsored by the Assembly of Canonical Orthodox Bishop, The United States Conference of Catholic Bishops and the Canadian Conference of Catholic Bishops. During the Forty-Eight years of its existence, the Dialogue has brought together theologians from both churches to meet twice each year. The Dialogue has produced twenty-six Joint Statements on various topics.

Another significant contribution of SCOBA to Orthodox ecumenical dialogue was the publication of *The Ecumenical Guidelines for Orthodox Christians* in 1966 and revised in 1973. The intent of this historic text was to guide Orthodox clergy in ecumenical activities. Attention was given to the proper expression of the doctrinal and ecclesiological principles of the Orthodox Church. Information about specific ecumenical organizations and other agencies also was provided. Suggestions about the degree and the manner of involvement in the various expressions of ecumenism were offered.

The SCOBA Guidelines recognized that Orthodox clergy and laity were becoming active in local and regional expressions of ecumenism with the approval of their bishop. At these levels, the Orthodox were involved in ecumenical prayer services, retreats, theological discussions, bible studies, social witness, pilgrimages, clergy associations and in Church Women United. The *Week of Prayer for Christian Unity,* 18-25 January, also provided in many places an opportunity for Orthodox to join with Catholics and Protestants in praying for unity. These expressions were complemented by the growing number of marriages of an Orthodox Christian with a member of another Church. Clearly, the call to ecumenical witness was not confined only to hierarchs and theologians. Indeed, the vast majority of Orthodox clergy and laity supported the various ecumenical efforts. They frequently felt the tragic consequences of disunity for families and the society.

The principal opposition to SCOBA and to its ecumenical witness came from the Russian Orthodox Church Outside of Russia (ROCOR), with headquarters in the United States since 1950. ROCOR separated from the Church of Russia in 1927. In the United States, ROCOR generally avoided pan-Orthodox activities. It was never a member of SCOBA. Throughout much of its history, it was viewed as uncanonical. The opposition of ROCOR to Orthodox ecumenical activities became especially intense in the period after 1965. ROCOR declared ecumenism to be a heresy in 1974. In 2007, however, ROCOR was reconciled with the Church of Russia. In addition to ROCOR, there have been a small number of uncanonical groups in the United States who have opposed the Orthodox participation in the ecumenical movement. While these small groups can be quite vocal, they have not captured the attention of most clergy and laity.

The importance of ecumenical witness was a major theme in the SCOBA *Pastoral Letter on the Occasion of the Third Christian Millennium (2000).* This is a remarkable and very distinctive text. As part of the Letter, the Bishops affirmed that the Church is meant to be a community of healing and reconciliation centered upon Christ and His Gospel. They recognized that "divisions among Christians are a tragedy which cannot be ignored. These divisions diminish the message of the Gospel of Salvation and impede the mission of the Church in the world. These divisions among Christians often divide families and contribute to alienation within our society." The bishops also affirmed that the "involvement of the Orthodox Church in the quest for the reconciliation of Christians and the restoration of the visible unity of the churches is an expression of our faithfulness to the Lord and His Gospel. By seeking the reconciliation of divided Christians, we are in fact sharing in our Lord's ministry of reconciliation."

Part IV: Ecumenical Dialogue in various Orthodox Churches and Settings

This Letter was published at a time when many Orthodox were questioning the direction that some Protestant denominations had taken with regards to Christian teaching and morals. Also of concern were directions in the WCC and NCCUSA which deemphasized the theological quest for reconciliation. The bishops recognized these significant concerns in their Letter. Yet, at the same time they affirmed the obligation of the Orthodox Church both to bear witness to the Apostolic Faith and to contribute to the process of reconciliation.

The ecumenical dialogues initiated by SCOBA were taken over by the Assembly of Canonical Orthodox Bishops which was established in 2010 in accordance with the decisions of the Fourth Pre-Conciliar Pan-Orthodox Conference in 2009.

The Orthodox ecumenical witness in the United States has been supported and sustained by many outstanding hierarchs and theologians. In addition to those already mentioned, the witness and writings of the following theologians deserve particular attention. These are: Metropolitan Maximos (Aghiorgoussis) of Pittsburgh, Fr. Georges Florovsky (+1979), Fr. John Meyendorff (+1992), and Fr. Alexander Schmemann (+1983). Many of their students include: Metropolitan Methodios of Boston, Fr. Robert Stephanopoulos, Fr. Leonid Kishkovsky, Fr. Emmanuel Gratsias (+2007) Fr. John Erickson, Fr. Emmanuel Clapsis, Fr. Nicholas Apostola, Dr. Kyriaki Karidoyanes FitzGerald, and Dr. Despina Prassas. At various times, most of these theologians have been active in the work of the WCC, the NCCUSA, and local ecumenical gatherings.

Holy Cross Greek Orthodox School of Theology in Brookline Massachusetts deserves particular mention with regard to Orthodox ecumenism. Founded in 1937, Holy Cross in the oldest and largest graduate level Orthodox School of Theology in the Americas. Founded and supported by the Greek Orthodox Archdiocese, Holy Cross continues the rich tradition of ecumenical engagement expressed by the Ecumenical Patriarchate. Many of its professors have been involved in ecumenical dialogues both at the local and international levels. Its graduate degree programs provide students with opportunities to study issues of Christian divisions and the advances in the ecumenical movement. Holy Cross has been a distinctive center for important ecumenical conferences and consultation. The Holy Cross Press and the Greek Orthodox Theological Review have published significant studies and documents related to the ecumenical movement. Holy Cross is also a full member of the Boston Theological Institute, a unique consortium of ten theological schools of different traditions in the Greater Boston area.

The Orthodox in the United States recognize the critical importance of ecumenical engagement and dialogue as an expression of the Gospel of Christ. This takes place through prayer, through theological dialogue and through common witness in the society. Living in a multi-religious society, the Orthodox are committed to affirming their distinctive faith convictions, to sharing their spiritual treasures with others and to seeking reconciliation in the Apostolic Faith.

Bibliography

John Borelli and John Erickson, (ed.), *The Quest for Unity: Orthodox and Catholics in Dialogue,* (Crestwood, NY: St. Vladimir's Press, 1996).

Thomas FitzGerald, "The Development of the Orthodox Parish in the United States", in Anton C. Vrame, *the Orthodox Parish in America*, (Brookline: Holy Cross Orthodox Press, 2003), 11-32.

-, "A Ministry of Reconciliation: The North American Orthodox-Catholic Theological Consultation," in M.S. Attridge and J.Z. Skira, eds., *In God's Hands: Essays on the Church and Ecumenism,* (Leuven: University Press, 2006).

-, *The Orthodox Church* (Westport, CN: Greenwood Press, 1995).

-, "Orthodoxy Theology and Ecumenical Witness," *St. Vladimir's Theological Quarterly* 42.3-4 (1998): 339-361.

Theodore Stylianopoulos, *Orthodox Perspectives on Pastoral Praxis* (Brookline: Holy Cross Orthodox Press, 1988).

(72) ECUMENICAL DIALOGUE IN THE PERSPECTIVE OF THE ORTHODOX CHURCHES IN LATIN (SOUTH) AMERICA

Bishop Iosif Bosch

Introduction

The description of the spiritual and religious landscape of South America has always been -and still is- a titanic undertaking. It is already a challenge to catalogue separately the different Christian denominations in the continent, from the oldest to the newest.

However, an even greater challenge is the description of the relationship between Christian denominations in the region.

We will, therefore, limit the enterprise, that far transcends the objectives, the intention and the limits of the document in hand. Our task, then, will be the identification of the linkages between Orthodoxy and other Christian denominations within the framework of ecumenical relationships in South America. This limitation, by all meanings logical, will allow us to deepen, even in part, in the Christian coexistence in the region.

Without doubt, the description and identification of linkages between Orthodoxy and other Christian denominations in South America, will allow us to lucubrate theologically on the linking process and to produce a synthesis on the subject.

In the body of the essay, we propose the development of the exposure discriminating doubly, at a descriptive and at a reflective level, in order to be more effective in the logical process as it is proposed.

Ars Dialectica

Paraphrasing philosophical dialectic art, we want to present the subject in a dialectical form, in order to clarify from the beginning our position.

I. Ὑπόθεσις: spaces of ecumenical dialogue do exist in South America

II. Θέσις: *It seems* that Orthodoxy does not interact altogether and systematically in the ecumenical movement in South America

III. Ἀντίθεσις: But Orthodoxy does participate in certain spaces of ecumenical interaction and has dialogue with the Roman Catholic Church

IV. Σύνθεσις: *So*, the development of ecumenical dialogue and interaction between Orthodoxy and other Christian denominations is still premature, and as such, insufficient and in process of progress.

Dialectic in progress

1. Hypothesis: The hypothesis of the proposed dialectical juncture is incontestable: *in South America ecumenical dialogue does exist between the various Christian denominations.* It is a fact. It is a reality. However, during the development of thinking we have to clarify ***how*** this dialogue exists between a portion of the universe of denominations and the rest of them.

Thesis 2: The hypothesis is followed by our thesis: *It seems that Orthodoxy does not interact altogether and systematically in the ecumenical movement through South America.*

In order to support our thesis, we must enter the descriptive level of reflexion.

2.1 Brief historical reference

Orthodox churches arrive to South America in order to supply the spiritual needs of the diverse communities that immigrated to the region because of various historical reasons, ethnic, economic, etc..

The presence of Orthodox churches in South America is noted since the late 19th century.

It must be well noticed that major purpose of the clergy sent from the mother churches is not ***missionary, but pastoral***. This pastoral attitude- will last until the late 20th and early 21st century, when the Orthodox Church leaders finally realize that the message of Orthodoxy should be shared with all people of good will, regardless of race, origin, economic, political, etc.

Immigrants, served by the Orthodox clergy sent by churches mothers, come from Russia, Ukraine, Greece, Asia Minor, Turkey, Syria, Lebanon, Palestine, Egypt, Serbia, and Romania. The various orthodox jurisdictions -mothers-churches- send their representatives in different historical periods. Gradually jurisdictions are organized and acquire "canonical form" with the presence of bishops, archbishops and metropolitans at different times.

2.2 Current Orthodox Presence

Currently, we find six (6) canonically recognized orthodox jurisdictions in South America:

I. Ecumenical Patriarchate of Constantinople.
a. Sacred Metropolis of Buenos Aires and Exarchate of South America
b. Sacred Metropolis of Mexico and Exarchate of Central America and the Caribbean islands

II. Patriarchate of Antioch
a. Metropolis of Buenos Aires and Argentina
b. Metropolis of Sao Paulo and Brazil
c. Metropolis of Mexico, Venezuela, Central America and the Caribbean
d. Metropolis of Santiago and Chile

III. Moscow Patriarchate
Metropolis of Buenos Aires and South America
Bishopric of Caracas and South America (ROCOR)

IV. Patriarchate of Serbia
a. Bishopric of Buenos Aires and South America

V. Patriarchate of Romania
a. Romanian Archdiocese in the Americas

VI. Autocephalous Church of Poland
a. Archdiocese of Rio
b. Diocese of Recife

2.3 Orthodox Interaction

Since the official formation of various orthodox jurisdictions in South America, a process that began at the late 50s, there has been no common area of pan-Orthodox dialogue in the region, neither globally nor locally.

The dialogue between the various Orthodox churches in the region has been informal and discontinuous.

Protestant churches held their first attempt to engage in dialogue on mission at Edinburgh in 1910, rectifying its approach to Latin America through a second attempt at the Panama Congress of 1916. The Catholic Church, meanwhile, in 1955 will wake up -if we may use the expression-, from a missionary lethargy at the region and will establish the Latin American Episcopal Conference (CELAM), and from since we should recall memorable meetings, as the one of Medellin (1968) and that of Puebla (1979). From the second half of the 20th century on, Protestant and Roman Catholic churches will start to create opportunities for dialogue within their structures, globally and locally[1].

---

[1] In Latin America there are -talking basically about the world-historic Protestant Evangelical- many spaces of "confessional families" at regional level: the CIEMAL (Council of Evangelical Methodist Churches of Latin America), the COP-COL (Conference of Bishops, Presidents and leaders churches of the Lutheran World Federation in Latin America and the Caribbean) and AIPRAL (Alliance of Presbyterian and Reformed Churches in Latin America, and the Caribbean).

What about the Orthodox Church? Unfortunately the Orthodox Church has never opened a pan-Orthodox space-for-dialogue in the region. The ethnic provincialism and jurisdictional conflict on the Diaspora continued to lessen the chances of meeting and dialoguing between the orthodox leaders in the region.

In consequence, it presents to the other churches an image of Orthodoxy disjointed and divided. But the worst thing is that this external image is rooted in a serious and sad reality: *Orthodoxy in South America is divided and disorganized.* It is not a mere image, a feeling, a ghost. This situation is factual.

Now, axiomatically: if Orthodoxy is divided and disjointed in South America, how can it interact with the Catholic Church or the Protestant Churches? If the churches that represent Orthodoxy do not dialogue between them, how can they dialogue with heterodox? There is not one voice. There is not one will. There are not common objectives. There is not a common perspective. How, then, can Orthodoxy be inserted into the larger picture of the ecumenical network in the region?

3. Antithesis: Reverse phenomenology

After the formation of local ecumenical organizations, the various orthodox churches tended to shy away from that ethnic provincialism, and joined these movements, usually of national character.

In Argentina, Brazil, Chile, Colombia, Peru, Venezuela, Uruguay certain Orthodox jurisdictions participate nationwide in these ecumenical commissions. They also participate at the provincial or local level. Participation in these spaces of ecumenical dialogue is conducted through the different jurisdictions.

According to our experience, this is the maximum level of ecumenical of interaction and commitment of the different Orthodox churches in South American context.

It is a presence:

- autonomous
- independent
- fragmented

and therefore *partial.*

Consequently, interaction in other areas of major geographic and confessional range -as CLAI, e.g., - is still infeasible.

The Orthodox, paradoxically, engage in dialogue between themselves in a field which is not their own: they get to know and interact with themselves, while are invited by other.

As be noted that, there are cases where an Orthodox jurisdiction belongs to a national or provincial ecumenical commission and others do not: that is why we speak about a fragmented and unsystematic orthodox presence.

3.1. The stone of scandal

In our humble opinion, the main -and perhaps veiled- obstacle to Orthodoxy in order to participate in a systematic, joint, associate, uniform, and full way in the South American ecumenical movement globally is the non-resolution of the jurisdictional issue on the Diaspora, which is extremely sensitive in the region, even altering the deeper uniformity of Orthodoxy inwards and outwards.

It is not a minor problem in the area. It prevents our common witness to other denominations; corrodes ecclesiastical communion *ad intra,* and finally, mortgage the bases of dialogue and understanding *ad extra.*

3.2. The Canonical Orthodox Bishops Assembly of South America

---

On the other hand, there is another major effort of unity among different confessional families: is the CLAI, The Latin American Council of Churches. *CLAI is, so far, the main effort of unity and walking together of churches and ecumenical bodies (184 in total) in Latin America and the Hispanic Caribbean* (Cuba, Puerto Rico and the Dominican Republic). These organizations are regional, and all of them have different pastoral work: women, youth, special programs, etc. At national level, we find *federations of churches* or *church councils.* These are also areas of rapprochement and dialogue between churches: in Argentina, e.g., the FAIE (Argentinean Federation of Evangelical Churches, which brings together 23 national churches) or in Uruguay, e.g., the FIEU (Federation of Evangelical Churches of Uruguay). In both spaces, are involved historical Protestant churches (not all of them) and some Pentecostals. Anglicans do not participate in the aforementioned ecumenical spaces.

Part IV: Ecumenical Dialogue in various Orthodox Churches and Settings

As an antidote to this major problematic was instituted *The Canonical Orthodox Bishops Assembly of South America*, obeying the resolutions of the Pan-Orthodox Pre-Synodal meeting in Chambesy, Geneva, 2009.

From an historical point of view, this is the first attempt to create a common space for dialogue and inter-action among all canonical hierarchs of the region. From the institutional point of view, it can be noted that the establishment of this Assembly responds to resolutions of a major pan-Orthodox body. It happened -*sine proprio motu*- but serving a superior resolution.

This assembly gathered three times (San Paulo 2010, Buenos Aires 2011, Caracas 2012). Only at the first meeting were all jurisdictions present.[2] Nevertheless, the activities of the assembly continue forward. At its last session, the assembly decided to make contact with the presidency of CELAM[3] and CLAI[4] to explore the methodologies of rapprochement and cooperation between these two spaces and our Assembly. *There is no doubt that, this initiative -voted unanimously by the members of the assembly- opens a new chapter in field of ecumenical relations between Orthodoxy and other confessions in South America.*

In addition, it provides the establishment of a *commission of ecumenical and interreligious dialogue,* in order to institutionalize the cooperation framework and to maintain an official dialogue of love and unity with

- the Roman Catholic Church, through CELAM and local Episcopal Conferences
- the Protestant churches, through CLAI and other councils or federations of local churches

From our point of view, the proper functioning of this assembly will directly affect the ecumenical and interreligious dialogue between Orthodoxy and other confessions in South America.

Respondeo

As the skilled reader can realize, we stand before a process: the process of re-meeting, re-uniting and dialogue. Paradoxically, we can define two processes with the same statement:

1 - the process of Orthodox Christians in a pan-Orthodox level (*ad intra*)

2 - the process of all Christians in an ecumenical context (*ad extra*)

We think that in the context of South America, the success of the second process depends on the success of the first. It is axiomatic.

In both cases the process is not simple. But it is absolutely necessary. It is part of the essence of being "Orthodox" and "Christian."

That is why we maintain our opinion that the participation of Orthodoxy in the South American global ec-umenical movement is not complete and unanimous. And it could not be yet. Just today we begin to observe this process to be extended and deepened; only now, we Orthodox, have the proper place for dialogue and interaction, that we needed: The Canonical Orthodox Bishops Assembly of South America; and that is why we can now open up our ecumenical agenda to another level, bigger, deeper, more diverse; now we begin to see each other and dialogue; if we do not dialogue between us, how can we dialogue with the other? If we do not unite ourselves, how we are going to unite with others?

I do not know whether the jurisdictional problem on the Diaspora will be solved some day, and this is irrelevant at this juncture: what we should be now concerned about is the fact that we, Orthodox, united and interacting, will still try to solve our problems jointly and not separately and so, in this way, come out "*in one voice and one heart*" to dialogue with the other Christian brothers.

---

[2] Already at the second and the third meeting, the jurisdiction of the Patriarchate of Antioch was absent. At the last meeting of Caracas was read by the president the expected apology of the antiochian hierarchs: *the Holy Synod of the Patriarchate of Antioch exempts the South American hierarchs to attend the meetings of the newly created pan-Orthodox body in the region.* I, *personally,* believe that this action once again threatens the union of Orthodoxy in the region, and not only: the consequences –sadly- will be of a greater spectrum. However, I deeply hope this situation soon will be solved, and the Assembly will count again its full membership!

[3] The Latin American Roman Catholic Episcopal Council.

[4] The Latin American Council of Churches.

The Patriarchate of Constantinople:
legitimate authority of ecumenical dialogue also in South America

The Patriarchate of Constantinople has not lost its identity in this region, and so remains a pioneer of dialogue and ecumenical cooperation. Therefore, the Mother Church sending her children as legitimate bearers of charisma ecumenical, confirm her most inner identity.

On behalf of the Orthodox Church, and specifically the Ecumenical Patriarchate, WCC constantly cooperates with two sons of this land: Mr. Elias C. Abramides and myself. We have both officially participated in official patriarchal delegations at WCC General Assemblies, as well as in other meetings and assemblies of the same organism. Currently, Mr. Abramides is a member of WCC's Working Committee on Climate Change, and the undersigned, a member of the WCC's Commission on Youth (Echos) and of the Joint Working Group between the WCC and the Roman Catholic Church.

The proposal and blessing of the Ecumenical Patriarchate for these two South American native people to serve on committees of the WCC is another an evidence of its commitment to ecumenical work worldwide and specifically in South America.

On the other hand, from an educational perspective, our Sacred Metropolis of Buenos Aires is cooperating with the Roman Catholic Church in Argentina and other countries in order to establish concrete collaboration at academic and educational level, having as a model some European and American Universities.

Final evaluation

According to our view, it is a primary need that the ecumenical dialogue in South America between the Orthodox Church and other denominations will be preceded by a fraternal pan-Orthodox dialogue within the framework of collaboration and dialogue of the Canonical Orthodox Bishops Assembly of South America.

Likewise, Orthodoxy must formalize and institutionalize dialogue and ecumenical cooperation at global and continental level through the *Commission of Ecumenical and Interreligious Dialogue* of the Canonical Orthodox Bishops Assembly of South America.

This action undoubtedly must be preceded by an imminent investigation, analysis and reflection on this important issue in the region, in order to proceed jointly and systematically.

Also each jurisdiction, in the same spirit, should continue its ecumenical cooperation at national and provincial/local level as part of the same process, which is still in its formative years.

Finally, we must emphasize what is primary and basic: *prayer!* Without prayer, without our most profound appeal to the Paraclete, it is impossible to reach Christian unity. We need to renounce religious individualism and abandon ourselves to divine Apocalypse, which includes all, unites all, and grants all a single destiny: Unity in multiplicity, as an extreme reflection of Uni-trine Deity, Divine *Eros*, Transcendent *Agape* diversified into absolute oneness.

Bibliography

Gonzalez Muñana, M., *Ecumenismo, Movimiento sin posible marcha atrás.* (Bugos: Editorial Monte Carmelo, 2008)

Kliewer, G.U., "Effervescent Diversity: Religious and Churches in Brazil today", *The Ecumenical Review*, 57.3 (2005): 314-321.

Quintero Perez M.; Sintado C., *Pasión y Compromiso con el Reino de Dios. El Testimonio Ecuménico de Emilio Castro*, (Buenos Aires: Kairos Ediciones, 2007).

Scampini, J., *La Iglesia Católica Apostólica Ortodoxa del Patriarcado de Antioquía y su presencia en Argentina*, http://www.san-pablo.com.ar/vidapastoral/?seccion=articulos&id=291 (last accessed at September, 2013).

-, *La participación de las iglesias reformadas en el movimiento ecuménico y las relaciones con la Iglesia católica.* http://www.san-pablo.com.ar/vidapastoral/?seccion=articulos&id=712 (last accessed at September 2013).

-, *Las relaciones católico-ortodoxas al inicio del tercer milenio.* http://www.san-pablo.com.ar/vidapastoral/?seccion=articulos&id=334 (last accessed at September 2013).

-, *Principales rasgos del perfil teológico, litúrgico, espiritual y disciplinar de las iglesias ortodoxas.* http://www.san-pablo.com.ar/vidapastoral/?seccion=articulos&id=318 (last accessed at September 2013).

-, *La Iglesia Ortodoxa Rusa y su presencia en nuestro país.* http://www.san pablo.com.ar/vidapastoral/?seccion=articulos&id=303(last accessed at September 2013).

-, *La Iglesia ortodoxa del Patriarcado ecuménico de Constantinopla y su presencia en Argentina.* http://www.san-pablo.com.ar/vidapastoral/?seccion=articulos&id=271(last accessed at September 2013).

-, *La Iglesia Apostólica Armenia y su presencia en la Argentina.* http://www.san-pablo.com.ar/vidapastoral/?seccion=articulos&id=235(last accessed at September 2013).

-, *Una presencia del cristianismo de origen arameo: la Iglesia siriana ortodoxa de Antioquía.* http://www.san-pablo.com.ar/vidapastoral/?seccion=articulos&id=223(last accessed at September 2013).

Von Sinner, R., "Trust and Convivência: Contributions to a Hermeneutics of Trust in Communal Interaction," in *The Ecumenical Review* 57.3 (2005): 322-341(last accessed at September 2013).

Chrysoulakis G., *The rugged course of my life*, (Athens, 2005) (in Greek).

(73) Ecumenical Dialogue in the Perspective of Orthodox Churches in Oceania

Bishop Irinej Dobrijevic

Historia magistra vitae est[1]

Introduction

To comprehend effectively the complexities of Orthodox Christianity in Oceania and its dialectical outreach, embracing ecumenical dialogue and wider engagement, is to note the efforts and endeavours of an immigrant people and their posterity, who through their Church and ethnic communities, interface with new societies and circumstances. Within the contextual paradigm of their new environmental and socio-political surrounds, they have attempted to create, more often than not to re-create, stabilise and develop a new life for their own generation and for succeeding generations in the remote lands of Australia and New Zealand, where even the "tyranny of distance"[2] is a causal factor.

Oceania, also known as Oceanica, is a loosely define geographical region centred on the islands of the tropical Pacific Ocean. Considerations of what constitutes Oceania, referred to as the "smallest of all the continents,"[3] range from its three subregions of Melanesia, Micronesia, and Polynesia to, more broadly, the entire insular region between Asia and the Americas, including Australasia and the Malay Archipelago. The term often connotes more specifically the Fifth Continent, comprising the mainland of the Australian continent as well as the island of Tasmania and proximate islands in the Indian and Pacific Oceans.[4]

The national history of Australia and New Zealand, lands which simultaneously embrace both the beginning of time and the ends of the earth, is a relatively young history. Confronted by an ancient landscape occupied by indigenous Aboriginal people for at least 40,000 years, the continuous migrant settlement of Australia began on 26 January 1788 with the arrival of the British "First Fleet" and the establishment of a penal colony consisting of 209 sailors and officers and 717 convicts, both male and female.[5] Originally cited by Captain James Cook, who sailed the complete east coast of Australia in 1770 stopping at the territory of today's city of Sydney, in a bay of dense vegetation which he named Botany Bay. One of the most remote lands of the earth, once called "The Unknown Land" (*Terra Australis Incognita*) or "The Great South Land", Australia is the sixth largest country in the world characterised by its ancient, semi-arid and worn landscape, enveloped by modern cities.

New Zealand, on the other hand, is a lush volcanic island which is also ancient yet preserved its purity and pristine nature. Due to its remoteness it was one of the last lands to be settled by humans. During its long period of isolation New Zealand developed and retained its distinctive biodiversity. Polynesians initially settled Aotearoa in 1250–1300 AD and advanced a distinctive Māori culture. Unlike the Aboriginal which remains a nominal, if not a marginalised culture the Māori peoples and their culture have been integrated into most areas of public life. Abel Tasman, a Dutch explorer, was the first European to sight New Zealand in 1642 and annexed the country for Holland under the name *Staten Landt*, later changed to New Zealand by Dutch mapmakers, though it was the British who ultimately colonised it.[6]

---

[1] Cicero, *De Oratore*, II, 36.

[2] Cf. Blainey, Geoffrey, *The Tyranny of Distance: How Distance Shaped Australia's History*, (Sydney: Pan Macmillan Australia Pty Limited, 1966, Rev. ed. 2001).

[3] *Scholastic Atlas of the World* (2003), "Oceania is the smallest of all the continents".

[4] Wikipedia: http://en.wikipedia.org/wiki/Oceania; and Australia: The Fifth Continent: http://www.dreamlike.info/aus/index.html.

[5] Spasovic, Stanimir and Miletic, Srboljub, *Историја Српске Православне Цркве у Аустралији, Новом Зеланду и Јужној Африци* (The History of the Serbian Orthodox Church in Australia, New Zealand and South Africa), (Belgrade: Academy of Sciences, 2007), 10-11.

[6] Wikipedia: http://en.wikipedia.org/wiki/New_Zealand; and Europeans arrive to Aotearoa: http://www.newzealand.com/au/feature/europeans-arrive-to-aotearoa/.

Early Orthodox Immigration

History records the arrival first of a Russian, John Potaskie, to Tasmania in 1804.[7] Thereafter a number of Greeks, forced into exile from the Ionian Islands for misdemeanours committed during British hegemony, sailed to Sydney in 1818.[8] Amongst the early Orthodox settlers were a number of Syrian-Lebanese. The first Orthodox liturgy was celebrated off the southern coast of New South Wales on Orthodox Easter Sunday in 1820 by Hieromonk Dionysii, a Russian Orthodox chaplain consigned to Captain Bellingshausen's round-the-world expedition of 1819 - 1821.[9] Subsequently docking at Kirribilli Point, regular services celebrated at a base-camp previously established by Russian naval visitors, popularly known as "Russian Point".[10] The next recorded service was held in Melbourne by another Russian naval chaplain under Captain Butakov, Fr Jerome, presumably a hieromonk, on Epiphany in January 1862. It is assumed that the Great Blessing of Water was celebrated at Port Phillip.[11]

Regular parish life was established with the arrival of the first permanent Orthodox priest, a Greek Archimandrite, Fr Dorotheos (Bakaliaros) in 1895.[12] He was soon followed in Sydney by the highly educated polyglot, Fr Seraphim Fokas and in Melbourne by Fr Athanasios Kantopoulos, both from the Jerusalem Patriarchate. Being bi-lingual they were readily able to service the needs of their mixed Greek and Arab parishes.[13] The first Orthodox parish church in Australia, dedicated to the Holy Trinity, was established in May 1898 in Surry Hills, Sydney, by Greeks and Syrian-Lebanese.[14] With the arrival of the first Arab priest in Australia, Fr Nicholas Shehadie in 1913, the Arab faithful severed themselves from the heretofore mixed parishes into ethnically separate parishes.[15] The many Russian refugees from Asia, due to the Russo-Japanese War, including a number of aristocrats and Chinese Orthodox, were briefly ministered to by a visiting priest from the United States in 1916. The first permanent Russian priest arrived in 1922 and their first parish church was erected in 1926 in Brisbane under the Russian Orthodox Church Outside of Russia (ROCOR).[16]

Ecumenical Patriarch Meletios III (Metaxakis) saw the first Metropolis of Australia and New Zealand established in 1924 with the very distinguished and highly cultivated Metropolitan Christophoros (Knetes) elected on 9 February of that year as its first hierarch.[17] In 1959 the Metropolis was elevated to the dignity of an Archdiocese.[18] Notwithstanding the cause and effect of the 'Venezelists' and the 'Royalists', Orthodoxy in Australia was already set in 1924 for a stormy confrontation between hierarchy and communities.[19] Through further inverted ecclesiastical beginnings, initiated by communities instead of the hierarchy, such confrontations continue to this very day.

---

[7] Cf. Lazarev, M.P., *Dokumenty I* (Moscow, 1952) in Simmons, H.L.N. "Eastern Orthodoxy in Australia: A Forgotten Chapter?" in *St Vladimir's Theological Quarterly* 23.3/4 (1979): 181, footnote 4.

[8] Simmons, Harry L.N., "Eastern Orthodoxy in Australia: A Forgotten Chapter?" in *St Vladimir's Theological Quarterly* 23.3/4 (1979): 181; and Simmons, Harry L.N., *Orthodoxy in Australia: Parallels and links with the USA*, (Brookline, MA: Hellenic College Press, 1986), 4.

[9] Lazarev, op cit., footnote 8 in Simmons, "Eastern Orthodoxy in Australia", op cit., 182 and ff.

[10] Simmons, "Eastern Orthodoxy in Australia", op cit., 183.

[11] Ibid, 183-184

[12] Quite possibly between the years 1896-1897.

[13] Ibid, 181-182, 184; and Simmons, *Orthodoxy in Australia*, op cit., 4-7.

[14] Godley, Stephen and Hughes, Philip J., *The Eastern Orthodox in Australia* (Canberra: Australian Government Publishing Service, 1996), 5.

[15] Simmons, "Eastern Orthodoxy in Australia", op cit., 184.

[16] Cf. Godley and Hughes, op cit.

[17] Simmons, *Orthodoxy in Australia*, op cit., 8-9.

[18] Godley and Hughes, op cit.

[19] Simmons, *Orthodoxy in Australia*, op cit.

The Ecumenical Patriarchate in January 1970 established a separate Metropolis for New Zealand and the Far East electing Bishop Dionysios (Psiachas), who had previously served in Australia, as its first Metropolitan. At the time the jurisdiction included missions in Korea.[20]

Later Orthodox Immigration

Largely, the Orthodox communities of Australia and New Zealand were brought into being with the massive arrival of displaced persons, escalating in the aftermath of World War II. Recruiting through the assistance of the International Refugee Organisation of the United Nations from the post-war refugee camps of Western Europe mostly Russians, Ukrainians, Serbians, Romanians and Bulgarians, including a lesser number of Bye-lorussians, Estonians and Georgians were brought to new shores.[21] A burgeoning history, beginning in the latter half of the 1940s, closely followed by the large numbers of Greeks after the Greek Civil War and the assisted passage of many more Greeks and numerous Serbs and other Yugoslavs in the 1950s to 1970s. By 1971 the Orthodox accounted for 340,000 or 2.6 percent of the Australian population. Today Eastern Orthodoxy is the fourth largest Christian denomination in Australia and consists of nearly 3 percent of the overall population[22] which presently stands at 23.34 million.[23]

The first Ukrainian Orthodox priest, Fr Anany Teodorovych, arrived in 1948 as a displaced person from the refugee camps in Germany to settle in Canberra.[24] He was followed by more clergy and faithful. Originally not part of the canonical hierarchy of the Orthodox Church, in the 1990s, they merged with the rest of the Ukrainian Orthodox Church in the Diaspora and eventually under the canonical protection of the Ecumenical Patriarchate of Constantinople.

Orthodox immigrants from Lebanon began arriving in substantial numbers following the 1967 Arab-Israeli War, augmented by another wave of Lebanese refugees beginning in 1975 with the outbreak of civil war, mostly Muslims, then Catholics, approximately 14 percent were Orthodox Christians.[25] This latter wave, given the composition of its immigrants, serves to explain the confused perception by the average Australian of the Christian identity of the Catholic and Orthodox Lebanese, at times erupting into violence. This, amongst all else, was cause for implementing the renaming of their jurisdiction from Syrian-Lebanese or, Syro-Arab, to Antiochian.

There were some Serbian settlers in Australia before World War I, such as Nikola Milovic, one of the gold miners mentioned around 1860 in Gold Field, Western Australia. Born in the coastal town of Boka Kotorska, he later grew fruit and had his own vineyard.[26] The great influx, however, came as displaced persons and refugees following World War II. More recent immigrants, primarily Serbian Orthodox, arrived from the successor republics of the Former Republic of Yugoslavia in the aftermath of its decade of civil wars in the 1990s.

With the organising of Serbian parishes, due to political differences, a schism erupted in the 1960s. This resulted in the formation of two rival dioceses, one loyal to the Patriarchate and the other, not canonically recognised, the "Free Serbian Orthodox Church", come New Gracanica Metropolitanate. Significant steps were taken towards reuniting them in the 1990s, culminating in full reconciliation in 2011 under Bishop Irinej

---

[20] Ibid, 15.

[21] There is also a substantial and influential number of immigrants from the Former Yugoslav Republic of Macedonia, who, albeit divided amongst themselves, belong to the self-proclaimed "Macedonian Orthodox Church" which is not recognised as canonical.

[22] Batrouney, Trevor, "Orthodoxy in Australia: Current and Future Perspectives" in Casiday, Augustine (Ed.), *The Orthodox Christian World*, (Routledge, 2012), 180.

[23] Australian Bureau of Statistics: http://www.abs.gov.au/ausstats/.

[24] Simmons, *Orthodoxy in Australia*, op cit., 26-27.

[25] Ibid.

[26] Spasovic and Miletic, op cit., 11.

(Dobrijevic) and the elevation of the previous two dioceses of Australia and New Zealand into a single unified Metropolitanate.

Tired and worn, at times near devastated, refugee families and individuals sought a new home and a new secure future. Their quest was and remains—as with all Diaspora communities—how to accept and interface with the unique culture, traditions and circumstances of their new homeland, without forgetting or betraying those of their fatherland which many have left behind, never again to return. Their only solace was the Church, the locus of both faith and heritage.

History and Consequences

Bereft of existent ecclesiastical structures, many of the newer Orthodox settlers sought the creation of a new life and a new home, a place to give birth, to raise children and to provide them with an adequate education, one which will emphasize the new and preserve from forgetfulness the old. Firstly, parish churches and then monasteries were raised by Orthodox laity, often without clergy or monastics, as a common home to retain their ancestral faith and provide places of worship, allowing settlers to become a viable part of sacred and secular history. Clergy were later summoned and then, in turn, the Mother Churches would appoint bishops to oversee these nascent extra-diocesan missionary territories.

In numerous cities, where there was neither an Orthodox Church nor an Orthodox priest, many felt the need to attend church services and compelled to enrol their children in local Roman Catholic or, more commonly, in Anglican churches and their schools. This early select interaction was characteristically dictated by past experience in their Fatherland. The Orthodox clearly felt more comfortable in turning toward the Anglican Communion as they were neither theologically liberal in the faith as the Protestants, nor were they dominated by the Papacy. In both Sydney and Melbourne, as well as in other cities, members of the Anglican Church would welcome Orthodox newcomers. Anglican clergy and monastics offered their churches for liturgical use and often for sale on favourable terms. Such individuals and groups were deemed "friends of the Orthodox". Eventually a significant number of 'friends of Orthodox' would convert to the Orthodox faith.[27]

Conversely this cause and effect also served to deprive Orthodoxy of many of its first born generations abroad. Without benefit of an Orthodox Christian upbringing and usually embarrassed by an ethnic heritage dismissed by society at large, they eventually left the Orthodox Church. Impeding upon future generations to come, this initial pragmatic resolve of the first settlers to retain at least their Christianity, resulted in subsequent estrangement from both faith and heritage. Such unintended consequences caused the second wave of arrivals to recoil from even practical engagement with other Christian communities, juxtaposing integration against assimilation.

Ecumenical relations were further strained with the arrival of many immigrants from Communist countries where such interaction was the only proverbial window to the outside world for their Church leaders and thereby denounced by the Communist leadership, playing upon the divergence of homogenisation and syncretism against differentiation. Ultimately such a mentality, complicated by an already isolated and distanced immigration, saw faith turning from subtle and flexible, breathing of divinely inspired freedom, to strict unimaginable dogma. Absolutism was more easily self-imposed than relativism. Eventually this lead to unintended sectarianism which became promoted as a vehicle for self-preservation, even internally amongst Orthodox.

Anti-Hierarchical Tendencies

Established to meet the pastoral needs of its people in a new and often times strange land, the Orthodox Churches in Australia and New Zealand have become the very pillar of their Diaspora communities. Yet the

[27] Batrouney, op cit., 183.

ecclesiastical history of the Church in the Fifth Continent has been and remains to a great extent, a turbulent history. This is essentially due to the fact that the Orthodox Church, a hierarchical church, instead of beginning with missions dispatched by the hierarchy, as in the historic development of its Mother Churches, began in this part of the world—as in other dispersions—with the laity establishing their communities and then seeking clergy to service their spiritual needs. However, in most cases, the laity, having lost almost all that they had strived to establish in their fatherlands to war and political machinations, displaced their anxieties toward the hierarchy, which they viewed as yet another authoritarian instance, by fiercely fighting to retain control of the church community assets and maintaining particular ownership.

The laws of both Australia and New Zealand served such purposes well in that property trusts were initially established, ostensibly to protect communal property rights of the first settlers who arrived to serve out prison terms in penal colonies. Trustees became variable owners of their entitlements and deemed it their task, on behalf of their community, to protect these investments even from the hierarchy of the Church. Such was always executed under the feeble yet effective guise that the bishops would sell their properties, albeit to whom and why is considered non-essential with determination and resolve, non-negotiable. Given such implacable motivation many hierarchs to this day have found themselves battling civil court cases to secure canonical and hierarchical rights and order.[28]

Egalitarianism and Secularism

This anti-hierarchical mentality is further undergirded by the after effect of penal colonisation in Australia, expressed through a strong sense of egalitarianism or at least the parity of all individuals. Natural or cultural diversity have, thereby, become obstacles that must be overcome or more so destroyed for the sake of society. The end result is the burdening of society in general and immigrants in particular with an inherent resentment towards those who are deemed "appointed" by favouring those who have been "elected". Such a mindset *a priori*, come intuitively, vehemently resents the imposition of "appointed leadership" such as clergy and hierarchs in particular, in favour of "elected leadership" such as church community boards. The result, ultimately, is rampant anti-clericalism.

In turn this anti-clericalism is complicated by prevalent secularism. In general the church is derided and the role of clergy, particularly in the public sector, is frowned upon. The intensity of this open resentment is further intensified by an underlying island mentality overtly complicated by distance. Despite such obstacles placed before communities of faith, 12.7 million or 64 per cent of Australians declared themselves as Christians in the 2006 Australian Bureau of Statistics Census. Over 2 million Australians continue to attend a place of worship every Sunday,[29] with a presumable majority being Orthodox and Asian Christians.

The Pivotal Role of Archbishop Stylianos of Australia

Many esteemed, erudite and dignified Orthodox hierarchs have diligently laboured in Oceania and attempted to make an impact against such numerous and complicated circumstances. Without exception Archbishop Dr Stylianos (Harkianakis), Primate of the Greek Orthodox Church in Australia, has had the greatest impact not only on the ongoing history of parochial, monastic and institutional expansion of the Greek Archdiocese, but also on the very prestige and viability of Orthodoxy itself in Australia.

Born in Rethymnon, Crete in 1935, he studied at the Theological School of Halki in Constantinople. In 1957, he was ordained to the diaconate and upon graduating he was ordained to the priesthood in 1958. Receiving a scholarship from the Ecumenical Patriarchate, he completed postgraduate studies in Systematic Theology

---

[28] Cf. "The Greek Hierarchs" in Simmons, Harry L.N., *Orthodoxy in Australia*, op cit., 9ff; and in Spasovic and Miletic, op cit.
[29] Australian Christian Lobby statistics: http://www.acl.org.au/about/.

Part IV: Ecumenical Dialogue in various Orthodox Churches and Settings

and Philosophy of Religion in Bonn from 1958-1966. Rather than earning a Doctorate of Divinity from an analogous western faculty, in 1965, he submitted his doctoral dissertation, titled "The Infallibility of the Church in Orthodox Theology", to the Theological Faculty of the University of Athens. In 1966, following his return from Germany, he was appointed Abbot of the historic Vlatadon Patriarchal Monastery in Thessaloniki. Therein he was requested by the Holy Synod of Constantinople to help establish, together with other scholars from the local Theological Faculty, a theological research centre. He soon became President of the newly-incepted Patriarchal Institute of Patristic Studies. Upon completing his post-doctoral dissertation, titled "The Dogmatic Constitution De Ecclesia of the Second Vatican Council" at the University of Thessaloniki, he became an Associate Professor at the same university in 1969. Subsequently, he also lectured at various faculties and academic institutions within Greece and abroad, most notably the University of Regensburg in 1973. He was unanimously elected by the Holy Synod of Constantinople as Titular Metropolitan of Militoupolis and Exarch of the Ecumenical Patriarchate for Mount Athos in 1970.

Five years later, he was again unanimously elected Archbishop of Australia, arriving in Sydney in April 1975. He is widely published in Systematic Theology and Ecclesiology in international theological journals. He has represented the Ecumenical Patriarchate to Assemblies of the World Council of Churches and in bilateral dialogues such as the Anglican-Orthodox Dialogue from 1969 to 1978.[30] From 1975 he also taught Orthodox Theology and Spirituality at the University of Sydney. He was unanimously elected in 1980 by all representatives of Orthodox Churches as their chairman to the official Theological Dialogue with the Roman Catholic Church, whilst his co-chair, Johannes Cardinal Willebrands, was appointed by the Vatican. After serving faithfully for more than two decades in this highly responsible and difficult position, he tendered his third and final resignation in 2003—having attempted this twice before without acceptance—when he published an extensive report, titled "The Misfortune of the Official Theological Dialogue between the Orthodox and the Roman Catholics."[31]

He is also a recognised essayist and poet, having published 37 collections of poetry.[32] For his outstanding contribution to European culture, having been nominated by the distinguished Philologist of the University of Vienna, Professor Albin Lesky, he received the prestigious international Gottfried von Herder Award in Vienna in 1973. Then in 1980, having been nominated by the renowned writer Pantelis Prevelakis, Archbishop Stylianos received the Award for Poetry from the Academy of Athens. The University of Lublin conferred on him an honorary doctorate in 1985, whilst the Sydney College of Divinity awarded him its first ever honorary doctorate in 2001. In 2005, he was acknowledged as a professor by an independent academic panel of the Sydney College of Divinity. Archbishop Stylianos is also Dean and Founder of St Andrew's Greek Orthodox Theological College where he lectures in Systematic Theology.[33]

Orthodox Theological Education

St Andrew's Theological College, established in Sydney in 1986, is the only civilly accredited Orthodox higher institution of its kind in the Southern Hemisphere. The opening of the Theological College was mandated by virtue of the very nature of the mission of the Church in Australia. There was need for an Orthodox theological school that would be primarily dedicated to theological study in co-operation with other theological colleges, as a centre of theological reflection and ecumenical dialogue, offering the Orthodox world-view and perspective.[34]

In his opening address on 23 February 1986, Archbishop Stylianos of Australia, succinctly noted:

---

[30] Simmons, *Orthodoxy in Australia*, op. cit., 16

[31] Theological School, Aristotelian University of Thessaloniki, Vol. 13, 2003.

[32] All of these are in Greek, with some translated Bilingual editions.

[33] Greek Orthodox Archdiocese of Australia: http://www.greekorthodox.org.au/general/aboutus/archbishopstylianos.

[34] St Andrew's Greek Orthodox Theological College (SAGOTC): http://www.sagotc.edu.au/about/establishment/.

"The establishment of the first Orthodox Theological College in the Southern Hemisphere is not and could not be simply an achievement of an ethnic group or of a denomination. Orthodoxy does not represent a certain number of Christians, a mere part of historical Christendom or an ideology dictated by geographical, racial or political conditions.

Orthodoxy is the faithful continuation of the undivided Christian Church of the first millennium, as decisively expressed in the Ecumenical Councils. Orthodoxy is a precious legacy for all of us. As such it belongs to all Christians and, through them, to the whole of mankind.

This is why the importance of the College is expressed not so much through the term 'Theological' as through the qualification 'Orthodox'. The Greek Orthodox Archdiocese of Australia had many years ago felt that its faithful would not be properly served and would not be creatively integrated in this multicultural and polyethnic society unless a Theological College were to be established...

Theology in Christianity cannot be a subject of individual thought and activities. Theology is the deeper breathing of the whole Church body as enlightened by the Holy Spirit who is promised only in the plurality of Church communion, and not in the isolation of the individual scholar...

We hope to be enabled to serve in a creative way not only our Church but also Australia and the universal society of peace, reconciliation, justice and sanctification which is God's ultimate will for His entire world."[35]

St Andrew's Greek Orthodox Theological College is accredited through the Sydney College of Divinity, a tertiary education institution providing high quality accredited awards in theology and related areas through the teaching colleges that are its member institutions.[36]

Separately, the Melbourne Institute for Orthodox Christian Studies, founded in 2004, provides both accredited and non-accredited study for anyone interested in studying Orthodoxy through the United Faculty of Theology of the Melbourne College of Divinity.[37]

Standing Council of Canonical Orthodox Churches in Australia

In addition to the founding of the St Andrew's Greek Orthodox Theological College, another hallmark events in the history of Orthodoxy in Australia was the founding of the Standing Council of Canonical Orthodox Churches in Australia (SCCOCA), also at the initiative of Archbishop Stylianos in 1979. The member churches consisted of the Greek, Antiochian, Serbian, Romanian and Bulgarian jurisdictions, including ROCOR.[38] The latter was received out of practical measures, given that almost all Russians in Australia belonged to this jurisdiction.[39] Though not in communion at that time with the majority of the member churches, the Church Abroad maintained canonical unity with wider Orthodoxy through inter-communion with the Serbian Church.

Predicated largely on the model of the Standing Conference of Canonical Orthodox Bishops in the Americas, SCCOCA provided a long needed common voice for Orthodoxy in Australia on various social issues. In addition to regular consultations, Pan-Orthodox liturgical celebrations were instituted for the Sunday of Orthodoxy and St Thomas Saturday, come Bright Friday of Pascha.

The anticipated aims of SCCOCA were formulated in the following:[40]

1. To work towards the full recognition of the Canonical Churches in Parliament through an Act of the Commonwealth Parliament;
2. To maximise consultations and cooperation between the Canonical Orthodox Churches in Australia;

---

[35] Published in the *Voice of Orthodoxy* (Sydney, March 1986), 22-23

[36] SAGOTC: http://www.sagotc.edu.au/about/accreditation/.

[37] MIOCS: http://www.miocs.net/ and http://uft.edu.au/.

[38] Also known as the Russian Orthodox Church Abroad (ROCA) or the "Synodal" Church, so named after the formation of the Holy Synod of ROCA in Sremski Karlovci, Serbia in 1922.

[39] Simmons, *Orthodoxy in Australia*, op. cit., 16.

[40] Ibid, 17-18, and cf. Godley and Hughes, op cit., 7.

3. To present the Orthodox Church's point of view on various moral and social issues to the legislators, governments and other relevant authorities, the media and the Australian Community at large;
4. To issue and distribute to government and instrumentalities, social agencies and other religious denominations, once every year, a Directory of the Canonical Orthodox Churches in Australia;
5. To present the common doctrinal position of the Canonical Orthodox Churches in Australia to the Australian Council of Churches[41]; and
6. To establish, in due course, a permanent Secretariat.

Unfortunately, following the pattern of both desirable and undesirable historical parallels with the Orthodox Churches in the United States, after an initial period of cooperation and success, the efficacy of SCCOCA was reduced by the boycotting of the newly-appointed isolationist, anti-ecumenical Bishop Pavel (Pavlov) of ROCOR.[42] Gratefully, this has been substantially overturned by Metropolitan Hilarion (Kapral), presently the First Hierarch of ROCOR, who has even sanctioned Western Rite clergy in Australia.

Important advances under the aegis of SCCOCA can be seen in the first time appointment of Orthodox university chaplains with Fr Militiades Chryssavgis to the University of New South Wales in 1979. This was expanded in 1981 to universities in Melbourne, Adelaide and Brisbane. That same year also witnessed the first Conference of Orthodox Tertiary Students at the University of New South Wales with others following suit in years to come.[43]

Another unique feature of SCCOCA was the prayer service held during the Opening of the Legal Year, primarily in Sydney but also in Melbourne. This unique endeavour brings together Orthodox hierarchs in Australia with Chief Justices and Justices of the Supreme Courts and the Attorney Generals of New South Wales and Melbourne, as well as members of the Phil-Hellenic Bar Association, eventually joined by members of the Serbian Bar Association.

National Councils of Churches in Australia and New Zealand

The contemporary ecumenical movement in Australia began to take its present shape as the 19th century drew to a close. Initiatives amongst students and between Church mission agencies led the way to the formation of the Australian Student Christian Movement in 1896 and the National Missionary Council in 1926. Thereafter, with the rapid increase in immigration following the devastation of World War II, the Australian Committee for the World Council of Churches was incepted in 1946. This developed into the Australian Council of Churches which in 1994 gave way to the current National Council of Churches in Australia (NCCA).

Initially the movement for Christian unity in Australia was an Anglican and Protestant undertaking. Eastern and Oriental Orthodox Churches joined as their numbers grew during the 1960s and 70s. As the Second Vatican Council opened new possibilities for relationships with other churches, in 1994 the National Council of Churches in Australia received the Roman Catholic Church as a full participant in Australia's national ecumenical movement.[44]

The NCCA consists of nineteen member churches. At present, of the Eastern Orthodox Churches, the Greek Orthodox Archdiocese, the Antiochian Orthodox Christian Archdiocese, the Serbian Orthodox Metropolitanate and the Romanian Orthodox Episcopate are member churches. The Serbian participation was withdrawn during the 1990s relative to what it viewed as discrimination, following a general tendency towards inversion, during the civil wars which followed the breakup of the Former Yugoslavia. At the initiative of Bishop Irinej, the same was reintegrated in 2008. As with many other local ecumenical endeavours, the Oriental Orthodox are more willing and active participants.

[41] Presently the National Council of Churches in Australia.
[42] Simmons, *Orthodoxy in Australia*, op. cit., 18, 24.
[43] Ibid, 18.
[44] NCCA: http://www.ncca.org.au/about/story.

The NCCA works in collaboration with state ecumenical councils throughout Australia, most notably the New South Wales Ecumenical Council and the Victorian Council of Churches. The NCCA is also an associate council of the World Council of Churches (WCC),[45] a member of the Christian Conference of Asia, as well as a partner of other international ecumenical bodies which include Eastern Orthodox participation.

The National Heads of Churches of Australia is a consultative body, comprised of the national heads or the chief executive officers of Christian Churches in Australia. Meeting twice annually, in tandem with and separate from the NCCA, this elite group convenes to openly discuss current ecclesial, theological and socio-political issues without drawing conclusions or publishing any findings or statements in common. Its chief aim is to foster good cooperation and mutual understanding amongst church leaders. Of the Eastern Orthodox jurisdictional heads, only the Greek and Antiochian archbishops, later joined by the Serbian bishop participate in the National Heads of Churches. For the first time in 2012, an Orthodox hierarch, Bishop Irinej (Dobrijevic), was unanimously elected chairman, a position he currently retains.

The National Council of Churches in New Zealand (NCCNZ) was formed in 1941 and comprises over 82 per cent of the membership of churches in New Zealand. The Greek Orthodox Metropolis of New Zealand is the only Eastern Orthodox member church in the NCCNZ.[46]

Dialogues Seeking Understanding

There have been ongoing theological discussions in the ecumenical movement, which have involved the Eastern Orthodox Churches both internationally and locally, since its inception. Fundamentally at the heart of all ecumenical enterprise is the very culture and spirit of dialogue, seeking mutual understanding and exchange.

Beginning at the Third World Conference on Faith and Order in Lund in 1952 and culminating at the Fourth in Montreal in 1963 many, especially the Orthodox, see a significant alteration in the methodological application of dialogue. By moving away from the comparative method to a form of theological dialogue which approaches controversial issues from a common biblical and Christological basis, ecumenical dialogue has advanced in unprecedented, productive ways.[47] The recent presentation of *The Church: Towards a Common Vision* during the 10th Assembly of the WCC in Busan in 2013, offers the promise of an eagerly anticipated ecclesiological foundation to more substantive theological dialogue.[48]

A vast dialectical variety also exists at almost every level in the life of the local church, both multilateral and bilateral. Internationally, multilateral dialogue is largely facilitated through the WCC. Theological dialogue is guided by the work of the Faith and Order Commission, with some very tangible results from this dialogue, most notably in *Baptism, Eucharist and Ministry*.[49] The same represented a remarkable degree of convergence on both theological and applicable matters, qualified by the question posed to the churches, *the extent to which your church can recognise in this text the faith of the Church through the ages*. That question remains essential to the "process of reception".[50]

---

[45] Bishop Irinej (Dobrijevic) currently serves in the WCC as a member of the Central Committee, its Public Issues Committee and the Permanent Committee on Consensus and Collaboration. At the 10th Assembly in 2013, Busan, Korea he held the position of Moderator of the Public Issues Committee.

[46] NCCNZ: http://www.teara.govt.nz/en/1966/national-council-of-churches.

[47] Cf. WCC: http://www.oikoumene.org/en/what-we-do/faith-and-order/history; and Williamson, op. cit., 1.

[48] "The Church: Towards a Common Vision," Faith and Order Paper No. 214, (Geneva: World Council of Churches, 2013): http://www.oikoumene.org/en/resources/documents/wcc-commissions/faith-and-order-commission/i-unity-the-church-and-its-mission/the-church-towards-a-common-vision.

[49] "Baptism, Eucharist and Ministry," Faith and Order Paper No. 111, (Geneva: World Council of Churches, 1982): http://www.oikoumene.org/en/resources/documents/wcc-commissions/faith-and-order-commission/i-unity-the-church-and-its-mission/baptism-eucharist-and-ministry-faith-and-order-paper-no-111-the-lima-text.

[50] Williamson, op. cit., 1.

Part IV: Ecumenical Dialogue in various Orthodox Churches and Settings

This diversity of dialogue, internationally, is also reflected in the ecumenical endeavours of the local churches within the Australian context. The aims of such dialogue differs, according to the Reverend Ray Williamson, former General Secretary of the New South Wales Ecumenical Council. All dialogues begin with an attempt to create better understanding between the partners. Many dialogues remain "dialogues seeking understanding". Others progress to a second level in seeking points of agreement in faith, order and mission. Such are "dialogues seeking theological convergence". Yet others go much further and seek the restoration of communion with one another, even full visible unity. These are "dialogues seeking mutual recognition".[51]

Thirteen bilateral dialogues were facilitated, at one point or another, in Australia.[52]

1. The Uniting Church of Australia (UCA) maintained such dialogues with the Anglican Church, the Armenian Apostolic Church, the Baptist Church, the Churches of Christ, the Greek Orthodox Church, the Lutheran Church, the Religious Society of Friends, the Roman Catholic Church and the Salvation Army.
2. The other dialogues are: Anglican-Lutheran, Anglican-Oriental Orthodox, Anglican-Roman Catholic; and Lutheran-Roman Catholic.

The bilateral dialogue between the Greek Orthodox Church and the Uniting Church was the only national dialogue in Australia in which there was Eastern Orthodox involvement. Having been initiated in 1981, its purpose was not doctrinal agreement, even less to seek intercommunion, rather building better relations. The dialogue partners meet one day per year to explore together mutually determined topics as were "Eucharist and Ministry" and "The Relationship between Authenticity and Authority in the Church". In 2003, the topic was to have been "Agreed Statements on the Holy Trinity". However, following the UCA Assembly's resolution concerning ordained ministry and sexuality, the meeting was never held.[53] The Uniting Church-Greek Orthodox Dialogue, co-chaired by Archbishop Stylianos for 20 years, was thereby discontinued due to irreconcilable differences.

The Greek Orthodox Archdiocese of Australia was also an avid participant in the Council of Christians and Jews. In time, however, this dimension of the interfaith dialogue lapsed into dormant status.

Outreach in a Foreign Land

Undergirded by his experience in London and as sub-dean of Holy Cross Seminary in Brookline, Massachusetts, Bishop Aristarchos (Mavrakis) of the Alexandrian Patriarchate, a graduate of both Halki in Constantinople and Durham University, joined the Greek Orthodox Archdiocese of Australia in 1969. It was through his persistence that Modern Greek studies were introduced to the Universities of Melbourne and West Australia.[54] Ongoing Modern Greek studies at universities and financial assistance to worthy causes and charities are sponsored in part by organisations such as the Greek Australian Professionals Association (GAPA), established in 1981 by George Liagras, a Greek born engineer, and Manuel Aroney, then professor of Mathematics at Sydney University. GAPA was the first organisation of its kind in Australia.[55]

The Antiochian Church is credited with being the first Orthodox jurisdiction in Oceania to have pioneered the liturgical use of the English language in Australia and New Zealand, largely due to two key factors: the early admission to the priesthood of a number of convert priests from the United States of America and the support of two hierarchs with American training and experience, Bishop Gibran (Ramlaoui) and presently, Metropolitan Paul (Saliba) who continues to move the church towards adopting the language of the country.[56]

---

[51] Williamson, op. cit., 2-6.

[52] Ibid, 1-2.

[53] Williamson, op. cit., 5.

[54] Simmons, *Orthodoxy in Australia*, op cit., 15-16.

[55] GAPA: http://www.gapa.com.au/index.php?option=com_content&view=article&id=6&Itemid=2.

[56] Simmons, *Orthodoxy in Australia*, op cit., 28-29 and in Batrouney, op cit., 183.

Entirely unlike the establishment of ethnic Orthodox communities in Australia and New Zealand, which were seen as internal missionary territories, the work of external ecclesiastical missions has been initiated by Metropolitan Amphilochios (Tsoukos), Archbishop of New Zealand and Exarch of Oceania, in 2006 to the indigenous peoples of the Pacific Islands: Fiji, Tonga and Samoa, which by the decision of the Ecumenical Patriarchate where incorporated into its Greek Orthodox Metropolis of New Zealand.[57] This stands in sharp contrast, substantially to avoid proselytism, to the question of Orthodox missionary endeavours to the Aboriginal communities of Australia and even to the Māori communities of New Zealand itself.

Conversely, an interesting historical anomaly is the person of Fr Seraphim Slade of Gunning, New South Wales, thus far the only Aborigine convert priest to Orthodoxy, serving in the Australian and New Zealand Diocese of ROCOR. Though it was known that the original Russian naval visitors of 1920 maintained extremely friendly relations with the local Aborigines, it was never recorded whether or not they attended those initial Orthodox liturgies or if matters of faith were discussed with them.

Certain unique particularities of the Orthodox migration in New Zealand include Serbian intellectuals that constitute the vast majority of the new Serbian immigration. Through the auspices of the Serbian Orthodox Metropolitanate of Australia and New Zealand, the Sts Cosmos and Damian Serbian-New Zealand Medical Society was founded in 2008. This elite group of medical professionals, many of whom are university professors, broadly interfaces with the wider New Zealand academic, medical, dental and pharmaceutical communities in scientific and philanthropic pursuits both in New Zealand and abroad in traditional Serbian lands.[58]

The Romanian Orthodox Episcopate of Australia and New Zealand, which formally came into existence with the appointment of Bishop Dr Mihail (Filimon) in 2008, is the only jurisdiction whose clergy all have theological degrees. The Romanian government assists in funding many of their missionary clergy. Disproportionate to their relatively small numbers, their contribution to theological education, inter-Orthodox and ecumenical endeavours has been substantial.[59] Most notable amongst the Romanian immigrants is the Reverend Dr Doru Kostache,[60] an exemplary multi-discipline senior lecturer, specialising in Patristics, at the St Andrew's Theological College in Sydney.

The Australian Government Organ and Tissue Authority in tandem with "DonateLife ... the greatest gift" launched a community education campaign in consultation with religious and community leaders for people from culturally, religiously and linguistically diverse communities, aimed at fostering awareness about organ and tissue donations. Ensuring access to appropriate information about organ and tissue donations to diverse communities is a priority for the Organ and Tissue Authority, which has produced a number of resources as part of the "DonateLife... the greatest gift campaign". Amongst the Orthodox resources available, statements concerning organ and tissue donations have been submitted by Archbishop Stylianos of the Greek Archdiocese and Bishop Irinej of the Serbian Metropolitanate.[61]

The Australian Christian Lobby (ACL) was established in 1995, originally as the Australian Christian Coalition. Its founder, John Gagliardi, a lay leader of a large Pentecostal church in Brisbane, also held journalistic positions as editor of the *Townsville Bulletin* and as a presenter for Channel 10 News. As a politically active and socially conservative lobbying organisation, it became known as the Australian Christian Lobby in 2001. It aims to see Christian principles and ethics accepted and influencing the way Australians are governed by seeking to have the positive public contributions of the Christian faith reflected in the political life of the nation. Based in Canberra, the ACL operates in the Federal Parliament and in all the state and territory parliaments,

---

[57] Greek Orthodox Metropolis of New Zealand: http://www.ecp-metnz.org.nz/home.htm.

[58] A common reference to the Serb populated areas of the new republics which have emerged from the Former Republic of Yugoslavia.

[59] Simmons, *Orthodox in Australia*, op cit., 28.

[60] A cleric of the Greek Orthodox Archdiocese.

[61] 'DonateLife': http://www.donatelife.gov.au/resources/culturally-and-linguistically-diverse-audiences/faith-language-and-cultural-resources/greek-orthodox; and http://www.donatelife.gov.au/resources/culturally-and-linguistically-diverse-audiences/faith-language-and-cultural-resources/serbian-orthodox.

Part IV: Ecumenical Dialogue in various Orthodox Churches and Settings

neither being party partisan nor denominationally-aligned. The ACL does not seek to be the peak political voice for the church, rather to facilitate a professional engagement of church with the state which allows for the voice of the church and individual Christians to be effective in the public square.[62] The only Eastern Orthodox participants numbered Metropolitan Paul of the Antiochian Archdiocese and currently, Bishop Irinej of the Serbian Metropolitanate.

Episcopal Assembly of Oceania

The Episcopal Assembly of Canonical Orthodox Bishops of Oceania began under the chairmanship *ex officio* of Archbishop Stylianos of Australia in 2010 in Sydney, as mandated by the Fourth Pre-Conciliar Pan-Orthodox Conference which met at the Patriarchal Centre in Chambésy, Geneva, from 6-9 June 2009. Convened at the initiative of Ecumenical Patriarch Bartholomew I with the active participation of delegates from the fourteen Autocephalous Orthodox Churches, this Conference was a direct result of the Synaxis of the Heads of Orthodox Churches, previously having met at the Ecumenical Patriarchate in Constantinople from 10-12 October 2008. The same had expressed its "desire for the swift healing of every canonical anomaly that has arisen from historical circumstances and pastoral requirements, such as in the so-called Orthodox Diaspora, with a view to overcome every possible influence that is foreign to Orthodox Ecclesiology."[63]

The Episcopal Assembly of Oceania consists of all local Orthodox hierarchs who are in canonical communion with all of the Orthodox Churches. According to the Chambésy Conference, the Assembly is chaired by the first amongst the prelates of the Church of Constantinople and, in the absence of thereof, in accordance with the order of the Diptychs. The Assembly is intended to be a temporary solution to the underlying Orthodox ecclesial principle of one bishop in one place at one time. Member bishops are not deprived of their administrative competencies and canonical character, nor are their rights restricted in the Diaspora. The aim is to form a common position of the Orthodox Church on various issues, whilst allowing members bishops to remain fully responsible to their own churches and to express the views of their own churches to the outside world.[64]

The current jurisdictions, whose hierarchs constitute the membership of the Oceania Assembly, include:
- The Patriarchate of Constantinople:
  - Greek Orthodox Archdiocese of Australia
  - Holy Metropolis of New Zealand and Exarchate of Oceania
  - Ukrainian Orthodox Church in the Diaspora
- The Patriarchate of Antioch:
  - Antiochian Orthodox Christian Archdiocese of Australia, New Zealand and the Philippines
- The Patriarchate of Moscow:
  - Australian and New Zealand Diocese of the Russian Orthodox Church Outside of Russia (including parishes in Indonesia)
- The Serbian Patriarchate:
  - Metropolitanate of Australia and New Zealand of the Serbian Orthodox Church
- The Romanian Patriarchate:
  - Romanian Orthodox Episcopate of Australia and New Zealand

---

[62] ACL: http://www.acl.org.au/about/ and Wikipedia: http://en.wikipedia.org/wiki/Australian_Christian_Lobby.

[63] Assembly of Canonical Orthodox Bishops of North and Central America: http://www.assemblyofbishops.org/about/documents/chambesy.

[64] "The Orthodox Diaspora: Decision" The Fourth Pre-Conciliar Pan-Orthodox Conference (The Orthodox Centre of the Ecumenical Patriarchate: Chambésy, 6-13 June 2009), 1-3: http://www.assemblyofbishops.org/assets/files/docs/chambesy/diasporadecision-pdf.pdf

- The Bulgarian Patriarchate:
  - Bulgarian Eastern Orthodox Diocese of USA, Canada and Australia

The First Episcopal Assembly of all canonical Orthodox Bishops of Oceania met in Sydney from 16-18 October 2010, commencing with a Hierarchical Divine Liturgy and manifesting its essential Eucharistic unity at the Greek Orthodox Cathedral of the Annunciation in Redfern, Sydney.

Lengthy and edifying discussion centered on issues of mutual concern, such as pastoral care, catechesis, liturgical life, reaffirmed the unity of all canonical Orthodox Churches; consequently, strongly condemning those who would attempt to destroy the precious unity of the Church through adherence to new or existing schismatic groups and sects in the region.

In order to safeguard and contribute to the unity of the Orthodox Church in Oceania, the members of the Assembly unanimously agreed on the formation of the following three Committees:[65]

1. Campus Ministry: cultivating the Orthodox faith amongst our University students and shielding them from the effects of proselytism, co-chaired by Bishop Irinej of the Serbian Church and Bishop Ezekiel (Kefalas) of Dervis of the Greek Archdiocese;
2. Inter-Orthodox Liturgical Services: embracing common Pan-Orthodox services and adopting a unified approach to pastoral and liturgical issues, co-chaired by Their Graces Bishop Mihail of the Romanian Church and Bishop Seraphim (Ginis) of Apollonias of the Greek Archdiocese; and
3. Canonical Issues: compiling a list of all canonical bishops and other clergy of Oceania and a secondary list of schismatic groups and sects which attempt to promote themselves as being canonical Orthodox. This Committee is chaired by Archbishop Stylianos and consists of representatives from each Orthodox Church.

Meeting in Sydney from 16-17 October 2011, the Second Episcopal Assembly, in order to inform the public of its work and provide a source of information, initiated the launching of an official website[66] that would include a catalogue of canonical clergy and thereby, knowledge of schismatic groups, as well as the promulgation of a Statute for the Episcopal Assembly of Oceania. In like manner, amongst all else, the Assembly rendered the following decisions:[67]

1. To pave the way for annual local Synaxis of the Clergy of all canonical jurisdictions for the purpose of forming brotherly relations and to have collaboration in carrying out the decisions of the Assembly on a local level;
2. The Assembly, importantly, decided to bring together prominent Orthodox theologians, medical doctors, psychologists, ethicists, legal and public policy experts to enable the Hierarchs of Oceania to issue responsible joint statements with regard to the ethical dimensions of proposed Government legislation;
3. The Assembly received a Report on the draft Act of Parliament, the 'Orthodox Bishops Empowering Bill' for the recognition of all canonical Orthodox Churches in New Zealand, and specifically with regard to the registration of Marriage Celebrants; and
4. Bishop Iakovos (Tsigounis) of Miletoupolis of the Greek Archdiocese was appointed to chair the Committee on Campus Ministry, the primary focus of which was to develop Orthodox Chaplaincy in tertiary educational institutions.

The Third Episcopal Assembly, convened from 14-15 October 2012, given the forthcoming historic 1,700th anniversary of the Edict of Milan in 2013, finalised plans for a common pan-Orthodox celebration within which to mark the same. Amongst other pertinent issues, the Assembly dealt with the following:[68]

1. The formation of the Orthodox Christian Chaplaincy Council of Victoria and subsequent appointment of Mr Daniel Bellis, its first co-ordinator for Hospital Chaplaincy in Victoria;

---

[65] Communiqué of the First Episcopal Assembly of Oceania (Sydney, 18 October 2010).
[66] Proposed Website: http://www.episcopalassembly.org.au/.
[67] Communiqué of the Second Episcopal Assembly of Oceania (Sydney, 17 October 2011).
[68] Communiqué of the Third Episcopal Assembly of Oceania (Sydney, 15 October 2012).

2. In accordance with the aim of issuing responsible joint statements on the ethical dimensions of proposed Government legislation, the Assembly issued on 22 March 2012 its first statement for the Senate Standing Committee on Legal and Constitutional Affairs in Canberra regarding the Marriage Equality Amendment Bill 2012; and

3. In concert with the Mother Churches, the Assembly sought to establish a common practice for the receiving of Orthodox Christians coming from ambiguous and/or non-canonical ecclesiastical circumstances.

Conclusion

The ongoing history of Orthodoxy and its dialectical outreach in Oceania is a grateful one, filled with unimaginable opportunities. Contextually, it is the history of a people and their ancient faith entering into new nations and a new epoch. Through their church, the faithful are transplanted beyond mere geography and time to a new reality which is not even remotely familiar, one that is constantly moving and progressing, changing and developing. The presence of Orthodoxy in Oceania is, therefore, not a stagnant history rather one which is vivified and exuberant.

Pausing to reflect on the history of the Orthodox Church and its outreach in Oceania, most sincere gratitude is herein offered to those historians, statisticians and analysts, who have graciously chosen to mark this history to date. By their endeavours, research and compilation, they have successfully preserved this nascent, yet significant history of the Orthodox Church and its people in distant lands for posterity and thereby prevented the same from lapsing into forgetfulness. In the words of T.S. Eliot: "The historical sense involves a perception, not only of the pastness of the past, but of its presence."[69]

Bibliography

Books

Godley, Stephen and Hughes, Philip J., *The Eastern Orthodox in Australia*, Series: Religious Community Profiles, (Canberra: Australian Government Publishing Service, 1996).
Hawkes, Olga and John, *Russian at Heart*, (Christchurch: Wily Publications, 2009).
Blainey, Geoffrey, *The Tyranny of Distance: How Distance Shaped Australia's History*, (Sydney: Pan Macmillan Australia Pty Limited, 1966, Rev. ed. 2001).
Protopopov, Michael A., *A Russian Presence: A History of the Russian Orthodox Church in Australia*, (Piscataway, New Jersey: Gorgias Press, 2006).
Simmons, Harry L.N., *Orthodoxy in Australia: Parallels and links with the USA*, Series: Nicholas E. Kulukundis Lectures in the History of Hellenism, (Brookline, MA: Hellenic College Press, 1986).
Spasovic, Stanimir and Miletic, Srboljub, *Историја Српске Православне Цркве у Аустралији, Новом Зеланду и Јужној Африци* (The History of the Serbian Orthodox Church in Australia, New Zealand and South Africa), (Belgrade: Academy of Sciences, 2007).
Williamson, Ray, *Bilateral Dialogues: An Overview*, (Sydney: New South Wales Ecumenical Council, 2004).

Journals

Anderson, Paul B., "Eastern Orthodox Migration with Special Reference to Australia" in *Eastern Churches Review* 2.3 (1969)
Batrouney, Trevor, "Orthodoxy in Australia: Current and Future Perspectives" in Casiday, Augustine (Ed.), *The Orthodox Christian World* (Routledge, 2012).

[69] Eliot, T.S., *Four Quartets*, (New York: Harcourt Publication, 1943).

Chryssavgis, Miltiades, "Greek Orthodoxy in Australia" in *Phronema* 1 (1986).

_____, Miltiades and Chryssavgis, John, "Australian Orthodoxy" in *Persons & Events in Orthodoxy: Historical Moments in the Development of Orthodox Christianity*, (Sydney: Greek Orthodox Archdiocese of Australia, 1985).

(Dobrijevic), Bishop Irinej, "An Overview of the Relationship between the Serbian Diaspora and the Serbian Orthodox Church" in *Western American Diocese 2011 Annual*, (Vasiljevic) Maxim and Ceko, Editors, (Alhambra, California: Sebastian Press, 2011).

(Dobrijevic), Bishop Irinej, "Наших руку дела: Епископ Митрополије аустралијско-новозеландске Иринеј ексклусивно за 'Србију-аустралијску ревију'" ("The Blessed Work of our Hands") in *Serbia—Australia Review* 1.1 (2013).

Doumanis, Nicholas, "Ecclesiastical Expansion of the Greek Diaspora: The Formative Years of the Greek Church in Australia" in *St Vladimir's Theological Quarterly* 37.1 (1993).

(Harkianakis), Archbishop Stylianos, "The Importance of Greek Culture for Australian Society" in *Phronema* 8 (1993)

Simmons, H.L.N., "Eastern Orthodoxy in Australia: A Forgotten Chapter?" in *St Vladimir's Theological Quarterly* 23.3/4 (1979).

_____, "Eastern Orthodoxy in Australia II: The Russians" in *St Vladimir's Theological Quarterly* 29.3 (1985).

Internet Presentations

Antiochian Orthodox Christian Archdiocese of Australia, New Zealand and the Philippines:

Assembly of Canonical Orthodox Bishops of North and Central America: http://www.assemblyofbishops.org/.

"Australia: The Fifth Continent": http://www.dreamlike.info/aus/index.html.

Australian Christian Lobby: http://www.acl.org.au/.

Bulgarian Eastern Orthodox Diocese of the USA, Canada and Australia: http://www.bulgariandiocese.org/.

'DonateLife': http://www.donatelife.gov.au/.

Episcopal Assembly of Oceania (Propose Website): http://www.episcopalassembly.org.au/.

Greek Australian Professionals Association: http://www.gapa.com.au/

Greek Orthodox Archdiocese of Australia: http://www.greekorthodox.org.au/.

Holy Metropolis of New Zealand: http://www.ecp-metnz.org.nz/.

Melbourne Institute of Orthodox Christian Studies: http://www.miocs.net/.

National Council of Churches in Australia: http://www.ncca.org.au/.

National Council of Churches in New Zealand: http://www.teara.govt.nz/en/1966/national-council-of-churches.

"New Zealand and Europeans arrive to Aotearoa" in Wikipedia: http://en.wikipedia.org/wiki/New_Zealand; and Europeans arrive to Aotearoa: http://www.newzealand.com/au/feature/europeans-arrive-to-aotearoa/.

"Oceania" in Wikipedia: http://en.wikipedia.org/wiki/Oceania.

Romanian Orthodox Episcopate of Australia and New Zealand: http://www.roeanz.com.au/.

Russian Orthodox Church Outside of Russia: http://www.rocor.org.au/.

Serbian Orthodox Church–Metropolitanate of Australia and New Zealand: http://www.soc.org.au.

St Andrew's Greek Orthodox Theological College: http://www.sagotc.edu.au/.

United Faculty of Theology, The: http://uft.edu.au/.

Ukrainian Orthodox Church in the Diaspora: http://www.uaoc-diaspora.com/.

World Council of Churches: http://www.oikoumene.org/en/.

Part IV: Ecumenical Dialogue in various Orthodox Churches and Settings

PART V

BILATERAL DIALOGUES BETWEEN EASTERN ORTHODOX CHURCHES AND OTHER CHURCHES AND CHRISTIAN TRADITIONS

(74) Bilateral Theological Dialogues of Orthodox Churches – A General Introduction [1]

Fr. Viorel Ionita

The Orthodox Church has a long standing experience of dialogue with other Christian traditions, although the dialogues or, more accurately the conversations, of the past have had a specific character, being either motivated by political interest or carried out by individual theologians. The theological dialogues initiated during the second half of the 20th century are specific, first of all because they are carried out on behalf and with the participation of all Autocephalous Orthodox Churches, as well as on the bilateral level with the respective partner churches. Of utmost importance for these theological dialogues were the decisions of the Pan-Orthodox Conferences, which began in 1961 after thorough preparation under the leadership of the Ecumenical Patriarchate. The original purpose of these conferences was to prepare for Orthodox Council, which would take path-finding new decisions for the life of the Orthodox churches. At the first Pan-Orthodox conference (24 September - 1 October 1961, Rhodes, Greece), the relations to the other churches were considered according to the position of the respective churches in relation to the Orthodox Church [2]:

1. Study ways of bringing closer and uniting the Churches in a Pan-Orthodox perspective, in other words promoting the inter-Orthodox co-operation.
2. Develop friendly relations to "the lesser Ancient Oriental Churches", that is to the Oriental Orthodox Churches, in view "of establishing union with them."
3. Orthodoxy and the Roman Catholic Church: a) Study the positive and negative points between the two Churches (in faith, in administration, in church activities – especially propaganda, proselytising, the *Uniatism*); and b) Cultivate relations in the spirit of Christian love, with particular reference to the points anticipated in the Patriarchal Encyclical of 1920.
4. Orthodoxy and the Churches and Confessions emanating from the Reformation: a) Confessions lying further from Orthodoxy (1. Lutheranism, 2. Calvinism; 3. Methodists and 4. Other Protestant Confessions), b) Confessions lying nearer to Orthodoxy (1. Anglican Church; 2. Episcopalians in general). Study the best relations to cultivate and draw them closer, especially the Episcopalian and Anglican Churches, to the Orthodox Church, in the light of existing definite assumptions,
5. Orthodoxy and Old Catholicism; Advancement of relations with them in the spirit of former theological discussions and their started intentions and inclinations to unite with the Orthodox Church;
6. Orthodoxy and the Ecumenical Movement.

At the 1966 preparatory conference in Belgrade, the foundation was laid for a dialogue between the Orthodox churches and the Anglican Communion, as well as between the Orthodox churches and the Old Catholic churches of the Union of Utrecht. The fourth Pan-Orthodox Conference (5-15 June 1968, Chambésy, Switzerland) decided to found an Inter-Orthodox Commission for dialogue with the Lutheran World Federation (LWF). The official visit of a delegation from the World Alliance of Reformed Churches (WARC) to the Ecumenical Patriarchate in Constantinople in July 1979 marked the preparation for the start of the official theological dialogue between the Orthodox churches and WARC. Thus the conditions for dialogue between the Orthodox

---

[1] See Pr. Prof. Dr. Viorel Ioniță, "The Vision of Unity in the Multilateral Dialogues and in the Bilateral Dialogues of the Orthodox Churches with other Churches", *Studii Teologice*, series 3a, 4.3 (2008): 7-58.

[2] *Ibid.,* 71-72.

churches and the churches of the Reformation were given, "continuing the many contacts and conversations between Orthodoxy and Protestantism since the 16th century."[3]

The most detailed as well as the most important decisions in relation to the bilateral theological dialogues of the Orthodox Church at the world level were taken by the third Pan-Orthodox Pre-Conciliar Conference (Chambésy, Switzerland, 20 October – 6 November 1986) through the text on the "Relations of the Orthodox Church with the Christian World." Although this text is to be finally adopted by the Great and Holy Synod of the Orthodox Church, it can and should already serve as a basis for the on-going theological dialogues of this church. This text sets a series of guidelines for how the bilateral dialogues shall be continued including the role and the responsibility of each Autocephalous Orthodox Church.

Based on these Pan-Orthodox decisions, initiatives were taken by the Ecumenical Patriarchate to enter into the following theological dialogues at the world wide level:

1) Orthodox - Anglican (since 1973);

2) Orthodox - Old Catholic (from 1975 to 1987);

3) Orthodox - Roman Catholic (since 1980);

4) Orthodox – Lutheran World Federation (since 1981);

5) Eastern Orthodox - Oriental Orthodox (from 1985 to 1993);

6) Orthodox – World Alliance of the Reformed Churches, since 2010 the World Communion of the Reformed Churches (since 1988).

The fourth Pan-Orthodox Conference also decided that the theological dialogue with the Lutheran churches in particular should be prepared, in a first phase, by the autocephalous Orthodox churches in bilateral conversations with various Evangelical churches. The first Pan-Orthodox Pre-Conciliar Conference reaffirmed this decision in 1976.[4] This laid down the pan-Orthodox basis for the bilateral theological dialogues between the various Orthodox churches and Evangelical ones on the regional level.[5] Besides these theological dialogues

---

[3] Athanasios Basdekis, *Die Orthodoxe Kirche. Eine Handreichung für nicht-orthodoxe und orthodoxe Christen und Kirchen (The Orthodox Church. A handbook for non-Orthodox and Orthodox Christians and Churches)*. (Frankfurt am Main, Otto Lembeck Press, 2001), 24.

[4] See *Irenikon*, 50.1 (1977): 99-100.

[5] In this category are the following bilateral theological dialogues:

1. Evangelical Church in Germany (EKD) and the Russian Orthodox Church, since 1959, known as the Arnoldshain conversations after the place where the first meeting was held. The most important topics in this dialogue have been: 1. Salvation; 2. Word and Sacrament; 3. Eucharistic Fellowship and 4. Service and Witness in the Church.

2. EKD and Ecumenical Patriarchate, since 1969, known also as the Constantinople Dialogue. Various aspects of Ecclesiology have been discussed, such as 1. Eucharist, Church and Ministry or 2. The Holy Spirit in the life of the church.

3. EKD and Bulgarian Orthodox Church, since 1992. This dialogue began in 1978 as a bilateral dialogue between the Bulgarian Orthodox Church and the Federation of Protestant Churches in the German Democratic Republic. Known as the Herrnhuter conversations, this dialogue dealt with topics as: 1. Proclamation of the Gospel; 2. the Source of Faith; 3. Baptism and Eucharist; and 4. the Ordained Ministry.

4. EKD and Romanian Orthodox Church, since 1979, known as the Goslar conversations. Topics discussed have been: 1. Scripture and Tradition; 2. Different aspects of the Sacraments; 3. Justification, *Theosis* and *Synergia*. The issue of ecclesiology was also discussed. At the 10th meeting between the two churches in Cluj (Romania, 14-20 November 2002), the theme was *"The Nature and the Unity of the Church of Christ - the Historical Difference between the Churches"*. The final statement of this meeting described the relation between the two churches as follows: Although our churches are still on the way towards full mutual recognition and therefore towards acceptance of eucharistic fellowship, neither wishes to deny that the other is, in principle, a church. So the Romanian Orthodox Church can clearly recognise in the EKD a way of being church. On the basis of our common faith in Jesus Christ, as authoritatively expressed in the Holy Scriptures and in our common Nicene-Constantinopolitan Creed, and especially on the basis of baptism, the Romanian Orthodox Church can also speak of a certain degree of fellowship with the EKD from which it is still divided. And, for its part, the EKD, despite the sometimes very different forms of expression of church life in the Orthodox churches, can see in these churches the realisation of essential elements of being church in accordance with the Gospel.

Orthodox Handbook on Ecumenism

at the regional level, it should be noted that there are also theological conversations between Orthodox and different other churches on the national level.[6]

Orthodox Anglican dialogue

The Anglican-Orthodox dialogue started in Oxford (1973) and decided from the beginning not to adopt statements at each meeting, but to work on the chosen themes until they are mature enough to be adopted as common statement. The meetings in between used to adopt reports, which constituted the basis for the agreed statements. According to this methodology from 1973 until 2006 three statements were adopted: 1. The Moscow Agreed Statement (1976); 2) the Dublin Agreed Statement (1984); and 3) the Cyprus Agreed Statement (2006). If the first statement is rather short (6 pages), the second and the third ones are well elaborated, with a preface, an introduction and footnotes, including the list of the participants during the whole period of work on the respective document.

At the end of the first meeting in Oxford "it was decided that the debates for 'common doctrinal discussions' between the Orthodox Church and the Anglican Church should be continued in three sub-commissions, in 1974 and 1975, each commission having the obligation to discuss one of the three proposed subjects: 1) inspiration and Revelation in Holy Scriptures; 2) the Synod's Authority; 3) the Church as Eucharistic Community.[7] In the light of this work, the Moscow statement contains the following topics: 1) the Knowledge of God; 2) The Inspiration and Authority of Holy Scripture; 3) Scripture and Tradition; 4) The Authority of the Council; 5) The *Filioque Clause*; 6) The Church as the Eucharistic Community, and 7) The Invocation of the Holy Spirit in the Eucharist. The Moscow statement ends with the following note: At their meeting in Thessaloniki in April 1977 the Orthodox members asked that it should be pointed out that, in regard to the words in paragraph 30 of the Moscow Agreed Statement it is inexact to call the *Epiclesis* a 'formula' since the Orthodox Church does not regard it as such.[8]

According to this statement, the Anglican-Orthodox dialogue started with some hermeneutical and introductory questions. Talking about matters of the authority of the council (that means of the Ecumenical Councils), the Anglican-Orthodox dialogue discussed the *Filioque* in the Nicene-Constantinopolitan creed. The result of these discussions was that the question of the origin of the Holy Spirit is to be distinguished from that of its mission to the world. It is with reference to the mission of the Spirit that we are to understand the biblical texts, which speak both of the Father (John 14.26) and of the Son (John 15.26) as sending *(pempein)* the Holy Spirit.[9]

In relation to the Moscow statement, we would like to underline also the chapter about the *Church as the Eucharistic Community*. First of all the statement notes the six points of the Bucharest Conference of 1935 about the validity of the Anglican ordinations. In the paragraph 24 of this statement we find a very good description of the relationship between the Eucharist and the Church: The Eucharist actualizes the Church. The Christian community has a basic sacramental character. The Church can be described as a *synaxis* or an *ecclesia*, which is, in its essence, a worshipping and eucharistic assembly. The Church is not only built up by the Eucharist, but is also a condition for it. Therefore one must be a believing member of the Church in order

---

5. The Russian Orthodox Church and the Evangelical Lutheran Church of Finland, since 1970. This dialogue, known as the Sinnappi conversations, has treated among others the following themes: 1. Eucharist; 2. Salvation; 3. Peace and Social Ethics.

[6] Such as:
- the dialogue between the Orthodox Church and Evangelical Lutheran Church in Finland;
- Lutheran, Reformed and Orthodox in Romania;
- Orthodox-Protestant in France;
- Orthodox-Protestant in Switzerland.

It should also be mentioned that theological conversations have taken place between Orthodox and Lutherans in the United States and in Australia (For all these dialogues, see Risto Saarinen, *Faith and Holiness. Lutheran Orthodox Dialogues 1959-1994.* (Göttingen: Vandenhoek & Ruprecht, 1997)).

[7] Rev. Prof. Dr. Ioan Mircea Ielciu, *Notes on the Anglican-Orthodox Theological Dialogue,* (Helsinki: Reseptio, 2006), 12.

[8] Available online: *www.anglicancommunion.org/ministry/ecumenical/resources/index.cfm* (last accessed September 2013).

[9] *Ibid.*

Part V: Bilateral Dialogues between Eastern Orthodox Churches
and other Churches and Christian Traditions

to receive the Holy Communion. The Church celebrating the Eucharist becomes fully itself; that is *koinonia,* fellowship - communion. The Church celebrates the Eucharist as the central act of its existence, in which the ecclesial community, as a living reality confessing its faith, receives its realization.[10] These considerations show that this dialogue reflected just from the beginning the new developments in the Orthodox theology especially in relation to the Eucharistic Ecclesiology.

The Dublin statement starts with a preface, in which a reference is made to the late Archbishop Basil of Brussels, who remarked that "the aim of our Dialogue is that we may eventually be visibly united in one Church." The introduction of about three pages explains then the whole process of this dialogue even from the beginning until 1984. The statement itself starts with the following explanation about the *Method and Approach:* "In our discussions since the adoption of the Moscow Agreed Statement, and especially during the last four years, our Joint Commission has endeavoured to keep constantly in mind the essential link that exists between theology and sanctification through prayer, between doctrine and the daily life of the Christian community. Keenly aware how dangerous it is to discuss the Christian faith in an abstract manner, we have sought always to understand how theological principles are expressed in the living experience of the people of God."[11] This is a very important reference for the spiritual atmosphere in this dialogue.

The Dublin statement deals with the following themes: I. The Mystery of the Church; II. Faith in the Trinity, Prayer and Holiness; III. Worship and Tradition and ends with an Epilogue. For this study the most important is the first part on the *Mystery of the Church*, out of which we will consider mainly the chapters: 1. The Mark of the Church and 2. Communion and Intercommunion. In the paragraph 8, there is a common confession of the two parts to the unity of the one Church in Christ: "In the Creed we proclaim the Church to be one, holy, catholic and apostolic. The Church is one, because there is a 'one Lord, one faith, one baptism, one God and Father of us all' (Eph. 4.5), and it participates in the life of the Holy Trinity, one God in three persons. The unity of the Church is expressed in common faith and in the fellowship of the Holy Spirit; it takes concrete and visible form as the Church, gathered round the bishop in the common celebration of the Holy Eucharist, proclaims Christ's death till he comes (1 Cor. 11.26). The unity of Christians with Christ in baptism is a unity of love and mutual respect which transcends all human division, of race, social status and sex (Gal. 3.28). This unity in Christ is God's gift to the world by which men and women may learn to live in unity with one another, accepting one another as Christ has accepted them."[12]

The theme of the Cyprus statement is *The Church of the Triune God*, as if the two partners in dialogue would have tried to go back to some more substantial debate on the unity of the Church they confess, before arriving at the debate about the unity they seek. After a preface and an introduction, very helpful as background information about the whole text, this statement contains the following nine sections: I. The Trinity and the Church; II. Christ, the Spirit and the Church; III. Christ, Humanity and the Church: Part 1; IV. Christ, Humanity and the Church: Part 2; V. Episcope, Episkopos and Primacy; VI. Priesthood, Christ and the Church; VII. Women and Men, Ministries and the Church; VIII. Heresy, Schism and the Church and IX. Reception in Communion.

First of all we value in this statement a close link between the Church and the Holy Trinity, as well as between Christology and Ecclesiology on one side, and between the Ecclesiology and Pneumatology on the other side. In the *Trinity and the Church* we would like to underline the link between the local and universal in the church: "The Church is both a local and a universal reality. As the one God is a communion of three persons, so the universal Church is one communion in Christ of many local churches. She is not a federation of separate parts. The relationship between the local church and the universal Church is determined by the revelation of

---

[10] *Ibid.*

[11] *Growth in Agreement II. Reports and Agreed Statements of Ecumenical Conversations on a World Level, 1982-1998.* Edited by Jeffrey Gros, FSC, Harding Meyer and William G. Rusch, (Geneva: WCC Publications, 2000), 84-85.

[12] *Ibid.* p. 85-86.

the life of the Holy Trinity."[13] The question is how Anglican and Orthodox could apply this ecclesiological view to their relationship as separate churches.

The Cyprus statement listed a series of issues for further discussion, first of all in relation to the ordination of women with the conclusion: that our theological differences with regard to the ordination of women do not undermine the agreement we have reached in the previous sections of this statement.[14] This clarification was not made by accident, because the practice of women's ordination in the Anglican Church created for many Orthodox an uncertainty about the continuation of this dialogue.

In the preface signed by the two co-chairmen of this joint commission,[15] the results of the Commission's deliberations are made available here in the hope that Anglicans and Orthodox will come to appreciate the things they have in common and to understand the nature of their disagreements.[16] In this perspective the contribution of this dialogue has been to clarify as many as possible doctrinal differences between the two theological traditions and to leave open the still existing differences. The two churches achieved a good deal of agreement on their way towards unity, but a lot of work is still to be done. Since 2009 the Anglican-Orthodox dialogue focussed at several meetings on the issue of Anthropology, on which a common statement is expected to be adopted at a next meeting of the plenary commission.

Orthodox - Old Catholic

There are five stages so far in the dialogue between the Orthodox Churches and the Old Catholic Churches gathered in the Union of Utrecht. The first phase from 1871-1888 was marked by the invitation addressed to the Orthodox Churches to send representatives to the Bonn reunion conferences of 1874 and 1875. During these encounters 'it was decided that agreement on the faith of the ecumenical councils, scripture and Tradition, the office of bishop and the seven sacraments was necessary for unity. Both the developments, which had led to the declaration of papal infallibility in the Roman Catholic Church and those, which in Protestantism had led to discontinuity with the early church, were rejected. As for the *Filioque,* it was agreed that the clause had been inserted wrongly into the creed but that it was possible to explain it in an orthodox way.'[17]

The second stage lasted from 1889 - 1917, that is from the establishment of the Union of Utrecht until the Russian revolution. During this period there was constituted a commission, which never met, but its members exchanged materials on *Filioque,* the Eucharist, and the canonical validity of the Old Catholic Episcopal orders.

The third stage (1920-1960) was marked by the relations between the Old Catholics and the Patriarchate of Constantinople. In that period of time the Old Catholics adopted an agreement of intercommunion with the Anglicans, which was then much criticised by the Orthodox.

The fourth stage lasted from 1961-1975, that is from the first Pan-orthodox Conference and the official presentation 'by the Old Catholics to the Ecumenical Patriarch on 21 June 1970 of the Homologia (which was first requested in 1904) till the actual beginning of the "dialogue of truth" by the joint commission of Old Catholic and Orthodox theologians in 1975.'[18] This *Homologia* (Confession) contained among others the Nicene-Constantinopolitan creed without *Filoque.*

The fifth phase comprised the official dialogue held between 1975-87 on the following topics: (1) the doctrine of God: divine revelation and its transmission, the canon of the Holy Scripture, the Holy Trinity; (2)

---

[13] *The Church of the Triune God.* The Cyprus Statement of the International Commission for Anglican Orthodox Theological Dialogue 2006, (London: Anglican Communion Office, 2006), 18.
[14] Ibid., 89.
[15] Bishop Mark Dyer and Metropolitan John of Pergamon.
[16] Ibid., 9.
[17] Available online: *www.utrechter-union.org/english/ecumenical.htm#The%20Old%20Catholic%20–%20Orthodox%20 dialogue* (last accessed September 2013).
[18] Ibid.

Christology: the incarnation of the Word of God, the hypostatic union, the Mother of God; (3) ecclesiology: the nature and marks of the church, the unity of the church and the local churches, the boundaries of the church, the authority of the church and in the church, the indefectibility of the church, the synods (councils) of the church, the necessity of apostolic succession, the head of the church; (4) soteriology: the redeeming work of Jesus Christ, the operation of the Holy Spirit in the church and the appropriation of salvation; (5) sacramental doctrine: the sacraments of the church, baptism, confirmation, the Eucharist, penance, the anointing of the sick, ordination, marriage; (6) eschatology: the church and the end of time, life after death, the resurrection of the dead and the renewal of the earth; and (7) ecclesial communion: conditions and consequences. Between 1975 and 1987 the two sides reached formal agreement on all these points.[19] According to this list we have here one of the most comprehensive dialogues with Orthodox participation.

Following a clear agenda and methodology, this dialogue was able to achieve its completion only in a period of 12 years. For us here of great interest are the two chapters in the section of Ecclesiology, namely: 1. The Unity of the Church and the Local Churches and 2. The Boundaries of the Church. The last common statement in this dialogue adopted at Kavala, Greece, in 1987, was on *Ecclesial Communion: Presuppositions and Consequences*. According to this statement 'the consequence and expression of reciprocally recognised fellowship in the faith is the full liturgical-canonical communion of Churches, the realization of organic unity in the one Body of Christ.'[20] If the two churches in dialogue achieve the 'reciprocally recognised fellowship in the faith' they will then enter in full communion with each other. Such an ecclesial fellowship has then to be 'elucidated and regulated by the Church on the basis of the tradition of the undivided Church.'[21]

We have to underline that all the statements in the dialogue between Orthodox and Old Catholics were adopted unanimously. That means that the two partners equally adopt all the affirmations exposed here. Meanwhile the Old Catholic Churches decided to introduce women's ordination, which made the implementation of the outcomes of this dialogue difficult for the Orthodox. This fact shows that the dialogue did not take enough into consideration the real differences between the two churches. This should be the task of future conversations.

Orthodox - Roman Catholic

The dialogue between the Orthodox Churches and the Roman Catholic Church is a specific one due first of all to the memory of the separation between the two churches. After the schism between Rome and Constantinople in 1054, the two churches tried on many occasions to restore their unity through different conversations, particularly the unionist councils in Lyon (1274) and in Ferrara-Florence (1448-1449). If the union adopted at Lyon was a rather political one, the union of Florence was based on four doctrinal points, which at that time summarised the doctrinal differences between the two churches: 1. The primate of the pope; 2. *Filioque;* 3. The use of unleavened bread in the Eucharist by the Catholics and 4. The catholic doctrine of the purgatory.

From the historical perspective, more problematic than the four points became the emergence of the Oriental Catholic Churches (OCC) after the Florence agreement, which actually was never accepted by the Orthodox Churches. The OCC appeared from the 15th to the 18th century and were parts of the Eastern Orthodox or of the Oriental Orthodox Churches. They recognised the authority of the pope, but continued to keep their Eastern/Oriental character. The Orthodox Churches considered the incorporation of the OCC into the Catholic Church as one of the most radical forms of proselytism. Therefore, from that perspective the relationship of the Orthodox Churches not only with the OCC but also with the Roman Catholic Church deteriorated more and more during the last centuries.

[19] Ibid.
[20] Ibid., 228.
[21] Ibid.

The relationships between the Orthodox and the Roman Catholic Churches changed in the context of the Second Vatican Council due first of all to the charismatic leaders of both churches at that time: the Ecumenical Patriarch Athenagoras and the Pope Paul VI. These two church leaders decided to lift the anathemas from 1054 on the same day in December 1965. This decision was a first radical step of the two churches towards a true dialogue on equal footing, as requested by the Orthodox. In the preparation for the official dialogue the Orthodox Churches pointed out from the beginning the problem of *Uniatism* that means the problem in relations to the OCC and the danger that the Roman Catholic Church may continue this practice.

The official dialogue between the Orthodox Churches and the Roman Catholic Church started in 1980. The first meeting of the Orthodox-Roman-Catholic Joint Commission (ORCJC) started on the island of Patmos and concluded its work on the island of Rhodes (29 May – 4 June, 1980). When the Orthodox participants noted that in the Catholic delegation there were representatives of the OCC, they asked that the question of the *Uniatism* be clarified at the next encounters of this joint commission. The representatives of the Church of Greece resigned from the meeting because of the presence at that meeting of the Eastern-rite Christians united with Rome. Finally the decision taken at Rhodes was to start this dialogue 'with what we have in common and, by developing it, to touch upon from inside and progressively all the points on which we are not in agreement.'[22]

It was only at the second meeting of the ORCJC (Munich, Germany, 30 June – 6 July 1982) when a statement was adopted on *The Mystery of the Church and of the Eucharist in the light of the Mystery of the Holy Trinity*. This statement comprises three sections without subtitles. This dialogue started straight away with the questions of Ecclesiology. The statement from Munich is a well-elaborated one and of profound theological reflection. One of the contributions of this statement is the link between the "Trinitarian *koinonia*", that means the relationship between the three Persons in the Holy Trinity, and the *koinonia* that takes shape in the church by celebrating the Eucharist. This *koinonia* is also eucharistic, eschatological, kerygmatic, ministerial and pneumatological. "While being a gift of the Trinitarian God, *koinonia* is also the response of men. In the faith which comes from the Spirit and the word, these put in practice the vocation and the mission received in baptism: to become living members, in one's proper rank, of the body of Christ."[23]

The second common statement in this dialogue was adopted in Bari, Italy (June 1987) on *Faith, Sacraments and Unity of the Church*.[24] This statement constitutes a continuation of the first one. After few lines of explanation about the preparatory process which lead to its adoption, the statement proceeded to an introduction about the work of the ORCJC since Munich; and then two parts follow: I. *Faith and communion in the sacraments*, with the following seven subchapters: 1. True faith is a divine gift and free response of the human person; 2. The liturgical expression of the faith; 3. The Holy Spirit and the sacraments; 4. The faith formulated and celebrated in the sacraments: the symbols of faith; 5. Conditions for communion of faith; 6. True faith and communion in the sacraments and 7. The unity of the church in faith and sacraments. The second part of the Bari document deals with *The sacraments of Christian initiation: their relation to the unity of the church*. From our perspective of specific interest are the subchapter 7 of the first part and the second part.

The third common statement of the ORCJC was adopted only a year after the previous one at the New Valamo Monastery, Finland (June 1988) under the title: *"The Sacrament of Order in the Sacramental Structure of the Church"*. The fact that this statement was adopted so quickly underlines the methodology of this dialogue, in which sub-commissions worked very hard between the plenary sessions. The document from 1988 makes the link to the previous statements in an Introductory note. The document itself starts with an indication that this theme is considered "in particular reference to the importance of Apostolic Succession for the Sanctification and Unity of the People of God."[25] The statement from 1988 comprises the following chapters: I. Christ and

---

[22] *Growth in Agreement II*, 652.

[23] Ibid., 655.

[24] Ibid., 660.

[25] Ibid., 672.

*Part V: Bilateral Dialogues between Eastern Orthodox Churches
and other Churches and Christian Traditions*

the Holy Spirit; II. The priesthood in the divine economy of salvation; III. The ministry of the bishop, presbyter and deacon; and IV. Apostolic succession.

In the aftermath of the political changes in Central and Eastern Europe (1989-1990) the relationship between the Orthodox Churches and the OCC in some former communist countries became more and more tense. This fact influenced the dialogue between Orthodox and Catholics at all levels including the work of the ORCJC. The sixth plenary meeting of the ORCJC (Freising, Germany, 1990) did not continue the discussion on the theological themes as it was the case until 1988, but focused on *Uniatism.* In relation to the question of *Uniatism* the Freising document stated that "we reject it as a method for the search for unity because it is opposed to the common tradition of our churches."[26]

The ORCJC decided to address this very delicate issue at its seventh plenary meeting in Balamand, Lebanon (June 1993), where a statement was adopted under the title: *Uniatism: Method of Union of the Past, and the Present Search for Full Communion.* The Balamand document is rather short and contains one introduction and two chapters: 1. Ecclesiological principles and 2. Practical rules. A first point to be underlined is the reference to the OCC in the following formulation: "concerning the Oriental Catholic Churches, it is clear that they, as part of the Catholic communion, have the right to exist and to act in answer to the spiritual needs of their faithful."[27] This declaration is probably the only official ecumenical recognition of the OCC by the Orthodox Churches at the world level, although not all of them approved the Balamand statement.

The second point to be underlined in the Balamand document is the fact that the two churches are considered as "Sister Churches" and that is also not accepted by all Orthodox Churches. For some Orthodox theologians the qualification "Sister Churches" is valid only for the inter-Orthodox relations, because this expression has a concrete ecclesiological significance. Church leaders on both sides have used this phrase before, but apparently without taking enough into consideration its ecclesiological implications. From the Orthodox perspective two churches, which are still divided and accordingly do not share the communion can not be "Sister Churches". In other words, in the light of the Balamand document the phrase "Sister Churches" obtained a very clear ecclesiological connotation, which created additional difficulties in this dialogue.

The ORCJC took again some years before continuing its work. The last statement adopted in this dialogue was on *Ecclesiological and canonical consequences of the sacramental nature of the Church. Ecclesial Communion, Conciliarity and Authority.* This statement adopted at the last meeting of the ORCJC in Ravenna, Italy (October, 2007) is introduced with a notice that "the document represents the outcome of the work of a Commission and should not be understood as an official declaration of the Church's teaching."[28]

The Ravenna document underlines finally that "Conciliarity at the universal level, exercised in the ecumenical councils, implies an active role of the bishop of Rome, as *protos* of the bishops of the major sees, in the consensus of the assembled bishops. Although the bishop of Rome did not convene the ecumenical councils of the early centuries and never personally presided over them, he nevertheless was closely involved in the process of decision-making by the councils."[29] We consider that in spite of the difficulties it had to face, the dialogue between the Orthodox Churches and the Roman Catholic Church achieved a great deal of consensus in some of the theological questions addressed and this fact should motivate the two churches to continue their dialogue.

Orthodox – Lutheran

The theological dialogue between the Orthodox churches and the Lutheran World Federation began in 1981 in Espoo, Finland. The theme of the first meeting was *The Mystery of the Church*; thus the ecclesiological

---

[26] Ibid., 680.

[27] Ibid.

[28] Available online: *www.vatican.va/roman_curia/pontifical_councils/chrstuni/ch_orthodox_docs/rc_pc_chrstuni_doc_20071013_documento-ravenna_en.html*

[29] Ibid.

question was to be tackled right from the beginning. However, there was no clear methodology, so that the conversation in Espoo, as well as the next one in Cyprus (Limassol, 1983) did not lead to any concrete result.[30] The first joint declaration in this dialogue was adopted at its third meeting in Allentown, PA. (USA, 1985) on the theme of *Divine Revelation*. The second common statement was adopted at the fourth meeting of the Joint Commission in Crete (1987), on *Scripture and Tradition*. The third common statement was adopted at the fifth meeting in Bad-Segeberg, (Germany, 1989), on *The Canon and the Inspiration of the Holy Scriptures*.[31]

After some initial difficulties, the dialogue between the Orthodox churches and the LWF moved into a second phase, in which "classic" themes for the encounter between two theological traditions were discussed, such as *Divine Revelation* or *Scripture and Tradition*. On the conclusions arrived at with regard to these topics, the third Pre-Conciliar Pan-Orthodox Conference in 1986, in Chambésy, Switzerland, noted that "this dialogue has begun with favourable prospects, and (this body) hopes that both the academic and the ecclesiological elements will be equally emphasised and developed."[32]

For a third phase in this dialogue, the meeting in Moscow (1990) proposed the theme *Authority in and of the Church*. This was to be regarded as an overall theme and to be dealt with through various sub-themes. The sixth meeting of the Orthodox-Lutheran dialogue (Sandbjerg, Denmark, 1993) discussed *The Ecumenical Councils and Authority in and of the Church*. In relation to this subject the common statement underlines first that for both Lutherans and Orthodox "the teachings of the ecumenical councils are authoritative for our churches. The ecumenical councils maintain the integrity of the teaching of the undivided Church concerning the saving, illuminating/justifying and glorifying acts of God and reject heresies which subvert the saving work of God in Christ."[33]

At the seventh encounter of the Lutheran-Orthodox Joint Commission (Limassol, Cyprus, 1995) the theme was *Authority in and of the Church: Understanding of Salvation in the Light of the Ecumenical Councils*. After different common reflections on this theme, the final statement adopted in Cyprus concluded that "Lutherans and Orthodox still need to explore further their different concepts of salvation as purification, illumination, and glorification, with the use of synergia, which is the Orthodox teaching and tradition and as justification and sanctification, with the use of *sola fide*, which is the Lutheran teaching and tradition."[34]

In the third phase of the Orthodox-Lutheran dialogue the topic of the nature of the church was dealt with only indirectly, through the issue of authority and from the perspective of salvation. However, this made it possible to reach a series of agreements, which can be very significant as basis for the further development of dialogue, precisely with regard to the discussion of ecclesiology.

Finally, a fourth phase of the theological dialogue between the Orthodox churches and the LWF began at the eighth meeting (Sigtuna, Sweden, 1998), when the joint Lutheran-Orthodox Commission chose the theme *The Mystery of the Church* for its further work. At its ninth meeting (Damascus, Syria, 2000), the Commission adopted a joint statement entitled *The Mystery of the Church: A. Word and Sacraments (mysteria) in the Life of the Church*. At the tenth meeting in this dialogue (Oslo, Norway, 2002) the topic *The Sacraments (mysteria) as Means of Salvation* was discussed, as a further aspect of the overall theme *The Mystery of the Church*.

The 12th Plenary of the International Lutheran-Orthodox Joint Commission (2004, in Durău, Romania, 2004) discussed the theme: *The Mystery of the Church. C. Baptism and Chrismation as Sacraments of initiation into the Church*. In the joint statement there was underlined that Orthodox and Lutherans "found that the three

---

[30] See the bibliography in *Orthodoxie im Dialog*, ed. Thomas Bremer, Johannes Oeldemann and Dagmar Stoltmann, Sophia series, vol. 32, (Paulinus Press, 1999), 225.

[31] See *Lutheran-Orthodox Dialogue. Agreed Statements, 1985-1989*, Geneva, 1992; see also The Revd Prof. Dr. Viorel Ionita, *Short Presentation of the Orthodox-Lutheran Dialogues*, in *Reseptio* 1 (2006): 18-26.

[32] Grigorios Larentzakis, *Die Orthodoxe Kirche. Ihr Leben und ihr Glaube (The Orthodox Church: its life and faith)*. (Graz: Styria Press, 2000), 201.

[33] Available online: www.helsinki.fi/%7Erisaarin/lutortjointtext.html#divi (last accessed September 2013).

[34] Ibid.

Part V: Bilateral Dialogues between Eastern Orthodox Churches
and other Churches and Christian Traditions

components of Christian initiation are to a large extent included in each other's rites. These components find their fulfilment in the Christian's full participation in the life of Christ and his church through eating his body and drinking his blood in the holy Eucharist." The 13th meeting of Lutheran - Orthodox Joint Commission (2-9 November 2006, Bratislava, Slovak Republic) discussed the theme: *The Mystery of the Church: D. The Holy Eucharist in the Life of the Church.* In relation to this topic the final statement from Bratislava underlined that "Orthodox and Lutherans agree that the Eucharist is also a gift of communion granted to us by Christ. In this communion we are fully united with him and with the members of his body."[35]

The 14th plenary of the International Joint Commission on the Theological Dialogue between the Orthodox Church and Lutherans was held from 30 May – 7 June 2008 at the St. George Hotel in Paphos, Cyprus, and discussed the following topic: *The Mystery of the Church. Preparation and the Social and Ecological Dimensions of the Eucharist.* Finally, the 15th plenary session of the Lutheran-Orthodox Joint Commission was held from 31 May to 7 June 2011 at Colleg Wittenberg in Lutherstadt Wittenberg, Germany and dealt with the theme: *The Mystery of the Church: The Nature, Attributes and Mission of the Church.* In Wittenberg-Lutherstadt this dialogue celebrated its 30th anniversary, an evaluation of the dialogue as a whole was undertaken including the issue of how this dialogue is received in the churches involved.

Eastern Orthodox - Oriental Orthodox

The family of the Oriental Orthodox Churches goes back to the rejection of the fourth Ecumenical Council (Chalcedon, 451), therefore, they used to be called non-Chalcedonian or Old-Oriental Churches. To this family belong the following five churches: the Coptic Orthodox Church, the Syrian Orthodox Patriarchate of Antioch and All the East, the Armenian Apostolic Church (the Supreme Catholicosate of All Armenians at Etchmiadzin and the Armenian Catholicosate of Cilicia); the Malankara Orthodox Syrian Church of the East and the Ethiopian Orthodox Church. The Eastern Orthodox Churches represent the family of the following 16 independent churches, which respect the seven Ecumenical councils: the Ecumenical Patriarchate, the Patriarchate of Alexandria, the Patriarchate of Antioch, the Patriarchate of Jerusalem, the Russian Patriarchate, the Romanian Patriarchate, the Serbian Patriarchate, the Bulgarian Patriarchate, the Georgian Patriarchate, the Church of Cyprus, the Church of Greece, the Church of Albania, the Orthodox Church of the Czech Lands and Slovakia, the Polish Orthodox Church, the Finnish Orthodox Church and the Orthodox Church of Estonia. Although these two families of churches have been separated since 451, they are close in their theology, spirituality and liturgy.

The official dialogue between these two families of churches was preceded by a series of four unofficial theological consultations: Aarhus (1964), Bristol (1967), Geneva (1970) and Addis Ababa (1971). These consultations were facilitated by the WCC Faith and Order Commission and focused their deliberations on Christology, which was the most controversial point between the two traditions. The unofficial conversations proved to be constructive and arrived at the common view that in spite of the different terminology used by the two theological traditions as well as the different emphasis in the Christological teaching of the two church families, they confess the same faith in the Person of Jesus Christ. One of the most encouraging achievements during the unofficial conversations was the agreement in regard to the two wills in Christ, which was the object of the sixth Ecumenical Council (680/681).[36] In this respect the unofficial conversations constituted an excellent basis for the official dialogue.

The first meeting of the Joint Commission for the official dialogue between the two church families (Chambésy, Geneva, December 1985) published only a communiqué, which indicated that the task of the first meeting was to establish a methodology for this dialogue. In this respect "a joint sub-committee of six theologians

---

[35] Ibid.

[36] Deacon Aisst. Viorel Ionita, *Sinodul al VI-lea Ecumenic si importanta sa pentru ecumenismul actual (The 6th Ecumenical Council and its importance for the today ecumenism)*, (Bucharest: doctoral thesis, 1978), 451-454.

was set up, three from each side, with the mandate to prepare common texts for our future work."[37] For the second meeting of the Joint Commission, the aim was "to rediscover our common grounds in Christology and ecclesiology, the following main theme and subsequent sub-themes were agreed upon: Towards Common Christology; 1. Problems of terminology; 2. Conciliar formulations; 3. Historical factors and 4. Interpretation of Christological dogmas today."[38]

The first agreed statement in this dialogue was adopted only at the second meeting of the Joint Committee at the Anba Bishoy Monastery (Egypt, June 1989). This statement underlines that "the four adverbs used to qualify the mystery of the hypostatic union belong to our common tradition - without commingling (or confusion) (asynchytos), without change (atreptos), without separation (achoristos) and without division (adiairetos). Those among us who speak of two natures in Christ, do not thereby deny their inseparable, indivisible union; those among us who speak of one united divine-human nature in Christ do not thereby deny the continuing dynamic presence in Christ of the divine and the human, without change, without confusion."[39] This paragraph shows how the two terminologies are combined and reconciled in one common statement. In the same statement it was also underlined that "Our mutual agreement is not limited to Christology, but encompasses the whole faith of the one undivided church of the early centuries. We are agreed also in our understanding of the Person and Work of God the Holy Spirit, Who proceeds from the Father alone, and is always adored with the Father and the Son."[40]

The second agreed statement between the Oriental and the Eastern Orthodox Churches (Chambésy, Geneva, September 1990) stressed the decisions of the first statement and formulated some recommendations to the churches. The first part of this statement, the common position of the two churches in relation to the first three Ecumenical Councils, is underlined including the condemnation of both Eutychian and Nestorian heresies. In this respect "Both families accept the first three Ecumenical Councils, which form our common heritage."[41] As for the last four Ecumenical Councils, the Orthodox stated that these are in concordance with the faith of the first three ones, "while the Oriental Orthodox consider this statement of the Orthodox as their interpretation. With this understanding, the Oriental Orthodox respond to it positively."[42]

Agreement is also achieved in relation to the teaching of two wills and two energies in the one Person of the Logos incarnate, that means content wise in concordance with the sixth Ecumenical Council. As for "the teaching of the Seventh Ecumenical Council of the Orthodox Church, the Oriental Orthodox agree that the theology and practice of the veneration of icons taught by that Council are in basic agreement with the teaching and practice of the Oriental Orthodox from ancient times, long before the convening of the Council, and that we have no disagreement in this regard."[43]

The statement concludes the doctrinal part as follows: "In the light of our Agreed Statement on Christology as well as of the above common affirmations, we have now clearly understood that both families have always loyally maintained the same authentic Orthodox Christological faith, and the unbroken continuity of the apostolic tradition, though they have used Christological terms in different ways. It is this common faith and continuous loyalty to the Apostolic Tradition that should be the basis for our unity and communion."[44]

The fourth and last encounter of the first stage of the dialogue between the Oriental and the Orthodox Churches took place again at Chambésy (November 1993), with a series of Proposals for Lifting of Anathemas. In the light of the first two agreements, "the representatives of both Church families agree that the lifting of anathemas

---

[37] *Growth in Agreement II*, 190.

[38] Ibid., 190.

[39] *Growth in Agreement II*, 193.

[40] Ibid., 193.

[41] Ibid., 196.

[42] Ibid., 196.

[43] Ibid., 196.

[44] Ibid., 196.

*Part V: Bilateral Dialogues between Eastern Orthodox Churches
and other Churches and Christian Traditions*

and condemnations of the past can be consummated on the basis of their common acknowledgement of the fact that the Councils and Fathers previously anathematized or condemned are Orthodox in their teachings. In the light of our four unofficial consultations (1964, 1967, 1970, 1971) and our three official meetings which followed on (1985, 1989, 1990), we have understood that both families have loyally maintained the authentic Orthodox Christological doctrine and the unbroken continuity of the apostolic tradition, though they may have used Christological terms in different ways."[45] It is also important that the lifting of anathemas "should be made unanimously and simultaneously by the Heads of all the Churches of both sides, through the signing of an appropriate ecclesiastical Act, the content of which will include acknowledgements from each side that the other one is Orthodox in all respects."[46]

Important for the continuation of this dialogue was the meeting of *the Inter-Orthodox Theological Committee for Dialogue between the Orthodox Church and the Oriental Orthodox Churches* held at the Orthodox Centre of the Ecumenical Patriarchate in Chambésy, Geneva, from 10-13 March 2005. This committee took into consideration:

a. the progress to date and the future prospects of this dialogue;
b. the criteria for evaluating the theological work of the Joint Theological Commission and on the reactions to these criteria;
c. the importance of the agreement that has been reached on the Christological issue, and on the refutation of those who objected to the interpretation of the recognition of the "Orthodoxy" of the non – Chalcedonians;
d. the obscurities of paragraph 8 of the 2nd Agreed Theological Statement, and on the need for these to be clarified;
e. the theological difficulties of Theological Dialogue with the Oriental Orthodox Churches, by the Professor of the Theological Academy of Moscow;
f. the bilateral relations of the Russian Orthodox Church with the Oriental Orthodox Churches, and on the reservations of the Russian Orthodox Church with respect to the text of the Agreed Statements and
g. the liturgical problems that have arisen in the rapprochement of the two ecclesiastical families and on ways to address them.

The committee considered that the "Theological Dialogue between the Orthodox Church and the pre-Chalcedonian Oriental Orthodox Churches is particularly important, as it was proclaimed by the relevant unanimous decision of the 3rd Pre-Conciliar Pan-Orthodox Conference (1986), and must therefore be continued to complete the work of both the Joint Theological Commission and the Sub Committees on the pastoral and liturgical issues."[47] The concrete recommendations[48] made by this committee should lead to a constructive continuation of this dialogue.

---

[45] Available online: www.monachos.net/library

[46] Ibid.

[47] Available online: *www.centreorthodoxe.org*

[48] 1. The Joint Theological Commission has to plan its work, on the one hand in reference to the reservations or criticism expressed, either justified or unjustified, on the ambiguous points in the two Agreed Theological Statements (1989, 1990) and to the consequences deriving from them, and on the other hand in reference to the still pending issues of the two Sub-Committees because only in this way will it be possible not only to demonstrate the significance of the agreement reached on the Christological issue, but to plan and prepare as required for the ecclesiastical body.

2. The ecclesiological importance of recognizing and including the doctrinal definitions of the IV, V, VI and VII Ecumenical Synods must be promoted more fully through special studies on their Cyrillian basis, and the Anathemas must be lifted in order to restore ecclesiastical communion; these measures presuppose thorough and integrated research of the theological heritage of both theological traditions and the clarification of the Christological terminology.

3. The planning of the future activities presupposes the immediate assembly, organization, and publication in an attractive special volume of all the presentations and studies, which refer to the disputed theological issues of the Agreed Theolog-

Orthodox – Reformed

The dialogue between the Orthodox Churches and the WARC/WCRC was prepared by a series of consultations between "Reformed and Greek Orthodox delegations" from 1979 to 1984. The *Concluding Affirmations* of this consultation process underlined that "deep soundings were taken on both sides to see if there were sufficient common ground regarding the canon of truth."[49] In the light of this experience a preparatory meeting for the official dialogue between the two church families took place in Chambésy, Geneva (March, 1986). This meeting suggested for the Orthodox – Reformed Joint Commission (ORJC)[50] the following theme: *The doctrine of the Holy Trinity on the basis of the Niceno-Constantinopolitan Creed.*[51] The first meeting of the ORJC took place in March 1988 at Leuenberg, Switzerland, where among others reports were presented "of recent national conversations between the two bodies."[52] As a first remark to this recommendation we underline the connection with the different levels of dialogue between the two theological traditions. The second remark is that the themes of this dialogue are following the structure of the Nicean – Constantinopolitan Creed that is the doctrine of the Holy Trinity and Christology. The theme of Ecclesiology was here debated on the basis of the achievement on the first themes. This approach expressed the experience accumulated in other dialogues by the Orthodox.

The theme of the Holy Trinity was then discussed at two consecutive plenary sessions (Leuenberg, 1988, and Minsk, 1990) and an agreement was adopted only during the third meeting of the ORJC at Kappel-am-Albis, Switzerland (1992). After a short introduction, this document contains the following chapters: 1. The Self-Revelation of God as Father, Son and Holy Spirit; 2. Three Divine Persons; 3. Eternal Relations in God; 4. The Order of Divine Persons in the Trinity; 5. Trinity in Unity and Unity in Trinity, the One Monarchy; 6. Perichoresis: the Mutual Indwelling of Father, Son and Holy Spirit; 7. One Being, Three Persons and 8. The Apostolic and Catholic Faith. At the suggestion of the Reformed delegation[53] an *Agreed Statement* on the *Holy Trinity, Significant Features* was also adopted in 1992, which underlined the ecumenical significance of this statement.[54]

The second agreed statement in this dialogue followed only two years later and addressed the doctrine of Christology (Limassol, Cyprus, January, 1994). In the statements adopted in this dialogue the position of the two traditions is very clearly exposed as well as the common view on some topics discussed. Talking about Christology, the Reformed-Orthodox dialogue came unavoidably to the discussion on the issue of icons. In this respect the statement from Limassol indicated that "The divergent conclusions drawn by the Orthodox and Reformed traditions on the subject of iconography is a subject related to the above statement which might well form a point of entry for discussion at a future dialogue."[55]

The fifth meeting of the ORJC (Aberdeen, UK, June 1996) started with the theme of Ecclesiology, respectfully of the *Identity and Unity of the Church*, but there was published only a summary of discussions. The discussions continued during the seventh meeting (Zakynthos, Greece, June, 1998), where a third common statement on *The Church as the Body of Christ* was adopted.

---

ical Statements, or to the refutation of the criticism against them, because in this way appropriate arguments will support not only the work that has already been accomplished, but also the future prospects of the work of the Joint Theological Commission and the two Sub-Committees. (*www.centreorthodoxe.org*)

[49] *Theological Dialogue between Orthodox and Reformed Churches*, Volume 2, edited by Thomas F. Torrance, (Edinburgh: Scottish Academic Press, 1993), ix.

[50] Which included representatives of all Orthodox churches, not only the Greek ones, as in the preparatory process?

[51] Ibid., x.

[52] Ibid., xi.

[53] Ibid., xxiii.

[54] See *Agreed Statements from the Orthodox-Reformed Dialogue*, edited by Lukas Vischer, (Geneva: World Alliance of Reformed Churches, 1988), 21-24.

[55] Ibid., 23.

The two partners agreed that the "Church founded upon Christ has a concrete, visible and historical form, the apostolic community. This community was expanded at Pentecost and from Jerusalem it spread to other places. As a historic community it was given a historic mission, to preach the good news of the Gospel and receive into membership of the One Body of Christ, the Church, all those who received the good news of the Gospel."[56] The believers are then "engrafted into Christ, put on Christ, are regenerated in Christ, so that in him they may be restored to their true nature and fulfilled in the Church. What Christ has done objectively for all in and through his humanity is now appropriated by those who believe and freely submit to him as their Lord and Saviour."[57] It is also to be noted that "Baptism is the great sacrament of entry into the Body of Christ, it is Christ's gracious gift to all human beings; it is a gift to be freely accepted and appropriated by each human being."[58] It is quite strange that in this text about the Church as the Body of Christ there is no reference to the Holy Spirit, which indicates that this text is only a stage on the way to a more complete statement.

The fourth common statement of the ORJC was adopted in Pittsburgh, USA (April 2000) and focused on the *Membership and Incorporation into the Body of Christ*. In this statement, the means for the incorporation into the Body of Christ are considered the Baptism and the Chrismation. For both sides the "baptism is a sacrament/mystery of divine grace freely given and freely received, which is not to be repeated."[59] It is also important to underline that for both Orthodox and Reformed the grace received in the Baptism "confers forgiveness of sins and rebirth of water and the Holy Spirit, which is necessary for entry into the Kingdom of Heaven. Nevertheless, there is a difference of understanding between the traditions as to whether this grace in baptism includes the seal of the Gift of the Spirit. The Orthodox believe that on the basis of Scripture and Tradition the seal of the Gift of the Spirit is granted through Chrismation. The Reformed include the fullness of the Spirit in the Baptismal grace. Both agree that they need to engage in fuller exploration of this issue, and especially the connection between baptism and eucharist."[60] We find here the missing part on the Holy Spirit from the previous statement.

Continuing discussion in the frame of the theme on Ecclesiology, the 8th plenary session of the ORJC adopted the fifth statement on *The Holiness of the Church* (Sibiu, Romania, September 2003). This statement is well structured and after a short introduction contains the following chapters: 1. The holiness of the Church; 2. Holiness as a divine gift and human task and 3. The Saints. The document concludes with some "Convergence and divergence."[61] There are four points of convergence and only one of divergence, namely related to "the understanding of the Holiness of the Church between the Reformed and the Orthodox", which "are clearly related to their divergence in the perception of the reality of the Church, which, they agree, needs to be explored further."[62]

The sixth statement adopted in this dialogue focused on *The Catholicity and Mission of the Church* (Beirut, Lebanon, October 2005). For both Orthodox and Reformed "the catholicity of the Church means being in communion with Christ and through Him with God and with one another. It also implies being committed to mission summoning the whole world to be reconciled to God. The intensive aspect of catholicity finds its manifestation and fulfilment in the extensive, which is realized through the mission of the Church in the world."[63] This summary linked catholicity with the mission of the Church.

The last plenary meeting of the ORJC so far took place at Volos, Greece (September, 2007) and addressed the topic of *Eschatology. Second Coming. The Resurrection of the dead. Last Judgment.* This is one of a few

---

[56] "Orthodox-Reformed Dialogue on the Doctrine of the Church," *Reformed World* 57.1 (March 2007): 89.

[57] Ibid., 89.

[58] Ibid.

[59] Ibid., 90.

[60] Ibid., 91.

[61] Ibid., 97.

[62] Ibid.

[63] Ibid., 100.

examples of dialogue, at least with Orthodox implications, which addressed the topic of Eschatology. This fact indicates that the dialogue discussed to the end the Creed. The common statement of the Orthodox and the Reformed on this topic is of great significance. We would like to underline one affirmation in this statement, which states that "The resurrection of our Saviour gives meaning not only to man's life, but also to the end of his life, because to Christians death is just a transition to the plenitude of eternal life. This plenitude of life is the fulfillment of a great purpose, that of intimate unification of the Son of God and humanity; man enjoys this plenitude spiritually first, after being found righteous at the particular judgment and then, also bodily, with his/her resurrected body and freed from corruption at the final judgment."[64]

The Orthodox-Reformed dialogue addressed extensively the question of Ecclesiology and reached in this respect a great deal of agreement. Nevertheless, there are many open questions, which must be clarified for the sake of the continuation of this dialogue. As for the theme of Church Unity we could not find here any substantial contribution. Probably the most successful part of this dialogue is the fact that each one of the two partners could identify the ecclesiological profile of the other and this fact is extremely important for these two church families on their way towards unity.

Conclusions

The purpose of all dialogues mentioned above was to investigate how the churches involved could achieve unity. From the Orthodox perspective, this is the main goal of all these dialogues. The Orthodox believe that the prayer of the Lord for the unity of all those who believe in Him is a mandate given to the Church throughout the centuries up to the end of the time.

The Orthodox view of the way towards unity appears quite coherent throughout all these dialogues. This view is that the unity cannot be achieved without clarifying all the dividing differences between the respective churches. The basis for the discussion about the visible unity - although the Orthodox do not use this concept much - is given in a concentrate form in the *Nicean - Constantinopolitan Creed*. This creed was taken as frame of discussions mainly in the Orthodox-Old Catholic and in the Orthodox-Reformed dialogues.

The experience made through these dialogues showed that the Creed cannot be taken separately from its liturgical context. Speaking about the faith confessed by the undivided Church, the Orthodox do not mean a theoretical exposition of the faith with no relation to the moral and liturgical life of the Church. In other words, the faith is confessed not simply mentally or theoretically but also liturgically, spiritually and practically. In this respect the Orthodox expect that what the churches confess doctrinally should be reflected in their practical life.

Taking this link into consideration we have to underline that one of the missing aspects in the dialogues we are talking about is the lack of references to the liturgical texts, to the prayers and hymns of the respective churches. There are very few such references in the dialogues we presented above. These references could help the dialogue to find a broader expression of the faith confessed by the churches.

The methodological approach in these dialogues so far focussed mainly on what unites the churches, in other words the consensus in doctrinal matters was the main purpose of these dialogues. This was a legitimate first step, but not helpful enough to provide a clear image of what really divides the churches, or of how near they were to each other. For a real breakthrough in these dialogues a necessary next step may be to identify the real dividing issues between the churches involved and to look for the solutions. Only in that moment could the churches really know how far they are from one another.

As for the methodology they followed, these dialogues differ from one another. Some of them adopted from the beginning a clear agenda, like the Orthodox-Old Catholic dialogue. There were other dialogues, which focussed on very specific issues, which divide the respective churches, as is the case with the Eastern Orthodox – Oriental Orthodox dialogue, which focussed mainly on Christology. Finally there were also dialogues,

---

[64] This statement was put at our disposal by Dr. Lecturer Ciprian Streza, member of the Orthodox Commission at the Volos meeting.

which did not adopt a long-term agenda, but developed their topics from one meeting to the other, as is the case with the Orthodox-LWF dialogue.

These practical aspects indicate that the dialogues presented above were adapted to the different situation and first of all to the different types of relations between the respective churches. It may be helpful for the Orthodox Churches to look at how the dialogues they have with different churches relate to the dialogues between these churches among themselves. The issue of accountability between all these dialogues may help them to advance one step forward on their way to unity.

Bibliography

1. Vezi *Koinonia auf altkatholischer Basis (The Koinonia on Old Catholic Basis),* edited by Urs von Arx, (Bern, 1989)

2. *Orthodoxie im Dialog. Bilaterale Dialoge der orthodoxen und der orientalisch-orthodoxen Kirchen 1945-1997. Eine Dokumentensammlung,* hrsg. von Thomas Bremer, Johannes Oeldemann und Dagmar Stoltmann, (Paulinus Verlag, 1999)

3. *Growth in Agreement II. Reports and Agreed Statements of Ecumenical Conversations on a World Level, 1982-1998.* Edited by Jeffrey Gros, FSC, Harding Meyer and William G. Rusch, (Geneva: WCC Publications, 2000)

4. Athanasios Basdekis, *Die Orthodoxe Kirche,* (Otto Lembeck Verlag, 2001)

5. *Agreed Statements from the Orthodox-Reformed Dialogue,* edited by Lukas Vischer, (Geneva: World Alliance of Reformed Churches, 1988)

6. "Orthodox-Reformed Dialogue on the Doctrine of the Church," *Reformed World* 57.1 (2007).

7. *Theological Dialogue between Orthodox and Reformed Churches,* Volume 2, edited by Thomas F. Torrance, (Edinburgh: Scottish Academic Press, 1993)

8. *Accords et dialogues oecuméniques,* Textes éditées par André Birmelé et Jaques Terme, (Paris, 1995)

9. Risto Saarinen, *Faith and Holiness. Lutheran-Orthodox Dialogue 1959-1994,* (Göttingen: Vandenhoeck & Ruprecht, 1997)

(75) Orthodox Dialogues with the Lutheran Churches

Konstantinos Delikostantis

The relations between Lutherans and Orthodox have a long history, starting with the birth of Protestantism. Martin Luther in 1519 made reference to the Orthodox Church in his conflict with Rome. Especially, the non-recognition of the primacy of the Pope by Orthodoxy served Luther as a point against Rome and as a proof for existence and legitimacy of the Christian Church outside of the papal jurisdiction. In his dispute with Eck, Luther defended the Eastern Church against the reproach of being schismatic or even heretical. He mentioned thousands of its martyrs and saints, the famous theologians and Church Fathers, and called the Eastern Church "the better part of the universal church", "*meliorem partem universalis ecclesiae*".[1]

Unfortunately, Luther could not develop his positive view of the Orthodox Church. In course of time he identified in the history of this church similar developments and problems as in the Roman Catholic tradition. Even in the Greek Church Luther saw the same powers in action, which led the West to the primacy of Rome, signs of a progressive decline.[2] Luther mentions the "endless quarrel" between Rome and Constantinople for "the worthless primacy" by means of "vain, week and useless twaddle".[3] Although Luther continues to make a distinction between the two Churches, and to refer to Eastern Church Fathers and to the accordance of the principles of the Reformation with the doctrine of the Ancient Church, generally his interest for Orthodoxy did not cross the limits of an apologetic attitude. Georges Florovsky regards Luther's knowledge of the history, doctrinal teaching of the early Church and of the Greek Fathers as insufficient.[4] "Luther has said much about the 'Fathers' of the Church, though he knew only a limited number of works from a small number of the Fathers."[5] Ioannis Karmiris notes that Luther could not enter deeply into 'the dogmatic system, the ecclesial order, the mystical nature, the spirit and the character' of the Eastern Church, even though he never ceased to use all the theological material which was accessible to him.[6] Certainly, Luther's limited interest for Orthodoxy proved to have a significant impact. The attitude of the Reformer influenced and formed the attitude of Protestantism to the Orthodox Church until today. Orthodoxy remained constantly "an object of attention for the Protestant point of view."[7] It was Phillip Melanchon who tried to establish first contacts between the new movement and the Orthodox Church. In 1559 he sent a letter and a Greek version of the *Confessio Augustana* to the Ecumenical Patriarch Joasaph II. This first attempt of contact did not lead to a success.[8]

Soon the Lutherans addressed the Greek Church in the Ottoman Empire to expose the insights of the Reformation and to hear its opinion about the new doctrine of the Reformation. The famous correspondence between the theologians of Württemberg - and the philologist Martinus Crusius - and the Ecumenical Patriarch Jeremias II, in the years 1573-1581, was an admirable attempt for contact and theological exchange.[9] The

---

[1] Luther M. (1519) *Disputatio Iohannis Eccii et Martini Lutheri Lipsiae habita.* WA, 2, 280, 5.

[2] Luther M. (1539) *Von den Konziliis und Kirchen.* WA, 50, 577, 30-578, 2.

[3] Ibid., 578, 31-579, 3.

[4] Florovsky G. The Byzantine Ascetic and Spiritual Fathers. In: Haugh R. S (ed.) *The Collected Works of Georges Florovsky*, volume 10, 92 and 95.

[5] Ibid., 94.

[6] Karmiris I., „Luther und Melanchton über die Orthodoxe Kirche," *Theologia* 34 (1963): 211-212.

[7] Gass G. W., *Symbolik der griechischen Kirche*, (Berlin, 1872), 41.

[8] See Karmiris I., "Luther und Melanchton über die Orthodoxe Kirche," 386-389.

[9] See Wendebourg D., *Reformation und Orthodoxie. Der ökumenische Briefwechsel zwischen der Leitung der Württembergischen Kirche und Patriarch Ieremias II. von Konstantinopel in den Jahren 1573-1581.* (Göttingen: Vandenhoeck & Ruprecht, 1986).

Lutheran scholars sent to the Patriarch a Greek version of the *Confessio Augustana* and asked for a comment on the main doctrines of the Reformation. The Patriarch answered with a detailed exposition of the Orthodox doctrine relating to some articles of *Confessio Augustana*.

The Lutherans, challenged by the response of the Patriarch wrote two letters with new explanations. The Patriarch answered to both texts using the same arguments. In his third response Patriarch Jeremias asked the Lutherans to correspond with him in the future not about dogmatic issues, but to write only "because of friendship".[10] At the end of his letter he complains about the fact that the westerners honour and praise the Church Fathers only in theory, but in practice and reality, they overlook and neglect them.

In this way ended this first significant attempt for approach between Protestantism and Orthodoxy. It has surely served to create a mutual acquaintance, but it could not lead to an authentic dialogue. The difficult questions, if the new Christian movement was able and ready to affirm the ancient original Christian doctrine, if the Orthodox could accept the theological principles of the Reformation exposed in the *Confessio Augustana*, were a serious obstacle. For Anastasios Kallis this correspondence was "a sign of good will and of the incapability to understand the partner. The aims of the Reformation remained closed for the Patriarch, while the Tübingen used such arguments, as if they spoke with a Roman theologian."[11] Dorothea Wendebourg sees as the "main difference" in the correspondence between Tübingen and Constantinople and the primary reason for the failure of this attempt, the "different evaluation of the ecclesial tradition."[12]

In my opinion, decisive in this correspondence was the fact that for the Patriarch, who registered the new movement not without sympathy, because of its criticism against the impasses of the Roman Church, it became quickly clear that Reformation was not a return to the doctrine and the practice of the Ancient Church and that its representatives were not ready or able for such a step. Patriarch Jeremias argues "the absence of calmness" of the mind, "the displeasure with tradition", the "ceaseless questioning and answering and also the desire for the new" were the sickness of the western spirit.[13]

In the following period a lot of unpleasant events occurred. Influenced by Calvinism, the 'Eastern Confession of the Christian Faith' of the Patriarch of Constantinople Cyril Loukaris provoked 'the first historical confessional reaction of Orthodoxy to the Reformation'.[14] The 17th century is a tragic time for the relations between East and West. The Orthodox East became the battlefield of Catholics and Protestants for more influence. A negative consequence of the struggle against the Calvinistic infiltration to Orthodoxy is that, up to this time, more and more Roman Catholic arguments have been used against Protestant doctrines, and all this damaged the proper articulation of the Orthodox theological tradition. Another negative side of this conflict was the psychological reserve against Protestantism, the Loukaris-complex, which influenced our attitude towards Protestantism until today.

The encyclical of the Synod of Constantinople 1836 against the Protestant missionaries,[15] which indicated the lowest point in the history of the relations between Orthodoxy and Protestantism, must be evaluated in the same context. In the first half of the 19th century, the Orthodox East had to resist strong Protestant missionarism, which mainly attacked the piety of the Orthodox and the practical dimension of the Eastern tradition. Facing this situation, the Ecumenical Patriarchate was obliged to react in a hard language against the Protestant missionaries and the leaders of the Reformation.

The 20th century was a turning point in the relations between Orthodox and Lutherans. The courageous initiatives of the Ecumenical Patriarchs and various contacts of both sides in the first half of this century culminated in the foundation of the World Council of Churches, which built a basis for the official dialogue

---

[10] Karmiris I., *The dogmatic and symbolic monuments of the Orthodox Catholic Church*, volume 2, (Graz, 1968), 569.
[11] Kallis A., *Das hätte ich gerne gewusst, 100 Fragen an einen orthodoxen Theologen*. (Münster: Theopano Verlag, 2003), 343.
[12] Wendebourg D., *Reformation und Orthodoxie*, 334.
[13] Karmiris I., *The dogmatic and symbolic monuments of the Orthodox Catholic Church*, volume 2, 556.
[14] Meyendorff J., *Catholicity and the Church*. (Crestwood, NY: St. Vladimir's Seminary Press, 1983), 79.
[15] For this text see Karmiris I., *The dogmatic and symbolic monuments of the Orthodox Catholic Church*, volume 2, 953-972.

between Orthodoxy and the Lutheran World Federation. This dialogue is considered a continuation of the first encounter in the 16th century responding to the claims of contemporary reality.[16]

The First Pan-Orthodox Conference in Rhodes (1961) put the ecumenical dialogue on the agenda of the Great Council of Orthodoxy. The Fourth Pan-Orthodox Conference (1968) suggested unanimously the inception of a bilateral dialogue with the Lutherans. Finally, the First Pre-Conciliar Pan-Orthodox Conference of 1976 decided "to promote the subject of the dialogue with the Lutherans and to constitute for this purpose, likely to the other theological dialogues, a special interorthodox committee."[17] This committee had to evaluate the former Orthodox / Lutheran contacts and to prepare the official bilateral dialogue.

The Ecumenical Patriarch sent on behalf of the whole Orthodoxy an invitation to the Lutheran World Federation to start of a dialogue on the global level. The Lutheran World Federation accepted in 1977 this invitation and after three separate preparatory meetings (1978, 1979 and 1980) the first official meeting of the Orthodox / Lutheran Joint Commission took place in Espoo / Helsinki 27 August – 4 September 1981.

This dialogue, aiming at 'full communion and full mutual recognition', is initially evaluated as an eminent event in the life of Orthodoxy and Lutheranism. The Report of the Orthodox / Lutheran Joint Commission from the meeting of Espoo States courageously:

> "We see it to be a momentous event in the life of our churches that for the first time in history official pan-Orthodox and pan-Lutheran delegations met for dialogue with the ultimate goal of full communion. Contacts and relations between our churches date from the 16th century. Regional theological dialogues between Orthodox and Lutheran churches have been going on for many years in various areas of the world. It was with this in mind that the pan-Orthodox Conference of 1968 decided to include in future planning a dialogue with Lutheran churches. The official invitation was extended in 1976 to the Lutheran churches through the Lutheran World Federation. The LWF Executive Committee accepted this invitation with joy in February 1977. During the following years preparatory meetings were held by the appointed representatives of the Orthodox churches who invited as guests the Lutheran observers. After this careful preparation the Orthodox churches and the Lutheran World Federation agreed to begin the official dialogue under the general theme 'Participation in the Mystery of the Church'. The subject of ecclesiology was chosen because we see the reality of our churches not only in theological terms, but also in light of their full life in the Body of Christ. We praise God that He brought us together for this first meeting, which fulfills the hopes of many eminent teachers in our churches since the 16th century. This surpasses human expectation when one looks at experiences of former centuries."[18]

This dialogue between Orthodox and Lutherans, despite the fact that it continues the former contacts and dialogues, is something new. It is not an occasional and particular encounter based on personal initiative, but for the first time in the history an official dialogue between the Orthodox Church as a whole and the Lutheran World Federation. A serious problem in this dialogue remains the fact that the Lutheran World Federation is a fellowship of Lutheran Churches, which does not include all the Lutheran Churches over the world and does not constitute a Church.

A first evaluation of this dialogue from the Orthodox side was made by the Third Preconciliar Panorthodox Conference (1986). The final text of this conference reads:

---

[16] See Karmiris I., *The Orthodox – Protestant Dialogue. Brief review of its development*, (Athens, 1988) (gr.); Saarinen. R, *Faith and Holiness. Lutheran – Orthodox Dialogue 1959-1994*, (Göttingen, 1997); Nikolaou Th., "Der Orthodox – Lutherische Dialog. Geschichtlicher Überblick und gemeinsame Texte." In: Bischof Eumenios von Lefka, *Die Orthodoxe Kirche. Ein Standortbestimmung an der Jahrtausendwende. Festgabe für Prof. Anastasios Kallis*, (Frankfurt a.M.: Verlag Otto Lembeck, 1999), 242-277; Martensen. D.F., "Lutheran- Orthodox Dialogue," in Lossky N. and others (eds.), *Dictionary of the Ecumenical Movement*. (Geneva: WCC Publications, 2002), 716-718; Delikostantis K., "Martin Luther and the Orthodox Church", *Lutheran Forum*, 45.3 (2011): 36-41.

[17] *Episkepsis* 158 (1976): 4.

[18] Bericht der Gemeinsamen Orthodoxen – Lutherischen Kommission Espoo / Finnland, 27 August – 4 September 1981. In: *Informationen aus der Orthodoxen Kirche* 2.10: 22.

Part V: Bilateral Dialogues between Eastern Orthodox Churches
and other Churches and Christian Traditions

"The Third Pre-Conciliar Pan-Orthodox Conference states with satisfaction the fact that the dialogue with the Lutherans started under a positive omen and with the right theme and that the partners chose as first subject to be treated Ecclesiology, which touches basically the most important issues and the core of theological differences. The conference expects that in the bilateral discourses as well as during the elaboration of the common texts, the same emphasis will be shown to the academic and to the ecclesiastical element. Although we can already preview future difficulties in the performance of the dialogue nevertheless we hope that with God's help it will prove to be fruitful and beneficial."[19]

The Orthodox / Lutheran Joint Commission produced significant texts and common statements reflecting convergences on the topics of divine Revelation, Scripture and Tradition, inspiration and canon, authority in and of the Church, conciliarity, salvation, grace, justification and synergy, and the "Mystery of the Church". These important texts affirm the commitment of the two sides to a serious theological discourse and contain many common issues, in spite of the newly arisen divergences.

In parallel to the pan-Orthodox dialogue with the Lutheran World Federation, many regional dialogues take place. We have regional dialogues of the Orthodox Church of Russia with the EKD and the Lutheran Church of Finland, of the Orthodox church of Bulgaria with the Lutherans of the former GDR, of the Orthodox Church of Romania with the Lutherans and the Reformed on their national level. Also in North America various dialogues on important theological topics have been organized between Lutherans and the Orthodox Churches. These regional dialogues, in combination with the worldwide dialogue of Orthodox and Lutherans, are a sign of hope, although the coordination of the two processes constitutes a major problem.

Although both sides of the dialogue received a better knowledge of each other and overcame a lot of prejudices and misunderstandings, some basic unsolved problems stand between them, as for instance for the Orthodox the subjection and the individualistic narrowing of ecclesial being in Lutheranism, and for the Lutheran side the Orthodox traditionalism. Another source of tension are the newly arisen anthropological and ethical questions. In addition to the problem of the ordination of women on all levels of clerical order, the new moral code concerning homosexual relations and their implications for the Christian anthropology cause new difficulties. These ecclesiogical and ethical innovations and the reactions of the Orthodox create new obstacles for the promotion of the relation between Orthodoxy and Lutheranism and endanger not only the final goal of the unity, but even the continuation of the dialogue.

Facing this change of paradigm in the ecumenical movement, it is necessary that the dialogues focus not only on the classical theological subjects, but also more strongly on the anthropological and moral issues. Perhaps in the future new strategies of dialogue will need to be applied. We have to rethink the methodology and strategy of ecumenism.

The Orthodox side has difficulties with the fact that although the Lutherans sincerely support rapprochement with the Orthodox Churches, they often act and make choices, which ignore major traditions of the undivided Church and hinder the aim of the Christian unity. The Orthodox Church, on the way to the Great Pan-Orthodox Council, has to act carefully to avoid hasty decisions. It is obvious that spectacular ecumenical gestures cannot be expected from the Orthodox side.

Nevertheless our dialogue has to continue in openness and without theological minimalism. In the words of Florovsky: "For the ecumenical dialogue to bear fruit, the very controversies that separate the churches must not be hushed up. Rather they must be brought into the open and discussed frankly, respectfully, and thoroughly."[20]

It is necessary to enforce the process of reception, to make clear to the faithful the achievements of the ecumenical dialogues, the amazing work and the significant theological and ecclesial output. It is very important that Christians discover the existential content and sense of the ecumenical movement, its significance for

---

[19] *Beschlüsse der III Panorthodoxen Vorkonziliaren Konferenz*, (Chambésy/Genf 1986). In: Basdekis A., *Orthodoxe Kirche und Ökumenische Bewegung. Dokumente – Erklärungen- Berichte 1900-2006.* (Frankfurt a.M/Paderborn: Lembeck/ Bonifatius, 2006), 386.
[20] Florovsky G., Op. cit., 21.

culture and society, for reconciliation and peace. We have to promote a fuller implementation of the theological achievements of the ecumenical dialogues in the life of our Churches, to create through the theological discourse a dialogue of life.

Sincere dialogue does not lead to a "pseudomorphosis" or to a loss of identity but primarily to a mutual enrichment, to a deeper comprehension of the other and also of our own tradition. Traditions can be understood properly only in their relation and openness to each other. Isolation produces stagnation. Only a Church open to the dialogue enables other Churches to participate in its precious heritage. In the openness to the others, Churches can discover and live more consciously their own tradition.

Part V: Bilateral Dialogues between Eastern Orthodox Churches
and other Churches and Christian Traditions

Fr. Dorin Oancea

The official theological dialogue between the Orthodox Churches and the Reformed Churches started in 1988 and has held ten sessions ever since. Their chronological order was: 1988 (Leuenberg, Switzerland), 1990 (Minsk, Belarus'), 1992 (Kappel-am-Albis, Switzerland), 1994 (Limassol, Cyprus), 1996 (Aberdeen, Scotland), 1998 (Zakynthos, Greece), 2000 (Pittsburgh, USA), 2003 (Sibiu, Romania), 2005 (Beirut, Lebanon) and 2007 (Volos, Greece). As one can see, nothing happened after 2007, and we are already in 2013. Why is this? Some people may think that the dialogue reached its goal and the participants eventually decided to put an end to it. But that was not so. In the very beginning it had been agreed by the two sides to start with the Nicene-Constantinopolitan Creed and to continue with other issues of common interest. In 2007 the last article of the Creed, on Eschatology, was discussed and by that the first aim of the dialogue reached. Nevertheless, analysing the Creed was not the first and only aim of those who agreed upon having this dialogue started. They actually had in mind an even broader theological understanding and after that a rapprochement between the two confessional families in their everyday experience of Christian existence. This second step of the dialogue is still waiting to be completed. I could enumerate certain objective causes of the delay, for example the developments within the Reformed world, which might have prevented them from concentrating on a theological dialogue. At the same time, I wonder whether some other reasons might not have been at work here; some internal reasons affecting not only this particular dialogue between the Orthodox and Reformed Churches, but also all theological/inter-confessional dialogues more generally.

It is not my intention to deal with different content aspects of the theological dialogue, mainly because I did this some years ago as part of an evaluation initiated and completed by the Study Commission of CEC.[1] At the same time, this particular dialogue is extremely significant because of the originally quite remote positions of the partners, demanding elaborate preliminaries, because of the results achieved and also because of its shortcomings. These three aspects shall be considered here, keeping in mind that the results of our analysis should be understood in the broader context of all kinds of ecumenical dialogues.[2]

Preliminaries

I dedicate a special part of my chapter to the preliminaries of the dialogue in order to reveal some difficulties encountered by dialogues between religious families and the importance of following a step-by-step agenda, in order to eliminate them.

Why did such a dialogue include special difficulties?

First of all because of the Orthodox perception of the initial Reformed Churches and their later development. For the standard Orthodox theologian, and by this I also mean the standard Orthodox priest, the Reformed were even more remote than the Lutherans. Such items as icons and saints, worshipped by the Orthodox but

---

[1] My evaluation of the different sessions of the dialogue entitled *The Theological Bilateral Dialogue between the Orthodox Churches and the World Alliance of Reformed Churches. An Evaluation from an Orthodox Point of View,* was published in the papers of the Member Churches Consultation on Dialogues between Orthodox and other CEC Member Churches, *Reseptio* 1 (2009): 32-43. An evaluation from the Reformed point of view was published in "Reformed World": *Orthodox-Reformed international dialogue: convergences on the doctrine of the Church (1886-2005),* Reformed World 57.1 (2007).

[2] With regard to the dialogues of the Orthodox Churches see V. Ionita, "The Vision of Unity in the Multilateral Dialogues and in the Bilateral Dialogues of the Orthodox Churches with the Other Churches", *Studii Teologice*, Bucharest, series 3, 4.3 (2008): 7-58.

rejected by the Reformed, are always remembered as differences not only by Orthodox theologians, but also by the average Orthodox faithful. Theologians would have added to that the problem of predestination, for example, which has been regarded as a major difference between the two traditions, with regard to the saving action of God. One should note that for centuries these differences were more or less academic for most of the Orthodox, as long as they did not live in one and the same country with Reformed Christians.

The one exception to this rule was Transylvania, the western province of present Romania, where the majority of the population had been for centuries Romanian and Orthodox, whereas the ruling class was Hungarian and to a great extent Reformed or Roman-Catholic. In the seventeenth century some of the Reformed Hungarian rulers of the province tried to impose upon the Orthodox Romanians Calvinistic ways of Christian experience and this led to the resistance of the Orthodox, who perceived this as a major threat to their identity. At the same time in the same province we can notice the positive results of this cohabiting of Hungarians and Romanians, a good example in this respect being the first translation of the New Testament into Romanian by the Orthodox Metropolitan Simion Ştefan in 1648, stimulated by the Reformed ruler of Transylvania.

As noted above, this unique, common experience had positive and negative sides, at least as it presents itself to the Orthodox mind. By introducing this example into a broader inter-confessional picture, one could say that the expectations the Orthodox and Reformed had from one another were more or less similar, up to the second half of the 20th century. Afterwards things changed rapidly on both sides. As parts of the same ecumenical bodies, the Orthodox and the Reformed learned to better know each other and to assume that behind all those differences, some of them already mentioned, there are a lot of similarities, which could lead to certain convergences.

During the Faith and Order Conferences held in Lausanne (1927), Edinburgh (1937), and Montreux (1962), some Orthodox and Reformed theologians discovered their mutual interest in the theology of the Church Fathers, especially of those belonging to the Alexandrian tradition.[3] This led to the idea that a theological dialogue between the Orthodox Churches and WARC might be possible and as early as 1972 an official letter for starting such a dialogue was sent to the Ecumenical Patriarchate by Jan Lochman, at that time head of the WARC theological department. This message led to several meetings, meant to make the necessary preparations for the dialogue. Such meetings were held in Istanbul (1979) and Geneva (1981, 1983). They dealt with important preliminaries. Maybe the most important was the one in 1972, when the two parties decided that the dialogue should be organized on the basis of the Nicean-Constantinopolitan Creed, because it was common to both confessional families.

From a methodological point of view I would like to note firstly the mutual interest, which led to this first consultation and then the decision to have a common element present in both traditions as a permanent base of understanding each other. The participants in the dialogue accepted from the very beginning the existence of this common element along with the differences between the two traditions. Starting from the existence of these common elements and their differences, they decided to reach a mutual understanding and to clarify the differences by deepening the common element we find in the Creed.

From the same point of view it is also important to note that besides the normal procedures of identifying common elements in the present articulations of faith, in this dialogue the importance of the common tradition is not only revealed, but this tradition becomes an instrument of articulating common elements of the contemporary Christian experience. As long as our languages are different, to a certain extent at least, mutual understanding becomes difficult. Therefore, retracing the historical threads of our contemporary models of thought and discovering the common basis from which they originate, might make us understand that the convergences between our two traditions are more significant than ever supposed.

The next consultations go two steps further in preparing the official dialogue. This time, they deal with the Church as related to God. It is interesting to notice here how solid ecumenical thinking develops. During

---

[3] With regard to the preparatory steps for the following dialogue sessions, see Thomas F. Torrance, *Theological dialogue between orthodox and reformed churches*, (Edinburgh: Clark Constable, 1985).

Part V: Bilateral Dialogues between Eastern Orthodox Churches
and other Churches and Christian Traditions

the first consultation in Geneva (1981), the papers dealt with *God's Incommunicability and Communicability* (Emilianos Tymiadis), *The Authority of the Church and in the Church according to the Reformed Tradition* (Hans-Helmut Esser), and *Authority in the Orthodox Church* (Chrysostomos Konstantinidis). It is quite obvious that the participants in the discussions could not understand each other well enough, that further deepening of the problem was necessary. Therefore, during the second consultation in Geneva (1983), both Orthodox and Reformed papers addressed the Authority of the Church in connection with the Holy Trinity: *The Trinitarian Foundation and Character of Faith and Authority in the Church* (Thomas Torrance), *The Trinitarian Structure of the Church and its Authority* (Emilianos Timiadis).

This should be understood on the one hand as a thorough research in and of itself. On the other hand, these two consultations expressed the conviction that the Creed should be understood in an ecclesiological context as a whole. Later on the necessity for such an approach became more and more evident, so that several further dialogue sessions were dedicated to the Creed article regarding the Church.

The Orthodox had usually thought that the differences between the two traditions are obvious in an ecclesiological context. Were they so important that no understanding was possible or were they not as important as originally supposed? It became quite clear that the second possibility was accepted, as long as the dialogue started on the basis of these two consultations.

Last but not least, one should note that the Orthodox were able to better understand who their partner in dialogue really was. They were confident now that both traditions had a similar understanding of authority in the Church and of its Trinitarian foundation.

Proceedings and Results of the Dialogue

As regards the content of the different sessions, they were summarized in several statements, according to the different articles of the Nicene Creed, the first objective of the dialogue agreed upon.

The Trinitarian articles of the Creed were carefully dealt with during the first three sessions, and this does not point only to their significance for Christian self-understanding but also to the dedication of the commission members, to the thoroughness of their theological work. The participants in these sessions even managed to put forward some new theological concepts, in order to avoid difficulties between the Eastern and Western tradition such as the whole *filioque* problem. According to this model, it is not possible to approach the monarchy of the Father apart from the perichoretical communion between all the three persons of the Holy Trinity. Therefore, one should not speak about a monarchy of the Father alone, but of a monarchy of the Father and the Spirit with regard to the Son and of the Father and the Son with regard to the Spirit. In my opinion, this concept offers a better understanding of the problem starting from the Holy Tradition and this should be welcomed as a theological achievement as such and as a pattern for the imperative creativity of ecumenical dialogues. At the same time, this perichoretical monarchy should by no means abandon the personal identity of the three persons and especially that of the Father: He is only *arche* in the Trinity and the two other persons do not participate in this action as its subjects. On the other hand, the Father does not stay alone when begetting the Son or proceeding the Spirit, but each time stays in communion with one of the two other persons.

The discussions on Christology took place in Kappel and Limassol and produced important convergences too, like the connection between Trinitarian and Christological theology, the history of salvation and the biblical history of Jesus of Nazareth as complementary approaches to Christology. In the context of the Lord's person, the participants in the dialogue were able to articulate convergences with regard to the common elements between the divine and the human as a necessary precondition of any communion, on the one hand, and on the dynamic character of the relation between *nature* and *hypostasis*, on the other. This last aspect reveals the creative dimension of ecumenical dialogues and demonstrates that convergences cannot be reached by reduction, but by searching for new possibilities to formulate a common point of view without any loss of confessional identity of the participants.

Having thoroughly discussed the Holy Trinity and the person of Jesus Christ, the commission was in the position to strive for a handle on the difficult issue of the Church, in which the Lord is being made present to the faithful through the *oikonomia* of the Holy Spirit, as one can read in the last chapter of the Limassol Agreed Statement. Aberdeen, Zakynthos, Pittsburgh, Sibiu, Beirut were the stations on this long journey. The participants in the dialogue succeeded in finding important convergences again, on issues like: the possibility of an ecclesiology "from above" and one "from below," reflecting the two natures of Christ; the understanding of the Church as an absolute reality of communion with God and his creation; the possibility to speak about "a first Church" referring to the primordial communion between God and the angels, which was extended upon the reality of Paradise; the incorporation through baptism into the Church which is the Body of Christ of those who receive the Gospel and freely believe in it; the reality of a communion between God and the departed; the intensive catholicity of the Church as experienced in the Eucharistic communion and its extensive dimension which means the all embracing communion with God of all those who experience, in the Church, the restoration of their image and likeness of God.

So many convergences! On everything? Almost, but not quite! For example, the two sides were able to express in one voice their conviction about God's communion with the departed, but could not make together the next logical step leading to a common understanding of the saints and of the *communio* sanctorum. Similarly it was not possible to have an agreement upon the meaning of apostolic succession or the unity of Baptism, Chrismation and Eucharist and upon the moment of their administration.

Beyond these fully or only partly reached convergences, I want to draw attention to a particular perspective opened at the end of the Common Statement adopted in Pittsburgh: "Both the Orthodox and the Reformed are certain that their convergence on the fundamental doctrines of the Trinity and Christology and their common acceptance of the Scriptures constitute a sufficient basis for building up greater convergence in the future by the Lord's grace and inspiration." First of all we notice here the image of an ecumenical process with several stages, the discussions concluded with the Common Statement being just a basis to build upon if the will of God be so. At the same time, the structure of the process is worth noticing: one agreement is the basis of another one and so on, within an architecture based upon different levels of mutual understanding.

The last meeting in the dialogue, Volos 2007, was dedicated to Eschatology and reached more convergences than one might have expected. This was possible because both sides share the same belief in the salvific communion with the Lord Jesus Christ in the Church. When I say that the Volos statement went beyond expectations I have in mind the acceptance by both sides of a communion with the Lord after earthly death. At the same time, some differences retained a certain significance since the intercession of the living for the departed could not be explained clearly enough to the Reformed to enable them to accept this possibility of communion between the two realms of existence.

In connection with the Trinitarian and Christological articles of the Creed, we noticed important attempts to find new models of understanding and of deepening the common experience. We also put forward the outstanding significance of such an enterprise for the progress of ecumenical discussions. In Volos, efforts of that kind were missing, the participants concentrated upon the first step of any ecumenical reflection, the common elements of faith, which can be articulated together. This is why some questions were left aside and have been waiting for a response ever since. I mention just one, which is of major importance in our globalized world where we meet people with various religious identities or with no religious commitment at all. Does God leave them outside the circuit of salvation, although He has decided the place of their birth or religious socialization? If not, how are they going to experience personal communion with Christ, according to Orthodox self-understanding a necessary condition of salvation? One might say that questions of the kind are collateral, at this stage of a dialogue, but I would with no hesitation reject such an argument, keeping in mind the tensions we have been confronted with in the Middle East for some time. Ecumenical dialogues should

Part V: Bilateral Dialogues between Eastern Orthodox Churches
and other Churches and Christian Traditions

bring us closer by deepening the understanding of our common faith in connection with the moment in time given to each of us. Having mentioned some of the questions, which are still to be raised, we can turn now to some shortcomings of the dialogue.

Shortcomings

The previous sections of this analysis outline some of the important achievements of this dialogue, both on the level of its actual content and with regard to the method of research the participants used. Nevertheless, the regular flow of sessions was abruptly interrupted. Why? The causes are various, most certainly, and we cannot open an exhaustive discussion on that. But it is possible for us to enumerate some of the shortcomings that emerged during the different stages of the dialogue.

The level of preliminaries

In the beginning of this analysis, we gave a positive appreciation of the preparations for the dialogue and we reaffirm it here. At the same time, we can identify a methodological deficiency at this level, without which the results of the discussions might have been even more fruitful. I mean the absence of discussions regarding the method of reading and understanding the Scriptures, the philosophical and historical background of Orthodox and Reformed theology and of the different understanding of contemporary society with its challenges.

The differences between the Orthodox and Western ways of new testamentary exegesis have been known for quite a long time, they are more or less taken for granted in any dialogue. Being aware of their existence is a good start for communication, but basing the discussions on them without an analysis of their origins, of the way they function and their outcome is something completely different. I do not want to say that the Orthodox methods are better than the Western ones or vice versa, each of them might be of an equal value. This is not the point. What is important is that they operate under different premises and have different results, all of them valuable according to one method or another. During theological discussions one should know which method is being used and on which level one should expect one or the other result. Let me give an example to make my point clear: Genesis 1 is regarded by the Orthodox as the broad framework of the whole history of salvation, whereas Western scholars regard it mainly as a document of the Hebrews and consider its significance from this narrow point of view. Without understanding the other's assumption and keeping in mind only one's own, his line of argument would seem totally wrong, although it actually deals with a completely different situation. Having mutually understood each other's premises, the arguments would not be contradictory anymore but complementary.

The differences regarding the philosophical and historical background of the theological discourse are of equal importance. It is not my intention to explore this idea now, but the problem is quite similar with the previous one. Without knowing these backgrounds and their terminological expression one might imagine differences, which actually are not there. What does an Orthodox theologian understand when a Reformed speaks about *signum*, or the Reformed theologian when the Orthodox speaks about *symbolon*? Is the Orthodox able to explain the theology of the icon in terms of the *signum* theology of Calvin? In my opinion, these different outlooks are usually not contradictory, but in order to reach convergences their specific logical structure should be made clear from the very beginning or at least when it obviously becomes necessary, so that the dialogue can continue successfully.

Last but not least, on the same level of preliminaries, the various accents specific to Orthodox and Reformed, to any Christian experience should be taken into account. The partners in dialogue do not come from an own ideal world; behind each of them lies a complex history, they live in non-identical environments; whilst they might have similar expectations, this is up to a certain point only. This dimension of identity cannot be severed from its spiritual counterpart, the two are complementary and it is not possible to understand one without the other. Theological dialogues do not consider this horizontal aspect of Christian life. On the contrary, keen to reach doctrinal and spiritual convergences, which have separated the two sides for longer or shorter periods of time, they usually ignore it as much as they can. The same happened during the dialogue between the Orthodox and the Reformed. The participants made great efforts with respect to the Nicean Creed, but did not pay attention to the changes in attitude brought about by the needs of contemporary society and by globalization. A direct cause for the temporary or permanent interruption of the dialogue was such a shift taking place within the Reformed family, on the level of internal organization and of theological interest. On the one hand, this led to the transition from the World Alliance of Reformed Churches to the World Communion of Reformed Churches, which wasn't purely formal.[4] On the other, this organizational change went hand in hand with an increased interest in the social dimension of Christian life and a decreased interest in fundamental theological reflection, as the one on the Creed had been. In my opinion, this last development has led to the, hopefully, short-term interruption of the dialogue sessions and could have been avoided from the very beginning by considering the complementarity of theological reflection and neighbourly love as inseparable dimensions of genuine Christian existence. At the same time, the new WCRC Constitution expresses its fidelity to the Tradition of the Church as formulated by the Ecumenical Councils[5] and encourages ecumenical dialogues,[6] so that this special dialogue might have a future, after all.

The Level of Theological Reflection

There are three main aspects in multilateral dialogues that I want to refer to. The first is related to a coherent theology of alterity, the second to the integration, by each sub-commission separately, of the, at times, different theological perspectives of its own members on certain items. They should be discussed in beforehand, so that each sub-commission can articulate unitary points of view during the dialogue session itself. The last problem refers to the mutual knowledge about the other's theological perspective.

As far as the theology of alterity is concerned, one can remark that the ecumenical movement has developed three models - "organic unity", "conciliar fellowship" and "reconciled diversity" – which refer directly to the unity of the Church/Churches. They have been useful, but not sufficient as a satisfactory basis of Christian efforts aiming for final unity mainly because the Orthodox and Roman-Catholics could not express the plenitude of their faith by means of these models. It is quite obvious that the participants in dialogues should take a step back and develop a general theology of alterity, acceptable for everybody, in order to have a new understanding of the three models of relation between the unity of the Church and the alterity of confessional experiences. Such a theology of alterity should refer to all kinds of diversities, going hand in hand with a complementary unity. A model of the kind was already put forward by the Orthodox Metropolitan Georges Khodr in 1971, in connection with religious pluralism.[7]

According to the Lebanese hierarch, the *oikonomia* of the Holy Spirit, related to the *oikonomia* of Jesus Christ, does not only achieve a balance between religious unity and diversity, with eschatological accomplishment, but should also lead to a Christian humbleness in relation to the faithful belonging to other religions.

---

[4] Details on the transition from WARC to WCRC can be found on the web-page of the new organization: http://www.wcrc.ch/

[5] We read in Article 2: 'The World Communion of Reformed Churches is committed to embody a Reformed identity as articulated in the historic Reformed confessions and the Ecumenical Creeds of the early church, and as continued in the life and witness of the Reformed community': http://www.wcrc.ch/sites/default/files [accessed September 4, 2013]

[6] Article III – Identity: 'Engaging other ecumenical organizations and churches of other traditions in the ecumenical movement through dialogue and cooperation in ministry.'

[7] Georges Khodr, 'Christianity in a Pluralistic World,' first time published in the *Ecumenical Review* in 1971 and four years later in the WCC collective volume *The Orthodox Church in the Ecumenical Movement. Documents and Statements 1902 - 1975*, (Geneva: World Council of Churches, 1978).

Part V: Bilateral Dialogues between Eastern Orthodox Churches
and other Churches and Christian Traditions

In my opinion, this model could be extrapolated for inter-Christian relations, in order to develop a similar attitude amongst Christians in dialogue. This would make it possible to include all efforts towards unity in everyone's communion with God, in one's Christian identity, where they actually belong. The reception of ecumenical efforts in Christian self-understanding could convey a new dimension to interconfessional theological dialogues on all levels, because their main purpose would not be discussions upon certain issues only, but equally and mainly communion with Christ within the *oikonomia* of the Holy Spirit. It is my belief that under such circumstances the already important results of the dialogue between the Orthodox and Reformed Churches would reach even higher levels of convergences and that the sessions themselves would not be interrupted anymore. Because which Christian theologian would consciously interrupt his communion with the Lord himself?

The theological discourse practiced within any denomination participates in this dialectic of unity and multiplicity. There is a common doctrinary body shared by all or at least the great majority of the theologians belonging to one denomination or another and the peculiar way to understand and express it by each theologian. Constant common reflection, or sharing publications within a specific linguistic space make sure that personal understanding is not separated from the unitary vision on different issues. It is even more important to have such permanent exchanges when theologians belong to different linguistic expressions of one and the same denomination. It is a well-known fact that differences in language always go along with differences in perception and expression of what is common. At the same time, human frailty tends to overvalue one's own expression and undervalue that of others. This obviously happened in the Ancient Church between the Orthodox and Old Oriental Churches, as the results of the contemporary dialogue between them clearly show. Differences in communication lead to divisions, they do not promote unity and give few opportunities for overcoming them. The only way to overcome this difficulty is to consciously share the common Christian experience of one's specific denominational identity by prayer and theological reflection.

These considerations refer to the unity and multiplicity of theological discourse as such and to the dialogue between the Orthodox and Reformed Churches. The discussions had fruitful results as long as the participants on each side shared the same understanding and were less fruitful when this common view was missing, to a certain extent at least. I might even say that one of the causes for the temporary interruption of the sessions has been this diminished common understanding or expression of confessional insights on each side. This leads me to the conclusion that preliminary thorough discussions between the commission members participating in dialogue are a necessary condition for ecumenical rapprochement.

Closely related to the problem of preliminary discussions is that of commission members being well informed about the positions defended by dialogue partners. As an Orthodox, for instance, it is necessary for me to have a clear idea of the Reformed position on the topics, which are to be discussed in beforehand, so that I can compare it with my own. This makes it possible to concentrate upon the accurateness of my understanding during the dialogue session itself, to correct it where necessary and to seek more elements of convergence than I might have originally expected.

I must confess that during the different dialogue sessions between the Orthodox and Reformed Churches I participated in, including the last one, this preliminary understanding of the other's position has almost never been practiced, with one or two exceptions. One may argue that knowing the other's theological arguments might induce preconceived notions with regard to one's dialogue partner, but I think that that the likelihood of this happening is small as long as commission members are nominated according to criteria of a well balanced personality, with enough communicatory experience.

An easy way of meeting this exigency might be the exchange of a minimal bibliography between the two sides in dialogue, with the possibility of discussing what one side thinks about the theological position of the other during those preliminary meetings I mentioned above.

The Spiritual Dimension of the Dialogue

There exists a general agreement about necessity of making efforts to achieve Christian unity. Because the Lord himself asked his disciples to experience unity as he does with the Father; and because the majority of Christians did experience such a unity during a long part of their history. One may think that these are good reasons for all participants in dialogues to do every possible effort to overcome apartness and achieve unity. And they do a lot, but most of them not enough. After hundreds of years Christians belonging to different traditions and denominations have got used to separation, they do not feel communion with the other as an absolute imperative, necessary for their own communion with God. The necessity of unity has become an important idea for Christians to grapple with, but not a reality to experience at all levels of their lives.

A solid theology of alterity, based on the *oikonomia* of the Holy Spirit, connected with the *oikonomia* of Jesus Christ, shows that I am able to experience communion with the Lord only through communion with the other Christian, even though he might have a different denominational identity. Under these circumstances, looking for communion with somebody belonging to a different Church means looking for communion with the Lord. Theological dialogue becomes an *askesis*, one could even say, together with the late Orthodox theologian of the Ecumenical Patriarchate of Romanian background, André Scrima, that there is an *askesis* of dialogue, of the encounter, and this means that we should try "to die for the other in order to resurrect together with him, that we should become the other, that we should not be afraid of him and lack confidence in him."[8]

From this point of view, during the dialogue sessions the participants in the dialogue between the Orthodox and the Reformed should first of all look for spiritual growth by means of their communion in Christ through the power of the Holy Spirit. I firmly believe that this is what the Lord himself expects from me, as an Orthodox member of this ecumenical body. I have not paid enough attention to the life of my Reformed brothers, have not been willing to understand well enough their communion with Christ the Lord in the Holy Spirit. I have not been able to experience my own communion with Christ by means of my communion with this Reformed partner in dialogue. With any partner in dialogue, irrespective of his/her denominational background. It is high time for a change in this respect so that the theological dialogue itself becomes a way to experience my communion with the Lord in the Holy Spirit.

As stated in the introduction to this analysis, when dealing with the theological dialogue between the Orthodox Churches and the Reformed Churches, it has been our intention to consider some problems of theological dialogues at a time when their effectiveness seized to be as obvious as it used to be. Having reflected upon preliminaries, proceedings, achievements and shortcomings, we suddenly discover that these dialogues are very much alive, that they go up and down, that they stop for a while, but not in order to give up but to prepare a new start. We feel in this dynamics something that surpasses our human good will and gives substance and perspective to our efforts. It is the Holy Spirit who drives us ahead and guides us towards a future when we shall be able to experience our communion with Christ explicitly by deepening our mutual theological understanding and communion. Along this path, we shall experience important achievements on a theological and human level, we shall be confronted with shortcomings originating in our sinful conditions, but in the end we shall be able to praise the Almighty God who opens His heart for us in Christ the Lord through the Holy Spirit.

Bibliography

Ioniţă Viorel, "The Vision of Unity in the Multilateral Dialogues and in the Bilateral Dialogues of the Orthodox Churches with the Other Churches," *Studii Teologice*, series 3, 4.3 (2008): 7-58.

---

[8] André Scrima , *Duhul Sfânt şi unitatea bisericii: "Jurnal" de conciliu,* (Bucharest: Ed. Anastasia, 2004), 214.

Part V: Bilateral Dialogues between Eastern Orthodox Churches
and other Churches and Christian Traditions

Khodr Georges, 'Christianity in a Pluralistic World,' first time published in the *Ecumenical Review* in 1971 and four years later in the WCC collective volume *The Orthodox Church in the Ecumenical Movement. Documents and Statements 1902 - 1975*, (Geneva: World Council of Churches, 1978).

Oancea Dorin, 'The Theological Bilateral Dialogue between the Orthodox Churches and the World Alliance of Reformed Churches. An Evaluation from an Orthodox Point of View,' was published in the papers of the Member Churches Consultation on Dialogues between Orthodox and other CEC Member Churches, Reseptio 1 (2009): 32-43.

'Orthodox-Reformed international dialogue: convergences on the doctrine of the Church (1886-2005),' *Reformed World* 57.1 (2007).

Scrima André, *Duhul Sfânt şi unitatea bisericii: "Jurnal" de conciliu*, (Bucharest: Ed. Anastasia, 2004), 214

Torrance Thomas F., *Theological dialogue between Orthodox and Reformed churches*, (Edinburgh: Clark Constable, 1985).

WORLD COMMUNION OF REFORMED CHURCHES (WCRC) *THE CONSTITUTION*: http://www.wcrc.ch/sites/default/files [accessed 4 September 2013].

Vachicouras Gary, *Historical Survey on the International Bilateral Dialogues of the Orthodox Church*, Orthodox Centre of the Ecumenical Patriarchate Chambésy/Geneva. Available online: http://www.deltapublicaciones.com/derechoyreligion/gestor/archivos [accessed 4 September 2013].

(77) Orthodox Dialogue with the Roman Catholic Church

Metropolitan Chrysostomos-Georges Savvatos

The official inauguration of the theological dialogue between the Orthodox and the Roman Catholic Church (Patmos-Rhodes, 1980) marked the transition from the "Dialogue of Charity" (1960-1980) to the "Dialogue on Truth" (1981). It builds on the decisions of the Third Pre-Conciliar Pan-Orthodox conference (Geneva 1986) and the Official document of the Second Vatican Council "Unitatis Redintegratio" (1965). The official theological dialogue in its present form differs from the past as regards both methodology and the conditions of the unifying efforts. The unifying efforts at the earlier stage were characterized either by serving expediency of political power and ecclesiastical administration, or by the methods that were different from what the canonical tradition of the Church teaches.

The theological dialogue between the Orthodox and the Roman Catholic Church at its present stage develops on the following principle:

1. Equal terms for all its participants.

2. Altough the issues for discussions favour commonalities between the two Churches, they do not exclude discussions on the topics, on which the two Churches have different views.

3. The discussions are confined to the first millennium before the schism 1054. They build on the common traditions (theological, liturgical, and canonical) of the historically undivided Church.

4. The final word in reception of the common theological texts of the dialogue belongs only to the Churches, not to their delegations to the dialogue.

The dialogue started with the discussions on the topics of ecclesiology: the identity of the Church (Munich, 1982), its relations with the Mysteries of the Church (Bari, 1987), and importance of sanctification and the 'apostolic succession' for the unity of the Church (New Valamo, 1988). Theological documents, which were produced during these sessions, constituted the theological basis for further discussions on issues in which the two ecclesiastic traditions converged and diverged. For example, paragraphs 53 and 55 of the document of New Valamo (1988) pointed out the primarily ecclesiological issue that differentiates the two Churches, the primacy of the bishop of Rome.

Preparations for the 6th plenary session (1990), which was to discuss the issue 'Ecclesiological and canonical conditions of the sacramental structure of the Church. Synodicity and authority in Church,' were impeded by the developments in the Eastern Europe, particularly the reemergence of the proselytizing activity of Unia. Those events modified the agenda of the dialogue. At the beginning of the second decade of the dialogue, the main subjects of the discussions were not ecclesiological, but political and inter-ecclesial: Unia and proselytism. Both of them were rejected by the Orthodox as method and as ecclesiastical phenomena. They were condemned as contrary to the principles of the Orthodox ecclesiology and the common theological and ecclesiological tradition of the two Churches. It was agreed that Unia cannot be a model of the union of the Churches.

The issues of Unia (Eastern Catholicism) and proselytism were discussed for the first time in New Valamo (1988) and then exclusively during the meetings in Vienna (1990), Freising - Munich (1990), Ariccia (1991), Balamand - Lebanon (1993), and Baltimore (USA) (2000). These meetings resulted in publication of the document entitled: 'The ecclesiological and normal effects of the Unia,' which was not accepted by all the Orthodox Churches.

Discussions on Unia and frictions between the Orthodox put the dialogue on hold from 2000 to 2005. During this period, the two Churches had time to assess its results and to decide about its future. In the meantime, the difficulties around Unia in the Eastern Europe and the Middle East aggravated. They caused an anti-ecumenical mood in some Orthodox Churches. Hyper-conservatism that grew on this grounds incured negative reception of the dialogue. It questioned the necessity of the dialogue and validity of the its common documents.

Five years of pause (2000-2005) helped the Churches to address these issues. Coordinated effort by the Ecumenical Patriarchate, and particularly its Orthodox co-chair Metropolitan John of Pergamon (Zizioulas) reestablished consensus of all the Primates of the Orthodox Churches about continuation of the dialogue. The Joint Theological Committee relaunched its work. It continued on the same principles that had been elaborated in the document of Moscow (1990). Later on, they were more clarified by the Coordinating Committee in Rome (2005) and during two plenary sessions in Belgrade (2006) and Ravenna (2007).

The document of Ravenna (2007) constituted continuity of the three previous documents (Munich 1982, Bari 1987, New Valamo 1988). It should not be considered an independent or autonomous theological document. It expresses the consensus of the Churches and at the same time reflects the ascertained or existing differences and divergences. The subject of the document of Ravenna is 'The Ecclesiological and Canonical Consequences of the Sacramental Nature of the Church. Ecclesiastical Communion, Synodality and Authority.'

The three previous texts discussed identity of the Church (Munich 1982: 'The Mystery of the Church and the Eucharist in the Light of the Mystery of the Holy Trinity'), the mystical structure of the Church (Bari 1987: 'Faith, Sacraments and the Unity of the Church in the light of the Mystery of the Holy Trinity'), and the importance of priesthood for the unity of the Church (New Valamo 1988: 'The Sacrament of Order in the Sacramental Structure of the Church, with particular Reference to the Importance of the Apostolic Succession for the Sanctification and Unity of the People of God'). The document of Ravenna (2007) went further and touched on the common tradition of the two Churches concerning the expressions of ecclesiastical unity, as well as three-levels synodality (local, regional, and universal). Synodality was defined on the basis of the 34th Apostolic canon. According to this canon, the first bishop of each church cannot act unless he has consent of the other bishops. The document of Ravenna gave a solution to the issues regarding the relationship of primacy and conciliarity at local and regional levels. At the same time, the role of the bishop of Rome as the 'first' among the Patriarchs on the universal level and in the frame of functioning of the seven Ecumenical Councils, was left for further discussions.

This issue was considered by the plenary of the Joint Commission (Vienna 2010). The discussions continued at the meetings of the new Constitutional and coordination committee (Rethymno 2011, Rome 2011), which worked according to the instructions from the Plenary Joint Theological Commission in Vienna. They concentrated on the role of the bishop of Rome in the Church during the first millennium. The work of the Joint Theological Commission for the Dialogue between the Orthodox and the Roman Catholic Churches continues in the same vein.

It has been rightly pointed out that 'the dialogue with the Roman Catholics will be definitively and irrevocably decided by the attitude of the Roman Catholics on the issue of Pope's primacy' and particularly by the way they understand its function and its implementation on the universal level, in relation to the institutions of the Patriarchs' Pentarchy and the Ecumenical Council. The primacy of the bishop of Rome should be examined in the context of the common tradition of the seven Ecumenical Councils, the canonical tradition of the Council of Constantinople (879-880), and the decisions of the Councils of Pisa (1409), Constance (1414-1418), Basel (1431-1442), and Trent (1545-1563). This will help determine a balanced outlook at the relations between the bishop of Rome as Primate and the body of bishops on the universal level. Interpretations of the primacy of the bishop of Rome as political or superior to other Churches will put the theological dialogue on hold. For the Orthodox Church, primacy is acceptable, provided that it differs from any authoritarianism. It should be understood as primacy of honour: first among equals - *primus inter pares*.

A second problem, which stays on the agenda of the dialogue is Uniatism. This issue interrupted the dialogue during its second decade (1990-2000). It requires further examination in the context of the discussions on the role of the bishop of Rome during the second millennium. At this point, the issue of the Unate Churches has to do with their own ecclesiological self-understanding and their historical origins. The question is whether these Churches accept their ecclesiological identity and how it can be grounded in the history of the undivided Church. The text of Freising can provide a basis for the discussions on this issue.

Finally, the question remains about the practical implementation of the texts of the dialogue, 'whether the two Churches want or are able to put into practice the joint decisions' and the common texts. This problem remains a concern not only for the dialogue between the Orthodox and the Roman Catholic Churches, but also for any other bilateral theological dialogue, as well as the entire ecumenical movement. As regards the Orthodox - Roman Catholic dialogue, its texts remain working papers. The process of their reception and approval by the two Churches depends on the structural differences of these Churches. For the Orthodox, acceptance of the common texts is a matter of the local Churches, which may have different positions. As for the Roman Catholic Church, it often applies either the tactics of 'prevention' or 'treatment'. Prior to the acceptance of common theological texts, committees and official bodies of this Church circulate 'interpretative guidelines' or 'interpretative letters', which 'preventively' suggest the content of the text as it should be. The Roman Catholic Church can also communicate its positions through papal encyclicals and decrees, which try to explain any theological divergences on the principles of the First and Second Vatican Councils. In the theological dialogue between the Orthodox and the Roman Catholic Church, there will always be problems, but we should not forget that we are involved in a dialogue 'for the sake of truth' and we cannot do anything 'against truth' (2 Cor 13:8).

Bibliography

Catholiques et Orthodoxes. Les enjeux de l'uniatisme dans le sillage de Balamand. Documents d'Eglise, (Paris: Comité mixte Catholique – Orthodoxe en France, 2004).

Vl. Pheidas, *Presupposes fontamentaux pour un dialogue thédogipus officiel entre l'Eglise Orthodoxe et l'Eglise Roman,* (Vienna 1976).

W. Kasper (ed). *Il ministero petrino. Cattolici e Orthodossi in dialogo,* (Citta Nuova-Roma 2004).

Gr. Liantas, *Inter-Orthodox Diaconate of the Ecumenical Patriarchate and the Church of Greece and the contribution of the two Churches in the bilateral theological dialogues with the Roman Catholic Church and the Church of Palaiokatholikon,* (Thessaloniki 2005) (in Greek).

Chrysostomos Savvatos, *The papal primacy in the dialogue between the Orthodox and the Roman Catholics,* (Athens 2006) (in Greek).

Idem, *The problem of the ecclesiastical acceptance of the joint texts of the Theological Dialogue between the Orthodox and the Roman Catholic Church,* (Athens 2008) (in Greek).

*Part V: Bilateral Dialogues between Eastern Orthodox Churches
and other Churches and Christian Traditions*

(78) ORTHODOX DIALOGUE WITH THE ANGLICAN CHURCH

Bogdan Lubardić

1. History and legacy

The official and unofficial relations between the Anglican and Orthodox Church, complex as they are, may be paradigmatically displayed by the work and results of the International Commission for Anglican-Orthodox Theological Dialogue (ICAOTD, the Commission, the Dialogue). Although specific in its own right, the Commission is a reflection of the long history of relations forged by the two Churches. The points of departure for the establishment of the mentioned relations may be sought in various historical events, not excluding the ecclesial and theological goals these events presuppose. These may be seen in the establishment, say, of the "Greek College" in Oxford (1699–1705); in the 19th-century Anglican missions to traditional Orthodox countries and *vice versa*; and the establishment of Anglican jurisdictions in Orthodox territories; in the mutual engagements during the 20th-century[1] – with their specific forms and contents that emerged before and after the two Great wars (*e.g.* the Anglican and Eastern Churches Association established in 1919, the ground-breaking Lambeth Conference of 1920[2], the arrival of Greek and Russian émigrés in England and the establishment of the Fellowship of St Albans and St Sergius since 1928 or, say, the Anglican-Orthodox Conference in Bucharest 1935 *etc*); and in other multifarious Anglican-Orthodox ecumenical events leading to the immediate present. In fact, the continuous interest of both Churches in the fundamentals of Christian life and doctrine – in living and re-living the sources (*pegai*) – does show that the point of departure is the Church itself: its history, teaching and tradition.

However, the inception of the Commission proper is a relatively recent event. It stems from the initiatives taken by both sides during the 1960s. The setting up of the Commission – which was initially named as the Anglican-Orthodox Joint Doctrinal Discussions (AOJDD), renamed as ICAOTD in 1990 at New Valamo – came to fruition officially in 1966. The key figures responsible for this remarkable event are the Archbishop of Canterbury, Dr Michael Ramsey, and the Ecumenical Patriarch, Athenagoras I of Constantinople. After the talks between the two distinguished primates of our Churches, in 1962, the initiative to *resume* dialogue was backed in 1964 by the Third Pan-Orthodox Conference at Rhodes. This was subsequently ratified by all the Orthodox Churches. A century[3] of prolonged official effort thus came to be summarized and reopened in view of hope for reaching reunion between the two Churches. As Archbishop Basil of Brussels, an eminent member of the AOJDD, notably remarked: "... the aim of our Dialogue is that we may eventually be visibly united in one Church" (AOD v). This has its corollary in the Lambeth Conference 1978 Resolution 35:2 which affirms that the aim is "... to explore the fundamental questions of doctrinal agreement and disagreement of our Churches" (AOD 3).

The Dialogue then entered a succession of organizational and theological stages. A series of changes regarding form and method followed suit. The main stages may be listed as follows: (1) the inceptive stage 1962–66 (*i.e.* the negotiations on resuming dialogue); (2) the preparatory stage 1966–72 (characterized by the fact that

---

[1] Colin Davey, "Anglican-Orthodox Dialogue 1920-1976," In: K. Ware and C. Davey (eds.), *Anglican Orthodox Dialogue: The Moscow Agreed Statement*, (London: SPCK, 1977), 4-36.

[2] Of special importance is Resolution 9 of this Lambeth Conference regarding Christian reunion.

[3] The Eastern Churches Association was founded in 1864. The latter then merged with the Anglican and Eastern Churches Union (founded in 1906) which in 1914 evolved into the Anglican and Eastern Churches Association.

the Anglican and Orthodox Commissions met separately); (3) the first series of joint conversations 1973–76 (these were discussions dedicated to the articulation and understanding of set theological topics): the latter resulted in the first agreed statement of the two Churches, namely *The Moscow Agreed Statement* (MAS 1976); (4) the second series of joint conversations 1976–84, with a particular interim "crisis period" 1976–78: these led to the second agreed statement, namely *The Dublin Agreed Statement* (DAS 1984); (5) the third series of joint conversations 1984–2006, again coupled with a "tense and fractious"[4] period (1984–89) followed by a "turning" point in 1990: these gave fruition in the third agreed statement, namely *The Cyprus Agreed Statement* (CAS 2006); (6) finally, the Dialogue is currently in its most recent stage, *i.e.* the fourth series of joint conversations, inaugurated as such in 2009, with the aim of reaching yet another agreed statement. Hence, in the post-60s era the Dialogue produced three officially accepted statements on the views that the Anglican and Orthodox Churches share regarding substantial matters of Christian and ecclesial identity, the prospects for reunion notwithstanding.

2. The Agreed Statements

If pressed for a succinct statement recapitulating the positive side of the results achieved in the Agreed statements mentioned, we could declare the following. Namely, a doubtlessly significant quality of mutual *agreement* was reached regarding the pivotal points of our common Christian heritage and ecclesial identity. That is to say, agreement on the:

1) knowledge of God in its trinitarian and ecclesial context (note: although the Orthodox stressed that the energies of God are "God himself in his self-manifestation" and, moreover, that it is through these that humanity may participate in God's divine love, on the way of "divinization by grace" in and through the Church, the Anglicans – while not rejecting this doctrine – cautioned that this language may be misleading and dangerous [MAS 50]);

2) inspiration and authority of Holy Scripture;

3) Scripture and Tradition (note: it was concluded that the relation between the two is intrinsic and correlative, yet the priority of the former was emphasized);

4) authority of the Ecumenical Councils (note: it was stated that the Anglican members of the Dialogue place more emphasis on the first four Councils, and believe that "an order or 'hierarchy' of truths" can be applied to the decisions of the Councils [MAS 53]; this was challenged by the Orthodox on the basis of the unity of faith as a whole; as to the Seventh Council, the Anglicans accept it as a defence of the doctrine of Incarnation, and they agree that the veneration of icons is not problematic, however, they do not hold the view that it can be required of all Christians);

5) *Filioque* clause (note: both sides agree that this clause should not be included in the Niceno-Constantinopolitan Creed [381], one of the reasons being that it was introduced without due catholic consent and without the authority of an Ecumenical Council [MAS 54-55]; however, under certain conditions it may be regarded as a *theologoumenon* of the Church, viz. St Maximus's interpretation of the view of St Augustine on this matter, and Bolotov's view on the matter as such [DAS 26-27]);

6) Church as the eucharistic community; and

7) invocation of the Holy Spirit in the Eucharist (note: the Orthodox found it necessary to stress that the "... deepest understanding of the hallowing of the elements rejects any theory of consecration by *formula**..." [MAS 57]).

All of these topics were gathered, discussed and then (mostly) agreed upon in the *Moscow Agreed Statement*. The ensuing Dublin and Cyprus agreed statements respectively may be regarded as further explications

---

[4] William B. Green, "The Anglican-Orthodox Dialogue and its Future," In: Peter M. Doll, ed., *Anglicanism and Orthodoxy: 300 years after the "Greek College" in Oxford*. (Oxford: Peter Lang, 2006), 383 = abbr. G.

and developments of the issues implicit and explicit in the Moscow statement. The *Dublin Agreed Statement* (1984) focused on the following main topics: (1) The Mystery of the Church, (2) Faith in the Trinity and (3) Worship and Tradition. As Canon Hugh Wybrew (a member of the dialogue since its inception) summarized: "Remarkable agreements were registered in the first section on the mystery of the Church, whose title was itself significant. There was much agreement on the nature of the Church, on the importance of the local church, and on the nature of wider leadership within the Church. Anglicans and Orthodox agreed in rejecting the Roman claim to universal jurisdiction and papal infallibility. There was agreement too on the witness and evangelism as aspects and worship."[5] The *Cyprus Agreed Statement* (2006) paid special heed to the following: (1) The Trinity and the Church, (2) Christ, the Spirit and the Church, (3, 4) Christ, Humanity and the Church, part 1 and 2, (5) *Episcope, Episcopos* and Primacy, (6) Priesthood, Christ and the Church, (7) Women and Men, Ministries in the Church, (8) Heresy, Schism and the Church, and (9) Reception in Communion.

Apart from further grounding the understanding of God as Trinity within an explicitly eucharistic context of the living Church, with the Christological and pneumatological dimensions clearly accentuated, the Cyprus statement is specific by its noteworthy reflection on the nature and effects of *reception* (CAS 98), particularly in view of its two aspects: namely, the Church receives (the divine love of God) and the Church is received (as the salvific event and content of our faith). That having been said, probably the most crucial aspect of the Cyprus document, as Canon Jonathan Goodall remarked, is that "... it was conceived as a means of setting the issue of the ordination of women in the context of all the key theological and ecclesiological considerations that might give the Churches best perspective on what kind of question it was and whether disagreement was (a) sufficient to require our continued sacramental separation and (b) whether the degree of agreement afforded any opportunities to grow closer together, despite the apparent blockage at a 'later' stage."[6] As the Archbishop of Canterbury Rowan Williams said at the press conference for Cyprus report at Lambeth in January 2007: "Based firmly on the scriptures and the Church's tradition, the report has returned to the wellsprings of faith, to take a long run up to the present problems between the Churches." At the same press conference the Orthodox co-chairman of the ICAOTD, Metropolitan John Zizioulas, said:

Neither side on the Commission had been convinced by the other's reasons on women's ordination. The Orthodox are not convinced that the reasons for the ordination of women given from the Anglican side are really so serious and so important as to lead to this change which is, as we all know, an innovation in the tradition. Ordination added nothing essential to women's status. These topics [women's ordination and homosexuality] must be handled with the utmost care so they do not become irremovable obstacles to our communion.

In short, apart from the thorny issues cited, especially during the 1973–76 and 1990–2006 period, the discussions revealed and affirmed, somewhat unexpectedly, a significant quality of agreement on some of the essential aspects of our common Christian identity. This sentiment was strongly affirmed by Metropolitan John of Pergamon (who served as Co-Chairman from 1989 till 2007, having succeeded Archbishop Methodios of Thyateira and Britain). It was Canon William B. Green who conveyed the promising words of Metropolitan John in relation to the Agreed statements (MAS, DAS). As the Metropolitan stated, the agreed statements are "... a mine of theological reflection which shows the extent to which the two Churches share a common faith in spite of their differences on many points" (G 386). But although agreement on some or many essential instances of doctrine is a necessary condition for reunion it is not a *sufficient* condition for reunion. Bearing all of this in mind, and not detracting from the positive results, nevertheless, we should make a note of the fact that the Dialogue and the work of the Commission were troubled by certain considerable problems and challenges. Shedding light on these will help us to further articulate both the positive and negative sides of the joint effort.

---

[5] Hugh Wybrew, "Anglican-Orthodox and Anglican-Roman Catholic Theological Dialogue," *Theoforum* 39.2 (2008): 217-233 = abbr. W.

[6] Shared in an email to the author, dated 15 July 2012.

3. Problems, tensions, breakthroughs

Perhaps the most divisive event, as regarded by the Orthodox members of the Dialogue, was Lambeth Conference's Resolution 21 passed in 1978 on the ordination of *women*. Coupled to this, although as a somewhat later happening, was the possibility in the North American Anglican provinces (in the US and Canada) of the liturgical blessing or ordination of persons in same-sex unions. The immediate reaction to the former was expressed by the Orthodox Co-Chairman Athenagoras I: "... the theological dialogue will continue, although now simply as an academic and informative exercise, and no longer as an ecclesial endeavour aiming at the union of the two churches" (AOD 3; G 382). The reaction was intense enough to warrant a particular meeting of the Commission in Athens (Monastery Pendeli 1978) dedicated solely to this burning issue (*pro et contra* arguments from both sides—reserved and dissenting Anglicans notwithstanding—were included in the Athens Report 1978 [AOD Appendix 2]). These problems, which demonstrably threaten to fracture permanently the ecclesial unity of the Anglican Communion itself, continue also to disturb Anglican-Orthodox relations to the present day. The case of the Episcopal Church in the US, *e.g.* its unilateral affirmative decisions on same-sex marriage and/or homosexuality since 2003, presents a vivid illustration of this problem.

The immediate effects of this development seemed to bear a rather negative outcome. Namely, in view of the new circumstances, it was suggested that "professors only" should take part in the Dialogue, without the higher clergy. However, after the initial "shock", which combined dismay and revolt, it was soon grasped that this need not be the case. Presently both the clergy and lay people take part in the Commission's work, including ordained Anglican women (e.g. Dn Christine Hall, and others). In fact, a new and deeper *understanding* of the nature, status and standing of the Dialogue itself was attained. In 1979 the Steering committee of the AOJDD decided that the Full Commission should persist in its work. Therefore, we may summarize the overall results of these processes as follows: (1) it was understood that the Commission is "not required to solve outstanding problems [...] as a *condition* of continuing the dialogue" (AOD 5); (2) it was understood, although painfully, that the goal of full visible union of the two Churches is not to be expected as something granted or as something that awaits us in the near future; and, nevertheless, (3) it was understood that since the Dialogue remains extremely valuable and substantial, new methods of work and reflection need to be conceptualized and procured. That is:

The ultimate aim remains the unity of the two Churches. But the method may need to change in order to emphasise the pastoral and practical dimensions of the subjects of theological discussions. Our conversations are concerned with the *search* for a unity in faith. They are *not* negotiations for immediate full communion. When this is understood the discovery of differences on various matters, though distressing, will be seen as a necessary step on the long road toward that unity which God wills for his Church (AOD 3).

Consequently, by virtue of the growing communal self-awareness, experience and maturity of the members of the Dialogue, qualitatively different levels *of* the "stages" of the Dialogue as such emerged: (1) the first stage, or what we might call the *preparatory* or *propedeutical* stage[7] of "exploring each other's faith and seeking co-operation in mission and service" (AOD 5), and (2) the second stage, or what we might call the *final* or *reunional* stage culminating in the hoped for consummation of full, visible and proper inter-communional unity. Needless to say, *all* the stages the Dialogue has gone through so far fall under the rubric of the *former* – propedeutical or preparatory stage (which is an *era* in its own right). Interestingly enough, and somewhat ironically, one of the areas of considerable rapprochement between the two Churches, attained before the Second World War, in the 1920s,[8] was covered by the willingness of the Orthodox to acknowledge the Anglican clerical orders and

---

[7] See: Anglican Consultative Council 1982 Consultation: Unity by Stages, Section III (a). Note: the Orthodox still reject any notion of this gradual growth through and by stages *if* this is meant to include any form of sacramental inter-communion. However, perhaps it would be truer to say that Anglicans, in fact, do not believe in sacramental communion by stages: but they do believe in ecclesial reconciliation and doctrinal affirmation by stages.

[8] Encyclical of the Ecumenical Patriarchate, 1920. In: Constantine G. Patelos, ed. *The Orthodox Church in the Ecumenical Movement*, (Geneva: WCC, 1978), 40-43.

ordination as expressions of authentic apostolic succession and ecclesial continuity. (A paradigmatic illustration of this is the Ecumenical Patriarchate's decision, inaugurated on 28 July 1922, followed by the Church of Cyprus and patriarchates of Jerusalem [1923], Alexandria [1930] and Romania [1936], to recognize that the rite of ordination [*hierothesia*] of the Anglican clergy and the apostolic succession of Anglican bishops – have "the same validity as those of the Roman, Old Catholic, and Armenian Churches..." In all truth, this decision soon met with opposition from other Orthodox churches and parties concerned, *i.e.* the Karlovci Synod 1935, the Moscow Conference 1948. In other words, it was never raised to a level of pan-Orthodox official approval. It seems that this favourable "agreement" is now even more remote, not least due to the aforementioned burning issues [even in 1922 the decision was conditioned by the expectation that Anglicans would become "fully" Orthodox in faith and substance, so as to make the decision valid *in practice*]). Still, in time, the Anglican-Orthodox dialogue has made other significant gains both in terms of the topical agreements listed previously and in terms of a new understanding of the goals and method themselves of the Dialogue.

4. Current challenges and future prospects

This new understanding may be seen as the emergence of a wholly new way of existence and operation of the ICAOTD, or Dialogue as such, prospects of which started to germinate in the post-Valamo 1990 period, leading to the present. We have moved from "wintry" and rather pessimistic – at times tumultuous – spells (especially after the events in 1977–78, and 1985–89) to more joyous and rather optimistic "summery" spells (especially after the meeting in New Valamo 1990, and during the fourth series of talks, commenced in Chania, Crete in 2009). As William Green had helped us to learn: before, in the pre-1990 period, as Bishop Max Thomas testified, it was "... as if each side had its massive filing system and when asked questions of one another, each goes into the relevant file and reveals its contents to the other" (G 393); yet now, in the post-1996 period it is different, as John Riches memorably put it: "... it is a conversation of delight and illumination. Like all true conversations, it has had its moments of surprise and strangeness. [...] But then it is good to be drawn into a conversation which engages in profound and sustained reflection on what it is that makes the Church the Church and to affirm, against all the appearances and signs of old age, the hidden life of the Trinity at the heart of our communities..." (G 393).

These words were stated in the paper Riches offered at the meeting in Llandaff (1996). In the meanwhile the Dialogue passed the Cyprus statement and, since the meeting in Crete in 2009, embarked on the mentioned fourth series of joint conversations – addressing the hugely important topic of Christian *anthropology*, or, what it is to be a human being in Christ?[9] This topic was already touched upon in the previous work of the Commission (*e.g.* DAS 9, 24, 26, 32; or Section 7 of CAS pp. 82-88). However, now the meaning of the human being – as created in the "image and likeness" of God – is at the centre of *all* discussions. This means that the next Agreed statement, which has entered its early drafting stage, will be dedicated to Anglo-Orthodox Christian anthropology, geared to address many old and new burning issues which affect our shared humanity in Christ, not least both our fallen and redeemed effects on the political-economic, cultural-social, scientific and cosmic environment, *etc.*

As in previous phases and periods, the newest series of talks have revealed how the Christian traditions of East and West, both spiritually and theologically, both ecclesially and academically, do come together for the betterment of both sides of one faith in our Lord Jesus Christ. The Orthodox, for example, have been thankful for being exposed to the phenomenon of the plurality of the Anglican schools of theological and ecclesiological commitment and political engagement. On the other side (respect to Anglican theology granted), the comprehensiveness of Anglicanism, the ambiguity of its doctrinal formularies, and the varied interpretations they receive, remain a sizeable problem for the Orthodox (and, on occasions, they are reserved to what some

---

[9] Duncan Reid, "Discussion of Theological Anthropology by The International Commission for Anglican-Orthodox Theological Dialogue," in *International Journal of Orthodox Theology* 2.4 (2011): 21-29.

of them think might be a potentially harmful theological liberalism); the Anglicans, for their part, have been appreciative for gaining insight into the balance between the deep spirituality or theological finesse of the Orthodox tradition and its catholic ecclesial expression (yet, on occasions, apart from viewing the Orthodox as tied to an apologetic and somewhat rigid conservatism, as "exclusivist", they have voiced their objections regarding what some of them deem to be a deficit of Orthodox engagement, say, with scriptural theology and hermeneutics, with the role of reason, as well as with political and social affairs and the rights and freedoms of individuals). Therefore, it is deeply significant that the representative of the Moscow Patriarchate, Fr. Cyril Hovorun, holds a view, which is intrinsically analogous to the spirit of the aforementioned words of John Riches. As Hovorun put it:

> „At the preliminary stage of the dialogue, between 1966 and 1972, when Orthodox and Anglicans met separately and shaped agenda for their discussions, one can see from the protocols of the meetings, how many stereotypes both sides had about each other. Then, when the first joint meeting took place in Oxford in 1973 and afterwards, it was interesting to see how both sides started getting rid of those stereotypes. Both sides realized that they need to learn much more about each other. Thus the dialogue turned into a process of learning. This process is continuing now. We still discover treasures in the traditions of each other. It means that our traditions are inexhaustible. When we realize this, it brings us to respecting each other even more. Learning and mutual respect are probably the most important achievements of the dialogue."[10]

Still, and in contrast, the hard fact remains that the hotly debated issues, say, of the ordination of women or same-sex marriage, and others too, in the final count tend to fade in light of the one and most essential point of divergence between the Anglican Communion and the Orthodox Church. Namely, it seems that most, if not all Orthodox participating in the Dialogue recur to the standpoint that it is the Orthodox Church which is *the* Church proper. The more collegial tone, the new understanding of the nature of the Dialogue, reached in recent times, has not been a sufficient tool (nor should it be) to overcome this fundamental point of division. This has been recognized by both sides. For instance, Wybrew is frank and true to the matter when he says that "These agreements, however, were necessarily coupled with a recognition that while Anglicans and Orthodox might broadly agree on the nature of the Church, they differ as to *where** the Church is to be found. Anglicans 'do not believe that they alone are the one true Church, but they believe that they belong to it.[11] Orthodox however believe that the Orthodox Church *is* the one true Church of Christ, which as his Body is not and cannot be divided" (W op. cit; also cf. G 392-393). Not avoiding tough talk and clear words, nevertheless, there is no doubt that we speak a common mind when we conclude that – in avoiding the confessionalist extremes of zealotic denial, of all colour and flavour – we remain together in dialogue, mutual respect and prayerful Christian love. We thus extend our bone naked *solidarity* to each other as a token of belief that it is God's will that we do become one having all things in common (Acts 2:44). Henceforth, against shadows of despondency, if such might arise, the Anglican-Orthodox Dialogue will proceed carefully and discerningly – guided by faith, sustained by hope that God will work his miracle of unity in the one Christ by the Spirit.

Abbreviations

AOD = Henry Hill, Methodios of Thyateira, eds. (1985) *Anglican-Orthodox Dialogue: The Dublin Agreed Statement.* SVSP, Crestwood, NY

---

[10] Shared in an email to the author, dated 9 July 2012.

[11] Or, updating Wybrew's statement, let us quote the most recent formulation—the Anglican Communion Covenant, currently in process of reception across the Communion (article 1.1.1)—each autonomous province of the Communion solemnly "affirms *its communion in* the one, holy, catholic, and apostolic Church, worshipping the one true God, Father, Son, and Holy Spirit".

*Part V: Bilateral Dialogues between Eastern Orthodox Churches
and other Churches and Christian Traditions*

AOJDD = Anglican-Orthodox Joint Doctrinal Discussions
DAS = The Dublin Agreed Statement
CAS = The Cyprus Agreed Statement
ICAOTD = International Commission for Anglican-Orthodox Theological Dialogue
G = Green, W. B. (2006) The Anglican-Orthodox Dialogue and its Future
MAS = The Moscow Agreed Statement
W = Wybrew, H. (2008) Anglican-Orthodox and Anglican-Roman Catholic Theological Dialogue

Bibliography

Ware, K., Davey, C. eds., *Anglican Orthodox Dialogue: The Moscow Agreed Statement*, (London: SPCK, 1977).

Hill, H., Methodios of Thyateira, eds., *Anglican-Orthodox Dialogue: The Dublin Agreed Statement*, (Crestwood, NY: SVSP, 1985).

ICAOTD, *The Cyprus Agreed Statement*, (London: The Anglican Communion Office, 2006)

Wybrew, H, "Anglican-Orthodox and Anglican-Roman Catholic Theological Dialogue," *Theoforum* 39.2 (2008).

Doll, P. M. ed., *Anglicanism and Orthodoxy: 300 years after the "Greek College" in Oxford*, (Oxford: Peter Lang, 2006).

Green, W. B., "The Anglican-Orthodox Dialogue and its Future."

Miller, E. C., *Toward a Fuller Vision: Orthodoxy and the Anglican Experience*, (Wilton, CT: Morehouse-Barlow Co., 1984).

Fouyas, M., *Orthodoxy, Roman Catholicism and Anglicanism*, (London: Oxford University Press, 1972).

Ioan Vasile Leb

It is a well known fact that the Old Catholic Church was born as a reaction to the new papal dogmas introduced by the Council of Vatican I in 1870: papal infallibility and the jurisdictional primacy of the Bishop of Rome, by which he considered himself the leader of the entire Christian world and the last instance of appeal.[1] The opponents who refused to accept these dogmatic innovations formed a separate Church, keeping the Catholic fundaments and eliminating the novelties, becoming a 'Catholicism without Rome.'[2] Having adopted the expression of Vincent of Lerin: 'Id teneamus, quod ubique, quod semper, quod ab omnibus creditum est'[3] as their fundamental principle, the Old Catholics considered themselves a bridge between Catholicism and Orthodoxy. As early as the Congress of Munich, of 22-24 September 1871, they expressed their hope for a reunification with the Eastern Greek and Russian Churches, 'whose separation was operated without sound reasons and is not based on any dogmatic difference that cannot be overcome.'[4] Furthermore, they also took the Anglicans and Protestants into consideration and in short time the first meeting of these denominations' representatives was held in Bonn in 1874.

Despite all the difficulties they were facing – as the Old Catholics had just formed a distinct Church – their relations with the Orthodox Church in view of their reunification were a constant priority in their ecumenical strategy. For them, Orthodoxy was the assurance and support they needed to attain their goal. In its turn, the Orthodox Church manifested a keen interest in the Old Catholics, from the very beginning, as it saw in them the key to the virtual reestablishment of the Old Undivided Church in the West. The Orthodox-Old Catholic relationships had a positive influence on both sides. On the one hand, the Old Catholics found support from the Orthodox, whereas on the other hand, the Orthodox were determined to have more intense discussions with the Western theologians and to study their teachings of faith in detail. The result of this relationship was a theological work produced by the Old Catholics, as well as by the Greek, Russian, Romanian, Bulgarian, Serb, Czech, Polish, Finnish and, lately, the American Orthodox.

Seen from the point of view of the commitment of the two Churches, the history of the effort put into their dialogue can be divided into two great phases, namely an unofficial and an official one. Chronologically, there are four periods to be discerned in the history of this dialogue that are more or less clearly outlined:

The first period (1871-1888)

This was a period for explorations that was later marked by the union conferences held in Bonn, from 1874 to 1875, summoned and presided by the great historian and theologian Ignaz von Döllinger.[5] In 1872, he had held

[1] J. Fr. von Schulte, *Der Altkatholizismus*, (Giessen, 1885, reed. Aalen, 1965); Urs Küry, *Die altkatholische Kirche. Ihre Geschichte, ihre Lehre, ihr Anliegen*, in col. *Die Kirchen der Welt*, Bd. III, (Evangelisches Verlagswerk Stuttgart, 1966); Ioan-Vasile Leb, *Ortodoxie și vechi-catolicism sau ecumenism înainte de Mișcarea Ecumenică* (Orthodoxy and Old-Catholicism or ecumenism before the Ecumenical Movement), (Cluj-Napoca: PUC, 1996).

[2] Victor Conzemius, *Katholizismus ohne Rom. Die altkatholische Kirchengemeinschaft*, (Zürich, Einsiedeln, Köln: Benziger Verlag, 1969).

[3] Gerhard Rauschen, *Des heiligen Vinzenz von Lerin Commonitorium*, in 'Bibliothek der Kirchenväter' (BKV), Bd.XX, 19 and 9, note 1; Marinus Kok, *Vincenz von Lerinum und sein Commonitorium*, in 'Internationale Kirchliche Zeitschrift' (IKZ) 52 (1962): 75–85.

[4] I.V. Leb, *Ortodoxie și vechi-catolicism*, 19.

[5] J. Finsterhölzl, *Ignaz von Döllinger*, (Graz, Wien, Köln: Styria Verlag, 1969); Peter Neuner, *Döllinger als Theologe der Ökumene*, (München: Paderborn, 1979).

his famous speeches in Munich On the reunification of the Christian Churches, which had a great echo in all the contemporary milieus.[6] Old Catholic, Orthodox, Anglican and Protestants theologians participated in the Bonn conferences without having an official commission from their churches. The topics of the discussions were a number of innovations in the ecclesiastical teachings and practices that the Roman Catholic Church had initiated, as well as some highly controversial issues that the Western Churches had had to deal with ever since the Reformation. These issues had to be settled in the spirit of the Tradition of the early Church. As a result of these deliberations held during the first Bonn conference of 1874, the Orthodox, the Anglicans and the Old Catholics agreed upon the following points: 1) the Holy Scripture and the Tradition; 2) the rejection of the 'immaculate conception'; 3) the confession of sins; 4) the penances; 5) the prayer for the dead and 6) the Holy Eucharist.[7]

During the same conference the Old Catholics proposed the adoption of yet another thesis, which stated that it should be acknowledged that the English Church and the churches born from it have kept an unbroken apostolic succession. However, the Orthodox responded that they could not accept this because they did not possess sufficient information in this matter. Finally, the thesis on the veneration of the saints was withdrawn because the Orthodox and the Old Catholics had different views, the latter believing that invoking the saints was not compulsory to every Christian.[8]

Although no accord was reached on all the points put forward, this first conference was a promising start. There was no agreement on the issues of Filioque and papal primacy either, a fact attesting to the inability of the westerners of those times to abandon the old Catholic tradition in which they had been formed. Because even though they agreed on eliminating the Filioque from the Credo, they did not forgo the Catholic understanding of Holy Trinity. On the other hand, the Orthodox manifested their conviction that the teaching of their Church was that which had always been preached by the Church and that they did not wish to make any compromises in this matter; for this reason the efforts had to be carried on by arranging new debates in view of reaching a full accord.[9]

The second union conference of Bonn held between 10-16 August 1875, dealt chiefly with the issue of Filioque.[10] Based on the teachings of Saint John of Damascus, the discussions resulted in the following theses: 1. The Holy Spirit proceeds from the Father as from a unique principle and cause of the Godhead. 2. The Holy Spirit does not proceed from the Son because within the Holy Trinity there is only one principle, one cause, by which all that is within the Godhead is being made manifest. 3. The Holy Spirit proceeds from the Father by the Son. 4. The Holy Spirit is the image of the Son, who is the image of the Father, proceeding from the Father and abiding with the Son, as his resplendent power. 5. The Holy Spirit is personally born from the Father, belongs to the Son, yet he is not from the Son, as he is the Spirit of God's mouth, who expresses the Word. 6. The Holy Spirit is the intercessor between the Father and the Son and is connected to the Father through the Son.[11] Although the proceedings should have also addressed the questions on the Anglican ordinations and the Purgatory, these issues were not discussed.[12] In spite of all this, the two conferences made extraordinary progress, considering those times and the circumstances under which the debates had been held. Although the results of these discussions did not have the desired impact, they did point the direction in which the Old

---

[6] Ignaz von Döllinger, *Über die Wiedervereinigung der christlichen Kirchen. Sieben Vorträge, gehalten zu München im Jahr 1872*, (Nördlingen, 1888). Soon these speeches were translated into English (1872) and French (1880).
[7] Friedrich Heinrich Reusch, *Bericht über die am 14., 15. und 16. September zu Bonn gehaltenen Unionskonferenzen. Im Auftrage des Vorsitzenden Dr. von Döllinger*, (Bonn, 1874), 33–50 (B.I.); I.V. Leb, *Ortodoxie și vechi-catolicism*, 35-36.
[8] *B.I.*, 34-50.
[9] I.V. Leb, *Ortodoxie și vechi-catolicism*, 36-37.
[10] Ibid., 40 and F.H. Reusch, *Bericht über die vom 10. bis 16. August zu Bonn gehaltenen Unionskonferenzen, im Auftrage des Vorsitzenden Dr. von Döllinger*, (Bonn, 1875) (*B.II*); Urs Küry, *Die altkatholische Kirche*, 462-465; Harald Rein, *Kirchengemeinschaft.* Band 2: *Die orthodox-altkatholischen Beziehungen*, (Bern: Peter Lang, 1994), 69-203.
[11] I.V. Leb, *op.cit.*, 45-46.
[12] *B.II*, 94-96.

Catholics had to channel their ecumenical endeavours, particularly turning to the teachings of the ancient, undivided Church.[13] Nevertheless, it seems that this criterion employed by the Old Catholics both in their talks with the Anglicans as well as with the Orthodox, provided them with varying results.[14]

The second phase (1889-1919)

This phase marks the beginning of the official dialogue between the Russian Orthodox Church and the Old Catholic Churches belonging to the Utrecht Union established in 1889 by a decision of the bishops of Holland, Germany and Switzerland, who were joined shortly thereafter by the vicar bishop of Austria.[15] This dialogue was lead by two commissions: The Commission of Sankt Petersburg designated in 1893 by the Holy Synod and The Commission of Rotterdam, established in 1894 by the International Conference of the Old Catholic Bishops (IBK). The two commissions have never met in a joined session, but did have an exchange of reports between 1894 and 1913, four of which had been drafted by the Orthodox, and three by the Old Catholics.[16] These documents repeatedly debated the issue of Filioque, deemed a theologumenon that did not stand in the way of achieving ecclesiastic unity, the terminology concerning the transformation of the Eucharistic Gifts and the statute of the Utrecht hierarchy from which the other Old Catholic churches and bishops received the apostolic succession. The last report of the Sankt Petersburg Commission considered, at that time, that the explanations provided thus far by the Old Catholics were sufficient elements for an agreement between the two churches. The Russian commission also expressed its belief that in its report there were not any point that the Old Catholics might consider hard to accept or that were inconsistent with the previously made declarations. The outbreak of the World War I and the subsequent establishment of the Bolshevik regime in Moscow impeded on the discussions from being continued any further. The task of reinitiating the dialogue now rested with the Ecumenical Patriarchate, which carried it out remarkably.[17] It should be noted that during this period a special contribution was brought by the International Old Catholic Congress, from 1890 onwards, and from 1893 by *Revue Internationale de Théologie*, which in 1911 became *Internationale Kirchliche Zeitschrift* (IKZ), published to this day.

The third phase (1920-1960)

The third phase bore the mark of the effort that the Ecumenical Patriarchate made to re-launch the dialogue in view of recreating the Orthodox-Old Catholic communion. The first step in this enterprise was the publication of the Synodal Encyclical of the Church of Constantinople to all the Churches of Christ in January 1920.[18]

---

[13] I.V. Leb, *op.cit.*, 29.

[14] Urs von Arx, "Kurze Einführung in die Geschichte des orthodox-altkatholischen Dialogs," in "Koinonia auf altkirchlicher Basis," IKZ 79.4 (1989): 13. (We have borrowed this structure from Urs von Arx).

[15] Nowadays the Utrecht Union reunites the bishops of the Old Catholic Churches in Holland, Germany, Switzerland, Austria, the Czech Republic, Slovakia, USA, Canada, Poland, and Croatia/Yugoslavia. - Cf. Urs von Arx, *Kurze Einführung*, 14, note 6.

[16] Here they are in chronological order: 1893/1894 - 1. *The report of the Sankt Petersburg Commission;* 1896 - 2. *The report of the Rotterdam Commission;* 1897 - 3. *The report of the Sankt Petersburg Commission;* 1898 - 4. *The report of the Rotterdam Commission;* 1907- 5. *The report of the Sankt Petersburg Commission;* 1908 - 6. *The report of the Rotterdam Commission;* 1912/1913 - 7. *The report of the Sankt Petersburg Commission.* See 'Revue Internationale de Theologie' (RITh), 5 (1897), p.1-7 and (1899), p.1-11; U.Küry, *Die letzte Antwort der orthodoxen Petersburger Kommission an die altkatholische Rotterdamer Kommission*, IKZ 58 (1968): 29-44.

[17] I.V. Leb, *op.cit.*, 48-65.

[18] Gennadios Zervos, *Il contributo del Patriarcato ecumenico per l'unità dei cristiani* (The contribution of the Ecumenical Patriarchate to the unity of the Christians), (Roma, 1974): 33-37.

Focusing on accomplishing a *koinonia* among the churches, the letter proposed an 11 points programme. There are three sides to its importance:

1. The Church of Constantinople was the first Church to suggest the creation of a permanent association or Council of Churches. 2. The letter was addressed to all the Churches, which are 'coheirs and members of the same body and equal partakers of Christ's promise' (Eph 3:6). This clearly showed that the Ecumenical Patriarchate was open towards all the Churches of the world. 3. The Church of Constantinople announced a principle of cooperation between the Churches which may open the way for their reunification. This became the fundamental principle of the Ecumenical Movement.[19] This principle allowed the Orthodox to enjoy a substantial participation in the ecumenical debates and also to closely follow the relations the other denominations established with one another. This is how in the autumn of 1931 – after almost four months since the intercommunion between the Old Catholics and the Anglicans had been achieved – a new conference for the unification of the Orthodox and the Old Catholics was convened in Bonn.[20] After two days of rather imprecise discussions on 13 topics regarding the teachings and the liturgical practices of the two sides, they reached the conclusion that there already was a sufficient base for the intercommunion and the union of the two Churches, respectively.[21] However, although both the Old Catholics and some of the Orthodox[22] believed that this union was going to become a reality soon, it never came to that. The causes thereof are believed to be the announcement that a future Orthodox Preparatory synod was to take place and officially decide on this matter. The Orthodox believed that the Old Catholic-Anglican intercommunion was achieved on the problematical dogmatical bases. To this respect, in his report addressed to the Holy Synod of the Orthodox Church of Greece Metropolitan Polykarpos of Trikke and Stagoi wrote the following, on 9 August 1932: 'We have been cautious not only because the sacramental communion needs to be preceded by dogmatical unity – a unity that now seems unattainable due to the dogmatical differences – but also because we are considering the fact that the Old Catholics have approved of and already practiced the sacramental communion with the Anglicans in their Church, although there are still some dogmatical differences.'[23] The same reserve was shared by the Archbishop Germanos of Thyatira.[24] It is understandable how such standpoints generated disappointment among the Old Catholics[25]. And even if the mutual relationships have not been completely severed, the dialogue would be reopened much later.

The fourth phase (from 1961 onwards)

The beginning of the new phase of the bilateral discussions was marked by the First Panorthodox Conference on Rhodes in 1961, which decided that the relationships with the Old Catholics were to be nurtured 'in the spirit of

---

[19] Constantine G. Patelos, *The Orthodox Church in the Ecumenical Movement*, (Geneva 1978), 41-43; *Dokumente zur kirchlichen Unionsbewegung. Enzyklika der Kirche von Konstantinopel an alle irchen der Welt* in *IKZ*, 12 (1922): 40-43; Grigorios Larentzakis, *Das ökumenische Patriarchat von Konstantinopel im Dienste der kirchlichen Einheit und der Vereinigung Europas*, in KNA-OKI 27 (1995): 5-11.

[20] A. Küry, *Bericht über die Verhandlungen der altkatholischen und der orthodoxen Kommission in Bonn am 27. und 82. Oktober 1931*, in IKZ 22 (1932): 18-27; U. Küry, *Die altkatholische Kirche*, 479-484. In Greek in *Ortodoxia* 7 (1932): 156-162, 210-211, in English in The Christian East 13 (1932): 91-98, and in Romanian in: *Biserica Ortodoxă Română (BOR)*, 3rd series, 50 (1932): 439ff.

[21] Urs von Arx, *Kurze Einführung*, 15.

[22] For instance prof. Nicholas Arseniev and the Romanian Metropolitan Nectarie Cotlarciuc. – Cf. I.V. Leb, *Ortodoxie şi vechi-catolicism*, 266, note 323.

[23] I. Karmiris, *Die dritte Panorthodoxe Konferenz von Rhodos. Der Dialog zwischen der orthodoxen und altkatholoschen Kirchen*, in IKZ 57 (1967): 81, note 1, and Maximos of Sardes, *Palaiokatholokismos kai Orthodoxia* (Old Catholicism and Orthodoxy), in *Orthodoxia* 37, (1962): 169.

[24] See Urs Küry, *Die altkatholische Kirche*, (Stuttgart, 1978), 477-478.

[25] Urs von Arx, *Kurze Einführung*, 16.

the discussions we have had so far.'[26] The two sides initially prepared separately for the negotiations' reopening.[27] At the Orthodox request demanding that the Old Catholics provide them with an official profession of faith, the latter published two declarations in 1970 regarding a number of teachings that remained unclear, namely: the letter on the Old Catholic faith which expounded on the teachings referring to the Revelation and its transmission; The Church and its Sacraments; On the principle of unity and The declaration on the issue of Filioque.[28] Furthermore, the Orthodox also paid close attention to the Declaration of the Old Catholic Bishops regarding primacy within the Church[29] in which they declared that they acknowledged the primacy of the Roman Bishop 'as it had been acknowledged according to the Holy Scripture, by the Holy Fathers and the Councils, in the old, undivided Church', namely as 'primus inter pares, without the recognition of the decrees on the Pope's infallibility and universal Episcopate.'

Here is a brief timeline of the preliminary stages of the dialogue, from 1961 to 1973[30]:

1961 The First Pan-Orthodox Conference in Rhodes.

1962 The visit of the IBK delegation to the Ecumenical Patriarchate in Constantinople.

1963 The Third Pan-Orthodox Conference on Rhodes (it was decided that an Inter-Orthodox Theological Commission was to be designated in order to launch the debates with the Old Catholics).

1966 The first meeting of the Inter-Orthodox Theological Commission for the dialogue with the Old Catholics at Belgrade (it issued a long list containing the points on which the Orthodox and the Old Catholics agreed or were in disagreement).

1966 The assembly of the Old Catholic bishops and theologians in Bonn (they temporarily formed an Old Catholic Theological Commission and drafted the project of a working programme for the common dialogue).

1967 The Fourth Pan-Orthodox Conference in Chambésy/Geneva (the Orthodox reiterated their wish that the Old Catholic provide a profession of faith).

1968 The publication, in agreement with the IBK, of a Memorandum written by Bishop Urs Küry regarding *The present state of the Orthodox-Old Catholic relations*, which all the leaders of the Orthodox Churches were presented with.[31]

1969 A delegation of the IBK presented the Ecumenical Patriarch Athenagoras I with the official declarations (*The letter of the Old Catholic faith* and *The declaration on the issue of the Filioque*); the second session of the Inter-Orthodox Theological Commission for the Dialogue with the Old Catholic Commission at Chambésy/Geneva (the list of coral issues reduced).

1970 The International Commission of the Utrecht Union for the Orthodox-Old Catholic Dialogue was constituted and approved by the IBK, in Bonn; the third session of the Inter-Orthodox Theological Commission for the Dialogue with the Old Catholics took place in Bonn (it was proposed that the two commissions meet in a common session).

1971 The first meeting of the Joined Orthodox-Old Catholic Theological Commission in Penteli/Athens (The completion of the separate preparations and the definition of the method and contents of the theological dialogue).

---

[26] I. Karmiris, *Die Panorthodoxe Konferenz von Rhodos*, in *Theologia,*Oct./Dec. 1961, p.517; L.Stan, *Soborul Panortodox de la Rhodos (24 sept.-4 oct. 1961)* (The Panorthodox Synod of Rhodes, 24 September-4 Oktober 1961), in *Mitropolia Olteniei* (MO) 13.10-12 (1961): 716-733.

[27] We should mention here the efforts of the Old Catholic Archbishop Andreas Rinkel of Utrecht (1889-1979, archbishop in 1937-1970) and those of the Bonn professor Werner Küppers (1905-1980, professor from 1939 to 1972), as well as the *Salutation of the International Conference of the Old Catholic bishops addressed to the Rhodes Conference*, in 1961. – Cf. Urs von Arx, *Kurze Einführung*, 16, note 10.

[28] For the texts see Urs Küry, *Die altkatholische Kirche*, p.485. *Dokumente zum orthodox-altkatholischen Dialog, Glaubensbrief der Internationalen Altkatholischen Bischofskonferenz*, in IKZ 61 (1971): 65, with a Romanian translation by I. Săbăduş and P.I.David in *Ortodoxia* 23.4 (1971): 658.

[29] *Erklärung der altkatholischen Bischöfe zum Primat in der Kirche*, in IKZ 60 (1960): 57-59.

[30] Urs von Arx, *Kurze Einführung*, 17-18 and I.V. Leb, *op.cit.*, 172-211.

[31] See IKZ 59 (1969): 89-99 and 63 (1973): 182-192.

*Part V: Bilateral Dialogues between Eastern Orthodox Churches
and other Churches and Christian Traditions*

1974 The first assembly of the Joint Committee for Coordination in Penteli/Athens; the working session of the Joint Orthodox-Old Catholic Theological Commission in Morschach/Switzerland (Presentation and discussions on the text projects);

1975 The second assembly of the Joint Committee for Coordination in Zürich; The first General Assembly of the Joint Orthodox-Old Catholic Theological Commission in Chambésy/Geneva. The adoption of the texts on: 1. The Holy Trinity; 2. The Divine Revelation and Its Transmission; 3. Canon of the Holy Scripture; 4. The Incarnation of the Word of God; 5. The Hypostatic Union.

1976 The Session of the Joint Sub-commission in Penteli/Athens.

1977 The Second General Assembly of the Joint Commission, in Chambésy/Geneva. The adoption of the texts regarding: 1. The Virgin Mary; 2. The Being and Characteristics of the Church;

1978 The Session of the Joint Sub-commission in Penteli/Athens.

1978 The Third General Assembly of the Joint Commission, in Bonn. The adoption of the following texts: 1. The Unity of the Church and the Local Churches; 2. The Boundaries of the Church.

1981 The Session of the Joint Sub-commission in Bern; The Fourth General Assembly of the Joint Commission in Zagorsk/Moscow. The adoption of the texts regarding: 1. The Authority of the Church and in the Church; 2. The Infallibility of the Church; 3. The Councils of the Church; 4. The Need for Apostolic Succession.

1983 The Session of the Joint Sub-commission in Penteli/Athens. The Fifth General Assembly of the Joint Commission in Chambésy/Geneva. The adoption of the texts regarding: 1. The Head of the Church; 2. The Lord's Work of Salvation; 3. The Work of the Holy Spirit in the Church and Gaining Salvation;

1984 The Session of the Joint Sub-commission on Thassos/Greece.

1985 The Sixth General Assembly of the Joint Commission in Amersfoort/Holland. The adoption of the texts concerning: 1. The Sacraments of the Church; 2. The Baptism; 3. The Chrismation; 4. The Holy Communion.

1986 The Session of the Joint Sub-commission in Minsk. The Seventh General Assembly of the Joint Commission in Kavala/Greece. The adoption of the texts on: 1. The Sacrament of Confession; 2. The Sacrament of the Holy Unction; 3. The Sacrament of Ordination; 4. The Sacrament of Marriage; 5. The Church and the End of the World; 6. The Afterlife; 7. The Resurrection of the Dead and the Renewal of the World; 8. Church Communion. Premises and Consequences.

That same year a delegation of the IBK visited the Ecumenical Patriarchate in Constantinople and the Seventh General Assembly of the Joint Commission completed the theological dialogue as planned.

Current status and perspectives

Nowadays, the leaders of the Orthodox and the Old Catholic Churches have 26 texts at their disposal documenting their substantial consensus. However, although the theological work is now over, severe problems remain pending. Metropolitan Damaskinos pointed them out in October 1986, at Chambésy: 'Do the theological agreements we reach actually engage the Churches we represent? How can they be incorporated in the life of the Church without risking a schism? Are we talking about the mutual relationship between the bilateral and multilateral dialogues and, if so, which are they? For instance, can an agreement between the Old Catholic Church and the Orthodox Church on church authority or the head of the Church actually fasten the official dialogue between the Orthodox and the Old Catholics? What may be the theological and ecclesiological consequences of the 1931 statements of the Old Catholic representatives and of those of the Anglican Communion for our dialogue, or even more so, what does the "Bonn Agreement Concerning Inter-communion" (1931) mean to us?'[32]

Although the Joint Commission answered these questions, 'the problem still stands with regard to how these answers will be incorporated in the teaching and life of our two Churches.'[33] Although this task exceeds the competence of the Joint Commission, as it is up to the officials of the Churches participating in the

---

[32] Damaskinos Papandreou, "Discours prononcé le 18 octobre 1987," in *Episkepsis* 387 (1987): 12.
[33] Ibid., 13.

dialogue to address it, the dialogue must be 'completed by a responsible report submitted to the Churches and showing the methods worth considering, in order to harness the theological consensus needed for the ecclesiastic communion.'[34] According to Metropolitan Damaskinos, such a report drafted by each group must 'reflect the spirit prevailing during the discussions of the seven General Assemblies of the Theological Commission and be the result of the common texts' contents which we all signed together.'[35] The successful completion of the theological dialogue between the Orthodox and Old Catholics gave the Orthodox hierarch the hope that the Joint Commission 'would have a positive multi-directional influence, so that the effort for unity should be harnessed within the Church with the same spirit of love and mutual understanding that guarded our dialogue.'[36]

Unfortunately, the hope expressed by Metropolitan Damaskinos remained a mere desire. We have mentioned only the problem of the relations between the Old Catholics and the Anglicans and Lutherans, and the ordination of women,[37] all of them generating disagreements even among the Old Catholics. And while much was written for or against this, so far there is no full consensus within the Utrecht Union.[38] Therefore, it is expected that the Old Catholics clarify their internal issues first, so as to then be able to discuss with the Orthodox.[39]

Bibliography

Arx, Urs von, "Koinonia auf altkirchlicher Basis," IKZ 79.4(1989).

Berlis, Angela, "Überlegungen zur Realisierung weiterer Schritte auf dem Weg zur sichtbaren Kirchengemeinschaft von Alt-Katholischer Kirche in Deutschalnd und Vereinigter Evangelisch-Lutherischer Kirche Deutschlands," in *Ökumenische Rundschau* 60.4 (2011): 500-512.

"Dokumente zur kirchlichen Unionsbewegung. Enzyklika der Kirche von Konstantinopel an alle Kirchen der Welt," in IKZ 12 (1922): 40-43.

Döllinger, Ignaz von, *Über die Wiedervereinigung der christlichen Kirchen. Sieben Vorträge, gehalten zu München im Jahr 1872*, (Nördlingen, 1888).

"Erklärung der altkatholischen Bischöfe zum Primat in der Kirche," in IKZ 60 (1960): 57-59.

Finsterhölzl, J. *Ignaz von Döllinger*, (Graz, Wien, Köln: Styria Verlag, 1969).

Larentzakis, Grigorios, "Das ökumenische Patriarchat von Konstantinopel im Dienste der kirchlichen Einheit und der Vereinigung Europas," in KNA-OKI 27 (1995): 5-11.

Leb, Ioan-Vasile, *Dialogul ortodoxo-vechi catolic – stadiul actual şi perspectivele sale (The Orthodox – Old Catholic Dialogue. Its current status and its perspectives),* (Cluj-Napoca: Renaşterea, 2000).

---

[34] Ibid.

[35] Ibid.

[36] Ibid., 14.

[37] For instance, ordination of Ms. Anne-Marie Kaufmann on 21 May 2005 and others. - Cf. *Présence. Mensuel des paroisses catholiques-chrétiennes de Suisse romande,* Supplément nr. 3/2005, I–III.

[38] Here are just a few articles published on the theme: *120 Session der Nationalsynode der Christkatholischen Kirche der Schweiz 7. und 8. Juni 1991 in Liestal,* 98–105; *121 Session der Nationalsynode der Christkatholischen Kirche der Schweiz 12. und 13. Juni in Starrkirch/Dulliken,* 83–103; Urs von Arx, „Koinonia auf altkirchlicher Basis," IKZ 79.4(1989). Urs von Arx und Anastasios Kallis (ed.), *Bild Christi und Geschlecht,* 'Gemeinsame Überlegungen' und Referate der Orthodox-Altkatholischen Konsultation zur Stellung der Frau in der Kirche und zur Frauenordination als ökumenischem Problem, 25 Februar – 1 März 1996 in Levadia (Griechenland) und 10–15 Dezember in Konstancin (Polen), Sonderdruck IKZ 88.2 (1998); Urs von Arx, „Der orthodox-altkatholische Dialog. Anmerkungen zu einer schwierigen Rezeption," IKZ 87.3 (1997): 184–185. Idem, „Eine verpasste Chance," IKZ, 87.4 (1997): 292–297; Idem, „Neuer Aufbruch? Bericht über die Anglikanisch – Altkatholische Theologenkonferenz von Guildford," IKZ 84.2 (1994): 66–76.

[39] For instance the recent debates of the Old-Catholics with the Catholics and the Lutherans of Germany: Ökumenische Rundschau 60.4 (2011): 500-512.

Part V: Bilateral Dialogues between Eastern Orthodox Churches
and other Churches and Christian Traditions

Leb, Ioan-Vasile, *Orthodoxie und Altkatholizismus. Eine hundert Jahre ökumenishe Zusammenarbeit (1870-1970)*, (Cluj-Napoca: PUC, 1995).

Leb, Ioan-Vasile, *Ortodoxie şi vechi-catolicism sau ecumenism înainte de Mişcarea Ecumenică* (Orthodoxy and Old-Catholicism or ecumenism before the Ecumenical Movement), (Cluj-Napoca: PUC, 1996).

Neuner, Peter, *Döllinger als Theologe der Ökumene*, (München: Paderborn, 1979).

Patelos, Constantin G., *The Orthodox Church in the Ecumenical Movement*, (Geneva, 1978).

Rein, Harald, *Kirchengemeinschaft. Die anglikanisch-altkatholisch-orthodoxen Beziehungen von 1870 bis 1990 und ihre ökumenische Relevanz*, B2. 1 u. 2, (Bern: Peter Lang Verlag, 1993).

Reusch, F.H., *Bericht über die vom 10. bis 16. August zu Bonn gehaltenen Unionskonferenzen, im Auftrage des Vorsitzenden Dr. von Döllinger*, (Bonn, 1875).

Reusch, Friedrich Heinrich, *Bericht über die am 14., 15. und 16. September zu Bonn gehaltenen Unionskonferenzen. Im Auftrage des Vorsitzenden Dr. von Döllinger*, (Bonn, 1874).

Schulte, J. Fr. von, *Der Altkatholizismus*, (Giessen, 1885, reed. Aalen, 1965).

Staffenberger, Franz Jörg, *Der orthodox – altakatholische Dialog*, (Graz: Diss. Theol., 1994).

Zervos, Gennadios, *Il contributo del Patriarcato ecumenico per l'unità dei cristiani* (The contribution of teh Ecumenical Patriarchate to the unity of the Christians), (Roma, 1974).

Petros Vassiliadis

Orthodoxy and Pectecostalism form two quite opposite Christian traditions. This is true, when one looks at their practice, spirituality and every day life, especially their mission praxis. And this is the reason why no official theological dialogue between Orthodox and Pentecostals has been launched as yet. If, however, one looks at their theological publications, one gets a completely different picture; the similarities even in theological terminology are tremendous. In the ecumenical theological discussions, the Orthodox are the main proponents of Pneumatology, an issue that is insistently brought into the the foreground also by Pentecostals.

In addition to various unofficial meetings and theological exchanges between Orthodox and Evangelicals of a Pentecostal type in the multilateral dialogue,[1] an important encounter has taken place in the last World Mission Conference of Athens (9-16 May 2005), as well as during the Edinburgh 2010 centinary celebration. At a *synaxis* (so the conventional workshops in the world mission conferences are called) under the title "Reconciliation and Mission. Orthodox and Pentecostal Perspectives", I was asked to introduce the subject from the Orthodox perspective.

The pneumatological dimension of our Christian identity is being slowly but steadily developed in ecumenical theology and in contemporary theology of mission. In the ecumenical dialogue, the consolidation of the trinitarian theology as a useful tool in almost all ecclesiological, sociological, moral etc., and above all missiological reflections was a further evidence. The trinitarian revolution in contemporary Christian theology is strongly felt across denominational boundaries – from post-Vatican II Catholicism to evangelicalism – and is in fact due to the rediscovery of the theology of the Holy Spirit of the undivided Christian Church. This rediscovery relulted in abandoning the old medieval (but also later) mission paradigm, which was founded on a Christocentric universalism, in some cases developed into a christomonistic expansionism and an aggresive imperialism.[2]

The second parameter is an increasing awareness of the *liturgical dimension* of our Christian self-understanding. The importance of liturgy is being underlined in post-modernity[3] as a significant element of the Christian witness – maybe not as central yet as the proclamation of the word, but certainly as a constitutive element. The exclusive emphasis of the old mission paradigm on the rational comprehension of truth, and as a result of it on the verbal proclamation of the Christian message, gave its place to a more holistic understanding of mission in post-modernity.[4] In addition, a new holistic understanding of healing, even of a miraculous healing, widely practiced by Pentecostals, challenges – and of course is challenged by – an overwhelming rational attitude of modernism, to which the majority of western Christianity was forced to surrender, or at least accommodate

---

[1] Cf. Huibert van Beek-Georges Lemopoulos (ed.), *Proclaiming Christ Today. Orthodox-Evangelical Consultation Alexandria, 10-15 July 1995,* (Geneva: WCC and Syndesmos, 1995); and Huibert van Beek-Georges Lemopoulos (ed.), *Turn to God. Orthodox Evangelical Consultation Hamburg, 30 March-4 April, 1998,*(Geneva: WCC, 1998).

[2] More on this in my "Beyond Christian Universalism: The Church's Witness in a Multicultural Society," in *Scholarly Annual of the Theological School of Thessaloniki,* n.s. Department of Theology 9 (1999): 309-320.

[3] Cf. my recently published books *Lex orandi. Liturgical Theology and Liturgical Renewal,* Idiomela 5: Indiktos, (Athens 2005); and *Post-modernity and the Church. The Challenge of Orthodoxy, (*Athens: Akritas, 2002) (both in Greek).

[4] Both of these dimensions are closely linked with the *eschatological* understanding of the Holy Spirit and the eschatological understanding of the Church. The *eschatology constitutes the central and primary aspect of the Church.* Hence the priority of the Kingdom of God in all ecclesiological considerations. Everything belongs to the Kingdom. The Church in her institutional expression does not administer all reality; she only prepares the way to the Kingdom, in the sense that she is an image if it.

itself.[5] The rapid growth of the Pentecostal movement will certainly challenge all secularized attitudes of Christianity. The rediscovery on the part of most Pentecostals of the traditional liturgical practice of exorcism, together with a renewed interest in demonology, will certainly be encountered with the Orthodox conception of healing (ἴασις) – beyond physical curing (θεραπεία) – and the openness of the Orthodox Churches to transcendent and awe inpiring realities.

Beyond all these issues that unite Orthodoxy and Pentecostalism, it is necessary to establish a sound theological basis. We need to examine whether we insist on a *universal proselytizing mission,* or on a *witness* to the world of the Church's eschatological experience. This was, in fact, made possible by the theology of the Holy Spirit. And this development was the result of the fundamental assumption of the *trinitarian theology,* "that God in God's own self is a life of communion and that God's involvement in history aims at drawing humanity and creation in general into this communion with God's very life."[6]

After all, one cannot overlook the fact that *the Holy Spirit,* in the Bible (but also in the early patristic tradition[7]) is first and foremost *eschatologically-* (Acts 2:17ff) and *communion-* (2 Cor 13:13) oriented. One cannot also ignore that from the time of the New Testament onwards two types of Pneumatology have been developed: one "historical" and one "eschatological". The first type, the "historical" is more familiar in the West to the present day, and understands the Holy Spirit as fully *dependent on* Christ, as being the agent of Christ to fulfill the task of mission. One clear result of this type of Pneumatology from the history of the Church is the famous *filioque* controversy, but also the aggressive and expansionist attitude of Christian witness in more recent mission activities. The second type of Pneumatology has been more consistently developed in the East and understands the Holy Spirit as the *source of* Christ. It also understands the Church in terms more of *coming together* (i.e as the eschatological *synaxis* of the people of God in his Kingdom) than of *going forth* for mission.[8]

Taking this second type of Pneumatology seriously into consideration and building upon the eschatological understanding of the Church,[9] one unavoidably concludes that the mission of the Church deals with the problem of ethics, i.e. the problem of overcoming the evil in the world, not primarily as a moral and social issue, but mainly – and for some even exclusively – as an *ecclesial* one. The moral and social responsibility of Christians, i.e. their mission in today's pluralistic world, is the logical consequence of their ecclesial (i.e. eschatological) self-consciousness. This means that mission is the *outcome,* not the primary goal of Christian theology. That is why for Orthodoxy what constitutes the essence of the Church is not her mission but the Eucharist, the Divine Liturgy;[10] the mission is the *meta-liturgy,* the Liturgy *after* the Liturgy, though it is obviously also the Liturgy *before* the Liturgy.[11]

[5] Peter Berger, a well-known sociologist, has described the attitude of the Church toward the modernist revolution in terms of two opposite positions: accomodation and resistance, see P. Berger, *The Sacred Canopy. Elements of a Sociological Theory of Religion,* (New York: Doubleday, 1967), 156ff and 106ff.

[6] I. Bria (ed.), *Go Forth in Peace,* (Geneva: WCC Publications, 1986): 3.

[7] This is evident in the Orthodox hymns of the Feast of Pentecost.

[8] J. Zizioulas, "Implications ecclésiologiques de deux types de pneumatologie," *Communio Sanctorum. Mélagnes offerts à Jean Jacques von Almen,* (Geneva: Labor et Fides, 1982), 141-154.

[9] In the Orthodox Church even the episcopocentric structure of the Church is seen as an essential part of the eschatological vision of the Church. The bishop e.g. as the presiding *primus inter pares* in love over the eucharistic community, has very seldom been understood as a vicar or representative, or ambassador of Christ, but as an *image* of Christ. So with the rest of the ministries of the Church: they are not *parallel to,* or *given by,* but *identical* with those of, Christ (J. Zizioulas, "The Mystery of the Church in Orthodox Tradition," *One in Christ* 24 (1988): 294-303.

[10] The imporance of Liturgy has been recently reaffirmed by cultural anthropologists as a constitutive element of all religious systems, and certainly of Christianity. The Eucharist, heart and center of Christian Liturgy, in its authentic perception is now widely accepted, especially in the ecumenical dialogues (multilateral and bilateral) as a proleptic manifestation of the Kingdom of God, as symbol and image of an alternative reality, which was conceived before all creation by God the Father in his mystical plan (the *mysterion* in the biblical sense), was inaugurated by our Lord, and is permanently sustained by the Holy Spirit.

[11] "Mission as ministry of reconciliation", *"You Are the Light of the World,* § 30 p. 114.

The above two types of Pneumatology, together with the two ecclesiological and missiological perspectives which came out of them, survived to the present ecumenical era. Today's world mission, in order to be consistent with the idea of "Common Christian Witness", and more importantly faithful to the tradition of the undivided Church, needs to proceed to a theological synthesis of the above two types of Pneumatology, of ecclesiology, and above all of missiology. And this is something, which a substantial Orthodox-Pentecostal theological dialogue can deal with. On my part I firmly believe that Pneumatology cannot be relegated to an isolated doctrine. Pneumatology was always, and should always be, in close connexion with Christology, to such an extend that one can now talk about a *Christology pneumatologically conditioned* and vice-versa.

The necessity of an honest theological dialogue, which has to be preceeded by a loving encounter, between Orthodoxy and Pentecostalism is clearly evidenced in the "Listeners' reports" of the Athens 2005 World Mission Conference.[12] The Reports expressed the spirit of the conference and constitute a source to discover the general feelings, the atmosphere and the main concerns of the participants. 8 out of 11 listeners – carefully selected "theologians and missiologists from all over the world and from various spiritual backgrounds to participate in the Athens conference with the intention to discern important trends"[13] – have underlined the importance of the Orthodox-Pentecostal encounter in the conference (five of them directly and another three indirectly), which was made manifest in more than one ways. Anastasia Vassiliadou, representing the Orthodox youth, stated her feeling as follows: "Another very important highlight of the conference was the encounter between Orthodox and Pentecostals. Although this issue was discussed at only one *synaxis* – and very late in the conference, and for this reason it was not visible enough to all – the preliminary theological debate between two quite distanced traditions left very important promises for the future."[14] The "institutional" bodies – if one can use such a term for the charismatic Pentecostals – are not ready to embark to this journey, mainly because of lack of appropriate structures. Their theologians fortunately realize that they need unofficially to take the theological discussion further.[15]

It was for this reason, and out of this awareness that five years later, immediately after the Edindurgh 2010 celebration, both the American and the European pentecostal groups made unofficial steps to request the Ecumenical Patriarchate to consider a launch of a more substantial encounter and to take an initiative to set up a Joint Theological Dialogue between Orthodox and Pentecostals.

One should never forget what the late Fr. Georges Florovsky, almost 60 years ago at the inaugural Assembly of WCC in Amsterdam, boldly stated:

"It is not enough to be moved towards ecumenical reconciliation by some sort of strategy, be it missionary, evangelistic, social or other, unless the Christian conscience has already become aware of the greater challenge, by the Divine challenge itself. We must seek unity or reunion not because it might make us more efficient or better equipped …, but because unity is the Divine imperative, the Divine purpose and design, because it belongs to the very essence of Christianity."[16]

---

[12] The entire July 2005 issue of the above *IRM* 374, was devoted to these reports under the general title "Athens 2005-Listeners' Reports", 352-439.

[13] From Jacques Matthey's "Editorial" of the *IRM* 94 (2005): 319-321, 320.

[14] Anastasia Vassiliadou, "Discerning the Spirit of Athens," *IRM* 94 (2005): 439.

[15] The (unofficial) Wesleyan-Orthodox theological dialogue, which has so far organized four meetings (cf. the preceedings of the first in S.T.Kimbrough, Jr [ed.], *Orthodox and Wesleyan Spirituality,* (New York: SVS Press, 2002), and earlier the (unofficial again) Eastern and Oriental Orthodox theological dialogue, have set a successful example.

[16] W.A.Visser't Hooft (ed.), *La Premiere Assemblee du Conseil Oecumenique des Eglises. Rapport officiel,* (Paris: Neuchatel, 1948). Also in G. Florovsky, "The Doctrine of the Church and the Ecumenical Movement", *The Ecumenical Review* 2 (1950): 152-161.

*Part V: Bilateral Dialogues between Eastern Orthodox Churches
and other Churches and Christian Traditions*

(81) Eastern Orthodox – Oriental Orthodox Dialogue – A Historical and Theological Survey

Ioan Ovidiu

1. Introduction

Whereas the appellation "Eastern Orthodox Churches" refers to those Churches belonging to the Byzantine tradition and following the seven Ecumenical Synods, the phrase "Oriental Orthodox Churches" is employed nowadays in order to indicate the smaller family of Churches formerly called with the misnomer "Monophysite" Churches, because they disagreed with the decisions of the Synod of Chalcedon (451) and afterwards went separate ways:

a. The Armenian Apostolic Church (Catholicate of Echmiadzin and Catholicate of Cilicia)
b. The Ethiopian Orthodox Church
c. The Erithrean Orthodox Church
d. The Coptic Orthodox Church (Patriarchate of Alexandria)
e. The Syrian Orthodox Church (Patriarchate of Antioch)
f. The Syrian Orthodox Church of Malankar

Not involved in this dialogue are the Assyrian Church of the East, i.e. the so-called Nestorian Church, and the Oriental Churches united with the Roman Catholic Church.

2. Premises

The dialogue between the Eastern Orthodox and the Oriental Orthodox Churches deals with one of the oldest divisions between the Christian Churches. Since the Synod of Chalcedon in 451, these Church families have been dogmatically separated and they have been confronting each other for more than 15 centuries. Theological and historical prejudices developed through this long period of time and were reflected in the liturgical and spiritual life of these Churches. The ecumenical dialogue is meant to enable them to overcome their resentments.

The first impulse and, at the same time, the legitimacy of this Ecumenical dialogue were given by the First Pan-Orthodox Consultation (Rhodes 1961) and by its specifications concerning the relationships with the Oriental Orthodox Churches. Thus, the representatives of all Eastern Orthodox Churches recommended that their Churches should "cultivate friendly relations with a view to establishing a union with them (i.e. with the Oriental Orthodox Churches)" and suggested some concrete actions in this respect: exchange of visits, exchange of teachers and students, theological encounters, study of the history, faith, worship and administration of the Oriental Churches, as well as cooperation in practical matters and ecumenical conferences.[1] This impulse was renewed and the dialogue was encouraged at the following Pan-orthodox Conferences.

These premises determined the whole approach. It was essential that the partners answer three important questions:

a. Is it possible for the Eastern Orthodox Churches to seek full communion and Church unity with Churches whose teaching was condemned at an Ecumenical Synod?

b. What are nowadays the differences and similarities between these two theological traditions as far as their belief is concerned?

---

[1] Gennadios Limouris, *Orthodox Visions of Ecumenism*, (Geneva 1994), 32.

c. What are nowadays the differences and similarities between these two Church families as far as Church life is concerned?

Here follows a presentation of the manner in which the two families of Orthodox Churches tackled these and other related issues.

3. Unofficial Consultations

The dialogue began with four unofficial theological consultations meant to prepare the actual dialogue of the above-mentioned Churches.

1964 - Aarhus, Denmark[2]

Between 11 and 15 of August 1964 fifteen representatives of the two Orthodox families met in Aarhus, Denmark, in the framework of Faith and Order Commission, in order to evaluate the relations between their Churches and especially the Christological teaching. On 14 August they adopted a common statement, which gave hope for future dialogue.

The first sentence of the statement mentioned the sporadic meetings between officials of the orthodox Churches occasioned by the Ecumenical movement since the second decade of the 20th century and especially the Pan-Orthodox Conference in Rhodes (1961), where "the desire to know each other and to restore our unity in the one church of Christ" was explicitly manifested. Already here is also mentioned that some Orthodox churches "accept seven ecumenical councils and others accept three." "Openness of charity" and "conviction of truth," mutual learning processes seem to have dominated the theological dialogue. "Inherited misunderstandings" began to clear up and both sides "recognized in each other the one orthodox faith," which has not gone astray from the faith of the Fathers even after 15 centuries of alienation.

The debate on Christology, curiously enough, started with an analysis of the Council of Chalcedon (451), i.e. the actual apple of discord between the two sides, while reaffirming commitment to the Christological expression of "our common father in Christ," St. Cyril of Alexandria (*mia physis* or *mia hypostasis tou Theou logou sesarkomene* / the one physis or hypostasis of God's Word Incarnate). The teaching of St. Cyril has constituted the common theological ground for the ecumenical dialogue since 1961 and up to these days. According to the statement, "both sides found themselves fundamentally following the Christological teaching of the one undivided church *as expressed by St. Cyril*." (author's emphasis).

The different developments of the Cyrillian Christology in the two theological traditions and the contrast between their expressions of faith were explained as a result of the different terminologies they employed. In spite of these differences, the theological commission declared that they "saw the same truth expressed" and that "on the essence of Christological dogma we found ourselves in full agreement." The inference that the theological diversity in expressing the Christological teaching is due to contrasting terminology and not to opposed teaching was confirmed by recent research and thorough studies. This conclusion is probably the most important result of the first unofficial dialogue, and it has determined the whole dialogue so far.

The positive theological agreement was followed by the dissociation from two heretical teachings: that of Eutyches and that of Nestorius. With this argument the commission also tried to solve the basic question whether it is necessary that the Oriental Churches formally accept the Council of Chalcedon. They asserted that "since we agree in rejecting without reservation the teaching of Eutyches as well as of Nestorius, the acceptance or non-acceptance of the Council of Chalcedon does not entail the acceptance of either heresy." Thus, if the Oriental Orthodox Churches officially reject the teaching of Eutyches and the Eastern Orthodox Churches publicly dissociate themselves from the teaching of Nestorius, there is no need for the Oriental Churches to formally adhere to the decisions of the forth Ecumenical Synod. This view is explained in the following

---

[2] Original English version in *Greek Orthodox Theological Review* 10 (1964-65): 7-160.

paragraph, which describes the ecumenical councils as "stages in an integral development," which "should not be studied in isolation." Therefore, also the Council of Chalcedon "can only be understood as reaffirming the decisions of Ephesus (431), and best understood in the light of the later Council of Constantinople (533)."

This text answers only indirectly the first general question of the dialogue, i.e. whether it is possible for the Eastern Orthodox Churches to seek full communion and Church unity with Churches whose teaching was condemned at an Ecumenical Synod. It points that the formal acceptance of the Council of Chalcedon is not necessary for the Oriental Churches, if the purpose of the Council, which is to reject the teaching of Eutyches, is fulfilled. Thus, these Churches confess another teaching than that condemned at Chalcedon, a fact that excludes them from the specific aim of the forth Ecumenical Synod. In the end of the statement the participants underlined "the significant role of political, sociological and cultural factors in creating tension between factions in the past," factors which should be studied together in the future, and expressed their hope, that these non-theological aspects "should not continue to divide us."

The document reviewing the theological discussions was signed by all representatives, among whom we recognise important theologians of both Orthodox Church families.[3]

1967 - Bristol, Great Britain[4]

After the successful meeting in Aarhus, another theological consultation took place two years later between 25 and 29 July 1967 in Bristol, Great Britain. The participants, who describe themselves as a study group gathered "with the blessing of the authorities of our respective Churches," intended to bring forth what they discovered in Aarhus as a "common ground for seeking closer ties among our Churches." The common statement emphasizes "several new areas of agreement" while accepting that "many questions still remain to be studied and settled."

The theological agreement from Aarhus on the Christological teaching of St. Cyril of Alexandria proves to be rather concise. Both Orthodox Church families confess that:

"God's infinite love for mankind, by which (He) has both created and saved us, is our starting point for apprehending the mystery of the union of perfect Godhead and perfect manhood in our Lord Jesus Christ. It is for our salvation that God the Word became one of us. Thus he who is consubstantial with the Father became by the Incarnation consubstantial also with us. By his infinite grace God has called us to attain to his uncreated glory. God became by nature man (so) that man may become by grace God. The manhood of Christ thus reveals and realizes the true vocation of man. God draws us into fullness of communion with himself in the body of Christ, (so) that we may be transfigured from glory to glory. It is in this soteriological perspective that we have approached the Christological question."

This Orthodox confession of faith proves that the dialogue was not a mere debate on Christological formulas and the agreement a simple compromise of Christological terminology, but a real reflection on the soteriological consequences of the Christological teaching. This way of dealing with matters of faith is traced back to the teaching of the common Church Fathers (St. Ignatius, St. Irenaeus, St. Anthony, St. Athanasius,

[3] Emilianos of Meloa, Ecumenical Patriarchate of Constantinople, Rev. Professor G. Florovsky, Greek Orthodox Archdiocese of North & South America- The Ecumenical Patriarchate of Constantinople, Rev. Professor J. S. Romanides, Greek Orthodox Archdiocese of North & South America- The Ecumenical Patriarchate of Constantinople, Rev. Professor Vitaly Borovoy, Russian Orthodox Church, Rev. Professor J. Meyendorff, Russian Orthodox Greek Catholic Church of North America, Professor J. Karmiris, Church of Greece, Professor G. Konidaris, Church of Greece, Archbishop Tiran Nersoyan, Armenian Apostolic Church, Bishop Karekin Sarkissian, Armenian Apostolic Church. Catholicate of Cilicia, Archbishop Mar Severius Zakka Iwas of Mosul, Syrian Orthodox Church, Metropolitan Mar Thoma Dionysius of Niranam, Orthodox Syrian Church of the East, Rev. Like Siltanat Habte Mariam Woroqineh, Ethiopian Orthodox Church, Rev. Professor V.C. Samuel, Orthodox Syrian Church of the East, Dr. Karam Nazir Khella, Coptic Orthodox Church, Dr. Getachew Haile, Ethiopian Orthodox Church.
[4] Original English version in *Greek Orthodox Theological Review* 13 (1968): 123-320.

St. Basil, St. Gregory of Nyssa and St. John Chrysostom, St. Ephraim the Syrian and St. Cyril of Alexandria). In the good patristic tradition, Christology is understood on the background not only of soteriology, but also of "the doctrine of God and the doctrine of man, ecclesiology and spirituality and the whole liturgical life of the Church." Thus, the participants managed to overcome the narrow Christological dispute and to consider this issue in the larger framework of soteriology, ecclesiology and anthropology, as well as of ecclesiastical liturgical and spiritual life. By doing this, they extended the common ground for the ecumenical dialogue and shifted the accent from the plain Christological debate to a wide area of theological dialogue where the two Church traditions are very close.

Still they came to express the Christological thinking of both traditions since the 5th century up to these days:

"Ever since the fifth century, we have used different formulae to confess our common faith in the One Lord Jesus Christ, perfect God and perfect man. Some of us affirm two natures, wills and energies hypostatically united in the One Lord Jesus Christ. Some of us affirm one united divine-human nature, will and energy in the same Christ. Both sides speak of a union without confusion, without change, without division, without separation. The four adverbs belong to our common tradition. Both affirm the dynamic permanence of the Godhead and the manhood, with all their natural properties and faculties, in the one Christ."

The unity in diversity is preserved by a precise differentiation and by clarifying additions. Thus, the Eastern Orthodox who speak in terms of "two" do not thereby divide or separate, while the Oriental Orthodox who speak in terms of "one" do not confuse or change.

The participants were aware of the differences in expressing the common faith, but they insisted on the shared essence of Christological teaching by underlining the four adverbs established at the Council of Chalcedon – "without confusion, without change, without division, without separation" – as belonging to the common tradition: the terms *without division* and *without separation* must be underlined for those who speak in terms of "two," while the terms *without confusion* and *without change* must be underlined for those who speak in terms of "one," so that "we may understand each other."

The Christological dialogue extended from the issues debated upon in Chalcedon to the aspects discussed during the next Ecumenical Synods "especially the monoenergetic and monothelete controversies of the seventh century."

> "All of us agree that the human will is neither absorbed nor suppressed by the divine will in the Incarnate Logos, nor are they contrary one to the other. The uncreated and created natures, with the fullness of their natural properties and faculties, were united without confusion or separation, and continue to operate in the one Christ, our Saviour. The position of those who wish to speak of one divine-human will and energy united without confusion or separation does not appear therefore to be incompatible with the decision of the Council of Constantinople (680-81), which affirms two natural wills and two natural energies in Him existing indivisibly, inconvertibly, inseparably, inconfusedly."

The theologians deal here with the consequences of accepting different expressions of the same faith. If the Eastern Orthodox theologians accept that the Miaphysite Christological formula of St. Cyril professed by the Oriental Orthodox Churches is as Orthodox and accurate as the formula of Chalcedon, then the Eastern Orthodox theologians must also accept the same expression when dealing with the question of the monoenergetic and monothelete controversies. Meanwhile it has become obvious that both expressions of faith always need some clarifying adverbs in order to exclude misunderstandings.

In the end of the document the participants inform us about the elaboration of a list of questions to be dealt with in future consultations and commit themselves to the common purpose of restoring "the full communion between our Churches," which is regarded as "a first priority for our Churches." However, "the difficulties *they* have encountered" are also mentioned.

Among the "preliminary actions" proposed by the participants is the "the formulation of a joint declaration in (which) we express together in the same formula our common faith in the One Lord Jesus Christ, whom we all acknowledge to be perfect God and perfect man." This joint declaration is not to be considered as a confession of faith or a creed, but a formula "drawn up by a group of theologians officially commissioned by the Churches, and submitted to the Churches for formal and authoritative approval, or for suggestions for modifications which will have to be considered by the commission before a final text is approved by the Churches."

The second proposed preliminary action was the examination of "the canonical, liturgical and jurisdictional problems involved." As examples for this kind of issues the document mentions "anathemas and liturgical deprecations by some Churches of theologians regarded by others as doctors and saints of the Church, and the jurisdictional assurance and agreements necessary before formal restoration of communion."

The representatives of the Churches entrusted the results of the dialogue to their Churches in order to give an impulse to the study group for further research.[5] Even though they prove aware of their status and of the limits of their mandate from the Churches, the participants show a certain precipitance determined by the enthusiasm generated by the dialogue results.

1970 - Geneva, Switzerland[6]

The third theological consultation between the Eastern Orthodox and Oriental Orthodox Churches was organised in Geneva, Switzerland, between 16 and 21 August 1970. The Summary of Conclusions agreed upon by the participants was divided in four parts:

I. Reaffirmation of Christological agreement

The document begins with the statement that in spite of a fifteen-century separation both Churches are still in full and deep agreement with the universal tradition of the one undivided Church. The Christological teaching of St. Cyril is declared as common theological ground, although the two traditions employ different terminologies in order to express it. The participants confess that the One, who is consubstantial with the Father because of His divine nature, became also consubstantial with us due to his human nature, which He assumed through the incarnation. He was born from the Father before time and in these last days He was born from the blessed Virgin Mary for us and for our salvation. This short profession is followed by the formula of Chalcedon: in Him both natures are united in the one hypostasis of the divine Logos, without confusion, without change, without division, without separation; thus, Jesus Christ is perfect God and perfect Man with all the properties and faculties which belong to the two natures. Concerning the two doctrines of monoenergism and monothelitism, the study group affirms the common belief, that the human will and energy of Christ were neither absorbed, nor suppressed by his divine will and energy, since they are not in contradiction to each other, but in complete harmony and unified without confusion and without division. They express the will and energy of the one hypostasis of the incarnated Logos, Emmanuel, God and Man, our Lord and Saviour.

The signatories then refer to the mutual visits and common studies by which the theologians rediscovered agreement in other theological matters than Christology: Triadology, Pneumatology, Ecclesiology, Eschatology; but also correspondences in liturgy and spirituality, doctrine and canonical practice. The document presents then the conclusion of the theological dialogue:

[5] Metropolitan Emilianos of Calabria, Ecumenical Patriarchate, Rev. Professor G. Florovsky, Ecumenical Patriarchate, Rev. Professor J. S. Romanides, Ecumenical Patriarchate, Rev. Professor Vitaly Borovoy, Russian Orthodox Church, Rev. Professor J. Meyendorff, Russian Orthodox Greek Catholic Church of North America, ArchimandriteDamaskinos Papandreou, Ecumenical Patriarchate, Professor G. Konidaris, Church of Greece, Professor N. Nissiotis, Church of Greece, Professor N. Chiţescu, Church of Romania, Bishop Nikodim Stiven, Church of Bulgaria, Professor E. Tsonievsky, Church of Bulgaria, Vardapet A. Berberian, Armenian Apostolic Church, Dr. N. Khella, Coptic Orthodox Church, Vardapet Mesrob Krikorian, Armenian Apostolic Church, Ato Merke Selassie Gebre Ammanuel, Ethiopian Orthodox Church, Metropolitan Philippos Mar Theophilos, Syrian Orthodox Church of the East, Professor V.C. Samuel, Syrian Orthodox Church of the East, Bishop Samuel, Coptic Orthodox Church, Rector Paul Verghese, Syrian Orthodox Church of the East.
[6] Original English version in *Greek Orthodox Theological Review* 16 (1971): 3-209.

"Our mutual agreement is not merely verbal or conceptual; it is a deep agreement that impels us to beg our Churches to consummate our union by bringing together again the two lines of tradition which have been separated from each other for historical reasons for such a long time. We work in the hope that our Lord will grant us full unity so that we can celebrate together that unity in the Common Eucharist. That is our strong desire and final goal."

It must be said that this reaffirmation of the Christological agreement not only points out the general positive results and its recommendations to the Churches, but it also details the actual content of the agreement. Nevertheless, it must be read in the framework of the previous theological dialogues in Aarhus and Bristol.

Very important for the dialogue itself and for the represented Churches is the fact that the theologians gathered in Geneva assumed these results and regarded them as compelling for the further dialogue and, even more important, for the full Eucharistic communion.

II. Some differences

This chapter proves the deep insight of the study group into the differences in teaching and practice between the two traditions, which occurred – as expected – during the 15 centuries of separation. These "ecclesiological issues" concern:

(a) The meaning and place of certain Councils

While the Eastern Orthodox Churches recognise seven Ecumenical Councils as a coherent and indivisible complex expressing one teaching of the Church, the Oriental Orthodox Churches only consider that it is they who have preserved so far the authentic Christological tradition on the basis of the three ecumenical Councils, completed by the liturgical and patristic tradition.

The study group expressed its conviction that the Ecumenical Synods should not be considered as an authority above the Church, but as "charismatic events in the Life of the Church" and proposed a sharp differentiation between definitions of faith and canonical law-making, as well as between the intention of the dogmatic definition and the terminology employed, since the latter has less authority than the intention.

(b) The anathematization or acclamation as Saints of certain controversial teachers

The study group neither recommends the lifting of the anathemas nor the canonization of the previously anathematized Fathers of the other Church, but proposes "that formal anathemas and condemnation of revered teachers of the other side should be discontinued as in the case of Leo, Dioscorus, Severus, and others." This passive action is regarded as implied by the restoration of full Communion.

(c) The jurisdictional questions related to uniting the Churches at local, regional and world levels

With respect to the restoration of the full communion, the study group also approached canonical and liturgical issues not only from an administrative perspective, but also from an ecclesiological one. They proposed a view of an open unity manifested not on the administrative level, but on the liturgical, Eucharistic level: "Most cities will need to have more than one bishop and more than one Eucharist, but it is important that the unity is expressed in Eucharistic Communion." This solution corresponds to the situation in the Eastern Orthodox Diaspora, where for pragmatic reasons several bishops belonging to different Eastern Orthodox Mother Churches were accepted into one city, even though this contravenes the ecclesiastical and canonical rules. On the other hand, the group stressed the necessity to clarify further aspects regarding the process of restoring the Church unity, even if we speak about a unity in diversity: "The universal tradition of the Church does not demand uniformity in all details of doctrinal formulation, forms of worship and canonical practice. But the limits of variability need to be more clearly worked out."

III. Towards a statement of reconciliation

The study group reaffirmed the need for an official joint commission delegated by the Churches and mandated to draft an explanatory statement of reconciliation, which could then be the fundament for restoring the Church unity. This statement of reconciliation, with a special accent on the common Christological agreement, could be centred on the theology of St. Cyril of Alexandria and on the *Formula Concordiae* with John of Antioch

Part V: Bilateral Dialogues between Eastern Orthodox Churches
and other Churches and Christian Traditions

(433). It should be worded in unambiguous terminology that would make it clear that the text would not be an innovation, but the teaching of both Churches which has been held by both sides for centuries, as is attested by the liturgical and patristic documents.

IV. Some practical steps

After mentioning the visits between the two families of Churches on the levels of bishops and theologians, as well as the exchange of students (Oriental Orthodox students studying at Eastern Orthodox Theological Institutions), the wish was expressed to proceed from the unofficial to the official level of dialogue.

The study group proposed that the participants should found a working group in order to continue the previous efforts and to form an Executive Committee[7] with the following objectives:

(a) Publication of a report on the last consultation in the *Greek Orthodox Theological Review*;

(b) Presenting the Churches with a summary of the three unofficial meetings;

(c) Publication of a handbook on both Church traditions with statistical, historical and theological information;

(d) Exploration of the possibility to found an association of all the Orthodox theological institutions;

(e) Publication of a periodical, which will continue to provide information about the Churches and to follow further discussions;

(f) Contribution to a better knowledge of the Churches by providing access to the original sources for an informed and accurate study of theological and spiritual developments;

(g) Encouragement of theological consultations on contemporary issues;

(h) Exploration of the possibilities to establish a common research centre for Orthodox theological and historical studies;

(i) Exploration of the possibility to create and employ common teaching material for children and youth.
The document ends with the signatories list.[8]

1971 - Addis Ababa, Ethiopia[9]

The forth and last unofficial consultation took place on 22 and 23 January 1971 in Addis Ababa, Ethiopia. The main topic of discussion was the lifting of the anathemas and the recognition of the saints.

This "indispensable step on the way to unity" has as its purpose the improvement of the communication between the two Church families. As a precondition for the lifting of the anathemas the study group emphasizes the unity in faith, which should be officially proclaimed by the Churches on the basis of the elaborated documents from Aarhus, Bristol and Geneva. The lifting of the anathemas does not lead to the canonisation

---

[7] Members of the Executive Committee: Metropolitan Emilianos of Calabria, Archpriest Vitalij Borovoj, Vardapet Mesrob Krikorian, Prof. Nikos Nissiotis, Rector Paul Verghese.

[8] Dr. Athanasios Arvanitis, Church of Greece, Archpriest Vitaly Borovoy, Russian Orthodox Church, Prof. Nicolae Chiţescu, Romanian Orthodox Church, Metropolitan Emilianos of Calabria, Ecumenical Patriarchate, Rev. Professor G. Florovsky, Ecumenical Patriarchate, Metropolitan Georges from Mt. Lebanon, Greek Orthodox Patriarchate of Antioch, Metropolitan Nikodim of Sliwen, Bulgarian Orthodox Church, Prof. Nikos Nissiotis, Church of Greece, ArchimandriteDamaskinos Papandreou, Ecumenical Patriarchate, Prof. Bojan Piperov, Bulgarian Orthodox Church, John S. Romanides, Church of Greece, Prof. L Voronov, Russian Orthodox Church, Bishop Petros of Cherson, Russian Orthodox Church, Prof. J. Karmiris, Church of Greece, Prof. Gerassimos I. Konidaris, Church of Greece, Prof. J. Meyendorff, Orthodox Church in America, Prof. N. Zabolotzky, Russian Orthodox Church, Dr. J.D. Zizioulas, Church of Greece, Prof. I. Zonewsky, Bulgarian Orthodox Church, Kahali Alemu, Ethiopian Orthodox Church, Nerses Bozabalian, Armenian Orthodox Church, Rector Paul Verghese, Syrian Orthodox Church of India, Liqe Siltanat Habte Mariam Worqneh, Ethiopian Orthodox Church, Abba G.E. Degou, Ethiopian Orthodox Church, Bishop Amba Gregorius, Coptic Orthodox Church, Metropolitan Severius Zakka Iwas, Syrian Orthodox Church, Dr. K.C. Joseph, Syrian Orthodox Church of India, Dr. Vardapet Mesrob Krikorian, Armenian Orthodox Church, Metropolitan Mar Theophilus Philippos, Syrian Orthodox Church of India. Advisor of the consultation on behalf of WCC was Dr. Lukas Vischer.

[9] Original English version in *Greek Orthodox Theological Review* 16 (1971): 210-259.

of those persons which were previously anathematized, but Churches have the right to keep their own list of saints and their liturgical praxis. The study group advocated the quiet dropping of the anathemas and proposed that a formal announcement should be made at the time of the union. The lifting of the anathema is the responsibility of the Church, which pronounced it upon certain persons or teachings at a certain time due to pastoral reasons.

The theological consequences of lifting the anathema were extensively discussed: it does not compromise the infallibility of the Church, it is not the exclusive function of an Ecumenical Synod, it is a theological process that should be preceded by a thorough study of the rejected teachings and the historical context of the anathematisation, as well as by a research of the methods for lifting the anathemas in the Church history.

This procedure should be followed by a process of actualisation and education, especially in those Churches that included the anathema in their liturgical texts and services: the revised texts should be explained to the believers. Also handbooks, textbooks and reference books should be revised according to the statement of reconciliation. Writings of Church history should be improved through objective research of the sources.

The study group noticed that the criteria for the canonisation of a Saint fluctuate from Church to Church and recommended a study of this differences which directly influence the lifting of the anathemas.

In the end of the common statement the representatives of the Churches expressed their hope that their 7-year work at an unofficial level will be continued at the official level by their churches.[10]

4. Official Dialogues

1985 - Chambésy, Switzerland[11]

In Chambésy, Switzerland between 10 and 15 December 1985 the first official consultation of the Joint Commission of the theological dialogue between the Orthodox Church and the Oriental Orthodox Churches took place. In the communiqué of the meeting the commission recalls the two decades of unofficial theological consultations and the reconciling grace of the Holy Spirit, which led the two families of the Orthodox Tradition[12] to take up the theological dialogue at an official level.

The common belief in one God, the Holy Trinity, Father, Son and Holy Spirit and the concern for the unity of the Body of Jesus Christ gave the impulse for this further step. The discussion about the proper appellation of the two families in the dialogue was followed by an evaluation of the unofficial consultations.

---

[10] Signatories: Metr. Parthenios of Carthage, Patriarchate of Alexandria, Metr. Nikodim of Leningrad, Russian Orthodox Church, Metr. Nikodim of Attica, Greek Orthodox Church, Metr. Methodios of Axum, Patriarchate of Alexandria, Archpr. L. Voronov, Russian Orthodox Church, Prof. S. Agouridis, Greek Orthodox Church, Prof. N. Nissiotis, Greek Orthodox Church, Prof. T. Sabev, Bulgarian Orthodox Church, Archpr. V. Borovoj, Russian Orthodox Church, Prof. P. Fouyas, Greek Orthodox Church, Dr. A. Mitsides, Orthodox Church of Cyprus, Fr. S. Hackel, Russian Orthodox Church, Fr. N. Osolin, Russian Orthodox Church, Bishop Samuel, Coptic Orthodox Church, Bishop Karekin Sarkissian, Armenian Orthodox Church, Paul Verghese, Syrian Orthodox Church of India, Liqe Siltanat Habte Mariam Workineh, Ethiopian Orthodox Church, Prof. Mikre Selassie Gebre Ammanue, Ethiopian Orthodox Church, Vardapet Nerses Bosabalian, Armenian Orthodox Church, Dr. K.M. Simon, Syrian Orthodox Patriarchate, Ato A. Yigzaw, Ethiopian Orthodox Church, Ato A. Amare, Ethiopian Orthodox Church, Ato A. Bekele, Ethiopian Orthodox Church, Ato W. Selassie, Ethiopian Orthodox Church, Ato A. Gulte, Ethiopian Orthodox Church, Archpr. M. Ketsela, Ethiopian Orthodox Church, Melake Berhanat Tesfa of Borana, Ethiopian Orthodox Church. Advisor of the consultation on behalf of WCC was Dr. Lukas Vischer; protocol: Fr. Philip Cousins. Also present were D.A. Aberra, Ethiopian Orthodox Church, Fr. N. Taffesse, Ethiopian Orthodox Church, Fr. G.I. Degou, Ethiopian Orthodox Church.

[11] Original English version in Christian Orient (Kottayam) 10 (1989): 188-189 and J. Gros, H. Meyer, W.G. Rusch (eds.), Growth in Agreement II, 190.

[12] The formula "two families of the Orthodox Tradition" was recurrent throughout the dialogue and in the common statements and shaped the understanding between the two sides, as well as the dialogue itself.

Part V: Bilateral Dialogues between Eastern Orthodox Churches
and other Churches and Christian Traditions

The agreed methodology presupposes the establishment of a Joint Subcommittee of six theologians, three from each side, with the mandate to prepare common texts for the discussions of the Joint Commission. The topics of the next meeting were focused upon the common ground in Christology and Ecclesiology under the generic title "Towards a common Christology."[13]

The participants expressed special thanks to the Ecumenical Patriarchate for convening and hosting the event and providing the necessary facilities. The document was signed by the two Co-Presidents of the Commission: Prof. Dr. Chrysostomos (Konstandinidis), Metropolitan of Myra, Ecumenical Patriarchate and Bishop Bishoy, Coptic Orthodox Church.

1989 – Anba Bishoy, Egypt[14]

With the meeting from the monastery Anba Bishoy in Wadi El Natrun, Egypt, held between 20 and 24 June, 1989 the Joint Commission began the actual dialogue and the elaboration of the agreements between the two Church families. Twenty three participants from 13 countries and 13 Churches attended the consultation. The Commission approached the report of the Joint Sub-Committee of six theologians on the present problems of terminology and interpretation of Christological dogmas, prepared during a special meeting in Corinth (1987). Based on this report, a brief statement of faith was elaborated,[15] which was later – after certain corrections – adopted by the Commission and transmitted to the Churches for their approval.

First Agreed Statement

The agreed statement refers to the one apostolic faith and tradition as a common heritage of the two families of Orthodox Churches from the Church Fathers in Christ. This legacy was preserved in spite of the centuries-long separation and is expressed in the common Creed. As already stated in the unofficial dialogues, the core of the common Christological teaching consists of the formula of St. Cyril of Alexandria, i.e. "*mia physis* (hypostasis) *tou Theou Logou sesarkomene*,"[16] and of his dictum according to which "it is sufficient for the confession of our true and irreproachable faith to say and to confess that the Holy Virgin is Theotokos (Hom : 15, cf. Ep. 39)."

The Christological mystery of the Incarnation is linked to the mystery of the Holy Trinity, "the Father, Son and Holy Spirit, one True God, one *ousia* in three *hypostaseis* or three *prosopa*," in order to express the common belief in the eternal Logos as the dynamic principle of the Incarnation:

> "The Logos, eternally consubstantial with the Father and the Holy Spirit in His Divinity, has in these last days, become incarnate of the Holy Spirit and Blessed Virgin Mary Theotokos, and thus became man, consubstantial with us in His humanity but without sin. He is true God and true Man at the same time, perfect in his Divinity, perfect in His humanity. Because the one she bore in her womb was at the same time fully God as well as fully human we call the Blessed Virgin Theotokos."

---

[13] Sub-themes: a) Problems of terminology; b) Conciliar formulations; c) Historical factors; d) Interpretation of Christological dogmas today. In his evaluation of the dialogue with the Oriental Churches Metropolitan Damaskinos of Switzerland states that already at this first official meeting four main points were regarded as decisive: a. The indissoluble unity between the "horos" of the 4th Ecumenical Council and the Christological decisions of other Ecumenical Councils; b. the recognition of the four post-Ephesian Ecumenical Councils by the Oriental Churches; c. the lifting of the anathemas; and d. common actions for current pastoral issues. See Episkepsis 516 (1995): 10-11.

[14] Original English version in *Christian Orient (Kottayam)* 10 (1989): 191-193; J. Gros, H. Meyer, W.G. Rusch (eds.), *Growth in Agreement* II, 191-193; *Greek Orthodox Theological Review* 34 (1989) 393-397.

[15] The drafting group was composed of Metropolitan Paulos Mar Gregorios of New Delhi, Professor Vlassios Pheidas, Prof. Fr. John Romanides, Prof. Dimitroff, and Mr. Joseph Moris Faltas.

[16] The term *hypostasis* was added by the signatories of the document as an explanation of their understanding of the Christological formula.

This Orthodox confession is followed by some clarifications concerning certain controversial Christological expressions. Thus, the Eastern Orthodox theologians gave explanations concerning the Neo-Chalcedonian concept of composite hypostasis (*synthetos hypostasis*): it does not express the union of two distinct hypostasis belonging to the two natures, but the real union between the two natures in the One hypostasis of the Son:

"When we speak of the one composite (*synthetos*) hypostasis of our Lord Jesus Christ, we do not say that in Him, a divine hypostasis and a human hypostasis came together. It is that the one eternal hypostasis of the Second Person of the Trinity has assumed our created human nature in that act uniting it with His own uncreated divine nature, to form an inseparably and unconfusedly united real divine-human being, the natures being distinguished from each other in contemplation (*theoria*) only."

Far from being a concession made to the Miaphysite side, the "distinction in contemplation (*en theoria*)" is a Christological expression of St. Cyril of Alexandria meant to emphasize the difference between his teaching and that of Nestorius.[17] The theologians went on explaining that the hypostasis of the Logos was not composite neither before nor after the Incarnation, but it was called so "on account of the natures which are united to form one composite unity":

"The hypostasis of the Logos before the incarnation, even with His divine nature, is of course not composite. The same hypostasis, as distinct from nature, of the Incarnate Logos is not composite either. The unique *theandric* person (*prosopon*) of Jesus Christ is one eternal hypostasis who has assumed human nature by the Incarnation. So we call that hypostasis composite, on account of the natures which are united to form one composite unity."

As for the terminology and its different employment in the Christology of the Church Fathers, the undertaken studies proved that

"it is not the case that our Fathers used *physis* and *hypostasis* always interchangeably and confused the one with the other. The term hypostasis can be used to denote both the person as distinct from nature, and also the person with the nature, for a hypostasis never in fact exists without a nature."

The mystery of the Incarnation, i.e. of the hypostatic union, is described as

"the real union of the divine with the human, with all the properties and functions of the uncreated divine nature, including natural will and natural energy, inseparably and unconfusedly united with the created human nature with all its properties and functions, including natural will and natural energy. It is the Logos Incarnate who is the subject of all the willing and acting of Jesus Christ."

The document refers again to the term hypostasis, which actually was the key-term of the theological dialogue. It is confessed once more that "it is the same hypostasis of the Second Person of the Trinity, eternally begotten from the Father who in these last days became a human being and was born of the Blessed Virgin."

This common confession of faith is presented as contrary to the teachings of Nestorius and Eutyches, the two heresies being condemned. In positive terms, this means that "we neither separate nor divide the human nature in Christ from His divine nature, nor do we think that the former was absorbed in the latter and thus ceased to exist."

The famous four adverbs used at the Council of Chalcedon in order to create a framework for expressing the unity of the natures in Christ – without commingling (or confusion, *asyngchytos*), without change (*atreptos*), without separation (*achoristos*) and without division (*adiairetos*) – are explicitly included in the common

---

[17] PG 77, 193-197.

theological tradition of both Orthodox Church families. The Commission states herewith that both traditions developed within the framework built up by the four adverbs:

> "Those among us who speak of two natures in Christ, do not thereby deny their inseparable, indivisible union; those among us who speak of one united divine-human nature in Christ do not thereby deny the continuing dynamic presence in Christ of the divine and the human, without change, without confusion."

Even though the Church separation was caused by the Christological controversy, the agreed statement "is not limited to Christology," but encompasses "the whole faith of the one undivided church of the early centuries." Special mention is made of the Pneumatology in contrast to the concept of *filioque* professed by the Roman Catholic Church: "We are agreed also in our understanding of the Person and Work of God the Holy Spirit, who proceeds from the Father alone, and is always adored with the Father and the Son."

The Joint Commission also appointed a joint Sub-Committee for Pastoral Problems between churches of the two families.[18] The joint Sub-Committee was supposed to meet from 5 to 9 of December 1989 in Anba Bishoy Monastery and to prepare a report for the next meeting of the joint Commission, which was decided to take place in September 1990 at Chambésy, Geneva. The agenda of the meeting in Chambésy included discussions about the report of the joint Subcommittee on Pastoral Problems, the Conciliar formulations and anathemas, the interpretation of Christological dogmas today, historical factors for the Church separation and future steps towards reconciliation.

The document ends with the proclamation of the established name of the Joint Commission – Joint Commission of the Orthodox Church and the Oriental Orthodox Churches – followed by the signatures of the officials.[19]

1990 - Chambésy, Switzerland[20]

As established in the previous meeting, the Joint-Commission of the Theological Dialogue between the Orthodox Church and the Oriental Orthodox Churches met in Chambésy, Geneva, from 23-28 September for the third official dialogue between the two Orthodox Church families.[21]

The Theological Sub-Committee, gathered at the Orthodox Centre, Chambésy (20-22 September 1990), and the Sub-Committee on Pastoral Relations, summoned at the Anba Bishoy Monastery, Egypt (31 January-4 February 1990) submitted their reports for evaluation and approval. The Theological Sub-Committee presented 6 papers on crucial topics like the dogmatic formulations, anathemas, terminology, historical factors for the Church separation and contemporary interpretation of dogmas.[22] The basis for the dialogue was completed with a "Summary of Conclusions" of the Fourth Unofficial Dialogue at Addis Ababa (1971). During the de-

---

[18] The Sub-Committee was composed of ten persons: Metropolitan Damaskinos, Bishop Bishoy, Prof. Vlassios Pheidas, Bishop Mesrob Krikorian, Metropolitan Georges Khodr of Mt Liban, Metropolitan Petros of Axum, Prof. Gosevic (Serbia), Prof. K.M. George (India), a nominee of Patriarch Ignatius Zakka Iwas of Syria, Metropolitan Gregorios of Shoa.

[19] Metropolitan Damaskinos Papandreou, Bishop Bishoy, Prof. Vlassios Phidas, Dr. Paulos Mar Gregorios, Dr. Joseph Moris Faltas.

[20] Original English version in *Greek Orthodox Theological Review* 36 (1991): 185-188; J. Gros, H. Meyer, W.G. Rusch (eds.), Growth in Agreement II, 194-199.

[21] The six-day meeting gathered 34 participants from 17 countries (Austria, Bulgaria, Cyprus, Czechoslovakia, Egypt, Ethiopia, Finland, Greece, India, Lebanon, Poland, Switzerland, Syria, U.K., U.S.A., U.S.S.R. – Russian Church, Georgian Church and Armenian Church –, and Yugoslavia).

[22] *Dogmatic Formulations and Anathemas by Local and Ecumenical Synods within their Social Context* - Revd Prof. John S. Romanides, Church of Greece; *Anathemas and Conciliar Decisions - Two issues to be settled for Restoration of Communion Among Oriental Orthodox and Eastern Orthodox Churches* - Dr. Paulos Mar Gregorios, Metropolitan of Delhi, Orthodox Syrian Church of the East; *Historical Factors and the Council of Chalcedon* - Fr. T. Malaty, Coptic Orthodox Church; *Historical Factors and the Terminology of the Synod of Chalcedon (451)* - Prof. Dr. Vlassios Pheidas, Greek Orthodox Patriarchate of Alexandria; *Interpretation of Christological Dogmas Today* - Metropolitan George Khodr - Greek

bates two drafting committees worked on the output of this meeting, i.e. the *Second Agreed Statement and Recommendations to the Churches*[23] and the *Recommendations on Pastoral issues.*[24]

Second Agreed Statement and Recommendations to the Churches

The basis for this statement is declared to be the first Agreed Statement on Christology adopted by the Joint Commission of the Theological Dialogue between the Orthodox and Oriental Orthodox Churches at Anba Bishoy Monastery, Egypt. The Second Agreed Statement is described as a sum of "affirmations of our common faith and understanding, and recommendations on steps to be taken for the communion of our two families of Churches in Jesus Christ our Lord, who prayed *that they all shall be one.*"

The document begins with the common rejection of the two Christological heresies condemned at the Councils of Chalcedon (451) and Ephesus (431): Eutychianism and Nestorianism together with "the crypto-Nestorianism of Theodoret of Cyrus."

The Eutychian heretical doctrine is rejected with the argument that "both families confess that the Logos, the Second Person of the Holy Trinity, only begotten of the Father before the ages and consubstantial with Him, was incarnate and was born from the Virgin Mary Theotokos; fully consubstantial with us, perfect man with soul, body and mind (νους); he was crucified, died, was buried, and rose from the dead on the third day, ascended to the Heavenly Father, where He sits on the right hand of the Father as Lord of all Creation. At Pentecost, by the coming of the Holy Spirit He manifested the Church as His Body. We look forward to His coming again in the fullness of His glory, according to the Scriptures."

The Nestorian heresy is rejected on the grounds of common confession: both Orthodox families profess "that it is not sufficient merely to say that Christ is consubstantial both with His Father and with us, by nature God and by nature man; it is necessary to affirm also that the Logos, Who is by nature God, became by nature Man, by His Incarnation in the fullness of time."

An interesting development in the theological dialogue is the adoption of the Neo-Chalcedonian term "composite hypostasis" by both traditions, after the thorough explanations given in the agreed statement of the Second Official Consultation in Anba Bishoy. Thus, "both families agree that the Hypostasis of the Logos became composite (συνθετος) by uniting to His divine uncreated nature with its natural will and energy, which He has in common with the Father and the Holy Spirit, (the) created human nature, which He assumed at the Incarnation and made His own, with its natural will and energy." At this stage, the Miaphysite family proved discernment in accepting the Eastern Orthodox understanding of the *synthethos hypostasis* as an expression of the union of the divine and human natures in Christ and not as an expression of a unity between two pre-existent hypostases. The key issue was here the confession that "He who wills and acts is always the one Hypostasis of the Logos incarnate."

As in the previous agreement the four adverbial constructions of Chalcedon are employed in order to create the framework of the hypostatic and natural union and to preserve for each nature its properties: "Both families agree that the natures with their proper energies and wills are united hypostatically and naturally without confusion, without change, without division and without separation, and that they are distinguished in thought alone (τη θεωρια μονη)." Again the Cyrillian expression "in contemplation" or "in theory" is used in order to distinguish between the common understanding of the "two natures" Christology and the Nestorian heresy. Nevertheless, the interpretation of the post-Ephesian Councils is restricted to the limits imposed by the "Horos of the Third Ecumenical Council and the letter (433) of Cyril of Alexandria to John of Antioch."

Orthodox Patriarchate of Antioch; *Interpretation of Christological Dogmas Today* - Bishop Mesrob Krikorian, Armenian Apostolic Church of Etchmiadzin.

[23] Metropolitan Georges Khodr, Metropolitan Paulos Mar Gregorios, Archbishop Kashishian, Archbishop Garima, Revd. Prof. John Romanides, Metropolitan Matta Mar Eustathius (Syria), Prof. Ivan Dimitrov (Bulgaria) with Prof. V. Pheidas and Bishop Krikorian as co-secretaries.

[24] Prof. Papavassiliou (Cyprus), Bishop Christoforos (Czechoslovakia), Metropolitan Paulos Mar Gregorios and Liqaselttanat Habtemariam (Ethiopia), with Fr. Dr. George Dragas as secretary.

Part V: Bilateral Dialogues between Eastern Orthodox Churches
and other Churches and Christian Traditions

These common dogmas are followed by the mutual recognition of the terminology employed by the two traditions in order to express the mystery of Incarnation:

"The Orthodox agree that the Oriental Orthodox will continue to maintain their traditional Cyrillian terminology of *one nature of the incarnate Logos* (μια φυσις του θεου λογου σεσαρκωμενη), since they acknowledge the double consubstantiality of the Logos which Eutyches denied. The Orthodox also use this terminology. The Oriental Orthodox agree that the Orthodox are justified in their use of the two-natures formula, since they acknowledge that the distinction is *in thought alone* (τη θεωρια μονη). Cyril interpreted correctly this use in his letter to John of Antioch and his letters to Acacius of Melitene (PG 77, 184-201), to Eulogius (PG 77, 224-228) and to Succensus (PG 77, 228-245)."

The two Orthodox families acknowledge the first three Ecumenical Synods as common heritage. While the Eastern Orthodox consider the following four Ecumenical Councils as professing the same belief as the first three and acknowledge them as normative, the Oriental Orthodox accept this opinion as a legitimate interpretation for their partners. Quite incomprehensible proves to be the last statement of this paragraph: "With this understanding, the Oriental Orthodox respond to it positively." It is not clear if the Oriental Orthodox acknowledge the last four Ecumenical Synods and their decisions or if they simply accept that these Councils rightfully belong to the Eastern Orthodox tradition and do not come into conflict with the teaching of the Oriental Orthodox.

However, the two traditions rediscovered their common belief in the praxis of the veneration of icons, as expressed by the 7th Ecumenical Council (787). Thus, "Oriental Orthodox agree that the theology and practice of the veneration of icons taught by that Council are in basic agreement with the teaching and practice of the Oriental Orthodox from ancient times, long before the convening of the Council, and that we have no disagreements in this regard." This issue is of vital importance also for the Christology, since the Incarnation is one of the theological arguments for the reverence, which Orthodox Christians show to the icons.

The 9th paragraph of the document formulates the conclusion of both Agreed Statements: "we have now clearly understood that both families have always loyally maintained the same authentic Orthodox Christological faith, and the unbroken continuity of the apostolic tradition, though they may have used Christological terms in different ways. It is this common faith and continuous loyalty to the Apostolic Tradition that should be the basis of our unity and communion." This conclusion proves that the dialogue partners managed to look beyond the terminological differences and to verify how the original intention and the meaning of the words are to be understood. In this way, they elaborated – based on the theological arguments of both traditions – a fundament for restoring the Church unity and the full communion between the two families of Churches. The consequence of the theological reconciliation is naturally the return to full communion, the lifting of the anathemas and condemnations of the Councils and Fathers sentenced in the past.

This conclusion is followed by three practical steps:

1. The Orthodox should lift all anathemas and condemnations against all Oriental Orthodox Councils and fathers whom they anathematised or condemned in the past.
2. The Oriental Orthodox should at the same time lift all anathemas and condemnations against all Orthodox Councils and fathers, whom they anathematised or condemned in the past.
3. The manner in which the anathemas are to be lifted should be decided by the Churches individually.

The signed[25] document was submitted to the Churches for "for their consideration and action."

[25] Metropolitan Damaskinos, Metropolitan Bishoy, Prof. Vlassios Pheidas, Bishop Dr. Mesrob Krikorian, Pro. Athanasios Arvanitis, Metropolitan Dr. Paulos Mar Gregorios, Metropolitan Chrysostomos of Peristerion, Dr Joseph M. Faltas, Prof. Father George Dragas, Bishop Serapion, Father Tadros Y. Malaty, Metropolitan Eustathius Matta Rouhm, Metropolitan George Khodr, Mr Nikolai Zabolotski, Mr. Grigorij Skobej, Archbishop Aram Keshishian, Professor Stojan Gosevic, Archbishop Mesrob Ashdjian, Father George Kondortha, Dr. Ivan Zhelev Dimitrov, Archbishop Abba Gerima Elvabur, Rev Habte Mariam Warkineh, Metropolitan David of Sukhum, Er Boris Gagua, Horepiskopos Barnabas of Salamis, Professor Andreas Papavasiliou, Metropolitan Meletios of Nikopolis, Prof. Father John Romanides, Bishop Jeremiasz of Wroclaw, Bishop Christoforos of Olomouc, Father Joseph Hauser, Father Heikki Huttunen.

Recommendations on Pastoral Issues

The Joint Pastoral Sub-Committee elaborated this approved document during a previous meeting at the Anba Bishoy Monastery in Egypt from 31 January-4 February 1990. It tackled four areas of pastoral care:

I. Relations between the two families of Orthodox Churches and the preparation for restoring the Church unity.

The starting point of the discussion was the need of the Orthodox clergy and faithful to benefit of "a period of intense preparation" for the restoration of full communion. The "practical procedure" proposed by the Commission involves exchanges of visits by the heads of Churches together with prelates, priests and lay people to their Orthodox brothers, exchange of theology professors and students for minimum one year, participation of people belonging to one congregation in the Eucharistic worship of the other Orthodox congregation on Sundays and feast days – it is not mentioned whether the document refers to the common feast days or it includes also the particular celebrations of each Church – in the places where the two families are both represented, publication of the key documents of the dialogue between the Eastern Orthodox and the Oriental Orthodox Churches, with explanations concerning the Christological agreement, editing booklets with historical information about all the Orthodox Churches and with new results of the research on the controversies of the fifth, sixth and seventh centuries. The Commission recommends to the Churches of both families to agree not to "re-baptize members of each other" and to recognize "the baptism of the Churches of our two families, if they have not already done so." Furthermore, the Churches are invited to initiate bilateral negotiations for sharing church premises in special cases when one of them is deprived of such means and for solving possible conflicts between them through bilateral agreements.[26]

Regarding theological education, the Churches are called to revise their theological curriculum and handbooks in order to promote "better understanding of the other family of Churches" and to instruct "the pastors and people in our congregations on the issues related to the union of the two families."

II. Relations of the Orthodox Churches with other Christian Churches and the common participation in the Ecumenical Movement.

This chapter is probably the most visible step towards unity, since it articulates the programme[27] of the preliminary discussion for a "better coordination" in order to fruitfully and effectively testify the "Faith, which was once delivered to the saints" in the framework of the Ecumenical Movement. The Orthodox family makes here the first attempt to speak with one voice in the Ecumenical dialogue. For the beginning some topics were proposed, "in which our two families agree fundamentally and have disagreements with the Roman Catholic and Protestant Churches": position and role of women in the Church life (with the aim of providing a common Orthodox response to the question of women's ordination); pastoral care for mixed marriages between Orthodox and heterodox Christians on the one hand, and between Orthodox Christians and non-Christians on the other hand; family issues (like divorce, annulment of marriage and separation of couples) and abortion. Special joint consultations were planned with regard to proselytism and the procedures for Christians to join another Christian church (special mention is made here of Catholic and Protestant churches), as well as concerning the "theology and practice of Uniatism in the Roman Catholic Church," as a "prelude" to a necessary discussion with the Church of Rome. The Commission also proposed a joint consultation meant to evaluate and coordinate the results of bilateral dialogues held by some of the Orthodox Churches with Protestant or Catholic Churches.

III. The common Orthodox service to the world of suffering, need, injustice and conflicts.

A small chapter is dedicated to the "need to think together" for "promoting our humanitarian and philanthropic projects." The Orthodox theologians merely proposed some areas of social commitment: (a) hunger and

---

[26] The Commission gives some examples of conflicts: marriages consecrated in one Church being annulled by a bishop of another Church; marriages between members of the two families, being celebrated in one church against the resolutions of the other; or children from such marriages being forced to join one church against the other.

[27] The commission proposed to begin the discussion at the 7th Assembly of WCC at Canberra, Australia, in February 1991 and to continue with regional and national councils of Churches and joint consultations.

Part V: Bilateral Dialogues between Eastern Orthodox Churches
and other Churches and Christian Traditions

poverty, (b) sickness and suffering, (c) political, religious and social discrimination, (d) refugees and victims of war, (e) youth, drugs and unemployment, (f) the mentally and physically handicapped, (g) the old and the aged.

IV. The Orthodox co-operation in the propagation of the common faith and tradition.

The last point on the agenda was the Church mission, both in the inner and outer dimensions. The Commission expressed the need of the Orthodox churches to cooperate "as far as possible" to instruct their believers in faith and teach them how to cope with the social and cultural transformations in their societies. Concrete mention is made of issues like secularism, materialism, AIDs, homosexuality, consumerism etc. Concerning the outer mission the Commission emphasised the "need to find a proper way for collaborating with each other and with other Christians in the Christian mission to the world without undermining the authority and integrity of the local Orthodox Churches."

1993 - Chambésy, Switzerland[28]

Three years later, between 1 and 6 November 1993, the Joint Commission of the theological dialogue between the Orthodox Church and the Oriental Orthodox Churches, "following the mandate of their Churches," met again in Chambésy, Switzerland, with the declared purpose to "consider the procedure for the restoration of full communion." The participants discussed "in an atmosphere of prayer and warm, cordial, Christian brotherly love."[29] The two chairmen of the meeting, Metropolitan Damaskinos of Switzerland and Metropolitan Bishoy of Damiette established the two dimensions of the dialogue: to evaluate correctly the truly historic theological work of the Commission accomplished in the previous meetings and to facilitate the necessary ecclesiastical procedures for the restoration of full communion.

The two delegations met separately and elaborated their position on the following issues:

1. What is the competent ecclesiastical authority from each side for the lifting of the anathemas and what are the presuppositions for the restoration of ecclesiastical communion?
2. Which anathemas of which synods and persons can be lifted in accordance with the proposal of paragraph 10 of the second Common Statement?
3. What is the canonical procedure of each side for the lifting of the anathemas and the restoration of ecclesiastical communion?
4. How can we understand and implement the restoration of ecclesiastical communion in the life of our Church?
5. What are the canonical and liturgical consequences of full communion?[30]

They summarized their conclusions in two different reports, which were presented to the plenary meeting for clarifications and discussion. The drafting committee[31] prepared appropriate *Proposals* to the two church families for lifting of mutual anathemas and restoring full communion among them.

The *Proposals* are particularly based on the *Agreed Statements on Christology* issued at St. Bishoy Monastery in 1989 and at Chambésy in 1990 and on "their common acknowledgement of the fact that the Councils and Fathers previously anathematized or condemned are orthodox in their teachings," but mention is also made of the four unofficial consultations (1964, 1967, 1970, 1971) and the three official meetings (1985, 1989, 1990), which led to the conclusion that "both families have loyally maintained the authentic orthodox Christological doctrine, and the unbroken continuity of the apostolic tradition, though they may have used Christological terms in different ways." The practical steps towards restoration of the full communion are thus based on an

---

[28] Original English version in J. Gros, T.F. Best, L.F. Fuchs (eds.), *Growth in Agreement* III, 4-7.

[29] The 30 participants came from Albania, Austria, Cyprus, the Czech Republic, Egypt, Ethiopia, Finland, Greece, India, Lebanon, Poland, Romania, Russia, Switzerland, Syria, United Kingdom and USA.

[30] J. Gros, T.F. Best, L.F. Fuchs (eds.), *Growth in Agreement* III, 4-5.

[31] Metropolitan Bishoy of Damiette, Metropolitan Gregorios Yohanna Ibrahim of Aleppo, Archbishop Mesrob Krikorian from the Oriental Orthodox side and Professors Fr. John Romanides, Fr. George Dragas and Vlassios Pheidas from the Eastern Orthodox side.

accurate review of Church history and especially on a theological reassessment of the Christological controversies of the 5th century.

Concerning the lifting of the anathemas, the Commission recommended that:

> "The lifting of the anathemas should be made unanimously and simultaneously by the Heads of all the Churches of both sides, through the signing of an appropriate ecclesiastical Act, the content of which will include acknowledgement from each side that the other one is orthodox in all respects."

This decision actually considers the issue of the reception of the dialogue in the partner Churches, since the signing of such an ecclesiastical act "unanimously and simultaneously" requires a positive response to the recommendations of the Commission *in all the Churches* and a thorough study concerning the theological and spiritual tradition of "the other" in order to acknowledge its Orthodoxy *in all respects*. That means that the Commission does not impose its conclusion on the Churches and that the lifting of the anathemas and implicitly the restoration of the full communion cannot be decided by certain Churches or Church representatives, but by all the Orthodox Churches by means of an unanimous and simultaneous ecclesiastical act. This is a very important decision, since according to the Commission the act of lifting the anathemas implies: a. that restoration of full communion for both sides is to be immediately implemented; b. that no past condemnation, synodical or personal, against each other is applicable anymore; c. that a catalogue of Diptychs of the Heads of the Churches should be agreed upon to be used liturgically.

Although it recommends such an ecclesiastical act, the Commission is aware of the necessary further work of the Joint Sub-Committee for Pastoral issues according to the agreement from 1990, as well as of the necessity to officially inform the Heads of the Churches about the outcome of the dialogue by direct visits of the two Co-Chairmen of the Joint Committee and by further publications for "explaining our common understanding of the orthodox faith which has led us to overcome the divisions of the past." An important result of this meeting is the appointment of a Liturgical Sub-Committee in order to "examine the liturgical implications arising from the restoration of communion and to propose appropriate forms of con-celebration." Other consequences of the ecclesiastical act of lifting the anathemas, such as matters relating to ecclesiastical jurisdiction, are "left to be arranged by the respective authorities of the local churches according to common canonical and synodical principles."

5. Further steps

In his report on the dialogue with the Oriental Churches from 1995,[32] Metropolitan Damaskinos of Switzerland states that following the fourth official theological consultation in 1993 the two co-presidents of the Joint Commission visited a large number of Churches in order to inform their Heads about the results of the dialogue.[33] The summits proved that the Orthodox Church hierarchy regarded with enthusiasm the achievements and were willing to continue the process of restoring the full communion. In this respect all of them adopted the Agreement proposed by the Joint Commission. They suggested that the ecclesiastical conscience should be thoroughly prepared for the next steps and that theological handbooks should be updated according to the new developments. Regarding the formal proclamation of the ecumenicity of all the seven ecumenical synods by the Oriental Churches it was decided that this was to be regarded as a natural consequence of the restoration of the full communion or be again evaluated in the future. Special mention is made of the criticism exerted by

---

[32] *Episkepsis* 516 (1995): 13-17.

[33] On the Eastern Orthodox side he names the Churches of Jerusalem, Antioch, Cyprus, Greece, Alexandria, Albania, Russia, Georgia, Poland, Romania, Bulgaria and Serbia. On the Oriental Orthodox side are mentioned the Coptic, Ethiopian, Syrian and Armenian Cilician Churches. The plan was to visit by the end of 1995 also the Eastern Orthodox Churches of Czech Republic, Slovakia, Finland, as well as the Syrian Church of India and the Church of Armenia.

some religious circles concerning certain paragraphs of the Second Agreement. The Metropolitan dismissed their arguments as based on unilateral and arbitrary arguments. Some reservations were expressed regarding the lifting of the anathemas for the condemnation of Dioscorus and Severus. The Russian and the Romanian Orthodox Churches also sent written communications to the Joint Commission.[34]

1994

Between 20-23 December 1994 the Joint Commission met at the Coptic monastery Anba Bishoy, in Egypt, to debate about the concrete measures to be taken in order to ensure a proper information of the "People of God" about the theological agreement and the perspectives of restoring the full communion, together with their canonical, liturgical and pastoral consequences. Since the canonical and pastoral aspects were appropriately settled at previous consultations, the main issue was now the liturgical aspect. The proposition of the Romanian Church, supported also by other participants, was to keep both liturgical traditions and in the case of con-celebration to use the local liturgical form. The liturgical Sub-Committee proposed a liturgical form based on the similarities between the Eastern Orthodox liturgies and the Oriental Orthodox liturgies (such as the Coptic liturgy of Saint Mark, the liturgy of the Church of Alexandria or the Armenian liturgy). The same Sub-Committee explored the methods to remove from the liturgical texts all elements, which provoked conflicts in the past or could create confusions concerning theological matters, to prove the validity of some old customs or adapt some feast days.

Three main resolutions were adopted:

a) to watch that the believers are well informed about the results of the dialogue by Church representatives and not misinformed by other circles;

b) to watch over the activity of the liturgical Sub-Committee concerning the consequences and the common liturgical form of con-celebration in the case of restoring the full communion;

c) to watch over the activity of the pastoral Sub-Committee.

1995

The two Sub-Committees for liturgical and pastoral issues came together at the Monastery of Pendeli, near Athens, between 15-19 March 1995. Both of them issued a set of proposals to the Churches. The liturgical Sub-Committee proposed to admit the diversity of liturgical forms "according to the spirit of the old undivided Church" as long as they are not expressions of a different faith than the common faith confessed by all the Orthodox Churches. This requires a further thorough study of those liturgical customs whose theological meaning is not clearly comprehensible yet. When all the Churches have signed the Document of Unification, two solemn con-celebrations should be organised (one in Constantinople and one in an Oriental Orthodox Church) using each time the local liturgical form. In order to avoid misunderstandings on any side, the Sub-Committee suggested that the liturgical diptychs should be kept as before and that any kind of mixture of liturgical customs "which could lead to something similar to the Uniate confusion of the ecclesial cult undertaken by Rome" are not acceptable. In order to achieve these tasks, the participants committed themselves to search for a method to eliminate the anathemas from the liturgical texts according to the view of the Joint Theological Commission and to find new ways to explain more clearly the new developments to the clergy and to the believers.

For its part, the pastoral Sub-Committee considered the proper information of the People of God about the importance, the meaning and the corollary of the dogmatic Christological consensus as groundwork towards the restoration of the full communion. In this respect, the participants proposed the publication of a "theological study" dealing with all the unclear and misunderstood paragraphs of the Christological Agreements and of a "Book of Edification" in which the premises, results and perspectives of the dialogue would be analytically and

---

[34] Both texts in French translation in *Episkepsis* 516 (1995): 15-17.

more simply presented. Each side should elaborate its own "Book of Edification" on the basis of a common text considering the following propositions: 1. to present the ecclesiastical identity of the other side (organisation, teaching, spiritual life, etc.); 2. to explain the reasons of the ecclesiastical separation in the light of the new developments in the framework of the dialogue; 3. to express the conscious pain caused by the fragmentation of the ecclesiastical body; 4. to evaluate the results of the dialogue and to clarify the confusions and misunderstandings about the agreed statements; and 5. to analyse the theological and ecclesiastical importance of restoring the full communion and the perspective of lifting the impediments for the unity of our Churches.

Both Sub-Committees expressed the necessity to meet more often and to evaluate the concrete steps to be undertaken in order to achieve the set goals, and established a subsequent meeting in Cairo for December 1995.

1998

Concrete steps towards a common Orthodox voice in the framework of the Ecumenical Movement, determined partially by the new developments in the Orthodox attitude towards the ecumenical dialogue, were taken in the form of three major consultations which took place in Thessaloniki (Greece April/May 1998), Damascus (Syria May 1998) and New Skete Monastery (near Cambridge, New York USA, 26 May–1 June 1998). On these occasions both families expressed their concerns about the ecclesiological and moral challenges which the new changes and developments in the WCC prepared for the Orthodox participation and articulated an Orthodox position on common worship, liturgical renewal and visible unity.

2001

As a direct outcome of the Recommendations on Pastoral Issues of the Official Theological Dialogue, a Meeting between Eastern Orthodox and Oriental Orthodox took place in Warburg, Germany between 27-29 July 2001 with the participation of more than 30 delegates.[35] The purpose of the meeting was "to know each other better as well as to discuss issues of mutual interest and of possible common action." Discussion sessions on social, liturgical, pastoral and cultural issues alternated with visiting of parishes and monasteries belonging to the Syrian and Coptic Orthodox Churches in Germany. Presentations were made about the Church life on the European continent of the Ethiopian and Armenian Orthodox Churches, as well as of the Finnish, Czech and Romanian Orthodox Churches. Special attention was given to Orthodox Youth Organisations and pastoral programmes for the Orthodox youth.

2005

After the submission of the Final report of the Special Commission on Orthodox Participation in the WCC from February 2005, which proved again that the two Orthodox families share the same opinion concerning their relationship to the WCC and their participation in the ecumenical movement, the Inter-Orthodox Theological Committee for Dialogue between the Orthodox Church and the Oriental Orthodox Churches was summoned at the Orthodox Centre of the Ecumenical Patriarchate in Chambésy, Geneva, from 10-13 March 2005.

Theologians, clergy and lay people involved in this field evaluated the results and prospected for the continuation of the work of the Joint Theological Commission. Several studies were presented and important issues were discussed (e.g. the criteria for evaluating the theological work of the Joint Theological Commission; the Christological agreement and "the refutation of those who objected to the interpretation of the recognition of the 'Orthodoxy' of the non-Chalcedonians by St. John of Damascus"; the obscurities of paragraph 8 of the Second Agreed Theological Statement and the necessity that these be clarified; the liturgical problems that have arisen in

---

[35] Among them Bishop Damian of the Coptic Orthodox Church in Germany; Metropolitan Seraphim, Romanian Orthodox Metropolitan of Western and Central Europe with seat in Germany, as well as Archbishop Mor Julius Cicek of the Syrian Orthodox Church.

Part V: Bilateral Dialogues between Eastern Orthodox Churches
and other Churches and Christian Traditions

the rapprochement of the two ecclesiastical families; the bilateral relations of the Russian Orthodox Church with the Oriental Orthodox Churches and the reservations of the Russian Orthodox Church with respect to the text of the Agreed Statements). Thus the Commission sought to respond to the critical reactions of certain theologians from both families to the developments in the ecumenical dialogue between Eastern and Oriental Orthodox Churches. By virtue of the "unanimous decision of the 3rd Pre-Conciliar Pan-Orthodox Conference (1986)" as the relevant voice of all Orthodox churches and of its conclusion that the theological Dialogue between the Orthodox Church and the pre-Chalcedonian Oriental Orthodox Churches is of particular importance, the Joint Theological Commission and the Sub-Committees on the pastoral and liturgical issues established as their mission in the future to mend the noticed obscurities and/or omissions. The target was to analyse "the reservations or criticism, either justified or unjustified, to the ambiguous points in the two Agreed Theological Statements (1989, 1990) and to the consequences deriving from them." The work of the two sub-committees was regarded as highly important as a way "to demonstrate the significance of the agreement reached on the Christological issue" and "to plan and prepare as required for the ecclesiastical body" a common pastoral and liturgical Church life.

From the theological perspective, one important decision was that "the ecclesiological importance of recognising and including the doctrinal definitions of the 1st, 5th, 6th and 7th Ecumenical Synods must be promoted more fully through special studies on their Cyrillian basis." It is a possible solution to solve the strong requirement of the Eastern Orthodox that the Oriental Orthodox recognise all the seven ecumenical councils on the one hand, and the desire of the Oriental Orthodox to faithfully preserve the Cyrillian theology on the other hand. The commission recommends once more the lifting of the anathemas as a concrete act of restoring the ecclesiastical communion. The participants consider that both "these measures presuppose thorough and integrated research of the theological heritage of both theological traditions and the clarification of the Christological terminology." The publication of "an attractive special volume of all the presentations and studies, which refer to the disputed theological issues of the Agreed Theological Statements, or to the refutation of the criticism against them" was planned as well.

6. Evaluation and Perspectives

It is not easy to provide a thorough evaluation of this ecumenical dialogue in a few lines. For some of the participants, their activities and initiatives in the framework of the Eastern Orthodox – Oriental Orthodox Dialogue represent their lifework. Still, in order to proceed to further discussions we need to be aware both of the achievements of this dialogue and of the issues that are yet to deal with.

The general impression is that much accent was put on the fifteen centuries of separation and alienation and too little on the fact that right after the Council of Chalcedon and until the fall of the Byzantine Empire there was an active dialogue between these two Orthodox Church families and countless attempts to re-establish the unity of the Church. At the same time, the two families have never completely ceased their relations altogether. Recent textual studies prove that in spite of the Christological conflict between them, these Churches continued to find inspiration in the writings and values of each other, especially in areas like mystical literature, which were not or only little explored by the participants to the dialogue.[36] Further research projects on such issues are necessary in order to explore both traditions and deepen our knowledge concerning the mutual influence and vivid exchange between our churches. Mainly unexplored also is the common theological ground shared by the two Church families which dates before the activity of St. Cyril of Alexandria, on whose teaching the dialogue is completely centred (e.g. St. Ignatius of Antioch). The impulse given in Bristol (1967) to extend the framework of the dialogue from the plain Christological dispute to a wider approach of soteriological, ecclesiological and anthropological, as well as ecclesiastical liturgical and spiritual matters has not been accordingly assumed.

---

[36] A good example, even beyond the borders of the two families, would be the work of St. Isaac the Syrian, the East-Syrian ("Nestorian") bishop of Niniveh whose writtings were adopted into the Miaphysite West-Syrian tradition by changing some names of the authors he was quoting, and then translated into Greek and spread all over in the Chalcedonian Byzantine and Western European world.

Instead of dealing with such aspects and under the strong influence of the great enthusiasm determined by the preliminary results, the responsible delegates established a rapid agenda of the steps towards the full communion, which led to controversies, since the "People of God" was not properly prepared with thorough information from the clerics, the actualisation of theological handbooks and up-to-date education of future theologians as well as with a careful familiarization of the believers with the results and prospects of the dialogue. This fact negatively influenced both the reception and the continuity of the dialogue and made room for anti-ecumenical circles to mislead the believers regarding the intent, procedures and results of the theological discussions.

The two families developed academic, pastoral and philanthropic cooperation only sporadically and these were limited to different areas and periods. This proves that the ecclesiastical conscience of the two Orthodox families, the fact that they belong together and have responsibilities towards one another, is still a desideratum.

At the same time, after adopting the two Christological Agreements it became obvious that practical, administrative, canonical and jurisdictional issues are as important as the theological concord and even more difficult to achieve. The fact that in spite of the theological agreement and the overcoming of the dogmatic barriers the full communion has not been restored yet is due exclusively to these aspects.

Nevertheless we have been dealing here with the most successful ecumenical dialogue since the grounding of the World Council of Churches, with two positive theological agreements (1989 and 1990) and good prospects for the restoration of the full communion. From the very beginning, this ecumenical dialogue was regarded with much enthusiasm by great theologians of the different Churches, even by some who were only seldom or not at all directly involved in this theological dialogue, such as the Romanian theologians Rev. Prof. Dumitru Stăniloae and Rev. Prof. Ion Bria.

The two Orthodox families managed to overcome dogmatic prejudices and even to express their common faith by using notions, concepts and terms previously employed by only one of the two theological traditions (e.g. on the one hand the four adverbs employed in the Horos of the Council from Chalcedon or the concept of the composite hypostasis; on the other hand the Cyrillian expression "in contemplation" extensively used in the Miaphysite tradition but not very common in the Chalcedonian tradition).

On the ecumenical level the two Church families were able to find their common Orthodox identity and share their views with One strong Orthodox Voice. This is one of the most important achievements of this dialogue and should be acknowledged as such. It created an Orthodox pole in the WCC able to effectively present the specific issues of the Orthodox theology and spirituality and to represent a community with specific values and ideals.

We can only hope that both the academic theology and the ecclesiastical authority will pay more attention to this important and already well developed historical dialogue so that the last hurdles may be overcome and the full communion restored. Only after a proper information of the "People of God," both clerics and believers, can it be assessed to what extent the restoration exists about the ecclesiastical communion and the reunification of the Body of Christ is the will of the entire Church.

7. Bibliography

a. General bibliography on the Oriental Orthodox Churches

Albert, M., Beylot, R., Coquin, R.-G., Outtier, B., and Renoux, Ch., *Christianismes orientaux. Intro-duction à l'étude des langues et des littératures*, (Paris 1993).

Aßfalg, J., and Krüger, P., *Kleines Wörterbuch zum Christlichen Orient*, (Wiesbaden 1975).

Atiya, A., *A History of Eastern Christianity*, (Millwood/N.Y. [2] 1980).

Betts, R.B., *Christians in the Arab East: A political study*, (Atlanta 1981).

Billioud, J.-M., *Histoire des chrétiens d'Orient*, (Paris 1995).

Hage, W., *Das orientalische Christentum*, (Stuttgart 2007).

*Part V: Bilateral Dialogues between Eastern Orthodox Churches
and other Churches and Christian Traditions*

Kaufhold, H. (Hg.), *Kleines Lexikon des Christlichen Orients*, (Wiesbaden 2007).

Lange, C. and Pingerra, K. (eds.), *Die altorientalischen Kirchen: Glaube und Geschichte*, (Darmstadt 2010).

Müller, C. D. G., *Geschichte der orientalischen Nationalkirchen* (Die Kirche in ihrer Ge-schichte; Bd. 1, D2), (Göttingen 1981).

Spuler, B., *Gegenwartslage der Ostkirchen in ihrer nationalen und staatlichen Umwelt*, (Frankfurt am Main 1968).

Parry, K., Brady, D., Melling, D.J., Griffith, S.H., and Healey, J.F., *The Blackwell Dictionary of Eastern Christianity*, (Malden – Oxford 2004).

Verghese, P. (eds.), *Koptisches Christentum. Die orthodoxen Kirchen Ägyptens*, (Stuttgart 1973).

b. Texts and studies on the dialogue

Basdekis, A., *Orthodoxe Kirche und Ökumenische Bewegung, Dokumente - Erklärungen - Berichte 1900-2006*, (Frankfurt am Main 2006).

Chaillot C., Belopopsky, A. (eds), *Towards Unity: The Theological Dialogue between the Orthodox Church and the Oriental Orthodox Churches*, (Geneva: Inter-Orthodox Dialogue, 1998).

FitzGerald, T., Bouteneff, P., *Turn to God. Rejoice in Hope. Orthodox Reflections on the Way to Harare*, (Geneva 1998).

Garijo-Guembe, M.M., Bremer, T., Oeldemann, J., Stoltmann, D., *Orthodoxie im Dialog: bilaterale Dialoge der orthodoxen und der orientalisch-orthodoxen Kirchen 1945-1997: eine Dokumentensammlung*, (Trier 1999).

Gregorios, P., Lazareth, W.H., and Nissiotis, N.A., *Does Chalcedon Divide or Unite? Towards Convergence in Orthodox Christology*, (Geneva 1981).

Gros, J., Meyer, H., and Rusch, W.G. (eds.), *Growth in Agreement II*, (Geneva 2000).

Gros, J., Best, T.F., Fuchs, L.F. (eds.), *Growth in Agreement III*, (Geneva 2007).

Kirchschläger, R. and Stirnemann, A. (eds), *Chalzedon und die Folgen. Festschrift 60. Geburtstag von Bischof Mesrob K. Krikorian*, Pro Oriente XIV, (Innsbruck 1992).

Limouris, G., *Orthodox Visions of Ecumenism. Statements, Messages and Reports on the Ecumenical Movement 1902-1992*, (Geneva 1994).

Lossky, N. *et al.*, *Dictionary of the Ecumenical Movement*, (Geneva 2002).

Methodius of Aksum, *Papers Referring to the Theological Dialogue between the Eastern and Oriental Orthodox Churches*, (Athens 1976).

Moraru, A., *Biserica Ortodoxă Română între anii 1885-2000. Dialog teologic şi ecumenic*, vol. III, Tom II, (Bucureşti 2006).

Samuel, V.C., *The Council of Chalcedon Re-examined: A Historical and Theological Survey*, Madras 1977.

Tsetsis, G., *Orthodox Thought, Reports of Orthodox Consultations organized by the World Council of Churches, 1975-1982*, (Geneva 1983).

Werner, D., Esterline, D., Kang, N., Raja, J., *Handbook of Theological Education in World Christianity. Theological Perspectives – Regional Surveys – Ecumenical Trends*, (Oxford 2010).

c. websites:

http://www.orthodoxunity.org/

http://www.orthodial.com/indexen.html

http://www.svots.edu/content/beyond-dialogue-quest-eastern-and-oriental-orthodox-unity-today

http://www.coptic.net/articles/orthodoxunitydialog.txt

http://www.pluralism.org/affiliates/student/allen/Oriental-Orthodox/Home.html

http://www.orientalorthodoxchurches.com/

http://orthodoxwiki.org/Oriental_Orthodox

(82) Eastern Orthodox – Oriental Orthodox Dialogue – A Historical and Theological Survey

George Martzelos

Introduction

One of the most comforting and promising ecclesiastical developments in recent years was the success of the theological dialogue between the Orthodox Church and the Non-Chalcedonian Churches of the East, i.e. the Coptic, Ethiopian, Jacobite Syrian, Armenian, and Indian Church of Malabar, which all together have around 60 million Christian adherents. After over 1,500 years of mutual suspicion and dogmatic confrontations since the Council of Chalcedon (451) and despite the differences in Christological terminology and the diametrically opposing positions regarding the Chalcedonian definition, the two ecclesiastical families surprisingly came to an agreement to sign a common dogmatic document stating their shared dogmatic faith and teaching throughout the ages. It should be noted that although many gaps and difficulties remain to be sorted out in this theological dialogue before full communion can be reached between the two Churches, the success even captured the attention of Western theologians, both Roman Catholic and Protestant, who were amazed at such an accomplishment.[1]

a. Key Milestones in the Theological Dialogue

The official dialogue was initiated by the Ecumenical Patriarchate at an ecclesiastical level in 1985 in Chambésy in Geneva, Switzerland and lasted until 1993.[2] This undertaking was preceded by fifteen years of unofficial contact and theological talks between the Orthodox and Non-Chalcedonians (1964-1979), during which both groups became acquainted and realized the proximity between their theological traditions in relation to the Christological dogma.

Significant stages in the official theological dialogue include the second general session of the ecclesiastical representatives of both traditions, which took place in June of 1989 at the Holy Monastery of Anba Bishoy in the desert of Nitria, and also the third general session, which was held in Chambésy in September of 1990. It was during these sessions that the common dogmatic statements, which clearly demonstrate total consensus on the essence of the Christological dogma, were signed. It is significant that the success of these above agreements is not limited to Christology only, but extends to the whole faith of the one and undivided Church of the first five centuries, as well as all the dogmatic teachings of the four Ecumenical Councils following the schism of 451. In other words, the Non-Chalcedonians now accept not only the first three Ecumenical Councils, which

---

[1] See A. M. Ritter, «Der gewonnene christologische Konzens zwischen orthodoxen Kirchen im Licht der Kirchenvätertradition», in *Logos. Festschrift für Luise Abramowski*, (Berlin - New York 1993), 469 ff. D. W. Winkler, *Koptische Kirche und Reichskirche. Altes Schisma und neuer Dialog*, (Innsbruck-Wien: Tyrolia-Verlag, 1997), 222 ff., 332; also D. Wendebourg, «Chalkedon in der ökumenischen Diskussion», in *Chalkedon: Geschichte und Aktualität. Studien zur Rezeption der christologischen Formel von Chalkedon*, hrsg. von J. van Oort und J. Roldanus, (Leuven: Peeters, 1998), 193.

[2] For more on the dialogue between Orthodox and Non-Chalcedonians see George Martzelos, Ὁ Θεολογικός Διάλογος τῆς Ὀρθόδοξης Καθολικῆς Ἐκκλησίας μέ τίς Μή-Χαλκηδόνιες Ἐκκλησίες τῆς Ἀνατολῆς. Χρονικό – Ἀξιολόγηση – Προοπτικές (The Theological Dialogue of the Orthodox Catholic Church with the Non-Chalcedonian Churches of the East. Timeline - Evaluation - Prospects), in *The Minutes of the 14th Theological Conference of the Holy Metropolis of Thessaloniki with the topic "I Mitir imon Orthodoxos Ekklisia" (Our Mother the Orthodox Church)» (10-13 November 1993)*, (Thessaloniki 1994), 293 ff.; ibid, Ὀρθόδοξο δόγμα καί θεολογικός προβληματισμός. Μελετήματα δογματικῆς θεολογίας, (Thessaloniki 2000), 247 ff.; Damaskinos Papandreou (Metropolitan of Switzerland), Λόγος Διαλόγου (On Dialogue) (Ἡ Ὀρθοδοξία ἐνώπιον τῆς τρίτης χιλιετίας/Orthodoxy in the the Third Millennium), (Athens: Kastanioti, 1997), 211 ff.(all in Greek).

are common to both traditions, but the dogmatic teachings of the four Councils that followed as well; although, without recognizing them as Ecumenical and equal with the first three.

The third general session mentioned above essentially fulfilled the purpose of the theological dialogue between the two committees as far as the Christological discussion was concerned; this being the main purpose of the dialogues. There remained, however, basic practical issues, which would need to be resolved in order to achieve full sacramental communion and unification between the Orthodox and the Non-Chalcedonians. Such issues include the recognition on the part of the Non-Chalcedonians of the last four Ecumenical Councils as holy and Ecumenical, the theological question of whether or not the Orthodox tradition allows the reversal of anathemas which were issued against certain people and Synods and which ecclesiastical authority would have the power to do so, and also the measure to which pastoral economy could be implemented in matters of liturgical and ecclesiastical administration for the realization of sacramental communion and unification between the two ecclesiastical families. Once more, the Ecumenical Patriarchate took the initiative to address these issues. A plenary session of the Mixed Theological Committee of the dialogue was convened in Chambésy in November of 1993 which, after meticulous considerations, drafted a mutually accepted text, which included specific proposals to both groups for the lifting of the anathemas and the restoration of full communion between them. Although this document does clearly define the way in which the anathemas could be lifted (taking into account the resulting ecclesiastical consequences) and specifically addresses the pastoral and liturgical issues of sacramental unification, it fails to mention the validation of the last four Ecumenical Councils as a presupposition for the sought after sacramental communion.

Having achieved the above-mentioned dogmatic agreements, the dialogue was then completely devolved from the Theological Committee to the level of the local Churches of both sides. Besides the signatures of ecclesiastical leaders who had taken part in the dialogue, the Patriarchates of Constantinople, Alexandria, Antioch, and Romania on the side of the Orthodox and by the Coptic, Jacobite Syrian, and Syro-Malabar Churches on the side of the Non-Chalcedonians upheld the dogmatic agreements with synodal decisions. The fact that the Non-Chalcedonians approved the agreements has especial dogmatic significance since with this action they recognized all the teachings of the seven Ecumenical Councils and the Church Fathers as completely Orthodox.

b. Problems Facing the Theological Dialogue

Despite the astonishing success of this dialogue as far as the Christological aspects were concerned, (which, as mentioned, drew the attention of Western theologians) it must be acknowledged that many obstacles still remain to be overcome before a full sacramental communion can be achieved between the two groups. Although the Non-Chalcedonians had recognized the orthodoxy of the teachings of all the Ecumenical Councils and Church Fathers, as attested to by the signed declarations, they had still not recognized the last four councils as Ecumenical and equal to the first three. This is the most fundamental problem that needs to be resolved before the goal of communion can be realized.

In order to overcome these obstacles, two subcommittees have been created, one for pastoral issues and one for liturgical matters, which meet from time to time, seeking out mutually acceptable solutions to the issues that arose from the success of the aforementioned dogmatic agreement. Specifically, these problems exist because of a lack of awareness regarding the successful dogmatic agreement. There are also steps that still need to be taken to guide us smoothly and certainly to full communion and unification. Regarding the issue of awareness of the proceedings, it must be mentioned that the plenary session of the Mixed Theological Committee confronted this topic during the fourth general assembly (November 1993) and decided that it was necessary for the two vice presidents of the committee to take the following actions: on the one hand they needed to visit the primates of both churches to fully inform them of the results of the dialogue, and on the other hand to collaborate with the two secretaries of the assembly to see to the drawing up of suitable documents that could explain the content of the dogmatic agreement, both at a scientific level and in a context understandable to laypeople, so that any potential misunderstandings could be avoided.

Orthodox Handbook on Ecumenism

However, while the joint vice presidents were very active in organizing the visits to the primates of both churches, very few steps were taken to create texts explaining the outcome of the dialogue. The texts and publications that did circulate were the result of people who took a personal interest and not due to an organized joint effort on the part of the Orthodox and Non-Chalcedonians. Besides this, these publications did not have the widespread impact that was needed to adequately and responsibly inform people regarding the outcome of the dialogue. Naturally the lack of proper and systematic reporting on the results - at least in the Greek Orthodox milieu - led to misinformation. If one excludes paragraph eight of the second joint declaration from 1990 (which needs clarification and better wording to avoid potential misinterpretations and to stop the doubts projected onto it by those who object), the fact remains that certain points of the dogmatic agreement that are indisputably orthodox and patristic in character were deliberately expressed in a vague manner with a clear dogmatic minimalism. This was allegedly done to facilitate a meretricious dogmatic agreement and an ecclesiastical union at the expense of the Orthodox faith.[3] There were, of course, documented responses to these highly critical and largely unwarranted assessments.[4] However, this created confusion in theological and ecclesiastical circles regarding the accomplishments and goals of the Theological Dialogue. In certain instances there were attempts to revive the past and the Fathers of the Church were being interpreted partially and at will in order to bring a halt to the continuation and success of the dialogue. Some considered any further continuation of the dialogue as cause for a split in Orthodoxy.[5] Within the context of these objections, the harmful instances of Orthodoxy digressing into fanaticism were, unfortunately, extremely disappointing. To avoid the reoccurrence of similar deplorable instances, not only is an efficient process of informing needed, but also productive inter-Orthodox deliberations and dialogue within the local Churches so as to create the

[3] See Th. Zisi, Ἡ "Ὀρθοδοξία" τῶν Ἀντιχαλκηδονίων Μονοφυσιτῶν (The "Orthodoxy" of Antichalcedonian Monophysites), (Thessaloniki: Vryennios, 1994). Ibid, Τά ὅρια τῆς Ἐκκλησίας (The Boundaries of the Church). Οἰκουμενισμός καί Παπισμός (Ecumenism and Papism), (Thessaloniki 2004), 104-125. Holy Monastery of Osios Gregory, Εἶναι οἱ Ἀντιχαλκηδόνιοι Ὀρθόδοξοι; Κείμενα τῆς Ἱερᾶς Κοινότητος τοῦ Ἁγίου Ὄρους καί ἄλλων ἁγιορειτῶν Πατέρων περί τοῦ διαλόγου Ὀρθοδόξων καί Ἀντιχαλκηδονίων (Μονοφυσιτῶν) (Texts of the Holy Community of Mount Athos and other hagiorite Fathers on the dialogue between Orthodox and Antichalcedonians (Monophysites), (Mount Athos 1995). Holy Community of Mount Athos, Παρατηρήσεις περί τοῦ Θεολογικοῦ Διαλόγου Ὀρθοδόξων καί Ἀντιχαλκηδονίων (Ἀπάντησις εἰς κριτικήν τοῦ Σεβ. Μητροπολίτου Ἐλβετίας κ. Δαμασκηνοῦ), Observations on the Theological Dialogue between the Orthodox and Antichalcedonians (Responses in critique of his Eminence Damaskinos Metropolitan of Switzerland), (Mount Athos 1996). S. N. Bozovitis, Τά αἰώνια σύνορα τῆς Ὀρθοδοξίας καί οἱ Ἀντιχαλκηδόνιοι (The Eternal borders of Orthodoxy and the Antichalcedonians), (Athens: Brotherhood of Theologians «O Sotir», 1999). A. N. Papavasileiou, Ὁ Θεολογικός Διάλογος μεταξύ Ὀρθοδόξων καί Ἀντιχαλκηδονίων, τόμ. A (The Theological Dialogue between Orthodox and Antichalcedonians), vol. A´, (Lefkosia: Center of Studies Holy Monastery of Kykkou, 2000). J. - C. Larchet, «Τό Χριστολογικό πρόβλημα περί τῆς μελετωμένης ἑνώσεως τῆς Ὀρθοδόξου Ἐκκλησίας καί τῶν Μή-Χαλκηδονίων Ἐκκλησιῶν: Ἐκκρεμοῦντα θεολογικά καί ἐκκλησιολογικά προβλήματα» (The Christological problem on the planned union of the Orthodox Churches and non-Chalcedonian Churches: outstanding theological and ecclesiological problems), in *Theologia* 74.1 (2003): 199-234; 74.2 (2003): 635-670; 75.1 (2004): 79-104 (all in Greek).

[4] See Damaskinos Papandreou (Metropolitan of Switzerland), «Ἀπάντησις εἰς τό Γράμμα τοῦ Ἁγίου Ὄρους περί τοῦ Θεολογικοῦ Διαλόγου πρός τάς Ἀρχαίας Ἀνατολικάς Ἐκκλησίας» (Response to the Letter of the Holy Mountain on the theological dialogue to the Ancient Eastern Church), in *Episkepsis* 521 (1995): 7 ff. ff. and in *Synaxi* 57 (1996): 69 ff. Ibid, Λόγος Διαλόγου (Ἡ Ὀρθοδοξία ἐνώπιον τῆς τρίτης χιλιετίας), (On Dialogue. Orthodoxy in the the Third Millennium), (Athens: Kastanioti, 1997), 237 ff. See also K. Papadopoulou, «Ὁ διάλογος μέ τούς Ἀντιχαλκηδονίους», (The Dialogue with the Antichalcedonians), in *Synaxi* 57 (1996): 43 ff (all in Greek).

[5] See Th. Zissis, Ἡ "Ὀρθοδοξία" τῶν Ἀντιχαλκηδονίων Μονοφυσιτῶν (The "Orthodoxy" of the Antichalcedonian Monophysites), (Thessaloniki: «Bryennios», 1994), 9ff. Ibid, Τά ὅρια τῆς Ἐκκλησίας. Οἰκουμενισμός καί Παπισμός, (The boundaries of the Church. Ecumenism and Papism), (Thessaloniki 2004), 108ff. S. N. Bozovitis, 171 ff. J.-C. Larchet, «Τό Χριστολογικό πρόβλημα περί τῆς μελετωμένης ἑνώσεως τῆς Ὀρθοδόξου Ἐκκλησίας καί τῶν Μή-Χαλκηδονίων Ἐκκλησιῶν: Ἐκκρεμοῦντα θεολογικά καί ἐκκλησιολογικά προβλήματα» (The Christological problem on the planned union of the Orthodox Churches and non-Chalcedonian Churches: outstanding theological and ecclesiological problems)», in *Theologia* 75.1 (2004): 100 (all in Greek).

Part V: Bilateral Dialogues between Eastern Orthodox Churches
and other Churches and Christian Traditions

greatest possible convergence and consensus between the ecclesiastical representatives in dialogue and the rest of the Orthodox flock. Without the greatest possible consensus, the sought after sacramental unification of the two ecclesiastical families poses a danger of creating internal splits among the local Churches, which would be the worst possible outcome.

Concerning the steps that still need to be taken to achieve sacramental unification between the two Churches in dialogue (besides the resolution of the liturgical matters, which the appointed liturgical subcommittees have responsibility for), we have the opinion that the most fundamental obstacle that needs to be surpassed is the question of the Non-Chalcedonians accepting the last four Ecumenical Councils and especially the Council of Chalcedon (451), which was the impetus for the schism in the first place. As was previously highlighted, the Non-Chalcedonians already fully accepted the dogmatic teaching of the last four Ecumenical Councils with the dogmatic agreement included in the common declarations. However, the Non-Chalcedonians have yet to recognize these Councils as Ecumenical and equal with the first three. This position of theirs, especially concerning the Council of Chalcedon, is due just as much to their traditional stance towards the definition of the Council and Pope Leo's Tome, which it approved (they considered the definition and the Tome to have Nestorian traits in the Christology due to the dyophysite wording), as it was to the condemnation by the Council of Dioscorus of Alexandria, whom they honor as a great Father of their Church.

Concerning the definition of Chalcedon, we must highlight the fact that modern academic research has proved very clearly that the theological nature of the definition not only is not Nestorian, but also is Cyrillian.[6] Indeed, the basis of the Dyophysite formula of the definition of Chalcedon has been proven outright to be not Leo's Tome, but the Christology of St. Cyril of Alexandria[7]; something which is acknowledged even by eminent Roman Catholic theologians,[8] who, as one can see, would have every reason to support the opposite opinion. Consequently, it must be understood by the Non-Chalcedonians that, based on modern theological scholarship, their reservation to accept the definition of Chalcedon is unjustifiable as long as they claim to be faithful adherents to the Christology of St. Cyril.

Also, regarding Leo's Tome, we must underline the fact that the Tome was accepted by the Council of Chalcedon, which is already apparent from the minutes of the Council, but only after they proved the orthodoxy and full agreement of the Tome with the epistles of St. Cyril and especially with the third epistle to Nestorius, after the well known intense challenges against its orthodoxy on the part of hierarchs from Eastern Illyricum

---

[6] See Th. Šagi-Bunić, «'Duo perfecta' et 'duae naturae' in definitione dogmatica chalcedonensi», in *Laurentianum* 5 (1964): 203 ff. Ibid, *«Deus perfectus et homo perfectus» a Concilio Ephesino (a. 431) ad Chalcedonense (a. 451)*, (Romae - Friburgi: Brisg. - Barcinone, 1965), 205 ff. A. de Halleux, «La définition christologique à Chalcédoine», in *Revue Théologique de Louvain* 7 (1976): 3ff., 155 ff., 155 ff. G. D. Martezlos, Γένεση καί πηγές τοῦ Ὅρου τῆς Χαλκηδόνας *(Origin and sources of the Definition of Chalcedon). Συμβολή στήν ἱστορικοδογματική διερεύνηση τοῦ Ὅρου τῆς Δ´ Οἰκουμενικῆς Συνόδου (Contribution to the historic dogmatic investigation of the definition of the 4th Ecumenical Council)*, (Thessaloniki 1986), 141ff., 197ff. (in Greek). See also A. M. Ritter, «Patristische Anmerkungen zur Frage "Lehrverurteilungen-kirchentrennend?" am Beispiel des Konzils von Chalkedon», in *Oecumenica et Patristica. Festschrift für Wilchelm Schneemelcher zum 75. Geburtstag*, hrsg. von D. Papandreou - W. A. Bienert - K. Schäferdiek, (Chambésy-Genf 1989), 269ff.

[7] For this subject see G. D. Martzelos, 172 ff. ibid, Ἡ Χριστολογία τοῦ Βασιλείου Σελευκείας καί ἡ οἰκουμενική σημασία της *(The Christology of Basil of Seleucia and its Ecumenical Significance)*, (Thessaloniki 1990), 235ff (in Greek). G. D. Martzelos, «Der Vater der dyophysitischen Formel von Chalkedon: Leo von Rom oder Basileios von Seleukeia?», in *Orthodoxes Forum* 6.1 (1992): 21ff. and in Ysabel de Andia / Peter Leander Hofrichter (Hsg.), *Christus bei den Vätern. Forscher aus dem Osten und Westen Europas an den Quellen des gemeinsamen Glaubens*, Pro Oriente, XXVII, Wiener patristische Tagungen 1 (PRO ORIENTE - Studientagung über „Christus bei den griechischen und lateinischen Kirchenvätern im ersten Jahrtausend" in Wien, 7.-9. Juni 2001), (Innsbruck - Wien: Tyrolia-Verlag, 2003), 272 ff.

[8] See Th. Šagi-Bunić, «'Duo perfecta' et 'duae naturae' in definitione dogmatica chalcedonensi», in *Laurentianum* 5 (1964): 325ff. ibid, *«Deus perfectus et homo perfectus» a Concilio Ephesino (a. 431) ad Chalcedonense (a. 451)*, (Romae-Friburgi; Brisg.-Barcinone, 1965), 219 ff. M. van Parys, «L' évolution de la doctrine christologique de Basile de Seléucie», in *Irénikon* 44 (1971): 405 ff. A. de Halleux, 160 ff. A. Grillmeier, *Jesus der Christus im Glauben der Kirche*, Bd. 1, (Freiburg - Basel - Wien 1982), 758.

and Palestine and the explanations given by the papal legates to the Council relating to the meaning of the dyophysite phrases in his Tome.[9] As a result, in this case, the reservations of the Non-Chalcedonians concerning the acceptance of the Leo's Tome are not justifiable with the commonly proposed argument that its acceptance by the Fourth Ecumenical Council allegedly entails violation of the Christology of St. Cyril.

In other words, the definition of Chalcedon, just as much as Leo's Tome, were accepted by the Council under the condition of their full dogmatic accordance with the Christology of St. Cyril, which means that in that aspect the theological character of the Council was absolutely in line with St. Cyril's theology. The Christological wording of St. Cyril comprised for the Council the highest dogmatic criteria both for the formulation and acceptance of the Definition and for the acceptance and signing of the Tome by the overwhelming majority of the Fathers of the Council. No reservations about the Cyrillian character of the Council of Chalcedon can be established scientifically based on the facts of modern historical theological research.[10]

Finally, regarding the question of the condemnation of Dioscorus of Alexandria at the Fourth Ecumenical Council, it is also clear from the minutes of the Council that Dioscorus was condemned not for dogmatic, but canonical reasons which are nevertheless real and incontestable.[11] As a result, the issue of his reinstatement, on which the Non-Chalcedonians insisted, can only be resolved in the context of the pastoral dispensation of the Church, and as such, the responsibility for this issue lies completely in the jurisdiction of the Church itself. The only thing which we must note from a theological perspective is that the imposed ecclesiastical punishments are first and foremost of a pastoral character with the aim of either correcting the faithful, or their preservation from the danger of heresies and, as such, these punishments are valid in the history of the Church through the principle of economy. Besides, in order for the Church to fulfill its ecumenical calling, it cannot be captive to historical occurrences and people when the truths of her faith are not affected by those historical occurrences. The examples of the great Fathers of the Church who confronted issues of a similar nature show the way in which even this matter can be approached. So, based on these facts, the acceptance of the Council of Chalcedon, and by extension the next three Ecumenical Councils, on the part of the Non-Chalcedonians should not constitute a problem.

Conclusion - Prospects

Taking this brief overview of the theological dialogue between the Orthodox and Non-Chalcedonians, we must emphasize in conclusion that despite the problems presented by this Theological Dialogue, its prospects for the realization of sacramental unification of the dialoguing Churches after the achievement of the dogmatic agreement are clearly favorable; provided that dialogue for the sake of dialogue is avoided and of course also provided that they do not simply seek out a hasty and fragile unification which would lead to internal divisions and further problems than they are already seeking to solve. To achieve this goal, both sides need to take sensible

[9] See VI, 972 ff.· VII, 9 ff.· ACO II, 1, 2, 81 [277] ff.· 94 [290] ff. See also J. S. Romanides, «St. Cyril's "One physis or hypostasis of God the Logos Incarnate" and Chalcedon», in *The Greek Orthodox Theological Review* 10.2 (1965): 88. P. Galtier, «Saint Cyrille d' Alexandrie et Saint Léon le Grand à Chalcédoine», in *Das Konzil von Chalkedon. Geschichte und Gegenwart*, (Würzburg 1973), 354. G. D. Martzelos, *Γένεση καί πηγές τοῦ Ὅρου τῆς Χαλκηδόνας (Origin and sources of the Definition of Chalcedon). Συμβολή στήν ἱστορικοδογματική διερεύνηση τοῦ Ὅρου τῆς Δ΄ Οἰκουμενικῆς Συνόδου (Contribution to the historic dogmatic investigation of the definition of the 4th Ecumenical Council)*, (Thessaloniki 1986), 44ff.

[10] See G. D. Martzelos, 197 ff. ibid, *Ἡ Χριστολογία τοῦ Βασιλείου Σελευκείας καί ἡ οἰκουμενική σημασία της (The Christology of Basil of Seleucia and its Ecumenical Significance)* 1990, 140 ff., 146 ff (in Greek).

[11] See G. D. Martzelos, Ἡ ἐπιστημονικότητα μιᾶς "ἐπιστημονικῆς κριτικῆς" στή διδακτορική διατριβή τοῦ Ἠλ. Κεσμίρη, "Ἡ Χριστολογία καί ἡ ἐκκλησιαστική πολιτική τοῦ Διοσκόρου Ἀλεξανδρείας" (The scientific approach of a "scientific review" in the doctoral thesis of IL. Kesmiri, "Christology and the ecclesiastical policy of Dioscorus of Alexandria", Thessaloniki, 2000», in *Grigorios o Palamas* 86 (798), Παντελεήμονι τῷ Β΄, τῷ Παναγιωτάτῳ Μητροπολίτῃ Θεσσαλονίκης, Τεῦχος ἀφιερωτήριον ἐπί τῇ εἰς Κύριον ἐκδημίᾳ αὐτοῦ (Panteleimon the 2nd All-holy Metropolitan of Thessaloniki, issue dedicated to his passing away), (Thessaloniki 2003), 598ff (in Greek).

Part V: Bilateral Dialogues between Eastern Orthodox Churches
and other Churches and Christian Traditions

and methodic steps based on the luminous examples of the great Fathers of the Church who overlooked all that was secondary and trivial as long as they saw that the unity of the faith was intact. The Fathers should not be perceived only as "canons of faith" and sure criteria of orthodoxy, but also as "canons" of pastoral prudence and ecclesiopolitical behavior in confronting similar problems of broken ecclesiastical unity. Only in this way can we properly understand the introductory phrase of the Definition of Chalcedon: "We, then, following the holy Fathers...", and what it means for us.

Bibliography

Galtier, P., «Saint Cyrille d' Alexandrie et Saint Léon le Grand à Chalcédoine», in *Das Konzil von Chalkedon. Geschichte und Gegenwart*, (Würzburg 1973), 345-387.

Grillmeier, A., *Jesus der Christus im Glauben der Kirche*, Bd. 1, (Freiburg – Basel – Wien 1982).

Halleux, A. de, «La définition christologique à Chalcédoine», in *Revue Théologique de Louvain* 7 (1976): 3-23. 155-170.

Ieras Koinotitos tou Agiou Orous Atho (Holy Community of Mount Athos), Ἁγίου Ὅρους Ἄθω, Παρατηρήσεις περί τοῦ Θεολογικοῦ Διαλόγου Ὀρθοδόξων καί Ἀντιχαλκηδονίων (Ἀπάντησις εἰς κριτικήν τοῦ Σεβ. Μητροπολίτου Ἑλβετίας κ. Δαμασκηνοῦ) (Observations on the Theological Dialogue between the Orthodox and Antichalcedonians, Responses in Critique of his Eminence Damaskinos Metropolitan of Switzerland), (Mount Athos 1996) (in Greek).

Holy Monastery of Osios Gregory, Εἶναι οἱ Ἀντιχαλκηδόνιοι Ὀρθόδοξοι; Κείμενα τῆς Ἱερᾶς Κοινότητος τοῦ Ἁγίου Ὅρους καί ἄλλων ἁγιορειτῶν Πατέρων περί τοῦ διαλόγου Ὀρθοδόξων καί Ἀντιχαλκηδονίων (Μονοφυσιτῶν) (Texts of the Holy Community of Mount Athos and other hagiorite Fathers on the dialogue between Orthodox and Antichalcedonians (Monophysites), (Mount Athos 1995) (in Greek).

Larchet, J.-C., 'Τό Χριστολογικό πρόβλημα περί τῆς μελετωμένης ἑνώσεως τῆς Ὀρθοδόξου Ἐκκλησίας καί τῶν Μή-Χαλκηδονίων Ἐκκλησιῶν: Ἐκκρεμοῦντα θεολογικά καί ἐκκλησιολογικά προβλήματα' (The Christological problem on the planned union of the Orthodox Churches and non-Chalcedonian Churches: outstanding theological and ecclesiological problems), in *Theologia* 74.1 (2003): 199-234; 74.2 (2003): 635-670; 75.1 (2004): 79-104 (in Greek).

Martezlos, G. D., Γένεση καί πηγές τοῦ Ὅρου τῆς Χαλκηδόνας. Συμβολή στήν ἱστορικοδογματική διερεύνηση τοῦ Ὅρου τῆς Δ΄ Οἰκουμενικῆς Συνόδου (Origin and sources of the Definition of Chalcedon. Contribution to the historic dogmatic investigation of the definition of the 4th Ecumenical Council), (Thessaloniki: Pournara, 1986) (in Greek).

— Ἡ Χριστολογία τοῦ Βασιλείου Σελευκείας καί ἡ οἰκουμενική σημασία της (The Christology of Basil of Seleucia and its Ecumenical Significance), (Thessaloniki: Pournara, 1990).

— Ὁ Θεολογικός Διάλογος τῆς Ὀρθοδόξης Καθολικῆς Ἐκκλησίας μέ τίς Μή-Χαλκηδόνιες Ἐκκλησίες τῆς Ἀνατολῆς. Χρονικό-Ἀξιολόγηση-Προοπτικές' (The Theological Dialogue of the Orthodox Catholic Church with the Non-Chalcedonian Churches of the East. Timeline - Evaluation - Prospects), in *The Minutes of the 14th Theological Conference of the Holy Metropolis of Thessaloniki with the topic "I Mitir imon Orthodoxos Ekklisia" (Our Mother the Orthodox Church)»* (10-13 Νοεμβρίου 1993), (Thessaloniki 1994), 293-319 (in Greek).

— Ὀρθόδοξο δόγμα καί θεολογικός προβληματισμός. Μελετήματα δογματικῆς θεολογίας Β (Orthodox Dogma and Theological Questions. Essays in Dogmatic Theology 2), (Thessaloniki 2000) (in Greek).

— Ἡ ἐπιστημονικότητα μιᾶς "ἐπιστημονικῆς κριτικῆς" στή διδακτορική διατριβή τοῦ Ἠλ. Κεσμίρη, "Ἡ Χριστολογία καί ἡ ἐκκλησιαστική πολιτική τοῦ Διοσκόρου Ἀλεξανδρείας (The scientific approach of a "scientific review" in the doctoral thesis of IL. Kesmiri, "Christology and the ecclesiastical policy of Dioscorus of Alexandria", Thessaloniki, 2000», in *Grigorios o Palamas* 86 (798), Παντελεήμονι τῷ Β΄, τῷ Παναγιωτάτῳ Μητροπολίτῃ Θεσσαλονίκης, Τεῦχος ἀφιερωτήριον ἐπί τῇ εἰς Κύριον ἐκδημίᾳ αὐτοῦ, (Panteleimon the 2nd, All-holy Metropolitan of Thessaloniki, issue dedicated to his passing away), (Thessaloniki 2003), 595-618 (in Greek).

Martzelos, G. D., «Der Vater der dyophysitischen Formel von Chalkedon: Leo von Rom oder Basileios von Seleukeia?», in *Orthodoxes Forum* 6.1 (1992): 21-39 and in Ysabel de Andia / Peter Leander Hofrichter (Hsg.), *Christus bei den Vätern. Forscher aus dem Osten und Westen Europas an den Quellen des gemeinsamen Glaubens*, Pro Oriente, XXVII, Wiener patristische Tagungen 1 (PRO ORIENTE - Studientagung über „Christus bei den griechischen und lateinischen Kirchenvätern im ersten Jahrtausend" in Wien, 7.-9. Juni 2001), (Innsbruck-Wien: Tyrolia-Verlag, 2003), 272-295.

Bozovitis, S. N., *Τά αἰώνια σύνορα τῆς Ὀρθοδοξίας καί οἱ Ἀντιχαλκηδόνιοι (The Eternal borders of Orthodoxy and the Antichalcedonians)*, (Athens: Brotherhood of Theologians «O Sotir», 1999) (in Greek).

Papavasileiou, A. N., *Ὁ Θεολογικός Διάλογος μεταξύ Ὀρθοδόξων καί Ἀντιχαλκηδονίων, τόμ. Α (The Theological Dialogue between Orthodox and Antichalcedonians)*, vol. Α´, (Lefkosia: Center of Studies Holy Monastery of Kykkou, 2000) (in Greek).

Papadopoulos, K., «Ὁ διάλογος μέ τούς Ἀντιχαλκηδονίους» (The Dialogue with the Antichalcedonians), in *Synaxi* 57 (1996): 43-53 (in Greek).

Papandreou, Damaskinou (Metropolitan of Switzerland), «Ἀπάντησις εἰς τό Γράμμα τῆς Ἱερᾶς Κοινότητος τοῦ Ἁγίου Ὄρους περί τοῦ Θεολογικοῦ Διαλόγου πρός τάς Ἀρχαίας Ἀνατολικάς Ἐκκλησίας», (Response to the Letter of the Holy Mountain on the theological dialogue to the Ancient Eastern Church), in *Episkepsis* 521 (1995): 7-18, and in *Synaxi* 57 (1996): (in Greek).

— *Logos Dialogou (On Dialogue) (I Orthodoxia enopion tis tritis chilietias/Orthodoxy in the the Third Millennium)*, (Athens: Kastanioti, 1997) (in Greek).

Parys, M. J. van, «L' évolution de la doctrine christologique de Basile de Séleucie», in *Irénikon* 44 (1971): 493-514.

Ritter, A. M., «Patristische Anmerkungen zur Frage "Lehrverurteilungen – kirchentrennend?" am Beispiel des Konzils von Chalkedon», in *Oecumenica et Patristica. Festschrift für Wilchelm Schneemelcher zum 75. Geburtstag*, hrsg. von D. Papandreou - W. A. Bienert - K. Schäferdiek, (Chambésy - Genf 1989), 269-279.

— «Der gewonnene christologische Konzens zwischen orthodoxen Kirchen im Licht der Kirchenvätertradition», in *Logos. Festschrift für Luise Abramowski*, (Berlin - New York 1993), 452-471.

Romanides, J. S., «St. Cyril's "One physis or hypostasis of God the Logos Incarnate" and Chalcedon», in *The Greek Orthodox Theological Review* 10.2 (1965): 82-102.

Šagi-Bunić, Th., «'Duo perfecta' et 'duae naturae' in definitione dogmatica chalcedonensi», in *Laurentianum* 5 (1964): 3-70, 203-244,

— *«Deus perfectus et homo perfectus» a Concilio Ephesino (a. 431) ad Chalcedonense (a. 451)*, (Romae - Friburgi: Brisg. - Barcinone 1965).

Wendebourg, D., «Chalkedon in der ökumenischen Diskussion», in *Chalkedon: Geschichte und Aktualität. Studien zur Rezeption der christologischen Formel von Chalkedon*, hrsg. von J. van Oort und J. Roldanus, (Leuven: Peeters, 1998), 190-223.

Winkler, D. W., *Koptische Kirche und Reichskirche. Altes Schisma und neuer Dialog*, (Innsbruck-Wien: Tyrolia - Verlag, 1997).

Zisis, Th., *Ἡ "Ὀρθοδοξία" τῶν Ἀντιχαλκηδονίων Μονοφυσιτῶν (The "Orthodoxy" of the Antichalcedonian Monophysites)*, pub. «Bryennios», (Thessaloniki: «Bryennios», 1994) (in Greek).

— *Τά ὅρια τῆς Ἐκκλησίας (The Boundaries of the Church). Οἰκουμενισμός καί Παπισμός (Ecumenism and Papism)*, (Thessaloniki 2004) (in Greek).

(translated by Stephanos Salzman)

Part V: Bilateral Dialogues between Eastern Orthodox Churches and other Churches and Christian Traditions

Bradley Nassif

In recent years, several positive theological encounters have taken place between Evangelical and Orthodox Christians at global, denominational, institutional, and personal levels. All have helped to foster greater understanding of our different traditions and created mutual trust and a growing commitment to find a way forward together as children of the Trinitarian God. This essay will attempt to summarize the accomplishments of the most important dialogues that have occurred since 1990 to the present, and then map the terrain through which future advances can be made toward unity-in-truth.

History of Orthodox-Evangelical Dialogues

From the Beginnings to 1990

As often happens, initial contacts between Orthodox and Evangelicals were characterized by a negative history of mutual suspicion, fear, hostility, and ignorance. Both proselytism and genuine conversions to Christ occurred, leading some Orthodox to leave their church and join one of the numerous Evangelical communities. Few, if any, formal dialogues seem to have occurred between Orthodox and Evangelical Christians, even though personal conversations took place at the grass roots level.

During the mid-1900s, a number of individual Evangelicals in the UK were involved in the Fellowship of St. Alban and St. Sergius. This Fellowship seeks to bringing together Eastern and Western Christians with the aim of discussing points of similarity and difference between their respective theological outlooks and church disciplines. Several Evangelicals are currently active members in the Fellowship. Also in the UK, a Russian Orthodox delegation headed by Metropolitan Anthony Bloom met with leaders from the Evangelical Alliance in the 1980s to discuss areas of common ground and share testimonies. However, no reports were published.

While Orthodox and Evangelicals remained (with a few exceptions) in a general state of tension prior to 1990, there existed at the same time the presence of renewal movements within the Orthodox Churches of Antioch (The Orthodox Youth Movement), Greece (Zoe), Romania (The Lord's Army), and the United States (The Brotherhood of St. Symeon the New Theologian), to name several of the more prominent ones. To the extent that these movements emphasized evangelical principles of renewal (such as Bible study, prayer, personal faith in Christ, evangelism, and social service), there was common ground with the Protestant Evangelicals. Nevertheless, the ecclesial and sacramental context of these various Orthodox renewal movements set them apart from their Protestant counterparts.

A major missiological event occurred in the United States in 1987, when the Antiochian Orthodox Archdiocese of North America welcomed into its church the mass conversion of 1,700 Evangelicals led by Peter Gillquist, a former Dallas Seminary graduate and leader of the Campus Crusade for Christ.[1] Under Metropolitan Philip Saliba and with the blessing of His Holiness Patriarch Ignatius IV, Gillquist became head of the Missions and Evangelism department in the Antiochian church. Under Gillquist, the Antiochian Archdiocese has chrismated

---

[1] "Evangelical Denomination Gains Official Acceptance into the Orthodox Church," *Christianity Today* (Feb. 6, 1987): 40; Timothy P. Weber, "Looking for Home: Evangelical Orthodoxy and the Search for the Original Church" in *New Perspectives on Historical Theology: Essays in Memory of John Meyendorff*, ed. Bradley Nassif (Grand Rapids, MI: Eerdmans, 1996), 95-121.

a sizeable number (never officially documented) of Evangelicals who joined the Orthodox since then. Today, many of those former Evangelicals have enlivened the faith and assisted the church in contextualizing Orthodoxy to the American culture.

From the 1990 to the Present

The year 1990 marks the formal beginning of the Orthodox-Evangelical dialogue with the founding of the Society for the Study of Eastern Orthodoxy and Evangelism in the United States (to be discussed below). A new paradigm of ecumenical relations emerged among professional theologians. With the fall of communism in Eastern Europe in the late 1980s, Western missionaries began flooding the former Soviet Union, Romania, and other Eastern European block countries. This necessitated additional theological training in Orthodox history and theology for Evangelical missionaries working in those countries.

Since 1990 to the present, there have been four major dialogues between the Orthodox and Evangelical communities:

1. The Society for the Study of Eastern Orthodoxy and Evangelicalism (SSEOE). Founded in the USA in 1990 by the present author along with five other Orthodox and Evangelical members, the primary focus of this group has been a deep and sustained dialogue over theological convergences and divergences. Subjects of discussion have included the authority of Scripture and tradition, the nature of the church, hermeneutics, proselytism *vs.* conversion, spirituality and others. The SSEOE met annually at the Billy Graham Center on the campus of Wheaton College until 1996 and has gathered at various times and places since its founding. Only a few of these papers have been published in serious theological journals while most remain archived and unpublished. The SSEOE has not met over the past few years, but new efforts are now underway to re-gather.

2. Beginning in 1997, the World Council of Churches (WCC) hosted a series of international and regional dialogues between the Orthodox and Evangelical communities. The dialogues initially began as relational meetings arising from Orthodox concerns over what they perceived as proselytism by Evangelicals in Russia and Eastern Europe after the fall of communism. The meetings eventually progressed to theological and missiological subjects within the context of continuing concerns over proselytism. Four seminars took place at the Ecumenical Institute in Bossey, Switzerland from 2000 to 2006. They covered the themes of salvation, the role and function of the Bible, the church, and theological anthropology. Statements were produced by groups of participants, but these were primarily for the participants' own benefit. It had been planned to continue these seminars, but financial and organizational constraints within the WCC have precluded it. Several of the papers, along with a complete history of the WCC dialogues, can be found in *Building Bridges: Between the Orthodox and Evangelical Traditions*, eds. Tim Grass, Jenny Rolph, Paul Rolph, Ioan Sauca (Geneva: WCC Publications, 2012).[2]

Evangelical Initiatives:

a. The Evangelical Alliance of the United Kingdom

In 2001, the Evangelical Alliance (UK) Commission on Unity and Truth among Evangelicals (ACUTE) published a 163-page book entitled *Evangelicalism and the Orthodox Church*. It is the product of a working group of Evangelical theologians in the UK and Wales that began in 1999. The book provides a broad overview of some of the key agreements and differences between the two traditions in the areas of history, doctrine, worship and spirituality. It is not a definitive or "official" document, since it was only produced by individual theologians who were interested in the subject; but it does make clear some of the central theological truths which Orthodox and Evangelicals hold in common, as well as several key differences in ecclesiology and sacramental theology.

---

[2] I am indebted to Fr. Ioan Sauca and Dr. Tim Grass for much of the information given in this paragraph.

Part V: Bilateral Dialogues between Eastern Orthodox Churches
and other Churches and Christian Traditions

b. World Vision Dialogue

An Orthodox-Evangelical Dialogue was hosted in 2009 by World Vision in Romania under the direction of Dr. Danut Manastireanu, Fr. Constantine Niclaud, and the Romanian Orthodox Patriarchate. A round-table discussion of Orthodox and Evangelical leaders occurred at the University of Cluj, but very little follow-through resulted.

c. The Lausanne-Orthodox Initiative (LOI)

This significant initiative was sponsored by senior leaders within the Oriental and Eastern Orthodox Churches and the Evangelical Churches who are part of the Lausanne Movement. Approximately 50 participants attended. Building on, and not repeating, the work which had already taken place at the theological level, the Lausanne-Orthodox Initiative brought together a select list of senior mission leaders from within the Orthodox Churches and the Lausanne Movement of Evangelical Christians. The consultation met at the monastery of St. Vlash in Albania under the host Archbishop Anastasios Yannoulatos from 2-6 September, 2013. Participants came from most parts of Europe, North America, Africa, and Asia. Their stated goals included, among others, the desire to build relationships of trust with one another; to benefit from the theological work already undertaken within their church traditions; to come to a greater understanding and appreciation of their different spiritual and theological heritages; to confront their differences honestly and in a spirit of desire that Christ's prayer for unity might be fulfilled; and to propose and plan any common actions which, guided by the Holy Trinity, they believe would honor God and help to overcome their past failings in mission.[3]

Lectureships, Fellowships, and Scholarly Publications

A significant variety of bridge-building efforts continue in small but fruitful ways on several fronts. Notable examples include (among others) lectures by Metropolitan Kallistos Ware at Wheaton College and North Park University (2011) on the topic, "Orthodox and Evangelicals: What Have We To Learn From Each Other?"[4] Since 2008, the Fellowship of St. Alban and St. Sergius continues to host a group of theologians, ecumenists, and church leaders who meet twice a year for a day in Oxford. Under the leadership of Fr. Stephen Platt and Dr. Tim Grass, speakers from each tradition cover themes such as the Bible, the church, sacramental theology, priesthood and mission (the papers may soon be published). Other fellowships that foster Orthodox-Evangelical dialogue include The Fellowship of St. James and *Touchstone* magazine (USA); and Act3 Network led by Dr. John Armstrong, a missions professor at Wheaton College.

Last, and perhaps the most fruitful area of ecumenical exchange, comes from the published work of individual scholars. I have documented much of this history through 2003 so will not repeat it here.[5] Since 2003, however, a virtual renaissance has occurred among Evangelical theologians who are exploring major theological themes within the Orthodox tradition. The titles are far too numerous to list in this brief précis, but a sample representation of the topics includes introductions to Orthodox theology, deification, ecclesiology, worship and Scripture, and tradition.[6] Evangelicals have done more research into Orthodox themes

---

[3] LOI invitational letter to the author from Dr. Mark Oxbrow in January, 2013.

[4] Available for download on www.ancientfaith.com

[5] "Eastern Orthodoxy and Evangelicalism: The Status of an Emerging Global Dialogue" in *Eastern Orthodox Theology: A Contemporary Reader*, 222 ff. The essay provides a fairly comprehensive documentation of Orthodox-Evangelical exchanges from 1990-2003.

[6] Examples include Tim Grass, "Evangelical – Orthodox Dialogue: Past, Present and Future", *Transformation* 27.3 (July 2010), 186-98; James R. Payton, *Light from the Christian East: An Introduction to the Orthodox Tradition*, (Downers Grove, IL: InterVarsity Press, 2007); Veli-Matti Karkkainen, *One with God: Salvation As Deification and Justification*, (Collegeville, MN: Unitas Books, Liturgical Press, 2004); Slavko Ezdenci, *Deification and Union with Christ: A Reformed Perspective on Salvation in Orthodoxy*, (Oxford: Latimer House, 2011); D.H. Williams, *Evangelicals and Tradition*, (Grand Rapids, MI: Baker Academic, 2005).

than Orthodox scholars have studied Evangelical theology. Orthodox research includes topics such as the centrality of the gospel in the life of the church, Scripture and tradition, and the evangelical character of Orthodox theology and spirituality.[7]

Mapping the Future

As we move into the future, common to all the above is the observation that Orthodox and Evangelicals agree that a sound basis for a common witness to the gospel rests on a common witness to Christian truth. This common conviction over the primacy of theology sets the dialogue on firm grounds that each side considers essential. However, Evangelicalism is a trans-denominational spiritual movement that is held together by a common set of theological *emphases*, and not a single denomination with a single set of doctrines.[8] This makes dialogue with Evangelicals decentralized and situational by its very nature. What, then, is an "Evangelical"? There are competing ways to define the movement, but a widely accepted definition of Evangelicalism comes from David Bebbington who identifies four unifying emphases[9]:

1. Through the life, death and resurrection of Jesus, God provided a way for the forgiveness of sins (crucicentrism).
2. The Bible is the inspired Word of God and is to be taken literally, word for word (biblicism).
3. People need to commit their lives to Jesus Christ and be converted (conversionism).
4. It is important to encourage non-Christians to become Christians and to engage in a life of service (activism).

The following observations may assist Orthodox communities in their future attempts to build bridges with groups who hold this set of Evangelical emphases:

1. Historic Evangelicalism is a moving target today. Contemporary Evangelicalism is rapidly questioning and reshaping its past identity due to postmodernist influences[10] and expanding definitions of the very meaning of the term "gospel."[11] Negatively, Evangelical postmodernism tends to undermine the theological moorings of the movement, which could significantly alter past areas of agreement with the Orthodox. Positively, a widening definition of an Evangelical understanding of the "gospel" is underway that comports well with Orthodox Christology. No longer is Evangelicalism restricted mainly to the primacy of justification by faith and substitutionary atonement, even though an influential Reformed body of Evangelicals still insists on the priority these emphases should have in defining Evangelical identity. A progressive wing in Evangelicalism is

---

[7] My best effort at comparing Orthodox and Evangelical theology is the essay entitled, "The Evangelical Theology of the Eastern Orthodox Church" in *Three Views on Eastern Orthodoxy and Evangelicalism*, ed. James Stamoolis, (Grand Rapids, MI: Zondervan, 2004). The book is translated into Romanian, *Ortodoxie evanghelism: Trei perspective*, (Iasi: Editura Adoramus, 2009). For the centrality of the gospel in the Orthodox liturgy, see Bradley Nassif, "Orthodox Spirituality: The Quest for a Transfigured Life" in *Four Views of Christian Spirituality*, ed. Bruce Demarest, (Grand Rapids, MI: Zondervan, 2012). For the centrality of the gospel in the whole of Orthodox life see Fr. Theodore Stylianopoulos, *The Way of Christ: Gospel, Spiritual Life and Renewal in Orthodoxy*, (Brookline, MA: Holy Cross Orthodox Press, 2002). For the biblical foundations for holy Tradition, Edith M. Humphrey, *Scripture and Tradition: What the Bible Really Says*, (Grand Rapids, MI: Baker Academic, 2013). For the centrality of the gospel in *The Philokalia*, see Bradley Nassif, "Concerning Those Who Imagine That They Are Justified By Works:" The Gospel According to St. Mark – the Monk" in *The Philokalia: A Classic Text of Orthodox Spirituality*, foreword Kallistos Ware, eds. Brock Bingaman and Bradley Nassif, (New York: Oxford University, 2012).

[8] *Why We Belong: Evangelical Unity and Denominational Diversity*, eds. Anthony L. Chute, Christopher W. Morgan, and Robert A. Peterson, (Wheaton, IL: Crossway, 2013).

[9] Cited by Mark Noll, *American Evangelical Christianity: An Introduction*, (Oxford, UK: Blackwell, 2001), 13, 31.

[10] Dr. Carl Raschke, *The Next Reformation: Why Evangelicals Must Embrace Postmodernity*, (Grand Rapids, MI: Baker, 2004); Brian McClaren, *A New Kind of Christianity: Ten Questions That Are Transforming the Faith*, (NY: HarperCollins, 2010).

[11] See Scot McKnight, *The King Jesus Gospel: The Original Good News Revisited*, (Grand Rapids, MI: Zondervan, 2011).

Part V: Bilateral Dialogues between Eastern Orthodox Churches and other Churches and Christian Traditions

beginning to see the gospel as embracing *the whole* of the Incarnation, life, death, resurrection, ascension and second coming while retaining its emphasis on the cross.

2. The four distinctions cited above are both embraced and transcended by the Orthodox faith through its Christological and Trinitarian theology. Whereas Evangelicalism is minimalistic in its approach to unity, Orthodoxy is maximalist in its vision of faith. These four distinctions of Evangelical identity have had far-reaching implications for the way historic Orthodoxy has interpreted their significance. Herein lies the crux of our known and continuing differences with Evangelicals. Even though we agree on these four distinctivenesses, we vary widely on their theological implications. Herein explains our differences in the areas of biblical interpretation, ecclesiology, sacramental theology, liturgy, iconography, and spiritual life.[12]

Cooperation between Orthodox and Evangelical believers should be explored in relation to common social action and, to a limited extent, evangelism, Bible study, and worship. In recent times, the World Evangelical Alliance has expressed concern about persecution by the Orthodox in places like Russia and other traditional Orthodox countries.[13] Likewise, the Orthodox have expressed concern that Evangelical missionaries have little appreciation for the religious and cultural heritage of Orthodox Christians, and that "folk religion" does not accurately represent the Orthodox faith. The Moscow Patriarchate, however, has demonstrated in the past that Orthodox and Evangelicals can work together successfully, as was done in earlier times under the Billy Graham evangelistic campaigns. Nominal Orthodox Christians who responded to the gospel under Billy Graham's preaching were not "proselytized," but directed to good Orthodox churches for discipleship. Similar cooperative ventures should be possible today, if there is a will to do so. A united voice that bears witness to historic Christian faith is urgently needed in areas of the gospel, human sexuality, marriage, human dignity, creation stewardship, and related areas.

In the area of church renewal, Orthodox theologians need to show how the church's incarnational Trinitarian faith challenges Evangelicals to reassess the limited comprehensiveness of their own incarnational Trinitarian beliefs. Evangelicals need to be shown how deeply "evangelical" the Orthodox Church really is (albeit in a much wider and richer sense than popular forms of Protestant Evangelicalism). The Gospel lies at the very heart of all the church's dogmatic definitions, ecumenical councils, liturgies, sacramental theology, patristic teachings, iconography, spirituality, and missions. Evangelicals should be able to affirm and support the Orthodox Church if we can express our "evangelical" theology in a vocabulary that is meaningful to our Evangelical brethren. We will not likely ever see full visible unity with Evangelicals, but we can manifest our spiritual unity with them in broken but visible ways. This should be possible since, as the late Fr. George Florovsky once wrote, "The true church [Orthodoxy] is not yet the perfect church."[14]

Finally – and most importantly – at the parish level, Evangelicals have much to offer the Orthodox Church today in terms of spiritual renewal. Theological dialogues can only do so much. There must come a time when dialogue is converted into action. *That is why the most urgent need in the Orthodox world today is the need for an aggressive internal mission of evangelizing our own nominal Orthodox people.* Nominalism is the number one problem that Orthodoxy faces today globally. Evangelicals challenge our bishops, priests, and lay leaders to make the gospel much clearer and more central to our parishioners' lives than we have done in the past. They remind us that just because the gospel is *in* the life of the church does not mean that our people have *understood and appropriated its message!* There is a tragic gap between Orthodox principles and Orthodox practice. All that we need for spiritual renewal is contained within our very own theology and church life. It

---

[12] For an Orthodox assessment of these distinctivenesses and the centrality of the gospel in the church's liturgy see my essays "The Evangelical Theology of the Eastern Orthodox Church" ibid., and "Orthodox Spirituality: The Quest for a Transfigured Life" ibid.

[13] Available online: http://www.worldea.org/news/4094/wea-rlc-research-and-analysis-report-why-russia-persecutes-non-orthodox-churches-1 (last accessed September 2013).

[14] George Florovsky, "The True Church is Not Yet the Perfect Church" in *Tuasend Jahre Christentum in Russland: Zum Millenium der Taufe der Kiever Rus'*, ed. K.C. Felmy et al., (Gottingen: Vandenhoeck und Ruprecht, 1988), 583-90.

is out of those rich resources that *the gospel must be made clear, central, and compelling to every person in each generation.* Whether through preaching, the confessional, personal conversations, or separate preaching sessions, Orthodox evangelism needs to take place much more aggressively than we have done to date, especially among the youth. It is possible for our young people to attend church, take communion, venerate the icons and end up *religious, but lost.* It is not without reason that the Book of the Gospels rests on the center of the altar in every Orthodox Church around the world. This liturgical symbolism tells us if we truly want to be people of the Gospel, we will need to constantly recover the personal and relational aspects of God in every life-giving action of the church. Perhaps if we humble ourselves before our Evangelical brothers and sisters and listen to the simplicity of their message we will rediscover the true meaning of our own faith and, in the process, bring them with us into the fullness of the Orthodox Church.

Bibliography

Tim Grass, Jenny Rolph, Paul Rolph, Ioan Sauca, editors. (2012) *Building Bridges: Between the Orthodox and Evangelical Traditions.* (Geneva: WCC Publications, 2012).

Tim Grass, "Evangelical – Orthodox Dialogue: Past, Present and Future." *Transformation* 27.3 (2010): 186-98.

Evangelicalism and the Orthodox Church. A Report by the Evangelical Alliance Commission on Unity and Truth among Evangelicals (ACUTE). (London: Whitfield House, 2001).

Bradley Nassif, "Eastern Orthodoxy and Evangelicalism: The Status of an Emerging Global Dialogue." *Eastern Orthodox Theology: A Contemporary Reader.* (Grand Rapids, Michigan: Zondervan, 2004), 222-48.

Bradley Nassif, "The Evangelical Theology of the Eastern Orthodox Church." *Three Views on Eastern Orthodoxy and Evangelicalism*, ed. James Stamoolis. (Grand Rapids, MI: Zondervan, 2004), 13-87. Translated into Romanian, *Ortodoxie evanghelism: Trei perspective.* (Iasi: Editura Adoramus, 2009), 27-92.

Theodore Stylianopoulos, *The Way of Christ: Gospel, Spiritual Life and Renewal in Orthodoxy.* (Brookline, MA: Holy Cross Orthodox Press, 2002).

*Part V: Bilateral Dialogues between Eastern Orthodox Churches
and other Churches and Christian Traditions*

PART VI

ECUMENICAL PERSPECTIVES OF ORIENTAL ORTHODOX CHURCHES

Fr. Kondothra M. George

The Oriental Orthodox family is comprised of the Ethiopian, Coptic, Armenian, Syrian, Indian and Eritrean Churches. Historically they have been referred to as non- or anti- or pre-Chalcedonian, Monophysite, Ancient Oriental or Lesser Eastern. Presently the generally accepted name is Oriental Orthodox. The majority of the members of these churches live in Ethiopia, Egypt, Eritrea, Armenia, India, Syria and Lebanon. There are also large diaspora communities in parts of the Middle East, Europe, Asia, North and South America, and Australia. The Oriental Orthodox churches are ancient churches which were founded in apostolic times, by apostles or by the apostles' earliest disciples. Their doctrinal position is based on the teachings of the first three ecumenical councils (Nicea 325, Constantinople 381 and Ephesus 431). The Alexandrian school of thought has guided and shaped their theological reflection. The teachings of Saint Cyril the Great constitute the foundation of their Christology. They are firmly attached to the Cyrilian formula of "One nature of the Word Incarnate." Their theology is biblical, liturgical and patristic, and is embodied in mysticism and spirituality.

The Oriental Orthodox churches, along with those of the Byzantine tradition or Eastern Orthodox, belong to the larger family of the Orthodox churches. The two groups are not in communion with each other. The breach, which occurred in 451, marking the first ecclesial division in church history, was about the Christological teaching of the Council of Chalcedon. Through the centuries confrontation and estrangement, but also dialogue and rapprochement have characterized the relations between the Oriental and Eastern Orthodox churches. In 1985, after two decades of unofficial meetings, the two groups engaged in an official theological dialogue, which has resulted in Christological agreements. The main remaining question is the reception of the agreements in the churches.

The history and life of the Oriental Orthodox churches has been marked by ceaseless persecution and massacres under the Byzantine, Persian, Muslim and Ottoman powers. The sufferings have had a profound impact on their life, witness, theology and spirituality. Yet this life of the cross has not led them to become entirely isolated and introverted. In spite of their continuous suffering, these churches have sustained themselves through constant efforts of renewal. Under the imperative of new realities and the demands of changing times, they have been able to challenge the strong traditionalism and inward-looking estate that prevailed for some time, due to the historical circumstances. While ancient traditions still dominate, a fresh vitality and creativity are blowing in these churches, both in their motherlands and in the diaspora. They have significantly revived monastic life as a rich source of spirituality, evangelism and diakonia for clergy as well as laity, men and women. They have reorganized theological education. Sunday schools have become centres of intense activities. Youth movements and student associations have been created. Bible study seminars, courses for the Christian formation of laity, fasting and daily celebrations of saints are vivid expressions of deep spirituality and of evangelistic inreach and outreach, which nurture and build these communities of faith. They are churches of the people, without the dichotomy between institution and community. The whole people of God participates actively in the life and witness of the church.

In early centuries the Oriental Orthodox churches have played a pivotal role in the expansion of Christianity beyond the borders of the Byzantine empire. The Christian faith was taken from Alexandria down to Africa, from Armenia to the North, from Antioch to the Far East. In later centuries, because of changing political and religious conditions, the missionary activities have been carried on mainly in terms of building and sustaining their own community. In today's context of a globalized world, and of pluralistic societies, there is an increasing awareness on the part of the Oriental Orthodox churches of the need to renew the methodologies and forms of mission and evangelism.

Although the Oriental Orthodox churches have suffered from Western missionary efforts in the Christian East, both Catholic and Protestant, they have taken the ecumenical challenge seriously. They firmly believe that meeting together, praying together and entering into frank and critical dialogue with their ecumenical partners is the will of the Lord. The World Council of Churches is for them the most comprehensive instrument of the ecumenical movement, providing them with a global framework for close and meaningful relationships and cooperation with other churches.

After centuries of isolation from each other, the Oriental Orthodox churches finally met in 1965 in Addis Ababa. At this historic meeting the church heads reaffirmed their belonging to one faith. They took several decisions which, for many reasons, have not fully materialized. The challenge remains to give more visibility and tangible expression to the unity of faith of the Oriental Orthodox churches. Among the issues they need to address together are the influence of secularism, the resurgence of religious fundamentalism and the increasing migration of the faithful from the motherlands to other parts of the world. The Oriental Orthodox family does not have an organized institution. Since 1996 the heads of the three churches in the Middle East (Coptic, Armenian and Syrian) have put in place a framework for annual meetings at which they discuss common concerns and issues. Several working groups have been formed to assist the patriarchs with this process. Besides the dialogue with the Eastern Orthodox, the Oriental Orthodox as a family is also engaged in a theological dialogue with the World Alliance of Reformed Churches, the Catholic Church and the Anglican Communion. The Oriental Orthodox churches have much to share with other churches. They have preserved a strong sense of history and tradition. They can make a unique contribution through their monastic tradition, oriental spirituality, rich liturgy and mystical theology.

The Oriental Orthodox churches, which are all members of the World Council of Churches, represent some 60 million Christians.

Bibliography

WCC website on Oriental Orthodox Churches: http://www.oikoumene.org

Geevarghese Mar Osthathios, "Oriental Orthodox Churches", in: Nicholas Lossky et al, *Dictionary of the Ecumenical Movement*, (Geneva: WCC, 2002), 857-859.

K.M. George, "Oriental Orthodox-Orthodox Dialogue", in: Nicholas Lossky et al, *Dictionary of the Ecumenical Movement*, (Geneva: WCC, 2002), 859-862.

Metropolitan Bishoy

Theological dialogue is the means for reaching Church unity, in order to fulfill the commandment of our Lord Jesus Christ in His commune with the Father *"that they may be one as We are"* (Jn 17:11). The Coptic Orthodox Church has never neglected or even delayed participation in any theological dialogue, eager to reach this unity based upon unity of faith.

Participation in the Middle East Council of Churches (MECC)

The Coptic Orthodox Church contributed in establishing the MECC, and participates in all its activities. The MECC includes now the four families of churches in the Middle East: Oriental Orthodox, Orthodox, Catholic, and Evangelical.

The Oriental Orthodox Churches in the Middles East

On 10-11 March 1998, a common declaration was signed by the heads of the Oriental Orthodox Churches in the Middle East: Pope Shenouda III Pope of Alexandria and Patriarch of the See of St. Mark (Coptic Orthodox Church), Mar Ignatius Zakka I Patriarch of the Antioch and all the East (Syrian Orthodox Church) and Catholicos Aram I (the Armenian Orthodox Church of Antelias, Lebanon). This historical incident took place at St. Bishoy's Monastery, Wadi El Natroon, Egypt, in the presence of a standing committee which consists of the delegated representatives of each church. The Common Declaration announced the oneness of faith among the three churches. The heads of these churches agreed on the necessity of maintaining a common position of faith in all theological dialogues. Thus, henceforth, they will engage as a family of Oriental Orthodox Churches in the Middle East in any theological dialogue with other churches and Christian world communions. Annual meetings are held between the heads of the three churches.

1. Dialogue with the Byzantine Orthodox

Under the supervision and encouragement of the World Council of Churches, unofficial dialogues commenced between the Orthodox Churches, sharing with our faith (i.e. Syrian, Armenian, Ethiopian and Indian) and the Byzantine Orthodox; being the two Orthodox families. The meetings were held as follows: 1964 in Arhus, Denmark, 1967 in Bristol, England, 1970 in Geneva, Switzerland, 1971 in Addis Ababa, Ethiopia.

In 1985 official dialogues commenced between both Orthodox families under the auspices of His Holiness Pope Shenouda III and the Ecumenical Patriarch Dimitrios. Dialogues have continued after the enthronement of Patriarch Bartholomaios of Constantinople.

In 1987 in Corinth, the first official theological agreement was formulated by a sub-committee which presented its report to the general plenary Committee of the Commission of the Dialogue. The commission met at Saint Bishoy Monastery in 1989 under the patronage of His Holiness Pope Shenouda III who urged the assembly to formulate an agreement that would terminate the disputes standing between the two families over the last fifteen centuries. According to the report from the sub-committee, they were indeed able to form a theological agreement on Christology based on the teachings of Saint Cyril I, Pope of Alexandria. The signing of this agreement produced a great echo throughout the entire world, as it was the first official agreement signed by the representatives of the Churches of both families.

On 28 September 1990, in Chambesy, Switzerland, an agreement was signed on the basis of the historical agreement of Saint Bishoy Monastery in 1989. The new agreement stated the lifting of anathemas issued against all the fathers and councils of the two Orthodox families. The official representatives of both families signed the agreement and forwarded it -as previously with the first agreement- to the Holy Synods of their respective churches, to take decisions. Our Church approved these agreements in the Holy Synod's sessions held on the Pentecost of 1990, and 12 November 1990, on condition that, this step from our behalf awaits a similar approval from the other churches; in order that the lifting of anathemas between the two families occurs unanimously and simultaneously.

The Holy Synod of the Indian Orthodox Church has also approved both agreements. Likewise, the Holy Synod of the Romanian Church approved both agreements. In February 1994, Patriarch Zaka I handed the approval of the Syrian Orthodox Church to all the executed agreements, to the Co-President of the Commission of the Dialogue. The responses of the churches follow in succession at the present time announcing that the fulfillment of the unity between the Orthodox Churches is near at hand. The Byzantine Orthodox Churches of Constantinople, Alexandria and Antioch have also approved.

In the first week of November 1993, the Dialogue Commission assembled in Switzerland to issue responses to the inquiries of some churches. It decided that the two co-Chairmen of the Commission, travel to all the Orthodox Churches of both families throughout the world to offer the required explanations for all the articles of the agreement, which they did. This decision was by general consent and fulfilled the wish that His Holiness Pope Shenouda III expressed since the second agreement of 1990. During the same meeting it was agreed to create a document for the unity of the Church and lifting of anathemas to be signed by all the heads of the Orthodox Churches of both parties, including confessions from both sides that the others are Orthodox in all their doctrines. Decisions were also taken for establishing a list of the heads of the Churches for use in the Diptychs. Decisions were taken to ensure the editing of books offering explanations of the agreements to the people, and for the establishment of a sub-committee for formulating the way of con-celebrating the liturgy after the union.

Later, in April 2007, Metropolitan Bishoy (co-chairman representing the Oriental Orthodox side) met Metropolitan Emmanuel of France (the new co-chairman representing the Orthodox side) in Lebanon in order to re-activate the job of *The Inter-Orthodox Theological Committee for Dialogue between the Orthodox Church and the Oriental Orthodox Churches* to help with the reception of the abovementioned agreed statements and its acceptance by the churches.

2. Consultation with the Russian Orthodox Church

In April 2000 Patriarch Alexy of Russia sent a letter inquiring the initiation of a dialogue with the Coptic Orthodox Church, in order to facilitate the reception of the agreed statements of the official dialogue between the two Orthodox families of churches. We responded that we maintain a common position with the Oriental Orthodox Churches of the Middle East, and the Russian Church agreed upon this condition. Consequently, a preparatory meeting was held in Russia in March 2001, followed by an official meeting in Moscow of *The Joint Commission for the Relations Between the Russian Orthodox Church and Oriental Orthodox Churches in the Middle East* in September 2001. Its aim was to deepen the ties of cooperation, exerting efforts to eradicate the obstacles facing their acceptance of the official theological agreements signed between the two Orthodox families.

In the first official meeting of Moscow, Metropolitan Bishoy, according to the request of the Russian Church, presented a paper interpreting the first agreed statement of the official dialogue between the Orthodox Churches and the Oriental Orthodox Churches. The second official meeting was held in Cairo in September

2004. Its subject was the Christology of St. Severus of Antioch. The third official meeting was held in Lebanon in December 2005. Its subject was the Council of Chalcedon. In each meeting papers were presented from both sides.

A new point was added to the points of discussion in the agenda with the Russian Church namely the *deification of man*, which occurred in a paper presented by one of the Russian participants and read by another. This paper stated that a hypostatic union between the divinity and humanity in Christ includes those who are saved in Christ and form the body of the church. This concept is completely rejected by our family of churches, and might be added to the agenda of *The Inter-Orthodox Theological Committee for Dialogue between the Orthodox Church and the Oriental Orthodox Churches*.

Presently, our dialogue with the Russian Church is stopped. However, when H. H. Patriarch Kyril of Russia visited H. H. Pope Shenouda III in Alexandria, in April 2010, they agreed to reactivate the work of the *Joint Commission*.

3. Dialogue with the Catholic Church

In September 1971, unofficial dialogues commenced between the Coptic Orthodox Church and the Catholic Churches. His Holiness Pope Shenouda III, then Bishop of Education, represented the Coptic Orthodox Church (during the time of the vacancy of the Coptic Orthodox Patriarchal throne). In this meeting, His Holiness formulated an Agreed Statement on Christology that was accepted by both the theologians of the family of churches sharing our faith (Oriental Orthodox Churches) and the Catholic Church theologians. The Formula of this Agreed Statement is as follows:

> "We believe that our Lord, God and Saviour Jesus Christ, the Incarnate Logos is perfect in His Divinity and perfect in His Humanity. He made His Humanity One with His Divinity without Mixture, nor Mingling, nor Change nor Confusion. His Divinity was not separated from His Humanity even for a moment or twinkling of an eye.

> At the same time, we anathematize the doctrines of both Nestorius and Eutyches".

The above Agreement was officially received in February 1988 when it was signed by H.H. Pope Shenouda III, some bishops and theologians of our church on one side and the representatives of the Roman Catholic Pope, the Patriarch of the Coptic Catholic Church in Egypt, some bishops and theologians on the other side. The Pope of Rome corresponded in writing to H.H. Pope Shenouda III expressing his rejoice at reaching such an Agreement befitting the well-known Coptic terminology.

Other Issues of the Dialogue :

The Holy Synod of the Coptic Orthodox Church, under the primacy of H.H. Pope Shenouda III, decided in its session dated 21 June 1986, that it is a necessity to reach solutions concerning doctrinal differences, prior to lifting the existing anathemas between both Churches. The foremost of these doctrinal differences are: Christology, Procession of the Holy Spirit (whereby the Catholic Church annexed the phrase "and the Son" to their Creed of Faith since 1054 AD), Purgatory, the Immaculate Conception (in the birth of the Virgin St. Mary), forgivenesses and excessiveness in virtues of the saints indulgences, marriages to non-believers (performed inside the Catholic Church, which the church blesses and absolves), the Catholic presence in Egypt.

The Holy Synod of the Coptic Orthodox Church dispatched official messages concerning the aforementioned subject to the Vatican dated 16 September 1986; including the proposed Statement of Agreement on Christology. Upon this foundation, the Vatican agreed to conduct dialogues. As previously mentioned the agreement on the first doctrinal difference was signed.

Part VI: Ecumenical Perspectives of Oriental Orthodox Churches

During the Holy Synod session dated 28 May 1988, under the primacy of H.H. Pope Shenouda III, the members were acquainted with the decisions of the Second Vatican council concerning the salvation of non-believers. Simultaneously, the Holy Synod decided to affix this fundamental issue to the other seven issues of the dialogue that should be solved, prior to lifting the anathemas with the Catholic Church. The Holy Synod dispatched an official letter dated 26 April 1990, to which the Vatican agreed and included this issue to the primary main points for dialogue.

Agreement on other Fundamental Doctrinal Differences should be reached:

Acquitting the Jews of the blood of Christ by a Vatican decision in the year 1965, the Primacy of Saint Peter the Apostle, infallibility of the Catholic Pope, the primacy of the Pope of Rome (Primacy of Jurisdiction) over the Christian churches of the whole world.

Secondary Doctrinal Differences:

Cancelling most of the fasts, not giving communion to children (ceremony for the first communion is at the age of eight), postponing the anointment with myroon (the Chrism) till the age of eight, not immersing the person in the baptismal font (only pouring a small amount of water on the child's head), not giving communion by bread, rather by unleavened bread, not giving blood of the communion to the congregation, the Latin Catholics do not permit the priests to marry, giving permission to the laity (both men and women) to enter into the sanctuary and to read the bible during the holy liturgy, entering the sanctuary with shoes, permitting nuns to dispense the Eucharist to sick people in the hospitals, permitting deacons to carry holy communion and to give it to the different priestly ranks, not permitting divorce in case of adultery, not facing the east during prayers, performing more than one liturgy on the same altar in one day, the priest prays and takes communion in more than one liturgy during the same day, not being cautious nine hours before communion but satisfied with two hours for food and half an hour for drinks, accepting anyone to perform the rite of baptism, even a non-Christian, giving communion to non-believers; this is practiced by Catholic bishops without an official clear decision from the Vatican.

No agreement was reached regarding Purgatory and the Procession of the Holy Spirit in spite of the studies and discussions. Then the dialogue stopped.

Several mailings and meetings re-occurred in 2001 between the Catholic Church and the Oriental Orthodox Churches (the Coptic, the Syrian, and the Armenian). According to the Common Declaration between the heads of the Oriental Orthodox Churches in the Middle East,[1] Cardinal Walter Casper, President of the Pontifical Council for Promoting Christian Unity, addressed a letter on 10 September 2002, to all of them in order to engage an official dialogue with the Catholic Church. A preparatory committee meeting was held in the Vatican, January 2003, to set up a work plan, agenda, membership, procedures, methodologies and timetable for the Joint Commission of the Official Theological Dialogue between the Catholic Church and the Oriental Orthodox Churches of the Middle East. The Agenda included the following topics: Christology, Procession of the Holy Spirit in a Trinitarian context, Ecclesiology (including the Councils and its dogma), the Mission of the Church, Sacraments, Purgatory, and Mariology. The dialogue has as its aim to foster a better understanding and relationship between the Catholic Church and the Oriental Orthodox Churches, addressing issues of common concern.

Annual official meetings of the Commission have been held since 2004, hosted alternatively by the Catholic Church and the Oriental Orthodox Churches. During these annual meeting studies and papers are presented from both sides to guide the Commission in its consideration and exploration of areas of convergence and

[1] Point 5 of the common declaration signed on 11 March 1998 states: We agreed on the necessity of maintaining a common position of faith in all theological dialogues. Thus, henceforth, we will engage as a family of Oriental Orthodox Churches in the Middle East in any theological dialogue with other churches and Christian world communions. We hope that this basic principle will also be accepted by other beloved churches of our family, as is happening now in many theological dialogues.

divergence. The meetings are co-chaired by the head of the pontifical council for promoting unity in the Vatican (Cardinal Walter Casper followed by Cardinal Kurt Koch) and Metropolitan Bishoy of Damiette (Coptic Orthodox Church).

During the first official meeting of the Joint Commission in Cairo, January 2005, the Oriental Orthodox side expressed that previous Christological official agreements with some of their churches have been challenged by the Christological Agreement between the Catholic church and the Assyrian Church of the East signed in Rome in November 1994, since that Church continued to defend the person and Christology of Nestorius and attack the Christology of St. Cyril of Alexandria on their official website on the internet at that time (2005). Consequently, the Joint Commission agreed to postpone discussions on Christology to a later stage while keeping the topic on its agenda.

In 2009, a common document was produced by the Commission entitled "*Nature, Constitution and Mission of the Church*" to be submitted to the authorities of the churches for consideration and action. The document describes broad areas of consensus regarding fundamental ecclesiological principles, and outlines areas that require further study and it is considered a major achievement. Our Holy Synod had some comments on this document to be conveyed to the Commission in its following meeting.

4. Dialogue with the Anglican Communion

The Anglican Communion was originally the Church of England, but it now encompasses a group of Churches (i.e. The Anglican Communion). Some of these churches refer to themselves as the Episcopal Church. The Anglican Communion originated through the independence of the Church of England from the Church of Rome in the era of King Henry VIII (1538). This occurrence followed the Reformation movement under the leadership of Martin Luther in Germany in 1521. The Anglican Communion is numbered among the family of Evangelical or Protestant Churches in many world assemblies. The Church of England apparently kept three of the seven Church Sacraments namely: Baptism, Eucharist and Priesthood (Ministry).

The World Council of Churches issued the Lima Document entitled B.E.M. (Baptism, Eucharist, Ministry) assuming that the churches could unite and reach a mutual recognition of one another on the basis of this Document. Our Church believes that unity is primarily estimated upon the basis of unity of thought and faith, prior to unity on the basis of baptism. It is stated in the Bible "*One Lord, one faith, one baptism*" (Eph. 4:5). The "*one faith*" is the basis for the "*one baptism*".

In addition to the belief of the Catholic Church in the procession of the Holy Spirit from the Father and the Son, the Anglican Communion add other variances, some of which are the following:

1- Cancelling four of the Church sacraments, namely Matrimony, Chrism, Confession, Unction of the Sick.

2- Abolishing monasticism, and subsequently allowing marriages to bishops.

3- Cancelling fasts.

4- Permitting the ordination of women to full ranking deacons and serving at the altar, the full priesthood rank accompanied by the sacramental services, the sub-episcopal rank, then the episcopal rank of a diocese bishop, having a Throne and a Bronze Snake. All women of these ranks are allowed to marry like men and some of them are divorced.

5- Believing in the salvation of non-believers regardless to the acceptance of faith or baptism.

6- A resolution in Lambeth Conference 1988 allowing polygamy for the Christians in Africa. If a man having more than one wife desires to become a Christian, they permit him and his wives baptism while all his wives remain with him, in a continued state of sexual relations with them all.

7- During Lambeth Conference 1988 defending homosexuals went on, under the pretense that God created some individuals with a tendency towards their own sex, so it is not their fault. Subsequently, some bishops ordained lesbians and gay persons to the priesthood ranks. This results in disgracing priesthood among all nations. The Lambeth Conference of 2008 readjusted its stance towards Christian marriage that it should be between male and female partners.

8- In many western dioceses, justification of Biblical criticism, the interference of the human mind as a source of theological teaching, has in its excessiveness reached a point that the Bishop of Salisbury in England, John Osten Backer published a book entitled The Foolishness of God. Not one of the members of his church questioned him for accusing God of foolishness, or for his criticism of the Bible, or for considering the Bible as a book that mostly counterfeits truth, in the history of humanity.

Many conservative bishops in the Anglican Communion refused the liberal trends and resolutions to the extent that they formed a conference of Global South bishops which declared its commitment to the biblical teachings. This conference involved the majority of the Anglican dioceses and bishops worldwide.

Our Holy Synod rejected some of the decisions of the Lambeth Conference 1988 which permitted ordination of women into priesthood even to episcopacy in some dioceses, allowed polygamy in Africa, and defended homosexuals. His Holiness Pope Shenouda III presented a paper on the "View Point of the Coptic Orthodox Church on the Ordination of Women."

In 2001, and as a result of the recommendations of the Lambeth Conference of 1988 and 1998 and the decisions of the Oriental Orthodox Churches, the Anglican-Oriental Orthodox dialogue was upgraded from a Forum (1985-1993) to a Commission. A preparatory meeting was held in Midhurst July 2001 in which a work plan agenda for the joint theological commission was set. It included all the important points and the serious differences that should be discussed. Christology is one of these points, especially after the Lambeth Conferences decisions accepting the Christology of the Assyrian Church, which our churches reject. The first meeting of the Commission was held in Etchmiadzin November 2002, where a Common Agreement on Christology was reached emphasizing the doctrines of the Assyrian Church, how they venerate Nestorius, Theodore of Mopsuestia, Diodore of Tarsus and follow the teachings of Nestorius. This agreed statement was submitted to the holy synods of the Oriental Orthodox Churches and to the next Lambeth Conference for consideration and action. The next meeting was scheduled on October 2003 but was postponed because of the ordination of a homosexual bishop in New Hampshire ECUSA.

The dialogue stopped for the same reason. In a special session dated 3 September 2003, our Holy Synod issued a Statement rejecting the legalization of homosexuality, same sex marriage, the ordination of homosexuals in different pastoral degrees and the process to ordain a homosexual bishop in the Episcopal Church of New Hampshire, USA. The Holy Synod of the Coptic Orthodox Church decided anonymously to strongly condemn these acts that violate the teachings of our Lord Jesus Christ and the Scriptures.

The ordination of the homosexual bishop caused a great division in the Anglican Communion. The Anglican Churches of the Global South strictly rejected this action and similar deviations from the biblical teachings. They held a meeting in Tanzania, September 2007 and another in Singapore 2010 to which H.H. Pope Shenouda III was invited and delegated H.G. Bishop Suriel of Melbourne to attend and present a lecture affirming the opinion of the Coptic Orthodox Church.

Later, our Holy Synod agreed upon starting a theological dialogue with the Global South of the Anglican Communion (2/3 of the Anglican Communion), upon condition that our family of churches receive an invitation from them. Metropolitan Monir, Bishop of Egypt and North Africa is the Horn Treasurer of the Global South Primates Committee.

Presently, it was agreed to resume the dialogue with the Anglican Communion on condition that their delegation should be uniformly conservative. The next meeting of the International Joint Commission is expected to be in England October 2013.

5. Dialogue with the World Alliance of Reformed Churches

The first meeting was held in St. Bishoy's Monastery, Wadi El Natroon, Egypt 2-5 May 1993. This was followed by a second dialogue in a forum held in Holland, 13 September 1994.

The Holland dialogue was based on Christology. His Holiness Pope Shenouda III presented a lecture on the doctrine of the family of our Orthodox Churches on Christology. The attendants agreed upon a common statement to be submitted to the authorities of the Oriental Orthodox Churches and to the Executive Committee of the World Alliance of Reformed Churches for their consideration and action.

We agreed upon the continuation for further dialogue on other numerous and important issues of differences. Dialogue will begin on the 'Concept of Inspiration in the Bible' and 'the Position of Church Tradition'.

The Reformed Churches, on its behalf, decided to issue advice to their publishing houses, not to continue referring to the family of our Churches as following the mono-physite doctrine, in their publications. The term mono-physite ('only nature' not 'one nature') implicitly denies the factual Human nature of Christ the Lord.

A third meeting was held in India, 10-15 January 1997. The main subject was "The Holy Bible-Inspiration-authority" another subject was "The Job of the Theologian in the Church".

Unfortunately, concerning the dialogue on 'Inspiration and the Bible', they presented a strange concept which denies that the Bible is the word of God Himself. Therefore the next dialogue will be dedicated to this concept; that our Church, as well as all the Churches, needs to preserve the Apostolic Tradition.

6. The Lutheran World Federation

In 2007 the Lutheran World Federation requested to start dialogue with the Oriental Orthodox Churches and their request was primarily welcomed by the heads of the Oriental Orthodox Churches.

7. The Assyrian Churches

The theological dialogue between the 'Middle East Council of Churches' and the 'Assyrian Church' that follows the new calendar (its Patriarch is (Mar) Dinkha), started in 1991 and continued till 1994. The Coptic Orthodox Church shared in this dialogue and presented some papers of theological researches.

In January 1995, and according to an invitation from His Holiness Pope Shenouda III, after nominating His Holiness as president for the Middle East Council of Churches, a dialogue took place between the Coptic Orthodox Church and the abovementioned Church in presence of delegates from the Syrian Orthodox Church and a representative of the Middle East Council of Churches. The Coptic Orthodox side was presided over by His Holiness Pope Shenouda III. The Assyrian side presented a proposed statement of faith on 'Christology and the Incarnation of the Word'. The statement was reviewed and changed to correspond with the teachings of the great Saint Cyril, and not contradict his twelve anathemas. Very frankly, the Coptic Church asked for the removal of the names of Diodore, Theodore, and Nestorius from the list of saints of this church, and in the meantime to remove all attacks against the saints of our church. Furthermore, it is necessary to address everything within the the Assyrian Church's teaching that contradicts this proposed statement, i.e. its refusal of the council of Ephesus and its decisions against Nestorius and his teaching…

The Assyrian side promised to work on executing these points. The Coptic Orthodox side asked that it should be stated in the agreed statement of the dialogue that the Assyrians should abolish from its liturgies and sources of teaching all that contradicts with the Christological statement. The two sides agreed upon forming a committee dialogue to follow-up executing these points and remove all church disagreements.

However, no agreement was reached and the issue was not presented to the Holy Synod because they decided to enter the Middle East Council of Churches via the Catholic family, especially after they signed a theological agreement with the Catholics in 1994 endorsed by the Pope of Rome from one side and the Assyrian Patriarch Dinkha from the other. We were surprised to find out that during the meeting of the ecumenical dialogue in February 1996 and July 1997 they presented papers (of which we have copies) in which unfortunately they considered Saint Cyril to have oppressed Nestorius, that the decision of Council of Ephesus against Nestorius was not just, and that anathemas against Nestorius together with Theodore and Diodore the fathers of Nestorianism, should be lifted. They defended the teachings of the three heretics speaking of two persons in Christ coming together only by an external conjoining.

The General Secretary of our Holy Synod, being the correspondent of the subcommittee of church relations, presented to the Holy Synod during its session of 1 June 1996 a report on the ecumenical dialogue with the Assyrians that he attended. Our Holy Synod found that the Assyrians are Nestorian and need to correct their doctrines and confess the doctrine and decisions of the third ecumenical council of Ephesus (431). This decision was issued in the book of the Decisions of the Holy Synod.

On 10 October 1998 His Holiness Pope Shenouda III presided over a session of the Executive Committee of the Middle East Council of Churches in Lebanon. All the documents about the reality of the Assyrian Church were accessed. Subsequently, knowing that the Assyrians are Nestorian in their doctrines, attacking the Council of Ephesus (431) and Saint Cyril, and in their liturgies referring to Nestorius as saint, it was decided that these churches are rejected from joining the Council since they do not belong to any of the four families of churches in the Council.

Conclusion

May our Lord aid us in our mission to reach the great goal i.e. church unity, on the basis of unity in faith, through the prayers of all the saints and defenders of faith throughout the ages in every place on earth. Asking for the prayers of everyone in order to fulfill our Lord's request from the Father "*that they may be one as We are*" (Jn 17:11).

Bibliography

The Truth Shall Make you Free, *Lambeth Conference 1988, the Reports, Resolutions & Pastoral Letteres from the Bishops*, Published for the Anglican Consultative Council, (Church House Publishing 1988).

Chaillot, C & Belopopsky, A, *Towards Unity, The Theological Dialogue between the orthodox Church and the Oriental Orthodox Churches*, (Geneva: Inter-Orthodox Dialogue, 1998).

Syriac Dialogue, First Non-Official Consultation of Dialogue within the Syriac Tradition, (Horn, Austria: Pro Oriente, Ferdinand Berger & sohne Ges.m.b.H., 1994).

Five Vienna Consultations between Theologians of the Oriental Orthodox Churches and the Roman Catholic Church, 1971, 1973, 1976, 1978, and 1988 Selected Papers in One Volume, (Vienna: Published and edited by the Ecumenical Poundation Pro Oriente, 1993).

Pro Oriente XXXVI, *Documents on Unity in Faith between the Oriental Orthodox Churches and the Roman Catholic Church*, edited by Peter Hofricher and Juhnann Marte, (Innsbruck-Wien: Tyrolia Verlag, 2013).

(86) Ecumenical Dialogue in the Orthodox Coptic Church

Wedak Tawfik

"…that they all may be one." (John 19:21)

It is certainly the Father's will that we all be one in Him (Gal. 3:28). For this end the Lord Jesus Christ prayed to the Father, *"… that they may be one as We are."* For this end He died, for each and every one of us, not for a certain nation or group. Ecumenism then is to fulfil the will of the Lord Christ that the Church His body may not be split or divided.

Ecumenism in the Coptic Orthodox view, as expressed by her holy patriarch late Pope Shenouda III and her great scholars and theologians, is the readiness to listen to the views of the others, to accept the others, to reach a common understanding with the others.

Ecumenism is openness to the others, without surrendering the Church dogmas out of courtesy or to satisfy the others. It is a space for dialogue and attempts to find points of convergence and agreement. Ecumenism does not mean that a church be swallowed in another, or that a church dominates over the other, but rather that all churches support each other towards benefiting from the gifts of the Holy Spirit to each. With such an understanding each church shall maintain her own self-governance according to her own traditions and systems. It is not an attempt to impose on the others certain views. This does not conflict with the need for mutual relationships and cooperation with other churches through regular meetings with a spirit of trust and avoiding any misunderstanding or hurting of the feelings of the other churches. Therefore the Coptic Church tries to implant within the young the idea of the oneness of the church as an essential requirement for a Christian life, without compromising the church dogmas. This is the role of the clergy and ministers in churches, besides the role of the church leaders and theologians on the higher level.

Church unity is not to gather people in the church building, not to bring people from other churches into our own church (proselytism), but it is rather to let the Holy Spirit work within everybody with one heart and one mind to bring everybody to witness to the Lord Christ under His leadership as the Head of the one catholic (universal) church.

H. E. Metropolitan Bishoy of Damiette[1] compares catholicity and conciliarity[2]: Catholicity as expressed by His Eminence means the communion and unity of faith of the church all over the world through Eucharistic Holy Communion, so long as we share the same heart, mind, and sacraments. Whereas conciliarity means that no one in the church shall impose his own views, but shall consider the other as a mirror that reveals to him the truth. The Catholicity of the church can be fulfilled by the conciliarity of the church. His Eminence gives examples from the Holy Scripture for the conciliarity as the spirit of readiness to listen to the others' views, when Saint Peter the apostle went to baptize the house of Cornelius, the church did not like it. But when he told them the story and through their readiness to hear his convincing words that God has accepted the nations to faith and that no one then can prevent those from getting baptized (Acts 10: 47), they accepted the idea. We also see how the universal church accepted the books of the Holy Scripture inspired by the Holy Spirit.

Actually the quarrels among the different Christian churches concerning the basic dogmas related to the Person of the Lord Jesus Christ are not a matter of factual substance, but of words and terminology, for they all confess Christ

---

[1] Metropolitan Bishoy of Damiette, Secretary of the Holy Synod of the Coptic Church, a great scholar and theologian, and an active ecumenist who co-chaired many of the official ecumenical meetings.

[2] Metropolitan Bishoy of Damiette, *Ecumenical Dialogues, and Sayings of the Fathers,* Lectures for the Institute of Pastoral Care and Seminaries, Edition 21, (2009): 200.

to be perfect God and perfect Man, without any commingling, mixing, or confusion of the natures. In other words, there is a common ground for faith. Satan is partly responsible for such divisions, and is still at work. He brings about disturbances, constantly encouraging new splits desiring the division of the body of Christ which is the Church.

Commitment of the Coptic Orthodox Church to Christian Unity

The Coptic Orthodox Church has a well known history concerning her ecumenical influence in the formation of the early church, and this has continued right up to the present day. The church has been forming and developing relationships with other churches, faiths and official organizations all over the world, as in the United Kingdom, in United States of America, in Australia and in all places where the Coptic Church has dioceses.

His Holiness late Pope Shenouda III, 117th Patriarch of the Coptic Orthodox Church, was known for his devotion to the unity of the church. He emphasized that Christian unity must be founded upon unity of faith not of jurisdiction.

He maintained good relations with the various Orthodox churches and with their patriarchs, and paid many visits to them, such as to the Patriarchs of Constantinople, Moscow, Romania, and Antioch. A full communion of these churches with the Oriental Orthodox Churches seems imminent. He also had good relations with the Anglican and Catholic Churches.

In 1971, while still a bishop, His Holiness attended the first meeting that was held with the Roman Catholic theologians in Vienna. In 1972 after his enthronement he became the first Coptic Orthodox Pope to visit the Vatican in over 1500 years. On 7 May 1973, together with Pope Paul VI of Rome, he signed a common declaration in which they expressed their mutual concern for church unity. Following that a joint committee was formed to follow up these efforts under his auspices. His Holiness wrote the Christological Statement agreed upon by both these churches.

In that historic visit to the Vatican, on 7 May 1973, and around the 1600th anniversary of the Feast of St. Athansius the Apostolic, the 20th Pope of Alexandria, His Holiness Pope Shenouda III, personally received this saint's relics from Pope Paul VI of Rome at St. Peter's Basilica at the Vatican.

In the year 2000, His Holiness received His Holiness Pope Paul of the Roman Catholic Church in Egypt. And in 2004, His Holiness met His Grace Dr. Rowan Williams Archbishop of Canterbury for the Church of England in the UK, as well as many other Church leaders throughout the world. Other visits were exchanged between His Holiness Pope Shenouda III and the Ecumenical Patriarch in Constantinople, the Orthodox Patriarch of Moscow, Romania, Bulgaria, and Antioch, and with the Catholic Patriarchs in the Middle Eastern Countries.

Moreover there have also been dialogues with various Protestant churches worldwide. Steps have been taken towards bringing about reconciliation with the Protestant Churches in Egypt. The first meeting of the churches took place at the Patriarchate in December 1976.

With a spirit of love His Holiness paid fraternal visits to several heads of churches in Europe and Asia in 1972. All this proves that the Coptic Church has a deep concept of ecumenism and the acceptance of others and a friendly attitude towards other churches in spite of the differences of views. The Coptic Orthodox Church extends her love to everybody in the world. This is also apparent in the friendly relations with the Moslems in Egypt represented in sharing their celebrations, in holding dialogues with them seeking common grounds of faith. His Holiness Pope Shenouda III was very esteemed by the Moslem leaders, and he was even invited to give a yearly lecture in a high standing Moslem meeting that was always met with great appreciation.

His Holiness was one of the presidents of World Council of Churches (WCC), and of the Middle East Council of Churches (MECC). The Coptic Church also is a member of the All Africa Conference of Churches (AACC), the National Council of Churches of Christ in the USA (NCC), the Canadian Council of Churches (CCC), the National Council of Churches in Australia (NCCA), and Churches Together in Britain and Ireland (CTBI).

His Holiness initiated a closely monitored theological dialogue with the Eastern Orthodox Churches, the Roman Catholic Church, Anglican, Swedish, Lutheran, and the World Alliance of Reformed Churches.

Orthodox Handbook on Ecumenism

The Unity of the Oriental Orthodox Churches

It is a longstanding unity based on common history and faith. This unity and the common view concerning the division of the Church was once expressed by H. H. Mar Igantius Zakka II. The Patriarch of Antioch, speaking in the University of Humboldt Berlin on 16 May 1995, stated that the split of the Christian Church is a big mistake, a blasphemy of the Holy Spirit and an ignoring of the existence of Christ who promised that the gates of hell will not prevail against it (Mt 16:18). He reminded us that throughout history thousands have shed blood and many suffered and were expelled for the sake of the one faith. Therefore there is a necessity of continuing the Christian dialogue on various levels. Unity can only happen in and around Christ who is the Head of the Church, and we with all our doctrines are only parts of the holy body of Christ.

There is therefore an Annual Meeting that has been founded since 1996 and continued up till now among the heads of the Oriental Orthodox Churches: His Holiness Pope Shenouda III of the Coptic Orthodox Church, His Holiness Patriarch Zakka I of the Syrian Orthodox Church, and His Holiness Catholicos Aram I of the Armenian Church – Holy See of Cilicia. The tenth meeting was that held 19-21 April 2007 at St. Ephraim Syrian Orthodox Monastery in Damascus, Syria, in which they signed a Common Declaration. In those annual meetings the heads of the three churches addressed issues related to the family of the Oriental Orthodox Churches and its theological dialogues with various churches. They discussed matters related to dialogue with the Eastern Orthodox Churches, the Roman Catholic Church, the Anglican Communion and the Lutheran World Federation Churches of the Reformation.

Relations with the Chalcedonian Churches (the Eastern Churches)
The First Fruits between the Two Families

Much has been accomplished in the past few decades especially in relationships with the Eastern Orthodox Churches. In addition to theological dialogue the church also actively hosts and participates in dialogue on topics such as inter-church marriages, setting a common date for Easter … etc.

But let us go back to the history of the division between the two families: for over 1500 years the Eastern (Byzantine) Orthodox Churches and the Oriental Orthodox Churches have remained separated. Both families, who have been long out of communion with each other, now pray and trust in God to restore that communion on the basis of the apostolic faith of the undivided church of the first centuries which we confess in our Common Creed. Only about forty years ago they came together for:

The Four Unofficial Theological Consultations:
- Aarhus (Denmark) in 1964   Bristol (England) in 1967
- Geneva (Switzerland) in 1970   Addis Ababa in 1971

The results were unexpectedly positive. As Bishop Timothy Kallistos Ware of Dioklea stated afterwards in 1993 in his book *The Orthodox Church*: "It became clear that on the basic question which had led historically to the division – the doctrine of the Person of Christ – there is no real disagreement … the divergence lies only on the level of Phraseology. On the essence of the Christological Dogma we found ourselves in full agreement."

This was clear in the statement of Bristol Consultation, which said:

"Some of us affirm two natures, wills and energies, hypostatically united in the One Lord Jesus Christ. Some of us affirm one united divine human nature, will, and energy in the same Christ. But both sides speak of a union without confusion, without change, without divisions, without separation. Both affirm the dynamic performance of the Godhead and the Manhood, with all their natural properties and faculties, in the One Christ."

These four Unofficial Conversations during the period 1964-1971, were followed up by the convening of:
The Official Joint Commission representing the two Church Families that met in:
- Geneva in 1985

Part VI: Ecumenical Perspectives of Oriental Orthodox Churches

- St. Bishoy Monastery in Egypt in 1989
- Geneva in 1990
- Geneva in 1993

Attempts for restoration of communion between the two Orthodox Families:

Joint Committees between both churches were formed and dealt in detail with almost every point of difference between the two families, providing suggestions for eliminating differences and reaching a common view concerning them. Among the subjects dealt with were:

- The matter of the different Christological formulations, which had been a stumbling block in the past: there was agreement that the underlying understanding of the Incarnation was the same.
- The reciprocal lifting of anathemas and condemnations: the meeting of 1993 agreed that the lifting of anathemas should be done unanimously and simultaneously by the heads of all the churches of both sides through the signing of an appropriate, ecclesiastical Act, the content of which will include acknowledgment from each side that the other one is Orthodox in all respects. Once the anathemas have been lifted, this should imply that the restoration of full communion for both sides is to be immediately implemented.
- However, difficulties still remain, for not everyone on the two sides is equally positive about the dialogue. Some in Greece for example continue to regard the Oriental Orthodox Churches as "monophysite heretics", and some Non-Chalcedonians continue to regard Chalcedon and the Tome of Leo as "Nestorian".
- The ritual differences such as the celebration of the Christmas-Epiphany Feast, making the sign of the cross, the Eucharist Bread, the Holy Chrism, Fasts, etc.

Again from 2- 4 February 1998 an Orthodox dialogue was held, where 30 theologians from the Eastern Orthodox and Oriental Orthodox Churches met in the halls of the Holy Cross Church of the Greek Orthodox Patriarchate of Antioch in Damascus, Syria. In the meeting among other presentations there were two papers from the Coptic Church: one by Metropolitan Bishoy on "Interpretation of the Christological Official Agreements" and the other by the Rev. Father Tadros Malaty on "Pastoral Efforts towards Unity".

Relations with the Roman Catholic Church

Dialogues were initiated under the auspices of Pro-Oriente, the Ecumenical Foundation in Vienna founded by Cardinal König Archbishop of Vienna in 1964. Unofficial Consultations were conducted in Vienna in 1971, 1976, 1988. These consultations focused particularly on the Christological doctrines resulting in what is known as "Vienna Christological Formulations", and paved the way for subsequent bilateral Christological Agreements between the heads of the churches.

A joint commission has been formed between Oriental Orthodox Churches and the Roman Catholic Churches. The third meeting was that held in Etchmiadzin, Armenia, under co-chairmanship of His Eminence Cardinal Walter Kasper, President of the Pontifical Council for Promoting Christian Unity, and His Eminence Metropolitan Bishoy of Damiette, General Secretary of the Holy Synod of the Coptic Orthodox Church.

The International Joint Commission for Theological Dialogue between the Catholic Church and the Oriental Orthodox Churches had its eighth meeting 25-28 January 2011 in Rome, hosted by the new president of the Pontifical Council for Promoting Christian Unity His Eminence Cardinal Kurt Kuch, and His Eminence Metropolitan Bishoy of Damiette, General Secretary of the Holy Synod of the Coptic Church.

Sessions began with common celebration of prayers, assuring the solid basis of faith, and study in a very friendly atmosphere of the ways in which the churches expressed their communion with one another that continued until the middle of the 5th century, and the role played by monasticism on this.

This meeting was followed by the 9th meeting in Addis Ababa, Ethiopia in January 16-23, 2012.

Ecumenical Services by the Coptic Orthodox Church
In Stevenage, the United Kingdom[3]

The Coptic Church in UK for the past thirty years and more intensively since the consecration of His Grace Bishop Angaelos as General Bishop in the UK in 1999 had fostered good working relationships with many ecumenical, official, charitable, and non-government bodies. The Church continues to work hard at developing connections with other religious and interfaith groups in that increasingly secular society. His Grace Bishop Angaelos is the official envoy on the official Anglican-Oriental Orthodox International Theological Commission.

- The Church is now a member of all official ecumenical instruments in the UK allowing it to develop and extend her role in serving our Lord Jesus Christ
- The Church is a member of Fellowship of Coptic Orthodox University Students as part of service for the youth and the community.
- The church is actively involved in a national multi-denominational conference for Christian Youth workers.
- The Coptic Orthodox Church acts as a focal point for official and ecumenical relations between the Coptic Church and other bodies in UK and abroad.
- The Oriental Orthodox Church Centre has hosted many visits from a variety of organizations, charities and interfaith groups and interested groups who wish to learn more about the church, her traditions, doctrines and the work that she does both in UK and all over the world.
- The Coptic Church plays an active part as a member of:
  - The Council of Oriental Orthodox Churches
  - Churches Together in England (CTE), since 1996
  - Membership of specialist group within CTE includes:
    - The Senior Representatives Forum
    - The Enabling Group
    - The Theology & Unity Group
    - The Spirituality Group
    - Minority and Ethnic Affairs Group
  - Membership of Anglican-Oriental Orthodox Regional Forum (AOORF). Members wish to publicize a new development in the ecumenical relationship between the Church of England and the Oriental Orthodox Churches

Ecumenical Services by the Coptic Orthodox Church in USA[4]

The ecumenical efforts of His Grace Bishop Serapion of the Coptic Orthodox Diocese of Los Angeles, Southern California and Hawaii are very distinguished:
- Friendly relations with other Orthodox Churches in US, sharing them their celebrations and events, as for example H.G. Bishop Serapion attending a service and reception at St. Nicholaos Cathedral honouring the Antioch Orthodox Archbishop Joseph who was promoted to the rank of Archbishop by His Beatitude Patriarch Ignatius IV on 11 December 2011.
- Copts and Russians discovering each other: The Coptic Church participates in the events of the Russian Church with spirit of love, as in 26 February 2009 when H.G. Bishop Serapion congratulated and attended the enthronement of His Eminence Metropolitan Kirill of Smolensk & Kaliningrad as the 16th Patriarch of Moscow & all Russia.

---

[3] www.stevenagechurches.org.uk ; www.churches_together.net
[4] The Coptic Orthodox Diocese of North America, in Pomona and Los Angeles

Part VI: Ecumenical Perspectives of Oriental Orthodox Churches

- There were theological dialogues between the Russian Church and the Coptic Church, as on 6 December 2006 when they discussed matters concerning the theological dialogue between the two Orthodox families, and the Orthodox cooperation at the ecumenical councils especially at the WCC, also the Orthodox joint responsibilities in confronting the liberty trends of some modern Christian groups in order to preserve the apostolic heritage and Christian ethics today.
- Joint Divine Liturgy celebrated annually by the Oriental Churches of the Western US. These days were filled with prayer, solidarity, and fellowship among over one hundred clergy members of the three sister churches.
- H.G. Bishop Serapion attended a Global Christian Forum (GCF) program Meeting in New Delhi in 2008 that focused on the evaluation of the organization's work throughout the past decade and a plan for the coming years.
- H.G. Bishop Serapion delivered a public lecture on "Christian Unity from an Orthodox Perspective" in the School of Religion and the Council for Coptic Studies at Claremont Graduate.
- Christian Churches Together CCT, formally launched in Passadena in 6-9 February 2007. The CCT is composed of 36 churches and national organizations from virtually all US Christian groups who have been seeking to come together for fellowship, worship and opportunities to share in important ministries. There was a consensus on the importance of evangelism and the need to eliminate domestic poverty marked the official formation of CCT. Somebody quoted the words "Remember that you belong to God and God does not belong to you." They said that this is the wisdom that will hold CCT group together.
- There are frequent Ecumenical Meetings of Orthodox Bishop celebrating Christian Feasts and events of each church.
- The Greek Orthodox Archdiocese of America expresses sincere support for the Coptic Christians of Egypt during their most difficult transition in the life of the Egyptian Nation.
- The Statement of Patriarch Kirill of Moscow and all Russia on 13 October 2011 on the Egyptian massacre of Copts, in which he defended their Egyptian brothers in faith and called upon the world community not to be indifferent to this lawlessness.
- The annual joint Orthodox meetings under the care of H.G. Bishop Serapion.
- The Diocese of Los Angeles, California expressed with a sense of love solidarity with the Russian people and church over the intense wildfires that afflicted the land of Russia which destroyed more than one hundred villages, leaving 50 people dead and thousands homeless. The Diocese also responded to the appeal by the Russian Church and made a contribution to the relief effort under the guidance of H.G. Bishop Serapion.
- In May 2000, His Holiness established the first ecumenical office in the Archdiocese in North America.

Middle East and Ecumenism

- Middle Eastern Oriental Orthodox Common Declaration at the 4th meeting of the Heads at St. Mark Centre for the Coptic Orthodox Church on 15-17 March 2001 and the members of the Standing Committee, H. E. Metropolitan Bishoy; H.G. Bishop Moussa; H. E. Metropoligan Theophilus George Saliba; H. G. Bishop Sebouh Sarkissian; Archimandrite Nareg Alemezian.
- Reaffirming unity in faith and firm attachment to the first three ecumenical councils: Nicaea 325, Constantinople 381, Ephesus 431 and to the teachings of the church fathers.
- Reconfirming the decisions adopted and guidelines set by them in the context of their common witness and service to their people, particularly in the Middle East, a region where the church of Christ was born and true faith was received and shaped by the fathers and martyrs through their teachings and martyrdom. This is our sacred heritage which was delivered to us and to be delivered in turn to the generations to come. They discussed among other things:

1. Theological dialogues between Oriental and Eastern Orthodox Churches which emphasized the importance of the dialogue for the full unity of the Orthodox churches
   - A committee is appointed to discuss the situation of theological dialogues between both churches. The Committee is to identify specific areas of closer ecumenical collaboration between our churches and the Russian Orthodox Church.
   - The Holy Synod of the Coptic Orthodox Church and the Permanent Holy Synod of the Greek Orthodox Patriarchate of Alexandria and All Africa in November 2000 have approved the Pastoral Agreement reached between them regarding the mutual recognition of the Sacrament of the Holy Matrimony blessed in their respective Churches in case of mixed marriages.

2. Oriental Orthodox Churches – Anglican Communion met concerning upgrading of the Theological Forum between them. The Oriental Churches decided to delegate their representatives to the next meeting to be held 27 July- 1 August 2001 in London. The purpose is to clarify matters pertaining to the agenda, procedures, and methodology.

3. Oriental Orthodox Churches – Roman Catholic Churches: Reflections on the document issued by the Roman Catholic Churches "Dominus Jesus" for the Doctrine of Faith of the Vatican.

4. Oriental Orthodox Churches – World Alliance of Reformed Churches: in January 2001, at the Armenian Catholicosate of Cilicia, Antelias Lebanon made a report that included among other things the Agreed Statement on Christology signed in 1994 and referred to the points of agreements and disagreements existing between the two families. The report was to be studied in the respective Holy Synods and considered further in next meetings.

5. WCC and the Special Commission for Orthodox Participation in the WCC: An interim report of the Special Commission was presented to the Central Committee of WCC in its meeting in Germany in February 2001. The report proposed that questions related to ecclesiology and as well as controversial theological matters be discussed in the Faith and Order Commission. MECC reaffirmed support to their regional ecumenical organization underlined the urgent need for making the ecumenical witness of the MECC more efficient and responsive to the new realities and expectations of the churches in the region.

6. Sub-Committees:
   - Sub-Committee for Theological Seminaries decided on 24-25 November 2000 in Damascus to establish a special department for Oriental Orthodox Studies in the Seminaries of the Oriental Orthodox Churches.
   - Sub-Committee for Youths.
   - Sub-Committee for Publications, aiming at exchange of information among churches as a vital task for the fellowship of the churches.

7. Peace in the Middle East: From the second half of the 20th century, Oriental Orthodox Churches have engaged in constructive dialogues among themselves and with other parties. Constructive Dialogue has begun with the Muslims with whom they share one homeland.

The WCC efforts for ecumenism

The Orthodox Churches members of the WCC are:

Six Oriental Orthodox Churches; namely: The Coptic Church, the Syrian Church, the Armenian Church, the Ethiopian Church, the Eriterian Church, and the Indian (Malankara) Church. These six Churches are in communion with each other. They accept the first three ecumenical councils, and do not accept the fourth of Chalcedon (451). The Ethiopian, Coptic and Indian Churches have been full members of the WCC since its inauguration in Amsterdam in 1948. The Syrian joined at the New Delhi Assembly of 1961. In Paris in 1962 the Central Committee admitted the Armenian Church.

Part VI: Ecumenical Perspectives of Oriental Orthodox Churches

Actually the efforts of the WCC in the field of ecumenism cannot be denied, for the WCC plays a very active role in bringing together churches for the sake of reaching the unity of the body of Christ. Through its programs and visits to the churches (the living letters) it succeeded to a great extent in improving understanding and deepening relationships within the ecumenical movement.

The Faith and Order Commission of the WCC paved the way for bilateral consultations between theologians of Byzantine and Oriental Churches in Aarhus (1964), Bristol (1967), Geneva (1971), and Addis Ababa (1971).

The WCC shares and supports the Christians in Egypt in the changing circumstances they experience, as for instance the message of solidarity sent by the WCC to the Christians in Egypt on 26 February 2010 concerning their security and encouraging the churches in Egypt to continue their involvement in the Moslem-Christian Dialogue. Until now with the same spirit the WCC shares the Egyptians the developments occurring in their country, ending with the message of congratulation sent to the new elect president of Egypt in June 2012.

Great Scholars and Theologians of the Coptic Orthodox Church

- The first and greatest who initiated the ecumenical work was His Holiness Late Pope Shenouda III.
- H. E. Metropolitan Bishoy of Damiette, Secretary General of the Holy Synod of the Coptic Orthodox Church and Director of the Institute of Coptic Studies in Cairo. H. E. is co-chair of almost all ecumenical commissions, an active worker in the field of Ecumenism, member of the WCC Executive Committee, member of the WCC Standing Commission of Faith & Order, Professor of Ecumenism and Ecumenical Dialogues at the Institute of Coptic Studies, Institute of Pastoral Care, and the Seminary with its various branches.
- H. G. Bishop Serapion of the Coptic Orthodox Diocese of Los Angeles, Southern California and Hawaii. H. G. is an active worker in the field of ecumenism, member of committees of the WCC, and initiator of many dialogues and friendly relationships with the various churches in his diocese.
- The Reverend Father Shenouda Maher Ishak, Professor of Theology and Biblical Studies in the Coptic Orthodox Theological College in Egypt and USA. His Rev. represents the church in many ecumenical meetings, and is member of various ecumenical committees.
- The Reverend Father Tadros Yacoub Malaty, Pastor of St. George Coptic Orthodox Church of Sporting, Alexandria. His Rev. is an active ecumenical worker and member of many committees. He wrote many books on the Coptic Orthodox Church and her main features including her spirituality, monasticism, education, ecumenism, as well as other books on the church dogmas.
- H. G. Bishop Angaelos of Stevenage, UK. H.G. is an active worker in the field of ecumenism in his diocese. He holds good and friendly relations with other churches, and is a member of many ecumenical bodies in UK.

Theological material and books from the Coptic Orthodox Church

- Metropolitan Bishoy of Damiette, (2008/2009) *The Council and Ecumenical Dialogues,* Lectures for the Institute of Coptic Studies, Department of Theology, 4th edition.
- Metropolitan Bishoy of Damiette, (2009/2010) *Ecumenical Dialogue, Sayings of the Fathers,* Lectures for the Institute of Pastoral Care and Seminary in Cairo and its branches, 21st Edition.
- Metropolitan Bishoy of Damiette and Secretary of the Holy Synod of the Coptic Orthodox Church, (2003) *The Eastern Assyrian Nestorian Church, A Documentary Book*, 1st Edition, published by St. Demiana Monastery.
- Deacon Dr. Emile Maher Ishak (now Fr. Shenouda Maher Ishak), (December 2000) *Studies in Comparative Theology I, Liturgical and Ritual Issues and Proposals Concerning the Restoration of Com-*

munion, submitted to The Joint Liturgical Sub-Committee of the dialogue between the Byzantine Orthodox Churches and the Oriental Orthodox Churches in its Meeting at Athens, 15-19 March, 1993 1st Edition, press Al Amba Ruweis (The aim of that meeting was to seek convergence between the two families of Orthodoxy) The book is the Paper presented by Deacon Dr. Emile Maher (now Father Shenouda) Professor of Theology and Biblical Studies in the Coptic Orthodox Theological College in USA. The Paper was entitled "Studies in Comparative Ritual Theology". It was first published in 1995 by the Byzantine side in the Periodical Kleronomia of the Patriarchal Institute for Patristic Studies in Thessaloniki, Greece, Tome 26, June - December 1994. The book is published with a foreword by Metropolitan Bishoy of Damiette.

- Father Tadros Yacoub Malaty, (1993) *Introduction to the Coptic Orthodox Church,* St. George's Coptic Orthodox Church, Sporting, Alexandia, Egypt.
- Father Tadros Yacoub Malaty, (1986) *The Coptic Orthodox Church and Spirituality,* (in Arabic), published by St. Mary Coptic Orthodox Church, Ottawa, Ontario, Canada.

To conclude with it is evident that the Coptic Orthodox Church longs for the unity of the body of Christ, trusting that God's Holy Spirit works and will always work within the hearts to bring such unity into reality. The Church is open and ready for constructive dialogue and for sharing views with the others and seeking convergence with them for the glory of God's Holy Name.

Bibliography

The World Council of Churches, *Together on the Way, Official Report of the Eighth Assembly of the World Council of Churches,* (Switzerland, 1999).

The World Council of Churches, *From Harare to Porto Alegre 1998- 2006,* (France 2005).

His Holiness Pope Shenouda III, *The Nature of Christ,* 1st edition, 1991.

His Holiness Pope Shenouda III, *The Divinity of Christ,* 1st edition, 1994.

Metropolitan Bishop of Damiette, *Ecumenical Dialogues and Sayings of the Fathers, Lectures for the Institute of Pastoral Care and Seminary,* 21st edition, 2009/2010.

Metropolitan Bishop of Damiette, *Councils and Ecumenical Dialogues, Part I, 4th edition, Lectures for the Institute of Coptic Studies, Department of Theology,* 2009/2010.

Metropolitan Bishop of Damiette, Secretary of the Holy Synod, and Co-Chairman of the Joint Commission of the Official Dialogue, "1992 Ecumenical Relations", an article in *Al Keraza* (Preaching) English Magazine, edited by The Coptic Orthodox Patriarchate, Vol. 1, No. 1

Father Tadros Yacoub Malaty, *Introduction to the Coptic Orthodox Church,* (Alexandria: St. George Coptic Orthodox Church in Sporting, 1993).

Father Tadros Yacoub Malaty, *The Coptic Orthodox Church and Spirituality,* (in Arabic), (Ottawa: St. Mary Coptic Orthodox Church, 1986).

Deacon Dr. Emile Maher Ishak (now Fr. Shenouda Maher), *Studies in Comparative Theology: Liturgical and Ritual Issues and Proposals Concerning the Restoration of Communion,* (Press of Al-amba Ruweis 2000).

Ayalkibet Berhanu

History, as well as the Old and the New Testament attest to the fact that Ethiopia is the first African nation to adhere to the Jewish religion (900 B.C)[1] and subsequently the Christian religion - from the era of the first apostles. Monotheism and Jewish religious beliefs and practices in Ethiopia date back to the reign of the Queen of Sheba and the reign of King Solomon of Israel. Christianity in Ethiopia at first came in about 34 A.D. through the Ethiopian Eunach who was baptized by the Apostle Philip, and then introduced this faith to his own country (Acts 8:26-40).[2] After this, St. Matthew, the evangelist, and later St. Andrew also came to Ethiopia and continued with their missionary activity of spreading the Christian faith.[3] It is because of all this evidence that the EOTC can be rightly regarded as an African indigenous church and one of the earliest apostolic churches in the world. Ethiopia was then transformed from Judaism to Christianity. This transformation gave Ethiopia a unique Christian identity in spite of the fact that the Christian world is a world in which people are divided by traditions, languages and continents. Although there are many Christian denominations and other religions within Ethiopia, such as Roman Catholicism, a number of Protestant groups, some Falashas (Bete Israel) who practice Judaism and a large Islamic community; the EOTC has remained the largest Christian denomination in the country. Gerima et al attest to this fact when they state thus: "the EOTC has more than 45 million members, 40,000 churches and monasteries, and about 500,000 clergymen, mainly in Ethiopia. It has been the dominant church in Ethiopia since the 4th century and is also the largest Oriental Orthodox Church in the world." [4]

Given this background it is important therefore to start the story of the EOTC's ecumenical relationship from the pre-Christian period.

Ethiopia in the Old Testament era

This story then begins with the relationship which was established between the Queen of Sheba (Queen Makeda) and King Solomon. The Queen of Sheba (Queen Makeda) visited Jerusalem to personally experience King Solomon's legendary wisdom, and that visit brought about a remarkable outcome for Ethiopia. The following are the main outcomes:

1. The birth of the Solomonic Dynasty in Ethiopia from Emperor Minlek I to Emperor Haile Silassie
2. The Levite clergy came to Ethiopia with Old Testament books and with the Ark of the Covenant, which enabled Ethiopians to worship the Monotheistic God in about 900 B.C.[5]

---

[1] For a historical perspective on the Christian religion in Ethiopia: http://eotc.faithweb.com/orth.html (last accessed, September 2013).
[2] The Ethiopian Eunuch who was a treasurer of Candace went to Jerusalem to partake in the annual feast as it was customary to those who accepted the Old Testament faith to be part of the annual feasts. Thus, the Ethiopian Eunuch who was a devoted religious person, a man of high rank in Ethiopia and the finance minister of Candace accepted Christianity, after meeting with apostle Philip, and got baptized. On his return, he preached the doctrine of Christ among his country people. He was the first to bring the Good News, although he was not called an apostle.
[3] Tesfaye, Ayalkibet B, "The Ethiopian Orthodox Tewahedo Church and its traditional theological education system." In *Handbook of Theological Education in Africa*, edited by Isabel Apawo Phiri and Dietrich Werner, 281-291 (Pietermaritzburg: Cluster Publications, 2013), 283.
[4] Gerima, Abuna et al, *The Ethiopian Orthodox Tewahedo Church History from the Birth of Christ up to 2000*: Ethiopia Stretches out her hands to God, (2008), xxi.
[5] Hancock, Graham. *The sign and the seal: the explosively controversial international best seller: a quest for the lost Ark of the Covenant.(* London: Arrow Books, 1992), 450, http://www.youtube.com/watch?v=tX2KbeD2_PE, http://www.youtube.com/watch?v=O97yb-UzXPs (last accessed on 08.08.2013).

3. The people of Ethiopia became accustomed to practising circumcision by which they followed Israel in terms of their relationship with God.

4. Ethiopia was transformed from being a nation whose religion was based on natural law (law of conscious) to one based on the Covenant law.[6]

5. *Axum* (Ethiopia's ancient capital) was founded by *Axsumawi* the great grandson of Ham and descendent of Noah. [7]

Moreover the name Ethiopia is mentioned several times in the Bible. Due to the journey of Queen Candace's Treasurer to Jerusalem, Ethiopia became the first region next to Jerusalem to accept Christianity.[8]

Ethiopia in the Christian era

Here it is important to note the fact that Christianity was not only limited to Ethiopia after being introduced by the Ethiopian Eunuch. It expanded to South Yemen and Nagran. During the reign of Emperor Caleb (514-42 A.D.) the Christians of Nagran in southern Arebia were persecuted by the Jews who were led by Phinhass. These Jews were the descendents of the settlers who fled away from Jerusalem when it was invaded and destroyed by Titus in 70 A.D.[9] Nagran Christians were bitterly persecuted by anti-Christian individuals. Those Christians who were persecuted appealed for help to their brothers in faith living in Constantinople, Alexandria and Axum (Ethiopia's ancient capital). Upon hearing about the tragedy of the Nagran Christians, Timothy the Patriarch of Alexandria wrote to Emperor Caleb (the Orthodox king of Ethiopia) who became very aggrieved and asked God in prayer to tell him how he could help the Christians of Nagarn. So the Emperor Caleb waged war against Phinhass (Dhu Nuwas). The King (Caleb) had enough men to fight, but he needed ships to transport his soldiers to Arabia. He wrote to the Emperor Justin I in Constantinople, and Justin sent him sixty ships, Caleb collected an army of 12,000 men. He attacked the Himyarites with success; he marched on and took the town of Takhar, the Yemenite capital. Phinhass was wounded, and he rode his horse into the sea and drowned. Kaleb then re-established Christianity in the land.[10]

In the 14th century Emperor Dawit or David (1380 – 1410) of Ethiopia communicated with John the Bishop of Jerusalem and received part of the True Cross on which Jesus was crucified, the Crown of thorns and an Icon of St. Mary which was painted by St. Luke.[11] The portion of the True Cross is kept in the *Geshen, Egziabher Ab* Church in Ethiopia, where people do a pilgrimage on every September 21st[12] of the Ethiopian calendar. People (even the Diaspora as well as global nationalities) come from all parts of the country to this place to get blessings and divine healing.

There is also a *Meskal* (Cross) celebration as a national holiday which has been taking place for more than 1600 years in Ethiopia. The word *Meskal* means "Cross," so this feast commemorates the discovery of the original cross by the Empress Helena (the mother of Constantine the Great). The original event took place on 19 March 326 A.D, but the feast is now celebrated on the 27th of September every year in Ethiopia.[13] It has become an international feast, because people are coming to see it from all over the world. *Meskal* also signifies the physical presence of part of the True Cross at the church of *Egziabher Ab*, the remote mountain

---

[6] When we say the law of conscious, it is believed that the one True God worship (the God of Noah) had been in existence in the early times, but it was confined to a limited number of families, that the Sun God was widely known in Axum, one of Ethiopia's earliest kingdom.

[7] Yesehaq, Abuna. *The Ethiopian Tewahedo Church: An Integrally African Church.* (New York: Vantage Press, 1989), 13.

[8] Yesehaq, Abuna. *The Ethiopian Tewahedo Church,* 13.

[9] Mekarios, Abuna. et al. *The Ethiopian Orthodox Tewahedo church Faith, Order of worship and Ecumenical Relations* (Addis Ababa:Tensae Publishing House, 1996), 130.

[10] Melaku, Lule. *The Ethiopian Orthodox Church history* (Addis Ababa 1997), 36.

[11] http://kweschn.wordpress.com/2012/09/26/meskel-festival-the-finding-of-the-true-cross/ (last accessed 28.07.2013).

[12] http://kweschn.wordpress.com/2012/09/26/meskel-festival-the-finding-of-the-true-cross/ (last accessed 28.07.2013).

[13] Melaku, Lule. *The Ethiopian Orthodox Church history* (Addis Ababa 1997), 86.

monastery of *Gishen Mariam*, located 483 km north of Addis Ababa in the *Wello* administrative zone. "In this monastery there is a massive volume of the book called the *Tefut*, written during the reign of Zara Yaqob (1434 – 1468). This text records the story of how the fragments of the cross were acquired."[14] From the legacy of Empress Helena and her son Constantine the Great, Ethiopians have learned to use the cross as a powerful weapon against evil or negative distress. The bishops and priests bless people by holding a cross in their hands, the people themselves put the cross mark on their houses, clothes and their bodies. During state visits to other countries, Ethiopian Emperors were in the habit of handing out Christian crosses to people under political oppression and racial domination. A Christian cross is perceived as a symbol of liberation. An example here would be Emperor Haile Silassie's visit to Jamaica in 1966.[15] Immediately after this visit the Emperor sent the EOTC Bishop Yesehaq with a cross on the basis of the belief that the blessing which comes from a Christian cross would lead to the liberation of the oppressed.[16] It may be in this sense that the processional cross of Emperor Adrar Seged which is found in South Africa, University of KwaZulu-Natal Pietermaritzburg main campus library contributed in some way towards black liberation in South Africa.

In the 15th century during the reign of Emperor ZeraYacob (1434 - 1468) an Ethiopian monk from the EOTC monastery in Jerusalem was delegated to participate in the international church council on the dialogue between Chalcedonian and non-Chalcedonian Churches held at Florence in Italy. This council was organised by the Roman Catholic Church and it is an indication of the continued willingness on the part of the EOTC to participate in ecumenical affairs.[17]

The EOTC's relationship with the Egyptian Coptic Church was started with the ordination of Permentius in 330 A.D. (as the first bishop of Ethiopia)[18] in order to bring the sacramental set up of the church of Christ. The relationship was continued in the 19th century when the Emperor Yohannes' requested the Egyptian church to bring four additional bishops to Ethiopia. Because of this, the work which was carried on by one bishop only expanded and the church services were increased.[19] This trend of bringing Egyptian bishops to Ethiopia continued for 1600 years until the EOTC became autocephalous (autonomy) in 1959. However, the relationship between the two churches is still in existence even now.[20]

Of great relevance was the arrival of the Nine Saints to Ethiopia in 480 A.D. from Constantinople and Syria. These saints contributed greatly to the spread of Christianity. They expanded monastic life and church schools in Ethiopia as well as outside the country.[21] The EOTC canonized them as saints and dedicated churches in their names. The coming of Gebremenfes kidus from Egypt also contributed to the strengthening of the EOTC faith, and the church canonized him as well and dedicated a monastery in his name.

We can see that Ethiopia has been an outgoing society willing to establish relationships with other countries and also open to receiving individuals from outside itself. This friendly nature of both the country as well as the Ethiopian Orthodox Church has been instrumental in advancing the course of ecumenism.

---

[14] Finding of the True cross (*Meskal*): http://www.wondersofethiopiatours.com/tour-to-finding-of-the-true-cross-meskal/ (last accessed 28.07.2013).

[15] http://anniepaul.net/2011/04/22/emperor-haile-selassies-1966-visit-to-jamaica-coral-gardens-kerala-etc/ (last accessed on 08.08.2013).

[16] http://www.youtube.com/watch?v=eI5eA67dN-o http://www.youtube.com/watch?v=GpRDtyPVgkg, http://www.youtube.com/watch?v=tnPZ1KTr1eU, http://www.youtube.com/watch?v=_ma3yBnD3P0, http://www.youtube.com/watch?v=aC0w-Jw0gouo (last accessed on 08.08.2013).

[17] Gerima, Abuna. *The Ethiopian Orthodox Tewahedo Church History from the Birth of Christ up to 2000*: Ethiopia Stretches out her hands to God, (2008), 297.

[18] Gerima, Abuna. *The Ethiopian Orthodox Tewahedo Church History*, 295.

[19] Chaillot, Christine. *The Ethiopian Orthodox Tewahedo Church tradition: a brief introduction to its life and spirituality*. Paris: Inter-Orthodox Dialogue, (2002), 38.

[20] Even though there was already a Christian presence in Ethiopia, the Apostle Mark later came to Egypt and decided to make his see there. Due to this, Ethiopia had to rely on the Egyptian Coptic church for about 1600 years in terms of the ordination of priests and bishops.

[21] Gerima, Abuna. *The Ethiopian Orthodox Tewahedo Church History*, 297.

The mutual relationship between Church and State

The EOTC has been the official religion in Ethiopia since 34 A.D. until the end of the monarchical era. Thus, the relationship between the church and state were so intertwined. The church and the state were the twin institutions which complemented each other. The abuna (bishop) was the most influential person in the Ethiopian nation. In ancient times, the abuna had even the power to crown the emperor, and he could effect excommunication in consultation with the emperor. He could influence the army and even the people to detach their allegiance from the ruler under certain circumstances.[22] At times of crisis the abuna acted as the mediator or the co- general with the emperor in the times of war. For instance, during the invasion of Ethiopia by Facist Italy, the Patriarch Basileos together with Emperor Hile Silassie went abroad to link the Ethiopian fight with the world community.[23]

Conversely, Ethiopian emperors played a significant role in the history of the church. King Lalibella for instance, like his forebears, played a prominent role in the continuation of the church by building those magnificent rock hewn churches known as the Churches of Lalibella. These churches are a big world tourist attraction that generates income for the country and the church today. They are also a magnet that pulls even Christendom into the EOTC. Therefore, it is not surprising that Nicholas, archbishop of the Greek community in Ethiopia, stated that "the state and the church are two faces of the same book. This book is Ethiopia."[24]

Even though the EOTC is no longer the official religion of Ethiopia since 1971, one can argue that the ethos and mores of the Ethiopian society have been deeply influenced by the EOTC. Further, one sees the state coming together with the church on political matters. In the hearts of most Ethiopians such a relationship of church and state is experienced even in crises. For instance, the near simultaneous deaths of Emperor Haile Silassie and the EOTC patriarch Thiophilos when the communist government came into power; the near simultaneous exile of the communist government president and the 4th patriarch of the EOTC; and the coincidental deaths of the 5th Patriarch of the EOTC and the Prime Minster of the country forced many people to interpret these as another dimension of Church - State relationship.[25]

The Participation of the Ethiopian Orthodox Tewahedo Church (EOTC) in the first millennium Ecumenical movement:

Before the advent of the WCC and AACC, the EOTC became an active participating member of the Ecumenical movement in existence during the first millennium. It was this Ecumenical stance which defined the identity of the EOTC in the history of its existence. The EOTC, by its involvement in the early Ecumenical councils, had effectively associated itself with a fellowship of Christian churches which confess the Lord Jesus Christ as God and Saviour according to the Scriptures. The following are the Ecumenical councils which the EOTC participated in. However, of the four Ecumenical councils mentioned here, the EOTC accepted only the decisions of the first three councils: Nicaea 325, Constantinople 381 and Ephesus 431, while it rejected the decision of the council of Chalcedon (451).

The Ecumenical Council of Nicaea (325 AD)

This council organized by Constantine the Great had to deal with the heretical teaching of Arius of Alexandria – that 'the Son of God is a created being, and did not co-exist with the Father.' The three hundred and eighteen

---

[22] Wondmagegnehu, Aymro. et al. *The Ethiopian Orthodox Church* (Addis Ababa: Ethiopian Orthodox Mission, 1970), 113.

[23] Wondmagegnehu, Aymro. et al. *The Ethiopian Orthodox Church,* 113.

[24] Wondmagegnehu, Aymro. et al. *The Ethiopian Orthodox Church,* 113.

[25] The EOTC Patriarch H.H. Abuna Paulos and PM Meless Zenawi have passed away in August, 2012.

bishops who attended this council condemned the teaching of Arius and his followers. The Nicene Creed was adopted by this council, and it became an important statement of the Orthodox Faith. [26]

The Ecumenical Council held in Constantinople (381 AD)

The Issue facing this council was the heresy of Macedonius who taught that 'the Holy Spirit has no form and no Divine nature.'

The one hundred and fifty church fathers who met at this council denounced this heresy and declared the Holy Spirit as the Lord and giver of life, who proceeds from the Father and this dogma of faith, was added to the Nicene Creed.[27]

The first Ecumenical Council of Ephesus (431 AD)

During this council two hundred church fathers had to deal with the heresy of Nestorious – who taught that 'Jesus had two persons and two natures, and that the Virgin Mary gave birth only to the human person of Jesus, and that therefore St. Mary should not be called the mother of God (*Theotokos*).'[28]

This council decreed Jesus Christ as one person and that the Virgin Mary should be called *Theotokos* – mother of God.[29]

The second Ecumenical Council of Ephesus (449 AD)

During the sitting of this council, the Issue at hand was the continuous teachings of Eutyches – that 'the humanity of Jesus Christ is absorbed by His Divinity.' After a denial and counter accusation the council finally upheld the decision of the first council of Ephesus (431).

The Ecumenical Council of Chalcedon (451 AD)

The teachings of Eutyches continued to disturb and to cast doubt on the declaration of Ephesus. Eutyches' teaching together with the teaching of the Roman Catholic 'Pope Leo' through his letters that 'Christ has two distinct natures in one person' provoked a schism within the then universal church. The EOTC and all those who rejected this notion of 'Christ having two distinct natures in one person' – the Coptic, the Armenian, the Syrian, the Indian and the Eritrean Orthodox churches became separated from the Byzantine and Latin body of churches.[30] The former were then called non-Chalcedonian Churches (the Oriental Orthodox churches) [31]and the later were referred to as the Chalcedonian Churches.[32]

The significance for the EOTC of participating in those early ecumenical councils helped the EOTC to be able to define its faith in a clear and unambiguous manner. Further participating in the early ecumenical councils

---

[26] Desta, Alemayehu. *Introduction to the Ethiopian Orthodox Faith* (USA: Author House 2012), 67.

[27] Ibid., 68.

[28] Ibid.

[29] Ibid.

[30] Ibid., 70.

[31] They do not accept the appellation 'Monophysite.' Ibid., 70.

[32] Wondmagegnehu, Aymro. et al. *The Ethiopian Orthodox Church,* 121. Alemayehu, 69, Following the council of Chalcedon in 451A.D which condemned the so-called Monophysites (one nature), there arose a division which caused the separation of the Copts, the Ethiopians, the Syrians and the Armenians from the Byzantine and Latin body of churches on the other. In 1054 came another Schism between the Latin Christians (Roman Catholics) and the Byzantines when the Byzantine Patriarchates in the East became known as the Eastern Orthodox Churches. This was over the issue of papal primacy over the other patriarchs and the filioque clause – a clause added to the Nicene Creed by Rome without the consent of an Ecumenical council, that 'the Holy Spirit proceeds from the Father and the Son.

also helped to prepare the EOTC for a meaningful contribution in the future of the ecumenical movement – the EOTC had then gained some experience on how things ought to be done at the ecumenical level.

The EOTC in the World Council of Churches (WCC) and in the All Africa Council of Churches (AACC)

With the advent of the WCC in 1948 in Amsterdam, the EOTC never hesitated to join the WCC as a founding member. The EOTC sought to fulfil together with the other WCC members what they believed was "their common calling to the glory of God the Father, the Son, and the Holy Spirit, one God."[33] When the AACC was formed in Nairobi in 1963, the EOTC accepted the challenge of being a founding member of the fellowship of churches within the African continent.[34]

The significance for the EOTC of joining the WCC:

- Notable successes have been achieved in the implementation of inter-church aid programmes.[35]
- From the department of the Inter-church Aid branch of the WCC in Ethiopia, the EOTC established the Development and Inter-church Aid Commission (EOTC - DICAC) in 1972, as a development wing of the church. It is the oldest organization in the country with a mission of "assisting the disadvantaged communities in Ethiopia to attain self reliance by tackling the root causes of poverty, drought, conflict, gender inequality and fighting the HIV/AIDS pandemic and by promoting sustainable development programs and community empowerment."[36]
- The EOTC's relationship with the WCC is further witnessed by the sharing of responsibilities. For instance, the late 5th Patriarch of the EOTC His Holiness Abuna Paulos, was one of the presidents of the World Council of Churches (WCC) and an Honorary President for the World Religions for peace at a global level.[37]
- The EOTC hosted the WCC meeting in Addis Ababa in 1963 E.C.[38]

The significance for the EOTC of joining the AACC facilitated:

- The provision of the common program of study and research.
- Close relations and mutual sharing of experience among the churches in Africa through visits, consultations, conferences and circulation of information.
- Assisting the churches in finding, sharing and placing personnel and utilizing other resources for the most effective way of undertaking their common tasks.
- Assisting the churches in their work of leadership training lay and clerical – personnel for the tasks of the churches today.
- Without prejudice to its own autonomy, collaboration with the WCC and appropriate agencies in such ways as may mutually be agreed.[39]

Most recently, one of the EOTC's bishops, (Archbishop Yacob), the Archbishop of All Africa Diocese, based in Johannesburg, South Africa has been nominated as a vice president of the AACC.[40] This is an attempt to have church leadership become engaged in ecumenical dialogues at different levels.

---

[33] Mekarios, Abuna. et al. *The Ethiopian Orthodox Tewahedo Church Faith, Order of worship and Ecumenical Relations.* Addis Ababa:Tensae Publishing House, (1996), 141.

[34] Ibid., 141.

[35] Ibid., 140.

[36] Act Alliance: http://www.actalliance.org/about/actmembers/ethiopian-orthodox-church-dicac (last accessed 29.07.2013).

[37] Tesfaye, Ayalkibet B, "The Ethiopian Orthodox Tewahedo Church and its traditional theological education system." In *Handbook of Theological Education in Africa*, 290.

[38] Gerima, Abuna. et al. *The Ethiopian Orthodox Tewahedo Church History*, 299-300.

[39] Mekarios, Abuna et al. The Ethiopian Orthodox Tewahedo Church, 142.

[40] Please see the letter attached on digital appendix.

Even though the EOTC is a patriarchal church, its involvement with the WCC and AACC has created an awareness of gender justice which in turn has allowed women to join in theological education as part time students.

The EOTC advanced its theological education systems besides its traditional educational system to a modern system by upgrading some of the theological clerical training centres to college level and University College level. This suggests a future possibility of allowing for a theological training of students from other church denominations within the continent and beyond.

Dialogue between Oriental and Roman Catholic Church

Despite a long standing separation between the EOTC and the Roman Catholic Church as a result inter alia of the differences in doctrinal understanding and exposition, there exist today examples of effective ecumenism between both the Roman Catholic and the Ethiopian Orthodox part of the universal church.

In Ethiopia for example, there is a joint evangelization programme conducted by a Roman Catholic Order – the Spiritan Congregation, based in Gamo Goffa and South Omo provinces together with the EOTC diocese in the area.

The Spiritan Congregation has also taken it upon itself to support the EOTC in clergy training programmes, in building new churches and renovating the old churches, and in supporting the formation of preachers for the purposes of spreading the Good News and attend to the spiritual needs of the EOTC's faithful in the remote areas of the abovementioned provinces. This kind of ecumenism is stated by St. Paul in these words "*For no one can lay any foundation other than the one that has been laid*" (1 Corinthians 3:11). The EOTC laid the foundation and the Roman Catholic through the Spiritan Congregation is providing support to that foundation.

The Roman Catholic priests (members of the Spiritan Congregation) who undertook this ecumenical venture with the EOTC diocese in the Gamo Goffa and South Omo, were inspired by the EOTC Fiath in the area coupled with their reflections based on that faith and the insights of the Vatican II council on ecumenism and the council's inclusive ecclesiology.[41]

The ecumenical dialogues between Oriental Orthodox churches including the EOTC and the Roman Catholic Church are favoured by the commonalities shared by the two churches:

> they confess the Apostolic faith as lived in the Tradition and as expressed in the Holy Scriptures, the first three Ecumenical Councils (Nicaea 325 – Constantinople 381 – Ephesus 431) and the Nicene-Constantinopolitan Creed; they believe in Jesus Christ the Incarnate Word of God, the same being true God and true man at the same time; they venerate the Holy Virgin Mary as Mother of God (*Theotokos*); they celebrate the seven sacraments (baptism, confirmation/chrismation, Eucharist, penance/reconciliation, ordination, matrimony, and anointing of the sick); they consider baptism as essential for salvation; with regard to the Eucharist, they believe that bread and wine become the true Body and Blood of Jesus Christ; they believe that the ordained ministry is transmitted through the bishops in apostolic succession; regarding the true nature of the Church, they confess together their belief in the "one, holy, catholic and apostolic Church," according to the Nicene-Constantinopolitan Creed.[42]

---

[41] Fr. Owen Lambert CSSP: http://www.cnewa.us/default.aspx?ID=793&pagetypeID=4&sitecode=US&pageno=2 (last accessed on 30.07.2013).

[42] http://www.vatican.va/roman_curia/pontifical_councils/chrstuni/anc-orient-ch- (accessed on 30.07.2013) docs/rc_pc_christuni_doc_20090129_mission-church_en.html (last accessed September 2013).

Based on the above mentioned commonalties the following are some of the dialogues between the Oriental Orthodox and the Roman Catholic Church that have taken place: [43]

- Cairo, Egypt: 27-30 January 2004
- Rome, Italy: 26-29 January 2005
- Etchmiadzin, Armenia: 27-30 January 2006
- Rome, Italy: 28 January-3 February 2007
- Maarrat Saydnaya, Syria: 27 January-2 February 2008
- Rome, Italy: 26-30 January 2009
- Antelias, Lebanon: 27-31 January 2010
- Rome, Italy: 25-28 January 2011
- Addis Ababa, Ethiopia: 17 -21 January 2012
- Rome, Italy: 23-27 January 2013

Gebremariam an EOTC writer says in his book *Merha Hiwot* that "the Orthodox church as it condemned Nestorius, it also condemns the heresy of Eutyches, and the Catholic Church as it condemns Eutyches, it also condemns the teaching of Nestorious, therefore, this is a common ground on which the original unity of Christ's church could be restored as long as both sides strive for unity out of good heart."[44] It is interesting to note that archbishop Yohannes of the Tigray diocese in Ethiopia said that the Orthodox Church and the Catholic Church are the two eyes of the world, but they are prevented by the Nose Bridge to see each other. The usage EOTC's liturgical rite by the Roman Catholic churches in Ethiopia is one of the favourable stances which can be used as driving force improving the ecumenical dialogue between the two churches.

Dialogue between Oriental and Eastern Orthodox Churches

The ecumenical relationship including the EOTC between Oriental Orthodox and Eastern Orthodox Churches has been on the level of official and unofficial dialogues. The following are some of the meetings which have taken place in this regard.[45]

1. Aarhus, Denmark: 11-15 August 1964
2. Bristol, England: 25-29 July 1967
3. Geneva, Switzerland, 16-21 August 1970
4. Addis Ababa, Ethiopia: 22-23 January 1971
5. Abba Bishoy Monastery, Egypt: 1989
6. Chambesy, Switzerland: 1990
7. Chambesy, Switzerland: 1-6 September 1993. [46]

Even though the Oriental and Eastern Orthodox churches are not yet in communion, the EOTC does have an ongoing relationship with the Eastern Orthodox Churches of Greece, Russia, Romania and with others whereby there are scholarships and other educational supports[47] that have been received by Ethiopian students from the above mentioned Eastern Orthodox churches. "In her relations with Chalcedonian Orthodox churches, the EOTC will continue to proceed from the desire to 'keep unity of the Spirit in the bond of

---

[43] Dialogue with the Oriental Orthodox Churches http://www.vatican.va/roman_curia/pontifical_councils/chrstuni/sub-index/index_ancient-oriental-ch.htm (last accessed September 2013).

[44] Gebeemariam, Asrat. *Merha Hiwot* 2nd book:(Addis Ababa, 1992), 192.

[45] Mekarios, Abuna. et al. *The Ethiopian Orthodox Tewahedo Church*, 144.

[46] Ibid., 146.

[47] Tesfaye, Ayalkibet B, "The Ethiopian Orthodox Tewahedo Church and its traditional theological education system." In *Handbook of Theological Education in Africa*, edited by Isabel Apawo Phiri and Dietrich Werner, 281-291 (Pietermaritzburg: Cluster Publications, 2013), 290.

Peace" (Eph 4: 3).[48] Generally speaking, Chalcedonian Churches (Roman Catholic and Eastern Orthodox) and non-Chalcedonian Churches (Oriental Orthodox Churches) need to engage in ecumenical dialogue in dogmatic matters. Timothy Ware, the Eastern Orthodox Church bishop stated in his book *The Orthodox Church* that "the [Chalcedonian Churches] decrees of Chalcedon from an Alexandrian point of view, and sought to explain in more constructive terms than Chalcedon (451) had used, how the two natures of Christ unite to form a single person."[49] According to him in discussions with Chalcedonian and non-Chalcedonian Orthodox Churches, it is more a question of semantic or the misunderstanding of words, but basically, they hold the same believe. Therefore, dialogue is of the greatest importance in order to understand each other's expression of the truth.[50]

Dialogue between the EOTC and other Oriental Orthodox Sister Churches

The EOTC has a close relationship with other Oriental Orthodox sister churches who explain how in the Incarnation of Jesus Christ the two natures of Godhead and Manhood are perfectly united and how Christ is thus one Person and one Nature from the two Natures.[51] These churces accept the three ecumenical councils of Nicaea 325, Constantinople 381 and Ephesus 431.[52]

The Oriental Orthodox churches met in Addis Ababa, Ethiopia in 1965, after a long time since the council of Ephesus 431. The meeting was organized by Emperor Haile Selassie and His Holiness Abuna Basil the patriarch of the EOTC. They discussed the following issues:[53]

- Secular civilization and the church
- Cooperation on providing theological education
- Fulfillment of the apostolic duty jointly
- Relationship with other Christian churches
- Establishment of an umbrella institution for permanent relationship with other churches
- Global peace and justice

They agreed on continually maintaining the dialogue with regard to the issues listed above. They vowed to remain together for all future endeavours by keeping the unity they have had since the ecumenical meetings of Nicaea 325, Constantinople 381 and Ephesus 431. They wished to fulfil the will of God - intended to accomplish through His Son Jesus Christ. Lastly, they declared Emperor Haile Silassie "the defender of faith."[54] Hence EOTC also brings scholars from other Oriental Orthodox sister Churches to lecture in the EOTC Seminaries. All these points indicate that there is indeed an accommodative ecumenical spirit within the EOTC -"the practice of churches and other Christian groups in which they seek and work for the unity that binds them together as Christians."[55]

[48] Wondmagegnehu, Aymro. et al. *The Ethiopian Orthodox Church*, 120.

[49] Ware, Timothy. *The Orthodox Church*. (London: Penguin Books, 1964), 37.

[50] Mekarios, Abuna. et al. *The Ethiopian Orthodox Tewahedo church Faith, Order of worship and Ecumenical Relations*, 144. In the meetings of the Oriental and Chalcedonian Orthodox Churches, the mystery of Incarnation of Christ became the common ground for both parties as it is based on the Christological teachings of the Oriental Orthodox Churches where it is postulated that the union of the two natures in Christ is without confusion, without change, without division and without separation. So it was equally accepted by the Chalcedonian side, because there they have realised that there is no doctrinal difference. Instead, their differences are in analytical interpretation.

[51] Wondmagegnehu, Aymro. et al. *The Ethiopian Orthodox Church*, 95.

[52] These churches are the Ethiopian, the Coptic, the Syrian, the Indian (Malankara), the Armenian and the Eritrean Orthodox Churches. The Eritrean Orthodox church become autocephalous after the independence of the country from Ethiopia in 1993.

[53] Wondmagegnehu, Aymro. et al. *The Ethiopian Orthodox Church*, 119.

[54] Wondmagegnehu, Aymro. et al. *The Ethiopian Orthodox Church*, 119.

[55] Karkkainen.V.M (eds). *Global Dictionary of Theology: A Resource for worldwide church.* (Intervarsity Christian Fellowship, 2008), 263.

Ecumenical dialogue is imperative because the division of the church is a stumbling block to Christ's World Mission – which is Unity and Peace. Thus, it is expressed "that they may all be one" (John 17:21). The scholars also agree with this idea of oneness when they argue for the unity of the church of Christ in this way "the whole Christian world is fully aware of the fact that there had been universal church until Chalcedon (451) and believes that it is still invisibly one since Christ is one and the church is one."[56] All this gives us a sense of the importance of ecumenism and ecumenical dialogue for the Christendom world.

Opportunities and Threats for Ecumenism in Ethiopia

The following are some of the pointers necessary to be considered by all those concerned with the future of ecumenism in Ethiopian.

1. Opportunities:

There are a number of internal and external factors or elements which could be seen as opportunities for promoting ecumenism among all Churches in Ethiopia. The following are the internal and external factors with huge potential for ecumenism.

1.1. One of the most notable elements that would indicate a very positive future for Ecumenism in the Christian Churches in Ethiopian is an *increasingly growing openness among the youth or the new generation towards the other*. In other words, young and educated believers from both Ethiopian Orthodox and Roman Catholic, as well as the Protestant churches are willing to accept each other as friends and brothers. This may enable them to discuss openly and positively common issues and to engage in dialogue on those matters they disagree on. In this, a civilized and rational way of discussion may be established by recognizing the existence and legitimacy of the other. In fact this should be nurtured by the more informed elites of both groups to maximize positive results.

1.2. The other point closely related to the first one is *an increasing awareness of the core values of the denomination they belong to or strong self-awareness*. This means, when one has a firm stand on their own viewpoint, there would be more openness to present oneself to the others without any threat of losing one's identity. In other words, as there is a growing tendency of self-awareness, which would enable them to defend themselves firmly, they would be willing to come together for a bigger and better engagement with others for greater results. As threats become minimized, cooperation and fellowship on the same ground would give more chance for mutual cooperation.

1.3. From on educational point of view, all Christian denominations have been *increasingly promoting and developing new higher theological education*. Such theological institutions are coming together to discuss some academic and theological matters which concern all parties. These preliminary relationships and fellowships would potentially grow to the much more firmly established ecumenical institutional networks in a manner that would in turn promote and facilitate ecumenism in an adequate and equal level.

1.4. A change in religio-political landscape in recent decades in Ethiopia has created a new opportunity to focus on mutual benefit rather than promoting animosity. For instance, the *aggressive attack of fundamentalist Islamic movements* a couple of years ago in the southwestern part of the country against all Christian churches that indiscrimately resulted in a number of casualties from both Orthodox and Protestants and turned a number of churches into ashes, brought churches together for a common cause. After such incidents, there has been a growing tendency of brotherhood and fellowship among all groups of Christians in the country.

1.5. In addition to the religious factor, there are so many other social, political, and cultural issues which all churches in Ethiopia would want to address and work together since they have been engaged in them independently up to this moment. *Poverty, justice, reconciliation, harmful cultural practices, HIV/AIDS, etc,*

---

[56] Mekarios, Abuna. et al. *The Ethiopian Orthodox Tewahedo church Faith, Order of worship and Ecumenical Relations*,143.

are areas where ecumenical unity is necessary among Christian Churches in Ethiopia. As they all would be working for the betterment of both the social and the spiritual well-being of the whole of society, cooperation would be indispensable.

1.6. Besides problems and openness within the country, there has been a growing tendency of ecumenism around the world, to come together and work for the same Goal and Mission. As part and parcel of the global Christendom, the Christian churches in Ethiopia are also becoming more and more influenced by such global movements. The EOTC and some of the Protestant Churches in Ethiopia are already (founding) members of some of the regional, continental and global Ecumenical Councils. So, such ecumenical *movements at global and regional levels would contribute to doing the same among themselves within the country.*

2. Threats:

There are as many threats as there are opportunities which would have the potential to distract or slow down any kind of meaningful ecumenism in the country. Bellow I mention only a few:

2.1. *Traditional animosity which has been developed throughout the last few centuries still has the potential* to keep the churches apart from each other. There are still "ministers/leaders/clergy/teachers" on all sides who are actively promoting such historical problems in an exaggerated manner. So, one cannot overemphasize the potential of the destructive elements in such a movement.

2.2. Similar to this threat would be *the wrong image about oneself and the other.* This is to say, on the one hand, the EOTC denies the legitimacy of the Protestant churches, and on the other hand, many Protestants deny that EOTC members are Christians as they target the EOTC members for conversion to Protestantism and they ignore the historical role that the EOTC has played in defending Christianity and its heritage in Ethiopia for three millennia and the apostolic originality of the EOTC. In other words, both groups give a wrong image of each other and this tendency still exists within some corners of each party. This would have a very strong power to destroy any kind of ecumenical unity.

2.3. *The fragmentation of the Protestant Churches* would have a huge drawback for any possible engagements of ecumenism as each Protestant denomination has their own independent stance, which may not be understood by EOTC. In other words, the EOTC generally considers all Protestants as one group, which in reality is not true. So, such fragmentation would make it difficult for any attempt at brining one voice from the Protestant side.

Bibliography

Chaillot, Christine. *The Ethiopian Orthodox Tewahedo Church tradition: a brief introduction to its life and spirituality. (Paris: Inter-Orthodox Dialogue, 2002).*

Desta, Alemayehu. 2012. *Introduction to the Ethiopian Orthodox Faith.* (USA: Author House, 2012).

Gebeemariam, Asrat. *Merha Hiwot,* 2nd book, (Addis Ababa 1992).

Gerima, Abuna. *The Ethiopian Orthodox Tewahedo Church History from the Birth of Christ up to 2000*: Ethiopia Stretches out her hands to God (2008).

Hancock, G. *The sign and the seal: the explosively controversial international best seller: a quest for the lost Ark of the Covenant.* (London: Arrow Books, 1992).

Karkkainen.V.M (eds). *Global Dictionary of Theology: A Resource for worldwide church.* (USA: Intervarsity Christian fellowship, 2008).

Mekarios, Abuna. et al. *The Ethiopian Orthodox Tewahedo church Faith, Order f worship and Ecumenical Relations.* (Addis Ababa: Tensae Publishing House, 1996).

Melaku, L. *The Ethiopian Orthodox church history.* (Addis Ababa 1997).

-. *History of the Ethiopian Orthodox Tewahedo Church. Part I.* (Addis Ababa 2008).

-. *The Ethiopian Orthodox Tewahedo Church History*. (Addis Ababa 1997)

The EOTC. *The Church of Ethiopia: A Panorama of History and Spiritual life*. (Addis Ababa: Ethiopian Orthodox Church, 1997).

Tesfaye, Ayalkibet B., "The Ethiopian Orthodox Tewahedo Church and its traditional theological education system." In *Handbook of Theological Education in Africa*, edited by Isabel Apawo Phiri and Dietrich Werner, (Pietermaritzburg: Cluster Publications, 2013), 281-291.

Wondmagegnehu, Aymro. et al. The Ethiopian Orthodox Church. (Addis Ababa: Ethiopian Orthodox Mission, 1970).

Ware, Timothy. *The Orthodox Church*. (London: Penguin Books, 1964).

Yesehaq, Abuna. *The Ethiopian Tewahedo Church: An Integrally African Church*. (New York: Vantage Press, 1989).

Act Alliance: http://www.actalliance.org/about/actmembers/ethiopian-orthodox-church-dicac (last accessed 29.07.2013).

Dialogue with the Oriental Orthodox Churches: http://www.vatican.va/roman_curia/pontifical_councils/chrstuni/sub-index/index_ancient-oriental-ch.htm (last accessed on 30.07.2013).

http://kweschn.wordpress.com/2012/09/26/meskel-festival-the-finding-of-the-true-cross/ (last accessed on 20.07.2013).

Fr. Owen Lambert CSSP: http://www.cnewa.us/default.aspx?ID=793&pagetypeID=4&sitecode=US&pageno=2

http://www.vatican.va/roman_curia/pontifical_councils/chrstuni/anc-orient-ch-docs/rc_pc_christuni_doc_20090129_mission-church_en.html (last accessed on 30.07.2013).

http://kweschn.wordpress.com/2012/09/26/meskel-festival-the-finding-of-the-true-cross/ (last accessed on 20.07.2013).

http://anniepaul.net/2011/04/22/emperor-haile-selassies-1966-visit-to-jamaica-coral-gardens-kerala-etc/ (last accessed on 08.08.2013).

http://www.youtube.com/watch?v=tX2KbeD2_PE

http://www.youtube.com/watch?v=O97yb-UzXPs (last accessed on 08.08.2013)

http://www.youtube.com/watch?v=eI5eA67dN-o

http://www.youtube.com/watch?v=GpRDtyPVgkg http://www.youtube.com/watch?v=tnPZ1KTr1eU

http://www.youtube.com/watch?v=_ma3yBnD3P0

http://www.youtube.com/watch?v=aC0wJw0gouo (last accessed on 08.08.2013).

Archbishop Philoxenos Mattias Nayis

"The split of the Christian church is a big mistake, a blasphemy of the Holy Spirit and an ignoring of the existence of Christ who promised: '... the gates of hell will not prevail against it.' (Mt 16:18). I invite you to stand before history for a moment to see the reason for our divisions. You will see that thousands of innocents have shed blood, righteous men have suffered and been expelled from their countries. We thank God that Christian churches in this generation have begun to feel the necessity of continuing the Christian dialogue and as a result they have drawn closer to each other and planned for continuous meetings at various levels to study different subjects. The unity of Christianity can only happen in and around Christ, who is the head of the Church and we with all our doctrines are only parts of the holy body of Christ.

Satan is still at work. He brings about disturbances, constantly encourages new splits and wants from that the division of the body of Christ which is the Church. We have to be careful. Politics usually uses religion to reach its worldly goals. We should limit our talks to spiritual themes because the kingdom of Christ is not of this world. We do not want the unity of Christianity to fight against other religions. Instead we want unity to reach our goal more quickly; that is the constructive dialogue with others who believe in God and here especially with the Muslims with whom we share one homeland. Let us learn from history. Let us avoid what splits us. Let us walk the way that leads to a better understanding, to a life in which love and peace rule."[1]

The quotation above from His Holiness Patriarch Ignatius Zakka I Iwas is a short summary of the vision and prophetic calling of His Holiness towards us all regarding our work for Christian unity.

The Syrian Orthodox Church, belonging to the Oriental Orthodox family, and the Byzantine and Roman Churches were separated from each other during the split at the fourth ecumenical council of Chalcedon 451.

This short article will deal with 3 major themes: (1) the current state of the Ecumenical movement in the Syrian Orthodox Church (SOC) with a short historical background; (2) major challenges and/or possibilities for the SOC in the Ecumenical movement together with (3) some reflections and thoughts from my humble-self, regarding the SOC and the Ecumenical movement.

The current state of the Ecumenical movement in the SOC
with a short historical background

After the synod of Chalcedon 451, the first great split occurred in the Church over the terminology of the Incarnation of Our Lord Jesus Christ. This split remains one of the greatest tragedies in the history of the Church. From a Syrian Orthodox perspective talk about two natures (*physis* in Greek and *kyono* in Syriac) in one hypostasis was ambiguous and our Church fathers rejected it. Since the Syriac word of *kyono*, that was translated from physis, has a greater meaning than its Greek equivalent the talks about two natures after the incarnation was rejected.[2]

For that reason the Syrian Orthodox Church was wrongly accused of the heresy of Monophysitism that originated from Eutyches. But the fact is that our Church has always rejected Eutyches and Monophysitism as well as Nestorius and Nestorianism. We believe that Jesus Christ is true God and true man without mixture or co-mingle.

In the years after Chalcedon no real talks ever took place between the Oriental Orthodox theologians with their Byzantine or Roman counterparts and the different sides held onto misconceptions, backbiting and even

---

[1] His Holiness Patriarch Ignatius Zakka I Iwas, Lecture at the University of Humboldt, Berlin on 16 May 1995
[2] On the Syriac meaning of *kyono* see Sebastian Brock and David Taylor, *The Hidden Pearl* - Volume III, 27

persecution of the other side. Some attempts to heal the division were made by emperors Justinian (532) and Heraclius (630) but they were unsuccessful.

Not until the publication of the Book of the Dove by saint Gregorius Yuhannon Bar 'Ebroyo († 1286), which he wrote during his last years and after writing numerous treaties and books on theology and spiritual life, did it become clear that perhaps the split at Chalcedon was not a theological split but a terminological split:

> "When I had given much thought and pondered on the matter, I became convinced that these quarrels among the different Christian Churches are not a matter of factual substance, but of words and terminology; for they all confess Christ our Lord to be perfect God and perfect human, without any commingling, mixing, or confusion of the natures... Thus I saw all the Christian communities, with their different Christological positions, as possessing a single common ground that is without any difference between them and I uprooted from my own heart the seed of hatred (Book of the Dove, Chapter IV).

With the insight of this saintly Church father a new phase was entered by the SOC. Unfortunately during many of the years after Bar 'Ebroyo the SOC endured many persecutions and hardships which in its turn also affected the Churches theological and ecumenical undertakings.

During the spring of the Ecumenical movement the Syrian Orthodox Church became a member of the WCC 1960 under the leadership of the thrice blessed Patriarch Ignatius Jakob III.

The SOC and the Eastern (Byzantine) Orthodox Churches

The SOC participated in the unofficial and official dialogues with the Eastern (Byzantine) Orthodox Churches from 1964 and onwards with the publication of different documents clarifying that *on the essence of the Christological dogma we found ourselves in full agreement. Through the different terminologies used by each side, we saw the same truth expressed"* (Communiqué of Aarhus 1964).

During the official meetings of 1985, 1989, 1990 and 1993 the former stumbling block of the Christological dogma was overcome, by acknowledging that the understanding of the incarnation was the same, although different formulas were used by the different Church traditions to speak about one or two natures.

The official meeting of 1993 that proposed a mutual lifting of the anathemas suggested a practical way to do this has not yet been formally accepted by all the Oriental and Eastern Churches involved.

On 22 July 1991, the Syrian Orthodox Patriarch Ignatius Zakka I was, together with the thrice blessed Patriarch Ignatius IV Hazim, of the Greek Orthodox patriarchate of Antioch, wrote a common declaration with 14 important issues.[3] Amongst them:

- We affirm the total and mutual respect of the spirituality, heritage and Holy Fathers of both Churches. The integrity of both the Byzantine and Syriac liturgies is to be preserved.
- In localities where there is only one priest, from either Church, he will celebrate services for the faithful of both Churches, including the Divine Liturgy, pastoral duties, and holy matrimony. He will keep an independent record for each Church and transmit that of the sister Church to its authorities.

Regarding the ecumenical relationship with the Eastern (Byzantine) Orthodox we are in need of a new emphasis or input in order to restore the full ecclesiastical unity between our sister Churches – a point I will discuss shortly further down.

The SOC and the Roman Catholic Church

The dialogue with the Roman Catholic Church started off on a non-official level. The initiative was taken by the Pro Oriente Foundation in Vienna, which had been founded by Cardinal König in 1964, during the Second Vatican Council. A series of meetings between SOC (and other Oriental Orthodox theologians) and Catholic

---

[3] Statement of the Orthodox Church of Antioch on the Relations between the Eastern and Syrian Orthodox Churches - 12 November 1991

Part VI: Ecumenical Perspectives of Oriental Orthodox Churches

theologians took place first 1971 and has been on-going since then. The biggest achievement with the Roman Catholic Church was the "Common declaration of Faith" that was signed by Patriarch Ignatius Zakka I Iwas and Pope John Paul II and included 10 different articles.[4] Among them:

- First of all, Their Holinesses confess the faith of their two Churches, formulated by Nicene Council of 325 A.D. and generally known as "the Nicene Creeds". The confusions and schisms that occurred between their Churches in the later centuries, they realize today, in no way affect or touch the substance of their faith, since these arose only because of differences in terminology and culture and in the various formulae adopted by different theological schools to express the same matter. Accordingly, we find today no real basis for the sad divisions and schisms that subsequently arose between us concerning the doctrine of Incarnation. In words and life we confess the true doctrine concerning Christ our Lord, notwithstanding the differences in interpretation of such a doctrine which arose at the time of the Council of Chalcedon.
- "Since it is the chief expression of Christian unity between the faithful and between Bishops and priests, the Holy Eucharist cannot yet be concelebrated by us. Such celebration supposes a complete identity of faith such as does not yet exist between us. Certain questions, in fact, still need to be resolved touching the Lord's will for His Church, as also the doctrinal implications and canonical details of the traditions proper to our communities which have been too long separated."

The declaration also concluded with a solemn obligation to work for full unity between the Syrian Orthodox Church and the Roman Catholic Church. It should also be mentioned here that fruitful talks and dialogue have been taking place between the Syrian Catholic Church and the SOC.

The SOC and Protestant Churches[5]

Amongst the different dialogues that have taken place between the SOC and different Protestant Churches, the dialogue with the Anglican Communion stands out. In 2002 a consensus was reached between the Oriental Orthodox Churches and the Anglican Communion regarding Christology and the report[6] stated:

> "In recent decades ecumenical conversations have gone a long way to resolving this ancient difference of understanding, and we rejoiced that in our own meeting Anglicans and Oriental Orthodox were able to agree a common statement on our understanding of Christ, and reach out to heal what is one of the most ancient Christian divisions."

However, in the aftermath of the consecration of a homosexual bishop for the Anglican Church in the US, the Oriental Orthodox Churches delayed the forthcoming meeting between the two Church families and until this day the dialogue has not been undertaken on a theological level but close friendly ties remain between many theologians of both Church families and representatives have met on different occasions and on different levels.

Major challenges and/or possibilities for the SOC in the Ecumenical movement together with some reflections and thoughts

After a short resume of the Ecumenical movement within the SOC, I will now try to list some challenges and/or possibilities for the SOC in the Ecumenical movement together with some of my reflections and thoughts on the matter. I will do this first with each Church-family separately and then say something about the WCC.

---

[4] The Common declaration of faith by Pope John Paul 2 and His Holiness Patriarch Ignatius Zakka I Iwas, 23 June 1984.
[5] Although the term "Churches" regarding the Protestant denominations is a source of discussion between the Orthodox theologians, I use the term "Churches" without taking any stance regarding the legitimacy or not in this paper.
[6] Report of The Right Rev Geoffrey Rowell Bishop of Gibraltar in Europe.

The Eastern (Byzantine) Orthodox

The close spiritual relationship with the Eastern (Byzantine) Orthodox Churches is the closest that SOC and the Oriental Orthodox family has to any other Churches. That is so because we all belong to the one and same Orthodox Tradition. Despite our cultural and linguistical differences, we believe that our Churches have minor issues to solve before a full communion can be restored between us.

The biggest issue is of course the split that occurred at the Council of Chalcedon 451, but as we have seen in the theological dialogues that have taken place, the split is not a theological split, but terminological. It seems as though we have the theoretical foundation for unity, but have not yet found its practical form.

The relationship between the SOC and the Greek Orthodox Church of Antioch is excellent and could work as a role model for unity between the Oriental and Byzantine Orthodox Churches.

A continued dialogue and close friendship in order to break the barriers that still divide us is necessary and also a willingness to read about the other Church family in a spirit of humility and love. A good step in this direction has taken place in Södertälje, Sweden, with the foundation of the Saint Ignatius Orthodox Theological Academy under the leadership of the Oriental Orthodox and Byzantine Orthodox bishops in Sweden. At Saint Ignatius they are working to provide an environment of brotherly understanding and love, and at the same time value and taking care of each specific Orthodox tradition (the Syriac, the Coptic, the Byzantine etc.). By providing for a natural environment where Oriental and Byzantine Orthodox faithful can meet each-other and pray and study together, the practical foundation for the healing of the split between the Churches is provided.

The Roman Catholic Church

A very close bond between the SOC and the Roman Catholic Church was made by their Holinesses, our present SOC Patriarch Ignatius Zakka I Iwas and the late Pope John Paul II. In a spirit of friendship and mutual respect their Holinesses wrote the Common Declaration of Faith 1984. The Common Declaration of Faith declared that in necessary cases the sacraments of the Holy Eucharist, Confession and Anointing of the Sick can be administered by a lawful priest of the other Church in the case when a priest of the faithful's own Church is not material or morally possible (9). It was also agreed upon that *"It would be a logical corollary of collaboration in pastoral care to cooperate in priestly formation and theological education. Bishops are encouraged to promote sharing of facilities for theological education where they judge it to be advisable"* (9).

The vision of the supremacy of the Roman Bishop is a subject of theological discussion and in order to find a solution I think that we need to go back to the first 400-years of Christianity and see the roles of the different Patriarchal Sees and the role of the bishop of Rome.

I think that before we can go into a deep theological discussion with the Roman Catholic Church and try to look for ways to restore full communion, the Oriental and Byzantine Orthodox Churches must themselves unite first, since today we do not have a common Orthodox voice as would be the case with a united Oriental and Byzantine Orthodox Church.

I believe that in a spirit of humbleness and love, with faithfulness to the Fathers of the Church, we can find practical ways towards a full communion.

The Protestant Churches

Many of the Protestant Churches have been of a great help to the SOC until this day, especially in Sweden and Germany. In these countries our faithful have received help in days of hardship and many of our parishes have lent a local Protestant Church for the liturgy before they could build their own Church. And for this we extend our whole heartedly thankfulness.

To make things a bit more complicated the Protestant Churches are between themselves divided into many different fractions with different viewpoints and teachings on theology.

Part VI: Ecumenical Perspectives of Oriental Orthodox Churches

Despite the close friendship with the Protestant Churches, the SOC sees major theological difficulties. To mention a few of them[7]: there is a difference in ethics and Christian values such as family and marriage; there is a liberalistic spirit that hovers over many of the Protestant Churches that has changed these Churches during the past 30 years in a way that we thought was unthinkable when our members first came to the western world; there is also a difference regarding the conception of the Divine Revelation and the Apostolic Tradition which in turn results in major theological differences.

Perhaps we have to realize that in some regards and with some Protestant Churches, we can be friends but not have a theological dialogue in the same sense that we have with the Eastern (Byzantine) Orthodox Churches and the Roman Catholic Church. I do think that Orthodox theologians have tried to express their views to the WCC on this matter and perhaps we Orthodox need to discuss and suggest practical ways forward in the Ecumenical movement with the Protestant Churches.

With all this said I cannot forget the many faithful Protestant Christians that have lived out the Gospel in many ways and shown a great love towards God and humanity, and of course the many martyrs of the Christian faith that deserves our deepest respect.

The WCC

The World Council of Churches (WCC) has served as a tool for uniting Christian leaders and faithful for over 60 years, and for this we must thank God. The SOC has found many friends within the WCC and we are very grateful for what we have been able to see, do and learn during our membership within the WCC.

Despite this, I believe that the WCC has major challenges that need to be tackled. Since many documents have been written and many statements have been made, I will not try to make a summary of them all here – but I would like to point to them and to refer to them for further reading. During the Inter-Orthodox pre-assembly consultation on the island of Kos, Greece 11-17 October 2012[8] many important points where made and I would like to quote here numbers 22 and 23.

22. Orthodox churches – both Eastern and Oriental – call for a stronger focus in the WCC on the search for Christian Unity. We often hear comments about the crisis in the ecumenical movement and about the lack of interest in unity or the lack of a clear vision about the nature of this unity. To a great extent, this is a consequence of the fact that the idea of visible unity is seen as unrealistic by many ecumenical partners, the Orthodox among them. We see this as a consequence of the developments taking place in some member churches over the last forty years (e.g., the ordination of women, different approaches to moral and ethical issues, etc.). The gap between member churches is thus growing wider. On the other hand, the growing participation in the ecumenical movement of churches which are not members of the WCC and which bring to the dialogue new ecclesiological considerations and new understandings of unity as mission, adds new challenges to the search for unity, particularly when such churches apply for WCC membership.

23. The most appropriate way to resolve this situation would be to go back to the theological and moral teachings and practices of the early Church, moving to a patristic understanding of the Holy Scriptures and ethical values. A re-reading together of the patristic heritage would enable us all to find common ground, and this will give the churches in the WCC the ability to move forward and to revitalize the whole ecumenical movement. It is our hope that the Faith and Order Commission will continue with such an approach.

Conclusion

As a conclusion to this short summery of a Syrian Orthodox perspective on Ecumenism, I would like to focus on the quotation from His Holiness Ignatius Zakka I Iwas in the opening lines: *"The unity of Christianity can only happen in and around Christ, who is the head of the Church."* In order to achieve the goal of a united

---

[7] The different points mentioned here is not applicable on all Protestant Churches, since there are Protestant Churches that have a strong belief in the traditional Christian ethics and family teaching.

[8] http://www.oikoumene.org/en/resources/documents/executive-committee/2013-03/orthodox-pre-assembly-report

Christianity we must focus on Our Lord and Saviour Jesus Christ and ask Him to lead us and help us. We must be humble and full of love, just like Our Lord, and at the same time remain faithful to the doctrines and life of the holy Orthodox Church, since there is no separation between Christ and the Church.

As a Syrian Orthodox metropolitan, I believe that the example of Bar 'Ebroyo is a very good one. After all his theological studies and treaties, he found that the Christological split between the Oriental and Byzantine Orthodox was a split of terminologies and not theology. And he saw that he had to start with the root of division that grew in his heart. When we have rooted out the root of hatred and division in our own hearts, we can meet each-other in the freedom of Christ and by the help and grace of the Holy Spirit find new ways of communication and a return to the undivided Church of the first 400-years.

Bibliography

Brock, Sebastian/Taylor, David G.K. (ed.s), *The Hidden Pearl: The Syrian Orthodox Church and Its Aramaic Heritage.* (Rome: Trans World Film Italia, 2001).

Chaillot, Christine/ Belopopsky, Alexander (eds.), *Toward Unity, The Theological Dialogue between the Orthodox Church and the Oriental Orthodox Churches,* (Geneva: Inter-Orthodox Dialogue, 1998).

Chediath, Geevarghese, *Syriac Churches in Dialogue, The Harp,* vol. XI-XII, (Kottayam 1998-99).

Fitzgerald, Thomas/ Bouteneff, Peter (ed.s), *Turn to God, Rejoice in hope – Orthodox reflections on the way to Harare,* (Geneva: Orthodox Task Force WCC, 1998).

Madey, John, *The Ecclesiological and Canonical Background of the So-Called Kerala Agreement, The Harp,* vol. XI-XII, (Kottayam 1998-99).

Paul, Daniel Babu, *The Quest for Unity.* (Damascus: Syrian Orthodox Patriarchate, 1985).

Samuel, V.C., *The Council of Chalcedon Re-examined.* (British Orthodox Press, 2001)

Ware, Timothy (Bishop Kallistos of Diokleia), *The Orthodox Church.* (London: Penguin Books, 1993).

Wensinck, A.J. *Bar Hebraeus's Book of the Dove.* (Leyden: Brill, 1919).

Part VI: Ecumenical Perspectives of Oriental Orthodox Churches

(89) Ecumenical Dialogue in the Malankara Orthodox Syrian Church[1]

Fr. Kondothra M. George

Any historical reflection on the Orthodox participation in the Ecumenical Movement in Asia will have to critically deal with various elements including the following:
- Asia and Christianity
- Emergence of the Asian Ecumenical Movement
- Orthodox presence in Asia and its ecumenical significance

1. Asia and Christianity

The very word Asia originated in the Graeco-Roman imperial geography which spoke of *Asia Minor* and *Asia Major*. However, many regions of present day Asia were simply *terra incognita* for the Romans. It was given a concrete geo-political form during the Western colonial movement beginning with the arrival of the Portuguese navigator Vasco da Gama who landed in an ancient port near Calicut on the Malabar cost in present-day Kerala, southwestern state of India. The Portuguese colonial invasion of Asia was followed up by other Western powers.

The idea of *Asia* as one entity was created by the European mind during this colonial period. The Western explorers and colonial authorities recognized the immense cultural, ethnic and linguistic diversity existing among the countries in Asia. However the people of Pakistan and India and those of China and Japan were all 'Asian' with a broad spectrum of other nations and cultures in between. There is a certain common ground of Asian-ness linking all these diverse cultures and nations. The overall approach to Reality in Asia, despite rich internal diversity and sometimes substantial divergence, is very different from the general western approach developed especially during the second millennium of the Christian era. One may be puzzled by the apparently very different world views represented, for example, between the philosophy of Advaita Vedanta in India and the Confucian ethics in China. Yet one may discern a certain common Asian ethos running through all ancient Asian systems of philosophy, spirituality and ethics. Religious roots and routes like that of Buddhism, for instance, are a connecting link that forged a certain cultural commonality in many of the Asian countries.

2. Eastern Christianity and Asia

In the first millennium of the Common Era there were two streams of the tradition of Christianity in Asia, one followed by the other chronologically, and the two merging subsequently until about the 16th century, that is, the time of the arrival of the Portuguese Roman Catholic and colonial power in Asia. The important point here is that both these streams were "oriental" in origin and character and reached Asia long before that continent came into contact with European Christianity. They are the following:

(i) The St Thomas Tradition

Thomas, one of the 12 Apostles of Jesus Christ, is traditionally believed to have arrived in India, precisely at the ancient port of Kodungalloor in present-day Kerala on the south west cost of India in AD 52. (Recent ex-

[1] Reprinted with kind permission from: K.M. George, "Orthodox Presence in the Asian Ecumenical Movement", in: Hope Antone, Wati Longchar, Hyunju Bae, Huang Po Ho, Dietrich Werner (eds), *Asian Handbook for Theological Education and Ecumenism*, (Oxford: Regnum Publishers, 2013), 60-65.

cavations have unearthed an ancient town called *Pattanam* not very far from Kodungalloor. It shows evidence of ancient trade and commerce between the Kerala cost *and* Romans, Greeks, Arabs and Jews before Christ, and in the early Christian period). The strong and living tradition of Indian Christians living in Kerala and in Diaspora has always been faithfully attested to the arrival of Thomas as the foundational event of Christianity in Asia. Circumstantial evidences for this event are prolific. The Christian tradition that survived in India from then on had a distinctly Eastern flavor.

In the 4th century there were several waves of immigration of Christians from the Persian empire due to persecution and trade to the Malabar cost (Kerala) where there were already Christians. These immigrants of old still retain to some extent their ethnic identity and generally practice endogamy though they live together with the other Kerala Christians in the same faith and practices.

Now divided between Oriental Orthodox, East Syrian, Roman Catholic and Protestant streams the St. Thomas Christians are a flourishing and influential community in Kerala. The efforts to overcome their division that occurred since the 16th century due to the aggressive missionary practices of the Portuguese Roman Catholic missionaries and then the rather soft mission of the British missionaries are as old as the division. Although the attribute 'ecumenical' for Church union efforts is of 20th century origin, some of the discerning and wise persons in the divided Indian Christian community always longed and worked for unity.

(ii) East Syrian Spiritual Connections

The other stream consisted in the arrival of East Syrian Christian traders and missionaries from the Mesopotamian region to India, China and greater Asia. China still retains the 7th century stele and the inscription commemorating the arrival of East Syrian "Alopen" and the "Nestorian" missionaries. In several countries in Asia from India to China, we have ancient stone crosses associated with East Syrian missionaries and traders. In India it is generally called "Persian Cross" or more recently as "St. Thomas Cross". However, while Indian Christian community in Kerala retained the continuity and live memory of this heritage, there was no trace of any living Christian community in China claiming this heritage when the western colonial and missionary bodies arrived there.

3. Asian Ecumenical Movement and Orthodox Presence.

The modern Ecumenical Movement has its origin in the early 20th century arising mainly from the missionary interests of Western Protestant Churches. In Asia, this was reflected naturally in the then young Churches founded by western missionary efforts. So it was, of course, confined to churches of the Reformation tradition.

The Orthodox presence in Asia, or rather Eastern Christianity, was mainly confined to the historic Malankara Orthodox Syrian Church (sometime wrongly called Jacobite) which traces its origin to the preaching of the Gospel of Christ by Thomas the Apostle. In fact, there is a group of churches based in Kerala, India, belonging to Roman Catholic, Orthodox and Protestant traditions, but jointly affirming the *St Thomas Tradition*. These Christians in general are locally called *Nazranis* (probably meaning 'the followers of the Nazarene'). Since the Portuguese colonial times a section of the Thomas Christians has been affiliated to the western tradition of the Roman Catholic Church. Heavily Latinized by the work of the Jesuit and Carmelite missionaries under Roman juridical and canonical authority and almost losing the eastern ecclesiological heritage, this section of the *Nazranis*, generally called Syro-Malabar Catholics, are now making serious efforts to regain their lost Eastern heritage. In the 16th century the Indian church of St Thomas, bitterly persecuted by the Portuguese authorities, sought help from Oriental patriarchates including the Syrian and Coptic Churches, in order to counter the efforts of proselytisation and inquisitorial oppression from the Western Roman Catholic authorities in the 16th and 17th centuries. In 1665, the arrival of a bishop called Mor Gregorios Abdul Jalil from Jerusalem in response to the request from India started a new chapter in the history of the St Thomas Christians. Instead of the gradually introduced East Syriac liturgy prevalent in the Indian church until then, the west Syrian or Antiochian liturgical tradition and practices were introduced. The present Orthodox Church in India now follows this liturgical heritage. It was welcomed by the people because it did not violate their original Eastern sense of the St Thomas Tradition nor did it challenge the sense of autonomy of the Indian Church. The ascetical spirituality of the Oriental Christian monks and bishops who occasionally visited India went very well with the Indian Hindu ethos of asceticism. However, towards the end of the 19th century, Syrian patriarchal authority making jurisdictional claims over the Indian Church began to be imposed on the church in the spirit and style of the then prevailing colonial regimes. This provoked the Indian Orthodox Church, and led to a series of legal wrangling and conflicts that still haunt the Church. Since all this is not about any doctrine of faith, but essentially a question of jurisdictional claims on the side of the patriarchate of Antioch over the Indian church *versus* the deep sense of autonomy of the church of St Thomas which had enjoyed freedom and self rule since ancient times, there is hope among the faithful that division would be healed and unity would be restored. In the 19th century with the arrival of the British missionaries and their missionary efforts, another section, though smaller, of the ancient community was attracted to the teachings of Reformation tradition. This eventually split the ancient church, and the separation between the Orthodox Church and newly the reformed *Marthoma* church on doctrinal grounds was the sad result of this division.

In modern times there are small Russian, Greek, Armenian, Coptic, Syrian and other Eastern traditions in different parts of Asia due to immigration and trade. There are small Asian Orthodox Churches like the Korean Orthodox Church of the Greek tradition. The Malankara Orthodox Church has strong Diaspora in Malaysia, Singapore and Australia. These Diaspora communities including those newly converted from local communities largely follow the liturgical and spiritual traditions of their mother churches. There is hardly anything called an "Asianization" happening in these Diaspora communities except perhaps in such areas as liturgical language and iconography.

These Diaspora Orthodox communities are generally open to ecumenical initiatives, mainly because their parent bodies are all members of the WCC and are committed to ecumenical collaboration. The Malankara (Indian) Orthodox Church became a founding member of the WCC in Amsterdam 1948.

If we take CCA as a major structural expression of Asian ecumenism, the Malankara Orthodox Church has been involved in it since the early 1970s. Metropolitan Mathews Mar Coorilos (later Catholicos Marthoma Mathews I), Fr. Paul Verghese (later Metropolitan Paulos Mar Gregorios), Fr. Philipose Thomas (later Metropolitan Mar Eusebios), to mention just a few, had been prominently involved in the ecumenical work of CCA and promoted its connections with the Malankara Orthodox Church of India.

4. Theological Significance of the Orthodox Presence in Asia

Unlike the Western Churches the Orthodox Eastern Churches have never been involved in any systematic proselytizing mission in Asia. Therefore, one does not find any significant Orthodox presence in Asia except in India where the historic Malankara Church existed since apostolic times. Therefore, as everywhere, it is not the quantitative but qualitative theological and spiritual presence of Orthodox Churches that is of any significance.

Let me mention three broad areas:

(a) Inter-faith Experience and Cooperation

While Christian churches in the West almost always lived in a rather mono-cultural European setting until about the second half of the 20th, century Asian Christians have always been living in the pluralistic context with a broad spectrum of religions, cultures, ethnicities and worldviews. Asia, being the home of some of the major religions, has been hospitable to Christianity as well, just as it has always been open to a vast array of greatly divergent spiritual and philosophical systems.

The Malankara Orthodox Church has developed a certain *modus vivendi* with the majority population of Hindus and others over the centuries. The implications of this long dialogue of life are important for the wider ecumenical concerns of global Christianity, especially since some prophets of doom foresee a clash of civilizations rooted in major religions of the world.

It is now generally perceived that the emergence of religious and cultural pluralism constitutes a major challenge for global Christianity, particularly for the classical mainline western churches which, with notable exceptions, continue to take their mono-cultural settings for granted. In this context the Asian experience of the Orthodox Church and its presence and mission on this continent acquire a paradigmatic character.

The first thing that strikes an outside observer is probably the minority status of the Christian Church in Asia. In India, for example, it is still less than 3% of the total population of more than 1.1 billion. In spite of the existence in India of a Christian community from the first century AD and the massive efforts of the Portuguese and the British missionaries since the 16th century to Christianize India, the Christian population has not registered any significant quantitative growth. It should also be noted that ancient Oriental Christianity in India has had no bitter memory of any persecution from local rulers or any aggressive opposition from other religions. (It may be a paradox that local Christians in Kerala suffered persecution not from non-Christian authorities or neighbors but from Christian brothers from the west during the Portuguese period). In fact, the centuries old experience of St Thomas tradition of Christianity in the Southern state of Kerala has, more or less, been that of acceptance and respect in a heavily caste-ridden society.

It is noteworthy that the Orthodox church in Asia or anywhere else does not give priority to any mission of conversion of non-Christians or proselytisation of other Christians. The mission emphasis is rather on bearing witness (*martyria*) to Christ in other ways rather than quantitative and numerical growth of the church. There are certainly occasional voluntary conversions to the Orthodox Church due to several factors like marriage, personal conviction of those who seek the apostolic faith, predilection for spiritual practices like fasting and emphasis on liturgical experience, attraction to monastic and acetic life and so on. However, the eastern Church attaches much importance to respecting other faiths and maintaining genuine friendliness to neighbors as forms of radiating Christ's love for the world. There is an obvious divergence in this respect between the Orthodox churches and the traditional western churches. The latter in general believe strongly in conversion as an integral part of preaching the Gospel of Christ and the mission of the Church.

Asia has the experience of two ancient missions far earlier to the western Christian mission. The Buddhist mission that started in India, some 2000 years before the west European colonial Christian missions began coming to Asia. That mission of the Buddha, the Enlightened One, changed the face of Asia in a considerable way, and it has generally been perceived to be peaceful and nonviolent, respecting local cultures and other faiths. Then Asia had the Christian mission of St Thomas and later the East Syrian ("Nestorian") mission in the first Christian millennium. This again was very peaceful though it lacked imperial might and the massive colonial outfit.

So the ecumenical question regarding Christian Mission and interfaith relations in Asia can be raised anew from this historical perspective. Christian Mission can be nothing but the dissemination of God's love for the world. The Gospel of Christ is the Gospel of Love. Whatever we think or do against this ultimate principle of love is against the Gospel. Any preaching of the gospel that undermines the Gospel message itself is not part of the Christian mission.

The Christian Church in Asia in its Eastern ethos has a lot of potential to enter deep into the spiritual genius of other Asian religions like Hinduism, Buddhism, Jainism and Taoism. Any common ground that appears to the genuine seekers in these religions need to be affirmed as our common human heritage endowed by the Creator to all humanity. Affirmation of commonality rather than the assertion of difference must be the rule in a genuine dialogue between different faiths.

The biblical question *who is your neighbor?* is still being raised in response to the ancient commandment *Love your neighbor as yourself.* The answer always points to a *Samaritan*, the one who is doctrinally heretical, culturally outcaste and spiritually out of communion with you. It is this despised, unredeemed and cast out stranger who becomes the true neighbor in a critical moment of your life. He has already shown supreme love to you in your pain and suffering, and is willing to do more for you. What would be your response?

When we consider the ultimate divine commandment to love one's neighbor in relation to interfaith dialogue and cooperation the parable of Jesus enlightens us with a new revolutionary insight. It is the Other who apparently does not share your doctrine of faith or worship your God who becomes your neighbor. As Asian Christians in general can acknowledge, they sometimes get more solid human support, true friendship and love from their neighbors of other faiths than from their own fold. An important ecumenical aspect of the mission of the Church in pluralistic Asia is to create, cherish and foster this genuine neighborliness. This is one significant manner in which we bear witness to Christ, the good Samaritan, who bore our sins and healed our wounds out of pure love and compassion.

(b) Ecclesiology

Orthodox Churches maintain an ecclesiology which they attribute to the spirit and structure of "the one undivided Church." "The local Church ecclesiology" of the Orthodox Churches rather than a "universal church ecclesiology" may go along more smoothly with the Asian spirit of plurality, harmony, hospitality and respect to the other. A *qualitative catholicity* is the Orthodox alternative to the claims of any *quantitative universality* of number or geographical extension. The Buddhist tradition, for instance, has created a new spirit in Asia of combining tolerance and compassion as well as diversity and unity across the Asian religious landscape.

The metaphor of the *Body of Christ* used by Apostle Paul is taken very seriously in the Orthodox tradition. There is a tendency in academic circles to minimize the importance of this Pauline image as merely a metaphor. However in the Patristic tradition of the Church it is a constitutive element of ecclesiology. The Church as the Body of Christ is One. The unity of the Church is affirmed by the Orthodox churches on the basis of the integral and holistic character of the Body of Christ. In the Ecumenical Movement, and its doctrinal arm of Faith and Order, the Orthodox Churches tirelessly stand for the undivided witness of the Church as one Body. It does not deny any true cultural, linguistic or liturgical diversity. In fact the Local Church Ecclesiology of the Orthodox tradition has always promoted all genuine diversity and distinct identities in the unity and wholeness of the Body of Christ. The ineffable perception of the Triune nature of Godhead in which the distinct identity or *Hypostasis* of the Father, of the Son and of the Holy Spirit share the one *Ousia* or Essence underlines the unity and catholicity of the Church, Body of Christ. This is to be newly interpreted and understood in Asia where the immense diversities can threaten its unity with fatal political and economic consequences. An ecclesiology for Asia requires the emphasis on the oneness of the body of humanity, the sacred character of that body, the inter-dependence of the limbs of the body, justice and peace in the mutual sharing and assistance within the body and the sense of oneness with all creation as the larger Body of Christ. The emphasis is not on legalistic authority structures or a pyramidical hierarchy or a simple linear perception of history and progress, but on the organic and holistic life of the Body continually renewed and perfected by the dynamic indwelling of the Holy Spirit.

An Asian ecclesiology rooted in the Body of Christ and drawing lessons from the harmony of religions in Asia and from the Eastern Christian tradition will be of great value to the wider world. It will be a radically new way of bearing witness to Christ.

(c) Spirituality and Ethics

Spirituality is an area of rich potential for the Orthodox presence in Asia. The Eastern Christian spiritual and ethical understanding of reality has a large common ground with Asian religious philosophies and spiritual mindset in general. The Orthodox understanding of *theosis* or divinization and the transfiguration of the created world rooted in a holistic, incarnational theology has openings to the Asian vision of unity, and diversity, transcendence, renunciation and compassion. The ascetic-monastic values in both Orthodox and Asian spiritual understanding have striking parallels.

The Asian ethical stand based on the integrity of the family and social bonds and values promoting justice, non-violence (*ahimsa*) and respect for creation can be further explored ecumenically by the Orthodox tradition and Asian religions together. There is great potential for a mutually enriching give and take here. Issues of poverty and injustice, marginalization and exploitation are to be addressed jointly by Eastern Christianity and Asian religions since there is a heavy emphasis in both on transcendence, ritual and meditative tranquility, sometimes at the expense of a prophetic commitment for the transformation of the economic, social and political structures aimed at common good and just socio-economic order. This broadens the ecumenical vocation of the Church in Asia as well as creates a domain of wider Asian Ecumenism that takes into account the profound Asian religious-spiritual heritage.

Bibliography

Koshy Ninan, *A History of the Ecumenical Movement in Asia*, Vol 1, (Hong Kong: WSCF, YMCA,CCA, 2004).

Daniel David, *The Orthodox Church of India*, (New Delhi, 1986)

Cherian C.V., *A History of Christianity in India: A History of the Orthodox Church AD 52-2002*, (Kottayam: Academic Publishers, 2003).

George Kondothra, "Theological Education in the Oriental Orthodox Tradition," in Dietrich Werner et al, *Handbook of Theological Education in World Christianity: Theological Perspectives, Regional Surveys, Ecumenical trends,* (Regnum Studies in Global Christianity, 2010), 623-628.

George K.M., *Interfacing theology with culture,* (Delhi 2010)

Thomas, Meladath Kurian, *The Indian Way of Christianity*, (Saarbruecken, Germany: Lambert Academic Publications, 2012).

Bishop Hovakim Manukyan

This article provides a brief description and information about the ecumenical activities carried out by the Mother See of Holy Etchmiadzin, Armenian Apostolic Church.

His Holiness Karekin II, Supreme Patriarch and Catholicos of All Armenia from the very beginning of His enthronement gave a great importance to inter-Church Relations and started to visit the leaders of sister Churches, signed agreements with them, and made joint statements. All these served as a good basis for a new and beneficial cooperation for the sake of mutual support, understanding and respect in the Christian World. The Armenian Apostolic Church is well aware that only such an attitude of the Church creates more favorable ways and possibilities for solving various issues concerning human progress, on which that human progress depends, this time full of challenges.

Due to these approaches and active contacts, not only leaders of traditional churches, but also leaders of other religions visited Armenia. These visits, in fact, form a great part of the inter-Church relations. Definitely, mutual visits, in their turn, strengthen not only the existing relations, but also create new ways to face the challenges rising day by day.

Relations with Oriental Orthodox Churches

During recent years, the relations with the Coptic, Syrian, Ethiopian and Malankara Orthodox Churches are marked with more activities.

In October 2000, His Holiness Karekin II, Supreme Patriarch and Catholicos of All Armenians made an official visit to Egypt and Ethiopia to meet the leaders of these Churches and to reinforce the relations among the Armenian, Coptic and Ethiopian Churches. Due to such visits between the heads of our Churches, the Mother See of Holy Etchmiadzin tried to show initiative and strengthen the historical friendship among the members of the Oriental Orthodox Churches, and this was confirmed by the agreements and messages between His Holiness and the heads of the Sister Churches.

Such relations were designed for the Syrian and Malankara Orthodox Churches. The proof of this is the visit of the leader of the Malankara Orthodox Church Patriarch Basilios Mar Thoma Matthews of blessed memory to the Mother See of Holy Etchmiadzin in 2001 and the visit of the head of the Syrian Orthodox Church to the Mother See of Holy Etchmiadzin in 2003. In 2008, representatives of almost all sister Churches participated in the ceremony of blessing the Holy Myron-chrism in the Mother See of Holy Etchmiadzin.

Relations with Eastern Orthodox Churches

Upon the invitation of the Ecumenical Patriarch His All Holiness Bartholomew I in 2006, the Catholicos of All Armenians left for Turkey to meet him in the Ecumenical Patriarchate in Fanar and to reestablish the existing cooperation between the two Churches. This meeting also aimed to discuss the issue of how to protect the rights of the religion and ethnic minorities in the territory of Turkey.

The created friendship resulted in various visits of the Ecumenical Patriarch Bartholomew I to Armenia. His first visit to Armenia was in 1997 during the enthronement of KAREKIN I of blessed memory. The second one was in 2001 for participating in the events held on the 1700th anniversary of adopting Christianity as the state religion, and the last one was in 2008 for participating in the Myron blessing ceremony in the Mother See of Holy Etchmiadzin.

Close relations have been created between the Armenian Apostolic and the Russian Orthodox Churches. One of the most important visits during the first years of the pontificate of His Holiness Karekin II was his visit to Alexy II of blessed memory, which was later followed by the participation of Alexy II in the events dedicated to the 1700th anniversary of adopting Christianity as the state religion in Armenia. The Armenian Diocese of New Nakhijevan and Russia and the Armenian Diocese of Southern Russia contributed greatly to the creation of these relations. In 2010, His Holiness Cyril visited Armenia and the Mother See of Holy Etchmiadzin and joint communiqué was signed.

Since 2001, active theological dialogue has been initiated between the Armenian Apostolic and Russian Orthodox Churches. The meeting of religious leaders of the Transcaucasia was held by the mediation of the Russian Orthodox Church, the result of which is the creation of the Inter-Religious Council, and His Holiness Karekin II is one of the co-chairmen.

Fruitful cooperation has also been created with the Romanian and Bulgarian Orthodox Churches. His Holiness Karekin II had personal meetings with the leaders of the above mentioned churches during his Pontifical visit to Bulgaria and Romania. It is important to mention that His Holiness was decorated with a medal of the state by Mr. Emil Constantinescu, President of Romania.

Important steps based on mutual understanding are undertaken to strengthen relations with our neighbor the Georgian Orthodox Church. During his visit to Georgia in 2000, His Holiness Karekin II signed an agreement with His Holiness Ilia II, Patriarch of the Georgian Orthodox Church. We hope that current problems will find solutions in the near future.

In fact, the Armenian Apostolic Church has good and continuous relations with all Orthodox Churches.

Relations with the Catholic Church

Relations with the Catholic Church are marked with great progress. The visit of His Holiness Karekin II to Rome and the visit of Pope John Paul II of blessed memory to Armenia were a promotion for further serious cooperation. In 2001, the Head of the Catholic Church visited Armenia for the first time in the history.

The fact that the Pope visited a country of the former Soviet Union not upon the invitation of the president, but upon the invitation of the Church leader was a unique phenomenon. The Head of the largest Christian Church visited the Genocide Memorial too.

It is noteworthy that the Pope was accommodated not in the apartment of the Apostolic Nuncio, according to the accepted tradition, but in the residence of His Holiness Karekin II. He celebrated Divine Liturgy not in an open-air stadium, but at the Open Altar, which is near the entrance to the Mother See of Holy Etchmiadzin and is a symbol of the 1700th anniversary of the adoption of Christianity as the state religion in Armenia

In 2005, His Holiness Karekin II participated in the funeral of Pope John Paul II, and in 2008, His Holiness had a four-day visit to the Vatican upon the fraternal invitation of His Holiness Pope Benedict XVI. During his visit, His Holiness Karekin II went to the tomb of John Paul II of blessed memory, prayed for the peace of his soul, and also visited the square named after St. Gregory the Illuminator. Together with His Holiness Pope Benedict XVI, he presided over the traditional audience held every Wednesday at St. Peter's Square. More than 35,000 faithful were present at the audience.

Salesian Pontifical University granted His Holiness Karekin II the degree of honorable Doctor as an appreciation of His Holiness' activities addressed towards Christian education for the youth.

This cooperation was also important from another point of view: the leaders of the Armenian Catholic Community in Armenia, Georgia and Europe began to be elected not among the representatives of the Armenian Catholic Patriarchate of Bzommar, but among the representatives of the Mekhitarist Congregation living and acting in St. Lazar Island in Venice.

Part VI: Ecumenical Perspectives of Oriental Orthodox Churches

According to the agreement signed between His Holiness Karekin II and Pope John Paul II in 2001, each year two or three members of the Brotherhood of Holy Etchmiadzin study in European Universities with the support of the Catholic Church.

One of the important achievements of this cooperation is the fact that St. Vlas Church was given to the Armenian Apostolic Church for meeting the spiritual needs of the Armenian Community in Rome. The Armenian Apostolic Church began an official dialogue with the Catholic Church as a member of the Oriental Orthodox Church Family. Some meetings of the official dialogue between the Catholic Church and the Oriental Orthodox Churches were held in the Mother See of Holy Etchmiadzin. It is also worth mentioning that in Armenian communities, where there is no Armenian Church, the Catholic Church provides churches to the Armenian Apostolic Church for offering Church services.

Relations with the Anglican and Protestant Churches

The relations with the Anglican Church are also friendly, which is best demonstrated by mutual visits of the leaders of both Churches. Many members of the Brotherhood of Holy Etchmiadzin have studied in spiritual institutions of the Anglican Church. The Archbishop of Canterbury has its representative in the Mother See of Holy Etchmiadzin.

The relations with the Lutheran Church of Finland began with mutual visits of the Church Heads.

There are more than 200 Protestant churches in the world, and the Armenian Apostolic Church keeps friendly relations with them. The relations with Protestant churches also develop in the framework of the ecumenical movement.

Relations with the WCC and CEC

During the years of the pontificate of His Holiness Karekin II, the Armenian Apostolic Church established constant relations with the WCC. The clergy of the Mother See of Holy Etchmiadzin began to participate in the events, meetings and charitable, educational projects realized by the WCC.

The WCC raised its voice concerning many issues that trouble our nation and Church, including the condemnation of the Armenian Genocide, and as a result, on 24 April commemoration ceremonies were held in all 347 member-churches of the WCC. This cooperation resulted in inviting clergymen of the Brotherhood of Holy Etchmiadzin to study at the Bossey Ecumenical Institute. The representatives of the Mother See of Holy Etchmiadzin are included in the Central Committee of the WCC, as well as in other WCC Committees.

As a continuation of this cooperation, Dr. Samuel Cobia, General Secretary of the WCC visited the Mother See of Holy Etchmiadzin in 2007, and later on members of the WCC Executive Committee visited Etchmiadzin to have a plenary meeting.

During the meeting with the Executive Committee members, His Holiness mentioned, "It is really a great joy for us that the Executive Committee holds its meeting in the Mother See of Holy Etchmiadzin. We take such relations as a blessing. Your presence is not only a good occasion to get acquainted with the Armenians and the Armenian Apostolic Church, but also it is a good occasion for our nation to get acquainted with the mission and activity of the WCC." The representatives of the Mother See of Holy Etchmiadzin also participate in the works of the ecumenical network of protecting the disables sponsored by the WCC. In 2011 the new General Secretary Olav Fykse Tveit also visited Armenia and the Mother See of Holy Etchmiadzin.

Since 2002, our Church has participated in the Global Ecumenical Forum initiated by the WCC.

Since 1977, the Mother See of Holy Etchmiadzin has been a member of the CEC. During the years of His Holiness' pontificate, relations with the CEC have been strengthened more.

Orthodox Handbook on Ecumenism

The representatives of the Mother See Holy Etchmiadzin not only actively participate in the works of the CEC, but also host its representatives in Holy Etchmiadzin, organize meetings and discussions.

During these years, the Mother See of Holy Etchmiadzin presented its official viewpoint concerning the membership of Turkey in the EU and the document entitled Carta Ecumenica.

The CEC was one of the first organizations to condemn the Armenian Genocide and the former general Secretary of the CEC participated in the events dedicated to the 90th anniversary of the Armenian Genocide.

The 13th Assembly of the CEC came out with calls to protect the right of religious minorities in Georgia. The Armenian Apostolic Church always delegates her representatives to participate in the works of the European Christian Ecological Network presenting ecological projects, which are realized in the Vaskenian Spiritual Seminary and in the Dioceses.

Inter-Religious Relations

The Mother See of Holy Etchmiadzin also promotes inter-religious dialogues and cooperation. In 2006, the Armenian Apostolic Church participated in the 8th conference of the "Religions in the World for Peace" International Organization in Kyoto, Japan. His Holiness Karekin II was elected as the co-president of this council.

Leaders and representatives of different churches come to Armenia with the mission to establish dialogue and cooperation among different religions.

By the way, all the religious figures visiting Armenia, whether Christian or not, visit the Genocide Memorial. His Holiness Karekin II also participated in many inter-religious conferances. He is one of the co-chairmen of the CIS Inter-Religious Council. During Pontifical visits to different countries, His Holiness Karekin II usually had meetings with representatives of different religions.

Bibliography

Bishop Hovakim Manukyan, *Ecumenism in the 20th century and the Armenian Church*, (Doctoral thesis, unpublished), (Etchmiadzin, Armenia, 2006).

Aram I, Catholicos of Cilicia, *The Challenge to be a Church in a Changing World*, (New York, USA, 1997).

Aram I, Catholicos of Cilicia, *In search of Ecumenical vision*, (Antelias, Lebanon, 2001).

Karekin I, (Karekin Sarkissian), *The Council of Chalcedon and the Armenia Church*, (London, UK, 1965).

Christine Chaillot, *Dialogue Between the Orthodox Church and the Oriental Orthodox Churches* (a compilation of the texts of the Theological Dialogue since 1964, with accompanying articles), (Geneva, 1998).

Archbishop Nareg Alemezian

1. Armenia: The First Christian Nation

On the seashore of Antelias, a suburb of Beirut-Lebanon, are located the headquarters of the Armenian Apostolic Orthodox Church – Holy See Catholicosate of Cilicia.

The origin of the Armenian Church dates back to the Apostolic Age. Christianity was preached in Armenia as early as the second half of the first century by the two apostles of Jesus Christ, St. Thaddeus and St. Bartholomew.

During the first three centuries, Christianity in Armenia was a hidden religion under heavy persecution. In 301, Armenians officially accepted Christianity as their state religion through the efforts of St. Gregory the Illuminator. Armenians became the first nation who formally adhered to Christianity.

The official line of the Heads of the Armenian Church, called "Catholicos," started with St. Gregory the Illuminator. St. Gregory chose as the site of the Catholicosate the capital of Armenia, Vagharshapat.

2. A Migrating Catholicosal See

The continuous upheavals in Armenia forced the kingdom to move to safer places. The Armenian Church center moved as well to different locations together with the political authority. Thus, in 485 the Catholicosate was transferred to Dvin, then to Dzoravank and Aghtamar (927), Arkina (947) and Ani (992). In 1045, after the fall of the Armenian Kingdom of Bagradits, masses of Armenians migrated to Cilicia and the Catholicosate settled there. It was first established in Tavblour (1062), then Dzamendav (1072), Dzovk (1116), Hromkla (1149) and Sis (1293), where it remained for seven centuries.

3. Two Catholicosates in the Armenian Church

The existence of two Catholicosates in the Armenian Church (the Catholicosate of All Armenians in Holy Etchmiadzin-Armenia and the Holy See Catholicosate of Cilicia in Antelias-Lebanon) is due to historical circumstances.

In the 10th century Armenia was devastated by Seljuks and many Armenians left their homeland and were settled in Cilicia. The Catholicosate also took refuge in Cilicia. For almost four centuries (10th-14th cent.) the center of the Armenian political, ecclesiastical and cultural life was in Cilicia.

In 1375 the Armenian Kingdom of Cilicia was destroyed and Cilicia became a battleground between invading foreign powers. In the meantime Armenia was having a relatively peaceful time, which led the bishops of Armenia to elect a Catholicos in Holy Etchmiadzin. Thus, in 1441 Giragos Virapetsi was elected Catholicos in Holy Etchmiadzin, meanwhile Krikor Moussabekiants continued to be the Catholicos in Cilicia. Since 1441 there have been two Catholicosates in the Armenian Church with equal rights and privileges, and with their respective jurisdictions. The Catholicosate of Cilicia has always recognized the primacy of honor of the Catholicosate of Holy Etchmiadzin.

4. The Catholicosate in Antelias-Lebanon

During the First World War, Turks perpetrated the first Genocide of the 20th century and massacred one million five hundred thousand Armenians. In 1921, when the French forces evacuated Cilicia, a second wave of massacres ordered by Kemalist Turkey took the lives of another 300.000 Armenians. The rest of the Armenians were forced to leave their homeland and found refuge mostly in Syria and Lebanon. The Catholicosate in Sis was also confiscated and ruined by the Turks. Catholicos Sahag II followed the exile of his flock and in 1930 he established the Catholicosate of Cilicia in Antelias.

The Catholicosate of Cilicia became the leading force in the worldwide Armenian Diaspora through its network of dioceses. Catholicoi Sahag II (1902-1939), Papken I (1930-1936), Bedros I (1940), Karekin I (1943-1952), Zareh I (1956-1963), Khoren I (1963-1983) and Karekin II (1977-1995) occupied the throne of the Catholicosate in Antelias.

The current Catholicos is His Holiness Aram I, who was elected and consecrated in 1995. During his many years of ecclesiastical service, he has assumed important responsibilities in the Armenian Church as well as in the ecumenical movement.

In 1972, he was appointed as the representative of the Catholicosate of Cilicia for ecumenical relations.

In 1974, he became a founding member of the Middle East Council of Churches and has served on its Executive Committee.

As delegate of his Church he participated in the World Council of Churches Nairobi (1975), Vancouver (1983), Canberra (1991), Harare (1998) and Porto Alegre (2006) Assemblies. In 1975, he was elected a member of the WCC Faith and Order Commission. At the Vancouver Assembly, he was elected member of the WCC Central Committee. At the Canberra Assembly, he was elected Moderator of the WCC Central and Executive Committees. He was the first Orthodox and the youngest person to be elected to the position of Moderator. After serving as Moderator for seven years, he was unanimously re-elected at the WCC Harare Assembly.

He is a founding member of the Joint Commission of the Theological Dialogue between the Orthodox and Oriental Orthodox Churches and the International Theological Dialogue between the Oriental Orthodox Family of Churches and the World Alliance of Reformed Churches. He has played an important role in the initiation of the International Joint Commission for Theological Dialogue between the Catholic Church and the Oriental Orthodox Churches.

In 1996, he was instrumental in creating the fellowship of the Three Heads (Coptic, Syrian, Armenian) of the Oriental Orthodox Churches in the Middle East.

He has played a significant role in promoting common values, mutual understanding and peaceful co-existence among religions, and especially among Christians and Muslims.

He is an honorary member of the Pro Oriente, the World Religions Museum Foundation and the Religions for Peace international organizations.

5. Ecumenical and Inter-Religious Initiatives and Activities

Ecumenism and inter-religious relations remain one of the main areas of mission and ministry of the Catholicosate of Cilicia. Since the 50s, its clergy and lay representatives have taken an active part in global and regional ecumenical and inter-religious meetings and conferences.

The ecumenical engagement of the Catholicosate was more organized after 1962, when it became a member of the World Council of Churches. In 1975, at the Nairobi Assembly, Bishop Karekin Sarkissian (later Catholicos Karekin II) was elected a Vice-Moderator of the WCC Central and Executive Committees. In 1991, at the Canberra Assembly, Archbishop Aram Keshishian (currently Catholicos Aram I) was elected Moderator of the WCC Central and Executive Committees. In 1998, at the Harare Assembly, His Holiness Aram I was re-elected Moderator of the WCC Central and Executive Committees.

Part VI: Ecumenical Perspectives of Oriental Orthodox Churches

The Catholicosate sent observers to the Second Vatican Council. The visits of the Catholicoi to Popes, as well as joint declarations, meetings and consultations with representatives of the Roman Catholic Church greatly contributed to the development of warm relations between the Armenian Church and the Roman Catholic Church on international, regional and local levels.

The relations of the Catholicosate with the Churches of the Middle East have always been fraternal. As one of the initiators of the ecumenical movement in the region, it took an active part in the foundation of the Middle East Council of Churches in 1974.

The Catholicosate has played a key role in promoting the theological dialogue between the Eastern and Oriental Orthodox Families. It had a significant part in the development of a more organized collaboration among the Oriental Orthodox Churches. Since 1997, the Heads of the Oriental Orthodox Churches in the Middle East and the Standing Committee appointed by them regularly meet and discuss ecumenical, inter-religious and inter-church issues.

The Catholicosate continues with growing impetus its ecumenical relations with the Anglican Communion and the other Churches of the Reformation, as well as with various ecumenical organizations.

In 1997, His Holiness Aram I established the Department for Ecumenical and Inter-religious Relations at the Catholicosate to further strengthen mutual collaboration with our ecumenical and inter-religious partners. Also, the Department organizes ecumenical formation seminars and coordinates the activities of the dioceses. Archbishop Nareg Alemezian is the Ecumenical Officer of the Department.

In 2002, the Ecumenical Relations Committee of the Catholicosate was formed with 7 ordained and lay men and women members.

In 2010, the Catholicosate became a member of the Christian Conference of Asia.

The Catholicosate participated in the meetings of the Co-ordinating Committee of the United Bible Societies and Eastern and Oriental Orthodox Churches Relations.

Armenian Church University Students Association of the Catholicosate is a member of Christian university and youth organizations.

On the local level, the Catholicosate has representatives in many committees such as the Religious Textbooks Editorial Committee, Humanitarian Assistance Committee and Christian-Muslim Committee.

The Catholicosate is seriously engaged in generating tolerance and building mutual confidence between Christian and Muslim communities in the Middle East and worldwide. It initiates a number of inter-religious dialogues and takes active part in important inter-religious conferences on regional and international levels and organizes meetings of the representatives of world religions.

The Catholicosate actively participates in the ecumenical movement and inter-religious dialogue through its clergy and laity represented in the commissions and committees of ecumenical councils and inter-religious organizations.

6. Theological Dialogues

The Catholicosate of Cilicia is involved in the following Theological Dialogues together with the other members of the Family of the Oriental Orthodox Churches[1]:

I. Joint Commission of the Theological Dialogue between the Orthodox and Oriental Orthodox Churches

For two decades (1964-85) unofficial theological consultations took place between the representatives of these two families and paved the way for the formation of the Joint Commission.

---

[1] The Family of the Oriental Orthodox Churches comprises of the Armenian Apostolic Orthodox Church-Catholicosate of All Armenians (Armenia), the Armenian Apostolic Orthodox Church – Catholicosate of Cilicia (Lebanon), the Coptic Orthodox Church (Egypt), the Syrian Orthodox Church (Syria), the Ethiopian Orthodox Church (Ethiopia), the Indian Orthodox Church (India) and the Eritrean Orthodox Church (Eritrea).

Orthodox Handbook on Ecumenism

The first meeting of the Joint Commission took place in Chambésy-Geneva, in December 1985. It identified four areas of discussion on Christology: 1) Problems of terminology, 2) Conciliar formulations, 3) Historical factors, 4) Interpretation of Christological dogmas today.

The second meeting of the Joint Commission took place in the Monastery of Anba Bishoy-Egypt in June 1989 and made a common statement, known as the First Agreed Statement (See Digital Appendix with the texts).

The third meeting of the Joint Commission took place in Chambésy-Geneva in September 1990 and produced the Second Agreed Statement and Recommendations to the Churches, and made recommendations to their Churches on the lifting of all anathemas and condemnations, and on pastoral issues, relations between the two Orthodox Families of Churches, relations of the two Orthodox Families of Churches with other Churches, their common service to the world of suffering, need, injustice and conflicts, and their cooperation in the propagation of the Christian faith.

On behalf of the Catholicosate of Cilicia Archbishop Aram Keshishian (currently Catholicos Aram I) and Archbishop Mesrob Ashjian participated in the dialogue.

The Co-presidents of the Joint Commission, Metropolitan Damaskinos of Switzerland and Metropolitan Bishoy of Damiette, embarked on a series of visitation to the Eastern and Oriental Orthodox Churches headquarters to ensure the facilitation of the outcome of the dialogue by the Holy Synods.

In 2007, Metropolitan Emmanuel of France, the Eastern Orthodox new Co-president, and Metropolitan Bishoy visited His Holiness Aram I in Antelias and discussed the practical steps to resume the official talks. Soon a core group will meet to secure the resuming of the full meeting of the Joint Commission.

II. International Joint Commission for Theological Dialogue between the Catholic Church and the Oriental Orthodox Churches

Catholic and Oriental Orthodox representatives, delegated by their Churches, met in January 2003, in Rome-Italy, as members of the Preparatory Committee for the Catholic Church-Oriental Orthodox Churches International Joint Commission for Dialogue. The Preparatory Committee established the rules of membership of the Joint Commission and set up the work plan, agenda, membership, procedures, methodologies and timetable of the Joint Commission.

Between 2004-2013, the Joint Commission had 10 meetings, each year alternating between Rome and an Oriental Orthodox Church headquarters. It held its 7th meeting in the Catholicosate of Cilicia, Antelias-Lebanon.

The Joint Commission has the following topics on its agenda: 1) Christology, 2) Procession of the Holy Spirit in a Trinitarian context, 3) Ecclesiology, 4) The Mission of the Church, 5) Sacraments, 6) Purgatory, 7) Mariology.

On behalf of the Catholicosate of Cilicia Archbishop Oshagan Choloyan and Archbishop Nareg Alemezian are members of the Commission.

III. Anglican-Oriental Orthodox International Commission

Anglican and Oriental Orthodox representatives, delegated by their Churches, held a preparatory meeting in Midhurst-England in July 2001. They considered the recommendations of the Lambeth Conferences of 1988 and 1998 and decisions of Oriental Orthodox Churches that the Anglican-Oriental Orthodox dialogue be upgraded from a Forum (1985-1993) to a Commission. They also established the agenda and clarified matters related to the membership, procedures, methodologies and timetable of the Commission. The agenda includes the following topics: 1) Christology, 2) Pneumatology, 3) Authority in the Church, 4) Holy Scripture and Holy Tradition, 5) Ecclesiology, 6) Sacraments, 7) Moral issues, 8) The place of women in the Church, 9) Matters of concern to the Churches in their mission and pastoral care.

Part VI: Ecumenical Perspectives of Oriental Orthodox Churches

The Commission had its first meeting in Holy Ejmiadzin-Armenia, in November 2002, signed an Agreed Statement on Christology (See Digital Appendix with the texts) and submitted it to the authorities of the Oriental Orthodox Churches and the Anglican Communion for their consideration.

On behalf of the Catholicosate of Cilicia Archbishop Kegham Khatcherian and Archbishop Nareg Alemezian participated in the meetings.

The work of the Commission has been interrupted since 2003, because of the ordination of homosexual clergy and the blessing of marriages of the homosexuals in the Anglican Communion.

Through the efforts of His Holiness Aram I a joint small group will meet in England, in 2013, to discuss the possibilities of restarting the full meeting of the Commission.

IV. International Theological Dialogue between the Oriental Orthodox Family of Churches and the World Alliance of Reformed Churches

A group of representatives of Oriental Orthodox and Reformed Churches held a preparatory meeting in Geneva-Switzerland in August 1992, and considered the possibility of embarking on a theological discussion on matters of common concern. Archbishop Aram Keshishian, then the Moderator of the World Council of Churches, played an important role in this initiative.

Between 1993-2001, the group had 7 meetings, alternatively hosted by a Reformed and an Oriental Orthodox Church.

One of the highlights of these meetings was the adoption of the Agreed Statement on Christology in Driebergen-The Netherlands, in September 1994 (See Digital Appendix with the texts).

During the meetings, 30 papers were presented and discussed on the following topics: 1) Tradition and Holy Scripture, 2) The Role of the Theologian in the Christian Community, 3) The Nature of the Church and Her Mission, 4) Priesthood/Ministry, 5) Sacraments.

In January 2001, at its last meeting in Antelias-Lebanon, the members prepared the report of the first phase of their discussion and submitted it to the authorities of their respective Churches for consideration.

On behalf of the Catholicosate of Cilicia Archbishop Dirayr Panossian and Archbishop Nareg Alemezian participated in the meetings.

The second phase of the dialogue is under consideration by both sides.

V. Conversation between The Lutheran World Federation and Churches of the Oriental Orthodox Family

Representatives of the Lutheran World Federation and Churches of the Oriental Orthodox family met in Geneva-Switzerland, in February 2008, to explore the possibility of establishing regular bilateral contact between their Churches.

On behalf of the Catholicosate of Cilicia Archbishop, Nareg Alemezian participated in the meeting.

Rev. Dr. Ishmael Noko, the LWF General Secretary, decided to make a visit to each of the Oriental Orthodox Churches in 2008 to discuss the matter with the heads of the Oriental Orthodox Churches, but because of leadership change in the LWF he could not do it.

Rev. Dr. Martin Junge, the LWF new General Secretary, will visit the Oriental Orthodox Churches in 2013.

Stanislau Paulau

Introduction

The Eritrean Orthodox Tewahedo Church is the youngest member of the Oriental Orthodox Church family, and it would not be an exaggeration to assert that it is also one of the least known Orthodox Churches worldwide. Although the Eritrean Orthodox Church was established only in the course of the last decade of the 20th century, it shares (together with the Ethiopian Orthodox Tewahedo Church) a heritage of a centuries-old tradition which goes back to the times of Late Antiquity. This young and simultaneously ancient Church is just making its first steps within the institutionalized ecumenical movement, but the interaction with other Christian denominations has already played a constitutive role in its formation.

Modern Eritrea is located along the south-western coast of the Red Sea, an area which once used to be the site of the ancient Kingdom of Aksum extending across the Red Sea into the Arabian Peninsula and beyond to the Gulf of Aden. Being a major player in the trade between the Roman Empire and Ancient India, China and Persia, the kingdom flourished from the 1st to the 7th century and attracted merchants and settlers from throughout the ancient world. It is therefore natural that the cosmopolite Kingdom of Aksum from the earliest times also had a number of Christians, but they were first of all foreigners and lived predominantly in the port city of Adulis. During the reign of Ezana (ca. 325–365), whose religious policy can be seen as an *imitatio imperii Romani*, the conversion of the kingdom to Christianity took place and was inaugurated by the ordination of its first bishop – St. Frumentius, a Syrian from Tyre, who is revered in Eritrea and Ethiopia as the 'Revealer of Light'. Thereby a long-standing ecclesiastic bond between the newly founded Church and the Holy See of St. Mark (the Coptic Orthodox Church) was established.

The Other as a Challenge: Early Contacts with the Western Christianity

"Encompassed on all sides by enemies of their religion, the Ethiopians slept for near a thousand years, forgetful of the world by whom they were forgotten."[1] This famous passage of the British historian Edward Gibbon transmits an idea which still dominates in the contemporary historiography – the idea that, since the rise of Islam in the neighbouring regions, Ethiopia (including Eritrea) was totally isolated from the wider world and the rest of Christianity throughout the centuries.[2] But as the new findings indicate, the Christians in the Horn of Africa were engaged in a rather active interaction with the Christian *oikumene* long before the advent of the Jesuit mission in the 16th century.[3] But in what follows we would like to focus on the interactions between the Orthodox Christians in Eritrea and the representatives of other Christian traditions in more recent times – close before and after the birth of the modern ecumenical movement.

---

[1] Edward Gibbon, *The Decline and Fall of the Roman Empire*, (New York, 1910), 176.
[2] For a critique of the contemporary historiographical discourse on the interaction between Ethiopia and the Western world see: Andreu Martínez d'Alòs-Moner, "Europe and Ethiopia's Isolation: the Ethio-Jesuit Paradigm Revised (17th cent.)," in Ludwig Gerhardt (Ed.), *Umbrüche in afrikanischen Gesellschaften und ihre Bewältigung*, (Berlin, 2006), 223–233.
[3] For the sources and literature on this mission see: Leonardo Cohen Shabot – Andreu Martínez d'Alòs-Moner, "The Jesuit Mission to Ethiopia (16th–17th centuries). An Analytical Bibliography," in *Aethiopica: International Journal of Ethiopian and Eritrean Studies* 9 (2006): 190–212. A historical overview of the Ethio-European contacts in the Middle Ages can be found in: Wilhelm Baum, *Äthiopien und der Westen im Mittelalter: die Selbstbehauptung der christlichen Kultur am oberen Nil zwischen dem islamischen Orient und dem europäischen Kolonialismus*, (Klagenfurt, 2001).

If an active interaction of Christians in Eritrea with the Catholic Church was established already in the Middle Ages, the first encounter with Protestantism happened first in the 19th century.[4] And this encounter was rather the result of a misfortune of Swedish Lutheran missionaries who came into the Eritrean city of Massawa in 1866 looking for a way to reach the land of the Oromo people, who were believed still to be "pagans".[5] But as they were successful neither in this undertaking, nor in the attempt to start a mission among Kunama and Barya in the north-west Ethiopia, they found no better idea than to propagate Lutheranism in Orthodox areas of Eritrea.[6] This inevitably led not just to an encounter, but to a certain clash between both traditions. Protestant proselytism among its members prompted the Orthodox Church to initiate a discussion with the missionaries and to give a theological response to this challenge.

Luckily enough, some Eritrean manuscripts have preserved echoes of these theological debates, whereby we have at our disposal not only a missionary perspective on the situation documented in their reports and diaries, but also – what is extremely rare – an indigenous African view on a Western mission. These manuscripts were composed by the monks of the Debre Bizen monastery, one of the main spiritual and educational centers of the Orthodox Church in Eritrea, in the beginning of the 20th century. The most important work is entitled *The Book of Wisdom* and is composed in the form of a dialogue between an Orthodox and a Protestant, discussing variety of theological issues, both theoretical and practical (here the question concerning fasting played an important role).[7] Nevertheless, this manuscript presenting an outstanding example of the Orthodox apologetic literature and an important document of the early Orthodox-Protestant dialogue is still awaiting its publication and a detailed analysis.

However important the dialogue with the Protestants might have been, the interaction with the Catholic Church received much more attention from the side of the Orthodox Eritreans, because from a certain point it exceeded a mere theological framework and became an issue of survival. It had to do with the political transformation of the region. Since the end of the 19th century, Eritrea started taking its modern shape in particularly through a series of small scale expansionist activities of Italy. As the culmination of this process the Italians declared the occupied territory to be its new colony, which they called with the word derived from the Latin name of the Red Sea – *Mare Eritreum* – 'Eritrea'.[8] The time of the Italian occupation (1890–1941) had not only a tremendous impact on all spheres of life, but played also a major role in the process of the Eritrean

---

[4] For general information on the political background to the missionary initiatives and their consequences in the 19th century see: Donald Crummey, *Priests and Politicians: Protestant and Catholic Missions in Orthodox Ethiopia (1830–1868)*, (Oxford, 1972). For the perspective of the first Protestant missionaries on the Ethiopian Church tradition see: Stanislau Paulau, "Encountering the Ethiopian Orthodox Church in the Pre-Ecumenical Age: First Protestant Missionaries in Ethiopia (1829–1843)," in E. Ficquet and A. Hassen (eds.), *Movements in Ethiopia, Ethiopia in Movement. Proceedings of the 18th International Conference of Ethiopian Studies*, (Addis Ababa: CFEE – IES, 2014). *Forthcoming.*

[5] For an overview of the history of the Evangelical Church in Eritrea see: Karl Johan Lundström – Ezra Gebremedhin, *Kenisha: The Roots and Development of the Evangelical Church of Eritrea 1866–1935*, (Trenton: The Red Sea Press, 2011). For the history of the educational work of the Swedish mission in Eritrea see: Jonas Iwarsson – Alberto Tron, *Notizie storiche e varie sulla missione evangelica svedese dell'Eritrea, 1866–1916*, (Asmara, 1918).

[6] Sven Rubenson, *The Survival of Ethiopian Independence*, (London, 1976), 288–289; Gustav Arén, *Evangelical Pioneers in Ethiopia*, (Stockholm, 1978), 127–148.

[7] EMML [Ethiopian Manuscript Microfilm Library] 1233, Ff. 5a–24b and ff. 29a–89b. The book was composed in 1905 E.C. (= 1912–1913 A.D.). The same manuscript contains also a report of a dialogue that took place on Maggābit 18, 1902 E.C. (= March 27, 1910 A.D.) between an Orthodox called Tasfā Śellāsē and the Protestant Abbā Māso, see: EMML 1233, Ff. 89b–96b. For the description of the manuscript see: Getatchew Haile (ed.), *A Catalogue of Ethiopian Manuscripts Microfilmed for the Ethiopian Manuscript Microfilm Library, Addis Ababa and for the Hill Monastic Manuscript Library, Collegeville. Vol. 4: Project numbers 1101–1500*, (Collegeville: Hill Monastic Ms. Libr., St. John's Abbey and Univ., 1979), 217.

[8] See: Haggai Erlich, "Pre-Colonial Eritrea", in Siegbert Uhlig (ed.), *Encyclopaedia Aethiopica*, Volume 2, D–Ha, (Wiesbaden: Harrassowitz Verlag, 2005), 358–359.

nation-building.[9] Obviously, the ecclesiastic landscape of the country under the new ruler could not remain the same – the Catholic missions in the region gained the momentum.[10] The colonial powers tried to use the Catholic mission as one of the tools in their propaganda of the new policy, connected with Italian national ideology.[11] Therefore the French Lazarists who were active in Eritrea prior to Italian colonization were suspected of disloyalty to the colonial state on the grounds of their nationality and replaced by the Italian Capuchins in 1894.[12] In order to strengthen the Catholic Church a new structure, the Apostolic Prefecture of Eritrea, was established.

At the same time, the Orthodox Church in Eritrea, being a diocese of the Ethiopian Orthodox Church, was the main bearer of the national identity and culture and was therefore seen by the Italians as a great threat. Owing to the proximity of the co-religionist Ethiopian Empire, where the Orthodox Church was still a pillar of the State, the danger of a potential resistance movement coming out of the Church and acting with Ethiopian help was very probable. Hence the colonial powers started to use various strategies to weaken the influence of Orthodoxy in Eritrea. First of all, the Italians undermined the economical power of the Orthodox Church and confiscated its lands. Second, they tried to challenge its religious authority through the educational policy – all the education was delegated to the missionaries, who became responsible not only for colonial teaching and the propagation of Italian culture, but also for lessons on religion.[13] In 1929, to counteract the potentially dangerous influence of the Church, the colonial government even abolished the Ethiopian ecclesiastic authority over Eritrea. However, both the Ethiopian Orthodox Tewahedo Church and the Coptic Orthodox Church, to whose jurisdiction the Ethiopian Church still belonged at that time, proclaimed this step uncanonical and correspondingly invalid. Another important element of the colonial religious policy was the support of Islam. As Federica Guazzini remarks, "the Italians actively encouraged the spread of Islam in Eritrea in order to achieve the support of their Muslim subjects and to set them against the Orthodox."[14]

All the attempts of the Italian government to weaken the Orthodox Church led neither to the extermination of its underground links with the Ethiopian empire, nor to a desirable number of Eritrean Orthodox conversions to Catholicism. And since the interaction between both Churches was very much instrumentalized for political aims and happened in a strictly power-related context, no significant attempt towards a real dialogue was made from either side. And if the encounter with Protestantism was a relatively new challenge for the Orthodox Church which demanded a theological response, the Catholic Church was already quite well known – Orthodox polemical literature against Catholicism had flourished already in the 16th and 17th centuries and could be further used for the apologetical purposes.[15]

---

[9] Cf.: Redie Bereketeab, *Eritrea: The making of a Nation, 1890–1991*, (Trenton, 2007); Bairu Tafla, "Independence through Independence: the Challenges of Eritrean Historiography," in Harold Golden Marcus (ed.), *New Trends in Ethiopian Studies. Papers of the 12th International Conference of Ethiopian Studies, Michigan State University, 5–10 September 1994*, (Lawrenceville, 1994), 497–514.

[10] The 19th century Catholic mission in Eritrea started with Father Giuseppe Sapeto who came in the late 1830s and was soon joined by Justin de Jacobis, appointed to be Perfect Apostolic of Ethiopia and neighboring regions. Donald Crummey, *Priests and Politicians: Protestant and Catholic Missions in Orthodox Ethiopia (1830–1868)*, (Oxford, 1972), 60; Kefelew Zelleke – Friedrich Heyer, *Das orthodoxe Äthiopien und Eritrea in jüngster Geschichte*, (Aachen, 2001), 156.

[11] Dirar, U. "Church-state Relations in Colonial Eritrea: Missionaries and the Development of Colonial Strategies (1869–1911)," in *Journal of Modern Italian Studies* 8.3 (2003): 391–410.

[12] See: Metodio da Nembro, *La missione dei Minori Cappuccini in Eritrea 1894–1952*, (Roma, 1953).

[13] For an analysis of the colonial textbooks (also regarding religion) in Eritrea see: Tekeste Negash, *Italian Colonialism in Eritrea, 1882–1941. Policies, Praxis and Impact*, (Uppsala, 1987), 72–79.

[14] Federica Guazzini, "Colonial history of Eritrea," in Siegbert Uhlig (ed.), *Encyclopaedia Aethiopica*, Volume 2, D–Ha, (Wiesbaden: Harrassowitz Verlag, 2005), 361.

[15] See Enrico Cerulli, *Scritti teologici etiopici dei secoli XVI–XVII. II: La storia dei quattro Concili ed puscoli monofisiti*, (Città del Vaticano, 1960). For a more recent Orthodox reaction on the Catholic mission see: Stéphane Ancel, "Discourse Against Catholic Doctrine in Təgray (Ethiopia): A Nineteenth Century Text," in *Aethiopica, International Journal for Ethiopian and Eritrean Studies* 15 (2012): 92–104.

From the Ethiopian Orthodox Church in Eritrea to the Eritrean Orthodox Church:
Inter-Orthodox Relations

In the course of the 20th century, the Eritrean political situation had been changing dramatically. After the defeat of the Italians, Eritrea was governed by the British (1941–1952), and subsequently federated with the Ethiopian Empire, only to be annexed in 1961. This led to the formation of an independence movement, which erupted into a 30-year war against successive Ethiopian governments that ended in 1991. Following a UN-supervised referendum in Eritrea in which the people overwhelmingly voted for separation from Ethiopia, Eritrea declared its independence and gained international recognition in 1993.

The Eritrean independence from Ethiopia became a huge challenge for the Orthodox Church which was still the Ethiopian Church. As it is often the case in the history, the Church decided to adjust to the utterly new political reality: "In view of the way the Orthodox Church in Eritrea had been co-opted by the imperial regime, it is understandable that the Eritrean Church felt obliged to dissociate itself from Ethiopia and become a patriotic national church."[16] But taking into consideration the canonical status of the Orthodox Church in Eritrea, this was not an easy undertaking. Here, several facts from the inter-Orthodox relations have to be re-called. Since the 4th century when St. Frumentius was ordained in Alexandria to be the first bishop of Aksum, all the Patriarchs of the Ethiopian Orthodox Church (including Eritrea) were sent from the Coptic Church. The situation changed only in the middle of the 20th century when the number of Ethiopian bishops was steadily increased until an independent Holy Synod could be formed. The culmination of the process took place in 1959 when the Coptic Patriarch granted Ethiopian Orthodox Tewahedo Church autocephaly and consecrated Abune Basilios was consecrated as the first Patriarch of the Ethiopian Church.

So being just a diocese of the Ethiopian Church, the Eritrean Orthodox community could not expect that the Ethiopian Church would give it autocephaly after the separation of Eritrea. So in order to obtain autocephaly, the Eritrean Orthodox hierarchs decided to make a detour and to appeal for an intervention of the Coptic Church. The Holy Synod of the Coptic Orthodox Church responded favourably to this request and authorized the training of as many as ten future bishops for the Eritrean Church in Coptic monasteries. And in 1994, five new Orthodox bishops for Eritrea were ordained in Cairo.[17] The clash with the Ethiopian Orthodox Tewahedo Church – which saw the actions of the Coptic Church as a violation of its canonical jurisdiction over Eritrea – was inescapable. Although the official documentation implies that there is a smooth transition to ecclesiastical independence, in reality things looked rather different. Initial reactions in Ethiopia upon hearing of the Coptic intervention were extremely negative and caused a rupture in Ethiopian-Coptic relations. Even though thereafter an agreement was signed in Addis Abeba that reaffirmed the autocephalous status of both the Ethiopian and the Eritrean Churches and recognized a primacy of honour of the Coptic Church among the Oriental Orthodox churches in Africa, the situation remained tense. And here the ecumenical movement became instrumental for the normalisation of the relationships between both Churches. As the Coptic journal *Glastonbury Bulletin* informed, "Relations between the Coptic and Ethiopian Churches have been strained since 1994... During the recent General assembly of the World Council of Churches in Harare, meetings between the two churches delegations produced hopeful signs that the problems between the two churches soon mighty be healed."[18] But these hopes were not to become

---

[16] Joachim G. Persoon, "The spiritual Legacy of the Ethio-Eritrean Conflict," in *Journal of Eastern Christian Studies* 57 (2005): 298.

[17] Fore more details on the negotiations between the Eritrean and the Coptic Churches see: Friedrich Heyer, "Die Einwirkung des koptischen Patriarchats auf die Gründung des orthodoxen Patriarchats von Eritrea," in Martin Tamcke (Ed.), *Daheim und in der Fremde. Beiträge zur jüngeren Geschichte und Gegenwartslage der orientalischen Christen*, (Hamburg: LIT, 2002), 252–259; Wolfram Reiss, "Vereinbarung zwischen der Koptisch-Orthodoxen und der Eritreisch-Orthodoxen Kirche," in Martin Tamcke (Ed.), *Daheim und in der Fremde. Beiträge zur jüngeren Geschichte und Gegenwartslage der orientalischen Christen*, (Hamburg: LIT, 2002), 261–265.

[18] "Hope For Improved Relations Between Coptic and Ethiopian Churches," in *Glastonbury Bulletin* 100 (1999): 71–72.

reality: in the very same year 1998 – against the will of the Orthodox Ethiopians – the last step in the process of creation of the autocephalous Eritrean Orthodox Church was undertaken and on 8 May the Pope of the Coptic Orthodox Church enthroned the bishop of Asmara Abba Philipos as the first Patriarch of the Eritrean Orthodox Tewahedo Church. Wolfgang Hage rightly points out that the Eritrean Church presents a remarkable example of the fact that the state-oriented model of obtaining autocephaly ("an independent Church for an independent state"), as it is often the case in Eastern Orthodoxy, can function also among the Oriental Churches.[19]

Of great ecumenical significance was the protocol signed between the Coptic and the Eritrean Orthodox Churches on the occasion of the granting autocephaly. It represents a unique example of the recognition of mutual independence and, at the same time, a commitment to common actions in all spheres of the Church life.[20] Declaring that the two Churches belong to the See of St. Mark and confess one Orthodox doctrine (article 3), the protocol stresses a need for a special liturgical expression of their closeness to each other (article 4): "In order to manifest and affirm the spiritual relations between the two Churches, His Holiness the Pope of Alexandria and His Holiness the Patriarch of Eritrea should be mentioned in all the liturgical prayers – the name of the Alexandrian Pope to be mentioned first."[21] This is an unparalleled practice within the Orthodox tradition. The protocol also anticipates further steps: a common general Synod of both Churches is to be convened together every three years (article 6), a common delegation for ecumenical dialogues on matters of faith is to be formed (article 10) and a standing committee to promote cooperation in such areas as theological education, social services, pastoral care and development projects is to be established (article 12). However this autocephaly and the program of cooperation defined in the protocol had ambivalent consequences. On the one hand, it set the groundwork for an unprecedentedly in the Orthodox world partnership between two (the Eritrean and the Coptic) Churches. On the other hand, totally neglecting the just claims of the Ethiopian Orthodox Church for jurisdiction over Eritrea, it intensified already existing inter-Orthodox tensions.[22] And political circumstances were not favorable for solving these tensions: in the beginning of May 1998 at the very same time as the Eritrean Orthodox Church celebrated the consecration of its first Patriarch, the Eritrean–Ethiopian War began.

Current State of the Eritrean Orthodox Church and its Engagement in the Ecumenical Movement

The war killed thousands of people, displaced hundreds of thousands and caused a serious humanitarian crisis. It was over only in June 2000, and the ecumenical movement played a key role in advocating for peace-making during the war and assisting in achieving reconciliation thereafter. Immediately after the outbreak of hostilities, the General Secretary of the World Council of Churches (WCC) wrote to the leaders of Ethiopia and Eritrea, imploring them to stop the fighting and to resolve the border issue, which was the immediate source of contention, by peaceful means. In 1999, an ecumenical delegation led by the WCC visited both countries to express the concerns of the Churches around the world and to offer its assistance.

---

[19] Wolfgang Hage, *Das orientalische Christentum*, (Stuttgart, 2007), 226.

[20] "Protocol between the Coptic Orthodox Church (COC) and the Eritrean Orthodox Church (EOC)," in Martin Tamcke (Ed.), *Daheim und in der Fremde. Beiträge zur jüngeren Geschichte und Gegenwartslage der orientalischen Christen*, (Hamburg: LIT, 2002), 266–275. See in the footnotes also the comparison of the similar agreement which was signed in 1994 between the Coptic Orthodox Church and the Ethiopian Orthodox Tewahedo Church. The text of this protocol can be found in: Klaus Schwarz (Ed.), *Überleben in Schwieriger Zeit. 4. Evangelisch/Orientalisch-Orthodoxe theologische Konsultationen*, (Hannover, 1995), 97–102.

[21] Ibid., 272.

[22] The conflict between the Coptic Orthodox and the Ethiopian Orthodox Tewahedo Churches was overcome only in July 2007 through the assistance of His Holiness Aram I, Armenian Catholicos of Cilicia.

With the help of Norwegian Church Aid (NCA) and other ecumenical partners, interfaith committees from Orthodox, Protestant, Roman Catholic and Muslim leaders had been formed in Eritrea and Ethiopia.[23] Particularly significant were six peace meetings of religious leaders held in Europe, the United States and Kenya, as there were no other contacts between Eritrea and Ethiopia. The culmination of the reconciliation process were visits of the Ethiopian religious leaders to Eritrea and of the Eritrean religious leaders to Ethiopia in 2002, described by Abune Paulos, the Patriarch of the Ethiopian Orthodox Church, as "a healing of wounds."[24] Apparently, this successful experience of a productive interfaith work encouraged the Eritrean Orthodox Church to extend its ecumenical involvement. Apart from the participation in the official theological dialogues within the Oriental Church family,[25] it obtained membership in the World Council of Churches and in the All Africa Conference of Churches (AACC).

However the Eritrean authoritarian regime did not excuse religious leaders from the criticism of the disastrous war – and consequently of its policy – and clearly considered it as threat for its authority. Also the participation of the Eritrean Orthodox Church in this ecumenical initiative was not passed over unnoticed by the Eritrean government. This resulted in a severe repression of civil society and in restrictions in the freedom of religious groups felt to undermine national integrity. In the course of this new religious policy, Eritrea became one of the world's worst persecutors of Christians. Since 2002, the Eritrean government acknowledges a right to exist for only four "recognized" religious groups, the Orthodox Church, the Roman Catholicism, the Lutheran Church, and the Sunni Islam. Members of all other religious groups are badly persecuted – arrested, held in oppressive conditions, and sometimes even tortured to compel them to recant their faith.

Even though the Eritrean Orthodox Church enjoys the status of an officially recognized religious group, it faces a great deal of restrictions. In May 2002, the desire of the Eritrean government to control the oldest and the most influential institution in the country brought the installation of a political appointee as the General Administrator of the Church. This position, similar to that of the Ober-Prokurator of the Russian Orthodox Holy Synod in Tsarist times, has full control over the decisions of the Synod. Besides this, in order to weaken the position of the Church and to reduce its role to a mere arm of the Department of the Religious Affairs, the government either arrested or unfrocked a great number of the leading clergy who could oppose the new course of the government. Yet this was not all: the finances of the Church fell under the control of the government,[26] the most precious artifacts and manuscripts were declared to be "the property of the Eritrean people" and confiscated.[27] But what makes the religious policy of the government even more dangerous for the future of the Eritrean Orthodox Church is that presently all deacons and priests below the age of fifty are obliged to undergo an indefinite military service. During the last several years, more than 1,500 Orthodox priests were forced to join the army and as a result of the shortage of clergy, Orthodox churches – and first of all in rural areas – are being shut down at an alarming rate in Eritrea.[28]

---

[23] *Minute on Peace and Reconciliation between Ethiopia and Eritrea,* adopted by the Central Committee of the World Council of Churches, Geneva, 26 August–3 September 1999. http://www.oikoumene.org/en/resources/documents/wcc-commissions/international-affairs/regional-concerns/africa/minute-on-peace-and-reconciliation-between-ethiopia-and-eritrea?set_language=en

[24] Cf. Joachim G. Persoon, "The spiritual Legacy of the Ethio-Eritrean Conflict," in *Journal of Eastern Christian Studies* 57 (2005): 300.

[25] Nareg Alemezian, "The Oriental Orthodox Family of Churches in Ecumenical Dialogue," in *The Ecumenical Review* 61.3 (2009): 315–327.

[26] See: "The Sufferings of the Eritrean Orthodox Church," in *Glastonbury Bulletin* 115 (2007). http://britishorthodox.org/glastonbury-review-archive/glastonbury-review-archive-issue-115/6/

[27] "The Detained Patriarch, Persecuted Christians and a Dying Church" (18 January 2012). http://theorthodoxchurch.info/blog/news/2012/01/the-detained-patriarch-persecuted-christians-and-a-dying-church/

[28] "Eritrean Orthodox Churches Closing Their Doors at an Alarming Rate" (13 October 2011), in *In Chains for Christ (ICFC). Voice of the Persecuted Church in Eritrea.* http://www.inchainsforchrist.org/index.php?view=article&id=70%3A eritrean-orthodox-churches-closing-their-doors-at-an-alarming-rate&option=com_content&Itemid=54

However the head of the Eritrean Orthodox Tewahedo Church, Patriarch Antonios, took an uncompromising stand against all encroachments by the government in the affairs of the Church and demanded the release of the imprisoned Christians. The reaction followed quite soon, and Patriarch Antonios was removed from his office by the Holy Synod which sided with the government. He was soon arrested and became one of around 2,000 Christians detained without trial or charge by the Eritrean government.[29] Since then, he has neither been seen nor heard from. In order to justify this uncanonical action, representatives of the Synod even sought the support of the Coptic Pope Shenouda III to excommunicate Abune Antonios, but the Pope refrained from this and expressed his support for the persecuted Patriarch.

The religious policy of the Eritrean regime found its anticipated turn on 27 May 2007 when a pro-government bishop Dioscoros of Mendefera was installed as a new Patriarch. Although all other Oriental Orthodox Churches still continue to recognize Abune Antonios as the genuine and canonical patriarch of Eritrean Orthodox Tweahedo Church,[30] the Eritrean Orthodox Community in Diaspora is divided into two groups: one (more numerous) supporting Abune Antonios and the other, Abune Dioscoros.

The severe restriction of religious freedom in Eritrea gained attention all around the world and this situation became a major concern not only for various NGO's, but also for Churches and ecumenical bodies worldwide. As the matter of fact, General Secretary of the WCC Konrad Raiser accompanied by an ecumenical team visited Eritrea in July 2002 and met there with Church leaders as well as government officials in order to advocate for the believers, whose fundamental human rights of freedom of religion, conscience, worship and organization had been violated.[31] Intensive work in this direction is being done also by the Eritrean Orthodox Church in Diaspora. Its recent appeal from May 2013 to the Secretary-General of the United Nations Ban Ki-moon could serve as an example of its activity.[32] In this letter the Archdioceses of the Eritrean Orthodox Church in North America, Europe and Middle East once again called upon the world community to help to release His Holiness Patriarch Antonios and all those who are in prison because of their faith.

As concerns the participation of the Eritrean Orthodox Tewahedo Church in the ecumenical movement, the situation is rather ambivalent. Although the official representatives of the Eritrean Orthodox Church participate in some ecumenical gatherings, their freedom of action is very much limited. Moreover after the forcible dismissal of Patriarch Antonios and the appointment of Abune Dioscoros, the canonical status of the Church in Eritrea is often questioned by other Churches. At the same time the Eritrean Orthodox Church consists not only of its members in Eritrea. It has already became an international body as the large number of refugees left Eritrea during the last decades established strong Orthodox parishes all around the world. These Eritrean Christians actively contribute to the ecumenical work at various levels, sharing both their ancient Christian tradition dating back to the first centuries and the experience of a dramatic history of the recent past.

---

[29] For more details see "Eritrean Patriarch Uncanonically Deposed," in *Glastonbury Bulletin* 113 (2006): 213–220. For the letter of the Abune Antonios to the Holy Synod after his removal from the position of the Patriarch see ibid., 216–218.For the current information about Patriarch Antonios and activities see: http://www.abuneantonios.com

[30] "The Eritrean Church," in *Standing Conference of Oriental Orthodox Churches in America.* http://www.scooch.org/member-churches/the-eritrean-church/

[31] Cf. *Letter of the Director of Commission of the Churches on International Affairs of the WCC to Mr Ali Ali Abdu, Minister of Information and Culture of Eritrea from 23 June,2003.* http://www.oikoumene.org/en/resources/documents/wcc-commissions/international-affairs/regional-concerns/africa/religious-freedom-and-liberty-in-eritrea

[32] "Letter to the Secretary-General of the United Nations Ban Ki-moon" (18 May 2013), in *Eritrean Orthodox Diocese of North America.* http://tewahdo.org/Pdf/Letter_051813-English.pdf

Part VI: Ecumenical Perspectives of Oriental Orthodox Churches

Bibliography

1. "Protocol between the Coptic Orthodox Church (COC) and the Eritrean Orthodox Church (EOC)," in Martin Tamcke (Ed.), *Daheim und in der Fremde. Beiträge zur jüngeren Geschichte und Gegenwartslage der orientalischen Christen*, (Hamburg, 2002), 266–275.

2. Joachim G. Persoon, "The spiritual Legacy of the Ethio-Eritrean Conflict," in *Journal of Eastern Christian Studies* 57 (2005): 291–315.

3. Wolfgang Hage, "Die Eritreisch-Orthodoxe Kirche," in *Das orientalische Christentum* (Stuttgart, 2007), 222–226.

4. Kefelew Zelleke – Friedrich Heyer, *Das orthodoxe Äthiopien und Eritrea in jüngster Geschichte*, (Aachen, 2001), 153–172.

5. Friedrich Heyer, "Die Einwirkung des koptischen Patriarchats auf die Gründung des orthodoxen Patriarchats von Eritrea," in Martin Tamcke (Ed.), *Daheim und in der Fremde. Beiträge zur jüngeren Geschichte und Gegenwartslage der orientalischen Christen*, (Hamburg, 2002), 252–259.

6. Wolfram Reiss, "Vereinbarung zwischen der Koptisch-Orthodoxen und der Eritreisch-Orthodoxen Kirche," in Martin Tamcke (Ed.), *Daheim und in der Fremde. Beiträge zur jüngeren Geschichte und Gegenwartslage der orientalischen Christen*, (Hamburg, 2002), 261–265.

7. Ernst Christoph Suttner, "Eritreas Eigenstaatlichkeit und die Kirchen," in *Una Sancta* 49 (1994): 106–124.

PART VII

PARTICULAR THEMES AND ISSUES
FOR ORTHODOX INVOLVEMENT IN ECUMENISM

(93) COMMON PRAYER AS AN ISSUE FOR ORTHODOX INVOLVEMENT IN ECUMENISM, ACCORDING TO THE CANON LAW[1]

Vlassios Pheidas

I. The Issue of Common Prayer in the Dialogue for the Unity of Christians

The issue of the participation of Orthodox clergy and laity in prayers with the heterodox is an inevitable consequence of the official decision of the Orthodox Church to take part, through the representatives of local Orthodox Churches, in the institutional organs and activities of the modern Ecumenical movement for the unity of Christians. This participation was approved on the initiative of the Ecumenical Patriarchate, *after lengthy discussions and on specific terms,* in order to serve clear ecclesiastical needs which became increasingly pressing because of the systematic or even violent questioning of the institutional role or spiritual mission of the Church, not only by secular ideology but also by the dynastic authority wielded by the state in the mainly Christian world.

So the participation of the Orthodox Church in the foundation, in 1948, of the *World Council of Churches* (WCC), as an organization for the coordination of cooperation of Christian Churches and Confessions in the face of a common attack on the whole of the Christian world, was not only beneficial but also a visionary initiative of the Ecumenical Patriarchate for the support of those Orthodox Churches which were then in dire straits.

Of course, the Ecumenical Patriarchate set *specific ecclesiological conditions* for the participation of the Orthodox Church in the WCC, which were included in its constitution, but the understanding of these conditions was dependent on the different ecclesiastical assumptions of the Orthodox Churches and the Protestant Confessions, which is why, in 1952, Patriarch Athenagoras, in a strictly-worded Patriarchal encyclical, clarified the *Orthodox criteria* for its participation, as these were set out in the famous Toronto Statement (1950). However, after the General Assembly of the WCC in New Delhi (1961), there was a change in the procedure for the *preparation and acceptance of joint texts*, while the cancellation of *separate Statements* from the Orthodox caused turmoil: on the one hand because of the indirect adoption of the *principle of the majority* in theological issues was unacceptable to the Orthodox; and, on the other, because the Orthodox proposals were mixed in with those of the Protestants as regards the *summaries* or *ambiguous theological terminology* of the joint texts. The Third Pre-Conciliar Pan-Orthodox Conference (1986), through a unanimous Pan-Orthodox resolution, made any further participation by the Orthodox Church in the Ecumenical movement contingent upon a radical reappraisal of the constitution of the WCC to reflect the Orthodox proposals. In the end, the question was brought before a *Special Committee*, consisting of equal numbers of representatives of the Orthodox Church and the WCC. The unanimous decisions of the Committee regarding the implementation of the *principle of unanimity* for the agreement of joint texts and for the *establishment of stricter theological and ecclesiological criteria* for the acceptance of new members were embodied in the Constitution by a unanimous decision of the General Assembly at Porto Alegre (2006) and allowed for positive prospects for the independent witness of Orthodoxy in the ecumenical dialogue on Christian unity.

The issue of *the Orthodox representatives praying together with the heterodox* at their ecumenical meetings was no more than a marginal problem in the participation of the Orthodox Church in the WCC, because it was felt to be a reasonable consequence of the dialogue. But it gained special significance after the collapse of the totalitarian regimes of existential socialism among the Orthodox peoples of Eastern Europe in the last decade of the previous century and the provocative development there of undesirable proselytizing activities,

---

[1] A full version of the present text was initially published in *Episkepsis*, no. 699 (30.04.2009) 11-33. Here it is re-published with the necessary adjustments (ed.).

on the part of both the Papal Uniates and of Protestant missionaries, which chafed the wounds of the past and struck a severe blow at the credibility of the Ecumenical movement. The challenge to the traditional spiritual relationship between the Orthodox Church and the suffering Orthodox peoples, as well as the characterization of Eastern Europe as "*terrae missionis*," for the re-evangelizing of the peoples there, presented conservative circles within Orthodoxy with the opportunity to voice sharp criticism against the Church hierarchy, both for its participation in the WCC and also for its collaboration with the Communist regimes.

It therefore escaped no one's attention that, in the last decade of the 20th century, the reason why the issue of common prayer with the heterodox at the multi- and bilateral theological dialogues of the Ecumenical movement was systematically raised was because of the unfraternal and assertive proselytizing activity of the heterodox to the detriment of the suffering Orthodox peoples. The opposition, however, is evidently inconsistent: on the one hand, as regards the decades-long, unreserved acceptance or tolerance of the established practice of common prayer, despite the supposedly serious canonical reasons for avoiding it; and, on the other, as regards the long-observed ecclesiastical practice of evaluating canonical issues with pastoral criteria, even if it is becoming increasingly clear that opposition to common prayer is directed mainly at the WCC and not to bilateral theological dialogues. Nevertheless, regardless of any assessment of this or that approach to the issue of praying in common with the heterodox, the *question of the true meaning* of the sacred canons quoted has always been, and remains, *the sole authentic criterion*, for the avoidance or deterrence of dangerous agitation on this issue which is crucial to the relations of the Orthodox Church with the heterodox.

II. The True Meaning of the Sacred Canons.

The fundamental principle in the investigation of the *true meaning* of one or more similar sacred canons is, on the one hand, *the precise grammatical interpretation* of the text transmitted, and on the other, the *consistent referral of its spirit* to the specific ecclesiastical problems of the particular time, because it is only in this way that the will of the sacred canons expresses the indissoluble pastoral connection between the solution proposed and the particular problem it addresses. Thus, the canons dealing with the problem of Orthodox praying with heretics cannot be understood, much less interpreted in their true dimensions, without a clear reference to the dangers which existed in the 4th century as regards the unity of the Church. These were:

First, the non-acceptance of the Nicene creed by the Arian-orientated bishops and clergy, who succeeded, through the support of like-minded emperors, both in exerting a decisive influence on Church affairs until the convocation of the Second Ecumenical Council (381) and in oppressing the Orthodox bishops.

Second, the *fragmentation of the Arians* after 341 into opposing groups which each developed its own hierarchy, at least in the major cities, and competed with one another, with the willing assistance of the authority of the state, both for the removal of the Orthodox bishops from these cities as well as for the control of the main churches.

Third, the *co-existence in the same city, of Arian bishops and of the main churches under their control* for the celebration of the divine liturgy for one and all (*Orthodox and Arians*), concerning which the Arians, on the one hand, restricted the protestations of the Orthodox parish clergy to a minimum, and, on the other, imposed common attendance of Orthodox and Arian clergy, to the obvious confusion of the ordinary Orthodox believers, who made up the overwhelming majority of the ecclesiastical body.

Fourth, the *complaisant* or even *compromising* attitude towards the Arian bishops on the part of certain Orthodox bishops, either because they were afraid of the well-known, harsh measures that the state might take against them (*deposition, exile*), or because they were unable to understand the theological profundity of the heretical aberration of the Arians, or because of both of these. They therefore tolerated *common attendance* or even *concelebration* between the Orthodox and Arians at the Orthodox liturgy and vice versa.

Fifth, the *exploitation by Arian bishops of the participation of Orthodox* clergy and laity in divine worship as celebrated by these bishops, especially at times of long absence of the Orthodox bishops due to exile, so that it could be claimed that the Orthodox flock was converting to the Arian heresy or, at least abandoning the

Nicene creed. This would have been to the obvious satisfaction of the declared opponents of this creed, the Arian emperors (Constantius and Valens).

Sixth, the urgent requirement *for an official ecclesiastical condemnation* of the transfer of the theological clashes between supporters and opponents of the Nicene creed to the sacred sphere of the celebration of the sacrament of the Divine Eucharist, because this transfer caused turmoil among ordinary Orthodox believers, with obvious and dangerous damage to the unity of the ecclesiastical body in the communion of the faith and in the association of love.

So the critical question *concerning the meaning of the prohibition by the sacred canons on common prayer with the heterodox and schismatics in relation to today's ecclesiastical reality* obviously has to do with our contemporary *appropriation* and *misappropriation* of certain canons which are used *indiscriminately*, or even *injudiciously* by some ecclesiastical circles in order to aim criticism at the Church hierarchy, under the pretext, indeed, of protecting endangered Orthodoxy from its participation in the Ecumenical movement or from the initiatives for the promotion of a constructive spirit in the way inter-Church relations are handled. The canons which refer directly or indirectly to this issue are numerous and cover a wide spectrum of pastoral matters, in order to prevent or counteract any enticement of the Orthodox faithful by the heterodox. In particular, however, regarding the specific question of common prayer with heterodox and schismatics, the 45th Apostolic canon and canon 33 of the Synod in Laodicea (4th c.) are quoted, because, on the basis of these, similar sacred canons referring indirectly to the issue are evaluated.

The 45th Apostolic canon declares that: "*Any bishop or priest or deacon who merely prays with heretics is to be excluded from communion, but if he permits them to act as clergy, he is to be deposed.*" Canon 33 of Laodicea states that: "*It is not permitted to pray with heretics or schismatics.*" In this sense, the correct interpretation of the holy canons requires a correct interpretation of the verb "to pray with," because the Apostolic canon makes the distinction between *praying with heretics* and *affording them the opportunity to celebrate* and it accompanies this distinction with a differentiation in the punishment in each of these cases: *exclusion from communion*, in the first and *defrocking* in the second. Therefore the verb *to pray with* refers to two different instances, either to mere common prayer or to concelebration, because in the second case, the proposed punishment is clearly more severe. Thus the eminent canonist Theodoros Valsamon, in his comment on this canon, although he expresses an unjustified, personal supposition regarding the purpose of the canon, correctly remarks on the multiple use of the verb *to pray with*, which is apparent from the different ecclesiastical punishments which are envisaged: *To the question why those bishops, priests and deacons who pray with heretics are not deposed, but merely excluded from communion, as is someone praying with such a person, according the 10th Apostolic canon. Answer: Here it does not mean that the bishop and the others pray* (i.e. concelebrate) *with heretics, because such are deposed, according to canon 66, as allowing them to act as clergy. But let it be taken to mean simply participating in and reciting at the prayer of the heretic* (participation in prayer) ..." G.Rallis-M. Potlis, *Constitution* II, 60).

The eminent canonist's reference to the 10th and 46th Apostolic canons was the foundation for the proposed distinction between the uses of the verb *to pray with*. The 10th Apostolic canon states that "*if anyone prays with someone excluded from communion, even in a house* (= not in a church), *let him be excluded also*"; while the related canon 11 declares: "*If any cleric joins in prayer with a deposed clergyman, as if he were a clergyman, let him also be deposed.*" The prominent canonist Ioannis Zonaras, in his comment on canon 10, notes that "*one should not communicate with these* (= who are excluded from communion), *for this would be contempt for the person who imposed the exclusion or even an implication that he had wrongly imposed it,*" while Theodoros Valsamon adds that "*we do not prevent conversation with those excluded from communion* (op. cit. II, 14). The comment on canon 11 broadens the circle of distinctions in the use of the verb *pray with*, because of the differences which arose in the understanding of the purpose of the canon. Thus, Ioannis Zonaras observes that: "*some of those who are deposed are prevented only from celebrating, not from taking communion or attending church, while others are deposed, not given communion and excluded from communion. Therefore if this canon refers to those deposed and excluded, let anyone praying with such also be under deposition, if praying together is understood rather than concelebrating. If not, and the person deposed is not also excluded, anyone concelebrating with him shall be deposed.*" Strangely, Valsamon does not take *praying together* as *concelebrating* and stresses that "*Some take praying together here as concelebrating, but it does not seem so to me... My understanding is that the aim in this canon is to chastise any cleric who prays with any cleric who has been deposed and, after deposition, continues to celebrate, which is why deposition is entailed for the former...*"

So the disagreement between the two eminent Byzantine canonists concerning the *true meaning* of the liturgical use of the verb *pray with* in the prohibition of common prayer with a deposed Orthodox cleric makes the *true canonical meaning* of the prohibition clearer. Zonaras' dilemma is rhetorical, because it is clear from the whole structure of the 11th Apostolic canon that the more correct choice is "*if praying together is understood rather than concelebrating and the person deposed is not also excluded, anyone concelebrating with him shall be deposed.*" Valsamon's stance on the above interpretation is less than scrupulous, because he introduces into the text of the canon a non-existent element concerning the deposed clergy (*after deposition, continues to celebrate*) and draws the baseless, subjective conclusion that "*the aim in this canon is to chastise any cleric who prays with any cleric who has been deposed,*" even though he knew that "*praying with*" a deposed clergyman was punishable in general only in the event that that the latter actually celebrated, because concelebrating was the reason for the punishment, not that the cleric who had been deposed had previously celebrated. So the real meaning of the canon associates "*praying with*" with "*concelebrating*" and is rendered fully by the succinct comment by Alexios Aristinos, that "*let anyone who prays with, that is concelebrates, with someone one has been deposed be deposed himself*" (Constitution, II, 15).

Focus on the reference to the *prohibition of "praying together"* in the Divine Liturgy is understandable, because all the services were linked to it, and, in the fourth century it was the same for the Orthodox and the heretics. The heretics were constantly pressing the Orthodox clergy for *common attendance* or even *concelebration*, in order to lead astray the ordinary believers. So the recourse to the comment by Valsamon on the 45th Apostolic canon is also important. This canon states that: "*we decree that any bishop or priest who accepts the baptism or sacrifice of heretics shall be deposed.*" This canon has been invoked to support the position that anyone "*praying with heretics in church*" is concelebrating with them, which is why the punishment of deposition is ordained. So if any bishop or priest arbitrarily consents to or participates in baptism or the Divine Eucharist (= sacrifice) by heretics for Orthodox faithful, in clear contempt of the established canonical order, the punishment is that he should be deposed for concelebrating with heretics. In his comment on this canon, Zonaras observes that "*should a bishop or priest receive someone baptized by them* (heretics) *or accept anyone brought by them to the sacrifice offered, he shall be deposed, either for giving the impression that he considers himself the same as them or for not hastening to correct their mistaken belief...*" (op. cit. II, 61). It is therefore obvious that the 45th and other relevant Apostolic canons always link "*praying with*" with the *concelebration* of Orthodox clerics and those of the heretics, because they condemn any such arbitrary action on the part of an Orthodox cleric as "*either for giving the impression that he considers himself the same as them or for not hastening to correct their mistaken belief....*"

Indeed, through their prohibition of *concelebration* with the heretics or the *acceptance of baptism performed by them*, the apostolic canons, on the one hand condemn any arbitrary action on the part of Orthodox clerics and on the other refer to heretics specifically recognized by the Church and who unrepentantly persist in their heresy. It is in this sense that canon 6 of Laodicea forbids "*the heretics to enter into the house of God, persisting in heresy.*" This prohibition, of course, refers to entry by the heretics into an Orthodox church, because Valsamon emphasizes that: "*the canon clearly does not permit heretics who persist in their heresy to attend church with the Orthodox*" (op. cit., III, 176). It follows that the canon forbids the attendance of those who persist in their heresy at the celebration of the Divine Liturgy. Canon 9 of Laodicea forbids the Orthodox to go to the *martyria* of heretics "*either to pray or for healing,*" that is to take part in the liturgy celebrated by them, though not, according to Valsamon, if they go "*to an assembly of heretics in order to spit upon it*" (ibid. III, 177-8). Canon 13 of Laodicea ("*That it is not permitted to pray with heretics or schismatics*") forbids *concelebration* or *common attendance,* in accordance with the spirit of the 45th Apostolic canon and is to be interpreted in conjunction with canons 31 and 32 of the same synod. Canon 31 forbids the Orthodox "*to marry any heretic or to give their sons or daughters, but only to accept them if they promise to become Christians*," whereas canon 32 forbids the Orthodox "*to receive the benedictions of heretics, which are mere mouthings rather than blessings,*" within the context, naturally, of heretical liturgical assemblies. It is therefore clear that the above canons used the verb "*pray together*" in the sense of "*concelebrate*" or "*attend church with*" in connection with officially recognized heretics, *who persist stubbornly and rigidly in their heresy,* and that these canons condemn any arbitrary activity on the part of Orthodox clerics or any ill-considered actions by the Orthodox faithful.

Therefore the true meaning of the above canon refers only to the obvious and self-evident *prohibition on concelebration* for Orthodox clergy with the heterodox, and not, of course, to *participation* in any other prayer. In this sense, all the eminent Byzantine commentators on the sacred canons mentioned above, as well as Saint Nikodimos in the *Rudder (Pedalion),* in his own commentary on the 45th Apostolic canon, specifically state their *agreement* with the 9th canon of Archbishop Timotheos of Alexandria, who expresses with the greatest possible clarity the *authentic meaning of the prohibition* in the relevant canons on *praying together* with heretics and even more so with schismatics: "Question nine: Should a cleric pray in the presence of Arians or other heretics, or does it do no harm when he makes the prayer, that is the offering? Answer: At the divine anaphora, the deacon proclaims, before the embrace, that those outside communion should leave. So they should not remain, unless they declare their repentance and rejection of the heresy." It follows that Arians and other heretics were allowed to be present at a liturgy celebrated by an Orthodox cleric, at least *until the embrace, while if they declare their repentance and rejection of the heresy, they could stay through the divine anaphora,* this is for the whole of the divine liturgy, though not of course be admitted as concelebrants or to holy communion.

Because he was of the opinion that "*we should hate heretics and turn away*" and not "*pray with*" them, Saint Nikodimos the Athonite *does not give the correct sense to the commentary on canon 9* by Timotheos. He *extends the condition of repentance on the part of the heretics to their participation even in the first part of the liturgy* because he also claimed, without substantiation, a general prohibition, that is, "*that the ninth canon of Timotheos does not permit heretics to be present at the time of the divine liturgy unless they promise to repent and abandon the heresy.*" It is clear that, with this view, Saint Nikodimos misinterprets or does not render the real meaning of the Archbishop of Alexandria's answer, through which the presence *of Arians and other heretics* at the Divine Liturgy is equated with that of *catechumens* or *penitents* that is those who have not yet the right to take communion. The full answer addressed the double question of whether: a) heretics could be present at the celebration of an Orthodox divine liturgy; and b) the specific issue of their presence at the sacramental part of the service ("Should a cleric pray in the presence of Arians or other heretics, or does it do no harm when he makes the prayer, that is the offering?").

The response of the Archbishop of Alexandria to the general question of the presence of heretics is given through the established ecclesiastical practice regarding all those outside communion (catechumens and penitents), which was that they could remain until the *embrace of love.* The specific issue of their continued presence at the celebration of the Divine Eucharist imposes the condition that the heretics could remain even after the embrace of love that is until the end of the liturgy, *if they declared their repentance and rejected their heresy,* in which case this "*did no harm.*" But the condition imposed (*if they declared*) clearly intimates a prior discussion with the heretics and an agreement during this dialogue for their return to the Church community, *because otherwise the distinction would be impossible.* Thus, according to the true interpretation of canon 9 by Timotheos of Alexandria, heretics were allowed *to attend church* with the Orthodox at the celebration of the divine liturgy for *the first part,* until the embrace, without any particular restrictions, and could remain for the *second part,* after the embrace, only on condition that they promised to show remorse for their heretical aberration. So if it *does no harm* for Orthodox and heretics to attend church together for part of the divine liturgy, how much *less harm does it do* for them to pray together at the theological dialogue for the unification of Christians which is being conducted today?

Part VII: Particular Themes and Issues for Orthodox Involvement in Ecumenism

III. The Church's interpretation of the sacred canons

On the basis of what has been said above, it has always been the practice of the Church that the 45th apostolic canon and canon 33 of Laodicea *were always applied only to prohibit Orthodox clerics from concelebrating with the heterodox*, because this is opposed to Orthodox ecclesiology. But *they were not applied to the presence of Orthodox* at heterodox services or to heterodox at those of the Orthodox, nor to *common prayer* for the unity of Christians in inter-Church encounters concerning the unity of the ecclesiastical body. Besides, at the period of the persecutions, the very participation of catechumens, or those who had lapsed, in the first part of the divine liturgy, at the various stages of their catechesis or repentance (canons 11, 12, 13, 14 of the 1st Ecumenical Council etc.) is sufficient confirmation of what was said above, because even those who invoke the 45th Apostolic canon are forced *to arbitrarily characterize as "concelebration" even the mere presence of Orthodox clerics at heterodox services*. Hence, according to the 9th canon of Timothy of Alexandria, *the sacred canons of the Synod in Carthage (419) concerning the dialogue with the Donatists are to be applied completely and at all times*. These canons express the enduring spirit of the Orthodox canonical tradition regarding all dialogue with the heterodox.

Thus, canon 66 states: "when all things had been considered and contemplated which seem conducive to the advantage of the church, with the Spirit of God guiding and admonishing us, we decided to act leniently and pacifically towards the people mentioned above [=Donatists], although they are cut off from the unity of the Lord's body by an unruly dissent, so that (as far as we can) it may become known to all those who have been caught in the net of their communion and society, throughout all the provinces of Africa, that they have been overcome by miserable error. Perhaps, as the Apostle says [*II Tim*. 2, 25], when we have corrected with gentleness those who hold different views, God will grant them repentance, so that they come to know the truth…" The response to this invitation on the part of the Donatists presupposed, on the one hand, a constructive theological dialogue on the documented theological differences, and, on the other, in the event of agreement being reached, the revocation of the old decision of the Synod of Carthage (251), which called the baptism, ordination and other sacraments of the Donatists *invalid*. This is why, instead of canonical exactitude, the Synod preferred the principle of *ecclesiastical flexibility* in order to encourage the return of those people to the bosom of the Church.

In this spirit, canon 57 of the synod states that: "those who as children were baptized by the Donatists, and not yet being able to know the disastrous nature of their error, and who afterwards, when they had come to the use of reason, had realized the truth, abhorred their former error, and were received, (in accordance with the ancient order) by the laying on of the hand, into the universal Church of God, which is spread throughout the world, for such men, recalling their error ought to be no impediment to the clerical office since they thought their own was the true Church to be their own... And it is not right to repeat that which should be given only once. If they have renounced the name of their former error, let them be received through the laying on of hands into the one Church… in which all these sacraments are received unto salvation and everlasting life; while the same sacraments obtain the heavy penalty of damnation for those who persist in heresy. So that which to those who are in the truth lightens to the obtaining of eternal life, the same to them who are in error brings darkness and damnation. With regard then to those who, having fled from error, acknowledge the correct teachings of their mother the universal Church, who believe and receive all these holy mysteries through the filter of the truth, and who have the testimony of a good life, they may certainly be raised to the clerical office, especially in such necessity as the present. There is no one who would not grant this…" Thus the synod, through canon 68, empowered individual bishops to accept clerics coming into the Church from the Donatists "in their own honours, if this appears to contribute to the peace of Christians…, so that there may be no rupture of unity over them…"

It is clear that, through these Synodal decisions, a proposal was being engineered for a constructive theological dialogue between the Church of North Africa and the Donatists, with a view to the removal of the reasons which had caused their secession. Canon 92 of the synod defines the *form*, the *manner* and the *aim* of the dialogue: "Sent by the authority of our universal synod, we have called you together, desiring to rejoice in your correction. For we bear in mind the love of the Lord who said: Blessed are the peacemakers, for they shall be called the children of God; and moreover he admonished through the prophet that we ought to say even to those who say they are not our brothers: You are our brethren. Therefore you ought not to despise this peaceful recollection which comes out of love, so that if you realize we have any part of the truth, you will not hesitate to say so: that is, when your synod is gathered together, you delegate certain of your number to whom you entrust the statement of your case, as we also will be able to do, so that those appointed by our synod, together with those delegated by you, may examine peacefully, at a determined place and time, whatever question there is which separates your communion from us; and that in the end, by the assistance of the Lord God, the old error may be brought to an end, lest through the stubbornness of people, weak souls, and inexperienced people should perish by sacrilegious division. If you accept this in a fraternal spirit, the truth will easily shine forth, but if you are not willing to do this, your distrust will be known." The Donatists, however, rejected the proposal for peaceful dialogue and engaged in violence against the Orthodox, and so the Synod in Carthage requested the intervention of the Emperor of the West, Honorius, in order to have the Edict of Theodosius the Great (380) enforced and for pressure to be brought to bear to make them enter into dialogue for the restoration of the unity of the Church in North Africa (canon 63).

Of course, the canons of the Synod in Carthage did not restrict the *ecclesiastical flexibility* merely to the recognition of the baptism and ordination of those Donatists returning to the bosom of the Church, because the Synodal proposal for a constructive dialogue on the reasons which caused the "*division*" involved an authorization for a discussion of other theological differences, which would lead to the achievement of the desired agreement. Thus, although Basil the Great did not accept the indiscriminate application of ecclesiastical flexibility for the recognition of the baptism of heretic *penitents* (canons 1 and 47) nevertheless, to the proposal for a constructive dialogue with moderate Arians, the Pneumatomachians, he extended, as the *least theological basis* for their acceptance into the community of the Church that they should not reject the *Nicene Creed* and should avoid calling the *Holy Spirit a creation*, in the sure hope that their other theological weaknesses would be cured within the community of the Church: "Let us then seek no more than this, but propose the Nicene Creed to all the brethren who are willing to join us. If they agree to that, let us further require that the Holy Spirit ought not to be called a creation, nor any of those who say so be received into communion. I do not think that we ought to insist upon anything beyond this. For it is my conviction that that by longer communication and mutual experience without strife, if anything more requires to be added by way of explanation, the Lord, Who works all things together for the good of those who love Him, will grant it" (Letter 113). The total consistency between the proposals of Basil the Great for the Pneumatomachians and those of the Synod of Carthage (419) concerning the Donatists is particularly significant, because it confirms that, in the case of constructive dialogue about the unity of the Church, the strict criteria of the canonical tradition can be relaxed, so that the maternal affection of the Church can function.

Thus, Basil calls the Pneumatomachians "brethren," while the synod in Carthage insists on according the appellation of "brethren" to the Donatists "even those who do not wish to be called our brethren" (canon 92), because the Church, as the mother of all Christians never abandons its errant children, which is why it prays "*for the union of all*." Saint Basil, in particular, was slandered by zealot monks in Cappadocia as being a *crypto-Pneumatomachian*, not only because of his previous spiritual relationship with the later head of the Pneumatomachians, Efstathios of Sevastia, but also because of the vague terminology of his teaching regarding the Holy Spirit. The zealot monks persisted in the slander against Saint Basil, despite the robust defence offered for him by Saint Gregory the Theologian, as regards both his unblemished Orthodox faith and his beneficial pastoral concern for the errant members of the body of the Church (Letter 58). These slurs even reached Athanasios the Great, who, in his letters to those clerics and monks who condemned Basil in writing, does not merely reject the slanders but praises the person of Basil and his efforts to find solutions necessary for the restoration of the unity of the Church, even if these efforts also involved *censorious epistolatory exhortations* to the powerful Archbishop of Alexandria regarding his passive or even injudicious attitude towards the Antiochean schism (362-398), which split the whole Church.

Part VII: Particular Themes and Issues for Orthodox Involvement in Ecumenism

According to Athanasios, the *ecclesiastical flexibility* ("economy") applied by Basil towards the Pneumatomachians was praiseworthy, not blameworthy, because it expressed the *sublime sense of his pastoral responsibility* towards the separated members of the body of the Church, an attitude which was not understood or correctly interpreted by his critics, the clerics and monks who wanted *an excuse to upset the pure* (PG 26, 1165). Thus, in writing to the priest Palladius, he stresses, with proper emphasis: "Since you have also told me of the monks at Cæsarea, and I have learned from our beloved Dianios that they are vexed, and are opposing our beloved Basil, the bishop. I welcome what you have told me, and I have pointed out to them their duty: that as children they should obey their father and not oppose what he approves. Now if he were to be suspected as regards the truth, they would be right to combat him. But if they are confident, as we all are, that he is the boast of the Church, contending rather on behalf of the truth and teaching those who require it [the Pneumatomachians], then it is not right to combat such a one, but rather to accept his good conscience. For from what our beloved Dianios tells us, they appear to be vexed in vain. For I am confident, that to the weak he has become weak to win over the weak. Let our beloved friends look at the aim and far-sightedness of his truth and glorify the Lord Who has given such a bishop to Cappadocia as any district must pray to have..." (PG 26, 1168-1169). Athanasios' words towards those zealot monks of Cappadocia who are fighting against are harsher: "I have been astonished at the audacity of those who dare to speak against our beloved bishop Basil, the true servant of God [or "the servant of the true God," the Greek, unusually, can be read both ways]. For this recklessness, they can be chastised as never having loved the confession of the Fathers..." (PG 26, 1168).

So the injudicious, condemnatory haste of the zealot monks, who "appear to be vexed in vain" as regards flexibility, as exercised by the Church authority responsible, towards those who had broken away from the unity of the Church body, risks being characterized as *irresponsible reckless speech* and also as *contempt for the example* of the recognized Fathers of the Church. On the basis of the above, it may clearly be concluded that the true meaning of the prohibition of the Orthodox praying with the heterodox, according to the 45th Apostolic canon, canon 33 of the Synod in Laodicea and other relevant sacred canons, on the one hand, expresses the beneficial pastoral concern of the Church as regards counteracting the undesirable methods of the heretics, applied to the detriment of the Orthodox faithful in the 4th century; and on the other, it does not have the meaning- wrongly attributed to them- of a general prohibition on all prayer in common with the heterodox, because both the letter and the spirit state [that this applied]:

First, only to the divine liturgy, which in the 4th century was one and the same for Orthodox and heretics and was the main service of the latter in their separate assemblies which had broken away from the body of the Church,

Second, only to concelebration of Orthodox clergy with those of the heretics at the Divine Liturgy, which was forbidden for serious ecclesiological reasons.

Third, the participation and even more so the communion of the Orthodox faithful in the divine liturgy celebrated by heretic clerics, and vice versa, which was forbidden for the same ecclesiological reasons.

Fourth, only to the attendance of heretics in the Orthodox Divine Liturgy after the embrace of love, *that is during the celebration of the sacrament of the Divine Eucharist*, unless their wish was accompanied by an express desire to return to the communion of the Church.

Fifth, the free attendance of both heretics and Orthodox together in the *first part of the liturgy*, that is until the embrace of love, according to the model of the participation of catechumens or penitents, in the hope that they (the heretics) would be encouraged to return to the bosom of the Church.

Sixth, the unbiased application of these canonical criteria in ecclesiastical practice over time, regarding any initiative for a dialogue aimed at the restoration of the unity of the Church, which, obviously, always involves common prayer on the part of the representatives of the Churches engaged in the talks.

Seven, the consistent application of these criteria to today's ecumenical dialogue concerning the unity of Christians, both as regards the strict prohibition on *concelebration* with the heterodox, as well as the unrestricted *participation in common prayer* for unity or *in the services* of the Churches conducting the official dialogue, in order to support or supplement these prospects, and

Eighth, the clear opposition to the scrupulous or unscrupulous interpretations regarding a supposed general prohibition on all common prayer with the heterodox, in order to demonstrate the true meaning of the sacred canons quoted, the letter of which is vague, but the spirit of which is clear: they do not merely tolerate but actively encourage common prayer to support the express inclination towards a constructive theological dialogue on the unity of the body of the Church.

It is therefore clear that the *canonical treatment* of the question was demanded by the responsibility for *consistent attention to the unity of the Church*: on the one hand, because the participation of those outside the ecclesiastical community (catechumens, penitents, schismatics and heretics) *in the first part of the divine liturgy*, that is until the embrace of love, was always encouraged by the Church in order to reinforce their express or potential inclination to be received into it; and on the other, because the participation of heretics *in the second part of the divine liturgy*, that is the sacrament of the Divine Eucharist, was allowed in the event that they declared that they wished to return to communion with the Orthodox Church. This perspective is highly relevant today as regards the bilateral and multilateral theological dialogues with the heterodox of the contemporary Ecumenical movement, because the real meaning of the sacred canons clearly covers *the life of worship* of the Churches involved in the dialogue, especially during the official meetings of the theological committees, not only because "*it does no harm*," but because *attendance at the Orthodox divine liturgy* greatly reinforces the desire of those people to participate also in the common Cup. So the feigned circumspection regarding this prospect is at odds not only with the real aim of the wording of the sacred canons, but also with the contemporary mission of the Orthodox Church, which is bound to offer freely a genuine account of the Orthodox tradition to anyone who asks. The idea and criterion behind this attitude is that the unity of the body of the Church, with all the positive consequences that this entails, is more likely to be achieved through the shining light of the Christian message in the modern world.

IV. The Temporality and Contemporality of the Sacred Canons

As the source of the sacred canons, then, the Church cannot be either the *subject* nor *object* of them, since all the sacred canons have as their object the members of the Church- clergy, laity and monastics- and as their purpose the functional cohesion of the body of the Church through the strict or lenient implementation of the spirit of the canons, as required. Indeed, despite the strictness of the Apostolic canons and of those of the Synod in Laodicea, the Church, in its relations with the heterodox, always applied the principle of *ecclesiastical flexibility* as appropriate to each case where heretics or schismatics were returning to its bosom, when it always recognized baptism as *valid*, even of those recognized by Ecumenical Council as heretics (canons 7 of the Second and 95 of the Quinisext Ecumenical Council), despite the fact that the 46th, 47th and 49th Apostolic canons reject all baptism by heretics as non-existent.

The relations of the Church towards those ecclesiastical bodies which had taken shape outside its confines were always assessed by reference to baptism and functioned always in relation to the sacrament of the *divine Eucharist*, that is the sacraments par excellence of the unity and community of the members of the body of the Church towards each other and towards the divine Head of the Church. As a rule, the graduation of the status of the baptism performed by those outside the Church (*non-existent, valid*, and *active*) defined not only the way the nomenclature applied with reference to the Church (*heresy, schism, rival assembly*), but also the *manner* in which they were to return to the ecclesiastical community (*rebaptism, re-chrismation, certificate of faith*). In this way, the status of the baptism performed by them was dealt with by the Church, on the one hand, at the time of their rupture from the whole body of the Church, through the strict application of the principle of *canonical exactitude*, in order to prevent the members of the Church from being lead astray (*invalid* or even *non-existent*); but, on the other hand, at the time of their return to the bosom of the Church, through the lenient application of the principle of *ecclesiastical flexibility*, which facilitated the restoration of the unity of the body of the Church (*existent* and *valid*).

Indeed, in the 4th century, *the divine liturgy was always one and the same, though the celebrants often changed*, depending on the preference of the Arianizing emperors who imposed on the local Churches bishops who were of the same mind as themselves, and other clergy, deposed or not, for example, bishops who were supporters of Arius and Arius himself. As a result, the strict *prohibition on the concelebration of Orthodox with heretics* was ignored, not only by the ordinary faithful but also by Orthodox clerics who, as we have seen, submitted to the pressures of the pro-Arian policies of the emperor and the administrative machine of the empire. So the prohibition of the 45th Apostolic canon on Orthodox clergy "*praying together*" with heretics or allowing heretical clergy to carry out priestly actions in a clearly Orthodox church also included the prohibition on the performance of these actions by Orthodox clergy in the churches of the heretics, because the multiple fracturing of the body of the Church into many heretical groups with parallel hierarchies was accompanied by the violent takeover of churches, which is why the Orthodox of Constantinople did not have their own church to worship in at the time when Saint Gregory the Theologian moved into the city (379).

The all-powerful heretics, then, supported by the machinery of state authority, concentrated their proselytizing propaganda on the [Orthodox] churches and services, which made it necessary [for the Orthodox] to focus their *pastoral concern* on making more evident their disparagement of the churches and services of the heretics. It is worth noting, however, that the removal of churches from the control of those who persisted in their heretical views, in accordance with the implementation of the edict of Theodosios the Great (380)- which imposed the Nicene Creed- and the subsequent transfer of these churches to the Orthodox, completely undermined the support of the heretics. Thus, once the churches had been returned to the Orthodox, the strict pastoral criteria of the canonical exactitude of the Apostolic canons and those of the Synod in Laodicea concerning the validity of baptism and relations with heretics were replaced by the more lenient canonical criteria of ecclesiastical flexibility, in order to facilitate the return to the bosom of the Church of the now weakened heretics. This can readily be understood from the lenient criteria expressed in canon 7 of the 2nd Ecumenical Synod (381).

In this sense, the 45th Apostolic canon and canon 33 of Laodicea have no more than a comparative significance for the contemporary question of the relations between the Orthodox Church and the Ecumenical movement for the unity of Christians, and then only in the matter of *concelebration*, which is why these canons are applied today *in accordance with their clear spirit and not of course, with their unclear letter.*

In the first place, they refer to *heretics officially recognized by the Church*, whereas the Roman Catholics, the Old Catholics, the Anglicans and the Protestants have not been condemned as heretics by the Orthodox Church through an official act, in an obvious example of the principle of ecclesiastical flexibility and in the hope of their restoration to the Church community. It is therefore baseless to call them heretics, as some people do, because *only the Church, through an official act, can declare Christian bodies outside its bounds to be heretical or schismatic.*

Second, they condemned *arbitrary, unilateral actions* on the part of certain bishops and priests as a departure from canonical order and without prior Synodal approval, whereas the participation of the Orthodox Church in the Ecumenical movement was under preparation for decades and *was approved by the ecclesiastical hierarchy of all the Orthodox Churches*, as serving their interests, in the best sense, in times of hardship. This is why it was unanimously supported not only by the Pan-Orthodox Conferences (1961, 1964, 1968), but also by the Pre-Conciliar Pan-Orthodox Conferences (1972, 1982, 1986).

Third, they were concerned principally with *heretics who adamantly refused to alter their beliefs*, who displayed absolutely no willingness to engage in dialogue with the Church with the aim of removing the causes of their separation from the Church community. The Ecumenical movement, on the other hand, has as a principle in its charter that *suitable conditions should be created for the promotion both of multi-lateral and bi-lateral theological dialogues*, aimed at the restoration of Church unity, against which the above canons have been invoked, either by guile or uncritically.

Fourth, the heretics mentioned in the above canons *were active within the boundaries of the local Churches*, and, being officially recognized, were known to one and all, *whereas the thousand-year estrangement between the Churches of the East and West* has been soured by the unfraternal proselytizing propaganda of the Papist Unia and of the Protestant Missionaries among the suffering members of the Orthodox Church. This is why support for a constructive theological dialogue among equals requires discreet or official contacts between Church leaders, much as these may trouble the self-styled defenders of the Orthodox faithful.

Fifth, by its *participation in the WCC* and through the official bi-lateral *theological dialogues* with other Christian Churches and Confessions, the Orthodox Church has not only been unscathed, but, on the contrary has always been able, with all due consistency and responsibility, to promote the enduring criteria of the Orthodox tradition to the Christian world in the West, *which has recognized the theological depth of the Patristic tradition, the liturgical experience and ascetic spirituality of the Orthodox Church*. This can be concluded from the Edicts *Lumen Gentium* and *Unitatis redintergratio* from the Second Vatican Council (1962-1965).

Sixth, the common theological texts from the Dialogues between the Orthodox Church and the Old Catholics and Anti-Chalcedonian Ancient Eastern Churches, the Roman Catholics, the Anglicans, the Lutherans and the Reformed Churches *highlight the established positions of the Orthodox tradition on critical issues, as well as the points of disagreement between it and the heterodox.* This reinforces their interest in the Patristic tradition and in Orthodox theology.

Seventh, the participation of the Orthodox Church in the Ecumenical movement has been greatly beneficial in a variety of ways *for the Orthodox Diaspora all over the world*, which has been supported by the heterodox, not only in the matter of the immediate need to deal with the problem of finding places of worship, and the various requirements of newly-established Orthodox communities, but also through the promotion of the Orthodox tradition in heterodox surroundings, especially the unbreakable link between the confession of the faith and the liturgical experience of the body of the Church. So for the Orthodox Diaspora, the Orthodox presence in the Christian world of the West has been highlighted more sharply and the contribution of Orthodox theology to multi- or bi-lateral discussions on Christian unity has been more significant, because the attendance of the heterodox at the Orthodox liturgies in dioceses in their area has presented a more tangible image of the mystagogical relationship of the liturgical experience and the whole spiritual life of the Orthodox faithful.

Therefore, the Church, in the maternal concern it is bound to show for those members who have seceded from its body, prays without ceasing for their return to the unity of the whole of the Church's body and exercises all consistent ecclesiastical flexibility towards this mission of salvation, in order to keep open the path of constructive dialogue for the facilitation of their attendance at the common Eucharistic Altar, at which the whole mystery of divine dispensation is celebrated for the salvation of the whole of the human race. The maternal filter of the love of the Church for all its members, especially those who have broken away from its body, links the exercise of ecclesiastical flexibility to its soteriological mission, through the action of the Holy Spirit, through which the sick are cured and those who are lacking are fulfilled. Because there is no room in this flexibility for injudicious or arrogant judgments against the heterodox in order to satisfy special interests or other expediencies which are foreign to the mission of the Church. The Church does not *"hate"* or *"despise"* the heterodox, but, on the contrary, constantly, in its own flesh, endures the wounding experience of their secession, and this is also why, praying without ceasing for the union of all, it always responds willingly to any proposal for constructive dialogue concerning unity. In this sense, the Orthodox Church, though it condemns in no uncertain terms the use of the Divine Liturgy by the heterodox in order to deceive the Orthodox faithful, nevertheless, through the proper interpretation of the canons mentioned above (10th, 11th, 45th, 46th and 64th Apostolic; 6 9, 31, 32 and 33 of Laodicea; 9th by Timothy of Alexandria and so on) accepts the presence of heterodox at the Orthodox Divine Liturgy and also considers it self-evident that there will be *common prayer* at the discussions for the restoration of the ecclesiastical community.

(translated by James Lillie)

Part VII: Particular Themes and Issues for Orthodox Involvement in Ecumenism

(94) COMMON PRAYER AS AN ISSUE FOR ORTHODOX INVOLVEMENT IN ECUMENISM. A SYSTEMATIC APPROACH

Peter Bouteneff

As a matter of history, the organized pursuit of unity among divided Christian churches has included prayer since its early twentieth-century roots. The First World Conference on Faith and Order (Lausanne, 1927) makes frequent references to prayer, taking note that the assembled delegates found themselves "...united in common prayer, in God our heavenly Father and His Son Jesus Christ, our Saviour, in the fellowship of the Holy Spirit."[1] As a matter of faith, it would only make sense that Christians — who are called to pray unceasingly (1 Thess. 5:17), to pray corporately (Matt. 18:20), and to pray for unity (John 17:11; 21) — should pray together as they engage the holy task of the pursuit of reconciliation.

Imperatives and Challenges

Indeed, it would seem natural that the delicate and sacred work of the quest for unity of divided Christians – work that involves thoughtful research, honest communication, and personal and corporate introspection and repentance – can only be pursued under the guidance of God the Father, in His Son, and by His Holy Spirit, whose name we invoke in prayer. And yet for many reasons the common prayer of divided Christians is fraught with complexities and difficulties. We are challenged theologically and canonically, as well as at the deepest level of our feelings about prayer. Common prayer is therefore an Orthodox Christian imperative, even as it can provoke tensions with Orthodox teaching and Orthodox sensibilities.

At the heart of common prayer lies the question as to whether it is indeed possible or appropriate. There is no universal answer to this question, especially since scriptural and patristic precedent does not easily translate to the present day. How do the divisions that we hear about in the New Testament, or even in the fourth century, apply to the present-day situation of a Christendom that has been divided for a millennium?

The prayer of Our Lord "that they may be one" – used (perhaps even a little too often) in the ecumenical setting – has been interpreted in a variety of ways that have different implications for the present situation. In one interpretation, Jesus prayed simply for the unity of his disciples, which relieves us of the responsibility to pray for any more complicated unity today. Yet John 17:20 forbids that limitation, for Jesus says specifically "I do not pray for these only, but also for those who believe in me through their word, that they may all be one..." Such a prayer would not have been necessary if there were no division or at least a threat of division that needed addressing, that elicited from Jesus an invitation into the most exalted inter-personal unity that could possibly exist: that between the divine Father and His co-eternal and consubstantial Son.

Still, some would interpret this prayer today as a prayer to maintain the unity among Orthodox Christians: only those who believe in exactly the right way. Likewise for the second petition of the Great Litany, where we prayer "for the welfare of the holy Churches of God, and for the union of all," some will say that this is for the union of the local Orthodox churches. It is true that we Orthodox, though united canonically by the grace of God, are also in constant threat of institutional disharmony and division, and must constantly pray that we [Orthodox] may be one. But is it not appropriate to pray in this very way for the union of divided churches? We do pray, in the anaphora of St. Basil's Liturgy, that

---

[1] H. N. Bate (ed.), *Faith and Order: Proceedings of the World Conference* (London: SCM, 1927), 459-75.

God "reunite the separated." St. Basil himself, as is well known, was an ardent worker for the reunion of separated Christians.[2]

Yet the fact remains that some Orthodox Christians believe that any person or group outside the canonical Orthodox Church is cut off from the body of Christ, and cannot even be properly called "Christian." Many of the same people call all non-Orthodox "heretics," using that word quite indiscriminately. (This view is expressed with such passion and emotion by those who hold it that it is difficult to see how rare it actually is.) More common, and arguably more patristic, is the view expressed by Fr. Georges Florovsky that the charismatic borders of the Church do not correspond with the canonical borders.[3] This is at least in part because the historical, doctrinal, spiritual divisions between Christian bodies have not all been of the same character, and do not all sever the bodies from each other completely. Otherwise St. Basil would not have recognized different *kinds* and different *extents* of division;[4] otherwise we would not receive converts to the Orthodox Church by a manifest variety of rites.[5]

All of this means that most Orthodox Christians recognize a certain bond that unites divided Christians – those who in faith call upon Jesus Christ as Lord and Savior – a bond that distinguishes them, for example, from non-Christians. This fellowship enjoyed by Christians (which the ecumenical movement calls "koinonia") does not nullify the historical, doctrinal, and spiritual divisions, neither does it free us from our responsibility to name and address those divisions. But it would be spiritual and theological madness to suggest that Roman Catholics, Lutherans, or Methodists, all reside on the dark side of a dividing wall, all together as a non-Orthodox block with pagans and atheists. No, they are Christians.

Canons and Ecclesiology

Opponents of "ecumenical common prayer" raise the issue of the Church's canonical tradition, which on more than one occasion has forbidden "prayer with heretics."[6] As the late professor Constantine Scouteris has helpfully pointed out on this issue, if we are to take the canons seriously and reverently, we must study their context so that we may apply them in the sense they were intended; likewise we must be attentive to what the term "heretic" actually means, for fear of falling into the "drastic simplification" of the applying that category to today's Roman Catholics and Protestants.[7] Heretics are those who willfully divide the Church from within it, or those who – like the "heretics" of St. Basil's canonical letter – hold to radically different understandings of God as did the Montanists, Valentinians of his day.

"Common prayer" in ecumenical settings rightly excludes concelebration or sacramental sharing. This results neither from others' "heretic" status, nor from elitism on our part. It is not a judgment on the activity or non-activity of the Holy Spirit in others' sacraments. It is simply Orthodox ecclesiology. We may not share in sacraments outside the Orthodox Church, for to do so would be to disregard the Church's canonical structure and its recognized ministry. And however close we may or may not feel to other Christians, sacraments are

---

[2] "I think then that the one great goal of all who are really and truly serving the Lord ought to be to bring back to union the churches who have "at sundry times and in divers manners" divided from one another" (*Epistle* 114).

[3] Specifically, Florovsky shows how St. Cyprian's equation of the charismatic and canonical borders of the Church was never received in the communal consciousness of the Church. See "The Limits of the Church" *Church Quarterly Review* in 1933. Anti-ecumenists, who nonetheless admire Fr. Georges, are at pains to ignore or argue away his fundamental sensibilities about Christian reality outside the Orthodox Church.

[4] See St Basil's *First Canonical Epistle,* also his *Epistle* 188.

[5] See John H. Erickson, "The Reception of Non-Orthodox into the Orthodox Church: Contemporary Practice," *St Vladimir's Theological Quarterly* 41 (1997): 1–17.

[6] See esp. Apostolic Canon 45: "Let a bishop, presbyter, or deacon, who has only prayed with heretics, be excommunicated: but if he has permitted them to perform any clerical office, let him be deposed."

[7] Constantine Scouteris, "Common Prayer," in *The Ecumenical Review* 54.1 (2002): 33–37.

not a matter of feeling, nor can they be administered based on what you and I may think about theological proximity with others. They are administered with respect to established ecclesiastical order.

That same order is based upon the historic succession, and accounts for historic divisions. The Orthodox Church understands itself as the body from which others have, to different extents, divided. It is in this and only this sense that the Orthodox Church identifies itself as the One Holy Catholic and Apostolic Church – because it takes these divisions seriously and sees them as yet unhealed. In many cases, these divisions are manifest in significant disagreements in both faith and ministry. Doctrines of prevenient grace and double predestination, total depravity in Reformed churches, the nature of papal jurisdiction as defined in the First Vatican Council, are examples of serious and so far unresolved differences – differences that justly divide our churches. Church divisions forbid sacramental concelebration and communion, but not common prayer.

The Character of Prayer

The canonical and ecclesiastical challenges to common prayer are important to clarify. But whatever arguments are offered that would justify common prayer in the face of church divisions, a greater challenge often presents itself in the sometimes deeply unfamiliar character of prayer across confessional lines. That discomfort can be universal. Most people, of any confession, are troubled by prayer traditions that are deeply unfamiliar, and this is because prayer is an intimate context, one where we are vulnerable, and where we therefore naturally recoil from the unfamiliar. It helps, in fact, to recall how unfamiliar and sometimes troubling Orthodox worship is to many people outside our tradition.

But we Orthodox are liable to feel alienated in a particular way by "common prayer". All Orthodox prayer, especially our corporate prayer, is normally done according to established rules and written prayers shared to a great extent across the entire Orthodox Church. We do not pray extemporaneously. We deliberately maintain a very sober character to our prayers, hymnography, and music. When confronted with prayer in more Evangelical (not to mention Pentecostal) traditions, we are liable to feel alienated. Emotional singing, music that generates rhythm and dance-like body movement, feels entirely foreign to us.

Apart from this gut-level reaction, there is the fact that Orthodox prayer life, based as it is on ancient and time-tested texts, is completely *dependable*. One knows that the prayer will be theologically and spiritually sound. We do not know the prayers from outside our tradition that are either chosen or written ad hoc for prayer services – and we appropriately fear singing or reciting texts that have not been theologically vetted. Corporate prayer that is said in unison, that is confirmed by the "Amen" of the people, must be genuinely agreed by the people gathered. This presents a serious challenge to common prayer in ecumenical settings, one that goes beyond the feeling of unfamiliarity.

This being said, there are times when allowing ourselves to participate in unfamiliar forms of prayer can, by God's grace, bring genuine spiritual joy and refreshment.

"Ecumenical Worship" and "Common Prayer"

We have reviewed canonical, theological, and visceral challenges to common prayer. From 1999-2002, the World Council of Churches convened a "Special Commission on Orthodox Participation in the WCC," part of whose work was to address the chronic tensions of ecumenical prayer. The Special Commission produced a set of recommendations that were "received" by the Central Committee.[8] They were not adopted as formal

---

[8] "A Framework For Common Prayer at WCC Gatherings," Appendix A of the Final Report of the Special Commission on Orthodox Participation in the WCC. See at http://www.oikoumene.org/en/resources/documents/assembly/2006-por-to-alegre/3-preparatory-and-background-documents/final-report-of-the-special-commission-on-orthodox-participation-in-the-wcc (last accessed 19 June 19 2013).

Orthodox Handbook on Ecumenism

rules, partly because they represented too sharp a departure from norms that were cherished by a great many Protestants, and possibly because they were too rational to address what was manifestly an emotional issue. But their logic is of interest in that they identify and attempt to address several issues at the heart of the debate on common prayer.

At the heart of the Special Commission's recommendations lay the articulation of a clear distinction that already existed in ecumenical practice. On the one hand, there have been "ecumenical prayer services" that often draw from the prayers and musical styles of multiple confessional traditions. (These have been likened to "fruit salad" – something seen either as refreshingly varied, or artificial and arbitrary.) On the other hand, there have been occasions where prayer has been according to one tradition, such as the celebration of an Anglican Evensong, a Lutheran Vespers service, or an Orthodox Matins service. (This has been likened to enjoying one fruit at a time – seen either as respectful of traditional integrity and richness, or staid.) Whatever the assets and liabilities of these two forms, the recommendations suggested that they should be kept as clearly distinct categories:

> "Ecumenical" or "interconfessional" prayer services do not "belong" to any church tradition, nor to a church hierarchy or structure. They are ad hoc services, and they should be conducted in the absence of anything that would indicate ecclesiastical identity (such as vestments, clergy who would offer blessings, etc.) They are not even properly called "worship" services, since the word "worship," in many of the native languages spoken by Orthodox Christians (notably Greek and Russian) bears the connotation of ecclesiastical, or even sacramental identity.
>
> "Confessional worship services," on the contrary, do by nature belong to a particular church tradition and are properly celebrated in accordance with that tradition, whether that tradition has an episcopate or any ordained ministry, male or female.

The logic of the recommendations is therefore especially sensitive to issues of ecclesiastical identity. Common prayer is just that: prayer said in common, not hosted or administered by any ecclesiastical body. Confessional worship is performed in the integrity of a particular confession.

A vital corollary of this logic is that, contrary to former practice, assemblies of the WCC no longer feature an "Ecumenical Eucharist." We Orthodox were at pains to explain that the very concept of "Ecumenical Eucharist" was for us a theological impossibility for the following reasons: (1) there are sharp limits to who can participate in such a Eucharist, (2) there is no such thing as an "ecumenical church" that can administer such a Eucharist, (3) even when one church does administer an "Ecumenical Eucharist" (such as Anglicans did at the Canberra Assembly in 1991), it inevitably conveys the misleading signal that the WCC is a "super-church" that administers the Eucharist.

As a result of Orthodox efforts, and to the relief of many like-minded non-Orthodox, subsequent assemblies did not have ecumenical Eucharist services; rather the participants went to local churches according to their respective confessional traditions. This practice is also enshrined in the recommendations of the Special Commission.

These recommendations address several of the theological and canonical problems at the heart of the endeavor of "common prayer." They attempt to respect the integrity of two modalities of common prayer, and as such are most effective in addressing issues of ecclesiastical identity, which in turn alleviate some significant canonical tensions. While the recommendations urge the organizers of prayer services to respect the sensitivities of the traditions represented at gatherings, they can not possibly prevent all personal and/or theological offense.

To conclude: common prayer in ecumenical settings remains – inevitably – a significant challenge for everyone. The theological and liturgical sensibilities of the Orthodox pose their own specific kinds of problems for common prayer that are worth identifying clearly. Yet, approached properly, common prayer is an imperative. Whether or not one abstains from attending, owing to matters of conscience, obedience, or preference, it is a vital and sustaining part of the inter-Christian encounter and the serious, hopeful, and repentant path towards unity. If we are serious about our encounters with divided Christians, if we see such encounters as anything more than a formal business meeting, if we see other Christians as human beings who call in faith upon God, His Christ, and His Spirit, then how can we possibly refrain from praying together?

Bibliography

Peter Bouteneff, Rolf Koppe, K.M. George, "How Should We Pray Together in the Future?" http://www.oikoumene.org/en/press-centre/news/how-should-we-pray-together-in-future-the-special-commission-on-orthodox-participation-in-the-wcc-is-preparing-its-final-report-part-3 (last accessed 20 June 2013).
Paul Meyendorff, "Ecumenical Prayer: An Orthodox Perspective," in *The Ecumenical Review* 54 (2002): 28-32.
Constantine Scouteris, "Common Prayer," in *The Ecumenical Review* 54.1 (2002): 33–37.

(95) ECUMENICAL IMPLICATIONS OF THE ORTHODOX UNDERSTANDING OF WORSHIP AND LITURGY[1]

Godfrey O' Donell

Abraham Joshua Heschel (1907-72) was a Polish born American rabbi and one of the leading Jewish theologians and Jewish philosophers of the 20th century. In a small book of his, he writes, we live in a world where 'God may be of no concern to man, but man is of much concern to God. The only way to discover this is the ultimate way, the way of worship. For worship is a way of living, a way of seeing the world in the light of God. To worship is to rise to a higher level of existence, to see the world from the point of view of God.... But to remember that the love of God is for all men, for all creatures; to remember His love and His claim to love in making a decision - this is the way He wants us to live. To worship God is to forget the self. It is in such instants of worship that man acts as a symbol of Him [God]... Of all things we do prayer is the least, the least worldly, the least practical. This why prayer is an act of self-purification. This is why prayer is an ontological necessity.'

Heschel feels that we are living through one of the greatest hours of history. The false gods are crumbling, and hearts are hungry for the voice of God. But the voice has been stifled. To recapture the echo, he insists that we must be honest in our willingness to listen; we must be unprejudiced in our readiness to listen. Acceptance of the spirit of God is prayer - prayer as a way of insight, not as a way of speaking. For him, prayer comes first of all the sacred acts. Religion is not 'what man does with his solitariness.' Religion is what man does with the presence of God. And the spirit of God is present whenever we are willing to accept it.[2]

An Orthodox preparatory group meeting in New York in 1998 on the way to the WCC Assembly in Harare Zimbabwe put it this way in their preamble: Every person is created with the capacity to praise God. It lies at the heart of our human existence; thus worship is universal. Yet worship is also surprisingly particular. It finds different expression in each human situation. Through worship we communicate with God. Just as language with its peculiarities of syntax, grammar and vocabulary can change through time, similarly worship with its gestures, symbols and style of a given time and place may not be readily grasped in another historical setting, and so the need for to critically assess this from time to time.[3]

Christianity right from the beginning was open to a variety of languages of worship as local churches developed their own forms of expressing and celebrating their faith. Through the centuries, in an effort to carry out its mission of bringing the Gospel to all nations, the Church continued to adapt its ways of worshipping in the new contexts. There was an openness and sensitivity among the Orthodox communities about inculturation. This is particularly evident in their use of the vernacular. The history of Orthodox mission copiously illustrates this. Yet in modern times we seem to be in danger of violating such a principle with the growing plethora of inward-looking ethnic churches with their unquestioning nationalism.

---

[1] In this article the term ecumenical is perceived in the original meaning of the word 'Oikoumene' and refers to the implications for the 'whole inhabited earth' and human experience (ed.).

[2] A. J Heschel, *Man's Quest for God: Studies in Prayer and Symbolism*, (Santa Fe: Aurora Press, 1998), xii-xiv. Having written a doctoral thesis on *The Prophets* (later expanded into modern classic) at the University of Berlin, he arrived in New York city in 1940. He was Professor of Ethics and Mysticism at the Jewish Theological Seminary of America at the time of his death. Extremely interested in spirituality, Heschel saw the teachings of the Hebrew prophets as a clarion call to social action in the States. He worked for black civil rights and against the Vietnam war. He also specifically criticised what he called an exclusive focus on religious moral behaviour to the neglect of the non-legalistic dimension of rabbinic tradition. Influential as a representative of American Jews at Vatican II in persuading the RC Church to eliminate or modify passages in their liturgy that demeaned Jews or expected their conversion to Christianity.

[3] T Fitzgerald & P. Bouteneff, (eds.), *Turn to God, Rejoice in Hope: Orthodox Reflections on the Way to Harare.* (Geneva: WCC, 1998), 139.

Liturgy is the source par excellence of theology. In 1966, Fr. Schmemann's *Introduction to Liturgical Theology* mooted the need for liturgical theology. For him, the essence of the Liturgy or *lex orandi* was simply nothing else but the Church's faith or, to put it more succinctly, the manifestation, communication and realisation of that faith. It is precisely faith as experience, the total and living experience of the Church that constitutes the source and the context of theology in the East, of that theology at least that characterised the patristic age. It is in this context that we are to understand the famous saying *lex orandi est lex credendi*. It certainly does not mean a reduction of the faith to Liturgy or cult, nor does it imply a confusion between faith and Liturgy, as for example with liturgical piety where 'liturgical experience', the experience of the 'sacred' simply replaces faith and has people indifferent to its doctrinal content. All this involves an organic and essential interdependence where faith, the source and cause of Liturgy, essentially needs the other for its self-understanding and self-fulfilment. Clearly, it is faith that gives birth to and 'shapes' Liturgy, but it is Liturgy, 'that by fulfilling and expressing faith, "bears testimony" to faith and thus becomes its true and adequate expression and norm: *lex orandi est lex credendi*.' Put another way, 'the Church's life has always been rooted in the *lex credendi*, the rule of faith, theology in the deepest sense of the word; and on the *lex orandi*, her rule of worship, the *leitourgia* which "always makes her what she is": the Body of Christ and the Temple of the Holy Spirit.' [4] So then for Schmemann, liturgical theology is not just another aspect of theology, a 'discipline', which deals with liturgy *in itself*, and has liturgy as *its specific object*. Rather it is about the effort to apprehend theology as revealed in and through Liturgy. [5]

Geoffrey Wainwright, an English Methodist theologian, would remark in summary: in Eastern Orthodoxy there is undoubtedly a close relationship between worship and doctrine. Certainly Orthodox Liturgy bears a high dogmatic density, and Orthodox theologians are expected to operate within and for the worshipping community. It is certainly true that Orthodoxy is enormously influenced by Evagrius of Pontus' adage in his *Chapters On Prayer*, 'If you are a theologian, you will pray truly, and if you pray truly, you are a theologian' (*Chapters on Prayer* 61). [6] Thus, 'there can be no theorising, no theologising without the practical impetus of prayer and faith.' But, unlike Hannah Hunt who surely overstates Evagrius' position that theology in this instance becomes an almost apophatic experience (perhaps influenced by Vladimir Lossky's stark interpretation of Orthodox theology), Evagrius, of all people, is saying that that there is a second movement here that necessitates the articulation and communication of the insights that come from the encounter with the Holy Spirit: there is still the need to theologise - to say something about the Incarnation of Our Saviour, the community of the Trinity and of the Church, etc. Of course humanity is not capable of comprehending the entirety of God. So the witness and why of Evagrius' own writings, the 'theologising' teachings of Symeon the New Theologian (949-1022) and Gregory Palamas (c.1296-1359) who she mentions.' [7] The heavy reliance on the part of Orthodox on inherited texts raises hermeneutical problems for Wainwright, but there is evidence from writers such as Alexander Schmemann that it is possible to elaborate the Tradition from within its own ongoing journey in ways that challenge rather than simply confirm the surrounding culture. [8] For his part, Schmemann would contend 'that for Orthodox theology, essentially different in this from western theology, the *sui generis* hermeneutical foundation is to be found in the *lex orandi*: the epiphany and experience by the Church of herself and her faith. This is what we mean when we state in accordance with our Tradition that the scripture is interpreted "by the Church," and that the Fathers are witnesses of the Catholic faith of the Church.

[4] A. Schmemann, *Liturgy and Tradition: Theological Reflections of Alexander Schmemann,* ed. T Fisch. (Crestwood, NY: St Vladimir's Seminary Press, 2003), 52.

[5] A. Schmemann, *Ibid.*, 38-39. See also his *Introduction to Liturgical Theology.* (Crestwood, NY: St Vladimir's Press, 2003).

[6] *The Philokalia: The Complete Text compiled by St Nikodimos of the Holy Mountain & St Makarios of Corinth,* trans. G E H Palmer, P Sherrard & K Ware, Vol I., (New York: Faber & Faber, 1983), 62.

[7] H Hunt, 'Byzantine Christianity', *The Blackwell Companion to Eastern Christianity,* ed. K. Parry, (Oxford: Wiley-Blackwell, 2010), 82.

[8] G Wainwright, 'Lex Orandi, Lex Credendi', *Dictionary of the Ecumenical Movement,* ed. N. Lossky et al, (Geneva: WCC Publications, 2002), 679-683, especially here at 680.

And as long, therefore, as this Orthodox "hermeneutics" is not acknowledged, rediscovered and practiced, the scrutiny of the most traditional "texts" will, alas, remain as irrelevant for our liturgical situation as in the past.'[9]

For Schmemann, questions asked by liturgical theologians about Liturgy and the whole liturgical tradition are in reality about theology (the faith of the Church as expressed, communicated and preserved in the Liturgy). 'Liturgy is viewed as the *locus theologicus par excellence* because it is its very function, its *leitourgia* in the original meaning of that word, to manifest and fulfill the Church's faith and to manifest it, not partially, not discursively, but as a living totality and catholic experience... For if theology, as the Orthodox Church maintains, is not a mere sequence of more or less individual interpretations of this or that "doctrine" in the light and thought forms of this or that "culture' and "situation," but the attempt to express Truth itself, to find words adequate to the mind and experience of the Church, then it must of necessity have its source where the faith, the mind, and the experience of the Church have their living focus and expression, where faith in both essential meanings of that word, as Truth revealed and given, and as Truth accepted and "lived," has its *epiphany,* and that is precisely the function of the *leitourgia.'*[10]

To sum up, Schmemann would contend that 'the purpose of worship is to constitute the Church, precisely to bring what is "private" into the new life, to transform it into what belongs to the Church, i.e. shared with all in Christ. In addition its purpose is always to express the Church, as the unity of that Body whose Head is Christ. And, finally, its purpose is that we should always "with one mouth and one heart" serve God, since it was only such worship which God commanded the Church to offer. In the same way it is impossible to justify the division of the Sacraments into separate liturgical departments, with the Eucharist regarded simply as "one among several." The Eucharist is *the* Sacrament of the Church, i.e. her eternal actualization as the Body of Christ, united in Christ by the Holy Spirit. Therefore the Eucharist is not only the "most important" of all the offices, it is also source and goal of the entire liturgical life of the Church. Any liturgical theology not having the Eucharist as the foundation of its whole structure is basically defective.'[11]

Another aspect of this is the great appreciation in Orthodoxy of language when it comes to Christology and the Trinity. It is the language of the Ecumenical Councils, and as such constitutes an enduring and definitive reference point. The same is equally true of Liturgy. It is constantly sung in our Liturgy giving it an ongoing deep acceptance in the life of the Church. This is the language of the Church - not just in technical mode, but when it is joyfully singing its doxology to God. The inference being, the two cannot be divorced: nor can they be divorced from piety which can be a problem. Secondly, this language was the vehicle by which a process took place that had life or death consequences for the Church. It was a language that adapted and developed in the service of a needed clear teaching, articulated with all the precision that can be mustered, about our relationship in and with God and our fellow humans, and the constant threat of error and misunderstanding.

Obviously here we must keep in mind that in contemplating the person of Christ, neither the Apostles, Fathers nor the Liturgy begin with technical language; 'Instead they begin with the vision of Christ, the King of Glory, crucified for our sake and risen from the dead. The technical language of Christology exists in the service of that confession.'[12] Thus, there is a clear appreciation of *Lex orandi lex credendi,* so too there is a strong reverence for the handed-down language of the services and reluctance among Orthodox to engage in syncretistic formulas.

According to Metropolitan John Zizioulas, 'Liturgical practice formed, and continues to form, the language in which the Church expresses this thesis. And we should pay attention to it.' This involves the biblical connection of the Eucharist and the Kingdom of God which is to come: it draws from it its being and truth.[13]

[9] A Schmemann, *Liturgy and Tradition: Theological Reflections of Alexander Schmemann,* ed. T Fisch. (Crestwood, NY: St Vladimir's Seminary Press, 2003), 44.

[10] A Schmemann, *Ibid.,* 40.

[11] A Schmemann, *Introduction to Liturgical Theology.* (Crestwood, NY: St Vladimir's Seminary Press, 2003) 24; see also n 23 for references to works by Archmandrite Kiprian Kern & Nicolas Afanasiev.

[12] P Bouteneff, 'Christ and Salvation', in *The Cambridge Companion to Orthodox Christian Theology.* (ed. M.B. Cunningham & E. Theokritoff), (New York: Cambridge University Press, 2008), 102-3.

[13] J D Zizioulas, *The Eucharistic Communion and The World* (ed. L Tallon). (London: T & T Clark, 2011), 45.

Leitourgia originally derived from the Greek meaning 'public service', though its use in ancient Greek had wider connotations of which 'religious service' was not one of its most immediate. Employed in the Septuagint bible to translate Hebrew terms such as 'charat' and 'avodah' (religious service and its ministers in the temple: Ex 38:27; 39:12; Joel 1:9; 2:17) saw it win acceptance in the Greek NT as 'worship' or 'service', 'rite', 'public ministry' or 'function.' From the 4th century it especially designated the Eucharistic Liturgy, its religious aspect being underlined by the added 'Divine' Liturgy.[14] Liturgy in the New Testament implies a life of service modelled on Jesus' self-giving. In Byzantium the term specifically refers to the ritual of the Eucharist, often called the Divine Liturgy *(theia leitourgia)* of which there were two parallel Constantinopolitan formularies, attributed to St John Chrysostom, who seemingly elaborated an existing anaphora of the Apostles, and to St Basil the Great, who is believed to have authored at least one of the redactions named after him. Each formulary consists of 19 prayers, the main one a borrowed Antiochene-type anaphora (Chrysostom's from Antioch, Basil's from Cappadocia), elaborated and embedded in a common ritual setting and structure of diaconal forms, Scripture readings, psalmody, and chants. Ten of these prayers are later additions to both Liturgies. The first attestation of the epiclesis is found in the Apostolic Tradition of St Hippolytus from the 3rd century. Within this text is a call for the Holy Spirit to descend and strengthen the Church through the sacrifice. There are also 4th century versions of the epiclesis in the Liturgy of St James, the *Euchologion* of Serapion of Deir Balyzeh, and the writings of St Cyril of Jerusalem. The theology that serves as a foundation for this prayer demonstrates the patristic teaching that God the Father's revelation and work comes through the Son and is completed by the Holy Spirit. The Church's call to the Spirit to sanctify and strengthen the community of believers (as well as consecrating the gifts) relates the Church and Holy Eucharist to the day of Pentecost and shows the eschatological nature of the Church's Trinitarian prayer. The epiclesis in the Liturgy of St John Chrysostom marks a shift from the Holy Spirit 'showing' the gifts to be the body of Christ to 'making' the gifts into the body of Christ.[15] The Liturgy of Basil predominated in Constantinople until circa 1000, when that of Chrysostom took over. Thereafter the Liturgy of Basil was celebrated only ten times a year, mainly during the Sundays of Great Lent.

In its full form, largely complete by the 12th century, the liturgy had four major parts (1) the prothesis rite, or preliminary preparation of the bread and wine; (2) the enarxis, or introductory services of three antiphons, litanies and prayers[16]; (3) the Liturgy of the Word which opened with the Little Entrance and Trisagion, comprising Scripture readings interspersed with psalmody and concluding with litanies and prayers[17]; (4) the Liturgy of the Eucharist which opened with the Great Entrance, included the pre-anaphoral rites, anaphoral dialogue, anaphora, pre-communion (including the fraction and zeon), communion, thanksgiving and the dismissal.

The early liturgy, described in the homilies of St John Chrysostom at Constantinople in 397-404 was a classical late antique Eucharist whose texts had been marked by the Arian controversy and the definitions of the First Council of Nicaea. In the 5th-6th century, especially with the construction of Hagia Sophia, the liturgy became 'imperial', acquiring greater ritual splendour. This period witnessed the addition of the Creed and three important chants: the Trisagion (c.438-9), Monogenes (535-6) and the Cherubikon (573-4).

In the 5th-7th centuries the liturgy was especially marked by the developing Constantinopolitan system of stational services.[18] In such a system the entire city was a 'liturgical space', and the principal liturgy of a feast, held a predetermined 'station', was preceded by a procession up to 10 km long. Though frequent in the 6th-7th centuries, such processions later took place in Constantinople only on certain important occasions.

[14] See I-H Dallas, 'Liturgy, I Christian Liturgy', *Encyclopedia of the Early Church*, Institutum Patristicum Augustinianum, ed. A Di Bernardino, ET. A Walford, Vol I. (Cambridge: James Clarke & Co, 1992), 494.

[15] T E French, 'Epiclesis', *The Encyclopaedia of Eastern Orthodox Christianity*, ed. J A McGuckin, Vol I A-M. (Chichester: Wiley-Blackwell, 2011), 221.

[16] J Mateos S.J., *La célébration de la parole dans la liturgie byzantine: étude historique*, OCA 191. (Rome: 1971), 27-90.

[17] J Mateos, *Ibid.*, 91-173.

[18] J Baldovin, *The Urban Character of Christian Worship*, OCA 227. (Rome: 1987), 167-226. See also R F Taft, *The Byzantine Liturgy: A Short History*, American Essays in Liturgy Series. (Collegeville, Minn: The Liturgical Press, 1992), 28-41, to whom I am much indebted for this next section of the article.

Several elements of the first half of the liturgy, however - the opening of the synapte litany, three antiphons, the Trisagion and its accompanying prayer, and the ektene litany after the Gospel - derive from these processions.

Other developments include the addition of litanies to cover the priests' silent recitation of the prayers, and in the 9th-12th centuries, the evolution of the prothesis rite and the addition of certain formulas to the pre-anaphoral rites.

Within a century of St Maximus Confessor's death (660), on the eve of the iconoclastic crisis, the traditional system of Maximus' 'cosmic' liturgical interpretation had begun to give way to a more literal and representational narrative vision based on the early story of Jesus' life. While not abandoning the cosmic, heavenly Liturgy typology inherited from Maximus' *Mystagogy,* Patriarch Germanus I (c.730) integrated another level of interpretation, also found, if less prominently, in earlier Byzantine writings: that of the Eucharist not only as a remembering of, but as representing actual moments of salvation history in Jesus. With Germanus, these two leitmotifs become an integral part of the Byzantine synthesis. This encroachment of a more literal historical tradition upon the earlier, mystical level of interpretation, coincided with the beginnings of the struggle against Iconoclasm, when Orthodoxy found itself locked in mortal combat to defend its icon worship, the expression of a radical incarnational realism against the conservative reaction promoting a more symbolic, iconoclastic spiritualism. The effect of the new mentality can be seen at once in the representational mystagogy integrated into the earlier Maximian tradition by Germanus.[19]

Especially characteristic of the liturgy are the entrances, which open and symbolise the two major parts of the service. The Little Entrance symbolises Christ's coming as Word (*Logos*); the Great Entrance prefigures his coming in the sacrament of his body and blood. Both these foreshadowings are fulfilled in two later appearances - when the deacon proceeds to the ambo for the proclamation of the Gospel, and when the priest comes out to distribute the consecrated gifts in communion - thus completing the symbolic structure of the Liturgy.

As the Liturgy underwent increased monastic influence, especially after iconoclasm and after the Latin occupation of Constantinople, these ritual processions were gradually compressed. Once functional entrances, they were increasingly confined to the interior space of the church and reduced to purely symbolic ritual that ended where they began. The churches themselves became smaller and smaller, and the ritual more private, retreating into the enclosed sanctuary with the templon (originally a low parapet or chancel barrier, a screen separating the nave from the sanctuary) that slowly evolved from the mid-5th to the 11th century into our iconostasis. The synthronon (one or more benches reserved for the bishop and priests and arranged in a semi-circular tier in the apse of a church, once elevated so that the clergy could see and be seen), disappeared from the apse. Readings and homilies became a ritualised formality, and communion, the point of the whole Liturgy, became a dead letter as fewer and fewer communicants approached to receive the sacrament.[20] Schmemann, too, concurs in this judgement, 'The Church orders the celebration of the Eucharist, and it will be a great step forward when we realise that the "Eucharistic individualism" which has transformed ninety percent of our Liturgies into Eucharist without communicants is the result of distorted piety and false humility.'

The Studite Typika (list of liturgical functions for those involved) introduced into the Liturgy some usages from the monastic hours, e.g. the Typika (liturgical calendar with added instructions for each day's services) and the dismissal formula. The mid-14th century diataxis (the rubric book) of Patriarch Philotheus and the Typika of the Lavra of St Sabas in the Judean desert, the intellectual and spiritual centre of the Patriarchate of Jerusalem and of Palestinian monasticism, ultimately determined the ceremonial and usage of the Liturgy in Byzantium.

The Liturgy of St James, the brother of the Lord, was once the standard Eucharistic prayer of the church of Jerusalem. The earliest extant manuscript of this Liturgy, a 9th century roll (Vat. gr. 2282) already shows

---

[19] R F Taft, 'Liturgy', *The Oxford University Handbook of Byzantine Studies.* (Oxford: Oxford University Press, ed. E Jeffreys et al., 2008), 601-2. See also Taft, 'The Liturgy of the Great Church: An Initial Synthesis of Structure and Interpretation on the Eve of Iconoclasm', Dumbarton Oaks Papers 34/35, (Dumbarton Oaks Research Library and Collection. Washington, DC: 1980-81), 58-66.

[20] R F Taft, 'Liturgy', *The Oxford Dictionary of Byzantium*, ed. A P Kazhdan et al., Vol 2. (Oxford: Oxford University Press, 1991), 1240-1.

unmistakable traces of Byzantine influence. In the first centuries of the second millennium the gradual liturgical byzantinism of the Orthodox patriarchates of Alexandria, Antioch, and Jerusalem, which had been weakened successively by Monophysitism, the Islamic conquests, and the crusades, proceeded apace, fostered especially by the canonist Theodore Balsamon (c.1130/40-died after 1195). By the end of the 13th century the process was more or less complete in Alexandria and Antioch, though the native hagiopolite Liturgy of St James remained in use for some further time in the patriarchate of Jerusalem.[21]

Pope St Gregory the Great (known in Orthodoxy as Gregory the Dialogist: c.540-604) is mainly known for the Liturgy attributed to him of the Pre-sanctified Gifts. This ritual is basically a communion service attached to a penitential form of Vespers, and served to allow the communion of the faithful on Wednesdays and Fridays during the Great Fast, and the first three days of Great Week leading to Pascha when the Divine Liturgy is not celebrated. The holy gifts are consecrated (pre-sanctified) at the Liturgy of the preceding Sunday.

The Liturgy of St Mark, also known as the Liturgy of St Cyril of Alexandria, is the only surviving Alexandrian Liturgy. Differences between the Coptic and Greek texts are due to translation from Greek to Coptic and to increasing variations which seem to have taken place in the period after the Chalcedonian schism. This Liturgy has several distinct features. Unlike other ancient anaphora, it has an offering immediately after the preface, followed by intercessions. After the Sanctus, instead of a Christological section, there is a primitive kind of epiclesis. This leads to the customary unit of institution narrative, anamnesis, offering and epiclesis, the latter completed by the doxology. Such is its medieval form. But thanks to the detective work of Geoffrey J Cuming, it is possible to demonstrate from surviving papyrus and other fragments, that it had assumed this form in a less wordy fashion by the time of the Council of Chalcedon (451).[22] From Cuming's analysis of the text of the oldest papyrus it appears likely that it had taken shape up to the Sanctus by the 3rd century, thus making it a contemporary of the anaphoras of Hippolytus, Addai and Mari, and the Egyptian Basil. The remainder of the medieval Liturgy has a structure differing in some ways from that of St James or St John Chrysostom, including one very ancient feature, the Three Prayers. As regards the Anaphora, it would seem that there was an early close relationship with St James, distinct from major borrowings of a later period. The epiclesis reflects Cyril of Alexandria's highly developed theology of the Holy Spirit. It is rarely used except during Lent, and in some modern editions of the Coptic *Euchologion* has been rearranged to follow the order of Basil and Gregory. The present order of the whole Coptic Liturgy has existed since 1411 when Patriarch Gabriel V edited and arranged it. The Greek Egyptian Liturgy of St Basil corresponds to the Coptic Liturgy of St Basil.[23]

The development of the Byzantine iconographic tradition, especially after the 8th century iconoclastic crisis, also stimulated reflection of church buildings as an earthly mirror of the heavenly cosmos. The pattern of depicting prophets and saints, with Christ in judgement typically occupying the central dome, and the Virgin with liturgical saints in the sanctuary area, attempted to mark a linear progressive movement (from the Narthex frescoes of the OT saints one entered deeper into the church with NT scenes until one arrived at Christ in glory), and also a vertical progressive movement (from the lower walls where ascetics and other saints gave way in an upward sweep to great martyrs, angels, and the Mother of God).[24] Interestingly Patriarch Germanus, in his *Historia Ecclesiastica,* reveals that particular parts of the church were seen in terms of evocative moments in the life of Christ, and so the apse was regarded as the cave of the nativity and the altar table as the place where Christ was laid in the tomb. Declining economic conditions after the 8th century made the typical village church in Orthodox lands usually a small and intimate affair (in marked contrast to Hagia Sophia which still served as

---

[21] R F Taft, 'Liturgy', *The Oxford University Handbook of Byzantine Studies.* (Oxford: Oxford University Press, ed. E Jeffreys et al., 2008), 608.

[22] G J Cuming, *The Liturgy of St Mark: edited from the Manuscripts with a Commentary,* OCA 234. (Rome: 1990), xiii.

[23] G Bebawi, 'The Liturgy of St Mark', *The Blackwell Dictionary of Eastern Christianity*, ed. K Parry et al. (Oxford: Blackwell Publishers, 2001), 138.

[24] J A McGuckin, 'Orthodox Church Architecture', *The Encyclopaedia of Eastern Orthodox Christianity,* ed. John A McGuckin, Vol I A-M. (Chichester: Wiley-Blackwell, 2011), 47.

model). In Orthodoxy the place of worship is called church (Gr: *Naos;* Slavonic: *Kram: Temple* in English). This double use of the word 'church' which means both the Christian community assembled and the house where it worships God, is in itself an indication of the function and nature of the Orthodox Temple: the place of the leitourgia, the place where the community of the faithful fulfils itself as the Church of God, the spiritual Temple. As we have seen Orthodox architecture has a liturgical meaning, a symbolism that completes that of the Liturgy. It has a long historical development and exists in a great variety of national expressions. But the common central idea is that of the temple as 'heaven on earth' the place where through our participation in the Liturgy of the Church, we enter into communion with the *age to come,* the Kingdom of God.[25]

Icons were being hung on the sanctuary barrier or a low parapet which eventually evolved into a taller partition by the 6th century, and on the templon by the 9th. It was only in the 12th to 14th centuries that rows of fixed icons began to obscure the sanctuary area, again reflecting changes in the byzantine liturgy and church architecture. In Byzantium two or three rows of icons were the norm, but a five-tiered iconostasis appears in Russia by the 15th century. In the Vladimir Dormition cathedral of 1408 Andrei Rublev and Daniil Cherny added a tier of prophets. In the 17th century another two rows were added.[26] The icon is to be considered as a doxological expression of the Divine Liturgy. It is a theology in images. The icons of the Orthodox Church graphically help believers to have a deeper understanding of the liturgical texts, and serve as aids for their reading so that it might become contemplative. This notion emphasises the theological and didactic role of icons in the spiritual understanding of the Divine Liturgy. In terms of what they represent, icons are an open bible or even a theological treatise. Throughout history they have spoken with power and beauty. Above all, through their transparency they manifest, they serve to open the spirit towards a profound longing for God.[27] The Liturgy, too, is a sacred action, a sequence of movement or rites, not just readings and prayers. The community just as the individual pray God not just in words, but through bodily movements. Kneeling, raising of hands, bowing of heads, prostrations, kisses, incensing are religious rites as old as humanity itself. The have been accepted into Christian worship, for they are direct and natural expressions of various religious states of humankind.[28]

And so by the middle of the 14th century the rubrical manuals of the Athonite hesychast monks dominated, giving a form to the Liturgy that has remained to our day. Yet there are implications for us in this historical sweep of 'Liturgy' and 'worship.' Liturgy has to be suited to the mentality of our times and still be in continuity with patristic times. There was an understanding in Orthodoxy that liturgy continues to develop. Our common heritage of the New Testament message and the liturgical tradition has us again pondering the meaning and direction of our liturgical worship. That Orthodox group that met in New York in 1998 on the way to the WCC Assembly in Harare have offered a balanced critique of Orthodoxy that still reads as fresh today - fourteen years later! Two of their recommendations are to be noted:

There is need to revaluate various practices related to confession, fasting & other forms of preparation for communion. This is particularly necessary when these practices not only obscure the ecclesial significance of the Eucharist but also discourage frequent communion, thus inhibiting the spiritual growth & nourishment of the faithful.

The study of worship is to be fostered. It will help free us of ritual formalism and help us discover and articulate the riches of our liturgical heritage. This will help to determine if our worship today inspires the faithful, young & old, to carry the message of the gospel into all areas of life and society and to bear witness to the compassion, justice, mercy and wisdom of God.

---

[25] A Schmemann, *Liturgy and Life: Christian Development through Liturgical Experience.* (New York: Department of Religious Education, Orthodox Church in America, 1993), 34-5.

[26] K Parry, 'Iconostasis', *The Blackwell Dictionary of Eastern Christianity*, ed. K Parry et al. (Oxford: Blackwell Publishers, 2001), 242-3.

[27] T Damian, 'Icons' ,*The Encyclopedia of Eastern Orthodox Christianity,* ed. J A McGuckin, Vol. I A-M. (Chichester: Wiley-Blackwell, 2011), 335-6.; also L Ph B, 'Templon', *The Oxford Dictionary of Byzantium,* ed. A P Kazhdan et al., Vol 3. (Oxford: Oxford University Press, 1991), 2023-4.

[28] A Schmemann, *Liturgy and Life: Christian Development through Liturgical Experience.* (New York: Department of Religious Education, Orthodox Church in America, 1993), 30-1.

Part VII: Particular Themes and Issues for Orthodox Involvement in Ecumenism

And their gentle reminders for Orthodox Ecumenical Worship:

(a) As the Third Pan-Orthodox Pre-Conciliar Conference in 1986 said: 'The Orthodox participation in the ecumenical movement does not run counter to the nature & history of the Orthodox Church: it constitutes the consistent expression of the Apostolic faith within new historical conditions, in order to respond to new existential demands.'

(b) From the beginnings of the Ecumenical Movement the Orthodox have participated in services of common prayer with Christians of other traditions.

We communicate with God through worship and language, as already stated. Again the 1998 New York preparatory team would have us jog our memories: language with its peculiarities of syntax, grammar and vocabulary can change through time, similarly worship with its gestures, symbols and style of a given time and place may not be readily grasped in another historical setting, and so the need for to critically assess this from time to time.[29] Recall Anton Baumstark's adages, quoted by Taft, that 'the forms of Liturgy are subject by their very nature to a process of continuous evolution', and it seems to be of the nature of Liturgy to relate itself to the concrete situations of times and places.'[30]

In the final analysis, the very variety of these liturgical types is a witness to the openness of liturgy in its attempt to embrace so many different cultural contexts and peoples as possible.

The Liturgy acclaims God thrice holy; it proclaims Christ as alone holy; it celebrates the feast of saints. We also speak of the holy gospels, of holy week; and we are called to be holy. Holiness then appears to be a complex reality which touches on the mystery of God, but also on worship and morality. It includes the notions of sacred and pure, but transcends them. It seems to be inaccessibly reserved to God, but constantly attributed to creatures.

Paul Evdokimov in an article entitled 'Nature' elaborates on creation, the fall, the sacred and the sacraments: 'God alone is holy. The sacred, the holiness of the creature is never such by its own nature, but always by participation in the holiness of God (Heb 12:10). The term *Qadosh, hagios, sanctus*, implies a relation of complete belonging to God.'[31] The Semitic word is derived from a root which means 'to cut off, separate' and points towards the idea of separation from the profane; holy things are those which are not to be touched or approached except under certain conditions of ritual purity. Something of Rudolf Otto's 'numinous': a mystery that is both terrifying (*tremendum*), presenting itself as an overwhelming power and purity, and fascinating (*fascinans*) at the same time by His love and grace. The transcendent God is experienced as 'wholly other', a condition entirely different from anything that we experience in ordinary life. 'The act of sanctifying makes us participants in the 'wholly other': to be the pure receptacle of a presence; the radiant power of God rests in it.'[32] This is what elicits worship from human beings at its manifestation, adds Wainwright.

It was God's choice 'set Israel apart' that had it become a 'holy nation'; and His choice of plan for the New Israel, that every baptised person, integrated into Christ, and becoming a bearer of the Holy Spirit, would be a 'partaker of the divine nature' (2 Peter 1:4), 'of the holiness of God' (Heb 12:10). And, above all, according to Nicholaos Cabasilas, 'the faithful are holy by reason of the holy thing in which they participate, the Eucharist.'

Evdokimov continues:

'From the single divine source: "You shall be holy, for I, the Lord your God, am holy"[33], flows a whole succession of consecrations by participation. They effect a 'de-secularisation', a 'de-popularisation' in the very being of this

---

[29] T FitzGerald & P. Bouteneff, (eds), *Turn to God, Rejoice in Hope: Orthodox Reflections on the Way to Harare,* (Geneva: WCC, 1998), 141-46.

[30] R F Taft, 'Liturgy', *The Oxford University Handbook of Byzantine Studies.* (Oxford: Oxford University Press, ed. E Jeffreys et al., 2008), 608.

[31] 'Nature', *Scottish Journal of Theology* 18.1 (1965): 1-22.

[32] See G Wainwright, 'Christian Worship: Scriptural Basis and Theological Frame', *The Oxford History of Christian Worship*, ed G Waintwright & K B Westerfield Tucker (Oxford: Oxford University Press, 2006), 2.

[33] Following the Jewish translation and commentary on Lev 19:2. 'Later interpreters often took it as a general command to emulate divine attributes such as compassion and forgiveness ("Imitatio Dei"). But 'holy' in the Bible does not refer to

world. This action of 'puncturing' the closed world by the in breaking of powers from the beyond belongs properly to the sacraments and the sacramentals, which teach us that everything is destined for its liturgical fulfilment. The blessing of the fruits of the earth at the feast of the Transfiguration or at Easter extends over all 'food' the sanctifying action contained in the word pronounced by the priest when he gives the Eucharist: 'for the healing of soul and body.' The destiny of the element of water is to participate in the mystery of the Epiphany; the destiny of the earth is to receive the body of the Lord for the repose of Great Saturday... ('What shall we offer you, O Christ...' every creature brings its token of gratitude:... 'the earth, its cave; the wilderness, the manger...')[34] Olive oil and water find their fulfilment as conductors of grace to regenerated man; the wheat and the vine culminate in the Eucharistic cup. *Everything* refers to the Incarnation, and *everything* (my emphasis) leads to the Lord... The Liturgy integrates the most elementary actions of life: drinking, eating, washing, speaking, acting, communicating, living – and restores to them their meaning and their true destiny; to be parts of the cosmic Temple of God's Glory... There is nothing in this world which has remained a stranger to His humanity and has not received the imprint of the Holy Spirit. It is for the Holy Spirit to bring that alive in all of us...'

If already the Old Testament inaugurates the sacredness of springs, mountains, stones, and holy nation, it is the Christian Liturgy which undertakes the consecration of the world. With Constantine, the place of worship forms part of the social structure of the city [35], and the Lord's Day coincides with the day on which men rest, and the temple offers an image of the organised cosmos.'

In all this we see how the Eucharist and worship encompass the whole world and the whole of creation. The universal impact of liturgical life, and its ecumenical relevance (in the sense of embracing everybody regardless of background – referring to the whole inhabited earth, but also the natural creation (creation symbolised and present in the elements of bread and wine).

Ultimately, Liturgy and sacraments are there to remind us of what we already have – the gift of life itself from God our Creator and the transforming presence of the Holy Spirit, healing our sinfulness and bringing us to full creative maturity; to reach out to others and to have them also touched by God's holiness (Ephes 4:11-13).

Perhaps as an adjustment to all this, the emphasis should rather be that Liturgy-Eucharist is not just a top down movement, but a movement towards each other, i.e. an organic whole where we accept God's 'gift', work the gift and make it happen. This in turn brings about Christ's living in us and being in His world; and where we contribute to the ongoing work of consecrating all mankind.

'This is right and acceptable in the sight of God our Saviour, who desires everyone to be saved and to come to the knowledge of the truth.' (1 Tim 2:4)

...And then there was *The Liturgy after the Liturgy* (Father Ion Bria)!

Bibliography

J F Baldovin, *The Urban Character of Christian Worship*, OCA 228. (Rome: 1987).

I Bria, *The Liturgy after the Liturgy: Mission and Witness from an Orthodox Perspective.* (Geneva: WCC Publications, 1996).

G J Cuming, *The Liturgy of St Mark: edited from the Manuscripts with a Commentary,* OCA 234. (Rome: 1990).

Dictionary of the Ecumenical Movement, ed N. Lossky et al. (Geneva: WCC Publications, 2002).

superior moral qualities. God's holiness is His essential 'otherness,' His being separate from all that is not divine; humans are not called upon to be holy in this sense (the text does not say 'as I am holy'). Holiness in humans, as in time, space, objects, and speech, is the state of belonging to the deity, being designated God's 'personal' property...In Priestly thought, holiness is the desired result of an effusion of God's immanent presence.' *The Jewish Study Bible*, eds A Berlin & M Z Brettler (Oxford: Oxford University Press, 1999), 253.

[34] Troparion of the Vespers of Christmas, *The Festal Menaion* (London, Faber & Faber, 1996), 254.

[35] M Low, *Celtic Christianity and Nature: Early Irish and Hebridean Traditions* (Belfast: The Blackstaff Press, 1996), 1-4, who reminds us of an initial stage of outdoor worship before the advent of (church) buildings with its implied social construct.

Encyclopedia of the Early Church, Institutum Patristicum Augustinianum, ed. A Di Bernardino, ET. A Walford, Vol I. (Cambridge: James Clarke & Co, 1992).

P Evdokimov, 'Nature', *Scottish Journal of Theology* 18.1 (March 1965): 1-22.

T FitzGerald & P. Bouteneff, (eds), *Turn to God, Rejoice in Hope: Orthodox Reflections on the Way to Harare*, (Geneva: WCC, 1998).

A J Heschel, *Man's Quest for God: Studies in Prayer and Symbolism*. (Santa Fe: Aurora Press,1998).

J Mateos S J, *La célébration de la parole dans la liturgie byzantine: étude historique*, OCA 191. (Rome: 1971).

A Schmemann, *Liturgy and Life: Christian Development through Liturgical Experience*. (New York: Department of Religious Education, Orthodox Church in America, 1993).

-, *Liturgy and Tradition: Theological Reflections of Alexander Schmemann*, ed. T Fisch. (Crestwood, NY: St Vladimir's Seminary Press, 2003).

-, *Introduction to Liturgical Theology*. (Crestwood, NY: St Vladimir's Seminary Press, 2003).

R F Taft, 'Liturgy' in *The Oxford Dictionary of Byzantium*, ed. A P Kazhdan et al., Vol 2. (Oxford: Oxford University Press, 1991), 1240-1.

-, 'Liturgy' in E Jeffreys et al. (ed.), *The Oxford University Handbook of Byzantine Studies*. (Oxford University Press 2008), 599-610.

-, *The Byzantine Liturgy: A Short History*, American Essays in Liturgy Series. (Collegeville, Minn: The Liturgical Press, 1992), 28-41.

-, *The Great Entrance. A History of the Transfer of Gifts and Other Preanaphoral Rites of the Liturgy of St John Chrysostom*, OCA 200. (Rome: 1975).

-, 'The Liturgy of the Great Church: An Initial Synthesis of Structure and Interpretation on the Eve of Iconoclasm', Dumbarton Oaks Papers 34/35, Dumbarton Oaks Research Library and Collection. (Washington, DC: 1980-81), 45-75.

The Blackwell Dictionary of Eastern Christianity, ed. K Parry et al. (Oxford: Blackwell Publishers, 2001).

The Cambridge Companion to Orthodox Christian Theology, ed. M.B. Cunningham & E. Theokritoff. (New York: Cambridge University Press, 2008).

The Encyclopaedia of Eastern Orthodox Christianity, ed. J A McGuckin, Vol. I A-M. (Chichester: Wiley-Blackwell, 2011).

J D Zizioulas, *The Eucharistic Communion and The World* (ed. L Tallon). (London: T & T Clark, 2011).

(96) Basic Elements of Church Unity/
Intercommunion according to Orthodox understanding[1]

Tamara Grdzelidze

The search for church unity has been the daily Orthodox prayer - 'for the union of all'. Therefore it is not surprising that from the very beginning of the Orthodox participation in the ecumenical movement the prevailing theme has been a desire for unity in spite of challenges due to different ecclesiologies.[2]

One of the important messages throughout the history of the Orthodox participation in the ecumenical movement is the Orthodox memorandum at the First World Conference of Faith and Order[3] in Lausanne 1927.[4] The Orthodox claimed that "reunion can take place only on the basis of the common faith and confession" of the undivided church, which they acknowledged as the reality of the first eight centuries of the Christian era. Real union is seen only as communio in sacris and the latter may happen only on the basis of the full agreement in faith. The Orthodox delegates expressed their readiness to continue the search for unity by means of the shared position which acknowledged "a partial reunion" of other Churches in anticipation of the "general union." Although fully conscious of the challenge of being divided by dogmatic differences, the Orthodox declared readiness to continue devotion to the rapprochement of the churches, with those who share the same faith in our Lord Jesus Christ. As Fr. George Florovsky expressed it in 1949, the Orthodox understood their mandate to participate in ecumenical movement "as a direct obligation which stems from the very essence of Orthodox consciousness."[5]

The main source of division between the churches, ecclesiology, has been treated at different points of Orthodox participation in the ecumenical movement but has not been solved to a great extent, at least as much as to help all Orthodox to pray with others, not to mention to share communion. Following the foundation of the World Council of Churches (1948) – and international ecumenical institution to serve and represent a fellowship of churches – the first 'concession' to the Orthodox ecclesiology was the so-called Toronto Statement (1950) on "The Church, the Churches, and the World Council of Churches."[6] The Orthodox concern was to avoid identifying the WCC as a church or super-church and its membership as implying a specific doctrine concerning the nature of church unity. The series of negations in the statement some called "provisional neutrality" which should be a starting-point dissolved with years.[7] The Toronto Statement 'allowed' the Orthodox

---

[1] The first following article on this subject is from Tamara Grdzelidze, while the second one from Petros Vassiliadis (ed.).

[2] See two patriarchal encyclicals, Patriarchal and Synodical Encyclical of 1902 (His Holiness Joachim III, Patriarch of Constantinople), *The Orthodox Church in the Ecumenical Movement, Documents and Statements*, edited by Constantin G. Patelos (Geneva, WCC Publications: 1978), 27-33. Even more explicitly ecumenical is the Encyclical of the Ecumenical Patriarchate of 1920, sent out by Archbishop Germanos, which is addressed "Unto the Churches of Christ everywhere" and sets the tune at the beginning by using a quote from the First letter of Peter as an epigraph: "Love one another earnestly from the heart." *Orthodox Visions of Ecumenism, Statements, Messages and Reports on the Ecumenical Movement, 1902-1992*, Compiled by Gennadios Limouris (Geneva, WCC Publications: 1994), 40-43.

[3] Faith and Order started as a movement of churches to combat church division and seek unity according to the will of Christ: "so that all may be one," John 17:21. At present it is a commission of nominees from different churches, 120 persons, coming together to reflect on divisive and non-divisive issues which keep the churches away from full communion.

[4] *Orthodox Visions of Ecumenism*, 12-14.

[5] Fr. Georges Florovsky, "The Orthodox Contribution to the Ecumenical Movement," in *Ecumenism I, A Doctrinal Approach* Collected works, Vol. 13 (Vaduz: 1989), 160.

[6] "The Church, the Churches, and the World Council of Churches," WCC Central Committee, Toronto, 1950 *The Ecumenical Movement, An Anthology of key texts and Voices*, 463-468.

[7] Ibid.

to participate in ecumenical movement. The very fact of the Orthodox participation in ecumenical movement, in spite of the huge ecclesiological challenges, can be considered as a contribution in itself.

At the outset of the ecumenical endeavour the Orthodox have been referring to the necessity for all to return to the bosom of the mother church of the first centuries. 'Return' to the ancient church will not be easy for any churches that are living bodies and have been exposed to historical changes. Nor does contemporary biblical scholarship accepts the idea that there was 'an ideal, homogenous church' in the ancient times." An acceptable formulation of such a demand must be a joint rediscovery of the common roots. This means that all churches are on the journey of rediscovering their common heritage which may bring the churches closer than it has been possible at present. The standpoint for the Orthodox in ecclesiological discussions is the Eucharistic ecclesiology: Koinonia does not know division; the unity exists only in Christ and is actualised in the Eucharist. But how far can the Orthodox Eucharistic ecclesiology embrace other ecclesiologies? Can the Orthodox pneumatology allow the full sharing of gifts with other churches?

At the third WCC Assembly in New Delhi (1963) the Orthodox voice became stronger in articulating the Orthodox ecclesiological self-understanding, and rejecting the notion of "parity of denominations." The idea of broken unity that is to be recovered was also a forceful declaration followed by the statement that the Orthodox Church is the church and not one among many, which claims the un-brokenness in tradition and sacramental life and faith. The Orthodox Church put apostolic succession of episcopacy and sacramental priesthood as essential and constitutive to the church which, on its own part, bears witness to the tradition of the undivided church. Then, modifying the above-mentioned idea concerning the provisional "reunion" between the non-Orthodox "churches," it recommended the Protestant churches to find a common ground in their common history. As for the future, the Orthodox modified again their statement by suggesting a movement neither towards uniformity nor restoration of old forms, but rather towards a recovery of apostolic tradition. (In this context it is recommended to read *On the Tradition in the Orthodox Church*).

The ecclesiological challenge begets one of the major obstacles for some Orthodox to participate in the ecumenical movement, that is common prayer. All partners in the ecumenical movement are aware of the difficulties related to common worship. There are theological, canonical, traditional, historical, ethical reasons behind, but in general from an Orthodox perspective, two sets of problems can be identified around the issue. Firstly, it is a canonical problem; "Do not pray with heretics" (Apostolic Constitutions 45, and Laodecean 33/34) interpreted as not praying or worshipping with the other Christians. Secondly, it is an ethical problem related to the nature of ecumenical prayer. There is not a single Orthodox approach to the matter of praying ecumenically with the exception of the "intercommunion" or "Eucharistic hospitality," which in the ecumenical context is excluded at once.

In spite of Orthodox concerns related to church unity stemming from their unique ecclesiology, there is an unceasing process of the Orthodox efforts in this direction – a search for visible unity.[8] This is very much in the spirit of teaching of the giants of the ecumenical movement such as Fr. Georges Florovsky or Prof. Nikos Nissiotis whose qualified eagerness to stay in the movement and witness to the world together with other fellow Christians can be understood as an imperative to the Orthodox worldwide.[9]

Orthodox ecclesiology has become an important question in the multilateral ecumenical conversations. The consciousness that the Orthodox Church is the "One, Holy, Catholic and Apostolic Church" has defined the participation of the Orthodox in the ecumenical movement. According to Metropolitan John Zizioulas, in the context of ecumenical dialogue four difficult aspects of Orthodox ecclesiology stand out: the church as

---

[8] The best and most vivid expression of this would be the Orthodox participation in and preference for the ecumenical work carried out by Faith and Order.

[9] See G. Florovsky, "The Limits of the Church," http://www.wcc-coe.org/wcc/who/crete-01-e.html (last accessed, September 2013).
N. Nissiotis, "Called to Unity The Significance of the Invocation of the Spirit for Church Unity," Lausanne 77, Fifty Years of Faith and Order, Faith and Order Paper no.82 (Geneva, WCC Publications: 1978), 48-64.

historical, as eschatological, as relational, and as a sacramental entity. Since the Orthodox find it impossible to separate the visible and the invisible aspects of the church, they "expect that the other Christians will take the visible unity of the Church seriously and it is indeed gratifying to see that since Nairobi at least the call to visible unity has become central in the ecumenical agenda and language."[10] The Church is called to be a sign of the Kingdom; it is an expression of the living tradition which is received in the Church by every generation.

The sacramental nature of the Church has been maintained through the central role of the sacraments, among which the primary significance of the Baptism and the Eucharist is taken for granted. The Orthodox for their part have been graciously carrying these ecclesiological principles within the ecumenical movement. Another difficulty faced by Orthodox theology, as it seeks to enter into an honest and constructive dialogue with fellow Christians, is the indivisible nature of this theology, seeking as it does to keep all aspects of the Christian faith and life together. Thus "ethics cannot be separated from faith anymore than Orthodoxia can be divorced from Orthopraxia."[11]

In the Orthodox view, the Church is a divine-human reality; the body of Christ does not know a separation between its invisible and visible aspects; it is both visible and invisible at once, and hence the Church does not sin. Its oneness and holiness is matched by its catholicity and apostolicity. The only way to full unity lies through sacramental communion, backed up by full sharing of faith in the Lord Jesus Christ, incarnate and resurrected, the founder of the Church. In this world, the Church is a sign of the Kingdom. Orthodox ecclesiology, therefore, sets limits as to the ways in which it can search towards unity: the Orthodox aim to arrive at a commonly shared ecclesiastical vision, rather than any other form of unity. This "common ecclesiastical vision" implies recovering the common faith and Tradition; the Church needs Tradition in order to exist as koinonia/communion. This ecclesiological understanding is deeply rooted in both the biblical and the patristic reality of the undivided church.

In the 90s, the Orthodox started expressing their dissatisfaction with the process and ethos of the ecumenical movement. One of the positive outcomes of their 'protest' has been the Special Commission on Orthodox Participation in the World Council of Churches.[12] Apart from other benefits, the Special Commission provided another opportunity to reflect more deeply on issues which the Orthodox have been raising for decades, most of all the nature and style of ecumenical prayer, the overall agenda of the WCC, questions of morality[13] and one of the central Orthodox concerns in ecumenical movement, the ecclesiological challenge expressed by the Special Commission Report in the following manner: "Is there space for other churches in Orthodox ecclesiology? How would this space and its limits be described?"[14]

The latest Orthodox contribution to the search for visible unity – through responding to the Faith and Order draft text, The Nature and Mission of the Church (2005) – highlights that "the Orthodox identify the Church with the Orthodox Church" (Inter-Orthodox Consultation, 2011, par.9) and points out (once more) the

---

[10] Metropolitan John of Pergamon, "The Self-understanding of the Orthodox and their Participation in the Ecumenical Movement," *The Ecumenical Movement, the Churches and the World Council of Churches*, An Orthodox contribution to the reflection process on "The Common Understanding and Vision of the WCC"; The proceedings of the Inter-Orthodox consultation on "The Common Understanding and Vision of the WCC," (Orthodox Centre of the Ecumenical Patriarchate, Chambésy, Geneva, 19 to 24 June 1995), Edited by George Lemopoulos, co-produced by the WCC and Syndesmos, 40.

[11] Ibid, 43.

[12] This was a committee of 60 persons, with equal Orthodox and non-Orthodox representation, consisting of high officials from churches and theologians. Although it started as a committee to meet particular Orthodox concerns, finally the Special Commission played a remarkable role in renewing various policies of the WCC. Thus it met the concerns of a wider constituency, and embraced a wider realm of issues, than had been initially considered (ecclesiology, common prayer, social-ethical issues, decision-making and membership).

[13] Anna Marie Aagard and Peter Bouteneff, *Beyond The East-West Divide, The World Council of Church and "the Orthodox Problem"* (Geneva: WCC Publications, 2001), 9.

[14] *The Ecumenical Review* 55.1 (2003): 7.

Part VII: Particular Themes and Issues for Orthodox Involvement in Ecumenism

inconsistency between a denominationalist ecclesiology and the Orthodox ecclesiology (par.12). The Church is the continuation of the mystery of Christ (par.14), reflecting the Trinitarian archetype (par.21); the holiness of the Church is one of its essential characteristics realized in the sacraments (par.16), and the fallen reality refers only to its members. The response also highlights a traditional position of the Orthodox towards the ministry in the Church which stresses a distinction between the ordained ministry and the ministry of all the faithful (par.28):

"Celebrating the Eucharist as one body, the Church rejects all fragmentation and discrimination on the basis of class and caste, race and gender, age and wealth. In upholding and constantly promoting the oneness of the Body, while respecting the identity and role of every particular organ, the Church sets the model for the unity of humanity and of all creation. Since all forms of injustice and discrimination, and all violence and war go against this God-given gift of unity, the Church is constantly called upon to struggle against every form of injustice and oppression, mistrust and conflict created by human beings" (par.39).[15]

Bibliography

The Ecumenical Patriarchate and Christian Unity, Third Revised and Enlarged Edition by Thomas FitzGerald, (Brookline, Massachusetts: Holy Cross Orthodox Press, 2009).

Florovsky, George, "The Orthodox Contribution to the Ecumenical Movement," *Ecumenism, A Doctrinal Approach*. Collected Works, Vol. 13 (Vaduz: 1989).

The Orthodox Church in the Ecumenical Movement, Documents and Statements, edited by Constantin G. Patelos (Geneva, WCC Publications: 1978).

Orthodox Visions of Ecumenism, Statements, Messages and Reports on the Ecumenical Movement, 1902-1992, Compiled by Gennadios Limouris (Geneva, WCC Publications: 1994).

Petros Vassiliadis

The main difference between the traditional Churches (Orthodox and Roman Catholic) and the rest of the Christian communities is the issue of the "exclusive" character of the Eucharist. It is on this issue exactly that all Eucharistic exchanges among them and between Orthodox-Catholics are unquestionably excluded, with no possibility to consider any way of extending among them some kind of "Eucharistic hospitality." In general the very idea of intercommunion is completely ruled out; the main argument being that the Eucharist, the Sacrament par excellence of the Church, is the culmination of unity, not a means towards unity. Yet, here and there, some isolated cases do exist in modern Orthodoxy, who expected that at least some sort of Eucharistic hospitality existed at least between the Eastern and the Oriental Orthodox Churches (I. Bria) or between the Orthodox and the Roman Catholic Church (O. Clement).

Others insist that on theological grounds Orthodoxy can move beyond the old dilemma "full communion vs. intercommunion." The key issue is how one can establish the "inclusive" or "exclusive" character of the Eucharist. If one ignores the biblical data, more precisely the undisputed Pauline Epistles, then exclusivity may come out as a possibility of erecting uncrossed barriers to anyone outside the canonical lines of the Church. If the Pauline Eucharistic theology is a sine qua non of all Orthodox consideration, then a new perspective enters into the discussion. The implications for ecclesiology, missiology and our ecumenical relations of such a Pauline theology are quite important.

[15]http://www.oikoumene.org/en/press-centre/news/an-orthodox-response-to-the-nature-and-mission-of-the-church (last accessed, September 2013).

According to almost all contemporary Orthodox theologians "there is an almost unanimous conviction... that the church must be defined in the framework of a Eucharistic ecclesiology."[16] It was, nevertheless, on this very theological articulation – rather the narrow interpretation of the Eucharist – that so many problems have emerged. A correct interpretation of the Pauline Epistles points to the conviction that from a strictly historical view "what distinguished Jesus among many of his rabbinic contemporaries was his practice of fellowship at meals."[17] This "open table fellowship" is clearly evidenced in the Epistle to Galatians, where St. Paul defended St. Peter's dining (before the arrival of St. James' people) with the Gentiles (cf. Gal 2:12 "ὅτι μετά των εθνών συνήσθιεν").[18] The "open table fellowship" and the absence of boundaries at meals are "characteristic and distinctive of the social-self-understanding that Jesus encouraged in his disciples."[19] No serious biblical scholar can deny today that the only reliable starting point in determining the very nature of the Eucharist is the "open table fellowship" and the "inclusiveness" underlined in Jesus' teaching of the coming Kingdom of God and the common meals, which he used to bless, and participate in, during his earthly ministry.

In few words the original, and by all means authentic, understanding of the Eucharist stems from the awareness of the early Christian community that they were God's eschatological people, who represented in their Eucharistic gatherings the expected Kingdom of God. As with the understanding of their mission, according to which the apostles were commissioned to proclaim not a set of given religious convictions, doctrines, moral commands etc., but the coming Kingdom and their resurrected Lord center and sovereign of it, so also with the Eucharist they actually expressed in deeds, i.e. around a common table, the Good News of a new eschatological reality.[20] That is why they were all called "holy," "royal priesthood," because in the eschatological era all of them (not just some special cast, such as the priests or Levites) believed to have priestly and spiritual authority to practice in the diaspora the work of the priestly class, reminded at the same time to be worthy of their election though their exemplary life and works.

In numerous cases the historical Jesus was actually challenging the social and religious validity of some Torah regulations on clean and unclean. Most of his healings were directed toward people who were considered unclean: lepers (Mk. 1:40-45; Mt. 8:1-4; cf. Lk. 17:11-19), the woman in bloodshed (Mk. 5:25-34; Mt. 9:20-22; Lk. 8:43-48), people possessed by daemons, blind, cripple etc. Whereas for the Jews the most important issue was "how and on what conditions can people approach God in order to be saved," the early Christians put more emphasis on "how God approaches people and offers salvation." To the former approaching God was accomplished only through the Law ("εν τω νόμω"), whereas to the latter through Christ ("εν Χριστώ").

The issue of inclusion within the community of faith of all people (clean and unclean – one can expand it in today's terms mutatis mutandis also to faithful and...heretics?) and therefore accepting them at the common (Eucharistic/ eschatological/messianic or otherwise) meals, received quite dangerous consequences for the emerging new Christian religion once it expanded beyond the boundaries of Judaism. Receiving new converts, of course, has never been an actual problem throughout the early Church. Even Judeo-Christians could accept and endorse it. The problem arose on the practical consequences of such a move: at the common (Eucharistic/ eschatological/messianic or otherwise) meals between circumcised Jews and former Gentiles. The expression

---

[16] Ion Bria, "Widening the Ecclesiological Basis of the Ecumenical Fellowship," The Ecumenical Review 56 (2004): 199ff, here at 119.

[17] B. Chilton, "Inclusion and Non-inclusion: The Practice of the Kingdom in Formative Christianity," in J. Neusner (ed.), *Religion and the Political Order*, (Scholars Press: Atlanta), 133-172, 137; also in his *Pure Kingdom: Jesus' Vision of God*, (Eerdmans: Grand Rapids, 1996).

[18] More in D. Passakos, "Μετά των εθνων συνήσθιεν..," Theology and Society in Dialogue, (Thessaloniki 2001), 96ff (in Greek).

[19] J. D. G. Dunn, *Jesus Remembered*, (Grand Rapids: Eerdmans, 2003), 599.

[20] Ion Bria extended this belief to the Trinity, defining the mission on the basis of Jn. 21 in terms of a mission dei, namely that "God in God's own self is a life of communion and that God's involvement in history aims at drawing humanity and creation in general into this communion with God's very life," which implies that this must also be the goal of mission (Ion Bria, *Go Forth in Peace*, (Geneva 1987), 3).

that before the arrival of representatives of the Jerusalem group Peter "ate with the Gentiles" (Gal 2:12) is quite characteristic. Obviously in the early Church there were leaders insisting on separate Eucharistic celebrations, so that the basic rules of cleanness are kept. This tendency followed the line of a "Eucharistic exclusiveness." Paul's line, on the contrary, understood the fundamental issue of salvation "in Christ" in a quite inclusive way. He considered the "separate" Eucharistic tables as an inconceivable practice, and he insisted on a "common" Eucharistic table for both Jews and Gentiles. In other words his view was that of a "Eucharistic inclusiveness." For Paul there was no other way; any compromise would destroy the basis of his faith and the legacy of Jesus of Nazareth.

St. Paul's "inclusive Eucharistic theology" does not by any means question the theological foundation of today's difficulty on the part of the Orthodox in accepting the idea of intercommunion, at least in the form it is generally presented by almost all Protestant theologians and their communities. The Eucharist is, and will remain, an expression of, not a means towards, Church unity. Nevertheless, Jesus of Nazareth's inclusive kerygma, and St. Paul's foundational teaching and praxis of a "Eucharistic inclusiveness," remind us that the original "open," "inclusive" and above all "unifying" character of the Eucharist somewhat challenges our contemporary views and demands a radical reconsideration of our Eucharistic ecclesiology.

(97) Orthodox Ecclesiology in Dialogue with other Understandings of the Nature of the Church

Athanasios Vletsis

Introductory Remarks

"There are ecclesiological presuppositions lying behind both the Basis and Constitution of the WCC. How do churches belonging to the fellowship of the WCC currently understand the commitment they make to the Trinitarian faith in the Basis? How do they understand the intention expressed in the Constitution 'to call one another to the goal of visible unity in one faith and in one eucharistic fellowship, expressed in worship and common life in Christ, through witness and service to the world and to advance towards this unity so that the world may believe'? The response to these questions is influenced by the existence of two basic ecclesiological self-understandings, namely of those churches (such as the Orthodox) which identify themselves with the One, Holy, Catholic and Apostolic Church, and those which see themselves as parts of the One, Holy, Catholic and Apostolic Church. These two ecclesiological positions affect whether or not churches recognize each other's baptism as well as their ability or inability to recognize one another as churches."[1]

Orthodox ecclesiology identifies the Church of Christ with one visible Church and concretely with the Orthodox Church. Thus it does not seem willing to accept the concept of an ideal, invisible Church, whose partial, visible appearances are the historical, institutionally organized Churches all around the world. But is this distinction of two types of ecclesiological self-understanding (according to the Final Report of the Special Commission on Orthodox Participation in the WCC) able to define correctly the problem of the relation between the one and the many Churches? If the models described in the text cited above represent the tradition of the Orthodox Church on the one side and the traditions of the Churches that emerged from the Reformation on the other, in what way is this distinction applicable to the Roman–Catholic Church? Does this distinction imply that the Orthodox model of unity proposes the return of the other Churches to the One (Orthodox) Church, which is believed to be identical with the Church of the Nicene–Constantinopolitan creed? Is really the Orthodox Church such a monolithic organism, or does it consist of a communion of Churches, which could expand – under presuppositions – its boundaries, so that it may include other (local) Churches, too?

In this article I will deal with the questions raised above, which mirror some central aspects of the general ecclesiological discussion. The question about the Church, the ecclesiological question, seems to monopolize the ecumenical inquiry since the very beginning of the 20th century: After about 100 years of rather general fruitful ecumenical pursuits, after at least 60 years of concrete and intense steps towards ecumenical reconcilement on a multilateral level on the basis of the WCC platform and after more than 30 years of intensive official bilateral dialogues with Orthodox participation, serious concerns are raising because of the difficulty to define concretely the next targets in our common way. The inability to harmonize the various suggested models of unity which represent the views of specific Churches and their theologies, reflects the puzzlement concerning the path the ecumenical movement should take in the future.

The first chapter of this article will provide a brief presentation of elementary principles of Orthodox ecclesiology and the problems surrounding it; in the second, one I will give a short overview of the models adopted

---

[1] Final Report of the Special Commission on Orthodox Participation in the WCC (1998–2002), §14-15. See the text in: Theodoros Meimaris, *The Holy and Great Council of the Orthodox Church and the Ecumenical Movement*, (Thessaloniki 2013), 282–346; at 286–287.

by the other (Roman–Catholic and Protestant) Churches. In the third, I will try to describe the Orthodox model of unity, as it is being reflected in Orthodox contributions in inter–Orthodox and inter–confessional forums of dialogue. In the last chapter, I will sketch some proposals for the future.

1. Eucharistic ecclesiology: precedence of the local Church?

"The Eucharist makes the Church"[2]: this principle summarizes the ecclesiological self–understanding of the Orthodox Church, or at least this is how the Orthodox – and not only – describe it in the 20th century. The celebration of the Eucharist is both the mystery and the image of communion and unity not only with the Triune God, but also with the brothers and sisters in Christ; it is both foretaste and manifestation of the Kingdom of God already in this world. The principle of Eucharistic ecclesiology gives evident precedence to the local Church, either we define this local Church as the parochial community or as the local diocese: From an Orthodox point of view the attribute of catholicity has not a quantitative, but primarily a qualitative meaning; it is rather an expression of the fullness of the truth of the Church.[3] This truth is being realized in every Eucharistic gathering; such a gathering does not merely constitute a part of the universal Church; moreover, it rather incarnates the fullness of ecclesial life. According to N. Afanassieff, who introduced eucharistic ecclesiology and provided its theoretical background, universalist ecclesiology (that is the view which understands the Church as primarily realized in its universal wholeness; according to this thinking, the local parochial or episcopal liturgical gathering is not but a part of this wholeness) was nothing else than a necessary adjustment to the new developments which took place within the Byzantine Empire (which was, at least according to its self–understanding, a Christian state) and which had certain consequences for the life of the Church.[4]

This equation of the Church and the Eucharist mirrors an idealization; it does not take sufficiently into account the presuppositions which are necessary, so that the local Eucharistic gathering may actually express the catholicity of the Church. It also overlooks the further consequences of the Eucharistic ecclesiology. Nowadays the impasses of an one–dimensional identification of the Church with the eucharist are visible in the Orthodox Churches: The eucharist is image of the eschaton and type of the Trinitarian unity only inasmuch as the unity of the faithful and the Eucharistic gathering "functions". This presupposes community not only in faith and life, but also in the order and structure of the ecclesial life. Orthodox Eucharistic ecclesiology is based upon the community of local Churches which built up their identity and their modes of communication during the first Christian millennium; this process owes a lot to the cultural communication and to the political framework of the eastern Hellenistic world and, later, of the Byzantine Empire. The rise of new kingdoms in the western regions and boundaries of the Western Roman Empire (and more concretely the rise of the kingdom of the Francs) shacked the structures of the Church and contributed in many ways to the mutual ecclesial alienation of East and West. As far as the Churches of the East are concerned, new conditions defined their context: the conquests of Muslim empires and afterwards the rise of new national states as successors of the Ottoman Empire led to the establishment of many autocephalous Churches. One may claim that, in the Orthodox tradition, the establishment of autocephalous Churches is generally compatible with the principle of the local–eucharistic gathering and that it should be regarded as a legitimate continuation of the Pentarchy. Nevertheless, when the structures which secure the harmonious communion of the local Churches (in this context I characterize the autocephalous

---

[2] See e.g. Paul McPartlan, *The Eucharist makes the Church. Henri de Lubac and John Zizioulas in Dialogue*, (Edinburgh 1993). For a spherical consideration of the problems of Eucharistic ecclesiology see the articles published in *International Journal for the Study of the Christian Church* 11.2/3 (2011).

[3] More in: Athanasios Vletsis, "Katholizität oder Ökumenizität der Kirche? Das Ringen um die dritte Eigenschaft der Kirche in der orthodoxen Theologie", in Silvia Hell (ed.), *Katholizität. Konfessionalismus oder Weltweite?*, (Innsbruck / Wien 2007), 49-91.

[4] Nicolas Afanassieff, "Das Hirtenamt der Kirche: In der Liebe der Gemeinde vorstehen", in Boris Bobrinskoy – Olivier Clément – B. Fize – Jean Meyendorff (eds.), *Der Primat des Petrus in der orthodoxen Kirche*, (Zürich 1961), 7-65.

Churches as local)[5] do not operate properly, the unity of Orthodoxy is continually threatened; thus it becomes problematic or rather impossible for these Churches to articulate a common witness towards the (always new) challenges of the world. These problems concerning the inter–Orthodox unity become apparent in the difficulty of calling a pan–Orthodox council, which a) would bear witness in a creative way considering a great amount of challenges for the faith (social ethics, bioethics, etc.), b) would organize the Orthodox missionary work and c) moreover would face the problems created in the ecclesial communities of the so–called Orthodox diaspora.[6] The difficulty I am talking about shows the limits of the eucharistic ecclesiology; because of such turbulences, Orthodoxy does not appear as a convincing interlocutor in the ecumenical dialogues for many of its partners.

2. The differing ecclesiological models of the western Churches

2.1. The ecclesiological model of the Roman–Catholic Church: inclusivistic ecclesiology?

In 2012, the Roman–Catholic Church celebrated the 50th anniversary from the beginning of the Second Vatican Council. According to many Roman–Catholic theologians this council signified a Copernican turn for the ecclesiology of their Church. The Dogmatic Constitution on the Church (Lumen Gentium), and more specifically its 8th paragraph, was the spearhead of the new articulation of the ecclesiological self–understanding of the Roman–Catholic Church. A dualism seems to be introduced here between the Church of Christ and the Roman–Catholic Church: the first is being realised (subsistit) in the Roman–Catholic Church, but there is no absolute identification and equation of the one with the other. Therefore the Roman–Catholic Church appeared willing to recognize elements of ecclesiality in the other Churches; it went further to regard these elements as possible contributions for the salvation of the faithful.[7] Thus the ecclesiology of the Second Vatican Council (1962-1965) renewed the hope that the Roman–Catholic Church will recognize the other Confessions as Churches. Nevertheless, this Church did not cease to repeat in various tones that the foundation of the catholicity of the Church is being realized only in communion with the bishop of Rome, who is the determining factor and guarantee of the unity of the Christian faithful; however, it does not specify what this communion with the bishop of Rome exactly means (or may mean) for the other Churches.

During the last years, and mainly after 2000, the hope raised by the ecclesiology of the Second Vatican Council is not really fulfilled. Nowadays the Roman–Catholic Church seems to interpret its great council from a much more narrow perspective: thus the famous *subsistit* reveals its systemic gaps; in its more recent documents the Vatican distances itself clearly from an interpretation of ecclesiology in the light of the principle of sister Churches; it rather prefers the principle of a mother Church and its daughters. Therefore the ecumenical approach is understood as a return of the daughters to the maternal bosom of the Roman–Catholic Church, which is claimed to be the only one able to guarantee the unity and the catholicity of the Church of Christ.

2.2. The ecclesial model of the Protestant world: reconciled diversity?

Although it is surely a simplification, it is not erroneous to summarize the Protestant model of ecclesial unity with the expression "reconciled diversity" (versöhnte Verschiedenheit).[8] Having overcome several subdivisions of their own, which took place during their historical past, such as the ones between the Reformed (Calvinist)

---

[5] Also according to the text of the Inter-Orthodox Consultation for a Response to the Faith and Order Study: The Nature and Mission of the Church (NMC), (Agia Napa / Paralimni Cyprus, 2.-9.03.2011).

[6] For the pan-Orthodox Council see Anastasios Kallis, *Auf dem Weg zum Konzil. Ein Quellen – und Arbeitsbuch zur orthodoxen Ekklesiologie*, (Münster 2013).

[7] For the Second Vatican Council see Otto Hermann Pesch, *Das Zweite Vatikanische Konzil. Vorgeschichte – Verlauf Ergebnisse – Nachgeschichte*, (Würzburg 1993).

[8] A Protestant Understanding of Ecclesial Communion. A statement on the Ordered Relations between Churches of Different Confessions from the Council of the Evangelical Church in Germany: http://www.ekd.de/english/1724-protestant_under-

and the Lutheran Churches, the Protestant Churches found (together with various Free Protestant Churches) a platform of unity that enables a reciprocal recognition of their sacraments and sacerdotal ministries. Within the European context this unity is expressed through the Council of CPCE (Community of Protestant Churches in Europe). [9]

The Evangelical Church of Germany (EKD) has expressed the opinion that the structure of Orthodoxy as a communion of autocephalous Churches may give impulses for establishment of communion among them and the Protestant Churches on the basis of the common acceptance of the Nicene-Constantinopolitan creed. [10]

The crucial question concerning the model of reconciled diversity is the following: where does the reconciliation end and where does the diversity which does not allow the sacramental communion begin? The Orthodox would undoubtedly ask to what extent the ordination of women or the recognition of the unions of same-sex couples (in various local Protestant Churches through a specific service) are expressions of legitimate diversity, or if they may lead to a break. [11] The two examples mentioned above cause serious concerns, which have already led to breaks between communities that are CEKE members (in the communities of Anglican Churches these concerns are exceptionally intense). A clear list of the unsolved problems which do not allow the coexistence of reconciled diversities, remains as a task for the ecumenical movement.

3. The Orthodox ecclesiological model: Return to Orthodoxy?

Orthodox ecclesiology, as it is articulated in the official documents of the Orthodox Churches in ecumenical or pan–Orthodox dialogues, seems to allow no dualism between an ideal image of the catholicity of the Church of Christ and its concrete, visible, institutional expression: according to the Third Pre-Conciliar Pan-Orthodox Conference (Geneva 1986, § 2) "the Orthodox Church is the One, Holy, Catholic and Apostolic Church which we confess in the creed of faith"; the Orthodox delegates at the third Assembly of the WCC in New Delhi use a more powerful expression: "For the Orthodox, the Orthodox Church is just the Church". [12]

The certainty of truth carried by the Orthodox Church as the Church of Jesus Christ is based on the certification of its continuity – and thus identification – with the undivided Church of the first millennium: "Indeed, for the Orthodox the apostolic succession of episcopacy and sacramental priesthood is an essential and constitutive, and therefore obligatory element of the Church's very existence" (1961). Therefore what the other Confessions have to do is to find the way back "to their common past" (1961); an older document

---

standing_1.html (last accessed, September 2013). Concerning the meaning of reconciled diversity see the works of Harding Meyer, (Versöhnte Verschiedenheit, 3 vol., Frankfurt a.M. 1998–2009).

[9] A Protestant Understanding (see footnote 8): "Otherwise, the majority of the Protestant churches in Europe are in full communion (altar and pulpit fellowship) as a consequence of the Leuenberg Agreement. This includes the inter-change-ability of ministries." For the Leuenberg Agreement see: www.leuenberg.net.

[10] A Protestant Understanding (see footnote 8): "On the other hand, as Orthodoxy is certainly familiar with ecclesial communion between autocephalous churches, one can ask whether this might not provide a basis for developing ecclesial communion with the Protestant churches" (III. 2.4)

[11] According to the text of the Inter-Orthodox Consultation for a Response to the Faith and Order Study: The Nature and Mission of the Church (NMC), Agia Napa / Paralimni Cyprus, 2.-9.03.2011: "Like nearly all ecumenical documents, the NMC text completely avoids the word 'heresy', and therefore fails to account for the possibility that some differences are indeed church-dividing, resulting from genuine disagreements. Diversity in faith, in worship and in moral and ethical practice has limits that the NMC text fails to help the churches identify for themselves or for each other" (§25–see the text in: http://archived.oikoumene.org/fileadmin/files/wcc-main/2011pdfs/NapaReport.pdf [last accessed on 24.8.2013]).

[12] For the texts of the pan–Orthodox decisions see Athanasios Basdekis, Orthodoxe Kirche und Ökumenische Bewegung. Dokumente – Erklärungen – Berichte 1900-2006, (Frankfurt – Paderborn 2006). The second part of the third pan–Orthodox pre-conciliar conference is published in English translation in Gennadios Limouris, Orthodox Visions of Ecumenism. Statements, Messages and Reports on the Ecumenical Movement 1902–1992, (Geneva 1994), 112–115. The text of 1961 is also published in Limouris, Orthodox Visions, 30–31.

(Ohio/USA 1957)[13] uses a stronger expression calling the other Confessions to find the way back "to the bosom of the Orthodox Church, which preserved its essential identity with early Christianity." However, neither these documents nor more recent ones clarify which are indeed these "important unalterable elements" of the ecclesial life, that the others are called to regain; the forms of ecclesial life which, as creatures of historical development (may) subject themselves to change are not specified, too. It is also known that the Orthodox Church avoids expressing itself on the ecclesial status of the non-Orthodox Churches.[14] If anybody wanted to acquire a concrete compulsory catalogue of points which the Orthodox regard as presuppositions for unity, then the confusion would be big: the range of the points that the heterodox Christians are called to accept in order to build up unity with Orthodoxy – according to the suggestions made by various Orthodox groups – is really broad: it extends from the abolition of Filioque and the papal dogmas (primacy and infallibility) to the acceptance of the teaching on the uncreated energies and the renunciation of the purgatorium. It is needless to observe that, concerning points such as the ones mentioned above, there is no common understanding and compulsory interpretation shared by all Orthodox Churches.

During the development of the ecumenical dialogue the terms expressing the ecclesiological self–understanding of Orthodoxy have experienced differentiations. According to my opinion, the claim of the Orthodox that they are the "bearer of and witness to the faith and the tradition of the One Holy Catholic and Apostolic Church" (text of Geneva 1986, B 1) may not be understood in a spirit of exclusivity, as an exclusion of the others, but in an atmosphere of openness which invites all for a new, joint, creative rediscovery of the common roots which may fruitfully graft the coordinates of the road to a new communion of the Christian Churches in their third millennium. It should also not be forgotten that the Orthodox are a communion of Churches with common coordinates concerning basic elements of doctrine, worship and Church order. Nevertheless, various differentiations are not missing: on the one side, in comparison to the early Church, the Church before Constantine the Great – differentiations which, nevertheless, did not serve as reasons of breaking the organic continuity of church life; on the other side, as far as various aspects of their own internal life are concerned. As we already noticed above, the question of their synodal pan–Orthodox communion and decision-making is still open. Therefore they still remain hostages of their past and are not regarded as convincing interlocutors, when they invite the other Churches to return to the undivided tradition and to Orthodoxy itself. Above these issues, the Orthodox are called to give convincing answers to the following crucial question: is the faithfulness to the common tradition of the first millennium enough for a fruitful confrontation with the new and more or less different problems of the third Christian millennium?

4. Vision for a common march of the Christian Churches in the third millennium

A creative march in the third millennium should surely not ignore the two thousand years of Church history. Those aspects of doctrine and daily – especially liturgical – praxis and life, shaped by the great Ecumenical Councils during the common march of the first millennium (above all on the basis of the creed of the Second Ecumenical Council) undoubtedly acquire great importance. In the fever of the bi– and multilateral ecumenical dialogues the official commissions usually devote themselves to a thorough investigation of the whole doctrine of their Churches, as if they were trying to write an extensive and very analytic "handbook of dogmatics". However, it is very doubtful if every one of these Churches already provides such a handbook for its own members regarded as compulsory. We usually overlook the fact that the common Christian faith of the

---

[13] Oberlin, Ohio, USA, 3.-10. September 1957, Nordamerikanische Regionalkonferenz über Fragen von Glauben und Kirchenverfassung zum Thema "Das Wesen der Einheit, die wir suchen", veranstaltet von der "US-Konferenz für den Ökumenischen Rat der Kirchen", in A. Basdekis, *Orthodoxe Kirche*, 74.

[14] See the text from the Meeting on "How Do the Orthodox Look at the Problem of Concepts of Unity and Models of Union", Geneva, Switzerland, 2-3 August 1973, in: *Orthodox Contributions to Nairobi, Papers Compiled and Presented by the Orthodox Task Force of the World Council of Churches*, (Geneva: WCC, 1975). Cited by Basdekis, *Orthodoxe Kirche*, 126.

first millennium has been articulated in very concrete and brief texts, which in the history of the Ecumenical Councils are called "Horoi" or creeds of faith. It would be surely useful for the future to write in common a brief catechetical handbook for the faithful;[15] it is also important for the credibility of the Christian churches to express themselves and work in common for a series of problems of the multifarious and so complicated modern human life, from the problems of bioethics to the issues concerning the environment. However, these are exactly future targets to be accomplished: namely the inquiry and reconfirmation *in every age* anew of the expression of the common Christian vision. What could serve as model of unity for the Churches in the direct future?

It does not seem that the current problem of the Churches is how much they are to identify themselves with the catholicity of the Church of Christ; all Churches claim that they express this catholicity, when this is understood as the truth of faith and as faithfulness to the early tradition of Christianity. Moreover, the most crucial question is how the Churches are related to each other on a global level.[16] At the end it appears that their problem is localized in the relations of the local Churches in terms of power and authority with those institutions that can (or are called) to guarantee the unity of the Church of Christ. Both the Orthodox and the Protestant Churches refuse to convey the certification and representation of their unity to a global institution, such as the bishop of Rome in the *current* Roman–Catholic understanding. Since the Orthodox experience their unity in actu (as it is built up in their long history and especially in their common liturgical rites, but also in various dogmatic documents), they probably feel no need for another institution as guarantee of their unity. However, as I briefly showed in the chapters 1 and 3 of this essay, this unity has been repeatedly challenged by the completely different conditions the Orthodox Churches had to face in their modern history. Thus one may observe that in the Orthodox Churches, too, the need is growing for the existence of an institution not only on a local and a regional, but also on a universal level, which will enable the harmonious collaboration of the Churches.[17] According to my opinion, this is the great challenge and responsibility of the Churches in their third millennium. It is self–evident that the institutions which may rise for the common expression of the Christian unity cannot guarantee this unity automatically, because this unity is a fruit of an intense effort so that we experience the truth of Lord 's word "that they all may be one" (John 17:21). How long are the Christian Churches allowed to prolong their divisions? In what other way could they express visibly the unity of the Christian faith?

The common participation in the sacrament of the Eucharist, as concrete visible expression of the unity of the Church, is surely a very high expression of the communion of the faithful in the Body of Christ; on the other side, it is surely not the only witness of faith, because faith is called to be incarnated in many other forms

---

[15] Going further in this direction, we should regard the already many common texts of bi – and multilateral dialogues as a precious help and secure basis. Concretely, concerning the ecclesiological question, I believe that the last version of the text for the Church (in: The Church. Towards a Common Vision, Faith and Order Paper No. 214, 2013) could become a starting point for the common march of the Churches.

[16] Concerning this point, revealing is the text of Agia Napa (2011): after having identified the autocephalous Orthodox Churches with the local Churches it is asking about the expression of unity on a global level: "The section on 'The Church as Communion of Local Churches' is a case in point. On the one hand, it speaks of local churches as expressions of the communion of the Church, leaving open the question of how each confession might read itself into the concept of 'local' and 'universal'. The Orthodox would understand 'local churches' first and foremost in the intra-Orthodox sense (the churches, e.g., of Constantinople, Alexandria, Antioch etc., and/or their local dioceses). Some non-Orthodox ecclesiologies understand 'local churches' in a denominational sense, incorporating Protestant, Catholic, Orthodox, etc., churches." (§11).

[17] This wish and need has been expressed by the official commision for the dialogue between Orthodox and Roman–Catholics in the document of Ravenna (2007), which has not yet been officially accepted by the Churches which participate in this dialogue (concerning the Orthodox side, the Russian Orthodox Church did not participate. See more in Athanasios Vletsis, "Asymmetrien und Hoffnungen in einer geschwisterlichen Beziehung. Der Orthodox-Katholische Dialog blickt zurück auf 30 bzw. 50 Jahre intensiver Beziehungen", in *Orthodoxes Forum* 25 (2011): 187-200.

of the common life of the Christian faithful in the world. I fear that, through the method we are following in the ecumenical dialogue, by leaving the eucharistic communion as the ultimately last ring of an endless chain of inquiry for the unity under various and, more or less, recent dogmatic and other conditions of faith and praxis, we instrumentalize the divine eucharist in order to achieve that highest possible common expression of the ecclesial life, which is undoubtedly an eschatological good.[18] Would it not be probably useful to think that the acceptance of the absolutely basic terms of faith (such as the acceptance of the doctrinal decisions of the Ecumenical Councils) and ecclesial order (such as the acceptance of the liturgical ministry and the value of the apostolic succession),[19] as they have been expressed in the Ecumenical Councils of the undivided Church, may suffice for the restoration of the sacramental communion? A necessary condition is, of course, according to the principle of consensus (which regulates the behaviour of the Churches in the context of the WCC), that no Church will raise a "matter of faith" (status confessionis) on behalf of more recent developments, which could in no way be accepted by other Churches. Nevertheless, such a demand (status confessionis) should be raised only for absolutely necessary and compulsory issues, which cause problems for the articulation of the common witness. The inquiry for a common statement on various new problems, from matters of social welfare and responsibility to the issues of the structures of the synodal life of the Church, could each time define new partial targets; thus the circles that the Church, centred in its eucharistic gatherings, draws will become greater and broader, till they experience their fulfilment in the great circle of the Kingdom of God, which will embrace everybody and everything, so "that God may be all in all" (1 Cor. 15:28).[20] However, during these two thousand years, Christians should have learnt not to confuse the limits of the Kingdom of God with the ones of their Church. Under this prism every season may become the beginning of a new fruition: the fruits of the Spirit should surely not deteriorate due to the "weather conditions" of the human weakness and opportunism. In every "ice age" (during the last years, the ecumenical movement talks a lot about it...) the faith to which the Holy Spirit leads the Church in its march may open new roads of communication and blossoming.

Bibliography

Aagaard, Anna Marie –Bouteneff, Peter, *Beyond the East – West Divide. The World Council of Churches and 'the Orthodox Problem'*, (Geneva: WCC, 2001).
Papandreou, Damaskinos, "Briefwechsel zwischen Metropolit Damaskinos und Kardinal Ratzinger", in: *Internationale Katholische Zeitschrift – Communio* 30 (2001): 282–96.

---

[18] While in the line of the Orthodox tradition, which does not want the nature of the Church to be defined in an obligatory and scholastic way, the common text of Orthodox and (ancient) Oriental Orthodox Churches in Agia Napa in 2011 (see footnote 10) regards the way the Churches relate themselves to the Kingdom of God as a point of (total?) differentiation among them: "The Church is a mystery in God's providence, and is not systematically defined in Holy Scripture and in the patristic teaching. The text provides various definitions from different Church traditions, but the text does not define how the Church is related to God's kingdom" (§42). If what is meant here is the symbolism of the Kingdom, as it is articulated especially in the liturgical tradition of the Orthodox Church, this surely cannot be obligatory for all the Churches, because the relation of the Church to the Kingdom of God is every time what we are asking for during the march of the Church towards its fulfillment.

[19] Concerning the apostolic succession, revealing is the text of the dialogue of the Roman–Catholic and the Lutheran Church in 2006, published in: Johannes Oeldemann / Friederike Nüssel / Uwe Swarat / Athanasios Vletsis (eds.), *Dokumente wachsender Übereinstimmung. Sämtliche Berichte und Konsenstexte interkonfessioneller Gespräche auf Weltebene, vol. 4: 2001–2010*, (Paderborn-Leipzig 2012), 527-678.

[20] The overcoming of the division between the local (autocephalous for the Orthodox) and the confessional Churches could be the long–term result of their common Eucharistic life: the Churches of every geographical location would finally be discerned according to their liturgical rites; by the passing of time the Eucharistic communion would allow them to articulate many other common expressions of ecclesial life. One may imagine that, speaking in long terms, the communion of this shared life would let the circles of communion grow even in the liturgical tradition.

Clapsis, Emmanuel, *Conversation – Orthodox Ecumenical Engagements*, (Geneva/ Brookline: WCC, 2000).

Kalaitzidis, Pantelis, "Challenges of Renewal and Reformation Facing the Orthodox Church", *The Ecumenical Review* 61 (2009): 136-164.

Larentzakis, Grigorios. "'The One Church and its Unity'. Consultations between the Conference of European Churches (CEC) and the Community of Protestant Churches in Europe (CPCE)", in: M. Beintker, M. Friedrich, and V. Ionita (ed.), *Leuenberg Documents 11* [in German and English]. (Frankfurt-am-Main: Otto Lembeck, 2007), 75-105.

Tsompanidis. Stylianos, "The Church and the churches in the ecumenical movement", in *International journal for the Study of the Christian Church* 12.2 (2012): 1-16.

(translated by Georgios Vlantis)

Adrian Lemeni

The dialogue between theology and science
from the Orthodox perspective in the actual epistemological context

There are certain assumed aspects of knowledge in the spirit of patristic and ecclesial Tradition that correspond in epistemological implications of the scientific research from contemporaneity. This fact is stimulating especially in the latest changes regarding contemporary science towards modernity, the actual epistemological mutations having the same spectacular and consistent openings regarding profound and unified world understanding. We are witnessing today by what means the unlimited trust in the power of knowledge explains reality, the science legitimation as the unique form of plausible knowledge, the complacency and triumphalism of positive thought are surpassed on an epistemological level by the contemporary science. This perspective sketches the renewing and favorable pattern of forming and cultivating a conscience of dialogue between theological and scientific knowledge.

To the degree that the efforts and searches of scientists that intuit the fact that the profound nature of reality cannot be worn-out in conceptual representations and formulations, there is a responsibility of theology to answer to such honest openings as far as scientific research concerns. The dialogue between theology and science does not mean that theology has to abdicate from the support of Revelation, but confessing the lived and revelatory Truth in the life of the Church, to assume requirements of culture and dialogue in which the specific competences of theology and science are respected. Distinct competences do not assume a separation, but a unitary vision in the plan of knowledge in which specific vocations of theological and scientific perspective are activated.

Between the paradigms of contemporary science there are significant epistemological mutations. Assuming limits as epistemological openings among scientific research, represents a chance for shaping a dialogue between theology and science. In this context, theology has a special responsibility, thus being called to generate and encourage a conscience of dialogue so necessary for the present society.

For an approach of dialogue between theology and science in an Orthodox perspective, assuming authentic theology is imperative. The mystery of theology is unraveling in the Holy Fathers' Tradition lived inside the Church. Theology is not to be understood only in its academic and rigorous concept explanation. Theology requires the experience in the light of personal prayer and liturgical life, lived in the plenitude of the Church. The living event that fundaments the identity of Christian theology is Jesus Christ, the Truth of the whole world and of each one of us. Jesus Christ, the Logos of whole creation, through His Incarnation in history, opens a possibility of incarnating a theology as an act of life based on the immediate experience of the Church. This is possible because in the Church, the mystic body of Christ, theology is being lived like a gift of God which anticipates the presence of kingdom of God in history. The dynamics of theology are special, given the fact that there is a permanent ecclesial Tradition in the eschatological coordinate.

Theology is not only a capitalization of autonomous reason, capable of analysis, synthesis, demonstration through a discursive capacity. The Holy Fathers of the Church made the distinction between *dianoia* and *nous*. Modern thinking lost the significance of this distinction, whereas modernity made us get used to an exclusivist mentality, with a sensibility disunited by the false and artificial conflict created between reason and faith. When the profound support of reason was weakened, the identity of reason was understood only as a natural and discursive faculty of the mind. For the ecclesial Tradition of the Church, the distinction between *dianoia* and *nous* in a united relation could help us understand today in an organic way, the link between reason and faith, between science and theology.

Dianoia explains the discursive capacity of the mind, the power of analysis and construction of coherent reasoning. The dimension of the mind explained by *dianoia* was harnessed especially in the occidental tradition, through deductive analysis of realities from creation, through serious and detailed investigations on the world. Exploration of God is not depleted through the capacity expressed by the *dianoia*. The *nous* is the faculty of the mind that expresses intuition, knowledge understood as a united way of seeing that the connoisseur is directly implicated in the known object. The *nous* meets more with faith, having a specific knowledge based on an inductive and implicative reason.

The adequate relation between *dianoia* and *nous*, specific to the Orthodox Tradition, is an extension in an epistemological plan of the indissoluble bond between natural and supernatural among the patristic ontology. A part of the approaches met in the occidental context regarding the dialogue between theology and science, understands that there is science that studies the world and theology that is occupied with the study of God's existence. In this way theology is understood only in its academic and conceptual side, detached from the life of the Church. On the contrary, the true identity of theology is supposed to come from being precisely anchored in the life of the Church. Likewise science is often reduced only to conceptions based on an instrumental reason which operates exclusively with discursive capacity.

This perspective has to be exceeded in the approach of dialogue between theology and science from the interior of the Orthodox Tradition. It demands that the confessing and dialogic conscience of the Holy Fathers of the Church be retrieved. Assuming from a theological perspective the existent openings from the science and realizing an honest dialogue between theology and science in fidelity to the Evangelic Truth represents a significant coordinate of Church mission in the contemporary context. In the dialogue between theology and science the specific potential of ecclesial Tradition has to be materialized.

This step being completed, at once assuming the demands of creating a dynamic and steadfast fidelity of Church Tradition, it can overpass the schematic understanding of dialogue between theology and science. A schematic understanding entrusted exclusively in the power of discursive reason cannot express the adequate relation between theology and science. "The step that places on the same level theology and science is possible thanks to discursive reason, detached through its ambition by its spiritual basis, thinking that it is capable of exceeding both theology and science through a comparative analysis between them. This step can be chosen by a variety of philosophies. In this understanding it is presumed that theology and science are uniform legally, epistemologically and ontologically. The naivety of this premise can be surpassed if theology is understood as an expression of the life of the Church and through her, as asymmetric with science. On the contrary, there is a risk that ambitious reason, forgetting about its spiritual basis, may have the pretention of trying to judge with authority these aspects of human existence that surpass the capacity of reason."[1]

The distinction between *nous* and *dianoia* - significant premise for contouring an adequate relation between theology and science from an Orthodox perspective

The recovery of Orthodox anthropology based on the patristic and ecclesial tradition, following on the one hand the actual epistemological context and contouring an adequate relation between theology and science in an Orthodox perspective on the other, requires assuming the distinction between *nous* and *dianoia*. The Holy Fathers identify *nous* with the spiritual intellect, with the faith that surpasses demonstration and requires cleric-ecclesial experience. The faith is associated with the one true knowledge that surpasses the finished demonstration. *Dianoia* represents the discursive capacity of understanding.

The *nous* indicates the reality of theology as a live and concrete experience of The One living God that is above all concepts. Through *nous*, the idolatry of concepts and unlimited trust in the axiomatic power of thinking are avoided. The *nous* is not reduced to faith, but expresses a center of the human existence; it indicates the

[1] Alexei Nesteruk, *Light from the East. Theology, Science and the Eastern Orthodox Tradition*, (Fortress Press, Minneapolis, 2003), 61-62.

core and fullness of the person, whereas it relates it to the supreme Logos. Between *nous* and *dianoia* there is a relation, but confirming a distinction in a relationship based on reciprocity requires confirmation and recovery of specific competences for theological and scientific knowledge.

From an Orthodox perspective, the relation between theology and science is asymmetrical because it assumes the distinction between *nous* and *dianoia*; thus, an epistemological monism is surpassed in which theology and science are placed on the same level of knowledge, through a homogeneity and equivalency of knowledge. From the patristic and ecclesial perspective of Tradition, theology is not consumed in the borders of theological science; therefore, the relation between theology and science, from this perspective, could bring a renewed wealth of senses and significations in consolidating the conscience of dialogue in this domain.

In the patristic gnoseology, the reason is not cancelled, but transfigured through faith. Knowledge is not reduced to its instrumental dimension, to its contingent and contextual facticity, but in the reciprocity between *nous* and *dianoia*, there is a priority of *nous* inasmuch as is observed a prevalence of faith in relation to reason. Faith is aprioristic towards knowledge based on analytic reason; it precedes it and it structures it including in the *dianoia* practice.

For example, the rational evidences of God's existence are either preceded by faith or they have no theological significance, whereas faith cannot be founded and structured on arguments. Even if from a methodological point of view, faith is not known as a reasonable option, it effectively structures and operates in a consequent mode inside a knowledge that the exclusive intentionality of legitimation exists through *dianoia*.

The *nous* highlights and accentuates the authority of knowledge structured through faith. The faith expects participation in the invoked and investigated reality; it also implies an impartation with someone or something in the act of thinking. Faith does not grow a knowledge based on the terms of an exterior relation. The God invoked by the believer is not a metaphysical construction, but it is the living God with whom he/she relates and kneels in front of and prays or brings doxology. Thinking about God and not having faith in Him means an abstract and artificial knowledge. Faith is irreducible in concept, and it generates a thinking about God through participation in His reality.

As much as faith is based on an implicative knowledge with an inside dimension, knowing through faith means to interiorize, to assume existentially the investigated reality. Faith directs one towards an experience that cannot be exhausted through explanations. Faith is expressed through a dialogic type of knowledge such as invitation-answer, exploring the mystery of the person. It is not a result of logical deductions.

The distinction between *nous* and *dianoia* shows the difference of intentionality inside the human subjectivity, in the plan of knowledge. There is a type of intentionality based on the discursive rationality and a spiritual type of intentionality structured through faith. In the relation between theology and science, starting from the distinction between *nous* and *dianoia*, from an Orthodox perspective, the spiritual intentionality is confirmed. This requires the ecclesial dimension. That is why the Orthodox perspective concening the relation between theology and science notes as a mandatory and definite element, the ecclesial aspect of attitude and reporting to this problem.

The ecclesial assumption of dialogue between theology and science requires the effort of tracing the spiritual intentionality in the scientific and philosophical knowledge. Theology as an expression of clerical and ecclesial living implicates the experience of the holy grace, but this experience of the holy grace through the Holy Spirit from the mystic body of Christ generates a knowledge that exceeds the logical intentionality and facticity. Although, knowledge based on *dianoia* is not despised, revaluation of the ecclesial dimension in the relation between theology and science it is insisted on the existential effort of guessing profound realities that are beyond the strict conceptual approach.

So "searching for the presence of the Spirit through science and philosophy, firstly means rediscovering humanity behind science, in a serious way: not through a simple statement that all the scientific theories are mental creations, but through disentangling the intentionalities implicated in different articulations of the world from science and theology. Practically, this implies the fact that science - and general scientific activity - must be appropriated not through analyzing the content of its theories and reality claims, but more likely through some sort of 'deconstruction' of its theoretic notions for discovering the structures of intentional human con-science (of which correspondent is interpreted by science as objective world) and the integrating capacity of sustaining the presence of the divine image in her and to confer this image to the world."[2]

The ecclesial perspective of the relation between theology and science points to the life of the Church, to the Holy Liturgy in which the descent of the Holy Spirit is experienced through epiclesis. Thus the entire creation is renewed through the Holy Spirit in Christ, and the presence of the Spirit is invoked through liturgical events. All these give sense to history and open it eschatologically towards the reality of the kingdom of God. The fact that the experience of the holy grace through the Holy Spirit is possible only inside the life of the Church shows the incompleteness of exclusively scientific approaches and institutions.

Assuming the comprehensive Patristic Tradition in the dialogue between theology and science

Assuming the Holy Fathers and Tradition imposes the requirements of an authentic ecclesial life in which the Nicene Creed cannot be seen as simple exterior speech, but as an act of life practiced in daily existence. The patristic perspective implies the dialogue between theology and culture, theology being called to answer human needs in a contextual way. The dialogue must not let itself be stopped by extreme attitudes such as intimidation or fear, or conversely by contempt and superiority. The dialogue between science and theology does not mean concordism or syncretism through which numerous confusions are made. A meeting between patristic gnosiology and scientific epistemology requires the existence and development of spiritual discernment.

Beyond mutual enrichment in the epistemological plan given by a complementary vision regarding scientific and theological knowledge, the dialogue between theology and science completed in an honest way could be a mode of developing personal relationships according to the respect of alterity. An open conscience to assume creatively the limits of human possibilities of research, reached by the profound mystery of creation, is a conscience ready for science. Theology could strengthen this conscience hired in the effort of assuming the world's truth.

Orthodoxy affirms the actualization of patristic thought as essential in contemporaneity. This actualization does not mean a simple textual appeal to our patristic writings, but more likely a mode that determines a true inner resurrection and sharing the Truth with the world. The Church understood as a lab of resurrection in which, through the Holy Liturgy, is foretasted here and now the kingdom of God, produces a radical *metanoia* through which the human mind is renewed and thus the knowledge does not remain the exclusive result of a critical and scholarly rationality which develops scholarly theories, hermetic towards the concrete needs of the human being. A theology based on Orthodox Tradition generates a creative thinking, that is open towards life and the needs of the contemporary world, and which gives answers by assuming the *same way of life* with the Holy Fathers.

Contemporary science recognizes the rationality and the mystery of the world. Theology, starting from epistemological mutations from the paradigm of contemporary science, can open an honest dialogue with science, but insisting towards the fundamental particularities existent in the Orthodox Tradition. A profound rationality of the world is not meeting its final purpose in the absence of a Person that generates and recapit-ulates all the deep reasons of creation. Knowing these final reasons above any scientific objectivity claims, means communion with the deified Logos, imitation of the accomplished communion between the Persons of the Holy Trinity.

The unifying perspective of the Orthodox Tradition requires an opening towards the other. But this opening is not only a formal relationship, animated and supported by mutual interests (and sometimes petty), but it is strengthened by the power of holiness. The effort to obtaining a holy life requires suddenly both delicacy manifested for the friend, but also the power of confessing the Truth of the Gospel. In the dialogue between

---

[2] Alexei Nesteruk, *Universul în comuniune*, (București: Ed. Curtea Veche, 2009), 243-244.

theology and science, theology must not be a victim of the concordist temptation or closed in a frustrating or aggressive way towards science. Orthodox theology does not have any ideological position to defend, but only to confess the redeeming Truth of the world. This way the risk of ideology can be surpassed, the one present both in theology and science, and through which the distances are invented and amplified.

Consequent to the patristic Tradition, Orthodox theology always hopes in God working through anyone, and does not give up the hope for fullness of conscience of the Truth which she is sharing. In this way one can talk about the catholicity of Orthodoxy given by a fullness of the Truth that guides to holiness. But at the same time this catholicity is open because the one who is raised in a real way on the Path of Truth and Life that guides to holiness, is a creature open to its friend and to the whole world. The Saint is praying for all his brethren and for the whole creation.

Ecclesial experience of the Truth – essential requirement of dialogue between Orthodox theology and science

As far as Orthodox Tradition is concerned, the Truth can be lived in the most authentic way in the spiritual and ecclesial experience. The Truth of the Orthodox Tradition is not accommodated to the requirements of a theory that belongs to some specific era. That is why Orthodoxy does not have any resentment towards scientific development and it does not feel the need to adjust its creed according to the rigors of a theory or another, which is perfectible in time. From the ecclesial perspective, apologetics or fundamental theology should be the path of an assuming dialogue in which Orthodoxy should be actualized. In this agreement, Orthodoxy is not a confession among others; neither is Christianity a simple religion among other religions. Orthodoxy is the path of ecclesial experience of the Truth through which the eternal Life is shared; the believer living the condition of son in relation with God, thanks to the Incarnation of Christ; the event that determines history to be assumed in the perspective of the Resurrection.

The specific identity of dialogue between Orthodox theology and science can be discerned only by assuming the integrating and unifying perspective of the Holy Fathers, for which the Truth is a central priority in their ecclesial knowledge, thus the Truth that is experimented in a clerical and ecclesial life becomes the fundamental criterion of apologetics. The autonomous intellect can only perceive forms of truth, pieces of conceptual truths, without having access to the unified contemplation of Truth. A partial knowledge free from the integrality of a clerical and ecclesial vision risks distorting the knowledge of the part. Only a knowledge understood as power of the Holy Spirit can move the hearts and minds of people to receive Jesus Christ as Truth of the world, possibly to experiment in the living experience of the Church.

The Truth cannot be owned, but shared. Knowledge is not only an effort of finding the truth through an intellect detached from the reality of the studied object, but it is the union of the knowing subject with the to-be-known object. That is why sharing the deified truth is possible only through deep love of the living community in the Church of Christ. In love, the true knowledge of Truth is possible and this knowledge is manifested as love, but outside the accomplished communion of the Holy Trinity extended in the life of the Church, there is no fullness of love. Thus, the Truth can be shared in the experience of clerical power of the ecclesial community. The Truth is revealed in the light of the Pentecost paradigm. Sharing the Truth requires passing from death to life, from a life encysted in the limits of decay to a life open to incorruption, of holy resurrection.

Christ is not a principal truth, quantifiable at the level of a concept and generator of doctrine systems or moral codes. Christ is the personal Truth, of each and everyone of us and of the entire world, which calls us from death to life and at the same time gives us the power to resurrect through his victory upon death. Jesus does not represent abstract doctrinal truths, but He is discovering Himself as The Path that takes one to the Father. "I am the light of the world" (John 8:72). Confessing the Truth is possible only by walking in the light of Christ. Any separation from Christ takes us away from the absolute reality of the discovered Truth in the Son of God. When Pilate asks Christ: "What is the truth?" the Savior does not give any definition, but he confesses: "To this end was I born, and for this cause came I into the world, that I should bear witness unto the truth. Every one that is of the truth heareth my voice." (John 18:37). The essence of the Gospel is confessing the Incarnated Truth that permits sharing the kingdom of God.

When Christ says that He is the Truth, He does it because He is the Life who saves the world. He frees it from the conditions of sin. This way the truth is not an ontological content, assuming that the true life consists in knowing God as a living communion with God. "And this is life eternal, that they might know thee the only true God, and Jesus Christ, whom thou hast sent." (John 17:3). Christ is the Truth because He does not only offer a solution for the temporary existence mode subject to biologic conditions, but He offers the path that takes one to eternal life, and makes it possible to foretaste it even in this existence, here and now.

Where the relation between theology and science tends to be associated only with the natural effort of proving religious truths through an exclusive rationalist path, for assuming the ecclesial perspective of knowledge, the confession of divine-humanity as a fundamental criterion is imperative. The experience in Christ, God-Human, as Truth of the world makes passing all delusions possible. Father Stăniloae says:

"In this way I knew the Truth. We no longer consider the world as ultimate truth, but Christ, the Son of God, Creator of the world and people, their Redeemer from the power of death and dark perspective of hell [...] I knew that Christ is the Truth from which and towards which all are carried. I knew that those who consider the world as an ultimate truth are in a lie, taking the darkness of an atheistic culture as light. I knew that those who don't know Christ as Son of God, incarnated and light of the world, but they judge it as a unique reality, they're living a big lie. I knew that all the words that sustain this false idea are lies. I knew that, only by having them, will we be in an eternal poverty and death."[3]

Bibliography

1. Alexei Nesteruk, *Light from the East. Theology, Science and the Eastern Orthodox Tradition*, (Minneapolis: Fortress Press, 2003).
2. Alexei Nesteruk, *Universul în comuniune (The Universe as Communion)*, (Bucureşti: Curtea Veche, 2009).
3. Adrian Lemeni, *Adevăr şi comuniune (Truth and Communiion)*, (Bucureşti: Editura Basilica, Patriarhia Română, 2011).
4. Adrian Lemeni, coordonator al volumului colectiv *Repere patristice în dialogul dintre teologie şi ştiinţă (Patristic References in the Dialogue between Theology and Science)*, (Bucureşti: Editura Basilica, Patriarhia Română, 2009).
5. Pr. Răzvan Ionescu, Adrian Lemeni, *Dicţionar de teologie ortodoxă-ştiinţă (Dictionary on Orthodox Theology-Science)*, (Bucureşti: Editura Curtea Veche, 2009).
6. Adrian Lemeni, Pr. Răzvan Ionescu, *Teologie ortodoxă şi ştiinţă (Orthodox Theology and Science)*, (Bucureşti: Editura Institutului Biblic şi de Misiune al Bisericii Ortodoxe Române, 2007).

---

[3] Pr. Dumitru Stăniloae, *Iisus Hristos, lumina lumii şi îndumnezeitorul omului*, Ed. Anastasia, (Bucureşti, 1993), 79.

(99) THE RELEVANCE OF ORTHODOX SPIRITUALITY FOR THE ECUMENICAL MOVEMENT[1]

Ciprian Toroczkai

According to Vladimir Lossky (1903-1958), one of the greatest Orthodox theologians of the twentieth century, there has never been a clear distinction in the Eastern tradition between mysticism and theology, between the personal experience of the divine mysteries and the dogma affirmed by the Church. In other words, there is no Christian mysticism without theology, but mostly, there is no theology without mysticism; mysticism is the completion of the entire theology or the theology *par excellence*.[2]

Drawing a parallel between mysticism and spirituality, Andrew Louth showed the interdependence of theology and spirituality. "Spirituality – prayer – is … that which keeps theology to its proper vocation, that which prevents theology from evading its own real object."[3] But the "object" of theology is actually a subject, or rather the supreme subject, God. "Theology is neither concerned exclusively with the truth of certain doctrines, nor with the validity of a certain way of life, but with the response of loving devotion to the revelation of God's love and God's glory in Jesus Christ – a response that involves an orientation of our whole being, a way of life, and the articulation of that glory in what we call doctrine."[4]

Dumitru Stăniloae (1903-1993) summarized the patristic teaching on spirituality and stressed that it presented the Christian advance on the path of perfection in Christ, by cleansing passions and acquiring virtues. It is a process that takes place in a specific order: first, man goes from cleansing a passion to cleansing another one, and thus acquires different virtues that fit a certain level of perfection; the peak of the process is love that means cleansing all the passions and acquiring all virtues. Moving toward this peak, man comes in union with Jesus Christ and in knowledge of Him through experience, i.e. deification (*theosis*). Deification or relentless increase of divine love is the third and final stage of apophatism[5] (the first step is rational knowledge of God through rational negation, in the sense that He is not to be attributed anything evil, the second step is "the mind rest"[6] when the words of the prayer become fewer and the gift of tears appears[7]).

Understanding Orthodox spirituality has its dangers. Thus, two opposite but equally false trends may be identified. The first may be called "Denzinger-Theology." The logic of such a theology is that it consists of a collection of true theological statements with reference to which any theological utterance may be checked. Apart from the objective criteria (such as the Scripture and the creeds), the appeal is to reason or, more exactly, to *discursive* reason.

The other tendency rejects such notions as prepositional truth; what is important is the *authenticity* of a certain attitude to life. Those who support the second tendency insist that something as deeply true as theology will not be easy to access (acceptance of God's revelation is more than a merely intellectual matter).

We deal here with an "apparent interior antinomy" that exists between the concrete experience, which moves us and helps us to determine our will, and abstract reasoning, which does not help directly to determine the will.

---

[1] The first following article on this subject was written by Ciprian Toroczkai while the second one was written by Christopher Savage (ed.)

[2] Vladimir Lossky, *Essai sur la théologie mystique de l'Eglise d'Orient*, (Les Editions du Cerf, 1990).

[3] Andrew Louth, *Theology and Spirituality*, (Oxford: SLG Press, Convent of the Incarnation, 1976), 4.

[4] Ibid., 7.

[5] Dumitru Stăniloae, *Ascetica şi Mistica Ortodoxă* [*Orthodox Ascetic and Mystic*] 2 vol., (Alba-Iulia: Deisis, 1993).

[6] See the prayer of the heart, which consists in repeating the words: "Lord Jesus Christ, have mercy on me a sinner," or just "Lord Jesus Christ."

[7] Irénée Hausherr, *Penthos: the Doctrine of Compunction in the Christian East*, (Kalamazoo: Cistercian Publications Inc., 1982).

This antinomy resolved in the saintly life.[8] It is not by chance that Evagrius said that "He who prays is a theologian; a theologian is one who prays." The saint proves that the theologian and the contemplative complement one another. The contemplative knows by experience, the theologian declares what is thus known. "Neither the contemplative nor the theologian is separated from the other: there is something of the theologian in the contemplative and of the contemplative in the theologian."[9] The true understanding of theology is "theology interpreting spirituality, and spirituality informing theology."[10]

We now understand the great appreciation that the saints have always enjoyed in Orthodoxy. The role of the spiritual father ("abba," called by the Greeks *gheron*, "elder" and by the Russians *starets*, "abbot") is to be a guide and companion for the other Christians towards salvation. The spiritual father received his ministry through the direct work of the Holy Spirit. Although retired from the world, he helps people not through what he says or does, but through his very existence, through the state of unceasing prayer. In this regard St. Seraphim of Sarov said: "Acquire inner peace and lots of people will find salvation around you." The saint achieves this precisely because of the gifts he receives from the Holy Spirit, to help his spiritual "children," i.e. 1) insight or discernment, 2) the ability to love others and to make the sufferings of others his own, and 3) the power to transform the human, material and immaterial environment (as e.g. in the case of the charisma of healing).[11]

In 1980, Professor Ion Bria published in Geneva a collective volume dedicated to the testimony of the Orthodox Churches at that time. He also reedited a small study which had been published by Fr. Stăniloae two years prior to the publication of the volume.[12] Although small in size, it has a special value because it exposes not only the main features of the Orthodox mission, but also the main contributions that Orthodoxy can bring in the future in the contemporary world.

The question that the Romanian theologian tried to answer was: why did the early Church experience a tremendous missionary success among non-Christians, while in the second Christian millennium it was not able to unfreeze the hardened hearts of the non-Christians? Is it about – asks Fr. Stăniloae – the very way that the Christian Church introduced itself in the second millennium?

The answers that Dumitru Stăniloae offers in an attempt to unravel the cause of the failure of the Church to be missionary, from both an internal and an external point of view, return to the present condition of the human being. Humans have experienced the dominant role of technology in their lives; technology met all their material needs, and led to the loss of spiritual interests. People today have tried to satisfy their spiritual needs through a series of substitutes such as the television and the internet, drugs, alcohol or sex, and some, unable to quench their spiritual thirst and hunger by means of material nature, turned to superficial religious forms of spirituality. Only the Orthodox spirituality can enable humans to discover and accomplish the full possibilities of their nature, and thus enter into a mystical and personal communion with the heavenly Father. Orthodox spirituality can help them rediscover a balanced and profound life, and this is achieved by receiving the uncreated power of God, which is accessible through Christ and in the Holy Spirit.

D. Stăniloae supported that the main concern of the Church in the contemporary world is to restore communion among people, especially since they experience, paradoxically, more loneliness: communion was lost in the life of the big cities, which is nothing but wilderness, now filled with great turmoil. He stressed that the fact that Orthodoxy attracts the attention of the Western world is not just because it is preaching a message of a personal, loving God, the only one who can save man forever by sharing this love, but also due to the fact that it offers people who live here and now that delicate presence of love, and communion of faith, which belong to a life of holiness.

---

[8] Andrew Louth, op. cit., 6-7.
[9] Ibid., 16.
[10] Ibid., 13.
[11] Kallistos Ware, "The Spiritual Father in Orthodox Christianity," *Cross Currents* 2-3 (1974): 296-313. see Irénée Hausherr, *Direction spirituelle en Orient autrefois* ("Orientalia Christiana Analecta" 144), (Roma, 1955).
[12] Dumitru Stăniloae, "Witness Through 'Holiness' of Life," in Ion Bria (ed.), *Martyria/Mission: the Witness of the Orthodox Churches Today*, Comission on World Mission and Evangelism, (Geneva: World Council of Churches, 1980), 45-51.

Orthodox mission therefore is superior to all other missions not because of the superiority of a particular type of message, but due to the very life of its preachers, saints and martyrs, who can truly awaken the thirst for holiness and immortality in people, and also give them confidence that this possibility can be realized. Their power comes not from certain human cultural and spiritual qualities, but from the divine grace that dwells in them. Stăniloae wrote in this respect that only the saints and martyrs can lead people to Christ, drawing their souls with the divine power that is shining in them. It is a power and capacity to love that makes them reach the stage of total self-sacrifice. People have the conviction that being a saint or martyr can be achieved through the divine grace, and they can acquire this grace too, and offer themselves to God and to their neighbor.

Consequently, the most important value of Orthodoxy consists in the possibility of holiness that it offers, combined with an understanding of the Church as a divine-human communion in Christ (not as a mere human institution). Thus, in order to prove its missionary orientation, the Orthodox Church must do nothing but be open towards the uncreated power of God, and believe that helped by this power it is possible for believers to live a life of holiness and sacrifice. Also, the Orthodox Church should be renewed as communion.

Fr. Dumitru Stăniloae points out that the efforts of the ancestors, the great hesychasts and saints or the charismatic people of Orthodoxy are to be mentioned in this respect. Without specifically intending it, they practiced mission through their very life and work. As St. Gregory Palamas affirmed in the 14th century, the hesychasts participated in the same grace as that manifested in the early Church by the Apostles and their immediate missionary successors. Since holiness and the absolute self-giving is the only way to do mission effectively, we should therefore search for the experience of the uncreated divine power, which offers both to humans.

The question then arises: are there saints in today's Orthodox Church anymore? If so, what is their ecumenical relevance? The answer to the first question is definitely yes. Let us recall Vladimir Lossky's definition of Tradition as "the life of the Holy Spirit in the Church."[13] The continuous presence of the Holy Spirit in the Church is shown both through the Holy Sacraments and the holy works and actions, and through the saints.

Concerning the second question, on the ecumenical relevance of contemporary Orthodox spirituality, we will focus on a single example and recall the Athonite Schimonach Silouan Ivanovich Antonov (1866-1938). Born in Russia, he reached the Holy Mountain in the fall of 1892. For 46 years, he lived in the Russikon monastery the common life of a monk of the Holy Mountain, marked by long services and vigils in the church, the rule of the personal prayer in his cell, frequent confessions and sharing, work and obedience. The long process of inner perfection, through which Silouan gradually reached the spiritual level of the great Fathers of the desert, is essential. It was a dramatic ascetic-mystical process, characterized by graceful illuminations and their loss, which made Silouan exclaim: "Keep your mind in Hell and do not despair."[14] Throughout his life, St. Silouan demonstrated that only with Christ can one descend to hell, meaning that he/she can overcome sin and death. To summarize, the center of his experience was universal love, the underpinning of all virtues, and access to it was provided by unceasing prayer and humility.[15] Hence Silouan's great gift for today's world: prayer for all people, including the enemies. "Our brother is our life," he said, showing that salvation is not only an ontological event (a change from the physical "old man," to the spiritual "new man"), but also a cosmic event (salvation of the whole humanity, the whole cosmos, is part of one's own, personal salvation).

The recognition of his holiness came in June 1988, when the Ecumenical Patriarchate canonized the blessed Silouan as "apostolic and prophetic teacher of the Church and of the Christian people." Moreover, Archiman-

---

[13] Vladimir Lossky, "Tradition and Traditions," in Idem, *In the Image and Likeness of God*, (Crestwood, NY: St Vladimir's Seminary Press, 1974), 141-168.

[14] Старец Силуан, *Жизнь и поучения* [Life andTeachings], Издательство „Православнаяобщина," (Москва – Ново-Казачье – Минск, 1991).

[15] Although a simple and unlearned peasant, Silouan was visited by many bishops, priests and lay people, including academics. One of the monks, surprised, asked another: "Why they go to him? It seems to me that still, he is not reading anything." The answer was: "He does not read anything but does everything, while others read everything but do nothing."

drite Iustin Popovici (1894-1979), the most important Serbian Orthodox theologian of the 20th century and author of the collection in 12 volumes *The Lives of the Saints*, did not hesitate to compare St. Silouan with St. Symeon the New Theologian.

The influential spirituality and spiritual fatherhood of the Blessed Silouan the Athonite manifested in different ways, one of which was the flourishing of his spiritual sons who continued his spiritual work. His most important disciple was Sophrony Sakharov (1896-1993). Born in Moscow, he went into exile in Paris in 1921. He reached Mount Athos in 1925, entering as a monk at the monastery Russikon. He was practiced obedience under Silouan the Blessed until the death of the latter in 1938. He was ordained priest in 1941. After a while, he got sick and had to return to Paris in 1947, where he was operated on. Miraculously, he survived the disease and in 1948 he wrote a book about "Abbot" Silouan.[16] He wanted to return to Athos, but he was denied a visa, which made him settle in England, where he set in 1959, the Orthodox monastic community in Maldon/ Essex. The first church dedicated to the Blessed Silouan was consecrated in 1988 at the monastery which is dedicated to St. John the Baptist. Father Sophrony's writings have been translated into several languages,[17] influencing people of different faiths.[18]

Member of the monastic community of Essex there was also monk Raphael Noica (b. 1942), of Romanian origin, who now lives as a hermit in Romania.[19] His life testifies the unity of the spiritual experience in the Orthodox Church, regardless of the context (Mount Athos or the West) and the origin of those who are leading a life of holiness: Russian, Greek, Romanian, etc.

One should notice that the recognition of Silouan's holiness was not limited in the Orthodox space. The expression: "and to the Christian people" in the act of canonization is not accidental. Silouan is considered a saint not only of the Orthodox Church *stricto sensu*, but of all Christians, regardless of confession. Thus, the famous American Cistercian monk Thomas Merton (1915-1968) wrote in 1958 that Silouan "was perhaps the most authentic monk of the 20th century" and Enzo Bianchi called him a real "saint without borders."[20] The great popularity that St. Silouan enjoyed is also affirmed by the establishment of the International Association of St. Silouan the Athonite in Switzerland, in 1993, by twelve members among which there was a Benedictine monk and two Protestant ministers. Today the Association has hundreds of members from over 20 countries, their activity being centered on "the organization of meetings" and editing of "Notebooks of St. Silouan the Athonite: The Burning Bush" (*Buisson Ardent*).

The circulation of *Buisson Ardent* led to the recognition of St. Silouan's holiness and to the reception of his thought (and that of Archimandrite Sophrony) beyond the visible boundaries of the Orthodox Church. For example, even before the official canonization of Silouan, the Roman Catholic monks of the abbeys of Saint-Wandrille, Lérins and Tamié were placed under the spiritual fatherhood of Abbot Silouan, adopting his name. In the Latin litany he is invoked with these words: "Holy Father Silouan the Athonite, pray to God for us."

The relevance of St. Silouan's thinking for Western monasticism is attested in the writings of a Benedictine monk.[21] Also, the experience of a prisoner sentenced to life imprisonment for murder who came to convert to

---

[16] This book is *Starets Silouan. Moine du Mont Athos (1886-1938). Vie – Doctrine – Ecrits*, (Paris: Editions Presence, 1973).

[17] We offer here the first edition of his main writing: *Sa vie est la mienne*, (Paris: Cerf, 1981); *Voir Dieu tel qu'Il est*, (Geneva: Labor et Fides, 1984); *La félicité de connaître la Voie*, (Geneva: Labor et Fides, 1988). On Sophrony's spirituality, see Nicholas V. Sakharov, *I Love Therefore I Am*, (Crestwood, NY: St. Vladimir's Seminary Press, 2003).

[18] An example here is the case of Klaus Kenneth, who describes the experience of conversion after meeting Abbot Sophrony in the book *Born to Hate, Reborn to Love: A Spiritual Odyssey from Head to Heart*, (Mount Thabor Publishing, 2012).

[19] Among his works we recall *Celălalt Noica* [*The Other Noica*], (Bucureşti: Anastasia: 1994); *Cultura Duhului* [*Culture of the Spirit*], (Alba Iulia: Reîntregirea, 2002).

[20] Likewise, Maxime Egger called him "a universal saint." Cf. Maxime Egger, "Starets Silouane: un saint actuel et universel," *Contacts* 171.3 (1995): 162-182.

[21] Dom Silouane, "Quand un moine bénédictin reçoit la paternité de saint Silouane," in *Buissont Ardent. Cahiers Saint-Silouane l'Athonite* nr. 1, (Pully: Ed. Le Sel de la Terre, 1995), 69-82. Worthy to be mentioned is also the conversion experience of David Balfour (1903-1989), an English Catholic monk who met Abbot Silouan and Fr. Sophronius during a visit to Athos

Orthodoxy after reading the writings of Silouan in prison, becoming even an icon painter and monk, verifies the same thing.[22]

A guide of the great religions published by Cerf in 1997 in France, considered Silouan the witness par excellence of the Orthodox tradition "who summarizes in himself all the aspects of the Eastern holiness" alongside Dalai Lama for Buddhism and Mahatma Gandhi for Hinduism. In 1998, Jean Biès published a book entitled *Les Grands Initiés du XXᵉ siècle* (Ed. Philippe Lebaud), where St. Silouan is remembered alongside great personalities like Sri Arobindo, Martin Buber, René Guénon, Georges Gurdjieff, Krishnamurti etc. Finally, in the article on "forgiveness" in the *Dictionnaire d'éthique et de philosophie moral* – a reference work published in 1996 by Presses Universitaires de France – Abbot Silouan is quoted alongside Plato, Aristotle, Cicero, Seneca, Rousseau, Kant, Hegel, Kierkegaard, Heidegger and Ricoeur.

All these examples reflect interest in St. Silouan in particular, but also in the Orthodox spirituality in general. It would be wrong to consider Silouan one of the "great Gnostic initiated people," regardless of his affiliation to the Church, and place him among the saints of the "universal Church," passing over in silence his adherence to the Orthodox faith and his ascetic-mystical practice inherited by the great tradition of the Fathers of the *Philokalia*.

I conclude by evoking a lecture on the occasion of the 10th congress of the Orthodox Brotherhood in Western Europe (30 October-1 November 1999, Paray-le-Monial, France) by Olivier Clément (published in *Service Orthodoxe du Presse* suppl. 243, December 1999). He outlined three basic requirements for a fruitful witness of Orthodoxy in the West: 1) "to try to make 'talking' coincide with 'doing'," 2) "to give back to history its open and creative dimension through the work of the Holy Spirit in it," and 3) "to try to think less against." Recalling examples of such attitudes of spiritual people like Metropolitan Anthony Bloom, Father Lev Gillet or Fathers Silouan and Sophrony, Clément said: "We are not here (in the West, n. n.) to condemn, but to bear witness and to share."

Bibliography

Vladimir Lossky, *Essai sur la théologie mystique de l'Eglise d'Orient*, (Les Editions du Cerf, 1990).

Andrew Louth, *Theology and Spirituality*, (Oxford: SLG Press, Convent of the Incarnation, 1976).

Dumitru Stăniloae, *Ascetica şi Mistica Ortodoxă* [*Orthodox Ascetic and Mystic*] 2 vol., (Alba-Iulia: Deisis, 1993).

Irénée Hausherr, *Penthos: the Doctrine of Compunction in the Christian East*, (Kalamazoo: Cistercian Publications Inc., 1982).

Irénée Hausherr, *Direction spirituelle en Orient autrefois* ("Orientalia Christiana Analecta" 144), (Roma, 1955).

Dumitru Stăniloae, "Witness Through «Holiness» of Life," in Ion Bria (ed.), *Martyria/Mission: the Witness of the Orthodox Churches Today*, (Geneva: Commission on World Mission and Evangelism, World Council of Churches, 1980), 45-51.

Vladimir Lossky, *In the Image and Likeness of God*, (Crestwood, NY: St. Vladimir's Seminary Press, 1974).

Archimandrite Sophrony, *Starets Silouan. Moine du Mont Athos (1886-1938). Vie – Doctrine – Ecrits*, (Paris: Editions Presence, 1973).

---

in 1932. He maintained an extensive correspondence with Fr. Sophronius which is important to understand the Orthodox spirituality of the 20th century. See for example Archimandrite Sophrony, "Lettre à un ami," in *Buisson Ardent. Cahiers Saint-Silouane l'Athonite* no. 5, (Pully: Ed. Sel de la Terre, 1999), 2-8.

[22] Dan Siluan, *Gotthinter Gittern. Mein Weg vom Straftäter zum Ikonenmaler*, (Freiburg-Basel-Wien: Herder Verlag, 1994). According to his own confession, the writer's encounter with St. Silouan's thinking totally changed his way of life: "behind the bars and the prison walls I became a free man."

Part VII: Particular Themes and Issues for Orthodox Involvement in Ecumenism

The Relevance of Orthodox Spirituality for the Ecumenical Movement

Christopher Savage

It is important to state from the outset that the following reflections on the relevance of Orthodox spirituality to ecumenism stem more from my lived experience as an Orthodox monk residing in an Orthodox monastery for over thirty years, than from disciplined, scholarly work. My monastery, New Skete, is located in an area of the United States that has a very small Orthodox population, and while we have a small but devout congregation that worships with us on weekends, the majority of visitors that come to the monastery are largely from different traditions. For many, their encounter with us has been their first experience of Orthodoxy, and the spiritual tradition they discover often encourages them to explore how it might link with and enrich their own spiritual journey. More than anything, this fact is what has shaped my convictions about how we share our heritage. My focus is decidedly from a grassroots perspective -- from the ground up -- and witnesses to the impact our spiritual tradition can have on ordinary people from other denominations, even other faiths.

As Christians, we are called by Jesus to love God with our whole mind, our whole heart, soul and strength, and to love our neighbor as ourself (cf. Mk 12:29-31). This commandment encompasses everything that is truly human, from that which is innermost in the heart, to that which we communicate by word, to the more external effects of our behavior. They form an indivisible unity that is meant to be a constant response through the ebb and flow of our everyday lives. Inevitably we will do this out of the perspective of a particular tradition, and each tradition has important lessons to share with the others. This is one of the bases, the rationales for ecumenical sharing. As the practice of our monastery is to welcome all without exception, we are simply following a perennial hallmark of Orthodox spirituality: hospitality. Not only did the early monks of the desert humbly welcome pilgrims in search of deeper understanding, we see the same warmth and openness manifest throughout the best expressions of the history of our church. There is the appreciation, the awareness that in welcoming the other, we welcome Christ.

For us, this has meant a willingness to share from the riches of our tradition, as well as being open to listening to the other. One cannot have one without the other. The only way other Christians (or more broadly individuals of other faiths) will be attracted to explore the deeper dimensions of Orthodoxy is if they encounter in us a respect and love that reflect the Gospel values we hope to live by. That sort of witness resists any sort of triumphalism, but is truly comfortable in its own ecclesial skin. We have nothing to be afraid of in such an encounter, no fear of watering down the faith, for we know who we are and that God's love extends to all. When people experience such an attitude, they are actually interested in what we believe.

Given this, I believe that one crucial insight that other believers discover in Orthodoxy is anthropological in nature: that Christian life is characterized by its organic wholeness. Orthodoxy resists any sort of artificial separation of sacred and secular. Rather, it understands that life is permeated by the presence of God and that fundamentally the human vocation is to come to share fully in the divine life, the process of theosis, or divinization. "God came human so that humans might become God"[23] wrote St Athanasius in the fourth century and St Basil echoes this when he wrote, "The human being is an animal who has received the vocation to become God."[24] Our vocation as human beings is to fulfill our humanity by becoming God through grace, that is to say through a life of deepening (and ultimately unending) communion with God. This is to fulfill our human nature in the most dynamic of ways, to live life in its abundance. It is to realize the freedom proper for a creature made in the image and likeness of God.

---

[23] *On the Incarnation*, sec 54.
[24] quoted by Gregory of Nazianzus, *Eulogy of Basil the Great, Oration 43*, 48

Three Gifts

While there is obviously a wealth of spiritual treasure from Orthodoxy that could be relevant to a living and vibrant ecumenism, in this short essay I would single out three gifts, three graces that the Orthodox tradition brings to the ecumenical table: a radically incarnate spirituality, a tradition of worship that is truly transcendent in character, and a tradition of prayer that emphasizes its continuous, unceasing nature, even in the midst of the busiest of lives. Each believer needs to unpack each gift and apply it to their own life, but it seems to me that the Orthodox tradition speaks from the wisdom of experience -- two millennia's worth -- and I believe all believers can benefit from its witness.

A radically incarnate spirituality

When we say 'radically incarnate', what do we mean? In a word, we go to God through matter. Orthodoxy has always highlighted the mystery in Christianity of bringing together the divine and human in the person of Jesus. This was the essential balancing theme of the Council of Chalcedon long ago in 451 C.E., and it supports the conviction that God, by his very nature and essence, communicates himself and has done so definitively in Jesus. Chalcedon embraces the paradox that Jesus can be fully God and fully human at the same time. As God, Jesus is the Word incarnate, who reveals God's inexhaustible love for humanity and for all creation, and the lengths God will go to bring us to salvation. As man, Jesus shares completely in the human experience, understanding from within all that a human being feels without succumbing to the alienating lure of sin. Jesus can be fully compassionate because he shares fully in our nature. Throughout his earthly life, at no time was Jesus "out of touch with the Father," and his example teaches us that life is not an impediment to living in God's presence, but is the very means we do so. We are not Platonists. Indeed, God can show Himself in every human situation if only we are open to it. This reinforces the understanding of the creation account where six times we find it affirmed that "God saw that it was good," and finally, upon finishing and viewing all that he had made, God saw that indeed it was very good (Gen 1: 4-31). God makes the entire created order good. Evil comes about only through what emerges from the human heart, and thus, our penetrating recognition of the created order can be the very means for living in the presence of God.

In today's world this message cannot be more relevant. We do not have to flee the material to be connected with the spiritual. Indeed, beyond the person of Jesus, Orthodoxy teaches that the whole of creation is permeated by the uncreated "energies of God" and are one of the means God uses to relate with the world, above all, with humanity. While unknowable in his essence, God is revealed to us through his energies in the created order and this leads to a reverent respect for creation. In an ecumenical context, it is extremely useful to be able to witness to the fact that the Christian tradition, in its most authentic expression, has always been world and life affirming and that concern for this is not simply the product of contemporary sensibilities. This is certainly something that visitors to our monastery deeply resonate with.

Transcendent Worship

One of the principal characteristics that Orthodoxy has always manifested is a deep concern for worship. When Prince Vladimir of Kiev sent envoys throughout the world to explore a fitting faith for his kingdom in the eleven4th century, the envoys reported back that when they had attended liturgy in Constantinople, "we did not know whether we were in heaven or on earth, for we have never experienced such beauty, nor do we know how to tell of it." Vladimir was so impressed by their witness that he chose Orthodoxy to be the religion of his realm.

What this famous story highlights is that worship and a concern for its transcendent beauty has always been a central concern of Orthodoxy. Worship, while using ritual, has nothing to do with mere ritualism nor is it seen in any sort of a magical way. Rather, when conducted with deep reverence and with the artistic components that have matured throughout the centuries, it expresses to its members the grandeur of God and the crucial message that God must increase while human beings decrease. The Russian writer Dostoevsky once said that 'beauty will save the world', and one could argue that the beauty of Orthodox liturgy, which rises to the Lord of the universe amidst incense, harmonious chant and gorgeous iconography and church architecture, gathers the faithful in its embrace and lifts them to an experience of the Living God that is transformative and salvific. This is why from the Orthodox perspective, the new life in Christ is always related to worship and liturgy, never detached from them. As important as prayer, ministry, and the other elements of Christian life are, they are never complete if they are not rooted in the experience of worship. Certainly the sacramental nature of Christian worship leaves an open ceiling to the experience of God, the experience of the Holy. It is also what binds the community together in a sense of 'oneness', of being part of the same body, making it a true 'mystagogy', something that progressively initiates us into the wonders of divine life.

Orthodoxy witnesses to this; it reminds the rest of the church of worship's importance on an existential level and offers the fruit of its own experience for deepening our sense of the Holy, the sacred. Over the course of many years of receiving guests here at New Skete, we are aware of the profound impact Orthodox worship has upon those who participate in it, Orthodox and non-Orthodox alike. For the many non-Orthodox, one of the constant comments we hear is how the beauty of the service made them forget themselves for a time, how it 'refreshed' them, and left them wondering how they might draw the same sort of spiritual nourishment from their own worship traditions. Beauty is surely not confined to one tradition. However, from our own experience of beauty in worship, I believe Orthodoxy can call our separated brothers and sisters in Christ to an appreciation and renewal of their own worship traditions, and the transforming place that each has in Christian life.

A tradition of continuous prayer

Within the tradition of Orthodoxy there has always been a fascination with the inner life, and the role that prayer has in being a follower of Christ. Orthodoxy possesses a vast literature on prayer that largely (though by no means exclusively) stems from monastic sources that try to articulate what a life that is increasingly contemplative might look like: not, let us be clear, a monastic, cloistered life (though a person's attraction could take them in that direction), but through realizing in whatever life one happens to be called to a prayerfulness that is increasingly constant, that seeks to express itself in the various rhythms of our lives. Believers from other denominations and traditions often look to Orthodoxy for guidance in this regard, and I believe we can speak helpfully out of our experience so long as we are honest and unpretentious. Prayer is a journey for everyone.

Yet prayer becomes more vital when we look at it less as an individual act than as a state that progressively deepens. This comes from the call to unceasing prayer, what St Paul exhorts us to in his first letter to the Thessalonians (5:17) when he writes, "Pray without ceasing." Though utterly central to Christian monastic tradition, East and West, we misunderstand this entirely if we conceive of it as applying only to monks. It is each Christian's vocation, indeed the fundamental human vocation, for prayer acknowledges and celebrates who we are in God. To pray without ceasing is simply becoming who we truly are, for it is only in relationship to God that we flourish.

But what would this look like? How would we avoid a practice that is fanatical and unnatural? St Basil the Great gives us a clue when he says, "this is how you pray continually – not by offering prayer in words, but by joining yourself to God through your whole way of life, so that your life becomes one continuous and uninterrupted prayer..."[25] You do not have to be sequestered in a monastery to feel the relevance of that text. Another desert father put it more tersely: "a person who prays only when they pray, is one who does not pray at all." What both of these fathers are getting at is prayerfulness, a climate of prayer in which we live and

[25] *Homily on the Martyr Julitta*, 3-4.

Orthodox Handbook on Ecumenism

breathe, and which expresses itself in a rich variety of ways, often without words. May it be said boldly and unambiguously: To pray without ceasing has little to do with always saying prayers, being artificially pious – in fact, to try to do that is the surest way to frustrate its development. While we may incorporate practices such as the Jesus Prayer to deepen our sense of prayerfulness, a literal application of it can be counterproductive. Instead, true prayerfulness is being absolutely in touch with reality, loving and serving the God of prayer in quiet, attentive openness. There is no divided consciousness here, no trying to do two things at once. We do not pay any less attention to daily realities or retreat from life's responsibilities. When we are living prayerfully we simply acknowledge God's presence in the demands of the now and cooperate with it, moment by moment.

I believe these three "gifts" are one example of how Orthodox spirituality can enrich the ecumenical movement by speaking out of its own experience in a way that touches the common concerns of Christians everywhere. Granted, they have an Orthodox flavor, but isn't that the desire of true ecumenical sharing?

Bibliography

Bulgakov, Sergius. *Orthodoxy*, (Crestwood, NY: St. Vladimir's Seminary Press, 1997).

Clement, Olivier, *The Roots of Christian Mysticism*, (London: New City Press, 1982).

Evdokimov, Paul, *Orthodoxy* (Hyde Park, New York: New City Press, 2011).

Monks of New Skete, *In the Spirit of Happiness* (New York: Little, Brown & Co., 1999).

Spidlik, Tomas, *Prayer: The Spirituality of the Christian East.* (Kalamazoo, Michigan: Cistercian Publications, 2005).

Part VII: Particular Themes and Issues for Orthodox Involvement in Ecumenism

(100) Theological Reflection on the Relationship of Scripture and Tradition as an Example of Ecumenical Learning

Daniel Ayuch

Introduction

The theological reflection about the place of Scripture in the Church has a long history in the writings of the Orthodox Church. The liturgical celebrations give a constitutional role to the Bible, and the Holy Fathers consecrate a major amount of their studies to interpret the word of God. Scripture has not been considered as a mere topic in theology, but rather as the true source to be consulted to discover the authentic contents of faith. Therefore, it is undisputable that Scripture and Tradition are one corpus in the life and thought of the Orthodox Church.

On the other hand, the dialectical relationship between Scripture and Tradition was first proposed in the context of the controversies between the rise of Protestantism and the apologetic answer to it by Catholicism. Within this framework the insistence on sola scriptura was understood as a Protestant doctrine, while Catholicism stressed on the importance of tradition. This simplistic exposition speaks above all about a situation that took place centuries ago. With the course of time and after Vatican II many things have changed. Protestants have their own liturgical and ecclesiastical traditions, while Catholics have reaffirmed the role of the Written Word in the Church.

Orthodoxy has interacted in this discussion from different points of view and in different periods of history. Modern theological and systematic writings dealing with this issue reflect a variety of standpoints depending on the writers' own approach and the particular questions they deal with. This is why this question of Scripture and Tradition seems to be one of the most discussed issues among Orthodox theologians. Some spheres reject the idea of stressing on the primacy of Scripture over Holy Tradition. Others prefer to bring up Holy Tradition since it also contains an oral Tradition that belongs to the apostles and it is not registered in the New Testament but later on in the canons and liturgical writings.

Undoubtedly this debate has been enriched by the ecumenical character of theological education in modern times. Orthodox theologians read other Christian writings and take benefit from the theological research worldwide. They also contribute to the ecumenical debates with their own points of view and with their research in their own Tradition. This article draws a modern way of understanding the question of Scripture and Tradition departing first of all from the writings of the Holy Fathers and the liturgical practice and considering the questions raised by modern authors.

Scripture is Divine and Communitarian

When the Apostle Paul teaches about his kerygmatic work in his epistles, he says: "Our gospel did not come to you in word only, but also in power and in the Holy Spirit and with full conviction;" (1Thes 1:5) and he adds, "for this reason we also constantly thank God that when you received from us the word of God's message, you accepted it not as the word of men, but for what it really is, the word of God, which also performs its work in you who believe" (1Thes 2:13). These two quotations, among others, inspire the Fathers to refer to the whole collection of scriptural Books in both the New and the Old Testaments as the Divine Scriptures (hai theiai graphai) in the sense that they are both the writings inspired by God and the writings that instruct about God. God has revealed his will to the prophets, apostles and saints so that men can attain salvation.

Furthermore, it is important to stress on the ecclesiastical aspect of Scripture, particularly in the first three centuries of Christianity. Christian daily life at the levels of liturgical organization, catechesis and community organization had the Bible as the sole source of divine revelation. The Church has never existed without

Scripture and Scripture has never existed without the Church. They are two inseparable realities that speak of a single identity. The Old Testament was always part of Christianity in its Greek version of the Septuagint, the Scripture on which the Fathers commented and interpreted. The early Church struggled to ensure that the Biblical canon be formed according to Christian doctrine. On the one hand they contested Marcionism, who cut the canon of the two Testaments, and on the other hand they struggled against Gnosticism, a movement that was particularly hostile to the Old Testament.

When one reads the Church Fathers in the context of Church history as a whole, one can see that the Bible was the sole document that was able to provide unity of the whole Church facing heresies and sociopolitical changes. Christians took the Bible in both Testaments as one source of revelation following mainly the school of interpretation that founded the apostles and that we find, for instance, in Saint Paul's approach to Genesis in his letters to Romans and Galatians. The centralizing and unifying power of the early Church comes from Scripture, which spreads among the faithful through its teachers and interpreters and who were able to find in the Bible every word of instruction and behavior.

Irenaeus of Lyons (+202) asseverates in his writings that Scripture must be understood within the Church. He clearly develops the concept of regula fidei (kanôn tês pisteôs) or analogia fidei (analogia tês pisteôs), which arises from Pauline texts such as Romans 12:6 and Galatians 6:16 and runs as a fundamental hermeneutical principle for the Fathers. The authors of the Bible are true members of the Church. Therefore, it is the Church who has the authentic authority of interpreting her writings. The Bible is a testimony of the Eucharistic faith and the believers are the ones who have the authority to interpret it.[1]

For the Fathers the Word of God is testimony of revelation by any given biblical author; this is why the biblical texts are always read in the Orthodox liturgy in reference to their source, which is mostly in direct relation to a witness' name: The prophets, the evangelists, the apostle Paul, and the other apostles. It is a person's witness, accepted and recognized by the reading community, which validates the contents of the text. The Eucharistic and communitarian dimension of revelation is manifested in this ritual of reading. Furthermore, the word of God is always present on the altar and is the basis of the Eucharist and, by extension, of every sacramental celebration. In any daily prayer other than the Eucharist, when there is neither chalice nor paten on the holy table, we find the Evangeliarion lying there. The word of God is present on the most sacred place of the Church having the key role of congregating people to meet in the presence of God. There is no sacrament in which this book should not be open to bless the service and to guide the celebration into the right sense and meaning. The centrality of the Evangeliarion in Orthodox liturgy expresses without doubt the assembly's conviction that the biblical canon is the inspired Word of God.

When reading the Fathers' understanding of the Bible, Georges Florovsky says that the Bible as a whole has been created by the community of believers. The Bible is not a collection, but a selection of writings that the community of faith has produced granting them a certain authority over the community.[2] Scripture gains the quality of inspired in the assembly of believers and in their act of reading. When Scripture sanctifies and renews the community by the force of its Word, it proves to have been inspired. The same Spirit that inspired the holy writers is the one that inspired the readers and still does. The Bible is a book and as such it proposes an open communication by its mere presence amidst the readers.

Scripture is the Backbone of Tradition

Frequently enough, Orthodox scholars are oblivious to the role of the Bible for the fundamentals of any given theological discipline. The Bible is the written source of revelation and the proof-text provider for every pastoral, liturgical, and dogmatic theory. Furthermore, the Bible serves often as a comparison pattern, when it comes to

---

[1] Cf. *Against Heresies* 3.2.2.
[2] Florovsky, Georges, *Bible, Church and Tradition: An Eastern Orthodox View*, CW vol. I (Massachusetts: Nordland Publishing Company, 1972), 18.

studying the historical behavior of the people of God throughout history. Far away from the saying *sola scriptura*, Orthodox theology should never forget that Scripture has always been seen as the backbone of our faith and the one which feeds any acceptable theological thought. Saint John of Damascus, who did not write biblical commentaries, sets high value to Scripture. He constructs his theological arguments out of Scripture and speaks of Divine Scripture as the source of God's revelation and God's mysteries. According to the Damascene, the Church is the one who interprets and comments on the Bible.[3] If we go back to John Chrysostom, one of the most assiduous interpreters among the Church Fathers, he approaches the Scriptures as an inexhaustible source of life. Wealth and abundance are predicatives used by the Saint to define the contents of the Holy Books. He affirms that the Divine Scriptures are "a never-failing spring".[4] In one of his sermons on Lazarus and the Rich Man, the Saint calls his audience five times in less than two columns to a persistent reading of Scripture.[5] Saint John Chrysostom belonged to one of the most relevant theological institutions in the classic times: the Antiochian School of Theology, which is worth mentioning here because of the prominent role given to biblical studies by its members. The Antiochian asketerion was a fellowship of men who dedicated their life to prayer, to study the Bible and to spiritual guidance. In this school we can see a clear example for the tradition of studying and teaching the Bible as one of the key activities in the history of Orthodox theological formation. The term askesis recuperates in the Antiochian pattern its close relation to the Latin word studium, in the sense of endeavor and training, not only for spiritual formation, but particularly for research and knowledge.

By consulting modern theologians, we can deduce that the Orthodox agree on the normative value of Scripture.[6] Scripture is the backbone of tradition, which it nourishes and sustains. As to how to interpret the biblical text, we also find a common hermeneutical principle in the modern Orthodox theological writings: Scriptures should be interpreted in the light of Holy Tradition. "Tradition provides the hermeneutic perspective by which any Biblical writing is to be properly interpreted," says John Breck.[7] Elias Oikonomos adds: "Tradition builds the fundament for an ecclesiological exegesis."[8] These are echoes of Georges Florovsky's understanding of the relationship existing between Tradition and Scripture. In his book *Bible, Church, Tradition*, Florovsky highlights the authority of Scripture as the source of revelation, while he considers Tradition as the authoritative hermeneutical principle for understanding the Bible.

However, there are two opposing views about how to interpret Holy Tradition and how to be part of the modern theological debate about Bible and its interpretation. On the one hand, there are those who see in Tradition a pattern for openness and a source of inspiration and challenge that encourages the dialogue with modern theories and methods.[9] On the other hand, there are those who see Tradition as the only accurate and reliable source to consult, when it comes to investigating the meaning of any paragraph in the Bible. The latter understand the continuity of tradition only through ritualism and encourage the repetition of the sayings of the Fathers,[10] while the former add to the sacramental life of the Church, the personal and communitarian effort, and emphasize the necessity of an open intellectual formation.

If we place emphasis on the dynamic character of tradition, there will be no impediment for seeking dialogue with modern scholars, no matter their origin or confession. This principle of dialogue is not only rooted in the Holy Tradition of the Orthodox Church but also in the message of the Bible.

---

[3] Studer, Basil, *Die theologische Arbeitsweise des Johannes von Damaskus*, (Ettal, Buch-Kunstverlag Ettal, 1956), 76-77.
[4] PG 48:1007: "pege gar estin oudepote epileipousa".
[5] PG 48:992, 58-60.
[6] Breck, John, *Scripture in Tradition. The Bible and its Interpretation in the Orthodox Church*, (Crestwood (N.Y.): St Vladimir Seminary Press, 2001), 11.
[7] Ibid., 10.
[8] Oikonomos, Elias, *Bibel und Bibelwissenschaft in der orthodoxen Kirche* (Stuttgarter Bibelstudien 81), (Stuttgart: KBW Verlag, 1976), 46.
[9] Karavidopoulos, Johannis, "The Exegetical Tradition of the Church and Modern Biblical Research Methods", in *St John of Damascus Institute of Theology Annals* 6 (2005-2006), 118-129 (in Arabic).
[10] Breck, John, ibid., 217-219.

Since the foundation of the WCC, the issue of Scripture and Tradition has been part of the theological dialogue agenda. A major agreement was reached at the Fourth World Conference on Faith and Order in Montreal in 1963. All churches proclaimed that their theological thought is rooted in Scripture (both Old and New Testament) and that there is a continuing attempt to interpret Scripture by the community of believers. The WCC consultative body Faith and Order issued in 1998 a document titled "A Treasure in Earthen Vessels" in which the representatives of the different Christian church families express their reflection on interpretation of Scripture in the Church. This document recalls the achievements of 1963 and goes further in analyzing the act of interpretation in diverse contexts. These two documents contain the principles of relation between Scripture and Tradition and reflect in great extent what is common to Orthodox doctrine. The distinction between Tradition and traditions is one of the most relevant points of discussion in this dialogue process. With Tradition is meant what is common to all Christians and has clear roots in Scripture, while the plural "traditions" represents the ways of living the faith in different cultural and historical contexts. This last point can be focused either as confessional – Protestant tradition, Catholic tradition or Orthodox tradition – or simply as the external customs in a given context.[11] This matter becomes essential when theologians discuss the role of history in the identity of the Church and when the assimilation of Christianity by new cultures is at stake. For the Orthodox it is very important to define to what extent the traditional Greek-Mediterranean cultures are supposed to influence new forms of Orthodoxy in the Americas, the Sub-Saharan Africa and Australia.

The Reading of Scripture

It belongs to Tradition that the Holy Fathers instructed people to read and listen to Scripture. Their commentaries, quotations and exegetical notes invite their readers and listeners to dedicate themselves to studying and reading the Bible. This is important to stress especially today when some Orthodox thinkers consider that reading the Fathers is more important than reading the Bible itself, because as they say, the Fathers would give us the content of revelation already "chewed" so that we could understand it better.[12]

Saint Irenaeus speaks of a careful reading to understand the mystery of Christ present in the Scriptures.[13] Those who read this way are the perfect disciples, who know how to interlace between the different Scriptural texts. Furthermore, if we follow the homilies of Origen, Chrysostom and many other writers and Fathers, we can appreciate that they used to follow the principles of a lectio continua rather than a lectio selecta of the Sacred Books, i.e. they used to choose a book according to the local church needs and read it in successive pericopes until it was finished.

Origen was the first to talk about theia anagnosis[14] a term that was translated into Latin as lectio divina and has had a great influence on the spirituality of the West. In this paragraph Origen urges Gregory to dedicate himself first of all to read Scripture and to do it with perseverance, with faith and in prayer. Saint John Chrysostom not only recommends that Christians read the Bible, but they should also make the reading of Scripture a permanent practice. In his above mentioned homilies on Lazarus and the rich man, Chrysostom uses two major key words: ceaselessly and continuously when he refers to the frequency of biblical reading by the common parishioner.[15] Chrysostom used to announce the subject of his coming sermon with the firm purpose that people prepare themselves by reading not only the announced paragraph, but also its context so that they can take a better profit from the Saint's words.[16]

---

[11] Cf. World Council of Churches, *A Treasure in Earthen Vessels: An Instrument for an Ecumenical Reflection on Hermeneutics* (Faith and Order Paper 182), (Geneva, 1998), # 32-37.

[12] Agourides, Savvas, "Biblical Studies in Orthodox Theology", *Greek Orthodox Theological Review* 17.1 (1972): 51.

[13] *Against Heresies* 4.26.1.

[14] See his *Letter to Gregory Thaumaturgus*, SC 148, 191.

[15] PG 48:992, 58-60.

[16] PG 48:991.

In his second homily on Matthew, Chrysostom admonishes his listeners, because they would not know to recite a single verse from the Psalms, while they would say by heart pagan poems and songs. The saint says that the Bible should be read in family and by all the faithful, not only by monks. The Word that has been heard in the Church is supposed to be read again at home because it is like a remedy for the wounds caused by our passing in the world. The saint says that even worse than not reading is to believe that reading is useless and vain.[17]

This categorical insistence of the Fathers to read the Bible in both its Testaments draws a compelling contrast with some modern tendencies in Orthodoxy that encourage the reading of classical and not so classical Fathers, the neo-monastic literature instead of the Bible itself, because they would fear misinterpretation.

Conclusions

The question of Scripture and Tradition has shown relevant theological implications in Orthodox modern thinking. As it has been shown above, this is a topic with roots in the Western Church but with an influence in contemporary Orthodox theology.

The questions raised in the context of this debate have provoked a new way of expressing the teachings of the Holy Fathers regarding the place of Scripture in the Church, as well as discussing the sense and meaning of Tradition in its diverse forms and contexts. From an ecumenical point of view, the Orthodox formulated in modern terms that Scripture is the vital and focal element in this complex body called Church. Even when Orthodox theology was sometimes reluctant to find a creative encounter with the significant topics of western theology, the issue of Scripture and Tradition was one of the most attractive themes of discussion.

A major agreement was achieved in the field of ecumenical dialogue. This agreement is a good fundament for further discussions on other issues such as sacramental theology and ecclesiology. Since theology is called to address the questions and the needs of Christians in a certain place and time, the issue on Scripture and traditions requests to be revisited now and then in order to explain, out of new contexts, what is one of the pillars of Christian faith.

Bibliography

Agourides, S. "Biblical Studies in Orthodox Theology", *Greek Orthodox Theological Review* 17.1 (1972): 51-62.

Breck, J, *Scripture in Tradition. The Bible and its Interpretation in the Orthodox Church,* (Crestwood, NY: St. Vladimir's Seminary Press, 2001).

Florovsky, Georges. *Bible, Church and Tradition: An Eastern Orthodox View.* Collected Works, vol. 1 (Massachusetts: Nordland Publishing Company, 1972).

Jeanrond, W.G., "History of Biblical Hermeneutics," in: *The Anchor Bible Dictionary* III, (1992), 433-443.

Kannengiesser, Ch. *Handbook of Patristic Exegesis. The Bible in Ancient Christianity.* (Leiden: Brill, 2006).

Karavidopoulos, J. "The Exegetical Tradition of the Church and Modern Biblical Research Methods", *St John of Damascus Institute of Theology Annals* 6 (2005-2006), 115-126 (in Arabic).

Nissiotis, N.A. "Unity of Scripture and Tradition: An Eastern Orthodox Contribution to the Prolegomena of Hermeneutics", *Greek Orthodox Theological Review* 11.2 (1966): 183-208.

Oikonomos, E. *Bibel und Bibelwissenschaft in der orthodoxen Kirche* (Stuttgarter Bibelstudien 81), (Stuttgart: KBW Verlag, 1976).

Stylianopoulos, T. *The New Testament: An Orthodox Perspective.* Volume One: *Scripture, Tradition, Hermeneutics.* (Brookline: Holy Cross Press, 1997).

Trevijano, R. *La Biblia en el cristianismo antiguo. Prenicenos. Gnósticos. Apócrifos* (IEB 10), (Estella: Verbo Divino, 2001).

World Council of Churches. *A Treasure in Earthen Vessels: An Instrument for an Ecumenical Reflection on Hermeneutics* (Faith and Order Paper 182). (Geneva, 1998).

---

[17] In his *Homily on Matthew* 1:1 in PG 57.30.

(101) Ethics and Ecology as an Issue for Joint Dialogue and Work with other Christian Traditions

Elizabeth Theokritoff

"There might be more East-West conversation were it not for uncertainty about how to understand an approach with all the trappings of ecological spirituality, yet insistently anthropocentric, even dominionist, and often methodologically conservative."[1] This observation by Anglican theologian Willis Jenkins encapsulates the paradox of Orthodox involvement in ecumenical eco-theology: the more Orthodoxy engages with its concerns and offers approaches eagerly accepted by Christians of other traditions, the harder it is to pigeon-hole. But rather than being an impediment to conversation, this could be seen as a challenge to the wider Christian world to accept paradox, and recognise the creative tension in approaches that might appear contradictory.

Faced with the call for a Christian response to environmental destruction, Orthodox for their part have embarked on a remarkable journey of discovery of their own tradition. It is easy to focus on the traditional sources thus uncovered and forget that ecumenical organisations, forums and publications were almost exclusively responsible for the early impetus to explore and articulate the tradition in new contexts. Furthermore, the practical and programmatic emphasis of ecumenical organisations still challenges the Orthodox to show how cosmic theology, liturgical practice and the example of the saints may bring forth fruit in the lives of Christians today.

Ethics or ethos?

The outspoken advocacy of Patriarch Bartholomew of Constantinople, with his insistence on the environmental aspect of the whole range of social and ethical concerns, has earned very wide respect and made it increasingly difficult to talk about ecumenical ecological concern without giving a prominent place to Orthodoxy. His approach is unusual in its concern with moral exhortation; he has even gained notice for talking about 'ecological sin', an idea applauded by some other Christians and environmentalists, and which at least underlines that our relationship with the rest of creation is not separable from our relationship with God. Patriarch Bartholomew also speaks, however, of ethos rather than ethics, a point discussed explicitly in Metropolitan John Zizioulas' seminal lectures 'Preserving God's creation'.[2] Zizioulas' critique of the 'moral rules' approach is perhaps even more relevant today, as the question of how to motivate people increasingly preoccupies those concerned about environmental *in*action, Christians among them. Many now feel that environmentalist attempts to motivate people through guilt are counterproductive, and this invites Christians too to look at their 'ethical strategies'. It suggests that there are advantages to the least moralistic approach, what Jenkins calls "ecological spirituality,"[3] of which the Orthodox ecological ethos would be an example. Zizioulas speaks of the need for 'a new culture in which the *liturgical dimension* would occupy the central place, and perhaps determine the ethical principle'; a sense of the world as 'cosmic liturgy', analogous to the lost pre-Enlightenment 'understanding of the world in which we live as a mysterious, sacred reality broader than the human mind can grasp or contain'.[4]

Central to introducing the spiritual and liturgical dimension into ecumenical ecological ethics was the 1990 publication by the Ecumenical Patriarchate of *Orthodoxy and the Ecological Crisis,* with a message from Patriarch Dimitrios calling for the dedication of 1 September as the Day of Protection of the Environment,

---

[1] *Ecologies of Grace: Environmental ethics and Christian theology* (Oxford: Oxford University Press, 2008), 108.
[2] Part 1; *Sourozh* 39 (March 1990): 2.
[3] *Ecologies,* 19.
[4] *op. cit.,* 2-3.

subsequently adopted by the WCC. In this booklet, used by the WCC Assembly in Canberra (1991), we find set out such key ideas as 'man as priest of creation' and "eucharistic and ascetic ethos." We will return to these themes; but first, to the idea of a 'new culture'.

Reclaiming the ecological tradition of Christianity

A number of Western Christians seem to have accepted and internalised the idea that "guilt" for environmental destruction lies with Christian tradition itself, which accordingly needs to be re-cast, with help from other religions and non-traditional ideas. Orthodox have not only noted that such accusations against "Christianity" take no account of the Christian East;[5] they also usually incline to the view that the problem stems not from the Christian tradition itself, but from its attenuation. The 'new' culture is not to be invented but rather rediscovered. Orthodoxy thus speaks not as a cluster of local traditions which happen to have a historical alibi, but as representative of a continuous Christian tradition in which all Christians are invited to recognise their own roots. Orthodox have taken part in the essentially ecumenical project of revisiting attitudes to creation in the church Fathers; as a result, it is today much harder to claim that an early cosmic vision failed to survive past Athanasius, or to survey the world view of Christian tradition without reference to the cosmic theology of St Maximus, with his vision of the Incarnation as the mystery for which all things exist, the 'cosmic liturgy' in which all things participate through their constitutive 'words' which inhere in the divine Word.

Such a theocentric cosmic vision has obvious ethical implications. No ethos that takes seriously the notion of God's 'words' or 'wills' in creation can make man the final arbiter of how creation is to be used; no vision of the Incarnation as a 'normative spiritual movement',[6] central to cosmic salvation, can see matter as mere resources for consumption. Many Christians today are struggling to recover a vision that holds together creation and salvation, matter and spirit – something that causes such difficulties especially for Christians of the Reformed tradition. For Orthodox, this unified vision is practically expressed and experienced in sacramental life, where matter becomes God's means for his gift of himself. A sacramental view of the world is by no means limited to Orthodox; it should strike some chord with all Christians who perform baptism and celebrate the Eucharist, reminding them that they do not have to invent or import forms of eco-worship in order to celebrate the openness of matter to the spiritual. Even those least comfortable with sacramental rites might be able to accept the world itself as 'the visible part of a universal and continuing sacrament'.[7]

Probably no manifestation of the Orthodox tradition is so widely embraced as the icon. For millions of contemporary Christians of all traditions, icons grace churches and homes in silent witness that salvation has been accomplished through matter, and that the material world is destined to be transfigured. And, at a time when many people are deeply ambivalent about human shaping of the world, it reminds us that human skill and work are able to make the world more and not less transparent to its Creator.

Perhaps the most persuasive evidence for the ecological implications of Christianity is that of those who practise their faith most consistently – the saints. There is a growing ecumenical awareness that St Francis of Assisi, far from being a luminous exception, is part of a very extensive pattern in which love for God spills over into love for all creatures and a profound sense of fellowship with them. Contemporary representatives of the same pattern, such as Elder Porphyrios, help us interpret earlier stories – from East and West - and see how they might serve as practical examples. The parallels between patterns of spiritual life in Eastern Christianity and in the early West may also help reclaim earlier traditions such as Celtic spirituality as deeply embedded in traditional Christianity, far from the New Age pastiche often presented in their name.

---

[5] Vigen Guroian, "Ecological Ethics: An ecclesial event" in *Ethics after Christendom* (Grand Rapids: Eerdmans, 1994); Issa J. Khalil, "The Ecological Crisis: An Eastern Christian Perspective," *St Vladimir's Theological Quarterly* 22.4 (1978): 193-211.
[6] J. Chryssavgis, *Beyond the Shattered Image* (Minneapolis: Light and Life Publishing, 1999), 54.
[7] D. Staniloae, "The World as Gift and Sacrament of God's Love," *Sobornost* 5.9 (1969): 667.

The human role

The ethical concern in modern ecotheology started by focussing on the Christian understanding of man's role in the world: is "let them have dominion" a license for exploitation? Does the exalted place accorded to man mean that human interests are all that count? The latter is described as an "anthropocentric" ethic, although Zizioulas and others have pointed out that "anthropomonistic" would be a more accurate label.

Writings from the early days of ecumenical creation theology already stake out a sense in which man is indeed "the creature in which all the planes of the world converge, a microcosm."[8] He is structurally central in the sense of being a creature at the boundary and thus a mid-point between creation and Creator.[9] *As an integral part of the creation he represents*, man participates in the priesthood of Christ;[10] his 'mastery' of nature is thus held within the eucharistic offering. Two points are evident here: the picture of man's place is complex and nuanced, and the general framework would be classed (or dismissed?) as "anthropocentric."

The writings of Patriarch Bartholomew are a prime example of unabashed commitment to human superiority – and a serious stumbling block to the assumption that 'anthropocentrism' in this sense entails any lack of reverence for the rest of creation. It is the very exaltation of man, as a creature in the divine image, that imposes a Godly ethos.[11] Such an approach sees Orthodox making common cause with Christians from the developing world in ecumenical meetings,[12] and can make a valuable contribution to thorny issues of balancing environment and development.

The effort to articulate man's proper relationship to the rest of creation is a continuing one, carried on very largely in dialogue with, and sometimes in counterpoint to, ecumenical efforts in the same direction. The search for a single appropriate image was catalysed by the ecumenical emphasis on "stewardship." After a brief dalliance with this imagery in the early days of ecumenical ecological problematic, it was increasingly realised that it is a poor fit for Orthodox theology of creation. Orthodox like to hold together paradox; Western Christian thinking often prefers to split the difference. For the Orthodox tradition, man is king and servant, frail and immortal; the earth praises the Lord and is cursed for man's sake. The 'stewardship' image splits the difference to produce a woefully impoverished world view. It gives some practical guidance for treatment of 'property' in a fallen world, but says nothing about the cosmic drama of salvation which gives meaning to our actions on earth.

For Orthodox, the natural starting point for reflection on the world is ecclesial, liturgical and sacramental; and this progressively leads to development of the image of "priest of creation" as an alternative to "steward." This language is favoured especially by Constantinople, and elaborated quite systematically by Metropolitan John Zizioulas, mostly in ecumenical settings. It finds favour with some other Christians, especially of the more sacramental traditions, but also wariness from others for whom "priesthood" implies clericalism, and priestly "mediation" is taken to mean that the "laity" have no direct relationship to God.[13] Even sympathetic commentators readily miss the point that priesthood *presupposes* kinship with and origin from the laity.[14] It may justly be pointed out that the 'priesthood' image lacks ethical precision;[15] but this is not necessarily a disadvantage. The notion of a priestly ethos can appeal even to those who would minimise the degree of actual environmental damage that we have to worry about, providing a common basis for evaluating behaviour between people who might find little agreement on environmental issues. Furthermore, Orthodox writers who use this language increasingly attach to this image an idea of great ethical significance, that of *sacrifice*. This has all the advantages of an approach that

---

[8] Paul Evdokimov, "Nature," *Scottish Journal of Theology* 18 (March 1965): 1-22 , at 1.

[9] Metropolitan Paulos mar Gregorio*s, The Human Presence* (Geneva: WCC, 1978)*.* 64ff.

[10] Mar Gregorios, 85.

[11] John Chryssavgis, ed., *Cosmic Grace, Humble Prayer: The Ecological Vision of the Green Patriarch Bartholomew I* (Grand Rapids, Michigan and Cambridge: Eerdmans, 2003), 140-1.

[12] See Larry L. Rasmussen, *Earth Community, Earth Ethics* (Geneva: WCC, 1996), 233.

[13] See further Elizabeth Theokritoff, "Creation and Priesthood in Modern Orthodox Thinking," *Ecotheology* 10.3 (December 2005): 344-363.

[14] E.g. Christopher Southgate, *The Groaning of Creation: God, Evolution and the Problem of Pain* (Louisville, KY: Westminster John Knox, 1998), 106 and n. 71.

[15] *Ibid.*

exalts human dignity, while identifying man's high calling of *making holy* (the literally meaning of 'sacrifice') with the antithesis of consuming the world.

Orthodox are good at producing inspiring imagery having a deep resonance with Christian tradition. In ecumenical discussions, such imagery is often challenged and refined by appeal to the empirical world and questions about practical meaning. So here: there are recurrent questions as to whether the emphasis on human 'priesthood' and mediation does justice to the antiquity, otherness and sheer scale of the creation.[16] Such reservations do not negate the possibility of "priesthood" imagery; but they do suggest that, *pace* Zizioulas, "man as priest of creation" should be not the over-all rubric but rather a *sub*-title for part of a much broader liturgical, eucharistic or sacramental picture. The metaphor of cosmic liturgy shifts the focus to the total worshipping *community,* in which priesthood is but one of several interdependent roles. A "liturgical"cosmos is one where all creatures "concelebrate" – in their own way, according to their own order. Something similar is conveyed when iconography depicts the elements with human faces - not that everything is humanised, but that everything has some personal, relational quality. Nothing can be treated merely as an object. This strand of Orthodox tradition clearly strikes a chord with indigenous people in many cultures. It also provides a compelling Christian alternative for those who are tempted to turn to neo-paganism in search of a God-filled world.

An awareness of God's presence in and to all creatures has a profound effect on all our dealings with other creatures; and, as is frequently remarked, Orthodoxy finds it much easier than does Western thought to embrace a radically panentheistic stance without compromising the absolute otherness of the Creator.[17] In striving to express the connectedness between God and creatures, both Orthodox and Western thought owes much to the cosmic vision of the great Orthodox ecumenist Fr. Sergei Bulgakov, with Western theologians being more inclined to use his explicit language of sophiology. Several Orthodox writers prefer to explore not the 'wisdom' but the "word" (logos) of God,[18] in conscious if not always explicit response to Western anxieties about human 'rationality' (*logos*) as an excuse for exploitation of 'irrational' nature. More than twenty years ago Patriarch Ignatius of Antioch, calling Christians to a common task, remarked that "those who like to stress the Word of God will need to recognise that the world also is a word of God";[19] Orthodox exploration of this idea and its ethical implications is still a work in progress.[20]

The image of 'cosmic Eucharist' depicts the world as gift rather than concelebrant, but it focuses on humble gratitude rather than mediation. Or, one might say, the mediation is in the opposite direction: God's good gifts in creation are there to be distributed, for the benefit of all (all people, and by extension all creatures). "Cosmic Eucharist" also provides a starting point for evaluating human creativity. The eucharistic elements, we are frequently reminded, are matter worked by humans; the sacramental world-view thus affirms human creativity in principle, through not necessarily to the degree that some ecumenical interlocutors might wish. But it also reminds us that after all our efforts, this worked matter is still wholly God's own gift, for his purposes and to his glory.

Whether we speak of our cosmological vision as eucharistic or sacramental, or in terms of divine words or wisdom, there is one constant: the path to its manifestation and fulfilment is one of asceticism. The reason is simple: the sacramental vision, as John Chryssavgis points out, encompasses three intuitions about the world. The world is created good, it is fallen into evil, and it is redeemed and re-created; and "there is an incalculable cost for the process of cosmic transfiguration because of the reality of evil."[21] It is remarkable how often the paradox gets lost in the transmission, so that the sacramental, liturgical vision is misread as static, "lost in wonder of what is," oblivious to evil and injustice.[22] The lesson, it seems, is always to speak of eucharistic *and ascetic* ethos in the same breath.

---

[16] E.g. Southgate, 106; Celia Deane-Drummond, *Eco-theology* (London: Darton, Longman and Todd, 2008), 60-61.

[17] Philip Clayton, "Panetheism today: A constructive systematic evaluation," in Philip Clayton and Arthur Peacocke (eds.), *In whom we live and move and have our being: Panentheistic Reflections on God's Presence in a Scientific World* (Grand Rapids/ Cambridge: Eerdmans, 2004), 257-8.

[18] E.g. Andrew Louth, "The cosmic vision of St Maximus the Confessor" in Clayton and Peacocke, op. cit. 189-191.

[19] "Three Sermons: A theology of creation; A spirituality of the creation; The responsibility of Christians," *Sourozh* 38 (Nov 1989): 1-14 (14).

[20] See further E. Theokritoff, "The Book of the Word: Reading God's creation" *Caring for Creation* (July 2012).

[21] *Beyond the Shattered Image*, 38-42, 39.

[22] E.g. Rasmussen, 240; cf. Southgate 113.

While a sacramental vision reveals the original and eschatological meaning of the world, realising that meaning in our lives requires a relentless battle with our fallen nature and the disordered relationships which it breeds.

The personal emphasis of asceticism might seem ill-matched to the scale of environmental problems, which undoubtedly require action at the national and international level. But the ascetic ethos has much potential for cutting though the tensions between rich and poor, developed and developing world. It embraces the call for humans to make sacrifices for the sake of other creatures – but demands that we ourselves should be those humans by whom the sacrifices are borne. As John Chryssavgis says, it is a way of learning 'to give and not simply to give up'; to offer, to share, to connect with the natural world and the neighbour.[23]

If this aspect of the Orthodox ethos gains so little ecumenical traction, it could be because in practice, it is usually honoured in the breach. Certainly, there are a number of impressive and inspiring examples of monasteries making a conscious connection between "ecological life-style" and traditional monastic life, sometimes working with environmental organisations. But their example is rarely followed in Orthodox parishes or local Churches. Orthodox writing on "ecological asceticism" thus serves a dual purpose. It reminds the wider Christian world that an ecological way of living that does not merely serve a practical necessity, is s traditional mainstay of spiritual life. But it also reminds Orthodox that asceticism is not merely a matter of traditional rules, but can properly be linked to social and environmental implications of our actions.

Some of the potential of these themes may be seen in the way they are taken up in recent work by the Protestant theologian Norman Wirzba; drawing extensively on Schmemann, Zizioulas and Staniloae, he links sacrifice, asceticism and gratitude in what he calls "a priestly approach."[24] By applying this approach to the basic act of eating - an ethical mine-field - he explores concrete and practical implications of Orthodox theology in a way that Orthodox writers almost never do for themselves. As Orthodox ecological theology reaches a wider audience and ventures further into dialogue with other traditions, there will be more such opportunities to explore the concrete ethical implications of the Orthodox theology of creation.

Bibliography

Olivier Clément, *On Human Being: A spiritual anthropology*, tr. Jeremy Hummerstone (London/New York: New City, 2000)

Metropolitan John (Zizioulas) of Pergamon, "Ecological Asceticism: A Cultural Revolution," *Sourozh* 67 (February 1997); reprinted from *One Planet* 7/6 (1996).

Metropolitan John (Zizioulas) of Pergamon, "Preserving God's creation," *King's Theological Review* 12 (1989): 1-5; 41-5; 13 (1990): 1-5.

Bishop Kallistos (Ware) of Diokleia, "Lent and the Consumer Society," in A. Walker and C. Carras (eds.), *Living Orthodoxy in the Modern World* (London: SPCK, 1996), 64-84.

Gennadios Limouris (ed.), *Justice, Peace and the Integrity of Creation: Insights from Orthodoxy* (Geneva: WCC, 1990)

Crina Gschwandtner, "Orthodox ecological theology: Bartholomew I and the Orthodox contribution to the ecological debate," *International Journal for the Study of the Christian Church* 10.2 (May 2010): 1-15.

Fr. Michael Oleksa, "Icons and the Cosmos: The missionary significance," *Sourozh* 16 (May 1984): 34-45; *Sacred Art Journal* 5.1 (1984): 5-13.

So that God's Creation might Live, Inter-Orthodox Conference on Environmental Protection (ET publ. Syndesmos, 1994).

Elizabeth Theokritoff, *Living in God's Creation: Orthodox Perspectives on Ecology* (St Vladimir's Seminary Press, 2009)

---

[23] *Cosmic Prayer,* Introduction, 32.

[24] "A priestly approach to environmental theology: Learning to receive and give again the gifts of creation," *Dialog* 50.5 (Winter 2011): 254-362; *Food and Faith: A theology of eating* (Cambridge: Cambridge University Press, 2011).

(102) Orthodox Perspectives on Mission[1]

Archbishop Anastasios Yannoulatos

Human pride, in its individual, social or racial expression, poisons and destroys life in the world at large or in the small communities in which we live. Human will obstinately exalts its autonomy. Loneliness is on the increase, nightmares multiply, and fears mount up. Old and new idols are being erected in the human consciousness. They dance around them. They offer them adulation and worship them ecstatically. And yet at the same time, every so often, new, sensitive voices speak out for a just and peaceful age. New initiatives are being undertaken; a new awareness of worldwide community is growing.

All of these facts come to light in our ecumenical gatherings, sometimes alarmingly, sometimes hopefully. Our problems overwhelm us. We describe them and try to solve them, but when we think we have solved one, three new ones spring up. Our mood keeps swinging, like a pendulum, between hope and despair.

In this world the faithful continue to pray: "Thy will be done, on earth as it is in heaven," proclaiming quietly, but resolutely, that above all human wills there is one will that is redemptive, life-giving, full of wisdom and power, that in the end will prevail. The choice of the theme for our meeting is essentially, I think, a protest and a refusal to accept that which militates against God's loving design, and, at the same time, is an expression of hope and optimism for the future of the world.

A. Reality and expectation

In the petition, "Thy will be done, on earth as it is in heaven," the firm certainty prevails that the Father's will is *already a reality.* Myriads of other beings, the angels and saints, are already in harmony with it. The realization of God's will is not simply a desire; it is *an event* that illuminates everything else. The center of reality is God and His Kingdom. On this, the realism of faith is grounded. On this ontology is based every Christian effort on earth.

---

[1] The present paper under the initial title *"Thy will be done." Mission in Christ's way* was the basic report to the World Missionary Conference of the World Council of Churches in San Antonio, Texas, 1989. · "Address by the Conference Moderator," (Conference on World Mission and Evangelism, San Antonio, TX, 1989) *International Review of Mission* 78 (1989): 316-328. · *The San Antonio Report, Your Will Be Done. Mission in Christ's Way,* ed., Fr. R. Wilson, (Geneva: WCC, 1990), 100-114. Address of the Moderator, Conference on World "Mission and Evangelism," San Antonio, 1989. · German: „Dein Wille geschehe—Mission in der Nachfolge Christi," *Dein Wille geschellte—Mission in der Nachfolge Jesu Christi.* Welt-missionskonferenz in San Antonio, 1989, (Frankfurt a. M.: Hrsg. J. Wietzke, Otto Lembeck, 1989), 217-235. *Jahrbuch 6 des Evangeleischen Missionswerkes in Sudwestdeutchland.* (Stuttgart: Mission bei uns gemeinsam mit den Partnern, 1989), 82-88. Greek: «Γενηθήτω τό θέλημά Σον - Ιεραποστολή στά ίχνη του Χρίστον,» Σάν Άντόνιο, Η.Π.Α., Πάντα τά Έθνη 9 (1990) 33, 3-7, 34, 35-38. · French: "Que ta volontée soit faite—Une mission conforme au Christ," *Supplement a SOP,* (Courbevoie, France, 1990), No. 140b. Swedish: «Ske Din vilja—Mission pa Kristi satt," *Till Heia Varlden— pa Kristii satt,* (Uppsala, Svenska: Mission radet, 1990), 7-17. *The Ecumenical Movement, An Anthology of Key Texts and Voices,* eds. M. Kinnamon and B.E. Cope, (Geneva: WCC, 1997), 388-393. This report was characterized as "the most solid theological contribution" to the aforementioned World Missionary Conference (Dr. Wietzke, Director of the Evangelisches Missionswerke in Hamburg). "It was Anastasios' presentation that provided the theological framework for the conference theme. Its overall thrust was truly ecumenical in the best sense of the word." (Prof. Dr. D. J. Bosch, Director of the International Academic Journal, *Missionalia,* "Your Will Be Done? Critical Reflection on San Antonio," *Missionalia* 17.2 (1989): 127.) *Mission in the footsteps of Christ. Theological essays and homilies,* (Athens 2007) (in Greek).

To some, to mention "heaven" might seem anachronistic. We usually look for immediate answers, down to earth and realistic—according to our own fixed ideas. We forget, however, that contemporary science and technology have made important leaps forward with regard to a material heaven. A few decades ago, we sought to solve humankind's communication problems by using wires stretched out over the earth's surface. Later on, we used wireless waves, still following the surface of our planet. With the new technology, however, we have discovered that we can communicate better above the earth, by sending wireless waves heavenwards. So in our theological, ecclesial and missionary thinking, if we turn our sight once more to the reality of "heaven," about which Scripture speaks constantly, we shall certainly find new answers to the world's problems and difficulties.

Our Church has not ceased to look in that direction, with prayer and celebration, affirming the supremacy of God's will. In order for this faith to shed light on the mass of problems that oppress us, a theological reference to the significance of the two proposals that form our theme is needed. I shall first attempt a synoptic approach, drawing on the Orthodox tradition of twenty centuries.

Permit me a parenthesis. In 1964, when for the first time the Orthodox were invited to a similar gathering of the Committee on World Mission and Evangelism in Mexico, I remember we were only three representatives. In San Antonio (Texas), we have altogether nearly one hundred participants. Already there has taken place a serious common theological search and an exchange of experience, which we hope will be continued creatively here as well.

1. "Thy will be done." In the prayer our Lord taught us that this petition follows two others, with which it forms a group: "Hallowed be Thy name, Thy kingdom come, Thy will be done." The chief characteristic of the three is the eschatological perspective. They all begin to be realized here below, in order to be perfected in the glory of the Kingdom that is to come.

The verb of the petition is in the passive voice. Who exactly is the subject of the action? A preliminary answer says, God. In this petition, God's intervention is sought for the implementation of His will, for the establishment of His Kingdom. He has the initiative; He carries out His own will. The chief and decisive role in what happens to humankind and the whole universe belongs to God. A second interpretation sees God's will be done on earth through humankind's conformity with God's commandments (cf. Matt 7:21; 12:50 and John 9:31). Humankind is called to "do" the Father's will. This is the point that is expressed in the insight that permeates the Old Testament and in the continuity that is a dominant feature of Jewish literature. In it, our participation in the fulfillment of God's will and the necessity of obedience is emphasized.

There is, however, yet a third interpretation, a composite one, that sees as the subject of the action both God and human beings, that considers that the divine will is realized by divine- human cooperation. Thus, the two preceding views are intertwined. Certainly, so that His will may be done, God's intervention is essential. But we, by conforming to His precepts, God's will in the here and now, contribute to the foretaste and coming of the Kingdom in historical time, until its final consummation at the last day.

"On earth as it is in heaven." In the next verse we can perhaps distinguish various closely connected aspects: ethical, social, missionary, ecumenical, and a further one, which we will call ontological. They summarize descriptively most of what Chrysostom meant when he said: "For he did not say, Thy will be done in me or in us'; but 'everywhere on earth,' so that error might be done away with and truth established, all evil be cast out, virtue return and so nothing henceforth separate heaven from earth."[2] The prayer that our Lord put on our lips and in our hearts aims at a more radical change: the "celestification" of the earth. "That all persons and all things may become heaven" (Origen).

By the phrase "Thy will be done," of the Lord's prayer, we beseech the Father that He will bring to completion His plan for the salvation of the whole world, and at the same time we ask for His grace that we may be freed from our own will and accept His will joyfully. Moreover, not only we as individuals, but that all of humankind may have fellowship in His will and share in its fulfillment.

---

[2] John Chrysostom, *Commentary on St. Matthew the Evangelist, Homily* 19, 5, PG 57:280, Paris. (J. P. Migne, ed., Patrologiae Cursus Completus, Series Graeca.)

Part VII: Particular Themes and Issues for Orthodox Involvement in Ecumenism

2. After Pentecost this prayer on the Church's lips is highlighted by the events of the Cross and the Resurrection. It becomes clear that the divine will has been revealed in its fullness by the word, life and sacrifice of Jesus Christ. Each member of the Church is called thenceforth to advance in its realization, "So to promote 'the' Father's 'will/ as Christ promoted it, who came to do 'the will' of his Father and finished it all; for it is possible by being united with him to become 'one spirit' with him" (Origen).[3] Christ is made the leader of the faithful in realizing the divine will.

The petition, "Thy will be done," is at the same time our guide in Gethsemane, at the decisive point in the history of the new Adam, our first-born brother. "My Father, if this cannot pass unless I drink it, thy will be done" (Matt 26:42). This prayer, in which the conformity of the human to the divine will reaches it culmination, illustrates *on a personal level* the meaning of the phrase "Thy will be done" of the Lord's Prayer. For all those who are determined to be conformed to God's will, who struggle for its realization on earth, the time will come to experience personally the pain, grief and humiliation that often accompany acceptance of God's will.

The repetition of "Thy will be done" by Christ in the context of His Passion sheds light on the second phase of our subject: Mission in Christ's way."

B. Mission in Christ's way

By this expression we often tend to concentrate our attention on some particular point in Christ's life, such as, the Passion, the Cross, and His compassion for the poor. It is certainly not strange to put particular emphasis at times on one aspect, especially when it is continually being overlooked in practice. However, the theological thinking and experience of the catholic Church insist on what is universal *(to katholou)*. The same is true of the person of Christ. This distinguishes the outlook and feeling of the "one, holy, catholic, and apostolic Church" from the schismatic, sectarian thought that adheres to that which is only a part. In this theological connection I would like to indicate five central points.

1. *Trinitarian relationship and reference.* Jesus Christ is seen in a continuous relationship to the Father and the Holy Spirit. He is the One sent *[Apestalmenos)* by the Father. The Holy Spirit opens the way for Him, works with Him, accompanies Him, sets the seal on His work and continues it from ages to ages.

Through Christ's preaching, we come to know the Father and the Holy Spirit. Nevertheless, even the preaching of Christ would remain incomprehensible without the enlightenment of the Holy Spirit, impossible to put into effect without the presence of the Paraclete.

In every expression of Christian life, but especially in mission, the work of Christ is done with the presence of the Holy Spirit; it is brought to completion within historical time by the uninterrupted action of the Holy Spirit. The Holy Spirit "recapitulates" all of us in Christ. He forms the Church. The source and bearing of our own apostolic activity resides in the promise and precept of the risen Lord in its Trinitarian perspective: "'As the Father has sent me, even so I send you.' And when he had said this, he breathed on them, and said to them, 'Receive the Holy Spirit'" (John 20:21-22).

The Christ-centeredness of the one Church is understandable only within the wider context of Trinitarian dogma. The one-sidedness of the Western type of Christocentrism was often caused by restriction of the image of Christ to the so-called "historical Jesus." However the Christ of the Church is the eternal Word, "the only Son, who is in the bosom of the Father" (John 1:18), who is ever present in the Church through the Holy Spirit, risen and ascended, the universal Judge, "the Alpha and the Omega, the first and the last, the beginning and the end" (Rev 22:13). The faith and experience of the Church are summed up in the phrase: The Father, through the Son, in the Holy Spirit, creates, provides, and saves. Essentially, mission in Christ's way is mission in the light of the Holy Trinity, in the mystical presence and working together of Father, Son and Holy Spirit.

2. *Assumption of the whole of humanity.* One of the favourite terms that Jesus Christ used to describe Himself was "Son of man." Jesus is the new Adam. The incarnation of the Word is the definitive event in the

[3] Origen, *On Prayer,* 26, 3,10:277. Cf. John 4:34; 1 Cor 6:17.

Orthodox Handbook on Ecumenism

history of humankind, and the Church has persisted in opposing any Docetist deviation; "incarnate by the Holy Spirit and the Virgin Mary" insists the Symbol of Faith. In His conception lies the human contribution, by the wholehearted acceptance of the divine will, in obedience, humility and joy, by His mother, the most pure representative of the human race. "Behold, I am the handmaid of the Lord; let it be to me according to your word" (Luke 1:38) was her decisive statement.

The absolute distinction between matter and spirit, as imagined by representatives of ancient Greek or Indian thought, is rejected, and humanity is raised up as a whole. Jesus Christ is not only the Savior of souls, but of the entire human being and the whole material-spiritual creation. This is as hard for classical thought to understand as the Trinitarian dogma. Often indeed, an attempt is made to simplify or pass it over, but then mission loses all its power and perspective. Christian mission does not mean taking refuge from our materiality, in one way or another, for the salvation of mere souls, but the transforming of present time, of society, and all matter in another way and by another dynamic. This perspective demands creative dialogue with contemporary cultures, with secular persons stuck in the materialism of this world, with the new options of physics about matter and energy and with every variety of human creation.

3. The radical and eternally new element: Love. Christ overthrows the established forms of authority, wisdom, glory, piety, success, traditional principles and values, and reveals that the living center of all is LOVE. The Father is love. The Son is love incarnate. The Spirit is the inexhaustible dynamic of love. This love is not a vague "principle." It is a "communion" of persons; it is the Supreme Being, the Holy Trinity. God is love because He is an eternal trinity, a communion of living, equal, distinct persons. The Son reveals this communion of love (koinonia agapes) in the world. In it He is not only the one who invites, but also the way.

Closely bound up with love are freedom, justice, liberation and the brotherhood of man, truth, harmony, joy and fullness of life. Every sincere utterance and endeavor for these things, anywhere in the world, in whatever age and culture, but above all in every loving, true expression of life, in a ray of God's grace and love. Jesus did not speak in vague and philosophical language about these great and holy things, but revealed them in power by clear signs and speech, and above all by His life.

Among the many surprises that Christ held in store was the fact that *He identified Himself with the humble,* the "least" of the people; from among whom He chose His companions and apostles. In the well-known saying about the universal Last Judgment He directly identified Himself with the despised, the infirm, the poor, the strangers and those in distress in the whole world. "As you did it to one of the least of these my brethren, you did it to me," He says, having "all the nations" assembled before Him (Matt 25:31-46).

This course remains determinative for His Church, His mystical body, for all ages. For this constitutes, in its authentic form, the most benevolent power that fights for human dignity, worth, relief, and the raising up of every human being throughout the length and breadth of the earth. Concern for all the poor and those unjustly treated, without exception—independent of race or creed—is not a fashion of the ecumenical movement, but a fundamental tradition of the united Church, an obligation that its genuine representatives have always seen as of first importance. "To the extent that you abound in wealth, you are lacking in love," declares St. Basil the Great, criticizing the predilection of many for a "piety that costs nothing."[4] He did not hesitate to call a "robber" not only the person who robs someone, but also the one who, though able to provide clothing and help, neglects to do so. Tersely he concludes: "You do injustice to so many, as many are those you could help."[5] The modern reality of the world's integration extends these judgments from the individual to the societal plane, from individuals to wider conglomerations, to peoples, and the rich nations. The saints of the Church did not simply speak for the poor, but, above all, shared their life. They voluntarily became poor out of love for Christ, in order to identify with Him, who made Himself poor.

4. The paradox of humility and the sacrifice of the Cross. From the first moment of His presence in humanity, Christ makes "kenosis" (self-emptying) the revelation of the power of the love of the Triune God.

---

[4] St. Basil the Great, *Homily*, To those who become wealthy, 1.
[5] St. Basil the Great, *Homily*, I will pull down my barns, 7.

Part VII: Particular Themes and Issues for Orthodox Involvement in Ecumenism

He spends the greater part of His human life in the simplicity of everyday labor. Later, in His short public life, He faces various disputes and serious accusations. The power of love is totally bound up with humility. The opposite of love we usually call hatred, but its real name is egoism. This is the denial of the Triune God who is a communion (koinonia) of love. Therein also lies the drama of Lucifer, that he can do everything except be humble, and that is precisely why he cannot love. Christ destroys the works of the devil (1 John 3:8), and ransoms us chained in our egoism, by accepting the ultimate humiliation, the Cross. By the excess of this humility He abolishes on the Cross demonic pride and self- centeredness. It is in that hour that the glory of His love shines forth, humankind is redeemed.

Christian life means continual assimilation of the mystery of the cross in the fight against individual and social egocentricity. This holy humility, which is ready to accept the ultimate sacrifice, is the mystical power behind Christian mission. Mission will always be a service that entails acceptance of dangers, sufferings and humiliations; experiencing simultaneously human powerlessness, and the power of God. Only those who are prepared to accept, with courage and trust in Christ, sacrifice, tribulation, contradiction and rejection for His sake, can withstand. One of the greatest dangers for Christian mission is that we become forgetful in the practice of the cross and create a comfortable type of Christian who wants the cross as an ornament, but who often prefers to crucify others than to be crucified himself.

5. Everything in the light of the Resurrection and eschatological hope. The basic precept of the universal mission is given within the light of the Resurrection. Before the event of the Cross and Resurrection, Jesus had not allowed His disciples to go out into the world. Unless one experiences the Resurrection, one cannot share in Christ's universal apostolate. If one experiences the Resurrection, one cannot help bearing witness to the risen Lord, setting one's sights on the whole world. "All authority in heaven and on earth has been given to me. Go therefore and make disciples of all the nations" (Matt 28:18-19). The first sentence takes our thought back to "on earth as it is in heaven" in the Lord's Prayer. Authority over the whole world has been given to the Son of man, who fully carried out the Father's will. He is the Lord, "who is and who was and who is to come, the Almighty" (Rev 1:8). The faith and power of the Church are founded precisely on this certainty. The Cross and the Resurrection go together. Conforming one's life to the crucified life of Christ involves the mystical power of the Resurrection. On the other side, the Resurrection is the glorious revelation of the mystery and power of the Cross, victory over selfishness and death.

A mission that does not put at its center the Cross and Resurrection ends up as a shadow and a fantasy. As do simple people, so also do the more cultivated, who wallow in wealth, comfort and honors, come at some moment of crisis face to face with the implacable, final question: What happens at death? In this problem that torments every thinking person in every corner of the world the Church has the task of revealing the mystery of Christ's word: "For this is the will of my Father, that everyone who sees the Son and believes in him should have eternal life; and I will raise him up at the last day" (John 6:40).

I recall a personal experience, in an out-of-the-way region of Western Kenya. We arrived at night at a house that was in mourning. The little girl, stricken mortally by malaria, was lying on a big bed, as if sleeping peacefully. "She was such a good child. She was always the first to greet me," whispered the afflicted father in perplexity. We read a short funeral prayer, and I said a few words of consolation. Alone in the room of the school house where we were staying, by the light of the oil lamp, with the sound of rain on the banana leaves and zinc roof, I remembered the events of the day. Away in the darkness a drum was beating. It was in the house of mourning. In my tiredness I wondered. Why are you here? There came confusedly to my mind the various things that are spoken about in connection with mission: preaching, love, education, civilization, peace, development. Suddenly a light flashed and lit up in the mist of my tired brain the essence of the matter: You bring the message, the hope of Resurrection. Every human person has a unique worth. They will rise again. Herein lays human dignity, value and hope. Christ is Risen! You teach them to celebrate the Resurrection in the mystery of the Church; to have a foretaste of it. As if in a fleeting vision, I saw the little African girl hurrying up to greet me first, as was her habit; helping me to determine more precisely the kernel of the Christian mission: That is, to infuse all with the truth and hope of the Resurrection; to teach them to celebrate it. And this we do in the Church.

What our brothers and sisters in the isolated corners of Africa and Asia or in the outskirts of our large and rich cities long for, in their depression and loneliness, is not vague words of consolation, a few material goods or the crumbs of civilization. They yearn, secretly or consciously, for human dignity, for hope, and to transcend death. In the end they are searching for the living Christ, the perfect God-man, the way, the truth and the life. All, of whatever age and class, rich or poor, obscure or famous, illiterate or learned, in their heart of hearts long to celebrate the Resurrection and the "certification" of life. In this the prospect of a mission "in Christ's way" reaches it culmination.

C. Fullness and Catholicity

The consequences of such a theological understanding are multifaceted. The important units, within which groups of critical problems for our time will be studied, have already been fixed: (a) turning to the living God; (b) participating in suffering and struggle; (c) the earth is the Lord's; and (d) towards renewed communities in mission. Before today much study, leavened with prayer, has taken place in small and larger groups, in conferences and congresses. The third part of this summary report will focus on only two points.

1. "Thy will be done," as it is repeated by Christ Himself in Gethsemane, helps us to overcome a great temptation: *The tendency for us to minimize the demands and cost of doing God's will in our personal life.* It is usually easier for us to rest in the general, in what concerns mostly others and in what suits us.

(a) The will of God, however, as it is revealed in Christ, is a single and indissoluble *WHOLE ("...*teaching them to observe all that I have commanded you"). "Thy will be done" entirely, not by halves. The various so-called corrections that have at times been made to make the Gospel easier and the Church more acceptable or, so to speak, more effective, do not strengthen but rob the Gospel of its power. While waiting at a European airport a couple of years ago there came into my hands an impressive leaflet in which, framed between other things, was written: "Blessed are those who are rich. Blessed are those who are handsome. Blessed are those who have power. Blessed are the smart. Blessed are the successful, for they will possess the earth." I thought to myself: How many times, even in our own communities, do we prefer, openly or secretly, these idols, this worldly topsy-turvy representation of the Beatitudes, making them the criteria of our way of life?

The name of the city in which this meeting of ours is taking place reminds us not only of St. Anthony of Padua, to which the toponymy refers, but also of St. Anthony the Great, one of the universal Church's great personalities, who traced a model of perfect acceptance of God's will. This great hermit, in perfect obedience to: "If you would be perfect, go, sell what you possess and give to the poor, and you will have treasure in heaven; and come, follow me" (Matt 19:21), went out in an adventure of freedom and love. This led to the outpouring of a new breath of the spirit in the Church at a time when it was in danger of compromising with secular power and the spirit of the world.

In the midst of our many sociopolitical concerns we have to bear in mind and act on the understanding that "this is the will of God, your sanctification" (1 Thess. 4:3). Our *sanctification,* by following the divine will in all things, in our daily obligations, in our personal endeavors, and in the midst of many and various difficulties and dilemmas. The simplistic anthropology that encourages a naive morality, overlooking our existential tragedy does not help at all. Human existence is an abyss. "I do not do what I want, but I do the very thing I hate. I see in my members another law at war with the law of my mind and making me captive to the law of sin which dwells in my members" (Rom 7:15-23). Unfortunately, many of us, in critical situations, while we easily say "Thy will be done," in practice add: "not as thou wilt, but as I will." This overt or secret reversal of the divine will in our decisions is the main reason and cause of the failure of many Christian missions and initiatives. The hard inner struggle for purification and sanctification is the premise and mystical power of the apostolate.

Part VII: Particular Themes and Issues for Orthodox Involvement in Ecumenism

The carrying out of God's will in the world will always be assisted by *continuous repentance,* so that we may be conformed to the model of Christ and be made one with Him. That is why in the Orthodox tradition monasteries have special importance, above all as centers of penitence. Everything that accompanies this struggle—worship, work, comforting the people, education, artistic creativity—follows, as a reflection of spiritual purification, of transformation, of a personal experience of repentance. The quest for new types of communities that will serve the contemporary apostolate must be closely bound up with the spiritual quest in the contemporary social reality for concrete forms of communities that will live out, profoundly and personally, repentance and longing for the coming of the Kingdom. The critical question for a mission in Christ's way is to what extent others can discern in our presence something, a ray, of His own presence.

(b) Conformity to God's will does not mean servile submission or fatalistic expectation. Nor is it achieved by a simple, moral, outward obedience. Joyful acceptance of God's will is an expression of love for a new relationship "in the Beloved"; it is a restoration of humanity's lost freedom. It means our communion in the mystery of the love of the Holy Trinity, communion within the freedom of love. Thus, we become "partakers of the divine nature" (2 Pet 1:4). Conformity to God's will is in the end a sharing in what the Orthodox tradition calls uncreated energies, by which we reach *theosis,* we become "god by grace."[6] The most blessed pages of Christian mission were written out of an excess of love for Christ, and identification with Him.

(c) The Church continually seeks to renew this holy intoxication of love, especially by the sacrament of the Holy Eucharist— which remains the pre-eminent missionary event—everywhere on earth. In the Divine Liturgy the celebrant, as representative of the whole community, prays: "Send thy Holy Spirit upon us and upon these gifts here present." Not "on the gifts only," but we beg that the Holy Spirit may be sent "upon us" also, so that we may be "moved by the Spirit." The whole prayer moves very clearly in a Trinitarian perspective. We beseech the Father to send the Spirit to change the precious gifts into Christ's Body and Blood, and in receiving Holy Communion we are united with Him; we become "of one body" and "of one blood" with Christ, that we may become fertile and bear the fruit of the Spirit, become "God's temple," receivers and transmitters of His blessed radiance.

The *enthusiasm for the acquisition of the Holy Spirit,* which is of late much sought after in the West, has always been strong in the East; but in a sober Christological context and in a Trinitarian perspective. The Church's experience is summed up in the well-known saying of St. Seraphim: "The purpose of Christian life is the *acquisition of* the Holy Spirit." The saint continues: "Prayer, fasting and almsgiving, and the other good works and virtues that are done for Christ, are simply, and only means of acquiring God's Holy Spirit."[7] This presence of the Holy Spirit has nothing at all to do with spiritual pride and self-satisfaction. It is at bottom connected with the continual exercise of penitence, with holy humility. "I tell you the truth," wrote a holy monk of Mount Athos, Starets Silouan, "I find nothing good in myself and I have committed many sins. But the grace of the Holy Spirit has blotted them out. And I know that to those who fight sin is afforded not only pardon, but also the grace of the Holy Spirit, which gladdens the soul and bestows a sweet and profound peace."[8]

2. The fact that the will of God refers to the whole world, the whole universe, *excludes isolating ourselves in an individualistic piety,* in a kind of *private Christianity.*

(a) The will of God covers the whole human reality; it is accomplished in the whole of history. It is not possible for the Christian to remain indifferent to historical happenings in the world, when faith is founded on two historical events: the Incarnation of the Word of God and the Second-coming of Christ. The social, the human reality is the place in which the Church unfolds. Every expression of human creativity, science, technology and the relationships of persons as individuals, peoples and various groupings are to be found among its concerns.

We are living at a critical, historic juncture in which a new universal culture, the electronic culture, is taking shape. The natural sciences, especially astronautics, biomedicine, and genetics are creating and posing

---

[6] St. Maximos the Confessor, *On various questions of Saints Dionysios and Gregorios,* PG 91:1084AC, 1092C, 1308.

[7] P.A. Botsis, *Philokalia of the Russian Vigilents,* (Athens 1983), 105 (in Greek).

[8] Archimandrite Sophrony, *Starets Silouan, Moine du Mont-Athos.* (Traduit du russe par le Hiéromoine Syméon) (Sisteron 1973), 318.

new problems. Half of the earth's population is crushed into huge urban centers; contemporary agnosticism is eating away at the thought and gifts (*charismata*) that every local Church possesses (personnel, knowledge, expertise, and financial facility), it can contribute to the development of the worldwide mission "to the end of the earth" (Acts 1:8). It is time for every Christian to realize that mission is our own obligation and to take part in it looking to the whole of humankind. Just as there is no Church without a worshipping life, so there cannot be a living Church without missionary life.

(b) Those outside the Christian faith, who still have no knowledge of the will of God in its fullness, do not cease to move in the mystical radiance of His glory. God's will is diffused throughout the whole of history and throughout the whole world. Consequently it influences their own lives, concerns them and embraces them. It is expressed in many ways— as divine providence, inspiration, and guidance. In recent time in the ecumenical movement, we have been striving hard for the theological understanding of people of other faiths; and this difficult, but hopeful dialogue very much deserves to continue at this present conference.

Certainly for the Church, God's will, as it was lived out in its fullness by Christ, remains its essential heritage and contribution in the world. It is not, therefore, a sign of respect for others to agree on a so-called common denominator that minimizes our convictions about Christ. Rather, it is an injustice if we are silent about the truth that constitutes the givenness of the Church's experience. It is one thing—imposition by force— that is unacceptable, and has always been anti-Christian and quite a different thing, a withholding or diminution, that leads to a double betrayal, both of our own faith and of others' right to know the whole truth.

Jesus Christ went about doing good among people of other faiths (let us recall the stories of the Canaanite woman and the centurion), admiring and praising their spontaneous faith and goodness. ("I say to you, not even in Israel have I found such faith" Matt 8:10.) He even used as a symbol of Himself a representative of another religious community, the good "Samaritan." His example remains determinative: beneficent service and sincere respect for whatever has been preserved from that which was made "in the image of God." Certainly in today's circumstances our duty is becoming more clear and extensive: a journey together in whatever does not militate against God's will; an understanding of the deepest religious insights that have developed in other civilizations by the assistance of the Spirit; a cooperation in the concrete applications of God's will, such as justice, peace, freedom, love, both in the universal community and on the local level.

(c) Not only the so-called spiritual, but also the whole physical universe moves within the sphere of God's will. Reverence for the animal and the vegetable kingdoms, the correct use of nature, concern for the conservation of the ecological balance, the struggle to prevent nuclear catastrophe and to preserve the integrity of creation, have become more important in the list of immediate ecclesiastical concerns. This is not a deviation, as asserted by some who see Christ as saving souls by choice and His Church as a traditional private religious concern of certain people. The whole world, not only "humankind," but the entire universe, has been called to share in the restoration that was accomplished by the redeeming work of Christ. "We wait for new heavens and a new earth in which righteousness dwells" (2 Pet 3:13). Christ, the Almighty and Logos of the Universe, remains the key to understanding the evolution of the world. All things will come to pass in Him who is their head. The surprising design, "the mystery of his will," which has been made known to us "according to his purpose," is "a plan for the fullness of time, to unite all things in him, things in heaven and things on earth" (Eph 1:9-10). The correspondence with the phrase of the Lord's Prayer is obvious. The transformation of creation, as victory over the disfigurement that sin brought to the world, is to be found in the wider perspective and immediate concerns of Christian mission. [...]

Through all the length and breadth of the earth, we millions of Christians of every race, class, culture and language repeat, "Thy will be done, on earth as it is in heaven." Sometimes painfully, faithfully and hopefully, sometimes mechanically and indifferently; but we seldom connect it intimately with the missionary obligation. The conjunction of the two phrases: "Thy will be done" and "Mission in Christ's way" gives a special dynamic to our conference. Understanding the missionary dimensions of this prayer will strengthen in the Christian world the conviction that mission is sharing in carrying out God's will on earth. Put the other way round, that God's will demands our own active participation, working with the Holy Trinity.

Part VII: Particular Themes and Issues for Orthodox Involvement in Ecumenism

By sharing the life of the risen Christ, living the Father's will, moved by the Holy Spirit, we have a decisive word and role in shaping the course of humankind. The Lord is at hand. The history of the world does not proceed in a vacuum. It is unfolding towards an end. There is a plan. God's will shall prevail on earth. The prayers of the saints will not remain unanswered! There will be a universal judgment by the Lord of love. At that last hour everything will have lost its importance and value, except for selfless love. The last word belongs to Christ; the mystery of God's will reaches its culmination in the recapitulation of all things in Him. We continue to struggle with fortitude. We celebrate the event that is coming. We enjoy a foretaste of that hour of the last things. Rejoicing in worship —with this vision—with this hope.

Lord, free us from our own will and incorporate us in your own. "Thy will be done."

(103) A Dynamic Understanding of Tradition and Mission and the Need for Contextualization

Petros Vassiliadis

Tradition (in Greek παράδοσις=paradosis) is the entire set of historical facts, beliefs, experiences, social and religious practices, and even philosophical doctrines or aesthetic conceptions, which form an entity transmitted from one generation to another either orally or in a written and even in artistic form. Thus, tradition - we may safely say - constitutes a fundamental element for the existence, coherence and advancement of human culture in any given context.

In the wider religious sphere – taking into consideration that *culture* is in some way connected with *cult* – tradition has to do more or less with the religious practices, i.e. with the *liturgy* of a given religious system, rather than with the religious *beliefs* that theoretically express or presuppose these practices, without of course excluding them.

In Christianity, paradoxically, tradition was for quite an extensive period of time confined only to the oral form of Christian faith, or more precisely the non-biblical part of it, both written in later Christian literature or transmitted in various ways from one generation to another. Thus, tradition has come to be determined by the post-reformation and post-Trentine dialectic opposition to the Bible, which has taken the oversimplified form: Bible and/or (even *versus*) Tradition. Only recently, from the beginning of the ecumenical era, has tradition acquired a new wider sense and understanding, which nevertheless has always been the authentic understanding in the ancient Church. Tradition no longer has a fragmented meaning connected to one only segment of Christian faith; it refers to the whole of Christian faith: not only the Christian doctrine but also to worship.

It is not a coincidence that the two main references in the Bible of the term in the sense of "receiving" (in Greek: παραλαμβάνειν) and "transmitting" (in Greek: παραδιδόναι) as recorded by St. Paul in his 1st epistle to Corinthians (ch.11 and 15) cover both the *kerygma* (doctrine in the wider sense) and the *Eucharist* (the heart of Christian worship).

Thus the importance of tradition in Christianity underlines a sense of a living continuity with the Church of the ancient times, of the apostolic period. Tradition in this sense is not viewed as something in addition to, or over against, the Bible. Scripture and Tradition are not treated as two different things, two distinct sources of the Christian faith. Scripture exists within Tradition, which although it gives a unique pre-eminence to the Bible, it also includes further developments - of course in the form of clarification and explication, not of addition - of the apostolic faith.

We exist as Christians by the *Tradition* (paradosis) of the *Gospel (evangellion, kerygma)*, testified in Scripture, and transmitted in and by the Church, through the power of the Holy Spirit. Tradition (with capital T) is distinguished from the various local or regional or even temporal traditions (with small t), which obviously cannot claim a universal authority in the life of the Church. Yet, there is a close connection between the two. "The traditions in Christian history are distinct from, yet connected with, the Tradition. They are expressions and manifestations in diverse historical terms of the one truth and reality which is in Christ" (IV World Conference on Faith and Order of WCC, Montreal, 1963).

At first glance the very concept of tradition, if it is connected only to the past, seems to be a contradiction, since the Holy Spirit who guides the Church to all truth (Jn. 16:13), cannot be limited by traditional past values only, for the "*pneuma* blows wherever he (or she) wishes" (Jn 3:8). If we take the Trinitarian and eschatological principles of Christian faith seriously into account, the Church as a koinonia proleptically manifesting the glory of the coming Kingdom of God, i.e. as a movement forward, toward the eschata, a movement of continuous renewal, can hardly be conditioned by what has been set in the past, with the exception of course of the living continuity and of the communion with all humanity - in fact with all the created world - both in space and in time.

Thus, tradition is not a static entity; it is rather a dynamic reality. It is not a dead acceptance of the past, but a living experience of the Holy Spirit in the present. In G. Florovsky's words, "Tradition is the witness of the Spirit; the Spirit's unceasing revelation and preaching of the Good news... It is not only a protective, conservative principle, but primarily the principle of growth and renewal."

Therefore, from an Orthodox perspective of mission, an authentic witness to the Gospel in any given context needs to be somehow differently connected to the "traditional" understanding of Tradition. The obvious variety of human experiences, formed in differing social, cultural, economic, political etc. contexts eliminates the very possibility of a single universal application of Christian mission. In a given situation, therefore, a true and effective mission has very little to do with any "local," "temporal" etc. tradition. Hence the importance of a theology of struggle (for liberation, for hope, for the integrity of creation etc.), or of a theology of spirituality and ascetic life, of liturgical theology, and so on and so forth. Tradition, as well as the theology of mission, become "contextual."

The question posed by contextual theology, in contrast to classical theology, is not so much whether and to what extent the theological positions are in agreement with any *local tradition*, but if these positions have any dynamic reference and relation at all to the given conditions of today's world. Consequently, therefore, the Churches that in the past were interested in *charitable diakonia*, with concrete expressions that were directed toward the *results* of social and environmental indifference and injustice, nowadays are more and more interested in *social diakonia*, beginning to shift toward the causes of social indifference and injustice.

The same holds true on a purely theological level: nothing can serve as an authoritative basis, at least in dialogue, or in mission, even if attested by "tradition" (Holy Scripture or Church tradition in general), since every past experience in the Church is conditioned by a certain (and therefore relative?) context. Some argue that the argument "from tradition" no longer constitutes an unshakable and unchangeable point of reference for any contested issue relevant to Christian witness (e.g. the question of the ordination of women, or of the inclusive language, or even the Trinitarian basis of Christian faith etc.). This also applies to the dialogue to achieve the visible unity, the minimum required for an effective and faithful to the divine call common Christian witness.

Contextual theology, taking as its point of departure the certainty that the Church is a "sign" of the Kingdom of God and of the "given by the triune God unity," calls into question the ability of the established institutions to advance on the road toward an egalitarian community of men and women, both within the Church and in the society at large. Similar questions might be raised both about the relationship between the eternal and inviolable "Gospel" and all finite "culture(s)," and even more pointedly about the dialogue of Christianity with other living religions, taking especially for granted that Christian mission is evolving in contexts that are heavily influenced by the presence of people of other faiths.

It is natural, then, that the understanding, and to some extent also the application, of mission can be better achieved as the natural consequence of the inner dynamics of the Triune God, i.e. of the communion and love that exists within the Holy Trinity. This Trinitarian basis cannot only have tremendous effect in helping the Church to overcome all kinds of imperialistic or confessionalistic attitudes, we experienced in the past; it also gives a new and liberating meaning to tradition. In Ion Bria's words,

> "the Trinitarian theology points to the fact that God's involvement in history aims at drawing humanity and creation in general into this communion with God's very life. The implications of this assertion for understanding mission are very important: mission does not aim primarily at the propagation or transmission of intellectual convictions, doctrines, moral commands etc. (i.e. does not depend on a static understanding of tradition), but at the transmission of the life of communion that exists in God."

This dynamic understanding of tradition has immensely helped contemporary world mission to move away from the old "universal proselytizing mission" concept. It was rather the natural consequence of the authentic identity of the Church and the rediscovery of the forgotten Trinity. More particularly it was the result of the reinforcement of Pneumatology into the missiological reflections.

Bibliography

D. J. Bosch, *Transforming Mission. Paradigm Schifts in Theology of Mission,* (New York 1991)

I.Bria, *The Sense of Ecumenical Tradition: The Ecumenical Witness and Vision of the Orthodox,* (Geneva 1991)

- (ed.), *Go forth in Peace. Orthodox Perspectives on Mission,* (Geneva: WCC Mission Series, 1986)

E.Clapsis, "Tradition: An Orthodox-Ecumenical View," *Orthodoxy in Conversation. Orthodox Ecumenical Engagements,* (Geneva: WCC Publications/HCO Press, 2000), 11-39.

Y.Congar, "Christianisme comme Foi et comme Culture," *Evangelizzatione e Culture. Atti del Congresso Internationale scientifico di Missiologica, Rome 1975,* vol. I, (1976), 83-103

G.Florovsky, "The Function of Tradition in the Ancient Church," *Greek Orthodox Theological Review* 9 (1963): 181-200;

K. Ware, "Tradition and Traditions," in N. Lossky and others (eds.), *Dictionary of the Ecumenical Movement,* 2nd Edition, (Geneva: WCC Publications, 2002), 1143-1148.

(104) COMMON MISSION AS A TASK FOR ORTHODOX INVOLVEMENT IN ECUMENISM[1]

Fr. John Njoroge

Introduction

Following the participation of the Orthodox Church in the ecumenical movement and especially in the World Council of Churches (WCC), it can be said that the Orthodox churches have had a profound impact on the life and work of the WCC. Orthodox participation has promoted Trinitarian theology, the unity of doctrine, ecclesiology of the local church, spirituality and sacramental life as well as the place of the liturgy in seeking visible unity.[2] This has been done in different forums in the life of the WCC, for example in the context of Faith and Order, and the Conference on World Mission and Evangelism. This article, will, therefore, focus on the participation of the Orthodox Church in the ecumenical movement and especially in the WCC and the Commission on World Mission and Evangelism (CWME). This is not only because the Orthodox churches have contributed soundly on this area, but because they have also learnt from the others. In doing that, this text will focus on the Pneumatological approach to mission. The article will conclude by highlighting the importance of mission in the life of the Church which, therefore, should be taught in the Orthodox theological institutions.

The participation of the Orthodox Churches in the WCC has greatly contributed to the enhancement of the Pneumatological mission paradigm in the ecumenical movement. It is observed that the coming of Trinitarian theology in ecumenism started appearing in articles following the WCC Third General Assembly in 1961 in New Delhi. This is when Orthodox churches started joining the WCC. Concerning the theology of mission, Prof. Petros Vassiliadis asserts that the decisive turning point was the 1963 World Mission Conference in Mexico, after which the mission agenda was enriched by a new understanding of mission, mostly represented by a variety of terms like *witness (martyria), dialogue* and *liberation.*[3] In addition, the Seventh WCC Assembly in Canberra, Australia with the theme "Come Holy Spirit-Renew the Whole Creation" was the first assembly to focus on the Holy Spirit. This was hailed not only by the Orthodox participants but also by others who acknowledged the importance of addressing world problems from a Pneumatological perspective. For the Orthodox, this was important because the theology of the Holy Spirit is addressed within the context of the Holy Trinity. This was a fundamental breakthrough in bringing into light the patristic thought that was essential to the ecumenical movement that, in all God's actions in regard to His creation and redemption of humanity are within the Trinity. Although each person in the Trinity got a definite role, they operate in unity.[4]As far as contemporary mission is concerned, the Pneumatological dimension of mission was fully articulated during the CWME conference in Athens in 2005 with the theme: "Come Holy Spirit, Heal and Reconcile."[5]

[1] The first following article on this subject is from Fr. John Njoroge while the second one from Valentin Kozhuharov.
[2] Michael Kinnamon & Brian E. Cope, *The Ecumenical Movement: An Anthology of Key Texts and Voices*, (Geneva: WCC Publications, 1997), 484.
[3] Petros Vassiliadis, "Reconciliation as a Pneumatological Mission Paradigm: Some Preliminary Reflections by an Orthodox" *International Review of Mission* 94.372 (January 2005): 30-42.
[4] Gennadios Limouris, *Orthodox Visions of Ecumenism: Statements, Messages and Reports* (Geneva: WCC Publications, 1994), 160.
[5] "Come Holy Spirit, Heal and Reconcile" Conference on World Mission and Evangelism of the (WCC, Athens 2005) Mission as Ministry of Reconciliation. Last accessed 17th June 2010. Available at: http://www.oikoumene.org/resources/documents/other-meetings/mission-and-evangelism/athens-2005-documents/preparatory-paper-n-1-mission-and-evangelism-in-unity-today.html (last accessed, September 2013).

Pneumatology and Mission of the Church

The Pneumatological approach to mission brings a new understanding of mission as the very nature of the Church based on sharing and witnessing God's love to His creation. *God so loved the world and gave his only begotten son so that he who believes in him may not perish but have eternal life* (John 3:16). God's love aims to restore the human being into the original state before the fall i.e. restoration of God's image in the human beings.[6] The process here is that of transforming the old person into a new person in Christ through the power of the Holy Spirit. Understanding mission from the Pneumatological dimension means the recovery of the theology of the Holy Spirit in mission. Theology of the Holy Spirit profoundly suggests the unity, inclusiveness and the reconciliatory nature of the Trinity.

According to the Orthodox theology, the doctrine of the Holy Spirit is inseparable from Christology and Ecclesiology. Therefore, the whole school of Orthodox Pneumatology is understood and practiced within the church doctrines and liturgical rites. Therefore, the Holy Spirit is in operation in the entire life of the Church. It is the Holy Spirit who operates all the church mysteries. It is through participation in the mysteries of the Church that the faithful become spiritual through the process of sanctification, *climbing from one degree of glory to another* (2 Cor 3:18) aiming for union with God (*Theosis*).

This is a daily experience of the Church and it is lived and witnessed by a worshiping community which is then called to witness to the world through the power of the Holy Spirit (Acts 1:8). This form of witnessing is an ideal missiological function of the Church and takes place through grace; hence the faith and the good works of Christians become visible '*with a demonstration of the spirit and the power*' (1 Cor. 2:4).[7] This asserts that mission brings what is experienced eschatologically into the visible and practical for the world to believe. This makes Metropolitan John Zizioulas' articulation of Pneumatology from an eschatological perspective profoundly ideal for mission today, because he understands the Church more as *coming together* as a community of worshippers.[8] The coming together as community reflects the Trinitarian communion of God the Father, the Son and the Holy Spirit. This approach has greatly enlightened the understanding of mission even in the ecumenical movement, making the former WCC General Secretary to suggest a radical shift to a "new paradigm," away from the "Christocentric universalism" and towards a "Trinitarian" understanding of the divine reality for the future of ecumenism and Christian mission.[9] This is because love, communion, unity and interdependence of the Trinity should also be lived by the whole humanity created in the image and likeness of the Triune God. This '*Trinitarianism*' is reflected or else manifested by the coming together of a worshiping community. A gathered community of believers through the sacrament of Eucharist becomes more self-conscious to witness the kingdom of God here in the world. This is why in the Orthodox Church the Eucharistic worship becomes the source of what Fr. Ion Bria calls 'Meta-*liturgy*' i.e. Mission as the Liturgy *after* the Liturgy.[10]

---

[6] Njoroge J. Ngige, *Orthodox Christian Witness in Africa: The Dynamics of the Orthodox Pneumatology as a Mission Paradigm Today*, (Unpublished Ph.D: Thessaloniki, 2011) (in Greek).

[7] Vassiliadis Petros, *Unity and Witness Orthodox Christian Witness and Interfaith Dialogue-Handbook on Missiology* (Athens: Epikentro, 2007), 325 (in Greek).

[8] Zizioulas John D., *Being As Communion; Studies in Personhood and the Church* (Crestwood, New York: St. Vladimir's Seminary Press, 2002) 130-31, 182.

[9] Konrad Raiser, *Ecumenism in Transition. A Paradigm Shift in the Ecumenical Movement,* (Geneva: WCC Publications, 1991) (translated with modifications from the German original *ÖkumeneimÜbergang,* C.Kaiser Verlag/München 1989), 79ff.

[10] Ion Bria, *The Liturgy after the Liturgy: Mission and Witness from an Orthodox Perspective*, (Geneva: WCC Publications, 1996), 19-35.

Part VII: Particular Themes and Issues for Orthodox Involvement in Ecumenism

The liturgy and Mission of the church

One of the greatest contributions of the Orthodox Church to the theology of mission is the Liturgy *after* the Liturgy by Fr.Ion Bria.[11] The Orthodox liturgy has a well-connected missionary structure and purpose.[12] The Divine Liturgy is basically celebrated as an event aiming to send the participants to a mission, to witness and share with the others what they have experienced in the liturgy of the Word and the liturgy of the faithful. The Orthodox understanding of worship is not only an expression representing Christ's saving ministry, death, resurrection and ascension but also it is a place where the members of the Church participate in the living anticipation of the kingdom of God. As a community they are entitled to fully participate in God's work (*Missio Dei*) of salvation of the world. This is why the celebrant at the end of the Divine Liturgy proclaims; *lets us go forth in peace.*[13] Fr. Ion Bria interprets this dismissal as a:

> Sending off [of] every believer to mission in the world where he or she lives and works, and whole community into the world, to witness by what they are that the kingdom is coming. Christians who have heard the word and received the bread of life should henceforth be living prophetic signs of the kingdom.[14]

This sending proclamation of the liturgy signals that liturgy is a basic spiritual preparatory form for mission for its participants. This comes along after following the ethos of the entire Orthodox theology surrounding the gathering of a worshiping community on the day of the Lord (*Κυριακή*). The act of gathering and the idea of the Eucharist are set within the framework of a communion, not only the communion between the living and the dead but also with the saints and the heavenly bodiless powers. This communion per *excellence* reflects the Trinitarian communion making the Eucharistic liturgy be the springboard for mission where everyone and everything is called into being.

Within the Eucharistic worship two major events take place that prepare participants to go forth in peace and witness. First, if we are convinced that liturgy is a missionary event where a true divine revelation becomes a reality, then the participants do par excellence witness a living anticipation of the kingdom.[15] Secondly, as we participate and become perfected as individuals through the Holy Communion, the whole community of believers is transformed into an authentic image of the kingdom of God. Through this transformation, however, the whole creation through the Church is also transformed. Here the Church becomes the "uncreated" light placed on a lamp stand to shine before the others (Mat 5:16). Therefore, it is this light Christians are sent to witness to all people for Christ who is the head of the Church said "*I am the light of the world. Whoever follows me will never walk in darkness but will have the light of life*" (John 8:12). The light here has to be interpreted as a continuous transfiguration of human lives into Christ Jesus with the power of the Holy Spirit. What is very important and connects this light to the liturgy is that this light is kept shining even brighter in our lives because of our continuous participation in the mysteries of the Church. Just as the light drives away the darkness and enlightens a darkened place, so does the light of Christ enlighten our spiritual consciousness making us more aware of the worthiness of life in the world and giving us hope for the eschaton. Spiritual consciousness makes individual members of the Church continue discovering various charismatic gifts received from the sacrament of Chrismation and are empowered to utilize these gifts in the diaconal life in the mission of the Church.

In every liturgical gathering we do not simply hear the words of 'anamnesis' but we participate in the very action of forgiveness of sins, sanctification and transformation of our very being (souls & bodies) into

---

[11] *International Review of Mission* 100.2 (Nov 2011): 190-192.

[12] Stamoolis J. James, *Eastern Orthodox Mission Theology Today* (Minneapolis: Light And Life Publishing Company, 1986), 86-102.

[13] Nicholas Cabasilas *A Commentary on the Divine Liturgy,* (London: S.P.C.K, 1960), 61.

[14] Bria Ion, Go Forth in Peace; *Orthodox Perspectives in Mission* (Geneva: WCC Mission Series, 1986), 38.

[15] Emmanuel Clapsis, *The Orthodox Churches in the pluralistic World; An Ecumenical Conversation* (Geneva: WCC Publications, 2004), 193.

the 'body of Christ' through the invocation of the Holy Spirit "epiclesis".[16] Archbishop Anastasios of Albania observes that, during the epiclesis the whole world is transformed into a Church, a Church which is in communion with the Triune God.[17] The communion takes place in the "Movement of Ascension" where the creation is called into the throne of God, into the kingdom. However, the movement does not end there; it takes a turn to descend into the world to put in place the *"liturgy after the* liturgy," i.e. to witness into the world the love of God. Within this movement of 'Ascending' and 'Descending' the Eucharist brings forth the relationship between the Church as a whole and the Church in mission.[18] Here mission is not just a mere proclamation of Christ's salvation for the world but a true revelation and calling into full participation in Christ's salvation through the Holy Spirit.

This means, although the Church is by nature a 'message of salvation' it has its apostolicity, to proclaim the kingdom of God, both by words of the gospel and the good works (James 2:14-20). The Church has just one 'apostolicity', because the Kingdom of God is one and this is why the Holy Apostles were not commissioned to proclaim a set of given religious beliefs and customs, doctrines and moral orders, but to proclaim the good news (ευαγγέλιον) which is the coming of the kingdom of God. So the Church has a great commission to proclaim by witnessing this eschatological reality to the world. Archbishop Anastasios affirms that, this creates a sense of mission responsibility to all who confess the apostolicity of the Church. When the faithful confesses that the Church is apostolic they simultaneously declare to share in her apostolic mission.[19]

Authentically, the Church gets into this eschatological reality during the celebration of the Eucharist where the Church becomes *par excellence* the icon of Kingdom. It is worthy to note that this reality of the Church is not intended only for a particular people, place or time but for everyone and everything and everywhere (John 4:21). Therefore, the apostolicity of the Church here becomes her mission to witness this reality to all people (πάντα τα έθνη) (Mt 28:19). This applies to all aspects of the human being which include social, economic, political and human relations and dependence to the environment. This unique understanding of the eschatological reality in the Eucharistic celebration has been well-developed by Maximus the Confessor who characterizes the events of the Old Testament as the 'shadow' of the future and that the present reality of the Church is only an 'image' of truth.[20]

Basically, if the reality of the Church is fully manifested within Eucharistic worship so is the mission of the Church. This is why the church Fathers in the Nicene Creed characterize the Church as "Apostolic."[21] Metropolitan Zizioulas argues that the apostolicity of the Church does not mean only the historical continuity and unbroken lineage of bishops to the apostles and the apostles to Christ, thus forming the Apostolic Succession; it also means and emphasizes a collegiality of persons with an eschatological function.[22] This eschatological function denotes the original apostolate of Christ's teachings and His 'calling and sending' of the twelve to proclaim the good news. The twelve form the inward layers of the *didascalias* of the Church and they even today remain in the Church as the pillars for *the wall of the city had twelve foundations, and on them were the twelve names of the twelve apostles of the Lamb* (Rev. 21:14). Further, Archbishop Anastasios of Albania enlightens: apostolicity of the Church implies having an "apostolic fire and zeal to preach the gospel 'to every creature' (Mk 16:15), because it nurtures its members so that they may become 'witnesses in Jerusalem and

---

[16] The liturgy of St. John Chrysostom, where the priest prays: once again we offer to you this spiritual worship without shedding of blood, and we ask you, pray and entreat you: send down your Holy Spirit upon us and upon these gifts here present.

[17] Yannoulatos Anastasios *Mission in the Steps of Christ, Theological Essays and Homilies*, (Athens: Apostoliki Diakonia of the Church of Greece, 2007) 167-68 (in Greek).

[18] Bassioudis George, *The power of Divine Liturgy The contribution of A. Schmemann to Liturgical theology* (Athens: Enplo Editions, 2008), 139 (in Greek).

[19] George Lemopoulos, *Your Will be Done; Orthodoxy in Mission*, (Katerini: Tertios, Geneva: WCC Publications 1989), 82.

[20] Μάξιμος Ομολογητής, *Περί διαφόρων αποριών*, PG 91 1084C-D.

[21] See the Nicene Creed where the church is characterized as One, Holy, Catholic and Apostolic.

[22] Zizioulas, *Being as communion*, 173.

in Judea and Samaria, and to the end of the earth' (Acts 1:8)."[23] This approach reminds all Christians that they are called to participate fully in witnessing the gospel because the gospel is for all peoples and therefore, never will the mission of the Church end unless all peoples (sheep) are brought into the fold (Church) of the good shepherd (Christ) (John 10:1-17).

Conclusion

Pneumatology is an important paradigm of mission in the ecumenical movement today. This is because it reminds churches and mission organizations that mission is rooted in the Triune God.[24] The Pneumatological approach to mission is based on the love, communion and conciliatory nature of the three persons of the Trinity. Because humanity has failed to actualize the love, communion and conciliatory nature of Trinity in the contemporary society, the notion of healing and reconciliation has become a paramount aspect of Christian mission. Christ has called His Church to be an icon of reconciliation. Christ did set the best example during His earthly ministry. St. Luke has perfectly cupped the whole notion of salvation in the miraculous healing of Christ. St. Paul in his letters is deeply concerned that those whom Christ has reconciled in His own body should always be united. Unity here expresses God's first plan to reconcile all things in Himself through Christ (2 Cor. 5:17-18). Unity for St. Paul is not only for the Jews and Gentiles expressed by Luke in the book of Acts, but also for the slave and free, male and female in Christ (Gal. 3:28).[25] John's gospel understands reconciliation from the point of view of truth and peace, which crowns Christ as a wonderful counselor and prince of peace (Isaiah 9:6).

The contemporary society is yearning for peace, justice and truth calling the churches to go back to the theology of the Holy Spirit as the source of forgiveness and reconciliation. In today's world, people are experiencing economic injustice, sexual exploitation, racism, political conflicts, religious proselytism and abuse of human rights. Those who are experiencing or have experienced in history any sort of injustice or exploitation may it be economic, political or religious are locked in a cycle of victimhood and aggression. Inability to break this cycle makes our societies to remain locked within the cycles of anger and revenge. It is the mission of the Church to make individuals and communities learn how to forgive and acceptance others. Forgiving and accepting one's self or even the other is the starting point of what Stanley Harakas characterizes as "the making of what one has into something other" or else, finding one's self to be a new person by virtue of the exchange of another.[26] For this to happen, the Church must advocate for justice and truth. Justice and truth makes the persons' involved to want to change their hearts i.e. forgiveness, making it possible to replace bad thoughts with good, anger with affection and bitterness with compassion.

Another important aspect of the Pneumatological approach to mission is that it reminds the faithful that the Church is not static but dynamic in nature. This is because the apostolicity of the Church is based on the kenotic energy of the Holy Spirit who always goes where it wills (John 3:8). The kenotic dynamic of the Holy Spirit guides the Church as it expands unlimitedly, culturally and geographically to all people. Within her expansion, the Church will not avoid meeting the cultural, social, economic and political challenges of today's world. Pneumatologically, the Church has to immerse into the depths of these realities and give hope to those who daily experience and are affected by these changes. For example focusing on Africa today, this approach and its dynamic nature will give answers to many pastoral needs of the local communities. It will

[23] See Anastasios Yannoulatos (Archbishop of Albania), Article; The missionary Activity of the Orthodox Church Church. Available at: http://jean.square7.ch/wolfcms/public/SyndesmosTexts/Text_95%20The%20missionary%20activity%20of%20the%20Orthodox%20Church,%20A%20Yannoulatos,%201964.pdf. Accessed on 10 July 2013.
[24] See the concept of Missio Dei well-articulated by D. J. Bosch, in his famous book, *Transforming Mission. Paradigm Shifts in Theology of Mission*, (New York: Orbis Books, 1991).
[25] Vasiliadis, *Unity and Witness*, 373-375.
[26] Stanley S. Harakas, "*Forgiveness and Reconciliation. An Orthodox Perspective*" in the *Orthodox Church in a Pluralistic World, an Ecumenical Conversation*, (Geneva/Brookline: WCC pub., Holy Cross Press, 2004), 114.

help the restoration of the once disregarded and disrespected elements of African culture(s). Christ through His incarnation embraced all cultures so that the message of salvation can reach every culture. Therefore, incarnation as a cosmic event will continue to humanity and its surroundings. St. Maximus the Confessor (7th c.) affirms that " God's Word, being God Himself i.e. the Son of God desires the mystery of His incarnation to be activated continuously and everywhere."[27] It is through the process of incarnation that man as the master of the cosmos is called by the creator to draw all creation to God.[28] Through the transformative energies of the Holy Spirit, the incarnation process brings meaning to the message of the gospel uniquely to every local context. These energies give balance between the universal meaning of the message and the contextualized interpretation and understanding of the gospel.

Bibliography

Bassioudis, George. *The Power of Divine Liturgy. The Contribution of A. Schmemann to Liturgical theology* (Athens: Enplo editions, 2008).

Bria, Ion. *Go Forth in Peace; Orthodox Perspectives in Mission*, (Geneva: WCC Mission Series, 1986).

Bria, Ion. *The Liturgy after the Liturgy: Mission and Witness from an Orthodox Perspective*, (Geneva: WCC Publications, 1996).

Cabasilas, Nicholas. *ACommentary on the Divine Liturgy*, (London: S.P.C.K, 1960).

Clapsis, Emmanuel. *The Orthodox Churches in the pluralistic World; An Ecuenical Conversation*, (Geneva: WCC Publications, 2004).

Harakas, Stanley. S., *Forgiveness and Reconciliation. An Orthodox Perspective in the Orthodox Church in a Pluralistic World, an Ecumenical Conversation*, (Geneva/Brookline: WCC pub., Holy Cross Press, 2004).

Kinnamon, Michael. & Brian E. Cope, *The Ecumenical Movement: An Anthology of Key Texts and Voices*, (Geneva: WCC Publications, 1997).

Lemopoulos, George. *Your Will be Done; Orthodoxy in Mission*, (Katerini: Tertios, Geneva: WCC Publications 1989).

Limouris, Gennadios. *Orthodox Visions of Ecumenism: Statements, Messages and Reports*, (Geneva: WCC Publications, 1994).

Meyendorff, John. *Byzantine Theology; Historical Trends and Doctrinal Themes*, (Fordham University Press: New York, 1974).

Raiser, Konrad. *Ecumenism in Transition. A Paradigm Shift in the Ecumenical Movement*, WCC Publications Geneva 1991 (translated with modifications from the German original *ÖkumeneimÜbergang*, (C.KaiserVerlagMünchen, 1989).

Stamoolis J. James. *Eastern Orthodox Mission Theology Today*, (Minneapolis: Light and Life Publishing Company, 1986).

Vassiliadis, Petros. *Unity and Witness: Orthodox Christian Witness and Interfaith Dialogue-Handbook on Missiology* (Athens: Epikentro, 2007) (in Greek).

Yannoulatos, Anastasios. *Mission in the steps of Christ, Theological essays and Homilies*, (Apostoliki Diakonia of the Church of Greece: Athens, 2007).

Zizioulas, John D., (Metropolitan). *Being As Communion; Studies in Personhood and the Church*, (Crestwood, New York: St. Vladimir's Seminary Press, 2002).

---

[27] Maximos the Confessor, *Περί διαφόρων αποριών*, PG 91 1084C-D.

[28] John Meyendorff, *Byzantine Theology*; Historical Trends and Doctrinal Themes (New York: Fordham University Press, 1974), 151.

Valentin Kozhuharov

Exploring contemporary mission issues as found in Orthodox theology and the practical life of the believers in the churches, and relating them to contemporary ecumenism, needs an extensive survey and reflection. In a brief account, as this essay is, only some main characteristics of the understanding of mission, theology and ecumenism from an Orthodox point of view can be pointed out. Let us consider the three – mission, theology, ecumenics – as they are understood and applied in contemporary Orthodoxy, most of all in (but not exclusively) the churches and the theological schools of Eastern Europe.

1. Mission and missiology in contemporary Orthodoxy

Most Orthodox churches experienced persecutions and destruction in the past, either by foreign oppressors (for example, the Ottoman rule in the Balkan region), or by home forces (i.e., the Communist regimes or other type of political oppression). This is one of the reasons that theology as an academic discipline was not well-developed in the past. Only in the 18th and 19th centuries did more systematic theological writings appear, and most of them were in some correspondence with the Western Christian theological thought. Surely, Orthodox theology widely used the Church Fathers' legacy, but this alone was not enough for the Orthodox churches and their schools to efficiently develop theology as an academic and scholarly discipline, hence the interactions with Western Christian theology.

Even today we can notice that in its structure and academic shape, theology in Orthodoxy is not much different from the theological reflections as found in any other main Christian church and their theological schools. It is well-known (though not always well-recognised) that in the last couple of centuries Orthodox theology has been in constant relations with the Roman Catholic and the Protestant theological thought,[29] where all Christian theology has been in constant dialogue with one another. This fact found its confirmation in almost the same structural function of theology in most of the theological schools in the Christian world where one could observe the teaching of several dozens of theological disciplines under the domain of Biblical, Historical, Systematic and Pastoral/Applied Theology. Today we can see that in the traditional Orthodox seminaries, spiritual academies and theological faculties within universities, most theological academic subjects fall into these four main theological domains.

In a similar way, mission has not been well-developed in Eastern Orthodoxy, at least not in the forms and methods of mission which have been employed by the western Christian non-Orthodox churches. Generally speaking, it was only the Greek and the Russian Orthodox churches which undertook missionary activities in the past; certainly, there have been exceptions, and the 9th century missions of the brothers St Cyril and St Methodius is only one example. In the period of forming of most Eastern European nations (mostly during the 19th and the beginning of the 20th century), we can hardly observe any missionary activity within Orthodoxy. Then the First World War and the Balkan wars put again the churches to the limits of mere existence, and this was followed by a series of coup d'état in some countries and the forceful establishment of Communist governments in most of the countries where Orthodoxy was in majority. These unfortunate circumstances pre-

---

[29] The Greek and the Russian Orthodox theology greatly influenced the theological developments in the rest of the Orthodox world in 18th century through the 20th century. Bearing in mind that these, on the other hand, have been influenced by the Roman Catholic and the Protestant theological reflections since the 17th century, we can assume that almost all Orthodox theology experienced a level of influence on the part of its Western counterpart. For the Greek theological development, there is a brief mention in Stamoolis, 12 (see bibliography), and in more detail in Christos Yannaras, "Theology in Present Day Greece," *St Vladimir's Theological Quarterly* 16.4 (1972): 195-214; for the Russian theology, see A. Schmemann and his "Russian Theology: An Introductory Survey." *St. Vladimir's Theological Quarterly* 16.4 (1972): 173-174.

vented the Orthodox churches in Eastern Europe from undertaking any missionary activity, with the exception of the Greek Church.[30]

The fact that Orthodox theology was slowly shaped in the 19th and 20th centuries, and the lack of missionary initiatives during this period, was the reason that Missiology as an academic theological discipline did not develop either. In many Orthodox theological schools there was a discipline called Mission, or Mission Studies, or Missiology, but its content was not much different from the content of a study of Christian sects where all the wrongs of Roman Catholicism, Protestantism and the other Christian communities were discussed on the pages of missiology textbooks. Time proved this approach inadequate and in many schools the teaching staff felt that Sectology was not the main content of Missiology. However, it was not until recently that Orthodox theologians started reflecting on truly missiological issues and have been trying to formulate the contents of a renewed Missiology, which was supposed to theoretically summarise the missionary practice of the Orthodox Church as found in the last two thousand years of existence of Christianity.

After the changes in Eastern Europe in 1989, new opportunities have arisen for the Orthodox churches and their theological schools. The theological disciplines taught obtained new content and new shape which aimed at providing theologically informed answers to the challenges that the contemporary societies have been experiencing. One would expect that Missiology would also obtain its proper theological content. Reshaping the subject, however, became a stumbling block for many theological schools, and this fact led to the situation that Missiology was either abandoned as a theological discipline and was withdrawn from the curricula of the schools, or it was left in its old-fashioned "clothing." With a few exceptions, today Missiology is taught in the traditional Orthodox theological schools as a type of Orthodox apologetics where the teachings of the other non-Orthodox churches and communities are discussed and widely criticised.

When looking at the curricula of the Orthodox theological schools, we can observe the following picture.

Missiology as a teaching discipline at the Orthodox theological schools of Eastern Europe (seminaries, academies and faculties within universities) is currently taught in five countries. In Russia it is taught in almost all schools; in Belarus it is present in 3 out of 4 theological schools; in Ukraine Missiology is taught in 8 out of 11 Orthodox theological schools under the Moscow Patriarchate, and within the Kiev Patriarchate it is taught in 2 schools out of 6; in Greece it is taught in 2 out of 6 schools, and in Romania Missiology is taught in all Orthodox theological schools.[31] There is no Missiology in the schools of Serbia, Bulgaria, Former Yugoslavic Republic of Macedonia and Moldova.[32] Even within the Finnish Orthodox Church and the Orthodox Church in America (which are churches that do mission), the discipline is not taught; it can be only found at St. Herman theological seminary at the third year of study, under the name "Missions and Evangelism."[33]

In seven out of 40 Orthodox theological schools, whose Missiology textbooks were briefly viewed, this academic discipline has recently embraced a more theologically grounded content, and the subject has been supported also by missiological research. These are the Moscow and St. Petersburg Orthodox theological seminaries and academies, the Belgorod missionary seminary, three of the Romanian Orthodox schools

---

[30] A brief but comprehensive exposition of the Greek missionary endeavours up to present day can be found in Athanasios N. Papathanasiou, "Missionary Experience and Academic Quest. The Research Situation in Greece." In: Frieder Ludvig & Afe Adogame (eds.). *European Traditions in the Study of Religion in Africa.* (Wiesbaden, Harrassowitz Verlag, 2004), 301-311.

[31] For references see the curricula of the respective Orthodox theological schools at the websites of the schools which are given below under point 2, where "Theology in Contemporary Orthodoxy" is discussed. (Providing websites as references seems more reliable than citing curricula books, most of which were published at least ten years ago, while the websites, on the other hand, reflect the dynamics of curricula changes which are quite often nowadays. Unfortunately, not all references are in English. All website links were last visited on 12 May 2013).

[32] In Bulgaria, an attempt was made in 2011, when for the first time since the changes of 1989, the author of this essay started teaching Missiology at the Orthodox theological department of Plovdiv university; then in the spring semester of 2013 the subject became elective and it is now taught by a theologian whose main subject is Apologetics; in the other 3 Orthodox theological schools there is no Missiology and the teaching staff are not willing, and feeling unprepared, to teach the subject.

[33] http://sthermanseminary.org/files/admissions/SHS-catalog--2012--updated.pdf, 22, 28 (last accessed June 2012).

Part VII: Particular Themes and Issues for Orthodox Involvement in Ecumenism

and the Theological Faculty of Athens. In all other schools Missiology is not supported by missiological research and is taught in the old-fashioned apologetic way. This can be evidenced even by the mission research done by Orthodox theologians and the books and articles on Orthodox mission recently published by authors from Russia, Greece, Romania, Albania and the Orthodox Church in America (there are some exceptions to this, too); it is not common to find missiological research published by the rest of Orthodox churches and their schools.

In some of the Orthodox churches there are mission departments within the Synods (for example, in the Russian, Greek, Romanian, Albanian, and Ukrainian Orthodox churches), the Finnish Orthodox Church has its Mission Agency, and the Orthodox Church in America has its Orthodox Christian Mission Centre (the last two missionary agencies closely cooperate with each other in the field of mission, especially in Africa). These departments and agencies appeared because the missionary activities and the missionaries themselves in the churches need guidance and advice, and furthermore, the mission of these churches is theologically reflected upon in the context of the subject of Missiology. The lack of missionary departments in the Orthodox churches in Bulgaria, Serbia, Former Yugoslavic Republic of Macedonia,[34] Moldova, Belarus and the other Orthodox churches indicates a lack of substantial missionary activity, and consequently – a lack of solid mission research and missiological reflection.

It is not strange that Missiology is poorly developed within Orthodoxy: it is a postulate that mission research reflects certain mission practice. Such mission practice has been observed in Greece, Russia, Albania/Africa, Romania and Finland, and these are the countries which also produce missiological research. In the cases where there are no research efforts concerning mission within an Orthodox church and her schools, this most probably indicates that there is no substantial mission practice to be reflected upon. Social and educational activities of the Church in schools, prisons, orphanages, etc. still does not constitute mission practice which needs reflection: something more is needed for a church to accumulate substantial missionary experience which at some point would urge the hierarchy and the theologians to reflect on it and present to Orthodox theology relevant missiological research, i.e. to theologically describe and explain the practical missionary life of the respective church.

We Orthodox recognise that our ecclesiastic life is very much centred in the liturgy, the Eucharist and the proclamation of the Good News. From this perspective, it seems strange that we often fail to do what the the liturgy and the Eucharist and the teachings of the Fathers require from us; to see the Church as fullness and as the Church of Christ. Don't we agree with Fr. Schmemann when he affirms: "Nothing reveals better the relation between the Church as fullness and the Church as mission than the Eucharist, the central act of the Church's *leitourgia,* the sacrament of the Church itself"?[35] As we are satisfied with our own "internal" church life and reject "going out" and preaching the Gospel, while we often limit Christianity to our local church, or ethnic group or nation, how can we understand and accept the truth in the words of Fr. Meyendorff: "A Church which ceases to be missionary, which limits itself to an introverted self-sustaining existence, or, even worse, places ethnic, racial, political, social, or geographic limitations upon the message of Christ, ceases to be authentically 'the Church of Christ'?"[36] If "prayer, worship and communion have always formed the context for the witness of faith, including evangelism, mission and church life,"[37] how do we understand and practice this witness if we are secluded and we shun the world around us? All these are missiological issues which we as believers in Jesus Christ need to properly address.

---

[34] The author here expresses his personal perception as regards the ecclesiastical situation and status in FYROM, since there is no any local Orthodox Church that has been officially and canonically recognized by the Ecumenical Patriarchate or other Orthodox Patriarchate or Autocephalus Churches yet (Ed.)

[35] Schmemann Alexander. *Church, World, Mission: Reflections on Orthodoxy in the West.* (Crestwood, NY: St Vladimir's Seminary Press, 1979), 214.

[36] Meyendorff John. *Living Tradition. Creswood,* (NY, St Vladimir's Seminary Press, 1978), 153.

[37] Bria Ion. *The Liturgy after the Liturgy: Mission and Witness from an Orthodox Perspective.* (Geneva: WCC Publications, 1996), 9.

In some of the Orthodox churches there are believers who tend to see mission in every aspect of their church life, to such an extent that they would consider mission such church activities as going to church every Sunday, or receiving the Holy Gifts during liturgy, or teaching at the parish Sunday school, or "consecrating" (in the rite of consecration of water) as many offices, clubs, businesses, etc. as possible. More than half a century ago Nissiotis clearly stated that the social and educational activities within the Church are not missionary activities: going into the world, preaching the Gospel and converting others to Christianity – this is mission.[38]

It may be this misunderstanding of the nature of the Church, of the role of the Eucharist, of the sacramental and social responsibility of the believers, that prevents the Orthodox in many countries from engaging in true mission, and then theologically reflecting on this practice within their missiological research, while helping Missiology to occupy its proper place in the theological schools. Sometimes one can hear Orthodox theologians saying that there is no such thing as mission or missiology: "Practical Ecclesiology," they affirm – this is mission as the Orthodox understand it. We could agree with this, but only if the Orthodox believers truly practice Orthodox ecclesiology. In addition to this, however, we need to see also practical activities where we preach the Gospel to others and convert them to Christianity, that is, to see acts of evangelism, as Fr. Hopko eloquently described what Christian evangelism is.[39] Many are the Orthodox who feel quite comfortable when they "theologize" and use the Greek words, which Fr. Hopko used in the quotation below (such as didaskalia, homologia, apologia, martyria, diakonia, etc.), but it seems that not so many are those who also practice their ecclesiology. Isn't better to speak of proclamation of the Gospel and the Kingdom, and of bringing others to Christ, that is, of mission, rather than speaking of "practical ecclesiology" while not practicing this ecclesiology?

Missiology is slowly trying to find its proper place among the other theological academic disciplines, and in order to better understand this process, and the question of what its connection is with the participation of the Orthodox in the ecumenical initiatives, let us briefly consider Orthodox theology and its function at the schools within Orthodoxy.

2. Theology in contemporary Orthodoxy

As mentioned above, Orthodox theology continues to be traditional where in most theological schools it functions under the domain of the four "departments": Biblical, Historic, Systematic and Practical Theology. As societies develop, and the needs of the people change, theology inevitably tries to adapt to these needs so that it better responds to the enquiries of the contemporary people and more adequately explains the modern social and world's developments. This has brought new tendencies which some Orthodox theological schools currently follow where we can see new theological disciplines emerging, or old ones being reformed or re-designed.

[38] Nissiotis writes: "It is a great mistake when we think that by discussing social questions, or by analysing the secular environment, or by helping in educational and material needs we are performing mission... There is one immediate need for those outside the Church: to be converted and become members of this community in a visible, concrete form." He also affirms that service, even the service done in the name of Christ, "is not absolutely necessary as a sign of the authenticity of the Christian mission," and that people do not believe because of service, "they are called to believe because they are converted by the power of the saving grace which is to be announced to them by word and shared by them through the sacraments in the Church." (in: Nissiotis, N. A. "The Ecclesiological Foundation of Mission from the Orthodox Point of View," *Greek Orthodox Theological Review* 7 (1961-62): 22-52, the quotes here on 31-32).

[39] Fr. Hopko writes: "This Christian *evangelism* is always accompanied by teaching (*didaskalia*) and confession (*homologia*) and defense (*apologia*) and witness (*martyria*). And, it is accomplished in *works of love* for human beings performed in concrete acts of mercy without condition or discrimination. This is Christian philanthropy understood not merely as various forms of charitable actions and almsgiving, but as sacrificial service (*diakonia*) and witness (*martyria*) in all areas of human existence that contribute to human dignity, freedom, justice, and peace on earth according to God's gospel in Jesus" (in: Hopko Thomas. *Speaking the Truth in Love: Education, Mission, and Witness in Contemporary Orthodoxy*. (Crestwood, NY: St. Vladimir's Seminary Press, 2004), 70.

Part VII: Particular Themes and Issues for Orthodox Involvement in Ecumenism

This process does not mean change in theology or in the teaching of the Church; it only means that the new reality needs new theological expressions and terms, which are rooted in the same theology and the same teaching of the Church and of the Church Fathers. It means that Orthodox theology is open to the world, as it always has been, and that the contemporary theologians try to pass on theological truths to others in contemporary forms and expressive contents. While providing below some examples of new theological academic disciplines in the Orthodox theological schools, we notice that this openness to the world can be observed in those schools which have embraced Missiology as an academic discipline reflecting specific missionary practice in the corresponding Orthodox churches, that is, the schools in Russia, Greece and Romania (and incidentally also in some of the schools in Ukraine and Belarus).

Along with the traditional theological disciplines taught at the Moscow spiritual academy, today we can find such subjects as: Challenges the Christian Faith Faces Today, Greek Paleography, Diakonia, Liturgical Legacy of the Old Testament, Byzantine Studies, Eastern Christian Theological Reflections, Russian Patristics, Contemporary Sects' Developments (in addition to Sectology), New Developments in Molecular Biomedicine, Russian Sects' Review, Catholic Theology, Protestant Theology (in addition to Comparative Theology dealing with the teachings of the main Christian denominations from an Orthodox point of view), Social Ethics, Ascetical Theology, Orthodox Ascetics, three new types of exegesis: Exegesis of the Antiochian Theological School, of the Text Related to the Messiah, and of Paul's Epistles.[40] In the Belgorod spiritual missionary seminary we find Pastoral Ethics and Aesthetics, Natural Science, Ethnography, Phenomenology of Religion, Theology of Apostle Paul, Orthodox Spirituality, Foundations of Prison Ministry, Catholic Missions, Protestant Missions.[41]

New theological academic disciplines have been introduced in the Minsk spiritual academy (Social Doctrine of the Orthodox Church and Study of Schisms[42]), and in the Minsk Institute of Theology St. Methodius and St. Cyril (Study of Holiness and Spiritual Guidance in the Russian Church, Foundations of Contemporary Natural Studies, Intercultural Communication, Social Ministry of the Church, Orthodox Feasts in Dogmatic Perspective, Principles of Intellectual Property's Management, History of European Calvinism, Science From the Point of View of Religion, Sociology of Religions).[43]

At the Kiev spiritual academy (under the Moscow Patriarchate) today we can find such academic disciplines as Orthodox Ecclesiology, Ascetics, Science and Religion, Social Doctrine of the Church, Orthodoxy and Youth, Liturgical Theology. The Kiev seminary also teaches Heortology (the Study of religious feasts), Cosmology, Religious Studies and Sacramentology.[44] The Chernovitsky Orthodox theological institute offers Christian Denominations (along with Comparative Theology), Soteriology and Eschatology, Principles of Intellectual Property, Political Studies, Sociology, Journalism, Ecology.[45] At the Kharkov spiritual seminary one can find Religious Economics, Sects and their Psychology.[46] At the Kiev Orthodox theological academy the new disciplines include Mystical Theology, Orthodox Ethical Code, Ecclesial Sociology, Christianity and Islam, History of the Ecumenical Movement, Cultural Studies, Political Studies, Ecology, Liturgical Tradition.[47]

In the Greek Orthodox theological schools one can observe greater diversity of academic disciplines, and this is mainly due to their more visible "theological openness" to the world. It is not possible to mention here all of them, we can only point to some of the new teaching subjects. At the theological faculty of Athens the subjects offered are Ancient Judaism and the World, The Dead Sea Scrolls, The Woman in the New Testament, Comparative Science of Religion, Entrepreneurship Development and the Art of Icon Painting, Contemporary

[40] http://www.mpda.ru/edu/plan/ (in Russian only).
[41] http://www.bel-seminaria.ru/node/16 (in Russian only).
[42] http://minds.by/academy/education_plan.html (in Russian only).
[43] http://www.inst.bsu.by/ru/student (in Russian only).
[44] http://www.kdais.kiev.ua/index.php?option=com_content&view=article&id=9&Itemid=9&lang=ru (in Russian only).
[45] http://www.cpbi.info/index.php?id=5 (in Ukrainian only).
[46] http://www.eparchia.kharkov.ua/stat/20 (in Russian only).
[47] http://www.kda.org.ua/plan.html (in Ukrainian only).

Ecclesiastic History of the Orthodox East, Sociology, Gender and Education, Religion and Gender, Orthodox Spirituality, Western Theology, Controversial Theologians after the 11th Century, Mystagogical Texts and Texts of Vigilant Theology (at the undergraduate level[48]), and Study of the Comparative Philosophy of Religion, The Dialogue Between Philosophy and Theology, The Study of Church and Dogma, Dialogue Between Theology, Psychology and Psychiatry, Study of the History of Doctrine and the Contemporary Ecumenical Dialogue (at the postgraduate level).[49]

At the Orthodox theological faculty of Thessaloniki, we can find such new disciplines like Computer Science and Theology, Sociology, Interpretation of the Poetical and Prophetical Books of the Old Testament from the Septuagint Text, Sociology of Religion, Sociology of Christianity, Interreligious Dialogue, Ecclesiastical Literature of the Slavs, The Ecumenical Movement, Old Testament Theology, Semiotics of Contemporary Culture, Interpretation and Misinterpretation in Patristic Tradition, The Interpretative Approach of the Filioque in the Patristic Tradition, Russian Spirituality, Mystic Thought in the Orthodox Slavic World, Theological Presuppositions of the Christian Deification of Man, The boundaries of the Church: The Discussion within the Ecumenical Movement, Church and Language, Historical Evolution and Theology of Sacraments, Volunteering, Diakonia, Solidarity: Theory and Praxis, Neo-Greek Alienation, Eros, Sexuality, Desire and Pleasure in Eastern Orthodox Theology, Churches and Religions in Dialogue to Promote Justice, Peace and Integrity of Creation, Conflict Management in Childhood and Parish Catechetical Service, Challenges of Bioethics, Religion and Migration (at the undergraduate level[50]), and Jewish Mysticism, The Eucharistic Ecclesiology of the New Testament, Slavic Philhellenism, Church literature of the Western Church, Dogmatic and Orthodox Tradition in Philosophy, Iconology, Dogmatic Theology in the West in Modern Times, The Moral Limits of the Doctrine and Art, Society and Sacrum, Heortology and Wishful Thinking, Cross-Field Ecumenical Theology, Eucharistic Ecclesiology in the Modern Christian Testimony, Human Sexuality and Biblical Soteriology, Islam, Contemporary Reality and Interreligious Dialogue, Bioethics, Pastoral Sociology, Theology of Worship and Contemporary Liturgical issues, Human Sexuality and Christian Testimony, Ecumenical Social Ethics (at the postgraduate level.)[51]

In the Bulgarian, Romanian, Moldovan and Serbian Orthodox theological schools we can find only a couple of new disciplines, and in the Orthodox schools of the Finnish Orthodox Church and the Orthodox Church in America, we mostly observe traditional theological curricula.

For centuries now Orthodox theology has accepted that it is not an abstract philosophical reflection but life itself: "theology is related to life. (…) Theology is something in which all believers can and must participate."[52] We need to remember that "all theology is mystical, inasmuch as it shows forth the divine mystery: the data of revelation."[53] "We must live the dogma expressing a revealed truth, which appears to us as an unfathomable mystery, in such a fashion that instead of assimilating the mystery to our mode of understanding, we should, on the contrary, look for a profound change, an inner transformation of spirit, enabling us to experience it mystically,"[54] and remember that "theology and mysticism support and complete each other. One is impossible without the other."[55]

These affirmations once more prove the importance of Orthodox theology for the lives of the believers in the churches and in their witness beyond the church's fence. In our liturgical life and in our prayers we

---

[48] http://en.theol.uoa.gr/undergraduate-studies/program-of-studies-ects.html, where the courses of the four departments of undergraduate level can be seen in separate windows; some of the courses are obligatory, some are mandatory-optional.

[49] http://en.theol.uoa.gr/postgraduate-studies/program-of-postgraduate-studies-ects.html, where the courses of the four departments of postgraduate level can be seen in separate windows; some of the courses are obligatory, some are mandatory-optional.

[50] http://www.theo.auth.gr/theo/en/Undergrad/Pages/Courses.aspx, including core disciplines and mandatory-elective subjects.

[51] http://www.theo.auth.gr/theo/en/Postgrad/Pages/Courses.aspx, including core disciplines and mandatory-elective subjects.

[52] Stamoolis James. *Eastern Orthodox Mission Theology Today*. (New York: Maryknoll, Orbis Books, 1986), 10.

[53] Lossky Vladimir. *The Mystical Theology of the Eastern Church*. (Crestwood, NY: St Vladimir's Seminary Press, 1976), 7.

[54] Lossky, *The Mystical Theology*, 8.

[55] Lossky, *The Mystical Theology*, 8.

practically experience what theology is, and in the Eucharistic participation we realise that "the whole life of the Church is rooted in the Eucharist, in the fruition of this eucharistic fullness in the time of this world whose 'image passeth by'."[56] From this understanding, in our life in the church we need to come to the conclusion which Fr. Schmemann noted while completing the above sentence: "This is indeed the *mission of the Church.*"[57]

We therefore need to be sure that our theology does not remain a secluded or isolated "teaching of the Church." It is our life as believers which must show others what theology is and what our witness (that is, our mission to and with others) is about. Through our church activities and eucharistic participation, through our life as a "liturgy after the liturgy," we need to "proclaim" our theology in the same way in which we declare our faith and our calling; we need to not only "satisfy" our spiritual needs but to obey God's calling and do our ministry in a true theological and missionary way. Otherwise we may be even sinning against our faith and against the calling of God to every faithful and to every follower of Christ. In the words of Fr. Schmemann, "Is it not a sin against this basic calling when the Church, the ecclesial community, locks herself in her 'inner' life and considers herself called only 'to attend to the spiritual needs' of her members and thus for all intents and purposes denies that mission is a basic ministry and task of the Church in 'this world?'."[58]

In the last few years in many Orthodox theological schools there has been the tendency to introduce various "liturgical" theologies, and this seems natural if we take into account the important role which liturgy plays in our life as Orthodox believers. In all these liturgical subjects we can find abundance of evidence that doctrine and personal experience of life in Christ are inseparable in the liturgy where the verbal proclamation is essential for the affirmation of our faith. "In the liturgy, the verbal proclamation of the gospel is inseparable from the doxological way of praying and symbolic ritual of the sacraments. This prevents the Orthodox from separating doctrine and prayer, biblical texts from hymnology, biblical stories from the life of saints. It overcomes the contradiction between doctrinal teachings and personal experiences. *Lex credendi* goes together with *lex orandi*," writes Fr. Bria.[59] If "the law of prayer is the law of the faith" (that is, if our liturgical life and the life of worshipping God is the foundation of our faith), then how can we separate our life as believers from our theology and from our witness to the world?

Theology (that is, our faith articulated in rational terms), and the mission we are called to do, need to be shared with others, both with other Christians and with non-Christians and the atheists. Many believers feel comfortable with sharing their faith only within the circle of Orthodox faithful in the Orthodox churches, and this feels right for them, and also right for the Church. Still, others are keen to "go out" and share the treasures of their Orthodox faith with others, and while doing so, according to the requirements of the Gospel and the teaching and the tradition of the Church, they do mission. But there is a difference; sharing your faith with other Christians (either Orthodox or non-Orthodox) seems different than sharing your faith with Muslims, Buddhists, new-age followers or atheists. If we cannot make this distinction, then we need to turn to our Orthodoxy and theology and seek the right answers.

From this perspective, the above consideration on mission and theology leads us to the issue of inter-Christian relations, or ecumenical relations, a term more widely circulated in the last several decades of the 20th and the beginning of the 21st century. Let us now turn to ecumenical relations, while keeping in mind the previous two points of this essay.

---

[56] Schmemann, *Church, World, Mission*, 212.

[57] Schmemann, *Church, World, Mission*, 212.

[58] Schmemann Alexander. *The Eucharist: Sacrament of the Kingdom.* (Crestwood, NY: St Vladimir's Seminary Press, 1988), 87.

[59] Bria Ion. *The Liturgy after the Liturgy*, 31. In fact, the original phrase of St Prosper is "*lex orandi, lex credendi, lex vivendi,*" that is, "what is prayed is what is believed, is what is lived,," or more literally, "the law of prayer is the law of belief is the law of life." (in: Prosper of Acquitaine, "Capitula Coelestini" Chapter 8 translated by Thomas M. Winger. *Studia Liturgica,* Volume 24 (1994).

3. Orthodoxy and ecumenism in a missionary perspective

We need to acknowledge that when Orthodox believers and theologians share their faith and theology and the whole teaching and tradition of the Church with non-Orthodox Christians, this is a specific case which is different from the calling to "go and make disciples of all nations," that is, from the mission of the Church. Some Orthodox are inclined to think that this is mission because through this activity non-Orthodox Christians may become Orthodox (and such affirmations we can occasionally see in Missiology textbooks). The assumption is that the non-Orthodox are not truly Christians, if we are to bring them to "our" Christianity. This inclination and assumption is incorrect, and in this case we speak of either proselytism or inter-Christian relations. If we leave aside the issue of proselytism (here is not the place to discuss it), then the inter-Christian dialogue and relations may be seen not as aspects of the mission of the Church, but as a communication or dialogue in connection with the mission of the Church. If ecumenism is seen from this perspective – as a dialogue between Christians in mutual understanding and love in the Lord – a way that is different to the understanding of ecumenism as it was shaped and proclaimed some decades ago, then the issue of inter-Christian relations becomes vital for all those who in their faith and church life profess the main postulates and doctrinal points of Christianity, i.e. the Holy Trinity, the nature of the Church, the Holy Scripture and the Tradition, the sacramental and mystical life of the Body of Christ, the Resurrection, the Redemption, the Salvation of believers and all the eschatological consequences for humanity in relation to Jesus Christ.

Along with the theologians who specialise in the field of inter-Christian and inter-religious dialogue and relations, it is the missionaries who seem to best understand the nature of the dialogue with others – both non-Christians (belonging to other religions or to other teachings or atheists) and Christians. Entering into dialogue with others is the most natural thing for the missionaries – this is how they share their faith and their theology, in addition to their exemplary life in Christ. This specific characteristic of the missionaries and the missiologists links – directly and inevitably – mission (as practical application of our faith in the dimension of difference[60]), with Missiology/Theology (as academic theological field of study), and ecumenism (the dialogue between Christians).

Where do the Orthodox stand in the efforts of theologians and missionaries to bring together Christians to discuss common inter-Christian issues? The Orthodox stand at different positions: some are willing to take part in ecumenical meetings and discussions and they do this openly and responsibly (the Greek, the Romanian, the Albanian and the Finnish Orthodox churches, and to some extent – the Russian Orthodox Church and the Orthodox Church in Ukraine); some have long ago withdrawn their participation from ecumenical organisations and meetings, and are not willing to enter into any dialogue with non-Orthodox Christians (the Bulgarian and the Georgian Orthodox churches); and others are quite inactive in inter-Christian meetings and forums, although they have not withheld their participation in ecumenical organisations (all other Orthodox churches, including the Orthodox Church in America).

Once again we can notice that the active members of ecumenical encounters are the churches which do mission and which also extensively engage in missiological research: the Greek, the Romanian, the Albanian, the Finnish and the Russian Orthodox churches. This fact once again indicates that engaging in ecumenical dialogue is not about "how Orthodox you are" (because the hierarchy and the believers in Greece, or Romania, or Russia, or Finland are not more or less Orthodox than those in other countries), but about how well you know your faith and tradition and are willing to share them with others responsibly and openly. This does not mean that the hierarchy and the believers of other Orthodox churches do not know their faith and do not want to share it with others – they do know their faith and tradition no less than all other Orthodox believers. One thing which they seem to lack, however, is the understanding of the role and importance of Orthodoxy in the inter-Christian encounter. And we need to affirm that Orthodoxy has a big role to play in the ecumenical

---

[60] An interesting and truly missiological understanding of doing mission as "ministry with a difference" was recently developed, see Presler Titus. "Mission Is Ministry in the Dimension of Difference: A Definition for the Twenty-first Century." *International Bulletin of Missionary Research* 34.4 (October 2010): 195-204.

dialogue where all Christian participants are enriched by the treasures and the deep mystical experience of the Orthodox Church. We may possess treasures and spiritual firmness but we ought to share these with others.

We need to accept the fact that in inter-Christian dialogue the representatives of different Christian communities use different "language" and terms which are loaded with much of their theology and doctrine. This prevents the participants from a true encounter with each other, not to mention coming to common agreement on doctrinal issues.[61] We need to also agree with the observation Schmemann made: "To explain this initial failure [i.e., no encounter happened between the Orthodox and the non-Orthodox participants in ecumenical meetings: my comment], two facts are of paramount importance. One is the isolation of the Orthodox church from the Christian West, the other a specifically Western character and ethos of the ecumenical movement."[62] The last point – that for many decades now the ecumenical movement has had a specifically western "disguise," makes many Orthodox quite hesitant to enter into dialogue with those who have long "forgotten" the "universal, or catholic, language" of the Church, as some Orthodox theologians assert.

Fr. Schmemann considers the ecumenical dialogue and the difficulties with the language in the framework of Orthodox mission which he also recognized as quite different in character and in spirit from the missionary efforts of the western Christian churches and mission agencies. He writes:

"In the ecumenical encounter, the Orthodox Church had to face a Christian world with several centuries of "autonomous" theological and spiritual development behind it, with a mind and thought-forms radically different from those of the East. The questions it asked of the Orthodox were formulated in Western terms, were conditioned very often by specifically Western experience and developments. The Orthodox answers were classified according to Western patterns, "reduced" to categories familiar to the West but hardly adequate to Orthodoxy. This situation, although years of contact and conversations have no doubt improved it, is still far from being overcome completely. The "catholic language" has not yet been recovered. All this, in addition to basic dogmatical differences, explains the "agony" of Orthodox participation in the ecumenical movement and constitutes a very real obstacle not only to agreement, but to simple understanding. One must remember this when trying to grasp the Orthodox approach to missions."[63]

In spite of these obstacles to a comprehensive dialogue between Christians, many Orthodox theologians and missiologists have tried to find the most appropriate language and terms to express the true meaning of the Orthodox teaching concerning specific theological and doctrinal issues which are discussed at ecumenical meetings.[64] Orthodox ecclesiology is one of the theological disciplines which has been extensively developed in the last decades. Theologians have repeatedly confirmed that understanding the nature of the Church is crucial to understand all (or at least many) doctrinal and denominational difficulties in our theology and in our Christian legacy as inherited from previous centuries. In Orthodoxy, Fr. Bria came to the understanding that

---

[61] Fr. Schmemann writes: "The ecumenical movement is by its very nature an encounter, a conversation, an accepted partnership in the search for Christian unity and wholeness. The encounter, however, is fruitful and meaningful only when it is founded on some degree of mutual understanding, on a common language, even if this language serves as a means of a sharp controversy. The tragedy of Orthodoxy is that from the very beginning of its ecumenical participation no such common language, no theological 'continuity' existed between her and her Western partners, within, at least, the organized and institutionally structured Ecumenical Movement." And he concludes: *There was no real encounter.* (in: Schmemann Alexander. „Moment of Truth for Orthodoxy," in Daniel B. Clendenin (ed.). *Eastern Orthodox Christianity: A Western Perspective.* 2nd edition, (Baker Academic & Paternoster Press, 2003), 203-210 (the citation here, on 203-204); italicized text in the original.

[62] Schmemann, "Moment of Truth," 205.

[63] Schmemann, *Church, World, Mission,* 211.

[64] In fact, it is the obstacles and the difficulties in explaining our faith or describing our theology that bear theological reflection and create appropriate language and terms. While discussing the mission of the Church in her early history, Stamoolis writes: "Serious theological reflection as to the nature and character of the missionary task of the Church did not arise in the earliest history of the Church... Reflection did not take place until obstacles were encountered." (in: Stamoolis, *Eastern Orthodox Mission Theology Today,* 48).

the Church "is the sign of the contemporary presence of Christ,"[65] Archbishop Yannoulatos clearly expressed the idea of the "global koinonia of love,"[66] and Fr. Hopko eloquently expressed the meaning of Church unity, while affirming that the Church "is not an organization with a gospel; it is a gospel with organizations; it is not an institution with mysteries; it is mystery with institutions. Church unity, in this perspective, is unity in the gospel of God and the mystery of Christ as revealed, known, proclaimed, celebrated, and witnessed in the formal ecclesiastical doctrines, sacramental structures, and liturgical rites of the Christian churches."[67]

The Orthodox churches are often criticised for their linguistic and national inclinations[68] where only the local expressions of faith, theology and church life seem to be the true ones. And we need to admit that there is much truth in this criticism and that we need to make every effort and try to listen to the Orthodox theologians who also expressed their dissatisfaction over the ethnic and the cultural features which we have ascribed to our belief and life in the church. "No nation has his [God's] exclusive love. Identifying the nation with the Church does damage to the 'One, Holy, Catholic, and Apostolic Church.' It ignores fundamental elements of the Christian creed. The fact that Orthodoxy has been accepted by and incorporated into the life of one or several nations in no way justifies the belief that it is their exclusive property. Respect for and preservation of our identity is natural and necessary, but if we limit Christ to an ethnic or national perspective we can indirectly end up denying him," writes Archbishop Yannoulatos.[69]

In terms of our missionary calling, we need to admit that seclusion is the antithesis of mission, and it is the antithesis of the Church herself. While insisting that only our own local church (our own "jurisdiction") is the truest and the most authentic one, we seem to deny authenticity to other Christian churches. How then do we interpret the oneness, the holiness, the catholicity and the apostolicity of the Church? "No 'jurisdiction' which limits itself by ethnic ties can be truly missionary, except in relation to the ethnic group with which it identifies itself. But then it ceases to be truly 'catholic,' since it places a limitation to its membership. The marks of the one, holy, catholic and apostolic Church are inconceivable if local churches are isolated from each other; together, they define what the Church of Christ truly is and what all of us together are called to become."[70]

For the Orthodox, the safest way to unity may be first through unity between the Orthodox churches themselves and then between Orthodoxy and the other Christian communities. For decades now, concerns have arisen as to how unified the voice of the different Orthodox churches is, and often appeals are made for closer cooperation between them: "Closer cooperation between all the autocephalous Orthodox Churches is essential: they must provide each other with mutual support, but they must also cultivate Orthodoxy's global consciousness. When we are united with Christ in his Church, we transcend our personal 'I' and our national

---

[65] Bria, *The Liturgy after the Liturgy*, 73.

[66] Yannoulatos Anastasios. *Facing the World: Orthodox Christian Essays on Global Concerns*. (Crestwood, NY: St. Vladimir's Press, 2003), 48, 203.

[67] Hopko, *Speaking the Truth in Love*, 139.

[68] In the most recent *Encyclopedia of Eastern Orthodox Christianity* the authors affirm that even today, language and ethnicity continue to form the foundation of Orthodoxy and of its mission. In the article about the establishment of the Orthodox Church in America, the authors notice the fact that in the aftermath of the Orthodox mission on this land, the first parishes showed much greater openness to society and involvement in social issues with the native people, but then most of them secluded in their own language and culture (initially, mostly Russian and Greek), to such an extent that in the late 19th and early 20th century even the relations between the local Orthodox churches were reduced to a minimum, not to speak of the relations with the wider society: "there was little contact among these parishes with other Orthodox groups and little sense of mission beyond the needs of a particular ethnic family. The large urban centers in the United States during the late 19th and early 20th centuries contained neighborhoods where the various immigrant groups could maintain their faith, culture and language, somewhat insulated from the wider society." ("Orthodoxy in the United States of America," in: McGuckin John Anthony (ed.) *The Encyclopedia of Eastern Orthodox Christianity*. Volume II, (Chichester, UK: Blackwell Publishing Ltd., 2011), 609-617

[69] Yannoulatos, *Facing the World*, 202-203.

[70] Meyendorff John. *The Vision of Unity*. (Crestwood, NY: St Vladimir's Seminary Press, 1987), 68.

Part VII: Particular Themes and Issues for Orthodox Involvement in Ecumenism

'we', so that we can join with all human beings and all peoples and nations in understanding and love,"[71] states Archbishop Yannoulatos.

This does not in any way mean that local expressions of faith and life in Christ should not be maintained and developed; quite the contrary: when we do mission in another country, our purpose must be to establish an authentic local church; from an Orthodox perspective, this should be a Church which is deeply eucharistic and liturgical.[72] When we go to Africa to build a church only for the Russians who speak Russian, or only for the Romanians who speak Romanian, or for the Greeks who speak Greek, etc., we need to ask ourselves what we have done so that also the local people may obtain an Orthodox church which is true to their culture, language and ways of expressions of life, without betraying the dogmatic and patristic value of Orthodoxy.

We would be ultimately led to admit that the Orthodox churches, through their sacramental and soteriological character, are called to play a substantial role in the world's events, and this we must do in a responsible and open way. Let us conclude this brief review with the words of Archbishop Yannoulatos: "If Orthodoxy is to be equal to its great mission in world events, it must maintain its sacramental, soteriological character intact, it must be open to humanity's constant quest, and it must conscientiously live its awareness of the Resurrection and live it up to its global responsibility."[73]

Bibliography

Bria Ion. *The Liturgy after the Liturgy: Mission and Witness from an Orthodox Perspective*. (Geneva: WCC Publications, 1996).

Hopko Thomas. *Speaking the Truth in Love: Education, Mission, and Witness in Contemporary Orthodoxy*. (Crestwood, NY: St. Vladimir's Seminary Press, 2004).

Lossky Vladimir. *The Mystical Theology of the Eastern Church*. (Crestwood, NY: St Vladimir's Seminary Press, 1976).

Meyendorff John. *Living Tradition*. (Crestwood, NY: St Vladimir's Seminary Press, 1978).

Meyendorff John. *The Vision of Unity*. (Crestwood, NY: St Vladimir's Seminary Press, 1987).

Schmemann Alexander. *Church, World, Mission: Reflections on Orthodoxy in the West*. (Crestwood, NY: St Vladimir's Seminary Press, 1979).

Schmemann Alexander. *The Eucharist: Sacrament of the Kingdom*. (Crestwood, NY: St Vladimir's Seminary Press, 1988).

Stamoolis James. *Eastern Orthodox Mission Theology Today*. (New York: Maryknoll, Orbis Books, 1986).

Veronis Luke. "Everything in Love: the Making of a Missionary," in: *Road to Emmaus: A Journal of Orthodox Faith and Culture*. Vol. VI, 4.23 (2005): 3-27.

Yannoulatos Anastasios. *Facing the World: Orthodox Christian Essays on Global Concerns*. (Crestwood, NY: St. Vladimir's Press, 2003).

---

[71] Yannoulatos, *Facing the World*, 203.

[72] As Fr. Luke Veronis affirms: "One has to be very clear about the purpose of missions. The goal of missions is to establish an authentic Eucharistic worshipping community in the people's own language and culture." (in: Veronis Luke. "Everything in Love: the Making of a Missionary," in: *Road to Emmaus: A Journal of Orthodox Faith and Culture*. Vol. VI, 4.23 (2005): 3-27, the quotation here on 13.

[73] Yannoulatos, *Facing the World*, 204.

Alina Patru

1. Brief overview of interfaith encounters of the Orthodox Church

Orthodox Christianity has been engaged in interfaith encounters and dialogue from its very beginning. The dialogue between Orthodoxy and Judaism is considered as probably one of the oldest dialogues in the civilized world.[1] Christianity, an offspring of Judaism, had to define itself primarily in relation to Judaism and thus engage in dialogue with the Jewish beliefs and teachings. Moreover, Christianity had to spread into a world full of different religious convictions and to engage implicitly in dialogue with them. Models of such a dialogue are given in Acts 17:16-34: the encounter of St. Paul the Apostle with the Athenian philosophers, but also in other New Testament fragments, like Acts 14:11-18: St. Paul and St. Barnabas the Apostles in dialogue with the pagans in Lystra. After the biblical era, the Church Fathers starting with St. Justin Martyr in the 2nd century have continued to engage in dialogue with the surrounding cultural and religious world.[2]

The dialogue between Eastern Christianity and Islam started immediately after the emergence of Islam in the 7th century.[3] The dialogue reaches a peak in 637, after the fall of Jerusalem to the caliph Umar I St. Sophronius, Patriarch of Jerusalem, reflects on the incident, enters in negotiations with the muslim leaders and even invites Umar I to pray in the Church of the Holy Sepulchre.[4] Archbishop Anastasios Yannoulatos speaks about three phases of the Byzantine-Islamic dialogue.[5] The first two phases are merely polemical, but later, St. Gregory Palamas and Emperor Manuel II Palaiologos in the 14th century, and Patriarch Gennadios Scholarios in the 15th century, the latest under the Ottoman rule, engage in a series of serious, profound dialogues with the Islam, reaching a new level of mutual understanding and respect between the two religions.[6]

The coexistence of Orthodox Christians and Muslims in the same territory has led to a "dialogue of life"[7] which has enriched both parts over the centuries. In recent times, the globalisation and the pluralisation of our societies have led to more frequent and diverse encounters between religions. The Orthodox Churches started to deal institutionally with the new forms of inter-religious encounters during the second half of the 20th century, either on their own or through participation in ecumenical initiatives. In 1972, Metropolitan Emilianos Timiadis noted that "in increasing measure our society appears as pluralistic. [...] The life and its realities oblige us to look attentively to the religious convictions of the others and to study them without prejudices and fanaticism."[8] In order to support his ideas, he pointed to the provisional "Guidelines on Dialogue with People of Living Faiths and Ideologies," discussed at the Central Committee of the WCC in 1971, signed and supported by the representatives of the Orthodox Churches, too.

---

[1] Rabbi Marc H. Tanenbaum, in the opening of the first National Colloquium on Greek Orthodox – Jewish Relations (New York, 1972). In *Thomas Kratzert, "Wir sind wie die Juden." Der griechisch-orthodoxe Beitrag zu einem jüdisch-christlichen Dialog*, (Berlin: Institut Kirche und Judentum, 1994), 195.

[2] George C. Papademetriou, *An Orthodox Christian View of Non-Christian Religions*, at http://www.goarch.org/ourfaith/ourfaith8089#_edn9, (last accessed at 1 June 2012).

[3] Grigorios Larentzakis, *Die Erklärung des II. Vatikanums Nostra Aetate über das Verhältnis der Kirche zu den nichtchristlichen Religionen aus orthodoxer Sicht*, in Hans Hermann Henrix (ed.), (Nostra Aetate – Ein zukunftsweisender Konzilstext, Aachen: Einhard, 2006), 112.

[4] See Steven Runciman, *A History of the Crusades, vol. 1 The First Crusade*, (Cambridge: Cambridge University Press, 1987), 3-4.

[5] See Anastasios (Yannoulatos), Bischof von Androussa, "Der Dialog mit dem Islam aus orthodoxer Sicht," in Rudolf Kirchschläger, Alfred Stirnemann, *Ein Laboratorium für Einheit, 25 Jahre Pro Oriente 1989*, (Innsbruck: Tyrolia 1991), 210.

[6] Ibidem, 210-212.

[7] Ibidem, 219.

[8] Metropolit Emilianos Timiadis, Die orthodoxen Väter und die nichtchristlichen Religionen, in *Una Sancta* 27 (1972), 163.

2. Modern ecumenical and Orthodox documents that established interfaith dialogue

"The desire of the World Council of Churches to open a dialogue with Hindus, Buddhists, Jews and Muslims resulted in the 1971 Dialogue with People of Living Faiths and Ideologies program."[9] Most Orthodox Churches were part of this process from its very beginning. The "Guidelines on Dialogue with People of Living Faiths and Ideologies" were first published in 1979[10] and serve as a basis for various bilateral and multilateral interfaith encounters of the churches which are members of the WCC. The document tries to define terms such as "community" and "dialogue," to reflect on the "theological significance of people of other faiths and ideologies" and to formulate basic rules for a honest, open, and mutually enriching encounter.

At the Third Pre-Conciliar Pan-Orthodox Conference held in 1986 in Chambésy, the Orthodox Chruches adopted a statement called "The Contribution of the Orthodox Local Churches to the Fulfilment of the Christian Ideals of Peace, Liberty, Fraternity, and Love among the Nations as well as to the Eradication of Racial Discrimination and Other Forms of Discriminations." This Pan-Orthodox document contains statements referring to the participation of the Orthodox Churches in interfaith encounters and dialogues:

> "The Orthodox local Churches see it as their duty to collaborate closely with believers from other religions who love peace for the peace on earth and the realisation of fraternal relations among nations. The Orthodox Churches are called to contribute to the interfaith understanding and cooperation and thus to the eradication of any fanaticism and therefore to the fraternization of the nations and to the enforcement of the goods of liberty and peace in the world, for the benefit of the contemporary man, independent of race and religion. It is obvious that this collaboration excludes any syncretism as well as any temptation to impose one religion to others."[11]

The 1986 document is not the first Pan-Orthodox statement in favour of the interfaith engagement. This form of engagement has been recommended at the First Pre-Conciliar Pan-Orthodox Conference (1976, Chambésy), too, where the participants drew up a list of ten themes to be discussed at the Holy and Great Council.[12] Besides that, several discourses of the Ecumenical Patriarchs Dimitrios I[13] and Bartholomaios I[14] are an invitation to interfaith dialogue and cooperation for the purpose of peace and freedom.

The Oriental Orthodox Churches have developed their own documents in favour of the interfaith dialogue and cooperation. E.g., the Malankara Orthodox Syrian Church has on its website its own statement about the "Dialogue with World Religions," signed by the leader of the Department of Ecumenical Relations, Metropolitan Dr. Paulos Mar Gregorios.[15]

---

[9] http://www.idcpublishers.com/pdf/479_brochure.pdf, (last accessed at 5 June 2012).

[10] http://www.oikoumene.org/en/resources/documents/wcc-programmes/interreligious-dialogue-and-cooperation/inter-religious-trust-and-respect/guidelines-on-dialogue-with-people-of-living-faiths-and-ideologies.html, (last accessed at 5 June 2012).

[11] Der Beitrag der Orthodoxen Kirche zur Verwirklichung des Friedens, der Gerechtigkeit, der Freiheit, der Brüderlichkeit und der Liebe zwischen den Völkern sowie zur Beseitigung der Rassen- und anderen Diskriminierungen, in *Una Sancta* 42.1 (1987): 16-17.

[12] Damaskinos Papandreou, Art. "Pan-Orthodox Conferences," in Erwin Fahlbusch (ed.), *The Encyclopedia of Christianity, Vol. 4*, (Grand Rapids: Eerdmans and Leiden-Brill, 2005), 26.

[13] See "1976 Patriarchal Christmas Encyclical," in *Episkepsis* (Special edition), (December 25, 1976).

[14] See the whole Chapter 5, "Interfaith Dialogue: Interreligious and Intercultural Dimensions" in Bartholomew I, John Chryssavgis (ed.), *In the World, Yet not of the World: Social and Global Initiatives of Ecumenical Patriarch Bartholomew*, (New York: Fordham University Press, 2010), 222-289.

[15] http://malankaraorthodoxchurch.in/index.php?Itemid=236&id=114&option=com_content&task=view, (last accessed at 6 June 2012).

3. Interfaith dialogues with Pan-Orthodox participation

Shortly after the First Pre-Conciliar Pan-Orthodox Conference, the first interfaith dialogue that was launched was the bilateral dialogue between Orthodoxy and Judaism that started in 1977, and counts seven meetings until today. Events which led to the establishment of this dialogue were the first National Colloquium on Greek Orthodox-Jewish Relations (New York, 1972), as well as a lecture held by Metropolitan Damaskinos Papandreou in Zurich in 1976.[16] It is worth noting that the sessions of these dialogues are called "academic consultations," and participants in them are experts who do not have an official mandate from their churches.[17] At the first consultation, Orthodoxy had been represented mainly by Greek theologians; later, the participation was gradually extended: Romanians and Bulgarians joined the Orthodox delegation at the second meeting in 1979; Russians, as well as representatives of the Oriental Orthodox Churches came to the 3rd meeting in 1993.[18] The organizers are, on the one hand, The International Jewish Committee for Inter-religious Consultations and, on the other, until 2001, The Orthodox Centre of the Ecumenical Patriarchate in Chambésy, and after 2001 onwards, The Office for Inter-religious and Intercultural Relations of the Ecumenical Patriarchate in Brussels.

Regarding the topics of interfaith dialogue, the first sessions addressed theological questions. During the fourth session, the participants dealt primarily with global and social concerns. Both on the theological and on the social levels, the dialogue has achieved important results. The Orthodox Christians learned that for the Jews, the law is not a dead letter, but has an internal dynamic and liveliness.[19] The Jews were surprised to hear "that there is a certain dynamic in the Orthodox theology and in the Orthodox community... This was new and encouraging to hear."[20] With regard to the relation between Scripture and Tradition, the Orthodox participants concluded that the Orthodox view is closer to the Jewish than to the Roman-Catholic or Evangelical thinking.[21] From perspective of practical results, it is worth mentioning the common condemnation of anti-Semitism: "an Orthodox participant stated that anti-Semitism is anti-Christian and the consultation adopted this as an abiding principle."[22] For both sides, every social initiative stands on "the pre-eminent value of the human person" and on the "respect for all forms of religious and secular expression, as long as they do not infringe upon or threaten the security and religious freedom of individuals, communities and societies."[23]

Another interfaith dialogue in which the Orthodox participated is the bilateral dialogue between Orthodoxy and Islam that started in 1986. The preliminary event was an Orthodox Christian-Muslim Symposium, held in 1985 at the Holy Cross Greek Orthodox School of Theology in Boston.[24] Ten international academic consultations have been organized until now. Before 2001, the organizers were The Royal Academy of Islamic Civilization Research (Al-Albait Foundation, Amman, Jordan), and The Orthodox Centre of the Ecumenical Patriarchate in Chambésy; after 2001, The Kingdom of Bahrain and The Office for Inter-religious and Intercultural Relations of the Ecumenical Patriarchate in Brussels are responsible for organizing this dialogue.

The goal of these conferences, as defined by Metropolitan Damaskinos Papandreou during the third consultation, was "to overcome the historical problems of conflict and to seek peaceful coexistence between the

---

[16] See Kratzert, 210-214.

[17] Ibid., 214.

[18] Alina Pătru, "Der bilaterale Dialog zwischen Orthodoxie und Judentum ab den 70-er Jahren," *RES – Revista Ecumenică Sibiu,* II, (1/2010) 73-74.

[19] See "Summary Minutes," *The Greek Orthodox Theological Review* 24 (1979), 289.

[20] Gerhart M. Riegner, "Closing Remarks" *Immanuel* 26/27 (1994), 189-190.

[21] Nifon Mihăiță, *The Christian Orthodox – Jewish Consultation II,* (Bucarest: EIBMBOR, no year), 30.

[22] *Communiqué, The 5th Academic Meeting between Judaism and Orthodox Christianity "Faithfulness to Our Sources: Our Common Commitment to Peace and Justice,"* Thessaloniki, May 27-29, 2003, (authors' manuscript, 2).

[23] *Communiqué, 6th Academic Meeting between Judaism and Orthodox Christianity, Jerusalem, March 14-15, 2007,* (authors' manuscript, 2).

[24] George C. Papademetriou, *Two Traditions, One Space: Orthodox Christians and Muslims in Dialogue,* (Boston: Somerset Hall Press, 2011) 209-210.

two religions."[25] He stressed "that giant preparation is needed for the two religions to stand against political systems, economic groups and social interests to eliminate violence."[26] This consultation, on "Peace and justice in the tradition of the two monotheistic religions," made a common reference to the content of the divine and human law, and the analogous understanding of the sacredness of the human person.[27] Two consultations (the sixth and the seventh) were dedicated to the problem of the education of the young generation. It was underlined, that education has to set as its goal to heal the healing of the wounds of the past and to eliminate the prejudices which exist among the believers of the two religions.[28]

4. Other interfaith initiatives

Besides these dialogues conducted with the participation of all Orthodox Churches, there are many other interfaith encounters and dialogues promoted by the local churches or developed as regional initiatives. It is not possible to enumerate them in the present frame. Therefore I will only provide a brief selection of examples.

The Ecumenical Patriarchate organized in February 1994 an interfaith Conference on Peace and Tolerance in Instabul, attended by Orthodox and Catholic Christians, Jews and Muslims, and which produced the "Bosphorus Declaration," a common condemnation of war and crimes committed in the name of religion.[29] Other interfaith conferences of the three monotheistic religions were organized by the Ecumenical Patriarchate in 2000 and 2001.[30] Also since 1995, the Russian Orthodox Church is in a bilateral dialogue with Iranian Islam.[31] The Joint Russian-Iranian Commission for Orthodoxy-Islam Dialogue has held eight meetings until now, discussing several themes of importance for today's world.[32] Lastly, from the side of the Oriental Orthodox Chruches, the Armenian Catholicos of the Great House of Cilicia is "actively involved in Inter-faith dialogues and relations with Islam and religions of the Far East"[33] as one reads on the website.

Bibliography

Contribution des Eglises orthodoxes locales à la réalisation des idéaux chrétiens de paix, de liberté, de fraternité et d'amour entre les peuples et à la suppression des discriminations raciales [in French], in *Episkepsis* 354 (Apr. 1986): 11-17. Greek Version: in *Episkepsis* 369 (Dec.1986): 18-26. German Version: "Der Beitrag der Orthodoxen Kirche zur Verwirklichung des Friedens, der Gerechtigkeit, der Freiheit, der Brüderlichkeit und der Liebe zwischen den Völkern sowie zur Beseitigung der Rassen- und anderen Diskriminierungen," in *Una Sancta* 42.1 (1987): 15-24.

Guidelines on Dialogue with People of Living Faiths and Ideologies, at http://www.oikoumene.org/en/resources/documents/wcc-programmes/interreligious-dialogue-and-cooperation/interreligious-trust-and-respect/guidelines-on-dialogue-with-people-of-living-faiths-and-ideologies.html. (last accessed at June 2012)

Adamakis, Emmanuel, "Involvement and Action of Orthodoxy in favour of Dialogue," in Marc Luyckx (ed.), *The Mediterranean Society: A Challenge for Islam, Judaism and Christianity*, (New York: St. Martin's Press, 1998), 29-32.

---

[25] George C. Papademetriou, "Two Traditions, One Space: Orthodox Christians and Muslims in Dialogue" *Islam and Christian-Muslim Relations* 15.1 (January 2004): 57.

[26] Ibidem, 60.

[27] Ibidem, 57.

[28] G. Larentzakis, 121.

[29] http://www.patriarchate.org/documents/joint-declaration, (last accessed at June 2012).

[30] G. Larentzakis, 119.

[31] http://www.mospat.ru/en/2011/10/21/news50153/, (last accessed at June 2012).

[32] http://abna.ir/data.asp?lang=3&Id=326006, (last accessed at June 2012).

[33] http://www.armenianorthodoxchurch.org/v10/index.htm, last accessed at June 2012).

Bartholomew I, Chryssavgis, John (ed.), *In the World, Yet not of the World: Social and Global Initiatives of Ecumenical Patriarch Bartholomew,* (New York: Fordham University Press, 2010).

[Yannoulatos], Bischof von Androussa, Anastasios, "Der Dialog mit dem Islam aus orthodoxer Sicht [germ. The Dialogue with the Islam from an Orthodox Perspective]," in Rudolf Kirchschläger, Alfred Stirnemann, *Ein Laboratorium für Einheit, 25 Jahre Pro Oriente (1989),* (Innsbruck: Tyrolia, 1991), 210-222.

Yannoulatos, Anastasios G., *Various Christian Approaches to Other Religions: A Historical Outline,* (Athens: Poreuthentes, 1971).

Kratzert, Thomas (evang.), *"Wir sind wie die Juden." Der griechisch-orthodoxe Beitrag zu einem jüdisch-christlichen Dialog* [germ.: "We are like the Jews." The Greek-Orthodox Contribution to a Jewish-Christian Dialogue], (Berlin: Institut Kirche und Judentum, 1994).

Larentzakis, Grigorios, "Die Erklärung des II. Vatikanums Nostra Aetate über das Verhältnis der Kirche zu den nichtchristlichen Religionen aus orthodoxer Sicht [germ.: The 2nd Vatican Declaration Nostra Aetate on the Relation of the Church with Non-Christian Religions from an Orthodox Perspective]," in Hans Hermann Henrix (ed.), *Nostra Aetate – Ein zukunftsweisender Konzilstext,* (Aachen: Einhard, 2006), 111-149.

Papademetriou, George C., *Essays on Orthodox Christian-Jewish Relations,* (Lima: Wyndham Hall Press, 1990).

Papademetriou, George C., *Two Traditions, One Space: Orthodox Christians and Muslims in Dialogue,* (Boston: Somerset Hall Press, 2011).

Papandreou, Damaskinos, *Logos Dialogou* (Athens: Kastaniotis, 1997) (in Greek). See also the German Version: *Dialog als Leitmotiv,* (Athens, 2000)

Timiadis, Metropolit Emilianos, "Die orthodoxen Väter und die nichtchristlichen Religionen [germ.: The Orthodox Fathers and the Non-Christian Religions]" *Una Sancta* 27 (1972): 163-167.

(106) THEOLOGY OF RELIGIONS
AS CONCERN FOR ECUMENICAL DIALOGUE OF ORTHODOX THEOLOGIANS [1]

Fr. Emmanuel Clapsis

Christian theologians in pluralistic societies have begun to formulate positive appreciative theological and practical stances toward other living faiths, and also towards the spiritual and ethical quality of life that is often found amongst secular people. Communities of all major world religious traditions can be found almost in all neighborhoods and places of work. Christians and religious others positively challenge each other's faith in their daily interaction as they become friends and even intermarry, by crossing their religious, ethnic, and cultural boundaries. The involvement of people of different religions in social action organizations – peace, human rights movements and environmental groups – exhibits a remarkable depth of social responsibility and dedication to peace, justice, dignity of human life and the wholeness of creation. Also many secular people exhibit an attractive personal wholeness, a quality of love and humility, which appears to be "of God." Both religious and secular non-Christians often appear to do God's work and contribute to the common good.

In the present world, religious freedom is an inalienable social right that all people must have, allowing them to make different faith statements or none at all. The most appropriate channels to overcome fragmentation and injustice to promote peace are communication and dialogue. Thus, it is important for all human beings and communities to develop conversational skills and to promote dialogue as liberation from parochialism, bigotry and violent urges that fear and misrecognition of the unknown "others" generate. Cultural and religious dialogue and communication presupposes respect for particularity and difference, building a sense of community in the midst of differences. From a theological perspective dialogue is a privileged medium by which the Spirit of God enables different people of different cultures, races, religions and ideologies to recognize their deeper unity in the midst of irreversible and irreducible diversity.

The Orthodox Churches have been involved in interfaith dialogue and have sought ways to collaborate in the public space with people of other living faiths to promote justice and peace in a turbulent world. The Third Pan-Orthodox Pre-Conciliar Conference (1986) has encouraged them to collaborate with people of other living faiths. It is their ethical duty, according the statement of the Third Pan-Orthodox Pre-Conciliar Conference, to collaborate with other religious communities in "joint efforts" for "reconciliation between peoples." The Orthodox churches must work with other religious communities for the triumph of "values represented by freedom and peace in the world, service to humanity today regardless of race or religion." In the mind of Orthodoxy, these ethical principles and values are expressions or consequences of its theology. If the same ethical principles and values can also be found in the theology of other religions, can we assume that they have a deeper common origin, perhaps in the presence of God's Spirit in them? The affirmative response to this question, I contend, must not be achieved at the expense of Christian particularity, namely the uniqueness of Jesus Christ as the Savior of the world.

The aim of this paper is to affirm the universal presence of God's Spirit that moves all and makes possible the unity of creation with God without minimizing or ignoring the particularity of the Christian faith about Jesus Christ and the importance of the Church in God's salvific presence and activity in the world. The affirmation of the presence of God's Spirit in the totality of the world and more particularly in other religious communities and in the secular world is a highly contentious issue in Orthodoxy since some do not recognize the presence of God's grace even in other Christian churches and communions. Thus, it is important to explore first the meaning of St. Cyprian's thesis: *extra ecclesiam nulla salus.*

---

[1] This article is part of a longer and fuller version of a paper which was presented during the International Conference that took place in Volos (June, 3-6, 2010) with the topic "Orthodoxy and Contextual Theology" and organized by Volos Academy for Theological Studies and several other Orthodox Institutions.

Extra ecclesiam nulla salus?

Interfaith dialogue and the participation of the Orthodox Churches in the Ecumenical movement are passionately disputed and have become divisive in the lives of the Orthodox Churches. However, the basic theological assumptions of those who repudiate the involvement of the Orthodox Church in ecumenical and interfaith dialogues are not different from those who favor the active participation of the Orthodox Church in the Ecumenical movement. What remains an unresolved and highly contentious issue is whether the salvific grace of God is actively present and limited only within the canonical boundaries of the Church or whether it is extended in different degrees and ways to other Christian churches, and to communities of other living faiths, to agnostics or even to atheists.

The refusal to acknowledge the salvific presence and operation of God's grace in other Christian churches/ communities and in other religious communities has its origins in the ecclesiological principle best expressed by St. Cyprian of Carthage's thesis that there is no salvation outside of the Church, *"Extra Ecclesiam Nulla Salus."* This principle reflects the belief of the early Church that since the plenitude of Christ and of the Holy Spirit can only be found in the Church, those who are situated outside of the Church cannot share the grace of God. The origins of this view can be traced back to the early Apostolic church: "there is salvation in no one else, for there is no other name under heaven given among men by which we must be saved" (Acts 4:12). Salvation, unity with God, is granted to those who believe in Jesus Christ and enter the Church through baptism (Jn. 3:5; cf. Heb. 11:6; Acts 2:37-41; Mk. 16:15-16). The understanding that salvific grace is granted only to baptized believers within the Church is repeated by later fathers and theologians - often with gradual modifications - leading to the belief that there is no salvation outside of the Church.

St. Cyprian, the bishop of Carthage in North Africa, who died as a martyr in 258 A.D, used this theological principle as a warning to Christians who were either in danger of being separated from the Church or who were already separated from it through either schism or heresy. It is interesting here to note that St. Cyprian did not apply this principle in any of his writings to pagans and Jews who were still the majority of the people in the Roman empire of his day. Those who had separated themselves from the Church, according to St. Cyprian, are the ones to blame for their separation and personally responsible for their exclusion from salvation that can be found in the Church. Given that the Church is Christ's body, anyone who is outside the Church is separated from Christ and is not saved.

While it was possible in situations of conflict and schism to identify canonically who is outside of the Church, a sacramental and charismatic perspective of the church does not allow God's salvific grace to be limited within the canonical boundaries of the Church. This does not deny the claim that the fullness of God's grace can only be found in the Church. The weakness of St. Cyprian's axiom is the absolute identification of the Church's charismatic boundaries with its canonical boundaries. His theology in its practical implications was never accepted in western Christianity. St. Augustine developed a theology of schism that significantly modified the Cyprianic principle. He differentiated the canonical and charismatic spheres of the Church and advocated that those who do not find themselves within the canonical boundaries of the church because of schism may be in the Church in variable degrees and ways. This was possible through the development of an expansive universal understanding of the Church's sacramental and charismatic boundaries. It led to the belief that aspects of the Church's life, faith, and practices can be found in the personal and communal life of those Christians who have been separated from the Church.

Western Christianity embraced wholeheartedly the Augustinian view of schism, while the Eastern Churches remained faithful to the Cyprianic ecclesiology because of its emphasis on the importance of the unity of the Church and its discouragement of schisms. However, the practical implications of this ecclesiology continue to generate theological controversies. Fr. Georges Florovsky, since 1933, has called the Orthodox Churches to embrace the Augustinian theology of schism for historical and theological reasons. He argues that although St. Cyprian was right in suggesting that the sacraments of the Church are accomplished only "in the Church," he defined this "in" hastily and too narrowly. In Florovsky's view, the communal consciousness of the Church never accepted the equation of its canonical limits with its charismatic boundaries. The Greek theologian Ioannis Karmires argues that the notion *extra ecclesiam nulla salus* does not have its origins in the biblical tradition and, although it has been taught by many Church Fathers, it lacks a basic and central characteristic of an Orthodox doctrine. He argues that historically this Cyprianic notion affirms the importance of the Church's unity in response to actual or imminent schisms. Karmires advocates that in a broader and invisible manner members of the church are not only the Orthodox and other baptized believers but also even believers of other religious faiths and all creation. In his opinion, God's salvific grace is not granted just to those who are members of the canonical church but it extends to all human beings and the world that God unconditionally loves. How the salvific grace of God is communicated to all human beings most especially to agnostics, seculars and believers of other religious faiths is an incomprehensible mystery that reflects God's freedom and love. However, if the Church is the body of Christ and the temple of the Holy Spirit, then it is through the Church that salvation is communicated to the world.

In 1971, the Preparatory Commission of the Great and Holy Council of the Orthodox Church produced a document on the issue of *Oikonomia* in the canonical tradition. Those who drafted this statement believed that through the principle of Oikonomia the Orthodox churches could move towards recognition of the ecclesial nature of other Christian churches/communions. The document insisted that in the lives of those outside of the Orthodox Church "Grace is not completely wanting… because they still maintain some form of relationship with Jesus Christ and the Church, and so the light of the divine grace in some ways still enlightens them."

In 1976, upon the recommendation of the secretariat for the preparation of the Holy Synod, the first pre-synodal Pan-Orthodox conference dropped the principle of *Oikonomia* from issues to be addressed at the coming Council of the Orthodox Church. The reason given was that the ensuing debate on this principle proved that the Orthodox Churches had not reached a consensus on the notion of *Oikonomia* that could permit a discussion without dangerous divisive consequences. Unfortunately, this action postponed a major and much needed internal Orthodox debate about the limits of the Church and the ecclesiological nature of other Christian churches/communions. However, one may also argue that this decision was wisely taken because the whole issue of recognizing the salvific presence of God's grace in other Christians was placed in the wrong context by invoking *Oikonomia*.

Addressing the same issues, Metropolitan John (Zizioulas) of Pergamon states that Orthodox theology continues to lack a satisfactory solution to the problem of the Church's limits. At the same time, he recognizes that the acknowledgement of the operation of God's spirit in other Christian churches cannot be affirmed at the expense of the importance of the canonical limits of the Church which, in his view, are "important but not absolute." The Church's canonical limits should not be conceived as fences or division, but as ways of relating the local Church to the rest of the world. They are primarily constituted by baptism. If baptism constitutes the boundaries of the Church, can we assume that salvation is granted only to the baptized Christians who have become ecclesial beings or is salvation (participation in God's life) extended through the Church to all human beings who live a life of openness towards God and relate in love with all creation and human beings? The cosmic dimension of the Eucharist by which creation - through Christ and God's Spirit - participates in God's being can be the basis of recognizing the salvific presence of God in the whole created world. This presence is a reflection of the unceasing work of God's Spirit that moves creation towards its eschatological fulfillment by uniting all in an explicit or hidden manner with the risen Christ.

The Church and the Salvation of the World

The universality of God's love as it is experienced in the Eucharist unites the entire creation with God. In the Eucharist, the Church is disclosed as the visible and effective sign of the coming reign of God, the ark of salvation. Humanity and creation constitute the body of Christ in its wider sense through the recapitulation of all in Christ and the indivisibility of humanity. In this wider sense of the Church's being, the Church is not just

Orthodox Christians but all Christians and people of other living faiths. The salvific presence of God expands beyond the distinct boundaries (Tit. 2: 11) of the Christian community offering salvation to all people of all ages throughout the world. What brings them into unity with God is their openness in desire and intention to live with God as well as their active love for all humanity and creation. None is excluded, in professor Karmires' view, from the gift of salvation that God grants to humanity regardless of the race, language, color, class, age and even of belief. Through Christ's redemptive sacrifice, the whole creation and humanity has been reconciled to God (I John. 2:2, 4:10).

How is it possible for those who do not believe in Jesus Christ to be saved? Does the Holy Spirit operating in the fullness of the world unite humanity and creation including nonbelievers or people of other living faiths with God? If the answer is affirmative, then how does this presence of God's Spirit in history relate to the salvific work of the incarnate Word of God and by extension to the Church?

Orthodox theologians, while they are reluctant to reflect on the exact patterns of God's presence beyond the narrowly defined "sacred space," affirm that God in His benevolence desires and unceasingly works for the salvation of the world. It is the unique ministry of the Holy Spirit to empower all human beings to overcome the limitations of their created nature moving towards unity and relationality. The Holy Spirit either precedes Christ preparing and moving all towards their eschatological fulfillment or follows Christ sustaining and continuing his mission in the world. Yet, how and in what specific ways the Holy Spirit is mystically present to those who live outside of the distinctive boundaries of the Church cannot be fully explained or discerned.

The incomprehensibility of God's active presence in the world beyond the boundaries of the Church is a sign of God's unconditional freedom and providential love. While God is actively present in the Church granting salvation to all who confess Jesus Christ as their Lord and Savior, God does not limit His presence and operation only within the distinctive boundaries of the Church.

St. John Chrysostom provides an example of how God had disclosed Himself to the nations before the incarnation of His Word by giving to the gentiles the natural ethical law and to the Jews the Mosaic Law. Both the natural ethical law and the written Mosaic Law, although they are different, prepared the gentiles and Jews for salvation "κοινά τά τῆς πρόνοιας ἦ, εἰ καὶ διαφόρως." What God had granted to both was of no less value or importance despite their difference. Here we have a disclosure of God's providence for all humanity and an expression of His freedom to act differently in different contexts. God, in His grace and philanthropy, has never ceased to do everything - since the beginning of time until the end - for the salvation of the human race.

The belief that there is salvation outside of the Church seems to contradict the axiom that that there is no salvation outside of the Church. The axiom "*extra Ecclesiam nulla salus*" excludes the possibility that schismatic or heretical communities can be salvific in themselves but it does not preclude the possibility that people in such communities can be saved either through their baptism and/or their righteous life as it is the case for non Christians. Megas Pharantos concludes his study on theology of religions by stating that the Fathers of the Church simultaneously affirm that there is divine grace before the incarnation of the Word and outside of the Church despite their belief that apart from Christ and the Church there in no salvation. The possibility of salvation for religious "others" and nonbelievers, according to Ioannis Karmires, expresses the Christian unshakeable hope and conviction, that God communicates His salvific grace through other unknown to us "incomprehensible ways" to those who live beyond the distinctive boundaries of the Church but possess the natural knowledge of God and faith as well as ethical consciousness. Their salvation originates in God's providence and is achieved through the incomprehensible workings of the Holy Spirit that brings all into unity with the risen Christ.

The recognition of the universal presence of God obliges the churches in their interfaith dialogue to be attentive to the insights, critique, and contributions of others. The Spirit of God may instruct the churches through religious others how to live in a more authentic and loving manner the Gospel of Jesus and how to deepen their unity with God and the world. In the context of the dialogue the churches may also guide the religious others towards a greater openness to God's love and enable them to recognize the fullness of God in

Jesus Christ. Thus, while the Holy Spirit may act in the world through the prayers and witness of the Church, it may also guide the churches, through its presence in communities of livings faiths and ideologies, to understand better how to live more authentically the Gospel and deepen their participation in God's mission for the salvation of the world. This latter possibility is difficult to accept for those who believe that the plenitude of God is actively present only within the distinctive boundaries of the Church, and they often view the world as the realm of darkness and sin.

The Church does not reject whatever is holy and true either in history or in other religious communities because it considers them as rays of the divine truth that enlightens and leads their people to God. The Church completes whatever is incomplete in others. It enhances those elements of faith and life that reflect God's love and will for His Creation. It completes those elements of truth that have their origins in God since Christ's mission is not to "abolish but to complete" (Mat. 5:17). Thus, the Church cannot be indifferent to those who are not Christians because they are also guided by God's Spirit. It is a fundamental belief of the Christian church that all creation is incessantly influenced by the *Dabar*, or Word of God, and by the *Ruah*, God's Spirit. The "two hands" of the Father, the Son and the Spirit, extend and bestow elements of divine truth to all human beings in ways conducive to their salvation. Even if the Church insists that its own preaching contains and promulgates divine truth in the least ambiguous and thus in the most adequate manner, Christians should never cease either to marvel at the spiritual force underlying the universal quest for truth or to invoke the Holy Spirit to rejuvenate the self-transcending impetus of this quest.

The Spirit of God in the World

Christian theologians with few exceptions have not yet sufficiently reflected on the work of the Holy Spirit in the world. The presence of God in secular order, programs of social transformation, public service, politics and other religious or humanistic systems of belief and communities remains an undeveloped aspect of the Christian theology of the Holy Spirit.

Christian theologians in light of the recognition of the universal presence of God's Spirit are discussing the vertical relationship of humanity's religious traditions with the mystery of Jesus Christ. Some of those who advocate the universal salvific presence of God's Spirit in the world view Jesus Christ to be the savior of the Christians but not necessarily the savior of believers of other religious faiths, of the seculars or even of atheists. They disassociate the salvific work of the Spirit from that of Christ. They argue that Christian theology should abandon its christo-centricity in favor either of theo-centricity or pneumato-centricity. On the other hand, some of those who adhere to the belief that *only* those who believe in Jesus Christ are saved resort to christomonism refusing to acknowledge the universal presence of God's Spirit because they considered it as opportunity for some to abandon the unique claims of Church about Jesus Christ. The real flaw with both of these positions is their deficient Trinitarian faith. Those who advocate that there are multiple ways to salvation tend to be pneumatomonists in their theology. Their focus on the Holy Spirit provides them with a universal framework to understand the operation of God in history without attributing any decisive salvific significance to what God has granted to the world through Jesus Christ for those who live outside of the Christian Church. On the other hand, those who believe that salvation is granted only to those who believe in Jesus Christ and have been baptized in His name tend to be christomonists in their theology. They limit the salvific work of Jesus Christ only within the distinctive boundaries of the Christian Church or of their particular confession without any acknowledgment of the universal aspect of the Christian faith by the omnipresence of God's Spirit. Adherence to the christocentricity of the Christian faith must be distinguished from a christomonism that fails to recognize the Trinitarian economy of God and the active participation and cooperation of the Holy Spirit with Christ in God's salvific work. On the other hand, the recognition of the presence of God's Spirit in the world, outside of the distinctive boundaries of the church, must not be disassociated from Christ. Pneumatomonism is not a substitute for Christomonism.

Orthodox Handbook on Ecumenism

God reveals and acts in the world through His Spirit and His Word. Hence, any attempt to limit and monopolize God in terms either solely of Jesus or of the Spirit turns to a binitarianism or unitarianism, which fails to account for the fullness of God's being. Orthodox theology in light of its Trinitarian faith simultaneously rejects exclusivism (christomonism) and pluralism (pneumatomonism or theocentrism) by dialectically relating the universal - through the omnipresence of God's spirit to the entire history of humankind - with the particular of God's self-disclosure in Jesus Christ. Thus, the Christian understanding of God cannot be divorced from the story of Jesus Christ and the universal operation mission of God's Spirit in the world. The Trinitarian faith anchors God's revelation in the particularities of history reaching its climax in Jesus Christ without limiting God to any particularity through the universal active presence of His Spirit in the world. Thus, the particularity of God's revelation in Jesus of Nazareth understood from a Trinitarian perspective cannot be disassociated from the universal presence and operation of God in the world through His Spirit.

The Orthodox Church acknowledges in prayer that the Spirit of God is everywhere present and fills all things. The one "who is everywhere present and fills all things" constantly works for the salvation of every person and the fulfillment and completion of the entire world. "Nothing can restrict the radiance of the Holy Spirit. Wherever we find love, goodness, peace, and the Spirit's other "fruits" (Gal. 5:22) there we discern the signs of its activity." All creation lives and moves and has its being in God (Acts 17:28). The salvific presence and work of that life-giving Spirit is not confined to Jews and Christians. Israel knew Yahweh's liberating work was not confined to its own salvation history. The Spirit of God, then, whom Christians identify as the Spirit of Christ, is persistently seen, in many parts of the Hebrew Scriptures, as the ever-present source, power, and life of all creation. The Spirit is to be found everywhere and amongst all people, giving and sustaining life. The Spirit's work, we may sure, is not for nothing; it is always salvific, creating wholeness and blessing. Of particular interest to us here is that the Spirit gives wisdom. This is an inherent part of Israel's understanding of the universality of God's presence to the whole world. The Wisdom Literature knows that humanity in general is endued with God's wisdom (Job 32:8). The Spirit of understanding is a gift to be sought in prayer. It is "a kindly Spirit" which "fills the world, is all embracing, and knows what a man says" (Wis. 1:5-7).

True human wisdom, we may conclude, is not mere foolishness, but a gift from God. The "wisdom of the world" may indeed be utterly false, but this cannot be said of all human wisdom as such, for all true *hokmah/ sophia* is of God. The "wisdom," the depth and wholeness which we discern in people of other religious traditions and in secular people, cannot be dismissed as idolatrous "wisdom of the world." Nor is it merely our contextual experience that pushes us to say this; as I have argued here, it is inherent in many parts of the biblical testimony that God is present to the whole world to grant wisdom, to bless, guide and shape the life of the whole human family and the whole earth.

In the Greek Patristic tradition, the energies of God's Spirit are active in all creation and history and indeed in all things. Despite the pervasiveness of evil in the fallen world, there is always a progressive force within it for the sanctification of everything and of everyone. The operation of the Holy Spirit in the whole universe and in the Church is incompatible with any personal and/or collective self-sufficiency and isolationism. The Church, as sign of the new creation, discloses the future of humanity and of creation as a community that transcends all its divisions and fragmentation by the power of God's Spirit and lives forever in unity in God's love.

The significance of the universality of the Spirit of God for dialogue lies not in *homo religiosus*. The point is not to establish a natural capacity of human beings to know God and therefore relativize the need for revelation, nor to find in "religion" as such the possibility of salvation. Rather, the truth and wisdom found in the religious "others" or in the "nonreligious" person, must be seen as God's gift. If the Spirit of God, whom Christians also name Spirit of Jesus Christ, is present and at work in all creation and with all people, we must eagerly expect to find truth and wisdom in many places. It is not for nothing that God's Spirit is omnipresent in the world. The presence of the Lord of exodus and resurrection is always for blessing, and for truth. That is why we listen intently to hear what God's wisdom has taught the people of other living faiths. That is why we thank God for the courage and love of justice which we find in many secular social activists; we may find in them too a risky and visionary thrust toward the future which is indeed an authentic "faith" response to the blowing of God's Spirit in history. The freedom of the wind of God to be at work everywhere should allow us to give thanks for signs of the presence of God's reign which often appear more dramatic and authentic in the lives and work of non-Christians than in Christians.

Since the universal Lordship and presence of Christ by the Holy Spirit pertain to the sphere of the world's living faiths as well as the secular sphere, true dialogue is indeed possible for the Christian with both secular and religious people.

Dialogue, however, also involves disagreement and discernment. If dialogue meant negotiated compromise, some dilution of Christian faith, it would in fact negate theology. But in true dialogue, Christians must not only listen but also bear witness. The Muslim, Sikh, or atheist is not interested in so-called "dialogue" with a *former* Christian. The Christian must bear witness to the crucified and risen Christ, in all his scandalous particularity, as Savior of the world. Jesus Christ cannot be reduced to "our Savior" or merely "our way" in some esoteric sense. In dialogue the Christian has something astounding to tell. It belongs not to the Christian, but to the Holy Spirit, already at work in our dialogue partner, to convince or convert.

The contribution of the Eastern Orthodox and Oriental Orthodox Consultation on the theme of the 9th Assembly of the World Council of Churches (1993) entitled "Come, Holy Spirit – Renew the Whole Creation: An Orthodox Approach" articulates premises for understanding the operation of the Holy Spirit in the history of the world. It states that Orthodox theology understands the presence and operation of the Holy Spirit in the world from the perspective of God's economy, which is intrinsically Trinitarian.

What does this recognition of the active presence of God's Spirit in the life of the world mean for the life and witness of the Church? The Orthodox contribution to the Seventh Assembly of WCC, expanding the presence and the operation of the Holy Spirit beyond the interior life of the believers and the sacramental life of the Church, recognizes the Holy Spirit's presence in all human efforts and movements toward the removal of all causes of injustice and oppression. It advocates that those who have been anointed by the Holy Spirit and through its guidance are united with God in Jesus Christ have the responsibility to participate in God's salvific and liberating ministry.

The participation of the Church in movements of social transformation is guided by its vision of what already is and what is becoming because of its identification with Christ by the grace of the Holy Spirit. If its life is "being as communion" then it is its essential mission in the world to be the "extension (and prolongation) of the communion of the Spirit." The identification of God's presence in movements of social transformation is critical since all efforts for human liberation are subject to corruptibility.

Orthodox theologians, here, while they affirm the universal presence of God's Spirit in religious and secular movements of social transformation and sustenance, note that these religious and secular movements cannot be fully identified with God's cause and actions because of their corruptibility cause by the pervasive presence of evil in them. Thus, it is crucial to reflect on how, for instance, the Spirit of God inspired and guided in positive and negative terms Buddha, Mohammed, Gandhi, Marx and others. The report has opted to identify the presence of God's Spirit in the religious and secular others not in conceptual terms that refer to their cognitive irreducible differences. It rather chose to affirm the universal operation and presence of God's Spirit through an existential language that points to its meaning in terms of life, communion, transcendence, and transformation in contrast to death, chaos and fragmentation.

While the Orthodox Church has a profound understanding of the active presence of God's Spirit in creation and in history, Orthodox theologians, perhaps for historical reasons, have limited the operation of God's Spirit within the sacred space of the Church and in the inner life of its members. They are reluctant to reflect on the concrete patterns of the salvific and transformative presence of God in the world.

Conclusions

The Orthodox churches in their contribution to the pneumatological theme of the Seventh Assembly of the World Council of Churches have recognized the active presence of God's Spirit in the world beyond the boundaries of the Church. Its presence in the world is not separate from Christ's, since both, in their distinctive but interdependent missions, disclose the active love of God the Father. The report while it recognized that the fullness of God's love for the world is revealed and experience in the Church, acknowledges that the Holy Spirit is working in the world for the unity of all and their participation in God's Kingdom. From a Trinitarian perspective, we assume that wherever and whenever we discern the operating presence of God's Spirit in aspects of the world's life, Christ is actively present in these situations in a hidden form and manner. Those who live the Christian pattern of life, openness to God and embrace in an active love all human beings even though they may not explicitly confess Jesus Christ, as their Lord and Savior, are not far from God.

Angeliki Ziaka

This paper will focus on the historic, ecclesiastic, and academic rapprochements between Orthodox Christianity and Islam from the 8th century until today. I will present a diachronic overview of the dialogue, controversies, and polemics between the two religious worlds, organized along three main axes: 1) by sketching the historical context and the theological terms with which the Eastern Roman (Byzantine) world met and tried to interpret and classify Islam; 2) by outlining the ambivalent relations between subjugate Orthodoxy and victorious Islam during the long Ottoman period, which lasted for many centuries, even up to the beginning of the 20th century, in South-East Europe; and 3) by discussing the agenda of an academic and ecclesiastic dialogue which hopes to foster mutual understanding with the Muslim world. I will employ historical, theological, as well as societal approaches to the issue, utilizing a European—and particularly Greek—bibliography.

Byzantium and Islam

The Orthodox Church's encounter with Islam begins with the latter's infancy in the East. Communication and dialogue with Islam, therefore, have always been vital to the Orthodox Church. Orthodox and Muslims have lived together in the East for fifteen centuries now. Great Fathers of the Church, such as John of Damascus (+749), *On Heresies* (*De Haeresibus*, PG 94, 764A-773A) and *Conversation Between a Saracen and a Christian* (*Disputatio Saraceni e Christiani*, PG 94, 1585-1596V and 96, 1336V-1348V) and Theodore Abû Qurra (+825), *Against the Heresies of the Jews and the Saracens* (*Contra Haereticos, Judaeos et Saracenos, Varia Opuscula*, PG 97, 1461A-1601B), were the first to engage with Islam and wrote dialogues—fabricated, of course—which demonstrate familiarity with Muslim teachings as they attempt to overturn them using Christian teachings.[1]

Shortly thereafter, the Byzantine Empire experienced a long period of controversy and polemic against Islamic literature, which, despite its acridity, created the conditions for knowledge of the Islamic world. Thus, the second phase of the Orthodox Church's and Byzantine Empire's engagement with Islam began around the middle of the 9th century and lasted until the end of the 14th century. The epicenter of this anti-Islamic literature was thenceforth Constantinople, the seat of the Byzantine Empire, and not, as in the previous phase, Damascus, the great Hellenistic center of learning and the arts, which became the first capital of the Islamic Caliphate of the Umayyads (661-750). During this period, many polemical texts against Islam

---

[1] The majority of the apologetic writings have been published in *Patrologia Graeca*, ed. and translated in Latin by J. P. Migne (*PG*); among the most important Greek and European works on this Byzantine literature are: C. H. Becker, "Christliche Polemik und islamische Dogmenbildun," *Islamstudien* I (Leipzig, 1912), 432-449. C. Güterbock, *Der Islam im Lichte der byzantinischen Polemic*, (Berlin, 1912), W. Eichner, « Die Nachrichten über den Islam bei den Byzantinern », *Der Islam* 23 (1936), 133-162 and 197-244, H.-G. Beck, *Kirche und theologische Literatur im byzantinischen Reich*, (Munich, 1959), E. D. Sdrakas, *Η κατά του Ισλάμ πολεμική των Βυζαντινών Θεολόγων (Byzantine's Polemic Theology against Islam)*, (Thessaloniki, 1961) (in Greek), G. C. Anawati, "Polémique, apologie et dialogue Islamo-Chrétiens. Positions classiques médiévales et positions contemporaines », *Euntes Docete* 22 (1969: Miscellanea in Honorem Card. Greg. P. Agagianian): 375-451. A. D. Karpozilos, "Byzantine Apologetic and Polemic Writings of the Paleologian Epoch against Islam," *Greek Orthodox Theological Review* 15 (1970): 213-248. A. Th. Khoury, *Les théologiens byzantins et l'Islam. Textes et Auteurs (VIIIᵉ-XIIIᵉ s.)*, (Nauwelaerts, Louvain-Paris, 1969), Idem, *Polémique byzantine contre l'Islam (VIIIᵉ-XIIIᵉ s.)*, (Leiden, ²1972), Idem, *Apologétique byzantine contre l'Islam (VIIIᵉ-XIIIᵉ s.)*, (Studien 1), (Altenberge, 1982), Idem, *Der theologische Streit der Byzantiner mit dem Islam*, (F. Schöningh, Paderborn, 1969).

were written in Greek, which were later edited and translated into Latin by J.P. Migne, the most significant of which were: Bishop Samonas of Gaza, *Conversation with Ahmed the Saracen* (*Disputatio cum Achmed Saraceno* PG 120, 821-832), Euthymius Zigabenus, *Dogmatic Armor* (*Panoplia Dogmatica*, § 28, PG 130, 1332D-1360D), Nicetas Choniates, *Treasure of Orthodoxy* (*Thesaurus Orthodoxae Fidei*, § 20, PG 140, 105A-121C), Bartholomeus of Edessa, *Refutation of the Hagarene* (*Elenchus et Confutatio Agareni*, PG 104, 1384A-1448), et al. Of particular importance is the work of Nicetas of Byzantium, *Refutation of the Book Forged by Muhammad the Arab* (*Confutatio falsi libri quem scripsit Mohamedes Arabs*, PG 105, 669A-805D). The text is, of course, polemical; Nicetas, however, undertakes a serious analysis and review of a large part of the Qur'an. This represented, at the end of the 9th century, the first attempt by Christians to translate the Qur'an into Greek, while the first Latin translation did not appear until 1141, by order of Peter Venerabilis, abbot of the Benedictine abbey of Cluny, under the title *The Religion of Muhammad the Pseudo-prophet* (*Lex Mahumet pseudoprophete*).[2]

The third stage of engagement with Islam began in the middle of the 14th century and ended with the overthrow of the Byzantine Empire in 1453. This phase is the most important because it was a period during which an attempt was made to better understand Islam and to effectively communicate and dialogue with it. That is why the works written during this period are distinguished for their moderate tone and—relatively speaking—objectivity. The most important figures during this period, who promoted communication between the two religious traditions, were the emperors Ioannis VI Cantacuzenus (1292-1383), *Four Apologies Against the Muslim Sect* (*Contra Sectam Mahometicam Apologiae IV*, PG 154, 372A -584A and *Contra Mahometem Orationes Quatuor*, PG 154, 584B-692C), and Manuel II Paleologus (1348-1425), *Dialogues Held With A Certain Persian, the Worthy Mouterizes, in Ankara of Galatia*, as well as the great theologians of the late Byzantine era, Gregory Palamas (1296-1359), *Letter to His Own Church in Thessaloniki*, b) *Letter to Anonymous "When Conquered"*, c) *Discourse with the Atheist Chionas*,[3] and the monk Joseph Vryenius (1350-1432).[4]

Orthodoxy and Islam during the Ottoman Period

Immediately after the fall of Constantinople on 29 May 1453, the enslaved Christians of the former Eastern Roman (Byzantine) Empire turned their hopes to God and hoped for divine intervention. During this period of the Ottoman Empire (15th-19th C.), a remarkable literature developed in the Greek language about Islam, with varied content: at first, an attempt at convergence and Greek-Turkish rapprochement and cooperation, followed

---

[2] On the knowledge of the Qur'an in Latin Christendom and the first Latin translation of the Qur'an by Robert of Ketton, a member of Peter's translation team, see Thomas E. Burman, *Reading the Qur'ân in Latin Christendom,* 1140-1560,(Philadelphia, 2009), 10, 15-16.

[3] Gregory Palamas' works were not published in PG. See the critical edition of these works by Anna Philippidis-Braat, "La captivité de Palamas chez les Turcs: dossier et commentaires", *Travaux et Mémoires* 7 (Paris 1979): 109-222. A second important edition has been done by professor P. K. Christou, Γρηγορίου τοῦ Παλαμᾶ, Συγγράμματα Δ΄, (Thessaloniki, 1986), 109-165. See also older editions: A. Sakellionos, Γρηγορίου τοῦ Παλαμᾶ, "Πρός τούς ἀθέους Χιόνας διάλεξις, συγγραφεῖσα παρὰ ἰατροῦ τοῦ Ταρωνείτου, παρόντος καὶ αὐτηκόου γεγονότος", *Soter* 15 (1892): 240-246. K. I. Dyovouniotis, "Ἐπιστολή, ἣν ἐξ Ἀσίας, αἰχμάλωτος ὤν, πρὸς τὴν ἑαυτοῦ Ἐκκλησίαν ἀπέστειλε", in Spryrou Lambrou, *NE* 16 (1922): 7-21. This edition was published by the "PI Κατάλοιπο τοῦ Σπύρου Λάμπρου". See also G. Georgiades-Arnakis, "Gregory Palamas among the Turks and Documents of his captivity as historical sources" *Speculum* 26 (1951): 104-118 and "Gregory Palamas, The Χιόνες and the Fall of Callipoli", *Byzantion* 22 (1952-53): 305-310.

[4] For a systematic presentation of the Byzantine literature on Islam, see my doctoral dissertation entitled *La recherche Grecque Contemporaine et l'Islam*, PhD, Université Marc Bloch de Strasbourg, 2002 (Lille: ANRT, 2004), 15-105; see also the augmented Greek edition *Μεταξύ Πολεμικής και Διαλόγου. Το Ισλάμ στη Βυζαντινή, Μεταβυζαντινή και Νεότερη ελληνική γραμματεία* (Between Polemics and Dialogue: Islam in Byzantine, Post-Byzantine and Modern Greek Literature, (Thessaloniki, 2010) (in Greek).

by polemics against the Ottoman Empire and Islam, and finally an apocalyptic literature, which comforted the Christians, prevented their Islamization, and looked forward to the end of Islam. A period of silence and endurance then began for the Christians of the former Christian empire. Of course, they were intimately familiar with Islam, but only in terms of subservience, under the domination of the Ottoman Empire, and according to the special status of Islamic subjugation (*dhimma* = protection). Nevertheless, there were always voices of reason and reconciliation, and from the very first years of the Ottoman Empire, to develop a dialogue and promote mutual understanding with Ottoman Islam. The pioneers of this new Christian attitude towards Islam were the very influential Patriarch George Scholarios (Gennadios II),[5] and the diplomat George Amiroutzes.[6] Their great difference from George of Trebizond, who also had a conciliatory demeanour towards Islam, was that after the fall of Constantinople they continued to live in the 'Dār al-Islam', the territory of the Ottoman Empire, and did not flee to the West.

The dire situation in which the Christianity of the former Eastern Roman Empire found itself was far from simple; Christians themselves were initially divided on how to react to this subjugation to the Ottoman Muslims, or the Mahometans, Agarins, Saracens, or Ismaelis, as they are referred to in the Byzantine sources. Some looked to the West for help, while others were firmly opposed to anything western or papal. One unfortunate consequence was the flight of Greek scholars to the West, which meant, on the one hand, the intellectual bankruptcy of the enslaved people, and, on the other, the intellectual enrichment of the West and the Western academia. Some of the church leaders, and the few intellectuals who remained after the conquest of Constantinople and the major centers of the East, accused the ruling class of scholars of abandoning their country, leaving it in darkness and ignorance, and securing for themselves a safe haven in the West. However, those scholars who sought refuge in Europe helped cultivate literature and the European Renaissance, and acted as ambassadors for the Greeks and the Christians of the East, often imploring the rulers of Europe to organize crusades against the Ottoman Empire in order to liberate the Christians from Islam. Scholars played a particularly important role in the conflict between the Islamic and Christian worlds during the 15th and 16th century. Figures such as Plethon Gemistos from Mystra, Manuel Chrysoloras, Cardinal John Bessarion, Janus Lascaris, Michael and Marcus Moussouros, Michael Apostolis, as well as Gazis and Kallistos Chalkokondilis were dedicated to ancient Greek beauty and conveying its light to the West. Being gripped by a spirit of unity between the two Churches, they fought against Ottoman rule and Islam, imploring the West for help. Many of them—in fact, the most eminent among them—believed that the growing Ottoman expansionism could be curtailed by sending the Christian forces of the West to aid the Christian populations in Greece and the Balkan Peninsula.

Of the many expatriate scholars from the period of Ottoman rule, who taught Greek in the West and became ambassadors to European countries for their enslaved compatriots, there are few who dealt specifically with Islam or the relations between Christians and Muslims in the Ottoman Empire. One of the first, just decades after the Fall of Constantinople, was George of Trebizond (1396-1484), who was born in Heraklion, Crete, although he descended from Trebizond. He studied in Italy and taught Greek in Venice, Rome, and Naples.

---

[5] Louis Petit - X. A. Sideridès - Martin Jugie (eds.), *Œuvres Complètes de Georges (Gennade) Scholarios*, 8 vols, (Paris, 1928-1936), vol 3, 434-475.

[6] Amiroutzes' work *Dialogue on Faith in Christ* was based on conversations that he had with the sultan himself. The Greek prototype of this text is lost, but has been preserved in a Latin translation from 1518 in the codex Bibliothèque nationale de France, MS Latinus, 3395, fol. 83-144, under the title *Dialogue on faith in Christ held with the King of Turks* (*Dialogus de fide in Christum habitus cum rege Turcarum*). Asterios Argyriou and Georges Lagarrigue published the full text of the MS Latinus, 3395, accompanied by a French translation; "Georges Amiroutzès et son *Dialogue sur la foi au Christ tenu avec le sultan des Turcs*", in *Byzantinische Forschungen*, 11, (Amsterdam, 1987). See also Oscar de la Cruz Palma, *Jorge Ameruzes de Trebisonda. El diálogo de la fe con el sultán de los turcos* (ed. crítica, traducción, estudio e índices), Colección "Nueva Roma" n. 9, (CSIC-UAB, Madrid, 2000), John Monfasani, 'The "Lost" final Part of George Amiroutzes Dialogus de Fide in Christum and Zanobi Acciaiuoli', in Christopher S. Celenza and Kenneth Gouwens, eds., *Humanism and Creativity in the Renaissance*, Essays in Honor of Ronald G. Witt, (Leiden 2006), 197-229.

He also served as a librarian in the Vatican Library. He wrote many works, the most notable for our purposes here being *On the Truth of the Christian Faith*, which attempted to bridge the differences between Christians and Muslims and create a climate of Greek-Turkish understanding.[7] He viewed Mehmed's rule as the historical continuation of the Roman Empire and thus understood that the sultan was called to restore the unity of the people in "one body," recreating the *pax romana*.[8]

Another very interesting form that developed during the period of Ottoman rule was that of apocalyptic and eschatological literature, which interpreted the reasons for Islam's ascension, foretold the end of Muslim power, and proclaimed the ultimate triumph of Christianity. The literature consists of legends, oracles, and prophecies, which speak about the revival of the Greek Christian empire, and includes interpretations of the Revelation of John, which had far-reaching political and social implications. This was the most popular form of literature during the Ottoman period, being directed against Islam and seeking to preserve the faith of the people and to nourish utopian discourse and hope for future salvation.[9]

The various oracles and prophecies spread not only among Greek Christians, but also to many Christian peoples in Europe and especially Russia. Thus was created the legend of a liberating "blond race." Original-ly, the "blond race" was thought to be the Franks and the Latins in general. But beginning in the early 16th century, the "blond race" became identified with the Russians. This was no doubt inspired by the marriage of Sophia-Zoe Palaiologina, niece of Constantine Palaiologus, to Ivan III (the Great). This symbolized that Russia was the heir and successor of the Byzantine Empire. As early as 1492, Metropolitan Zosimus of Moscow named Ivan III "the new Tsar Constantine of the new Constantinople—Moscow." The enslaved Greeks could not, of course, foresee the subsequent political and ecclesiastical implications of this theory, and pinned their hopes for liberation on this "blond race," without, however, abandoning the original idea of turning to the great powers of Europe. Later, when both proved fruitless, they realized the value of relying on their own forces.[10]

The literary genre of apocalyptic and eschatological literature that developed during the Ottoman Empire was predominantly apologetic and polemic, turning openly against Islam. Many such apocalyptic works were written between 1453 and 1825. The main body of work began with the translation *The Revelation of John the Theologian and Evangelist into Vernacular Greek by Maximos the Peloponnesian* around 1600, and continued with an assortment of interpretations of the Revelation of John, the most characteristic being those by George Koressios (1645), Gordios (1717), Pantazes from Larissa (1767) and Cyril Lavriotis (1825).[11]

This hermeneutical and eschatological literature was not only religious, but also had political and social ramifications. It sought: a) to comfort and encourage the Orthodox Christian world during its slavery to Mus-lims, b) to provide the necessary moral, spiritual, and theological means by which the Church and its people

---

[7] A special edition on this work has been made by G. Th. Zoras, *Γεώργιος Τραπεζούντιος και αι προς ελληνοτουρκικήν συνεννόησιν προσπάθειαι αυτού [George of Trapezond and His Efforts at Greek-Turkish Rapprochement]*, (Athens, 1954) (in Greek). See also John Monfasani, *George of Trebizond: a Biography and a Study of his Rhetoric and Logic*, (Leiden, 1976), 3-237. According to Monfasani, George's approach to Islam must be considered not only within its political context but also in light of his apocalyptic views.

[8] G. Th. Zoras, *Γεώργιος Τραπεζούντιος και αι προς ελληνοτουρκικήν συνεννόησιν προσπάθειαι αυτού*, 95.

[9] The research pioneer in this field is Asterios Argyriou; among his many writings, of particular note are: *«Sur Mahomet et contre les Latins», un Traité inédit d'Anastassios Gordios (1656-1729), religieux et Professeur grec*. Ed. critique du texte grec, accompagné d'une traduction française, d'une introduction et de notes (thèse pour le doctorat de troisième cycle) (Strasbourg, 1967), 2 vol., 122+438 pages ronéotypées; «Anastassios Gordios et l'Islam», Strasbourg, *RSR* 43 (1969): 58-87 ; *Les Exégèses grecques de l'Apocalypse à l'époque turque (1453-1821). Equisse d'une histoire des courants idéologiques au sein du peuple grec asservi*, Doctorat d'Etat ès Lettres, vols. II, Strasbourg, 1977 ; *Macaire Macrès et la polèmique contre l'Islam. Edition critique de cinq œuvres anti-islamiques inédites de Macaire Makrès ainsi que d'un « Eloge à Macaire » de la même époque (XVe s.) également inédit, accompagnée d'une longue introduction sur les questions soulevées par les textes*. Studi e Testi, 314, (Vatican, 1986), 346 pages.

[10] Angeliki Ziaka, *La Recherche Grecque contemporaine et l'Islam*, 148-152 and 208-211.

[11] Ibid, 148-211.

Part VII: Particular Themes and Issues for Orthodox Involvement in Ecumenism

could become grounded in the Orthodox faith and meet the challenges of Islam (which is why these were also apologetic texts aimed against Islam), c) to tackle, religiously, the vaunted problem of theodicy and explain, with various rationalizations, the meaning of the subjugation of the Orthodox Christians to the power of Islam, d) to define, according to the biblical conception of history, the age in which humanity was living, i.e., whether it was living in the eschatological age which leads to the end of the world, or the age leading to the triumph of Christ and his "thousand-year reign," which, according to the dominant view of the time, would precede the world's end, e) to describe, in light of the eschatological images contained in the book of Revelation, the Antichrist, who is identified with Islam and the person of Muhammad, and to determine when the reign of the Antichrist started and when it would end, and finally f) to reinvigorate Christians' minds, endurance, and hope for future freedom.

The combination of this kind of history with theology, and the human need to interpret history and the future of humankind through predictions and prophecies from the past, is well known throughout the Christian world, and over time crept into the Islamic world as well, giving rise to numerous myths, beliefs, and expectations.[12] The humans of every era dress their fears and concerns with eschatological images and await, under these symbols, a better future. In times of war and adverse social situations, they interpret the images as eschatological prophecies that foretell the punishment of believers for their apostasy, as well as their future redemption.

Orthodoxy and Islam in Modern and Postmodern Times

The aforementioned are some of the key aspects of the life of Greek Orthodox Christians during the period of Ottoman Empire, and their struggle for the survival of their religion, languages, and traditions. With the gradual decline of the Ottoman Empire, much of the Orthodox world of the Balkan Peninsula achieved independence, both politically and religiously, while another part of the Christianity of the East remained largely under Islamic control. Interest in Islam gradually developed among the Orthodox peoples of South-Eastern Europe. Among Greek historians and scholars, particular interest in Islam first developed at the end of the 19th and beginning of the 20th century, especially regarding Greek-Turkish relations, primarily those during the period of Ottoman rule and the Byzantine period. An independent field of Islamic Studies, an objective and impartial inquiry into the principles of Islam, began after 1960 in the Theological Schools in both Thessaloniki and Athens. In the Department of Theology at Aristotle University of Thessaloniki in particular, scholars investigated virtually all aspects of Islam, including early Islamic times and the spread of Islam, the relationship with biblical teaching, the various schools of Muslim theology (*Kalam*) and Islamic law (*Shari'ah*), Islamic mysticism, the transmission of Greek literature and Aristotelian philosophy from the 8th AD century onwards to the Islamic world, as well as the newer and modern reformist trends and the various manifestations of political Islam.[13] The contemporary religious studies approach to Islam focuses more on specific aspects of Islam, such as Shi'a Islam, the early sectarian movements, such as the Alides, Kharijites, Ibadites, etc., Islamic Messianism and its political ramifications, and the Byzantine and post-Byzantine polemical and apologetic literature against Islam.[14]

---

[12] On Messianic ideas in early Islam, see Angeliki Ziaka, "Μεσσιανικές προσδοκίες στο σιιτικό Ισλάμ" ("Messianic Expectations in Shi'a Islam"), Stavros Zoumpoulakis (ed.), *Η Μεσσιανική Ιδέα και οι Μεταμορφώσεις της (The Messianic Idea and its Transformations),* (Athens: Artos Zois, 2011), 211-236 (in Greek).

[13] The pioneers in this field are Archbishop Anastasios Yannoulatos and Professor Grigorios Ziakas, with numerous publications and lectures on Islam, interreligious dialogue, and the major world religions in general.

[14] See my aforementioned works on footnotes 12 and 13. See also my works on *Shi'a Islam. Its political and Social Dimensions in the Middle East* (Thessaloniki 2004); *Apocalyptical and Messianic Movements in Islam. Mahdi the Eschatological Savior* (London, 2012); *Interreligious Dialogues: The meeting of Christianity with Islam* (Thessaloniki, 2010), all written in Greek. See also the doctoral dissertation of Michalis Marioras, on *Shari'a, Το Ισλαμικό Νομικό Σύστημα (Shari'a. The Islamic Legal System)*, (Athens, 2005) (in Greek, unpublished).

The Ecumenical Patriarchate and Inter-Religious Overtures and Dialogues

The Orthodox Churches of the East thus carry out a substantial and necessary dialogue with Islam based on current academic research and their experience of living with Islam. Specifically, the Ecumenical Patriarchate of Constantinople and the ancient Patriarchates of Alexandria, Antioch, and Jerusalem all live and converse with both the Muslim world of the East, as well as with other Christian Churches and Judaism. For the Orthodox, the basis of modern dialogue is both the conciliar encyclicals of the Ecumenical Patriarchate of Constantinople, those of 1902 and 1904, in which then-Patriarch Joachim III invited the metropolitans and bishops of the territory of the Ecumenical Throne to intensify their efforts at dialogue and interdenominational communication, and to work toward the closer unity of the Orthodox Churches. Those encyclical letters are some of the key texts in the history of the ecumenical movement. The Ecumenical Patriarchate's initiatives are crucial not only for the unity of the Christian churches but the whole world. The aforementioned patriarchal documents, as well as the encyclical of 1920, express the "Mother Church's" anguish for the breakdown amongst the churches and throughout the world.

The Ecumenical Patriarchate's first major overtures to other religions were the First Pan-Orthodox Conference in Rhodes, 1961, and the First Pre-Conciliar Pan-Orthodox Conference held at the Orthodox Center of the Ecumenical Patriarchate in Chambésy in 1976, in which the Church clearly decided to work toward interreligious understanding and cooperation through the elimination of fanaticism on all sides, reconciliation among peoples, and the promotion of the ideals of freedom and peace in the world, all in the service of contemporary humankind, irrespective of race or religion.

Today this dialogue is championed by the Ecumenical Patriarchate, which regards it as essential. Following firmly in the footsteps of its past, the Patriarchate offers itself and its centuries of knowledge in matters of coexistence to open a new and modern dialogue with the religions of the world, and especially with the two other Abrahamic religions, Judaism and Islam.

The dialogue with Judaism began in 1976 and was followed, in 1986, by the dialogue with Islam. The late Metropolitan Damaskinos of Switzerland (and later Adrianople), in describing his experience of interreligious dialogue with Judaism and Islam, noted that the Orthodox Center of the Ecumenical Patriarchate's initiatives in organizing academic meetings with both Judaism and Islam reflect the Ecumenical Patriarchate's broader disposition toward Orthodoxy's positive contribution to the peaceful coexistence of the faithful of the three religions who live in the same geographical area and face common challenges.[15]

Orthodoxy and Judaism

The academic series of meetings between Orthodoxy and Judaism has focused on the biblical tradition and the sources of the two religions as a common commitment to defend peace and justice in the world. The Ecumenical Patriarchate—through its representatives, both priests and academics—has engaged in dialogue on these issues with the International Jewish Committee, the Jewish community of Romania, the World Jewish Council of Jerusalem and the International Jewish Committee for Interreligious Consultations in New York. Metropolitan Emmanuel of France, who is in charge of interreligious dialogue and the Office of the Ecumenical Patriarchate at the E.U., has characterized the meetings as a waypoint in the continuation of the dialogue between the two religious traditions and in the understanding of the common values not only in the past but also in the modern reality of the multiple ideological, spiritual, and social confusions and divisions of the world. "The Spiritual and Physical Environment: Respecting Our World, Respecting One Another," marked the eighth such conference between Christian Orthodoxy and Judaism in the city of Thessaloniki in June 2013.

---

[15] Bishop Damaskinos Papandreou, (+2010) "The Interreligious Dialogues of the Orthodox Church", *Ο Διάλογος Χριστιανισμού-Ισλάμ ως κοινό Καθήκον* (Christian-Muslim Dialogue like a Commun Duty), M. Konstantinou-A. Stirnemann (eds.), (Thessaloniki: Paratiritis, 1998), 31-51, 35.

Orthodoxy and Islam

A prominent place has been occupied by the dialogue between Christians and Muslims, which has been promoted by the Ecumenical Patriarchate and the Theological Schools in Greece. Under the aegis of the Ecumenical Patriarchate since their inception in 1986, these meetings were led by the late Metropolitan Damaskinos of Switzerland until 1998. Damaskinos was the heart and soul of the interreligious dialogue with Islam, supported primarily by Prince Hassan of Jordan. For many years, the two worked together toward mutual understanding and peaceful coexistence between Muslims and Christians. The Muslim world of the Middle East, in any event, has always felt a close proximity and historical affinity with Orthodoxy. The Ecumenical Patriarchate's interreligious initiatives continue today under the leadership of Metropolitan Emmanuel of France. There were eleven meetings between 1986-2008, which covered a wide variety of issues: *authority and religion in the traditions of the two religions; models of historical coexistence between Muslims and Christians and shared humanistic ideals; the concept of peace in the traditions of the two monotheistic religions; the problem of religious pluralism and its limits in Islam and Christianity; young people and the value of moderation; the importance of education for understanding and cooperation between the two religious traditions; the educational system in Islam and Christianity; the prospects for cooperation between Christians and Muslims in the third millennium; the role of Muslims and Christians in modern society; the image of the Other and the meaning of equality before the law; the role of religion in peaceful coexistence in modern society;* and, finally, *the ability to build up interreligious dialogue to ensure joint training opportunities for young religious leaders, priests, imams, theologians, and students of the respective Muslim and Orthodox Christian communities.* Such initiatives encourage the participation of intellectuals and young religious leaders in dialogues and therefore in the process of mutual interreligious understanding and rapprochement between religious and cultural communities, facilitating dialogues and interreligious partnerships and allowing participants to act locally as well as ecumenically, contributing thus to mutual understanding and the advancement of reconciliation.

The Ecumenical Patriarchate also organizes or participates in conferences at local, regional, and global conferences related to religious, humanitarian, social, and ecological issues.[16]

The Department of Theology of Aristotle University of Thessaloniki and the Dialogues with Islam

Parallel to the aforementioned activities of the Churches are the important initiatives undertaken by the Department of Theology at Aristotle University of Thessaloniki, which has attributed great significance to the study of world religions and continues to promote dialogue with other religions, especially Islam.

In order to facilitate a better understanding of the ancient, historical, spiritual, and academic links between Greek and Arab-Islamic thinking, and thus between the Eastern Christians and Islamic traditions, the *Society for Greek-Arabic Studies* was founded in June 1980 in Thessaloniki. It publishes the journal *Graeco-Arabica*, and has organized a series of international conferences to advance the study of the Greek-Arabic sources and to promote research and communication between the Greek and Arab-Islamic world.

The *Orthodoxy and Islam* movement began in 1990, which seeks to bring together the Greek Orthodox and Iranian Shi'i worlds. This was extremely significant, since it represented the first time, since the Islamic revolution of 1979, that the Islamic Republic of Iran made an overture toward the "West," choosing—it should be noted—Greece and Orthodoxy. This movement organized four remarkable and productive academic conferences, of which the first two and the fourth were hosted in Athens (1990, 1992, and 1997), and the third in Tehran (1994).

---

[16] For a detailed account of the Ecumenical Patriarchate's activities and dialogues with Islam, see the study by Grigorios Ziakas, «Το Οικουμενικό Πατριαρχείο και ο Διάλογος με το Ισλάμ» (The Ecumenical Patriarchate and the Dialogue with Islam"), *Φανάρι 400 χρόνια (Fanari 400 years)*, (Εκδόσεις Οικουμενικου Πατριαρχείου (Ecumenical Patriarchate Publication), 2001). Re-edition under the title *Interreligious Dialogues*, v. I., (Thessaloniki: Pournaras, 2010) (in Greek).

The Department of Theology of the Theological Faculty of Thessaloniki has also hosted numerous occasional workshops and lectures related to the interreligious dialogue and relations between Christians and Muslims. In this framework, a workshop was organized in September 1993 on *Islamic Studies in Greece and Islam's Place in Greek Public School Textbooks*, which was attended by professors from the University of Cologne, professors of the Theological Faculty of Thessaloniki, and teachers of religion in the secondary school system of Northern Greece and Thessaly. The proceedings of the conference were published a few years later.[17]

On 15 May 1995, Thessaloniki hosted *Islam in Greece: Meeting with the Evangelical Church of Germany's Representatives for Islam (KEK)*, in which members of the evangelical delegation were guided by professors from the Faculty of Theology of Aristotle University to what was then the *Special Pedagogical Academy of Thessaloniki* for the education of Muslims, as well as the Theological School. This was then followed by a tour of the Islamic foundations and a meeting with representatives of the Muslim community of Thrace.[18]

In November 2009, the Section on Biblical Literature and Religious Studies of Thessaloniki's Department of Theology organized a major international conference on *Ibadism, Ibadi Studies, and the Sultanate of Oman*, which was headlined by the most respected professors in the Western world for research on the Middle East and Islam, as well as by prominent Muslim academics. Interdisciplinary relations with the Sultanate of Oman have continued with a bilateral academic agreement between the Department of Theology of Aristotle University, led by the present author, and the Institute for Islamic Law in the Sultanate of Oman (http://ibadhism-conference. web.auth.gr/). Within this framework, the academic head for the Sultanate of Oman, Dr. Abdulrahman al-Salimi, delivered a lecture at the Department of Theology on 29 March 2012, entitled, "Christians and Muslims and the Issue of the Middle East."

University professors have also participated in conferences pertaining to interreligious dialogue, and the Department of Theology of the Theological Faculty of Aristotle University of Thessaloniki is particularly well known for its interest in interreligious dialogue, including it in a related course, which is divided into two sections a) mission and ecumenical dialogue, and b) interreligious dialogue. The Department of Theology has been the pioneer in promoting knowledge of—as well as communication and dialogue with—Islam within the Greek educational and theological milieu since the 1970s.[19]

In the Theological Faculty of Athens, interreligious dialogue was promoted by Anastasios Yannoulatos, Professor of Religious Studies and now Archbishop of the Orthodox Church of Albania. His rich life and work has sprung not so much from the Theological Faculty itself as from his missionary work in Africa (with the blessing of the Patriarchate of Alexandria), his multifaceted involvement in the inter-Orthodox, inter-Christian, and interreligious dialogues of the World Council of Churches (WCC), and his monumental work in Albania, where, in exceedingly difficult historical times, he helped resurrect the local Church, which now plays a leading role in fostering a peaceful coexistence between Christians and Muslims. His work there is complemented by his enormous academic contributions and publications, which cover important aspects of the interreligious dialogue.

---

[17] "Το Ισλάμ στα σχολικά εγχειρίδια της Ελλάδος. Μια προσέγγιση στο διάλογο φιλίας Χριστιανισμού και Ισλάμ", in N. Zacharopoulos and Gr. Ziakas (eds.), *Επιστημονική Επετηρίς Θεολογικής Σχολής Αριστοτελείου Πανεπιστημίου Θεσσαλονίκης*, Annexe n° 2, vol. 2, 1991-1992, (Thessaloniki 1996), 149-191 (in Greek).

[18] On the dialogues between Aristotle University's Dept. of Theology and Muslims representatives from various countries and institutions, see the aforementioned works by Grigorios Ziakas, *Θρησκειολογικά Μελετήματα. Ζώντας αρμονικά με ανθρώπους διαφορετικής πίστης (Studies on Religions); Interreligious Dialogues*, v. I., (Thessaloniki: Pournaras, 2010) (in Greek).

[19] Professor Petros Vassiliadis inaugurated missionary studies from an Orthodox perspective and has served for many years as a representative of Thessaloniki's Dept. of Theology, the Church of Greece, as well the Ecumenical Patriarchate of Constantinople, in many ecumenical initiatives, such as the WCC. Among his numerous works, see particularly: "Reconciliation as a Pneumatological Mission Paradigm: Some Preliminary Reflections by an Orthodox", *International Review of Mission* 94.372 (January 2005): 30-42; *Ενότητα και Μαρτυρία (Unity and Witness)*, (Thessaloniki: Epikentro, 2007) (in Greek).

Part VII: Particular Themes and Issues for Orthodox Involvement in Ecumenism

The Challenges and Difficulties of the Interreligious Dialogues

A basic prerequisite for conducting a peaceful and constructive dialogue with the religious "other" is good will. The primary goal of interreligious dialogue is the understanding of this "other," based on the conviction that, through their diversity, people, religions, and universal values can come together on a common point, which is, first and foremost, respect for the human person and creation. And while the interreligious dialogue from the 1970s through the 1990s was primarily theoretical and academic, concerning the sources and principles of each religion—in order to better understand the beliefs and the person of the religious "other"—, there was a turn at the dawn of the new millennium toward more practical and pressing issues. The dialogue is now more focused on cultivating friendly and peaceful relations between peoples and nations, and overcoming misunderstandings and religious conflicts.

The *raison d'être* of the interreligious dialogue is thus first and foremost the peaceful coexistence of religious communities, which are called to live together in the same space. Lack of dialogue can lead to tensions and conflicts between different religious groups, and religion itself can facilitate war as well as peace. The contemporary interreligious dialogue is most concerned with social and economic issues, as well as immigration, global poverty, and—by extension—human suffering and the increase of fundamentalism, which is a danger to religions themselves. Therefore, the most appropriate lens through which to view these vital issues is not the dogmatic one—relying on our preconceived notions of the religious convictions of the "other" and our fear of losing our own doctrines, a stance which can lead to war between religions or proselytizing—but primarily the social and humanitarian one. It is a dialogue of religious cultures, an effort to meet and work together in service of universal values that lead to harmony between cultures in the name of humanism, which is founded on the conciliatory values of the religious traditions. In this way, representatives of the world religions and academic teachers cannot be confined within insulated "theological" boundaries, but are open to the religious concerns of others, willing to listen to their views, and reconcile with them. To this end, it is essential to change the curricula to include the teaching of interreligious dialogue, in order to mitigate religious misunderstandings and conflicts, and to promote proper understanding of the religious other. This leads to the inevitable question about the relationship between this new positive approach to the religious "other" and the current missionary methods and programs.

The question today for the Orthodox and more generally for all Christians is how they will manage to respond to the new historical reality, and the challenges of the times, and especially that of today's multi-religious environment. How will they go about discovering new theological avenues of mutual understanding and coexistence with the "other," the non-Christian? The Christian faith is called to converse with the great religions of the world and to take into account the following factors: a) that cultural and religious diversity is a social good, b) that participation in interreligious dialogue is, according to Christ's teachings, one of the Church's obligations to humankind, and c) that the path of interreligious dialogue leads closer to the mutual understanding and harmonious coexistence of peoples and is a step toward the spread of "peace on earth," in accordance with the Gospel maxim.[20]

It is possible, in this sense, for systematic theology to make a contribution to interreligious dialogue. A *theology of religions*, from an Orthodox perspective, would help Orthodox faithful and Churches to approach and reflect upon the people of other religions. Christians, on the basis of Scripture and the life of the Church, must come to see God's grace and providence abounding throughout the world, the whole of divine creation. This is the meaning of the mystery of the Divine Economy in Christ. The salvific work of Jesus Christ is for all humankind. And this is the sense of the ecumenicity or universality of the Church, which subsumes within it every particularity and locality, the one and the many, indivisibly. Its "special" grace is its "universal" grace. The breath of God is one and blows everywhere: "in Him we live and move and have our being" (Acts 17:28

---

[20] On the interreligious dialogue, the Churches' initiatives, and the challenges today, see Angeliki Ziaka "Interreligious Dialogue in Promoting Peace and Overcoming Religious Conflicts", in E. Eynikel, A. Ziaka (et al.) (eds.) *Religion and Conflict. Essays on the Origins of Religious Conflicts and Resolution Approaches*, (London: Harptree, 2010), 543-561.

RSV). It is in this sense that we can understand the presence of Christ in the universal church and the history of the world, and thus we can experience the grace of God, which spreads across the world. If the grace of God is confined to the narrow boundaries of a single organization, a church bound within the world, the work of the Divine Economy and salvation in Christ would lose its universality.

In a recent workshop on interreligious dialogue entitled "Mission and Modern Religions," which took place at Aristotle University of Thessaloniki, in cooperation with the Department of Theology of Holy Cross in Boston, USA (11 May 2012), Fr. Emmanuel Clapsis emphasized that God's love for humanity would not permit the delimitation of his saving grace to the narrow framework of the Orthodox Church. Fr. Clapsis presented a brief overview of the literature on the Orthodox understanding of other religions. He referred to systematic and biblical theologians (Karmiris, Agourides, Khodr) as well as experts on religious studies (Yannoulatos, Ziakas). In fact, he noted that, according to Karmiris, "the limits of salvation are independent of the Church." Fr. Clapsis then noted the "particularity of Religions," a concept which has been emphasized in recent research, observing at the same time that an overemphasis on "particularity" can lead to a loss of religions' global dimensions. The question is then how people's particular faith can be open to world affairs and not remain closed in on itself. Professor Stelios Tsompanidis, who teaches ecumenical theology in the Department of Theology, recalled the words of the late Kostis Moskov concerning the "encounter of the great Word." The challenge therefore today for the Orthodox world is to emphasize that the catholicity of the Church is found in the Local Church (the concept of conciliarity, which is characteristic of Orthodoxy). When, however, the Church closes in on itself and restricts itself to the local, the catholic and universal automatically ceases to exist. The challenge for Orthodoxy, then, is to open itself to its catholicity and to dialog with other religions in a spirit of love in Christ.

Christians are called to join together in understanding God's work in the world and his will, which allows each of us to live according to our traditions. Law or force cannot achieve such progress. It requires rather changes in disposition, education, and mutuality, in the sense of forming relationships with mutual respect, aid and—primarily—love.

Bibliography

Yannoulatos Anastasios (Archbishop), Ἰσλάμ, Θρησκειολογικὴ Ἐπισκόπησις *(Islam. An Overview from the History of Religions,* (Athens: Nations and Peoples, 1971) (re-edition 2001) (in Greek).

-, *Facing the World. Orthodox Christian Essay on Global Concerns,* (Geneva: W.C.C., 2004).

Damaskinos Papandreou (Bishop), "Due Rolle der Orthodoxie im Dialog zwischen Christentum und Islam", *Una Sancta* 49 (1994): 357-359.

-, "The Interreligious Dialogues of the Orthodox Church", Ο Διάλογος Χριστιανισμού-Ισλάμ ως κοινό Καθῆκον (Christian-Muslim Dialogue like a Commun Duty), M. Konstantinou-A. Stirnemann (eds.), (Thessaloniki: Paratiritis, 1998), 31-51, 35 (in Greek).

Damascinos Papandreou (Bishop), Λόγος Διαλόγου. Η Ορθοδοξία ενώπιον της τρίτης χιελιετίας *(Reason of Dialogue. Orthodoxie befor the third millennium)* (Athens: Kastaniotis, 1997) (in Greek).

Vassiliadis Petros, "Reconciliation as a Pneumatological Mission Paradigm: Some Preliminary Reflections by an Orthodox", *International Review of Mission* 94.372 (January 2005): 30-42.

Ziaka Angeliki, *La recherche Grecque Contemporaine et l'Islam,* PhD, Université Marc Bloch de Strasbourg, 2002 (Lille: ANRT, 2004), 15-105.

-, "Muslims and Muslim Education in Greece", *Islamic Education in Europe,* Ednan Aslan (ed.), (Vienna: Bohlau Verlag, 2009), 141-178.

-, "Interreligious Dialogue in Promoting Peace and overcoming religious Conflicts", *Religion and Conflict. Essays on the Origins of Religious Conflicts and Resolution Approaches,* E. Eynikel, A. Ziaka (et al) (eds.), (London: Harptree, 2010), 543-561.

Part VII: Particular Themes and Issues for Orthodox Involvement in Ecumenism

Ziakas Grigorios, «Το Οικουμενικό Πατριαρχείο και ο Διάλογος με το Ισλάμ» (The Ecumenical Patriarchate and the Dialogue with Islam"), *Φανάρι 400 χρόνια (Fanari 400 years)*, (Ecumenical Patriarchate's Editons, 2001) (in Greek).

-, *Θρησκειολογικά Μελετήματα. Ζώντας αρμονικά με ανθρώπους διαφορετικής πίστης (Studies on Religions)*, P. Pachis (ed.), t. Α΄, Thessaloniki: Vanias, 2004 (re-edition under the title *Interreligious Dialogues*, v. I., Thessaloniki: Pournaras, 2010) (in Greek).

-, *Τα Ελληνικά Γράμματα και ο Αριστοτέλης στην Αραβική Παράδοση (Greek Letters and Aristotle in the Arab Tradition)*, (Athens: Agra, 2007). (in Greek).

-, *Ιστορία των Θρησκευμάτων. Β΄ Το Ισλάμ (History of Religions II. Islam)*, (Thessaloniki: Pournaras, 1997, 2001 (1983)) (in Greek).

(Translated by Fr. Gregory Edwards)

(108) ORTHODOX CONTRIBUTIONS FOR THE UNDERSTANDING AND PRACTICE OF DIAKONIA (THE 'LITURGY AFTER LITURGY')

Dragica Tadic-Papanikolaou

The first Christians, whose life was distinctly based on Christ's example, avoided using terms that stand for authority and power, and gave preference to those referring to fraternal life and activity, and serving. This is how the term *liturgy* entered into general use. It derives from the Greek *leitourgia* – a compound word made of *leitos* = public (from *laos* = people), and *ergon* = work. Therefore, in the Ancient world *liturgy* meant 'public, common work for the benefit of community.' In the Christian tradition, it takes on the meaning of worship and denotes exclusively the celebration of the eucharist, since the 'breaking of bread' was the most important work of a local Christian community.[1]

The other frequent term in the early Christian vocabulary was *diakonia*, which derives from the Greek verb *diakonein* – to serve (from which comes *diakonos* – male or female servant).[2] Nowadays, it refers to service as a permanent activity of the Church throughout history. *Diakonia* is also the name of an international organization networking among those involved in service ministries of different churches. The term *diakonate* refers to practicing the service of *diakonia*, but also to a specific order of ministry in the churches.[3] Although the term *diakonia* includes these different basic meanings – the service of the church, a specific church order of ministry, and the organized, institutional help to the those in need, its essence is summed up in one – serving the neighbor, rooted and modeled on Christ's service and teachings.[4]

Already the Old Testament law provided a variety of ways of helping and supporting the poor, widows and orphans. But with the New Testament, *diakonia* became the way of life of the Church (Acts 11:27ff.; 2 Cor. 8). This attitude was motivated by Christ's teaching. At the Last Supper, Jesus washed the feet of his disciples, which was at the time, the job of a servant. And He told them: "So if I, your Lord and Teacher, have washed your feet, you also ought to wash one another's feet. For I have set you an example, that you also should do as I have done to you" (John 13:14-15). Thus Christ asks us to follow his example, to serve each other in love.

Jesus defines himself as one who did not come to be served, but to serve (Matt 20:28; Mark 10:45). In that way, he gives to *diakonia*, which in the Ancient world was mainly a synonym for slavery,[5] a messianic and

---

[1] *A Greek-English Lexicon*, H.G. Liddell-R.Scott, revised by H.S. Jones, (Oxford: Clarendon Press, 1996), 1036-1037. Cf. *A Patristic Greek Lexicon*, G.W.H. Lampe, (Oxford: Clarendon Press, 1961), 795.

[2] *A Greek-English Lexicon*, H.G. Liddell-R.Scott, revised by H.S. Jones, (Oxford: Clarendon Press, 1996), 398. Cf. *A Patristic Greek Lexicon*, G.W.H. Lampe, (Oxford: Clarendon Press, 1961), 350-351.

[3] Teresa Joan White, "*Diakonia*," entry in the *Dictionary of ecumenical movement*, http://www.oikoumene.org/en/resources/themes/christian-service-diakonia/ecumenical-dictionary-diakonia.html (last accessed September, 2013)

[4] The Greek word *diakonia* is usually translated and conceived as *service*. Therefore the central idea of diaconal ministry is that of helping the needy, after the model of Jesus. J.N. Collins conducts the comprehensive study of that word in different Christian and non-Christian sources from about 200 BCE to 200 CE, and he concludes that the word *diakonia* used to mean also *acting as someone's representative* or *transferring the message*. Therefore, *deacon* was to be conceived as *messenger* or *emissary*. This challenges the traditional concept of *diakonia* in terms of humble service. Instead, the role of the deacon is associated with the carrying out of a task commissioned by God and Church, represented in the person of Bishop. V. John N. Collins, *Diakonia – Re-interpreting the Ancient Sources*, (New York: Oxford University Press, 1990). For the different aspects of notion *diakonia* and their implementation in ecclesiological context, v. Здравко Јовановић, "*Представљајући* аспекти појма διακονία"(Zdravko Jovanovic, "*Representational* aspects of the notion *diakonia*"), *Богословље* (*Bogoslovlje*) 71.1 (2012): 74-94. Since this concept introduced by Collins refers mainly to the ministry of ordained deacons, I will not develop it further. I will present one aspect of the term *diakonia*, that of humble, loving care for one's neighbor, which is the task of all baptized members of the Church and one of the main characteristics of Christian life.

[5] But not exclusively. V. John N. Collins, *Diakonia – Re-interpreting the Ancient Sources*, 194.

eschatological meaning. Namely, Jesus Christ puts the service of brother/sister and neighbor as the ultimate criterion of entering the kingdom of God (Matt 25:34-46). Since Jesus identifies himself with every man, the love for God is tested and showed through the love for man (1 Jn. 4:20). For that reason, the acts of love became the very centre of Christian life; not a secondary thing, or instrument to attain something more important.[6]

Jesus is placing two commandments of love – to love God with all one's heart, and to love one's neighbor as oneself – in immediate juxtaposition. The ways we love our neighbor reveal the authenticity of our faith in God: "We know love by this, that he laid down his life for us—and we ought to lay down our lives for one another. How does God's love abide in anyone who has the world's goods and sees a brother or sister in need and yet refuses help? Little children, let us love, not in word or speech, but in truth and action" (1 Jn. 3:16-18). This conception of love is constantly present in the New Testament (cf. par example Gal. 5:13-14, or James 2:14-15).[7]

The first institutional form of *diakonia* is described in Acts 6:1-6. Seven men were elected and by imposition of hands, they were introduced in specific service. Their main concern was the distributing of alms. In the ancient churches, the funds used for *diakonia* were collected from the whole congregation at the Eucharist.[8] In the Roman Church male deacons, and in the Eastern Church both men and women in the diaconate, were the key administrators of practical care in the name of the Church. It is important to note that in the early Church even a fast had the meaning of diaconal service. The very essence of the fast was to eat less in order to give what remains to the poor. In *The Shepherd of Hermas*, e.g. it is advised: "Having fulfilled what is written, on that day on which thou fastest thou shalt taste nothing but bread and water; and from thy meats, which thou wouldest have eaten, thou shalt reckon up the amount of that day's expenditure, which thou wouldest have incurred, and shalt give it to a widow, or an orphan, or to one in want…"[9]

At the beginning of the 4th century, the bishop Rabbula of Edessa in Syria built a hostel and arranged for a female deacon and nuns to provide care for the women in need and a male deacon and monks to care for men. This aspect of *diakonia* as an institution to care for the sick and poor, spread from Syria throughout the Byzantine Empire. At the height of their ministry, the deacons of the Eastern churches were involved in social care, liturgical-pastoral care, teaching, administrative-juridical duties and burial *diakonia*. Emperor Justinian (483-565) stressed philanthropy and promulgated philanthropic legislation which covered not only the capital but also the provinces. He established separate residential institutions to care for the various types of people in need. During his reign institutions were set up to care for poor pilgrims in Jerusalem; through the pilgrims the idea of hospices reached the Western Church.

As concerns the monasteries, both Basil and Benedict, main writers of regulations of monastic life, expected monks to practice *diakonia*; each guest was to be received like Christ. The monasteries tended mainly to provide food for the poor at their gates.

When the diaconate came chiefly to be a transitional office to the priesthood, the duties of deacons became more limited to the formal liturgical ones; and during the Middle Ages responsibility for the care of the poor shifted from the bishop to the parish clergy, who coped with needs mainly on an ad hoc, local basis. At the same time, the social care passes manly in the hands of monks. So for many years we see monasteries as places

---

[6] Ante Crnčević, "Sklad u raznolikosti liturgijskih službi" ("Harmony in the Diversity of Liturgical Services"), *Bogoslovska Smotra* 72.2-3 (2002): 338:335-365, Stipe Nimac, "Služba dijakonije u postmodernom društvu" ("The Service of *diakonia* in post-modern society"), *Bogoslovska Smotra 76.4 (2006):* 1001-1002:1001-1012.

[7] Emmanuel Clapsis, "Wealth and Poverty in Christian Tradition," Paper presented at Orthodox Diakonia: International Conference on the Social Witness and Service of the Orthodox Churches, 30. April – 5 May 2004, Valamo Lay Academy, Finland, 7:1-11. Quoted by http://www.iocc.org/orthodoxdiakonia/content/revclapsis.pdf (last accessed at September 2013).

[8] For the very important early Christian institution – the Pauline *Collection* – and its social and ecumenical dimension, see Πέτρος Βασιλειάδης, *Χάρις-Κοινωνία-Διακονία. Ο κοινωνικός χαρακτήρας του παύλειου προγράμματος της λογείας: Εισαγωγή και ερμηνευτικό υπόμνημα στο Β´ Κορ 8-9*, Θεσσαλονίκη 1985 (Petros Vassiliadis, *Xaris-Koinonia-Diakonia. The Social Character of the Pauline Collection. Introduction and Commentary on 2 Cor 8-9*, Thessaloniki 1985) (in Greek).

[9] *The Shepherd of Hermas, Parable 5*, 3,7 (J. B. Lightfoot translation).

where the hungry and those who suffer find consolation. Hospitals, orphanages and guest-houses were built next to so many of them. Monasteries were also the centers of literacy and culture.

Changes in life-style and the economy, but also the crisis of the Black Death greatly increased the necessity for care. Hence by the 16th century, the diaconal system was no longer able to cope with the needs. In England the breakdown of the medieval provisions resulted in the Poor Law, by which minimal relief was provided to residents through a poor tax levied on all householders. The reformers recalled the role of deacons in the New Testament Church: Luther recommended that deacons "keep a register of poor people and care for them"; Calvin stressed that the proper function of a deacon was not liturgy but collecting alms from the faithful and distributing them to the poor. This was put into practice in some Reformed churches: male deacons administered the affairs of the poor; the women cared for the poor themselves. The 1662 Ordinal of the Church of England directed the deacon to search out the sick and poor of the parish and inform the curate, so that "by his exhortation they may be relieved with the alms of the parishioners, or others." The most extensive diaconal concern was shown by the radical reformers.

Meanwhile in the Roman Catholic Church new religious orders, especially those inspired by St. Vincent de Paul specialized in various aspects of *diakonia*. At the same period, the Eastern churches under Turkish rule found themselves severely restricted from public *diakonia*, as more recently did a number of Orthodox churches under various communist governments.

The rise of the capitalist system in the 19th century provoked many social problems. Secular and Christian social reformers made many people conscious of the plight of their neighbors. Public charities increased, and secular movements produced a philanthropy not tied to any religion or denomination (e.g. the Red Cross). Meanwhile, the idea of the professional social worker began to emerge.[10]

In the frame of the ecumenical movement, *diakonia* emerged in 1922 with the founding of the European Central Bureau for Inter-Church Aid under the auspices of the Federal Council of the Churches of Christ in America and the Federation of Swiss Protestant Churches, later joined by other European churches. The direct involvement of the World Council of Churches (WCC) in *diakonia* began during the years of the Second World War in the form of ministry to refugees and prisoners of war, working closely with a variety of other churches and church-related organizations, as well as the Red Cross. Plans for post-war involvement in reconstruction were laid already in 1942. From that period the WCC broadened its diaconal service to different forms of emergency relief and service worldwide. The meeting of the WCC Central Committee in Chichester, in 1949, underscored that interchurch aid is a permanent obligation of the WCC, not a temporary engagement that would come to an end with the completion of reconstruction after the war, and that this is a spiritual and not just a material task. There was also a widespread agreement that the most effective *diakonia* is that which is rendered ecumenically, rather than bilaterally between churches of the same tradition.

Nowadays, with changes in the world, the *diakonia* service changes as well. In the second half of the 20th century, as governments in Western Europe tended to take on more responsibility for social security, some churches left *diakonia* in the hands of the social services and welfare and saw their diaconal role as one of only "plugging the gaps." A number of churches established "boards of social responsibility" or similar bodies to influence government policy and thus practice prophetic *diakonia*. Especially in Eastern Europe, Christians were asking what it means to be a Christian in a socialist and communist state. Others reflected on what it means to be a Christian and to be a church in a capitalist state. Does it mean evangelizing the government as well as those in private companies? In the global village is *diakonia* to be exercised only towards the Christian neighbor, or is it for all?

Individual churches in different cultures vary immensely in their degree of articulation of *diakonia* and in their practice. There is also great variation concerning who has primary responsibility for *diakonia*: central church offices (bishops or specialized national agencies), local presbyters, deacons, professional social workers or laity.[11]

---

[10] Teresa Joan White, "Diakonia," *Dictionary of Ecumenical Movement.*
[11] Teresa Joan White, "Diakonia," *Dictionary of Ecumenical movement.*

Part VII: Particular Themes and Issues for Orthodox Involvement in Ecumenism

The restructuring of the religious congregations of the Roman Catholic Church has greatly affected their *diakonia*. Fewer religious and more lay professionals are now involved in the diminished institutional work, the former taking on new forms of work. The theoretical bases for this social engagement are the Papal encyclicals. Since 1891 when Pope Leo XIII published the encyclical "Rerum novarum" by which he criticized the social status of the working class, the bishops of Rome have communicated officially their positions on various social issues and problems.

The Orthodox Churches have often been criticized for concentrating too much on the doctrinal and ritual aspect, while neglecting *diakonia*. The criticism was mostly well-founded, but the truth is that this practice of Orthodox Churches was caused by unfavourable historical circumstances. During the period of the Ottoman Empire, the activities and influence of Orthodox churches were limited. Similar situation occurred again in the 20th century when most Orthodox churches of the Central and Eastern Europe found themselves again in an adverse position. During the 1990s, the collapse of the socialist system brought to the surface a wide range of unmet needs in society, but the churches, having been prevented from undertaking diaconal activities for more than 40 years (and in Russia for more than 70 years), had few structures and little experience to deal with this. The only thing that they could do was the foundation of a parish-church based *diakonia* and the restoration of some diaconal houses.

In the case of the Orthodox churches, significant reflection on *diakonia* emerged in the mid-1970s. In 1974 in Bucharest and in 1975 in Etchmiadzin, at the preparatory Consultations of Orthodox member churches for the WCC's fifth Assembly in Nairobi in 1975, the idea arose of the "liturgy after liturgy." First, in discussions of how theology of mission (missiology) and the theology of the church (ecclesiology) are related, it was underlined that "mission is ultimately possible only in and through an event of communion which reflects in history the trinitarian existence of God himself." In other words, when the Church is distorted or divided, or suffers of any ecclesiological heresy that makes its identification with communion no longer possible, then the mission of the church is impossible. Afterwards, it was highlighted that the eucharistic liturgy has implications not only for the being and identity of the Church, but also for its mission in the world. "Prayer and the Eucharist, whereby Christians overcome their selfish ways, impel them also to become involved in the social and political life of their respective countries." Out of this idea of the extension of the liturgical celebration into the daily life of the faithful in the world arose the concept of the "liturgy after the Liturgy."[12] This theological approach linking *diakonia* with *leitourgia* was formulated at a Consultation in Crete, in 1978: "Christian *diakonia* is not an optional action ... but an indispensable expression of that community, which has its source in the eucharistic and liturgical life of the church. It is a 'liturgy after the Liturgy.'"[13]

The concept of *diakonia* as "liturgy after the Liturgy," developed by Orthodox theologians in the context of ecumenical dialogue, could lead to two main problems – to the collapsing of Orthodoxy into a kind of sacramentalism that disconnects eschatology from history, or to giving preeminence to the ethical implications of the eucharist at the expense of its ontological and doxological character.[14] Preventing these problems lies only in the correct understanding of the expression "liturgy after liturgy" and of the relation of liturgical and diaconal worship.

"People may confess faith in God through the creeds of the Church but, who they are in relation to God is revealed in what they love the most and in what they worship."[15] In the life of a Christian, the object of love and the object of worship are not to be separated. Following Christ's commandment, a Christian should express his love for God through the practice of concrete love for the brother. The same goes for worship.

[12] Ion Bria, *The Liturgy after the Liturgy. Mission and Witness form an Orthodox Perspective*, (Geneva: WCC Publications, 1996), 19-20.

[13] Teresa Joan White, "Diakonia," *Dictionary of Ecumenical movement*.

[14] Emmanuel Clapsis, "Wealth and Poverty in Christian Tradition," 8:1-11. On problems provoked by one-sided interpretations, v. Bria, 22-23.

[15] Emmanuel Clapsis, "Wealth and Poverty in Christian Tradition," 3:1-11.

"The ethos of the Church is simultaneously shaped through the celebration of Eucharist, the proclamation of the Word of God and the mystery of the poor brethren. None of them should be considered as a substitute for the other or that in itself and apart from the other can communicate the fullness of the Church's ethos."[16] The inseparable unity of those three elements is testified already in the *Apology* of Justin the Martyr. In describing the Eucharist of the 2nd century, he says that first the writings of the apostles (gospels) were read; after that, they had eucharistic thanksgiving and communion in bread and wine, and at the end of worship the Christians collected things for those that were in need.[17] As we see, diaconal dimension of the worship was integrated in the very liturgy.

For many centuries, the liturgy of St. John Chrysostom has been celebrated most frequently in Orthodox churches. The text of this liturgy originates from Syria. Over time it has been modified and reshaped, and one of its most significant redactions was done by St. John Chrysostom, whose name it carries. The Orthodox churches celebrate this liturgy, but they are not familiar with the pastoral recommendations of its redactor. Namely, St. John Chrysostom is, among the Church Fathers, the one who spoke most prominently about the inevitability of *diakonia* in the life of every Christian and its distinctly liturgical aspect.

Christians, based on Matthew 25:34-46, believe that Christ is sacramentally present in the poor and the needy. That is the faith expressed by many Church Fathers. John Chrysostom draws a similar conclusion from the identification of Christ with the poor, and in his homilies he suggests specific ways to express the recognition that Christ lives and is actively present in the poor and needy:

"Do you wish to see his altar? ... This altar is composed of the very members of Christ, and the body of the Lord becomes your altar... venerable because it is itself Christ's body... This altar you can see lying everywhere, in the alleys and in the agoras and you can sacrifice upon it anytime... invoke the spirit not with words, but with deeds."[18]
"Do you really wish to pay homage to Christ's body? Then do not neglect him when he is naked. At the same time that you honor him here [in church] with hangings made of silk, do not ignore him outside when he perishes from cold and nakedness. For the One who said 'This is my body' ... also said 'When I was hungry you gave me nothing to eat.'"[19]

According to Chrysostom's homilies, the poor become the liturgical images of the most holy elements in all of Christian worship: the altar and the body of Christ. As so, they are bearers of salvation.[20] Also, for St. John Chrysostom, the identification of the poor with the body of Christ is based on His words and commandments. The creative words of Jesus establish this double sacramental identity, of the bread with the body of Christ and of Christ glorified with the most humble of His brothers.[21] This is also testified in the Bible. In the gospel accounts of the last supper, we have the testimony of God's commandment to break the bread and drink the cup in memory of Him (Matt. 26:26-28; Mark 14:22-24; Luke 22:17-20). In the gospel according to St. John, however, that commandment is replaced with the washing of the disciples' feet by Christ and the commandment of mutual love (John 13:13-16). Both the Eucharist and *diakonia* are based on Christ's commandment during the Supper. For this reason, love for the brethren cannot be something exterior to the Eucharist, or something secondary to the consecration of the gifts. And St. Chrysostom does not hesitate to confirm in many homilies that the service of love and *diakonia* are inscribed in the very heart of the eucharistic mystery![22]

---

[16] Emmanuel Clapsis, "Wealth and Poverty in Christian Tradition," 8:1-11.
[17] Justin Martyr, *First Apology* 67.
[18] John Chrysostom, *On the Second Epistle to the Corinthians, Homily* 20.3.
[19] John Chrysostom, *On Matthew, Homily* 50.4.
[20] Emmanuel Clapsis, "Wealth and Poverty in Christian Tradition," 9-10.
[21] Boris Bobrinskoy, "L'Esprit du Christ dans les sacrements chez Jean Chrysostome et Augustin," in: *Communion du Saint-Esprit*, (Bégrolles-en-Mauges: Abbaye de Bellefontaine), 1992, 305:279-311.
[22] Boris Bobrinskoy, "L'Esprit du Christ dans les sacrements chez Jean Chrysostome et Augustin,» 304-305:279-311.

In order to better explain the reasons for the service to the brethren, St. John Chrysostom put the following words in the mouth of Jesus:

"I want to be nourished by you, that much I love you. I want to be invited at your table, as to a friend."[23]

Our God loves us that much that He sent His Son for our salvation. Jesus Christ became one of us because He loves us, and He would like that we love Him also as our brother. He would like us to love every man, because every man is His, and also our brother.

"The service at the altar, the eucharistic sacrifice, does not take its full signification if the charity, sacrificed and sourced from the sacrifice of the Christ, does not help in the real way to the poor, who are also the altar of God and the body of Christ."[24] Those two services are in fact two dimensions of the same thing, of the same Christ who is present in the liturgy and in our neighbor. This twofold presence of Christ, as also the fact that the Eschaton is already present in history, but still not in its fullness, further determinate the main structure of the liturgy which is based on two moments: first the people gather for worship, to hear the word of God and to eat the bread of life; then, at the end of the liturgy, they are sent out to testify the Eschatological event by spreading the love of Christ.[25]

> "The sending forth of the faithful at the end of the liturgy has a profound symbolic and sacramental significance. The *Ite, missa est* of the Roman mass or *let us go in peace* of the Byzantine liturgies, this 'sending out' of the faithful, is only the announcement of the end of the first stage of the Eucharist ... What follows is not so much an 'exit' from the church, as an entrance by the church into the world, continuing the sending forth of the disciples by the risen Lord in the power of the Spirit of Pentecost. When we leave the church, we enter another mode of the liturgy which is the 'liturgy after the Liturgy.'"[26]

In that way "The dynamics of the liturgy go beyond the boundaries of the Eucharistic assembly to serve the community at large. The Eucharistic liturgy is not an escape into an inner realm of prayer, a pious turning away from social realities; rather it calls and sends the faithful to celebrate 'the sacrament of the brother' outside the temple in the public marketplace, where the cries of the poor and marginalized are heard."[27]

In both parts of our service – eucharistic and *diaconal* – we are doing a single thing. We are standing in front of the altar and "Thine own of Thine own we offer unto Thee, in behalf of all, and for all." Having taken them of God's gifts, we are offering bread and wine in celebrating the Eucharist, according to God's commandment. In the same way, we are offering to the brother the goods that we took from God's creation, fulfilling again God's commandment.

Diakonia was established by the commandment of Christ, and in everyday life of the church, it springs, as a sacrament of the brother, from the sacrament of the eucharist.[28] This is the eschatological and eternal base of *diakonia*. But, since we live in history, *diakonia* took (and still takes) different forms, adapted to the historical context and circumstances. At the apostolic times, small church communities gathered the goods and shared them to the poor people, or with other church communities. The age of the Fathers was characterized by theological explanations of *diakonia*, in the frame of pastoral exhortations. The ascetic trinôme – fast, prayer and charity – was also present, as the main characteristic of monastic life. In the Middle ages, we had charity

---

[23] John Chrysostom, *On the Epistle to the Romans, Homily* 16.6.

[24] Adalbert Hamman, *Vie liturgique et vie sociale*, Paris-Tournai: Desclée, 1968, 284. The identification of the poor with Christ in the context of Eucharist is present already in Paul's epistles. V. Растко Јовић, „Недостојни хришћани" (Rastko Jovic, "Undignified Christians"), *Видослов (Vidoslov)* 55 (2012): 159-172.

[25] Ion Bria, *The Liturgy after the Liturgy*, 24.

[26] Boris Bobrinskoy, « Prière du cœur et eucharistie », in : *Persoana si comunione-Prinos de cinstire, Preotului Profesor Academician Dumitru Staniloae (1903-1993)*, ed. I.I. Ica, Sibiu 1993, 631ff.:627-634.

[27] Ion Bria, *The Liturgy after the Liturgy*, 20.

[28] Cf. Cf. Boris Bobrinskoy, "La liturgie et la vie de tous les jours," in: *Communion du Saint-Esprit*, (Bégrolles-en-Mauges: Abbaye de Bellefontaine, 1992), 337-348.

work and helping the poor, ill, orphans and captives. In modern times, institutions for charity, education and care appeared.[29]

The postmodern society is characterized by plurality, individualization and globalization. As a consequence, problems have arisen to which individual acts of charity cannot provide a satisfactory solution, and which require institutionalized and expert help. Such problems include drug addiction, or care for the sick and elderly. Therefore, in the postmodern society, active Christian love should be implemented on three levels, based on the Bible story of the merciful Samaritan (Luke 10:29-37). According to the model of this story, Christian *diakonia* is carried out in the following way:

• Direct help – Samaritan
• Institution - Innkeeper
• Structural *diakonia* – society.[30]

However, *diakonia* should be always based on liturgy, in the way described by the Church Fathers. Due to different historical circumstances, the unification with Christ in the Eucharist was separated from communicating with Him through serving of the neighbor. Therefore the WCC's sixth Assembly in Vancouver in 1983 underlined the urgent need to recover the unity between worship and daily Christian life: "For the sake of witnessing vocation of the church we need to find a true rhythm of Christian involvement in the world. The church is gathered for worship and scattered for everyday life... It must be stressed that there is no Christian service to the world unless it is rooted in the service of worship."[31]

The life of every Christian has to be a constant *diakonia* and everyday personal sacrifice for the people in need. This sacrifice is the temporal extension of the Eucharist and by character it should be *liturgical*, which means that it is energized by participation in Eucharist, it constitutes the best preparation for a more conscious participation in the Eucharist, and that it is the clear and living expression of the real transformation of men and women in Christ.[32] From this perspective, every Christian and every church have the power and possibility to witness the living God, by expressing in everyday life His love that they adopted sacramentally. And this theoretical and practical connection of *diakonia* with liturgy is the main contribution of Orthodoxy to the ecumenical *diakonia*.

Bibliography

"Christianity and the Social Order," in *The Truth Shall Make You Free: The Lambeth Conference 1988*, (London: Church House, 1988).

Bobrinskoy, Boris, "L'Esprit du Christ dans les sacrements chez Jean Chrysostome et Augustin," in: *Communion du Saint-Esprit*, (Bégrolles-en-Mauges: Abbaye de Bellefontaine, 1992), 305:279-311.

Bobrinskoy, Boris, "La liturgie et la vie de tous les jours," in: *Communion du Saint-Esprit*, (Bégrolles-en-Mauges: Abbaye de Bellefontaine, 1992), 337-348.

Bopp, Karl, "Diakonie in der postmodern Gesellschaft," in: *Kirchesein in der Welt von heute. Pastoraltheologisches Lehrbuch*, Konferenz der Bayerischen Pastoraltheologen (ed.), (Munchen: Don Bosco Verlag, 2004), 118-132.

Bria, Ion, *The Liturgy after the Liturgy. Mission and Witness form an Orthodox Perspective*, (Geneva: WCC Publications, 1996), 19-20.

---

[29] Stipe Nimac, "Služba dijakonije u postmodernom društvu" („The Service of *diakonia* in post-modern society"), *Bogoslovska Smotra* 76.4 (2006): 1003-1004:1001-1012.

[30] Karl Bopp, "Diakonie in der postmodern Gesellschaft," in: *Kirchesein in der Welt von heute. Pastoraltheologisches Lehrbuch*, Konferenz der Bayerischen Pastoraltheologen (ed.), (Munchen: Don Bosco Verlag, 2004), 118-132.

[31] *Gathered for Life: Official Report of the WCC's Sixth Assembly*, David Gill (ed.), (Geneva: WCC, 1983), 35; Ion Bria, *The Liturgy after the Liturgy*, 21.

[32] Ion Bria, *The Liturgy after the Liturgy*, 21; Anastasios Yannoulatos, "Discovering the Orthodox Missionary Ethos," in: *Martyria-Mission. The Witness of the Orthodox Churches Today*, ed. I.Bria, (Geneva: WCC Publications, 1980), 20-37.

Clapsis, Emmanuel, "Wealth and Poverty in Christian Tradition," Paper presented at Orthodox Diakonia: International Conference on the Social Witness and Service of the Orthodox Churches, 30. April – 5 May 2004, Valamo Lay Academy, Finland. Quoted by http://www.iocc.org/orthodoxdiakonia/content/revclapsis. pdf (last accessed at September, 2013).

Collins, John N., *Diakonia – Re-interpreting the Ancient Sources*, (New York: Oxford University Press, 1990).

Hamman, Adalbert, *Vie liturgique et vie sociale*, (Paris-Tournai: Desclée, 1968), 284.

Joan White, Teresa, *"Diakonia,"* entry in the *Dictionary of ecumenical movement*, http://www.oikoumene. org/en/resources/themes/christian-service-diakonia/ecumenical-dictionary-diakonia.html (last accessed at September, 2013)

Βασιλειάδης, Πέτρος, *Χάρις-Κοινωνία-Διακονία. Ο κοινωνικός χαρακτήρας του παύλειου προγράμματος της λογείας: Εισαγωγή και ερμηνευτικό υπόμνημα στο Β΄ Κορ 8-9*, Θεσσαλονίκη 1985 (Vassiliadis, Petros, *Xaris-Koinonia-Diakonia. The Social Character of the Pauline Collection. Introduction and Commentary on 2 Cor 8-9*, Thessaloniki 1985) (in Greek).

Fr. Vasileios Thermos

Being a lay member of the Church has been traditionally (and erroneously) considered by the folk as a *'lack'*, as a quality that is marked by something missing. Lay faithful quite often distinguish themselves from clergy by attributing to the ordained members of the Church a property which the former do not possess. This attitude eventually results in *clericalism*, a stance that undermines the very meaning of the Church.

It has not been a coincidence that voices who favor the upgrading of lay members of the Church inside the Orthodox world have remarkably increased since the theological renewal of the second half of the twentieth century. Such a revision has been possible only by revisiting patristic sources and by re-interpreting them in the light of ecclesiology. Yet theory has not adequately turned into actual reality of the Churches. The ecclesiological turn of theology still waits for its implementation.

A. The gift of being a lay member of the Church

Early Christian sources highlight the position of lay members of the Church by declaring the nature of their Chrismation as an *ordination*. What follows after the sacrament of Baptism which makes the 'gate' for a new Christian to enter the Body of Christ, is the gift of the Holy Spirit. By this sacrament one becomes a bearer of divine grace, albeit in the form of a 'seed' which is expected to be cultivated with awe and attention throughout life so that it can grow and give fruits in the form of virtues.

Thus, during the first centuries, the newly enlightened through the Baptism was ordained by the bishop into the order of laity, at the beginnings by his hand and later by the holy myrrh. It is by virtue of this ordination that the new member of the Church participates in the Eucharist. Actually the Eucharist is being celebrated *in front of* the ordained gifted faithfuls, *by* them, and *for* them.

The 'areopagitic' writings epitomize: "Next, they throw garments, white as light, over the man initiated... But the perfecting unction of the Myrrh makes the man initiated of good odour, for the holy perfecting of the Divine birth unites those who have been perfected to the supremely Divine Spirit... At the conclusion of all, the Hierarch calls the man initiated to the most Holy Eucharist, and imparts to him the communion of the perfecting mysteries."[1] The process was similar to that of ordination: liturgical prayers of initiation with bishop's hand on the head, vesting, kiss, participation in the Eucharist as a member of the appropriate order.

As an ordained member the lay Christian becomes an indispensable part of the integral ecclesiastical Body and is invited to contribute to its health and progress. All ordinations find their place in the Eucharist as it is still today the case with the three highest ecclesiastical diakonias (bishop, presbyter, deacon), because it is in the Eucharist that they are justified and they derive their very meaning; thus there has been a distortion with serious theological and psychological impacts that the sacraments of Baptism and Chrismation have nowadays been disconnected from the Eucharist.

B. The aim of the gift: worship, unity, mission

A divine gift is never bestowed without a purpose; the assignment now is three-fold. All three tasks serve the glory of God and the salvation of the world.

---

[1] Dionysius Areopagite, *Ecclesiastical Hierarchy*, 2, II, 8.

First, the new members of the Church are invited to join the full *worship*, without the limitations applied in their previous status as catechumenoi. They are welcomed in the kiss of peace by the present congregation, they are expected to hear the liturgical prayers and respond to them loudly together with the people of God, and they are invited to participate in the Holy Sacraments. By doing so, what becomes manifest is that they are in communion with the entire Church, that they have been blessed by the fullness of grace, and that they start now proclaiming in worship the Kingdom of God and the Lord's Cross and Resurrection.

Second, a major consequence of worship is *unity*. A certain degree of unity is required in order that someone be allowed to participate in worship, but a true worship, 'in Spirit', further strengthens unity. The new members of the Church have been credited with the duty to preserve unity in all their thoughts, emotions, and deeds, and are fully responsible for wounds in unity that occur because of their own faults. Even when disruptive conditions take place in the flock, one is responsible to intervene and try to restore them, obviously with respect to one's age, abilities, diakonias, and context.

Unity has two dimensions: unity of love (disrupted by indifference, prejudice, exploitation, resentment, hate etc.) and unity of truth (disrupted by heresy). Both are subject to the responsibility of the laity, therefore they are called to be vigilant in their hearts and their minds. The task of unity is not limited to the Church's interior; instead lay members of the ecclesiastical body should pray and long for 'the unity of all', and never forget the Lord's vision and wish "that they be one" (John 17: 11). Saint Paul in 1 Cor 12: 12-27 describes vividly the idea that Church makes the unified Body of Christ, a schema from which personal responsibility stems.

The various differences among the members of the Church (personal, ethnic, cultural etc.) are a detail compared to our embodiment into the mystical Body of Christ. Saint Basil the Great put it: "Our Lord Jesus Christ, Who has deigned to style the universal Church of God His body, and has made us individually members one of another, has moreover granted to all of us to live in intimate association with one another, as befits the agreement of the members. Wherefore, although we dwell far away from one another, yet, as regards our close conjunction, we are very near."[2]

Third, *mission* complements what was described above, by being an active journey in the world in order to continue the work of Christ. Missionary work has historically been undertaken by both clergy and lay members of the Church, and the latter have greatly contributed to the expansion of the Church. This mission, in any of its various forms (preaching, catechesis, philanthropy, justice, asceticism, sanctity), reflects the testimony of Lord's witnesses throughout His world. Thus mission makes a genuine product of the self-consciousness of chrismated faithfuls that they are valuable members of His Body and that they share the same desire for His beloved creation.

C. Shortcomings and misperceptions inside the Orthodox Churches

The Orthodox Churches have experienced a variety of painful historical adventures which have left their marks in mentalities and practices. The position and the mission of lay members of the Church have definitely been a 'victim' in those 'accidents'.

"The word *laikos* 'a layman' in the East c. A.D. 300 still meant 'one of the People (laos) of God', with all the rights and high duties and destinies that implied. By c. A.D. 450 it had almost come to mean 'profane' as opposed to 'sacred.'"[3] This has been a serious shift with lasting consequences that have not been adequately estimated so far.

The theology of Baptism and Chrismation does not support this old turn that exerts its impact even on our era. According to Saint Gregory the Theologian, there are no 'prohibited' areas for the faithful: "As long as you are a Catechumen you are but in the porch of religion; you must come inside, and cross the court, and observe the Holy Things, and look into the Holy of Holies, and be in company with the Trinity. Great are the

---

[2] Basil, *To the bishops of Italy and Gaul concerning the condition and confusion of the Churches*, 1.
[3] Gregory Dix *The shape of the liturgy*, (Dacre Press, 1952), 480.

interests for which you are fighting, great too the stability which you need. Protect yourself with the shield of faith."[4] Namely, with both the quality of the chrismated one and with the active faith.

Although lay Orthodox Christians participate in various ecclesiastical activities and essentially help the Church carry out particular tasks, the underlying idea about their ecclesiological status seems to fall short of the theological standards. Many lay members of the Church think of their marginalization as quite natural, as 'the way it should be', as almost a revealed truth and a divine will. This misperception is part of a customary way of thinking in our Church throughout centuries, which is poorly informed by historical knowledge or does not consider it necessary. Clergy share the basic responsibility for this misperception, as they continue teaching, through words and deeds, the laity's marginalization.

Worship and ecclesiastical life seem to follow the same 'monopoly' of the clergy, in terms of depriving the lay members of the Church of their appropriate contribution. In the vast majority of cases worldwide the lay congregation do not chant or recite together, leaving this task to their 'representatives', chanters or choirs, which frequently turn to behave as mere 'professionals', isolated from the body and ignoring their assignment. Meanwhile decision-makers in the Church are almost exclusively priests and basically bishops, thus forming a condition that reasonably discourages the lay members of the Church from caring about their own Church and from dedicating themselves to her progress. As worship is the central function of the Church, its defects influence all other aspects of ecclesiastical life, so it is not to wonder why those two fundamental dysfunctions coexist. Persons who lack the self-consciousness of having been blessed by the ordination of Holy Spirit tend to behave in withdrawal or reluctance too when liturgical praxis or administrative issues are at stake. So the Church and her tasks have become a business for the 'experts'.

A renewal of the position and mision of the lay members of the Church unavoidably gets through the 'rediscovering' of Holy Chrismation. Such a movement will for sure require drastic changes in the way our Churches worship and are organized. Lay theologians (theology remains today the only aspect of ecclesiastical life which has not succumbed to clericalism) are capable of contributing essentially to this indispensable renewal.

D. Implications for ecumenical activity

The first and fundamental implication for ecumenical life and activity is that a local Orthodox Church whose the lay members have regained their proper status prays far more for 'the unity of all'. When the awareness of the gift of the Holy Spirit is alive, prayer becomes one of His fruits. And the more the heart is motivated by the Spirit, the more inclusive prayer is.

Ecumenical activity has now informed academic curricula, but it still does not seem linked to the sacrament of Chrismation. However, to the degree this activity is pneumatologically founded it can be more reliable in its didactic and ecumenical aims. A deepening into the theology of Chrismation will pave the way for a solid ecumenical work (as this task should not be reduced to only sentimental motivations), and will make the common effort safer and more effective. The vivid feeling and voice of a living Body inspired by the Spirit will bring fresh air into an ecumenism that has somehow been stagnated among 'experts'.

Besides, a long experience has shown that strong resistances against ecumenical activity have developed across Orthodox Churches. Parts of the ecclesiastical body refuse to accept efforts for dialogue and cooperation, and sometimes tend to react with a dynamism that is fueled by suspicion. An appropriate ecclesiastical response to these opponents has not to be merely defensive but to resort to applied theology. By fostering structures and habits in the Church which are in resonance with her theological inheritance on Holy Spirit and on human nature, we put aside secularized habits accumulated through centuries and we discover the core of ecclesiastical experience. Actually by doing so we allow more space for the Holy Spirit to act, as 'unity of all' is His very mission and wish.

---

[4] Gregory the Theologian, *The Oration on Holy Baptism*, 16.

Bibliography

Nikolai Afanassieff, *Ministry of the Laity*. http://philotimo-leventia.blogspot.gr/2011/02/ministry-of-laity-by-fr-n-afanassieff.html (last accessed September 2013).

Radu Bordeianu, *Staniloae, Dimitru: An Ecumenical Ecclesiology* (T&T Clark, 2011)

Paul Evdokimov, *The Struggle with God.* (Paulist Press, 1966).

Alexander Schmemann, *Clergy and Laity in the Orthodox Church.* www.schmemann.org/byhim/clergyandlaityinthechurch.html (last accessed 19 September 2013)

Alexander Schmemann, *Of Water and the Spirit: A Liturgical Study of Baptism* (St Vladimir's Seminary Press, 1974)

Alexander Schmemann, *Church, World, Mission* (St Vladimir's Seminary Press, 1979)

Anthony Scott (Ed.), *Good and Faithful Servant: Stewardship in the Orthodox Church* (St Vladimir's Seminary Press, 2003)

Eleni Kasselouri-Hatzivassiliadi

Women in Church and society has been one of the main areas of concern in the ecumenical movement from its very beginning.

At the world conference on *Faith and Order* (1927), seven women presented a statement demanding that the issue of women's participation be central in the life and work of the World Council of Churches (WCC). Before the WCC's 1st Assembly (Amsterdam 1948) a questionnaire was sent out to obtain information about the life and work of women in the churches. In Evanston (1954) the will clearly existed "to help women find the right balance between their family responsibilities and their professional life." It was in 1974 at the women's consultation in Berlin on "sexism in the 1970s," in preparation of the WCC's Nairobi Assembly, where the structures of injustice and sexism in the Church were fundamentally challenged. The problem of sexism in the Church was dealt in a study on the 'Community of women and men in the Church'. The crucial aspect of this study was that it focused not on what Christian men and women ought to think, but on their experience. This priority especially on women's experience was given mostly in the WCC activities and programs that followed.

The development of feminist theologies in the 70s created a worldwide ecumenical network of systematic scholarship. The biblical and ecclesiological dimension of this systematic work has clear implications for the modern ecumenical movement. According to Diane Brewster, "not only has received historical tradition about patterns of ministry and leadership been challenged by feminist scholars (and has obvious relevance to the debate within some churches regarding the ordination of women), but there is also a creative re-visioning of what is to *be* church."[1]

Through the 80s there was an attempt to connect theology with social practice. There were studies on issues of women and work, women in poverty, and violence against women. The WCC declared the *Ecumenical Decade of the Churched in Solidarity with women* (EDCSW) from 1988 to 1998. A major post-decade initiative, *On being Church: Women's voices and visions* sought to sustain solidarity noting that the mid-Decade teams heard not only stories of violence and exclusion, but also 'stories of women standing in solidarity with each other, of their commitment to their churches and their efforts to develop their own ways of being church together.'

There has been a vivid – yet not enough – work and involvement of Orthodox women in raising issues of women's participation, human sexuality and ministry in the Orthodox Church, since the first ecumenical study on women in the church was presented to the inaugural Assembly of the WCC in 1948, through the Istanbul Consultation held in May 1997, the presentation of the EDCSW to the 8th WCC Assembly in Harare (1998), and the participation in the 9th Assembly of WCC, Porto Alegre (2006).

In this historical and theological journey, one has to observe certain crucial moments. In 1976, 40 participants arrived at the Agapia Monastery for the first Orthodox Women's Consultation to discuss their participation in the Orthodox Church. As Elizabeth Behr-Sigel observed some years later: "for the first time in Christian history women were called to reflect together, in dialogue with bishops and theologians, on their vocation and specific ministry."

One of the main themes and obstacles in ecumenical dialogue was and still is the ordination of women. The position of the Roman Catholic and the Orthodox churches has been unchanged. In 1988, the Orthodox churches held a Consultation in Rhodes to set out their reasons for maintaining the unbroken tradition of the Church. However, the 25th conclusion of the consultation points out and admits that: "while recognizing these

---

[1] "Theology, Feminist," *Dictionary of the Ecumenical Movement*, Nicholas Lossky, Jose Miguez Bonino, John Pobee, Tom F. Stransky, Goffrey Wainwright, Pauline Webb (eds.), (Geneva: WCC Publications, 2002), 1114.

facts, which witness to the promotion through the Church of the equality of honor between men and women, it is necessary to confess in honesty and with humility, that, owing to human weakness and sinfulness, the Christian communities have not always and in all places been able to suppress effectively ideas, manners, customs, historical developments and social conditions which have resulted in practical discrimination against women." This is maybe the most sincere conclusion of the conference and a starting point for reflection.

The consultation in Rhodes opened the debate on the arguments against and for the ordination of women. Elisabeth Behr-Sigel and Kallistos Ware in their book *The ordination of women in the Orthodox Church* have made a sincere effort to provide a response. After outlining the historical context, Elisabeth Behr-Sigel, a well-known ecumenical figure, philosopher and theologian, describes the ups and downs of the difficult growth of consciousness, coupled with a creative return to the sources of genuine ecclesial Tradition called for by frank ecumenical dialogue. On the other hand, Kallistos Ware, Bishop of Diokleia, sets the question of the ordination of women in the light of patristic anthropology and Orthodox theology.

In the period during the Ecumenical Decade – Churches in Solidarity with Women (1988-1998) – two main gatherings were held among many other Bossey Seminars and inter-Christian meetings. The first was hosted by the Greek Orthodox Patriarchate of Antioch and all the East in Damascus (1996), and the second by the Ecumenical Patriarchate of Constantinople in Istanbul (1997), both under the theme: *"Discerning the Signs of the Times" (Matt. 16:3): Women in the life of the Orthodox Church."* The final documents reflect the fact that: "there are some occasions when the role and the presence of women, as well as their work, is not always validated for the value it has....we recognize with deep concern how social injustices such as poverty, illiteracy and invisibility may affect Orthodox women and women in general in our part of the world."

After the EDCSW, in the frame of the WCC Programme *Women's Voices and Visions on being Church*, Orthodox women had the opportunity to discuss and reflect not only in their context but also in cooperation with sisters from other Christian traditions. One of the many meetings between 2000 and 2005 was held in Geneva from 11-16 October 2001. Thirteen Orthodox women from Albania, Australia, Bulgaria, Cyprus, France, Greece, Lebanon, Romania, the USA, and the WCC gathered together. Throughout the four days they discussed their understanding of the Church. As in previous meetings held in Greece, Istanbul, Damascus/Syria, Rumania etc, their concerns and expectations regarding their churches and the ecumenical movement were reflected in the following:

- They encouraged Orthodox women theologians, historians, sociologists, psychologists, and health-care providers to publish their writings, at the same time encouraging the editors of scholarly journals to be more receptive to their research and writings.
- Depending on geographical location, many women in the Orthodox Church felt excluded from the decision-making process of the Church.
- They would like to see women organize themselves on an international level into a formal network, and they would like this network to have a close relationship with the bishops and priests of the Church.
- In certain contexts, women who were theologically educated had great difficulty in being appointed to positions in the Church that corresponded to their level of education.

At the end of the Programme, a small book was published in 2006 under the title *Women's Voices and Visions on Being Church. Reflections of Orthodox Women.*

There were three women theologians – coming from different national backgrounds – who contributed to this volume and shared their vision of the Church. The first contributor is Leonie Liveris, an Australian Orthodox theologian, well-known in the ecumenical circles as the editor of the Orthodox Bulletin *Martha and Maria* and her book *Ancient Taboos and Gender Prejudice. Challenges for Orthodox Women and the Church.* Leonie Liveris raised the question:

"Can it be too bold, too modern that Orthodox Ecclesiology might begin to re-examine and renew many aspects of church life that do adversely affect the lives of women? Can there not be a new alignment of hierarchy, of including women in decision-making in order to meet the new needs of this century acknowledging many women of faith are competent, qualified and educated and immensely committed to their Orthodox Church? Can not the experiences of women and their knowledge of contemporary society and family life better inform the church hierarchy?"

The second woman who contributed to the publication was Teva Regule, a Rumanian Orthodox theologian and member of the editorial Board of the Bulletin *St. Nina Quarterly*. Regule stressed that

"The Orthodox Church's theology of God and our relationship to Him is life-giving. However, there are times when certain practices in the Church fail to reflect this life-giving theology. One area that has been particularly painful to many girls and women is the practice of only allowing males to serve within the altar in parishes. Although many bishops, priests, and theologians admit that there is no good theological reason for such a practice (women have served in the past as female deacons in Byzantium and as altar servers in Russia and elsewhere as well as in monastic settings), it persists. Within the past few years, a small number of parishes have taken tentative steps to include girls as altar servers. Anecdotal evidence suggests that this has been a welcome development in those settings. It is my fervent hope that this practice, which can have such an important impact on the spiritual development of a young girl, be allowed to continue and grow…We are all called to give glory to God to the best of our abilities within the community of the Church. However, a community whose members are hurt is deformed. We need to be the Church, a therapeutic, healing community. It is then that we can experience the love of God more fully in this world as in the next."

The third contributor was Niki Papageorgiou, Professor of Sociology at the Department of Theology of Aristotle University of Thessaloniki, who enquired:

"Which type of woman is preferred within the frame of the ecclesiastical community, Martha or Mary? Christ seems to be accepting the second role, that of Mary. But the Church seems to be preferring the role of Martha. The differentiation of the roles of Martha and Mary reflects a struggle within the Church between institution and charisma. The institutional role of woman appears different from the charismatic one. The distinction between institution and charisma -likable in the field of Sociology- doesn't leave the Orthodox Church unaffected. While the role of Mary is praised, progressively, the role of Martha seems to be getting greater importance over the centuries, following a course parallel to the one of the institutionalization of the Church. Whereas at the charismatic - theological level the equal place of Mary in the ecclesiastical community is acknowledged, at the institutional-sociological level Martha survives through specific roles, roles of discrimination and underestimation that become broader accepted and get established."

In the 9th Assembly of the WCC in Porto Alegre (2006), the participation of Orthodox women was more than visible. They participated as delegates, official observers, lectures, co-opted staff members, stewards, mutirão participants. Many factors had contributed to that progress: historical, political and economic changes, especially in Eastern Europe, which influenced not only the social, but also the cultural and religious reality; theological challenges that came from other Christian traditions about the role of women in the churches and the foremost issue of women's ordination; many initiatives that had been taken by ecumenical bodies and organizations in the direction of encouraging and improving the participation of women in their decision-making bodies.

The participation of Orthodox women in the 9th Assembly created a sense of optimism for the future, and on the other hand, an obligation for a deep self-criticism. But really, how much progress and change has there been in the last decades, after the Agapia Consultation (1976)? Are the changes sufficient to ensure that the progress will continue in the future?

In this frame, and in order to answer these question, a consultation was held in Volos, Greece, in June 2008 on the theme: *Many Women were also there…the Participation of Orthodox women in the ecumenical movement* organized by the WCC Programme *Women in Church and Society*, and hosted by the Volos Academy for Theological Studies. The Volos Consultation brought together three generations of Orthodox women: the generation that worked in the EDCSW and participated in the inter-Orthodox consultation in Rhodes, the Crete Consultation, the Damascus and Istanbul conferences; the generation that continued with the WCC Programme *Women's Voices and visions on being church*; and last, but not least, the third generation of young theologians who are active today in various ecumenical bodies, giving witness to their tradition and faith. During the Consultation, all the so-called 'open issues' were discussed; those, in other words that require a deeper theological analysis and comprehension by the Orthodox: the revival of the female diaconate and the ordination of women, the more active participation of women in the administrative and pastoral work of the Church, the empowerment of women in theological research and study, and the language and content of some liturgical texts connected with women.

Have these concerns of Orthodox women modified their churches in order to reform attitudes and practices that for centuries deemed women to be the 'other'? What kind of theological word do we need as Church? What is the role of Orthodox women theologians? How can Orthodox women discuss and answer the various questions raised or created by post-modernity that influenced the local contexts? Where can Orthodox women theologians find the necessary resources for empowering other women? Is there a necessity of re-discovering and re-defining the 'healing' witness of our written and oral tradition in order to take care of the wounds of injustice, fear and violence? How can we move from communities of authority and injustice to communities of love and respect? It is imperative that the Orthodox churches should break the silence on gender discrimination and inequality and challenge all the patriarchal ideas and stereotypes that deny women a full participation in the life of the community. The message of the 'good news' is clear:

> When anyone is united to Christ, there is a new world; the old order has gone, and the new order has already begun (II Cor. 5:17).

Bibliography

Genadios Limouris (ed.), *The place of the Woman in the Orthodox Church and the question of the ordination of women*, (Katerini: Tertios Publications, 1992) (in Greek).

Kyriaki Karidoyannes FitzGerald, *Orthodox Women Speak. Discerning the 'Signs of the Times'*, (Geneva: WCC Publications, 1999).

Elisabeth Behr-Sigel, *The Ordination of Women in the Orthodox Church,* (Geneva: WCC Publications, 2000).

Christina Breaban, Sophie Deicha, Eleni Kasselouri-Hatzivassiliadi (eds.), *Women's Voices and Visions of the Church. Reflections of Orthodox Women,* (WCC, 2006).

Leonie Liveris, *Ancient Taboos and Gender Prejudice. Challenges for Orthodox Women and the Church,* (Hampshire: Ashgate, 2005).

Aristotle Papanikolaou & Elizabeth Prodromou (eds.), *Thinking through Faith. New Perspectives from Orthodox Christian Scholars,* (Crestwood, NY: St. Vladimir's Seminary Press, 2008).

Eleni Kasselouri-Hatzivassiliadi, Fulata Mbano Moyo, Aikaterini Pekridou (eds.), *Many women were also there...the participation of Orthodox women in the ecumenical movement,* (Geneva/Volos: WCC & Volos Academy for Theological Study Publications, 2010).

Stavros Yangazoglou

1. The Anthropology of Modernity

Modernity does not consist of simply a sociological, philosophical or political meaning. It is not characterized only by a historical period, but rather complete culture, a way of seeing and evaluating the world. This culture started creeping within the Renaissance, formed mainly by the Enlightenment, the rapid progress of science, the industrial revolution and received almost universal dimensions with the technological boom of the 20th century. Modernity gradually overturned the traditional worldview which was unaltered for centuries, and every metaphysical authority, initiating a new system of values in all fields of human life.

With sound reason and the use of empirical example as the main tools, modernity signaled a new epoch in the relationship between man and nature. The break in the assumed meanings of every mythical and religious sense brought the absolute value of scientific knowledge and domination of man over nature to the epicenter of modernity. Knowledge and use of the natural world through scientific knowledge attempted to demystify the phenomena of nature and replace any metaphysical preoccupation, highlighting the earthly happiness of man against religious metaphysical bliss. The transition from traditional to urban and industrialized society, the unshackling of any transcendent authority, the autonomy of the human subject, the rational criteria for understanding the human past, the secularization of society and the state, the declaration of the rights of the individual as a foundational and primary axiom, constitute some of the key features of modernity. Myth and reality, novelty became the new consciousness of man and spread to all areas of human life and culture. A modern state, secular society, dizzying scientific progress, modernist art, music, painting, morals, ideas and values, modernity has evolved into the dominant ideology of modern man.[1]

However, that which makes modernity so radically different from other previous epochs is precisely that the present is now more thoroughly defined by a secularized conception of history. The traditional 'history of salvation' of Christianity is replaced by the 'progress' of humanity. Time does not carry out God's plan for the world and man, but is a purely human and worldly process. Historical time is human time par excellence. The world of history, the only intelligible world, is a creation of man. After the end of transcendence, history not only becomes autonomous and the unique world of man, but gradually replaces God.[2] The declaration of the rejection of the Christian past of Europe was the primary instrument of the Renaissance and the Enlightenment. Seeking cultural norms beyond the medieval tradition, modernity turned rapidly to classical antiquity and yet paradoxically raised the nostalgia of this as a future realization of a fully anthropological era.

Now that man is the sole source of truth, he can recognize himself as the only God and human history as the only reality. The conquest of the world of history, "the age of the image of the world," was indeed a founding principle of the new age, but also a new ontology in relations between world and man. The Cartesian version of the thinking subject has turned the world into an object of knowledge. The world is found inside man, who in this way can rightfully become its "lord and master." The world became the object and man the subject, the universe was split in 'nature' and in 'history', historical time is being juxtaposed to the natural world, paving the way for the tragic experience of the contrast between nature and spirit. Man, the only protagonist in the

---

[1] For Modernity cf. Charles Taylor, *Sources of the Self: The Making of the Modern Identity*, (Cambridge, MA: Harvard University Press, 1989). For the relationship of Orthodoxy with Modernity cf. P. Kalaitzidis-N. Dontos, (eds.) *Orthodoxy and Modernity*, (Athens: Indiktos, 2007) (in Greek).

[2] Cf. Kostas Papaioannou, *La Consécration de l'Histoire*, avant-propos d'Alain Pons, (Paris: Éditions Champ libre, 1983).

theater of history, free from any metaphysical obligation, discovers endless possibilities. The deification of man as the purpose of history provides the only possible ontological definition of history. History as a progressive realization of freedom is ultimately the place of the 'theophany' of man.

2. Anthropological Aspects of Post-modernity

However, by the last quarter of the 20th century, modernity had already begun to lose its original luster and soteriological halo. The first cracks appeared with the experience of two world wars centralized in Europe. Deadlocks multiplied with the emergence of the ecological crisis, the problems of the third world, the techno-logical revolution in cybernetics and informatics, the consumerism and the need for perpetual euphoria, and finally, the phenomenon of globalization. In the era of 'late' modernity or post-modernity,[3] the idea of a linear progression of history, the Cartesian pursuit of certain objectives, absolute faith in the imperatives of rationality, the urban culture, the nation-state (ethnic-state), the various ideologies, the visions of general wellbeing, the great narratives of humanity, the human subject, and even history itself and the time of man began to falter and reveal a great impasse and show signs of the 'end' of an entire culture, at least in the form that modernity has lent in the last three centuries.

Now scientific knowledge and the imposition of an absolute and objective truth about the world, man and history not only is being challenged, but is considered the same in relation to religious knowledge. Secularism is no longer seen as a development, which will inevitably eliminate the religious phenomenon, which dynam-ically and diversely reappears on the historical scene. All the fundamental imperatives of modernity, such as omnipotence of reason, the overturning of sanctity, the priority of the thinking subject, and the relationship of man with nature are being placed in an unrelenting criticism. However, a pervasive nihilism and a new fuzzy religiosity in the form of a neo-Gnosticism tend to replace both the Christian faith and the sound-mindedness of modernity. In this new understanding the almost metaphysical faith of man is perpetuated in the endless progress of technology. And while it unrestrainedly dominates the market economy and the consumer happi-ness of the masses, the practical nihilism shapes the society of indifference and automated man as an extreme individualistic conclusion of the thinking subject of modernity. In the evolving new society indifference is expressed toward any spiritual and cultural heritage of the past, and slowly but surely the new communication technologies transform the culture of reason (speech) toward a global dominance of electronic images.

But what especially characterizes the post-modern man is the anonymity of existence and of life in modern mega-cities. The modern world is a 'world of foreigners,'[4] a world in which fluidity dominates and speed and fragmentation act as a catalyst in the depths of man's being. Precisely this eclipse of the subject leads many to think that the 21st century will prove to be the century of anthropology as a radical reevaluation of the unique and unparalleled value of human existence.[5] Man's loneliness is accentuated by the fundamental choices of post-modernity. Indeed, the postmodern thought vehemently denied the possibility of the existence of an anthropology with universal validity for all people and for all times. The characteristic of post-mo-dernity incredulity towards meta-narratives, the proclamation of the death of grand narratives, limit the meaning of human existence to individual cultural and historical references, which are necessarily transitory

---

[3] For a discussion of post-modernity in relation with Orthodox theology cf. Petros Vassiliadis, *Post-Modernity and Church: The Challenge of Orthodoxy*, (Athens: Akritas, 2002) (in Greek). Christos Yannaras, *Postmodern Metaphysics*, (Brook-line, MA: H.C. Press, 2004). Stavros Yangazoglou, "Philosophy of History and Theology of History" in *Orthodoxy and Post-Modernity*, (Patras: Hellenic Open University Press, 2008), 15-80 (in Greek).

[4] For the anthropological implications of post-modernity cf. Marc Augé, *Non-Places; Introduction to an Anthropology of Super-modernity,* (New York: Vesro Books, 1995), Zygmunt Bauman, *Globalization: The Human Consequences*, (New York: Columbia University Press, 1998).

[5] Kallistos Ware, "Orthodox theology in the new millennium: what is the most important question?" *Sobornost* 26.2 (2004): 7-23.

and disposable, each with its own dependent truths.[6] Everything is relative and an interpretation of the era.[7] Here emerges anew the primordial philosophical problem of the dialectic between the one and the many, the struggle between partial and universal. In the postmodern condition Squires avers that the "death of Man, History and Metaphysics. This implies the rejection of all of essentialism - transcendent understanding of human nature ... man is a social, historical and linguistic structure."[8] In such a perspective of degradation there exists no meaning, neither in history nor in the life of man. The point is this "currency," i.e. a temporary construction of man.

This context includes the uncovering of relational postmodern anthropology and contradictions. The human subject is interpreted inter-subjectively now.[9] However, his relationship with the other becomes almost impossible, since social structures as a ground for the emergence of relations decomposes continuously and public space has been eclipsed and subsides gradually in favor of private and consumer choices. Modern man seems to vary increasingly energized his private desire: "each is tempted when he is drawn away by his own desires and enticed" (Jas.1:14). The narcissism of this man of post-modernity ultimately is defined as a self-referential anthropology of the relations between the subject with his own components.[10] This brings about a regression into extreme individualism. These concepts overtly or discreetly seem to diffuse into the modern conceptions of man in philosophy, psychology, sociology, economy, as well as in biotechnological research and applications, at the same time dulling the very criteria of social justice and ethics. The practical nihilism of man exacerbates social alienation, massively expands the problem of poverty, and is unable to control or even to interpret the evil and violence from man to man or man against the natural enviroment. In order to simplify a very complex world and the acceleration of market trade, a new way of life made an appearance, changing people's everyday lives. Human life becomes more simple and effective which, as long as each man thinks only of himself and his interests. Thus, in the era of information capitalism and mass consumption, the man without realizing it has entrusted the organization of his life and soul to the economists. Everything is subordinated to private desire, the aggressive interest of the individual. At the same time, the undefined relationship of identity and otherness in our rapidly changing world propagates several local outbreaks of nationalism and fundamentalism.

3. Toward a dynamic and relational anthropology: the meaning of Orthodox anthropology today

In times of late modernity, when all the grand narratives and traditions are in fact on the sidelines, what critical and existential meaning of life for the world, man and history conveys a debate in anthropology from the standpoint of orthodox theology? Under the new environment of pluralism, Orthodox theology is called upon to articulate a resolution and meaning of life for the world, man and history. In this way, a new interpretive theory to Christian anthropology must be realized, distinguishing what is fundamental and unchanging and what is merely cultural and cosmological verbiage of a given era. In this theological hermeneutics as a re-measuring of pluralism and diversity in the ecumenical dimension, Orthodox theology must highlight the potential meaning of human existence in dialogue with the anxieties and problems of modern man.

For Orthodox theology the human is not to be defined statically. Man is not merely biological or spiritual existence, but a being in relation and en route. The fullness of existence is not its self-referentiality but the

[6] Lyotard, Jean-François, *The Post-Modern Condition, A Report of Knowledge*, (University of Minnesota Press, 1984)
[7] Cf. Zygmunt Bauman, *Life in fragments*, (Oxford: Blackwell, 1995).
[8] Judith Squires, "Indroduction," in Judith Squires (ed.), *Principled Positions. Postmodernism and Rediscovery of Value*, (London: Lawrence and Wishart, 1993), 2.
[9] Cf. Christos Yannaras, "Psychoanalysis and Orthodox anthropology," in John T. Chirban (Ed.), *Personhood: Orthodox Christianity and the Connection between Body, Mind and Soul, Bergin and Garvey*, (Westport, CT, 1996) 83-89. Vasileios Thermos, *In Search of the Person: "True" and "False Self" according to Donald Winnicott and St. Gregory Palamas*, (Quebec, Canada: Alexander Press, 2002).
[10] Christopher Lash, *The Culture of Narcissism*, (New York: W.W. Norton, 1978).

encounter and communion with the absolute Other, with an existence radically beyond and outside his own. In light of the Christology of the Church this means that man can the opening and communion of his being with the Triune God, in Christ and through the Holy Spirit. i.e. with the One Being who is *communion* and *otherness* par excellence; becoming by grace that which it is not by nature, becoming a son of God in by way of relation, and gaining a *new way of being* beyond decay and death. Original sin and the problem of evil in the orthodox tradition is not defined by the concept of predestination, but the tragic exercise of human freedom.

The Metropolitan of Pergamon John Zizioulas key notes that "the essence of sin is the fear of the Other, a thing which is a part of the rejection of God. If the confirmation of our 'self' is made through the rejection rather than acceptance of others – that which Adam has chosen to do freely – then it is only normal and inevitable for the other to become an enemy and a threat. Reconciliation with God is a prerequisite for reconciliation with any 'other' ... The fact that the fear of the other is pathologically inherent in our existence leads to fear not only of the other, but *every otherness.*"[11] In each case the freedom proves to be a key of anthropology.

The other is a necessary condition of my existence. But this is not for anyone else, but for the eminently Other. This means that the relationship with God and the relationship in Christ with the fellowman and the world becomes the new way of human existence, beyond his conventional and corrupted life. The Church is not just any historical institution, but becomes the eminently anthropological place and way, the eschatological root and substance of true life for humans. Modern Orthodox theology has to present hermeneutically not only the *theological ontology of the person* but also the conscious and free act of man, composing theory and practice, the eschatological glory of man with the ethos of ascesis and Eucharistic communion. Otherwise, such a person-centered anthropology can easily be seen as an excuse for an unhistorical escape.

In the person of Christ, man experiences theosis, transcending the boundaries of creation not only psychologically or "naturally," but through a person.[12] The link of the communion of the uncreated God and created man expressed "in person," as a reflection, i.e. personal existence of God toward man as much from the biblical as from the patristic tradition of the "image and likeness." The anthropological problem of the ontology of the person is found, moreover, in the priority and absoluteness of otherness in relation to the general, i.e. the problem of the relationship of the "one" and the "many." The solution of this problem has been given, in patristic theology, by the Incarnation of the Son and Word of God, which is moreover an iconological and eschatological reality. The truth of the person as the ultimate truth of existence is an icon of the future in the sense that it is experienced as a dialectical relationship between the eschatological character of a person who enters into story, without being converted into history.

Christ through the Holy Spirit takes on His body, the Church, the many different human faces, and instills whatever constitutes the inseparable relationship with the way of existence of the persons of the Holy Trinity mutually co-indwelling in freedom and love. Thus, the life of every person is weaving together of freedom with love, since the cohesion does not militate against or eliminate the heterogeneity, just as different human faces do not deprive the identity from the individual and finite selves. In the society of His body, the Church, the knowledge of God is possible, which passes only through love towards each other. Without the relationship with the other the self does not exist that knows and loves God. In Christ we find others interpersonally without being alienated, in Christ we cease to exist as enclosed and divided individualities that rush toward decay and demise, in Christ we attain to the ethos of the person, which leads "that unity which possesses teaching the Holy Trinity ."[13] The non-static direction of the person allows the integration of the *many* in *one* Christ, making the Church the Body of Christ and each of His members becomes himself Christ and Church. This truth of the person which transcends individuality, division and death of being, is not just a conceptual and abstract metaphysical proposition, but a historical and empirical event in the life of the Church, it is the Holy Eucharist.

---

[11] John Zizioulas, "Communion and Otherness," *St Vladimir's Theological Quarterly* 38.4 (1994): 348.

[12] Cf. Stavros Yangazoglou, *Communion of Theosis. The synthesis of Christology and Pneumatology in the work of St. Gregory Palamas*, (Athens: Domos, 2001) (in Greek).

[13] St. Isaac in the Syrian, *Ascetical Orat. 22,* 477.

Therefore, the ethos of the person and the society is not the result of a moral teaching, even the most high, but the ability and experiential achievement within a *community* that has become inside of history the truth of the person as an existential demeanor and attitude towards life. Man is restored as a priest and cosmic minister of Creation and of the ethos of freedom that is realized in the image of divine freedom. For Orthodox anthropology moral responsibility as a practical attitude with respect to history and everyday life is contained in the ethos of the Eucharistic communion and culture of the person.

At this point it is necessary to point out that descriptive anthropology and the human sciences are one thing and the work of theology another, which offers an existential interpretation of the fact of human existence, beyond objective justification. For Orthodox theology both the uncreated God and the created man are perceived as 'under-principle' (lit. translation of Greek υπό άρχη). Man is "animal being made God"[14] in the perspective of the dialectical relationship between created and uncreated, as manifested in Patristic Christology. Male and female, body-soul, the whole man is the image of God. He is not immortal, neither in the body nor in soul, he is immortal in the perspective of the life in Christ, when he is open to communion with others and with the eminent Other. If now in history the ontology of the human person in Christ is iconic, "in a mirror, dimly" (*Cor.* 13, 12), to the eschaton of the kingdom will the fullness of the "likeness of God" shall be revealed.

Bibliography

Vladimir Lossky, *In the Image and Likeness of God*, (Crestwood, NY: St Vladimir's Seminary Press, 1997).

Panayotis Nellas, *Deification in Christ: Orthodox Perspectives on the Nature of the Human Person*, (Crestwood, NY: St Vladimir's Seminary Press, 1987).

Athanasios Papathanassiou, "Christian anthropology for a culture of peace: considering the Church in mission and dialogue today," in Emmanuel Clapsis (ed.), *Violence and the Christian spirituality*, (Geneva/Brookline: WCC/Holy Cross Orthodox Press, 2007), 87-106.

Vasileios Thermos, *In Search of the Person: "True" and "False Self" according to Donald Winnicott and St. Gregory Palamas*, (Quebec, Canada: Alexander Press, 2002).

Kallistos Ware, "The Human Person as an Icon of the Trinity," *Sobornost incorporating Eastern Churches Review* 8.2 (1986): 6-23.

-, *Orthodox Theology in the Twenty-First Century*, Doxa & Praxis series, (Geneva: WCC Publications/Volos Academy, 2012).

Stavros Yangazoglou, "The person in the Trinitarian Theology of Grogory Palamas. The Palamite Synthesis of a Prosopocentric Ontology," *Philotheos, International Journal for Philosophy and Theology* 1 (2001): 137-143.

Christos Yannaras, *The Freedom of Morality*, (Crestwood, NY: St Vladimir's Seminary Press, 1984).

-, *Person and Eros*, (Brookline, MA: H.C. Press, 2008).

John Zizioulas, *Being as Communion: Studies in Personhood and the Church*, (London: Darton, Longman & Todd, 1985)

-, *Communion and Otherness: Further Studies in Personhood and the Church*, (London: T&T Clark, 2006).

(translated by Christopher Henson)

---

[14] St. Gregory the Theologian, *Orat. On Theophania* PG 36, 324, 13.

Fr. Christophe D'Aloisio

The title for this short piece covers an extremely broad range of topics which could easily fill a whole book. There are a number of ways in which it could be addressed: perhaps by offering direct testimonies, or else through scientific analysis – be it historical, ecclesiological or canonical. Either way, this theme is likely to be polemical, depending on the strength and perspective of the differing points of view. The aim of our contribution here is certainly not to offer a definitive opinion on Orthodox youth in the ecumenical movement. We seek rather to highlight some questions which arise both from our empirical knowledge as representative of youth movements in various ecumenical gatherings over a number of years, and from our experience as simple Orthodox believers who feel concerned about the ecclesiological challenges of today. May this short contribution be an occasion for debate between young people and their local pastoral authorities about the functioning of the local Churches, and the progress of ecumenism in other Orthodox contexts.

Orthodox Youth in the Ecumenical Movement. Wouldn't some observers be puzzled by this title? *Is there an Orthodox Youth,* organised as such and committed in Church life? And *what possibility, if any, do they have of making a contribution* in the ecumenical movement, whether in parallel with, or from within the range of official delegations from the Orthodox Church in ecumenical organisations?

In fact, there has been and there could still be an input from Orthodox Youth in the ecumenical movement. But in order to present our thesis, we need first of all to clarify the terms of the title.

1. *What is the Ecumenical Movement, for an Orthodox believer?* This question, repeatedly raised today, has so far not found an appropriate answer for the Orthodox faithful. Of course, the big ecumenical organisations established during the 20th century appear as the major actors of the ecumenical movement today. However, one has to admit that ecumenism in the 21st century must *also* explore other paths beyond the reconfiguration of existing ecumenical organisations. It must aim to serve not the structured organisations of the current ecumenical movement, but Christ and his Church, in the assumption of her apostolic Mission in History, towards unity and love.

In this respect, we can distinguish the Orthodox ecumenical involvement on the one hand in the integrated structures of the organised ecumenical movement (WCC, Regional Councils of Churches, National Councils of Churches, etc., all of them subject to constant reconfiguration in order to be closer to their initial mission), and on the other hand in informal ecumenical meetings which, in today's rapidly changing and communicating world, tend more and more to be the focus of daily grass-root ecumenism.

Furthermore, there is another aspect of ecumenical dialogue which needs to be taken into deeper consideration. For Orthodox Ecclesiology, any advances in the instituted ecumenical dialogues can be considered as *official* achievements only if they are *received* by the People of God, in the *consensus fidelium*. Recent administrative developments within the World Council of Churches (implemented for the first time during the General Assembly in Porto Alegre, Brazil in 2006, following the recommendations of the Special Commission on Orthodox Participation) adopted the decision-making process through *consensus*, in order to foster in particular Orthodox integration into the structure of the WCC. This same decision-making process through *consensus*, almost imposed upon other Christians by the Orthodox, is still an unknown practice inside most of the Orthodox Churches themselves and, therefore, remains a great challenge.

Hence, a huge work is still to be done to submit the fruit of the dialogues brought by the ecumenical organisations to the reception of the *consensus fidelium* in the Orthodox Churches. Our basic knowledge of the pastoral situations in the Orthodox Church makes us quite pessimistic about such a process. Indeed, the achievements of the ecumenical dialogues need to be *positively received*; however, *indifference* is sometimes the best result one can expect, in several Orthodox contexts. In fact, hostile manifestations against ecumenism are quite common nowadays, coming sometimes from very prominent persons or groups in the Orthodox Church. Such attitudes are, it has to be said, *rarely rejected* by the pastoral authorities: this *lack of disavowal* could almost be seen as a *negative reception*.

In some Orthodox contexts today, the mere fact of mentioning the name of some ecumenical organisations or the name of the Pope of Rome is enough to create a wave of protest against any kind of brotherly contacts with non-Orthodox Christians.

Consequently, in addition to the vital role which the ecumenical organisations take on, it is also crucial that committed young Orthodox people explore *new ways of ecumenism* which could help to achieve a positive reception of the dialogues by the entire Church body.

2. And there comes a second clarification about our title: what is the Orthodox *Youth*? Ecclesiologically, the Church constituency consists of Christ – as the head of the Body – and the whole people of God – as the rest of the Body. Within the people of God, the *pastors* are, among other tasks, elected to minister the unity of the whole body. In the Orthodox Church, the bishops should be seen as the pastors *par excellence*, not considered as individuals, of course, but surrounded by the presbyteral college of their local Church (in the sense of the *episkopē*), in a permanent and living conciliarity (in the sense of *sobornost'*, simultaneously catholicity and synodality).

The ordination of bishops and presbyters among the people of God does not mean that the unity of the Church is operated only by those ministers: they are the coordinators of the work towards unity, which is a fundamental aspect of the Church, but *all* members of the Church are to be committed to the service of unity. Beside this differentiation between the ordained ministers and the rest of the people, there is no other *order* within the Church constituency; there is no *Orthodox Youth* as a distinct group *per se*, apart from the rest of the people.

However, Church pastors, when they represent their local Churches in an ecumenical dialogue, need the advice of specific groups as representatives of the people of God: academic theologians, committed young adults, canonists and lawyers, etc., according to the type of questions which are to be discussed.

3. During the 20th century, mostly thanks to the freedom of speech – which was previously not so developed in the societies where the Orthodox were living – a theological renewal enabled informal groups to establish Church movements in some Orthodox contexts. The basic characteristic of a Church movement lies in the term itself: a *mov*ement *moves*. It tries to re*move* from Church life what is extrinsic to catholicity and to pro*mote* dormant aspects of the ecclesial Tradition.

The various movements which were established during the 20th century have not necessarily all had the same motivation. It is even likely that some of them have not tried to contribute to Church unity. Others, however, not only fostered dialogues, but also created spaces for dialogues when dialogues were not yet in place.

If one examines recent Church history, it appears obvious that almost *all* theologians of the Orthodox Church, who committed themselves to the ecumenical initiatives which founded the existing ecumenical organisations of the 20th century, were trained and sent by Church movements, mostly youth movements.

In this respect, Syndesmos, the World Fellowship of Orthodox Youth, which was established in 1953, always understood itself as an organ of dialogue between Orthodoxy and other Christians. The role played by active members of the Fellowship in various ecumenical organisations, beginning with the WCC, is far too significant to be expounded here. Church pastors of all Orthodox Churches relied on the zeal for unity of Syndesmos to witness Orthodox catholicity in the ecumenical movement and to provide ecumenical organisations with competent officers and speakers. Orthodox youth was not considered merely as a category of age, but as a way of being: "young Orthodox" could sometimes be quite old, but with a spirit of boldness and enthusiasm which is not easy to cultivate when one has taken on official pastoral responsibilities. In a sense, the "youth" were those who were not elders (*presbuteroi*).

4. Today, both youth movements and official Church delegations have evolved to something new: the youth is now often strictly defined by age (e.g. 15-25 or 18-30 years old); Church delegates are mostly professional Church

officers, so utterly devoted to ecumenical meetings that they can not possibly be present on a regular basis in the local Churches where they are pastors. It sometimes also happens that Orthodox Churches are represented by titular bishops who, by definition, are not ecclesiologically pastors of the respective Churches which send them.

This fact is not secondary and is only one example, among others, of awkward situations in the current ecumenical movement. It does not meet the ecclesiological requirements of Church reception: only the canonical – single – bishop of a given local Church can speak on behalf of his community. The spiritual gift *to make his Church present* in a dialogue of Churches is given only to him; the gift is conveyable to nobody else, even temporarily, because the gift is not an object which is held sovereignly by the bishop: it was entrusted to him by the Holy Spirit at his ordination, through the invocation of the plenary Church assembly.

Any other delegate – whether an ordained titular bishop or any other deputy representative – acts as representative not of the local Church, but of the canonical bishop of the local Church. Therefore, the ecumenical dialogue changes in its essence, and becomes a dialogue of individuals, not a dialogue of Churches through the charismatic ministry of their canonical local bishops strictly understood in the living conciliarity of the clergy and laity.

Another ecclesiologically puzzling situation in the representation of the Orthodox Church today in the ecumenical movement, is the fact that, despite the Orthodox ecclesiology which is strictly territorial, the ecumenical organisations (at least, the WCC) recognise several "Orthodox World Communions."

This fact is problematic for the Orthodox faithful. Indeed, there can only be either regional communions of Orthodox local Churches (i.e. Patriarchal, Autocephalous or Autonomous Churches) or a single Orthodox Church worldwide, with a single coordinator of the communion among all Orthodox Churches. Considering two or more "Orthodox World Communions" simply divides the Orthodox Church which is supposed to be taking part in the ecumenical movement to promote unity. If some Autocephalous Orthodox Churches have a pastoral presence outside their canonical boundaries, this should not be considered as being in accordance with Orthodox ecclesiological principles and should not last in the long-term.

If one bishop has to be considered as the single representative of the whole Orthodox Church worldwide, only the Ecumenical Patriarch of Constantinople can be recognised as such, being the first among all Orthodox pastors worldwide. There exist no arguments to oppose this historical and, moreover, ecclesiological fact. If there is a second bishop who claims to be a representative of an "Orthodox World Communion," then *any* Orthodox diocesan bishop should be allowed to do so too – but that of course would be absurd. Communion and conciliarity necessarily go hand in hand with the recognition of primacies.

So far, the logic of the Orthodox official representatives in ecumenical organisations has not been clarified and creates confusion in the eyes of other Christians about what Orthodoxy truly is. It also gives the impression to Orthodox observers that the ecumenical organisations are sanctioning Orthodox disorder.

5. What can Orthodox movements bring to enrich the current situation in the ecumenical movement? Those who *really represent specific sensitivities* in the local Churches are the Church movements, especially the youth movements, in the sense explained above, which are characterised by their boldness towards Church hierarchy – a boldness which does not exclude but rather implies respect. In an ideal Church situation, those sensitivities would be conveyed by the local bishops (always serving in the conciliarity of the clergy and laity of their local Church); however, the Church situation is far from being ideal.

The palliative, which is the existence of *real* Youth Movements, could be terminated if the ecclesial ministries were aligned in reality with their theological definition.

Until then, all ecumenical dialogues should include youth participation. That would ensure that the dialogues were public, open and closer to the reality of the local Churches.

Instead of that, one has sometimes the impression that official Orthodox representations take less and less into consideration organised Church movements, sometimes preventing them locally to attend ecumenical meetings.

Again, we would like to emphasise that the input of a youth movement is not to be limited to a category of age, but to a way of understanding Church realities. The youth movements have to dare to be critical towards their own pastors, in order to help them not to remove themselves too far from the consciousness of their local community; and pastors should be thankful to youth movements which try, with respect and love, to remind them of the challenges of the world of today. The absence of a critical view from inside the Orthodox Church would be anything but healthy for the life of the body.

The 20th century, which has been the century of all big ecumenical meetings, has also been the century of the morbid silence of some peoples from Eastern Europe during several decades. Humankind has painfully learned that not allowing critical voices can be damaging for the circulation of love in a community; allowing even very critical voices to be heard shows the wisdom of the pastors, and is a sign of the health of the whole body.

6. Let us conclude this contribution with some concrete perspectives by way of two practical suggestions. Firstly, within the ecumenical organisations, a transparent discussion should take place as to how the Orthodox Church is represented. The Ecumenical Patriarchate has to be recognised as the only competent centre of co-ordination of Orthodoxy and could then ensure that only bishops of real cities would represent the Church in ecumenical meetings. We know that tensions exist among the Orthodox hierarchies, but one has to acknowledge that it is likely that tensions have always existed; either we abandon the idea of being one single Orthodox Church, or we comply with our ecclesiological principles which are the expressions of the catholicity of our faith.

Secondly, it must be understood that the future of ecumenism in the 21st century has to be plural and belongs to nobody but to the Lord. The continuation of the ecumenical organisations is vital and their experience is essential in witnessing the progress towards the unity of Christians. In parallel, an ecumenism of Church movements is also vital and should be encouraged, to open new ways towards unity. One important project – probably the most important project today – of this kind has been the initiative of many Church movements (more than 250 movements and communities) called "Together for Europe," mainly initiated by the late Chiara Lubich. The reception by the people of God is very active when Church movements meet with each other; this is indeed the case in the "Together for Europe" meetings. The aim of these ecclesiological events is complementary to those of ecumenical organisations. "It is right for you to do these, and not to let the others be undone" (Matt 23:23).

Bibliography

1. Sergius BULGAKOV, *The Bride of the Lamb*, (Grand Rapids, MI: Eerdmans, 2002).
2. Nicholas AFANASIEV, *The Church of the Holy Spirit*, (Notre Dame, IN: University of Notre Dame Press, 2007).
3. John ZIZIOULAS, *Informal Groups in the Church: An Orthodox Viewpoint*, in R. METZ and J. SCHLICK (eds.), *Informal Groups in the Church – Papers of the Second Cerdic Colloquium Strasbourg – May 13-15, 1971*, (Pittsburgh, PA: The Pickwick Press, 1975), 275-298.
4. Alexander SCHMEMANN, *Church, World, Mission – Reflections on Orthodoxy In the West*, (Crestwood, NY: St. Vladimir's Seminary Press, 1979).
5. John MEYENDORFF, *The vision of unity*, (Crestwood, NY: St. Vladimir's Seminary Press, 1987).
6. (Paul ADELHEIM) Павел Адельгейм, *Догмат о Церкви в канонах и практике* (*Dogmatic teaching of the Church, in the Canons and in the practice*), (Pskov, 2002);
7. www.syndesmos.org (with a database of relevant texts from past activities).

Part VII: Particular Themes and Issues for Orthodox Involvement in Ecumenism

Teva Regule

Orthodox Christian worship and life are marked by the use of icons. They fill public and private worship spaces and are symbols[1] through which the faithful have an opportunity to encounter God and participate in Trinitarian life. The use of icons affirms the goodness of creation, the historicity and Truth of God becoming human in the Incarnation, and the ultimate consummation of all things in God. This paper will briefly introduce Orthodox iconography and highlight some of the ways that one can grow in relationship with God through the iconic encounter. I will begin by presenting some of the theology of the icon from the received tradition of the Orthodox Church. I will then explore briefly the ways that an iconic theology can speak to the wider Christian realm of today. Lastly, I will outline some implications of the use of icons and the iconic encounter for ecumenical dialogue, in particular by using icons to expand our understanding of Christian education, invite us to prayer with the living God, appreciate the beauty of creation, and draw us and all of creation into communion with the Trinity.

Theology of the Icon

Symbols have been a part of the Christian experience since the time of Jesus Christ. Early believers used the Fish (Ἰχθύς, *ichthus*— an acronym in Greek for "Jesus Christ, Son of God, Savior") to identify themselves as Christians and mark their gathering places, the Lamb to represent the sacrifice of Christ (e.g. Rev. 5:6), and the Good Shepherd to represent His care and guidance (e.g. Jn. 10:11, 14). Later, the Church adopted more elaborate renderings to illustrate the experience of the Christian life. For instance, in the baptistery of the house church at Dura Europos, the walls were covered with paintings of biblical themes. They told the story of the Christian experience from the Hebrew Scriptures to the Gospel accounts, including scenes of Adam and Eve, David and Goliath, the Healing of the Paralytic, and three women approaching an empty sarcophagus (most likely, the Myrrh-bearing women). It is likely that these stories helped to instruct the initiate and provided the background for the theological understanding of baptism as a new life in Christ.

In late antiquity, the Church struggled with the idea of actually depicting Christ, Himself, in visual form. Emperor Constantine V (741–775) rejected images of Christ, claiming that the divine nature could not be depicted. He found icons to be idolatrous and posited that the only acceptable image of Christ was in the bread and wine of the Eucharist.[2] Other theologians, most notably John of Damascus, argued for a visual representation of Christ. They reasoned that God used images to reveal Himself (e.g. the Burning Bush) and even made an image of Himself in His Son. Furthermore, the Incarnation transformed the Mosaic injunction found in the Decalogue. Although God the Father still could not be depicted in material form, the Son could be so rendered because of the Incarnation. In His Third Apology, John of Damascus explained the nature of the image. He says, "An image is a likeness, or a model, or a figure of something, showing in itself what it depicts."[3] Although distinction remains, for him, there was a close relationship between the image and its prototype in the icon. Icons of Christ affirm Christ's humanity and show forth His divinity, the understanding of Christ as one person (*hypostasis*) with two natures as articulated by the Council of Chalcedon (451). According to John

---

[1] I use the term "symbol" in its classic sense—that which participates in what it represents.

[2] Anton C. Vrame, *The Educating Icon: Teaching Wisdom and Holiness in the Orthodox Way* (Brookline, Mass.: Holy Cross Orthodox Press, 1999), 24. Henceforth: Vrame, *The Educating Icon*.

[3] John of Damascus, "Third Apology, 16" in *On the Divine Images*. Translated by David Anderson (Crestwood, New York, 1980), 73. Henceforth: *On the Divine Images*.

of Damascus, "Fleshly nature was not lost when it became part of the Godhead, but just as the Word made flesh remained the Word, so also flesh became the Word, yet remained flesh, being united to the person of the Word."[4] Icons of Christ can, therefore, be aids to worship as they lead the believer to the prototype of what is depicted. As Dr. Anthony Vrame, a Greek Orthodox educator, explains, "The appropriate encounter with the icon, despite its powerful presence as a visual image, is an encounter that goes beyond the icon itself to the greater transcendent reality of God."[5]

God is both radically transcendent and yet, permeates everything by His divine energies. The Greek fathers distinguished between these "energies" and the "essence" of God. Although God in God's essence is unknowable, we are called to union with God through His energies.[6] In the Greek patristic mind, there is no sharp line between the spiritual and the material. The icon is part of this continuum. According to Fr. John Chryssavgis, a Greek Orthodox theologian, "The icon constitutes the epiphany of God in wood and the existence of the wood in the presence of God."[7] Furthermore, it can help to bridge the distance between God and us. God invites us to engagement and participation in Him. Icons can provide a focal point for our response and the encounter with the Divine energies of God.

Artistically, icons provide this focal point through the use of inverse perspective. The focal point is not some distant point on the horizon, but lies within our immediate space, opening the horizon to us. It reverses the viewer-image relation. We are not just subjects and the image an object within our gaze. The image is both to be looked at and looks at us; we are put into relationship with each other. In our physical presence in front of an icon, we are both subjects and objects. According to Davor Dzalto, director of the Institute for the Study of Culture and Christianity (Belgrade), "In other words, the icon appears as a window which enables communication; it becomes a way to enter a dialogue with a personal reality revealed in its gaze. Icons inspire activity and constant attention as they signify a personal presence of the portrayed person [or event]."[8]

An emerging Christian Worldview

The 20th century was a time of great ecumenical convergence within Christianity.[9] Many Western Christian theologians "returned to the sources" (ressourcement), rediscovering the writings of the Early Church fathers, especially the Greek fathers. As a result, they grew in their appreciation of the early church and its expression within Eastern Christianity. In addition, as the wider literary, philosophical, and cultural milieu was moving from a "modern" world to what has been described as a "post modern" one, theologians began to mine the wider Christian tradition for categories and ways of articulating the Christian message within this new paradigm. There was less emphasis on defined, declaratory Truth and more emphasis on the Mystery of God. In addition, there was an appreciation for both an apophatic dimension in knowing, as well as a relational way of understanding that included our experience. An iconic theology can speak to these aspects of post-modern thought particularly.

---

[4] John of Damascus, "First Apology, 4" as quoted in *On the Divine Images.*
[5] Vrame, *The Educating Icon,* 44.
[6] Gregory of Palamas articulated more fully the patristic understanding of the distinction between the "energies" and "essence" of God. Excerpts of his thought can be found in John Meyendorff, ed., *Gregory Palamas: The Triads.* (New York: Paulist Press, 1983).
[7] John Chryssavgis, "The World of the Icon" in *Phronema* 7 (1992): 35. Henceforth: Chryssavgis, "The World of the Icon."
[8] Davor Dzalto, "How to be a Human Being" in *Red Egg Review.* (Last accessed on 4/9/13). http://www.redeggreview.org/how-to-be-a-human-being. Henceforth: Dzalto, "How to be a Human Being."
[9] For instance, the establishment of the World Council of Churches in 1948.

Implications of the Icon and Iconic Encounter

What can we learn from the early iconographic debates within the Church that can speak to our world today? What can we share from the understanding of icons in the received tradition with our brothers and sisters for whom the use of icons is either not a part of their tradition or a recent addition?

Expand our Understanding of Christian Education—"Iconic Catechesis"

From the early church, we see that icons have been used to educate the faithful. John of Damascus says that they are "books of the illiterate… teaching without using words those who gaze upon them, and sanctifying the sense of sight…"[10] Icons are images that proclaim the Gospel. However, for the Damascene, icons are not just tools for narration, but function to sanctify the vision of those who look upon them. They allow us to acquire a "spiritual vision"—to see the world as God sees it—in its eschatological fullness. We can see a scene from the past (or future) and yet can experience it in the present. It is not a static remembrance, but a living, active presence, one that we can encounter. For instance, the Transfiguration icon is often rendered with Moses and Elijah, figures before the time of the historical Jesus yet present at the time and place of the event. They are part of the story. Their presence in the icon teaches us that for God, history *is* present, all are together in the same time and place. Time and space are sanctified.[11]

To encounter an icon is to be taught by it through personal engagement. Knowledge of an event is continually deepened by our participation in the event through the icon. Icons have the potential not only to inform, but form the believer. In the Transfiguration icon, we are not just to learn about Jesus Christ and the saints, but are to strive to become like them, those imbued with God through the Holy Spirit. In fact, the process of Christian living is continually to be and become an icon of God (i.e. *theosis*). Vrame describes the process of learning through the use of icons as "iconic catechesis." He emphasizes that as "'iconic catechesis' becomes praxis, the act of education can become sacramental."[12]

Invite us to Prayer with the Living God

Although the icon can be pedagogical, the primary value of an icon is sacramental. It is not uncommon to see an Orthodox believer, talking to or praying with the referent in an icon, exercising the iconic catechesis mentioned above. In doing so, they are communicating and growing in relationship with that referent. The more we open ourselves up to the other, even losing our individual "self," the more we find our true selves. It is the double movement of *kenosis* (self emptying) and *ekstasis* (standing outside oneself) of relational life, an icon of Trinitarian Life. In the words of Dzalto, "They [icons] express the message that the only way that human beings can realize their true identity is through communication, interaction, and ultimately communion [with God]."[13] In our example of the Transfiguration icon we get a glimpse of who we are called to be as icons of God. Praying with an icon invites us to move gradually from cognitive knowledge of God to knowledge of the heart from gathering information to formation and, ultimately, transformation.

Appreciate the Beauty of Creation

In the Orthodox world icons adorn the worship space. They invite us to appreciate the beauty of creation and of its creator. The language of iconography frequently uses proportion to give us a glimpse of Divine Mystery. Perhaps, the most intriguing ratio found within many icons is the "Golden Mean" or "Golden Spiral."[14] This

[10] John of Damascus, "Commentary on a sermon on the Forty Holy Martyrs of St. Basil" in *On Divine Images*, 39.
[11] Western Christians are often familiar with a similar "icon." The Christmas pageant is usually a contemporary demonstration of the gospel accounts of the Nativity of Jesus Christ merging into one event.
[12] Vrame, *The Educating Icon*, 17.
[13] Dzalto, "How to be a Human Being."
[14] The Golden Mean (phi) is 1.618… The fractional part of the ratio never ends and never repeats.

is a ratio that is found throughout creation— in the curve of a wave, our ear, a galaxy, etc. These proportions, found in nature and in art (in particular, iconography), point to a Truth that exists beyond our comprehension.

Like any painting, the aesthetic quality of the icon allows us to experience another dimension or plane of existence. In the Transfiguration icon to which I have referred, we not only see the human figure of Jesus Christ, but a figure transfigured. We experience a glimpse of a world imbued with the energies of God. According to Chryssavgis, "Gradually the experience of awe and wonder is replaced with the certainty of the knowledge and recognition of God in all things created."[15] Iconography connects Beauty and Truth.

Draw Us and All of Creation into Communion with God

One of the main dogmatic disagreements between Christians is how we understand the elements of bread and wine in the Eucharist. Many Roman Catholics, following Thomas Aquinas, attempt to explain the change of bread and wine into the Body and Blood of Christ during the Mass in Aristotelian categories of substance and accidents, an explanation commonly known as "transubstantiation." For Orthodox Christians, the nature of this transformation remains a "mystery." For many Protestants, the bread and wine are simply mimetic devices, recalling the Last Supper.[16] Perhaps, looking at the bread and wine through an iconic lens will help to open up our understanding of these elements and our relationship to them. Instead of simply thinking in categories of objective "presence" or "non-presence," we can also understand the bread and wine as "icons," viewing them through categories of encounter, journey, and ascent to God.

All of life is a gift from God and is destined to return to God. All of life is sacramental. Bread and wine are symbols of our life. We offer them to God and in return God gives us Life. In the received text of the Liturgy of Basil, after offering our gifts to God, we ask the Holy Spirit to come upon them *and* us "… και αναδειξαι τον αρτον τουτον αυτο το τιμιον Σωμα του κυριου, και θεου, και Σωτηρος ημων Ιησου Χριστου" (kai *anadeixai* ton men arton touton auto to timion Swma tou Kiriou, kai Theou, kai Swtiros imwn Isou Christou) — and [show forth] this bread to be the precious Body of our Lord and God and Savior Jesus Christ….[17] The Greek word, *anadeixai* ("to declare" or "show forth") implies an encounter through the elements that are "transfigured" by the Holy Spirit. By the agency of the Holy Spirit, we, too, are changed. Just like the disciples at the Transfiguration, we are able to encounter Jesus Christ is His glory, but now through the symbols of bread and wine. According to the Fr. Alexander Schmemann, one of the foremost liturgical theologians of the 20th century, "Only in Christ and by His power can matter be liberated and become again the symbol of God's glory and presence, the sacrament of His action and communion with man (sic)… Christ came not to replace "natural" matter with some "supernatural" and sacred matter, but to restore it and to fulfill it as a means of communion with God."[18] In the Eucharistic gift, the bread and wine become the Bread of Life (re: Jn. 6: 32–58), a means of union with Christ into whom we are incorporated. Each time we receive it, we grow in relationship with Him and are further transformed. Schmemann emphasizes this ultimate goal of the Eucharist. In his words, "… the fulfillment of the Eucharist is in the communion and transformation of man (sic) for which it is given… [it is] a means to an end, which is man's (sic) deification—knowledge of God and communion with God."[19]

Whether through the painted icon or through the icons of the bread and wine, we are drawn into relationship with the Transfigured One, in and through whom we participate in Trinitarian Life.

---

[15] Chryssavgis, "The World of the Icon,"41.

[16] This is an overly broad generalization, but used for the purposes of illustration.

[17] This construction is also found in the Blessing of the Water in the Baptismal rite: "But do You, O Master of All, [show forth] this water to be water of redemption, water of sanctification, a cleansing of flesh and spirit, a loosing of bonds, a forgiveness of sins, an illumination of soul, a laver of regeneration, a renewal of spirit, a gift of Son-ship, a garment of incorruption, a fountain of life." (Vaporis, Fr. N.M., ed., *An Orthodox Prayer Book*, (Brookline, Mass.: Holy Cross Orthodox Press), 60.

[18] Alexander Schmemann, *Of Water and the Spirit*, (Crestwood, New York: St. Vladimir's Seminary Press), 49.

[19] Ibid., 50.

Part VII: Particular Themes and Issues for Orthodox Involvement in Ecumenism

Bibliography

Chryssavgis, John, "The World of the Icon" *Phronema* 7 (1992), 35–43.

Damascus, John *Three Treatises on the Divine Images*. Translated by Andrew Louth, (Crestwood, NY: St. Vladimir's Seminary Press, 2003).

Evdokimov, Michael, *Light from the East: Icons in Liturgy and Prayer*. Translated by Robert Smith (New York: Paulist Press, 2004).

Evdokimov, Paul. *The Art of the Icon: A Theology of Beauty*, (Redondo Beach: Oakwood Publications, 1990).

Kalokyris Constantine D, *The Essence of Orthodox Iconography*, Translated by Peter A. Chamberas. (Brookline, Mass.: Holy Cross Orthodox Press, 1971). (Chapters of the book found in the *Greek Orthodox Theological Review* 12.2 (Winter 1966–67): 168–204, 13.1 (Spring 1968): 65–102, 14.1 (Spring 1969): 42–64).

Lossky, Vladimir, *The Mystical Theology of the Eastern Church*, (Crestwood, NY: St. Vladimir's Seminary Press, 1998).

Mango, Cyril, *The Art of the Byzantine Empire 312–1453*, (Medieval Academy of America, Toronto: University of Toronto Press, 1986). (Contains a compendium of patristic writings both for and against iconoclasm.)

Ouspensky, Leonide, *Theology of the Icon*, (Crestwood, NY: St. Vladimir's Seminary Press, 1978).

Quenot, Michel, *The Icon: Windows on the Kingdom*, (Crestwood, NY: St. Vladimir's Seminary Press, 1991).

Regule, Teva "Babette's Feast: An Icon of the Beautiful" in Natalia Ermolaev, ed., *Beauty and the Beautiful in Eastern Christian Culture*, (New York: Theotokos Press, 2012).

Vrame, Anton C, *The Educating Icon: Teaching Wisdom and Holiness in the Orthodox Way*, (Brookline, Mass.: Holy Cross Orthodox Press, 1999).

(114) LOCAL ECUMENISM FROM ORTHODOX PERSPECTIVES

Fr. Heiki Huttunen

1. The local church

The Church is a key concept in describing the Orthodox Christian experience. The Church is mentioned in the Creed, as an object of faith. Thus for the Orthodox it is primarily a spiritual category, part of God's action for the salvation of humanity and the world. Our participation in God's saving action happens through our membership in the Church. Being part of God's activity and His Church, and growing in this reality, will also change our relation to other humans and the world. In our everyday life as Christians, the Church is a local and communal reality.

Membership in the Church is actualized in the Eucharistic community. As described in the Gospel, the Eucharistic meal is the basic Christian experience from the beginning, since the first evening on the day of Christ's resurrection (Mark 16, Luke 24, John 20, 21). This experience is actualized in each place where a concrete group of people is gathered together in order to celebrate this mystery, and thus the Church becomes a concrete reality in each locality. The entire spirituality and life-style of Orthodox Christianity springs forth from this source. Our faith and life need to be renewed through participation in the Eucharist every Sunday, the day of the resurrection. This is how the Church has lived through all of its history. Even when nothing else was possible, Sunday Eucharist confirmed the Church's continued existence. This was proven true in the recent persecutions of the 20th century. The Eucharistic celebration is also the criterion by which our life and witness as a community is constantly scrutinized challenged, strengthened and rejuvenated.

In the Eucharistic community everyone needs each other. Mutual love, respect, dialogue and service characterize the followers of Christ. In the Christian community there are various tasks that function in relation to each other, with the Risen Lord as the Shepherd. The office of the bishop needs to be performed in dialogue with the community, as well as those of the presbyter and the deacon, and the other tasks in the local Church. Such a dialogical nature of the Eucharistic community is the basis for the synodal structure of the Church universal. The essential expressions of the Orthodox Christian faith as creeds and creedal statements were arrived at through a synodal process in local and ecumenical councils. Similar mutuality and dialogue should also characterize the relationship with those outside the Church community.

The Church has the task to be the icon of genuine life for the entire human community. The Church is a divine-human community and in its life it should reflect the koinonia of the Holy Trinity, and the Triune God's love and care for all creation. Therefore the local Church community reaches out to all around it, in witness and in service. The task of the Church is to be the model of real life for the society. In its prayer to God the Church embraces the town or village where it is located, as well as all humanity and all creation.

This concept of the Church, on the one hand, includes all Christians in a given locality, and on the other, it determines the relationship of Christians with people of other faith or no faith. To discover other followers of Christ outside the Church community causes the Orthodox Christian a spiritual and intellectual contradiction. Orthodoxy – defined as the genuine praise and the correct belief – signifies fidelity to the faith of the Apostles. It excludes those who willingly fall away from the apostolic continuity of the One Church and its faith. At the same time, it is inclusive for those who profess their spiritual belonging to that continuity. Therefore, Orthodoxy, correctly understood, presents the challenge to overcome the spiritual and intellectual contradiction of division by recovering Christian unity according to the Apostolic origins. The Church intercedes for the township or village where it lives, and for the whole world. This intercession is essential because it expresses the Church's nature as the revelation of God's care for all people and the entire world. The mission of the Church is the dialogue of love with all humans and the ultimate unity of all according to God's will.[1]

2. Being Orthodox and Ecumenical

Ecumenical engagement should be seen as a natural part of the life of an Orthodox Christian. It should not be regarded as something separate from essential Church life. It should not be something that only "ecumenists" are concerned about.

Ecumenism does not have its own essence, in theology or spirituality. It does not represent an ideology that would be different from or additional to the ethos of the Church. There is no other ecumenical vision than God's revelation in the Gospel, the faith as expressed in the Creed and experienced in the life of the Church, and lived out in the life of the person and of the community.

The accusations that "ecumenism" is based on the so-called "branch theory" and aims at a federated "world church" are false. Christian unity cannot be achieved through combining differing theological components, or negotiating and compromising on issues of faith. It does not aim at a creed formed by the smallest common denominator of various Christian traditions. Equally, to claim that ecumenism aims at syncretism or mixing of religions is a misunderstanding or disinformation.

Compromise is not a method of ecumenical dialogue, because the common aim is nothing less than the truth. Ecumenical co-operation does not imply denominational relativism or giving up of the Orthodox emphasis on the One Church. It does not signify doctrinal reductionism or minimalism. In the words of the Gospel (John 14), the Lord himself is the truth, and this is confessed and adhered to by the participating Christian groups. The best contribution the Orthodox can bring to ecumenical work is their insistence on the wholeness and unity in the theology and life of the undivided Church.

Ecumenical attitude, correctly understood, has been an intrinsic dimension of the Orthodox Christian conviction throughout the 2000 years of Church history. The Church has always interceded for the whole world, and its mission and service have been directed to all people of the *oikoumene*, the whole inhabited earth. Christians outside of the visible boundaries of the Church or people of other or no faith are included in this concern.

The task of openness and of sharing the Christian hope (1 Peter 3:15) is given by the risen Lord Himself in His Universal Missionary Commandment (Matthew 28, Mark 16). The aim is that the entire humanity might become partakers of the salvation wrought by the cross and resurrection of Christ. Christ's salvific work extends to all people and all God's creation. That needs to be also the scope of the mission of the Church, and of each Orthodox Christian.

To include all *oikoumene* in our prayers and to consider all our neighbors as brothers and sisters needs to be part and parcel of our faith and life style. The unity of all Disciples of Christ is a self-evident gift that comes with membership in the body of Christ. When we see that this unity is broken, it is our unquestionable task to engage in making it whole. Were this is not the case, our own fidelity to Christ would come under serious doubt. Thus, to have an ecumenical attitude towards fellow Christians and all humanity is a *sine qua non* part of our Orthodox Christian calling.

We should not be contented with a self-sufficient parish-life, which is not concerned about the life and death of all those human brothers and sisters of other faith communities or no faith, that the parishioners share their everyday life with, in workplaces, schools, in other situations, and in their families. The parish

[1] The Ecumenical movement aims at the visible unity of the Church of Christ. It involves all who follow Christ, and it is a response to Christ's expressed will (John 17). Dialogue and cooperation with people of other faiths and of no faith is based on the respect due to all humans as images of God. For Christians, God's love, which is most perfectly expressed in Christ, is the ultimate motivation for seeking both Christian unity and unity of all humankind. These goals are not separate but inter-related and mutually nested, and will be fully revealed at the *eschaton* according to God's will.

needs to realize its place in the surrounding society and recognize opportunities for Christian witness and service in it.

Such an ecumenical perspective is clear in the Orthodox tradition, although it has been impeded by historical developments that have shrouded our ability to fully discern the Orthodox Christian faith. We remember the love of Christ in our thoughts and ideas but we do not always practice it.

3. The Ecumenical Basis

In the beginning of the modern Ecumenical Movement, the pioneering Christians from different churches, who discovered each other as brothers and sisters, soon realized that they needed some theological definition for their common conviction. They also needed to draw some limits to those who did not share the same Christian faith. That is how the so-called *ecumenical basis* was first drafted by ecumenical youth and student movements in the 19th century, and later adopted and amended by the World Council of Churches. The National Councils of Churches, the Regional Ecumenical Organizations as well as many other inter-church bodies define them-selves as follows: *a fellowship of churches which confess the Lord Jesus Christ as God and Savior according to the scriptures and therefore seek to fulfill together their common calling to the glory of the one God, Father, Son and Holy Spirit.* According to some classical Church fathers, those who share these basic elements of the Orthodox faith should not be called heretics.[2]

Our Orthodox attitude towards Christians outside the visible canonical limits of the Church stems from the principles of the early, undivided Church. In the first Christian millennium, it was unthinkable to suggest that the Church could be more than one in terms of several churches professing different "confessions." Even during divisive controversies with heretical sects, parallel Church structures were not usually established by the Orthodox. Their consistent aim was the restoration of Church Unity. It is only in the modern era that the Christians have begun to think of churches in the plural, as if different confessions were competing brands in a supermarket of beliefs. For Orthodox thinking, the idea of many churches with differing theologies and basic structures, even with an abstract Church of Christ above them, is not acceptable. The oneness of the Church of Christ is to be incarnated in the concrete reality of plurality in cultural expressions and unity in faith and life. Faithfulness to Christ's will for His disciples to be one (John 17) must influence the words and deeds of His disciples. Ecumenical involvement is a response to this fundamental requirement of the Gospel.

We believe that the Orthodox Church is the visible, historical realization of the One Church. It is at the same time a Divine institution and a community of humans. In its human aspect, it is influenced also by the sin of its members. Therefore, the Orthodox should always look truthfully at our own life as parishes, monasteries, families and persons, and be ready to recognize our mistakes and shortcomings in an attitude of humility. Truthful self-examination and self-criticism is an indispensable prerequisite for any spiritual growth. This applies also to the Church as a community of humans. The discrepancy between our Orthodox faith and our Orthodox praxis is a sin that needs to be confessed so that we can look for repentance and a change for the better.

To present the Orthodox Church as an institution that administers all reality and has monopoly of the divine truth reflects neither the spirit of the Gospel and the teaching of the Fathers, nor the reality of our communities as perceived at present. While our Orthodox history has kept the core of the Eucharistic celebration and the definitions of the faith intact, we must admit that their expressions in concrete witness and service are often almost unrecognizable – or non-existent. According to our spiritual tradition, being Orthodox is a calling to grow ever closer to the Risen Lord. As Orthodox Christians we have not reached that goal, but we are con-stantly challenged to repent and to change in the direction of that calling. The Orthodox faith does not present

---

[2] St. Basil the Great differentiates between schismatics, parasynagogoi and heretics. The Orthodox are obliged to seek dialogue and unity with the two groups mentioned first, because the disputes with them do not involve essentials of the faith. The ones called heretics, however, hold a differing view and faith regarding God, and therefore unity with them is not within the reach of dialogue. Letter no. 188 of St. Basil *to Amfilochios of Ikonion.* P.G. 32, 665 AB and V.E.P. 55, page 202.

a comprehensive philosophical system or an ideological plan for the world, but rather it prepares the way for the Kingdom at hand, shows the way and invites into an eternally increasing participation in the reality opened by Christ's cross and resurrection.

Orthodox ecumenical involvement is formed by the same evangelical attitude and principles about the Church in different situations. Be it on the level of Church leaders, academic theologians, local parishes or any Church members, the Orthodox message should be the same. This is a global process, involving the world-wide Orthodox Church. Orthodox Christians in different local situations have their particular contributions to the quest for unity, and they need to learn from others in other situations. Real and lasting progress, however, can only be achieved with the unanimity of all Orthodox.

4. Prayer together with neighbors

Liturgical life and prayer belong to the most valuable gifts the Orthodox can bring to ecumenical encounters. This is concretely experienced when Christian congregations learn to know each other in the local setting, and are able to come together to pray for each other and the surrounding community. More than anything else, experiencing the liturgical life of the Orthodox Church can help other Christians to appreciate and grasp the witness and depth of the Orthodox Tradition. Orthodox liturgical theology reflects a holistic view on the Eucharist, the sanctification of time and the dogma of the Church in a unique way, and thus it offers renewing inspiration for Christians of other traditions.

Prayer is considered to be the core of the Ecumenical endeavor. When it expresses a common Christian faith in shared biblical terms, it is a blessing and an inspiration for the participants. Prayer helps to re-focus all ecumenical activity on Christ, the basis and goal of our commitment for Christian Unity. Prayer in the proper sense is possible when the participants share the same faith in Jesus Christ and God in Trinity, as expressed in the Ecumenical Basis. Spiritual readings and meditations together with people of other religions is a different concern.

The Special Commission on Orthodox Participation in the World Council of Churches (WCC) deliberated seriously on the question of common prayer. Its recommendations give renewed accuracy and depth for confessional and inter-confessional ecumenical prayer from the Orthodox point of view. These recommendations were officially received and decided upon by the Central Committee and the 9th General Assembly of the WCC, and are now the generally accepted directives for ecumenical worship.[3]

Prayer in ecumenical encounters is a question that invites differing responses among the Orthodox. Some are suspicious towards common prayer because of the canonical restrictions regarding prayer together with those outside the communion of the Church. When the Orthodox in the beginning of the modern Ecumenical movement decided to pray together with other Christians they took a conscious step. It has been described as a conviction that an ecumenical situation does not compromise the canonical definition of the Church, and instead of creating more division, it is directed towards Christian unity. It should be kept in mind that for some Church Fathers the Christological and Trinitarian faith expressed in the ecumenical basis precludes the accusation of heresy.[4] It goes without saying that for the Orthodox, prayer in an ecumenical setting and style is different from the sanctification of time and the holy mysteries as they are celebrated the actual liturgical life of the Church.

Prayer in local ecumenical situations should reflect the genuine theological and liturgical traditions of the participating Christians. In that way an atmosphere of prayer is created and learning from the spiritual riches

[3] Final report of the Special Commission on Orthodox Participation in the WCC. www.oikoumene.org
[4] See note 2 on St. Basil. A nuanced approach to Christians outside the canonical limits of the Church is expressed also e.g. in the stipulations of the Fifth-Sixth Synod (*Penthekte Synodos, Concilium Quinisextum*) known as that of the Trullo A.D. 692 in Constantinople regarding the need to baptize those already baptized by various schismatic and heretical groups. Quinisext council, canon 95.

of each other is possible. Ecumenical prayer should not be mistaken for some kind of liturgy of an anticipated united "world church." Rather, it is earnest and humble prayer for Unity by Christians still separated. The aim is not to create an "ecumenical spirituality" or "ecumenical liturgics," but to discover the common biblical language and the original Apostolic expression in the core of the various liturgical and spiritual traditions.

Celebrating the Eucharist together needs to be kept in mind as the final goal of the quest for Christian unity. It is not a means, or "a snack on the ecumenical way." The goal of the ecumenical endeavor is the visible unity of the Church of Christ. This implies unity in faith, which is expressed in the worship, witness and service of the Church. The Eucharist is the paramount expression of the life of the Church and its unity.

5. Friendship as the ecumenical method

The ecumenical adventure is for many opened by a surprising experience. It involves seeing the non-Orthodox Christian as a genuine disciple of Christ, with real faith and a life-style in accordance with that faith. This experience clarifies our perception of the other, clearing our prejudices, but it also helps to see better our own tradition and how we follow it. Most importantly, this ecumenical opening points to the reality of Christ as the common Savior, and how, in accordance with Orthodox spiritual experience, those who come closer to Him, also come closer to each other. This experience is the starting point for ecumenical friendship. It requires respect for the other spiritual tradition, even the aspects I cannot embrace or even understand. It challenges us always to check our facts and to base our attitudes on true and up-to-date knowledge about other Christians. It is best expressed in ecumenical hospitality, e.g. when migrant Orthodox Christians are welcomed to serve their Liturgy in rooms offered by other Christians. Such friendship is based on the love of Christ and the shared love for Him which leads to a growing trust and a will to remain together and look for deeper communion.

The local situation is the real test of ecumenical progress. What the different Christians could in principle do together, they should in fact practice in the local situation. Whatever is said and agreed in the polite atmosphere of international meetings must be tested in the home situation of the hierarchs and theologians. Without application in the local situation, ecumenical agreements remain theoretical constructions. If they cannot be applied in the local context, what should be said about their theological or spiritual credibility? When the ideas of theological dialogue can be put into practice by the local communities of the various traditions, they prove their genuinity and validity. The local situation is where the reception process takes place by the people of God with regard to the theology expressed by their leaders.

Ecumenical cooperation is different in each situation. It is defined by the political and cultural situation of Christianity, as majority or minority, and by the relations of the different majority and minority Churches, as well as the various cultural, social and economic factors defining the life of the people. It is healthy for Orthodox Churches that represent traditional majorities to know the situation of Orthodox minorities. Their relations to the neighboring majority Churches, Catholic or Protestant, may help the Orthodox majorities to develop their good relations with their smaller neighbor Churches, Catholic or Protestant. It is a basic spiritual discovery to see that practicing Christians are in minority everywhere, also in nations who may pride themselves with a glorious Christian history. This discovery helps Christians to see each other having the same basis and the same aims.

Orthodox Christians living in different local situations have different experiences of other Christians. The more distant other people are, the more distorted our ideas about their lives and beliefs can become. What can be presented as a theological fact in a textbook may have since some time developed in practice, e.g. as a result of ecumenical dialogue. In many instances, local ecumenical cooperation includes the challenge to understand the other Christians in their responses to the challenges of modernity. Living in the same society often gives valuable insight into the theology, and especially into concrete pastoral solutions of a neighboring Church. Some aspects that seem incomprehensible from a geographical and cultural distance may be much more understandable when regarded within the same cultural and political circumstances. Understanding does not, however, mean that the Orthodox solutions in the same situation would necessarily be similar.

Part VII: Particular Themes and Issues for Orthodox Involvement in Ecumenism

There are experiences in each ecumenical situation that others can learn from. Congregations and Christians living in the same cultural context may find unique ways to communicate and cooperate. Such cooperation should not compromise the theological or ecclesial identity of the participants, but rather ensure them a safe space of Christian friendship to express their particular spirituality and their attachment to the Gospel.

Friendship as the ecumenical method applies also to relations with people of other faith or no faith. From the Christian point of view, it is based on our faith in God's image in every human being. Communities representing different religions in the same locality can contribute to the well-being of all people by maintaining good relations and by cooperating for common spiritual and social goals.

Friendship with the other Christians and their Churches in the same local situation leads to common Christian witness and service, for the well-being of the surrounding community. As citizens of the community, the Christians should have solidarity, not only towards each other, but in true imitation of Christ, to the most vulnerable and marginalized people. Such ecumenical cooperation enhances the Christian presence and witness in the society, and opens new ways of faithfulness to the very calling of the Gospel. The Christians who are not members in the same Church cannot share the Eucharistic sacrament, but they can share the Sacrament of the Brother and the Sister, when they render service to the needy. St. John Chrysostom emphasizes that in both ways we encounter Christ. [5]

Friendship and trust is in some instances expressed in ecumenical agreements between churches. For example, the *Charta Oecumenica* is a statement on cooperation and respect signed by most European Churches since 2001. The *Charta* has become a symbol of the way in which theological principles are translated into action in mutual respect among the European Churches. In the Nordic countries, its principles have been crystallized in a set of headings – unity, faith, respect, trust, dialogue, Church leadership, and the simultaneously global and local character of the Ecumenical movement. These documents conclude with the commitment to speak the truth and to speak well of each other, as well as an affirmation to proclaim the Gospel and to refrain from proselytism. These principles spell out clearly the best features of effective local ecumenical relations.

Good relations among Churches in the same country and region should inspire appreciation and interest in others. It can be argued, that in the spirit of the early Church, each local Church in its ecumenical endeavors should be seriously listened to by the other Churches. Local rapprochement and agreement with non-Orthodox Christians should be taken as an opening and an initiative for the global process. Thus ecumenical friendship in a local context carries real potential for Christian Unity everywhere.

Bibliography

Anna Marie Aagaard & Peter Bouteneff, *Beyond the East-West Divide*, (Geneva: WCC, 2001).

Archimandrite Cyril Argenti, "Christian Unity", *The Ecumenical Review* 28.1 (January 1976): 1.

Olivier Clément, *Petite boussolle spirituelle pour notre temps.* (Paris: Desclée de Brouwer, 2008).

Emmanuel Clapsis, *Orthodoxy in Conversation*, (Geneva: WCC Publications, 2000).

Metropolitan Daniel Ciobotea, *Confessing the Truth as Love*, (Iasi: Trinitas, 2001).

Georges Florovsky, "The Orthodox Church and the Ecumenical Movement Prior to 1910" in *Christianity and Culture* Collected Works vol. 2 (Nordland, 1974), 161-231.

-, *Bible, Church, Tradition: An Eastern Orthodox View*, Collected Works vol. 1 (Nordland, 1972).

---

[5] P.G. 43, 396.

(115) Proselytism as an Issue for Orthodox Engagement in Ecumenism

Alexei Dikarev

1. The origin of the term

The term 'proselytism' originates from the word 'proselyte.' It comes from a Greek verb that means 'to approach' and it appears only in Jewish and Christian literature. Historically, the word 'proselyte' (Heb. מִיַּרג) means a stranger, foreigner, newcomer, settler. This term was used to denote first a newcomer, but later anyone who moved from one land to another, from one community to another, especially from one faith to another, that is a new convert.

This was the name used in particular for new converts from paganism to Judaism. Proselytes who embraced Judaism fully were called 'proselytes of the truth,' 'proselyte sons of the covenant,' 'perfect Israeli.' Other newcomers might have not accepted the Law of Moses and circumcision in full (Num. 10:29; Judg. 1:16; 1 Sam. 15:5; Jer. 35). These proselytes, known as 'proselytes of the gates,' were to observe the so-called 'Noah's law.'

Since the time of the Maccabees, the zeal with which heathens were converted to Judaism grew, and the number of proselytes began to increase. There were even cases of forced conversion to Judaism. In the Roman Empire as a whole, the adoption of Judaism became popular. Jews who lived in diaspora actively championed Judaic religious concepts. In fact, the whole Jewish Hellenistic literature represents to a considerable extent propagandistic religious literature.

By the time of the coming of Jesus Christ, many sensible heathens dissatisfied with either heathen religious rituals or heathen philosophy were thirsty for the divine truth concealed in the Old Testament. During great feasts, these heathens would come to Jerusalem for worship. The outer court of the temple was open for them (cf. Acts 21:28); also they could come to synagogues (Acts 13:42-44). The centurion who built a synagogue for Jews was probably one of these heathens who worshiped God (Lk. 7:2-10).

In the New Testament the word 'proselyte' appears only in four passages and, with the exception of Matthew 23:15, in the description of the new church in the missionary field (Acts 2:11; 6:5, 13:43). In the case of Matthew, interpreters have different views on whether Jesus is criticizing the missionary zeal of the Pharisees, or the fact that once they win one person they impose on them their formalistic understanding of the law.

2. The contemporary notion of proselytism

At present, the notion of 'proselytism' as used in the Christian context is solely negative since it denotes purposeful efforts to convert Christians of other confessions into one's own denomination. This is the common understanding of proselytism found, first of all, in inter-Christian documents. At the same time, proselytism is normally associated with not quite correct and even downright reprehensible methods used for the purpose of converting others into one's own faith. In 1970, The Joint Working Group between the Roman Catholic Church and the World Council of Churches, in its document *Common Witness and Proselytism,* gave this overall definition of proselytism: 'Proselytism. Here is meant improper attitudes and behaviour in the practice of Christian witness. Proselytism embraces whatever violates the right of the human person, Christian or non-Christian, to be free from external coercion in religious matters, or whatever, in the proclamation of the Gospel, does not conform to the ways God draws free men to himself in response to his calls to serve in spirit and in truth.'[1]

---

[1] *Common Witness and Proselytism. A Study Document*, in Pontifical Council for Promoting Christian Unity, *Information Service* 14.2 (1971): 14. See also: Loeffler, P., *Proselytism*, in *Dictionary of the Ecumenical Movement*, (Geneva: WCC, 1991), 829.

The 1995 document of the Joint Working Group *The Challenge of Proselytism and the Calling to Common Witness* enumerated methods falling under the definition of proselytism in more detail:

- making unjust or uncharitable references to other churches' beliefs and practices and even ridiculing them;
- comparing two Christian communities by emphasizing the achievements and ideals of one, and the weaknesses and practical problems of the other;
- employing any kind of physical violence, moral compulsion and psychological pressure, e.g. the use of certain advertising techniques in mass media that might bring undue pressure on readers/viewers;
- using political, social and economic power as a means of winning new members for one's own church;
- extending explicit or implicit offers of education, health care or material inducements or using financial resources with the intent of making converts;
- manipulative attitudes and practices that exploit people's needs, weaknesses or lack of education especially in situations of distress, and fail to respect their freedom and human dignity.[2]

3. Proselytism and relations between Churches

Proselytism had free scope already after the Great Schism between East and West in the 11th century. By the time of the 4th Crusade in 1204, which ended in the barbaric plunder of Constantinople by Crusaders, the Western Church had formed her view of Eastern Christians as schismatics separated from the true Church of Christ pastured by the Pope of Rome as successor of St. Peter. The Roman Catholic Church did not recognize the validity and saving nature of sacramental and spiritual life in any Churches separated from her. This view found its ultimate expression in the principle declared by the Pope Pius IX (1846-1878): 'Outside the Roman Catholic Church there is no salvation.' Quite understandably, the efforts of Catholic missionaries were aimed at 'returning' schismatics into the fold of the true Church. In doing so, missionaries often used methods commonly defined as 'proselytism' today: in Catholic countries, such as Poland and Austria-Hungary, and countries under the influence of Catholic states, such as those in the Middle East in the era of protectorates, wide usage was made of political, social and economic resources to convert Eastern Christians to Catholicism.

Proselytism carried out by Catholic missionaries among Orthodox and non-Chalcedonian Christians in the 16th-18th centuries led to the formation of the so-called Eastern Catholic Churches in unity with Rome. This kind of 'unity' effected on terms dictated by Rome was called *unia* (from Lat. *unio* – unity). Not based on real agreement as to the truth of Christ and faithfulness to the Tradition, *unias* did not unite but rather sowed distrust and disunity among Eastern and Western Christians. Protopresbyter Alexander Schmemann, a well-known church historian, wrote, 'Precisely these attempts at union reinforced the division more than any others, for the very question of church unity was mixed for a long time with lies and calculations and poisoned it with non-ecclesiastical and low motives. The Church knows of unity alone and for this reason does not know of 'unia.' Virtually, *unia* is unbelief in unity.'[3]

The Second Vatican Council of the Roman Catholic Church (1962-1965) initiated a fundamentally new approach to building relations with Christians of other Churches. There was no longer the call to 'return' to the fold of 'the Mother Church' but to equal dialogue to become decisive in relations with the Orthodox Church and Oriental Churches. For the first time since the 1054 division, the Roman Catholic Church officially recognized that Orthodox Churches possessed the apostolic succession and sacraments necessary for salvation.[4]

---

[2] *The Challenge of Proselytism and the Calling to Common Witness,* 19, in http://www.oikoumene.org/en/resources/documents/wcc-commissions/joint-working-group-between-the-roman-catholic-church-and-the-wcc/challenge-of-proselytism.html (last accessed at September 2013)

[3] Шмеман, А., протопр., *Исторический путь Православия*, Париж 1989, с. 301 [Schmemann, A., protopr., *Historical Way of the Orthodox Church*, (Paris 1989), 301] (in Russian).

[4] See, Decree of the Second Vatican Council on Ecumenism *Unitatis redintegratio,* 15.3.

In contacts between the Roman Catholic Church and the Orthodox Churches, the term 'sister Churches' began to be used more and more often. It was natural in the new situation that the justification of mission among the Orthodox should have been challenged, and the conversion of the Orthodox to Catholicism began to be seen now as proselytism. In this spirit, Pope John Paul II and Ecumenical Patriarch Dimitrios I together stated clearly: "We reject every form of proselytism, every attitude which would be or could be perceived to be a lack of respect" (December 7th, 1987).[5]

The problem of proselytism emerged with a new force in the late 1980s-early 1990s with the fall of the communist regimes together with the ideological curtain in Eastern European countries. Along with the political freedom in these countries came numerous missionaries, mostly from Protestant sects, Pentecostals and new religious movements, such as the Jehovah's Witnesses and the Mormons. Seeing the former communist countries as a spiritual *tabula rasa* and a 'territory of mission,' foreign preachers often used their considerable financial resources to attract local people who experienced financial difficulties.

In the same period, the revival of Greek Catholic church structures in Ukraine and Romania brought about the problem of *unia* in Orthodox-Catholic relations in all its sharpness. This problem was the sole subject of plenary sessions of the Joint International Commission for theological dialogue between the Roman Catholic Church and the Orthodox Church in Freising (Germany, 1990), Balamand (Lebanon, 1993) and Baltimore (USA, 2000). In joint documents adopted by these meetings, proselytism was not interpreted merely as mission using methods incompatible with the preaching of the Gospel, but as preaching to a population belonging historically to another Church. Thus, the Communiqué of the 6th plenary session of the Joint International Commission (Freising, 15 June 1990) states: "Every effort aimed at having the faithful of one Church pass to another, which is commonly called 'proselytism,' should be excluded as a misuse of pastoral energy" (7. c).[6]

The principle of immunity of 'the canonical territory' of a local Orthodox Church for non-Orthodox mission was underscored when four Catholic dioceses of Latin Rite were established in the territory of Russia in February 2002 and when the structures of the Ukrainian Greek Catholic Church spread to southern and eastern Ukraine in July of the same year 2002. The Statement of the Holy Synod of the Russian Orthodox Church of 17 July 2002, reads: 'The Catholic proselytism carried out among the traditionally Orthodox population in Russia and other countries of the Commonwealth of the Independent States presents a serious obstacle for normalizing Orthodox-Catholic relations... We believe to be proselytistic the very fact of the conduct of Catholic mission among Christians of the Apostolic faith who have neither historical nor cultural relation to the Catholic Church... [The Roman Catholic Church] should abandon her theoretical condemnation of proselytism 'in general' and recognize the missionary effort in a territory of pastoral responsibility of another Church as inadmissible.'[7] The Roman Catholic Church, in her turn, refusing to agree with the definition of proselytism based on the notion of 'canonical territory,' upheld her right and even duty to preach the gospel to non-believers though baptized in the Orthodox Church or living in the territory of her 'pastoral responsibility.'

At the same time, the Roman Catholic Church herself experienced considerable difficulties caused by the growing proselytism carried out by Pentecostals among traditionally Catholic populations, especially in Latin American countries. This problem became a subject of discussion in the Pentecostal-Roman Catholic dialogue, which published in 1998 a document on *Evangelization, Proselytism and Common Witness.*

---

[5] See, *Uniatism, Method of Union of the Past, and the Present Search for Full Communion,* 18 (Balamand, June 23, 1993), in Pontifical Council for Promoting Christian Unity, *Information Service* 83.2 (1993): 97.

[6] Pontifical Council for Promoting Christian Unity, *Information Service* 73.2 (1990): 53.

[7] *Заявление Патриарха Московского и всея Руси Алексия II и Священного Синода Русской Православной Церкви от 17 июля 2002 года// «Церковь и время»* 20.3 (2002), сс. 10, 11. [*Statement of Alexy II, Patriarch of Moscow and All Russia, and the Holy Synod of the Russian Orthodox Church (17 July 2002)*, in "Church and Time", 20.3 (2002): 10, 11] (in Russian).

Part VII: Particular Themes and Issues for Orthodox Involvement in Ecumenism

4. The problem of proselytism in the ecumenical perspective

The joint documents of inter-Christian dialogue place the problems of religious freedom and proselytism in the ecumenical framework of church unity and common witness.

It should be emphasized from the very beginning that everyone is free to adhere to particular beliefs, to belong to this or that religious community or to change one's affiliation. Churches recognize their members' full right to religious freedom. They are concerned, however, not for this right of the free individual but for the conscious desire of particular Churches and communities to draw in believers of other traditions. Proselytism is especially painful when its actions are directed to a partner Church in long-standing dialogue or a sister Church.

The mutual, though partial, recognition reached in relations between Churches after years of ecumenical dialogue, should rather lead to inter-church cooperation, including in the area of Christian witness. 'This existing communion should be an encouragement for further efforts to overcome the barriers that still prevent churches from reaching full communion. It should also provide a basis for avoiding all rivalry and antagonistic competition in mission because the use of coercive or manipulative methods in evangelism distorts koinonia.'[8] Proselytism aggravates the scandal generated by the division between Christians who are called to unity in Christ. In the prayer of Jesus 'that they all may be one so that the world may believe' (John 17:21), we are reminded that the unity of Christians and the mission of the Church are intrinsically related.

It is not sufficient merely to condemn proselytism. Churches active in the ecumenical movement should join their efforts to overcome mutual alienation, the feeling of one's own exclusiveness and the practice of rivalry as causes of proselytism. The Joint Working Group between the Roman Catholic Church and the WCC in its document adopted in 1995 recommends 'to continue to prepare ourselves for genuine common Christian witness through common prayer, common retreats, Bible courses, Bible sharing, study and action groups, religious education jointly or in collaboration, joint or coordinated pastoral and missionary activity, a common service (diakonia) in humanitarian matters and theological dialogue.'[9]

The provision of the JWG document of 1970 is still relevant as it emphasizes the difference between mission and proselytism from the ecumenical point of view. In the ecumenical perspective, Christian mission has as its main goal the preaching of the gospel among non-Christians: 'Missionary action should be carried out in an ecumenical spirit which takes into consideration the priority of the announcement of the Gospel to non-Christians. The missionary effort of one Church in an area or milieu where another Church is already at work depends on an honest answer to the question: what is the quality of the Christian message proclaimed by the Church already at work, and in what spirit is it being proclaimed and lived? Here frank discussion between the Churches concerned would be highly desirable, in order to have a clear understanding of each other's missionary and ecumenical convictions, and with the hope that it would help to determine the possibilities of cooperation, of common witness, of fraternal assistance, or of complete withdrawal.'[10]

Bibliography

Bria, I., "Evangelism, Proselytism, and Religious Freedom in Romania: An Orthodox Point of View", *Journal of Ecumenical Studies* 36.1-2 (1999).

Joint International Commission for Theological Dialogue between the Roman Catholic Church and the Orthodox Church, *Communiqué of the VI Plenary Session (Freising, 15 June 1990)*, in Pontifical Council for Promoting Christian Unity, *Information Service* 73.2 (1990).

[8] *The Challenge of Proselytism and the Calling to Common Witness,* 12, in http://www.oikoumene.org/en/resources/documents/wcc-commissions/joint-working-group-between-the-roman-catholic-church-and-the-wcc/challenge-of-proselytism.html (last accessed at September, 2013)
[9] Ibidem, 35.
[10] *Common Witness and Proselytism. A Study Document*, in Pontifical Council for Promoting Christian Unity, *Information Service* 14.2 (1971): 23.

Idem, *Uniatism, Method of Union of the Past, and the Present Search for Full Communion (Balamand, June 23, 1993)*, in Pontifical Council for Promoting Christian Unity, *Information Service* 83 (1993).

Joint Working Group between the Roman Catholic Church and the WCC, *Common Witness and Proselytism. A Study Document*, in Pontifical Council for Promoting Christian Unity, *Information Service* 14 (1971).

Idem, *The Challenge of Proselytism and the Calling to Common Witness*, in http://www.oikoumene.org/en/resources/documents/wcc-commissions/joint-working-group-between-the-roman-catholic-church-and-the-wcc/challenge-of-proselytism.html (last accessed at September, 2013)

Karkkainen, V.-M., "Proselytism and Church Relations", *Ecumenical Review* July (2000).

Loeffler, P., "Proselytism", in *Dictionary of the Ecumenical Movement*, (Geneva: WCC, 1991), 829.

Mirus, J., *Understanding Proselytism*, in http://www.catholicculture.org

Witte, J., and Bourdeaux, M., *Proselytism and Orthodoxy in Russia: the New War for Souls*, (Maryknoll NY, 1999).

Алексий II, Патриарх Московский и всея Руси, *О миссии Русской Православной Церкви в современном мире*// «Церковь и время», 4 (1, 1998) [Alexy II, Patriarch of Moscow and All Russia, *On the Mission of the Russian Orthodox Church in the Contemporary World*, in "Church and Time", 4.1 (1998)] (in Russian).

Заявление Патриарха Московского и всея Руси Алексия II и Священного Синода Русской Православной Церкви от 12 февраля 2002 года и другие документы// «Церковь и время», 20.3 (2002).

[*Statement of Alexy II, Patriarch of Moscow and All Russia, and the Holy Synod of the Russian Orthodox Church (12 February 2002), and other documents*, in "Church and Time", 20.3 (2002)] (in Russian).

(116) Orthodox Perspectives on the Historical Role of Church Unions

Fr. Vaclav Jezek

"The difference in language....did not allow us to converse, as we had wished, with really good men who were extremely anxious to show us favour."[1]

A desire for unity of the Church or the koinonia was present from the beginning of the existence of Christianity. However, unity is a tricky and elusive notion. There can be various degrees and forms of unity, including unity of faith, institutional unity, and unity in common characteristics and so on. In fact many theologians and philosophers pondered on the notion of unity itself and reached diverging conclusions. This has serious implications, since before seeking unity, one has to be clear on what he or she understands by "unity." This is even more important in the Church, where unity cannot be an obstacle to diversity. On the basic Gospel level, it seems that unity is an expression of love. Without love there is no unity. This in fact seems to be the most important criterion for ecclesial unity.

If one looks at the early church one can see two important facets. First of all, there was a strong passion and belief that dogma, "the correct faith," or faith generally are directly linked to spirituality and to one's spiritual disposition. There is no such thing as theory divorced from practice; a notion, which was already present in Greek philosophy. One's spiritual life determines and is the mark of one's expression of faith and vice versa. This is a feature which has somewhat moved to the background in our period, where theoretical theology lives a life of its own often divorced from any personal spiritual experience. This is one of the reasons why it is so difficult to "stick" to the agreements in ecumenical meetings, since the "soul wants one thing, while the body something else." Secondly, we can see that a plurality of opinions and theologies, just as the plurality of spiritual experiences was a common feature in the early church and was not necessary an obstacle to unity in the general sense. Undoubtedly influenced by secular humanism and secular institutional theories of unity, the modern churches have often sought unity through concepts and ideas and structures which are foreign to an authentic communion of love in the Holy Spirit.

The present contribution presents a brief overview of attempts to arrive at ecclesial unity in the context of various church unions.

The liberation of Christianity after Constantine presented new possibilities for Christianity but also challenges. If one looks at the early Byzantine Empire, one has to conclude, that the primary force supporting ecclesial unity was the Roman emperor and government. Thus early on, the church was pushed towards unity from the "outside." This itself is not negative, since the emperors (apart from some), together with others in the government were mainly Christians and naturally desired Christian unity. However, it needs to be said, that politics did not always contribute to ecclesial unity, especially when notions of ecclesial unity coincided with the secular desire for power and centrality.

In this regard one of the biggest tests of church unity, with more or less unfortunate consequences was the "Monophysite controversy." Here the imperial initiative in the end proved unsuccessful in promoting ecclesial unity, with unfortunate consequences.

The Monophysite controversy was not only about theology, but about pride, tradition and personalities, again illustrating the link between theology and "life," so strongly present in the early church. It was also about the competition between emerging and traditionally strong centres of culture and Christianity, such as

---

[1] Letter of Manuel II Paleologus to Chrysolarus sent from Paris, Manuel II Paleologus, Letters, 37, In: Dennis, G.T., *The letters of Manuel II Paleologus, Corpus Fontium Historiae Byzantium VIII*, (Washington, 1977), 98, 99, 4-6.

Alexandria and Constantinople. Just as later with the Iconoclastic controversies in Byzantium so in the context of monophysite controversies we can observe, that the further one was from the power of the Byzantine emperor the lesser power the government had in implementing its idea of ecclesial unity and the stronger the opposition to it. Alexandria being a powerful city in its own right could more easily mount opposition to the relatively distant capital. But not only distance and power was leverage to the capital. Monasteries as strong cohesive communal structures could mount formidable opposition to the policies even if they were close to the capital geographically.

The monophysite controversy was linked to a long standing debate on who Christ was, and on the relationship between the divine and human in Him, which was all linked to the issue of how Christ saves us. The reason why this debate ended up in the first major schism in the church has as much to do with differing opinions as with personal ambitions and political pressure.

In this context various theologians presented various opinions about Christ and the line of what was and what was not orthodox was a thin one and often delineated afterwards. Figures such as Theodore of Mopsuestia[2] who was associated with Nestorius were often deemed orthodox but at the same time could also be severely condemned depending on various developments and retrospective views. Paul of Samosata doubted the distinction between the pre-existent Christ and God, understanding the historical Jesus as merely a unique man. Paul of Samosata claimed that Jesus did not have a human rational soul but a divine one instead. Diodor from Tarsus rejected the idea of hypostasis, since according to his opinion it occasioned the mixture of the divine and human in Christ. Theologians such as Gregory the Theologian reasoned that Christ's salvific role would be severely limited if he was not fully human, not sharing fully in humanity arguing that "what has not been assumed has not been healed." (Cf. his famous Epistle. 101).

Various theological positions and traditions where more or less associated with particular important centres of Christianity, notably, Antioch, Alexandria and Constantinople. In this regard, Constantinople had an important position and could act as a kind of leverage point between rival cities and theological traditions. Thus the elevation of Nestorius in Constantinople to the patriarchate in 428 was not welcomed by Cyril and provided fuel to the existing rivalry between Antioch and Alexandria. Nestorius in his famous homily of 428 argued that the Mother of God should be called Christotokos instead of Theotokos. Nestorius further preferred the term prosopon (face, appearance) to designate the individual Jesus rather than hypostasis, which was said to be associated with the essence or abstract principle of an individual or personal nature.[3] For the Alexandrians, the term physis was more or less synonymous with hypostasis. The discussions centred on terms, which themselves were subject to a fluidity of meaning and associations, depending on the schools and traditions involved.

In his third letter to Nestorius, Cyril introduced his famous sentence, which later became the basis of monophysite aspirations "one hypostasis of the Word incarnate" (mia physis tou Theou Logon sesarkomene). Interestingly, Cyril thought his phrase was in line with Athanasius' conceptions, whereas it was based on Apollinarius' phrase.[4] These developments have to be seen in the context of Alexandria, where tradition and respect to ones previous spiritual leaders and theologians was of paramount importance, just as it is today. In this regard Cyril was and is highly respected in the Alexandrian context, as much as for his theology as for the fact of being a "home-born" figure. Cyril's phrase did not solve the issues and Theodosius II convoked the council in Ephesus (430). It is perhaps possible to state, that if the government did not intervene, the issue would have taken its natural course. However by intervening the government directly or indirectly favoured

---

[2] Grillmeier characterises him in this way "he had at least dimly guessed at the idea of an ontic unity in Christ, even though he lacked the right concepts to show the metaphysical level on which it was achieved" Grillmeier, S.J., *Christ in Christian Tradition: from the Apostolic Age to Chalcedon*, (New York: Sheed and Ward, 1964), 348.

[3] Irvin D. T. and Sunquist, S.W. *History of the World Christian Movement, vol. 1, Earliest Christianity to 1453* (New York: Maryknoll, 2002), 190.

[4] The phrase of Apollinarius:, *mia physis kai mia hypostasis tou Theou Logou sesarkomene*. See Hans Lietzmanns' discussion of the issue in Young, Frances M. *From Nicaea to Chalcedon, a Guide to the Literature and its Background*, (Philadelphia, 1983), 183.

Part VII: Particular Themes and Issues for Orthodox Involvement in Ecumenism

one position over the other and it is not important whether it was right or wrong, since it led to a polarisation of the conflict, which could have died out naturally. The situation was complicated due to political, cultural and national issues. The Byzantine Empire at that time was multi-cultural, and Semitic traditions in Christianity played a strong role. The controversies provoked the emergence of a Nestorian church based on Syro-antiochian theology, which was persecuted by the imperial forces and found refuge especially in areas with Persian influence. In 410 a Persian church was established.

The debate on Christ continued as well as attempts at reconciliation of the various positions from the government. A council in Ephesus II (the 449 "robber" council) vindicated the position of a certain Eutyches who believed, that after the incarnation only one nature existed, whereas before the incarnation there was a human and divine nature. Christ was different from the human being. This was in a certain way giving support to Alexandrian concerns (over the Antiochian position) which placed emphasis on preserving the unity in Christ.

In this context the council of Chalcedon was very important, as it was a council which not only dealt with important issues, but it was a council, which deliberately sought to find a compromise between the various Christological camps, especially between the traditions of Alexandria and Antioch. Chalcedon affirmed Christ in two natures without confusion (en duo physes in asygchytos), two natures united in one single person-prosopon and one single hypostasis. It upheld the synodical letters of Cyril (to Nestorius and the Orientals) to placate the Alexandrians. Bishops were deposed and exonerated on this council to satisfy all sides. As if to show the various groups who is in charge, this council interestingly enough, also in its 28th canon affirmed the precedence of Constantinople over Antioch and Alexandria. Especially in Alexandria the council of Chalcedon was not widely accepted; there were riots. Allegiance to respected figures played a role in the conflict. The deposition of Dioscorus sparked troubles in Alexandria and Proterius the bishop of Alexandria was killed. The context of Alexandria was especially more complex due to its ethnic and cultural multiformity, not speaking of the various religious influences. In a way, looking back seeking unity in such a multiform environment would be very difficult if not impossible.

Later the emperor Zeno issued the Henoticon (482), which was a document seeking a compromise solution, supporting the teaching of Chalcedon but attempting to satisfy the Cyrillians. The Henoticon was not accepted in the West resulting in the first West-East schism when Acacius was excommunicated in the West in 484. The imperial administration lost patience and under Justin I, monophysite bishops as Severus of Antioch were removed. The later formula of Hormisdas (518) was conciliation between the East and West.

The monophysite controversy was not elevated by Chalcedon and continued to be a divisive issue on all levels including the imperial couple. Justinian himself seems to have been more of a Chalcedonian than his wife Theodora who was more pro-Cyrillian. The differences in theoretical theology went hand in hand with overall differences of spiritual tradition and mentality. There were differences between the monastic traditions of Egypt and other areas, conditioned by natural surroundings and religious history. Differences in theology began to be associated with differences in culture and ethnic contexts and aspirations. When an Arab ruler in the Ghassanid kingdom desired a Cyrillian bishop, Theodora sent the deposed Theodosius to take care of the shortage of clergy in the region. He ordained Jacob Baradai as Bishop of Edessa (ordained in 541), who became a successful missionary spreading Cyrillian Christianity all over the Far East.[5] Jacob in turn ordained Sergius of Tela (544-546), the last common patriarch of Antioch for the Byzantine and Syriac churches. The persecution of the monophysites on all levels only served to enhance the development of a "monophysite" identity, which included the development of ethnical identity and autonomous spiritual traditions. The rivalry between Alexandria and Antioch did not abate as is witnessed by the arguments between Severus of Antioch and the Alexandrian Julian of Halicarnasus.

The situation did not improve even after 531, when monophysites were allowed to return from exile. A coloqium held between 532 and 533 at Hormisdas palace did not help to resolve the issue. Justinian's at-

---

[5] The term "Jacobite" was until recently still used in relation to the Syriac Church of Antioch, and is still now associated with one of the two Indian Catholicates of the Indian churches, which are jurisdictionally dependent on Syrian Antioch.

tempts at reconciliation did not work, and individuals such as Menas the patriarch of Constantinople were not as conciliatory and Cyrillians were banished from the capital. New terms were introduced to help settle the issue such as for example "enhypostasis" developed by Leontius of Byzantium which attempted to find middle ground. Later it was dealt with by Maximos the Confessor. Politics were played out to suit the ends of unity. Pope Vigilius was placed at the throne with the support of Theodora to strengthen support for unity (537).

The fifth and sixth ecumenical councils were apart from other things attempts to reach a compromise with the monophysites. Constantinople II (553) condemned Theodore of Mopsuestia, to placate Alexandria; and Origen from Alexandria, to placate others. Efforts continued to find a compromise by searching for commonalities. Thus for example, the afthartodocetist idea was developed under Justinian. Justinian further suggested the theopaschites idea,which had a background in Cyrillian theology, and later ended up as the hymn "O only begotten Son" used in the liturgy. While Justin II (565-578) sought compromises, under Maurice and John Scholasticos, the policy reverted to persecution of monophysites. Egypt and areas at the fringe of the Byzantine Empire became safe-havens for free-thinkers and monophysites. Monophysitism did not merely become a theological movement but a movement associated with cultural and national aspirations.

Theological issues coincided with increasing political problems. The loss of vast territories on the part of Byzantium from the seventh century onwards would change the structure and make up of Byzantium. Efforts at reconciliation occurred through a theology of energies and wills.[6] An attempt to promulgate union by Heraclius (the Ecthesis of 638) and Constans II (Typos 648) was not successful. Later these documents would be rejected. Later Constantinople III, (680-681) would offer a correction of the doctrine of energy and will in Christ, by stating that in Christ there are two wills and energies.

The Monophysite controversy was one of the first major challenges to Christian unity, and as such provides interesting and important insights into the mechanics of how unity was sought. It clearly demonstrates the intrinsic relationship between politics, ethnic and cultural aspirations, spirituality and theology. The controversy also shows the importance of personalities and the reception of theology. In general terms, it also shows a historical irony. The controversy essentially broke out as a "Greek affair" in that in its basis lay solely Greek theological and philosophical concepts. Interestingly enough those peoples and contexts which were later mostly associated with Cyrillian Christology did not belong to the Hellenic conceptual tradition. For example, the Ethiopian Christians who became associated with Monophysitism through the Coptic tradition have little conceptual affinity with Greek terms such as hypostasis or prosopon. In fact, it is almost impossible to find equivalents to these words. While the modern Coptic tradition adheres to the Cyrillian context, it expresses itself in radically different contexts, using Arabic. The emperor's adamant desire for unity was linked to the fundamental fact that in those periods religion was linked to all facets of society. However, it also illustrates that fundamental tragedy of seeking unity at all costs, and not cherishing the rich Christian spiritualities and traditions which were developing in that period. Ironically progress in Christological issues (Egypt 1989; Geneva 1990) made by the two families have been reached in a context, totally different from the one they emerged from.

Lyon

Efforts to seek union with the West had a direct relationship with the development of Latin ecclesiology and ecclesiology in the East. As the centuries past, Latin ecclesiology, especially in relation to the position of the pope, had undergone change. On the other hand, in the East the Patriarchate of Constantinople became the main representative of Orthodoxy before the nascent of other Orthodox Churches later.

The coronation of Charlemagne by Pope Leo III in 800 as the Roman Emperor signalled new aspirations for the papacy. This was coupled with the appearance of forged documents such as the Donation of Constantine, claiming various rights for the Roman papacy supposedly given by the Emperor Constantine. Rome was left

---

[6] After Constantinople II an idea emerged of one will in Christ advanced by Sergius I of Constantinople (610-638). This was an attempt to reach the Cyrillians.

to the Popes and the Popes received insignia of quasi-imperial authority.[7] In the same century personal disliking of Patriarch Photius went hand in hand with doctrinal disputes provoking reactions from the Latin Pope.

In the Dictatus papae (1075), Gregory VII asserted, that only the pope had the right to employ imperial insignia.[8] Clause XII of this document enabled the pope to depose emperors. Despite this document, Gregory VII preferred the concept of concordia and not union between the churches. Things seemed to improve. In 1073, Gregory told Emperor Michael, that "we not only desire to renew (innovare) the ancient concordia that God ordained between the Roman church and its Constantinopolitan daughter, but also, if it may be, so far as in us lies, we desire to have peace with all men" (Gregory is citing Rom. 12: 18).[9] According to Gregory, the apostle Peter should decide among the differences of opinion.[10] Concorde (omonia) is a word used also by Urban II.[11] A Synod in 1089 held in Constantinople, which was presided by Alexius viewed the letter of Urban seeking peace and concord (omonian) positively. The Synod asked Urban to send a systatic letter together with a profession of faith that would confirm the common union (ten koinen enosin). The Synod also stated that the name of the pope (Urban) was accidentally omitted from the diptychs at Constantinople.[12] This positive development was brought to an end by the negative impact of the First Crusade.

Under Pope Innocent III the concept of the translatio imperii matured. In his letter from 1202, Venerabilem fratrem, it is claimed that in the person of Charlemagne the apostolic see by legal right transferred the Roman Empire from the Greeks to the Germans.[13] The year of 800 was seen as a point where the empire went from the Greeks to the Franks and then subsequently to the Germans.

Regardless of the liberation of Constantinople from Latin rule in 1261, the Byzantine emperor Michael VIII sought unity with the Latin Church, partly because he realised that co-operation with the West was important for the survival of the empire as such. Michael VIII approached Urban IV, who at that time also needed allies against enemies such as Manfred Hohenstaufen. The desire for union on Michael VIII's part was perhaps also linked to the desire to avoid the recapture of Constantinople and to buy time. His efforts did not bare sufficient fruits and after the treaty of Viterbo, the Latins with Pope Clement IV's assent were prepared to attack the Byzantine Empire. Later pope Gregory X was more congenial to the Byzantine approaches and decided to convene a council in Lyon. In fact the events show how Michael VIII had shown a personal initiative for union. As the unionist Imperial Tome suggests (reconstructed from various surviving texts) the issue of papal primacy was very important. However, as is shown from the meeting with Patriarch Joseph, where the Tome was read, the Byzantines understood that accepting the pope meant also accepting the entire teaching of the Westerners.[14]

The events around Lyon demonstrate a great division between an individual emperor and his supporters and the rest of the population in dealing with ecclesial issues. Michael VIII had mounted little support for the union often resorting to persecution of anti-unionists. A document of union was signed in Lyon on 24 June 1274.

[7] See Constitutum Constantini, In: Fuhrmann H ed., MGH, Fontes iuris Germanici antiqui, (Hanover 1968), x.

[8] Gregorii VII Registrum, Caspar, E., ed. In: *MGH, Epistolae selectae*. Reg. 2, 55a, cap.8, (1920-3), 204.

[9] Cowdrey H. E. J. "The Gregorian Papacy: Byzantium, and the First Crusade," 145-169, In: *Byzantium and the West c. 850-c.1200, proceedings of the XVIII Spring Symposium of Byzantine Studies*, Howard Johnston J.D. ed. (Oxford: Adolf M. Hakkert Publishers, 1988),153,149.

[10] Ibid. Reg. 1.18, 2.31, s. 29-30, 166-67.

[11] Cowdrey H. E. J. "The Gregorian Papacy: Byzantium, and the First Crusade," 145-169, In: *Byzantium and the West c. 850-c.1200, proceedings of the XVIII Spring Symposium of Byzantine Studies*, Howard Johnston J.D. ed. (Oxford: Adolf M. Hakkert Publishers, 1988) 161.

[12] Ibid. 162.

[13] Patrologiae Latina, Migne J.P. (1865), Paris, ccxvi, col. 1065C; Regestum Innocentii III papae super negotio Romani imperii, no. 62, In: Kempf F. Ed. (1947), *Miscellanea historiae pontificiae*, xxii, (Rome), 168-69.

[14] Pachymeres book 5, ch. 14, 487, In: Kolbaba Tia M. Repercussions of the second council of Lyon (1274): Theological polemic and the boundaries of orthodoxy, In: Hinterberger M., Schabel C., *Greeks, Latins and Intellectual History,1204-1500*, (Peeters, 2011), 43-69. See also Failler, A and Laurent V. Eds. and trans. *Georges Pachyméres, Relations Historiques*, (Paris, 1984), vol.2.

Importantly, there was no general council and Michael VIII wrote a letter repeating the profession of faith sent to him by Pope Clement IV which contained the filioque, and which was brought to Lyon. It acknowledges the supreme authority of the pope.

The division between the government, the Church at large and the common folk is nicely shown by Pachymeres who implies that the people were not interested in these unionist or anti-unionist issues. Pachymeres notes that attempts to gain support from the common people were futile, since the common person was not interested in these matters. The common person was not left alone "to work out his salvation without trouble....knowing nothing more than the pickaxe, the mattock, and a life without problems."[15]

In any event the crusades had revealed sharp cultural distinctions between the two sides and anti-unionist opposition was also linked to a hatred of Latins as a whole. This hatred was also related to an increasing genre of misinformation. Thus in a Libellus of 1274, the Latins are accused of opening their veins in their glasses and washing them and drinking from them.[16] Odo of Deuil the witness of the Second Crusade (1147), who was a chaplain to the French king Louis VII mentions the hatred the Greeks have shown to the Latins, by purifying altars where the Latins served. Even before the sack of Constantinople by the Latins there were expressions of mutual violence. For example, there was a Greek attack against Latins in 1182 and 1185, or the sack of Thessaloniki in 1185 by the Normans.

It appears, that in Byzantium opposition towards the Union of Lyon, was especially strong in the provinces and among monks, which shows a marked disparity between cities and provinces in Byzantium.[17] The cities saw a milder anti-Western reaction. Many of the aristocrats were more pro-Latin due to profits and business opportunities. However, the inability to find compromise was also centred on diverging national and cultural elements on both sides.

Florence-Ferrara

The attempts to reach union in the fourteenth and fifteenth centuries coincided with a difficult period for Byzantium. In comparison to earlier periods, Byzantium and the Church had changed. The Church was more and more identified on ethnic lines. The Church of Byzantium owed its character to the Greek culture. Whereas in previous centuries, the unity of the Church in a way transcended borders and cultures, in this period, it was a question of the unity between two more or less concrete worlds, the Latin (West) and the Greek (East). The instigation for union in this period came from the emperors, who took an active role. However, the pope also needed to solidify his position in this period. Andronicus III sent Barlaam the Calabrian to Avignon in order to discuss plans related to Church Union (1339). In 1369 John V Paleologus was converted to the Roman faith in Rome.[18] The motives for union were not only related to expectations of political and economical help, but in contrast to earlier periods, the Byzantines were more and more conscious of the technical, military and scientific advances in the West. Byzantine scholars such as Demetrius Kydones and Bessarion were aware of the intellectual power of the West and admired it. Interestingly, protagonists of this period were conscious of the fact, that in order for the union to be successful it had to be sought not only on the level of scholars, but of people. Thus Barlaam observed that no process can

---

[15] Pachymeres book 5, ch. 23, 513, pg. 57, In: *Kolbaba Tia M. Repercussions of the second council of Lyon (1274): Theological polemic and the boundaries of orthodoxy*, In: Hinterberger M., Schabel C., *Greeks, Latins and Intellectual History,1204-1500*, (Peeters, 2011), 43-69.

[16] *Libellus* of 1274, In:Vassilife, A, *Anecdota Graeco-byzantina*, (Moscow 1893), 179-88.

[17] Oikonomides argues that during the Palaiologon period, Byzantine cities resembled Western cities, while the countryside remained traditional, which accounts for much of the ideological positions. See Oikonomides, N., (1988) "Byzantium between East and west (XIII-XV cent.)," In: *Byzantium and the West c. 850-c.1200, proceedings off the XVIII Spring Symposium of Byzantine Studies*, Howard Johnston J.D. ed. (Amsterdam: Adolf M. Hakkert- publishers, 1988), 319-332; 321.

[18] Vasiliev, A. *Il viaggio di Giovanni V Paleologo in Italia et l,unione di Roma, S.B. III*, (Rome, 1931), 153-193.

be made if union is sought only on the level of scholars. The people will only trust a general council held in the East.[19]

On 24 November 1437, Emperor John VIII departed with a group of theologians and clerics to Rome. Sylvester Syropoulos who wrote memoirs and who attended the council in Florence gives us a picture of the passionate quarrels in the Byzantine camp.[20] He shows how intrigues and sycophancy of the bishops to the emperor was present,[21] and who were capable of changing their affiliation if the emperor showed them his inclination. Bribery also played a role at this council. The council was attended by two important figures, Bessarion and Mark Eugenicos (metropolitan of Ephesus). Bessarion was a renaissance man, educated and civilised who had great admiration for statehood. Mark was a monastic and Palamite. Both had prominent positions at the council and the emperor gave them the right to give answers to the Latins.[22] For the monastics such as Mark, the spiritual life and truth was more important than the survival of the Byzantine state. This is not surprising if one realises that in this period the monasteries served as the backbone of the Byzantine state both in cultural and other ways.

Often commentators on this council neglect to mention the important fact that the council was set against the backdrop of the political problems of Pope Eugene IV and the Council of Basil. The Council of Basil was an important test case on the power of the council or the idea of conciliarity as such, as against the power of the pope. The events would determine whether conciliarity would predominate in the Latin Church or whether the idea of the pope as the supreme authority would prevail. In fact, the council rejected the authority of the pope, who dissolved it by a bull (18 December 1431). Later a compromise was reached by Sigismund (crowned Roman emperor on 31 May 1433 in Rome) and the pope recognised the council as ecumenical. The pope however rejected the canon, which placed the authority of the council above the pope. The council of Ferrara convened by the pope (8 January 1438), was also an effort to offset the council at Basil. The Pope excommunicated the prelates at Basil, while he was deposed by the council in Basil (25 June 1439).

It is interesting to note that papal primacy was not such an important issue at Florence-Ferrara as other issues such as the Filioque. In terms of the papacy the East did not have a problem in recognising the important role of Peter, but it had a problem in recognising the Western claim that authority continued from Peter to the Western popes. Further, Western claims that Rome had a special position due to the presence of the apostle's tombs, or that it was special due to its apostolic foundation were not valid arguments, since in the East many sees could have claimed apostolic foundation.

In fact, especially in this period the discussions moved increasingly away from a unity based on faith towards a unity based on "submission" to the pope. This is reflected by emperor Cantacuzenos who wrote: "Since the beginning of the separation you (Westerners) have never sought unity in a courteous, fraternal manner. Instead, in your peremptory, high-handed way you have habitually ordered us never to challenge or contradict what the pope says or will say, since he is Peter's successor, which is to say Christ's. Everyone must yield and bow down before him as if Christ himself is speaking. Know this, your Grace, as long as that approach prevails among you, church unity will never be possible."[23]

---

[19] See Geanakoplos, D. "Byzantium and the Crusades," In: Setton, S. *A history fo the Crusades*, (Madison, Wis, 1975), vol. 3, ch. 3, pg. 55-56. Citing MPG vol. 151, cols.1332ff.

[20] Laurent, V. *Les Memoires du grand ecclésiarque de l,Eglise de Constantinople, Sylvestre Syropoulos, sur le concile de Florence, Éditions du Centre national de la Recherche Scientifique*, (Paris, 1971). See also Tsirpanlis C.N. *Mark Eugenicus and the Council of Florence*, (Thessaloniki: Center of Byzantine Studies, 1974), 48.

[21] Ibid. VII,parag. 9, 358. See also Tsirpanlis C.N. *Mark Eugenicus and the Council of Florence*, (Thessaloniki: Center of Byzantine Studies, 1974), 48.

[22] Ibid. V, 262; VI, 306, 320. See also Tsirpanlis C.N., *Mark Eugenicus and the Council of Florence*, (Thessaloniki: Center of Byzantine Studies, 1974), 45.

[23] Meyendorff, J. Projets de concile oecuménique en 1367: un dialogue inédit entre Jean Cantacuzene et légat Paul, In: *Dumbarton Oaks papers 14*, (Washington, 1960), 172.

Eastern Europe and Central Europe

Ideas of ecclesial union in the region of Eastern Europe at least in their initial phases were also linked to Byzantine policies of union. Further, the marriage of Ivan III with Zoe (who was called Sophia in Russia) Paleologos in the fifteenth century paved the way for Russia to claim special status as the Third Rome, a kind of translatio imperium analogous to the Western idea of the Roman emperor in the Medieval period.

Coinciding with the fall of Byzantium to the Latins, efforts of ecclesial union in Eastern Europe were becoming a facet of religious policy for many reasons. Nations became increasingly identified with their confession, and denominational affiliation was an important mark of political power, especially in the contexts of Poland, Central Europe and the area under the supervision of Kiev. The popes made approaches to various rulers in this region. For example, the ruler of Halych Roman Mstislavovich was offered the crown by Pope Innocent III in 1204 on the condition of accepting Rome's protection (possibly against the devout Roman Catholic Polish king Leszek I). Roman's son Danil Romanovich (ruler of Volhynia and Halych) accepted Roman Catholicism in order to seek help against the Mongol invasion.

The union of Poland and Lithuania in 1385 (Krewo union) brought a commitment from the ruler Jagaylo the Grand duke of Lithuania to Christianise his lands according to the Roman Catholic faith. In a decree of 1387 (20 February), Vladislav-Jagaylo ascertains the property rights of the Roman Catholic aristocracy and states that anyone converting from Catholicism would lose these rights.[24] Roman catholic female aristocrats were forbidden to marry non-Catholics in Lithuania.[25] These and other steps obviously contributed to a religious polarisation in this area. Religious boundaries, which were more or less unclear, had now been firmly set.

Even though the union at Florence was signed by metropolitan Isidor (the Byzantine-Greek representative of Moscow and Kiev), the council of Moscow (1459) rejected this union. After the Florentine union, tensions between the Orthodox and Roman Catholics intensified. Western missions arrived often supported by the rulers. For example, the Polish-Lituanian ruler Kazimir IV Jagello supported the Bernardines in Vilno for whom he established a monastery, while at the same time forbidding to build new Orthodox churches in Vilno and Vitebsk.[26] Roman-Catholic missionary activities intensified under the Polish-Lithuanian ruler Alexander Kazimirovich (1460-1506). A Bernardine monastery emerged in Polotsk (1498). Dominicans arrived in Vilno in 1501. Pope Alexander VI gave rights to Voytech Shabor to punish enemies of Catholicism.[27]

The polarisation of religious confession was coupled with other issues, which contributed to problems. The king awarded religious property and offices without consideration of spiritual worthiness. Thus, for example, in one decree Sigismund II awarded a monastery with all its servants and affiliated staff, for life, to an aristocrat. While the decree states that he should place a worthy spiritual person to head the monastery this undoubtedly did not alleviate the problem.[28] The Polish-Lithuanian rulers could award ecclesial appointments or property to secular people, compromising the position of the churches. A great period of confusion and immorality ensued with people bargaining with ecclesial offices. There was great irresponsible fluidity and, for example, priests moved from a diocese/eparchy to another where they became patrons of property etc.[29]

Christian unity was subjected to the political whims and tumults in Eastern Europe. Significant events included the unity of Lithuania and Poland after Lublin (1569), creating the idea of one nation and pre-

---

[24] *Gramota* (decree) of Polish king and Grand duke of Lithuania Vladislav about feudal privileges given after the acceptance of the Catholic faith In: Теплов, В.А. Зуев, З.И., *УНИЯ В ДОКУМЕНТАХ*, (Minsk: Luchi Sofii, 1997), 64.

[25] Stipulations from 2 October, 1413, from the Gorodelsk Seym, about the union, of the great duchy of Lithuania with Poland, and about the rights and privileges of Catholic feudals in Lithuania and Belarus. Ibid., 68-69.

[26] Ibid., 32.

[27] Ibid.

[28] *Gramota*, October 20, King Sigismund II, to the aristocrat Borkulab Korsak, and his gift of the Polotsk John the Baptist monastery. Ibid., 78.

[29] Ibid. 34.

Part VII: Particular Themes and Issues for Orthodox Involvement in Ecumenism

sumably one religion. While the Warsaw confederation (28 January 1573) proclaimed religious tolerance in Poland, it met with opposition from the Latin hierarchy and the hardliner theologian Piotr Skarga, who had a very depreciative view of the laity generally. Jesuits arrived in Poland in 1564 invited by Cardinal Stanislav Gozi. In 1571 they affirmed themselves in Galicia.[30] Their arrival and zeal instigated by the reformation again contributed to a religious polarisation in the areas involved. King Stephen affirmed religious freedom in his letter from 21 January 1584.[31] Also, religious freedom is upheld in his letter from 18 May 1585.[32]

The idea of submission to the pope is present strongly in this period. It was claimed that this submission would liberate the peoples from various problems such as foreign invasion. This idea was advanced by people like Piotr Scarga.[33] The Kievan metropolitan Michail Ragoza in one of his decrees supports that the union is a protection against the spread of heresy and sects.[34] Further theology advanced notions that those not in union with Rome are not part of the body of Christ.[35] This was a specifically Jesuit theme at the time.

Coinciding with the issue of ecclesial union was the problem of scandals in the Church, which were also related to lay patronage. Ecclesial union became an element in an ever-growing division between the laity and the hieararchy. In the aftermath of the Livonian war of 1558-1583, a new lay movement appeared which can be subsumed under the name Orthodox Brotherhoods. It would be fair to say that one of the reasons for the division between the hierarchy and the laity in this period lies in the fact that the hierarchy was interested more in profit and income from their ecclesial dependencies, partly due to the system of ecclesial appointments which was set by the governments. Perhaps also their motivation for union and therefore financial harmony and stability would lie in this area. Interestingly, even patriarch Jeremiah of Constantinople supported these Brotherhoods in their struggle with the hierarchs. Jeremiah visited Kiev in 1589 and further complicated the relationships between the various hierarchs and laity, by making some disciplinary and jurisdictional measures, which perhaps contributed to the fact that some hierarchs decided to go to the union, thus getting rid of the patriarch's authority and also the laity.

Positions changed; some formerly had supported the unionist tendencies and later changed their position. One was bishop of Lviv Gedeon Balaban, who was also in conflict with his Brotherhood and initially supported the union and organised a council to this effect in Lviv (25 January 1595). The council stipulated apart from other things that disunity in the Church is the consequence of heresy and disorder. However, later Gedeon Balaban saw that the union was more or less a one-sided process dominated by Latin positions and became a staunch supporter of Orthodoxy.

One of the most pronounced defenders of the anti-union position in this period was the aristocrat Konstantin Ostrozhskiy, who in 1595 wrote an encyclical to Orthodox believers in Poland. The encyclical implies the that hierarchy is interested merely in money and that one has to preserve the purity of the one faith.[36]

---

[30] Ibid. 35.

[31] No author or date given. Journal *Акта Западной России т.* 3.139: 280.

[32] Journal no author given, Бѣлорусскій Архивѣ, 1.15 (1824): 42.

[33] For example his work "About the unity of God's Church under one pastor and about the Greek departure from this unity, and warning and exhortation to the Russian people" published in 1577.

[34] Common *Gramota* (decree) of the Metropolitan of Kiev Michail Ragozo and Orthodox bishops, and their wish to submit to the Roman Pope (1594, 2 dec.). In: Теплов, В.А. Зуев, З.И., УНИЯ В ДОКУМЕНТАХ, (Minsk: Luchi Sofii, 1997), 88. Signed also by Ipatiy, Bishop of Vladimir and Brest, Cyril Terletskiy, exarch o metropolitan of Kiev, bishop of Lutsk and Ostrozh. The concern with sects and heresies is also strongly felt in the letter of the bishop of Vladimir and Brest Ipatiy Potiy to the Kiev *voyevod* and *knaz* Constantine of Ostrozh, about his wish to conclude a church union. Ibid., 95. The letter also indicates, that the bishops were accused of heresy by the common people.

[35] Bulla of pope Clement VIII concerning the submission of higher Orthodox hieararchy to the Roman Pope (23 Dec. 1595), Ibid., 118.

[36] Circular epistle of Constantine Ostrozh, Kiev *Voevod* and *knaz*, to Orthodox clerics and people in the kingdom of Poland and great duchy of Lithuania, with the exhortation to them to remain steadfast in the Orthodox faith (24 June 1595). Ibid., 97.

The discussions related to the union were not the result of a general ecclesial reflection but were often related to individual efforts of various hierarchs or individuals. Thus for example in 1595 Ipatiy Potiy and Kiril Terleckiy visited Clement VIII affirming their desire for union. Clement VIII did not give away any concessions and fell short of their expectations in terms of preserving Eastern rite elements.[37] These then had to "sell" this idea of union back home.

Rulers such as Sigismund III played a coercive role in the union. Sigismund III did not have a positive view of the Eastern Church.[38] Misfortunes of the Eastern Church were seen as the consequence of their schismatic position.[39] Sigismund III (Ruler of the Polish-Lithuanian commonwealth in 1587-1632. From 1592 to 1599 king of Sweden) together with the active role of the Jesuits played an important part in the organisation of the Council of Brest (6 October 1596). This council was a strong affirmation of the authority of the pope and his monarchical governance. Non-submission to the pope was understood as one of the reasons why the Turks were winning militarily and heresies were spreading.[40] Apologies written after the council argue that the pope historically was always the highest authority in the Church.[41]

Parallel to the council of Brest an Orthodox council was held under the auspices of Constantine Ostrozh. While the council of Brest was dominated by the hierarchy, this council was dominated by the lower hierarchy and the laity. It was held in a Protestant prayer house, since all Orthodox churches in Brest were closed by Potiy.[42] The anonymous defence of the Brest synod claims that this synod was not valid, since apart from other reasons it was not allowed by the king.[43]

The council of Brest found support from the king and only the Uniate Church was recognised as truly existing. In a letter from December 1596, the king urged all people to accept the union.[44] Interestingly, in the Script of the Synod of Berestensko, (singed by a group of laity and clerics), it is said that the Brest unionist council had no authority from the Eastern Church.[45] Apologetic works, in opposition to Brest often criticised the hierarchy for betraying Orthodoxy.[46]

The union increased the divisions between the hierarchy and the laity. The common folk, the laity were associated with the defence of Orthodoxy and the truth. This was to become a strong feature later on in many contexts. It was not easy to convert the people to the union as is suggested by the various

---

[37] Conditions for the unity of the Catholic and Orthodox churches in the Polish Lithuanian commonwealth, accepted by Ipatij Potij and Cyril Terletskij in Rome 1595 and their subsequent changes. (23 December 1595-1744), Ibid., 136.

[38] Sigismund III forbade entry to any people carrying any epistles or documents from Greek patriarchs. Circular epistle of Sigismund III, to the border mayors, not to let in the country embassies from the patriarch of Constantinople and to send their epistles indirectly to the king., (28 July 1595). Ibid., 102.

[39] Epistle of Sigismund III to the Kiev *Voyevod* and *knaz* Constantine Ostrozh with the exhortation to accept the union and help to spread it among spiritual people.

[40] The list of the Holy Union, in 412, secretary and writers of the holy synod, ordered by the elders, 9 October 1596. In: Anonymous, Исторія о Листрійском то есть разбойническом или флорентійском соборѣ, (collection of documents), (Sankt Petersburg 1856).

[41] Ibid. "Defence of the Synod in Brest," 428.

[42] Теплов, В.А. Зуев, З.И., *УНИЯ В ДОКУМЕНТАХ*, (Minsk: Luchi Sofii, 1997), 42.

[43] In: anonymous (1856), *Исторія о Листрійском то есть разбойническом или флорентійском соборѣ*, (collection of documents), Sankt Petersburg. "Defence of the Synod in Brest," 428.

[44] Encyclical epistle of the king to the Orthodox laity and clerics encouraging them to accept the union, (15 December 1596).

[45] Anonymous author and date not indicated. *Journal Архивѣ Югозападной Россія* 1.128: 519-530.

[46] For example, the work *Apokrisis*, which was a polemical work against the Brest union written by an anonymous author and published in Polish in 1597 in Vilnius. It was written by a person, who called himself Christoforos Filalethes. It criticises the higher Orthodox hierarchy for cooperation with the governments and upholds the conciliar attitued and the laity. Similarly, also the work by M. Smotritskiy (1578-1633) called *Frinos*, or the "Cry of the Eastern Church" (1610). This work complains about the leaders of the Church, who were entrusted to lead but instead have fallen into the service of hell, and asks the leaders why they have betrayed the people.

Part VII: Particular Themes and Issues for Orthodox Involvement in Ecumenism

documents. Since there "is not hope, that these proud and sincere people, will en masse submit to the union."[47]

Difficult times for the non-unionists ensued under the metropolitan of Kiev Potiy, who wanted to close Orthodox monasteries and churches. This situation continued under Josif Rutskiy (1613-1637), who founded the order of Basilians (1617), whose goal was to support the union. The work Synopsis describes the many Orthodox churches destroyed or turned into inns.[48] In his work Palinodia, Zacharias Kopistenskiy complains about the various forms of violence and torture used by the uniates.[49]

The situation between the uniates and non-uniates somewhat improved under Vladislav IV, who in the beginning of his reign attempted to achieve reconciliation.[50] He issued a diploma of rights for the Orthodox (14 March 1633). However the arguments continued and there are numerous documents of mutual complaints and intrigues in cities such as Vitebsk. This touched all walks of life including day to day business activities. Later the Seym (council) of 1635 calmed the tensions. After the treaty of Zbiriv (1649), Jan Kazimir issued a diploma to the Orthodox affirming their rights.[51]

After the Russian-Polish-Lithuanian war in 1654-1667, Jan Kazimir ordered that only Catholics could have positions in the government in Polotsk and awarded other privileges to them.[52] Until 1676 the rights of uniates were upheld very strongly and the Orthodox suffered serious persecution in the Polish-Lithuanian common-wealth. For example, Voevod of Vitebsk forbade the people to attend Orthodox churches in Vitebsk.[53] Only after 1686 and the peace with Russia did the situation of the the Orthodox improve. However, only in areas that were not under the rule of the Polish king, where a systematic eradication of Orthodoxy had begun. Many complaints about this systematic destruction were voiced.[54]

These events and others illustrate that the fortunes of the uniates[55] and Orthodox directly depended on the political circumstances and political will. It can be further stated that slowly from the beginning of the eighteenth century, the uniates began to build their own identity, which was obviously influenced by the Latin tradition, and which began to diverge from the Orthodox cultural millieu. We can thus speak of an ecclesial tradition independent of the Orthodox and Latin traditions, although the issue of Latin influence at this point remained a prominent one. The nascent uniate structures had to constantly struggle with latinising policies. The uniate council of Zamoshtch in 1720, carried with it strong latinising policies, paving the way for a great-er latinisation of uniatism.[56]

In the period of the struggles with the union the Orthodox Church in Russia struggled with its own issues related to liturgical practice. In 1667 (13 May) the great council condemned all those who opposed the deci-

---

[47] Instruction to the papal nuncios in Poland Lanchelotii, about the spreading of ňthe union and Catholicism in Belarus and Ukraine. (14 Dec. 1622). In: Теплов, В.А. Зуев, З.И., *УНИЯ В ДОКУМЕНТАХ*, (Luchi Sofii, Minsk, 1997) 193.

[48] *Sinopsis* of the religious persecution of the Orthodox from the uniates and Catholics, (1632). Ibid., 199.

[49] *Palinodia*, Zacharias Kopistensky, concerning violence done to the Belarusian population with the aim of affirming the union and Catholicism. Ibid., 151. (end of XVI to XVII century).

[50] Epistle of Vladislav IV, given to the Orthodox inhabitants in the Polish-Lithuaniana Commonwealth at the Sejm when he was chosen as king. Ibid., 200.

[51] Diploma of Jan Kazimir given as affirmation of the Zbiriv treaty (1649) about the destruction of the union and the rein-troduction of ancient rights of the Orthodox. Ibid., 242.

[52] Epistle of Jan Kazimir to the Polotsk voevod, magister and city aristocracy of Polotsk, about strict establsihmed of order in elections to magsiterial positions of only Catholics and uniates. (17 April 1668). Ibid., 248.

[53] Universal (copy) of the Vitebsk voevod Ivan Chrapovitskiy, to the inhabitants of Vitebsk, forbiding the enty to Orthodox churches for liturgy, and norm of behaviour on religious feast days. (21 April 1672), Ibid., 254.

[54] For example, a list of activities in the Remark by the chancellor of count Golovkin to Rome to the name of cardinal Sinoli about the persecution of the Orthodox inhabitants of the Polish-Lithuanian Commonwealth, with a brief list of the persecutions. Ibid., 270.

[55] By the term "uniate" I do not mean a pejorative definition, but use it simply to discern between later designations, as for example "Greek-Catholics" which was awarded to people, who accepted the Latin Church.

[56] 26 August 1720 dogmatic formulations, acceped on the Zamoy seym, Ibid., 262.

sions of patriarch Nikon (1652-1666) who "recovered" the pristine purity of the liturgical books. These events are very important, because they bear similar traits as other issues relating to the union with the Latin Church and ecclesial life. Reforms of Nikon, who sought liturgical reform and with the help of Alexiy Michailovich (1645-1676) achieved this goal in a rather harsh and unnecessarily quick manner, had brought to the fore the division between the official Church and the laity. The "raskol," as it is called, showed a division between the official Church and hierarchy together with the state and the laity or nation as such. The official Church was termed the Babylonian whore.

In the area of Russia, the division between the laity and the hierarchy and clergy appeared often as is shown by the various heretical movements. These include the movement of the Strigolniks who appeared in Pskov in 1371 and who argued for greater morality for the clergy. The Moscovite Matvey Semenovich Bashkin (16th century) believed that anyone can interpret the Scriptures and denied the efficacy of the official Church.

The Warsaw Seym in 1732 curtailed the rights of the Orthodox paving the way for their destruction. Monasteries were systematically taken into union. In the eparchy of Belarus and Turov from 1732 to 1743, 128 monasteries were taken into the union.[57] Jesuit students were accused of beating and chasing away clergy, including throwing human excrement in holy water and throwing the dead body of an Orthodox around.[58] Coinciding with the persecution of the Orthodox there was a persecution of the uniates from the aristocracy, which was keen on latinisation. The Orthodox and uniate faiths were viewed as *chlopska wiara*, as the religion of the primitive folk.[59] In 1766 the Cracow bishop Soltik on the Warsaw Seym stated that all those who support other beliefs than the Catholic one are betrayers of the fatherland.[60] These facts are important, since they illustrate a tendency, which was to play a significant role further in other contexts as well. This is the association of religion with national aspirations and identity, which was to be pronounced, especially in the nineteenth century. Further, importantly, the Uniate church was viewed as offering greater educational and intellectual possibilities. A split emerged between the Roman Catholic advanced West and the backward Orthodox East.

After the first partition of the Commonwealth, the Russian Empress Catherine II expounded a policy of religious freedom, affirming the rights of the Orthodox and non-Orthodox.[61] Ironically, Catherine II even supported the Jesuit order, when it fell into problems elsewhere. It is important to state, that the Russian tsars were not automatic enemies of the uniate or Latin cause as it is often portrayed. For example, Tsar Paul I, did not encourage the movement from uniatism to Orthodoxy. In 1798, the Emperor established two new uniate eparchies in Brest and Lutsk.

The union struggled with latinising tendencies, which was a constant issue in the area of Russia. In 1803, in the Polotsk uniate eparchy 100,000 people joined the Latin Church.[62] Many figures sought to top this latinising process like for example, Archbishop Irakliy Lisovskiy, who in 1803 managed to get official support for the cessation of proselytism of Latins among uniates.[63] The prelate Joseph Semashko notes the increasing assimilation policy of uniates to the Latins.[64] Interestingly enough the authorities moved to protect the integrity of

---

[57] Ibid., 50.

[58] Report of priestmonk Silvester Kochov to the Russian minister resident in Warsaw Golembevsk on the suffering and persecution of the Orthodox in Belarus, Ibid., 279.

[59] Ibid., 50.

[60] Ibid., 51.

[61] Stipulation of Catherine II about the situion in the Polish-Lithuanian Commonwealth (1768), Ibid., 413.

[62] Ibid., 55.

[63] Notes of Metropolitan Iraklios Lisovskiy to the *oberprokuror* of the holy Synod about the solution regarding the situation of the Uniate Church, (1805), Ibid., 427.

[64] Notes of the assessor of the Greek-Uniate collegium of the prelate Joseph Semashko about the situation of the Uniate Church, Ibid., 430.

the uniates and a commission of uniates and Orthodox was established for harmonious relations. In fact, the uniates were claimed to be valuable assets of the Russian cultural context.[65]

Nicholas I, in 1826 issued a decree forbidding Catholics to build churches in areas, where only Orthodox where present.[66] He also issued measures protecting the Slavonic and Eastern elements in the uniate churches and to curtail latinising elements. After the Polish rebelion in 1831, the Russian government sought to bring the uniates closer to Orthodoxy. A commission was established outlining the steps and conditions for a union between Orthodox and uniates.[67] In 1839, the effort for unity between Orthodox and uniates came to fruition in the Polotsk agreement (12 February 1839). Interestingly, the agreement stipulates that the existence of the Catholic union was a "Polish intrigue."[68] After this uniates still remained in some parts of Cholm eparchy. After the Polish uprising (1863) these remaining unitates were also rejoined to Orthodoxy in 1875.[69]

The momentum for union reached in Brest spread elsewhere and it would be true to state, that all efforts for union where solely dependent on political interests of the reigning powers. Territories dominated by the Habsburgs, were characterised by a strong inclination to implement unionist policies. This desire for union was partly influenced by the spread of the Reformation. In any event, the seventeenth century witnessed further local unions which were pretty much based on the model achieved in Brest.

In the context of Austria-Hungary the uniates became to be termed "Greek-Catholics" in the reign of Maria Theresia (1740-1780). As an official name it was adopted on 24 April 1773. The union spread especially among the Ruthenian Orthodox, who were living under harsh conditions in Austria-Hungary. The clergy had no means of economical support and had to work on the land. The Ruthenian bishop who lived in the monastery of St. Nicholas in Mukatchevo, though protected by various royal patents, faced constant pressure from his feudal overlords.[70] Writing in 1654 the Latin Archbishop G. Lippay pretty much summed up the situation, when he wrote in his report to Rome: "Those priests as well as the people were of the Greek rite, but in other respects were most ignorant, rough, uneducated- the bishop first, and then the priests and the people, lay like brute beasts sunk in great evils and ignorance of things divine. They were not even rightly divided into parishes, but in some villages there were no priests, in others 4, 5, 10 priests with their wives and children lived like peasants, and they were subject to all the servitudes and tasks of the peasant, in favour of the land-lords, to which they were dragged away even from the very altar."[71]

The Brest union found support in Austria-Hungary. Local Roman Catholic aristocracy sought to advance this unionist policy in their territories. This was true also for the Druget aristocratic family, which is associated with the so-called Uzhorod union. Just as in other contexts, some individuals were persuaded to accept the union. These could have been intellectuals or others, who saw in the union the possibility of gaining equal rights and educational and economical possibilities. In the context of the Uzhorod union one such advocate of the union was the Mukatchevo bishop Vasil Tarasovitch, who made a confession of the Catholic faith. However, his fate typically displays the character of conversions in this period. While the union took place,

---

[65] An announcement of the minister of internal affairs Bludov to the metropolitan Joseph, about the establishment of a secret committee regarding uniate issues. Ibid., 465.

[66] Ibid., 56.

[67] The secret committee steps needed to abolish the union, (26 January 1839).

[68] Common act of the unification of the Uniate Church with the Orthodox Church in Polotsk, (12 Feb. 1839). Ibid., 487.

[69] Ibid., 59.

[70] Hodinka A., A munkácsi gör. Szert. Püspökség története. Ferdinandus I, 9 Oct. 1551; Isabella, 3 July 1558; John Sigismund Zápolya, 18 Feb. 1567; Maximilian II, 13 Oct. 1569; Rudolph II, 29 March 1597 etc. Cited In: Lacko M.,The Union of Užhorod, (Rome 1976), 24.

[71] Hodinka A., *A munkácsi gör. Szert. Püspökség története.* No.126. In: Ibid., 25. George Lippay, archbishop of Esztergom, in his report to Rome of 1651 writes: "In that part of the Kingdom of Hungary that borders on Poland, in the dioceses of Esztergom and Eger, there dwells a large number of schismatical Ruthenians…This favour of Your Holiness will bring about the accession to the bosom of holy Mother Church and to the obedience to Your Holiness of at least 100000 souls." Hodinka A., A munkácsi gör. Szert. Püspökség története. No.116. In: Ibid., 18.

acceptance of the union by the Latin officials was not so forthcoming and Tarasovitch alternated between Orthodoxy and the union, later again becoming Orthodox. The union of Uzhorod consisted of 63 priests who accepted the union with Rome in the chapel of the Uzhorod castle on 24 April 1646. These priests were part of the Druget family holdings in the zhupa of Uzh. This was followed by some other priests from other zhupa such as the Spish, Sharish, Zemplin, Uzhorod and Sabolch ones on 15 January 1652. Although there is no official record from this union (apart from stipulations appearing later in 1652) the union was pretty much in line with the union of Brest.

At the turn of the twentieth century, among the uniates there was a movement of return to Orthodoxy, which was further stimulated by a return to Orthodoxy of uniate migrants in the USA. Reasons for conversion to Orthodoxy included the alleged immorality of the uniate clergy, economical exploitation by the uniates, and association of the uniates with the Hungarian oppression.[72]

Unionism spread in other parts of Austria-Hungary and in 1611 a uniate eparchy was created for Croatian uniates in Karlovac and Varazhdin.

In Transylvania, a union was promulgated in 1700 in Alba Julia.[73] The union was built on the Ferraro-Florentine idea. Similarly to other contexts in Austria-Hungary, economical issues and issues of equal rights were the motivating factors for union. Emperor Leopold-I offered to those accepting the union the same rights as the Catholics had, including that the clergy would not have to work hard labour and there would be new fiscal rights. However, these new rights offered to those accepting the union did not materialise and in 1740 there was a movement of return to Orthodoxy.

It is important to note that in the context of Romania and the Ruthenian contexts, the uniate churches were associated with great intellectual and cultural activity and stood at the beginning of a process of national and cultural self-consciousness, supporting Romanian and Ruthenian national aspirations. This was true especially in the nineteenth century.

After the communist takeover in Eastern Europe the uniate churches found themselves in disgrace from the communist rulers. The primary reason for this was that the communist governments accused the uniates of supporting national ideas and independence in areas of Western Ukraine and others and especially due to their alleged support of Nazi Germany, which was a sensitive issue after the Second World War. The communists accused the Slovakian Uniate bishop Goyditch of supporting Ukrainian fascists.[74] They accused him of co-operating with the Nazi regime sending uniate missionaries to occupied regions of Ukraine to facilitate the spread of the union.[75]

The communist ideology saw in the uniates betrayers of Slavic culture, (due to their association with Latinism) and thus, betrayers of Slavic unity. The uniate hierarchy was seen as oppressing the simple "believing peasant folk." The communist stimulated a return to Orthodoxy which in the context of Czechoslovakia materialised in the so-called Preshov Sobor (1950), in the Soviet Union in the so-called Lviv "Synod" (1946), and in Romania (1948) in Alba Julia in a declaration of return to Orthodoxy. Many uniates were arrested and there was wide-scale persecution of the uniate organisations. This issue remains of great contention between the Orthodox churches and the Uniate churches. Since some uniates remained Orthodox even after the fall of communism, some Orthodox argue that the validity of these anti-union councils cannot be rejected outright, whereas the uniate position is that these should be rejected entirely as invalid, even if some decided to remain Orthodox. Some writers argue that all unionist councils were

[72] Hrabec M., Marmarošský proces a jeho podstata In: Zatloukal J. Ed. *Podkarpatská Rus*, (Bratislava: Klub přátel Podkarpatské Rusi, 1936), 58.
[73] In 1697 a Declaration of Union was signed by metropolitan Teofil and 12 archpriests, in 1698 the Book of Testimony was signed by bishop Atanasie Anghel and 38 archpriests and in 1700 bishop Atanasie Anghel and 54 archpriests signed the Leaflet of Union.
[74] No author given *Proces proti Vlastizradným Biskupom Jánovi Vojtaššákovi, Michalovi Buzalkovi Pavlovi Gojdičovi*, (Juridicial process against the betrayers of the fatherland bishops...), (Tatran, Slovakia, 1951), 118.
[75] Ibid. 12.

violent and that if we do not accept the validity of these anti-unionist councils then the uniate churches should reject their own forced unionist councils. Any solid objective self-reflection and self- criticisim on both sides is still lacking.

Oriental Churches

In the context of the "Oriental Orthodox" it is fair to say that the unionist tendencies after the Ferraro-Florentine council were largely centred on personal initiatives and jurisdictional complexities. Some Oriental Orthodox present at Ferraro-Florence accepted the union together with other Orthodox delegates, but this act fell into oblivion.

In the Coptic context, negotiations for union stimulated partly by Jesuit missionary activites took place especially in relation to individual Coptic hierarchs. However most of the period after the seventeenth century, when intensive Jesuit missionary activity began, the dialogue centred solely on the ideal of total submission to the pope and the neglect of the spiritual heritage of the Copts on the part of the Roman Church.[76] Some Coptic hierarchs were sympathetic to the union, but this did not materialise in any significant results.

The heavy-handed arrogant and latinising approach of the Portuguese also led to the disenchantment among the Thomas Christians in India, and in 1653 some decided to break away from the authority of the Catholic archbishop eventually joining the Syrian church.

Internal problems could have stimulated efforts at union, which is the case of the Assyrian Christians. A practice of hereditary leadership developed there, which provoked a schism, and some Assyrian bishops rather chose to accept union with Rome than to tolerate this. Thus in 1553 Pope Julius III ordained Yuhannan Sulaka as Patriarch Simon VIII. Similarly, in the context of the Melkite tradition a schism broke out in 1724 in relation to the acceptance or non-acceptance of a pro-Catholic candidate for the patriarchal throne in Antioch. The term Melkite originally designated Christians of Antioch, Alexandria and Jerusalem who accepted Chalcedon. Eventually the Orthodox candidate, Sylvester, became Patriarch of Antioch, while Pope Bene-dict XIII recognised the pro-Catholic candidate Cyril VI (in 1729), splitting the Catholic segment into the "Melkite Church." Analogous is the Syriac Catholic patriarch of Antioch, which emerged as a split between the Orthodox party and the pro-Catholic party. Ignatius Andrew Akijan (1622-1677) was supported by the Ottomans as the head of the Syrian Christian millet regardless of his pro-Catholic identity. Ignatius Michael III Jarweh became the Catholic Syrian Patriarch (enthroned in 1783). He himself personally converted to Catholicism. The context of Oriental Churches was influenced by effective missionary activity on the part of Catholic orders.

An interesting case is the union of the Ethiopian Church with Rome. It is similar to the Byzantine context, in that the ruler of Ethiopia was motivated by fear of the Muslim invasions to accept union. The Ethiopians were present at the council of Florence. The Portuguese came to Ethiopia in 1520 and thought they had discovered the legendary kingdom of Prester John. They viewed the Ethiopian tradition with its strong Judaic inclinations as highly suspicious. King Galawdewos gained military support from the Portuguese and was under pressure to come through with a close union with Rome. An idea of submission to Rome was again prevalent. In 1539 Cardinal Alfonso sent a letter to ruler Dawit (Lebna Dengel) calling for total submission to the authority of the Roman Pontiff, who was acknowledged even by the "Greeks" at Florence.[77] Under Ruler Susneyos (1607-

---

[76] For example, in 1590, Pope Sixtus V writing to the Coptic hierarch Gabriel VIII emphasises the necessity of submission to the Roman See and the Vicar of Christ.

[77] Cohen L, "The Portuguese Context of the Confesio Fide of King Claudius," In: Baye Yimam, Richard Pankhurst, David Chapple, Yonas Admassu, Alula Pankhurst, Birhanu Teferra (eds.) *Ethiopian Studies at the End of the Second Millennium*, vol. I, (Institute of Ethiopian Studies Addis Ababa University, 2000), 155. See also Beccari, C., *Aethiopicarum Scriptores Occidentales Inediti a Saeculo XVI ad XIX*, vol. 10 (Roma 1903-1919).

1632) an edict was published in 1626 (11 February), where Roman Catholicism became the official religion. This was rejected by the people and Susneyos was forced to recant his edict.[78] Later during Mussolini and the Italian invasion, the Church in Ethiopia was subjected to persecution.

The union with the Armenian Church had been arranged between the king of Armenia and the crusaders in Cilicia in 1198, but did not have any consequence outside of Cilicia. Later the union was enlivened by missionary activity.

Conclusions

The preceding account in a way offers its own conclusions. In the early Church we have seen, that often "natural" and "innocent" theological debates have been polarised and turned into irreconcilable positions through the action or pressure from the outside (government-emperor). While surely, the role of the state in the early Church was positive, in that it contributed to a clarification and victory over heresy, action from the state was not always fortunate and perhaps some things would have sorted out themselves without this intervention.

Efforts for union were directly dependent on ecclesiological positions. Here it is important to emphasise, that these were constantly developing. In the West, a notion developed emphasising the submission to the pope as a necessary prerequisite for unity and an idea of the Church as a mystical body of Christ, (Ignatius of Loyola), with exclusive rights to salvation. In the East, the changing character of Byzantium from a multicultural empire to a Hellenic empire and the later developing notions of "national" autocephalous churches presented new developments.

Efforts for ecclesial union became the result of political whims and policies of competing empires. In this context we have to discard the modern idea that there can be a total separation between church and state. It is hardly possible to claim, that there can be a total separation of the state and ideology. Each person brings with them his or her ideologies into every walk of life. The unions offered national and cultural identity to aspiring nations, which then enforced this union using extreme violence and used it not as an instrument of unity but on the contrary of identifying oneself in contrast to the other.

Most importantly, the unions reveal an incredible disparity between the hierarchy and those it represented, especially in the context of the Orthodox Church. It displays the fundamental fact, that ecclesial unity cannot be ordained from above and that rather it is an event of love coming from below.

The motives for union were various most of them however, having little to do with a true desire for unity. This is related to the question of theological awareness among the faithful. The faithful were rather driven by inclusive "spiritual" intuitivism than theory.

Generally it can be stated, that the classical models of church unions are historically conditioned and can hardly serve as a basis of unity in our period. It also has to be said, that both ecclesial families, that is the Roman Catholic tradition and the Orthodox, have to approach future union without opportunism and proselytism. It would be rather fair if the churches did not recognise any unions which would not encompass the "totality" of faithful from any church and this would avoid historical problems with partial unions, partial conversions and so on. Those seeking union bring with them their own contexts, which have to be critically judged through the prism of love in order for any effective union to take place.

Bibliography

Cowdrey, H.E.J. "The Gregorian Papacy: Byzantium, and the First Crusade," Oxford, 145-169, In: *Byzantium and the West c. 850-c.1200, proceedings off the XVIII Spring Symposium of Byzantine Studies*, Howard Johnston J.D ed., (Adolf M. Hakkert-publishers, Amsterdam, 1988).

[78] Trimingham J., S., *Islam in Ethiopia*, (London, 1972), 99.

Part VII: Particular Themes and Issues for Orthodox Involvement in Ecumenism

Grillmeier S.J., *Christ in Christian Tradition: from the Apostolic Age to Chalcedon*, (New York, Sheed and Ward, 1964).

Tsirpanlis C.N., *Mark Eugenicus and the Council of Florence*, (Thassaloniki: Center of Byzantine Studies, 1974) (in Greek).

Oikonomides, N., "Byzantium between East and west (XIII-XV cent.)," In: *Byzantium and the West c. 850-c.1200*, proceedings off the XVIII Spring Symposium of Byzantine Studies, Howard Johnston J.d. ed. Adolf (Amsterdam: M. Hakkert-publishers, 1988).

Lacko M., *The Union of Užhorod*, (Rome, 1976).

Теплов, В.А, Зуев З.И УНИЯ В ДОКУМЕНТАХ, (Minsk: Luchi Sofii, 1977).

Irvin D. T. And Sunquist, S. W., *History of the World Christian Movement, vol. 1, Earliest Christianity to 1453* (Minsk: Luchi Sofii, 2002).

Young, F. M., *From Nicaea to Chalcedon, a Guide to the Literature and its Background* (Philadelphia, 1983)

(117) ECUMENICAL DIMENSION IN THE ORTHODOX CHRISTIAN EDUCATION

Natallia Vasilevich

It is not possible to disconnect the development of Orthodox theology and theological education in the present day from its ecumenical context, which is recognized and reflected upon both by Orthodox theologians involved in the ecumenical movement, and those who avoid such involvement. Stating the necessity for Orthodox theological education to be ecumenical in its academic and religious dimension could sound in different ecclesial and social contexts either too radical or too self-evident.

When in 1920 the Encyclical of the Ecumenical Patriarchate called for theological cooperation between different Christian communities, studying the theological doctrines, traditions and practices of other Christian churches was not an innovative idea for Orthodox theological educational establishments. However, this ecumenical document of the Orthodox Church elaborated a new way, significantly contrasting the widely spread exclusively apologetical, polemical and comparative approach employed by Orthodox seminaries and faculties. That approach aimed rather to equip future ministers for their pastoral work in areas where other Christians and ecclesial communities were present. It often encouraged them to understand their own identity as Orthodox pushing off the confessional differences, while presenting other Christian beliefs and traditions' "mistakes" in a polemical, often inadequate way, that did not reflect enough on the contextuality of their own theological concepts and practices. In the beginning of the twentieth century, Fr. Heorhi Šavielski[1], a famous theologian of Belarusian origin, who in his doctoral dissertation tried to be sincere and critically reflect on the sensitive issue of Uniatism and the reunification of the Uniate churches with the Orthodox, grieved for this misleading approach: "We, Orthodox, also were not always right in our attitude towards the heterodox churches and confessions. We stood aloof of lively communication with them and judged them with outdated scholastic seminarian handbooks not checked with neutral and accurate research on their modern state, religious moods and Christian life; in grand scale we imagined them other than in reality."[2]

This criticized polemical approach starting with the self-evident affirmation of the deficiency of other Christian theologies and therefore picturing other Christian churches in a specific way, is still widely used in theological education, and it is not exclusively an Orthodox problem in the ecumenical movement. It is strongly judged as a "scandal" in the recent ecumenical document on theological education and ecumenical formation, the so-called "Magna Charta": "churches remaining in disunity and using distorted images of sister churches in one's own educational materials and publication needs to be overcome with foremost priority in the area of theological education and ministerial formation."[3] Still, the polemical attitude does not prevent inter-Christian contacts and cooperation in theological education, but rather forms a special ecumenical ethos which can be named as a polemical ecumenical ethos, where the necessity of such contacts are seen as studies for future apologetics, which is two-dimensional. On the one hand, that means studying the theological concepts of other Christian traditions to discover their "mistakes," and on the other, witnessing to them the truth of the Orthodox faith. Such an approach was rejected in a statement of the recent conference on ecumenical education in Sibiu:

---

[1] Fr. Heorhi Šavielski was one of the key figures of the Russian Orthodox Church Outside of Russia, an ecclesial body later known for its strong skepticism towards the ecumenical movement.

[2] Heorhi Šavielski, prot., translated from Russian: Георгий Шавельский, прот. Государственный Архив Российской Федерации. ф.1486. Оп.1. д.13. л.6., Quoted from: Кострюков А.А. Протопресвитер Георгий Шавельский и Карловацкий Синод, *Церковь и время* 1.34 (2006): 138.

[3] Dietrich Werner, "Magna Charta on Ecumenical Formation in Theological Education in the 21st Century – 10 Key Convictions." *International Review of Mission* 98.1(2009): 161. This paper is republished here in the next chapter of the present Handbook, under the same title.

"It was agreed that the study of other Christian churches, other faiths and the ecumenical movement only in the framework of comparative or even polemical apologetics, although still widely practiced is insufficient."[4]

The prophetic Encyclical of 1920 saw theological education as central to improving the relations between the Christian churches, by maintaining "a friendship and kindly disposition towards each other" through particularly the following:

[...] Relationships between theological schools and professors of theology; by the exchange of theological and ecclesiastical reviews, and of other works published in each church.

... Exchanging students for further training between seminaries of different churches.

[...] Impartial and deeper historical study of doctrinal differences both by seminaries and in books.[5]

In the twentieth century the theological relationships, exchanges and studies became more intensive than before which helped Orthodox theology to overcome isolationism and be present in the global theological discourse. But in the West, theological academia is still dominated by Protestant and Catholic theological schools, while the presence of Orthodox scholars is more sporadic than systematic. Orthodox theology both institutionally and thematically is assigned to heterodox faculties and research projects with few exceptions of Orthodox theological institutions which emerged in the West during the last century. Moreover, the Orthodox Church itself is a minority of the Christian oikoumene, often with a strong migrant background. In such circumstances, the Orthodox presence in the theological framework is a presence rather of a guest kindly hosted by other Christian traditions, often marked with what Nikos Nissiotis names as "sentimental pro-Orthodox attitude, which narrows ecumenism into sympathy, an appreciation of the symbolism and richness of liturgy, and an admiration of the exotic or extravagant elements."[6] Therefore, Orthodox theology in the Western context is of secondary importance compared to the dominant traditions which determines her "shadowing" character and underlines the necessity to produce theological concepts that compete with the respective Western theological traditions. Doing research and studies in the Catholic or Protestant faculties, participating in scholarship programmes, being invited to deliver lectures on specific "Orthodox" topics, Orthodox professors and students see ecumenical involvement and openness of the Orthodox theological education as not only natural, but unavoidable.

The first concept of such a two-dimensional learning can be described as "learning about each other" and is the first step of the Orthodox theological education in ecumenical dialogue. Such a model is presented, for example, in the Russian Orthodox Church's document on "The Main Principles of the Attitude to Heterodoxy" which presupposes a two-directional movement: firstly, "to explain to heterodox partners the ecclesiological self-consciousness of the Orthodox church, basics of its doctrine, canonical order and spiritual tradition, to allay perplexities and existing stereotypes,"[7] and secondly, to listen as "witness cannot be just a monologue - it presupposes those who hear, presupposes communication... being ready to understand."[8] Comparative theology,

---

[4] Communique of the Inter-Orthodox Consultation on the Ecumenical Movement in Theological Education and Orthodox Church Life. - Sibiu, Romania, 9-12 November 2010. - Official web-page of WCC: <http://www.oikoumene.org/en/resources/documents/wcc-programmes/ecumenical-movement-in-the-21st-century/member-churches/inter-orthodox-consultation-on-the-ecumenical-movement-in-theological-education-and-orthodox-church-life>, (last accessed 28 June 2012). The Sibiu Communique is re-published in the next chapter of the present Handbook.

[5] Encyclical of the Ecumenical Patriarchate "Unto the Churches of the Christ Everywhere," 1920 in Gennadios Limouris (compl.) *Orthodox Visions of Ecumenism: Statements, Messages and Reports in the Ecumenical Movement: 1902-1992*, (Geneva: WCC Publications, 1994), 10.

[6] Nikos A. Nissiotis, "Orthodox Principles in the Service of an Ecumenical Theological Education" in *Orthodox Theology and Diakonia*, (Brookline, MA: Hellenic College Press, 1981), 329-338.

[7] Основные принципы отношения Русской Православной Церкви к инославию. (2000) [The Main Principles of the Russian Orthodox Church's Attitude to Heterodoxy]. Approved by Bishops Council of the Russian Orthodox Church. - Official web-page of the Russian Orthodox Church <http://www.patriarchia.ru/db/text/418840.html>, (last accessed 28 June 2012). §4.2.

[8] Ibid. §4.5.

however, helps to find a common language and translates different theological concepts of one tradition into a language understandable in the framework of the other.

Despite its positive implications, such an externally forced ecumenical awareness, based on non-theological factors, seen as a necessity rather than a choice, does not help Orthodox theological education to flourish in the Western inter-Christian context. First of all, Orthodox theology is reduced to a specific set of topics and disciplines (patristic studies, ascetic and neptic tradition, studies of Eastern liturgical tradition), while in the other areas it is marginalized. However, this tendency is not a result of exclusively external factors. As Pantelis Kalaitzidis argues, it is a consequence of the internal identity issue of Orthodox theology and the "return to the fathers" movement in order to release itself "from its 'Babylon captivity' to Western theology in terms of its language, its presupposition and its thinking,"[9] which resulted, according to the Greek scholar, in the neglect of biblical studies, a non-critical approach to Patristics, the absence of Orthodox theology from theological developments and trends of the twentieth century, and to a weak theological response to social issues.[10]

Orthodox theology, having its indisputable advantages in the ecumenical context, among which is the "experience of an intense liturgical life, with very strong emphasis on eschatology and cosmic salvation,"[11] as Nikos Nissiotis noted, in a certain way it becomes hostage to them. This happens despite its potential to contribute to academic theology and the ecumenical movement through its sacramental ecclesiology, Eucharistic theology, the centrality of liturgy and pneumatology, and "understanding of the Church as the presupposition of all sacraments and the word of God," "professing an absolute unity between Scripture and tradition," "the importance of the liturgical-sacramental life centered on the Eucharist," "understanding of the unity of the Church... [as] both gift of the Spirit and a goal," the "insistence that unity in faith and praxis, with the bond of love and peace, is the condition for sacramental communion."[12] Overemphasis of the advantages and a non-critical approach to them can lead to a closed theological discourse, focused on internal Orthodox issues; however, they should not be neglected either.

In Eastern and Central Europe, where the Orthodox Church has a strong presence, Orthodox theological education enjoys, in turn, a dominant position among other Christian traditions. But it still experiences marginalization at the academic level. This has to do with the communistic past, when theological education was marginalized, if not completely absent from the academic field and often reduced exclusively to the priestly formation. During the last decades due to political and social changes in Eastern and Central Europe, where the majority of Orthodox theological education institutions are concentrated, due to the involvement of several countries in the European Union family and the Bologna process, the gap between Eastern and Western theological institutions diminished. However, the latter still experience the effects of communist isolation in terms of theological education, and reflect an ecumenical ethos whose context needs special reflection.

In the Eastern predominantly Orthodox context an approach is widely spread as an alternative to the ecumenicity of the theological education, which Fr. Ion Bria called "defend orthodoxy principle."[13] He supported that it leads to "fundamentalism and nationalism,"[14] and as Fr. Constantin Coman, another Romanian theologian, argued it results in the situation where "theology seems to be a-temporal and irremediably locked in the past."[15] Another theologian actively involved in the ecumenical movement, Fr. Vladimir Fedorov from Russia, is also

---

[9] Pantelis Kalaitzidis, "From the 'Return to the Fathers' to the Need for a Modern Orthodox Theology" *Saint Vladimir's Theological Quarterly* 54.1 (2010): 5-36.

[10] Ibid.

[11] Nikos A. Nissiotis, "Orthodox Principles in the Service of an Ecumenical Theological Education," in *Orthodox Theology and Diakonia*, (Brookline, MA: Hellenic College Press, 1981), 329- 338.

[12] Ibid.

[13] Ion Bria, *Orthodox Theological Education: the Case of Romania*, (Geneva: WCC, 1993), 11.

[14] Ibid.

[15] Constantin Coman, "Teologia ortodoxă românească în epoca post-Stăniloae," in *Studii Teologice* III-a, I.1 (2005): 162, Quotation from: Dan Sandu. Romanian Orthodoxy at the Crossroads: Past and Present in the Higher Theological Education. - <http://www.dansandu.ro/pdf/carti/orthodox-education-at-the-crossroads.pdf> (last accessed, September 2013).

Part VII: Particular Themes and Issues for Orthodox Involvement in Ecumenism

critical about the contemporary approach to theological education: "Many think fundamentalism is the under-lying principle of Orthodoxy... Fundamentalism ardently stands for traditionalism while opposing modernism and liberalism,"[16] and in fact makes Orthodoxy "deeply enmeshed in its cultural and national backgrounds as well as in specific ethical choices the Orthodox have to make... popular religiosity, simplicity, uncritical acceptance of sacramental life."[17]

This fundamentalistic tendency is not an exclusively Orthodox phenomenon; all regions and Christian traditions are subject to parochialism. According to Dietrich Werner, a theologian dealing specifically with theological education, it is one among three main trends which threat theological education not only in its ecumenical dimension but in general: fundamentalism, confessionalism (denominational parochialism and ecclesial self-centeredness), and privatization (absence from the public sphere).[18]

Nevertheless, it was the Orthodox theological education which played a key role in reviving the ecumenical ethos in the Orthodox churches, overcoming the tendency of parochialism, and strengthening the Orthodox participation in the ecumenical movement in general, "[...] articulating an Orthodox theological discourse re-sponding... to the ecumenical agenda; ... assessing developments... and keeping... churches... informed; and... teaching ecumenical studies in educational institutions...."[19] However, being mainly oriented to an academic level, Orthodox theology which is ecumenically sensitive did not reach all levels of the church community, and oftentimes, as Fr. Dan Sandu skeptically observed, it was challenged by the "popular charismatic theology of elders" which is often opposed to scientific and accurate theology,[20] and is not only non-ecumenical in its ethos, but even anti-ecumenical.

An urgent need to overcome this gap between academic theology and ecclesial communities, can be met, as suggested by Petros Vassiliadis, by placing theological education again to its Eucharistic/liturgical framework and its ecclesial, community, local context and making it liturgical-centered.[21] This two-way process will not only warm communities up with an ecumenical ethos, balancing the preservation of faith, by "concentrating on ... church life 'internally', 'mystically', 'liturgically' with a dynamic presence in the world – 'ecumenically'."[22] It will also "feed" theology with "a sacramental-ecclesiological vision of the world."[23] The concept of Fr. Ion Bria of the "liturgy after the liturgy" that warns against over-emphasizing a truly Eucharistic and liturgical understanding of the Church as an "exclusive worshipping community,"[24] while promoting the centeredness of liturgy, must also result in the ecumenical witness.

Orthodox theological thought, nourished with asceticism and liturgical sacramental life, should avoid the one extreme of pure ecumenical socio-political activism, placing social activity "after the liturgy," and also the other extreme of focusing on the "liturgy within liturgy," proposing a vision which transcends

---

[16] Vladimir Fedorov, "Eastern and Central Europe Context: Problem of Theological and Religious Education in the 21st Century." *Ministerial Formation* 100 (2003): 50.

[17] Nikos A. Nissiotis, "Orthodox Principles in the Service of an Ecumenical Theological Education" *Orthodox Theology and Diakonia*, (Brookline, MA: Hellenic College Press, 1981), 329- 338.

[18] Dietrich Werner, "Magna Charta on Ecumenical Formation in Theological Education in the 21st Century – 10 Key Convictions" *International Review of Mission* 98.1 (2009): 168.

[19] Communique of the Inter-Orthodox Consultation on the Ecumenical Movement in Theological Education and Ortho-dox Church Life. - Sibiu, Romania, 9-12 November 2010. - Official web-page of WCC: <http://www.oikoumene.org/en/ resources/documents/wcc-programmes/ecumenical-movement-in-the-21st-century/member-churches/inter-orthodox-con-sultation-on-the-ecumenical-movement-in-theological-education-and-orthodox-church-life>, (last accessed 28 June 2012).

[20] Dan Sandu. Romanian Orthodoxy at the Crossroads: Past and Present in the Higher Theological Education. - <http:// www.dansandu.ro/pdf/carti/orthodox-education-at-the-crossroads.pdf> (last accessed, September 2013).

[21] Petros Vassiliadis, "Ecumenical Theological Education and Orthodox Issues for the 3rd Millennium," *Ministerial For-mation* 90 (2000): 1-2.

[22] Nissiotis "Orthodox Principles in the Service of an Ecumenical Theological Education" in *Orthodox Theology and Diakonia*, (Brookline, MA: Hellenic College Press, 1981), 329-338.

[23] Ibid.

[24] Ion Bria, "The Liturgy after the Liturgy," *International Review of Mission* 67.2 (1978): 87.

liturgy as exclusively worship. Moreover, as Vassiliadis argues, "Orthodox ecumenical education must allow itself to be affected by contemporary trends of ecumenical activism... But this does not mean to copy or imitate."[25] Indeed, Orthodox theology has benefited from its ecumenical involvement not only in being open to this ecumenical activism, but also in a theological sense by "the insistence of the Western reformed theologians on the centrality of the Bible and the kerygma of the Church; the critical approach which is wary of an easy acceptance of church history as the unique criterion and norm of the present church life; the work of the historical critical method applied to biblical texts; the need of permanent renewal of church life and theology; the continuous concern for man's daily life and the sharing of human efforts to improve the human condition; the missionary character of theology as contextual and inductive methodology."[26] This ecumenical exchange from different sides can be described by the concept of "learning from each other," which understands the ecumenical openness of Orthodox education not only in the sense of finding a common language and adequate interpretations of theological concepts, but also the ability to import developments and creatively rework them. That would be the second step of Orthodox theological education in the ecumenical context.

Nevertheless, a cooperative ecumenical ethos also has the danger of being reduced just to pragmatic ethos using facilities, infrastructure and developments in theological education of other Christian traditions and the ecumenical movement, enjoying participation in conferences, scholarships, academic programmes and so on. Or it could be reduced to perceiving ecumenical awareness as deriving from the need to equip Orthodox theologians for Christian dialogue or ecumenical involvement. This pragmatic ethos paradoxically often goes hand in hand with a polemical approach, the risk of which was described at the beginning of this text. Both of these derive from a genuine idea of dialogue, where partners are fundamentally equal.

A shift in the theory of theological education in general was marked by a concept of ecumenical learning which postulated a new methodology of education alternative to the simply instructive one. Konrad Raiser, theologian and former General Secretary of the WCC, argued for the need of this shift distinguishes ecumenical learning as "the process of empowerment for a holistic and responsible life that is able to integrate new and conflicting experiences and to connect them with what is considered reliable and trustworthy." The new methodology was developed "to nurture ecumenical awareness on all levels of the churches' life" starting from the concept of education "as a formalized and institution-based process by which people are being introduced into the traditions and order of a given community."[27]

The idea of dialogue nurtures ecumenical cooperation, and has allowed Orthodox theology to share its treasures, while also benefiting. However, the concept of ecumenical education is mutual learning, dialogue as a "learning about each other" and "learning from each other" that shall be completed with the next step which is "learning with each other." Learning with each other allows not only to produce and reinterpret knowledge in the confessionally based theological system and presenting the results to other traditions, but also to cooperate in planting common theological trees, and enjoy common theological fruits.

Bibliography

Vladimir Fedorov, "Challenges to the Theological Education in Central and Eastern Europe: Education as Liturgy Before Liturgy." *Ministerial Formation* 101 (2003): 13-23

Vladimir Fyodorov. *Perspectives of Ecumenical Cooperation in Theological Education in Eastern and Central Europe* (2008).

[25] Nikos A. Nissiotis "Orthodox Principles in the Service of an Ecumenical Theological Education," *Orthodox Theology and Diakonia*, (Brookline, MA: Hellenic College Press, 1981), 329- 338.
[26] Ibid.
[27] Konrad Raiser. "The Future of Theological Education in Central and Eastern Europe: Challenges for Ecumenical Learning in the 21st Century." *International Review of Mission* 98.1 (2009): 56-58.

Part VII: Particular Themes and Issues for Orthodox Involvement in Ecumenism

Thomas FitzGerald, "Orthodox Theology and Ecumenical Witness: An Introduction to Major Themes," *Saint Vladimir's Theological Quarterly* 42.3-4 (1998): 339-61.

Pantelis Kalaitzidis, "From the 'Return to the Fathers' to the Need for a Modern Orthodox Theology", *Saint Vladimir's Theological Quarterly* 54.1 (2010): 5-36.

Eleni Kasselouri-Hatzivassiliadi, "Orthodox Women in Theological Education: From a Greek Orthodox Perspective" *Paper presented at Sambata Seminar on Ecumenical Theological Education in Eastern and Central Europe - September 2008. -* http://www.oikoumene.org/fileadmin/files/wcc-main/documents/p5/ete/Women_and_Orthodox_Theological_Education_-_Eleni_Kasseluri.pdf (last accessed, September 2013).

Natalie Maxson, Katerina Pekridou. Ecumenical Youth Formation as as Integral Part of Theological Education. - http://www.oikoumene.org/fileadmin/files/wcc-main/documents/p5/ete/Natalie%20Maxson-Katerina%20Pekridou%20-%20%20Ecumenical%20youth%20formation%20as%20an%20integral%20part%20of%20theological%20education.pdf (2009) (last accessed, September 2013).

Radu Constantin Miron "Über das Wahrnehmen: Beobachtungen zur Begegnung zwischen Ost- und Westkirche" *Orthodoxes Forum* 23 (2009), 53 – 64.

Nikos Nissiotis, "Orthodox Principles in the Service of an Ecumenical Theological Education" in *Orthodox Theology and Diakonia: Essays in Honour of Archbishop Iakovos,* (Brookline, MA: Hellenic College Press, 1981), 329-38.

John S. Pobee, "Perspectives For Ecumenical Formation Tomorrow" *Ecumenical Review* 48.4 (1996): 483-90.

Dan Sandu. Romanian Orthodoxy at the Crossroads: Past and Present in the Higher Theological Education. - http://www.dansandu.ro/pdf/carti/orthodox-education-at-the-crossroads.pdf (last accessed, September 2013).

Petros Vassiliadis *Ecumenical Theological Education and Orthodox Issues for the 3rd Millenium. Ministerial Formation* 90 (2000): 14-21.

- "Contextuality and Catholicity: The Task of Orthodox Theology in Ecumenical Theological Education" *International Review of Mission* 98.1 (2009): 37-48

Dietrich Werner, "Magna Charta on Ecumenical Formation in Theological Education in the 21st Century – 10 Key Convictions" *International Review of Mission* 98.1(2009).

John Zizioulas, "The Ecumenical Dimensions of Orthodox Theological Education, in *Orthodox Theological Education for the Life and Witness of the Church,* (Geneva: WCC, 1978), 33-40 (this paper is re-published in the next chapter of the present Handbook, under the same title).

Perry Hamalis

Introduction

Since the 1980s, participants in the ecumenical movement have increasingly recognized the impact of moral questions and issues upon their efforts to promote visible unity and common witness among Christians. The potential for ethical claims both to unite and to divide churches has prompted church leaders to express the need for study and discussion of moral discernment, the process through which churches and their members develop responses to moral questions and issues. The aim of this essay is to provide an introduction to Orthodox perspectives on the subject of moral discernment within ecumenical dialogue. I begin with a brief discussion of the significance and meaning of moral discernment within ecumenism. After this, I focus on the WCC study document, "Moral Discernment in the Churches (2013)," offering some analysis of the contributions made to the document and of the reservations expressed about it by Orthodox representatives. Finally, I will comment on the value of continued ecumenical debate on moral discernment by members of the Orthodox Church.

The Increasing Significance of Moral Discernment in Ecumenical Dialogue

In recent decades, social injustices like segregation in the United States and apartheid in South Africa have prompted effective cooperation and constructive dialogue between and within churches. Notwithstanding theological differences, Christians have collaborated across denominational lines on several moral issues in order to provide a shared witness, promote the common good, and help reform unjust social structures. While the Orthodox Church has participated enthusiastically in many collaborations of this kind on local, national, and international levels, Orthodox representatives in the ecumenical movement have stressed repeatedly that Christian unity will not come through "ethics" alone. From an Orthodox perspective, resolving theological or doctrinal differences must remain the basis and core of ecumenism's unifying mission.[1]

Furthermore, while Christians have cooperated effectively at times on shared social concerns, many of the greatest current obstacles either to increasing Christian unity or to preventing further divisions seem to be grounded less in doctrinal issues and more in moral or ethical issues. To be sure, doctrinal and ethical claims cannot be separated sharply. On the one hand, ethical responses draw upon and apply doctrinal convictions about God, human persons, and all creation. On the other hand, moral situations and a church's experience as a "moral community" influence doctrinal reflection on the personal and communal levels. Yet doctrinal teachings and moral teachings are also different kinds of claims, with different degrees of linguistic precision and different expectations for how they are appropriated by a church's members.[2] Such differences between doctrine and

---

[1] See the excellent discussion of this point in Stanley Harakas, "What Orthodox Christian Ethics Can Offer Ecumenism," *Journal of Ecumenical Studies* 45.3 (Summer 2010): 376-378.

[2] A full treatment of this point lies beyond our present scope. However, we can note that doctrinal claims, which pertain more to *theoria* than to *praxis*, typically are articulated with a higher degree of linguistic precision than moral claims in order to protect the saving truths of the faith against heresies and false teachers. In addition, all members of a church generally are expected to confess the same doctrines as a matter of shared ecclesial identity. For example, one cannot be an Orthodox Christian in good standing while expressing the Arian belief that Jesus Christ was created, not begotten. Yet the same is not true of moral claims. Faith traditions may not expect all of their members to express moral claims with universal consensus; in addition, the development of a moral response typically allows for some freedom in order to take into account the uniqueness of each person and each historical-cultural context. For example, some Orthodox may argue

ethics have, at times, facilitated ecumenical cooperation on moral challenges both between and within churches; however, more frequently, the divisive potential of moral claims has prevailed when Christians have struggled to respond to major moral dilemmas like economic injustice in developed and developing nations, war and terrorism, racism, environmental degradation, gender inequality, proselytism, issues of sexuality and marriage, and developments in biotechnology. As these moral debates have unfolded, it has become apparent that differences among Christians and churches are often rooted in a much more complex set of causes than many might suspect. It is not simply a matter of applying the Lord's teaching "accurately," to a question like 'should I voluntarily participate in my nation's military?' or 'as the Church, should we advocate for new legislation restricting or allowing same-sex marriage?' Some leaders and members of churches may agree on many premises, but reach different conclusions; others utilize a methodology for ethical decision-making that is foreign and incomprehensible to their interlocutors; still others may arrive at the same position on an issue, but for significantly different reasons, undermining oneness of mind and long-term stability. The tensions and accusations experienced by partners in ecumenical and intra-church dialogue during such exchanges have highlighted the significance of and need for a better understanding of moral discernment as it is practiced within one's own and others' traditions.

The Meaning of "Moral Discernment"

"Moral discernment" refers to the spiritual and intellectual *process* through which a person or community of faith develops a response to a moral question, challenge, or issue. Since moral questions pertain to claims about what is "right" and "wrong" or what is "good" and "bad," *moral* discernment is the manner in which believers and faith communities arrive at judgments about what is, or is not, right and good. Complementarily, while all communities and all human persons engage in "moral decision making," the term moral *discernment* typically refers to an explicitly Christian approach, one that employs authoritative sources and is governed by beliefs and practices that non-Christians generally do not embrace. Thus, while the Bible's status as divinely-inspired and the decision-making authority of an episcopal synod are points about which Christians may disagree, there are few—if any—non-Christians whose method for moral decision-making includes such convictions. To examine "moral discernment" is to study how and why Christian communities arrive at the moral stances they hold. Ecumenical debate on moral discernment is, therefore, a type of second-order thinking that identifies, articulates, and analyzes the different forms that moral discernment takes in an effort to better understand and minimize the divisive effects of moral disagreements.

The WCC Study Document, "Moral Discernment in the Churches"

Within the World Council of Churches (WCC), the most significant effort to date toward advancing such understanding was undertaken by the Faith and Order Commission in 2007 and generated a study document in 2013 entitled, "Moral Discernment in the Churches."[3] The fact that Faith and Order undertook this project highlights the increasing awareness of connections between doctrine, ecclesiology, and ethics within ecumenism. While a full discussion of this landmark text lies beyond our present scope, a few of its core features merit our consideration.

that following Christ faithfully and serving in a voluntary national military are not mutually exclusive, while other Orthodox may hold to a more strictly pacifist standard. Neither faces excommunication for their moral disagreement. Similarly, while lying is regarded generally as sinful, there are celebrated cases of Orthodox saints telling lies in order to protect the lives of others (St. Dionysios of Zakynthos, St Maria (Skobstova) of Paris, etc.). For a helpful treatment of these issues, see Christos Yannaras, *The Freedom of Morality*, trans. Elizabeth Briere (Crestwood, NY: St Vladimir's Seminary Press, 1984).
[3] "Moral Discernment in the Churches, A Faith and Order Study Document," Faith & Order Paper 215, (Geneva: WCC, 2013). Available online at: http://www.oikoumene.org/en/resources/documents/wcc-commissions/faith-and-order-commission/i-unity-the-church-and-its-mission/moral-discernment-in-the-churches-a-study-document. Hereafter "MDC" followed by section number. For an account of the document's development, see MDC § 7-12 (last accessed September 2013).

First, from the start, the Standing Commission decided to utilize a "case study" approach in order to provide specific content, or examples, for the conversations and to facilitate constructive discussion of how and why moral disagreements generate and exacerbate divisions between different churches, within churches or church families, among churches in the global North and the global South, and between Christians in different cultures.[4] The cases were read, discussed, and reported on by the study's working group members, by attendees of the 2009 Plenary Commission on Faith and Order, and by university and seminary students in multiple cultural contexts. The final version of the study paper draws upon the reports and insights that were gained through the case study phase of the project.[5]

Second, the study document "Moral Discernment in the Churches" makes an important distinction between "normative ethics" and "descriptive ethics." The former centers on determining what is right or good and why, while the latter centers on the context of moral dilemmas and on giving an account of what is going on in a moral situation, of what is believed to be right or wrong by those involved, and of the basis for the different moral positions.[6] Put differently, normative ethics yields prescriptive claims about how persons and communities *ought* to respond to moral challenges (what is the right, or appropriate, Christian response to proselytism, economic injustices, same sex marriage, stem cell research, etc.), while descriptive ethics yields claims about how and why persons and communities are *in fact* responding to the moral challenges they confront (what are the different stances held by Christians on, for example, stem cell research, what are the bases of these differences, and what factors are fueling the conflict between those involved). Building upon this distinction, the document emphasizes strongly that the "Moral Discernment in the Churches" project is an exercise in *descriptive ethics*, not in *normative ethics*. It states:

> [T]his study aims to engage in descriptive ethics to identify and describe the factors that contribute to differences regarding moral issues. This descriptive task is in no way normative in that it does not seek to develop prescriptive norms about what should be done about particular moral issues or about church-dividing situations. Rather, the purpose of a descriptive study [like this] is to help the churches gain deeper insight into the causative factors of disagreement with the hope that a deeper understanding of difference and division can pave the way for improved ecumenical dialogue about moral issues.[7]

If there is any normative content to the study document, it comes in the concluding section, where recommendations are offered for those involved in moral discernment debates within ecumenical settings.[8]

Third, in a section titled, "Sources for Moral Discernment," the study document describes the various authoritative sources from which Christians and churches draw when engaged in moral discernment. It identifies "faith sources," which are specifically Christian and include: Guidance of the Holy Spirit, the Bible, Tradition, teaching authority, spirituality, and church culture. It also identifies "human reason and other sapiential sources," which are not exclusively Christian and include: reason, natural law, moral philosophy, science, conscience, experience, civil law and human rights, and culture.[9] The text notes that not all churches regard all

---

[4] Toward this end, four case study narratives were written, one on each of the following topics: (1) the use of stem cell in research, focusing on debates between Catholics and Protestants in Germany, (2) the struggle over homosexuality within the Anglican Communion, (3) the identification of neo-liberal economic globalization as a "sin" at the General Council meeting of the World Alliance of Reformed Churches, and (4) the practices of proselytism and evangelism in Russia after the fall of communism. I was invited to participate in this study process as an outside consultant and, at the invitation of the WCC, authored one of the four case studies. See Perry T. Hamalis, "Proselytism in Russia: Case Study and Commentary," *Commission on Faith and Order 2009 Plenary Documents* (Geneva: World Council of Churches, 2009).

[5] MDC § 27-29.

[6] MDC § 25.

[7] MDC § 25.

[8] MDC § 87-110.

[9] MDC § 31-48.

Part VII: Particular Themes and Issues for Orthodox Involvement in Ecumenism

of the above-listed sources as being authoritative and that those sources from which churches do draw are not all ranked equally. By describing the various sources from which at least some Christians draw, the document hopes to increase understanding between ecumenical dialogue partners.

Finally, in a section titled, "Causative Factors in the Disagreements between and within Churches," the study document identifies and describes thirteen factors that historically have fuelled conflicts over moral issues.[10] Here, especially, the descriptive purpose of the study document is evident. For each of the thirteen factors, the document provides both a short historical example and a descriptive account of the factor's dynamics and impact upon churches. Merely identifying and giving historical examples of these major and common causative factors of moral disagreement is a significant accomplishment, one that carries much potential for promoting constructive ecumenical dialogue and preventing unnecessary divisions.

Orthodox representatives were involved in and contributed to all aspects of the development of this study document; however, there were times when Orthodox representatives expressed serious reservations about either the study process being employed or the style and content of the text itself. Roman Catholic representatives expressed some similar reservations. Thus, the study document includes an "Orthodox Addendum" and a Roman Catholic notation of shared concern.[11] The content of this addendum exemplifies some of the perspectives Orthodox hold regarding the broader ecumenical debate on moral discernment. Three Orthodox concerns should be discussed briefly.

First, echoing an earlier point, Orthodox ecumenical representatives expressed reservations regarding the study document's "non-theological academic approach" and "lack of spiritual and theological aspects." This concern reflects their belief that ecumenism should center on theological or doctrinal issues, since resolving such issues is essential to achieving the ecumenical aim of Christian unity. While the Orthodox do not deny the significance of moral issues, and Orthodox Christians collaborate with other Christians on issues of shared moral concern (marching alongside Dr. Martin Luther King, Jr. for civil rights, advocating for environmental protection laws, etc.), the Orthodox do not see ethical endeavors as a viable path to Christian unity. Some Orthodox contend that ecumenical efforts to resolve moral differences and, even, to study the moral discernment process amount to 'putting the cart before the horse.' Theological claims ground moral claims, they argue, therefore theological differences must be worked out before ecumenical dialogue on moral issues can proceed with integrity.

Second, Orthodox representatives expressed concern regarding the study's "relativistic approach" both in its methodology and in its account of authoritative sources. This point exemplifies, in my judgment, a confusion regarding the difference between *normative* and *descriptive* ethics. The Orthodox who hold this perspective seem to object to the use of a case study approach that both acknowledges Christians' different moral stances and solicits input from a wide range of readers, including many who are not experts in moral theology or ethics. Regarding authoritative sources, the Orthodox concern is stated as follows, "for the Orthodox there are three initial capital sources for moral discernment: the Holy Trinity, the Holy Scriptures, and the Holy Tradition. These sources cannot be placed at the same level with the other sources." Thus the objection seems to be that that study document endorses or encourages the equal use and authority of all sources in moral discernment. If the document's aim was to suggest the goodness, rightness, or appropriateness of (1) many different ethical stances or (2) many different uses and orderings of authoritative sources, then the concern expressed here by

[10] The thirteen factors are grouped under two main headings, "Social and Ecclesial Factors" and "Factors Stemming from Different Approaches to Moral Discernment." The factors listed under the first heading include: (1) influence of historical and cultural contexts, (2) differing understandings of what is at stake, (3) emotional intensity of moral issues, (4) cultural protocol in debating moral concerns, (5) different structural characteristics of churches, (6) power, (7) stereotypes, and (8) attitudes towards otherness. The factors listed under the latter heading include: (1) using different sources and weighing them differently, (2) interpreting sources differently, (3) conflict between competing principles, (4) applying the same principle differently, and (5) conflict between different approaches towards moral reasoning. See MDC § 49-84.
[11] See MDC "Introduction."

some Orthodox would be legitimate. However, the study document clearly states that its aim is *descriptive*; it provides an account of what *is* the case—not of what *ought to be* the case—when Church leaders and members confront moral challenges. The fact that the Orthodox felt compelled to state that, for them, three sources are "capital" only proves the point that differences exist in how churches understand and practice moral discernment.

Third, "Orthodox Ethics" is young discipline, and some Orthodox thinkers even deny that such a discipline exists.[12] Simply put, the historical ethos of the Orthodox Church does not include a highly developed and systematic methodology of moral discernment. Moral positions and counsel have traditionally been discerned on a more local and personal level, between bishops, priests, and their flocks or between spiritual fathers or mothers and their spiritual children. Even canon law has been interpreted with "economy," sensitive to the unique situation and spiritual needs of each person. Thus many Orthodox feel unprepared or ill-equipped to participate in ecumenical dialogues that center on moral issues and methodologies.

Conclusion: The Value of Continued Debate on Moral Discernment

Notwithstanding their reservations, representatives of the Orthodox Church have contributed significantly to the ecumenical debate on moral discernment. They have endorsed ongoing participation in the WCC study process and in other ecumenical efforts aimed at deepening our understanding of moral discernment. While the Orthodox Church has been less inclined that other churches to systematize its discernment process and to articulate detailed positions on social and moral issues, the seriousness of such issues for the lives of Christians and for the whole world, as well as the challenges Orthodox face as they encounter other churches and other religions in a culture of increasing diversity and globalization, underscore the need for and value of continued Orthodox reflection on moral discernment.

Bibliography

Guroian, Vigen, *Incarnate Love.* (Notre Dame, IN: University of Notre Dame Press, 1987).

Gustafson, James M., *Discernment in the Christian Life: Essays in Theological Ethics.* Edited by Theo Boer and Paul Capetz. (Louisville: Westminster John Knox Press, 2007).

Hamalis, Perry, "Ethics." In *The Orthodox Christian World*, edited by Augustine Casiday, (London and New York: Routledge, 2012), 419-431.

Harakas, Stanley, "What Orthodox Christian Ethics Can Offer Ecumenism." *Journal of Ecumenical Studies* 45.3 (Summer 2010): 376-384.

-. *Toward Transfigured Life: The* Theoria *of Eastern Orthodox Ethics* (Minneapolis: Light & Life, 1983).

Mantzaridis, Georgios. "How We Arrive at Moral Judgments: An Orthodox Perspective," *Phronema* 3 (1988), 11-20.

Russian Orthodox Church, "The Basis of the Social Concept." Moscow: Moscow Patriarchate, 2000. https://mospat.ru/en/documents/social-concepts/ (last accessed 19 September 2013)

Williams, Rowan, "Making Moral Decisions." In *The Cambridge Companion to Christian Ethics*. Edited by Robin Gill, (Cambridge and New York: Cambridge University Press, 2001), 3-15

Woodill, Joseph, *The Fellowship of Life: Virtue Ethics and Orthodox Christianity* (Washington, DC: Georgetown University Press, 1998).

Yannaras, Christos, *The Freedom of Morality.* Translated by Elizabeth Briere (Crestwood, NY: St. Vladimir's seminary Press, 1984).

---

[12] See the discussion of this point in Perry Hamalis, "Ethics," in *The Orthodox Christian World*, ed. Augustine Casiday (London and New York: Routledge, 2012), especially 421-424.

(119) The Issue of Mixed Marriages - Canonical and Pastoral Perspectives[1]

Bassam Nassif

Introduction

The Christian faith is primarily nurtured in the family household. During the past fifty years, human lifestyle has radically changed, seriously affecting personal and family life. The Middle Eastern world has been exposed to the influence of the new world order characterized by globalization and technological advancement. As a result, societies have become increasingly pluralistic. In this era of postmodernism, the individual's freedom of choice has been upheld as the primary value of society. As a result, a change occurred in the social view of marriage and family life.

Marriages between spouses of various religious and ethnic groups have significantly increased. Two kinds of mixed marriages are notably seen to occur in the Middle East: marriages between spouses of the same culture, but having different religious affiliations (Orthodox with Catholic/Protestant affiliation or Orthodox with Muslim/Jewish background, for example); and marriages between two spouses having different religious affiliations and coming from different cultures (such as African, Far Eastern, European, American, to name a few).

Sociologists have observed that marriages between spouses of different faiths are peaceful enough provided that both spouses are indifferent to their respective religions and cultures. This is not the case in the Middle East, since people in general are religiously oriented. For many, faith is not just a personal matter, but it is related to family belonging, and even to demographic belonging and ethnic existence. Thus, mixed marriages have become a source of tension between religions, cultures, and traditions.

Some Christian "ecumenical" figures view the mixed marriage experience as religiously enriching. It is often not the case. The mixed family needs to develop particular religious norms that affect their various relationships: the spouses (the husband and wife) and their immediate families (their in-laws). If the Orthodox spouse is devout and sincerely tries to live his or her faith, sooner or later this will be perceived by his or her non-Orthodox partner as an imposition. Others choose to overlook their personal spiritual needs and religious convictions for the sake of domestic tranquility. How can the children absorb opposing or disharmonious views or values coming from their mixed marriage parents? This situation creates confusion in the family's Christian identity and weakens the faith. It even destabilizes the unity and stability of the family and its growth. The consequences of mixed marriages have a great effect on the future of the Church.

The Orthodox Church, however, has been always keen to help all family members in their marital journey towards holiness and salvation in Christ. This includes the support that the Church ought to offer to the couple for their religious education and the formation of their children, and for helping them to develop their Christian identity and activate their church membership. Thinking about this challenge, we ask: *what are the possible pastoral approaches that ought to be used by the Orthodox Church in order to support a mixed marriage couple?* First, we need to review the Biblical and recent canonical considerations and ecumenical views on mixed marriages and their social and religious challenges. Then, we shall propose an educational solution to the issue.

The Religious Unity of the Couple in a Mixed Marriage

In Mathew 19:5 and Mark 10:8, we read that the Lord Jesus Christ emphasizes the words of Genesis 2:24 by quoting them: "The two shall become one flesh." The expression "one flesh" in the Hebrew sense means one being, including unity in body and spirit, mind and heart. The verse of Malachi 2:24 states: "Has not [the Lord]

---

[1] The first following article on this subject was written by Bassam Nassif (dealing implicitly with Middle East), while the second one was written by Pekka Metso (ed.) (dealing implicitly with the Western perspective).

made them one? In flesh and spirit they are his. And why one? Because he was seeking godly offspring." So the relationship of a man and a woman joined in marriage is humanly unique, since each one of the spouses strives to have perfect harmony with the other. In elaborating the importance of communion and unity in marriage, the Apostle Paul spoke against mixed marriages, saying: "Be ye not unequally yoked together with unbelievers: for what fellowship hath righteousness with unrighteousness? And what communion hath light with darkness?" (2 Cor. 6:14-15). In mixed marriages, the Church faces the dilemma of *sacramentally* uniting "in one flesh" a man and a woman who are religiously disunited! As a result, we often see a tension developing within the family.

Concerning the primacy of the unity of faith in marriage, a different attitude was developed in the West. In the Roman Catholic tradition, a Catholic woman or man is given a special permission to marry a non-Catholic or even a non-Christian spouse, based on a particular understanding of the words of St. Paul in 1 Cor. 7:12-13 that the Catholic spouse sanctifies both the marriage and his or her non-Catholic or even non-Christian spouse, and that the Catholic spouse becomes a witness of the faith and a preacher.

On the other hand, these Pauline words were not interpreted by the Eastern Church Fathers as giving permission to believers to marry non-believers. In the early church, Christians were newly baptized adults who have come into the Church of their own volition. Many of these new believers were already married and had families before they were baptized. It was not usually case that the whole family converted to Christianity upon the conversion of one of its members. Very often, there were individual conversions. The remaining family members converted later on, as a result of the witness and love shown by the Christian member within the family. A mixed marriage was tolerated only when both partners were outside the Church when the marriage took place. This is the common view of the Eastern Church Fathers, represented as follows by the words of St. John Chrysostom: "The question now is not about those who have never yet come together, but about those who are already joined. He did not say, If any one wishes to take an unbelieving wife, but, If anyone has an unbelieving wife…" (Homily 19) [2]

In 691 A.D., the Quinisext Ecumenical Council held in Trullo discussed several issues related to church life, in a time when Byzantine society was becoming more liberal and open. The very question of mixed marriages was one of many hot topics. In Canon LXXII, the holy fathers spoke out against marriages between Orthodox and "heretics" as follows:

> An Orthodox man is not permitted to marry an heretical woman, nor is an Orthodox woman to be joined to an heretical man. But if anything of this kind appear to have been done by any, we require them to consider the marriage null, and that the marriage be dissolved. For it is not fitting to mingle together what should not be mingled… [3]

Since the nineteenth century, however, mixed marriages between Orthodox and other Christian spouses have become openly allowed in the Orthodox Church through *oikonomia*. [4] The non-Christian spouse was obliged to receive baptism in the Orthodox Church before getting married to his or her Orthodox spouse. The issue of intercommunion is raised when the mixed marriage couple participates in a Divine Liturgy in an Orthodox parish. Canonically, communion is reserved to baptized people in the Orthodox Church. Another dimension of the issue is how should the Church deal with those believers who were baptized and confirmed in the Orthodox faith, but not married in the Church? Would the Church allow administering the Sacrament of Holy Communion to them as well? Canonically, they are not considered in good standing with the Orthodox Church, since they must have taken the sacrament of marriage in the Orthodox Church.

---

[2] St. John Chrysostom, *Homilies on the Epistle of St Paul to the Corinthians, A Select Library of the Nicene and Post-Nicene Fathers of the Christian Church*, First Series, ed. Philip Schaff, vol. 12, (Grand Rapids: Eerdmans, 1889), 107.

[3] *Seven Ecumenical Councils. A Select Library of the Nicene and Post-Nicene Fathers of the Christian Church*, Second Series, ed. Philip Schaff and Henry Wace, vol. 14, (Grand Rapids: Eerdmans, 1971), 397.

[4] A detailed article on how the Orthodox Church came to tolerate the blessing of mixed marriages is found in Dr Demetrios Constantelos, "Marriage in the Greek Orthodox Church" *Journal of Ecumenical Studies* 22.1 (Winter 1985): 21-27.

Part VII: Particular Themes and Issues for Orthodox Involvement in Ecumenism

Sources of Religious Tension in an Orthodox/Catholic Mixed Marriage

Both the Orthodox and Catholic churches view marriage as a sacrament instituted by God, wherein the grace of the Holy Spirit comes on both spouses leading them to union with each other and with God in Christ Jesus. Nevertheless, the Orthodox and Catholic churches differ on a number of issues regarding marital life. The Roman Catholic theologians emphasize the idea that sexual relations are a part of the fallen world and considered sinful if not for the sole purpose of begetting children within marriage. In general, the Orthodox Church views sexual relations not only for begetting children, but also as an expression of mutual love and harmony among spouses. Also, the Catholic Church forbids the use of birth control in all circumstances, while the Orthodox is not against a mature and responsible use of birth control by married spouses in some circumstances under the direction of the couple's spiritual father. Thus, a married couple that did not beget children because of a certain physical sterility which was discovered after contracting marriage is not legally permitted to get a divorce in the Orthodox Church. This, however, is a case for the annulment of marriage for the Catholic Canon Law. Moreover, Catholic theology is generally influenced by the Augustinian teaching on the original sin as inherited through the sexual act. The most complicated issue revolves around the matters of divorce in the case of a mixed marriage couple. There are differences in views between various Christian churches about what constitutes a cause for a legal divorce.

The question of such mixed marriages is not just limited to canonical laws, but has several other dimensions, namely the pastoral dimension. In Lebanon, religion was often used as a tool to fight others. The children became the victims of the religious tension between spouses. Sometimes during their clashes as a result of their continuous disagreements, one of the spouses may use some issues within the religious affiliation of the other spouse in order to attack their religious affiliation and humiliate them. If sometimes sarcastic or even funny comments are said by one of the spouses about the other spouse's religious or social customs or traditions, a kind of injury is caused to the other spouse's feelings and emotions. Thus, both have to know very well each other's faith in order to be sensitive to any spoken word that could open the way to quarrels and disputes. This knowledge lessens the actual points of tension between the spouses.

The Shift in Society Affecting Married Life

The traditional family structure has undergone tremendous pressures, which led to a slow but steady change in gender roles, religious adherence, and family values. The marriage age, roles of husbands and wives, child-rearing policies within the household, and attitude to marriage, all have changed significantly. The change started in the last quarter of the last century and continues with large leaps today.[5]

A major reason for this change is that women have entered the workforce and become equally involved in the educational, social, political, cultural, and economic life. As a result, women are not dependent on their parents' household. In earning their living through their work salaries, they became more detached from their family household. Their career brought them self-fulfillment. The major involvement of women of different religious backgrounds led them to be in direct contact with men in society every day. In addition, young women at work and in universities came into direct contact with young men. Marriages motivated by love increased. Young men and women became involved in sexual relationships before marriage, a matter which was unacceptable in society in the past. Consequently, family-arranged marriages that were the normal marriage arrangement in the twentieth century slowly declined. It became a sort of social shame to declare that an engagement was pre-arranged.

All this resulted in a great increase in mixed marriage. In Lebanon, for example, statistics drawn from spiritual courts reveal an increase in mixed marriages from ten percent in the year 1960 to sixty percent today.

---

[5] Much information on this issue is given in the book by Edwin Terry Prothro and Najib Diab Lutfy, *Changing family patterns in the Arab East*, (Beirut: American University of Beirut, 1974).

Orthodox Handbook on Ecumenism

The majority of mixed marriages in Lebanon are between Orthodox and Maronite spouses. This situation is not just limited to the Christians living in Lebanon, but also extends to those living abroad, in the Americas, Europe, Australia and the Far East.

The Ecumenical Dimension of Mixed Marriages

There is no "ecumenical marriage," for the marriage belongs to the Church that conducts it. The Catholic Church desires to have the sole right to work on marital conflicts and divorce in case that the Catholic spouse is willing to divorce even though the marriage may have been conducted in an Orthodox Church, and requires the couple to raise the children in the Catholic Church. In the case of the Middle East, up to the year 1996, the Eastern Catholic churches used to require a signed pledge from the Catholic spouse, marrying a non-Catholic spouse, to baptize and raise his or her children in the Catholic Church parishes.[6] In 14 October 1996, a meeting was held in *Deir Sayedat al Najat – Shurfa,* Lebanon, between the primates of the Orthodox and Catholic Churches in the Middle East. The agreement that was issued upon this meeting declared that the Christian identity of the family is based on the father's denomination, since we live in a patriarchal society.

After taking the approval of the Vatican, the Catholic churches in the Middle East no more require taking the pledge of the Catholic spouse marrying an Orthodox. Thus, the groom who is Orthodox has the responsibility to baptize his children in the Orthodox Church and raise them in an Orthodox parish, helping them to develop an Orthodox Christian identity.[7] This important document reminded the faithful that intercommunion is not yet achieved, since the churches have not yet reached this state of unity. So the mixed marriages could not be a way of practicing eucharistic communion. Marriage is neither a way to Christian unity nor to having syncretistic views about faith and religious practice! Also, one cannot avoid talking about doctrinal issues which are not agreed upon among various Christian denominations.[8] The spouse has to follow her husband's denomination and parish. Having these religious, cultural, and social obstacles, the question is how the Orthodox Church could help two Christian spouses coming from different Christian backgrounds or cultures to actually create a family, live in one faith and be committed to a single parish.

The Challenging Education on Mixed Marriages

We live in a consumer, pluralistic and materialistic society that favours individualism and looks for temporal satisfaction. Studying various social factors and degrees of religious influence on people helps clarify human behaviour. A study on mixed marriages done by Father Charles Joanides led to an "Orthodox ecological developmental grounded theory of interfaith marriages."[9] The aim of a grounded theory is to generate or discover a

---

[6] See the *Codex Canonum Ecclesiarum Orientalium* (= *CCEO*), promulgated in 1990 (*Code of Canons for the Catholic Oriental Churches*). The canons that deal with mixed marriages are 813-816 as found in http://www.intratext.com/IXT/ ENG1199/_INDEX.HTM, (last accessed 20 April 2013).

[7] Emil Kabba, ed., *Mixed Marriages: Theological Basis, Challenges, and Pastoral Horizons,* (Beirut: Publications of La Sagesse University, 2012), 241-244.

[8] This method is now used within the Ecumenical dialogues, especially with the Orthodox-Catholic dialogue: The plan is to avoid conflicting issues and to work on strengthening the common understandings in faith and practice, in an atmosphere of mutual respect and appreciation. Many see this attitude as a positive way of dealing with the issue of mixed marriages. However, some doctrinal issues, such as original sin, cannot be avoided, since they are reflected in the way spouses live out, for example, their intimate relationship.

[9] Father Charles Joanides, "A Systematic Conceptualization of Intermarriages in the Greek Orthodox Archdiocese of America," in *The Orthodox Parish in America: Faithfulness to the Past and Responsibility for the Future*, ed. Anton C. Vrame, (Brookline, MA: Holy Cross Press, 2003), 191-208.

theory from data systematically obtained from social research. Certainly such a solid study would contribute to a better understanding of the problem and its solution.

The new social situation affects present and future generations of Orthodox Christians. To deal with it, one may suggest that special classes ought to be organized for the non-Orthodox Christian women who marry Orthodox men. Will this, however, really alter the preset outlook (various social customs and religious convictions) that has been gradually formed in the mind of the spouse? Another crucial question related to mixed marriages is whether we need to recall canons from the first millennium requiring a non-Orthodox spouse to be baptized before his or her marriage to an Orthodox spouse. Such baptisms have occurred in the past, but the church's experience proved that in many cases the baptized spouse did not undergo inner change in his or her religious convictions.[10]

Father John Meyendorff calls for the re-establishment of an old practice which conducts the wedding service within the eucharistic celebration (the Divine Liturgy).[11] This is a theological solution, as it reflects the deep meaning of marriage as unity "in Christ" through the partaking of the Holy Communion. In doing so, Father John insists that the non-Orthodox spouse needs to be catechized and baptized before marriage. Practically, however, some of the problems related to conflicts in a mixed marriage are due to the differences in views that the spouses have concerning marriage according to their religious, social, and cultural environment, especially with regard to child-rearing. It is important that the church accompany the mixed marriage couple. How can the Church properly care for the couple, not just before marriage, but also after the wedding ceremony, and be present in their daily challenges and journeys of faith?

An Educational Approach

Mixed marriages continue to be a source of anxiety for Orthodox Church leaders, and a significant pastoral challenge facing the Orthodox Church. What are the conditions upon which harmony is established between spouses in a mixed marriage, leading them to build a happy family? What are the rights and responsibilities of the spouses in a mixed marriage in order to succeed? A request that always comes from a mixed marriage couple is: "We love each other, but please teach us how to live our Christian faith in our family, since we come from different Christian backgrounds and/or cultures." Why do mixed marriages constitute a challenging pastoral issue in the Orthodox Church? Most importantly, what is the role of the priest and the parish where the couple belongs?

The Orthodox Christian parish priest does not have the legal, cultural or religious power or tools to change the whole social fabric. What are then the educational methods that need to be sought and explored? Part of the education includes the need to explain to the spouses the rules and laws of the church that the marriage is being held at. This explanation includes the church's views on unity, divorce, child-rearing, inheritance laws, fidelity, indissolubility of marriage, etc. These are important to prevent conflicts between the spouses, as it is important to explore the key to real unity. Dealing with this issue is an experience of learning and growth.

Orthodoxy does not oblige anyone to follow its teaching and practice. The Church respects and preserves the dignity of each person and their joy and well-being. But if a spouse is willing to explore the Orthodox faith, this could serve as the needed key to overcome the challenge that a mixed marriage brings. Then the door may open widely for the spouses to have a change of mind with regard to the Orthodox faith. This change, or *metanoia,* must occur in the depth of their inner heart and mind. This alternative educational method should lead the spouses to undergo a personal transformation, directing them to love the Orthodox faith and worship. So, what is the tool that a parish priest may use in achieving this special purpose?

---

[10] A recent discussion on this issue is found in the article written by Archimandrite Grigorios Papathomas, "Un communautarisme ecclésial ouvert: Mariages dispars-mixtes et conversions d'adultes," *Annals of St. John of Damascus Institute of Theology* 7 (Balamand, Lebanon: St. John of Damascus Institute of Theology, 2006): 71-90.

[11] John Meyendorff, *Marriage: An Orthodox Perspective,* (Crestwood, N. Y.: St. Vladimir's Seminary Press, 1975), 58-59.

The model of iconographic education is the best model for this challenging issue in parish life. "The aim of iconic catechesis is to nurture, instruct, and direct each member of the community of faith in Christian living... so that each person grows 'in the grace and knowledge of our Lord and Savior Jesus Christ' (2 Pet. 3:18)... to become an icon, a living image of God... reflecting in a particular way – the Christ like way – of knowing and living in the world, hence 'iconic knowing and living.'"[12] So this iconic *knowing and living* leads to the needed transformation.

What is the process to achieve the "transformation" of the spouses? It is a process similar to the one of creating an icon, since it involves using successive layers which could be cultural, social, personal, etc. In iconography, this process ends by creating an icon of God's Kingdom. In anthropology, this process leads to the growth of both spouses in knowing and living the Orthodox faith, transforming them into living icons of Christ's Kingdom. What are the different layers of this process? We have the social, personal and parochial levels.

In the social layer, the iconic model calls for a very relational and interactive action. For example, the priest ought to strive to create a Christ-centered parish or community which reflects the life in Christ. In the parish, the priest ought to create an atmosphere of variety and unity through a strong community life. In the parish, the priest offers various interesting opportunities that the couple may choose from. These things could be various ministries and occasions for fellowship and service, both social and religious. Calling the parishioners to be involved in these various ministries in the Church is inviting them to action and to activate their role as the people of God and the body of Christ through vibrant relationships and community service.

One example could be the following. The parish may organize workshops on family living skills that teach couples how to establish a family with healthy relationships. Couples are usually attracted to these kinds of workshops, since they help heal certain misunderstandings of the spouses in the beginning of their married life, allowing them to grow in love. Other workshops could include child-rearing policies within the household, which is a very important topic especially for mothers in modern Lebanese society. Also these workshops help develop a sense of community and fellowship within the parish.

In the personal layer, the parish priest, as part of his outreach ministry to his faithful, ought to organize personal visits to the couples, consecrating a special time for them. These visits ought not to have, at first, the purpose of classical education, detailing the tenets of the Orthodox Church. Rather, the priest's aim ought to be the establishment of a closer personal relationship with the couple, knowing more about their life, talents, challenges, successes, hobbies, expressing his care and love to them, and answering any personal needs they may have. Iconic living is having an active presence of both the human and the divine, and a dynamic interaction. The active presence of the priest, by virtue of his priestly function, brings both the human and the divine, as the icon does.

In his visit, the priest may inform them about the different programs the parish may organize that are of interest to them. Although he may not find an immediate positive reaction from them, the pastor must not push them to participate in the parochial activities, workshops, or worship of the Church. In Christ's spirit of freedom, the priest may kindly call them to "come and see." His main goal is to reach the couple *where they are* and touch their hearts through his active presence and care, accepting them *where they are on their terms*, even if their terms are not where he desires them to be.

As each icon is unique, so also each couple's relationship is unique, and each partner's personality and character as well. Every person is made in God's image, having the gift of freedom. Each person, however, is living in a fallen world and growing in His likeness. Living a married life means living a relational life, and sharing in God's creativity, and being in His love. Growing in God-likeness, through a life of prayer and witness is a continuous process of transformation toward divinization or *theosis*. So another way of icon living is

---

[12] Anton Vrame, *The Educating Icon: Teaching Wisdom and Holiness in the Orthodox Way*, (Brookline, MA: Holy Cross Orthodox Press, 1999), 63.

Part VII: Particular Themes and Issues for Orthodox Involvement in Ecumenism

inciting a successful "icon" of one joyful, faithful and committed married couple from the parish to befriend the mixed marriage couple. This living icon of a happy married couple committed to the parish may attract the mixed marriage couple to know more about the beauty and depth of the Orthodox faith and life. As looking at an icon may kindle and awaken the heart, so also a living icon of married couple may transform other couples, leading them to the love of the Church.

Finally, as an icon is written by prayer and the creativity/inspiration and perseverance of the icon writer, so is the work of the priest with the couple. This pastoral work demands a lot of creativity, personal attention, patience, and most especially continuous prayer. Asking for God's help, allowing Him to work through His grace and love, is essential so that He may write this marital icon of the spouses and hang it in the abode of His Kingdom. The sacramental act of unity given to the spouses in the liturgical service of matrimony is a potential, a divine seed sown in grace, and formed in lives of the spouses through this holistic, iconic model of education. I believe that this pastoral and educational model presented above, if well practiced in the Orthodox Church in Lebanon, can yield much fruits, transforming mixed marriages, and turning them from a problematic issue to a cause for invigorating parish life, and making the couple's home a little church.

Bibliography

Chrysostom, St. John. *On Marriage and Family Life*. (Crestwood, N. Y.: St. Vladimir's Seminary Press, 1986).

Constantelos, Demetrios. "Marriage in the Greek Orthodox Church." *Journal of Ecumenical Studies* 22.1 (Winter 1985): 21-27.

Evdokimov, Paul. *The Sacrament of Love: The Nuptial Mystery in the Light of the Orthodox Tradition*. (Crestwood, N. Y.: St. Vladimir's Seminary Press, 1985).

Joanides, Charles. *Ministering to Intermarried Couples: A Resource for Clergy and Lay Workers*. (Brookline, MA: Holy Cross Orthodox Press, 2003).

Kabba, Emil, ed. *Mixed Marriages: Theological Basis, Challenges, and Pastoral Horizons*. Conference Proceedings. (Beirut: Publications of La Sagesse University, 2012). [in Arabic].

Meyendorff, John. *Marriage: An Orthodox Perspective*. (Crestwood, N. Y.: St. Vladimir's Seminary Press, 1975).

National Conference of Catholic Bishops; Standing Conference of Oriental Orthodox Churches. *Oriental Orthodox - Roman Catholic inter church marriages: and other pastoral relationships*. (Washington, D.C.: United States Catholic Conference, 1995).

Papathomas, Archimandrite Grigorios. "Un communautarisme ecclésial ouvert: Mariages dispars-mixtes et conversions d'adultes." *Annals of St. John of Damascus Institute of Theology* 7 (Balamand, Lebanon: St. John of Damascus Institute of Theology, 2006): 71-90.

Prothro, Edwin Terry, and Lutfy Najib Diab. *Changing family patterns in the Arab East*. (Beirut : American University of Beirut, 1974).

Vrame, Anton C., editor. *Intermarriage: Orthodox Perspectives*. (Brookline, MA: Holy Cross Orthodox Press, 1997).

Pekka Metso

The concept of mixed marriage refers to marriage between an Orthodox Christian and a non-Orthodox Christian. The terms 'ecumenical marriage', 'inter-Christian marriage' and 'interchurch marriage' are also nowadays occasionally used alongside 'mixed marriage'. In an ecumenical context, as in this handbook, a marriage with a spouse coming from a non-Orthodox Christian tradition can properly be designated as a mixed marriage. Interfaith or interreligious marriages (between a Christian and a non-Christian) do not namely fall into the conventional ecumenical context of mixed marriages, but are rather part of Christian dialogue with world religions. Naturally, there are common pastoral issues involved in interchurch marriages and interfaith marriages. In this article the emphasis is profusely on mixed marriage, specifically as an ecumenical marriage, whereas the issue of interfaith marriage is dealt with briefly.

A mixed marriage is usually formed when an Orthodox marries a non-Orthodox Christian. Mixed marriages originate also from conversions to Orthodoxy. When a person joins the Orthodox Church but the rest of the family remains outside its canonical boundaries, a mixed marriage comes about at the same time. The family of the newly converted Orthodox may belong to another Christian church, another religion altogether, or they may be irreligious or atheist. Thus, the beginnings and manifestations of mixed marriages are manifold.

There are significant differences among the local Orthodox churches concerning the ways and attitudes toward issues and problems relating to mixed marriages. The question may seem proportionally irrelevant in predominantly Orthodox societies, such as Greece and Romania. Nonetheless, mixed marriage is nowadays a reality for many Orthodox from traditionally Orthodox countries. In Russia, for example, the annual number of mixed marriages with non-Russian citizens is around 60,000, approximately half of them with spouses from traditionally non-Orthodox regions and countries. This figure is suggestive of the reality in the Russian Orthodox Church, where mixed marriages pose a pastoral concern especially in predominantly Muslim areas due to an increasing number of interfaith marriages with Muslims. For the local churches operating in culturally and religiously heterogeneous contexts, such as North Europe, the United States and other non-traditional Orthodox territories, the question of mixed marriages is a notable everyday concern. For example, it is estimated that in the United States the portion of mixed marriages among the Orthodox is between 70 to 80%.[13] Due to different contexts, there are also considerable differences in the needs and capacity in dealing with pastoral urges relating to mixed marriages in Orthodox local churches. These examples show that, through mixed marriages, ecumenism is an everyday reality for several local Orthodox Churches and their faithful.[14]

Evidently, a sincere will to secure stability of marital and family life of Orthodox faithful living in interchurch marriages orientates the Orthodox Church to reconsider its ecumenical involvement and inquiry . Where there is a tendency to understand compassionately the unique pastoral needs caused by mixed marriages, there is more responsiveness to ecumenical involvement in general.

---

[13] Patsavos & Joanides (2000), 438.

[14] The author of this article is a member of the Finnish Orthodox Church, a small autonomous church with slightly more than 60,000 faithful. The percentage of the Orthodox population in Finland is only 1%, with the majority of the Finnish population (76 % in 2012) belonging to the Evangelical Lutheran Church. The next largest Christian group (with approximately the same number of faithful as the Orthodox) is the Pentecostals. A pronounced minority status makes meeting ecumenical realities compulsory to the Finnish Orthodox faithful in everyday life – especially since the percentage of mixed marriages among the Orthodox population is over 90%.

Canonical and historical attitudes towards mixed marriages:
The non-Orthodox as the modern heretics?

Mixed marriages are not a new phenomena brought about only recently with modern ecumenism or the Orthodox diaspora. From the very beginning, the Church has faced the situation where her members share marital
and family life with people outside the Church. Already St. Paul deals with the issue in his First Letter to the
Corinthians (7:12-16) when he instructs believers to continue their pre-existing marriages with non-believing
spouses. It was not uncommon for Christians in the early apostolic community to have non-Christian spouses,
especially since many entered the Church through adult conversion. As St. Paul's directions demonstrate, the
family of a convert did not automatically embrace Christianity. Moreover, St. Paul takes a positive stance
towards the spiritual arrangement of such (interfaith) marriages: the believer sanctifies his or her unbelieving
spouse through the former's faith.

As Christianity prospered and the Church took a strong root in Roman society, mixed marriages of any
sort were approached censoriously. Once the marriage between two faithful Orthodox Christians had become
the ecclesial and cultural standard, opinions on deviations from the norm became discouraging. In the ancient
canons of the Orthodox Church, the issue of mixed marriages was elaborated with a critical attitude: mixed
marriages were not regarded favourably.

There is a group of canons that explicitly address marriage with a non-Orthodox Christian or a non-Christian.
In these canons, the issue of mixed marriages is considered to epitomize the border between Orthodoxy and
heterodoxy. In canons 10 & 31 of the council of Laodicea (343), the Orthodox are therefore discouraged to
let their children marry heretics indifferently, unless they are willing to convert to Orthodoxy. The council of
Carthage (419) considers a marriage of children of the clergy with non-Orthodox altogether impossible (canon
21). In case an Orthodox has married someone outside of the Church, they are urged in the 14th canon of the
council of Chalcedon (451) to bring the entire family to Orthodoxy. The 72nd canon of the council of Trullo
(692) combines early Pauline policy with a later tendency to rebut mixed marriages entirely. While pre-existing
marriages before conversion to Christianity with non-Orthodox are tolerated, marriage with a non-Orthodox is
considered void and punishable.[15] Consequently, the council of Trullo takes an explicitly negative stance against
marrying a non-Orthodox. Over the Byzantine era, toleration of mixed marriages petered out. For example, in
the 14th century canonical commentary, Matthew Blastares considers it impossible for an Orthodox to co-habit
with a non-believing or unbaptized spouse – contrary to the earlier reading still witnessed by Trullo. [16]

Until our times these canons have regulated the official attitude of the Orthodox Church towards her members
marrying someone outside her canonical boundaries. For example, marriages with non-Orthodox were heavily
regulated in pre-revolutionary Russia; although from the 18th century onward, they were considered possible
on some occasions. In modern day Greece, civil law still bans marriages with non-Christians.

How then should we read the canons in our modern day ecumenical setting? Can present day Protestants,
Catholics and Pentecostals be identified with 4th or 7th century heretics? This cannot possibly be the case. The
current context calls for interpretations that avoid anachronistic and perverted readings of the canons. The
general mindset behind the canons, which is expressed through them, accentuates the uncontested value of
an intact and harmonious Christian life. The canons dealing with mixed marriages, as harsh as they may look
on the surface, aim to promote the eligible and beautiful concept of sharing one faith and flawless life in holy
matrimony. One and the same faith shared by the spouses is a self evident Christian value, deeply rooted in the
Orthodox view of sacramental nature of marriage. Common faith as a norm has been historically manifested
in the wedding service, which, until the 9th century, took place in the Eucharistic liturgy. Since the heterodox

---

[15] For exact phrasing of the mentioned canons see *The Rudder of the Orthodox Catholic Church. Compilation of the Holy
Canons by Saints Nicodemus and Agapius*, (Chicago: The Orthodox Christian Educational Society, 1983).

[16] Viscuso, Patrick Demetrios, *Sexuality, Marriage and Celibacy in Byzantine Law: Selections from a Foutheenth-Century
Encyclopedia of Canon Law and Theology: The Alphabetical Collection of Matthew Blastares*, (Brookline, MA: Holy
Cross Orthodox Press, 2008), 113-114.

did not share the Orthodox faith, they could not receive communion and be wed in the church. In the historical context of the canons, therefore, it was heresies and schisms which threatened the intact theory and practice of marriage and constituted marrying a non-Orthodox a canonical anomaly.

Even though major historical non-Orthodox Christian churches and confessions of the present day cannot be seen to originate from the ancient heresies, and should not therefore be labeled as such, marrying someone from those non-Orthodox ecclesial bodies still fails to achieve the ideal Orthodox understanding of marriage as life in unity of faith. Although in the current practice the wedding service takes place outside the Eucharistic context, mixed marriage fails to establish full sacramental communion between the spouses. A non-Orthodox spouse cannot receive Holy Communion in the Orthodox Church and have admittance to other mysteries, e.g. confession and ointment of the sick. Nor is he or she permitted to receive an Orthodox funeral. Consequently, mixed marriage falls short of the ideal Orthodox understanding of marriage. In our present ecumenical state, it is important to acknowledge that unwillingness to encourage mixed marriages does not imply that non-Orthodox Christians are considered to be heretics – albeit such opinions are not uncommon among the Orthodox. Rather, reluctance is based more on the theological and canonical understanding of marriage as a common life of the spouses shared in the Church in all its fullness. Since marital unity in the one Orthodox faith simply cannot be manifested through mixed marriage, it leads to cautious and sometimes negative attitudes towards it. Where mixed marriage is more or less the norm, the Orthodox Church assimilated more permissive attitudes.

Even though the Church prefers that Orthodox Christians marry from inside the Church, it does not insist on it in practice. For the spiritual welfare of the faithful, the Church will conduct marriage with non-Orthodox Christians coming from a Trinitarian Christian tradition, i.e. with faith and baptism in the name of the Holy Trinity. However, mixed marriages with non-Trinitarian Christians, with Unitarian beliefs, and persons from other religions (Islam, Judaism, Buddhism), or sectarian groups (Scientology, Mormonism) are not possible. Such categorization proves that the paradigm of heresy, inherited from the canons, yet prevails: the Orthodox Church blesses marriage with Christians coming, for example, from Catholic and Protestant traditions, but does not approve interfaith marriage. Consequently, an Orthodox willing to marry a non-Christian cannot have an Orthodox priest conduct the wedding. In the case of interfaith marriage, the Orthodox Christian partner also loses his or her sacramental privileges, thus ending up outside of the Eucharistic communion.[17]

Possibilities and boundaries of the mixed marriage wedding service in the Orthodox Church

In local Orthodox churches, quite consistent principals have been acquired for coping with conducting a wedding of interchurch couples. Basic guidelines can be captured as follows:
- The wedding needs to take place in an Orthodox Church and must be performed by an Orthodox priest
- The non-Orthodox partner must have been baptized in water in the name of Holy Trinity, and in a Christian church.
- The couple agrees to baptize and raise their children in the Orthodox church

A mixed marriage is thus conducted in a similar manner as a normative Orthodox wedding; there is no difference in the service whether both spouses are Orthodox or just one of them. An interchurch wedding service should also take place in an Orthodox church, conducted by an Orthodox priest. Since active participation of non-Orthodox clergy in conducting the wedding service is not allowed, co-celebration of the wedding service between Orthodox and non-Orthodox clergy is not possible.[18] Nevertheless, depending on an approval of the local Orthodox bishop (whose opinion usually reflects the local ecumenical attitude of the Orthodox church),

---

[17] Harakas, Stanley, *Contemporary Moral Issues Facing the Orthodox Christian,* revised and expanded edition, (Minneapolis: Light and Life Publishing, 1982), 105-106.

[18] The general approach of the Orthodox Church towards mixed marriages and celebration of wedding service is exemplified in the guidelines given by the Orthodox Church of America (OCA). See *Guidelines for Clergy. Compiled under the Guidance of the Holy Synod of the Orthodox Church of America,* (New York 1998), 14-15.

celebration of a separate non-Orthodox blessing or prayer may yet be performed before or at the conclusion of the Orthodox ceremony.

In reality, the life of the Orthodox faithful is not always adjustable to the above standards. Orthodox Christians do get married to non-Orthodox Christians in non-Orthodox churches, and their children are not necessary baptized in the Orthodox Church and nurtured in the Orthodox faith. Actually, the recommendation to baptize children as Orthodox sets forth the ideal of unity in faith as an aim for the marital life in a mixed marriage as well. As desirable as the norm is for interchurch marriage set by the Church, in many cases reality is far from it.

What if an Orthodox Christian is wed in some other Christian church? Even if the Orthodox spouse wishes, an Orthodox priest cannot participate in a non-Orthodox ritual. He may of course attend the wedding service, but only as a guest. The Orthodox Church does not allow combining parts of Orthodox services with non-Orthodox rites – even in the case where an Orthodox member is being married in another church. According to the prevailing practice, an Orthodox priest may not even offer a prayer on behalf of the couple in a non-Orthodox church.

What room, then, do the given boundaries leave for recognition of a mixed marriage which is conducted in a non-Orthodox church? This is a matter of utmost importance, because if the marriage is not solemnized by the Orthodox Church, the Orthodox partner is not any more in good standing with the Church. So the question is what constitutes sufficient ecclesial claim? The answer very much depends on demography. Where Orthodoxy is the main form of Christianity, the Orthodox Church might not discuss recognition of the marriage, but instead insist that the couple should have an Orthodox wedding service. Accordingly, if an Orthodox Christian is married outside the Orthodox Church and wishes to attain good relations with the church, a wedding service is celebrated. Through performance of the Sacrament of Marriage he or she once again becomes canonically and spiritually in good standing with the Orthodox Church.

However, in areas where Orthodoxy is not the prevailing faith, the Orthodox Church has occasionally adopted other ways of dealing with the issue. For example, in the guidelines of the Orthodox Church of America, the restoration of Eucharistic fellowship requires confirmation of the marriage through a rite approved by the hierarch. Not only in America but also elsewhere, a *moleben*, i.e. a prayer service, has been perceived as sufficient rite on some occasions when an Orthodox Christian asks for Orthodox recognition of a marriage conducted in a non-Orthodox church. The *moleben* is distinct from the sacrament of marriage and without sacramental validity, and it does not include any of the central elements of the wedding service, such as the wedding crowns and the common cup. When giving a blessing to a mixed marriage through this prayer service, the Orthodox Church recognizes the lawful status of such marriage, restores the Orthodox partner to good standing with the Church, and gifts the couple with prayerful consolation. However, blessing a mixed marriage in this way may seem compromising and dubious to Orthodox Christians not familiar with the challenges caused by being in a minority position.

The Orthodox Church also accepts – though with hesitation – a double performance of the wedding service. The wedding service is then celebrated in both the Orthodox church and the non-Orthodox church. Even if it is not ecumenically the most satisfactory solution, it enables full celebration wedding services according to the respective traditions of the spouses. Having two separate wedding services also meets the Orthodox requirement of appropriate ecclesial solemnization of marriage.

Pastoral concerns relating to mixed marriages

Occasionally mixed marriages are seen as a threat to Orthodoxy which explains some shortcomings in Orthodox prosperity especially in heterogeneous contexts where the Orthodox Church is in a minority position. Such a fear seems to be wrongly directed. Is it really the non-Orthodox spouses that risk Orthodox identity? Or rather, is it the Orthodox themselves – whether in mixed marriages or not – who expose their faith to real danger by being negligent and becoming worldly? It must be noted, that depending on the context, mixed marriages can and should raise a concern in the Orthodox Church with regard to the reality in which many of the faithful carry out their daily lives in the frame of a mixed marriage. Reflection on this particular ecumenical reality that a number of Orthodox believers experience, should pierce all strategic church activities and teaching. Supporting the religious upbringing of Orthodox children in mixed marriages should be of special concern, as through them issues relating to mixed marriages extend to the next generation, since these children are more likely to have mixed marriages themselves.

Why do the Orthodox faithful marry non-Orthodox Christians in the first place? There are various factors that explain the growing number of mixed marriages, especially in multicultural and multi-religious contexts. To begin with, the fewer the possible partners in the Orthodox faith group, the more likely the spouse is sought outside. Even though the Church can offer opportunities for single individuals to meet and mix with other Orthodox, in diverse societies the youth simply have more social contacts outside their own faith and are more likely to date persons of a different Christian tradition or religion. Nowadays young people from different faith backgrounds have increasing social contacts, and thus social barriers between them are being broken down. Another reason that explains mixed marriages is connected to the commitment to faith experienced at home which has a great impact on young peoples' identity. If faith loses its significance among Orthodox youth, the importance of their own and their partner's church affiliation declines. Lastly, when tolerance to religious diversity is promoted, Orthodox are also more willing to consider a mixed marriage. Entering a mixed marriage does not, however, automatically equal diminishing the Orthodox tradition. Thus, the Orthodox partners in mixed marriages should not be reproached for disregarding the Orthodox Tradition simply due to the fact that they married a non-Orthodox Christian.

In the last resort, canonical definitions and rules of conducting a wedding service, as important as they are, manage to resonate only with the outer limits of marriage. As any marriage, a mixed marriage also demonstrates the fullness of human life and experiences, regardless of canonical, spiritual and sacramental flaws the Orthodox ecclesial interpretation finds in "the case of mixed marriage." However, no one should be perceived as just a case or arrangement defined by canonical legislation. No matter how troublesome the Orthodox Church finds mixed marriages, indifference and hostile stiffness should not mark her pastoral approach. Instead, compassion and sensitivity are required in meeting the particular problems and needs of the faithful living in mixed marriages.

Mixed marriage as a family challenge

Proper pastoral support cannot be offered unless the Church sympathizes with those living in inter-Christian marriages. The Orthodox Church is expected to promote a pastoral understanding of mixed marriages. The question then arises: do Orthodox clergy really understand the reality of mixed marriages? For example, in the case of a married priest, his wife and children who are all Orthodox, their life is (in principle at least) spiritually intact and thoroughly Orthodox. It may, therefore, be challenging for them to identify with someone living in a different family setting.

Depending on the attitude of the partners of mixed marriage, differences in their ecclesial traditions may lead to diverse outcomes. The encounter of two Christian traditions within the marriage certainly can be a source of tensions. That said, some couples experience it as a positive and enriching element for the family. Against all the odds set by canonical and theological reluctance, a mixed marriage can be spiritually fruitful for both partners alike. The effect on the couple themselves of the different faith convictions depends on how they treat their own religious convictions and the kind of beliefs they have concerning faith groups other than their own. As a consequence, the impact of religious differences on mixed marriages may lead to various outcomes. Statistically speaking, the religious factor is a destabilizing one. Problems arise when either one or both of the spouses find the interchurch setting troubling, and when there is no room to compromise on their beliefs. Awareness of the Orthodox ideal of the unity of faith can already be stressful if the Orthodox spouse feels he or she is not meeting the normative requirements set by the church. However, in principle there is nothing that prevents a successful mixed marriage from having a positive influence on the local community and the Orthodox parish. In addition to the quality of relationship that the couple communicates, the influence that the mixed marriage has on the community also depends on the attitude of the community itself towards other Christian traditions and faith communities in general.

The respective families of the partners may also add tension with their attitudes and expectations. Both families may find it hard to accept that foreign religious and cultural elements enter their sphere of life through marriage. In a 'homogenous' Orthodox setting, it is normally the non-Orthodox partner who faces prejudices, whereas for the Orthodox in a minority situation, it is the Orthodox partner's tradition which is the unfamiliar element. The Orthodox aspiration to have the children baptized in the Orthodox Church alone easily causes regret in the non-Orthodox partner's side, especially if he or she is from a practicing Christian family. Tensions arising from personal and family traditions and expectations primarily require support and understanding by the Orthodox Church.

If the Orthodox partner chooses the children to be baptized in the non-Orthodox partner's church, the Orthodox Church interprets the decision as a sign which calls into question the desire to live according to the Orthodox lifestyle. Is this really the only motive behind such a decision? It is true that some Orthodox Christians are indifferent towards Orthodoxy or embarrassed of it? Oftentimes the Orthodox partner, sadly enough, is not at all aware of the canonical consequences of their decisions on family issues, like baptism of children. In those cases an embryonic Orthodox identity often explains the decision. When the canonical unawareness of a spiritually immature Orthodox is revealed, should he or she be turned away from the Church? What if the non-Orthodox spouse simply refuses Orthodox baptism of the children? In these cases, especially if the person has maintained a close relation to the Church, tender pastoral approach is needed instead of rigid punishment. Of course, all proposed settlements should aim to re-establish good standing with the Orthodox Church and the favourable continuation of marriage and family life.

Peaceful religious life within family as a pastoral goal

When an Orthodox believer has entered a mixed marriage and is in need of consolation, there is not much help if the Church just voices her verdict instead of offering sincere pastoral guidance. What, then, should be the main guiding principle for mixed marriages in pastoral care? The answer is simple: fostering the good relationship of the spouses. This does not mean that the Orthodox ideal needs to be compromised; quite the contrary. Suitable solutions for peaceful life in a mixed marriage usually contribute, in time, to faithful Orthodox witness. What the Orthodox Christians in mixed marriages need from their Church is protection from unnecessary and damaging religious harm. This means that the Orthodox Church should approve the couple, both the Orthodox and the non-Orthodox partner alike. They are welcome to partake in the life of the Orthodox Church as they are (sacramental restrictions for non-Orthodox maintained), without any pressure to become someone else. A warm response will make a positive impact in the couple's support and involvement in the life of the Orthodox Church. In other words, a conversion mentality should not be encouraged in any way. An Orthodox husband does not need to be a missionary to his wife, nor should an Orthodox wife see her husband's family as objects of proselytism. A conversion attitude does not only make a mockery of ecumenical tolerance, but also falsifies and disrespects the foundations of marriage. In the course of life, harmonious family life occasionally can lead to the non-Orthodox spouse embracing Orthodoxy. Naturally, if the Orthodox Church greets such conversions with joy, she cannot expect and accept them to happen by force. Even as a desired outcome, a sole possibility of future conversion simply does not qualify as an adequate reason to accept mixed marriages.

The Orthodox Church has to some extent, mainly locally, dealt with the issue of mixed marriages wherever necessary. As a result, pastoral guidelines have been expressed in various fora for the support of Orthodox Christians entering into and living in mixed marriages. Preliminary pan-Orthodox input was given some decades ago as part of the preparation of the Great and Holy Synod. The Greek Orthodox Church has recently made bilateral agreements with Oriental Orthodox churches in Antioch and Alexandria on conducting mixed marriages. These agreements give evidence of an increasing ecumenical understanding between the Eastern Orthodox and Oriental Orthodox traditions. In America, the pastoral needs of believers in mixed marriages have been a major concern in the dialogue between the North-American Eastern Orthodox and Catholic Churches. The two churches voiced an essential principle in their agreed statement already in 1971: "Each partner should be reminded of the obligation to respect the religious convictions and practice of the other and mutually to support and encourage the other in growing into the fullness of the Christian life."[19] The Greek Orthodox Archdiocese of America has managed to establish an interfaith marriage website to serve and guide Orthodox faithful in intermarriages.[20] In Finland, the 1992 bilateral national-level Lutheran-Orthodox dialogue gave practical pastoral suggestions to support life in intermarriage. The suggestions deserve to be presented for international Orthodox reflection here. The two churches gave three recommendations:

1. Prior to the wedding service (conducted either in the Lutheran or Orthodox church) there should be a pastoral discussion on the nature of Christian marriage and special issues relating to baptism of children and their religious education in the context of the mixed marriage.

2. Local parishes of the two churches should support prayer life of both traditions at home and participation of the entire family in the services in both churches.

3. All the children of the family should be baptized as members of the same church. In addition, early childhood religious education should be according to that one tradition. Later on the ecclesial tradition of the other parent should be introduced.[21]

Despite the apparent conciliatory ecumenical spirit of the guidelines, the Orthodox reading still prefers mixed marriages to be conducted and the children baptized in the Finnish Orthodox Church. Nevertheless, the sight of the churches in dialogue is set on a peaceful co-existence of the respective traditions of both spouses. The compassionate suggestions clearly aim to stabilize the religious setting of family life in mixed marriages. As simple as these suggestions may seem, they nevertheless exceptionally reach out to the partners, balancing on two church traditions. The American Orthodox-Catholic dialogue has also highlighted the duty of the respective churches in supporting the family in finding "as much unity as possible in the faith and morals of the family."[22] Too often the instructions on mixed marriages by Orthodox Churches settle with the minimum; the pastoral demands of mixed marriages are not met by simply spelling out the requirements for the appropriate conducting of the wedding service.

The issue of mixed marriages makes Christian division a personal and a family matter. Circumstances relating to mixed marriages vividly illustrate that the dividing lines between Christian churches and confessions cannot be considered to sweep somewhere in the external sphere of ecclesial bodies. Quite the contrary, divisional boundaries intersect personal life of many Orthodox Christians in a most significant manner. Mixed marriages verify that ecumenism cannot be considered by Orthodox Church as a foreign affair; it is a home affair.

---

[19] *Agreed Statement on Mixed Marriage. U.S. Theological Consultation, 1971.* In *The Quest for Unity. Orthodox and Catholics in Dialogue*, eds. John Borelli & John H. Ericson, (Crestwood, NY: SVS Press, 1996), 198-199.

[20] Greek Orthodox Archdiocese of America, Department of Interfaith Marriage website: http://www.goarch.org/archdiocese/departments/marriage/interfaith/

[21] "The Finnish Orthodox-Lutheran Dialogue. Communiqué Valamo 1990" in *The Finnish Lutheran - Orthodox Dialogue. Conversations in 1989 and 1990.* Documents of the Evangelical Lutheran Church of Finland, No 4. 1993, 62.

[22] "Agreed Statement on Orthodox-Roman Catholic Marriages. Metropolitan New York/New Jersey Orthodox-Roman Catholic Dialogue, 1986" in *The Quest for Unity. Orthodox and Catholics in Dialogue*, eds. John Borelli & John H. Ericson, (Crestwood, NY: SVS Press, 1996), 219.

Bibliography

The Finnish Lutheran - Orthodox Dialogue. Conversations in 1989 and 1990. Documents of the Evangelical Lutheran Church of Finland, No 4. Helsinki, 1993.

Gratsias, Emmanuel, "Effect of Mixed Marriage on the Parish" in *Greek Orthodox Theological Review* 40.3-4 (1995): 365-370.

Intermarriage. Orthodox Perspectives, ed. Anton Vrame, (Brookline, MA: Holy Cross Orthodox Press, 1997).

Joanides, Charles, *When You Intermarry. A Resource for Inter-Christian, Intercultural Couples, Parents and Families*, (Greek Orthodox Archdiocese of America, 2002).

_____. *Ministering to Intermarried Couples. A Resource for Clergy and Lay Workers*, (Greek Orthodox Archdiocese of America, 2003).

Patsavos, Lewis, "Canonical Response to Intra-Christian Marriage" in *Greek Orthodox Theological Review* 40.3-4 (1995): 287-298.

Patsavos, Lewis & Joanides, Charles, "Interchurch Marriages. An Orthodox Perspective" in *Greek Orthodox Theological Review* 45.4 (2000): 433-442.

The Quest For Unity. Orthodox and Catholics in Dialogue, eds. John Borelli & John H. Erickson, (Crestwood, NY: SVS Press, 1996), 191-250.

Tsetsis, George, "The Pastoral Dimension of Mixed Marriages" in Ἐκκλησία-Οἰκουμένη-Πολιτική, *(Athens 2007)*, 599-611.

(120) Orthodox Perspectives on Ecumenical Hermeneutics[1]

Metropolitan Gennadios Limouris

Ecumenical history calls for a reflection on hermeneutics

Churches and Christians are in the midst of a decade-long crisis - a stagnation in the ecumenical movement and in the search for the unity of the church. Some churches, "traditional" or not, make strong complaints about the ecumenical movement. Others have abandoned their original commitment. Some cite new issues related to worldwide political, economic, socio-political and ethnic problems. Some, such as the Orthodox churches of Bulgaria and Georgia, have withdrawn their membership of the World Council of Churches. Amid all this is the recognition that at the eve of the third millennium Christendom - the church of Christ, his church, which we all proclaim and confess as the one, holy, catholic and apostolic church - is still divided.

This is a reality and a fact. It is true that many efforts have been undertaken during past decades on the part of the churches, through their multilateral and bilateral theological conversations and official dialogues, as well as on the part of the WCC, and the Faith and Order commission in particular. But the situation still remains unchanged. Is the quest for Christian unity still among the churches' priorities?

During the 1980s, and even before, there were many hopes that the convergence document on *Baptism, Eucharist and Ministry* would attract the churches to a closer rapprochement and to the study of divisive issues which could be identified with the help of that document. There was a hope, a deep desire that something very significant and important might happen within the churches at the close of the 20th century. Others looked towards the recent eighth assembly, marking fifty years of the WCC's existence. Unfortunately, because of the *kairos* of human hostilities, these hopes as well as many others, emerging in theological multilateral conversations, have collapsed. Churches adhere still very strongly and solidly to their respective ecclesiological, confessional and denominational positions and presuppositions.

Nearly forty years ago, at the New Delhi assembly of 1961, the Orthodox[2] delegates suggested that the ecumenical endeavor could be characterized as *ecumenism in space,* aiming at agreement between various denominations, as they exist at present. They affirmed that the common ground, or rather the common background, of existing denominations, can and must be found in their common past history, in that common, ancient and apostolic tradition from which they all derive their existence.

This kind of ecumenical endeavor can properly be called an *ecumenism in time.* The Faith and Order report to the New Delhi assembly speaks of agreement (in faith) with all ages, as one of the normative prerequisites of unity. The Orthodox in that report suggested a new method - which is still true for today - of ecumenical inquiry, and this new criterion on ecumenical evaluation, as a kingly rock, with the hope that unity may be recovered by the divided denominations by their return to their common past. In this way divergent denominations may meet each other on the unity of common tradition. No static restoration of old forms is anticipated, but rather a dynamic recovery of *perennial ethos,* which only can secure the true agreement of all ages. Nor should there be a rigid uniformity, since the same faith, mysterious in its essence and unfathomable adequately in the formulas of human reason, can be expressed accurately in different manners. The immediate objective of the ecumenical search, according to the traditional understanding, a reintegration of Christian mind, a recovery of apostolic tradition, a fullness of Christian vision and belief, in agreement with all ages.

---

[1] This article of Metropolitan Gennadios which republished here with the necessary title and content adjustments was first appeared in P. Bouteneff-D. Heller (eds.) *Interpreting together. Essays in Hermeneutics* (Geneva: WCC Publications, 2001), under the title "Hermeneutics: An instrument for an Ecumenical Reflection on the search for Church Unity."

[2] Cf. third assembly of the World Council of Churches, New Delhi, India, 1961, in Gennadios Limouris, (ed.), *Orthodox Visions of Ecumenism,* (GenevaŞ WCC, 1994), 30-31.

The fifth world conference on Faith and Order at Santiago de Compostela, Spain, in 1993 initiated and encouraged Faith and Order to undertake a study on "Hermeneutics in Ecumenical Perspective." This new ecumenical venture created new difficulties for the churches and for theologians, at least those considered traditional, because the notion and the understanding of hermeneutics (*hermeneutiki* or *hermeneutica*) itself needs to be explored. The proposed studies for an ecumenical hermeneutics raised more important doctrinal issues, because the various church traditions have a different understanding, interpretation and ecclesial experience on hermeneutics on the one hand, and the expectations engendered by such studies on the other.

In Orthodox understanding, hermeneutics is considered to be the whole life of the church. There is not one hermeneutic for scripture and another for the patristic teachings, or another for the understanding of the church and holy sacraments. The "hermeneutics" of the Orthodox understanding is a holistic approach realizing the oneness of doctrine and dogma. On the other hand, if by interpretation we would try precisely to identify hermeneutics in this context we would be involved in an overly scholastic approach inappropriate to Orthodox theology.

Has the ecumenical reality expressed forty years ago in New Delhi changed? I do not think so, at any rate not completely. In the reports mentioned, what stands out is that the search for Christian unity identifies a *perennial ethos*, demanding the return of the churches to their common roots of the apostolic tradition which constitute our common background.

The French philosopher Ramonet describes today's world situation in terms of a certain *chaos*[3] but he identifies *good* and *bad* chaos. Confronted by bad chaos, humankind can avoid isolation only through all possible efforts, supported by strong existential ideological and metaphysical presuppositions.

The dawn of a new century heralds the dawn of a new period for humanity, with hopes and expectations for the whole world. Likewise, the new period from Harare and beyond demands new efforts from all of us - church leaders and all those people committed to the sacred goal of the search for Christian unity. It demands new efforts on the part of Faith and Order, for its programmes are instruments for moving together in the pilgrimage towards a full communion/koinonia of humankind and the church of Christ.

First of all, existing programmes must continue in order to be finalized and to reach their convergence stage in the near future. But *how* must they continue? It is our duty to give them much-needed fresh blood, to offer new theological visions and new programmatic directions, not so much to satisfy our ecclesial and denominational traditions but rather in order to find ways of bringing the good news to people in their contemporary context and reality.

We need to rediscover Christ, to discover whether He as the Lord and Saviour is in the midst of us, somewhere where each of us can call upon him for very personal and human needs. Today, a christological crisis exists, a crisis of faith. Jesus Christ is neglected, his salvation is questioned and, even more, his existence as a divine-human person is questioned. A renewal of faith is demanded a faith to be reaffirmed, which emerges from the ecclesial tradition, rooted in apostolic times and teachings. Our spiritual commitment should be enriched by our *metanoia,* a repentance for our divisions. Churches and Christians cannot continue to be divided; at the very least they should be able to share the common treasures and richness of our common roots of the ancient undivided church.

We must not continue to confess the divided body of Christ and to drink his blood which is the life of the church. Isolation and stagnation are bringing a kind of schizophrenia to human minds, and people are becoming eternal "earthen vessels" of a new paranoiac world which continues on another road - not the one leading to Emmaus and the kingdom of God, but to death. Ecumenical history teaches us that we must learn to distinguish between the unity which exists and the fuller unity which should characterize the church of Christ and which it is our task to realize. There is the unity which holds us together right now and obliges us to go forward together. And there is the unity which is promised to us and which will be given to us in God's time if we respond obediently to do his will, to do his work of gathering. There is unity on the road and there is unity

---

[3] Cf. Ignacio Ramonet, *Le chaos et le monde*, (Paris, 1999), 45.

as the goal. The full unity of the church is something which still requires work, action and prayer. But there exists a unity in allegiance to our Lord for the manifestation of which we are all responsible. To paraphrase Archbishop William Temple, we should act upon it insofar as it is already a reality.[4]

Does a real unity exist already? The churches would not have declared that they "intend to stay together" if their common faith in Jesus Christ as God and Saviour, the bond of their common calling, was not real. The Amsterdam message to the churches and to the world describes that unity in these words: "... we are divided from one another, but Christ has made us his own and he is not divided." In a resolution concerning the nature of the World Council of Churches, also adopted by the first assembly, it was said of the churches: "They find their unity in him. They have not to create their unity; it is the gift of God."

Spirit and church: a hermeneutical Pentecostal image

The *unity of the church* is the *necessary* corollary to its calling. The church is the community of those who are called (1 Cor. 1:23). Thus, in the New Testament, calling does not refer only to individual callings, or vocations, but to the common calling in Christ (Rom. 8:30, 2 Tim. 1:9). And it is this common calling which binds Christians in an indestructible fellowship. They are united because they "share in a heavenly call" (Heb. 3:1), and there is one body because it can be said of them: "You were called to the one hope that belongs to your call" (Eph. 4:4). This calling could be considered as a biblical and ecclesiological hermeneutic. And it is not simply a privilege to be enjoyed; it demands a constantly renewed response (cf. 2 Pet. 1:10) in order to have a wider affirmation and implementation.

In the New Testament, from a hermeneutical perspective, unity is never static. Unity is always the result of the gathering and the search for the truth and love of our common roots in the Lord of the church. But in thinking of the church christologically, as the body of Christ, it is necessary to keep in mind the "image" of the church as the kingdom of the Holy Spirit. St Irenaeus spoke of the Son and the Spirit as the "two hands of God" which always work together. If the church is eucharistic, it is at the same time Pentecostal: it is an extension of the incarnation and of Pentecost.

In this gift of the Spirit at Pentecost, there are three elements of special importance. First, the Spirit is not conferred solely upon a particular hierarchical order. It is a gift to the whole people of God: "they were all filled with the Holy Spirit." It is helpful to recall the distinction, emphasized by the Russian Orthodox theologian Vladimir Lossky, between the two givings of the Spirit. The first occurs on Easter day, when Jesus - risen but not yet ascended - breathes upon the disciples and says to them: "Receive the Holy Spirit. Whatsoever sins you remit, they are remitted; and whatsoever sins you retain, they are retained" (John 20:22-23). At this moment the apostles represent the hierarchy of the church: the gift of the Spirit is specifically linked with the authority to bind and loosen, and this particular power is not conferred upon the whole body of Christ but is transmitted through the apostolic college to the later form of the episcopate.

In the second giving *of* the Spirit, recorded in Acts 2 and following, the apostles no longer represent the hierarchy, but rather they constitute the entire body of the church as it then existed. The Spirit descends at Pentecost upon each and every member of the redeemed community, and this universality of the Pentecostal gift continues in the church throughout all ages. We are all baptized in the Holy Spirit and are spirit bearers: "You have been anointed by the Holy One and you all know" (1 John 2:20). Just as the Eucharist is an action performed by all alike, so the Spirit is a gift to all alike.

Secondly, the gift of the Spirit at Pentecost is a gift of unity: in the words of Acts 2:1, "they were all with one accord in one place." It is the special task of the Spirit to draw humankind together. This aspect of the Spirit's work is vividly emphasized in Greek hymnography, when it contrasts God's descent at Pentecost with his descent at the building of the tower of Babel (Gen. 11:7). The God of old came down in order to divide humanity, but at Pentecost he came down in order to unite it. The festal hymn of Pentecost says the same:

---

[4] Cf. his *The World Council of Churches: Its Process of Formation*, (London, 1946), 172-73.

Part VII: Particular Themes and Issues for Orthodox Involvement in Ecumenism

"When the Most High descended and confused the tongues, He divided the nations; but when He distributed the tongues of the fire, He called all to unity."

Yet the gift of the Spirit not only calls humankind to unity but it is also, and thirdly, a gift of differentiation. The tongues of fire are "divided" so that they rest upon each one personally. The Holy Spirit is a Spirit of freedom, and He bestows upon humankind an infinite diversity.

Unity and differentiation: such are the two aspects - contrasted but not opposed - of the gift of the Spirit to the church. The church is a mystery of unity in diversity and of diversity in unity. In the church a multitude of persons are united in one, and yet each of them preserves his *personal* integrity unimpaired. In our association on the purely human level there will always exist a tension between individual liberty and the demands of corporate solidarity. Only within the church, and through the gift of the Spirit, is the conflict between these two resolved. In the kingdom of the Holy Spirit there is neither totalitarianism nor individualism, neither dictatorship nor anarchy, but harmony and unanimity. Russian Orthodox thinkers since Khomiakov have used the word *sobornost,* "catholicity" to express this notion of unanimity in freedom.

The Pentecostal "image" or "icon" of the church and, together with it, our eucharistic "icon" form a salutary corrective to the first and inexact image, the image of earthly power and jurisdiction. "It shall not be so among you" because the church is not a kingdom of this world, but of the kingdom of the Holy Spirit, and therefore its rules and principles are not those of human government.

There is no way for churches which are neither fully united nor completely separated to arrive at real, concrete, manifest unity except the way of common obedience to the common calling. The ecumenical task is to go forward together in making a common response to the one christological calling. To act on unity, without using symbols or images, is to work towards the growth of this calling, which does not imply that any pressure is brought upon the churches other than the pressure which is inherent in their common calling and to which every church must make its own free response in accordance with the Tradition and the teaching of the undivided church.

The already existing "unity" which is expressed in various forms between churches yet divided, gives an opportunity to the World Council of Churches to be a unique ecumenical channel for the common witness and action of the churches in those matters in which they have to come to a common mind. In the words of Lesslie Newbigin, "we are in a transitory phase of the journey from disunity to unity."[5]

---

[5] *The Household of God,* (London, 1953), 21.

Georgios Vlantis

During the last 5 decades "reception" has been gradually established as *terminus technicus* in ecumenical theology, signifying processes of appropriation and integration of results of the bi- or multilateral ecumenical dialogue in the various levels of the churches' life (doctrinal, liturgical, juridical, pastoral, etc.).[1]

Vatican Council II (1962–1965) gave decisive impulses for modern, ecumenically oriented Roman–Catholic approaches to a theology of reception.[2] Many churches and ecumenical institutions have initiated more or less successful processes of adoption of numerous inter–confessional agreed statements; there are also documents which have not been positively received by the people of God or they evoked no significant echo within the churches. Inspired by both positive and negative experiences, a considerable literature on ecumenical reception has emerged.[3] In this short essay I will focus upon some aspects of a theology of reception from an Orthodox point of view; I will also comment on the experience of the Orthodox world concerning this crucial issue, and describe some of the challenges that have to be faced.

I. Towards a theology of reception

Ecumenical reception constitutes to a certain extent a novelty in the history of Christianity, because it is taking place in a context of separation, of deficient communion among churches, which during the previous centuries gradually alienated from each other, going their own way in history and developing their own theologies, creeds, structures, etc.[4] Therefore the texts of the ecumenical dialogues are not only bi- or multilateral manifestations of faith, but also instruments for the restoration of ecclesial unity.

---

[1] For the various meanings of reception see e.g. Günther Gaßmann, "Rezeption, Kirchliche. I. Kirchengeschichtlich," *Theologische Realenzyklopädie [TRE]* 29 (1998): 131–142; Hermann Fischer, "Rezeption, Kirchliche. II. Systematisch–Theologisch," *ibid.,* 143–149); William G. Rusch, *Ecumenical Reception. Its Challenge and Opportunity*, (Grand Rapids, MI: Eerdmans, 2007); Viorel Ionita, "Die Rezeption ökumenischer Entscheidungen. Beispiele aus verschiedenen kirchlichen Traditionen": Anna Briskina–Müller / Armenuhi Drost–Abgarian / Axel Meisner (ed.), *Logos im Dialogos. Auf der Suche nach der Orthodoxie. Gedenkschrift für Hermann Goltz (1946–2010)*, [Forum Orthodoxe Theologie 11], (Berlin: LIT, 2011), 375–386.

[2] Yves Congar's article "La 'réception' comme réalité ecclésiologique" (*Revue des sciences philosophiques et théologiques* 56 (1972): 369–403) is one of the most valuable Roman–Catholic contribution. Cf. Johannes Willebrands, "The Ecumenical Dialogue and its Reception," *One in Christ* 21 (1985): 217–225; Wolfgang Beinert (ed.), *Glaube als Zustimmung. Zur Interpretation kirchlicher Rezeptionsvorgänge*, [Quaestiones disputatae 131], (Basel: Herder, 1991); Wolfgang Beinert, "Die Rezeption und ihre Bedeutung für Leben und Lehre der Kirche": Wolfhart Pannenberg / Theodor Schneider (ed.), *Verbindliches Zeugnis*, II [Dialog der Kirchen 9], (Göttingen: Vanderhoeck & Rupprecht, 1995), 193–218.

[3] A great amount of publications on reception appeared in relation to the WCC convergence text of Lima (1982) on Baptism, Eucharist and Ministry (BEM). BEM set indeed the most important landmark in the theological elaboration on this topic. On the basis of this document the WCC initiated the broadest reception process in the history of the ecumenical movement. See the special issue of the journal *Una Sancta* 67 (2012): 3, „Taufe, Eucharistie und Amt–30 Jahre Lima-Dokument." Cf. Nikos Nissiotis, "The Meaning of Reception in Relation to the Results of Ecumenical Dialogue on the Basis of the Faith and Order Document 'Baptism, Eucharist and Ministry'": Gennadios Limouris / Nomikos Michael Vaporis (eds.), *Orthodox Perspectives on Baptism, Eucharist and Ministry*, [Faith and Order Papers Nr. 128], *The Greek Orthodox Theological Review* 30 (1985): 47–74.

[4] There are certain parallels between ecumenical reception and the reception of a council in the early Church. One of the crucial differences is the ecclesial unity presupposed in the second case. See Ulrich Kühn, "Reception – An Imperative

i. The biblical background

Reception comes from the latin verb *recipere*, whose equivalents in Greek are the verbs λαμβάνειν and δέχεσθαι; terms such as ἀπολαμβάνειν, παραλαμβάνειν, παραδιδόναι, ἀποδέχεσθαι, δοχή, ἀποδοχή, etc. are related to them, too.[5] Being itself a product of a long reception process (the construction of the biblical Canon), the Bible refers to a great variety of reception processes. The creation itself receives its being from God. The whole history of Israel is focused on the way this people receives God's word and the covenant. Jesus Christ calls the people to receive him, his word and his eschatological kingdom (e.g. John 1:11ff; Mark 4:20; 10:15). The *Acts of the Apostles* and the Pauline texts present the birth of Christian communities as acts of reception of the message of the new covenant.[6] What is being received is finally the person of the Lord (Col. 2:6). Paul describes his preaching as both result of and initiation for reception and also "speaks of the Eucharist as something received and transmitted"[7] (1 Cor. 11:23).

ii. Christology and reception

Christology serves as touchstone of every ecumenical activity. Source of inspiration for the reception processes in the Church is its own Head, namely God himself in Jesus Christ. The divine Logos received the human nature in a "critical" way ("without sin" – Hebr. 4:15), recapitulating, healing it and providing an eschatological perspective for the humankind. By revealing the will of the Father and by inviting all nations to adopt his salvific message, Jesus Christ comes out as the initiator and also the way of a reception whose content is truth and whose gift is life, life in abundance (cf. John 14:4). A real reception of his message cannot be dissociated from the reception of his person and of the whole Trinity; it is an act of authentic personal encounter (Matt. 10:40; John 13:20).[8]

Being understood as response and service to Jesus Christ, reception cannot take place at the expense of the truth of faith. It is rather a continuous incorporation of this truth, shared in personal communion. Seeking for unity in faith, the separated Christians are longing for fuller communion with each other and with the Lord. As the transcendental–eschatological truth of the Church, that cannot be enclosed in human formulations, Jesus Christ questions steadily the existing images of the truth and warns against their mythologizing; a christologically rooted apophaticism as recognition of the incapacity of the human word to express the fullness of the divine reality could serve liberatingly against the frequent short circuits of the ecumenical dialogues and their reception processes.

iii. The Spirit of reception

Christological views on reception presuppose an adequate pneumatology: "no one can say that Jesus is the Lord, but by the Holy Spirit" (1. Cor. 12:3). As Spirit of Truth and communion, the Comforter guides the fellowship of the faithful "into all Truth" (John 16:13) and establishes unity among them. The Church initiates reception

and an Opportunity": Max Thurian (ed.), *Ecumenical Perspectives on Baptism, Eucharist and Ministry*, [Faith and Order Papers Nr. 116], (Geneva: WCC, 1983), 163–174: 168; John Zizioulas, "The Theological Problem of Reception," *One in Christ* 21 (1985): 187–193: 188; Nissiotis, "Meaning," 47–48, 51–56; André Birmelé, "Die Rezeption als ökumenisches Erfordernis. Das Beispiel der theologischen Dialoge zwischen den christlichen Kirchen," *Una Sancta* 51 (1996): 342–360: 343–349. For a historical overview of reception see Edward Killmartin, "Reception in History: An Ecclesiological Phenomenon and Its Significance," *Journal of Ecumenical Studies* 21 (1984): 34–54; Gaßmann, "Rezeption." Kirhengeschichtlich.

[5] For the concept of reception in the Bible with numerous references see Gaßmann, "Rezeption." Kirchengeschichtlich, 132–134. See also Kühn, "Reception," 165–166; Zizioulas, "Theological Problem," 190; Beinert, "Rezeption," 193.

[6] See e.g. Acts 2:37–42; 1 Cor. 15:1. Cf. Beinert, "Rezeption", 199–200.

[7] Zizioulas, "Theological Problem," 190. Cf. Beinert, "Rezeption," 200.

[8] Cf. Günther Gaßmann, "Rezeption im ökumenischen Kontext," *Ökumenische Rundschau* 26 (1977): 314–327:326–327; Kühn, "Reception," 165; Zizioulas, "Theological Problem," 190–191; Nissiotis, "Meaning," 51–52; Beinert, "Rezeption," 200.

processes (the ecumenical ones included) believing and praying that the Spirit may inspire, lead and fulfill them, sending the divine grace which heals the ill and fills in what is missing.

Emphasizing the soteriological importance of the synergy of God and human beings, Orthodox theology would never underestimate the importance of human contribution to ecumenical reception. The alternative of a magic or thoughtless automatism contradicts the teaching of a tradition which insists on free will and calls for active participation in the event of redemption. On the other hand, this very tradition is conscious of the unsurpassable limits of every human act and of the decisive importance of the divine aid. Therefore it principally considers every fruitful reception as a gift of the Paraclete. By enabling the Church to receive constantly the divine revelation, the grace of God and the gift of communion, the Spirit donates life to the Body of Christ. A receiving church is a living church, the Church of the life-giving Spirit.[9]

iv. The Church as receiving community

The Body of Christ is nothing less than a receiving community, a community receiving God's revelation in terms of doxological acceptance and integration of its salvific content in all existential and communal aspects of the ecclesial life.[10] The Church is per se the positive response to the inviting act of its Head; this response is taking place both in the individual and the communal level, both in the personal life of each faithful and in the common experience of Jesus' redeeming presence in his Church.

1. Eucharistic ecclesiology and the challenge of reception

The Eastern Church insists upon the importance of synodal structures for every receptive procedure. It regards the bishops as the guarantors of orthodoxy (=the right faith) of their local churches. Their synodal gathering mirrors the communion of their churches in the one faith. As governing body, the synod of an Orthodox church plays a decisive role in its ecumenical activity: it is the authority which determines the attitude of a church in the ecumenical dialogue; it names official delegates, evaluates the results, decides for or against their reception and takes consequential pastoral initiatives.

In accordance to Orthodox ecclesiology, the eucharistic-liturgical expression of ecclesial unity is an essential way of demonstrating the fruitfulness of an ecumenical reception process on the highest level. A really successful ecumenical dialogue between two churches is crowned with the restoration of their eucharistic communion; the common participation in the Eucharist is being regarded as the strongest sacramental expression of the experience of unity, which is also unity in faith.[11]

---

[9] As N. Nissiotis remarks: "the Spirit of God [...] is the Spirit of reception insofar as he is the Spirit of newness and renewal in the Church and the world" ("Meaning," 74). On the pneumatological components of reception see also Congar, "Réception," 392–395; Gaßmann, Rezeption, 325–326. Especially on the Orthodox point of view, discussing the views of Khomiakov and others, see Waclaw Hryniewicz, "Die ekklesiale Rezeption in der Sicht der orthodoxen Theologie," *Theologie und Glaube* 65 (1975): 250–266: 251–256.

[10] Anton Houtepen, "Reception, Tradition, Communion": Max Thurian (ed.), *Ecumenical Perspectives*, 140–160: 149ff.; Zizioulas, "Theological Problem"; Nissiotis, "Meaning," 51–53; Beinert, "Rezeption," 209–210; Birmelé, "Erfordernis," 345.

[11] Cf. Zizioulas, "Theological Problem," 191–193; Wiebke Köhler, *Rezeption in der Kirche. Begriffsgeschichtliche Studien bei Sohm, Afanas'ev, Dombois und Congar*, [Kirche und Konfession 41], (Göttingen: Vanderhoeck & Rupprecht, 1998), 95–112. Eucharistic communion among churches that have not yet reached full theological agreement with each other (intercommunio) is a practice not welcome by the Orthodox Cchurches (see e.g. Athanasios Basdekis, "Eucharistie–Kirchengemeinschaft aus orthodoxer Sicht. Unter besonderer Berücksichtigung der Ergebnisse des theologischen Dialogs zwischen der orthodoxen und der römisch–katholischen Kirche": Bernt Jochen Hilberath / Dorothea Sattler [eds.], *Vorgeschmack. Ökumenische Bemühungen um die Eucharistie. Festschrift für Theodor Schneider*, (Mainz: Matthias Grünewald, 1995), 457–472. In the gap between separating theological views and unifying sacramental expressions one sees a questioning of the character of the Eucharist as sacrament of unity. For the Orthodox, it is exactly the longing for common participation in the Eucharist which motivates them to contribute to ecumenical dialogues and to activate processes to receive their fruits.

2. The consciousness of the Church and the eschatological anticipation

In spite of the importance of a synodal approval of e.g. an ecumenical text, from an Orthodox point of view this does not suffice for a full reception.[12] The synod ought to express the conscience of the Church, but it does not substitute it. Numerous historical examples of failed reception testify that typical criteria are not enough for the recognition of an ecclesial document (or of a Council as a whole) by the conscience of the Church: the 'robber' council of Ephesus (449), the iconoclastic council of Iereia (754), and the council of Ferrara-Florence have been rejected from the people of God, who exercised their prophetic - critical function in the Body of the Church. With their involvement in the reception process clergymen and laity together mirror the permanent conciliarity of the Church, reveal the Church as a conciliar being.[13] As far as Orthodoxy is concerned, lay people still play a secondary role in decision-making; the challenge of reception offers them the possibility of a more active involvement, it gives them the opportunity to unfold their potential in the life of the Church.[14]

It is impossible to develop a-priory a theory of ecumenical reception.[15] The dynamic self-consciousness of the Church cannot be deteriorated in juridical formulas. The Body of Christ is living in the tension of old and new, continuity and novelty, thanksgiving acceptance of the past and creative elaboration of the future. Therefore all reception processes are ex natura endless;[16] every generation is called to receive anew what has been given and to elaborate it in a fruitful and creative way.[17] Several examples from various Christian traditions show that the evaluation of ecumenical texts varies even in the same Church, depending on each specific historical period and cultural context:[18] Documents welcomed in the past are being read in a more critical way today and vice versa. Orthodox churches in multicultural societies are much more open than others acting in an almost mono-confessional atmosphere.

Inspired and assisted by God in their ecumenical journey, the churches live in the expectation of the eschatological completion of the reception processes. Overcoming the range of human capacities, unity in its fullness is a gift of the world to come. Attempting to receive the gifts of their common ecumenical commitment, the churches attempt to foretaste eschatological qualities; they act against frustration and disappointments which are not absent from history – and from every receptive activity.

v. The ethos of reception

Reception presupposes a corresponding ecumenical ethos. Orthodox ecumenists insist on the importance of spirituality for the inter–Christian dialogue, referring to the patristic–ascetic tradition of the Eastern

---

[12] Olivier Clément, "Ecclésiologie orthodoxe er dialogue oecumenique," *Contacts* 15.42 (1963): 89–106:102; Hryniewicz, "Ekklesiale Rezeption," 252; Athanasios Vletsis, "Autorität oder Authentizität? Das Ringen der orthodoxen Theologie um die Erkenntnis und die Träger der kirchlichen Lehre vor der Herausforderung des dritten Milleniums": Christoph Böttigheimer / Johannes Hofmann (eds.), *Autorität und Synodalität. Eine interdisziplinäre und interkonfessionelle Umschau nach ökumenischen Chancen und ekklesiologischen Desideraten*, (Frankfurt a.M.: Lembeck, 2008), 147–167.

[13] See Orthodox perspectives summarized in Hryniewicz, "Ekklesiale Rezeption," 251, footnote 7; Ion Bria, "La 'réception' des résultats des dialogues": Papandreou, Damaskinos (ed.), *Les dialogues oecuméniques hier et aujourd'hui*, [Les études théologiques de Chambésy 5], (Chambésy–Genève: Centre Orthodoxe du Patriarcat Oecumenique, 1985), 286–293: 289–291. Cf. Congar, "Recéption," 396; Gaßmann, "Rezeption," 314; Houtepen, "Reception, Tradition, Communion," 145; Beinert, "Rezeption," 213.

[14] For the involvement of the whole Church in the reception process see: Hryniewicz, Ekklesiale Rezeption (he presents the view of Alexis Khomiakov and the critique against him); Alexandros Papaderos, "Some Thoughts on Reception: Not Forgetting the People and Life," *Mid–Stream* 23 (1984): 51–63; Bria, "Réception," 286–287.

[15] Killmartin, "Reception in History," 37–38; Beinert, "Rezeption," 199.

[16] Gaßmann, "Rezeption," 322; Houtepen, "Reception, Tradition, Communion," 144–149; Beinert, "Rezeption," 195; Birmelé, "Erfordernis," 343.

[17] Therefore we speak also of a re–reception of the already received (Zizioulas, "Theological Problem," 193; Beinert, "Rezeption," 195). Cf. Kühn, "Reception," 169; Killmartin, "Reception in History," 37; Birmelé, "Erfordernis," 344.

[18] On the importance of contextuality see also Beinert, "Rezeption," 212.

Church.[19] A receptive attitude presupposes a resignation from the narcissistic spirit of self-sufficiency. It promotes the adoption of an apophatic ethos of discipleship and creates an atmosphere of anticipation that the gifts of the Other will enrich our own tradition. Unburdened by the polemic confrontation of the past, the churches have to show mutually a self-critical readiness for sincere penitence and to work for the healing of memories which still hamper their relations. Authentic reception is impossible without confession.[20]

II. Reception in the Orthodox world: achievements and challenges

The historical road of Orthodoxy has not been easy in the 20th century. Nevertheless, the Orthodox Church has been one of most important initiators of the modern ecumenical movement.[21] It has not only followed, but also actively co-shaped decisive developments, participating in numerous multi- and bilateral dialogues in local, national and global level. The documents that the Orthodox Church is called to receive are texts co-authored by Orthodox delegates, officially appointed by their Churches. Therefore, Orthodoxy is invited to receive not something exogenous, but something which emerged through her cooperation and contribution.[22]

i. Achievements (some examples)

Concrete sacramental and juridical acts are indeed necessary as visible signs of the adoption of the fruits of the ecumenical effort. But even if Orthodoxy has not yet restored eucharistic communion with its dialogue partners, certain developments bear witness to vital achievements in the reception processes. By focusing exclusively on what has still to be achieved (and this is undoubtedly a lot) one overlooks the importance of what has already been achieved. Moreover, one might underestimate the character of reception not as an event, but as a process taking place in various levels, as a process which presupposes and contributes to the gradual growing of the "unity of the Spirit" among churches "in the bond of peace" (Eph. 4:3).[23]

1. Orthodoxy and inter-church relations

A sign of positive reception of the ecumenical dialogue in the Orthodox world is the establishment of fraternal relations with churches with which there is yet no full communion. On the level of ecclesial authorities these relations are expressed through official visits of the leadership of one church to the other, common declarations and initiatives, etc. Commonly planned projects (conferences, publications, charitable work, etc.) speak of the overcoming of the prejudices of the past and the growing trust among the churches.

2. Pastoral arrangements and the receptive potential of the "diaspora"

The so-called Orthodox diaspora, namely the Orthodox presence in traditionally non-Orthodox countries, has developed a receptive potential, which has to be used further and more efficiently in the future. Based upon the experience of daily co-existence with the heterodox brothers and sisters, the diaspora communities could provide convincing examples for the reception of inter-Christian dialogue. This co-existence has led to pastoral arrangements between the Orthodox and other churches on a series of issues (e.g. mixed marriages) or coura-

---

[19] Thomas FitzGerald, "Spirituality and Reception," *Orthodoxes Forum* 11 (1997): 157–168; Kallistos Ware, "Receptive Ecumenism. An Orthodox Perspective," *Louvain Studies* 33 (2008): 46–53.
[20] Killmartin, "Reception in History," 46; Willebrands, "Ecumenical Dialogue," 224; Paul Murray, *Receptive Ecumenism and the Call to Catholic Learning. Exploring a Way or Contemporary Ecumenism*, (Oxford: Oxford University Press, 2008).
[21] Theodoros Meimaris, *The Holy and Great Council of the Orthodox Church and the Ecumenical Movement*, (Thessaloniki: Ant. Stamoulis, 2013), esp. 19–40.
[22] Cf. Kühn, "Reception," 169; Nissiotis, "Meaning," 50.
[23] Cf. Bria, "Réception," 292.

geous ecumenical steps (e.g. the declaration of mutual recognition of Baptism in Magdeburg 2007, co-signed by the Orthodox churches in Germany)[24] are visible signs of successful reception of theological agreements.

3. Two dialogues

The Eastern Orthodox Church held official bilateral dialogues with the Oriental Orthodox and the Old Catholic Churches. In both cases the churches reached doctrinal agreement in a series of crucial points; this raised great expectations for a restoration of full communion in the near future. Nevertheless, the reception of their results remains insufficient. Doctrinal, canonical, etc. issues seem to impede further steps towards fuller communion.

In spite on their theological agreement on Christology, the Eastern and Oriental Orthodox have not yet reached a common ground concerning the status of councils that are accepted by the Chalcedonian Orthodoxy as ecumenical. The most vital challenge is the possibility of restoration of persons - who are heretics, anathematized by ecumenical councils for the one church family, while for the other are highly respected saints. The Eastern Orthodox Churches are reluctant to the restoration of full communion with the Old Catholic Church, mainly because this Church accepts the ordination of women and practices intercommunion.

Historical and cultural reasons contribute to this deceleration of the reception process. Twenty-five years after the fall of communism the Eastern Orthodox churches are still trying to define their identity and role in a new political and social order, with inevitable consequences for the pan-Orthodox and inter-Christian relations, too. The political and social instability in the Middle East, which has dramatically increased during the last years, obliged the Oriental Orthodox Churches to set other priorities. Serious turbulences in the Old Catholic world concerning the ordination of women, the evaluation of homosexuality, etc. are hindrances to the reception processes.[25]

4. Orthodoxy and BEM

The Orthodox churches did not ignore the invitation of the WCC to receive BEM. Official responses, conferences and publications mirrored the interest of the Orthodox world in this valuable document. Observations and critical questions contributed to the ecumenical discussion on the theology of the sacraments. Nevertheless, rather confessionalist readings dominated in the end, overlooking the character of BEM as a convergence document and hampering further ecumenical steps.[26]

ii. Challenges

In spite of the positive developments, one cannot be satisfied with the rhythm and the fruits of reception processes in the Orthodox world. Their optimization and intensification presupposes the confrontation with problems and deficits which impede the ecumenical road of Orthodoxy in general.

---

[24] Georgios Basioudis, "Die Konsequenzen aus der gemeinsamen Taufe für das Verständnis von Kirche und für das ökumenische Bemühen um die sichtbare Einheit der Kirchen aus orthodoxer Sicht," *Ökumenische Rundschau* 57 (2008): 363–370.

[25] Despite the problems, the success of both dialogues has initiated processes of mutual approach and close ecumenical cooperation, which permit a sense of optimism. On the Eastern Orthodox-Oriental Orthodox Dialogue see Georgios Martzelos, "Probleme und Perspektiven des theologischen Dialogs zwischen den Orthodoxen und Nicht-Chalzedonensern," *Una Sancta* 66 (2011): 42-49. On the Orthodox–Old Catholic dialogue: Urs von Arx, "Der orthodox–altkatholische Dialog. Anmerkungen zu einer schwierigen Rezeption," *Internationale Kirchliche Zeitschrift [IKZ]* 87 (1997): 184–224; Angela Berlis, "Zur Rezeption der orthodox / altkatholischen Dialogtexte von 1975–1987 in den Niederlanden," *IKZ* 94 (2004): 135–139; Anastasios Kallis, "Erfolgreicher Dialog ohne Folgen. Zur Rezeptionsproblematik im Hinblick auf die altkatholisch–orthodoxe Gemeinschaft," *IKZ* 96 (2006): 1–8.

[26] Georgios Vlantis, "Die vermisste Apophatik. 30 Jahre BEM und die Orthodoxie," *Una Sancta* 67 (2012): 226–240. Cf. Nissiotis, "Meaning," 62–74. This attitude was not genuinely Orthodox; many other Churches reacted similarly. See Birmelé, "Erfordernis," 347.

1. Matters of ecclesiology

After more than a century of intense ecumenical work Orthodoxy has not provided an official response concerning the issue of the limits of the Church and the ecclesiological status of the other Churches. This ecclesiological vagueness deteriorates the effects of a reception process. The whole dynamics of an agreement with a partner cannot be sufficiently unfolded if this partner is not clearly defined. On the other hand, it is to expect that the reception process, as a process of mutual knowledge and understanding, may constructively contribute to the articulation of this expected definition or description of the Other.[27]

What should be the structural expressions of the unity we seek? Which are the doctrinal, canonical, etc. conditions for the re-establishment of full communion among the churches? Which are the points that still separate the churches and which ones have lost their separating effect?[28] A successful ecumenical reception presupposes a clear vision concerning the model of unity we seek. As long as the expectations from the ecumenical dialogue are not concretized, its results cannot be sufficiently evaluated.[29]

The discussion around the prerogatives of the Ecumenical Patriarch, who is regarded as primus inter pares among the Orthodox hierarchs, and the barriers on the way to a pan-Orthodox council mirror serious problems in inter-Orthodox communication which prevent the Orthodox Church from adopting a common voice, attitude and strategy in the ecumenical dialogue and in the reception processes.[30]

2. Contextuality and hermeneutics

Reception is influenced by historical-cultural contexts.[31] Processes of self-definition taking place in the Orthodox world have been already mentioned: the confrontation of the churches with their own past, the introvert tendencies, the financial, political and social instability are all factors which play a serious role to the construction of an ecumenical profile and influence reception processes. Churches present in strongly patriarchal societies or in contexts characterized by their deficient confrontation with the challenges of modernity are normally more reluctant to follow ecumenical developments than other churches of the same confession, who are acting in more pluralistic and liberal contexts. Reception is to a certain extend a matter of hermeneutics; its principles have usually strong contextual connotations.[32]

---

[27] See the remarks of Kühn, "Reception," 70; Nissiotis, "Meaning," 64–66, 71–73 and by the same author, "The Credible Reception of the Lima Document as the Ecumenical Conversion of the Churches": Max Thurian (ed.), *Churches respond to BEM. Official Responses to the "Baptism, Eucharist and Ministry" Text*, Vol. 3, [Faith and Order Papers Nr. 135], (Geneva: World Council of Churches, 1987), xi–xvii: xiii; Peter Bouteneff, "Ecclesiology and Ecumenism": Augustine Casiday (ed.), *The Orthodox Christian World*, [The Routledge Worlds], (New York: Routledge, 2012), 369–382: 377–381 .

[28] This last question is directly associated with the theological challenge of a continuous re-reception of one's own tradition. Cf. Beinert, "Rezeption," 216.

[29] Cf. Houtepen, "Reception, Tradition, Communion," 153–155.

[30] See Athanasios Vletsis, "Wer ist der erste in der Orthodoxie? Das Ringen der Orthodoxen Kirchen um die Gestaltung einer panorthodoxen Rangsordnung," *Una Sancta* 66 (2011): 2-4; Meimaris, "Great Council." For the relation of local and universal level with regard to reception cf. Gaßmann, "Rezeption," 323–324. John Zizioulas sees exactly in this point a possibility for an Orthodox acceptance of a kind of primacy for the bishop of Rome: "Reception cannot be limited to the local level but has to be universal. A ministry of universal reception is needed which should meet the requirements of communion. Such requirements would involve the following: (a) that this ministry should be episcopal in nature: i.e. it should be exercised by the head of a local church. This would assure that universal catholicity does not bypass or contradict the catholicity of the local church. (b) That a consensus of the faithful should be obtained in every case of reception and that his should pass through the local bishops and not be a matter of individual. In these circumstances one should not hesitate to seek such a ministry in the Bishop of Rome" ("Theological Problem," 192).

[31] Cf. Alois Grillmeier, "Konzil und Rezeption. Methodische Bemerkungen zu einem Thema der ökumenischen Diskussion der Gegenwart," *Theologie und Philosophie* 45 (1970): 321–352: 347–348.

[32] In May 2013 the Volos Academy for Theological Studies in collaboration with several other Orthodox Theological Faculties and Institutions organized an international conference in Cluj-Napoca, Romania with the title: "Can Orthodox Theology Be Contextual? Concrete Approaches from the Orthodox Tradition." Its very interesting proceedings are to be published soon.

3. Anti-ecumenical tendencies

Due to the ecumenical movement the churches begin to realize the role that the mutual ignorance has played in the establishment and continuation of separation between them. The unknown Other becomes easily the project area of fears and negative images. The knowledge of Western and Oriental Christianity in traditionally Eastern Orthodox countries still remains insufficient. A lot of work has to be done for the deconstruction of prejudices in order to facilitate the reception of ecumenical texts.

This deficit in ecumenical education sustains anti-ecumenical currents, setting a serious barrier to the reception processes. Based on a radically exclusivist ecclesiology of strongly dualistic nuances (mythologized Orthodoxy against demonized heresy, etc.) anti–ecumenists develop a broad activity (preaching, books, journals, newspapers, websites, etc.) questioning the orthodoxy of the ecumenically active church leadership, clergymen and laity and daunting the congregations against the ecumenical dialogue and its achievements.[33]

4. Anti-Westernism

Various versions of Orthodox anti-Westernism have in common the adoption of dualistic schemata, which in an undifferentiated way interpret the historical paths of the Western churches and theologies as a fall from the Orthodox authenticity of the East. Even if serving other priorities than the polemic against the ecumenical dialogue, the spreading of caricature images of the West does not contribute to a mutual understanding of the church traditions and to a fruitful reception of their common achievements.[34]

Reception justifies the scope of the ecumenical movement, offering the possibility of integration of its attainments in the life of the participating churches, and thus decisively promoting ecclesial unity. Otherwise inter-Christian dialogue could be degenerated to a sort of inter-Christian bureaucracy, to a self-referential church diplomacy with no importance for the people of God.

There is a great potential for further and more fruitful reception of ecumenical dialogues in the Orthodox world. This presupposes an ecumenical openness and generosity, the overcome of anxieties associated with the construction, the authenticity and preservation of one's own identity. Some concrete steps may assist the realization of this difficult target: more intense theological work on ecclesiological challenges; ecumenical educational projects (e.g. exchange of students and scholars); conferences; publications; missionary initiatives; ecumenical pastoral initiatives for the parishes (ecumenical courses, fraternization of parishes of different denominations); cooperation of youth fellowships; deeper involvement of lay people, etc.[35]

Ecumenical reception is both a mandate and a challenge. Even if it is not easy, it is a crucial matter. For as Nikos Nissiotis writes: "Ecumenicity concerns the authenticity of Orthodoxy."[36]

Bibliography[37]

Bria, Ion, "La 'réception' des résultats des dialogues": Papandreou, Damaskinos (ed.), *Les dialogues oecuméniques hier et aujourd'hui*, [Les études théologiques de Chambésy 5], (Chambésy–Genève: Centre Orthodoxe du Patriarcat Oecumenique, 1985), 286–293.

---

[33] Cf. e.g. Bouteneff, "Ecclesiology and ecumenism," 378–381.
[34] See Pantelis Kalaitzidis, *Greekness and Antiwesternism in the Greek Theology of '60s*, Unpublished Doctoral Dissertation, School of Theology, (Aristotle University of Thessaloniki, 2008) [in Greek].
[35] For various proposals see Sabine Pensel–Meier, *Rezeption. Schwierigkeiten und Chancen. Eine Untersuchung zur Aufnahme und Umsetzung ökumenischer Konsensdokumente in den Ortskirchen*, (Würzburg: Echter, 1993).
[36] Nissiotis, "Meaning," 68.
[37] In this short bibliography I list only *ad hoc* studies on reception from an Orthodox point of view to provide the reader with a short overview.

Hryniewicz, Waclaw, "Die ekklesiale Rezeption in der Sicht der orthodoxen Theologie," *Theologie und Glaube* 65 (1975): 250–266.

Ionita, Viorel, "Die Rezeption ökumenischer Entscheidungen. Beispiele aus verschiedenen kirchlichen Traditionen": Anna Briskina–Müller / Armenuhi Drost–Abgarian / Axel Meisner (ed.), *Logos im Dialogos. Auf der Suche nach der Orthodoxie. Gedenkschrift für Hermann Goltz (1946–2010)*, [Forum Orthodoxe Theologie 11], (Berlin: LIT, 2011), 375–386.

Nissiotis, Nikos, "The Meaning of Reception in Relation to the Results of Ecumenical Dialogue on the Basis of the Faith and Order Document 'Baptism, Eucharist and Ministry'": Gennadios Limouris / Nomikos Michael Vaporis (eds.), *Orthodox Perspectives on Baptism, Eucharist and Ministry*, [Faith and Order Papers Nr. 128], *The Greek Orthodox Theological Review* 30 (1985): 47–74.

Nissiotis, Nikos, "The Credible Reception of the Lima Document as the Ecumenical Conversion of the Churches": Max Thurian (ed.), *Churches respond to BEM. Official Responses to the "Baptism, Eucharist and Ministry" Text*, Vol. 3, [Faith and Order Papers Nr. 135], (Geneva: World Council of Churches, 1987), xi–xvii.

Papaderos, Alexandros, "Some Thoughts on Reception: Not Forgetting the People and Life," *Mid–Stream* 23 (1984): 51–63.

Ware, Kallistos, "Receptive Ecumenism. An Orthodox Perspective," *Louvain Studies* 33 (2008): 46–53.

Zizioulas, John, "The Theological Problem of Reception," *One in Christ* 21 (1985): 187–193.

Aikaterini Pekridou

The present text argues that disability is a question for ecumenical dialogue and therefore must be taken seriously within the ecumenical movement. It briefly unfolds the difficulties around definition, terminology and the development of Christian theological thinking around disability particularly within the framework of the WCC, and attempts to highlight crucial points for future ecumenical dialogue to which Orthodox theology can make a substantial contribution.

People living with some form of physical or mental disability are members of every church and society. United Nations statistics affirm that "around 15% of the world's population, or estimated 1 billion people, live with disabilities. They are the world's largest minority."[1] Thus, whether as churches we acknowledge it or not, disabilities are part of our community life, no matter what our doctrinal teachings and liturgical practices may be. Disability, therefore, is a question that concerns all of us as a community, not just 'them'; it is not a question of the "disabled" and the "abled", but a matter that concerns all of us as members of the Church of God and as the One body of Christ.

There are specific understandings of disability that stem from societal or cultural constructions and interpretations that mingle with understandings of disability coming from faith. The faith of a particular community relates to its ways of interpreting the Bible and also its interpretation of doctrine and ways of doing theology. It also relates to social action and decision-making mechanisms, the full inclusion (or non-inclusion) of persons with disabilities in the life of the community, and the attitude of those considered "abled" towards them. From this perspective, disability is a question for every Christian community and needs to be explored and discussed in depth within the community, but also in relation to other Christian (and other faith) communities. In this sense, disability is an ecumenical matter that needs to be studied carefully in the context of multilateral dialogue.

What is disability?

Definitions around disability have been reflecting different understandings and interests of those providing them at different historical moments. In the bibliography concerning disability definitions are classified according to two models, the medical and the social one. The former has been supported mainly by academics and health workers, whereas the latter has been promoted mostly by persons with disabilities. Medical definitions focus on the individual impairments, which they see as the cause of the problems of persons with disabilities. It has been argued that this approach sustains traditional social structures and disregards that the problem lies with discriminatory societies that make persons with disabilities outcasts and treat them in demeaning ways.[2] Recent definitions emerged through the disability rights movement and the struggle of persons with disabilities against segregation and in order that their full value as human beings be acknowledged. These definitions are of political significance, because they come out of the direct experience of disability. They locate the cause of disability with society and measure the relevance of current service structures. They view disability positively and expose the discrimination experienced by persons with disabilities in society (and the church).[3]

---

[1] http://www.un.org/disabilities/default.asp?id=18 (lastly accessed 10 Jan 2014).
[2] Fritzson Arne, "Preface" in Interpreting Disability, *A Church of All and for All*, Risk Series, eds. Fritson Arne, Kabue Samuel, (Geneva: WCC Publications, 2004), viii-ix.
[3] Ibid. x.

But what is disability in Christian theology and the Church? In certain Christian traditions disability was seen as punishment for the sins of the individual or his/her parents, or was thought to be connected to demonic possession. In some, it was considered as a test of faith, or as an act of God; people with disabilities were often told they are special in the eyes of God and that's why they were given their disability. Sometimes they were told not to worry about their pain and suffering now, because in heaven they would be made whole.[4] Despite the significant work they offered, some churches treated persons with disabilities as objects of pity and saw in their disability a chance to exercise their charity. Other churches failed to see disability as a priority, and therefore, they did not study it seriously or reflect upon it theologically, and failed to develop specific ministries and services relating to disability.

Despite the varied approaches and attitudes (mainly negative) of churches toward disability that tend to see people with disabilities as a homogenous group (and therefore disregard the special contributions an individual can make and the special needs he/she may have), contemporary biblical scholarship has claimed that the Judeo-Christian tradition provided no classification for the experiences of the persons with disabilities or a single term to describe them, as is the case with the term disability itself. Instead, the Bible portrays people who suffer from specific infirmities. A close examination of the terms used in Greek literature to denote what the modern world classified as disability (such as *astheneia, adunatos, anapeiros*), shows that "there was no overarching concept of disability in the ancient world."[5] Definitions of disability are subject to cultural and historical changes, as well as the advancement of science. This is evident in the case of definitions used within the ecumenical movement which moved from the area of theological reflection to practical questions of inclusion within the church. Since interpretations of disability vary, we need to note that the terms "persons with disabilities" and "people with disabilities" used by WCC since 1997, might be considered controversial in other circles.[6] In my opinion, definitions of disability are part of the ongoing study and debate on disability in light of new medical advancements and fresh theological thinking.

Disability as discussed within the WCC framework

Under the influence of liberation and feminist theology, the question of disability has been treated within the WCC as an issue of justice and of full participation in the community. The multilateral dialogue showed that churches working on disability start from different points and have different perspectives that are based largely on culture. It became apparent that theological understandings of the cause of a disabling condition vary tremendously in different societies, and this affects how societies view and treat persons with a disability, and also how the latter participate in the life and work of local churches.[7]

Serious theological work on disability started in 1971 at the Faith and Order Commission meeting in Louvain. Four years later, the Fifth Assembly in Nairobi came up with a statement entitled "The Handicapped and the Wholeness of the Family of God." Consultancy work related to the United Nations International Year of the Disabled Persons led to high visibility of persons with disabilities in the Sixth Assembly in Vancouver in 1983. From 1984 to 1991 the work on disability within WCC and its member churches was promoted by a full-time consultant. This led to a big group of persons with disabilities participating as delegates, advisers or visitors in the Seventh Assembly of 1991 in Canberra. From 1994 to 1996 emphasis was given on networking among the member churches and promoting the work on local and national level through regional consultations.

---

[4] Eiesland Nancy, "Liberation, Inclusion, and Justice: A Faith Response to Persons with Disabilities" in *EDAN Quarterly Newsletter* (January-March 2009): 4-5.

[5] Frances Bruce Patricia, "'A daughter of Abraham': Luke 13:10-17 and the inclusion of people with disabilities" in the *Journal of Constructive Theology* 11.1 (July 2005): 8-11.

[6] Fritzson Arne, "Preface", x.

[7] Katsuno Lynda and Fritzson Arne, "Disability" in *The Dictionary of the Ecumenical Movement*, Nicholas Lossky et all (eds), 2nd edition, (Geneva: WCC, 2010), 327.

Part VII: Particular Themes and Issues for Orthodox Involvement in Ecumenism

The Programme on Lay Participation towards Inclusive Community that followed played an important role in giving visibility to ten advisers with disabilities who participated in the Eighth Assembly in Harare in 1998. This group formed the Ecumenical Disability Advisers Network that later became the Ecumenical Disability Advocates Network (EDAN), which links with the WCC though its coordinator who was originally based at the National Council of Churches in Nairobi, and was also staff member of the WCC.[8] Today, the All Africa Conference of Churches (AACC) provides hospitality to EDAN.

The disability advisers of Harare formed the Global Network which sustains the vision of EDAN. It is from this group that the Regional Coordinators are chosen. Both in Porto Alegre in 2006 and in Busan in 2013, EDAN Pre-Assembly meetings were held to facilitate better the work of EDAN participants in both Assemblies.[9] In the Tenth WCC Assembly more than sixty members of EDAN from all Regions participated as advisers in the Ecumenical Conversations, plenaries and workshops, including fifteen members from Korea. Their larger number compared to previous Assemblies raised awareness for the full participation of persons with disabilities in the life of the church and the ecumenical structures.

EDAN is an active network with its own website (http://www.edan-wcc.org/) and quarterly bulletin, EDAN Newsletter, which stimulates theological reflection on issues concerning persons with disabilities. Among other things, the network organizes consultations and promotes publications on disability questions, works with different ecumenical partners and disability organizations worldwide, and shapes the work of the WCC through appointing advisers in Central Committee and in all major meetings of the Council. The theological work of EDAN in recent decades is summed up in its 2003 interim statement entitled "A Church of All and for All,"[10] which was prepared for the Central Committee and was commended to the churches for study, feedback and action. The statement starts with Eph. 2:14 and is based on the conviction that Christ came to tear down the walls that shut people out and to offer a ministry of reconciliation. It develops the commonalities and differences of persons with disabilities, and addresses hermeneutical issues relating to disability, examining the question of how we can interpret theologically the fact that some people live with disabilities, and what this tells us about human life in God's world. It then analyses the idea that humanity is made in the image of God (imago Dei), and studies disability vis-à-vis healing and forgiveness. Lastly, the statement focuses on the giftedness of every human being and promotes the church as a community for all.

The 2003 statement does not claim to be the final word on disability. Instead it raises questions and poses some of the challenges to our Christian theologies. To name a few, the challenge to our ways of interpreting stories about healing in the gospels (§ 56), the challenge to human notions of perfection, purpose, reward, success and status; the challenge to the notion of a God who rewards virtue with health and prosperity (§ 57), the challenge to accept Christ as a God of vulnerability and woundedness who rose from the dead with his wounds (§59, 60), the challenge to serve God's image instead of a worldly image, "where ideal perfection is valued and weakness criticized, and where virtues alone are emphasized and failures are concealed" (§ 63), the challenge to disconnect disability from shame, sin, or lack of faith (§ 64), the challenge to re-consider forgiveness as "fitting together" (synchoresis) and disassociate it from sin and guilt (§ 65). These and more challenges and questions are currently studied by EDAN through consultations and with the contributions of experts in the area of disability in view of the preparation of a new statement on disability.

Crucial points for future dialogue

The meeting organized by EDAN and Faith and Order in May 2013 reconsidered the 2003 statement in an attempt to provide a theological response to the reality of disability in the context of theological anthropology

---

[8] Ibid.

[9] More on the recent history of EDAN on http://www.edan-wcc.org/index.php/about-us/from-harare-to-porto-alegre (lastly accessed on 10 Jan 2014).

[10] The text is available on http://www2.wcc-coe.org/ccdocuments2003.nsf/index/plen-1.1-en.html.

and in light of the vision of the church and its mission in the world. Participants discussed what it means to live with a disability in view of the meaning of being human. What does it mean to be created in God's image and likeness? Does God's image and likeness cease to exist in cases of profound intellectual disabilities or dementia? The group also discussed the connections that are made between disability, sin and suffering in different Christian traditions, and challenged traditional interpretations of the healing narratives of the bible. Other questions raised during the meeting were: Is disability really a weakness or a loss? Does vulnerability characterize the persons with disabilities or all humans? What does it mean for church members to be united in the body of Christ? What does it mean for them to build up the church of God each one according to their gifts?

I think that Orthodox theological reflection can make a significant contribution untangling aspects of these questions relating to disability. First of all, Orthodox theology on creation emphasizes the distinction between the uncreated God and the created humans which demonstrates that compared to God, (who is the actual Being), humans are imperfect, even though created as good – an idea constantly repeated in Genesis, as God created only good. Humans *are* (considered beings) to the extent that they participate in the life of the Triune God through faith and the mysteries of the Church. Thus, compared to God, all humans – not just the persons with disabilities – are imperfect and all are sinners. Their perfection lies in their participation in the grace of God, not in the abilities that the society they live in thinks they have. This implies a dynamic and constantly evolving process that starts from birth and continues to the Kingdom; a struggle to fulfill the 'likeness' of God. Because they are created human beings are changeable and corruptible, i.e. weak and vulnerable, and subject to mortality. Thus, they live and have to choose between perfection and alienation from God. These ideas were developed by the Cappadocians and explored further by John Damascene.

The story of creation, and especially the fall and its consequences, was interpreted in different ways in the West and the East. The Eastern Church maintained the view that the goodness of creation was not lost after the fall, and also the ability of humans to reach "likeness". Corruptibility and death had been inherited by the next generations because of the fall. Sin was seen as failure of the human being to reach salvation, or as illness, and evil was not associated with guilt and punishment. This interpretation of the fall and its consequences need to be kept in mind as they are crucial for the debate concerning the image and likeness of God in human beings.

Another theological presupposition in Orthodox thinking is the participation of humans in the uncreated energies of God. The human being participates in the energies of God as a whole, with its soul and body. The veneration of relics, or the emphasis on the senses participating in the liturgy (music, icons, incense, flowers, myrrh, liturgical gestures), testify to the fact that God is known by the human being as a whole, not only the human intellect or soul. This is a point to be considered when profound impairment is discussed.

These are just a few examples of areas where Orthodox theology could make a contribution in the ongoing debate on disability. Disability poses a challenge to the Orthodox Church to actively engage in ecumenical dialogue, benefit from policies, services and structures of other churches that promote full inclusion of persons with disabilities, and contribute its own experience and resources in order to respond to questions relating to disability. Disability studies seem to be an unexplored area for Orthodox theology and it's relatively new for the ecumenical movement. Persons with disabilities need to be heard in churches and ecumenical organizations to set the tone for future work on disability.

Bibliography

World Report on Disability (Introduction, Chapters 1, 2 & 9) published by World Health Organization and the World Bank in 2011, http://whqlibdoc.who.int/publications/2011/9789240685215_eng.pdf

United Nations Convention on the Rights of Persons with Disabilities (CRPD), http://www.un.org/disabilities/default.asp?id=150

A Church of All and for All, http://www2.wcc-coe.org/ccdocuments2003.nsf/index/plen-1.1-en.html

Brian Brock and John Swinton (eds), *Disability in the Christian Tradition: A Reader*, (Grand Rapids/Cambridge: W. B. Eerdmans Publishing Co, 2012).

John Chryssavgis, *The Body of Christ: A Place of Welcome for People with Disabilities*, (Light & Life Publishing Company, 2002).

Nancy L. Eiseland, *The Disabled God: Toward a Liberatory Theology of Disability*, (Abingdon Press, 1994).

Fritson Arne and Kabue Samuel (eds), *Interpreting Disability, A Church of All and for All*, Risk Series, (Geneva: WCC Publications, 2004).

Henri J.M. Nouwen, *Adam: God's Beloved,* (Maryknoll, NY: Orbis Books, 2012).

David A. Pailin, *A Gentle Touch: From a theology of handicap to a theology of human being,* (London: SPCK, 1992).

Hans S. Reinders, *Receiving the Gift of Friendship: Profound Disability, Theological Anthropology, and Ethics*, (Grand Rapids/Cambridge: W.B. Eerdmans Publishing Company, 2008).

_____, *The future of the disabled in liberal society: an ethical analysis,* (South Bend, IN: University of Notre Dame Press, 2000).

_____, *The Paradox of Disability Responses to Jean Vanier and the L'Arce Communities from Theology and the Sciences*, (Grand Rapids/Cambridge: W. B. Eerdmans Publishing Company, 2010).

Amos Yong, *Theology and Down Syndrome: Reimagining Disability in Late Modernity*, (Texas: Baylor University Press, 2007).

(123) THE ORTHODOX CHURCHES AND THE GEOGRAPHICAL REDISTRIBUTION OF CHRISTIANITY[1]

Stavros Zoumboulakis

Not long ago, a religious atlas was published in France (*L'Atlas des religions*, [2007], pp. 196), a joint production of the periodical *La Vie* and the daily newspaper *Le Monde,* with the stated intention that it would be brought up to date and republished regularly. It includes two hundred maps and analytical numerical data on all the religions and confessions on the planet. As regards the objection that the measurement and plotting of religious faith are impossible, those responsible for the publication have dealt with this as follows: they do not measure faith, but religious affiliation, or more precisely, the declaration of religious allegiance (and, of course, many other measurable facets of religious life). We do not, then, learn about the faith of the Swedes, for example, or about its depth and intensity, but it is important that we know that more than 80% declare themselves to be Lutherans and that fewer than 5% of them go to church at least once a month. The ultimate goal of this *Atlas* is to record the geopolitical dimension of the religious phenomenon, a dimension which is of exceptional importance and fluidity today.

So there is much useful information which is provided by this *Atlas*, in particular how the various religions and confessions are distributed by country. We learn, for example, that Nigeria is, after America, the second most Protestant country on the planet (or third, if we take into account the Anglican United Kingdom, though Nigeria is still above Germany, the home of Protestantism); that there are more Christians than Buddhists in South Korea; that, in India, Buddhism represents a mere 1% of the overall population (in the twentieth century, Buddhism and Orthodox Christianity suffered the greatest setbacks as Communism either spread or was imposed in their countries); that, while in Asia generally, Christians are a minority (4%), in the Philippines in particular they account for 90% of the population; that Indonesia, the first Muslim nation in the world, Pakistan, India and Bangladesh make up half the Muslim population of the planet; that, in Africa, one in three people is a Muslim (there, Egypt and Nigeria are the first Muslim nations; in the case of Nigeria, 50% of the population are Muslim, who often clash with Christians); and finally, we learn how the trends amongst the Jews of Israel and those of America (where the Reform Jews are in a majority of 35%, that is 1,500,000, with more than two hundred female rabbis, compared to only four in Israel) are split. Anyone who thought that the largest Christian pilgrimage is that of Our Lady at Lourdes (6,000,000 pilgrims in 2006) will learn that it is far smaller than Our Lady of Guadeloupe, in Mexico (15,000,000), while the largest pilgrimage of any in the world is the Hindu *Kumbh Mela*, which attracts 24,000,000 pilgrims (the famous Mecca pilgrimage draws no more than 2,500,000). I could continue at length with this gleaning of very interesting or merely curious numerical data; my object, however, is not to demonstrate the utility of the *Atlas* in question, but rather, in the light of it, to discuss the position of Orthodox Christianity in today's world.

Christianity, then, is not doing at all badly in the world today. Christians of all confessions number two billion and, in 2050, this figure is expected to rise to three billion (as against 2.229 billion Muslims). Christianity is the only really global religion- Islam, the next largest, may number 4,000,000 believers in North America, but is entirely absent from Latin America.

A substantial change has occurred, however, in the geography of Christianity: the axis has moved from Europe and North America to Africa, Asia and Latin America. The uneasy question asked by many Christians

[1] The present article has been initially published under the same title in the leading Greek literary journal *Nea Hestia* 1806 (December 2007) and republished in Stavros Zoumboulakis, *Christians in the Public Sphere: Faith or Cultural Identity*, (Athens: Hestia, 2010), 107-117 [in Greek], reflecting the wider socio-political context and the demographic data of Christianity and the Orthodox Churches of that era (2007-2010).

a few decades ago as to whether Christianity would survive or die- *Le Christianisme va-t-il mourir?* was the title of a widely read book by Jean Delumeau in 1977- really only concerned European countries. In Europe, we are certainly experiencing the collapse of Christianity as an institution, as a dogmatic structure, as a system of values. The secularization of European societies, which has been very rapid in the last three or four decades, has not merely led to a tremendous drop in the number of Christians, but has demolished the centuries-old structure of Christian tradition and culture, a whole spiritual universe which cannot any longer be transmitted from the old to the young, from parents to children and which is now languishing in oblivion. Europe refuses even to mention its Christian roots in its constitutional charter.[2]

Christianity is, however, expanding elsewhere, it is alive and well in the Third World, in the South. Christianity is now no longer European or American, but African, Latin American and Asiatic. There are 300 million Christians in Africa (out of a total population of 800 million), 530 million in Latin America (Brazil is the first Catholic country in the world, with 153 million believers), and 67 million in the Philippines. The path to China has not yet opened, though there are there 15 million Catholics and at least as many Protestants.[3]

But apart from the shift in the geographical axis, another move has begun to become apparent in the confessional situation, away from Catholicism and towards neo-Protestantism. Even though the Catholic Church continues to dominate numerically and the traditional Protestant confessions are holding up well, the neo-Protestant confessions of the Evangelical, Pentecostal and Charismatic type are exhibiting an impressive dynamic: they certainly constitute, together with the Islamic movements, the most interesting religious phenomenon of our times. Without institutional ties, centred on a self-declared pastor, they set up communities everywhere at a rapid rate, and these communities are enthusiastic (intense bodily participation in the services), morally strict (precise observation of the commandments), fundamentalist (literal interpretation of the Bible), and with a zealous missionary outlook. In Brazil, for example, the bastion of Catholicism, 600,000 believers leave the Catholic Church every year, so that membership has dropped one-quarter in twenty-five years and has fallen to 70% of the total population, whereas the neo-Protestants already account for 18%. There are 14,000 Catholic priests in Brazil (that is, one for every 90,000 inhabitants), while the neo-Protestant pastors already number more than three times this. We might add, without further ado for fear of becoming long-winded, that this Christianity of the Third World, of the South, this "third Christianity", is clearly different from that of Europe: it is often syncretistic and definitely far-removed from its roots in Hellenism and Judaism which nourished the dogma and worship of European Christianity.

And what is Orthodox Christianity doing about all this? Where is it to be found? As the twentieth century drew to a close, Orthodox Christianity was granted an unexpected gift: the collapse of Communism gave it the opportunity to regain its historical heartlands (Russia and the Balkans) and to re-evangelize people there.

---

[2] Of exceptional interest from this point of view is the research on the Catholics in France published in *Le Monde des Religions* 21 (January-February 2007). 51% of the French population declare themselves to be Catholic (before 1975-1980 the percentage was 80%). But what kind of Catholic? It is only half of them, i.e. of that 51% of the French population, that believe in God! Again, it is only 18% of half of that 51% that believe in a personal God (the rest believe in a certain power, energy or spirit). Only 58% of French Catholics believe in the Resurrection of Christ; only 37% in the triunity of God; only 10% in the resurrection of the dead. In short, that research demonstrated in numbers what we already knew empirically: in Europe, the Christian faith is being de-institutionalized (i.e., Christians keep turning away from the Church as an institution), it has become a personal issue, has been subjected to relativism (Christianity constitutes one truth among others), has become selective (noone subscribes to the whole of Christian teaching; the faithful choose what suits them best and supplement their faith from other sources). We are dealing with a *religion à la carte*, as Jean-Louis Schlegel has so aptly put it.

[3] In the end of November 2007, an official delegation from the Vatican arrived in Beijing: a few days later, two newly-elected Chinese bishops, who belong to the official (known as the "patriotic") Catholic Church of China, were canonically recognized by the Vatican, since they had, in any case, been elected with its approval (next to the official, or "patriotic", Church, there is an unofficial, or "underground", one, which accounts exclusively to the Papal authority). These are signs, on the one hand, of the improvement in the relations between the two branches, the patriotic and the underground, of the Catholic Church of China since 2006; and, on the other, of a warming in relations between the Vatican and Beijing which brings closer the prospect of the restoration of full diplomatic ties, which were broken off in 1951.

Beyond this, nothing. The Orthodox are entirely absent from the rest of the world.[4] The reason is simple: there is, in essence, no Orthodox missionary activity. Those of us who read Πάντα τὰ ἔθνη, the quarterly of the Office of External Mission of *Apostolike Diakonia*, may be moved by the often heroic efforts made by a few, unaided Orthodox clergymen and lay people, but, unfortunately, the quantifiable final result is negligible and statistically insignificant. It is also true that, in recent years, we have developed an important theology of mission. This year [2007], two very good books have been published on the subject, one by Archbishop Anastasios (Yannoulatos) of Tirana and All Albania (Ἱεραποστολή. Στὰ ἴχνη τοῦ Χριστοῦ [Mission: In the Footsteps of Christ], *Apostolike Diakonia*, Athens, 2007); and the other by Petros Vasileiadis, Professor of New Testament Studies at the Theological School of the University of Thessaloniki (Ἑνότητα καὶ μαρτυρία. Ὀρθόδοξη Χριστιανικὴ μαρτυρία καὶ διαθρησκειακὸς διάλογος: Ἐγχειρίδιο Ἱεραποστολῆς [Unity and Witness. Orthodox Christian Witness and Inter-Religious Dialogue: A Manual of Mission], *Epikentro*, Thessaloniki, 2007). Agreed, we now have a theology of mission, but we do not have mission. We shall mention only one example- there will be no need for another- posed as a question requiring our answer. We have drawn it from the article "Orthodox Mission: Past, Present, and Future", by Archbishop Anastasios, published in 1989, which is included in his book mentioned above. On page 250, he writes: "Why is it that, while the Orthodox mission in Korea began at just about the same time as that of the Protestants, today [1989], there are 5.5 million Protestants and the Orthodox hardly number 2,000?" Indeed, according to the *Atlas* which provided the stimulus for this article, in 2007, the Orthodox continued to number about 2,000 and are not included in any statistical study, whereas there are some 20,000,000 Protestants now (40% of the total population of the country). I would add that there are 16,500 neo-Protestant Korean missionaries active in 173 countries and that 126 of these have lost their lives, between 1999 and today, in carrying out their missions.

The absence of Orthodox Christianity from the Third World is certainly attributable to historical reasons. The spread of Christianity there was initially linked to military or cultural expansion on the part of the West, aimed at the discovery of new territories or markets (especially in the sixteenth century, with the discovery of the New World, which took Spanish and Portuguese conquerors to South America, and in the nineteenth century, with the foundation of the colonial empires of France and England in particular). The expansion of the West automatically meant the spread of Christianity, too. Historical attribution, however, cannot be a comfortable alibi for the missionary torpidity of Orthodoxy today. Orthodox Christianity today does not have any mission, primarily because it has been crushed by national ideas and has dedicated itself to every kind of national struggle. National claims have absorbed all its energies and nothing has been left for the spread of the Gospel. Not only has the nationalistic ideology, which all the Orthodox Churches have espoused, brought them into conflict among themselves; it has also hindered any permanent and co-ordinated Orthodox missionary collaboration (of the sort which the Protestants have broadly achieved). Moreover, it has distorted the very evangelic nature of their missionary enterprise, wherever and however faintly this is attested, and has often turned that enterprise into little more than exporting nationalism.

Orthodox Christians have not been mission-conscious. They are willing to respond to any national call, even the most outrageous, but do not have ears to hear the command of the risen Christ: "Go therefore and make disciples of all nations, baptizing them in the name of the Father and of the Son and of the Holy Spirit, and teaching them to observe all that I have commanded you", perhaps because they do not have faith in His assurance: "And remember, I am with you always, to the end of the age" (Matt 28:19-20). We believe that the command to engage in missionary witness is relevant only to the history of the early Church, not to its present

---

[4] We should note here that the Christians of the Middle East, i.e. of the historic cradle of Christianity, where the Orthodox Patriarchates are located, are rapidly and violently disappearing amid general, world-wide indifference. On 16-17 November 2007, a conference concerning these Christians was held in Paris, in the presence of the French Foreign Minister, Bernard Kouchner. The President of the *Institut Européen en Sciences des Religions* and organizer of this event, Régis Debray, announced the formation of a watch-dog institution (observatoire) for the Christians of the (Middle) East, with the Franco-Lebanese academic Joseph Maïla as its chairman. Too late, we fear.

condition each time. We are more moved by the national anthem or the flag than by the Cross of Christ and His Gospel. Now we have to pay the price. What do I mean? Today, when Christianity is collapsing in Europe and is moving elsewhere, the shrinking of Orthodoxy to the geographical bounds of the European continent will, sooner or later (probably sooner than later, when the dynamic of re-evangelizing the former Communist countries is exhausted), result in a historic decay.

"Orthodox Christianity in the Modern World" is a common and popular subject for many ecclesiastical lectures, where words of theological fatuousness are often heard, such as that the modern world is thirsting for the message of salvation that only Orthodox Christianity preserves in its authentic, unaltered form and so on. In order to transmit a message, first and foremost you have to exist. Mission for Christians in general has always meant obeying Christ's commands ("as the Father sent me, so I send you" [John 20:21], or "you will be witnesses to me [...] to the ends of the earth" [Acts 1:8]); conforming to the missionality of the Church; witnessing to truth and love. But particularly for Orthodox Christianity today, given the way the new global Christian reality is being shaped, it is a *sine qua non* for its survival.

(translated by James Lillie)

Metropolitan Geevarghese Coorilos

Introduction

Much has been said about mission and inter-religious dialogue. Orthodox theology has also made significant contributions in this area. The co-existence of Orthodox churches alongside other faiths and secular ideologies historically has, in a way, necessitated inter-faith dialogues, both as an existential imperative as well as a mission inclination. From very early on, the missionary being of the Church had also been in dialogue with other faiths, especially Judaism and Hellenism. A major part of the Patristic age was thus characterized by profound theological encounters with the then religious and metaphysical world views. However, as George Martzelos observes, the earliest theological encounters of Orthodoxy with these faiths were of a refutational and apologetic nature.[1] With the subsequent conquest of the Byzantine world by the Arab and Ottoman empires, dialogue with Islam also became an existential necessity. In the Oriental Orthodox world, co-existence of Orthodox churches with religious traditions such has Hinduism, Buddhism and Jainism has been and continues to be, for the most part, a smooth affair. Therefore, it could be said that Orthodoxy has exhibited consistent commitment to inter-religious dialogue. The Primates of the Orthodox churches in their festal message during their first co-celebration in Bethlehem in 2000 underlined the importance of dialogue and their commitment to it when they said, "We look to other great religions, particularly the monotheistic ones of Judaism and Islam, and we are prepared to build up even further the presuppositions for dialogue with them, looking to achieve a peaceful co-existence of all peoples...The Orthodox Church condemns religious fanaticism wherever these phenomena may appear."[2]

The post-2011 global scenario, if anything, has once again reiterated the urgency of the need for greater cooperation among and co-existence of world religions. The recent vicious conflicts in Egypt, Syria and elsewhere also point to this critical challenge. The importance of dialogue in such contexts is highlighted in the following words of Archbishop Anastasios of Tirana and All Albania. "To abandon inter-religious dialogue is to give new impetus to the formation of ghettos, to ethnic or religious 'cleansing' and to the development of various new expressions of religious fanaticism that lead finally to another terrible 'dialogue'- a dialogue between bombs of terrorists and rockets of the powerful."[3]

"Dialogue or perish" seems to be the warning of the times that churches, Christians, and indeed all people of good will can ill afford to ignore. This essay is an attempt to offer some perspectives on mission and inter-religious dialogue from an Orthodox theological perspective.

Theo(Trinito)- centric understanding of Mission and Dialogue in Orthodoxy

Mission and Dialogue theologies have over the years adopted various approaches such as Christo-centrism, Ecclesio-centrism, and Theo-centrism. In my own view, Orthodoxy would find a natural affinity with a Theo-centric perspective vís-a-vís mission and dialogue theologies. Genuine mission ultimately belongs to God (*Missio Dei*) and genuine dialogue originates in God.

One of the fundamental tenets of Orthodox theology is its apophatic nature. This means that God is essentially ineffable and beyond full human comprehension. Human language is inadequate to describe the totality of the mystery of God. One could, at best, describe God only through negation. Indian philosophical systems

---

[1] See George Martzelos, "Orthodoxy and Interreligious Dialogue", www.apostoliki-diakonia.gr
[2] Archbishop Anastasios, *Mission in Christ's Way*, (Boston: Holy Cross Orthodox Press, 2010), 226.
[3] Anastasios (Yannoulatos), "Problems and Prospects of Interreligious Dialogue," in *Ecumenical Review* 52.3 (2000): 6-7.

call it "*neti, neti*", meaning "God is neither this nor that...." The underlying principle of apophatic theology is that God is beyond human categories and comprehension.[4] One of the implications of apophatic theology is that since God is beyond human intelligence, then none can make exclusive claims about the knowledge of God, let alone God's saving power. This is why San Antonio CWME Mission Conference would go only as far as it could and affirm that although we could not point to any other way except that of Jesus Christ, we could not set limits to God's saving power. Apophatic theology would prompt us to be humble and inclusive, both in essence and methodology, in our mission and dialogue endeavors. Mission, as it belongs primarily to God, cannot be an enterprise which is essentially driven by some feverish human motives, let alone by those of Christians or churches. All God's peoples can be partakers in God's mission. God, being beyond human reasoning, none can claim monopoly over the divine truth in encounters of inter-faith dialogues. Having said that, it must be added that although God remains inconceivable and ineffable, humanity can still participate in the divine energies, themselves manifested as theophanies. As George C. Papadametriou puts it,[5] the revealed glory of God, God's energies, penetrate the entire humanity and the whole creation, suggesting the universal appeal and availability of God's presence and gifts, including the gift of salvation.

The universality of the availability of the divine presence and grace is also linked to the concept of *imago Dei*. That all human beings carry the same image of God in them is the basis for universal parenthood of God and universal brother/sisterhood of all humanity. Orthodox theology holds that every human being by virtue of possessing the divine likeness in him/her has access to revelation of and salvation from God. As one of the thematic papers of Edinburgh 2010 Mission Conference, prepared by Orthodox theologians, extracts the missiological pertinence of "image of God", "A theology which recognizes the dignity of human beings as created by the one God cannot deny such dignity and respect to others...it will therefore want to honor their faith."[6]

Whilst God is conceived in an apophatic manner, the most profound expression of the divine in Orthodox theology is its Trinitarian conception of God. One of the most important advantages of a Trinitarian theology is that it can resolve the tension that is often felt between mission and dialogue. There is a general perception that the two cannot be held together. There are those who hold that inter-religious dialogue can only happen by compromising one's commitment to mission and evangelism, and that commitment to dialogue is incompatible with commitment to mission. There have been various approaches to deal with this conundrum. Exclusivism, fulfillment approach, inclusivism, and pluralism have been some of them, to name just a few. The tension is not completely resolved in several circles. For the Orthodox Church, this tension is perceived as a dialectical one and the task is to "live wisely in the middle of this tension with Christ's humility and attitude."[7] The Holy Trinity has the innate potential to resolve this seeming tension between mission and dialogue, as the Holy Trinity is concurrently a missionary and a dialogical community. Mission originates in the dialogue among the three persons of the Holy Trinity, itself the source and fountain of mission. The missionary God who sends the Son and the Holy Spirit also sends God's people for mission (Jn:20:21). God in the Holy Trinitarian community becomes both the sender and the one sent, and this process of sending and being sent is essentially a dialogical process (more precisely a trialogical process) that happens within the pluralistic community of the Holy Trinity. Dialogue, then, ought to be the ideal ethos of all mission. Trinitarian divine Truth is conceived as a plural category. It is multi-facetted as the three persons within the Trinitarian Godhead exist with individual identities and qualities. What characterizes the Trinitarian God is *perichoresis* or mutual indwelling. Sharing among one another is the distinct hallmark of the Holy Trinity. This would imply then that both mission and

[4] Apophatic theology is held in balance with Kataphatic theology in Orthodoxy which holds that God has made itself comprehensible through the revelation in and through the person of Jesus Christ.
[5] See George C. Papademetriou, "An Orthodox View of Non-Christian Religions" in www.goarch.org>Our Faith.
[6] See Theme 2 "Christian Mission among Other Faiths" in Daryl Balia and Kirsteen Kim (eds), *Witnessing to Christ Today* 11 (2010): 45.
[7] See Mihai Himcinschi, "Orthodox Insights for a Contemporary Inter-religious Dialogue," in *International Journal of Orthodox Theology* 4.1 (2013): 83-111.

inter-religious dialogue must be guided by and oriented towards mutual sharing of different understandings of God, spiritualities, and resources between and amongst various faith communities. The Trinitarian community of God is also known for it's sense of egalitarianism and non hierarchical order. This means that the three persons of the Trinity are coequal members of the divine family. Differently put, relationalism, not relativism is the bottom line and defining feature of the divine Trinity. This too has ramifications for inter-faith dialogue and mission as it negates the subject-object binaries and instead enables, as Petros Vassiliadis holds, us to understand "the other" in mission and dialogue as co-workers and co-walkers in our common pilgrimage towards discovering the divine Truth.[8] The Trinity is also governed by love which is at the heart of the Trinitarian Godhead. When we participate in the mission of the Triune God, we actually respond to the outpouring of the love of God which is offered as a free gift to the whole creation. This mission is in itself a process of sharing God's love- a dialogue of love.

Economy of the Holy Spirit: Towards a Trinitarian Pneumatology

"Christocentric universalism" has been, by and large, the overarching theological principle in much of mission and dialogue theology, particularly in their Protestant versions. As a result, the role of the Holy Spirit, Pneumatology has not received much attention in such theological discourses. Even when the Holy Spirit was engaged in some form, it was done from the perspective of "historical Pneumatology" which would understand the Holy Spirit as being the agent of Christ to fulfill the missionary task in which the person of the Holy Spirit is fully dependent on the person of Christ. However, there is another view of the Holy Spirit, the "eschatological Pneumatology" which affirms the independent individuality of the Holy Spirit. The Orthodox theology tends to follow the latter perception of Pneumatology, which is also highlighted in the new WCC Affirmation on Mission and Evangelism entitled "Together Towards Life: Mission and Evangelism in Changing Landscapes."[9] The eschatological pneumatology proclaims the Holy Spirit as the "source of Christ" and the Church as the eschatological coming together (synaxis) of the people of God in God's reign. One could recall here the 'Filioque' controversy in which the Orthodox Church held the position that adding the clause 'Filioque', meaning "and the Son" and therefore the notion of "double procession of the Holy Spirit" would effectively subordinate the role and identity of the Holy Spirit within the Holy Trinity. The social Trinity, thus, offers a collegial, as opposed to a pyramidal, vision of a community where particular identities are affirmed with integrity and freedom.[10] The accent on a Trinitarian Pneumatology in Orthodox theology helps her to avoid the reductionism of Christo-monism, the proclivity to equate God's self exclusively with the person of Christ, without reference to the totality of the Holy Trinity. A Trinitarian perspective would also resist the other extreme of reducing Christ to the historical Jesus of Nazareth. As Samartha observes,[11] an impoverished notion of "Jesuology" and a narrow "Christo-monism" are both temptations to be resisted. The Orthodox Christology and Pnuematology, understood from a Trinitarian viewpoint, overcome such risks. This, in no way, takes the centrality of Jesus Christ away from Christian faith, but places both Christ and the Holy Spirit clearly in the Trinitarian framework of Christian faith.

A pneumatological approach, understood within a Trinitarian perspective, can be a helpful paradigm for mission and dialogue theologies for our times. The "economy of the Holy Spirit" can liberate us from

---

[8] Quoted in Petros N. Toulis, "Orthodox Understanding of Religions: The Role of Contextual Theology" in www.academia. edu/...Orthodox_understanding_

[9] See Jooseop Keum (Ed), *Together Towards Life: Mission and Evangelism in Changing Landscapes With a Practical Guide*, (Geneva: WCC, 2013), para. 17.

[10] See George Mathew Nalunnakkal (presently Geevarghese Coorilos), "Come Holy Spirit, Heal and Reconcile, Called in Christ to be healing and reconciling communities" in *International Review of Mission* 94.372 (January 2005): 11.

[11] S. J. Samartha, "The Cross and the Rainbow:Christ in a Multi-Religious Context" in Somen Das (Ed), *Christian Faith and Multiform Culture in India*, (Bangalore: UTC, 1987), 37.

various reductionism, be it epistemological, metaphysical, post-modernist or any other type.[12] In Orthodox theology, the "economy of the Word/Christ" is held alongside the "economy of the Spirit" within the Trinitarian framework.[13] This would imply that God uses people (synergy) from all faiths and persuasions, not just Christians and churches, for the salvation of the world. It is the Spirit of Truth that leads us to the "whole truth" and the Spirit of God blows where she/it wills (Jn.3:8). The "unbound Spirit" cannot be domesticated and monopolized by any one or any one religion. We cannot control the pervasive wind of the Holy Spirit from blowing everywhere. To paraphrase the San Antonio position, we cannot set limits to the omniscient presence and functioning of God. The positive consequence for such a wider pneumatological perspective for mission and inter-faith encounters is that: "With the 'economy of the Spirit,' the narrow boundaries of the Church are widened, and the cultural (and religious) syndromes give their place to 'common witness' and a humble 'inter-faith dialogue.'"[14]

This is because the Holy Spirit operates in ways that are mysterious and unimaginable. (Lk 1:34-35; Jn.3:8; Acts 2:16-21). Since the Spirit blows everywhere, it also inspires human cultures and creativity. Therefore, it is incumbent upon us, as the WCC document *Together Towards Life* would infer: "to acknowledge, respect, and cooperate with life-giving wisdoms in every culture and context."[15] Or as Nifon Mihaita opines, "On the basis of the reciprocity that exists between "the economy of the Son" and "the economy of the Holy Spirit" who blows where she wills (Jn.3:8), one cannot exclude the other religions as points where the Holy Spirit acts upon."[16]

All this suggests that the Orthodox focus on "the economy of the Holy Spirit" provides us with an inclusive and open framework that would inspire mission in humility and dialogue with openness.

Unfortunately, much of the Western "imperial" projects of mission in the past often turned out to be detrimental to the local indigenous wisdom and spiritualities, in that the missionaries with a colonial mindset approached them with utter disdain, even to the extent of having demonized them. The Trinitarian economy the Holy Spirit offers a corrective to such negative and dismissive positions and provides us with an inclusive and liberative vision of mission and dialogue. As the Spirit works in mysterious ways, we are not able to fully comprehend the workings of the Spirit in other faiths and cultures. As the Spirit of God brings fullness of Life, the same Spirit of God can be encountered in other traditions and religions that affirm life in its fullness. The new WCC Mission Affirmation, therefore, would say with conviction, "We acknowledge that there is inherent value and wisdom in diverse life-giving spiritualities. Therefore, authentic mission makes the 'other' a partner in, not an "object" of mission."[17]

This brings home the point that it is fullness of Life -- life in the Holy Spirit -- Trinitarian Life, that is the goal and purpose of all mission and dialogue. The theological principle of Life then can bring mission and inter-faith dialogue together because mission essentially is to affirm Life and dialogue is about sharing this Life. The Holy Spirit is discernible in contexts where fullness of life is affirmed, where the oppressed are set free, where the broken communities find reconciliation and healing, and where integrity of creation is restored. It follows then that the mission of the Holy Spirit, "the economy of the Holy Spirit", cannot be confined to churches alone, but wherever people struggle for fullness of life, justice and human rights.

[12] Felix Wilfred talks about three kinds of reductionism vís-a-vís inter-religious dialogue. "Epistemological reductionism" tends to make dialogue among faiths as an issue of Truth and relativism. "Metaphysical reductionism" is about reconciling "one" with "many" conceptually. In "Postmodernist reductionism," though, "everything goes." See Felix Wilfred "Our Neighbors and Our Christian Mission" in Philip Wickeri (Ed), *The People of God among All God's Peoples: Frontiers in Christian Mission*, (London: CCA-CWM, 2000), 98.

[13] Even when "Logos Christology" is engaged in Orthodox theology, it tends to do it in an inclusive manner. For instance, Justin Martyr, the 2nd century apologist, delineates the concept of "spermatikos logos" in an inclusive manner. According to him, the seed of reason (Word) implanted in every human race makes God's revelation accessible to all.

[14] See Theme 2 "Mission among Other Faiths: An Orthodox Perspective" in Daryl Balia and Kirsteen Kim (eds), op.cit, 50.

[15] See *Together Towards Life*, op.cit, para. 27.

[16] See Nifon Mihaita, "Dialogue and Orthodox Mission Today", in www.onlinelibrary.Wiley.com/doi/10.1111/irom.12010/pdf

[17] See *Together Towards Life*, op.cit, para 93.

Towards a Mission of dialogue that affirms Life

One of the limitations of both mission and dialogue theologies has been the fact that much of it (this is more true of dialogue theology than missiology) has remained at the level of the intellect. There have been several instances where theological reflections in the arena of inter-faith dialogue tended to be pure academic exercises in the discipline of "comparative religion". To put it differently, theological articulations in the arena of inter-faith dialogue have been more 'heady' than 'hearty' exercises. As Stackhouse would argue, we should explore these concerns with the aid of *poiesis* rather than of *theoria*.[18] Klaus Klostermaier follows the way of the heart in his *Hinduism and Christianity in Vrindaban* (1969) where he maintains that both dialogue and mission should "manifest themselves in a meeting of hearts rather than of minds."[19]

Orthodox theology would sit comfortably with a theological position that would hold a balance between the head and the heart, theory and praxis, orthodoxy and orthopraxis. St. Maximus the Confessor said: "A theology without action is a theology of the Devil." "Liturgy after liturgy" or the living out of the faith is an integral aspect of Orthodoxy. This is expressed through certain ways of living, spirituality or *askesis,* often exemplified in monastic and ascetic kind of spiritualities and life styles. This can also be manifested in concrete actions for justice, human rights and so on. Mission and dialogue get applied in concrete life contexts of people of various faiths and no faiths. Here the values of God's reign, principles such as freedom, justice, human rights, dignity and love enter into dialogue and get witnessed to, by people of all religions, races, gender, classes and castes together. According to Archbishop Anastasios this type of mission and inter-faith dialogue are more relevant and conducive to the contemporary contexts as these "would not demand common agreements on faith aspects, but can be based on acceptance and respect for the religious freedom of others and their right to decide what their ultimate visions and goals are."[20]

The Bible also narrates stories of mission and dialogue that are oriented towards the head and the heart. Much of Pauline mission enterprise through dialogue were intellectually oriented. A classic example would be that of the Areopagus event in Acts 17: 16-34. To the Athenians, Paul said, "For as I walked around and looked carefully at the objects of your worship, I even found an altar with this inscription: *To an unknown God.* Now what you worship as something unknown I am going to proclaim to you". (Acts 17:23)

Athens was known for its religious pluralism and its galaxy of deities, the pantheon. Paul encountered the phenomenon of religious pluriformity through an intellectual discourse with the people of Athens. As Anastasios holds,[21] Paul here, after having dialogued with the Athenians, proceeds directly to witness and proclamation. He offered an alternative system to the Hellenistic wisdom by introducing Jesus Christ to them as the centre of creation and the *entelechy*, the goal and purpose of the created order. To the Athenians who followed a philosophical system that was essentially self contained and closed, Paul brought the message of the personal God in Christ. All along, Paul engaged metaphysical categories and systems to get them on board in mission and dialogue. As already indicated, this approach has dominated much of inter-religious dialogue in the ecumenical circles until recently. Jesus' own approach in dialogue was quite different in that he engaged more of life situations of ordinary people rather than philosophical concepts and postulates. He encountered individuals and communities of people at the level of their hearts, not so much at the academic level. His conversation with the Samaritan woman (Jn. 4) is a classic example of a dialogue of life. I would like to cite an illustration of a contemporary instance of dialogue of life in an inter-religious context.

The story of Basheer is narrated in a book authored by Dr. V. P. Gangadharan,[22] a leading oncologist in India, who is also known for his philanthropic activities. Basheer, a young Muslim, was being treated for

---

[18] Quoted in David J. Bosch, *Transforming Mission: Paradigm Shifts in Theology of Mission,* (Bangalore: Centre for Contemporary Christianity, 2006), 607.

[19] Ibid.

[20] Anastasios, *Ecumenical Review* 52.3: 6-7.

[21] Archbishop Anastasios, *Mission in Christ's Way,* op.cit, 229.

[22] V. P. Gangadharan, Jeevithamenna Maha Albhutham (Malayalam) (Life, a great Miracle), (Kottayam: DC Books, 2000),12-15.

leukemia. Being a jovial person, Basheer would ensure that the other patients in the hospital were kept happy. Even when he was in acute pain, he would have a smile on his face and make others smile as well. One day he went to the office of Dr. Gangadharan to seek permission to go out to attend the wedding of one of his close friends. Because this was in a distant place he wasn't sure if the doctor would let him travel that far, especially given the fact that he had just received a major doze of chemotherapy. The risk of infection was very high. Nevertheless, Dr. Gangadharan gave him permission to go under strict conditions. Upon his return from the wedding, Basheer went straight to the office of the doctor and said: "Doctor, there is something within me that tells me that my days are numbered and my hunch is that I will not survive beyond a few days. These few days that are left are going to be very special for me. So when I came back from the wedding, I brought you a gift. You know I love you like my brother and I cannot thank you enough for the love and care I received from you. Therefore, I wanted to give you this small token of my love and gratitude to you before I depart from this world." Then he opened the box that he was carrying and gave the gift to Dr. Gangadharan and told him: "Doctor, I would like you to keep this gift of mine in your showcase. Every time you happen to look at this gift, I want you to remember me and say a prayer for me". Basheer then asked the doctor to open the packet. To his pleasant surprise Dr. Gangadharan found a lovely picture of Lord Krishna. As he said good bye to the doctor with a warm embrace, he said: "Doctor, please know that this gift comes from the bottom of the heart of a devout Muslim who prays five times a day."

To me, this story is a poignant illustration of a genuine dialogue of life that took place at the heart level. This is quite unlike the Pauline witness and dialogue at the Areopagus. Here, Basheer, a devout Muslim is able to share the religiosity and sense of divinity of his friend, his neighbor. Basheer could have given something from his own religious tradition as a gift to the Hindu doctor. But he chose otherwise. It is when one is able to appreciate and even share the divine in other faiths that one's own spirituality and faith assumes greater maturity. This is an example of a lived out dialogue. Daily life experiences of ordinary people, especially of the marginalized, can provide us with more meaningful starting points than abstract notions of God for our witness and dialogue. In other words, it is at the interjections of lived out experiences of people of all faiths and no faith that one encounters religiosity and spirituality in their profound sense.

Participation in the struggles of people to affirm life in dignity is a genuine form of witness and inter-faith dialogue. This is often called *diapraxis,* bringing together dialogue and praxis (witness). Here "dialogue aims at joining hands, of developing relationships across the barriers of race, gender and cultural background and ... common action for the sake of society."[23] This is where the Orthodox notion of *synergy* comes in handy. God chooses to work through God's people (of all faiths and no faith). No one is excluded from God's choice for partnership in mission (*Missio Dei*) and dialogue of Life. Peter was given this inclusive vision in Acts 10 and he proclaimed the new vision with bold conviction when he said, "Truly I know that God shows no partiality, but in every nation anyone who fears Him and does what is just is acceptable to Him (Acts 10:34-35)."

This would suggest that it is one's commitment to the values of God's reign such as justice and peace (Fullness of Life), expressed in concrete manifestations of identification with the poor and the oppressed that ultimately matters to God. The Matthean narrative of the last judgment (Mt.25) also reinforces God's prefer-ence for a Life-centric mission and dialogue. Mission that affirms fullness of life and dialogue of life is not the sole prerogative of Christians or churches. On the other hand, common witness and inter-faith dialogue do not aim at the creation of a new "pan-religion" either. Instead, common endeavors in mission and dialogue are aimed at creating "communities of faithful from different religious traditions." Such an approach would consider "the other" as a partner in mission and dialogue, never as a target or object. "through participation with the faithful from other faiths, Christians synergetically assists in the realization of the work of the Holy Spirit for a new world reality-- a global communion of love."[24]

---

[23] Daryl Balia and Kirsteen Kim (eds), op.cit, 47.

[24] Ibid.

Conclusion

Alongside contextual compulsions such as imperial conquests and religious persecution, the innate inclusive theological perspective of Orthodoxy has also been instrumental in enhancing open dialogue and sensitive mission practices by Orthodox churches worldwide. Orthodox theology with its essential apophatic nature is bound to adopt honesty in mission and humility in inter-faith dialogue. A Theo-centric orientation, guided by a Trinitarian world view prompts Orthodox theology to go beyond reductionism of either "Jesuologies" or "Christo-monism". God is the common ground and mission belongs to God (*Missio Dei)* who is also the source and fountain of dialogue. The Orthodox theological accent on *Imago Dei* contributes towards a wider humanitarian perspective on mission and dialogue because the *Imago Dei* affirms that every human being by virtue of possessing God's image has access to divine grace and salvation. The distinct Orthodox emphasis on the "economy of the Spirit" held alongside the "economy of the Son", again applied within the overarching Trinitarian ambit, is a helpful parameter both in mission and inter-religious dialogue. The energies of the Spirit of God cannot be contained and confined to any one faith community as the Spirit blows where She/it wills (Jn. 3:8). The Holy Trinity, the centre of gravity of Orthodox theology and ecclesial life, is perhaps the most conducive framework for authentic mission and credible inter-faith dialogue and relations. *Missio Trinitatis*, the mission of the Holy Trinity is one that affirms Trinitarian Life, Life in it's fulness, Life defined by the values of justice, love and mutual sharing that characterize the Trinitarian community of God. The Holy Trinity also represents a community of dialogue, (trialogue to be more precise), where the members co-exist in a relationship of *perichoresis,* perpetual communication or mutual indwelling. One couldn't possibly think of a better framework other than Trinity for inter-faith encounters and common witness. Whilst it promotes missions that affirm and promote Fullness of Life, it also enhances dialogues that are grounded in integrity, equality and genuine partnership where "the other" is an equal partner and subject, not a target or object. Mission of affirming Life and a dialogue of Life, therefore, are the natural results of these Orthodox theological insights when they are contextually and authentically applied. When that happens, liturgy and "liturgy after liturgy" will embrace each other; orthodoxy and orthopraxis will join hands; and dialogue and dia(tria)praxis will find perfect synthesis.

(125) Reconciliation, Peace and Forgiveness, as a task for Orthodox Involvement in Ecumenism

Fr. Leonid Kishkovsky

In Orthodox assessments of involvement in ecumenism, the emphasis is often on the "problems" and "challenges" of ecumenism. Although a discussion of problems and challenges has its reasons and place, when ecumenism is "reduced" in this way the result is a deadly lack of joy. The Gospel of Christ is the gift of joy. When we seek to convey our faith in Christ, in Christ's truth and love, in a joyless manner we betray the Gospel.

Orthodox involvement in ecumenism is correctly understood as a response to the task of living alongside other Christians. The term ecumenism, indeed, is properly used to describe the quest for Christian unity. Today we cannot ignore our interaction with people of other faiths. How do we as Orthodox Christians adhere faithfully to the Orthodox tradition and teaching while building reconciliation, peace, and forgiveness?

The tasks of ecumenism and of interfaith relations are often perceived as an "external" challenge. The standard treatment of religion in the pluralist setting is a study "from the outside looking in." It is commonly suggested that religious communities must strive to observe human rights and civil society standards. In other terms, faith communities are expected to rise to what is presumed to be the high level of political of the political and international understanding of human rights, tolerance, and peace.

Yet the images and parables by which most people live are not civil society images and stories. The worldview of people of religious faith is informed by religious teachings, holy writings, and experiences of worship and spirituality. The Orthodox faith has rich spiritual and liturgical resources. The piety of Orthodox people often "reduces" and "spiritualizes" the Orthodox faith and practice, isolating faith and practice from life in society. When we "connect" the Orthodox liturgy and sacramental acts to the questions and difficulties we face in society we will discover the theological and practical guidance we need.

The Gospel lessons read on Sundays during the weeks before the beginning of Great Lent convey important teaching and guidance. No Orthodox Christian is completely unfamiliar with these texts. The images presented by the texts shape a Christian worldview and offer a moral framework for the appropriate ordering of relationships – with God and with all fellow human beings. The story of Zacchaeus the Tax Collector (Luke 19:1-10) speaks of a sinner's repentance and how repentance leads to making amends, to setting this right – to returning what has been fraudulently taken from others and sharing riches with the poor. The parable of the Publican and Pharisee (Luke 18: 9-14) commends the virtue of humility. The parable of the Prodigal Son (Luke 15:11-32) explores the rhythm of human life – a selfish departure from the Father's house, and prodigal and wasteful life in a foreign land, a return to the Father in repentance, culminating in the joyful reception by the Father. The parable of the Last Judgment (Matthew 25: 31-46) teaches that mercy and compassion towards those who suffer and are in need will be the criterion of God's judgment when the Lord comes in glory and the nations are summoned before him. And finally on the last Sunday before Great Lent, the Gospel lesson (Matthew 6:14-21) calls for mutual forgiveness, pointing out that God's forgiveness comes to those who forgive their brothers and sisters.

These Gospel lessons are all relevant to daily living as a moral vocation, giving insight and guidance for the relationship of the Christian with all human beings. The story of the Last Judgment is especially vivid and relevant, insistently offering a radical and universal commandment. Those who give food to the hungry and drink to the thirsty, who welcomed the stranger and clothed the naked and visited the sick and imprisoned – did this to the Son of Man himself. And those who did not minister to their neighbor in need have refused to minister to the Lord himself. The Son of Man who sits in the judgment seat does not inquire about religion or race or nationality. Whoever is in need is closely identified with the Son of Man. The commandment of mercy, compassion, and love is not confined to the household of faith. The household of faith is commanded to see the Lord in every human, and to minister to every human who is in need as if ministering to Christ himself.

Orthodox Christians, like other Christians, indeed like all human beings, are inclined and tempted to confine religious lessons and commandments to the comfortable circle of their own household of faith. Yet it is clear that the parable of the Last Judgment commands mercy towards all who suffer and enjoins ministry to the suffering neighbor. This means that the Orthodox Christian who heeds this Gospel prescription is under orders to minister to members of other Christian communities, and Jews, Muslims, Buddhists, Hindus, indeed every person of every religion and also every atheist and agnostic – when there is human need or human suffering.

Another Gospel lesson which is instructive in its radical teaching is the parable of the Good Samaritan (Luke 10:25-37). Answering a question about wht must be done to inherit eternal life, and who is the neighbor God commands us to love, Jesus tells the story of the Good Samaritan. The priest and the Levite pass by on the other side, averting their eyes when they encounter the wounded and robbed man on the road to Jericho. The Samaritan – an adherent of another religious community – is the one who takes care of the wounded man, binds up his wounds, arranges for lodging in an inn, pays the innkeeper what is owed and promises to pay any other expenses that may be incurred. The Jew to whom Jesus is speaking, a lawyer, is told that this Samaritan who showed mercy is the one to imitate, he is the one who exemplifies the love of neighbor commanded by God. It is interesting that Jesus is here going even further than saying that a faithful Israelite should show love of all human beings, including those of another religion. He offers the Samaritan – one whose religion is repugnant to the faithful Israelites – as the model of ethical behavior.

In the sacramental practice of the Orthodox Church it is instructive that this Gospel lesson is prescribed for the service of healing. The sacrament of healing, while analogous in some respects to extreme unction in some Western Christian traditions, has a very different place in the liturgy and spirituality of Orthodox Christianity. While it is possible to perform this sacrament for those who are near death, for the healing of soul and body, it is equally customary to offer the sacrament to those who are sick and suffering in prayer and hope of healing and recovery. In the prayers of the service of healing the themes of forgiveness and reconciliation are emphasized, and are seen as dimensions of healing. Thus, the Good Samaritan takes care of the wounded man, and in doing so embodies mutual forgiveness and reconciliation by erasing the dividing wall between Jews and Samaritans. In its deepest reality, healing is relevant to all of human life – the healing of the soul and body of the suffering person, the healing of relationships and the healing of communities.

The Gospel lessons prescribed for the services and sacraments of the Orthodox Church provide central reference points of meaning and teaching. The worship of the Orthodox Church also offers a treasure of teaching in the texts and hymns of services. Great Lent is certainly a time of personal reflection and serious inner spiritual effort. Yet it is also a time for the overcoming of selfishness in order to love and serve others. The texts of Great Lent are full of admonitions for the healing of relationships in human community.

> While fasting physically, brothers,
> Let us also fast spiritually.
> Let us loose every knot of iniquity.
> Let us tear up every unrighteous bond.
> Let us distribute bread to the hungry
> And welcome to our homes
> those who have no roof over their heads,
> So that we may receive great mercy from Christ our God.

> Come O faithful,
> Let us perform the works of God in the light:
> Let us walk honestly as in the day,

Part VII: Particular Themes and Issues for Orthodox Involvement in Ecumenism

Let us rid ourselves of unjust accusations against our neighbors
    So that we place no stumbling block in their way.
Let us put aside the pleasures of the flesh,
    So that we may increase the grace of our souls.
Let us give bread to those in need.
Let us draw near in repentance to Christ and say:
    O, our God! Have mercy on us.

Even in the midst of Holy Week, when the liturgical texts meditate on the last days of Christ's ministry, and on his death and burial, the theme of serving the "other" is woven into the liturgical tapestry.

Come, ye faithful, and let us serve the Master eagerly,
    For He gives riches to His servants.
Each of us according to the measure that we have received,
    Let us increase the talent of grace.
    Let one gain wisdom through good deeds;
    Let another celebrate the Liturgy with beauty;
    Let another share his faith by preaching to the uninstructed;
    Let another give his wealth to the poor.
So shall we increase what is entrusted to us,
    And as faithful stewards of His grace,
    We shall be counted worthy of the Master's joy.
Bestow this joy upon us, O Christ our God
    In Thy love for mankind.

The biblical teaching that the human person is created in the image and likeness of God is fundamental to the proper ordering of human relationships. *"Let us make man in our image, after our likeness....So God created man in his own image, in the image of God he created him, male and female he created them"* (Genesis 1:26–27). This biblical account unequivocally asserts that every human without exception bears the imprint of God. The implications this has for our theme is uncomplicated, yet profound. We are commanded to respect and honor the image of God in every human being. No matter what beliefs and convictions others hold, no matter how mistaken or even perverse I may consider their views to be – nevertheless they bear within them the image of God. Thus, my fellow human beings must not be abused or assaulted or treated violently. In their faces I see the very face of Christ. It is my religious duty to honor and protect the freedom and dignity of the "other" person. And though I feel also the duty to pray that Christ may draw this man or this woman to Himself, I am duty-bound not to coerce, not to manipulate, not to insult this image of God in any way.

The doctrine of the image and likeness of God affirms two essential realities. One reality is the uniqueness and and unique value of each person. The other reality is human community. If the image and likeness of God are at the heart of what it means to be human, then the unique integrity of every man and woman is fulfilled in community.

For Orthodox Christians, the story of the hospitality of Abraham and Sarah in the eighteenth chapter of Genesis offers the first glimpse or suggestion of God as Trinity.

The biblical narrative begins by announcing the appearance of the Lord to Abraham as he sits in his tent at the oak of Mamre in the heat of the day. Abraham and Sarah offer hospitality to three men, yet Abraham address the three in the singular as "my Lord." The great Russian iconographer, St. Andrei Rublev, left for us a profound iconographic meditation on the Holy Trinity by depicting three angels sitting at a table (suggesting a Eucharistic table), with the oak of Mamre hinted in the background. The image is one of three persons united in a community of harmony and love.

The Greek word for hospitality is *philoxenia* or love of the stranger. The opposite of *philoxenia* is *xenophobia* (fear or hatred of the stranger), and now a universally-recognized term describing hateful attitudes and actions towards aliens, foreigners, strangers.

The meaning of the person and the meaning of community are not in contradiction to one another. The doctrine of the image and likeness affirms the integrity and meaning of both.

In the light of the image and likeness of God, Christians are called to show respect and even reverence for every man and woman, every child and adult. The more difficult it is to see the image of God in distorted human lives, the more important it is to discern God's image in suffering human persons. Our vision of the image of God is not a weapon we are given to judge and condemn our neighbor. Our vision of the image of God is an invitation to hope and to healing. The image of God is Trinitarian, which means that the image of God in humanity opens each person to communion and community. Humanity is not composed of individuals who are closed in upon themselves. Humanity is composed of persons who are open to God and to one another. Just as the "content" of the life of the Trinity is love, so the "content" of the human person is love. Some of the Eastern Fathers of the Church spoke of a distinction between the image and likeness of God. They described the image as the gift of God to each human person and to humanity as a whole, a gift which can be defaced, but not lost or taken away. And they spoke of the likeness of God as the vocation and calling of the human person, as the goal of the spiritual life. In this teaching, the image and likeness of God is a dynamic reality, not a static concept.

St. Seraphim of Sarov, the great 19th century Russian Orthodox mystic, gives to us another dimension of joy in the recognition of Christ in the "other." St. Seraphim was a man of prayer and solitude. After living for years as a hermit, he returned to his monastic community and opened his doors to any who wanted to come to him. Many came, seeking healing in his counsel, his prayers, his blessing. Whether it was the season of the celebration of of the Resurrection of Christ or not, it was habit to greet all who came to him with the words "Christ is Risen, my joy!" For him, the "other" human being was not a burden, not an intrusion, not an imposition – but joy. In each person St. Seraphim recognized the presence of the Risen Christ. In his teaching he stressed that the goal of the Christian life is the acquisition of the Holy Spirit. This suggests it is by acquiring the Holy Spirit that we are empowered to recognize the Risen Christ in our neighbor.

Let us recall that an influential philosopher of the 20th century Jean-Paul Sartre asserted that "hell is other people." St. Seraphim of Sarov offers us the antidote to this assertion in his conviction and experience that "heaven is other people" through the Resurrection of Christ.

The Orthodox tradition has much to offer humanity in the common quest for reconciliation, peace, and forgiveness. The Orthodox task must not be reduced to a defensive stance, a policy of "protecting" Orthodoxy against heterodoxy. Such defensiveness is often expressed in hostility to others, and does not bring anyone to the Good News of Christ.

All of the above shows that the task of Orthodox involvement in ecumenism is not reducible to pragmatic collaboration with other Christian communities. Our task in today's world is not merely to co-exist peaceably with other Christians and members of other faith communities. We are entrusted with the holy task of joyful witness to Christ. The quest for Christian unity is an expression of this joyful witness. The commitment to recognize the face of Christ in every person is an expression of this joyful witness.

The following passage provides us a fitting conclusion to the present reflections.

From the very beginning Christianity has been the proclamation of joy, of the only possible joy on earth.... Without the proclamation of this joy Christianity is incomprehensible. It is only as joy that the Church was victorious in the world, and it lost the world when it lost the joy, when it ceased to be a credible witness to it. Of all accusations against Christians, the most terrible one was uttered by Nietzsche when he said that Christians had no joy.

Let us, therefore, forget for a while the technical discussions about the Church, its mission its methods. Not that these discussions are wrong or unnecessary – but they can be useful or meaningful only within a fundamental context, and that context is the "great joy" from which everything else in Christianity developed and acquired its meaning. "For behold, I bring you tidings of great joy" – thus begins the Gospel, and its end is: "And they worshipped him and returned to Jerusalem with great joy…" (Luke 2:10; 24:52). And we must recover the meaning of this great joy.

Father Alexander Schmemann, *For the Life of the World*

(126) Orthodox Social Theology
as a task for the Orthodox Engagement in Ecumenism[1]

Radu Preda

By way of introduction:
the demise of communism and the new post-secular paradigm

The demise of communism two decades ago, throughout most Eastern European countries, entailed, among other long-term results, the fact that religion had changed its quasi-clandestine status imposed by a political regime professing atheism, by proclaiming its own ideology as *Ersatzreligion*.[2] Thus the year 1989 marked a shift not only in the political history of the world, but equally in the religious history as well.[3] Leaving aside the on-going debate among sociologists of religion on the phenomenon of religious revival ("God's return"), especially following the attacks of 11 September 2001, the metaphor became reality in the Eastern European countries with a significant religious majority, such as Roman-Catholic Poland or Orthodox Romania.[4] In these countries, as well as others like Slovenia or Croatia, we witness a massive comeback of the Churches in public life, resulting in a highly dynamic post-communist religious culture.[5] It is also true that the legacy of communism in terms of religious identity is manifest, in the number of East Europeans declaring themselves to be non-religious, as it happens for instance in the Czech Republic or in the eastern Lands of the unified Germany.

---

[1] The article by Associate Professor Radu Preda which is re-published here with the necessary adjustments, was first published in V. Ionita (ed.), *The 20ᵗʰ Century and Early 21ˢᵗ Century. A Romanian Orthodox Perspective*, (Bucuresti: Editura Basilica a Patriarchiei Romane, 2011), 726-770 under the title: "Orthodox Social Theology. Prolegomena to an Eastern perspective on today's world."

[2] To understand the genesis and significance of the *secular religion* peculiar to totalitarianisms, all of them brought forth by the secularization process, see the 1938 seminal study of Eric Voegelin, *Die politischen Religionen*, 3., *mit einem neuen Nachwort versehene Auflage*, (München: Wilhelm Fink, 2007). For an updated interpretation of the relationship between political ideology and its tendency towards self-dogmatizing, by turning itself into a quasi-religious institution, see Emilio Gentile, *Le religioni della politica. Fra democrazie e totalitarismi*, (Bari/Roma: Laterza, 2007). On the *communist religion*, see the classic exegesis of Nicolai Berdiaev, Истоки и смысл русского коммунизма [The Origins and Significance of Russian Communism], (Paris: YMCA-Press, 1955). See also the recent analysis of Michail Ryklin, *Kommunismus als Religion. Die Intelektuellen und die Oktoberrevolution*, (Frankfurt am Main: Verlag der Weltreligionen, 2008).

[3] An overview on the impact of the year 1989 on the history of (European and non-European) Christianity, is provided by the volume published by Klaus KOSCHORKE (ed.), *Falling Walls. The Year 1989/90 as a Turning Point in the History of World Christianity/ Einstürzende Mauern. Das Jahr 1989/90 als Epochenjahr in der Geschichte des Weltchristentums* (Studien zur Außereuropäischen Christentumsgeschichte 15), Harrassowitz, Wiesbaden, 2009.

[4] See also the analysis of Radu PREDA, "*Revenirea lui Dumnezeu. Ambiguitățile unui diagnostic*" [God's return. The Ambiguities of a diagnose], *Studii Teologice* V, 1 (2009), p. 103-125. In the current pages you can find some observations from the study.

[5] On the religious landscape in post-communist Europe, see the sociological investigation carried out during 1997-2007, by Miklós Tomka, Paul M. Zulehner, *Religionen und Kirchen in Ost (Mittel) Europa. Entwicklungen seit der Wende. Aufbruch 2007, Tabellenband (mit den vergleichbaren Daten von AUFBRUCH 1997)*, f.e., (Wien, Budapest, 2008); Paul M. Zulehner, Miklós Tomka, Inna Naleova, *Religionen und Kirchen in Ost(Mittel) Europa. Entwicklungen seit der Wende*, (Ostfildern: Schwabenverlag, 2008). The first volume presents the data of the sociological survey, while the second provides their evaluation. Orthodoxy is discussed in the second volume, pp. 138-179. See also the recent sociological study, with results published by Gert Pickel, Olaf Müller (eds.), *Church and Religion in Contemporary Europe. Results from Empirical and Comparative Research* (Veröffentlichungen der Sektion Religionssoziologie der Deutschen Gesellschaft für Soziologie), (Wiesbade: VS-Verlag, 2009).

Broadly speaking, the fall of communism strengthened the European religious profile due to the return of the former communist communities to their original pattern after the estrangement from religion during the Cold War decades; thus cultural adherence anticipated the political one, and the ideas prevailed over, and were one step ahead of, interests. Since regained liberty also entails new responsibilities, Eastern European Churches and denominations acquired their new social role in an extremely complex context. The last two decades have clearly demonstrated that the pace at which mind-sets, thought categories, horizons of expectations, principles and values change is much slower than that of transitioning between forms of government, political statuses, or from a legal system based on false justice to one based on actual rights. At various points and intensities, all former communist countries endeavoured to harmonize forms with content, ideals with reality, calendar with history. Transition put the greatest possible strain on social structures, challenged every person's ability to adjust, vexed some (generally the elderly) and favoured others (especially the young), altered the value criteria radically, affected the self-perceptions of identity in Eastern Europe, released both creative and pernicious energies, constructed and demolished, stirred enthusiasm and disappointment alike. The scope of this phenomenon is demonstrated by its perpetuation after the symbolic dates of accession, in 2004 and 2007, of the ten Eastern-European states to the European Union. Just as the fall of political communist did not make the effects of communism (as a way of living and thinking) disappear overnight, neither did the EU accession put a definitive, complete end to transition.[6]

As for their own public responsibility, the Churches and denominations in post-communist Europe have undergone a paradoxical stage characterized, on the one hand, by the reassertion of their symbolic status as sources of tradition and collective identity, and on the other hand, by the necessity to adapt to political and social changes, in order to bring their distinctive contribution (more or less acknowledged as such) to post-totalitarian therapy. The pressure to *adapt* was at times just as intense as the pressure to *resist*.[7] Predictably, from such an uncomfortable position, the religious answer to the challenges of freedom has not always been coherent. Religion has either encouraged, explicitly or implicitly, the reference to the past as a unique solution for the crises of the present, which partly explains the re-emergence of all kinds of post-communist nationalisms which have a strong denominational aspect; or adhered to the new trends and fashions, mistaking imitation for renewal. The religious factor in Eastern Europe has been constantly in search of – usually unaware and unacknowledged – the contact points with the new historical epoch and with its political-juridical paradigm. The social involvement of some religious denominations proved to be more problematic than it seemed in the first months of freedom, which had been marked by a pseudo-spiritual enthusiasm. Legally, in various countries of Eastern Europe the generic relationship between Church and State went through a process of a partial and conditional restoration of the situation previous to the appearance of communism, more than half a century ago. Comparable to the political post-communist evolution, very little or even nothing was "restored", as the religious environment cannot return to a different historical time.[8] Systematically, the vision about the role and the place of the main

---

[6] A few words on this overused term. The investigation into the transition from a political regime to the next, for instance in the case of post-war (or post-reunification) Germany, or the Latin American countries has given birth to an academic discipline: *Transitology*. The situation after 1989/ 90 in Eastern European countries provided it with rich material for research. For an introduction to the matter, see Wolfgang Merkel, *Systemtransformation*, (Oplade: Leske + Budrich, 1999). See also the correlation between theory and case studies, in Petra Bendel, Aurel Croissant, Friedbert W. Rüb (Hg.), *Hybride Regime. Zur Konzeption und Empirie demokratischer Grauzonen*, (Opladen: Leske + Budrich, 2002). See also the article of Rudolf L. Tökés, "*Transitology*. Global Dreams and Post-Communist Realities," in: *Central Europe Review* 2.10 (2000); this text is available online at the address: www.ce_review.org100/10/tokes10.htl\ml, posted on 15 July 2009.
[7] See the investigation carried out by Detlef Pollack, Irena Borowik, Wolfgang Jagodzinski (Hg.), *Religiöser Wandel in den postkommunistischen Ländern Ost- und Mitteleuropas* (Religion in der Gesellschaft), (Würzburg: Ergon, 2001).
[8] About the new legal framework concerning religion in the post-communist era see the overview edited by W. Cole Durham Jr, Silvio Ferrari (eds.), *Law and Religion in Post-Communist Europe* (European Consortium of Church and State Research 1), (Leuven: Peeters, 2003). Such overviews with more than one author should be read attentively since some countries are represented by better or lesser renowned scholars, whose expertise might be questionable, as it was the case with the

denominations in post-communist societies, had to face the rigours imposed by the definite pluralism of the actual epoch, the stronger secular consciousness and generally the juridical background, which, in this area, is far more complex than five or six decades ago. Such hardship will not only be seen in countries where the population is mostly Orthodox or Catholic, but also in those which are "mixt" (Catholic and Protestant), like Hungary, and even more in those which are profoundly secularised, like Czech Republic. Furthermore, these substantial modifications, in vision regarding the relationship between religious denominations and state are characteristic not only to the East-European area, but also in time they will mark the entire continent.[9]

Despite the hesitations and uncertainty – accentuated by the aggressive secularism,[10] combined with the offensive of neo-atheism that aims to revive the older conflict between faith and science[11]– that characterize the period of transition, one thing is certain for the Churches and for the religions from the post-communist countries, and not only: they have regained the relevance of their social involvement. This extremely valuable acquisition does only confirm – even if indirectly and with the above-mentioned obstacles – the new post-secular paradigm, regarding the relationship between the political power and the religious authority of the early 21st century.[12] Briefly stated, leaving aside the triumphal tonality of the presumed 'victory' of religion over secularisation, and mentioning that *secularity*, as a value obtained in spite of the excesses of *secularism*, is an advantage that our society should not give up, we must say that the post-secular matter must be, in turn, included in the wider dynamic of the philosophical (and theological) critique to which the project of modernity and the counter-offer of post-modernity have been subjected to during the past two decades. Therefore, after the acknowledgement of the immense failure of the modern faith in reason and after the failure of post-modern relativism, which was incapable of providing solutions for the integration of the otherness within a coherent social project,[13] the post-secular paradigm assumes the mission of a substantial correctness by giving up all the

chapter about Romania in the volume mentioned above. The analysis of the religious life and the public perception regarding religion is one of the vulnerable research areas, since the researcher needs not only precise knowledge, but also an ethical standard which can help him against a the tendency to interpret the events in biased way.

[9] For a short presentation of the relationship between Church and State in Europe see: Silvio Ferrari, "The transformation of the European religious landscape. A legal perspective," which was delivered at the International Congress on Justice and Human Values in Europe, Karlsruhe, 2007. The text can be found at: werturteile.de/customize/pdf/Ferrari.pdf, accessed 10 April 2009. Analyses of the situation in Romania, before the actual legal framework was completed, can be found in two collective volumes: Ioan-Vasile Leb, Radu Preda (eds.), *Cultele şi statul în România. Colocviul internaţional desfăşurat la Cluj-Napoca în zilele de 10-11 mai 2002. Acta* [Religious denominations and State in Romania. International Colloquium in Cluj-Napoca 10-11 May 2002. Acta], (Cluj-Napoca: Renaşterea, 2003); Adrian Lemeni, Florin Frunză, Viorel Dima (eds.), *Libertatea religioasă în context românesc şi european, Simpozion internaţional, Bucureşti, 12-13 septembrie 2005. Acta* [Religious Liberty in Romanian and European Context, International Symposium, Bucharest, 12-13 September 2005. Acta], (Bucharest: Bizantină, 2005).

[10] See here the diagnosis given by one of the most lucid analysts of contemporary European secularism: Marcello Pera, *Perché dobbiamo dirci cristiani. Il liberalismo, l'Europa, l'etica. Con una lettera di Benedetto XVI*, (Milano: Mondadori, 2008).

[11] See here one of the answers to the current atheism, which claims to be scientific, just like the one that dominated the early period of modernity did: Richard Schröder, *Abschaffung der Religion? Wissenschaftlicher Fanatismus und die Folgen*, (Freiburg: Herder, 2008).

[12] The term 'post-secular' was semantically marked during the conference from the autumn of 2001, held immediately after 9/11 by the popular German social philosopher Jürgen HABERMAS, "Glauben und Wissen. Friedenspreisrede," in: Jürgen Habermas, *Zeitdiagnosen. Zwölf Essays 1980-2001*, (Frankfurt am Main: Suhrkamp, 2003), 249-262. See the development of the theme in some other gathered texts: Jürgen Habermas , *Zwischen Naturalismus und Religion. Philosophische Aufsätze*, (Frankfurt am Main: Suhrkamp, 2005). A theologically lucid and succinct analysis of the new paradigm: Hans-Joachim Höhn, *Postsäkular. Gesellschaft im Umbruch – Religion im Wandel*, (Paderborn: Schöningh, 2007). Also see José Casanova, *Public Religions in the Modern World*, (Chicago: The University of Chicago Press, 1994). See here the religious and inter-religious evaluations by Peter L. Berger (ed.), *The Desecularization of the World. Resurgent Religion and World Politics*, (Washington, D.C./Grand Rapids, MI: Ethics and Public Policy Center and Wm. B. Erdmans Publishing Co., 1999).

[13] For a review of the current challenges implied by the increasing and poignant plurality of identities in Europe, see the volume edited by Antonela Capelle-Pogăcean, Patrick Michel, Enzo Pace (sous la direction de), *Religion(s) et identité(s)*

previous excesses and simplifications. If secularisation, a characteristic of modernity, was a project of forced modernisation of the world's data of thought, the post-secular approach was rather a diagnosis or an observation. Therefore, we can say that the revival of the discussion concerning the place and role of religion within the public space is less (or not at all) a result of its great comeback, and more the direct effect of an inventory made after almost three centuries following the debut of the paradigm of modernity and the acknowledgement of the fact that without a real ethical-moral basis – not that of consumerism – a pluralist society is not capable of dealing with its extended crises or of responding to the current challenges.[14]

In order to prevent the voluntary or involuntary misunderstandings, we must note the fact that the post-secular paradigm does not at all represent an offensive towards the principle of separation between the political and religious spheres or between the profane power and the religious authority, principle which is healthy, even from a theological point of view. The paradigm is a nuanced interpretation of this principle, done by rejecting the hypostasis of the aggressive and irrational laicism.[15] In concrete terms, the post-secular paradigm confirms the "Böckenförde paradox", which has been intensely commented upon in the specialized literature for almost half a century. We are dealing with a statement of the brilliant German jurist who, analysing the bases of the modern and secular state, comes to observe a fact that is simple, but amazing, and important because of its consequences: "the liberal and secularised state lives on the basis of some conditions that even itself cannot guarantee."[16]

Böckenförde made this statement in 1964, in the context of the on-going dispute at that time between Blumenberg and Löwith, concerning the meanings of secularisation; this statement set the road towards overcoming the dilemma of secularisation through distinction versus secularisation through elimination, or of secularisation as emancipation (Blumenberg) and the one that views the same phenomenon as an instrument of usurping religion (Löwith). Moreover, the analysis of the mentioned jurist reformulates the fundamental problem concerning the ethos that guarantees the functional homogeneity of a society, from the perspective of the state itself. In this interpretation, the modern state must accept the lack of neutrality of some wide groups and structures of society which, together, guarantee, through their values that have practical consequences the conditions of existence of the state itself, even if the state's role is that of remaining secular and neutral. The "Böckenförde paradox" takes an opposing stance towards the absolutist variant of the modern state (including the communist one) and against its tendency to monopolise the public space and manipulate the social consciousness on the one hand, and, on the other hand, it encourages those citizens who hold religious beliefs which are compatible with the basic data of society to participate in the enrichment of the moral and ethical resources of the public space by practicing religion. Thus, an active partnership between the state and the religious denominations (meant to exemplify the post-secular paradigm) does not represent the transgression of the basic principles of modernity; it represents their application in a constructive manner, which is useful to the general social corpus; this means

---

en Europe. L'épreuve du pluriel, (Paris: Presses de la Fondation Nationale des Sciences Politiques, 2008).

[14] Concerning the process of secularisation, see two remarkable syntheses: René Rémond, *Religion et société en Europe aux XIème et XXème siècles. Essai sur la sécularisation*, (Paris: Seuil, 1996); Charles Taylor, *A Secular Age*, (Cambridge: The Belknap Press of Harvard University Press, 2007).

[15] Concerning the metamorphoses of laicism, especially in its French variant, see Jean-Paul Willaime, *Le retour du religieux dans la sphère publique. Vers une laïcité de reconnaissance et de dialogue*, (Lyon: Olivétan, 2008).

[16] For the terminological specification, the quote in original: "Der freiheitliche, säkularisierte Staat lebt von Voraussetzungen, die er selbst nicht garantieren kann." Further see the context of the sentence: "Das ist das große Wagnis, das er, um der Freiheit willen, eingegangen ist. Als freiheitlicher Staat kann er einerseits nur bestehen, wenn sich die Freiheit, die er seinen Bürgern gewährt, von innen her, aus der moralischen Substanz des einzelnen und der Homogenität der Gesellschaft, reguliert. Andererseits kann er diese inneren Regulierungskräfte nicht von sich aus, das heißt mit den Mitteln des Rechtszwanges und autoritativen Gebots, zu garantieren suchen, ohne seine Freiheitlichkeit aufzugeben." Ernst-Wolfgang Böckenförde, *Recht, Staat, Freiheit. Studien zur Rechtsphilosophie, Staatstheorie und Verfassungsgeschichte*, (Frankfurt am Main: Suhrkamp, 1991), 111; Conference from 1964 – title: "Die Entstehung des Staates als Vorgang der Säkularisation" – recently re-brought to discussion: Ernst-Wolfgang Böckenförde, *Kirche und christlicher Glaube in den Herausforderungen der Zeit. Beiträge zur politisch-theologischen Verfassungsgeschichte 1957-2002* (Wissenschaftliche Paperbacks 25), 2. erweiterte Auflage, fortgeführt bis 2006, (Berlin: LIT, 2007), 213-230.

that it aims towards the establishment of the common good and not *against* religion, but *together* with it.[17] We must admit that this is a significant step towards normalising a relationship that was caused by modernity founding atheism and, in the case of post-totalitarian societies, it is a call to revive the social dialogue, with all the complexity and variety of its actors, *y compris* the Church (generically speaking). Moreover, if we were to talk about "God's return" in the early 20th century, this aspect of the revived dialogue would be the most serious indication and at the same time, the one that mostly provides hope.

The Church between the World and the Kingdom of God.
The Constitutive Social Dimension of Orthodox Thought

What has been shortly characterised above represents the wide context in which the Orthodox Church of Eastern Europe has been consolidating its public presence, getting involved socially and trying to maintain that difficult equilibrium between the (unofficial) status of power and its part of the civil society for the last two decades. After 1989, Orthodoxy has been facing insistent questionings concerning the manner in which it perceives the social phenomena, the crisis situations, or the personal and communitarian diseases, which are quite common within the societies with an Orthodox majority. We must not forget that one of the accusations constantly brought against Orthodoxy is its presumed lack of social involvement, or the tendency towards contemplative refuge and isolation from the rest of the world. The choice for Christ the God seems to undermine the one for Christ the Human Being. The Orthodox Church is viewed as being indifferent to the immediate needs of the community and, at the same time, as being ready to symbolically serve the state, especially the authoritarian one.[18] In fact, the authority of the post-communist state and the credibility of the political class are more than fragile, and the risks of a slip continue to latently exist within a social corpus that is shaken by the rhythm and the magnitude of the never before seen changes, which are, in turn, amplified by the international context. This, in turn, is marked by the instability resulted from a phenomenon of globalisation with a huge social toll; the question of whether and how the main symbolic and identifying depositary, which enjoys the trust of the majority of population, understands to get involved in the effort of articulating a project of society is more than just a mere challenge and goes beyond the level of Huntington's clichés about the "Orthodox cultural circle/ space", which is hard to distinguish from the Muslim one.[19]

Beyond the preconceived ideas, it is clear that the Eastern European Orthodoxy, which has meanwhile become the most consistent part of Orthodoxy worldwide, answers these questions and challenges endowed with resources that differ from those of the Western religions. As we know, the main difference resides in the fact that Orthodox theology has not taken the same road of modernity, it has not been systematically faced with the challenges of Enlightenment, it has not been forced to prove the pertinence of its discourse in comparison to that of the post-scholastic philosophy and that of the natural sciences, it has not been put in a situation in which it needed to impose itself in an inter-confessional and political competition like the one between Catholicism and Protestantism and it has not had the chance to formulate a complete vision on the separation between

---

[17] See a more complete analysis: Radu Preda, "Parteneriatul social dintre stat şi cultele religioase. Marginalii la un proiect actual de lege" [Social Partnership between State and Religious denominations. Annexes to an actual Law Project], in: *Tabor* 5 (2009): 19-33.

[18] On the Western stereotypes concerning the presumed incapacity of Orthodoxy to positively model the social structures in which it holds the majority, see, as an example, the analysis carried out by the theoretician of social and market economy, Alfred Müller-Armack, *Religion und Wirtschaft. Geistesgeschichtliche Hintergründe unserer europäischen Lebensform*, (Stuttgart: Kohlhammer, 1959). For an up-to-date diagnosis, this time form a more nuanced theological perspective, see Basilio Petrá, *Tra cielo e terra. Introduzione alla teologia morale ortodossa contemporanea*, (Bologna: Dehoniane, 1991).

[19] The theory of the existence of a line separating the Occidental civilised, Catholic and Protestant societies from the retarded Orthodox one has been circulating for centuries. The revival of this theory is only one of the several questionable aspects of the analysis carried out by Samuel Huntington, *The Clash of Civilizations and the Remaking of World Order*, (New York: Simon & Schuster, 1996).

Part VII: Particular Themes and Issues for Orthodox Involvement in Ecumenism

the Church and the state. If we are to summarise the main points of its evolution, we can say that the modern experience of Orthodoxy is different from the one of the European West. On the one hand, it is different due to the simple fact that its history had been marked by abuses, from the Tsarist authority to the communist one, going through the Ottoman domination or through the Habsburg control and, on the other hand, it is different due to the absence of periods characterised by reflective critique and self-critique. Put simply, ever since the fall of Constantinople, the local Orthodoxies did not even have one century of self-diagnosis and they did not get the historical respite needed in order to establish themselves as independent structures in relationship to the profane power that they had either supported – this applies especially to the fight for national survival – or had been persecuted by, especially during the communist decades, but also during the precedent decades of ethnical and political marginalisation. Such is the case of Hungary, where religious tolerance was possible only among equals, or Ukraine, country which was subjected to a process of forced Westernisation. Of course, these points of intersection of the cultural and political historiography are not just convenient justifications; they facilitate a better understanding of the complexity of an intra-European dialogue, which is too often simplified and reduced to an East-West (or Orient-Occident) opposition, to the Protestant-Catholic cultural circle versus the Orthodox one, to a freedom-dictatorship dichotomy, to civilisation versus barbarism, or to superiority versus inferiority. Without being "stunted", Orthodoxy simply comes into dialogue with modernity holding another type of perception, possessing other sensitivities, having a different historical memory, and, consequently, having a different kind of expectations. This explains why, before some consensual results, the dialogue between Orthodoxy and modernity – carried out even on an inter-confessional level – gives birth, at the time being, to a series of communicational misunderstandings. Paradoxically, these misunderstandings, if regarded without any ideological implications and without a rather widespread superficiality, can represent an enrichment of the discourse of Western modernity itself, but also of the manner of relating the Orthodox thought to history.[20]

In order to get a clear idea of the problem concerning the way in which Orthodoxy perceives its own social dimension in modernity and in the current post-secular horizon, we must go back to its ecclesiological bases and question them, especially from the perspective of the process known during the recent centuries.[21] So is the theological tradition of the Eastern Church "prone" to historical escapism? Does the spiritual ideal of the God-like becoming of man (gr. θέωσις) lie in contradiction with social involvement? Does the mystical *vision* (gr. θεωρία) exclude the social vision? Is contemplation the opposite of engagement? Within the limited space of these pages, we can provide an answer to these questions, basing ourselves exactly on the Biblical data that Orthodoxy applies in its internal life and in its relationship to the world. Well, the biblical discourse possesses an often disregarded salutary ambivalence, which makes both *social involvement* and *heavenly involvement* possible at the same time, and solves from the start the tension between the two, which is inevitable for the limited nature of rational thought. Therefore, it is clearly and repeatedly specified that His Kingdom is not identical and does not overlap this world (cf. John 18:36), fact which will disappoint those who hoped for an exclusively or, primarily, political Messiah. Christ indicates just as clearly, in the Sermon on the Mount (cf. Matthew 5), the virtues needed in order to obtain the spiritual citizenship, all of which have direct social implications: poverty in spirit, with the meaning provided by the patristic exegesis, that is to say the absence of pride, or, in today's language, the capacity to communicate directly, to take your interlocutor seriously and to exit the boundaries of the ego;

---

[20] For a recent and synthetic analysis of the themes of dialogue between Orthodoxy and modernity, with everything implied by this ample hermeneutic process, see, for example, Παντελής Καλαϊτζιδης, *Ορθοδοξία καὶ Νεωτερικότητα. Προλεγόμενα* [Orthodoxy and Modernity. An Introduction], (Athens: Ἰνδικτος, 2007). Also see the collective volume with the same title, in fact the *acta* of a theological symposium held at the Volos Academy for Theological Studies, edited by Παντελής Καλαϊτζιδης, Νίκος Ντοντος (eds.), *Ορθοδοξία καὶ Νεωτερικότητα*, (Athens: Ἰνδικτος, 2007).

[21] As a starting point, see the well-known text by Georges Florovsky, "The Social Problem in the Eastern Orthodox Church," in Georges Florovsky, *Christianity and Culture*, Collected Works, vol. 2, (Belmont, 1972), 131-142. Also see John Meyendorff, "The Christian Gospel and Social Responsibility. The Eastern Orthodox Tradition in History," in F. Forrester Church, Timothy George (eds.), *Continuity and Discontinuity in Church History* (Studies in the History of Christian Thought 19), (Leiden: Brill, 1979), 118-130.

the assuming of hardships in life, including by means of sadness and tears, as concrete forms of empathy with the fallen creation, which means affective and effective solidarity with all those who are in critical situations; kindness as a foundation for communion; the thirst and hunger for righteousness – thus we can see that poverty in spirit and kindness are not synonymous to fatalism or resignation and that there is an ethical imperative in any spiritual attitude; mercy in all the most varied forms in which it may manifest itself, from material to spiritual aid – this also implies that a kind word, uttered at the right moment, is an act of mercy; cleanliness of heart or honesty, which further turns the social work of Christianity into a non-ideological and disinterested fact; the irenic vocation, which shows that the pacifist mandate of the Church is not an invention of the "fight for peace" from the communist period; the eschatological desire for the fulfilment of complete justice only beyond the horizon of history, which takes the spiritual desire for justice out of the limited frames of legalism and prevents the nourishment of the illusion of achieving social equity through forceful methods; optimism in the face of all calumnies and persecutions – this attitude is far from encouraging resignation and shows that all evil in the world, no matter how heavy it may be, is limited and this further contradicts the tendency shown by many of our contemporaries to render evil as an absolute presence and thus to view the imminent conditions of the Apocalypse fulfilled. Those deeds which, according to Christ, are gestures towards Him, done however by assisting the hungry, the thirsty, the strangers, those who need clothes, the sick and those who are in prison (cf. Matthew 25:34-46) are deeds of social and anthropological nature. All these deeds, being explicitly centred on man, give the measure of faith which has God in its centre. In other words, in perfect symmetry to His own incarnation, but in an opposite direction – from the created to the Creator – the beginning of Redemption *in beyond* is done *here*; one can get to God only through people. God's philanthropy is in a fundamental disagreement with the misanthropy or egoism of those who want to earn Redemption by themselves.

The fundamental dialectic of being in the world, but *not belonging to the world* and of doing the deeds of faith in order to gain the Kingdom, but only through concrete involvement, transforms the commandment of love from a theoretical principle into a direct one; this is a departure point in the proximity of God, through and with those created by Him – humans and nature alike. After all, this is the most direct manner of concretising that *imitatio Christi* shared equally by both Christian hemispheres: just like Christ has taken a human face and assumed everything specific to humanity, except for sin, the human being is called to assume his own condition – primarily the limitations of sin – and to transfigure it in and through divine grace. In other words, the vocation of man's deification does not imply the abandonment of the concrete environment in which he resides. On the contrary, the Christological consistency of Incarnation renders the authentic spiritual road *above* or *near* history impossible. Only *through* history, in the same way as the Resurrection is possible only *through* death, can one reach the horizon that lies beyond it. This is the source of the deeply inauthentic character of all sectarian movements and tendencies which, along the centuries, have had the ambition to redeem themselves through a complete independence from the world, as if the latter were of no relevance in the work of God's love towards His creation.[22] In other words, spiritual maturity is verifiable, above all, according to the manner in which we relate ourselves to our historic and human frame and to the religious and civil community to which we belong. Highly personal, redemption is, at the same time, the reward for communion. The fact that the entire Orthodox theology underlines the defining communitarian character of the Church, expressed visibly in the religious services, and especially in the Divine Liturgy,[23] is not at all haphazard. The development of

---

[22] An example in this sense is represented by the eschatological uncertainty of some of the Christians belonging to the first generations, which periodically reoccurs even today. As an example, see the historical presentation of Peter Brown, *The Body and Society. Men, Women and Sexual Renunciation in Early Christianity*, (New York: Columbia University Press, 1988).
[23] See here the Liturgical-ecclesiological commentary of Dumitru Stăniloae, *Spiritualitate și comuniune în liturghia ortodoxă* [Spirituality and Communion in Orthodox Liturgy], (Craiova: Mitropolia Olteniei, 1986). Father Stăniloae underlines, throughout his works, the intimate relationship between celebration and communion or between the interpersonal dialogue between man and God and the personal relationships between human beings: "The fact that the Liturgy is experienced by the believers together, as an ascension or as a movement forward in the ambiance of the communion of the Trinity makes it the most effective way of establishment, maintenance and strengthening of the community of people as an anticipation of the

one's status as a person and the reaching of the spiritual maturity[24] depend, in a decisive manner, on the way in which one lives in communion. Even the askesis, or solitude, is impossible to understand without the constant prayer done with and for the people. After all, only together with the other persons can we reflect in our life the triple communion of the Father, Son and the Holy Spirit.

Without insisting upon some common points, we must remember the essential fact that, in a Biblical-patristic interpretation, the spiritual vocation belonging to the Orthodox tradition cannot justify the precise ignorance towards the environment in which the Incarnation, the Death and the Resurrection of Christ have historically taken place and in which they have always taken place, from an Eucharistic point of view, as well as from one related to the anamnesis. This concomitant placement of the Christian both in the world and on the path towards the Kingdom of God, illustrated by the creative tension between *already* but *not yet,* or by the definition of the Church as an antechamber or as a pre-tasting of the Kingdom, is best expressed in the *Epistle to Diognetus,* where the Christians belonging to late Ancient society are considered to be, for their world, the same thing that 'the soul is for the body'[25]. If s crisis of identity schizophrenia is to be avoided, the theme of the two citizenships – spiritual and historical – can only be formulated in complementary terms, which makes it possible for the anthropological coordinates to become sublime through deification; this also makes the social involvement for the sake of the desire for peace and for the sake of the thirst for justice (which are, in turn, reflections of the divine peace and justice[26]) possible. The status of the Christian community of Israel (cf. Romans 3:1) does not concretise itself as a ghetto mentality, but it covers as many ways of participating in humanity as there exist. For this reason, we can say that nothing that is human is unknown or indifferent to the Church. The chosen part of the creation – or the unleavened batch (cf. 1 Corinthians 5:7-8) – the Christians prove their character not by isolating themselves from the world, but by assuming the world. Thus, the sacredness of Christ's life is inseparable from the testimony of the Christians in front of their contemporaries. Moreover, the involvement of Christians in worldly matters is the essential condition needed in order to bring the profound reasons put by the Creator in the most intimate strata of His creation to the surface of the consciousness, which has been alienated by sin. This capacity to see the divine reason in worldly matters – as we prominently find in the apologetic discourse of St. Justin the Martyr and Philosopher and later on in that of Origen or St. Maximus the Confessor, culminating with the teachings of St. Gregory Palamas on the increase energies – implies a dynamic theology of history, orientated towards the eschatological horizon, just as much as it is focussed upon the present moment, understood as the chance to achieve salvation and not as material captivity or Gnostic punishment for the fall from the pure spirit.[27]

Kingdom of God. The believers who, together, in communion go to the same Church every Sunday for the Divine Liturgy, feel increasingly integrated within the God of Triple love, thus increasing the communion between them as well" (9-10).

[24] Concerning the relationship between communion and person in the Orthodox thought, see John D. Zizioulas, *Being as Communion. Studies in Personhood and the Church,* (Crestwood, NY: St Vladimir's Seminary Press, 1997).

[25] *Epistle to Diognetus 6, 1:* "ὅπερ ἐστὶν ἐν σώματι ψυχή, τοῦτ' εἰσὶν ἐν κόσμῳ Χριστιανοί". See the critical edition by Andreas Lindemann, Henning Paulsen (neu übersetzt und herausgegeben von), *Die Apostolischen Väter,* Griechisch-deutsche Parallelausgabe auf der Grundlage der Ausgaben von Franz Xaver Funk, Karl Bihlmeyer und Molly Whittaker mit Übersetzungen von M. Dibelius und D.-A. Koch, Mohr (Paul Siebeck), (Tübingen, 1992), 312.

[26] For the two citizenships – a *topos* introduced in the ideological and terminological core of patristic literature during the first centuries – see the philological analysis of Dirk Schinkel, *Die himmlische Bürgerschaft. Untersuchungen zu einem urchristlichen Sprachmotiv im Spannungsfeld von religiöser Integration und Abgrenzung im 1. und 2. Jahrhundert* (Forschungen zur Religion und Literatur des Alten und Neuen Testaments 220), (Göttingen: Vandenhoeck & Ruprecht, 2007).

[27] Concerning the reasoning at the basis of creation and, in general, concerning the manner in which Christian theology of the first centuries (here St. Justin and Origen) articulated, in a permanent and fertile dialogue, even if it was not one without polemical accents, with ancient philosophy and his own vision on the sense of the world restored by Christ, see, as an example, Christopher Stead, *Philosophy in Christian antiquity,* (Cambridge: Cambridge University Press, 1994). Concerning the vision of St. Maximus on the relationship between the spiritual sense of the work done by the Church and its historical one, see a monograph of reference, such as Hans Urs von Balthasar, *Kosmische Liturgie. Das Weltbild Maximus'des Bekenners,* (Einsiedeln: Johannes, 1988). Concerning the theology of St. Gregory Palamas, see the two basic

In conclusion, we can say that, Orthodox thought is based on the belief that despite the sin of our ancestors, no ontological gap has been established between the world and its Creator – a fact which gives even to the Incarnation of Christ a more important meaning, different from a simple divine satisfaction or a restoration of the pre-existent order as if the original sin had not taken place. According to this belief, the Orthodox approach to history is based on the most concrete fact, namely: the complete human freedom to ascend unburdened from the image of God to the likeliness of God. The religious re-establishment of the world through the sacrifice of Christ (the new Adam), only confirms this privileged status of man as a free being who gains redemption through love while possessing a full knowledge of the facts. This is a defining characteristic of an authentic inter-personal relationship. Furthermore, the permanent dialogue between the Creator and the creation has direct consequences. Thus, the world and the Kingdom of God are placed against one another as two completely different realities, impossible to be known through the other. They overlap in a synergetic manner, the church as a space for practicing religion being the place where the boundaries between the two are partially eliminated. The mirror-like relationship between the earthly and the heavenly spheres allows us to further identify, within the geographical order of this world, privileged spaces; that is to say, these are spaces that are exempted from the profane laws; similarly and symmetrically, the world thereafter becomes closer to us through the prolongation of our knowledge from this world into it. Despite the difference of regime, the two realities prepare each other. Κένωσις is the fundamental step towards θέωσις. With the risk of repeating what has been stated above, we must say that if we are to "take God seriously", we cannot ignore an equal attention paid to the world created and held by Him, the social involvement of the Christian being an inevitable part of the road to transfiguration. The conditioning of the spiritual vocation from the historical one, or, in better words, the inclusion of the social dimension in the religious one does not only render the involvement of the Christian in the worldly matters explicable, but it also projects it on the real eschatological horizon, showing that the good done here will truly and completely fulfil itself in the Kingdom of God, fact which is often disregarded. Only in this way and with an awakened eschatological consciousness can we prevent the public engagement of the Christian from degenerating into political activism and the Gospel from becoming an instrument for the conquest of profane power. By inspiring, correcting or criticising the decisions of the worldly leaders and by playing an active role in the normative debate of society, the Church traces the path of humanity, which goes far beyond the succession of electoral cycles. In other words, assuming the historical citizenship is not done in the detriment of the spiritual one, just like the latter cannot be gained without assuming the former. By serving the world, the Christians serve Christ in His most humble hypostases – from that of a humble man to that of a naked one. These small transfigurations (such as feeding the hungry or clothing the naked), thus realised, announce the final transfiguration of the entire creation, filled with the love of God and wrapped in His grace. On a mystagogic level, just like the Church as a space for the practice of religion is a tabernacle in the altar of the world, the good deed is a small scale pre-figuration of the goodness which will overflow the creation at the end of all times.

The Orthodox Church between state and society.
The dissonance of the symphonic score

As we have already seen that the social involvement of a Christian is in need of a double equilibrium: the one between the ideal of redemption and his personal role in the world, on the one hand, and the one between the commitment to creation and the eschatological horizon of the Kingdom of God, on the other hand. In other words, firstly, one must overcome the possible tendency to understand the call to Redemption by following Christ as a rejection of the fallen creation, and, secondly, one must accept his role in history without falling into the temptation

introductions: Dumitru Stănilaoe, *Viața și învățătura Sfântului Grigorie Palama. Cu patru tratate traduse* [Gregory Palamas' Life and Teaching. With four translated Treatises], second edition, (Bucharest: Scripta, 1993 (¹1938)); Jean Meyendorff, *St. Grégoire Palamas et la mystique orthodoxe*, (Paris: Seuil, 1959).

Part VII: Particular Themes and Issues for Orthodox Involvement in Ecumenism

of expecting the perfect peace and righteousness in this world. If spiritual balance and maturity are indispensable for one's relation to the developing history, this is also true for the Orthodox Church in its institutional, theological and pastoral hypostases. From this point of view, the Orthodox Church has accumulated a great experience. Without going into detail, for which there is no space here, we must mention the fact that Orthodoxy has constantly been facing a widespread cliché which negatively conditions its social involvement. Therefore, not only is the lack of interest of Orthodoxy towards the needs of the believers who have reached crisis situations presumed, but it has also been given as an example of combining the political and theological spheres for centuries. The frequently used term is caesaropapism. Due to its recurrence, we must focus on it for longer, in order to see what kind of ecclesiastic principle and social reality it implied in the past and what it implies now.

The term caesaropapism has a strong pejorative connotation, referring to the domination of the material power over the ecclesiastic authority; in this case, we are dealing with that of the Byzantine emperor over the Church. The term is often used in inappropriate constructions. The fact that the extremely complicated and subtle balance between political power and spiritual authority is often disregarded or insufficiently known has led to the grounding of a common place in the specialised Western literature, according to which Orthodoxy has the great genetic defect of not having defended itself in front of the instrumentalisation carried out by the Byzantine emperors. It is for the same reason that later on, under the authority of the Tsars, then of the Turks, or even more so of the communists, it did not have the resources needed for a systematic resistance from a theological and human point of view. From such a perspective, this deficit of independence could further explain even the difficulties encountered by the mainly Orthodox countries[28] in the process of post-communist democratisation. This process is characterised by the enforcement of some principles born in the modern culture, which is dominated by the generic separation between the Church and the state, by religious freedom and by pluralism of beliefs.[29]

Genealogically, the term caesaropapism was first used in the 18th century, in order to describe the new relationships between religion and politics that appeared in the era of the Reformation. It is well-known that they have been marked by the *Landeskirchenregiment* model, that is to say, by the total dependence of the ecclesiastic structure on the will of the local political master. Applied abusively to the Byzantine society, caesaropapism proved to be a pseudo-elucidating term, in the sense that it did not facilitate an understanding of the situation, or, in most cases, it simply falsified the access to an objective reading.[30] In the meantime, the sense of the term has fortunately undergone a process of clarification and the vision of the Occidental historiography has been considerably corrected in this case. One sign of this change in perspective is represented by the dictionary entries on this subject. We should at least insist on one example, since it is known that the circulation of corrupt meanings leads to similar conclusions. Therefore, the 1957 third edition of the impor-

---

[28] This is the core of Huntington's already-mentioned theory on Orthodoxy. The thesis was taken up and recycled in various forms until today. The major defect of an analysis that starts from this premise is based, on the one hand, on the democratic rules absolute rendering of rules, forgetting that the imposition and consolidation are very complex processes, and on the other hand, on the identification of the entire Orthodox message with its excesses of all kinds. For such a premeditated analysis, see, for example, Lavinia Stan, Lucian Turcescu, *Religion and Politics in Post-communist Romania*, (Oxford: Oxford University Press, 2007). On the poor methodology of this book, see Radu Carp's review in *Inter* 1.2 (2008): 551-557.

[29] In this sense, see the nuanced and applied analysis of Vasilios N. Makrides, "Orthodoxes Christentum, Pluralismus, Zivilgesellschaft," in Andreas Gotzmann, Vasilios N. Makrides, Jamal Malik, Jörg Rüpke, *Pluralismus in der europäischen Religionsgeschichte. Religionswissenschaftliche Antrittsvorlesungen*, (Marburg: Diagonal, 2001), 53-78.

[30] Fact also confirmed by Henry Chadwick, *Die Kirche in der antiken Welt* (Berlin: Walter de Gruyter, 1972); see p. 191: "Der Begriff *Cäsaropapismus* ist kein nützliches oder erhellendes Wort für breite Verallgemeinungen über die politische Theorie des griechischen Ostens." A few decades earlier, the same conclusion was reached by Ernest Barker, *Social and Political Thought in Byzantium. From Justinian I to the last Palaeologos*, (London: Oxford at the Clarendon Press, 1957); p. 7: "The division between the spiritual and the temporal was conceived by the Eastern Church, and by the general community of the East Roman Empire, in a way which differed from that in which it was conceived by the West. Some scholars have invented the short-hand term 'Caesaropapism' to express the difference, and to denote the peculiar power of Byzantine emperors. It is true that the emperors were 'Caesars', or rather *autocratores* (the term 'Caesar' was used in a peculiar sense in Constantinople); but it is *not* true that they were 'popes'."

tant theological dictionary *Die Religion in Geschichte und Gegenwart* presents the nature of the "Byzantine caesaropapism" as being derived from Constantine the Great's status of king and priest (βασιλεὺς καὶ ἱερεύς/ rex-sacerdos), and later related this model to the ecclesiastical-political system of Tsarist Russia, which was installed by Peter the Great in 1727 by the abolishment of patriarchy, the instalment of the synod regime and its submission to the authority of the state.[31] In the first place, the author of the article disregards the fundamental difference of political vision between the Constantine paradigm (a tribute to an imperial Latinity, adapted to the political theology of early Christianity) and that of Peter (related to the Enlightenment and to the influence of Protestantism on the state-Church relationship). This is where the second inconsistency of thought arises: not any form of imposing political power on ecclesiastic matters is automatically an act of caesaropapism. If it were so, the role of the religious authority would be reduced to a strictly passive one and the intervention of the political power would automatically be, in a symmetrical way, an act of religious significance. The author of the article points to the fact that the East has cultivated the unity of the worldly kingdom under an autocrat, whereas the West rejected this model and promoted the separation of the two powers. In other words, if we were to give credit to this article, the different development of the Christian West represents the materialization of the rejection of the Byzantine and post-Byzantine model. Or, as it is well-known, the reasons, ingredients and visions promoted in the West indicate an image that is far more complex than a simple opposition between the East and the West when it comes to the generic relation between the Church and the state, since, in a way, the "Byzantine caesaropapism" is successfully matched by pontifical monarchy. Simplifying the meanings of the terms too much, the author fails to point out the essence of the real difference between the two hemispheres of the Christian world and, even more so, he does not elucidate us on the Byzantine particularities.

Published three decades later than the article from 1957, the article on Byzantium from *Evangelisches Kirchenlexikon* introduces delimitations and specifications concerning the given meaning of "Byzantine ceasaropapism"[32] and its real one. The author observes the low degree of applicability of the term, despite the historical and judicial ground offered by Justinian I's *Novella 6,* for example. It underlines the fact that the Byzantine sources offer no notable reference to the theory of "political dyophysitism" – a political sacredness embodied by the priest-emperor. Moreover, as the author of the article states, as opposed to the Occident, Byzantium does not have a clergy that forms a homogenous class, that detains the cultural-shaping monopoly and that is capable of expanding itself over the state structures. Quite the contrary! As the historical experience shows, priesthood was more a sort of Byzantine "civil society" rather than a mechanism of leadership and has systematically come into conflict with the heads of the profane power. Moreover, as the author rightly states, in Byzantium, the entrance in an ecclesiastic structure implied giving up any other worldly role. In other words, the two spheres – religious and political – have never really overlapped, despite their attempts to subvert each other; for this reason, a term such as "caesaropapism" is not very helpful, if at all, in understanding the social-theological phenomenon of the Byzantine world.[33]

The criticism against the undifferentiated usage of the term "caesaropapism" has finally been heard. Only the application of a Western reading to some Eastern cultural-historical phenomena can explain the long-lived usage of the term. According to this perspective, the role of the Byzantine emperor was exaggerated, his exceptional intervention in dogmatic matters being transformed into a rule.[34] Moreover, whether they were

---

[31] U. Scheuner, Art. "Cäsaropapismus," in: Kurt Galling, et al. (Ed.), *Die Religion in Geschichte und Gegenwart. Handwörterbuch für Theologie und Religionswissenschaft,* Dritte, völlig neu bearbeitete Auflage, J.C.B. Mohr (Paul Siebeck), (Tübingen, 1957), col. 1582.

[32] Karl-Heinz Uthemann, Art. "Byzanz," in Erwin Fahlbusch, et al. (Ed.), *Evangelisches Kirchenlexikon. Internationale theologische Enzyklopädie,* (Göttingen: Vandenhoeck & Ruprecht, 1986), Erster Band, coll. 610-616.

[33] Related to the Byzantine particularities and to the confusion of the modern exegetes who make use of inappropriate categories, see Hélène Ahrweiler, *L'Idéologie politique de l'Empire Byzantin,* (Paris: Presses Universitaires de France, 1975).

[34] See the observation of Hans-Georg Beck, *Das byzantinische Jahrtausend,* 2. Auflage, (München: C.H. Beck, 1994); see p. 102: "Im Ganzen bleibt es erstaunlich, wie selten – entgegen landläufiger Meinung – die byzantinischen Kaiser es in die Hand nehmen, von sich aus und autokratisch einen dogmatischen Streit zu entscheiden oder gar vom Zaun zu brechen."

Part VII: Particular Themes and Issues for Orthodox Involvement in Ecumenism

aware of it or not, the majority of Occidental historians who have focused on the Byzantine world have held the relationship between the papal institution and the monarchy as a reference-image and have transferred it, *tale quale*, on the shores of the Bosphorus. Being based upon the false premise of a similitude of relationship between the relation Pope-king in the West and emperor-patriarch in the East, the analyses in the field have induced conclusions, instead of drawing them after an objective research of the Byzantine particularities.[35] In other words, prejudice has triumphed over evidence.[36]

In the absence of a vicarial theory, meaning a theory of terrestrial incarnation by means of a delegation from the Kingdom of God, just like the Episcope of Rome somewhat "embodies" Christ by representation, the political Byzantium is aware of its limitations; it does not aim for more than the maintenance of the course of history towards the eschatological horizon. The ambition to be a Christian empire and a society of the Gospel remains the guiding ideal and is only partially transposed in a reality that always shows signs of imperfection.[37] This fact can thoroughly explain why the political power and the spiritual authority do not overlap, in spite of the fact that the former symbolically feeds itself off the aura of the latter, while the latter, awaiting the Kingdom of God, is making use of the terrestrial goods. Incomplete and unclear in some instances, the synthesis between the prototype that the royalty related to the Old Testament and the Christ-related royalty has not created any univocal model of establishment or, even more so, of power guarantee. The succession of a rather high number of emperors, the external social dynamic (the road that led from the stables to the purple decorated apartments was shorter than we might imagine), the frequent ascensions to power and the voices that spoke against those who detained the power (through the demes, or the Byzantine parties, "disguised" as sport camps with a hippodrome) and the difficulties of imposing dynasties on the long term are all elements that prove one fact: the relative character of the emperor as a *person*, which was completely compensated for by the ceremonial luxury and complexity of the imperial *institution* – a veritable "profane Liturgy", held primarily at the imperial place which was called the "sacred palace". Liutprand of Cremona recounted it critically towards the end of the 10th century, when he was sent to the palace of Nikephoros Phokas[38] by Otto I. In order to better understand the relationship between the emperor as a person and his position, we could compare it to the relationship between the bishop as a person, and his duty during the Liturgy: after all, it is a monk who is wearing the gold robes. He is a Christian who has taken the oath of poverty and the difference and tension between his person and the "sacramental" decoration are equal to those between the generic ideal of sacredness and the concrete sanctification of one's own life. In other words, the particularities of the Byzantine world reside in the manner in which the persons – belonging to the political or ecclesiastic environment – are engaged or engage themselves in the service of a vision with which they cannot and, in fact, are not allowed to identify themselves.

[35] See Herbert Hunger, "Byzantinismus. Nachwirkungen byzantinischer Verhaltensweisen bis in die Gegenwart," in Herbert Hunger, Epidosis. *Gesammelte Schriften zur byzantinischen Geistes- und Kulturgeschichte*, (München: Maris, 1989); see p. 4: "Was das Verhältnis von Kirche und Staat betrifft, stoßen wir hier auf die immer wieder auftretende Meinung, Byzanz habe einen ausgeprägten Caesaropapismus besessen. Gerade das aber beruht auf einer falschen Interpretation der Stellung des Kaisers, der in Byzanz nicht außerhalb der Kirche stand, sondern als deren Herr zugleich der erste Vorkämpfer der Orthodoxie war; dies gehörte zu seinen vornehmsten Pflichten. Konfrontationen zwischen Kaiser und Patriarch, die es auch in Byzanz wiederholt gab, beruhten auf anderen Voraussetzungen als jene zwischen Kaiser und Papst im Westen, wo man mit Recht auch von Caesaropapismus sprechen konnte." A compulsory reading for the understanding of the so-called Byzantine caeseropapism: Gilbert Dagron, *Empereur et prêtre. Étude sur le "césaropapisme" byzantin* (Bibliothèque des Histoires), (Paris: Gallimard, 1996).

[36] The lack of historical evidence for caesaropapism in Byzantium is the foundation of the study by Deno J. Geanakoplos, "Church and State in the Byzantine Empire: A Reconsideration of the Problem of Caesaropapism," in *Church History* 34 (1965): 381-403.

[37] The Byzantine history as an ideal of social Incarnation of a Christian ideal is presented by Alain Duchellier, *Le Drame de Byzance. Idéal et échec d'une société chrétienne*, (Paris: Hachette, 1976).

[38] For a complete and detailed image of the imperial ceremony of Byzantium, which is a veritable culture in itself, see the contributions edited in the collective volume by Henry Maguire (ed.), *Byzantine Court Culture from 829 to 1204*, (Washington D.C.: Dumbarton Oaks, 1997).

Trying to draw a conclusion of this short presentation of the usage of a central concept of the social-theological history of Orthodoxy, we can say that a research of the Byzantine Empire, done without any ideological involvements, shows that, in fact, the charge with caesaropapism is not valid, the ecclesiastic and profane testimonials leading to a much more nuanced conclusion. First of all, the role of the Emperor within the Church life was more restricted than we might be tempted to think. Emperors such as Constantine, Justinian or Theodosius (all of them preserved carefully in the social memory as "the Great") who were greatly involved in the theological debate, approaching the edge of authority abuse or even crossing it, stand out rather as exceptions to the rule. Furthermore, the position of the patriarchs of Constantinople towards the Imperial Court is disregarded, and so is the fact that a considerable number of ecclesiastical personalities have opposed the Court, most often on dogmatic grounds, due to discipline matters or simply because of the architecture of power at a certain moment. One paradigmatic case is that of Saint John Chrysostom, who was exiled for political reasons, unskilfully masked as some assumed doctrinal deviations.[39] Even the final centuries of the Byzantine Empire marked by the quest for an anti-Ottoman alliance at any price, even at that of the union with Rome, proves the ecclesiastic dissidence in the face of political will and the fact that the tension between the Church and the Imperial Institution was not solved through a "synthesis" similar to the presumed "Byzantine caesaropapism".

If caesaropapism is not the right term to describe Byzantium from the point of view of designating the relationship between the Church and the state, then what is the most appropriate term? Well, another term that inevitably arises within the debate is that of *symphony*. Through its defining character and through its ulterior influence, the symphony is the identity mark of the Byzantine political theory. It is a recurrent term, despite the different accents and exegeses known throughout a millennium characterized by the permanent resettling of the relationships between the ecclesiastic authority and the political power.[40] Even if just theoretically, the Byzantine symphony can be regarded as the Eastern solution to the Western dilemma. Instead of aiming at establishing the value hierarchy and at drawing practical consequences from it – the submission of one authority to the other, namely of the king/emperor to the Pope/Patriarch – the symphonic Byzantine concept views the spiritual authority and the political power as being part of a relationship of distinction and completion at the same time. As we know, the first step towards the formation of a strong Byzantine political theology was taken by Eusebius of Caesarea, the Byzantine Bishop and religious historian who was close to Constantine the Great. The symphonic trend in thought – for which we do not have space to present in this paper – was carried on until much later, long after the disappearance of the historical body that had given birth to it. Even the Romanian leaders[41] made use of it. In the same way, the Russian tsars[42] were ascribed and legitimized to the same category, as a continuation of the symphonic ideal, but one 'enriched' with autocratic tendencies.

In its fundamental aim, the Byzantine symphony is a direct consequence of being aware of Latinity as a life philosophy and accepting a rightful order or a hierarchy of instances, the *nomocanonical* tradition being its concrete transposition. The religious right is directly linked to the profane one and the latter represents the secular expression of the divine order, fact which did not exclude the possibility of a discrepancy between the two. If in Latin Catholicism, the ecclesiastic institution turns into a sort of state, with the avowed finality of

---

[39] Related to this case which is symbolic for the relation between political power and spiritual authority in Byzantium, see the excellent monograph of Claudia Tiersch, *Johannes Chrysostomus in Konstantinopel (398-404). Weltsicht und Wirken eines Bischofs in der Hauptstadt des Oströmischen Reiches* (Studien und Texte zu Antike und Christentum 6), (Tübingen: Mohr Siebeck, 2002).

[40] See here the short presentation of the political theory of Byzantium: I.E. ΚΑΡΑΓΙΑΝΝΟΠΟΥΛΟΣ, Ἡ πολιτικὴ θεωρία τῶν Βυζαντινῶν (Ἑταιρεία βυζαντινῶν ἐρευνῶν), (Θεσσαλονίκη: Βανιας, 1992).

[41] See a synthesis of the Romanian medieval and pre-modern political thought: Andrei Pippidi, *Tradiția politică bizantină în țările române în secolele XVI-XVIII* [Byzantine Political Tradition in the Romanian Countries between the 16th and 18th centuries], (Bucharest: Corint, 2001).

[42] A history of theological Russian politics of Orthodox tradition is provided by Konstantin Kostjuk, *Der Begriff des Politischen in der russisch-orthodoxen Tradition. Zum Verhältnis von Kirche, Staat und Gesellschaft in Rußland* (Politik- und Kommunikationswissenschaftliche Veröffentlichungen der Görres-Gesellschaft 24), (Paderborn: Ferdinand Schöningh, 2005).

establishing a *societas perfecta,* in Byzantium, which is marked by a permanent political mirror, the Church wanted to gain and maintain its autonomy as much as possible, precisely through its demarcation from the state structure, no matter how close the ideas and interests of the two major institutions[43] might have been at a certain time, especially from the point of view of a historical theology. It is true that, in the tradition established by Eusebius, an identification of destiny would take place between the Church and the Empire, but this wouldn't lead to the annihilation of the rightful distinction. The *kanon* would never take the place of the *nomos* and the *nomos* would never replace the canonical establishment, but this does not mean that it has never tried to. Otherwise, reiterating the lack of intervention of the worldly officials in Church matters at every Synod, local or ecumenical, wouldn't have made any sense. Essentially, this is the signification of symphony according to the already quoted Eusebius of Caesarea, the religious man who was unfairly charged with the ideological enslaving of the Eastern Church to the Byzantine imperial power. The view of Eusebius on the relationship between bishop of the interior matters (the archbishop/patriarch) and the bishop of foreign matters (the emperor) made possible the coexistence of two powers, both divinely legitimated, but with two different missions. It was impossible to replace one with the other, and the two of them were twice intersected: at the core of the common source of spiritual legitimacy and in the everyday character of a state that was not and could not become the earthly materialisation of the Kingdom of God. This is the source of a course of action that is surprising for the Western analyst. Despite the spiritual source of legitimacy of the state, the Church did not perceive all political decisions as expressions of divine will; otherwise, the firm rejection of the intervention of the political sphere in the ecclesiastic life would have been pointless. This fact further meant that the symphony did not abolish the character of radical distinction of the ecclesiastic sphere in relation to the political men. It was a veritable exercise of power autonomy, in the modern sense of the term, which allowed the Church to assume a critical role in relation to the state. Without that distance dictated by the difference between the two entities, the ecclesiastical critique would have been, after all, impossible.

Unfortunately, the critical dimension of theology in Byzantium, exerted precisely due to the fidelity to the project of a Christian society, but which can only be completely and definitively realised on an eschatological level, is often disregarded by the Orthodox believers of today, who are used to understand the divine plan as a justification of compromise. The Byzantine authors interpreted the words from the Sermon on the Mount: "No one can serve two masters" (Matthew 6:24), by using an equally Biblical context: "So give back to Caesar what is Caesar's, and to God what is God's" (Matthew 22:21).

Thus they accomplished the balance between the respect towards the order of the world and the submission to God (cf. The Acts of the Apostles), meaning that faith provides a consciousness that is immune to any outer discretionary controls. Respecting the order of the temporary establishment means understanding that which God has permitted (cf. Romans 13:1-7): the Christian cannot lead a permanent protest against the world, for the world is held, led and endured by He Who created it. The role of the Christian and of the Church is to bear witness to the divine providence. This is the reason why Christians pray for constraint and for those in authority (cf. 1 Timothy 2:1-2). The spiritual legitimisation of power is a mirror in which the political decision-maker gazes. It is not just an approval of his deeds that does not take into account their moral quality or their consequences.

Without encouraging civic passivity or alienation from the immediate responsibility of the man endowed with freedom and reason, the political theology of Byzantium, formulated on these Biblical foundations and enriched with a millennium of work done by the Orthodox Church in society, is characterised by the practice of any situation of rightful thought or civic reflex of rightful faith. This fact makes it possible for the imperfect present to be read from an eschatological perspective and to view limitation from the perspective of fulfilment. In the light of such a spiritual realism, the Church and the State are not perceived as two competing powers. As Eusebius of Caesarea puts it, the power of the state is exterior, while the religious

---

[43] See here the parallel evolution of the Byzantine system of law and the Latin one: Onorato Bucci, „La genesi della struttura del diritto della Chiesa latina e del diritto delle Chiese cristiane orientali in rapporto allo svolgimento storico del diritto romano e del diritto bizantino," *Apollinarius* 65 (1992): 93-135.

authority is one that resonates within. The everyday life of the work specific to each of the collective spheres that overlap on an individual level takes place between the *potestas* of one and the *auctoritas* of the other, between the *nomos* and the *kanon*. Their main harmony rules out the confusion concerning their roles. The worldly citizenship is transitory and that means that it evolves towards the priestly one. As history clearly shows us, this vision does not exclude the tension between the state and the Church or the one between one's interests and his vision.[44]

The history of the Byzantine Empire has known plenty of moments when symphony turned into cacophony either through the intervention of the political power in the ecclesiastic life, or through the worldly ambitions of the spiritual authority. If Isidore of Pelusium wrote that the priest, through his pastoral work, has to educate and to punish the errors of the political service because the priest has to be the immediate judge of the monarch,[45] Hosius de Coroba unequivocally draw Emperor Constantine's attention on the relationship between the spiritual authority and the secular power: "Just like we are not allowed to rule the world, you are not allowed to interfere with the internal matters of the Church, Emperor!" It was to the same emperor that Leontius of Tripoli addressed similarly clear words: "I wonder at your aspiration to things other than the ones you are called for, interfering with matters that are supposed to be dealt with by the Bishops, while your role is to look over the military and political affairs of the state."[46]

As I have already mentioned, we do not have here the space to present thoroughly the stages of the political Byzantine theory, or all the articulations of the Orthodox political theology. What remains fundamental is the acknowledgement as a reference point of the fact that Byzantium does not have that programmatic conflict between the political power and the spiritual authority that characterises the West. The absence of this institutional and ideological competition can further explain why the political emancipation is not assimilated, in the predominantly Orthodox societies, to the revolt against the ecclesiastic domination, just like the role of the Church is not defined through delimitation from the state in terms of a rupture or of an irremediable antagonism. The state is not threatened by the weight of the spiritual authority of the Church, which does not aspire to be the ideal variant of a society that resides under the mark of the sin, an anti-world or even a sort of state within a state; the Church aspires to be a service within the world and therefore, within the core of the existent establishment. This is where the popular character of Orthodoxy, materialised in the form of a national Church and the countries in which Orthodoxy has given birth to the national character and has shaped personal choices. Similarly, this is where the almost natural inclination to render the national or local dimension, in the detriment of the universal one comes from, as a consequence. This is, in fact, the great problem of yesterday's and today's Orthodoxy when it comes to establishing a constructive balance between the local and the universal sphere, between the ethnical particularities and that which overpasses them in spiritual importance. The multi-ethnic Byzantium has made this experience of universality possible by incorporating the ethnic differences, at least in its historical period of maximum geographical expansion. The ulterior limitation of the Byzantine heritage to a strictly Greek one has drastically reduced the capacity of Byzantium as a model of *de facto* universality for Orthodoxy. For this reason, local Churches view their canonical independence in relationship with the Greek element, which is perceived as being the dominant one. The "anti-Greek affect" can also be found in other variants of the ecclesiastic nationalism of the past centuries.

Aside from a good framing of the relationship with the political power, the Byzantine model also shows that the presence of the Church serving within the world makes critical consciousness possible, or even mandatory. Precisely because it is a witness to the historical path of the social and religious community, within which it preaches the Gospel of Christ, the Church formulates its critique possessing a full knowledge of the facts. An

---

[44] Far from being an unchallengeable and sacrosanct whole, the profane Byzantine power is questioned every now and then. See, for example, Jean-Claude Cheynet, *Pouvoir et contestations à Byzance (963-1210)* (Byzantina Sorbonensia 9), (Paris: Presses Universitaires de Paris, 1990).

[45] *Epist. 268*, PG 78, 1492 D.

[46] According to St. Athanasius the Great, *Hist. Arian.* 44, PG 25, 745.

essential part of its role is to read carefully the signals of the historical period in cause.[47] The prophetic role of the Church is thus exerted both on a social level and on a purely ecclesiastic one, the critical sense being applied to weaknesses of all kinds and from any place. As I have already mentioned, the lucid and critical aspect is often ignored nowadays, being replaced by a certain spiritually argued historical fatalism. The long period of communism has encouraged this kind of interpretation of the role assumed by the Church throughout history, which was a reason to restart the theological debate in order to formulate a social vision of Orthodoxy in today's world, one that should be faithful to Tradition as it is creative.

Between charity and "Weltanschauung".
From Social Work to the Orthodox social theology

The short mentioning of the Biblical-patristic foundations of the historical experience and of some of its stages helps us get a view of how we can articulate a specific theological vision on the contemporary challenges, or a sort of Eastern *Weltanschauung*, in the context of the modern era to which the traditional Orthodox societies already belong. I have previously insisted upon the elucidation of the meaning of the so-called Byzantine caesaropapism, but also upon the one of the cacophonies inherent to the symphony between the Church and the state. I have done this precisely to underline the territorial freedom that Orthodox theology has always had. It must always remember this freedom and make use of it without any reservation and more systematically than it has until now. To begin with, we must provide some short explanations of the genealogy and sense of modernity.

Born out of the gesture of opposition towards the ideological forces of Western Europe, which was seeking political emancipation in relation to Rome, anticipated in this sense by Luther's Reformation and comprising more factors, from the new geographical discoveries to those in the exact sciences, based upon a juridical system situated above the moral-religious categories, postulating the territorial freedom of the human being, even (or precisely) when it comes to religious belief, placing reason above faith and cultivating the experiment as an ultimate proof of reality, the project of modernity which has been going on over the past three centuries, has meanwhile become the identity mark of Europe, but also of North America. This project meant, above all, a deep rupture from the religiously and culturally dominated vision of the world which has marked a whole millennium.[48] As it is easy to imagine, the inversion of the criteria and of the vision was a significant one, practically comprising the entire social structure. The power relations between the political power and the spiritual authority would undergo great changes, the everyday values would grow to be interpreted in a different manner, the traditions would be understood in a different way and lifestyles would be changed. In short, the history of Europe (and that of North America), in the totality of its actors, from people and institutions to laws and mentalities, would take a completely new course.[49]

---

[47] This is how the following statement made by the Orthodox theologian Vladimir Lossky should be understood: "Les Eglises dans l'Europe nouvelle," in *Service orthodoxe de presse* 195 (1995): 32: "[...] il me paraît important de retirer de l'expérience des orthodoxes l'idée positive que l'Eglise est appelée à s'identifier aux destinées du peuple. Mais cette identification doit rester fidèle à sa véritable nature qui est que l'Eglise s'identifier aux destinées d'un peuple, non pas sous une forme quelconque de servilité, mais comme la conscience de ce peuple, donc parfois comme une conscience critique qui rappelle le respect de la personne humaine en toutes circonstances."

[48] For a more complete presentation of the birth of European modernity, provided by an expert in the domain, see Paul Hazard, *La crise de la conscience européenne 1680-1715*, (Paris: Fayard, 1961). As far as the change of scientific paradigm is concerned, see Amos Funkenstein, *Theology and the Scientific Imagination from the Middle Ages to the Seventeenth Century*, (Princeton: Princeton University Press, 1986).

[49] An exemplary, even schematic history of these mutations within the collective European mentality, from Antiquity and up to modernity and including the medieval period see the collective volume edited by Peter Dinzelbacher (Ed.), *Europäische Mentalitätsgeschichte. Hauptthemen in Einzeldarstellungen*, 2. durchgesehene und ergänzte Auflage, (Stuttgart: Alfred Kröner, 2008).

Due to their genesis and complexity, the discoveries of modernity are inevitably ambivalent. Therefore, not everything that would be rejected because of belonging to the "dark medieval world", as opposed to the light of reason, would prove to be bad. Similarly, not all the proposed innovations would unequivocally prove useful or beneficial. Without attempting an inventory or an evaluation, we must note that it is certain that many characteristics of modernity as an era, ideological trend, cultural proposal, economical system or political desiderate lead to what we call today the life standard of the early 21st century man. The long list of technical conveniences, the ways of social organisation, of welfare and support, many of them based on the profane variant of the eschatological principle of subsidiarity, the formative facilities, the options of personal fulfilment and the basic rights and liberties are all acquisitions meant to guarantee and support human life in a decent manner a lot more efficiently than the system based on casts, blood privileges or inherited titles, or, put simply, on invariable hierarchies and in general on an evaluation and on a possible recognition of human dignity on outer reasons. In other words, the theological dilemma when it comes to the results of modernity resides in the necessity to honestly admit that, apart from the excesses, notable changes have taken place. These changes are numerous and culminate with the doctrine of human rights which is directly fed with the Christian ethos.[50] This is also the conclusion of a careful reader of the signs of the period like Antonio Rosmini. He opposed the officially negative attitude of the Roman Church from the mid-19th century and became an interpreter of the good part of modernity. According to him, the positive aspect of modernity can be understood and accepted through a comparison with the defunct feudalism and the Christian values: "Feudalism induces a personal servitude and even this single fact is repulsive to the (fundamental) ecclesiastic characteristic that bases itself on liberty."[51]

On the other hand, it is just as true that the same modernity has triggered a series of changes which are deeply questionable from a theological and ecclesiastic point of view. The project of modernity is decisively anti-Christian, especially in the variant promoted by the French Revolution of 1789. The violence with which religious faith has been eliminated from the public space and the aggressiveness with which the proclaimed laic state wanted to impose its ideological monopoly are two aspects that did not bring any progress, but that have influenced the profile of the so-called modern society on the long term.[52] Sticking to the example of France, we can see that, after 1789, a policy of obliteration of the religious sphere and not of separation between the religious sphere and the public one has been carried out. Taking into account the proportions, we can say that it was a sort of atheist 'Reformation' during which the establishments changed their initial role and the religious personnel is forced, for the promise of a convenient pension, to "reconvert". Later on, the religious officials and the Christian supporters would be eliminated from the public system; being a clerk implied abjuring faith. Repeating what I have said before, this vision has nothing in common with tolerance, with religious freedom or with the healthy principle of distinguishing between religion and politics. We are facing a complete anti-religious attack and not a process of establishing the neutrality of a state that is claimed to be the warrant of its citizens' rights, including that to practice religion freely, publicly or privately.[53] In order to preserve the

---

[50] The bibliography on ethical kinship between the Gospel and human rights, based on the concept of personal dignity, is extremely vast. For an introductory guideline, see Wolfgang Huber's article "Menschenrechte/Menschenwürde", in: Gerhard Müller, et al. (Ed.), *Theologische Realenzyklopädie*, (Berlin: Walter de Gruyter, 1992), Band XXII, 577-602. A standard introduction in the modern and cultural history of rights is provided by Norberto Bobbio, *L'età dei diritti. Dodici saggi sul tema dei diritti*, (Torino: Einaudi, 1990).

[51] Antonio Rosmini, *Delle Cinque Piaghe della Santa Chiesa*, Testo ricostruito nella forma ultima voluta dall'Autore con saggio introduttivo e note di Nunzio Galantino, (San Paolo: Cinisello Balsamo, 1997); here: p. 332. Also see the recent monograph: Markus Krienke, *Antonio Rosmini. Ein Philosoph zwischen Tradition und Moderne*, (Freiburg: Karl Alber, 2008).

[52] See Peter Gay, *The Enlightenment. The Rise of Modern Paganism*, (The Norton Library 870), (New York: Norton, 1977).

[53] For a historical and ideological introduction in the events of 1789, see Roland Desné, *L'année 1789* (Société Française d'Etude du Dix-Huitième Siècle 20), (Paris: Presses Universitaires de France, 1988). Also see the analysis of an expert historian: François Furet, *Penser la révolution française* (Folio. Histoire 3), (Paris: Gallimard, 1988). See also another useful dictionary François Furet, Mona Ozouf, *Dictionnaire critique de la révolution française*, (Paris: Flammarion, 1988). As far as the religious matter and the magnitude of the systematic persecution are concerned, see Serge Bonin (ed.), *Atlas*

balance of this short presentation, we must not forget that the emergence of modernity had not been stained by the blood of anti-religious attacks, which remains a historical reality supposed to encourage the critical interpretation of yesterday's or even today's secular excesses.[54] Moreover, as we have seen in the first part of the present analysis, the fundamentally anti-religious data of the cultural and political modernity have, in the meantime, undergone corrections and gradations that make the on-going discussion on secularization possible.

Due to space limitations, we shall not insist upon other more or less visible negative effects of the project of modernity, like the ones systematically mentioned in its critiques, such as individualism and materialism, as if such phenomena were the exclusive luggage of one model of society. It is important for our understanding to remember firstly that the anti-religious affect of modernity (especially in its laic French hypostasis) led to the resistance of Catholicism in front of the principles of modern reality, for over two centuries. This process ended only during the Second Vatican Council, when the compatibility between the fundamental human rights and liberties with the Christian anthropology was proclaimed.[55] Secondly, the same constitutive and permanently latent anti-religious affect continues to feed the fundamental reservation of Orthodoxy towards the same modernity, despite the post-secular corrections that have taken place lately.

The Orthodox attitude towards modernity has not always been unambiguously negative. It has varied from embracing the national cause – which was possible precisely due to the new principles of self-determination and the right to national existence – to fervent critique of secularisation – which acted more as a patrimonial policy of the modern state and less as a cultural offer. This ambivalent relation has characterised primarily the 19th century; during the following century, the decisive factor would be the global experience made possible by Orthodoxy through the development of the diaspora in Western Europe and the establishment of new communities on other continents, primarily in North and South America, but also in Australia. The immense geographical opening beyond the Mediterranean horizon concretely implied the dialogue or at least the placement near the effects of modernity. The Orthodox believers would fully enjoy its technical and judicial advantages, even if only in an insufficiently reflected manner. During the past century and especially during its first half, a series of modern "revolutions" took place in the traditionally Orthodox countries of Eastern Europe: a distinct culture appeared and it was somewhat reserved in front of the Christian values, the political scene became diversified (at least through the forceful instauration of communism), the rise of the living standards in the urban environment triggered notable changes in the rural area which began being idealised and promoted to the status of identity matrix and the clergy was more and more often forced to resort to rational arguments and only to those of authority. Theology became integrated in the academic environment, as was the case of Romania and Greece, or, if it remained under the exclusive control of the Church, as was the case of Russia, it was at least related to the above-mentioned environment and tried to confirm its academic and scientific status.

Despite the adaptation to the *realities of modernity*, which happened primarily due to the modernisation of the state and of the society, the theme of modernity continues to remain controversial up to this day for the Orthodox theology. The range of theologians is very large from those who restrict modernity to the West and the West to the amount of its sins (like Yannaras lately) to those who state that modernity, ecumenism and heresy are equal (like Popovici and his direct and indirect disciples) from the authentic and critical seekers of dialogue between, for example, Orthodox anthropology and human rights (like Delikostantis) or between theological theory and social practice (like Khodr), to the admirers of Western theology, from which they

---

de la Révolution Française (Librairie du bicentenaire de la Révolution Française), vol. 6: Claude Langlois (direction scientifique), *Religion*, (Paris: Éditions de l'École des Hautes Études en Sciences Sociales, 1996).

[54] For a very useful comparative presentation of the manner of instalment of modernity in different cultural and geographical spaces, see Gertrude Himmelfarb, *The Roads to Modernity. The British, French, and American Enlightenments*, (New York: Alfred A. Knopf, 2005).

[55] A complete view of the long path towards the critical and constructive assumption of modernity by the Catholic theology and by the Magisterium: Neuner, *Der Streit um den katholischen Modernismus*, (Frankfurt am Main: Verlag der Weltreligionen, 2009). Also see the important analysis from the perspective of religious sociology of Émile Poulat, *Histoire, dogme et critique dans la crise moderniste*, (Tournai: Casterman, 1979).

constructively extract working methods such as the domain of Biblical exegesis (like Men), from those who present Orthodoxy in its universal dimension (like the theologians of exile such as Meyendorff, Schmemann or Lossky, but also Stăniloae or Trembelas) to the followers of local or past inclined tradition (like Romanides), from those who practice the transfer of ideas and knowledge between the two confessional and cultural hemispheres (like Ică Jr.) to those who view the faults of other in the first place and never their own (like Zizis), from those who place Orthodoxy in dialogue with the exact sciences and with the philosophical discourse of the time (like Bodrov) to those who, finally, do not need anything or anyone, exalting the lack of culture and the closure as virtues that are sufficient for redemption and whose only alternative to Orthodoxy is death, the spectre is very wide.[56]

This diversity, confusing to those who are outside the sphere of theological preoccupations or/and to those who belong to other religions, can be interpreted in two ways. Firstly, it points to the salutary absence of a doctrinal centre of the Orthodox world. The emphasis laid by the Eastern Church upon communion and Synod character materialises itself in the form of the rejection of a pyramidal ecclesiastic construction, no matter what its tip might be: Rome, Constantinople or Moscow. The primatial theology of Orthodox thought does not have jurisdictional consequences, the universality of the Church not being identified with its organisation in a centralist manner, but with the sharing of the same beliefs (dogmatic unity) celebrated in the same way (liturgical unity) and following the same disciplinary canons (canonical unity). The lack of a formal central authority is made up for in Orthodoxy. This is shown by numerous Synods that have taken place over the past two millenniums and by consensus. Unfortunately, this is precisely what is being impacted in the historical life of modern and contemporary Orthodoxy.[57] The ignorance towards it, under the pretext of nationalist interests, can also explain the absence, at the highest pan-Orthodox level, of some systematic documents of position referring to the public, ecclesiastic and social agenda of the moment in our theology.[58] In other words, not just ecclesiology, but also the social message of Orthodoxy faces the consequences of an unsolved tension between the local plan and the universal one. Then, such a plurality of approaches can also be understood as an expression of uncertainty when it comes to the theological – meaning both spiritual and intellectual – relation to modernity.

---

[56] For an understanding of these debates from the point of view of national Orthodoxies, but also from an inter-Orthodox point of view, we need theological syntheses. In Romania, we don't have an up-to-date one. For Greece, see the wider panorama of Yannis Spiteris, *La teologia ortodossa neo-greca*, (Bologna: Dehoniane, 1992). The only free Orthodoxy in Eastern Europe in the aftermath of the Second World War, namely the Greek one, has provided a thematic synthesis of the trends of modernity. For this, see the contributions of the Volos Symposium of 2005 on the theme of Greek theology during the sixth decade of the past century: Π. ΚΑΛΛΑΪΤΖΙΔΗΣ, Θ. Ν. ΠΑΠΑΘΑΝΑΣΙΟΥ, Θ. ΑΜΠΑΤΖΙΔΗΣ (eds.), *Αναταράξεις στη μεταπολεμική θεολογία. Η "θεολογία του '60"*, (Ἀθήναι: ΙΝΔΙΚΤΟΣ, 2009). Related to Russian theology, consult an expert in the domain, even if the theme of modernity is not central: Georges Florovsky, *Ways of Russian Theology*, (Nordland, 1979). Further see the article of Alexander Schmemann, "Russian Theology: 1920-1972. An Introductory Survey," in *St Vladimir's Theological Quarterly* 16.4 (1972): 172-194. Also see Kristina Stöckl, "Modernity and its critique in 20th century Russian orthodox thought", in *Studies in East European Thought* 58.4 (2006): 243-269.

[57] Concerning the present divergence that undermines the unity of Orthodoxy on the surface of history: Radu Preda, "Die orthodoxen Kirchen zwischen nationaler Identität und *babylonischer Gefangenschaft* in der EU," in Ingeborg Gabriel (Ed.), *Politik und Theologie in Europa. Perspektiven ökumenischer Sozialethik*, (Ostfildern: Matthias-Grünewald, 2008), 285-305. Also see Radu Preda, *Ortodoxia & ortodoxiile. Studii social-teologice* [Orthodoxy & Orthodoxies. Social-Theological Studies] (*Theologia Socialis* 10), (Cluj-Napoca: Eikon, 2010). Also see the article by Athanasios Vletsis, "Der Letzte macht das Licht aus: Orthodoxie vor dem Kollaps? Die Grenzen und die Belastbarkeit panorthodoxer Einheit," in *Una Sancta* 3 (2008): 234-247.

[58] The pan-Orthodox documents on social themes are few in number and, unfortunately, they are not taken into account enough. See such a collection of texts with social-theological character and more (the majority are related to Orthodox participation on the ecumenical dialogue of the last century): Athanasios Basdekis (Ed.), *Orthodoxe Kirche und Ökumenische Bewegung. Dokumente – Erklärungen – Berichte (1900-2006)*, (Frankfurt am Main: Otto Lembeck, 2006). Also consult the collection of the official publication of the Center of the Ecumenical Patriarchate Chambésy-Geneva, *Episkepsis*. Also see the official website of the Center: www.centreorthodoxe.org, accessed on 15 October 2009.

Part VII: Particular Themes and Issues for Orthodox Involvement in Ecumenism

If the first impasse can only have an ecclesiological solution, which is nonetheless predictable on the relatively distant horizon of a general Synod of Orthodoxy, the second one needs a sustained theological approach. The social interpretation of Orthodoxy can have a substantial contribution in this case. Why? Because when we proclaim the necessity of a message of Orthodoxy to the contemporary man, we cannot disregard the fact that he is marked by modernity and by the social-cultural phenomena that follow the so-called post-modernity or radical modernity, which is delayed. In other words, the pastoral, missionary, apologetic, normative, social and cultural dialogue of contemporary Orthodoxy has to take into account what the Germans call *der Sitz im Leben,* meaning the complex of realities (some of them secondary) that facilitates the correct understanding of the moment. As far as modernity is concerned, while sticking to this generic term, we must say that our theological reflection should accept the irreversible character of its project. The irreversible character is in fact the trait of historical theology, the vision of a circular repetition of the major human events that flagrantly contradicts the eschatological perspective of Christianity. Without being determined, this perspective insists upon the fact that the Incarnation of Christ – a unique event – confirms the plan of God (cf. Genesis 1:26-27). This further implies the confirmation of the superior reason of everything that happens in the plan of creation. Therefore, admitting the irreversible character of modernity, that is to say admitting that pre-modernity cannot be reconstructed, not even in laboratory or sect-like conditions, is the first step towards understanding it. Even the philosophers who criticise modernity, like Habermas or Adorno, only do it from the perspective of modernity itself. The two cited authors blame modernity for not being modern enough. If we take into account a basic theological example, we see that even the Church Fathers referred to the syncretic and pagan late Antiquity, as to a given situation. This means that they did not set off on their mission with a model of ideal society dating from the time of Moses or even from the historical time of Christ's life on Earth on their mind. Their fundamental spiritual motivation did not belong to the past, no matter how ideal and moral that past might have been, but to the future of redemption, which is prepared during the time of the present generations. The continuity with all past generations, expressed liturgically in the clearest manner, is materialised by bringing those generations to our present and not by the illusory effort of regressing to their time. From this point of view, history is not a refuge, but an advice to assume our present just like the ones before us had done it. According to this logic, Tradition is, as Lossky put it, "the critical memory of the Church." This means that it is necessary for the assuming of the present challenges, because it provides a foundation for the factual state of our world, it guides us and it enlightens us, while the direction is always facing the Eschaton.[59] The dogmatic authority is not an end in itself and the Church's statements of faith ultimately serve this personal and communitarian ideal. Similarly, by means of comparison, the Holy Scripture is a "closed" text from an editorial point of view, but it is "open" from a hermeneutical point of view so that we can feed ourselves with it in any situation. In other words, the argument of authority is not meant to freeze us within a time that has been proclaimed ideal and thus to render theological thought and debate useless, but to provide them with a frame within which they can exercise their freedom to the fullest, while remaining Orthodox.

In short, turning back to modernity, we can say that rejecting it on the basis that it is bad does not indicate a strong theological state of spirit, but it rather shows a spiritual deficit of faith actualisation or an unnatural inclosing within the dogma data that are meant to help us assume the present and not run away from it, as we have seen. It is useless to further insist upon the fact that this rather widespread attitude makes it possible for all abnormalities to portray themselves as competing, "salvific" solutions which claim to provide answers

---

[59] See Vladimir Lossky, "Tradition and Traditions," in Vladimir Lossky, *In the Image and Likeness of God*, translated by Anca Manolache, Humanitas, (Bucharest, 1998), 134-162. For the patristic manner of relating to the argument of dogmatic authority, see, for example, Michael Fiedrowicz, *Theologie der Kirchenväter. Grundlagen frühchristlicher Glaubensreflexion*, (Freiburg: Herder, 2007). Regarding the way in which the Fathers have integrated contemporary culture in their apologetic (towards the outer sphere) and dogmatic (related to clearing the ecclesiastic space from within) demarche see, as an example, the analysis carried out over several volumes by Christian Gnilka, Χρῆσις. *Die Methode der Kirchenväter im Umgang mit der antiken Kultur*, (Stuttgart: Schwabe, 1984 (vol. I – *Der Begriff des „rechten Gebrauchs"*), 1993 (vol. II – *Kultur und Conversion*)).

for questions whose contents they do not want to hear, and even less, understand. Once the irreversibility of modernity is accepted as a given fact – this does not at all mean that its unchangeableness should be accepted, a proof of this being the fact that it is contested by post-modernity, which in turn is questioned by a post-post-modernity and so on and thus modernity, no matter how well "installed" in history it might seem, is far from being the final stage of humanity – the Orthodox critique of the project can authentically unravel itself by accepting the challenge with an equal lack of inhibitions and with an equal cultural aplomb, based on a healthy pastoral institution, just like the Church Fathers did when they were faced with their "modernity".

Finally, we get to the matter of completing social work with a social theology, or, in other words, of completing practice with vision and charity with mission. We can state that, in the context of the irreversible modernity and of the manner in which the human being, the society and the state from the countries with Orthodox majorities have meanwhile become part of this project that is unique in its own way, the matter of a contribution from the part of a specialized theology to the social project is based on solid grounds. Even if only for the simple and sufficient reason that the redemption of man cannot blot out the social environment in which he is shaped and grows spiritually, Orthodox social theology fully proves its "utility". Moreover, if we take into account the fact that the traditional Churches and confessions have at least one theological discipline meant to analyse the points of contact between faith – personal and institutional – and society (the Catholic social doctrine or Protestant ethics), it once again becomes obvious that we need an equivalent both in the inter-confessional and in the inter-Orthodox dialogue. As far as the term itself is concerned, we need to provide some explanations.

The formula of Orthodox social theology started circulating here when the homogenisation of the state University education was commenced by the enforcement of the Bologna Declaration of June 1999; the faculties of Orthodox theology were part of it. This structural reform has triggered the obligation of the Romanian academic theology to specify its own mechanism, in the case of a double specialisation.[60] Advocating the abolishment of double specialisations in the way in which they used to be practiced until recently, the Bologna system made it possible for the Theology - Social Work department to no longer be a mere association of two discipline branches from two different faculties. This is how a department of Social Theology was created (later renamed due to a certain unclearness concerning the assimilation of its graduate on the labour market). At the same time, a new discipline was established; this discipline is the one that provides the essence of the specialisation: Social Theology. This involuntary positive effect, present at the time being only at a lexical level, practically means the opening of a new and interesting horizon for the articulation of the Orthodox social theological discourse, with a full knowledge of the facts and with an academic legitimacy. A very important fact is that this syntax also means taking the social preoccupations out of the exclusive sphere of the deacons and rendering it as an assistance of social outcasts; it also means re-establishing a relationship between theology and the other profane disciplines that study the phenomena of the public space.

As one might easily suspect, in order to speak about an Eastern *Weltanschauung,* we still have a long road ahead of us and we still have to face a lot of prejudices that have grown strong especially during the last half of century, when theology has been rather an *Orchideenfach.* This means that it was lacking a social impact and a dialogue with the world, in the non-liturgical and profane sense of the word. On the basis of historical experience of Church life within the limits of a ghetto, we can explain why the Orthodox theology taught in school still preserves the vision according to which the social problem – no matter how complex it might be – is either secondary or localized somewhere in the area of competence of moral theology. Therefore, people forget that moral theology should be specialised in teaching the virtues and the manner of practicing them on a personal level; this means that some implicit or explicit references to the social aspects of the individual moral choice can only be included in the moral discourse in an adjacent manner. Projected in inappropriate terms, Moral Theology turns, from a spiritual and philokalic theology, into a sort of universal model of interpretation

---

[60] The Bologna Process also has consequences in the sphere of ethical theology of other religions. See the study of symptomatic character carried out by Reiner Anselm, Johannes Fischer, Wolfgang Lienemann, Hans-Richard Reuter, "Der Bologna-Prozess als Herausforderung für die theologische Ethik," in *Zeitschrift für Evangelische Ethik* 49 (2005): 169-189.

of all phenomena, crises and problems for which it does not provide solutions or normative alternatives on a public level. Pushed aside from its spiritual role because of the intrusion of the secondary element, which is not supported on a secondary level by its specific criteria of interpretation, Moral Theology becomes moralism. It becomes a paradoxical theological support of Christian lack of adaptation to the world, which is a reason to stop any missionary zeal to spread the faith. Thus, the Church appears to want to teach the world what is right before understanding the world as it is. The inconsistency between the message and the audience thus underlines not only the missionary clumsiness of the Church workers, but it also provides the sceptics and the anti-ecclesiastic people with ammunition. The exit of this methodological trap, in which some fellow theologians continue to reside out of intellectual and spiritual comfort, can only be provided by a social theology conceived as being complementary to the moral theology and generally aimed at hermeneutically transporting theological themes to the social space of debate, as well as "profane" aspects to the theological debate, a fact which is proven by the last Orthodox documents on the subject.[61]

Briefly and as a general conclusion, Orthodox social theology must be regarded as a necessary challenge that must be faced after the Orthodox Churches of Eastern Europe regained their freedom of expression within the public space two decades ago. As freedom means responsibility and as the assumption of the latter is actually desirable in the context of the post-secular paradigm, social theology answers the call of time, without being a trend or a concession. It translates the genuine apostolic mandate of a Church that exists in the concrete world and also announces the Kingdom of God into contemporary terms. Such a theology, carefully and competently inclined towards the social life, without transforming it into a vehicle of auto-secularisation through an excess of sociology, challenges us all to an acquisitive return to the Biblical and patristic sources of faith, in order to give an adequate answer to its critics (who are more and more numerous). Most of all it has to give an answer to those who, despite the fact that accept the teaching of the Church, do not know how to lead a harmonious Orthodox life in the 21st century.

---

[61] In addition to the few pan-Orthodox documents with social-theological subjects, we are currently witnessing the intensification of the preoccupations with this matter shown by local Orthodoxies. An example is provided by Russia. See the document, dating from 2000, on the social vision of the Russian Orthodox Church; in original: Основы социальной концепции Русской Православной Церкви – on the official website http://www.patriarhia.ru/db/text/428616.html, accessed on 1 March 2009; *Fundamentele concepţiei sociale a Bisericii Ortodoxe Ruse* [Basis for the Social Concepts of The Russian Orthodox Church] translated into Romanian in: Ioan Ică jr., Germano Marani (ed.), *Gândirea socială a Bisericii. Fundamente — documente — analize — perspective* [The Social Thought of the Church. Bases – Documents – Analyses], (Sibiu: Deisis, 2002), 185-266. The electronic variant of the document in Romanian translation can be found at www.teologia-sociala.ro. This document was quite quickly translated in several international languages. See the German version: Josef Thesing, Rudolf Uertz (Ed.), *Die Grundlagen der Sozialdoktrin der Russisch-Orthodoxen Kirche*, (Sankt Augustin: Deutsche Übersetzung mit Einführung und Kommentar, Konrad-Adenauer-Stiftung, 2001). See the French version: Église Orthodoxe Russe, *Les fondements de la doctrine sociale*, Introduction par le Métropolite Cyrille de Smolensk et de Kaliningrad, Traduction du russe par Hyacinthe Destivelle, Alexandre Siniakov, Claire Jouniévy, (Paris: Cerf, 2007). Further, see the 2008 document on human rights. The original text – „Основы учения Русской Православной Церкви о достоинстве, свободе и правах человека" – can be found at the same address, http://www.patriarhia.ru/db/text/428616.html, accessed on 1 March 2009. Shortly after, the German translation was published: *Die Grundlagen der Lehre der Russischen Orthodoxen Kirche über die Würde, die Freiheit und die Menschenrechte*, Veröffentlicht in deutscher Sprache durch das Auslandsbüro der Konrad-Adenauer-Stiftung, (Moskau, 2008). See the Romanian translation of this last document in the annex of Radu Preda, "Ortodoxia şi drepturile omului. Aspecte social-teologice" [Orthodoxy and human rights. Social-Theological Aspects], *Analele ştiinţifice ale Facultăţii de Teologie Ortodoxă*, Cluj XI (2007-2008), (Cluj-Napoca: Renaşterea, 2009), 181-214.

PART VIII

ECUMENICAL FORMATION IN ORTHODOX THEOLOGICAL EDUCATION

(127) Orthodox Theological Education and the Need for Ecumenical Formation – An Introduction

Fr. Thomas FitzGerald

The historic Encyclical of 1920 from the Ecumenical Patriarchate is frequently cited as one of the major impetuses for the contemporary ecumenical movement. Written only a few short years after the conclusion of the First World War, this encyclical was addressed "Unto All the Churches of Christ Everywhere." The letter was probably the first official correspondence of this century to be addressed from one church to all other Christian churches. It was a time when formal contacts between the churches were limited and generally polemical.

This Patriarchal encyclical sent greetings to all the churches and invited them to consider seriously the establishment of a "Fellowship of Churches" which would be a vehicle of Christian reconciliation. Cognizant of the tragic consequences of the Balkan Wars and the First World War, the Patriarchate boldly called upon the churches to come together in common service and in theological study. Echoing the tone of an earlier Encyclical of 1902, this encyclical said:

> Our own Church holds that rapprochement between the various Christian Churches and fellowship between them is not excluded by doctrinal differences which exist between them. In our opinion such a rapprochement is highly desirable and necessary. It would be useful in many ways for the real interest of each particular Church and of the whole Christian body, and also for the preparation and advancement of that blessed union which will be completed in the future in accordance with the will of God. We therefore consider that the present time is most favorable for bringing forward this important question and studying it together.[1]

The encyclical recognized that two actions would immediately contribute greatly to this rapprochement. First, the Patriarchate saw that it was necessary to remove "all the mistrust and bitterness between the different churches which arise from the tendency of some of them to entice and proselytize adherents of other confessions." And secondly, the letter affirmed that "love should be rekindled and strengthened among churches, so that they should no more consider one another as strangers and foreigners, but as relatives, and as being part of the household of Christ and 'fellow heirs, members of the same body and partakers of the promise of God in Christ' " (Eph. 3:6).[2] The Encyclical reflected both profound theological affirmations and the need of theological reflection to advance the cause of reconciliation.

This encyclical was also significant, because it identified a number of areas through which contact among the churches could be immediately begun. Of the many substantial proposals, it is quite significant that the Patriarchate called for new relationships between the theological schools and the professors of theology of various traditions. The Encyclical called for the exchange of theological and ecclesiastical reviews, and of other works published in each church. The encyclical also proposed the exchange of students for further training among the seminaries of the different churches.

In these brief but significant proposals, the Patriarchate recognized that professors and students from the divided churches could come together for study of issues of divisions and for mutual understanding. The Patriarchate also recognized that literature from the churches needed to be shared. As with many of its dramatic proposals contained in the Encyclical, the Patriarchate recognized that the advancement of reconciliation and

---

[1] "Encyclical to the Churches of Christ Everywhere," in *The Orthodox Church and the Ecumenical Movement*, ed. Constantin G. Patelos (Geneva: WCC Publications, 1978), 40.

[2] Ibid., 41.

unity could be profoundly affected by positive relationship among professors and student of theological schools of different churches. A remarkable insight for the time![3]

The Patriarchal Encyclical of 1920 was unprecedented. Clearly, the tone and the content of this encyclical were remarkable for its day. At a time when official contact among the Churches was nearly nonexistent, the Patriarchate proposed a "Fellowship of Churches." When mutual mistrust and accusations were common, the Patriarchate advocated mutual respect and joint theological study. At a time when it was more common to emphasize the differences between the churches, the Patriarchate reminded all Christians of their common allegiance to Christ and his Gospel of reconciliation.

A Commitment to Dialogue

Since the publication of the Encyclical of 1920, the Ecumenical Patriarchate has continued to play a decisive role both in advocating greater cooperation among the Autocephalous Orthodox Churches and in guiding them in the stages of the ecumenical movement.[4]

The contributions of Orthodox theologians to the process of Christian reconciliation and the restoration of the visible unity of the churches have been profound and multifarious. This contribution to ecumenical witness has been made especially during the past fifty years and has been expressed through personal encounters, formal dialogues, lectures, publications, and through worship. It is a witness which is expressed in local ecumenical settings, in regional and national councils of churches, at the World Council of Churches and in formal bilateral dialogues.

Certainly, Orthodox theologians in recent years have raised legitimate concerns about the direction and character of certain ecumenical organizations. Yet, Orthodox theologians have contributed in a positive manner both to bilateral and to multilateral theological dialogues. They have contributed to the insights of theologians from other churches. The perspectives of Orthodox worship, spirituality, and iconography have contributed to the liturgical renewal movement in the Western Churches. All of this has advanced the process of reconciliation and the unity of the churches. And, it is an offering which has contributed to a deeper and richer understanding of "the knowledge of God's mystery that is Christ himself (Col 2:2)."

A Renewal of Theology

Closely related to Orthodox involvement in the early ecumenical movement has been the renewal of Orthodox theology. In the past fifty years especially, we have witnessed a gradual renewal of Orthodox theology which has moved it far beyond its captivity to the arid systematic "manuals" of theology which were influenced by the Reformation and Counter-Reformation debates of the 16th and 17th centuries. The Reformation and Catholic Reformation raised critical questions about scripture and tradition, faith and works, sacraments and ministry. For the Orthodox, the period between the 15th century and the early 20th century was a time when limited centers of advanced theological study and educational resources were available. It is frequently described as a time of theological pseudomorphosis.

This renewal is expressed in an approach to theology which transcends the arid scholasticism and polemicism coming out of periods of oppression and limited educational opportunities. It is an approach to theology which integrates Orthodoxia and Orthopraxia, which relates theology, spirituality, and philanthropy. It is an approach which has an ecclesial context centered upon the Eucharist. It is an approach which recognizes that all authentic theology has a pastoral character because it is concerned with salvation.

This renewal is reflected not only in Orthodox involvement in bilateral and multilateral dialogues, but also in a gradual engagement among Orthodox theologians from the various Autocephalous Churches and

[3] Ibid.

[4] Thomas FitzGerald, *The Ecumenical Patriarchate and Christian Unity,* (Brookline: Holy Cross Orthodox Press, 2009).

theological institutions. Encouraged by the Ecumenical Patriarchate, the Orthodox were coming out of their isolation from one another. Old ecclesiastical tensions and nationalistic barriers were beginning to soften in favor of cooperation and dialogue. Let us remember that the first Conference of Orthodox Theological Schools was held in Athens in 1936.

Through ecumenical meetings, theological dialogues, and consultations Western Christian theologians have come into a living contact with the Orthodox Church and her theologians. This encounter has enabled many Western Christians to move beyond a distorted and stereotypical perception of Orthodoxy which was popularized in the late 19th and early 20th centuries. This false perception of Orthodoxy, which portrays it as essentially exotic, decadent and moribund, was rooted especially in the writings of Edward Gibbon and Adolf von Harnack. Regretfully, their influence can still be found in more recent theological and historical studies which continue to ignore so many of the developments in non-Western Christianity. At the same time, the scholarly writings of Orthodox theologians and historians have done much to provide a more balanced and accurate picture of Orthodox Christianity. It is against this backdrop, with its limitations and possibilities, that the Orthodox have made their contribution to ecumenical witness.

Aspects of Ecumenical Formation

Today, there are well over one hundred Orthodox theological institutions throughout the world. They have a variety of titles: seminaries, institutes, faculties, academies, and Schools of Theology. Some are small institutions concerned primarily with the preparation of future clergy. Some are related to state universities and are concerned with the preparation of future teachers, theologians and clergy. Some have a rich history. Others are only recently established. In addition, there are Orthodox theologians who teach at universities and institutes which are not directly related to the Orthodox Church.

Viewed from a global perspective, Orthodox theological institutions are quite diverse. They reflect the needs of the Church in a specific place. Each reflects the particular history and culture of the Church in a specific context. Each reflects the educational methodology in a specific place. Each may reflect the relationship of Church and state in a specific context. Here, let us not forget that the famous Theological School of Halki of the Ecumenical Patriarchate remains closed.

There are three major characteristics which bind these diverse Orthodox theological institutions together.

First, each school is obliged to provide its students with an appreciation of the breath and depth of Orthodox Christian theology and life. Whether the program lasts one year or four years of graduate level study, this is no small task. It is a great challenge to convey the various disciplines of Orthodox theology in a manner which is both comprehensive and understandable within a given context.

Second, each school is obliged to provide its students with an appreciation of the wider theological world and the issues of the society. In today's world, Orthodox theology must be done in relationship with other theological trends and with an appreciation of the issues of society. The Orthodox do not live on islands. The great fathers and teachers of the Church were not reluctant to address theological topics. They also addressed the political and moral challenges facing their people. They were concerned with morality, philanthropy, peace, and social justice. (Of course, these were theological as well!) They sought to engage their culture and to apply the Gospel perspectives to their challenges because they knew that Christ had come "for the life of the world" (John 6:51).

With this patristic spirit, Orthodox theology must address contemporary concerns about the loving God, the dignity of the human person, and the blessing of the creation. The message of the Gospel must have contemporary application. As the great Fathers did in their time, Orthodox theologians must address the issues of our day. With the guidance of the Spirit, authentic theology provides perspectives on our relationships and responsibilities as believers today. Authentic theology bears witness to the healing and reconciling activity of the Living God who "desires all to be saved and come to knowledge of truth" (1 Tim. 2:4).

Part VIII: Ecumenical Formation in Orthodox Theological Education

Within the Orthodox churches today, there is an unhealthy tendency towards isolation and self-sufficiency. There is a tendency to avoid critical issues facing the Church and the societies in which we live. For many, the reality of pluralism and a growing secularism is overwhelming.

Moreover, there is a sectarian movement within certain circles of Church life which distorts Orthodox teachings and misleads the faithful.

We cannot be frozen in our witness to the love of God. We cannot become victims of fanaticism or narrow mindedness. Here, we cannot hide our face in the sand. Orthodox theologians need to address critical contemporary challenges from the perspective of the historic Apostolic Faith.

Theologians need to do more theological reflection on a number of critical issues. These include issues of internal Church life. These also include issues such as the dignity of women in Church and society, human rights and responsibilities, poverty, world religions, bioethics, moral issues, technological developments and the environment.

Many of these issues and other related ones were raised in Conferences on Orthodox theological education held in Basil in 1978, Athens/Penteli in 2000, and in Sibiu in 2012.[5] These texts are available in this handbook,

Because of the challenges we face today, therefore, there is a tremendous need for Orthodox leaders and theologians to have the opportunity to meet together to identify and to discuss these concerns.

And thirdly, this theological reflection must be done in a community which encourages a deepened personal relationship with God and one another. Orthodox theology is best done within the context of a believing community of faith and worship. One of the great dangers of Orthodox theology today is that it can become an academic pursuit with little connection to the community of faith and worship. Knowledge without love has little lasting value.

When we speak about ecumenical formation, we are referring to at least three dimensions of teaching and learning.

First, Orthodox theologians have an obligation to transmit to the wider Orthodox population the advances in theological discussions and common understanding which have been reached in ecumenical dialogues. The story of the ecumenical dialogues cannot be the domain solely of academic theologians and hierarchs who are chief among the participants in such encounters. In order to involve the wider church and theological institutions, the themes of the dialogues, the consensus documents produced, the difficulties, and the goals of these discussions must be clearly disseminated among younger theologians, clergy and laity. In so doing, this will contribute to the process of reception by the entire Church. It will also prevent misunderstanding and misrepresentation of the ecumenical dialogues.[6]

Second, Orthodox theologians have an obligation to convey to the wider church community and theological institutions an accurate picture of developments which have taken place in the Catholic and Protestant theological worlds. The other churches must be studied with integrity. This requires honesty and humility. It is important, for example, to identify the historic factors in the divisions between the Chalcedonian and non Chalcedonians. It is important to identify the historic factors contributing to the 'Great Schism' between the Christian East and the Christian West. It is important to identify the historic factors contributing to the Protestant Reformation and subsequent developments.

Yet, we cannot remain in the realm of distant history regardless of how important it may be. Each of these historical events has been studied extensively over the past fifty years, especially within the context of the ecumenical movement. Scholars have placed new light on these historic divisions and the theological perspectives behind them. Bilateral dialogues have studied the issues and have provided areas of new consensus. Let us simply recall the extensive dialogues, both unofficial and official, between Orthodox and Oriental Orthodox. Let

---

[5] The full reports of these meetings are available in this chapter of the Handbook, see below.

[6] John D. Zizioulas "The Ecumenical Dimensions of Orthodox Theological Education," in Fr. Gregory Edwards (ed.) *The One and the Many: Studies on God, Man, the Church, and the World Today*, (Alhambra, California: Sebastian Press, 2010), 349-359. (The paper of Metropolitan John is re-published in this section of the present Handbook).

us recall the extensive contemporary studies on the Filioque question. Let us recall the Second Vatican Council and subsequent developments in the Catholic Church. Let us recall the document on *Baptism, Eucharist, and Ministry*. Let us recall the *Joint Declaration* between the Catholic Church and the Lutheran World Federation.

These are no small matters. And there are many others which could be mentioned. The question is whether Orthodox theologians have presented these and other contemporary documents when discussing the present stage of Orthodox relationships with the Catholic Church and the Protestant Churches as well as the ecumenical movement in general. There have been critical developments in the theological world, both positive and negative, which must be honestly presented and analyzed.

Finally, we cannot fail to mention the importance of personal relationships among theologians from different traditions. In the course of bilateral and multilateral dialogues, Orthodox theologians have come 'face to face' with the colleagues from other churches. A personal face is placed on the representatives of another tradition. In a sense, these personal relationships do much to overcome past prejudices and misunderstandings. These personal relationships provide a foundation to examine in a new light issue of division and directions for reconciliation.

Conclusion

The Patriarchal Encyclical of 1920 recognized the critical importance of theologians and theological schools in fostering reconciliation among the divided churches. The Patriarchate envisioned meetings of theologians from the various churches. The Patriarchate envisioned students of theology from the various churches meeting together. Certainly, history shows that the insight of the Patriarchate was profound. Over the past nine decades, Orthodox theologians have been engaged in the renewal of Orthodox theology. They have addressed issues of reconciliation and church unity. And at the same time, they have joined with colleagues from other churches in both formal and informal settings. They have come to know one another. They are no longer strangers. In many places, there has been a genuine encounter of theologians from various churches. These encounters have strengthened Christian witness, enriched the participants and contributed to the unity which Christ wills for his Church (John 17:21).

Bibliography

Metropolitan Maximos Aghiorgoussis, *Together in Christ: Studies in Ecclesiology and Ecumenism*, (Brookline: Holy Cross Orthodox Press, 2012).

Kyriaki Karidoyanes FitzGerald, *Persons in Communion: A Theology of Authentic Relationships*, (Berkeley: InterOrthodox Press, 2006).

Thomas FitzGerald, *The Ecumenical Patriarchate and Christian Unity*, (Brookline: Holy Cross Orthodox Press, 2009).

Gennadios Limouris, (ed.), *Orthodox Vision of Ecumenism*, (Geneva: World Council of Churches, 1994).

Constantin G. Patelos, (ed.), *The Orthodox Church and the Ecumenical Movement*, (Geneva: World Council of Churches, 1978).

Metropolitan John Zizioulas of Pergamon, *Being as Communion*, (Crestwood, NY: St. Vladimir's Press, 1985), 67-122.

(128) A short global Survey on Orthodox Theological Institutions[1]

Fr. Viorel Ionita

The Orthodox theological schools of the 19th and 20th centuries represented one of the decisive factors in promoting the theological thinking during this span of time. As from the Middle Ages up to the threshold of the modern times, Orthodox theological education was carried out especially in monasteries, and as such, their role in preserving and conveying accurately the Orthodox theology and particularly the Orthodox spirituality should not be underestimated. Proper institutions for theological education in the current sense of the word appeared no earlier than the 17th century and evolved during the next century. We mention to this end the royal academies in Bucharest and Jassy, with Greek as the teaching language, as the students of these schools were recruited from all over southeastern Europe. These academies were not intended for the formation of future clergy only, since along with humanistic and theological sciences real sciences were also taught.[2] On this account these academies may be considered among the first institutions of Orthodox education, which entertained if not a dialogue, at least a creative debate with the western thinking of the time.

During the same period mention should be made of the theological academies of the Russian Orthodox Church, namely those in Moscow, St. Petersburg, Kiev and Kazan. Due to the influence exerted by Tsar Peter I on the Russian culture, these academies ended up by using intensively the Latin language. In this way the Russian theologians had a direct access to the Western theological writings, while the Orthodox theological thought was permeated by scholastic thinking. We should also remember that the penetration of the Western scholastic thought into Orthodox theology using Greek language had taken place during the last centuries of the Byzantine Empire, through the activity of the so-called latinofroni, a term designating those thinkers who were influenced by the Latin philosophy in the 14th century.[3] Following these influences the Orthodox theology began its scholastic period. It was able to free itself from these influences only in the 20th century. Certainly this scholastic period of the Orthodox theology was severely criticized in the 20th century, mainly because it represented the element from which the Orthodox theological thought in the previous century was trying to break free.

The first Orthodox theological schools were founded in the 19th century in framework of the state universities in Greece, Romania, Serbia, etc. In addition to the theological schools incorporated in the public system, higher theological schools continued to exist in all Orthodox Churches, either as academies or as institutes. Even though these institutions which developed throughout the 20th century faced serious difficulties in several countries, they became real strongholds, and without them the extraordinary development of the Orthodox theological thought cannot be imagined. Finally, let us recall that, owing to the emigration of a great number of Orthodox believers and theologians - in the first place from the Soviet Union following the establishment of the Bolshevik dictatorship in Russia, and then from other countries with an Orthodox majority - several

---

[1] This article by Fr. Viorel Ionita, which is re-published here with the necessary adjustments, was first published in Viorel Ionita (ed.) *The 20th century and early 21st century. A Romanian Orthodox Perspective*, (Bucureşti: Editura BASILICA a Patriarhiei Române, 2011) under the title "Orthodox Institutions of Theological Education: Key Factors in promoting Orthodox theology," trans. Carmen Bobocescu, 151-177.

[2] Rev. Viorel Ionită, "Der Unterricht der exakten Wissenschaften an der Fürstlichen Hochschule von Bukarest im XVII.-XVIII. Jahrhundert und die Kirche in der Walachei," in: Olivier Fatio (ed.), *Les Eglises Face aux sciences du Moyen Age au XXème siècle. Actes du Colloque de la Commission international d'histoire ecclésiastique comparée tenu à Genève en août 1989*, (Genève: Droz, 1991), 109-117.

[3] See the chapter: "Encounter with the West," in John Meyendorff, *Byzantine Theology. Historical Trends and Doctrinal Themes*, (New York: Fordham University Press, 1979), 103 ff.

institutions Orthodox theological schools were set up in the West. The first one was the Saint Serge Institute in Paris, followed by Saint Vladimir's Seminary in New York, and others.

Until the mid-20th century, Orthodox theology was virtually unknown in the West. At the beginning of that century highly authoritative theologians like Adolf von Harnack or Hans Lietzmann considered that the Orthodox Church in their time was nothing but the petrified Church from the time of Constantine the Great. That is why in the Protestant as well as in the Catholic world one would give credit to the information about the Orthodox Church or theology only if it came from Western specialized authors. It was only in the second half of the previous century that the Westerners started to be interested in Orthodox theology and to grant more and more credit to Orthodox theologians. Thus the Orthodox theologians were to become equal partners to the Western theologians so that the former came to exert an increasing influence on the Western theological thought of different confessional traditions. This change was largely due to the contribution of the Orthodox theologians in Diaspora, forbidden in their home countries, but highly appreciated in the West. We have in mind especially the theologians of the two institutes we mentioned above. The role played by these theologians in asserting the Orthodox theology in the Western world is still little known, and the reception of their work in the traditional Orthodox theological Institutes has just started. In addition to the contribution by the Orthodox theologians from the Diaspora towards promoting their theology among theologians belonging to different denominations, we must recall another important factor, i.e., the translation of an ever-growing number of representative Orthodox theological works into Western languages.

This worldwide presence of the Orthodox Theology, which was facilitated particularly by Orthodox participation in inter-Christian meetings on different levels, especially from the second half of the last century, led to the creation of departments or chairs of Orthodox Theology at Faculties of Western Theology, as it happened in München and Münster in Germany, Graz in Austria, Glasgow and Oxford in the UK, and so on. A special example is that of the Ecumenical Institute in Bossey, Switzerland, set up by the World Council of Churches soon after the Second World War, which has a chair for an Orthodox theologian, held, among others, by Nikos Nissiotis, His Beatitude Patriarch Daniel of Romania (at the time a young lay theologian), Metropolitan Athanasios of Achaia (Archimandrite Athanasios Chatzopoulos at that time), Rev. Prof. Dr. Ioan Sauca, and so on.

As far as the current theological education is concerned, there are at present more than 30 Higher Theological Schools throughout the world, be they academies, institutes or schools. They function in the public or private system and belong to different autocephalous Orthodox Churches. In addition to these schools, there over 120 Theological Seminaries and at least 10 special institutions where Church Music or Sacred Art is being taught.[4] One must not overlook the fact that three decades ago there were only a third of such institutions of Orthodox Theological Education and that a large number of them have been set up over the past few years; a testimony to the development of Orthodox theology during this period of time.

In the following pages we are going to present some of the most important schools of higher education, active during the 20th century, in order to highlight the way in which Orthodox theological thought developed during this period of time. It is not our purpose to outline here a history of Orthodox theological education, even though such a history would be worth writing. Since Orthodox theological education is mainly provided in the language employed by each Orthodox Church, we will refer to a few of these institutions according to their teaching language: Greek, Arabic, Russian, Serbian, Romanian, Bulgarian, etc.

I. Institutions of Orthodox Theological Education in Greek Language

I.1. *The Theological School of Halki (Turkey)* was for a long period of time one of the most important theological school of the Ecumenical Patriarchate. It was set up in 1844 on the island of Halki and provided both high and higher education. The school functioned until 1971 when it was closed by order of the Turkish government.

[4] http://orthodoxwiki.org/Seminaries_and_Theological_Schools (last accessed at September 2013).

Part VIII: Ecumenical Formation in Orthodox Theological Education

In spite of multiple interventions at an international level, the Halki School has not yet reopened. Some of the professors of theology from Halki have drafted many theological documents of pan-Orthodox importance during the 20th century. The Ecumenical Patriarchs Maximus V, Athenagoras I, Demetrios I, as well as His Holiness the Patriarch Bartholomew I were among the students of this school.[5]

I.2. *The School of Theology at the National and Kapodistrian University of Athens (Greece)*[6] was founded in 1837 by decree of King Otho I of Greece. In 1862, the name of the university was changed from *Othonian* to *National*. At the beginning of the previous century, the School of Theology became part of the newly-founded Kapodistrian University (1911), and since 1932 it has been part of the National Kapodistrian University of Athens. The school's structure was homogenous until 1974 when, beside Theology, a Pastoral Department for clergy education was set up. In 1975, this department was replaced by a section for "clergy qualification" for a period of two years. In 1977, the Pastoral Department was introduced again in the structure of the school and ever since it functioned uninterruptedly. The 1982 law sanctions the current status of the School of Theology in Athens with two Faculties: Theological and Pastoral. In 1994, the Pastoral Department became a section of Social Theology. Among the most notable Athenian professors we can mention Christos Androutsos, Chrysostomos Papadopoulos, Amilkas Alivizatos, Ioannis Karmiris, K. Bonis, G. Konidaris, Savvas Agourides, Panayotis N. Trembelas, Konstantinos Belezos, Constantinos Diovouniotis, Evangelos Theodorou, Megas L. Farantos, Konstantinos Scouteris, Vlasios Pheidas, Georgios Metallinos, Konstantinos Delikostantis, and others.

I.3. The foundation of *the School of Theology at the Aristotle University of Thessaloniki (Greece)*[7] was envisaged in the 1925 law of the Hellenic government, which stipulated the establishment of a University in Thessaloniki. Nevertheless, it was only in the spring of 1942 that the school started to function and in the autumn of the same year the courses were suspended only to be resumed three years later. From 1945 until today the faculty had functioned uninterruptedly, having a unitary structure until 1964, when the courses would be organized into three sections: (a) Theology; (b) Pastoral; and (c) Church and Social Service. The last section was dissolved a few years later. The two departments had common professors until 1983, but different curricula. In the academic year 1975-1976 the documents mention the existence of a department for Clergy Formation in Thessaloniki. The current condition of the Faculty was regulated by the 1982 law, which stipulates that the two departments *(Pastoral Theology* and *Social Theology)* were to function as distinct entities academically and administratively, while belonging to the same institution. In the two schools, courses are held in several departments: five at the School of Theology and four at the School of Pastoral Theology. Among the best-known professors who taught here we should mention Georgios Mantzaridis, V. Christoforidis, Ioannis Anastasiou, Fr. Ioannis Romanides, V. Stravridis, Christos Oikonomou, George Martzelos, Fr. Theodoros Zisis, Petros Vassiliadis, Anestis Kesselopoulos, Dimitra Koukoura etc. Since 1971, the School functions on its own premises inside the campus of the Aristotle University. From 1963 onwards the School of Theology in Thessaloniki has provided postgraduate as well as doctoral studies.

---

[5] http://orthodoxwiki.org/Theological_School_of_Halki (last accessed at September 2013)
[6] Chapter written on the basis of information conveyed by Rev. Assistant professor Dr. Ionut Moldoveanu and PhD Candidate Sorin Stoian. See also: *University Course Guide. National and Kapodistrian University of Athens. School of Theology. Faculty of Theology* [in Greek], academic year 2009-2010, (Athens, 2009); Dimitrios Balanos, *The History of the School of Theology,* (Athens: National and Kapodistrian University of Athens, 1937), as well as http://deantheol.uoa.gr/ (last accessed at September 2013).
[7] Chapter written on the basis of information conveyed by Rev. Assistant professor PhD Ionut Moldoveanu and PhDC Sorin Stoian. Also see the *Annuary of the Academic Year* [in Greek], University of Thessaloniki, the academic years 1948-1984; Theodoros Zisis, *The School of Theology in Thessaloniki: An Homage (1942-1992)* [in Greek], (Thessaloniki, 1999); as well as: http://www.auth.gr/faculties (last accessed at September 2013).

II. Institutions of Theological Education in Arabic language

Saint John of Damascus Institute of Theology in Balamand (Lebanon)[8] was set up in 1970 and was officially inaugurated on 7 October 1971 by his Holiness Patriarch Elias IV of Antioch and All East. This institute is the most important institution of Orthodox Theological Higher Education in Arabic language. Among the most representative professors we can mention: Isaac Barakat, Daniel Ayuch, Georgi Fadi, Georges Nahas, Ramy Wannous.

III. Institutions of Theological Education in Russian language

III.1. *The Theological Academy of Moscow (Russia)*[9] had its origin in the Greco-Latin School founded in Moscow in 1687 as the first higher education institution of this city. In 1701, Tsar Peter the Great transformed this school into a state academy, in the pattern of the Western universities. In 1775, the name of the Academy was officially changed into Slavonic Greek and Latin Academy, and in 1814 the latter was transformed into the Ecclesiastical Academy and was transferred from Moscow to the Holy Trinity Monastery (St. Sergius Lavra). In 1918, the Academy was closed by the Bolshevik government and it was reopened in Moscow in 1943. In 1949, it moved back to St. Sergius Lavra where it has hitherto functioned. In 1947, the Academy achieved the right to grant the academic degrees of PhD Candidate, PhD and Professor. Among the professors of this institution we can mention: Fjodor Posdejewsky, Metropolitan Arsenii Stadnitkii, Filaret Gumilevsky, Alexander Gorsky, E. Golubinsky, Ioan Popov, Veniamin Platonov, Dimitrii Bogoliubov, Nicolai Kolcitkii, Peter Knedici, Serghei A. Volkov, A. Lebedev, Veniamin Platonov, Serghei V. Troitskii, Archbishop Sergius, Metropolitan Nicolai Kytepov, Archbishop Alexander Timofeev, Aleksej I. Osipov, Konstantin E. Skurat, Vladislav Cypin, and others.

III.2. *St. Petersburg Orthodox Theological Academy (Russia)*[10]. Its forerunner is the Slavonic school which functioned in the Alexander Nevskji Monastery and was founded in 1721. In 1726, the school was transformed into the Slavonic-Greco-Latin Seminary; in 1788, into the St Persburg Principal Seminary and, in 1797, it became an academy. The academy was closed by the Bolshevik government in 1918. Among the most notable professors of the 19th century were Metropolitan Filaret Drozdov, Vasily Vasilievitch Bolotov, Nikolai Nikanorovitch Glubokovsky, A.P. Lopukhin, I.A. Chistovitch, A.I. Brilliantov, Evgeny Bolkhovitinov, Makary Bulgakov, Innokenty Borisov, Anthony Vadkovsky, A.A. Dmitrievsky and among the best-known alumni: St. John of Kronstadt, St. Tikhon (Bellavin), St Nicholas of Japan, Varnava (Rosich) the Patriarch of Serbia, St. Theophanus the Recluse and St. Metropolitan Benjamin (Kasansky), N.D. Uspenskij. The Orthodox Theological Academy of St. Petersburg was reopened in 1946. The professors of the latest period included His Holiness Cyril Patriarch of Moscow and All Russia, as well as Vitaly Borovoj, Vladimir Mustafin, Iannuarij Iuliev, Vladimir Khulap, and others.

III.3. *The Kiev Theological Academy*[11] was founded in 1632 by the son of a Romanian ruler, Archimandrite Peter Mogila. To start with, it functioned as an Orthodox school on the grounds of Lavra Pecerska Monastery, with Latin and Polish as teaching languages. In 1701, the school became *Peter Mogila Academy;* throughout the 18th century a whole series of famous professors taught there: A.A. Dimitrievski, F.A. Smirnov, V.D. Priluczkiy, N.N. Palmov, M.N. Skaballanovic and others. In 1819, the academy was closed by a decree of Tsar Alexander I and two years later it was reopened on the same premises under the name of Theological Academy, closed again by a decree of the Bolshevik government. In 1992, the Theological Academy was reopened and has hitherto functioned under the jurisdiction of the Ukrainian Orthodox Church (Patriarchate of Moscow).

---

[8] http://www.balamand.edu.lb/theology/Introduction.htm#History (last accessed at September 2013).

[9] http://www.mpda.ru/history/faces/ (last accessed at September 2013).

[10] Information conveyed by Rev. Prof. Dr. Vladimir Khulap from Saint Petersburg Theological Academy; see also: www.spbda.ru.

[11] http://orthodox.org.ua/eng/node/71 (last accessed at September 2013).

III.4. The Kazan Theological Academy[12] was originally a school for the education of children of the clergy in this city, set up in 1718. In 1723, this school was transformed into the Slavonic-latin School, and in turn was reorganized as the Kazan Theological Seminary in 1732. It was not until 1842 that the Kazan Theological Academy was set up and it became the fourth Theological Academy of the Tsarist Empire, after Moscow, St. Petersburg and Kiev. Among the professors of this academy we should mention Veniamin Snegirev, Nikolai Petrov, Nikanor Brovkovic, Ioan Sokolov, V.A. Snegirevs, P.P. Ponomarev, L.I. Pisarev; N.F. Krasnoselcev,V.A. narbekov, Victor Ivanovich Nesmelov, Ilia Berdnikov, Peter Vasilievich Znamensky, Gordiy Semenovich Sablukov. In its early stages, the Kazan Academy was noted especially for its missionary activity among non-Christians. This academy was closed by the Bolsheviks in 1918. Among its alumni, several died as martyrs during the Communist regime: Metropolitan Anatoly Grisyuk, Archbishop Athanasios Malinin, Victor Ostrovidov, Gavrill Abolimov, German Ryashentsev, Gury Stepanov, Bishop Ioasaf Udalov, Juvenaly Maslovsky, Ioann Poyarkov and Iov Rogozhin. In September 1997, a theological seminary was opened on the premises of the former academy.

III.5. St. Tikhon's Theological Institute in Moscow was set up in 1992 and provides theological education especially to those who previously graduated from other fields of study. The study programs involve: Pastoral Theology; Catechetics, History-Philology, the education of professors of Religion, Ecclesiastical Iconography, Painting, and Architecture.[13]

III.6. St. Andrew's Biblical Institute in Moscow was founded in 1995, as an institution of theological education based on a university curriculum. As its name implies, Saint Andrew Biblical Institute offers the possibility to study theology, especially biblical studies, not only for future clergy, but also for larger circles of people interested in this kind of studies. The institute organizes summer courses, seminars, public conferences, etc. In addition, St Andrew Institute is noted for its theological publications.[14]

III.7.The Orthodox Theological Academy of Minsk (Belarus)[15] was set up in 1996 as a private institution of the Russian Orthodox Church, with a three-year period of studies.

IV. Institutions of Theological Education in Serbian Language

IV.1. *The Faculty of Orthodox Theology in the University of Belgrade*[16] was founded in 1920, although attempts had been made to set up a higher school of education as early as the last decade of the 19th century. In 1952, the School of Theology was ousted from the University, but it continued to function as an institution of the Church. The school was received again into the structure of the State University after the change of the political regime in Belgrade, in January 2004, with the annulment of the Act of 15 February 1952, by virtue of which the faculty was expelled from the university. Among the professors who taught in this school we mention: Cedomir Drashkovitch, St. Nicholas Velimirovitch, St. Justin (Popovitch) of Celije, Bishop Athanasios Jevtici, Bishop Irinaeus (Bulovitch), Bishop Ignatie D. Mititch, Vladan Perisici, Radomir Popovici, Predrag Puzovitch, Radovan Bigovitch, Zoran Krstitch, Porfirie Peritch, Dragan Milin, Ksenija Koncerevitch.

IV.2. *Saint Basil of Ostrog Theological Academy* was founded in 1992 in Srbinje (Foca, Bosnia-Herzegovina). After its incorporation into the structure of the University of Sarajevo in 1994, the Academy became a Faculty of Theology in 2004.[17] Among its professors we mention: Milan Radulovic, Boris Brajovic, Radomir Popovic.

---

[12] http://orthodoxwiki.org/Kazan_Theological_Academy (last accessed at September 2013).

[13] http://kuz1.pstbi.ccas.ru/institut/insteng.htm (last accessed at September, 2013).

[14] http://standrews.ru/(last accessed at September, 2013).

[15] http://www.minds.by(last accessed at September, 2013).

[16] http://www.bfspc.bg.ac.rs/ (last accessed September 2013).

[17] Pedrag Puzovic, "Histoire abregée de l'Église Orthodoxe Serbe en Ex-Yougoslavie au XXème," in: Christine Chaillot (ed.), *L'Eglise Orthodoxe en Europe Occidentale au XXème siècle,* (Paris : Les Editions du Cerf, 2009), 129.

V. Institutions of Orthodox Theological Education in Romanian Language[18]

V.1. *The Orthodox Theological School of Czernowitz*[19] continued the activity of the Theological Institute which had functioned in this city from 1827 until 1875. It became a Theological Faculty and it functioned until 1940, when the Northern Bukovina including Czernowitz was occupied by the Soviet army, and ever since remained in the Republic of Ukraine. After 1940 this faculty first moved to Suceava, then to Jassy and Râmnic. In 1948, what has survived from it was incorporated into the Theological Institute in Bucharest. Until 1918 the courses at this School were delivered mostly in German and Polish. The use of German language offered two major benefits: firstly, the courses could be attended by Orthodox students from all over the Habsburg Empire: Romanians, Serbians, Ukrainians, etc, and secondly, it provided teaching and research at European standards. Many theologians who were to have a decisive contribution to the development of the Orthodox theological thought during the 20th century were educated in this school, such as Orest Bucevschi, Vasile Loichită, Liviu Stan, Vladimir Prelipceanu and, last but not least, Dumitru Stăniloae. When the school in Czernowitz was dissolved, several professors took refuge first in Jassy and then in Bucharest. They brought with them a part of the famous library of the school. Among the most representative professors of the school in Czernowitz we should mention Çtefan Saghin, Vasile Tarnavschi, Eusebiu Popovici, Vasile Gheorghiu, Nicolae Cotoş, Vasile Loichită, Valerian Çesan, Simion Relli, and others.

V.2. *The Orthodox Theological School of Kishinev*[20] was set up in 1926, and employed several professors of theology from Bucharest, such as Ioan Mihălcescu, the first dean of the school, later on Metropolitan of Moldavia, Vasile Radu, Gala Galaction, Nichifor Crainic, Toma Bulat, Constantin N. Tomescu, Ioan Savin, Cicerone and Valeriu Iordachescu; Iuliu Scriban, Nicolae Popescu-Prahova, and some local professors: Serghie Bejan, Ilie Tocan, Çtefan Ciobanu and Alexandru Boldur. When the Soviet troops invaded Moldavia, on 28 June 1940, the School moved to Jassy and merged with the Theological School from Czernowitz, which had been transferred to Jassy. In 1948, what was left of this school was moved to the newly-founded Higher Theological Institute, the successor of the Faculty of Orthodox Theology in Bucharest.

V.3. *"Patriarch Justinian" Faculty of Orthodox Theology in the University of Bucharest*[21] was founded on 12 November 1881 and functioned in the University of Bucharest until 4 August 1948, when it was ousted from the university by the communist regime. It carried on its activity as a Higher Theological Institute until 1991, when it was reinstated in the University of Bucharest. Currently the Faculty offers four specializations: Pastoral Orthodox Theology, Didactical Orthodox Theology, Social Theology and Sacred Arts, and three academic degrees: Bachelor's (three years), Master's (two years) and Doctoral (three years). Pastoral Theology still has a four-year program of study. Among the most representative professors we mention: Dumitru Stăniloae, Dimitrie Boroianu, Ioan G. Coman, Nichifor Crainic, Gala Galaction, Teodor M. Popescu, Petre Vintilescu, Liviu Stan, Nicolae Nicolaescu, Petru Rezuş, Nicolae Chitescu, Ene Braniçte, Alexandra Elian, Niculae M. Popescu, Vasile Ispir, Niculae Çerbânescu, Dumitru Fecioru, Nicolae Balcă, Dumitru Popescu, and others.

V.4. *"Andrei Şaguna" Faculty of Orthodox Theology in the "Lucian Blaga" University (Sibiu)* is one of the oldest institutions of theological education in Romanian language. It has functioned ever since 1786. From the 19th century to 1948 it functioned as a Theological Academy, from 1948 to 1990, as a Higher Theological Institute, and from 1991 onwards, as a Faculty of Theology in the University of Sibiu. Nowadays the Faculty has three departments: Pastoral Theology, Social Theology and Didactic Theology.[22] Among the most represen-

---

[18] In this chapter we made use of information conveyed by Rev. Assist. Prof. Dr. Ioan Moldoveanu from the "Patriarch Justinian" Faculty of Theology, Bucharest.

[19] http://www.princeradublog.ro/jurnal/orasul-cernauti/ (last accessed September 2013).

[20] Rev. Assist. prof. Vasile Seckieru, *Facultatea de Teologie din Chisinau [Theological Faculty of Kishinev]*, available at: http://www.teologie.net/?file=secrieru_02. pdf&action=down (last accessed at September 2013).

[21] http://www.ftoub.ro/.

[22] http://www.ulbsibiu.ro/ro/facultati/teologie/.

Part VIII: Ecumenical Formation in Orthodox Theological Education

tative professors we mention: Nicolae Colan, Dumitru Stăniloae, Nicolae Popovici, Grigorie Marcu, Spiridon Cândea, Liviu Stan, Teodor Bodogae, Corneliu Sârbu, Nicolae Mladin, Gheorghe Çoima, Dumitru Călugăr, Nicolae Neaga, Sofron Vlad, Grigorie T. Marcu, Dumitru Belu, Isidor Todoran, Teodor Bodogae, Milan Sesan, Mircea Păcurariu, Dumitru Abrudan, and others.

V.5. *"Dumitru Stăniloae" Faculty of Orthodox Theology in the "Al.I. Cuza" University (Jassy)* is the successor of the first Romanian School of Orthodox Theology, founded in 1860, and functioned in the first Romanian university of this city; the school founded in 1860 was active for a very short period of time. The current Faculty was set up in the autumn of 1990 by His Beatitude Patriarch Daniel, at the time Metropolitan of Moldavia and Bucovina. To start with it was a Higher Theological Institute, and a year later it became a Faculty of Theology in the state university of the city. This school trains not only priests, but also experts in several fields of its four departments: Pastoral Theology, Social Theology, Didactic Theology and Sacred Arts, and it provides degrees, such as: Bachelor's, Master's and PhD in Theology.[23]

V.6. *The Faculty of Orthodox Theology in the "Babeş-Bolyai" University (Cluj-Napoca)* dates back to 1924 when the Theological Institute in Cluj was set up. It provided a three-year study program for students coming from other Theological Academies in Transylvania. In the following academic year, the length of studies was extended to four years and the Institute was organized as a Theological Academy, with the confessed intention of transforming it into a Faculty of Theology, and in due course to be incorporated into the university. The Theological Academy of Cluj functioned from 1925 to 1948, when it was dissolved by the communist regime. The Orthodox Theology Institute of Higher Studies in Cluj-Napoca was reestablished on 1 July 1990 and during the 1992-1993 academic year it was incorporated in the "Babeş-Bolyai" University under the name of the Faculty of Orthodox Theology of Cluj-Napoca,[24] with the following sections: Pastoral Theology, Didactic Theology, Social Theology and Sacred Arts. Among the most representative professors we should mention Andrei Buzdug, Orest Bucevschi, Liviu Galaction Munteanu, Ioan Paçca, Gheorghe Stănescu, Isidor Todoran, Bishop Nicolae Colan, Ioan Zăgrean, etc.

V.7. *The Faculty of Orthodox Theology in Arad* was founded in 1991, and it was incorporated in the Aurel Vlaicu University in Arad. It wishes to continue the theological tradition in this part of the country, illustrated by the Theological Institute (1822-1927) and the Theological Academy (1927-1948) which functioned in this city. Among the professors of the Theological Academy we mention: Teodor Botiç, Ilarion V. Felea, Petru Deheleanu, Simion Çiclovan, Vintilă Popescu, and others. During this academic year the Faculty of Orthodox Theology in Arad received a new name, i.e., *"Ilarion V. Felea" Faculty of Orthodox Theology,* and provides the following fields of studies: Pastoral Theology, Didactic Theology and Social Theology. Since 1997 the Faculty in Arad edited its own journal, *Teologia,* and since April 2000 the weekly missionary-pastoral magazine *The Path to Salvation.*[25]

V.8. *The Faculty of Orthodox Theology in the University of Oradea*[26] was set up in May 1990. It continues the activity of the former Theological Academy which was founded in May 1923. After the Vienna Diktate (30 August 1940), the Theological Academy took refuge to Caransebes, and in the autumn of 1941 moved to Timisoara, where it functioned until 1948 when it was dissolved. Among the professors of this academy we mention: Vasile Lăzarescu, later Metropolitan of the Banat, Mihail Bulacu, Çtefan Lupça, Dumitru Belu, Sofron Vlad and Teodor Savu. To start with, the Faculty of Orthodox Theology in Oradea provided two fields of study, namely, Orthodox Pastoral Theology and Letters-Theology, with a four year period of study, and 5 years for correspondence courses, providing a Bachelor's Degree in Theology. Currently this faculty offers three fields of study, namely, Orthodox Pastoral Theology, Orthodox Didactic Theology and Orthodox Social Theology. The Orthodox Pastoral Theology extends over a four-year period of study, whereas the other two over a three-year period.

---

[23] http://www.teologie.uaic.ro/istoric (last accessed at September, 2013).

[24] http://ot.ubbcluj.ro/istoric(last accessed at September, 2013).

[25] Information received from Rev. Professor Dr. Ioan Tulcan, Dean of the School; see also http://www.teologiearad.ro/index.html(last accessed at September, 2013).

[26] http://teologie.uoradea.ro(last accessed at September, 2013).

V.9. *The Faculty of Orthodox Theology in the University of Craiova* was founded on 1 October 1992. As a result of the new organization of the Romanian Higher Education System, the Faculty of Orthodox Theology has three departments: Pastoral Theology, Didactic Theology, Social Theology, with the following academic structure accredited by the National Council for Academic Evaluation and Assessment: *(a)* Graduate Studies; *(b)* Master's Studies, and *(c)* The Doctoral School.[27]

V.10. *The Faculty of Orthodox Theology in 'The December 1, 1918' University (Alba Iulia)* was founded in 1990. To start with, it had only one department: Theology-Social Assistance. In 1995 it was set up as a regular Faculty with the following departments: Pastoral Theology, Theology-English Letters, Theology-Romanian Letters and Theology-History. Following the reform of the Higher Education in 2005 (when the number of programs were reduced in accordance with Bologna Declaration), the five departments were reduced to three: Pastoral Theology (for future priests), Didactic Theology (for teachers of religion in the public schools) and Social Theology.[28]

V.11. *The Faculty of Orthodox Theology in The 'Ovid' University in Constanta* opened with the academic year 1992-1993. Since 2001 the Faculty offers a Master's program in Theology and since 2004 a Doctoral program. Currently the Faculty provides the following fields of study: Pastoral Theology, Didactic Theology, Social Theology, Theology and Sacred Art - Mural Painting, and Theology Sacred Art - Music. In 2005, a Centre for Theological, Ecumenical and Intercultural Research was set up at the faculty and steps are taken to place this centre under the aegis of the Department of Philosophy, Theology, Pedagogy, Psychology of the Romanian Academy.[29]

V.12. *"The Saint Martyr Philothea" Faculty of Orthodox Theology in the University of Pitești* was set up in 1990 when the University itself was founded. Currently, this Faculty offers the following fields of studies: Pastoral Theology, Didactic Theology and Social Theology. In 1999, the department of "Communication and Religious Service in Sign Language" was opened; since 2000, a Master's program in Theology is being offered, and since 2005, a Master's program in "The Management of Health and Social Services." Starting with the academic year 2005-2006, the Faculty of Orthodox Theology has provided special courses in Musical Pedagogy and Sacred Art.[30]

V.13. *Faculty of Orthodox Theology with degrees in Theology- Letters at the "Valahia" University of Târgoviște,* founded in 1992, follows the tradition of the Greco-Latin School which functioned in this city in the 17th century. Two other degrees were added to the former degrees of this Faculty, i.e. Theology-Letters, Theology-Social Assistance (1993) and Pastoral Theology (1995). After giving up the double degree Theology-Letters in accordance with the Bologna Educational System in 1995, this specialization became a department of Letters in the Faculty of Humanistic Studies, so that at present the Faculty of Orthodox Theology offers the following specializations: Pastoral Theology and Theology-Social Assistance. From 2000 onwards the school has also provided Master's programs. The Faculty of Theology in Târgoviçte houses the following Research Centers: *The Holy Apostle Paul National Centre for Ecumenical and Missionary Studies, St. Maximus the Confessor Centre for Interdisciplinary Research in Science and Religion* and *Dumitru Staniloae Centre for Research and Humanistic Studies.*[31]

V.14. *The Department of Orthodox Theology-History* of the Faculty of Economic and Administrative Science, "Eftimie Murgu" University in Reçita. Its field of study is Didactic Theology. It was founded in 1998 as a successor of the *Theological Academy in Caransebeş.* This academy had its roots in the Clerical School of Vârçet, which was transferred to Reçita in 1865 and changed into a Diocesan Theological Institute. In 1927, the Theological Institute was turned into a Theological Academy and functioned as such until 1948, when it was dissolved and turned into a School for Church Singers. It functioned as such until 1955, "when it was upgraded to a Theological Seminary with a 5-year period of studies (the first two years for church singers, the

---

[27] http://teologie.central.ucv.ro/index.php/prezentare/prezentare/istoric.html(last accessed at September, 2013).

[28] http://www.reintregirea.ro/index.php?cid=pagina-facultate(last accessed at September, 2013).

[29] http://teologie.univ-ovidius.ro/(last accessed at September, 2013).

[30] http://www.upit.ro/index.php?lang=ro-utf-8&i=59(last accessed at September, 2013).

[31] http://www.patriarhia.ro/ro/administratia_patriarhala/Iuditu.html(last accessed at September, 2013).

last three years for seminary students)".[32] This seminary is still functioning. Among the professors who taught at the Institute and then at the Theological Academy of Caransebeç, we mention first those who became bishops, such as Ioan Popasu, Nicolae Popea, Ilie Miron Cristea, Vasile Lăzărescu, Veniamin Nistor. In the second place we recall the following: George Peştean, Mihail Velcean, George Petrescu, Andrei Ghidiu, George Dragomir, Vasile Loichită, Dumitru Cioloca, Ştefan Pop, George Popovici, Ioan David, George Cotoşman, Iova Firca, Petru Rezuş, Mircea Chialda, Constantin Vladu, and others.

V.15. *The Department of Orthodox Theology* of the Faculty of Letters and Theology in the University 'Dunărea de Jos' in Galati was set up in 1991 and offers degrees in Didactic Theology and Social Assistance.[33]

V.16. *The Department of Orthodox Theology* of the Faculty of Letters, History and Theology in the *West University* of Timişoara was founded in 2003 with two fields of study: Pastoral Theology and Didactic Theology.[34]

V.17. *The Department of Orthodox Theology* of the Faculty of Letters in the *North University* of Baia Mare provides degrees in the following fields: Pastoral Theology, Didactic Theology and Social Theology.[35]

VI. Institutions of Theological Education in Bulgarian Language[36]

VI.1. *Saint Clement of Ohrid Faculty of Theology in the University of Sofia*[37] was founded in 1923; in 1950, it was eliminated from the University and from 1950 to 1991 it functioned as a Theological Academy under the auspices of the Bulgarian Orthodox Church. In 1991 it was integrated in the University of Sophia. This faculty is made up of three departments: *(1)* Bible Studies; *(2)* Historical and Systematical Theology, and *(3)* Practical Theology. Among the most representative professors of the faculty University we mention: Nicolae Glubokovsky (of Russian origin), Stefan Zankov, Ivan Goçev, Ivan Panchovsky, Theodor Sabev, Evthymiy Sapundzhiev, Christo Stoyanov, Nikolay Shivarov, Ivan Zhelev Dimitrov, and others.

VI.2. *'Saints Cyril and Methodius' Faculty of Orthodox Theology in the University of Veliko Trnovo*[37] was set up in 1991 and has four departments: 1. Biblical and Systematical Theology; 2. Historical and Practical Theology; 3. Church Arts, and 4. Social Theology (a recently founded department). Among the professors of this faculty we mention: Totyu Koev, Dimitar Popmarinov Kirov, Marian Stoyadinov, and others.

VI.3. *The Department of Theology* of the Faculty of Humanistic Sciences in the *'Bishop Constantin Preslavski' University in Sumen* was set up in 1991; among its professors we recall Archimandrite Pavel Stefanov.

VI.4. *The Department of Theology* of the Faculty of Philosophy and History in *'Saint Paisy of Hilandar University, Plovdiv* was set up in 1991. Among the professors we can mention Dimitar Stankov Kirov.

VII. Institutions of Theological Education in Georgian Language

The Theological Academy of Tbilisi was established in 1988, and in 1996 the *Theological Academy of Gelatti,* founded as early as the 12th century and dissolved during the Communist regime, was reopened near Kutaissi. This academy represents one of the most important centers of culture and spirituality of the Orthodox Church of Georgia. In 2005, the Church of Georgia set up an international foundation of charity with a view to renewing and developing the Georgian spirituality, culture and science. In 2006, a center of Georgian liturgical music[38] was opened at the Theological Academy of Tbilisi.

---

[32] http://www.episcopiacaransebesului.ro/pagini/invatamantul-teologic.php(last accessed at September, 2013).

[33] http://www.lit.ugal.ro/(last accessed at September, 2013).

[34] http://www.litere.uvt.ro/(last accessed at September, 2013).

[35] http://www.patriarhia.ro/ro/administratia_patriarhala/luditu.html; http://www.ubm.ro/(last accessed at September, 2013).

[36] Chapter edited by Prof. Dr. Ivan Zhelev Dimitrov from the Faculty of Orthodox Theology of Sofia.

[37] http://portal.uni-sofia.bg/index.php/eng/faculties/faculty_of_theology2(last accessed at September, 2013).

[38] Cf. Zaza Abashidze, "L'Église Orthodoxe de Géorgie au XXᵉ siècle," in Christine Chaillot (ed.), *L'Eglise Orthodoxe en Europe Orientale au XXᵉ siècle,* (Paris: Les Éditions du Cerf, 2009), 400.

VIII. Institutions of Theological Education in Albanian Language

'The Resurrection of Christ Theological Academy was founded in 1922 in Tirana, Albania, and in 1996 was transferred to the newly built premises near Saint Blas Monastery of Durres.[39] This academy ensures the spiritual and academic education of the clergy and lay people through theological studies, liturgical life and practical activity.[40] Among the professors of this academy a special mention deserves its founder Archbishop Athanasios of Tirana and All Albania, as well as Bishop Nicholas, Luke Veronis, Nathan Hope, and others.

IX. Institutions of Theological Education in Polish Language

The Christian Theological Academy of Warsaw (Poland) is an ecumenical state institution with three departments of theology: *(1)* Lutheran, *(2)* Orthodox, and *(3)* Old Catholic. The study of Orthodox theology was provided in an independent department in the University of Warsaw until 1945, when it was no longer granted the right to continue its activity. As of 1957 the study of Orthodox theology was again permitted along with the other two theological traditions, which make up the Academy of Warsaw. The academy has a single theological school, with two departments: one of theology with three sections and one for social sciences. In 1991, an ecumenical pedagogical-catechetical institute was set up at the Academy and since 1996 social studies have also been taught. In 1994, the Theological Academy of Warsaw received the right to grant the degree of Doctor in Theology. Apart from the Department of Theology of this academy, the Orthodox Church of Poland has its own Theological Seminary in Warsaw, a school of icon painting in Bielsk Podalski, and a school of church music at Hajnowka.[41]

X. Institutions of Theological Education in Czech and Slovak Languages

The Faculty of Orthodox Theology with Czech and Slovak as teaching languages was founded in Prague in 1950. It was transferred to Presov[42] in 1951 and in 1997 it was incorporated in the Presov University, Slovakia. Currently, the Faculty grants Bachelor's and Master's degrees in Orthodox Theology, Religious Education, Ethical Education and Social Activity. The Faculty of Presov has a branch in Olomouc, in the Czech Republic. The Faculty of Husite Theology in the *Karlovy University* of Prague offers a program of Orthodox Theology studies.

XI. Institutions of Orthodox Theological Education in Finnish Language

The Faculty of Theology in the University of Joensuu (Finland)[43] was set up in 1992 and it includes two departments: a department of Western Theology, namely, Lutheran and a second department of Orthodox Theology. This school provides study programs for Bachelor's, Master's and Doctoral degrees, and is the only school to ensure the study of Orthodox theology in Finland and all Scandinavian countries. The students of the two departments attend some common courses, whereas the students from the department of Orthodox Theology also attend the courses at the Orthodox Theological Seminary, transferred from Kuopio to Joensuu in 1988.

---

[39] Anastasios Yannoulatos, "Quelques notes sur l'histoire de l'Église Orthodoxe d'Albanie au XXᵉ siècle et sa résurrection depuis 1991," in: C. Chaillot (ed.), *L'Eglise Orthodoxe en Europe Orientale au XXᵉ siècle*, 142.

[40] http://www.orthodoxalbania.org/English/akademteo/ATFrame.htm(last accessed at September, 2013).

[41] http://de.wikipedia.org/wiki/Christliche_Theologische_Akademie_Warschau(last accessed at September, 2013).

[42] Christophe PuLEC, Georges Stransky, "L'Église Orthodoxe en République Tchèque et en Slovaquie au XXᵉ siècle," in: C. Chaillot (ed.), *L'Eglise Orthodoxe en Europe Orientale au XXᵉ siècle*, 227-228.

[43] http://www.uef.fi/en/filtdk/teologia/(last accessed at September, 2013).

XII. Theological Education Institutions of the Orthodox Diaspora

XII.1. *St Vladimir's Orthodox Theological Seminary, New-York* (USA)[44] functions under the jurisdiction of the Orthodox Church of America (OCA).

The first Orthodox theological institute in America was founded in Minneapolis in 1905. In 1912, it moved to Tenafly, on the eastern coast, much more populated by Orthodox emigrants, who provided most of its students. The seminary went through very difficult times after the Bolshevik Revolution of 1917, as it was deprived of the material support from Russia and it was affected by the internal divisions which were tearing apart the American Orthodoxy. So in 1923 Metropolitan Platon (1866-1934) took the inevitable decision to close the school.[45] The Institute resumed its activity on 3 October 1938, under the name of Saint Vladimir,[46] in a modest location in Brooklyn, New York.[47] The first years proved to be extremely difficult, and in 1942 the admission to the seminary was temporarily discontinued for lack of funds. New prospects opened up unexpectedly after the Second World War. Although the financial crisis threatened ever more the functioning of the school, the arrival of several outstanding theologians from the Old World gave new thrust to this seminary. The revival of the Seminary is connected particularly with the names of former professors from the Saint Serge Institute in Paris: Georges Florovsky (1893-1979, dean from 1949 to 1955), Alexander Schmemann (1921-1983, dean from 1962 to 1983) and John Meyendorff (1929-1992, dean from 1984 to 1992). Several other professors such as George P. Fedotov (1886-1951), Nicolas O. Lossky (1870-1965), Nicolas S. Arseniev (1888-1977), Alexander A. Bogolepov (1886-1980), Serge S. Verhovskoy (1907-1986), Sophie Koulomzin (1903-2000), John Breck (b. 1939), Thomas Hopko (b. 1939, dean from 1992 to 2002), John H. Erickson (dean from 2002 to 2007), John Behr (dean since 2007) have contributed to the school's high academic level and prestige. Since 1963, the Seminary has its own campus in Crestwood, New York. *St. Vladimir's* represents nowadays one of the most outstanding Orthodox educational centers in the Western World. It is famous for its academic journal, *St. Vladimir's Theological Quarterly,* as well as for *St. Vladimir's Seminary Press,* the most prolific Orthodox publishing house in English language.

XII.2. *St. Sergius Institute of Orthodox Theology (Institut de Théologie Orthodoxe Saint-Serge)*[48] founded in Paris in 1925 is the oldest Orthodox institution of higher education in the West, and functions currently under the jurisdiction of the Ecumenical Patriarchate. The founder of this institute was Metropolitan Eulogius, at the time exarch of the patriarchate of Moscow for Western Europe.

The purpose behind the foundation of this institute, which played in time an important role in promoting Orthodox thinking during the 20th century, was to bring together the Russian theologians who left Russia when the Communist regime came to power in Moscow. Among the most notable professors of this Institute we recall: Sergei Bulgakov, A.W. Kartaschev, Basilius Zenkowskij, Kassian Besobrasov, G. Florovsky, G. Fedotov, L. Zander, N. Afanassjev, Kiprian Kern, V. Iljin, Paul Evdokimov, A. Kniazeff, Boris Bobrinskoy, Olivier Clément, Ilya Melia, N. Kulomzin, V.A. Firillas, K. Eltschaninov. We should also point out that a number

---

[44] Chapter drafted by Rev. Ilie Toader; see also Alexander Schmemann, "St Vladimir's Twentieth Anniversary, 1938-1958," in: *St Vladimir's Theological Quarterly* 2.3 (1958): 1-10; John Meyendorff, Vladimir Bokichevsky, William Schneirla, *A legacy of excellence: St Vladimir's Orthodox Theological Seminary, 1938-1988,* (Crestwood, N.Y.: St Vladimir's Seminary Press, 1988), 96pp; Constance J. Tarasar (ed.), *Orthodox America: 1794-1976. Development of the Orthodox Church in America,* (Syosset, New York: The Orthodox Church in America - Department of History and Archives, 1975), 352pp.

[45] Constance J. Tarasar (ed.), *Orthodox America: 1794-1976,* 110.

[46] Saint Vladimir's election as patron saint of the Institute was doubly motivated: commemorating 950 years from the Christianization of Russians by Prince Vladimir in 1938 and emphasizing the school's missionary profile.

[47] At the beginning the institution had no permanent premises of its own, being hosted by parishes. On account of the difficult conditions of that time students were boarded at the *Union Theological (Evangelical) Seminary,* attending courses at Columbia University in the morning and professors' of theology lectures at the rectory of 'Christ the Savior' Church on East Street in the afternoon; cf. John Meyendorff, "St Vladimir's Faculty," in J. Meyendorff, Vl. Borichevsky, W. Schneirla, *A legacy of excellence,* 208.

[48] http://www.saint-serge.net/(last accessed at September, 2013).

of Orthodox theologians, such as John Meyendorff and Alexander Schmemann, studied in this institute and became notable at Saint Vladimir Orthodox Theological Seminary of New York.

XII.3. *Holy Cross Greek Orthodox School of Theology (USA)*[49] is an outstanding Institute for Higher Theological Education under the jurisdiction of the Ecumenical Patriarchate. It was founded in 1937 in Pomfret Connecticut as a seminary of the Greek Orthodox Diocese of America. In 1946, the school was moved to Brookline, Massachusetts, where it functioned as an institution of higher theological education. Holy Cross also houses a Hellenic College, distinct from the Seminary, although the students of the two institutions make up a single student community. Among the most representative professors of this school we can mention George Bebis, Alkiviadis Calivas, Stanley S. Harakas, George C. Papademetriou, Thomas Fitzgerald, Emmanuel Clapsis, George Dion. Dragas, Lewis Patsavos, Eugen J. Pentiuc, James C. Skedros, Theodore Stylianopoulos, Evie Zachariades-Holmberg.

XII.4. *The Institute of Orthodox Theology in München University*[50] was founded at the proposal of the Faculty of Catholic Theology in this university in 1979, turning the chair of "Mission and Religious Sciences" into a Chair of Orthodox Theology. The first to hold the chair was Prof. Dr. Theodor Nikolaou. He started his work in München on 1 November 1994. A few months later, the Bavarian ministry commissioned Prof. Nikolau to set up an institute named Institute of Orthodox Theology. This school started its activity in the autumn of 1995, under the jurisdiction of the Ecumenical Patriarchate. Nevertheless it has a pan-Orthodox character, as far as its professors and students are concerned. The institute offers the following programs of studies: *(1)* Bachelor's degree - for a period of 4 and 1/2 years (9 semesters); *(2)* Doctoral studies (since 1999); and *(3)* Minor degree in theology (Nebenfach). The institute has also been noted for its particular publishing activity. We mention in this context its review *The Orthodox Forum (Orthodoxes Forum)*. Among the professors active here we mention: Theodor Nikolaou, Vladimir Ivanov, Konstantinos Nikolakopoulos, Athanasios Vletsis, and others.

XII.5. *The Institute for Orthodox Christian Studies* (IOCS)[51] was set up in 1999 in Cambridge, Great Britain, under the jurisdiction of the Ecumenical Patriarchate. Among the Professors of this Institute we mention the Metropolitans Anthony of Suroj, Kallistos of Diokleias, and John Zizioulas; Thomas Hopko, Andrew Louth, the Archimandrites Simon and Zacharias from Saint John the Baptist Monastery in Essex (Great Britain).

XII.6. *The Institute of Orthodox Theology of the Orthodox Center of the Ecumenical Patriarchate of Chambésy (Switzerland)* was founded on 12 June 1996, when an agreement was signed between Damascene, at the time Metropolitan of Switzerland, the School of Protestant Theology in the University of Geneva and the School of Catholic Theology in the University of Fribourg. According to the patriarchal act of foundation, the institute has the following goals:

(1) to inform the Western Christian world, especially in Europe, about the Orthodox worship, teachings, tradition and theology; (2) to ensure the contacts between different Orthodox Churches in order to promote Orthodox Unity; and (3) to develop the ecumenical spirit and cultivate the relationships between Orthodoxy and other Churches and Christian denominations and thus to contribute to the final goal, which is Christian unity[52]. The two-year postgraduate courses offered by this Institute are attended by students belonging to different Orthodox Churches. Among the professors who taught at this institute we mention Constantin Scouteris, Vlassios Pheidas, the Archimandrite Athanasios Hatzopoulos, Constantin Delikostantis and Archimandrite Job Getcha.

---

[49] http://www.hchc.edu/holycross.html(last accessed at September, 2013).

[50] http://www.orththeol.uni-muenchen.de/index.html(last accessed at September, 2013). Also see: Theodor Nikolau, Konstantin Nikolakopoulos, Anargyros Anapliotis (eds.), *Ost-und Westerweiterung in Theologie. 20 Jahre Orthodoxe Theologie in München* (Veröffentlichungen des Instituts für Orthodoxe Theologie, Bd 9), (Erzabtei St. Otilien: EOS Verlag, 2006), 315pp.

(129) TEACHING ORTHODOX THEOLOGY IN THE CONTEXT OF CHRISTIAN DIVERSITY[1]

Dn Paul Gavrilyuk

At the beginning of the twentieth century, those Westerners who knew about the Orthodox Church tended to think it exotic and theologically and culturally irrelevant. Orthodox theology was very little known and even less understood, and perhaps even less valued than understood. The Bolshevik Revolution changed this. By the direct order of Lenin, at the beginning of the 1920s, the leading Russian religious thinkers were exiled to the West. With the arrival in Western Europe of the leaders of what became known as the Russian Religious Renaissance on the "philosophy steamer" (since most of them traveled by sea) and the establishment of the St. Sergius Orthodox Theological Institute in Paris in 1925, Orthodox émigré theologians began to speak with distinctive and recognizable, if at times discordant, voices in the West.

The Russian Religious Renaissance was an attempt to interpret all aspects of human existence— culture, politics, even economics—in Christian terms, brought about by the generation of Nicholas Berdyaev, Sergius Bulgakov, Nicholas Lossky, and Lev Shestov. This older generation built upon the main currents of nineteenth-century western European and Russian religious thought. For example, Berdyaev's religious existentialism and personalism had its roots in German mystics, especially Jacob Boehme, as well as in the religious questions raised by Tolstoy and Dostoevsky. Bulgakov took as his point of departure the German Idealist tradition, especially Schelling, as worked out in the sophiology of Vladimir Solovyov. Lossky developed religious and philosophical intuitivism, whereas Shestov worked out a form of antirationalist existentialism akin to the religious vision of Soren Kierkegaard. The movement was interrupted midstream in Russia, but it continued with renewed vigor in the diaspora.

The younger generation, whose thought matured in the emigration, was led by Georges Florovsky and Nicholas Lossky's son Vladimir. This generation rebelled against the previous generation's perceived theological "modernism" and was concerned to free Orthodox theology from its centuries-old "Western captivity." They announced a reform of Orthodox theology through a return to the patristic sources. By the second half of the twentieth century, this theology had become the dominant paradigm of Orthodox theology.

In Florovsky's works, this reform program received the name of a "neopatristic synthesis," which, he wrote, "should be more than just a collection of patristic sayings or statements; it must truly be a synthesis, a creative reassessment of those insights which were granted to the holy men of old. It must be Patristic, faithful to the spirit and vision of the Fathers, ad mentem Patrum. Yet, it also must be neo-Patristic, since it is to be addressed to the new age, with its own problems and queries." For Florovsky, this involved a Christocentric approach to theology, rooted in the Chalcedonian definition, whereas for Lossky it was a rediscovery of the apophatic theology of Pseudo-Dionysius the Areopagite. Along with Basil Krivocheine and Myrrha Lot-Borodine, Lossky participated in the retrieval of the theology of Gregory Palamas. The Palamite distinction between the incommunicable divine essence and the communicable divine energies, and the attendant theological anthropology, became a trademark of an important expression of neopatristic theology called Neo-Palamism.

In the course of this development, those who tended to present Orthodox theology as something universal—for example, Bulgakov and Berdyaev— ultimately lost the battle of ideas to those who emphasized Orthodoxy's particularity and distinctiveness. The generation involved in expanding the boundaries of Orthodoxy lost its battle to the generation involved in defining the same boundaries. Even those Orthodox theologians who

[1] The present article was initially published in *First Things* (2012): 33-38 under the title "Orthodox Renaissance." (The author's focus in this article is on the North-American reality) (Ed.).

resisted a self-imposed intellectual isolation from the West tended to highlight the differences, rather than the points of resemblance, between the Eastern and Western modes of theologizing.

Orthodox theologians often "orientalized" Orthodox theology by presenting it primarily as an antithesis to Western theology. To simplify the frequently invoked dichotomies, the allegedly individualistic, legalistic, rationalistic, positivistic, and anthropocentric Western religious thought was contrasted with the allegedly communitarian, holistic, mystical, and theocentric Orthodox thought. Such dichotomies reveal as much about the internal tensions within various expressions of Western intellectual history as they do about the alleged contrast between the East and the West. Along with constructing modern Orthodox theology as an alternative to its Western counterpart, Orthodox intellectuals could not resist producing an idealized picture of their Church, a "book version" of Orthodoxy, in the interest of apologetics. Often it is this sanitized picture of Orthodoxy that has the greatest initial appeal to Western inquirers.

After World War II, the second steamer sailed across the Atlantic. The most important migrants on the "theology steamer" first included Nicholas Lossky (his son Vladimir stayed in France) and Georges Florovsky (who became the first Orthodox to teach at Harvard Divinity School), who were followed shortly thereafter by Alexander Schmemann, John Meyendorff, Serges Verkhovskoy, and others. Although other theologians, primarily Greek theologians like John Zizioulas, John Romanides, and Christos Yannaras, exercised theological leadership in the historically Orthodox countries, Orthodox theology remained largely a phenomenon of the diaspora. Behind the Iron Curtain, communist governments stifled theological thought, although some heroic attempts were made in the Soviet Union and Romania to pass on this nearly extinguished light. One may mention in this regard the names of such scholars as Alexei Losev, Sergei Averintsev, and Dumitru Staniloae.

It is true that only a few first-rate minds could rival the extraordinary spiritual boldness, learning, and resourcefulness of the Renaissance thinkers, but the standard of Orthodox theology remained high. For example, under Schmemann's influence, Orthodox liturgical theology acquired its maturity. Creative works in Orthodox moral theology began to emerge, including, for example, the contributions of Paul Evdokimov and Vigen Guroian, followed by forays into the field of Orthodox biblical studies, such as the works of Theodore Stylianopoulos, Paul Tarazi, and John Breck.

Presently, Orthodox theology in the West is changing fundamentally. It can even be said to have been transformed already, and in five important ways.

First, Orthodox theology has developed from an unknown commodity into a respectable minority theology. In the beginning of the twentieth century, Orthodox theology inspired little sympathy in the West. Harnack, for example, construed Greek patristic theology as a result of the corruption of the gospel by Greek metaphysics. Writing in the 1930s, Florovsky noted that "in the West one has become accustomed to regard Orthodoxy as a sort of exhumed Christianity, retrograde and stagnant, to think that the Christian East, at best, is in a state of historic coma. Historic separation and estrangement account for this deceptive interpretation."

Today, many universities in the United States pride themselves on having at least one "token" Orthodox faculty member in their departments of religion, theology, or philosophy. For example, Harvard Divinity School has Kimberley Patton, Princeton Theological Seminary George Lewis Parsenios, Brown University Susan Ashbrook Harvey, Pittsburgh Theological Seminary Edith Humphrey, and Baruch College Michael Plekon. Remarkably, the theology departments of Fordham and Duquesne universities each have two full-time Orthodox faculty members. It is not unreasonable to expect that where two or three Orthodox theologians are gathered, there could emerge a small center or a program to promote Orthodoxy's intellectual legacy, like the Orthodox Christian Studies Center that George Demacopoulos and Aristotle Papanikolaou have established at Ford- ham in 2007, hardly possible even thirty years ago.

In most cases, Orthodox theologians enjoy considerable intellectual freedom and little ideological pressure at the non-Orthodox schools that employ them. Our Catholic hosts, as a rule, accept us as potentially offering a corrective to what they perceive as the limitations of "Latin" theology. Our Protestant colleagues often regard the representatives of Orthodoxy as offering the goods of Catholic Christianity without the historical traumas of the Reformation. As a minority, we enjoy a unique, politically non-threatening status and are respected for who we are.

Second, Orthodox theologians have moved from teaching mainly in Orthodox seminaries to teaching in non-Orthodox schools. A century ago, the majority of Orthodox theologians who relocated to Europe either held posts at the established Orthodox schools like the University of Belgrade and Sofia University or had to create new Orthodox institutions like the St. Sergius and St. Denys theological institutes in Paris. After the war, in the United States, most Orthodox theologians taught at the recently established Orthodox schools. Today the situation is quite different. The total number of full-time faculty at the Holy Cross Greek Orthodox School of Theology, St. Vladimir's Orthodox Theological Seminary, and St. Tikhon's Orthodox Theological Seminary is around fifty. At least twice as many now teach religion-related subjects at non-Orthodox institutions and seminaries.

Due to the financial challenges and relatively slow growth of the Orthodox Church in the U.S., the number of full-time faculty at the Orthodox schools is not going to increase considerably in the near future. Yet the number of Orthodox students pursuing doctoral work has been steadily growing, and these often very gifted young scholars are more likely to find teaching posts at mainstream academic institutions than at Orthodox schools. They will interact regularly with their non-Orthodox peers as well as the non-Orthodox students, and their thinking, teaching, and writing will naturally turn into an implicit dialogue with the non-Orthodox. Any act of accountable and serious scholarship becomes in some sense an ecumenical act, whether or not they actually engage in formal ecumenical negotiations.

Third, Orthodox theology is shifting from engaging in ecumenical dialogue to addressing the post-denominational condition. In the beginning of the twentieth century, the ecumenical dialogue was predicated on the assumption of clear and rigid denominational boundaries. Those outside one's own group were typically regarded as heretics or schismatics. While the traditionalist Orthodox may still use this language, the denominational boundaries in America have become increasingly porous and flexible.

On one level, a century after the beginning of the ecumenical movement, Christians have become even more divided. On another, the dividing lines no longer coincide neatly with the ecclesiastical boundaries but with positions on controversial issues of human sexuality, the ministry of women, and other social issues. On yet another level, non-Orthodox theologians are more and more willing to engage with and incorporate into their own work the insights of Orthodox theology. For example, apophatic theology and the concept of deification are no longer perceived as exclusively Eastern ideas. Postmodern theologians of all stripes are captivated by the via negativa, and more remarkably, Catholic and Protestant theologians, both mainstream and Evangelical, have recently offered very appreciative accounts of deification.

There is a growing awareness that the Orthodox tradition has been previously neglected in the curriculum of Western theological institutions and has to be more effectively represented. Forward-looking deans of various theological schools are considering concrete ways of institutionalizing such changes. For example, Union Theological Seminary created the endowed chair in Late Antique and Byzantine Christian History for the renowned Orthodox patristic scholar and theologian John Anthony McGuckin and provided the resources for the establishment of the Orthodox Sophia Institute. Fordham University will soon establish an endowed chair in Orthodox Theology and Culture. More institutional determination will be required in the future for this trend to continue.

Fourth, Orthodox theology has shifted from diaspora theology to convert theology. Only thirty years ago, almost without exception, Orthodox scholarship in the United States was dominated by Slavs like Schmemann and Meyendorff and Greeks like Romanides. Some were educated and even born outside of their countries of ethnic origin, but their roots still ran deep in their respective ethnic traditions. Now, a deep immersion in the Orthodox tradition has led a number of noted scholars to join the Orthodox Church. These include McGuckin, Humphrey, Harvey, the late Jaroslav Pelikan, Richard Swinburne, Andrew Louth, and David Bentley Hart. All of them teach or have taught primarily at non-Orthodox schools. Converts also predominate among Orthodox graduate students. For example, the ten Orthodox students currently pursuing their doctorates at Fordham are all either converts or come from the families of converts.

As a Slavic immigrant and an Orthodox Levite myself—the maternal side of my family includes several generations of Russian Orthodox clergymen, albeit with a hiatus during the Soviet time—I welcome this new development. At the annual meetings of the Orthodox Theological Society in America, the contributions of the converts are at least as substantial as those of the ethnic Orthodox. As for the sessions of the Eastern Orthodox Studies Group at the annual meetings of the American Academy of Religion, recent years have witnessed increasing attendance by Roman Catholics, Evangelicals, and others. Sociologically, the increasing intellectual presence of converts—I predict that their influence will grow exponentially in the years ahead—will create some new identity challenges for the Orthodox. Having received the elephants like Pelikan, Swinburne, Hart, and McGuckin into the house of contemporary Orthodox theology, the walls are bound to shift in unpredictable ways. One cannot, of course, just shrug one's shoulders and declare that any given theological contribution counts as Orthodox theology if the author intends it as such. Some damage control and boundary making will be inevitable, as the gifts of the convert theologians are received and unwrapped.

How, for example, are we to fit Richard Swinburne's defense of Christian theism, written before his entry into the Orthodox Church, into the body of modern Orthodox theology? With trepidation or with admiration? Swinburne's use of probabilistic arguments to defend the rationality of Christian beliefs is without precedent in Orthodox theology. Such a move challenges Orthodox theologians to reconsider the role of reason. Swinburne's work, widely read by philosophers in Russia, is awaiting its reception in Orthodoxy.

Moreover, consider the exchange a few years ago between McGuckin and Hart in the pages of the Scottish Journal of Theology. McGuckin argued that Hart's engagement of postmodernism in The Beauty of the Infinite did not authentically speak for Orthodoxy. Hart replied that Orthodoxy does not offer one paradigm for doing theology and cited precedents of other paradigms besides the neopatristic one. This was an argument between two convert theologians regarding the boundaries of Orthodoxy.

Some converts prefer to draw more clearly defined boundaries between the East and the West than do many cradle Orthodox, especially those of my generation. After all, the converts made a conscious decision to move from non-Orthodoxy to Orthodoxy, something that the ethnic Orthodox have not experienced. For some converts, joining the Orthodox Church is a bit like a happy second marriage: the hairs are gray, the feelings mature, but the bliss of the honeymoon is not over yet.

Finally, Orthodox theology is shifting from the dominance of neopatristics to a re-emerging plurality of theological paradigms. The Russian Religious Renaissance was an enormous explosion of different theological visions of the world, in which no aspect of human endeavor was to remain outside of the framework of Christian teaching (it is somewhat akin in its breadth to the Radical Orthodoxy movement). In contrast, the post-war generation accepted Florovsky's and Lossky's critique of the Renaissance and expanded most of its scholarly efforts on patristic theology and church history. However, pace Florovsky, not all theological problems can be successfully resolved by recourse to the history of patristic ideas. For example, many questions in the contemporary discussion of theology and science should be addressed on strictly philosophical, rather than exclusively historical, grounds. The same applies to Orthodox bioethics and political theology.

In the years ahead, neopatristic theology will remain a leading direction of Orthodox theology. Indeed, Orthodox theology cannot become post-patristic if it is to remain Orthodox. Yet the time is ripe to explore the paradigms that engage modernity and post-modernity in a more robust and direct manner. Orthodox theology is at the crossroads, and there is a growing dissatisfaction with the hegemony of the neopatristic paradigm, at least as practiced by Florovsky's generation.

The emerging diversity of paradigms must not deteriorate into a cacophony in which Orthodox theologians lose their common language, or their common ontological assumptions, or their common goal of coming to know more profoundly the reality of the triune God. There are many ways in which our ivory towers could be turned into a tower of Babel. The emerging pluriform Orthodox theology must avoid this fate. Fortunately, however, contemporary Orthodox theologians have exactly the right amount of common ground required to move forward.

Part VIII: Ecumenical Formation in Orthodox Theological Education

I left the September 2011 meeting of the Orthodox Theological Society in America with a strong premonition that we are at the threshold of a new theological renaissance. In this renaissance, the United States, not Europe, is more likely to be the center of gravity, though I also expect some groundbreaking work to come from Greece as well as from Russia, Ukraine, and Romania, as they continue to emerge out of the ruins of their communist past.

I had felt this already at the Orthodox theological conferences in Moscow in 2007 and in Volos in 2010. Orthodox theologians are making a clear attempt to break out of the neopatristic paradigm in very creative ways. In the common internet space that Orthodox theologians now share, the ethnic and geographic boundaries are going to matter less and less. The international exchange between Orthodox theologians will grow, even if the bishops—conspicuously absent from the theological societies' meetings—have no immediate plans for resolving our enduring and scandalous jurisdictional divisions in the United States and elsewhere. In this regard, the pan-Orthodox character of the Orthodox Theological Society in America is another powerful sign of Orthodox unity in America.

Whatever the theologians produce in the years ahead—and the harvest, I predict, will be plentiful— will have to be received, rejected, or ignored by the Church at large. It appears to be increasingly clear that we are presently witnessing the first signs of a theological earthquake that will bring about the new and more potent wave of the world-wide Orthodox theological renaissance. The epicenter is likely to be North America, the main areas affected are likely to be non-Orthodox schools, and the sources of the most potent shockwaves are likely to be converts to Orthodoxy. Even if my prediction errs in its details, for the earthquakes of the Spirit are more difficult to predict than natural events, we are soon likely to enjoy an embarrassment of theological riches not seen since the heyday of the Russian Religious Renaissance of the previous century.

Bored to Death

(Based on the story of Eutychus, Acts 20:7-12)

As Paul's words droned on like the furry buzz of bees, I unfolded off the floor,
crammed myself into a window. The sun crawled down
onto the horizon and stared at me, as if to say, pay attention, you
whose time is so short, you who have no idea on what day
your thread will be cut. I stared until the sky purpled, until
the darkness swept its broom through the sky, scattering shards of dust
winking at me in the blackness.
Then the words lulled me. I tried as best I could to listen, to hear what miracles he described, only, I admit,
I was painfully bored.
What were these other than fairy tales I would tell my little cousins on a long night? The air thickened, and
I found myself dreaming
of lying out in a tall field of grain. In the distance someone was reaping.
I could hear the whisper of the scythe intoning through the wheat, could hear its urgency, saying something
about this moment. Only I lay back and closed my eyes and fell.
When I woke, he was standing over me whispering.
A crowd stared down at me, their mouths, their eyes wide, as if they could not decide whether or not
this was a moment of horror or triumph. "Don't be alarmed," he said,
"He's alive!"
Afterwards, we climbed the stairs, broke bread. I stared at him, surprised not just at the oddity of being
alive but also understanding everything
he had said was true: a heavy yoke I shouldered that night slipping his words now ringing true around my
unwilling neck.

—David Holper

(130) TEACHING ORTHODOX THEOLOGY IN THE CONTEXT OF CHRISTIAN DIVERSITY

Fr. Radu Bordeianu

It is possible to teach Ecumenism without a single reference to Orthodoxy. It is also possible to teach Orthodoxy without a single reference to Catholics or Protestants and the movement that attempts their visible union, namely Ecumenism. Even worse, it is possible to teach Ecumenism and caricaturize Orthodoxy, just as it is possible to teach Orthodoxy and have a confrontational attitude towards the West. The result is an impoverishment—even a distortion—of both Ecumenism and Orthodoxy: Ecumenism is not truly ecumenical if it does not embrace Orthodoxy, and Orthodoxy is not truly Orthodox if it does not define its identity dialogically, in relationship with Catholic and Protestant churches. In this brief essay I intend to provide a succinct description of Orthodox ecumenical theological teaching today, several suggestions for change, and a sample syllabus outline for a class on "Primacies," in order to make the case for an explicit inclusion of Ecumenism in Orthodox theological teaching and of Orthodox theology in Catholic and Protestant education.

Assessment

The state of ecumenical teaching in Orthodox schools and of Orthodox education in Western institutions is promising, and yet far from ideal. It is encouraging to look, for example, at major Faculties of Orthodox Theology in Romania and see that they require all students to take classes in "Missiology and Ecumenism" in order to gain an appreciation for the ecumenical relevance of Orthodox theology, the gifts that Western churches contribute to the Christian family, and the need for visible reunion. It is equally encouraging to consider institutions in countries where Orthodoxy is a minority, such as St. Vladimir's Orthodox Theological Seminary or Holy Cross Greek Orthodox School of Theology in the United States of America; their professors write explicitly about Ecumenism, are involved in ecumenical institutions, and teach Ecumenism proper as well as various subjects from an ecumenical perspective. In other cases Orthodox students preparing for Ordination are allowed to take classes at non-Orthodox institutions and students from other schools take classes together with Orthodox seminarians. Such is the case of Holy Cross Seminary, which is part of a consortium of ten theological institutions in Boston, MA, which facilitate cross-registrations and share resources.[1] The Cambridge Theological Federation in England is even more intentionally ecumenical in its educational approach, offering joint courses and degrees among the various denominational schools that form it.[2]

Other similar situations exist in Orthodox schools around the world, which leads to the following question: Why do Orthodox institutions of higher education include Ecumenism in their curricula? This question becomes even more intriguing when considering that the main purpose of most of these schools is not the exploration of various theological disciplines primarily for academic purposes, but the education of future generations of Orthodox priests and lay ministers, often in countries that are majority Orthodox. It means—and I will further analyze these statements— that Orthodox life, including at parish level, is richer when lived in communion

---

[1] See the websites of the two American institutions mentioned above, as well as the Faculties of Orthodox Theology in Bucharest, Sibiu, Iasi, and Cluj – Romania.

[2] The Cambridge Theological Federation "brings together the teaching and learning of eleven institutions through which people of different churches, including Anglican, Methodist, Orthodox, Reformed and Roman Catholic, train for various forms of Christian ministry and service." For further information, see http://www.theofed.cam.ac.uk/.

with other Christian churches, and it also means that ecumenism is a theological discipline necessary for a proper and substantial pastoral education. Furthermore, as this essay begins to show, Orthodox theology is intrinsically ecumenical.

Most countries in which the Orthodox population represents the majority are situated in what used to be the Eastern Block. In varying degrees, Orthodox theologians under Soviet domination were forbidden to have meaningful engagements with the West. Moreover, during the years of militant-atheism, Orthodox theology was primarily concerned with its survival. Both of these factors resulted in an Orthodox theology that was not receptive to the recent developments in the West and was unable to fully appreciate the gifts of other churches. After the fall of the Iron Curtain, a period of opening towards the West followed, in which many Orthodox theologians engaged with the latest developments in Protestant and Catholic theology. Their encounters were quickly reflected in their teaching: professors educated in the West or familiar with Western theology taught Ecumenism or other subjects from an ecumenical perspective. Orthodoxy in the diaspora seems to have followed a similar journey earlier on.

In contrast with this open attitude, anti-Western feelings are on the rise among the general Orthodox population, including in the academia.[3] The influences that such an attitude could have on theological teaching are worrisome. Orthodox education could lose the ecumenical dimension that is absolutely necessary in today's pluralistic world, as I discuss shortly.

Attitudes and pastoral life are mutually interdependent. When Western churches contribute to the restoration of Orthodox churches persecuted by Communism, Orthodox teaching is favorable to the West, future priests or lay ministers are taught to collaborate with non-Orthodox churches in various pastoral settings, and the West testifies to its riches in a most constructive way. When Orthodoxy is confronted with Western proselytism, however, Orthodoxy adopts a defensive stance, in order to protect its faithful from other churches. Furthermore, proselytism encourages the unfair binary where the West is set up against the East, even though, obviously, not all Western churches actually proselytize. Instead of a fair comparison of best with best and worst with worst, such binary projects false identities upon both East (defensive) and West (aggressive). Unfortunately, some Orthodox theologians treat the West as an easy target for their unjustified attacks, even though Orthodoxy does not need to put down the other in order to show its greatness. Even worse, putting down the other is usually unfair in the sense that Catholic and Protestant positions that are very complex and contextual become caricaturized and then blamed for the failures of Orthodoxy. What might have originated as a justified, constructive criticism stands no chance of being heard and applied by the West, so theology becomes a polemic meant to put down the other, rather than a loving dialogue intended to build up the other and be mutually enriched. Such attitudes are detrimental to the academic integrity of Orthodox theology and to pastoral life. Even when faced with proselytism, Orthodox teaching needs to remain ecumenical in order to remain true to its nature and to have a positive impact on a pastoral context marked by plurality and globalization.

In a world that is becoming more and more a global village, ideas and beliefs circulate without much restriction. It is virtually impossible for Orthodox theology to be enclosed within itself, without describing its identity dialogically and reshaping itself in reference to the other. Pastoral life—even in countries that are majority Orthodox, not to mention places where Orthodoxy is a minority—is equally marked by diversity today.

---

[3] In this regard, the "Thessaloniki Statement" (1 May 1998) of the representatives of all the Orthodox Churches gathered to discuss their relationship with the World Council of Churches, states in par. 4: "The delegates unanimously denounced those groups of schismatics, as well as certain extremist groups within the local Orthodox Churches themselves, that are using the theme of ecumenism in order to criticize the Church leadership and undermine its authority, thus attempting to create divisions and schisms within the Church. They also use non-factual material and misinformation in order to support their unjust criticism." http://www.oikoumene.org/en/resources/documents/wcc-programmes/ecumenical-movement-in-the-21st-century/member-churches/special-commission-on-participation-of-orthodox-churches/first-plenary-meeting-documents-december-1999/thessaloniki-statement (last accessed 19 June 2013).

Society in general and families in particular lack the (relative) homogeneity of past centuries, so preparation for ministry must include an ecumenical component.

Despite the pluralism of contemporary societies, Orthodox institutions sometimes remain enclosed. I do not know of any Orthodox Seminary or Faculty that offered tenure to a non-Orthodox professor who teaches a theological discipline necessary towards Ordination. In the new climate of rising anti-Western feelings, the attitudes of many students and professors seem to be that of indifference at best and confrontation at worst. It is not uncommon to find schools that continue to offer lectures and use books written in the manual tradition, reminiscent of the "Western captivity" of Orthodox theology. Orthodoxy was not creative enough and preferred to adopt Calvinist polemical arguments against Roman Catholic theology or Roman Catholic positions crystal-lized during the Counter-Reformation.[4] This manual tradition was formative for many Orthodox professors who find in the West an easy target, without giving a voice to the best Catholic and Protestant voices, especially as those have evolved over time. Early in my studies I have attended an ecumenically open Romanian Orthodox Faculty, and yet I was never required to read a single Western author; Western positions were always discussed through the lens of Orthodox interpreters.

In countries where Orthodoxy is a minority, it is not surprising that Orthodox theologians are more inclined to approach their faith from an ecumenical perspective. Moreover, their pastoral setting is marked by a diversity that does not exist to the same extent in countries that are majority Orthodox. Seminaries in the West, faced with being situated as a minority among substantial diversity, maintain an Orthodox identity in a non-Orthodox context. They also provide their students with realistic descriptions of other churches so as to equip them with the necessary tools to minister to mixed families, to engage in common initiatives with other Christians, and to teach Orthodoxy to seekers. Orthodoxy cannot afford to work with self-created images of the West. And yet, there is a danger that Orthodox theologians could misuse their minority status and become self-enclosed for fear of compromising the purity of their faith in ecumenical encounters or, even worst, see themselves as persecuted and adopt a defensive attitude, unable to see the good that it could learn from the other.

Countries where Orthodoxy forms a minority exemplify an additional facet of ecumenism in that some Or-thodox scholars have found a home in non-Orthodox institutions. It is not uncommon for Catholic, Protestant, and secular universities to hire Orthodox theologians to teach Orthodox theology. Faced with such generosity, Orthodox theology should not take a confrontational attitude, but should seek cooperation and understanding with the West. Teaching Orthodox theology, however, is hampered when one is forced to assign sources composed in a polemical tone. The professor is tasked with distinguishing valid criticism of the West from caricatures of it and with explaining how ideas evolved both within Eastern and Western theologies.

Suggestions

The above description, while extremely brief, is meant to support the case for an explicit inclusion of Ecumenism in Orthodox theological teaching and of Orthodox theology in non-Orthodox institutions by identifying both promising situations open to further development and remaining challenges. There are several concrete ways in which Orthodox teaching could become even more ecumenical in character.

Ecumenical implications for effective ministry in a pluralistic world

First, seminaries need to commit themselves to equipping ordained and lay ministers with the tools for an effec-tive ministry in a pluralistic world, both in countries where Orthodoxy is the majority and where it is a minority. Ecumenical education is urgently needed, since the reality in the parish is already marked by a diversity that

---

[4] For various aspects of the interaction between East and West, see *Orthodox Constructions of the West*, edited by George E. Demacopoulos and Aristotle Papanikolaou. (New York: Fordham University Press, 2013), including my own contribution on Dumitru Staniloae's interaction with the West on pages 240-253; 348-355.

Part VIII: Ecumenical Formation in Orthodox Theological Education

was less prevalent in the past; there are now more converts to Orthodoxy and inter-faith or mixed marriages than ever before. These individuals and families need guidance on concrete aspects of religious life and its ecumenical implications: Should they baptize their children in the Orthodox Church even when the spouse's faith prohibits infant Baptism? Do they need to have their non-Orthodox Marriage blessed in the Orthodox Church? In the case of mixed marriages, which community will they support? Which church calendar will they follow when their churches observe differing feast days and fasting periods? Will they be able to have icons in their home or will prayers to the saints and Virgin Mary be allowed?

Pastoral care of Orthodox parishes is increasingly marked by such ecumenical concerns and the Orthodox attitude has to be rooted in the Orthodox faith, open to the other, and presented with love and pastoral tact. At the same time, converts to Orthodoxy and mixed marriages should be encouraged to contribute to Orthodox life, whether they teach the rest of the community enthusiasm in worship, interest in preaching, sustained Biblical study—areas in which many Protestant faithful could contribute—or whether they share their concern for universal unity and collaboration among various world regions, just to give two examples in which the Catholic Church excels. Only through strong theological education in ecumenism can the Orthodox Church have a meaningful pastoral contact with other churches and have the confidence to accept the gifts of other communities. Otherwise, converts would adopt a wholesale adversarial attitude towards their previous faiths and would be attracted to a triumphalist Orthodoxy; further, mixed marriages would be split along faith lines and, instead of cherishing the opportunity to present Orthodoxy at its best, a situation of animosity and mistrust would be created; and Orthodoxy would be impoverished by rejecting the gifts that other churches could contribute to its life in Christ. A solid ecumenical education could certainly curtail such consequences.

Honest dialogue of Orthodox theology with the West

Second, Orthodox theology needs to engage in an honest dialogue with the West, which would contribute to the mutual enrichment of all faiths. Listening is of utmost importance, so Protestant and Catholic theologians should be received as they speak in their own voice, rather than according to Orthodox interpretation alone. Educators know that the best students are the ones who combine an analytic spirit with a thirst for new information. Orthodox churches in general, and Orthodox institutions of higher education in particular, are encouraged to become good students. Educators need to be educated.

A complete education involves knowledge and love of both East and West. If the instructor is interested in learning from other faiths, so will their students who later become lay or ordained ministers. For example, a professor of history should teach the writings of Western Fathers, Catholic and Protestant historians, and Eastern Fathers who had a direct and constructive exposure to the West, such as Maximus the Confessor in the matter of the *Filioque*. [5] Professors of Old Testament should require their students to read Rabbinic interpretations, while those who teach the New Testament should focus on the Eastern history of biblical interpretation engaged in dialogue with traditional and recent Western biblical scholarship, so rich especially in its historical-critical approach, much of which would no doubt be endorsed by the early Antiochian school of interpretation. Other examples of the benefits of an ecumenical approach to education and its positive benefits for the life of the Orthodox Church will be mentioned later in this essay.

Before continuing with a third suggestion, a brief clarification is necessary. In the previous paragraph, I have advocated for teaching theology from a denominational perspective with ecumenical openness, as opposed to presenting a theology that claims to be objective and free of denominational influences. In my opinion, the second type of theology does not exist, but rather all theological discourse takes place within a certain

---

[5] In 2003, the American Orthodox-Catholic Theological Consultation issued "The *Filioque*: A Church-Dividing Issue? An Agreed Statement," which provides an excellent example of ecumenical theology. In their historical analysis, the members of the Consultation mention the case of Maximus the Confessor who, in his *Letter to Marinus* (PG 91:133-136) considers that the conflict over the *Filioque* is due "to a misunderstanding on both sides of the different ranges of meaning implied in the Greek and Latin terms for 'procession'."

context that dictates the lenses through which one understands reality and speaks. The dichotomy between a purely academic approach to theology and a denominational approach is false. That is not to say that there is no distinction between "Religious Studies" and "Theology," but the ideas analyzed from the perspective of Religious Studies have been generated and are meant for specific contexts, which need to be acknowledged. The illusion of ontological objectivism should make way for a phenomenological approach to theology. The latter allows room for both the belief in the truthfulness of Revelation and an irenic dialogue with the other, including when teaching History and Biblical Studies.

Anti-ecumenical attitudes as a distortion of Orthodoxy

Third, anti-ecumenical attitudes and Orthodox isolationism result in the distortion of Orthodoxy itself. True, Orthodoxy is related to the other Christian churches. Other chapters in the present volume support this affirmation more fully, but several directions can be sketched here, as well. Georges Florovsky argued that the canonical boundaries of the Orthodox Church do not coincide with the charismatic boundaries of the Church of Christ; Orthodoxy represents the fullness of the Church *Una Sancta*, but not its totality, so Orthodox Christians need to live their ecclesial life in relation to other Christians.[6] Dumitru Staniloae added that Orthodoxy should engage in "spiritual intercommunion" with other churches, namely growing in a common understanding of the spiritual core of our churches' dogmas, common prayer, and concerted efforts to be a healing presence in society; Staniloae also proposed "open sobornicity," which is the acceptance of Western concepts into the Orthodox faith, as long as there is sufficient biblical and patristic basis to do so; enclosed in itself, Orthodoxy would not benefit from the various instances in which God revealed himself in non-Orthodox contexts.[7] Many other Orthodox theologians support the view that Orthodoxy is intrinsically related to other Christians in a common *martyria*, *diakonia*, and *leitourgia*: even though dogmatic differences still divide our communities, we share in the core of our beliefs; even though love is sometimes lacking, we need to engage more in common initiatives to manifest the Kingdom of God; even though we do not share in the sacraments, we can pray together and continue to pray the Divine Liturgy "for the union of all."[8]

Ecumenical orientation in vision statements of Orthodox theological schools

Fourth, the theoretical affirmation that an anti-ecumenical attitude is tantamount to a distortion of Orthodoxy has practical consequences for theological education. Orthodox schools should adopt vision statements that include ecumenical references. Such statements could vary anywhere from "teach Orthodox theology and its ecumenical relevance" to "educate Orthodox priests for a pluralistic society" or "offer an ecumenical perspective on Orthodox theology." These vision statements would dictate both hiring decisions and curricular offerings. One implication would be that Orthodox seminaries both in the West and East should offer tenure to non-Orthodox professors who teach theological disciplines required for lay and ordained ministries. A humble beginning would be to hire non-Orthodox professors in the areas of Old Testament, New Testament, and History

---

[6] Florovsky, Georges. " The Boundaries of the Church." In *Ecumenism I: A Doctrinal Approach* (Belmont, Mass.: Nordland Publishing Company, 1989), 36-45. See also his article, "St. Cyprian and St. Augustine on Schism." In *Ecumenism II: A Historical Approach* (Belmont, Mass.: Nordland Publishing Company, 1989), 48-51.

[7] Dumitru Staniloae. "Sobornicitate deschisa [Open Sobornicity]." Ortodoxia 23.2 (1971): 165-80. See also Lucian Turcescu. "Eucharistic Ecclesiology or Open Sobornicity?" In *Dumitru Staniloae: Tradition and Modernity in Theology*, edited by Lucian Turcescu, *83-103. Iasi, Romania; Palm Beach, FL: Center for Romanian Studies, 2002.*

[8] See for example the 1920 encyclical of the Ecumenical Patriarchate of Constantinople "Unto the Churches of Christ Everywhere," in which the Patriarch proposes the formation of a fellowship (*koinonia*) of churches and affirms that some degree of rapprochement need not await the resolution of dogmatic differences, recommending various ways to foster unity, including exchange of students and professors and adopting an irenic tone in theological discussions. Gennadios Limouris, ed. *Orthodox Visions of Ecumenism: Statements, Messages and Reports of the Ecumenical Movement 1902-1992.* (Geneva: WCC, 1994), 9-11.

Part VIII: Ecumenical Formation in Orthodox Theological Education

(including Patristics and Spirituality), since many Catholic and Protestant scholars are leaders in these fields today and since many of them show sensitivity and respect to the history of interpretation of the Bible in the Orthodox Church or to Orthodox life as it has been shaped by its history and spirituality. Similarly, Catholic and Protestant institutes in countries that are majority Orthodox should hire Orthodox scholars, thus following the example of their sister institutions in the West and benefiting from the same fruitful ecumenical exchanges.

Teaching theological courses with ecumenical sensitivity

An ecumenical vision should influence the curriculum, as well. All courses can be taught with ecumenical sensitivity. History certainly looks different through ecumenical lenses, especially when assessing the long string of schisms and when applauding ecumenical progress. Spirituality unifies Christians in their quest for union with God, as Metropolitan Evlogy wrote: "On the heights of their spiritual lives have not the saints passed beyond the walls that separate us, walls which, according to the grand saying of Metropolitan Platon of Kiev, do not mount up as far as heaven?"[9] Biblical Theology is an ideal platform for ecumenical collaboration given the differing histories of biblical reception in the East and West. Pastoral Theology warns against the dangers of proselytism while at the same time encouraging common missions. Shared principles of Moral Theology become a necessity in an increasingly secularized world in need of a common Christian testimony. Orthodox Dogmatics also has to take into account the positive developments in the West, and testify with love to the Eastern tradition. Last but not least, Orthodox institutions need to offer classes in Ecumenism and highlight its accomplishments, especially when they are directly relevant to Orthodoxy. Foremost in this sense would be the theological agreements between the Eastern and Oriental Orthodox Churches on issues of Christology, which mark an enormous step towards the healing of a schism that lasted fifteen centuries.[10] Seminaries should place special emphasis on other significant accomplishments of the ecumenical movement, such as the decisions of the World Council of Churches to adopt the unanimity system of voting at the insistence of Orthodox representatives[11] and the North American Orthodox-Catholic Theological Consultation's conclusion that the *Filioque* "need no longer divide us."[12]

Adopting an ecumenical teaching philosophy and methodology

Fifth, and related to the previous point, Orthodox professors need to adopt an ecumenical teaching philosophy and methodology. An Orthodox educator should help his or her students to understand intrinsically the positions of Catholic and Protestant theologians and appreciate the contributions of the West. Professors and students usually adopt reconciliatory and appreciative attitudes when those of different faiths are present. Such an exercise would be even more effective if all students were asked to attend worship at two churches to which they do not belong and then write a report comparing the two experiences. Another suggestion would be to construct a reading list based on the best representatives of various traditions, as opposed to outdated,

---

[9] Quoted in Timothy (Kallistos) Ware. *The Orthodox Church.* New ed. (London, New York: Penguin Books, 1997), 307. In regard to the similarities between Eastern Orthodox and Oriental Orthodox spiritualties, see Alexander Golitzin. "Anathema! Some Historical Perspectives on the Athonite Statement of May, 1995." *St. Nersess Theological Review* 3.1-2 (1998): 103-17.

[10] The dialogue between the Eastern and Oriental Orthodox Churches started informally in 1964, but since 1985 it has continued at the level of a Joint Theological Commission. The Commission's most important statements of Anba Bishoi (1989) and Chambésy (1990) show that, despite centuries of alienation and terminological confusion, the two churches share the same Orthodox faith. See Thomas FitzGerald and Peter Bouteneff, eds. *Turn to God, Rejoice in Hope: Orthodox Reflections on the Way to Harare.* (Geneva: WCC, 1998), 145.

[11] In order to alleviate the tensions generated by unfair voting procedures, the WCC has adopted in 2002 the consensus decision-making procedure.

[12] http://www.usccb.org/beliefs-and-teachings/ecumenical-and-interreligious/ecumenical/orthodox/filioque-church-dividing-issue-english.cfm, accessed 19 June 2013.

caricaturist, polemical writings that become easy targets and do not correspond to the current reality. Orthodox students should be exposed to primary Western sources, and not only Eastern analyses of the West. As an Orthodox professor teaching in a Catholic university, I have experienced the joy of teaching Catholic and Protestant students whom I regard as well-intended, receptive, sincere in their faith, and committed to dialogue. I also enjoy numerous conversations with my colleagues who do not share my faith, but who are excited to have an Orthodox partner of discussions. One also notices how scholars criticize each other differently when the person being criticized is in the audience. It would be beneficial to invite non-Orthodox lecturers to present their positions in their own terms, and thus give the West its own voice. This suggestion applies to all Orthodox institutions, whether they are in majority Orthodox countries or not.

Syllabus Outline

In what follows, I would like to suggest several syllabus components for a doctoral-level course on the subject of "Primacies in the Church." Orthodox theology, in particular, needs to articulate its understanding of primacy more clearly, since it presently works with several models, depending on the level at which it is being applied—local, regional, or universal. The class would reflect on the primacy of Christ, the local bishop over his local church, the primate of a region or a national Church, universal primacy, infallibility in/of the Church, and reception of doctrine. While approaching these issues with respect for Tradition and responsibility for Church unity, the class should be aware that contemporary theologians did not find a satisfactory solution to all these aspects of primacy.

Expected learning outcomes:

By the end of the course, students should expect to:

1. identify the ecclesiological themes most relevant for contemporary ecumenical discussion of primacy and infallibility.

2. know the most significant contemporary works on primacies.

3. understand the ways in which theologians interact with each other within or outside their theological traditions.

4. suggest potential solutions to the present ecumenical crisis.

5. distinguish different methods of theological investigation and be able to implement them, discerning what methods are most appropriate for a certain type of text.

6. develop the skills of written and oral communication necessary to approach ecclesiological issues related to primacies at a doctoral level.

7. acquire the competence necessary to comprehend multiple points of view in the global community.

Required Readings (Select sources, some books should not be assigned in their entirety):

Afanassieff, Nicolas. *The Church of the Holy Spirit.* (South Bend, IN: Notre Dame University Press, 2007).

-. "Una Sancta" and "The Eucharist: Principal Link Between the Catholics and the Orthodox." In *Tradition Alive: On the Church and the Christian Life in Our Time: Readings from the Eastern Church,* edited by Michael Plekon, (Lanham, MD: Rowan & Littlefield, 2003), 3-30, 47-49.

Clément, Olivier. *You Are Peter: An Orthodox Theologian's Reflection on the Exercise of Papal Primacy.* (New York: New City Press, 2003).

de Lubac, Henri. *The Motherhood of the Church followed by Particular Churches in the Universal Church and an interview conducted by Gwendoline Jarczyk.* Translated by Sergia Englund. (San Francisco: Ignatius Press, 1982).

DeVille, Adam A. J. *Orthodoxy and the Roman Papacy:* Ut Unum Sint *and the Prospects of East-West Unity.* (South Bend, IN: University of Notre Dame Press, 2011).

Doyle, Dennis M. *Communion Ecclesiology: Vision and Versions.* (Maryknoll, NY: Orbis Books, 2000).

Florovsky, Georges. "The 'Doctrine' of the Church: Schism and the Branch Theory." In *Ecumenism I: A Doctrinal Approach*, CW 13, (Belmont, Mass.: Nordland Publishing Company, 1989), 34-35.

-. "The Boundaries of the Church." In *Ecumenism I*, 36-45.

-. "St. Cyprian and St. Augustine on Schism." In *Ecumenism II: A Historical Approach*, (Belmont, Mass.: Nordland Publishing Company, 1989), 48-51.

Hinze, Bradford E. *Practices of Dialogue in the Roman Catholic Church: Aims and Obstacles, Lessons and Laments.* (New York: Continuum, 2006).

Kasper, Walter. *That They May All Be One: The Call to Unity.* (New York: Burns & Oates, 2004).

-, ed. *The Petrine Ministry: Catholics and Orthodox in Dialogue.* (Mahwah, NJ: Newman Press, 2006).

-. "On the Church: A Friendly Reply to Cardinal Ratzinger." *America* 184.14 (2001): 8-14.

Meyendorff, John, ed. *The Primacy of Peter: Essays in Ecclesiology and the Early Church.* (Crestwood, NY: St. Vladimir's Seminary Press, 1992).

Murphy, Francesca A. and Christopher Asprey, eds. *Ecumenism Today: The Universal Church in the 21st Century.* (Burlington, VT: Ashgate, 2008).

Orsy, Ladislas. *Receiving the Council: Theological and Canonical Insights and Debates.* (Collegeville, MN: Liturgical Press, 2009).

Phan, Peter C., ed. *The Gift of the Church: A Textbook on Ecclesiology in Honor of Patrick Granfield, O.S.B..* (Collegeville, MN: Liturgical Press, 2000).

Powell, Mark E. *Papal Infallibility: A Protestant Evaluation of an Ecumenical Issue.* (Grand Rapids, MI: Eerdmans, 2009).

Puglisi, James F., ed. *Petrine Ministry and the Unity of the Church: "Toward a Patient and Fraternal Dialogue": A Symposium Celebrating the 100th Anniversary of the Foundation of the Society of the Atonement, Rome, December 4-6, 1997.* (Collegeville, MN: Liturgical Press, 1999.)

Ratzinger, Joseph Cardinal. *Church, Ecumenism and Politics: New Essays in Ecclesiology.* (New York: Crossroad, 1988.)

-. "The Local Church and the Universal Church: A Response to Walter Kasper." *America* 185.16 (2001): 7-11.

Staniloae, Dumitru. *Theology and the Church*, translated by Robert Barringer (New York: St. Vladimir's Seminary Press, 1980).

Tillard, J.-M.-R. *Church of Churches: The Ecclesiology of Communion.* Translated by R. C. De Peaux. (Collegeville, MN: Liturgical Press, 1992).

Zizioulas, John D. "The Development of Conciliar Structures to the Time of the First Ecumenical Council." In *Councils and the Ecumenical Movement*, edited by Faith and Order Secretariat, (Geneva: WCC, 1968), 34-51.

-. *Being as Communion: Studies in Personhood and the Church, Contemporary Greek Theologians; no. 4.* (Crestwood, NY: St. Vladimir's Seminary Press, 1985).

-. "The Theological Problem of 'Reception'." *One in Christ* 21.3 (1985): 187-93.

-. "The Institution of Episcopal Conferences: An Orthodox Reflection." *The Jurist* 48 (1988): 376-83.

-. *Eucharist, Bishop, Church: The Unity of the Church in the Divine Eucharist and the Bishop During the First Three Centuries.* Translated by Elizabeth Theokritoff. (Brookline, Mass.: Holy Cross Orthodox Press, 2001).

Various documents (ordered chronologically):

"*Pastor Aeternus*" in Tanner, Norman P., ed. *Decrees of the Ecumenical Councils.* Vol. 2, (Washington, DC: Georgetown University Press / Sheed & Ward, 1990), 811-816.

Vatican Council II. *Vatican Council II: The Conciliar and Postconciliar Documents.* Edited by Austin Flannery O.P. New Revised ed. Vol. 1. (Northport, NY: Costello Publishing Company, 1998).

ARCIC III: "Agreed Statement on Authority in the Church (1976)."

North American Orthodox-Catholic Theological Consultation. "An Agreed Statement on Conciliarity and Primacy in the Church (1989)." In *The Quest for Unity: Orthodox and Catholics in Dialogue*, edited by John Borelli and John H. Erickson, (Crestwood, NY: St. Vladimir's Seminary Press, 1996), 152-55.

French Joint Roman Catholic – Orthodox Committee. "The Roman Primacy within the Communion of Churches (1991)." *One in Christ* 29.2 (1993): 156-64.

Ravenna Document, 2007.

"Pew Report on Global Christianity", 2011.

Conclusion

This essay was intended to make a case for an explicit inclusion of ecumenism in theological teaching, primarily in Orthodox institutions of higher education. Classes on Ecumenism, as well as ecumenical perspectives on other theological subjects are necessary in a pluralistic, globalized society, both in countries that are majority Orthodox and in other parts of the world with an Orthodox presence. Orthodox teaching needs to be ecumenical and ecumenical teaching needs an Orthodox component in order to maintain the integrity of both Orthodoxy and ecumenical education.

Bibliography

Bird, Darlene L. and Simon G. Smith, eds. *Theology and Religious Studies in Higher Education: Global Perspectives*. (New York, London: Continuum, 2009).

Bezzerides, Ann, ed. *Orthodox Christianity, Higher Education, and the University: Theological, Historical, and Contemporary Reflections*. (South Bend: University of Notre Dame Press) [Forthcoming].

Demacopoulos, George E. and Aristotle Papanikolaou, eds. *Orthodox Constructions of the West*. (New York: Fordham University Press, 2013).

Elias, John L. *The History of Christian Education: Protestant, Catholic and Orthodox Perspectives* (Krieger Publishing: Malabar, FL, 2002).

Kelsey, David H. *Between Athens and Berlin: The Theological Education Debate*, (Eerdmans: Grand Rapids, 1993).

Kinnamon, Michael. *The Vision of the Ecumenical Movement and How It Has Been Impoverished by Its Friends*. (St. Louis: Chalice Press, 2003).

(131) Methods of Teaching About and With Other Christian Denominations in Ecumenical Theological Education of Orthodox Institutions

Fr. Grigorios Papathomas

Ecumenical Movement, as a theological stance as well as a theological attempt, is called to follow the *course* (historical integration) along with the *perspective* (eschatological reception) of Christ's Incarnation. Indeed, the Incarnation of Christ is nothing else than *the hypostatical exodus from the Trinitarian communion of the Divinity*, or, using biblical language, the Pauline *kenosis* of Christ,[1] the initiative the Uncreated took, based on unselfconscious free will, *to get into the place of the created [reception], to take his place [integration],* so as to *meet* with the created [communion] that had been dissociated from Him, remaining in a state of detachment, which was caused by an erroneous choice, having broken every form of communion with Him. In other words, Christ's kenosis of His divinity takes place in order for Him to take man's place, to get into his place so as to re-establish His communion both with man and the created. This way we are left with an everlasting legacy as well as with a *didactic "paradigm,"* among other things, "to follow in His footsteps."[2] However, the weakness the Christians display nowadays, not only towards other Christians but also towards people in general, lies in the fact that we do not manifest a *willingness similar* to that of Christ, as well as the consequent *action* to get into the place of the other, understand him and meet with him. In practice, such a disposition means that in our Christian and Ecumenical everyday life, while we embrace and proclaim Christ's Incarnation, we actually fall into *"Docetism,"* just because we do not do what Christ Himself substantiated. We do not embrace the *perspective of a communion based interpersonal integration,* but instead we remain aloof, thus becoming potential *"docetic* Christians."

Therefore, it is quite significant, for the envisaged as well as the attempted teaching of other Christians within the frame of the Ecumenical Movement, to look at Incarnation's features under the scope of this teaching.

The Uncreated:

- is not incarnated in order to pass judgment on the created and have a *critical stance* towards it;
- is not incarnated in order to reproach the created about *some historical responsibility* it bears, on the grounds that the created is solely responsible for *its own fall and its alienation from the communion*;
- is not incarnated in order to ascribe *any liability and punish*;
- is not incarnated in order to *assume a provocative stance* towards the created and *impeach it* into a *factual legal penance,* due to its phenomenal self-evident responsibility,
- but,
- is incarnated, i.e. becoming "integrated" ("*εν-σωματώνεται*"), part of the Creation, in order to *acquire* the created after the fall and turn it into His *own flesh*;
- is incarnated in order to take up, under Its new (divine-) human form, the responsibility for the fall, our *misguided behavior* (= sin);
- is incarnated in order to take our place by our side, among us, thus showing the way[3] and the footsteps,[4] left to follow, so as to recover the now lost, original and complete [holistic] communion with Him;
- is incarnated in order to defeat – within the scope of the created – death, which is the cause as well as the consequence of the interrupted communion, by becoming the [New] Adam, in Adam's place, leading to a hypostatical *communion*, both with man and the created.

---

[1] Phil 2:7.
[2] 1 Pet 2:21.
[3] Cf. John 14:6.
[4] Cf. 1 Pet 2:21.

Through these widely known characteristic parameters, the one thing that constitutes the definition of the course (*historical integration, along with everything that is brought by it*) and the perspective (*eschatological reception, along with everything that is brought by it*) of Christ's Incarnation becomes clear. The fruit of this attempt is an *en-hypostatical communion* with His creation. Therefore, Christ assumes man's place, moves towards the other, the *man-other*, the human otherness, so as to become *hypostatically* indistinguishable. This feature is what the envisaged teaching presupposes and pre-requires as an existing base, prior to setting off to examine parts of its methodology. Putting it in a different way, the one who teaches the "other Christians" is called to put himself in the place of the other/others in order to understand their otherness, i.e. to participate receptively in the *opposite otherness*, always under the criterion of communion's perspective. This means that teaching methodology goes through, let us symbolically call it, "itinerary of Incarnation": "Reception-Integration-Communion." This is exactly what Christ through His word-*lapis Lydius* gives meaning to, when He says "Treat others just as you want to be treated."[5]

Therefore, here we can discern three steps which constitute the trifold outline of the anticipated teaching on an ecumenical level: 1) Affirmation of the *otherness*, 2) *Fusion of otherness' diversity*, and 3) Attainment of *communion* through this teaching. These three aspects constitute at the same time both the axes, and possibly the plans for this teaching.

1) Affirmation of the *otherness*

As is the case with Trinitarian God, in order for *communion* to exist, we need to have different types of otherness, such as personal or collective. Communion does not necessarily coincide with "*co-identifying*" of the otherness, but *affirming* it instead. In other words, this affirmation constitutes the beginning of communion. Affirmation of the otherness, either personal or collective, still remains a prerequisite as well as a presupposition in order for us to reach communion. Una persona, nulla persona, was a motto used by the early Christians, therefore, una persona, nulla communio. Communion goes through the otherness and is attained only along with the otherness. God would not be *communion*, as we will point out later, if He were not a Trinity of Persons. Therefore, the teaching "other Christians" cannot be established, unless this is done so on the grounds of a *communion with the otherness*.

Regarding the verification of this, we can refer back to our two thousand year Church life. Let us give a historical example of a case when the Church displayed an exemplary affirmation of the otherness in terms of universality on a world wide scale. In the times, when Christianity was the "official" main prevailing religion of the Roman Empire and enjoyed its full benevolence (4th-8th century), a fact which actually meant it could exert what is theologically charged with a negative meaning, i.e. "tolerance" (*sic*) of religious otherness, which is something clearly theologically derogatory for the ontological equivalence of the otherness within the one, complete and whole Creation. The Church of the 8th century teaches fragmented Christians for over two thousand years, especially divided Christians of our times, on a level of ecumenical behavior and attitude towards deviating situations. The incident brings us back to the Iconoclastic period of the emperor Leo III the Isaurian.

The emperor of the Eastern Empire Leo III the Isaurian (717-741), despite what has been erroneously recorded in history that he had Jewish advisors who inspired him through their uniconic tradition to become involved in iconoclasm, actually fought against iconophiles and casted them away, along with the Jewish people, who later on faced a great deal of hardship. Emperor Leo's threat instilled in the Jewish people quite logical fears for their extinction, who according to the proceedings of the Seventh Ecumenical Council (Canon 8) of Nicaea-787 to "*christianize*" [once mentioned-"*ἅπαξ λεγόμενον*"], i.e. they began behaving in two different ways: officially they were considered as "Christians," but actually, unofficially they still remained Jewish.

---

[5] Lk 6:31; cf. Mt 7:12.

Part VIII: Ecumenical Formation in Orthodox Theological Education

When the Church, 50 years later, both theologically and synodically dealt with the issue of the empire policy regarding iconoclasm, theologically reinstated he icons after the Seventh Ecumenical Council (787), but at the same time displayed exemplary behavior of ecumenical stance towards people of different religious beliefs (and just towards people of different denominations). This exceptional synodical stance, since it can be considered as an answer to the people of different religious beliefs, it can even more, or better yet proportionally, apply to the "other" [*heterodox*] Christians, the Christians belonging to different denominations.

The 8th canon of the Seventh Ecumenical Council mentions: "[…]. We decree, state the Church Fathers, that the Jewish people, since they pretend to "*christianize*," to be Christians, to let them be openly Hebrews according to their religion, and let them not bring their children to baptism, nor purchase or possess a slave. […]"[6]. As we can see from this synodical canon, the Church has nothing to be envious of the Declaration of the Human Rights, not even of the more recent Declarations of Religious Freedom. Indeed, as early as the 8th century, i.e. over a millennium ago, the Church takes actions, especially during an Ecumenical Council, an extraordinary synodical event reflecting the unity of the Church consciousness, *distinctively* (under the perspective of otherness), *subtly* (by merging, as we will see later on, into an ecumenical perspective any form of otherness or distinction and contrast) and *under the sense of communion* (by preserving Creation's unity).

Next to this distinctive historical paradigm and model of the attempted teaching, let us mention a contemporary example as well, one that highlights the transcendence of otherness. In recent years, in the period of World War II and the Holocaust (1940-1945), the Archbishop of Athens of the Orthodox Church of Greece, Damaskinos Papandreou displayed a similar behavior. When, during the German occupation, he had to face the possibility of the Jewish community of Athens being persecuted and killed, he suggested that they should just be …"baptized" so as they be enrolled as Christians on the official Church name catalogues and thus be able to prove their innocence and be exempted. He was sincere towards them, bearing in mind his responsibility on such a historical moment, and cleared out that they would still remain Jewish in faith and worship practices and would not be obliged to have any participation in the liturgical practices of the Church. Such a mutual understanding and sincerity was the main factor which made their secret plan successful and averted the danger of many Athenian Jewish people being killed.

In this part, we mentioned two distinctive timeless examples that reveal an inclination to get into somebody else's place, the same thing Christ succeeded through His Incarnation, by also taking the other person's responsibilities, visions, reflections and perspectives and sharing them with the other, *whoever they may be*, especially when this action takes place within the Ecumenical Movement, where such a vision is not only *commonly* shared but also *distinctively* Christian. These paradigms are quite characteristic and we could have more of them through the common ecumenical experience of those Christians teaching and those being taught before moving on to the second step of the attempted teaching, the step dealing with the fusion of the otherness' diversity.

2) The fusion of the otherness' [alterities'] diversity

The after-the-fall created exists bearing all the characteristics of susceptibility and [after-the-fall] contrasts. When all these types of diversity are objectified, then the distance between collective diversification/alterity becomes longer. This is the main characteristic of the fall and the divisions existing among the Christians: each one adheres to their own beliefs and to their vested cultural gains of the second millennium denominational-confessionalistic past. These are the "new [at first] and old [then],"[7] that Christ through His teaching calls

---

[6] P.-P. JOANNOU, *Discipline générale antique (IVe-IXe siècles). Les Canons des Conciles œcuméniques (IIe-IXe siècles)*, édition critique du texte grec, version latine et traduction française, [Pontificia Commissione per la Redazione del Codice di Diritto Canonico Orientale], Fonti fascicolo IX, t. I, 1, (Grottaferrata (Rome), Tipografia Italo-Orientale «S. Nilo,» 1962), 261-263 (trilingual).
[7] Mt 13:52.

us to abandon, exactly because we have found "the valuable pearl."[8] This dual movement, the "outcome"[9] of historical objectifications as well as the willing acceptance of the "valuable pearl," becomes a starting point for this *fusion of the otherness' diversity*, something proper teaching is called to take into consideration as an equally important methodological prerequisite.

However, here is where we have to be really careful about teaching fulfillment. All the above-mentioned, cannot be applied by using violence, conversion practices, proselytism, powerful methods of attraction or abusive corporate-like arguments. Instead, they should be applied through freedom of communion, the exact same freedom God applied, when He called into being the created, the exact same freedom He let the created use, when taking initiatives of either positive or negative freedom. When Christ freed us, through His Incarnation, from the tyrannizing existence of the after-the-fall created, it was given to us as an ontological legacy: "Christ has set us free, stand firm, then, and do not be subject again to the yoke of slavery."[10] Then the teaching (will) become(s) a beacon lighting on the right path we should follow, and (will) act(s) as a medium fulfilling the teaching vision St. Gregory the Theologian (4th century) suggested: «Πτερῶσαι ψυχήν, αρπάσαι κόσμου και δοῦναι Θεώ», "Give wings to the soul, take it away from this world and offer it to God,"[11] i.e. exactly what the vision of Incarnation stands for. In other words, this means that the teacher is supposed to offer *theological wings* to the one being taught, since teaching on an *ecumenical level* cannot differ from the one followed on a *theological level [identical teaching perspective]*. The "soul" here stands for every different type of otherness that remains in an after-the-fall state, which by definition alone can cause centrifugal forces. These are the diversities of the other on a communal level, diversifications of the otherness' diversities, opposite types of existence, something like *heteronym fractions that cannot "commune" unless they become homonym fractions*. However, this does not involve existence *identification*; instead it stands for *affirmation* of the otherness' diversities and their fusion. When, according to Gregory of Nazianzus, the ones teaching give such wings to the ones being taught, then they will be able to fly off having a solid sense of orientation. Once they acquire such wings [only after the acquisition, *never before*], then the teaching itself will "take them away" from this world,[12] set them free from culturalistic slavery where fragmented Christians are kept nowadays, giving them a single perspective: offer them to God, i.e. to the Trinitarian communion, to the [*christic*] communion of the created and the uncreated under Christ, to the *complete communion*, to Christ's "ontological one."[13]

Christ is the only one who can fuse all this otherness' diversities. He does so in an ontological manner in order to lead them to commune with Him. He does not abolish otherness; instead He applies a "fusion of their otherness and their diversities" in order to create the right presuppositions for a communion with Him as well as with each other. Therefore, a definition of *theological Ecumenism within teaching* would be that of a fusion of the otherness under the perspective of successful communion. It is not only a form but also an attempt of "incarnation" within the "body of the otherness, either personal or collective." In this case, the, what could be called, voluntary *communional* integration provides us, among other things, a possibility of inner teaching instead of some form of practical teaching that remains arrogantly external, bearing elements of disregarding the other under the possibility of their "ignorance" or their different perceptions, even under their *hetero-oriented* approach. In that case, one would get involved in teaching inclined to put it into practice within a *dialectic*, as well as an *exchangeable*, approach ("to offer and receive"), within the frame of solid dialogue, due to the fact that positive dialogues do not result in victors and defeated. It is something like Socrates' method of *maieutic*, only in this case it is not shaped under the *cognitive perspective,* but under the *communional perspective* where knowledge and love are actually identified. The more you get to know the other, the more you get to love them, eventually the more you get to love them the more you get to know them. This is what teaching dialectics and exchangeability should be on an ecumenical level.

---

[8] Mt 13:46.
[9] Cf. Mt 13:52.
[10] Gal. 5:1.
[11] Gregory the Theologian, "*Oration B, Apologet.*" 22, in *P.G.*, vol. 35, 431B-432B.
[12] Precisely because "you do not belong to the world" (John 15:19).
[13] Cf. John 17:21 and 23.

Therefore, communion's aim is to for us to get to know the different types of otherness, personal or collective, through each parameter that constitutes their mere existence: what they are, where they are, how they are, since when and why they are. We should make an effort to get to know them, exactly the way they are, the way they think, the way they write, being precise and objective, distancing ourselves from personal and collective eccentricities. This will signal the beginning of the otherness' fusion, will lead to *communion* with the help of ecumenical perspective's theological teaching.

3) Attainment of *communion* through teaching

One commonly shared Church Father, St. John Chrysostom (5th century), defined first the relationship that could be developed between the one teaching and the one being taught, a practice, as well as a dimension of Education, that today, unfortunately, has been significantly weakened. He states: «Ουδέν ούτω προς διδασκαλίαν επαγωγόν, ως το φιλείν και το φιλείσθαι», "There is nothing better that will help teaching than for the teacher and the one being taught to love each other."[14] The only motive Chrysostom sees in a successful teaching is *love for the one being taught*. Here is where the singularity of the teacher lies. In the beginning, the teacher is the one who loves; his love focuses towards properly orientating the ones being taught from being theologically "ignorant" to developing broad horizons, not only regarding their knowledge but also their *way of life* and *communion*. Precisely, this way of life and *communion*, to which the one teaching will inure the one being taught, is nothing else but *love*! The meaning of the word "love" in this case is referring to the "Pre-Age," "Pre-Eternal," to the state prior to the "Created" being brought into existence, to the creative Trinity, which both *exists* and *is* as *communion*. In the once mentioned "God is love,"[15] the word "love" does not imply a "biological sentiment," as it is usually perceived, instead the word entails the meaning of "communion," the kind of ontological communion, which defines the Trinity's mode of existence, that creates man "in his own image, in the image of God," not just to place him, to make him last forever in the course of history, but to keep him close until *Eschaton* in an everlasting *communion*. Therefore "love" means "commune." It means that I "display an inclination to *commune* with the other," "affirm the otherness under the perspective *commune* with it." This is, among other things, that is implied in the phrase of Maximus the Confessor (7th century) about Christ: "Θεολογίαν γάρ διδάσκει σαρκούμενος ο του Θεού Λόγος," "*by becoming flesh the Word teaches Theo-logy*,"[16] i.e. that the Word through *His Incarnation* talks to us about God (Θεο-λογία), *teaches* us about "God's being," how God, the Trinitarian-three Persons God, is described by the Johannine expression as "love,"[17] precisely because He is *communion*. Let us take this opportunity and clarify something which may "shock," but it gives an answer to a longstanding philosophical-theological question: the Trinitarian God *does not exist* (υπάρχει) and *does not sustain* (υφίσταται)! We did not expect philosophers or atheists over the centuries to inform us about that. The Bible itself as well as the Church proclaims that. If He *existed* (υπ-ήρχε), if He *was* (υφ-ίστατο), we would have to accept the fact that the Trinitarian God *rules under* (άρχει κάτω από) someone else's divine authority and decision making other, but Him, God. However, God "is" (είναι) [cf. «Εγώ ειμι ο Ων», "I am that I am"[18] (we witness here a case of tautology: "God is that God is," the "being Being" → *ontology*], "*just is*," infinite, no time boundaries (past, present, future), just like Apostle Paul says: "Jesus Christ never changes! He is the same *yesterday, today*, and *forever*."[19] In the same context, he adds: "Do not be fooled by any kind of strange teachings,"[20] i.e. do not get carried away by different and foreign *teachings*. Here we can understand how important *teaching* is on various levels, so we can connect it to the subject we are examining.

[14] John the Chrysostom, "Commentary on I Timothy" *P.G.*, 62, 529-530.
[15] 1 Jn 4:8, 16.
[16] Maximus the Confessor, "On the Prayer 'Our Father', in *P.G.* 90, 876D; our own highlighting.
[17] 1 Jn 4:8, 16.
[18] Ex 3:14.
[19] Heb 13:8.
[20] Heb 13:9.

So, when we succeed in orienting the ones being taught towards an *ontological* perception of *love*, at the same time we inure them into being inclined to *commune*, not only transcendally but also *ontologically*. This kind of love, however, has as a starting point the one who teaches. He should be the one that loves the teaching he puts into practice, precisely because he loves and longs to *commune* with the ones being taught. At this point, we can discern why this kind of *love* and *communion* can be described as *ontological* [*categories*-classifications]. Under this perspective, the ones being taught will not only learn how to put to good and *Christian* use their gained knowledge, but also how to live realistically, *christically* and harmoniously, being oriented towards a church and ecumenical, as well as a family and social environment. We often consider that the one teaching is expressing his views from the standpoint of superiority and authority. However, St. John Chrysostom radically suggest an entirely different *standpoint*, that of the *heart of the one being taught*! The one being taught can easily realize his teacher's love, when the teacher truly loves, and then he can embrace him without being able to hide his love. Accepting the one who teaches means that the one being taught instantly accepts what the teacher professes along with their perspective. That is the reason why love always precedes any kind of theological knowledge offering, or any other kind of knowledge for that matter. Anyone who has ever tried to follow a diverse course either did not manage to love the ones they were teaching, or failed significantly into their every teaching attempt, much more on an ecumenical level. The most beautiful moment for anyone involved in teaching is when he feels that his theological pedagogical seeds finally bring fruits not only of knowledge but of love/communion as well. When he feels that the ones being taught love him back. And those who are taught actually know how to love. Maybe that is the time when the one who teaches realizes, that the one who was taught, whoever that may be, becomes an integral part of himself, a mind out of his own mind and a heart out of his own heart, part of his mere existence. That is when they begin to reach the boundaries of ontological communion. Therefore, the relationship established between the ones teaching and the ones being taught is a relationship of *love, personal* as well as *mutual*. It is a relationship of communion based upon theological presuppositions and ecumenical perspectives. Teaching *under communion perspective* leads to *"incarnation" on the part of the one being taught*. Then, teaching becomes a path towards knowing the other and of course of communion with the other, and vice versa. Therefore, teaching becomes clearly reciprocal on a communion level. "There is nothing better that will help teaching than for the teacher and the one being taught to love each other."[21]

Let us examine, though, this envisaged teaching on a more practical ecumenical level. During the 20th century, ever since the Ecumenical Movement was clearly and theological systematized, two main axes of ecumenical practices have been solidified followed by two main teaching methodologies wherever these methodologies had to be applied:

1. Every Christian denomination displays *Church exclusivity*; therefore, every other denomination-confession is treated as existing *outside* this Church.

2. Church is considered as one body; therefore, every other denomination is treated as existing *inside* the Church.

• The first methodology presupposes the existence of a *schism* among Churches (since 1054), which means that we deal with clearly set and defined boundaries which exclude the Christians that are not considered members of this Church.

• The second methodology is based upon the *disruption of communion*[22] (since 1054) among the Churches, along with openness and an inclination to developing dialectic relationships and communion.

---

[21] John Chrysostom, "Commentary.." *op.cit.*

[22] Cf. Archim. Grig. D. Papathomas, "Au temps de la post-ecclésialité. La naissance de la modernité post-ecclésiologique : de l'Église une aux nombreuses Églises, de la dispersion de l'Église à l'anéantissement du Corps du Christ,» in *Kanon* [Vienna], 19 (2006): 3-21, *Istina* [Paris], 51.1 (2006): 64-84, *Irénikon* [Chevetogne-Belgium], 79.4 (2006): 491-522 (in French), in *Overdruk uit Collationes* [Belgium] 37 (2007): 407-428 (in Flemish), in *The Messenger* [London], 1.2 (2007): 26-47, *Derecho y Religión* [Madrid], 3 (2008): 133-150, *Inter* [Cluj-Napoca], 2.1-2 (2008): 40-54 (in English), in *Usk ja Elu*, 3.1 (2007): 31-56 (in Estonian and Russian), and in *Μέτρον-Mira* [Lviv], 5-6 (2009): 63-88 (in Ukrainian).

The first practice is dated back to the Vatican Council II (1962-1965) and is a distinctive perception characterizing Roman Catholic theology as well as Orthodox theology, which could be considered as a methodological follower in many steps; the first one follows. The post-Vatican period has significantly changed the way of approach; still, the fundamental values remain the same, especially on an Ecclesiological level.

The second practice, which dictates the corresponding teaching methodology, is based upon the ecclesio-canonical notion of *disruption of communion*, which deals with *denominational diversification* as an event within the Church, therefore teaching takes place on a *dialectic level of communion* among brothers, within a communion *"in Christ,"* even if die to the *disruption of communion*, they have not [yet] come to *communion in "body of Christ."* Christ Himself makes a similar distinction, addressing it to every Christian when He says: "I have other sheep that are not in this sheep pen. I must also bring them together, when they hear my voice. Then there will be one flock of sheep and one shepherd."[23] However, this is precisely what becomes a teaching model, the *Christic* approach of "the other sheep," "the other children" of the same Father, the "other Christians" of the one and the same Church of Christ.

Additionally,

• The first methodology has an apologetic function, under exclusive uniqueness, obvious, or not so obvious polemics, distinctive disdain of the otherness, due to the fact that Church ecclesiology has been distorted. This Ecclesiology of Church has been distorted indeed during the second millennium. Its fundamental feature is a *prismatic ecclesiality under a denominational mentality*, or, in other simple words, the *confessional multi-ecclesiality* in a specific place. That is why we speak of Ecclesiology in plural or *plural Ecclesiologies.* Therefore, during the second millennium, most of the partial ecclesiologies are marked by the history of fragmentation, their ontological autonomy and isolation. This is exactly why, during this period, the Churches have clearly defined and endorsed their identity on the basis of their *denominational differences.* This is what brought about *Ecclesial confessiocracy (denomination-archy)* of the second millennium along with its corresponding Ecclesiology. Under this new and newly looking perspective, any occurring Ecclesial confession-denomination, which was self defined as [*aggressive-denominational*] *Church,* did not acknowledge any other Church outside its own *confession-ecclesial communion* and described the "other" Churches as schismatic or even occasionally heretic, following the well known scholastic western methodology of dividing the "other" Churches in concentric circles around one single center. This adopted anti-ecclesiological gradation is what caused friction and conflict among these denominational Churches. These conflicts are still happening nowadays and they have created the theologically objectionable configuration "we are on one side, and on the other side, there are the *others*, the *heterodox* [Christians]," a configuration that must be surpassed by any envisaged teaching.

• The second methodology by following a more appropriate mode, the mode of teaching, is making an effort to take double consecutive actions (démarches), before opening a broader common educational field. The *first* action involves the distinctive emergence of their otherness, as it was above mentioned and analyzed, so that their ontological boundaries along with their hypostatic features are made clear, and their dialectic counterparts of their common theological educational field – along with the ones that are actively participating in it – are aware of the presuppositions. At the same time, through these presuppositions they will become aware of their common or variant points as well as of their convergences or divergences. At this point, we should point to Fr. George Florovsky's well-known quote, that whoever is not familiar with history, cannot do [teach or be taught] Theology. Therefore, the best teaching subject would be *theological history,* which of course should be taught in ways that do not remind us of the aforementioned "first methodological approach." This action will help the fulfillment of the consecutive one. The *second* action involves the identity of these different types of otherness, their ontological content, the knowledge completeness of their content, as well as the methodology they apply. Therefore, when these two actions precede and are complete, then we can more easily schedule a common study field, which by being common to everyone, and under mutual love and inclination to commune, will, on one hand, offer objectivity to the one teaching and, on the other hand, will abort any mechanism of denominational

---

[23] Jn 10:16.

defense from the one being taught. Thus, by setting these two actions as a prerequisite the second methodology (will) act(s) under the scope of a dialectic theology, bearing receptive features and being open to every research possibility. This is exactly what Christ means by openly stating "search the Scriptures"[24]; only, in this case, it will be worth adding, with a sense of mutual-assistance in the attempted research. Such a teaching perspective along with love can also turn the ones teaching and the ones being taught, to a single body, to a single body of communion. Thereby, teaching functions as and is turned into an open, inclusive stance towards the other.

However, besides *theological* history, of which the Bible is considered an integrated part, Ecclesiology constitutes another teaching subject. Ecclesiology is a highly important matter for Christian theology, both for the Church body and its universal and ecumenical perspective. In other words, Ecclesiology cannot be detached or separated by Church's testimony and mission within History and all over the world. Ecclesiology's most important testimony is that the Church can exist as *one* and that, according to this consideration, which should also be an integral part of the teaching, this specific *theological* Ecclesiology aims, by extension, at an *ontological transcendence* of the after-the-fall divergences and to an *ontological unity*.

In conclusion, what applies on the Incarnation perspective, also applies on "methods of teaching other Christians in Ecumenical Movement." This teaching should first and foremost take place in the sense that our common Church Father, St. John Chrysostom, proposes. When we teach Ecumenical Theology in such a manner, the Ecumenical Movement will be recorded in the *prophetic category-classification of Theology* and will constitute an attempt to renew Christianity at the face of all the de facto new evidence of Christian plurality and open multicultural society of the third millennium. It will also constitute a well-founded hope that the Christians, as *one Church*, will be all the more able to fulfill Sunday's vision of "being one with each other"[25].

Bibliography

Agoras K., "Sacramental 'Christology', Cultural Modernity and Eschatological 'Gospel'," in P. Kalaitzidis-N. Dontos (eds.), *Orthodoxy and Modernity*, (Athens: Indiktos Publications, 2007), 263-291 (in Greek).

Agoras K., «Nature and Person, History and Eschata in Metropolitan John Zizioulas and Christos Yannaras. Eucharistic hermeneutics and Cultural hermeneutics in theology" in P. Kalaitzidis-Th. N. Papathanasiou-Th. Ampatzidis (eds.) *Turbulences in post-War theology. The generation of 60s"* (Athens: Indiktos Publications, 2009), 165-233 (in Greek).

Zizioulas J., Metropolitan of Pergamon, "Engagement œcuménique et recherche théologique," in *Istina* 53.1 (2006): 13-22.

Zizioulas J., Metropolitan of Pergamon, "Tradition liturgique et unité chrétienne," in *Revue de l'Institut Catholique de Paris* (oct.-dec. 1990): 157-170.

Nissiotis Nik. A., *Interpreting Orthodoxy*, (USA: Light & Life Pub Co, 1980).

Papathomas Gr. D., (Archim.), "Au temps de la post-ecclésialité. La naissance de la modernité post-ecclésiologique : de l'Église une aux nombreuses Églises, de la dispersion de l'Église à l'anéantissement du Corps du Christ," in *Kanon* 19 (2006): 3-21, in *Istina* 51.1 (2006): 64-84, in *Irénikon* 79.4 (2006): 491-522 (in French), in *The Messenger* 1.2 (2007): 26-47, in *Derecho y Religión* 3 (2008):133-150, in *Inter* [Cluj-Napoca], 2.1-2 (2008): 40-54 (in English).

(translated by Paraskeyi Arapoglou)

---

[24] Jn 5:39.
[25] Cf. Jn 17:21, 23.

Fr. Aurel Pavel/Fr. Daniel Buda

Introduction

This article tries to articulate a few ideas about how ecumenism and aspects related to other Christian confessions should be taught in Orthodox theological institutions in order to facilitate a proper understanding of the ecumenical movement and to nurture an "ecumenical spirit" among all constituencies of the Orthodox Churches. These thoughts are based on guideline documents issued by different meetings concerned with theological-ecumenical education in Orthodox theological institutions, on ideas of experienced ecumenists expressed in different studies, as well as on the experience of the authors in teaching ecumenism or other theological specialities. The first part is an attempt to articulate the importance of phrasing the "ecumenical message" in terms that will speak to and inspire Orthodox theologians, while the second one tries to identify the other theological disciplines which in their context imply extensive references to other Christian traditions and might influence the way they are perceived within Orthodox circles. It will also propose certain approaches which can contribute to improving an ecumenical understanding.

Teaching of Ecumenism

Some of the Orthodox theological institutions have established the teaching of Ecumenism as a separate and independent discipline, being part of their curriculum,[1] while others have elements of teaching ecumenism only as part of their teaching of Church History, Missiology, Systematic or even Practical theology. Ideally it would be appropriate to have Ecumenism as an independent discipline taught for at least one semester. Teaching of ecumenism as part of another theological discipline hinders an authentic and balanced approach. Special aspects of ecumenical theology could be approached in additional optional courses proposed to students.

Too often the teaching of ecumenism means only a dry and boring presentation of an endless list of assemblies and meetings organized by different ecumenical organizations or details about structures and programs of several ecumenical organizations which are undergoing continual restructuring, without any logic and sense, which makes the discipline of ecumenism unattractive to students. In other cases, the teaching of ecumenism is reduced to a history of the modern ecumenical movement or to a handful of information of different kinds to which the students are supposed to provide standard responses in order to pass the exam.

A coherent curriculum of teaching ecumenism in Orthodox theological schools shall include:

---

[1] Already the consultation on *Orthodox Theological Education for the Life and Witness of the Church* (Basel, Switzerland, 4-7 July 1978), which was "the very first consultation organized by in that time the newly established WCC "Program on Theological Education" (the predecessor of the actual "Ecumenical Theological Education" Program) and enjoyed a large participation of the leadership of several Orthodox theological institutions, welcomed "a widening of curricula to include ecumenical concerns." In several Orthodox schools, this meeting was the starting point for developing independent courses on ecumenism. For the text of the communiqué of the Basel consultation see Georges Tsetsis (ed.), *Orthodox Thought*, (Geneva: WCC Publications, 1983), 29-34; here 30. A German translation was published in Athanasios Basdekis (ed.), *Orthodoxe Kirche und ökumenische Bewegung. Dokumente – Erklärungen –Berichte*, (Frankfurt am Main: Verlag Otto Lembeck, 2006), document 39, 249-257. For a detailed report of the meeting see Paul Lazor, "Consultation on Orthodox Theological Education" *St. Vladimir's Theological Quarterly* 22.4 (1978): 213-225.

- A clear notional and terminological definition of the terms used in ecumenical theology;
- A coherent presentation of the biblical, historical, patristic and ecclesiological foundations of the ecumenical movement;
- A clear emphasis on the basic idea "that the participation of the Orthodox in the ecumenical movement of today is not, in principle, a revolution in the history of Orthodoxy, but it is a natural consequence of the constant prayer of the Church 'for the unity of all.' It constitutes another attempt, like those made in Patristic period, to apply the apostolic faith to new historical situation and existential demands. What is in a sense new today, is the fact that this attempt is being made together with other Christian bodies with whom there is no full unity. It is here that the difficulties arise, but it is precisely here that there also are many signs of real hope for growing fellowship and cooperation."[2] With other works, it is important to underline that the ecumenical movement is not a result of modernity, but the desire for Christian unity existed always within the Church and was expressed in different forms since Apostolic times;
- A brief presentation of the types of ecumenical institutions with their history, mandates and achievements: global, regional, national etc. with their scopes and specifics;
- An objective presentation of the positive impact of the participation of Orthodox churches in the modern ecumenical movement;
- Aspects related to the importance of ecumenism for the daily life of Orthodox communities;
- Specific local, regional or national opportunities and challenges related with ecumenism, making the teaching of ecumenism relevant for the immediate context in which the students are living.

Part of the objectivity in teaching ecumenism is to avoid cheap propaganda for ecumenical engagement or an idealistic presentation of the ecumenical movement without any basis on reality. Such a non-objective approach can create damages to an authentic ecumenical approach and erect unrealistic expectations or even to deliver argumentation to fundamentalists or anti-ecumenists. As Orthodox fundamentalism within some Orthodox groups is becoming a significant problem - being caused by several reasons like narrow reading of church history, a legalistic approach to the canons, failure to appreciate the spirit of Scripture, liturgy and patristic literature - the teaching of ecumenism in Orthodox theological schools shall include the following:

- Well articulated presentations of Orthodox positions on major ecumenical themes like Orthodox understanding of unity, Orthodox understanding of the role of ecclesiology and Eucharist in struggling for a genuine unity of the Church of Jesus Christ.[3]
- Extensive presentations of the Orthodox positions on critical issues related with ecumenism like proselytism, women ordination, inclusive language etc. or on last developments within other Christian traditions which discount Orthodox engagement in ecumenical work, like acceptance of same sex marriages or of abortion (see chapter 18 *On the Critical Role of Orthodox Churches in the Ecumenical Movement* of this Handbook);
- Emphasis of the ecumenical priorities for the Orthodox, like the theological dialogue with the Oriental Orthodox Churches. A consultation on Orthodox Theological Education and Ecumenical Themes held in the Penteli monastery (2-9 February 2000) stated that: "At this moment in the history of the universal Church, the task of theological schools is to convey the positive results of these bilateral dialogues (i.e. the one with the Oriental Orthodox Churches) in order to convince the Churches to take the final steps in restoring full sacramental communion."[4]

---

[2] See *Report of an Inter-Orthodox Consultation „The Ecumenical Nature of Orthodox Witness," New Valamo, Finland, 24-20 September 1977* in Gennadios Limouris (ed.), *Orthodox Visions of Ecumenism. Statements, Messages and Reports on the Ecumenical Movement 1902-1992*, (Geneva: WCC Publications, 1994), 66-69.

[3] The Basel consultation (see footnote 1) discussed " the affirmation that the real Orthodox understanding of the church is basically ecumenical in that all humanity is called to share in the same Eucharist", 31.

[4] See *Report of the consultation of Orthodox Theological Education and ecumenical themes* in *St. Vladimir's Theological Quarterly* 44.2 (2000): 181-194, here 185.

Part VIII: Ecumenical Formation in Orthodox Theological Education

- Emphasis on the fact that leadership of the Orthodox Churches as well as widely-recognized personalities, including saints, were and are involved in the modern ecumenical movement;
- Formulation of clear responses to the main accusations formulated by Orthodox anti-ecumenists to the ecumenical movement and especially to Orthodox involvement in it.

Teaching about other Christian traditions

First of all, it should be underlined that a positive ecumenical approach is needed in teaching all theological disciplines in order to make the teaching of ecumenism meaningful. If the main theological disciplines like the biblical, historical, systematic and practical ones are taught in a polemic way, without coherence with what are presented in the curriculum of teaching ecumenism, students will get confused. In some Orthodox theological institutions, the teaching of different theological disciplines is still determined by confessionalism[5] which is a late development and a contradiction to the genuine Orthodox way of theological education.[6] The remains of confessionalism determined a polemical approach regarding other Christian traditions in the context of teaching other theological specialities.

For a few ideas of how Church history (Historical theology in general) could be thought, see chapter 11 *Foundations for ecumenism in Patristic Theology and Church History* of this Handbook. Additional valuable recommendations were formulated by the consultation on Orthodox Theological Education held in the Penteli Monastery: "The time is ripe for Orthodox educators at all levels to review how we understand and speak about our past. Our Orthodox Christian history is a rich tapestry of varying colours and textures. Perhaps forgotten champions of the faith need to be remembered. Inspiring women should be held up for all to know. Holy people from marginalized groups can serve to comfort and instruct today's faithful. Christ showed indescribable courage in the course of his passion and death. Modern Orthodox are in a position where they must display a similar humility and courage in speaking honesty and forthrightly about their own histories. Not every historical figure was perfect and heroic; not every decision was inspired by the Spirit of God, yet the saving Spirit of God is best seen in the context of fallen humanity struggling to grow into God's likeness. Good and holy people existed on both sides – even in the most painful of theological disputes – we owe it to them and to Jesus Christ who died for all to honour their faith and commitment. Responsible stewardship of our historical memory is integral in the task of moving from frozen traditionalism to a living tradition."[7]

It is crucial to have Systematic Theology and especially the teaching of dogmatics done in a non-polemical way, focusing primarily on presenting the Orthodox doctrine. Doctrinal differences between different Christian confessions should be clearly underlined, but presented in an irenic way and explained historically. There are

---

[5] According to John Zizioulas who presented in the Basel consultation a paper on "The Ecumenical Dimension in Orthodox Theological Education," "Confessionalism was seen as an external imposition on Orthodox theology arising from conflicts between Roman Catholics and Protestants in the 16th and 17th centuries. This spirit of confessionalism tended to make faith into a merely intellectual pursuit characterized by a propositional understanding of the faith. As a result, theology derived its content from the confessional statement and promoted this as a criterion of faith and the condition of ecclesial existence. The Church as a whole then acquired its identity by creedal assertion. This view must be rejected if one considers ancient Church practice, which did not define the Church in creedal terms, but rather maintained that the Church was and is constituted by the local Eucharistic celebration, based on the mystery of the divine reality manifested in the ecclesial community. Such a view is open to ecumenical potential, while the confessional approach merely separates and will forever divide." (See footnote 1, here 33). (The paper of Metropolitan John Zizioulas is re-published in this section).

[6] For the lessons that the Orthodox theological education of modern times could learn from the Patristic and Byzantine past see John Meyendorff, "Theological Education in the Patristic and Byzantine Eras and its Lessons for Today" in *St. Vladimir's Theological Quarterly* 31.3 (1987): 197-213.

[7] See footnote 4, 187.

two good examples of this kind of approach: Ion Bria`s *Dogmatic and Ecumenical Theology*[8] and Karl Christian Felmy's *Introduction in the contemporary Orthodox theology.*[9]

Pastoral theology shall include lectures on how to relate to "our pluralistic and secularized world."[10] Part of this approach should be also an honest treatment of ecumenical challenges in the practical life and pastoral praxis of Orthodox Churches like mixed marriages, common prayer, participation in funeral worship or other services provided by other churches, etc. Liturgical studies shall emphasize that the Orthodox Liturgy contents "ecumenical invocation for the peace and unity of all,"[11] without excluding anyone. It should be also underlined that some Christian traditions kept genuine elements of the liturgies and worship orders of the Early Church.

Missiological studies can contribute significantly to a better understanding of the role of ecumenism in developing a common understanding of Christian mission. According to a final statement of a meeting on The Ecumenical Movement in the Twenty Century: The role of Theology in Ecumenical Thought and Life, one of the reasons for the foundation of WCC was "missionary." The WCC founders realized "that only a common witness could give credibility to the proclamation of the Good News."[12] Along with the two-thousand years of experience of Orthodox tradition in mission, the work on mission and evangelism developed by several ecumenical organizations, with significant contribution of Orthodox participants, should be presented to Orthodox students for their misiological formation.

Most of the curricula of Orthodox theological institutions do not include introduction in different Christian confessions (germ. *Konfessionskunde*) where students can learn, in a non-polemical way the history, doctrine and actual situation of main-line churches, but also of newly established Christian traditions developed after the Reformation. Traditional theological disciplines can provide only a very limited knowledge about the actual situation of Christianity with its confessional diversity. Traditionally, Orthodox students are taught about Roman-Catholicism, churches of the Reformation (Lutheran and Reformed) and probably about the existence of Old-Catholics. There is presently almost no information provided to Orthodox students about Methodism, Presbyterianism, Congregationalism, Pentecostalism, African Instituted Churches (AICs) etc. The necessity of teaching about these Christian traditions is at least twofold: Orthodox are, together with churches of this tradition, part of the fellowship of the ecumenical movement; because of migration and globalization, Orthodox Christians live more and more together with Christians of all Christian traditions.

Last but not least, a line should be added here about the teaching of the *history or philosophy of religions* which is part of the curriculum of some Orthodox theological schools. The way in which other religions are presented to students influences directly the approach of *inter-religious dialogue*, which is a very real issue and a priority for some ecumenical organizations and the way in which daily life with people of other faiths is understood. Archbishop Anastasios mentions two fundamental dimensions of the Orthodox approach regarding other religions: respect and love for everyone, independently of the individual belief and the fact that Christians' contact and dialogue with other religions is as old as Christianity itself.[13] In academic settings, first of all, the history and teaching of other religions need to be taught in a non-polemic way, highlighting the common

---

[8] Ion Bria, *Tratat de Teologie dogmatică și ecumenică*, (România creștină: Bucharest, 1999) (available only in Romanian).

[9] Karl Christian Felmy, *Die orthodoxe Theologie der Gegenwart. Eine Einführung*, (Wissentschaftliche Buchgesellschft: Darmstadt, 1990). In the introduction, the author mentions that he „presents the Orthodox theology with the eyes of love ... but without idealization." (XII).

[10] Thomas Hopko, "The Legacy of Fr. Alexander Schmemann: Theological Education for Pastoral Ministry" *St. Vladimir's Theological Quarterly*, 53:2-3 (2009), 331-339, here 331.

[11] Dan-Ilie Ciobotea, *The Role of liturgy in Orthodox theological education St. Vladimir's Theological Quarterly*, 31:2 (1987), 101-122, here 115.

[12] "The Ecumenical Movement in the Twentieth Century: The Role of Theology in Ecumenical Thought and Life in Romania" in Thomas fitzGerard and Peter Bouteneff (eds.), *Turn to God Rejoice in Hope. Orthodox Reflections on the Way to Harare*, (WCC Publications: Geneva, 1998), 130-135.

[13] Archbishop Anastasios, *Mission in Christ's Way. An Orthodox Understanding of Mission*, (Holy Cross Orthodox Press, Brookline, Massachusetts, WCC Publications: Geneva, 2010), 225.

elements and values with Christianity and objectively presenting the differences (if any), especially in terms of world understanding and salvation. An important dimension of Orthodox understanding of other religions seems to be their role in preparing the way to Christ's salvation. Such an emphasis, if done in a non-polemical way and following a certain Patristic understanding in this matter, might be helpful and meaningful. Those religions with whom Christianity shares many common values (especially monotheism) and which have a long history of living together with Christianity, unfortunately not always peaceful, i. e. Judaism and Islam, should be presented in an especially careful way. Historical objectivity is absolutely needed, approaching in a balanced way positive and negative experiences of the past, but highlighting especially future potentials for improving inter-religious dialogue between the three Abrahamitic religions.

As the landscapes in which the Orthodox Churches are living in is going through radical changes, a lot of wisdom[14] is needed for shaping the Orthodox theological education in a way that can be in line with our authentic tradition and at the same time responding to the needs and challenges of the present time and especially of those of the future.

Bibliography

Archbishop Anastasios, *Mission in Christ's Way. An Orthodox Understanding of Mission,* (Brookline, MA: Holy Cross Orthodox Press, 2010), 225-228.

Dan-Ilie Ciobotea, "The Role of liturgy in Orthodox theological education" *St. Vladimir's Theological Quarterly* 31.2 (1987): 101-122.

- "The Ecumenical Movement in the Twentieth Century: The Role of Theology in Ecumenical Thought and Life in Romania" in Thomas FitzGerard and Peter Bouteneff (eds.), *Turn to God Rejoice in Hope. Orthodox Reflections on the Way to Harare,* (Geneva: WCC Publications, 1998), 130-135.

Karl Christian Felmy, *Die orthodoxe Theologie der Gegenwart. Eine Einführung*, (Darmstadt: Wissentschaftliche Buchgesellschft, 1990).

Thomas Hopko, "The Legacy of Fr. Alexander Schmemann : theological education for pastoral Ministry" *St. Vladimir's Theological Quarterly* 53.2-3 (2009): 331-339.

Meinhold, P., *Ökumenische Kirchenkunde. Lebensformen d. Christenheit heute.* (Stuttgart: Kreuz, 1962), 652 S. (as an example of a Protestant introduction into 'Christian confessions').

Nikos Nissiotis, "Orthodox principles in the service of an ecumenical theological education" in *Orthodox Theology and Diakonia,* (Brookline, Massachusetts, 1981), 319-338.

- "Orthodox Theological Education for the Life and witness of the Church" in Georges Tsetsis (ed.), *Orthodox Thought,* (Geneva: WCC Publications, 1983), 29-34.

- "Report of the consultation of Orthodox Theological Education and ecumenical themes" *St. Vladimir's Theological Quarterly* 44.2 (2000): 181-194.

John A. McGuckin, "Seeking Learning, and the Grace of Insightfulness : The Issue of Wisdom in Orthodox Tradition" *St. Vladimir's Theological Quarterly* 51.4 (2007): 423-434.

Report of an Inter-Orthodox Consultation "The Ecumenical Nature of Orthodox Witness," New Valamo, Finland, 24-20 September 1977 in Gennadios Limouris (ed.), *Orthodox Visions of Ecumenism. Statements, Messages and Reports on the Ecumenical Movement 1902-1992,* (Geneva: WCC Publications, 1994), 66-69.

.

---

[14] See John A. McGuckin, "Seeking Learning, and the Grace of Insightfulness: The Issue of Wisdom in Orthodox Tradition" *St. Vladimir's Theological Quarterly* 51.4 (2007): 423-434.

(133) Magna Charta on Ecumenical Formation in Theological Education in the 21st century – A WCC/ETE Reference Document

Dietrich Werner

1) Ecumenism as an urgent need in theological education

The basis of the WCC affirms: "The World Council of Churches is a fellowship of churches which confess the Lord Jesus Christ as God and Saviour according to the scriptures and therefore seek to fulfill together their common calling to the glory of the one God, Father, Son and Holy Spirit." In the constitution of WCC the concern for ecumenical theological education therefore receives a high priority: It is defined as one of the primary purposes and functions of the WCC to "nurture the growth of an ecumenical consciousness through processes of education and a vision of life in community rooted in each particular cultural context"(WCC constitution par. III). The ecumenical movement from its very beginning and even before the founding of the WCC 1948 (comp. history of World Council of Christian Education) had a profound impact on the understanding of Christian education in general and ministerial formation for future ministers and priests in particular. If the ecumenical movement as a whole is about strengthening common witness and promoting new forms of the visible unity between churches of different denominational and confessional traditions then the scandal of churches remaining in disunity and using distorted images of sister churches in one's own educational materials and publications needs to be overcome with foremost priority in the area of theological education and ministerial formation. The strengthening and pursuit of church unity in theological education is a Gospel imperative for any church joining in the affirmation of the church as being "one, holy, catholic and apostolic"in its essence (The Nicene-Constantinopolitan Creed [381]) (*interdenominational or ecclesial dimension of ecumenical formation*). The emergence of interdenominational or non-denominational institutions of theological education in the 50s and 60s which was intentionally supported by the Theological Education Fund (TEF) of the IMC as well as the introduction of distinct courses and curriculum models on ecumenism and the ecumenical movement was a consequence of this ecclesiological insight. The emphasis on interdenominational cooperation in theological education as well as the development of proper teaching materials on ecumenism remains an indispensable and in many places still lacking component of the theological education of pastors and ministers. There is no future for the ecumenical movement as a whole if there is no commitment to ecumenical formation processes in formal and non-formal theological education programmes of WCC member churches. If theological education fails to be guided by an ecumenical vision of a church renewed in mission and service to the whole of humankind there will be a serious shortage in terms of a new generation of Christian leaders, pastors and theological teachers carrying on the ecumenical vision and commitment into the 21st century and a widening gap and estrangement between the majority clergy and ever fewer experts on the ecumenical movement and ecumenical theological discourse which can already be observed in a number of member churches.

2) Contextualization of theological education

Ecumenical formation in theological education is guided by the vision of the church truly united and serving the renewal of the human community. Therefore, ecumenical formation reaches beyond the realm of issues of inner church unity in addressing fundamental questions of the human family and the survival of the whole earth. Being inspired by the ecumenical vision of God as the owner of the whole earth (oikumene) as well as the eschatological vision of a new heaven and a new earth, theological education in ecumenical understanding will always try to respond to the pressing needs of social contexts and to be related to issues of human survival both in global and in local environments. Relating theological education to the realities of particular social and cultural contexts, liberating theological education from any captivity of certain social milieus, cultural one-sidedness and spiritual blindness to religious values existing in certain indigenous traditions has been a major emphasis of the WCC in the programme on theological education (PTE) since the sixties (*social or contextual dimension in ecumenical formation of theological education*). The demand for contextualization of theological education in terms of opening its agenda to the realities and challenges of different church contexts, cultural identities and living situations both in the global South as well as in churches in the West facing consequences of globalization and pluralization of life-styles and religious orientations in their own midst remains an ongoing task for theological education worldwide. Some of the areas in which contextualization of curriculum designs were most prominent and successful for ETE in recent past was the development of HIV/AIDS curriculum and doing theology from disability perspective.

3) Theological education for the whole people of God

Ecumenical formation in theological education since the rediscovery of the importance of the laity and their missionary role in church and society (Evanston Assembly 1954) is also guided by the rediscovery of the comprehensive character of the ministry of the whole people of God, to which all are called who have received baptism. Ministerial formation in the ecumenical debate on theological education since the 70s was understood as a particular expression and a specific part of the more comprehensive task of equipping the whole people of God for the multiple forms of ministries of and in the Christian community. New forms of lay theological formation like non-residential forms of theological education both for lay people as well as for future ministers have been a fundamental contribution to broadening theological education for the whole people of God which is an essential demand for a holistic and participatory understanding of the mission of the church as a body of Christ (*missionary or participatory dimension of ecumenical formation in theological education*). What has changed theological education most dramatically in the past decades is also the growing participation of women in teaching, researching and theological networking in many regions of the world. Feminist and womanist theological networks, the deepening of feminist hermeneutics as well as the promotion of women in leadership positions of theological teaching and research is an indispensable part of ecumenical formation in theological education today. How to support women in theological education and theological research and how to maintain a proper balance between lay formation programmes and ministerial formation programmes (and to secure sufficient interaction between both) remain two major concerns in the work towards theological education education for the whole people of God. Talking about theological education for the whole people of God in recent years also involves inventing and strengthening new models of academic ecumenical theological training for migrants and churches with migration background (for instance African churches in Europe) as often established systems of theological education cannot easily adapt to their needs.

4) Interfaith dialogue in theological education

Ecumenical formation in theological education fourthly is guided by a vision of sharing and mutual discoveries reaching beyond the realm of Christianity to the human community in the whole inhabited earth (Oikoumene) and taking into account the challenges of Christians living in close neighbourhoods and experiencing mutual sharing and solidarity with people of other faith traditions in many church contexts. Thus interfaith encounter and learning about what can be affirmed in common action for peace, justice and human dignity with people of other living faith traditions is an integral component of ecumenical formation (*interfaith dimension of ecu-*

menical formation) which is not endangering one's own Christian identity but rather deepening it in processes of communication and sharing with people of different faiths. With the recent Letter of some 140 Muslim Leaders ("A Common Word between Us and You,") to Leaders of Christian Churches around the world at the feast of "Eid al-Fitr al-Mubarak" 2007, which marks the end of Ramadan, and the answer from WCC this whole dimension again becomes an urgent priority also for institutions of theological education.

5) Spiritual formation in theological educaction

Very often ecumenical formation processes have been described as having a profound spiritual basis and character referring back to the very biblical understanding as the church as learning community (*spiritual dimension of ecumenical formation*). "Learning in the Bible is a process by which people relate to God and God's way of truth, righteousness and peace, that they may in obedience practice that way in relation to each other and extending to the nations…Learning does not simply mean acquiring knowledge or skills, or being intellectually equipped, or just memorizing some catechism of faith. Rather it means so entering with our whole being and with all the people into a relationship with God through God's self-revelation, that our horizons are widened and our wills are strengthened to be right with God and with one another in word and deed" (Philip Potter in Vancouver 1983). If ecumenical formation is about becoming open and responsive to the will of God in the whole of our own existence, ecumenical formation is not just a cheap way of adding some additional pieces of information to the theological curriculum, but involves a certain aspect of deep and spiritual conversion and metanoia in the understanding of both one's own Christian existence as well as one's own confessional identity, a conversion from denominational self-centredness and cultural captivities to the realities of God's mission in the whole of the inhabited earth. "Having ecumenical spirituality in common prayer and other forms as the underpinning of ecumenical formation invites all to conversion and change of heart which is the very soul of the work for restoring unity."(Study document on "Ecumenical Formation" of the Joint Working Group between the Roman Catholic Church and the WCC Geneva, 1993).

6) Ecumenical formation as informed participation in the ecumenical movement

There finally is a certain methodological principle at work in the understanding of ecumenical formation which is due to the appropriation and integration of much of the didactical and catechetical revolutions and fundamental paradigm changes occurring in the 'pedagogy of the oppressed', methods of conscientization and the methods of learning by involvement in common action which have come up strongly in the ecumenical debate of learning during the 70s and 80s (*didactical, practical or liberational dimension in ecumenical formation in theological education*). Already in the early and first statement of WCC in 1957 on ecumenical education the emphasis was put on concrete practical involvement as a prerogative of proper ecumenical learning: "Ecumenical education can no longer be limited to the history of attempts to reunite churches or the growth of ecumenical organizations. Ecumenical education essentially means fostering understanding of, commitment to and informed participation in this whole ecumenical process" (Central Comittee 1957). Ecumenical formation is not possible without a didactical and pedagogical approach which fosters practical involvement in both local, regional and global projects of ecumenical cooperation and human struggles for dignity, reconciliation and social justice. What in certain areas is referred to as "globalization in theological education" (though this term is not without ambivalence) can be understood in terms of equipping both future ministers, church workers and lay people for informed and theologically reflected participation in the global ecumenical movement by deepening their formation in intercultural theology, ecumenical biblical hermeneutics, interreligious dialogue, history of ecumenism, ecumenical Missiology and ecumenical social ethics while at the same time remaining faithful to their own contextual demands for relating the Gospel to a given culture and situation.

Part VIII: Ecumenical Formation in Orthodox Theological Education

7) Major goals and principles of ecumenical formation

What follows from these six fundamental dimensions of ecumenical formation for understanding the *goals and principles of ecumenical formation* has been spelled out in the 1989 key WCC document on "Alive together – a practical guide to Ecumenical Learning" in certain alternative key formulations for principles of ecumenical learning, namely:

"a) Learning which enables people, while remaining rooted in one tradition of the church, to become open and responsive to the richness and perspectives of other churches, so that they may become more active in seeking unity, openness and collaboration between churches;

b) Learning which enables people of one country, language, ethnic group, class or political and economic system, to become sensitive and responsive to those of other countries, ethnic groups, political and economic situations, so that they may become active participants in action for a more just world;

c) Learning which happens when diverse persons, rooted in their own faith traditions and complex experiences of culture, gender, nationality, race, call etc. become open and responsive to the richness of perspectives in the struggle of others, together seeking to know God and to be faithful to God's intention for them in their world.

d) Learning by which:
- diverse groups and individuals,
- well rooted in their own faith, traditions, cultures and contexts,
- are enabled to risk honest encounters with one another before God,
- as they study and struggle together in community,
- with personally relevant issues,
- in the light of the Scriptures, the traditions of their faith, worship and global realities,
- resulting in communal action in faithfulness to God's intention for the unity of the church and humankind, and for justice, peace and integrity of creation."

Or, to recall a formulation which was used during the Vancouver Assembly in 1983: Ecumenical learning both in theological education as well as in Christian education as whole is characterised by the essential marks that

"a) it *transcends barriers* – of origin and biography, individual as well as community limitations, because it responds to the exhortation of the word of God and the far-reaching horizons of God's promise

b) it is *action-oriented*, not satisfied with information but seeking to enable Christians to act in order to learn, to be right with God and with one another, in word and deed

c) it is *done in community*, in which people are asked to establish relationships with one another and also with those who are far away and with what is unfamiliar

d) it means *learning together*, detecting the global in the local, the unfamiliar in the context of one's own environment, in order to become aware of one's own limited horizons and implications

e) it is *inter-cultural*, promoting the encounter of different cultures, traditions and forms of life because only a widening of perspectives will bring about experiences of the riches in creation in nature, in history and culture

f) it is a *total process, social and religious learning are not separated from each* other but constitute a unity."

8) Theological competence redefined for an ecumenical age of global Christianity

This can be summarized: theological education of the church as a whole cannot be complete without unfolding itself and being directed towards equipping a future generation of both ordained and non-ordained partakers of the manifold ministries of the church with:

a) a *pastoral competence* which is about enabling and building up individuals as well as Christian communities so as to become living witnesses of the life-giving power of the Gospel and the transforming power of the Holy Spirit in word, liturgy and sacrament;

Orthodox Handbook on Ecumenism

b) a *competence of leadership* which empowers rather than controls the manifold gifts of a given Christian community and helps to enable, equip and discern these gifts and charismata for the benefit of both the upbuilding the local congregation (oikodome) as well as peace and justice for the whole of the human community;

c) *a theological competence* which is about the ability to give a voice to the spiritual experiences of a Christian community, interpreting both biblical and church tradition in ways meaningful to contemporaries and to relate the faith insights of a local community to the treasures and challenges of the church universal and the contemporary discourse in culture and society;

d) a *missionary competence* which is about the ability to discern and to give shape to the demands and promises of the Gospel in relation to the missionary and evangelizing vocation of the church and the longing for healing and wholeness, peace and reconciliation in the human community;

e) an *ecumenical competence* which while including the other dimensions emphazises particularly that no church can be the church for itself alone and each church is becoming truly the church in the full sense of the word if and so far it is related to the fellowship of Christian churches truly united both locally and globally in prayer, witness and service. This means that theological education is taking seriously the basic nature of both the catholicity and apostolicity, oneness and holiness of the church universal.

In essence, what is at stake therefore in ecumenical formation in theological education today is nothing less than rediscovering and adjusting to the truly global and ecumenical nature of the church, existing within the manifold forms of global Christianity which has become a new reality only after the gradual shift of centre of gravity from the North to the South and meanwhile presents itself as a multi-centered global Christianity of the South or the "two-thirds-world". For most of the past centuries of the history of Christianity, theological reflection, interpretation of Christian tradition and the perception of cultures and living conditions in the "peripheries" was heavily influenced and carried out from the viewpoint of one or several dominating centres of global Christianity (Jerusalem in the first century, Rome up to the fourth century and much beyond, Western Christianity over against Eastern Christianity in the Middle Ages, North Atlantic Christianity over against Christianity in the South for some 200-300 years during colonial expansion and domination). While dominance and cultural and economic ethnocentrism are still continuing with regard to American and/or Western culture and life-styles at many levels in theology and theological education, global Christianity of the South for the last 30 years or so (comp. the role of the Bangkok world mission conference in the ecumenical debate on mission 1974) has entered into a stage in which a truly multi-centered understanding of Christianity has emerged and an unprecedented genuine plurality of Christian of interpretations has been developed and is promoted. Ecumenical formation (or globalization in theological education) is the unfinished theological and didactical process by which churches worldwide are aligning and opening up themselves to the realities of a truly multi-centered and multi-faceted global Christianity in the 21st century thereby challenging any attitude, hidden prejudices or overt practices of cultural, theological and interpretative domination by any assumed majority culture within global Christianity. This means that ecumenical formation is about reappropriating the ecumenical nature of the church as confessed in the creed (one, holy, catholic and apostolic) though under new and unprecedented historical conditions.

9) New challenges for ecumenical formation in the beginning 21st century

In the beginning of the 21st century we find ourselves in a new historical situation where we both need a fresh articulation of the ecumenical vision (which has lost some of its momentum and support at the local level) as well as a significant and relevant new commitment for ecumenical education and formation in the member churches of WCC as a whole if the ecumenical movement is to remain a vital force of renewal and conversion in global Christianity. The new situation is particularly marked by the fact that the rapid globalization of markets, media and technologies has given rise to counter-reactions in terms of different forms of growing fundamentalism affirming exclusive and closed national, ethnic, cultural and religious identities. These factors of increased fragmentation and fundamentalist trends in the midst of globalization oblige us to renew and rethink our commitment to ecumenical formation as an urgent necessity and priority for safeguarding the continuation of the ecumenical movement and ecumenical witness as a whole. To promote an ecumenical orientation in theological education is the only possible option to maintain an "alternative and ecumenically responsible vision of globalization" over against growing trends towards either withdrawing Christian faith from public responsibility and dialogue altogether (privatization), or turn to denominational provincialism and ecclesial self-centredness (confessionalization) or to seek refuge in religious fundamentalism (simplification) within the christian family or in relation to other religions. Thus ecumenical formation is not only a "constitutive mark of the church being the church" (Vancouver 1983) but also an essential priority of new urgency at the beginning of the 21st century.

10) Costly ecumenical learning – suggestions for practical implementation in theological education

There is no cheap way of adding ecumenical formation into existing schemes of theological education and curriculum plans. Rather introducing ecumenical formation has a certain price as it can entail a reordering of priorities in theological education in terms of both contents, methods and working principles applied – but the costly way of integrating ecumenical formation is rewarded by a profound process of truly broadening and deepening theological education:

a) powerful and dominant cultures as well as theological perceptions are called to give up their sense of control, allow for more inclusivity and processes of reorientation by minority cultures and theological perceptions which contribute to the holistic character of the body of Christ truly united;

b) majority denominational traditions of a certain region are challenged to include proper presentations and truly participation of Christian minority traditions within their own context as well as from other contexts in their theological curriculum and theological teaching materials (handbooks);

c) theological education institutions of one context and denominational background are challenged to develop long-term partnership and exchange programmes with theological education institutions from a different context and church background;

d) students are challenged to learn at least one language different from their own native language and the dominant language of their context to be immersed and introduced into the challenges and dynamics of proper intercultural communication (for instance with immigrant cultures in their context);

e) crossing cultural and denominational boundaries for a certain period within a certain period of one's own theological education programme becomes an obligatory component of any programme of theological education;

f) participating in ecumenical stewardship and ecumenical sharing of financial resources for theological education worldwide in the context of grave and persistent inequalities in terms of financial means for theological education becomes a structural component for each theological colleges/faculty/university (either by giving scholarships to a college in another context or extending ecumenical journal subcriptions for other colleges, providing placements for international students and lectures in one's own college);

g) ecumenism, intercultural theology and ecumenical missiology are both necessary dimensions and horizons within the classical five disciplns of theological science as well as deserve and demand for a distinct place and realm of study and research in the composition of theological faculties;

h) individualism, voluntarism and onesided denominationalism in college life are challenged by the deliberate introduction of ecumenical elements into the regular worship life of any given college (e.g. intercessions for other churches; statements of faith from other traditions; music and hymns from global Christianity);

i) mutuality and reciprocity are supported in the partnership relations between colleges/faculties in one context to colleges/faculties of another context (in order to avoid onesided dependency, one-directional giving mentalities; lack of respect and mutuality in processes of sharing between contexts of inequality);

Orthodox Handbook on Ecumenism

j) churches are challenged to stengthen their sense of responsibility and ownership for institutions of theological education as a vital source for their own renewal by accompanying theological education institutions properly, making provisions in church budgets for relevant and appropritae financial support for institutions of theological education, creating scholarship endowment funds particularly for Master's and PhD-programmes and embarking on proper regional development plans for the future of theological education.

k) support and enhancement of bilateral and multilateral initiatives for the recognition and accreditation of institutions of theological education in the global South in other countries (both in the South as well as in the North) is an urgent task for mutual cooperation between associations of theological schools in WOCATI and beyond.

The WCC assembly in Porto Alegre has highlighted the centrality of ecumenical formation for all aspects of the work of the WCC as well as for theological education in its member churches. The process to unfold the concrete implications of this overarching and manifold task has only just begun.

(134) RECOMMENDATIONS FOR ECUMENICAL LEARNING IN ORTHODOX THEOLOGICAL EDUCATION. REPORTS FROM BASEL (1978) AND PENTELI (2000)

Report of the Consultation on Orthodox Theological Education[1]

Theologians representing Orthodox Theological Education gathered at the Missionshaus in Basel, Switzerland, from 4-7 July 1978, to share information and to discuss some of the problems involved in ministerial formation, especially those relating to their own programmes, as well as certain challenges raised by contemporary issues. The meeting was organized by the Programme on Theological Education and is probably the first such consultation under the auspices of the World Council of Churches. Present and participating in the discussion were P.T.E. Commission members and Roman Catholic observers.

I. The Status of Theological Education in Orthodoxy Today

The first item on the agenda was a review of all the reports prepared by participating institutions. Reports were received from the following Orthodox theological schools:

- Armenian Orthodox Seminary, Etchmiadzin, Armenian S.S.R.
- Theological Faculty of Preshov, Czechoslovakia
- Institut théologique orthodoxe de Saint-Serge, Paris, France
- Theological Academy, Mcheti, Georgian S.S.R.
- Faculty of Theology, University of Athens, Greece Faculty of Theology, University of Thessalonica, Greece
- Greece Orthodox Seminary of Kottayam, India
- Theological School of the Armenian Patriarchate, Jerusalem
- Armenian Orthodox Seminary, Bikfaya, Lebanon
- The University Institute of Theology, Bucharest, Roumania
- The University Institute of Theology, Sibiu, Roumania
- Holy Cross Greek Orthodox School of Theology, Brookline, U.S.A.
- St. Vladimir's Orthodox Theological Seminary, Tuckahoe, U.S.A.
- Leningrad Theological Academy, Russia
- Moscow Theological Academy, Zagorsk, Russia
- Odessa Theological Seminary, Russia
- Theological Faculty, Belgrade, Yugoslavia

The common concerns arising out of the reports from these institutions were then summarized by the Rev. Aharon Sapsezian, Director of the P.T.E., and a lively discussion ensued, generated by these findings, and touching on the following points:

    a. All the schools of theology maintain a close identity with the history of the churches and the people they serve.

    b. The primary concern of all is the education of the clergy for leadership roles in the Church, while not excluding a measure of concern for lay theological education.

    c. Spiritual formation of the future clergyman was found to be central to the process of theological education. The general consensus was that this aspect of formation is accomplished primarily through liturgical life and the example of the teacher.

---

[1] This report of the consultation on Orthodox theological Education has been initially published in *Orthodox Theological Education for Life and Witness of the Church: Report on the Consultation at Basel, Switzerland,* 4-8 July 1978 (Geneva: WCC, 1978).

d. Although it was universally affirmed that theology is to touch on all of life, there was no wide-spread expression of concern about social and political problems as part of the curriculum of a theological school.

e. On the other hand, a widening of curricula to include ecumenical concerns appeared to be welcomed and under serious consideration in nearly all of the schools.

f. Theological creativity was generally understood as the rediscovery and reapplication to contemporary situations of the patristic heritage, as well as re-presentation of this heritage.

g. The summary-comment raised certain questions, i.e. the place of women in Orthodox theological education, the issue of education for mission, and the relative lack of inter-Orthodox co-operation in theological education.

The discussion of these points ranged far and wide, and included:

- theological school/Church hierarchy relations;
- the importance of the Divine Liturgy to theological education;
- the fact that some women are being educated in Orthodox theology schools;
- inadequate theological knowledge among the people of the Church and the need for widespread education efforts;
- the ancient sense of theology as witness to the ministry of God rather than as intellectualism;
- the need, as well for the intellectual dimension in theology;
- the cultivation of mission-mindedness in the Church;
- Field education as an important part of theological education;
- the close relationship of theology with the life of the Church;
- the distinction between teaching students about ecumenism as opposed to introducing into the curriculum an ecumenical approach to theological matters;
- the affirmation that the real Orthodox understanding of the Church is basically ecumenical in that all humanity is called to share in the same Eucharist.

II. The Place and Function of Theological Education in the Church

On the place and function of theological education in the life of the Church, there was a strong consensus which, it was felt, should be more sharply delineated, as follows:

a. The main purpose of theological education is the education and formation of young men for the priesthood. All agreed that this preparation requires spiritual and liturgical formation as well as academic instruction.

b. Other considerations were lay education and the continuing education of the clergy. Most participants felt that these are important, though derived, aspects of theological education.

c. The schools agree that their faculties are properly involved in scholarly research and that they serve as the Churches' thinkers, especially as regards the development and enrichment of the life of the Church.

III. Aspects of Theological Education

The subsequent agenda, presented to the Orthodox theological educators by the Programme on Theological Education Planning Committee (which included both Orthodox and non-Orthodox members), consisted of three topics designed to challenge and stretch the understandings and practices in Orthodox theological education today.

1. The first of these was entitled Ministry of the Eucharistic Liturgy and the Ministry of the "Liturgy after the Liturgy."

Its purpose was to challenge present Orthodox theological education in the light of the implications of Orthodox theology for a "ministry of transforming and sanctifying witness in society and in the world." Professor Jan Anchimiuk of the Orthodox Department, Chrzescijanska Akademia Teologiczna, Warsaw, presented a

Part VIII: Ecumenical Formation in Orthodox Theological Education

reflection on this topic. He pointed out that in the Eucharist man brings to God an offering, the thanksgiving and the praise of the whole cosmos, thus becoming an agent of the world's transformation.

Church, social and political structures are subject to the transfiguring mission of the Church in the world. This mission, Professor Anchimiuk cautioned, is endangered when the practice of theological education is separated from the whole body and life of the Church. A further danger cited was the old Scholastic system which turned theology into a system of ideas rather than a living reality.

Much discussion followed on the place of the Liturgy in the life of the Church. A need for liturgical education and the renewal of the liturgical life was expressed. Other topics were:
- the role of some churches in the national life of their -people and culture;
- the need for a broader base of social concerns in Orthodox theology rather than the Eucharist alone
- the possible value of the Orthodox theology of "epiclesis";
- sacrifice and "agapai" for the development of an effective social witness;
- a question on the adequacy of the formula "the Liturgy after the Liturgy."

2. The question of the mission of the theological school for lay education was the second issue addressed on the agenda. Fr. Stanley Harakas of Holy Cross School of Theology, Brookline, Massachusetts, presented a paper on the assigned topic, extending the Benefit of Theological Education Beyond the Ordained Ministry to the People of God.

Fr. Harakas focused on adult lay education, noting that some work is already being done in this area, as indicated above. His main point was to provide some biblically based guidance so as to improve and direct this work in its substance rather than in its form. Thus, adult lay education should strive to proclaim the Christian message as a serious and life-important message.

It should lead to and expect personal commitment to Christ and to the Church.

Focusing on the Orthodox view of Christian life as growth toward theosis, adult lay education should affirm the specificity of Christian truth as teaching and life. In addition, it should be concerned with an ongoing up-building of both the personal and corporate life in the Church. Such proposals challenge the theological schools to develope new and fresh approaches to adult lay leadership education far from simplistic, impersonal and authoritarian ideas. It was proposed that these should be sacramental in character, participatory, personal and productive of spiritual growth toward theosis.

The discussion involved the place of the Eucharist in the actual life of the faithful as an educative force. The *ad hoc* character of much adult lay theological education was mentioned, as well as the need for renewal of the people for participation in the eucharistie life. In general, the participants saw the training of priests by theological schools as essential, for it includes preparing the priest for an educative ministry in the community. From the Orthodox perspective, the laity, clergy, theologians and hierarchs form one body of Christ, sharing the whole task of up-building the Church in the liturgical, spiritual and educational life. This view depicts a process of interaction rather than an agent acting upon a passive recipient.

3. The third and final agenda topic addressed the question of The Ecumenical Dimension in Orthodox Theological Education.

In this paper, Professor John Zizioulas of the Department of Divinity, University of Glasgow, focused on two aspects:
- Orthodox confessionalism and theology as a specialized discipline;
- the current view that theology is an isolated and specialized subject;

Confessionalism was seen as an external imposition on Orthodox theology arising from conflicts between Roman Catholics and Protestants in the 16th and 17th centuries. This spirit of confessionalism tended to make faith into a merely intellectual pursuit characterized by a propositional understanding of the faith. As a result, theology derived its content from the confessional statement and promoted this as the criterion of faith and the condition of ecclesial existence. The Church as a whole then acquired its identity by creedal assertion. This view must be rejected if one considers ancient Church practice, which did not define the Church in creedal terms, but rather maintained that the Church was and is constituted by the local Eucharist celebration, based on the mystery of the divine reality manifest in the ecclesial community. Such a view is open to ecumenical potential, while the confessional approach merely separates and will forever divide.

On the second topic, Dr. Zizioulas (now Metropolitan of Pergamon) emphasized that the scholastic and analytic view of the university, rather than unifying the vision of the whole cosmos, separates and particularizes it. This is a disastrous for Orthodox theology, in which the cosmic and integrative doctrines of Transfiguration and theosis imply an all-inclusive and ecumenical vision of theology and theological education.

In connection with the above, new approaches to curriculum are needed; a de- confessionalization of theology is required; faculties and student bodies must be made in fact, ecumenical; theology must point not to confessions of doctrine but to the mystery of salvation.

Some of the discussion which followed raised the question whether it is possible to admit to Orthodox theological schools non-Orthodox faculty members and students, since they cannot share in the Eucharistic life of the school community, so vital in the process of Orthodox theological education. Another subject of discussion was the relationship between confessionalism and the concern for truth in Orthodox theology. Some members strongly objected to the attack on confessionalism in this paper, interpreting it as a lack of concern with the articulation of Orthodox theological truth. This was related to the historical concern of the Church with Orthodoxy of faith, both as teaching and as life. Some members, however, did not agree with these objections.

Recommendations

1. It would appear that the most valuable part of the Consultation has been the exchange among the participants, Orthodox and non-Orthodox. It is recommended, therefore, that the WCC further enhance this experience by publishing and distributing reports and papers related to the Consultation, especially for all Orthodox faculties.

2. The WCC Programme on Theological Education should facilitate the planning of other consultations that bring together Orthodox theological educators to discuss specific topics like:
   a. the teaching of particular disciplines in the curriculum;
   b. curricular development and teaching methods;
   c. spiritual life and educational programmes.
In some cases, preliminary conferences may be needed to clarify theological issues.

3. Theological education has been shown to be in need of examination in the light of the best of Orthodox tradition. How can it free itself from the mold of academism and scholasticism in which it seems to have cast itself? Orthodox theological schools are urged to undertake the study of this issue and share the results so as to permit joint changes in curriculum and methodology.

4. Orthodox theological schools are urged to deal seriously with the need to be open to ecumenical demands both inherent in the Orthodox tradition and as they are present in contemporary situations. If needed, the WCC Programme on Theological Education should be asked to provide opportunities for promoting such efforts.

5. The Consulation participants are encouraged to submit to the Hierarchy of the Orthodox Churches the advisability of setting up an Orthodox Theological Commission to promote permanent relationships among the Orthodox theological schools. This should be an essentially Orthodox body with consultants from WCC and its Programme on Theological Education.

6. All of the proceeding should be brought to the attention of the Hierarchies of the Orthodox Churches for study and attention.

Part VIII: Ecumenical Formation in Orthodox Theological Education

Report of the Consultation on Orthodox Theological Education and Ecumenical Themes

Penteli Monastery, Athens, Greece / 2-9 February 2000

Introduction

My eyes have seen your salvation, which was prepared in the presence of all peoples (Lk 2:29—32)

On the great feast of the Presentation of our Lord, the Consultation on Orthodox Theological Education met (2-9 February 2000) at the Inter-Orthodox Centre, located in the historic Penteli Monastery in the suburbs of Athens, Greece. Following the righteous and devout Symeon, they were prepared to receive the incarnate Lord in spiritual joy; as the prophet Anna, they rejoiced in the opportunity to speak about the child to all who were looking for redemption (cf. Lk 2:38).

At the invitation of the World Council of Churches, with the assistance of the Society for Ecumenical Studies and Inter-Orthodox Relations (Thessaloniki, Greece), and the blessing of His Beatitude Christodoulos, Archbishop of Athens and All Greece, 40 delegates met, representing the Oriental Orthodox and Eastern Orthodox Churches, as well as a number of other Christian traditions. Coming from Africa, Asia, former Communist countries in Southeastern and Eastern Europe, the Middle East, North America, and Western Europe, the assembled theological educators provided an inspiring witness to the great diversity of Orthodox Christian educational ministries. His Beatitude underlined the importance of their mission in his initial greeting at the first plenary session, as well as in his introduction of the Consultation and its work at the end of an Archepiscopal Divine Liturgy celebrated in the monastery's church on the Feast of St Photios (6 February), attended by university professors from throughout Greece and scores of local faithful. His Beatitude further blessed the Consultation by meeting with them privately after the Divine Liturgy.

As a hierarch deeply concerned with proclaiming the Gospel of Salvation in modern society, His Beatitude reminded the group that it is wrong to relegate Theological Education to the simple transmission of theoretical knowledge, thereby falling into the pitfall of turning Theology into a philosophical and abstract discipline. ... For Orthodox, Theology is life, life in Christ, life in His Body, life in the Church. It is experiential, not rational or speculative. ... Theology cannot be viable if it is not rooted in the experience of God, if it is not born in the Church and does not lead one to catharsis, illumination, and theosis. Should this not be the case, then its impact and influence will out of necessity be weak and sorely limited. And certainly one cannot be a true and genuine teacher of Orthodox Theology if his [or her] life is devoid of this experience.

The theme of the Consultation was elaborated by a series of four plenary presentations treating "The Ministry of the Theologian" (Fr. Thomas FitzGerald), "Contextual Issues and Orthodox Theological Education" (Fr. Kondothra M. George), "Orthodox Involvement in Regional Theological Associations" (Prof. Michel Nseir), and "Ecumenical Theological Education and Orthodox Issues for the 3rd Millennium" (Prof. Petros Vassiliadis). Mr. George Lemopoulos, Deputy General Secretary of the WCC, offered reflections on the Special Commission on Orthodox Participation in the WCC. The Reverend Simon Oxley introduced the Consultation to the Councils work on education and ecumenical formation. Additionally, four panel discussions allowed 20 participants to share their own experiences with the group. These discussions focused on "Teaching Orthodox Theology in Particular Educational and Cultural Contexts," "Addressing 'Ecumenical Themes' in Courses and Curricula and Associations," "Ecumenical Themes which deserve more attention from Orthodox Theologians and Faculties," and "Theological Education in Protestant Seminaries." From the outset, delegates were able to see the vast diversity of theological educational programs connected with the Orthodox Churches—catechism classes, theological academies, seminaries, Church-operated schools, theological faculties associated with state-governed universities, programs in majority-Orthodox contexts, and courses taught in settings where Orthodoxy is a minority Faith.

Coming together in Christian love and inspired by the movement of the Spirit even in today's troubled world, the Consultation proclaimed with one heart that progress is impossible in isolation. Only by bearing one another's burdens can we move forward on our pilgrimage into the Heavenly Kingdom.

The Consultation is thankful to the Council for facilitating this most valuable meeting. Most welcome was the opportunity for both families of the Orthodox Churches—the Eastern and the Oriental—to work together in harmony, addressing issues of common concern and discussing a unified witness to Christ's reconciling love in our strife-torn world.

Background

The relationship of the Orthodox Churches to the World Council of Churches is presently a major concern and challenge. In the period before the Harare Assembly, a number of Orthodox Churches, which are members of the Council, began to express more intensely their concerns about the structure, ethos, and priorities of the WCC. Many of these concerns were not new. Orthodox representatives identified them in varying degrees over the years in a variety of settings.

In light of this increasing Orthodox "malaise" and critique, the WCC initiated a process of intense consultation with its Orthodox and other member churches. This process culminated in the decision of the Harare Assembly to create a "Special Commission on Orthodox Participation in the WCC." According to the Assembly resolution, the Commission was established "to study and analyze the whole spectrum of questions related to Orthodox participation in the WCC, recognizing that many of these concerns are of importance to other member churches as well." The Special Commission, therefore, was given the mandate "to devote a period of at least three years to studying the full range of issues related to participation of Orthodox Churches in the WCC and to present proposals about changes in structure, working style, and ethos to the Central Committee for decision."[2]

The primary intention of the Consultation was to help the Programme on Ecumenical Theological Education (ETE) of the World Council of Churches design programs to identify and address needs of Orthodox Christian theological education worldwide. Additionally, it was also hoped that the Consultation's work would also contribute to the ongoing discussion concerning Orthodox participation in the WCC.

Purpose

The purpose of this Consultation was threefold. First, the Consultation was to identify key theological issues related to ecumenical themes which are of concern to Orthodox Theological Institutions. Secondly, it was asked to identify areas where the ETE can be of service to Orthodox Theological Schools and Institutions as they relate to the Council and to the wider ecumenical movement and as they struggle to fulfill their mission. Finally, the delegates quickly realized the need to discuss ways in which Orthodox Schools, Institutes, and Organizations can support and further the work of other Orthodox institutions as well as facilitate the work of the WCC/ETE. These issues of concern and concrete proposals are intended primarily for the Programme on Ecumenical Theological Education, but should also be shared with Orthodox Churches and Institutions, other offices of the Council, and members of the Special Commission on Orthodox Participation in the WCC.

Issues

From the first presentation, theological reflection guided the group in its deliberations. Delegates took as a starting point the understanding that they were acting as members of a deeply-roo ted faith community, speaking about and in the presence of the life-giving God, for the glory of God and the salvation of God's people.

---

[2] Diane Kessler (ed.), *Together on the Way: Official Report of the Eighth Assembly of the WCC,* (Geneva: WCC, 1999), 160f.

Issue One: Restoration of Communion between Eastern and Oriental Churches

The tragic division between the Oriental and Eastern families of Orthodoxy at the Council of Chalcedon continues to be an issue of the most profound importance for the teaching of Orthodox theology. Although the differing theological orientations were reconciled within local churches from the tenth century, and in spite of the official agreed statements issued in the past two decades, it is to the shame of Orthodox Christians that these two families of Orthodox Churches remain separated. At this moment in the history of the universal Church, the task of theological schools is to convey the positive results of these bilateral dialogues in order to convince the Churches to take the final steps in restoring full sacramental communion.

Issue Two: Self-Identity

Limits of the Church. This line of theological reflection led naturally to very significant issues of Self-Identity. Much theological reflection is needed on how to understand the limits of the Church. Can we continue to speak of the Church using language taken exclusively from canon law while ignoring more inclusive scriptural and liturgical images? Acknowledging that "the Spirit blows where it chooses, and you hear the sound of it, but you do not know where it comes from or where it goes" (Jn 3:8), Orthodox theologians need to reflect on what dimensions of the faith are core and apostolic and which characteristics are peripheral and cultural. Simply put: what is transcendent truth and what is its temporal expression? This sort of theological inquiry will allow the Orthodox Church to recognize Christ's beloved sheep who belong to other folds (cf. Jn 10:16). Only by removing centuries of exclusivist debris from our own eyes will we be able to recognize others as the children of God that they are. A challenging dimension of this process is re-visioning ourselves using positive concepts rather than continually defining ourselves over and against others. We must relearn how to think of ourselves in positive terms instead of depending on negative characterizations of others.

Inculturation and Diversity. Recent work in the areas of Sociology and Anthropology enables us to deepen our appreciation of the reality of inculturation within the various local churches. With a clearer understanding of what is fundamental to Orthodox Christianity, we will be able to address the issue of how catholicity can be rescued from a dominant culture—whether that culture be modern or ancient. Closely related to this is the urgent need to behold the diversity of Orthodox Churches throughout the world. Besides forming a strong bond between the believer and the Church, regional diversity is indicative of the fact that the Gospel has been received and expressed by a wide variety of people in a multitude of cultural contexts.

Influences on Orthodox self identity. Recognizing the human dimension of the evolution of the Church prompts the inquisitive person to ask "Who and what shapes the views of the Orthodox?" To what degree are modern women and men formed in their faith by participation in the liturgical life of the Church, classroom instruction, living within pious families, or (mis) representations provided by various media outlets? What are the voices that the faithful find most persuasive: hierarchs, parish priests, monastics, spiritual fathers, catechists, theologians, professors, friends, or family? Only by assessing the factors that form modern Orthodox can we begin to think about the impact of theological education on formation of self-identity.

History and Tradition. Similarly, the time is ripe for Orthodox educators at all levels to review how we understand and speak about our past. Our Orthodox Christian history is a rich tapestry of varying colors and textures. Perhaps forgotten champions of the faith need to be remembered. Inspiring women should be held up for all to know. Holy people from marginalized groups can serve to comfort and instruct today's faithful. Christ showed indescribable courage in the course of his passion and death. Modern Orthodox are in a position where they must display a similar humility and courage in speaking honestly and forthrightly about their own histories. Not every historical figure was perfect and heroic; not every decision was inspired by the Spirit of God, yet the saving Spirit of God is best seen in the contexts of fallen humanity struggling to grow into God s likeness. Good and holy people existed on both sides—even in the most painful of theological disputes—we owe it to them and to Jesus Christ who died for all to honor their faith and commitment. Responsible steward-ship of our historical memory is integral in the task of moving from frozen traditionalism to a living tradition.

The Situation in Post-Communist Europe. An urgent challenge before the ETE is the matter of Orthodox theological education and ministerial formation in post-Communist Europe. Theological schools are in a key position to analyze the new ecumenical contexts in this region, and facilitate theological dialogue on the local level. Attention must be given to the major changes in theological education, namely the status of schools, the intellectual framework of the societies, the democratic states, and civil society.

These are the issues which will contribute to a revitalized and transfigured image of who we are as children of the merciful and life-giving God.

Issue Three: Relations between Churches

Once Orthodox theological reflection and education has enabled us to see ourselves more clearly, it will be possible to address key Relational Issues.

Relations among the Orthodox. As noted above, the most pressing of these is restoring full communion between the Oriental and Eastern Orthodox. Beyond that, divisions need to be healed between all local Orthodox Churches and jurisdictions. It is unthinkable that brothers and sisters who share the same Eucharistic Meal can also engage in hateful, hurtful, and sinful actions against one another. The holy Apostle Paul had harsh words for those Christians who insulted the Eucharist by their own shameful factionalism and treatment of one another (cf. 1 Cor 1 1:17ff).

Support in marginalized areas. Fundamental to the integrity of the Body of Christ is the obligation to support and to help our sisters and brothers struggling to do God's work under difficult conditions. "How does God s love abide in anyone who has the world's goods and sees a brother or sister in need and yet refuses to help?" (1 Jn 3:17). In spite of overwhelming circumstances, Orthodox education continues to flourish and share the Gospel of Christ the world. It is important to highlight all schools and institutions engaged in this important work and develop a network capable of sharing information in a timely manner and facilitating all types of support.

Presenting the Relationships between Orthodox and other Christian Communities. In every session of the Consultation, members emphasized the importance of phrasing the "ecumenical message" in terms that will speak to and inspire Orthodox Christians. Similarly, Orthodox theological education needs to be expressed in a way that is accessible to other Christians. Rather than to use jargon and language that are at best foreign and at worst offensive, Orthodox theological educators in every context are encouraged to speak of the need for "the stability of the Churches of God and the unity of all" (petition from the Byzantine Synapte) using scriptural, patristic, and liturgical language that affects people's minds by touching their hearts. The laudable goal of reconciling all God's children will be greatly furthered if spiritually powerful terms are substituted for phrases that provoke negative reactions.

A Common Ecumenical Vision. " Closely related is the pressing need to articulate a common "ecumenical vision." On the one hand, the Orthodox themselves need to reflect on how they envision Christian unity. On the other hand (and necessarily dependent on their own common vision) the Orthodox Churches need to engage other member churches in an honest, forthright, and charitable discussion of how all people who have clothed themselves with Christ (cf. Gal 3:27) can work together toward the fulfillment of Christ's prayer that all may be one as He and the Father are one (cf. Jn 17).

Issue Four: Pressing Concerns

Communicating the Message. As discussed above, making the message of inter-Christian love and unity accessible to all people is imperative. In terms of this and other messages communicated through theological education, it clear that in order for a message to be effective, it must be directed to a particular audience. Theological educators must work to identify their various constituencies and to present the Gospel message in a way that will be intelligible and persuasive. Furthermore, in planning their curricula and lessons, all Orthodox educators are strongly encouraged to present material that is naturally conducive to the work of restoring Christian unity.

Women's Issues. Women's issues demand thorough consideration combining intellectual honesty, theological integrity, and pastoral sensitivity. Some issues are of vital importance within the Orthodox Church itself (e.g., the opportunity for all women to pursue theological education without restriction; study and evaluation of the language and images applied to women in liturgical and educational texts; restoration of women to the ordained diaconate, and further recognition of the fact that the call to minister to God's people extends beyond the boundaries of ordained ministry, making full use of God's gifts to persons within the Church [cf. Rom 12]) and injustice within the Church must be rectified immediately. Other social issues concerning women (e.g., abuse, denial of full human rights, and freedom to pursue justice) require the Church of God to assume an advocacy role just as Christ defended the woman who was being stoned (cf. Jn 8:1-11). Certain theological issues (e.g., the ordination of women to the presbyterate and episcopacy) may not be of immediate concern to Orthodox Churches, but they undeniably affect relationships with other churches, demanding that the Orthodox address them seriously and fairly.

The Consultation felt that these and other gender issues can only be addressed in light of a thorough reconsideration of Christian anthropology.

Orthodox Fundamentalism. Fundamentalism within some Orthodox groups is becoming a significant problem throughout the world. An excessively narrow reading of church history, a legalistic approach to the canons, and a failure to appreciate the spirit of scripture, liturgy, and patristic literature has prompted certain communities to embrace a form of Orthodoxy that is at odds with both the apostolic faith and Christian temperament. At best these groups make it difficult for God's saving love to be experienced; at worst people are being manipulated and deprived of the Gospel of life.

Proselytism. In many contexts, most notably the former Communist nations and the developing counties, proselytism by fundamentalist Protestant churches and some over-zealous missionaries are robbing the Church of the sheep entrusted to it by Christ (cf. Jn 21:15ff). Moreover, it is fostering an atmosphere of open hostility between people who claim to be God's children. Efforts must be made to educate faithful women and men, providing them with the foundation to remain firm in the Orthodox faith. At the same time, however, theological educators should be open to serious dialogue with these groups.

Facing Controversial Issues. Finally, in a world daily encountering societal, scientific, and technological change, the Orthodox must not shy away from controversial topics of the modern world in a clear and direct manner. Some of these issues are: secularism, bioethics, globalization, postmodernism, gender and sexuality, status of the family, reproduction issues, politics, drugs, AIDS. Men and women of good will are struggling to make the right decisions when faced with hard situations; it is incumbent upon the Church of God to provide strong moral leadership based on responsible use of scriptures and tradition, remaining faithful to the spirit of Orthodox Christianity.

Recommendations

An Orthodox Consultant to the WCC. The consultation very strongly suggests that an Orthodox Consultant be appointed to the ETE. The role of this consultant should be to bring Orthodox theological reflection to the WCC/ETE and to bring ecumenical affairs to the Orthodox theological institutions. The consultant would thus help and facilitate the work of ETE in assisting Orthodox theological schools to do their work. The consultant should work with a steering committee made of representatives of various Orthodox theological schools and Institutions. While the scope of responsibility of the post is global, because of the present situation, this Consultation recommends that the consultant initially be located in and primarily concerned for Central and Eastern Europe.

Institutional Support. The Consultation also strongly encourages the Orthodox Schools and Institutes to support their sibling institutions. Creative means of non-financial support may be valuable in assisting theological education around the world especially in Africa, Eastern Europe, and other areas. Support should also be provided for new initiatives in theological education. All churches, schools, and institutions are exhorted to make some tangible efforts to support Orthodox theological education financially; even the widow's mite is praiseworthy (cf. Lk 21:1-4). Earmarked scholarship funds may be an attractive option for both individuals and institutions within the Church.

Other Recommendations. Besides the recommendations discussed above, the Consultation was able to offer other recommendations. Discussion began with the idea that the WCC/ETE would be the primary source for support and assistance, but as the Consultation progressed, members began to see ways in which Orthodox institutions could become involved in tasks intended to further theological education and ministerial formation.

—Developing networks and producing a global directory of Orthodox educational institutions, both Eastern and Oriental. A joint project of the Patriarch Athenagoras Orthodox Institute (Berkeley, California, USA) and SYNDESMOS is well under way; data has been collected and converted into an electronic format. Every effort should be made to see this project to completion in the very near future.

—Production of resource materials for (1) classes on Christian unity and (2) for all classes incorporating a dimension of Christian unity.

—Adapting distance education to the needs of Orthodox schools and theological institutions.

—Developing and coordinating scholarship and cooperative education programs. This includes programs for students, faculty, and exchange programs. Besides their current practice of providing scholarships for faculty development and advocacy, the ETE may be able to help draft guidelines for granting scholarships, thereby encouraging Orthodox schools and institutions who might be willing to provide their own scholarship assistance. Furthermore, it may be fruitful to help establish some structure to provide information about programs and scholarship opportunities. These could assist schools and institutions insure that resources are allocated in the most equitable way possible.

—Intensified efforts to include representatives of Orthodox theological schools and institutions in WCC consultations and work. Not only would this allow for theological educators to have more input into Council deliberations, but it would expose students to the ecumenical scene.

—Plan and host conferences on several different levels: with other Orthodox churches, regional inter-church meetings, and special gatherings focused on specific issues (e.g., church-state relationships in various regions, moral and ethical issues especially related to sexuality, bioethics, proselytism and mission, liturgical renewal, other living faiths, secularism and non-Christian ideologies).

—Assist in acquiring technological assistance, especially for marginalized areas and emerging programs. This may include computer and teleconferencing equipment.

—Developing plans to share library resources. Creating online catalogues, sharing extra books, providing grants to purchase needed books, and setting-up a distribution network may be dimensions of such plans. Especially encouraged are materials from a wide variety of Christian communions since this will increase inter-Christian familiarity.

—Assisting in the development, production, and distribution of materials to foster faculty and curriculum development.

—Help in producing "translated" ecumenical materials. Beyond translation into different languages, this effort would also address phrasing the message itself in a form more understandable and acceptable to Orthodox. Care should be taken to make Orthodox statements more understandable to others. This would involve a dimension of coordinating translation efforts.

—Production of Internet resources designed by and for Orthodox audiences, but accessible to other Christian churches.

—Distribution of pertinent ecumenical materials, insuring that they get to libraries and key faculty members.

—Publicizing existing programs, events, and structures that involve Orthodox theological educators in inter-church experiences. This would not only broaden knowledge of the WCC's initiative in and support of Orthodox theological education, but it would inform educators of opportunities open to them.

—Promotion of creative approaches to theological education both in the classroom and in the wider community. These methods should include incorporating the viewpoints of people from other traditions, promotion of debate among faculties, and emphasize diversity within the Orthodox tradition. Such efforts will result in a greater appreciation for the variety of contexts and charismata affecting the Church, its life, and its work.

Part VIII: Ecumenical Formation in Orthodox Theological Education

—Engaging in an analysis of Communisms effects on interchurch relations, on Orthodox world-views, and its continuing legacy. Attention should also be given to the current situation in post-Communist countries. This line of inquiry will assist theological educators in their work.

—Fostering an ongoing inter-faith dialogue. Theological educators can have a positive influence on the understanding of Islam and other non-Christian religions.

—Promotion of language training to facilitate meetings and cross-cultural exchange of ideas.

Conclusion

The Consultation on Orthodox Theological Education came together by the Grace of God, doing their part as faithful servants of God to address the Apostle Pauls concern: "How are [women and men] to believe in one of whom they have never heard? And how are they to hear without someone to proclaim him?" (Rom 10:14). It is important today, more than ever, to confess, proclaim, and teach Jesus Christ and him crucified (cf. 1 Cor 2:2). Theological schools and institutions must address the many challenges of the modern world. It is our prayer that the Holy Spirit continue to inspire all those involved in Orthodox theological education, teaching them in every hour what they ought to say (cf. Lk 12:12).

When the Most High came down and confused the tongues, he divided the nations; but when He distributed the tongues of fire, He called all to unity. Therefore with one voice, we glorify the all-holy Spirit. (Kontakion of Pentecost)

Heavenly King, keep your Church undivided and steadfast, preserve the peace of all believers who worship you. (Oriental Orthodox Eucharistic liturgy)

(135) The Ecumenical Dimensions of Orthodox Theological Education[1]

Metropolitan John Zizioulas

My object in this brief paper is to offer for discussion some personal remarks concerning the ecumenical nature of Orthodox theology and the way it is expressed in the actual theological education of the Orthodox Churches. It is the first time in the history of the Ecumenical Movement that the Orthodox, among other participants in this Movement, are asked to examine their own theological education methods and programmes in the light first of all of their own tradition and secondly of the fact that they participate in the Ecumenical Movement. So far Orthodox theological education has taken for granted its method and practice of teaching theology, as if there were no points that needed reconsideration and revision. And yet, there is a great deal to be reconsidered. The opportunity offered to us by the Programme on Theological Education of the World Council of Churches to re-think on this matter should be welcome. I am personally glad that the World Council of Churches has at last paid attention to the importance of theological education for the unity of the Church and is trying to see how Orthodox tradition and theology can be of help to and be helped by other theological traditions in this respect.

Introduction

I have stressed that the Orthodox are asked to examine their theological education first of all in the light of their own tradition. This may sound too arrogant on the part of an Orthodox theologian: do we not have a lot to learn from the non-Orthodox as to how to do and teach theology?

Why take such an introspective attitude in the framework of the Ecumenical Movement? The answer is simply that the Orthodox more than anyone else have allowed themselves to learn a lot from the non-Orthodox concerning theological education, and this has taken place to such an extent that almost the entire system of theological education which prevails throughout the Orthodox world is a copy of the theological education systems which are found in Protestant and Roman Catholic theological institutions. One need simply be reminded of the way the German Protestant and Roman Catholic Universities of the last century acted as the pattern and the prototype in the establishment of the theological Faculties in the Universities of Athens and Thessaloniki in Greece, not to speak of what happened in the theological Academies in Russia and throughout the rest of the Orthodox world.[2] The Orthodox, in establishing their theological institutions, have looked for inspiration everywhere else except their own theology. This is unfortunate for two reasons:

a) The first reason is that by so doing the Orthodox have inevitably brought about a crisis between method and content in theology. As long as the content of Orthodox theology was basically a variation of Western Scholasticism, the crisis was not felt. As soon, however, as Orthodox theology began to liberate itself from the "Scholastic Captivity", it became apparent that something was wrong in the relation between content and method in Orthodox theological education. You cannot return to the Patristic ethos of theology and still keep your scholastic methodology.

---

[1] This article of Metropolitan John Zizioulas which is re-published here with the necessary adjustments, first appeared in *Orthodox Theological Education for Life and Witness of the Church: Report on the Consultation at Basel, Switzerland,* July 4-8 1978 (Geneva: WCC, 1978), 33-40.

[2] See G. Florovsky "Orthodoxe Theologie" in *Die Religion in Geschichte und Genwart* vol. 6 (Stuttgart: UTB, 1986); A. Schmemann, *The Historical Road of Eastern Orthodoxy,* trans. Lydia W. Kesich (London: Harvill Press, 1963), 289ff. Cf. C. Yannaras "Theology in Present-Day Greece" *St. Vladimir's Seminary Theological Quarterly* 16.4 (1972): 195, 207.

This crisis between form and content in theological education is responsible for the tendency in our time to look for theology outside the theological Faculties in private reading of literature not used in theological courses or even in monastic circles and secular literature.[3]

b) The second reason why this is unfortunate is that by neglecting their own tradition in theological education the Orthodox have lost sight of the ecumenical dimensions of their theology. This may sound strange, but I hope to make it clearer in the course of what I am going to say further. Two main areas are involved when we speak of "ecumenical dimensions" of theology in this context. The first area covers the relation between differing theological traditions or ecclesiastically divided groups of Christians. This is the narrow sense of "ecumenical" in our contemporary ecclesiastical and theological language. The second area concerns the relationship between theology and the rest of disciplines in science, research and reflection, or indeed the rest of human life as a whole. This is not usually referred to with the word "ecumenical", but it is, as we shall see, not unrelated to it. It is with regard to these two areas that, I think, Orthodox theological education has impoverished itself and the others by not looking primarily into its own traditions with regard to its method of theological education. This has resulted in two concrete forms of theological education. With regard to the first area theological education took the form of a confessionalist theology. With regard to the second, it became an area of specialization existing side by side with other fields of specialized disciplines such as Law, Medicine, Philosophy, etc. The question that arises now is the following: if we look into the nature of Orthodox theology as it was formed in the Patristic period, to what extent can we justify these two forms which theological education has taken? This, I think, is the fundamental question that an Orthodox should ask himself in considering the ecumenical dimensions of Orthodox theological education.

Let me raise this twofold question in the very way I have put the problem here and try to offer my views to you for discussion.

1. Can you do Orthodox Theology in a Confessional way?

Confessionalism as a historical phenomenon appeared for the first time mainly in 17th century Protestantism and caught the Orthodox by surprise. The question which Confessionalism raised to the Churches was: What books or definitions and formulations of your faith do you possess which you regard as expressing your proper identity as a Christian? The Orthodox were caught by surprise because - and this is in itself significant - they could not answer this question out of their tradition. As a result and in order to conform with the spirit of that time they started producing their own confessional books, such as the Confession of Dositheos of Jerusalem, of Peter Mogila, etc. These Confessions were written as responses to issues which were at stake at that time in the debate between Roman Catholics and Protestants and attempted to show the "Orthodox position" on the various problems. As the problematic was already set by the Roman Catholic-Protestant debate, the so-called Orthodox position consisted mainly of an attempt to follow the "middle way" between the two,[4] and in fact was nothing but borrowing arguments from Roman Catholicism in order to face Protestantism and vice-versa according to the particular problem at stake or to the inclinations of the author. Thus Peter Mogila was inclined favorably towards Roman Catholicism, whereas Cyril Lucaris, towards Calvinism. Neither of the two, however, thought of questioning the very problematic with which they were presented or, what is even more important, the very spirit and the idea of Confessionalism. The result of this has been that ever since that time Orthodox theology has been engaged in an attempt to define its own confessional sources. Even when criticism was raised against the Confessional books of the 17th century as not constituting sources of Orthodox theology,[5] it was

---

[3] Such a tendency is to be found in Greece today. The monasteries are gradually becoming centers of theology that attract more and more people.

[4] See J. Karmiris *Heterodox Influences on the Confessions of the Seventeenth Century* (1949), 4: "The Eastern Church and theology in defending Orthodoxy against the attack of Roman Catholicism and Protestantism...occupied a sort of middle position between these the two churches of the West."

[5] This was the case, for example, in the First Congress of the Orthodox Theological Faculties, which took place in Athens in 1936.

still maintained that some such Confessional books ought to exist because Orthodoxy ought to have its own Confessional books. It was as recently as our own days that a renowned dogmatic theologian of Athens, Prof. J. Karmiris, published a monumental two-volume book containing what he calls "The Dogmatic and Symbolic Monuments of the Orthodox Church", in which are included not only the Creeds of the ancient Church but even the modern Confessions of Faith (Dositheos, Mogila, etc.). To indicate this subjection to Confessionalism even further, Orthodox Theological Faculties, copying mainly German prototypes, established chairs of what they call Symbolics which exist up to this moment and which aim at comparing Orthodoxy with other confessions on the basis of such confessional books. Even those Orthodox who would not accept any of these modern Confessions as expressing faithfully the Orthodox faith, still look for confessional sources which they usually identify with the definitions of the seven Ecumenical Councils. The Spirit of Confessionalism is still alive in Orthodox Theological education.

But what do we mean by the spirit of Confessionalism? And why is it not compatible with the ecumenical dimensions which are contained in the genuine Orthodox tradition? Confessionalism bears the following characteristics: a) It assumes that faith is mainly an intellectual process through which one's mind is illuminated so that it can formulate the truth of revelation in the form of *propositions*. Truth is essentially a matter of propositions. Once you agree on these propositions you can be regarded as agreeing on faith itself.[6] b) Because of that, tradition is understood as handing down from generation to generation the original faith of the Apostles mainly in the form of creeds and theological statements, usually but not necessarily written. These have to be subscribed to be each generation; c) Theology draws its content from these propositions or becomes itself the promoter of such propositions through its systematic work. It thus becomes the criterion of faith, more or less identical with it, and the *condition* of ecclesiality. d) Finally in the spirit of Confesionalism the Church acquires her identity on the basis of these propositions which are formulated though theology. Thus, as a result of Confessionalism, Christendom consists of confessional bodies, identified with the help of some *credo*, written or unwritten, explicit or inexplicit, to which the members of this body adhere as to a condition of faith.

Now, what is wrong with all this? What is incompatible in this with the ecumenical spirit of the ancient Orthodox tradition? The following points may serve as an answer to this question.

The non-existence of confessional bodies in the ancient Church is not a mere historical accident. It was rather inconceivable at that time that faith would be a matter of accepting certain propositions and that the acceptance of these propositions could in itself be the basis of what was called *the Church*. It is true that credal conditions were from the beginning attached to Baptism and that as the Church became more and more preoccupied with the danger of heresy these creeds were given a prominent place in the Church. But it was never the case that credal statements could be the basis either for theology or for the Church. The Church was always understood as the great mystery of the plan of God for the final destiny of the world, a mystery which was celebrated in the Eucharist and of which one became partaker as a member of a concrete local community. It was membership in this community that determined both theology and belonging to the Church. No theology could identify itself on the basis of a creed but on the basis of its conformity to this great mystery of the salvation of the world manifested and experienced in the Eucharistic community. It is for this reason that just as there were no confessional Churches but simply, in cases of division, separated communities needing unity on the level of the local community; equally there were no confessional theologies existing side by side on the basis of credal statements. It is a different matter that today looking into the ancient Church through confessional eyes we can speak of various theologies (Alexandrian, Antiochene, etc.) But in the ancient Church itself the term "theology" was not based on creeds or propositions of faith; it

---

[6] According to C. Androutsos, *Dogmatics of the Orthodox Eastern Church* (Athens, 1907) (in Greek), 2-12, the truth of faith consists of concepts that are defined by the human intellect, which is the instrument of the formulation of dogma. On the intellectualism of seventeenth – century Orthodoxy in the West, see K. Heussi and E. Peter, *Precis d'Histoire de l'Eglise* (Neuchatel, 1967), para. 94,1. Cf C. Yannaras, "Theology in Present-Day Greece".

was used to denote a grasp of the mystery of divine existence as it is offered to the world and experienced in the ecclesial community.[7] These were the ecumenical dimensions which Confessionalism tends to take away from theology by making it a matter of identifying oneself with certain confessional statements.

If we put Orthodox theological education in the light of this tradition, we realize how far we have moved from it in our actual situation. It was only a few years ago that a non-Orthodox student deeply and genuinely interested in Patristic and Orthodox theology decided to receive his doctorate from an Orthodox Theological Faculty and wrote to the Dean of one such Faculty to that effect. The answer he received in an official letter was that the Faculty was in the Dean's word's "a Confessional Faculty" and would not grant doctoral degrees to non-Orthodox, since a particular oath of confessional allegiance was attached as a condition to the granting of the degree. I refer to this case not in order to criticize any particular Faculty nor in order to limit my criticism to the case of granting doctorates. This case may well not apply to other Orthodox Faculties and may not even apply to this Faculty any more. What applies, however, to almost all Orthodox Faculties is their confessional character which this particular Faculty had the courage to admit. For is there any Orthodox Faculty which does not regard its purpose as primarily consisting in training ministers and teachers for its own confessional body? Orthodox Theological Schools on the whole educate not for *the Church* but for a "confessional" Church. They do not take into account either in their curriculum or in their teaching staff the needs of the Church as a whole but of a particular confessional Church. What could be done to change this is a matter for later consideration. For the moment let it suffice to take note of it, as a situation that stands out in contrast with the spirit of the earliest Orthodox tradition.

Related to all this is the second fundamental question that emerges from a consideration of the ecumenical dimensions of Orthodox theology, namely:

2. Can you do Orthodox Theology as a Specialized Subject?

Here the problem is a complex one and requires clarification to avoid misunderstandings. Theology as we know it today, i.e. as a special discipline existing side by side with other disciplines, is a fairly modern thing and as such it is unknown to the ancient Orthodox tradition. Theology in the ancient Church was taught either in the so-called Catechetical Schools which were originally connected with the preparation of the Catechumens for Baptism to become eventually centers of highly developed theological reflection, or in the bishop's house under the personal guidance of the bishop, as was the case with the theological education of people like Athanasius of Alexandria; or finally in the Monasteries which have produced most of the great theologians of the ancient Orthodox tradition. Now, the fact that there were no theological Faculties at that time, as we have today, is not again a matter of mere historical accident. The main reason why the actual form of theological education which we have today would not fit easily into the pattern of theology at that time is a profoundly epistemological one. It has to do with the fact that at that time Truth was regarded as indivisible and One and that the various scientific disciplines were not unrelated to each other but ought somehow to converge in this one Truth. Theology did not claim access to a special branch of knowledge but addressed itself to the mystery of existence in general, and as such no area of knowledge was indifferent to it.

This concept of Truth was seriously challenged by later analytical approaches to epistemology which resulted in what is known as specialization in science. The idea of the University[8] which originally stemmed

---

[7] Significantly enough, the Orthodox Church has chosen the commemoration of the Seventh Ecumenical Council to be the Sunday of Orthodoxy. As is well known, this Council dealt with the issue of the icons and did not put forth any propositional definition of the faith. In declaring, "This is the faith of the Fathers; this is the faith which has sustained the oecumene," the Council was pointing to a form of "theology", the icon, which was a form of liturgical experience of the community and did not require any subscription to conceptual statements.

[8] See the discussion of the problem in W. Pannenberg, *Theology and the Philosophy of Science*, trans. F. McDonagh (Philadelphia: Westminster Press, 1973), passim and pp. 3-14 and 228ff.

from the ancient conception of Truth as an unbreakable totality was meant to promote the co-operation of various disciplines so that they might converge in the one Truth. In fact, however, it has ended up as the place where each discipline attains its autonomy and self-sufficiency in the most negative way. To be a Faculty in a University means to be independent and self-sufficient; it means not to be interdependent except in matters of finance, administration and professional interests.

The effect that this situation has had on theology is evident when we consider above all the confusion it has created as to the exact content of theology itself. Most of what is taught in a theological Faculty is not theology and what is supposed to be theology is so specialized with regard to other disciplines that it is not theology in the proper sense. In order to maintain its self-sufficiency a theological Faculty includes in its curriculum historical and linguistic courses which could be done by non-theologians. This is not just a matter of curriculum but reaches the very concept of what theology is. A doctoral dissertation can pass, let us say, in the area of Canon Law having as its subject a historical or legal problem dealt with methodologically without reference whatsoever to theology. Thus it is difficult to tell what makes one a theologian. In our present day system the very intention of making theology a distinctive discipline has led us to denying it any distinctiveness. The self-sufficiency of theology vis-à-vis other disciplines has deprived it of its specific contribution to knowledge. The fact that no Orthodox theological Faculty bothers to send its students to hear what the biologists or the physicists or the medical scientists say, and the fact that these other disciplines do not bother to relate their research to theology points to a malaise in education which escapes the boundaries and the control of theology, but for which theology is not entirely without any responsibility. Orthodox theology in particular must think again on this matter. The claim to Truth throughout the Patristic period and the liturgical experience of Orthodoxy contains cosmological and sociological implications so profound that it is inconceivable to do Orthodox theology without reference to the problems facing other sciences, both natural and human. A theology which through its Patristic and liturgical foundations claims to have a vision of cosmic transformation - of a Transfiguration of the World - which includes such matters as the overcoming of death - not of "spiritual" but of physical death - and the conversion of the human individual into a true person living in the image of the Holy Trinity, cannot ignore either the natural sciences or sociological concerns. We cannot train Orthodox theologians without opening up their eyes to all the aspects of existence. We cannot of course turn our students into doctors and chemists, but we can perhaps hope that their teachers will present theology to them as a matter for which no aspect of human existence is irrelevant.

This will require of course fundamental changes not only in the curriculum but also in the entire method of doing Theology. We cannot aim in such a brief paper at a programme of reformation for Orthodox Theological Faculties. Nor do I regard myself as a competent person to give advice to the Orthodox Faculties and Academies on any matter, least of all on such a serious matter which would require serious study and co-operation among the Orthodox Theological Schools. The only thing I can do is to touch upon certain matters that come to my mind as possible points of reform in the light of what I have tried to say in this paper.

If Orthodox theology is by its very nature ecumenical in the double sense which I underlined here, namely in its concern not with a particular confession but with the Church as a whole and with the salvation and existence of the World in its totality, then the following concrete steps seem to me to be suggested with regard to theological education.

1. The first point concerns the basic methodological principles underlying theological education. If theology aims at opening up the vision of its students to the mystery of the whole Church and of existence in its totality, there should be no specific part, department or chair of theology, which would not contribute directly to this global and ecclesial vision. This would require a radical revision of the traditional Western division of theology into Biblical, Historical, Systematic and Practical. New schemes must be found to express more adequately this global and existential character of theology. It would also mean introducing new subjects into the curriculum, which would require more inter-disciplinary and ecumenical co-operation.

Part VIII: Ecumenical Formation in Orthodox Theological Education

2. An attempt should be made to de-confessionalize the various branches of theology. Much of what is written and taught in theological schools is done so from the old traditional viewpoint of Confessionalism. This is true not only of dogmatic theology which undoubtedly suffers most from Confessionalism. It is also true of other areas such as Church History which helps to perpetuate confessional identities instead of transcending them. Equally it is true of Biblical Theology which in Orthodox theology at least calls for a lot of work in order to integrate into the global vision of theology the disintegrating tendencies of modern Biblical scholarship.

3. Equally we must increasingly feel the need to open up the confessional boundaries of Orthodox theological schools from the point of view of teaching staff and students. It is of course true that in the last decades more and more non-Orthodox students are accepted for studies in Orthodox theological schools. This trend should be encouraged until the point is reached where a non-Orthodox student will be regarded as a full member of the academic family in whatever refers to academic work. With regard to teaching staff it is to be regretted that almost nothing has happened so far to de-confessionalize Orthodox theological schools in this respect. Apart from invitations to non-Orthodox to give sporadic lectures, Orthodox theological schools remain insularly closed to themselves. When those who gave us Confessionalism take steps to renounce it in our time by opening up their theological schools to Orthodox teachers and students, is it not to be regretted that the Orthodox to whom confessional ism is by nature a stranger should do nothing in this direction?

Conclusions

In bringing my remarks to their conclusion let me emphasize that the concern behind these remarks is not to facilitate ecumenical progress at all costs. On the contrary, it may well be the case that by taking a confessio-lialistic line we may arrive more easily at some kind of union of divided Christendom. My concern is rather to arrive at an ecumenical progress which would be firmly based on the true nature of the Church.[9] The Orthodox claim in the Ecumenical Movement that they are not a confessional body but the Church. And yet in so many ways they seem to act as a confessional body - not least in theological education. I personally believe that the greatest contribution the Orthodox can make to the Ecumenical Movement consists of insisting on the point that we are not saved by belonging to a confessional body but to a concrete ecclesial community, to the Church. And theology exists only as a pointer to this mystery of salvation which is the Church.

---

[9] Cf. my remarks on this subject in "The Local Church in a Eucharistic Perspective", in *In Each Place: Towards a Fellowship of Local Churches Truly United*, (Geneva: WCC, 1977), 50-61, especially 60ff.

(136) ORTHODOXY AND ECUMENICAL THEOLOGICAL EDUCATION[1]

Nikos Nissiotis

Between the efforts of humanity to preserve and develop its identity by respecting the human person, and the efforts of the separated Christian traditions to restore the wholeness of the Gospel message through their fellowship in the ecumenical movement, there exists a relationship which is implied in all definitions of "ecumenical" and "ecumenical education". The world is looking to the Church to contribute, through her own oneness and renewal, to the task of building one human family, liberating peoples from all kinds of historical injustice and domination, from exploitation, from discrimination based on race or sex, eliminating the divisions between the rich and the poor that separate classes of society and nations.

In using the term "ecumenical", we are referring to that which "helps to describe everything that relates to the whole task of the whole Church to bring the Gospel to the whole world." The main element of this definition - the search for the unity and renewal of the Church in her relationship to the world - implies for ecumenical education a threefold task:

• first, an affirmation of the wholeness of the Gospel, comprising the good news of salvation for all human beings;

• second, an emphasis on the need of the Churches to renew their lives and commitment as they grow together within one fellowship;

• and third, a call to students of theology to confess Christ through involvement in the struggle to build a just, participatory and sustainable society.

It is of paramount importance for the renewal of theological thinking today that we undertake a critical self-appraisal of our application of these principles of renewal, unity and involvement. Each theology needs to examine its ability to build up an authentic ecumenical education on this threefold basis, seeking to alert theological educators, students and church people to their ecumenical vocation.

I

Eastern Orthodox theology possesses sound principles for contributing to such an ecumenical education, being nourished by the experience of an intense liturgical life, with a very strong emphasis on eschatology and cosmic salvation. These include:

1. a global vision of the divine economy in relation to the whole of history. The Church is a pars pro toto, a miniature of Creation in the process of renewal and salvation, as the "Koine ktisis". The oneness of the Church is the vehicle for the re-gathering of all things into the Oneness of the whole universe. The liturgy invites everybody to pray for the "union of all" and the faithful share in the foretaste of the restoration of the whole Creation.

2. Orthodox theology, thus, does not allow any simple division between sacred and secular and does not favor any kind of sectarianism in the Church, either within herself or in opposition to the world. Or account of its fundamental principle of universal salvation, the world is seen as potentially saved. The historical reality has, therefore, a primary importance and the Church does not alienate herself from any world situation.

---

[1] This article of Nikos Nissiotis which is re-published here with the necessary adjustments, first appeared in *Orthodox Theological Education for Life and Witness of the Church: Report on the Consultation at Basel, Switzerland*, July 4-8 1978, (Geneva: WCC, 1978), 41-48.

3. This attitude affects the understanding of the Church as the world that has been already saved and transformed, or the new Creation, with the implication that the Church cannot but be One throughout the centuries. For the Orthodox, a particular confessional identity separating a local church as a new ecclesia/community is totally impossible. The Church is identical only with the One, Holy, Catholic and Apostolic Church in unbroken continuity right from the beginning of the Christian era.

4. In this sense every local church possesses the fullness of divine grace and catholicity within all different cultures as part of the whole Church belonging to all times and all places. The local church is never foreign to the prevailing culture of the place where she exists and yet retains her identity with the One Catholic and Apostolic Church.

5. The Church is permanently renewed by the cleansing operation of the Paraclete, the Spirit of truth promised by Christ and given to her on the day of Pentecost. Being able to invoke the Spirit of God is the only assurance which the Church has for remaining in full communication with Christ and maintaining at the same time a positive and constructive relationship with the world.

Guided by these fundamental principles in the understanding of the threefold task described above, Orthodox theology is by its very nature ecumenical and has contributed, especially through its fellowship in the World Council of Churches, in the following ways to the ecumenical movement:

a. by a fuller understanding of the Church as the presupposition of al sacraments and of the word of God. The Church is not only identical with the gathering of the local congregation but also with the body of Christ as enacted again and again in her sacramental life and kerygma by the Holy Spirit. The Church is not simply an association of believers whose life can be modified by the application of new administrative rules. She is the Body of Christ and her nature is a mystery in which one shares only by faith and full commitment. Although the Church is composed of repenting sinners, she is Holy, being continually cleansed by the Spirit;

b. by professing an absolute unity between Scriptures and Tradition, defeating the dualism in western theology of the so-called two sources of revelation which led to the problem of authority in the Church; the acceptance or rejection of magisterium, and the acceptance or rejection of the tradition, the opposition between Bible and tradition;

c. by the importance of the liturgical-sacramental life centered around the Eucharist, the event which reaffirms the Church as the Body of Christ, renewed by the Spirit and preserving her identity in all world situations. The Church, thus understood, does not depend on confessional statements or scholastic definitions. She is her Own life in Christ. Ecclesiology is a commentary on the operation of the Holy Spirit. Church structure, apostolic ministry and succession have to be interpreted through a charismatic pneumatology, Church orders are not de jure derived from divine "potestas" or a pyramidal hierarchy, but are a communal event, a gift of grace to the Ecclesia, which guarantees its authenticity. That means that there is no qualitative difference "in essence" between a general and a special ministry. Instead there is a particular, indispensable diakonia incarnating not an order and a discipline but rather a love of the Spirit, binding the members of the church community into one Body. There cannot be an organic unity in the Church without one mutually recognized ministry, and each local church is recognizable through the one who presides at the liturgy and who thus unites it with the Universal Church.

d. by its understanding of the unity of the Church which is given in one faith, one baptism and one spirit, and which is gradually being realized in the life of the Church. Unity is both a gift of the spirit and also goal which the faithful must strive to achieve so as to grow into mature manhood and womanhood in the image of Christ. This dynamic concept of unity is a sine qua non condition for authentic church life and the indispensable precondition of the presence and action of the Church and her ministry in and to the world.

e. by the insistence that unity in faith and praxis with the bond of love and peace are conditions for sacramental communion. The non- acceptance of intercommunion by the Orthodox in ecumenical gatherings should not be interpreted as a judgment against other churches. It is the expression of an attitude consistent with the fundamental principle that unity is full union and communion. The practice of intercommunion must presuppose this kind of full union or should lead to the immediate abolition of church divisions between those who practice it. The Orthodox without passing any judgment on those practicing intercommunion play the necessary role for the ecumenical movement of a reminder of the final requirements for re-establishing a full church communion. The rejection of intercommunion by a church like the Orthodox is in the end a rather positive contribution to a realistic, hopeful and authentic vision of the unity to come.

On the whole one can say that the Orthodox have helped ecumenical theological circles to regain their sacramental ecclesiology, the centrality of the liturgy in Christian life and the theology of the Holy Spirit. At the same time, controversial theological issues between Roman Catholicism and Protestantism, like the question of ministry and apostolic succession, have been discussed in a more flexible manner with the broader Orthodox vision of Eucharistic theology, which can overcome a unilateral, confessional theology.

On the other hand, Orthodox theology has certainly benefited from:

a. the insistence of the Western reformed theologies on the centrality of the Bible and the kerygma of the Church;
b. the critical approach which is wary of an easy acceptance of Church history as the unique criterion and norm of present church life;
c. the work of the historical critical method applied to Biblical texts;
d. the need for permanent renewal of Church life and theology;
e. the continuous concern for man's daily life and the sharing in human efforts to improve the human condition;
f. the missionary character of Christian theology as contextual and inductive, i.e. in permanent relationship with a changing cultural and social environment, which has to be taken seriously as a norm for theological thinking and methodology.

II

While the contribution of Orthodox theology is undeniable regarding ecclesiological subjects in the realm of ecumenical education, it appears that its contribution in the field of renewal and social ethics is not proportionately high. The Orthodox appear to be reactionary toward certain recent trends in the WCC which are considered by many to be vital to an authentic and full ecumenism, for example: attempts to create new forms of Church life, to readapt Church structures in conformity with the modern world, and, especially, the recent trends in the WCC to assist in liberation movements of all kinds.

It is true that the Orthodox by their total devotion to the "Inner" sacramental life of the Church, are tempted to neglect this other dimension of ecumenism. It seems that their fidelity to their distinctive Church life has led them to a one sided and partial interpretation and application of their ecumenical vocation. There is a kind of esoteric language developing in Orthodox circles which proves to be more and more incompatible with the ecumenical mandate in its emphasis on the world situation. Unless the Orthodox accept this mandate with a sense of profound responsibility, they are not, in fact, fully and rightly interpreting their ecumenical tradition.

Social ethics and liberation movements which serve to help to create a just, participatory and sustainable society, by eliminating the power center of unjust structures and of racial and sex discrimination, are not a politics programme, nor are they a reflection of the outlook of certain very revolutionary societies in the so-called Third World. This action is implied in the doctrine of the Trinity as communion, revealing the communal nature of the whole Creation; in the mystery of the Incarnation, the Cross and the Resurrection pointing to the human-centered world reality which needs continual restructuring, defeating all kinds of attempts against human dignity; in the operation of the Holy Spirit renewing the whole world by liberating it from the forces of evil which disrupt its peace. For the Orthodox, the liturgy itself is linked with all aspects of daily life, and history is taken into serious consideration. The role of the Christian and of the Churches is not simply reconci liatory, passively irenic, assisting the poor and the sick a posteriori, but also revolutionary in the face of injustice and exploitation, preventive in the face of threats of famine and sickness, and creative of new, more just and participatory structures.

Confessing Christ today as an ecumenical task does not only imply fidelity to creeds of the past and spiritual devotion to the sacramental life. It is precisely the confession of the faith through ancient creeds and churchly devotion that forces Christians into a dynamic presence in the world. This is not another modern, politicized, activistic and human- centered act of confessing Christ, but precisely the other side of the same coin, the other indispensible, inseparable dimension of the one and the same confession.

Under difficult historical circumstances, among enemies of the Christian faith, the Orthodox churches were obliged to preserve their faith by concentrating on their church life "internally", "mystically", "liturgically".

Nor were they allowed to interpret and apply their faith in the way that the ecumenical nature of their church life and theology would imply. But these restrictions of the past should not lead them now to a one sided fulfillment of their ecumenical vocation. Orthodox patristic thought, as it must be followed up and re-iinterpreted today, is equally as pro-activistic, creative and revolutionary (in a positive sense), as other kinds of theology which profess a strong social gospel of liberation today. The difference perhaps is only that patristic thought is continually fed by a sacramental - ecclesiological vision of the world which does not allow any kind of absolutization of socio-political action.

Certainly, here, Orthodox ecumenical education must allow itself to be affected by contemporary trends of ecumenical activism in the world. Orthodox ecumenical education must be willing to accept a beneficial exchange, with non-Orthodox ecumenical teachers and students, of the elements missing from their respective ecumenical education. This does not signify that they are to copy or imitate a type of social Gospel which is foreign to the principles of Orthodox ecumenical theology. In this connection the following remarks can be made:

1. Socio-political action cannot become a substitute for the sacramental life, but is its natural and self-evident outcome.

2. Liberation church activism is not another confession of faith, uniting Christians of separated traditions into a new type of church commitment and reality, but the same ancient act of confessing the faith in its right and indispensible application.

3. There are not different kinds of Gospel message to be applied in a pluralistic society by a pluriform human-centered activism, but it is the One all-embracing and all-uniting Gospel in all world situations.

4. Though the need to change the world's political, social and economic structures may be a priority in the agenda of a local church if human dignity is under immediate threat, it cannot become a criterion of church life by which those who cannot share in this activism are excluded; socio-political puritanism should not replace the old ethical puritanism, leading the Church to further divisions and schisms.

5. Socio-political action cannot become the unique and final Christian confession and shape the core of ecumenical education, but it must always be authorized, cleansed from human absolutisms by a serious Christian discernment of the spirits.

Thus the Orthodox may regain from other church traditions a dimension missing from their ecumenical theological education and at the same time they contribute a certain restraint to all any extremist tendencies in the application of the Christian social gospel.

III

As a matter of fact, an enriching exchange is taking place between Orthodox theological education and non-Orthodox traditions within the ecumenical movement. The signs of this development are clearly to be seen in all realms of ecumenical education and practice.

To favor and foster this exchange, several chairs in ecumenics have been established in Orthodox faculties, and far more chairs in Orthodox theology have been created in Protestant and Roman Catholic universities and in Church institutions in non-Orthodox countries.

It is true, however, that in most cases this exchange is not really taking place. It remains one more dimension in theological education.

It is also descriptive and informative in character. No deeper influence is exercised on the way of thinking about our theological task today. Though there are some interesting exceptions, theologies remain untouched in their traditional vision. There are only specialized theologians who are better able to interpret more authentically the others' traditions. In this respect, however, a certain progress has taken place. There is also more readiness to include the others' approach while preparing books on theology, without a defensive attitude.

Theological chairs on ecumenism are of great help and we should wish that their numbers continue to increase. What is more necessary, however, is :

   a. a more frequent exchange of a greater number of students and teachers in a two-way traffic (not only Orthodox students studying in non-Orthodox faculties);
   b. the establishment of institutes of an ecumenical character for creating possibilities of life and prayer together;
   c. attempts to teach theology through teams of lecturers of Orthodox and non-Orthodox backgrounds;
   d. the introduction of extension programmes in theological faculties with the participation of non-theological educators.

Especially if we want to promote a deeper knowledge of Orthodoxy, we should organize special courses of intensive study of Orthodox theology and church life. May I refer to the annual liturgical seminar for non-Orthodox students, initiated at Bossey 20 years ago, as an example. This 15-day intensive course combines theoretical instruction with attendance at the Holy Week offices of the Orthodox Church, thereby giving the students a double enrichment.

In all the methods we use to promote ecumenical education, we should try to bear in mind that ecumenics is not just one more theological discipline for specialists. Rather, it is intended to permeate the whole theological curriculum with an ecumenical spirit of awareness and alertness. This is especially true in the interaction of Orthodox and non- Orthodox undertakings. Here, however, we cannot say that there has been satisfactory progress. In particular in the area of studies of Orthodoxy there is among some non-Orthodox a sentimental pro-Orthodox attitude which narrows down ecumenism to a sympathy, an appreciation of the symbolism and richness of liturgy and an admiration of the exotic or extravagant elements. On the other hand, the Orthodox must appreciate the ethos of the non-Orthodox and be ready to listen and comprehend attitudes and positions that may appear to be unilateral or extremist. Here, ecumenical education must be concerned with very profound problems, not necessarily all of a theological nature. There are prejudices derived from cultural, political and ethical presuppositions which affect the theological attitude of an Orthodox vis- à-vis a Roman Catholic or a Protestant; a certain psychological barrier often renders the possibility of a new open horizon towards a non-Orthodox very difficult. Education, in the narrow sense of increasing knowledge about subject matter, does not help to change attitudes at this point. What is needed is a thorough-going exchange of experience and sharing of community life. This must have priority when we talk of exchanging theological programmes with traditions foreign to the Orthodox.

The same difficulties exist with those non-Orthodox who are eager to penetrate the Eastern Orthodox tradition. Orthodoxy is very deeply interrelated with its cultural and national backgrounds, as well as with specific ethical choices that the Orthodox have to make in their particular environment. One cannot study an Orthodoxy

Part VIII: Ecumenical Formation in Orthodox Theological Education

disassociated from these non- theological elements. That is why a non-Orthodox can enter into the life and mind of the Orthodox churches only if he is ready to appreciate the popular religiosity of their members, and the simplicity of their appreciation of national and church history, as well as their uncritical acceptance of the sacramental life that sanctifies their entire social, family and professional life.

In the end what is necessary is not to overemphasize the need for a special Orthodox/non-Orthodox axis, thereby intensifying one particular branch of ecumenical education. Although we accept this as an area requiring special attention, experience has convinced us that this "specialization" should be treated as an integral part of the broad ecumenical concern. It would be a tactical error to isolate the Orthodox/non-Orthodox axis as if this were a special area on account of the particularity (strangeness, extravagance, conservativism) of Ortho-doxy. The Orthodox must be involved in ecumenical education as a whole, feeling that they are making their contribution to shaping it from within. There cannot be a true exchange of educational experiences, nor can ecumenical education in the service of the Church be truly authentic without the whole-hearted participation of the Orthodox. Unless the Orthodox are accepted without the slightest open or hidden discrimination - aris-ing from the fact that they appear at first sight to be conservative, past-oriented and politically hesitant when confronted with radical liberation theologies - they cannot, however, share to the full extent of their potential in the promotion of ecumenical theological education. Their contribution towards developing a more compre-hensive programme could be most fruitful, due to their global vision of the relationship between nature and grace, Church and world, Church and state. There is a particular qualitative catholicity that Orthodox devotion presupposes and professes in very simply, non-theological terms. Such an existential approach can be of some importance for ecumenical education today.

(137) Ecumenical Formation as a Priority for the Churches in Eastern and Central Europe-Document from Sambata de Sus, Romania Consultation (2008)[1]

Dietrich Werner/Fr. Viorel Ionita

The issue of Ecumenical Formation is a top priority not only for ecumenical organisations but also for all churches. Learning about the relationship to other churches, as well as about the challenges all churches are facing in the world of today is a priority not only for church leaders and ministers, but also for the people of God as a whole. This task is mainly the responsibility of the theological training institutions, which often have other priorities. All these aspects were discussed at a Seminar organised jointly by the Conference of European Churches (CEC) with the Ecumenical Theological Education (ETE) programme of the WCC and in cooperation with the Orthodox Academy from Volos, Greece, from 24-28 September 2008 at the Orthodox Academy of the Brancoveanu Monastery, Sambata de Sus, Romania. Some forty representatives of institutions for theological education, ecumenical institutes and theological educators from 12 different countries of Eastern and Central Europe showed a remarkably new interest, passion and enthusiasm for interdenominational dialogue and ecumenical cooperation in theological education and research. This seminar aimed at bringing together important centres and institutions of ecumenical theological education and to continue some work which had begun with earlier attempts both in the work of ETE in Eastern Europe and with the CEC initiative in the so called Graz process which brings together theological faculties and colleges in both Western and Eastern Europe.

Regarding the historical context of such a seminar in Eastern and Central Europe, it certainly was not easy to arrive at a common understanding of the purpose of it. All participating countries – except Greece – shared more or less a common political history as having come from past decades of communist rule and struggle with recent transformation processes in their societies as well as reviewing and discerning their past. Certainly the social, political und ecclesial realities in Eastern and Central Europe vary considerably from country to country and there is no homogeneous setting at all: the majority churches are either Orthodox or Roman-Catholic or Protestant. The minority churches often do not have an equal status and play different roles in the various national contexts. The process of secularization and de-christianization in some countries is much more advanced or differently shaped than in other countries. There are also great varieties in terms of relationships between church and state in this part of the world which in turn also leads to different models and settings of theological education: there are church-related theological colleges with or without recognition of theological degrees by the state authorities; there are denominational theological faculties at state universities and there are some departments of interdenominational religious studies in state related universities. What has emerged in terms of the institutional framework for theological education, very much depends from different national conditions and also cultural and political contexts.

There was also a genuine feeling that there is a certain *kairos* and new longing for ecumenical cooperation and learning in theological education in many countries of Eastern and Central Europe today. After having suffered for several decades from anti-religious persecutions during the Soviet time and from atheistic policies of communist regimes there is some longing of Christians to go beyond all of that and leave their closed survival mentality and small niche existence. There are new openings, innovative projects and a new openness for dialogue beyond the boundaries of denominational and national identities in almost all of the Eastern and Central European churches – though in several instances these new openings are still a minority phenomenon and not yet a broad popular movement. Despite painful experiences with some culturally and spiritually

[1] This text is from the introduction to: *The Future of Ecumenical Theological Education in Eastern and Central Europe.* Report of the International Seminar for Young Lecturers and professors of theology. Sambata Monastery, Romania, 24-28 September 2008, (Geneva: CEC/WCC/ETE, 2009), 7-13, reprinted with kind permission.

insensitive proselytism, many Christians of all traditions meanwhile have started to work together in social programs, in education programs and in common ecumenical research projects, which also involve Orthodox Churches or their theologians. Concepts which allow only for limited interdenominational cooperation like the concept of 'canonical territory' are reinterpreted afresh from both Protestant, Roman-Catholic and Orthodox perspectives. This concept is now brought into contact with ecumenical ecclesiological dialogues and the tradition of ecclesiology within the Ancient Church of the first centuries in which this concept was grounded in a pastoral, personal and indefectible relation between the bishop and his community.

A key-concept raised at that seminar was the question of how to understand ecumenical learning in terms of deepening a "culture of ecumenical friendship in theological education." "Friendship" was viewed as a category which has some deeper meaning and relevance beyond just a personal relationship. Friendship was seen as rooted in biblical tradition and describing an essential element of what it means to be the church: *"I do not call you servants any longer, because the servants do not know what the master is doing; but I have called you friends, because I have made known to you everything that I have heard from my father."(John 15:15)* This biblical passage is a reminder of the intimate relationship between knowledge and friendship, between theological learning and dialogue with each other. The acquisition of knowledge has been a double edged sword for the history of humanity. It was its arbitrary accumulation that drove human beings to distortion and disruption. Yet in the context of incarnation which restores the fallen creation, knowledge becomes the great gift from God to humanity, leading back to a community of blessedness and inspiration. The gift of knowledge about God thus springs up from a relation and demands a relation to the totally "other" who at the same time can become a friend and this could lead to a *koinonia of friends*. Thus this kind of knowledge, which is rooted in a growing community of friends, will be able to bear fruits of blessing for future generations.

The demand of sharing and communion, in learning and education, becomes an imperative in an era that experiences the challenges of grave tensions and polarizations between religious, political and cultural identities in a globalized world. The gift of knowledge of God, the source of all koinonia, entrusted and handed over to human beings, calls us, perhaps as never before, to come closer to each other as Christians from different confessional and cultural backgrounds. Seen in this perspective, the cooperation and dialogue of theological educators from Eastern and Central Europe was seen as an affirmation that Christianity in its very essence is about unity and reconciliation and only by realizing this can it become a vital source of new energies and inspiring visions for a better future also in a predominantly atheist society like many of those in Eastern and Central Europe. Developing a culture of ecumenical friendship in theological education and deepening processes of ecumenical formation in theological learning and research thus were viewed as a priority vision for the future of theological education in this part of the world which in its history in many ways was marked by extraordinary and manifold religious and cultural, ecclesial and national divisions and fragmentations.

When using the term "ecumenical learning" or "ecumenical education" the seminar in Romania referred to an understanding and manner of theological learning, which
- allows learning from each other beyond our denominational traditions;
- encourages the development of friendship with all members of the wider Christian family;
- prevents us from becoming guided and mislead by readymade stereotypes and distorted images about "the others";
- seeks to understand the others as they understand themselves;
- recognizes that our traditions only together reach the width and depth of Christian theology and contribute to a missionary presence of Christian churches in modern societies;
- is not confusing proper ecumenism with any distorted and false concept of creating a monolithic super-church which would rule over all churches – a concept which never was promoted by the WCC;
- integrates the concern for justice, peace and integrity of creation into the curricula of theological learning.

If it is true that Christian unity, as Karl Barth said, is not a construction of human beings, but a gift which is there already and only needs to be discovered, and that – like the Orthodox Metropolitan Plato (Levchine) of Kiev affirmed powerfully - the walls separating the churches do not go up to heaven, this has consequences for theological education in Eastern European contexts both in its structures and its contents. Ecumenism therefore, before being an academic discipline with its own texts of reference, its epistemological field and its basic concepts, and before being a given set of theological insights and concepts, has some basic spiritual dimensions and is rooted in a basic attitude of an ecumenical ethos or spirituality of ecumenical friendship with the totally "other," who will be recognized as a neighbour and as a friend. Ecumenical Education and Learning from an Eastern European perspective can be practised and deepened only if both are understood as a spiritual attitude, if they relate to a particular personal experience with the living God in the fullness of the fellowship of his churches around the world.

This attitude of ecumenical openness and dialogue needs to be at the root of studying the history of the deep national, confessional and cultural divisions in the Eastern European context and of any attempt to start a process of healing memories and to overcome the damage these divisions have caused for generations. Being students and teachers of theology together requires practical steps and involves some helpful methodological elements, such as

- attending theological courses together with students of different confessional backgrounds;
- exchanges of students and teachers of different confessional backgrounds;
- theological resource books of theologians representing viewpoints from different confessional traditions;
- common projects of theological research and dialogue;
- sharing in each other's diaconical work and social witness;
- attending worship and experiencing spiritual life in other Christian traditions as a way of dialogue and learning.

Participants in the Sambata seminar were convinced that engaging in such ways of ecumenical learning in theological education is not endangering or diluting our individual confessional identities but rather it is deepening our own Christian vocation and affirming our spiritual roots in the wider catholic heritage of the Christian church. In meeting the other we more fully realize who we are ourselves. Therefore participants in this seminar were aware of the fact that in the context of rapid social and political changes in Eastern and Central Europe institutions of theological education can be attentive to their historic responsibility at present only if they seek more common cooperation and more ecumenical commitment. Ecumenical theological education is vital for the future of the church and the dialogue between churches and societies in Eastern and Central Europe. Participants therefore recognized the need to promote ecumenical dialogue in theological education in the curricula of their universities and seminaries as well as in the life of the churches of that region.

There are several pioneering centres of ecumenical education which were created during the last fifteen years in Central and Eastern Europe in order to face and answer the new developments of ecclesial and civil consciousness. If in Georgia and Bulgaria the relation with ecumenism remains conflictual, many teachers in theology or social sciences are sharing in a creative and individual way their interest for the question of Christian unity. In Belarus, the Institute of Saints Methodius and Cyril was created very early in the year of 1990, more or less directly after the political changes in that region, in order to make known the significant ecumenical heritage accumulated by the churches during the Soviet time when the communist governments were not allowing these churches to spread their experiences of the Christian otherness. In Romania, in addition to the constitution of faculties of Orthodox, Catholic or Protestant theology, the Institute of Ecumenical Studies of Sibiu was created in 2005.

In Poland, from Opole to Lublin, many denominational faculties of theology integrated the teaching of ecumenism. In Russia the Theological Institute Saint Andrews in Moscow set up very quickly a vast program of publications in ecumenical research issues and has reached a number of some one hundred annual titles of theological publications each year until today. In the Czech Republic, the Ecumenical Institute affiliated to the University of Prague has about sixty students to whom it offers a master degree in ecumenical studies. In Greece the Orthodox Academy of Volos initiated a vast program of seminars and international conferences on ecumenical issues like the relation between the Church and the world. In Estonia, there is a fascinating project of writing the ecumenical history of the different churches in this country, which would not have been possible during the Soviet time. In Ukraine the Institute of Ecumenical Studies at the Ukrainian Catholic University launched a master program in ecumenical studies in cooperation with the State University Ivan Franco of Lviv. Rejecting at the same time a denominational approach (which the State university does not accept) and an agnostic approach (about which the churches would be worried) the Catholic, Protestant and Orthodox theological teachers of this program propose an open, dialogical and comprehensive formation in the Christian faith. The recognition of the degree by the regional branch of the Ukrainian ministry of education allows the students to teach Christian ethics in the governmental schools. The Institute of Ecumenical Studies also created two distant learning master programs in ecumenical studies in Ukrainian and English languages. This distant learning program in ecumenism could become and constitute a basis of mutual cooperation between the different newly created institutes of ecumenical learning and research in Eastern and Central Europe.

Following the traditional teaching of conciliarity or catholicity ('sobornost') of the Church, these new initiatives and foundations for ecumenical educational programs and research institutes in Eastern and Central Europe develop a remarkable openness and interest to pick up new themes which are relating churches of these regions to global challenges and learning movements like subjects as different as the global warming of the planet, the history of the feminist movement, human rights or the right way of communicating. Today the various new ecumenical structures existing in Central and Eastern Europe seem to look beyond their present stage and further want to explore how to establish a proper network of ecumenical institutes and theological educators in Eastern Europe. The task of such a network should be to promote the contextualization and transformation of theological education in this part of the world, a new "ecumenical awakening" in Eastern Europe, which needs to be recognized and supported by partners from other churches and educational institutions in the West.[2]

European Christianity has been the result of a mission and a plea for help (Acts 16:9). No matter the differences in character, historical and cultural contexts, Eastern and Western Christianity share this common inheritance. This unique theological and historical reality is the fountain of spiritual strength challenging the dominance of materialism, consumerism and secularism of our era. An important number of the theological schools of Eastern and Central Europe – this became obvious in Sambata – have recognized that the Christian vocation requires, more than ever before, working together in mutual understanding and establishing a genuine common basis for mutual cooperation in order to be faithful to the Christian mission. In a fragmented and self-centred world, Christian theology is called to offer the truth of the most genuine friendship, Christ's friendship. The Christian truth which comes as a "sound of sheer silence"(1 Kings 19:12) is called to heal and to reconcile, to support and to encourage the vision of healing and hope for the world.

---

[2] The Network for Ecumenical Learning in Central and Eastern Europe (NELCEE) was created in 2008 and is assisted by the Ecumenical Institute of Sibiu. Contact: Institut für Ökumenische Foschung, Str. Mitropoliei 30, 550179 Sibiu, Romania. Website: www.ecum.ro; Mail-adress: nelcee@ecum.ro. Since 2014 NELCEE network is coordinated by Nikolaos Asproulis, representing the Volos Academy for Theological Studies: e-mail: asprou@acadimia.gr, Contact details:Volos Academy for Theological Studies: P.O Box 1308, Zip Code 38001, Volos-Greece, info@acadimia.gr.

(138) The Future of Orthodox Theological Education and Ecumenism. Communiqué of Sibiu Consultation (2010)

> *...Love should be rekindled and strengthened among the churches,*
> *so that they should no more consider one another as strangers and foreigners,*
> *but as relatives, and as being a part of the household of Christ*
> *and "fellow heirs, members of the same body*
> *and partakers of the promise of God in Christ" (Eph. 3:6).*
> Encyclical of the Ecumenical Patriarchate (1920):
> "To the Churches of Christ Everywhere"

At the initiative of the World Council of Churches, with the blessing of H.B. Patriarch Daniel of Romania and the gracious hospitality of H.E. Metropolitan Prof. Dr Laurentiu of Ardeal, with the collaboration of the Orthodox Theological Faculty "Andrei Saguna" of Sibiu and with H.E. Metropolitan Prof. Dr Gennadios of Sassima (Ecumenical Patriarchate) serving as moderator, representatives from various Eastern Orthodox Churches (Ecumenical Patriarchate, Patriarchate of Alexandria, Patriarchate of Antioch, Moscow Patriarchate, Patriarchate of Romania, Patriarchate of Bulgaria, Church of Cyprus, Church of Greece, Church of Poland, Church of Albania and the Orthodox Church in America), from Oriental Orthodox Churches (Syrian Orthodox Patriarchate of Antioch and All the East, Ethiopian Orthodox Tewahedo Church), from the Conference of European hurches (CEC) and theological institutions met in Sibiu to reflect on and make proposals concerning *"The Ecumenical Movement in Theological Education and in the Life of Orthodox Churches."*

The main purpose of the meeting was to consider how the Orthodox Churches and theological schools have been involved in the modern ecumenical movement from its very beginning, and what steps forward they might take today.

Indeed theological institutions through their professors, educators and graduates, have played a crucial role in the Orthodox participation in the ecumenical movement, and they have contributed significantly in:

a. developing an ecumenical ethos within the Orthodox Churches, by participating in ecumenical gatherings as representatives of their Churches;

b. articulating an Orthodox theological discourse, responding to the major issues and challenges included in the ecumenical agenda;

c. assessing the developments within the ecumenical movement and keeping their Churches, their colleagues and their students regularly informed; and

d. teaching ecumenical studies in educational institutions at different levels.

Theological educators are entrusted by the Churches with the ecumenical- theological formation of the next generations of clergy, church leaders and experienced staff involved in ecumenical work. The future involvement of Orthodox Churches in the ecumenical movement largely depends on the methods, levels and—most crucially—inspiration that theological education will equip future generations.

Thirty hierarchs, priests, university professors, and lay men and women, gathered at the Orthodox Theological Faculty *"Andrei Saguna"* in Sibiu, Romania, 9-12 November 2010 to address this topic.

Conference Proceedings

The Consultation opened in the Chapel of the Orthodox Theological Faculty *"Andrei Saguna"* with a Te Deum service celebrated by H.E. Metropolitan Laurentiu and with the participation of all members, including the Professors and the students of the Faculty. Metropolitan Laurentiu then welcomed the Consultation very warmly. He underlined the important role played by the historical Theological School with its predominant academic and spiritual personalities and teachers of ecumenical theology such as the late Metropolitan Nicolae Bălan, the late Metropolitan Antonie, Fr. Dumitru Stăniloae, Fr. Ioan Bria, all of blessed memory, and many others. He spoke as well about the Faculty's contribution to ecumenical theology and learning over many decades.

Metropolitan Gennadios conveyed the paternal wishes and patriarchal blessings of His All Holiness the Ecumenical Patriarch Bartholomew and wholeheartedly thanked Metropolitan Laurentiu for his generous hospitality. He greeted the participants and expressed the hope that this encounter would become another occasion to further strengthen the existing fraternal links between the Orthodox Churches and that it would enable them to act and speak in a coordinated way as they reflect on the issue of ecumenical education and the deeper participation of the Orthodox Churches in the ecumenical movement. In addition, he mentioned that we are gathered in a historical place, Sibiu, which three years ago as one of the cultural capitals of Europe, a crossroad of cultures and history, a bridge between East and West, had the great privilege to host the Third European Ecumenical Assembly in 2007. The Metropolitanate of Ardeal has a long history of hosting ecumenical gatherings and meetings and this is due to the fact that it has always been open to promoting and facilitating dialogue among the Christian Churches. Metropolitan Gennadios concluded by pointing out that regardless of the unresolved difficulties the Churches face in ecumenical dialogue concerning issues of an ecclesiological, theological and moral nature, they should deliver a clear common witness to the world and to secularized society. This could be done on the basis of the common denominator that is faith in the Triune God and in the saving action of our Lord Jesus Christ. In this way Churches could become agents for renewal and co-builders for the construction of society in whatever part of the world God has placed them.

Along with the discussion and various presentations, the program included prayer and visits to the famous Museums of traditional glass icons.

The conference opened with presentations by Mr George Lemopoulos (Deputy General Secretary, WCC) on "Orthodox Participation in the Ecumenical Movement: Some Questions to Theological Education for Today and Tomorrow/' Very Rev. Prof. Dr Viorel Ionita (Interim General Secretary of CEC) on "The Graz Process and the Implications for Orthodox Theological Institutions," Rev. Dr Dietrich Werner (Ecumenical Theological Education coordinator, WCC) on "Ecumenical Perspectives in Theological Education in Orthodox Contexts," and Rev. Dr. K.M. George on "Theological Education in the Oriental Orthodox Tradition and the Ecumenical Movement," (presented in his absence).

On the last day in the main Hall of the Theological Faculty two keynote addresses were presented by H.E. Metropolitan Prof. Dr Gennadios of Sassima "The Ecumenical Movement in the Life of the Orthodox Churches" and Very Rev. Dr John Jillions (Orthodox Church in America), "The Future of Orthodox Theological Engagement: Traditionalist, Mainstream or Prophetic?", with the participation of Professors of Theological Faculties teaching ecumenical studies from all over Romania. The session raised challenging questions for discussion and further reflection.

Input From Participants

The Consultation invited participants to present a reflection on the following questions:

(1) how are ecumenical studies taught in different Orthodox Churches? There are different ways of teaching ecumenical studies in Orthodox theological institutions. In some countries ecumenical studies are taught as an independent discipline, while elsewhere they are combined with other theological disciplines (e.g. dogmatics, mission) or are included as part of Church history.

The conference also explored different teaching models in order to learn from each other, but also suggested the development of a common model for teaching ecumenical studies.

Each Church is the arena where the results of the ecumenical movement are shared, thought about and debated. The Consultation considered how participation of the Orthodox Churches in the ecumenical movement is presented at the different levels of the Church. This includes how it appears in the Church press and other publications, and how the ecumenical commitment of Orthodox Churches is determined by their contextual reality and *"local ecumenical involvement"*.

(2) the future of ecumenical studies and ecumenical engagement in Orthodox Churches. There has been an Orthodox involvement in the modern ecumenical movement for approximately one century. This involvement provides a certain ecumenical experience that helps us to look to the future. At the same time there are new and burning challenges facing the Orthodox churches as well as the ecumenical movement.

Participants presented the position and experience of their Church in responding to these questions, and this was followed by discussion.

Observations and Suggestions

Inter-Christian and inter-faith issues are at the heart of a lively debate within the Orthodox Churches and touch many aspects not only of theological education, but of global, national, community, family and parish life. While these debates can become polarized, they also reveal a healthy tension between faithfulness to what has been received from Holy Tradition in the past and discerning where the Holy Spirit may be leading the Churches in the present and future. However, while the reports and discussions demonstrated a number of positive developments in the Orthodox Churches and theological schools concerning relations with other Christians and other faiths, there remain serious gaps to address.

1. There is a broad official agreement among the Orthodox Churches concerning the general direction of Orthodox ecumenical engagement. However, at many levels of Church life there is a wide diversity of opinion among the Orthodox concerning inter-Christian and inter-faith issues. This demonstrates that there is as yet no unanimous Orthodox theological understanding of how to relate to other Christians and other faiths. Orthodox Churches should use their theological faculties and seminaries as academic laboratories to generate discussion on acute issues debated in ecumenical circles. An attempt should be made to engage all Orthodox voices in this, especially those who may be most opposed to dialogue. Synergy between Church leadership and theological schools is necessary for the meaningful and credible witness of our churches in society today.

2. Adopting a self-critical approach to its own ecclesial life, in a spirit of humility, is essential for authentic Orthodox dialogue and engagement with other Christians and the faithful of other religions.

3. The Orthodox Churches have profoundly benefitted from the ecumenical movement. It has allowed them to overcome possible temptations to isolation, to meet other Christians and each other and to strengthen fraternal relations, to be introduced to the living thought of other Christians, to explore their own Orthodox mind and voice, to engage in reflection on major global events and social changes, to follow developments in Christian missions worldwide, and to engage in common work for the material and moral betterment of humanity as a whole.

4. In order to improve the level of inter-Christian and inter-faith studies in Orthodox theological schools, to promote understanding and eradicate prejudice, the general level of theological studies must be raised. It is through an objective academic approach and critical analysis that the aims of the ecumenical movement can be better understood and received by Orthodox students of theology. High-level Orthodox theological education was emphasized as testimony to the catholicity of Orthodoxy and a corrective to sectarianism.

5. It was agreed that the study of other Christian churches, other faiths and the ecumenical movement only in the framework of comparative or even polemical apologetics, although still widely practiced, is insufficient for an academically balanced understanding.

Part VIII: Ecumenical Formation in Orthodox Theological Education

6. There is a clear need to develop appropriate, fair-minded, non-polemical Orthodox resources and methodologies for teaching about other Christian churches, other religions and the ecumenical movement.

7. Orthodox theological schools should seek out faculty members from the theological schools of other Christian churches and other religions to present their own perspective on their faith and to interact, dialogue, discuss and debate with Orthodox students and faculty. Visits of Orthodox theological students to the places of worship and theological schools of other churches and faiths should be encouraged.

8. Careful analysis of the particular inter-Christian and inter-faith issues facing Orthodox Churches in specific contexts will mean that the exact shape of ecumenical education will differ from place to place. Even within a single Orthodox Church there can be vastly differing needs in this regard.

9. The importance of including theological students as future pastors and teachers of the church in the process of ecumenical theological reflection, education and exposure was underlined.

10. It is necessary to prepare an Essay book about the history of the ecumenical movement from the Orthodox point of view to be introduced as a part of the teaching curriculum in our theological schools and seminaries.

11. The activities of the WCC, regional ecumenical organizations, national councils of churches and bilateral dialogues must be publicized more thoroughly in local church publications, TV and radio stations, websites etc..

12. Conferences and seminars about inter-Christian and inter-faith dialogue should continue to be organized on national, local, regional and continental levels with attention paid to more effective communication about these meetings to the clergy and faithful of the churches.

13. Initiatives are needed for the training of Orthodox teachers, clergy and laity to be involved competently and with dedication in inter-Christian and inter-faith conversation and activities on behalf of the local Orthodox Churches.

14. Theological institutions should be encouraged to support events on a local and parish level that engage as many people as possible in the Week of Prayer for Christian Unity and other inter-Christian and inter-faith initiatives, including visits to other places of worship. They should also encourage initiatives in organizing common Christian and interfaith ministries addressing social problems and protecting human rights and democracy.

15. More opportunities should be created for Orthodox from as many local Churches as possible to serve in staff positions in ecumenical organizations.

16. The ground-breaking 1920 encyclical of the Ecumenical Patriarchate, *"Unto the Churches of Christ Everywhere"* made special mention of the role that theological schools could play in promoting greater mutual understanding:
    - by relationships between the theological schools and the professors of theology; by the exchange of theological and ecclesiastical reviews, and of other works published in each church.
    - by exchanging students for further training among the seminaries of the different churches.

    This encyclical was produced in collaboration with the faculty of the Patriarchal Theological School at Halki. The consultation expressed the hope that Halki would soon be re-opened so that it could be allowed to once again make a contribution to efforts of inter-Christian and inter-faith collaboration and reconciliation.

17. The Consultation strongly recommends that the WCC in collaboration with Holy Cross Greek Orthodox School of Theology (Boston, USA) coordinate a meeting in the near future to bring together representatives of all Orthodox theological faculties and schools and seminaries of theology to continue to make progress on collaboratively addressing these issues of ecumenical education.

PART IX

APPENDIX:
BIBLIOGRAPHICAL SURVEY ON KEY-TEXTS OF ECUMENISM

(139) INTRODUCTION TO THE BIBLIOGRAPHICAL LIST
OF OFFICIAL ORTHODOX TEXTS ON ECUMENISM

Vassiliki Stathokosta

The Orthodox Church has been active since the very beginning of the ecumenical movement in the early 20th century taking serious initiatives for the rapprochement between Eastern and Western Christianity. At the same time, she has been a decisive factor and a guarantee for the "ecumenical" character of this movement, preventing it from being just a "pan-Protestant" endeavour of the West. Furthermore, the Orthodox participation in the WCC justifies its name as Council of Churches. For the Orthodox the WCC is recognized mostly as a forum where they can give witness of the Orthodox faith, the faith of the One Holy, Catholic and Apostolic Church and work for church unity.

In this Section the official documents of the Orthodox are selected and presented, giving the reader the possibility to study directly and in full detail the position the Orthodox Church kept all these years towards the WCC. We propose an arrangement of these texts according their origin and their context as following:

I. Patriarchic Letters (Encyclicals) on the ecumenical movement
II. Decisions of Pan-Orthodox Conferences and decisions of Pre-Conciliar Pan-Orthodox Conferences
III. Orthodox Statements and Orthodox Contributions in General Assemblies and FO meetings
IV. Other significant Messages and Declarations by Orthodox Churches or Prelates
V. Reports of Inter-Orthodox Consultations
VI. Documents related to the Special Commission on the Orthodox participation in the WCC

I. Patriarchal Letters (Encyclicals) on the Ecumenical Movement

Despite the difficult situation Orthodoxy experienced in the East from the 15th to 19th century, as subjected to Turkish occupation, the Ecumenical Patriarchate was always aware of the developments and the process of Christianity in the West, waiting for the right time, the "kairos," to come for their rapprochement.

It was in the begging of the 20th century that the Ecumenical Patriarchate undertook the initiative to act on matters of Christian unity: two official letters were addressed to the Orthodox Patriarchates and the Autocephalous Churches during the Patriarchate of Joachim III, known as the Patriarchal and Synodical Encyclicals of 1902-1904, that due to their content are considered and studied as one.

Although the primary purpose of this Encyclical was to ensure canonical order and unity within Orthodoxy, a careful study shows another important dimension concerning inter-Christian relations and Church unity.[1] This Encyclical of 1902-1904 expresses disapproval for the fragmentation of Christianity, demonstrates the Orthodox perception of the Church and puts forward the question of finding ways to facilitate the meeting of the Churches. Furthermore, the Encyclical determines the method that the Orthodox Churches should follow approaching the heterodox 'walking in wisdom and in the spirit of gentleness towards those who disagree with us, and remembering that they too believe in the All-Holy

---

[1] Vassiliki El. Stathokosta, *The relationship between the Church of Greece and the World Council of Churches, 1948-1961, based on the Archives of the WCC*, (PhD diss. in Greek, University of Thessaloniki, 1999) (in Greek). See also Vassiliki El. Stathokosta, "Relations between the Orthodox and the Anglicans in the Twentieth Century: A Reason to Consider the Present and the Future of the Theological Dialogue," in *Ecclesiology* 8 (2012): 350-374.

Trinity and glory, in the name of our Lord Jesus Christ and hope to be saved by the grace of God.'[2] Serious obstacles as proselytism are underlined as well, yet not inhibiting and not insurmountable for inter-Christian relations.[3]

A similar approach is noticed once again, and in a more systematic way on behalf of the Ecumenical Patriarchate almost twenty years later, in 1920, when it addresses a new Encyclical to "all Churches of Christ." With this new Encyclical the Ecumenical Patriarchate went further and urged the issue of inter-Christian cooperation as it introduced a certain plan for the formation of a "Koinonia of Churches" according the example of the "Koinonia (League) of Nations," offering at the same time concrete suggestions for Church cooperation. This Encyclical is considered the Constitution of the Orthodox participation in the ecumenical movement.

In 1952, another Encyclical was addressed by the Ecumenical Patriarchate prior to the 3nd Conference of FO in Lund. This time the Patriarchal Encyclical aimed to deal with the question of the character of the Orthodox participation in the WCC. It takes into consideration that already in 4 February 1945, the Orthodox Churches had replied positively to the fundamental question "whether our Most Holy Orthodox Church should or should not participate in the work and conferences of the World Council."[4] Based on this positive decision and on the study of all the documents and reactions following the 1st Assembly in Amsterdam (1948), the Encyclical of 1952 deals with certain questions and reservations expressed concerning the way the WCC was developed and the position of the Orthodox towards it. Moreover, it urges for responsible participation and it defines the method of inter-Orthodox cooperation for a most effective Orthodox participation in the WCC.

These three Patriarchal Encyclicals (1902-1904, 1920 and 1952) are invitations the Ecumenical Patriarchate addressed to "all Churches of Christ":

- to work together for Church unity
- to evaluate problems and perspectives on inter-Church relation
- to offer a certain method for inter-Church cooperation
- to express reservations, put the limits and presuppositions concerning the Orthodox participation in the ecumenical movement and the WCC
- to manifest certain expectations the Orthodox have from the WCC and the member churches, and last but not least
- to reflect and manifest the consciousness of the Orthodox Church as the One, Holy, Catholic and Apostolic Church.

We include in the same section the "Declaration of the Ecumenical Patriarchate on the Occasion of the Twenty-Fifth Anniversary of the WCC, 1973," the Message of the Ecumenical Patriarchate on the Occasion of the Fortieth Anniversary of the WCC, Phanar, 1988 and the Message of the Primates of the Most Holy Orthodox Churches, Phanar, 1992, as these three texts have mostly the same characteristics as an Encyclical.

All these are documents of the Ecumenical Patriarchate and they express the Orthodox official attitude towards the WCC.

---

[2] Op. cit.

[3] See V. Stathokosta, *Η διαμόρφωση των οικουμενικών σχέσεων στην Ελλάδα. Ζητήματα προσηλυτισμού και θρησκευτικής ελευθερίας στη μεταπολεμική Ελλάδα (από το 1948 έως τα μέσα της δεκαετίας του '60)*, (εκδόσεις Παρατηρητής, Θεσσαλονίκη 2003) [The formation of the ecumenical relations in Greece. Issues of proselytism and religious liberty in post-war Greece (1948 until the mid-sixties), ("Parateretis," Thessaloniki, 2003)] (in Greek).

[4] See the text of the "Encyclical of the Ecumenical Patriarchate, 1952" in Limouris Gennadios (ed.), *Orthodox Visions of Ecumenism, Statements, Messages and Reports on the Ecumenical Movememnt, 1902-1992*, (Geneva: WCC Publications, 1994), 20-22. Original text in Greek in V. Istavridis and Ev. Varella (eds), Ιστορία της Οικουμενικής Κινήσεως (History of the Ecumenical Movement) (Thessaloniki: Patriarchal Institute of Patristic Studies, 1996), 336-339

II. Decisions of Pan-Orthodox Conferences
and Pre-Conciliar Pan-Orthodox Conferences

The second section of this chapter includes the decisions of:

a) *Pan-Orthodox Conferences*:

These were meetings held by the initiative of the Ecumenical Patriarchate in order to improve inter-Orthodox relations and inter-church cooperation as well. These Conferences were held in Rhodos/Greece (1961, 1962 and 1963) and in Chambesy/Geneva (1968). Of great importance for the Orthodox participation in the ecumenical movement are the decisions of the First and the Fourth Pan-Orthodox Conferences, held in 1961 (Rhodes) and in 1968 (Chambesy) respectively.

b) *Pre-Conciliar Pan-Orthodox Conferences*:

Following to the Pan-Orthodox Conferences, the Pre-Conciliar Pan-Orthodox Conferences are occasional meetings of the Orthodox Church the Ecumenical Patriarchate invites having the consensus of the Prelates of the local Autocephalous and Autonomous Orthodox Churches. The purpose of these Conferences is the preparation of the Holy and Great Synod that is going to be held in a future time[5] and in an appropriate "kairos."

The importance of their decisions is of great importance as they express the Orthodox tradition and consensus on certain matters and they shape the Orthodox position towards the ecumenical movement. Still, it is the Holy and Great Synod who has the authority to confirm these decisions. Of great importance are the ones of the Third Pre-conciliar Pan-Orthodox Conference on the Orthodox Church and the Ecumenical Movement, held in Chambesy, Switzerland, 1986.

III. Orthodox Statements and Contributions

A. *Orthodox Statements to FO and WCC General Assemblies*:

Orthodox Statements are certain texts the Orthodox representatives in the FO and WCC Assemblies used to submit, in order to express the Orthodox point of view with clarity and to differentiate themselves from the Protestant understanding concerning Church unity. Evidently, this need was urgent mostly at the congresses of FO and its dogmatic discussions. The first Orthodox Statement was submitted at the first congress of FO (Lausanne 1927). The Orthodox delegations kept on this same method for some years up to the 3nd General Assembly in New Delhi (1961).

In order to understand better what the Statements are about, it is necessary to underline that there were several good reasons in ecumenical gatherings dictating the submission of a separate Statement by the Orthodox representatives. In general, those reasons were as following:

a) The Orthodox had a special sense of responsibility: the absence of the greater part of Orthodox Churches until 1961 from the WCC and until 1963 from the FO left the Greek Orthodox alone to represent Orthodoxy. They were not numerically enough to participate in all sections and committees of the WCC so the Orthodox point of view was not possible to be heard enough. It was this sense of responsibility that dictated the submission of an Orthodox Statement at least at the early steps of the FO movement and the WCC.

b) The anglo-saxon way of thought and work of the majority of the participants that prevailed during the meetings and it was much different than the Eastern - Orthodox way. The submission of a Statement was often necessary in order to reinforce the Orthodox presence and voice in the midst of a majority of the other participants who were of Protestant origin.

---

[5] See Κανονισμός Λειτουργία Προσυνοδικών Πανορθοδόξων Διασκέψεων στα Τελικά κείμενα-αποφάσεις της Γ› Προσυνοδικής Πανορθοδόξου Διασκέψεως (28 Οκτωβρίου - 6 Νοεμβρίου *1986*), "Επίσκεψις," Αριθμ. 366 (15.12.1989), σ. 21 κ.ε. (in Greek) ["Regulation of the Pre-Conciliar Pan-Orthodox Conferences in *Final Texts – Decisions of the III Pre-Conciliar Pan-Orthodox Conferences* (28 Oct. – 6 Nov. 1986)", in *Episkepsis* 366 (1989): 21ff.

Part IX: Appendix: Bibliographical Survey on Key-Texts of Ecumenism

c) The use of an "ecumenical language and disposition," that could be interpreted either as an intentional effort to cover up disagreements among the Churches, or as a "compromise of things that could not be compromised."[6] Furthermore, there was always a risk of inability for true communication due to different mentalities of the participants. Often it was noticed that certain terms could have a different meaning for Protestants and Orthodox. So, the Orthodox had to clarify in a separate document their point of view.

d) The difficulty of a proper preparation of the Orthodox delegation plus the one of the selection and nomination of the right persons as representatives, at least concerning the Church of Greece, made a hard situation even harder.[7] At a moment of a strict criticism on behalf of the Orthodox, this method of Statements followed until the New Delhi Assembly was interpreted as "a consequence of inconsistencies and discontinuity … an easy solution … -what could be more easy- disapproval of every non-Orthodox." According to the same point of view, the Orthodox contribution would be more positive if, instead of submitting a Statement, the Orthodox participants in the theological discussions had taken care to be adequately prepared in advance.[8]

e) Strong scaremongering on the part of anti-ecumenical cycles contributed to the consolidation of this method of writing and submitting a separate Statement, as no one risked the possibility to have his Orthodox belief under question.[9]

Eventually, all the above mentioned reasons led to the adoption of this special method of Statements for a certain time, as the only means for the presentation of the Orthodox point of view and the preservation of its specific characteristics. Anyhow, this certain method was not against the rules of the WCC, according to which there could be a possibility for a member church to differentiate and to point out its opinions and write them down at the minutes of the Assembly.

Certainly, the texts of the Statements:

- constitute a presentation of the Orthodox principles and official positions towards the ecumenical movement and the endeavour for Church unity as well as for individual doctrinal issues discussed in ecumenical conferences.
- express the settled position of the Orthodox, that a safe basis for any discussion is the doctrine of the ancient Church, "as it is found in the Holy Scripture, the Creed, the decisions of the ecumenical Synods and the teaching of the Fathers and in the worship and whole life of the undivided Church."[10]
- their main characteristic is that they provide affirmation for the positive attitude of the Orthodox Church towards the whole effort.[11]

---

[6] A Greek theologian of that time, Prof. V. Ioannidis considered as "ecumenical language and disposition" the use of certain ambiguous expressions in order to disguise the differences. According to Prof. Ioannidis, this was an explicit application of saying "si duo dicunt idem non est idem". See Vassileios Ioannidis, Η εν Ν. Δελχί Συνέλευσις του ΠΣΕ, *16 Νοεμβ. – 6 Δεκ. 1961*, Ανάτυπον εκ του περιοδικού "Εκκλησία," Αθήνα 1963, σ. 74 (The New Delhi Assembly of the WCC, 16 Nov. – 6 Dec. 1961, Offprint of "Ecclesia," Athens 1963) (in Greek).

[7] It is a common appreciation of almost all Greek theologians of that period, who served as members of the delegation of the Church of Greece in Assemblies of the WCC, who usually noticed that some Orthodox delegates were not well prepared for such a duty. See indicatively Ger. Konidaris, Η θέσις της Καθολικής Ορθοδόξου Εκκλησίας εν τη «Κοινωνία των Εκκλησιών» (Ανάτυπον εκ της "Θεολογίας", τόμ. Κ´ 1949), (Αθήνα 1949), 37 (The place of the Catholic Orthodox Church in the "Koinonia of Churches," Offprint of "Ecclesia," Athens 1949) (in Greek). Besides, a similar remark was the one of Metropolitan of Theiatyron Germanos Strenopoulos at Amsterdam. See V. Istavridis and Ev. Varella (eds), Ιστορία της Οικουμενικής Κινήσεως (*History of the Ecumenical Movement*) (Thessaloniki: Patriarchal Institute of Patristic Studies, 1996), 79-80 (in Greek).

[8] Δεσμευτικαί υποχρεώσεις, στο "Μηνιαίο Δελτίο της Αντιπροσωπείας του Οικουμενικού Πατριαρχείου παρά του Π.Σ.Ε.", αριθ. 47, Νοέμ.-Δεκ. 1961

[9] See Vassiliki Stathokosta, 'The relationship between the Church of Greece and the World Council of Churches, 1948-1961, based on the Archives of the WCC' (PhD diss. in Greek, University of Thessaloniki, 1999, 299 ff.)

[10] See the Statement of the Orthodox in Edinburgh, 1937.

[11] See the Statement of the Orthodox in Lausanne (1927): "we beg to assure the Conference that we have derived much comfort here from the experience that, although divided by dogmatic differences, we are one with our brethren here in

- do not include any accusation against other church members of the WCC. A possible exception might be the Statement submitted in the FO meeting during the Evanston Assembly that ends like this: "we are bound to declare our profound conviction that the Holy Orthodox Church alone has preserved in full and intact 'the faith once delivered unto the saints.' It is not because of our human merit, but because it pleases God to preserve 'his treasure in earthen vessels, that the excellency of the power may be of God'" (2 Cor. 4:7).[12]

Other characteristics of the Statements[13] are the following:

a) Reference to the conviction that the Orthodox Church is the unbroken continuation of the apostolic and undivided Church,

b) the Orthodox opposition to the use of vague and abstract language,

c) the disagreement to references concerned an "invisible" Church as the one united and holy, and the presentation of the Orthodox teaching that "the Orthodox Church believes that by its essential characteristic, the Church on earth is visible and that only one true Church can be visible and exist on earth,"[14]

d) the proclamation of faith in the tradition of the ancient undivided Church of the seven Ecumenical Councils and the first eight centuries,

e) the position that " intercommunio" should be understood as the crowning of genuine and real unity through the agreement in faith and church administration,[15]

e) the conviction that the "general reunion of Christian Churches may possibly be hastened if union is first achieved between those Churches which present features of great similarity with one another" (Statement of 1937),

f) the opinion that individual theological opinions have no absolute value themselves, but it is mostly the whole Church, clergy and laity, and especially the Hierarchy as it is expressed in the Holy Synod and under the guidance of the Holy Spirit,[16]

g) the demand for condemnation of proselytism among the member churches of the WCC.[17]

In general, the method of Statements caused the reaction of the heterodox, either positive[18] or negative.[19] depending on their confessional background. It is certain that the Statements underlined that churches had a long way to walk until their unity. However, the Statements should not be interpreted as being against neither the ecumenical movement nor the other member churches. Instead, they should be understood as reminding them all about their common heritage.[20]

The above estimation is confirmed by the fact that this method of Statements was abandoned from N. Delhi onwards. The year 1961 is considered as a landmark in the history of the ecumenical movement as the Orthodox presence in WCC was reinforced on the one hand and many misunderstandings were solved on the other. For example, it was made clear that FO programme was a "call for unity" and not an effort for union in a new confessional form.

---

faith in our Lord and Saviour Lord Jesus Christ." Also in the Statement of the Orthodox in Edinburgh, 1937 they declared that "we are constrained and rejoice to utter a few words by which to emphasize the great spiritual profit which we have drawn from our daily intercourse with you, the representatives of other Christian Churches".

[12] Statement concerning FO in Evanston Assembly (1954) see Patelos, Patelos (ed.), *The Orthodox Church in the Ecumenical Movement, Documents and Statements 190-1975)*, (WCC, 1978), 93-96.

[13] Cf. Nikos A. Nissiotis, *The programme of the Faith and Order*, (1986), 135-159; Nikos Matsoukas, *Ecumenical Movement, History - Theology*, (Thessloniki: P. Pournaras, 1986), 243 (in Greek).

[14] See the Statement of the Orthodox in Edinburgh (1937), in Constantin Patelos (ed.), *The Orthodox Church in the Ecumenical Movement, Documents and Statements 190-1975)*, (WCC, 1978), 83-86 (84).

[15] See the Statement of the Orthodox in Edinburgh (1937), op.cit, 139.

[16] See the Statement of the Orthodox in Lund (1952), op.cit, 142.

[17] See the Statement of the Orthodox in Lund (1952), op.cit, 143.

[18] See Vassiliki Stathokosta, 'The relationship between the Church of Greece and the World Council of Churches, 1948-1961, based on the Archives of the WCC' (PhD diss. in Greek, University of Thessaloniki, 1999, 304.

[19] Op.cit.

[20] Cf. N. Nissiotis, *The programme of the Faith and Order*, 135-159 (151).

Part IX: Appendix: Bibliographical Survey on Key-Texts of Ecumenism

Furthermore, we should underline that the Orthodox managed to contribute essentially to all critical discussions and they avoided the risk of submitting a Statement in really crucial discussions even as the ones related to BEM. Their work has been marvelous as they even managed to introduce their own theological terminology in the official FO documents, so that it was some Protestants feeling marginalized that time and thinking of submitting a statement of their own.[21] Another factor for this Orthodox attitude should be taken into consideration and it has to do with a change in the position of the Roman Catholic Church that it turned to be positive towards FO.

B. *Orthodox Contributions to WCC General Assemblies*:

The Orthodox abandoned the method of Statements in 1961, as in New Delhi their participation was numerically larger than before, due to the entrance of the Orthodox Churches of the Eastern countries. It was their common decision to present the Orthodox point of view at the various sections and committees of the Assembly rather than writing them down at a separate document.

Actually, several other factors had contributed to this decision: a self criticism of the Orthodox according to which their contribution in the ecumenical movement should not be limited to grand declarations about the good will of the Orthodox Church to participate. But, it was necessary that certain initiatives for active involvement and substantial contribution to the effort for collaboration with other Christians should be undertaken.[22]

It was in this context that a solution was found in New Delhi so that the Orthodox did not submit a Statement on the one hand, and at the same time present the Orthodox position on Church unity. That solution was the submission by certain Orthodox delegates -those participated in one of its Committees, the one on Unity- of a text called Contribution that was not included in the official report of the Assembly. And this was exactly the difference of a Statement.[23]

From New Delhi (1961) to Canberra (1991) the Orthodox managed to avoid submitting a separate text. They worked mostly on presenting the Orthodox point of view in the various sections and committees of the WCC General Assemblies. It is worth mentioning that in Canberra the Orthodox had to express their concern that the discussion on Pneumatology, as it was developed by a certain group in the WCC still a minority, was misleading and long distanced from the teaching of the Church. That very text was called "Reflections of the Orthodox participants."[24]

Later on, the Orthodox would find other methods to empower their presence and point out the Orthodox perception of Church unity: inter-Orthodox meetings organized in order to study certain issues of the WCC agenda are a significant contribution to its work; similarly, the work of the Special Commission on Orthodox participation in the WCC aims to the same direction.

IV. Other Significant Messages and Declarations by Orthodox Churches or Prelates

In this Section significant messages and declarations by Orthodox Churches and Prelates, mostly on behalf of the Ecumenical Patriarchate and the Russian Orthodox Church, are included as representing serious estimations on the Orthodox – WCC relation.

[21] N. Nissiotis, *The programme of the Faith and Order*, 135-159 (152).

[22] "Orthodox Christians should realize that it is time to stop advertising their "ecumenical disposition" and the democratic way of church administration and start working in order to meet their brothers". See Αρχιεπίσκοπος Βορείου και Νοτίου Αμερικής Ιάκωβος (Archbishop of North and South America Iakovos), Η ενότης των χριστιανικών Εκκλησιών (The unity of Christian Churches) (Offsprint from "Orthodoxos Paratiritis", vol Apr. 1961), (New York 1961), 23.

[23] See Vassiliki Stathokosta, 'The relationship between the Church of Greece and the World Council of Churches, 1948-1961, based on the Archives of the WCC' (PhD diss. in Greek, University of Thessaloniki, 1999), 301-302.

[24] «Σκέψεις των ορθοδόξων συνέδρων»: Δήλωση των Ορθοδόξων και μη Χαλκηδονίων Ορθοδόξων στην Ζ΄ Γενική Συνέλευση του Π.Σ.Ε., in Yorgo Lemopoulos (ed.), *Η Ζ΄ Γενική Συνέλευση*, (The 7th Assembly of the WCC), 77-82 (§ 5, 80-81) (in Greek).

V. Reports of Inter-Orthodox Consultations

In this Section are reports on various Orthodox meetings organized mostly on the initiative of the WCC in collaboration with the Orthodox Church, in order to enable the Orthodox to study and express their Orthodox perspective in matters of common interest such as unity, mission, women participation in the Church etc.

Usually, these meetings are held before an important meeting or Assembly of the WCC and at a different place that one of the Assembly. There are several such meetings called "Orthodox Contribution" referring actually to the impact the Orthodox study done prior to the Assembly could bring in its main theme, by stimulating reflection on it. It is evident that these contributions are different than the "Contribution" the Orthodox submitted to Assemblies like the one in New Dehli.

VI. Documents Related to the Special Commission
on Orthodox Participation in the WCC

These documents reflect the concerns, problems and claims the Orthodox had related to their participation in the WCC since its very beginning.

Mostly, it was following the Harare Assembly and the way Pneumatology was understood and expressed by certain participants that urged the submission of an Orthodox text called "Reflections of the Orthodox participants." That was the time the Orthodox decided not only to express their concern and bring to the surface their disagreements with certain aspects of the WCC but to move further asking for certain changes in the WCC structure and way of work in order to cope with the Orthodox demands.

In 1999, a Special Commission was set up with equal Orthodox and WCC representatives who worked on issues related to what the WCC is and what its task should be, as well as of ecclesiology, social and ethical issues, common prayer, the way of taking decisions and membership.[25] The documents of these meetings are presented in this section.

---

[25] Grand Protopresbyter Georges Tsetsis, *Introduction to the "Special Commission": The Origins and the Work of the "Special Commission on the Orthodox Participation in the WCC"*; Yorgo Lemopoulos, *Special Commission on the Orthodox Participation in the World Council of Churches: Theological Evaluation of its Individual Issues*, Papers presented at the International Scientific Conference "Theological Studies and Ecumene - With reference to the participation of the Orthodox Church to the Inter-Christian Dialogues and their future," Inter-Orthodox Center of Penteli/Athens, 12-13 March 2012 (not published yet).

Part IX: Appendix: Bibliographical Survey on Key-Texts of Ecumenism

(140) Official Orthodox Texts on Ecumenism – A Bibliographical List (Digital Reader of Official Reference Texts - CD ROM)[1]

Vassiliki Stathokosta

I. Patriarchal Letters (Encyclicals) on the Ecumenical Movement

- The Patriarchal Encyclicals of 1902-1904
  a. Patriarchal and Synodical Encyclical of 1902 (Limouris, pp. 1-5)
  b. Response to the Reactions of the local Orthodox Churches, 1904 (Limouris, pp. 5-8)
- Encyclical of the Ecumenical Patriarchate "Unto the Churches of Christ everywhere", 1920 (Limouris, pp. 9-11)
- Encyclical of the Ecumenical Patriarchate, 1952 (Limouris, pp. 20-22)
- Declaration of the Ecumenical Patriarchate on the Occasion of the Twenty-Fifth Anniversary of the WCC, 1973 (Limouris, pp. 50-54)
- Message of the Ecumenical Patriarchate on the Occasion of the Fortieth Anniversary of the WCC, Phanar, 1988 (Limouris, pp. 131-132)
- Message of the Primates of the Most Holy Orthodox Churches, Phanar, 1992 (Limouris, pp. 195-198)

II. Decisions of Pan-Orthodox Conferences and Decisions of Pre-Conciliar Pan-Orthodox Conferences

- First Pan-Orthodox Conference, Rhodes, 1961 (Limouris, pp. 32-33)
- Fourth Pan-Orthodox Conference, Chambesy, 1968 (Limouris, pp. 38-39)
- Decisions of the Third Pre-Conciliar Pan-Orthodox Conference on the Orthodox Church and the Ecumenical Movement, Chambesy, Switzerland, 1986 (Limouris, pp. 112-115, also in WCC website: *Third Pan-Orthodox Pre-Conciliar Conference, Chambésy, 1986, Section III of the report*, http://www.oikoumene.org/en/resources/documents/wcc-programmes/ecumenical-movement-in-the-21st-century/member-churches/special-commission-on-participation-of-orthodox-churches/first-plenary-meeting-documents-december-1999/third-panorthodox-preconciliar-conference.html)

III. Orthodox Statements and Orthodox Contributions

A. Orthodox Statements to FO and WCC Assemblies:

- First World Conference on Faith and Order, Lausanne, 1927 (Patelos, pp. 79-82)
- Second World Conference on Faith and Order, Edinburgh, 1937 (Patelos, pp. 83-86)
- Third World Conference on Faith and Order, Lund, 1952 (Patelos, pp. 87-90)
- Second Assembly of the World Council of Churches, Evanston, 1954
  a. General Statement on the main theme of the Assembly, "Christ – the Hope of the World" (Patelos, pp. 91-93)
  b. Statement concerning the Faith and Order (Patelos, pp. 94-96)

---

[1] In the attached Digital Reader of Official Texts, a broader selection of historical orthodox reference texts is available.

B. Orthodox Contributions to WCC Assemblies:

- Contribution to the Section of the Assembly dealing with the unity of the Church (Third Assembly of the World Council of Churches, New Delhi, 1961) (Patelos, pp. 97-98)
- Reflections of Orthodox Participants Addressed to the Seventh Assembly of the WCC, Canberra, Australia, 1991 (Limouris, pp. 177-179)

IV. Other Significant Messages and Declarations by Orthodox Churches or Prelates

- Resolution on the Ecumenical Question, Moscow, USSR, 1948 (Limouris, pp. 18-19)
- Address by His All Holiness Athenagoras I, Ecumenical Patriarch, on the Occasion of His Visit to WCC Headquarters, 1967 (Limouris, pp. 34-37)
- The Russian Orthodox Church and the Ecumenical Movement by Metropolitan Nikodim (1969) (Limouris, pp. 40-49)
- Statement addressed by the Ecumenical Patriarch Dimitrios to Rev. Dr Ph. Potter, General Secretary of WCC, on the Occasion of the Twenty-Fifth Anniversary of the WCC, 1973 (Patelos, pp. 57-58)
- Message of Patriarch Pimen of Moscow and All Russia and the Holy Synod of the Russian Orthodox Church to the Central Committee of the WCC, 1973 (Patelos, pp. 47-52)
- Address by His Holiness Dimitrios I, Ecumenical Patriarch, on the Occasion of His Visit to the WCC, 1987 (Limouris, pp. 127-130)
- Basic Principles of the Attitude of the Russian Orthodox Church toward the other Christian Confessions', 2000 (http://www.orthodox.cn/contemporary/20000814basicprinciples/basicprinciples_encn.pdf)
- Speech of His Beatitude Archbishop Christodoulos of Athens and All Greece, 30 may 2006, Embargoed against delivery, Given at the dinner in his honour by the general secretary of the WCC, Rev. Dr Samuel Kobia http://www.oikoumene.org/es/documentacion/documents/other-meetings/visits/archbishop-christodoulos/archbishop-christodoulos-speech-at-wcc-dinner.html
- Homily by the Ecumenical Patriarch H.A.H. Bartholomew at the 60th anniversary of the World Council of Churches, Saint Pierre Cathedral, Geneva, 17 February 2008, http://www.oikoumene.org/en/resources/documents/central-committee/geneva-2008/reports-and-documents/homily-by-the-ecumenical-patriarch-hah-bartholomew.html

V. Reports of Inter-Orthodox Consultations

- Reports of three Orthodox Consultations organized on the initiative of the WCC in cooperation with the Orthodox Church as preparatory for the Fifth Assembly of the WCC, Nairobi, Kenya, 1975, as following:
  a. Consultation on "Education in the Orthodox Church", Holland, 1972 (Patelos, pp. 101-102)
  b. Consultation on "Confessing Christ Today", Rumania, 1974 (Patelos, 103-115)
  c. Consultation on "the Church's Struggle for Justice and Unity", Crete/Greece, 1975 (Patelos, 116-124)
- Report of an Inter-Orthodox Consultation on "Confessing Christ through the Liturgical Life of the Church Today", Etchmiadzine, Armenia, 1975 (Limouris, pp. 55-59)
- Report of an Inter-Orthodox Consultation on "Orthodox Women: Their Role and Participation in the Orthodox Church", Agapia, Romania, 1976 (Limouris, pp. 60-65)
- Report of an Inter-Orthodox Consultation on "The Ecumenical Nature of Orthodox Witness", New Valamo, Finland, 1977 (Limouris, pp. 66-69)
- Report from the Work Groups of an Inter-Orthodox Consultation on "An Orthodox Approach to Diaconia", Chania, Crete, 1978 (Limouris, pp. 69-73)

Part IX: Appendix: Bibliographical Survey on Key-Texts of Ecumenism

- Summary of the Conclusions of an Inter-Orthodox Consultation on "The Place of the Monastic Life within the Witness of the Church Today", Amba Bishoy Monastery, Egypt, 1979 (Limouris, pp. 74-78)
- "Your Kingdom Come!": Orthodox Contribution to the Theme of the World Conference on Mission and Evangelism, Melbourne, 1980 (Limouris, pp. 79-86)
- Report of an Eastern Orthodox-WCC Consultation on "Orthodox Involvement in the World Council of Churches", Sofia, Bulgaria, 1981 (Limouris, pp. 87-94 and http://www.oikoumene.org/en/resources/documents/wcc-programmes/ecumenical-movement-in-the-21st-century/member-churches/special-commission-on-participation-of-orthodox-churches/first-plenary-meeting-documents-december-1999/sofia-consultation.html
- "Jesus Christ – the Life of the Word". Orthodox Contribution to the Theme of the Sixth Assembly of the WCC, Damascus 1982 – Vancouver 1983 (Limouris, pp. 95-104)
- Report of an Inter-Orthodox Symposium on "Baptism, Eucharist and Ministry", Boston, USA, 1985 (Limouris, pp. 105-109)
- An Orthodox Statement on the Prague Consultation by the V. Rev. Dr. G. Dragas, Dr D. Koukoura and V. Rev. Dr. G. Limouris (Limouris, pp. 110-111)
- Report of an Inter-Orthodox Consultation on "Orthodox Perspectives on Creation", Sofia, Bulgaria, 1987 (Limouris, pp. 116-126)
- Conclusions of an Inter-Orthodox Consultation on "The Place of the Woman in the Orthodox Church and the Question of the Ordination of Women", Rhodes, Greece, 1988 (Limouris, pp. 133-140)
- Report of an Inter-Orthodox Consultation "Your will be done: Orthodoxy in Mission", Neapolis/Greece, 1988 (Limouris, pp. 141-149)
- Report of an Inter-Orthodox Consultation on Orthodox Perspectives on Justice and Peace, Minsk, USSR, 1989 (Limouris, pp. 150-157)
- Orthodox Letter to the WCC Conference on Mission and Evangelism, San Antonio, USA, 1989 (Limouris, pp. 158)
- Report of an Inter-Orthodox Consultation on "Come, Holy Spirit – Renew the Whole Creation: An Orthodox Approach", Crete, Greece, 1989 (Limouris, pp. 159-170)
- Message of His Holiness Dimitrios I, Ecumenical Patriarch, on the Day of the Protection of the Environment, 1989 (Limouris, pp. 171-172)
- Eastern and Oriental Orthodox Contribution at the World Convocation on Justice, Peace and the Integrity of Creation, Seoul, Korea, 1990 (Limouris, pp. 173-176)
- Report of an Inter-Orthodox Consultation on "Renewal in Orthodox Worship", Bucharest, Romania, 1991 (Limouris, pp. 180-185)
- Conclusions and Recommendations of an Inter-Orthodox Conference on Environmental Protection, Chania, Greece, 1991 (Limouris, pp. 186-188)
- Report of an Inter-Orthodox Consultation of Orthodox WCC Member Churches on "The Orthodox Churches and the WCC", Chambesy, Switzerland, 1991 (Limouris, pp. 189-194)
- Inter - Orthodox Consultation for a Response to the Faith and Order Study: The Nature And Mission of the Church, A Stage on the Way to a Common Statement (Faith and Order Paper 198, 2005 WCC), Agia Napa/Paralimni, Cyprus, 2-9 March 2011, http://www.oikoumene.org/en/press-centre/news/NapaReport.pdf

VI. Documents Related to the Special Commission
on Orthodox Participation in the WCC

- The Thessaloniki statement, Thessaloniki, Greece, May 1998 *http://www.oikoumene.org/en/resources/documents/wcc-programmes/ecumenical-movement-in-the-21st-century/member-churches/special-com-*

mission-on-participation-of-orthodox-churches/first-plenary-meeting-documents-december-1999/thessaloniki-statement.html
- The Damascus report Orthodox Pre-Assembly meeting, Ma'arat Saydnaya, Syria, May 1998 http://www.oikoumene.org/en/resources/documents/wcc-programmes/ecumenical-movement-in-the-21st-century/member-churches/special-commission-on-participation-of-orthodox-churches/first-plenary-meeting-documents-december-1999/damascus-report.html
- Orthodox participation in the WCC. The current situation: issues and ways forward Orthodox Task Force, September 1998, http://www.oikoumene.org/en/resources/documents/wcc-programmes/ecumenical-movement-in-the-21st-century/member-churches/special-commission-on-participation-of-orthodox-churches/first-plenary-meeting-documents-december-1999/orthodox-participation-in-the-wcc.html
- Foundations for the Special Commission Executive Committee Doc. 5.1, Harare, Zimbabwe, December 1998, http://www.oikoumene.org/en/resources/documents/wcc-programmes/ecumenical-movement-in-the-21st-century/member-churches/special-commission-on-participation-of-orthodox-churches/first-plenary-meeting-documents-december-1999/foundations-for-the-special-commission.html
- Preliminary Orthodox proposals for an unimpeded participation in the WCC A record of the proposals emerging from the preparatory meeting of the Orthodox Participants by H.E. Metropolitan Chrysostomos of Ephesus Thessaloniki, Greece, May 1998, http://www.oikoumene.org/en/resources/documents/wcc-programmes/ecumenical-movement-in-the-21st-century/member-churches/special-commission-on-participation-of-orthodox-churches/first-plenary-meeting-documents-december-1999/morges-preliminary-orthodox-proposals.html
- Report of the Meeting of the Orthodox (Eastern and Oriental) members of the WCC Special Commission, Chambésy, Switzerland, 2-5 December 1999, http://www.oikoumene.org/en/resources/documents/wcc-programmes/ecumenical-movement-in-the-21st-century/member-churches/special-commission-on-participation-of-orthodox-churches/first-plenary-meeting-documents-december-1999/meeting-of-the-orthodox-members-of-the-wcc-special-commission.html
- *Interim Report of The Special Commission on Orthodox Participation in the WCC*: Report to the WCC Central Committee, Potsdam, Germany, 2001, http://www.wcc-coe.org/wcc/who/cc2001/gs4-e.html
- *Final report of the Special Commission on Orthodox Participation in the WCC (14.02.2006)* http://www.oikoumene.org/en/resources/documents/assembly/porto-alegre-2006/3-preparatory-and-background-documents/final-report-of-the-special-commission-on-orthodox-participation-in-the-wcc.html
- Also available in print: Final Report of the Special Commission on Orthodox Participation in the WCC. The Ecumenical Review 55.1 (2003): 4-38 on-line:

VII. Documents and Reports of Oriental Orthodox Consultations

- Report of the Joint International Commission for Theological Dialogue between the Catholic Church and the Oriental Orthodox Churches (Jan, 2012, Addis Ababa, Ethiopia)
- Agreed Statement of Joint Commission of the Theological Dialogue between the Orthodoxy and Oriental Orthodox Churches (Monastery of Anba Bishoy-Egypt, 24 June 1989)
- Christology, Anglican-Oriental Orthodox International Commission (Holy Etchmiadzin, Armenia, 5-10 November 2012)
- Agreed Statement of Christology International Theological Dialogue between the Oriental Orthodox family and the World Alliance of Reformed Churches (Driebergen-The Netherlands, 13 September 1994)

Part IX: Appendix: Bibliographical Survey on Key-Texts of Ecumenism

VIII. Bibliography of Some Major Sources in Text Collections

Athanasios Basdekis, *Orthodoxe Kirche und Ökumenische Bewegung.* Dokumente - Erklärungen - Berichte 1900-2006, (Lembeck-Bonifatius 2006)

Bria, Ion: *The Sense Of Ecumenical Tradition: The Ecumenical Witness And Vision Of The Orthodox,* (Geneva: WCC Publications, 1991)

FitzGerald, Thomas: *The Ecumenical Patriarchate and Christian Unity* (Brookline: Holy Cross Orthodox Press, 2009).

Michael Kinnamon and Brian E Cope (eds), *Ecumenical Movement: An Anthology of Keytexts and Voices, Eerdmanns 1997*

Limouris, Gennadios (ed.): *Orthodox Vision on Ecumenism: Statements, Messages and Reports on the Ecumenical Movement, 1902-1992.* (Geneva: WCC Publications, 1994).

Limouris, G - Vaporis, N. M. (eds.): *Orthodox Perspectives on Baptism, Eucharist and Ministry.* FO/128. (Boston: Holy Cross Orthodox Press, 1985).

Patelos, Constantin George (ed.): *The Orthodox Church in the Ecumenical Movement*: Documents and Statements 1902-1975. (Geneva: WCC, 1978).

Sabev, Todor: *The Orthodox Churches in the WCC. Towards the Future.* (Geneva: WCC Publications - Bialystock: Syndesimos, 1996).

Metropolitan Maximos Aghiorgoussis, *Together in Christ: Studies in Ecclesiology and Ecumenism* (Brookline: Holy Cross Orthodox Press, 2012).